America's
Top-Rated Smaller Cities:
A Statistical Handbook

Volume 2: Nebraska - Wyoming

2008/09

Seventh Edition

America's Top-Rated Smaller Cities: A Statistical Handbook

Volume 2: Nebraska - Wyoming

A Universal Reference Book

Grey House Publishing

PUBLISHER: Leslie Mackenzie
EDITORIAL DIRECTOR: Laura Mars-Proietti
EDITOR: David Garoogian
CONTRIBUTING WRITERS: Brian Fier; Jonna Goreham; Breanna Koval; Chelsey Klinger; Jessica Leifeld; Courtney E. Taylor; Sebastian Marturana; Carl Pedersen
PRODUCTION MANAGER: Karen Stevens
MARKETING DIRECTOR: Jessica Moody

A Universal Reference Book
Grey House Publishing, Inc.
185 Millerton Road
Millerton, NY 12546
FAX 518.789.0545
www.greyhouse.com
e-mail: books @greyhouse.com

Seventh Edition
Printed in the USA

America's top-rated smaller cities : a statistical handbook. - 1st ed. (1994-1995)-

v.;27.5 cm.
Biennial
Title varies.
ISSN: 1094-4893

1. Cities and towns-Ratings-United States-Statistics. 2. Cities and towns-United States-Statistics. 3. Social indicators-United States. 4. Quality of life-United States-Statistics.
HT123.A6692
307.76/0973/05

ISBN: 978-1-59237-284-3

Bellevue, Nebraska

Sparks, Nevada

Merrimack, New Hampshire

Bernards, New Jersey

Evesham, New Jersey

Marlboro, New Jersey

Rockaway, New Jersey

South Brunswick, New Jersey

West Windsor, New Jersey

Rio Rancho, New Mexico

Santa Fe, New Mexico

Bethlehem, New York

Greenburgh, New York

Apex, North Carolina

Cary, North Carolina

Huntersville, North Carolina

Matthews, North Carolina

Fargo, North Dakota

Beavercreek, Ohio

Dublin, Ohio

Hilliard, Ohio

Stow, Ohio

Edmond, Oklahoma

Bend, Oregon

Tualatin, Oregon

West Linn, Oregon

Cranberry, Pennsylvania

Hampden, Pennsylvania

Lower Providence, Pennsylvania

Northampton, Pennsylvania

South Kingstown, Rhode Island

Mount Pleasant, South Carolina

Rapid City, South Dakota

Brentwood, Tennessee

Collierville, Tennessee

Allen, Texas

Flower Mound, Texas

Frisco, Texas

Keller, Texas

League City, Texas

Pflugerville, Texas

Round Rock, Texas

Southlake, Texas

Sugar Land, Texas

Draper, Utah

Lehi, Utah

South Jordan, Utah

Spanish Fork, Utah

Burlington, Vermont

Leesburg, Virginia

Redmond, Washington

Richland, Washington

Sammamish, Washington

Morgantown, West Virginia

Brookfield, Wisconsin

Sun Prairie, Wisconsin

Casper, Wyoming

Appendices

Cities profiled in this edition of *America's Top-Rated Smaller Cities*

By City

Allen, TX
Ankeny, IA
Apex, NC
Bangor, ME
Beavercreek, OH
Bellevue, NE
Bend, OR
Bernards, NJ
Bethlehem, NY
Bozeman, MT
Brentwood, TN
Brookfield, WI
Broomfield, CO
Burlington, VT
Carmel, IN
Cary, NC
Casper, WY
Cheshire, CT
Chino Hills, CA
Collierville, TN
Conway, AR
Coronado, CA
Cranberry, PA
Dover, DE
Draper, UT
Dublin, OH
Edmond, OK
Evesham, NJ
Fargo, ND
Farmington, CT
Fishers, IN
Flower Mound, TX
Franklin, MA
Frederick, MD
Frisco, TX
Goodyear, AZ
Grand Blanc, MI
Greenburgh, NY
Greenwich, CT
Hampden, PA
Hilliard, OH
Hoover, AL
Huntersville, NC
Juneau, AK
Keller, TX
Kenner, LA
Kennesaw, GA
League City, TX
Leawood, KS
Lee's Summit, MO
Leesburg, VA
Lehi, UT
Lower Providence, PA
Madison, AL
Manhattan Beach, CA
Maple Grove, MN
Marion, IA
Marlboro, NJ
Matthews, NC
Meridian, ID
Merrimack, NH
Morgantown, WV
Mount Pleasant, SC
Northampton, PA
Northville, MI
Novi, MI
O'Fallon, MO
Oro Valley, AZ
Oviedo, FL
Palm Beach Gardens, FL
Parker, CO
Peachtree City, GA
Pflugerville, TX
Pleasanton, CA
Rapid City, SD
Redmond, WA
Richland, WA
Richmond, KY
Rio Rancho, NM
Rockaway, NJ
Rocklin, CA
Rogers, AR
Round Rock, TX
Sammamish, WA
San Ramon, CA
Santa Fe, NM
Saratoga, CA
Savage, MN
Schererville, IN
Shawnee, KS
Shrewsbury, MA
South Brunswick, NJ
South Jordan, UT
South Kingstown, RI
Southaven, MS
Southlake, TX
Spanish Fork, UT
Sparks, NV
Stow, OH
Sugar Land, TX
Sun Prairie, WI
Tualatin, OR
Waimalu, HI
Wellington, FL
West Des Moines, IA
West Linn, OR
West Windsor, NJ
Weston, FL
Woodbury, MN
Woodridge, IL
Yorba Linda, CA

By State

Hoover, AL
Madison, AL
Juneau, AK
Goodyear, AZ
Oro Valley, AZ
Conway, AR
Rogers, AR
Chino Hills, CA
Coronado, CA
Manhattan Beach, CA
Pleasanton, CA
Rocklin, CA
San Ramon, CA
Saratoga, CA
Yorba Linda, CA
Broomfield, CO
Parker, CO
Cheshire, CT
Farmington, CT
Greenwich, CT
Dover, DE
Oviedo, FL
Palm Beach Gardens, FL
Wellington, FL
Weston, FL
Kennesaw, GA
Peachtree City, GA
Waimalu, HI
Meridian, ID
Woodridge, IL
Carmel, IN
Fishers, IN
Schererville, IN
Ankeny, IA
Marion, IA
West Des Moines, IA
Leawood, KS
Shawnee, KS
Richmond, KY
Kenner, LA
Bangor, ME
Frederick, MD
Franklin, MA
Shrewsbury, MA
Grand Blanc, MI
Northville, MI
Novi, MI
Maple Grove, MN
Savage, MN
Woodbury, MN
Southaven, MS
Lee's Summit, MO
O'Fallon, MO
Bozeman, MT
Bellevue, NE
Sparks, NV
Merrimack, NH
Bernards, NJ
Evesham, NJ
Marlboro, NJ
Rockaway, NJ
South Brunswick, NJ
West Windsor, NJ
Rio Rancho, NM
Santa Fe, NM
Bethlehem, NY
Greenburgh, NY
Apex, NC
Cary, NC
Huntersville, NC
Matthews, NC
Fargo, ND
Beavercreek, OH
Dublin, OH
Hilliard, OH
Stow, OH
Edmond, OK
Bend, OR
Tualatin, OR
West Linn, OR
Cranberry, PA
Hampden, PA
Lower Providence, PA
Northampton, PA
South Kingstown, RI
Mount Pleasant, SC
Rapid City, SD
Brentwood, TN
Collierville, TN
Allen, TX
Flower Mound, TX
Frisco, TX
Keller, TX
League City, TX
Pflugerville, TX
Round Rock, TX
Southlake, TX
Sugar Land, TX
Draper, UT
Lehi, UT

Introduction

This is the seventh edition of *America's Top-Rated Smaller Cities* — current, concise statistical profiles of top U.S. cities with populations between 25,000 and 125,000. The 2008/09 edition features 111 cities, 35 never before included, representing all 50 states. Comprehensive geographic representation is important for several reasons, most compelling is that while some of us have the luxury of choosing where to live, others move for a specific reason — employment, family, weather — and therefore to a specific area. And businesses on the move look for other things, like business climate and specific markets for their product or service. *America's Top-Rated Smaller Cities* is now more valuable to more users, with data that helps individuals and businesses choose a top-rated smaller city anywhere in the country.

> "…its coverage is [far more] thorough, focused and detailed. A useful addition to public and academic library reference collections."
> *Choice*

> "A quick and handy reference tool, this work will have a wide and grateful audience…recommended for public and academic libraries."
> *ARBA*

> "…additional coverage and updated data makes [America's Top-Rated Smaller Cities] an appealing purchase."
> *Columbia University Libraries*

There are many ways to research new places to live. The Internet can provide important details, like the cost of your lifestyle in various cities, and which schools are top rated, but only *America's Top-Rated Smaller Cities* gives you a complete picture. We've done the extensive research necessary to compile comprehensive profiles and comparative statistics that will educate and prepare you for relocation.

To expand our available city choices, the selection was not limited to incorporated cities, but also included towns and townships. This availed us many top-rated communities not designated as cities. Final selection was based on our unique rating system, using five key criteria: population growth, income, crime rate, educational attainment, and unemployment.

FEATURES

The city rankings for each of the 111 city chapters now comprise information from more than 240 books, magazines, newspapers and research reports — dozens more than the last edition. Interesting new "top-city" rankings include . . . **Organic Consumers, Identity Theft, Best Teeth, Commuters,** and **Foreclosure Rates**. You'll also learn which cities are the most . . . **Wired, Greedy, Rainy, Lustful, Clean, Obese, Sun-smart,** and more!

Each city chapter in this edition has nine new tables: **State Business Tax Climate; Grocery Prices; House Price Valuations; Health Risks; Mortality Rates; Best Colleges/Business Schools; Air Quality Index Trends;** and **Maximum Air Pollutant Concentrations**.

ARRANGEMENT

America's Top-Rated Smaller Cities is arranged in two volumes - Volume 1 has 54 city chapters, Alabama to Montana, and Volume 2 has 57 city chapters, Nebraska to Wyoming. Each city chapter is divided into three sections: **Background & Rankings; Business Environment;** and **Living Environment**. Both volumes include **80 Honorable Mention Cities,** four **Regional Maps** that indicate the location of each of the 111 cities, and six **Appendices**, with comparative rankings and resource information on all cities. Here is a detailed look:

City Background
Each of the 111 city chapters begins with an informative background. These page-long narratives combine history with current events, and touch on the city's environment, politics, employment, and cultural offerings, along with some interesting trivia:

- West Windsor, NJ is the reported landing spot of alien spacecraft in the October 30, 1938 "War of the Worlds" broadcast, meant to be a Halloween special but, in fact, had residents fleeing from their homes;
- Shrewsbury, MA is where 400 residents began their march to the Worcester courthouse, protesting unfair debt collection and foreclosures, known as Shay's Rebellion;

- Saratoga, CA is where the 1998 movie "The Horse Whisper" was filmed, and also home to film director Steven Spielberg's high school;
- Lower Providence, RI was the first American home to John James Audubon, now a wildlife refuge and museum commemorating the namesake of the Audubon Society;
- Farmington, CT is the birthplace of Sarah Porter, founder of Miss Porter's School for Girls in 1843, which is still housed in the town's many historical buildings saved from destruction by Porter;
- Dover, DE is home to Dover International Speedway, the first concrete super speedway in the nation, and host of the annual NASCAR Nextel Cup series.

Rankings
This section is significantly expanded from the previous edition, with 11 ranking categories, including *Business/Finance, Health, Women/Minorities, Retirement, Family, Safety, Recreation,* and *Dating/Romance.* It contains data from more than 240 books, articles, and research reports, and is presented in an easy-to-read, bulleted format. You'll find rankings — and several scores and figures — on a wide variety of topics, such as Best Cities for Seniors; America's Most Literate Cities; Best Cities for Relocating Families; Best Cities for Hispanics; Best Places for Artists; Best Cities for Latinas; Best Cities for Dogs; Best Sports Cities; Fittest Cities; Best Places for Business and Career, and hundreds more.

Sources for these Rankings include both well-known magazines and other media, including *Field & Stream, Forbes, Fortune, Inc. Magazine, Working Mother, Prevention, Business Week, Men's Journal,* and *Travel & Leisure,* as well as resources not as well known, such as *Inside Triathlon, Black Enterprise, The National Coalition for the Homeless, Center for Digital Government, U.S. Conference of Mayors, Partners for Livable Communities,* and *Mercer Human Resources Consulting.*

Business Environment — Statistical Tables
Each city chapter in *America's Top-Rated Smaller Cities, 2008/09* includes 34 tables with business related data for 7 topics. Here is where you will find hard facts and figures on city finances, population demographics, income, bankruptcy rates, employment, and taxes. Again, our editors have used sources that are obvious, such as the *U.S. Census Bureau* and the *Bureau of Labor Statistics,* and more obscure ones, like *The Tax Foundation* and the *Glenmary Research Center.* Some data is drawn from other Grey House titles, such as *The Grey House Performing Arts Directory.*

Living Environment — Statistical Tables
The business tables are followed by 42 tables with data related to 12 living environment topics. These include information on housing, healthcare, cost-of-living, education, recreation, and climate. Sources include the *U.S. Environmental Protection Agency, Federal Bureau of Investigation, Centers for Disease Control,* and *National Center for Education Statistics.*

The availability of statistics is related to both a city's size and how data is gathered. Some statistics represent the Metropolitan Statistical Area the city is part of, and some are not available at all, indicated by n/a.

Six Appendices
- **A/B — Current and Historical Metropolitan Statistical Areas (MSAs):** In straight alpha-by-city order, this includes the counties that combine to form each city's Metropolitan Statistical Area.
- **C — Counties:** Includes an alphabetical list of cites and the county they are a part of.
- **D — Chambers of Commerce and Economic Development Organizations:** Alpha-by-city, includes address, phone numbers and fax numbers of additional city resources.
- **E — State Departments of Labor and Employment:** Another source for additional economic and employment data for each city, with address and phone number for easy access.
- **F — Comparative Statistics:** A city-by city comparison of hundreds of variables spread out over 72 tables that offers both an overview of the city, and a broad geographical profile.

The material provided by public and private agencies and organizations was supplemented by library sources and Internet sites. This edition is designed for individuals considering relocating a residence or business; professionals considering expanding a business or changing careers; corporations considering relocation or additional offices; government agencies; general and market researchers; real estate consultants; human resource personnel; urban planners; investors; and urban government students. With more content and more coverage, this edition is our strongest and most informative to date.

Honorable Mention Cities

These cities did not make our editor's final cut, however, they were on our preliminary list.

By City

Alabaster, AL	Dublin, CA	Livermore, CA	Rancho Santa Margarita, CA
Aliso Viejo, CA	East Brunswick, NJ	Londonderry, NH	Randolph, NJ
Alpharetta, GA	Eden Prairie, MN	Los Altos, CA	Richardson, TX
American Fork, UT	Folsom, CA	Manalapan, NJ	Rockwall, TX
Apple Valley, MN	Foster City, CA	Mansfield, TX	Roswell, GA
Auburn, AL	Franklin, NJ	Marana, AZ	San Clemente, CA
Aventura, FL	Franklin, TN	McKinney, TX	San Juan Capistrano, CA
Bellevue, WA	Freehold, NJ	Middletown, PA	Shakopee, MN
Blaine, MN	Friendswood, TX	Mission Viejo, CA	Sierra Vista, AZ
Bothell, WA	Georgetown, TX	Missouri City, TX	South Pasadena, CA
Brea, CA	Glastonbury, CT	Mount Olive, NJ	South Windsor, CT
Bridgewater, NJ	Grapevine, TX	Murrieta, CA	Surprise, AZ
Canton, MI	Hillsborough, NJ	Newport Beach, CA	The Colony, TX
Carlsbad, CA	La Quinta, CA	Noblesville, IN	Upper Merion, PA
Castle Rock, CO	Laguna Niguel, CA	Olathe, KS	Urbandale, IA
Cedar City, UT	Lake Oswego, OR	Orem, UT	Walnut, CA
Cedar Park, TX	Lakeville, MN	Palo Alto, CA	Washington, NJ
Claremont, CA	Lawrence, NJ	Pearland, TX	West Jordan, UT
Coppell, TX	Lenexa, KS	Plymouth, MN	Westfield, NJ
Danville, CA	Lewisville, TX	Rancho Palos Verdes, CA	Wylie, TX

By State

Alabaster, AL	Palo Alto, CA	Eden Prairie, MN	Cedar Park, TX
Auburn, AL	Rancho Palos Verdes, CA	Lakeville, MN	Coppell, TX
Marana, AZ	Rancho Santa Margarita, CA	Plymouth, MN	Friendswood, TX
Sierra Vista, AZ	San Clemente, CA	Shakopee, MN	Georgetown, TX
Surprise, AZ	San Juan Capistrano, CA	Londonderry, NH	Grapevine, TX
Aliso Viejo, CA	South Pasadena, CA	Bridgewater, NJ	Lewisville, TX
Brea, CA	Walnut, CA	East Brunswick, NJ	Mansfield, TX
Carlsbad, CA	Castle Rock, CO	Franklin, NJ	McKinney, TX
Claremont, CA	Glastonbury, CT	Freehold, NJ	Missouri City, TX
Danville, CA	South Windsor, CT	Hillsborough, NJ	Pearland, TX
Dublin, CA	Aventura, FL	Lawrence, NJ	Richardson, TX
Folsom, CA	Alpharetta, GA	Manalapan, NJ	Rockwall, TX
Foster City, CA	Roswell, GA	Mount Olive, NJ	The Colony, TX
La Quinta, CA	Noblesville, IN	Randolph, NJ	Wylie, TX
Laguna Niguel, CA	Urbandale, IA	Washington, NJ	American Fork, UT
Livermore, CA	Lenexa, KS	Westfield, NJ	Cedar City, UT
Los Altos, CA	Olathe, KS	Lake Oswego, OR	Orem, UT
Mission Viejo, CA	Canton, MI	Middletown, PA	West Jordan, UT
Murrieta, CA	Apple Valley, MN	Upper Merion, PA	Bellevue, WA
Newport Beach, CA	Blaine, MN	Franklin, TN	Bothell, WA

Western United States

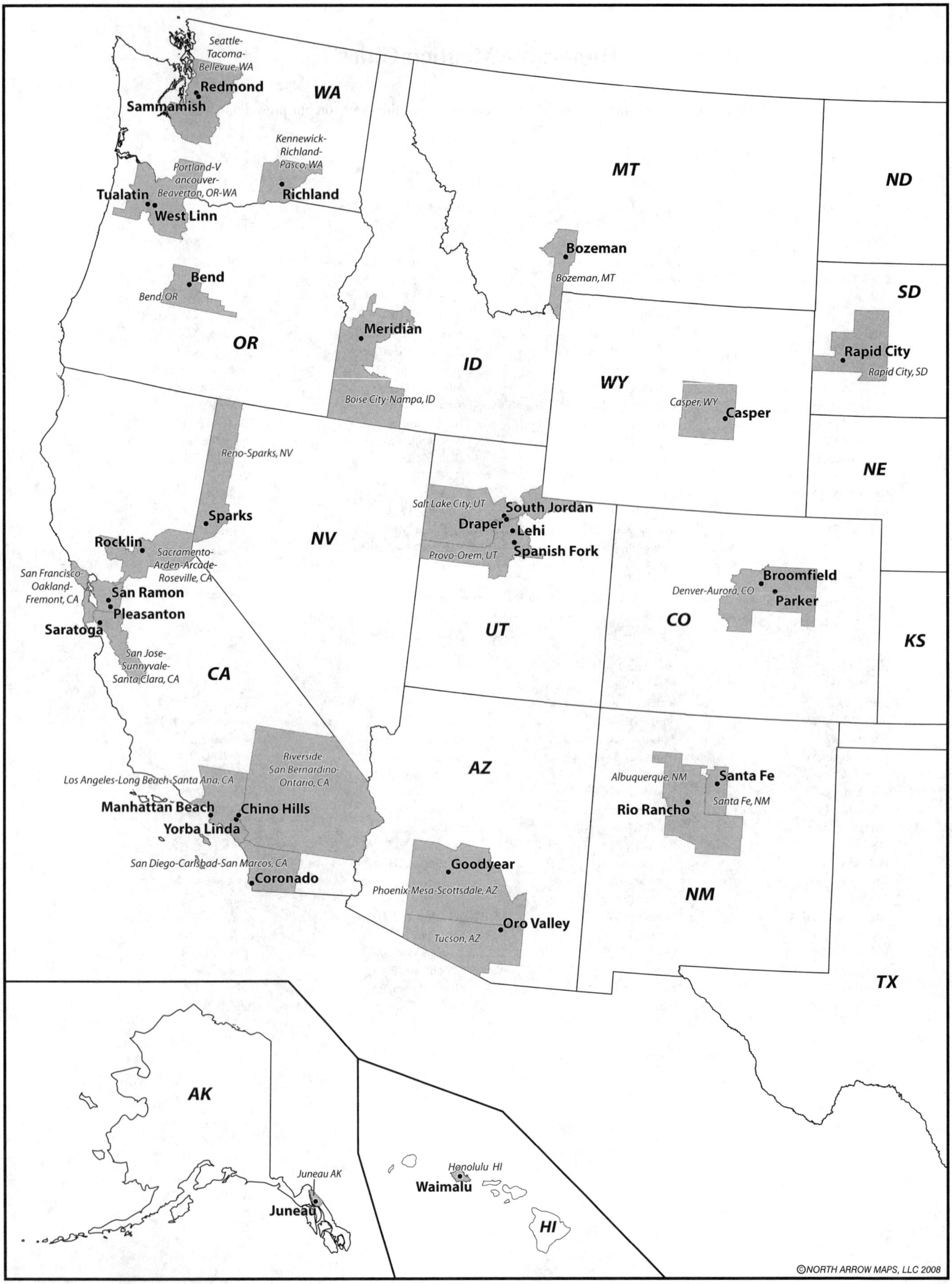
WA
Seattle-Tacoma-Bellevue, WA
Redmond
Sammamish
Kennewick-Richland-Pasco, WA
Richland
Portland-Vancouver-Beaverton, OR-WA
Tualatin
West Linn
MT
ND
Bozeman
Bozeman, MT
SD
Bend
Bend, OR
OR
Meridian
ID
Boise City-Nampa, ID
WY
Rapid City
Rapid City, SD
Casper, WY
Casper
Reno-Sparks, NV
NE
Salt Lake City, UT
South Jordan
Draper
Lehi
Spanish Fork
Provo-Orem, UT
Sparks
NV
Rocklin
Sacramento-Arden-Arcade-Roseville, CA
San Francisco-Oakland-Fremont, CA
San Ramon
Pleasanton
Saratoga
Broomfield
Denver-Aurora, CO
Parker
CO
UT
KS
San Jose-Sunnyvale-Santa Clara, CA
CA
Riverside-San Bernardino-Ontario, CA
AZ
Los Angeles-Long Beach-Santa Ana, CA
Manhattan Beach
Chino Hills
Yorba Linda
San Diego-Carlsbad-San Marcos, CA
Coronado
Albuquerque, NM
Santa Fe
Rio Rancho
Santa Fe, NM
Goodyear
Phoenix-Mesa-Scottsdale, AZ
NM
Oro Valley
Tucson, AZ
TX
AK
Juneau AK
Juneau
Honolulu HI
Waimalu
HI
©NORTH ARROW MAPS, LLC 2008

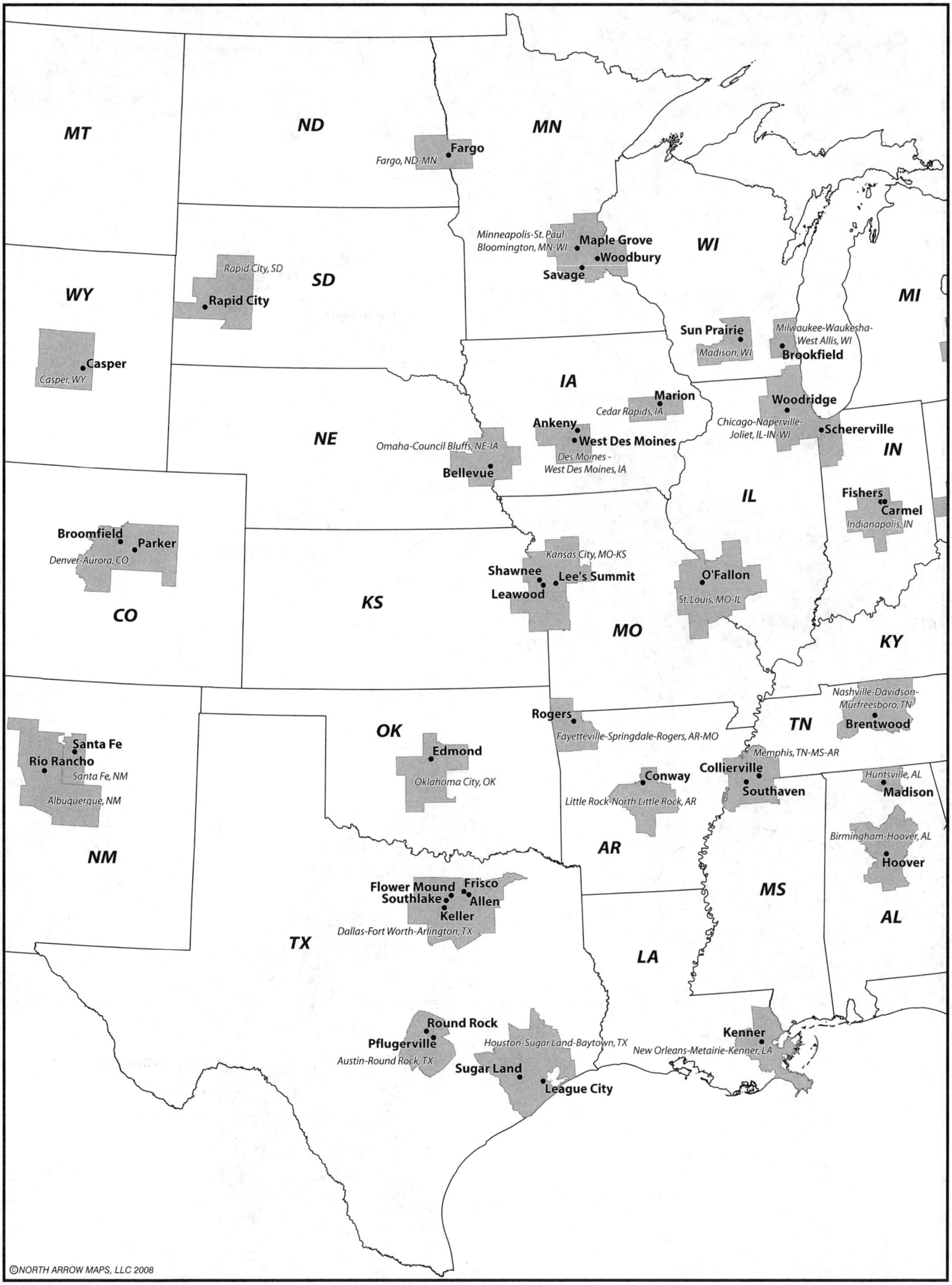
MT
ND
MN
Fargo
Fargo, ND-MN
WY
SD
Rapid City, SD
Rapid City
Casper
Casper, WY
Minneapolis-St. Paul-Bloomington, MN-WI
Maple Grove
Woodbury
Savage
WI
MI
Sun Prairie
Madison, WI
Milwaukee-Waukesha-West Allis, WI
Brookfield
IA
Marion
Cedar Rapids, IA
Woodridge
Chicago-Naperville-Joliet, IL-IN-WI
Schererville
NE
Omaha-Council Bluffs, NE-IA
Bellevue
Ankeny
West Des Moines
Des Moines - West Des Moines, IA
IN
IL
Fishers
Carmel
Indianapolis, IN
Broomfield
Parker
Denver-Aurora, CO
CO
KS
Kansas City, MO-KS
Shawnee
Lee's Summit
Leawood
MO
O'Fallon
St. Louis, MO-IL
KY
Nashville-Davidson-Murfreesboro, TN
Brentwood
TN
Rogers
Fayetteville-Springdale-Rogers, AR-MO
OK
Edmond
Oklahoma City, OK
Santa Fe
Rio Rancho
Santa Fe, NM
Albuquerque, NM
NM
Memphis, TN-MS-AR
Collierville
Southaven
Conway
Little Rock-North Little Rock, AR
Huntsville, AL
Madison
Birmingham-Hoover, AL
Hoover
AR
MS
AL
Flower Mound
Frisco
Southlake
Allen
Keller
Dallas-Fort Worth-Arlington, TX
TX
LA
Round Rock
Pflugerville
Austin-Round Rock, TX
Houston-Sugar Land-Baytown, TX
Sugar Land
League City
Kenner
New Orleans-Metairie-Kenner, LA

Southeastern United States

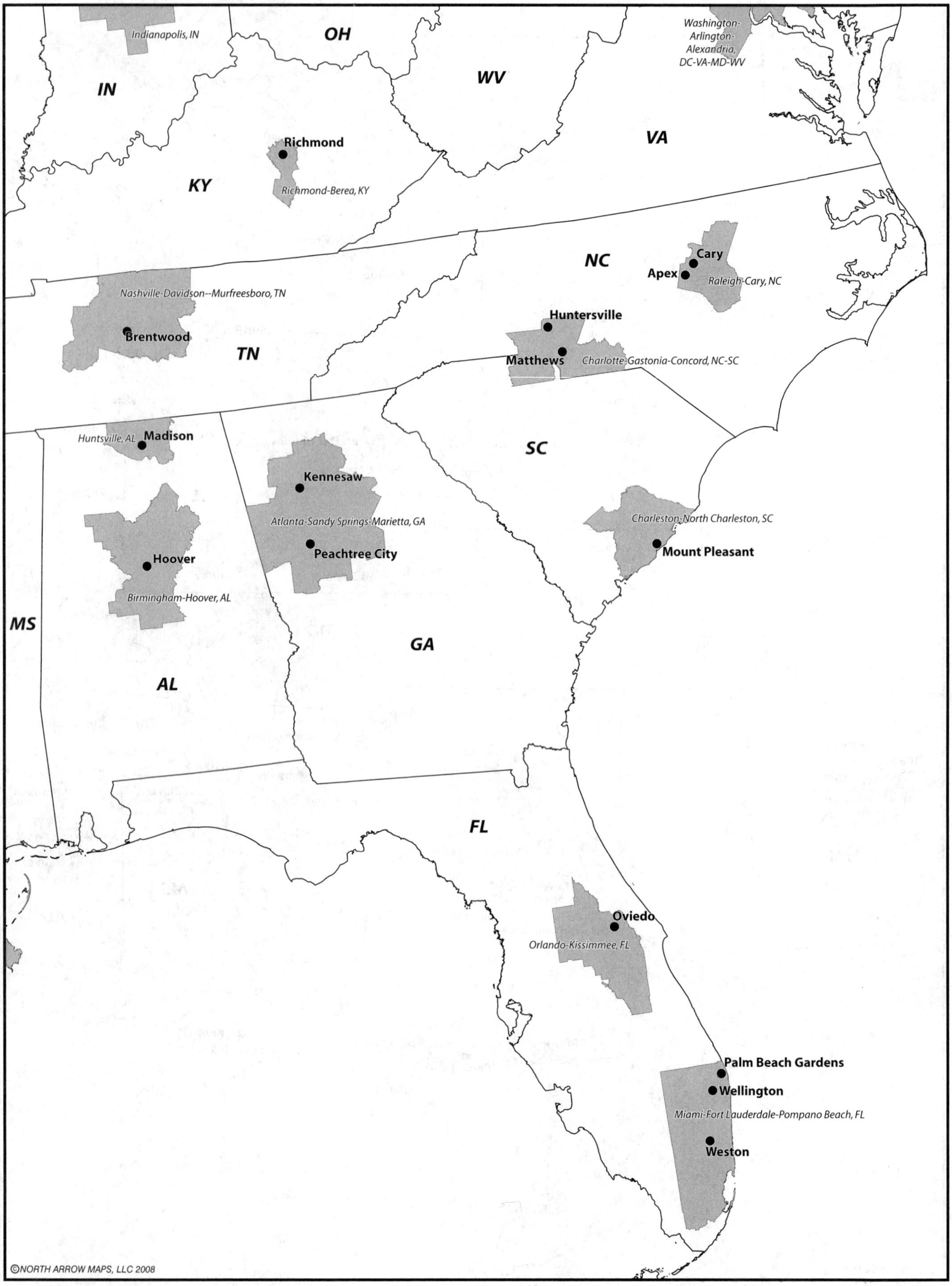

Northeastern United States

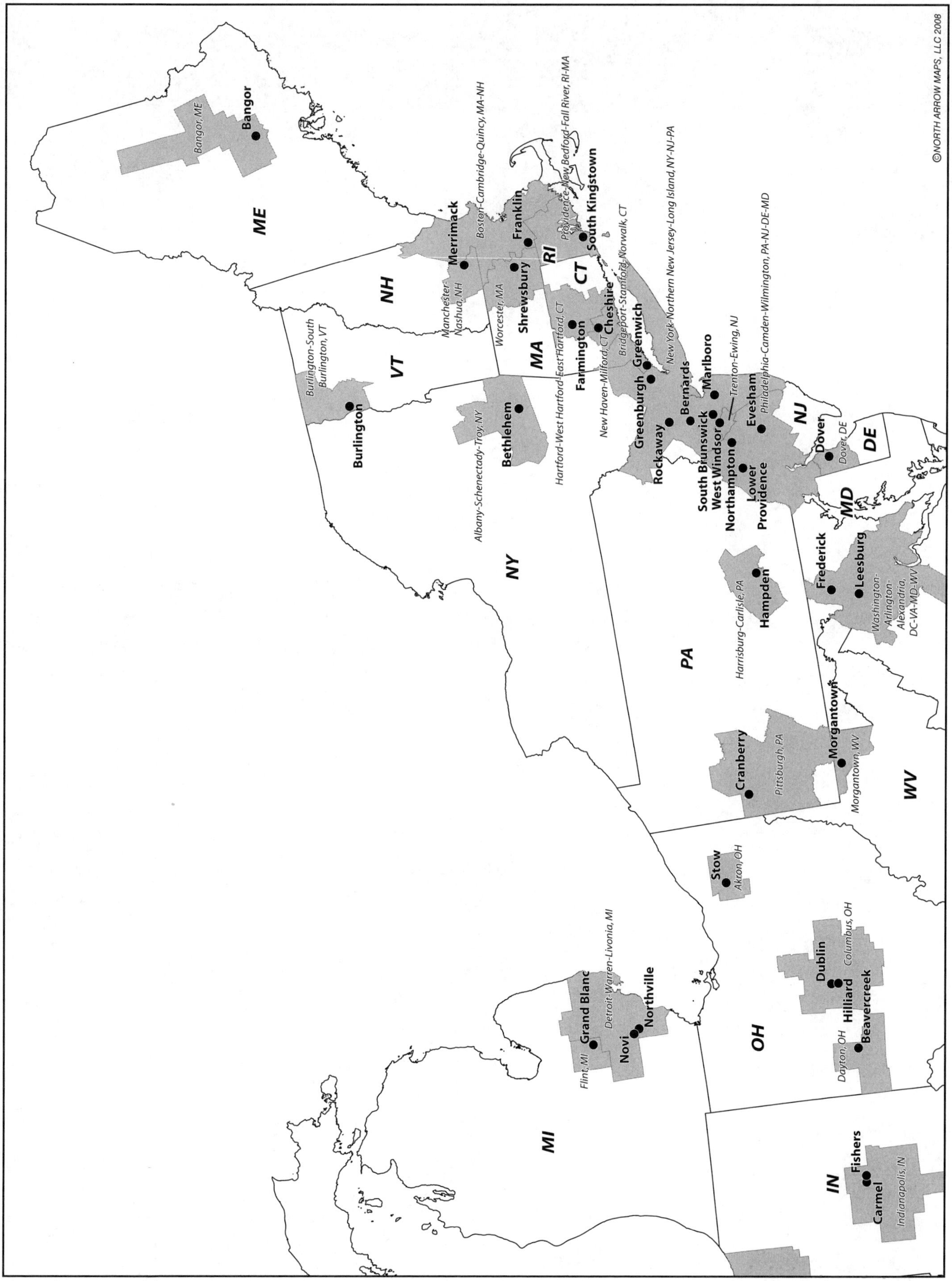

©NORTH ARROW MAPS, LLC 2008
ME
Bangor
Bangor, ME
NH
Merrimack
Manchester-Nashua, NH
Boston-Cambridge-Quincy, MA-NH
Franklin
Shrewsbury
Worcester, MA
MA
RI
Providence-New Bedford-Fall River, RI-MA
South Kingstown
CT
Farmington
Cheshire
Hartford-West Hartford-East Hartford, CT
New Haven-Milford, CT
Bridgeport-Stamford-Norwalk, CT
Greenwich
Greenburgh
New York-Northern New Jersey-Long Island, NY-NJ-PA
VT
Burlington
Burlington-South Burlington, VT
NY
Bethlehem
Albany-Schenectady-Troy, NY
Rockaway
Bernards
Marlboro
South Brunswick
West Windsor
Trenton-Ewing, NJ
Northampton
Lower Providence
Evesham
Philadelphia-Camden-Wilmington, PA-NJ-DE-MD
NJ
Dover
Dover, DE
DE
MD
Frederick
Leesburg
Washington-Arlington-Alexandria, DC-VA-MD-WV
PA
Hampden
Harrisburg-Carlisle, PA
Cranberry
Pittsburgh, PA
Morgantown
Morgantown, WV
WV
Stow
Akron, OH
OH
Dublin
Hilliard
Columbus, OH
Beavercreek
Dayton, OH
MI
Grand Blanc
Flint, MI
Novi
Northville
Detroit-Warren-Livonia, MI
IN
Fishers
Carmel
Indianapolis, IN

Bellevue, Nebraska

Background

Bellevue, the third largest city in Nebraska, bordered to its north by the state capital, Omaha, has maintained valuable elements of its small town past. The city's southern section adjoins Offutt Air Force Base, which is a vital strategic military center for the nation, creating a talented and resourceful labor and entrepreneurial population.

The area around Bellevue had been explored in the late eighteenth century by trappers and traders, mostly of French descent, from St. Louis, New Orleans, or Canada, and Lewis and Clark are said to have come through the site. The town itself was first established in 1822, as a trading post for the Missouri Fur Company. It functioned as an important hub for trade with members of the Omaha, Oto, and Pawnee Indian tribes. The French "Bellevue" was chosen as the name because of the beautiful view it afforded of the Missouri River.

The fur trade was a rich one, and drew many adventurers from afar, including Prince Maximillian of Germany in 1831, who sought to bolster his family's fortunes through the exploitation of an abundant new world resource. As furs moved east and manufactured goods moved west though Bellevue, the town grew at a rapid pace. By the middle of the nineteenth century, the town boasted churches, banks, inns, a major hotel, and many richly appointed private homes.

The town's residents had confidently expected that Bellevue would be chosen as the capital of the Nebraska Territory. The territorial governor, Francis Burt, had even purchased a home in Bellevue. However, he died suddenly and unexpectedly, and his replacement quickly selected rival Omaha as the capital city.

Bellevue was incorporated in 1855, making it the oldest city in Nebraska, but it nevertheless lost population for the next several decades, at one point nearly disappearing. However, Bellevue College was established in 1876, and Fort Crook was built in the 1890s, both of which stimulated new settlement and economic growth.

Fort Crook was destined, ultimately, to become Offutt Air Force Base, and when that base became home to a Martin aircraft factory, during World War II, Bellevue's fortunes changed dramatically. The city's new prosperity was accelerated after the war, when the United States Strategic Air Command chose Bellevue as its headquarters. This development attracted many new workers, both civilian and military.

Other than the base, major employers include Albertsons, Ameritrade, BAE Systems, Inc., Computer Cable Connection, Metz Baking Company, Pendelton Woolen Mills, Sterling Software and TRW.

The Bellevue Public School district is the fourth largest in Nebraska, and it operates eighteen highly regarded schools. Bellevue also hosts a variety of religiously affiliated schools. Institutions of higher learning in the area include Bellevue University, College of St. Mary, Creighton University, Grace University, Metropolitan Community College, Southern Illinois University, and the University of Nebraska at Omaha.

Bellevue operates many parks, with swimming pools, playing fields for baseball and soccer tennis courts, jogging and walking trails, ice skating rinks, children's playgrounds, camping facilities, and an equestrian center. The town's recreation department offers almost fifty different activities throughout the year, providing many recreational outlets for children, youth and adults.

Bellevue is governed by a mayor, with a four -year term, and by a ten-member city council, two each from five wards.

Rankings

General Rankings

- Omaha* was ranked #127 out of 375 metro areas in *Cities Ranked & Rated*. Criteria: cost of living; climate; crime; transportation; economy and jobs; education; arts and culture; health and healthcare; leisure; quality of life. *Cities Ranked & Rated, 2nd Edition, 2007*
- Omaha* was ranked #65 out of 379 metro areas in *Places Rated Almanac*. Criteria: health care; education; recreation; transportation; ambience; climate; crime; housing costs; jobs. *Places Rated Almanac, 7th Edition, 2007*
- The Omaha* metro area was selected one of America's "Best Cities to Live, Work and Play" by *Kiplinger Personal Finance*. Criteria: population growth; percentage of workforce in the creative class (scientists, engineers, educators, writers, artists, entertainers, etc.); job quality; income growth; cost of living. *Kiplinger Personal Finance, "Best Cities to Live, Work and Play," July 2008*
- *Expansion Management* rated 362 metro areas to find out which offer the best middle class lifestyle for manufacturing and service companies. The Omaha* metro area was selected as a "5-Star Quality of Life Metro" (a distinction the magazine awards to the top 20 percent of metro areas studied). The annual "Quality of Life Quotient" measures dozens of indicators across nine major categories and compares them among 362 metropolitan statistical areas in the United States. The categories are: affordable housing; good public schools; low crime levels; adult education level; standard of living; traffic and commuting; continuing education opportunities; commercial air access; labor market. *Expansion Management, June 2007*

Business/Finance Rankings

- The nation's 100 largest metro areas were analysed in terms of the percentage of households entering some stage of foreclosure in 2007. The Omaha* metro area ranked #57 out of 100 (#1 = highest foreclosure rate). *RealtyTrac, "Year-End 2007 Metropolitan Foreclosure Report"*
- The Omaha* metro area was identified as one of the "10 Best Cities for Jobs in 2008" by *Forbes*. The metro area ranked #8. Criteria: state unemployment rate; job growth; income growth; median household income; cost of living. *Forbes.com, "Best Cities for Jobs in 2008," January 10, 2008*
- The Omaha* metro area was selected one of America's "Top 50 Business Opportunity Metros" by *Expansion Management* in their 5th annual Mayor's Challenge ranking of metro areas that have achieved solid ratings across the board in numerous *EM* studies during the past 12 months. The area ranked #8. Criteria: public schools; quality of life; college educated workers; logistics infrastructure; healthcare costs; taxes and government spending; reputation among site consultants. *Expansion Management, August 2007*
- Omaha* was selected as one of the best places to start and grow a company by *Entrepreneur* and the National Policy Research Council. The Omaha* metro area ranked #10 out of 63 mid-size metro areas. Criteria: business formation and growth (firms started four to 14 years ago that still employ at least 5 people and experienced rapid growth over the last four years). *Entrepreneur/National Policy Research Council, "Hot Cities for Entrepreneurs," September 2006*
- Omaha* was cited as one of America's top mid-size metros (population 200,000 to 1 million) for new and expanded facility projects in 2007. The area appeared in the top 10 with 29 projects. *Site Selection, "Top Metropolitan Area Awards," March 2008*
- The Omaha* metro area was selected as one of the "Top 20 Real Estate Markets" for expanding or relocating companies. The area ranked #15. Criteria: low rental costs; low purchase prices; high vacancy rates of office and warehouse space. *Expansion Management, October 2007*

- Intel, in partnership with Sperling's BestPlaces, ranked the 80 "Best Cities for Teleworking" in America. The Omaha* metro area ranked #14 among mid-sized metro areas. The study identifies cities that hold the greatest potential for teleworking based on a host of factors including typical commuting times, fuel prices, availability of broadband Internet access and percentage of the population in telework friendly jobs. The study also factored in extreme climate and natural hazards. *Intel, "Best Cities for Teleworking," March 30, 2006*

- The Omaha* metro area appeared on the Milken Institute "2007 Best Performing Cities" index. Rank: #104 out of 200 large metro areas. Criteria: job growth; wage and salary growth; high-tech output growth. *Milken Institute, "2007 Best Performing Cities"*

- Omaha* was identified as one of the 100 "Most Unwired Cities" in the U.S. The area ranked #60 out of the 100 largest metro areas in the U.S. Criteria: number of public and commercial wireless access points (hotspots); airports with wireless Internet access; broadband availability; local wireless networks; and wireless email devices. *Intel, "Most Unwired Cities Survey," June 7, 2005*

- *Forbes* ranked the 200 most populous metro areas in the U.S. in terms of the "Best Places for Business and Careers." The Omaha* metro area was ranked #34. Criteria: business costs (labor, energy, tax and office space expenses); living costs (housing, transportation, food and other household expenditures); education levels of the work force; job growth; income growth; migration trends; crime rates; and culture/leisure. *Forbes, "Best Places for Business and Careers," March 19, 2008*

- *Fortune* ranked the 100 largest metro areas in the U.S. in terms of projected median home price change in 2007. The Omaha* metro area ranked #35. *Fortune.com, "Hot Spots, Cold Spots"*

Health/Environment Rankings

- 100 of the largest metro areas in the U.S. were analyzed in terms of their current drought severity. The Omaha* metro area ranked #90 (#1 = driest). The rankings were based on statistics such as long-term precipitation trends and patterns and the Palmer drought indices. *Sperling's BestPlaces, www.BestPlaces.net, "America's Drought-Riskiest Cities," November 2007*

- The Omaha* metro area appeared in *Country Home's* "2008 Best Green Places" report. The area ranked #142 out of 379. Criteria: official energy policies; green power; green buildings; availability of fresh, locally grown food. *Country Home, "2008 Best Green Places"*

- The American Podiatric Medical Association and *Prevention* magazine ranked America's 100 most populated cities based on fitness-walker friendliness. The best cities have safe streets, beautiful places to walk, mild weather and good air quality. Bellevue ranked #363. *Prevention, "The Best Walking Cities of 2008," April 2008; American Podiatric Medical Association, "2008 Best Fitness-Walking Cities, "April 2008*

- Omaha* was identified as a "2008 Asthma Capital." The area ranked #75 out of the nation's 100 largest metropolitan areas. Twelve factors were used to identify the most challenging places to live for people with asthma: estimated prevalence; self-reported prevalence; crude death rate for asthma; annual pollen score; annual air quality; public smoking laws; number of board-certified asthma specialists; school inhaler access laws; rescue medication use; controller medication use; uninsured rate; poverty rate. *Asthma and Allergy Foundation of America, "2008 Asthma Capitals"*

- Omaha* was identified as a "Spring Allergy Capital." The area ranked #64 out of 100. Three groups of factors were used to identify the most severe cities for people with allergies during the spring season: annual pollen levels; medicine utilization; access to board-certified allergists. *Asthma and Allergy Foundation of America, "2007 Spring Allergy Capital Rankings"*

- Omaha* was identified as a "Fall Allergy Capital." The area ranked #67 out of 100. Three groups of factors were used to identify the most severe cities for people with allergies during the fall season: annual pollen levels; medicine utilization; access to board-certified allergists. *Asthma and Allergy Foundation of America, "2007 Fall Allergy Capital Rankings"*

- Ortho-McNeil Neurologics, in partnership with Sperling's BestPlaces, analyzed 110 metro areas and identified those U.S. cities with the highest prevalence of factors that are most commonly associated with migraine headaches. The Omaha* metro area ranked #17. Criteria: number of migraine-related drug prescriptions per capita; lifestyle factors that can contribute to migraines; environmental factors that can trigger migraines; and consumption of migraine-triggering foods. *Ortho-McNeil Neurologics, "America's Migraine Hot Spots," March 14, 2006*

- Sperling's BestPlaces ranked 331 metro areas and identified the most and least stressful U.S. cities. The Omaha* metro area ranked #94 out of the 100 largest metro areas (#1 = most stressful). Criteria: divorce rate; unemployment rate; violent and property crime; suicide rate; commute time; mental health; alcohol consumption; cloudy days. *Sperling's BestPlaces, www.BestPlaces.net, "America's Most (and Least) Stressful Cities," January 9, 2004*

- Omaha* was highlighted as one of the cleanest metro areas for ozone air pollution in the U.S. The list represents cities with no monitored ozone air pollution in unhealthful ranges. *American Lung Association, State of the Air: 2007*

Women/Minorities Rankings

- Omaha* was ranked #46 out of 100 metro areas in *SELF Magazine's* ranking of "America's Best Places for Women." A panel of experts came up with more than 50 criteria including death and disease rates, environmental indicators, community resources, and lifestyle habits. *SELF Magazine, "America's Best Places for Women 2007," December 2007*

Seniors/Retirement Rankings

- A.G. Edwards ranked America's 500 top-performing communities based on their residents' personal savings and investing behavior. The Omaha* metro area ranked #223 with an index score of 102.34 (national average = 100.00). A dozen statistical factors were measured including: participation in retirement savings plans; personal debt levels; and home ownership. *A.G. Edwards, "2007 Nest Egg Index", September 12, 2007*

Children/Family Rankings

- The Omaha* metro area was selected as one of the "Best Cities for Relocating Families" by Worldwide ERC and Primacy Relocation. The 2007 study placed a special emphasis on the housing market, which has significantly impacted the relocation industry and an employer's ability to transfer employees. The variables which weigh heavily in this category include home price, home affordability index, appreciation rates, and property tax. Other criteria include cost of living, crime rates, education, climate, focus on diversity, physicians per capita, recreation and leisure, arts and culture, air quality, watershed quality, sales tax, unemployment rate, job growth, high school and higher education index, school expenditures per student, students in public school, SAT/ACT percentile, and population growth. *Worldwide ERC and Primacy Relocation, "2007 Best Cities for Relocating Families"*

Safety Rankings

- The National Insurance Crime Bureau ranked 361 metro areas in the U.S. in terms of per capita rates of vehicle theft. The Omaha* metro area ranked #57 (#1 = highest rate). Criteria: number of vehicle theft offenses per 100,000 inhabitants. *National Insurance Crime Bureau, "NICB Vehicle Theft Study," April 22, 2008*

- Farmers Insurance Group of Companies, in partnership with Sperling's BestPlaces, ranked 379 metro areas and identified the "Most Secure U.S. Place to Live." The Omaha* metro area ranked #77 out of 114 in the large metro area category (500,000 or more residents). Criteria: crime rates; extreme weather; risk of natural disasters; environmental hazards; terrorism threats; air quality; life expectancy; job loss numbers. *Farmers Insurance Group, "Most Secure U.S. Places to Live 2007"*

Sports/Recreation Rankings

- The Omaha* metro area appeared on the *Sporting News* list of the "Best Sports Cities 2007". The area ranked #110 out of 150 cities in the U.S. *Sporting News* takes a 12-month snapshot, roughly July to July, of each city's sports, putting a heavy premium on regular-season won-lost records (from the most recently completed season). Other criteria include: playoff berths, bowl appearances and tournament bids; championships; applicable power ratings; quality of competition; overall fan fervor as measured in part by attendance as percentage of venue capacity; abundance of teams (rewarding quality over quantity); stadium and arena quality; ticket availability and prices; franchise ownership; and marquee appeal of athletes. *SportingNews.com, "Best Sports Cities 2007," August 1, 2007*

- The Omaha* metro area was selected by *Cranium* as one of the "Top 50 Fun Cities" in America. The area ranked #30. Criteria includes: number of sports teams, restaurants, and dance performances; number of toy stores; city budget spent on recreation. *Cranium, November 4, 2003*

- *Golf Digest* ranked 330 metro areas in the U.S. in terms of golf. The Omaha* metro area was ranked #96. Criteria: access to golf; weather; value of golf; and quality of golf. *Golf Digest, "Metro Golf Rankings," August 2005*

Dating/Romance Rankings

- The Omaha* metro area was selected as one of the "Best Cities for Relocating Singles" by Worldwide ERC and Primacy Relocation. The area ranked #68 out of the 100 largest metro areas in the U.S. Areas were selected based on the following criteria: a robust cost-of-living index; adventure and outdoor recreation opportunities; violent crime and property crime rates; percentage of the population that is unmarried (ages 25-34); ratio of single men and single women; affordability of quality higher education, including in-state and out-of-state tuition requirements and rates; number of newcomers to the area; commute times; tax rates; fee and occupancy rates for temporary housing and mini-storage; quality and quantity of collegiate and professional sporting events and fun, fan-friendly venues. *Worldwide ERC and Primacy Relocation, "2007 Best Cities for Relocating Singles," October 25, 2007*

- Sperling's BestPlaces in partnership with AXE Deodorant Bodyspray ranked 80 metro areas and identified "America's Best (and Worst) Cities for Dating." The Omaha* metro area ranked #37 (#1 = best). Criteria: percentage of singles ages 18-24; population density; dating venues per capita. *AXE Deodorant Bodyspray, "America's Best (and Worst) Cities for Dating," May 2004*

Miscellaneous Rankings

- Bellevue was selected as one of the "50 Best Affordable Suburbs" in the U.S. by *Business Week.*. The 50 suburbs were chosen based on dozens of factors including: median home prices; population growth; crime rates; levels of education; unemployment rate; commute times; and affordability. One suburb from each state was selected. *BusinessWeek, "Where the Affordable Suburbs Are," December 13, 2007*

- Sperling's BestPlaces in partnership with Pep Boys ranked 77 metro areas and identified "America's Most Drivable Cities." The Omaha* metro area ranked #47. Criteria: climate; road roughness; urban mobility; gas prices. *Pep Boys, "America's Most Drivable Cities," April 9, 2003*

- A study by Sperling's BestPlaces examined which U.S. metro areas were most affected by high fuel prices in 2006. The Omaha* metro area was ranked #75 out of 80 (#1 = most expensive city for driving). Rankings are based on the average dollars spent on gas per year by two driver households. Criteria: cost of regular-grade gasoline; average miles driven per day; average number of gallons each driver uses and wastes in traffic congestion each day. *Sperling's BestPlaces, www.bestplaces.net, "Pain at the Pump," May 18, 2006*

Bellevue is located within the Omaha-Council Bluffs, NE-IA Metropolitan Statistical Area.

Business Environment

CITY FINANCES

City Government Finances

Component	2004-2005 ($000)	2004-2005 ($ per capita)
Total Revenues	37,825	799
Total Expenditures	40,915	864
Debt Outstanding	48,170	1,018
Cash and Securities	12,283	259

Source: U.S Census Bureau, Government Finances 2004-2005

City Government Revenue by Source

Source	2004-2005 ($000)	2004-2005 ($ per capita)
General Revenue		
From Federal Government	0	0
From State Government	3,264	69
From Local Governments	1,202	25
Taxes		
Property	8,400	177
Sales	7,947	168
Personal Income	0	0
License	0	0
Charges	9,353	198
Liquor Store	0	0
Utility	0	0
Employee Retirement	0	0
Other	7,659	162

Source: U.S Census Bureau, Government Finances 2004-2005

City Government Expenditures by Function

Function	2004-2005 ($000)	2004-2005 ($ per capita)	2004-2005 (%)
General Expenditures			
Airports	0	0	0.0
Corrections	0	0	0.0
Education	0	0	0.0
Fire Protection	3,940	83	9.6
Governmental Administration	17,960	379	43.9
Health	0	0	0.0
Highways	3,466	73	8.5
Hospitals	0	0	0.0
Housing and Community Development	1,081	23	2.6
Interest on General Debt	1,870	40	4.6
Libraries	0	0	0.0
Parking	0	0	0.0
Parks and Recreation	2,978	63	7.3
Police Protection	5,910	125	14.4
Public Welfare	0	0	0.0
Sewerage	2,410	51	5.9
Solid Waste Management	1,300	27	3.2
Liquor Store	0	0	0.0
Utility	0	0	0.0
Employee Retirement	0	0	0.0
Other	0	0	0.0

Source: U.S Census Bureau, Government Finances 2004-2005

Municipal Bond Ratings

Area	Moody's
City	n/a

Source: Mergent Bond Record, January 2008 (unless noted otherwise)

DEMOGRAPHICS

Population Growth

Area	1990 Census	2000 Census	2007 Estimate	2012 Projection	Population Growth (%) 1990-2000	Population Growth (%) 2000-2012
City	43,698	44,382	46,425	48,202	1.6	8.6
MSA[1]	685,797	767,041	827,708	869,447	11.8	13.4
U.S.	248,709,873	281,421,906	301,045,522	314,920,978	13.2	11.9

Note: (1) Metropolitan Statistical Area - see Appendix B for areas included
Source: Claritas, Inc.

Number of Households and Average Household Size

Area	2007 Estimate	2007 Average Household Size
City	18,227	2.55
MSA[1]	322,040	2.57
U.S.	113,668,003	2.65

Note: (1) Metropolitan Statistical Area - see Appendix B for areas included
Source: Claritas, Inc.

Race and Ethnicity

Area	White Alone[2]	Black Alone[2]	Asian Alone[2]	Other Race Alone[2]	Hispanic[3]
City	84.6	5.7	2.2	7.5	8.0
MSA[1]	84.5	7.7	1.8	6.0	7.2
U.S.	73.1	12.4	4.3	10.3	14.9

Note: Figures are 2007 estimates; (1) Metropolitan Statistical Area - see Appendix B for areas included (2) Alone is defined as not being in combination with one or more other races; (3) May be of any race.
Source: Claritas, Inc.

Ancestry

Area	German	Irish[2]	English	American	Italian	Polish	French[3]	Scottish
City	28.6	15.5	10.8	5.2	5.0	5.9	3.2	1.7
MSA[1]	32.3	16.3	9.6	4.2	4.5	4.5	2.8	1.4
U.S.	15.2	10.9	8.7	7.3	5.6	3.2	3.0	1.7

Note: Figures include multiple ancestry (e.g. if a person reported being Irish and Italian, they were included in both columns); (1) Metropolitan Statistical Area - see Appendix A for areas included; (2) Includes Celtic; (3) Includes Alsatian but excludes Basque
Source: Census 2000, Summary File 3

Foreign-Born Population

Area	Percent of Population Born in							
	Any Foreign Country	Europe	Asia	Africa	Oceania[2]	Canada	Mexico	Latin America[3]
City	5.7	1.7	2.0	0.3	0.0	0.2	0.8	0.7
MSA[1]	4.8	0.8	1.3	0.3	0.0	0.1	1.8	0.5
U.S.	11.1	1.7	2.9	0.3	0.1	0.3	3.3	2.5

Note: (1) Metropolitan Statistical Area - see Appendix A for areas included; (2) Includes Australia, New Zealand subregion, Melanesia, Micronesia, Polynesia, and Oceania n.e.c; (3) Includes Central America (excluding Mexico), South America, and the Caribbean.
Source: Census 2000, Summary File 3

Marriage Status

Area	Never Married	Now Married (excluding Separated)	Separated	Widowed	Divorced
City	25.1	57.4	1.5	4.7	11.4
MSA[1]	27.6	54.8	1.4	5.7	10.5
U.S.	27.1	54.4	2.2	6.6	9.7

Note: Figures are percentages and cover the population 15 years of age and older; (1) Metropolitan Statistical Area - see Appendix A for areas included
Source: Census 2000, Summary File 3

Age Distribution

Area	Percent of Population						
	Under Age 5	Age 5 to 17	Age 18 to 34	Age 35 to 49	Age 50 to 64	Age 65 to 79	80 Years and Over
City	7.0	20.2	24.9	23.2	15.3	7.8	1.5
MSA[1]	7.3	19.8	24.6	23.7	13.9	7.9	2.8
U.S.	6.8	18.9	23.7	23.5	14.8	9.2	3.2

Note: (1) Metropolitan Statistical Area - see Appendix A for areas included
Source: Census 2000, Summary File 3

Male/Female Ratio

Area	Males	Females	Males per 100 Females
City	23,072	23,353	98.8
MSA[1]	408,561	419,147	97.5
U.S.	148,320,305	152,725,217	97.1

Note: Figures are 2007 estimates; (1) Metropolitan Statistical Area - see Appendix B for areas included
Source: Claritas, Inc.

Religion

Area	Catholic	Southern Baptist	United Meth-odist	ELCA[1]	LDS[2]	Presby-terian Church USA	Jewish Est.	Muslim Est.
County	17.2	2.6	2.8	4.2	1.2	1.5	0.0	0.0
U.S.	22.0	7.1	3.7	1.8	1.5	1.1	2.2	0.6

Note: Figures are the number of adherents as a percentage of the total population; Adherents are defined as all members, including full members, their children and the estimated number of other participants who are not considered members (e.g. the baptized, those not confirmed, those regularly attending services, etc.); (1) Evangelical Lutheran Church in America; (2) The Church of Jesus Christ of Latter Day Saints
Source: Reprinted with permission from Religious Congregations and Membership in the United States 2000 (Nashville, Glenmary Research Center, 2002) Copyright Association of Statisticians of American Religious Bodies. All rights reserved.

ECONOMY

Gross Metropolitan Product

Area	2002	2003	2004	2005	2005 Rank[2]
MSA[1]	28.5	30.5	31.7	33.5	60

Note: Figures are in billions of dollars; (1) Omaha-Council Bluffs, NE-IA Metropolitan Statistical Area - see Appendix A for areas included; (2) Rank ranges from 1 to 361
Source: The U.S. Conference of Mayors, "U.S. Metro Economies: GMP - The Engines of America's Growth," January 2007

Economic Growth

Area	1995 GMP	2005 GMP	Average Annual Growth Rate	Growth Rate Rank[2]
MSA[1]	21.3	33.5	4.7	259

Note: Figures are in billions of dollars; GMP = Gross Metropolitan Product; (1) Omaha-Council Bluffs, NE-IA Metropolitan Statistical Area - see Appendix A for areas included; (2) Rank ranges from 1 to 361
Source: The U.S. Conference of Mayors, "U.S. Metro Economies: GMP - The Engines of America's Growth," January 2007

INCOME

Per Capita/Median/Average Income

Area	Per Capita ($)	Median Household ($)	Average Household ($)
City	25,266	54,916	64,155
MSA[1]	26,544	53,433	67,682
U.S.	25,495	49,280	66,670

Note: Figures are 2007 estimates; (1) Metropolitan Statistical Area - see Appendix B for areas included
Source: Claritas, Inc.

Household Income Distribution

Area	Percent of Households Earning							
	Under $15,000	$15,000 -24,999	$25,000 -34,999	$35,000 -49,999	$50,000 -74,999	$75,000 -99,000	$100,000 -149,999	$150,000 and up
City	6.7	8.3	11.8	17.9	25.7	14.5	11.8	3.3
MSA[1]	9.6	9.8	11.3	16.1	21.7	13.6	12.3	5.6
U.S.	13.1	10.9	11.2	15.6	19.5	11.9	11.3	6.6

Note: Figures are 2007 estimates; (1) Metropolitan Statistical Area - see Appendix B for areas included
Source: Claritas, Inc.

Poverty Rates by Age

Area	All Ages	Under 5 Years Old	5 to 17 Years Old	18 to 64 Years Old	65 Years and Over
City	5.9	0.6	1.7	3.2	0.3
MSA[1]	8.4	0.9	2.2	4.7	0.7
U.S.	12.4	1.2	3.0	6.9	1.2

Note: Figures are percent of population with income in 1999 below poverty level and only include population for whom poverty status is determined; (1) Metropolitan Statistical Area - see Appendix A for areas included
Source: Census 2000, Summary File 3

Personal Bankruptcy Filing Rate

Area	2004	2005	2006
Sarpy County	5.45	7.27	2.48
U.S.	5.31	6.82	2.00

Note: Numbers are per 1,000 population and include Chapter 7 and Chapter 13 filings
Source: Federal Deposit Insurance Corporation (FDIC), Regional Economic Conditions (RECON), 8/23/2007

EMPLOYMENT

Labor Force and Employment

Area	Civilian Labor Force			Workers Employed		
	Dec. 2006	Dec. 2007	% Chg.	Dec. 2006	Dec. 2007	% Chg.
City	25,640	25,745	0.4	24,885	25,045	0.6
MSA[1]	447,220	449,040	0.4	432,928	435,011	0.5
U.S.	152,571,000	153,705,000	0.7	146,081,000	146,334,000	0.2

Note: Data is not seasonally adjusted and covers workers 16 years of age and older;
(1) Metropolitan Statistical Area - see Appendix B for areas included
Source: Bureau of Labor Statistics, http://stats.bls.gov

Unemployment Rate

Area	2007											
	Jan.	Feb.	Mar.	Apr.	May	Jun.	Jul.	Aug.	Sep.	Oct.	Nov.	Dec.
City	4.0	3.7	3.1	2.7	2.9	3.3	3.7	3.3	3.1	3.0	3.0	2.7
MSA[1]	4.1	3.7	3.3	3.1	3.3	3.6	3.7	3.3	3.1	3.1	3.3	3.1
U.S.	5.0	4.9	4.5	4.3	4.3	4.7	4.9	4.6	4.5	4.4	4.5	4.8

Note: Data is not seasonally adjusted and covers workers 16 years of age and older; All figures are percentages; (1) Metropolitan Statistical Area - see Appendix B for areas included
Source: Bureau of Labor Statistics, http://stats.bls.gov

Employment by Occupation

Occupation Classification	City (%)	MSA[1] (%)	U.S. (%)
Sales and Office	30.7	30.1	26.7
Professional and Related	19.6	20.2	20.2
Service	15.2	13.7	14.9
Production, Transportation, and Material Moving	11.6	12.3	14.6
Management, Business, and Financial	12.8	14.8	13.5
Construction, Extraction, and Maintenance	9.8	8.6	9.4
Farming, Forestry, and Fishing	0.3	0.2	0.7

Note: Figures cover employed civilians 16 years of age and older;
(1) Metropolitan Statistical Area - see Appendix A for areas included
Source: Census 2000, Summary File 3

Employment by Industry

Sector	MSA[1] Number of Employees	MSA[1] Percent of Total	U.S. Percent of Total
Government	63,100	13.4	16.3
Education and Health Services	67,700	14.4	13.4
Professional and Business Services	64,700	13.7	13.1
Retail Trade	55,100	11.7	11.6
Manufacturing	33,800	7.2	9.9
Leisure and Hospitality	44,300	9.4	9.6
Financial Activities	39,300	8.3	5.9
Construction	n/a	n/a	5.3
Wholesale Trade	18,200	3.9	4.4
Other Services	16,400	3.5	3.9
Transportation and Utilities	30,400	6.5	3.7
Information	12,600	2.7	2.2
Natural Resources and Mining	n/a	n/a	0.5

Note: Figures cover non-farm employment as of December 2007 and are not seasonally adjusted; (1) Metropolitan Statistical Area - see Appendix B for areas included; n/a not available
Source: Bureau of Labor Statistics, http://stats.bls.gov

Average Wages

Occupation	$/Hr.	Occupation	$/Hr.
Accountants and Auditors	29.32	Maids and Housekeeping Cleaners	8.96
Automotive Mechanics	17.96	Maintenance and Repair Workers	15.89
Bookkeepers	14.94	Marketing Managers	48.23
Carpenters	16.38	Nuclear Medicine Technologists	28.75
Cashiers	8.46	Nurses, Licensed Practical	17.96
Clerks, General Office	12.25	Nurses, Registered	26.45
Clerks, Receptionists/Information	11.77	Nursing Aides/Orderlies/Attendants	11.61
Clerks, Shipping/Receiving	14.19	Packers and Packagers, Hand	9.33
Computer Programmers	32.69	Physical Therapists	30.10
Computer Support Specialists	19.01	Postal Service Mail Carriers	21.58
Computer Systems Analysts	34.46	Real Estate Brokers	22.06
Cooks, Restaurant	9.79	Retail Salespersons	12.39
Dentists	n/a	Sales Reps., Exc. Tech./Scientific	27.52
Electrical Engineers	36.17	Sales Reps., Tech./Scientific	35.47
Electricians	21.28	Secretaries, Exc. Legal/Med./Exec.	13.73
Financial Managers	48.80	Security Guards	13.01
First-Line Supervisors/Mgrs., Sales	19.83	Surgeons	67.93
Food Preparation Workers	8.75	Teacher Assistants	9.50
General and Operations Managers	47.85	Teachers, Elementary School	19.60
Hairdressers/Cosmetologists	12.38	Teachers, Secondary School	20.10
Internists	78.53	Telemarketers	10.82
Janitors and Cleaners	10.26	Truck Drivers, Heavy/Tractor-Trailer	19.07
Landscaping/Groundskeeping Workers	11.55	Truck Drivers, Light/Delivery Svcs.	13.73
Lawyers	49.03	Waiters and Waitresses	7.54

Note: Wage data covers the Omaha-Council Bluffs, NE-IA Metropolitan Statistical Area - see Appendix B for areas included. Hourly wages for elementary/secondary school teachers and teacher assistants were calculated by the editors from annual wage data assuming a 40 hour work week; n/a not available.
Source: Bureau of Labor Statistics, May 2007 Metro Area Occupational Employment and Wage Estimates

RESIDENTIAL REAL ESTATE

Building Permits

Area	Single-Family 2006	Single-Family 2007p	Single-Family Pct. Chg.	Multi-Family 2006	Multi-Family 2007p	Multi-Family Pct. Chg.	Total 2006	Total 2007p	Total Pct. Chg.
City	317	354	11.7	20	248	1,140.0	337	602	78.6
U.S.	1,378,200	973,300	-29.4	460,700	407,200	-11.6	1,838,900	1,380,500	-24.9

Note: (p) preliminary; figures cover and represent new, privately-owned housing units authorized (unadjusted data); All permit data are based on estimates with imputation; U.S. figures are based on the new 20,000-place series.
Source: U.S. Census Bureau, Manufacturing, Mining, and Construction Statistics

Homeownership and Housing Vacancies

Area	Homeownership Rate[2] (%)			Rental Vacancy Rate[3] (%)			Homeowner Vacancy Rate[4] (%)		
	2005	2006	2007	2005	2006	2007	2005	2006	2007
MSA[1]	69.7	68.1	67.9	8.5	11.3	11.9	1.5	2.8	2.5
U.S.	68.9	68.8	68.1	9.8	9.8	9.7	1.9	2.4	2.7

Note: (1) Metropolitan Statistical Area - see Appendix B for areas included; (2) The proportion of households that are owners; (3) The proportion of the rental inventory that is vacant for rent; (4) The proportion of the homeowner inventory that is vacant for sale; n/a not available
Source: U.S. Census Bureau, Housing Vacancies and Homeownership Annual Statistics: 2007

TAXES

State Corporate Income Tax Rates

State	Rates and Tax Brackets
Nebraska	5.58% > $0; 7.81% > 50K

Note: Tax rates as of January 1, 2008
Source: Tax Foundation, www.taxfoundation.org

State Individual Income Tax Rates

State	Federal Deductibility	Marginal Rates (%)	Standard Deduction ($)		Personal Exemptions ($)[1]	
			Single	Joint	Single	Dependents
Nebraska	No	2.56 - 6.84 (x)(y)	5,350 (r)	10,700 (r)	106 (c)(n)	106 (c)(n)

Note: Tax rates as of January 1, 2008; Local- and county-level taxes are not included; n/a not applicable; (1) Married joint filers generally receive double the single exemption; (c) Tax Credit; (n) The $106 personal exemption credit no longer phases out for filers with higher adjusted gross incomes; (r) State adjusts its bracket levels for inflation at the end of each year before printing tax forms; (x) If adjusted gross income is $150,500 or more ($75,250 if married filing separate), Nebraska itemized deductions are reduced and marginal tax rates are phased out; (y) Brackets are not double for married taxpayers.
Source: Tax Foundation, www.taxfoundation.org

Various State and Local Tax Rates

State and Local Sales and Use (%)	State Sales and Use (%)	Gasoline[1,2] ($/gal.)	Cigarette ($/pack)	Spirits ($/gal.)	Table Wine ($/gal.)	Beer ($/gal.)
7.0	5.5	0.239	0.64	3.75	0.95	0.31

Note: Tax rates as of January 1, 2008; (1) In addition to the 18.4 cpg Federal gasoline tax; (2) Rates may include additional state sales taxes, environmental protection and storage fees/taxes, and local taxes. When necessary, the volume-weighted average of all local taxes is used to approximate the typical statewide rate including local tax
Source: Tax Foundation, www.taxfoundation.org; Original research

State Tax Burdens

Area	Combined State and Local Tax Burden		Combined Federal, State and Local Tax Burden	
	Percent	Rank	Percent	Rank
Nebraska	11.9	9	31.8	22
U.S. Average	11.0	-	32.7	-

Note: Figures cover 2007 and measure taxes as a percentage of income
Source: Tax Foundation, www.taxfoundation.org

State Business Tax Climate Index Rankings

State	Overall Rank	Corporate Tax Index Rank	Individual Income Tax Index Rank	Sales Tax Index Rank	Unemployment Insurance Tax Index Rank	Property Tax Index Rank
Nebraska	43	33	33	46	17	42

Note: Rankings range from 1 to 50 where 1 is best. Rankings do not average across to Overall Rank. States without a given tax are given a ranking of 1.
Source: Tax Foundation, State Business Tax Climate Index 2008

TRANSPORTATION

Means of Transportation to Work

Area	Car/Truck/Van		Public Transportation			Bicycle	Walked	Other Means	Worked at Home
	Drove Alone	Car-pooled	Bus	Subway	Railroad				
City	85.1	10.7	0.2	0.0	0.0	0.1	1.1	0.4	2.4
MSA[1]	82.9	10.5	1.1	0.0	0.0	0.1	1.9	0.6	2.9
U.S.	75.7	12.2	2.5	1.5	0.5	0.4	2.9	1.0	3.3

Note: Figures are percentages and cover workers 16 years of age and older;
(1) Metropolitan Statistical Area - see Appendix A for areas included
Source: Census 2000, Summary File 3

Travel Time to Work

Area	Less Than 15 Minutes	15 to 29 Minutes	30 to 44 Minutes	45 to 59 Minutes	60 Minutes or More
City	31.7	50.2	14.1	2.0	2.0
MSA[1]	33.9	48.4	12.9	2.2	2.5
U.S.	29.4	36.1	19.1	7.4	8.0

Note: Figures are percentages and include workers 16 years old and over; (1) Metropolitan Statistical Area - see Appendix A for areas included
Source: Census 2000, Summary File 3

Travel Time Index

Area	1982	1995	2004	2005
Urban Area[1]	1.04	1.11	1.16	1.16
Average[2]	1.11	1.22	1.29	1.30

Note: Travel Time Index - The ratio of travel time in the peak period to the travel time at free-flow conditions. A value of 1.35 indicates a 20-minute free-flow trip takes 27 minutes in the peak. Free-flow speeds (60 mph on freeways and 35 mph on principal arterials) are used as the comparison threshold; (1) Covers the Omaha, NE-IA urban area; (2) average of 85 urban areas
Source: Texas Transportation Institute, The 2007 Urban Mobility Report, September 2007

Living Environment

COST OF LIVING

Cost of Living Index

Composite Index	Groceries	Housing	Utilities	Trans-portation	Health Care	Misc. Goods/ Services
88.9	87.2	79.3	88.3	101.0	94.7	93.2

Note: U.S. = 100; Figures cover the Omaha NE urban area.
Source: The Council for Community and Economic Research (formerly ACCRA), Cost of Living Index, 2007

Grocery Prices

Area[1]	T-Bone Steak ($/pound)	Frying Chicken ($/pound)	Whole Milk ($/half gal.)	Eggs ($/dozen)	Orange Juice ($/64 oz.)	Coffee ($/11.5 oz.)
City[2]	8.33	1.04	1.84	1.17	2.96	3.07
Avg.	8.93	1.12	2.13	1.52	3.26	3.31
Min.	5.88	0.71	1.33	0.83	2.30	2.20
Max.	12.80	2.07	3.43	3.54	5.79	6.20

Note: (1) Values for the local area are compared with the average, minimum and maximum values for all 331 areas in the Cost of Living Index report; (2) Figures cover the Omaha NE urban area; **T-Bone Steak** *(price per pound);* **Frying Chicken** *(price per pound, whole fryer);* **Whole Milk** *(half gallon carton);* **Eggs** *(price per dozen, Grade A, large);* **Orange Juice** *(64 oz. Tropicana or Florida Natural);* **Coffee** *(11.5 oz. can, vacuum-packed, Maxwell House, Hills Bros, or Folgers).*
Source: The Council for Community and Economic Research (formerly ACCRA), Cost of Living Index, 2007

Housing and Utility Costs

Area[1]	New Home Price ($)	Apartment Rent ($/month)	All Electric ($/month)	Part Electric ($/month)	Other Energy ($/month)	Telephone ($/month)
City[2]	240,408	690	-	59.92	78.98	24.31
Avg.	309,605	782	146.13	78.67	90.16	26.14
Min.	189,877	n/a	82.03	37.41	33.15	17.08
Max.	1,202,800	3,481	271.14	150.60	257.67	37.45

Note: (1) Values for the local area are compared with the average, minimum and maximum values for all 331 areas in the Cost of Living Index report; (2) Figures cover the Omaha NE urban area; **New Home Price** *(2,400 sf living area, 8,000 sf lot, in urban area with full utilities);* **Apartment Rent** *(950 sf 2 bedroom/1.5 or 2 bath, unfurnished, excluding all utilities except water);* **All Electric** *(average monthly cost for an all-electric home);* **Part Electric** *(average monthly cost for a part-electric home);* **Other Energy** *(average monthly cost for natural gas, fuel oil, coal, wood, and any other forms of energy except electricity);* **Telephone** *(price includes basic monthly rate for a private residential line plus additional local usage charges incurred by a family of four).*
Source: The Council for Community and Economic Research (formerly ACCRA), Cost of Living Index, 2007

Health Care, Transportation, and Other Costs

Area[1]	Doctor ($/visit)	Dentist ($/visit)	Optometrist ($/visit)	Gasoline ($/gallon)	Beauty Salon ($/visit)	Men's Shirt ($)
City[2]	87.33	61.27	66.73	2.70	23.89	23.13
Avg.	79.48	71.93	79.55	2.64	29.52	25.77
Min.	52.08	44.80	43.95	2.19	15.58	16.19
Max.	148.44	126.27	158.83	3.48	60.62	48.53

Note: (1) Values for the local area are compared with the average, minimum and maximum values for all 331 areas in the Cost of Living Index report; (2) Figures cover the Omaha NE urban area; **Doctor** *(general practitioners routine exam of an established patient);* **Dentist** *(adult teeth cleaning and periodic oral examination);* **Optometrist** *(full vision eye exam for established adult patient);* **Gasoline** *(one gallon regular unleaded, national brand, including all taxes, cash price at self-service pump if available);* **Beauty Salon** *(woman's shampoo, trim, and blow-dry);* **Men's Shirt** *(cotton/polyester dress shirt, pinpoint weave, long sleeves).*
Source: The Council for Community and Economic Research (formerly ACCRA), Cost of Living Index, 2007

HOUSING

House Price Index (HPI)

Area	National Ranking[2]	Quarterly Change (%)	One-Year Change (%)	Five-Year Change (%)
MSA[1]	160	0.53	1.35	17.68
U.S.[3]	-	0.10	0.84	41.37

Note: The HPI is a weighted repeat sales index. It measures average price changes in repeat sales or refinancings on the same properties. This information is obtained by reviewing repeat mortgage transactions on single-family properties whose mortgages have been purchased or securitized by Fannie Mae or Freddie Mac in January 1975; (1) Metropolitan Statistical Area - see Appendix B for areas included; (2) Rankings are based on annual percentage change for all metro areas containing at least 15,000 transactions over the last 10 years and ranges from 1 to 291; (3) figures based on a weighted average of Census Division estimates; all figures are for the period ending December 31, 2007
Source: Office of Federal Housing Enterprise Oversight, House Price Index, February 26, 2008

House Price Valuations

Area	Q1 2000	Q1 2001	Q1 2002	Q1 2003	Q1 2004	Q1 2005	Q1 2006	Q1 2007	Q1 2008
MSA[1]	-3.5	-5.0	-7.0	-6.0	-7.6	-6.8	-8.5	-11.5	-19.2

Note: Figures show the percentage of over- or under-valuation of single family homes relative to statistically normal house values (e.g. a value of 23.6 indicates that house values are 23.6% overvalued). Statistically normal house values are based on house prices, interest rates, household incomes, population densities, and any historical premiums or discounts metropolitan areas have exhibited over time; (1) Figures cover the Metropolitan Statistical Area - see Appendix B for areas included
Source: Global Insight/National City Corporation, House Prices in America, May 2008

Median Home Prices

Area	2005	2006	2007[r]	Percent Change 2006 to 2007
MSA[1]	136.2	138.4	138.0	-0.3
U.S. Average	219.0	221.9	217.9	-1.8

Note: Figures are median sales prices of existing single-family homes in thousands of dollars; (r) revised; n/a not available; (1) Metropolitan Statistical Area - see Appendix B for areas included
Source: National Association of Realtors, Metropolitan Area Prices, 1st Quarter 2008

Housing: Year Structure Built

Area	1990 -2000	1980 -1989	1970 -1979	1960 -1969	1950 -1959	1940 -1949	Before 1940	Median Year
City	9.3	13.2	30.2	23.6	13.6	4.8	5.2	1971
MSA[1]	15.8	11.8	19.5	15.8	11.9	6.1	19.1	1968
U.S.	17.0	15.8	18.5	13.7	12.7	7.3	15.0	1971

Note: Figures are percentages; (1) Metropolitan Statistical Area - see Appendix A for areas included
Source: Census 2000, Summary File 3

HEALTH

Health Risk Data

Category	Area[1] (%)	U.S. (%)
Adults who have been told they have high blood pressure[3]	23.0	25.5
Adults who have been told they have high blood cholesterol[3]	34.1	35.6
Adults who have been told they have diabetes[2]	8.2	7.5
Adults who have been told they have arthritis[3]	24.8	27.0
Adults who have been told they currently have asthma	8.9	8.5
Adults who are current smokers	20.4	20.1
Adults who are heavy drinkers[4]	3.5	4.9
Adults who are overweight (BMI 25.0 - 29.9)	36.9	36.5
Adults who are obese (BMI 30.0 - 99.8)	27.0	25.1

Note: Data as of 2006 unless otherwise noted; (1) Figures cover the Metropolitan Statistical Area - see Appendix B for areas included; (2) Figures do not include pregnancy-related diabetes, pre-diabetes or borderline diabetes; (3) 2005 data; (4) Heavy drinkers are classified as adult men having more than two drinks per day or adult women having more than one drink per day
Source: Centers for Disease Control and Prevention, Behaviorial Risk Factor Surveillance System, SMART: Selected Metropolitan/Micropolitan Area Risk Trends, 2005, 2006

Mortality Rates for the Top 10 Causes of Death in the U.S.

ICD-10[a] Sub-Chapter	ICD-10[a] Code	Age-Adjusted Mortality Rate[1] per 100,000 population	
		County[2]	U.S.
Malignant neoplasms	C00-C97	171.4	186.5
Ischaemic heart diseases	I20-I25	111.8	152.3
Other forms of heart disease	I30-I51	70.8	51.5
Cerebrovascular diseases	I60-I69	55.8	50.0
Chronic lower respiratory diseases	J40-J47	50.9	42.6
Diabetes mellitus	E10-E14	14.6	24.8
Other degenerative diseases of the nervous system	G30-G31	18.0	22.6
Other external causes of accidental injury	W00-X59	24.9	21.4
Influenza and pneumonia	J10-J18	33.6	20.7
Hypertensive diseases	I10-I13	14.5	18.2

Note: (a) ICD-10 = International Classification of Diseases 10th Revision; (1) Mortality rates are a three year average covering 2003-2005; (2) Figures cover Sarpy County
Source: Centers for Disease Control and Prevention, National Center for Health Statistics. Compressed Mortality File 1999-2004. CDC WONDER On-line Database, compiled from Compressed Mortality File 1999-2005 Series 20 No. 2K, 2008.

Mortality Rates for Selected Causes of Death

ICD-10[a] Sub-Chapter	ICD-10[a] Code	Age-Adjusted Mortality Rate[1] per 100,000 population	
		County[2]	U.S.
Assault	X85-Y09	*1.4	5.9
Human immunodeficiency virus (HIV) disease	B20-B24	*0.2	4.5
Intentional self-harm	X60-X84	8.3	10.8
Malnutrition	E40-E46	*1.1	1.0
Obesity and other hyperalimentation	E65-E68	*0.2	1.4
Organic, including symptomatic, mental disorders	F01-F09	17.0	16.8
Transport accidents	V01-V99	7.5	16.1
Viral hepatitis	B15-B19	*0.2	1.8

Note: (a) ICD-10 = International Classification of Diseases 10th Revision; (1) Mortality rates are a three year average covering 2003-2005; (2) Figures cover Sarpy County; (*) Unreliable data as per CDC
Source: Centers for Disease Control and Prevention, National Center for Health Statistics. Compressed Mortality File 1999-2004. CDC WONDER On-line Database, compiled from Compressed Mortality File 1999-2005 Series 20 No. 2K, 2008.

Distribution of Physicians[1]

Area	Total	Family/ General Practice	Specialties	
			Medical	Surgical
Sarpy County (number)	136	64	43	31
Sarpy County (rate per 10,000 pop.)	9.8	4.6	3.1	2.2
U.S. (rate per 10,000 pop.)	17.7	4.6	6.9	4.3

Note: Data as of 2005; (1) Includes all non-federal, patient-care, office-based MDs
Source: Area Resource File (ARF). June 2007. U.S. Department of Health and Human Services, Health Resources and Services Administration, Bureau of Health Professions, Rockville, MD.

Hospitals

There were no hospitals listed within the city limits.
AHA Guide to the Healthcare Field 2008

EDUCATION

Public School District Statistics

District Name	Schls	Pupils	Pupil/ Teacher Ratio	Minority Pupils[1] (%)	Free Lunch Eligible[2] (%)	IEP[3] (%)
Bellevue Public Schools	19	9,227	15.3	21.7	13.6	14.0
Papillion-La Vista Public Schools	18	8,743	15.3	12.1	10.3	13.1

Note: Table includes regular local school districts with 2,000 or more students; (1) Percentage of students that are not white, non-Hispanic; (2) Percentage of students that are eligible for the free lunch program; (3) Percentage of students that have an Individualized Education Program.
Source: U.S. Department of Education, National Center for Education Statistics, Common Core of Data, Local Education Agency (School District) Universe Survey: School Year 2005-2006; U.S. Department of Education, National Center for Education Statistics, Common Core of Data, Public Elementary/Secondary School Universe Survey: School Year 2005-2006

Highest Level of Education

Area	Less than H.S.	H.S. Diploma	Some College, No Deg.	Associate Degree	Bachelors Degree	Masters Degree	Profess. School Degree	Doctorate Degree
City	8.2	27.5	30.1	8.4	17.4	6.7	1.2	0.5
MSA[1]	11.6	28.4	25.0	6.9	19.6	5.8	2.0	0.8
U.S.	19.4	28.4	21.2	6.4	15.7	5.9	2.0	1.0

Note: Figures are 2007 estimated percentages and cover persons age 25 and over; (1) Metropolitan Statistical Area - see Appendix B for areas included
Source: Claritas, Inc.

Educational Attainment by Race

Area	High School Graduate (%)					Bachelor's Degree (%)				
	Total	White	Black	Asian	Hisp.[2]	Total	White	Black	Asian	Hisp.[2]
City	91.5	92.4	90.7	82.6	76.5	25.2	25.3	26.8	36.6	8.8
MSA[1]	88.0	89.9	78.2	85.8	53.7	28.0	29.3	13.5	51.1	11.6
U.S.	80.4	83.6	72.3	80.4	52.4	24.4	26.1	14.3	44.1	10.4

Note: Figures shown cover persons 25 years old and over; (1) Metropolitan Statistical Area - see Appendix A for areas included; (2) people of Hispanic origin can be of any race
Source: Census 2000, Summary File 3

School Enrollment by Type

Area	Grades KG to 8				Grades 9 to 12			
	Public		Private		Public		Private	
	Enrollment	%	Enrollment	%	Enrollment	%	Enrollment	%
City	5,032	84.2	943	15.8	2,744	91.7	247	8.3
MSA[1]	82,606	83.0	16,937	17.0	37,494	86.1	6,066	13.9
U.S.	33,526,011	88.7	4,285,121	11.3	14,848,628	90.6	1,532,323	9.4

Note: Figures shown cover persons 3 years old and over; (1) Metropolitan Statistical Area - see Appendix A for areas included
Source: Census 2000, Summary File 3

School Enrollment by Race

Area	Grades KG to 8 (%)				Grades 9 to 12 (%)			
	White	Black	Asian	Hisp.[1]	White	Black	Asian	Hisp.[1]
City	84.0	6.2	0.5	8.7	82.5	8.4	2.1	8.7
MSA[2]	80.5	11.0	1.2	7.2	82.0	10.7	1.4	5.6
U.S.	68.5	15.5	3.3	16.8	68.8	15.5	3.8	15.7

Note: Figures shown cover persons 3 years old and over; (1) people of Hispanic origin can be of any race; (2) Metropolitan Statistical Area - see Appendix A for areas included
Source: Census 2000, Summary File 3

Average Salaries of Public School Classroom Teachers

District	2005-06		2006-07		Percent Change 2005-06 to 2006-07
	Dollars	Rank[1]	Dollars	Rank[1]	
Nebraska	40,382	43	42,044	43	4.12
U.S. Average	49,026	-	50,816	-	3.65

Note: (1) State rank ranges from 1 to 51.
Source: National Education Association, Rankings & Estimates: Rankings of the States 2006 and Estimates of School Statistics 2007, December 2007

Higher Education

Four-Year Colleges			Two-Year Colleges			Medical Schools[1]	Law Schools[2]	Voc/ Tech[3]
Public	Private Non-profit	Private For-profit	Public	Private Non-profit	Private For-profit			
0	1	0	0	0	0	0	0	0

Note: Figures cover institutions located within the city limits; (1) includes schools accredited by the Liaison Committee on Medical Education and the American Osteopathic Association; (2) includes American Bar Association-accredited law schools; (3) includes all schools with programs that are less than 2 years.
Source: National Center for Education Statistics, The Integrated Postsecondary Education System (IPEDS) Peer Analysis System, 2007; www.usnews.com, Law and Medical School Directories, 2009

PRESIDENTIAL ELECTION

2004 Presidential Election Results

Area	Bush	Kerry	Nader	Other
Sarpy County	68.9	29.9	0.6	0.7
U.S.	50.7	48.3	0.4	0.6

Note: Results are percentages and may not add to 100% due to rounding
Source: Dave Leip's Atlas of U.S. Presidential Elections, www.uselectionatlas.org

EMPLOYERS

Major Employers

Company Name	Industry	Type of Site
Air Combat Command	National security	Branch
Alabama Processors Inc	Meat packing plants	Single
Alegent Hlth - Immnuel Med Ctr	General medical and surgical hospitals	Headquarters
City of Omaha	Executive offices	Headquarters
Creighton University	Colleges and universities	Headquarters
First Data	Data processing and preparation	Headquarters
Kiewit Offshore Services Ltd	Fabricated structural metal	Single
Lockheed Martin Intgrt Sys Sol	Search and navigation equipment	Branch
Mutual of Omaha	Life insurance	Headquarters
Nebraska Furniture Mart Inc	Furniture stores	Headquarters
OPPD	Electric services	Headquarters
Purchasing Department	Colleges and universities	Branch
Terrys Village	Hobby, toy, and game shops	Headquarters
US Dept of the Air Force	National security	Branch
Valmont Industries Inc	Farm machinery and equipment	Single
Werner Enterprises Inc	Local trucking, without storage	Single

Note: Companies shown are located within the Omaha metropolitan area; nec = not elsewhere classified.
Source: www.zapdata.com, May 2008

PUBLIC SAFETY

Crime Rate

Area	All Crimes	Violent Crimes				Property Crimes		
		Murder	Forcible Rape	Robbery	Aggrav. Assault	Burglary	Larceny -Theft	Motor Vehicle Theft
City	2,737.9	0.0	21.0	42.0	77.7	292.1	2,078.1	226.9
Metro[1]	4,495.5	4.8	37.6	118.0	255.9	642.9	2,880.5	555.9
U.S.	3,808.1	5.7	30.9	149.4	287.5	729.4	2,206.8	398.4

Note: Figures are crimes per 100,000 population; (1) Metropolitan Statistical Area - see Appendix B for areas included
Source: FBI Uniform Crime Reports, 2006

Hate Crimes

Area	Number of Quarters Reported	Bias Motivation				
		Race	Religion	Sexual Orientation	Ethnicity	Disability
City	4	0	0	0	0	0

Source: Federal Bureau of Investigation, Hate Crime Statistics 2006

RECREATION

Culture

Dance[1]	Theatre[1]	Instrumental Music[1]	Vocal Music[1]	Series/ Festivals	Museums	Zoos and Aquariums[2]
0	1	0	0	0	1	0

Note: (1) Number of professional perfoming groups; (2) AZA-accredited
Source: The Grey House Performing Arts Directory, 2007; Official Museum Directory, 2008; Association of Zoos & Aquariums, AZA Member Zoos & Aquariums, June 2008

Professional Sports Teams

Team Name	League
No teams are located in the metro area	

Source: Original research

MEDIA

Newspapers

Name	News Focus	Frequency	Circulation
Bellevue Leader	Community	Weekly	25,650

Note: Includes newspapers with offices located in the city
Source: MediaContactsPro, March 2008

Television Stations

Name	Ch.	Network(s)	Type	Ownership
KMTV	3	CBS	Commercial	Emmis Communications Corporation
WOWT	6	NBC	Commercial	Chronicle Broadcasting Inc.
KETV	7	ABC	Commercial	Hearst-Argyle Broadcasting
KXVO	15	WBN	Commercial	Mitts Telecasting Co.
KPTM	42	Fox	Commercial	Pappas Telecasting Companies

Note: Stations included cover the Omaha DMA (Designated Market Area)
BurrellesLuce, MediaContacts Online, January 2007

Major AM Radio Stations

Call Letters	Freq. (kHz)	Station Type	Target Audience	Station Format	Music Format
KOMJ	590	Commercial	General	Music/News	Adult Standards
KCRO	660	Commercial	General/Religious	Music/Talk	Christian
KTIC	840	Commercial	General	Music/News/Sports	Country
KJSK	900	Commercial	General	Educational/News/Sports	n/a
KYFR	920	Non-Comm	General/Religious	Educational/Talk	n/a
KMA	960	Commercial	General	Sports/Talk	n/a
KOAK	1080	n/a	General	Music/News/Sports	n/a
KFAB	1110	Commercial	General	Talk	n/a
KOIL	1180	Commercial	Children/General	Educational/Music	Country
KJAN	1220	Commercial	General	Music/Talk	Soft Rock
KTNC	1230	n/a	General	Music	n/a
KKAR	1290	Commercial	General	News/Talk	n/a
KHUB	1340	n/a	General	News/Sports/Talk	n/a
KBBX	1420	n/a	Hispanic	Music	n/a
KOSR	1490	Commercial	General/Men	Sports	n/a
KTTT	1510	n/a	General	Music/News/Sports	Latin
KDSN	1530	Commercial	General	Music/Talk	Contemp. Country
KLNG	1560	Commercial	General/Religious	News/Talk	n/a
KNCY	1600	Commercial	General	Educational/Music/News	Country
KOZN	1620	Commercial	General	Sports/Talk	n/a

Note: Stations included cover the Omaha DMA (Designated Market Area); n/a not available
Source: BurrellesLuce, MediaContacts Online, January 2007

Major FM Radio Stations

Call Letters	Freq. (mHz)	Station Type	Target Audience	Station Format	Music Format
KIWR	89.7	College	General	Educational/Music/News	Modern Rock
KVNO	90.7	Public	General	News/Talk	n/a
KDCV	91.1	College	General	Educational/Sports/Talk	Album Rock
KIOS	91.5	Public	General	Educational/News/Talk	n/a
KEZO	92.3	Commercial	General	Music	Modern Rock
KKOT	93.5	Commercial	General	Music/News	International
KCSI	95.3	n/a	General	Music/News/Sports	n/a
KSWI	95.7	n/a	General	Music	n/a
KEFM	96.1	Commercial	General	Music	Adult Contemp.
KSOM	96.5	n/a	General	Music/News	n/a
KQCH	97.7	Commercial	General	Music/News/Sports/Talk	Urban Contemp.
KQKQ	98.5	Commercial	General	Music	Top 40
KKBZ	99.3	Commercial	General	Music	Adult Contemp.
KGOR	99.9	n/a	General	Music	n/a
KZEN	100.3	n/a	General	Music	n/a
KGBI	100.7	College	General/Religious	Music/News	Christian
KLIR	101.1	Commercial	General	Music/News	Adult Contemp.
KLTQ	101.9	Commercial	General	Music/News/Talk	Soft Rock
KXKT	103.7	n/a	General	Music	n/a
KSRZ	104.5	Commercial	General/Women	Music	Adult Contemp.
KNOD	105.3	Commercial	General	Music/News	Oldies
KFMT	105.5	n/a	General	Music/News/Sports	n/a
KNCY	105.5	Commercial	General/Religious	Music/News	Country
KKCD	105.9	Commercial	General	Music/Talk	Classic Rock
KCTY	106.9	Commercial	General	Music	Alternative
KDSN	107.1	Commercial	General	n/a	n/a
KWPN	107.9	n/a	General	Music/News/Sports	n/a

Note: Stations included cover the Omaha DMA (Designated Market Area); n/a not available
BurrellesLuce, MediaContacts Online, January 2007

CLIMATE

Average and Extreme Temperatures

Temperature	Jan	Feb	Mar	Apr	May	Jun	Jul	Aug	Sep	Oct	Nov	Dec	Yr.
Extreme High (°F)	67	77	89	97	98	105	110	107	103	95	80	69	110
Average High (°F)	31	37	48	64	74	84	88	85	77	66	49	36	62
Average Temp. (°F)	22	27	38	52	63	73	77	75	66	54	39	27	51
Average Low (°F)	11	17	27	40	52	61	66	64	54	42	29	17	40
Extreme Low (°F)	-23	-21	-16	5	27	38	44	43	25	13	-9	-23	-23

Note: Figures cover the years 1948-1992
Source: National Climatic Data Center, International Station Meteorological Climate Summary, 9/96

Average Precipitation/Snowfall/Humidity

Precip./Humidity	Jan	Feb	Mar	Apr	May	Jun	Jul	Aug	Sep	Oct	Nov	Dec	Yr.
Avg. Precip. (in.)	0.8	0.9	2.0	2.8	4.3	4.0	3.7	3.8	3.4	2.1	1.5	0.9	30.1
Avg. Snowfall (in.)	7	6	7	1	Tr	0	0	0	Tr	Tr	3	6	29
Avg. Rel. Hum. 6am (%)	78	80	79	77	80	82	84	86	85	81	79	80	81
Avg. Rel. Hum. 3pm (%)	61	59	54	46	49	50	51	53	51	47	55	61	53

Note: Figures cover the years 1948-1992; Tr = Trace amounts (<0.05 in. of rain; <0.5 in. of snow)
Source: National Climatic Data Center, International Station Meteorological Climate Summary, 9/96

Weather Conditions

Temperature			Daytime Sky			Precipitation		
5°F & below	32°F & below	90°F & above	Clear	Partly cloudy	Cloudy	0.01 inch or more precip.	0.1 inch or more snow/ice	Thunder-storms
23	139	35	100	142	123	97	20	46

Note: Figures are average number of days per year and cover the years 1948-1992
Source: National Climatic Data Center, International Station Meteorological Climate Summary, 9/96

HAZARDOUS WASTE

Superfund Sites

Bellevue has no sites on the EPA's Superfund Final National Priorities List.
U.S. Environmental Protection Agency, Final National Priorities List, June 23, 2008

AIR & WATER QUALITY

Air Quality Index

Area	Percent of Days when Air Quality was...[2]				AQI Statistics	
	Good	Moderate	Unhealthy for Sensitive Groups	Unhealthy	Maximum	Median
MSA[1]	46.6	51.5	1.9	0.0	123	52

Note: The Air Quality Index (AQI) is an index for reporting daily air quality. EPA calculates the AQI for five major air pollutants regulated by the Clean Air Act: ground-level ozone, particle pollution (also known as particulate matter), carbon monoxide, sulfur dioxide, and nitrogen dioxide. The AQI runs from 0 to 500. The higher the AQI value, the greater the level of air pollution and the greater the health concern. There are six AQI categories: "Good" The AQI is between 0 and 50. Air quality is considered satisfactory; "Moderate" The AQI is between 51 and 100. Air quality is acceptable; "Unhealthy for Sensitive Groups" When AQI values are between 101 and 150, members of sensitive groups may experience health effects; "Unhealthy" When AQI values are between 151 and 200 everyone may begin to experience health effects; "Very Unhealthy" AQI values between 201 and 300 trigger a health alert; "Hazardous" AQI values over 300 trigger health warnings of emergency conditions; (1) Metropolitan Statistical Area - see Appendix A for areas included; (2) Based on 365 days with AQI data in 2007.
Source: U.S. Environmental Protection Agency, Air Quality Index Report, 2007

Air Quality Index Pollutants

Area	Percent of Days when AQI Pollutant was...[2]					
	Carbon Monoxide	Nitrogen Dioxide	Ozone	Sulfur Dioxide	Particulate Matter 2.5	Particulate Matter 10
MSA[1]	0.3	0.0	11.2	1.4	67.7	19.5

Note: The Air Quality Index (AQI) is an index for reporting daily air quality. EPA calculates the AQI for five major air pollutants regulated by the Clean Air Act: ground-level ozone, particle pollution (also known as particulate matter), carbon monoxide, sulfur dioxide, and nitrogen dioxide. The AQI runs from 0 to 500. The higher the AQI value, the greater the level of air pollution and the greater the health concern; (1) Metropolitan Statistical Area - see Appendix A for areas included; (2) Based on 365 days with AQI data in 2007.
Source: U.S. Environmental Protection Agency, Air Quality Index Report, 2007

Air Quality Index Trends

Area	Trend Sites (14)								All Sites (38)
	1999	2000	2001	2002	2003	2004	2005	2006	2006
MSA[1]	5	1	2	0	1	1	1	0	0

Note: An AQI value greater than 100 indicates that air quality would have been in the unhealthful range on that day. Data from exceptional events are not included. These counts are presented in two ways. First, the counts are based on sites having an adequate record of monitoring data during the trend period (trend sites). These counts represent the relative change in the number of days with AQI values greater than 100. In the last column, the counts are based on all sites with data in the most recent year (because it is possible for a site to have data in the most recent year but not enough data to be a trend site); (1) Metropolitan Statistical Area - see Appendix A for areas included.
Source: U.S. Environmental Protection Agency, Office of Air and Radiation, Air Trends, Factbook and Related Information, Air Pollution Trends in Selected Metropolitan Areas 2006

Maximum Air Pollutant Concentrations

	Particulate Matter 10 (ug/m³)	Particulate Matter 2.5 (ug/m³)	Ozone (ppm)	Carbon Monoxide (ppm)	Sulfur Dioxide (ppm)	Nitrogen Dioxide (ppm)	Lead (ug/m³)
MSA[1] Level	129	26	0.08	2	0.019	n/a	n/a
NAAQS[2]	150	35	0.125	9	0.140	0.053	1.50
Met NAAQS[2]	Yes	Yes	Yes	Yes	Yes	n/a	n/a

Note: Data from exceptional events are not included; (1) Metropolitan Statistical Area - see Appendix A for areas included; (2) National Ambient Air Quality Standards; n/a not available
Concentrations: Particulate Matter 10 (coarse particulate) - highest second maximum 24-hour concentration; Particulate Matter 2.5 (fine particulate) - highest 98th percentile 24-hour concentration; Ozone - highest second daily maximum 1-hour concentration; Carbon Monoxide - highest second maximum non-overlapping 8-hour concentration; Sulfur Dioxide - highest second maximum 24-hour concentration; Nitrogen Dioxide - highest arithmetic mean concentration; Lead - highest quarterly maximum concentration
Units: ppm = parts per million; ug/m³ = micrograms per cubic meter
Source: U.S. Environmental Protection Agency, MSA Factbook 2006, Air Quality Statistics by City

Drinking Water

Water System Name	Pop. Served	Primary Water Source Type	Violations[1]	
			Health Based	Monitoring/ Reporting
Metropolitan Utilities District	506,420	Surface	0	0

Note: (1) Based on violation data from January 1, 2007 to December 31, 2007 (includes unresolved violations from earlier years)
Source: U.S. Environmental Protection Agency, Office of Ground Water and Drinking Water, Safe Drinking Water Information System (based on data extracted April 15, 2008)

Sparks, Nevada

Background

At an elevation of nearly 4,500 feet, Sparks lies just north of Reno. Situated along Interstate 80 in Washoe County on the banks of the Truckee River, Sparks is Nevada's fifth-largest city, with a strong downtown business core and expanding residential neighborhoods. The city is a major center for distribution, warehousing, and light manufacturing, harboring the business facilities of more than 100 national companies, including General Motors, Kmart Corporation, Ralston-Purina, Federal Express, and United Parcel Service.

Sparks was created in 1904 to replace Wadsworth as the large switching yard on that section of the Southern Pacific Railroad. The city was incorporated in 1905. Originally named Harriman after the railroad tycoon, Sparks was quickly renamed in honor of Governor John T. Sparks to cool the anti-railroad sentiment brewing in the state legislature over uncontrolled railroad tariffs.

For the first half of the twentieth century, Sparks was a very sleepy, unassuming place. In the 1950s, the city's northeast pasturelands became covered with subdivisions built to entice more families to the area. They served the purpose; Sparks became an even quieter, more residential community. By the 1970s, however, businesses became attracted to the city's potential, sparking truly dynamic growth.

Schools in Sparks are managed by the Washoe County School District, and comprise two high schools, three middle schools, and 14 elementary schools. Truckee Meadows Community College and the University of Nevada, Reno, are within an easy commute of the city.

The convenience of nearby Reno Tahoe International Airport is an added boon to Sparks residents. It is among the fastest-growing airports n the nation, serving major carriers such as American, Southwest, United, and Continental. The region is served by eight medical facilities, including the Nevada Mental Health Institute, Northern Nevada Medical Center, and Tahoe Pacific Hospital, with nearly 700 physicians and surgeons, and 200 dentists. Nursing homes and licensed child care centers are also available in the city.

Magnificent surroundings provide myriad outdoor activities. Sparks is less than an hour's drive from Lake Tahoe, with over 20 alpine ski areas and some of the best Nordic skiing in the country. Sparks itself contains numerous neighborhood parks and sports facilities, the newest being Sparks Marina Lake Park, encompassing 80 acres of water for swimming, boating, fishing and scuba diving, along with picnic areas, all affording spectacular mountain views.

The Sparks Heritage Foundation and Museum features early regional and railroad memorabilia, and Wild Island offers outdoor water rides, an arcade, and a 36-hole miniature golf course. The Reno metropolitan area has 40 casinos, eight of which are located in Sparks.

Located on a semi-arid plateau east of the Sierra Nevada, Sparks has a mild climate, with 80% sunshine throughout the year, accompanied by low humidity. Temperatures vary widely from day to night.

Rankings

General Rankings

- Reno* was ranked #64 out of 375 metro areas in *Cities Ranked & Rated*. Criteria: cost of living; climate; crime; transportation; economy and jobs; education; arts and culture; health and healthcare; leisure; quality of life. *Cities Ranked & Rated, 2nd Edition, 2007*
- Reno* was ranked #45 out of 379 metro areas in *Places Rated Almanac*. Criteria: health care; education; recreation; transportation; ambience; climate; crime; housing costs; jobs. *Places Rated Almanac, 7th Edition, 2007*

Business/Finance Rankings

- Reno* was selected as one of the best places to start and grow a company by *Entrepreneur* and the National Policy Research Council. The Reno* metro area ranked #36 out of 63 mid-size metro areas. Criteria: business formation and growth (firms started four to 14 years ago that still employ at least 5 people and experienced rapid growth over the last four years). *Entrepreneur/National Policy Research Council, "Hot Cities for Entrepreneurs," September 2006*
- The Reno* metro area was selected as one of "America's 50 Hottest Cities" for business relocations and expansions. Criteria: industry's most prominent site selection consultants were asked to list their top city choices for relocating and expanding manufacturing companies, taking into consideration such factors as the business climate, work force quality, operating costs, incentive programs, and the ease of working with local political and economic development officials. *Expansion Management, January-February 2007*
- The Reno* metro area appeared on the Milken Institute "2007 Best Performing Cities" index. Rank: #26 out of 200 large metro areas. Criteria: job growth; wage and salary growth; high-tech output growth. *Milken Institute, "2007 Best Performing Cities"*
- The Reno* metro area was selected as one of the hottest cities for entrepreneurs in America by *Inc. Magazine.* Criteria: job-growth data for 393 metro was analyzed for current-year employment growth, average annual employment growth over past three years, and employment growth by industry sector. The Reno* metro area ranked #8 among mid-sized metro areas and #36 overall. *Inc. Magazine, May 2007*
- *Forbes* ranked the 200 most populous metro areas in the U.S. in terms of the "Best Places for Business and Careers." The Reno* metro area was ranked #137. Criteria: business costs (labor, energy, tax and office space expenses); living costs (housing, transportation, food and other household expenditures); education levels of the work force; job growth; income growth; migration trends; crime rates; and culture/leisure. *Forbes, "Best Places for Business and Careers," March 19, 2008*
- Reno* was identified as one of the top 20 metro areas with the lowest rate of house price appreciation in 2007. The area ranked #19 with a one-year price appreciation of -7.8% through the 4th quarter 2007. *Office of Federal Housing Enterprise Oversight, House Price Index, 4th Quarter 2007*

Health/Environment Rankings

- The Reno* metro area appeared in *Country Home's* "2008 Best Green Places" report. The area ranked #109 out of 379. Criteria: official energy policies; green power; green buildings; availability of fresh, locally grown food. *Country Home, "2008 Best Green Places"*
- The American Podiatric Medical Association and *Prevention* magazine ranked America's 100 most populated cities based on fitness-walker friendliness. The best cities have safe streets, beautiful places to walk, mild weather and good air quality. Sparks ranked #193. *Prevention, "The Best Walking Cities of 2008," April 2008; American Podiatric Medical Association, "2008 Best Fitness-Walking Cities, "April 2008*

- Sperling's BestPlaces ranked 331 metro areas and identified the most and least stressful U.S. cities. The Reno* metro area ranked #64 out of 114 mid-size metro areas (#1 = most stressful). Criteria: divorce rate; unemployment rate; violent and property crime; suicide rate; commute time; mental health; alcohol consumption; cloudy days. *Sperling's BestPlaces, www.BestPlaces.net, "America's Most (and Least) Stressful Cities," January 9, 2004*

- Reno* was highlighted as one of the top 25 cleanest metro areas for long-term particle pollution (PM 2.5) in the U.S. The area ranked #25. *American Lung Association, State of the Air: 2007*

Seniors/Retirement Rankings

- A.G. Edwards ranked America's 500 top-performing communities based on their residents' personal savings and investing behavior. The Reno* metro area ranked #179 with an index score of 103.84 (national average = 100.00). A dozen statistical factors were measured including: participation in retirement savings plans; personal debt levels; and home ownership. *A.G. Edwards, "2007 Nest Egg Index", September 12, 2007*

Children/Family Rankings

- The Reno* metro area was selected as one of the "Best Cities for Relocating Families" by Worldwide ERC and Primacy Relocation. The 2007 study placed a special emphasis on the housing market, which has significantly impacted the relocation industry and an employer's ability to transfer employees. The variables which weigh heavily in this category include home price, home affordability index, appreciation rates, and property tax. Other criteria include cost of living, crime rates, education, climate, focus on diversity, physicians per capita, recreation and leisure, arts and culture, air quality, watershed quality, sales tax, unemployment rate, job growth, high school and higher education index, school expenditures per student, students in public school, SAT/ACT percentile, and population growth. *Worldwide ERC and Primacy Relocation, "2007 Best Cities for Relocating Families"*

Safety Rankings

- The National Insurance Crime Bureau ranked 361 metro areas in the U.S. in terms of per capita rates of vehicle theft. The Reno* metro area ranked #72 (#1 = highest rate). Criteria: number of vehicle theft offenses per 100,000 inhabitants. *National Insurance Crime Bureau, "NICB Vehicle Theft Study," April 22, 2008*

- Farmers Insurance Group of Companies, in partnership with Sperling's BestPlaces, ranked 379 metro areas and identified the "Most Secure U.S. Place to Live." The Reno* metro area ranked #91 out of 127 in the mid-size city category (150,000 to 500,000 residents). Criteria: crime rates; extreme weather; risk of natural disasters; environmental hazards; terrorism threats; air quality; life expectancy; job loss numbers. *Farmers Insurance Group, "Most Secure U.S. Places to Live 2007"*

Sports/Recreation Rankings

- The Reno* metro area appeared on the *Sporting News* list of the "Best Sports Cities 2007". The area ranked #80 out of 150 cities in the U.S. *Sporting News* takes a 12-month snapshot, roughly July to July, of each city's sports, putting a heavy premium on regular-season won-lost records (from the most recently completed season). Other criteria include: playoff berths, bowl appearances and tournament bids; championships; applicable power ratings; quality of competition; overall fan fervor as measured in part by attendance as percentage of venue capacity; abundance of teams (rewarding quality over quantity); stadium and arena quality; ticket availability and prices; franchise ownership; and marquee appeal of athletes. *SportingNews.com, "Best Sports Cities 2007," August 1, 2007*

- *Golf Digest* ranked 330 metro areas in the U.S. in terms of golf. The Reno* metro area was ranked #141. Criteria: access to golf; weather; value of golf; and quality of golf. *Golf Digest, "Metro Golf Rankings," August 2005*

***Sparks is located within the Reno-Sparks, NV Metropolitan Statistical Area.**

Business Environment

CITY FINANCES

City Government Finances

Component	2004-2005 ($000)	2004-2005 ($ per capita)
Total Revenues	109,869	1,339
Total Expenditures	91,867	1,120
Debt Outstanding	76,835	936
Cash and Securities	72,734	886

Source: U.S Census Bureau, Government Finances 2004-2005

City Government Revenue by Source

Source	2004-2005 ($000)	2004-2005 ($ per capita)
General Revenue		
From Federal Government	923	11
From State Government	27,324	333
From Local Governments	1,008	12
Taxes		
Property	21,147	258
Sales	4,365	53
Personal Income	0	0
License	11,080	135
Charges	33,960	414
Liquor Store	0	0
Utility	0	0
Employee Retirement	0	0
Other	10,062	123

Source: U.S Census Bureau, Government Finances 2004-2005

City Government Expenditures by Function

Function	2004-2005 ($000)	2004-2005 ($ per capita)	2004-2005 (%)
General Expenditures			
Airports	0	0	0.0
Corrections	0	0	0.0
Education	0	0	0.0
Fire Protection	12,470	152	13.6
Governmental Administration	10,280	125	11.2
Health	0	0	0.0
Highways	8,871	108	9.7
Hospitals	0	0	0.0
Housing and Community Development	2,817	34	3.1
Interest on General Debt	2,966	36	3.2
Libraries	0	0	0.0
Parking	552	7	0.6
Parks and Recreation	8,119	99	8.8
Police Protection	16,889	206	18.4
Public Welfare	111	1	0.1
Sewerage	13,894	169	15.1
Solid Waste Management	0	0	0.0
Liquor Store	0	0	0.0
Utility	0	0	0.0
Employee Retirement	0	0	0.0
Other	14,898	182	16.2

Source: U.S Census Bureau, Government Finances 2004-2005

Municipal Bond Ratings

Area	Moody's
City	n/a

Source: Mergent Bond Record, January 2008 (unless noted otherwise)

DEMOGRAPHICS

Population Growth

Area	1990 Census	2000 Census	2007 Estimate	2012 Projection	Population Growth (%) 1990-2000	Population Growth (%) 2000-2012
City	54,716	66,346	86,298	100,168	21.3	51.0
MSA[1]	257,193	342,885	408,722	456,898	33.3	33.3
U.S.	248,709,873	281,421,906	301,045,522	314,920,978	13.2	11.9

Note: (1) Metropolitan Statistical Area - see Appendix B for areas included
Source: Claritas, Inc.

Number of Households and Average Household Size

Area	2007 Estimate	2007 Average Household Size
City	31,178	2.77
MSA[1]	157,092	2.60
U.S.	113,668,003	2.65

Note: (1) Metropolitan Statistical Area - see Appendix B for areas included
Source: Claritas, Inc.

Race and Ethnicity

Area	White Alone[2]	Black Alone[2]	Asian Alone[2]	Other Race Alone[2]	Hispanic[3]
City	75.1	2.6	5.5	16.9	24.3
MSA[1]	77.2	2.2	4.9	15.8	20.5
U.S.	73.1	12.4	4.3	10.3	14.9

Note: Figures are 2007 estimates; (1) Metropolitan Statistical Area - see Appendix B for areas included (2) Alone is defined as not being in combination with one or more other races; (3) May be of any race.
Source: Claritas, Inc.

Ancestry

Area	German	Irish[2]	English	American	Italian	Polish	French[3]	Scottish
City	16.5	13.8	12.6	3.7	7.3	1.9	4.0	2.1
MSA[1]	17.1	13.8	12.6	4.6	6.8	1.9	3.9	2.6
U.S.	15.2	10.9	8.7	7.3	5.6	3.2	3.0	1.7

Note: Figures include multiple ancestry (e.g. if a person reported being Irish and Italian, they were included in both columns); (1) Metropolitan Statistical Area - see Appendix A for areas included; (2) Includes Celtic; (3) Includes Alsatian but excludes Basque
Source: Census 2000, Summary File 3

Foreign-Born Population

Area	Percent of Population Born in							
	Any Foreign Country	Europe	Asia	Africa	Oceania[2]	Canada	Mexico	Latin America[3]
City	15.6	1.3	3.7	0.2	0.3	0.5	7.6	2.1
MSA[1]	14.1	1.4	3.4	0.1	0.3	0.5	6.7	1.7
U.S.	11.1	1.7	2.9	0.3	0.1	0.3	3.3	2.5

Note: (1) Metropolitan Statistical Area - see Appendix A for areas included; (2) Includes Australia, New Zealand subregion, Melanesia, Micronesia, Polynesia, and Oceania n.e.c; (3) Includes Central America (excluding Mexico), South America, and the Caribbean.
Source: Census 2000, Summary File 3

Marriage Status

Area	Never Married	Now Married (excluding Separated)	Separated	Widowed	Divorced
City	23.9	53.5	1.6	5.7	15.2
MSA[1]	25.7	52.1	1.9	5.4	14.9
U.S.	27.1	54.4	2.2	6.6	9.7

Note: Figures are percentages and cover the population 15 years of age and older; (1) Metropolitan Statistical Area - see Appendix A for areas included
Source: Census 2000, Summary File 3

Age Distribution

Area	Percent of Population						
	Under Age 5	Age 5 to 17	Age 18 to 34	Age 35 to 49	Age 50 to 64	Age 65 to 79	80 Years and Over
City	7.2	19.4	23.8	25.0	14.3	8.1	2.2
MSA[1]	6.8	18.0	24.1	24.8	15.9	8.3	2.3
U.S.	6.8	18.9	23.7	23.5	14.8	9.2	3.2

Note: (1) Metropolitan Statistical Area - see Appendix A for areas included
Source: Census 2000, Summary File 3

Male/Female Ratio

Area	Males	Females	Males per 100 Females
City	42,688	43,610	97.9
MSA[1]	207,050	201,672	102.7
U.S.	148,320,305	152,725,217	97.1

Note: Figures are 2007 estimates; (1) Metropolitan Statistical Area - see Appendix B for areas included
Source: Claritas, Inc.

Religion

Area	Catholic	Southern Baptist	United Meth-odist	ELCA[1]	LDS[2]	Presby-terian Church USA	Jewish Est.	Muslim Est.
County	16.2	1.1	0.8	0.6	3.5	0.5	0.6	0.2
U.S.	22.0	7.1	3.7	1.8	1.5	1.1	2.2	0.6

Note: Figures are the number of adherents as a percentage of the total population; Adherents are defined as all members, including full members, their children and the estimated number of other participants who are not considered members (e.g. the baptized, those not confirmed, those regularly attending services, etc.); (1) Evangelical Lutheran Church in America; (2) The Church of Jesus Christ of Latter Day Saints
Source: Reprinted with permission from Religious Congregations and Membership in the United States 2000 (Nashville, Glenmary Research Center, 2002) Copyright Association of Statisticians of American Religious Bodies. All rights reserved.

ECONOMY

Gross Metropolitan Product

Area	2002	2003	2004	2005	2005 Rank[2]
MSA[1]	15.4	16.6	18.2	19.9	94

Note: Figures are in billions of dollars; (1) Reno-Sparks, NV Metropolitan Statistical Area - see Appendix A for areas included; (2) Rank ranges from 1 to 361
Source: The U.S. Conference of Mayors, "U.S. Metro Economies: GMP - The Engines of America's Growth," January 2007

Economic Growth

Area	1995 GMP	2005 GMP	Average Annual Growth Rate	Growth Rate Rank[2]
MSA[1]	10.7	19.9	6.5	78

Note: Figures are in billions of dollars; GMP = Gross Metropolitan Product; (1) Reno-Sparks, NV Metropolitan Statistical Area - see Appendix A for areas included; (2) Rank ranges from 1 to 361
Source: The U.S. Conference of Mayors, "U.S. Metro Economies: GMP - The Engines of America's Growth," January 2007

INCOME

Per Capita/Median/Average Income

Area	Per Capita ($)	Median Household ($)	Average Household ($)
City	25,147	55,562	68,563
MSA[1]	27,754	54,199	71,518
U.S.	25,495	49,280	66,670

Note: Figures are 2007 estimates; (1) Metropolitan Statistical Area - see Appendix B for areas included
Source: Claritas, Inc.

Household Income Distribution

Area	Percent of Households Earning							
	Under $15,000	$15,000 -24,999	$25,000 -34,999	$35,000 -49,999	$50,000 -74,999	$75,000 -99,000	$100,000 -149,999	$150,000 and up
City	7.8	8.7	11.5	16.6	22.1	14.2	13.6	5.4
MSA[1]	9.7	9.4	11.3	15.7	21.2	13.3	12.6	6.9
U.S.	13.1	10.9	11.2	15.6	19.5	11.9	11.3	6.6

Note: Figures are 2007 estimates; (1) Metropolitan Statistical Area - see Appendix B for areas included
Source: Claritas, Inc.

Poverty Rates by Age

Area	All Ages	Under 5 Years Old	5 to 17 Years Old	18 to 64 Years Old	65 Years and Over
City	8.0	1.0	1.8	4.8	0.5
MSA[1]	10.0	1.1	2.1	6.1	0.6
U.S.	12.4	1.2	3.0	6.9	1.2

Note: Figures are percent of population with income in 1999 below poverty level and only include population for whom poverty status is determined; (1) Metropolitan Statistical Area - see Appendix A for areas included
Source: Census 2000, Summary File 3

Personal Bankruptcy Filing Rate

Area	2004	2005	2006
Washoe County	6.08	7.62	1.47
U.S.	5.31	6.82	2.00

Note: Numbers are per 1,000 population and include Chapter 7 and Chapter 13 filings
Source: Federal Deposit Insurance Corporation (FDIC), Regional Economic Conditions (RECON), 8/23/2007

EMPLOYMENT

Labor Force and Employment

Area	Civilian Labor Force			Workers Employed		
	Dec. 2006	Dec. 2007	% Chg.	Dec. 2006	Dec. 2007	% Chg.
City	47,759	49,063	2.7	45,974	46,587	1.3
MSA[1]	225,076	231,510	2.9	216,355	219,238	1.3
U.S.	152,571,000	153,705,000	0.7	146,081,000	146,334,000	0.2

Note: Data is not seasonally adjusted and covers workers 16 years of age and older;
(1) Metropolitan Statistical Area - see Appendix B for areas included
Source: Bureau of Labor Statistics, http://stats.bls.gov

Unemployment Rate

Area	2007											
	Jan.	Feb.	Mar.	Apr.	May	Jun.	Jul.	Aug.	Sep.	Oct.	Nov.	Dec.
City	4.7	4.5	4.3	4.2	3.9	4.1	4.3	4.1	4.2	4.1	4.4	5.0
MSA[1]	5.0	4.8	4.5	4.5	4.2	4.4	4.5	4.3	4.5	4.4	4.7	5.3
U.S.	5.0	4.9	4.5	4.3	4.3	4.7	4.9	4.6	4.5	4.4	4.5	4.8

Note: Data is not seasonally adjusted and covers workers 16 years of age and older; All figures are percentages; (1) Metropolitan Statistical Area - see Appendix B for areas included
Source: Bureau of Labor Statistics, http://stats.bls.gov

Employment by Occupation

Occupation Classification	City (%)	MSA[1] (%)	U.S. (%)
Sales and Office	30.1	28.9	26.7
Professional and Related	12.9	16.6	20.2
Service	20.4	19.9	14.9
Production, Transportation, and Material Moving	15.2	12.1	14.6
Management, Business, and Financial	11.3	12.9	13.5
Construction, Extraction, and Maintenance	10.0	9.5	9.4
Farming, Forestry, and Fishing	0.1	0.2	0.7

Note: Figures cover employed civilians 16 years of age and older;
(1) Metropolitan Statistical Area - see Appendix A for areas included
Source: Census 2000, Summary File 3

Employment by Industry

Sector	MSA[1] Number of Employees	MSA[1] Percent of Total	U.S. Percent of Total
Government	30,400	13.4	16.3
Education and Health Services	21,100	9.3	13.4
Professional and Business Services	29,900	13.2	13.1
Retail Trade	25,700	11.3	11.6
Manufacturing	14,800	6.5	9.9
Leisure and Hospitality	40,100	17.6	9.6
Financial Activities	10,000	4.4	5.9
Construction	20,100	8.8	5.3
Wholesale Trade	10,800	4.8	4.4
Other Services	7,300	3.2	3.9
Transportation and Utilities	13,900	6.1	3.7
Information	2,800	1.2	2.2
Natural Resources and Mining	400	0.2	0.5

Note: Figures cover non-farm employment as of December 2007 and are not seasonally adjusted; (1) Metropolitan Statistical Area - see Appendix B for areas included
Source: Bureau of Labor Statistics, http://stats.bls.gov

Average Wages

Occupation	$/Hr.	Occupation	$/Hr.
Accountants and Auditors	26.29	Maids and Housekeeping Cleaners	9.38
Automotive Mechanics	19.65	Maintenance and Repair Workers	16.58
Bookkeepers	16.55	Marketing Managers	38.43
Carpenters	22.38	Nuclear Medicine Technologists	n/a
Cashiers	9.89	Nurses, Licensed Practical	22.09
Clerks, General Office	12.77	Nurses, Registered	32.82
Clerks, Receptionists/Information	13.21	Nursing Aides/Orderlies/Attendants	12.72
Clerks, Shipping/Receiving	14.54	Packers and Packagers, Hand	11.33
Computer Programmers	31.08	Physical Therapists	36.64
Computer Support Specialists	18.74	Postal Service Mail Carriers	21.19
Computer Systems Analysts	33.99	Real Estate Brokers	n/a
Cooks, Restaurant	11.40	Retail Salespersons	12.57
Dentists	n/a	Sales Reps., Exc. Tech./Scientific	27.67
Electrical Engineers	37.08	Sales Reps., Tech./Scientific	42.45
Electricians	25.22	Secretaries, Exc. Legal/Med./Exec.	16.28
Financial Managers	40.12	Security Guards	11.35
First-Line Supervisors/Mgrs., Sales	19.70	Surgeons	98.94
Food Preparation Workers	8.91	Teacher Assistants	13.10
General and Operations Managers	48.39	Teachers, Elementary School	n/a
Hairdressers/Cosmetologists	11.15	Teachers, Secondary School	n/a
Internists	96.83	Telemarketers	12.53
Janitors and Cleaners	10.18	Truck Drivers, Heavy/Tractor-Trailer	19.98
Landscaping/Groundskeeping Workers	12.37	Truck Drivers, Light/Delivery Svcs.	14.92
Lawyers	65.63	Waiters and Waitresses	7.31

Note: Wage data covers the Reno-Sparks, NV Metropolitan Statistical Area - see Appendix B for areas included. Hourly wages for elementary/secondary school teachers and teacher assistants were calculated by the editors from annual wage data assuming a 40 hour work week; n/a not available.
Source: Bureau of Labor Statistics, May 2007 Metro Area Occupational Employment and Wage Estimates

RESIDENTIAL REAL ESTATE

Building Permits

Area	Single-Family 2006	Single-Family 2007p	Single-Family Pct. Chg.	Multi-Family 2006	Multi-Family 2007p	Multi-Family Pct. Chg.	Total 2006	Total 2007p	Total Pct. Chg.
City	1,126	610	-45.8	28	13	-53.6	1,154	623	-46.0
U.S.	1,378,200	973,300	-29.4	460,700	407,200	-11.6	1,838,900	1,380,500	-24.9

Note: (p) preliminary; figures cover and represent new, privately-owned housing units authorized (unadjusted data); All permit data are based on estimates with imputation; U.S. figures are based on the new 20,000-place series.
Source: U.S. Census Bureau, Manufacturing, Mining, and Construction Statistics

Homeownership and Housing Vacancies

Area	Homeownership Rate[2] (%)			Rental Vacancy Rate[3] (%)			Homeowner Vacancy Rate[4] (%)		
	2005	2006	2007	2005	2006	2007	2005	2006	2007
MSA[1]	n/a	n/a	n/a	n/a	n/a	n/a	n/a	n/a	n/a
U.S.	68.9	68.8	68.1	9.8	9.8	9.7	1.9	2.4	2.7

Note: (1) Metropolitan Statistical Area - see Appendix B for areas included; (2) The proportion of households that are owners; (3) The proportion of the rental inventory that is vacant for rent; (4) The proportion of the homeowner inventory that is vacant for sale; n/a not available
Source: U.S. Census Bureau, Housing Vacancies and Homeownership Annual Statistics: 2007

TAXES

State Corporate Income Tax Rates

State	Rates and Tax Brackets
Nevada	None

Note: Tax rates as of January 1, 2008
Source: Tax Foundation, www.taxfoundation.org

State Individual Income Tax Rates

State	Federal Deductibility	Marginal Rates (%)	Standard Deduction ($)		Personal Exemptions ($)[1]	
			Single	Joint	Single	Dependents
Nevada	No	None	n/a	n/a	n/a	n/a

Note: Tax rates as of January 1, 2008; Local- and county-level taxes are not included; n/a not applicable; (1) Married joint filers generally receive double the single exemption
Source: Tax Foundation, www.taxfoundation.org

Various State and Local Tax Rates

State and Local Sales and Use (%)	State Sales and Use (%)	Gasoline[1,2] ($/gal.)	Cigarette ($/pack)	Spirits ($/gal.)	Table Wine ($/gal.)	Beer ($/gal.)
7.375	6.5	0.325	0.80	3.60	0.70	0.16

Note: Tax rates as of January 1, 2008; (1) In addition to the 18.4 cpg Federal gasoline tax; (2) Rates may include additional state sales taxes, environmental protection and storage fees/taxes, and local taxes. When necessary, the volume-weighted average of all local taxes is used to approximate the typical statewide rate including local tax
Source: Tax Foundation, www.taxfoundation.org; Original research

State Tax Burdens

Area	Combined State and Local Tax Burden		Combined Federal, State and Local Tax Burden	
	Percent	Rank	Percent	Rank
Nevada	10.1	36	35.2	4
U.S. Average	11.0	-	32.7	-

Note: Figures cover 2007 and measure taxes as a percentage of income
Source: Tax Foundation, www.taxfoundation.org

State Business Tax Climate Index Rankings

State	Overall Rank	Corporate Tax Index Rank	Individual Income Tax Index Rank	Sales Tax Index Rank	Unemployment Insurance Tax Index Rank	Property Tax Index Rank
Nevada	3	1	1	43	41	13

Note: Rankings range from 1 to 50 where 1 is best. Rankings do not average across to Overall Rank. States without a given tax are given a ranking of 1.
Source: Tax Foundation, State Business Tax Climate Index 2008

TRANSPORTATION

Means of Transportation to Work

Area	Car/Truck/Van		Public Transportation			Bicycle	Walked	Other Means	Worked at Home
	Drove Alone	Car-pooled	Bus	Subway	Railroad				
City	76.3	14.2	2.8	0.0	0.0	0.7	2.5	1.2	2.2
MSA[1]	75.3	13.8	3.0	0.0	0.0	0.7	3.2	1.2	2.9
U.S.	75.7	12.2	2.5	1.5	0.5	0.4	2.9	1.0	3.3

Note: Figures are percentages and cover workers 16 years of age and older; (1) Metropolitan Statistical Area - see Appendix A for areas included
Source: Census 2000, Summary File 3

Travel Time to Work

Area	Less Than 15 Minutes	15 to 29 Minutes	30 to 44 Minutes	45 to 59 Minutes	60 Minutes or More
City	35.4	51.7	8.3	1.9	2.7
MSA[1]	35.2	49.2	9.5	2.7	3.3
U.S.	29.4	36.1	19.1	7.4	8.0

Note: Figures are percentages and include workers 16 years old and over; (1) Metropolitan Statistical Area - see Appendix A for areas included
Source: Census 2000, Summary File 3

Living Environment

COST OF LIVING

Cost of Living Index

Composite Index	Groceries	Housing	Utilities	Trans-portation	Health Care	Misc. Goods/ Services
108.3	104.3	115.1	86.8	111.3	109.0	109.4

Note: U.S. = 100; Figures cover the Reno-Sparks NV urban area.
Source: The Council for Community and Economic Research (formerly ACCRA), Cost of Living Index, 2007

Grocery Prices

Area[1]	T-Bone Steak ($/pound)	Frying Chicken ($/pound)	Whole Milk ($/half gal.)	Eggs ($/dozen)	Orange Juice ($/64 oz.)	Coffee ($/11.5 oz.)
City[2]	9.09	1.13	2.09	1.80	3.38	4.24
Avg.	8.93	1.12	2.13	1.52	3.26	3.31
Min.	5.88	0.71	1.33	0.83	2.30	2.20
Max.	12.80	2.07	3.43	3.54	5.79	6.20

Note: (1) Values for the local area are compared with the average, minimum and maximum values for all 331 areas in the Cost of Living Index report; (2) Figures cover the Reno-Sparks NV urban area; **T-Bone Steak** *(price per pound);* **Frying Chicken** *(price per pound, whole fryer);* **Whole Milk** *(half gallon carton);* **Eggs** *(price per dozen, Grade A, large);* **Orange Juice** *(64 oz. Tropicana or Florida Natural);* **Coffee** *(11.5 oz. can, vacuum-packed, Maxwell House, Hills Bros, or Folgers).*
Source: The Council for Community and Economic Research (formerly ACCRA), Cost of Living Index, 2007

Housing and Utility Costs

Area[1]	New Home Price ($)	Apartment Rent ($/month)	All Electric ($/month)	Part Electric ($/month)	Other Energy ($/month)	Telephone ($/month)
City[2]	371,493	705	-	73.83	86.10	18.04
Avg.	309,605	782	146.13	78.67	90.16	26.14
Min.	189,877	n/a	82.03	37.41	33.15	17.08
Max.	1,202,800	3,481	271.14	150.60	257.67	37.45

Note: (1) Values for the local area are compared with the average, minimum and maximum values for all 331 areas in the Cost of Living Index report; (2) Figures cover the Reno-Sparks NV urban area; **New Home Price** *(2,400 sf living area, 8,000 sf lot, in urban area with full utilities);* **Apartment Rent** *(950 sf 2 bedroom/1.5 or 2 bath, unfurnished, excluding all utilities except water);* **All Electric** *(average monthly cost for an all-electric home);* **Part Electric** *(average monthly cost for a part-electric home);* **Other Energy** *(average monthly cost for natural gas, fuel oil, coal, wood, and any other forms of energy except electricity);* **Telephone** *(price includes basic monthly rate for a private residential line plus additional local usage charges incurred by a family of four).*
Source: The Council for Community and Economic Research (formerly ACCRA), Cost of Living Index, 2007

Health Care, Transportation, and Other Costs

Area[1]	Doctor ($/visit)	Dentist ($/visit)	Optometrist ($/visit)	Gasoline ($/gallon)	Beauty Salon ($/visit)	Men's Shirt ($)
City[2]	75.42	90.43	91.54	2.94	29.25	24.25
Avg.	79.48	71.93	79.55	2.64	29.52	25.77
Min.	52.08	44.80	43.95	2.19	15.58	16.19
Max.	148.44	126.27	158.83	3.48	60.62	48.53

Note: (1) Values for the local area are compared with the average, minimum and maximum values for all 331 areas in the Cost of Living Index report; (2) Figures cover the Reno-Sparks NV urban area; **Doctor** *(general practitioners routine exam of an established patient);* **Dentist** *(adult teeth cleaning and periodic oral examination);* **Optometrist** *(full vision eye exam for established adult patient);* **Gasoline** *(one gallon regular unleaded, national brand, including all taxes, cash price at self-service pump if available);* **Beauty Salon** *(woman's shampoo, trim, and blow-dry);* **Men's Shirt** *(cotton/polyester dress shirt, pinpoint weave, long sleeves).*
Source: The Council for Community and Economic Research (formerly ACCRA), Cost of Living Index, 2007

HOUSING

House Price Index (HPI)

Area	National Ranking[2]	Quarterly Change (%)	One-Year Change (%)	Five-Year Change (%)
MSA[1]	273	-2.39	-7.83	65.05
U.S.[3]	-	0.10	0.84	41.37

Note: The HPI is a weighted repeat sales index. It measures average price changes in repeat sales or refinancings on the same properties. This information is obtained by reviewing repeat mortgage transactions on single-family properties whose mortgages have been purchased or securitized by Fannie Mae or Freddie Mac in January 1975; (1) Metropolitan Statistical Area - see Appendix B for areas included; (2) Rankings are based on annual percentage change for all metro areas containing at least 15,000 transactions over the last 10 years and ranges from 1 to 291; (3) figures based on a weighted average of Census Division estimates; all figures are for the period ending December 31, 2007
Source: Office of Federal Housing Enterprise Oversight, House Price Index, February 26, 2008

House Price Valuations

Area	Q1 2000	Q1 2001	Q1 2002	Q1 2003	Q1 2004	Q1 2005	Q1 2006	Q1 2007	Q1 2008
MSA[1]	-18.7	-21.9	-14.1	-5.8	0.9	29.4	40.6	25.3	-0.2

Note: Figures show the percentage of over- or under-valuation of single family homes relative to statistically normal house values (e.g. a value of 23.6 indicates that house values are 23.6% overvalued). Statistically normal house values are based on house prices, interest rates, household incomes, population densities, and any historical premiums or discounts metropolitan areas have exhibited over time; (1) Figures cover the Metropolitan Statistical Area - see Appendix B for areas included
Source: Global Insight/National City Corporation, House Prices in America, May 2008

Median Home Prices

Area	2005	2006	2007[r]	Percent Change 2006 to 2007
MSA[1]	349.9	347.2	321.4	-7.4
U.S. Average	219.0	221.9	217.9	-1.8

Note: Figures are median sales prices of existing single-family homes in thousands of dollars; (r) revised; n/a not available; (1) Metropolitan Statistical Area - see Appendix B for areas included
Source: National Association of Realtors, Metropolitan Area Prices, 1st Quarter 2008

Housing: Year Structure Built

Area	1990 -2000	1980 -1989	1970 -1979	1960 -1969	1950 -1959	1940 -1949	Before 1940	Median Year
City	21.8	22.6	28.1	14.1	7.8	2.9	2.7	1978
MSA[1]	27.3	20.6	25.0	13.0	7.3	3.5	3.3	1979
U.S.	17.0	15.8	18.5	13.7	12.7	7.3	15.0	1971

Note: Figures are percentages; (1) Metropolitan Statistical Area - see Appendix A for areas included
Source: Census 2000, Summary File 3

HEALTH

Health Risk Data

Category	Area[1] (%)	U.S. (%)
Adults who have been told they have high blood pressure[3]	22.1	25.5
Adults who have been told they have high blood cholesterol[3]	35.3	35.6
Adults who have been told they have diabetes[2]	7.5	7.5
Adults who have been told they have arthritis[3]	23.5	27.0
Adults who have been told they currently have asthma	8.6	8.5
Adults who are current smokers	19.8	20.1
Adults who are heavy drinkers[4]	9.4	4.9
Adults who are overweight (BMI 25.0 - 29.9)	38.0	36.5
Adults who are obese (BMI 30.0 - 99.8)	23.6	25.1

Note: Data as of 2006 unless otherwise noted; (1) Figures cover the Metropolitan Statistical Area - see Appendix B for areas included; (2) Figures do not include pregnancy-related diabetes, pre-diabetes or borderline diabetes; (3) 2005 data; (4) Heavy drinkers are classified as adult men having more than two drinks per day or adult women having more than one drink per day
Source: Centers for Disease Control and Prevention, Behaviorial Risk Factor Surveillance System, SMART: Selected Metropolitan/Micropolitan Area Risk Trends, 2005, 2006

Mortality Rates for the Top 10 Causes of Death in the U.S.

ICD-10[a] Sub-Chapter	ICD-10[a] Code	Age-Adjusted Mortality Rate[1] per 100,000 population	
		County[2]	U.S.
Malignant neoplasms	C00-C97	184.7	186.5
Ischaemic heart diseases	I20-I25	133.8	152.3
Other forms of heart disease	I30-I51	49.7	51.5
Cerebrovascular diseases	I60-I69	52.5	50.0
Chronic lower respiratory diseases	J40-J47	73.0	42.6
Diabetes mellitus	E10-E14	14.0	24.8
Other degenerative diseases of the nervous system	G30-G31	16.2	22.6
Other external causes of accidental injury	W00-X59	20.0	21.4
Influenza and pneumonia	J10-J18	18.4	20.7
Hypertensive diseases	I10-I13	48.1	18.2

Note: (a) ICD-10 = International Classification of Diseases 10th Revision; (1) Mortality rates are a three year average covering 2003-2005; (2) Figures cover Washoe County
Source: Centers for Disease Control and Prevention, National Center for Health Statistics. Compressed Mortality File 1999-2004. CDC WONDER On-line Database, compiled from Compressed Mortality File 1999-2005 Series 20 No. 2K, 2008.

Mortality Rates for Selected Causes of Death

ICD-10[a] Sub-Chapter	ICD-10[a] Code	Age-Adjusted Mortality Rate[1] per 100,000 population	
		County[2]	U.S.
Assault	X85-Y09	4.3	5.9
Human immunodeficiency virus (HIV) disease	B20-B24	2.2	4.5
Intentional self-harm	X60-X84	21.7	10.8
Malnutrition	E40-E46	*1.1	1.0
Obesity and other hyperalimentation	E65-E68	*0.4	1.4
Organic, including symptomatic, mental disorders	F01-F09	12.5	16.8
Transport accidents	V01-V99	16.5	16.1
Viral hepatitis	B15-B19	2.6	1.8

Note: (a) ICD-10 = International Classification of Diseases 10th Revision; (1) Mortality rates are a three year average covering 2003-2005; (2) Figures cover Washoe County; (*) Unreliable data as per CDC
Source: Centers for Disease Control and Prevention, National Center for Health Statistics. Compressed Mortality File 1999-2004. CDC WONDER On-line Database, compiled from Compressed Mortality File 1999-2005 Series 20 No. 2K, 2008.

Distribution of Physicians[1]

Area	Total	Family/ General Practice	Specialties	
			Medical	Surgical
Washoe County (number)	831	216	235	215
Washoe County (rate per 10,000 pop.)	21.3	5.5	6.0	5.5
U.S. (rate per 10,000 pop.)	17.7	4.6	6.9	4.3

Note: Data as of 2005; (1) Includes all non-federal, patient-care, office-based MDs
Source: Area Resource File (ARF). June 2007. U.S. Department of Health and Human Services, Health Resources and Services Administration, Bureau of Health Professions, Rockville, MD.

Hospitals

Sparks has the following hospitals: 1 general medical and surgical; 1 psychiatric.
AHA Guide to the Healthcare Field 2008

EDUCATION

Public School District Statistics

District Name	Schls	Pupils	Pupil/ Teacher Ratio	Minority Pupils[1] (%)	Free Lunch Eligible[2] (%)	IEP[3] (%)
Washoe County School District	98	64,246	18.0	42.7	n/a	13.1

Note: Table includes regular local school districts with 2,000 or more students; (1) Percentage of students that are not white, non-Hispanic; (2) Percentage of students that are eligible for the free lunch program; (3) Percentage of students that have an Individualized Education Program.
Source: U.S. Department of Education, National Center for Education Statistics, Common Core of Data, Local Education Agency (School District) Universe Survey: School Year 2005-2006; U.S. Department of Education, National Center for Education Statistics, Common Core of Data, Public Elementary/Secondary School Universe Survey: School Year 2005-2006

Top Public High Schools

High School Name	Index[1]	Rank[1]	Subsidized Lunch (%)[2]	E&E (%)[3]
Edward Reed	1.219	1,199	15.0	15.9
Spanish Springs	1.020	1,407	15.4	18.6
Sparks	1.664	745	44.7	10.2

Note: (1) Public schools are ranked according to a ratio that is the number of Advanced Placement, International Baccalaureate, and/or Cambridge tests taken by all students at a school in 2007 divided by the number of graduating seniors. All of the schools on the list have an index of at least 1.000; they are in the top five percent of public schools measured this way. The rankings range from 1 to 1,422; (2) Percentage of students receiving federally subsidized meals; (3) E & E stands for equity and excellence percentage: the portion of all graduating seniors at a school that had at least one passing grade on one AP or IB test; (**) Gave both IB and AP tests. AP and IB participation are indicators of a school's efforts to get students to excel and prepare for college.
Source: Newsweek Online, "Top High Schools 2008"

Highest Level of Education

Area	Less than H.S.	H.S. Diploma	Some College, No Deg.	Associate Degree	Bachelors Degree	Masters Degree	Profess. School Degree	Doctorate Degree
City	16.3	27.4	29.0	7.6	13.9	3.8	1.5	0.6
MSA[1]	15.4	25.1	28.3	7.2	16.1	5.1	1.9	1.0
U.S.	19.4	28.4	21.2	6.4	15.7	5.9	2.0	1.0

Note: Figures are 2007 estimated percentages and cover persons age 25 and over; (1) Metropolitan Statistical Area - see Appendix B for areas included
Source: Claritas, Inc.

Educational Attainment by Race

Area	High School Graduate (%)					Bachelor's Degree (%)				
	Total	White	Black	Asian	Hisp.[2]	Total	White	Black	Asian	Hisp.[2]
City	82.2	86.4	86.1	80.5	46.2	17.8	18.6	15.9	27.5	7.0
MSA[1]	83.9	87.3	84.2	83.2	45.9	23.7	25.2	16.7	34.2	6.9
U.S.	80.4	83.6	72.3	80.4	52.4	24.4	26.1	14.3	44.1	10.4

Note: Figures shown cover persons 25 years old and over; (1) Metropolitan Statistical Area - see Appendix A for areas included; (2) people of Hispanic origin can be of any race
Source: Census 2000, Summary File 3

School Enrollment by Type

Area	Grades KG to 8				Grades 9 to 12			
	Public		Private		Public		Private	
	Enrollment	%	Enrollment	%	Enrollment	%	Enrollment	%
City	8,769	94.0	558	6.0	3,604	94.2	220	5.8
MSA[1]	41,138	94.0	2,646	6.0	17,229	93.4	1,216	6.6
U.S.	33,526,011	88.7	4,285,121	11.3	14,848,628	90.6	1,532,323	9.4

Note: Figures shown cover persons 3 years old and over; (1) Metropolitan Statistical Area - see Appendix A for areas included
Source: Census 2000, Summary File 3

School Enrollment by Race

Area	Grades KG to 8 (%)				Grades 9 to 12 (%)			
	White	Black	Asian	Hisp.[1]	White	Black	Asian	Hisp.[1]
City	72.4	3.2	4.6	28.0	75.3	3.0	4.7	23.4
MSA[2]	74.2	2.0	3.8	25.1	74.0	3.0	4.4	22.4
U.S.	68.5	15.5	3.3	16.8	68.8	15.5	3.8	15.7

Note: Figures shown cover persons 3 years old and over; (1) people of Hispanic origin can be of any race; (2) Metropolitan Statistical Area - see Appendix A for areas included
Source: Census 2000, Summary File 3

Average Salaries of Public School Classroom Teachers

District	2005-06		2006-07		Percent Change 2005-06 to 2006-07
	Dollars	Rank[1]	Dollars	Rank[1]	
Nevada	44,426	26	45,342	28	2.06
U.S. Average	49,026	-	50,816	-	3.65

Note: (1) State rank ranges from 1 to 51.
Source: National Education Association, Rankings & Estimates: Rankings of the States 2006 and Estimates of School Statistics 2007, December 2007

Higher Education

Four-Year Colleges			Two-Year Colleges			Medical Schools[1]	Law Schools[2]	Voc/ Tech[3]
Public	Private Non-profit	Private For-profit	Public	Private Non-profit	Private For-profit			
0	0	0	0	0	0	0	0	1

Note: Figures cover institutions located within the city limits; (1) includes schools accredited by the Liaison Committee on Medical Education and the American Osteopathic Association; (2) includes American Bar Association-accredited law schools; (3) includes all schools with programs that are less than 2 years.
Source: National Center for Education Statistics, The Integrated Postsecondary Education System (IPEDS) Peer Analysis System, 2007; www.usnews.com, Law and Medical School Directories, 2009

PRESIDENTIAL ELECTION

2004 Presidential Election Results

Area	Bush	Kerry	Nader	Other
Washoe County	51.3	47.0	0.6	1.1
U.S.	50.7	48.3	0.4	0.6

Note: Results are percentages and may not add to 100% due to rounding
Source: Dave Leip's Atlas of U.S. Presidential Elections, www.uselectionatlas.org

EMPLOYERS

Major Employers

Company Name	Industry	Type of Site
152nd Tctcal Rcnnissance Group	National security	Branch
Atlantis Casino Resort	Hotels and motels	Headquarters
Boomtown Casino & Hotel Inc	Amusement and recreation, nec	Single
Club Cal-Neva	Hotels and motels	Single
County of Washoe	Social services, nec	Headquarters
El Dorado Hotel & Casino	Hotels and motels	Single
Hilton	Hotels and motels	Single
Hyatt Hotel	Hotels and motels	Branch
IGT	Manufacturing industries, nec	Headquarters
Ichem	Building maintenance services, nec	Single
Nevada System Higher Education	Colleges and universities	Branch
Peppermill Hotel Casino	Hotels and motels	Branch
Saint Marys Eye Institute	General medical and surgical hospitals	Headquarters
Sierra Nevada Healthcare Sys	Administration of veterans' affairs	Branch
Sierra Pacific Power Company	Electric services	Headquarters
UPS	Business services, nec	Branch
US Post Office	U.S. postal service	Branch
University of Nevada Reno	Colleges and universities	Single
Washoe County Sheriffs Office	Police protection	Branch

Note: Companies shown are located within the Reno metropolitan area; nec = not elsewhere classified.
Source: www.zapdata.com, May 2008

PUBLIC SAFETY

Crime Rate

Area	All Crimes	Violent Crimes				Property Crimes		
		Murder	Forcible Rape	Robbery	Aggrav. Assault	Burglary	Larceny -Theft	Motor Vehicle Theft
City	4,519.2	3.5	47.2	146.2	251.2	1,053.1	2,481.3	536.6
Metro[1]	4,522.6	7.4	34.6	164.8	302.9	889.4	2,553.3	570.1
U.S.	3,808.1	5.7	30.9	149.4	287.5	729.4	2,206.8	398.4

Note: Figures are crimes per 100,000 population; (1) Metropolitan Statistical Area - see Appendix B for areas included
Source: FBI Uniform Crime Reports, 2006

Hate Crimes

Area	Number of Quarters Reported	Bias Motivation				
		Race	Religion	Sexual Orientation	Ethnicity	Disability
City	4	0	0	0	0	0

Source: Federal Bureau of Investigation, Hate Crime Statistics 2006

RECREATION

Culture

Dance[1]	Theatre[1]	Instrumental Music[1]	Vocal Music[1]	Series/ Festivals	Museums	Zoos and Aquariums[2]
0	0	0	0	0	0	0

Note: (1) Number of professional perfoming groups; (2) AZA-accredited
Source: The Grey House Performing Arts Directory, 2007; Official Museum Directory, 2008; Association of Zoos & Aquariums, AZA Member Zoos & Aquariums, June 2008

Professional Sports Teams

Team Name	League
No teams are located in the metro area	

Source: Original research

MEDIA

Newspapers

Name	News Focus	Frequency	Circulation
Daily Sparks Tribune	Community	Daily	3,800

Note: Includes newspapers with offices located in the city
Source: MediaContactsPro, March 2008

Television Stations

Name	Ch.	Network(s)	Type	Ownership
KTVN	2	CBS	Commercial	Sarkes Tarzian Inc.
KRNV	4	NBC	Commercial	Sierra Broadcasting Company
KNPB	5	PBS	Public	Channel 5 Public Broadcasting Inc.
KOLO	8	ABC	Commercial	Stephens Group Inc.
KRXI	11	Fox	Commercial	Cox Enterprises Inc.
KAME	21	Fox/UPN	Commercial	Broadcast Development L.L.C.
KREN	27	WBN	Commercial	Pappas Telecasting Companies

Note: Stations included cover the Reno DMA (Designated Market Area)
BurrellesLuce, MediaContacts Online, January 2007

Major AM Radio Stations

Call Letters	Freq. (kHz)	Station Type	Target Audience	Station Format	Music Format
KHIT	630	Commercial	General	Music	Country
KKOH	780	Commercial	General	Talk	n/a
KVLV	980	Commercial	General	Music/News	Country
KPLY	1230	Commercial	General	News	n/a
KSUE	1240	Commercial	General	News/Sports/Talk	n/a
KPTL	1300	Commercial	General	Music/News	Oldies
KWNA	1400	Commercial	General	Music/News	Oldies
KOZZ	1450	n/a	General	Sports	n/a
KOWL	1490	Commercial	General	News/Talk	n/a
KIHM	1590	Non-Comm	General/Religious	Educational/Music	Christian
KQLO	1590	Commercial	General/Hispanic	Educational/Music	Top 40

Note: Stations included cover the Reno DMA (Designated Market Area); n/a not available
Source: BurrellesLuce, MediaContacts Online, January 2007

Major FM Radio Stations

Call Letters	Freq. (mHz)	Station Type	Target Audience	Station Format	Music Format
KUNR	88.7	College	General	Music/News	Jazz
KNIS	91.3	Non-Comm	General/Religious	Educational/Music	Christian
KJZS	92.1	Commercial	General	Music	Jazz
KNHK	92.9	Commercial	General	Music/News/Talk	Classic Rock
KJDX	93.3	Commercial	General	Music/News	Country
KWYL	93.7	Commercial	General	Music	Urban Contemp.
KRLT	93.9	Commercial	General	Music	Adult Contemp.
KNEV	95.5	Commercial	General	Music	Alternative
KLCA	96.5	Commercial	General	Music	Adult Contemp.
KWNZ	97.3	Commercial	General	Music	Urban Contemp.
KVLV	99.3	Commercial	General	Music/News	Adult Contemp.
KGVM	99.3	Commercial	General	Music/News	Adult Contemp.
KRZQ	100.9	Commercial	General	Music/Talk	Alternative
KRNV	101.7	Commercial	General/Hispanic	Music/News	Latin
KHJQ	102.1	Commercial	General	Music	Top 40
KODS	103.7	Commercial	General	Music	Oldies
KDOT	104.5	Commercial	General	Music	Modern Rock
KOZZ	105.7	n/a	General	Music	n/a
KMMT	106.5	Commercial	General	Music/News	Adult Contemp.
KRNO	106.9	Commercial	General	Music	Soft Rock

Note: Stations included cover the Reno DMA (Designated Market Area); n/a not available
BurrellesLuce, MediaContacts Online, January 2007

CLIMATE

Average and Extreme Temperatures

Temperature	Jan	Feb	Mar	Apr	May	Jun	Jul	Aug	Sep	Oct	Nov	Dec	Yr.
Extreme High (°F)	70	75	83	89	96	103	104	105	101	91	77	70	105
Average High (°F)	45	51	56	64	73	82	91	89	81	70	55	46	67
Average Temp. (°F)	32	38	41	48	56	63	70	68	61	51	40	33	50
Average Low (°F)	19	23	26	31	38	44	49	47	40	32	25	20	33
Extreme Low (°F)	-16	-16	0	13	18	25	33	24	20	8	1	-16	-16

Note: Figures cover the years 1949-1992
Source: National Climatic Data Center, International Station Meteorological Climate Summary, 9/96

Average Precipitation/Snowfall/Humidity

Precip./Humidity	Jan	Feb	Mar	Apr	May	Jun	Jul	Aug	Sep	Oct	Nov	Dec	Yr.
Avg. Precip. (in.)	1.0	0.9	0.7	0.4	0.7	0.4	0.3	0.2	0.3	0.4	0.8	1.0	7.2
Avg. Snowfall (in.)	6	5	4	1	1	Tr	0	0	Tr	Tr	2	4	24
Avg. Rel. Hum. 7am (%)	79	77	71	61	55	51	49	55	64	72	78	80	66
Avg. Rel. Hum. 4pm (%)	51	41	34	27	26	22	19	19	22	27	41	51	32

Note: Figures cover the years 1949-1992; Tr = Trace amounts (<0.05 in. of rain; <0.5 in. of snow)
Source: National Climatic Data Center, International Station Meteorological Climate Summary, 9/96

Weather Conditions

Temperature			Daytime Sky			Precipitation		
10°F & below	32°F & below	90°F & above	Clear	Partly cloudy	Cloudy	0.01 inch or more precip.	0.1 inch or more snow/ice	Thunder-storms
14	178	50	143	139	83	50	17	14

Note: Figures are average number of days per year and cover the years 1949-1992
Source: National Climatic Data Center, International Station Meteorological Climate Summary, 9/96

HAZARDOUS WASTE

Superfund Sites

Sparks has no sites on the EPA's Superfund Final National Priorities List.
U.S. Environmental Protection Agency, Final National Priorities List, June 23, 2008

AIR & WATER QUALITY

Air Quality Index

Area	Percent of Days when Air Quality was...[2]				AQI Statistics	
	Good	Moderate	Unhealthy for Sensitive Groups	Unhealthy	Maximum	Median
MSA[1]	75.3	24.7	0.0	0.0	100	42

Note: The Air Quality Index (AQI) is an index for reporting daily air quality. EPA calculates the AQI for five major air pollutants regulated by the Clean Air Act: ground-level ozone, particle pollution (also known as particulate matter), carbon monoxide, sulfur dioxide, and nitrogen dioxide. The AQI runs from 0 to 500. The higher the AQI value, the greater the level of air pollution and the greater the health concern. There are six AQI categories: "Good" The AQI is between 0 and 50. Air quality is considered satisfactory; "Moderate" The AQI is between 51 and 100. Air quality is acceptable; "Unhealthy for Sensitive Groups" When AQI values are between 101 and 150, members of sensitive groups may experience health effects; "Unhealthy" When AQI values are between 151 and 200 everyone may begin to experience health effects; "Very Unhealthy" AQI values between 201 and 300 trigger a health alert; "Hazardous" AQI values over 300 trigger health warnings of emergency conditions; (1) Metropolitan Statistical Area - see Appendix A for areas included; (2) Based on 365 days with AQI data in 2007.
Source: U.S. Environmental Protection Agency, Air Quality Index Report, 2007

Air Quality Index Pollutants

Area	Percent of Days when AQI Pollutant was...[2]					
	Carbon Monoxide	Nitrogen Dioxide	Ozone	Sulfur Dioxide	Particulate Matter 2.5	Particulate Matter 10
MSA[1]	4.9	0.0	84.9	0.0	5.2	4.9

Note: The Air Quality Index (AQI) is an index for reporting daily air quality. EPA calculates the AQI for five major air pollutants regulated by the Clean Air Act: ground-level ozone, particle pollution (also known as particulate matter), carbon monoxide, sulfur dioxide, and nitrogen dioxide. The AQI runs from 0 to 500. The higher the AQI value, the greater the level of air pollution and the greater the health concern; (1) Metropolitan Statistical Area - see Appendix A for areas included; (2) Based on 365 days with AQI data in 2007.
Source: U.S. Environmental Protection Agency, Air Quality Index Report, 2007

Air Quality Index Trends

Area	Trend Sites								All Sites
	1999	2000	2001	2002	2003	2004	2005	2006	2006
MSA[1]	n/a	n/a	n/a	n/a	n/a	n/a	n/a	n/a	n/a

Note: An AQI value greater than 100 indicates that air quality would have been in the unhealthful range on that day. Data from exceptional events are not included. These counts are presented in two ways. First, the counts are based on sites having an adequate record of monitoring data during the trend period (trend sites). These counts represent the relative change in the number of days with AQI values greater than 100. In the last column, the counts are based on all sites with data in the most recent year (because it is possible for a site to have data in the most recent year but not enough data to be a trend site); (1) Metropolitan Statistical Area - see Appendix A for areas included; n/a not available.
Source: U.S. Environmental Protection Agency, Office of Air and Radiation, Air Trends, Factbook and Related Information, Air Pollution Trends in Selected Metropolitan Areas 2006

Maximum Air Pollutant Concentrations

	Particulate Matter 10 (ug/m^3)	Particulate Matter 2.5 (ug/m^3)	Ozone (ppm)	Carbon Monoxide (ppm)	Sulfur Dioxide (ppm)	Nitrogen Dioxide (ppm)	Lead (ug/m^3)
MSA[1] Level	104	27	0.092	3	n/a	n/a	n/a
NAAQS[2]	150	35	0.125	9	0.140	0.053	1.50
Met NAAQS[2]	Yes	Yes	Yes	Yes	n/a	n/a	n/a

Note: Data from exceptional events are not included; (1) Metropolitan Statistical Area - see Appendix A for areas included; (2) National Ambient Air Quality Standards; n/a not available
Concentrations: Particulate Matter 10 (coarse particulate) - highest second maximum 24-hour concentration; Particulate Matter 2.5 (fine particulate) - highest 98th percentile 24-hour concentration; Ozone - highest second daily maximum 1-hour concentration; Carbon Monoxide - highest second maximum non-overlapping 8-hour concentration; Sulfur Dioxide - highest second maximum 24-hour concentration; Nitrogen Dioxide - highest arithmetic mean concentration; Lead - highest quarterly maximum concentration
Units: ppm = parts per million; ug/m^3 = micrograms per cubic meter
Source: U.S. Environmental Protection Agency, MSA Factbook 2006, Air Quality Statistics by City

Drinking Water

Water System Name	Pop. Served	Primary Water Source Type	Violations[1]	
			Health Based	Monitoring/ Reporting
Truckee Meadows Water Auth.	315,200	Surface	0	0

Note: (1) Based on violation data from January 1, 2007 to December 31, 2007 (includes unresolved violations from earlier years)
Source: U.S. Environmental Protection Agency, Office of Ground Water and Drinking Water, Safe Drinking Water Information System (based on data extracted April 15, 2008)

Merrimack, New Hampshire

Background

The town of Merrimack is located in southern New Hampshire, just north and adjacent to Nashua along the west bank of the Merrimack River. The township includes four villages: Reeds Ferry in the north; Merrimack (originally Souhegan Village) near the Souhegan River; and Thorntons Ferry and South Merrimack in the southern border. Thorntons Ferry was named after Matthew Thornton, a signer of the Declaration of Independence.

Originally the town was in Massachusetts: In 1734, the Commonwealth of Massachusetts granted the town organization under the name Naticook. In 1746, after the border between Massachusetts and New Hampshire was redrawn to its present line, Governor Wentworth of New Hampshire signed a charter awarding the lands between the Pennichuck and Souhegan Rivers to the town of "Merrymac." In 1750 the charter was ratified with the addition of lands north of the Souhegan River.

At first the four villages were fairly autonomous, each with its own schools, stores, and social life. Most of the people were farmers; what industry there was consisted of sawmills and grist mills. Later on, a central meetinghouse was built. In the nineteenth century, sawmills and grist mills gave way to brickyards: Bricks were floated down the Merrimack River on barges, to the city of Lowell.

In 1839, when Henry David Thoreau and his brother passed by Merrimack on the journey described in *A Week on the Concord and Merrimack Rivers*, the town was placid and rural, and it retained its character well into the twentieth century. After the 1950s, the pace of life picked up and the town grew quickly, as the Everett Turnpike was built and travel to and from Nashua, Lowell, and Boston became easier. During the 1960s, and later during the prosperous 1980s, the town became a more and more of a bedroom community for Nashua and cities in Massachusetts, as hundreds of high-tech firms sprang up, especially along Route 128 and I-495 around Boston. Merrimack, along with southeastern New Hampshire in general, was among the fastest-growing areas in the nation. New roads and housing developments now occupied what had once been farm or woodland.

In addition, major businesses moved to town. The Anheuser-Busch Company built a bottling plant and moved its famous Clydesdale horses to Merrimack, where they remain a popular attraction for visitors. PC Connection, a leading provider of electronics and computer equipment, has its headquarters in Merrimack, as does Brookstone, the specialty retailer.

To serve this knowledgeable and sophisticated work force, the town has gourmet restaurants, specialty shops, and other features.

Merrimack, like the rest of New England, enjoys a four-season climate, with pleasant summers and falls, cold winters, and late springs. Located in the low-lying Merrimack River valley, the town enjoys warmer temperatures than the hills and mountains of western and northern New Hampshire; its climate more closely resembles that of northeastern Massachusetts and Boston. Snow can begin in late November and December, but consistent ground cover is not expected until January.

Rankings

General Rankings

- Manchester* was ranked #71 out of 375 metro areas in *Cities Ranked & Rated*. Criteria: cost of living; climate; crime; transportation; economy and jobs; education; arts and culture; health and healthcare; leisure; quality of life. *Cities Ranked & Rated, 2nd Edition, 2007*
- Manchester* was ranked #130 out of 379 metro areas in *Places Rated Almanac*. Criteria: health care; education; recreation; transportation; ambience; climate; crime; housing costs; jobs. *Places Rated Almanac, 7th Edition, 2007*
- *Expansion Management* rated 362 metro areas to find out which offer the best middle class lifestyle for manufacturing and service companies. The Boston* metro area was selected as a "5-Star Quality of Life Metro" (a distinction the magazine awards to the top 20 percent of metro areas studied). The annual "Quality of Life Quotient" measures dozens of indicators across nine major categories and compares them among 362 metropolitan statistical areas in the United States. The categories are: affordable housing; good public schools; low crime levels; adult education level; standard of living; traffic and commuting; continuing education opportunities; commercial air access; labor market. *Expansion Management, June 2007*

Business/Finance Rankings

- The nation's 100 largest metro areas were analysed in terms of the percentage of households entering some stage of foreclosure in 2007. The Boston* metro area ranked #69 out of 100 (#1 = highest foreclosure rate). *RealtyTrac, "Year-End 2007 Metropolitan Foreclosure Report"*
- The Boston* metro area was identified as one of the most expensive places to rent in the U.S. The area ranked #69 out of 10 markets with an average effective rent of $1,590 per month. The rental figures cover apartment properties in complexes with 40 or more units (20 or more units in California and Arizona). The figures are blended average rents, which include all unit sizes. Effective rents include free rent incentives and other landlord concessions. *Wall Street Journal Online, January 17, 2008*
- The Boston* metro area was identified as one of the "Top 12 Nano Metros" in the U.S. by the Woodrow Wilson International Center for Scholars. The metro area is home to 36 companies, universities, government laboratories and/or organizations working in nanotechnology. *Woodrow Wilson International Center for Scholars, May 17, 2007*
- The Boston* metro area was selected one of America's "Top 50 Business Opportunity Metros" by *Expansion Management* in their 5th annual Mayor's Challenge ranking of metro areas that have achieved solid ratings across the board in numerous *EM* studies during the past 12 months. The area ranked #32. Criteria: public schools; quality of life; college educated workers; logistics infrastructure; healthcare costs; taxes and government spending; reputation among site consultants. *Expansion Management, August 2007*
- The Boston* metro area was selected as one of "America's Most Wired Cities" by *Forbes*. The metro area was ranked #13 out of 30. Criteria: percentage of Internet users with high-speed access; the range of service providers within a city; availability of public wireless hot spots. *Forbes, "America's Most Wired Cities," January 10, 2008*
- Manchester* was selected as one of the best places to start and grow a company by *Entrepreneur* and the National Policy Research Council. The Manchester* metro area ranked #32 out of 50 large metro areas. Criteria: business formation and growth (firms started four to 14 years ago that still employ at least 5 people and experienced rapid growth over the last four years). *Entrepreneur/National Policy Research Council, "Hot Cities for Entrepreneurs," September 2006*
- The Boston* metro area was selected as one of "America's Greediest Cities" by *Forbes*. The area was ranked #5 out of 10. Criteria: number of Forbes 400 (*Forbes* annual list of the richest Americans) members per capita. *Forbes, "America's Greediest Cities," December 7, 2007*

- The Boston* metro area was selected one of America's "Top 10 Knowledge Worker Metros." The area ranked #4. Criteria: degree holders (bachelors, masters, professional, and Ph.D.) as a percent of the workforce; science and engineering workers as a percent of the workforce; number of patents issued; number and type of colleges in each metro area. *Expansion Management, April 2007*

- Intel, in partnership with Sperling's BestPlaces, ranked the 80 "Best Cities for Teleworking" in America. The Boston* metro area ranked #2 among extra large metro areas. The study identifies cities that hold the greatest potential for teleworking based on a host of factors including typical commuting times, fuel prices, availability of broadband Internet access and percentage of the population in telework friendly jobs. The study also factored in extreme climate and natural hazards. *Intel, "Best Cities for Teleworking," March 30, 2006*

- The Manchester* metro area appeared on the Milken Institute "2007 Best Performing Cities" index. Rank: #126 out of 200 large metro areas. Criteria: job growth; wage and salary growth; high-tech output growth. *Milken Institute, "2007 Best Performing Cities"*

- The Boston* metro area was selected as one of "The Top 20 Boom Towns in America." *Business 2.0* magazine and econometric research firm Global Insight compared 319 metropolitan areas in the U.S. and ranked the 61 with populations over 1 million. Criteria: a weighted formula that includes forecast growth rates in sectors that contain the economy's 10 most skilled occupational clusters; the prevalence of college degrees in the local workforce; median salary. The area ranked #10 among large metro areas. *Business 2.0 Magazine, March 2004*

- Boston* was identified as one of the 100 "Most Unwired Cities" in the U.S. The area ranked #13 out of the 100 largest metro areas in the U.S. Criteria: number of public and commercial wireless access points (hotspots); airports with wireless Internet access; broadband availability; local wireless networks; and wireless email devices. *Intel, "Most Unwired Cities Survey," June 7, 2005*

- Boston* was ranked #2 out of 125 regions worldwide in terms of its "Knowledge Competitiveness Index." The index attempts to measure the knowledge-based development taking place throughout the world and is based on 19 measures of economic performance that indicate a region's ability to translate its knowledge capacity into economic value. *Robert Huggins Associates, World Knowledge Competitiveness Index 2005*

- *Forbes* ranked the 200 most populous metro areas in the U.S. in terms of the "Best Places for Business and Careers." The Manchester* metro area was ranked #134. Criteria: business costs (labor, energy, tax and office space expenses); living costs (housing, transportation, food and other household expenditures); education levels of the work force; job growth; income growth; migration trends; crime rates; and culture/leisure. *Forbes, "Best Places for Business and Careers," March 19, 2008*

- *Fortune* ranked the 100 largest metro areas in the U.S. in terms of projected median home price change in 2007. The Boston* metro area ranked #72. *Fortune.com, "Hot Spots, Cold Spots"*

- The Boston* metro area was identified as one of "America's Most Overpriced Real Estate Markets." The area ranked #9 out of 10. Criteria: housing "P/E" ratio (a market's median home price divided by annual rents minus taxes and insurance); housing affordability. *Forbes.com, "America's Most Overpriced Real Estate Markets," May 11, 2007*

Health/Environment Rankings

- 100 of the largest metro areas in the U.S. were analyzed in terms of their current drought severity. The Boston* metro area ranked #64 (#1 = driest). The rankings were based on statistics such as long-term precipitation trends and patterns and the Palmer drought indices. *Sperling's BestPlaces, www.BestPlaces.net, "America's Drought-Riskiest Cities," November 2007*

- Tahitian Noni International Hiro™, in partnership with Sperling's BestPlaces, ranked the nation's 50 largest metro areas in terms of the "Most Energetic Cities." The Boston* metro area ranked #3. Criteria: percentage of population that walk or bicycle to work; BMI score; number of food co-ops; number of farmers markets. *Tahitian Noni International Hiro™, "Most Energetic Cities," March 13, 2007*

- Doctors at the Harvard School of Public Health ranked 40 metropolitan areas based on data from the government-sponsored Hospital Quality Alliance program. The program tracks the performance of individual hospitals in treating patients for three common health problems: heart attacks, congestive heart failure, and pneumonia. The Boston* metro area ranked #1 in quality of care for heart attacks, #1 for congestive heart failure, and #30 for pneumonia. *New England Journal of Medicine, July 21, 2005*

- Scarborough Research, a leading market research firm, identified the top local markets for organic consumers. The Boston* DMA (Designated Market Area) ranked in the top 15 with 21% of adults reporting that they used any organic food product in their household during the past month. *Scarborough Research, October 10, 2007*

- *Reader's Digest* ranked the 50 largest metro areas in the U.S. in terms of how "clean" they are. The Boston* metro area ranked #43. Criteria: air quality; water quality; toxic industrial pollution; Superfund sites; and sanitation. *Reader's Digest, "The 50 Cleanest (and Dirtiest) Cities in America," July 2005*

- The American Academy of Dermatology ranked 32 U.S. metropolitan regions in terms of their residents knowledge, attitude and behaviors towards tanning and sun protection. The Manchester* metro area ranked #21. The results of the study are based on an online national survey of 3,342 respondents. *American Academy of Dermatology, "RAYS: Your Grade," May 7, 2007*

- The Manchester* metro area appeared in *Country Home's* "2008 Best Green Places" report. The area ranked #212 out of 379. Criteria: official energy policies; green power; green buildings; availability of fresh, locally grown food. *Country Home, "2008 Best Green Places"*

- Wyeth Consumer Healthcare, in partnership with Sperling's BestPlaces, ranked the nation's 50 most populous metro areas in terms of five key health factors. The Boston* metro area ranked #11. Criteria: physical activity; health status; nutrition; lifestyle pursuits; and mental wellness. *Wyeth Consumer Healthcare, "Centrum Healthiest Cities Study," April 19, 2005*

- HealthGrades surveyed over 41,000 individuals on doctor satisfaction and ranked the 20 largest metro areas based on the highest "definitely yes" responses to the question "Do you trust the physician to make decisions/recommendations that are in your best interest?" The Boston* metro area ranked #3. *HealthGrades.com, "Top Cities in Doctor-Trust," September 7, 2006*

- Boston* was identified as a "2008 Asthma Capital." The area ranked #49 out of the nation's 100 largest metropolitan areas. Twelve factors were used to identify the most challenging places to live for people with asthma: estimated prevalence; self-reported prevalence; crude death rate for asthma; annual pollen score; annual air quality; public smoking laws; number of board-certified asthma specialists; school inhaler access laws; rescue medication use; controller medication use; uninsured rate; poverty rate. *Asthma and Allergy Foundation of America, "2008 Asthma Capitals"*

- Boston* was identified as a "Spring Allergy Capital." The area ranked #99 out of 100. Three groups of factors were used to identify the most severe cities for people with allergies during the spring season: annual pollen levels; medicine utilization; access to board-certified allergists. *Asthma and Allergy Foundation of America, "2007 Spring Allergy Capital Rankings"*

- Boston* was identified as a "Fall Allergy Capital." The area ranked #99 out of 100. Three groups of factors were used to identify the most severe cities for people with allergies during the fall season: annual pollen levels; medicine utilization; access to board-certified allergists. *Asthma and Allergy Foundation of America, "2007 Fall Allergy Capital Rankings"*

- Ortho-McNeil Neurologics, in partnership with Sperling's BestPlaces, analyzed 110 metro areas and identified those U.S. cities with the highest prevalence of factors that are most commonly associated with migraine headaches. The Boston* metro area ranked #109. Criteria: number of migraine-related drug prescriptions per capita; lifestyle factors that can contribute to migraines; environmental factors that can trigger migraines; and consumption of migraine-triggering foods. *Ortho-McNeil Neurologics, "America's Migraine Hot Spots," March 14, 2006*

- Sperling's BestPlaces ranked 331 metro areas and identified the most and least stressful U.S. cities. The Manchester* metro area ranked #84 out of 114 mid-size metro areas (#1 = most stressful). Criteria: divorce rate; unemployment rate; violent and property crime; suicide rate; commute time; mental health; alcohol consumption; cloudy days. *Sperling's BestPlaces, www.BestPlaces.net, "America's Most (and Least) Stressful Cities," January 9, 2004*

- An analysis of the "Best & Worst Cities for Sleep" was conducted by Sperling's BestPlaces. The study ranked America's 50 most populated metro areas. The Boston* metro area ranked #12 (#1 = best city for sleep). Criteria: number of days residents didn't get enough rest or sleep during the past month; average length of daily commute; divorce rate; unemployment rate. *Sperling's BestPlaces, www.BestPlaces.net, "Best & Worst Cities for Sleep," 2006*

- HealthGrades evaluated the performance of America's 25 most populous metropolitan areas by measuring the outcomes of five of the highest volume and most widely studied procedures and diagnoses: coronary artery bypass graft surgery; percutaneus coronary interventions; acute myocardial infarction/heart attack in angioplasty-capable hospitals; congestive heart failure; and community acquired pneumonia. The Boston* metro area ranked #18. *HealthGrades, "HealthGrades Hospital Quality in America Study," October 12, 2004*

- Boston* was selected as one of "America's Pet Healthiest Cities" by Purina. The city ranked #13 out of 50. Criteria: veterinary services; environment; legislation; preventative care; obesity/body condition. *Purina Pet Institute, "America's Pet Healthiest Cities," May 20, 2003*

Women/Minorities Rankings

- Boston* was ranked #19 out of 100 metro areas in *SELF Magazine's* ranking of "America's Best Places for Women." A panel of experts came up with more than 50 criteria including death and disease rates, environmental indicators, community resources, and lifestyle habits. *SELF Magazine, "America's Best Places for Women 2007," December 2007*

- Boston* appeared on a list of the top 10 metro areas with the highest concentration of African-American same-sex couples among all African-American households. The area ranked #8. *Urban Institute Press, The Gay and Lesbian Atlas, May 2004*

Seniors/Retirement Rankings

- Sperling's BestPlaces in partnership with Bankers Life & Casualty Company designed a survey to identify the top 50 metro areas in the U.S. that offer the best overall qualities for senior living. The Boston* metro area ranked #8. The following criteria were statistically weighted to reflect the needs of the senior population: health; disease; economics; social; environment; spiritual; transportation; housing; and crime. *Bankers Life & Casualty Company, "Best Cities for Seniors 2005"*

- A.G. Edwards ranked America's 500 top-performing communities based on their residents' personal savings and investing behavior. The Manchester* metro area ranked #33 with an index score of 111.66 (national average = 100.00). A dozen statistical factors were measured including: participation in retirement savings plans; personal debt levels; and home ownership. *A.G. Edwards, "2007 Nest Egg Index", September 12, 2007*

Children/Family Rankings

- The Manchester* metro area was selected as one of the "Best Cities for Relocating Families" by Worldwide ERC and Primacy Relocation. The 2007 study placed a special emphasis on the housing market, which has significantly impacted the relocation industry and an employer's ability to transfer employees. The variables which weigh heavily in this category include home price, home affordability index, appreciation rates, and property tax. Other criteria include cost of living, crime rates, education, climate, focus on diversity, physicians per capita, recreation and leisure, arts and culture, air quality, watershed quality, sales tax, unemployment rate, job growth, high school and higher education index, school expenditures per student, students in public school, SAT/ACT percentile, and population growth. *Worldwide ERC and Primacy Relocation, "2007 Best Cities for Relocating Families"*

Safety Rankings

- The National Insurance Crime Bureau ranked 361 metro areas in the U.S. in terms of per capita rates of vehicle theft. The Manchester* metro area ranked #314 (#1 = highest rate). Criteria: number of vehicle theft offenses per 100,000 inhabitants. *National Insurance Crime Bureau, "NICB Vehicle Theft Study," April 22, 2008*

- Boston* appeared on Sperling's BestPlaces list of the "Riskiest Cities for Identity Theft." The area ranked #26 out of the nations 50 largest metro areas. Over 80 criteria were analyzed across four major categories: technology impact; crime; transactions; and risk profile. *Sperling's BestPlaces, www.BestPlaces.net, "Riskiest Cities for Identity Theft," July 2006*

- Farmers Insurance Group of Companies, in partnership with Sperling's BestPlaces, ranked 379 metro areas and identified the "Most Secure U.S. Place to Live." The Manchester* metro area ranked #21 out of 127 in the mid-size city category (150,000 to 500,000 residents). Criteria: crime rates; extreme weather; risk of natural disasters; environmental hazards; terrorism threats; air quality; life expectancy; job loss numbers. *Farmers Insurance Group, "Most Secure U.S. Places to Live 2007"*

- Boston* was identified as one of the most dangerous large metro areas for pedestrians in the U.S. The area ranked #50 out of the nations 50 largest metro areas. Criteria: average yearly pedestrian fatalities per capita (for the years 2002 and 2003) adjusted for the number of walkers. *Surface Transportation Policy Project, "Mean Streets 2004"*

Sports/Recreation Rankings

- The Boston* metro area appeared on the *Sporting News* list of the "Best Sports Cities 2007". The area ranked #6 out of 150 cities in the U.S. *Sporting News* takes a 12-month snapshot, roughly July to July, of each city's sports, putting a heavy premium on regular-season won-lost records (from the most recently completed season). Other criteria include: playoff berths, bowl appearances and tournament bids; championships; applicable power ratings; quality of competition; overall fan fervor as measured in part by attendance as percentage of venue capacity; abundance of teams (rewarding quality over quantity); stadium and arena quality; ticket availability and prices; franchise ownership; and marquee appeal of athletes. *SportingNews.com, "Best Sports Cities 2007," August 1, 2007*

- The Boston* metro area was selected by *Cranium* as one of the "Top 50 Fun Cities" in America. The area ranked #42. Criteria includes: number of sports teams, restaurants, and dance performances; number of toy stores; city budget spent on recreation. *Cranium, November 4, 2003*

- *Golf Digest* ranked 330 metro areas in the U.S. in terms of golf. The Manchester* metro area was ranked #325. Criteria: access to golf; weather; value of golf; and quality of golf. *Golf Digest, "Metro Golf Rankings," August 2005*

Dating/Romance Rankings

- Eli Lily and Company, in partnership with Sperling's BestPlaces, ranked the nation's 50 largest metro areas in terms of the "Most Romantic Cities for Baby Boomers." The Boston* metro area ranked #12. Criteria: marriage and divorce rates among "baby boomers" age 45 to 60; great restaurants; dance studios; chocolate, jewelry and flower sales. *Eli Lily and Company, "Most Romantic Cities for Baby Boomers," April 20, 2007*
- The Boston* metro area was selected as one of the "Top Ten U.S. Cities for Finding a Rich, Single Man" by Teasley, a Manhattan-based marketing consulting firm. The area ranked #8. Criteria: high single-male to single-female ratios; higher income to cost-of-living ratios. *Teasley, "Top Ten U.S. Cities for Finding a Rich, Single Man," February 10, 2004*
- The Boston* metro area was selected as one of the "Top Ten U.S. Cities for Finding a Rich, Single Woman" by Teasley, a Manhattan-based marketing consulting firm. The area ranked #3. Criteria: high single-female to single-male ratio; higher income to cost-of-living ratio; percentage of population that is single. *Teasley, "Where to Find a Rich, Single Woman in the United States," 2005*
- The Boston* metro area was selected as one of the "Best Cities for Relocating Singles" by Worldwide ERC and Primacy Relocation. The area ranked #21 out of the 100 largest metro areas in the U.S. Areas were selected based on the following criteria: a robust cost-of-living index; adventure and outdoor recreation opportunities; violent crime and property crime rates; percentage of the population that is unmarried (ages 25-34); ratio of single men and single women; affordability of quality higher education, including in-state and out-of-state tuition requirements and rates; number of newcomers to the area; commute times; tax rates; fee and occupancy rates for temporary housing and mini-storage; quality and quantity of collegiate and professional sporting events and fun, fan-friendly venues. *Worldwide ERC and Primacy Relocation, "2007 Best Cities for Relocating Singles," October 25, 2007*
- *Forbes* ranked the 40 most populous urbanized areas in the U.S. in terms of the "Best Cities for Singles." The Boston* metro area ranked #11. Criteria: number of singles; cost of living alone; nightlife; culture; job growth; coolness; and online dating. *Forbes.com, August 21, 2007*
- Sperling's BestPlaces in partnership with AXE Deodorant Bodyspray ranked 80 metro areas and identified "America's Best (and Worst) Cities for Dating." The Boston* metro area ranked #63 (#1 = best). Criteria: percentage of singles ages 18-24; population density; dating venues per capita. *AXE Deodorant Bodyspray, "America's Best (and Worst) Cities for Dating," May 2004*

Culture/Performing Arts Rankings

- Scarborough Research, a leading market research firm, identified the top local markets for rock concert attendance. The Boston* DMA (Designated Market Area) ranked in the top 25 with 16% of consumers, 18 years old and over, reporting that they have attended a rock concert during the past year. *Scarborough Research, June 14, 2004*

Miscellaneous Rankings

- The Boston* metro area was identified as one of "The 10 Worst Commuter Cities" in the U.S. by the *U.S. News and World Report*. The mean travel time to work is 30 minutes. *U.S. News and World Report, May 7, 2007*
- Avis Rent-A-Car and Motorola, in partnership with Sperling's BestPlaces, ranked the nation's 75 most populous metro areas in terms of how difficult they are to navigate. The Boston* metro area ranked #1 with #1 being the most challenging. Criteria: street layouts; overall design and layout; travel time index; percent of congested freeway and street lane miles; bodies of water; complexity of directions needed to travel from major airports to city center; annual delay per person; days of snow exceeding 1.5 inches; and days of rain exceeding 0.5 inch. *Avis Rent-A-Car and Motorola, "America's Most Challenging Cities to Navigate," August 3, 2004*

- The Boston* metro area appeared on *Forbes* list of "America's Drunkest Cities". The area ranked #4. Criteria: 35 of the largest continental U.S. metro areas were chosen based on availability of data and geographic diversity. Each metro was ranked in five areas: state laws; drinkers; heavy drinkers; binge drinkers; and alcoholism. *Forbes.com, "America's Drunkest Cities," August 22, 2006*
- Sperling's BestPlaces in partnership with Pep Boys ranked 77 metro areas and identified "America's Most Drivable Cities." The Boston* metro area ranked #73. Criteria: climate; road roughness; urban mobility; gas prices. *Pep Boys, "America's Most Drivable Cities," April 9, 2003*
- State Farm Insurance, in partnership with Sperling's BestPlaces, analyzed several key factors that contribute to overall family preparedness. The Boston* metro area ranked #40 out of the nation's 50 most populous metro areas. Criteria: quality of life; life insurance coverage; and investments. *State Farm Life Insurance, "Fiscally Fit Cities Report," July 20, 2004*
- Scarborough Research, a leading market research firm, identified the top local markets for grocery coupon use. The Boston* DMA (Designated Market Area) ranked in the top 25 with 37% of consumers reporting that they use grocery coupons at least once per week. *Scarborough Research, December 8, 2004*
- A study by Sperling's BestPlaces examined which U.S. metro areas were most affected by high fuel prices in 2006. The Boston* metro area was ranked #32 out of 80 (#1 = most expensive city for driving). Rankings are based on the average dollars spent on gas per year by two driver households. Criteria: cost of regular-grade gasoline; average miles driven per day; average number of gallons each driver uses and wastes in traffic congestion each day. *Sperling's BestPlaces, www.bestplaces.net, "Pain at the Pump," May 18, 2006*

Merrimack is located within the Manchester-Nashua, NH Metropolitan Statistical Area and.

Business Environment

CITY FINANCES

City Government Finances

Component	2004-2005 ($000)	2004-2005 ($ per capita)
Total Revenues	27,049	1,015
Total Expenditures	22,259	835
Debt Outstanding	6,414	241
Cash and Securities	51,259	1,923

Source: U.S Census Bureau, Government Finances 2004-2005

City Government Revenue by Source

Source	2004-2005 ($000)	2004-2005 ($ per capita)
General Revenue		
From Federal Government	316	12
From State Government	1,708	64
From Local Governments	4	0
Taxes		
Property	18,072	678
Sales	0	0
Personal Income	0	0
License	506	19
Charges	5,430	204
Liquor Store	0	0
Utility	0	0
Employee Retirement	0	0
Other	1,013	38

Source: U.S Census Bureau, Government Finances 2004-2005

City Government Expenditures by Function

Function	2004-2005 ($000)	2004-2005 ($ per capita)	2004-2005 (%)
General Expenditures			
Airports	0	0	0.0
Corrections	0	0	0.0
Education	0	0	0.0
Fire Protection	3,902	146	17.5
Governmental Administration	2,362	89	10.6
Health	0	0	0.0
Highways	3,107	117	14.0
Hospitals	0	0	0.0
Housing and Community Development	0	0	0.0
Interest on General Debt	284	11	1.3
Libraries	1,115	42	5.0
Parking	0	0	0.0
Parks and Recreation	1,221	46	5.5
Police Protection	3,962	149	17.8
Public Welfare	82	3	0.4
Sewerage	2,681	101	12.0
Solid Waste Management	1,923	72	8.6
Liquor Store	0	0	0.0
Utility	0	0	0.0
Employee Retirement	0	0	0.0
Other	1,620	61	7.3

Source: U.S Census Bureau, Government Finances 2004-2005

Municipal Bond Ratings

Area	Moody's
City	Aaa

Source: Mergent Bond Record, January 2008 (unless noted otherwise)

DEMOGRAPHICS

Population Growth

Area	1990 Census	2000 Census	2007 Estimate	2012 Projection	Population Growth (%) 1990-2000	Population Growth (%) 2000-2012
City	22,156	25,119	26,837	27,933	13.4	11.2
MSA[1]	336,073	380,841	406,243	422,426	13.3	10.9
U.S.	248,709,873	281,421,906	301,045,522	314,920,978	13.2	11.9

Note: (1) Metropolitan Statistical Area - see Appendix B for areas included
Source: Claritas, Inc.

Number of Households and Average Household Size

Area	2007 Estimate	2007 Average Household Size
City	9,639	2.78
MSA[1]	155,658	2.61
U.S.	113,668,003	2.65

Note: (1) Metropolitan Statistical Area - see Appendix B for areas included
Source: Claritas, Inc.

Race and Ethnicity

Area	White Alone[2]	Black Alone[2]	Asian Alone[2]	Other Race Alone[2]	Hispanic[3]
City	95.6	0.7	2.2	1.5	1.4
MSA[1]	91.8	1.5	3.0	3.7	4.4
U.S.	73.1	12.4	4.3	10.3	14.9

Note: Figures are 2007 estimates; (1) Metropolitan Statistical Area - see Appendix B for areas included (2) Alone is defined as not being in combination with one or more other races; (3) May be of any race.
Source: Claritas, Inc.

Ancestry

Area	German	Irish[2]	English	American	Italian	Polish	French[3]	Scottish
City	11.5	19.8	16.3	4.2	11.4	5.3	13.9	4.7
MSA[1]	9.4	21.0	15.3	5.0	9.4	4.5	13.6	3.6
U.S.	15.2	10.9	8.7	7.3	5.6	3.2	3.0	1.7

Note: Figures include multiple ancestry (e.g. if a person reported being Irish and Italian, they were included in both columns); (1) Metropolitan Statistical Area - see Appendix A for areas included; (2) Includes Celtic; (3) Includes Alsatian but excludes Basque
Source: Census 2000, Summary File 3

Foreign-Born Population

Area	Percent of Population Born in: Any Foreign Country	Europe	Asia	Africa	Oceania[2]	Canada	Mexico	Latin America[3]
City	5.0	1.4	1.6	0.1	0.0	1.5	0.0	0.4
MSA[1]	6.9	1.7	2.1	0.3	0.0	1.3	0.3	1.2
U.S.	11.1	1.7	2.9	0.3	0.1	0.3	3.3	2.5

Note: (1) Metropolitan Statistical Area - see Appendix A for areas included; (2) Includes Australia, New Zealand subregion, Melanesia, Micronesia, Polynesia, and Oceania n.e.c; (3) Includes Central America (excluding Mexico), South America, and the Caribbean.
Source: Census 2000, Summary File 3

Marriage Status

Area	Never Married	Now Married (excluding Separated)	Separated	Widowed	Divorced
City	20.9	66.4	1.2	3.0	8.5
MSA[1]	23.9	60.2	1.7	4.7	9.6
U.S.	27.1	54.4	2.2	6.6	9.7

Note: Figures are percentages and cover the population 15 years of age and older; (1) Metropolitan Statistical Area - see Appendix A for areas included
Source: Census 2000, Summary File 3

Age Distribution

Area	Percent of Population						
	Under Age 5	Age 5 to 17	Age 18 to 34	Age 35 to 49	Age 50 to 64	Age 65 to 79	80 Years and Over
City	6.8	22.2	19.0	29.0	17.1	4.5	1.4
MSA[1]	6.9	20.4	20.8	27.2	15.5	6.9	2.4
U.S.	6.8	18.9	23.7	23.5	14.8	9.2	3.2

Note: (1) Metropolitan Statistical Area - see Appendix A for areas included
Source: Census 2000, Summary File 3

Male/Female Ratio

Area	Males	Females	Males per 100 Females
City	13,382	13,455	99.5
MSA[1]	201,221	205,022	98.1
U.S.	148,320,305	152,725,217	97.1

Note: Figures are 2007 estimates; (1) Metropolitan Statistical Area - see Appendix B for areas included
Source: Claritas, Inc.

Religion

Area	Catholic	Southern Baptist	United Meth-odist	ELCA[1]	LDS[2]	Presby-terian Church USA	Jewish Est.	Muslim Est.
County	45.5	0.2	1.0	0.4	0.5	0.4	1.6	0.0
U.S.	22.0	7.1	3.7	1.8	1.5	1.1	2.2	0.6

Note: Figures are the number of adherents as a percentage of the total population; Adherents are defined as all members, including full members, their children and the estimated number of other participants who are not considered members (e.g. the baptized, those not confirmed, those regularly attending services, etc.); (1) Evangelical Lutheran Church in America; (2) The Church of Jesus Christ of Latter Day Saints
Source: Reprinted with permission from Religious Congregations and Membership in the United States 2000 (Nashville, Glenmary Research Center, 2002) Copyright Association of Statisticians of American Religious Bodies. All rights reserved.

ECONOMY

Gross Metropolitan Product

Area	2002	2003	2004	2005	2005 Rank[2]
MSA[1]	15.3	16.1	17.3	18.3	102

Note: Figures are in billions of dollars; (1) Manchester-Nashua, NH Metropolitan Statistical Area - see Appendix A for areas included; (2) Rank ranges from 1 to 361
Source: The U.S. Conference of Mayors, "U.S. Metro Economies: GMP - The Engines of America's Growth," January 2007

Economic Growth

Area	1995 GMP	2005 GMP	Average Annual Growth Rate	Growth Rate Rank[2]
MSA[1]	10.7	18.3	5.6	152

Note: Figures are in billions of dollars; GMP = Gross Metropolitan Product; (1) Manchester-Nashua, NH Metropolitan Statistical Area - see Appendix A for areas included; (2) Rank ranges from 1 to 361
Source: The U.S. Conference of Mayors, "U.S. Metro Economies: GMP - The Engines of America's Growth," January 2007

INCOME

Per Capita/Median/Average Income

Area	Per Capita ($)	Median Household ($)	Average Household ($)
City	32,940	79,899	91,644
MSA[1]	29,843	62,027	77,121
U.S.	25,495	49,280	66,670

Note: Figures are 2007 estimates; (1) Metropolitan Statistical Area - see Appendix B for areas included
Source: Claritas, Inc.

Household Income Distribution

Area	Percent of Households Earning							
	Under $15,000	$15,000 -24,999	$25,000 -34,999	$35,000 -49,999	$50,000 -74,999	$75,000 -99,000	$100,000 -149,999	$150,000 and up
City	3.0	4.0	5.5	10.1	23.5	19.3	22.7	11.8
MSA[1]	8.2	8.0	8.9	14.1	21.7	15.3	15.4	8.3
U.S.	13.1	10.9	11.2	15.6	19.5	11.9	11.3	6.6

Note: Figures are 2007 estimates; (1) Metropolitan Statistical Area - see Appendix B for areas included
Source: Claritas, Inc.

Poverty Rates by Age

Area	All Ages	Under 5 Years Old	5 to 17 Years Old	18 to 64 Years Old	65 Years and Over
City	1.9	0.1	0.7	0.9	0.2
MSA[1]	4.6	0.4	1.1	2.5	0.5
U.S.	12.4	1.2	3.0	6.9	1.2

Note: Figures are percent of population with income in 1999 below poverty level and only include population for whom poverty status is determined; (1) Metropolitan Statistical Area - see Appendix A for areas included
Source: Census 2000, Summary File 3

Personal Bankruptcy Filing Rate

Area	2004	2005	2006
Hillsborough County	3.62	4.34	1.32
U.S.	5.31	6.82	2.00

Note: Numbers are per 1,000 population and include Chapter 7 and Chapter 13 filings
Source: Federal Deposit Insurance Corporation (FDIC), Regional Economic Conditions (RECON), 8/23/2007

EMPLOYMENT

Labor Force and Employment

Area	Civilian Labor Force			Workers Employed		
	Dec. 2006	Dec. 2007	% Chg.	Dec. 2006	Dec. 2007	% Chg.
City	16,642	16,668	0.2	16,193	16,241	0.3
NECTA[1]	179,695	179,719	0.0	173,427	173,813	0.2
U.S.	152,571,000	153,705,000	0.7	146,081,000	146,334,000	0.2

Note: Data is not seasonally adjusted and covers workers 16 years of age and older;
(1) New England City and Town Area Division - see Appendix B for areas included
Source: Bureau of Labor Statistics, http://stats.bls.gov

Unemployment Rate

Area	2007											
	Jan.	Feb.	Mar.	Apr.	May	Jun.	Jul.	Aug.	Sep.	Oct.	Nov.	Dec.
City	3.4	3.5	3.2	3.0	3.2	3.3	3.1	3.0	2.7	2.5	2.6	2.6
NECTA[1]	4.3	4.2	3.9	3.6	3.5	3.6	3.6	3.6	3.2	3.0	3.1	3.3
U.S.	5.0	4.9	4.5	4.3	4.3	4.7	4.9	4.6	4.5	4.4	4.5	4.8

Note: Data is not seasonally adjusted and covers workers 16 years of age and older; All figures are percentages; (1) New England City and Town Area Division - see Appendix B for areas included
Source: Bureau of Labor Statistics, http://stats.bls.gov

Employment by Occupation

Occupation Classification	City (%)	MSA[1] (%)	U.S. (%)
Sales and Office	29.3	26.5	26.7
Professional and Related	25.8	25.0	20.2
Service	10.9	10.7	14.9
Production, Transportation, and Material Moving	10.6	14.1	14.6
Management, Business, and Financial	17.4	16.0	13.5
Construction, Extraction, and Maintenance	6.0	7.5	9.4
Farming, Forestry, and Fishing	0.1	0.2	0.7

Note: Figures cover employed civilians 16 years of age and older;
(1) Metropolitan Statistical Area - see Appendix A for areas included
Source: Census 2000, Summary File 3

Employment by Industry

Sector	NECTA[1] Number of Employees	NECTA[1] Percent of Total	U.S. Percent of Total
Government	15,700	11.5	16.3
Education and Health Services	17,200	12.6	13.4
Professional and Business Services	14,900	11.0	13.1
Retail Trade	21,300	15.7	11.6
Manufacturing	25,400	18.7	9.9
Leisure and Hospitality	10,500	7.7	9.6
Financial Activities	8,900	6.5	5.9
Construction	n/a	n/a	5.3
Wholesale Trade	6,200	4.6	4.4
Other Services	4,400	3.2	3.9
Transportation and Utilities	4,100	3.0	3.7
Information	2,200	1.6	2.2
Natural Resources and Mining	n/a	n/a	0.5

Note: Figures cover non-farm employment as of December 2007 and are not seasonally adjusted;
(1) New England City and Town Area Division - see Appendix B for areas included; n/a not available
Source: Bureau of Labor Statistics, http://stats.bls.gov

Average Wages

Occupation	$/Hr.	Occupation	$/Hr.
Accountants and Auditors	28.45	Maids and Housekeeping Cleaners	10.42
Automotive Mechanics	18.97	Maintenance and Repair Workers	17.70
Bookkeepers	16.21	Marketing Managers	52.96
Carpenters	18.97	Nuclear Medicine Technologists	n/a
Cashiers	8.93	Nurses, Licensed Practical	18.83
Clerks, General Office	14.28	Nurses, Registered	28.86
Clerks, Receptionists/Information	12.06	Nursing Aides/Orderlies/Attendants	12.37
Clerks, Shipping/Receiving	15.45	Packers and Packagers, Hand	10.59
Computer Programmers	28.22	Physical Therapists	30.64
Computer Support Specialists	23.69	Postal Service Mail Carriers	21.33
Computer Systems Analysts	37.51	Real Estate Brokers	n/a
Cooks, Restaurant	11.28	Retail Salespersons	11.53
Dentists	n/a	Sales Reps., Exc. Tech./Scientific	32.69
Electrical Engineers	39.94	Sales Reps., Tech./Scientific	37.87
Electricians	23.21	Secretaries, Exc. Legal/Med./Exec.	14.42
Financial Managers	49.63	Security Guards	14.04
First-Line Supervisors/Mgrs., Sales	18.84	Surgeons	94.87
Food Preparation Workers	8.73	Teacher Assistants	11.80
General and Operations Managers	51.15	Teachers, Elementary School	23.60
Hairdressers/Cosmetologists	13.14	Teachers, Secondary School	24.70
Internists	n/a	Telemarketers	13.92
Janitors and Cleaners	11.70	Truck Drivers, Heavy/Tractor-Trailer	20.51
Landscaping/Groundskeeping Workers	13.61	Truck Drivers, Light/Delivery Svcs.	14.51
Lawyers	43.17	Waiters and Waitresses	9.62

Note: Wage data covers the Nashua, NH-MA NECTA Division - see Appendix B for areas included. Hourly wages for elementary/secondary school teachers and teacher assistants were calculated by the editors from annual wage data assuming a 40 hour work week; n/a not available.
Source: Bureau of Labor Statistics, May 2007 Metro Area Occupational Employment and Wage Estimates

RESIDENTIAL REAL ESTATE

Building Permits

Area	Single-Family 2006	Single-Family 2007[p]	Single-Family Pct. Chg.	Multi-Family 2006	Multi-Family 2007[p]	Multi-Family Pct. Chg.	Total 2006	Total 2007[p]	Total Pct. Chg.
City	59	18	-69.5	24	0	-100.0	83	18	-78.3
U.S.	1,378,200	973,300	-29.4	460,700	407,200	-11.6	1,838,900	1,380,500	-24.9

Note: (p) preliminary; figures cover and represent new, privately-owned housing units authorized (unadjusted data); All permit data are based on estimates with imputation; U.S. figures are based on the new 20,000-place series.
Source: U.S. Census Bureau, Manufacturing, Mining, and Construction Statistics

Homeownership and Housing Vacancies

Area	Homeownership Rate[2] (%)			Rental Vacancy Rate[3] (%)			Homeowner Vacancy Rate[4] (%)		
	2005	2006	2007	2005	2006	2007	2005	2006	2007
MSA[1]	63.0	64.7	64.8	5.1	5.3	5.0	1.2	2.0	1.9
U.S.	68.9	68.8	68.1	9.8	9.8	9.7	1.9	2.4	2.7

Note: (1) Metropolitan Statistical Area - see Appendix B for areas included; (2) The proportion of households that are owners; (3) The proportion of the rental inventory that is vacant for rent; (4) The proportion of the homeowner inventory that is vacant for sale; n/a not available
Source: U.S. Census Bureau, Housing Vacancies and Homeownership Annual Statistics: 2007

TAXES

State Corporate Income Tax Rates

State	Rates and Tax Brackets
New Hampshire	8.5% > $50K; 9.25% > 150K

Note: Tax rates as of January 1, 2008; Its two corporate taxes - the Business Profits Tax (BPT) and the Business Enterprise Tax (BET) - have different rates and bases. The BPT rate is 8.5% on gross income over $50K. The BET rate is either 0.75% on gross income over $150K, or 0.75% on total compensation paid out, including dividends and interest, over $75K, making 9.25% the top rate a corporation may face.
Source: Tax Foundation, www.taxfoundation.org

State Individual Income Tax Rates

State	Federal Deductibility	Marginal Rates (%)	Standard Deduction ($)		Personal Exemptions ($)[1]	
			Single	Joint	Single	Dependents
New Hampshire	No	5.0 (h)	2,400	4,800	n/a	n/a

Note: Tax rates as of January 1, 2008; Local- and county-level taxes are not included; n/a not applicable; (1) Married joint filers generally receive double the single exemption; (h) Applies to interest and dividend income only.
Source: Tax Foundation, www.taxfoundation.org

Various State and Local Tax Rates

State and Local Sales and Use (%)	State Sales and Use (%)	Gasoline[1,2] ($/gal.)	Cigarette ($/pack)	Spirits ($/gal.)	Table Wine ($/gal.)	Beer ($/gal.)
None	(f)	0.196	1.08	(q)	(p)	0.30

Note: Tax rates as of January 1, 2008; (1) In addition to the 18.4 cpg Federal gasoline tax; (2) Rates may include additional state sales taxes, environmental protection and storage fees/taxes, and local taxes. When necessary, the volume-weighted average of all local taxes is used to approximate the typical statewide rate including local tax; (f) New Hampshire has no sales tax but does have a GRT called the business enterprise tax (BET). It has a rate of 0.75% on gross income over $150,000 or base (total compensation, interest and dividends paid) over $75,000. Businesses must also pay the b

iness profits tax (BPT), an 8.5% income tax on businesses with gross income over $50,000; (p) All wine sales are through state-run stores. Revenue in these states is generated from various taxes, fees and net profits; (q) Control state where the implied excise tax rate as calculated by DISCUS is less then zero.
Source: Tax Foundation, www.taxfoundation.org; Original research

State Tax Burdens

Area	Combined State and Local Tax Burden		Combined Federal, State and Local Tax Burden	
	Percent	Rank	Percent	Rank
New Hampshire	8.0	49	30.8	29
U.S. Average	11.0	-	32.7	-

Note: Figures cover 2007 and measure taxes as a percentage of income
Source: Tax Foundation, www.taxfoundation.org

State Business Tax Climate Index Rankings

State	Overall Rank	Corporate Tax Index Rank	Individual Income Tax Index Rank	Sales Tax Index Rank	Unemployment Insurance Tax Index Rank	Property Tax Index Rank
New Hampshire	7	50	9	1	38	36

Note: Rankings range from 1 to 50 where 1 is best. Rankings do not average across to Overall Rank. States without a given tax are given a ranking of 1.
Source: Tax Foundation, State Business Tax Climate Index 2008

TRANSPORTATION

Means of Transportation to Work

Area	Car/Truck/Van		Public Transportation			Bicycle	Walked	Other Means	Worked at Home
	Drove Alone	Car-pooled	Bus	Subway	Railroad				
City	87.5	7.8	0.1	0.0	0.0	0.2	0.5	0.4	3.5
MSA[1]	84.8	8.7	0.3	0.0	0.2	0.1	1.6	0.7	3.5
U.S.	75.7	12.2	2.5	1.5	0.5	0.4	2.9	1.0	3.3

Note: Figures are percentages and cover workers 16 years of age and older;
(1) Metropolitan Statistical Area - see Appendix A for areas included
Source: Census 2000, Summary File 3

Travel Time to Work

Area	Less Than 15 Minutes	15 to 29 Minutes	30 to 44 Minutes	45 to 59 Minutes	60 Minutes or More
City	23.0	45.4	14.5	7.3	9.8
MSA[1]	29.5	33.8	17.9	8.4	10.4
U.S.	29.4	36.1	19.1	7.4	8.0

Note: Figures are percentages and include workers 16 years old and over; (1) Metropolitan Statistical Area - see Appendix A for areas included
Source: Census 2000, Summary File 3

Travel Time Index

Area	1982	1995	2004	2005
Urban Area[1]	1.08	1.20	1.27	1.27
Average[2]	1.11	1.22	1.29	1.30

Note: Travel Time Index - The ratio of travel time in the peak period to the travel time at free-flow conditions. A value of 1.35 indicates a 20-minute free-flow trip takes 27 minutes in the peak. Free-flow speeds (60 mph on freeways and 35 mph on principal arterials) are used as the comparison threshold; (1) Covers the Boston, MA-NH-RI urban area; (2) average of 85 urban areas
Source: Texas Transportation Institute, The 2007 Urban Mobility Report, September 2007

Living Environment

COST OF LIVING

Cost of Living Index

Composite Index	Groceries	Housing	Utilities	Trans-portation	Health Care	Misc. Goods/ Services
114.7	106.3	124.4	107.0	102.4	125.2	114.5

Note: U.S. = 100; Figures cover the Manchester NH urban area.
Source: The Council for Community and Economic Research (formerly ACCRA), Cost of Living Index, 2007

Grocery Prices

Area[1]	T-Bone Steak ($/pound)	Frying Chicken ($/pound)	Whole Milk ($/half gal.)	Eggs ($/dozen)	Orange Juice ($/64 oz.)	Coffee ($/11.5 oz.)
City[2]	9.51	1.14	2.10	1.47	3.03	3.04
Avg.	8.93	1.12	2.13	1.52	3.26	3.31
Min.	5.88	0.71	1.33	0.83	2.30	2.20
Max.	12.80	2.07	3.43	3.54	5.79	6.20

Note: (1) Values for the local area are compared with the average, minimum and maximum values for all 331 areas in the Cost of Living Index report; (2) Figures cover the Manchester NH urban area; **T-Bone Steak** *(price per pound);* **Frying Chicken** *(price per pound, whole fryer);* **Whole Milk** *(half gallon carton);* **Eggs** *(price per dozen, Grade A, large);* **Orange Juice** *(64 oz. Tropicana or Florida Natural);* **Coffee** *(11.5 oz. can, vacuum-packed, Maxwell House, Hills Bros, or Folgers).*
Source: The Council for Community and Economic Research (formerly ACCRA), Cost of Living Index, 2007

Housing and Utility Costs

Area[1]	New Home Price ($)	Apartment Rent ($/month)	All Electric ($/month)	Part Electric ($/month)	Other Energy ($/month)	Telephone ($/month)
City[2]	378,952	1,014	-	75.57	91.72	29.93
Avg.	309,605	782	146.13	78.67	90.16	26.14
Min.	189,877	n/a	82.03	37.41	33.15	17.08
Max.	1,202,800	3,481	271.14	150.60	257.67	37.45

Note: (1) Values for the local area are compared with the average, minimum and maximum values for all 331 areas in the Cost of Living Index report; (2) Figures cover the Manchester NH urban area; **New Home Price** *(2,400 sf living area, 8,000 sf lot, in urban area with full utilities);* **Apartment Rent** *(950 sf 2 bedroom/1.5 or 2 bath, unfurnished, excluding all utilities except water);* **All Electric** *(average monthly cost for an all-electric home);* **Part Electric** *(average monthly cost for a part-electric home);* **Other Energy** *(average monthly cost for natural gas, fuel oil, coal, wood, and any other forms of energy except electricity);* **Telephone** *(price includes basic monthly rate for a private residential line plus additional local usage charges incurred by a family of four).*
Source: The Council for Community and Economic Research (formerly ACCRA), Cost of Living Index, 2007

Health Care, Transportation, and Other Costs

Area[1]	Doctor ($/visit)	Dentist ($/visit)	Optometrist ($/visit)	Gasoline ($/gallon)	Beauty Salon ($/visit)	Men's Shirt ($)
City[2]	148.44	89.04	82.59	2.49	35.00	34.09
Avg.	79.48	71.93	79.55	2.64	29.52	25.77
Min.	52.08	44.80	43.95	2.19	15.58	16.19
Max.	148.44	126.27	158.83	3.48	60.62	48.53

Note: (1) Values for the local area are compared with the average, minimum and maximum values for all 331 areas in the Cost of Living Index report; (2) Figures cover the Manchester NH urban area; **Doctor** *(general practitioners routine exam of an established patient);* **Dentist** *(adult teeth cleaning and periodic oral examination);* **Optometrist** *(full vision eye exam for established adult patient);* **Gasoline** *(one gallon regular unleaded, national brand, including all taxes, cash price at self-service pump if available);* **Beauty Salon** *(woman's shampoo, trim, and blow-dry);* **Men's Shirt** *(cotton/polyester dress shirt, pinpoint weave, long sleeves).*
Source: The Council for Community and Economic Research (formerly ACCRA), Cost of Living Index, 2007

HOUSING

House Price Index (HPI)

Area	National Ranking[2]	Quarterly Change (%)	One-Year Change (%)	Five-Year Change (%)
MSA[1]	208	1.04	-1.09	31.30
U.S.[3]	-	0.10	0.84	41.37

Note: The HPI is a weighted repeat sales index. It measures average price changes in repeat sales or refinancings on the same properties. This information is obtained by reviewing repeat mortgage transactions on single-family properties whose mortgages have been purchased or securitized by Fannie Mae or Freddie Mac in January 1975; (1) Metropolitan Statistical Area - see Appendix B for areas included; (2) Rankings are based on annual percentage change for all metro areas containing at least 15,000 transactions over the last 10 years and ranges from 1 to 291; (3) figures based on a weighted average of Census Division estimates; all figures are for the period ending December 31, 2007
Source: Office of Federal Housing Enterprise Oversight, House Price Index, February 26, 2008

House Price Valuations

Area	Q1 2000	Q1 2001	Q1 2002	Q1 2003	Q1 2004	Q1 2005	Q1 2006	Q1 2007	Q1 2008
MSA[1]	-25.5	-13.8	-2.0	8.5	9.7	21.1	19.6	13.9	2.9

Note: Figures show the percentage of over- or under-valuation of single family homes relative to statistically normal house values (e.g. a value of 23.6 indicates that house values are 23.6% overvalued). Statistically normal house values are based on house prices, interest rates, household incomes, population densities, and any historical premiums or discounts metropolitan areas have exhibited over time; (1) Figures cover the Metropolitan Statistical Area - see Appendix B for areas included
Source: Global Insight/National City Corporation, House Prices in America, May 2008

Median Home Prices

Area	2005	2006	2007[r]	Percent Change 2006 to 2007
MSA[1]	413.2	402.2	395.6	-1.6
U.S. Average	219.0	221.9	217.9	-1.8

Note: Figures are median sales prices of existing single-family homes in thousands of dollars; (r) revised; n/a not available; (1) Metropolitan Statistical Area - see Appendix B for areas included (data from the New Hampshire part of the metro area was not available);
Source: National Association of Realtors, Metropolitan Area Prices, 1st Quarter 2008

Housing: Year Structure Built

Area	1990 -2000	1980 -1989	1970 -1979	1960 -1969	1950 -1959	1940 -1949	Before 1940	Median Year
City	16.4	33.8	27.9	13.5	4.1	0.8	3.6	1980
MSA[1]	12.9	25.3	21.8	12.5	7.1	3.7	16.7	1975
U.S.	17.0	15.8	18.5	13.7	12.7	7.3	15.0	1971

Note: Figures are percentages; (1) Metropolitan Statistical Area - see Appendix A for areas included
Source: Census 2000, Summary File 3

HEALTH

Health Risk Data

Category	Area[1] (%)	U.S. (%)
Adults who have been told they have high blood pressure[3]	21.6	25.5
Adults who have been told they have high blood cholesterol[3]	35.5	35.6
Adults who have been told they have diabetes[2]	6.7	7.5
Adults who have been told they have arthritis[3]	25.1	27.0
Adults who have been told they currently have asthma	9.5	8.5
Adults who are current smokers	17.8	20.1
Adults who are heavy drinkers[4]	5.5	4.9
Adults who are overweight (BMI 25.0 - 29.9)	38.3	36.5
Adults who are obese (BMI 30.0 - 99.8)	22.3	25.1

Note: Data as of 2006 unless otherwise noted; (1) Figures cover the Metropolitan Statistical Area - see Appendix B for areas included; (2) Figures do not include pregnancy-related diabetes, pre-diabetes or borderline diabetes; (3) 2005 data; (4) Heavy drinkers are classified as adult men having more than two drinks per day or adult women having more than one drink per day
Source: Centers for Disease Control and Prevention, Behaviorial Risk Factor Surveillance System, SMART: Selected Metropolitan/Micropolitan Area Risk Trends, 2005, 2006

Mortality Rates for the Top 10 Causes of Death in the U.S.

ICD-10[a] Sub-Chapter	ICD-10[a] Code	Age-Adjusted Mortality Rate[1] per 100,000 population	
		County[2]	U.S.
Malignant neoplasms	C00-C97	185.5	186.5
Ischaemic heart diseases	I20-I25	143.2	152.3
Other forms of heart disease	I30-I51	44.6	51.5
Cerebrovascular diseases	I60-I69	38.4	50.0
Chronic lower respiratory diseases	J40-J47	41.6	42.6
Diabetes mellitus	E10-E14	23.4	24.8
Other degenerative diseases of the nervous system	G30-G31	28.5	22.6
Other external causes of accidental injury	W00-X59	17.9	21.4
Influenza and pneumonia	J10-J18	20.8	20.7
Hypertensive diseases	I10-I13	12.5	18.2

Note: (a) ICD-10 = International Classification of Diseases 10th Revision; (1) Mortality rates are a three year average covering 2003-2005; (2) Figures cover Hillsborough County
Source: Centers for Disease Control and Prevention, National Center for Health Statistics. Compressed Mortality File 1999-2004. CDC WONDER On-line Database, compiled from Compressed Mortality File 1999-2005 Series 20 No. 2K, 2008.

Mortality Rates for Selected Causes of Death

ICD-10[a] Sub-Chapter	ICD-10[a] Code	Age-Adjusted Mortality Rate[1] per 100,000 population	
		County[2]	U.S.
Assault	X85-Y09	2.0	5.9
Human immunodeficiency virus (HIV) disease	B20-B24	*1.0	4.5
Intentional self-harm	X60-X84	9.6	10.8
Malnutrition	E40-E46	*0.8	1.0
Obesity and other hyperalimentation	E65-E68	1.7	1.4
Organic, including symptomatic, mental disorders	F01-F09	16.1	16.8
Transport accidents	V01-V99	11.0	16.1
Viral hepatitis	B15-B19	*0.5	1.8

Note: (a) ICD-10 = International Classification of Diseases 10th Revision; (1) Mortality rates are a three year average covering 2003-2005; (2) Figures cover Hillsborough County; (*) Unreliable data as per CDC
Source: Centers for Disease Control and Prevention, National Center for Health Statistics. Compressed Mortality File 1999-2004. CDC WONDER On-line Database, compiled from Compressed Mortality File 1999-2005 Series 20 No. 2K, 2008.

Distribution of Physicians[1]

Area	Total	Family/ General Practice	Specialties	
			Medical	Surgical
Hillsborough County (number)	720	178	283	164
Hillsborough County (rate per 10,000 pop.)	17.9	4.4	7.1	4.1
U.S. (rate per 10,000 pop.)	17.7	4.6	6.9	4.3

Note: Data as of 2005; (1) Includes all non-federal, patient-care, office-based MDs
Source: Area Resource File (ARF). June 2007. U.S. Department of Health and Human Services, Health Resources and Services Administration, Bureau of Health Professions, Rockville, MD.

Hospitals

There were no hospitals listed within the city limits.
AHA Guide to the Healthcare Field 2008

According to *U.S. News,* the Boston-Cambridge-Quincy, MA-NH metro area is home to 11 of the best hospitals in the U.S.: **Beth Israel Deaconess Medical Center**; **Boston Medical Center**; **Brigham and Women's Hospital**; **Children's Hospital Boston**; **Dana-Farber Cancer Institute**; **Lahey Clinic**; **Massachusetts Eye and Ear Infirmary**; **Massachusetts General Hospital**; **McLean Hospital**; **New England Baptist Hospital**; **Spaulding Rehabilitation Hospital**. *U.S. News Online, "America's Best Hospitals 2007"*

EDUCATION

Public School District Statistics

District Name	Schls	Pupils	Pupil/ Teacher Ratio	Minority Pupils[1] (%)	Free Lunch Eligible[2] (%)	IEP[3] (%)
Merrimack School District	6	4,751	13.9	5.6	3.5	16.0

Note: Table includes regular local school districts with 2,000 or more students; (1) Percentage of students that are not white, non-Hispanic; (2) Percentage of students that are eligible for the free lunch program; (3) Percentage of students that have an Individualized Education Program.
Source: U.S. Department of Education, National Center for Education Statistics, Common Core of Data, Local Education Agency (School District) Universe Survey: School Year 2005-2006; U.S. Department of Education, National Center for Education Statistics, Common Core of Data, Public Elementary/Secondary School Universe Survey: School Year 2005-2006

Highest Level of Education

Area	Less than H.S.	H.S. Diploma	Some College, No Deg.	Associate Degree	Bachelors Degree	Masters Degree	Profess. School Degree	Doctorate Degree
City	7.0	24.8	22.0	11.2	25.2	8.3	1.0	0.5
MSA[1]	13.0	27.4	20.4	9.1	20.1	7.6	1.6	0.8
U.S.	19.4	28.4	21.2	6.4	15.7	5.9	2.0	1.0

Note: Figures are 2007 estimated percentages and cover persons age 25 and over; (1) Metropolitan Statistical Area - see Appendix B for areas included
Source: Claritas, Inc.

Educational Attainment by Race

Area	High School Graduate (%)					Bachelor's Degree (%)				
	Total	White	Black	Asian	Hisp.[2]	Total	White	Black	Asian	Hisp.[2]
City	92.9	92.9	94.2	90.7	94.6	35.0	34.5	34.5	59.7	60.0
MSA[1]	89.4	89.7	93.7	90.1	67.9	33.2	32.7	29.5	67.2	23.8
U.S.	80.4	83.6	72.3	80.4	52.4	24.4	26.1	14.3	44.1	10.4

Note: Figures shown cover persons 25 years old and over; (1) Metropolitan Statistical Area - see Appendix A for areas included; (2) people of Hispanic origin can be of any race
Source: Census 2000, Summary File 3

School Enrollment by Type

Area	Grades KG to 8				Grades 9 to 12			
	Public		Private		Public		Private	
	Enrollment	%	Enrollment	%	Enrollment	%	Enrollment	%
City	3,659	87.8	508	12.2	1,419	88.2	190	11.8
MSA[1]	25,037	86.9	3,776	13.1	9,813	89.6	1,145	10.4
U.S.	33,526,011	88.7	4,285,121	11.3	14,848,628	90.6	1,532,323	9.4

Note: Figures shown cover persons 3 years old and over; (1) Metropolitan Statistical Area - see Appendix A for areas included
Source: Census 2000, Summary File 3

School Enrollment by Race

Area	Grades KG to 8 (%)				Grades 9 to 12 (%)			
	White	Black	Asian	Hisp.[1]	White	Black	Asian	Hisp.[1]
City	94.9	0.5	2.4	0.5	93.4	3.7	2.5	0.0
MSA[2]	92.3	1.2	2.0	5.0	92.0	1.8	1.9	4.3
U.S.	68.5	15.5	3.3	16.8	68.8	15.5	3.8	15.7

Note: Figures shown cover persons 3 years old and over; (1) people of Hispanic origin can be of any race; (2) Metropolitan Statistical Area - see Appendix A for areas included
Source: Census 2000, Summary File 3

Average Salaries of Public School Classroom Teachers

District	2005-06		2006-07		Percent Change 2005-06 to 2006-07
	Dollars	Rank[1]	Dollars	Rank[1]	
New Hampshire	45,263	23	46,527	24	2.79
U.S. Average	49,026	-	50,816	-	3.65

Note: (1) State rank ranges from 1 to 51.
Source: National Education Association, Rankings & Estimates: Rankings of the States 2006 and Estimates of School Statistics 2007, December 2007

Higher Education

Four-Year Colleges			Two-Year Colleges			Medical Schools[1]	Law Schools[2]	Voc/ Tech[3]
Public	Private Non-profit	Private For-profit	Public	Private Non-profit	Private For-profit			
0	1	0	0	0	0	0	0	0

Note: Figures cover institutions located within the city limits; (1) includes schools accredited by the Liaison Committee on Medical Education and the American Osteopathic Association; (2) includes American Bar Association-accredited law schools; (3) includes all schools with programs that are less than 2 years.
Source: National Center for Education Statistics, The Integrated Postsecondary Education System (IPEDS) Peer Analysis System, 2007; www.usnews.com, Law and Medical School Directories, 2009

PRESIDENTIAL ELECTION

2004 Presidential Election Results

Area	Bush	Kerry	Nader	Other
Hillsborough County	51.0	48.2	0.6	0.2
U.S.	50.7	48.3	0.4	0.6

Note: Results are percentages and may not add to 100% due to rounding
Source: Dave Leip's Atlas of U.S. Presidential Elections, www.uselectionatlas.org

EMPLOYERS

Major Employers

Company Name	Industry	Type of Site
Anthem	Accident and health insurance	Headquarters
Catholic Medical Center	General medical and surgical hospitals	Headquarters
Citizens Bank	Investment advice	Headquarters
Comcast New Hampshire Inc	Cable and other pay television services	Single
Elliot Hospital	General medical and surgical hospitals	Headquarters
Framatome Group	Electronic connectors	Single
Freudenberg-Nok General Partnr	Plastics materials and resins	Branch
GE	Aircraft engines and engine parts	Branch
Insight Technology Inc	Optical instruments and lenses	Single
Manchester Vamc 608	Administration of veterans' affairs	Branch
Nynex	Telephone communication, except radio	Branch
Osram Sylvania Inc	Electric lamps	Branch
Oxford Health Plans Inc	Hospital and medical service plans	Branch
Roman Cthlic Docese Manchester	Religious organizations	Headquarters
St Anselm College	Colleges and universities	Single
Summit Packaging Systems Inc	Fabricated metal products, nec	Headquarters
Unitrode Corporation	Semiconductors and related devices	Headquarters
Velcro Inc	Narrow fabric mills	Headquarters

Note: Companies shown are located within the Manchester metropolitan area; nec = not elsewhere classified.
Source: www.zapdata.com, May 2008

PUBLIC SAFETY

Crime Rate

Area	All Crimes	Violent Crimes				Property Crimes		
		Murder	Forcible Rape	Robbery	Aggrav. Assault	Burglary	Larceny -Theft	Motor Vehicle Theft
City	1,132.6	0.0	0.0	3.7	7.5	112.1	990.5	18.7
Metro[1]	2,212.0	1.2	23.3	57.3	75.5	376.4	1,548.1	130.1
U.S.	3,808.1	5.7	30.9	149.4	287.5	729.4	2,206.8	398.4

Note: Figures are crimes per 100,000 population; (1) Metropolitan Statistical Area - see Appendix B for areas included
Source: FBI Uniform Crime Reports, 2006

Hate Crimes

Area	Number of Quarters Reported	Bias Motivation				
		Race	Religion	Sexual Orientation	Ethnicity	Disability
City	4	0	1	0	0	0

Source: Federal Bureau of Investigation, Hate Crime Statistics 2006

RECREATION

Culture

Dance[1]	Theatre[1]	Instrumental Music[1]	Vocal Music[1]	Series/ Festivals	Museums	Zoos and Aquariums[2]
0	0	0	0	0	0	0

Note: (1) Number of professional perfoming groups; (2) AZA-accredited
Source: The Grey House Performing Arts Directory, 2007; Official Museum Directory, 2008; Association of Zoos & Aquariums, AZA Member Zoos & Aquariums, June 2008

Professional Sports Teams

Team Name	League
Boston Red Sox	Major League Baseball (MLB)
New England Revolution	Major League Soccer (MLS)
Boston Celtics	National Basketball Association (NBA)
New England Patriots	National Football League (NFL)
Boston Bruins	National Hockey League (NHL)

Note: Includes teams located in the Boston metro area.
Source: Original research

MEDIA

Newspapers

Name	News Focus	Frequency	Circulation
Merrimack News Connection	Community	Weekly	10,000

Note: Includes newspapers with offices located in the city
Source: MediaContactsPro, March 2008

Television Stations

Name	Ch.	Network(s)	Type	Ownership
WGBH	2	PBS	Public	WGBH Educational Foundation
WBZ	4	CBS	Commercial	Viacom International Inc.
WCVB	5	ABC	Commercial	Hearst Corporation
WHDH	7	NBC	Commercial	Sunbeam Corporation
WMUR	9	ABC	Commercial	Hearst Broadcasting Group
WENH	11	PBS	Public	New Hampshire Public Television
WCEA	19	n/a	Commercial	WCEA-TV
WPXG	21	Pax	Commercial	Paxson Communications Corporation
WFXT	25	Fox	Commercial	Fox Television Stations Inc.
WUNI	27	Univision	Commercial	Entravision Communications
WSBK	38	UPN	Commercial	Viacom International Inc.
WGBX	44	PBS	Public	WGBH Educational Foundation
WLED	49	PBS	Public	New Hampshire Public Television
WNDS	50	n/a	Commercial	C.T.V. of Derry Inc.
WEKW	52	PBS	Public	New Hampshire Public Television
WLVI	56	WBN	Commercial	Tribune Broadcasting Company
WDPX	58	Pax	Commercial	Paxson Communications Corporation
WNEU	60	Telemundo	Commercial	Paxson Communications Corporation
WMFP	62	n/a	Commercial	Shop at Home Inc.
WUTF	66	n/a	Commercial	Univision Inc.
WBPX	68	Pax	Commercial	Paxson Communications Corporation

Note: Stations included cover the Boston DMA (Designated Market Area)
BurrellesLuce, MediaContacts Online, January 2007

Major AM Radio Stations

Call Letters	Freq. (kHz)	Station Type	Target Audience	Station Format	Music Format
WTAG	580	Commercial	General	News/Sports/Talk	n/a
WEZE	590	n/a	General/Religious	Educational	n/a
WGIR	610	Commercial	General	News/Talk	n/a
WRKO	680	n/a	General	Music/News/Talk	n/a
WVNE	760	Commercial	General/Religious	News/Talk	n/a
WCRN	830	n/a	General	Music/News/Talk	n/a
WEEI	850	n/a	General/Men	Music/News/Sports/Talk	n/a
WGIN	930	Commercial	General	News/Sports/Talk	n/a
WROL	950	Commercial	Religious	Music/Talk	Christian
WCAP	980	Commercial	General	News/Sports/Talk	n/a
WNTK	1020	Commercial	General	Music	Blues
WBZ	1030	Commercial	General	Sports/Talk	n/a
WBIX	1060	Commercial	General	Music/News/Talk	Contemp. Country
WILD	1090	Commercial	General	Music/News/Sports	Urban Contemp.
WNNW	1110	Commercial	Hispanic	Music/News	Latin
WAMG	1150	n/a	General/Hispanic	Music/Talk	n/a
WKOX	1200	n/a	General/Hispanic	Educational	n/a
WMKI	1260	n/a	Children/General	Music/News	n/a
WTSN	1270	n/a	General	News/Sports/Talk	n/a
WEIM	1280	Commercial	General	Talk	n/a
WPNH	1300	Commercial	General	Music	Middle Road
WORC	1310	Commercial	General	News/Talk	n/a
WDER	1320	n/a	General/Religious	Talk	n/a
WRCA	1330	Commercial	General/Hispanic	Educational/Music	World Music
WWNH	1340	n/a	General/Religious	Music	n/a
WEZS	1350	Commercial	General	Music/News	Easy Listening
WFEA	1370	Commercial	General	Music	Adult Standards
WPLM	1390	Commercial	General	Music/News	Easy Listening
WXKS	1430	Commercial	General	Music/News	Oldies
WVEI	1440	Commercial	General	Sports/Talk	n/a
WBET	1460	n/a	General	Music/News/Talk	n/a
WSRO	1470	Commercial	General	News/Talk	n/a
WNTN	1550	Commercial	General	Music/Talk	Middle Road
WSMN	1590	n/a	General	Talk	n/a
WUNR	1600	n/a	General/Hispanic	Music/News/Sports	n/a

Note: Stations included cover the Boston DMA (Designated Market Area); n/a not available
Source: BurrellesLuce, MediaContacts Online, January 2007

Major FM Radio Stations

Call Letters	Freq. (mHz)	Station Type	Target Audience	Station Format	Music Format
WGBH	89.7	n/a	General	Educational/Music/News	Blues

Note: Stations included cover the Boston DMA (Designated Market Area); n/a not available
BurrellesLuce, MediaContacts Online, January 2007

CLIMATE

Average and Extreme Temperatures

Temperature	Jan	Feb	Mar	Apr	May	Jun	Jul	Aug	Sep	Oct	Nov	Dec	Yr.
Extreme High (°F)	68	66	85	95	97	98	102	101	98	90	80	68	102
Average High (°F)	31	34	43	57	69	77	83	80	72	61	48	35	57
Average Temp. (°F)	20	23	33	44	56	65	70	68	59	48	38	25	46
Average Low (°F)	9	11	22	32	42	51	57	55	46	35	28	15	34
Extreme Low (°F)	-33	-27	-16	8	21	30	35	29	22	10	-5	-22	-33

Note: Figures cover the years 1948-1990
Source: National Climatic Data Center, International Station Meteorological Climate Summary, 9/96

Average Precipitation/Snowfall/Humidity

Precip./Humidity	Jan	Feb	Mar	Apr	May	Jun	Jul	Aug	Sep	Oct	Nov	Dec	Yr.
Avg. Precip. (in.)	2.8	2.5	2.9	3.1	3.2	3.1	3.1	3.3	2.9	3.1	3.8	3.2	36.9
Avg. Snowfall (in.)	18	15	11	2	Tr	0	0	0	0	Tr	4	14	63
Avg. Rel. Hum. 7am (%)	76	76	76	75	75	80	82	87	89	86	83	79	80
Avg. Rel. Hum. 4pm (%)	59	55	52	46	47	52	51	53	55	53	61	63	54

Note: Figures cover the years 1948-1990; Tr = Trace amounts (<0.05 in. of rain; <0.5 in. of snow)
Source: National Climatic Data Center, International Station Meteorological Climate Summary, 9/96

Weather Conditions

Temperature			Daytime Sky			Precipitation		
5°F & below	32°F & below	90°F & above	Clear	Partly cloudy	Cloudy	0.01 inch or more precip.	0.1 inch or more snow/ice	Thunder-storms
32	171	12	87	131	147	125	32	19

Note: Figures are average number of days per year and cover the years 1948-1990
Source: National Climatic Data Center, International Station Meteorological Climate Summary, 9/96

HAZARDOUS WASTE

Superfund Sites

Merrimack has one hazardous waste site on the EPA's Superfund Final National Priorities List: **New Hampshire Plating Co.**. *U.S. Environmental Protection Agency, Final National Priorities List, June 23, 2008*

AIR & WATER QUALITY

Air Quality Index

Area	Percent of Days when Air Quality was...[2]				AQI Statistics	
	Good	Moderate	Unhealthy for Sensitive Groups	Unhealthy	Maximum	Median
MSA[1]	94.7	5.0	0.3	0.0	127	21

Note: The Air Quality Index (AQI) is an index for reporting daily air quality. EPA calculates the AQI for five major air pollutants regulated by the Clean Air Act: ground-level ozone, particle pollution (also known as particulate matter), carbon monoxide, sulfur dioxide, and nitrogen dioxide. The AQI runs from 0 to 500. The higher the AQI value, the greater the level of air pollution and the greater the health concern. There are six AQI categories: "Good" The AQI is between 0 and 50. Air quality is considered satisfactory; "Moderate" The AQI is between 51 and 100. Air quality is acceptable; "Unhealthy for Sensitive Groups" When AQI values are between 101 and 150, members of sensitive groups may experience health effects; "Unhealthy" When AQI values are between 151 and 200 everyone may begin to experience health effects; "Very Unhealthy" AQI values between 201 and 300 trigger a health alert; "Hazardous" AQI values over 300 trigger health warnings of emergency conditions; (1) Metropolitan Statistical Area - see Appendix A for areas included; (2) Based on 359 days with AQI data in 2007.
Source: U.S. Environmental Protection Agency, Air Quality Index Report, 2007

Air Quality Index Pollutants

Area	Percent of Days when AQI Pollutant was...[2]					
	Carbon Monoxide	Nitrogen Dioxide	Ozone	Sulfur Dioxide	Particulate Matter 2.5	Particulate Matter 10
MSA[1]	25.6	0.0	51.0	15.9	0.0	7.5

Note: The Air Quality Index (AQI) is an index for reporting daily air quality. EPA calculates the AQI for five major air pollutants regulated by the Clean Air Act: ground-level ozone, particle pollution (also known as particulate matter), carbon monoxide, sulfur dioxide, and nitrogen dioxide. The AQI runs from 0 to 500. The higher the AQI value, the greater the level of air pollution and the greater the health concern; (1) Metropolitan Statistical Area - see Appendix A for areas included; (2) Based on 359 days with AQI data in 2007.
Source: U.S. Environmental Protection Agency, Air Quality Index Report, 2007

Air Quality Index Trends

Area	Trend Sites (13)								All Sites (85)
	1999	2000	2001	2002	2003	2004	2005	2006	2006
MSA[1]	4	0	3	9	8	1	4	1	4

Note: An AQI value greater than 100 indicates that air quality would have been in the unhealthful range on that day. Data from exceptional events are not included. These counts are presented in two ways. First, the counts are based on sites having an adequate record of monitoring data during the trend period (trend sites). These counts represent the relative change in the number of days with AQI values greater than 100. In the last column, the counts are based on all sites with data in the most recent year (because it is possible for a site to have data in the most recent year but not enough data to be a trend site); (1) Metropolitan Statistical Area - see Appendix A for areas included.
Source: U.S. Environmental Protection Agency, Office of Air and Radiation, Air Trends, Factbook and Related Information, Air Pollution Trends in Selected Metropolitan Areas 2006

Maximum Air Pollutant Concentrations

	Particulate Matter 10 (ug/m^3)	Particulate Matter 2.5 (ug/m^3)	Ozone (ppm)	Carbon Monoxide (ppm)	Sulfur Dioxide (ppm)	Nitrogen Dioxide (ppm)	Lead (ug/m^3)
MSA[1] Level	31	n/a	0.086	3	0.014	0.01	n/a
NAAQS[2]	150	35	0.125	9	0.140	0.053	1.50
Met NAAQS[2]	Yes	Yes	Yes	Yes	Yes	Yes	n/a

Note: Data from exceptional events are not included; (1) Metropolitan Statistical Area - see Appendix A for areas included; (2) National Ambient Air Quality Standards; n/a not available
Concentrations: Particulate Matter 10 (coarse particulate) - highest second maximum 24-hour concentration; Particulate Matter 2.5 (fine particulate) - highest 98th percentile 24-hour concentration; Ozone - highest second daily maximum 1-hour concentration; Carbon Monoxide - highest second maximum non-overlapping 8-hour concentration; Sulfur Dioxide - highest second maximum 24-hour concentration; Nitrogen Dioxide - highest arithmetic mean concentration; Lead - highest quarterly maximum concentration
Units: ppm = parts per million; ug/m^3 = micrograms per cubic meter
Source: U.S. Environmental Protection Agency, MSA Factbook 2006, Air Quality Statistics by City

Drinking Water

Water System Name	Pop. Served	Primary Water Source Type	Violations[1]	
			Health Based	Monitoring/ Reporting
Merrimack Village District	23,000	Ground	0	0

Note: (1) Based on violation data from January 1, 2007 to December 31, 2007 (includes unresolved violations from earlier years)
Source: U.S. Environmental Protection Agency, Office of Ground Water and Drinking Water, Safe Drinking Water Information System (based on data extracted April 15, 2008)

Bernards, New Jersey

Background

Bernards is located in North-Central New Jersey, 25 miles west of Newark in Somerset County. It includes the communities of Basking Ridge, Liberty Corner and Lyons.

Bernards was formed in 1760 by a royal charter from King George II of England. The township was named for Sir Francis Bernard, who was the royal governor of New Jersey from 1758 until 1760 when he left to take a similar position in Massachusetts. At the time, the area was under the control of the Rev. Samuel Kennedy, fourth pastor of the Presbyterian Church in Basking Ridge. The territory was known as "The Ridge" and was the cultural center for the surrounding villages and hamlets.

In December 1776, the Township Continental Army General Charles Lee, second in command to George Washington, was captured by the British. Bernard's history is still evident today in many parts of the township.

Bernards architecture is eclectic, with many recognized historic sites. The Basking Ridge Presbyterian Church , an example of Greek Revival architecture was constructed in 1839 and its exterior has changed very little. The Coffee House, built in 1804 and a wonderful example of a New Jersey frame farmhouse, has been a residence, crossroads tavern, and community center for local farms in the early 19th century. Lyons Station, a one-story Tudor Revival-style structure, was designed and built by noted architect D.T. Mack in 1931.

Other places of interest include the Penn Brook Golf Course, Day Camp Sunshine, Lord Sterling Park, and Schmidt Park.

Somerset county is one of the fastest growing counties in New Jersey. Major employers in Bernards include Affinity Federal Credit Union and Barnes and Noble College Booksellers, the college textbook division of the retail giant.

The Mountain View Corporate Center, an 821,000 square foot campus will feature six buildings ranging from 58,000 to 212,000 square feet; several structures are already completed and occupied.

Bernards has a seasonal climate with hot summers and cold winters. Median summer temperatures average 70 degrees, while winter averages can be as low as 20 degrees during of December and January. The city averages 4.5 inches of rainfall per month from April to October and 7 inches of snowfall per month from December to March.

Rankings

General Rankings

- Edison* was ranked #161 out of 375 metro areas in *Cities Ranked & Rated*. Criteria: cost of living; climate; crime; transportation; economy and jobs; education; arts and culture; health and healthcare; leisure; quality of life. *Cities Ranked & Rated, 2nd Edition, 2007*
- Edison* was ranked #50 out of 379 metro areas in *Places Rated Almanac*. Criteria: health care; education; recreation; transportation; ambience; climate; crime; housing costs; jobs. *Places Rated Almanac, 7th Edition, 2007*

Business/Finance Rankings

- The nation's 100 largest metro areas were analysed in terms of the percentage of households entering some stage of foreclosure in 2007. The Edison* metro area ranked #61 out of 100 (#1 = highest foreclosure rate). *RealtyTrac, "Year-End 2007 Metropolitan Foreclosure Report"*
- The New York* metro area was identified as one of the most expensive places to rent in the U.S. The area ranked #61 out of 10 markets with an average effective rent of $2,720 per month. The rental figures cover apartment properties in complexes with 40 or more units (20 or more units in California and Arizona). The figures are blended average rents, which include all unit sizes. Effective rents include free rent incentives and other landlord concessions. *Wall Street Journal Online, January 17, 2008*
- The New York* metro area was selected as one of "America's Most Wired Cities" by *Forbes*. The metro area was ranked #9 out of 30. Criteria: percentage of Internet users with high-speed access; the range of service providers within a city; availability of public wireless hot spots. *Forbes, "America's Most Wired Cities," January 10, 2008*
- Middlesex* was selected as one of the best places to start and grow a company by *Entrepreneur* and the National Policy Research Council. The Middlesex* metro area ranked #35 out of 50 large metro areas. Criteria: business formation and growth (firms started four to 14 years ago that still employ at least 5 people and experienced rapid growth over the last four years). *Entrepreneur/National Policy Research Council, "Hot Cities for Entrepreneurs," September 2006*
- The New York* metro area was selected as one of "America's Greediest Cities" by *Forbes*. The area was ranked #6 out of 10. Criteria: number of Forbes 400 (*Forbes* annual list of the richest Americans) members per capita. *Forbes, "America's Greediest Cities," December 7, 2007*
- Edison* was cited as one of America's top large metros (population over 1 million) for new and expanded facility projects in 2007. The area appeared in the top 10 with 72 projects. *Site Selection, "Top Metropolitan Area Awards," March 2008*
- Intel, in partnership with Sperling's BestPlaces, ranked the 80 "Best Cities for Teleworking" in America. The New York* metro area ranked #6 among extra large metro areas. The study identifies cities that hold the greatest potential for teleworking based on a host of factors including typical commuting times, fuel prices, availability of broadband Internet access and percentage of the population in telework friendly jobs. The study also factored in extreme climate and natural hazards. *Intel, "Best Cities for Teleworking," March 30, 2006*
- The Edison* metro area appeared on the Milken Institute "2007 Best Performing Cities" index. Rank: #133 out of 200 large metro areas. Criteria: job growth; wage and salary growth; high-tech output growth. *Milken Institute, "2007 Best Performing Cities"*
- The Middlesex* metro area was selected as one of "The Top 20 Boom Towns in America." *Business 2.0* magazine and econometric research firm Global Insight compared 319 metropolitan areas in the U.S. and ranked the 61 with populations over 1 million. Criteria: a weighted formula that includes forecast growth rates in sectors that contain the economy's 10 most skilled occupational clusters; the prevalence of college degrees in the local workforce; median salary. The area ranked #8 among large metro areas. *Business 2.0 Magazine, March 2004*

- Middlesex* was identified as one of the 100 "Most Unwired Cities" in the U.S. The area ranked #76 out of the 100 largest metro areas in the U.S. Criteria: number of public and commercial wireless access points (hotspots); airports with wireless Internet access; broadband availability; local wireless networks; and wireless email devices. *Intel, "Most Unwired Cities Survey," June 7, 2005*

- New York* was ranked #12 out of 125 regions worldwide in terms of its "Knowledge Competitiveness Index." The index attempts to measure the knowledge-based development taking place throughout the world and is based on 19 measures of economic performance that indicate a region's ability to translate its knowledge capacity into economic value. *Robert Huggins Associates, World Knowledge Competitiveness Index 2005*

- *Forbes* ranked the 200 most populous metro areas in the U.S. in terms of the "Best Places for Business and Careers." The Edison* metro area was ranked #51. Criteria: business costs (labor, energy, tax and office space expenses); living costs (housing, transportation, food and other household expenditures); education levels of the work force; job growth; income growth; migration trends; crime rates; and culture/leisure. *Forbes, "Best Places for Business and Careers," March 19, 2008*

- *Fortune* ranked the 100 largest metro areas in the U.S. in terms of projected median home price change in 2007. The Edison* metro area ranked #75. *Fortune.com, "Hot Spots, Cold Spots"*

- The New York* metro area was identified as one of "America's Most Overpriced Real Estate Markets." The area ranked #7 out of 10. Criteria: housing "P/E" ratio (a market's median home price divided by annual rents minus taxes and insurance); housing affordability. *Forbes.com, "America's Most Overpriced Real Estate Markets," May 11, 2007*

Health/Environment Rankings

- 100 of the largest metro areas in the U.S. were analyzed in terms of their current drought severity. The New York* metro area ranked #75 (#1 = driest). The rankings were based on statistics such as long-term precipitation trends and patterns and the Palmer drought indices. *Sperling's BestPlaces, www.BestPlaces.net, "America's Drought-Riskiest Cities," November 2007*

- Doctors at the Harvard School of Public Health ranked 40 metropolitan areas based on data from the government-sponsored Hospital Quality Alliance program. The program tracks the performance of individual hospitals in treating patients for three common health problems: heart attacks, congestive heart failure, and pneumonia. The New York* metro area ranked #17 in quality of care for heart attacks, #8 for congestive heart failure, and #34 for pneumonia. *New England Journal of Medicine, July 21, 2005*

- *Reader's Digest* ranked the 50 largest metro areas in the U.S. in terms of how "clean" they are. The New York* metro area ranked #49. Criteria: air quality; water quality; toxic industrial pollution; Superfund sites; and sanitation. *Reader's Digest, "The 50 Cleanest (and Dirtiest) Cities in America," July 2005*

- The American Academy of Dermatology ranked 32 U.S. metropolitan regions in terms of their residents knowledge, attitude and behaviors towards tanning and sun protection. The New York* metro area ranked #2. The results of the study are based on an online national survey of 3,342 respondents. *American Academy of Dermatology, "RAYS: Your Grade," May 7, 2007*

- The Edison* metro area appeared in *Country Home's* "2008 Best Green Places" report. The area ranked #265 out of 379. Criteria: official energy policies; green power; green buildings; availability of fresh, locally grown food. *Country Home, "2008 Best Green Places"*

- Wyeth Consumer Healthcare, in partnership with Sperling's BestPlaces, ranked the nation's 50 most populous metro areas in terms of five key health factors. The New York* metro area ranked #43. Criteria: physical activity; health status; nutrition; lifestyle pursuits; and mental wellness. *Wyeth Consumer Healthcare, "Centrum Healthiest Cities Study," April 19, 2005*

- HealthGrades surveyed over 41,000 individuals on doctor satisfaction and ranked the 20 largest metro areas based on the highest "definitely yes" responses to the question "Do you trust the physician to make decisions/recommendations that are in your best interest?" The New York* metro area ranked #10. *HealthGrades.com, "Top Cities in Doctor-Trust," September 7, 2006*

- New York* was identified as a "2008 Asthma Capital." The area ranked #38 out of the nation's 100 largest metropolitan areas. Twelve factors were used to identify the most challenging places to live for people with asthma: estimated prevalence; self-reported prevalence; crude death rate for asthma; annual pollen score; annual air quality; public smoking laws; number of board-certified asthma specialists; school inhaler access laws; rescue medication use; controller medication use; uninsured rate; poverty rate. *Asthma and Allergy Foundation of America, "2008 Asthma Capitals"*

- New York* was identified as a "Spring Allergy Capital." The area ranked #79 out of 100. Three groups of factors were used to identify the most severe cities for people with allergies during the spring season: annual pollen levels; medicine utilization; access to board-certified allergists. *Asthma and Allergy Foundation of America, "2007 Spring Allergy Capital Rankings"*

- New York* was identified as a "Fall Allergy Capital." The area ranked #69 out of 100. Three groups of factors were used to identify the most severe cities for people with allergies during the fall season: annual pollen levels; medicine utilization; access to board-certified allergists. *Asthma and Allergy Foundation of America, "2007 Fall Allergy Capital Rankings"*

- Ortho-McNeil Neurologics, in partnership with Sperling's BestPlaces, analyzed 110 metro areas and identified those U.S. cities with the highest prevalence of factors that are most commonly associated with migraine headaches. The Middlesex* metro area ranked #106. Criteria: number of migraine-related drug prescriptions per capita; lifestyle factors that can contribute to migraines; environmental factors that can trigger migraines; and consumption of migraine-triggering foods. *Ortho-McNeil Neurologics, "America's Migraine Hot Spots," March 14, 2006*

- Sperling's BestPlaces ranked 331 metro areas and identified the most and least stressful U.S. cities. The Middlesex* metro area ranked #84 out of the 100 largest metro areas (#1 = most stressful). Criteria: divorce rate; unemployment rate; violent and property crime; suicide rate; commute time; mental health; alcohol consumption; cloudy days. *Sperling's BestPlaces, www.BestPlaces.net, "America's Most (and Least) Stressful Cities," January 9, 2004*

- An analysis of the "Best & Worst Cities for Sleep" was conducted by Sperling's BestPlaces. The study ranked America's 50 most populated metro areas. The Middlesex* metro area ranked #15 (#1 = best city for sleep). Criteria: number of days residents didn't get enough rest or sleep during the past month; average length of daily commute; divorce rate; unemployment rate. *Sperling's BestPlaces, www.BestPlaces.net, "Best & Worst Cities for Sleep," 2006*

- HealthGrades evaluated the performance of America's 25 most populous metropolitan areas by measuring the outcomes of five of the highest volume and most widely studied procedures and diagnoses: coronary artery bypass graft surgery; percutaneus coronary interventions; acute myocardial infarction/heart attack in angioplasty-capable hospitals; congestive heart failure; and community acquired pneumonia. The New York* metro area ranked #17. *HealthGrades, "HealthGrades Hospital Quality in America Study," October 12, 2004*

- New York* was highlighted as one of the 25 metro areas most polluted by year-round particle pollution (PM 2.5) in the U.S. The area ranked #17. *American Lung Association, State of the Air: 2007*

- New York* was highlighted as one of the 25 most ozone-polluted metro areas in the U.S. The area ranked #10. *American Lung Association, State of the Air: 2007*

- New York* was selected as one of "America's Top 10 Low-Carb Cities" by *LowCarbiz Magazine*. Criteria: abundance of low-carb products; restaurants with low-carb menu items; health practitioners supportive of carb-cutting regimens; local culture generally conducive to exercise and health. *LowCarbiz Magazine, April 2004*

- New York* was selected as one of "America's Pet Healthiest Cities" by Purina. The city ranked #14 out of 50. Criteria: veterinary services; environment; legislation; preventative care; obesity/body condition. *Purina Pet Institute, "America's Pet Healthiest Cities," May 20, 2003*

Women/Minorities Rankings

- Middlesex* was ranked #11 out of 100 metro areas in *SELF Magazine's* ranking of "America's Best Places for Women." A panel of experts came up with more than 50 criteria including death and disease rates, environmental indicators, community resources, and lifestyle habits. *SELF Magazine, "America's Best Places for Women 2007," December 2007*
- New York* appeared on a list of the top 10 metro areas with the highest concentration of same-sex households. The area ranked #6. *Urban Institute Press, The Gay and Lesbian Atlas, May 2004*
- New York* appeared on a list of the top 10 metro areas with the highest concentration of gay male couples. The area ranked #5. *Urban Institute Press, The Gay and Lesbian Atlas, May 2004*

Seniors/Retirement Rankings

- Sperling's BestPlaces in partnership with Bankers Life & Casualty Company designed a survey to identify the top 50 metro areas in the U.S. that offer the best overall qualities for senior living. The New York* metro area ranked #7. The following criteria were statistically weighted to reflect the needs of the senior population: health; disease; economics; social; environment; spiritual; transportation; housing; and crime. *Bankers Life & Casualty Company, "Best Cities for Seniors 2005"*
- A.G. Edwards ranked America's 500 top-performing communities based on their residents' personal savings and investing behavior. The New York* metro area ranked #241 with an index score of 101.69 (national average = 100.00). A dozen statistical factors were measured including: participation in retirement savings plans; personal debt levels; and home ownership. *A.G. Edwards, "2007 Nest Egg Index", September 12, 2007*

Children/Family Rankings

- The Edison* metro area was selected as one of the "Best Cities for Relocating Families" by Worldwide ERC and Primacy Relocation. The 2007 study placed a special emphasis on the housing market, which has significantly impacted the relocation industry and an employer's ability to transfer employees. The variables which weigh heavily in this category include home price, home affordability index, appreciation rates, and property tax. Other criteria include cost of living, crime rates, education, climate, focus on diversity, physicians per capita, recreation and leisure, arts and culture, air quality, watershed quality, sales tax, unemployment rate, job growth, high school and higher education index, school expenditures per student, students in public school, SAT/ACT percentile, and population growth. *Worldwide ERC and Primacy Relocation, "2007 Best Cities for Relocating Families"*

Safety Rankings

- The National Insurance Crime Bureau ranked 361 metro areas in the U.S. in terms of per capita rates of vehicle theft. The New York* metro area ranked #224 (#1 = highest rate). Criteria: number of vehicle theft offenses per 100,000 inhabitants. *National Insurance Crime Bureau, "NICB Vehicle Theft Study," April 22, 2008*
- New York* appeared on Sperling's BestPlaces list of the "Riskiest Cities for Identity Theft." The area ranked #29 out of the nations 50 largest metro areas. Over 80 criteria were analyzed across four major categories: technology impact; crime; transactions; and risk profile. *Sperling's BestPlaces, www.BestPlaces.net, "Riskiest Cities for Identity Theft," July 2006*

- Farmers Insurance Group of Companies, in partnership with Sperling's BestPlaces, ranked 379 metro areas and identified the "Most Secure U.S. Place to Live." The Edison* metro area ranked #13 out of 114 in the large metro area category (500,000 or more residents). Criteria: crime rates; extreme weather; risk of natural disasters; environmental hazards; terrorism threats; air quality; life expectancy; job loss numbers. *Farmers Insurance Group, "Most Secure U.S. Places to Live 2007"*

- Middlesex* was identified as one of the most dangerous large metro areas for pedestrians in the U.S. The area ranked #47 out of the nations 50 largest metro areas. Criteria: average yearly pedestrian fatalities per capita (for the years 2002 and 2003) adjusted for the number of walkers. *Surface Transportation Policy Project, "Mean Streets 2004"*

Sports/Recreation Rankings

- The New York* metro area appeared on the *Sporting News* list of the "Best Sports Cities 2007". The area ranked #2 out of 150 cities in the U.S. *Sporting News* takes a 12-month snapshot, roughly July to July, of each city's sports, putting a heavy premium on regular-season won-lost records (from the most recently completed season). Other criteria include: playoff berths, bowl appearances and tournament bids; championships; applicable power ratings; quality of competition; overall fan fervor as measured in part by attendance as percentage of venue capacity; abundance of teams (rewarding quality over quantity); stadium and arena quality; ticket availability and prices; franchise ownership; and marquee appeal of athletes. *SportingNews.com, "Best Sports Cities 2007," August 1, 2007*

- The New York* metro area was selected by *Cranium* as one of the "Top 50 Fun Cities" in America. The area ranked #41. Criteria includes: number of sports teams, restaurants, and dance performances; number of toy stores; city budget spent on recreation. *Cranium, November 4, 2003*

- *Golf Digest* ranked 330 metro areas in the U.S. in terms of golf. The Middlesex* metro area was ranked #306. Criteria: access to golf; weather; value of golf; and quality of golf. *Golf Digest, "Metro Golf Rankings," August 2005*

Dating/Romance Rankings

- Eli Lily and Company, in partnership with Sperling's BestPlaces, ranked the nation's 50 largest metro areas in terms of the "Most Romantic Cities for Baby Boomers." The New York* metro area ranked #16. Criteria: marriage and divorce rates among "baby boomers" age 45 to 60; great restaurants; dance studios; chocolate, jewelry and flower sales. *Eli Lily and Company, "Most Romantic Cities for Baby Boomers," April 20, 2007*

- The New York* metro area was selected as one of the "Top Ten U.S. Cities for Finding a Rich, Single Woman" by Teasley, a Manhattan-based marketing consulting firm. The area ranked #2. Criteria: high single-female to single-male ratio; higher income to cost-of-living ratio; percentage of population that is single. *Teasley, "Where to Find a Rich, Single Woman in the United States," 2005*

- The Edison* metro area was selected as one of the "Best Cities for Relocating Singles" by Worldwide ERC and Primacy Relocation. The area ranked #17 out of the 100 largest metro areas in the U.S. Areas were selected based on the following criteria: a robust cost-of-living index; adventure and outdoor recreation opportunities; violent crime and property crime rates; percentage of the population that is unmarried (ages 25-34); ratio of single men and single women; affordability of quality higher education, including in-state and out-of-state tuition requirements and rates; number of newcomers to the area; commute times; tax rates; fee and occupancy rates for temporary housing and mini-storage; quality and quantity of collegiate and professional sporting events and fun, fan-friendly venues. *Worldwide ERC and Primacy Relocation, "2007 Best Cities for Relocating Singles," October 25, 2007*

- *Forbes* ranked the 40 most populous urbanized areas in the U.S. in terms of the "Best Cities for Singles." The New York* metro area ranked #2. Criteria: number of singles; cost of living alone; nightlife; culture; job growth; coolness; and online dating. *Forbes.com, August 21, 2007*

- Sperling's BestPlaces in partnership with AXE Deodorant Bodyspray ranked 80 metro areas and identified "America's Best (and Worst) Cities for Dating." The New York* metro area ranked #18 (#1 = best). Criteria: percentage of singles ages 18-24; population density; dating venues per capita. *AXE Deodorant Bodyspray, "America's Best (and Worst) Cities for Dating," May 2004*

Culture/Performing Arts Rankings

- The New York* metro area was selected as one of the "Best Places for Artists in America" by *BusinessWeek.com.* Criteria: percentage of young people age 25 to 34; population diversity; concentration of museums, philharmonic orchestras, dance companies, theater troupes, library resources, and college arts programs. *BusinessWeek.com, "Best Places for Artists in America," February 26, 2007*
- Scarborough Research, a leading market research firm, identified the top local markets for rock concert attendance. The New York* DMA (Designated Market Area) ranked in the top 25 with 14% of consumers, 18 years old and over, reporting that they have attended a rock concert during the past year. *Scarborough Research, June 14, 2004*

Miscellaneous Rankings

- The New York* metro area was identified as one of "The 10 Worst Commuter Cities" in the U.S. by the *U.S. News and World Report.* The mean travel time to work is 39 minutes. *U.S. News and World Report, May 7, 2007*
- Scarborough Research, a leading market research firm, identified the top local markets for bloggers. The New York* DMA (Designated Market Area) ranked in the top 13 with 10% of adults reporting that they had read or contributed to a blog within the past 30 days. *Scarborough Research, October 24, 2007*
- The New York* metro area was selected as one of the "Top 10 Most Independent Cities for Homesellers". The area ranked #1. The cities listed had more consumers choosing to sell their homes without the help of a real-estate agent than anywhere else. Data was based on geographical information for listings posted on ForSaleByOwner.com from January 1, 2007 through June 30, 2007. *ForSaleByOwner.com, October 1, 2007*
- Avis Rent-A-Car and Motorola, in partnership with Sperling's BestPlaces, ranked the nation's 75 most populous metro areas in terms of how difficult they are to navigate. The New York* metro area ranked #5 with #1 being the most challenging. Criteria: street layouts; overall design and layout; travel time index; percent of congested freeway and street lane miles; bodies of water; complexity of directions needed to travel from major airports to city center; annual delay per person; days of snow exceeding 1.5 inches; and days of rain exceeding 0.5 inch. *Avis Rent-A-Car and Motorola, "America's Most Challenging Cities to Navigate," August 3, 2004*
- The New York* metro area appeared on *Forbes* list of "America's Drunkest Cities". The area ranked #32. Criteria: 35 of the largest continental U.S. metro areas were chosen based on availability of data and geographic diversity. Each metro was ranked in five areas: state laws; drinkers; heavy drinkers; binge drinkers; and alcoholism. *Forbes.com, "America's Drunkest Cities," August 22, 2006*
- Sperling's BestPlaces in partnership with Pep Boys ranked 77 metro areas and identified "America's Most Drivable Cities." The New York* metro area ranked #70. Criteria: climate; road roughness; urban mobility; gas prices. *Pep Boys, "America's Most Drivable Cities," April 9, 2003*
- State Farm Insurance, in partnership with Sperling's BestPlaces, analyzed several key factors that contribute to overall family preparedness. The New York* metro area ranked #44 out of the nation's 50 most populous metro areas. Criteria: quality of life; life insurance coverage; and investments. *State Farm Life Insurance, "Fiscally Fit Cities Report," July 20, 2004*

- Scarborough Research, a leading market research firm, identified the top local markets for grocery coupon use. The New York* DMA (Designated Market Area) ranked in the top 25 with 38% of consumers reporting that they use grocery coupons at least once per week. *Scarborough Research, December 8, 2004*

- A study by Sperling's BestPlaces examined which U.S. metro areas were most affected by high fuel prices in 2006. The New York* metro area was ranked #64 out of 80 (#1 = most expensive city for driving). Rankings are based on the average dollars spent on gas per year by two driver households. Criteria: cost of regular-grade gasoline; average miles driven per day; average number of gallons each driver uses and wastes in traffic congestion each day. *Sperling's BestPlaces, www.bestplaces.net, "Pain at the Pump," May 18, 2006*

Bernards is located within the New York-Northern New Jersey-Long Island, NY-NJ-PA Metropolitan Statistical Area, Edison, NJ Metropolitan Division, and Middlesex-Somerset-Hunterdon, NJ metro area.

Business Environment

CITY FINANCES

City Government Finances

Component	2004-2005 ($000)	2004-2005 ($ per capita)
Total Revenues	30,960	1,149
Total Expenditures	27,701	1,028
Debt Outstanding	14,670	545
Cash and Securities	36,587	1,358

Source: U.S Census Bureau, Government Finances 2004-2005

City Government Revenue by Source

Source	2004-2005 ($000)	2004-2005 ($ per capita)
General Revenue		
From Federal Government	100	4
From State Government	2,618	97
From Local Governments	609	23
Taxes		
Property	19,936	740
Sales	263	10
Personal Income	0	0
License	827	31
Charges	5,378	200
Liquor Store	0	0
Utility	0	0
Employee Retirement	0	0
Other	1,229	46

Source: U.S Census Bureau, Government Finances 2004-2005

City Government Expenditures by Function

Function	2004-2005 ($000)	2004-2005 ($ per capita)	2004-2005 (%)
General Expenditures			
Airports	0	0	0.0
Corrections	0	0	0.0
Education	0	0	0.0
Fire Protection	544	20	2.0
Governmental Administration	2,698	100	9.7
Health	788	29	2.8
Highways	2,641	98	9.5
Hospitals	0	0	0.0
Housing and Community Development	0	0	0.0
Interest on General Debt	621	23	2.2
Libraries	1,607	60	5.8
Parking	0	0	0.0
Parks and Recreation	4,004	149	14.5
Police Protection	3,953	147	14.3
Public Welfare	0	0	0.0
Sewerage	3,470	129	12.5
Solid Waste Management	439	16	1.6
Liquor Store	0	0	0.0
Utility	0	0	0.0
Employee Retirement	0	0	0.0
Other	6,936	257	25.0

Source: U.S Census Bureau, Government Finances 2004-2005

Municipal Bond Ratings

Area	Moody's
City	Aaa

Source: Mergent Bond Record, January 2008 (unless noted otherwise)

DEMOGRAPHICS

Population Growth

Area	1990 Census	2000 Census	2007 Estimate	2012 Projection	Population Growth (%) 1990-2000	Population Growth (%) 2000-2012
City	17,199	24,575	27,401	29,222	42.9	18.9
MSA[1]	16,845,992	18,323,002	18,887,605	19,111,248	8.8	4.3
U.S.	248,709,873	281,421,906	301,045,522	314,920,978	13.2	11.9

Note: (1) Metropolitan Statistical Area - see Appendix B for areas included
Source: Claritas, Inc.

Number of Households and Average Household Size

Area	2007 Estimate	2007 Average Household Size
City	10,105	2.71
MSA[1]	6,870,593	2.75
U.S.	113,668,003	2.65

Note: (1) Metropolitan Statistical Area - see Appendix B for areas included
Source: Claritas, Inc.

Race and Ethnicity

Area	White Alone[2]	Black Alone[2]	Asian Alone[2]	Other Race Alone[2]	Hispanic[3]
City	83.6	1.7	12.9	1.9	3.4
MSA[1]	59.5	17.6	8.8	14.1	21.2
U.S.	73.1	12.4	4.3	10.3	14.9

Note: Figures are 2007 estimates; (1) Metropolitan Statistical Area - see Appendix B for areas included (2) Alone is defined as not being in combination with one or more other races; (3) May be of any race.
Source: Claritas, Inc.

Ancestry

Area	German	Irish[2]	English	American	Italian	Polish	French[3]	Scottish
City	18.7	23.6	11.0	3.3	19.1	7.1	1.9	3.2
MSA[1]	12.8	15.0	5.7	2.9	17.2	9.8	1.5	1.3
U.S.	15.2	10.9	8.7	7.3	5.6	3.2	3.0	1.7

Note: Figures include multiple ancestry (e.g. if a person reported being Irish and Italian, they were included in both columns); (1) Metropolitan Statistical Area - see Appendix A for areas included; (2) Includes Celtic; (3) Includes Alsatian but excludes Basque
Source: Census 2000, Summary File 3

Foreign-Born Population

Area	Percent of Population Born in: Any Foreign Country	Europe	Asia	Africa	Oceania[2]	Canada	Mexico	Latin America[3]
City	12.5	4.4	5.9	0.3	0.0	0.6	0.2	1.1
MSA[1]	20.8	4.4	8.9	1.1	0.0	0.2	1.1	5.1
U.S.	11.1	1.7	2.9	0.3	0.1	0.3	3.3	2.5

Note: (1) Metropolitan Statistical Area - see Appendix A for areas included; (2) Includes Australia, New Zealand subregion, Melanesia, Micronesia, Polynesia, and Oceania n.e.c; (3) Includes Central America (excluding Mexico), South America, and the Caribbean.
Source: Census 2000, Summary File 3

Marriage Status

Area	Never Married	Now Married (excluding Separated)	Separated	Widowed	Divorced
City	19.4	67.1	0.9	5.8	6.8
MSA[1]	26.3	58.8	1.6	6.2	7.0
U.S.	27.1	54.4	2.2	6.6	9.7

Note: Figures are percentages and cover the population 15 years of age and older; (1) Metropolitan Statistical Area - see Appendix A for areas included
Source: Census 2000, Summary File 3

Age Distribution

Area	Under Age 5	Age 5 to 17	Age 18 to 34	Age 35 to 49	Age 50 to 64	Age 65 to 79	80 Years and Over
	Percent of Population						
City	8.0	19.7	13.0	30.5	16.4	9.0	3.4
MSA[1]	6.7	17.6	22.8	26.1	15.0	8.9	2.9
U.S.	6.8	18.9	23.7	23.5	14.8	9.2	3.2

Note: (1) Metropolitan Statistical Area - see Appendix A for areas included
Source: Census 2000, Summary File 3

Male/Female Ratio

Area	Males	Females	Males per 100 Females
City	13,418	13,983	96.0
MSA[1]	9,117,706	9,769,899	93.3
U.S.	148,320,305	152,725,217	97.1

Note: Figures are 2007 estimates; (1) Metropolitan Statistical Area - see Appendix B for areas included
Source: Claritas, Inc.

Religion

Area	Catholic	Southern Baptist	United Meth-odist	ELCA[1]	LDS[2]	Presby-terian Church USA	Jewish Est.	Muslim Est.
County	39.9	0.3	1.5	0.6	0.2	2.1	3.7	0.6
U.S.	22.0	7.1	3.7	1.8	1.5	1.1	2.2	0.6

Note: Figures are the number of adherents as a percentage of the total population; Adherents are defined as all members, including full members, their children and the estimated number of other participants who are not considered members (e.g. the baptized, those not confirmed, those regularly attending services, etc.); (1) Evangelical Lutheran Church in America; (2) The Church of Jesus Christ of Latter Day Saints
Source: Reprinted with permission from Religious Congregations and Membership in the United States 2000 (Nashville, Glenmary Research Center, 2002) Copyright Association of Statisticians of American Religious Bodies. All rights reserved.

ECONOMY

Gross Metropolitan Product

Area	2002	2003	2004	2005	2005 Rank[2]
MSA[1]	820.9	847.1	902.4	952.6	1

Note: Figures are in billions of dollars; (1) New York-Northern New Jersey-Long Island, NY-NJ-PA Metropolitan Statistical Area - see Appendix A for areas included; (2) Rank ranges from 1 to 361
Source: The U.S. Conference of Mayors, "U.S. Metro Economies: GMP - The Engines of America's Growth," January 2007

Economic Growth

Area	1995 GMP	2005 GMP	Average Annual Growth Rate	Growth Rate Rank[2]
MSA[1]	585.5	952.6	5.0	221

Note: Figures are in billions of dollars; GMP = Gross Metropolitan Product; (1) New York-Northern New Jersey-Long Island, NY-NJ-PA Metropolitan Statistical Area - see Appendix A for areas included; (2) Rank ranges from 1 to 361
Source: The U.S. Conference of Mayors, "U.S. Metro Economies: GMP - The Engines of America's Growth," January 2007

INCOME

Per Capita/Median/Average Income

Area	Per Capita ($)	Median Household ($)	Average Household ($)
City	62,910	125,848	169,789
MSA[1]	30,292	58,080	82,491
U.S.	25,495	49,280	66,670

Note: Figures are 2007 estimates; (1) Metropolitan Statistical Area - see Appendix B for areas included
Source: Claritas, Inc.

Household Income Distribution

Area	Percent of Households Earning							
	Under $15,000	$15,000 -24,999	$25,000 -34,999	$35,000 -49,999	$50,000 -74,999	$75,000 -99,000	$100,000 -149,999	$150,000 and up
City	2.9	3.1	2.4	6.1	11.6	11.5	20.8	41.7
MSA[1]	14.0	8.8	8.7	12.6	17.1	12.3	14.5	12.0
U.S.	13.1	10.9	11.2	15.6	19.5	11.9	11.3	6.6

Note: Figures are 2007 estimates; (1) Metropolitan Statistical Area - see Appendix B for areas included
Source: Claritas, Inc.

Poverty Rates by Age

Area	All Ages	Under 5 Years Old	5 to 17 Years Old	18 to 64 Years Old	65 Years and Over
City	1.3	0.2	0.2	0.6	0.3
MSA[1]	5.4	0.4	1.1	3.3	0.6
U.S.	12.4	1.2	3.0	6.9	1.2

Note: Figures are percent of population with income in 1999 below poverty level and only include population for whom poverty status is determined; (1) Metropolitan Statistical Area - see Appendix A for areas included
Source: Census 2000, Summary File 3

Personal Bankruptcy Filing Rate

Area	2004	2005	2006
Somerset County	2.29	2.93	0.81
U.S.	5.31	6.82	2.00

Note: Numbers are per 1,000 population and include Chapter 7 and Chapter 13 filings
Source: Federal Deposit Insurance Corporation (FDIC), Regional Economic Conditions (RECON), 8/23/2007

EMPLOYMENT

Labor Force and Employment

Area	Civilian Labor Force			Workers Employed		
	Dec. 2006	Dec. 2007	% Chg.	Dec. 2006	Dec. 2007	% Chg.
City	14,233	14,114	-0.8	13,939	13,803	-1.0
MD[1]	1,199,770	1,190,736	-0.8	1,157,810	1,146,507	-1.0
U.S.	152,571,000	153,705,000	0.7	146,081,000	146,334,000	0.2

Note: Data is not seasonally adjusted and covers workers 16 years of age and older; (1) Metropolitan Division - see Appendix B for areas included
Source: Bureau of Labor Statistics, http://stats.bls.gov

Unemployment Rate

Area	2007											
	Jan.	Feb.	Mar.	Apr.	May	Jun.	Jul.	Aug.	Sep.	Oct.	Nov.	Dec.
City	2.4	2.3	2.3	2.1	2.2	2.3	2.5	2.1	2.2	2.1	2.2	2.2
MD[1]	4.4	4.2	4.0	3.6	3.6	3.8	4.3	3.7	3.7	3.4	3.6	3.7
U.S.	5.0	4.9	4.5	4.3	4.3	4.7	4.9	4.6	4.5	4.4	4.5	4.8

Note: Data is not seasonally adjusted and covers workers 16 years of age and older; All figures are percentages; (1) Metropolitan Division - see Appendix B for areas included
Source: Bureau of Labor Statistics, http://stats.bls.gov

Employment by Occupation

Occupation Classification	City (%)	MSA[1] (%)	U.S. (%)
Sales and Office	23.7	27.3	26.7
Professional and Related	30.2	25.9	20.2
Service	5.3	10.4	14.9
Production, Transportation, and Material Moving	3.8	11.2	14.6
Management, Business, and Financial	33.9	18.1	13.5
Construction, Extraction, and Maintenance	3.2	7.0	9.4
Farming, Forestry, and Fishing	0.0	0.1	0.7

Note: Figures cover employed civilians 16 years of age and older; (1) Metropolitan Statistical Area - see Appendix A for areas included
Source: Census 2000, Summary File 3

Employment by Industry

Sector	MSA[1] Number of Employees	MSA[1] Percent of Total	U.S. Percent of Total
Government	152,800	14.6	16.3
Education and Health Services	139,600	13.3	13.4
Professional and Business Services	180,200	17.2	13.1
Retail Trade	136,200	13.0	11.6
Manufacturing	73,200	7.0	9.9
Leisure and Hospitality	78,400	7.5	9.6
Financial Activities	60,400	5.8	5.9
Construction	n/a	n/a	5.3
Wholesale Trade	60,800	5.8	4.4
Other Services	48,200	4.6	3.9
Transportation and Utilities	41,000	3.9	3.7
Information	30,400	2.9	2.2
Natural Resources and Mining	n/a	n/a	0.5

Note: Figures cover non-farm employment as of December 2007 and are not seasonally adjusted; (1) Metropolitan Statistical Area - see Appendix B for areas included; n/a not available
Source: Bureau of Labor Statistics, http://stats.bls.gov

Average Wages

Occupation	$/Hr.	Occupation	$/Hr.
Accountants and Auditors	36.27	Maids and Housekeeping Cleaners	9.77
Automotive Mechanics	18.30	Maintenance and Repair Workers	18.27
Bookkeepers	17.66	Marketing Managers	66.08
Carpenters	24.94	Nuclear Medicine Technologists	37.95
Cashiers	9.35	Nurses, Licensed Practical	23.49
Clerks, General Office	13.14	Nurses, Registered	33.79
Clerks, Receptionists/Information	12.50	Nursing Aides/Orderlies/Attendants	12.60
Clerks, Shipping/Receiving	14.55	Packers and Packagers, Hand	9.76
Computer Programmers	40.08	Physical Therapists	37.21
Computer Support Specialists	24.41	Postal Service Mail Carriers	21.31
Computer Systems Analysts	42.13	Real Estate Brokers	50.65
Cooks, Restaurant	11.99	Retail Salespersons	12.69
Dentists	n/a	Sales Reps., Exc. Tech./Scientific	35.27
Electrical Engineers	45.42	Sales Reps., Tech./Scientific	44.40
Electricians	28.34	Secretaries, Exc. Legal/Med./Exec.	16.38
Financial Managers	59.33	Security Guards	12.84
First-Line Supervisors/Mgrs., Sales	21.41	Surgeons	n/a
Food Preparation Workers	10.15	Teacher Assistants	12.40
General and Operations Managers	70.21	Teachers, Elementary School	27.40
Hairdressers/Cosmetologists	14.36	Teachers, Secondary School	29.00
Internists	87.25	Telemarketers	15.72
Janitors and Cleaners	12.10	Truck Drivers, Heavy/Tractor-Trailer	19.53
Landscaping/Groundskeeping Workers	12.61	Truck Drivers, Light/Delivery Svcs.	16.22
Lawyers	57.95	Waiters and Waitresses	11.25

Note: Wage data covers the Edison, NJ Metropolitan Division - see Appendix B for areas included. Hourly wages for elementary/secondary school teachers and teacher assistants were calculated by the editors from annual wage data assuming a 40 hour work week; n/a not available.
Source: Bureau of Labor Statistics, May 2007 Metro Area Occupational Employment and Wage Estimates

RESIDENTIAL REAL ESTATE

Building Permits

Area	Single-Family 2006	Single-Family 2007p	Single-Family Pct. Chg.	Multi-Family 2006	Multi-Family 2007p	Multi-Family Pct. Chg.	Total 2006	Total 2007p	Total Pct. Chg.
City	21	22	4.8	0	0	-	21	22	4.8
U.S.	1,378,200	973,300	-29.4	460,700	407,200	-11.6	1,838,900	1,380,500	-24.9

Note: (p) preliminary; figures cover and represent new, privately-owned housing units authorized (unadjusted data); All permit data are based on estimates with imputation; U.S. figures are based on the new 20,000-place series.
Source: U.S. Census Bureau, Manufacturing, Mining, and Construction Statistics

Homeownership and Housing Vacancies

Area	Homeownership Rate[2] (%)			Rental Vacancy Rate[3] (%)			Homeowner Vacancy Rate[4] (%)		
	2005	2006	2007	2005	2006	2007	2005	2006	2007
MSA[1]	54.6	53.6	53.8	5.0	5.4	5.7	1.9	1.8	2.1
U.S.	68.9	68.8	68.1	9.8	9.8	9.7	1.9	2.4	2.7

Note: (1) Metropolitan Statistical Area - see Appendix B for areas included; (2) The proportion of households that are owners; (3) The proportion of the rental inventory that is vacant for rent; (4) The proportion of the homeowner inventory that is vacant for sale; n/a not available
Source: U.S. Census Bureau, Housing Vacancies and Homeownership Annual Statistics: 2007

TAXES

State Corporate Income Tax Rates

State	Rates and Tax Brackets
New Jersey	6.5% > $0; 7.5 > 50K; 9.0% > 100K

Note: Tax rates as of January 1, 2008; Companies with income greater than $100K pay 9% on all income, companies with income greater than $50K but less than $100K pay 7.5 % on all income and companies with income under $50K pay 6.5%. The minimum tax is $500. An Alternative Minimum Assessment based on Gross Receipts applies if greater than corporate franchise tax for out-of-state companies with New Jersey sales. 4% surtax for 2007.
Source: Tax Foundation, www.taxfoundation.org

State Individual Income Tax Rates

State	Federal Deductibility	Marginal Rates (%)	Standard Deduction ($)		Personal Exemptions ($)[1]	
			Single	Joint	Single	Dependents
New Jersey	No	1.4 - 8.97 (y)	n/a	n/a	1,000	1,500

Note: Tax rates as of January 1, 2008; Local- and county-level taxes are not included; n/a not applicable; (1) Married joint filers generally receive double the single exemption; (y) Brackets are not double for married taxpayers.
Source: Tax Foundation, www.taxfoundation.org

Various State and Local Tax Rates

State and Local Sales and Use (%)	State Sales and Use (%)	Gasoline[1,2] ($/gal.)	Cigarette ($/pack)	Spirits ($/gal.)	Table Wine ($/gal.)	Beer ($/gal.)
7.0	7.0	0.145	2.575	4.40	0.70	0.12

Note: Tax rates as of January 1, 2008; (1) In addition to the 18.4 cpg Federal gasoline tax; (2) Rates may include additional state sales taxes, environmental protection and storage fees/taxes, and local taxes. When necessary, the volume-weighted average of all local taxes is used to approximate the typical statewide rate including local tax
Source: Tax Foundation, www.taxfoundation.org; Original research

State Tax Burdens

Area	Combined State and Local Tax Burden		Combined Federal, State and Local Tax Burden	
	Percent	Rank	Percent	Rank
New Jersey	11.6	10	35.6	3
U.S. Average	11.0	-	32.7	-

Note: Figures cover 2007 and measure taxes as a percentage of income
Source: Tax Foundation, www.taxfoundation.org

State Business Tax Climate Index Rankings

State	Overall Rank	Corporate Tax Index Rank	Individual Income Tax Index Rank	Sales Tax Index Rank	Unemployment Insurance Tax Index Rank	Property Tax Index Rank
New Jersey	49	41	49	44	24	49

Note: Rankings range from 1 to 50 where 1 is best. Rankings do not average across to Overall Rank. States without a given tax are given a ranking of 1.
Source: Tax Foundation, State Business Tax Climate Index 2008

TRANSPORTATION

Means of Transportation to Work

Area	Car/Truck/Van: Drove Alone	Car/Truck/Van: Car-pooled	Public Transportation: Bus	Public Transportation: Subway	Public Transportation: Railroad	Bicycle	Walked	Other Means	Worked at Home
City	83.0	5.0	0.8	0.2	4.5	0.1	0.7	0.3	5.3
MSA[1]	77.2	9.9	2.7	0.2	3.6	0.2	2.4	0.9	2.9
U.S.	75.7	12.2	2.5	1.5	0.5	0.4	2.9	1.0	3.3

Note: Figures are percentages and cover workers 16 years of age and older; (1) Metropolitan Statistical Area - see Appendix A for areas included
Source: Census 2000, Summary File 3

Travel Time to Work

Area	Less Than 15 Minutes	15 to 29 Minutes	30 to 44 Minutes	45 to 59 Minutes	60 Minutes or More
City	21.5	32.2	21.5	9.6	15.2
MSA[1]	23.3	31.2	20.7	10.3	14.6
U.S.	29.4	36.1	19.1	7.4	8.0

Note: Figures are percentages and include workers 16 years old and over; (1) Metropolitan Statistical Area - see Appendix A for areas included
Source: Census 2000, Summary File 3

Travel Time Index

Area	1982	1995	2004	2005
Urban Area[1]	1.10	1.24	1.36	1.39
Average[2]	1.11	1.22	1.29	1.30

Note: Travel Time Index - The ratio of travel time in the peak period to the travel time at free-flow conditions. A value of 1.35 indicates a 20-minute free-flow trip takes 27 minutes in the peak. Free-flow speeds (60 mph on freeways and 35 mph on principal arterials) are used as the comparison threshold; (1) Covers the New York-Newark, NY-NJ-CT urban area; (2) average of 85 urban areas
Source: Texas Transportation Institute, The 2007 Urban Mobility Report, September 2007

Living Environment

COST OF LIVING

Cost of Living Index

Composite Index	Groceries	Housing	Utilities	Trans-portation	Health Care	Misc. Goods/ Services
127.5	113.2	169.1	107.3	103.7	110.6	114.2

Note: U.S. = 100; Figures cover the Middlesex-Monmouth NJ urban area.
Source: The Council for Community and Economic Research (formerly ACCRA), Cost of Living Index, 2007

Grocery Prices

Area[1]	T-Bone Steak ($/pound)	Frying Chicken ($/pound)	Whole Milk ($/half gal.)	Eggs ($/dozen)	Orange Juice ($/64 oz.)	Coffee ($/11.5 oz.)
City[2]	9.68	1.09	2.24	2.25	3.07	3.46
Avg.	8.93	1.12	2.13	1.52	3.26	3.31
Min.	5.88	0.71	1.33	0.83	2.30	2.20
Max.	12.80	2.07	3.43	3.54	5.79	6.20

Note: (1) Values for the local area are compared with the average, minimum and maximum values for all 331 areas in the Cost of Living Index report; (2) Figures cover the Middlesex-Monmouth NJ urban area; **T-Bone Steak** *(price per pound);* **Frying Chicken** *(price per pound, whole fryer);* **Whole Milk** *(half gallon carton);* **Eggs** *(price per dozen, Grade A, large);* **Orange Juice** *(64 oz. Tropicana or Florida Natural);* **Coffee** *(11.5 oz. can, vacuum-packed, Maxwell House, Hills Bros, or Folgers).*
Source: The Council for Community and Economic Research (formerly ACCRA), Cost of Living Index, 2007

Housing and Utility Costs

Area[1]	New Home Price ($)	Apartment Rent ($/month)	All Electric ($/month)	Part Electric ($/month)	Other Energy ($/month)	Telephone ($/month)
City[2]	531,339	1,321	-	82.61	85.27	29.75
Avg.	309,605	782	146.13	78.67	90.16	26.14
Min.	189,877	n/a	82.03	37.41	33.15	17.08
Max.	1,202,800	3,481	271.14	150.60	257.67	37.45

Note: (1) Values for the local area are compared with the average, minimum and maximum values for all 331 areas in the Cost of Living Index report; (2) Figures cover the Middlesex-Monmouth NJ urban area; **New Home Price** *(2,400 sf living area, 8,000 sf lot, in urban area with full utilities);* **Apartment Rent** *(950 sf 2 bedroom/1.5 or 2 bath, unfurnished, excluding all utilities except water);* **All Electric** *(average monthly cost for an all-electric home);* **Part Electric** *(average monthly cost for a part-electric home);* **Other Energy** *(average monthly cost for natural gas, fuel oil, coal, wood, and any other forms of energy except electricity);* **Telephone** *(price includes basic monthly rate for a private residential line plus additional local usage charges incurred by a family of four).*
Source: The Council for Community and Economic Research (formerly ACCRA), Cost of Living Index, 2007

Health Care, Transportation, and Other Costs

Area[1]	Doctor ($/visit)	Dentist ($/visit)	Optometrist ($/visit)	Gasoline ($/gallon)	Beauty Salon ($/visit)	Men's Shirt ($)
City[2]	70.73	93.52	88.50	2.52	31.67	35.87
Avg.	79.48	71.93	79.55	2.64	29.52	25.77
Min.	52.08	44.80	43.95	2.19	15.58	16.19
Max.	148.44	126.27	158.83	3.48	60.62	48.53

Note: (1) Values for the local area are compared with the average, minimum and maximum values for all 331 areas in the Cost of Living Index report; (2) Figures cover the Middlesex-Monmouth NJ urban area; **Doctor** *(general practitioners routine exam of an established patient);* **Dentist** *(adult teeth cleaning and periodic oral examination);* **Optometrist** *(full vision eye exam for established adult patient);* **Gasoline** *(one gallon regular unleaded, national brand, including all taxes, cash price at self-service pump if available);* **Beauty Salon** *(woman's shampoo, trim, and blow-dry);* **Men's Shirt** *(cotton/polyester dress shirt, pinpoint weave, long sleeves).*
Source: The Council for Community and Economic Research (formerly ACCRA), Cost of Living Index, 2007

HOUSING

House Price Index (HPI)

Area	National Ranking[2]	Quarterly Change (%)	One-Year Change (%)	Five-Year Change (%)
MD[1]	214	-0.27	-1.48	54.92
U.S.[3]	-	0.10	0.84	41.37

Note: The HPI is a weighted repeat sales index. It measures average price changes in repeat sales or refinancings on the same properties. This information is obtained by reviewing repeat mortgage transactions on single-family properties whose mortgages have been purchased or securitized by Fannie Mae or Freddie Mac in January 1975; (1) Metropolitan Division - see Appendix B for areas included; (2) Rankings are based on annual percentage change for all metro areas containing at least 15,000 transactions over the last 10 years and ranges from 1 to 291; (3) figures based on a weighted average of Census Division estimates; all figures are for the period ending December 31, 2007
Source: Office of Federal Housing Enterprise Oversight, House Price Index, February 26, 2008

House Price Valuations

Area	Q1 2000	Q1 2001	Q1 2002	Q1 2003	Q1 2004	Q1 2005	Q1 2006	Q1 2007	Q1 2008
MD[1]	-26.4	-21.9	-13.1	0.2	9.5	22.2	26.6	18.8	11.3

Note: Figures show the percentage of over- or under-valuation of single family homes relative to statistically normal house values (e.g. a value of 23.6 indicates that house values are 23.6% overvalued). Statistically normal house values are based on house prices, interest rates, household incomes, population densities, and any historical premiums or discounts metropolitan areas have exhibited over time; (1) Figures cover the Metropolitan Division - see Appendix B for areas included
Source: Global Insight/National City Corporation, House Prices in America, May 2008

Median Home Prices

Area	2005	2006	2007[r]	Percent Change 2006 to 2007
MD[1]	375.5	387.7	380.3	-1.9
U.S. Average	219.0	221.9	217.9	-1.8

Note: Figures are median sales prices of existing single-family homes in thousands of dollars; (r) revised; n/a not available; (1) Metropolitan Division - see Appendix B for areas included
Source: National Association of Realtors, Metropolitan Area Prices, 1st Quarter 2008

Housing: Year Structure Built

Area	1990 -2000	1980 -1989	1970 -1979	1960 -1969	1950 -1959	1940 -1949	Before 1940	Median Year
City	35.9	25.8	8.8	12.2	6.5	3.7	7.0	1985
MSA[1]	15.2	18.7	13.3	16.8	16.2	6.8	13.0	1968
U.S.	17.0	15.8	18.5	13.7	12.7	7.3	15.0	1971

Note: Figures are percentages; (1) Metropolitan Statistical Area - see Appendix A for areas included
Source: Census 2000, Summary File 3

HEALTH

Health Risk Data

Category	Area[1] (%)	U.S. (%)
Adults who have been told they have high blood pressure[3]	25.7	25.5
Adults who have been told they have high blood cholesterol[3]	38.5	35.6
Adults who have been told they have diabetes[2]	7.0	7.5
Adults who have been told they have arthritis[3]	25.7	27.0
Adults who have been told they currently have asthma	6.4	8.5
Adults who are current smokers	16.4	20.1
Adults who are heavy drinkers[4]	3.3	4.9
Adults who are overweight (BMI 25.0 - 29.9)	37.9	36.5
Adults who are obese (BMI 30.0 - 99.8)	21.6	25.1

Note: Data as of 2006 unless otherwise noted; (1) Figures cover the Metropolitan Division - see Appendix B for areas included; (2) Figures do not include pregnancy-related diabetes, pre-diabetes or borderline diabetes; (3) 2005 data; (4) Heavy drinkers are classified as adult men having more than two drinks per day or adult women having more than one drink per day
Source: Centers for Disease Control and Prevention, Behaviorial Risk Factor Surveillance System, SMART: Selected Metropolitan/Micropolitan Area Risk Trends, 2005, 2006

Mortality Rates for the Top 10 Causes of Death in the U.S.

ICD-10[a] Sub-Chapter	ICD-10[a] Code	Age-Adjusted Mortality Rate[1] per 100,000 population	
		County[2]	U.S.
Malignant neoplasms	C00-C97	166.2	186.5
Ischaemic heart diseases	I20-I25	126.5	152.3
Other forms of heart disease	I30-I51	45.5	51.5
Cerebrovascular diseases	I60-I69	42.5	50.0
Chronic lower respiratory diseases	J40-J47	30.9	42.6
Diabetes mellitus	E10-E14	26.5	24.8
Other degenerative diseases of the nervous system	G30-G31	16.7	22.6
Other external causes of accidental injury	W00-X59	14.4	21.4
Influenza and pneumonia	J10-J18	22.9	20.7
Hypertensive diseases	I10-I13	12.7	18.2

Note: (a) ICD-10 = International Classification of Diseases 10th Revision; (1) Mortality rates are a three year average covering 2003-2005; (2) Figures cover Somerset County
Source: Centers for Disease Control and Prevention, National Center for Health Statistics. Compressed Mortality File 1999-2004. CDC WONDER On-line Database, compiled from Compressed Mortality File 1999-2005 Series 20 No. 2K, 2008.

Mortality Rates for Selected Causes of Death

ICD-10[a] Sub-Chapter	ICD-10[a] Code	Age-Adjusted Mortality Rate[1] per 100,000 population	
		County[2]	U.S.
Assault	X85-Y09	*1.6	5.9
Human immunodeficiency virus (HIV) disease	B20-B24	2.5	4.5
Intentional self-harm	X60-X84	5.9	10.8
Malnutrition	E40-E46	*0.9	1.0
Obesity and other hyperalimentation	E65-E68	*1.3	1.4
Organic, including symptomatic, mental disorders	F01-F09	17.8	16.8
Transport accidents	V01-V99	5.9	16.1
Viral hepatitis	B15-B19	*1.1	1.8

Note: (a) ICD-10 = International Classification of Diseases 10th Revision; (1) Mortality rates are a three year average covering 2003-2005; (2) Figures cover Somerset County; (*) Unreliable data as per CDC
Source: Centers for Disease Control and Prevention, National Center for Health Statistics. Compressed Mortality File 1999-2004. CDC WONDER On-line Database, compiled from Compressed Mortality File 1999-2005 Series 20 No. 2K, 2008.

Distribution of Physicians[1]

Area	Total	Family/ General Practice	Specialties	
			Medical	Surgical
Somerset County (number)	964	160	393	211
Somerset County (rate per 10,000 pop.)	30.1	5.0	12.3	6.6
U.S. (rate per 10,000 pop.)	17.7	4.6	6.9	4.3

Note: Data as of 2005; (1) Includes all non-federal, patient-care, office-based MDs
Source: Area Resource File (ARF). June 2007. U.S. Department of Health and Human Services, Health Resources and Services Administration, Bureau of Health Professions, Rockville, MD.

Hospitals

There were no hospitals listed within the city limits.
AHA Guide to the Healthcare Field 2008

According to *U.S. News,* the New York-Northern New Jersey-Long Island, NY-NJ-PA metro area is home to 14 of the best hospitals in the U.S.: **Hackensack University Medical Center**; **Hospital for Special Surgery**; **Kessler Institute for Rehabilitation**; **Lenox Hill Hospital**; **Long Island Jewish Medical Center**; **Memorial Sloan-Kettering Cancer Center**; **Montefiore Medical Center**; **Mount Sinai Medical Center**; **New York Eye and Ear Infirmary**; **New York-Presbyterian Univ. Hosp. of Columbia and Cornell**; **NYU Medical Center**; **Robert Wood Johnson University Hospital**; **Saint Francis Hospital**; **University Hospital**. *U.S. News Online, "America's Best Hospitals 2007"*

EDUCATION

Public School District Statistics

District Name	Schls	Pupils	Pupil/ Teacher Ratio	Minority Pupils[1] (%)	Free Lunch Eligible[2] (%)	IEP[3] (%)
Somerset Hills Regional	3	2,005	13.0	17.0	2.1	26.0

Note: Table includes regular local school districts with 2,000 or more students; (1) Percentage of students that are not white, non-Hispanic; (2) Percentage of students that are eligible for the free lunch program; (3) Percentage of students that have an Individualized Education Program.
Source: U.S. Department of Education, National Center for Education Statistics, Common Core of Data, Local Education Agency (School District) Universe Survey: School Year 2005-2006; U.S. Department of Education, National Center for Education Statistics, Common Core of Data, Public Elementary/Secondary School Universe Survey: School Year 2005-2006

Top Public High Schools

High School Name	Index[1]	Rank[1]	Subsidized Lunch (%)[2]	E&E (%)[3]
Bernards **	1.994	518	5.0	36.4

Note: (1) Public schools are ranked according to a ratio that is the number of Advanced Placement, International Baccalaureate, and/or Cambridge tests taken by all students at a school in 2007 divided by the number of graduating seniors. All of the schools on the list have an index of at least 1.000; they are in the top five percent of public schools measured this way. The rankings range from 1 to 1,422; (2) Percentage of students receiving federally subsidized meals; (3) E & E stands for equity and excellence percentage: the portion of all graduating seniors at a school that had at least one passing grade on one AP or IB test; (**) Gave both IB and AP tests. AP and IB participation are indicators of a school's efforts to get students to excel and prepare for college.
Source: Newsweek Online, "Top High Schools 2008"

Highest Level of Education

Area	Less than H.S.	H.S. Diploma	Some College, No Deg.	Associate Degree	Bachelors Degree	Masters Degree	Profess. School Degree	Doctorate Degree
City	4.1	11.5	11.7	4.9	36.5	22.2	5.3	3.7
MSA[1]	21.5	26.4	16.5	5.6	17.7	8.2	3.0	1.2
U.S.	19.4	28.4	21.2	6.4	15.7	5.9	2.0	1.0

Note: Figures are 2007 estimated percentages and cover persons age 25 and over; (1) Metropolitan Statistical Area - see Appendix B for areas included
Source: Claritas, Inc.

Educational Attainment by Race

Area	High School Graduate (%)					Bachelor's Degree (%)				
	Total	White	Black	Asian	Hisp.[2]	Total	White	Black	Asian	Hisp.[2]
City	95.8	96.7	69.6	94.9	78.1	67.4	66.2	43.5	89.5	45.6
MSA[1]	86.5	87.6	83.3	91.3	61.9	37.4	35.0	27.2	71.5	13.3
U.S.	80.4	83.6	72.3	80.4	52.4	24.4	26.1	14.3	44.1	10.4

Note: Figures shown cover persons 25 years old and over; (1) Metropolitan Statistical Area - see Appendix A for areas included; (2) people of Hispanic origin can be of any race
Source: Census 2000, Summary File 3

School Enrollment by Type

Area	Grades KG to 8				Grades 9 to 12			
	Public		Private		Public		Private	
	Enrollment	%	Enrollment	%	Enrollment	%	Enrollment	%
City	3,187	87.9	439	12.1	1,074	91.3	102	8.7
MSA[1]	129,755	87.7	18,130	12.3	53,556	88.7	6,806	11.3
U.S.	33,526,011	88.7	4,285,121	11.3	14,848,628	90.6	1,532,323	9.4

Note: Figures shown cover persons 3 years old and over; (1) Metropolitan Statistical Area - see Appendix A for areas included
Source: Census 2000, Summary File 3

School Enrollment by Race

Area	Grades KG to 8 (%)				Grades 9 to 12 (%)			
	White	Black	Asian	Hisp.[1]	White	Black	Asian	Hisp.[1]
City	87.4	0.2	9.3	2.7	87.2	2.6	6.9	3.0
MSA[2]	70.1	9.4	11.4	13.9	68.2	10.9	10.7	14.7
U.S.	68.5	15.5	3.3	16.8	68.8	15.5	3.8	15.7

Note: Figures shown cover persons 3 years old and over; (1) people of Hispanic origin can be of any race; (2) Metropolitan Statistical Area - see Appendix A for areas included
Source: Census 2000, Summary File 3

Average Salaries of Public School Classroom Teachers

District	2005-06		2006-07		Percent Change 2005-06 to 2006-07
	Dollars	Rank[1]	Dollars	Rank[1]	
New Jersey	58,156	5	59,920	3	3.03
U.S. Average	49,026	-	50,816	-	3.65

Note: (1) State rank ranges from 1 to 51.
Source: National Education Association, Rankings & Estimates: Rankings of the States 2006 and Estimates of School Statistics 2007, December 2007

Higher Education

Four-Year Colleges			Two-Year Colleges			Medical Schools[1]	Law Schools[2]	Voc/ Tech[3]
Public	Private Non-profit	Private For-profit	Public	Private Non-profit	Private For-profit			
0	0	0	0	0	0	0	0	0

Note: Figures cover institutions located within the city limits; (1) includes schools accredited by the Liaison Committee on Medical Education and the American Osteopathic Association; (2) includes American Bar Association-accredited law schools; (3) includes all schools with programs that are less than 2 years.
Source: National Center for Education Statistics, The Integrated Postsecondary Education System (IPEDS) Peer Analysis System, 2007; www.usnews.com, Law and Medical School Directories, 2009

PRESIDENTIAL ELECTION

2004 Presidential Election Results

Area	Bush	Kerry	Nader	Other
Somerset County	51.7	47.4	0.6	0.4
U.S.	50.7	48.3	0.4	0.6

Note: Results are percentages and may not add to 100% due to rounding
Source: Dave Leip's Atlas of U.S. Presidential Elections, www.uselectionatlas.org

EMPLOYERS

Major Employers

Company Name	Industry	Type of Site
A T & T Corp	Telephone communication, except radio	Branch
Air Safety Equipment Inc	Airports, flying fields, and services	Branch
Community Medical Center Inc	General medical and surgical hospitals	Headquarters
Doon Technologies Inc	Business consulting, nec	Single
Ethicon Inc	Surgical appliances and supplies	Headquarters
Fort Monmouth Training Center	National security	Branch
In Ventive Commercial Services	Management consulting services	Single
JFK Medical Center	General medical and surgical hospitals	Headquarters
Larson & Toubro Infotech Ltd	Computer related services, nec	Headquarters
Rehabilitation Medicine	Specialty outpatient clinics, nec	Single
School of Public Health	Colleges and universities	Branch
St Peters University Hospital	General medical and surgical hospitals	Headquarters
Telcordia Technologies Inc	Custom computer programming services	Headquarters
US Post Office	U.S. postal service	Branch
Veterans Health Administration	Offices and clinics of medical doctors	Branch

Note: Companies shown are located within the Edison metropolitan area; nec = not elsewhere classified.
Source: www.zapdata.com, May 2008

PUBLIC SAFETY

Crime Rate

Area	All Crimes	Violent Crimes				Property Crimes		
		Murder	Forcible Rape	Robbery	Aggrav. Assault	Burglary	Larceny -Theft	Motor Vehicle Theft
City	630.6	3.7	11.1	0.0	11.1	155.8	426.6	22.3
Metro[1]	2,085.6	2.0	10.1	69.3	103.0	365.7	1,408.9	126.5
U.S.	3,808.1	5.7	30.9	149.4	287.5	729.4	2,206.8	398.4

Note: Figures are crimes per 100,000 population; (1) Metropolitan Division - see Appendix B for areas included
Source: FBI Uniform Crime Reports, 2006

Hate Crimes

Area	Number of Quarters Reported	Bias Motivation				
		Race	Religion	Sexual Orientation	Ethnicity	Disability
City	4	0	0	0	0	0

Source: Federal Bureau of Investigation, Hate Crime Statistics 2006

RECREATION

Culture

Dance[1]	Theatre[1]	Instrumental Music[1]	Vocal Music[1]	Series/ Festivals	Museums	Zoos and Aquariums[2]
0	0	0	0	0	0	0

Note: (1) Number of professional perfoming groups; (2) AZA-accredited
Source: The Grey House Performing Arts Directory, 2007; Official Museum Directory, 2008; Association of Zoos & Aquariums, AZA Member Zoos & Aquariums, June 2008

Professional Sports Teams

Team Name	League
New York Mets	Major League Baseball (MLB)
New York Yankees	Major League Baseball (MLB)
New York Red Bulls	Major League Soccer (MLS)
New Jersey Nets	National Basketball Association (NBA)
New York Knicks	National Basketball Association (NBA)
New York Giants	National Football League (NFL)
New York Jets	National Football League (NFL)
New Jersey Devils	National Hockey League (NHL)
New York Islanders	National Hockey League (NHL)
New York Rangers	National Hockey League (NHL)

Note: Includes teams located in the New York-Northern New Jersey metro area.
Source: Original research

MEDIA

Newspapers

Name	News Focus	Frequency	Circulation
No newspapers have an office in the city			

Note: Includes newspapers with offices located in the city
Source: MediaContactsPro, March 2008

Television Stations

Name	Ch.	Network(s)	Type	Ownership
WCBS	2	CBS	Commercial	CBS
WNBC	4	NBC	Commercial	General Electric Corporation
WNYW	5	Fox	Commercial	Fox Television Stations Inc.
WABC	7	ABC	Commercial	ABC Inc.
WWOR	9	UPN	Commercial	Fox Television Stations Inc.
WPIX	11	WBN	Commercial	Tribune Broadcasting Company
WNET	13	PBS	Public	Educational Broadcasting Corporation
WLIW	21	PBS	Public	Long Island Educational TV Council Inc.
WNYE	25	PBS	Public	New York City Board of Education
WPXN	31	Pax	Commercial	Paxson Communications Corporation
WXTV	41	Univision	Commercial	Univision Holding
WNJU	47	Telemundo	Commercial	Telemundo Group Inc.
WTBY	54	n/a	Commercial	Trinity Broadcasting Network
WLNY	55	n/a	Commercial	Michael C. Pascucci
WRNN	62	n/a	Commercial	WRNN-TV Associates L.P.
WMBC	63	n/a	Commercial	Mountain Broadcasting Corporation
WHSI	67	n/a	Commercial	USA Broadcasting Group
WHSE	68	n/a	Commercial	USA Broadcasting Group

Note: Stations included cover the New York DMA (Designated Market Area); n/a not available
BurrellesLuce, MediaContacts Online, January 2007

Major AM Radio Stations

Call Letters	Freq. (kHz)	Station Type	Target Audience	Station Format	Music Format
WMCA	570	n/a	General/Religious	Music/News/Talk	n/a
WFAN	660	n/a	General	News/Sports/Talk	n/a
WOR	710	n/a	General	Music/News	Reggae
WABC	770	n/a	General	n/a	n/a
WNYC	820	Public	General	Music/Talk	Blues
WCBS	880	Commercial	General	Music/News/Sports	Reggae
WGHQ	920	n/a	General	Music	n/a
WWDJ	970	n/a	General/Religious	Music/Talk	n/a
WINS	1010	n/a	General	News	n/a
WHLI	1100	Commercial	General	Music	Adult Standards
WBBR	1130	n/a	General/Men	Music/News	Reggae
WVNJ	1160	n/a	General	n/a	n/a
WOBM	1160	n/a	General	Music	n/a
WLIB	1190	n/a	General	News/Talk	n/a
WGNY	1220	n/a	General	News/Talk	n/a
WMTR	1250	Commercial	General	Music	Adult Standards
WADO	1280	Commercial	General/Hispanic	News/Sports/Talk	n/a
WWRV	1330	n/a	General/Hisp/Rel	Music/News/Talk	n/a
WELV	1370	n/a	General	Music	n/a
WEOK	1390	Commercial	General/Hispanic	Music/Sports	Latin
WLNA	1420	n/a	General	Music/News/Sports/Talk	n/a
WNSW	1430	n/a	Ethnic/General	Music/News/Talk	n/a
WZRC	1480	n/a	Asian	Talk	n/a
WQEW	1560	n/a	Child/Gen/Yng Adlt	Educational	n/a
WLIM	1580	Commercial	Ethnic/General	Music/News	World Music
WWRL	1600	n/a	General	Music/Talk	Reggae
WWRU	1660	n/a	Asian/General/Hispanic	News/Talk	n/a

Note: Stations included cover the New York DMA (Designated Market Area); n/a not available
Source: BurrellesLuce, MediaContacts Online, January 2007

Major FM Radio Stations

Call Letters	Freq. (mHz)	Station Type	Target Audience	Station Format	Music Format
WFSO	88.3	n/a	Religious	Educational/Music/News	n/a
WFDU	89.1	College	General	Music	n/a
WFUV	90.7	College	General	Music/News/Sports	Folk
WPAT	93.1	Commercial	General/Hispanic	News/Talk	n/a
WRKI	95.1	n/a	General	Music/News/Talk	n/a
WQHT	97.1	n/a	General	Music/News/Talk	n/a
WSKQ	97.9	Commercial	General/Hispanic	Music/News/Talk	Latin
WRKS	98.7	n/a	General/Women	News/Talk	Rhythm & Blues
WBAI	99.5	Non-Comm	General	Music/Talk	Reggae
WHUD	100.7	n/a	General	Music/News/Talk	n/a
WPDH	101.5	Commercial	General	Music	Classic Rock
WKTU	103.5	n/a	General/Women	Music/News/Talk	Urban Contemp.
WAXQ	104.3	n/a	General	Music/Talk	n/a
WSPK	104.7	n/a	General	Music/News/Talk	n/a
WWPR	105.1	Commercial	General	Music	Rhythm & Blues
WBLI	106.1	Commercial	General	Music/Talk	Top 40
WLTW	106.7	n/a	General	Music	n/a
WBLS	107.5	n/a	Black/General	Music	n/a
WEBE	107.9	n/a	General	Music/News	n/a

Note: Stations included cover the New York DMA (Designated Market Area); n/a not available
BurrellesLuce, MediaContacts Online, January 2007

CLIMATE

Average and Extreme Temperatures

Temperature	Jan	Feb	Mar	Apr	May	Jun	Jul	Aug	Sep	Oct	Nov	Dec	Yr.
Extreme High (°F)	74	76	89	94	98	102	105	103	105	93	85	72	105
Average High (°F)	38	41	50	61	72	81	86	84	77	66	54	42	63
Average Temp. (°F)	32	33	42	52	63	72	77	76	68	57	47	36	55
Average Low (°F)	24	25	33	43	53	62	68	67	59	48	39	28	46
Extreme Low (°F)	-8	-7	6	16	33	41	52	45	35	25	15	-1	-8

Note: Figures cover the years 1935-1995
Source: National Climatic Data Center, International Station Meteorological Climate Summary, 9/96

Average Precipitation/Snowfall/Humidity

Precip./Humidity	Jan	Feb	Mar	Apr	May	Jun	Jul	Aug	Sep	Oct	Nov	Dec	Yr.
Avg. Precip. (in.)	3.4	3.0	4.0	3.7	3.9	3.3	4.2	4.1	3.6	3.0	3.8	3.4	43.5
Avg. Snowfall (in.)	8	8	5	1	Tr	0	0	0	0	Tr	1	5	27
Avg. Rel. Hum. 7am (%)	73	71	69	67	70	71	72	76	79	78	76	74	73
Avg. Rel. Hum. 4pm (%)	58	54	51	48	51	51	52	54	55	53	57	59	54

Note: Figures cover the years 1935-1995; Tr = Trace amounts (<0.05 in. of rain; <0.5 in. of snow)
Source: National Climatic Data Center, International Station Meteorological Climate Summary, 9/96

Weather Conditions

Temperature			Daytime Sky			Precipitation		
5°F & below	32°F & below	90°F & above	Clear	Partly cloudy	Cloudy	0.01 inch or more precip.	0.1 inch or more snow/ice	Thunder-storms
2	90	24	80	146	139	122	16	46

Note: Figures are average number of days per year and cover the years 1935-1995
Source: National Climatic Data Center, International Station Meteorological Climate Summary, 9/96

HAZARDOUS WASTE

Superfund Sites

Bernards has no sites on the EPA's Superfund Final National Priorities List.
U.S. Environmental Protection Agency, Final National Priorities List, June 23, 2008

AIR & WATER QUALITY

Air Quality Index

Area	Percent of Days when Air Quality was...[2]				AQI Statistics	
	Good	Moderate	Unhealthy for Sensitive Groups	Unhealthy	Maximum	Median
MSA[1]	71.0	20.8	7.4	0.8	166	39

Note: The Air Quality Index (AQI) is an index for reporting daily air quality. EPA calculates the AQI for five major air pollutants regulated by the Clean Air Act: ground-level ozone, particle pollution (also known as particulate matter), carbon monoxide, sulfur dioxide, and nitrogen dioxide. The AQI runs from 0 to 500. The higher the AQI value, the greater the level of air pollution and the greater the health concern. There are six AQI categories: "Good" The AQI is between 0 and 50. Air quality is considered satisfactory; "Moderate" The AQI is between 51 and 100. Air quality is acceptable; "Unhealthy for Sensitive Groups" When AQI values are between 101 and 150, members of sensitive groups may experience health effects; "Unhealthy" When AQI values are between 151 and 200 everyone may begin to experience health effects; "Very Unhealthy" AQI values between 201 and 300 trigger a health alert; "Hazardous" AQI values over 300 trigger health warnings of emergency conditions; (1) Metropolitan Statistical Area - see Appendix A for areas included; (2) Based on 365 days with AQI data in 2007.
Source: U.S. Environmental Protection Agency, Air Quality Index Report, 2007

Air Quality Index Pollutants

Area	Percent of Days when AQI Pollutant was...[2]					
	Carbon Monoxide	Nitrogen Dioxide	Ozone	Sulfur Dioxide	Particulate Matter 2.5	Particulate Matter 10
MSA[1]	0.0	0.0	64.1	0.0	35.9	0.0

Note: The Air Quality Index (AQI) is an index for reporting daily air quality. EPA calculates the AQI for five major air pollutants regulated by the Clean Air Act: ground-level ozone, particle pollution (also known as particulate matter), carbon monoxide, sulfur dioxide, and nitrogen dioxide. The AQI runs from 0 to 500. The higher the AQI value, the greater the level of air pollution and the greater the health concern; (1) Metropolitan Statistical Area - see Appendix A for areas included; (2) Based on 365 days with AQI data in 2007.
Source: U.S. Environmental Protection Agency, Air Quality Index Report, 2007

Air Quality Index Trends

Area	Trend Sites (4)								All Sites (17)
	1999	2000	2001	2002	2003	2004	2005	2006	2006
MSA[1]	23	9	13	20	8	6	12	5	10

Note: An AQI value greater than 100 indicates that air quality would have been in the unhealthful range on that day. Data from exceptional events are not included. These counts are presented in two ways. First, the counts are based on sites having an adequate record of monitoring data during the trend period (trend sites). These counts represent the relative change in the number of days with AQI values greater than 100. In the last column, the counts are based on all sites with data in the most recent year (because it is possible for a site to have data in the most recent year but not enough data to be a trend site); (1) Metropolitan Statistical Area - see Appendix A for areas included.
Source: U.S. Environmental Protection Agency, Office of Air and Radiation, Air Trends, Factbook and Related Information, Air Pollution Trends in Selected Metropolitan Areas 2006

Maximum Air Pollutant Concentrations

	Particulate Matter 10 (ug/m^3)	Particulate Matter 2.5 (ug/m^3)	Ozone (ppm)	Carbon Monoxide (ppm)	Sulfur Dioxide (ppm)	Nitrogen Dioxide (ppm)	Lead (ug/m^3)
MSA[1] Level	n/a	33	0.125	2	0.014	0.014	n/a
NAAQS[2]	150	35	0.125	9	0.140	0.053	1.50
Met NAAQS[2]	Yes	Yes	Yes	Yes	Yes	Yes	n/a

Note: Data from exceptional events are not included; (1) Metropolitan Statistical Area - see Appendix A for areas included; (2) National Ambient Air Quality Standards; n/a not available
Concentrations: Particulate Matter 10 (coarse particulate) - highest second maximum 24-hour concentration; Particulate Matter 2.5 (fine particulate) - highest 98th percentile 24-hour concentration; Ozone - highest second daily maximum 1-hour concentration; Carbon Monoxide - highest second maximum non-overlapping 8-hour concentration; Sulfur Dioxide - highest second maximum 24-hour concentration; Nitrogen Dioxide - highest arithmetic mean concentration; Lead - highest quarterly maximum concentration
Units: ppm = parts per million; ug/m^3 = micrograms per cubic meter
Source: U.S. Environmental Protection Agency, MSA Factbook 2006, Air Quality Statistics by City

Drinking Water

Water System Name	Pop. Served	Primary Water Source Type	Violations[1]	
			Health Based	Monitoring/ Reporting
NJ American Water Company	n/a	n/a	n/a	n/a

Note: (1) Based on violation data from January 1, 2007 to December 31, 2007 (includes unresolved violations from earlier years); n/a not available

Source: U.S. Environmental Protection Agency, Office of Ground Water and Drinking Water, Safe Drinking Water Information System (based on data extracted April 15, 2008)

Evesham, New Jersey

Background

Evensham is located in Burlington County, 13 miles southwest of Camden and 17 miles southwest of Philadelphia. The city borders Mount Laurel, Medford, and Camden County.

Present-day Evesham was settled by Quakers in 1672 and probably named for a town in England of the same name. The city was divided twice in its history, in 1847 and 1872, creating Medford and Mount Laurel, respectively. In 1955, the United States Army opened the PH-32 Nike Ajax facility in Evesham, one of 12 facilities intended to shield Philadelphia from an aerial assault during the Cold War. The facility was decommissioned in the mid-1960s and is currently used as a civil defense center. It is also the site of an upscale housing development.

The commercial center of Evesham is the historic Marlton Village, easily accessible from routes 70 and 73. This center offers businesses modern office space and upscale shopping, while still maintaining its old-time beauty.

Each fall, Evesham hosts the Olde Marlton Fall Festival, which features arts, crafts, food, and live entertainment in the city's historic downtown. Another major attraction in Evesham is the Indian Spring Country Club, with a 141-acre, 18-hole public golf course established in 1952.

A 14,000-square foot office building in the Evesham Corporate Center industrial park, is home to Lot Two, LLC, and the Elmwood Village Office Center along Route 70. More exciting to some than office space, however, is the state sponsored bikeway transportation system in the planning stages.

Evesham has a moderate climate with hot summers and cold winters. Median summer temperatures average 70 degrees, while winter averages are as low as 35 degrees during of December and January. The city averages 4.5 inches of rainfall per month from April to August and 6 inches of snowfall per month from December to March.

Rankings

General Rankings

- Camden* was ranked #163 out of 375 metro areas in *Cities Ranked & Rated*. Criteria: cost of living; climate; crime; transportation; economy and jobs; education; arts and culture; health and healthcare; leisure; quality of life. *Cities Ranked & Rated, 2nd Edition, 2007*
- Camden* was ranked #192 out of 379 metro areas in *Places Rated Almanac*. Criteria: health care; education; recreation; transportation; ambience; climate; crime; housing costs; jobs. *Places Rated Almanac, 7th Edition, 2007*

Business/Finance Rankings

- The nation's 100 largest metro areas were analysed in terms of the percentage of households entering some stage of foreclosure in 2007. The Camden* metro area ranked #37 out of 100 (#1 = highest foreclosure rate). *RealtyTrac, "Year-End 2007 Metropolitan Foreclosure Report"*
- The Camden* metro area was selected one of America's "Top 50 Business Opportunity Metros" by *Expansion Management* in their 5th annual Mayor's Challenge ranking of metro areas that have achieved solid ratings across the board in numerous *EM* studies during the past 12 months. The area ranked #28. Criteria: public schools; quality of life; college educated workers; logistics infrastructure; healthcare costs; taxes and government spending; reputation among site consultants. *Expansion Management, August 2007*
- The Philadelphia* metro area was selected as one of "America's Most Wired Cities" by *Forbes*. The metro area was ranked #26 out of 30. Criteria: percentage of Internet users with high-speed access; the range of service providers within a city; availability of public wireless hot spots. *Forbes, "America's Most Wired Cities," January 10, 2008*
- Philadelphia* was selected as one of the best places to start and grow a company by *Entrepreneur* and the National Policy Research Council. The Philadelphia* metro area ranked #45 out of 50 large metro areas. Criteria: business formation and growth (firms started four to 14 years ago that still employ at least 5 people and experienced rapid growth over the last four years). *Entrepreneur/National Policy Research Council, "Hot Cities for Entrepreneurs," September 2006*
- The Camden* metro area was selected as one of "America's 50 Hottest Cities" for business relocations and expansions. Criteria: industry's most prominent site selection consultants were asked to list their top city choices for relocating and expanding manufacturing companies, taking into consideration such factors as the business climate, work force quality, operating costs, incentive programs, and the ease of working with local political and economic development officials. *Expansion Management, January-February 2007*
- Intel, in partnership with Sperling's BestPlaces, ranked the 80 "Best Cities for Teleworking" in America. The Philadelphia* metro area ranked #7 among extra large metro areas. The study identifies cities that hold the greatest potential for teleworking based on a host of factors including typical commuting times, fuel prices, availability of broadband Internet access and percentage of the population in telework friendly jobs. The study also factored in extreme climate and natural hazards. *Intel, "Best Cities for Teleworking," March 30, 2006*
- The Camden* metro area appeared on the Milken Institute "2007 Best Performing Cities" index. Rank: #62 out of 200 large metro areas. Criteria: job growth; wage and salary growth; high-tech output growth. *Milken Institute, "2007 Best Performing Cities"*
- The Philadelphia* metro area was selected as one of "The Top 20 Boom Towns in America." *Business 2.0* magazine and econometric research firm Global Insight compared 319 metropolitan areas in the U.S. and ranked the 61 with populations over 1 million. Criteria: a weighted formula that includes forecast growth rates in sectors that contain the economy's 10 most skilled occupational clusters; the prevalence of college degrees in the local workforce; median salary. The area ranked #20 among large metro areas. *Business 2.0 Magazine, March 2004*

- Philadelphia* was identified as one of the 100 "Most Unwired Cities" in the U.S. The area ranked #50 out of the 100 largest metro areas in the U.S. Criteria: number of public and commercial wireless access points (hotspots); airports with wireless Internet access; broadband availability; local wireless networks; and wireless email devices. *Intel, "Most Unwired Cities Survey," June 7, 2005*

- Philadelphia* was ranked #17 out of 125 regions worldwide in terms of its "Knowledge Competitiveness Index." The index attempts to measure the knowledge-based development taking place throughout the world and is based on 19 measures of economic performance that indicate a region's ability to translate its knowledge capacity into economic value. *Robert Huggins Associates, World Knowledge Competitiveness Index 2005*

- *Forbes* ranked the 200 most populous metro areas in the U.S. in terms of the "Best Places for Business and Careers." The Camden* metro area was ranked #75. Criteria: business costs (labor, energy, tax and office space expenses); living costs (housing, transportation, food and other household expenditures); education levels of the work force; job growth; income growth; migration trends; crime rates; and culture/leisure. *Forbes, "Best Places for Business and Careers," March 19, 2008*

- *Fortune* ranked the 100 largest metro areas in the U.S. in terms of projected median home price change in 2007. The Camden* metro area ranked #48. *Fortune.com, "Hot Spots, Cold Spots"*

Health/Environment Rankings

- The Philadelphia* metro area was identified as one of "America's 20 Most Sedentary Cities" by *Forbes*. The metro area ranked #20. Criteria: percentage of overweight or obese people; percentage of people who had not engaged in any physical activity in the past 30 days; average number of hours of TV watched per week. *Forbes.com, "America's Most Sedentary Cities," October 29, 2007*

- 100 of the largest metro areas in the U.S. were analyzed in terms of their current drought severity. The Camden* metro area ranked #57 (#1 = driest). The rankings were based on statistics such as long-term precipitation trends and patterns and the Palmer drought indices. *Sperling's BestPlaces, www.BestPlaces.net, "America's Drought-Riskiest Cities," November 2007*

- Doctors at the Harvard School of Public Health ranked 40 metropolitan areas based on data from the government-sponsored Hospital Quality Alliance program. The program tracks the performance of individual hospitals in treating patients for three common health problems: heart attacks, congestive heart failure, and pneumonia. The Camden* metro area ranked #7 in quality of care for heart attacks, #4 for congestive heart failure, and #4 for pneumonia. *New England Journal of Medicine, July 21, 2005*

- *Reader's Digest* ranked the 50 largest metro areas in the U.S. in terms of how "clean" they are. The Philadelphia* metro area ranked #44. Criteria: air quality; water quality; toxic industrial pollution; Superfund sites; and sanitation. *Reader's Digest, "The 50 Cleanest (and Dirtiest) Cities in America," July 2005*

- The American Academy of Dermatology ranked 32 U.S. metropolitan regions in terms of their residents knowledge, attitude and behaviors towards tanning and sun protection. The Philadelphia* metro area ranked #9. The results of the study are based on an online national survey of 3,342 respondents. *American Academy of Dermatology, "RAYS: Your Grade," May 7, 2007*

- The Camden* metro area appeared in *Country Home's* "2008 Best Green Places" report. The area ranked #270 out of 379. Criteria: official energy policies; green power; green buildings; availability of fresh, locally grown food. *Country Home, "2008 Best Green Places"*

- Wyeth Consumer Healthcare, in partnership with Sperling's BestPlaces, ranked the nation's 50 most populous metro areas in terms of five key health factors. The Philadelphia* metro area ranked #24. Criteria: physical activity; health status; nutrition; lifestyle pursuits; and mental wellness. *Wyeth Consumer Healthcare, "Centrum Healthiest Cities Study," April 19, 2005*

- HealthGrades surveyed over 41,000 individuals on doctor satisfaction and ranked the 20 largest metro areas based on the highest "definitely yes" responses to the question "Do you trust the physician to make decisions/recommendations that are in your best interest?" The Philadelphia* metro area ranked #5. *HealthGrades.com, "Top Cities in Doctor-Trust," September 7, 2006*

- Philadelphia* was identified as a "2008 Asthma Capital." The area ranked #12 out of the nation's 100 largest metropolitan areas. Twelve factors were used to identify the most challenging places to live for people with asthma: estimated prevalence; self-reported prevalence; crude death rate for asthma; annual pollen score; annual air quality; public smoking laws; number of board-certified asthma specialists; school inhaler access laws; rescue medication use; controller medication use; uninsured rate; poverty rate. *Asthma and Allergy Foundation of America, "2008 Asthma Capitals"*

- Philadelphia* was identified as a "Spring Allergy Capital." The area ranked #33 out of 100. Three groups of factors were used to identify the most severe cities for people with allergies during the spring season: annual pollen levels; medicine utilization; access to board-certified allergists. *Asthma and Allergy Foundation of America, "2007 Spring Allergy Capital Rankings"*

- Philadelphia* was identified as a "Fall Allergy Capital." The area ranked #58 out of 100. Three groups of factors were used to identify the most severe cities for people with allergies during the fall season: annual pollen levels; medicine utilization; access to board-certified allergists. *Asthma and Allergy Foundation of America, "2007 Fall Allergy Capital Rankings"*

- Ortho-McNeil Neurologics, in partnership with Sperling's BestPlaces, analyzed 110 metro areas and identified those U.S. cities with the highest prevalence of factors that are most commonly associated with migraine headaches. The Camden* metro area ranked #88. Criteria: number of migraine-related drug prescriptions per capita; lifestyle factors that can contribute to migraines; environmental factors that can trigger migraines; and consumption of migraine-triggering foods. *Ortho-McNeil Neurologics, "America's Migraine Hot Spots," March 14, 2006*

- Sperling's BestPlaces ranked 331 metro areas and identified the most and least stressful U.S. cities. The Philadelphia* metro area ranked #49 out of the 100 largest metro areas (#1 = most stressful). Criteria: divorce rate; unemployment rate; violent and property crime; suicide rate; commute time; mental health; alcohol consumption; cloudy days. *Sperling's BestPlaces, www.BestPlaces.net, "America's Most (and Least) Stressful Cities," January 9, 2004*

- An analysis of the "Best & Worst Cities for Sleep" was conducted by Sperling's BestPlaces. The study ranked America's 50 most populated metro areas. The Philadelphia* metro area ranked #32 (#1 = best city for sleep). Criteria: number of days residents didn't get enough rest or sleep during the past month; average length of daily commute; divorce rate; unemployment rate. *Sperling's BestPlaces, www.BestPlaces.net, "Best & Worst Cities for Sleep," 2006*

- HealthGrades evaluated the performance of America's 25 most populous metropolitan areas by measuring the outcomes of five of the highest volume and most widely studied procedures and diagnoses: coronary artery bypass graft surgery; percutaneus coronary interventions; acute myocardial infarction/heart attack in angioplasty-capable hospitals; congestive heart failure; and community acquired pneumonia. The Philadelphia* metro area ranked #23. *HealthGrades, "HealthGrades Hospital Quality in America Study," October 12, 2004*

- Camden* was highlighted as one of the 25 metro areas most polluted by year-round particle pollution (PM 2.5) in the U.S. The area ranked #24. *American Lung Association, State of the Air: 2007*

- Camden* was highlighted as one of the 25 most ozone-polluted metro areas in the U.S. The area ranked #12. *American Lung Association, State of the Air: 2007*

- Philadelphia* was selected as one of "America's Pet Healthiest Cities" by Purina. The city ranked #9 out of 50. Criteria: veterinary services; environment; legislation; preventative care; obesity/body condition. *Purina Pet Institute, "America's Pet Healthiest Cities," May 20, 2003*

Women/Minorities Rankings

- Philadelphia* was ranked #81 out of 100 metro areas in *SELF Magazine's* ranking of "America's Best Places for Women." A panel of experts came up with more than 50 criteria including death and disease rates, environmental indicators, community resources, and lifestyle habits. *SELF Magazine, "America's Best Places for Women 2007," December 2007*

Seniors/Retirement Rankings

- Sperling's BestPlaces in partnership with Bankers Life & Casualty Company designed a survey to identify the top 50 metro areas in the U.S. that offer the best overall qualities for senior living. The Philadelphia* metro area ranked #6. The following criteria were statistically weighted to reflect the needs of the senior population: health; disease; economics; social; environment; spiritual; transportation; housing; and crime. *Bankers Life & Casualty Company, "Best Cities for Seniors 2005"*
- A.G. Edwards ranked America's 500 top-performing communities based on their residents' personal savings and investing behavior. The Camden* metro area ranked #73 with an index score of 107.82 (national average = 100.00). A dozen statistical factors were measured including: participation in retirement savings plans; personal debt levels; and home ownership. *A.G. Edwards, "2007 Nest Egg Index", September 12, 2007*

Children/Family Rankings

- The Camden* metro area was selected as one of the "Best Cities for Relocating Families" by Worldwide ERC and Primacy Relocation. The 2007 study placed a special emphasis on the housing market, which has significantly impacted the relocation industry and an employer's ability to transfer employees. The variables which weigh heavily in this category include home price, home affordability index, appreciation rates, and property tax. Other criteria include cost of living, crime rates, education, climate, focus on diversity, physicians per capita, recreation and leisure, arts and culture, air quality, watershed quality, sales tax, unemployment rate, job growth, high school and higher education index, school expenditures per student, students in public school, SAT/ACT percentile, and population growth. *Worldwide ERC and Primacy Relocation, "2007 Best Cities for Relocating Families"*

Safety Rankings

- The National Insurance Crime Bureau ranked 361 metro areas in the U.S. in terms of per capita rates of vehicle theft. The Camden* metro area ranked #110 (#1 = highest rate). Criteria: number of vehicle theft offenses per 100,000 inhabitants. *National Insurance Crime Bureau, "NICB Vehicle Theft Study," April 22, 2008*
- Camden* appeared on Sperling's BestPlaces list of the "Riskiest Cities for Identity Theft." The area ranked #30 out of the nations 50 largest metro areas. Over 80 criteria were analyzed across four major categories: technology impact; crime; transactions; and risk profile. *Sperling's BestPlaces, www.BestPlaces.net, "Riskiest Cities for Identity Theft," July 2006*
- Farmers Insurance Group of Companies, in partnership with Sperling's BestPlaces, ranked 379 metro areas and identified the "Most Secure U.S. Place to Live." The Camden* metro area ranked #52 out of 114 in the large metro area category (500,000 or more residents). Criteria: crime rates; extreme weather; risk of natural disasters; environmental hazards; terrorism threats; air quality; life expectancy; job loss numbers. *Farmers Insurance Group, "Most Secure U.S. Places to Live 2007"*
- Camden* was identified as one of the most dangerous large metro areas for pedestrians in the U.S. The area ranked #38 out of the nations 50 largest metro areas. Criteria: average yearly pedestrian fatalities per capita (for the years 2002 and 2003) adjusted for the number of walkers. *Surface Transportation Policy Project, "Mean Streets 2004"*

Sports/Recreation Rankings

- The Philadelphia* metro area appeared on the *Sporting News* list of the "Best Sports Cities 2007". The area ranked #9 out of 150 cities in the U.S. *Sporting News* takes a 12-month snapshot, roughly July to July, of each city's sports, putting a heavy premium on regular-season won-lost records (from the most recently completed season). Other criteria include: playoff berths, bowl appearances and tournament bids; championships; applicable power ratings; quality of competition; overall fan fervor as measured in part by attendance as percentage of venue capacity; abundance of teams (rewarding quality over quantity); stadium and arena quality; ticket availability and prices; franchise ownership; and marquee appeal of athletes. *SportingNews.com, "Best Sports Cities 2007," August 1, 2007*

- The Philadelphia* metro area was selected by *Cranium* as one of the "Top 50 Fun Cities" in America. The area ranked #22. Criteria includes: number of sports teams, restaurants, and dance performances; number of toy stores; city budget spent on recreation. *Cranium, November 4, 2003*

- *Golf Digest* ranked 330 metro areas in the U.S. in terms of golf. The Philadelphia* metro area was ranked #322. Criteria: access to golf; weather; value of golf; and quality of golf. *Golf Digest, "Metro Golf Rankings," August 2005*

Dating/Romance Rankings

- Eli Lily and Company, in partnership with Sperling's BestPlaces, ranked the nation's 50 largest metro areas in terms of the "Most Romantic Cities for Baby Boomers." The Philadelphia* metro area ranked #14. Criteria: marriage and divorce rates among "baby boomers" age 45 to 60; great restaurants; dance studios; chocolate, jewelry and flower sales. *Eli Lily and Company, "Most Romantic Cities for Baby Boomers," April 20, 2007*

- The Philadelphia* metro area was selected as one of the "Top Ten U.S. Cities for Finding a Rich, Single Woman" by Teasley, a Manhattan-based marketing consulting firm. The area ranked #6. Criteria: high single-female to single-male ratio; higher income to cost-of-living ratio; percentage of population that is single. *Teasley, "Where to Find a Rich, Single Woman in the United States," 2005*

- The Camden* metro area was selected as one of the "Best Cities for Relocating Singles" by Worldwide ERC and Primacy Relocation. The area ranked #16 out of the 100 largest metro areas in the U.S. Areas were selected based on the following criteria: a robust cost-of-living index; adventure and outdoor recreation opportunities; violent crime and property crime rates; percentage of the population that is unmarried (ages 25-34); ratio of single men and single women; affordability of quality higher education, including in-state and out-of-state tuition requirements and rates; number of newcomers to the area; commute times; tax rates; fee and occupancy rates for temporary housing and mini-storage; quality and quantity of collegiate and professional sporting events and fun, fan-friendly venues. *Worldwide ERC and Primacy Relocation, "2007 Best Cities for Relocating Singles," October 25, 2007*

- *Forbes* ranked the 40 most populous urbanized areas in the U.S. in terms of the "Best Cities for Singles." The Philadelphia* metro area ranked #10. Criteria: number of singles; cost of living alone; nightlife; culture; job growth; coolness; and online dating. *Forbes.com, August 21, 2007*

- Sperling's BestPlaces in partnership with AXE Deodorant Bodyspray ranked 80 metro areas and identified "America's Best (and Worst) Cities for Dating." The Philadelphia* metro area ranked #64 (#1 = best). Criteria: percentage of singles ages 18-24; population density; dating venues per capita. *AXE Deodorant Bodyspray, "America's Best (and Worst) Cities for Dating," May 2004*

Culture/Performing Arts Rankings

- Scarborough Research, a leading market research firm, identified the top local markets for rock concert attendance. The Philadelphia* DMA (Designated Market Area) ranked in the top 25 with 16% of consumers, 18 years old and over, reporting that they have attended a rock concert during the past year. *Scarborough Research, June 14, 2004*

Miscellaneous Rankings

- The Philadelphia* metro area was identified as one of "The 10 Worst Commuter Cities" in the U.S. by the *U.S. News and World Report*. The mean travel time to work is 32 minutes. *U.S. News and World Report, May 7, 2007*
- The Philadelphia* metro area appeared on *Forbes* list of "America's Drunkest Cities". The area ranked #9. Criteria: 35 of the largest continental U.S. metro areas were chosen based on availability of data and geographic diversity. Each metro was ranked in five areas: state laws; drinkers; heavy drinkers; binge drinkers; and alcoholism. *Forbes.com, "America's Drunkest Cities," August 22, 2006*
- Sperling's BestPlaces in partnership with Pep Boys ranked 77 metro areas and identified "America's Most Drivable Cities." The Philadelphia* metro area ranked #44. Criteria: climate; road roughness; urban mobility; gas prices. *Pep Boys, "America's Most Drivable Cities," April 9, 2003*
- State Farm Insurance, in partnership with Sperling's BestPlaces, analyzed several key factors that contribute to overall family preparedness. The Philadelphia* metro area ranked #16 out of the nation's 50 most populous metro areas. Criteria: quality of life; life insurance coverage; and investments. *State Farm Life Insurance, "Fiscally Fit Cities Report," July 20, 2004*
- Scarborough Research, a leading market research firm, identified the top local markets for grocery coupon use. The Philadelphia* DMA (Designated Market Area) ranked in the top 25 with 42% of consumers reporting that they use grocery coupons at least once per week. *Scarborough Research, December 8, 2004*
- A study by Sperling's BestPlaces examined which U.S. metro areas were most affected by high fuel prices in 2006. The Philadelphia* metro area was ranked #72 out of 80 (#1 = most expensive city for driving). Rankings are based on the average dollars spent on gas per year by two driver households. Criteria: cost of regular-grade gasoline; average miles driven per day; average number of gallons each driver uses and wastes in traffic congestion each day. *Sperling's BestPlaces, www.bestplaces.net, "Pain at the Pump," May 18, 2006*

Evesham is located within the Philadelphia-Camden-Wilmington, PA-NJ-DE-MD Metropolitan Statistical Area and Camden, NJ Metropolitan Division.

Business Environment

CITY FINANCES

City Government Finances

Component	2004-2005 ($000)	2004-2005 ($ per capita)
Total Revenues	39,584	843
Total Expenditures	40,322	859
Debt Outstanding	91,826	1,955
Cash and Securities	37,300	794

Source: U.S Census Bureau, Government Finances 2004-2005

City Government Revenue by Source

Source	2004-2005 ($000)	2004-2005 ($ per capita)
General Revenue		
From Federal Government	0	0
From State Government	4,754	101
From Local Governments	70	1
Taxes		
Property	15,854	338
Sales	151	3
Personal Income	0	0
License	874	19
Charges	9,225	196
Liquor Store	0	0
Utility	4,419	94
Employee Retirement	0	0
Other	4,237	90

Source: U.S Census Bureau, Government Finances 2004-2005

City Government Expenditures by Function

Function	2004-2005 ($000)	2004-2005 ($ per capita)	2004-2005 (%)
General Expenditures			
Airports	0	0	0.0
Corrections	0	0	0.0
Education	0	0	0.0
Fire Protection	18	< 1	< 0.1
Governmental Administration	3,177	68	7.9
Health	25	1	0.1
Highways	1,417	30	3.5
Hospitals	0	0	0.0
Housing and Community Development	0	0	0.0
Interest on General Debt	2,305	49	5.7
Libraries	0	0	0.0
Parking	0	0	0.0
Parks and Recreation	6,512	139	16.1
Police Protection	5,465	116	13.6
Public Welfare	0	0	0.0
Sewerage	5,761	123	14.3
Solid Waste Management	2,790	59	6.9
Liquor Store	0	0	0.0
Utility	5,049	108	12.5
Employee Retirement	0	0	0.0
Other	7,803	166	19.4

Source: U.S Census Bureau, Government Finances 2004-2005

Municipal Bond Ratings

Area	Moody's
City	n/a

Source: Mergent Bond Record, January 2008 (unless noted otherwise)

DEMOGRAPHICS

Population Growth

Area	1990 Census	2000 Census	2007 Estimate	2012 Projection	Population Growth (%) 1990-2000	Population Growth (%) 2000-2012
City	35,309	42,275	47,843	51,265	19.7	21.3
MSA[1]	5,435,470	5,687,147	5,862,653	5,970,852	4.6	5.0
U.S.	248,709,873	281,421,906	301,045,522	314,920,978	13.2	11.9

Note: (1) Metropolitan Statistical Area - see Appendix B for areas included
Source: Claritas, Inc.

Number of Households and Average Household Size

Area	2007 Estimate	2007 Average Household Size
City	18,026	2.65
MSA[1]	2,221,104	2.64
U.S.	113,668,003	2.65

Note: (1) Metropolitan Statistical Area - see Appendix B for areas included
Source: Claritas, Inc.

Race and Ethnicity

Area	White Alone[2]	Black Alone[2]	Asian Alone[2]	Other Race Alone[2]	Hispanic[3]
City	88.9	3.5	5.6	2.0	2.6
MSA[1]	70.2	20.5	4.1	5.2	6.2
U.S.	73.1	12.4	4.3	10.3	14.9

Note: Figures are 2007 estimates; (1) Metropolitan Statistical Area - see Appendix B for areas included (2) Alone is defined as not being in combination with one or more other races; (3) May be of any race.
Source: Claritas, Inc.

Ancestry

Area	German	Irish[2]	English	American	Italian	Polish	French[3]	Scottish
City	20.4	27.8	9.9	3.1	26.6	9.2	2.2	1.8
MSA[1]	17.1	20.6	8.3	3.2	14.4	5.7	1.6	1.4
U.S.	15.2	10.9	8.7	7.3	5.6	3.2	3.0	1.7

Note: Figures include multiple ancestry (e.g. if a person reported being Irish and Italian, they were included in both columns); (1) Metropolitan Statistical Area - see Appendix A for areas included; (2) Includes Celtic; (3) Includes Alsatian but excludes Basque
Source: Census 2000, Summary File 3

Foreign-Born Population

Area	Percent of Population Born in: Any Foreign Country	Europe	Asia	Africa	Oceania[2]	Canada	Mexico	Latin America[3]
City	6.5	2.4	3.0	0.2	0.0	0.3	0.1	0.4
MSA[1]	7.0	2.3	2.8	0.4	0.0	0.2	0.3	1.1
U.S.	11.1	1.7	2.9	0.3	0.1	0.3	3.3	2.5

Note: (1) Metropolitan Statistical Area - see Appendix A for areas included; (2) Includes Australia, New Zealand subregion, Melanesia, Micronesia, Polynesia, and Oceania n.e.c; (3) Includes Central America (excluding Mexico), South America, and the Caribbean.
Source: Census 2000, Summary File 3

Marriage Status

Area	Never Married	Now Married (excluding Separated)	Separated	Widowed	Divorced
City	23.3	61.7	1.8	5.3	7.8
MSA[1]	30.6	51.3	2.7	7.6	7.8
U.S.	27.1	54.4	2.2	6.6	9.7

Note: Figures are percentages and cover the population 15 years of age and older; (1) Metropolitan Statistical Area - see Appendix A for areas included
Source: Census 2000, Summary File 3

Age Distribution

Area	Percent of Population						
	Under Age 5	Age 5 to 17	Age 18 to 34	Age 35 to 49	Age 50 to 64	Age 65 to 79	80 Years and Over
City	7.2	19.5	20.7	28.0	15.7	6.9	2.0
MSA[1]	6.4	18.9	22.2	23.9	14.9	10.0	3.6
U.S.	6.8	18.9	23.7	23.5	14.8	9.2	3.2

Note: (1) Metropolitan Statistical Area - see Appendix A for areas included
Source: Census 2000, Summary File 3

Male/Female Ratio

Area	Males	Females	Males per 100 Females
City	23,189	24,654	94.1
MSA[1]	2,831,289	3,031,364	93.4
U.S.	148,320,305	152,725,217	97.1

Note: Figures are 2007 estimates; (1) Metropolitan Statistical Area - see Appendix B for areas included
Source: Claritas, Inc.

Religion

Area	Catholic	Southern Baptist	United Meth-odist	ELCA[1]	LDS[2]	Presby-terian Church USA	Jewish Est.	Muslim Est.
County	31.0	0.2	2.4	1.7	0.3	1.4	3.1	2.0
U.S.	22.0	7.1	3.7	1.8	1.5	1.1	2.2	0.6

Note: Figures are the number of adherents as a percentage of the total population; Adherents are defined as all members, including full members, their children and the estimated number of other participants who are not considered members (e.g. the baptized, those not confirmed, those regularly attending services, etc.); (1) Evangelical Lutheran Church in America; (2) The Church of Jesus Christ of Latter Day Saints
Source: Reprinted with permission from Religious Congregations and Membership in the United States 2000 (Nashville, Glenmary Research Center, 2002) Copyright Association of Statisticians of American Religious Bodies. All rights reserved.

ECONOMY

Gross Metropolitan Product

Area	2002	2003	2004	2005	2005 Rank[2]
MSA[1]	227.1	236.5	250.3	264.8	6

Note: Figures are in billions of dollars; (1) Philadelphia-Camden-Wilmington, PA-NJ-DE-MD Metropolitan Statistical Area - see Appendix A for areas included; (2) Rank ranges from 1 to 361
Source: The U.S. Conference of Mayors, "U.S. Metro Economies: GMP - The Engines of America's Growth," January 2007

Economic Growth

Area	1995 GMP	2005 GMP	Average Annual Growth Rate	Growth Rate Rank[2]
MSA[1]	164.1	264.8	4.9	230

Note: Figures are in billions of dollars; GMP = Gross Metropolitan Product; (1) Philadelphia-Camden-Wilmington, PA-NJ-DE-MD Metropolitan Statistical Area - see Appendix A for areas included; (2) Rank ranges from 1 to 361
Source: The U.S. Conference of Mayors, "U.S. Metro Economies: GMP - The Engines of America's Growth," January 2007

INCOME

Per Capita/Median/Average Income

Area	Per Capita ($)	Median Household ($)	Average Household ($)
City	35,607	80,070	94,068
MSA[1]	29,121	57,357	75,797
U.S.	25,495	49,280	66,670

Note: Figures are 2007 estimates; (1) Metropolitan Statistical Area - see Appendix B for areas included
Source: Claritas, Inc.

Household Income Distribution

Area	Percent of Households Earning							
	Under $15,000	$15,000 -24,999	$25,000 -34,999	$35,000 -49,999	$50,000 -74,999	$75,000 -99,000	$100,000 -149,999	$150,000 and up
City	4.1	4.2	5.4	12.8	19.8	17.8	23.5	12.3
MSA[1]	11.8	8.9	9.4	13.9	19.0	13.4	14.6	8.9
U.S.	13.1	10.9	11.2	15.6	19.5	11.9	11.3	6.6

Note: Figures are 2007 estimates; (1) Metropolitan Statistical Area - see Appendix B for areas included
Source: Claritas, Inc.

Poverty Rates by Age

Area	All Ages	Under 5 Years Old	5 to 17 Years Old	18 to 64 Years Old	65 Years and Over
City	2.8	0.2	0.6	1.7	0.3
MSA[1]	11.1	1.0	2.8	6.1	1.3
U.S.	12.4	1.2	3.0	6.9	1.2

Note: Figures are percent of population with income in 1999 below poverty level and only include population for whom poverty status is determined; (1) Metropolitan Statistical Area - see Appendix A for areas included
Source: Census 2000, Summary File 3

Personal Bankruptcy Filing Rate

Area	2004	2005	2006
Burlington County	6.40	6.10	2.16
U.S.	5.31	6.82	2.00

Note: Numbers are per 1,000 population and include Chapter 7 and Chapter 13 filings
Source: Federal Deposit Insurance Corporation (FDIC), Regional Economic Conditions (RECON), 8/23/2007

EMPLOYMENT

Labor Force and Employment

Area	Civilian Labor Force			Workers Employed		
	Dec. 2006	Dec. 2007	% Chg.	Dec. 2006	Dec. 2007	% Chg.
City	27,561	27,529	-0.1	26,854	26,722	-0.5
MD[1]	663,461	661,003	-0.4	636,850	633,724	-0.5
U.S.	152,571,000	153,705,000	0.7	146,081,000	146,334,000	0.2

Note: Data is not seasonally adjusted and covers workers 16 years of age and older;
(1) Metropolitan Division - see Appendix B for areas included
Source: Bureau of Labor Statistics, http://stats.bls.gov

Unemployment Rate

Area	2007											
	Jan.	Feb.	Mar.	Apr.	May	Jun.	Jul.	Aug.	Sep.	Oct.	Nov.	Dec.
City	3.2	3.0	2.8	2.7	2.9	3.2	3.3	2.7	2.9	2.7	2.8	2.9
MD[1]	4.8	4.7	4.3	4.1	4.1	4.3	4.9	4.1	4.2	3.9	3.9	4.1
U.S.	5.0	4.9	4.5	4.3	4.3	4.7	4.9	4.6	4.5	4.4	4.5	4.8

Note: Data is not seasonally adjusted and covers workers 16 years of age and older; All figures are percentages; (1) Metropolitan Division - see Appendix B for areas included
Source: Bureau of Labor Statistics, http://stats.bls.gov

Employment by Occupation

Occupation Classification	City (%)	MSA[1] (%)	U.S. (%)
Sales and Office	31.1	28.9	26.7
Professional and Related	26.8	23.2	20.2
Service	9.7	13.9	14.9
Production, Transportation, and Material Moving	6.1	11.5	14.6
Management, Business, and Financial	21.2	14.6	13.5
Construction, Extraction, and Maintenance	5.1	7.7	9.4
Farming, Forestry, and Fishing	0.0	0.2	0.7

Note: Figures cover employed civilians 16 years of age and older;
(1) Metropolitan Statistical Area - see Appendix A for areas included
Source: Census 2000, Summary File 3

Employment by Industry

Sector	MSA[1] Number of Employees	MSA[1] Percent of Total	U.S. Percent of Total
Government	90,300	16.4	16.3
Education and Health Services	79,500	14.5	13.4
Professional and Business Services	73,800	13.4	13.1
Retail Trade	75,100	13.7	11.6
Manufacturing	45,100	8.2	9.9
Leisure and Hospitality	40,800	7.4	9.6
Financial Activities	33,000	6.0	5.9
Construction	n/a	n/a	5.3
Wholesale Trade	32,200	5.9	4.4
Other Services	24,800	4.5	3.9
Transportation and Utilities	21,000	3.8	3.7
Information	9,500	1.7	2.2
Natural Resources and Mining	n/a	n/a	0.5

Note: Figures cover non-farm employment as of December 2007 and are not seasonally adjusted; (1) Metropolitan Statistical Area - see Appendix B for areas included; n/a not available
Source: Bureau of Labor Statistics, http://stats.bls.gov

Average Wages

Occupation	$/Hr.	Occupation	$/Hr.
Accountants and Auditors	31.23	Maids and Housekeeping Cleaners	9.66
Automotive Mechanics	19.04	Maintenance and Repair Workers	18.10
Bookkeepers	17.35	Marketing Managers	59.38
Carpenters	23.99	Nuclear Medicine Technologists	34.80
Cashiers	9.30	Nurses, Licensed Practical	22.75
Clerks, General Office	13.09	Nurses, Registered	31.33
Clerks, Receptionists/Information	12.12	Nursing Aides/Orderlies/Attendants	12.33
Clerks, Shipping/Receiving	15.83	Packers and Packagers, Hand	10.57
Computer Programmers	36.98	Physical Therapists	34.89
Computer Support Specialists	21.69	Postal Service Mail Carriers	21.27
Computer Systems Analysts	35.28	Real Estate Brokers	50.94
Cooks, Restaurant	11.30	Retail Salespersons	12.32
Dentists	n/a	Sales Reps., Exc. Tech./Scientific	33.54
Electrical Engineers	43.85	Sales Reps., Tech./Scientific	38.64
Electricians	32.31	Secretaries, Exc. Legal/Med./Exec.	16.18
Financial Managers	52.60	Security Guards	11.36
First-Line Supervisors/Mgrs., Sales	20.44	Surgeons	n/a
Food Preparation Workers	9.66	Teacher Assistants	10.80
General and Operations Managers	64.05	Teachers, Elementary School	28.20
Hairdressers/Cosmetologists	15.22	Teachers, Secondary School	28.90
Internists	84.98	Telemarketers	12.39
Janitors and Cleaners	12.31	Truck Drivers, Heavy/Tractor-Trailer	21.19
Landscaping/Groundskeeping Workers	12.18	Truck Drivers, Light/Delivery Svcs.	13.42
Lawyers	57.44	Waiters and Waitresses	10.52

Note: Wage data covers the Camden, NJ Metropolitan Division - see Appendix B for areas included. Hourly wages for elementary/secondary school teachers and teacher assistants were calculated by the editors from annual wage data assuming a 40 hour work week; n/a not available.
Source: Bureau of Labor Statistics, May 2007 Metro Area Occupational Employment and Wage Estimates

RESIDENTIAL REAL ESTATE

Building Permits

Area	Single-Family 2006	Single-Family 2007p	Single-Family Pct. Chg.	Multi-Family 2006	Multi-Family 2007p	Multi-Family Pct. Chg.	Total 2006	Total 2007p	Total Pct. Chg.
City	30	26	-13.3	0	0	-	30	26	-13.3
U.S.	1,378,200	973,300	-29.4	460,700	407,200	-11.6	1,838,900	1,380,500	-24.9

Note: (p) preliminary; figures cover and represent new, privately-owned housing units authorized (unadjusted data); All permit data are based on estimates with imputation; U.S. figures are based on the new 20,000-place series.
Source: U.S. Census Bureau, Manufacturing, Mining, and Construction Statistics

Homeownership and Housing Vacancies

Area	Homeownership Rate[2] (%)			Rental Vacancy Rate[3] (%)			Homeowner Vacancy Rate[4] (%)		
	2005	2006	2007	2005	2006	2007	2005	2006	2007
MSA[1]	73.5	73.1	73.1	11.6	11.6	12.6	1.7	1.7	1.9
U.S.	68.9	68.8	68.1	9.8	9.8	9.7	1.9	2.4	2.7

Note: (1) Metropolitan Statistical Area - see Appendix B for areas included; (2) The proportion of households that are owners; (3) The proportion of the rental inventory that is vacant for rent; (4) The proportion of the homeowner inventory that is vacant for sale; n/a not available
Source: U.S. Census Bureau, Housing Vacancies and Homeownership Annual Statistics: 2007

TAXES

State Corporate Income Tax Rates

State	Rates and Tax Brackets
New Jersey	6.5% > $0; 7.5 > 50K; 9.0% > 100K

Note: Tax rates as of January 1, 2008; Companies with income greater than $100K pay 9% on all income, companies with income greater than $50K but less than $100K pay 7.5 % on all income and companies with income under $50K pay 6.5%. The minimum tax is $500. An Alternative Minimum Assessment based on Gross Receipts applies if greater than corporate franchise tax for out-of-state companies with New Jersey sales. 4% surtax for 2007.
Source: Tax Foundation, www.taxfoundation.org

State Individual Income Tax Rates

State	Federal Deductibility	Marginal Rates (%)	Standard Deduction ($)		Personal Exemptions ($)[1]	
			Single	Joint	Single	Dependents
New Jersey	No	1.4 - 8.97 (y)	n/a	n/a	1,000	1,500

Note: Tax rates as of January 1, 2008; Local- and county-level taxes are not included; n/a not applicable; (1) Married joint filers generally receive double the single exemption; (y) Brackets are not double for married taxpayers.
Source: Tax Foundation, www.taxfoundation.org

Various State and Local Tax Rates

State and Local Sales and Use (%)	State Sales and Use (%)	Gasoline[1,2] ($/gal.)	Cigarette ($/pack)	Spirits ($/gal.)	Table Wine ($/gal.)	Beer ($/gal.)
7.0	7.0	0.145	2.575	4.40	0.70	0.12

Note: Tax rates as of January 1, 2008; (1) In addition to the 18.4 cpg Federal gasoline tax; (2) Rates may include additional state sales taxes, environmental protection and storage fees/taxes, and local taxes. When necessary, the volume-weighted average of all local taxes is used to approximate the typical statewide rate including local tax
Source: Tax Foundation, www.taxfoundation.org; Original research

State Tax Burdens

Area	Combined State and Local Tax Burden		Combined Federal, State and Local Tax Burden	
	Percent	Rank	Percent	Rank
New Jersey	11.6	10	35.6	3
U.S. Average	11.0	-	32.7	-

Note: Figures cover 2007 and measure taxes as a percentage of income
Source: Tax Foundation, www.taxfoundation.org

State Business Tax Climate Index Rankings

State	Overall Rank	Corporate Tax Index Rank	Individual Income Tax Index Rank	Sales Tax Index Rank	Unemployment Insurance Tax Index Rank	Property Tax Index Rank
New Jersey	49	41	49	44	24	49

Note: Rankings range from 1 to 50 where 1 is best. Rankings do not average across to Overall Rank. States without a given tax are given a ranking of 1.
Source: Tax Foundation, State Business Tax Climate Index 2008

TRANSPORTATION

Means of Transportation to Work

Area	Car/Truck/Van: Drove Alone	Car/Truck/Van: Car-pooled	Public Transportation: Bus	Public Transportation: Subway	Public Transportation: Railroad	Bicycle	Walked	Other Means	Worked at Home
City	83.2	7.4	0.5	2.2	1.9	0.0	1.2	0.5	3.1
MSA[1]	72.3	10.1	5.5	1.8	2.1	0.3	4.1	0.9	2.9
U.S.	75.7	12.2	2.5	1.5	0.5	0.4	2.9	1.0	3.3

Note: Figures are percentages and cover workers 16 years of age and older; (1) Metropolitan Statistical Area - see Appendix A for areas included
Source: Census 2000, Summary File 3

Travel Time to Work

Area	Less Than 15 Minutes	15 to 29 Minutes	30 to 44 Minutes	45 to 59 Minutes	60 Minutes or More
City	21.9	35.2	20.4	10.6	11.9
MSA[1]	23.7	33.2	22.6	10.4	10.0
U.S.	29.4	36.1	19.1	7.4	8.0

Note: Figures are percentages and include workers 16 years old and over; (1) Metropolitan Statistical Area - see Appendix A for areas included
Source: Census 2000, Summary File 3

Travel Time Index

Area	1982	1995	2004	2005
Urban Area[1]	1.12	1.18	1.27	1.28
Average[2]	1.11	1.22	1.29	1.30

Note: Travel Time Index - The ratio of travel time in the peak period to the travel time at free-flow conditions. A value of 1.35 indicates a 20-minute free-flow trip takes 27 minutes in the peak. Free-flow speeds (60 mph on freeways and 35 mph on principal arterials) are used as the comparison threshold; (1) Covers the Philadelphia, PA-NJ-DE-MD urban area; (2) average of 85 urban areas
Source: Texas Transportation Institute, The 2007 Urban Mobility Report, September 2007

Living Environment

COST OF LIVING

Cost of Living Index

Composite Index	Groceries	Housing	Utilities	Trans-portation	Health Care	Misc. Goods/ Services
124.1	124.4	146.1	116.5	105.9	110.9	115.3

Note: U.S. = 100; Figures cover the Philadelphia PA urban area.
Source: The Council for Community and Economic Research (formerly ACCRA), Cost of Living Index, 2007

Grocery Prices

Area[1]	T-Bone Steak ($/pound)	Frying Chicken ($/pound)	Whole Milk ($/half gal.)	Eggs ($/dozen)	Orange Juice ($/64 oz.)	Coffee ($/11.5 oz.)
City[2]	9.62	1.53	2.16	1.94	4.33	3.81
Avg.	8.93	1.12	2.13	1.52	3.26	3.31
Min.	5.88	0.71	1.33	0.83	2.30	2.20
Max.	12.80	2.07	3.43	3.54	5.79	6.20

Note: (1) Values for the local area are compared with the average, minimum and maximum values for all 331 areas in the Cost of Living Index report; (2) Figures cover the Philadelphia PA urban area; **T-Bone Steak** *(price per pound);* **Frying Chicken** *(price per pound, whole fryer);* **Whole Milk** *(half gallon carton);* **Eggs** *(price per dozen, Grade A, large);* **Orange Juice** *(64 oz. Tropicana or Florida Natural);* **Coffee** *(11.5 oz. can, vacuum-packed, Maxwell House, Hills Bros, or Folgers).*
Source: The Council for Community and Economic Research (formerly ACCRA), Cost of Living Index, 2007

Housing and Utility Costs

Area[1]	New Home Price ($)	Apartment Rent ($/month)	All Electric ($/month)	Part Electric ($/month)	Other Energy ($/month)	Telephone ($/month)
City[2]	424,647	1,385	-	55.44	112.57	35.89
Avg.	309,605	782	146.13	78.67	90.16	26.14
Min.	189,877	n/a	82.03	37.41	33.15	17.08
Max.	1,202,800	3,481	271.14	150.60	257.67	37.45

Note: (1) Values for the local area are compared with the average, minimum and maximum values for all 331 areas in the Cost of Living Index report; (2) Figures cover the Philadelphia PA urban area; **New Home Price** *(2,400 sf living area, 8,000 sf lot, in urban area with full utilities);* **Apartment Rent** *(950 sf 2 bedroom/1.5 or 2 bath, unfurnished, excluding all utilities except water);* **All Electric** *(average monthly cost for an all-electric home);* **Part Electric** *(average monthly cost for a part-electric home);* **Other Energy** *(average monthly cost for natural gas, fuel oil, coal, wood, and any other forms of energy except electricity);* **Telephone** *(price includes basic monthly rate for a private residential line plus additional local usage charges incurred by a family of four).*
Source: The Council for Community and Economic Research (formerly ACCRA), Cost of Living Index, 2007

Health Care, Transportation, and Other Costs

Area[1]	Doctor ($/visit)	Dentist ($/visit)	Optometrist ($/visit)	Gasoline ($/gallon)	Beauty Salon ($/visit)	Men's Shirt ($)
City[2]	100.28	80.89	94.67	2.70	54.67	37.35
Avg.	79.48	71.93	79.55	2.64	29.52	25.77
Min.	52.08	44.80	43.95	2.19	15.58	16.19
Max.	148.44	126.27	158.83	3.48	60.62	48.53

Note: (1) Values for the local area are compared with the average, minimum and maximum values for all 331 areas in the Cost of Living Index report; (2) Figures cover the Philadelphia PA urban area; **Doctor** *(general practitioners routine exam of an established patient);* **Dentist** *(adult teeth cleaning and periodic oral examination);* **Optometrist** *(full vision eye exam for established adult patient);* **Gasoline** *(one gallon regular unleaded, national brand, including all taxes, cash price at self-service pump if available);* **Beauty Salon** *(woman's shampoo, trim, and blow-dry);* **Men's Shirt** *(cotton/polyester dress shirt, pinpoint weave, long sleeves).*
Source: The Council for Community and Economic Research (formerly ACCRA), Cost of Living Index, 2007

HOUSING

House Price Index (HPI)

Area	National Ranking[2]	Quarterly Change (%)	One-Year Change (%)	Five-Year Change (%)
MD[1]	163	-0.54	1.01	63.65
U.S.[3]	-	0.10	0.84	41.37

Note: The HPI is a weighted repeat sales index. It measures average price changes in repeat sales or refinancings on the same properties. This information is obtained by reviewing repeat mortgage transactions on single-family properties whose mortgages have been purchased or securitized by Fannie Mae or Freddie Mac in January 1975; (1) Metropolitan Division - see Appendix B for areas included; (2) Rankings are based on annual percentage change for all metro areas containing at least 15,000 transactions over the last 10 years and ranges from 1 to 291; (3) figures based on a weighted average of Census Division estimates; all figures are for the period ending December 31, 2007
Source: Office of Federal Housing Enterprise Oversight, House Price Index, February 26, 2008

House Price Valuations

Area	Q1 2000	Q1 2001	Q1 2002	Q1 2003	Q1 2004	Q1 2005	Q1 2006	Q1 2007	Q1 2008
MD[1]	-17.0	-18.9	-15.3	-7.1	1.5	12.1	18.8	18.0	13.2

Note: Figures show the percentage of over- or under-valuation of single family homes relative to statistically normal house values (e.g. a value of 23.6 indicates that house values are 23.6% overvalued). Statistically normal house values are based on house prices, interest rates, household incomes, population densities, and any historical premiums or discounts metropolitan areas have exhibited over time; (1) Figures cover the Metropolitan Division - see Appendix B for areas included
Source: Global Insight/National City Corporation, House Prices in America, May 2008

Median Home Prices

Area	2005	2006	2007[r]	Percent Change 2006 to 2007
MSA[1]	215.3	230.2	234.9	2.0
U.S. Average	219.0	221.9	217.9	-1.8

Note: Figures are median sales prices of existing single-family homes in thousands of dollars; (r) revised; n/a not available; (1) Metropolitan Statistical Area - see Appendix B for areas included
Source: National Association of Realtors, Metropolitan Area Prices, 1st Quarter 2008

Housing: Year Structure Built

Area	1990 -2000	1980 -1989	1970 -1979	1960 -1969	1950 -1959	1940 -1949	Before 1940	Median Year
City	25.0	35.2	21.3	12.3	4.4	0.9	1.1	1983
MSA[1]	9.4	10.0	13.0	13.9	17.3	11.1	25.3	1958
U.S.	17.0	15.8	18.5	13.7	12.7	7.3	15.0	1971

Note: Figures are percentages; (1) Metropolitan Statistical Area - see Appendix A for areas included
Source: Census 2000, Summary File 3

HEALTH

Health Risk Data

Category	Area[1] (%)	U.S. (%)
Adults who have been told they have high blood pressure[3]	24.7	25.5
Adults who have been told they have high blood cholesterol[3]	37.0	35.6
Adults who have been told they have diabetes[2]	8.0	7.5
Adults who have been told they have arthritis[3]	25.8	27.0
Adults who have been told they currently have asthma	8.5	8.5
Adults who are current smokers	20.7	20.1
Adults who are heavy drinkers[4]	6.0	4.9
Adults who are overweight (BMI 25.0 - 29.9)	35.2	36.5
Adults who are obese (BMI 30.0 - 99.8)	26.5	25.1

Note: Data as of 2006 unless otherwise noted; (1) Figures cover the Metropolitan Division - see Appendix B for areas included; (2) Figures do not include pregnancy-related diabetes, pre-diabetes or borderline diabetes; (3) 2005 data; (4) Heavy drinkers are classified as adult men having more than two drinks per day or adult women having more than one drink per day
Source: Centers for Disease Control and Prevention, Behaviorial Risk Factor Surveillance System, SMART: Selected Metropolitan/Micropolitan Area Risk Trends, 2005, 2006

Mortality Rates for the Top 10 Causes of Death in the U.S.

ICD-10[a] Sub-Chapter	ICD-10[a] Code	Age-Adjusted Mortality Rate[1] per 100,000 population	
		County[2]	U.S.
Malignant neoplasms	C00-C97	195.9	186.5
Ischaemic heart diseases	I20-I25	172.7	152.3
Other forms of heart disease	I30-I51	53.2	51.5
Cerebrovascular diseases	I60-I69	44.7	50.0
Chronic lower respiratory diseases	J40-J47	42.4	42.6
Diabetes mellitus	E10-E14	23.7	24.8
Other degenerative diseases of the nervous system	G30-G31	25.2	22.6
Other external causes of accidental injury	W00-X59	17.6	21.4
Influenza and pneumonia	J10-J18	15.8	20.7
Hypertensive diseases	I10-I13	9.5	18.2

Note: (a) ICD-10 = International Classification of Diseases 10th Revision; (1) Mortality rates are a three year average covering 2003-2005; (2) Figures cover Burlington County
Source: Centers for Disease Control and Prevention, National Center for Health Statistics. Compressed Mortality File 1999-2004. CDC WONDER On-line Database, compiled from Compressed Mortality File 1999-2005 Series 20 No. 2K, 2008.

Mortality Rates for Selected Causes of Death

ICD-10[a] Sub-Chapter	ICD-10[a] Code	Age-Adjusted Mortality Rate[1] per 100,000 population	
		County[2]	U.S.
Assault	X85-Y09	2.6	5.9
Human immunodeficiency virus (HIV) disease	B20-B24	2.5	4.5
Intentional self-harm	X60-X84	7.2	10.8
Malnutrition	E40-E46	*1.1	1.0
Obesity and other hyperalimentation	E65-E68	*1.2	1.4
Organic, including symptomatic, mental disorders	F01-F09	19.4	16.8
Transport accidents	V01-V99	11.2	16.1
Viral hepatitis	B15-B19	*1.3	1.8

Note: (a) ICD-10 = International Classification of Diseases 10th Revision; (1) Mortality rates are a three year average covering 2003-2005; (2) Figures cover Burlington County; (*) Unreliable data as per CDC
Source: Centers for Disease Control and Prevention, National Center for Health Statistics. Compressed Mortality File 1999-2004. CDC WONDER On-line Database, compiled from Compressed Mortality File 1999-2005 Series 20 No. 2K, 2008.

Distribution of Physicians[1]

Area	Total	Family/ General Practice	Specialties	
			Medical	Surgical
Burlington County (number)	900	190	347	180
Burlington County (rate per 10,000 pop.)	20.0	4.2	7.7	4.0
U.S. (rate per 10,000 pop.)	17.7	4.6	6.9	4.3

Note: Data as of 2005; (1) Includes all non-federal, patient-care, office-based MDs
Source: Area Resource File (ARF). June 2007. U.S. Department of Health and Human Services, Health Resources and Services Administration, Bureau of Health Professions, Rockville, MD.

Hospitals

There were no hospitals listed within the city limits.
AHA Guide to the Healthcare Field 2008

According to *U.S. News,* the Philadelphia-Camden-Wilmington, PA-NJ-DE-MD metro area is home to 10 of the best hospitals in the U.S.: **Children's Hospital of Philadelphia**; **Christiana Care Health System**; **Fox Chase Cancer Center**; **Hahnemann University Hospital**; **Hospital of the University of Pennsylvania**; **Magee Rehabilitation Hospital**; **Moss Rehab**; **Pennsylvania Hospital**; **Thomas Jefferson University Hospital**; **Wills Eye Hospital**. *U.S. News Online, "America's Best Hospitals 2007"*

EDUCATION

Public School District Statistics

District Name	Schls	Pupils	Pupil/ Teacher Ratio	Minority Pupils[1] (%)	Free Lunch Eligible[2] (%)	IEP[3] (%)
Evesham Township	9	5,186	12.7	12.2	2.8	33.4

Note: Table includes regular local school districts with 2,000 or more students; (1) Percentage of students that are not white, non-Hispanic; (2) Percentage of students that are eligible for the free lunch program; (3) Percentage of students that have an Individualized Education Program.
Source: U.S. Department of Education, National Center for Education Statistics, Common Core of Data, Local Education Agency (School District) Universe Survey: School Year 2005-2006; U.S. Department of Education, National Center for Education Statistics, Common Core of Data, Public Elementary/Secondary School Universe Survey: School Year 2005-2006

Highest Level of Education

Area	Less than H.S.	H.S. Diploma	Some College, No Deg.	Associate Degree	Bachelors Degree	Masters Degree	Profess. School Degree	Doctorate Degree
City	6.9	25.4	20.2	7.9	27.3	8.6	3.0	0.8
MSA[1]	17.3	31.4	17.5	5.8	17.4	6.8	2.5	1.3
U.S.	19.4	28.4	21.2	6.4	15.7	5.9	2.0	1.0

Note: Figures are 2007 estimated percentages and cover persons age 25 and over; (1) Metropolitan Statistical Area - see Appendix B for areas included
Source: Claritas, Inc.

Educational Attainment by Race

Area	High School Graduate (%)					Bachelor's Degree (%)				
	Total	White	Black	Asian	Hisp.[2]	Total	White	Black	Asian	Hisp.[2]
City	93.3	93.8	95.4	83.3	80.7	39.7	39.4	34.1	57.9	41.2
MSA[1]	82.2	85.7	71.9	77.2	55.5	27.7	31.1	12.8	46.7	12.8
U.S.	80.4	83.6	72.3	80.4	52.4	24.4	26.1	14.3	44.1	10.4

Note: Figures shown cover persons 25 years old and over; (1) Metropolitan Statistical Area - see Appendix A for areas included; (2) people of Hispanic origin can be of any race
Source: Census 2000, Summary File 3

School Enrollment by Type

Area	Grades KG to 8				Grades 9 to 12			
	Public		Private		Public		Private	
	Enrollment	%	Enrollment	%	Enrollment	%	Enrollment	%
City	5,186	86.6	801	13.4	2,095	88.9	261	11.1
MSA[1]	544,674	79.7	138,763	20.3	248,356	81.5	56,489	18.5
U.S.	33,526,011	88.7	4,285,121	11.3	14,848,628	90.6	1,532,323	9.4

Note: Figures shown cover persons 3 years old and over; (1) Metropolitan Statistical Area - see Appendix A for areas included
Source: Census 2000, Summary File 3

School Enrollment by Race

Area	Grades KG to 8 (%)				Grades 9 to 12 (%)			
	White	Black	Asian	Hisp.[1]	White	Black	Asian	Hisp.[1]
City	91.1	2.2	3.8	2.5	91.0	3.5	3.5	2.4
MSA[2]	65.6	24.9	3.1	7.0	64.8	25.6	3.7	6.4
U.S.	68.5	15.5	3.3	16.8	68.8	15.5	3.8	15.7

Note: Figures shown cover persons 3 years old and over; (1) people of Hispanic origin can be of any race; (2) Metropolitan Statistical Area - see Appendix A for areas included
Source: Census 2000, Summary File 3

Average Salaries of Public School Classroom Teachers

District	2005-06 Dollars	2005-06 Rank[1]	2006-07 Dollars	2006-07 Rank[1]	Percent Change 2005-06 to 2006-07
New Jersey	58,156	5	59,920	3	3.03
U.S. Average	49,026	-	50,816	-	3.65

Note: (1) State rank ranges from 1 to 51.
Source: National Education Association, Rankings & Estimates: Rankings of the States 2006 and Estimates of School Statistics 2007, December 2007

Higher Education

Four-Year Colleges			Two-Year Colleges			Medical Schools[1]	Law Schools[2]	Voc/ Tech[3]
Public	Private Non-profit	Private For-profit	Public	Private Non-profit	Private For-profit			
0	0	0	0	0	0	0	0	0

Note: Figures cover institutions located within the city limits; (1) includes schools accredited by the Liaison Committee on Medical Education and the American Osteopathic Association; (2) includes American Bar Association-accredited law schools; (3) includes all schools with programs that are less than 2 years.
Source: National Center for Education Statistics, The Integrated Postsecondary Education System (IPEDS) Peer Analysis System, 2007; www.usnews.com, Law and Medical School Directories, 2009

PRESIDENTIAL ELECTION

2004 Presidential Election Results

Area	Bush	Kerry	Nader	Other
Burlington County	46.1	53.1	0.5	0.3
U.S.	50.7	48.3	0.4	0.6

Note: Results are percentages and may not add to 100% due to rounding
Source: Dave Leip's Atlas of U.S. Presidential Elections, www.uselectionatlas.org

EMPLOYERS

Major Employers

Company Name	Industry	Type of Site
Abington Memorial Hospital	General medical and surgical hospitals	Headquarters
Childrens Hosp of Philadelphia	Specialty hospitals, except psychiatric	Headquarters
Clinical Practices of Univ PA	Colleges and universities	Headquarters
Comcast Holdings Corporation	Cable and other pay television services	Headquarters
Glaxosmithkline	Commercial physical research	Branch
Lockheed Martin	Search and navigation equipment	Branch
Lockheed Martin	Transportation services, nec	Headquarters
Lockheed Martin Integrated TEC	Management services	Single
Mercy Hlth Corp Sutheastern PA	Management services	Headquarters
Navy Aviation Supply Office	National security	Branch
Our Lady of Lourdes Health	Management services	Single
Police Dept	Police protection	Branch
Temple University Hospital	General medical and surgical hospitals	Single
The Vanguard Group Inc	Management investment, open-ended	Headquarters
Thomas Jefferson Univ Hosp	General medical and surgical hospitals	Headquarters
Toll Bros Inc	Residential construction, nec	Single
Tyco Electronics Corporation	Electronic connectors	Headquarters
University of Pennsylvania	General medical and surgical hospitals	Branch

Note: Companies shown are located within the Philadelphia metropolitan area; nec = not elsewhere classified.
Source: www.zapdata.com, May 2008

PUBLIC SAFETY

Crime Rate

Area	All Crimes	Violent Crimes: Murder	Violent Crimes: Forcible Rape	Violent Crimes: Robbery	Violent Crimes: Aggrav. Assault	Property Crimes: Burglary	Property Crimes: Larceny -Theft	Property Crimes: Motor Vehicle Theft
City	1,627.8	0.0	12.8	17.0	59.6	195.8	1,291.6	51.1
Metro[1]	3,008.6	4.7	24.5	134.3	188.5	530.8	1,886.0	240.0
U.S.	3,808.1	5.7	30.9	149.4	287.5	729.4	2,206.8	398.4

Note: Figures are crimes per 100,000 population; (1) Metropolitan Division - see Appendix B for areas included
Source: FBI Uniform Crime Reports, 2006

Hate Crimes

Area	Number of Quarters Reported	Bias Motivation				
		Race	Religion	Sexual Orientation	Ethnicity	Disability
City	4	1	0	0	0	0

Source: Federal Bureau of Investigation, Hate Crime Statistics 2006

RECREATION

Culture

Dance[1]	Theatre[1]	Instrumental Music[1]	Vocal Music[1]	Series/ Festivals	Museums	Zoos and Aquariums[2]
0	0	0	0	0	0	0

Note: (1) Number of professional perfoming groups; (2) AZA-accredited
Source: The Grey House Performing Arts Directory, 2007; Official Museum Directory, 2008; Association of Zoos & Aquariums, AZA Member Zoos & Aquariums, June 2008

Professional Sports Teams

Team Name	League
Philadelphia Phillies	Major League Baseball (MLB)
Unnamed Expansion Team (2010)	Major League Soccer (MLS)
Philadelphia 76ers	National Basketball Association (NBA)
Philadelphia Eagles	National Football League (NFL)
Philadelphia Flyers	National Hockey League (NHL)

Note: Includes teams located in the Philadelphia metro area.
Source: Original research

MEDIA

Newspapers

Name	News Focus	Frequency	Circulation
No newspapers have an office in the city			

Note: Includes newspapers with offices located in the city
Source: MediaContactsPro, March 2008

Television Stations

Name	Ch.	Network(s)	Type	Ownership
KYW	3	CBS	Commercial	CBS
WPVI	6	ABC	Commercial	ABC Inc.
WCAU	10	NBC	Commercial	General Electric Corporation
WHYY	12	PBS	Public	WHYY Inc.
WPHL	17	WBN	Commercial	Tribune Broadcasting Company
WNJS	23	PBS	Public	New Jersey Public Broadcasting Authority
WZBN	25	n/a	Public	n/a
WTXF	29	Fox	Commercial	Fox Television Stations Inc.
WYBE	35	PBS	Public	Independence Public Media of Philadelphia Inc.
WLVT	39	PBS	Public	Lehigh Valley Public Telecommunications
WMGM	40	NBC	Commercial	The Greene Group
WGTW	48	n/a	Commercial	Brunson Communications
WNJN	50	PBS	Public	New Jersey Public Broadcasting Authority
WTVE	51	n/a	Commercial	Reading Broadcasting Inc.
WNJT	52	PBS	Public	New Jersey Public Broadcasting Authority
WMCN	53	n/a	Commercial	WWAC
WPSG	57	UPN	Commercial	Paramount Communications Inc.
WNJB	58	n/a	Public	New Jersey Public Broadcasting Authority
WBPH	60	n/a	Commercial	Sonshine Family Television Inc.
WPPX	61	Pax	Commercial	Paxson Communications Corporation
WWSI	62	Telemundo	Commercial	Hispanic Broadcasters of Philadelphia
WUVP	65	n/a	Commercial	Univision Inc.
WFMZ	69	n/a	Commercial	Maranatha Broadcasting

Note: Stations included cover the Philadelphia DMA (Designated Market Area); n/a not available
BurrellesLuce, MediaContacts Online, January 2007

Major AM Radio Stations

Call Letters	Freq. (kHz)	Station Type	Target Audience	Station Format	Music Format
WFIL	560	n/a	General	Ed/Music/News/Talk	Easy Listening
WIP	610	Commercial	General	Sports/Talk	n/a
WTMR	800	n/a	General/Religious	Music	n/a
WPEN	950	Commercial	General	Music/Talk	Big Band
WJHR	1040	Commercial	General	News/Talk	n/a
KYW	1060	n/a	General	Music/News	n/a
WDEL	1150	Commercial	General	Sports/Talk	n/a
WPHT	1210	Commercial	General	Talk	n/a
WBUD	1260	n/a	General	Music/News/Talk	n/a
WMIZ	1270	n/a	General/Hispanic	Music/News	n/a
WIMG	1300	n/a	Black/General	Music/News/Talk	n/a
WTKZ	1320	Commercial	Hispanic	Music	Latin
WHWH	1350	n/a	General	News/Sports/Talk	n/a
WDOV	1410	Commercial	General	News/Talk	n/a
WCOJ	1420	n/a	General	Music/News/Talk	n/a
WIFI	1460	Commercial	General/Religious	Music/News/Talk	Christian
WKAP	1470	n/a	General	Music	n/a
WDAS	1480	n/a	Black/Gen/Rel/Women	Sports	n/a
WNWR	1540	n/a	General/Religious	Music/News/Sports	n/a
WISP	1570	n/a	Catholic/General	Educational/Talk	n/a
WHOL	1600	n/a	General/Hisp/Rel	Music/News/Sports	n/a

Note: Stations included cover the Philadelphia DMA (Designated Market Area); n/a not available
Source: BurrellesLuce, MediaContacts Online, January 2007

Major FM Radio Stations

Call Letters	Freq. (mHz)	Station Type	Target Audience	Station Format	Music Format
WXPH	88.1	College	General	Music/News/Sports/Talk	Adult Contemp.
WXTU	92.5	n/a	General	Music	n/a
WSTW	93.7	Commercial	General	Music/News	Adult Top 40
WRDX	94.7	Commercial	General	Music	Alternative
WAYV	95.1	Commercial	General	Music/Talk	Top 40
WCTO	96.1	n/a	General	Music	n/a
WFPG	96.9	n/a	General	News/Talk	n/a
WPST	97.5	n/a	General	Music	n/a
WJBR	99.5	Commercial	General	Music/News/Sports/Talk	Adult Contemp.
WODE	99.9	n/a	General	Music	n/a
WLEV	100.7	Commercial	General/Women	Music	Soft Rock
WBEB	101.1	Commercial	General	Music	Soft Rock
WKXW	101.5	n/a	General	Music/News/Sports/Talk	n/a
WMGM	103.7	Commercial	General	Music/Talk	Classic Rock
WAEB	104.1	n/a	General	Music	n/a
WBYN	107.5	n/a	General/Religious	Ed/Music/News/Talk	n/a

Note: Stations included cover the Philadelphia DMA (Designated Market Area); n/a not available
BurrellesLuce, MediaContacts Online, January 2007

CLIMATE

Average and Extreme Temperatures

Temperature	Jan	Feb	Mar	Apr	May	Jun	Jul	Aug	Sep	Oct	Nov	Dec	Yr.
Extreme High (°F)	74	74	85	94	96	100	104	101	100	89	84	72	104
Average High (°F)	39	42	51	63	73	82	86	85	78	67	55	43	64
Average Temp. (°F)	32	34	42	53	63	72	77	76	68	57	47	36	55
Average Low (°F)	24	26	33	43	53	62	67	66	59	47	38	28	45
Extreme Low (°F)	-7	-4	7	19	28	44	51	44	35	25	15	1	-7

Note: Figures cover the years 1948-1990
Source: National Climatic Data Center, International Station Meteorological Climate Summary, 9/96

Average Precipitation/Snowfall/Humidity

Precip./Humidity	Jan	Feb	Mar	Apr	May	Jun	Jul	Aug	Sep	Oct	Nov	Dec	Yr.
Avg. Precip. (in.)	3.2	2.8	3.7	3.5	3.7	3.6	4.1	4.0	3.3	2.7	3.4	3.3	41.4
Avg. Snowfall (in.)	7	7	4	Tr	Tr	0	0	0	0	Tr	1	4	22
Avg. Rel. Hum. 7am (%)	74	73	73	72	75	77	80	82	84	83	79	75	77
Avg. Rel. Hum. 4pm (%)	60	55	51	48	51	52	54	55	55	54	57	60	54

Note: Figures cover the years 1948-1990; Tr = Trace amounts (<0.05 in. of rain; <0.5 in. of snow)
Source: National Climatic Data Center, International Station Meteorological Climate Summary, 9/96

Weather Conditions

Temperature			Daytime Sky			Precipitation		
10°F & below	32°F & below	90°F & above	Clear	Partly cloudy	Cloudy	0.01 inch or more precip.	0.1 inch or more snow/ice	Thunder-storms
5	94	23	81	146	138	117	14	27

Note: Figures are average number of days per year and cover the years 1948-1990
Source: National Climatic Data Center, International Station Meteorological Climate Summary, 9/96

HAZARDOUS WASTE

Superfund Sites

Evesham has one hazardous waste site on the EPA's Superfund Final National Priorities List: **Ellis Property**. *U.S. Environmental Protection Agency, Final National Priorities List, June 23, 2008*

AIR & WATER QUALITY

Air Quality Index

Area	Percent of Days when Air Quality was...[2]				AQI Statistics	
	Good	Moderate	Unhealthy for Sensitive Groups	Unhealthy	Maximum	Median
MSA[1]	44.9	44.1	9.0	1.9	203	54

Note: The Air Quality Index (AQI) is an index for reporting daily air quality. EPA calculates the AQI for five major air pollutants regulated by the Clean Air Act: ground-level ozone, particle pollution (also known as particulate matter), carbon monoxide, sulfur dioxide, and nitrogen dioxide. The AQI runs from 0 to 500. The higher the AQI value, the greater the level of air pollution and the greater the health concern. There are six AQI categories: "Good" The AQI is between 0 and 50. Air quality is considered satisfactory; "Moderate" The AQI is between 51 and 100. Air quality is acceptable; "Unhealthy for Sensitive Groups" When AQI values are between 101 and 150, members of sensitive groups may experience health effects; "Unhealthy" When AQI values are between 151 and 200 everyone may begin to experience health effects; "Very Unhealthy" AQI values between 201 and 300 trigger a health alert; "Hazardous" AQI values over 300 trigger health warnings of emergency conditions; (1) Metropolitan Statistical Area - see Appendix A for areas included; (2) Based on 365 days with AQI data in 2007.
Source: U.S. Environmental Protection Agency, Air Quality Index Report, 2007

Air Quality Index Pollutants

Area	Percent of Days when AQI Pollutant was...[2]					
	Carbon Monoxide	Nitrogen Dioxide	Ozone	Sulfur Dioxide	Particulate Matter 2.5	Particulate Matter 10
MSA[1]	0.8	0.0	47.7	0.0	50.4	1.1

Note: The Air Quality Index (AQI) is an index for reporting daily air quality. EPA calculates the AQI for five major air pollutants regulated by the Clean Air Act: ground-level ozone, particle pollution (also known as particulate matter), carbon monoxide, sulfur dioxide, and nitrogen dioxide. The AQI runs from 0 to 500. The higher the AQI value, the greater the level of air pollution and the greater the health concern; (1) Metropolitan Statistical Area - see Appendix A for areas included; (2) Based on 365 days with AQI data in 2007.
Source: U.S. Environmental Protection Agency, Air Quality Index Report, 2007

Air Quality Index Trends

Area	Trend Sites (45)								All Sites (98)
	1999	2000	2001	2002	2003	2004	2005	2006	2006
MSA[1]	33	21	34	35	19	9	21	18	20

Note: An AQI value greater than 100 indicates that air quality would have been in the unhealthful range on that day. Data from exceptional events are not included. These counts are presented in two ways. First, the counts are based on sites having an adequate record of monitoring data during the trend period (trend sites). These counts represent the relative change in the number of days with AQI values greater than 100. In the last column, the counts are based on all sites with data in the most recent year (because it is possible for a site to have data in the most recent year but not enough data to be a trend site); (1) Metropolitan Statistical Area - see Appendix A for areas included.
Source: U.S. Environmental Protection Agency, Office of Air and Radiation, Air Trends, Factbook and Related Information, Air Pollution Trends in Selected Metropolitan Areas 2006

Maximum Air Pollutant Concentrations

	Particulate Matter 10 (ug/m^3)	Particulate Matter 2.5 (ug/m^3)	Ozone (ppm)	Carbon Monoxide (ppm)	Sulfur Dioxide (ppm)	Nitrogen Dioxide (ppm)	Lead (ug/m^3)
MSA[1] Level	159	39	0.124	3	0.024	0.021	0.05
NAAQS[2]	150	35	0.125	9	0.140	0.053	1.50
Met NAAQS[2]	No	No	Yes	Yes	Yes	Yes	Yes

Note: Data from exceptional events are not included; (1) Metropolitan Statistical Area - see Appendix A for areas included; (2) National Ambient Air Quality Standards; n/a not available
Concentrations: Particulate Matter 10 (coarse particulate) - highest second maximum 24-hour concentration; Particulate Matter 2.5 (fine particulate) - highest 98th percentile 24-hour concentration; Ozone - highest second daily maximum 1-hour concentration; Carbon Monoxide - highest second maximum non-overlapping 8-hour concentration; Sulfur Dioxide - highest second maximum 24-hour concentration; Nitrogen Dioxide - highest arithmetic mean concentration; Lead - highest quarterly maximum concentration
Units: ppm = parts per million; ug/m^3 = micrograms per cubic meter
Source: U.S. Environmental Protection Agency, MSA Factbook 2006, Air Quality Statistics by City

Drinking Water

Water System Name	Pop. Served	Primary Water Source Type	Violations[1]	
			Health Based	Monitoring/ Reporting
Evesham MUA	47,784	Ground	n/a	n/a

Note: (1) Based on violation data from January 1, 2007 to December 31, 2007 (includes unresolved violations from earlier years)
Source: U.S. Environmental Protection Agency, Office of Ground Water and Drinking Water, Safe Drinking Water Information System (based on data extracted April 15, 2008)

Marlboro, New Jersey

Background

Marlboro rests 43 miles south of New York City in Monmouth County and less than 18 miles west of the Jersey shore, making it accessible to both a bustling urban center and peaceful seaside recreational opportunities.

The Township was established in 1848, largely as a farming community. From its earliest settlements until fairly recently, Marlboro was a rural community composed of a number of small hamlets. Although each had small inns or taverns, the hub of activity centered around what is still referred to today as Marlboro Village. Historical research reveals that the name came from the discovery of marl on a farm just east of the village in 1768. Marl, composed of the remains of prehistoric fish, clams, etc., dates back to the period when New Jersey was part of the ocean bed. Farmers used the heavily demanded marl to improve the soil in the days before commercial fertilizers, and the export of marl to all parts of the country became one of Marlboro's first industries.

During the Revolutionary War, Marlboro was the scene of many skirmishes between British and American forces. When retreating from the Battle of Monmouth in 1778, the British troops passed through Marlboro on their way to ships at nearby Sandy Hook. They were attacked by American militiamen who mobilized along their route.

Today, Marlboro is a largely residential suburban community which, although surrounded by urban sprawl, continues to encourage reclamation of its remaining open spaces. The 378-acre Big Brook Park, once part of the Marlboro State Hospital facility, was recently acquired by the county to help protect the Navesink Watershed. This protected open space is adjacent to Camp Arrowhead Reserves, and includes a piece of the Henry Hudson Trail along its westerly edge.

In 2004, Marlboro Township launched an education and government television station. Informational and educational programming, produced by Marlboro Township, can be seen in households throughout the municipality. The video messaging system features public information from the Township, the Board of Education, and local not-for-profit entities.

The school systems in Marlboro offers several innovative opportunities. The Marlboro Early Learning Center serves all pre-school handicapped, as well as all kindergarten children in the district. Students in grades one through five attend one of five elementary schools in the district. A district wide approach to curriculum development results in a common and equal teaching guide in all the schools. Each school, however, is unique in its implementation of the curricula.

Marlboro Middle School and the district's newest school, Marlboro Memorial Middle School houses all students in sixth, seventh, and eighth grades. Seventh and eighth grade students are offered an Enrichment Opportunity Period, which enables them to select several electives throughout the year.

Rankings

General Rankings

- Edison* was ranked #161 out of 375 metro areas in *Cities Ranked & Rated*. Criteria: cost of living; climate; crime; transportation; economy and jobs; education; arts and culture; health and healthcare; leisure; quality of life. *Cities Ranked & Rated, 2nd Edition, 2007*
- Edison* was ranked #50 out of 379 metro areas in *Places Rated Almanac*. Criteria: health care; education; recreation; transportation; ambience; climate; crime; housing costs; jobs. *Places Rated Almanac, 7th Edition, 2007*
- Marlboro was selected as one of the "2007 Best Places to Live" by *Money* magazine. The city ranked #33 out of 100. Methodology: Places on the list had to have populations above 7,500 and under 50,000. Retirement-oriented communities, places where income is less than 90% or more than 180% of the state median and towns that were more than 95% white were screened out. Towns with low education scores, high crime rates, declines or sharp increases in population, projected job losses or lack of access to airports or teaching hospitals were eliminated. The remaining places were ranked based on job, income and cost-of-living data; housing affordability; school quality; arts and leisure opportunities; ease of living; health-care access; and racial diversity. Finally, the sense of community, vibrancy of town center, natural surroundings, amenities, real estate and congestion were assessed.
CNNMoney.com, "Best Places to Live 2007"

Business/Finance Rankings

- The nation's 100 largest metro areas were analysed in terms of the percentage of households entering some stage of foreclosure in 2007. The Edison* metro area ranked #61 out of 100 (#1 = highest foreclosure rate). *RealtyTrac, "Year-End 2007 Metropolitan Foreclosure Report"*
- The New York* metro area was identified as one of the most expensive places to rent in the U.S. The area ranked #61 out of 10 markets with an average effective rent of $2,720 per month. The rental figures cover apartment properties in complexes with 40 or more units (20 or more units in California and Arizona). The figures are blended average rents, which include all unit sizes. Effective rents include free rent incentives and other landlord concessions. *Wall Street Journal Online, January 17, 2008*
- The New York* metro area was selected as one of "America's Most Wired Cities" by *Forbes*. The metro area was ranked #9 out of 30. Criteria: percentage of Internet users with high-speed access; the range of service providers within a city; availability of public wireless hot spots. *Forbes, "America's Most Wired Cities," January 10, 2008*
- Monmouth* was selected as one of the best places to start and grow a company by *Entrepreneur* and the National Policy Research Council. The Monmouth* metro area ranked #35 out of 50 large metro areas. Criteria: business formation and growth (firms started four to 14 years ago that still employ at least 5 people and experienced rapid growth over the last four years). *Entrepreneur/National Policy Research Council, "Hot Cities for Entrepreneurs," September 2006*
- The New York* metro area was selected as one of "America's Greediest Cities" by *Forbes*. The area was ranked #6 out of 10. Criteria: number of Forbes 400 (*Forbes* annual list of the richest Americans) members per capita. *Forbes, "America's Greediest Cities," December 7, 2007*
- Edison* was cited as one of America's top large metros (population over 1 million) for new and expanded facility projects in 2007. The area appeared in the top 10 with 72 projects. *Site Selection, "Top Metropolitan Area Awards," March 2008*
- Intel, in partnership with Sperling's BestPlaces, ranked the 80 "Best Cities for Teleworking" in America. The New York* metro area ranked #6 among extra large metro areas. The study identifies cities that hold the greatest potential for teleworking based on a host of factors including typical commuting times, fuel prices, availability of broadband Internet access and percentage of the population in telework friendly jobs. The study also factored in extreme climate and natural hazards. *Intel, "Best Cities for Teleworking," March 30, 2006*

- The Edison* metro area appeared on the Milken Institute "2007 Best Performing Cities" index. Rank: #133 out of 200 large metro areas. Criteria: job growth; wage and salary growth; high-tech output growth. *Milken Institute, "2007 Best Performing Cities"*

- Monmouth* was identified as one of the 100 "Most Unwired Cities" in the U.S. The area ranked #88 out of the 100 largest metro areas in the U.S. Criteria: number of public and commercial wireless access points (hotspots); airports with wireless Internet access; broadband availability; local wireless networks; and wireless email devices. *Intel, "Most Unwired Cities Survey," June 7, 2005*

- New York* was ranked #12 out of 125 regions worldwide in terms of its "Knowledge Competitiveness Index." The index attempts to measure the knowledge-based development taking place throughout the world and is based on 19 measures of economic performance that indicate a region's ability to translate its knowledge capacity into economic value. *Robert Huggins Associates, World Knowledge Competitiveness Index 2005*

- *Forbes* ranked the 200 most populous metro areas in the U.S. in terms of the "Best Places for Business and Careers." The Edison* metro area was ranked #51. Criteria: business costs (labor, energy, tax and office space expenses); living costs (housing, transportation, food and other household expenditures); education levels of the work force; job growth; income growth; migration trends; crime rates; and culture/leisure. *Forbes, "Best Places for Business and Careers," March 19, 2008*

- *Fortune* ranked the 100 largest metro areas in the U.S. in terms of projected median home price change in 2007. The Edison* metro area ranked #75. *Fortune.com, "Hot Spots, Cold Spots"*

- The New York* metro area was identified as one of "America's Most Overpriced Real Estate Markets." The area ranked #7 out of 10. Criteria: housing "P/E" ratio (a market's median home price divided by annual rents minus taxes and insurance); housing affordability. *Forbes.com, "America's Most Overpriced Real Estate Markets," May 11, 2007*

Health/Environment Rankings

- 100 of the largest metro areas in the U.S. were analyzed in terms of their current drought severity. The New York* metro area ranked #75 (#1 = driest). The rankings were based on statistics such as long-term precipitation trends and patterns and the Palmer drought indices. *Sperling's BestPlaces, www.BestPlaces.net, "America's Drought-Riskiest Cities," November 2007*

- Doctors at the Harvard School of Public Health ranked 40 metropolitan areas based on data from the government-sponsored Hospital Quality Alliance program. The program tracks the performance of individual hospitals in treating patients for three common health problems: heart attacks, congestive heart failure, and pneumonia. The New York* metro area ranked #17 in quality of care for heart attacks, #8 for congestive heart failure, and #34 for pneumonia. *New England Journal of Medicine, July 21, 2005*

- *Reader's Digest* ranked the 50 largest metro areas in the U.S. in terms of how "clean" they are. The New York* metro area ranked #49. Criteria: air quality; water quality; toxic industrial pollution; Superfund sites; and sanitation. *Reader's Digest, "The 50 Cleanest (and Dirtiest) Cities in America," July 2005*

- The American Academy of Dermatology ranked 32 U.S. metropolitan regions in terms of their residents knowledge, attitude and behaviors towards tanning and sun protection. The New York* metro area ranked #2. The results of the study are based on an online national survey of 3,342 respondents. *American Academy of Dermatology, "RAYS: Your Grade," May 7, 2007*

- The Edison* metro area appeared in *Country Home's* "2008 Best Green Places" report. The area ranked #265 out of 379. Criteria: official energy policies; green power; green buildings; availability of fresh, locally grown food. *Country Home, "2008 Best Green Places"*

- Wyeth Consumer Healthcare, in partnership with Sperling's BestPlaces, ranked the nation's 50 most populous metro areas in terms of five key health factors. The New York* metro area ranked #43. Criteria: physical activity; health status; nutrition; lifestyle pursuits; and mental wellness. *Wyeth Consumer Healthcare, "Centrum Healthiest Cities Study," April 19, 2005*

- HealthGrades surveyed over 41,000 individuals on doctor satisfaction and ranked the 20 largest metro areas based on the highest "definitely yes" responses to the question "Do you trust the physician to make decisions/recommendations that are in your best interest?" The New York* metro area ranked #10. *HealthGrades.com, "Top Cities in Doctor-Trust," September 7, 2006*
- New York* was identified as a "2008 Asthma Capital." The area ranked #38 out of the nation's 100 largest metropolitan areas. Twelve factors were used to identify the most challenging places to live for people with asthma: estimated prevalence; self-reported prevalence; crude death rate for asthma; annual pollen score; annual air quality; public smoking laws; number of board-certified asthma specialists; school inhaler access laws; rescue medication use; controller medication use; uninsured rate; poverty rate. *Asthma and Allergy Foundation of America, "2008 Asthma Capitals"*
- New York* was identified as a "Spring Allergy Capital." The area ranked #79 out of 100. Three groups of factors were used to identify the most severe cities for people with allergies during the spring season: annual pollen levels; medicine utilization; access to board-certified allergists. *Asthma and Allergy Foundation of America, "2007 Spring Allergy Capital Rankings"*
- New York* was identified as a "Fall Allergy Capital." The area ranked #69 out of 100. Three groups of factors were used to identify the most severe cities for people with allergies during the fall season: annual pollen levels; medicine utilization; access to board-certified allergists. *Asthma and Allergy Foundation of America, "2007 Fall Allergy Capital Rankings"*
- Ortho-McNeil Neurologics, in partnership with Sperling's BestPlaces, analyzed 110 metro areas and identified those U.S. cities with the highest prevalence of factors that are most commonly associated with migraine headaches. The Monmouth* metro area ranked #106. Criteria: number of migraine-related drug prescriptions per capita; lifestyle factors that can contribute to migraines; environmental factors that can trigger migraines; and consumption of migraine-triggering foods. *Ortho-McNeil Neurologics, "America's Migraine Hot Spots," March 14, 2006*
- Sperling's BestPlaces ranked 331 metro areas and identified the most and least stressful U.S. cities. The Monmouth* metro area ranked #72 out of the 100 largest metro areas (#1 = most stressful). Criteria: divorce rate; unemployment rate; violent and property crime; suicide rate; commute time; mental health; alcohol consumption; cloudy days. *Sperling's BestPlaces, www.BestPlaces.net, "America's Most (and Least) Stressful Cities," January 9, 2004*
- An analysis of the "Best & Worst Cities for Sleep" was conducted by Sperling's BestPlaces. The study ranked America's 50 most populated metro areas. The New York* metro area ranked #47 (#1 = best city for sleep). Criteria: number of days residents didn't get enough rest or sleep during the past month; average length of daily commute; divorce rate; unemployment rate. *Sperling's BestPlaces, www.BestPlaces.net, "Best & Worst Cities for Sleep," 2006*
- HealthGrades evaluated the performance of America's 25 most populous metropolitan areas by measuring the outcomes of five of the highest volume and most widely studied procedures and diagnoses: coronary artery bypass graft surgery; percutaneus coronary interventions; acute myocardial infarction/heart attack in angioplasty-capable hospitals; congestive heart failure; and community acquired pneumonia. The New York* metro area ranked #17. *HealthGrades, "HealthGrades Hospital Quality in America Study," October 12, 2004*
- New York* was highlighted as one of the 25 metro areas most polluted by year-round particle pollution (PM 2.5) in the U.S. The area ranked #17. *American Lung Association, State of the Air: 2007*
- New York* was highlighted as one of the 25 most ozone-polluted metro areas in the U.S. The area ranked #10. *American Lung Association, State of the Air: 2007*
- New York* was selected as one of "America's Top 10 Low-Carb Cities" by *LowCarbiz Magazine*. Criteria: abundance of low-carb products; restaurants with low-carb menu items; health practitioners supportive of carb-cutting regimens; local culture generally conducive to exercise and health. *LowCarbiz Magazine, April 2004*

- New York* was selected as one of "America's Pet Healthiest Cities" by Purina. The city ranked #14 out of 50. Criteria: veterinary services; environment; legislation; preventative care; obesity/body condition. *Purina Pet Institute, "America's Pet Healthiest Cities," May 20, 2003*

Women/Minorities Rankings

- Monmouth* was ranked #25 out of 100 metro areas in *SELF Magazine's* ranking of "America's Best Places for Women." A panel of experts came up with more than 50 criteria including death and disease rates, environmental indicators, community resources, and lifestyle habits. *SELF Magazine, "America's Best Places for Women 2007," December 2007*
- New York* appeared on a list of the top 10 metro areas with the highest concentration of same-sex households. The area ranked #6. *Urban Institute Press, The Gay and Lesbian Atlas, May 2004*
- New York* appeared on a list of the top 10 metro areas with the highest concentration of gay male couples. The area ranked #5. *Urban Institute Press, The Gay and Lesbian Atlas, May 2004*

Seniors/Retirement Rankings

- Sperling's BestPlaces in partnership with Bankers Life & Casualty Company designed a survey to identify the top 50 metro areas in the U.S. that offer the best overall qualities for senior living. The New York* metro area ranked #7. The following criteria were statistically weighted to reflect the needs of the senior population: health; disease; economics; social; environment; spiritual; transportation; housing; and crime. *Bankers Life & Casualty Company, "Best Cities for Seniors 2005"*
- A.G. Edwards ranked America's 500 top-performing communities based on their residents' personal savings and investing behavior. The New York* metro area ranked #241 with an index score of 101.69 (national average = 100.00). A dozen statistical factors were measured including: participation in retirement savings plans; personal debt levels; and home ownership. *A.G. Edwards, "2007 Nest Egg Index", September 12, 2007*

Children/Family Rankings

- The Edison* metro area was selected as one of the "Best Cities for Relocating Families" by Worldwide ERC and Primacy Relocation. The 2007 study placed a special emphasis on the housing market, which has significantly impacted the relocation industry and an employer's ability to transfer employees. The variables which weigh heavily in this category include home price, home affordability index, appreciation rates, and property tax. Other criteria include cost of living, crime rates, education, climate, focus on diversity, physicians per capita, recreation and leisure, arts and culture, air quality, watershed quality, sales tax, unemployment rate, job growth, high school and higher education index, school expenditures per student, students in public school, SAT/ACT percentile, and population growth. *Worldwide ERC and Primacy Relocation, "2007 Best Cities for Relocating Families"*

Safety Rankings

- The National Insurance Crime Bureau ranked 361 metro areas in the U.S. in terms of per capita rates of vehicle theft. The New York* metro area ranked #224 (#1 = highest rate). Criteria: number of vehicle theft offenses per 100,000 inhabitants. *National Insurance Crime Bureau, "NICB Vehicle Theft Study," April 22, 2008*
- New York* appeared on Sperling's BestPlaces list of the "Riskiest Cities for Identity Theft." The area ranked #29 out of the nations 50 largest metro areas. Over 80 criteria were analyzed across four major categories: technology impact; crime; transactions; and risk profile. *Sperling's BestPlaces, www.BestPlaces.net, "Riskiest Cities for Identity Theft," July 2006*

- Farmers Insurance Group of Companies, in partnership with Sperling's BestPlaces, ranked 379 metro areas and identified the "Most Secure U.S. Place to Live." The Edison* metro area ranked #13 out of 114 in the large metro area category (500,000 or more residents). Criteria: crime rates; extreme weather; risk of natural disasters; environmental hazards; terrorism threats; air quality; life expectancy; job loss numbers. *Farmers Insurance Group, "Most Secure U.S. Places to Live 2007"*

- Monmouth* was identified as one of the most dangerous large metro areas for pedestrians in the U.S. The area ranked #47 out of the nations 50 largest metro areas. Criteria: average yearly pedestrian fatalities per capita (for the years 2002 and 2003) adjusted for the number of walkers. *Surface Transportation Policy Project, "Mean Streets 2004"*

Sports/Recreation Rankings

- The New York* metro area appeared on the *Sporting News* list of the "Best Sports Cities 2007". The area ranked #2 out of 150 cities in the U.S. *Sporting News* takes a 12-month snapshot, roughly July to July, of each city's sports, putting a heavy premium on regular-season won-lost records (from the most recently completed season). Other criteria include: playoff berths, bowl appearances and tournament bids; championships; applicable power ratings; quality of competition; overall fan fervor as measured in part by attendance as percentage of venue capacity; abundance of teams (rewarding quality over quantity); stadium and arena quality; ticket availability and prices; franchise ownership; and marquee appeal of athletes. *SportingNews.com, "Best Sports Cities 2007," August 1, 2007*

- The New York* metro area was selected by *Cranium* as one of the "Top 50 Fun Cities" in America. The area ranked #41. Criteria includes: number of sports teams, restaurants, and dance performances; number of toy stores; city budget spent on recreation. *Cranium, November 4, 2003*

- *Golf Digest* ranked 330 metro areas in the U.S. in terms of golf. The Monmouth* metro area was ranked #264. Criteria: access to golf; weather; value of golf; and quality of golf. *Golf Digest, "Metro Golf Rankings," August 2005*

Dating/Romance Rankings

- Eli Lily and Company, in partnership with Sperling's BestPlaces, ranked the nation's 50 largest metro areas in terms of the "Most Romantic Cities for Baby Boomers." The New York* metro area ranked #16. Criteria: marriage and divorce rates among "baby boomers" age 45 to 60; great restaurants; dance studios; chocolate, jewelry and flower sales. *Eli Lily and Company, "Most Romantic Cities for Baby Boomers," April 20, 2007*

- The New York* metro area was selected as one of the "Top Ten U.S. Cities for Finding a Rich, Single Woman" by Teasley, a Manhattan-based marketing consulting firm. The area ranked #2. Criteria: high single-female to single-male ratio; higher income to cost-of-living ratio; percentage of population that is single. *Teasley, "Where to Find a Rich, Single Woman in the United States," 2005*

- The Edison* metro area was selected as one of the "Best Cities for Relocating Singles" by Worldwide ERC and Primacy Relocation. The area ranked #17 out of the 100 largest metro areas in the U.S. Areas were selected based on the following criteria: a robust cost-of-living index; adventure and outdoor recreation opportunities; violent crime and property crime rates; percentage of the population that is unmarried (ages 25-34); ratio of single men and single women; affordability of quality higher education, including in-state and out-of-state tuition requirements and rates; number of newcomers to the area; commute times; tax rates; fee and occupancy rates for temporary housing and mini-storage; quality and quantity of collegiate and professional sporting events and fun, fan-friendly venues. *Worldwide ERC and Primacy Relocation, "2007 Best Cities for Relocating Singles," October 25, 2007*

- *Forbes* ranked the 40 most populous urbanized areas in the U.S. in terms of the "Best Cities for Singles." The New York* metro area ranked #2. Criteria: number of singles; cost of living alone; nightlife; culture; job growth; coolness; and online dating. *Forbes.com, August 21, 2007*

- Sperling's BestPlaces in partnership with AXE Deodorant Bodyspray ranked 80 metro areas and identified "America's Best (and Worst) Cities for Dating." The New York* metro area ranked #18 (#1 = best). Criteria: percentage of singles ages 18-24; population density; dating venues per capita. *AXE Deodorant Bodyspray, "America's Best (and Worst) Cities for Dating," May 2004*

Culture/Performing Arts Rankings

- The New York* metro area was selected as one of the "Best Places for Artists in America" by *BusinessWeek.com*. Criteria: percentage of young people age 25 to 34; population diversity; concentration of museums, philharmonic orchestras, dance companies, theater troupes, library resources, and college arts programs. *BusinessWeek.com, "Best Places for Artists in America," February 26, 2007*

- Scarborough Research, a leading market research firm, identified the top local markets for rock concert attendance. The New York* DMA (Designated Market Area) ranked in the top 25 with 14% of consumers, 18 years old and over, reporting that they have attended a rock concert during the past year. *Scarborough Research, June 14, 2004*

Miscellaneous Rankings

- The New York* metro area was identified as one of "The 10 Worst Commuter Cities" in the U.S. by the *U.S. News and World Report*. The mean travel time to work is 39 minutes. *U.S. News and World Report, May 7, 2007*

- Scarborough Research, a leading market research firm, identified the top local markets for bloggers. The New York* DMA (Designated Market Area) ranked in the top 13 with 10% of adults reporting that they had read or contributed to a blog within the past 30 days. *Scarborough Research, October 24, 2007*

- The New York* metro area was selected as one of the "Top 10 Most Independent Cities for Homesellers". The area ranked #1. The cities listed had more consumers choosing to sell their homes without the help of a real-estate agent than anywhere else. Data was based on geographical information for listings posted on ForSaleByOwner.com from January 1, 2007 through June 30, 2007. *ForSaleByOwner.com, October 1, 2007*

- Avis Rent-A-Car and Motorola, in partnership with Sperling's BestPlaces, ranked the nation's 75 most populous metro areas in terms of how difficult they are to navigate. The New York* metro area ranked #5 with #1 being the most challenging. Criteria: street layouts; overall design and layout; travel time index; percent of congested freeway and street lane miles; bodies of water; complexity of directions needed to travel from major airports to city center; annual delay per person; days of snow exceeding 1.5 inches; and days of rain exceeding 0.5 inch. *Avis Rent-A-Car and Motorola, "America's Most Challenging Cities to Navigate," August 3, 2004*

- The New York* metro area appeared on *Forbes* list of "America's Drunkest Cities". The area ranked #32. Criteria: 35 of the largest continental U.S. metro areas were chosen based on availability of data and geographic diversity. Each metro was ranked in five areas: state laws; drinkers; heavy drinkers; binge drinkers; and alcoholism. *Forbes.com, "America's Drunkest Cities," August 22, 2006*

- Sperling's BestPlaces in partnership with Pep Boys ranked 77 metro areas and identified "America's Most Drivable Cities." The New York* metro area ranked #70. Criteria: climate; road roughness; urban mobility; gas prices. *Pep Boys, "America's Most Drivable Cities," April 9, 2003*

- State Farm Insurance, in partnership with Sperling's BestPlaces, analyzed several key factors that contribute to overall family preparedness. The New York* metro area ranked #44 out of the nation's 50 most populous metro areas. Criteria: quality of life; life insurance coverage; and investments. *State Farm Life Insurance, "Fiscally Fit Cities Report," July 20, 2004*

- Scarborough Research, a leading market research firm, identified the top local markets for grocery coupon use. The New York* DMA (Designated Market Area) ranked in the top 25 with 38% of consumers reporting that they use grocery coupons at least once per week.
  Scarborough Research, December 8, 2004

- A study by Sperling's BestPlaces examined which U.S. metro areas were most affected by high fuel prices in 2006. The New York* metro area was ranked #64 out of 80 (#1 = most expensive city for driving). Rankings are based on the average dollars spent on gas per year by two driver households. Criteria: cost of regular-grade gasoline; average miles driven per day; average number of gallons each driver uses and wastes in traffic congestion each day.
  Sperling's BestPlaces, www.bestplaces.net, "Pain at the Pump," May 18, 2006

Marlboro is located within the New York-Northern New Jersey-Long Island, NY-NJ-PA Metropolitan Statistical Area, Edison, NJ Metropolitan Division, and Monmouth-Ocean, NJ metro area.

Business Environment

CITY FINANCES

City Government Finances

Component	2004-2005 ($000)	2004-2005 ($ per capita)
Total Revenues	32,659	823
Total Expenditures	35,194	887
Debt Outstanding	40,354	1,017
Cash and Securities	32,227	812

Source: U.S Census Bureau, Government Finances 2004-2005

City Government Revenue by Source

Source	2004-2005 ($000)	2004-2005 ($ per capita)
General Revenue		
From Federal Government	58	1
From State Government	3,591	91
From Local Governments	79	2
Taxes		
Property	18,535	467
Sales	100	3
Personal Income	0	0
License	1,235	31
Charges	935	24
Liquor Store	0	0
Utility	6,555	165
Employee Retirement	0	0
Other	1,571	40

Source: U.S Census Bureau, Government Finances 2004-2005

City Government Expenditures by Function

Function	2004-2005 ($000)	2004-2005 ($ per capita)	2004-2005 (%)
General Expenditures			
Airports	0	0	0.0
Corrections	0	0	0.0
Education	0	0	0.0
Fire Protection	143	4	0.4
Governmental Administration	3,312	83	9.4
Health	197	5	0.6
Highways	2,026	51	5.8
Hospitals	0	0	0.0
Housing and Community Development	0	0	0.0
Interest on General Debt	913	23	2.6
Libraries	33	1	0.1
Parking	0	0	0.0
Parks and Recreation	1,748	44	5.0
Police Protection	7,836	198	22.3
Public Welfare	0	0	0.0
Sewerage	0	0	0.0
Solid Waste Management	826	21	2.3
Liquor Store	0	0	0.0
Utility	6,121	154	17.4
Employee Retirement	0	0	0.0
Other	12,039	304	34.2

Source: U.S Census Bureau, Government Finances 2004-2005

Municipal Bond Ratings

Area	Moody's
City	n/a

Source: Mergent Bond Record, January 2008 (unless noted otherwise)

DEMOGRAPHICS

Population Growth

Area	1990 Census	2000 Census	2007 Estimate	2012 Projection	Population Growth (%) 1990-2000	Population Growth (%) 2000-2012
City	27,974	36,398	40,193	42,410	30.1	16.5
MSA[1]	16,845,992	18,323,002	18,887,605	19,111,248	8.8	4.3
U.S.	248,709,873	281,421,906	301,045,522	314,920,978	13.2	11.9

Note: (1) Metropolitan Statistical Area - see Appendix B for areas included
Source: Claritas, Inc.

Number of Households and Average Household Size

Area	2007 Estimate	2007 Average Household Size
City	12,711	3.16
MSA[1]	6,870,593	2.75
U.S.	113,668,003	2.65

Note: (1) Metropolitan Statistical Area - see Appendix B for areas included
Source: Claritas, Inc.

Race and Ethnicity

Area	White Alone[2]	Black Alone[2]	Asian Alone[2]	Other Race Alone[2]	Hispanic[3]
City	79.3	1.7	17.2	1.8	3.6
MSA[1]	59.5	17.6	8.8	14.1	21.2
U.S.	73.1	12.4	4.3	10.3	14.9

Note: Figures are 2007 estimates; (1) Metropolitan Statistical Area - see Appendix B for areas included (2) Alone is defined as not being in combination with one or more other races; (3) May be of any race.
Source: Claritas, Inc.

Ancestry

Area	German	Irish[2]	English	American	Italian	Polish	French[3]	Scottish
City	6.7	10.6	2.9	6.4	20.1	10.6	0.7	0.6
MSA[1]	16.1	23.3	7.7	3.4	24.1	8.1	2.0	1.8
U.S.	15.2	10.9	8.7	7.3	5.6	3.2	3.0	1.7

Note: Figures include multiple ancestry (e.g. if a person reported being Irish and Italian, they were included in both columns); (1) Metropolitan Statistical Area - see Appendix A for areas included; (2) Includes Celtic; (3) Includes Alsatian but excludes Basque
Source: Census 2000, Summary File 3

Foreign-Born Population

Area	Percent of Population Born in: Any Foreign Country	Europe	Asia	Africa	Oceania[2]	Canada	Mexico	Latin America[3]
City	15.4	5.2	8.7	0.3	0.0	0.2	0.1	1.0
MSA[1]	8.6	3.2	2.3	0.2	0.0	0.2	0.8	1.9
U.S.	11.1	1.7	2.9	0.3	0.1	0.3	3.3	2.5

Note: (1) Metropolitan Statistical Area - see Appendix A for areas included; (2) Includes Australia, New Zealand subregion, Melanesia, Micronesia, Polynesia, and Oceania n.e.c; (3) Includes Central America (excluding Mexico), South America, and the Caribbean.
Source: Census 2000, Summary File 3

Marriage Status

Area	Never Married	Now Married (excluding Separated)	Separated	Widowed	Divorced
City	19.3	72.2	0.6	5.0	2.8
MSA[1]	23.3	58.6	1.6	8.9	7.6
U.S.	27.1	54.4	2.2	6.6	9.7

Note: Figures are percentages and cover the population 15 years of age and older; (1) Metropolitan Statistical Area - see Appendix A for areas included
Source: Census 2000, Summary File 3

Age Distribution

Area	Under Age 5	Age 5 to 17	Age 18 to 34	Age 35 to 49	Age 50 to 64	Age 65 to 79	80 Years and Over
	Percent of Population						
City	7.3	22.8	14.7	28.7	17.5	7.3	1.7
MSA[1]	6.6	18.2	18.3	24.1	15.8	12.2	4.8
U.S.	6.8	18.9	23.7	23.5	14.8	9.2	3.2

Note: (1) Metropolitan Statistical Area - see Appendix A for areas included
Source: Census 2000, Summary File 3

Male/Female Ratio

Area	Males	Females	Males per 100 Females
City	19,916	20,277	98.2
MSA[1]	9,117,706	9,769,899	93.3
U.S.	148,320,305	152,725,217	97.1

Note: Figures are 2007 estimates; (1) Metropolitan Statistical Area - see Appendix B for areas included
Source: Claritas, Inc.

Religion

Area	Catholic	Southern Baptist	United Meth-odist	ELCA[1]	LDS[2]	Presby-terian Church USA	Jewish Est.	Muslim Est.
County	47.0	0.2	2.1	1.3	0.2	1.3	10.6	1.5
U.S.	22.0	7.1	3.7	1.8	1.5	1.1	2.2	0.6

Note: Figures are the number of adherents as a percentage of the total population; Adherents are defined as all members, including full members, their children and the estimated number of other participants who are not considered members (e.g. the baptized, those not confirmed, those regularly attending services, etc.); (1) Evangelical Lutheran Church in America; (2) The Church of Jesus Christ of Latter Day Saints
Source: Reprinted with permission from Religious Congregations and Membership in the United States 2000 (Nashville, Glenmary Research Center, 2002) Copyright Association of Statisticians of American Religious Bodies. All rights reserved.

ECONOMY

Gross Metropolitan Product

Area	2002	2003	2004	2005	2005 Rank[2]
MSA[1]	820.9	847.1	902.4	952.6	1

Note: Figures are in billions of dollars; (1) New York-Northern New Jersey-Long Island, NY-NJ-PA Metropolitan Statistical Area - see Appendix A for areas included; (2) Rank ranges from 1 to 361
Source: The U.S. Conference of Mayors, "U.S. Metro Economies: GMP - The Engines of America's Growth," January 2007

Economic Growth

Area	1995 GMP	2005 GMP	Average Annual Growth Rate	Growth Rate Rank[2]
MSA[1]	585.5	952.6	5.0	221

Note: Figures are in billions of dollars; GMP = Gross Metropolitan Product; (1) New York-Northern New Jersey-Long Island, NY-NJ-PA Metropolitan Statistical Area - see Appendix A for areas included; (2) Rank ranges from 1 to 361
Source: The U.S. Conference of Mayors, "U.S. Metro Economies: GMP - The Engines of America's Growth," January 2007

INCOME

Per Capita/Median/Average Income

Area	Per Capita ($)	Median Household ($)	Average Household ($)
City	46,497	121,029	146,878
MSA[1]	30,292	58,080	82,491
U.S.	25,495	49,280	66,670

Note: Figures are 2007 estimates; (1) Metropolitan Statistical Area - see Appendix B for areas included
Source: Claritas, Inc.

Household Income Distribution

Area	Percent of Households Earning							
	Under $15,000	$15,000 -24,999	$25,000 -34,999	$35,000 -49,999	$50,000 -74,999	$75,000 -99,000	$100,000 -149,999	$150,000 and up
City	3.4	3.5	3.6	6.2	10.7	12.5	23.2	36.8
MSA[1]	14.0	8.8	8.7	12.6	17.1	12.3	14.5	12.0
U.S.	13.1	10.9	11.2	15.6	19.5	11.9	11.3	6.6

Note: Figures are 2007 estimates; (1) Metropolitan Statistical Area - see Appendix B for areas included
Source: Claritas, Inc.

Poverty Rates by Age

Area	All Ages	Under 5 Years Old	5 to 17 Years Old	18 to 64 Years Old	65 Years and Over
City	3.5	0.3	0.9	2.1	0.2
MSA[1]	6.6	0.7	1.5	3.4	1.0
U.S.	12.4	1.2	3.0	6.9	1.2

Note: Figures are percent of population with income in 1999 below poverty level and only include population for whom poverty status is determined; (1) Metropolitan Statistical Area - see Appendix A for areas included
Source: Census 2000, Summary File 3

Personal Bankruptcy Filing Rate

Area	2004	2005	2006
Monmouth County	3.60	4.37	1.25
U.S.	5.31	6.82	2.00

Note: Numbers are per 1,000 population and include Chapter 7 and Chapter 13 filings
Source: Federal Deposit Insurance Corporation (FDIC), Regional Economic Conditions (RECON), 8/23/2007

EMPLOYMENT

Labor Force and Employment

Area	Civilian Labor Force			Workers Employed		
	Dec. 2006	Dec. 2007	% Chg.	Dec. 2006	Dec. 2007	% Chg.
City	20,579	20,366	-1.0	20,073	19,878	-1.0
MD[1]	1,199,770	1,190,736	-0.8	1,157,810	1,146,507	-1.0
U.S.	152,571,000	153,705,000	0.7	146,081,000	146,334,000	0.2

Note: Data is not seasonally adjusted and covers workers 16 years of age and older; (1) Metropolitan Division - see Appendix B for areas included
Source: Bureau of Labor Statistics, http://stats.bls.gov

Unemployment Rate

Area	2007											
	Jan.	Feb.	Mar.	Apr.	May	Jun.	Jul.	Aug.	Sep.	Oct.	Nov.	Dec.
City	3.0	2.7	2.5	2.4	2.6	2.8	3.3	2.8	2.7	2.4	2.5	2.4
MD[1]	4.4	4.2	4.0	3.6	3.6	3.8	4.3	3.7	3.7	3.4	3.6	3.7
U.S.	5.0	4.9	4.5	4.3	4.3	4.7	4.9	4.6	4.5	4.4	4.5	4.8

Note: Data is not seasonally adjusted and covers workers 16 years of age and older; All figures are percentages; (1) Metropolitan Division - see Appendix B for areas included
Source: Bureau of Labor Statistics, http://stats.bls.gov

Employment by Occupation

Occupation Classification	City (%)	MSA[1] (%)	U.S. (%)
Sales and Office	28.7	29.3	26.7
Professional and Related	28.7	22.2	20.2
Service	6.3	13.9	14.9
Production, Transportation, and Material Moving	5.7	9.5	14.6
Management, Business, and Financial	26.5	15.4	13.5
Construction, Extraction, and Maintenance	4.2	9.4	9.4
Farming, Forestry, and Fishing	0.0	0.2	0.7

Note: Figures cover employed civilians 16 years of age and older; (1) Metropolitan Statistical Area - see Appendix A for areas included
Source: Census 2000, Summary File 3

Employment by Industry

Sector	MSA[1] Number of Employees	MSA[1] Percent of Total	U.S. Percent of Total
Government	152,800	14.6	16.3
Education and Health Services	139,600	13.3	13.4
Professional and Business Services	180,200	17.2	13.1
Retail Trade	136,200	13.0	11.6
Manufacturing	73,200	7.0	9.9
Leisure and Hospitality	78,400	7.5	9.6
Financial Activities	60,400	5.8	5.9
Construction	n/a	n/a	5.3
Wholesale Trade	60,800	5.8	4.4
Other Services	48,200	4.6	3.9
Transportation and Utilities	41,000	3.9	3.7
Information	30,400	2.9	2.2
Natural Resources and Mining	n/a	n/a	0.5

Note: Figures cover non-farm employment as of December 2007 and are not seasonally adjusted; (1) Metropolitan Statistical Area - see Appendix B for areas included; n/a not available
Source: Bureau of Labor Statistics, http://stats.bls.gov

Average Wages

Occupation	$/Hr.	Occupation	$/Hr.
Accountants and Auditors	36.27	Maids and Housekeeping Cleaners	9.77
Automotive Mechanics	18.30	Maintenance and Repair Workers	18.27
Bookkeepers	17.66	Marketing Managers	66.08
Carpenters	24.94	Nuclear Medicine Technologists	37.95
Cashiers	9.35	Nurses, Licensed Practical	23.49
Clerks, General Office	13.14	Nurses, Registered	33.79
Clerks, Receptionists/Information	12.50	Nursing Aides/Orderlies/Attendants	12.60
Clerks, Shipping/Receiving	14.55	Packers and Packagers, Hand	9.76
Computer Programmers	40.08	Physical Therapists	37.21
Computer Support Specialists	24.41	Postal Service Mail Carriers	21.31
Computer Systems Analysts	42.13	Real Estate Brokers	50.65
Cooks, Restaurant	11.99	Retail Salespersons	12.69
Dentists	n/a	Sales Reps., Exc. Tech./Scientific	35.27
Electrical Engineers	45.42	Sales Reps., Tech./Scientific	44.40
Electricians	28.34	Secretaries, Exc. Legal/Med./Exec.	16.38
Financial Managers	59.33	Security Guards	12.84
First-Line Supervisors/Mgrs., Sales	21.41	Surgeons	n/a
Food Preparation Workers	10.15	Teacher Assistants	12.40
General and Operations Managers	70.21	Teachers, Elementary School	27.40
Hairdressers/Cosmetologists	14.36	Teachers, Secondary School	29.00
Internists	87.25	Telemarketers	15.72
Janitors and Cleaners	12.10	Truck Drivers, Heavy/Tractor-Trailer	19.53
Landscaping/Groundskeeping Workers	12.61	Truck Drivers, Light/Delivery Svcs.	16.22
Lawyers	57.95	Waiters and Waitresses	11.25

Note: Wage data covers the Edison, NJ Metropolitan Division - see Appendix B for areas included. Hourly wages for elementary/secondary school teachers and teacher assistants were calculated by the editors from annual wage data assuming a 40 hour work week; n/a not available.
Source: Bureau of Labor Statistics, May 2007 Metro Area Occupational Employment and Wage Estimates

RESIDENTIAL REAL ESTATE

Building Permits

Area	Single-Family 2006	Single-Family 2007p	Single-Family Pct. Chg.	Multi-Family 2006	Multi-Family 2007p	Multi-Family Pct. Chg.	Total 2006	Total 2007p	Total Pct. Chg.
City	71	51	-28.2	0	0	-	71	51	-28.2
U.S.	1,378,200	973,300	-29.4	460,700	407,200	-11.6	1,838,900	1,380,500	-24.9

Note: (p) preliminary; figures cover and represent new, privately-owned housing units authorized (unadjusted data); All permit data are based on estimates with imputation; U.S. figures are based on the new 20,000-place series.
Source: U.S. Census Bureau, Manufacturing, Mining, and Construction Statistics

Homeownership and Housing Vacancies

Area	Homeownership Rate[2] (%)			Rental Vacancy Rate[3] (%)			Homeowner Vacancy Rate[4] (%)		
	2005	2006	2007	2005	2006	2007	2005	2006	2007
MSA[1]	54.6	53.6	53.8	5.0	5.4	5.7	1.9	1.8	2.1
U.S.	68.9	68.8	68.1	9.8	9.8	9.7	1.9	2.4	2.7

Note: (1) Metropolitan Statistical Area - see Appendix B for areas included; (2) The proportion of households that are owners; (3) The proportion of the rental inventory that is vacant for rent; (4) The proportion of the homeowner inventory that is vacant for sale; n/a not available
Source: U.S. Census Bureau, Housing Vacancies and Homeownership Annual Statistics: 2007

TAXES

State Corporate Income Tax Rates

State	Rates and Tax Brackets
New Jersey	6.5% > $0; 7.5 > 50K; 9.0% > 100K

Note: Tax rates as of January 1, 2008; Companies with income greater than $100K pay 9% on all income, companies with income greater than $50K but less than $100K pay 7.5 % on all income and companies with income under $50K pay 6.5%. The minimum tax is $500. An Alternative Minimum Assessment based on Gross Receipts applies if greater than corporate franchise tax for out-of-state companies with New Jersey sales. 4% surtax for 2007.
Source: Tax Foundation, www.taxfoundation.org

State Individual Income Tax Rates

State	Federal Deductibility	Marginal Rates (%)	Standard Deduction ($)		Personal Exemptions ($)[1]	
			Single	Joint	Single	Dependents
New Jersey	No	1.4 - 8.97 (y)	n/a	n/a	1,000	1,500

Note: Tax rates as of January 1, 2008; Local- and county-level taxes are not included; n/a not applicable; (1) Married joint filers generally receive double the single exemption; (y) Brackets are not double for married taxpayers.
Source: Tax Foundation, www.taxfoundation.org

Various State and Local Tax Rates

State and Local Sales and Use (%)	State Sales and Use (%)	Gasoline[1,2] ($/gal.)	Cigarette ($/pack)	Spirits ($/gal.)	Table Wine ($/gal.)	Beer ($/gal.)
7.0	7.0	0.145	2.575	4.40	0.70	0.12

Note: Tax rates as of January 1, 2008; (1) In addition to the 18.4 cpg Federal gasoline tax; (2) Rates may include additional state sales taxes, environmental protection and storage fees/taxes, and local taxes. When necessary, the volume-weighted average of all local taxes is used to approximate the typical statewide rate including local tax
Source: Tax Foundation, www.taxfoundation.org; Original research

State Tax Burdens

Area	Combined State and Local Tax Burden		Combined Federal, State and Local Tax Burden	
	Percent	Rank	Percent	Rank
New Jersey	11.6	10	35.6	3
U.S. Average	11.0	-	32.7	-

Note: Figures cover 2007 and measure taxes as a percentage of income
Source: Tax Foundation, www.taxfoundation.org

State Business Tax Climate Index Rankings

State	Overall Rank	Corporate Tax Index Rank	Individual Income Tax Index Rank	Sales Tax Index Rank	Unemployment Insurance Tax Index Rank	Property Tax Index Rank
New Jersey	49	41	49	44	24	49

Note: Rankings range from 1 to 50 where 1 is best. Rankings do not average across to Overall Rank. States without a given tax are given a ranking of 1.
Source: Tax Foundation, State Business Tax Climate Index 2008

TRANSPORTATION

Means of Transportation to Work

Area	Car/Truck/Van		Public Transportation			Bicycle	Walked	Other Means	Worked at Home
	Drove Alone	Car-pooled	Bus	Subway	Railroad				
City	68.9	8.9	10.3	0.3	6.4	0.0	0.4	0.6	4.1
MSA[1]	78.7	9.8	3.0	0.1	2.3	0.3	1.8	1.1	3.0
U.S.	75.7	12.2	2.5	1.5	0.5	0.4	2.9	1.0	3.3

Note: Figures are percentages and cover workers 16 years of age and older; (1) Metropolitan Statistical Area - see Appendix A for areas included
Source: Census 2000, Summary File 3

Travel Time to Work

Area	Less Than 15 Minutes	15 to 29 Minutes	30 to 44 Minutes	45 to 59 Minutes	60 Minutes or More
City	17.4	18.6	16.0	10.5	37.4
MSA[1]	26.3	28.3	16.7	9.0	19.8
U.S.	29.4	36.1	19.1	7.4	8.0

Note: Figures are percentages and include workers 16 years old and over; (1) Metropolitan Statistical Area - see Appendix A for areas included
Source: Census 2000, Summary File 3

Travel Time Index

Area	1982	1995	2004	2005
Urban Area[1]	1.10	1.24	1.36	1.39
Average[2]	1.11	1.22	1.29	1.30

Note: Travel Time Index - The ratio of travel time in the peak period to the travel time at free-flow conditions. A value of 1.35 indicates a 20-minute free-flow trip takes 27 minutes in the peak. Free-flow speeds (60 mph on freeways and 35 mph on principal arterials) are used as the comparison threshold; (1) Covers the New York-Newark, NY-NJ-CT urban area; (2) average of 85 urban areas
Source: Texas Transportation Institute, The 2007 Urban Mobility Report, September 2007

Living Environment

COST OF LIVING

Cost of Living Index

Composite Index	Groceries	Housing	Utilities	Trans-portation	Health Care	Misc. Goods/ Services
127.5	113.2	169.1	107.3	103.7	110.6	114.2

Note: U.S. = 100; Figures cover the Middlesex-Monmouth NJ urban area.
Source: The Council for Community and Economic Research (formerly ACCRA), Cost of Living Index, 2007

Grocery Prices

Area[1]	T-Bone Steak ($/pound)	Frying Chicken ($/pound)	Whole Milk ($/half gal.)	Eggs ($/dozen)	Orange Juice ($/64 oz.)	Coffee ($/11.5 oz.)
City[2]	9.68	1.09	2.24	2.25	3.07	3.46
Avg.	8.93	1.12	2.13	1.52	3.26	3.31
Min.	5.88	0.71	1.33	0.83	2.30	2.20
Max.	12.80	2.07	3.43	3.54	5.79	6.20

Note: (1) Values for the local area are compared with the average, minimum and maximum values for all 331 areas in the Cost of Living Index report; (2) Figures cover the Middlesex-Monmouth NJ urban area; **T-Bone Steak** *(price per pound);* **Frying Chicken** *(price per pound, whole fryer);* **Whole Milk** *(half gallon carton);* **Eggs** *(price per dozen, Grade A, large);* **Orange Juice** *(64 oz. Tropicana or Florida Natural);* **Coffee** *(11.5 oz. can, vacuum-packed, Maxwell House, Hills Bros, or Folgers).*
Source: The Council for Community and Economic Research (formerly ACCRA), Cost of Living Index, 2007

Housing and Utility Costs

Area[1]	New Home Price ($)	Apartment Rent ($/month)	All Electric ($/month)	Part Electric ($/month)	Other Energy ($/month)	Telephone ($/month)
City[2]	531,339	1,321	-	82.61	85.27	29.75
Avg.	309,605	782	146.13	78.67	90.16	26.14
Min.	189,877	n/a	82.03	37.41	33.15	17.08
Max.	1,202,800	3,481	271.14	150.60	257.67	37.45

Note: (1) Values for the local area are compared with the average, minimum and maximum values for all 331 areas in the Cost of Living Index report; (2) Figures cover the Middlesex-Monmouth NJ urban area; **New Home Price** *(2,400 sf living area, 8,000 sf lot, in urban area with full utilities);* **Apartment Rent** *(950 sf 2 bedroom/1.5 or 2 bath, unfurnished, excluding all utilities except water);* **All Electric** *(average monthly cost for an all-electric home);* **Part Electric** *(average monthly cost for a part-electric home);* **Other Energy** *(average monthly cost for natural gas, fuel oil, coal, wood, and any other forms of energy except electricity);* **Telephone** *(price includes basic monthly rate for a private residential line plus additional local usage charges incurred by a family of four).*
Source: The Council for Community and Economic Research (formerly ACCRA), Cost of Living Index, 2007

Health Care, Transportation, and Other Costs

Area[1]	Doctor ($/visit)	Dentist ($/visit)	Optometrist ($/visit)	Gasoline ($/gallon)	Beauty Salon ($/visit)	Men's Shirt ($)
City[2]	70.73	93.52	88.50	2.52	31.67	35.87
Avg.	79.48	71.93	79.55	2.64	29.52	25.77
Min.	52.08	44.80	43.95	2.19	15.58	16.19
Max.	148.44	126.27	158.83	3.48	60.62	48.53

Note: (1) Values for the local area are compared with the average, minimum and maximum values for all 331 areas in the Cost of Living Index report; (2) Figures cover the Middlesex-Monmouth NJ urban area; **Doctor** *(general practitioners routine exam of an established patient);* **Dentist** *(adult teeth cleaning and periodic oral examination);* **Optometrist** *(full vision eye exam for established adult patient);* **Gasoline** *(one gallon regular unleaded, national brand, including all taxes, cash price at self-service pump if available);* **Beauty Salon** *(woman's shampoo, trim, and blow-dry);* **Men's Shirt** *(cotton/polyester dress shirt, pinpoint weave, long sleeves).*
Source: The Council for Community and Economic Research (formerly ACCRA), Cost of Living Index, 2007

HOUSING

House Price Index (HPI)

Area	National Ranking[2]	Quarterly Change (%)	One-Year Change (%)	Five-Year Change (%)
MD[1]	214	-0.27	-1.48	54.92
U.S.[3]	-	0.10	0.84	41.37

Note: The HPI is a weighted repeat sales index. It measures average price changes in repeat sales or refinancings on the same properties. This information is obtained by reviewing repeat mortgage transactions on single-family properties whose mortgages have been purchased or securitized by Fannie Mae or Freddie Mac in January 1975; (1) Metropolitan Division - see Appendix B for areas included; (2) Rankings are based on annual percentage change for all metro areas containing at least 15,000 transactions over the last 10 years and ranges from 1 to 291; (3) figures based on a weighted average of Census Division estimates; all figures are for the period ending December 31, 2007
Source: Office of Federal Housing Enterprise Oversight, House Price Index, February 26, 2008

House Price Valuations

Area	Q1 2000	Q1 2001	Q1 2002	Q1 2003	Q1 2004	Q1 2005	Q1 2006	Q1 2007	Q1 2008
MD[1]	-26.4	-21.9	-13.1	0.2	9.5	22.2	26.6	18.8	11.3

Note: Figures show the percentage of over- or under-valuation of single family homes relative to statistically normal house values (e.g. a value of 23.6 indicates that house values are 23.6% overvalued). Statistically normal house values are based on house prices, interest rates, household incomes, population densities, and any historical premiums or discounts metropolitan areas have exhibited over time; (1) Figures cover the Metropolitan Division - see Appendix B for areas included
Source: Global Insight/National City Corporation, House Prices in America, May 2008

Median Home Prices

Area	2005	2006	2007[r]	Percent Change 2006 to 2007
MD[1]	375.5	387.7	380.3	-1.9
U.S. Average	219.0	221.9	217.9	-1.8

Note: Figures are median sales prices of existing single-family homes in thousands of dollars; (r) revised; n/a not available; (1) Metropolitan Division - see Appendix B for areas included
Source: National Association of Realtors, Metropolitan Area Prices, 1st Quarter 2008

Housing: Year Structure Built

Area	1990 -2000	1980 -1989	1970 -1979	1960 -1969	1950 -1959	1940 -1949	Before 1940	Median Year
City	32.4	33.3	16.4	11.9	2.5	0.8	2.6	1985
MSA[1]	14.7	18.3	19.9	17.2	13.4	5.8	10.8	1971
U.S.	17.0	15.8	18.5	13.7	12.7	7.3	15.0	1971

Note: Figures are percentages; (1) Metropolitan Statistical Area - see Appendix A for areas included
Source: Census 2000, Summary File 3

HEALTH

Health Risk Data

Category	Area[1] (%)	U.S. (%)
Adults who have been told they have high blood pressure[3]	25.7	25.5
Adults who have been told they have high blood cholesterol[3]	38.5	35.6
Adults who have been told they have diabetes[2]	7.0	7.5
Adults who have been told they have arthritis[3]	25.7	27.0
Adults who have been told they currently have asthma	6.4	8.5
Adults who are current smokers	16.4	20.1
Adults who are heavy drinkers[4]	3.3	4.9
Adults who are overweight (BMI 25.0 - 29.9)	37.9	36.5
Adults who are obese (BMI 30.0 - 99.8)	21.6	25.1

Note: Data as of 2006 unless otherwise noted; (1) Figures cover the Metropolitan Division - see Appendix B for areas included; (2) Figures do not include pregnancy-related diabetes, pre-diabetes or borderline diabetes; (3) 2005 data; (4) Heavy drinkers are classified as adult men having more than two drinks per day or adult women having more than one drink per day
Source: Centers for Disease Control and Prevention, Behaviorial Risk Factor Surveillance System, SMART: Selected Metropolitan/Micropolitan Area Risk Trends, 2005, 2006

Mortality Rates for the Top 10 Causes of Death in the U.S.

ICD-10[a] Sub-Chapter	ICD-10[a] Code	Age-Adjusted Mortality Rate[1] per 100,000 population	
		County[2]	U.S.
Malignant neoplasms	C00-C97	200.5	186.5
Ischaemic heart diseases	I20-I25	168.1	152.3
Other forms of heart disease	I30-I51	51.8	51.5
Cerebrovascular diseases	I60-I69	41.5	50.0
Chronic lower respiratory diseases	J40-J47	34.7	42.6
Diabetes mellitus	E10-E14	28.6	24.8
Other degenerative diseases of the nervous system	G30-G31	23.2	22.6
Other external causes of accidental injury	W00-X59	14.8	21.4
Influenza and pneumonia	J10-J18	15.8	20.7
Hypertensive diseases	I10-I13	11.9	18.2

Note: (a) ICD-10 = International Classification of Diseases 10th Revision; (1) Mortality rates are a three year average covering 2003-2005; (2) Figures cover Monmouth County
Source: Centers for Disease Control and Prevention, National Center for Health Statistics. Compressed Mortality File 1999-2004. CDC WONDER On-line Database, compiled from Compressed Mortality File 1999-2005 Series 20 No. 2K, 2008.

Mortality Rates for Selected Causes of Death

ICD-10[a] Sub-Chapter	ICD-10[a] Code	Age-Adjusted Mortality Rate[1] per 100,000 population	
		County[2]	U.S.
Assault	X85-Y09	1.6	5.9
Human immunodeficiency virus (HIV) disease	B20-B24	4.4	4.5
Intentional self-harm	X60-X84	7.0	10.8
Malnutrition	E40-E46	1.3	1.0
Obesity and other hyperalimentation	E65-E68	1.4	1.4
Organic, including symptomatic, mental disorders	F01-F09	15.5	16.8
Transport accidents	V01-V99	10.2	16.1
Viral hepatitis	B15-B19	1.3	1.8

Note: (a) ICD-10 = International Classification of Diseases 10th Revision; (1) Mortality rates are a three year average covering 2003-2005; (2) Figures cover Monmouth County
Source: Centers for Disease Control and Prevention, National Center for Health Statistics. Compressed Mortality File 1999-2004. CDC WONDER On-line Database, compiled from Compressed Mortality File 1999-2005 Series 20 No. 2K, 2008.

Distribution of Physicians[1]

Area	Total	Family/ General Practice	Specialties	
			Medical	Surgical
Monmouth County (number)	1,734	144	771	421
Monmouth County (rate per 10,000 pop.)	27.3	2.3	12.1	6.6
U.S. (rate per 10,000 pop.)	17.7	4.6	6.9	4.3

Note: Data as of 2005; (1) Includes all non-federal, patient-care, office-based MDs
Source: Area Resource File (ARF). June 2007. U.S. Department of Health and Human Services, Health Resources and Services Administration, Bureau of Health Professions, Rockville, MD.

Hospitals

There were no hospitals listed within the city limits.
AHA Guide to the Healthcare Field 2008

According to *U.S. News,* the New York-Northern New Jersey-Long Island, NY-NJ-PA metro area is home to 14 of the best hospitals in the U.S.: **Hackensack University Medical Center**; **Hospital for Special Surgery**; **Kessler Institute for Rehabilitation**; **Lenox Hill Hospital**; **Long Island Jewish Medical Center**; **Memorial Sloan-Kettering Cancer Center**; **Montefiore Medical Center**; **Mount Sinai Medical Center**; **New York Eye and Ear Infirmary**; **New York-Presbyterian Univ. Hosp. of Columbia and Cornell**; **NYU Medical Center**; **Robert Wood Johnson University Hospital**; **Saint Francis Hospital**; **University Hospital**. *U.S. News Online, "America's Best Hospitals 2007"*

EDUCATION

Public School District Statistics

District Name	Schls	Pupils	Pupil/ Teacher Ratio	Minority Pupils[1] (%)	Free Lunch Eligible[2] (%)	IEP[3] (%)
Freehold Regional High School	6	11,440	14.6	15.3	3.6	22.3
Marlboro Township	8	6,143	14.8	25.2	1.0	24.6

Note: Table includes regular local school districts with 2,000 or more students; (1) Percentage of students that are not white, non-Hispanic; (2) Percentage of students that are eligible for the free lunch program; (3) Percentage of students that have an Individualized Education Program.
Source: U.S. Department of Education, National Center for Education Statistics, Common Core of Data, Local Education Agency (School District) Universe Survey: School Year 2005-2006; U.S. Department of Education, National Center for Education Statistics, Common Core of Data, Public Elementary/Secondary School Universe Survey: School Year 2005-2006

Highest Level of Education

Area	Less than H.S.	H.S. Diploma	Some College, No Deg.	Associate Degree	Bachelors Degree	Masters Degree	Profess. School Degree	Doctorate Degree
City	6.0	18.9	16.1	6.5	29.9	16.9	3.6	2.2
MSA[1]	21.5	26.4	16.5	5.6	17.7	8.2	3.0	1.2
U.S.	19.4	28.4	21.2	6.4	15.7	5.9	2.0	1.0

Note: Figures are 2007 estimated percentages and cover persons age 25 and over; (1) Metropolitan Statistical Area - see Appendix B for areas included
Source: Claritas, Inc.

Educational Attainment by Race

Area	High School Graduate (%)					Bachelor's Degree (%)				
	Total	White	Black	Asian	Hisp.[2]	Total	White	Black	Asian	Hisp.[2]
City	94.0	94.4	85.4	92.2	82.8	52.3	49.4	30.3	76.1	34.9
MSA[1]	85.6	86.5	76.7	87.7	65.8	27.6	27.6	14.9	60.3	14.9
U.S.	80.4	83.6	72.3	80.4	52.4	24.4	26.1	14.3	44.1	10.4

Note: Figures shown cover persons 25 years old and over; (1) Metropolitan Statistical Area - see Appendix A for areas included; (2) people of Hispanic origin can be of any race
Source: Census 2000, Summary File 3

School Enrollment by Type

Area	Grades KG to 8				Grades 9 to 12			
	Public		Private		Public		Private	
	Enrollment	%	Enrollment	%	Enrollment	%	Enrollment	%
City	5,394	91.4	505	8.6	2,181	88.5	284	11.5
MSA[1]	127,771	85.7	21,328	14.3	52,824	88.1	7,144	11.9
U.S.	33,526,011	88.7	4,285,121	11.3	14,848,628	90.6	1,532,323	9.4

Note: Figures shown cover persons 3 years old and over; (1) Metropolitan Statistical Area - see Appendix A for areas included
Source: Census 2000, Summary File 3

School Enrollment by Race

Area	Grades KG to 8 (%)				Grades 9 to 12 (%)			
	White	Black	Asian	Hisp.[1]	White	Black	Asian	Hisp.[1]
City	82.3	1.0	13.9	4.0	84.9	2.8	8.7	4.9
MSA[2]	84.8	7.5	3.0	7.3	85.1	7.5	3.1	6.7
U.S.	68.5	15.5	3.3	16.8	68.8	15.5	3.8	15.7

Note: Figures shown cover persons 3 years old and over; (1) people of Hispanic origin can be of any race; (2) Metropolitan Statistical Area - see Appendix A for areas included
Source: Census 2000, Summary File 3

Average Salaries of Public School Classroom Teachers

District	2005-06 Dollars	2005-06 Rank[1]	2006-07 Dollars	2006-07 Rank[1]	Percent Change 2005-06 to 2006-07
New Jersey	58,156	5	59,920	3	3.03
U.S. Average	49,026	-	50,816	-	3.65

Note: (1) State rank ranges from 1 to 51.
Source: National Education Association, Rankings & Estimates: Rankings of the States 2006 and Estimates of School Statistics 2007, December 2007

Higher Education

Four-Year Colleges			Two-Year Colleges					
Public	Private Non-profit	Private For-profit	Public	Private Non-profit	Private For-profit	Medical Schools[1]	Law Schools[2]	Voc/ Tech[3]
0	0	0	0	0	0	0	0	0

Note: Figures cover institutions located within the city limits; (1) includes schools accredited by the Liaison Committee on Medical Education and the American Osteopathic Association; (2) includes American Bar Association-accredited law schools; (3) includes all schools with programs that are less than 2 years.
Source: National Center for Education Statistics, The Integrated Postsecondary Education System (IPEDS) Peer Analysis System, 2007; www.usnews.com, Law and Medical School Directories, 2009

PRESIDENTIAL ELECTION

2004 Presidential Election Results

Area	Bush	Kerry	Nader	Other
Monmouth County	54.6	44.6	0.6	0.3
U.S.	50.7	48.3	0.4	0.6

Note: Results are percentages and may not add to 100% due to rounding
Source: Dave Leip's Atlas of U.S. Presidential Elections, www.uselectionatlas.org

EMPLOYERS

Major Employers

Company Name	Industry	Type of Site
A T & T Corp	Telephone communication, except radio	Branch
Air Safety Equipment Inc	Airports, flying fields, and services	Branch
Community Medical Center Inc	General medical and surgical hospitals	Headquarters
Doon Technologies Inc	Business consulting, nec	Single
Ethicon Inc	Surgical appliances and supplies	Headquarters
Fort Monmouth Training Center	National security	Branch
In Ventive Commercial Services	Management consulting services	Single
JFK Medical Center	General medical and surgical hospitals	Headquarters
Larson & Toubro Infotech Ltd	Computer related services, nec	Headquarters
Rehabilitation Medicine	Specialty outpatient clinics, nec	Single
School of Public Health	Colleges and universities	Branch
St Peters University Hospital	General medical and surgical hospitals	Headquarters
Telcordia Technologies Inc	Custom computer programming services	Headquarters
US Post Office	U.S. postal service	Branch
Veterans Health Administration	Offices and clinics of medical doctors	Branch

Note: Companies shown are located within the Edison metropolitan area; nec = not elsewhere classified.
Source: www.zapdata.com, May 2008

PUBLIC SAFETY

Crime Rate

Area	All Crimes	Violent Crimes: Murder	Violent Crimes: Forcible Rape	Violent Crimes: Robbery	Violent Crimes: Aggrav. Assault	Property Crimes: Burglary	Property Crimes: Larceny -Theft	Property Crimes: Motor Vehicle Theft
City	1,045.5	0.0	2.5	20.2	17.6	183.9	788.5	32.7
Metro[1]	2,085.6	2.0	10.1	69.3	103.0	365.7	1,408.9	126.5
U.S.	3,808.1	5.7	30.9	149.4	287.5	729.4	2,206.8	398.4

Note: Figures are crimes per 100,000 population; (1) Metropolitan Division - see Appendix B for areas included
Source: FBI Uniform Crime Reports, 2006

Hate Crimes

Area	Number of Quarters Reported	Bias Motivation: Race	Religion	Sexual Orientation	Ethnicity	Disability
City	4	2	4	0	0	0

Source: Federal Bureau of Investigation, Hate Crime Statistics 2006

RECREATION

Culture

Dance[1]	Theatre[1]	Instrumental Music[1]	Vocal Music[1]	Series/ Festivals	Museums	Zoos and Aquariums[2]
0	0	0	0	0	0	0

Note: (1) Number of professional perfoming groups; (2) AZA-accredited
Source: The Grey House Performing Arts Directory, 2007; Official Museum Directory, 2008; Association of Zoos & Aquariums, AZA Member Zoos & Aquariums, June 2008

Professional Sports Teams

Team Name	League
New York Mets	Major League Baseball (MLB)
New York Yankees	Major League Baseball (MLB)
New York Red Bulls	Major League Soccer (MLS)
New Jersey Nets	National Basketball Association (NBA)
New York Knicks	National Basketball Association (NBA)
New York Giants	National Football League (NFL)
New York Jets	National Football League (NFL)
New Jersey Devils	National Hockey League (NHL)
New York Islanders	National Hockey League (NHL)
New York Rangers	National Hockey League (NHL)

Note: Includes teams located in the New York-Northern New Jersey metro area.
Source: Original research

MEDIA

Newspapers

Name	News Focus	Frequency	Circulation
No newspapers have an office in the city			

Note: Includes newspapers with offices located in the city
Source: MediaContactsPro, March 2008

Television Stations

Name	Ch.	Network(s)	Type	Ownership
WCBS	2	CBS	Commercial	CBS
WNBC	4	NBC	Commercial	General Electric Corporation
WNYW	5	Fox	Commercial	Fox Television Stations Inc.
WABC	7	ABC	Commercial	ABC Inc.
WWOR	9	UPN	Commercial	Fox Television Stations Inc.
WPIX	11	WBN	Commercial	Tribune Broadcasting Company
WNET	13	PBS	Public	Educational Broadcasting Corporation
WLIW	21	PBS	Public	Long Island Educational TV Council Inc.
WNYE	25	PBS	Public	New York City Board of Education
WPXN	31	Pax	Commercial	Paxson Communications Corporation
WXTV	41	Univision	Commercial	Univision Holding
WNJU	47	Telemundo	Commercial	Telemundo Group Inc.
WTBY	54	n/a	Commercial	Trinity Broadcasting Network
WLNY	55	n/a	Commercial	Michael C. Pascucci
WRNN	62	n/a	Commercial	WRNN-TV Associates L.P.
WMBC	63	n/a	Commercial	Mountain Broadcasting Corporation
WHSI	67	n/a	Commercial	USA Broadcasting Group
WHSE	68	n/a	Commercial	USA Broadcasting Group

Note: Stations included cover the New York DMA (Designated Market Area); n/a not available
BurrellesLuce, MediaContacts Online, January 2007

Major AM Radio Stations

Call Letters	Freq. (kHz)	Station Type	Target Audience	Station Format	Music Format
WMCA	570	n/a	General/Religious	Music/News/Talk	n/a
WFAN	660	n/a	General	News/Sports/Talk	n/a
WOR	710	n/a	General	Music/News	Reggae
WABC	770	n/a	General	n/a	n/a
WNYC	820	Public	General	Music/Talk	Blues
WCBS	880	Commercial	General	Music/News/Sports	Reggae
WGHQ	920	n/a	General	Music	n/a
WWDJ	970	n/a	General/Religious	Music/Talk	n/a
WINS	1010	n/a	General	News	n/a
WHLI	1100	Commercial	General	Music	Adult Standards
WBBR	1130	n/a	General/Men	Music/News	Reggae
WVNJ	1160	n/a	General	n/a	n/a
WOBM	1160	n/a	General	Music	n/a
WLIB	1190	n/a	General	News/Talk	n/a
WGNY	1220	n/a	General	News/Talk	n/a
WMTR	1250	Commercial	General	Music	Adult Standards
WADO	1280	Commercial	General/Hispanic	News/Sports/Talk	n/a
WWRV	1330	n/a	General/Hisp/Rel	Music/News/Talk	n/a
WELV	1370	n/a	General	Music	n/a
WEOK	1390	Commercial	General/Hispanic	Music/Sports	Latin
WLNA	1420	n/a	General	Music/News/Sports/Talk	n/a
WNSW	1430	n/a	Ethnic/General	Music/News/Talk	n/a
WZRC	1480	n/a	Asian	Talk	n/a
WQEW	1560	n/a	Child/Gen/Yng Adlt	Educational	n/a
WLIM	1580	Commercial	Ethnic/General	Music/News	World Music
WWRL	1600	n/a	General	Music/Talk	Reggae
WWRU	1660	n/a	Asian/General/Hispanic	News/Talk	n/a

Note: Stations included cover the New York DMA (Designated Market Area); n/a not available
Source: BurrellesLuce, MediaContacts Online, January 2007

Major FM Radio Stations

Call Letters	Freq. (mHz)	Station Type	Target Audience	Station Format	Music Format
WFSO	88.3	n/a	Religious	Educational/Music/News	n/a
WFDU	89.1	College	General	Music	n/a
WFUV	90.7	College	General	Music/News/Sports	Folk
WPAT	93.1	Commercial	General/Hispanic	News/Talk	n/a
WRKI	95.1	n/a	General	Music/News/Talk	n/a
WQHT	97.1	n/a	General	Music/News/Talk	n/a
WSKQ	97.9	Commercial	General/Hispanic	Music/News/Talk	Latin
WRKS	98.7	n/a	General/Women	News/Talk	Rhythm & Blues
WBAI	99.5	Non-Comm	General	Music/Talk	Reggae
WHUD	100.7	n/a	General	Music/News/Talk	n/a
WPDH	101.5	Commercial	General	Music	Classic Rock
WKTU	103.5	n/a	General/Women	Music/News/Talk	Urban Contemp.
WAXQ	104.3	n/a	General	Music/Talk	n/a
WSPK	104.7	n/a	General	Music/News/Talk	n/a
WWPR	105.1	Commercial	General	Music	Rhythm & Blues
WBLI	106.1	Commercial	General	Music/Talk	Top 40
WLTW	106.7	n/a	General	Music	n/a
WBLS	107.5	n/a	Black/General	Music	n/a
WEBE	107.9	n/a	General	Music/News	n/a

Note: Stations included cover the New York DMA (Designated Market Area); n/a not available
BurrellesLuce, MediaContacts Online, January 2007

CLIMATE

Average and Extreme Temperatures

Temperature	Jan	Feb	Mar	Apr	May	Jun	Jul	Aug	Sep	Oct	Nov	Dec	Yr.
Extreme High (°F)	74	76	89	94	98	102	105	103	105	93	85	72	105
Average High (°F)	38	41	50	61	72	81	86	84	77	66	54	42	63
Average Temp. (°F)	32	33	42	52	63	72	77	76	68	57	47	36	55
Average Low (°F)	24	25	33	43	53	62	68	67	59	48	39	28	46
Extreme Low (°F)	-8	-7	6	16	33	41	52	45	35	25	15	-1	-8

Note: Figures cover the years 1935-1995
Source: National Climatic Data Center, International Station Meteorological Climate Summary, 9/96

Average Precipitation/Snowfall/Humidity

Precip./Humidity	Jan	Feb	Mar	Apr	May	Jun	Jul	Aug	Sep	Oct	Nov	Dec	Yr.
Avg. Precip. (in.)	3.4	3.0	4.0	3.7	3.9	3.3	4.2	4.1	3.6	3.0	3.8	3.4	43.5
Avg. Snowfall (in.)	8	8	5	1	Tr	0	0	0	0	Tr	1	5	27
Avg. Rel. Hum. 7am (%)	73	71	69	67	70	71	72	76	79	78	76	74	73
Avg. Rel. Hum. 4pm (%)	58	54	51	48	51	51	52	54	55	53	57	59	54

Note: Figures cover the years 1935-1995; Tr = Trace amounts (<0.05 in. of rain; <0.5 in. of snow)
Source: National Climatic Data Center, International Station Meteorological Climate Summary, 9/96

Weather Conditions

Temperature			Daytime Sky			Precipitation		
5°F & below	32°F & below	90°F & above	Clear	Partly cloudy	Cloudy	0.01 inch or more precip.	0.1 inch or more snow/ice	Thunder-storms
2	90	24	80	146	139	122	16	46

Note: Figures are average number of days per year and cover the years 1935-1995
Source: National Climatic Data Center, International Station Meteorological Climate Summary, 9/96

HAZARDOUS WASTE

Superfund Sites

Marlboro has one hazardous waste site on the EPA's Superfund Final National Priorities List: **Burnt Fly Bog.** *U.S. Environmental Protection Agency, Final National Priorities List, June 23, 2008*

AIR & WATER QUALITY

Air Quality Index

Area	Percent of Days when Air Quality was...[2]				AQI Statistics	
	Good	Moderate	Unhealthy for Sensitive Groups	Unhealthy	Maximum	Median
MSA[1]	76.7	17.5	5.8	0.0	140	36

Note: The Air Quality Index (AQI) is an index for reporting daily air quality. EPA calculates the AQI for five major air pollutants regulated by the Clean Air Act: ground-level ozone, particle pollution (also known as particulate matter), carbon monoxide, sulfur dioxide, and nitrogen dioxide. The AQI runs from 0 to 500. The higher the AQI value, the greater the level of air pollution and the greater the health concern. There are six AQI categories: "Good" The AQI is between 0 and 50. Air quality is considered satisfactory; "Moderate" The AQI is between 51 and 100. Air quality is acceptable; "Unhealthy for Sensitive Groups" When AQI values are between 101 and 150, members of sensitive groups may experience health effects; "Unhealthy" When AQI values are between 151 and 200 everyone may begin to experience health effects; "Very Unhealthy" AQI values between 201 and 300 trigger a health alert; "Hazardous" AQI values over 300 trigger health warnings of emergency conditions; (1) Metropolitan Statistical Area - see Appendix A for areas included; (2) Based on 365 days with AQI data in 2007.
Source: U.S. Environmental Protection Agency, Air Quality Index Report, 2007

Air Quality Index Pollutants

Area	Percent of Days when AQI Pollutant was...[2]					
	Carbon Monoxide	Nitrogen Dioxide	Ozone	Sulfur Dioxide	Particulate Matter 2.5	Particulate Matter 10
MSA[1]	6.0	0.0	54.8	0.0	39.2	0.0

Note: The Air Quality Index (AQI) is an index for reporting daily air quality. EPA calculates the AQI for five major air pollutants regulated by the Clean Air Act: ground-level ozone, particle pollution (also known as particulate matter), carbon monoxide, sulfur dioxide, and nitrogen dioxide. The AQI runs from 0 to 500. The higher the AQI value, the greater the level of air pollution and the greater the health concern; (1) Metropolitan Statistical Area - see Appendix A for areas included; (2) Based on 365 days with AQI data in 2007.
Source: U.S. Environmental Protection Agency, Air Quality Index Report, 2007

Air Quality Index Trends

Area	Trend Sites (4)								All Sites (5)
	1999	2000	2001	2002	2003	2004	2005	2006	2006
MSA[1]	27	11	21	32	13	8	16	10	10

Note: An AQI value greater than 100 indicates that air quality would have been in the unhealthful range on that day. Data from exceptional events are not included. These counts are presented in two ways. First, the counts are based on sites having an adequate record of monitoring data during the trend period (trend sites). These counts represent the relative change in the number of days with AQI values greater than 100. In the last column, the counts are based on all sites with data in the most recent year (because it is possible for a site to have data in the most recent year but not enough data to be a trend site); (1) Metropolitan Statistical Area - see Appendix A for areas included.
Source: U.S. Environmental Protection Agency, Office of Air and Radiation, Air Trends, Factbook and Related Information, Air Pollution Trends in Selected Metropolitan Areas 2006

Maximum Air Pollutant Concentrations

	Particulate Matter 10 (ug/m^3)	Particulate Matter 2.5 (ug/m^3)	Ozone (ppm)	Carbon Monoxide (ppm)	Sulfur Dioxide (ppm)	Nitrogen Dioxide (ppm)	Lead (ug/m^3)
MSA[1] Level	n/a	33	0.125	2	0.014	0.014	n/a
NAAQS[2]	150	35	0.125	9	0.140	0.053	1.50
Met NAAQS[2]	Yes	Yes	Yes	Yes	Yes	Yes	n/a

Note: Data from exceptional events are not included; (1) Metropolitan Statistical Area - see Appendix A for areas included; (2) National Ambient Air Quality Standards; n/a not available
Concentrations: Particulate Matter 10 (coarse particulate) - highest second maximum 24-hour concentration; Particulate Matter 2.5 (fine particulate) - highest 98th percentile 24-hour concentration; Ozone - highest second daily maximum 1-hour concentration; Carbon Monoxide - highest second maximum non-overlapping 8-hour concentration; Sulfur Dioxide - highest second maximum 24-hour concentration; Nitrogen Dioxide - highest arithmetic mean concentration; Lead - highest quarterly maximum concentration
Units: ppm = parts per million; ug/m^3 = micrograms per cubic meter
Source: U.S. Environmental Protection Agency, MSA Factbook 2006, Air Quality Statistics by City

Drinking Water

Water System Name	Pop. Served	Primary Water Source Type	Violations[1]	
			Health Based	Monitoring/ Reporting
Marlboro MUA	30,058	Ground	n/a	n/a

Note: (1) Based on violation data from January 1, 2007 to December 31, 2007 (includes unresolved violations from earlier years)
Source: U.S. Environmental Protection Agency, Office of Ground Water and Drinking Water, Safe Drinking Water Information System (based on data extracted April 15, 2008)

Rockaway, New Jersey

Background

Rockaway is located in northwestern Morris County, 35 miles west of New York City and 35 minutes from Newark International Airport.

In 1715, Dutch settlers who came to the area named it Rockaway, based on the Indian word, "Rechouwakie," meaning, "the place of sands." Also in 1715, the earliest land grants in the area were recorded between William Penn and the Delaware Tribe of Indians. In 1844, Morris County divided some of its larger townships and formed Rockway township.

Rockaway became the first place in America to work and mine iron ore. In 1730, an early forge was constructed by Job Allen in Rockaway Village. By 1740, forges were operating along the Rockaway River, close to the ore, waterpower, and thick forests, which supplied huge amounts of charcoal to the ironworks. By 1776, Morris County was the principal smelting center of the United States. The forges and furnaces at nearby Hibernia and Mount Hope furnished the Continental Army with shovels, axes, cannons, cannon balls, grapeshot and other supplies. Despite the large need for soldiers in the Continental Army, in 1777 the state legislature passed a resolution exempting seventy-five men from entering the service because they were needed to mine the iron necessary for the war.

Much of the business in Rockaway is generated by Picatinny Arsenal, a 6,500 acre military research and manufacturing facility. The company employs over 3,000 and is the township's largest employer. Other major business comes from the Rockaway Townsquare Mall, one of the largest and most modern shopping malls in New Jersey.

Other major attractions include recently developed lake resorts at Green Pond, Lake Telemark, and White Meadow Lake.

The Townsquare Mall recently expansion project is under way. Major stores and a Loew's 18-screen movie theatre are complete. Next is renovation of the outer mall's facades, construction of new wing, and additional new stores.

Rockaway has a seasonal climate with hot summers and cold winters. Median summer temperatures average 70 degrees, while winter averages can be as low as 15 degrees during December and January. The city averages 4.5 inches of rainfall per month from April to October and 7 inches of snowfall per month from December to March.

Rankings

General Rankings

- Newark* was ranked #180 out of 375 metro areas in *Cities Ranked & Rated*. Criteria: cost of living; climate; crime; transportation; economy and jobs; education; arts and culture; health and healthcare; leisure; quality of life. *Cities Ranked & Rated, 2nd Edition, 2007*
- Newark* was ranked #15 out of 379 metro areas in *Places Rated Almanac*. Criteria: health care; education; recreation; transportation; ambience; climate; crime; housing costs; jobs. *Places Rated Almanac, 7th Edition, 2007*

Business/Finance Rankings

- The nation's 100 largest metro areas were analysed in terms of the percentage of households entering some stage of foreclosure in 2007. The Newark* metro area ranked #45 out of 100 (#1 = highest foreclosure rate). *RealtyTrac, "Year-End 2007 Metropolitan Foreclosure Report"*
- The New York* metro area was identified as one of the most expensive places to rent in the U.S. The area ranked #45 out of 10 markets with an average effective rent of $2,720 per month. The rental figures cover apartment properties in complexes with 40 or more units (20 or more units in California and Arizona). The figures are blended average rents, which include all unit sizes. Effective rents include free rent incentives and other landlord concessions. *Wall Street Journal Online, January 17, 2008*
- The New York* metro area was selected as one of "America's Most Wired Cities" by *Forbes*. The metro area was ranked #9 out of 30. Criteria: percentage of Internet users with high-speed access; the range of service providers within a city; availability of public wireless hot spots. *Forbes, "America's Most Wired Cities," January 10, 2008*
- Newark* was selected as one of the best places to start and grow a company by *Entrepreneur* and the National Policy Research Council. The Newark* metro area ranked #35 out of 50 large metro areas. Criteria: business formation and growth (firms started four to 14 years ago that still employ at least 5 people and experienced rapid growth over the last four years). *Entrepreneur/National Policy Research Council, "Hot Cities for Entrepreneurs," September 2006*
- The New York* metro area was selected as one of "America's Greediest Cities" by *Forbes*. The area was ranked #6 out of 10. Criteria: number of Forbes 400 (*Forbes* annual list of the richest Americans) members per capita. *Forbes, "America's Greediest Cities," December 7, 2007*
- Newark* was cited as one of America's top large metros (population over 1 million) for new and expanded facility projects in 2007. The area appeared in the top 10 with 72 projects. *Site Selection, "Top Metropolitan Area Awards," March 2008*
- Intel, in partnership with Sperling's BestPlaces, ranked the 80 "Best Cities for Teleworking" in America. The Newark* metro area ranked #6 among extra large metro areas. The study identifies cities that hold the greatest potential for teleworking based on a host of factors including typical commuting times, fuel prices, availability of broadband Internet access and percentage of the population in telework friendly jobs. The study also factored in extreme climate and natural hazards. *Intel, "Best Cities for Teleworking," March 30, 2006*
- The Newark* metro area appeared on the Milken Institute "2007 Best Performing Cities" index. Rank: #168 out of 200 large metro areas. Criteria: job growth; wage and salary growth; high-tech output growth. *Milken Institute, "2007 Best Performing Cities"*
- Newark* was identified as one of the 100 "Most Unwired Cities" in the U.S. The area ranked #21 out of the 100 largest metro areas in the U.S. Criteria: number of public and commercial wireless access points (hotspots); airports with wireless Internet access; broadband availability; local wireless networks; and wireless email devices. *Intel, "Most Unwired Cities Survey," June 7, 2005*

- New York* was ranked #12 out of 125 regions worldwide in terms of its "Knowledge Competitiveness Index." The index attempts to measure the knowledge-based development taking place throughout the world and is based on 19 measures of economic performance that indicate a region's ability to translate its knowledge capacity into economic value. *Robert Huggins Associates, World Knowledge Competitiveness Index 2005*
- *Forbes* ranked the 200 most populous metro areas in the U.S. in terms of the "Best Places for Business and Careers." The Newark* metro area was ranked #107. Criteria: business costs (labor, energy, tax and office space expenses); living costs (housing, transportation, food and other household expenditures); education levels of the work force; job growth; income growth; migration trends; crime rates; and culture/leisure. *Forbes, "Best Places for Business and Careers," March 19, 2008*
- *Fortune* ranked the 100 largest metro areas in the U.S. in terms of projected median home price change in 2007. The Newark* metro area ranked #71. *Fortune.com, "Hot Spots, Cold Spots"*
- The New York* metro area was identified as one of "America's Most Overpriced Real Estate Markets." The area ranked #7 out of 10. Criteria: housing "P/E" ratio (a market's median home price divided by annual rents minus taxes and insurance); housing affordability. *Forbes.com, "America's Most Overpriced Real Estate Markets," May 11, 2007*

Health/Environment Rankings

- 100 of the largest metro areas in the U.S. were analyzed in terms of their current drought severity. The Newark* metro area ranked #75 (#1 = driest). The rankings were based on statistics such as long-term precipitation trends and patterns and the Palmer drought indices. *Sperling's BestPlaces, www.BestPlaces.net, "America's Drought-Riskiest Cities," November 2007*
- Doctors at the Harvard School of Public Health ranked 40 metropolitan areas based on data from the government-sponsored Hospital Quality Alliance program. The program tracks the performance of individual hospitals in treating patients for three common health problems: heart attacks, congestive heart failure, and pneumonia. The New York* metro area ranked #17 in quality of care for heart attacks, #8 for congestive heart failure, and #34 for pneumonia. *New England Journal of Medicine, July 21, 2005*
- *Reader's Digest* ranked the 50 largest metro areas in the U.S. in terms of how "clean" they are. The New York* metro area ranked #49. Criteria: air quality; water quality; toxic industrial pollution; Superfund sites; and sanitation. *Reader's Digest, "The 50 Cleanest (and Dirtiest) Cities in America," July 2005*
- The American Academy of Dermatology ranked 32 U.S. metropolitan regions in terms of their residents knowledge, attitude and behaviors towards tanning and sun protection. The New York* metro area ranked #2. The results of the study are based on an online national survey of 3,342 respondents. *American Academy of Dermatology, "RAYS: Your Grade," May 7, 2007*
- The Newark* metro area appeared in *Country Home's* "2008 Best Green Places" report. The area ranked #202 out of 379. Criteria: official energy policies; green power; green buildings; availability of fresh, locally grown food. *Country Home, "2008 Best Green Places"*
- Wyeth Consumer Healthcare, in partnership with Sperling's BestPlaces, ranked the nation's 50 most populous metro areas in terms of five key health factors. The Newark* metro area ranked #25. Criteria: physical activity; health status; nutrition; lifestyle pursuits; and mental wellness. *Wyeth Consumer Healthcare, "Centrum Healthiest Cities Study," April 19, 2005*
- HealthGrades surveyed over 41,000 individuals on doctor satisfaction and ranked the 20 largest metro areas based on the highest "definitely yes" responses to the question "Do you trust the physician to make decisions/recommendations that are in your best interest?" The New York* metro area ranked #10. *HealthGrades.com, "Top Cities in Doctor-Trust," September 7, 2006*

- New York* was identified as a "2008 Asthma Capital." The area ranked #38 out of the nation's 100 largest metropolitan areas. Twelve factors were used to identify the most challenging places to live for people with asthma: estimated prevalence; self-reported prevalence; crude death rate for asthma; annual pollen score; annual air quality; public smoking laws; number of board-certified asthma specialists; school inhaler access laws; rescue medication use; controller medication use; uninsured rate; poverty rate. *Asthma and Allergy Foundation of America, "2008 Asthma Capitals"*

- New York* was identified as a "Spring Allergy Capital." The area ranked #79 out of 100. Three groups of factors were used to identify the most severe cities for people with allergies during the spring season: annual pollen levels; medicine utilization; access to board-certified allergists. *Asthma and Allergy Foundation of America, "2007 Spring Allergy Capital Rankings"*

- New York* was identified as a "Fall Allergy Capital." The area ranked #69 out of 100. Three groups of factors were used to identify the most severe cities for people with allergies during the fall season: annual pollen levels; medicine utilization; access to board-certified allergists. *Asthma and Allergy Foundation of America, "2007 Fall Allergy Capital Rankings"*

- Ortho-McNeil Neurologics, in partnership with Sperling's BestPlaces, analyzed 110 metro areas and identified those U.S. cities with the highest prevalence of factors that are most commonly associated with migraine headaches. The Newark* metro area ranked #106. Criteria: number of migraine-related drug prescriptions per capita; lifestyle factors that can contribute to migraines; environmental factors that can trigger migraines; and consumption of migraine-triggering foods. *Ortho-McNeil Neurologics, "America's Migraine Hot Spots," March 14, 2006*

- Sperling's BestPlaces ranked 331 metro areas and identified the most and least stressful U.S. cities. The Newark* metro area ranked #55 out of the 100 largest metro areas (#1 = most stressful). Criteria: divorce rate; unemployment rate; violent and property crime; suicide rate; commute time; mental health; alcohol consumption; cloudy days. *Sperling's BestPlaces, www.BestPlaces.net, "America's Most (and Least) Stressful Cities," January 9, 2004*

- An analysis of the "Best & Worst Cities for Sleep" was conducted by Sperling's BestPlaces. The study ranked America's 50 most populated metro areas. The Newark* metro area ranked #29 (#1 = best city for sleep). Criteria: number of days residents didn't get enough rest or sleep during the past month; average length of daily commute; divorce rate; unemployment rate. *Sperling's BestPlaces, www.BestPlaces.net, "Best & Worst Cities for Sleep," 2006*

- HealthGrades evaluated the performance of America's 25 most populous metropolitan areas by measuring the outcomes of five of the highest volume and most widely studied procedures and diagnoses: coronary artery bypass graft surgery; percutaneus coronary interventions; acute myocardial infarction/heart attack in angioplasty-capable hospitals; congestive heart failure; and community acquired pneumonia. The New York* metro area ranked #17. *HealthGrades, "HealthGrades Hospital Quality in America Study," October 12, 2004*

- Newark* was highlighted as one of the 25 metro areas most polluted by year-round particle pollution (PM 2.5) in the U.S. The area ranked #17. *American Lung Association, State of the Air: 2007*

- Newark* was highlighted as one of the 25 most ozone-polluted metro areas in the U.S. The area ranked #10. *American Lung Association, State of the Air: 2007*

- New York* was selected as one of "America's Top 10 Low-Carb Cities" by *LowCarbiz Magazine*. Criteria: abundance of low-carb products; restaurants with low-carb menu items; health practitioners supportive of carb-cutting regimens; local culture generally conducive to exercise and health. *LowCarbiz Magazine, April 2004*

- Newark* was selected as one of "America's Pet Healthiest Cities" by Purina. The city ranked #24 out of 50. Criteria: veterinary services; environment; legislation; preventative care; obesity/body condition. *Purina Pet Institute, "America's Pet Healthiest Cities," May 20, 2003*

Women/Minorities Rankings

- Newark* was ranked #36 out of 100 metro areas in *SELF Magazine's* ranking of "America's Best Places for Women." A panel of experts came up with more than 50 criteria including death and disease rates, environmental indicators, community resources, and lifestyle habits. *SELF Magazine, "America's Best Places for Women 2007," December 2007*
- New York* appeared on a list of the top 10 metro areas with the highest concentration of same-sex households. The area ranked #6. *Urban Institute Press, The Gay and Lesbian Atlas, May 2004*
- New York* appeared on a list of the top 10 metro areas with the highest concentration of gay male couples. The area ranked #5. *Urban Institute Press, The Gay and Lesbian Atlas, May 2004*

Seniors/Retirement Rankings

- Sperling's BestPlaces in partnership with Bankers Life & Casualty Company designed a survey to identify the top 50 metro areas in the U.S. that offer the best overall qualities for senior living. The Newark* metro area ranked #33. The following criteria were statistically weighted to reflect the needs of the senior population: health; disease; economics; social; environment; spiritual; transportation; housing; and crime. *Bankers Life & Casualty Company, "Best Cities for Seniors 2005"*
- A.G. Edwards ranked America's 500 top-performing communities based on their residents' personal savings and investing behavior. The New York* metro area ranked #241 with an index score of 101.69 (national average = 100.00). A dozen statistical factors were measured including: participation in retirement savings plans; personal debt levels; and home ownership. *A.G. Edwards, "2007 Nest Egg Index", September 12, 2007*

Children/Family Rankings

- The Newark* metro area was selected as one of the "Best Cities for Relocating Families" by Worldwide ERC and Primacy Relocation. The 2007 study placed a special emphasis on the housing market, which has significantly impacted the relocation industry and an employer's ability to transfer employees. The variables which weigh heavily in this category include home price, home affordability index, appreciation rates, and property tax. Other criteria include cost of living, crime rates, education, climate, focus on diversity, physicians per capita, recreation and leisure, arts and culture, air quality, watershed quality, sales tax, unemployment rate, job growth, high school and higher education index, school expenditures per student, students in public school, SAT/ACT percentile, and population growth. *Worldwide ERC and Primacy Relocation, "2007 Best Cities for Relocating Families"*

Safety Rankings

- The National Insurance Crime Bureau ranked 361 metro areas in the U.S. in terms of per capita rates of vehicle theft. The New York* metro area ranked #224 (#1 = highest rate). Criteria: number of vehicle theft offenses per 100,000 inhabitants. *National Insurance Crime Bureau, "NICB Vehicle Theft Study," April 22, 2008*
- New York* appeared on Sperling's BestPlaces list of the "Riskiest Cities for Identity Theft." The area ranked #29 out of the nations 50 largest metro areas. Over 80 criteria were analyzed across four major categories: technology impact; crime; transactions; and risk profile. *Sperling's BestPlaces, www.BestPlaces.net, "Riskiest Cities for Identity Theft," July 2006*
- Farmers Insurance Group of Companies, in partnership with Sperling's BestPlaces, ranked 379 metro areas and identified the "Most Secure U.S. Place to Live." The Newark* metro area ranked #41 out of 114 in the large metro area category (500,000 or more residents). Criteria: crime rates; extreme weather; risk of natural disasters; environmental hazards; terrorism threats; air quality; life expectancy; job loss numbers. *Farmers Insurance Group, "Most Secure U.S. Places to Live 2007"*

- Newark* was identified as one of the most dangerous large metro areas for pedestrians in the U.S. The area ranked #47 out of the nations 50 largest metro areas. Criteria: average yearly pedestrian fatalities per capita (for the years 2002 and 2003) adjusted for the number of walkers. *Surface Transportation Policy Project, "Mean Streets 2004"*

Sports/Recreation Rankings

- The New York* metro area appeared on the *Sporting News* list of the "Best Sports Cities 2007". The area ranked #2 out of 150 cities in the U.S. *Sporting News* takes a 12-month snapshot, roughly July to July, of each city's sports, putting a heavy premium on regular-season won-lost records (from the most recently completed season). Other criteria include: playoff berths, bowl appearances and tournament bids; championships; applicable power ratings; quality of competition; overall fan fervor as measured in part by attendance as percentage of venue capacity; abundance of teams (rewarding quality over quantity); stadium and arena quality; ticket availability and prices; franchise ownership; and marquee appeal of athletes. *SportingNews.com, "Best Sports Cities 2007," August 1, 2007*
- The Newark* metro area was selected by *Cranium* as one of the "Top 50 Fun Cities" in America. The area ranked #45. Criteria includes: number of sports teams, restaurants, and dance performances; number of toy stores; city budget spent on recreation. *Cranium, November 4, 2003*
- *Golf Digest* ranked 330 metro areas in the U.S. in terms of golf. The Newark* metro area was ranked #316. Criteria: access to golf; weather; value of golf; and quality of golf. *Golf Digest, "Metro Golf Rankings," August 2005*

Dating/Romance Rankings

- Eli Lily and Company, in partnership with Sperling's BestPlaces, ranked the nation's 50 largest metro areas in terms of the "Most Romantic Cities for Baby Boomers." The New York* metro area ranked #16. Criteria: marriage and divorce rates among "baby boomers" age 45 to 60; great restaurants; dance studios; chocolate, jewelry and flower sales. *Eli Lily and Company, "Most Romantic Cities for Baby Boomers," April 20, 2007*
- The New York* metro area was selected as one of the "Top Ten U.S. Cities for Finding a Rich, Single Woman" by Teasley, a Manhattan-based marketing consulting firm. The area ranked #2. Criteria: high single-female to single-male ratio; higher income to cost-of-living ratio; percentage of population that is single. *Teasley, "Where to Find a Rich, Single Woman in the United States," 2005*
- The Newark* metro area was selected as one of the "Best Cities for Relocating Singles" by Worldwide ERC and Primacy Relocation. The area ranked #81 out of the 100 largest metro areas in the U.S. Areas were selected based on the following criteria: a robust cost-of-living index; adventure and outdoor recreation opportunities; violent crime and property crime rates; percentage of the population that is unmarried (ages 25-34); ratio of single men and single women; affordability of quality higher education, including in-state and out-of-state tuition requirements and rates; number of newcomers to the area; commute times; tax rates; fee and occupancy rates for temporary housing and mini-storage; quality and quantity of collegiate and professional sporting events and fun, fan-friendly venues. *Worldwide ERC and Primacy Relocation, "2007 Best Cities for Relocating Singles," October 25, 2007*
- *Forbes* ranked the 40 most populous urbanized areas in the U.S. in terms of the "Best Cities for Singles." The New York* metro area ranked #2. Criteria: number of singles; cost of living alone; nightlife; culture; job growth; coolness; and online dating. *Forbes.com, August 21, 2007*
- Sperling's BestPlaces in partnership with AXE Deodorant Bodyspray ranked 80 metro areas and identified "America's Best (and Worst) Cities for Dating." The New York* metro area ranked #18 (#1 = best). Criteria: percentage of singles ages 18-24; population density; dating venues per capita. *AXE Deodorant Bodyspray, "America's Best (and Worst) Cities for Dating," May 2004*

Culture/Performing Arts Rankings

- The New York* metro area was selected as one of the "Best Places for Artists in America" by *BusinessWeek.com.* Criteria: percentage of young people age 25 to 34; population diversity; concentration of museums, philharmonic orchestras, dance companies, theater troupes, library resources, and college arts programs. *BusinessWeek.com, "Best Places for Artists in America," February 26, 2007*

- Scarborough Research, a leading market research firm, identified the top local markets for rock concert attendance. The New York* DMA (Designated Market Area) ranked in the top 25 with 14% of consumers, 18 years old and over, reporting that they have attended a rock concert during the past year. *Scarborough Research, June 14, 2004*

Miscellaneous Rankings

- The Newark* metro area was identified as one of "The 10 Worst Commuter Cities" in the U.S. by the *U.S. News and World Report*. The mean travel time to work is 32 minutes. *U.S. News and World Report, May 7, 2007*

- Scarborough Research, a leading market research firm, identified the top local markets for bloggers. The New York* DMA (Designated Market Area) ranked in the top 13 with 10% of adults reporting that they had read or contributed to a blog within the past 30 days. *Scarborough Research, October 24, 2007*

- The New York* metro area was selected as one of the "Top 10 Most Independent Cities for Homesellers". The area ranked #1. The cities listed had more consumers choosing to sell their homes without the help of a real-estate agent than anywhere else. Data was based on geographical information for listings posted on ForSaleByOwner.com from January 1, 2007 through June 30, 2007. *ForSaleByOwner.com, October 1, 2007*

- Avis Rent-A-Car and Motorola, in partnership with Sperling's BestPlaces, ranked the nation's 75 most populous metro areas in terms of how difficult they are to navigate. The New York* metro area ranked #5 with #1 being the most challenging. Criteria: street layouts; overall design and layout; travel time index; percent of congested freeway and street lane miles; bodies of water; complexity of directions needed to travel from major airports to city center; annual delay per person; days of snow exceeding 1.5 inches; and days of rain exceeding 0.5 inch. *Avis Rent-A-Car and Motorola, "America's Most Challenging Cities to Navigate," August 3, 2004*

- The New York* metro area appeared on *Forbes* list of "America's Drunkest Cities". The area ranked #32. Criteria: 35 of the largest continental U.S. metro areas were chosen based on availability of data and geographic diversity. Each metro was ranked in five areas: state laws; drinkers; heavy drinkers; binge drinkers; and alcoholism. *Forbes.com, "America's Drunkest Cities," August 22, 2006*

- Sperling's BestPlaces in partnership with Pep Boys ranked 77 metro areas and identified "America's Most Drivable Cities." The Newark* metro area ranked #60. Criteria: climate; road roughness; urban mobility; gas prices. *Pep Boys, "America's Most Drivable Cities," April 9, 2003*

- State Farm Insurance, in partnership with Sperling's BestPlaces, analyzed several key factors that contribute to overall family preparedness. The Newark* metro area ranked #34 out of the nation's 50 most populous metro areas. Criteria: quality of life; life insurance coverage; and investments. *State Farm Life Insurance, "Fiscally Fit Cities Report," July 20, 2004*

- Scarborough Research, a leading market research firm, identified the top local markets for grocery coupon use. The New York* DMA (Designated Market Area) ranked in the top 25 with 38% of consumers reporting that they use grocery coupons at least once per week. *Scarborough Research, December 8, 2004*

- A study by Sperling's BestPlaces examined which U.S. metro areas were most affected by high fuel prices in 2006. The Newark* metro area was ranked #64 out of 80 (#1 = most expensive city for driving). Rankings are based on the average dollars spent on gas per year by two driver households. Criteria: cost of regular-grade gasoline; average miles driven per day; average number of gallons each driver uses and wastes in traffic congestion each day. *Sperling's BestPlaces, www.bestplaces.net, "Pain at the Pump," May 18, 2006*

Rockaway is located within the New York-Northern New Jersey-Long Island, NY-NJ-PA Metropolitan Statistical Area and Newark-Union, NJ-PA Metropolitan Division.

Business Environment

CITY FINANCES

City Government Finances

Component	2004-2005 ($000)	2004-2005 ($ per capita)
Total Revenues	n/a	n/a
Total Expenditures	n/a	n/a
Debt Outstanding	n/a	n/a
Cash and Securities	n/a	n/a

Source: U.S Census Bureau, Government Finances 2004-2005

City Government Revenue by Source

Source	2004-2005 ($000)	2004-2005 ($ per capita)
General Revenue		
From Federal Government	n/a	n/a
From State Government	n/a	n/a
From Local Governments	n/a	n/a
Taxes		
Property	n/a	n/a
Sales	n/a	n/a
Personal Income	n/a	n/a
License	n/a	n/a
Charges	n/a	n/a
Liquor Store	n/a	n/a
Utility	n/a	n/a
Employee Retirement	n/a	n/a
Other	n/a	n/a

Source: U.S Census Bureau, Government Finances 2004-2005

City Government Expenditures by Function

Function	2004-2005 ($000)	2004-2005 ($ per capita)	2004-2005 (%)
General Expenditures			
Airports	n/a	n/a	n/a
Corrections	n/a	n/a	n/a
Education	n/a	n/a	n/a
Fire Protection	n/a	n/a	n/a
Governmental Administration	n/a	n/a	n/a
Health	n/a	n/a	n/a
Highways	n/a	n/a	n/a
Hospitals	n/a	n/a	n/a
Housing and Community Development	n/a	n/a	n/a
Interest on General Debt	n/a	n/a	n/a
Libraries	n/a	n/a	n/a
Parking	n/a	n/a	n/a
Parks and Recreation	n/a	n/a	n/a
Police Protection	n/a	n/a	n/a
Public Welfare	n/a	n/a	n/a
Sewerage	n/a	n/a	n/a
Solid Waste Management	n/a	n/a	n/a
Liquor Store	n/a	n/a	n/a
Utility	n/a	n/a	n/a
Employee Retirement	n/a	n/a	n/a
Other	n/a	n/a	n/a

Source: U.S Census Bureau, Government Finances 2004-2005

Municipal Bond Ratings

Area	Moody's
City	Aaa

Source: Mergent Bond Record, January 2008 (unless noted otherwise)

DEMOGRAPHICS

Population Growth

Area	1990 Census	2000 Census	2007 Estimate	2012 Projection	Population Growth (%) 1990-2000	Population Growth (%) 2000-2012
City	19,668	22,930	26,073	27,966	16.6	22.0
MSA[1]	16,845,992	18,323,002	18,887,605	19,111,248	8.8	4.3
U.S.	248,709,873	281,421,906	301,045,522	314,920,978	13.2	11.9

Note: (1) Metropolitan Statistical Area - see Appendix B for areas included
Source: Claritas, Inc.

Number of Households and Average Household Size

Area	2007 Estimate	2007 Average Household Size
City	9,320	2.80
MSA[1]	6,870,593	2.75
U.S.	113,668,003	2.65

Note: (1) Metropolitan Statistical Area - see Appendix B for areas included
Source: Claritas, Inc.

Race and Ethnicity

Area	White Alone[2]	Black Alone[2]	Asian Alone[2]	Other Race Alone[2]	Hispanic[3]
City	85.0	3.4	7.6	4.0	8.8
MSA[1]	59.5	17.6	8.8	14.1	21.2
U.S.	73.1	12.4	4.3	10.3	14.9

Note: Figures are 2007 estimates; (1) Metropolitan Statistical Area - see Appendix B for areas included (2) Alone is defined as not being in combination with one or more other races; (3) May be of any race.
Source: Claritas, Inc.

Ancestry

Area	German	Irish[2]	English	American	Italian	Polish	French[3]	Scottish
City	15.2	19.3	7.9	3.9	23.4	10.0	1.7	1.6
MSA[1]	10.8	12.9	5.2	3.1	15.8	5.9	1.3	1.3
U.S.	15.2	10.9	8.7	7.3	5.6	3.2	3.0	1.7

Note: Figures include multiple ancestry (e.g. if a person reported being Irish and Italian, they were included in both columns); (1) Metropolitan Statistical Area - see Appendix A for areas included; (2) Includes Celtic; (3) Includes Alsatian but excludes Basque
Source: Census 2000, Summary File 3

Foreign-Born Population

Area	Percent of Population Born in							
	Any Foreign Country	Europe	Asia	Africa	Oceania[2]	Canada	Mexico	Latin America[3]
City	13.3	4.3	4.6	0.6	0.0	0.2	0.1	3.5
MSA[1]	19.0	4.9	3.3	0.9	0.0	0.2	0.4	9.2
U.S.	11.1	1.7	2.9	0.3	0.1	0.3	3.3	2.5

Note: (1) Metropolitan Statistical Area - see Appendix A for areas included; (2) Includes Australia, New Zealand subregion, Melanesia, Micronesia, Polynesia, and Oceania n.e.c; (3) Includes Central America (excluding Mexico), South America, and the Caribbean.
Source: Census 2000, Summary File 3

Marriage Status

Area	Never Married	Now Married (excluding Separated)	Separated	Widowed	Divorced
City	20.7	67.0	1.2	4.4	6.7
MSA[1]	29.8	53.1	2.8	7.1	7.2
U.S.	27.1	54.4	2.2	6.6	9.7

Note: Figures are percentages and cover the population 15 years of age and older; (1) Metropolitan Statistical Area - see Appendix A for areas included
Source: Census 2000, Summary File 3

Age Distribution

Area	Percent of Population						
	Under Age 5	Age 5 to 17	Age 18 to 34	Age 35 to 49	Age 50 to 64	Age 65 to 79	80 Years and Over
City	7.6	19.4	18.4	28.5	16.5	7.8	1.9
MSA[1]	7.0	18.5	22.0	24.9	15.5	8.9	3.3
U.S.	6.8	18.9	23.7	23.5	14.8	9.2	3.2

Note: (1) Metropolitan Statistical Area - see Appendix A for areas included
Source: Census 2000, Summary File 3

Male/Female Ratio

Area	Males	Females	Males per 100 Females
City	12,923	13,150	98.3
MSA[1]	9,117,706	9,769,899	93.3
U.S.	148,320,305	152,725,217	97.1

Note: Figures are 2007 estimates; (1) Metropolitan Statistical Area - see Appendix B for areas included
Source: Claritas, Inc.

Religion

Area	Catholic	Southern Baptist	United Meth-odist	ELCA[1]	LDS[2]	Presby-terian Church USA	Jewish Est.	Muslim Est.
County	38.1	0.1	2.0	0.9	0.3	2.5	7.1	0.5
U.S.	22.0	7.1	3.7	1.8	1.5	1.1	2.2	0.6

Note: Figures are the number of adherents as a percentage of the total population; Adherents are defined as all members, including full members, their children and the estimated number of other participants who are not considered members (e.g. the baptized, those not confirmed, those regularly attending services, etc.); (1) Evangelical Lutheran Church in America; (2) The Church of Jesus Christ of Latter Day Saints
Source: Reprinted with permission from Religious Congregations and Membership in the United States 2000 (Nashville, Glenmary Research Center, 2002) Copyright Association of Statisticians of American Religious Bodies. All rights reserved.

ECONOMY

Gross Metropolitan Product

Area	2002	2003	2004	2005	2005 Rank[2]
MSA[1]	820.9	847.1	902.4	952.6	1

Note: Figures are in billions of dollars; (1) New York-Northern New Jersey-Long Island, NY-NJ-PA Metropolitan Statistical Area - see Appendix A for areas included; (2) Rank ranges from 1 to 361
Source: The U.S. Conference of Mayors, "U.S. Metro Economies: GMP - The Engines of America's Growth," January 2007

Economic Growth

Area	1995 GMP	2005 GMP	Average Annual Growth Rate	Growth Rate Rank[2]
MSA[1]	585.5	952.6	5.0	221

Note: Figures are in billions of dollars; GMP = Gross Metropolitan Product; (1) New York-Northern New Jersey-Long Island, NY-NJ-PA Metropolitan Statistical Area - see Appendix A for areas included; (2) Rank ranges from 1 to 361
Source: The U.S. Conference of Mayors, "U.S. Metro Economies: GMP - The Engines of America's Growth," January 2007

INCOME

Per Capita/Median/Average Income

Area	Per Capita ($)	Median Household ($)	Average Household ($)
City	41,360	95,282	115,612
MSA[1]	30,292	58,080	82,491
U.S.	25,495	49,280	66,670

Note: Figures are 2007 estimates; (1) Metropolitan Statistical Area - see Appendix B for areas included
Source: Claritas, Inc.

EMPLOYMENT

Household Income Distribution

Area	Percent of Households Earning							
	Under $15,000	$15,000 -24,999	$25,000 -34,999	$35,000 -49,999	$50,000 -74,999	$75,000 -99,000	$100,000 -149,999	$150,000 and up
City	3.6	3.6	4.3	7.1	16.9	17.9	26.3	20.4
MSA[1]	14.0	8.8	8.7	12.6	17.1	12.3	14.5	12.0
U.S.	13.1	10.9	11.2	15.6	19.5	11.9	11.3	6.6

Note: Figures are 2007 estimates; (1) Metropolitan Statistical Area - see Appendix B for areas included
Source: Claritas, Inc.

Poverty Rates by Age

Area	All Ages	Under 5 Years Old	5 to 17 Years Old	18 to 64 Years Old	65 Years and Over
City	2.4	0.3	0.4	1.3	0.3
MSA[1]	9.7	0.9	2.3	5.4	1.0
U.S.	12.4	1.2	3.0	6.9	1.2

Note: Figures are percent of population with income in 1999 below poverty level and only include population for whom poverty status is determined; (1) Metropolitan Statistical Area - see Appendix A for areas included
Source: Census 2000, Summary File 3

Personal Bankruptcy Filing Rate

Area	2004	2005	2006
Morris County	2.31	2.80	0.79
U.S.	5.31	6.82	2.00

Note: Numbers are per 1,000 population and include Chapter 7 and Chapter 13 filings
Source: Federal Deposit Insurance Corporation (FDIC), Regional Economic Conditions (RECON), 8/23/2007

Labor Force and Employment

Area	Civilian Labor Force			Workers Employed		
	Dec. 2006	Dec. 2007	% Chg.	Dec. 2006	Dec. 2007	% Chg.
City	14,741	14,648	-0.6	14,462	14,332	-0.9
MD[1]	1,097,724	1,089,849	-0.7	1,055,293	1,045,749	-0.9
U.S.	152,571,000	153,705,000	0.7	146,081,000	146,334,000	0.2

Note: Data is not seasonally adjusted and covers workers 16 years of age and older;
(1) Metropolitan Division - see Appendix B for areas included
Source: Bureau of Labor Statistics, http://stats.bls.gov

Unemployment Rate

Area	2007											
	Jan.	Feb.	Mar.	Apr.	May	Jun.	Jul.	Aug.	Sep.	Oct.	Nov.	Dec.
City	2.6	2.4	2.4	2.2	2.2	2.2	2.7	2.3	2.2	2.0	2.1	2.2
MD[1]	4.8	4.6	4.4	4.1	4.1	4.3	4.8	4.1	4.1	3.9	3.9	4.0
U.S.	5.0	4.9	4.5	4.3	4.3	4.7	4.9	4.6	4.5	4.4	4.5	4.8

Note: Data is not seasonally adjusted and covers workers 16 years of age and older; All figures are percentages; (1) Metropolitan Division - see Appendix B for areas included
Source: Bureau of Labor Statistics, http://stats.bls.gov

Employment by Occupation

Occupation Classification	City (%)	MSA[1] (%)	U.S. (%)
Sales and Office	28.2	28.2	26.7
Professional and Related	26.3	22.5	20.2
Service	9.8	13.3	14.9
Production, Transportation, and Material Moving	8.2	12.2	14.6
Management, Business, and Financial	21.2	16.3	13.5
Construction, Extraction, and Maintenance	6.2	7.5	9.4
Farming, Forestry, and Fishing	0.0	0.1	0.7

Note: Figures cover employed civilians 16 years of age and older;
(1) Metropolitan Statistical Area - see Appendix A for areas included
Source: Census 2000, Summary File 3

Employment by Industry

Sector	MSA[1] Number of Employees	MSA[1] Percent of Total	U.S. Percent of Total
Government	168,500	16.1	16.3
Education and Health Services	148,200	14.1	13.4
Professional and Business Services	162,000	15.4	13.1
Retail Trade	108,700	10.4	11.6
Manufacturing	87,900	8.4	9.9
Leisure and Hospitality	67,600	6.4	9.6
Financial Activities	75,300	7.2	5.9
Construction	n/a	n/a	5.3
Wholesale Trade	54,400	5.2	4.4
Other Services	48,400	4.6	3.9
Transportation and Utilities	58,800	5.6	3.7
Information	24,700	2.4	2.2
Natural Resources and Mining	n/a	n/a	0.5

Note: Figures cover non-farm employment as of December 2007 and are not seasonally adjusted; (1) Metropolitan Statistical Area - see Appendix B for areas included; n/a not available
Source: Bureau of Labor Statistics, http://stats.bls.gov

Average Wages

Occupation	$/Hr.	Occupation	$/Hr.
Accountants and Auditors	37.05	Maids and Housekeeping Cleaners	10.91
Automotive Mechanics	18.93	Maintenance and Repair Workers	18.38
Bookkeepers	18.48	Marketing Managers	62.55
Carpenters	25.61	Nuclear Medicine Technologists	37.51
Cashiers	9.46	Nurses, Licensed Practical	23.64
Clerks, General Office	13.55	Nurses, Registered	35.63
Clerks, Receptionists/Information	12.56	Nursing Aides/Orderlies/Attendants	12.34
Clerks, Shipping/Receiving	15.52	Packers and Packagers, Hand	9.65
Computer Programmers	43.47	Physical Therapists	40.68
Computer Support Specialists	23.16	Postal Service Mail Carriers	21.18
Computer Systems Analysts	43.80	Real Estate Brokers	29.99
Cooks, Restaurant	11.82	Retail Salespersons	12.70
Dentists	n/a	Sales Reps., Exc. Tech./Scientific	33.22
Electrical Engineers	n/a	Sales Reps., Tech./Scientific	37.22
Electricians	31.84	Secretaries, Exc. Legal/Med./Exec.	16.96
Financial Managers	61.75	Security Guards	13.59
First-Line Supervisors/Mgrs., Sales	22.55	Surgeons	96.86
Food Preparation Workers	10.27	Teacher Assistants	11.20
General and Operations Managers	69.48	Teachers, Elementary School	28.00
Hairdressers/Cosmetologists	15.37	Teachers, Secondary School	29.90
Internists	78.14	Telemarketers	15.30
Janitors and Cleaners	12.49	Truck Drivers, Heavy/Tractor-Trailer	19.44
Landscaping/Groundskeeping Workers	13.47	Truck Drivers, Light/Delivery Svcs.	15.30
Lawyers	59.41	Waiters and Waitresses	11.16

Note: Wage data covers the Newark-Union, NJ-PA Metropolitan Division - see Appendix B for areas included. Hourly wages for elementary/secondary school teachers and teacher assistants were calculated by the editors from annual wage data assuming a 40 hour work week; n/a not available.
Source: Bureau of Labor Statistics, May 2007 Metro Area Occupational Employment and Wage Estimates

RESIDENTIAL REAL ESTATE

Building Permits

Area	Single-Family 2006	Single-Family 2007p	Single-Family Pct. Chg.	Multi-Family 2006	Multi-Family 2007p	Multi-Family Pct. Chg.	Total 2006	Total 2007p	Total Pct. Chg.
City	23	21	-8.7	19	96	405.3	42	117	178.6
U.S.	1,378,200	973,300	-29.4	460,700	407,200	-11.6	1,838,900	1,380,500	-24.9

Note: (p) preliminary; figures cover and represent new, privately-owned housing units authorized (unadjusted data); All permit data are based on estimates with imputation; U.S. figures are based on the new 20,000-place series.
Source: U.S. Census Bureau, Manufacturing, Mining, and Construction Statistics

Homeownership and Housing Vacancies

Area	Homeownership Rate[2] (%)			Rental Vacancy Rate[3] (%)			Homeowner Vacancy Rate[4] (%)		
	2005	2006	2007	2005	2006	2007	2005	2006	2007
MSA[1]	54.6	53.6	53.8	5.0	5.4	5.7	1.9	1.8	2.1
U.S.	68.9	68.8	68.1	9.8	9.8	9.7	1.9	2.4	2.7

Note: (1) Metropolitan Statistical Area - see Appendix B for areas included; (2) The proportion of households that are owners; (3) The proportion of the rental inventory that is vacant for rent; (4) The proportion of the homeowner inventory that is vacant for sale; n/a not available
Source: U.S. Census Bureau, Housing Vacancies and Homeownership Annual Statistics: 2007

TAXES

State Corporate Income Tax Rates

State	Rates and Tax Brackets
New Jersey	6.5% > $0; 7.5 > 50K; 9.0% > 100K

Note: Tax rates as of January 1, 2008; Companies with income greater than $100K pay 9% on all income, companies with income greater than $50K but less than $100K pay 7.5 % on all income and companies with income under $50K pay 6.5%. The minimum tax is $500. An Alternative Minimum Assessment based on Gross Receipts applies if greater than corporate franchise tax for out-of-state companies with New Jersey sales. 4% surtax for 2007.
Source: Tax Foundation, www.taxfoundation.org

State Individual Income Tax Rates

State	Federal Deductibility	Marginal Rates (%)	Standard Deduction ($)		Personal Exemptions ($)[1]	
			Single	Joint	Single	Dependents
New Jersey	No	1.4 - 8.97 (y)	n/a	n/a	1,000	1,500

Note: Tax rates as of January 1, 2008; Local- and county-level taxes are not included; n/a not applicable; (1) Married joint filers generally receive double the single exemption; (y) Brackets are not double for married taxpayers.
Source: Tax Foundation, www.taxfoundation.org

Various State and Local Tax Rates

State and Local Sales and Use (%)	State Sales and Use (%)	Gasoline[1,2] ($/gal.)	Cigarette ($/pack)	Spirits ($/gal.)	Table Wine ($/gal.)	Beer ($/gal.)
7.0	7.0	0.145	2.575	4.40	0.70	0.12

Note: Tax rates as of January 1, 2008; (1) In addition to the 18.4 cpg Federal gasoline tax; (2) Rates may include additional state sales taxes, environmental protection and storage fees/taxes, and local taxes. When necessary, the volume-weighted average of all local taxes is used to approximate the typical statewide rate including local tax
Source: Tax Foundation, www.taxfoundation.org; Original research

State Tax Burdens

Area	Combined State and Local Tax Burden		Combined Federal, State and Local Tax Burden	
	Percent	Rank	Percent	Rank
New Jersey	11.6	10	35.6	3
U.S. Average	11.0	-	32.7	-

Note: Figures cover 2007 and measure taxes as a percentage of income
Source: Tax Foundation, www.taxfoundation.org

State Business Tax Climate Index Rankings

State	Overall Rank	Corporate Tax Index Rank	Individual Income Tax Index Rank	Sales Tax Index Rank	Unemployment Insurance Tax Index Rank	Property Tax Index Rank
New Jersey	49	41	49	44	24	49

Note: Rankings range from 1 to 50 where 1 is best. Rankings do not average across to Overall Rank. States without a given tax are given a ranking of 1.
Source: Tax Foundation, State Business Tax Climate Index 2008

TRANSPORTATION

Means of Transportation to Work

Area	Car/Truck/Van		Public Transportation			Bicycle	Walked	Other Means	Worked at Home
	Drove Alone	Car-pooled	Bus	Subway	Railroad				
City	85.1	9.3	0.8	0.0	1.2	0.1	0.8	0.3	2.5
MSA[1]	71.8	10.6	6.1	0.7	3.6	0.2	3.0	1.0	3.0
U.S.	75.7	12.2	2.5	1.5	0.5	0.4	2.9	1.0	3.3

Note: Figures are percentages and cover workers 16 years of age and older; (1) Metropolitan Statistical Area - see Appendix A for areas included
Source: Census 2000, Summary File 3

Travel Time to Work

Area	Less Than 15 Minutes	15 to 29 Minutes	30 to 44 Minutes	45 to 59 Minutes	60 Minutes or More
City	21.1	30.8	24.2	13.0	10.9
MSA[1]	22.8	31.6	21.3	10.0	14.2
U.S.	29.4	36.1	19.1	7.4	8.0

Note: Figures are percentages and include workers 16 years old and over; (1) Metropolitan Statistical Area - see Appendix A for areas included
Source: Census 2000, Summary File 3

Travel Time Index

Area	1982	1995	2004	2005
Urban Area[1]	1.10	1.24	1.36	1.39
Average[2]	1.11	1.22	1.29	1.30

Note: Travel Time Index - The ratio of travel time in the peak period to the travel time at free-flow conditions. A value of 1.35 indicates a 20-minute free-flow trip takes 27 minutes in the peak. Free-flow speeds (60 mph on freeways and 35 mph on principal arterials) are used as the comparison threshold; (1) Covers the New York-Newark, NY-NJ-CT urban area; (2) average of 85 urban areas
Source: Texas Transportation Institute, The 2007 Urban Mobility Report, September 2007

Living Environment

COST OF LIVING

Cost of Living Index

Composite Index	Groceries	Housing	Utilities	Trans-portation	Health Care	Misc. Goods/ Services
127.1	111.2	165.9	107.8	104.1	107.0	116.2

Note: U.S. = 100; Figures cover the Newark-Elizabeth NJ urban area.
Source: The Council for Community and Economic Research (formerly ACCRA), Cost of Living Index, 2007

Grocery Prices

Area[1]	T-Bone Steak ($/pound)	Frying Chicken ($/pound)	Whole Milk ($/half gal.)	Eggs ($/dozen)	Orange Juice ($/64 oz.)	Coffee ($/11.5 oz.)
City[2]	9.72	1.14	2.22	2.18	3.13	3.22
Avg.	8.93	1.12	2.13	1.52	3.26	3.31
Min.	5.88	0.71	1.33	0.83	2.30	2.20
Max.	12.80	2.07	3.43	3.54	5.79	6.20

Note: (1) Values for the local area are compared with the average, minimum and maximum values for all 331 areas in the Cost of Living Index report; (2) Figures cover the Newark-Elizabeth NJ urban area; **T-Bone Steak** *(price per pound);* **Frying Chicken** *(price per pound, whole fryer);* **Whole Milk** *(half gallon carton);* **Eggs** *(price per dozen, Grade A, large);* **Orange Juice** *(64 oz. Tropicana or Florida Natural);* **Coffee** *(11.5 oz. can, vacuum-packed, Maxwell House, Hills Bros, or Folgers).*
Source: The Council for Community and Economic Research (formerly ACCRA), Cost of Living Index, 2007

Housing and Utility Costs

Area[1]	New Home Price ($)	Apartment Rent ($/month)	All Electric ($/month)	Part Electric ($/month)	Other Energy ($/month)	Telephone ($/month)
City[2]	518,648	1,322	-	84.58	84.80	29.75
Avg.	309,605	782	146.13	78.67	90.16	26.14
Min.	189,877	n/a	82.03	37.41	33.15	17.08
Max.	1,202,800	3,481	271.14	150.60	257.67	37.45

Note: (1) Values for the local area are compared with the average, minimum and maximum values for all 331 areas in the Cost of Living Index report; (2) Figures cover the Newark-Elizabeth NJ urban area; **New Home Price** *(2,400 sf living area, 8,000 sf lot, in urban area with full utilities);* **Apartment Rent** *(950 sf 2 bedroom/1.5 or 2 bath, unfurnished, excluding all utilities except water);* **All Electric** *(average monthly cost for an all-electric home);* **Part Electric** *(average monthly cost for a part-electric home);* **Other Energy** *(average monthly cost for natural gas, fuel oil, coal, wood, and any other forms of energy except electricity);* **Telephone** *(price includes basic monthly rate for a private residential line plus additional local usage charges incurred by a family of four).*
Source: The Council for Community and Economic Research (formerly ACCRA), Cost of Living Index, 2007

Health Care, Transportation, and Other Costs

Area[1]	Doctor ($/visit)	Dentist ($/visit)	Optometrist ($/visit)	Gasoline ($/gallon)	Beauty Salon ($/visit)	Men's Shirt ($)
City[2]	76.17	84.13	78.93	2.52	34.33	33.55
Avg.	79.48	71.93	79.55	2.64	29.52	25.77
Min.	52.08	44.80	43.95	2.19	15.58	16.19
Max.	148.44	126.27	158.83	3.48	60.62	48.53

Note: (1) Values for the local area are compared with the average, minimum and maximum values for all 331 areas in the Cost of Living Index report; (2) Figures cover the Newark-Elizabeth NJ urban area; **Doctor** *(general practitioners routine exam of an established patient);* **Dentist** *(adult teeth cleaning and periodic oral examination);* **Optometrist** *(full vision eye exam for established adult patient);* **Gasoline** *(one gallon regular unleaded, national brand, including all taxes, cash price at self-service pump if available);* **Beauty Salon** *(woman's shampoo, trim, and blow-dry);* **Men's Shirt** *(cotton/polyester dress shirt, pinpoint weave, long sleeves).*
Source: The Council for Community and Economic Research (formerly ACCRA), Cost of Living Index, 2007

HOUSING

House Price Index (HPI)

Area	National Ranking[2]	Quarterly Change (%)	One-Year Change (%)	Five-Year Change (%)
MD[1]	170	0.38	0.83	54.03
U.S.[3]	-	0.10	0.84	41.37

Note: The HPI is a weighted repeat sales index. It measures average price changes in repeat sales or refinancings on the same properties. This information is obtained by reviewing repeat mortgage transactions on single-family properties whose mortgages have been purchased or securitized by Fannie Mae or Freddie Mac in January 1975; (1) Metropolitan Division - see Appendix B for areas included; (2) Rankings are based on annual percentage change for all metro areas containing at least 15,000 transactions over the last 10 years and ranges from 1 to 291; (3) figures based on a weighted average of Census Division estimates; all figures are for the period ending December 31, 2007
Source: Office of Federal Housing Enterprise Oversight, House Price Index, February 26, 2008

House Price Valuations

Area	Q1 2000	Q1 2001	Q1 2002	Q1 2003	Q1 2004	Q1 2005	Q1 2006	Q1 2007	Q1 2008
MD[1]	-23.3	-19.6	-10.7	0.9	6.4	17.7	20.8	15.3	9.8

Note: Figures show the percentage of over- or under-valuation of single family homes relative to statistically normal house values (e.g. a value of 23.6 indicates that house values are 23.6% overvalued). Statistically normal house values are based on house prices, interest rates, household incomes, population densities, and any historical premiums or discounts metropolitan areas have exhibited over time; (1) Figures cover the Metropolitan Division - see Appendix B for areas included
Source: Global Insight/National City Corporation, House Prices in America, May 2008

Median Home Prices

Area	2005	2006	2007[r]	Percent Change 2006 to 2007
MD[1]	416.8	433.0	443.7	2.5
U.S. Average	219.0	221.9	217.9	-1.8

Note: Figures are median sales prices of existing single-family homes in thousands of dollars; (r) revised; n/a not available; (1) Metropolitan Division - see Appendix B for areas included
Source: National Association of Realtors, Metropolitan Area Prices, 1st Quarter 2008

Housing: Year Structure Built

Area	1990 -2000	1980 -1989	1970 -1979	1960 -1969	1950 -1959	1940 -1949	Before 1940	Median Year
City	15.5	10.2	12.2	25.7	20.8	6.5	9.0	1965
MSA[1]	7.5	8.1	11.2	15.7	19.4	13.0	25.1	1956
U.S.	17.0	15.8	18.5	13.7	12.7	7.3	15.0	1971

Note: Figures are percentages; (1) Metropolitan Statistical Area - see Appendix A for areas included
Source: Census 2000, Summary File 3

HEALTH

Health Risk Data

Category	Area[1] (%)	U.S. (%)
Adults who have been told they have high blood pressure[3]	23.1	25.5
Adults who have been told they have high blood cholesterol[3]	34.5	35.6
Adults who have been told they have diabetes[2]	7.3	7.5
Adults who have been told they have arthritis[3]	21.5	27.0
Adults who have been told they currently have asthma	6.9	8.5
Adults who are current smokers	16.5	20.1
Adults who are heavy drinkers[4]	4.7	4.9
Adults who are overweight (BMI 25.0 - 29.9)	37.0	36.5
Adults who are obese (BMI 30.0 - 99.8)	21.7	25.1

Note: Data as of 2006 unless otherwise noted; (1) Figures cover the Metropolitan Division - see Appendix B for areas included; (2) Figures do not include pregnancy-related diabetes, pre-diabetes or borderline diabetes; (3) 2005 data; (4) Heavy drinkers are classified as adult men having more than two drinks per day or adult women having more than one drink per day
Source: Centers for Disease Control and Prevention, Behaviorial Risk Factor Surveillance System, SMART: Selected Metropolitan/Micropolitan Area Risk Trends, 2005, 2006

Mortality Rates for the Top 10 Causes of Death in the U.S.

ICD-10[a] Sub-Chapter	ICD-10[a] Code	Age-Adjusted Mortality Rate[1] per 100,000 population	
		County[2]	U.S.
Malignant neoplasms	C00-C97	182.5	186.5
Ischaemic heart diseases	I20-I25	146.1	152.3
Other forms of heart disease	I30-I51	52.3	51.5
Cerebrovascular diseases	I60-I69	40.1	50.0
Chronic lower respiratory diseases	J40-J47	29.1	42.6
Diabetes mellitus	E10-E14	22.1	24.8
Other degenerative diseases of the nervous system	G30-G31	18.9	22.6
Other external causes of accidental injury	W00-X59	15.0	21.4
Influenza and pneumonia	J10-J18	19.6	20.7
Hypertensive diseases	I10-I13	12.3	18.2

Note: (a) ICD-10 = International Classification of Diseases 10th Revision; (1) Mortality rates are a three year average covering 2003-2005; (2) Figures cover Morris County
Source: Centers for Disease Control and Prevention, National Center for Health Statistics. Compressed Mortality File 1999-2004. CDC WONDER On-line Database, compiled from Compressed Mortality File 1999-2005 Series 20 No. 2K, 2008.

Mortality Rates for Selected Causes of Death

ICD-10[a] Sub-Chapter	ICD-10[a] Code	Age-Adjusted Mortality Rate[1] per 100,000 population	
		County[2]	U.S.
Assault	X85-Y09	*0.8	5.9
Human immunodeficiency virus (HIV) disease	B20-B24	1.3	4.5
Intentional self-harm	X60-X84	5.4	10.8
Malnutrition	E40-E46	*1.1	1.0
Obesity and other hyperalimentation	E65-E68	1.4	1.4
Organic, including symptomatic, mental disorders	F01-F09	18.0	16.8
Transport accidents	V01-V99	6.8	16.1
Viral hepatitis	B15-B19	1.4	1.8

Note: (a) ICD-10 = International Classification of Diseases 10th Revision; (1) Mortality rates are a three year average covering 2003-2005; (2) Figures cover Morris County; (*) Unreliable data as per CDC
Source: Centers for Disease Control and Prevention, National Center for Health Statistics. Compressed Mortality File 1999-2004. CDC WONDER On-line Database, compiled from Compressed Mortality File 1999-2005 Series 20 No. 2K, 2008.

Distribution of Physicians[1]

Area	Total	Family/ General Practice	Specialties	
			Medical	Surgical
Morris County (number)	1,369	131	617	314
Morris County (rate per 10,000 pop.)	27.9	2.7	12.6	6.4
U.S. (rate per 10,000 pop.)	17.7	4.6	6.9	4.3

Note: Data as of 2005; (1) Includes all non-federal, patient-care, office-based MDs
Source: Area Resource File (ARF). June 2007. U.S. Department of Health and Human Services, Health Resources and Services Administration, Bureau of Health Professions, Rockville, MD.

Hospitals

There were no hospitals listed within the city limits.
AHA Guide to the Healthcare Field 2008

According to *U.S. News,* the New York-Northern New Jersey-Long Island, NY-NJ-PA metro area is home to 14 of the best hospitals in the U.S.: **Hackensack University Medical Center**; **Hospital for Special Surgery**; **Kessler Institute for Rehabilitation**; **Lenox Hill Hospital**; **Long Island Jewish Medical Center**; **Memorial Sloan-Kettering Cancer Center**; **Montefiore Medical Center**; **Mount Sinai Medical Center**; **New York Eye and Ear Infirmary**; **New York-Presbyterian Univ. Hosp. of Columbia and Cornell**; **NYU Medical Center**; **Robert Wood Johnson University Hospital**; **Saint Francis Hospital**; **University Hospital**. *U.S. News Online, "America's Best Hospitals 2007"*

EDUCATION

Public School District Statistics

District Name	Schls	Pupils	Pupil/ Teacher Ratio	Minority Pupils[1] (%)	Free Lunch Eligible[2] (%)	IEP[3] (%)
Morris County Vocational	3	549	11.1	22.4	2.0	40.3
Morris Hills Regional	2	2,795	12.0	23.4	5.0	27.1
Rockaway Borough	2	611	13.8	29.8	10.0	20.9
Rockaway Township	6	2,844	11.1	22.3	4.6	27.8

Note: Table includes regular local school districts with 2,000 or more students; (1) Percentage of students that are not white, non-Hispanic; (2) Percentage of students that are eligible for the free lunch program; (3) Percentage of students that have an Individualized Education Program.
Source: U.S. Department of Education, National Center for Education Statistics, Common Core of Data, Local Education Agency (School District) Universe Survey: School Year 2005-2006; U.S. Department of Education, National Center for Education Statistics, Common Core of Data, Public Elementary/Secondary School Universe Survey: School Year 2005-2006

Highest Level of Education

Area	Less than H.S.	H.S. Diploma	Some College, No Deg.	Associate Degree	Bachelors Degree	Masters Degree	Profess. School Degree	Doctorate Degree
City	7.1	24.9	19.1	7.2	29.2	9.5	2.1	0.8
MSA[1]	21.5	26.4	16.5	5.6	17.7	8.2	3.0	1.2
U.S.	19.4	28.4	21.2	6.4	15.7	5.9	2.0	1.0

Note: Figures are 2007 estimated percentages and cover persons age 25 and over; (1) Metropolitan Statistical Area - see Appendix B for areas included
Source: Claritas, Inc.

Educational Attainment by Race

Area	High School Graduate (%)					Bachelor's Degree (%)				
	Total	White	Black	Asian	Hisp.[2]	Total	White	Black	Asian	Hisp.[2]
City	93.0	93.1	81.8	93.6	91.4	41.4	39.7	42.1	72.6	32.6
MSA[1]	81.6	85.3	73.7	90.4	60.2	31.5	36.0	15.5	65.0	12.8
U.S.	80.4	83.6	72.3	80.4	52.4	24.4	26.1	14.3	44.1	10.4

Note: Figures shown cover persons 25 years old and over; (1) Metropolitan Statistical Area - see Appendix A for areas included; (2) people of Hispanic origin can be of any race
Source: Census 2000, Summary File 3

School Enrollment by Type

Area	Grades KG to 8				Grades 9 to 12			
	Public		Private		Public		Private	
	Enrollment	%	Enrollment	%	Enrollment	%	Enrollment	%
City	2,714	84.5	499	15.5	1,073	93.6	73	6.4
MSA[1]	234,826	86.3	37,148	13.7	99,591	86.8	15,189	13.2
U.S.	33,526,011	88.7	4,285,121	11.3	14,848,628	90.6	1,532,323	9.4

Note: Figures shown cover persons 3 years old and over; (1) Metropolitan Statistical Area - see Appendix A for areas included
Source: Census 2000, Summary File 3

School Enrollment by Race

Area	Grades KG to 8 (%)				Grades 9 to 12 (%)			
	White	Black	Asian	Hisp.[1]	White	Black	Asian	Hisp.[1]
City	86.2	3.0	6.8	6.5	90.9	1.1	4.8	7.1
MSA[2]	60.3	26.3	4.0	15.0	58.2	27.5	4.1	15.7
U.S.	68.5	15.5	3.3	16.8	68.8	15.5	3.8	15.7

Note: Figures shown cover persons 3 years old and over; (1) people of Hispanic origin can be of any race; (2) Metropolitan Statistical Area - see Appendix A for areas included
Source: Census 2000, Summary File 3

Average Salaries of Public School Classroom Teachers

District	2005-06		2006-07		Percent Change 2005-06 to 2006-07
	Dollars	Rank[1]	Dollars	Rank[1]	
New Jersey	58,156	5	59,920	3	3.03
U.S. Average	49,026	-	50,816	-	3.65

Note: (1) State rank ranges from 1 to 51.
Source: National Education Association, Rankings & Estimates: Rankings of the States 2006 and Estimates of School Statistics 2007, December 2007

Higher Education

Four-Year Colleges			Two-Year Colleges			Medical Schools[1]	Law Schools[2]	Voc/ Tech[3]
Public	Private Non-profit	Private For-profit	Public	Private Non-profit	Private For-profit			
0	0	0	0	0	0	0	0	0

Note: Figures cover institutions located within the city limits; (1) includes schools accredited by the Liaison Committee on Medical Education and the American Osteopathic Association; (2) includes American Bar Association-accredited law schools; (3) includes all schools with programs that are less than 2 years.
Source: National Center for Education Statistics, The Integrated Postsecondary Education System (IPEDS) Peer Analysis System, 2007; www.usnews.com, Law and Medical School Directories, 2009

PRESIDENTIAL ELECTION

2004 Presidential Election Results

Area	Bush	Kerry	Nader	Other
Morris County	57.5	41.7	0.5	0.3
U.S.	50.7	48.3	0.4	0.6

Note: Results are percentages and may not add to 100% due to rounding
Source: Dave Leip's Atlas of U.S. Presidential Elections, www.uselectionatlas.org

EMPLOYERS

Major Employers

Company Name	Industry	Type of Site
Atlantic Health System	General medical and surgical hospitals	Single
Budget Rent-A-Car	Passenger car rental	Single
County Hall of Records	Courts	Branch
County of Essex	Executive offices	Headquarters
Domestic Telecom	Telephone communication, except radio	Single
Gateway Security Inc	Detective and armored car services	Single
Hoffmann-La Roche Inc	Noncommercial research organizations	Headquarters
Horizon BC/BS of NJ	Hospital and medical service plans	Headquarters
Linde Inc	Industrial gases	Headquarters
National Envelope	Envelopes	Single
New Jrsey Trnst Rail Operations	Colleges and universities	Headquarters
Novartis Pharmaceuticals Corp	Analystical instruments	Headquarters
Obgyn	Miscellaneous personal services	Branch
Onegci Inc	Computer related services, nec	Single
Overlook Hospital Association	General medical and surgical hospitals	Headquarters
Picatinny Army Arsenal	National	Branch
Prudential	Life insurance	Headquarters
Saint Clares Health System	General medical and surgical hospitals	Headquarters
Tacom-Ardec	National security	Branch
Umdnj	Colleges and universities	Headquarters

Note: Companies shown are located within the Newark metropolitan area; nec = not elsewhere classified.
Source: www.zapdata.com, May 2008

PUBLIC SAFETY

Crime Rate

Area	All Crimes	Violent Crimes				Property Crimes		
		Murder	Forcible Rape	Robbery	Aggrav. Assault	Burglary	Larceny -Theft	Motor Vehicle Theft
City	1,944.5	0.0	11.7	23.5	23.5	148.7	1,658.9	78.3
Metro[1]	2,759.4	8.7	13.8	198.2	194.6	442.2	1,384.0	517.9
U.S.	3,808.1	5.7	30.9	149.4	287.5	729.4	2,206.8	398.4

Note: Figures are crimes per 100,000 population; (1) Metropolitan Division - see Appendix B for areas included
Source: FBI Uniform Crime Reports, 2006

Hate Crimes

Area	Number of Quarters Reported	Bias Motivation				
		Race	Religion	Sexual Orientation	Ethnicity	Disability
City	4	2	2	0	0	0

Source: Federal Bureau of Investigation, Hate Crime Statistics 2006

RECREATION

Culture

Dance[1]	Theatre[1]	Instrumental Music[1]	Vocal Music[1]	Series/ Festivals	Museums	Zoos and Aquariums[2]
0	0	0	0	0	0	0

Note: (1) Number of professional perfoming groups; (2) AZA-accredited
Source: The Grey House Performing Arts Directory, 2007; Official Museum Directory, 2008; Association of Zoos & Aquariums, AZA Member Zoos & Aquariums, June 2008

Professional Sports Teams

Team Name	League
New York Mets	Major League Baseball (MLB)
New York Yankees	Major League Baseball (MLB)
New York Red Bulls	Major League Soccer (MLS)
New Jersey Nets	National Basketball Association (NBA)
New York Knicks	National Basketball Association (NBA)
New York Giants	National Football League (NFL)
New York Jets	National Football League (NFL)
New Jersey Devils	National Hockey League (NHL)
New York Islanders	National Hockey League (NHL)
New York Rangers	National Hockey League (NHL)

Note: Includes teams located in the New York-Northern New Jersey metro area.
Source: Original research

MEDIA

Newspapers

Name	News Focus	Frequency	Circulation
Suburban Life	Community	Weekly	20,000

Note: Includes newspapers with offices located in the city
Source: MediaContactsPro, March 2008

Television Stations

Name	Ch.	Network(s)	Type	Ownership
WCBS	2	CBS	Commercial	CBS
WNBC	4	NBC	Commercial	General Electric Corporation
WNYW	5	Fox	Commercial	Fox Television Stations Inc.
WABC	7	ABC	Commercial	ABC Inc.
WWOR	9	UPN	Commercial	Fox Television Stations Inc.
WPIX	11	WBN	Commercial	Tribune Broadcasting Company
WNET	13	PBS	Public	Educational Broadcasting Corporation
WLIW	21	PBS	Public	Long Island Educational TV Council Inc.
WNYE	25	PBS	Public	New York City Board of Education
WPXN	31	Pax	Commercial	Paxson Communications Corporation
WXTV	41	Univision	Commercial	Univision Holding
WNJU	47	Telemundo	Commercial	Telemundo Group Inc.
WTBY	54	n/a	Commercial	Trinity Broadcasting Network
WLNY	55	n/a	Commercial	Michael C. Pascucci
WRNN	62	n/a	Commercial	WRNN-TV Associates L.P.
WMBC	63	n/a	Commercial	Mountain Broadcasting Corporation
WHSI	67	n/a	Commercial	USA Broadcasting Group
WHSE	68	n/a	Commercial	USA Broadcasting Group

Note: Stations included cover the New York DMA (Designated Market Area); n/a not available
BurrellesLuce, MediaContacts Online, January 2007

Major AM Radio Stations

Call Letters	Freq. (kHz)	Station Type	Target Audience	Station Format	Music Format
WMCA	570	n/a	General/Religious	Music/News/Talk	n/a
WFAN	660	n/a	General	News/Sports/Talk	n/a
WOR	710	n/a	General	Music/News	Reggae
WABC	770	n/a	General	n/a	n/a
WNYC	820	Public	General	Music/Talk	Blues
WCBS	880	Commercial	General	Music/News/Sports	Reggae
WGHQ	920	n/a	General	Music	n/a
WWDJ	970	n/a	General/Religious	Music/Talk	n/a
WINS	1010	n/a	General	News	n/a
WHLI	1100	Commercial	General	Music	Adult Standards
WBBR	1130	n/a	General/Men	Music/News	Reggae
WVNJ	1160	n/a	General	n/a	n/a
WOBM	1160	n/a	General	Music	n/a
WLIB	1190	n/a	General	News/Talk	n/a
WGNY	1220	n/a	General	News/Talk	n/a
WMTR	1250	Commercial	General	Music	Adult Standards
WADO	1280	Commercial	General/Hispanic	News/Sports/Talk	n/a
WWRV	1330	n/a	General/Hisp/Rel	Music/News/Talk	n/a
WELV	1370	n/a	General	Music	n/a
WEOK	1390	Commercial	General/Hispanic	Music/Sports	Latin
WLNA	1420	n/a	General	Music/News/Sports/Talk	n/a
WNSW	1430	n/a	Ethnic/General	Music/News/Talk	n/a
WZRC	1480	n/a	Asian	Talk	n/a
WQEW	1560	n/a	Child/Gen/Yng Adlt	Educational	n/a
WLIM	1580	Commercial	Ethnic/General	Music/News	World Music
WWRL	1600	n/a	General	Music/Talk	Reggae
WWRU	1660	n/a	Asian/General/Hispanic	News/Talk	n/a

Note: Stations included cover the New York DMA (Designated Market Area); n/a not available
Source: BurrellesLuce, MediaContacts Online, January 2007

Major FM Radio Stations

Call Letters	Freq. (mHz)	Station Type	Target Audience	Station Format	Music Format
WFSO	88.3	n/a	Religious	Educational/Music/News	n/a
WFDU	89.1	College	General	Music	n/a
WFUV	90.7	College	General	Music/News/Sports	Folk
WPAT	93.1	Commercial	General/Hispanic	News/Talk	n/a
WRKI	95.1	n/a	General	Music/News/Talk	n/a
WQHT	97.1	n/a	General	Music/News/Talk	n/a
WSKQ	97.9	Commercial	General/Hispanic	Music/News/Talk	Latin
WRKS	98.7	n/a	General/Women	News/Talk	Rhythm & Blues
WBAI	99.5	Non-Comm	General	Music/Talk	Reggae
WHUD	100.7	n/a	General	Music/News/Talk	n/a
WPDH	101.5	Commercial	General	Music	Classic Rock
WKTU	103.5	n/a	General/Women	Music/News/Talk	Urban Contemp.
WAXQ	104.3	n/a	General	Music/Talk	n/a
WSPK	104.7	n/a	General	Music/News/Talk	n/a
WWPR	105.1	Commercial	General	Music	Rhythm & Blues
WBLI	106.1	Commercial	General	Music/Talk	Top 40
WLTW	106.7	n/a	General	Music	n/a
WBLS	107.5	n/a	Black/General	Music	n/a
WEBE	107.9	n/a	General	Music/News	n/a

Note: Stations included cover the New York DMA (Designated Market Area); n/a not available
BurrellesLuce, MediaContacts Online, January 2007

CLIMATE

Average and Extreme Temperatures

Temperature	Jan	Feb	Mar	Apr	May	Jun	Jul	Aug	Sep	Oct	Nov	Dec	Yr.
Extreme High (°F)	74	76	89	94	98	102	105	103	105	93	85	72	105
Average High (°F)	38	41	50	61	72	81	86	84	77	66	54	42	63
Average Temp. (°F)	32	33	42	52	63	72	77	76	68	57	47	36	55
Average Low (°F)	24	25	33	43	53	62	68	67	59	48	39	28	46
Extreme Low (°F)	-8	-7	6	16	33	41	52	45	35	25	15	-1	-8

Note: Figures cover the years 1935-1995
Source: National Climatic Data Center, International Station Meteorological Climate Summary, 9/96

Average Precipitation/Snowfall/Humidity

Precip./Humidity	Jan	Feb	Mar	Apr	May	Jun	Jul	Aug	Sep	Oct	Nov	Dec	Yr.
Avg. Precip. (in.)	3.4	3.0	4.0	3.7	3.9	3.3	4.2	4.1	3.6	3.0	3.8	3.4	43.5
Avg. Snowfall (in.)	8	8	5	1	Tr	0	0	0	0	Tr	1	5	27
Avg. Rel. Hum. 7am (%)	73	71	69	67	70	71	72	76	79	78	76	74	73
Avg. Rel. Hum. 4pm (%)	58	54	51	48	51	51	52	54	55	53	57	59	54

Note: Figures cover the years 1935-1995; Tr = Trace amounts (<0.05 in. of rain; <0.5 in. of snow)
Source: National Climatic Data Center, International Station Meteorological Climate Summary, 9/96

Weather Conditions

Temperature			Daytime Sky			Precipitation		
5°F & below	32°F & below	90°F & above	Clear	Partly cloudy	Cloudy	0.01 inch or more precip.	0.1 inch or more snow/ice	Thunder-storms
2	90	24	80	146	139	122	16	46

Note: Figures are average number of days per year and cover the years 1935-1995
Source: National Climatic Data Center, International Station Meteorological Climate Summary, 9/96

HAZARDOUS WASTE

Superfund Sites

Rockaway has four hazardous waste sites on the EPA's Superfund Final National Priorities List: **Picatinny Arsenal (USARMY)**; **Rockaway Township Wells**; **Rockaway Borough Well Field**; **Radiation Technology, Inc.**. *U.S. Environmental Protection Agency, Final National Priorities List, June 23, 2008*

AIR & WATER QUALITY

Air Quality Index

Area	Percent of Days when Air Quality was...[2]				AQI Statistics	
	Good	Moderate	Unhealthy for Sensitive Groups	Unhealthy	Maximum	Median
MSA[1]	54.8	39.2	5.5	0.5	151	47

Note: The Air Quality Index (AQI) is an index for reporting daily air quality. EPA calculates the AQI for five major air pollutants regulated by the Clean Air Act: ground-level ozone, particle pollution (also known as particulate matter), carbon monoxide, sulfur dioxide, and nitrogen dioxide. The AQI runs from 0 to 500. The higher the AQI value, the greater the level of air pollution and the greater the health concern. There are six AQI categories: "Good" The AQI is between 0 and 50. Air quality is considered satisfactory; "Moderate" The AQI is between 51 and 100. Air quality is acceptable; "Unhealthy for Sensitive Groups" When AQI values are between 101 and 150, members of sensitive groups may experience health effects; "Unhealthy" When AQI values are between 151 and 200 everyone may begin to experience health effects; "Very Unhealthy" AQI values between 201 and 300 trigger a health alert; "Hazardous" AQI values over 300 trigger health warnings of emergency conditions; (1) Metropolitan Statistical Area - see Appendix A for areas included; (2) Based on 365 days with AQI data in 2007.
Source: U.S. Environmental Protection Agency, Air Quality Index Report, 2007

Air Quality Index Pollutants

Area	Percent of Days when AQI Pollutant was...[2]					
	Carbon Monoxide	Nitrogen Dioxide	Ozone	Sulfur Dioxide	Particulate Matter 2.5	Particulate Matter 10
MSA[1]	0.0	0.0	42.2	0.0	57.8	0.0

Note: The Air Quality Index (AQI) is an index for reporting daily air quality. EPA calculates the AQI for five major air pollutants regulated by the Clean Air Act: ground-level ozone, particle pollution (also known as particulate matter), carbon monoxide, sulfur dioxide, and nitrogen dioxide. The AQI runs from 0 to 500. The higher the AQI value, the greater the level of air pollution and the greater the health concern; (1) Metropolitan Statistical Area - see Appendix A for areas included; (2) Based on 365 days with AQI data in 2007.
Source: U.S. Environmental Protection Agency, Air Quality Index Report, 2007

Air Quality Index Trends

Area	Trend Sites (17)								All Sites (46)
	1999	2000	2001	2002	2003	2004	2005	2006	2006
MSA[1]	26	12	18	29	11	7	11	13	14

Note: An AQI value greater than 100 indicates that air quality would have been in the unhealthful range on that day. Data from exceptional events are not included. These counts are presented in two ways. First, the counts are based on sites having an adequate record of monitoring data during the trend period (trend sites). These counts represent the relative change in the number of days with AQI values greater than 100. In the last column, the counts are based on all sites with data in the most recent year (because it is possible for a site to have data in the most recent year but not enough data to be a trend site); (1) Metropolitan Statistical Area - see Appendix A for areas included.
Source: U.S. Environmental Protection Agency, Office of Air and Radiation, Air Trends, Factbook and Related Information, Air Pollution Trends in Selected Metropolitan Areas 2006

Maximum Air Pollutant Concentrations

	Particulate Matter 10 (ug/m^3)	Particulate Matter 2.5 (ug/m^3)	Ozone (ppm)	Carbon Monoxide (ppm)	Sulfur Dioxide (ppm)	Nitrogen Dioxide (ppm)	Lead (ug/m^3)
MSA[1] Level	n/a	41	0.114	3	0.034	0.034	0.02
NAAQS[2]	150	35	0.125	9	0.140	0.053	1.50
Met NAAQS[2]	Yes	No	Yes	Yes	Yes	Yes	Yes

Note: Data from exceptional events are not included; (1) Metropolitan Statistical Area - see Appendix A for areas included; (2) National Ambient Air Quality Standards; n/a not available
Concentrations: Particulate Matter 10 (coarse particulate) - highest second maximum 24-hour concentration; Particulate Matter 2.5 (fine particulate) - highest 98th percentile 24-hour concentration; Ozone - highest second daily maximum 1-hour concentration; Carbon Monoxide - highest second maximum non-overlapping 8-hour concentration; Sulfur Dioxide - highest second maximum 24-hour concentration; Nitrogen Dioxide - highest arithmetic mean concentration; Lead - highest quarterly maximum concentration
Units: ppm = parts per million; ug/m^3 = micrograms per cubic meter
Source: U.S. Environmental Protection Agency, MSA Factbook 2006, Air Quality Statistics by City

Drinking Water

Water System Name	Pop. Served	Primary Water Source Type	Violations[1]	
			Health Based	Monitoring/ Reporting
Rockaway Twp Water Dept	15,000	Ground	n/a	n/a

Note: (1) Based on violation data from January 1, 2007 to December 31, 2007 (includes unresolved violations from earlier years)
Source: U.S. Environmental Protection Agency, Office of Ground Water and Drinking Water, Safe Drinking Water Information System (based on data extracted April 15, 2008)

South Brunswick, New Jersey

Background

South Brunswick is located in Middlesex County, 33 miles southwest of Newark and 46 miles from New York City.

South Brunswick was incorporated in 1798. In the 18th century, it was a rural agricultural region with small clustered settlements located on major transportation routes. Early settlers took advantage of fertile soils and favorable growing conditions. The 19th century brought increased commercial and residential growth, which coincided with new transportation routes. The Straight Turnpike, now Route 1, was built in 1804. In 1872, the state Legislature reduced the size of South Brunswick with the creation of Cranbury from the southern portion of South Brunswick. In 1919, the size of South Brunswick was further reduced with the formation of Plainsboro.

By 1980, South Brunswick's population approached 18,000; by 1990, it was over 25,000. Despite its rapid growth, much of South Brunswick's 42 square miles remain undeveloped with significant amounts of wetlands, woodlands and open space.

Manufacturing and wholesale trade make up most of the economic activity in South Brunswick. The township also benefits from its location along the Route 1 corridor between Princeton and New Brunswick, which has recently become popular with high tech companies.

There are over 2,000 acres of municipal, county and state park land within South Brunswick. Recreational facilities include a Community Center and Senior Center. The township is also close to many art and music centers in nearby Princeton and New Brunswick.

Recent development includes a Volunteers of America project, aided by a grant from the South Brunswick Township Affordable Housing Trust Fund, that includes renovation of an existing apartment complex.

South Brunswick has a seasonal climate with hot summers and cold winters. Median summer temperatures average 70 degrees, while winter averages can be as low as 20 degrees during December and January. The city averages 4.5 inches of rainfall per month from April to October and 7.5 inches of snowfall per month from December to March.

Rankings

General Rankings

- Edison* was ranked #161 out of 375 metro areas in *Cities Ranked & Rated*. Criteria: cost of living; climate; crime; transportation; economy and jobs; education; arts and culture; health and healthcare; leisure; quality of life. *Cities Ranked & Rated, 2nd Edition, 2007*

- Edison* was ranked #50 out of 379 metro areas in *Places Rated Almanac*. Criteria: health care; education; recreation; transportation; ambience; climate; crime; housing costs; jobs. *Places Rated Almanac, 7th Edition, 2007*

Business/Finance Rankings

- The nation's 100 largest metro areas were analysed in terms of the percentage of households entering some stage of foreclosure in 2007. The Edison* metro area ranked #61 out of 100 (#1 = highest foreclosure rate). *RealtyTrac, "Year-End 2007 Metropolitan Foreclosure Report"*

- The New York* metro area was identified as one of the most expensive places to rent in the U.S. The area ranked #61 out of 10 markets with an average effective rent of $2,720 per month. The rental figures cover apartment properties in complexes with 40 or more units (20 or more units in California and Arizona). The figures are blended average rents, which include all unit sizes. Effective rents include free rent incentives and other landlord concessions. *Wall Street Journal Online, January 17, 2008*

- The New York* metro area was selected as one of "America's Most Wired Cities" by *Forbes*. The metro area was ranked #9 out of 30. Criteria: percentage of Internet users with high-speed access; the range of service providers within a city; availability of public wireless hot spots. *Forbes, "America's Most Wired Cities," January 10, 2008*

- Middlesex* was selected as one of the best places to start and grow a company by *Entrepreneur* and the National Policy Research Council. The Middlesex* metro area ranked #35 out of 50 large metro areas. Criteria: business formation and growth (firms started four to 14 years ago that still employ at least 5 people and experienced rapid growth over the last four years). *Entrepreneur/National Policy Research Council, "Hot Cities for Entrepreneurs," September 2006*

- The New York* metro area was selected as one of "America's Greediest Cities" by *Forbes*. The area was ranked #6 out of 10. Criteria: number of Forbes 400 (*Forbes* annual list of the richest Americans) members per capita. *Forbes, "America's Greediest Cities," December 7, 2007*

- Edison* was cited as one of America's top large metros (population over 1 million) for new and expanded facility projects in 2007. The area appeared in the top 10 with 72 projects. *Site Selection, "Top Metropolitan Area Awards," March 2008*

- Intel, in partnership with Sperling's BestPlaces, ranked the 80 "Best Cities for Teleworking" in America. The New York* metro area ranked #6 among extra large metro areas. The study identifies cities that hold the greatest potential for teleworking based on a host of factors including typical commuting times, fuel prices, availability of broadband Internet access and percentage of the population in telework friendly jobs. The study also factored in extreme climate and natural hazards. *Intel, "Best Cities for Teleworking," March 30, 2006*

- The Edison* metro area appeared on the Milken Institute "2007 Best Performing Cities" index. Rank: #133 out of 200 large metro areas. Criteria: job growth; wage and salary growth; high-tech output growth. *Milken Institute, "2007 Best Performing Cities"*

- The Middlesex* metro area was selected as one of "The Top 20 Boom Towns in America." *Business 2.0* magazine and econometric research firm Global Insight compared 319 metropolitan areas in the U.S. and ranked the 61 with populations over 1 million. Criteria: a weighted formula that includes forecast growth rates in sectors that contain the economy's 10 most skilled occupational clusters; the prevalence of college degrees in the local workforce; median salary. The area ranked #8 among large metro areas. *Business 2.0 Magazine, March 2004*

- Middlesex* was identified as one of the 100 "Most Unwired Cities" in the U.S. The area ranked #76 out of the 100 largest metro areas in the U.S. Criteria: number of public and commercial wireless access points (hotspots); airports with wireless Internet access; broadband availability; local wireless networks; and wireless email devices. *Intel, "Most Unwired Cities Survey," June 7, 2005*

- New York* was ranked #12 out of 125 regions worldwide in terms of its "Knowledge Competitiveness Index." The index attempts to measure the knowledge-based development taking place throughout the world and is based on 19 measures of economic performance that indicate a region's ability to translate its knowledge capacity into economic value. *Robert Huggins Associates, World Knowledge Competitiveness Index 2005*

- *Forbes* ranked the 200 most populous metro areas in the U.S. in terms of the "Best Places for Business and Careers." The Edison* metro area was ranked #51. Criteria: business costs (labor, energy, tax and office space expenses); living costs (housing, transportation, food and other household expenditures); education levels of the work force; job growth; income growth; migration trends; crime rates; and culture/leisure. *Forbes, "Best Places for Business and Careers," March 19, 2008*

- *Fortune* ranked the 100 largest metro areas in the U.S. in terms of projected median home price change in 2007. The Edison* metro area ranked #75. *Fortune.com, "Hot Spots, Cold Spots"*

- The New York* metro area was identified as one of "America's Most Overpriced Real Estate Markets." The area ranked #7 out of 10. Criteria: housing "P/E" ratio (a market's median home price divided by annual rents minus taxes and insurance); housing affordability. *Forbes.com, "America's Most Overpriced Real Estate Markets," May 11, 2007*

Health/Environment Rankings

- 100 of the largest metro areas in the U.S. were analyzed in terms of their current drought severity. The New York* metro area ranked #75 (#1 = driest). The rankings were based on statistics such as long-term precipitation trends and patterns and the Palmer drought indices. *Sperling's BestPlaces, www.BestPlaces.net, "America's Drought-Riskiest Cities," November 2007*

- Doctors at the Harvard School of Public Health ranked 40 metropolitan areas based on data from the government-sponsored Hospital Quality Alliance program. The program tracks the performance of individual hospitals in treating patients for three common health problems: heart attacks, congestive heart failure, and pneumonia. The New York* metro area ranked #17 in quality of care for heart attacks, #8 for congestive heart failure, and #34 for pneumonia. *New England Journal of Medicine, July 21, 2005*

- *Reader's Digest* ranked the 50 largest metro areas in the U.S. in terms of how "clean" they are. The New York* metro area ranked #49. Criteria: air quality; water quality; toxic industrial pollution; Superfund sites; and sanitation. *Reader's Digest, "The 50 Cleanest (and Dirtiest) Cities in America," July 2005*

- The American Academy of Dermatology ranked 32 U.S. metropolitan regions in terms of their residents knowledge, attitude and behaviors towards tanning and sun protection. The New York* metro area ranked #2. The results of the study are based on an online national survey of 3,342 respondents. *American Academy of Dermatology, "RAYS: Your Grade," May 7, 2007*

- The Edison* metro area appeared in *Country Home's* "2008 Best Green Places" report. The area ranked #265 out of 379. Criteria: official energy policies; green power; green buildings; availability of fresh, locally grown food. *Country Home, "2008 Best Green Places"*

- Wyeth Consumer Healthcare, in partnership with Sperling's BestPlaces, ranked the nation's 50 most populous metro areas in terms of five key health factors. The New York* metro area ranked #43. Criteria: physical activity; health status; nutrition; lifestyle pursuits; and mental wellness. *Wyeth Consumer Healthcare, "Centrum Healthiest Cities Study," April 19, 2005*

- HealthGrades surveyed over 41,000 individuals on doctor satisfaction and ranked the 20 largest metro areas based on the highest "definitely yes" responses to the question "Do you trust the physician to make decisions/recommendations that are in your best interest?" The New York* metro area ranked #10. *HealthGrades.com, "Top Cities in Doctor-Trust," September 7, 2006*
- New York* was identified as a "2008 Asthma Capital." The area ranked #38 out of the nation's 100 largest metropolitan areas. Twelve factors were used to identify the most challenging places to live for people with asthma: estimated prevalence; self-reported prevalence; crude death rate for asthma; annual pollen score; annual air quality; public smoking laws; number of board-certified asthma specialists; school inhaler access laws; rescue medication use; controller medication use; uninsured rate; poverty rate. *Asthma and Allergy Foundation of America, "2008 Asthma Capitals"*
- New York* was identified as a "Spring Allergy Capital." The area ranked #79 out of 100. Three groups of factors were used to identify the most severe cities for people with allergies during the spring season: annual pollen levels; medicine utilization; access to board-certified allergists. *Asthma and Allergy Foundation of America, "2007 Spring Allergy Capital Rankings"*
- New York* was identified as a "Fall Allergy Capital." The area ranked #69 out of 100. Three groups of factors were used to identify the most severe cities for people with allergies during the fall season: annual pollen levels; medicine utilization; access to board-certified allergists. *Asthma and Allergy Foundation of America, "2007 Fall Allergy Capital Rankings"*
- Ortho-McNeil Neurologics, in partnership with Sperling's BestPlaces, analyzed 110 metro areas and identified those U.S. cities with the highest prevalence of factors that are most commonly associated with migraine headaches. The Middlesex* metro area ranked #106. Criteria: number of migraine-related drug prescriptions per capita; lifestyle factors that can contribute to migraines; environmental factors that can trigger migraines; and consumption of migraine-triggering foods. *Ortho-McNeil Neurologics, "America's Migraine Hot Spots," March 14, 2006*
- Sperling's BestPlaces ranked 331 metro areas and identified the most and least stressful U.S. cities. The Middlesex* metro area ranked #84 out of the 100 largest metro areas (#1 = most stressful). Criteria: divorce rate; unemployment rate; violent and property crime; suicide rate; commute time; mental health; alcohol consumption; cloudy days. *Sperling's BestPlaces, www.BestPlaces.net, "America's Most (and Least) Stressful Cities," January 9, 2004*
- An analysis of the "Best & Worst Cities for Sleep" was conducted by Sperling's BestPlaces. The study ranked America's 50 most populated metro areas. The Middlesex* metro area ranked #15 (#1 = best city for sleep). Criteria: number of days residents didn't get enough rest or sleep during the past month; average length of daily commute; divorce rate; unemployment rate. *Sperling's BestPlaces, www.BestPlaces.net, "Best & Worst Cities for Sleep," 2006*
- HealthGrades evaluated the performance of America's 25 most populous metropolitan areas by measuring the outcomes of five of the highest volume and most widely studied procedures and diagnoses: coronary artery bypass graft surgery; percutaneus coronary interventions; acute myocardial infarction/heart attack in angioplasty-capable hospitals; congestive heart failure; and community acquired pneumonia. The New York* metro area ranked #17. *HealthGrades, "HealthGrades Hospital Quality in America Study," October 12, 2004*
- New York* was highlighted as one of the 25 metro areas most polluted by year-round particle pollution (PM 2.5) in the U.S. The area ranked #17. *American Lung Association, State of the Air: 2007*
- New York* was highlighted as one of the 25 most ozone-polluted metro areas in the U.S. The area ranked #10. *American Lung Association, State of the Air: 2007*
- New York* was selected as one of "America's Top 10 Low-Carb Cities" by *LowCarbiz Magazine*. Criteria: abundance of low-carb products; restaurants with low-carb menu items; health practitioners supportive of carb-cutting regimens; local culture generally conducive to exercise and health. *LowCarbiz Magazine, April 2004*

- New York* was selected as one of "America's Pet Healthiest Cities" by Purina. The city ranked #14 out of 50. Criteria: veterinary services; environment; legislation; preventative care; obesity/body condition. *Purina Pet Institute, "America's Pet Healthiest Cities," May 20, 2003*

Women/Minorities Rankings

- Middlesex* was ranked #11 out of 100 metro areas in *SELF Magazine's* ranking of "America's Best Places for Women." A panel of experts came up with more than 50 criteria including death and disease rates, environmental indicators, community resources, and lifestyle habits. *SELF Magazine, "America's Best Places for Women 2007," December 2007*
- New York* appeared on a list of the top 10 metro areas with the highest concentration of same-sex households. The area ranked #6. *Urban Institute Press, The Gay and Lesbian Atlas, May 2004*
- New York* appeared on a list of the top 10 metro areas with the highest concentration of gay male couples. The area ranked #5. *Urban Institute Press, The Gay and Lesbian Atlas, May 2004*

Seniors/Retirement Rankings

- Sperling's BestPlaces in partnership with Bankers Life & Casualty Company designed a survey to identify the top 50 metro areas in the U.S. that offer the best overall qualities for senior living. The New York* metro area ranked #7. The following criteria were statistically weighted to reflect the needs of the senior population: health; disease; economics; social; environment; spiritual; transportation; housing; and crime. *Bankers Life & Casualty Company, "Best Cities for Seniors 2005"*
- A.G. Edwards ranked America's 500 top-performing communities based on their residents' personal savings and investing behavior. The New York* metro area ranked #241 with an index score of 101.69 (national average = 100.00). A dozen statistical factors were measured including: participation in retirement savings plans; personal debt levels; and home ownership. *A.G. Edwards, "2007 Nest Egg Index", September 12, 2007*

Children/Family Rankings

- The Edison* metro area was selected as one of the "Best Cities for Relocating Families" by Worldwide ERC and Primacy Relocation. The 2007 study placed a special emphasis on the housing market, which has significantly impacted the relocation industry and an employer's ability to transfer employees. The variables which weigh heavily in this category include home price, home affordability index, appreciation rates, and property tax. Other criteria include cost of living, crime rates, education, climate, focus on diversity, physicians per capita, recreation and leisure, arts and culture, air quality, watershed quality, sales tax, unemployment rate, job growth, high school and higher education index, school expenditures per student, students in public school, SAT/ACT percentile, and population growth. *Worldwide ERC and Primacy Relocation, "2007 Best Cities for Relocating Families"*

Safety Rankings

- The National Insurance Crime Bureau ranked 361 metro areas in the U.S. in terms of per capita rates of vehicle theft. The New York* metro area ranked #224 (#1 = highest rate). Criteria: number of vehicle theft offenses per 100,000 inhabitants. *National Insurance Crime Bureau, "NICB Vehicle Theft Study," April 22, 2008*
- New York* appeared on Sperling's BestPlaces list of the "Riskiest Cities for Identity Theft." The area ranked #29 out of the nations 50 largest metro areas. Over 80 criteria were analyzed across four major categories: technology impact; crime; transactions; and risk profile. *Sperling's BestPlaces, www.BestPlaces.net, "Riskiest Cities for Identity Theft," July 2006*

- Farmers Insurance Group of Companies, in partnership with Sperling's BestPlaces, ranked 379 metro areas and identified the "Most Secure U.S. Place to Live." The Edison* metro area ranked #13 out of 114 in the large metro area category (500,000 or more residents). Criteria: crime rates; extreme weather; risk of natural disasters; environmental hazards; terrorism threats; air quality; life expectancy; job loss numbers. *Farmers Insurance Group, "Most Secure U.S. Places to Live 2007"*
- Middlesex* was identified as one of the most dangerous large metro areas for pedestrians in the U.S. The area ranked #47 out of the nations 50 largest metro areas. Criteria: average yearly pedestrian fatalities per capita (for the years 2002 and 2003) adjusted for the number of walkers. *Surface Transportation Policy Project, "Mean Streets 2004"*

Sports/Recreation Rankings

- The New York* metro area appeared on the *Sporting News* list of the "Best Sports Cities 2007". The area ranked #2 out of 150 cities in the U.S. *Sporting News* takes a 12-month snapshot, roughly July to July, of each city's sports, putting a heavy premium on regular-season won-lost records (from the most recently completed season). Other criteria include: playoff berths, bowl appearances and tournament bids; championships; applicable power ratings; quality of competition; overall fan fervor as measured in part by attendance as percentage of venue capacity; abundance of teams (rewarding quality over quantity); stadium and arena quality; ticket availability and prices; franchise ownership; and marquee appeal of athletes. *SportingNews.com, "Best Sports Cities 2007," August 1, 2007*
- The New York* metro area was selected by *Cranium* as one of the "Top 50 Fun Cities" in America. The area ranked #41. Criteria includes: number of sports teams, restaurants, and dance performances; number of toy stores; city budget spent on recreation. *Cranium, November 4, 2003*
- *Golf Digest* ranked 330 metro areas in the U.S. in terms of golf. The Middlesex* metro area was ranked #306. Criteria: access to golf; weather; value of golf; and quality of golf. *Golf Digest, "Metro Golf Rankings," August 2005*

Dating/Romance Rankings

- Eli Lily and Company, in partnership with Sperling's BestPlaces, ranked the nation's 50 largest metro areas in terms of the "Most Romantic Cities for Baby Boomers." The New York* metro area ranked #16. Criteria: marriage and divorce rates among "baby boomers" age 45 to 60; great restaurants; dance studios; chocolate, jewelry and flower sales. *Eli Lily and Company, "Most Romantic Cities for Baby Boomers," April 20, 2007*
- The New York* metro area was selected as one of the "Top Ten U.S. Cities for Finding a Rich, Single Woman" by Teasley, a Manhattan-based marketing consulting firm. The area ranked #2. Criteria: high single-female to single-male ratio; higher income to cost-of-living ratio; percentage of population that is single. *Teasley, "Where to Find a Rich, Single Woman in the United States," 2005*
- The Edison* metro area was selected as one of the "Best Cities for Relocating Singles" by Worldwide ERC and Primacy Relocation. The area ranked #17 out of the 100 largest metro areas in the U.S. Areas were selected based on the following criteria: a robust cost-of-living index; adventure and outdoor recreation opportunities; violent crime and property crime rates; percentage of the population that is unmarried (ages 25-34); ratio of single men and single women; affordability of quality higher education, including in-state and out-of-state tuition requirements and rates; number of newcomers to the area; commute times; tax rates; fee and occupancy rates for temporary housing and mini-storage; quality and quantity of collegiate and professional sporting events and fun, fan-friendly venues. *Worldwide ERC and Primacy Relocation, "2007 Best Cities for Relocating Singles," October 25, 2007*
- *Forbes* ranked the 40 most populous urbanized areas in the U.S. in terms of the "Best Cities for Singles." The New York* metro area ranked #2. Criteria: number of singles; cost of living alone; nightlife; culture; job growth; coolness; and online dating. *Forbes.com, August 21, 2007*

- Sperling's BestPlaces in partnership with AXE Deodorant Bodyspray ranked 80 metro areas and identified "America's Best (and Worst) Cities for Dating." The New York* metro area ranked #18 (#1 = best). Criteria: percentage of singles ages 18-24; population density; dating venues per capita. *AXE Deodorant Bodyspray, "America's Best (and Worst) Cities for Dating," May 2004*

Culture/Performing Arts Rankings

- The New York* metro area was selected as one of the "Best Places for Artists in America" by *BusinessWeek.com*. Criteria: percentage of young people age 25 to 34; population diversity; concentration of museums, philharmonic orchestras, dance companies, theater troupes, library resources, and college arts programs. *BusinessWeek.com, "Best Places for Artists in America," February 26, 2007*
- Scarborough Research, a leading market research firm, identified the top local markets for rock concert attendance. The New York* DMA (Designated Market Area) ranked in the top 25 with 14% of consumers, 18 years old and over, reporting that they have attended a rock concert during the past year. *Scarborough Research, June 14, 2004*

Miscellaneous Rankings

- The New York* metro area was identified as one of "The 10 Worst Commuter Cities" in the U.S. by the *U.S. News and World Report*. The mean travel time to work is 39 minutes. *U.S. News and World Report, May 7, 2007*
- Scarborough Research, a leading market research firm, identified the top local markets for bloggers. The New York* DMA (Designated Market Area) ranked in the top 13 with 10% of adults reporting that they had read or contributed to a blog within the past 30 days. *Scarborough Research, October 24, 2007*
- The New York* metro area was selected as one of the "Top 10 Most Independent Cities for Homesellers". The area ranked #1. The cities listed had more consumers choosing to sell their homes without the help of a real-estate agent than anywhere else. Data was based on geographical information for listings posted on ForSaleByOwner.com from January 1, 2007 through June 30, 2007. *ForSaleByOwner.com, October 1, 2007*
- Avis Rent-A-Car and Motorola, in partnership with Sperling's BestPlaces, ranked the nation's 75 most populous metro areas in terms of how difficult they are to navigate. The New York* metro area ranked #5 with #1 being the most challenging. Criteria: street layouts; overall design and layout; travel time index; percent of congested freeway and street lane miles; bodies of water; complexity of directions needed to travel from major airports to city center; annual delay per person; days of snow exceeding 1.5 inches; and days of rain exceeding 0.5 inch. *Avis Rent-A-Car and Motorola, "America's Most Challenging Cities to Navigate," August 3, 2004*
- The New York* metro area appeared on *Forbes* list of "America's Drunkest Cities". The area ranked #32. Criteria: 35 of the largest continental U.S. metro areas were chosen based on availability of data and geographic diversity. Each metro was ranked in five areas: state laws; drinkers; heavy drinkers; binge drinkers; and alcoholism. *Forbes.com, "America's Drunkest Cities," August 22, 2006*
- Sperling's BestPlaces in partnership with Pep Boys ranked 77 metro areas and identified "America's Most Drivable Cities." The New York* metro area ranked #70. Criteria: climate; road roughness; urban mobility; gas prices. *Pep Boys, "America's Most Drivable Cities," April 9, 2003*
- State Farm Insurance, in partnership with Sperling's BestPlaces, analyzed several key factors that contribute to overall family preparedness. The New York* metro area ranked #44 out of the nation's 50 most populous metro areas. Criteria: quality of life; life insurance coverage; and investments. *State Farm Life Insurance, "Fiscally Fit Cities Report," July 20, 2004*

- Scarborough Research, a leading market research firm, identified the top local markets for grocery coupon use. The New York* DMA (Designated Market Area) ranked in the top 25 with 38% of consumers reporting that they use grocery coupons at least once per week. *Scarborough Research, December 8, 2004*

- A study by Sperling's BestPlaces examined which U.S. metro areas were most affected by high fuel prices in 2006. The New York* metro area was ranked #64 out of 80 (#1 = most expensive city for driving). Rankings are based on the average dollars spent on gas per year by two driver households. Criteria: cost of regular-grade gasoline; average miles driven per day; average number of gallons each driver uses and wastes in traffic congestion each day. *Sperling's BestPlaces, www.bestplaces.net, "Pain at the Pump," May 18, 2006*

South Brunswick is located within the New York-Northern New Jersey-Long Island, NY-NJ-PA Metropolitan Statistical Area, Edison, NJ Metropolitan Division, and Middlesex-Somerset-Hunterdon, NJ metro area.

Business Environment

CITY FINANCES

City Government Finances

Component	2004-2005 ($000)	2004-2005 ($ per capita)
Total Revenues	52,523	1,294
Total Expenditures	76,442	1,883
Debt Outstanding	89,852	2,213
Cash and Securities	40,274	992

Source: U.S Census Bureau, Government Finances 2004-2005

City Government Revenue by Source

Source	2004-2005 ($000)	2004-2005 ($ per capita)
General Revenue		
From Federal Government	0	0
From State Government	7,679	189
From Local Governments	250	6
Taxes		
Property	21,893	539
Sales	463	11
Personal Income	0	0
License	2,626	65
Charges	8,249	203
Liquor Store	0	0
Utility	9,034	223
Employee Retirement	0	0
Other	2,329	57

Source: U.S Census Bureau, Government Finances 2004-2005

City Government Expenditures by Function

Function	2004-2005 ($000)	2004-2005 ($ per capita)	2004-2005 (%)
General Expenditures			
Airports	0	0	0.0
Corrections	0	0	0.0
Education	0	0	0.0
Fire Protection	489	12	0.6
Governmental Administration	4,138	102	5.4
Health	694	17	0.9
Highways	8,632	213	11.3
Hospitals	0	0	0.0
Housing and Community Development	429	11	0.6
Interest on General Debt	1,599	39	2.1
Libraries	6,563	162	8.6
Parking	0	0	0.0
Parks and Recreation	5,938	146	7.8
Police Protection	8,449	208	11.1
Public Welfare	36	1	0.0
Sewerage	11,107	274	14.5
Solid Waste Management	2,822	70	3.7
Liquor Store	0	0	0.0
Utility	13,427	331	17.6
Employee Retirement	0	0	0.0
Other	12,119	299	15.9

Source: U.S Census Bureau, Government Finances 2004-2005

Municipal Bond Ratings

Area	Moody's
City	Aaa

Source: Mergent Bond Record, January 2008 (unless noted otherwise)

DEMOGRAPHICS

Population Growth

Area	1990 Census	2000 Census	2007 Estimate	2012 Projection	Population Growth (%) 1990-2000	Population Growth (%) 2000-2012
City	25,792	37,734	41,168	43,268	46.3	14.7
MSA[1]	16,845,992	18,323,002	18,887,605	19,111,248	8.8	4.3
U.S.	248,709,873	281,421,906	301,045,522	314,920,978	13.2	11.9

Note: (1) Metropolitan Statistical Area - see Appendix B for areas included
Source: Claritas, Inc.

Number of Households and Average Household Size

Area	2007 Estimate	2007 Average Household Size
City	14,352	2.87
MSA[1]	6,870,593	2.75
U.S.	113,668,003	2.65

Note: (1) Metropolitan Statistical Area - see Appendix B for areas included
Source: Claritas, Inc.

Race and Ethnicity

Area	White Alone[2]	Black Alone[2]	Asian Alone[2]	Other Race Alone[2]	Hispanic[3]
City	60.7	8.9	25.7	4.8	6.6
MSA[1]	59.5	17.6	8.8	14.1	21.2
U.S.	73.1	12.4	4.3	10.3	14.9

Note: Figures are 2007 estimates; (1) Metropolitan Statistical Area - see Appendix B for areas included (2) Alone is defined as not being in combination with one or more other races; (3) May be of any race.
Source: Claritas, Inc.

Ancestry

Area	German	Irish[2]	English	American	Italian	Polish	French[3]	Scottish
City	13.4	14.1	5.8	2.6	19.2	8.1	1.5	2.0
MSA[1]	12.8	15.0	5.7	2.9	17.2	9.8	1.5	1.3
U.S.	15.2	10.9	8.7	7.3	5.6	3.2	3.0	1.7

Note: Figures include multiple ancestry (e.g. if a person reported being Irish and Italian, they were included in both columns); (1) Metropolitan Statistical Area - see Appendix A for areas included; (2) Includes Celtic; (3) Includes Alsatian but excludes Basque
Source: Census 2000, Summary File 3

Foreign-Born Population

Area	Percent of Population Born in							
	Any Foreign Country	Europe	Asia	Africa	Oceania[2]	Canada	Mexico	Latin America[3]
City	21.6	3.4	14.0	1.6	0.0	0.4	0.1	2.1
MSA[1]	20.8	4.4	8.9	1.1	0.0	0.2	1.1	5.1
U.S.	11.1	1.7	2.9	0.3	0.1	0.3	3.3	2.5

Note: (1) Metropolitan Statistical Area - see Appendix A for areas included; (2) Includes Australia, New Zealand subregion, Melanesia, Micronesia, Polynesia, and Oceania n.e.c; (3) Includes Central America (excluding Mexico), South America, and the Caribbean.
Source: Census 2000, Summary File 3

Marriage Status

Area	Never Married	Now Married (excluding Separated)	Separated	Widowed	Divorced
City	22.2	64.5	1.4	4.4	7.5
MSA[1]	26.3	58.8	1.6	6.2	7.0
U.S.	27.1	54.4	2.2	6.6	9.7

Note: Figures are percentages and cover the population 15 years of age and older; (1) Metropolitan Statistical Area - see Appendix A for areas included
Source: Census 2000, Summary File 3

Age Distribution

Area	Under Age 5	Age 5 to 17	Age 18 to 34	Age 35 to 49	Age 50 to 64	Age 65 to 79	80 Years and Over
	Percent of Population						
City	7.6	20.8	21.2	29.6	13.4	5.9	1.5
MSA[1]	6.7	17.6	22.8	26.1	15.0	8.9	2.9
U.S.	6.8	18.9	23.7	23.5	14.8	9.2	3.2

Note: (1) Metropolitan Statistical Area - see Appendix A for areas included
Source: Census 2000, Summary File 3

Male/Female Ratio

Area	Males	Females	Males per 100 Females
City	20,025	21,143	94.7
MSA[1]	9,117,706	9,769,899	93.3
U.S.	148,320,305	152,725,217	97.1

Note: Figures are 2007 estimates; (1) Metropolitan Statistical Area - see Appendix B for areas included
Source: Claritas, Inc.

Religion

Area	Catholic	Southern Baptist	United Meth-odist	ELCA[1]	LDS[2]	Presby-terian Church USA	Jewish Est.	Muslim Est.
County	45.7	0.1	0.8	0.6	0.2	1.0	6.0	0.9
U.S.	22.0	7.1	3.7	1.8	1.5	1.1	2.2	0.6

Note: Figures are the number of adherents as a percentage of the total population; Adherents are defined as all members, including full members, their children and the estimated number of other participants who are not considered members (e.g. the baptized, those not confirmed, those regularly attending services, etc.); (1) Evangelical Lutheran Church in America; (2) The Church of Jesus Christ of Latter Day Saints
Source: Reprinted with permission from Religious Congregations and Membership in the United States 2000 (Nashville, Glenmary Research Center, 2002) Copyright Association of Statisticians of American Religious Bodies. All rights reserved.

ECONOMY

Gross Metropolitan Product

Area	2002	2003	2004	2005	2005 Rank[2]
MSA[1]	820.9	847.1	902.4	952.6	1

Note: Figures are in billions of dollars; (1) New York-Northern New Jersey-Long Island, NY-NJ-PA Metropolitan Statistical Area - see Appendix A for areas included; (2) Rank ranges from 1 to 361
Source: The U.S. Conference of Mayors, "U.S. Metro Economies: GMP - The Engines of America's Growth," January 2007

Economic Growth

Area	1995 GMP	2005 GMP	Average Annual Growth Rate	Growth Rate Rank[2]
MSA[1]	585.5	952.6	5.0	221

Note: Figures are in billions of dollars; GMP = Gross Metropolitan Product; (1) New York-Northern New Jersey-Long Island, NY-NJ-PA Metropolitan Statistical Area - see Appendix A for areas included; (2) Rank ranges from 1 to 361
Source: The U.S. Conference of Mayors, "U.S. Metro Economies: GMP - The Engines of America's Growth," January 2007

INCOME

Per Capita/Median/Average Income

Area	Per Capita ($)	Median Household ($)	Average Household ($)
City	39,603	96,951	113,403
MSA[1]	30,292	58,080	82,491
U.S.	25,495	49,280	66,670

Note: Figures are 2007 estimates; (1) Metropolitan Statistical Area - see Appendix B for areas included
Source: Claritas, Inc.

Household Income Distribution

Area	Percent of Households Earning							
	Under $15,000	$15,000 -24,999	$25,000 -34,999	$35,000 -49,999	$50,000 -74,999	$75,000 -99,000	$100,000 -149,999	$150,000 and up
City	3.4	3.2	4.3	7.8	16.2	17.1	26.6	21.3
MSA[1]	14.0	8.8	8.7	12.6	17.1	12.3	14.5	12.0
U.S.	13.1	10.9	11.2	15.6	19.5	11.9	11.3	6.6

Note: Figures are 2007 estimates; (1) Metropolitan Statistical Area - see Appendix B for areas included
Source: Claritas, Inc.

Poverty Rates by Age

Area	All Ages	Under 5 Years Old	5 to 17 Years Old	18 to 64 Years Old	65 Years and Over
City	3.1	0.2	0.7	1.9	0.3
MSA[1]	5.4	0.4	1.1	3.3	0.6
U.S.	12.4	1.2	3.0	6.9	1.2

Note: Figures are percent of population with income in 1999 below poverty level and only include population for whom poverty status is determined; (1) Metropolitan Statistical Area - see Appendix A for areas included
Source: Census 2000, Summary File 3

Personal Bankruptcy Filing Rate

Area	2004	2005	2006
Middlesex County	3.23	4.29	0.98
U.S.	5.31	6.82	2.00

Note: Numbers are per 1,000 population and include Chapter 7 and Chapter 13 filings
Source: Federal Deposit Insurance Corporation (FDIC), Regional Economic Conditions (RECON), 8/23/2007

EMPLOYMENT

Labor Force and Employment

Area	Civilian Labor Force			Workers Employed		
	Dec. 2006	Dec. 2007	% Chg.	Dec. 2006	Dec. 2007	% Chg.
City	23,435	23,248	-0.8	22,869	22,645	-1.0
MD[1]	1,199,770	1,190,736	-0.8	1,157,810	1,146,507	-1.0
U.S.	152,571,000	153,705,000	0.7	146,081,000	146,334,000	0.2

Note: Data is not seasonally adjusted and covers workers 16 years of age and older; (1) Metropolitan Division - see Appendix B for areas included
Source: Bureau of Labor Statistics, http://stats.bls.gov

Unemployment Rate

Area	2007											
	Jan.	Feb.	Mar.	Apr.	May	Jun.	Jul.	Aug.	Sep.	Oct.	Nov.	Dec.
City	3.0	2.8	2.6	2.5	2.7	2.9	3.4	2.9	2.9	2.7	2.7	2.6
MD[1]	4.4	4.2	4.0	3.6	3.6	3.8	4.3	3.7	3.7	3.4	3.6	3.7
U.S.	5.0	4.9	4.5	4.3	4.3	4.7	4.9	4.6	4.5	4.4	4.5	4.8

Note: Data is not seasonally adjusted and covers workers 16 years of age and older; All figures are percentages; (1) Metropolitan Division - see Appendix B for areas included
Source: Bureau of Labor Statistics, http://stats.bls.gov

Employment by Occupation

Occupation Classification	City (%)	MSA[1] (%)	U.S. (%)
Sales and Office	26.2	27.3	26.7
Professional and Related	31.1	25.9	20.2
Service	8.0	10.4	14.9
Production, Transportation, and Material Moving	6.5	11.2	14.6
Management, Business, and Financial	22.7	18.1	13.5
Construction, Extraction, and Maintenance	5.4	7.0	9.4
Farming, Forestry, and Fishing	0.0	0.1	0.7

Note: Figures cover employed civilians 16 years of age and older; (1) Metropolitan Statistical Area - see Appendix A for areas included
Source: Census 2000, Summary File 3

Employment by Industry

Sector	MSA[1] Number of Employees	MSA[1] Percent of Total	U.S. Percent of Total
Government	152,800	14.6	16.3
Education and Health Services	139,600	13.3	13.4
Professional and Business Services	180,200	17.2	13.1
Retail Trade	136,200	13.0	11.6
Manufacturing	73,200	7.0	9.9
Leisure and Hospitality	78,400	7.5	9.6
Financial Activities	60,400	5.8	5.9
Construction	n/a	n/a	5.3
Wholesale Trade	60,800	5.8	4.4
Other Services	48,200	4.6	3.9
Transportation and Utilities	41,000	3.9	3.7
Information	30,400	2.9	2.2
Natural Resources and Mining	n/a	n/a	0.5

Note: Figures cover non-farm employment as of December 2007 and are not seasonally adjusted; (1) Metropolitan Statistical Area - see Appendix B for areas included; n/a not available
Source: Bureau of Labor Statistics, http://stats.bls.gov

Average Wages

Occupation	$/Hr.	Occupation	$/Hr.
Accountants and Auditors	36.27	Maids and Housekeeping Cleaners	9.77
Automotive Mechanics	18.30	Maintenance and Repair Workers	18.27
Bookkeepers	17.66	Marketing Managers	66.08
Carpenters	24.94	Nuclear Medicine Technologists	37.95
Cashiers	9.35	Nurses, Licensed Practical	23.49
Clerks, General Office	13.14	Nurses, Registered	33.79
Clerks, Receptionists/Information	12.50	Nursing Aides/Orderlies/Attendants	12.60
Clerks, Shipping/Receiving	14.55	Packers and Packagers, Hand	9.76
Computer Programmers	40.08	Physical Therapists	37.21
Computer Support Specialists	24.41	Postal Service Mail Carriers	21.31
Computer Systems Analysts	42.13	Real Estate Brokers	50.65
Cooks, Restaurant	11.99	Retail Salespersons	12.69
Dentists	n/a	Sales Reps., Exc. Tech./Scientific	35.27
Electrical Engineers	45.42	Sales Reps., Tech./Scientific	44.40
Electricians	28.34	Secretaries, Exc. Legal/Med./Exec.	16.38
Financial Managers	59.33	Security Guards	12.84
First-Line Supervisors/Mgrs., Sales	21.41	Surgeons	n/a
Food Preparation Workers	10.15	Teacher Assistants	12.40
General and Operations Managers	70.21	Teachers, Elementary School	27.40
Hairdressers/Cosmetologists	14.36	Teachers, Secondary School	29.00
Internists	87.25	Telemarketers	15.72
Janitors and Cleaners	12.10	Truck Drivers, Heavy/Tractor-Trailer	19.53
Landscaping/Groundskeeping Workers	12.61	Truck Drivers, Light/Delivery Svcs.	16.22
Lawyers	57.95	Waiters and Waitresses	11.25

Note: Wage data covers the Edison, NJ Metropolitan Division - see Appendix B for areas included. Hourly wages for elementary/secondary school teachers and teacher assistants were calculated by the editors from annual wage data assuming a 40 hour work week; n/a not available.
Source: Bureau of Labor Statistics, May 2007 Metro Area Occupational Employment and Wage Estimates

RESIDENTIAL REAL ESTATE

Building Permits

Area	Single-Family			Multi-Family			Total		
	2006	2007p	Pct. Chg.	2006	2007p	Pct. Chg.	2006	2007p	Pct. Chg.
City	145	184	26.9	0	0	-	145	184	26.9
U.S.	1,378,200	973,300	-29.4	460,700	407,200	-11.6	1,838,900	1,380,500	-24.9

Note: (p) preliminary; figures cover and represent new, privately-owned housing units authorized (unadjusted data); All permit data are based on estimates with imputation; U.S. figures are based on the new 20,000-place series.
Source: U.S. Census Bureau, Manufacturing, Mining, and Construction Statistics

Homeownership and Housing Vacancies

Area	Homeownership Rate[2] (%)			Rental Vacancy Rate[3] (%)			Homeowner Vacancy Rate[4] (%)		
	2005	2006	2007	2005	2006	2007	2005	2006	2007
MSA[1]	54.6	53.6	53.8	5.0	5.4	5.7	1.9	1.8	2.1
U.S.	68.9	68.8	68.1	9.8	9.8	9.7	1.9	2.4	2.7

Note: (1) Metropolitan Statistical Area - see Appendix B for areas included; (2) The proportion of households that are owners; (3) The proportion of the rental inventory that is vacant for rent; (4) The proportion of the homeowner inventory that is vacant for sale; n/a not available
Source: U.S. Census Bureau, Housing Vacancies and Homeownership Annual Statistics: 2007

TAXES

State Corporate Income Tax Rates

State	Rates and Tax Brackets
New Jersey	6.5% > $0; 7.5 > 50K; 9.0% > 100K

Note: Tax rates as of January 1, 2008; Companies with income greater than $100K pay 9% on all income, companies with income greater than $50K but less than $100K pay 7.5 % on all income and companies with income under $50K pay 6.5%. The minimum tax is $500. An Alternative Minimum Assessment based on Gross Receipts applies if greater than corporate franchise tax for out-of-state companies with New Jersey sales. 4% surtax for 2007.
Source: Tax Foundation, www.taxfoundation.org

State Individual Income Tax Rates

State	Federal Deductibility	Marginal Rates (%)	Standard Deduction ($)		Personal Exemptions ($)[1]	
			Single	Joint	Single	Dependents
New Jersey	No	1.4 - 8.97 (y)	n/a	n/a	1,000	1,500

Note: Tax rates as of January 1, 2008; Local- and county-level taxes are not included; n/a not applicable; (1) Married joint filers generally receive double the single exemption; (y) Brackets are not double for married taxpayers.
Source: Tax Foundation, www.taxfoundation.org

Various State and Local Tax Rates

State and Local Sales and Use (%)	State Sales and Use (%)	Gasoline[1,2] ($/gal.)	Cigarette ($/pack)	Spirits ($/gal.)	Table Wine ($/gal.)	Beer ($/gal.)
7.0	7.0	0.145	2.575	4.40	0.70	0.12

Note: Tax rates as of January 1, 2008; (1) In addition to the 18.4 cpg Federal gasoline tax; (2) Rates may include additional state sales taxes, environmental protection and storage fees/taxes, and local taxes. When necessary, the volume-weighted average of all local taxes is used to approximate the typical statewide rate including local tax
Source: Tax Foundation, www.taxfoundation.org; Original research

State Tax Burdens

Area	Combined State and Local Tax Burden		Combined Federal, State and Local Tax Burden	
	Percent	Rank	Percent	Rank
New Jersey	11.6	10	35.6	3
U.S. Average	11.0	-	32.7	-

Note: Figures cover 2007 and measure taxes as a percentage of income
Source: Tax Foundation, www.taxfoundation.org

State Business Tax Climate Index Rankings

State	Overall Rank	Corporate Tax Index Rank	Individual Income Tax Index Rank	Sales Tax Index Rank	Unemployment Insurance Tax Index Rank	Property Tax Index Rank
New Jersey	49	41	49	44	24	49

Note: Rankings range from 1 to 50 where 1 is best. Rankings do not average across to Overall Rank. States without a given tax are given a ranking of 1.
Source: Tax Foundation, State Business Tax Climate Index 2008

TRANSPORTATION

Means of Transportation to Work

Area	Car/Truck/Van		Public Transportation			Bicycle	Walked	Other Means	Worked at Home
	Drove Alone	Car-pooled	Bus	Subway	Railroad				
City	81.1	7.7	3.3	0.3	3.0	0.1	1.1	0.4	2.9
MSA[1]	77.2	9.9	2.7	0.2	3.6	0.2	2.4	0.9	2.9
U.S.	75.7	12.2	2.5	1.5	0.5	0.4	2.9	1.0	3.3

Note: Figures are percentages and cover workers 16 years of age and older; (1) Metropolitan Statistical Area - see Appendix A for areas included
Source: Census 2000, Summary File 3

Travel Time to Work

Area	Less Than 15 Minutes	15 to 29 Minutes	30 to 44 Minutes	45 to 59 Minutes	60 Minutes or More
City	19.0	32.0	21.2	9.3	18.5
MSA[1]	23.3	31.2	20.7	10.3	14.6
U.S.	29.4	36.1	19.1	7.4	8.0

Note: Figures are percentages and include workers 16 years old and over; (1) Metropolitan Statistical Area - see Appendix A for areas included
Source: Census 2000, Summary File 3

Travel Time Index

Area	1982	1995	2004	2005
Urban Area[1]	1.10	1.24	1.36	1.39
Average[2]	1.11	1.22	1.29	1.30

Note: Travel Time Index - The ratio of travel time in the peak period to the travel time at free-flow conditions. A value of 1.35 indicates a 20-minute free-flow trip takes 27 minutes in the peak. Free-flow speeds (60 mph on freeways and 35 mph on principal arterials) are used as the comparison threshold; (1) Covers the New York-Newark, NY-NJ-CT urban area; (2) average of 85 urban areas
Source: Texas Transportation Institute, The 2007 Urban Mobility Report, September 2007

Living Environment

COST OF LIVING

Cost of Living Index

Composite Index	Groceries	Housing	Utilities	Trans-portation	Health Care	Misc. Goods/ Services
127.5	113.2	169.1	107.3	103.7	110.6	114.2

Note: U.S. = 100; Figures cover the Middlesex-Monmouth NJ urban area.
Source: The Council for Community and Economic Research (formerly ACCRA), Cost of Living Index, 2007

Grocery Prices

Area[1]	T-Bone Steak ($/pound)	Frying Chicken ($/pound)	Whole Milk ($/half gal.)	Eggs ($/dozen)	Orange Juice ($/64 oz.)	Coffee ($/11.5 oz.)
City[2]	9.68	1.09	2.24	2.25	3.07	3.46
Avg.	8.93	1.12	2.13	1.52	3.26	3.31
Min.	5.88	0.71	1.33	0.83	2.30	2.20
Max.	12.80	2.07	3.43	3.54	5.79	6.20

Note: (1) Values for the local area are compared with the average, minimum and maximum values for all 331 areas in the Cost of Living Index report; (2) Figures cover the Middlesex-Monmouth NJ urban area; **T-Bone Steak** *(price per pound);* **Frying Chicken** *(price per pound, whole fryer);* **Whole Milk** *(half gallon carton);* **Eggs** *(price per dozen, Grade A, large);* **Orange Juice** *(64 oz. Tropicana or Florida Natural);* **Coffee** *(11.5 oz. can, vacuum-packed, Maxwell House, Hills Bros, or Folgers).*
Source: The Council for Community and Economic Research (formerly ACCRA), Cost of Living Index, 2007

Housing and Utility Costs

Area[1]	New Home Price ($)	Apartment Rent ($/month)	All Electric ($/month)	Part Electric ($/month)	Other Energy ($/month)	Telephone ($/month)
City[2]	531,339	1,321	-	82.61	85.27	29.75
Avg.	309,605	782	146.13	78.67	90.16	26.14
Min.	189,877	n/a	82.03	37.41	33.15	17.08
Max.	1,202,800	3,481	271.14	150.60	257.67	37.45

Note: (1) Values for the local area are compared with the average, minimum and maximum values for all 331 areas in the Cost of Living Index report; (2) Figures cover the Middlesex-Monmouth NJ urban area; **New Home Price** *(2,400 sf living area, 8,000 sf lot, in urban area with full utilities);* **Apartment Rent** *(950 sf 2 bedroom/1.5 or 2 bath, unfurnished, excluding all utilities except water);* **All Electric** *(average monthly cost for an all-electric home);* **Part Electric** *(average monthly cost for a part-electric home);* **Other Energy** *(average monthly cost for natural gas, fuel oil, coal, wood, and any other forms of energy except electricity);* **Telephone** *(price includes basic monthly rate for a private residential line plus additional local usage charges incurred by a family of four).*
Source: The Council for Community and Economic Research (formerly ACCRA), Cost of Living Index, 2007

Health Care, Transportation, and Other Costs

Area[1]	Doctor ($/visit)	Dentist ($/visit)	Optometrist ($/visit)	Gasoline ($/gallon)	Beauty Salon ($/visit)	Men's Shirt ($)
City[2]	70.73	93.52	88.50	2.52	31.67	35.87
Avg.	79.48	71.93	79.55	2.64	29.52	25.77
Min.	52.08	44.80	43.95	2.19	15.58	16.19
Max.	148.44	126.27	158.83	3.48	60.62	48.53

Note: (1) Values for the local area are compared with the average, minimum and maximum values for all 331 areas in the Cost of Living Index report; (2) Figures cover the Middlesex-Monmouth NJ urban area; **Doctor** *(general practitioners routine exam of an established patient);* **Dentist** *(adult teeth cleaning and periodic oral examination);* **Optometrist** *(full vision eye exam for established adult patient);* **Gasoline** *(one gallon regular unleaded, national brand, including all taxes, cash price at self-service pump if available);* **Beauty Salon** *(woman's shampoo, trim, and blow-dry);* **Men's Shirt** *(cotton/polyester dress shirt, pinpoint weave, long sleeves).*
Source: The Council for Community and Economic Research (formerly ACCRA), Cost of Living Index, 2007

HOUSING

House Price Index (HPI)

Area	National Ranking[2]	Quarterly Change (%)	One-Year Change (%)	Five-Year Change (%)
MD[1]	214	-0.27	-1.48	54.92
U.S.[3]	-	0.10	0.84	41.37

Note: The HPI is a weighted repeat sales index. It measures average price changes in repeat sales or refinancings on the same properties. This information is obtained by reviewing repeat mortgage transactions on single-family properties whose mortgages have been purchased or securitized by Fannie Mae or Freddie Mac in January 1975; (1) Metropolitan Division - see Appendix B for areas included; (2) Rankings are based on annual percentage change for all metro areas containing at least 15,000 transactions over the last 10 years and ranges from 1 to 291; (3) figures based on a weighted average of Census Division estimates; all figures are for the period ending December 31, 2007
Source: Office of Federal Housing Enterprise Oversight, House Price Index, February 26, 2008

House Price Valuations

Area	Q1 2000	Q1 2001	Q1 2002	Q1 2003	Q1 2004	Q1 2005	Q1 2006	Q1 2007	Q1 2008
MD[1]	-26.4	-21.9	-13.1	0.2	9.5	22.2	26.6	18.8	11.3

Note: Figures show the percentage of over- or under-valuation of single family homes relative to statistically normal house values (e.g. a value of 23.6 indicates that house values are 23.6% overvalued). Statistically normal house values are based on house prices, interest rates, household incomes, population densities, and any historical premiums or discounts metropolitan areas have exhibited over time; (1) Figures cover the Metropolitan Division - see Appendix B for areas included
Source: Global Insight/National City Corporation, House Prices in America, May 2008

Median Home Prices

Area	2005	2006	2007[r]	Percent Change 2006 to 2007
MD[1]	375.5	387.7	380.3	-1.9
U.S. Average	219.0	221.9	217.9	-1.8

Note: Figures are median sales prices of existing single-family homes in thousands of dollars; (r) revised; n/a not available; (1) Metropolitan Division - see Appendix B for areas included
Source: National Association of Realtors, Metropolitan Area Prices, 1st Quarter 2008

Housing: Year Structure Built

Area	1990 -2000	1980 -1989	1970 -1979	1960 -1969	1950 -1959	1940 -1949	Before 1940	Median Year
City	34.7	27.6	14.1	9.1	10.4	1.0	3.1	1984
MSA[1]	15.2	18.7	13.3	16.8	16.2	6.8	13.0	1968
U.S.	17.0	15.8	18.5	13.7	12.7	7.3	15.0	1971

Note: Figures are percentages; (1) Metropolitan Statistical Area - see Appendix A for areas included
Source: Census 2000, Summary File 3

HEALTH

Health Risk Data

Category	Area[1] (%)	U.S. (%)
Adults who have been told they have high blood pressure[3]	25.7	25.5
Adults who have been told they have high blood cholesterol[3]	38.5	35.6
Adults who have been told they have diabetes[2]	7.0	7.5
Adults who have been told they have arthritis[3]	25.7	27.0
Adults who have been told they currently have asthma	6.4	8.5
Adults who are current smokers	16.4	20.1
Adults who are heavy drinkers[4]	3.3	4.9
Adults who are overweight (BMI 25.0 - 29.9)	37.9	36.5
Adults who are obese (BMI 30.0 - 99.8)	21.6	25.1

Note: Data as of 2006 unless otherwise noted; (1) Figures cover the Metropolitan Division - see Appendix B for areas included; (2) Figures do not include pregnancy-related diabetes, pre-diabetes or borderline diabetes; (3) 2005 data; (4) Heavy drinkers are classified as adult men having more than two drinks per day or adult women having more than one drink per day
Source: Centers for Disease Control and Prevention, Behaviorial Risk Factor Surveillance System, SMART: Selected Metropolitan/Micropolitan Area Risk Trends, 2005, 2006

Mortality Rates for the Top 10 Causes of Death in the U.S.

ICD-10[a] Sub-Chapter	ICD-10[a] Code	Age-Adjusted Mortality Rate[1] per 100,000 population	
		County[2]	U.S.
Malignant neoplasms	C00-C97	173.2	186.5
Ischaemic heart diseases	I20-I25	155.4	152.3
Other forms of heart disease	I30-I51	47.5	51.5
Cerebrovascular diseases	I60-I69	34.4	50.0
Chronic lower respiratory diseases	J40-J47	26.8	42.6
Diabetes mellitus	E10-E14	24.4	24.8
Other degenerative diseases of the nervous system	G30-G31	12.1	22.6
Other external causes of accidental injury	W00-X59	13.8	21.4
Influenza and pneumonia	J10-J18	16.4	20.7
Hypertensive diseases	I10-I13	11.0	18.2

Note: (a) ICD-10 = International Classification of Diseases 10th Revision; (1) Mortality rates are a three year average covering 2003-2005; (2) Figures cover Middlesex County
Source: Centers for Disease Control and Prevention, National Center for Health Statistics. Compressed Mortality File 1999-2004. CDC WONDER On-line Database, compiled from Compressed Mortality File 1999-2005 Series 20 No. 2K, 2008.

Mortality Rates for Selected Causes of Death

ICD-10[a] Sub-Chapter	ICD-10[a] Code	Age-Adjusted Mortality Rate[1] per 100,000 population	
		County[2]	U.S.
Assault	X85-Y09	2.3	5.9
Human immunodeficiency virus (HIV) disease	B20-B24	3.0	4.5
Intentional self-harm	X60-X84	5.3	10.8
Malnutrition	E40-E46	*0.7	1.0
Obesity and other hyperalimentation	E65-E68	1.1	1.4
Organic, including symptomatic, mental disorders	F01-F09	12.4	16.8
Transport accidents	V01-V99	7.8	16.1
Viral hepatitis	B15-B19	1.2	1.8

Note: (a) ICD-10 = International Classification of Diseases 10th Revision; (1) Mortality rates are a three year average covering 2003-2005; (2) Figures cover Middlesex County; (*) Unreliable data as per CDC
Source: Centers for Disease Control and Prevention, National Center for Health Statistics. Compressed Mortality File 1999-2004. CDC WONDER On-line Database, compiled from Compressed Mortality File 1999-2005 Series 20 No. 2K, 2008.

Distribution of Physicians[1]

Area	Total	Family/ General Practice	Specialties	
			Medical	Surgical
Middlesex County (number)	1,746	206	872	359
Middlesex County (rate per 10,000 pop.)	22.1	2.6	11.0	4.5
U.S. (rate per 10,000 pop.)	17.7	4.6	6.9	4.3

Note: Data as of 2005; (1) Includes all non-federal, patient-care, office-based MDs
Source: Area Resource File (ARF). June 2007. U.S. Department of Health and Human Services, Health Resources and Services Administration, Bureau of Health Professions, Rockville, MD.

Hospitals

There were no hospitals listed within the city limits.
AHA Guide to the Healthcare Field 2008

According to *U.S. News,* the New York-Northern New Jersey-Long Island, NY-NJ-PA metro area is home to 14 of the best hospitals in the U.S.: **Hackensack University Medical Center**; **Hospital for Special Surgery**; **Kessler Institute for Rehabilitation**; **Lenox Hill Hospital**; **Long Island Jewish Medical Center**; **Memorial Sloan-Kettering Cancer Center**; **Montefiore Medical Center**; **Mount Sinai Medical Center**; **New York Eye and Ear Infirmary**; **New York-Presbyterian Univ. Hosp. of Columbia and Cornell**; **NYU Medical Center**; **Robert Wood Johnson University Hospital**; **Saint Francis Hospital**; **University Hospital**. *U.S. News Online, "America's Best Hospitals 2007"*

EDUCATION

Public School District Statistics

District Name	Schls	Pupils	Pupil/ Teacher Ratio	Minority Pupils[1] (%)	Free Lunch Eligible[2] (%)	IEP[3] (%)
South Brunswick Township	10	8,783	12.9	48.3	3.7	20.9

Note: Table includes regular local school districts with 2,000 or more students; (1) Percentage of students that are not white, non-Hispanic; (2) Percentage of students that are eligible for the free lunch program; (3) Percentage of students that have an Individualized Education Program.
Source: U.S. Department of Education, National Center for Education Statistics, Common Core of Data, Local Education Agency (School District) Universe Survey: School Year 2005-2006; U.S. Department of Education, National Center for Education Statistics, Common Core of Data, Public Elementary/Secondary School Universe Survey: School Year 2005-2006

Highest Level of Education

Area	Less than H.S.	H.S. Diploma	Some College, No Deg.	Associate Degree	Bachelors Degree	Masters Degree	Profess. School Degree	Doctorate Degree
City	6.6	20.7	16.6	6.8	29.2	14.5	3.0	2.6
MSA[1]	21.5	26.4	16.5	5.6	17.7	8.2	3.0	1.2
U.S.	19.4	28.4	21.2	6.4	15.7	5.9	2.0	1.0

Note: Figures are 2007 estimated percentages and cover persons age 25 and over; (1) Metropolitan Statistical Area - see Appendix B for areas included
Source: Claritas, Inc.

Educational Attainment by Race

Area	High School Graduate (%)					Bachelor's Degree (%)				
	Total	White	Black	Asian	Hisp.[2]	Total	White	Black	Asian	Hisp.[2]
City	93.3	93.3	92.4	94.1	85.4	49.0	43.5	36.0	78.5	29.8
MSA[1]	86.5	87.6	83.3	91.3	61.9	37.4	35.0	27.2	71.5	13.3
U.S.	80.4	83.6	72.3	80.4	52.4	24.4	26.1	14.3	44.1	10.4

Note: Figures shown cover persons 25 years old and over; (1) Metropolitan Statistical Area - see Appendix A for areas included; (2) people of Hispanic origin can be of any race
Source: Census 2000, Summary File 3

School Enrollment by Type

Area	Grades KG to 8				Grades 9 to 12			
	Public		Private		Public		Private	
	Enrollment	%	Enrollment	%	Enrollment	%	Enrollment	%
City	5,224	90.3	564	9.7	2,038	96.5	75	3.5
MSA[1]	129,755	87.7	18,130	12.3	53,556	88.7	6,806	11.3
U.S.	33,526,011	88.7	4,285,121	11.3	14,848,628	90.6	1,532,323	9.4

Note: Figures shown cover persons 3 years old and over; (1) Metropolitan Statistical Area - see Appendix A for areas included
Source: Census 2000, Summary File 3

School Enrollment by Race

Area	Grades KG to 8 (%)				Grades 9 to 12 (%)			
	White	Black	Asian	Hisp.[1]	White	Black	Asian	Hisp.[1]
City	69.3	8.8	17.8	6.6	65.0	9.0	16.2	10.2
MSA[2]	70.1	9.4	11.4	13.9	68.2	10.9	10.7	14.7
U.S.	68.5	15.5	3.3	16.8	68.8	15.5	3.8	15.7

Note: Figures shown cover persons 3 years old and over; (1) people of Hispanic origin can be of any race; (2) Metropolitan Statistical Area - see Appendix A for areas included
Source: Census 2000, Summary File 3

Average Salaries of Public School Classroom Teachers

District	2005-06 Dollars	2005-06 Rank[1]	2006-07 Dollars	2006-07 Rank[1]	Percent Change 2005-06 to 2006-07
New Jersey	58,156	5	59,920	3	3.03
U.S. Average	49,026	-	50,816	-	3.65

Note: (1) State rank ranges from 1 to 51.
Source: National Education Association, Rankings & Estimates: Rankings of the States 2006 and Estimates of School Statistics 2007, December 2007

Higher Education

Four-Year Colleges			Two-Year Colleges			Medical Schools[1]	Law Schools[2]	Voc/ Tech[3]
Public	Private Non-profit	Private For-profit	Public	Private Non-profit	Private For-profit			
0	0	0	0	0	0	0	0	0

Note: Figures cover institutions located within the city limits; (1) includes schools accredited by the Liaison Committee on Medical Education and the American Osteopathic Association; (2) includes American Bar Association-accredited law schools; (3) includes all schools with programs that are less than 2 years.
Source: National Center for Education Statistics, The Integrated Postsecondary Education System (IPEDS) Peer Analysis System, 2007; www.usnews.com, Law and Medical School Directories, 2009

PRESIDENTIAL ELECTION

2004 Presidential Election Results

Area	Bush	Kerry	Nader	Other
Middlesex County	42.8	56.3	0.6	0.3
U.S.	50.7	48.3	0.4	0.6

Note: Results are percentages and may not add to 100% due to rounding
Source: Dave Leip's Atlas of U.S. Presidential Elections, www.uselectionatlas.org

EMPLOYERS

Major Employers

Company Name	Industry	Type of Site
A T & T Corp	Telephone communication, except radio	Branch
Air Safety Equipment Inc	Airports, flying fields, and services	Branch
Community Medical Center Inc	General medical and surgical hospitals	Headquarters
Doon Technologies Inc	Business consulting, nec	Single
Ethicon Inc	Surgical appliances and supplies	Headquarters
Fort Monmouth Training Center	National security	Branch
In Ventive Commercial Services	Management consulting services	Single
JFK Medical Center	General medical and surgical hospitals	Headquarters
Larson & Toubro Infotech Ltd	Computer related services, nec	Headquarters
Rehabilitation Medicine	Specialty outpatient clinics, nec	Single
School of Public Health	Colleges and universities	Branch
St Peters University Hospital	General medical and surgical hospitals	Headquarters
Telcordia Technologies Inc	Custom computer programming services	Headquarters
US Post Office	U.S. postal service	Branch
Veterans Health Administration	Offices and clinics of medical doctors	Branch

Note: Companies shown are located within the Edison metropolitan area; nec = not elsewhere classified.
Source: www.zapdata.com, May 2008

PUBLIC SAFETY

Crime Rate

Area	All Crimes	Violent Crimes: Murder	Violent Crimes: Forcible Rape	Violent Crimes: Robbery	Violent Crimes: Aggrav. Assault	Property Crimes: Burglary	Property Crimes: Larceny -Theft	Property Crimes: Motor Vehicle Theft
City	1,550.7	0.0	4.9	29.5	41.8	349.5	1,028.9	96.0
Metro[1]	2,085.6	2.0	10.1	69.3	103.0	365.7	1,408.9	126.5
U.S.	3,808.1	5.7	30.9	149.4	287.5	729.4	2,206.8	398.4

Note: Figures are crimes per 100,000 population; (1) Metropolitan Division - see Appendix B for areas included
Source: FBI Uniform Crime Reports, 2006

Hate Crimes

Area	Number of Quarters Reported	Bias Motivation				
		Race	Religion	Sexual Orientation	Ethnicity	Disability
City	4	3	0	1	2	0

Source: Federal Bureau of Investigation, Hate Crime Statistics 2006

RECREATION

Culture

Dance[1]	Theatre[1]	Instrumental Music[1]	Vocal Music[1]	Series/ Festivals	Museums	Zoos and Aquariums[2]
0	0	0	0	0	0	0

Note: (1) Number of professional perfoming groups; (2) AZA-accredited
Source: The Grey House Performing Arts Directory, 2007; Official Museum Directory, 2008; Association of Zoos & Aquariums, AZA Member Zoos & Aquariums, June 2008

Professional Sports Teams

Team Name	League
New York Mets	Major League Baseball (MLB)
New York Yankees	Major League Baseball (MLB)
New York Red Bulls	Major League Soccer (MLS)
New Jersey Nets	National Basketball Association (NBA)
New York Knicks	National Basketball Association (NBA)
New York Giants	National Football League (NFL)
New York Jets	National Football League (NFL)
New Jersey Devils	National Hockey League (NHL)
New York Islanders	National Hockey League (NHL)
New York Rangers	National Hockey League (NHL)

Note: Includes teams located in the New York-Northern New Jersey metro area.
Source: Original research

MEDIA

Newspapers

Name	News Focus	Frequency	Circulation
No newspapers have an office in the city			

Note: Includes newspapers with offices located in the city
Source: MediaContactsPro, March 2008

Television Stations

Name	Ch.	Network(s)	Type	Ownership
WCBS	2	CBS	Commercial	CBS
WNBC	4	NBC	Commercial	General Electric Corporation
WNYW	5	Fox	Commercial	Fox Television Stations Inc.
WABC	7	ABC	Commercial	ABC Inc.
WWOR	9	UPN	Commercial	Fox Television Stations Inc.
WPIX	11	WBN	Commercial	Tribune Broadcasting Company
WNET	13	PBS	Public	Educational Broadcasting Corporation
WLIW	21	PBS	Public	Long Island Educational TV Council Inc.
WNYE	25	PBS	Public	New York City Board of Education
WPXN	31	Pax	Commercial	Paxson Communications Corporation
WXTV	41	Univision	Commercial	Univision Holding
WNJU	47	Telemundo	Commercial	Telemundo Group Inc.
WTBY	54	n/a	Commercial	Trinity Broadcasting Network
WLNY	55	n/a	Commercial	Michael C. Pascucci
WRNN	62	n/a	Commercial	WRNN-TV Associates L.P.
WMBC	63	n/a	Commercial	Mountain Broadcasting Corporation
WHSI	67	n/a	Commercial	USA Broadcasting Group
WHSE	68	n/a	Commercial	USA Broadcasting Group

Note: Stations included cover the New York DMA (Designated Market Area); n/a not available
BurrellesLuce, MediaContacts Online, January 2007

Major AM Radio Stations

Call Letters	Freq. (kHz)	Station Type	Target Audience	Station Format	Music Format
WMCA	570	n/a	General/Religious	Music/News/Talk	n/a
WFAN	660	n/a	General	News/Sports/Talk	n/a
WOR	710	n/a	General	Music/News	Reggae
WABC	770	n/a	General	n/a	n/a
WNYC	820	Public	General	Music/Talk	Blues
WCBS	880	Commercial	General	Music/News/Sports	Reggae
WGHQ	920	n/a	General	Music	n/a
WWDJ	970	n/a	General/Religious	Music/Talk	n/a
WINS	1010	n/a	General	News	n/a
WHLI	1100	Commercial	General	Music	Adult Standards
WBBR	1130	n/a	General/Men	Music/News	Reggae
WVNJ	1160	n/a	General	n/a	n/a
WOBM	1160	n/a	General	Music	n/a
WLIB	1190	n/a	General	News/Talk	n/a
WGNY	1220	n/a	General	News/Talk	n/a
WMTR	1250	Commercial	General	Music	Adult Standards
WADO	1280	Commercial	General/Hispanic	News/Sports/Talk	n/a
WWRV	1330	n/a	General/Hisp/Rel	Music/News/Talk	n/a
WELV	1370	n/a	General	Music	n/a
WEOK	1390	Commercial	General/Hispanic	Music/Sports	Latin
WLNA	1420	n/a	General	Music/News/Sports/Talk	n/a
WNSW	1430	n/a	Ethnic/General	Music/News/Talk	n/a
WZRC	1480	n/a	Asian	Talk	n/a
WQEW	1560	n/a	Child/Gen/Yng Adlt	Educational	n/a
WLIM	1580	Commercial	Ethnic/General	Music/News	World Music
WWRL	1600	n/a	General	Music/Talk	Reggae
WWRU	1660	n/a	Asian/General/Hispanic	News/Talk	n/a

Note: Stations included cover the New York DMA (Designated Market Area); n/a not available
Source: BurrellesLuce, MediaContacts Online, January 2007

Major FM Radio Stations

Call Letters	Freq. (mHz)	Station Type	Target Audience	Station Format	Music Format
WFSO	88.3	n/a	Religious	Educational/Music/News	n/a
WFDU	89.1	College	General	Music	n/a
WFUV	90.7	College	General	Music/News/Sports	Folk
WPAT	93.1	Commercial	General/Hispanic	News/Talk	n/a
WRKI	95.1	n/a	General	Music/News/Talk	n/a
WQHT	97.1	n/a	General	Music/News/Talk	n/a
WSKQ	97.9	Commercial	General/Hispanic	Music/News/Talk	Latin
WRKS	98.7	n/a	General/Women	News/Talk	Rhythm & Blues
WBAI	99.5	Non-Comm	General	Music/Talk	Reggae
WHUD	100.7	n/a	General	Music/News/Talk	n/a
WPDH	101.5	Commercial	General	Music	Classic Rock
WKTU	103.5	n/a	General/Women	Music/News/Talk	Urban Contemp.
WAXQ	104.3	n/a	General	Music/Talk	n/a
WSPK	104.7	n/a	General	Music/News/Talk	n/a
WWPR	105.1	Commercial	General	Music	Rhythm & Blues
WBLI	106.1	Commercial	General	Music/Talk	Top 40
WLTW	106.7	n/a	General	Music	n/a
WBLS	107.5	n/a	Black/General	Music	n/a
WEBE	107.9	n/a	General	Music/News	n/a

Note: Stations included cover the New York DMA (Designated Market Area); n/a not available
BurrellesLuce, MediaContacts Online, January 2007

CLIMATE

Average and Extreme Temperatures

Temperature	Jan	Feb	Mar	Apr	May	Jun	Jul	Aug	Sep	Oct	Nov	Dec	Yr.
Extreme High (°F)	74	76	89	94	98	102	105	103	105	93	85	72	105
Average High (°F)	38	41	50	61	72	81	86	84	77	66	54	42	63
Average Temp. (°F)	32	33	42	52	63	72	77	76	68	57	47	36	55
Average Low (°F)	24	25	33	43	53	62	68	67	59	48	39	28	46
Extreme Low (°F)	-8	-7	6	16	33	41	52	45	35	25	15	-1	-8

Note: Figures cover the years 1935-1995
Source: National Climatic Data Center, International Station Meteorological Climate Summary, 9/96

Average Precipitation/Snowfall/Humidity

Precip./Humidity	Jan	Feb	Mar	Apr	May	Jun	Jul	Aug	Sep	Oct	Nov	Dec	Yr.
Avg. Precip. (in.)	3.4	3.0	4.0	3.7	3.9	3.3	4.2	4.1	3.6	3.0	3.8	3.4	43.5
Avg. Snowfall (in.)	8	8	5	1	Tr	0	0	0	0	Tr	1	5	27
Avg. Rel. Hum. 7am (%)	73	71	69	67	70	71	72	76	79	78	76	74	73
Avg. Rel. Hum. 4pm (%)	58	54	51	48	51	51	52	54	55	53	57	59	54

Note: Figures cover the years 1935-1995; Tr = Trace amounts (<0.05 in. of rain; <0.5 in. of snow)
Source: National Climatic Data Center, International Station Meteorological Climate Summary, 9/96

Weather Conditions

Temperature			Daytime Sky			Precipitation		
5°F & below	32°F & below	90°F & above	Clear	Partly cloudy	Cloudy	0.01 inch or more precip.	0.1 inch or more snow/ice	Thunder-storms
2	90	24	80	146	139	122	16	46

Note: Figures are average number of days per year and cover the years 1935-1995
Source: National Climatic Data Center, International Station Meteorological Climate Summary, 9/96

HAZARDOUS WASTE

Superfund Sites

South Brunswick has no sites on the EPA's Superfund Final National Priorities List.
U.S. Environmental Protection Agency, Final National Priorities List, June 23, 2008

AIR & WATER QUALITY

Air Quality Index

Area	Percent of Days when Air Quality was...[2]				AQI Statistics	
	Good	Moderate	Unhealthy for Sensitive Groups	Unhealthy	Maximum	Median
MSA[1]	71.0	20.8	7.4	0.8	166	39

Note: The Air Quality Index (AQI) is an index for reporting daily air quality. EPA calculates the AQI for five major air pollutants regulated by the Clean Air Act: ground-level ozone, particle pollution (also known as particulate matter), carbon monoxide, sulfur dioxide, and nitrogen dioxide. The AQI runs from 0 to 500. The higher the AQI value, the greater the level of air pollution and the greater the health concern. There are six AQI categories: "Good" The AQI is between 0 and 50. Air quality is considered satisfactory; "Moderate" The AQI is between 51 and 100. Air quality is acceptable; "Unhealthy for Sensitive Groups" When AQI values are between 101 and 150, members of sensitive groups may experience health effects; "Unhealthy" When AQI values are between 151 and 200 everyone may begin to experience health effects; "Very Unhealthy" AQI values between 201 and 300 trigger a health alert; "Hazardous" AQI values over 300 trigger health warnings of emergency conditions; (1) Metropolitan Statistical Area - see Appendix A for areas included; (2) Based on 365 days with AQI data in 2007.
Source: U.S. Environmental Protection Agency, Air Quality Index Report, 2007

Air Quality Index Pollutants

Area	Percent of Days when AQI Pollutant was...[2]					
	Carbon Monoxide	Nitrogen Dioxide	Ozone	Sulfur Dioxide	Particulate Matter 2.5	Particulate Matter 10
MSA[1]	0.0	0.0	64.1	0.0	35.9	0.0

Note: The Air Quality Index (AQI) is an index for reporting daily air quality. EPA calculates the AQI for five major air pollutants regulated by the Clean Air Act: ground-level ozone, particle pollution (also known as particulate matter), carbon monoxide, sulfur dioxide, and nitrogen dioxide. The AQI runs from 0 to 500. The higher the AQI value, the greater the level of air pollution and the greater the health concern; (1) Metropolitan Statistical Area - see Appendix A for areas included; (2) Based on 365 days with AQI data in 2007.
Source: U.S. Environmental Protection Agency, Air Quality Index Report, 2007

Air Quality Index Trends

Area	Trend Sites (4)								All Sites (17)
	1999	2000	2001	2002	2003	2004	2005	2006	2006
MSA[1]	23	9	13	20	8	6	12	5	10

Note: An AQI value greater than 100 indicates that air quality would have been in the unhealthful range on that day. Data from exceptional events are not included. These counts are presented in two ways. First, the counts are based on sites having an adequate record of monitoring data during the trend period (trend sites). These counts represent the relative change in the number of days with AQI values greater than 100. In the last column, the counts are based on all sites with data in the most recent year (because it is possible for a site to have data in the most recent year but not enough data to be a trend site); (1) Metropolitan Statistical Area - see Appendix A for areas included.
Source: U.S. Environmental Protection Agency, Office of Air and Radiation, Air Trends, Factbook and Related Information, Air Pollution Trends in Selected Metropolitan Areas 2006

Maximum Air Pollutant Concentrations

	Particulate Matter 10 (ug/m^3)	Particulate Matter 2.5 (ug/m^3)	Ozone (ppm)	Carbon Monoxide (ppm)	Sulfur Dioxide (ppm)	Nitrogen Dioxide (ppm)	Lead (ug/m^3)
MSA[1] Level	n/a	33	0.125	2	0.014	0.014	n/a
NAAQS[2]	150	35	0.125	9	0.140	0.053	1.50
Met NAAQS[2]	Yes	Yes	Yes	Yes	Yes	Yes	n/a

Note: Data from exceptional events are not included; (1) Metropolitan Statistical Area - see Appendix A for areas included; (2) National Ambient Air Quality Standards; n/a not available
Concentrations: Particulate Matter 10 (coarse particulate) - highest second maximum 24-hour concentration; Particulate Matter 2.5 (fine particulate) - highest 98th percentile 24-hour concentration; Ozone - highest second daily maximum 1-hour concentration; Carbon Monoxide - highest second maximum non-overlapping 8-hour concentration; Sulfur Dioxide - highest second maximum 24-hour concentration; Nitrogen Dioxide - highest arithmetic mean concentration; Lead - highest quarterly maximum concentration
Units: ppm = parts per million; ug/m^3 = micrograms per cubic meter
Source: U.S. Environmental Protection Agency, MSA Factbook 2006, Air Quality Statistics by City

Drinking Water

Water System Name	Pop. Served	Primary Water Source Type	Violations[1]	
			Health Based	Monitoring/ Reporting
South Brunswick Twp WDI	35,000	Ground	n/a	n/a

Note: (1) Based on violation data from January 1, 2007 to December 31, 2007 (includes unresolved violations from earlier years)
Source: U.S. Environmental Protection Agency, Office of Ground Water and Drinking Water, Safe Drinking Water Information System (based on data extracted April 15, 2008)

West Windsor, New Jersey

Background

West Windsor is centrally located on the eastern border of Mercer County. Princeton lies to the north, East Windsor and Plainsboro to the east, Hamilton and Lawrence to the west, and Robbinsville to the south.

The area was originally inhabited by the Lenni Lenape ("true people") Indians, also known as the Delaware Indians. Captain Thomas Yong of England discovered what is now known as West Windsor, during his exploration of the Delaware Bay area in 1634. In 1682, after many Europeans settled in this area, William Penn signed a treaty with the Lenni Lenape Indians to purchase the land and established West Windsor. In 1737, William Penn's heirs sold the property to the Dutch farming families of Scheck and Covenhoven. In 1751 it became the Town of Windsor. Finally, in 1797 it was officially incorporated.

West Windsor is an area rich in history and culture, with part of the prestigious Princeton University campus located within West Windsor's borders. On October 30, 1938, however, a radio broadcast of H.G. Welles' War of The Worlds, put West Windsor in a different national spotlight. Performed as a Halloween special aired over the CBS Radio network, narrator Orson Wells began telling the story of an alien spacecraft that landed on a farm near Grovers Mill, located in West Windsor. Terrified listeners, thinking that news of an impending Martian attack was real, began fleeing their homes to seek shelter. Today, a monument at Grovers Mill commemorates the broadcast and is a popular tourist stop.

For the more conservative history buff, The Schenck House (circa 1750) shows what life was like in early-day West Windsor. Max Zaitz gifted it to West Windsor Historical Society in 1995, with a mission to preserve and document the farming past of West Windsor. It has housed the Historical Society of West Windsor since its founding in 1983.

The McCarter Theatre Center for the Performing Arts is West Windsor's theatrical gem, built for the Princeton University Triangle Club. Since opening night, on February 21, 1930, it has served as an endless avenue of fine productions with appearances of many well-known companies and actors. "Our Town" had its world premiere there and such actors as Catherine Hepburn and James Stewart have performed at the McCarter in the 1930s. More recently, its diverse program has included such artists as Bill Cosby, James Taylor, Billy Joel, Carol Burnett, Bob Dylan, Bette Midler, George Winston and many more.

Another popular attraction is the "Dinky" which is a one-car train shuttle. It runs between Princeton Junction and Princeton stations, in the history books as the shortest and most expensive per-mile, regularly scheduled train passenger route in the United States, traveling 2.7 miles each way.

Since 1993, West Windsor's government is made up of an elected Mayor and five City Council members. Some of the many educational institutions that serve West Windsor are Princeton University, Mercer Community College, Westminster Choir College of Rider University, Princeton Theological Seminary, as well as many high ranking high schools and elementary schools.

Rankings

General Rankings

- Trenton* was ranked #81 out of 375 metro areas in *Cities Ranked & Rated*. Criteria: cost of living; climate; crime; transportation; economy and jobs; education; arts and culture; health and healthcare; leisure; quality of life. *Cities Ranked & Rated, 2nd Edition, 2007*
- Trenton* was ranked #173 out of 379 metro areas in *Places Rated Almanac*. Criteria: health care; education; recreation; transportation; ambience; climate; crime; housing costs; jobs. *Places Rated Almanac, 7th Edition, 2007*

Business/Finance Rankings

- The Trenton* metro area was identified as one of the "25 Hottest Housing Markets" in the U.S. The area ranked #173 out of 156 markets with a home price appreciation rate of 6.2%. Criteria: year-over-year change of median sales price of existing single-family homes between the 4th quarter of 2006 and the 4th quarter of 2007. *National Association of Realtors, Median Sales Price of Existing Single-Family Homes for Metropolitan Areas, 4th Quarter 2007*
- The Trenton* metro area appeared on the Milken Institute "2007 Best Performing Cities" index. Rank: #55 out of 200 large metro areas. Criteria: job growth; wage and salary growth; high-tech output growth. *Milken Institute, "2007 Best Performing Cities"*

Health/Environment Rankings

- The Trenton* metro area appeared in *Country Home's* "2008 Best Green Places" report. The area ranked #153 out of 379. Criteria: official energy policies; green power; green buildings; availability of fresh, locally grown food. *Country Home, "2008 Best Green Places"*

Seniors/Retirement Rankings

- A.G. Edwards ranked America's 500 top-performing communities based on their residents' personal savings and investing behavior. The Trenton* metro area ranked #18 with an index score of 114.35 (national average = 100.00). A dozen statistical factors were measured including: participation in retirement savings plans; personal debt levels; and home ownership. *A.G. Edwards, "2007 Nest Egg Index", September 12, 2007*

Children/Family Rankings

- The Trenton* metro area was selected as one of the "Best Cities for Relocating Families" by Worldwide ERC and Primacy Relocation. The 2007 study placed a special emphasis on the housing market, which has significantly impacted the relocation industry and an employer's ability to transfer employees. The variables which weigh heavily in this category include home price, home affordability index, appreciation rates, and property tax. Other criteria include cost of living, crime rates, education, climate, focus on diversity, physicians per capita, recreation and leisure, arts and culture, air quality, watershed quality, sales tax, unemployment rate, job growth, high school and higher education index, school expenditures per student, students in public school, SAT/ACT percentile, and population growth. *Worldwide ERC and Primacy Relocation, "2007 Best Cities for Relocating Families"*

Safety Rankings

- The National Insurance Crime Bureau ranked 361 metro areas in the U.S. in terms of per capita rates of vehicle theft. The Trenton* metro area ranked #171 (#1 = highest rate). Criteria: number of vehicle theft offenses per 100,000 inhabitants. *National Insurance Crime Bureau, "NICB Vehicle Theft Study," April 22, 2008*

- Farmers Insurance Group of Companies, in partnership with Sperling's BestPlaces, ranked 379 metro areas and identified the "Most Secure U.S. Place to Live." The Trenton* metro area ranked #59 out of 127 in the mid-size city category (150,000 to 500,000 residents). Criteria: crime rates; extreme weather; risk of natural disasters; environmental hazards; terrorism threats; air quality; life expectancy; job loss numbers. *Farmers Insurance Group, "Most Secure U.S. Places to Live 2007"*

Sports/Recreation Rankings

- *Golf Digest* ranked 330 metro areas in the U.S. in terms of golf. The Trenton* metro area was ranked #317. Criteria: access to golf; weather; value of golf; and quality of golf. *Golf Digest, "Metro Golf Rankings," August 2005*

West Windsor is located within the Trenton-Ewing, NJ Metropolitan Statistical Area.

Business Environment

CITY FINANCES

City Government Finances

Component	2004-2005 ($000)	2004-2005 ($ per capita)
Total Revenues	27,990	1,077
Total Expenditures	27,178	1,046
Debt Outstanding	30,653	1,180
Cash and Securities	13,787	531

Source: U.S Census Bureau, Government Finances 2004-2005

City Government Revenue by Source

Source	2004-2005 ($000)	2004-2005 ($ per capita)
General Revenue		
From Federal Government	0	0
From State Government	3,428	132
From Local Governments	214	8
Taxes		
Property	17,454	672
Sales	420	16
Personal Income	0	0
License	1,434	55
Charges	3,412	131
Liquor Store	0	0
Utility	0	0
Employee Retirement	0	0
Other	1,628	63

Source: U.S Census Bureau, Government Finances 2004-2005

City Government Expenditures by Function

Function	2004-2005 ($000)	2004-2005 ($ per capita)	2004-2005 (%)
General Expenditures			
Airports	0	0	0.0
Corrections	0	0	0.0
Education	0	0	0.0
Fire Protection	1,128	43	4.2
Governmental Administration	3,505	135	12.9
Health	474	18	1.7
Highways	3,063	118	11.3
Hospitals	0	0	0.0
Housing and Community Development	32	1	0.1
Interest on General Debt	1,149	44	4.2
Libraries	0	0	0.0
Parking	0	0	0.0
Parks and Recreation	1,083	42	4.0
Police Protection	5,026	193	18.5
Public Welfare	45	2	0.2
Sewerage	2,552	98	9.4
Solid Waste Management	1,670	64	6.1
Liquor Store	0	0	0.0
Utility	0	0	0.0
Employee Retirement	0	0	0.0
Other	7,451	287	27.4

Source: U.S Census Bureau, Government Finances 2004-2005

Municipal Bond Ratings

Area	Moody's
City	n/a

Source: Mergent Bond Record, January 2008 (unless noted otherwise)

DEMOGRAPHICS

Population Growth

Area	1990 Census	2000 Census	2007 Estimate	2012 Projection	Population Growth (%) 1990-2000	Population Growth (%) 2000-2012
City	16,021	21,907	27,392	30,743	36.7	40.3
MSA[1]	325,804	350,761	370,167	382,207	7.7	9.0
U.S.	248,709,873	281,421,906	301,045,522	314,920,978	13.2	11.9

Note: (1) Metropolitan Statistical Area - see Appendix B for areas included
Source: Claritas, Inc.

Number of Households and Average Household Size

Area	2007 Estimate	2007 Average Household Size
City	8,955	3.06
MSA[1]	133,646	2.77
U.S.	113,668,003	2.65

Note: (1) Metropolitan Statistical Area - see Appendix B for areas included
Source: Claritas, Inc.

Race and Ethnicity

Area	White Alone[2]	Black Alone[2]	Asian Alone[2]	Other Race Alone[2]	Hispanic[3]
City	60.7	2.6	33.2	3.5	4.9
MSA[1]	63.6	19.9	7.9	8.6	12.3
U.S.	73.1	12.4	4.3	10.3	14.9

Note: Figures are 2007 estimates; (1) Metropolitan Statistical Area - see Appendix B for areas included (2) Alone is defined as not being in combination with one or more other races; (3) May be of any race.
Source: Claritas, Inc.

Ancestry

Area	German	Irish[2]	English	American	Italian	Polish	French[3]	Scottish
City	12.8	15.3	10.0	2.4	14.5	5.5	2.1	1.7
MSA[1]	11.8	13.1	8.0	2.9	15.4	8.0	1.5	1.4
U.S.	15.2	10.9	8.7	7.3	5.6	3.2	3.0	1.7

Note: Figures include multiple ancestry (e.g. if a person reported being Irish and Italian, they were included in both columns); (1) Metropolitan Statistical Area - see Appendix A for areas included; (2) Includes Celtic; (3) Includes Alsatian but excludes Basque
Source: Census 2000, Summary File 3

Foreign-Born Population

Area	Percent of Population Born in: Any Foreign Country	Europe	Asia	Africa	Oceania[2]	Canada	Mexico	Latin America[3]
City	22.4	3.6	14.7	0.9	0.1	0.3	0.4	2.4
MSA[1]	13.9	3.8	3.8	0.9	0.0	0.3	0.4	4.7
U.S.	11.1	1.7	2.9	0.3	0.1	0.3	3.3	2.5

Note: (1) Metropolitan Statistical Area - see Appendix A for areas included; (2) Includes Australia, New Zealand subregion, Melanesia, Micronesia, Polynesia, and Oceania n.e.c; (3) Includes Central America (excluding Mexico), South America, and the Caribbean.
Source: Census 2000, Summary File 3

Marriage Status

Area	Never Married	Now Married (excluding Separated)	Separated	Widowed	Divorced
City	19.5	71.0	1.2	3.3	5.0
MSA[1]	29.9	52.9	2.4	7.0	7.8
U.S.	27.1	54.4	2.2	6.6	9.7

Note: Figures are percentages and cover the population 15 years of age and older; (1) Metropolitan Statistical Area - see Appendix A for areas included
Source: Census 2000, Summary File 3

Age Distribution

Area	Percent of Population: Under Age 5	Age 5 to 17	Age 18 to 34	Age 35 to 49	Age 50 to 64	Age 65 to 79	80 Years and Over
City	6.7	24.9	14.3	31.9	16.0	5.1	1.2
MSA[1]	6.3	17.5	24.2	24.5	14.9	9.1	3.4
U.S.	6.8	18.9	23.7	23.5	14.8	9.2	3.2

Note: (1) Metropolitan Statistical Area - see Appendix A for areas included
Source: Census 2000, Summary File 3

Male/Female Ratio

Area	Males	Females	Males per 100 Females
City	13,568	13,824	98.1
MSA[1]	181,394	188,773	96.1
U.S.	148,320,305	152,725,217	97.1

Note: Figures are 2007 estimates; (1) Metropolitan Statistical Area - see Appendix B for areas included
Source: Claritas, Inc.

Religion

Area	Catholic	Southern Baptist	United Meth-odist	ELCA[1]	LDS[2]	Presby-terian Church USA	Jewish Est.	Muslim Est.
County	31.2	0.0	1.6	1.2	0.2	2.8	2.6	3.3
U.S.	22.0	7.1	3.7	1.8	1.5	1.1	2.2	0.6

Note: Figures are the number of adherents as a percentage of the total population; Adherents are defined as all members, including full members, their children and the estimated number of other participants who are not considered members (e.g. the baptized, those not confirmed, those regularly attending services, etc.); (1) Evangelical Lutheran Church in America; (2) The Church of Jesus Christ of Latter Day Saints
Source: Reprinted with permission from Religious Congregations and Membership in the United States 2000 (Nashville, Glenmary Research Center, 2002) Copyright Association of Statisticians of American Religious Bodies. All rights reserved.

ECONOMY

Gross Metropolitan Product

Area	2002	2003	2004	2005	2005 Rank[2]
MSA[1]	19.0	19.7	21.1	22.4	86

Note: Figures are in billions of dollars; (1) Trenton-Ewing, NJ Metropolitan Statistical Area - see Appendix A for areas included; (2) Rank ranges from 1 to 361
Source: The U.S. Conference of Mayors, "U.S. Metro Economies: GMP - The Engines of America's Growth," January 2007

Economic Growth

Area	1995 GMP	2005 GMP	Average Annual Growth Rate	Growth Rate Rank[2]
MSA[1]	13.6	22.4	5.1	212

Note: Figures are in billions of dollars; GMP = Gross Metropolitan Product; (1) Trenton-Ewing, NJ Metropolitan Statistical Area - see Appendix A for areas included; (2) Rank ranges from 1 to 361
Source: The U.S. Conference of Mayors, "U.S. Metro Economies: GMP - The Engines of America's Growth," January 2007

INCOME

Per Capita/Median/Average Income

Area	Per Capita ($)	Median Household ($)	Average Household ($)
City	58,426	142,859	178,147
MSA[1]	33,474	67,440	91,166
U.S.	25,495	49,280	66,670

Note: Figures are 2007 estimates; (1) Metropolitan Statistical Area - see Appendix B for areas included
Source: Claritas, Inc.

Household Income Distribution

Area	Percent of Households Earning							
	Under $15,000	$15,000 -24,999	$25,000 -34,999	$35,000 -49,999	$50,000 -74,999	$75,000 -99,000	$100,000 -149,999	$150,000 and up
City	2.5	2.2	2.5	5.1	8.5	9.9	22.8	46.5
MSA[1]	9.7	7.4	7.8	12.2	17.9	14.0	17.1	13.8
U.S.	13.1	10.9	11.2	15.6	19.5	11.9	11.3	6.6

Note: Figures are 2007 estimates; (1) Metropolitan Statistical Area - see Appendix B for areas included
Source: Claritas, Inc.

Poverty Rates by Age

Area	All Ages	Under 5 Years Old	5 to 17 Years Old	18 to 64 Years Old	65 Years and Over
City	2.5	0.2	0.6	1.6	0.1
MSA[1]	8.6	0.8	1.9	4.9	1.1
U.S.	12.4	1.2	3.0	6.9	1.2

Note: Figures are percent of population with income in 1999 below poverty level and only include population for whom poverty status is determined; (1) Metropolitan Statistical Area - see Appendix A for areas included
Source: Census 2000, Summary File 3

Personal Bankruptcy Filing Rate

Area	2004	2005	2006
Mercer County	4.49	5.13	1.50
U.S.	5.31	6.82	2.00

Note: Numbers are per 1,000 population and include Chapter 7 and Chapter 13 filings
Source: Federal Deposit Insurance Corporation (FDIC), Regional Economic Conditions (RECON), 8/23/2007

EMPLOYMENT

Labor Force and Employment

Area	Civilian Labor Force			Workers Employed		
	Dec. 2006	Dec. 2007	% Chg.	Dec. 2006	Dec. 2007	% Chg.
City	14,348	14,339	-0.1	14,137	14,102	-0.2
MSA[1]	196,855	196,495	-0.2	189,807	189,343	-0.2
U.S.	152,571,000	153,705,000	0.7	146,081,000	146,334,000	0.2

Note: Data is not seasonally adjusted and covers workers 16 years of age and older; (1) Metropolitan Statistical Area - see Appendix B for areas included
Source: Bureau of Labor Statistics, http://stats.bls.gov

Unemployment Rate

Area	2007											
	Jan.	Feb.	Mar.	Apr.	May	Jun.	Jul.	Aug.	Sep.	Oct.	Nov.	Dec.
City	1.9	1.7	1.7	1.7	1.9	2.1	2.3	2.0	2.2	1.8	1.8	1.7
MSA[1]	4.4	4.1	3.9	3.6	3.6	3.9	4.4	3.7	3.7	3.4	3.5	3.6
U.S.	5.0	4.9	4.5	4.3	4.3	4.7	4.9	4.6	4.5	4.4	4.5	4.8

Note: Data is not seasonally adjusted and covers workers 16 years of age and older; All figures are percentages; (1) Metropolitan Statistical Area - see Appendix B for areas included
Source: Bureau of Labor Statistics, http://stats.bls.gov

Employment by Occupation

Occupation Classification	City (%)	MSA[1] (%)	U.S. (%)
Sales and Office	20.5	26.5	26.7
Professional and Related	39.0	26.8	20.2
Service	4.5	14.3	14.9
Production, Transportation, and Material Moving	2.4	9.7	14.6
Management, Business, and Financial	32.0	16.5	13.5
Construction, Extraction, and Maintenance	1.6	6.1	9.4
Farming, Forestry, and Fishing	0.0	0.2	0.7

Note: Figures cover employed civilians 16 years of age and older; (1) Metropolitan Statistical Area - see Appendix A for areas included
Source: Census 2000, Summary File 3

Employment by Industry

Sector	MSA[1] Number of Employees	MSA[1] Percent of Total	U.S. Percent of Total
Government	67,600	28.1	16.3
Education and Health Services	42,900	17.8	13.4
Professional and Business Services	36,800	15.3	13.1
Retail Trade	22,800	9.5	11.6
Manufacturing	8,000	3.3	9.9
Leisure and Hospitality	13,900	5.8	9.6
Financial Activities	17,100	7.1	5.9
Construction	n/a	n/a	5.3
Wholesale Trade	5,400	2.2	4.4
Other Services	9,600	4.0	3.9
Transportation and Utilities	4,800	2.0	3.7
Information	5,800	2.4	2.2
Natural Resources and Mining	n/a	n/a	0.5

Note: Figures cover non-farm employment as of December 2007 and are not seasonally adjusted; (1) Metropolitan Statistical Area - see Appendix B for areas included; n/a not available
Source: Bureau of Labor Statistics, http://stats.bls.gov

Average Wages

Occupation	$/Hr.	Occupation	$/Hr.
Accountants and Auditors	35.00	Maids and Housekeeping Cleaners	10.35
Automotive Mechanics	19.59	Maintenance and Repair Workers	18.22
Bookkeepers	18.62	Marketing Managers	64.09
Carpenters	29.73	Nuclear Medicine Technologists	36.90
Cashiers	9.21	Nurses, Licensed Practical	22.87
Clerks, General Office	13.61	Nurses, Registered	31.97
Clerks, Receptionists/Information	12.53	Nursing Aides/Orderlies/Attendants	13.21
Clerks, Shipping/Receiving	14.80	Packers and Packagers, Hand	9.76
Computer Programmers	36.50	Physical Therapists	36.45
Computer Support Specialists	22.64	Postal Service Mail Carriers	21.22
Computer Systems Analysts	39.20	Real Estate Brokers	n/a
Cooks, Restaurant	12.58	Retail Salespersons	13.04
Dentists	n/a	Sales Reps., Exc. Tech./Scientific	31.16
Electrical Engineers	40.47	Sales Reps., Tech./Scientific	39.62
Electricians	35.05	Secretaries, Exc. Legal/Med./Exec.	18.56
Financial Managers	59.01	Security Guards	16.36
First-Line Supervisors/Mgrs., Sales	22.80	Surgeons	n/a
Food Preparation Workers	9.75	Teacher Assistants	12.20
General and Operations Managers	71.72	Teachers, Elementary School	27.50
Hairdressers/Cosmetologists	14.70	Teachers, Secondary School	29.40
Internists	62.30	Telemarketers	19.95
Janitors and Cleaners	12.16	Truck Drivers, Heavy/Tractor-Trailer	19.05
Landscaping/Groundskeeping Workers	13.04	Truck Drivers, Light/Delivery Svcs.	14.13
Lawyers	48.80	Waiters and Waitresses	10.89

Note: Wage data covers the Trenton-Ewing, NJ Metropolitan Statistical Area - see Appendix B for areas included. Hourly wages for elementary/secondary school teachers and teacher assistants were calculated by the editors from annual wage data assuming a 40 hour work week; n/a not available.
Source: Bureau of Labor Statistics, May 2007 Metro Area Occupational Employment and Wage Estimates

RESIDENTIAL REAL ESTATE

Building Permits

Area	Single-Family 2006	Single-Family 2007p	Single-Family Pct. Chg.	Multi-Family 2006	Multi-Family 2007p	Multi-Family Pct. Chg.	Total 2006	Total 2007p	Total Pct. Chg.
City	154	62	-59.7	0	0	-	154	62	-59.7
U.S.	1,378,200	973,300	-29.4	460,700	407,200	-11.6	1,838,900	1,380,500	-24.9

Note: (p) preliminary; figures cover and represent new, privately-owned housing units authorized (unadjusted data); All permit data are based on estimates with imputation; U.S. figures are based on the new 20,000-place series.
Source: U.S. Census Bureau, Manufacturing, Mining, and Construction Statistics

Homeownership and Housing Vacancies

Area	Homeownership Rate[2] (%)			Rental Vacancy Rate[3] (%)			Homeowner Vacancy Rate[4] (%)		
	2005	2006	2007	2005	2006	2007	2005	2006	2007
MSA[1]	n/a	n/a	n/a	n/a	n/a	n/a	n/a	n/a	n/a
U.S.	68.9	68.8	68.1	9.8	9.8	9.7	1.9	2.4	2.7

Note: (1) Metropolitan Statistical Area - see Appendix B for areas included; (2) The proportion of households that are owners; (3) The proportion of the rental inventory that is vacant for rent; (4) The proportion of the homeowner inventory that is vacant for sale; n/a not available
Source: U.S. Census Bureau, Housing Vacancies and Homeownership Annual Statistics: 2007

TAXES

State Corporate Income Tax Rates

State	Rates and Tax Brackets
New Jersey	6.5% > $0; 7.5 > 50K; 9.0% > 100K

Note: Tax rates as of January 1, 2008; Companies with income greater than $100K pay 9% on all income, companies with income greater than $50K but less than $100K pay 7.5 % on all income and companies with income under $50K pay 6.5%. The minimum tax is $500. An Alternative Minimum Assessment based on Gross Receipts applies if greater than corporate franchise tax for out-of-state companies with New Jersey sales. 4% surtax for 2007.
Source: Tax Foundation, www.taxfoundation.org

State Individual Income Tax Rates

State	Federal Deductibility	Marginal Rates (%)	Standard Deduction ($)		Personal Exemptions ($)[1]	
			Single	Joint	Single	Dependents
New Jersey	No	1.4 - 8.97 (y)	n/a	n/a	1,000	1,500

Note: Tax rates as of January 1, 2008; Local- and county-level taxes are not included; n/a not applicable; (1) Married joint filers generally receive double the single exemption; (y) Brackets are not double for married taxpayers.
Source: Tax Foundation, www.taxfoundation.org

Various State and Local Tax Rates

State and Local Sales and Use (%)	State Sales and Use (%)	Gasoline[1,2] ($/gal.)	Cigarette ($/pack)	Spirits ($/gal.)	Table Wine ($/gal.)	Beer ($/gal.)
7.0	7.0	0.145	2.575	4.40	0.70	0.12

Note: Tax rates as of January 1, 2008; (1) In addition to the 18.4 cpg Federal gasoline tax; (2) Rates may include additional state sales taxes, environmental protection and storage fees/taxes, and local taxes. When necessary, the volume-weighted average of all local taxes is used to approximate the typical statewide rate including local tax
Source: Tax Foundation, www.taxfoundation.org; Original research

State Tax Burdens

Area	Combined State and Local Tax Burden		Combined Federal, State and Local Tax Burden	
	Percent	Rank	Percent	Rank
New Jersey	11.6	10	35.6	3
U.S. Average	11.0	-	32.7	-

Note: Figures cover 2007 and measure taxes as a percentage of income
Source: Tax Foundation, www.taxfoundation.org

State Business Tax Climate Index Rankings

State	Overall Rank	Corporate Tax Index Rank	Individual Income Tax Index Rank	Sales Tax Index Rank	Unemployment Insurance Tax Index Rank	Property Tax Index Rank
New Jersey	49	41	49	44	24	49

Note: Rankings range from 1 to 50 where 1 is best. Rankings do not average across to Overall Rank. States without a given tax are given a ranking of 1.
Source: Tax Foundation, State Business Tax Climate Index 2008

TRANSPORTATION

Means of Transportation to Work

Area	Car/Truck/Van		Public Transportation			Bicycle	Walked	Other Means	Worked at Home
	Drove Alone	Car-pooled	Bus	Subway	Railroad				
City	66.5	4.4	0.6	0.4	20.6	0.3	1.2	0.4	5.5
MSA[1]	73.3	11.0	2.9	0.1	3.7	0.5	4.5	0.8	3.2
U.S.	75.7	12.2	2.5	1.5	0.5	0.4	2.9	1.0	3.3

Note: Figures are percentages and cover workers 16 years of age and older; (1) Metropolitan Statistical Area - see Appendix A for areas included
Source: Census 2000, Summary File 3

Travel Time to Work

Area	Less Than 15 Minutes	15 to 29 Minutes	30 to 44 Minutes	45 to 59 Minutes	60 Minutes or More
City	21.8	27.7	10.5	6.9	33.1
MSA[1]	28.4	38.3	15.7	6.3	11.3
U.S.	29.4	36.1	19.1	7.4	8.0

Note: Figures are percentages and include workers 16 years old and over; (1) Metropolitan Statistical Area - see Appendix A for areas included
Source: Census 2000, Summary File 3

Living Environment

COST OF LIVING

Cost of Living Index

Composite Index	Groceries	Housing	Utilities	Trans-portation	Health Care	Misc. Goods/ Services
n/a	n/a	n/a	n/a	n/a	n/a	n/a

Note: U.S. = 100; n/a not available
Source: The Council for Community and Economic Research (formerly ACCRA), Cost of Living Index, 2007

Grocery Prices

Area[1]	T-Bone Steak ($/pound)	Frying Chicken ($/pound)	Whole Milk ($/half gal.)	Eggs ($/dozen)	Orange Juice ($/64 oz.)	Coffee ($/11.5 oz.)
City[2]	n/a	n/a	n/a	n/a	n/a	n/a
Avg.	8.93	1.12	2.13	1.52	3.26	3.31
Min.	5.88	0.71	1.33	0.83	2.30	2.20
Max.	12.80	2.07	3.43	3.54	5.79	6.20

Note: (1) Values for the local area are compared with the average, minimum and maximum values for all 331 areas in the Cost of Living Index report; n/a not available; (2) Figures cover the West Windsor NJ urban area; **T-Bone Steak** *(price per pound);* **Frying Chicken** *(price per pound, whole fryer);* **Whole Milk** *(half gallon carton);* **Eggs** *(price per dozen, Grade A, large);* **Orange Juice** *(64 oz. Tropicana or Florida Natural);* **Coffee** *(11.5 oz. can, vacuum-packed, Maxwell House, Hills Bros, or Folgers).*
Source: The Council for Community and Economic Research (formerly ACCRA), Cost of Living Index, 2007

Housing and Utility Costs

Area[1]	New Home Price ($)	Apartment Rent ($/month)	All Electric ($/month)	Part Electric ($/month)	Other Energy ($/month)	Telephone ($/month)
City[2]	n/a	n/a	n/a	n/a	n/a	n/a
Avg.	309,605	782	146.13	78.67	90.16	26.14
Min.	189,877	n/a	82.03	37.41	33.15	17.08
Max.	1,202,800	3,481	271.14	150.60	257.67	37.45

Note: (1) Values for the local area are compared with the average, minimum and maximum values for all 331 areas in the Cost of Living Index report; n/a not available; (2) Figures cover the West Windsor NJ urban area; **New Home Price** *(2,400 sf living area, 8,000 sf lot, in urban area with full utilities);* **Apartment Rent** *(950 sf 2 bedroom/1.5 or 2 bath, unfurnished, excluding all utilities except water);* **All Electric** *(average monthly cost for an all-electric home);* **Part Electric** *(average monthly cost for a part-electric home);* **Other Energy** *(average monthly cost for natural gas, fuel oil, coal, wood, and any other forms of energy except electricity);* **Telephone** *(price includes basic monthly rate for a private residential line plus additional local usage charges incurred by a family of four).*
Source: The Council for Community and Economic Research (formerly ACCRA), Cost of Living Index, 2007

Health Care, Transportation, and Other Costs

Area[1]	Doctor ($/visit)	Dentist ($/visit)	Optometrist ($/visit)	Gasoline ($/gallon)	Beauty Salon ($/visit)	Men's Shirt ($)
City[2]	n/a	n/a	n/a	n/a	n/a	n/a
Avg.	79.48	71.93	79.55	2.64	29.52	25.77
Min.	52.08	44.80	43.95	2.19	15.58	16.19
Max.	148.44	126.27	158.83	3.48	60.62	48.53

Note: (1) Values for the local area are compared with the average, minimum and maximum values for all 331 areas in the Cost of Living Index report; n/a not available; (2) Figures cover the West Windsor NJ urban area; **Doctor** *(general practitioners routine exam of an established patient);* **Dentist** *(adult teeth cleaning and periodic oral examination);* **Optometrist** *(full vision eye exam for established adult patient);* **Gasoline** *(one gallon regular unleaded, national brand, including all taxes, cash price at self-service pump if available);* **Beauty Salon** *(woman's shampoo, trim, and blow-dry);* **Men's Shirt** *(cotton/polyester dress shirt, pinpoint weave, long sleeves).*
Source: The Council for Community and Economic Research (formerly ACCRA), Cost of Living Index, 2007

HOUSING

House Price Index (HPI)

Area	National Ranking[2]	Quarterly Change (%)	One-Year Change (%)	Five-Year Change (%)
MSA[1]	199	0.07	-0.51	51.25
U.S.[3]	-	0.10	0.84	41.37

Note: The HPI is a weighted repeat sales index. It measures average price changes in repeat sales or refinancings on the same properties. This information is obtained by reviewing repeat mortgage transactions on single-family properties whose mortgages have been purchased or securitized by Fannie Mae or Freddie Mac in January 1975; (1) Metropolitan Statistical Area - see Appendix B for areas included; (2) Rankings are based on annual percentage change for all metro areas containing at least 15,000 transactions over the last 10 years and ranges from 1 to 291; (3) figures based on a weighted average of Census Division estimates; all figures are for the period ending December 31, 2007
Source: Office of Federal Housing Enterprise Oversight, House Price Index, February 26, 2008

House Price Valuations

Area	Q1 2000	Q1 2001	Q1 2002	Q1 2003	Q1 2004	Q1 2005	Q1 2006	Q1 2007	Q1 2008
MSA[1]	-23.7	-20.6	-17.0	-7.7	0.5	12.9	13.2	4.2	-1.4

Note: Figures show the percentage of over- or under-valuation of single family homes relative to statistically normal house values (e.g. a value of 23.6 indicates that house values are 23.6% overvalued). Statistically normal house values are based on house prices, interest rates, household incomes, population densities, and any historical premiums or discounts metropolitan areas have exhibited over time; (1) Figures cover the Metropolitan Statistical Area - see Appendix B for areas included
Source: Global Insight/National City Corporation, House Prices in America, May 2008

Median Home Prices

Area	2005	2006	2007[r]	Percent Change 2006 to 2007
MSA[1]	261.1	289.6	307.1	6.0
U.S. Average	219.0	221.9	217.9	-1.8

Note: Figures are median sales prices of existing single-family homes in thousands of dollars; (r) revised; n/a not available; (1) Metropolitan Statistical Area - see Appendix B for areas included
Source: National Association of Realtors, Metropolitan Area Prices, 1st Quarter 2008

Housing: Year Structure Built

Area	1990 -2000	1980 -1989	1970 -1979	1960 -1969	1950 -1959	1940 -1949	Before 1940	Median Year
City	28.7	35.1	12.1	9.9	6.9	1.6	5.6	1984
MSA[1]	10.2	12.4	12.5	15.2	16.6	9.6	23.5	1960
U.S.	17.0	15.8	18.5	13.7	12.7	7.3	15.0	1971

Note: Figures are percentages; (1) Metropolitan Statistical Area - see Appendix A for areas included
Source: Census 2000, Summary File 3

HEALTH

Health Risk Data

Category	Area[1] (%)	U.S. (%)
Adults who have been told they have high blood pressure[3]	24.2	25.5
Adults who have been told they have high blood cholesterol[3]	39.3	35.6
Adults who have been told they have diabetes[2]	7.0	7.5
Adults who have been told they have arthritis[3]	26.5	27.0
Adults who have been told they currently have asthma	11.3	8.5
Adults who are current smokers	13.6	20.1
Adults who are heavy drinkers[4]	3.1	4.9
Adults who are overweight (BMI 25.0 - 29.9)	38.2	36.5
Adults who are obese (BMI 30.0 - 99.8)	20.3	25.1

Note: Data as of 2006 unless otherwise noted; (1) Figures cover the Metropolitan Statistical Area - see Appendix B for areas included; (2) Figures do not include pregnancy-related diabetes, pre-diabetes or borderline diabetes; (3) 2005 data; (4) Heavy drinkers are classified as adult men having more than two drinks per day or adult women having more than one drink per day
Source: Centers for Disease Control and Prevention, Behaviorial Risk Factor Surveillance System, SMART: Selected Metropolitan/Micropolitan Area Risk Trends, 2005, 2006

Mortality Rates for the Top 10 Causes of Death in the U.S.

ICD-10[a] Sub-Chapter	ICD-10[a] Code	Age-Adjusted Mortality Rate[1] per 100,000 population	
		County[2]	U.S.
Malignant neoplasms	C00-C97	173.6	186.5
Ischaemic heart diseases	I20-I25	153.1	152.3
Other forms of heart disease	I30-I51	44.2	51.5
Cerebrovascular diseases	I60-I69	35.7	50.0
Chronic lower respiratory diseases	J40-J47	33.2	42.6
Diabetes mellitus	E10-E14	25.7	24.8
Other degenerative diseases of the nervous system	G30-G31	15.2	22.6
Other external causes of accidental injury	W00-X59	16.3	21.4
Influenza and pneumonia	J10-J18	16.7	20.7
Hypertensive diseases	I10-I13	15.3	18.2

Note: (a) ICD-10 = International Classification of Diseases 10th Revision; (1) Mortality rates are a three year average covering 2003-2005; (2) Figures cover Mercer County
Source: Centers for Disease Control and Prevention, National Center for Health Statistics. Compressed Mortality File 1999-2004. CDC WONDER On-line Database, compiled from Compressed Mortality File 1999-2005 Series 20 No. 2K, 2008.

Mortality Rates for Selected Causes of Death

ICD-10[a] Sub-Chapter	ICD-10[a] Code	Age-Adjusted Mortality Rate[1] per 100,000 population	
		County[2]	U.S.
Assault	X85-Y09	6.6	5.9
Human immunodeficiency virus (HIV) disease	B20-B24	7.3	4.5
Intentional self-harm	X60-X84	5.8	10.8
Malnutrition	E40-E46	1.8	1.0
Obesity and other hyperalimentation	E65-E68	2.1	1.4
Organic, including symptomatic, mental disorders	F01-F09	12.5	16.8
Transport accidents	V01-V99	7.5	16.1
Viral hepatitis	B15-B19	1.8	1.8

Note: (a) ICD-10 = International Classification of Diseases 10th Revision; (1) Mortality rates are a three year average covering 2003-2005; (2) Figures cover Mercer County
Source: Centers for Disease Control and Prevention, National Center for Health Statistics. Compressed Mortality File 1999-2004. CDC WONDER On-line Database, compiled from Compressed Mortality File 1999-2005 Series 20 No. 2K, 2008.

Distribution of Physicians[1]

Area	Total	Family/ General Practice	Specialties	
			Medical	Surgical
Mercer County (number)	967	93	417	229
Mercer County (rate per 10,000 pop.)	26.4	2.5	11.4	6.3
U.S. (rate per 10,000 pop.)	17.7	4.6	6.9	4.3

Note: Data as of 2005; (1) Includes all non-federal, patient-care, office-based MDs
Source: Area Resource File (ARF). June 2007. U.S. Department of Health and Human Services, Health Resources and Services Administration, Bureau of Health Professions, Rockville, MD.

Hospitals

There were no hospitals listed within the city limits.
AHA Guide to the Healthcare Field 2008

EDUCATION

Public School District Statistics

District Name	Schls	Pupils	Pupil/ Teacher Ratio	Minority Pupils[1] (%)	Free Lunch Eligible[2] (%)	IEP[3] (%)
West Windsor-Plainsboro	10	9,290	12.5	52.1	2.3	20.2

Note: Table includes regular local school districts with 2,000 or more students; (1) Percentage of students that are not white, non-Hispanic; (2) Percentage of students that are eligible for the free lunch program; (3) Percentage of students that have an Individualized Education Program.
Source: U.S. Department of Education, National Center for Education Statistics, Common Core of Data, Local Education Agency (School District) Universe Survey: School Year 2005-2006; U.S. Department of Education, National Center for Education Statistics, Common Core of Data, Public Elementary/Secondary School Universe Survey: School Year 2005-2006

Highest Level of Education

Area	Less than H.S.	H.S. Diploma	Some College, No Deg.	Associate Degree	Bachelors Degree	Masters Degree	Profess. School Degree	Doctorate Degree
City	3.1	7.7	10.1	5.2	35.0	25.4	6.7	6.8
MSA[1]	17.9	25.4	16.8	5.4	18.8	9.9	2.9	3.0
U.S.	19.4	28.4	21.2	6.4	15.7	5.9	2.0	1.0

Note: Figures are 2007 estimated percentages and cover persons age 25 and over; (1) Metropolitan Statistical Area - see Appendix B for areas included
Source: Claritas, Inc.

Educational Attainment by Race

Area	High School Graduate (%)					Bachelor's Degree (%)				
	Total	White	Black	Asian	Hisp.[2]	Total	White	Black	Asian	Hisp.[2]
City	96.9	97.8	96.7	95.8	81.0	73.9	73.8	60.7	79.7	44.8
MSA[1]	81.8	86.0	69.8	91.3	55.5	34.0	38.3	12.8	72.2	11.6
U.S.	80.4	83.6	72.3	80.4	52.4	24.4	26.1	14.3	44.1	10.4

Note: Figures shown cover persons 25 years old and over; (1) Metropolitan Statistical Area - see Appendix A for areas included; (2) people of Hispanic origin can be of any race
Source: Census 2000, Summary File 3

School Enrollment by Type

Area	Grades KG to 8				Grades 9 to 12			
	Public		Private		Public		Private	
	Enrollment	%	Enrollment	%	Enrollment	%	Enrollment	%
City	3,586	91.1	351	8.9	1,250	86.6	194	13.4
MSA[1]	37,980	86.3	6,027	13.7	16,206	85.8	2,692	14.2
U.S.	33,526,011	88.7	4,285,121	11.3	14,848,628	90.6	1,532,323	9.4

Note: Figures shown cover persons 3 years old and over; (1) Metropolitan Statistical Area - see Appendix A for areas included
Source: Census 2000, Summary File 3

School Enrollment by Race

Area	Grades KG to 8 (%)				Grades 9 to 12 (%)			
	White	Black	Asian	Hisp.[1]	White	Black	Asian	Hisp.[1]
City	70.8	2.3	22.3	4.7	63.0	3.3	27.1	5.7
MSA[2]	59.9	25.8	5.2	11.6	58.1	27.2	5.2	11.8
U.S.	68.5	15.5	3.3	16.8	68.8	15.5	3.8	15.7

Note: Figures shown cover persons 3 years old and over; (1) people of Hispanic origin can be of any race; (2) Metropolitan Statistical Area - see Appendix A for areas included
Source: Census 2000, Summary File 3

Average Salaries of Public School Classroom Teachers

District	2005-06		2006-07		Percent Change 2005-06 to 2006-07
	Dollars	Rank[1]	Dollars	Rank[1]	
New Jersey	58,156	5	59,920	3	3.03
U.S. Average	49,026	-	50,816	-	3.65

Note: (1) State rank ranges from 1 to 51.
Source: National Education Association, Rankings & Estimates: Rankings of the States 2006 and Estimates of School Statistics 2007, December 2007

Higher Education

Four-Year Colleges			Two-Year Colleges			Medical Schools[1]	Law Schools[2]	Voc/Tech[3]
Public	Private Non-profit	Private For-profit	Public	Private Non-profit	Private For-profit			
0	0	0	1	0	0	0	0	0

Note: Figures cover institutions located within the city limits; (1) includes schools accredited by the Liaison Committee on Medical Education and the American Osteopathic Association; (2) includes American Bar Association-accredited law schools; (3) includes all schools with programs that are less than 2 years.
Source: National Center for Education Statistics, The Integrated Postsecondary Education System (IPEDS) Peer Analysis System, 2007; www.usnews.com, Law and Medical School Directories, 2009

PRESIDENTIAL ELECTION

2004 Presidential Election Results

Area	Bush	Kerry	Nader	Other
Mercer County	37.9	61.3	0.6	0.3
U.S.	50.7	48.3	0.4	0.6

Note: Results are percentages and may not add to 100% due to rounding
Source: Dave Leip's Atlas of U.S. Presidential Elections, www.uselectionatlas.org

EMPLOYERS

Major Employers

Company Name	Industry	Type of Site
Administration Hall	Management services	Branch
Capital Hlth Systems at Mercer	General medical and surgical hospitals	Branch
ETS	Business consulting, nec	Headquarters
Environmental Protection Agency	Air, water, and solid waste management	Branch
Helene Fuld Medical Center	General medical and surgical hospitals	Headquarters
James Kerney Campus	Junior colleges	Headquarters
Judicary Curts of the State of NJ	Courts	Headquarters
Michael J Baker Jr Inc	Commercial physical research	Branch
NJ Dept Labor & Workforce Dev	Regulation, miscellaneous commercial sectors	Headquarters
New Jersey Dept Transportation	Regulation, administration of transportation	Headquarters
New Jersey Mfrs Insur Group	Fire, marine, and casualty insurance	Headquarters
Pharmanet Dev Group Inc	Commercial physical research	Headquarters
Presbyterian Homes & Services	Residential care	Single
RWJ University Hosp Hamilton	General medical and surgical hospitals	Single
University Med Ctr at Prnceton	Business consulting, nec	Headquarters

Note: Companies shown are located within the Trenton metropolitan area; nec = not elsewhere classified.
Source: www.zapdata.com, May 2008

PUBLIC SAFETY

Crime Rate

Area	All Crimes	Violent Crimes				Property Crimes		
		Murder	Forcible Rape	Robbery	Aggrav. Assault	Burglary	Larceny -Theft	Motor Vehicle Theft
City	2,157.3	3.8	3.8	26.9	30.8	203.8	1,815.0	73.1
Metro[1]	2,692.0	5.7	18.0	236.5	225.6	507.5	1,474.1	224.5
U.S.	3,808.1	5.7	30.9	149.4	287.5	729.4	2,206.8	398.4

Note: Figures are crimes per 100,000 population; (1) Metropolitan Statistical Area - see Appendix B for areas included
Source: FBI Uniform Crime Reports, 2006

RECREATION

Hate Crimes

Area	Number of Quarters Reported	Bias Motivation: Race	Religion	Sexual Orientation	Ethnicity	Disability
City	4	1	0	0	0	1

Source: Federal Bureau of Investigation, Hate Crime Statistics 2006

Culture

Dance[1]	Theatre[1]	Instrumental Music[1]	Vocal Music[1]	Series/ Festivals	Museums	Zoos and Aquariums[2]
0	0	0	0	0	0	0

Note: (1) Number of professional perfoming groups; (2) AZA-accredited
Source: The Grey House Performing Arts Directory, 2007; Official Museum Directory, 2008; Association of Zoos & Aquariums, AZA Member Zoos & Aquariums, June 2008

Professional Sports Teams

Team Name	League
No teams are located in the metro area	

Source: Original research

MEDIA

Newspapers

Name	News Focus	Frequency	Circulation
No newspapers have an office in the city			

Note: Includes newspapers with offices located in the city
Source: MediaContactsPro, March 2008

Television Stations

Name	Ch.	Network(s)	Type	Ownership
KYW	3	CBS	Commercial	CBS
WPVI	6	ABC	Commercial	ABC Inc.
WCAU	10	NBC	Commercial	General Electric Corporation
WHYY	12	PBS	Public	WHYY Inc.
WPHL	17	WBN	Commercial	Tribune Broadcasting Company
WNJS	23	PBS	Public	New Jersey Public Broadcasting Authority
WZBN	25	n/a	Public	n/a
WTXF	29	Fox	Commercial	Fox Television Stations Inc.
WYBE	35	PBS	Public	Independence Public Media of Philadelphia Inc.
WLVT	39	PBS	Public	Lehigh Valley Public Telecommunications
WMGM	40	NBC	Commercial	The Greene Group
WGTW	48	n/a	Commercial	Brunson Communications
WNJN	50	PBS	Public	New Jersey Public Broadcasting Authority
WTVE	51	n/a	Commercial	Reading Broadcasting Inc.
WNJT	52	PBS	Public	New Jersey Public Broadcasting Authority
WMCN	53	n/a	Commercial	WWAC
WPSG	57	UPN	Commercial	Paramount Communications Inc.
WNJB	58	n/a	Public	New Jersey Public Broadcasting Authority
WBPH	60	n/a	Commercial	Sonshine Family Television Inc.
WPPX	61	Pax	Commercial	Paxson Communications Corporation
WWSI	62	Telemundo	Commercial	Hispanic Broadcasters of Philadelphia
WUVP	65	n/a	Commercial	Univision Inc.
WFMZ	69	n/a	Commercial	Maranatha Broadcasting

Note: Stations included cover the Philadelphia DMA (Designated Market Area); n/a not available
BurrellesLuce, MediaContacts Online, January 2007

Major AM Radio Stations

Call Letters	Freq. (kHz)	Station Type	Target Audience	Station Format	Music Format
WFIL	560	n/a	General	Ed/Music/News/Talk	Easy Listening
WIP	610	Commercial	General	Sports/Talk	n/a
WTMR	800	n/a	General/Religious	Music	n/a
WPEN	950	Commercial	General	Music/Talk	Big Band
WJHR	1040	Commercial	General	News/Talk	n/a
KYW	1060	n/a	General	Music/News	n/a
WDEL	1150	Commercial	General	Sports/Talk	n/a
WPHT	1210	Commercial	General	Talk	n/a
WBUD	1260	n/a	General	Music/News/Talk	n/a
WMIZ	1270	n/a	General/Hispanic	Music/News	n/a
WIMG	1300	n/a	Black/General	Music/News/Talk	n/a
WTKZ	1320	Commercial	Hispanic	Music	Latin
WHWH	1350	n/a	General	News/Sports/Talk	n/a
WDOV	1410	Commercial	General	News/Talk	n/a
WCOJ	1420	n/a	General	Music/News/Talk	n/a
WIFI	1460	Commercial	General/Religious	Music/News/Talk	Christian
WKAP	1470	n/a	General	Music	n/a
WDAS	1480	n/a	Black/Gen/Rel/Women	Sports	n/a
WNWR	1540	n/a	General/Religious	Music/News/Sports	n/a
WISP	1570	n/a	Catholic/General	Educational/Talk	n/a
WHOL	1600	n/a	General/Hisp/Rel	Music/News/Sports	n/a

Note: Stations included cover the Philadelphia DMA (Designated Market Area); n/a not available
Source: BurrellesLuce, MediaContacts Online, January 2007

Major FM Radio Stations

Call Letters	Freq. (mHz)	Station Type	Target Audience	Station Format	Music Format
WXPH	88.1	College	General	Music/News/Sports/Talk	Adult Contemp.
WXTU	92.5	n/a	General	Music	n/a
WSTW	93.7	Commercial	General	Music/News	Adult Top 40
WRDX	94.7	Commercial	General	Music	Alternative
WAYV	95.1	Commercial	General	Music/Talk	Top 40
WCTO	96.1	n/a	General	Music	n/a
WFPG	96.9	n/a	General	News/Talk	n/a
WPST	97.5	n/a	General	Music	n/a
WJBR	99.5	Commercial	General	Music/News/Sports/Talk	Adult Contemp.
WODE	99.9	n/a	General	Music	n/a
WLEV	100.7	Commercial	General/Women	Music	Soft Rock
WBEB	101.1	Commercial	General	Music	Soft Rock
WKXW	101.5	n/a	General	Music/News/Sports/Talk	n/a
WMGM	103.7	Commercial	General	Music/Talk	Classic Rock
WAEB	104.1	n/a	General	Music	n/a
WBYN	107.5	n/a	General/Religious	Ed/Music/News/Talk	n/a

Note: Stations included cover the Philadelphia DMA (Designated Market Area); n/a not available
BurrellesLuce, MediaContacts Online, January 2007

CLIMATE

Average and Extreme Temperatures

Temperature	Jan	Feb	Mar	Apr	May	Jun	Jul	Aug	Sep	Oct	Nov	Dec	Yr.
Extreme High (°F)	74	74	85	94	96	100	104	101	100	89	84	72	104
Average High (°F)	39	42	51	63	73	82	86	85	78	67	55	43	64
Average Temp. (°F)	32	34	42	53	63	72	77	76	68	57	47	36	55
Average Low (°F)	24	26	33	43	53	62	67	66	59	47	38	28	45
Extreme Low (°F)	-7	-4	7	19	28	44	51	44	35	25	15	1	-7

Note: Figures cover the years 1948-1990
Source: National Climatic Data Center, International Station Meteorological Climate Summary, 9/96

Average Precipitation/Snowfall/Humidity

Precip./Humidity	Jan	Feb	Mar	Apr	May	Jun	Jul	Aug	Sep	Oct	Nov	Dec	Yr.
Avg. Precip. (in.)	3.2	2.8	3.7	3.5	3.7	3.6	4.1	4.0	3.3	2.7	3.4	3.3	41.4
Avg. Snowfall (in.)	7	7	4	Tr	Tr	0	0	0	0	Tr	1	4	22
Avg. Rel. Hum. 7am (%)	74	73	73	72	75	77	80	82	84	83	79	75	77
Avg. Rel. Hum. 4pm (%)	60	55	51	48	51	52	54	55	55	54	57	60	54

Note: Figures cover the years 1948-1990; Tr = Trace amounts (<0.05 in. of rain; <0.5 in. of snow)
Source: National Climatic Data Center, International Station Meteorological Climate Summary, 9/96

Weather Conditions

Temperature			Daytime Sky			Precipitation		
10°F & below	32°F & below	90°F & above	Clear	Partly cloudy	Cloudy	0.01 inch or more precip.	0.1 inch or more snow/ice	Thunder-storms
5	94	23	81	146	138	117	14	27

Note: Figures are average number of days per year and cover the years 1948-1990
Source: National Climatic Data Center, International Station Meteorological Climate Summary, 9/96

HAZARDOUS WASTE

Superfund Sites

West Windsor has no sites on the EPA's Superfund Final National Priorities List.
U.S. Environmental Protection Agency, Final National Priorities List, June 23, 2008

AIR & WATER QUALITY

Air Quality Index

Area	Percent of Days when Air Quality was...[2]				AQI Statistics	
	Good	Moderate	Unhealthy for Sensitive Groups	Unhealthy	Maximum	Median
MSA[1]	70.7	24.3	4.4	0.6	177	40

Note: The Air Quality Index (AQI) is an index for reporting daily air quality. EPA calculates the AQI for five major air pollutants regulated by the Clean Air Act: ground-level ozone, particle pollution (also known as particulate matter), carbon monoxide, sulfur dioxide, and nitrogen dioxide. The AQI runs from 0 to 500. The higher the AQI value, the greater the level of air pollution and the greater the health concern. There are six AQI categories: "Good" The AQI is between 0 and 50. Air quality is considered satisfactory; "Moderate" The AQI is between 51 and 100. Air quality is acceptable; "Unhealthy for Sensitive Groups" When AQI values are between 101 and 150, members of sensitive groups may experience health effects; "Unhealthy" When AQI values are between 151 and 200 everyone may begin to experience health effects; "Very Unhealthy" AQI values between 201 and 300 trigger a health alert; "Hazardous" AQI values over 300 trigger health warnings of emergency conditions; (1) Metropolitan Statistical Area - see Appendix A for areas included; (2) Based on 362 days with AQI data in 2007.
Source: U.S. Environmental Protection Agency, Air Quality Index Report, 2007

Air Quality Index Pollutants

Area	Percent of Days when AQI Pollutant was...[2]					
	Carbon Monoxide	Nitrogen Dioxide	Ozone	Sulfur Dioxide	Particulate Matter 2.5	Particulate Matter 10
MSA[1]	0.0	0.0	62.7	0.0	36.7	0.6

Note: The Air Quality Index (AQI) is an index for reporting daily air quality. EPA calculates the AQI for five major air pollutants regulated by the Clean Air Act: ground-level ozone, particle pollution (also known as particulate matter), carbon monoxide, sulfur dioxide, and nitrogen dioxide. The AQI runs from 0 to 500. The higher the AQI value, the greater the level of air pollution and the greater the health concern; (1) Metropolitan Statistical Area - see Appendix A for areas included; (2) Based on 362 days with AQI data in 2007.
Source: U.S. Environmental Protection Agency, Air Quality Index Report, 2007

Air Quality Index Trends

Area	Trend Sites								All Sites
	1999	2000	2001	2002	2003	2004	2005	2006	2006
MSA[1]	n/a	n/a	n/a	n/a	n/a	n/a	n/a	n/a	n/a

Note: An AQI value greater than 100 indicates that air quality would have been in the unhealthful range on that day. Data from exceptional events are not included. These counts are presented in two ways. First, the counts are based on sites having an adequate record of monitoring data during the trend period (trend sites). These counts represent the relative change in the number of days with AQI values greater than 100. In the last column, the counts are based on all sites with data in the most recent year (because it is possible for a site to have data in the most recent year but not enough data to be a trend site); (1) Metropolitan Statistical Area - see Appendix A for areas included; n/a not available.
Source: U.S. Environmental Protection Agency, Office of Air and Radiation, Air Trends, Factbook and Related Information, Air Pollution Trends in Selected Metropolitan Areas 2006

Maximum Air Pollutant Concentrations

	Particulate Matter 10 (ug/m³)	Particulate Matter 2.5 (ug/m³)	Ozone (ppm)	Carbon Monoxide (ppm)	Sulfur Dioxide (ppm)	Nitrogen Dioxide (ppm)	Lead (ug/m³)
MSA[1] Level	44	36	0.118	n/a	n/a	0.012	n/a
NAAQS[2]	150	35	0.125	9	0.140	0.053	1.50
Met NAAQS[2]	Yes	No	Yes	n/a	n/a	Yes	n/a

Note: Data from exceptional events are not included; (1) Metropolitan Statistical Area - see Appendix A for areas included; (2) National Ambient Air Quality Standards; n/a not available
Concentrations: Particulate Matter 10 (coarse particulate) - highest second maximum 24-hour concentration; Particulate Matter 2.5 (fine particulate) - highest 98th percentile 24-hour concentration; Ozone - highest second daily maximum 1-hour concentration; Carbon Monoxide - highest second maximum non-overlapping 8-hour concentration; Sulfur Dioxide - highest second maximum 24-hour concentration; Nitrogen Dioxide - highest arithmetic mean concentration; Lead - highest quarterly maximum concentration
Units: ppm = parts per million; ug/m³ = micrograms per cubic meter
Source: U.S. Environmental Protection Agency, MSA Factbook 2006, Air Quality Statistics by City

Drinking Water

Water System Name	Pop. Served	Primary Water Source Type	Violations[1]	
			Health Based	Monitoring/ Reporting
NJ American Water Company	n/a	n/a	n/a	n/a

Note: (1) Based on violation data from January 1, 2007 to December 31, 2007 (includes unresolved violations from earlier years); n/a not available
Source: U.S. Environmental Protection Agency, Office of Ground Water and Drinking Water, Safe Drinking Water Information System (based on data extracted April 15, 2008)

Rio Rancho, New Mexico

Background

Rio Rancho is located at the top of West Mesa, close to Albuquerque and Santa Fe, and 19 miles north of Albuquerque International Airport. Surrounded by majestic views of Albuquerque, the Sandia Mountains, and the Rio Grande Valley, Rio Rancho is one of the nation's fastest-growing communities, offering both a magnificent setting and a mild climate, as well as low land costs, high-quality education, and affordable housing. Major companies located here include Intel and Sprint.

The area was originally inhabited by Pueblo Indians, who farmed the rich soil and hunted along the Rio Grande. In 1540, Don Francisco Vasquez de Coronado explored the region in search of the fabled Seven Cities of Gold. However, the beginning of Rio Rancho occurred over 300 years later, in the early 1960s, when AMREP Corporation purchased 55,000 acres of land on the outskirts of Albuquerque, originally called Rio Rancho Estates. AMREP marketed the area to residents in the East and Midwest. Many of the first residents were retirees; 1966 saw the hundredth family move in. Through another purchase of land in 1971, Rio Rancho Estates grew to 92,000 acres, becoming larger geographically than Albuquerque. By the early 1980s, Rio Rancho was incorporated. A new financing program, offering low-interest home loans, transformed Rio Rancho from a retirement community to a city attracting young families.

The Rio Rancho Public School System includes one high school, six elementary and three middle schools. There are approximately 50 private and/or parochial schools in the greater Albuquerque area, covering levels from elementary through high school.

The abundance of higher-education choices is one of the many benefits of living in Rio Rancho. Albuquerque-based Technical-Vocational Institute offers 35 classes in technology, arts and sciences, and business. The University of New Mexico is one of the top institutions in the Southwest, offering 4,000 courses in 150 disciplines, along with highly regarded business and law schools, and a school of medicine that is ranked among the country's 10 best primary-care learning centers. The University of Phoenix offers degrees in business management, technology, and nursing, while the College of Santa Fe in Albuquerque awards bachelor's and master's degrees in business, psychology, and teacher education. Aztech College trains students in computer-aided design, architecture, and mechanical drafting.

Rio Rancho offers some of the most varied and interesting historical and recreational attractions in the country: Bandelier National Monument on Jemez Mountain Trail features twelfth-century Indian pueblos and breathtaking scenery; Petroglyph National Monument, created in 1990, protects 15,000 ancient petroglyphs and other archaeological sites just west of Albuquerque; The Sandia Peak Tramway provides a ride up to Sandia Peak — over 11,000 feet — on the world's longest aerial tramway. Indoor recreation includes several casinos, the Albuquerque Aquarium, and New Mexico's largest shopping center, the Cottonwood Mall, with movie theaters and hundreds of shops.

One of the biggest events in Rio Rancho is the Highland Games & Scottish/Irish Festival in June. This includes competitions in Highland dancing, individual piping and drumming, Scottish/Irish dancing, and athletic contents, as well as Celtic foods and other cultural attractions. And not far away is the annual Albuquerque International Balloon Festival, held each August.

Numerous medical facilities are located in the area, such as St. Joseph West Mesa Hospital, a 128-bed family-centered hospital offering everything from general medical and surgical services and pediatric care to obstetrics. Other facilities include Lovelace Primary Care Center and St. Joseph's Urgent Care. Senior communities comprise Talbert Medical Group Nursing Homes, Ancantilado Vista Independent Living, Rio Rancho Nursing and Rehabilitation Center, and Sandia Springs Assisted Living.

Rio Rancho enjoys a dry, arid climate with plenty of sunshine, low humidity, and scant rainfall. More than three-fourths of the daylight hours have sunshine, summer and winter. As in all desert climates, temperatures can fluctuate widely between day and night. Precipitation is meager during the winter, more abundant in summer with afternoon and evening thunderstorms.

Rankings

General Rankings

- Albuquerque* was ranked #145 out of 375 metro areas in *Cities Ranked & Rated*. Criteria: cost of living; climate; crime; transportation; economy and jobs; education; arts and culture; health and healthcare; leisure; quality of life. *Cities Ranked & Rated, 2nd Edition, 2007*
- Albuquerque* was ranked #64 out of 379 metro areas in *Places Rated Almanac*. Criteria: health care; education; recreation; transportation; ambience; climate; crime; housing costs; jobs. *Places Rated Almanac, 7th Edition, 2007*
- Rio Rancho was selected as one of the "2006 Best Places to Live" by *Money* magazine. Places were ranked using 38 quality-of-life indicators and six economic opportunity measures in the following categories: ease of living; health; education; crime; park space; arts and leisure. *CNNMoney.com, "Best Places to Live 2006"*

Business/Finance Rankings

- The nation's 100 largest metro areas were analysed in terms of the percentage of households entering some stage of foreclosure in 2007. The Albuquerque* metro area ranked #71 out of 100 (#1 = highest foreclosure rate). *RealtyTrac, "Year-End 2007 Metropolitan Foreclosure Report"*
- Albuquerque* was selected as one of the best places to start and grow a company by *Entrepreneur* and the National Policy Research Council. The Albuquerque* metro area ranked #14 out of 63 mid-size metro areas. Criteria: business formation and growth (firms started four to 14 years ago that still employ at least 5 people and experienced rapid growth over the last four years). *Entrepreneur/National Policy Research Council, "Hot Cities for Entrepreneurs," September 2006*
- The Albuquerque* metro area was selected as one of "America's 50 Hottest Cities" for business relocations and expansions. Criteria: industry's most prominent site selection consultants were asked to list their top city choices for relocating and expanding manufacturing companies, taking into consideration such factors as the business climate, work force quality, operating costs, incentive programs, and the ease of working with local political and economic development officials. *Expansion Management, January-February 2007*
- Intel, in partnership with Sperling's BestPlaces, ranked the 80 "Best Cities for Teleworking" in America. The Albuquerque* metro area ranked #15 among mid-sized metro areas. The study identifies cities that hold the greatest potential for teleworking based on a host of factors including typical commuting times, fuel prices, availability of broadband Internet access and percentage of the population in telework friendly jobs. The study also factored in extreme climate and natural hazards. *Intel, "Best Cities for Teleworking," March 30, 2006*
- Rio Rancho was selected as one of the "100 Best Places to Live and Launch" in the U.S. The city ranked #83. The editors at *Fortune Small Business* ranked 296 Census-designated metro areas by business friendliness (Launching Score, % New Businesses) and lifestyle offerings (Living Score). Then, through reporting, they picked the town within each of the top 100 metro areas that best blends business and pleasure. *Fortune Small Business, "100 Best Places to Live and Launch 2008," April 2008*
- The Albuquerque* metro area appeared on the Milken Institute "2007 Best Performing Cities" index. Rank: #31 out of 200 large metro areas. Criteria: job growth; wage and salary growth; high-tech output growth. *Milken Institute, "2007 Best Performing Cities"*
- The Albuquerque* metro area was selected as one of the hottest cities for entrepreneurs in America by *Inc. Magazine*. Criteria: job-growth data for 393 metro was analyzed for current-year employment growth, average annual employment growth over past three years, and employment growth by industry sector. The Albuquerque* metro area ranked #19 among mid-sized metro areas and #84 overall. *Inc. Magazine, May 2007*

- Albuquerque* was identified as one of the 100 "Most Unwired Cities" in the U.S. The area ranked #30 out of the 100 largest metro areas in the U.S. Criteria: number of public and commercial wireless access points (hotspots); airports with wireless Internet access; broadband availability; local wireless networks; and wireless email devices. *Intel, "Most Unwired Cities Survey," June 7, 2005*

- *Forbes* ranked the 200 most populous metro areas in the U.S. in terms of the "Best Places for Business and Careers." The Albuquerque* metro area was ranked #13. Criteria: business costs (labor, energy, tax and office space expenses); living costs (housing, transportation, food and other household expenditures); education levels of the work force; job growth; income growth; migration trends; crime rates; and culture/leisure. *Forbes, "Best Places for Business and Careers," March 19, 2008*

- *Fortune* ranked the 100 largest metro areas in the U.S. in terms of projected median home price change in 2007. The Albuquerque* metro area ranked #3. *Fortune.com, "Hot Spots, Cold Spots"*

Health/Environment Rankings

- 100 of the largest metro areas in the U.S. were analyzed in terms of their current drought severity. The Albuquerque* metro area ranked #92 (#1 = driest). The rankings were based on statistics such as long-term precipitation trends and patterns and the Palmer drought indices. *Sperling's BestPlaces, www.BestPlaces.net, "America's Drought-Riskiest Cities," November 2007*

- Scarborough Research, a leading market research firm, identified the top local markets for organic consumers. The Albuquerque* DMA (Designated Market Area) ranked in the top 15 with 21% of adults reporting that they used any organic food product in their household during the past month. *Scarborough Research, October 10, 2007*

- The Albuquerque* metro area appeared in *Country Home's* "2008 Best Green Places" report. The area ranked #102 out of 379. Criteria: official energy policies; green power; green buildings; availability of fresh, locally grown food. *Country Home, "2008 Best Green Places"*

- The American Podiatric Medical Association and *Prevention* magazine ranked America's 100 most populated cities based on fitness-walker friendliness. The best cities have safe streets, beautiful places to walk, mild weather and good air quality. Rio Rancho ranked #377. *Prevention, "The Best Walking Cities of 2008," April 2008; American Podiatric Medical Association, "2008 Best Fitness-Walking Cities, "April 2008*

- Albuquerque* was identified as a "2008 Asthma Capital." The area ranked #78 out of the nation's 100 largest metropolitan areas. Twelve factors were used to identify the most challenging places to live for people with asthma: estimated prevalence; self-reported prevalence; crude death rate for asthma; annual pollen score; annual air quality; public smoking laws; number of board-certified asthma specialists; school inhaler access laws; rescue medication use; controller medication use; uninsured rate; poverty rate. *Asthma and Allergy Foundation of America, "2008 Asthma Capitals"*

- Albuquerque* was identified as a "Spring Allergy Capital." The area ranked #38 out of 100. Three groups of factors were used to identify the most severe cities for people with allergies during the spring season: annual pollen levels; medicine utilization; access to board-certified allergists. *Asthma and Allergy Foundation of America, "2007 Spring Allergy Capital Rankings"*

- Albuquerque* was identified as a "Fall Allergy Capital." The area ranked #36 out of 100. Three groups of factors were used to identify the most severe cities for people with allergies during the fall season: annual pollen levels; medicine utilization; access to board-certified allergists. *Asthma and Allergy Foundation of America, "2007 Fall Allergy Capital Rankings"*

- Ortho-McNeil Neurologics, in partnership with Sperling's BestPlaces, analyzed 110 metro areas and identified those U.S. cities with the highest prevalence of factors that are most commonly associated with migraine headaches. The Albuquerque* metro area ranked #83. Criteria: number of migraine-related drug prescriptions per capita; lifestyle factors that can contribute to migraines; environmental factors that can trigger migraines; and consumption of migraine-triggering foods. *Ortho-McNeil Neurologics, "America's Migraine Hot Spots," March 14, 2006*

- Sperling's BestPlaces ranked 331 metro areas and identified the most and least stressful U.S. cities. The Albuquerque* metro area ranked #29 out of the 100 largest metro areas (#1 = most stressful). Criteria: divorce rate; unemployment rate; violent and property crime; suicide rate; commute time; mental health; alcohol consumption; cloudy days. *Sperling's BestPlaces, www.BestPlaces.net, "America's Most (and Least) Stressful Cities," January 9, 2004*

- Sperling's BestPlaces in partnership with Vistakon ranked the 100 largest metro areas and identified "America's 10 Worst Cities for Comfortable Eyes." The Albuquerque* metro area ranked #2. Criteria: altitude; sunny days; wind; extreme temperatures; humidity; pollution; commute time; computer use. *Vistakon, "America's Best and Worst Cities for Comfortable Eyes," June 15, 2004*

- Albuquerque* was highlighted as one of the top 25 cleanest metro areas for long-term particle pollution (PM 2.5) in the U.S. The area ranked #10. *American Lung Association, State of the Air: 2007*

Women/Minorities Rankings

- Albuquerque* was ranked #35 out of 100 metro areas in *SELF Magazine's* ranking of "America's Best Places for Women." A panel of experts came up with more than 50 criteria including death and disease rates, environmental indicators, community resources, and lifestyle habits. *SELF Magazine, "America's Best Places for Women 2007," December 2007*

- Albuquerque* appeared on a list of the top 10 metro areas with the highest concentration of same-sex households. The area ranked #8. *Urban Institute Press, The Gay and Lesbian Atlas, May 2004*

Seniors/Retirement Rankings

- Rio Rancho was profiled in the book *Where to Retire: America's Best and Most Affordable Places.* Cities were selected based on personal visits by the author and interviews with local residents coupled with statistics from various government agencies. *Where to Retire: America's Best and Most Affordable Places, 2006*

- Rio Rancho was identified as one of the "100 Most Popular Places to Retire" by *Where to Retire* magazine. The city ranked #84. Criteria: net retirees received from 1995-2000 (derived by subtracting all outbound retirees from inbound retirees for the county or county group - includes interstate moves only). *Where to Retire, "100 Most Popular Places to Retire," January/February 2007*

- Rio Rancho was identified as one of the best places to retire in *Retirement Places Rated.* Criteria: population above 10,000; attractiveness to older adults; affordability; climate and natural endowments; personal safety. The city was ranked #51 out of 200. *Retirement Places Rated, 7th Edition, 2007*

- A.G. Edwards ranked America's 500 top-performing communities based on their residents' personal savings and investing behavior. The Albuquerque* metro area ranked #405 with an index score of 96.95 (national average = 100.00). A dozen statistical factors were measured including: participation in retirement savings plans; personal debt levels; and home ownership. *A.G. Edwards, "2007 Nest Egg Index", September 12, 2007*

Children/Family Rankings

- The Albuquerque* metro area was selected as one of the "Best Cities for Relocating Families" by Worldwide ERC and Primacy Relocation. The 2007 study placed a special emphasis on the housing market, which has significantly impacted the relocation industry and an employer's ability to transfer employees. The variables which weigh heavily in this category include home price, home affordability index, appreciation rates, and property tax. Other criteria include cost of living, crime rates, education, climate, focus on diversity, physicians per capita, recreation and leisure, arts and culture, air quality, watershed quality, sales tax, unemployment rate, job growth, high school and higher education index, school expenditures per student, students in public school, SAT/ACT percentile, and population growth. *Worldwide ERC and Primacy Relocation, "2007 Best Cities for Relocating Families"*

Safety Rankings

- The National Insurance Crime Bureau ranked 361 metro areas in the U.S. in terms of per capita rates of vehicle theft. The Albuquerque* metro area ranked #7 (#1 = highest rate). Criteria: number of vehicle theft offenses per 100,000 inhabitants. *National Insurance Crime Bureau, "NICB Vehicle Theft Study," April 22, 2008*
- Farmers Insurance Group of Companies, in partnership with Sperling's BestPlaces, ranked 379 metro areas and identified the "Most Secure U.S. Place to Live." The Albuquerque* metro area ranked #75 out of 114 in the large metro area category (500,000 or more residents). Criteria: crime rates; extreme weather; risk of natural disasters; environmental hazards; terrorism threats; air quality; life expectancy; job loss numbers. *Farmers Insurance Group, "Most Secure U.S. Places to Live 2007"*

Sports/Recreation Rankings

- The Albuquerque* metro area appeared on the *Sporting News* list of the "Best Sports Cities 2007". The area ranked #107 out of 150 cities in the U.S. *Sporting News* takes a 12-month snapshot, roughly July to July, of each city's sports, putting a heavy premium on regular-season won-lost records (from the most recently completed season). Other criteria include: playoff berths, bowl appearances and tournament bids; championships; applicable power ratings; quality of competition; overall fan fervor as measured in part by attendance as percentage of venue capacity; abundance of teams (rewarding quality over quantity); stadium and arena quality; ticket availability and prices; franchise ownership; and marquee appeal of athletes. *SportingNews.com, "Best Sports Cities 2007," August 1, 2007*
- *Golf Digest* ranked 330 metro areas in the U.S. in terms of golf. The Albuquerque* metro area was ranked #267. Criteria: access to golf; weather; value of golf; and quality of golf. *Golf Digest, "Metro Golf Rankings," August 2005*

Dating/Romance Rankings

- The Albuquerque* metro area was selected as one of the "Best Cities for Relocating Singles" by Worldwide ERC and Primacy Relocation. The area ranked #76 out of the 100 largest metro areas in the U.S. Areas were selected based on the following criteria: a robust cost-of-living index; adventure and outdoor recreation opportunities; violent crime and property crime rates; percentage of the population that is unmarried (ages 25-34); ratio of single men and single women; affordability of quality higher education, including in-state and out-of-state tuition requirements and rates; number of newcomers to the area; commute times; tax rates; fee and occupancy rates for temporary housing and mini-storage; quality and quantity of collegiate and professional sporting events and fun, fan-friendly venues. *Worldwide ERC and Primacy Relocation, "2007 Best Cities for Relocating Singles," October 25, 2007*
- Sperling's BestPlaces in partnership with AXE Deodorant Bodyspray ranked 80 metro areas and identified "America's Best (and Worst) Cities for Dating." The Albuquerque* metro area ranked #65 (#1 = best). Criteria: percentage of singles ages 18-24; population density; dating venues per capita. *AXE Deodorant Bodyspray, "America's Best (and Worst) Cities for Dating," May 2004*

Culture/Performing Arts Rankings

- Scarborough Research, a leading market research firm, identified the top local markets for rock concert attendance. The Albuquerque* DMA (Designated Market Area) ranked in the top 25 with 14% of consumers, 18 years old and over, reporting that they have attended a rock concert during the past year. *Scarborough Research, June 14, 2004*

Miscellaneous Rankings

- Sperling's BestPlaces in partnership with Pep Boys ranked 77 metro areas and identified "America's Most Drivable Cities." The Albuquerque* metro area ranked #33. Criteria: climate; road roughness; urban mobility; gas prices. *Pep Boys, "America's Most Drivable Cities," April 9, 2003*

- A study by Sperling's BestPlaces examined which U.S. metro areas were most affected by high fuel prices in 2006. The Albuquerque* metro area was ranked #45 out of 80 (#1 = most expensive city for driving). Rankings are based on the average dollars spent on gas per year by two driver households. Criteria: cost of regular-grade gasoline; average miles driven per day; average number of gallons each driver uses and wastes in traffic congestion each day. *Sperling's BestPlaces, www.bestplaces.net, "Pain at the Pump," May 18, 2006*

Rio Rancho is located within the Albuquerque, NM Metropolitan Statistical Area.

Business Environment

CITY FINANCES

City Government Finances

Component	2004-2005 ($000)	2004-2005 ($ per capita)
Total Revenues	80,553	1,210
Total Expenditures	64,106	963
Debt Outstanding	183,310	2,752
Cash and Securities	143,422	2,154

Source: U.S Census Bureau, Government Finances 2004-2005

City Government Revenue by Source

Source	2004-2005 ($000)	2004-2005 ($ per capita)
General Revenue		
From Federal Government	840	13
From State Government	17,787	267
From Local Governments	0	0
Taxes		
Property	7,534	113
Sales	15,753	237
Personal Income	0	0
License	389	6
Charges	14,654	220
Liquor Store	0	0
Utility	12,149	182
Employee Retirement	0	0
Other	11,447	172

Source: U.S Census Bureau, Government Finances 2004-2005

City Government Expenditures by Function

Function	2004-2005 ($000)	2004-2005 ($ per capita)	2004-2005 (%)
General Expenditures			
Airports	0	0	0.0
Corrections	133	2	0.2
Education	0	0	0.0
Fire Protection	292	4	0.5
Governmental Administration	4,758	71	7.4
Health	28	< 1	< 0.1
Highways	6,464	97	10.1
Hospitals	0	0	0.0
Housing and Community Development	720	11	1.1
Interest on General Debt	956	14	1.5
Libraries	536	8	0.8
Parking	0	0	0.0
Parks and Recreation	6,676	100	10.4
Police Protection	14,310	215	22.3
Public Welfare	0	0	0.0
Sewerage	8,003	120	12.5
Solid Waste Management	6	< 1	< 0.1
Liquor Store	0	0	0.0
Utility	14,306	215	22.3
Employee Retirement	0	0	0.0
Other	6,918	104	10.8

Source: U.S Census Bureau, Government Finances 2004-2005

Municipal Bond Ratings

Area	Moody's
City	Aa2

Source: Mergent Bond Record, January 2008 (unless noted otherwise)

DEMOGRAPHICS

Population Growth

Area	1990 Census	2000 Census	2007 Estimate	2012 Projection	Population Growth (%) 1990-2000	Population Growth (%) 2000-2012
City	32,674	51,765	71,284	84,681	58.4	63.6
MSA[1]	599,416	729,649	819,948	885,373	21.7	21.3
U.S.	248,709,873	281,421,906	301,045,522	314,920,978	13.2	11.9

Note: (1) Metropolitan Statistical Area - see Appendix B for areas included
Source: Claritas, Inc.

Number of Households and Average Household Size

Area	2007 Estimate	2007 Average Household Size
City	26,500	2.69
MSA[1]	324,089	2.53
U.S.	113,668,003	2.65

Note: (1) Metropolitan Statistical Area - see Appendix B for areas included
Source: Claritas, Inc.

Race and Ethnicity

Area	White Alone[2]	Black Alone[2]	Asian Alone[2]	Other Race Alone[2]	Hispanic[3]
City	75.8	2.6	1.4	20.3	32.0
MSA[1]	67.8	2.6	1.7	27.9	43.5
U.S.	73.1	12.4	4.3	10.3	14.9

Note: Figures are 2007 estimates; (1) Metropolitan Statistical Area - see Appendix B for areas included (2) Alone is defined as not being in combination with one or more other races; (3) May be of any race.
Source: Claritas, Inc.

Ancestry

Area	German	Irish[2]	English	American	Italian	Polish	French[3]	Scottish
City	16.4	11.2	10.5	5.7	6.6	2.7	3.5	2.3
MSA[1]	11.8	8.5	8.5	4.3	3.5	1.6	2.4	1.9
U.S.	15.2	10.9	8.7	7.3	5.6	3.2	3.0	1.7

Note: Figures include multiple ancestry (e.g. if a person reported being Irish and Italian, they were included in both columns); (1) Metropolitan Statistical Area - see Appendix A for areas included; (2) Includes Celtic; (3) Includes Alsatian but excludes Basque
Source: Census 2000, Summary File 3

Foreign-Born Population

Area	Percent of Population Born in: Any Foreign Country	Europe	Asia	Africa	Oceania[2]	Canada	Mexico	Latin America[3]
City	4.8	1.4	1.3	0.0	0.1	0.2	1.0	0.8
MSA[1]	7.9	1.0	1.2	0.1	0.0	0.3	4.7	0.6
U.S.	11.1	1.7	2.9	0.3	0.1	0.3	3.3	2.5

Note: (1) Metropolitan Statistical Area - see Appendix A for areas included; (2) Includes Australia, New Zealand subregion, Melanesia, Micronesia, Polynesia, and Oceania n.e.c; (3) Includes Central America (excluding Mexico), South America, and the Caribbean.
Source: Census 2000, Summary File 3

Marriage Status

Area	Never Married	Now Married (excluding Separated)	Separated	Widowed	Divorced
City	22.1	60.5	1.1	5.7	10.5
MSA[1]	28.6	51.5	1.6	5.6	12.6
U.S.	27.1	54.4	2.2	6.6	9.7

Note: Figures are percentages and cover the population 15 years of age and older; (1) Metropolitan Statistical Area - see Appendix A for areas included
Source: Census 2000, Summary File 3

Age Distribution

Area	Percent of Population						
	Under Age 5	Age 5 to 17	Age 18 to 34	Age 35 to 49	Age 50 to 64	Age 65 to 79	80 Years and Over
City	7.4	21.9	20.1	26.3	12.6	8.6	3.0
MSA[1]	7.0	19.2	23.6	24.3	14.6	8.4	2.8
U.S.	6.8	18.9	23.7	23.5	14.8	9.2	3.2

Note: (1) Metropolitan Statistical Area - see Appendix A for areas included
Source: Census 2000, Summary File 3

Male/Female Ratio

Area	Males	Females	Males per 100 Females
City	34,534	36,750	94.0
MSA[1]	402,639	417,309	96.5
U.S.	148,320,305	152,725,217	97.1

Note: Figures are 2007 estimates; (1) Metropolitan Statistical Area - see Appendix B for areas included
Source: Claritas, Inc.

Religion

Area	Catholic	Southern Baptist	United Meth-odist	ELCA[1]	LDS[2]	Presby-terian Church USA	Jewish Est.	Muslim Est.
County	37.5	2.2	0.4	0.0	2.5	0.7	0.0	0.0
U.S.	22.0	7.1	3.7	1.8	1.5	1.1	2.2	0.6

Note: Figures are the number of adherents as a percentage of the total population; Adherents are defined as all members, including full members, their children and the estimated number of other participants who are not considered members (e.g. the baptized, those not confirmed, those regularly attending services, etc.); (1) Evangelical Lutheran Church in America; (2) The Church of Jesus Christ of Latter Day Saints
Source: Reprinted with permission from Religious Congregations and Membership in the United States 2000 (Nashville, Glenmary Research Center, 2002) Copyright Association of Statisticians of American Religious Bodies. All rights reserved.

ECONOMY

Gross Metropolitan Product

Area	2002	2003	2004	2005	2005 Rank[2]
MSA[1]	24.7	27.0	29.9	32.3	65

Note: Figures are in billions of dollars; (1) Albuquerque, NM Metropolitan Statistical Area - see Appendix A for areas included; (2) Rank ranges from 1 to 361
Source: The U.S. Conference of Mayors, "U.S. Metro Economies: GMP - The Engines of America's Growth," January 2007

Economic Growth

Area	1995 GMP	2005 GMP	Average Annual Growth Rate	Growth Rate Rank[2]
MSA[1]	20.4	32.3	4.7	253

Note: Figures are in billions of dollars; GMP = Gross Metropolitan Product; (1) Albuquerque, NM Metropolitan Statistical Area - see Appendix A for areas included; (2) Rank ranges from 1 to 361
Source: The U.S. Conference of Mayors, "U.S. Metro Economies: GMP - The Engines of America's Growth," January 2007

INCOME

Per Capita/Median/Average Income

Area	Per Capita ($)	Median Household ($)	Average Household ($)
City	24,050	55,331	64,576
MSA[1]	24,571	46,368	61,538
U.S.	25,495	49,280	66,670

Note: Figures are 2007 estimates; (1) Metropolitan Statistical Area - see Appendix B for areas included
Source: Claritas, Inc.

Household Income Distribution

Area	Percent of Households Earning							
	Under $15,000	$15,000 -24,999	$25,000 -34,999	$35,000 -49,999	$50,000 -74,999	$75,000 -99,000	$100,000 -149,999	$150,000 and up
City	6.3	8.3	10.3	18.0	27.6	15.4	11.0	3.1
MSA[1]	13.1	11.9	12.1	16.8	19.6	11.1	10.4	5.1
U.S.	13.1	10.9	11.2	15.6	19.5	11.9	11.3	6.6

Note: Figures are 2007 estimates; (1) Metropolitan Statistical Area - see Appendix B for areas included
Source: Claritas, Inc.

Poverty Rates by Age

Area	All Ages	Under 5 Years Old	5 to 17 Years Old	18 to 64 Years Old	65 Years and Over
City	5.1	0.4	1.1	2.9	0.7
MSA[1]	13.8	1.5	3.4	7.9	1.0
U.S.	12.4	1.2	3.0	6.9	1.2

Note: Figures are percent of population with income in 1999 below poverty level and only include population for whom poverty status is determined; (1) Metropolitan Statistical Area - see Appendix A for areas included
Source: Census 2000, Summary File 3

Personal Bankruptcy Filing Rate

Area	2004	2005	2006
Sandoval County	6.03	7.43	1.27
U.S.	5.31	6.82	2.00

Note: Numbers are per 1,000 population and include Chapter 7 and Chapter 13 filings
Source: Federal Deposit Insurance Corporation (FDIC), Regional Economic Conditions (RECON), 8/23/2007

EMPLOYMENT

Labor Force and Employment

Area	Civilian Labor Force			Workers Employed		
	Dec. 2006	Dec. 2007	% Chg.	Dec. 2006	Dec. 2007	% Chg.
City	36,528	36,554	0.1	35,419	35,316	-0.3
MSA[1]	409,444	407,506	-0.5	396,231	395,075	-0.3
U.S.	152,571,000	153,705,000	0.7	146,081,000	146,334,000	0.2

Note: Data is not seasonally adjusted and covers workers 16 years of age and older;
(1) Metropolitan Statistical Area - see Appendix B for areas included
Source: Bureau of Labor Statistics, http://stats.bls.gov

Unemployment Rate

Area	2007											
	Jan.	Feb.	Mar.	Apr.	May	Jun.	Jul.	Aug.	Sep.	Oct.	Nov.	Dec.
City	3.6	3.5	3.1	3.2	3.1	3.9	4.0	3.2	3.9	3.5	3.6	3.4
MSA[1]	3.8	3.6	3.3	3.3	3.3	3.8	4.0	3.5	3.4	3.2	3.3	3.1
U.S.	5.0	4.9	4.5	4.3	4.3	4.7	4.9	4.6	4.5	4.4	4.5	4.8

Note: Data is not seasonally adjusted and covers workers 16 years of age and older; All figures are percentages; (1) Metropolitan Statistical Area - see Appendix B for areas included
Source: Bureau of Labor Statistics, http://stats.bls.gov

Employment by Occupation

Occupation Classification	City (%)	MSA[1] (%)	U.S. (%)
Sales and Office	30.9	28.1	26.7
Professional and Related	21.5	23.7	20.2
Service	15.1	15.7	14.9
Production, Transportation, and Material Moving	9.9	9.9	14.6
Management, Business, and Financial	13.0	13.1	13.5
Construction, Extraction, and Maintenance	9.5	9.4	9.4
Farming, Forestry, and Fishing	0.1	0.2	0.7

Note: Figures cover employed civilians 16 years of age and older;
(1) Metropolitan Statistical Area - see Appendix A for areas included
Source: Census 2000, Summary File 3

Employment by Industry

Sector	MSA[1] Number of Employees	MSA[1] Percent of Total	U.S. Percent of Total
Government	81,300	20.4	16.3
Education and Health Services	49,400	12.4	13.4
Professional and Business Services	63,900	16.0	13.1
Retail Trade	47,000	11.8	11.6
Manufacturing	23,000	5.8	9.9
Leisure and Hospitality	39,400	9.9	9.6
Financial Activities	19,300	4.8	5.9
Construction	n/a	n/a	5.3
Wholesale Trade	13,300	3.3	4.4
Other Services	12,200	3.1	3.9
Transportation and Utilities	11,300	2.8	3.7
Information	9,300	2.3	2.2
Natural Resources and Mining	n/a	n/a	0.5

Note: Figures cover non-farm employment as of December 2007 and are not seasonally adjusted; (1) Metropolitan Statistical Area - see Appendix B for areas included; n/a not available
Source: Bureau of Labor Statistics, http://stats.bls.gov

Average Wages

Occupation	$/Hr.	Occupation	$/Hr.
Accountants and Auditors	28.23	Maids and Housekeeping Cleaners	7.91
Automotive Mechanics	16.96	Maintenance and Repair Workers	13.92
Bookkeepers	14.47	Marketing Managers	44.75
Carpenters	15.73	Nuclear Medicine Technologists	20.37
Cashiers	8.29	Nurses, Licensed Practical	25.26
Clerks, General Office	10.83	Nurses, Registered	29.56
Clerks, Receptionists/Information	10.91	Nursing Aides/Orderlies/Attendants	11.17
Clerks, Shipping/Receiving	12.29	Packers and Packagers, Hand	8.46
Computer Programmers	37.38	Physical Therapists	29.38
Computer Support Specialists	21.82	Postal Service Mail Carriers	21.02
Computer Systems Analysts	34.19	Real Estate Brokers	n/a
Cooks, Restaurant	9.72	Retail Salespersons	11.68
Dentists	n/a	Sales Reps., Exc. Tech./Scientific	23.60
Electrical Engineers	41.09	Sales Reps., Tech./Scientific	30.37
Electricians	19.56	Secretaries, Exc. Legal/Med./Exec.	13.04
Financial Managers	38.02	Security Guards	11.23
First-Line Supervisors/Mgrs., Sales	18.34	Surgeons	102.33
Food Preparation Workers	8.77	Teacher Assistants	9.00
General and Operations Managers	44.73	Teachers, Elementary School	20.90
Hairdressers/Cosmetologists	8.79	Teachers, Secondary School	23.40
Internists	n/a	Telemarketers	10.55
Janitors and Cleaners	9.31	Truck Drivers, Heavy/Tractor-Trailer	18.79
Landscaping/Groundskeeping Workers	9.54	Truck Drivers, Light/Delivery Svcs.	12.72
Lawyers	43.08	Waiters and Waitresses	7.11

Note: Wage data covers the Albuquerque, NM Metropolitan Statistical Area - see Appendix B for areas included. Hourly wages for elementary/secondary school teachers and teacher assistants were calculated by the editors from annual wage data assuming a 40 hour work week; n/a not available.
Source: Bureau of Labor Statistics, May 2007 Metro Area Occupational Employment and Wage Estimates

RESIDENTIAL REAL ESTATE

Building Permits

Area	Single-Family 2006	Single-Family 2007p	Single-Family Pct. Chg.	Multi-Family 2006	Multi-Family 2007p	Multi-Family Pct. Chg.	Total 2006	Total 2007p	Total Pct. Chg.
City	1,935	1,147	-40.7	3	132	4,300.0	1,938	1,279	-34.0
U.S.	1,378,200	973,300	-29.4	460,700	407,200	-11.6	1,838,900	1,380,500	-24.9

Note: (p) preliminary; figures cover and represent new, privately-owned housing units authorized (unadjusted data); All permit data are based on estimates with imputation; U.S. figures are based on the new 20,000-place series.
Source: U.S. Census Bureau, Manufacturing, Mining, and Construction Statistics

Homeownership and Housing Vacancies

Area	Homeownership Rate[2] (%)			Rental Vacancy Rate[3] (%)			Homeowner Vacancy Rate[4] (%)		
	2005	2006	2007	2005	2006	2007	2005	2006	2007
MSA[1]	69.2	70.0	70.5	7.9	8.3	8.8	1.8	2.0	2.6
U.S.	68.9	68.8	68.1	9.8	9.8	9.7	1.9	2.4	2.7

Note: (1) Metropolitan Statistical Area - see Appendix B for areas included; (2) The proportion of households that are owners; (3) The proportion of the rental inventory that is vacant for rent; (4) The proportion of the homeowner inventory that is vacant for sale; n/a not available
Source: U.S. Census Bureau, Housing Vacancies and Homeownership Annual Statistics: 2007

TAXES

State Corporate Income Tax Rates

State	Rates and Tax Brackets
New Mexico	4.8% > $0; 6.4% > 500K; 7.6% > 1,000,000

Note: Tax rates as of January 1, 2008
Source: Tax Foundation, www.taxfoundation.org

State Individual Income Tax Rates

State	Federal Deductibility	Marginal Rates (%)	Standard Deduction ($)		Personal Exemptions ($)[1]	
			Single	Joint	Single	Dependents
New Mexico	No	1.7 - 5.3 (s)	5,150 (s)	10,300 (s)	3,300 (s)	3,300 (s)

Note: Tax rates as of January 1, 2008; Local- and county-level taxes are not included; n/a not applicable; (1) Married joint filers generally receive double the single exemption; (s) Deductions and exemptions tied to federal tax system. Federal deductions and exemptions are indexed for inflation.
Source: Tax Foundation, www.taxfoundation.org

Various State and Local Tax Rates

State and Local Sales and Use (%)	State Sales and Use (%)	Gasoline[1,2] ($/gal.)	Cigarette ($/pack)	Spirits ($/gal.)	Table Wine ($/gal.)	Beer ($/gal.)
6.688	5.0 (g)	0.18	0.91	6.06	1.70	0.41

Note: Tax rates as of January 1, 2008; (1) In addition to the 18.4 cpg Federal gasoline tax; (2) Rates may include additional state sales taxes, environmental protection and storage fees/taxes, and local taxes. When necessary, the volume-weighted average of all local taxes is used to approximate the typical statewide rate including local tax; (g) New Mexico has no sales tax but does have a 5% GRT.
Source: Tax Foundation, www.taxfoundation.org; Original research

State Tax Burdens

Area	Combined State and Local Tax Burden		Combined Federal, State and Local Tax Burden	
	Percent	Rank	Percent	Rank
New Mexico	9.8	40	28.8	45
U.S. Average	11.0	-	32.7	-

Note: Figures cover 2007 and measure taxes as a percentage of income
Source: Tax Foundation, www.taxfoundation.org

State Business Tax Climate Index Rankings

State	Overall Rank	Corporate Tax Index Rank	Individual Income Tax Index Rank	Sales Tax Index Rank	Unemployment Insurance Tax Index Rank	Property Tax Index Rank
New Mexico	23	36	17	41	13	1

Note: Rankings range from 1 to 50 where 1 is best. Rankings do not average across to Overall Rank. States without a given tax are given a ranking of 1.
Source: Tax Foundation, State Business Tax Climate Index 2008

TRANSPORTATION

Means of Transportation to Work

Area	Car/Truck/Van		Public Transportation			Bicycle	Walked	Other Means	Worked at Home
	Drove Alone	Car-pooled	Bus	Subway	Railroad				
City	84.4	10.5	0.4	0.0	0.0	0.2	0.4	0.8	3.1
MSA[1]	77.7	13.3	1.2	0.0	0.0	0.8	2.3	0.9	3.9
U.S.	75.7	12.2	2.5	1.5	0.5	0.4	2.9	1.0	3.3

Note: Figures are percentages and cover workers 16 years of age and older;
(1) Metropolitan Statistical Area - see Appendix A for areas included
Source: Census 2000, Summary File 3

Travel Time to Work

Area	Less Than 15 Minutes	15 to 29 Minutes	30 to 44 Minutes	45 to 59 Minutes	60 Minutes or More
City	23.8	31.7	27.1	11.4	5.9
MSA[1]	26.9	45.1	18.4	5.3	4.3
U.S.	29.4	36.1	19.1	7.4	8.0

Note: Figures are percentages and include workers 16 years old and over; (1) Metropolitan Statistical Area - see Appendix A for areas included
Source: Census 2000, Summary File 3

Travel Time Index

Area	1982	1995	2004	2005
Urban Area[1]	1.05	1.16	1.16	1.17
Average[2]	1.11	1.22	1.29	1.30

Note: Travel Time Index - The ratio of travel time in the peak period to the travel time at free-flow conditions. A value of 1.35 indicates a 20-minute free-flow trip takes 27 minutes in the peak. Free-flow speeds (60 mph on freeways and 35 mph on principal arterials) are used as the comparison threshold; (1) Covers the Albuquerque, NM urban area; (2) average of 85 urban areas
Source: Texas Transportation Institute, The 2007 Urban Mobility Report, September 2007

Living Environment

COST OF LIVING

Cost of Living Index

Composite Index	Groceries	Housing	Utilities	Trans-portation	Health Care	Misc. Goods/ Services
95.8	100.9	90.0	86.5	100.2	106.0	98.7

Note: U.S. = 100; Figures cover the Rio Rancho NM urban area.
Source: The Council for Community and Economic Research (formerly ACCRA), Cost of Living Index, 2007

Grocery Prices

Area[1]	T-Bone Steak ($/pound)	Frying Chicken ($/pound)	Whole Milk ($/half gal.)	Eggs ($/dozen)	Orange Juice ($/64 oz.)	Coffee ($/11.5 oz.)
City[2]	8.37	1.05	2.04	1.62	3.25	3.44
Avg.	8.93	1.12	2.13	1.52	3.26	3.31
Min.	5.88	0.71	1.33	0.83	2.30	2.20
Max.	12.80	2.07	3.43	3.54	5.79	6.20

Note: (1) Values for the local area are compared with the average, minimum and maximum values for all 331 areas in the Cost of Living Index report; (2) Figures cover the Rio Rancho NM urban area; **T-Bone Steak** *(price per pound);* **Frying Chicken** *(price per pound, whole fryer);* **Whole Milk** *(half gallon carton);* **Eggs** *(price per dozen, Grade A, large);* **Orange Juice** *(64 oz. Tropicana or Florida Natural);* **Coffee** *(11.5 oz. can, vacuum-packed, Maxwell House, Hills Bros, or Folgers).*
Source: The Council for Community and Economic Research (formerly ACCRA), Cost of Living Index, 2007

Housing and Utility Costs

Area[1]	New Home Price ($)	Apartment Rent ($/month)	All Electric ($/month)	Part Electric ($/month)	Other Energy ($/month)	Telephone ($/month)
City[2]	274,224	720	-	60.41	73.39	24.38
Avg.	309,605	782	146.13	78.67	90.16	26.14
Min.	189,877	n/a	82.03	37.41	33.15	17.08
Max.	1,202,800	3,481	271.14	150.60	257.67	37.45

Note: (1) Values for the local area are compared with the average, minimum and maximum values for all 331 areas in the Cost of Living Index report; (2) Figures cover the Rio Rancho NM urban area; **New Home Price** *(2,400 sf living area, 8,000 sf lot, in urban area with full utilities);* **Apartment Rent** *(950 sf 2 bedroom/1.5 or 2 bath, unfurnished, excluding all utilities except water);* **All Electric** *(average monthly cost for an all-electric home);* **Part Electric** *(average monthly cost for a part-electric home);* **Other Energy** *(average monthly cost for natural gas, fuel oil, coal, wood, and any other forms of energy except electricity);* **Telephone** *(price includes basic monthly rate for a private residential line plus additional local usage charges incurred by a family of four).*
Source: The Council for Community and Economic Research (formerly ACCRA), Cost of Living Index, 2007

Health Care, Transportation, and Other Costs

Area[1]	Doctor ($/visit)	Dentist ($/visit)	Optometrist ($/visit)	Gasoline ($/gallon)	Beauty Salon ($/visit)	Men's Shirt ($)
City[2]	80.27	79.94	97.26	2.63	32.33	25.29
Avg.	79.48	71.93	79.55	2.64	29.52	25.77
Min.	52.08	44.80	43.95	2.19	15.58	16.19
Max.	148.44	126.27	158.83	3.48	60.62	48.53

Note: (1) Values for the local area are compared with the average, minimum and maximum values for all 331 areas in the Cost of Living Index report; (2) Figures cover the Rio Rancho NM urban area; **Doctor** *(general practitioners routine exam of an established patient);* **Dentist** *(adult teeth cleaning and periodic oral examination);* **Optometrist** *(full vision eye exam for established adult patient);* **Gasoline** *(one gallon regular unleaded, national brand, including all taxes, cash price at self-service pump if available);* **Beauty Salon** *(woman's shampoo, trim, and blow-dry);* **Men's Shirt** *(cotton/polyester dress shirt, pinpoint weave, long sleeves).*
Source: The Council for Community and Economic Research (formerly ACCRA), Cost of Living Index, 2007

HOUSING

House Price Index (HPI)

Area	National Ranking[2]	Quarterly Change (%)	One-Year Change (%)	Five-Year Change (%)
MSA[1]	49	0.27	4.66	56.29
U.S.[3]	-	0.10	0.84	41.37

Note: The HPI is a weighted repeat sales index. It measures average price changes in repeat sales or refinancings on the same properties. This information is obtained by reviewing repeat mortgage transactions on single-family properties whose mortgages have been purchased or securitized by Fannie Mae or Freddie Mac in January 1975; (1) Metropolitan Statistical Area - see Appendix B for areas included; (2) Rankings are based on annual percentage change for all metro areas containing at least 15,000 transactions over the last 10 years and ranges from 1 to 291; (3) figures based on a weighted average of Census Division estimates; all figures are for the period ending December 31, 2007
Source: Office of Federal Housing Enterprise Oversight, House Price Index, February 26, 2008

House Price Valuations

Area	Q1 2000	Q1 2001	Q1 2002	Q1 2003	Q1 2004	Q1 2005	Q1 2006	Q1 2007	Q1 2008
MSA[1]	-6.9	-14.3	-12.7	-9.6	-7.7	-3.1	7.6	13.4	10.4

Note: Figures show the percentage of over- or under-valuation of single family homes relative to statistically normal house values (e.g. a value of 23.6 indicates that house values are 23.6% overvalued). Statistically normal house values are based on house prices, interest rates, household incomes, population densities, and any historical premiums or discounts metropolitan areas have exhibited over time; (1) Figures cover the Metropolitan Statistical Area - see Appendix B for areas included
Source: Global Insight/National City Corporation, House Prices in America, May 2008

Median Home Prices

Area	2005	2006	2007[r]	Percent Change 2006 to 2007
MSA[1]	169.2	184.2	198.5	7.8
U.S. Average	219.0	221.9	217.9	-1.8

Note: Figures are median sales prices of existing single-family homes in thousands of dollars; (r) revised; n/a not available; (1) Metropolitan Statistical Area - see Appendix B for areas included
Source: National Association of Realtors, Metropolitan Area Prices, 1st Quarter 2008

Housing: Year Structure Built

Area	1990 -2000	1980 -1989	1970 -1979	1960 -1969	1950 -1959	1940 -1949	Before 1940	Median Year
City	42.0	38.2	16.4	2.8	0.3	0.1	0.2	1988
MSA[1]	24.3	20.3	22.0	12.5	12.0	5.1	3.7	1978
U.S.	17.0	15.8	18.5	13.7	12.7	7.3	15.0	1971

Note: Figures are percentages; (1) Metropolitan Statistical Area - see Appendix A for areas included
Source: Census 2000, Summary File 3

HEALTH

Health Risk Data

Category	Area[1] (%)	U.S. (%)
Adults who have been told they have high blood pressure[3]	22.0	25.5
Adults who have been told they have high blood cholesterol[3]	28.0	35.6
Adults who have been told they have diabetes[2]	6.4	7.5
Adults who have been told they have arthritis[3]	22.5	27.0
Adults who have been told they currently have asthma	8.6	8.5
Adults who are current smokers	19.5	20.1
Adults who are heavy drinkers[4]	4.4	4.9
Adults who are overweight (BMI 25.0 - 29.9)	37.4	36.5
Adults who are obese (BMI 30.0 - 99.8)	20.9	25.1

Note: Data as of 2006 unless otherwise noted; (1) Figures cover the Metropolitan Statistical Area - see Appendix B for areas included; (2) Figures do not include pregnancy-related diabetes, pre-diabetes or borderline diabetes; (3) 2005 data; (4) Heavy drinkers are classified as adult men having more than two drinks per day or adult women having more than one drink per day
Source: Centers for Disease Control and Prevention, Behaviorial Risk Factor Surveillance System, SMART: Selected Metropolitan/Micropolitan Area Risk Trends, 2005, 2006

Mortality Rates for the Top 10 Causes of Death in the U.S.

ICD-10[a] Sub-Chapter	ICD-10[a] Code	Age-Adjusted Mortality Rate[1] per 100,000 population	
		County[2]	U.S.
Malignant neoplasms	C00-C97	166.6	186.5
Ischaemic heart diseases	I20-I25	97.0	152.3
Other forms of heart disease	I30-I51	37.8	51.5
Cerebrovascular diseases	I60-I69	44.1	50.0
Chronic lower respiratory diseases	J40-J47	36.4	42.6
Diabetes mellitus	E10-E14	28.0	24.8
Other degenerative diseases of the nervous system	G30-G31	15.8	22.6
Other external causes of accidental injury	W00-X59	30.3	21.4
Influenza and pneumonia	J10-J18	11.1	20.7
Hypertensive diseases	I10-I13	14.3	18.2

Note: (a) ICD-10 = International Classification of Diseases 10th Revision; (1) Mortality rates are a three year average covering 2003-2005; (2) Figures cover Sandoval County
Source: Centers for Disease Control and Prevention, National Center for Health Statistics. Compressed Mortality File 1999-2004. CDC WONDER On-line Database, compiled from Compressed Mortality File 1999-2005 Series 20 No. 2K, 2008.

Mortality Rates for Selected Causes of Death

ICD-10[a] Sub-Chapter	ICD-10[a] Code	Age-Adjusted Mortality Rate[1] per 100,000 population	
		County[2]	U.S.
Assault	X85-Y09	*5.8	5.9
Human immunodeficiency virus (HIV) disease	B20-B24	*1.0	4.5
Intentional self-harm	X60-X84	11.2	10.8
Malnutrition	E40-E46	*0.4	1.0
Obesity and other hyperalimentation	E65-E68	*0.0	1.4
Organic, including symptomatic, mental disorders	F01-F09	18.9	16.8
Transport accidents	V01-V99	19.5	16.1
Viral hepatitis	B15-B19	*0.7	1.8

Note: (a) ICD-10 = International Classification of Diseases 10th Revision; (1) Mortality rates are a three year average covering 2003-2005; (2) Figures cover Sandoval County; (*) Unreliable data as per CDC
Source: Centers for Disease Control and Prevention, National Center for Health Statistics. Compressed Mortality File 1999-2004. CDC WONDER On-line Database, compiled from Compressed Mortality File 1999-2005 Series 20 No. 2K, 2008.

Distribution of Physicians[1]

Area	Total	Family/ General Practice	Specialties	
			Medical	Surgical
Sandoval County (number)	119	64	36	11
Sandoval County (rate per 10,000 pop.)	11.1	6.0	3.4	1.0
U.S. (rate per 10,000 pop.)	17.7	4.6	6.9	4.3

Note: Data as of 2005; (1) Includes all non-federal, patient-care, office-based MDs
Source: Area Resource File (ARF). June 2007. U.S. Department of Health and Human Services, Health Resources and Services Administration, Bureau of Health Professions, Rockville, MD.

Hospitals

There were no hospitals listed within the city limits.
AHA Guide to the Healthcare Field 2008

EDUCATION

Public School District Statistics

District Name	Schls	Pupils	Pupil/ Teacher Ratio	Minority Pupils[1] (%)	Free Lunch Eligible[2] (%)	IEP[3] (%)
Rio Rancho Public Schools	16	13,655	15.3	48.9	18.4	18.2

Note: Table includes regular local school districts with 2,000 or more students; (1) Percentage of students that are not white, non-Hispanic; (2) Percentage of students that are eligible for the free lunch program; (3) Percentage of students that have an Individualized Education Program.
Source: U.S. Department of Education, National Center for Education Statistics, Common Core of Data, Local Education Agency (School District) Universe Survey: School Year 2005-2006; U.S. Department of Education, National Center for Education Statistics, Common Core of Data, Public Elementary/Secondary School Universe Survey: School Year 2005-2006

Highest Level of Education

Area	Less than H.S.	H.S. Diploma	Some College, No Deg.	Associate Degree	Bachelors Degree	Masters Degree	Profess. School Degree	Doctorate Degree
City	8.1	27.0	29.7	9.5	17.7	6.3	1.1	0.6
MSA[1]	15.8	25.9	23.9	6.1	16.6	7.9	2.1	1.6
U.S.	19.4	28.4	21.2	6.4	15.7	5.9	2.0	1.0

Note: Figures are 2007 estimated percentages and cover persons age 25 and over; (1) Metropolitan Statistical Area - see Appendix B for areas included
Source: Claritas, Inc.

Educational Attainment by Race

Area	High School Graduate (%)					Bachelor's Degree (%)				
	Total	White	Black	Asian	Hisp.[2]	Total	White	Black	Asian	Hisp.[2]
City	91.2	92.0	80.1	77.0	87.9	24.8	26.0	22.0	31.6	17.7
MSA[1]	83.9	87.3	85.3	81.1	70.4	28.4	32.8	22.5	39.4	13.2
U.S.	80.4	83.6	72.3	80.4	52.4	24.4	26.1	14.3	44.1	10.4

Note: Figures shown cover persons 25 years old and over; (1) Metropolitan Statistical Area - see Appendix A for areas included; (2) people of Hispanic origin can be of any race
Source: Census 2000, Summary File 3

School Enrollment by Type

Area	Grades KG to 8				Grades 9 to 12			
	Public		Private		Public		Private	
	Enrollment	%	Enrollment	%	Enrollment	%	Enrollment	%
City	7,178	90.3	768	9.7	3,079	92.1	264	7.9
MSA[1]	84,412	88.0	11,536	12.0	37,748	89.6	4,358	10.4
U.S.	33,526,011	88.7	4,285,121	11.3	14,848,628	90.6	1,532,323	9.4

Note: Figures shown cover persons 3 years old and over; (1) Metropolitan Statistical Area - see Appendix A for areas included
Source: Census 2000, Summary File 3

School Enrollment by Race

Area	Grades KG to 8 (%)				Grades 9 to 12 (%)			
	White	Black	Asian	Hisp.[1]	White	Black	Asian	Hisp.[1]
City	73.6	2.5	1.2	34.5	75.3	0.6	2.0	32.9
MSA[2]	61.5	2.6	1.2	50.4	62.9	2.5	1.5	49.0
U.S.	68.5	15.5	3.3	16.8	68.8	15.5	3.8	15.7

Note: Figures shown cover persons 3 years old and over; (1) people of Hispanic origin can be of any race; (2) Metropolitan Statistical Area - see Appendix A for areas included
Source: Census 2000, Summary File 3

Average Salaries of Public School Classroom Teachers

District	2005-06 Dollars	2005-06 Rank[1]	2006-07 Dollars	2006-07 Rank[1]	Percent Change 2005-06 to 2006-07
New Mexico	41,637	36	42,780	41	2.75
U.S. Average	49,026	-	50,816	-	3.65

Note: (1) State rank ranges from 1 to 51.
Source: National Education Association, Rankings & Estimates: Rankings of the States 2006 and Estimates of School Statistics 2007, December 2007

Higher Education

Four-Year Colleges			Two-Year Colleges			Medical Schools[1]	Law Schools[2]	Voc/ Tech[3]
Public	Private Non-profit	Private For-profit	Public	Private Non-profit	Private For-profit			
0	0	1	0	0	0	0	0	0

Note: Figures cover institutions located within the city limits; (1) includes schools accredited by the Liaison Committee on Medical Education and the American Osteopathic Association; (2) includes American Bar Association-accredited law schools; (3) includes all schools with programs that are less than 2 years.
Source: National Center for Education Statistics, The Integrated Postsecondary Education System (IPEDS) Peer Analysis System, 2007; www.usnews.com, Law and Medical School Directories, 2009

PRESIDENTIAL ELECTION

2004 Presidential Election Results

Area	Bush	Kerry	Nader	Other
Sandoval County	50.8	48.1	0.5	0.6
U.S.	50.7	48.3	0.4	0.6

Note: Results are percentages and may not add to 100% due to rounding
Source: Dave Leip's Atlas of U.S. Presidential Elections, www.uselectionatlas.org

EMPLOYERS

Major Employers

Company Name	Industry	Type of Site
Athletics Deperment	Colleges and universities	Branch
CNM	Vocational schools, nec	Single
Central NM Cmnty College	Vocational schools, nec	Headquarters
City of Albuquerque	Executive offices	Headquarters
Dept of Surgery	Offices and clinics of medical doctors	Branch
Kirtland AFB	National security	Branch
Mediplex	Nursing and personal care, nec	Single
NM Dept Children Yuth Families	Administration of social & manpower programs	Branch
NM Veterans Medical Center	Administration of veterans' affairs	Branch
Police Department	Police protection	Branch
Rio Rancho Public Schools	Elementary and secondary schools	Single
SNL	Noncommercial research organizations	Headquarters
United States Dept of Energy	Administration of general economic programs	Branch
University Hospital	Colleges and universities	Branch
University Hospital	General medical and surgical hospitals	Branch
V A Medical Center	Administration of veterans' affairs	Branch

Note: Companies shown are located within the Albuquerque metropolitan area; nec = not elsewhere classified.
Source: www.zapdata.com, May 2008

PUBLIC SAFETY

Crime Rate

Area	All Crimes	Violent Crimes: Murder	Violent Crimes: Forcible Rape	Violent Crimes: Robbery	Violent Crimes: Aggrav. Assault	Property Crimes: Burglary	Property Crimes: Larceny -Theft	Property Crimes: Motor Vehicle Theft
City	2,746.5	0.0	23.7	22.2	346.6	717.0	1,370.3	266.7
Metro[1]	5,602.7	8.9	51.9	174.3	542.7	1,109.3	2,885.3	830.3
U.S.	3,808.1	5.7	30.9	149.4	287.5	729.4	2,206.8	398.4

Note: Figures are crimes per 100,000 population; (1) Metropolitan Statistical Area - see Appendix B for areas included
Source: FBI Uniform Crime Reports, 2006

Hate Crimes

Area	Number of Quarters Reported	Bias Motivation				
		Race	Religion	Sexual Orientation	Ethnicity	Disability
City	n/a	n/a	n/a	n/a	n/a	n/a

Note: n/a not available.
Source: Federal Bureau of Investigation, Hate Crime Statistics 2006

RECREATION

Culture

Dance[1]	Theatre[1]	Instrumental Music[1]	Vocal Music[1]	Series/ Festivals	Museums	Zoos and Aquariums[2]
0	0	0	0	0	0	0

Note: (1) Number of professional perfoming groups; (2) AZA-accredited
Source: The Grey House Performing Arts Directory, 2007; Official Museum Directory, 2008; Association of Zoos & Aquariums, AZA Member Zoos & Aquariums, June 2008

Professional Sports Teams

Team Name	League
No teams are located in the metro area	

Source: Original research

MEDIA

Newspapers

Name	News Focus	Frequency	Circulation
Kirtland Air Force Base Nucleus	Community	Weekly	14,000
Rio Rancho Observer	Community	Weekly	18,100

Note: Includes newspapers with offices located in the city
Source: MediaContactsPro, March 2008

Television Stations

Name	Ch.	Network(s)	Type	Ownership
KASA	2	Fox	Commercial	Raycom Media Inc.
KOFT	3	ABC	Commercial	Hearst-Argyle Broadcasting
KOB	4	NBC	Commercial	Hubbard Broadcasting Inc.
KNME	5	PBS	Public	n/a
KOCT	6	ABC	Commercial	Hearst-Argyle Broadcasting
KREZ	6	CBS	Commercial	Lee Enterprises Inc.
KOAT	7	ABC	Commercial	Hearst-Argyle Broadcasting
KOBR	8	NBC	Commercial	Hubbard Broadcasting Inc.
KBIM	10	CBS	Commercial	Emmis Communications
KOVT	10	ABC	Commercial	Hearst-Argyle Broadcasting
KCHF	11	n/a	Commercial	Son Broadcasting
KOBF	12	NBC	Commercial	Hubbard Broadcasting Inc.
KRQE	13	CBS	Commercial	Lee Enterprises Inc.
KWBQ	19	WBN	Commercial	n/a
KNAT	23	n/a	Non-comm.	All American Network
KAZQ	32	n/a	Non-comm.	Alpha Omega Broadcasting of Albuquerque
KLUZ	41	Univision	Commercial	Entravision Communications
KRPV	42	n/a	Non-comm.	Prime Time Christian Broadcasting Inc.
KASY	50	UPN	Commercial	Acme Broadcasting Inc.

Note: Stations included cover the Albuquerque-Santa Fe DMA (Designated Market Area)
BurrellesLuce, MediaContacts Online, January 2007

Major AM Radio Stations

Call Letters	Freq. (kHz)	Station Type	Target Audience	Station Format	Music Format
KLLV	550	Non-Comm	General/Religious	Educational/Music	Gospel
KNML	610	Commercial	General	Sports/Talk	n/a
KTNN	660	Commercial	Gen/Nat Amer/Nat Can	Educational/Music/News	Country
KKOB	770	n/a	General	Music/News	n/a
KSWV	810	Commercial	General/Hispanic	Educational/Music/News	Latin
KHAC	880	Commercial	Gen/Nat Amer/Rel	Educational/Music	Christian
KBIM	910	Commercial	General	News/Sports/Talk	n/a
KIUP	930	Commercial	General	Music/News/Sports/Talk	Oldies
KNFT	950	Commercial	General/Hispanic	Music/Talk	Blues
KNDN	960	Commercial	General/Native Amer	Music/News	World Music
KKIM	1000	Commercial	General/Religious	Talk	n/a
KINF	1020	Commercial	General/Hispanic	Music	Oldies
KYKK	1110	Commercial	General	News/Talk	n/a
KXKS	1190	Commercial	Hispanic	Music/News/Talk	Latin
KVSF	1260	n/a	General	Talk	n/a
KRDD	1320	Commercial	General/Hispanic	Educational/Music	Latin
KGAK	1330	Commercial	General/Native Amer	Music	International
KABQ	1350	Commercial	Hispanic	Music/News/Talk	Latin
KBUY	1360	Commercial	General	Music	Oldies
KENN	1390	Commercial	General	Talk	n/a
KCRX	1430	n/a	General	Music	Classical

Note: Stations included cover the Albuquerque-Santa Fe DMA (Designated Market Area); n/a not available
Source: BurrellesLuce, MediaContacts Online, January 2007

Major FM Radio Stations

Call Letters	Freq. (mHz)	Station Type	Target Audience	Station Format	Music Format
KFLQ	91.5	Non-Comm	General/Religious	Educational/Music/News	Christian
KRST	92.3	Commercial	General	Music/News/Talk	Country
KTZA	92.9	Commercial	General	Music	Contemp. Country
KRWN	92.9	Commercial	General	Music	Modern Rock
KXXI	93.7	Commercial	General	Music	Classic Rock
KZRR	94.1	Commercial	General	Music/News/Talk	Modern Rock
KKOR	94.5	Commercial	General	Music	Top 40
KBOM	94.7	n/a	General	Music/News/Talk	n/a
KBIM	94.9	Commercial	General	Music/News/Sports/Talk	Adult Contemp.
KWYK	94.9	Commercial	General	Music	Adult Contemp.
KWRK	96.1	Commercial	General	Music	Adult Top 40
KDAG	96.9	Commercial	General	Music	Classic Rock
KBCQ	97.1	Commercial	General	Music	Top 40
KKSS	97.3	Commercial	General	Music/News/Talk	Rhythm & Blues
KLVO	97.7	Commercial	General/Hispanic	Music/News/Talk	Latin
KISZ	97.9	Commercial	General	Music	Contemp. Country
KABG	98.5	Commercial	General	Music/News/Talk	Oldies
KRSJ	100.5	Commercial	General	Music	Contemp. Country
KKIT	100.7	Commercial	General	Music/News/Sports/Talk	Modern Rock
KIQX	101.3	Commercial	General	Music	Alternative
KTRA	102.1	n/a	General	Music/News	n/a
KIXN	102.9	Commercial	General	Music	Contemp. Country
KNFT	102.9	Commercial	General	Music	Country
KTZO	103.3	Commercial	General	Music/News/Talk	Alternative
KYVA	103.7	Commercial	General	Music/News	Oldies
KBAC	104.1	Commercial	General	Music	Alternative
KCDY	104.1	Commercial	General	Music	Adult Contemp.
KKFG	104.5	Commercial	General	Music	Oldies
KTEG	104.7	n/a	Asian/Hispanic	Talk	n/a
KMOU	104.7	Commercial	General	Ed/Music/News/Sports/Talk	Country
KYLZ	106.3	Commercial	General	Music/News/Talk	Urban Contemp.
KZNM	106.7	n/a	General	Music/News/Sports	n/a

Note: Stations included cover the Albuquerque-Santa Fe DMA (Designated Market Area); n/a not available
BurrellesLuce, MediaContacts Online, January 2007

CLIMATE

Average and Extreme Temperatures

Temperature	Jan	Feb	Mar	Apr	May	Jun	Jul	Aug	Sep	Oct	Nov	Dec	Yr.
Extreme High (°F)	69	76	85	89	98	105	105	101	100	91	77	72	105
Average High (°F)	47	53	61	71	80	90	92	89	83	72	57	48	70
Average Temp. (°F)	35	40	47	56	65	75	79	76	70	58	45	36	57
Average Low (°F)	23	27	33	41	50	59	65	63	56	44	31	24	43
Extreme Low (°F)	-17	-5	8	19	28	40	52	50	37	21	-7	-7	-17

Note: Figures cover the years 1948-1992
Source: National Climatic Data Center, International Station Meteorological Climate Summary, 9/96

Average Precipitation/Snowfall/Humidity

Precip./Humidity	Jan	Feb	Mar	Apr	May	Jun	Jul	Aug	Sep	Oct	Nov	Dec	Yr.
Avg. Precip. (in.)	0.4	0.4	0.5	0.4	0.5	0.5	1.4	1.5	0.9	0.9	0.4	0.5	8.5
Avg. Snowfall (in.)	3	2	2	1	Tr	0	0	0	Tr	Tr	1	3	11
Avg. Rel. Hum. 5am (%)	68	64	55	48	48	45	60	65	61	60	63	68	59
Avg. Rel. Hum. 5pm (%)	41	33	25	20	19	18	27	30	29	29	35	43	29

Note: Figures cover the years 1948-1992; Tr = Trace amounts (<0.05 in. of rain; <0.5 in. of snow)
Source: National Climatic Data Center, International Station Meteorological Climate Summary, 9/96

Weather Conditions

Temperature			Daytime Sky			Precipitation		
10°F & below	32°F & below	90°F & above	Clear	Partly cloudy	Cloudy	0.01 inch or more precip.	0.1 inch or more snow/ice	Thunder-storms
4	114	65	140	161	64	60	9	38

Note: Figures are average number of days per year and cover the years 1948-1992
Source: National Climatic Data Center, International Station Meteorological Climate Summary, 9/96

HAZARDOUS WASTE

Superfund Sites

Rio Rancho has no sites on the EPA's Superfund Final National Priorities List.
U.S. Environmental Protection Agency, Final National Priorities List, June 23, 2008

AIR & WATER QUALITY

Air Quality Index

Area	Percent of Days when Air Quality was...[2]				AQI Statistics	
	Good	Moderate	Unhealthy for Sensitive Groups	Unhealthy	Maximum	Median
MSA[1]	34.2	63.8	1.6	0.3	178	54

Note: The Air Quality Index (AQI) is an index for reporting daily air quality. EPA calculates the AQI for five major air pollutants regulated by the Clean Air Act: ground-level ozone, particle pollution (also known as particulate matter), carbon monoxide, sulfur dioxide, and nitrogen dioxide. The AQI runs from 0 to 500. The higher the AQI value, the greater the level of air pollution and the greater the health concern. There are six AQI categories: "Good" The AQI is between 0 and 50. Air quality is considered satisfactory; "Moderate" The AQI is between 51 and 100. Air quality is acceptable; "Unhealthy for Sensitive Groups" When AQI values are between 101 and 150, members of sensitive groups may experience health effects; "Unhealthy" When AQI values are between 151 and 200 everyone may begin to experience health effects; "Very Unhealthy" AQI values between 201 and 300 trigger a health alert; "Hazardous" AQI values over 300 trigger health warnings of emergency conditions; (1) Metropolitan Statistical Area - see Appendix A for areas included; (2) Based on 365 days with AQI data in 2007.
Source: U.S. Environmental Protection Agency, Air Quality Index Report, 2007

Air Quality Index Pollutants

Area	Percent of Days when AQI Pollutant was...[2]					
	Carbon Monoxide	Nitrogen Dioxide	Ozone	Sulfur Dioxide	Particulate Matter 2.5	Particulate Matter 10
MSA[1]	0.0	0.0	43.0	0.0	23.8	33.2

Note: The Air Quality Index (AQI) is an index for reporting daily air quality. EPA calculates the AQI for five major air pollutants regulated by the Clean Air Act: ground-level ozone, particle pollution (also known as particulate matter), carbon monoxide, sulfur dioxide, and nitrogen dioxide. The AQI runs from 0 to 500. The higher the AQI value, the greater the level of air pollution and the greater the health concern; (1) Metropolitan Statistical Area - see Appendix A for areas included; (2) Based on 365 days with AQI data in 2007.
Source: U.S. Environmental Protection Agency, Air Quality Index Report, 2007

Air Quality Index Trends

Area	Trend Sites (18)								All Sites (70)
	1999	2000	2001	2002	2003	2004	2005	2006	2006
MSA[1]	1	0	2	4	2	2	0	1	5

Note: An AQI value greater than 100 indicates that air quality would have been in the unhealthful range on that day. Data from exceptional events are not included. These counts are presented in two ways. First, the counts are based on sites having an adequate record of monitoring data during the trend period (trend sites). These counts represent the relative change in the number of days with AQI values greater than 100. In the last column, the counts are based on all sites with data in the most recent year (because it is possible for a site to have data in the most recent year but not enough data to be a trend site); (1) Metropolitan Statistical Area - see Appendix A for areas included.
Source: U.S. Environmental Protection Agency, Office of Air and Radiation, Air Trends, Factbook and Related Information, Air Pollution Trends in Selected Metropolitan Areas 2006

Maximum Air Pollutant Concentrations

	Particulate Matter 10 (ug/m^3)	Particulate Matter 2.5 (ug/m^3)	Ozone (ppm)	Carbon Monoxide (ppm)	Sulfur Dioxide (ppm)	Nitrogen Dioxide (ppm)	Lead (ug/m^3)
MSA[1] Level	266	28	0.091	3	n/a	0.016	n/a
NAAQS[2]	150	35	0.125	9	0.140	0.053	1.50
Met NAAQS[2]	No	Yes	Yes	Yes	n/a	Yes	n/a

Note: Data from exceptional events are not included; (1) Metropolitan Statistical Area - see Appendix A for areas included; (2) National Ambient Air Quality Standards; n/a not available
Concentrations: Particulate Matter 10 (coarse particulate) - highest second maximum 24-hour concentration; Particulate Matter 2.5 (fine particulate) - highest 98th percentile 24-hour concentration; Ozone - highest second daily maximum 1-hour concentration; Carbon Monoxide - highest second maximum non-overlapping 8-hour concentration; Sulfur Dioxide - highest second maximum 24-hour concentration; Nitrogen Dioxide - highest arithmetic mean concentration; Lead - highest quarterly maximum concentration
Units: ppm = parts per million; ug/m^3 = micrograms per cubic meter
Source: U.S. Environmental Protection Agency, MSA Factbook 2006, Air Quality Statistics by City

Drinking Water

Water System Name	Pop. Served	Primary Water Source Type	Violations[1]	
			Health Based	Monitoring/ Reporting
Rio Rancho Sewer & Wastewater	56,000	Ground	0	0

Note: (1) Based on violation data from January 1, 2007 to December 31, 2007 (includes unresolved violations from earlier years)
Source: U.S. Environmental Protection Agency, Office of Ground Water and Drinking Water, Safe Drinking Water Information System (based on data extracted April 15, 2008)

Santa Fe, New Mexico

Background

Santa Fe is located in the foothills of the Rocky Mountains in Santa Fe County, 59 miles northeast of Albuquerque and 445 miles northeast of Phoenix. Unique in the way it embraces its extraordinary high desert landscape, Santa Fe is America's oldest capital city.

Before becoming part of the United States, Santa Fe was a province of New Spain, discovered by Coronado in 1598. After the 1810 Mexican War of Independence, the territory became the Mexican capital. After a military excursion to gain control of the Santa Fe Trail, the United States eventually acquired the territory that would become New Mexico. The Atchison, Topeka and Santa Fe Railway reached the city in 1880 and, with the help of the telegraph, started an economic revolution in the area. In 1912, New Mexico became the country's 47th state, with Santa Fe as its capital.

Tourism makes up most of the city's economy, with wholesale trade and manufacturing next in importance. Santa Fe has the third largest art market in the United States, behind New York and Los Angeles. Its Canyon Road galleries showcase a wide variety of contemporary Southwestern, indigenous American, and experimental art.

In addition to its truly unique art industry, Santa Fe offers visitors and residents a wide variety of cultural and historic attractions. Music includes the Santa Fe Opera, the Santa Fe Chamber Music Festival, and the Lensic Theatre, a major performing arts venue. The city's word-class museums, located in the Museum Hill district, include the Georgia O'Keeffe Museum, the Museum of New Mexico, The Museum of Fine Arts, and the Museum of International Folk Art. Historically significant landmarks include the Cathedral Basilica of Saint Francis of Assisi, the Loretto Chapel, the Palace of the Governors, the San Miguel Mission, and the Santuario de Guadalupe.

New development in the city includes the Las Soleras Project, with more than 2,000 new homes and nearly one million square feet of commercial space. Important to this and all Santa Fe development, is staying true to its Mexican heritage, so that its typical brown adobe architecture is a visual statement all its own.

Despite its southern location, Santa Fe has an average temperate climate thanks to its high altitude; at nearly 7,000 feet above sea level it is the highest state capital in the country. The average temperate in Santa Fe ranges from 14 to 40 in winter and from 55 to 86 in summer. Santa Fe receives 1-2 inches of rain per month in summer and about 5 inches of snow per month in winter.

Rankings

General Rankings

- Santa Fe* was ranked #20 out of 375 metro areas in *Cities Ranked & Rated*. Criteria: cost of living; climate; crime; transportation; economy and jobs; education; arts and culture; health and healthcare; leisure; quality of life. *Cities Ranked & Rated, 2nd Edition, 2007*
- Santa Fe* was ranked #259 out of 379 metro areas in *Places Rated Almanac*. Criteria: health care; education; recreation; transportation; ambience; climate; crime; housing costs; jobs. *Places Rated Almanac, 7th Edition, 2007*
- Santa Fe was selected as one of the "2006 Best Places to Live" by *Money* magazine. Places were ranked using 38 quality-of-life indicators and six economic opportunity measures in the following categories: ease of living; health; education; crime; park space; arts and leisure. *CNNMoney.com, "Best Places to Live 2006"*
- Santa Fe appeared on *Travel & Leisure's* list of the ten best cities in the continental U.S. and Canada. The city was ranked #4. Criteria: activities/attractions; culture/arts; restaurants/food; people; and value. *Travel & Leisure, "The World's Best Awards 2007"*
- *Condé Nast Traveler* polled thousands of readers for travel satisfaction. American cities were ranked based on the following criteria: friendliness; ambiance; culture/sites; restaurants; lodging; and shopping. Santa Fe appeared in the top 10, ranking #4. *Condé Nast Traveler, Readers' Choice Awards 2007*

Business/Finance Rankings

- The Santa Fe* metro area was identified as one of 10 "Top Up-and-Coming Tech Cities" by *Forbes*. The metro area ranked #2. Criteria: regional innovation trends; important patents. *Forbes.com, "Top Up-and-Coming Tech Cities," March 11, 2008*
- Santa Fe* was selected as one of the best places to start and grow a company by *Entrepreneur* and the National Policy Research Council. The Santa Fe* metro area ranked #90 out of 162 small metro areas. Criteria: business formation and growth (firms started four to 14 years ago that still employ at least 5 people and experienced rapid growth over the last four years). *Entrepreneur/National Policy Research Council, "Hot Cities for Entrepreneurs," September 2006*
- Santa Fe was selected as one of the "100 Best Places to Live and Launch" in the U.S. The city ranked #17. The editors at *Fortune Small Business* ranked 296 Census-designated metro areas by business friendliness (Launching Score, % New Businesses) and lifestyle offerings (Living Score). Then, through reporting, they picked the town within each of the top 100 metro areas that best blends business and pleasure. *Fortune Small Business, "100 Best Places to Live and Launch 2008," April 2008*
- The Santa Fe* metro area appeared on the Milken Institute "2007 Best Performing Cities" index. Rank: #81 out of 179 small metro areas. Criteria: job growth; wage and salary growth; high-tech output growth. *Milken Institute, "2007 Best Performing Cities"*
- The Santa Fe* metro area was selected as one of "The Top 10 Boom Villages in America." *Business 2.0* magazine and econometric research firm Global Insight compared 319 metropolitan areas in the U.S. Criteria: a weighted formula that includes forecast growth rates in sectors that contain the economy's 10 most skilled occupational clusters; the prevalence of college degrees in the local workforce; median salary. The area ranked #3 among small metro areas. *Business 2.0 Magazine, March 2004*
- *Forbes* ranked 179 smaller metro areas in the U.S. in terms of the "Best Places for Business and Careers." The Santa Fe* metro area was ranked #29. Criteria: business costs (labor, energy, tax and office space expenses); living costs (housing, transportation, food and other household expenditures); education levels of the work force; job growth; income growth; migration trends; crime rates; and culture/leisure. *Forbes, "Best Places for Business and Careers," March 19, 2008*

Health/Environment Rankings

- Scarborough Research, a leading market research firm, identified the top local markets for organic consumers. The Santa Fe* DMA (Designated Market Area) ranked in the top 15 with 21% of adults reporting that they used any organic food product in their household during the past month. *Scarborough Research, October 10, 2007*

- The Santa Fe* metro area appeared in *Country Home's* "2008 Best Green Places" report. The area ranked #39 out of 379. Criteria: official energy policies; green power; green buildings; availability of fresh, locally grown food. *Country Home, "2008 Best Green Places"*

- Santa Fe was identified as one of "America's Heart-Healthiest Cities" by *Men's Journal.* The city ranked #6 out of 8. Criteria: easy access to the outdoors; strong park and trail system; clear culture of activity (i.e. outdoor festivals, street fairs, bike racks and local distance races); city should be dense (good walkability), but not big (too stressful). *Men's Journal, "Where You Live is Key," August 2006*

- The American Podiatric Medical Association and *Prevention* magazine ranked America's 100 most populated cities based on fitness-walker friendliness. The best cities have safe streets, beautiful places to walk, mild weather and good air quality. Santa Fe ranked #22. *Prevention, "The Best Walking Cities of 2008," April 2008; American Podiatric Medical Association, "2008 Best Fitness-Walking Cities, "April 2008*

- Sperling's BestPlaces ranked 331 metro areas and identified the most and least stressful U.S. cities. The Santa Fe* metro area ranked #42 out of the 117 smallest metro areas (#1 = most stressful). Criteria: divorce rate; unemployment rate; violent and property crime; suicide rate; commute time; mental health; alcohol consumption; cloudy days. *Sperling's BestPlaces, www.BestPlaces.net, "America's Most (and Least) Stressful Cities," January 9, 2004*

- Santa Fe* was highlighted as one of the top 25 cleanest metro areas for long-term particle pollution (PM 2.5) in the U.S. The area ranked #2. *American Lung Association, State of the Air: 2007*

Women/Minorities Rankings

- Santa Fe was profiled in the book *50 Fabulous Gay-Friendly Places to Live.* Criteria: an active gay community; positive gay health programs; youth outreach; gay-friendly politics; gay-owned and gay-friendly businesses; employment opportunities; fun nightlife; cultural opportunities; recreational opportunities; housing options. *50 Fabulous Gay-Friendly Places to Live, 2005*

- Santa Fe* appeared on a list of the top 10 metro areas with the highest concentration of gay male couples. The area ranked #8. *Urban Institute Press, The Gay and Lesbian Atlas, May 2004*

- Santa Fe* appeared on a list of the top 10 metro areas with the highest concentration of lesbian couples. The area ranked #3. *Urban Institute Press, The Gay and Lesbian Atlas, May 2004*

Seniors/Retirement Rankings

- Santa Fe was profiled in the book *America's 100 Best Places to Retire*. Criteria: comfortable climate; nearby health-care facilities; affordable housing; access to shopping and cultural venues; opportunities for community involvement and continuing education. *America's 100 Best Places to Retire, 4th Edition, 2007*

- Santa Fe was profiled in the book *Where to Retire: America's Best and Most Affordable Places.* Cities were selected based on personal visits by the author and interviews with local residents coupled with statistics from various government agencies. *Where to Retire: America's Best and Most Affordable Places, 2006*

- Santa Fe was identified as one of the 50 best places to retire in America. Criteria: climate; taxes; cost of living; jobs; medical care; services for seniors; continuing education; crime and safety; transportation; culture and recreation. *50 Fabulous Places to Retire in America, 3rd Edition, 2006*

- Santa Fe was profiled in the book *Retire in Style: 60 Outstanding Places Across the USA and Canada.* Criteria: landscape; climate; quality of life; cost of living; transportation; retail services; health care; community services; cultural and educational activities; recreational activities; work and volunteer activities; crime rates and public safety. *Retire in Style: 60 Outstanding Places Across the USA and Canada, 2nd Edition, 2005*

- Santa Fe was identified as one of the best places to retire in *Retirement Places Rated.* Criteria: population above 10,000; attractiveness to older adults; affordability; climate and natural endowments; personal safety. The city was ranked #75 out of 200. *Retirement Places Rated, 7th Edition, 2007*

- A.G. Edwards ranked America's 500 top-performing communities based on their residents' personal savings and investing behavior. The Santa Fe* metro area ranked #147 with an index score of 104.62 (national average = 100.00). A dozen statistical factors were measured including: participation in retirement savings plans; personal debt levels; and home ownership. *A.G. Edwards, "2007 Nest Egg Index", September 12, 2007*

Safety Rankings

- The National Insurance Crime Bureau ranked 361 metro areas in the U.S. in terms of per capita rates of vehicle theft. The Santa Fe* metro area ranked #146 (#1 = highest rate). Criteria: number of vehicle theft offenses per 100,000 inhabitants. *National Insurance Crime Bureau, "NICB Vehicle Theft Study," April 22, 2008*

- Farmers Insurance Group of Companies, in partnership with Sperling's BestPlaces, ranked 379 metro areas and identified the "Most Secure U.S. Place to Live." The Santa Fe* metro area ranked #59 out of 138 in the small town category (fewer than 150,000 residents). Criteria: crime rates; extreme weather; risk of natural disasters; environmental hazards; terrorism threats; air quality; life expectancy; job loss numbers. *Farmers Insurance Group, "Most Secure U.S. Places to Live 2007"*

- Santa Fe* was identified as one of the safest places in the U.S. in terms of its vulnerability to natural disasters and weather extremes. The city ranked #3 out of 10. Sperling's BestPlaces analyzed data to show a metro areas' relative tendency to experience natural disasters (hail, tornados, high winds, hurricanes, earthquakes, and brush fires) or extreme weather (abundant rain or snowfall or days that are below freezing or above 90 degrees Fahrenheit). *Forbes, "Safest and Least Safe Places in the U.S.," August 30, 2005*

Sports/Recreation Rankings

- Santa Fe was selected as one of the best towns in the U.S. Editors at *Outside Magazine* asked the best adventure athletes in America where they live and why. *Outside Magazine, "Best Towns 2007," August 2007*

- *Golf Digest* ranked 330 metro areas in the U.S. in terms of golf. The Santa Fe* metro area was ranked #268. Criteria: access to golf; weather; value of golf; and quality of golf. *Golf Digest, "Metro Golf Rankings," August 2005*

Culture/Performing Arts Rankings

- The Santa Fe* metro area was selected as one of the "Best Places for Artists in America" by *BusinessWeek.com.* Criteria: percentage of young people age 25 to 34; population diversity; concentration of museums, philharmonic orchestras, dance companies, theater troupes, library resources, and college arts programs. *BusinessWeek.com, "Best Places for Artists in America," February 26, 2007*

- Santa Fe was selected as one of "America's Favorite Cities." The city ranked #8 in the "Culture" category. Travelandleisure.com and CNN Headline News polled travelers and residents on what they like (and don't like) about 25 top urban destinations in the U.S. Criteria: classical music; theater; museums/galleries; underground arts scene; historical sites/monuments; architecture/notable buildings. *Travelandleisure.com and CNN Headline News, "America's Favorite Cities 2007"*

- Santa Fe was selected as one of America's 10 best large (population 30,000 - 100,000) art towns. The city ranked #1. Criteria: number of art galleries; affordability; natural beauty; local support for the arts; availability of suitable studio and rehearsal space; frequency and impact of art festivals; cohesiveness of the local arts community; diversity of creative statements being made by local visual and performing artists; number of theaters, art schools, art museums, and alternative exhibition and performance venues. *The 100 Best Art Towns in America: A Guide to Galleries, Museums, Festivals, Lodging, and Dining, 4th Edition, 2005*

- Santa Fe was selected as one of "America's Top 25 Arts Destinations." The city ranked #1 in the small city (population under 100,000) category. Criteria: readers' top choices for arts travel destinations based on the richness and variety of visual arts sites, activities and events. *American Style, June 2007*

- Scarborough Research, a leading market research firm, identified the top local markets for rock concert attendance. The Santa Fe* DMA (Designated Market Area) ranked in the top 25 with 14% of consumers, 18 years old and over, reporting that they have attended a rock concert during the past year. *Scarborough Research, June 14, 2004*

Miscellaneous Rankings

- Santa Fe was selected as one of "America's Favorite Cities." The city ranked #11 in the "Cityscape" category. Travelandleisure.com and CNN Headline News polled travelers and residents on what they like (and don't like) about 25 top urban destinations in the U.S. Criteria: notable neighborhoods; skyline/views; public parks/spaces; cleanliness; access to outdoors; pedestrian friendliness. *Travelandleisure.com and CNN Headline News, "America's Favorite Cities 2007"*

- Santa Fe was selected as one of "America's Favorite Cities." The city ranked #13 in the "People" category. Travelandleisure.com and CNN Headline News polled travelers and residents on what they like (and don't like) about 25 top urban destinations in the U.S. Criteria: attractive; friendly; stylish; intelligent; worldly; athletic/active; fun; diverse. *Travelandleisure.com and CNN Headline News, "America's Favorite Cities 2007"*

- Santa Fe was selected as one of "America's Favorite Cities." The city ranked #25 in the "Food/Dining" category. Travelandleisure.com and CNN Headline News polled travelers and residents on what they like (and don't like) about 25 top urban destinations in the U.S. Criteria: big-name restaurants; ethnic food; cheap eats; farmers' markets; coffee; pizza; barbeque. *Travelandleisure.com and CNN Headline News, "America's Favorite Cities 2007"*

- Santa Fe was selected as one of "America's Favorite Cities." The city ranked #3 in the "Characteristics" category. Travelandleisure.com and CNN Headline News polled travelers and residents on what they like (and don't like) about 25 top urban destinations in the U.S. Criteria: people watching; peace and quiet; weather; safety; ease of getting around/public transportation; affordability; gay-friendliness; environmental awareness. *Travelandleisure.com and CNN Headline News, "America's Favorite Cities 2007"*

- Santa Fe was identified one of America's smartest cities" by *Forbes*. The area ranked #23out of 25. Criteria: percentage of the population age 25 and over with at least a bachelor's degree. *Forbes.com, "The Smartest Cities in America," February 8, 2008*

Santa Fe is located within the Santa Fe, NM Metropolitan Statistical Area.

Business Environment

CITY FINANCES

City Government Finances

Component	2004-2005 ($000)	2004-2005 ($ per capita)
Total Revenues	174,992	2,478
Total Expenditures	157,516	2,230
Debt Outstanding	233,166	3,301
Cash and Securities	121,715	1,723

Source: U.S Census Bureau, Government Finances 2004-2005

City Government Revenue by Source

Source	2004-2005 ($000)	2004-2005 ($ per capita)
General Revenue		
From Federal Government	7,938	112
From State Government	54,839	776
From Local Governments	0	0
Taxes		
Property	1,646	23
Sales	40,364	571
Personal Income	0	0
License	2,779	39
Charges	33,524	475
Liquor Store	0	0
Utility	28,610	405
Employee Retirement	0	0
Other	5,292	75

Source: U.S Census Bureau, Government Finances 2004-2005

City Government Expenditures by Function

Function	2004-2005 ($000)	2004-2005 ($ per capita)	2004-2005 (%)
General Expenditures			
Airports	482	7	0.3
Corrections	0	0	0.0
Education	0	0	0.0
Fire Protection	10,782	153	6.8
Governmental Administration	20,641	292	13.1
Health	14	< 1	< 0.1
Highways	10,551	149	6.7
Hospitals	0	0	0.0
Housing and Community Development	8,243	117	5.2
Interest on General Debt	10,327	146	6.6
Libraries	2,782	39	1.8
Parking	3,662	52	2.3
Parks and Recreation	16,894	239	10.7
Police Protection	20,715	293	13.2
Public Welfare	12,054	171	7.7
Sewerage	6,366	90	4.0
Solid Waste Management	7,470	106	4.7
Liquor Store	0	0	0.0
Utility	12,587	178	8.0
Employee Retirement	0	0	0.0
Other	13,946	197	8.9

Source: U.S Census Bureau, Government Finances 2004-2005

Municipal Bond Ratings

Area	Moody's
City	Aaa

Source: Mergent Bond Record, January 2008 (unless noted otherwise)

DEMOGRAPHICS

Population Growth

Area	1990 Census	2000 Census	2007 Estimate	2012 Projection	Population Growth (%) 1990-2000	Population Growth (%) 2000-2012
City	56,919	62,203	70,863	76,629	9.3	23.2
MSA[1]	98,928	129,292	143,831	153,765	30.7	18.9
U.S.	248,709,873	281,421,906	301,045,522	314,920,978	13.2	11.9

Note: (1) Metropolitan Statistical Area - see Appendix B for areas included
Source: Claritas, Inc.

Number of Households and Average Household Size

Area	2007 Estimate	2007 Average Household Size
City	31,770	2.23
MSA[1]	59,497	2.42
U.S.	113,668,003	2.65

Note: (1) Metropolitan Statistical Area - see Appendix B for areas included
Source: Claritas, Inc.

Race and Ethnicity

Area	White Alone[2]	Black Alone[2]	Asian Alone[2]	Other Race Alone[2]	Hispanic[3]
City	76.1	1.0	1.5	21.3	48.7
MSA[1]	72.7	1.0	1.0	25.3	49.4
U.S.	73.1	12.4	4.3	10.3	14.9

Note: Figures are 2007 estimates; (1) Metropolitan Statistical Area - see Appendix B for areas included (2) Alone is defined as not being in combination with one or more other races; (3) May be of any race.
Source: Claritas, Inc.

Ancestry

Area	German	Irish[2]	English	American	Italian	Polish	French[3]	Scottish
City	10.7	8.8	10.2	4.0	2.8	1.9	2.7	2.5
MSA[1]	11.8	8.4	10.2	4.3	2.8	1.8	2.5	2.4
U.S.	15.2	10.9	8.7	7.3	5.6	3.2	3.0	1.7

Note: Figures include multiple ancestry (e.g. if a person reported being Irish and Italian, they were included in both columns); (1) Metropolitan Statistical Area - see Appendix A for areas included; (2) Includes Celtic; (3) Includes Alsatian but excludes Basque
Source: Census 2000, Summary File 3

Foreign-Born Population

Area	Percent of Population Born in: Any Foreign Country	Europe	Asia	Africa	Oceania[2]	Canada	Mexico	Latin America[3]
City	11.6	2.1	0.9	0.2	0.0	0.3	7.1	1.0
MSA[1]	9.7	1.8	0.9	0.1	0.1	0.3	5.7	0.8
U.S.	11.1	1.7	2.9	0.3	0.1	0.3	3.3	2.5

Note: (1) Metropolitan Statistical Area - see Appendix A for areas included; (2) Includes Australia, New Zealand subregion, Melanesia, Micronesia, Polynesia, and Oceania n.e.c; (3) Includes Central America (excluding Mexico), South America, and the Caribbean.
Source: Census 2000, Summary File 3

Marriage Status

Area	Never Married	Now Married (excluding Separated)	Separated	Widowed	Divorced
City	30.3	44.7	1.6	6.6	16.9
MSA[1]	26.6	53.3	1.4	5.0	13.7
U.S.	27.1	54.4	2.2	6.6	9.7

Note: Figures are percentages and cover the population 15 years of age and older; (1) Metropolitan Statistical Area - see Appendix A for areas included
Source: Census 2000, Summary File 3

Age Distribution

Area	Under Age 5	Age 5 to 17	Age 18 to 34	Age 35 to 49	Age 50 to 64	Age 65 to 79	80 Years and Over
	Percent of Population						
City	5.4	14.7	22.1	24.5	19.1	10.5	3.7
MSA[1]	6.0	18.2	20.1	26.2	18.6	8.5	2.4
U.S.	6.8	18.9	23.7	23.5	14.8	9.2	3.2

Note: (1) Metropolitan Statistical Area - see Appendix A for areas included
Source: Census 2000, Summary File 3

Male/Female Ratio

Area	Males	Females	Males per 100 Females
City	34,169	36,694	93.1
MSA[1]	70,713	73,118	96.7
U.S.	148,320,305	152,725,217	97.1

Note: Figures are 2007 estimates; (1) Metropolitan Statistical Area - see Appendix B for areas included
Source: Claritas, Inc.

Religion

Area	Catholic	Southern Baptist	United Meth-odist	ELCA[1]	LDS[2]	Presby-terian Church USA	Jewish Est.	Muslim Est.
County	39.2	2.2	1.2	0.3	1.0	0.6	1.3	0.0
U.S.	22.0	7.1	3.7	1.8	1.5	1.1	2.2	0.6

Note: Figures are the number of adherents as a percentage of the total population; Adherents are defined as all members, including full members, their children and the estimated number of other participants who are not considered members (e.g. the baptized, those not confirmed, those regularly attending services, etc.); (1) Evangelical Lutheran Church in America; (2) The Church of Jesus Christ of Latter Day Saints
Source: Reprinted with permission from Religious Congregations and Membership in the United States 2000 (Nashville, Glenmary Research Center, 2002) Copyright Association of Statisticians of American Religious Bodies. All rights reserved.

ECONOMY

Gross Metropolitan Product

Area	2002	2003	2004	2005	2005 Rank[2]
MSA[1]	3.6	3.9	4.3	4.6	292

Note: Figures are in billions of dollars; (1) Santa Fe, NM Metropolitan Statistical Area - see Appendix A for areas included; (2) Rank ranges from 1 to 361
Source: The U.S. Conference of Mayors, "U.S. Metro Economies: GMP - The Engines of America's Growth," January 2007

Economic Growth

Area	1995 GMP	2005 GMP	Average Annual Growth Rate	Growth Rate Rank[2]
MSA[1]	2.7	4.6	5.2	195

Note: Figures are in billions of dollars; GMP = Gross Metropolitan Product; (1) Santa Fe, NM Metropolitan Statistical Area - see Appendix A for areas included; (2) Rank ranges from 1 to 361
Source: The U.S. Conference of Mayors, "U.S. Metro Economies: GMP - The Engines of America's Growth," January 2007

INCOME

Per Capita/Median/Average Income

Area	Per Capita ($)	Median Household ($)	Average Household ($)
City	29,679	46,730	65,312
MSA[1]	29,096	50,532	69,718
U.S.	25,495	49,280	66,670

Note: Figures are 2007 estimates; (1) Metropolitan Statistical Area - see Appendix B for areas included
Source: Claritas, Inc.

Household Income Distribution

Area	Percent of Households Earning							
	Under $15,000	$15,000 -24,999	$25,000 -34,999	$35,000 -49,999	$50,000 -74,999	$75,000 -99,000	$100,000 -149,999	$150,000 and up
City	13.0	10.9	11.9	17.7	18.4	11.3	10.5	6.4
MSA[1]	12.3	9.9	10.9	16.4	18.8	11.8	12.3	7.6
U.S.	13.1	10.9	11.2	15.6	19.5	11.9	11.3	6.6

Note: Figures are 2007 estimates; (1) Metropolitan Statistical Area - see Appendix B for areas included
Source: Claritas, Inc.

Poverty Rates by Age

Area	All Ages	Under 5 Years Old	5 to 17 Years Old	18 to 64 Years Old	65 Years and Over
City	12.3	1.2	2.4	7.4	1.3
MSA[1]	10.9	0.9	2.4	6.5	1.0
U.S.	12.4	1.2	3.0	6.9	1.2

Note: Figures are percent of population with income in 1999 below poverty level and only include population for whom poverty status is determined; (1) Metropolitan Statistical Area - see Appendix A for areas included
Source: Census 2000, Summary File 3

Personal Bankruptcy Filing Rate

Area	2004	2005	2006
Santa Fe County	3.34	5.05	1.00
U.S.	5.31	6.82	2.00

Note: Numbers are per 1,000 population and include Chapter 7 and Chapter 13 filings
Source: Federal Deposit Insurance Corporation (FDIC), Regional Economic Conditions (RECON), 8/23/2007

EMPLOYMENT

Labor Force and Employment

Area	Civilian Labor Force			Workers Employed		
	Dec. 2006	Dec. 2007	% Chg.	Dec. 2006	Dec. 2007	% Chg.
City	41,497	41,202	-0.7	40,526	40,338	-0.5
MSA[1]	79,300	78,727	-0.7	77,220	76,863	-0.5
U.S.	152,571,000	153,705,000	0.7	146,081,000	146,334,000	0.2

Note: Data is not seasonally adjusted and covers workers 16 years of age and older;
(1) Metropolitan Statistical Area - see Appendix B for areas included
Source: Bureau of Labor Statistics, http://stats.bls.gov

Unemployment Rate

Area	2007											
	Jan.	Feb.	Mar.	Apr.	May	Jun.	Jul.	Aug.	Sep.	Oct.	Nov.	Dec.
City	2.9	2.8	2.5	2.6	2.7	2.9	3.0	2.5	2.5	2.3	2.3	2.1
MSA[1]	3.2	3.1	2.8	2.8	2.8	3.1	3.3	2.7	2.7	2.5	2.6	2.4
U.S.	5.0	4.9	4.5	4.3	4.3	4.7	4.9	4.6	4.5	4.4	4.5	4.8

Note: Data is not seasonally adjusted and covers workers 16 years of age and older; All figures are percentages; (1) Metropolitan Statistical Area - see Appendix B for areas included
Source: Bureau of Labor Statistics, http://stats.bls.gov

Employment by Occupation

Occupation Classification	City (%)	MSA[1] (%)	U.S. (%)
Sales and Office	26.2	24.1	26.7
Professional and Related	27.2	28.9	20.2
Service	16.7	15.5	14.9
Production, Transportation, and Material Moving	5.5	6.0	14.6
Management, Business, and Financial	15.8	16.2	13.5
Construction, Extraction, and Maintenance	8.3	9.0	9.4
Farming, Forestry, and Fishing	0.2	0.2	0.7

Note: Figures cover employed civilians 16 years of age and older;
(1) Metropolitan Statistical Area - see Appendix A for areas included
Source: Census 2000, Summary File 3

Employment by Industry

Sector	MSA[1] Number of Employees	MSA[1] Percent of Total	U.S. Percent of Total
Government	16,700	25.3	16.3
Education and Health Services	9,800	14.8	13.4
Professional and Business Services	5,700	8.6	13.1
Retail Trade	9,200	13.9	11.6
Manufacturing	1,100	1.7	9.9
Leisure and Hospitality	9,100	13.8	9.6
Financial Activities	3,000	4.5	5.9
Construction	n/a	n/a	5.3
Wholesale Trade	1,200	1.8	4.4
Other Services	2,800	4.2	3.9
Transportation and Utilities	800	1.2	3.7
Information	1,800	2.7	2.2
Natural Resources and Mining	n/a	n/a	0.5

Note: Figures cover non-farm employment as of December 2007 and are not seasonally adjusted; (1) Metropolitan Statistical Area - see Appendix B for areas included; n/a not available
Source: Bureau of Labor Statistics, http://stats.bls.gov

Average Wages

Occupation	$/Hr.	Occupation	$/Hr.
Accountants and Auditors	24.56	Maids and Housekeeping Cleaners	10.21
Automotive Mechanics	19.43	Maintenance and Repair Workers	13.57
Bookkeepers	16.15	Marketing Managers	n/a
Carpenters	18.56	Nuclear Medicine Technologists	n/a
Cashiers	9.93	Nurses, Licensed Practical	20.59
Clerks, General Office	12.03	Nurses, Registered	27.65
Clerks, Receptionists/Information	12.49	Nursing Aides/Orderlies/Attendants	11.91
Clerks, Shipping/Receiving	13.09	Packers and Packagers, Hand	10.50
Computer Programmers	n/a	Physical Therapists	35.57
Computer Support Specialists	20.49	Postal Service Mail Carriers	21.16
Computer Systems Analysts	29.20	Real Estate Brokers	52.51
Cooks, Restaurant	10.80	Retail Salespersons	11.90
Dentists	n/a	Sales Reps., Exc. Tech./Scientific	26.14
Electrical Engineers	38.70	Sales Reps., Tech./Scientific	n/a
Electricians	18.41	Secretaries, Exc. Legal/Med./Exec.	13.35
Financial Managers	45.08	Security Guards	13.51
First-Line Supervisors/Mgrs., Sales	19.34	Surgeons	n/a
Food Preparation Workers	9.73	Teacher Assistants	9.40
General and Operations Managers	43.97	Teachers, Elementary School	20.00
Hairdressers/Cosmetologists	11.14	Teachers, Secondary School	n/a
Internists	n/a	Telemarketers	n/a
Janitors and Cleaners	10.91	Truck Drivers, Heavy/Tractor-Trailer	15.15
Landscaping/Groundskeeping Workers	11.79	Truck Drivers, Light/Delivery Svcs.	12.04
Lawyers	52.30	Waiters and Waitresses	9.03

Note: Wage data covers the Santa Fe, NM Metropolitan Statistical Area - see Appendix B for areas included. Hourly wages for elementary/secondary school teachers and teacher assistants were calculated by the editors from annual wage data assuming a 40 hour work week; n/a not available.
Source: Bureau of Labor Statistics, May 2007 Metro Area Occupational Employment and Wage Estimates

RESIDENTIAL REAL ESTATE

Building Permits

Area	Single-Family 2006	Single-Family 2007p	Single-Family Pct. Chg.	Multi-Family 2006	Multi-Family 2007p	Multi-Family Pct. Chg.	Total 2006	Total 2007p	Total Pct. Chg.
City	417	277	-33.6	0	0	-	417	277	-33.6
U.S.	1,378,200	973,300	-29.4	460,700	407,200	-11.6	1,838,900	1,380,500	-24.9

Note: (p) preliminary; figures cover and represent new, privately-owned housing units authorized (unadjusted data); All permit data are based on estimates with imputation; U.S. figures are based on the new 20,000-place series.
Source: U.S. Census Bureau, Manufacturing, Mining, and Construction Statistics

Homeownership and Housing Vacancies

Area	Homeownership Rate[2] (%)			Rental Vacancy Rate[3] (%)			Homeowner Vacancy Rate[4] (%)		
	2005	2006	2007	2005	2006	2007	2005	2006	2007
MSA[1]	n/a	n/a	n/a	n/a	n/a	n/a	n/a	n/a	n/a
U.S.	68.9	68.8	68.1	9.8	9.8	9.7	1.9	2.4	2.7

Note: (1) Metropolitan Statistical Area - see Appendix B for areas included; (2) The proportion of households that are owners; (3) The proportion of the rental inventory that is vacant for rent; (4) The proportion of the homeowner inventory that is vacant for sale; n/a not available
Source: U.S. Census Bureau, Housing Vacancies and Homeownership Annual Statistics: 2007

TAXES

State Corporate Income Tax Rates

State	Rates and Tax Brackets
New Mexico	4.8% > $0; 6.4% > 500K; 7.6% > 1,000,000

Note: Tax rates as of January 1, 2008
Source: Tax Foundation, www.taxfoundation.org

State Individual Income Tax Rates

State	Federal Deductibility	Marginal Rates (%)	Standard Deduction ($)		Personal Exemptions ($)[1]	
			Single	Joint	Single	Dependents
New Mexico	No	1.7 - 5.3 (s)	5,150 (s)	10,300 (s)	3,300 (s)	3,300 (s)

Note: Tax rates as of January 1, 2008; Local- and county-level taxes are not included; n/a not applicable; (1) Married joint filers generally receive double the single exemption; (s) Deductions and exemptions tied to federal tax system. Federal deductions and exemptions are indexed for inflation.
Source: Tax Foundation, www.taxfoundation.org

Various State and Local Tax Rates

State and Local Sales and Use (%)	State Sales and Use (%)	Gasoline[1,2] ($/gal.)	Cigarette ($/pack)	Spirits ($/gal.)	Table Wine ($/gal.)	Beer ($/gal.)
7.938	5.0 (g)	0.18	0.91	6.06	1.70	0.41

Note: Tax rates as of January 1, 2008; (1) In addition to the 18.4 cpg Federal gasoline tax; (2) Rates may include additional state sales taxes, environmental protection and storage fees/taxes, and local taxes. When necessary, the volume-weighted average of all local taxes is used to approximate the typical statewide rate including local tax; (g) New Mexico has no sales tax but does have a 5% GRT.
Source: Tax Foundation, www.taxfoundation.org; Original research

State Tax Burdens

Area	Combined State and Local Tax Burden		Combined Federal, State and Local Tax Burden	
	Percent	Rank	Percent	Rank
New Mexico	9.8	40	28.8	45
U.S. Average	11.0	-	32.7	-

Note: Figures cover 2007 and measure taxes as a percentage of income
Source: Tax Foundation, www.taxfoundation.org

State Business Tax Climate Index Rankings

State	Overall Rank	Corporate Tax Index Rank	Individual Income Tax Index Rank	Sales Tax Index Rank	Unemployment Insurance Tax Index Rank	Property Tax Index Rank
New Mexico	23	36	17	41	13	1

Note: Rankings range from 1 to 50 where 1 is best. Rankings do not average across to Overall Rank. States without a given tax are given a ranking of 1.
Source: Tax Foundation, State Business Tax Climate Index 2008

TRANSPORTATION

Means of Transportation to Work

Area	Car/Truck/Van		Public Transportation			Bicycle	Walked	Other Means	Worked at Home
	Drove Alone	Car-pooled	Bus	Subway	Railroad				
City	72.4	13.3	1.1	0.0	0.0	0.8	4.1	1.0	7.3
MSA[1]	72.7	15.0	0.5	0.0	0.0	0.7	3.0	1.0	6.9
U.S.	75.7	12.2	2.5	1.5	0.5	0.4	2.9	1.0	3.3

Note: Figures are percentages and cover workers 16 years of age and older;
(1) Metropolitan Statistical Area - see Appendix A for areas included
Source: Census 2000, Summary File 3

Travel Time to Work

Area	Less Than 15 Minutes	15 to 29 Minutes	30 to 44 Minutes	45 to 59 Minutes	60 Minutes or More
City	50.6	33.1	8.6	4.2	3.5
MSA[1]	37.3	37.0	15.0	6.3	4.6
U.S.	29.4	36.1	19.1	7.4	8.0

Note: Figures are percentages and include workers 16 years old and over; (1) Metropolitan Statistical Area - see Appendix A for areas included
Source: Census 2000, Summary File 3

Living Environment

COST OF LIVING

Cost of Living Index

Composite Index	Groceries	Housing	Utilities	Trans-portation	Health Care	Misc. Goods/ Services
n/a	n/a	n/a	n/a	n/a	n/a	n/a

Note: U.S. = 100; n/a not available
Source: The Council for Community and Economic Research (formerly ACCRA), Cost of Living Index, 2007

Grocery Prices

Area[1]	T-Bone Steak ($/pound)	Frying Chicken ($/pound)	Whole Milk ($/half gal.)	Eggs ($/dozen)	Orange Juice ($/64 oz.)	Coffee ($/11.5 oz.)
City[2]	n/a	n/a	n/a	n/a	n/a	n/a
Avg.	8.93	1.12	2.13	1.52	3.26	3.31
Min.	5.88	0.71	1.33	0.83	2.30	2.20
Max.	12.80	2.07	3.43	3.54	5.79	6.20

Note: (1) Values for the local area are compared with the average, minimum and maximum values for all 331 areas in the Cost of Living Index report; n/a not available; (2) Figures cover the Santa Fe NM urban area; **T-Bone Steak** *(price per pound);* **Frying Chicken** *(price per pound, whole fryer);* **Whole Milk** *(half gallon carton);* **Eggs** *(price per dozen, Grade A, large);* **Orange Juice** *(64 oz. Tropicana or Florida Natural);* **Coffee** *(11.5 oz. can, vacuum-packed, Maxwell House, Hills Bros, or Folgers).*
Source: The Council for Community and Economic Research (formerly ACCRA), Cost of Living Index, 2007

Housing and Utility Costs

Area[1]	New Home Price ($)	Apartment Rent ($/month)	All Electric ($/month)	Part Electric ($/month)	Other Energy ($/month)	Telephone ($/month)
City[2]	n/a	n/a	n/a	n/a	n/a	n/a
Avg.	309,605	782	146.13	78.67	90.16	26.14
Min.	189,877	n/a	82.03	37.41	33.15	17.08
Max.	1,202,800	3,481	271.14	150.60	257.67	37.45

Note: (1) Values for the local area are compared with the average, minimum and maximum values for all 331 areas in the Cost of Living Index report; n/a not available; (2) Figures cover the Santa Fe NM urban area; **New Home Price** *(2,400 sf living area, 8,000 sf lot, in urban area with full utilities);* **Apartment Rent** *(950 sf 2 bedroom/1.5 or 2 bath, unfurnished, excluding all utilities except water);* **All Electric** *(average monthly cost for an all-electric home);* **Part Electric** *(average monthly cost for a part-electric home);* **Other Energy** *(average monthly cost for natural gas, fuel oil, coal, wood, and any other forms of energy except electricity);* **Telephone** *(price includes basic monthly rate for a private residential line plus additional local usage charges incurred by a family of four).*
Source: The Council for Community and Economic Research (formerly ACCRA), Cost of Living Index, 2007

Health Care, Transportation, and Other Costs

Area[1]	Doctor ($/visit)	Dentist ($/visit)	Optometrist ($/visit)	Gasoline ($/gallon)	Beauty Salon ($/visit)	Men's Shirt ($)
City[2]	n/a	n/a	n/a	n/a	n/a	n/a
Avg.	79.48	71.93	79.55	2.64	29.52	25.77
Min.	52.08	44.80	43.95	2.19	15.58	16.19
Max.	148.44	126.27	158.83	3.48	60.62	48.53

Note: (1) Values for the local area are compared with the average, minimum and maximum values for all 331 areas in the Cost of Living Index report; n/a not available; (2) Figures cover the Santa Fe NM urban area; **Doctor** *(general practitioners routine exam of an established patient);* **Dentist** *(adult teeth cleaning and periodic oral examination);* **Optometrist** *(full vision eye exam for established adult patient);* **Gasoline** *(one gallon regular unleaded, national brand, including all taxes, cash price at self-service pump if available);* **Beauty Salon** *(woman's shampoo, trim, and blow-dry);* **Men's Shirt** *(cotton/polyester dress shirt, pinpoint weave, long sleeves).*
Source: The Council for Community and Economic Research (formerly ACCRA), Cost of Living Index, 2007

HOUSING

House Price Index (HPI)

Area	National Ranking[2]	Quarterly Change (%)	One-Year Change (%)	Five-Year Change (%)
MSA[1]	40	0.90	4.99	57.28
U.S.[3]	-	0.10	0.84	41.37

Note: The HPI is a weighted repeat sales index. It measures average price changes in repeat sales or refinancings on the same properties. This information is obtained by reviewing repeat mortgage transactions on single-family properties whose mortgages have been purchased or securitized by Fannie Mae or Freddie Mac in January 1975; (1) Metropolitan Statistical Area - see Appendix B for areas included; (2) Rankings are based on annual percentage change for all metro areas containing at least 15,000 transactions over the last 10 years and ranges from 1 to 291; (3) figures based on a weighted average of Census Division estimates; all figures are for the period ending December 31, 2007

Source: Office of Federal Housing Enterprise Oversight, House Price Index, February 26, 2008

House Price Valuations

Area	Q1 2000	Q1 2001	Q1 2002	Q1 2003	Q1 2004	Q1 2005	Q1 2006	Q1 2007	Q1 2008
MSA[1]	-2.4	-4.4	-2.1	5.7	11.3	12.2	15.6	17.4	12.2

Note: Figures show the percentage of over- or under-valuation of single family homes relative to statistically normal house values (e.g. a value of 23.6 indicates that house values are 23.6% overvalued). Statistically normal house values are based on house prices, interest rates, household incomes, population densities, and any historical premiums or discounts metropolitan areas have exhibited over time; (1) Figures cover the Metropolitan Statistical Area - see Appendix B for areas included

Source: Global Insight/National City Corporation, House Prices in America, May 2008

Median Home Prices

Area	2005	2006	2007[r]	Percent Change 2006 to 2007
MSA[1]	n/a	n/a	n/a	n/a
U.S. Average	219.0	221.9	217.9	-1.8

Note: Figures are median sales prices of existing single-family homes in thousands of dollars; (r) revised; n/a not available; (1) Metropolitan Statistical Area - see Appendix B for areas included

Source: National Association of Realtors, Metropolitan Area Prices, 1st Quarter 2008

Housing: Year Structure Built

Area	1990 -2000	1980 -1989	1970 -1979	1960 -1969	1950 -1959	1940 -1949	Before 1940	Median Year
City	19.2	21.6	18.8	13.0	10.8	6.9	9.7	1975
MSA[1]	27.7	21.8	18.3	11.1	9.2	5.5	6.4	1980
U.S.	17.0	15.8	18.5	13.7	12.7	7.3	15.0	1971

Note: Figures are percentages; (1) Metropolitan Statistical Area - see Appendix A for areas included

Source: Census 2000, Summary File 3

HEALTH

Health Risk Data

Category	Area[1] (%)	U.S. (%)
Adults who have been told they have high blood pressure[3]	19.3	25.5
Adults who have been told they have high blood cholesterol[3]	31.0	35.6
Adults who have been told they have diabetes[2]	5.1	7.5
Adults who have been told they have arthritis[3]	27.3	27.0
Adults who have been told they currently have asthma	8.9	8.5
Adults who are current smokers	18.3	20.1
Adults who are heavy drinkers[4]	5.9	4.9
Adults who are overweight (BMI 25.0 - 29.9)	34.9	36.5
Adults who are obese (BMI 30.0 - 99.8)	14.1	25.1

Note: Data as of 2006 unless otherwise noted; (1) Figures cover the Metropolitan Statistical Area - see Appendix B for areas included; (2) Figures do not include pregnancy-related diabetes, pre-diabetes or borderline diabetes; (3) 2005 data; (4) Heavy drinkers are classified as adult men having more than two drinks per day or adult women having more than one drink per day

Source: Centers for Disease Control and Prevention, Behaviorial Risk Factor Surveillance System, SMART: Selected Metropolitan/Micropolitan Area Risk Trends, 2005, 2006

Mortality Rates for the Top 10 Causes of Death in the U.S.

ICD-10[a] Sub-Chapter	ICD-10[a] Code	Age-Adjusted Mortality Rate[1] per 100,000 population	
		County[2]	U.S.
Malignant neoplasms	C00-C97	154.7	186.5
Ischaemic heart diseases	I20-I25	95.7	152.3
Other forms of heart disease	I30-I51	34.4	51.5
Cerebrovascular diseases	I60-I69	28.1	50.0
Chronic lower respiratory diseases	J40-J47	36.5	42.6
Diabetes mellitus	E10-E14	22.0	24.8
Other degenerative diseases of the nervous system	G30-G31	23.7	22.6
Other external causes of accidental injury	W00-X59	39.4	21.4
Influenza and pneumonia	J10-J18	9.9	20.7
Hypertensive diseases	I10-I13	12.4	18.2

Note: (a) ICD-10 = International Classification of Diseases 10th Revision; (1) Mortality rates are a three year average covering 2003-2005; (2) Figures cover Santa Fe County
Source: Centers for Disease Control and Prevention, National Center for Health Statistics. Compressed Mortality File 1999-2004. CDC WONDER On-line Database, compiled from Compressed Mortality File 1999-2005 Series 20 No. 2K, 2008.

Mortality Rates for Selected Causes of Death

ICD-10[a] Sub-Chapter	ICD-10[a] Code	Age-Adjusted Mortality Rate[1] per 100,000 population	
		County[2]	U.S.
Assault	X85-Y09	*4.2	5.9
Human immunodeficiency virus (HIV) disease	B20-B24	*2.2	4.5
Intentional self-harm	X60-X84	19.1	10.8
Malnutrition	E40-E46	*0.5	1.0
Obesity and other hyperalimentation	E65-E68	*1.3	1.4
Organic, including symptomatic, mental disorders	F01-F09	16.6	16.8
Transport accidents	V01-V99	21.8	16.1
Viral hepatitis	B15-B19	*2.4	1.8

Note: (a) ICD-10 = International Classification of Diseases 10th Revision; (1) Mortality rates are a three year average covering 2003-2005; (2) Figures cover Santa Fe County; (*) Unreliable data as per CDC
Source: Centers for Disease Control and Prevention, National Center for Health Statistics. Compressed Mortality File 1999-2004. CDC WONDER On-line Database, compiled from Compressed Mortality File 1999-2005 Series 20 No. 2K, 2008.

Distribution of Physicians[1]

Area	Total	Family/ General Practice	Specialties	
			Medical	Surgical
Santa Fe County (number)	374	152	103	70
Santa Fe County (rate per 10,000 pop.)	26.6	10.8	7.3	5.0
U.S. (rate per 10,000 pop.)	17.7	4.6	6.9	4.3

Note: Data as of 2005; (1) Includes all non-federal, patient-care, office-based MDs
Source: Area Resource File (ARF). June 2007. U.S. Department of Health and Human Services, Health Resources and Services Administration, Bureau of Health Professions, Rockville, MD.

Hospitals

Santa Fe has the following hospitals: 2 general medical and surgical.
AHA Guide to the Healthcare Field 2008

EDUCATION

Public School District Statistics

District Name	Schls	Pupils	Pupil/ Teacher Ratio	Minority Pupils[1] (%)	Free Lunch Eligible[2] (%)	IEP[3] (%)
Pojoaque Valley Public Schools	4	1,985	15.2	92.4	36.3	20.5
Santa Fe Public Schools	37	13,624	14.8	77.9	50.1	18.5

Note: Table includes regular local school districts with 2,000 or more students; (1) Percentage of students that are not white, non-Hispanic; (2) Percentage of students that are eligible for the free lunch program; (3) Percentage of students that have an Individualized Education Program.
Source: U.S. Department of Education, National Center for Education Statistics, Common Core of Data, Local Education Agency (School District) Universe Survey: School Year 2005-2006; U.S. Department of Education, National Center for Education Statistics, Common Core of Data, Public Elementary/Secondary School Universe Survey: School Year 2005-2006

Highest Level of Education

Area	Less than H.S.	H.S. Diploma	Some College, No Deg.	Associate Degree	Bachelors Degree	Masters Degree	Profess. School Degree	Doctorate Degree
City	15.9	17.3	22.3	5.3	21.2	11.1	4.0	2.8
MSA[1]	16.1	19.6	22.0	5.7	20.1	10.3	3.4	2.7
U.S.	19.4	28.4	21.2	6.4	15.7	5.9	2.0	1.0

Note: Figures are 2007 estimated percentages and cover persons age 25 and over; (1) Metropolitan Statistical Area - see Appendix B for areas included
Source: Claritas, Inc.

Educational Attainment by Race

Area	High School Graduate (%)					Bachelor's Degree (%)				
	Total	White	Black	Asian	Hisp.[2]	Total	White	Black	Asian	Hisp.[2]
City	84.6	87.0	89.6	83.6	69.9	40.0	45.2	36.4	57.4	15.4
MSA[1]	86.0	88.6	83.6	91.0	71.0	39.9	45.1	28.2	65.5	14.6
U.S.	80.4	83.6	72.3	80.4	52.4	24.4	26.1	14.3	44.1	10.4

Note: Figures shown cover persons 25 years old and over; (1) Metropolitan Statistical Area - see Appendix A for areas included; (2) people of Hispanic origin can be of any race
Source: Census 2000, Summary File 3

School Enrollment by Type

Area	Grades KG to 8				Grades 9 to 12			
	Public		Private		Public		Private	
	Enrollment	%	Enrollment	%	Enrollment	%	Enrollment	%
City	5,501	85.6	926	14.4	2,334	82.6	490	17.4
MSA[1]	16,469	87.1	2,449	12.9	7,133	86.2	1,143	13.8
U.S.	33,526,011	88.7	4,285,121	11.3	14,848,628	90.6	1,532,323	9.4

Note: Figures shown cover persons 3 years old and over; (1) Metropolitan Statistical Area - see Appendix A for areas included
Source: Census 2000, Summary File 3

School Enrollment by Race

Area	Grades KG to 8 (%)				Grades 9 to 12 (%)			
	White	Black	Asian	Hisp.[1]	White	Black	Asian	Hisp.[1]
City	67.9	0.2	0.8	63.8	69.2	0.6	0.9	64.1
MSA[2]	69.0	0.4	1.2	54.8	69.7	1.3	1.3	54.1
U.S.	68.5	15.5	3.3	16.8	68.8	15.5	3.8	15.7

Note: Figures shown cover persons 3 years old and over; (1) people of Hispanic origin can be of any race; (2) Metropolitan Statistical Area - see Appendix A for areas included
Source: Census 2000, Summary File 3

Average Salaries of Public School Classroom Teachers

District	2005-06		2006-07		Percent Change 2005-06 to 2006-07
	Dollars	Rank[1]	Dollars	Rank[1]	
New Mexico	41,637	36	42,780	41	2.75
U.S. Average	49,026	-	50,816	-	3.65

Note: (1) State rank ranges from 1 to 51.
Source: National Education Association, Rankings & Estimates: Rankings of the States 2006 and Estimates of School Statistics 2007, December 2007

Higher Education

Four-Year Colleges			Two-Year Colleges			Medical Schools[1]	Law Schools[2]	Voc/ Tech[3]
Public	Private Non-profit	Private For-profit	Public	Private Non-profit	Private For-profit			
1	3	1	1	0	0	0	0	0

Note: Figures cover institutions located within the city limits; (1) includes schools accredited by the Liaison Committee on Medical Education and the American Osteopathic Association; (2) includes American Bar Association-accredited law schools; (3) includes all schools with programs that are less than 2 years.
Source: National Center for Education Statistics, The Integrated Postsecondary Education System (IPEDS) Peer Analysis System, 2007; www.usnews.com, Law and Medical School Directories, 2009

PRESIDENTIAL ELECTION

2004 Presidential Election Results

Area	Bush	Kerry	Nader	Other
Santa Fe County	27.9	71.1	0.5	0.5
U.S.	50.7	48.3	0.4	0.6

Note: Results are percentages and may not add to 100% due to rounding
Source: Dave Leip's Atlas of U.S. Presidential Elections, www.uselectionatlas.org

EMPLOYERS

Major Employers

Company Name	Industry	Type of Site
Camel Rock Casino	Public order and safety	Branch
Energy Mineral & Nat RES	Administration of social and manpower programs	Branch
Fish and Wildlife Service US	Correctional institutions	Branch
Genzyme Corporation	Administration of social and manpower programs	Branch
Golden West Telecommunications	Legal counsel and prosecution	Branch
NM Cyfd Office General Council	Medical laboratories	Branch
NM Dept Children Yuth Families	Administration of public health programs	Headquarters
NM Dept Taxation and Revenue	Amusement and recreation	Single
NM Dept Taxation and Revenue	Theatrical producers and services	Headquarters
National Guard of New Mexico	Regulation	Branch
New Mexico Department Health	Regulation	Headquarters
New Mexico Dept Environment	Finance	Branch
New Mexico Dept Human Services	Finance	Headquarters
New Mexico Dept Human Services	Regulation	Branch
New Mexico Dept Public Safety	Junior colleges	Single
New Mexico Dept Transportation	General medical and surgical hospitals	Single
New Mexico Education Dept	Land	Branch
Office of The Secretary	Public building and related furniture	Branch
Procurement Services Bureau	Land	Branch
Santa Fe Opera	National security	Headquarters
St Vincent Regional Med Ctr	Public order and safety	Branch
Transportation Dept	Air	Branch
Western Dakota Tech Institute	Administration of educational programs	Branch

Note: Companies shown are located within the Santa Fe metropolitan area; nec = not elsewhere classified.
Source: www.zapdata.com, May 2008

PUBLIC SAFETY

Crime Rate

Area	All Crimes	Violent Crimes				Property Crimes		
		Murder	Forcible Rape	Robbery	Aggrav. Assault	Burglary	Larceny -Theft	Motor Vehicle Theft
City	6,520.4	12.6	58.7	145.3	368.8	3,085.6	2,547.8	301.7
Metro[1]	4,182.3	6.3	47.6	81.2	310.3	2,084.5	1,493.3	159.0
U.S.	3,808.1	5.7	30.9	149.4	287.5	729.4	2,206.8	398.4

Note: Figures are crimes per 100,000 population; (1) Metropolitan Statistical Area - see Appendix B for areas included
Source: FBI Uniform Crime Reports, 2006

Hate Crimes

Area	Number of Quarters Reported	Bias Motivation				
		Race	Religion	Sexual Orientation	Ethnicity	Disability
City	n/a	n/a	n/a	n/a	n/a	n/a

Note: n/a not available.
Source: Federal Bureau of Investigation, Hate Crime Statistics 2006

RECREATION

Culture

Dance[1]	Theatre[1]	Instrumental Music[1]	Vocal Music[1]	Series/ Festivals	Museums	Zoos and Aquariums[2]
1	0	3	4	3	14	0

Note: (1) Number of professional perfoming groups; (2) AZA-accredited
Source: The Grey House Performing Arts Directory, 2007; Official Museum Directory, 2008; Association of Zoos & Aquariums, AZA Member Zoos & Aquariums, June 2008

Professional Sports Teams

Team Name	League
No teams are located in the metro area	

Source: Original research

MEDIA

Newspapers

Name	News Focus	Frequency	Circulation
La Voz de Nuevo Mexico	Local	n/a	13,960
Santa Fe New Mexican	Local	Daily	28,000

Note: Includes newspapers with offices located in the city; n/a not available
Source: MediaContactsPro, March 2008

Television Stations

Name	Ch.	Network(s)	Type	Ownership
KASA	2	Fox	Commercial	Raycom Media Inc.
KOFT	3	ABC	Commercial	Hearst-Argyle Broadcasting
KOB	4	NBC	Commercial	Hubbard Broadcasting Inc.
KNME	5	PBS	Public	n/a
KOCT	6	ABC	Commercial	Hearst-Argyle Broadcasting
KREZ	6	CBS	Commercial	Lee Enterprises Inc.
KOAT	7	ABC	Commercial	Hearst-Argyle Broadcasting
KOBR	8	NBC	Commercial	Hubbard Broadcasting Inc.
KBIM	10	CBS	Commercial	Emmis Communications
KOVT	10	ABC	Commercial	Hearst-Argyle Broadcasting
KCHF	11	n/a	Commercial	Son Broadcasting
KOBF	12	NBC	Commercial	Hubbard Broadcasting Inc.
KRQE	13	CBS	Commercial	Lee Enterprises Inc.
KWBQ	19	WBN	Commercial	n/a
KNAT	23	n/a	Non-comm.	All American Network
KAZQ	32	n/a	Non-comm.	Alpha Omega Broadcasting of Albuquerque
KLUZ	41	Univision	Commercial	Entravision Communications
KRPV	42	n/a	Non-comm.	Prime Time Christian Broadcasting Inc.
KASY	50	UPN	Commercial	Acme Broadcasting Inc.

Note: Stations included cover the Albuquerque-Santa Fe DMA (Designated Market Area)
BurrellesLuce, MediaContacts Online, January 2007

Major AM Radio Stations

Call Letters	Freq. (kHz)	Station Type	Target Audience	Station Format	Music Format
KLLV	550	Non-Comm	General/Religious	Educational/Music	Gospel
KNML	610	Commercial	General	Sports/Talk	n/a
KTNN	660	Commercial	Gen/Nat Amer/Nat Can	Educational/Music/News	Country
KKOB	770	n/a	General	Music/News	n/a
KSWV	810	Commercial	General/Hispanic	Educational/Music/News	Latin
KHAC	880	Commercial	Gen/Nat Amer/Rel	Educational/Music	Christian
KBIM	910	Commercial	General	News/Sports/Talk	n/a
KIUP	930	Commercial	General	Music/News/Sports/Talk	Oldies
KNFT	950	Commercial	General/Hispanic	Music/Talk	Blues
KNDN	960	Commercial	General/Native Amer	Music/News	World Music
KKIM	1000	Commercial	General/Religious	Talk	n/a
KINF	1020	Commercial	General/Hispanic	Music	Oldies
KYKK	1110	Commercial	General	News/Talk	n/a
KXKS	1190	Commercial	Hispanic	Music/News/Talk	Latin
KVSF	1260	n/a	General	Talk	n/a
KRDD	1320	Commercial	General/Hispanic	Educational/Music	Latin
KGAK	1330	Commercial	General/Native Amer	Music	International
KABQ	1350	Commercial	Hispanic	Music/News/Talk	Latin
KBUY	1360	Commercial	General	Music	Oldies
KENN	1390	Commercial	General	Talk	n/a
KCRX	1430	n/a	General	Music	Classical

Note: Stations included cover the Albuquerque-Santa Fe DMA (Designated Market Area); n/a not available
Source: BurrellesLuce, MediaContacts Online, January 2007

Major FM Radio Stations

Call Letters	Freq. (mHz)	Station Type	Target Audience	Station Format	Music Format
KFLQ	91.5	Non-Comm	General/Religious	Educational/Music/News	Christian
KRST	92.3	Commercial	General	Music/News/Talk	Country
KTZA	92.9	Commercial	General	Music	Contemp. Country
KRWN	92.9	Commercial	General	Music	Modern Rock
KXXI	93.7	Commercial	General	Music	Classic Rock
KZRR	94.1	Commercial	General	Music/News/Talk	Modern Rock
KKOR	94.5	Commercial	General	Music	Top 40
KBOM	94.7	n/a	General	Music/News/Talk	n/a
KBIM	94.9	Commercial	General	Music/News/Sports/Talk	Adult Contemp.
KWYK	94.9	Commercial	General	Music	Adult Contemp.
KWRK	96.1	Commercial	General	Music	Adult Top 40
KDAG	96.9	Commercial	General	Music	Classic Rock
KBCQ	97.1	Commercial	General	Music	Top 40
KKSS	97.3	Commercial	General	Music/News/Talk	Rhythm & Blues
KLVO	97.7	Commercial	General/Hispanic	Music/News/Talk	Latin
KISZ	97.9	Commercial	General	Music	Contemp. Country
KABG	98.5	Commercial	General	Music/News/Talk	Oldies
KRSJ	100.5	Commercial	General	Music	Contemp. Country
KKIT	100.7	Commercial	General	Music/News/Sports/Talk	Modern Rock
KIQX	101.3	Commercial	General	Music	Alternative
KTRA	102.1	n/a	General	Music/News	n/a
KIXN	102.9	Commercial	General	Music	Contemp. Country
KNFT	102.9	Commercial	General	Music	Country
KTZO	103.3	Commercial	General	Music/News/Talk	Alternative
KYVA	103.7	Commercial	General	Music/News	Oldies
KBAC	104.1	Commercial	General	Music	Alternative
KCDY	104.1	Commercial	General	Music	Adult Contemp.
KKFG	104.5	Commercial	General	Music	Oldies
KTEG	104.7	n/a	Asian/Hispanic	Talk	n/a
KMOU	104.7	Commercial	General	Ed/Music/News/Sports/Talk	Country
KYLZ	106.3	Commercial	General	Music/News/Talk	Urban Contemp.
KZNM	106.7	n/a	General	Music/News/Sports	n/a

Note: Stations included cover the Albuquerque-Santa Fe DMA (Designated Market Area); n/a not available
BurrellesLuce, MediaContacts Online, January 2007

CLIMATE

Average and Extreme Temperatures

Temperature	Jan	Feb	Mar	Apr	May	Jun	Jul	Aug	Sep	Oct	Nov	Dec	Yr.
Extreme High (°F)	69	76	85	89	98	105	105	101	100	91	77	72	105
Average High (°F)	47	53	61	71	80	90	92	89	83	72	57	48	70
Average Temp. (°F)	35	40	47	56	65	75	79	76	70	58	45	36	57
Average Low (°F)	23	27	33	41	50	59	65	63	56	44	31	24	43
Extreme Low (°F)	-17	-5	8	19	28	40	52	50	37	21	-7	-7	-17

Note: Figures cover the years 1948-1992
Source: National Climatic Data Center, International Station Meteorological Climate Summary, 9/96

Average Precipitation/Snowfall/Humidity

Precip./Humidity	Jan	Feb	Mar	Apr	May	Jun	Jul	Aug	Sep	Oct	Nov	Dec	Yr.
Avg. Precip. (in.)	0.4	0.4	0.5	0.4	0.5	0.5	1.4	1.5	0.9	0.9	0.4	0.5	8.5
Avg. Snowfall (in.)	3	2	2	1	Tr	0	0	0	Tr	Tr	1	3	11
Avg. Rel. Hum. 5am (%)	68	64	55	48	48	45	60	65	61	60	63	68	59
Avg. Rel. Hum. 5pm (%)	41	33	25	20	19	18	27	30	29	29	35	43	29

Note: Figures cover the years 1948-1992; Tr = Trace amounts (<0.05 in. of rain; <0.5 in. of snow)
Source: National Climatic Data Center, International Station Meteorological Climate Summary, 9/96

Weather Conditions

Temperature			Daytime Sky			Precipitation		
10°F & below	32°F & below	90°F & above	Clear	Partly cloudy	Cloudy	0.01 inch or more precip.	0.1 inch or more snow/ice	Thunder-storms
4	114	65	140	161	64	60	9	38

Note: Figures are average number of days per year and cover the years 1948-1992
Source: National Climatic Data Center, International Station Meteorological Climate Summary, 9/96

HAZARDOUS WASTE

Superfund Sites

Santa Fe has no sites on the EPA's Superfund Final National Priorities List.
U.S. Environmental Protection Agency, Final National Priorities List, June 23, 2008

AIR & WATER QUALITY

Air Quality Index

Area	Percent of Days when Air Quality was...[2]				AQI Statistics	
	Good	Moderate	Unhealthy for Sensitive Groups	Unhealthy	Maximum	Median
MSA[1]	95.3	4.7	0.0	0.0	71	27

Note: The Air Quality Index (AQI) is an index for reporting daily air quality. EPA calculates the AQI for five major air pollutants regulated by the Clean Air Act: ground-level ozone, particle pollution (also known as particulate matter), carbon monoxide, sulfur dioxide, and nitrogen dioxide. The AQI runs from 0 to 500. The higher the AQI value, the greater the level of air pollution and the greater the health concern. There are six AQI categories: "Good" The AQI is between 0 and 50. Air quality is considered satisfactory; "Moderate" The AQI is between 51 and 100. Air quality is acceptable; "Unhealthy for Sensitive Groups" When AQI values are between 101 and 150, members of sensitive groups may experience health effects; "Unhealthy" When AQI values are between 151 and 200 everyone may begin to experience health effects; "Very Unhealthy" AQI values between 201 and 300 trigger a health alert; "Hazardous" AQI values over 300 trigger health warnings of emergency conditions; (1) Metropolitan Statistical Area - see Appendix A for areas included; (2) Based on 365 days with AQI data in 2007.
Source: U.S. Environmental Protection Agency, Air Quality Index Report, 2007

Air Quality Index Pollutants

Area	Percent of Days when AQI Pollutant was...[2]					
	Carbon Monoxide	Nitrogen Dioxide	Ozone	Sulfur Dioxide	Particulate Matter 2.5	Particulate Matter 10
MSA[1]	1.6	0.0	49.9	0.0	44.4	4.1

Note: The Air Quality Index (AQI) is an index for reporting daily air quality. EPA calculates the AQI for five major air pollutants regulated by the Clean Air Act: ground-level ozone, particle pollution (also known as particulate matter), carbon monoxide, sulfur dioxide, and nitrogen dioxide. The AQI runs from 0 to 500. The higher the AQI value, the greater the level of air pollution and the greater the health concern; (1) Metropolitan Statistical Area - see Appendix A for areas included; (2) Based on 365 days with AQI data in 2007.
Source: U.S. Environmental Protection Agency, Air Quality Index Report, 2007

Air Quality Index Trends

Area	Trend Sites								All Sites
	1999	2000	2001	2002	2003	2004	2005	2006	2006
MSA[1]	n/a	n/a	n/a	n/a	n/a	n/a	n/a	n/a	n/a

Note: An AQI value greater than 100 indicates that air quality would have been in the unhealthful range on that day. Data from exceptional events are not included. These counts are presented in two ways. First, the counts are based on sites having an adequate record of monitoring data during the trend period (trend sites). These counts represent the relative change in the number of days with AQI values greater than 100. In the last column, the counts are based on all sites with data in the most recent year (because it is possible for a site to have data in the most recent year but not enough data to be a trend site); (1) Metropolitan Statistical Area - see Appendix A for areas included; n/a not available.
Source: U.S. Environmental Protection Agency, Office of Air and Radiation, Air Trends, Factbook and Related Information, Air Pollution Trends in Selected Metropolitan Areas 2006

Maximum Air Pollutant Concentrations

	Particulate Matter 10 (ug/m^3)	Particulate Matter 2.5 (ug/m^3)	Ozone (ppm)	Carbon Monoxide (ppm)	Sulfur Dioxide (ppm)	Nitrogen Dioxide (ppm)	Lead (ug/m^3)
MSA[1] Level	29	9	n/a	1	n/a	n/a	n/a
NAAQS[2]	150	35	0.125	9	0.140	0.053	1.50
Met NAAQS[2]	Yes	Yes	n/a	Yes	n/a	n/a	n/a

Note: Data from exceptional events are not included; (1) Metropolitan Statistical Area - see Appendix A for areas included; (2) National Ambient Air Quality Standards; n/a not available
Concentrations: Particulate Matter 10 (coarse particulate) - highest second maximum 24-hour concentration; Particulate Matter 2.5 (fine particulate) - highest 98th percentile 24-hour concentration; Ozone - highest second daily maximum 1-hour concentration; Carbon Monoxide - highest second maximum non-overlapping 8-hour concentration; Sulfur Dioxide - highest second maximum 24-hour concentration; Nitrogen Dioxide - highest arithmetic mean concentration; Lead - highest quarterly maximum concentration
Units: ppm = parts per million; ug/m^3 = micrograms per cubic meter
Source: U.S. Environmental Protection Agency, MSA Factbook 2006, Air Quality Statistics by City

Drinking Water

Water System Name	Pop. Served	Primary Water Source Type	Violations[1]	
			Health Based	Monitoring/ Reporting
Santa Fe Water System	70,001	Surface	0	0

Note: (1) Based on violation data from January 1, 2007 to December 31, 2007 (includes unresolved violations from earlier years)
Source: U.S. Environmental Protection Agency, Office of Ground Water and Drinking Water, Safe Drinking Water Information System (based on data extracted April 15, 2008)

Bethlehem, New York

Background

The town of Bethlehem, on the Hudson river six miles from the capital of New York state at Albany, is comprised of seven historic hamlets: Delmar, Elsmere, Glenmont, Selkirk, Slingerlands, and North and South Bethlehem. The area in general, was initially settled by the Dutch, and this early heritage is reflected in the town's annual spring "Feestelijk" arts and entertainment festival.

Incorporated in 1793, Bethlehem is a prosperous and modern community that maintains a comfortable sense of its small-town past. With excellent schools, convenient access to the greater Albany metropolitan area, excellent recreational resources, and consistently higher median incomes and employment rates than the state as a whole, Bethlehem is a model of careful planning and development.

Bethlehem Central School District is widely held to be one of the state's best. An unusually high percentage of graduating high school seniors are college-bound. Many institutions of higher education are in the area, including Siena College, The College of St. Rose, Maria College, Rensselaer Polytechnic Institute, Union College, The Sage Colleges, State University at Albany, Hudson Valley Community College, Skidmore College, Schenectady County Community College, Albany Law School, Albany Medical College and Albany College of Pharmacy.

Bethlehem operates a number of its own parks and recreational facilities, and many other recreational resources are available in the surrounding area. Elm Avenue Park is a year-round 160-acre recreational center that offers swimming, tennis, basketball and volleyball courts, baseball, softball and soccer fields, a fitness trail, ice skating rinks, sledding, playground, supervised programs and picnic facilities.

There is an Audubon Society sanctuary in the immediate area, plus John Boyd Thatcher State Park, and Five Rivers Environmental Education Center, a 350-acre environmental and natural history state-run learning center. Skiers and hikers enjoy the nearby Adirondack, Catskill and Berkshire mountains, while water sports enthusiasts are close to Lake George and Lake Placid.

Major medical facilities in the area, all less than half an hour away, include Albany Medical Center, Memorial Hospital, St. Peter's Hospital, a major Veteran's Administration Hospital, and the Capital District Psychiatric Center. In Bethlehem itself there are two large privately run medical centers.

Although it retains its small-town ambiance, Bethlehem is efficiently connected to the greater metropolitan region, with an average commute of just over twenty minutes. The town is also conveniently located for travel, via road or rail, to major northeast coast destinations, including New York City, Boston and Montreal, with Albany International Airport less than twenty minutes away, and four smaller regional airports nearby.

The Bethlehem Town Board is comprised of a Supervisor and four Board Members. The Supervisor is elected every two years and town board members serve four year terms, with two of the seats elected every two years.

Rankings

General Rankings

- Albany* was ranked #235 out of 375 metro areas in *Cities Ranked & Rated*. Criteria: cost of living; climate; crime; transportation; economy and jobs; education; arts and culture; health and healthcare; leisure; quality of life. *Cities Ranked & Rated, 2nd Edition, 2007*
- Albany* was ranked #28 out of 379 metro areas in *Places Rated Almanac*. Criteria: health care; education; recreation; transportation; ambience; climate; crime; housing costs; jobs. *Places Rated Almanac, 7th Edition, 2007*
- *Expansion Management* rated 362 metro areas to find out which offer the best middle class lifestyle for manufacturing and service companies. The Albany* metro area was selected as a "5-Star Quality of Life Metro" (a distinction the magazine awards to the top 20 percent of metro areas studied). The annual "Quality of Life Quotient" measures dozens of indicators across nine major categories and compares them among 362 metropolitan statistical areas in the United States. The categories are: affordable housing; good public schools; low crime levels; adult education level; standard of living; traffic and commuting; continuing education opportunities; commercial air access; labor market. *Expansion Management, June 2007*

Business/Finance Rankings

- The nation's 100 largest metro areas were analysed in terms of the percentage of households entering some stage of foreclosure in 2007. The Albany* metro area ranked #94 out of 100 (#1 = highest foreclosure rate). *RealtyTrac, "Year-End 2007 Metropolitan Foreclosure Report"*
- The Albany* metro area was selected one of America's "Top 50 Business Opportunity Metros" by *Expansion Management* in their 5th annual Mayor's Challenge ranking of metro areas that have achieved solid ratings across the board in numerous *EM* studies during the past 12 months. The area ranked #36. Criteria: public schools; quality of life; college educated workers; logistics infrastructure; healthcare costs; taxes and government spending; reputation among site consultants. *Expansion Management, August 2007*
- Albany* was selected as one of the best places to start and grow a company by *Entrepreneur* and the National Policy Research Council. The Albany* metro area ranked #46 out of 63 mid-size metro areas. Criteria: business formation and growth (firms started four to 14 years ago that still employ at least 5 people and experienced rapid growth over the last four years). *Entrepreneur/National Policy Research Council, "Hot Cities for Entrepreneurs," September 2006*
- Intel, in partnership with Sperling's BestPlaces, ranked the 80 "Best Cities for Teleworking" in America. The Albany* metro area ranked #7 among mid-sized metro areas. The study identifies cities that hold the greatest potential for teleworking based on a host of factors including typical commuting times, fuel prices, availability of broadband Internet access and percentage of the population in telework friendly jobs. The study also factored in extreme climate and natural hazards. *Intel, "Best Cities for Teleworking," March 30, 2006*
- The Albany* metro area appeared on the Milken Institute "2007 Best Performing Cities" index. Rank: #166 out of 200 large metro areas. Criteria: job growth; wage and salary growth; high-tech output growth. *Milken Institute, "2007 Best Performing Cities"*
- Albany* was identified as one of the 100 "Most Unwired Cities" in the U.S. The area ranked #46 out of the 100 largest metro areas in the U.S. Criteria: number of public and commercial wireless access points (hotspots); airports with wireless Internet access; broadband availability; local wireless networks; and wireless email devices. *Intel, "Most Unwired Cities Survey," June 7, 2005*
- *Forbes* ranked the 200 most populous metro areas in the U.S. in terms of the "Best Places for Business and Careers." The Albany* metro area was ranked #94. Criteria: business costs (labor, energy, tax and office space expenses); living costs (housing, transportation, food and other household expenditures); education levels of the work force; job growth; income growth; migration trends; crime rates; and culture/leisure. *Forbes, "Best Places for Business and Careers," March 19, 2008*

- *Fortune* ranked the 100 largest metro areas in the U.S. in terms of projected median home price change in 2007. The Albany* metro area ranked #22. *Fortune.com, "Hot Spots, Cold Spots"*

Health/Environment Rankings

- 100 of the largest metro areas in the U.S. were analyzed in terms of their current drought severity. The Albany* metro area ranked #91 (#1 = driest). The rankings were based on statistics such as long-term precipitation trends and patterns and the Palmer drought indices. *Sperling's BestPlaces, www.BestPlaces.net, "America's Drought-Riskiest Cities," November 2007*

- Doctors at the Harvard School of Public Health ranked 40 metropolitan areas based on data from the government-sponsored Hospital Quality Alliance program. The program tracks the performance of individual hospitals in treating patients for three common health problems: heart attacks, congestive heart failure, and pneumonia. The Albany* metro area ranked #4 in quality of care for heart attacks, #11 for congestive heart failure, and #12 for pneumonia. *New England Journal of Medicine, July 21, 2005*

- The Albany* metro area appeared in *Country Home's* "2008 Best Green Places" report. The area ranked #66 out of 379. Criteria: official energy policies; green power; green buildings; availability of fresh, locally grown food. *Country Home, "2008 Best Green Places"*

- Albany* was identified as a "2008 Asthma Capital." The area ranked #59 out of the nation's 100 largest metropolitan areas. Twelve factors were used to identify the most challenging places to live for people with asthma: estimated prevalence; self-reported prevalence; crude death rate for asthma; annual pollen score; annual air quality; public smoking laws; number of board-certified asthma specialists; school inhaler access laws; rescue medication use; controller medication use; uninsured rate; poverty rate. *Asthma and Allergy Foundation of America, "2008 Asthma Capitals"*

- Albany* was identified as a "Spring Allergy Capital." The area ranked #88 out of 100. Three groups of factors were used to identify the most severe cities for people with allergies during the spring season: annual pollen levels; medicine utilization; access to board-certified allergists. *Asthma and Allergy Foundation of America, "2007 Spring Allergy Capital Rankings"*

- Albany* was identified as a "Fall Allergy Capital." The area ranked #98 out of 100. Three groups of factors were used to identify the most severe cities for people with allergies during the fall season: annual pollen levels; medicine utilization; access to board-certified allergists. *Asthma and Allergy Foundation of America, "2007 Fall Allergy Capital Rankings"*

- Ortho-McNeil Neurologics, in partnership with Sperling's BestPlaces, analyzed 110 metro areas and identified those U.S. cities with the highest prevalence of factors that are most commonly associated with migraine headaches. The Albany* metro area ranked #55. Criteria: number of migraine-related drug prescriptions per capita; lifestyle factors that can contribute to migraines; environmental factors that can trigger migraines; and consumption of migraine-triggering foods. *Ortho-McNeil Neurologics, "America's Migraine Hot Spots," March 14, 2006*

- Sperling's BestPlaces ranked 331 metro areas and identified the most and least stressful U.S. cities. The Albany* metro area ranked #100 out of the 100 largest metro areas (#1 = most stressful). Criteria: divorce rate; unemployment rate; violent and property crime; suicide rate; commute time; mental health; alcohol consumption; cloudy days. *Sperling's BestPlaces, www.BestPlaces.net, "America's Most (and Least) Stressful Cities," January 9, 2004*

Women/Minorities Rankings

- Albany* was ranked #17 out of 100 metro areas in *SELF Magazine's* ranking of "America's Best Places for Women." A panel of experts came up with more than 50 criteria including death and disease rates, environmental indicators, community resources, and lifestyle habits. *SELF Magazine, "America's Best Places for Women 2007," December 2007*

Seniors/Retirement Rankings

- A.G. Edwards ranked America's 500 top-performing communities based on their residents' personal savings and investing behavior. The Albany* metro area ranked #188 with an index score of 103.52 (national average = 100.00). A dozen statistical factors were measured including: participation in retirement savings plans; personal debt levels; and home ownership. *A.G. Edwards, "2007 Nest Egg Index", September 12, 2007*

Children/Family Rankings

- The Albany* metro area was selected as one of the "Best Cities for Relocating Families" by Worldwide ERC and Primacy Relocation. The 2007 study placed a special emphasis on the housing market, which has significantly impacted the relocation industry and an employer's ability to transfer employees. The variables which weigh heavily in this category include home price, home affordability index, appreciation rates, and property tax. Other criteria include cost of living, crime rates, education, climate, focus on diversity, physicians per capita, recreation and leisure, arts and culture, air quality, watershed quality, sales tax, unemployment rate, job growth, high school and higher education index, school expenditures per student, students in public school, SAT/ACT percentile, and population growth. *Worldwide ERC and Primacy Relocation, "2007 Best Cities for Relocating Families"*

Safety Rankings

- The National Insurance Crime Bureau ranked 361 metro areas in the U.S. in terms of per capita rates of vehicle theft. The Albany* metro area ranked #298 (#1 = highest rate). Criteria: number of vehicle theft offenses per 100,000 inhabitants. *National Insurance Crime Bureau, "NICB Vehicle Theft Study," April 22, 2008*

- Farmers Insurance Group of Companies, in partnership with Sperling's BestPlaces, ranked 379 metro areas and identified the "Most Secure U.S. Place to Live." The Albany* metro area ranked #29 out of 114 in the large metro area category (500,000 or more residents). Criteria: crime rates; extreme weather; risk of natural disasters; environmental hazards; terrorism threats; air quality; life expectancy; job loss numbers. *Farmers Insurance Group, "Most Secure U.S. Places to Live 2007"*

Sports/Recreation Rankings

- The Albany* metro area appeared on the *Sporting News* list of the "Best Sports Cities 2007". The area ranked #132 out of 150 cities in the U.S. *Sporting News* takes a 12-month snapshot, roughly July to July, of each city's sports, putting a heavy premium on regular-season won-lost records (from the most recently completed season). Other criteria include: playoff berths, bowl appearances and tournament bids; championships; applicable power ratings; quality of competition; overall fan fervor as measured in part by attendance as percentage of venue capacity; abundance of teams (rewarding quality over quantity); stadium and arena quality; ticket availability and prices; franchise ownership; and marquee appeal of athletes. *SportingNews.com, "Best Sports Cities 2007," August 1, 2007*

- *Golf Digest* ranked 330 metro areas in the U.S. in terms of golf. The Albany* metro area was ranked #290. Criteria: access to golf; weather; value of golf; and quality of golf. *Golf Digest, "Metro Golf Rankings," August 2005*

Dating/Romance Rankings

- The Albany* metro area was selected as one of the "Best Cities for Relocating Singles" by Worldwide ERC and Primacy Relocation. The area ranked #11 out of the 100 largest metro areas in the U.S. Areas were selected based on the following criteria: a robust cost-of-living index; adventure and outdoor recreation opportunities; violent crime and property crime rates; percentage of the population that is unmarried (ages 25-34); ratio of single men and single women; affordability of quality higher education, including in-state and out-of-state tuition requirements and rates; number of newcomers to the area; commute times; tax rates; fee and occupancy rates for temporary housing and mini-storage; quality and quantity of collegiate and professional sporting events and fun, fan-friendly venues. *Worldwide ERC and Primacy Relocation, "2007 Best Cities for Relocating Singles," October 25, 2007*

- Sperling's BestPlaces in partnership with AXE Deodorant Bodyspray ranked 80 metro areas and identified "America's Best (and Worst) Cities for Dating." The Albany* metro area ranked #33 (#1 = best). Criteria: percentage of singles ages 18-24; population density; dating venues per capita. *AXE Deodorant Bodyspray, "America's Best (and Worst) Cities for Dating," May 2004*

Culture/Performing Arts Rankings

- Scarborough Research, a leading market research firm, identified the top local markets for rock concert attendance. The Albany* DMA (Designated Market Area) ranked in the top 25 with 16% of consumers, 18 years old and over, reporting that they have attended a rock concert during the past year. *Scarborough Research, June 14, 2004*

Miscellaneous Rankings

- Sperling's BestPlaces in partnership with Pep Boys ranked 77 metro areas and identified "America's Most Drivable Cities." The Albany* metro area ranked #52. Criteria: climate; road roughness; urban mobility; gas prices. *Pep Boys, "America's Most Drivable Cities," April 9, 2003*

- Scarborough Research, a leading market research firm, identified the top local markets for grocery coupon use. The Albany* DMA (Designated Market Area) ranked in the top 25 with 38% of consumers reporting that they use grocery coupons at least once per week. *Scarborough Research, December 8, 2004*

- A study by Sperling's BestPlaces examined which U.S. metro areas were most affected by high fuel prices in 2006. The Albany* metro area was ranked #11 out of 80 (#1 = most expensive city for driving). Rankings are based on the average dollars spent on gas per year by two driver households. Criteria: cost of regular-grade gasoline; average miles driven per day; average number of gallons each driver uses and wastes in traffic congestion each day. *Sperling's BestPlaces, www.bestplaces.net, "Pain at the Pump," May 18, 2006*

Bethlehem is located within the Albany-Schenectady-Troy, NY Metropolitan Statistical Area.

Business Environment

CITY FINANCES

City Government Finances

Component	2004-2005 ($000)	2004-2005 ($ per capita)
Total Revenues	32,244	980
Total Expenditures	29,369	893
Debt Outstanding	19,733	600
Cash and Securities	17,060	518

Source: U.S Census Bureau, Government Finances 2004-2005

City Government Revenue by Source

Source	2004-2005 ($000)	2004-2005 ($ per capita)
General Revenue		
From Federal Government	388	12
From State Government	534	16
From Local Governments	9,026	274
Taxes		
Property	10,000	304
Sales	414	13
Personal Income	0	0
License	1,886	57
Charges	1,687	51
Liquor Store	0	0
Utility	5,659	172
Employee Retirement	0	0
Other	2,650	81

Source: U.S Census Bureau, Government Finances 2004-2005

City Government Expenditures by Function

Function	2004-2005 ($000)	2004-2005 ($ per capita)	2004-2005 (%)
General Expenditures			
Airports	0	0	0.0
Corrections	0	0	0.0
Education	0	0	0.0
Fire Protection	13	< 1	< 0.1
Governmental Administration	2,320	71	7.9
Health	850	26	2.9
Highways	5,323	162	18.1
Hospitals	0	0	0.0
Housing and Community Development	0	0	0.0
Interest on General Debt	817	25	2.8
Libraries	0	0	0.0
Parking	0	0	0.0
Parks and Recreation	1,464	44	5.0
Police Protection	4,572	139	15.6
Public Welfare	0	0	0.0
Sewerage	2,522	77	8.6
Solid Waste Management	765	23	2.6
Liquor Store	0	0	0.0
Utility	5,791	176	19.7
Employee Retirement	0	0	0.0
Other	4,932	150	16.8

Source: U.S Census Bureau, Government Finances 2004-2005

Municipal Bond Ratings

Area	Moody's
City	Aaa

Source: Mergent Bond Record, January 2008 (unless noted otherwise)

DEMOGRAPHICS

Population Growth

Area	1990 Census	2000 Census	2007 Estimate	2012 Projection	Population Growth (%) 1990-2000	Population Growth (%) 2000-2012
City	27,552	31,304	33,063	34,057	13.6	8.8
MSA[1]	809,443	825,875	855,337	872,264	2.0	5.6
U.S.	248,709,873	281,421,906	301,045,522	314,920,978	13.2	11.9

Note: (1) Metropolitan Statistical Area - see Appendix B for areas included
Source: Claritas, Inc.

Number of Households and Average Household Size

Area	2007 Estimate	2007 Average Household Size
City	12,996	2.54
MSA[1]	348,278	2.46
U.S.	113,668,003	2.65

Note: (1) Metropolitan Statistical Area - see Appendix B for areas included
Source: Claritas, Inc.

Race and Ethnicity

Area	White Alone[2]	Black Alone[2]	Asian Alone[2]	Other Race Alone[2]	Hispanic[3]
City	93.7	2.5	2.2	1.6	2.2
MSA[1]	87.0	7.1	2.8	3.1	3.0
U.S.	73.1	12.4	4.3	10.3	14.9

Note: Figures are 2007 estimates; (1) Metropolitan Statistical Area - see Appendix B for areas included (2) Alone is defined as not being in combination with one or more other races; (3) May be of any race.
Source: Claritas, Inc.

Ancestry

Area	German	Irish[2]	English	American	Italian	Polish	French[3]	Scottish
City	21.5	24.3	13.7	4.1	16.0	6.2	5.0	2.4
MSA[1]	16.9	22.6	10.7	4.2	16.9	7.5	7.6	2.1
U.S.	15.2	10.9	8.7	7.3	5.6	3.2	3.0	1.7

Note: Figures include multiple ancestry (e.g. if a person reported being Irish and Italian, they were included in both columns); (1) Metropolitan Statistical Area - see Appendix A for areas included; (2) Includes Celtic; (3) Includes Alsatian but excludes Basque
Source: Census 2000, Summary File 3

Foreign-Born Population

Area	Percent of Population Born in							
	Any Foreign Country	Europe	Asia	Africa	Oceania[2]	Canada	Mexico	Latin America[3]
City	4.8	2.2	1.5	0.1	0.0	0.5	0.0	0.6
MSA[1]	4.7	1.9	1.5	0.2	0.0	0.3	0.1	0.7
U.S.	11.1	1.7	2.9	0.3	0.1	0.3	3.3	2.5

Note: (1) Metropolitan Statistical Area - see Appendix A for areas included; (2) Includes Australia, New Zealand subregion, Melanesia, Micronesia, Polynesia, and Oceania n.e.c; (3) Includes Central America (excluding Mexico), South America, and the Caribbean.
Source: Census 2000, Summary File 3

Marriage Status

Area	Never Married	Now Married (excluding Separated)	Separated	Widowed	Divorced
City	19.8	64.2	1.8	7.0	7.2
MSA[1]	28.3	52.9	2.8	7.6	8.5
U.S.	27.1	54.4	2.2	6.6	9.7

Note: Figures are percentages and cover the population 15 years of age and older; (1) Metropolitan Statistical Area - see Appendix A for areas included
Source: Census 2000, Summary File 3

Age Distribution

Area	Under Age 5	Age 5 to 17	Age 18 to 34	Age 35 to 49	Age 50 to 64	Age 65 to 79	80 Years and Over
	Percent of Population						
City	6.4	21.0	15.0	26.1	17.1	9.6	4.7
MSA[1]	6.0	17.8	22.4	23.8	15.7	10.2	4.1
U.S.	6.8	18.9	23.7	23.5	14.8	9.2	3.2

Note: (1) Metropolitan Statistical Area - see Appendix A for areas included
Source: Census 2000, Summary File 3

Male/Female Ratio

Area	Males	Females	Males per 100 Females
City	15,875	17,188	92.4
MSA[1]	417,318	438,019	95.3
U.S.	148,320,305	152,725,217	97.1

Note: Figures are 2007 estimates; (1) Metropolitan Statistical Area - see Appendix B for areas included
Source: Claritas, Inc.

Religion

Area	Catholic	Southern Baptist	United Meth-odist	ELCA[1]	LDS[2]	Presby-terian Church USA	Jewish Est.	Muslim Est.
County	47.0	0.1	2.6	1.1	0.2	1.1	4.1	0.2
U.S.	22.0	7.1	3.7	1.8	1.5	1.1	2.2	0.6

Note: Figures are the number of adherents as a percentage of the total population; Adherents are defined as all members, including full members, their children and the estimated number of other participants who are not considered members (e.g. the baptized, those not confirmed, those regularly attending services, etc.); (1) Evangelical Lutheran Church in America; (2) The Church of Jesus Christ of Latter Day Saints
Source: Reprinted with permission from Religious Congregations and Membership in the United States 2000 (Nashville, Glenmary Research Center, 2002) Copyright Association of Statisticians of American Religious Bodies. All rights reserved.

ECONOMY

Gross Metropolitan Product

Area	2002	2003	2004	2005	2005 Rank[2]
MSA[1]	39.5	41.1	44.0	46.4	47

Note: Figures are in billions of dollars; (1) Albany-Schenectady-Troy, NY Metropolitan Statistical Area - see Appendix A for areas included; (2) Rank ranges from 1 to 361
Source: The U.S. Conference of Mayors, "U.S. Metro Economies: GMP - The Engines of America's Growth," January 2007

Economic Growth

Area	1995 GMP	2005 GMP	Average Annual Growth Rate	Growth Rate Rank[2]
MSA[1]	28.2	46.4	5.1	208

Note: Figures are in billions of dollars; GMP = Gross Metropolitan Product; (1) Albany-Schenectady-Troy, NY Metropolitan Statistical Area - see Appendix A for areas included; (2) Rank ranges from 1 to 361
Source: The U.S. Conference of Mayors, "U.S. Metro Economies: GMP - The Engines of America's Growth," January 2007

INCOME

Per Capita/Median/Average Income

Area	Per Capita ($)	Median Household ($)	Average Household ($)
City	38,385	74,438	96,744
MSA[1]	27,300	51,760	66,055
U.S.	25,495	49,280	66,670

Note: Figures are 2007 estimates; (1) Metropolitan Statistical Area - see Appendix B for areas included
Source: Claritas, Inc.

Household Income Distribution

Area	Under $15,000	$15,000 -24,999	$25,000 -34,999	$35,000 -49,999	$50,000 -74,999	$75,000 -99,000	$100,000 -149,999	$150,000 and up
	Percent of Households Earning							
City	3.4	6.0	7.3	14.7	19.0	14.8	20.8	14.0
MSA[1]	11.5	10.4	11.0	15.5	20.3	13.1	12.4	5.8
U.S.	13.1	10.9	11.2	15.6	19.5	11.9	11.3	6.6

Note: Figures are 2007 estimates; (1) Metropolitan Statistical Area - see Appendix B for areas included
Source: Claritas, Inc.

Poverty Rates by Age

Area	All Ages	Under 5 Years Old	5 to 17 Years Old	18 to 64 Years Old	65 Years and Over
City	3.1	0.2	0.9	1.6	0.4
MSA[1]	9.4	0.9	2.1	5.5	1.0
U.S.	12.4	1.2	3.0	6.9	1.2

Note: Figures are percent of population with income in 1999 below poverty level and only include population for whom poverty status is determined; (1) Metropolitan Statistical Area - see Appendix A for areas included
Source: Census 2000, Summary File 3

Personal Bankruptcy Filing Rate

Area	2004	2005	2006
Albany County	4.84	6.05	2.26
U.S.	5.31	6.82	2.00

Note: Numbers are per 1,000 population and include Chapter 7 and Chapter 13 filings
Source: Federal Deposit Insurance Corporation (FDIC), Regional Economic Conditions (RECON), 8/23/2007

EMPLOYMENT

Labor Force and Employment

Area	Civilian Labor Force			Workers Employed		
	Dec. 2006	Dec. 2007	% Chg.	Dec. 2006	Dec. 2007	% Chg.
City	17,736	17,576	-0.9	17,272	17,035	-1.4
MSA[1]	454,658	451,335	-0.7	438,693	432,686	-1.4
U.S.	152,571,000	153,705,000	0.7	146,081,000	146,334,000	0.2

Note: Data is not seasonally adjusted and covers workers 16 years of age and older;
(1) Metropolitan Statistical Area - see Appendix B for areas included
Source: Bureau of Labor Statistics, http://stats.bls.gov

Unemployment Rate

Area	2007											
	Jan.	Feb.	Mar.	Apr.	May	Jun.	Jul.	Aug.	Sep.	Oct.	Nov.	Dec.
City	3.3	3.2	3.0	2.7	2.9	3.0	3.1	2.7	3.0	2.8	3.0	3.1
MSA[1]	4.5	4.4	4.0	3.7	3.6	3.9	4.1	3.7	3.8	3.6	3.8	4.1
U.S.	5.0	4.9	4.5	4.3	4.3	4.7	4.9	4.6	4.5	4.4	4.5	4.8

Note: Data is not seasonally adjusted and covers workers 16 years of age and older; All figures are percentages; (1) Metropolitan Statistical Area - see Appendix B for areas included
Source: Bureau of Labor Statistics, http://stats.bls.gov

Employment by Occupation

Occupation Classification	City (%)	MSA[1] (%)	U.S. (%)
Sales and Office	24.3	27.9	26.7
Professional and Related	36.7	24.5	20.2
Service	9.9	14.2	14.9
Production, Transportation, and Material Moving	5.8	11.3	14.6
Management, Business, and Financial	18.6	14.0	13.5
Construction, Extraction, and Maintenance	4.5	7.7	9.4
Farming, Forestry, and Fishing	0.1	0.3	0.7

Note: Figures cover employed civilians 16 years of age and older;
(1) Metropolitan Statistical Area - see Appendix A for areas included
Source: Census 2000, Summary File 3

Employment by Industry

Sector	MSA[1] Number of Employees	MSA[1] Percent of Total	U.S. Percent of Total
Government	110,300	24.3	16.3
Education and Health Services	82,200	18.1	13.4
Professional and Business Services	54,800	12.1	13.1
Retail Trade	52,600	11.6	11.6
Manufacturing	22,700	5.0	9.9
Leisure and Hospitality	32,200	7.1	9.6
Financial Activities	25,900	5.7	5.9
Construction	n/a	n/a	5.3
Wholesale Trade	14,800	3.3	4.4
Other Services	18,200	4.0	3.9
Transportation and Utilities	13,600	3.0	3.7
Information	9,800	2.2	2.2
Natural Resources and Mining	n/a	n/a	0.5

Note: Figures cover non-farm employment as of December 2007 and are not seasonally adjusted; (1) Metropolitan Statistical Area - see Appendix B for areas included; n/a not available
Source: Bureau of Labor Statistics, http://stats.bls.gov

Average Wages

Occupation	$/Hr.	Occupation	$/Hr.
Accountants and Auditors	29.53	Maids and Housekeeping Cleaners	9.65
Automotive Mechanics	19.14	Maintenance and Repair Workers	16.50
Bookkeepers	15.93	Marketing Managers	54.44
Carpenters	19.56	Nuclear Medicine Technologists	33.16
Cashiers	8.88	Nurses, Licensed Practical	18.43
Clerks, General Office	12.87	Nurses, Registered	26.94
Clerks, Receptionists/Information	12.27	Nursing Aides/Orderlies/Attendants	11.78
Clerks, Shipping/Receiving	13.36	Packers and Packagers, Hand	11.87
Computer Programmers	29.86	Physical Therapists	29.26
Computer Support Specialists	21.14	Postal Service Mail Carriers	21.03
Computer Systems Analysts	32.68	Real Estate Brokers	26.53
Cooks, Restaurant	11.60	Retail Salespersons	12.12
Dentists	n/a	Sales Reps., Exc. Tech./Scientific	26.24
Electrical Engineers	41.51	Sales Reps., Tech./Scientific	31.12
Electricians	20.82	Secretaries, Exc. Legal/Med./Exec.	15.51
Financial Managers	49.70	Security Guards	12.56
First-Line Supervisors/Mgrs., Sales	19.96	Surgeons	97.53
Food Preparation Workers	9.39	Teacher Assistants	11.90
General and Operations Managers	51.23	Teachers, Elementary School	28.50
Hairdressers/Cosmetologists	11.80	Teachers, Secondary School	28.20
Internists	80.21	Telemarketers	11.47
Janitors and Cleaners	11.91	Truck Drivers, Heavy/Tractor-Trailer	21.06
Landscaping/Groundskeeping Workers	11.96	Truck Drivers, Light/Delivery Svcs.	14.88
Lawyers	47.40	Waiters and Waitresses	10.56

Note: Wage data covers the Albany-Schenectady-Troy, NY Metropolitan Statistical Area - see Appendix B for areas included. Hourly wages for elementary/secondary school teachers and teacher assistants were calculated by the editors from annual wage data assuming a 40 hour work week; n/a not available.
Source: Bureau of Labor Statistics, May 2007 Metro Area Occupational Employment and Wage Estimates

RESIDENTIAL REAL ESTATE

Building Permits

Area	Single-Family 2006	Single-Family 2007p	Single-Family Pct. Chg.	Multi-Family 2006	Multi-Family 2007p	Multi-Family Pct. Chg.	Total 2006	Total 2007p	Total Pct. Chg.
City	71	64	-9.9	14	10	-28.6	85	74	-12.9
U.S.	1,378,200	973,300	-29.4	460,700	407,200	-11.6	1,838,900	1,380,500	-24.9

Note: (p) preliminary; figures cover and represent new, privately-owned housing units authorized (unadjusted data); All permit data are based on estimates with imputation; U.S. figures are based on the new 20,000-place series.
Source: U.S. Census Bureau, Manufacturing, Mining, and Construction Statistics

Homeownership and Housing Vacancies

Area	Homeownership Rate[2] (%)			Rental Vacancy Rate[3] (%)			Homeowner Vacancy Rate[4] (%)		
	2005	2006	2007	2005	2006	2007	2005	2006	2007
MSA[1]	66.3	67.0	68.0	3.1	4.8	4.9	2.0	1.5	2.1
U.S.	68.9	68.8	68.1	9.8	9.8	9.7	1.9	2.4	2.7

Note: (1) Metropolitan Statistical Area - see Appendix B for areas included; (2) The proportion of households that are owners; (3) The proportion of the rental inventory that is vacant for rent; (4) The proportion of the homeowner inventory that is vacant for sale; n/a not available
Source: U.S. Census Bureau, Housing Vacancies and Homeownership Annual Statistics: 2007

TAXES

State Corporate Income Tax Rates

State	Rates and Tax Brackets
New York	7.1%

Note: Tax rates as of January 1, 2008; Businesses pay greatest of regular income tax, 1.5% AMT, 0.178% of capital base, or a fixed dollar minimum tax between $100 and $1500. There is an additional 0.09% tax on subsidiary capital.
Source: Tax Foundation, www.taxfoundation.org

State Individual Income Tax Rates

State	Federal Deductibility	Marginal Rates (%)	Standard Deduction ($)		Personal Exemptions ($)[1]	
			Single	Joint	Single	Dependents
New York	No	4.0 - 6.85	7,500	15,000	n/a	1,000

Note: Tax rates as of January 1, 2008; Local- and county-level taxes are not included; n/a not applicable; (1) Married joint filers generally receive double the single exemption
Source: Tax Foundation, www.taxfoundation.org

Various State and Local Tax Rates

State and Local Sales and Use (%)	State Sales and Use (%)	Gasoline[1,2] ($/gal.)	Cigarette ($/pack)	Spirits ($/gal.)	Table Wine ($/gal.)	Beer ($/gal.)
8.0	4.0	0.412	1.50	6.44	0.19	0.11

Note: Tax rates as of January 1, 2008; (1) In addition to the 18.4 cpg Federal gasoline tax; (2) Rates may include additional state sales taxes, environmental protection and storage fees/taxes, and local taxes. When necessary, the volume-weighted average of all local taxes is used to approximate the typical statewide rate including local tax
Source: Tax Foundation, www.taxfoundation.org; Original research

State Tax Burdens

Area	Combined State and Local Tax Burden		Combined Federal, State and Local Tax Burden	
	Percent	Rank	Percent	Rank
New York	13.8	3	37.1	2
U.S. Average	11.0	-	32.7	-

Note: Figures cover 2007 and measure taxes as a percentage of income
Source: Tax Foundation, www.taxfoundation.org

State Business Tax Climate Index Rankings

State	Overall Rank	Corporate Tax Index Rank	Individual Income Tax Index Rank	Sales Tax Index Rank	Unemployment Insurance Tax Index Rank	Property Tax Index Rank
New York	48	23	41	49	46	43

Note: Rankings range from 1 to 50 where 1 is best. Rankings do not average across to Overall Rank. States without a given tax are given a ranking of 1.
Source: Tax Foundation, State Business Tax Climate Index 2008

TRANSPORTATION

Means of Transportation to Work

Area	Car/Truck/Van		Public Transportation			Bicycle	Walked	Other Means	Worked at Home
	Drove Alone	Car-pooled	Bus	Subway	Railroad				
City	86.2	6.4	1.8	0.1	0.2	0.2	1.4	0.3	3.5
MSA[1]	79.4	9.9	2.8	0.0	0.1	0.2	3.8	0.8	3.0
U.S.	75.7	12.2	2.5	1.5	0.5	0.4	2.9	1.0	3.3

Note: Figures are percentages and cover workers 16 years of age and older; (1) Metropolitan Statistical Area - see Appendix A for areas included
Source: Census 2000, Summary File 3

Travel Time to Work

Area	Less Than 15 Minutes	15 to 29 Minutes	30 to 44 Minutes	45 to 59 Minutes	60 Minutes or More
City	28.1	52.5	14.6	1.7	3.1
MSA[1]	30.8	41.0	18.4	5.5	4.2
U.S.	29.4	36.1	19.1	7.4	8.0

Note: Figures are percentages and include workers 16 years old and over; (1) Metropolitan Statistical Area - see Appendix A for areas included
Source: Census 2000, Summary File 3

Travel Time Index

Area	1982	1995	2004	2005
Urban Area[1]	1.02	1.04	1.08	1.08
Average[2]	1.11	1.22	1.29	1.30

Note: Travel Time Index - The ratio of travel time in the peak period to the travel time at free-flow conditions. A value of 1.35 indicates a 20-minute free-flow trip takes 27 minutes in the peak. Free-flow speeds (60 mph on freeways and 35 mph on principal arterials) are used as the comparison threshold; (1) Covers the Albany-Schenectady, NY urban area; (2) average of 85 urban areas
Source: Texas Transportation Institute, The 2007 Urban Mobility Report, September 2007

Living Environment

COST OF LIVING

Cost of Living Index

Composite Index	Groceries	Housing	Utilities	Trans-portation	Health Care	Misc. Goods/ Services
n/a	n/a	n/a	n/a	n/a	n/a	n/a

Note: U.S. = 100; n/a not available
Source: The Council for Community and Economic Research (formerly ACCRA), Cost of Living Index, 2007

Grocery Prices

Area[1]	T-Bone Steak ($/pound)	Frying Chicken ($/pound)	Whole Milk ($/half gal.)	Eggs ($/dozen)	Orange Juice ($/64 oz.)	Coffee ($/11.5 oz.)
City[2]	n/a	n/a	n/a	n/a	n/a	n/a
Avg.	8.93	1.12	2.13	1.52	3.26	3.31
Min.	5.88	0.71	1.33	0.83	2.30	2.20
Max.	12.80	2.07	3.43	3.54	5.79	6.20

Note: (1) Values for the local area are compared with the average, minimum and maximum values for all 331 areas in the Cost of Living Index report; n/a not available; (2) Figures cover the Bethlehem NY urban area; **T-Bone Steak** *(price per pound);* **Frying Chicken** *(price per pound, whole fryer);* **Whole Milk** *(half gallon carton);* **Eggs** *(price per dozen, Grade A, large);* **Orange Juice** *(64 oz. Tropicana or Florida Natural);* **Coffee** *(11.5 oz. can, vacuum-packed, Maxwell House, Hills Bros, or Folgers).*
Source: The Council for Community and Economic Research (formerly ACCRA), Cost of Living Index, 2007

Housing and Utility Costs

Area[1]	New Home Price ($)	Apartment Rent ($/month)	All Electric ($/month)	Part Electric ($/month)	Other Energy ($/month)	Telephone ($/month)
City[2]	n/a	n/a	n/a	n/a	n/a	n/a
Avg.	309,605	782	146.13	78.67	90.16	26.14
Min.	189,877	n/a	82.03	37.41	33.15	17.08
Max.	1,202,800	3,481	271.14	150.60	257.67	37.45

Note: (1) Values for the local area are compared with the average, minimum and maximum values for all 331 areas in the Cost of Living Index report; n/a not available; (2) Figures cover the Bethlehem NY urban area; **New Home Price** *(2,400 sf living area, 8,000 sf lot, in urban area with full utilities);* **Apartment Rent** *(950 sf 2 bedroom/1.5 or 2 bath, unfurnished, excluding all utilities except water);* **All Electric** *(average monthly cost for an all-electric home);* **Part Electric** *(average monthly cost for a part-electric home);* **Other Energy** *(average monthly cost for natural gas, fuel oil, coal, wood, and any other forms of energy except electricity);* **Telephone** *(price includes basic monthly rate for a private residential line plus additional local usage charges incurred by a family of four).*
Source: The Council for Community and Economic Research (formerly ACCRA), Cost of Living Index, 2007

Health Care, Transportation, and Other Costs

Area[1]	Doctor ($/visit)	Dentist ($/visit)	Optometrist ($/visit)	Gasoline ($/gallon)	Beauty Salon ($/visit)	Men's Shirt ($)
City[2]	n/a	n/a	n/a	n/a	n/a	n/a
Avg.	79.48	71.93	79.55	2.64	29.52	25.77
Min.	52.08	44.80	43.95	2.19	15.58	16.19
Max.	148.44	126.27	158.83	3.48	60.62	48.53

Note: (1) Values for the local area are compared with the average, minimum and maximum values for all 331 areas in the Cost of Living Index report; n/a not available; (2) Figures cover the Bethlehem NY urban area; **Doctor** *(general practitioners routine exam of an established patient);* **Dentist** *(adult teeth cleaning and periodic oral examination);* **Optometrist** *(full vision eye exam for established adult patient);* **Gasoline** *(one gallon regular unleaded, national brand, including all taxes, cash price at self-service pump if available);* **Beauty Salon** *(woman's shampoo, trim, and blow-dry);* **Men's Shirt** *(cotton/polyester dress shirt, pinpoint weave, long sleeves).*
Source: The Council for Community and Economic Research (formerly ACCRA), Cost of Living Index, 2007

HOUSING

House Price Index (HPI)

Area	National Ranking[2]	Quarterly Change (%)	One-Year Change (%)	Five-Year Change (%)
MSA[1]	59	1.22	4.31	64.06
U.S.[3]	-	0.10	0.84	41.37

Note: The HPI is a weighted repeat sales index. It measures average price changes in repeat sales or refinancings on the same properties. This information is obtained by reviewing repeat mortgage transactions on single-family properties whose mortgages have been purchased or securitized by Fannie Mae or Freddie Mac in January 1975; (1) Metropolitan Statistical Area - see Appendix B for areas included; (2) Rankings are based on annual percentage change for all metro areas containing at least 15,000 transactions over the last 10 years and ranges from 1 to 291; (3) figures based on a weighted average of Census Division estimates; all figures are for the period ending December 31, 2007
Source: Office of Federal Housing Enterprise Oversight, House Price Index, February 26, 2008

House Price Valuations

Area	Q1 2000	Q1 2001	Q1 2002	Q1 2003	Q1 2004	Q1 2005	Q1 2006	Q1 2007	Q1 2008
MSA[1]	-17.4	-23.0	-15.1	-9.8	-5.5	3.0	6.5	2.6	3.5

Note: Figures show the percentage of over- or under-valuation of single family homes relative to statistically normal house values (e.g. a value of 23.6 indicates that house values are 23.6% overvalued). Statistically normal house values are based on house prices, interest rates, household incomes, population densities, and any historical premiums or discounts metropolitan areas have exhibited over time; (1) Figures cover the Metropolitan Statistical Area - see Appendix B for areas included
Source: Global Insight/National City Corporation, House Prices in America, May 2008

Median Home Prices

Area	2005	2006	2007[r]	Percent Change 2006 to 2007
MSA[1]	183.5	195.4	198.9	1.8
U.S. Average	219.0	221.9	217.9	-1.8

Note: Figures are median sales prices of existing single-family homes in thousands of dollars; (r) revised; n/a not available; (1) Metropolitan Statistical Area - see Appendix B for areas included
Source: National Association of Realtors, Metropolitan Area Prices, 1st Quarter 2008

Housing: Year Structure Built

Area	1990 -2000	1980 -1989	1970 -1979	1960 -1969	1950 -1959	1940 -1949	Before 1940	Median Year
City	17.6	14.4	13.0	13.3	15.7	8.8	17.2	1966
MSA[1]	11.1	11.4	13.2	10.9	11.9	8.7	32.9	1957
U.S.	17.0	15.8	18.5	13.7	12.7	7.3	15.0	1971

Note: Figures are percentages; (1) Metropolitan Statistical Area - see Appendix A for areas included
Source: Census 2000, Summary File 3

HEALTH

Health Risk Data

Category	Area[1] (%)	U.S. (%)
Adults who have been told they have high blood pressure[3]	n/a	25.5
Adults who have been told they have high blood cholesterol[3]	n/a	35.6
Adults who have been told they have diabetes[2]	n/a	7.5
Adults who have been told they have arthritis[3]	n/a	27.0
Adults who have been told they currently have asthma	n/a	8.5
Adults who are current smokers	n/a	20.1
Adults who are heavy drinkers[4]	n/a	4.9
Adults who are overweight (BMI 25.0 - 29.9)	n/a	36.5
Adults who are obese (BMI 30.0 - 99.8)	n/a	25.1

Note: Data as of 2006 unless otherwise noted; n/a not available; (1) Figures cover the Metropolitan Statistical Area - see Appendix B for areas included; (2) Figures do not include pregnancy-related diabetes, pre-diabetes or borderline diabetes; (3) 2005 data; (4) Heavy drinkers are classified as adult men having more than two drinks per day or adult women having more than one drink per day
Source: Centers for Disease Control and Prevention, Behaviorial Risk Factor Surveillance System, SMART: Selected Metropolitan/Micropolitan Area Risk Trends, 2005, 2006

Mortality Rates for the Top 10 Causes of Death in the U.S.

ICD-10[a] Sub-Chapter	ICD-10[a] Code	Age-Adjusted Mortality Rate[1] per 100,000 population	
		County[2]	U.S.
Malignant neoplasms	C00-C97	188.2	186.5
Ischaemic heart diseases	I20-I25	202.9	152.3
Other forms of heart disease	I30-I51	49.7	51.5
Cerebrovascular diseases	I60-I69	41.8	50.0
Chronic lower respiratory diseases	J40-J47	40.5	42.6
Diabetes mellitus	E10-E14	16.9	24.8
Other degenerative diseases of the nervous system	G30-G31	25.2	22.6
Other external causes of accidental injury	W00-X59	13.6	21.4
Influenza and pneumonia	J10-J18	17.0	20.7
Hypertensive diseases	I10-I13	11.6	18.2

Note: (a) ICD-10 = International Classification of Diseases 10th Revision; (1) Mortality rates are a three year average covering 2003-2005; (2) Figures cover Albany County
Source: Centers for Disease Control and Prevention, National Center for Health Statistics. Compressed Mortality File 1999-2004. CDC WONDER On-line Database, compiled from Compressed Mortality File 1999-2005 Series 20 No. 2K, 2008.

Mortality Rates for Selected Causes of Death

ICD-10[a] Sub-Chapter	ICD-10[a] Code	Age-Adjusted Mortality Rate[1] per 100,000 population	
		County[2]	U.S.
Assault	X85-Y09	2.8	5.9
Human immunodeficiency virus (HIV) disease	B20-B24	4.1	4.5
Intentional self-harm	X60-X84	6.2	10.8
Malnutrition	E40-E46	*0.6	1.0
Obesity and other hyperalimentation	E65-E68	*1.7	1.4
Organic, including symptomatic, mental disorders	F01-F09	13.1	16.8
Transport accidents	V01-V99	6.1	16.1
Viral hepatitis	B15-B19	*1.2	1.8

Note: (a) ICD-10 = International Classification of Diseases 10th Revision; (1) Mortality rates are a three year average covering 2003-2005; (2) Figures cover Albany County; (*) Unreliable data as per CDC
Source: Centers for Disease Control and Prevention, National Center for Health Statistics. Compressed Mortality File 1999-2004. CDC WONDER On-line Database, compiled from Compressed Mortality File 1999-2005 Series 20 No. 2K, 2008.

Distribution of Physicians[1]

Area	Total	Family/ General Practice	Specialties	
			Medical	Surgical
Albany County (number)	979	111	370	279
Albany County (rate per 10,000 pop.)	32.9	3.7	12.4	9.4
U.S. (rate per 10,000 pop.)	17.7	4.6	6.9	4.3

Note: Data as of 2005; (1) Includes all non-federal, patient-care, office-based MDs
Source: Area Resource File (ARF). June 2007. U.S. Department of Health and Human Services, Health Resources and Services Administration, Bureau of Health Professions, Rockville, MD.

Hospitals

There were no hospitals listed within the city limits.
AHA Guide to the Healthcare Field 2008

EDUCATION

Public School District Statistics

District Name	Schls	Pupils	Pupil/ Teacher Ratio	Minority Pupils[1] (%)	Free Lunch Eligible[2] (%)	IEP[3] (%)
Bethlehem Central School District	7	5,178	14.2	8.6	2.1	10.1

Note: Table includes regular local school districts with 2,000 or more students; (1) Percentage of students that are not white, non-Hispanic; (2) Percentage of students that are eligible for the free lunch program; (3) Percentage of students that have an Individualized Education Program.
Source: U.S. Department of Education, National Center for Education Statistics, Common Core of Data, Local Education Agency (School District) Universe Survey: School Year 2005-2006; U.S. Department of Education, National Center for Education Statistics, Common Core of Data, Public Elementary/Secondary School Universe Survey: School Year 2005-2006

Highest Level of Education

Area	Less than H.S.	H.S. Diploma	Some College, No Deg.	Associate Degree	Bachelors Degree	Masters Degree	Profess. School Degree	Doctorate Degree
City	6.8	18.1	15.1	10.0	22.8	16.7	7.5	3.0
MSA[1]	13.7	29.5	17.4	10.1	16.3	9.0	2.5	1.5
U.S.	19.4	28.4	21.2	6.4	15.7	5.9	2.0	1.0

Note: Figures are 2007 estimated percentages and cover persons age 25 and over; (1) Metropolitan Statistical Area - see Appendix B for areas included
Source: Claritas, Inc.

Educational Attainment by Race

Area	High School Graduate (%)					Bachelor's Degree (%)				
	Total	White	Black	Asian	Hisp.[2]	Total	White	Black	Asian	Hisp.[2]
City	93.1	93.2	92.4	91.2	88.3	50.0	49.9	45.2	59.8	67.6
MSA[1]	85.6	86.5	72.6	88.7	69.6	28.2	28.4	15.5	65.4	23.6
U.S.	80.4	83.6	72.3	80.4	52.4	24.4	26.1	14.3	44.1	10.4

Note: Figures shown cover persons 25 years old and over; (1) Metropolitan Statistical Area - see Appendix A for areas included; (2) people of Hispanic origin can be of any race
Source: Census 2000, Summary File 3

School Enrollment by Type

Area	Grades KG to 8				Grades 9 to 12			
	Public		Private		Public		Private	
	Enrollment	%	Enrollment	%	Enrollment	%	Enrollment	%
City	3,700	83.5	731	16.5	1,815	88.2	242	11.8
MSA[1]	99,443	89.7	11,383	10.3	43,264	91.7	3,921	8.3
U.S.	33,526,011	88.7	4,285,121	11.3	14,848,628	90.6	1,532,323	9.4

Note: Figures shown cover persons 3 years old and over; (1) Metropolitan Statistical Area - see Appendix A for areas included
Source: Census 2000, Summary File 3

School Enrollment by Race

Area	Grades KG to 8 (%)				Grades 9 to 12 (%)			
	White	Black	Asian	Hisp.[1]	White	Black	Asian	Hisp.[1]
City	92.5	3.8	1.7	1.5	94.6	1.7	1.1	0.6
MSA[2]	85.2	8.5	1.7	4.0	86.1	7.9	2.0	3.6
U.S.	68.5	15.5	3.3	16.8	68.8	15.5	3.8	15.7

Note: Figures shown cover persons 3 years old and over; (1) people of Hispanic origin can be of any race; (2) Metropolitan Statistical Area - see Appendix A for areas included
Source: Census 2000, Summary File 3

Average Salaries of Public School Classroom Teachers

District	2005-06 Dollars	2005-06 Rank[1]	2006-07 Dollars	2006-07 Rank[1]	Percent Change 2005-06 to 2006-07
New York	57,354	6	58,537	6	2.06
U.S. Average	49,026	-	50,816	-	3.65

Note: (1) State rank ranges from 1 to 51.
Source: National Education Association, Rankings & Estimates: Rankings of the States 2006 and Estimates of School Statistics 2007, December 2007

Higher Education

Four-Year Colleges			Two-Year Colleges			Medical Schools[1]	Law Schools[2]	Voc/ Tech[3]
Public	Private Non-profit	Private For-profit	Public	Private Non-profit	Private For-profit			
0	0	0	0	0	0	0	0	0

Note: Figures cover institutions located within the city limits; (1) includes schools accredited by the Liaison Committee on Medical Education and the American Osteopathic Association; (2) includes American Bar Association-accredited law schools; (3) includes all schools with programs that are less than 2 years.
Source: National Center for Education Statistics, The Integrated Postsecondary Education System (IPEDS) Peer Analysis System, 2007; www.usnews.com, Law and Medical School Directories, 2009

PRESIDENTIAL ELECTION

2004 Presidential Election Results

Area	Bush	Kerry	Nader	Other
Albany County	37.3	60.7	1.8	0.3
U.S.	50.7	48.3	0.4	0.6

Note: Results are percentages and may not add to 100% due to rounding
Source: Dave Leip's Atlas of U.S. Presidential Elections, www.uselectionatlas.org

EMPLOYERS

Major Employers

Company Name	Industry	Type of Site
Administration	Legal counsel and prosecution	Branch
Albany Medical Center	General medical and surgical hospitals	Headquarters
Center Health Care	Individual and family services	Single
Deputy Commissioner & Counsel	Finance, taxation and monetary policy	Branch
Director Human Resources MGT	General government, nec	Branch
Division Investments Cash MGT	Finance, taxation and monetary policy	Branch
GE	Medical laboratories	Branch
Health New York State Dept	Administration of public health programs	Branch
Information Technology Svcs	Finance, taxation and monetary policy	Branch
Lockheed Martin	Commercial physical research	Headquarters
NY Dept Correctional Services	Correctional institutions	Branch
NY Dept Taxation and Finance	Finance, taxation and monetary policy	Headquarters
New York Department of Labor	Administration of social and manpower programs	Branch
New York Dept Motor Vehicles	Regulation, administration of transportation	Headquarters
New York State Dept Health	Administration of public health programs	Headquarters
Office for Administration	Finance, taxation and monetary policy	Branch
Operations Support Bureau	Finance, taxation and monetary policy	Branch
Price Chopper Supermarkets	Grocery stores	Headquarters
St Peters Hospital	General medical and surgical hospitals	Headquarters
The Comptroller Office of	Finance, taxation and monetary policy	Headquarters

Note: Companies shown are located within the Albany metropolitan area; nec = not elsewhere classified.
Source: www.zapdata.com, May 2008

PUBLIC SAFETY

Crime Rate

Area	All Crimes	Violent Crimes				Property Crimes		
		Murder	Forcible Rape	Robbery	Aggrav. Assault	Burglary	Larceny -Theft	Motor Vehicle Theft
City	1,794.4	0.0	3.0	15.2	54.6	263.7	1,406.4	51.5
Metro[1]	3,115.1	2.1	24.3	113.3	232.2	569.7	2,034.2	139.3
U.S.	3,808.1	5.7	30.9	149.4	287.5	729.4	2,206.8	398.4

Note: Figures are crimes per 100,000 population; (1) Metropolitan Statistical Area - see Appendix B for areas included
Source: FBI Uniform Crime Reports, 2006

Hate Crimes

Area	Number of Quarters Reported	Bias Motivation				
		Race	Religion	Sexual Orientation	Ethnicity	Disability
City	n/a	n/a	n/a	n/a	n/a	n/a

Note: n/a not available.
Source: Federal Bureau of Investigation, Hate Crime Statistics 2006

RECREATION

Culture

Dance[1]	Theatre[1]	Instrumental Music[1]	Vocal Music[1]	Series/ Festivals	Museums	Zoos and Aquariums[2]
0	0	0	0	0	0	0

Note: (1) Number of professional perfoming groups; (2) AZA-accredited
Source: The Grey House Performing Arts Directory, 2007; Official Museum Directory, 2008; Association of Zoos & Aquariums, AZA Member Zoos & Aquariums, June 2008

Professional Sports Teams

Team Name	League
No teams are located in the metro area	

Source: Original research

MEDIA

Newspapers

Name	News Focus	Frequency	Circulation
No newspapers have an office in the city			

Note: Includes newspapers with offices located in the city
Source: MediaContactsPro, March 2008

Television Stations

Name	Ch.	Network(s)	Type	Ownership
WRGB	6	CBS	Commercial	Freedom Communications Inc.
WNCE	8	UPN	Commercial	Northern Broadcasting
WTEN	10	ABC	Commercial	Young Broadcasting Inc.
WNYT	13	NBC	Commercial	Hubbard Broadcasting Inc.
WMHT	17	PBS	Public	WMHT Educational Telecommunications Inc.
WXXA	23	Fox	Commercial	Clear Channel Communications Inc.
WEWB	45	WBN	Commercial	Tribune Broadcasting Company
WMHQ	45	WBN/PBS	Public	WMHT Educational Telecommunications Inc.
WYPX	55	Pax	Commercial	Paxson Communications Corporation

Note: Stations included cover the Albany-Schenectady-Troy DMA (Designated Market Area)
BurrellesLuce, MediaContacts Online, January 2007

Major AM Radio Stations

Call Letters	Freq. (kHz)	Station Type	Target Audience	Station Format	Music Format
WCKL	560	Commercial	General	Music	Adult Standards
WROW	590	Commercial	General	News/Talk	n/a
WGY	810	Commercial	General	Talk	n/a
WSBS	860	Commercial	General	Ed/News/Sports/Talk	n/a
WIZR	930	n/a	General	Music/News	n/a
WOFX	980	Commercial	General	Sports/Talk	n/a
WUHN	1110	Commercial	General	Music/Talk	Country
WXBH	1190	Commercial	General	Talk	n/a
WMML	1230	Commercial	General	Sports/Talk	n/a
WNAW	1230	Commercial	General	Music	Easy Listening
WHUC	1230	n/a	General	Music/News	n/a
WVKZ	1240	Commercial	General	Music	Country
WTMM	1300	Commercial	General	Talk	n/a
WHAZ	1330	Commercial	General/Religious	Educational/Talk	n/a
WBRK	1340	Commercial	General	Music/News/Sports	Adult Standards
WENT	1340	Commercial	General	Music/News	Adult Contemp.
WBTN	1370	Commercial	General	Music/News/Sports/Talk	Adult Standards
WENU	1410	Commercial	General	Music/News	Adult Standards
WBEC	1420	Commercial	General	News/Talk	n/a
WWSC	1450	Commercial	General	Music/News/Talk	Oldies
WGNA	1460	n/a	General	Music/News	n/a
WCSS	1490	Commercial	General	Music/News/Sports/Talk	Adult Standards
WPTR	1540	Commercial	General	Music	Oldies

Note: Stations included cover the Albany-Schenectady-Troy DMA (Designated Market Area); n/a not available
Source: BurrellesLuce, MediaContacts Online, January 2007

Major FM Radio Stations

Call Letters	Freq. (mHz)	Station Type	Target Audience	Station Format	Music Format
WFLY	92.3	n/a	General	Music	n/a
WYJB	95.5	Commercial	General	Music	Adult Contemp.
WJIV	101.9	Commercial	General/Religious	Educational/Music/Talk	Christian
WEQX	102.7	Commercial	General	Music/News	Jazz
WAMQ	105.1	Public	General	Ed/Music/News/Talk	Country
WPYX	106.5	Commercial	General	Music	Classic Rock
WGNA	107.7	n/a	General	Music	n/a

Note: Stations included cover the Albany-Schenectady-Troy DMA (Designated Market Area); n/a not available
BurrellesLuce, MediaContacts Online, January 2007

CLIMATE

Average and Extreme Temperatures

Temperature	Jan	Feb	Mar	Apr	May	Jun	Jul	Aug	Sep	Oct	Nov	Dec	Yr.
Extreme High (°F)	64	67	86	92	94	99	100	99	100	89	82	71	100
Average High (°F)	31	33	43	58	69	78	83	81	73	62	48	35	58
Average Temp. (°F)	22	24	34	47	58	67	72	70	61	51	40	27	48
Average Low (°F)	13	14	25	36	46	55	60	58	50	39	31	19	37
Extreme Low (°F)	-28	-21	-21	10	26	36	40	34	24	16	5	-22	-28

Note: Figures cover the years 1945-1990
Source: National Climatic Data Center, International Station Meteorological Climate Summary, 9/96

Average Precipitation/Snowfall/Humidity

Precip./Humidity	Jan	Feb	Mar	Apr	May	Jun	Jul	Aug	Sep	Oct	Nov	Dec	Yr.
Avg. Precip. (in.)	2.4	2.3	2.8	2.9	3.6	3.4	3.1	3.3	3.1	2.9	3.1	2.9	35.8
Avg. Snowfall (in.)	16	14	11	3	Tr	0	0	0	0	Tr	4	14	63
Avg. Rel. Hum. 7am (%)	77	77	76	72	74	77	80	85	88	86	82	80	79
Avg. Rel. Hum. 4pm (%)	64	60	54	49	51	53	53	55	57	56	64	67	57

Note: Figures cover the years 1945-1990; Tr = Trace amounts (<0.05 in. of rain; <0.5 in. of snow)
Source: National Climatic Data Center, International Station Meteorological Climate Summary, 9/96

Weather Conditions

Temperature			Daytime Sky			Precipitation		
5°F & below	32°F & below	90°F & above	Clear	Partly cloudy	Cloudy	0.01 inch or more precip.	0.1 inch or more snow/ice	Thunder-storms
22	147	11	58	149	158	133	36	24

Note: Figures are average number of days per year and cover the years 1945-1990
Source: National Climatic Data Center, International Station Meteorological Climate Summary, 9/96

HAZARDOUS WASTE

Superfund Sites

Bethlehem has no sites on the EPA's Superfund Final National Priorities List.
U.S. Environmental Protection Agency, Final National Priorities List, June 23, 2008

AIR & WATER QUALITY

Air Quality Index

Area	Percent of Days when Air Quality was...[2]				AQI Statistics	
	Good	Moderate	Unhealthy for Sensitive Groups	Unhealthy	Maximum	Median
MSA[1]	74.5	21.4	4.1	0.0	135	37

Note: The Air Quality Index (AQI) is an index for reporting daily air quality. EPA calculates the AQI for five major air pollutants regulated by the Clean Air Act: ground-level ozone, particle pollution (also known as particulate matter), carbon monoxide, sulfur dioxide, and nitrogen dioxide. The AQI runs from 0 to 500. The higher the AQI value, the greater the level of air pollution and the greater the health concern. There are six AQI categories: "Good" The AQI is between 0 and 50. Air quality is considered satisfactory; "Moderate" The AQI is between 51 and 100. Air quality is acceptable; "Unhealthy for Sensitive Groups" When AQI values are between 101 and 150, members of sensitive groups may experience health effects; "Unhealthy" When AQI values are between 151 and 200 everyone may begin to experience health effects; "Very Unhealthy" AQI values between 201 and 300 trigger a health alert; "Hazardous" AQI values over 300 trigger health warnings of emergency conditions; (1) Metropolitan Statistical Area - see Appendix A for areas included; (2) Based on 365 days with AQI data in 2007.
Source: U.S. Environmental Protection Agency, Air Quality Index Report, 2007

Air Quality Index Pollutants

Area	Percent of Days when AQI Pollutant was...[2]					
	Carbon Monoxide	Nitrogen Dioxide	Ozone	Sulfur Dioxide	Particulate Matter 2.5	Particulate Matter 10
MSA[1]	0.0	0.0	66.6	0.0	33.4	0.0

Note: The Air Quality Index (AQI) is an index for reporting daily air quality. EPA calculates the AQI for five major air pollutants regulated by the Clean Air Act: ground-level ozone, particle pollution (also known as particulate matter), carbon monoxide, sulfur dioxide, and nitrogen dioxide. The AQI runs from 0 to 500. The higher the AQI value, the greater the level of air pollution and the greater the health concern; (1) Metropolitan Statistical Area - see Appendix A for areas included; (2) Based on 365 days with AQI data in 2007.
Source: U.S. Environmental Protection Agency, Air Quality Index Report, 2007

Air Quality Index Trends

Area	Trend Sites (5)								All Sites (27)
	1999	2000	2001	2002	2003	2004	2005	2006	2006
MSA[1]	6	1	11	8	5	2	3	1	2

Note: An AQI value greater than 100 indicates that air quality would have been in the unhealthful range on that day. Data from exceptional events are not included. These counts are presented in two ways. First, the counts are based on sites having an adequate record of monitoring data during the trend period (trend sites). These counts represent the relative change in the number of days with AQI values greater than 100. In the last column, the counts are based on all sites with data in the most recent year (because it is possible for a site to have data in the most recent year but not enough data to be a trend site); (1) Metropolitan Statistical Area - see Appendix A for areas included.
Source: U.S. Environmental Protection Agency, Office of Air and Radiation, Air Trends, Factbook and Related Information, Air Pollution Trends in Selected Metropolitan Areas 2006

Maximum Air Pollutant Concentrations

	Particulate Matter 10 (ug/m^3)	Particulate Matter 2.5 (ug/m^3)	Ozone (ppm)	Carbon Monoxide (ppm)	Sulfur Dioxide (ppm)	Nitrogen Dioxide (ppm)	Lead (ug/m^3)
MSA[1] Level	n/a	n/a	0.086	2	0.014	n/a	n/a
NAAQS[2]	150	35	0.125	9	0.140	0.053	1.50
Met NAAQS[2]	Yes	Yes	Yes	Yes	Yes	n/a	n/a

Note: Data from exceptional events are not included; (1) Metropolitan Statistical Area - see Appendix A for areas included; (2) National Ambient Air Quality Standards; n/a not available
Concentrations: Particulate Matter 10 (coarse particulate) - highest second maximum 24-hour concentration; Particulate Matter 2.5 (fine particulate) - highest 98th percentile 24-hour concentration; Ozone - highest second daily maximum 1-hour concentration; Carbon Monoxide - highest second maximum non-overlapping 8-hour concentration; Sulfur Dioxide - highest second maximum 24-hour concentration; Nitrogen Dioxide - highest arithmetic mean concentration; Lead - highest quarterly maximum concentration
Units: ppm = parts per million; ug/m^3 = micrograms per cubic meter
Source: U.S. Environmental Protection Agency, MSA Factbook 2006, Air Quality Statistics by City

Drinking Water

Water System Name	Pop. Served	Primary Water Source Type	Violations[1]	
			Health Based	Monitoring/ Reporting
Bethlehem WD #1 - New Salem	31,000	Surface	0	0

Note: (1) Based on violation data from January 1, 2007 to December 31, 2007 (includes unresolved violations from earlier years)
Source: U.S. Environmental Protection Agency, Office of Ground Water and Drinking Water, Safe Drinking Water Information System (based on data extracted April 15, 2008)

Greenburgh, New York

Background

Greenburgh is located in southwestern Westchester County, along the Huson River, and a very manageable 28 miles north of New York City — giving it the enviable combination of urban proximity with small-town lifestyle. Greenburgh includes the villages of Ardsley, Dobbs Ferry, Elmsford, Hastings-on-Hudson, Tarrytown, and Irvington.

Greenburgh was originally inhabited by the Weckquaesgeek Native Americans, a branch of the Mohican tribe. It was incorporated as a city in 1788. The area was mainly agricultural, and concentrated on raising wheat for the large brewery in Dobbs Ferry and vegetables for nearby New York City. In the late 19th century, the city's striking vistas and cool breezes attracted wealthy estate owners Jay Gould and Jasper Cropsey, who both built houses that quickly encouraged brisk suburban development.

A building boom in the 1990s brought a wave of new residents and businesses, the effects of which are still being felt today. The city's school districts have been building new classrooms to handle the burgeoning population, and elected officials are working on open-space regulations.

Because of its desirable location and palatable feeling of community, Greenburgh has become a popular site for business startup and relocation. Major companies in the city include Kraft Foods and the Dannon Company.

Main attractions include the Greenburgh Nature Center and Ridge Road Park. The nature center is a 33-acre preserve featuring a live animal museum, a discovery room, a greenhouse, changing nature-arts exhibits, and a nature store. The grounds include a pond and gardens. Ridge Road Park offers 170 acres with group picnicking facilities, three pavilions, ball fields and playgrounds.

In May 2006, the City Council approved plans to build a new Greenburgh Public Library, that began in 2007. A new Catskill-Delaware Ultraviolet Light Disinfection Facility was recently built in the city. The project, designed to disinfect the region's north-based water supply, was commissioned by the New York City Department of Environmental Protection.

Greenburgh has a typically northeastern climate with hot summers, cold winters and moderate snowfalls. Median summer temperatures average 68 degrees, while winter averages can be as low as 20 degrees during of December and January. The city averages 4.5 inches of rainfall per month from April to October and 7 inches of snowfall per month from December to March.

Rankings

General Rankings

- New York* was ranked #251 out of 375 metro areas in *Cities Ranked & Rated.* Criteria: cost of living; climate; crime; transportation; economy and jobs; education; arts and culture; health and healthcare; leisure; quality of life. *Cities Ranked & Rated, 2nd Edition, 2007*
- New York* was ranked #18 out of 379 metro areas in *Places Rated Almanac.* Criteria: health care; education; recreation; transportation; ambience; climate; crime; housing costs; jobs. *Places Rated Almanac, 7th Edition, 2007*

Business/Finance Rankings

- The nation's 100 largest metro areas were analysed in terms of the percentage of households entering some stage of foreclosure in 2007. The New York* metro area ranked #76 out of 100 (#1 = highest foreclosure rate). *RealtyTrac, "Year-End 2007 Metropolitan Foreclosure Report"*
- The New York* metro area was identified as one of the most expensive places to rent in the U.S. The area ranked #76 out of 10 markets with an average effective rent of $2,720 per month. The rental figures cover apartment properties in complexes with 40 or more units (20 or more units in California and Arizona). The figures are blended average rents, which include all unit sizes. Effective rents include free rent incentives and other landlord concessions. *Wall Street Journal Online, January 17, 2008*
- The New York* metro area was selected as one of "America's Most Wired Cities" by *Forbes.* The metro area was ranked #9 out of 30. Criteria: percentage of Internet users with high-speed access; the range of service providers within a city; availability of public wireless hot spots. *Forbes, "America's Most Wired Cities," January 10, 2008*
- Westchester County* was selected as one of the best places to start and grow a company by *Entrepreneur* and the National Policy Research Council. The Westchester County* metro area ranked #35 out of 50 large metro areas. Criteria: business formation and growth (firms started four to 14 years ago that still employ at least 5 people and experienced rapid growth over the last four years). *Entrepreneur/National Policy Research Council, "Hot Cities for Entrepreneurs," September 2006*
- The New York* metro area was selected as one of "America's Greediest Cities" by *Forbes.* The area was ranked #6 out of 10. Criteria: number of Forbes 400 (*Forbes* annual list of the richest Americans) members per capita. *Forbes, "America's Greediest Cities," December 7, 2007*
- New York* was cited as one of America's top large metros (population over 1 million) for new and expanded facility projects in 2007. The area appeared in the top 10 with 72 projects. *Site Selection, "Top Metropolitan Area Awards," March 2008*
- Intel, in partnership with Sperling's BestPlaces, ranked the 80 "Best Cities for Teleworking" in America. The New York* metro area ranked #6 among extra large metro areas. The study identifies cities that hold the greatest potential for teleworking based on a host of factors including typical commuting times, fuel prices, availability of broadband Internet access and percentage of the population in telework friendly jobs. The study also factored in extreme climate and natural hazards. *Intel, "Best Cities for Teleworking," March 30, 2006*
- The Westchester County* metro area appeared on the Milken Institute "2007 Best Performing Cities" index. Rank: #148 out of 200 large metro areas. Criteria: job growth; wage and salary growth; high-tech output growth. *Milken Institute, "2007 Best Performing Cities"*
- New York* was identified as one of the 100 "Most Unwired Cities" in the U.S. The area ranked #21 out of the 100 largest metro areas in the U.S. Criteria: number of public and commercial wireless access points (hotspots); airports with wireless Internet access; broadband availability; local wireless networks; and wireless email devices. *Intel, "Most Unwired Cities Survey," June 7, 2005*

- New York* was ranked #12 out of 125 regions worldwide in terms of its "Knowledge Competitiveness Index." The index attempts to measure the knowledge-based development taking place throughout the world and is based on 19 measures of economic performance that indicate a region's ability to translate its knowledge capacity into economic value. *Robert Huggins Associates, World Knowledge Competitiveness Index 2005*
- *Forbes* ranked the 200 most populous metro areas in the U.S. in terms of the "Best Places for Business and Careers." The New York* metro area was ranked #121. Criteria: business costs (labor, energy, tax and office space expenses); living costs (housing, transportation, food and other household expenditures); education levels of the work force; job growth; income growth; migration trends; crime rates; and culture/leisure. *Forbes, "Best Places for Business and Careers," March 19, 2008*
- *Fortune* ranked the 100 largest metro areas in the U.S. in terms of projected median home price change in 2007. The New York* metro area ranked #74. *Fortune.com, "Hot Spots, Cold Spots"*
- The New York* metro area was identified as one of "America's Most Overpriced Real Estate Markets." The area ranked #7 out of 10. Criteria: housing "P/E" ratio (a market's median home price divided by annual rents minus taxes and insurance); housing affordability. *Forbes.com, "America's Most Overpriced Real Estate Markets," May 11, 2007*

Health/Environment Rankings

- 100 of the largest metro areas in the U.S. were analyzed in terms of their current drought severity. The New York* metro area ranked #75 (#1 = driest). The rankings were based on statistics such as long-term precipitation trends and patterns and the Palmer drought indices. *Sperling's BestPlaces, www.BestPlaces.net, "America's Drought-Riskiest Cities," November 2007*
- Doctors at the Harvard School of Public Health ranked 40 metropolitan areas based on data from the government-sponsored Hospital Quality Alliance program. The program tracks the performance of individual hospitals in treating patients for three common health problems: heart attacks, congestive heart failure, and pneumonia. The New York* metro area ranked #17 in quality of care for heart attacks, #8 for congestive heart failure, and #34 for pneumonia. *New England Journal of Medicine, July 21, 2005*
- *Reader's Digest* ranked the 50 largest metro areas in the U.S. in terms of how "clean" they are. The New York* metro area ranked #49. Criteria: air quality; water quality; toxic industrial pollution; Superfund sites; and sanitation. *Reader's Digest, "The 50 Cleanest (and Dirtiest) Cities in America," July 2005*
- The American Academy of Dermatology ranked 32 U.S. metropolitan regions in terms of their residents knowledge, attitude and behaviors towards tanning and sun protection. The New York* metro area ranked #2. The results of the study are based on an online national survey of 3,342 respondents. *American Academy of Dermatology, "RAYS: Your Grade," May 7, 2007*
- The New York* metro area appeared in *Country Home's* "2008 Best Green Places" report. The area ranked #103 out of 379. Criteria: official energy policies; green power; green buildings; availability of fresh, locally grown food. *Country Home, "2008 Best Green Places"*
- Wyeth Consumer Healthcare, in partnership with Sperling's BestPlaces, ranked the nation's 50 most populous metro areas in terms of five key health factors. The New York* metro area ranked #43. Criteria: physical activity; health status; nutrition; lifestyle pursuits; and mental wellness. *Wyeth Consumer Healthcare, "Centrum Healthiest Cities Study," April 19, 2005*
- HealthGrades surveyed over 41,000 individuals on doctor satisfaction and ranked the 20 largest metro areas based on the highest "definitely yes" responses to the question "Do you trust the physician to make decisions/recommendations that are in your best interest?" The New York* metro area ranked #10. *HealthGrades.com, "Top Cities in Doctor-Trust," September 7, 2006*

- New York* was identified as a "2008 Asthma Capital." The area ranked #38 out of the nation's 100 largest metropolitan areas. Twelve factors were used to identify the most challenging places to live for people with asthma: estimated prevalence; self-reported prevalence; crude death rate for asthma; annual pollen score; annual air quality; public smoking laws; number of board-certified asthma specialists; school inhaler access laws; rescue medication use; controller medication use; uninsured rate; poverty rate. *Asthma and Allergy Foundation of America, "2008 Asthma Capitals"*

- New York* was identified as a "Spring Allergy Capital." The area ranked #79 out of 100. Three groups of factors were used to identify the most severe cities for people with allergies during the spring season: annual pollen levels; medicine utilization; access to board-certified allergists. *Asthma and Allergy Foundation of America, "2007 Spring Allergy Capital Rankings"*

- New York* was identified as a "Fall Allergy Capital." The area ranked #69 out of 100. Three groups of factors were used to identify the most severe cities for people with allergies during the fall season: annual pollen levels; medicine utilization; access to board-certified allergists. *Asthma and Allergy Foundation of America, "2007 Fall Allergy Capital Rankings"*

- Ortho-McNeil Neurologics, in partnership with Sperling's BestPlaces, analyzed 110 metro areas and identified those U.S. cities with the highest prevalence of factors that are most commonly associated with migraine headaches. The Westchester County* metro area ranked #106. Criteria: number of migraine-related drug prescriptions per capita; lifestyle factors that can contribute to migraines; environmental factors that can trigger migraines; and consumption of migraine-triggering foods. *Ortho-McNeil Neurologics, "America's Migraine Hot Spots," March 14, 2006*

- Sperling's BestPlaces ranked 331 metro areas and identified the most and least stressful U.S. cities. The New York* metro area ranked #5 out of the 100 largest metro areas (#1 = most stressful). Criteria: divorce rate; unemployment rate; violent and property crime; suicide rate; commute time; mental health; alcohol consumption; cloudy days. *Sperling's BestPlaces, www.BestPlaces.net, "America's Most (and Least) Stressful Cities," January 9, 2004*

- An analysis of the "Best & Worst Cities for Sleep" was conducted by Sperling's BestPlaces. The study ranked America's 50 most populated metro areas. The New York* metro area ranked #47 (#1 = best city for sleep). Criteria: number of days residents didn't get enough rest or sleep during the past month; average length of daily commute; divorce rate; unemployment rate. *Sperling's BestPlaces, www.BestPlaces.net, "Best & Worst Cities for Sleep," 2006*

- HealthGrades evaluated the performance of America's 25 most populous metropolitan areas by measuring the outcomes of five of the highest volume and most widely studied procedures and diagnoses: coronary artery bypass graft surgery; percutaneus coronary interventions; acute myocardial infarction/heart attack in angioplasty-capable hospitals; congestive heart failure; and community acquired pneumonia. The New York* metro area ranked #17. *HealthGrades, "HealthGrades Hospital Quality in America Study," October 12, 2004*

- New York* was highlighted as one of the 25 metro areas most polluted by year-round particle pollution (PM 2.5) in the U.S. The area ranked #17. *American Lung Association, State of the Air: 2007*

- New York* was highlighted as one of the 25 most ozone-polluted metro areas in the U.S. The area ranked #10. *American Lung Association, State of the Air: 2007*

- New York* was selected as one of "America's Top 10 Low-Carb Cities" by *LowCarbiz Magazine*. Criteria: abundance of low-carb products; restaurants with low-carb menu items; health practitioners supportive of carb-cutting regimens; local culture generally conducive to exercise and health. *LowCarbiz Magazine, April 2004*

- New York* was selected as one of "America's Pet Healthiest Cities" by Purina. The city ranked #14 out of 50. Criteria: veterinary services; environment; legislation; preventative care; obesity/body condition. *Purina Pet Institute, "America's Pet Healthiest Cities," May 20, 2003*

Women/Minorities Rankings

- New York* was ranked #8 out of 100 metro areas in *SELF Magazine's* ranking of "America's Best Places for Women." A panel of experts came up with more than 50 criteria including death and disease rates, environmental indicators, community resources, and lifestyle habits. *SELF Magazine, "America's Best Places for Women 2007," December 2007*
- New York* appeared on a list of the top 10 metro areas with the highest concentration of same-sex households. The area ranked #6. *Urban Institute Press, The Gay and Lesbian Atlas, May 2004*
- New York* appeared on a list of the top 10 metro areas with the highest concentration of gay male couples. The area ranked #5. *Urban Institute Press, The Gay and Lesbian Atlas, May 2004*

Seniors/Retirement Rankings

- Sperling's BestPlaces in partnership with Bankers Life & Casualty Company designed a survey to identify the top 50 metro areas in the U.S. that offer the best overall qualities for senior living. The New York* metro area ranked #7. The following criteria were statistically weighted to reflect the needs of the senior population: health; disease; economics; social; environment; spiritual; transportation; housing; and crime. *Bankers Life & Casualty Company, "Best Cities for Seniors 2005"*
- A.G. Edwards ranked America's 500 top-performing communities based on their residents' personal savings and investing behavior. The New York* metro area ranked #241 with an index score of 101.69 (national average = 100.00). A dozen statistical factors were measured including: participation in retirement savings plans; personal debt levels; and home ownership. *A.G. Edwards, "2007 Nest Egg Index", September 12, 2007*

Children/Family Rankings

- The New York* metro area was selected as one of the "Best Cities for Relocating Families" by Worldwide ERC and Primacy Relocation. The 2007 study placed a special emphasis on the housing market, which has significantly impacted the relocation industry and an employer's ability to transfer employees. The variables which weigh heavily in this category include home price, home affordability index, appreciation rates, and property tax. Other criteria include cost of living, crime rates, education, climate, focus on diversity, physicians per capita, recreation and leisure, arts and culture, air quality, watershed quality, sales tax, unemployment rate, job growth, high school and higher education index, school expenditures per student, students in public school, SAT/ACT percentile, and population growth. *Worldwide ERC and Primacy Relocation, "2007 Best Cities for Relocating Families"*

Safety Rankings

- The National Insurance Crime Bureau ranked 361 metro areas in the U.S. in terms of per capita rates of vehicle theft. The New York* metro area ranked #224 (#1 = highest rate). Criteria: number of vehicle theft offenses per 100,000 inhabitants. *National Insurance Crime Bureau, "NICB Vehicle Theft Study," April 22, 2008*
- New York* appeared on Sperling's BestPlaces list of the "Riskiest Cities for Identity Theft." The area ranked #29 out of the nations 50 largest metro areas. Over 80 criteria were analyzed across four major categories: technology impact; crime; transactions; and risk profile. *Sperling's BestPlaces, www.BestPlaces.net, "Riskiest Cities for Identity Theft," July 2006*
- Farmers Insurance Group of Companies, in partnership with Sperling's BestPlaces, ranked 379 metro areas and identified the "Most Secure U.S. Place to Live." The New York* metro area ranked #43 out of 114 in the large metro area category (500,000 or more residents). Criteria: crime rates; extreme weather; risk of natural disasters; environmental hazards; terrorism threats; air quality; life expectancy; job loss numbers. *Farmers Insurance Group, "Most Secure U.S. Places to Live 2007"*

- Westchester County* was identified as one of the most dangerous large metro areas for pedestrians in the U.S. The area ranked #47 out of the nations 50 largest metro areas. Criteria: average yearly pedestrian fatalities per capita (for the years 2002 and 2003) adjusted for the number of walkers. *Surface Transportation Policy Project, "Mean Streets 2004"*

Sports/Recreation Rankings

- The New York* metro area appeared on the *Sporting News* list of the "Best Sports Cities 2007". The area ranked #2 out of 150 cities in the U.S. *Sporting News* takes a 12-month snapshot, roughly July to July, of each city's sports, putting a heavy premium on regular-season won-lost records (from the most recently completed season). Other criteria include: playoff berths, bowl appearances and tournament bids; championships; applicable power ratings; quality of competition; overall fan fervor as measured in part by attendance as percentage of venue capacity; abundance of teams (rewarding quality over quantity); stadium and arena quality; ticket availability and prices; franchise ownership; and marquee appeal of athletes. *SportingNews.com, "Best Sports Cities 2007," August 1, 2007*
- The New York* metro area was selected by *Cranium* as one of the "Top 50 Fun Cities" in America. The area ranked #41. Criteria includes: number of sports teams, restaurants, and dance performances; number of toy stores; city budget spent on recreation. *Cranium, November 4, 2003*
- *Golf Digest* ranked 330 metro areas in the U.S. in terms of golf. The New York* metro area was ranked #329. Criteria: access to golf; weather; value of golf; and quality of golf. *Golf Digest, "Metro Golf Rankings," August 2005*

Dating/Romance Rankings

- Eli Lily and Company, in partnership with Sperling's BestPlaces, ranked the nation's 50 largest metro areas in terms of the "Most Romantic Cities for Baby Boomers." The New York* metro area ranked #16. Criteria: marriage and divorce rates among "baby boomers" age 45 to 60; great restaurants; dance studios; chocolate, jewelry and flower sales. *Eli Lily and Company, "Most Romantic Cities for Baby Boomers," April 20, 2007*
- The New York* metro area was selected as one of the "Top Ten U.S. Cities for Finding a Rich, Single Woman" by Teasley, a Manhattan-based marketing consulting firm. The area ranked #2. Criteria: high single-female to single-male ratio; higher income to cost-of-living ratio; percentage of population that is single. *Teasley, "Where to Find a Rich, Single Woman in the United States," 2005*
- The New York* metro area was selected as one of the "Best Cities for Relocating Singles" by Worldwide ERC and Primacy Relocation. The area ranked #39 out of the 100 largest metro areas in the U.S. Areas were selected based on the following criteria: a robust cost-of-living index; adventure and outdoor recreation opportunities; violent crime and property crime rates; percentage of the population that is unmarried (ages 25-34); ratio of single men and single women; affordability of quality higher education, including in-state and out-of-state tuition requirements and rates; number of newcomers to the area; commute times; tax rates; fee and occupancy rates for temporary housing and mini-storage; quality and quantity of collegiate and professional sporting events and fun, fan-friendly venues. *Worldwide ERC and Primacy Relocation, "2007 Best Cities for Relocating Singles," October 25, 2007*
- *Forbes* ranked the 40 most populous urbanized areas in the U.S. in terms of the "Best Cities for Singles." The New York* metro area ranked #2. Criteria: number of singles; cost of living alone; nightlife; culture; job growth; coolness; and online dating. *Forbes.com, August 21, 2007*
- Sperling's BestPlaces in partnership with AXE Deodorant Bodyspray ranked 80 metro areas and identified "America's Best (and Worst) Cities for Dating." The New York* metro area ranked #18 (#1 = best). Criteria: percentage of singles ages 18-24; population density; dating venues per capita. *AXE Deodorant Bodyspray, "America's Best (and Worst) Cities for Dating," May 2004*

Culture/Performing Arts Rankings

- The New York* metro area was selected as one of the "Best Places for Artists in America" by *BusinessWeek.com*. Criteria: percentage of young people age 25 to 34; population diversity; concentration of museums, philharmonic orchestras, dance companies, theater troupes, library resources, and college arts programs. *BusinessWeek.com, "Best Places for Artists in America," February 26, 2007*

- Scarborough Research, a leading market research firm, identified the top local markets for rock concert attendance. The New York* DMA (Designated Market Area) ranked in the top 25 with 14% of consumers, 18 years old and over, reporting that they have attended a rock concert during the past year. *Scarborough Research, June 14, 2004*

Miscellaneous Rankings

- The New York* metro area was identified as one of "The 10 Worst Commuter Cities" in the U.S. by the *U.S. News and World Report*. The mean travel time to work is 39 minutes. *U.S. News and World Report, May 7, 2007*

- Scarborough Research, a leading market research firm, identified the top local markets for bloggers. The New York* DMA (Designated Market Area) ranked in the top 13 with 10% of adults reporting that they had read or contributed to a blog within the past 30 days. *Scarborough Research, October 24, 2007*

- The New York* metro area was selected as one of the "Top 10 Most Independent Cities for Homesellers". The area ranked #1. The cities listed had more consumers choosing to sell their homes without the help of a real-estate agent than anywhere else. Data was based on geographical information for listings posted on ForSaleByOwner.com from January 1, 2007 through June 30, 2007. *ForSaleByOwner.com, October 1, 2007*

- Avis Rent-A-Car and Motorola, in partnership with Sperling's BestPlaces, ranked the nation's 75 most populous metro areas in terms of how difficult they are to navigate. The New York* metro area ranked #5 with #1 being the most challenging. Criteria: street layouts; overall design and layout; travel time index; percent of congested freeway and street lane miles; bodies of water; complexity of directions needed to travel from major airports to city center; annual delay per person; days of snow exceeding 1.5 inches; and days of rain exceeding 0.5 inch. *Avis Rent-A-Car and Motorola, "America's Most Challenging Cities to Navigate," August 3, 2004*

- The New York* metro area appeared on *Forbes* list of "America's Drunkest Cities". The area ranked #32. Criteria: 35 of the largest continental U.S. metro areas were chosen based on availability of data and geographic diversity. Each metro was ranked in five areas: state laws; drinkers; heavy drinkers; binge drinkers; and alcoholism. *Forbes.com, "America's Drunkest Cities," August 22, 2006*

- Sperling's BestPlaces in partnership with Pep Boys ranked 77 metro areas and identified "America's Most Drivable Cities." The New York* metro area ranked #70. Criteria: climate; road roughness; urban mobility; gas prices. *Pep Boys, "America's Most Drivable Cities," April 9, 2003*

- State Farm Insurance, in partnership with Sperling's BestPlaces, analyzed several key factors that contribute to overall family preparedness. The New York* metro area ranked #44 out of the nation's 50 most populous metro areas. Criteria: quality of life; life insurance coverage; and investments. *State Farm Life Insurance, "Fiscally Fit Cities Report," July 20, 2004*

- Scarborough Research, a leading market research firm, identified the top local markets for grocery coupon use. The New York* DMA (Designated Market Area) ranked in the top 25 with 38% of consumers reporting that they use grocery coupons at least once per week. *Scarborough Research, December 8, 2004*

- A study by Sperling's BestPlaces examined which U.S. metro areas were most affected by high fuel prices in 2006. The New York* metro area was ranked #64 out of 80 (#1 = most expensive city for driving). Rankings are based on the average dollars spent on gas per year by two driver households. Criteria: cost of regular-grade gasoline; average miles driven per day; average number of gallons each driver uses and wastes in traffic congestion each day. *Sperling's BestPlaces, www.bestplaces.net, "Pain at the Pump," May 18, 2006*

***Greenburgh is located within the New York-Northern New Jersey-Long Island, NY-NJ-PA Metropolitan Statistical Area and New York-White Plains-Wayne, NY-NJ Metropolitan Division.**

Business Environment

CITY FINANCES

City Government Finances

Component	2004-2005 ($000)	2004-2005 ($ per capita)
Total Revenues	72,067	805
Total Expenditures	75,931	848
Debt Outstanding	38,803	433
Cash and Securities	87,490	977

Source: U.S Census Bureau, Government Finances 2004-2005

City Government Revenue by Source

Source	2004-2005 ($000)	2004-2005 ($ per capita)
General Revenue		
From Federal Government	326	4
From State Government	1,048	12
From Local Governments	5,742	64
Taxes		
Property	42,846	479
Sales	572	6
Personal Income	0	0
License	6,922	77
Charges	4,434	50
Liquor Store	0	0
Utility	5,415	60
Employee Retirement	0	0
Other	4,762	53

Source: U.S Census Bureau, Government Finances 2004-2005

City Government Expenditures by Function

Function	2004-2005 ($000)	2004-2005 ($ per capita)	2004-2005 (%)
General Expenditures			
Airports	0	0	0.0
Corrections	0	0	0.0
Education	0	0	0.0
Fire Protection	1,426	16	1.9
Governmental Administration	6,289	70	8.3
Health	844	9	1.1
Highways	3,734	42	4.9
Hospitals	0	0	0.0
Housing and Community Development	0	0	0.0
Interest on General Debt	1,452	16	1.9
Libraries	3,026	34	4.0
Parking	57	1	0.1
Parks and Recreation	12,116	135	16.0
Police Protection	11,937	133	15.7
Public Welfare	0	0	0.0
Sewerage	443	5	0.6
Solid Waste Management	3,529	39	4.6
Liquor Store	0	0	0.0
Utility	7,055	79	9.3
Employee Retirement	0	0	0.0
Other	24,023	268	31.6

Source: U.S Census Bureau, Government Finances 2004-2005

Municipal Bond Ratings

Area	Moody's
City	Aa1

Source: Mergent Bond Record, January 2008 (unless noted otherwise)

DEMOGRAPHICS

Population Growth

Area	1990 Census	2000 Census	2007 Estimate	2012 Projection	Population Growth (%) 1990-2000	Population Growth (%) 2000-2012
City	83,816	86,764	89,457	90,770	3.5	4.6
MSA[1]	16,845,992	18,323,002	18,887,605	19,111,248	8.8	4.3
U.S.	248,709,873	281,421,906	301,045,522	314,920,978	13.2	11.9

Note: (1) Metropolitan Statistical Area - see Appendix B for areas included
Source: Claritas, Inc.

Number of Households and Average Household Size

Area	2007 Estimate	2007 Average Household Size
City	34,116	2.62
MSA[1]	6,870,593	2.75
U.S.	113,668,003	2.65

Note: (1) Metropolitan Statistical Area - see Appendix B for areas included
Source: Claritas, Inc.

Race and Ethnicity

Area	White Alone[2]	Black Alone[2]	Asian Alone[2]	Other Race Alone[2]	Hispanic[3]
City	70.0	12.8	10.4	6.9	11.0
MSA[1]	59.5	17.6	8.8	14.1	21.2
U.S.	73.1	12.4	4.3	10.3	14.9

Note: Figures are 2007 estimates; (1) Metropolitan Statistical Area - see Appendix B for areas included (2) Alone is defined as not being in combination with one or more other races; (3) May be of any race.
Source: Claritas, Inc.

Ancestry

Area	German	Irish[2]	English	American	Italian	Polish	French[3]	Scottish
City	7.7	13.6	4.6	3.3	17.9	5.4	1.1	1.1
MSA[1]	3.9	6.7	2.0	3.1	10.4	2.9	0.8	0.5
U.S.	15.2	10.9	8.7	7.3	5.6	3.2	3.0	1.7

Note: Figures include multiple ancestry (e.g. if a person reported being Irish and Italian, they were included in both columns); (1) Metropolitan Statistical Area - see Appendix A for areas included; (2) Includes Celtic; (3) Includes Alsatian but excludes Basque
Source: Census 2000, Summary File 3

Foreign-Born Population

Area	Percent of Population Born in: Any Foreign Country	Europe	Asia	Africa	Oceania[2]	Canada	Mexico	Latin America[3]
City	21.0	5.3	7.5	0.7	0.1	0.3	0.8	6.2
MSA[1]	33.7	6.8	7.9	1.1	0.1	0.2	1.5	16.1
U.S.	11.1	1.7	2.9	0.3	0.1	0.3	3.3	2.5

Note: (1) Metropolitan Statistical Area - see Appendix A for areas included; (2) Includes Australia, New Zealand subregion, Melanesia, Micronesia, Polynesia, and Oceania n.e.c; (3) Includes Central America (excluding Mexico), South America, and the Caribbean.
Source: Census 2000, Summary File 3

Marriage Status

Area	Never Married	Now Married (excluding Separated)	Separated	Widowed	Divorced
City	24.8	60.1	1.6	6.8	6.8
MSA[1]	36.2	45.3	4.0	7.0	7.6
U.S.	27.1	54.4	2.2	6.6	9.7

Note: Figures are percentages and cover the population 15 years of age and older; (1) Metropolitan Statistical Area - see Appendix A for areas included
Source: Census 2000, Summary File 3

Age Distribution

Area	Percent of Population						
	Under Age 5	Age 5 to 17	Age 18 to 34	Age 35 to 49	Age 50 to 64	Age 65 to 79	80 Years and Over
City	6.4	17.3	18.0	26.2	17.7	10.8	3.7
MSA[1]	6.7	17.6	25.9	23.2	14.7	8.8	3.2
U.S.	6.8	18.9	23.7	23.5	14.8	9.2	3.2

Note: (1) Metropolitan Statistical Area - see Appendix A for areas included
Source: Census 2000, Summary File 3

Male/Female Ratio

Area	Males	Females	Males per 100 Females
City	42,658	46,799	91.2
MSA[1]	9,117,706	9,769,899	93.3
U.S.	148,320,305	152,725,217	97.1

Note: Figures are 2007 estimates; (1) Metropolitan Statistical Area - see Appendix B for areas included
Source: Claritas, Inc.

Religion

Area	Catholic	Southern Baptist	United Meth-odist	ELCA[1]	LDS[2]	Presby-terian Church USA	Jewish Est.	Muslim Est.
County	50.9	0.1	1.2	0.6	0.2	1.2	10.2	0.6
U.S.	22.0	7.1	3.7	1.8	1.5	1.1	2.2	0.6

Note: Figures are the number of adherents as a percentage of the total population; Adherents are defined as all members, including full members, their children and the estimated number of other participants who are not considered members (e.g. the baptized, those not confirmed, those regularly attending services, etc.);
(1) Evangelical Lutheran Church in America; (2) The Church of Jesus Christ of Latter Day Saints
Source: Reprinted with permission from Religious Congregations and Membership in the United States 2000 (Nashville, Glenmary Research Center, 2002) Copyright Association of Statisticians of American Religious Bodies. All rights reserved.

ECONOMY

Gross Metropolitan Product

Area	2002	2003	2004	2005	2005 Rank[2]
MSA[1]	820.9	847.1	902.4	952.6	1

Note: Figures are in billions of dollars; (1) New York-Northern New Jersey-Long Island, NY-NJ-PA Metropolitan Statistical Area - see Appendix A for areas included; (2) Rank ranges from 1 to 361
Source: The U.S. Conference of Mayors, "U.S. Metro Economies: GMP - The Engines of America's Growth," January 2007

Economic Growth

Area	1995 GMP	2005 GMP	Average Annual Growth Rate	Growth Rate Rank[2]
MSA[1]	585.5	952.6	5.0	221

Note: Figures are in billions of dollars; GMP = Gross Metropolitan Product; (1) New York-Northern New Jersey-Long Island, NY-NJ-PA Metropolitan Statistical Area - see Appendix A for areas included; (2) Rank ranges from 1 to 361
Source: The U.S. Conference of Mayors, "U.S. Metro Economies: GMP - The Engines of America's Growth," January 2007

INCOME

Per Capita/Median/Average Income

Area	Per Capita ($)	Median Household ($)	Average Household ($)
City	50,392	93,433	131,190
MSA[1]	30,292	58,080	82,491
U.S.	25,495	49,280	66,670

Note: Figures are 2007 estimates; (1) Metropolitan Statistical Area - see Appendix B for areas included
Source: Claritas, Inc.

Household Income Distribution

Area	Percent of Households Earning							
	Under $15,000	$15,000 -24,999	$25,000 -34,999	$35,000 -49,999	$50,000 -74,999	$75,000 -99,000	$100,000 -149,999	$150,000 and up
City	5.0	4.9	5.9	9.4	15.0	13.2	19.2	27.3
MSA[1]	14.0	8.8	8.7	12.6	17.1	12.3	14.5	12.0
U.S.	13.1	10.9	11.2	15.6	19.5	11.9	11.3	6.6

Note: Figures are 2007 estimates; (1) Metropolitan Statistical Area - see Appendix B for areas included
Source: Claritas, Inc.

Poverty Rates by Age

Area	All Ages	Under 5 Years Old	5 to 17 Years Old	18 to 64 Years Old	65 Years and Over
City	3.9	0.2	0.8	2.2	0.7
MSA[1]	19.5	1.8	4.9	10.9	1.9
U.S.	12.4	1.2	3.0	6.9	1.2

Note: Figures are percent of population with income in 1999 below poverty level and only include population for whom poverty status is determined; (1) Metropolitan Statistical Area - see Appendix A for areas included
Source: Census 2000, Summary File 3

Personal Bankruptcy Filing Rate

Area	2004	2005	2006
Westchester County	2.25	3.39	0.72
U.S.	5.31	6.82	2.00

Note: Numbers are per 1,000 population and include Chapter 7 and Chapter 13 filings
Source: Federal Deposit Insurance Corporation (FDIC), Regional Economic Conditions (RECON), 8/23/2007

EMPLOYMENT

Labor Force and Employment

Area	Civilian Labor Force			Workers Employed		
	Dec. 2006	Dec. 2007	% Chg.	Dec. 2006	Dec. 2007	% Chg.
City	51,000	51,052	0.1	49,579	49,380	-0.4
MD[1]	5,532,850	5,580,260	0.9	5,306,749	5,313,071	0.1
U.S.	152,571,000	153,705,000	0.7	146,081,000	146,334,000	0.2

Note: Data is not seasonally adjusted and covers workers 16 years of age and older; (1) Metropolitan Division - see Appendix B for areas included
Source: Bureau of Labor Statistics, http://stats.bls.gov

Unemployment Rate

Area	2007											
	Jan.	Feb.	Mar.	Apr.	May	Jun.	Jul.	Aug.	Sep.	Oct.	Nov.	Dec.
City	3.5	3.3	3.0	2.8	3.0	3.2	3.5	3.2	3.3	3.2	3.3	3.3
MD[1]	5.0	4.8	4.4	4.3	4.4	4.7	5.4	4.9	4.7	4.8	4.6	4.8
U.S.	5.0	4.9	4.5	4.3	4.3	4.7	4.9	4.6	4.5	4.4	4.5	4.8

Note: Data is not seasonally adjusted and covers workers 16 years of age and older; All figures are percentages; (1) Metropolitan Division - see Appendix B for areas included
Source: Bureau of Labor Statistics, http://stats.bls.gov

Employment by Occupation

Occupation Classification	City (%)	MSA[1] (%)	U.S. (%)
Sales and Office	24.0	27.2	26.7
Professional and Related	34.0	23.9	20.2
Service	10.6	17.9	14.9
Production, Transportation, and Material Moving	4.7	10.2	14.6
Management, Business, and Financial	22.1	14.2	13.5
Construction, Extraction, and Maintenance	4.6	6.6	9.4
Farming, Forestry, and Fishing	0.1	0.1	0.7

Note: Figures cover employed civilians 16 years of age and older; (1) Metropolitan Statistical Area - see Appendix A for areas included
Source: Census 2000, Summary File 3

Employment by Industry

Sector	MSA[1] Number of Employees	MSA[1] Percent of Total	U.S. Percent of Total
Government	790,000	14.8	16.3
Education and Health Services	972,900	18.2	13.4
Professional and Business Services	813,500	15.2	13.1
Retail Trade	496,500	9.3	11.6
Manufacturing	200,300	3.7	9.9
Leisure and Hospitality	409,900	7.7	9.6
Financial Activities	583,600	10.9	5.9
Construction	n/a	n/a	5.3
Wholesale Trade	247,400	4.6	4.4
Other Services	225,600	4.2	3.9
Transportation and Utilities	190,400	3.6	3.7
Information	211,100	4.0	2.2
Natural Resources and Mining	n/a	n/a	0.5

Note: Figures cover non-farm employment as of December 2007 and are not seasonally adjusted; (1) Metropolitan Statistical Area - see Appendix B for areas included; n/a not available
Source: Bureau of Labor Statistics, http://stats.bls.gov

Average Wages

Occupation	$/Hr.	Occupation	$/Hr.
Accountants and Auditors	38.15	Maids and Housekeeping Cleaners	14.67
Automotive Mechanics	18.68	Maintenance and Repair Workers	18.01
Bookkeepers	18.44	Marketing Managers	69.31
Carpenters	27.76	Nuclear Medicine Technologists	34.59
Cashiers	9.64	Nurses, Licensed Practical	22.54
Clerks, General Office	13.42	Nurses, Registered	37.94
Clerks, Receptionists/Information	13.66	Nursing Aides/Orderlies/Attendants	15.29
Clerks, Shipping/Receiving	14.18	Packers and Packagers, Hand	9.70
Computer Programmers	37.83	Physical Therapists	37.06
Computer Support Specialists	26.98	Postal Service Mail Carriers	21.12
Computer Systems Analysts	42.64	Real Estate Brokers	61.95
Cooks, Restaurant	13.59	Retail Salespersons	12.68
Dentists	n/a	Sales Reps., Exc. Tech./Scientific	34.35
Electrical Engineers	43.02	Sales Reps., Tech./Scientific	41.28
Electricians	33.75	Secretaries, Exc. Legal/Med./Exec.	16.30
Financial Managers	71.16	Security Guards	12.96
First-Line Supervisors/Mgrs., Sales	22.70	Surgeons	89.78
Food Preparation Workers	10.84	Teacher Assistants	12.50
General and Operations Managers	69.08	Teachers, Elementary School	30.30
Hairdressers/Cosmetologists	14.86	Teachers, Secondary School	31.90
Internists	77.20	Telemarketers	15.56
Janitors and Cleaners	13.14	Truck Drivers, Heavy/Tractor-Trailer	21.15
Landscaping/Groundskeeping Workers	13.87	Truck Drivers, Light/Delivery Svcs.	16.73
Lawyers	70.39	Waiters and Waitresses	13.25

Note: Wage data covers the New York-White Plains-Wayne, NY-NJ Metropolitan Division - see Appendix B for areas included. Hourly wages for elementary/secondary school teachers and teacher assistants were calculated by the editors from annual wage data assuming a 40 hour work week; n/a not available.
Source: Bureau of Labor Statistics, May 2007 Metro Area Occupational Employment and Wage Estimates

RESIDENTIAL REAL ESTATE

Building Permits

Area	Single-Family 2006	Single-Family 2007p	Single-Family Pct. Chg.	Multi-Family 2006	Multi-Family 2007p	Multi-Family Pct. Chg.	Total 2006	Total 2007p	Total Pct. Chg.
City	11	9	-18.2	0	0	-	11	9	-18.2
U.S.	1,378,200	973,300	-29.4	460,700	407,200	-11.6	1,838,900	1,380,500	-24.9

Note: (p) preliminary; figures cover and represent new, privately-owned housing units authorized (unadjusted data); All permit data are based on estimates with imputation; U.S. figures are based on the new 20,000-place series.
Source: U.S. Census Bureau, Manufacturing, Mining, and Construction Statistics

Homeownership and Housing Vacancies

Area	Homeownership Rate[2] (%)			Rental Vacancy Rate[3] (%)			Homeowner Vacancy Rate[4] (%)		
	2005	2006	2007	2005	2006	2007	2005	2006	2007
MSA[1]	54.6	53.6	53.8	5.0	5.4	5.7	1.9	1.8	2.1
U.S.	68.9	68.8	68.1	9.8	9.8	9.7	1.9	2.4	2.7

Note: (1) Metropolitan Statistical Area - see Appendix B for areas included; (2) The proportion of households that are owners; (3) The proportion of the rental inventory that is vacant for rent; (4) The proportion of the homeowner inventory that is vacant for sale; n/a not available
Source: U.S. Census Bureau, Housing Vacancies and Homeownership Annual Statistics: 2007

TAXES

State Corporate Income Tax Rates

State	Rates and Tax Brackets
New York	7.1%

Note: Tax rates as of January 1, 2008; Businesses pay greatest of regular income tax, 1.5% AMT, 0.178% of capital base, or a fixed dollar minimum tax between $100 and $1500. There is an additional 0.09% tax on subsidiary capital.
Source: Tax Foundation, www.taxfoundation.org

State Individual Income Tax Rates

State	Federal Deductibility	Marginal Rates (%)	Standard Deduction ($)		Personal Exemptions ($)[1]	
			Single	Joint	Single	Dependents
New York	No	4.0 - 6.85	7,500	15,000	n/a	1,000

Note: Tax rates as of January 1, 2008; Local- and county-level taxes are not included; n/a not applicable; (1) Married joint filers generally receive double the single exemption
Source: Tax Foundation, www.taxfoundation.org

Various State and Local Tax Rates

State and Local Sales and Use (%)	State Sales and Use (%)	Gasoline[1,2] ($/gal.)	Cigarette ($/pack)	Spirits ($/gal.)	Table Wine ($/gal.)	Beer ($/gal.)
7.375	4.0	0.412	1.50	6.44	0.19	0.11

Note: Tax rates as of January 1, 2008; (1) In addition to the 18.4 cpg Federal gasoline tax; (2) Rates may include additional state sales taxes, environmental protection and storage fees/taxes, and local taxes. When necessary, the volume-weighted average of all local taxes is used to approximate the typical statewide rate including local tax
Source: Tax Foundation, www.taxfoundation.org; Original research

State Tax Burdens

Area	Combined State and Local Tax Burden		Combined Federal, State and Local Tax Burden	
	Percent	Rank	Percent	Rank
New York	13.8	3	37.1	2
U.S. Average	11.0	-	32.7	-

Note: Figures cover 2007 and measure taxes as a percentage of income
Source: Tax Foundation, www.taxfoundation.org

State Business Tax Climate Index Rankings

State	Overall Rank	Corporate Tax Index Rank	Individual Income Tax Index Rank	Sales Tax Index Rank	Unemployment Insurance Tax Index Rank	Property Tax Index Rank
New York	48	23	41	49	46	43

Note: Rankings range from 1 to 50 where 1 is best. Rankings do not average across to Overall Rank. States without a given tax are given a ranking of 1.
Source: Tax Foundation, State Business Tax Climate Index 2008

TRANSPORTATION

Means of Transportation to Work

Area	Car/Truck/Van		Public Transportation			Bicycle	Walked	Other Means	Worked at Home
	Drove Alone	Car-pooled	Bus	Subway	Railroad				
City	63.3	7.5	3.1	0.7	17.5	0.1	2.7	0.7	4.3
MSA[1]	31.4	8.3	10.4	31.8	3.0	0.4	9.3	2.5	3.0
U.S.	75.7	12.2	2.5	1.5	0.5	0.4	2.9	1.0	3.3

Note: Figures are percentages and cover workers 16 years of age and older; (1) Metropolitan Statistical Area - see Appendix A for areas included
Source: Census 2000, Summary File 3

Travel Time to Work

Area	Less Than 15 Minutes	15 to 29 Minutes	30 to 44 Minutes	45 to 59 Minutes	60 Minutes or More
City	20.9	30.4	18.9	9.6	20.1
MSA[1]	13.3	24.0	24.4	14.9	23.5
U.S.	29.4	36.1	19.1	7.4	8.0

Note: Figures are percentages and include workers 16 years old and over; (1) Metropolitan Statistical Area - see Appendix A for areas included
Source: Census 2000, Summary File 3

Travel Time Index

Area	1982	1995	2004	2005
Urban Area[1]	1.10	1.24	1.36	1.39
Average[2]	1.11	1.22	1.29	1.30

Note: Travel Time Index - The ratio of travel time in the peak period to the travel time at free-flow conditions. A value of 1.35 indicates a 20-minute free-flow trip takes 27 minutes in the peak. Free-flow speeds (60 mph on freeways and 35 mph on principal arterials) are used as the comparison threshold; (1) Covers the New York-Newark, NY-NJ-CT urban area; (2) average of 85 urban areas
Source: Texas Transportation Institute, The 2007 Urban Mobility Report, September 2007

Living Environment

COST OF LIVING

Cost of Living Index

Composite Index	Groceries	Housing	Utilities	Trans-portation	Health Care	Misc. Goods/ Services
n/a	n/a	n/a	n/a	n/a	n/a	n/a

Note: U.S. = 100; n/a not available
Source: The Council for Community and Economic Research (formerly ACCRA), Cost of Living Index, 2007

Grocery Prices

Area[1]	T-Bone Steak ($/pound)	Frying Chicken ($/pound)	Whole Milk ($/half gal.)	Eggs ($/dozen)	Orange Juice ($/64 oz.)	Coffee ($/11.5 oz.)
City[2]	n/a	n/a	n/a	n/a	n/a	n/a
Avg.	8.93	1.12	2.13	1.52	3.26	3.31
Min.	5.88	0.71	1.33	0.83	2.30	2.20
Max.	12.80	2.07	3.43	3.54	5.79	6.20

Note: (1) Values for the local area are compared with the average, minimum and maximum values for all 331 areas in the Cost of Living Index report; n/a not available; (2) Figures cover the Greenburgh NY urban area; **T-Bone Steak** *(price per pound);* **Frying Chicken** *(price per pound, whole fryer);* **Whole Milk** *(half gallon carton);* **Eggs** *(price per dozen, Grade A, large);* **Orange Juice** *(64 oz. Tropicana or Florida Natural);* **Coffee** *(11.5 oz. can, vacuum-packed, Maxwell House, Hills Bros, or Folgers).*
Source: The Council for Community and Economic Research (formerly ACCRA), Cost of Living Index, 2007

Housing and Utility Costs

Area[1]	New Home Price ($)	Apartment Rent ($/month)	All Electric ($/month)	Part Electric ($/month)	Other Energy ($/month)	Telephone ($/month)
City[2]	n/a	n/a	n/a	n/a	n/a	n/a
Avg.	309,605	782	146.13	78.67	90.16	26.14
Min.	189,877	n/a	82.03	37.41	33.15	17.08
Max.	1,202,800	3,481	271.14	150.60	257.67	37.45

Note: (1) Values for the local area are compared with the average, minimum and maximum values for all 331 areas in the Cost of Living Index report; n/a not available; (2) Figures cover the Greenburgh NY urban area; **New Home Price** *(2,400 sf living area, 8,000 sf lot, in urban area with full utilities);* **Apartment Rent** *(950 sf 2 bedroom/1.5 or 2 bath, unfurnished, excluding all utilities except water);* **All Electric** *(average monthly cost for an all-electric home);* **Part Electric** *(average monthly cost for a part-electric home);* **Other Energy** *(average monthly cost for natural gas, fuel oil, coal, wood, and any other forms of energy except electricity);* **Telephone** *(price includes basic monthly rate for a private residential line plus additional local usage charges incurred by a family of four).*
Source: The Council for Community and Economic Research (formerly ACCRA), Cost of Living Index, 2007

Health Care, Transportation, and Other Costs

Area[1]	Doctor ($/visit)	Dentist ($/visit)	Optometrist ($/visit)	Gasoline ($/gallon)	Beauty Salon ($/visit)	Men's Shirt ($)
City[2]	n/a	n/a	n/a	n/a	n/a	n/a
Avg.	79.48	71.93	79.55	2.64	29.52	25.77
Min.	52.08	44.80	43.95	2.19	15.58	16.19
Max.	148.44	126.27	158.83	3.48	60.62	48.53

Note: (1) Values for the local area are compared with the average, minimum and maximum values for all 331 areas in the Cost of Living Index report; n/a not available; (2) Figures cover the Greenburgh NY urban area; **Doctor** *(general practitioners routine exam of an established patient);* **Dentist** *(adult teeth cleaning and periodic oral examination);* **Optometrist** *(full vision eye exam for established adult patient);* **Gasoline** *(one gallon regular unleaded, national brand, including all taxes, cash price at self-service pump if available);* **Beauty Salon** *(woman's shampoo, trim, and blow-dry);* **Men's Shirt** *(cotton/polyester dress shirt, pinpoint weave, long sleeves).*
Source: The Council for Community and Economic Research (formerly ACCRA), Cost of Living Index, 2007

HOUSING

House Price Index (HPI)

Area	National Ranking[2]	Quarterly Change (%)	One-Year Change (%)	Five-Year Change (%)
MD[1]	169	0.07	0.85	60.20
U.S.[3]	-	0.10	0.84	41.37

Note: The HPI is a weighted repeat sales index. It measures average price changes in repeat sales or refinancings on the same properties. This information is obtained by reviewing repeat mortgage transactions on single-family properties whose mortgages have been purchased or securitized by Fannie Mae or Freddie Mac in January 1975; (1) Metropolitan Division - see Appendix B for areas included; (2) Rankings are based on annual percentage change for all metro areas containing at least 15,000 transactions over the last 10 years and ranges from 1 to 291; (3) figures based on a weighted average of Census Division estimates; all figures are for the period ending December 31, 2007

Source: Office of Federal Housing Enterprise Oversight, House Price Index, February 26, 2008

House Price Valuations

Area	Q1 2000	Q1 2001	Q1 2002	Q1 2003	Q1 2004	Q1 2005	Q1 2006	Q1 2007	Q1 2008
MD[1]	-23.5	-20.3	-10.3	2.4	6.5	10.9	12.4	3.9	0.5

Note: Figures show the percentage of over- or under-valuation of single family homes relative to statistically normal house values (e.g. a value of 23.6 indicates that house values are 23.6% overvalued). Statistically normal house values are based on house prices, interest rates, household incomes, population densities, and any historical premiums or discounts metropolitan areas have exhibited over time; (1) Figures cover the Metropolitan Division - see Appendix B for areas included

Source: Global Insight/National City Corporation, House Prices in America, May 2008

Median Home Prices

Area	2005	2006	2007[r]	Percent Change 2006 to 2007
MD[1]	495.2	539.4	540.3	0.2
U.S. Average	219.0	221.9	217.9	-1.8

Note: Figures are median sales prices of existing single-family homes in thousands of dollars; (r) revised; n/a not available; (1) Metropolitan Division - see Appendix B for areas included

Source: National Association of Realtors, Metropolitan Area Prices, 1st Quarter 2008

Housing: Year Structure Built

Area	1990 -2000	1980 -1989	1970 -1979	1960 -1969	1950 -1959	1940 -1949	Before 1940	Median Year
City	6.7	7.1	10.4	16.4	23.7	11.0	24.7	1956
MSA[1]	4.5	5.4	9.2	15.5	16.2	14.6	34.7	1950
U.S.	17.0	15.8	18.5	13.7	12.7	7.3	15.0	1971

Note: Figures are percentages; (1) Metropolitan Statistical Area - see Appendix A for areas included

Source: Census 2000, Summary File 3

HEALTH

Health Risk Data

Category	Area[1] (%)	U.S. (%)
Adults who have been told they have high blood pressure[3]	24.0	25.5
Adults who have been told they have high blood cholesterol[3]	33.7	35.6
Adults who have been told they have diabetes[2]	7.3	7.5
Adults who have been told they have arthritis[3]	23.0	27.0
Adults who have been told they currently have asthma	7.9	8.5
Adults who are current smokers	15.6	20.1
Adults who are heavy drinkers[4]	4.7	4.9
Adults who are overweight (BMI 25.0 - 29.9)	35.7	36.5
Adults who are obese (BMI 30.0 - 99.8)	20.3	25.1

Note: Data as of 2006 unless otherwise noted; (1) Figures cover the Metropolitan Division - see Appendix B for areas included; (2) Figures do not include pregnancy-related diabetes, pre-diabetes or borderline diabetes; (3) 2005 data; (4) Heavy drinkers are classified as adult men having more than two drinks per day or adult women having more than one drink per day

Source: Centers for Disease Control and Prevention, Behaviorial Risk Factor Surveillance System, SMART: Selected Metropolitan/Micropolitan Area Risk Trends, 2005, 2006

Mortality Rates for the Top 10 Causes of Death in the U.S.

ICD-10[a] Sub-Chapter	ICD-10[a] Code	Age-Adjusted Mortality Rate[1] per 100,000 population	
		County[2]	U.S.
Malignant neoplasms	C00-C97	168.8	186.5
Ischaemic heart diseases	I20-I25	164.3	152.3
Other forms of heart disease	I30-I51	38.8	51.5
Cerebrovascular diseases	I60-I69	32.3	50.0
Chronic lower respiratory diseases	J40-J47	29.1	42.6
Diabetes mellitus	E10-E14	14.4	24.8
Other degenerative diseases of the nervous system	G30-G31	6.7	22.6
Other external causes of accidental injury	W00-X59	11.1	21.4
Influenza and pneumonia	J10-J18	18.4	20.7
Hypertensive diseases	I10-I13	15.0	18.2

Note: (a) ICD-10 = International Classification of Diseases 10th Revision; (1) Mortality rates are a three year average covering 2003-2005; (2) Figures cover Westchester County
Source: Centers for Disease Control and Prevention, National Center for Health Statistics. Compressed Mortality File 1999-2004. CDC WONDER On-line Database, compiled from Compressed Mortality File 1999-2005 Series 20 No. 2K, 2008.

Mortality Rates for Selected Causes of Death

ICD-10[a] Sub-Chapter	ICD-10[a] Code	Age-Adjusted Mortality Rate[1] per 100,000 population	
		County[2]	U.S.
Assault	X85-Y09	3.5	5.9
Human immunodeficiency virus (HIV) disease	B20-B24	3.4	4.5
Intentional self-harm	X60-X84	3.8	10.8
Malnutrition	E40-E46	*0.2	1.0
Obesity and other hyperalimentation	E65-E68	*0.6	1.4
Organic, including symptomatic, mental disorders	F01-F09	8.3	16.8
Transport accidents	V01-V99	7.3	16.1
Viral hepatitis	B15-B19	1.4	1.8

Note: (a) ICD-10 = International Classification of Diseases 10th Revision; (1) Mortality rates are a three year average covering 2003-2005; (2) Figures cover Westchester County; (*) Unreliable data as per CDC
Source: Centers for Disease Control and Prevention, National Center for Health Statistics. Compressed Mortality File 1999-2004. CDC WONDER On-line Database, compiled from Compressed Mortality File 1999-2005 Series 20 No. 2K, 2008.

Distribution of Physicians[1]

Area	Total	Family/ General Practice	Specialties	
			Medical	Surgical
Westchester County (number)	4,199	323	1,878	911
Westchester County (rate per 10,000 pop.)	44.6	3.4	20.0	9.7
U.S. (rate per 10,000 pop.)	17.7	4.6	6.9	4.3

Note: Data as of 2005; (1) Includes all non-federal, patient-care, office-based MDs
Source: Area Resource File (ARF). June 2007. U.S. Department of Health and Human Services, Health Resources and Services Administration, Bureau of Health Professions, Rockville, MD.

Hospitals

There were no hospitals listed within the city limits.
AHA Guide to the Healthcare Field 2008

According to *U.S. News,* the New York-Northern New Jersey-Long Island, NY-NJ-PA metro area is home to 14 of the best hospitals in the U.S.: **Hackensack University Medical Center**; **Hospital for Special Surgery**; **Kessler Institute for Rehabilitation**; **Lenox Hill Hospital**; **Long Island Jewish Medical Center**; **Memorial Sloan-Kettering Cancer Center**; **Montefiore Medical Center**; **Mount Sinai Medical Center**; **New York Eye and Ear Infirmary**; **New York-Presbyterian Univ. Hosp. of Columbia and Cornell**; **NYU Medical Center**; **Robert Wood Johnson University Hospital**; **Saint Francis Hospital**; **University Hospital**. *U.S. News Online, "America's Best Hospitals 2007"*

EDUCATION

Public School District Statistics

District Name	Schls	Pupils	Pupil/ Teacher Ratio	Minority Pupils[1] (%)	Free Lunch Eligible[2] (%)	IEP[3] (%)
Greenburgh Central School District	6	1,826	10.4	87.8	23.9	16.0

Note: Table includes regular local school districts with 2,000 or more students; (1) Percentage of students that are not white, non-Hispanic; (2) Percentage of students that are eligible for the free lunch program; (3) Percentage of students that have an Individualized Education Program.
Source: U.S. Department of Education, National Center for Education Statistics, Common Core of Data, Local Education Agency (School District) Universe Survey: School Year 2005-2006; U.S. Department of Education, National Center for Education Statistics, Common Core of Data, Public Elementary/Secondary School Universe Survey: School Year 2005-2006

Highest Level of Education

Area	Less than H.S.	H.S. Diploma	Some College, No Deg.	Associate Degree	Bachelors Degree	Masters Degree	Profess. School Degree	Doctorate Degree
City	9.1	17.1	14.9	5.5	26.2	17.5	7.0	2.7
MSA[1]	21.5	26.4	16.5	5.6	17.7	8.2	3.0	1.2
U.S.	19.4	28.4	21.2	6.4	15.7	5.9	2.0	1.0

Note: Figures are 2007 estimated percentages and cover persons age 25 and over; (1) Metropolitan Statistical Area - see Appendix B for areas included
Source: Claritas, Inc.

Educational Attainment by Race

Area	High School Graduate (%)					Bachelor's Degree (%)				
	Total	White	Black	Asian	Hisp.[2]	Total	White	Black	Asian	Hisp.[2]
City	91.0	92.3	85.2	95.2	74.6	53.7	55.6	34.6	73.6	32.8
MSA[1]	74.0	81.2	70.8	70.9	53.9	29.2	37.9	16.3	38.1	11.0
U.S.	80.4	83.6	72.3	80.4	52.4	24.4	26.1	14.3	44.1	10.4

Note: Figures shown cover persons 25 years old and over; (1) Metropolitan Statistical Area - see Appendix A for areas included; (2) people of Hispanic origin can be of any race
Source: Census 2000, Summary File 3

School Enrollment by Type

Area	Grades KG to 8				Grades 9 to 12			
	Public		Private		Public		Private	
	Enrollment	%	Enrollment	%	Enrollment	%	Enrollment	%
City	9,644	88.0	1,320	12.0	3,612	84.7	653	15.3
MSA[1]	965,235	80.8	229,009	19.2	450,178	81.9	99,330	18.1
U.S.	33,526,011	88.7	4,285,121	11.3	14,848,628	90.6	1,532,323	9.4

Note: Figures shown cover persons 3 years old and over; (1) Metropolitan Statistical Area - see Appendix A for areas included
Source: Census 2000, Summary File 3

School Enrollment by Race

Area	Grades KG to 8 (%)				Grades 9 to 12 (%)			
	White	Black	Asian	Hisp.[1]	White	Black	Asian	Hisp.[1]
City	67.1	15.0	10.0	9.7	63.6	17.4	9.2	11.9
MSA[2]	39.1	30.1	8.0	32.0	37.2	31.2	9.0	31.3
U.S.	68.5	15.5	3.3	16.8	68.8	15.5	3.8	15.7

Note: Figures shown cover persons 3 years old and over; (1) people of Hispanic origin can be of any race; (2) Metropolitan Statistical Area - see Appendix A for areas included
Source: Census 2000, Summary File 3

Average Salaries of Public School Classroom Teachers

District	2005-06		2006-07		Percent Change 2005-06 to 2006-07
	Dollars	Rank[1]	Dollars	Rank[1]	
New York	57,354	6	58,537	6	2.06
U.S. Average	49,026	-	50,816	-	3.65

Note: (1) State rank ranges from 1 to 51.
Source: National Education Association, Rankings & Estimates: Rankings of the States 2006 and Estimates of School Statistics 2007, December 2007

Higher Education

Four-Year Colleges			Two-Year Colleges			Medical Schools[1]	Law Schools[2]	Voc/ Tech[3]
Public	Private Non-profit	Private For-profit	Public	Private Non-profit	Private For-profit			
0	0	0	0	0	0	0	0	0

Note: Figures cover institutions located within the city limits; (1) includes schools accredited by the Liaison Committee on Medical Education and the American Osteopathic Association; (2) includes American Bar Association-accredited law schools; (3) includes all schools with programs that are less than 2 years.
Source: National Center for Education Statistics, The Integrated Postsecondary Education System (IPEDS) Peer Analysis System, 2007; www.usnews.com, Law and Medical School Directories, 2009

PRESIDENTIAL ELECTION

2004 Presidential Election Results

Area	Bush	Kerry	Nader	Other
Westchester County	40.3	58.1	1.4	0.2
U.S.	50.7	48.3	0.4	0.6

Note: Results are percentages and may not add to 100% due to rounding
Source: Dave Leip's Atlas of U.S. Presidential Elections, www.uselectionatlas.org

EMPLOYERS

Major Employers

Company Name	Industry	Type of Site
AIG Inc	Detective and armored car services	Headquarters
American Express	Business services, nec	Headquarters
American International Group	Fire, marine, and casualty insurance	Headquarters
Brookfield Asset MGT LLC	Management services	Single
Citicorp	Business services, nec	Headquarters
Cornell University Medical Col	Colleges and universities	Branch
Deloitte Consulting LLP	Management consulting services	Headquarters
Department Ecnmic Scial Affirs	International affairs	Branch
Dr Paul Appelbaum	Offices and clinics of medical doctors	Branch
Ernst & Young LLP	Accounting, auditing, and bookkeeping	Headquarters
Housing Budget Office	Housing programs	Branch
M T A Long Island Rail Road	Local and suburban transit	Headquarters
MDC Partners Inc	Holding companies, nec	Single
MW Custom Papers LLC	Pulp mills	Single
McGraw-Hill Companies Inc	Credit reporting services	Branch
Merrill Lynch	Security brokers and dealers	Headquarters
Mount Sinai Hospital	General medical and surgical hospitals	Headquarters
NBC	Medical laboratories	Branch
NEC USA Inc	Telephone and telegraph apparatus	Single
New York Life	Life insurance	Single
New York and Presbyterian Hosp	General medical and surgical hospitals	Headquarters
Paramount Communications	Holding companies, nec	Single
Time Magazine	Periodicals	Headquarters
United Nations	International affairs	Headquarters
Wellchoice Inc	Accident and health insurance	Headquarters

Note: Companies shown are located within the New York metropolitan area; nec = not elsewhere classified.
Source: www.zapdata.com, May 2008

PUBLIC SAFETY

Crime Rate

Area	All Crimes	Violent Crimes				Property Crimes		
		Murder	Forcible Rape	Robbery	Aggrav. Assault	Burglary	Larceny -Theft	Motor Vehicle Theft
City	1,882.2	0.0	0.0	43.8	39.2	184.5	1,503.9	110.7
Metro[1]	2,422.6	5.9	12.0	250.7	282.9	289.2	1,382.2	199.7
U.S.	3,808.1	5.7	30.9	149.4	287.5	729.4	2,206.8	398.4

Note: Figures are crimes per 100,000 population; (1) Metropolitan Division - see Appendix B for areas included
Source: FBI Uniform Crime Reports, 2006

Hate Crimes

Area	Number of Quarters Reported	Bias Motivation				
		Race	Religion	Sexual Orientation	Ethnicity	Disability
City	n/a	n/a	n/a	n/a	n/a	n/a

Note: n/a not available.
Source: Federal Bureau of Investigation, Hate Crime Statistics 2006

RECREATION

Culture

Dance[1]	Theatre[1]	Instrumental Music[1]	Vocal Music[1]	Series/ Festivals	Museums	Zoos and Aquariums[2]
0	0	0	0	0	0	0

Note: (1) Number of professional perfoming groups; (2) AZA-accredited
Source: The Grey House Performing Arts Directory, 2007; Official Museum Directory, 2008; Association of Zoos & Aquariums, AZA Member Zoos & Aquariums, June 2008

Professional Sports Teams

Team Name	League
New York Mets	Major League Baseball (MLB)
New York Yankees	Major League Baseball (MLB)
New York Red Bulls	Major League Soccer (MLS)
New Jersey Nets	National Basketball Association (NBA)
New York Knicks	National Basketball Association (NBA)
New York Giants	National Football League (NFL)
New York Jets	National Football League (NFL)
New Jersey Devils	National Hockey League (NHL)
New York Islanders	National Hockey League (NHL)
New York Rangers	National Hockey League (NHL)

Note: Includes teams located in the New York-Northern New Jersey metro area.
Source: Original research

MEDIA

Newspapers

Name	News Focus	Frequency	Circulation
No newspapers have an office in the city			

Note: Includes newspapers with offices located in the city
Source: MediaContactsPro, March 2008

Television Stations

Name	Ch.	Network(s)	Type	Ownership
WCBS	2	CBS	Commercial	CBS
WNBC	4	NBC	Commercial	General Electric Corporation
WNYW	5	Fox	Commercial	Fox Television Stations Inc.
WABC	7	ABC	Commercial	ABC Inc.
WWOR	9	UPN	Commercial	Fox Television Stations Inc.
WPIX	11	WBN	Commercial	Tribune Broadcasting Company
WNET	13	PBS	Public	Educational Broadcasting Corporation
WLIW	21	PBS	Public	Long Island Educational TV Council Inc.
WNYE	25	PBS	Public	New York City Board of Education
WPXN	31	Pax	Commercial	Paxson Communications Corporation
WXTV	41	Univision	Commercial	Univision Holding
WNJU	47	Telemundo	Commercial	Telemundo Group Inc.
WTBY	54	n/a	Commercial	Trinity Broadcasting Network
WLNY	55	n/a	Commercial	Michael C. Pascucci
WRNN	62	n/a	Commercial	WRNN-TV Associates L.P.
WMBC	63	n/a	Commercial	Mountain Broadcasting Corporation
WHSI	67	n/a	Commercial	USA Broadcasting Group
WHSE	68	n/a	Commercial	USA Broadcasting Group

Note: Stations included cover the New York DMA (Designated Market Area); n/a not available
BurrellesLuce, MediaContacts Online, January 2007

Major AM Radio Stations

Call Letters	Freq. (kHz)	Station Type	Target Audience	Station Format	Music Format
WMCA	570	n/a	General/Religious	Music/News/Talk	n/a
WFAN	660	n/a	General	News/Sports/Talk	n/a
WOR	710	n/a	General	Music/News	Reggae
WABC	770	n/a	General	n/a	n/a
WNYC	820	Public	General	Music/Talk	Blues
WCBS	880	Commercial	General	Music/News/Sports	Reggae
WGHQ	920	n/a	General	Music	n/a
WWDJ	970	n/a	General/Religious	Music/Talk	n/a
WINS	1010	n/a	General	News	n/a
WHLI	1100	Commercial	General	Music	Adult Standards
WBBR	1130	n/a	General/Men	Music/News	Reggae
WVNJ	1160	n/a	General	n/a	n/a
WOBM	1160	n/a	General	Music	n/a
WLIB	1190	n/a	General	News/Talk	n/a
WGNY	1220	n/a	General	News/Talk	n/a
WMTR	1250	Commercial	General	Music	Adult Standards
WADO	1280	Commercial	General/Hispanic	News/Sports/Talk	n/a
WWRV	1330	n/a	General/Hisp/Rel	Music/News/Talk	n/a
WELV	1370	n/a	General	Music	n/a
WEOK	1390	Commercial	General/Hispanic	Music/Sports	Latin
WLNA	1420	n/a	General	Music/News/Sports/Talk	n/a
WNSW	1430	n/a	Ethnic/General	Music/News/Talk	n/a
WZRC	1480	n/a	Asian	Talk	n/a
WQEW	1560	n/a	Child/Gen/Yng Adlt	Educational	n/a
WLIM	1580	Commercial	Ethnic/General	Music/News	World Music
WWRL	1600	n/a	General	Music/Talk	Reggae
WWRU	1660	n/a	Asian/General/Hispanic	News/Talk	n/a

Note: Stations included cover the New York DMA (Designated Market Area); n/a not available
Source: BurrellesLuce, MediaContacts Online, January 2007

Major FM Radio Stations

Call Letters	Freq. (mHz)	Station Type	Target Audience	Station Format	Music Format
WFSO	88.3	n/a	Religious	Educational/Music/News	n/a
WFDU	89.1	College	General	Music	n/a
WFUV	90.7	College	General	Music/News/Sports	Folk
WPAT	93.1	Commercial	General/Hispanic	News/Talk	n/a
WRKI	95.1	n/a	General	Music/News/Talk	n/a
WQHT	97.1	n/a	General	Music/News/Talk	n/a
WSKQ	97.9	Commercial	General/Hispanic	Music/News/Talk	Latin
WRKS	98.7	n/a	General/Women	News/Talk	Rhythm & Blues
WBAI	99.5	Non-Comm	General	Music/Talk	Reggae
WHUD	100.7	n/a	General	Music/News/Talk	n/a
WPDH	101.5	Commercial	General	Music	Classic Rock
WKTU	103.5	n/a	General/Women	Music/News/Talk	Urban Contemp.
WAXQ	104.3	n/a	General	Music/Talk	n/a
WSPK	104.7	n/a	General	Music/News/Talk	n/a
WWPR	105.1	Commercial	General	Music	Rhythm & Blues
WBLI	106.1	Commercial	General	Music/Talk	Top 40
WLTW	106.7	n/a	General	Music	n/a
WBLS	107.5	n/a	Black/General	Music	n/a
WEBE	107.9	n/a	General	Music/News	n/a

Note: Stations included cover the New York DMA (Designated Market Area); n/a not available
BurrellesLuce, MediaContacts Online, January 2007

CLIMATE

Average and Extreme Temperatures

Temperature	Jan	Feb	Mar	Apr	May	Jun	Jul	Aug	Sep	Oct	Nov	Dec	Yr.
Extreme High (°F)	68	75	85	96	97	101	104	99	99	88	81	72	104
Average High (°F)	38	41	50	61	72	80	85	84	76	65	54	43	62
Average Temp. (°F)	32	34	43	53	63	72	77	76	68	58	48	37	55
Average Low (°F)	26	27	35	44	54	63	68	67	60	49	41	31	47
Extreme Low (°F)	-2	-2	8	21	36	46	53	50	40	29	17	-1	-2

Note: Figures cover the years 1962-1992
Source: National Climatic Data Center, International Station Meteorological Climate Summary, 9/96

Average Precipitation/Snowfall/Humidity

Precip./Humidity	Jan	Feb	Mar	Apr	May	Jun	Jul	Aug	Sep	Oct	Nov	Dec	Yr.
Avg. Precip. (in.)	3.5	3.1	4.0	3.9	4.5	3.8	4.5	4.1	4.1	3.3	4.5	3.8	47.0
Avg. Snowfall (in.)	7	8	4	Tr	Tr	0	0	0	0	Tr	Tr	3	23
Avg. Rel. Hum. 7am (%)	67	67	66	64	72	74	74	76	78	75	72	69	71
Avg. Rel. Hum. 4pm (%)	55	53	50	45	52	55	53	54	56	55	57	58	53

Note: Figures cover the years 1962-1992; Tr = Trace amounts (<0.05 in. of rain; <0.5 in. of snow)
Source: National Climatic Data Center, International Station Meteorological Climate Summary, 9/96

Weather Conditions

Temperature			Daytime Sky			Precipitation		
32°F & below	45°F & below	90°F & above	Clear	Partly cloudy	Cloudy	0.01 inch or more precip.	0.1 inch or more snow/ice	Thunder-storms
75	170	18	85	166	114	120	11	20

Note: Figures are average number of days per year and cover the years 1962-1992
Source: National Climatic Data Center, International Station Meteorological Climate Summary, 9/96

HAZARDOUS WASTE

Superfund Sites

Greenburgh has no sites on the EPA's Superfund Final National Priorities List.
U.S. Environmental Protection Agency, Final National Priorities List, June 23, 2008

AIR & WATER QUALITY

Air Quality Index

Area	Percent of Days when Air Quality was...[2]				AQI Statistics	
	Good	Moderate	Unhealthy for Sensitive Groups	Unhealthy	Maximum	Median
MSA[1]	52.1	40.3	6.6	1.1	164	49

Note: The Air Quality Index (AQI) is an index for reporting daily air quality. EPA calculates the AQI for five major air pollutants regulated by the Clean Air Act: ground-level ozone, particle pollution (also known as particulate matter), carbon monoxide, sulfur dioxide, and nitrogen dioxide. The AQI runs from 0 to 500. The higher the AQI value, the greater the level of air pollution and the greater the health concern. There are six AQI categories: "Good" The AQI is between 0 and 50. Air quality is considered satisfactory; "Moderate" The AQI is between 51 and 100. Air quality is acceptable; "Unhealthy for Sensitive Groups" When AQI values are between 101 and 150, members of sensitive groups may experience health effects; "Unhealthy" When AQI values are between 151 and 200 everyone may begin to experience health effects; "Very Unhealthy" AQI values between 201 and 300 trigger a health alert; "Hazardous" AQI values over 300 trigger health warnings of emergency conditions; (1) Metropolitan Statistical Area - see Appendix A for areas included; (2) Based on 365 days with AQI data in 2007.
Source: U.S. Environmental Protection Agency, Air Quality Index Report, 2007

Air Quality Index Pollutants

Area	Percent of Days when AQI Pollutant was...[2]					
	Carbon Monoxide	Nitrogen Dioxide	Ozone	Sulfur Dioxide	Particulate Matter 2.5	Particulate Matter 10
MSA[1]	0.0	0.0	40.0	0.0	60.0	0.0

Note: The Air Quality Index (AQI) is an index for reporting daily air quality. EPA calculates the AQI for five major air pollutants regulated by the Clean Air Act: ground-level ozone, particle pollution (also known as particulate matter), carbon monoxide, sulfur dioxide, and nitrogen dioxide. The AQI runs from 0 to 500. The higher the AQI value, the greater the level of air pollution and the greater the health concern; (1) Metropolitan Statistical Area - see Appendix A for areas included; (2) Based on 365 days with AQI data in 2007.
Source: U.S. Environmental Protection Agency, Air Quality Index Report, 2007

Air Quality Index Trends

Area	Trend Sites (20)								All Sites (135)
	1999	2000	2001	2002	2003	2004	2005	2006	2006
MSA[1]	22	19	19	27	11	6	15	11	12

Note: An AQI value greater than 100 indicates that air quality would have been in the unhealthful range on that day. Data from exceptional events are not included. These counts are presented in two ways. First, the counts are based on sites having an adequate record of monitoring data during the trend period (trend sites). These counts represent the relative change in the number of days with AQI values greater than 100. In the last column, the counts are based on all sites with data in the most recent year (because it is possible for a site to have data in the most recent year but not enough data to be a trend site); (1) Metropolitan Statistical Area - see Appendix A for areas included.
Source: U.S. Environmental Protection Agency, Office of Air and Radiation, Air Trends, Factbook and Related Information, Air Pollution Trends in Selected Metropolitan Areas 2006

Maximum Air Pollutant Concentrations

	Particulate Matter 10 (ug/m^3)	Particulate Matter 2.5 (ug/m^3)	Ozone (ppm)	Carbon Monoxide (ppm)	Sulfur Dioxide (ppm)	Nitrogen Dioxide (ppm)	Lead (ug/m^3)
MSA[1] Level	n/a	41	0.114	3	0.034	0.034	0.02
NAAQS[2]	150	35	0.125	9	0.140	0.053	1.50
Met NAAQS[2]	Yes	No	Yes	Yes	Yes	Yes	Yes

Note: Data from exceptional events are not included; (1) Metropolitan Statistical Area - see Appendix A for areas included; (2) National Ambient Air Quality Standards; n/a not available
Concentrations: Particulate Matter 10 (coarse particulate) - highest second maximum 24-hour concentration; Particulate Matter 2.5 (fine particulate) - highest 98th percentile 24-hour concentration; Ozone - highest second daily maximum 1-hour concentration; Carbon Monoxide - highest second maximum non-overlapping 8-hour concentration; Sulfur Dioxide - highest second maximum 24-hour concentration; Nitrogen Dioxide - highest arithmetic mean concentration; Lead - highest quarterly maximum concentration
Units: ppm = parts per million; ug/m^3 = micrograms per cubic meter
Source: U.S. Environmental Protection Agency, MSA Factbook 2006, Air Quality Statistics by City

Drinking Water

Water System Name	Pop. Served	Primary Water Source Type	Violations[1]	
			Health Based	Monitoring/ Reporting
Greenburgh Consolidated WD #1	38,489	Purchased Surface	0	1

Note: (1) Based on violation data from January 1, 2007 to December 31, 2007 (includes unresolved violations from earlier years)

Source: U.S. Environmental Protection Agency, Office of Ground Water and Drinking Water, Safe Drinking Water Information System (based on data extracted April 15, 2008)

Apex, North Carolina

Background

Apex is located in Wake County, 15 miles southwest of Raleigh. Other neighboring cities include Cary to the northeast and Holly Springs to the south.

Apex was incorporated in 1873. Its name resulted from it being the highest point on the Chatham Railroad between Richmond, VA and Jacksonville, FL. The city grew slowly through its first few decades, partially due to several devastating fires, including a 1912 blaze that destroyed most of the downtown business district. The town center was rebuilt and still stands today. After a period of slowed growth during the Depression, the 1950s saw a population boom. A more recent growth explosion during the 1990s resulted, in large part, to the city's proximity to Research Triangle Park (RTP) — the largest science and technology research park in the world.

Today, Apex is one of the most intact railroad towns in the state. At the heart of the downtown region stands the Apex Union Depot which was originally a passenger station for the Seaboard Air Line Railroad until becoming the home of the Apex Community Library. Apex prides itself in maintaining small town character while experiencing rapid growth.

Since 1990, with a population of 5,000, the city has more than quadrupled. Demands on the town's infrastructure and housing market have been tremendous and nearly constant construction is taking place to support the growth. RTP, located between Duke University in Durham, North Carolina State University in Raleigh, and the University of North Carolina at Chapel Hill, is often compared to Silicon Valley in California. It is considered one of the most prominent high-tech research and development centers in the world, and has played an enormous part in Apex's growth. IBM and GlaxoSmithKline, the National Institute of Environmental Health Services and the North Carolina Biotechnology Center are some of its more than 100 tenants. RTP employs more than 37,000 individuals.

The restored downtown area of Apex is on the National Register of Historic Places and offers antique and specialty gift shops, an old-fashioned soda shop, an ice cream parlor, and fine dining. Additionally, the city boasts the New Hope Valley Railway, which offers rides on restored trains, and the North Carolina Railway Museum. The annual PeakFest is held the first Saturday in May with hundreds of crafters, fine arts, food, and entertainment.

Still under construction is the expansion of the Beaver Creek Crossing shopping complex, with new restaurants and stores. A new multiplex movie theatre opened on the site in May 2006.

Apex has a temperate southern climate with hot summers and cold winters. Median summer temperatures average 75 degrees, while winter averages can be as low as 30 degrees during December and January. The city averages 4 inches of rainfall per month from April to October and 1.5 inches of snowfall per month from December to March.

Rankings

General Rankings

- Raleigh* was ranked #63 out of 375 metro areas in *Cities Ranked & Rated*. Criteria: cost of living; climate; crime; transportation; economy and jobs; education; arts and culture; health and healthcare; leisure; quality of life. *Cities Ranked & Rated, 2nd Edition, 2007*

- Raleigh* was ranked #57 out of 379 metro areas in *Places Rated Almanac*. Criteria: health care; education; recreation; transportation; ambience; climate; crime; housing costs; jobs. *Places Rated Almanac, 7th Edition, 2007*

- The Raleigh* metro area was selected one of America's "Best Cities to Live, Work and Play" by *Kiplinger Personal Finance.* Criteria: population growth; percentage of workforce in the creative class (scientists, engineers, educators, writers, artists, entertainers, etc.); job quality; income growth; cost of living. *Kiplinger Personal Finance, "Best Cities to Live, Work and Play," July 2008*

- *Expansion Management* rated 362 metro areas to find out which offer the best middle class lifestyle for manufacturing and service companies. The Raleigh* metro area was selected as a "5-Star Quality of Life Metro" (a distinction the magazine awards to the top 20 percent of metro areas studied). The annual "Quality of Life Quotient" measures dozens of indicators across nine major categories and compares them among 362 metropolitan statistical areas in the United States. The categories are: affordable housing; good public schools; low crime levels; adult education level; standard of living; traffic and commuting; continuing education opportunities; commercial air access; labor market. *Expansion Management, June 2007*

- Apex was selected as one of the "2007 Best Places to Live" by *Money* magazine. The city ranked #14 out of 100. Methodology: Places on the list had to have populations above 7,500 and under 50,000. Retirement-oriented communities, places where income is less than 90% or more than 180% of the state median and towns that were more than 95% white were screened out. Towns with low education scores, high crime rates, declines or sharp increases in population, projected job losses or lack of access to airports or teaching hospitals were eliminated. The remaining places were ranked based on job, income and cost-of-living data; housing affordability; school quality; arts and leisure opportunities; ease of living; health-care access; and racial diversity. Finally, the sense of community, vibrancy of town center, natural surroundings, amenities, real estate and congestion were assessed. *CNNMoney.com, "Best Places to Live 2007"*

Business/Finance Rankings

- The nation's 100 largest metro areas were analysed in terms of the percentage of households entering some stage of foreclosure in 2007. The Raleigh* metro area ranked #53 out of 100 (#1 = highest foreclosure rate). *RealtyTrac, "Year-End 2007 Metropolitan Foreclosure Report"*

- The Raleigh* metro area was identified as one of the "10 Best Cities for Jobs in 2008" by *Forbes*. The metro area ranked #9. Criteria: state unemployment rate; job growth; income growth; median household income; cost of living. *Forbes.com, "Best Cities for Jobs in 2008," January 10, 2008*

- The Raleigh* metro area was selected one of America's "Top 50 Business Opportunity Metros" by *Expansion Management* in their 5th annual Mayor's Challenge ranking of metro areas that have achieved solid ratings across the board in numerous *EM* studies during the past 12 months. The area ranked #3. Criteria: public schools; quality of life; college educated workers; logistics infrastructure; healthcare costs; taxes and government spending; reputation among site consultants. *Expansion Management, August 2007*

- The Raleigh* metro area was selected as one of "America's Most Wired Cities" by *Forbes*. The metro area was ranked #3 out of 30. Criteria: percentage of Internet users with high-speed access; the range of service providers within a city; availability of public wireless hot spots. *Forbes, "America's Most Wired Cities," January 10, 2008*

- Raleigh* was selected as one of the best places to start and grow a company by *Entrepreneur* and the National Policy Research Council. The Raleigh* metro area ranked #3 out of 50 large metro areas. Criteria: business formation and growth (firms started four to 14 years ago that still employ at least 5 people and experienced rapid growth over the last four years). *Entrepreneur/National Policy Research Council, "Hot Cities for Entrepreneurs," September 2006*

- The Raleigh* metro area was selected as one of "America's 50 Hottest Cities" for business relocations and expansions. Criteria: industry's most prominent site selection consultants were asked to list their top city choices for relocating and expanding manufacturing companies, taking into consideration such factors as the business climate, work force quality, operating costs, incentive programs, and the ease of working with local political and economic development officials. *Expansion Management, January-February 2007*

- Raleigh* was cited as one of America's top mid-size metros (population 200,000 to 1 million) for new and expanded facility projects in 2007. The area appeared in the top 10 with 25 projects. *Site Selection, "Top Metropolitan Area Awards," March 2008*

- The Raleigh* metro area was selected as one of the "Top 20 Real Estate Markets" for expanding or relocating companies. The area ranked #16. Criteria: low rental costs; low purchase prices; high vacancy rates of office and warehouse space. *Expansion Management, October 2007*

- Intel, in partnership with Sperling's BestPlaces, ranked the 80 "Best Cities for Teleworking" in America. The Raleigh* metro area ranked #2 among mid-sized metro areas. The study identifies cities that hold the greatest potential for teleworking based on a host of factors including typical commuting times, fuel prices, availability of broadband Internet access and percentage of the population in telework friendly jobs. The study also factored in extreme climate and natural hazards. *Intel, "Best Cities for Teleworking," March 30, 2006*

- The Raleigh* metro area appeared on the Milken Institute "2007 Best Performing Cities" index. Rank: #10 out of 200 large metro areas. Criteria: job growth; wage and salary growth; high-tech output growth. *Milken Institute, "2007 Best Performing Cities"*

- The Raleigh* metro area was selected as one of the hottest cities for entrepreneurs in America by *Inc. Magazine.* Criteria: job-growth data for 393 metro was analyzed for current-year employment growth, average annual employment growth over past three years, and employment growth by industry sector. The Raleigh* metro area ranked #7 among large metro areas and #50 overall. *Inc. Magazine, May 2007*

- The Raleigh* metro area was selected as one of "The Top 20 Boom Towns in America." *Business 2.0* magazine and econometric research firm Global Insight compared 319 metropolitan areas in the U.S. and ranked the 61 with populations over 1 million. Criteria: a weighted formula that includes forecast growth rates in sectors that contain the economy's 10 most skilled occupational clusters; the prevalence of college degrees in the local workforce; median salary. The area ranked #1 among large metro areas. *Business 2.0 Magazine, March 2004*

- Raleigh* was identified as one of the 100 "Most Unwired Cities" in the U.S. The area ranked #8 out of the 100 largest metro areas in the U.S. Criteria: number of public and commercial wireless access points (hotspots); airports with wireless Internet access; broadband availability; local wireless networks; and wireless email devices. *Intel, "Most Unwired Cities Survey," June 7, 2005*

- Raleigh* was ranked #31 out of 125 regions worldwide in terms of its "Knowledge Competitiveness Index." The index attempts to measure the knowledge-based development taking place throughout the world and is based on 19 measures of economic performance that indicate a region's ability to translate its knowledge capacity into economic value. *Robert Huggins Associates, World Knowledge Competitiveness Index 2005*

- *Forbes* ranked the 200 most populous metro areas in the U.S. in terms of the "Best Places for Business and Careers." The Raleigh* metro area was ranked #1. Criteria: business costs (labor, energy, tax and office space expenses); living costs (housing, transportation, food and other household expenditures); education levels of the work force; job growth; income growth; migration trends; crime rates; and culture/leisure. *Forbes, "Best Places for Business and Careers," March 19, 2008*

- *Fortune* ranked the 100 largest metro areas in the U.S. in terms of projected median home price change in 2007. The Raleigh* metro area ranked #32. *Fortune.com, "Hot Spots, Cold Spots"*

Health/Environment Rankings

- 100 of the largest metro areas in the U.S. were analyzed in terms of their current drought severity. The Raleigh* metro area ranked #17 (#1 = driest). The rankings were based on statistics such as long-term precipitation trends and patterns and the Palmer drought indices. *Sperling's BestPlaces, www.BestPlaces.net, "America's Drought-Riskiest Cities," November 2007*

- Scarborough Research, a leading market research firm, identified the top local markets for diabetes medication purchasers. The Raleigh* DMA (Designated Market Area) ranked in the top 13 with 10% of consumers reporting that they purchased medication for diabetes within the past 12 months. *Scarborough Research, March 19, 2007*

- The Raleigh* metro area appeared in *Country Home's* "2008 Best Green Places" report. The area ranked #235 out of 379. Criteria: official energy policies; green power; green buildings; availability of fresh, locally grown food. *Country Home, "2008 Best Green Places"*

- Wyeth Consumer Healthcare, in partnership with Sperling's BestPlaces, ranked the nation's 50 most populous metro areas in terms of five key health factors. The Raleigh* metro area ranked #17. Criteria: physical activity; health status; nutrition; lifestyle pursuits; and mental wellness. *Wyeth Consumer Healthcare, "Centrum Healthiest Cities Study," April 19, 2005*

- Raleigh* was identified as a "2008 Asthma Capital." The area ranked #42 out of the nation's 100 largest metropolitan areas. Twelve factors were used to identify the most challenging places to live for people with asthma: estimated prevalence; self-reported prevalence; crude death rate for asthma; annual pollen score; annual air quality; public smoking laws; number of board-certified asthma specialists; school inhaler access laws; rescue medication use; controller medication use; uninsured rate; poverty rate. *Asthma and Allergy Foundation of America, "2008 Asthma Capitals"*

- Raleigh* was identified as a "Spring Allergy Capital." The area ranked #48 out of 100. Three groups of factors were used to identify the most severe cities for people with allergies during the spring season: annual pollen levels; medicine utilization; access to board-certified allergists. *Asthma and Allergy Foundation of America, "2007 Spring Allergy Capital Rankings"*

- Raleigh* was identified as a "Fall Allergy Capital." The area ranked #56 out of 100. Three groups of factors were used to identify the most severe cities for people with allergies during the fall season: annual pollen levels; medicine utilization; access to board-certified allergists. *Asthma and Allergy Foundation of America, "2007 Fall Allergy Capital Rankings"*

- Ortho-McNeil Neurologics, in partnership with Sperling's BestPlaces, analyzed 110 metro areas and identified those U.S. cities with the highest prevalence of factors that are most commonly associated with migraine headaches. The Raleigh* metro area ranked #37. Criteria: number of migraine-related drug prescriptions per capita; lifestyle factors that can contribute to migraines; environmental factors that can trigger migraines; and consumption of migraine-triggering foods. *Ortho-McNeil Neurologics, "America's Migraine Hot Spots," March 14, 2006*

- Sperling's BestPlaces ranked 331 metro areas and identified the most and least stressful U.S. cities. The Raleigh* metro area ranked #91 out of the 100 largest metro areas (#1 = most stressful). Criteria: divorce rate; unemployment rate; violent and property crime; suicide rate; commute time; mental health; alcohol consumption; cloudy days. *Sperling's BestPlaces, www.BestPlaces.net, "America's Most (and Least) Stressful Cities," January 9, 2004*

- An analysis of the "Best & Worst Cities for Sleep" was conducted by Sperling's BestPlaces. The study ranked America's 50 most populated metro areas. The Raleigh* metro area ranked #3 (#1 = best city for sleep). Criteria: number of days residents didn't get enough rest or sleep during the past month; average length of daily commute; divorce rate; unemployment rate. *Sperling's BestPlaces, www.BestPlaces.net, "Best & Worst Cities for Sleep," 2006*

Women/Minorities Rankings

- Raleigh* was ranked #27 out of 100 metro areas in *SELF Magazine's* ranking of "America's Best Places for Women." A panel of experts came up with more than 50 criteria including death and disease rates, environmental indicators, community resources, and lifestyle habits. *SELF Magazine, "America's Best Places for Women 2007," December 2007*

- Raleigh* appeared on a list of the top 10 metro areas with the highest concentration of Hispanic same-sex couples among all Hispanic households. The area ranked #8. *Urban Institute Press, The Gay and Lesbian Atlas, May 2004*

- Raleigh* appeared on *Black Enterprise's* list of the "Ten Best Cities for African Americans." The top picks were culled from more than 2,000 interactive surveys completed on www.blackenterprise.com and by editorial staff evaluation. The editors weighed the following criteria as it pertained to African Americans in each city: median household income; percentage of households earning more than $100,000; percentage of businesses owned; percentage of college graduates; unemployment rates; home loan rejections; and homeownership rates. *Black Enterprise, May 2007*

Seniors/Retirement Rankings

- Sperling's BestPlaces in partnership with Bankers Life & Casualty Company designed a survey to identify the top 50 metro areas in the U.S. that offer the best overall qualities for senior living. The Raleigh* metro area ranked #26. The following criteria were statistically weighted to reflect the needs of the senior population: health; disease; economics; social; environment; spiritual; transportation; housing; and crime. *Bankers Life & Casualty Company, "Best Cities for Seniors 2005"*

- A.G. Edwards ranked America's 500 top-performing communities based on their residents' personal savings and investing behavior. The Raleigh* metro area ranked #98 with an index score of 106.67 (national average = 100.00). A dozen statistical factors were measured including: participation in retirement savings plans; personal debt levels; and home ownership. *A.G. Edwards, "2007 Nest Egg Index", September 12, 2007*

Children/Family Rankings

- The Raleigh* metro area was selected as one of the "Best Cities for Relocating Families" by Worldwide ERC and Primacy Relocation. The 2007 study placed a special emphasis on the housing market, which has significantly impacted the relocation industry and an employer's ability to transfer employees. The variables which weigh heavily in this category include home price, home affordability index, appreciation rates, and property tax. Other criteria include cost of living, crime rates, education, climate, focus on diversity, physicians per capita, recreation and leisure, arts and culture, air quality, watershed quality, sales tax, unemployment rate, job growth, high school and higher education index, school expenditures per student, students in public school, SAT/ACT percentile, and population growth. *Worldwide ERC and Primacy Relocation, "2007 Best Cities for Relocating Families"*

Safety Rankings

- The National Insurance Crime Bureau ranked 361 metro areas in the U.S. in terms of per capita rates of vehicle theft. The Raleigh* metro area ranked #173 (#1 = highest rate). Criteria: number of vehicle theft offenses per 100,000 inhabitants. *National Insurance Crime Bureau, "NICB Vehicle Theft Study," April 22, 2008*
- Farmers Insurance Group of Companies, in partnership with Sperling's BestPlaces, ranked 379 metro areas and identified the "Most Secure U.S. Place to Live." The Raleigh* metro area ranked #21 out of 114 in the large metro area category (500,000 or more residents). Criteria: crime rates; extreme weather; risk of natural disasters; environmental hazards; terrorism threats; air quality; life expectancy; job loss numbers. *Farmers Insurance Group, "Most Secure U.S. Places to Live 2007"*
- Raleigh* was identified as one of the most dangerous large metro areas for pedestrians in the U.S. The area ranked #23 out of the nations 50 largest metro areas. Criteria: average yearly pedestrian fatalities per capita (for the years 2002 and 2003) adjusted for the number of walkers. *Surface Transportation Policy Project, "Mean Streets 2004"*

Sports/Recreation Rankings

- The Raleigh* metro area appeared on the *Sporting News* list of the "Best Sports Cities 2007". The area ranked #38 out of 150 cities in the U.S. *Sporting News* takes a 12-month snapshot, roughly July to July, of each city's sports, putting a heavy premium on regular-season won-lost records (from the most recently completed season). Other criteria include: playoff berths, bowl appearances and tournament bids; championships; applicable power ratings; quality of competition; overall fan fervor as measured in part by attendance as percentage of venue capacity; abundance of teams (rewarding quality over quantity); stadium and arena quality; ticket availability and prices; franchise ownership; and marquee appeal of athletes. *SportingNews.com, "Best Sports Cities 2007," August 1, 2007*
- The Raleigh* metro area was selected by *Cranium* as one of the "Top 50 Fun Cities" in America. The area ranked #6. Criteria includes: number of sports teams, restaurants, and dance performances; number of toy stores; city budget spent on recreation. *Cranium, November 4, 2003*
- *Golf Digest* ranked 330 metro areas in the U.S. in terms of golf. The Raleigh* metro area was ranked #200. Criteria: access to golf; weather; value of golf; and quality of golf. *Golf Digest, "Metro Golf Rankings," August 2005*

Dating/Romance Rankings

- Eli Lily and Company, in partnership with Sperling's BestPlaces, ranked the nation's 50 largest metro areas in terms of the "Most Romantic Cities for Baby Boomers." The Raleigh* metro area ranked #3. Criteria: marriage and divorce rates among "baby boomers" age 45 to 60; great restaurants; dance studios; chocolate, jewelry and flower sales. *Eli Lily and Company, "Most Romantic Cities for Baby Boomers," April 20, 2007*
- The Raleigh* metro area was selected as one of the "Top Ten U.S. Cities for Finding a Rich, Single Woman" by Teasley, a Manhattan-based marketing consulting firm. The area ranked #8. Criteria: high single-female to single-male ratio; higher income to cost-of-living ratio; percentage of population that is single. *Teasley, "Where to Find a Rich, Single Woman in the United States," 2005*
- The Raleigh* metro area was selected as one of the "Best Cities for Relocating Singles" by Worldwide ERC and Primacy Relocation. The area ranked #5 out of the 100 largest metro areas in the U.S. Areas were selected based on the following criteria: a robust cost-of-living index; adventure and outdoor recreation opportunities; violent crime and property crime rates; percentage of the population that is unmarried (ages 25-34); ratio of single men and single women; affordability of quality higher education, including in-state and out-of-state tuition requirements and rates; number of newcomers to the area; commute times; tax rates; fee and occupancy rates for temporary housing and mini-storage; quality and quantity of collegiate and professional sporting events and fun, fan-friendly venues. *Worldwide ERC and Primacy Relocation, "2007 Best Cities for Relocating Singles," October 25, 2007*

- Sperling's BestPlaces in partnership with AXE Deodorant Bodyspray ranked 80 metro areas and identified "America's Best (and Worst) Cities for Dating." The Raleigh* metro area ranked #4 (#1 = best). Criteria: percentage of singles ages 18-24; population density; dating venues per capita. *AXE Deodorant Bodyspray, "America's Best (and Worst) Cities for Dating," May 2004*

Miscellaneous Rankings

- Apex was identified as one of the 100 fastest-growing suburbs in America by "Forbes." The city ranked #63. Criteria: suburban cities, townships and villages with more than 10,000 people in 2000 were ranked by their population growth from 2000 to 2006. *Forbes.com, "America's Fastest-Growing Suburbs," July 16, 2007*

- State Farm Insurance, in partnership with Sperling's BestPlaces, analyzed several key factors that contribute to overall family preparedness. The Raleigh* metro area ranked #42 out of the nation's 50 most populous metro areas. Criteria: quality of life; life insurance coverage; and investments. *State Farm Life Insurance, "Fiscally Fit Cities Report," July 20, 2004*

- Scarborough Research, a leading market research firm, identified the top local markets for reality television. The Raleigh* DMA (Designated Market Area) ranked in the top 10 with 27% of consumers reporting that they "typically watch" reality-dating, reality-talent, or reality- adventure television shows. *Scarborough Research, January 11, 2005*

- Scarborough Research, a leading market research firm, identified the top local markets for frequent fast food restaurant patronage. The Raleigh* DMA (Designated Market Area) ranked in the top 10 with consumers reporting an average of 6.2 visits within the past 30 days. *Scarborough Research, May 31, 2006*

- A study by Sperling's BestPlaces examined which U.S. metro areas were most affected by high fuel prices in 2006. The Raleigh* metro area was ranked #6 out of 80 (#1 = most expensive city for driving). Rankings are based on the average dollars spent on gas per year by two driver households. Criteria: cost of regular-grade gasoline; average miles driven per day; average number of gallons each driver uses and wastes in traffic congestion each day. *Sperling's BestPlaces, www.bestplaces.net, "Pain at the Pump," May 18, 2006*

Apex is located within the Raleigh-Cary, NC Metropolitan Statistical Area.

Business Environment

CITY FINANCES

City Government Finances

Component	2004-2005 ($000)	2004-2005 ($ per capita)
Total Revenues	51,586	1,807
Total Expenditures	47,469	1,663
Debt Outstanding	8,095	284
Cash and Securities	49,579	1,737

Source: U.S Census Bureau, Government Finances 2004-2005

City Government Revenue by Source

Source	2004-2005 ($000)	2004-2005 ($ per capita)
General Revenue		
From Federal Government	127	4
From State Government	2,604	91
From Local Governments	5,707	200
Taxes		
Property	10,471	367
Sales	20	1
Personal Income	0	0
License	111	4
Charges	9,482	332
Liquor Store	0	0
Utility	20,369	713
Employee Retirement	0	0
Other	2,695	94

Source: U.S Census Bureau, Government Finances 2004-2005

City Government Expenditures by Function

Function	2004-2005 ($000)	2004-2005 ($ per capita)	2004-2005 (%)
General Expenditures			
Airports	0	0	0.0
Corrections	0	0	0.0
Education	0	0	0.0
Fire Protection	2,404	84	5.1
Governmental Administration	3,724	130	7.8
Health	80	3	0.2
Highways	2,351	82	5.0
Hospitals	0	0	0.0
Housing and Community Development	0	0	0.0
Interest on General Debt	265	9	0.6
Libraries	0	0	0.0
Parking	0	0	0.0
Parks and Recreation	4,386	154	9.2
Police Protection	4,074	143	8.6
Public Welfare	0	0	0.0
Sewerage	2,758	97	5.8
Solid Waste Management	2,276	80	4.8
Liquor Store	0	0	0.0
Utility	23,267	815	49.0
Employee Retirement	0	0	0.0
Other	1,884	66	4.0

Source: U.S Census Bureau, Government Finances 2004-2005

Municipal Bond Ratings

Area	Moody's
City	n/a

Source: Mergent Bond Record, January 2008 (unless noted otherwise)

DEMOGRAPHICS

Population Growth

Area	1990 Census	2000 Census	2007 Estimate	2012 Projection	Population Growth (%) 1990-2000	Population Growth (%) 2000-2012
City	7,092	20,212	28,400	34,004	185.0	68.2
MSA[1]	541,081	797,071	994,403	1,134,243	47.3	42.3
U.S.	248,709,873	281,421,906	301,045,522	314,920,978	13.2	11.9

Note: (1) Metropolitan Statistical Area - see Appendix B for areas included
Source: Claritas, Inc.

Number of Households and Average Household Size

Area	2007 Estimate	2007 Average Household Size
City	10,460	2.72
MSA[1]	384,764	2.58
U.S.	113,668,003	2.65

Note: (1) Metropolitan Statistical Area - see Appendix B for areas included
Source: Claritas, Inc.

Race and Ethnicity

Area	White Alone[2]	Black Alone[2]	Asian Alone[2]	Other Race Alone[2]	Hispanic[3]
City	84.8	4.9	6.2	4.0	4.4
MSA[1]	69.7	20.2	3.6	6.5	8.2
U.S.	73.1	12.4	4.3	10.3	14.9

Note: Figures are 2007 estimates; (1) Metropolitan Statistical Area - see Appendix B for areas included (2) Alone is defined as not being in combination with one or more other races; (3) May be of any race.
Source: Claritas, Inc.

Ancestry

Area	German	Irish[2]	English	American	Italian	Polish	French[3]	Scottish
City	17.7	13.5	15.0	8.3	9.0	3.7	2.8	3.2
MSA[1]	10.4	8.6	11.8	9.9	3.5	1.8	2.1	2.7
U.S.	15.2	10.9	8.7	7.3	5.6	3.2	3.0	1.7

Note: Figures include multiple ancestry (e.g. if a person reported being Irish and Italian, they were included in both columns); (1) Metropolitan Statistical Area - see Appendix A for areas included; (2) Includes Celtic; (3) Includes Alsatian but excludes Basque
Source: Census 2000, Summary File 3

Foreign-Born Population

Area	Percent of Population Born in: Any Foreign Country	Europe	Asia	Africa	Oceania[2]	Canada	Mexico	Latin America[3]
City	7.3	1.6	3.1	0.5	0.0	0.7	0.3	1.2
MSA[1]	9.2	1.2	2.5	0.7	0.1	0.4	3.2	1.3
U.S.	11.1	1.7	2.9	0.3	0.1	0.3	3.3	2.5

Note: (1) Metropolitan Statistical Area - see Appendix A for areas included; (2) Includes Australia, New Zealand subregion, Melanesia, Micronesia, Polynesia, and Oceania n.e.c; (3) Includes Central America (excluding Mexico), South America, and the Caribbean.
Source: Census 2000, Summary File 3

Marriage Status

Area	Never Married	Now Married (excluding Separated)	Separated	Widowed	Divorced
City	20.0	68.9	1.9	2.4	6.9
MSA[1]	30.0	54.2	2.5	4.9	8.4
U.S.	27.1	54.4	2.2	6.6	9.7

Note: Figures are percentages and cover the population 15 years of age and older; (1) Metropolitan Statistical Area - see Appendix A for areas included
Source: Census 2000, Summary File 3

Age Distribution

Area	Percent of Population						
	Under Age 5	Age 5 to 17	Age 18 to 34	Age 35 to 49	Age 50 to 64	Age 65 to 79	80 Years and Over
City	10.2	20.4	28.2	28.5	8.5	3.1	1.1
MSA[1]	6.9	17.3	29.0	24.9	13.3	6.5	2.1
U.S.	6.8	18.9	23.7	23.5	14.8	9.2	3.2

Note: (1) Metropolitan Statistical Area - see Appendix A for areas included
Source: Census 2000, Summary File 3

Male/Female Ratio

Area	Males	Females	Males per 100 Females
City	14,148	14,252	99.3
MSA[1]	495,512	498,891	99.3
U.S.	148,320,305	152,725,217	97.1

Note: Figures are 2007 estimates; (1) Metropolitan Statistical Area - see Appendix B for areas included
Source: Claritas, Inc.

Religion

Area	Catholic	Southern Baptist	United Meth-odist	ELCA[1]	LDS[2]	Presby-terian Church USA	Jewish Est.	Muslim Est.
County	9.5	12.6	7.4	0.9	0.6	2.7	1.0	0.5
U.S.	22.0	7.1	3.7	1.8	1.5	1.1	2.2	0.6

Note: Figures are the number of adherents as a percentage of the total population; Adherents are defined as all members, including full members, their children and the estimated number of other participants who are not considered members (e.g. the baptized, those not confirmed, those regularly attending services, etc.); (1) Evangelical Lutheran Church in America; (2) The Church of Jesus Christ of Latter Day Saints
Source: Reprinted with permission from Religious Congregations and Membership in the United States 2000 (Nashville, Glenmary Research Center, 2002) Copyright Association of Statisticians of American Religious Bodies. All rights reserved.

ECONOMY

Gross Metropolitan Product

Area	2002	2003	2004	2005	2005 Rank[2]
MSA[1]	31.2	32.8	35.3	38.4	55

Note: Figures are in billions of dollars; (1) Raleigh-Cary, NC Metropolitan Statistical Area - see Appendix A for areas included; (2) Rank ranges from 1 to 361
Source: The U.S. Conference of Mayors, "U.S. Metro Economies: GMP - The Engines of America's Growth," January 2007

Economic Growth

Area	1995 GMP	2005 GMP	Average Annual Growth Rate	Growth Rate Rank[2]
MSA[1]	18.8	38.4	7.4	22

Note: Figures are in billions of dollars; GMP = Gross Metropolitan Product; (1) Raleigh-Cary, NC Metropolitan Statistical Area - see Appendix A for areas included; (2) Rank ranges from 1 to 361
Source: The U.S. Conference of Mayors, "U.S. Metro Economies: GMP - The Engines of America's Growth," January 2007

INCOME

Per Capita/Median/Average Income

Area	Per Capita ($)	Median Household ($)	Average Household ($)
City	36,968	88,470	100,123
MSA[1]	29,177	58,800	74,884
U.S.	25,495	49,280	66,670

Note: Figures are 2007 estimates; (1) Metropolitan Statistical Area - see Appendix B for areas included
Source: Claritas, Inc.

Household Income Distribution

Area	Percent of Households Earning							
	Under $15,000	$15,000 -24,999	$25,000 -34,999	$35,000 -49,999	$50,000 -74,999	$75,000 -99,000	$100,000 -149,999	$150,000 and up
City	2.1	3.8	3.7	10.1	20.2	18.8	26.5	14.8
MSA[1]	9.3	8.3	9.8	14.9	20.6	14.1	14.7	8.3
U.S.	13.1	10.9	11.2	15.6	19.5	11.9	11.3	6.6

Note: Figures are 2007 estimates; (1) Metropolitan Statistical Area - see Appendix B for areas included
Source: Claritas, Inc.

Poverty Rates by Age

Area	All Ages	Under 5 Years Old	5 to 17 Years Old	18 to 64 Years Old	65 Years and Over
City	1.9	0.2	0.2	1.2	0.3
MSA[1]	10.2	1.0	1.9	6.4	1.0
U.S.	12.4	1.2	3.0	6.9	1.2

Note: Figures are percent of population with income in 1999 below poverty level and only include population for whom poverty status is determined; (1) Metropolitan Statistical Area - see Appendix A for areas included
Source: Census 2000, Summary File 3

Personal Bankruptcy Filing Rate

Area	2004	2005	2006
Wake County	4.21	5.75	1.81
U.S.	5.31	6.82	2.00

Note: Numbers are per 1,000 population and include Chapter 7 and Chapter 13 filings
Source: Federal Deposit Insurance Corporation (FDIC), Regional Economic Conditions (RECON), 8/23/2007

EMPLOYMENT

Labor Force and Employment

Area	Civilian Labor Force			Workers Employed		
	Dec. 2006	Dec. 2007	% Chg.	Dec. 2006	Dec. 2007	% Chg.
City	16,610	16,609	0.0	16,197	16,210	0.1
MSA[1]	541,158	542,390	0.2	522,867	523,302	0.1
U.S.	152,571,000	153,705,000	0.7	146,081,000	146,334,000	0.2

Note: Data is not seasonally adjusted and covers workers 16 years of age and older; (1) Metropolitan Statistical Area - see Appendix B for areas included
Source: Bureau of Labor Statistics, http://stats.bls.gov

Unemployment Rate

Area	2007											
	Jan.	Feb.	Mar.	Apr.	May	Jun.	Jul.	Aug.	Sep.	Oct.	Nov.	Dec.
City	2.8	2.8	2.5	2.4	2.7	2.9	2.8	2.4	2.5	2.5	2.5	2.4
MSA[1]	3.7	3.7	3.4	3.3	3.5	3.8	3.8	3.5	3.4	3.5	3.5	3.5
U.S.	5.0	4.9	4.5	4.3	4.3	4.7	4.9	4.6	4.5	4.4	4.5	4.8

Note: Data is not seasonally adjusted and covers workers 16 years of age and older; All figures are percentages; (1) Metropolitan Statistical Area - see Appendix B for areas included
Source: Bureau of Labor Statistics, http://stats.bls.gov

Employment by Occupation

Occupation Classification	City (%)	MSA[1] (%)	U.S. (%)
Sales and Office	21.4	24.8	26.7
Professional and Related	38.2	28.2	20.2
Service	7.5	11.8	14.9
Production, Transportation, and Material Moving	5.8	9.8	14.6
Management, Business, and Financial	23.0	16.1	13.5
Construction, Extraction, and Maintenance	3.9	9.0	9.4
Farming, Forestry, and Fishing	0.2	0.3	0.7

Note: Figures cover employed civilians 16 years of age and older; (1) Metropolitan Statistical Area - see Appendix A for areas included
Source: Census 2000, Summary File 3

Employment by Industry

Sector	MSA[1] Number of Employees	MSA[1] Percent of Total	U.S. Percent of Total
Government	96,800	18.3	16.3
Education and Health Services	51,500	9.7	13.4
Professional and Business Services	93,000	17.6	13.1
Retail Trade	61,100	11.5	11.6
Manufacturing	33,000	6.2	9.9
Leisure and Hospitality	48,500	9.2	9.6
Financial Activities	26,800	5.1	5.9
Construction	n/a	n/a	5.3
Wholesale Trade	22,700	4.3	4.4
Other Services	25,400	4.8	3.9
Transportation and Utilities	12,900	2.4	3.7
Information	16,600	3.1	2.2
Natural Resources and Mining	n/a	n/a	0.5

Note: Figures cover non-farm employment as of December 2007 and are not seasonally adjusted; (1) Metropolitan Statistical Area - see Appendix B for areas included; n/a not available
Source: Bureau of Labor Statistics, http://stats.bls.gov

Average Wages

Occupation	$/Hr.	Occupation	$/Hr.
Accountants and Auditors	28.50	Maids and Housekeeping Cleaners	8.67
Automotive Mechanics	17.75	Maintenance and Repair Workers	16.95
Bookkeepers	15.64	Marketing Managers	52.72
Carpenters	15.46	Nuclear Medicine Technologists	27.80
Cashiers	8.43	Nurses, Licensed Practical	17.64
Clerks, General Office	12.14	Nurses, Registered	27.57
Clerks, Receptionists/Information	12.06	Nursing Aides/Orderlies/Attendants	11.84
Clerks, Shipping/Receiving	13.35	Packers and Packagers, Hand	10.02
Computer Programmers	34.06	Physical Therapists	34.87
Computer Support Specialists	22.45	Postal Service Mail Carriers	21.12
Computer Systems Analysts	36.64	Real Estate Brokers	24.13
Cooks, Restaurant	10.48	Retail Salespersons	11.26
Dentists	n/a	Sales Reps., Exc. Tech./Scientific	25.86
Electrical Engineers	39.57	Sales Reps., Tech./Scientific	31.86
Electricians	16.82	Secretaries, Exc. Legal/Med./Exec.	14.19
Financial Managers	43.89	Security Guards	11.43
First-Line Supervisors/Mgrs., Sales	17.46	Surgeons	n/a
Food Preparation Workers	8.69	Teacher Assistants	9.00
General and Operations Managers	56.84	Teachers, Elementary School	19.30
Hairdressers/Cosmetologists	16.94	Teachers, Secondary School	21.70
Internists	90.17	Telemarketers	11.27
Janitors and Cleaners	9.89	Truck Drivers, Heavy/Tractor-Trailer	17.38
Landscaping/Groundskeeping Workers	10.29	Truck Drivers, Light/Delivery Svcs.	14.17
Lawyers	52.93	Waiters and Waitresses	8.50

Note: Wage data covers the Raleigh-Cary, NC Metropolitan Statistical Area - see Appendix B for areas included. Hourly wages for elementary/secondary school teachers and teacher assistants were calculated by the editors from annual wage data assuming a 40 hour work week; n/a not available.
Source: Bureau of Labor Statistics, May 2007 Metro Area Occupational Employment and Wage Estimates

RESIDENTIAL REAL ESTATE

Building Permits

Area	Single-Family 2006	Single-Family 2007p	Single-Family Pct. Chg.	Multi-Family 2006	Multi-Family 2007p	Multi-Family Pct. Chg.	Total 2006	Total 2007p	Total Pct. Chg.
City	324	567	75.0	19	0	-100.0	343	567	65.3
U.S.	1,378,200	973,300	-29.4	460,700	407,200	-11.6	1,838,900	1,380,500	-24.9

Note: (p) preliminary; figures cover and represent new, privately-owned housing units authorized (unadjusted data); All permit data are based on estimates with imputation; U.S. figures are based on the new 20,000-place series.
Source: U.S. Census Bureau, Manufacturing, Mining, and Construction Statistics

Homeownership and Housing Vacancies

Area	Homeownership Rate[2] (%)			Rental Vacancy Rate[3] (%)			Homeowner Vacancy Rate[4] (%)		
	2005	2006	2007	2005	2006	2007	2005	2006	2007
MSA[1]	71.4	71.1	72.8	10.7	9.0	11.2	2.3	1.6	1.6
U.S.	68.9	68.8	68.1	9.8	9.8	9.7	1.9	2.4	2.7

Note: (1) Metropolitan Statistical Area - see Appendix B for areas included; (2) The proportion of households that are owners; (3) The proportion of the rental inventory that is vacant for rent; (4) The proportion of the homeowner inventory that is vacant for sale; n/a not available
Source: U.S. Census Bureau, Housing Vacancies and Homeownership Annual Statistics: 2007

TAXES

State Corporate Income Tax Rates

State	Rates and Tax Brackets
North Carolina	6.9%

Note: Tax rates as of January 1, 2008; The franchise tax rate is $1.50 per $1,000, with a minimum of $35.
Source: Tax Foundation, www.taxfoundation.org

State Individual Income Tax Rates

State	Federal Deductibility	Marginal Rates (%)	Standard Deduction ($)		Personal Exemptions ($)[1]	
			Single	Joint	Single	Dependents
North Carolina	No	6.0 - 8.0 (y)(dd)	3,000	6,000	1,300 (o)(r)	1,300 (o)(r)

Note: Tax rates as of January 1, 2008; Local- and county-level taxes are not included; n/a not applicable; (1) Married joint filers generally receive double the single exemption; (o) Exemptions are based on federal Adjusted Gross Income (AGI) and are adjusted according to income and filing status. Taxpayer's filing single with AGI less than $60,000 receive $800 per exemption, if they earn over $60,000 they get $1,300 per exempt

n. Taxpayers married filing jointly with AGI under $100,000 get $1,600 per exemption and $2,600 for AGI over $100,00; (r) State adjusts its bracket levels for inflation at the end of each year before printing tax forms; (y) Brackets are not double for married taxpayers; (dd) North Carolina will finally allow the expiration of the temporary increase of its top income tax rate as of January 1, 2008 when the top rate will return to 7.75 percent.
Source: Tax Foundation, www.taxfoundation.org

Various State and Local Tax Rates

State and Local Sales and Use (%)	State Sales and Use (%)	Gasoline[1,2] ($/gal.)	Cigarette ($/pack)	Spirits ($/gal.)	Table Wine ($/gal.)	Beer ($/gal.)
6.75	4.25	0.302	0.35	10.36 (n)	0.79	0.53

Note: Tax rates as of January 1, 2008; (1) In addition to the 18.4 cpg Federal gasoline tax; (2) Rates may include additional state sales taxes, environmental protection and storage fees/taxes, and local taxes. When necessary, the volume-weighted average of all local taxes is used to approximate the typical statewide rate including local tax; (n) The state government controls all sales. The implied excise tax rate is calculated using methodology designed by the Distilled Spirits Council of the United States (DISCUS).
Source: Tax Foundation, www.taxfoundation.org; Original research

State Tax Burdens

Area	Combined State and Local Tax Burden		Combined Federal, State and Local Tax Burden	
	Percent	Rank	Percent	Rank
North Carolina	11.0	19	31.3	24
U.S. Average	11.0	-	32.7	-

Note: Figures cover 2007 and measure taxes as a percentage of income
Source: Tax Foundation, www.taxfoundation.org

State Business Tax Climate Index Rankings

State	Overall Rank	Corporate Tax Index Rank	Individual Income Tax Index Rank	Sales Tax Index Rank	Unemployment Insurance Tax Index Rank	Property Tax Index Rank
North Carolina	40	25	44	39	6	34

Note: Rankings range from 1 to 50 where 1 is best. Rankings do not average across to Overall Rank. States without a given tax are given a ranking of 1.
Source: Tax Foundation, State Business Tax Climate Index 2008

TRANSPORTATION

Means of Transportation to Work

Area	Car/Truck/Van		Public Transportation			Bicycle	Walked	Other Means	Worked at Home
	Drove Alone	Car-pooled	Bus	Subway	Railroad				
City	87.5	7.4	0.3	0.0	0.0	0.1	0.5	0.8	3.4
MSA[1]	78.5	12.9	1.5	0.0	0.0	0.4	2.3	0.9	3.5
U.S.	75.7	12.2	2.5	1.5	0.5	0.4	2.9	1.0	3.3

Note: Figures are percentages and cover workers 16 years of age and older; (1) Metropolitan Statistical Area - see Appendix A for areas included
Source: Census 2000, Summary File 3

Travel Time to Work

Area	Less Than 15 Minutes	15 to 29 Minutes	30 to 44 Minutes	45 to 59 Minutes	60 Minutes or More
City	19.8	39.3	32.5	5.5	2.8
MSA[1]	24.7	40.4	22.3	7.4	5.2
U.S.	29.4	36.1	19.1	7.4	8.0

Note: Figures are percentages and include workers 16 years old and over; (1) Metropolitan Statistical Area - see Appendix A for areas included
Source: Census 2000, Summary File 3

Travel Time Index

Area	1982	1995	2004	2005
Urban Area[1]	1.04	1.11	1.17	1.18
Average[2]	1.11	1.22	1.29	1.30

Note: Travel Time Index - The ratio of travel time in the peak period to the travel time at free-flow conditions. A value of 1.35 indicates a 20-minute free-flow trip takes 27 minutes in the peak. Free-flow speeds (60 mph on freeways and 35 mph on principal arterials) are used as the comparison threshold; (1) Covers the Raleigh-Durham, NC urban area; (2) average of 85 urban areas
Source: Texas Transportation Institute, The 2007 Urban Mobility Report, September 2007

Living Environment

COST OF LIVING

Cost of Living Index

Composite Index	Groceries	Housing	Utilities	Trans-portation	Health Care	Misc. Goods/ Services
99.7	102.1	97.8	91.6	95.7	103.7	103.2

Note: U.S. = 100; Figures cover the Raleigh NC urban area.
Source: The Council for Community and Economic Research (formerly ACCRA), Cost of Living Index, 2007

Grocery Prices

Area[1]	T-Bone Steak ($/pound)	Frying Chicken ($/pound)	Whole Milk ($/half gal.)	Eggs ($/dozen)	Orange Juice ($/64 oz.)	Coffee ($/11.5 oz.)
City[2]	9.44	1.21	2.58	1.74	3.45	2.91
Avg.	8.93	1.12	2.13	1.52	3.26	3.31
Min.	5.88	0.71	1.33	0.83	2.30	2.20
Max.	12.80	2.07	3.43	3.54	5.79	6.20

Note: (1) Values for the local area are compared with the average, minimum and maximum values for all 331 areas in the Cost of Living Index report; (2) Figures cover the Raleigh NC urban area; **T-Bone Steak** *(price per pound);* **Frying Chicken** *(price per pound, whole fryer);* **Whole Milk** *(half gallon carton);* **Eggs** *(price per dozen, Grade A, large);* **Orange Juice** *(64 oz. Tropicana or Florida Natural);* **Coffee** *(11.5 oz. can, vacuum-packed, Maxwell House, Hills Bros, or Folgers).*
Source: The Council for Community and Economic Research (formerly ACCRA), Cost of Living Index, 2007

Housing and Utility Costs

Area[1]	New Home Price ($)	Apartment Rent ($/month)	All Electric ($/month)	Part Electric ($/month)	Other Energy ($/month)	Telephone ($/month)
City[2]	301,390	739	141.03	-	-	26.00
Avg.	309,605	782	146.13	78.67	90.16	26.14
Min.	189,877	n/a	82.03	37.41	33.15	17.08
Max.	1,202,800	3,481	271.14	150.60	257.67	37.45

Note: (1) Values for the local area are compared with the average, minimum and maximum values for all 331 areas in the Cost of Living Index report; (2) Figures cover the Raleigh NC urban area; **New Home Price** *(2,400 sf living area, 8,000 sf lot, in urban area with full utilities);* **Apartment Rent** *(950 sf 2 bedroom/1.5 or 2 bath, unfurnished, excluding all utilities except water);* **All Electric** *(average monthly cost for an all-electric home);* **Part Electric** *(average monthly cost for a part-electric home);* **Other Energy** *(average monthly cost for natural gas, fuel oil, coal, wood, and any other forms of energy except electricity);* **Telephone** *(price includes basic monthly rate for a private residential line plus additional local usage charges incurred by a family of four).*
Source: The Council for Community and Economic Research (formerly ACCRA), Cost of Living Index, 2007

Health Care, Transportation, and Other Costs

Area[1]	Doctor ($/visit)	Dentist ($/visit)	Optometrist ($/visit)	Gasoline ($/gallon)	Beauty Salon ($/visit)	Men's Shirt ($)
City[2]	80.88	74.02	77.14	2.58	34.02	27.67
Avg.	79.48	71.93	79.55	2.64	29.52	25.77
Min.	52.08	44.80	43.95	2.19	15.58	16.19
Max.	148.44	126.27	158.83	3.48	60.62	48.53

Note: (1) Values for the local area are compared with the average, minimum and maximum values for all 331 areas in the Cost of Living Index report; (2) Figures cover the Raleigh NC urban area; **Doctor** *(general practitioners routine exam of an established patient);* **Dentist** *(adult teeth cleaning and periodic oral examination);* **Optometrist** *(full vision eye exam for established adult patient);* **Gasoline** *(one gallon regular unleaded, national brand, including all taxes, cash price at self-service pump if available);* **Beauty Salon** *(woman's shampoo, trim, and blow-dry);* **Men's Shirt** *(cotton/polyester dress shirt, pinpoint weave, long sleeves).*
Source: The Council for Community and Economic Research (formerly ACCRA), Cost of Living Index, 2007

HOUSING

House Price Index (HPI)

Area	National Ranking[2]	Quarterly Change (%)	One-Year Change (%)	Five-Year Change (%)
MSA[1]	24	0.73	6.04	26.41
U.S.[3]	-	0.10	0.84	41.37

Note: The HPI is a weighted repeat sales index. It measures average price changes in repeat sales or refinancings on the same properties. This information is obtained by reviewing repeat mortgage transactions on single-family properties whose mortgages have been purchased or securitized by Fannie Mae or Freddie Mac in January 1975; (1) Metropolitan Statistical Area - see Appendix B for areas included; (2) Rankings are based on annual percentage change for all metro areas containing at least 15,000 transactions over the last 10 years and ranges from 1 to 291; (3) figures based on a weighted average of Census Division estimates; all figures are for the period ending December 31, 2007

Source: Office of Federal Housing Enterprise Oversight, House Price Index, February 26, 2008

House Price Valuations

Area	Q1 2000	Q1 2001	Q1 2002	Q1 2003	Q1 2004	Q1 2005	Q1 2006	Q1 2007	Q1 2008
MSA[1]	-11.4	-14.3	-9.5	-6.9	-7.9	-7.6	-6.7	-6.4	-7.9

Note: Figures show the percentage of over- or under-valuation of single family homes relative to statistically normal house values (e.g. a value of 23.6 indicates that house values are 23.6% overvalued). Statistically normal house values are based on house prices, interest rates, household incomes, population densities, and any historical premiums or discounts metropolitan areas have exhibited over time; (1) Figures cover the Metropolitan Statistical Area - see Appendix B for areas included

Source: Global Insight/National City Corporation, House Prices in America, May 2008

Median Home Prices

Area	2005	2006	2007[r]	Percent Change 2006 to 2007
MSA[1]	194.9	213.8	224.2	4.9
U.S. Average	219.0	221.9	217.9	-1.8

Note: Figures are median sales prices of existing single-family homes in thousands of dollars; (r) revised; n/a not available; (1) Metropolitan Statistical Area - see Appendix B for areas included

Source: National Association of Realtors, Metropolitan Area Prices, 1st Quarter 2008

Housing: Year Structure Built

Area	1990 -2000	1980 -1989	1970 -1979	1960 -1969	1950 -1959	1940 -1949	Before 1940	Median Year
City	78.5	10.6	3.5	3.1	1.8	0.6	1.8	1997
MSA[1]	33.2	22.9	16.6	10.9	7.2	3.9	5.4	1983
U.S.	17.0	15.8	18.5	13.7	12.7	7.3	15.0	1971

Note: Figures are percentages; (1) Metropolitan Statistical Area - see Appendix A for areas included

Source: Census 2000, Summary File 3

HEALTH

Health Risk Data

Category	Area[1] (%)	U.S. (%)
Adults who have been told they have high blood pressure[3]	23.2	25.5
Adults who have been told they have high blood cholesterol[3]	33.3	35.6
Adults who have been told they have diabetes[2]	7.4	7.5
Adults who have been told they have arthritis[3]	20.3	27.0
Adults who have been told they currently have asthma	5.4	8.5
Adults who are current smokers	14.9	20.1
Adults who are heavy drinkers[4]	3.7	4.9
Adults who are overweight (BMI 25.0 - 29.9)	39.1	36.5
Adults who are obese (BMI 30.0 - 99.8)	24.5	25.1

Note: Data as of 2006 unless otherwise noted; (1) Figures cover the Metropolitan Statistical Area - see Appendix B for areas included; (2) Figures do not include pregnancy-related diabetes, pre-diabetes or borderline diabetes; (3) 2005 data; (4) Heavy drinkers are classified as adult men having more than two drinks per day or adult women having more than one drink per day

Source: Centers for Disease Control and Prevention, Behaviorial Risk Factor Surveillance System, SMART: Selected Metropolitan/Micropolitan Area Risk Trends, 2005, 2006

Mortality Rates for the Top 10 Causes of Death in the U.S.

ICD-10[a] Sub-Chapter	ICD-10[a] Code	Age-Adjusted Mortality Rate[1] per 100,000 population	
		County[2]	U.S.
Malignant neoplasms	C00-C97	172.8	186.5
Ischaemic heart diseases	I20-I25	115.9	152.3
Other forms of heart disease	I30-I51	49.1	51.5
Cerebrovascular diseases	I60-I69	62.8	50.0
Chronic lower respiratory diseases	J40-J47	35.5	42.6
Diabetes mellitus	E10-E14	25.0	24.8
Other degenerative diseases of the nervous system	G30-G31	24.4	22.6
Other external causes of accidental injury	W00-X59	18.8	21.4
Influenza and pneumonia	J10-J18	14.2	20.7
Hypertensive diseases	I10-I13	18.1	18.2

Note: (a) ICD-10 = International Classification of Diseases 10th Revision; (1) Mortality rates are a three year average covering 2003-2005; (2) Figures cover Wake County
Source: Centers for Disease Control and Prevention, National Center for Health Statistics. Compressed Mortality File 1999-2004. CDC WONDER On-line Database, compiled from Compressed Mortality File 1999-2005 Series 20 No. 2K, 2008.

Mortality Rates for Selected Causes of Death

ICD-10[a] Sub-Chapter	ICD-10[a] Code	Age-Adjusted Mortality Rate[1] per 100,000 population	
		County[2]	U.S.
Assault	X85-Y09	3.7	5.9
Human immunodeficiency virus (HIV) disease	B20-B24	4.1	4.5
Intentional self-harm	X60-X84	8.3	10.8
Malnutrition	E40-E46	*0.9	1.0
Obesity and other hyperalimentation	E65-E68	1.3	1.4
Organic, including symptomatic, mental disorders	F01-F09	16.9	16.8
Transport accidents	V01-V99	12.7	16.1
Viral hepatitis	B15-B19	1.1	1.8

Note: (a) ICD-10 = International Classification of Diseases 10th Revision; (1) Mortality rates are a three year average covering 2003-2005; (2) Figures cover Wake County; (*) Unreliable data as per CDC
Source: Centers for Disease Control and Prevention, National Center for Health Statistics. Compressed Mortality File 1999-2004. CDC WONDER On-line Database, compiled from Compressed Mortality File 1999-2005 Series 20 No. 2K, 2008.

Distribution of Physicians[1]

Area	Total	Family/ General Practice	Specialties	
			Medical	Surgical
Wake County (number)	1,575	376	610	364
Wake County (rate per 10,000 pop.)	21.0	5.0	8.1	4.9
U.S. (rate per 10,000 pop.)	17.7	4.6	6.9	4.3

Note: Data as of 2005; (1) Includes all non-federal, patient-care, office-based MDs
Source: Area Resource File (ARF). June 2007. U.S. Department of Health and Human Services, Health Resources and Services Administration, Bureau of Health Professions, Rockville, MD.

Hospitals

There were no hospitals listed within the city limits.
AHA Guide to the Healthcare Field 2008

EDUCATION

Public School District Statistics

District Name	Schls	Pupils	Pupil/ Teacher Ratio	Minority Pupils[1] (%)	Free Lunch Eligible[2] (%)	IEP[3] (%)
Wake County Schools	138	120,996	14.8	44.7	23.1	14.7

Note: Table includes regular local school districts with 2,000 or more students; (1) Percentage of students that are not white, non-Hispanic; (2) Percentage of students that are eligible for the free lunch program; (3) Percentage of students that have an Individualized Education Program.
Source: U.S. Department of Education, National Center for Education Statistics, Common Core of Data, Local Education Agency (School District) Universe Survey: School Year 2005-2006; U.S. Department of Education, National Center for Education Statistics, Common Core of Data, Public Elementary/Secondary School Universe Survey: School Year 2005-2006

Highest Level of Education

Area	Less than H.S.	H.S. Diploma	Some College, No Deg.	Associate Degree	Bachelors Degree	Masters Degree	Profess. School Degree	Doctorate Degree
City	4.1	11.7	17.0	8.3	41.9	12.5	2.0	2.6
MSA[1]	13.5	20.9	20.1	7.7	26.0	8.3	1.9	1.7
U.S.	19.4	28.4	21.2	6.4	15.7	5.9	2.0	1.0

Note: Figures are 2007 estimated percentages and cover persons age 25 and over; (1) Metropolitan Statistical Area - see Appendix B for areas included
Source: Claritas, Inc.

Educational Attainment by Race

Area	High School Graduate (%)					Bachelor's Degree (%)				
	Total	White	Black	Asian	Hisp.[2]	Total	White	Black	Asian	Hisp.[2]
City	96.0	98.2	79.5	89.5	80.8	58.8	61.5	29.1	74.6	43.3
MSA[1]	85.4	89.4	76.6	91.6	43.0	38.9	43.7	22.2	70.0	15.3
U.S.	80.4	83.6	72.3	80.4	52.4	24.4	26.1	14.3	44.1	10.4

Note: Figures shown cover persons 25 years old and over; (1) Metropolitan Statistical Area - see Appendix A for areas included; (2) people of Hispanic origin can be of any race
Source: Census 2000, Summary File 3

School Enrollment by Type

Area	Grades KG to 8				Grades 9 to 12			
	Public		Private		Public		Private	
	Enrollment	%	Enrollment	%	Enrollment	%	Enrollment	%
City	2,857	94.5	166	5.5	887	90.8	90	9.2
MSA[1]	134,391	89.7	15,408	10.3	51,033	90.4	5,428	9.6
U.S.	33,526,011	88.7	4,285,121	11.3	14,848,628	90.6	1,532,323	9.4

Note: Figures shown cover persons 3 years old and over; (1) Metropolitan Statistical Area - see Appendix A for areas included
Source: Census 2000, Summary File 3

School Enrollment by Race

Area	Grades KG to 8 (%)				Grades 9 to 12 (%)			
	White	Black	Asian	Hisp.[1]	White	Black	Asian	Hisp.[1]
City	86.5	6.5	3.6	2.7	83.2	11.0	2.1	2.1
MSA[2]	63.0	28.2	2.6	6.1	64.9	27.9	2.6	4.7
U.S.	68.5	15.5	3.3	16.8	68.8	15.5	3.8	15.7

Note: Figures shown cover persons 3 years old and over; (1) people of Hispanic origin can be of any race; (2) Metropolitan Statistical Area - see Appendix A for areas included
Source: Census 2000, Summary File 3

Average Salaries of Public School Classroom Teachers

District	2005-06 Dollars	2005-06 Rank[1]	2006-07 Dollars	2006-07 Rank[1]	Percent Change 2005-06 to 2006-07
North Carolina	43,922	27	46,410	25	5.66
U.S. Average	49,026	-	50,816	-	3.65

Note: (1) State rank ranges from 1 to 51.
Source: National Education Association, Rankings & Estimates: Rankings of the States 2006 and Estimates of School Statistics 2007, December 2007

Higher Education

Four-Year Colleges			Two-Year Colleges			Medical Schools[1]	Law Schools[2]	Voc/ Tech[3]
Public	Private Non-profit	Private For-profit	Public	Private Non-profit	Private For-profit			
0	0	0	0	0	0	0	0	0

Note: Figures cover institutions located within the city limits; (1) includes schools accredited by the Liaison Committee on Medical Education and the American Osteopathic Association; (2) includes American Bar Association-accredited law schools; (3) includes all schools with programs that are less than 2 years.
Source: National Center for Education Statistics, The Integrated Postsecondary Education System (IPEDS) Peer Analysis System, 2007; www.usnews.com, Law and Medical School Directories, 2009

PRESIDENTIAL ELECTION

2004 Presidential Election Results

Area	Bush	Kerry	Nader	Other
Wake County	50.8	48.7	0.1	0.4
U.S.	50.7	48.3	0.4	0.6

Note: Results are percentages and may not add to 100% due to rounding
Source: Dave Leip's Atlas of U.S. Presidential Elections, www.uselectionatlas.org

EMPLOYERS

Major Employers

Company Name	Industry	Type of Site
Applebees	Eating places	Single
Carolina Power & Light Company	Electric services	Headquarters
Dorthea Dix Hospital	Management services	Branch
Executive Office State of NC	Executive offices	Headquarters
Forest Resources	Land, mineral, and wildlife conservation	Branch
NC Dept Transportation	Regulation, administration of transportation	Headquarters
North Carolina Dept Justice	Legal services	Single
Pricewaterhousecoopers LLP	Accounting, auditing, and bookkeeping	Branch
Progress Energy Inc	Electric services	Single
Rex Health Care	Home health care services	Headquarters
Software Media Consultants	Prepackaged software	Headquarters
Verizon Bus Netwrk Svcs Inc	Telephone communication, except radio	Branch
Wake County	Executive offices	Headquarters
Wake County Transportation Sys	School buses	Branch
Wake Medical Center	General medical and surgical hospitals	Branch
Wake Technical Community	Junior colleges	Headquarters

Note: Companies shown are located within the Raleigh metropolitan area; nec = not elsewhere classified.
Source: www.zapdata.com, May 2008

PUBLIC SAFETY

Crime Rate

Area	All Crimes	Violent Crimes: Murder	Violent Crimes: Forcible Rape	Violent Crimes: Robbery	Violent Crimes: Aggrav. Assault	Property Crimes: Burglary	Property Crimes: Larceny -Theft	Property Crimes: Motor Vehicle Theft
City	2,013.2	3.6	7.2	25.0	128.7	332.5	1,426.7	89.4
Metro[1]	3,249.1	3.3	20.9	112.1	194.6	778.4	1,934.0	205.8
U.S.	3,900.5	5.6	31.8	140.8	290.8	726.9	2,287.8	416.8

Note: Figures are crimes per 100,000 population; (1) Metropolitan Statistical Area - see Appendix B for areas included
Source: FBI Uniform Crime Reports, 2005

Hate Crimes

Area	Number of Quarters Reported	Bias Motivation				
		Race	Religion	Sexual Orientation	Ethnicity	Disability
City	4	0	0	0	0	0

Source: Federal Bureau of Investigation, Hate Crime Statistics 2006

RECREATION

Culture

Dance[1]	Theatre[1]	Instrumental Music[1]	Vocal Music[1]	Series/ Festivals	Museums	Zoos and Aquariums[2]
0	0	0	0	0	0	0

Note: (1) Number of professional perfoming groups; (2) AZA-accredited
Source: The Grey House Performing Arts Directory, 2007; Official Museum Directory, 2008; Association of Zoos & Aquariums, AZA Member Zoos & Aquariums, June 2008

Professional Sports Teams

Team Name	League
Carolina Hurricanes	National Hockey League (NHL)

Note: Includes teams located in the Raleigh-Durham metro area.
Source: Original research

MEDIA

Newspapers

Name	News Focus	Frequency	Circulation
Apex Herald	Community	Weekly	3,600

Note: Includes newspapers with offices located in the city
Source: MediaContactsPro, March 2008

Television Stations

Name	Ch.	Network(s)	Type	Ownership
WUNC	4	PBS	Public	University of North Carolina
WRAL	5	CBS	Commercial	Capitol Broadcasting Company Inc.
WTVD	11	ABC	Commercial	ABC Inc.
WUND	12	PBS	Public	University of North Carolina
WNCN	17	NBC	Commercial	General Electric Corporation
WUNE	17	PBS	Public	University of North Carolina
WUNM	19	PBS	Public	University of North Carolina
WLFL	22	WBN	Commercial	Sinclair Broadcast Group
WUNK	25	PBS	Public	University of North Carolina
WUNL	26	PBS	Public	University of North Carolina
WRDC	28	UPN	Commercial	Sinclair Broadcast Group
WRAY	30	n/a	Commercial	Shop at Home Inc.
WUNU	31	PBS	Public	University of North Carolina
WUNF	33	PBS	Public	University of North Carolina
WUNP	36	PBS	Public	University of North Carolina
WUNJ	39	PBS	Public	University of North Carolina
WRPX	47	Pax	Commercial	Paxson Communications Corporation
WRAZ	50	Fox	Commercial	Capital Broadcasting Inc.
WUNG	58	n/a	Public	University of North Carolina
WFPX	62	Pax	Commercial	Paxson Communications Corporation

Note: Stations included cover the Raleigh-Durham DMA (Designated Market Area)
BurrellesLuce, MediaContacts Online, January 2007

Major AM Radio Stations

Call Letters	Freq. (kHz)	Station Type	Target Audience	Station Format	Music Format
WETC	540	Commercial	General/Hispanic	Music	International
WGTM	590	Commercial	General/Religious	Music	Gospel
WDNC	620	Commercial	General	News/Talk	n/a
WFNC	640	n/a	General	Music/News/Sports/Talk	n/a
WPTF	680	n/a	General	News/Talk	n/a
WRBZ	850	Commercial	General/Men	n/a	n/a
WEEB	990	Commercial	General	Sports/Talk	n/a
WGBR	1150	Commercial	General/Hispanic	Educational/News/Talk	n/a
WCLN	1170	Commercial	General/Religious	Music/Sports	Oldies
WMPM	1270	n/a	Christian/General	Educational/Music/News	n/a
WYAL	1280	Commercial	Black/General/Rel	Music	Christian
WCHL	1360	Commercial	General	Music/News/Sports/Talk	Adult Contemp.
WLLN	1370	n/a	Hispanic/Religious	Music/News/Sports/Talk	n/a
WSHV	1370	n/a	General/Religious	News	n/a
WEED	1390	Commercial	General/Religious	Music/Talk	Gospel
WSRC	1410	n/a	General/Religious	Music/Talk	n/a
WRTP	1530	n/a	General/Rel/Women	Music	n/a
WHPY	1590	Non-Comm	General/Religious	Music/Talk	Christian

Note: Stations included cover the Raleigh-Durham DMA (Designated Market Area); n/a not available
Source: BurrellesLuce, MediaContacts Online, January 2007

Major FM Radio Stations

Call Letters	Freq. (mHz)	Station Type	Target Audience	Station Format	Music Format
WZRU	88.5	Public	General	Music/News/Talk	Adult Standards
WCPE	89.7	Public	General	Educational/Music	Classical
WUNC	91.5	College	General	Educational/News/Talk	n/a
WFSS	91.9	College	General/Hispanic	Music/News	n/a
WRSN	93.9	Commercial	General/Women	Music/News/Sports/Talk	Adult Contemp.
WQDR	94.7	Commercial	General	Music	Country
WKML	95.7	Commercial	General	Music/Talk	Contemp. Country
WFLB	96.5	Commercial	General	Music/News/Sports/Talk	Oldies
WQOK	97.5	n/a	Black/General	Music/News/Talk	n/a
WQSM	98.1	n/a	General	Music	n/a
WZFX	99.1	Commercial	General	Music/Talk	Urban Contemp.
WTRG	100.7	Commercial	General	Music/News/Talk	Oldies
WRAL	101.5	Commercial	General	Music	Adult Contemp.
WYMY	102.9	n/a	Hispanic	Music	n/a
WRCQ	103.5	Commercial	General	Music/News/Talk	Album Rock
WFXK	104.3	Commercial	Black/General	Music/News/Talk	Oldies
WDCG	105.1	Commercial	General	Music/News/Talk	Contemp. Country
WRDU	106.1	Commercial	General	Music/Sports	Classic Rock
WKQB	106.9	Commercial	General	Music/Talk	Urban Contemp.

Note: Stations included cover the Raleigh-Durham DMA (Designated Market Area); n/a not available
BurrellesLuce, MediaContacts Online, January 2007

CLIMATE

Average and Extreme Temperatures

Temperature	Jan	Feb	Mar	Apr	May	Jun	Jul	Aug	Sep	Oct	Nov	Dec	Yr.
Extreme High (°F)	79	84	90	95	97	104	105	105	104	98	88	79	105
Average High (°F)	50	53	61	72	79	86	89	87	81	72	62	53	71
Average Temp. (°F)	40	43	50	59	67	75	78	77	71	60	51	42	60
Average Low (°F)	29	31	38	46	55	63	68	67	60	48	39	32	48
Extreme Low (°F)	-9	5	11	23	29	38	48	46	37	19	11	4	-9

Note: Figures cover the years 1948-1990
Source: National Climatic Data Center, International Station Meteorological Climate Summary, 9/96

Average Precipitation/Snowfall/Humidity

Precip./Humidity	Jan	Feb	Mar	Apr	May	Jun	Jul	Aug	Sep	Oct	Nov	Dec	Yr.
Avg. Precip. (in.)	3.4	3.6	3.6	2.9	3.9	3.6	4.4	4.4	3.2	2.9	3.0	3.1	42.0
Avg. Snowfall (in.)	2	3	1	Tr	0	0	0	0	0	0	Tr	1	8
Avg. Rel. Hum. 7am (%)	79	79	79	80	84	86	88	91	91	90	84	81	84
Avg. Rel. Hum. 4pm (%)	53	49	46	43	51	54	57	59	57	53	51	53	52

Note: Figures cover the years 1948-1990; Tr = Trace amounts (<0.05 in. of rain; <0.5 in. of snow)
Source: National Climatic Data Center, International Station Meteorological Climate Summary, 9/96

Weather Conditions

Temperature			Daytime Sky			Precipitation		
32°F & below	45°F & below	90°F & above	Clear	Partly cloudy	Cloudy	0.01 inch or more precip.	0.1 inch or more snow/ice	Thunder-storms
77	160	39	98	143	124	110	3	42

Note: Figures are average number of days per year and cover the years 1948-1990
Source: National Climatic Data Center, International Station Meteorological Climate Summary, 9/96

HAZARDOUS WASTE

Superfund Sites

Apex has no sites on the EPA's Superfund Final National Priorities List.
U.S. Environmental Protection Agency, Final National Priorities List, June 23, 2008

AIR & WATER QUALITY

Air Quality Index

Area	Percent of Days when Air Quality was...[2]				AQI Statistics	
	Good	Moderate	Unhealthy for Sensitive Groups	Unhealthy	Maximum	Median
MSA[1]	53.7	38.1	8.2	0.0	142	47

Note: The Air Quality Index (AQI) is an index for reporting daily air quality. EPA calculates the AQI for five major air pollutants regulated by the Clean Air Act: ground-level ozone, particle pollution (also known as particulate matter), carbon monoxide, sulfur dioxide, and nitrogen dioxide. The AQI runs from 0 to 500. The higher the AQI value, the greater the level of air pollution and the greater the health concern. There are six AQI categories: "Good" The AQI is between 0 and 50. Air quality is considered satisfactory; "Moderate" The AQI is between 51 and 100. Air quality is acceptable; "Unhealthy for Sensitive Groups" When AQI values are between 101 and 150, members of sensitive groups may experience health effects; "Unhealthy" When AQI values are between 151 and 200 everyone may begin to experience health effects; "Very Unhealthy" AQI values between 201 and 300 trigger a health alert; "Hazardous" AQI values over 300 trigger health warnings of emergency conditions; (1) Metropolitan Statistical Area - see Appendix A for areas included; (2) Based on 365 days with AQI data in 2007.
Source: U.S. Environmental Protection Agency, Air Quality Index Report, 2007

Air Quality Index Pollutants

Area	Percent of Days when AQI Pollutant was...[2]					
	Carbon Monoxide	Nitrogen Dioxide	Ozone	Sulfur Dioxide	Particulate Matter 2.5	Particulate Matter 10
MSA[1]	0.0	0.0	52.3	0.0	47.7	0.0

Note: The Air Quality Index (AQI) is an index for reporting daily air quality. EPA calculates the AQI for five major air pollutants regulated by the Clean Air Act: ground-level ozone, particle pollution (also known as particulate matter), carbon monoxide, sulfur dioxide, and nitrogen dioxide. The AQI runs from 0 to 500. The higher the AQI value, the greater the level of air pollution and the greater the health concern; (1) Metropolitan Statistical Area - see Appendix A for areas included; (2) Based on 365 days with AQI data in 2007.
Source: U.S. Environmental Protection Agency, Air Quality Index Report, 2007

Air Quality Index Trends

Area	Trend Sites (6)								All Sites (58)
	1999	2000	2001	2002	2003	2004	2005	2006	2006
MSA[1]	27	8	4	18	5	1	3	0	3

Note: An AQI value greater than 100 indicates that air quality would have been in the unhealthful range on that day. Data from exceptional events are not included. These counts are presented in two ways. First, the counts are based on sites having an adequate record of monitoring data during the trend period (trend sites). These counts represent the relative change in the number of days with AQI values greater than 100. In the last column, the counts are based on all sites with data in the most recent year (because it is possible for a site to have data in the most recent year but not enough data to be a trend site); (1) Metropolitan Statistical Area - see Appendix A for areas included.

Source: U.S. Environmental Protection Agency, Office of Air and Radiation, Air Trends, Factbook and Related Information, Air Pollution Trends in Selected Metropolitan Areas 2006

Maximum Air Pollutant Concentrations

	Particulate Matter 10 (ug/m^3)	Particulate Matter 2.5 (ug/m^3)	Ozone (ppm)	Carbon Monoxide (ppm)	Sulfur Dioxide (ppm)	Nitrogen Dioxide (ppm)	Lead (ug/m^3)
MSA[1] Level	43	41	0.097	3	0.006	n/a	n/a
NAAQS[2]	150	35	0.125	9	0.140	0.053	1.50
Met NAAQS[2]	Yes	No	Yes	Yes	Yes	n/a	n/a

Note: Data from exceptional events are not included; (1) Metropolitan Statistical Area - see Appendix A for areas included; (2) National Ambient Air Quality Standards; n/a not available

Concentrations: Particulate Matter 10 (coarse particulate) - highest second maximum 24-hour concentration; Particulate Matter 2.5 (fine particulate) - highest 98th percentile 24-hour concentration; Ozone - highest second daily maximum 1-hour concentration; Carbon Monoxide - highest second maximum non-overlapping 8-hour concentration; Sulfur Dioxide - highest second maximum 24-hour concentration; Nitrogen Dioxide - highest arithmetic mean concentration; Lead - highest quarterly maximum concentration

Units: ppm = parts per million; ug/m^3 = micrograms per cubic meter

Source: U.S. Environmental Protection Agency, MSA Factbook 2006, Air Quality Statistics by City

Drinking Water

Water System Name	Pop. Served	Primary Water Source Type	Violations[1]	
			Health Based	Monitoring/ Reporting
Town of Apex	26,100	Purchased Surface	0	0

Note: (1) Based on violation data from January 1, 2007 to December 31, 2007 (includes unresolved violations from earlier years)

Source: U.S. Environmental Protection Agency, Office of Ground Water and Drinking Water, Safe Drinking Water Information System (based on data extracted April 15, 2008)

Cary, North Carolina

Background

Nicknamed "Technology Town of North Carolina," Cary is in the heart of the Research Triangle, nestled between the cities of Durham, Raleigh and Chapel Hill. The Research Triangle was developed in the 1950s as a center for technology and research, based on three of the nation's most prestigious universities located in these major metro areas: Duke University; The University of North Carolina; and North Carolina State University.

As one of the fastest growing cities in the country, Cary is frequently recognized as one of the safest and best places to live. The careful planning of this city contributes to its small town feel, with expansive parks and tree lined streets.

Settlers first came to Cary in 1770, which was named for a general in the Union army, Samuel Fenton Cary. Businessman Allison Francis "Frank" Page opened the Page Hotel to service the recently built railroad and it was under his guidance that the town was incorporated in 1871. Although the Page family sold the hotel in 1884 they continued to live in Cary and one of Page's eight children, Walter Hines Page, distinguished himself as an ambassador to Great Britain and one of the founders of North Carolina State University. The full history of the city, as well as the influence of technology in modern-day Cary, is celebrated at The Cary-Heritage Museum at the Page-Walker Arts and History Center.

The Cary Parks, Recreation and Cultural Resources Department is a nationally accredited organization, committed to enhancing the lives of Cary's residents and visitors. The town has over 20 parks with trails ranging in size and skill levels, and a wide range of sports facilities from softball fields to parks specifically designed for dog lovers and most everything in between. Public celebrations are held in beautifully maintained community space, including holiday festivities, the Dog Days of June, the Lazy Daze Arts and Crafts Festival, and the Cary Cycling Celebration. The Booth Amphitheater is one of the cities must-see venues. With capacity for 7,000, musical events are enhanced by the natural setting venue. Located at the edge of Symphony Lake, amid 14 acres of towering trees, concert-goers sit on the lawn or in deck seating to performances by nationally known artists, the North Carolina Symphony, and family movies throughout the summer months.

The people of Cary are a diverse mix of racial, religious and cultural backgrounds. The high tech industry attracts some of the best and brightest to settle in the area. The population of Cary has doubled every decade since 1960. Of those who call Cary home, 61 percent have bachelor's degrees or higher and 25 percent hold a masters or doctorate degree. This strong emphasis on education can be seen in the Wake County Public School System, which offers both traditional and year round schooling and provides a strong foundation for graduates to build on.

Being in the Research Triangle not only provides business and educational opportunities but also offers world class healthcare, with WakeMed Cary Hospital in the city, but the medical schools and hospitals of UNC and Duke a short drive away.

Cary offers businesses looking to relocate a highly educated, motivated workforce, and a pro-business environment that includes one of the lowest unemployment tax rates in the nation at 0.4 percent, and lower than average self-insurance and employer insurance rates. Leading employers in Cary include SAS International Inc., Kellogg's, John Deere Company, Caterpillar Inc., Oxford University Press, and American Airlines.

Cary's growth has not been restricted to population; city leaders are committed to maintaining infrastructure, with over $550 million budgeted for infrastructure projects since 1990, including transportation related projects and parks, recreation and cultural activities.

Cary is serviced by the Raleigh-Durham International Airport and Amtrak personal train service at the Cary Depot.

Rankings

General Rankings

- Raleigh* was ranked #63 out of 375 metro areas in *Cities Ranked & Rated*. Criteria: cost of living; climate; crime; transportation; economy and jobs; education; arts and culture; health and healthcare; leisure; quality of life. *Cities Ranked & Rated, 2nd Edition, 2007*
- Raleigh* was ranked #57 out of 379 metro areas in *Places Rated Almanac*. Criteria: health care; education; recreation; transportation; ambience; climate; crime; housing costs; jobs. *Places Rated Almanac, 7th Edition, 2007*
- The Raleigh* metro area was selected one of America's "Best Cities to Live, Work and Play" by *Kiplinger Personal Finance*. Criteria: population growth; percentage of workforce in the creative class (scientists, engineers, educators, writers, artists, entertainers, etc.); job quality; income growth; cost of living. *Kiplinger Personal Finance, "Best Cities to Live, Work and Play," July 2008*
- *Expansion Management* rated 362 metro areas to find out which offer the best middle class lifestyle for manufacturing and service companies. The Raleigh* metro area was selected as a "5-Star Quality of Life Metro" (a distinction the magazine awards to the top 20 percent of metro areas studied). The annual "Quality of Life Quotient" measures dozens of indicators across nine major categories and compares them among 362 metropolitan statistical areas in the United States. The categories are: affordable housing; good public schools; low crime levels; adult education level; standard of living; traffic and commuting; continuing education opportunities; commercial air access; labor market. *Expansion Management, June 2007*
- Cary was selected as one of the "2006 Best Places to Live" by *Money* magazine. Places were ranked using 38 quality-of-life indicators and six economic opportunity measures in the following categories: ease of living; health; education; crime; park space; arts and leisure. *CNNMoney.com, "Best Places to Live 2006"*

Business/Finance Rankings

- The nation's 100 largest metro areas were analysed in terms of the percentage of households entering some stage of foreclosure in 2007. The Raleigh* metro area ranked #53 out of 100 (#1 = highest foreclosure rate). *RealtyTrac, "Year-End 2007 Metropolitan Foreclosure Report"*
- The Raleigh* metro area was identified as one of the "10 Best Cities for Jobs in 2008" by *Forbes*. The metro area ranked #9. Criteria: state unemployment rate; job growth; income growth; median household income; cost of living. *Forbes.com, "Best Cities for Jobs in 2008," January 10, 2008*
- The Raleigh* metro area was selected one of America's "Top 50 Business Opportunity Metros" by *Expansion Management* in their 5th annual Mayor's Challenge ranking of metro areas that have achieved solid ratings across the board in numerous *EM* studies during the past 12 months. The area ranked #3. Criteria: public schools; quality of life; college educated workers; logistics infrastructure; healthcare costs; taxes and government spending; reputation among site consultants. *Expansion Management, August 2007*
- The Raleigh* metro area was selected as one of "America's Most Wired Cities" by *Forbes*. The metro area was ranked #3 out of 30. Criteria: percentage of Internet users with high-speed access; the range of service providers within a city; availability of public wireless hot spots. *Forbes, "America's Most Wired Cities," January 10, 2008*
- Raleigh* was selected as one of the best places to start and grow a company by *Entrepreneur* and the National Policy Research Council. The Raleigh* metro area ranked #3 out of 50 large metro areas. Criteria: business formation and growth (firms started four to 14 years ago that still employ at least 5 people and experienced rapid growth over the last four years). *Entrepreneur/National Policy Research Council, "Hot Cities for Entrepreneurs," September 2006*

- The Raleigh* metro area was selected as one of "America's 50 Hottest Cities" for business relocations and expansions. Criteria: industry's most prominent site selection consultants were asked to list their top city choices for relocating and expanding manufacturing companies, taking into consideration such factors as the business climate, work force quality, operating costs, incentive programs, and the ease of working with local political and economic development officials. *Expansion Management, January-February 2007*

- Raleigh* was cited as one of America's top mid-size metros (population 200,000 to 1 million) for new and expanded facility projects in 2007. The area appeared in the top 10 with 25 projects. *Site Selection, "Top Metropolitan Area Awards," March 2008*

- The Raleigh* metro area was selected as one of the "Top 20 Real Estate Markets" for expanding or relocating companies. The area ranked #16. Criteria: low rental costs; low purchase prices; high vacancy rates of office and warehouse space. *Expansion Management, October 2007*

- Intel, in partnership with Sperling's BestPlaces, ranked the 80 "Best Cities for Teleworking" in America. The Raleigh* metro area ranked #2 among mid-sized metro areas. The study identifies cities that hold the greatest potential for teleworking based on a host of factors including typical commuting times, fuel prices, availability of broadband Internet access and percentage of the population in telework friendly jobs. The study also factored in extreme climate and natural hazards. *Intel, "Best Cities for Teleworking," March 30, 2006*

- The Raleigh* metro area appeared on the Milken Institute "2007 Best Performing Cities" index. Rank: #10 out of 200 large metro areas. Criteria: job growth; wage and salary growth; high-tech output growth. *Milken Institute, "2007 Best Performing Cities"*

- The Raleigh* metro area was selected as one of the hottest cities for entrepreneurs in America by *Inc. Magazine.* Criteria: job-growth data for 393 metro was analyzed for current-year employment growth, average annual employment growth over past three years, and employment growth by industry sector. The Raleigh* metro area ranked #7 among large metro areas and #50 overall. *Inc. Magazine, May 2007*

- The Raleigh* metro area was selected as one of "The Top 20 Boom Towns in America." *Business 2.0* magazine and econometric research firm Global Insight compared 319 metropolitan areas in the U.S. and ranked the 61 with populations over 1 million. Criteria: a weighted formula that includes forecast growth rates in sectors that contain the economy's 10 most skilled occupational clusters; the prevalence of college degrees in the local workforce; median salary. The area ranked #1 among large metro areas. *Business 2.0 Magazine, March 2004*

- Raleigh* was identified as one of the 100 "Most Unwired Cities" in the U.S. The area ranked #8 out of the 100 largest metro areas in the U.S. Criteria: number of public and commercial wireless access points (hotspots); airports with wireless Internet access; broadband availability; local wireless networks; and wireless email devices. *Intel, "Most Unwired Cities Survey," June 7, 2005*

- Raleigh* was ranked #31 out of 125 regions worldwide in terms of its "Knowledge Competitiveness Index." The index attempts to measure the knowledge-based development taking place throughout the world and is based on 19 measures of economic performance that indicate a region's ability to translate its knowledge capacity into economic value. *Robert Huggins Associates, World Knowledge Competitiveness Index 2005*

- *Forbes* ranked the 200 most populous metro areas in the U.S. in terms of the "Best Places for Business and Careers." The Raleigh* metro area was ranked #1. Criteria: business costs (labor, energy, tax and office space expenses); living costs (housing, transportation, food and other household expenditures); education levels of the work force; job growth; income growth; migration trends; crime rates; and culture/leisure. *Forbes, "Best Places for Business and Careers," March 19, 2008*

- *Fortune* ranked the 100 largest metro areas in the U.S. in terms of projected median home price change in 2007. The Raleigh* metro area ranked #32. *Fortune.com, "Hot Spots, Cold Spots"*

Health/Environment Rankings

- 100 of the largest metro areas in the U.S. were analyzed in terms of their current drought severity. The Raleigh* metro area ranked #17 (#1 = driest). The rankings were based on statistics such as long-term precipitation trends and patterns and the Palmer drought indices. *Sperling's BestPlaces, www.BestPlaces.net, "America's Drought-Riskiest Cities," November 2007*

- Scarborough Research, a leading market research firm, identified the top local markets for diabetes medication purchasers. The Raleigh* DMA (Designated Market Area) ranked in the top 13 with 10% of consumers reporting that they purchased medication for diabetes within the past 12 months. *Scarborough Research, March 19, 2007*

- The Raleigh* metro area appeared in *Country Home's* "2008 Best Green Places" report. The area ranked #235 out of 379. Criteria: official energy policies; green power; green buildings; availability of fresh, locally grown food. *Country Home, "2008 Best Green Places"*

- Wyeth Consumer Healthcare, in partnership with Sperling's BestPlaces, ranked the nation's 50 most populous metro areas in terms of five key health factors. The Raleigh* metro area ranked #17. Criteria: physical activity; health status; nutrition; lifestyle pursuits; and mental wellness. *Wyeth Consumer Healthcare, "Centrum Healthiest Cities Study," April 19, 2005*

- The American Podiatric Medical Association and *Prevention* magazine ranked America's 100 most populated cities based on fitness-walker friendliness. The best cities have safe streets, beautiful places to walk, mild weather and good air quality. Cary ranked #293. *Prevention, "The Best Walking Cities of 2008," April 2008; American Podiatric Medical Association, "2008 Best Fitness-Walking Cities, "April 2008*

- Raleigh* was identified as a "2008 Asthma Capital." The area ranked #42 out of the nation's 100 largest metropolitan areas. Twelve factors were used to identify the most challenging places to live for people with asthma: estimated prevalence; self-reported prevalence; crude death rate for asthma; annual pollen score; annual air quality; public smoking laws; number of board-certified asthma specialists; school inhaler access laws; rescue medication use; controller medication use; uninsured rate; poverty rate. *Asthma and Allergy Foundation of America, "2008 Asthma Capitals"*

- Raleigh* was identified as a "Spring Allergy Capital." The area ranked #48 out of 100. Three groups of factors were used to identify the most severe cities for people with allergies during the spring season: annual pollen levels; medicine utilization; access to board-certified allergists. *Asthma and Allergy Foundation of America, "2007 Spring Allergy Capital Rankings"*

- Raleigh* was identified as a "Fall Allergy Capital." The area ranked #56 out of 100. Three groups of factors were used to identify the most severe cities for people with allergies during the fall season: annual pollen levels; medicine utilization; access to board-certified allergists. *Asthma and Allergy Foundation of America, "2007 Fall Allergy Capital Rankings"*

- Ortho-McNeil Neurologics, in partnership with Sperling's BestPlaces, analyzed 110 metro areas and identified those U.S. cities with the highest prevalence of factors that are most commonly associated with migraine headaches. The Raleigh* metro area ranked #37. Criteria: number of migraine-related drug prescriptions per capita; lifestyle factors that can contribute to migraines; environmental factors that can trigger migraines; and consumption of migraine-triggering foods. *Ortho-McNeil Neurologics, "America's Migraine Hot Spots," March 14, 2006*

- Sperling's BestPlaces ranked 331 metro areas and identified the most and least stressful U.S. cities. The Raleigh* metro area ranked #91 out of the 100 largest metro areas (#1 = most stressful). Criteria: divorce rate; unemployment rate; violent and property crime; suicide rate; commute time; mental health; alcohol consumption; cloudy days. *Sperling's BestPlaces, www.BestPlaces.net, "America's Most (and Least) Stressful Cities," January 9, 2004*

- An analysis of the "Best & Worst Cities for Sleep" was conducted by Sperling's BestPlaces. The study ranked America's 50 most populated metro areas. The Raleigh* metro area ranked #3 (#1 = best city for sleep). Criteria: number of days residents didn't get enough rest or sleep during the past month; average length of daily commute; divorce rate; unemployment rate. *Sperling's BestPlaces, www.BestPlaces.net, "Best & Worst Cities for Sleep," 2006*

Women/Minorities Rankings

- Raleigh* was ranked #27 out of 100 metro areas in *SELF Magazine's* ranking of "America's Best Places for Women." A panel of experts came up with more than 50 criteria including death and disease rates, environmental indicators, community resources, and lifestyle habits. *SELF Magazine, "America's Best Places for Women 2007," December 2007*
- Raleigh* appeared on a list of the top 10 metro areas with the highest concentration of Hispanic same-sex couples among all Hispanic households. The area ranked #8. *Urban Institute Press, The Gay and Lesbian Atlas, May 2004*
- Raleigh* appeared on *Black Enterprise's* list of the "Ten Best Cities for African Americans." The top picks were culled from more than 2,000 interactive surveys completed on www.blackenterprise.com and by editorial staff evaluation. The editors weighed the following criteria as it pertained to African Americans in each city: median household income; percentage of households earning more than $100,000; percentage of businesses owned; percentage of college graduates; unemployment rates; home loan rejections; and homeownership rates. *Black Enterprise, May 2007*

Seniors/Retirement Rankings

- Sperling's BestPlaces in partnership with Bankers Life & Casualty Company designed a survey to identify the top 50 metro areas in the U.S. that offer the best overall qualities for senior living. The Raleigh* metro area ranked #26. The following criteria were statistically weighted to reflect the needs of the senior population: health; disease; economics; social; environment; spiritual; transportation; housing; and crime. *Bankers Life & Casualty Company, "Best Cities for Seniors 2005"*
- A.G. Edwards ranked America's 500 top-performing communities based on their residents' personal savings and investing behavior. The Raleigh* metro area ranked #98 with an index score of 106.67 (national average = 100.00). A dozen statistical factors were measured including: participation in retirement savings plans; personal debt levels; and home ownership. *A.G. Edwards, "2007 Nest Egg Index", September 12, 2007*

Children/Family Rankings

- Cary was selected as one of the ten "Best of the Best" places to raise a family in the U.S. The city was ranked #7.Criteria: demographic characteristics; standard of living; education; lifestyle; health and safety. *Best Place to Raise Your Family: The Top 100 Affordable Communities in the U.S., 1st Edition, 2006*
- The Raleigh* metro area was selected as one of the "Best Cities for Relocating Families" by Worldwide ERC and Primacy Relocation. The 2007 study placed a special emphasis on the housing market, which has significantly impacted the relocation industry and an employer's ability to transfer employees. The variables which weigh heavily in this category include home price, home affordability index, appreciation rates, and property tax. Other criteria include cost of living, crime rates, education, climate, focus on diversity, physicians per capita, recreation and leisure, arts and culture, air quality, watershed quality, sales tax, unemployment rate, job growth, high school and higher education index, school expenditures per student, students in public school, SAT/ACT percentile, and population growth. *Worldwide ERC and Primacy Relocation, "2007 Best Cities for Relocating Families"*

Safety Rankings

- The National Insurance Crime Bureau ranked 361 metro areas in the U.S. in terms of per capita rates of vehicle theft. The Raleigh* metro area ranked #173 (#1 = highest rate). Criteria: number of vehicle theft offenses per 100,000 inhabitants. *National Insurance Crime Bureau, "NICB Vehicle Theft Study," April 22, 2008*
- Farmers Insurance Group of Companies, in partnership with Sperling's BestPlaces, ranked 379 metro areas and identified the "Most Secure U.S. Place to Live." The Raleigh* metro area ranked #21 out of 114 in the large metro area category (500,000 or more residents). Criteria: crime rates; extreme weather; risk of natural disasters; environmental hazards; terrorism threats; air quality; life expectancy; job loss numbers. *Farmers Insurance Group, "Most Secure U.S. Places to Live 2007"*
- Raleigh* was identified as one of the most dangerous large metro areas for pedestrians in the U.S. The area ranked #23 out of the nations 50 largest metro areas. Criteria: average yearly pedestrian fatalities per capita (for the years 2002 and 2003) adjusted for the number of walkers. *Surface Transportation Policy Project, "Mean Streets 2004"*
- Cary was identified as one of the safest cities in America by Morgan Quitno. All 371 cities with populations over 75,000 that reported crime rates in 2006 for murder, rape, robbery, aggravated assault, burglary, and motor vehicle thefts were ranked. The city ranked #14 out of the top 25. *www.morganquitno.com, 14th Annual America's Safest (and Most Dangerous) Cities Awards*
- Cary was identified as one of the safest mid-size cities in America by Morgan Quitno. All 213 cities with populations of 100,000 to 499,999 that reported crime rates in 2006 for murder, rape, robbery, aggravated assault, burglary, and motor vehicle thefts were ranked. The city ranked #4 out of the top 10. *www.morganquitno.com, 14th Annual America's Safest (and Most Dangerous) Cities Awards*

Sports/Recreation Rankings

- The Raleigh* metro area appeared on the *Sporting News* list of the "Best Sports Cities 2007". The area ranked #38 out of 150 cities in the U.S. *Sporting News* takes a 12-month snapshot, roughly July to July, of each city's sports, putting a heavy premium on regular-season won-lost records (from the most recently completed season). Other criteria include: playoff berths, bowl appearances and tournament bids; championships; applicable power ratings; quality of competition; overall fan fervor as measured in part by attendance as percentage of venue capacity; abundance of teams (rewarding quality over quantity); stadium and arena quality; ticket availability and prices; franchise ownership; and marquee appeal of athletes. *SportingNews.com, "Best Sports Cities 2007," August 1, 2007*
- The Raleigh* metro area was selected by *Cranium* as one of the "Top 50 Fun Cities" in America. The area ranked #6. Criteria includes: number of sports teams, restaurants, and dance performances; number of toy stores; city budget spent on recreation. *Cranium, November 4, 2003*
- *Golf Digest* ranked 330 metro areas in the U.S. in terms of golf. The Raleigh* metro area was ranked #200. Criteria: access to golf; weather; value of golf; and quality of golf. *Golf Digest, "Metro Golf Rankings," August 2005*

Dating/Romance Rankings

- Eli Lily and Company, in partnership with Sperling's BestPlaces, ranked the nation's 50 largest metro areas in terms of the "Most Romantic Cities for Baby Boomers." The Raleigh* metro area ranked #3. Criteria: marriage and divorce rates among "baby boomers" age 45 to 60; great restaurants; dance studios; chocolate, jewelry and flower sales. *Eli Lily and Company, "Most Romantic Cities for Baby Boomers," April 20, 2007*

- The Raleigh* metro area was selected as one of the "Top Ten U.S. Cities for Finding a Rich, Single Woman" by Teasley, a Manhattan-based marketing consulting firm. The area ranked #8. Criteria: high single-female to single-male ratio; higher income to cost-of-living ratio; percentage of population that is single. *Teasley, "Where to Find a Rich, Single Woman in the United States," 2005*

- The Raleigh* metro area was selected as one of the "Best Cities for Relocating Singles" by Worldwide ERC and Primacy Relocation. The area ranked #5 out of the 100 largest metro areas in the U.S. Areas were selected based on the following criteria: a robust cost-of-living index; adventure and outdoor recreation opportunities; violent crime and property crime rates; percentage of the population that is unmarried (ages 25-34); ratio of single men and single women; affordability of quality higher education, including in-state and out-of-state tuition requirements and rates; number of newcomers to the area; commute times; tax rates; fee and occupancy rates for temporary housing and mini-storage; quality and quantity of collegiate and professional sporting events and fun, fan-friendly venues. *Worldwide ERC and Primacy Relocation, "2007 Best Cities for Relocating Singles," October 25, 2007*

- Sperling's BestPlaces in partnership with AXE Deodorant Bodyspray ranked 80 metro areas and identified "America's Best (and Worst) Cities for Dating." The Raleigh* metro area ranked #4 (#1 = best). Criteria: percentage of singles ages 18-24; population density; dating venues per capita. *AXE Deodorant Bodyspray, "America's Best (and Worst) Cities for Dating," May 2004*

Miscellaneous Rankings

- Cary was determined to be one of America's smartest cities. The city ranked #7 in the small city category (50,000 to 100,000 adults 25 years and older). Criteria: the editors rated the collective brainpower of U.S communities based on the educational attainment of its residents. *American City Business Journals, www.bizjournals.com, June 12, 2006*

- State Farm Insurance, in partnership with Sperling's BestPlaces, analyzed several key factors that contribute to overall family preparedness. The Raleigh* metro area ranked #42 out of the nation's 50 most populous metro areas. Criteria: quality of life; life insurance coverage; and investments. *State Farm Life Insurance, "Fiscally Fit Cities Report," July 20, 2004*

- Scarborough Research, a leading market research firm, identified the top local markets for reality television. The Raleigh* DMA (Designated Market Area) ranked in the top 10 with 27% of consumers reporting that they "typically watch" reality-dating, reality-talent, or reality- adventure television shows. *Scarborough Research, January 11, 2005*

- Scarborough Research, a leading market research firm, identified the top local markets for frequent fast food restaurant patronage. The Raleigh* DMA (Designated Market Area) ranked in the top 10 with consumers reporting an average of 6.2 visits within the past 30 days. *Scarborough Research, May 31, 2006*

- A study by Sperling's BestPlaces examined which U.S. metro areas were most affected by high fuel prices in 2006. The Raleigh* metro area was ranked #6 out of 80 (#1 = most expensive city for driving). Rankings are based on the average dollars spent on gas per year by two driver households. Criteria: cost of regular-grade gasoline; average miles driven per day; average number of gallons each driver uses and wastes in traffic congestion each day. *Sperling's BestPlaces, www.bestplaces.net, "Pain at the Pump," May 18, 2006*

Cary is located within the Raleigh-Cary, NC Metropolitan Statistical Area.

Business Environment

CITY FINANCES

City Government Finances

Component	2004-2005 ($000)	2004-2005 ($ per capita)
Total Revenues	151,326	1,422
Total Expenditures	158,561	1,490
Debt Outstanding	204,102	1,918
Cash and Securities	268,293	2,521

Source: U.S Census Bureau, Government Finances 2004-2005

City Government Revenue by Source

Source	2004-2005 ($000)	2004-2005 ($ per capita)
General Revenue		
From Federal Government	3,919	37
From State Government	8,282	78
From Local Governments	18,949	178
Taxes		
Property	49,328	463
Sales	649	6
Personal Income	0	0
License	2,641	25
Charges	28,840	271
Liquor Store	0	0
Utility	9,855	93
Employee Retirement	0	0
Other	28,863	271

Source: U.S Census Bureau, Government Finances 2004-2005

City Government Expenditures by Function

Function	2004-2005 ($000)	2004-2005 ($ per capita)	2004-2005 (%)
General Expenditures			
Airports	0	0	0.0
Corrections	0	0	0.0
Education	0	0	0.0
Fire Protection	13,525	127	8.5
Governmental Administration	14,008	132	8.8
Health	0	0	0.0
Highways	30,544	287	19.3
Hospitals	0	0	0.0
Housing and Community Development	857	8	0.5
Interest on General Debt	4,013	38	2.5
Libraries	0	0	0.0
Parking	0	0	0.0
Parks and Recreation	9,968	94	6.3
Police Protection	12,468	117	7.9
Public Welfare	0	0	0.0
Sewerage	13,471	127	8.5
Solid Waste Management	4,939	46	3.1
Liquor Store	0	0	0.0
Utility	33,735	317	21.3
Employee Retirement	0	0	0.0
Other	21,033	198	13.3

Source: U.S Census Bureau, Government Finances 2004-2005

Municipal Bond Ratings

Area	Moody's
City	n/a

Source: Mergent Bond Record, January 2008 (unless noted otherwise)

DEMOGRAPHICS

Population Growth

Area	1990 Census	2000 Census	2007 Estimate	2012 Projection	Population Growth (%) 1990-2000	Population Growth (%) 2000-2012
City	49,835	94,536	109,793	121,357	89.7	28.4
MSA[1]	541,081	797,071	994,403	1,134,243	47.3	42.3
U.S.	248,709,873	281,421,906	301,045,522	314,920,978	13.2	11.9

Note: (1) Metropolitan Statistical Area - see Appendix B for areas included
Source: Claritas, Inc.

Number of Households and Average Household Size

Area	2007 Estimate	2007 Average Household Size
City	40,117	2.74
MSA[1]	384,764	2.58
U.S.	113,668,003	2.65

Note: (1) Metropolitan Statistical Area - see Appendix B for areas included
Source: Claritas, Inc.

Race and Ethnicity

Area	White Alone[2]	Black Alone[2]	Asian Alone[2]	Other Race Alone[2]	Hispanic[3]
City	77.6	6.4	11.3	4.7	5.6
MSA[1]	69.7	20.2	3.6	6.5	8.2
U.S.	73.1	12.4	4.3	10.3	14.9

Note: Figures are 2007 estimates; (1) Metropolitan Statistical Area - see Appendix B for areas included (2) Alone is defined as not being in combination with one or more other races; (3) May be of any race.
Source: Claritas, Inc.

Ancestry

Area	German	Irish[2]	English	American	Italian	Polish	French[3]	Scottish
City	17.3	12.3	14.3	7.4	6.5	3.6	3.0	3.2
MSA[1]	10.4	8.6	11.8	9.9	3.5	1.8	2.1	2.7
U.S.	15.2	10.9	8.7	7.3	5.6	3.2	3.0	1.7

Note: Figures include multiple ancestry (e.g. if a person reported being Irish and Italian, they were included in both columns); (1) Metropolitan Statistical Area - see Appendix A for areas included; (2) Includes Celtic; (3) Includes Alsatian but excludes Basque
Source: Census 2000, Summary File 3

Foreign-Born Population

Area	Percent of Population Born in: Any Foreign Country	Europe	Asia	Africa	Oceania[2]	Canada	Mexico	Latin America[3]
City	14.0	2.8	6.5	1.1	0.1	0.8	1.8	1.0
MSA[1]	9.2	1.2	2.5	0.7	0.1	0.4	3.2	1.3
U.S.	11.1	1.7	2.9	0.3	0.1	0.3	3.3	2.5

Note: (1) Metropolitan Statistical Area - see Appendix A for areas included; (2) Includes Australia, New Zealand subregion, Melanesia, Micronesia, Polynesia, and Oceania n.e.c; (3) Includes Central America (excluding Mexico), South America, and the Caribbean.
Source: Census 2000, Summary File 3

Marriage Status

Area	Never Married	Now Married (excluding Separated)	Separated	Widowed	Divorced
City	23.5	65.7	1.5	2.5	6.7
MSA[1]	30.0	54.2	2.5	4.9	8.4
U.S.	27.1	54.4	2.2	6.6	9.7

Note: Figures are percentages and cover the population 15 years of age and older; (1) Metropolitan Statistical Area - see Appendix A for areas included
Source: Census 2000, Summary File 3

Age Distribution

Area	Percent of Population						
	Under Age 5	Age 5 to 17	Age 18 to 34	Age 35 to 49	Age 50 to 64	Age 65 to 79	80 Years and Over
City	8.1	21.0	23.3	29.9	12.3	4.1	1.2
MSA[1]	6.9	17.3	29.0	24.9	13.3	6.5	2.1
U.S.	6.8	18.9	23.7	23.5	14.8	9.2	3.2

Note: (1) Metropolitan Statistical Area - see Appendix A for areas included
Source: Census 2000, Summary File 3

Male/Female Ratio

Area	Males	Females	Males per 100 Females
City	54,786	55,007	99.6
MSA[1]	495,512	498,891	99.3
U.S.	148,320,305	152,725,217	97.1

Note: Figures are 2007 estimates; (1) Metropolitan Statistical Area - see Appendix B for areas included
Source: Claritas, Inc.

Religion

Area	Catholic	Southern Baptist	United Meth-odist	ELCA[1]	LDS[2]	Presby-terian Church USA	Jewish Est.	Muslim Est.
County	9.5	12.6	7.4	0.9	0.6	2.7	1.0	0.5
U.S.	22.0	7.1	3.7	1.8	1.5	1.1	2.2	0.6

Note: Figures are the number of adherents as a percentage of the total population; Adherents are defined as all members, including full members, their children and the estimated number of other participants who are not considered members (e.g. the baptized, those not confirmed, those regularly attending services, etc.); (1) Evangelical Lutheran Church in America; (2) The Church of Jesus Christ of Latter Day Saints
Source: Reprinted with permission from Religious Congregations and Membership in the United States 2000 (Nashville, Glenmary Research Center, 2002) Copyright Association of Statisticians of American Religious Bodies. All rights reserved.

ECONOMY

Gross Metropolitan Product

Area	2002	2003	2004	2005	2005 Rank[2]
MSA[1]	31.2	32.8	35.3	38.4	55

Note: Figures are in billions of dollars; (1) Raleigh-Cary, NC Metropolitan Statistical Area - see Appendix A for areas included; (2) Rank ranges from 1 to 361
Source: The U.S. Conference of Mayors, "U.S. Metro Economies: GMP - The Engines of America's Growth," January 2007

Economic Growth

Area	1995 GMP	2005 GMP	Average Annual Growth Rate	Growth Rate Rank[2]
MSA[1]	18.8	38.4	7.4	22

Note: Figures are in billions of dollars; GMP = Gross Metropolitan Product; (1) Raleigh-Cary, NC Metropolitan Statistical Area - see Appendix A for areas included; (2) Rank ranges from 1 to 361
Source: The U.S. Conference of Mayors, "U.S. Metro Economies: GMP - The Engines of America's Growth," January 2007

INCOME

Per Capita/Median/Average Income

Area	Per Capita ($)	Median Household ($)	Average Household ($)
City	39,555	89,187	107,966
MSA[1]	29,177	58,800	74,884
U.S.	25,495	49,280	66,670

Note: Figures are 2007 estimates; (1) Metropolitan Statistical Area - see Appendix B for areas included
Source: Claritas, Inc.

Household Income Distribution

Area	Percent of Households Earning							
	Under $15,000	$15,000 -24,999	$25,000 -34,999	$35,000 -49,999	$50,000 -74,999	$75,000 -99,000	$100,000 -149,999	$150,000 and up
City	3.1	4.5	5.5	10.0	17.7	16.3	23.8	19.2
MSA[1]	9.3	8.3	9.8	14.9	20.6	14.1	14.7	8.3
U.S.	13.1	10.9	11.2	15.6	19.5	11.9	11.3	6.6

Note: Figures are 2007 estimates; (1) Metropolitan Statistical Area - see Appendix B for areas included
Source: Claritas, Inc.

Poverty Rates by Age

Area	All Ages	Under 5 Years Old	5 to 17 Years Old	18 to 64 Years Old	65 Years and Over
City	3.4	0.2	0.6	2.4	0.2
MSA[1]	10.2	1.0	1.9	6.4	1.0
U.S.	12.4	1.2	3.0	6.9	1.2

Note: Figures are percent of population with income in 1999 below poverty level and only include population for whom poverty status is determined; (1) Metropolitan Statistical Area - see Appendix A for areas included
Source: Census 2000, Summary File 3

Personal Bankruptcy Filing Rate

Area	2004	2005	2006
Wake County	4.21	5.75	1.81
U.S.	5.31	6.82	2.00

Note: Numbers are per 1,000 population and include Chapter 7 and Chapter 13 filings
Source: Federal Deposit Insurance Corporation (FDIC), Regional Economic Conditions (RECON), 8/23/2007

EMPLOYMENT

Labor Force and Employment

Area	Civilian Labor Force			Workers Employed		
	Dec. 2006	Dec. 2007	% Chg.	Dec. 2006	Dec. 2007	% Chg.
City	61,948	62,051	0.2	60,456	60,503	0.1
MSA[1]	541,158	542,390	0.2	522,867	523,302	0.1
U.S.	152,571,000	153,705,000	0.7	146,081,000	146,334,000	0.2

Note: Data is not seasonally adjusted and covers workers 16 years of age and older;
(1) Metropolitan Statistical Area - see Appendix B for areas included
Source: Bureau of Labor Statistics, http://stats.bls.gov

Unemployment Rate

Area	2007											
	Jan.	Feb.	Mar.	Apr.	May	Jun.	Jul.	Aug.	Sep.	Oct.	Nov.	Dec.
City	2.8	2.8	2.5	2.5	2.7	2.9	2.8	2.5	2.6	2.5	2.6	2.5
MSA[1]	3.7	3.7	3.4	3.3	3.5	3.8	3.8	3.5	3.4	3.5	3.5	3.5
U.S.	5.0	4.9	4.5	4.3	4.3	4.7	4.9	4.6	4.5	4.4	4.5	4.8

Note: Data is not seasonally adjusted and covers workers 16 years of age and older; All figures are percentages; (1) Metropolitan Statistical Area - see Appendix B for areas included
Source: Bureau of Labor Statistics, http://stats.bls.gov

Employment by Occupation

Occupation Classification	City (%)	MSA[1] (%)	U.S. (%)
Sales and Office	24.0	24.8	26.7
Professional and Related	36.0	28.2	20.2
Service	7.4	11.8	14.9
Production, Transportation, and Material Moving	4.7	9.8	14.6
Management, Business, and Financial	23.9	16.1	13.5
Construction, Extraction, and Maintenance	3.9	9.0	9.4
Farming, Forestry, and Fishing	0.1	0.3	0.7

Note: Figures cover employed civilians 16 years of age and older;
(1) Metropolitan Statistical Area - see Appendix A for areas included
Source: Census 2000, Summary File 3

Employment by Industry

Sector	MSA[1] Number of Employees	MSA[1] Percent of Total	U.S. Percent of Total
Government	96,800	18.3	16.3
Education and Health Services	51,500	9.7	13.4
Professional and Business Services	93,000	17.6	13.1
Retail Trade	61,100	11.5	11.6
Manufacturing	33,000	6.2	9.9
Leisure and Hospitality	48,500	9.2	9.6
Financial Activities	26,800	5.1	5.9
Construction	n/a	n/a	5.3
Wholesale Trade	22,700	4.3	4.4
Other Services	25,400	4.8	3.9
Transportation and Utilities	12,900	2.4	3.7
Information	16,600	3.1	2.2
Natural Resources and Mining	n/a	n/a	0.5

Note: Figures cover non-farm employment as of December 2007 and are not seasonally adjusted; (1) Metropolitan Statistical Area - see Appendix B for areas included; n/a not available
Source: Bureau of Labor Statistics, http://stats.bls.gov

Average Wages

Occupation	$/Hr.	Occupation	$/Hr.
Accountants and Auditors	28.50	Maids and Housekeeping Cleaners	8.67
Automotive Mechanics	17.75	Maintenance and Repair Workers	16.95
Bookkeepers	15.64	Marketing Managers	52.72
Carpenters	15.46	Nuclear Medicine Technologists	27.80
Cashiers	8.43	Nurses, Licensed Practical	17.64
Clerks, General Office	12.14	Nurses, Registered	27.57
Clerks, Receptionists/Information	12.06	Nursing Aides/Orderlies/Attendants	11.84
Clerks, Shipping/Receiving	13.35	Packers and Packagers, Hand	10.02
Computer Programmers	34.06	Physical Therapists	34.87
Computer Support Specialists	22.45	Postal Service Mail Carriers	21.12
Computer Systems Analysts	36.64	Real Estate Brokers	24.13
Cooks, Restaurant	10.48	Retail Salespersons	11.26
Dentists	n/a	Sales Reps., Exc. Tech./Scientific	25.86
Electrical Engineers	39.57	Sales Reps., Tech./Scientific	31.86
Electricians	16.82	Secretaries, Exc. Legal/Med./Exec.	14.19
Financial Managers	43.89	Security Guards	11.43
First-Line Supervisors/Mgrs., Sales	17.46	Surgeons	n/a
Food Preparation Workers	8.69	Teacher Assistants	9.00
General and Operations Managers	56.84	Teachers, Elementary School	19.30
Hairdressers/Cosmetologists	16.94	Teachers, Secondary School	21.70
Internists	90.17	Telemarketers	11.27
Janitors and Cleaners	9.89	Truck Drivers, Heavy/Tractor-Trailer	17.38
Landscaping/Groundskeeping Workers	10.29	Truck Drivers, Light/Delivery Svcs.	14.17
Lawyers	52.93	Waiters and Waitresses	8.50

Note: Wage data covers the Raleigh-Cary, NC Metropolitan Statistical Area - see Appendix B for areas included. Hourly wages for elementary/secondary school teachers and teacher assistants were calculated by the editors from annual wage data assuming a 40 hour work week; n/a not available.
Source: Bureau of Labor Statistics, May 2007 Metro Area Occupational Employment and Wage Estimates

RESIDENTIAL REAL ESTATE

Building Permits

Area	Single-Family 2006	Single-Family 2007p	Single-Family Pct. Chg.	Multi-Family 2006	Multi-Family 2007p	Multi-Family Pct. Chg.	Total 2006	Total 2007p	Total Pct. Chg.
City	1,982	2,326	17.4	1,004	754	-24.9	2,986	3,080	3.1
U.S.	1,378,200	973,300	-29.4	460,700	407,200	-11.6	1,838,900	1,380,500	-24.9

Note: (p) preliminary; figures cover and represent new, privately-owned housing units authorized (unadjusted data); All permit data are based on estimates with imputation; U.S. figures are based on the new 20,000-place series.
Source: U.S. Census Bureau, Manufacturing, Mining, and Construction Statistics

Homeownership and Housing Vacancies

Area	Homeownership Rate[2] (%)			Rental Vacancy Rate[3] (%)			Homeowner Vacancy Rate[4] (%)		
	2005	2006	2007	2005	2006	2007	2005	2006	2007
MSA[1]	71.4	71.1	72.8	10.7	9.0	11.2	2.3	1.6	1.6
U.S.	68.9	68.8	68.1	9.8	9.8	9.7	1.9	2.4	2.7

Note: (1) Metropolitan Statistical Area - see Appendix B for areas included; (2) The proportion of households that are owners; (3) The proportion of the rental inventory that is vacant for rent; (4) The proportion of the homeowner inventory that is vacant for sale; n/a not available
Source: U.S. Census Bureau, Housing Vacancies and Homeownership Annual Statistics: 2007

TAXES

State Corporate Income Tax Rates

State	Rates and Tax Brackets
North Carolina	6.9%

Note: Tax rates as of January 1, 2008; The franchise tax rate is $1.50 per $1,000, with a minimum of $35.
Source: Tax Foundation, www.taxfoundation.org

State Individual Income Tax Rates

State	Federal Deductibility	Marginal Rates (%)	Standard Deduction ($)		Personal Exemptions ($)[1]	
			Single	Joint	Single	Dependents
North Carolina	No	6.0 - 8.0 (y)(dd)	3,000	6,000	1,300 (o)(r)	1,300 (o)(r)

Note: Tax rates as of January 1, 2008; Local- and county-level taxes are not included; n/a not applicable; (1) Married joint filers generally receive double the single exemption; (o) Exemptions are based on federal Adjusted Gross Income (AGI) and are adjusted according to income and filing status. Taxpayer's filing single with AGI less than $60,000 receive $800 per exemption, if they earn over $60,000 they get $1,300 per exempt

n. Taxpayers married filing jointly with AGI under $100,000 get $1,600 per exemption and $2,600 for AGI over $100,00; (r) State adjusts its bracket levels for inflation at the end of each year before printing tax forms; (y) Brackets are not double for married taxpayers; (dd) North Carolina will finally allow the expiration of the temporary increase of its top income tax rate as of January 1, 2008 when the top rate will return to 7.75 percent.
Source: Tax Foundation, www.taxfoundation.org

Various State and Local Tax Rates

State and Local Sales and Use (%)	State Sales and Use (%)	Gasoline[1,2] ($/gal.)	Cigarette ($/pack)	Spirits ($/gal.)	Table Wine ($/gal.)	Beer ($/gal.)
6.75	4.25	0.302	0.35	10.36 (n)	0.79	0.53

Note: Tax rates as of January 1, 2008; (1) In addition to the 18.4 cpg Federal gasoline tax; (2) Rates may include additional state sales taxes, environmental protection and storage fees/taxes, and local taxes. When necessary, the volume-weighted average of all local taxes is used to approximate the typical statewide rate including local tax; (n) The state government controls all sales. The implied excise tax rate is calculated using methodology designed by the Distilled Spirits Council of the United States (DISCUS).
Source: Tax Foundation, www.taxfoundation.org; Original research

State Tax Burdens

Area	Combined State and Local Tax Burden		Combined Federal, State and Local Tax Burden	
	Percent	Rank	Percent	Rank
North Carolina	11.0	19	31.3	24
U.S. Average	11.0	-	32.7	-

Note: Figures cover 2007 and measure taxes as a percentage of income
Source: Tax Foundation, www.taxfoundation.org

State Business Tax Climate Index Rankings

State	Overall Rank	Corporate Tax Index Rank	Individual Income Tax Index Rank	Sales Tax Index Rank	Unemployment Insurance Tax Index Rank	Property Tax Index Rank
North Carolina	40	25	44	39	6	34

Note: Rankings range from 1 to 50 where 1 is best. Rankings do not average across to Overall Rank. States without a given tax are given a ranking of 1.
Source: Tax Foundation, State Business Tax Climate Index 2008

TRANSPORTATION

Means of Transportation to Work

Area	Car/Truck/Van		Public Transportation			Bicycle	Walked	Other Means	Worked at Home
	Drove Alone	Car-pooled	Bus	Subway	Railroad				
City	84.2	8.9	0.2	0.0	0.0	0.1	0.8	0.8	4.9
MSA[1]	78.5	12.9	1.5	0.0	0.0	0.4	2.3	0.9	3.5
U.S.	75.7	12.2	2.5	1.5	0.5	0.4	2.9	1.0	3.3

Note: Figures are percentages and cover workers 16 years of age and older;
(1) Metropolitan Statistical Area - see Appendix A for areas included
Source: Census 2000, Summary File 3

Travel Time to Work

Area	Less Than 15 Minutes	15 to 29 Minutes	30 to 44 Minutes	45 to 59 Minutes	60 Minutes or More
City	23.7	47.6	21.5	4.1	3.1
MSA[1]	24.7	40.4	22.3	7.4	5.2
U.S.	29.4	36.1	19.1	7.4	8.0

Note: Figures are percentages and include workers 16 years old and over; (1) Metropolitan Statistical Area - see Appendix A for areas included
Source: Census 2000, Summary File 3

Travel Time Index

Area	1982	1995	2004	2005
Urban Area[1]	1.04	1.11	1.17	1.18
Average[2]	1.11	1.22	1.29	1.30

Note: Travel Time Index - The ratio of travel time in the peak period to the travel time at free-flow conditions. A value of 1.35 indicates a 20-minute free-flow trip takes 27 minutes in the peak. Free-flow speeds (60 mph on freeways and 35 mph on principal arterials) are used as the comparison threshold; (1) Covers the Raleigh-Durham, NC urban area; (2) average of 85 urban areas
Source: Texas Transportation Institute, The 2007 Urban Mobility Report, September 2007

Living Environment

COST OF LIVING

Cost of Living Index

Composite Index	Groceries	Housing	Utilities	Trans-portation	Health Care	Misc. Goods/ Services
99.7	102.1	97.8	91.6	95.7	103.7	103.2

Note: U.S. = 100; Figures cover the Raleigh NC urban area.
Source: The Council for Community and Economic Research (formerly ACCRA), Cost of Living Index, 2007

Grocery Prices

Area[1]	T-Bone Steak ($/pound)	Frying Chicken ($/pound)	Whole Milk ($/half gal.)	Eggs ($/dozen)	Orange Juice ($/64 oz.)	Coffee ($/11.5 oz.)
City[2]	9.44	1.21	2.58	1.74	3.45	2.91
Avg.	8.93	1.12	2.13	1.52	3.26	3.31
Min.	5.88	0.71	1.33	0.83	2.30	2.20
Max.	12.80	2.07	3.43	3.54	5.79	6.20

Note: (1) Values for the local area are compared with the average, minimum and maximum values for all 331 areas in the Cost of Living Index report; (2) Figures cover the Raleigh NC urban area; **T-Bone Steak** *(price per pound);* **Frying Chicken** *(price per pound, whole fryer);* **Whole Milk** *(half gallon carton);* **Eggs** *(price per dozen, Grade A, large);* **Orange Juice** *(64 oz. Tropicana or Florida Natural);* **Coffee** *(11.5 oz. can, vacuum-packed, Maxwell House, Hills Bros, or Folgers).*
Source: The Council for Community and Economic Research (formerly ACCRA), Cost of Living Index, 2007

Housing and Utility Costs

Area[1]	New Home Price ($)	Apartment Rent ($/month)	All Electric ($/month)	Part Electric ($/month)	Other Energy ($/month)	Telephone ($/month)
City[2]	301,390	739	141.03	-	-	26.00
Avg.	309,605	782	146.13	78.67	90.16	26.14
Min.	189,877	n/a	82.03	37.41	33.15	17.08
Max.	1,202,800	3,481	271.14	150.60	257.67	37.45

Note: (1) Values for the local area are compared with the average, minimum and maximum values for all 331 areas in the Cost of Living Index report; (2) Figures cover the Raleigh NC urban area; **New Home Price** *(2,400 sf living area, 8,000 sf lot, in urban area with full utilities);* **Apartment Rent** *(950 sf 2 bedroom/1.5 or 2 bath, unfurnished, excluding all utilities except water);* **All Electric** *(average monthly cost for an all-electric home);* **Part Electric** *(average monthly cost for a part-electric home);* **Other Energy** *(average monthly cost for natural gas, fuel oil, coal, wood, and any other forms of energy except electricity);* **Telephone** *(price includes basic monthly rate for a private residential line plus additional local usage charges incurred by a family of four).*
Source: The Council for Community and Economic Research (formerly ACCRA), Cost of Living Index, 2007

Health Care, Transportation, and Other Costs

Area[1]	Doctor ($/visit)	Dentist ($/visit)	Optometrist ($/visit)	Gasoline ($/gallon)	Beauty Salon ($/visit)	Men's Shirt ($)
City[2]	80.88	74.02	77.14	2.58	34.02	27.67
Avg.	79.48	71.93	79.55	2.64	29.52	25.77
Min.	52.08	44.80	43.95	2.19	15.58	16.19
Max.	148.44	126.27	158.83	3.48	60.62	48.53

Note: (1) Values for the local area are compared with the average, minimum and maximum values for all 331 areas in the Cost of Living Index report; (2) Figures cover the Raleigh NC urban area; **Doctor** *(general practitioners routine exam of an established patient);* **Dentist** *(adult teeth cleaning and periodic oral examination);* **Optometrist** *(full vision eye exam for established adult patient);* **Gasoline** *(one gallon regular unleaded, national brand, including all taxes, cash price at self-service pump if available);* **Beauty Salon** *(woman's shampoo, trim, and blow-dry);* **Men's Shirt** *(cotton/polyester dress shirt, pinpoint weave, long sleeves).*
Source: The Council for Community and Economic Research (formerly ACCRA), Cost of Living Index, 2007

HOUSING

House Price Index (HPI)

Area	National Ranking[2]	Quarterly Change (%)	One-Year Change (%)	Five-Year Change (%)
MSA[1]	24	0.73	6.04	26.41
U.S.[3]	-	0.10	0.84	41.37

Note: The HPI is a weighted repeat sales index. It measures average price changes in repeat sales or refinancings on the same properties. This information is obtained by reviewing repeat mortgage transactions on single-family properties whose mortgages have been purchased or securitized by Fannie Mae or Freddie Mac in January 1975; (1) Metropolitan Statistical Area - see Appendix B for areas included; (2) Rankings are based on annual percentage change for all metro areas containing at least 15,000 transactions over the last 10 years and ranges from 1 to 291; (3) figures based on a weighted average of Census Division estimates; all figures are for the period ending December 31, 2007
Source: Office of Federal Housing Enterprise Oversight, House Price Index, February 26, 2008

House Price Valuations

Area	Q1 2000	Q1 2001	Q1 2002	Q1 2003	Q1 2004	Q1 2005	Q1 2006	Q1 2007	Q1 2008
MSA[1]	-11.4	-14.3	-9.5	-6.9	-7.9	-7.6	-6.7	-6.4	-7.9

Note: Figures show the percentage of over- or under-valuation of single family homes relative to statistically normal house values (e.g. a value of 23.6 indicates that house values are 23.6% overvalued). Statistically normal house values are based on house prices, interest rates, household incomes, population densities, and any historical premiums or discounts metropolitan areas have exhibited over time; (1) Figures cover the Metropolitan Statistical Area - see Appendix B for areas included
Source: Global Insight/National City Corporation, House Prices in America, May 2008

Median Home Prices

Area	2005	2006	2007[r]	Percent Change 2006 to 2007
MSA[1]	194.9	213.8	224.2	4.9
U.S. Average	219.0	221.9	217.9	-1.8

Note: Figures are median sales prices of existing single-family homes in thousands of dollars; (r) revised; n/a not available; (1) Metropolitan Statistical Area - see Appendix B for areas included
Source: National Association of Realtors, Metropolitan Area Prices, 1st Quarter 2008

Housing: Year Structure Built

Area	1990 -2000	1980 -1989	1970 -1979	1960 -1969	1950 -1959	1940 -1949	Before 1940	Median Year
City	54.1	24.9	13.8	4.5	1.5	0.4	0.8	1991
MSA[1]	33.2	22.9	16.6	10.9	7.2	3.9	5.4	1983
U.S.	17.0	15.8	18.5	13.7	12.7	7.3	15.0	1971

Note: Figures are percentages; (1) Metropolitan Statistical Area - see Appendix A for areas included
Source: Census 2000, Summary File 3

HEALTH

Health Risk Data

Category	Area[1] (%)	U.S. (%)
Adults who have been told they have high blood pressure[3]	23.2	25.5
Adults who have been told they have high blood cholesterol[3]	33.3	35.6
Adults who have been told they have diabetes[2]	7.4	7.5
Adults who have been told they have arthritis[3]	20.3	27.0
Adults who have been told they currently have asthma	5.4	8.5
Adults who are current smokers	14.9	20.1
Adults who are heavy drinkers[4]	3.7	4.9
Adults who are overweight (BMI 25.0 - 29.9)	39.1	36.5
Adults who are obese (BMI 30.0 - 99.8)	24.5	25.1

Note: Data as of 2006 unless otherwise noted; (1) Figures cover the Metropolitan Statistical Area - see Appendix B for areas included; (2) Figures do not include pregnancy-related diabetes, pre-diabetes or borderline diabetes; (3) 2005 data; (4) Heavy drinkers are classified as adult men having more than two drinks per day or adult women having more than one drink per day
Source: Centers for Disease Control and Prevention, Behaviorial Risk Factor Surveillance System, SMART: Selected Metropolitan/Micropolitan Area Risk Trends, 2005, 2006

Mortality Rates for the Top 10 Causes of Death in the U.S.

ICD-10[a] Sub-Chapter	ICD-10[a] Code	Age-Adjusted Mortality Rate[1] per 100,000 population	
		County[2]	U.S.
Malignant neoplasms	C00-C97	172.8	186.5
Ischaemic heart diseases	I20-I25	115.9	152.3
Other forms of heart disease	I30-I51	49.1	51.5
Cerebrovascular diseases	I60-I69	62.8	50.0
Chronic lower respiratory diseases	J40-J47	35.5	42.6
Diabetes mellitus	E10-E14	25.0	24.8
Other degenerative diseases of the nervous system	G30-G31	24.4	22.6
Other external causes of accidental injury	W00-X59	18.8	21.4
Influenza and pneumonia	J10-J18	14.2	20.7
Hypertensive diseases	I10-I13	18.1	18.2

Note: (a) ICD-10 = International Classification of Diseases 10th Revision; (1) Mortality rates are a three year average covering 2003-2005; (2) Figures cover Wake County
Source: Centers for Disease Control and Prevention, National Center for Health Statistics. Compressed Mortality File 1999-2004. CDC WONDER On-line Database, compiled from Compressed Mortality File 1999-2005 Series 20 No. 2K, 2008.

Mortality Rates for Selected Causes of Death

ICD-10[a] Sub-Chapter	ICD-10[a] Code	Age-Adjusted Mortality Rate[1] per 100,000 population	
		County[2]	U.S.
Assault	X85-Y09	3.7	5.9
Human immunodeficiency virus (HIV) disease	B20-B24	4.1	4.5
Intentional self-harm	X60-X84	8.3	10.8
Malnutrition	E40-E46	*0.9	1.0
Obesity and other hyperalimentation	E65-E68	1.3	1.4
Organic, including symptomatic, mental disorders	F01-F09	16.9	16.8
Transport accidents	V01-V99	12.7	16.1
Viral hepatitis	B15-B19	1.1	1.8

Note: (a) ICD-10 = International Classification of Diseases 10th Revision; (1) Mortality rates are a three year average covering 2003-2005; (2) Figures cover Wake County; (*) Unreliable data as per CDC
Source: Centers for Disease Control and Prevention, National Center for Health Statistics. Compressed Mortality File 1999-2004. CDC WONDER On-line Database, compiled from Compressed Mortality File 1999-2005 Series 20 No. 2K, 2008.

Distribution of Physicians[1]

Area	Total	Family/ General Practice	Specialties	
			Medical	Surgical
Wake County (number)	1,575	376	610	364
Wake County (rate per 10,000 pop.)	21.0	5.0	8.1	4.9
U.S. (rate per 10,000 pop.)	17.7	4.6	6.9	4.3

Note: Data as of 2005; (1) Includes all non-federal, patient-care, office-based MDs
Source: Area Resource File (ARF). June 2007. U.S. Department of Health and Human Services, Health Resources and Services Administration, Bureau of Health Professions, Rockville, MD.

Hospitals

Cary has the following hospitals: 1 general medical and surgical.
AHA Guide to the Healthcare Field 2008

EDUCATION

Public School District Statistics

District Name	Schls	Pupils	Pupil/ Teacher Ratio	Minority Pupils[1] (%)	Free Lunch Eligible[2] (%)	IEP[3] (%)
Wake County Schools	138	120,996	14.8	44.7	23.1	14.7

Note: Table includes regular local school districts with 2,000 or more students; (1) Percentage of students that are not white, non-Hispanic; (2) Percentage of students that are eligible for the free lunch program; (3) Percentage of students that have an Individualized Education Program.
Source: U.S. Department of Education, National Center for Education Statistics, Common Core of Data, Local Education Agency (School District) Universe Survey: School Year 2005-2006; U.S. Department of Education, National Center for Education Statistics, Common Core of Data, Public Elementary/Secondary School Universe Survey: School Year 2005-2006

Highest Level of Education

Area	Less than H.S.	H.S. Diploma	Some College, No Deg.	Associate Degree	Bachelors Degree	Masters Degree	Profess. School Degree	Doctorate Degree
City	4.6	10.6	15.9	7.2	38.7	16.2	3.0	3.9
MSA[1]	13.5	20.9	20.1	7.7	26.0	8.3	1.9	1.7
U.S.	19.4	28.4	21.2	6.4	15.7	5.9	2.0	1.0

Note: Figures are 2007 estimated percentages and cover persons age 25 and over; (1) Metropolitan Statistical Area - see Appendix B for areas included
Source: Claritas, Inc.

Educational Attainment by Race

Area	High School Graduate (%)					Bachelor's Degree (%)				
	Total	White	Black	Asian	Hisp.[2]	Total	White	Black	Asian	Hisp.[2]
City	95.1	96.2	93.8	92.5	59.4	60.7	61.1	47.7	74.0	33.4
MSA[1]	85.4	89.4	76.6	91.6	43.0	38.9	43.7	22.2	70.0	15.3
U.S.	80.4	83.6	72.3	80.4	52.4	24.4	26.1	14.3	44.1	10.4

Note: Figures shown cover persons 25 years old and over; (1) Metropolitan Statistical Area - see Appendix A for areas included; (2) people of Hispanic origin can be of any race
Source: Census 2000, Summary File 3

School Enrollment by Type

Area	Grades KG to 8				Grades 9 to 12			
	Public		Private		Public		Private	
	Enrollment	%	Enrollment	%	Enrollment	%	Enrollment	%
City	13,377	91.4	1,252	8.6	4,691	89.2	566	10.8
MSA[1]	134,391	89.7	15,408	10.3	51,033	90.4	5,428	9.6
U.S.	33,526,011	88.7	4,285,121	11.3	14,848,628	90.6	1,532,323	9.4

Note: Figures shown cover persons 3 years old and over; (1) Metropolitan Statistical Area - see Appendix A for areas included
Source: Census 2000, Summary File 3

School Enrollment by Race

Area	Grades KG to 8 (%)				Grades 9 to 12 (%)			
	White	Black	Asian	Hisp.[1]	White	Black	Asian	Hisp.[1]
City	81.3	6.3	7.9	4.2	81.6	7.6	6.9	3.3
MSA[2]	63.0	28.2	2.6	6.1	64.9	27.9	2.6	4.7
U.S.	68.5	15.5	3.3	16.8	68.8	15.5	3.8	15.7

Note: Figures shown cover persons 3 years old and over; (1) people of Hispanic origin can be of any race; (2) Metropolitan Statistical Area - see Appendix A for areas included
Source: Census 2000, Summary File 3

Average Salaries of Public School Classroom Teachers

District	2005-06		2006-07		Percent Change 2005-06 to 2006-07
	Dollars	Rank[1]	Dollars	Rank[1]	
North Carolina	43,922	27	46,410	25	5.66
U.S. Average	49,026	-	50,816	-	3.65

Note: (1) State rank ranges from 1 to 51.
Source: National Education Association, Rankings & Estimates: Rankings of the States 2006 and Estimates of School Statistics 2007, December 2007

Higher Education

Four-Year Colleges			Two-Year Colleges			Medical Schools[1]	Law Schools[2]	Voc/ Tech[3]
Public	Private Non-profit	Private For-profit	Public	Private Non-profit	Private For-profit			
0	0	0	0	0	1	0	0	0

Note: Figures cover institutions located within the city limits; (1) includes schools accredited by the Liaison Committee on Medical Education and the American Osteopathic Association; (2) includes American Bar Association-accredited law schools; (3) includes all schools with programs that are less than 2 years.
Source: National Center for Education Statistics, The Integrated Postsecondary Education System (IPEDS) Peer Analysis System, 2007; www.usnews.com, Law and Medical School Directories, 2009

PRESIDENTIAL ELECTION

2004 Presidential Election Results

Area	Bush	Kerry	Nader	Other
Wake County	50.8	48.7	0.1	0.4
U.S.	50.7	48.3	0.4	0.6

Note: Results are percentages and may not add to 100% due to rounding
Source: Dave Leip's Atlas of U.S. Presidential Elections, www.uselectionatlas.org

EMPLOYERS

Major Employers

Company Name	Industry	Type of Site
Applebees	Eating places	Single
Carolina Power & Light Company	Electric services	Headquarters
Dorthea Dix Hospital	Management services	Branch
Executive Office State of NC	Executive offices	Headquarters
Forest Resources	Land, mineral, and wildlife conservation	Branch
NC Dept Transportation	Regulation, administration of transportation	Headquarters
North Carolina Dept Justice	Legal services	Single
Pricewaterhousecoopers LLP	Accounting, auditing, and bookkeeping	Branch
Progress Energy Inc	Electric services	Single
Rex Health Care	Home health care services	Headquarters
Software Media Consultants	Prepackaged software	Headquarters
Verizon Bus Netwrk Svcs Inc	Telephone communication, except radio	Branch
Wake County	Executive offices	Headquarters
Wake County Transportation Sys	School buses	Branch
Wake Medical Center	General medical and surgical hospitals	Branch
Wake Technical Community	Junior colleges	Headquarters

Note: Companies shown are located within the Raleigh metropolitan area; nec = not elsewhere classified.
Source: www.zapdata.com, May 2008

PUBLIC SAFETY

Crime Rate

Area	All Crimes	Violent Crimes				Property Crimes		
		Murder	Forcible Rape	Robbery	Aggrav. Assault	Burglary	Larceny -Theft	Motor Vehicle Theft
City	2,137.0	0.0	12.9	38.7	69.1	510.3	1,400.1	105.9
Metro[1]	3,295.3	3.8	21.0	111.4	223.6	777.1	1,947.1	211.3
U.S.	3,808.1	5.7	30.9	149.4	287.5	729.4	2,206.8	398.4

Note: Figures are crimes per 100,000 population; (1) Metropolitan Statistical Area - see Appendix B for areas included
Source: FBI Uniform Crime Reports, 2006

Hate Crimes

Area	Number of Quarters Reported	Bias Motivation				
		Race	Religion	Sexual Orientation	Ethnicity	Disability
City	4	1	1	0	0	0

Source: Federal Bureau of Investigation, Hate Crime Statistics 2006

RECREATION

Culture

Dance[1]	Theatre[1]	Instrumental Music[1]	Vocal Music[1]	Series/ Festivals	Museums	Zoos and Aquariums[2]
0	0	0	0	0	0	0

Note: (1) Number of professional perfoming groups; (2) AZA-accredited
Source: The Grey House Performing Arts Directory, 2007; Official Museum Directory, 2008; Association of Zoos & Aquariums, AZA Member Zoos & Aquariums, June 2008

Professional Sports Teams

Team Name	League
Carolina Hurricanes	National Hockey League (NHL)

Note: Includes teams located in the Raleigh-Durham metro area.
Source: Original research

MEDIA

Newspapers

Name	News Focus	Frequency	Circulation
Cary News	Community	Weekly	12,500

Note: Includes newspapers with offices located in the city
Source: MediaContactsPro, March 2008

Television Stations

Name	Ch.	Network(s)	Type	Ownership
WUNC	4	PBS	Public	University of North Carolina
WRAL	5	CBS	Commercial	Capitol Broadcasting Company Inc.
WTVD	11	ABC	Commercial	ABC Inc.
WUND	12	PBS	Public	University of North Carolina
WNCN	17	NBC	Commercial	General Electric Corporation
WUNE	17	PBS	Public	University of North Carolina
WUNM	19	PBS	Public	University of North Carolina
WLFL	22	WBN	Commercial	Sinclair Broadcast Group
WUNK	25	PBS	Public	University of North Carolina
WUNL	26	PBS	Public	University of North Carolina
WRDC	28	UPN	Commercial	Sinclair Broadcast Group
WRAY	30	n/a	Commercial	Shop at Home Inc.
WUNU	31	PBS	Public	University of North Carolina
WUNF	33	PBS	Public	University of North Carolina
WUNP	36	PBS	Public	University of North Carolina
WUNJ	39	PBS	Public	University of North Carolina
WRPX	47	Pax	Commercial	Paxson Communications Corporation
WRAZ	50	Fox	Commercial	Capital Broadcasting Inc.
WUNG	58	n/a	Public	University of North Carolina
WFPX	62	Pax	Commercial	Paxson Communications Corporation

Note: Stations included cover the Raleigh-Durham DMA (Designated Market Area)
BurrellesLuce, MediaContacts Online, January 2007

Major AM Radio Stations

Call Letters	Freq. (kHz)	Station Type	Target Audience	Station Format	Music Format
WETC	540	Commercial	General/Hispanic	Music	International
WGTM	590	Commercial	General/Religious	Music	Gospel
WDNC	620	Commercial	General	News/Talk	n/a
WFNC	640	n/a	General	Music/News/Sports/Talk	n/a
WPTF	680	n/a	General	News/Talk	n/a
WRBZ	850	Commercial	General/Men	n/a	n/a
WEEB	990	Commercial	General	Sports/Talk	n/a
WGBR	1150	Commercial	General/Hispanic	Educational/News/Talk	n/a
WCLN	1170	Commercial	General/Religious	Music/Sports	Oldies
WMPM	1270	n/a	Christian/General	Educational/Music/News	n/a
WYAL	1280	Commercial	Black/General/Rel	Music	Christian
WCHL	1360	Commercial	General	Music/News/Sports/Talk	Adult Contemp.
WLLN	1370	n/a	Hispanic/Religious	Music/News/Sports/Talk	n/a
WSHV	1370	n/a	General/Religious	News	n/a
WEED	1390	Commercial	General/Religious	Music/Talk	Gospel
WSRC	1410	n/a	General/Religious	Music/Talk	n/a
WRTP	1530	n/a	General/Rel/Women	Music	n/a
WHPY	1590	Non-Comm	General/Religious	Music/Talk	Christian

Note: Stations included cover the Raleigh-Durham DMA (Designated Market Area); n/a not available
Source: BurrellesLuce, MediaContacts Online, January 2007

Major FM Radio Stations

Call Letters	Freq. (mHz)	Station Type	Target Audience	Station Format	Music Format
WZRU	88.5	Public	General	Music/News/Talk	Adult Standards
WCPE	89.7	Public	General	Educational/Music	Classical
WUNC	91.5	College	General	Educational/News/Talk	n/a
WFSS	91.9	College	General/Hispanic	Music/News	n/a
WRSN	93.9	Commercial	General/Women	Music/News/Sports/Talk	Adult Contemp.
WQDR	94.7	Commercial	General	Music	Country
WKML	95.7	Commercial	General	Music/Talk	Contemp. Country
WFLB	96.5	Commercial	General	Music/News/Sports/Talk	Oldies
WQOK	97.5	n/a	Black/General	Music/News/Talk	n/a
WQSM	98.1	n/a	General	Music	n/a
WZFX	99.1	Commercial	General	Music/Talk	Urban Contemp.
WTRG	100.7	Commercial	General	Music/News/Talk	Oldies
WRAL	101.5	Commercial	General	Music	Adult Contemp.
WYMY	102.9	n/a	Hispanic	Music	n/a
WRCQ	103.5	Commercial	General	Music/News/Talk	Album Rock
WFXK	104.3	Commercial	Black/General	Music/News/Talk	Oldies
WDCG	105.1	Commercial	General	Music/News/Talk	Contemp. Country
WRDU	106.1	Commercial	General	Music/Sports	Classic Rock
WKQB	106.9	Commercial	General	Music/Talk	Urban Contemp.

Note: Stations included cover the Raleigh-Durham DMA (Designated Market Area); n/a not available
BurrellesLuce, MediaContacts Online, January 2007

CLIMATE

Average and Extreme Temperatures

Temperature	Jan	Feb	Mar	Apr	May	Jun	Jul	Aug	Sep	Oct	Nov	Dec	Yr.
Extreme High (°F)	79	84	90	95	97	104	105	105	104	98	88	79	105
Average High (°F)	50	53	61	72	79	86	89	87	81	72	62	53	71
Average Temp. (°F)	40	43	50	59	67	75	78	77	71	60	51	42	60
Average Low (°F)	29	31	38	46	55	63	68	67	60	48	39	32	48
Extreme Low (°F)	-9	5	11	23	29	38	48	46	37	19	11	4	-9

Note: Figures cover the years 1948-1990
Source: National Climatic Data Center, International Station Meteorological Climate Summary, 9/96

Average Precipitation/Snowfall/Humidity

Precip./Humidity	Jan	Feb	Mar	Apr	May	Jun	Jul	Aug	Sep	Oct	Nov	Dec	Yr.
Avg. Precip. (in.)	3.4	3.6	3.6	2.9	3.9	3.6	4.4	4.4	3.2	2.9	3.0	3.1	42.0
Avg. Snowfall (in.)	2	3	1	Tr	0	0	0	0	0	0	Tr	1	8
Avg. Rel. Hum. 7am (%)	79	79	79	80	84	86	88	91	91	90	84	81	84
Avg. Rel. Hum. 4pm (%)	53	49	46	43	51	54	57	59	57	53	51	53	52

Note: Figures cover the years 1948-1990; Tr = Trace amounts (<0.05 in. of rain; <0.5 in. of snow)
Source: National Climatic Data Center, International Station Meteorological Climate Summary, 9/96

Weather Conditions

Temperature			Daytime Sky			Precipitation		
32°F & below	45°F & below	90°F & above	Clear	Partly cloudy	Cloudy	0.01 inch or more precip.	0.1 inch or more snow/ice	Thunder-storms
77	160	39	98	143	124	110	3	42

Note: Figures are average number of days per year and cover the years 1948-1990
Source: National Climatic Data Center, International Station Meteorological Climate Summary, 9/96

HAZARDOUS WASTE

Superfund Sites

Cary has no sites on the EPA's Superfund Final National Priorities List.
U.S. Environmental Protection Agency, Final National Priorities List, June 23, 2008

AIR & WATER QUALITY

Air Quality Index

Area	Percent of Days when Air Quality was...[2]				AQI Statistics	
	Good	Moderate	Unhealthy for Sensitive Groups	Unhealthy	Maximum	Median
MSA[1]	53.7	38.1	8.2	0.0	142	47

Note: The Air Quality Index (AQI) is an index for reporting daily air quality. EPA calculates the AQI for five major air pollutants regulated by the Clean Air Act: ground-level ozone, particle pollution (also known as particulate matter), carbon monoxide, sulfur dioxide, and nitrogen dioxide. The AQI runs from 0 to 500. The higher the AQI value, the greater the level of air pollution and the greater the health concern. There are six AQI categories: "Good" The AQI is between 0 and 50. Air quality is considered satisfactory; "Moderate" The AQI is between 51 and 100. Air quality is acceptable; "Unhealthy for Sensitive Groups" When AQI values are between 101 and 150, members of sensitive groups may experience health effects; "Unhealthy" When AQI values are between 151 and 200 everyone may begin to experience health effects; "Very Unhealthy" AQI values between 201 and 300 trigger a health alert; "Hazardous" AQI values over 300 trigger health warnings of emergency conditions; (1) Metropolitan Statistical Area - see Appendix A for areas included; (2) Based on 365 days with AQI data in 2007.
Source: U.S. Environmental Protection Agency, Air Quality Index Report, 2007

Air Quality Index Pollutants

Area	Percent of Days when AQI Pollutant was...[2]					
	Carbon Monoxide	Nitrogen Dioxide	Ozone	Sulfur Dioxide	Particulate Matter 2.5	Particulate Matter 10
MSA[1]	0.0	0.0	52.3	0.0	47.7	0.0

Note: The Air Quality Index (AQI) is an index for reporting daily air quality. EPA calculates the AQI for five major air pollutants regulated by the Clean Air Act: ground-level ozone, particle pollution (also known as particulate matter), carbon monoxide, sulfur dioxide, and nitrogen dioxide. The AQI runs from 0 to 500. The higher the AQI value, the greater the level of air pollution and the greater the health concern; (1) Metropolitan Statistical Area - see Appendix A for areas included; (2) Based on 365 days with AQI data in 2007.
Source: U.S. Environmental Protection Agency, Air Quality Index Report, 2007

Air Quality Index Trends

Area	Trend Sites (6)								All Sites (58)
	1999	2000	2001	2002	2003	2004	2005	2006	2006
MSA[1]	27	8	4	18	5	1	3	0	3

Note: An AQI value greater than 100 indicates that air quality would have been in the unhealthful range on that day. Data from exceptional events are not included. These counts are presented in two ways. First, the counts are based on sites having an adequate record of monitoring data during the trend period (trend sites). These counts represent the relative change in the number of days with AQI values greater than 100. In the last column, the counts are based on all sites with data in the most recent year (because it is possible for a site to have data in the most recent year but not enough data to be a trend site); (1) Metropolitan Statistical Area - see Appendix A for areas included.
Source: U.S. Environmental Protection Agency, Office of Air and Radiation, Air Trends, Factbook and Related Information, Air Pollution Trends in Selected Metropolitan Areas 2006

Maximum Air Pollutant Concentrations

	Particulate Matter 10 (ug/m^3)	Particulate Matter 2.5 (ug/m^3)	Ozone (ppm)	Carbon Monoxide (ppm)	Sulfur Dioxide (ppm)	Nitrogen Dioxide (ppm)	Lead (ug/m^3)
MSA[1] Level	43	41	0.097	3	0.006	n/a	n/a
NAAQS[2]	150	35	0.125	9	0.140	0.053	1.50
Met NAAQS[2]	Yes	No	Yes	Yes	Yes	n/a	n/a

Note: Data from exceptional events are not included; (1) Metropolitan Statistical Area - see Appendix A for areas included; (2) National Ambient Air Quality Standards; n/a not available
Concentrations: Particulate Matter 10 (coarse particulate) - highest second maximum 24-hour concentration; Particulate Matter 2.5 (fine particulate) - highest 98th percentile 24-hour concentration; Ozone - highest second daily maximum 1-hour concentration; Carbon Monoxide - highest second maximum non-overlapping 8-hour concentration; Sulfur Dioxide - highest second maximum 24-hour concentration; Nitrogen Dioxide - highest arithmetic mean concentration; Lead - highest quarterly maximum concentration
Units: ppm = parts per million; ug/m^3 = micrograms per cubic meter
Source: U.S. Environmental Protection Agency, MSA Factbook 2006, Air Quality Statistics by City

Drinking Water

Water System Name	Pop. Served	Primary Water Source Type	Violations[1]	
			Health Based	Monitoring/ Reporting
Town of Cary	130,000	Surface	0	0

Note: (1) Based on violation data from January 1, 2007 to December 31, 2007 (includes unresolved violations from earlier years)
Source: U.S. Environmental Protection Agency, Office of Ground Water and Drinking Water, Safe Drinking Water Information System (based on data extracted April 15, 2008)

Huntersville, North Carolina

Background

Located about 14 miles north of Charlotte, Huntersville is a former small town that has seen plenty of growth. In north Mecklenburg County, near Lake Norman, the city watched its population explode since 1990.

In 1996, the city threw out its old zoning ordinances and adopted new planning measures designed to coordinate growth, rather that allow their town to be overtaken by suburban sprawl. Originally incorporated in 1873, Huntersville was named for a notable local land owner and cotton farmer. This was farm country, and a cotton mill operated by the Virgin Manufacturing Company later helped stake out a mill town area on the east side of the town's railroad tracks.

The town continues to work to maintain a community spirit, hosting events such as a Christmas and spring festival. In addition, Lake Norman offers plenty of recreational opportunities for boaters and fishermen. As North Carolina's largest manmade lake, it has a 32,510-acre surface area when filled to capacity. And Huntersville residents can pay homage to their city's roots at the Historic Latta Plantation, an early cotton plantation that is now a living history museum replete with pigs and sheep.

Major employers operate in the area, including GE Polymerland, Rubbermaid, Irwin Industrial Tools, Max Daetwyler Corporation, and American Tire Distributors Inc. The Huntersville Business Park comprises 650 acres.

Students attend the Charlotte-Mecklenburg Schools. Davidson College, a four-year liberal arts college, is in nearby Davidsonville.

Huntersville regularly cooperates with other towns in the North Mecklenburg Municipal area, offering arts and cultural opportunities. In meeting these needs, the town actively encourages ongoing citizen participation.

And, of course, Huntersville residents are only a short drive from the benefits of Charlotte, with its Museum of the New South, Mint Museum of Craft, Charlottesville Symphony Orchestra and Charlotte Philharmonic Orchestra, to name a few. The National Football League's Carolina Panthers are based here as well.

With its location in the Piedmont Plateau region of the Carolinas, Huntersville enjoys a moderate climate characterized by cool winters and long, warm summers. Winter weather is changeable, but seldom extremely cold, owing to the protection afforded by the mountains to the northwest. Summer afternoons can be hot, and thunderstorms occur. When hurricanes strike the Carolina coast, they may produce heavy rain in Huntersville, but they seldom cause dangerous winds.

Rankings

General Rankings

- Charlotte* was ranked #85 out of 375 metro areas in *Cities Ranked & Rated*. Criteria: cost of living; climate; crime; transportation; economy and jobs; education; arts and culture; health and healthcare; leisure; quality of life. *Cities Ranked & Rated, 2nd Edition, 2007*
- Charlotte* was ranked #52 out of 379 metro areas in *Places Rated Almanac*. Criteria: health care; education; recreation; transportation; ambience; climate; crime; housing costs; jobs. *Places Rated Almanac, 7th Edition, 2007*

Business/Finance Rankings

- The nation's 100 largest metro areas were analysed in terms of the percentage of households entering some stage of foreclosure in 2007. The Charlotte* metro area ranked #34 out of 100 (#1 = highest foreclosure rate). *RealtyTrac, "Year-End 2007 Metropolitan Foreclosure Report"*
- The Charlotte* metro area was selected as one of "America's Most Wired Cities" by *Forbes*. The metro area was ranked #7 out of 30. Criteria: percentage of Internet users with high-speed access; the range of service providers within a city; availability of public wireless hot spots. *Forbes, "America's Most Wired Cities," January 10, 2008*
- Charlotte* was selected as one of the best places to start and grow a company by *Entrepreneur* and the National Policy Research Council. The Charlotte* metro area ranked #2 out of 50 large metro areas. Criteria: business formation and growth (firms started four to 14 years ago that still employ at least 5 people and experienced rapid growth over the last four years). *Entrepreneur/National Policy Research Council, "Hot Cities for Entrepreneurs," September 2006*
- The Charlotte* metro area was selected as one of "America's 50 Hottest Cities" for business relocations and expansions. Criteria: industry's most prominent site selection consultants were asked to list their top city choices for relocating and expanding manufacturing companies, taking into consideration such factors as the business climate, work force quality, operating costs, incentive programs, and the ease of working with local political and economic development officials. *Expansion Management, January-February 2007*
- The Charlotte* metro area was selected as one of the "Top 20 Real Estate Markets" for expanding or relocating companies. The area ranked #8. Criteria: low rental costs; low purchase prices; high vacancy rates of office and warehouse space. *Expansion Management, October 2007*
- Intel, in partnership with Sperling's BestPlaces, ranked the 80 "Best Cities for Teleworking" in America. The Charlotte* metro area ranked #12 among mid-sized metro areas. The study identifies cities that hold the greatest potential for teleworking based on a host of factors including typical commuting times, fuel prices, availability of broadband Internet access and percentage of the population in telework friendly jobs. The study also factored in extreme climate and natural hazards. *Intel, "Best Cities for Teleworking," March 30, 2006*
- The Charlotte* metro area appeared on the Milken Institute "2007 Best Performing Cities" index. Rank: #23 out of 200 large metro areas. Criteria: job growth; wage and salary growth; high-tech output growth. *Milken Institute, "2007 Best Performing Cities"*
- The Charlotte* metro area was selected as one of "The Top 20 Boom Towns in America." *Business 2.0* magazine and econometric research firm Global Insight compared 319 metropolitan areas in the U.S. and ranked the 61 with populations over 1 million. Criteria: a weighted formula that includes forecast growth rates in sectors that contain the economy's 10 most skilled occupational clusters; the prevalence of college degrees in the local workforce; median salary. The area ranked #19 among large metro areas. *Business 2.0 Magazine, March 2004*

- Charlotte* was identified as one of the 100 "Most Unwired Cities" in the U.S. The area ranked #17 out of the 100 largest metro areas in the U.S. Criteria: number of public and commercial wireless access points (hotspots); airports with wireless Internet access; broadband availability; local wireless networks; and wireless email devices. *Intel, "Most Unwired Cities Survey," June 7, 2005*
- Charlotte* was ranked #41 out of 125 regions worldwide in terms of its "Knowledge Competitiveness Index." The index attempts to measure the knowledge-based development taking place throughout the world and is based on 19 measures of economic performance that indicate a region's ability to translate its knowledge capacity into economic value. *Robert Huggins Associates, World Knowledge Competitiveness Index 2005*
- *Forbes* ranked the 200 most populous metro areas in the U.S. in terms of the "Best Places for Business and Careers." The Charlotte* metro area was ranked #37. Criteria: business costs (labor, energy, tax and office space expenses); living costs (housing, transportation, food and other household expenditures); education levels of the work force; job growth; income growth; migration trends; crime rates; and culture/leisure. *Forbes, "Best Places for Business and Careers," March 19, 2008*
- *Fortune* ranked the 100 largest metro areas in the U.S. in terms of projected median home price change in 2007. The Charlotte* metro area ranked #17. *Fortune.com, "Hot Spots, Cold Spots"*

Health/Environment Rankings

- 100 of the largest metro areas in the U.S. were analyzed in terms of their current drought severity. The Charlotte* metro area ranked #13 (#1 = driest). The rankings were based on statistics such as long-term precipitation trends and patterns and the Palmer drought indices. *Sperling's BestPlaces, www.BestPlaces.net, "America's Drought-Riskiest Cities," November 2007*
- Doctors at the Harvard School of Public Health ranked 40 metropolitan areas based on data from the government-sponsored Hospital Quality Alliance program. The program tracks the performance of individual hospitals in treating patients for three common health problems: heart attacks, congestive heart failure, and pneumonia. The Charlotte* metro area ranked #21 in quality of care for heart attacks, #12 for congestive heart failure, and #11 for pneumonia. *New England Journal of Medicine, July 21, 2005*
- *Reader's Digest* ranked the 50 largest metro areas in the U.S. in terms of how "clean" they are. The Charlotte* metro area ranked #20. Criteria: air quality; water quality; toxic industrial pollution; Superfund sites; and sanitation. *Reader's Digest, "The 50 Cleanest (and Dirtiest) Cities in America," July 2005*
- The Charlotte* metro area appeared in *Country Home's* "2008 Best Green Places" report. The area ranked #213 out of 379. Criteria: official energy policies; green power; green buildings; availability of fresh, locally grown food. *Country Home, "2008 Best Green Places"*
- Wyeth Consumer Healthcare, in partnership with Sperling's BestPlaces, ranked the nation's 50 most populous metro areas in terms of five key health factors. The Charlotte* metro area ranked #32. Criteria: physical activity; health status; nutrition; lifestyle pursuits; and mental wellness. *Wyeth Consumer Healthcare, "Centrum Healthiest Cities Study," April 19, 2005*
- Charlotte* was identified as a "2008 Asthma Capital." The area ranked #7 out of the nation's 100 largest metropolitan areas. Twelve factors were used to identify the most challenging places to live for people with asthma: estimated prevalence; self-reported prevalence; crude death rate for asthma; annual pollen score; annual air quality; public smoking laws; number of board-certified asthma specialists; school inhaler access laws; rescue medication use; controller medication use; uninsured rate; poverty rate. *Asthma and Allergy Foundation of America, "2008 Asthma Capitals"*

- Charlotte* was identified as a "Spring Allergy Capital." The area ranked #9 out of 100. Three groups of factors were used to identify the most severe cities for people with allergies during the spring season: annual pollen levels; medicine utilization; access to board-certified allergists. *Asthma and Allergy Foundation of America, "2007 Spring Allergy Capital Rankings"*

- Charlotte* was identified as a "Fall Allergy Capital." The area ranked #26 out of 100. Three groups of factors were used to identify the most severe cities for people with allergies during the fall season: annual pollen levels; medicine utilization; access to board-certified allergists. *Asthma and Allergy Foundation of America, "2007 Fall Allergy Capital Rankings"*

- Ortho-McNeil Neurologics, in partnership with Sperling's BestPlaces, analyzed 110 metro areas and identified those U.S. cities with the highest prevalence of factors that are most commonly associated with migraine headaches. The Charlotte* metro area ranked #46. Criteria: number of migraine-related drug prescriptions per capita; lifestyle factors that can contribute to migraines; environmental factors that can trigger migraines; and consumption of migraine-triggering foods. *Ortho-McNeil Neurologics, "America's Migraine Hot Spots," March 14, 2006*

- Sperling's BestPlaces ranked 331 metro areas and identified the most and least stressful U.S. cities. The Charlotte* metro area ranked #22 out of the 100 largest metro areas (#1 = most stressful). Criteria: divorce rate; unemployment rate; violent and property crime; suicide rate; commute time; mental health; alcohol consumption; cloudy days. *Sperling's BestPlaces, www.BestPlaces.net, "America's Most (and Least) Stressful Cities," January 9, 2004*

- An analysis of the "Best & Worst Cities for Sleep" was conducted by Sperling's BestPlaces. The study ranked America's 50 most populated metro areas. The Charlotte* metro area ranked #16 (#1 = best city for sleep). Criteria: number of days residents didn't get enough rest or sleep during the past month; average length of daily commute; divorce rate; unemployment rate. *Sperling's BestPlaces, www.BestPlaces.net, "Best & Worst Cities for Sleep," 2006*

- Charlotte* was highlighted as one of the 25 most ozone-polluted metro areas in the U.S. The area ranked #16. *American Lung Association, State of the Air: 2007*

- Charlotte* was selected as one of "America's Pet Healthiest Cities" by Purina. The city ranked #48 out of 50. Criteria: veterinary services; environment; legislation; preventative care; obesity/body condition. *Purina Pet Institute, "America's Pet Healthiest Cities," May 20, 2003*

Women/Minorities Rankings

- Charlotte* was ranked #73 out of 100 metro areas in *SELF Magazine's* ranking of "America's Best Places for Women." A panel of experts came up with more than 50 criteria including death and disease rates, environmental indicators, community resources, and lifestyle habits. *SELF Magazine, "America's Best Places for Women 2007," December 2007*

- Charlotte* appeared on *Black Enterprise's* list of the "Ten Best Cities for African Americans." The top picks were culled from more than 2,000 interactive surveys completed on www.blackenterprise.com and by editorial staff evaluation. The editors weighed the following criteria as it pertained to African Americans in each city: median household income; percentage of households earning more than $100,000; percentage of businesses owned; percentage of college graduates; unemployment rates; home loan rejections; and homeownership rates. *Black Enterprise, May 2007*

Seniors/Retirement Rankings

- Sperling's BestPlaces in partnership with Bankers Life & Casualty Company designed a survey to identify the top 50 metro areas in the U.S. that offer the best overall qualities for senior living. The Charlotte* metro area ranked #40. The following criteria were statistically weighted to reflect the needs of the senior population: health; disease; economics; social; environment; spiritual; transportation; housing; and crime. *Bankers Life & Casualty Company, "Best Cities for Seniors 2005"*

- A.G. Edwards ranked America's 500 top-performing communities based on their residents' personal savings and investing behavior. The Charlotte* metro area ranked #182 with an index score of 103.61 (national average = 100.00). A dozen statistical factors were measured including: participation in retirement savings plans; personal debt levels; and home ownership. *A.G. Edwards, "2007 Nest Egg Index", September 12, 2007*

Children/Family Rankings

- The Charlotte* metro area was selected as one of the "Best Cities for Relocating Families" by Worldwide ERC and Primacy Relocation. The 2007 study placed a special emphasis on the housing market, which has significantly impacted the relocation industry and an employer's ability to transfer employees. The variables which weigh heavily in this category include home price, home affordability index, appreciation rates, and property tax. Other criteria include cost of living, crime rates, education, climate, focus on diversity, physicians per capita, recreation and leisure, arts and culture, air quality, watershed quality, sales tax, unemployment rate, job growth, high school and higher education index, school expenditures per student, students in public school, SAT/ACT percentile, and population growth. *Worldwide ERC and Primacy Relocation, "2007 Best Cities for Relocating Families"*

Safety Rankings

- The National Insurance Crime Bureau ranked 361 metro areas in the U.S. in terms of per capita rates of vehicle theft. The Charlotte* metro area ranked #38 (#1 = highest rate). Criteria: number of vehicle theft offenses per 100,000 inhabitants. *National Insurance Crime Bureau, "NICB Vehicle Theft Study," April 22, 2008*
- Charlotte* appeared on Sperling's BestPlaces list of the "Riskiest Cities for Identity Theft." The area ranked #19 out of the nations 50 largest metro areas. Over 80 criteria were analyzed across four major categories: technology impact; crime; transactions; and risk profile. *Sperling's BestPlaces, www.BestPlaces.net, "Riskiest Cities for Identity Theft," July 2006*
- Farmers Insurance Group of Companies, in partnership with Sperling's BestPlaces, ranked 379 metro areas and identified the "Most Secure U.S. Place to Live." The Charlotte* metro area ranked #107 out of 114 in the large metro area category (500,000 or more residents). Criteria: crime rates; extreme weather; risk of natural disasters; environmental hazards; terrorism threats; air quality; life expectancy; job loss numbers. *Farmers Insurance Group, "Most Secure U.S. Places to Live 2007"*
- Charlotte* was identified as one of the most dangerous large metro areas for pedestrians in the U.S. The area ranked #13 out of the nations 50 largest metro areas. Criteria: average yearly pedestrian fatalities per capita (for the years 2002 and 2003) adjusted for the number of walkers. *Surface Transportation Policy Project, "Mean Streets 2004"*

Sports/Recreation Rankings

- The Charlotte* metro area appeared on the *Sporting News* list of the "Best Sports Cities 2007". The area ranked #37 out of 150 cities in the U.S. *Sporting News* takes a 12-month snapshot, roughly July to July, of each city's sports, putting a heavy premium on regular-season won-lost records (from the most recently completed season). Other criteria include: playoff berths, bowl appearances and tournament bids; championships; applicable power ratings; quality of competition; overall fan fervor as measured in part by attendance as percentage of venue capacity; abundance of teams (rewarding quality over quantity); stadium and arena quality; ticket availability and prices; franchise ownership; and marquee appeal of athletes. *SportingNews.com, "Best Sports Cities 2007," August 1, 2007*
- The Charlotte* metro area was selected by *Cranium* as one of the "Top 50 Fun Cities" in America. The area ranked #29. Criteria includes: number of sports teams, restaurants, and dance performances; number of toy stores; city budget spent on recreation. *Cranium, November 4, 2003*
- *Golf Digest* ranked 330 metro areas in the U.S. in terms of golf. The Charlotte* metro area was ranked #288. Criteria: access to golf; weather; value of golf; and quality of golf. *Golf Digest, "Metro Golf Rankings," August 2005*

Dating/Romance Rankings

- Eli Lily and Company, in partnership with Sperling's BestPlaces, ranked the nation's 50 largest metro areas in terms of the "Most Romantic Cities for Baby Boomers." The Charlotte* metro area ranked #5. Criteria: marriage and divorce rates among "baby boomers" age 45 to 60; great restaurants; dance studios; chocolate, jewelry and flower sales. *Eli Lily and Company, "Most Romantic Cities for Baby Boomers," April 20, 2007*

- The Charlotte* metro area was selected as one of the "Best Cities for Relocating Singles" by Worldwide ERC and Primacy Relocation. The area ranked #38 out of the 100 largest metro areas in the U.S. Areas were selected based on the following criteria: a robust cost-of-living index; adventure and outdoor recreation opportunities; violent crime and property crime rates; percentage of the population that is unmarried (ages 25-34); ratio of single men and single women; affordability of quality higher education, including in-state and out-of-state tuition requirements and rates; number of newcomers to the area; commute times; tax rates; fee and occupancy rates for temporary housing and mini-storage; quality and quantity of collegiate and professional sporting events and fun, fan-friendly venues. *Worldwide ERC and Primacy Relocation, "2007 Best Cities for Relocating Singles," October 25, 2007*

- Sperling's BestPlaces in partnership with AXE Deodorant Bodyspray ranked 80 metro areas and identified "America's Best (and Worst) Cities for Dating." The Charlotte* metro area ranked #71 (#1 = best). Criteria: percentage of singles ages 18-24; population density; dating venues per capita. *AXE Deodorant Bodyspray, "America's Best (and Worst) Cities for Dating," May 2004*

Miscellaneous Rankings

- Huntersville was identified as one of the 100 fastest-growing suburbs in America by "Forbes." The city ranked #46. Criteria: suburban cities, townships and villages with more than 10,000 people in 2000 were ranked by their population growth from 2000 to 2006. *Forbes.com, "America's Fastest-Growing Suburbs," July 16, 2007*

- The Charlotte* metro area appeared on *Forbes* list of "America's Drunkest Cities". The area ranked #34. Criteria: 35 of the largest continental U.S. metro areas were chosen based on availability of data and geographic diversity. Each metro was ranked in five areas: state laws; drinkers; heavy drinkers; binge drinkers; and alcoholism. *Forbes.com, "America's Drunkest Cities," August 22, 2006*

- Sperling's BestPlaces in partnership with Pep Boys ranked 77 metro areas and identified "America's Most Drivable Cities." The Charlotte* metro area ranked #27. Criteria: climate; road roughness; urban mobility; gas prices. *Pep Boys, "America's Most Drivable Cities," April 9, 2003*

- State Farm Insurance, in partnership with Sperling's BestPlaces, analyzed several key factors that contribute to overall family preparedness. The Charlotte* metro area ranked #24 out of the nation's 50 most populous metro areas. Criteria: quality of life; life insurance coverage; and investments. *State Farm Life Insurance, "Fiscally Fit Cities Report," July 20, 2004*

- Scarborough Research, a leading market research firm, identified the top local markets for grocery coupon use. The Charlotte* DMA (Designated Market Area) ranked in the top 25 with 38% of consumers reporting that they use grocery coupons at least once per week. *Scarborough Research, December 8, 2004*

- A study by Sperling's BestPlaces examined which U.S. metro areas were most affected by high fuel prices in 2006. The Charlotte* metro area was ranked #18 out of 80 (#1 = most expensive city for driving). Rankings are based on the average dollars spent on gas per year by two driver households. Criteria: cost of regular-grade gasoline; average miles driven per day; average number of gallons each driver uses and wastes in traffic congestion each day. *Sperling's BestPlaces, www.bestplaces.net, "Pain at the Pump," May 18, 2006*

Huntersville is located within the Charlotte-Gastonia-Concord, NC-SC Metropolitan Statistical Area.

Business Environment

CITY FINANCES

City Government Finances

Component	2004-2005 ($000)	2004-2005 ($ per capita)
Total Revenues	n/a	n/a
Total Expenditures	n/a	n/a
Debt Outstanding	n/a	n/a
Cash and Securities	n/a	n/a

Source: U.S Census Bureau, Government Finances 2004-2005

City Government Revenue by Source

Source	2004-2005 ($000)	2004-2005 ($ per capita)
General Revenue		
From Federal Government	n/a	n/a
From State Government	n/a	n/a
From Local Governments	n/a	n/a
Taxes		
Property	n/a	n/a
Sales	n/a	n/a
Personal Income	n/a	n/a
License	n/a	n/a
Charges	n/a	n/a
Liquor Store	n/a	n/a
Utility	n/a	n/a
Employee Retirement	n/a	n/a
Other	n/a	n/a

Source: U.S Census Bureau, Government Finances 2004-2005

City Government Expenditures by Function

Function	2004-2005 ($000)	2004-2005 ($ per capita)	2004-2005 (%)
General Expenditures			
Airports	n/a	n/a	n/a
Corrections	n/a	n/a	n/a
Education	n/a	n/a	n/a
Fire Protection	n/a	n/a	n/a
Governmental Administration	n/a	n/a	n/a
Health	n/a	n/a	n/a
Highways	n/a	n/a	n/a
Hospitals	n/a	n/a	n/a
Housing and Community Development	n/a	n/a	n/a
Interest on General Debt	n/a	n/a	n/a
Libraries	n/a	n/a	n/a
Parking	n/a	n/a	n/a
Parks and Recreation	n/a	n/a	n/a
Police Protection	n/a	n/a	n/a
Public Welfare	n/a	n/a	n/a
Sewerage	n/a	n/a	n/a
Solid Waste Management	n/a	n/a	n/a
Liquor Store	n/a	n/a	n/a
Utility	n/a	n/a	n/a
Employee Retirement	n/a	n/a	n/a
Other	n/a	n/a	n/a

Source: U.S Census Bureau, Government Finances 2004-2005

Municipal Bond Ratings

Area	Moody's
City	n/a

Source: Mergent Bond Record, January 2008 (unless noted otherwise)

DEMOGRAPHICS

Population Growth

Area	1990 Census	2000 Census	2007 Estimate	2012 Projection	Population Growth (%) 1990-2000	Population Growth (%) 2000-2012
City	9,131	24,960	38,378	47,223	173.4	89.2
MSA[1]	1,024,331	1,330,448	1,580,079	1,758,436	29.9	32.2
U.S.	248,709,873	281,421,906	301,045,522	314,920,978	13.2	11.9

Note: (1) Metropolitan Statistical Area - see Appendix B for areas included
Source: Claritas, Inc.

Number of Households and Average Household Size

Area	2007 Estimate	2007 Average Household Size
City	14,446	2.66
MSA[1]	614,864	2.57
U.S.	113,668,003	2.65

Note: (1) Metropolitan Statistical Area - see Appendix B for areas included
Source: Claritas, Inc.

Race and Ethnicity

Area	White Alone[2]	Black Alone[2]	Asian Alone[2]	Other Race Alone[2]	Hispanic[3]
City	86.2	7.7	1.9	4.2	7.3
MSA[1]	68.3	23.5	2.6	5.7	8.0
U.S.	73.1	12.4	4.3	10.3	14.9

Note: Figures are 2007 estimates; (1) Metropolitan Statistical Area - see Appendix B for areas included (2) Alone is defined as not being in combination with one or more other races; (3) May be of any race.
Source: Claritas, Inc.

Ancestry

Area	German	Irish[2]	English	American	Italian	Polish	French[3]	Scottish
City	18.0	14.0	13.5	8.6	6.1	2.7	3.4	2.9
MSA[1]	11.7	8.1	8.4	12.4	2.7	1.3	1.7	2.2
U.S.	15.2	10.9	8.7	7.3	5.6	3.2	3.0	1.7

Note: Figures include multiple ancestry (e.g. if a person reported being Irish and Italian, they were included in both columns); (1) Metropolitan Statistical Area - see Appendix A for areas included; (2) Includes Celtic; (3) Includes Alsatian but excludes Basque
Source: Census 2000, Summary File 3

Foreign-Born Population

Area	Percent of Population Born in							
	Any Foreign Country	Europe	Asia	Africa	Oceania[2]	Canada	Mexico	Latin America[3]
City	4.5	0.8	0.8	0.2	0.0	0.4	1.7	0.6
MSA[1]	6.7	0.9	1.5	0.4	0.0	0.2	2.3	1.4
U.S.	11.1	1.7	2.9	0.3	0.1	0.3	3.3	2.5

Note: (1) Metropolitan Statistical Area - see Appendix A for areas included; (2) Includes Australia, New Zealand subregion, Melanesia, Micronesia, Polynesia, and Oceania n.e.c; (3) Includes Central America (excluding Mexico), South America, and the Caribbean.
Source: Census 2000, Summary File 3

Marriage Status

Area	Never Married	Now Married (excluding Separated)	Separated	Widowed	Divorced
City	19.3	67.9	2.2	3.6	7.0
MSA[1]	25.5	57.0	2.7	5.8	8.9
U.S.	27.1	54.4	2.2	6.6	9.7

Note: Figures are percentages and cover the population 15 years of age and older; (1) Metropolitan Statistical Area - see Appendix A for areas included
Source: Census 2000, Summary File 3

Age Distribution

Area	Under Age 5	Age 5 to 17	Age 18 to 34	Age 35 to 49	Age 50 to 64	Age 65 to 79	80 Years and Over
	Percent of Population						
City	9.7	18.6	26.2	27.8	11.5	4.0	2.3
MSA[1]	7.1	18.3	25.7	24.4	14.5	7.8	2.4
U.S.	6.8	18.9	23.7	23.5	14.8	9.2	3.2

Note: (1) Metropolitan Statistical Area - see Appendix A for areas included
Source: Census 2000, Summary File 3

Male/Female Ratio

Area	Males	Females	Males per 100 Females
City	19,021	19,357	98.3
MSA[1]	778,817	801,262	97.2
U.S.	148,320,305	152,725,217	97.1

Note: Figures are 2007 estimates; (1) Metropolitan Statistical Area - see Appendix B for areas included
Source: Claritas, Inc.

Religion

Area	Catholic	Southern Baptist	United Methodist	ELCA[1]	LDS[2]	Presbyterian Church USA	Jewish Est.	Muslim Est.
County	8.5	10.8	6.7	1.2	0.5	6.0	1.2	1.1
U.S.	22.0	7.1	3.7	1.8	1.5	1.1	2.2	0.6

Note: Figures are the number of adherents as a percentage of the total population; Adherents are defined as all members, including full members, their children and the estimated number of other participants who are not considered members (e.g. the baptized, those not confirmed, those regularly attending services, etc.); (1) Evangelical Lutheran Church in America; (2) The Church of Jesus Christ of Latter Day Saints
Source: Reprinted with permission from Religious Congregations and Membership in the United States 2000 (Nashville, Glenmary Research Center, 2002) Copyright Association of Statisticians of American Religious Bodies. All rights reserved.

ECONOMY

Gross Metropolitan Product

Area	2002	2003	2004	2005	2005 Rank[2]
MSA[1]	60.6	63.1	66.1	71.3	35

Note: Figures are in billions of dollars; (1) Charlotte-Gastonia-Concord, NC-SC Metropolitan Statistical Area - see Appendix A for areas included; (2) Rank ranges from 1 to 361
Source: The U.S. Conference of Mayors, "U.S. Metro Economies: GMP - The Engines of America's Growth," January 2007

Economic Growth

Area	1995 GMP	2005 GMP	Average Annual Growth Rate	Growth Rate Rank[2]
MSA[1]	36.5	71.3	6.9	45

Note: Figures are in billions of dollars; GMP = Gross Metropolitan Product; (1) Charlotte-Gastonia-Concord, NC-SC Metropolitan Statistical Area - see Appendix A for areas included; (2) Rank ranges from 1 to 361
Source: The U.S. Conference of Mayors, "U.S. Metro Economies: GMP - The Engines of America's Growth," January 2007

INCOME

Per Capita/Median/Average Income

Area	Per Capita ($)	Median Household ($)	Average Household ($)
City	36,503	83,171	96,668
MSA[1]	27,995	53,758	71,403
U.S.	25,495	49,280	66,670

Note: Figures are 2007 estimates; (1) Metropolitan Statistical Area - see Appendix B for areas included
Source: Claritas, Inc.

Household Income Distribution

Area	Percent of Households Earning							
	Under $15,000	$15,000 -24,999	$25,000 -34,999	$35,000 -49,999	$50,000 -74,999	$75,000 -99,000	$100,000 -149,999	$150,000 and up
City	5.2	4.7	6.2	11.6	16.7	17.4	25.3	13.0
MSA[1]	10.4	9.1	10.9	16.1	21.1	13.0	12.0	7.3
U.S.	13.1	10.9	11.2	15.6	19.5	11.9	11.3	6.6

Note: Figures are 2007 estimates; (1) Metropolitan Statistical Area - see Appendix B for areas included
Source: Claritas, Inc.

Poverty Rates by Age

Area	All Ages	Under 5 Years Old	5 to 17 Years Old	18 to 64 Years Old	65 Years and Over
City	3.1	0.1	0.6	1.9	0.4
MSA[1]	9.3	0.9	2.2	5.3	1.0
U.S.	12.4	1.2	3.0	6.9	1.2

Note: Figures are percent of population with income in 1999 below poverty level and only include population for whom poverty status is determined; (1) Metropolitan Statistical Area - see Appendix A for areas included
Source: Census 2000, Summary File 3

Personal Bankruptcy Filing Rate

Area	2004	2005	2006
Mecklenburg County	3.47	5.07	1.61
U.S.	5.31	6.82	2.00

Note: Numbers are per 1,000 population and include Chapter 7 and Chapter 13 filings
Source: Federal Deposit Insurance Corporation (FDIC), Regional Economic Conditions (RECON), 8/23/2007

EMPLOYMENT

Labor Force and Employment

Area	Civilian Labor Force			Workers Employed		
	Dec. 2006	Dec. 2007	% Chg.	Dec. 2006	Dec. 2007	% Chg.
City	21,418	21,228	-0.9	20,838	20,572	-1.3
MSA[1]	841,508	837,004	-0.5	804,473	796,443	-1.0
U.S.	152,571,000	153,705,000	0.7	146,081,000	146,334,000	0.2

Note: Data is not seasonally adjusted and covers workers 16 years of age and older;
(1) Metropolitan Statistical Area - see Appendix B for areas included
Source: Bureau of Labor Statistics, http://stats.bls.gov

Unemployment Rate

Area	2007											
	Jan.	Feb.	Mar.	Apr.	May	Jun.	Jul.	Aug.	Sep.	Oct.	Nov.	Dec.
City	3.1	3.0	2.7	2.7	2.9	3.3	3.4	3.2	3.1	3.1	3.1	3.1
MSA[1]	4.8	4.7	4.3	4.4	4.6	4.9	5.1	4.8	4.6	4.6	4.8	4.8
U.S.	5.0	4.9	4.5	4.3	4.3	4.7	4.9	4.6	4.5	4.4	4.5	4.8

Note: Data is not seasonally adjusted and covers workers 16 years of age and older; All figures are percentages; (1) Metropolitan Statistical Area - see Appendix B for areas included
Source: Bureau of Labor Statistics, http://stats.bls.gov

Employment by Occupation

Occupation Classification	City (%)	MSA[1] (%)	U.S. (%)
Sales and Office	28.9	27.4	26.7
Professional and Related	23.0	17.9	20.2
Service	9.1	12.1	14.9
Production, Transportation, and Material Moving	7.0	16.9	14.6
Management, Business, and Financial	24.9	15.1	13.5
Construction, Extraction, and Maintenance	6.9	10.4	9.4
Farming, Forestry, and Fishing	0.1	0.3	0.7

Note: Figures cover employed civilians 16 years of age and older;
(1) Metropolitan Statistical Area - see Appendix A for areas included
Source: Census 2000, Summary File 3

Employment by Industry

Sector	MSA[1] Number of Employees	MSA[1] Percent of Total	U.S. Percent of Total
Government	107,600	12.3	16.3
Education and Health Services	79,500	9.1	13.4
Professional and Business Services	135,300	15.5	13.1
Retail Trade	100,200	11.5	11.6
Manufacturing	80,800	9.3	9.9
Leisure and Hospitality	83,800	9.6	9.6
Financial Activities	77,900	8.9	5.9
Construction	n/a	n/a	5.3
Wholesale Trade	49,400	5.7	4.4
Other Services	39,400	4.5	3.9
Transportation and Utilities	36,600	4.2	3.7
Information	22,200	2.5	2.2
Natural Resources and Mining	n/a	n/a	0.5

Note: Figures cover non-farm employment as of December 2007 and are not seasonally adjusted; (1) Metropolitan Statistical Area - see Appendix B for areas included; n/a not available
Source: Bureau of Labor Statistics, http://stats.bls.gov

Average Wages

Occupation	$/Hr.	Occupation	$/Hr.
Accountants and Auditors	29.49	Maids and Housekeeping Cleaners	8.53
Automotive Mechanics	19.44	Maintenance and Repair Workers	17.79
Bookkeepers	15.42	Marketing Managers	52.05
Carpenters	16.09	Nuclear Medicine Technologists	30.34
Cashiers	8.59	Nurses, Licensed Practical	18.99
Clerks, General Office	12.19	Nurses, Registered	27.81
Clerks, Receptionists/Information	11.98	Nursing Aides/Orderlies/Attendants	10.87
Clerks, Shipping/Receiving	13.98	Packers and Packagers, Hand	9.44
Computer Programmers	38.36	Physical Therapists	33.80
Computer Support Specialists	21.92	Postal Service Mail Carriers	21.00
Computer Systems Analysts	36.11	Real Estate Brokers	28.24
Cooks, Restaurant	10.49	Retail Salespersons	11.53
Dentists	n/a	Sales Reps., Exc. Tech./Scientific	29.39
Electrical Engineers	36.13	Sales Reps., Tech./Scientific	30.02
Electricians	17.73	Secretaries, Exc. Legal/Med./Exec.	13.82
Financial Managers	56.20	Security Guards	10.86
First-Line Supervisors/Mgrs., Sales	17.63	Surgeons	n/a
Food Preparation Workers	8.52	Teacher Assistants	9.70
General and Operations Managers	56.26	Teachers, Elementary School	19.50
Hairdressers/Cosmetologists	13.95	Teachers, Secondary School	20.60
Internists	87.33	Telemarketers	14.87
Janitors and Cleaners	9.98	Truck Drivers, Heavy/Tractor-Trailer	19.51
Landscaping/Groundskeeping Workers	10.51	Truck Drivers, Light/Delivery Svcs.	14.92
Lawyers	52.52	Waiters and Waitresses	8.21

Note: Wage data covers the Charlotte-Gastonia-Concord, NC-SC Metropolitan Statistical Area - see Appendix B for areas included. Hourly wages for elementary/secondary school teachers and teacher assistants were calculated by the editors from annual wage data assuming a 40 hour work week; n/a not available.
Source: Bureau of Labor Statistics, May 2007 Metro Area Occupational Employment and Wage Estimates

RESIDENTIAL REAL ESTATE

Building Permits

Area	Single-Family			Multi-Family			Total		
	2006	2007p	Pct. Chg.	2006	2007p	Pct. Chg.	2006	2007p	Pct. Chg.
City	n/a	n/a	n/a	n/a	n/a	n/a	n/a	n/a	n/a
U.S.	1,378,200	973,300	-29.4	460,700	407,200	-11.6	1,838,900	1,380,500	-24.9

Note: (p) preliminary; figures cover and represent new, privately-owned housing units authorized (unadjusted data); All permit data are based on estimates with imputation; U.S. figures are based on the new 20,000-place series.
Source: U.S. Census Bureau, Manufacturing, Mining, and Construction Statistics

Homeownership and Housing Vacancies

Area	Homeownership Rate[2] (%)			Rental Vacancy Rate[3] (%)			Homeowner Vacancy Rate[4] (%)		
	2005	2006	2007	2005	2006	2007	2005	2006	2007
MSA[1]	65.8	66.1	66.5	11.1	13.5	11.0	2.3	2.9	3.1
U.S.	68.9	68.8	68.1	9.8	9.8	9.7	1.9	2.4	2.7

Note: (1) Metropolitan Statistical Area - see Appendix B for areas included; (2) The proportion of households that are owners; (3) The proportion of the rental inventory that is vacant for rent; (4) The proportion of the homeowner inventory that is vacant for sale; n/a not available
Source: U.S. Census Bureau, Housing Vacancies and Homeownership Annual Statistics: 2007

TAXES

State Corporate Income Tax Rates

State	Rates and Tax Brackets
North Carolina	6.9%

Note: Tax rates as of January 1, 2008; The franchise tax rate is $1.50 per $1,000, with a minimum of $35.
Source: Tax Foundation, www.taxfoundation.org

State Individual Income Tax Rates

State	Federal Deductibility	Marginal Rates (%)	Standard Deduction ($)		Personal Exemptions ($)[1]	
			Single	Joint	Single	Dependents
North Carolina	No	6.0 - 8.0 (y)(dd)	3,000	6,000	1,300 (o)(r)	1,300 (o)(r)

Note: Tax rates as of January 1, 2008; Local- and county-level taxes are not included; n/a not applicable; (1) Married joint filers generally receive double the single exemption; (o) Exemptions are based on federal Adjusted Gross Income (AGI) and are adjusted according to income and filing status. Taxpayer's filing single with AGI less than $60,000 receive $800 per exemption, if they earn over $60,000 they get $1,300 per exempt

n. Taxpayers married filing jointly with AGI under $100,000 get $1,600 per exemption and $2,600 for AGI over $100,00; (r) State adjusts its bracket levels for inflation at the end of each year before printing tax forms; (y) Brackets are not double for married taxpayers; (dd) North Carolina will finally allow the expiration of the temporary increase of its top income tax rate as of January 1, 2008 when the top rate will return to 7.75 percent.
Source: Tax Foundation, www.taxfoundation.org

Various State and Local Tax Rates

State and Local Sales and Use (%)	State Sales and Use (%)	Gasoline[1,2] ($/gal.)	Cigarette ($/pack)	Spirits ($/gal.)	Table Wine ($/gal.)	Beer ($/gal.)
7.25	4.25	0.302	0.35	10.36 (n)	0.79	0.53

Note: Tax rates as of January 1, 2008; (1) In addition to the 18.4 cpg Federal gasoline tax; (2) Rates may include additional state sales taxes, environmental protection and storage fees/taxes, and local taxes. When necessary, the volume-weighted average of all local taxes is used to approximate the typical statewide rate including local tax; (n) The state government controls all sales. The implied excise tax rate is calculated using methodology designed by the Distilled Spirits Council of the United States (DISCUS).
Source: Tax Foundation, www.taxfoundation.org; Original research

State Tax Burdens

Area	Combined State and Local Tax Burden		Combined Federal, State and Local Tax Burden	
	Percent	Rank	Percent	Rank
North Carolina	11.0	19	31.3	24
U.S. Average	11.0	-	32.7	-

Note: Figures cover 2007 and measure taxes as a percentage of income
Source: Tax Foundation, www.taxfoundation.org

State Business Tax Climate Index Rankings

State	Overall Rank	Corporate Tax Index Rank	Individual Income Tax Index Rank	Sales Tax Index Rank	Unemployment Insurance Tax Index Rank	Property Tax Index Rank
North Carolina	40	25	44	39	6	34

Note: Rankings range from 1 to 50 where 1 is best. Rankings do not average across to Overall Rank. States without a given tax are given a ranking of 1.
Source: Tax Foundation, State Business Tax Climate Index 2008

TRANSPORTATION

Means of Transportation to Work

Area	Car/Truck/Van		Public Transportation			Bicycle	Walked	Other Means	Worked at Home
	Drove Alone	Car-pooled	Bus	Subway	Railroad				
City	84.0	10.0	0.4	0.0	0.0	0.0	0.5	0.5	4.6
MSA[1]	80.9	12.9	1.3	0.0	0.0	0.1	1.2	0.8	2.8
U.S.	75.7	12.2	2.5	1.5	0.5	0.4	2.9	1.0	3.3

Note: Figures are percentages and cover workers 16 years of age and older;
(1) Metropolitan Statistical Area - see Appendix A for areas included
Source: Census 2000, Summary File 3

Travel Time to Work

Area	Less Than 15 Minutes	15 to 29 Minutes	30 to 44 Minutes	45 to 59 Minutes	60 Minutes or More
City	17.8	31.2	29.7	13.5	7.7
MSA[1]	23.8	38.7	23.0	8.5	6.1
U.S.	29.4	36.1	19.1	7.4	8.0

Note: Figures are percentages and include workers 16 years old and over; (1) Metropolitan Statistical Area - see Appendix A for areas included
Source: Census 2000, Summary File 3

Travel Time Index

Area	1982	1995	2004	2005
Urban Area[1]	1.07	1.13	1.25	1.23
Average[2]	1.11	1.22	1.29	1.30

Note: Travel Time Index - The ratio of travel time in the peak period to the travel time at free-flow conditions. A value of 1.35 indicates a 20-minute free-flow trip takes 27 minutes in the peak. Free-flow speeds (60 mph on freeways and 35 mph on principal arterials) are used as the comparison threshold; (1) Covers the Charlotte, NC-SC urban area; (2) average of 85 urban areas
Source: Texas Transportation Institute, The 2007 Urban Mobility Report, September 2007

Living Environment

COST OF LIVING

Cost of Living Index

Composite Index	Groceries	Housing	Utilities	Trans-portation	Health Care	Misc. Goods/ Services
90.0	99.2	76.5	83.5	92.4	104.3	96.9

Note: U.S. = 100; Figures cover the Charlotte NC urban area.
Source: The Council for Community and Economic Research (formerly ACCRA), Cost of Living Index, 2007

Grocery Prices

Area[1]	T-Bone Steak ($/pound)	Frying Chicken ($/pound)	Whole Milk ($/half gal.)	Eggs ($/dozen)	Orange Juice ($/64 oz.)	Coffee ($/11.5 oz.)
City[2]	9.41	1.04	2.59	1.65	3.26	2.92
Avg.	8.93	1.12	2.13	1.52	3.26	3.31
Min.	5.88	0.71	1.33	0.83	2.30	2.20
Max.	12.80	2.07	3.43	3.54	5.79	6.20

Note: (1) Values for the local area are compared with the average, minimum and maximum values for all 331 areas in the Cost of Living Index report; (2) Figures cover the Charlotte NC urban area; **T-Bone Steak** *(price per pound);* **Frying Chicken** *(price per pound, whole fryer);* **Whole Milk** *(half gallon carton);* **Eggs** *(price per dozen, Grade A, large);* **Orange Juice** *(64 oz. Tropicana or Florida Natural);* **Coffee** *(11.5 oz. can, vacuum-packed, Maxwell House, Hills Bros, or Folgers).*
Source: The Council for Community and Economic Research (formerly ACCRA), Cost of Living Index, 2007

Housing and Utility Costs

Area[1]	New Home Price ($)	Apartment Rent ($/month)	All Electric ($/month)	Part Electric ($/month)	Other Energy ($/month)	Telephone ($/month)
City[2]	235,835	658	130.06	-	-	23.29
Avg.	309,605	782	146.13	78.67	90.16	26.14
Min.	189,877	n/a	82.03	37.41	33.15	17.08
Max.	1,202,800	3,481	271.14	150.60	257.67	37.45

Note: (1) Values for the local area are compared with the average, minimum and maximum values for all 331 areas in the Cost of Living Index report; (2) Figures cover the Charlotte NC urban area; **New Home Price** *(2,400 sf living area, 8,000 sf lot, in urban area with full utilities);* **Apartment Rent** *(950 sf 2 bedroom/1.5 or 2 bath, unfurnished, excluding all utilities except water);* **All Electric** *(average monthly cost for an all-electric home);* **Part Electric** *(average monthly cost for a part-electric home);* **Other Energy** *(average monthly cost for natural gas, fuel oil, coal, wood, and any other forms of energy except electricity);* **Telephone** *(price includes basic monthly rate for a private residential line plus additional local usage charges incurred by a family of four).*
Source: The Council for Community and Economic Research (formerly ACCRA), Cost of Living Index, 2007

Health Care, Transportation, and Other Costs

Area[1]	Doctor ($/visit)	Dentist ($/visit)	Optometrist ($/visit)	Gasoline ($/gallon)	Beauty Salon ($/visit)	Men's Shirt ($)
City[2]	79.40	81.33	80.65	2.60	24.70	22.39
Avg.	79.48	71.93	79.55	2.64	29.52	25.77
Min.	52.08	44.80	43.95	2.19	15.58	16.19
Max.	148.44	126.27	158.83	3.48	60.62	48.53

Note: (1) Values for the local area are compared with the average, minimum and maximum values for all 331 areas in the Cost of Living Index report; (2) Figures cover the Charlotte NC urban area; **Doctor** *(general practitioners routine exam of an established patient);* **Dentist** *(adult teeth cleaning and periodic oral examination);* **Optometrist** *(full vision eye exam for established adult patient);* **Gasoline** *(one gallon regular unleaded, national brand, including all taxes, cash price at self-service pump if available);* **Beauty Salon** *(woman's shampoo, trim, and blow-dry);* **Men's Shirt** *(cotton/polyester dress shirt, pinpoint weave, long sleeves).*
Source: The Council for Community and Economic Research (formerly ACCRA), Cost of Living Index, 2007

HOUSING

House Price Index (HPI)

Area	National Ranking[2]	Quarterly Change (%)	One-Year Change (%)	Five-Year Change (%)
MSA[1]	23	0.06	6.08	27.81
U.S.[3]	-	0.10	0.84	41.37

Note: The HPI is a weighted repeat sales index. It measures average price changes in repeat sales or refinancings on the same properties. This information is obtained by reviewing repeat mortgage transactions on single-family properties whose mortgages have been purchased or securitized by Fannie Mae or Freddie Mac in January 1975; (1) Metropolitan Statistical Area - see Appendix B for areas included; (2) Rankings are based on annual percentage change for all metro areas containing at least 15,000 transactions over the last 10 years and ranges from 1 to 291; (3) figures based on a weighted average of Census Division estimates; all figures are for the period ending December 31, 2007
Source: Office of Federal Housing Enterprise Oversight, House Price Index, February 26, 2008

House Price Valuations

Area	Q1 2000	Q1 2001	Q1 2002	Q1 2003	Q1 2004	Q1 2005	Q1 2006	Q1 2007	Q1 2008
MSA[1]	-9.3	-9.4	-11.9	-9.6	-12.0	-12.6	-11.8	-10.5	-10.1

Note: Figures show the percentage of over- or under-valuation of single family homes relative to statistically normal house values (e.g. a value of 23.6 indicates that house values are 23.6% overvalued). Statistically normal house values are based on house prices, interest rates, household incomes, population densities, and any historical premiums or discounts metropolitan areas have exhibited over time; (1) Figures cover the Metropolitan Statistical Area - see Appendix B for areas included
Source: Global Insight/National City Corporation, House Prices in America, May 2008

Median Home Prices

Area	2005	2006	2007[r]	Percent Change 2006 to 2007
MSA[1]	180.9	190.6	204.3	7.2
U.S. Average	219.0	221.9	217.9	-1.8

Note: Figures are median sales prices of existing single-family homes in thousands of dollars; (r) revised; n/a not available; (1) Metropolitan Statistical Area - see Appendix B for areas included
Source: National Association of Realtors, Metropolitan Area Prices, 1st Quarter 2008

Housing: Year Structure Built

Area	1990 -2000	1980 -1989	1970 -1979	1960 -1969	1950 -1959	1940 -1949	Before 1940	Median Year
City	70.2	13.5	5.4	4.0	2.6	2.1	2.2	1995
MSA[1]	30.3	19.1	16.3	12.7	10.0	5.5	6.1	1980
U.S.	17.0	15.8	18.5	13.7	12.7	7.3	15.0	1971

Note: Figures are percentages; (1) Metropolitan Statistical Area - see Appendix A for areas included
Source: Census 2000, Summary File 3

HEALTH

Health Risk Data

Category	Area[1] (%)	U.S. (%)
Adults who have been told they have high blood pressure[3]	26.7	25.5
Adults who have been told they have high blood cholesterol[3]	35.2	35.6
Adults who have been told they have diabetes[2]	7.7	7.5
Adults who have been told they have arthritis[3]	25.0	27.0
Adults who have been told they currently have asthma	5.3	8.5
Adults who are current smokers	19.3	20.1
Adults who are heavy drinkers[4]	4.1	4.9
Adults who are overweight (BMI 25.0 - 29.9)	37.5	36.5
Adults who are obese (BMI 30.0 - 99.8)	23.3	25.1

Note: Data as of 2006 unless otherwise noted; (1) Figures cover the Metropolitan Statistical Area - see Appendix B for areas included; (2) Figures do not include pregnancy-related diabetes, pre-diabetes or borderline diabetes; (3) 2005 data; (4) Heavy drinkers are classified as adult men having more than two drinks per day or adult women having more than one drink per day
Source: Centers for Disease Control and Prevention, Behaviorial Risk Factor Surveillance System, SMART: Selected Metropolitan/Micropolitan Area Risk Trends, 2005, 2006

Mortality Rates for the Top 10 Causes of Death in the U.S.

ICD-10[a] Sub-Chapter	ICD-10[a] Code	Age-Adjusted Mortality Rate[1] per 100,000 population	
		County[2]	U.S.
Malignant neoplasms	C00-C97	178.3	186.5
Ischaemic heart diseases	I20-I25	104.7	152.3
Other forms of heart disease	I30-I51	58.7	51.5
Cerebrovascular diseases	I60-I69	55.5	50.0
Chronic lower respiratory diseases	J40-J47	38.3	42.6
Diabetes mellitus	E10-E14	19.9	24.8
Other degenerative diseases of the nervous system	G30-G31	47.2	22.6
Other external causes of accidental injury	W00-X59	19.2	21.4
Influenza and pneumonia	J10-J18	17.5	20.7
Hypertensive diseases	I10-I13	19.0	18.2

Note: (a) ICD-10 = International Classification of Diseases 10th Revision; (1) Mortality rates are a three year average covering 2003-2005; (2) Figures cover Mecklenburg County
Source: Centers for Disease Control and Prevention, National Center for Health Statistics. Compressed Mortality File 1999-2004. CDC WONDER On-line Database, compiled from Compressed Mortality File 1999-2005 Series 20 No. 2K, 2008.

Mortality Rates for Selected Causes of Death

ICD-10[a] Sub-Chapter	ICD-10[a] Code	Age-Adjusted Mortality Rate[1] per 100,000 population	
		County[2]	U.S.
Assault	X85-Y09	9.6	5.9
Human immunodeficiency virus (HIV) disease	B20-B24	10.5	4.5
Intentional self-harm	X60-X84	9.3	10.8
Malnutrition	E40-E46	1.6	1.0
Obesity and other hyperalimentation	E65-E68	1.4	1.4
Organic, including symptomatic, mental disorders	F01-F09	36.6	16.8
Transport accidents	V01-V99	11.2	16.1
Viral hepatitis	B15-B19	1.5	1.8

Note: (a) ICD-10 = International Classification of Diseases 10th Revision; (1) Mortality rates are a three year average covering 2003-2005; (2) Figures cover Mecklenburg County
Source: Centers for Disease Control and Prevention, National Center for Health Statistics. Compressed Mortality File 1999-2004. CDC WONDER On-line Database, compiled from Compressed Mortality File 1999-2005 Series 20 No. 2K, 2008.

Distribution of Physicians[1]

Area	Total	Family/ General Practice	Specialties	
			Medical	Surgical
Mecklenburg County (number)	1,851	389	702	466
Mecklenburg County (rate per 10,000 pop.)	23.2	4.9	8.8	5.9
U.S. (rate per 10,000 pop.)	17.7	4.6	6.9	4.3

Note: Data as of 2005; (1) Includes all non-federal, patient-care, office-based MDs
Source: Area Resource File (ARF). June 2007. U.S. Department of Health and Human Services, Health Resources and Services Administration, Bureau of Health Professions, Rockville, MD.

Hospitals

Huntersville has the following hospitals: 1 general medical and surgical.
AHA Guide to the Healthcare Field 2008

According to *U.S. News,* the Charlotte-Gastonia-Concord, NC-SC metro area is home to one of the best hospitals in the U.S.: **Carolinas Medical Center**. *U.S. News Online, "America's Best Hospitals 2007"*

EDUCATION

Public School District Statistics

District Name	Schls	Pupils	Pupil/ Teacher Ratio	Minority Pupils[1] (%)	Free Lunch Eligible[2] (%)	IEP[3] (%)
Charlotte-Mecklenburg Schools	142	124,005	14.4	62.4	39.5	11.6
Lake Norman Charter	1	635	n/a	7.7	n/a	6.6

Note: Table includes regular local school districts with 2,000 or more students; (1) Percentage of students that are not white, non-Hispanic; (2) Percentage of students that are eligible for the free lunch program; (3) Percentage of students that have an Individualized Education Program.
Source: U.S. Department of Education, National Center for Education Statistics, Common Core of Data, Local Education Agency (School District) Universe Survey: School Year 2005-2006; U.S. Department of Education, National Center for Education Statistics, Common Core of Data, Public Elementary/Secondary School Universe Survey: School Year 2005-2006

Top Public High Schools

High School Name	Index[1]	Rank[1]	Subsidized Lunch (%)[2]	E&E (%)[3]
Hopewell	1.964	543	24.0	30.6
North Mecklenburg **	2.850	193	n/a	30.5

Note: (1) Public schools are ranked according to a ratio that is the number of Advanced Placement, International Baccalaureate, and/or Cambridge tests taken by all students at a school in 2007 divided by the number of graduating seniors. All of the schools on the list have an index of at least 1.000; they are in the top five percent of public schools measured this way. The rankings range from 1 to 1,422; (2) Percentage of students receiving federally subsidized meals; (3) E & E stands for equity and excellence percentage: the portion of all graduating seniors at a school that had at least one passing grade on one AP or IB test; (**) Gave both IB and AP tests. AP and IB participation are indicators of a school's efforts to get students to excel and prepare for college.
Source: Newsweek Online, "Top High Schools 2008"

Highest Level of Education

Area	Less than H.S.	H.S. Diploma	Some College, No Deg.	Associate Degree	Bachelors Degree	Masters Degree	Profess. School Degree	Doctorate Degree
City	7.8	15.6	22.2	7.3	34.7	9.8	1.9	0.7
MSA[1]	17.9	24.6	21.9	6.9	20.8	5.7	1.6	0.6
U.S.	19.4	28.4	21.2	6.4	15.7	5.9	2.0	1.0

Note: Figures are 2007 estimated percentages and cover persons age 25 and over; (1) Metropolitan Statistical Area - see Appendix B for areas included
Source: Claritas, Inc.

Educational Attainment by Race

Area	High School Graduate (%)					Bachelor's Degree (%)				
	Total	White	Black	Asian	Hisp.[2]	Total	White	Black	Asian	Hisp.[2]
City	91.6	93.4	78.7	86.4	68.5	46.5	47.5	36.7	42.4	26.3
MSA[1]	80.5	83.0	74.7	76.4	48.6	26.5	29.1	16.5	37.8	11.9
U.S.	80.4	83.6	72.3	80.4	52.4	24.4	26.1	14.3	44.1	10.4

Note: Figures shown cover persons 25 years old and over; (1) Metropolitan Statistical Area - see Appendix A for areas included; (2) people of Hispanic origin can be of any race
Source: Census 2000, Summary File 3

School Enrollment by Type

Area	Grades KG to 8				Grades 9 to 12			
	Public		Private		Public		Private	
	Enrollment	%	Enrollment	%	Enrollment	%	Enrollment	%
City	2,744	81.5	622	18.5	1,235	94.6	70	5.4
MSA[1]	176,153	88.3	23,233	11.7	71,217	91.1	6,951	8.9
U.S.	33,526,011	88.7	4,285,121	11.3	14,848,628	90.6	1,532,323	9.4

Note: Figures shown cover persons 3 years old and over; (1) Metropolitan Statistical Area - see Appendix A for areas included
Source: Census 2000, Summary File 3

School Enrollment by Race

Area	Grades KG to 8 (%)				Grades 9 to 12 (%)			
	White	Black	Asian	Hisp.[1]	White	Black	Asian	Hisp.[1]
City	88.4	5.5	0.9	4.3	83.5	12.0	1.6	3.4
MSA[2]	67.2	26.1	1.8	5.0	67.2	27.1	2.2	3.8
U.S.	68.5	15.5	3.3	16.8	68.8	15.5	3.8	15.7

Note: Figures shown cover persons 3 years old and over; (1) people of Hispanic origin can be of any race; (2) Metropolitan Statistical Area - see Appendix A for areas included
Source: Census 2000, Summary File 3

Average Salaries of Public School Classroom Teachers

District	2005-06		2006-07		Percent Change 2005-06 to 2006-07
	Dollars	Rank[1]	Dollars	Rank[1]	
North Carolina	43,922	27	46,410	25	5.66
U.S. Average	49,026	-	50,816	-	3.65

Note: (1) State rank ranges from 1 to 51.
Source: National Education Association, Rankings & Estimates: Rankings of the States 2006 and Estimates of School Statistics 2007, December 2007

Higher Education

Four-Year Colleges			Two-Year Colleges			Medical Schools[1]	Law Schools[2]	Voc/ Tech[3]
Public	Private Non-profit	Private For-profit	Public	Private Non-profit	Private For-profit			
0	0	0	0	0	0	0	0	0

Note: Figures cover institutions located within the city limits; (1) includes schools accredited by the Liaison Committee on Medical Education and the American Osteopathic Association; (2) includes American Bar Association-accredited law schools; (3) includes all schools with programs that are less than 2 years.
Source: National Center for Education Statistics, The Integrated Postsecondary Education System (IPEDS) Peer Analysis System, 2007; www.usnews.com, Law and Medical School Directories, 2009

PRESIDENTIAL ELECTION

2004 Presidential Election Results

Area	Bush	Kerry	Nader	Other
Mecklenburg County	48.0	51.6	0.1	0.3
U.S.	50.7	48.3	0.4	0.6

Note: Results are percentages and may not add to 100% due to rounding
Source: Dave Leip's Atlas of U.S. Presidential Elections, www.uselectionatlas.org

EMPLOYERS

Major Employers

Company Name	Industry	Type of Site
Bank of America	National commercial banks	Headquarters
Carlisle Companies Inc	Asphalt felts and coatings	Headquarters
Carolinas Healthcare System	General medical and surgical hospitals	Headquarters
Caromont Health	General medical and surgical hospitals	Single
Chancellors Office	Colleges and universities	Branch
Chrysler Freight Line	Truck and bus bodies	Branch
Duke Power	Electric services	Headquarters
IBM	Calculating and accounting equipment	Branch
IBM	Office equipment	Branch
Insource Contract Services LLC	Help supply services	Single
M C A	Business consulting, nec	Single
Medcath Incorporated	Specialty hospitals, except psychiatric	Headquarters
Northeast Medical Ctr	General medical and surgical hospitals	Headquarters
PGI Nonwovens	Nonwoven fabrics	Headquarters
Rohr Inc Credit Corporation	Aircraft engines and engine parts	Single
University NC At Chapel Hl	Schools and educational services	Branch
Wachovia	Bank holding companies	Headquarters
Wachovia	Management consulting services	Branch

Note: Companies shown are located within the Charlotte metropolitan area; nec = not elsewhere classified.
Source: www.zapdata.com, May 2008

PUBLIC SAFETY

Crime Rate

Area	All Crimes	Violent Crimes				Property Crimes		
		Murder	Forcible Rape	Robbery	Aggrav. Assault	Burglary	Larceny -Theft	Motor Vehicle Theft
City	3,452.6	0.0	29.6	80.9	161.7	722.3	2,312.5	145.5
Metro[1]	n/a	8.3	36.7	269.5	n/a	1,405.5	3,220.5	622.0
U.S.	3,808.1	5.7	30.9	149.4	287.5	729.4	2,206.8	398.4

Note: Figures are crimes per 100,000 population; (1) Metropolitan Statistical Area - see Appendix B for areas included
Source: FBI Uniform Crime Reports, 2006

Hate Crimes

Area	Number of Quarters Reported	Bias Motivation				
		Race	Religion	Sexual Orientation	Ethnicity	Disability
City	4	0	0	0	0	0

Source: Federal Bureau of Investigation, Hate Crime Statistics 2006

RECREATION

Culture

Dance[1]	Theatre[1]	Instrumental Music[1]	Vocal Music[1]	Series/ Festivals	Museums	Zoos and Aquariums[2]
0	0	0	0	0	1	0

Note: (1) Number of professional perfoming groups; (2) AZA-accredited
Source: The Grey House Performing Arts Directory, 2007; Official Museum Directory, 2008; Association of Zoos & Aquariums, AZA Member Zoos & Aquariums, June 2008

Professional Sports Teams

Team Name	League
Charlotte Bobcats	National Basketball Association (NBA)
Carolina Panthers	National Football League (NFL)

Note: Includes teams located in the Charlotte metro area.
Source: Original research

MEDIA

Newspapers

Name	News Focus	Frequency	Circulation
The Huntersville Star	Regional	Monthly	n/a

Note: Includes newspapers with offices located in the city; n/a not available
Source: MediaContactsPro, March 2008

Television Stations

Name	Ch.	Network(s)	Type	Ownership
WBTV	3	CBS	Commercial	Jefferson-Pilot Communications Company
WSOC	9	ABC	Commercial	Cox Enterprises Inc.
WHKY	14	n/a	Commercial	Long Family Partnership
WCCB	18	Fox	Commercial	Bahakel Communications Inc.
WNSC	30	PBS	Public	South Carolina Educational Television Commission
WCNC	36	NBC	Commercial	Belo Corporation
WTVI	42	PBS	Public	Charlotte-Mecklenburg Public Broadcasting Authority
WJZY	46	UPN	Commercial	Capitol Broadcasting Company Inc.
WWWB	55	WBN	Commercial	Capitol Broadcasting Company Inc.
WAXN	64	n/a	Commercial	Cox Enterprises Inc.

Note: Stations included cover the Charlotte DMA (Designated Market Area); n/a not available
BurrellesLuce, MediaContacts Online, January 2007

Major AM Radio Stations

Call Letters	Freq. (kHz)	Station Type	Target Audience	Station Format	Music Format
WFNZ	610	n/a	General	News/Sports/Talk	n/a
WLWL	770	Commercial	General	Educational/Music/Talk	Oldies
WYFQ	930	n/a	Religious	Music/News/Talk	n/a
WNOW	1030	Commercial	General/Hispanic	Music/News	Latin
WKGX	1080	Commercial	General	Music	Country
WBT	1110	Commercial	General	News/Talk	n/a
WCXN	1170	Commercial	General/Hisp/Rel	Music/News	Latin
WCGC	1270	Commercial	General	Educational/Music/News	Gospel
WHKY	1290	Commercial	General	News/Talk	n/a
WLTC	1370	Commercial	Religious	Music/News	Christian
WMNC	1430	Commercial	General	Music	Country
WGFY	1480	Commercial	Children/General	Ed/Music/News/Sports/Talk	Top 40
WAGL	1560	Commercial	General/Hisp/Rel	Music/Talk	Latin

Note: Stations included cover the Charlotte DMA (Designated Market Area); n/a not available
Source: BurrellesLuce, MediaContacts Online, January 2007

Major FM Radio Stations

Call Letters	Freq. (mHz)	Station Type	Target Audience	Station Format	Music Format
WPIR	88.1	Non-Comm	General/Religious	Educational/Music	Gospel
WGWG	88.3	College	General/Religious	Educational/Music/Talk	Blues
WDAV	89.9	College	General	Music/Talk	Classical
WFAE	90.7	College	General	Educational/Talk	n/a
WMNC	92.1	Commercial	General	Music	Contemp. Country
WNKS	95.1	Commercial	Young Adult	Music/News/Talk	Top 40
WXRC	95.7	Commercial	General	Music	Classic Rock
WKKT	96.9	Commercial	General	Music	Contemp. Country
WPEG	97.9	Commercial	General	Music/News/Talk	Urban Contemp.
WBT	99.3	Commercial	General	News/Sports/Talk	n/a
WRFX	99.7	Commercial	General	Music	Classic Rock
WZJS	100.7	Commercial	General	Music	Country
WBAV	101.9	Commercial	General	Music	Urban Contemp.
WECR	102.3	Commercial	General	Music	Oldies
WLYT	102.9	Commercial	General	Music/News/Talk	Adult Contemp.
WKVS	103.3	Commercial	General	Music	Country
WSOC	103.7	Commercial	General	Music/News/Talk	Country
WSSS	104.7	Commercial	General	Music/Talk	80's
WFMX	105.7	n/a	General	Music/News	n/a
WNMX	106.1	Commercial	General	Music/News/Talk	Adult Standards
WEND	106.5	n/a	General	Music/News/Talk	n/a
WRHM	107.1	Commercial	General	Music/News	Country
WLNK	107.9	Commercial	General	Music/News/Talk	Adult Contemp.

Note: Stations included cover the Charlotte DMA (Designated Market Area); n/a not available
BurrellesLuce, MediaContacts Online, January 2007

CLIMATE

Average and Extreme Temperatures

Temperature	Jan	Feb	Mar	Apr	May	Jun	Jul	Aug	Sep	Oct	Nov	Dec	Yr.
Extreme High (°F)	78	81	86	93	97	103	103	103	104	98	85	77	104
Average High (°F)	51	54	62	72	80	86	89	88	82	72	62	53	71
Average Temp. (°F)	41	44	51	61	69	76	79	78	72	61	51	43	61
Average Low (°F)	31	33	40	48	57	65	69	68	62	50	40	33	50
Extreme Low (°F)	-5	5	4	25	32	45	53	53	39	24	11	2	-5

Note: Figures cover the years 1948-1990
Source: National Climatic Data Center, International Station Meteorological Climate Summary, 9/96

Average Precipitation/Snowfall/Humidity

Precip./Humidity	Jan	Feb	Mar	Apr	May	Jun	Jul	Aug	Sep	Oct	Nov	Dec	Yr.
Avg. Precip. (in.)	3.6	3.8	4.5	3.0	3.7	3.4	3.9	3.9	3.4	3.2	3.1	3.4	42.8
Avg. Snowfall (in.)	2	2	1	Tr	0	0	0	0	0	0	Tr	1	6
Avg. Rel. Hum. 7am (%)	78	77	78	78	82	83	86	89	89	87	83	79	82
Avg. Rel. Hum. 4pm (%)	53	49	46	43	49	51	54	55	54	50	50	54	51

Note: Figures cover the years 1948-1990; Tr = Trace amounts (<0.05 in. of rain; <0.5 in. of snow)
Source: National Climatic Data Center, International Station Meteorological Climate Summary, 9/96

Weather Conditions

Temperature			Daytime Sky			Precipitation		
10°F & below	32°F & below	90°F & above	Clear	Partly cloudy	Cloudy	0.01 inch or more precip.	0.1 inch or more snow/ice	Thunderstorms
1	65	44	98	142	125	113	3	41

Note: Figures are average number of days per year and cover the years 1948-1990
Source: National Climatic Data Center, International Station Meteorological Climate Summary, 9/96

HAZARDOUS WASTE

Superfund Sites

Huntersville has no sites on the EPA's Superfund Final National Priorities List.
U.S. Environmental Protection Agency, Final National Priorities List, June 23, 2008

AIR & WATER QUALITY

Air Quality Index

Area	Percent of Days when Air Quality was...[2]				AQI Statistics	
	Good	Moderate	Unhealthy for Sensitive Groups	Unhealthy	Maximum	Median
MSA[1]	40.8	43.8	13.7	1.6	205	55

Note: The Air Quality Index (AQI) is an index for reporting daily air quality. EPA calculates the AQI for five major air pollutants regulated by the Clean Air Act: ground-level ozone, particle pollution (also known as particulate matter), carbon monoxide, sulfur dioxide, and nitrogen dioxide. The AQI runs from 0 to 500. The higher the AQI value, the greater the level of air pollution and the greater the health concern. There are six AQI categories: "Good" The AQI is between 0 and 50. Air quality is considered satisfactory; "Moderate" The AQI is between 51 and 100. Air quality is acceptable; "Unhealthy for Sensitive Groups" When AQI values are between 101 and 150, members of sensitive groups may experience health effects; "Unhealthy" When AQI values are between 151 and 200 everyone may begin to experience health effects; "Very Unhealthy" AQI values between 201 and 300 trigger a health alert; "Hazardous" AQI values over 300 trigger health warnings of emergency conditions; (1) Metropolitan Statistical Area - see Appendix A for areas included; (2) Based on 365 days with AQI data in 2007.
Source: U.S. Environmental Protection Agency, Air Quality Index Report, 2007

Air Quality Index Pollutants

Area	Percent of Days when AQI Pollutant was...[2]					
	Carbon Monoxide	Nitrogen Dioxide	Ozone	Sulfur Dioxide	Particulate Matter 2.5	Particulate Matter 10
MSA[1]	0.0	0.0	59.2	0.0	40.8	0.0

Note: The Air Quality Index (AQI) is an index for reporting daily air quality. EPA calculates the AQI for five major air pollutants regulated by the Clean Air Act: ground-level ozone, particle pollution (also known as particulate matter), carbon monoxide, sulfur dioxide, and nitrogen dioxide. The AQI runs from 0 to 500. The higher the AQI value, the greater the level of air pollution and the greater the health concern; (1) Metropolitan Statistical Area - see Appendix A for areas included; (2) Based on 365 days with AQI data in 2007.
Source: U.S. Environmental Protection Agency, Air Quality Index Report, 2007

Air Quality Index Trends

Area	Trend Sites (11)								All Sites (70)
	1999	2000	2001	2002	2003	2004	2005	2006	2006
MSA[1]	34	22	13	27	4	5	11	8	18

Note: An AQI value greater than 100 indicates that air quality would have been in the unhealthful range on that day. Data from exceptional events are not included. These counts are presented in two ways. First, the counts are based on sites having an adequate record of monitoring data during the trend period (trend sites). These counts represent the relative change in the number of days with AQI values greater than 100. In the last column, the counts are based on all sites with data in the most recent year (because it is possible for a site to have data in the most recent year but not enough data to be a trend site); (1) Metropolitan Statistical Area - see Appendix A for areas included.
Source: U.S. Environmental Protection Agency, Office of Air and Radiation, Air Trends, Factbook and Related Information, Air Pollution Trends in Selected Metropolitan Areas 2006

Maximum Air Pollutant Concentrations

	Particulate Matter 10 (ug/m^3)	Particulate Matter 2.5 (ug/m^3)	Ozone (ppm)	Carbon Monoxide (ppm)	Sulfur Dioxide (ppm)	Nitrogen Dioxide (ppm)	Lead (ug/m^3)
MSA[1] Level	62	32	0.115	2	0.013	0.013	0
NAAQS[2]	150	35	0.125	9	0.140	0.053	1.50
Met NAAQS[2]	Yes	Yes	Yes	Yes	Yes	Yes	Yes

Note: Data from exceptional events are not included; (1) Metropolitan Statistical Area - see Appendix A for areas included; (2) National Ambient Air Quality Standards; n/a not available
Concentrations: Particulate Matter 10 (coarse particulate) - highest second maximum 24-hour concentration; Particulate Matter 2.5 (fine particulate) - highest 98th percentile 24-hour concentration; Ozone - highest second daily maximum 1-hour concentration; Carbon Monoxide - highest second maximum non-overlapping 8-hour concentration; Sulfur Dioxide - highest second maximum 24-hour concentration; Nitrogen Dioxide - highest arithmetic mean concentration; Lead - highest quarterly maximum concentration
Units: ppm = parts per million; ug/m^3 = micrograms per cubic meter
Source: U.S. Environmental Protection Agency, MSA Factbook 2006, Air Quality Statistics by City

Drinking Water

Water System Name	Pop. Served	Primary Water Source Type	Violations[1]	
			Health Based	Monitoring/ Reporting
Charlotte-Mecklenburg Utility	750,000	Surface	0	0

Note: (1) Based on violation data from January 1, 2007 to December 31, 2007 (includes unresolved violations from earlier years)
Source: U.S. Environmental Protection Agency, Office of Ground Water and Drinking Water, Safe Drinking Water Information System (based on data extracted April 15, 2008)

Matthews, North Carolina

Background

Matthews is a quaint, historic, smaller city within a stone's throw of the excitement and lure of a big city. Via the I-485 beltway, the 17-square-mile Matthews easily connect to Charlotte 10 miles away, for both commuters and entertainment seekers.

Matthews was first known as Stumptown, named for the tree stumps left after the area was cleared to grow cotton. In 1825, Stumptown became known as Fullwood, named after the town's first postmaster and operator of the Stagecoach Inn.

The city was incorporated in 1879 and named Matthews in honor of Edward W. Matthews one of the directors of the Carolina Central Railway-the town's lifeline to the outside world. The railroad facilitated growth and economic security by allowing for the easy export of cotton and the import of needed supplies. The railroad's imprint on the town is reflected in the town seal, town mascot, and a mural at the local library.

Cotton farming was the base of the economy until after World War II. After the war, nearby Charlotte grew, rapidly as did Matthews. Eight Fortune 500 companies are headquartered in Mecklenburg County and one, Family Dollar, is headquartered in Matthews and is one of the city's largest employer.

Matthews consistently receives high marks by residents for being safe, a good place to raise children, a good environment for business and responsive to citizens' needs. The city carefully plans its growth so to preserve its southern charm and open spaces. Much of the city is thoughtfully landscaped with gardens and art exhibits, and most of its homes are single-family houses.

Matthews Athletic & Recreation Association facilitates sports programs for local area youth year round, and a variety of classes, from exercise to wellness to art, are available at the Matthews Community Center and Crews Road Recreation Center. Summer activities for children include Forensics 101 Science Camp, Gymstars, Art in the Park, Super Hero Camp, and Afternoon Activity Camps. Matthews Playhouse for the Performing Arts offers free performances during the summer months. Stumptown Park offers Summer Concert and Movie Series, and Matthews Alive! Festival is held each Labor Day weekend.

Students in the public school system consistently perform well above state averages. Central Piedmont Community College, Wingate University Metro College, and University of North Carolina Charlotte are nearby institutions of higher education.

Presbyterian Hospital, with the first health library open to the public, is located in Matthews. Mercy Hospital Inc, Presbyterian-Orthopedic Hospital, and the Charlotte Institute of Rehabilitation are also all within 12 miles of he city.

Charlotte/Douglas International Airport is seventeen miles from Matthews, and there is an Amtrak station twelve miles away.

Rankings

General Rankings

- Charlotte* was ranked #85 out of 375 metro areas in *Cities Ranked & Rated*. Criteria: cost of living; climate; crime; transportation; economy and jobs; education; arts and culture; health and healthcare; leisure; quality of life. *Cities Ranked & Rated, 2nd Edition, 2007*
- Charlotte* was ranked #52 out of 379 metro areas in *Places Rated Almanac*. Criteria: health care; education; recreation; transportation; ambience; climate; crime; housing costs; jobs. *Places Rated Almanac, 7th Edition, 2007*

Business/Finance Rankings

- The nation's 100 largest metro areas were analysed in terms of the percentage of households entering some stage of foreclosure in 2007. The Charlotte* metro area ranked #34 out of 100 (#1 = highest foreclosure rate). *RealtyTrac, "Year-End 2007 Metropolitan Foreclosure Report"*
- The Charlotte* metro area was selected as one of "America's Most Wired Cities" by *Forbes*. The metro area was ranked #7 out of 30. Criteria: percentage of Internet users with high-speed access; the range of service providers within a city; availability of public wireless hot spots. *Forbes, "America's Most Wired Cities," January 10, 2008*
- Charlotte* was selected as one of the best places to start and grow a company by *Entrepreneur* and the National Policy Research Council. The Charlotte* metro area ranked #2 out of 50 large metro areas. Criteria: business formation and growth (firms started four to 14 years ago that still employ at least 5 people and experienced rapid growth over the last four years). *Entrepreneur/National Policy Research Council, "Hot Cities for Entrepreneurs," September 2006*
- The Charlotte* metro area was selected as one of "America's 50 Hottest Cities" for business relocations and expansions. Criteria: industry's most prominent site selection consultants were asked to list their top city choices for relocating and expanding manufacturing companies, taking into consideration such factors as the business climate, work force quality, operating costs, incentive programs, and the ease of working with local political and economic development officials. *Expansion Management, January-February 2007*
- The Charlotte* metro area was selected as one of the "Top 20 Real Estate Markets" for expanding or relocating companies. The area ranked #8. Criteria: low rental costs; low purchase prices; high vacancy rates of office and warehouse space. *Expansion Management, October 2007*
- Intel, in partnership with Sperling's BestPlaces, ranked the 80 "Best Cities for Teleworking" in America. The Charlotte* metro area ranked #12 among mid-sized metro areas. The study identifies cities that hold the greatest potential for teleworking based on a host of factors including typical commuting times, fuel prices, availability of broadband Internet access and percentage of the population in telework friendly jobs. The study also factored in extreme climate and natural hazards. *Intel, "Best Cities for Teleworking," March 30, 2006*
- The Charlotte* metro area appeared on the Milken Institute "2007 Best Performing Cities" index. Rank: #23 out of 200 large metro areas. Criteria: job growth; wage and salary growth; high-tech output growth. *Milken Institute, "2007 Best Performing Cities"*
- The Charlotte* metro area was selected as one of "The Top 20 Boom Towns in America." *Business 2.0* magazine and econometric research firm Global Insight compared 319 metropolitan areas in the U.S. and ranked the 61 with populations over 1 million. Criteria: a weighted formula that includes forecast growth rates in sectors that contain the economy's 10 most skilled occupational clusters; the prevalence of college degrees in the local workforce; median salary. The area ranked #19 among large metro areas. *Business 2.0 Magazine, March 2004*

- Charlotte* was identified as one of the 100 "Most Unwired Cities" in the U.S. The area ranked #17 out of the 100 largest metro areas in the U.S. Criteria: number of public and commercial wireless access points (hotspots); airports with wireless Internet access; broadband availability; local wireless networks; and wireless email devices. *Intel, "Most Unwired Cities Survey," June 7, 2005*

- Charlotte* was ranked #41 out of 125 regions worldwide in terms of its "Knowledge Competitiveness Index." The index attempts to measure the knowledge-based development taking place throughout the world and is based on 19 measures of economic performance that indicate a region's ability to translate its knowledge capacity into economic value. *Robert Huggins Associates, World Knowledge Competitiveness Index 2005*

- *Forbes* ranked the 200 most populous metro areas in the U.S. in terms of the "Best Places for Business and Careers." The Charlotte* metro area was ranked #37. Criteria: business costs (labor, energy, tax and office space expenses); living costs (housing, transportation, food and other household expenditures); education levels of the work force; job growth; income growth; migration trends; crime rates; and culture/leisure. *Forbes, "Best Places for Business and Careers," March 19, 2008*

- *Fortune* ranked the 100 largest metro areas in the U.S. in terms of projected median home price change in 2007. The Charlotte* metro area ranked #17. *Fortune.com, "Hot Spots, Cold Spots"*

Health/Environment Rankings

- 100 of the largest metro areas in the U.S. were analyzed in terms of their current drought severity. The Charlotte* metro area ranked #13 (#1 = driest). The rankings were based on statistics such as long-term precipitation trends and patterns and the Palmer drought indices. *Sperling's BestPlaces, www.BestPlaces.net, "America's Drought-Riskiest Cities," November 2007*

- Doctors at the Harvard School of Public Health ranked 40 metropolitan areas based on data from the government-sponsored Hospital Quality Alliance program. The program tracks the performance of individual hospitals in treating patients for three common health problems: heart attacks, congestive heart failure, and pneumonia. The Charlotte* metro area ranked #21 in quality of care for heart attacks, #12 for congestive heart failure, and #11 for pneumonia. *New England Journal of Medicine, July 21, 2005*

- *Reader's Digest* ranked the 50 largest metro areas in the U.S. in terms of how "clean" they are. The Charlotte* metro area ranked #20. Criteria: air quality; water quality; toxic industrial pollution; Superfund sites; and sanitation. *Reader's Digest, "The 50 Cleanest (and Dirtiest) Cities in America," July 2005*

- The Charlotte* metro area appeared in *Country Home's* "2008 Best Green Places" report. The area ranked #213 out of 379. Criteria: official energy policies; green power; green buildings; availability of fresh, locally grown food. *Country Home, "2008 Best Green Places"*

- Wyeth Consumer Healthcare, in partnership with Sperling's BestPlaces, ranked the nation's 50 most populous metro areas in terms of five key health factors. The Charlotte* metro area ranked #32. Criteria: physical activity; health status; nutrition; lifestyle pursuits; and mental wellness. *Wyeth Consumer Healthcare, "Centrum Healthiest Cities Study," April 19, 2005*

- Charlotte* was identified as a "2008 Asthma Capital." The area ranked #7 out of the nation's 100 largest metropolitan areas. Twelve factors were used to identify the most challenging places to live for people with asthma: estimated prevalence; self-reported prevalence; crude death rate for asthma; annual pollen score; annual air quality; public smoking laws; number of board-certified asthma specialists; school inhaler access laws; rescue medication use; controller medication use; uninsured rate; poverty rate. *Asthma and Allergy Foundation of America, "2008 Asthma Capitals"*

- Charlotte* was identified as a "Spring Allergy Capital." The area ranked #9 out of 100. Three groups of factors were used to identify the most severe cities for people with allergies during the spring season: annual pollen levels; medicine utilization; access to board-certified allergists. *Asthma and Allergy Foundation of America, "2007 Spring Allergy Capital Rankings"*

- Charlotte* was identified as a "Fall Allergy Capital." The area ranked #26 out of 100. Three groups of factors were used to identify the most severe cities for people with allergies during the fall season: annual pollen levels; medicine utilization; access to board-certified allergists. *Asthma and Allergy Foundation of America, "2007 Fall Allergy Capital Rankings"*

- Ortho-McNeil Neurologics, in partnership with Sperling's BestPlaces, analyzed 110 metro areas and identified those U.S. cities with the highest prevalence of factors that are most commonly associated with migraine headaches. The Charlotte* metro area ranked #46. Criteria: number of migraine-related drug prescriptions per capita; lifestyle factors that can contribute to migraines; environmental factors that can trigger migraines; and consumption of migraine-triggering foods. *Ortho-McNeil Neurologics, "America's Migraine Hot Spots," March 14, 2006*

- Sperling's BestPlaces ranked 331 metro areas and identified the most and least stressful U.S. cities. The Charlotte* metro area ranked #22 out of the 100 largest metro areas (#1 = most stressful). Criteria: divorce rate; unemployment rate; violent and property crime; suicide rate; commute time; mental health; alcohol consumption; cloudy days. *Sperling's BestPlaces, www.BestPlaces.net, "America's Most (and Least) Stressful Cities," January 9, 2004*

- An analysis of the "Best & Worst Cities for Sleep" was conducted by Sperling's BestPlaces. The study ranked America's 50 most populated metro areas. The Charlotte* metro area ranked #16 (#1 = best city for sleep). Criteria: number of days residents didn't get enough rest or sleep during the past month; average length of daily commute; divorce rate; unemployment rate. *Sperling's BestPlaces, www.BestPlaces.net, "Best & Worst Cities for Sleep," 2006*

- Charlotte* was highlighted as one of the 25 most ozone-polluted metro areas in the U.S. The area ranked #16. *American Lung Association, State of the Air: 2007*

- Charlotte* was selected as one of "America's Pet Healthiest Cities" by Purina. The city ranked #48 out of 50. Criteria: veterinary services; environment; legislation; preventative care; obesity/body condition. *Purina Pet Institute, "America's Pet Healthiest Cities," May 20, 2003*

Women/Minorities Rankings

- Charlotte* was ranked #73 out of 100 metro areas in *SELF Magazine's* ranking of "America's Best Places for Women." A panel of experts came up with more than 50 criteria including death and disease rates, environmental indicators, community resources, and lifestyle habits. *SELF Magazine, "America's Best Places for Women 2007," December 2007*

- Charlotte* appeared on *Black Enterprise's* list of the "Ten Best Cities for African Americans." The top picks were culled from more than 2,000 interactive surveys completed on www.blackenterprise.com and by editorial staff evaluation. The editors weighed the following criteria as it pertained to African Americans in each city: median household income; percentage of households earning more than $100,000; percentage of businesses owned; percentage of college graduates; unemployment rates; home loan rejections; and homeownership rates. *Black Enterprise, May 2007*

Seniors/Retirement Rankings

- Sperling's BestPlaces in partnership with Bankers Life & Casualty Company designed a survey to identify the top 50 metro areas in the U.S. that offer the best overall qualities for senior living. The Charlotte* metro area ranked #40. The following criteria were statistically weighted to reflect the needs of the senior population: health; disease; economics; social; environment; spiritual; transportation; housing; and crime. *Bankers Life & Casualty Company, "Best Cities for Seniors 2005"*

- A.G. Edwards ranked America's 500 top-performing communities based on their residents' personal savings and investing behavior. The Charlotte* metro area ranked #182 with an index score of 103.61 (national average = 100.00). A dozen statistical factors were measured including: participation in retirement savings plans; personal debt levels; and home ownership. *A.G. Edwards, "2007 Nest Egg Index", September 12, 2007*

Children/Family Rankings

- Matthews was selected as one of the top 100 best places to raise a family in the U.S. Criteria: demographic characteristics; standard of living; education; lifestyle; health and safety. *Best Place to Raise Your Family: The Top 100 Affordable Communities in the U.S., 1st Edition, 2006*

- The Charlotte* metro area was selected as one of the "Best Cities for Relocating Families" by Worldwide ERC and Primacy Relocation. The 2007 study placed a special emphasis on the housing market, which has significantly impacted the relocation industry and an employer's ability to transfer employees. The variables which weigh heavily in this category include home price, home affordability index, appreciation rates, and property tax. Other criteria include cost of living, crime rates, education, climate, focus on diversity, physicians per capita, recreation and leisure, arts and culture, air quality, watershed quality, sales tax, unemployment rate, job growth, high school and higher education index, school expenditures per student, students in public school, SAT/ACT percentile, and population growth. *Worldwide ERC and Primacy Relocation, "2007 Best Cities for Relocating Families"*

Safety Rankings

- The National Insurance Crime Bureau ranked 361 metro areas in the U.S. in terms of per capita rates of vehicle theft. The Charlotte* metro area ranked #38 (#1 = highest rate). Criteria: number of vehicle theft offenses per 100,000 inhabitants. *National Insurance Crime Bureau, "NICB Vehicle Theft Study," April 22, 2008*

- Charlotte* appeared on Sperling's BestPlaces list of the "Riskiest Cities for Identity Theft." The area ranked #19 out of the nations 50 largest metro areas. Over 80 criteria were analyzed across four major categories: technology impact; crime; transactions; and risk profile. *Sperling's BestPlaces, www.BestPlaces.net, "Riskiest Cities for Identity Theft," July 2006*

- Farmers Insurance Group of Companies, in partnership with Sperling's BestPlaces, ranked 379 metro areas and identified the "Most Secure U.S. Place to Live." The Charlotte* metro area ranked #107 out of 114 in the large metro area category (500,000 or more residents). Criteria: crime rates; extreme weather; risk of natural disasters; environmental hazards; terrorism threats; air quality; life expectancy; job loss numbers. *Farmers Insurance Group, "Most Secure U.S. Places to Live 2007"*

- Charlotte* was identified as one of the most dangerous large metro areas for pedestrians in the U.S. The area ranked #13 out of the nations 50 largest metro areas. Criteria: average yearly pedestrian fatalities per capita (for the years 2002 and 2003) adjusted for the number of walkers. *Surface Transportation Policy Project, "Mean Streets 2004"*

Sports/Recreation Rankings

- The Charlotte* metro area appeared on the *Sporting News* list of the "Best Sports Cities 2007". The area ranked #37 out of 150 cities in the U.S. *Sporting News* takes a 12-month snapshot, roughly July to July, of each city's sports, putting a heavy premium on regular-season won-lost records (from the most recently completed season). Other criteria include: playoff berths, bowl appearances and tournament bids; championships; applicable power ratings; quality of competition; overall fan fervor as measured in part by attendance as percentage of venue capacity; abundance of teams (rewarding quality over quantity); stadium and arena quality; ticket availability and prices; franchise ownership; and marquee appeal of athletes. *SportingNews.com, "Best Sports Cities 2007," August 1, 2007*

- The Charlotte* metro area was selected by *Cranium* as one of the "Top 50 Fun Cities" in America. The area ranked #29. Criteria includes: number of sports teams, restaurants, and dance performances; number of toy stores; city budget spent on recreation. *Cranium, November 4, 2003*

- *Golf Digest* ranked 330 metro areas in the U.S. in terms of golf. The Charlotte* metro area was ranked #288. Criteria: access to golf; weather; value of golf; and quality of golf. *Golf Digest, "Metro Golf Rankings," August 2005*

Dating/Romance Rankings

- Eli Lily and Company, in partnership with Sperling's BestPlaces, ranked the nation's 50 largest metro areas in terms of the "Most Romantic Cities for Baby Boomers." The Charlotte* metro area ranked #5. Criteria: marriage and divorce rates among "baby boomers" age 45 to 60; great restaurants; dance studios; chocolate, jewelry and flower sales. *Eli Lily and Company, "Most Romantic Cities for Baby Boomers," April 20, 2007*

- The Charlotte* metro area was selected as one of the "Best Cities for Relocating Singles" by Worldwide ERC and Primacy Relocation. The area ranked #38 out of the 100 largest metro areas in the U.S. Areas were selected based on the following criteria: a robust cost-of-living index; adventure and outdoor recreation opportunities; violent crime and property crime rates; percentage of the population that is unmarried (ages 25-34); ratio of single men and single women; affordability of quality higher education, including in-state and out-of-state tuition requirements and rates; number of newcomers to the area; commute times; tax rates; fee and occupancy rates for temporary housing and mini-storage; quality and quantity of collegiate and professional sporting events and fun, fan-friendly venues. *Worldwide ERC and Primacy Relocation, "2007 Best Cities for Relocating Singles," October 25, 2007*

- Sperling's BestPlaces in partnership with AXE Deodorant Bodyspray ranked 80 metro areas and identified "America's Best (and Worst) Cities for Dating." The Charlotte* metro area ranked #71 (#1 = best). Criteria: percentage of singles ages 18-24; population density; dating venues per capita. *AXE Deodorant Bodyspray, "America's Best (and Worst) Cities for Dating," May 2004*

Miscellaneous Rankings

- The Charlotte* metro area appeared on *Forbes* list of "America's Drunkest Cities". The area ranked #34. Criteria: 35 of the largest continental U.S. metro areas were chosen based on availability of data and geographic diversity. Each metro was ranked in five areas: state laws; drinkers; heavy drinkers; binge drinkers; and alcoholism. *Forbes.com, "America's Drunkest Cities," August 22, 2006*

- Sperling's BestPlaces in partnership with Pep Boys ranked 77 metro areas and identified "America's Most Drivable Cities." The Charlotte* metro area ranked #27. Criteria: climate; road roughness; urban mobility; gas prices. *Pep Boys, "America's Most Drivable Cities," April 9, 2003*

- State Farm Insurance, in partnership with Sperling's BestPlaces, analyzed several key factors that contribute to overall family preparedness. The Charlotte* metro area ranked #24 out of the nation's 50 most populous metro areas. Criteria: quality of life; life insurance coverage; and investments. *State Farm Life Insurance, "Fiscally Fit Cities Report," July 20, 2004*

- Scarborough Research, a leading market research firm, identified the top local markets for grocery coupon use. The Charlotte* DMA (Designated Market Area) ranked in the top 25 with 38% of consumers reporting that they use grocery coupons at least once per week. *Scarborough Research, December 8, 2004*

- A study by Sperling's BestPlaces examined which U.S. metro areas were most affected by high fuel prices in 2006. The Charlotte* metro area was ranked #18 out of 80 (#1 = most expensive city for driving). Rankings are based on the average dollars spent on gas per year by two driver households. Criteria: cost of regular-grade gasoline; average miles driven per day; average number of gallons each driver uses and wastes in traffic congestion each day. *Sperling's BestPlaces, www.bestplaces.net, "Pain at the Pump," May 18, 2006*

Matthews is located within the Charlotte-Gastonia-Concord, NC-SC Metropolitan Statistical Area.

Business Environment

CITY FINANCES

City Government Finances

Component	2004-2005 ($000)	2004-2005 ($ per capita)
Total Revenues	14,898	589
Total Expenditures	14,595	577
Debt Outstanding	15,768	623
Cash and Securities	10,438	412

Source: U.S Census Bureau, Government Finances 2004-2005

City Government Revenue by Source

Source	2004-2005 ($000)	2004-2005 ($ per capita)
General Revenue		
From Federal Government	0	0
From State Government	1,995	79
From Local Governments	2,509	99
Taxes		
Property	7,698	304
Sales	645	25
Personal Income	0	0
License	248	10
Charges	266	11
Liquor Store	0	0
Utility	0	0
Employee Retirement	0	0
Other	1,537	61

Source: U.S Census Bureau, Government Finances 2004-2005

City Government Expenditures by Function

Function	2004-2005 ($000)	2004-2005 ($ per capita)	2004-2005 (%)
General Expenditures			
Airports	0	0	0.0
Corrections	0	0	0.0
Education	0	0	0.0
Fire Protection	196	8	1.3
Governmental Administration	1,590	63	10.9
Health	387	15	2.7
Highways	1,689	67	11.6
Hospitals	0	0	0.0
Housing and Community Development	0	0	0.0
Interest on General Debt	698	28	4.8
Libraries	0	0	0.0
Parking	0	0	0.0
Parks and Recreation	247	10	1.7
Police Protection	4,466	176	30.6
Public Welfare	0	0	0.0
Sewerage	1,694	67	11.6
Solid Waste Management	1,229	49	8.4
Liquor Store	0	0	0.0
Utility	537	21	3.7
Employee Retirement	0	0	0.0
Other	1,862	74	12.8

Source: U.S Census Bureau, Government Finances 2004-2005

Municipal Bond Ratings

Area	Moody's
City	n/a

Source: Mergent Bond Record, January 2008 (unless noted otherwise)

DEMOGRAPHICS

Population Growth

Area	1990 Census	2000 Census	2007 Estimate	2012 Projection	Population Growth (%) 1990-2000	Population Growth (%) 2000-2012
City	14,681	22,127	25,128	27,369	50.7	23.7
MSA[1]	1,024,331	1,330,448	1,580,079	1,758,436	29.9	32.2
U.S.	248,709,873	281,421,906	301,045,522	314,920,978	13.2	11.9

Note: (1) Metropolitan Statistical Area - see Appendix B for areas included
Source: Claritas, Inc.

Number of Households and Average Household Size

Area	2007 Estimate	2007 Average Household Size
City	9,149	2.75
MSA[1]	614,864	2.57
U.S.	113,668,003	2.65

Note: (1) Metropolitan Statistical Area - see Appendix B for areas included
Source: Claritas, Inc.

Race and Ethnicity

Area	White Alone[2]	Black Alone[2]	Asian Alone[2]	Other Race Alone[2]	Hispanic[3]
City	85.7	7.9	3.2	3.3	4.4
MSA[1]	68.3	23.5	2.6	5.7	8.0
U.S.	73.1	12.4	4.3	10.3	14.9

Note: Figures are 2007 estimates; (1) Metropolitan Statistical Area - see Appendix B for areas included (2) Alone is defined as not being in combination with one or more other races; (3) May be of any race.
Source: Claritas, Inc.

Ancestry

Area	German	Irish[2]	English	American	Italian	Polish	French[3]	Scottish
City	17.8	12.2	15.4	10.4	5.0	3.2	2.6	2.9
MSA[1]	11.7	8.1	8.4	12.4	2.7	1.3	1.7	2.2
U.S.	15.2	10.9	8.7	7.3	5.6	3.2	3.0	1.7

Note: Figures include multiple ancestry (e.g. if a person reported being Irish and Italian, they were included in both columns); (1) Metropolitan Statistical Area - see Appendix A for areas included; (2) Includes Celtic; (3) Includes Alsatian but excludes Basque
Source: Census 2000, Summary File 3

Foreign-Born Population

Area	Percent of Population Born in							
	Any Foreign Country	Europe	Asia	Africa	Oceania[2]	Canada	Mexico	Latin America[3]
City	5.8	1.8	1.5	0.5	0.0	0.4	0.1	1.4
MSA[1]	6.7	0.9	1.5	0.4	0.0	0.2	2.3	1.4
U.S.	11.1	1.7	2.9	0.3	0.1	0.3	3.3	2.5

Note: (1) Metropolitan Statistical Area - see Appendix A for areas included; (2) Includes Australia, New Zealand subregion, Melanesia, Micronesia, Polynesia, and Oceania n.e.c; (3) Includes Central America (excluding Mexico), South America, and the Caribbean.
Source: Census 2000, Summary File 3

Marriage Status

Area	Never Married	Now Married (excluding Separated)	Separated	Widowed	Divorced
City	19.6	68.4	1.2	4.5	6.4
MSA[1]	25.5	57.0	2.7	5.8	8.9
U.S.	27.1	54.4	2.2	6.6	9.7

Note: Figures are percentages and cover the population 15 years of age and older; (1) Metropolitan Statistical Area - see Appendix A for areas included
Source: Census 2000, Summary File 3

Age Distribution

Area	Under Age 5	Age 5 to 17	Age 18 to 34	Age 35 to 49	Age 50 to 64	Age 65 to 79	80 Years and Over
	Percent of Population						
City	7.0	21.9	17.7	28.8	15.3	6.5	2.7
MSA[1]	7.1	18.3	25.7	24.4	14.5	7.8	2.4
U.S.	6.8	18.9	23.7	23.5	14.8	9.2	3.2

Note: (1) Metropolitan Statistical Area - see Appendix A for areas included
Source: Census 2000, Summary File 3

Male/Female Ratio

Area	Males	Females	Males per 100 Females
City	12,242	12,886	95.0
MSA[1]	778,817	801,262	97.2
U.S.	148,320,305	152,725,217	97.1

Note: Figures are 2007 estimates; (1) Metropolitan Statistical Area - see Appendix B for areas included
Source: Claritas, Inc.

Religion

Area	Catholic	Southern Baptist	United Meth-odist	ELCA[1]	LDS[2]	Presby-terian Church USA	Jewish Est.	Muslim Est.
County	8.5	10.8	6.7	1.2	0.5	6.0	1.2	1.1
U.S.	22.0	7.1	3.7	1.8	1.5	1.1	2.2	0.6

Note: Figures are the number of adherents as a percentage of the total population; Adherents are defined as all members, including full members, their children and the estimated number of other participants who are not considered members (e.g. the baptized, those not confirmed, those regularly attending services, etc.); (1) Evangelical Lutheran Church in America; (2) The Church of Jesus Christ of Latter Day Saints
Source: Reprinted with permission from Religious Congregations and Membership in the United States 2000 (Nashville, Glenmary Research Center, 2002) Copyright Association of Statisticians of American Religious Bodies. All rights reserved.

ECONOMY

Gross Metropolitan Product

Area	2002	2003	2004	2005	2005 Rank[2]
MSA[1]	60.6	63.1	66.1	71.3	35

Note: Figures are in billions of dollars; (1) Charlotte-Gastonia-Concord, NC-SC Metropolitan Statistical Area - see Appendix A for areas included; (2) Rank ranges from 1 to 361
Source: The U.S. Conference of Mayors, "U.S. Metro Economies: GMP - The Engines of America's Growth," January 2007

Economic Growth

Area	1995 GMP	2005 GMP	Average Annual Growth Rate	Growth Rate Rank[2]
MSA[1]	36.5	71.3	6.9	45

Note: Figures are in billions of dollars; GMP = Gross Metropolitan Product; (1) Charlotte-Gastonia-Concord, NC-SC Metropolitan Statistical Area - see Appendix A for areas included; (2) Rank ranges from 1 to 361
Source: The U.S. Conference of Mayors, "U.S. Metro Economies: GMP - The Engines of America's Growth," January 2007

INCOME

Per Capita/Median/Average Income

Area	Per Capita ($)	Median Household ($)	Average Household ($)
City	30,428	72,598	83,226
MSA[1]	27,995	53,758	71,403
U.S.	25,495	49,280	66,670

Note: Figures are 2007 estimates; (1) Metropolitan Statistical Area - see Appendix B for areas included
Source: Claritas, Inc.

Household Income Distribution

Area	Percent of Households Earning							
	Under $15,000	$15,000 -24,999	$25,000 -34,999	$35,000 -49,999	$50,000 -74,999	$75,000 -99,000	$100,000 -149,999	$150,000 and up
City	5.6	5.0	5.5	12.2	24.0	18.5	21.0	8.2
MSA[1]	10.4	9.1	10.9	16.1	21.1	13.0	12.0	7.3
U.S.	13.1	10.9	11.2	15.6	19.5	11.9	11.3	6.6

Note: Figures are 2007 estimates; (1) Metropolitan Statistical Area - see Appendix B for areas included
Source: Claritas, Inc.

Poverty Rates by Age

Area	All Ages	Under 5 Years Old	5 to 17 Years Old	18 to 64 Years Old	65 Years and Over
City	4.0	0.2	0.7	2.4	0.7
MSA[1]	9.3	0.9	2.2	5.3	1.0
U.S.	12.4	1.2	3.0	6.9	1.2

Note: Figures are percent of population with income in 1999 below poverty level and only include population for whom poverty status is determined; (1) Metropolitan Statistical Area - see Appendix A for areas included
Source: Census 2000, Summary File 3

Personal Bankruptcy Filing Rate

Area	2004	2005	2006
Mecklenburg County	3.47	5.07	1.61
U.S.	5.31	6.82	2.00

Note: Numbers are per 1,000 population and include Chapter 7 and Chapter 13 filings
Source: Federal Deposit Insurance Corporation (FDIC), Regional Economic Conditions (RECON), 8/23/2007

EMPLOYMENT

Labor Force and Employment

Area	Civilian Labor Force			Workers Employed		
	Dec. 2006	Dec. 2007	% Chg.	Dec. 2006	Dec. 2007	% Chg.
City	14,336	14,195	-1.0	13,926	13,749	-1.3
MSA[1]	841,508	837,004	-0.5	804,473	796,443	-1.0
U.S.	152,571,000	153,705,000	0.7	146,081,000	146,334,000	0.2

Note: Data is not seasonally adjusted and covers workers 16 years of age and older; (1) Metropolitan Statistical Area - see Appendix B for areas included
Source: Bureau of Labor Statistics, http://stats.bls.gov

Unemployment Rate

Area	2007											
	Jan.	Feb.	Mar.	Apr.	May	Jun.	Jul.	Aug.	Sep.	Oct.	Nov.	Dec.
City	3.3	3.4	3.1	3.0	3.2	3.4	3.6	3.2	3.2	3.3	3.3	3.1
MSA[1]	4.8	4.7	4.3	4.4	4.6	4.9	5.1	4.8	4.6	4.6	4.8	4.8
U.S.	5.0	4.9	4.5	4.3	4.3	4.7	4.9	4.6	4.5	4.4	4.5	4.8

Note: Data is not seasonally adjusted and covers workers 16 years of age and older; All figures are percentages; (1) Metropolitan Statistical Area - see Appendix B for areas included
Source: Bureau of Labor Statistics, http://stats.bls.gov

Employment by Occupation

Occupation Classification	City (%)	MSA[1] (%)	U.S. (%)
Sales and Office	28.0	27.4	26.7
Professional and Related	25.1	17.9	20.2
Service	10.2	12.1	14.9
Production, Transportation, and Material Moving	5.4	16.9	14.6
Management, Business, and Financial	23.7	15.1	13.5
Construction, Extraction, and Maintenance	7.5	10.4	9.4
Farming, Forestry, and Fishing	0.1	0.3	0.7

Note: Figures cover employed civilians 16 years of age and older; (1) Metropolitan Statistical Area - see Appendix A for areas included
Source: Census 2000, Summary File 3

Employment by Industry

Sector	MSA[1] Number of Employees	MSA[1] Percent of Total	U.S. Percent of Total
Government	107,600	12.3	16.3
Education and Health Services	79,500	9.1	13.4
Professional and Business Services	135,300	15.5	13.1
Retail Trade	100,200	11.5	11.6
Manufacturing	80,800	9.3	9.9
Leisure and Hospitality	83,800	9.6	9.6
Financial Activities	77,900	8.9	5.9
Construction	n/a	n/a	5.3
Wholesale Trade	49,400	5.7	4.4
Other Services	39,400	4.5	3.9
Transportation and Utilities	36,600	4.2	3.7
Information	22,200	2.5	2.2
Natural Resources and Mining	n/a	n/a	0.5

Note: Figures cover non-farm employment as of December 2007 and are not seasonally adjusted; (1) Metropolitan Statistical Area - see Appendix B for areas included; n/a not available
Source: Bureau of Labor Statistics, http://stats.bls.gov

Average Wages

Occupation	$/Hr.	Occupation	$/Hr.
Accountants and Auditors	29.49	Maids and Housekeeping Cleaners	8.53
Automotive Mechanics	19.44	Maintenance and Repair Workers	17.79
Bookkeepers	15.42	Marketing Managers	52.05
Carpenters	16.09	Nuclear Medicine Technologists	30.34
Cashiers	8.59	Nurses, Licensed Practical	18.99
Clerks, General Office	12.19	Nurses, Registered	27.81
Clerks, Receptionists/Information	11.98	Nursing Aides/Orderlies/Attendants	10.87
Clerks, Shipping/Receiving	13.98	Packers and Packagers, Hand	9.44
Computer Programmers	38.36	Physical Therapists	33.80
Computer Support Specialists	21.92	Postal Service Mail Carriers	21.00
Computer Systems Analysts	36.11	Real Estate Brokers	28.24
Cooks, Restaurant	10.49	Retail Salespersons	11.53
Dentists	n/a	Sales Reps., Exc. Tech./Scientific	29.39
Electrical Engineers	36.13	Sales Reps., Tech./Scientific	30.02
Electricians	17.73	Secretaries, Exc. Legal/Med./Exec.	13.82
Financial Managers	56.20	Security Guards	10.86
First-Line Supervisors/Mgrs., Sales	17.63	Surgeons	n/a
Food Preparation Workers	8.52	Teacher Assistants	9.70
General and Operations Managers	56.26	Teachers, Elementary School	19.50
Hairdressers/Cosmetologists	13.95	Teachers, Secondary School	20.60
Internists	87.33	Telemarketers	14.87
Janitors and Cleaners	9.98	Truck Drivers, Heavy/Tractor-Trailer	19.51
Landscaping/Groundskeeping Workers	10.51	Truck Drivers, Light/Delivery Svcs.	14.92
Lawyers	52.52	Waiters and Waitresses	8.21

Note: Wage data covers the Charlotte-Gastonia-Concord, NC-SC Metropolitan Statistical Area - see Appendix B for areas included. Hourly wages for elementary/secondary school teachers and teacher assistants were calculated by the editors from annual wage data assuming a 40 hour work week; n/a not available.
Source: Bureau of Labor Statistics, May 2007 Metro Area Occupational Employment and Wage Estimates

RESIDENTIAL REAL ESTATE

Building Permits

Area	Single-Family 2006	Single-Family 2007p	Single-Family Pct. Chg.	Multi-Family 2006	Multi-Family 2007p	Multi-Family Pct. Chg.	Total 2006	Total 2007p	Total Pct. Chg.
City	n/a	n/a	n/a	n/a	n/a	n/a	n/a	n/a	n/a
U.S.	1,378,200	973,300	-29.4	460,700	407,200	-11.6	1,838,900	1,380,500	-24.9

Note: (p) preliminary; figures cover and represent new, privately-owned housing units authorized (unadjusted data); All permit data are based on estimates with imputation; U.S. figures are based on the new 20,000-place series.
Source: U.S. Census Bureau, Manufacturing, Mining, and Construction Statistics

Homeownership and Housing Vacancies

Area	Homeownership Rate[2] (%)			Rental Vacancy Rate[3] (%)			Homeowner Vacancy Rate[4] (%)		
	2005	2006	2007	2005	2006	2007	2005	2006	2007
MSA[1]	65.8	66.1	66.5	11.1	13.5	11.0	2.3	2.9	3.1
U.S.	68.9	68.8	68.1	9.8	9.8	9.7	1.9	2.4	2.7

Note: (1) Metropolitan Statistical Area - see Appendix B for areas included; (2) The proportion of households that are owners; (3) The proportion of the rental inventory that is vacant for rent; (4) The proportion of the homeowner inventory that is vacant for sale; n/a not available
Source: U.S. Census Bureau, Housing Vacancies and Homeownership Annual Statistics: 2007

TAXES

State Corporate Income Tax Rates

State	Rates and Tax Brackets
North Carolina	6.9%

Note: Tax rates as of January 1, 2008; The franchise tax rate is $1.50 per $1,000, with a minimum of $35.
Source: Tax Foundation, www.taxfoundation.org

State Individual Income Tax Rates

State	Federal Deductibility	Marginal Rates (%)	Standard Deduction ($)		Personal Exemptions ($)[1]	
			Single	Joint	Single	Dependents
North Carolina	No	6.0 - 8.0 (y)(dd)	3,000	6,000	1,300 (o)(r)	1,300 (o)(r)

Note: Tax rates as of January 1, 2008; Local- and county-level taxes are not included; n/a not applicable; (1) Married joint filers generally receive double the single exemption; (o) Exemptions are based on federal Adjusted Gross Income (AGI) and are adjusted according to income and filing status. Taxpayer's filing single with AGI less than $60,000 receive $800 per exemption, if they earn over $60,000 they get $1,300 per exempt

n. Taxpayers married filing jointly with AGI under $100,000 get $1,600 per exemption and $2,600 for AGI over $100,00; (r) State adjusts its bracket levels for inflation at the end of each year before printing tax forms; (y) Brackets are not double for married taxpayers; (dd) North Carolina will finally allow the expiration of the temporary increase of its top income tax rate as of January 1, 2008 when the top rate will return to 7.75 percent.
Source: Tax Foundation, www.taxfoundation.org

Various State and Local Tax Rates

State and Local Sales and Use (%)	State Sales and Use (%)	Gasoline[1,2] ($/gal.)	Cigarette ($/pack)	Spirits ($/gal.)	Table Wine ($/gal.)	Beer ($/gal.)
6.75	4.25	0.302	0.35	10.36 (n)	0.79	0.53

Note: Tax rates as of January 1, 2008; (1) In addition to the 18.4 cpg Federal gasoline tax; (2) Rates may include additional state sales taxes, environmental protection and storage fees/taxes, and local taxes. When necessary, the volume-weighted average of all local taxes is used to approximate the typical statewide rate including local tax; (n) The state government controls all sales. The implied excise tax rate is calculated using methodology designed by the Distilled Spirits Council of the United States (DISCUS).
Source: Tax Foundation, www.taxfoundation.org; Original research

State Tax Burdens

Area	Combined State and Local Tax Burden		Combined Federal, State and Local Tax Burden	
	Percent	Rank	Percent	Rank
North Carolina	11.0	19	31.3	24
U.S. Average	11.0	-	32.7	-

Note: Figures cover 2007 and measure taxes as a percentage of income
Source: Tax Foundation, www.taxfoundation.org

State Business Tax Climate Index Rankings

State	Overall Rank	Corporate Tax Index Rank	Individual Income Tax Index Rank	Sales Tax Index Rank	Unemployment Insurance Tax Index Rank	Property Tax Index Rank
North Carolina	40	25	44	39	6	34

Note: Rankings range from 1 to 50 where 1 is best. Rankings do not average across to Overall Rank. States without a given tax are given a ranking of 1.
Source: Tax Foundation, State Business Tax Climate Index 2008

TRANSPORTATION

Means of Transportation to Work

Area	Car/Truck/Van		Public Transportation			Bicycle	Walked	Other Means	Worked at Home
	Drove Alone	Car-pooled	Bus	Subway	Railroad				
City	85.1	8.7	0.8	0.0	0.0	0.1	0.8	0.4	4.2
MSA[1]	80.9	12.9	1.3	0.0	0.0	0.1	1.2	0.8	2.8
U.S.	75.7	12.2	2.5	1.5	0.5	0.4	2.9	1.0	3.3

Note: Figures are percentages and cover workers 16 years of age and older;
(1) Metropolitan Statistical Area - see Appendix A for areas included
Source: Census 2000, Summary File 3

Travel Time to Work

Area	Less Than 15 Minutes	15 to 29 Minutes	30 to 44 Minutes	45 to 59 Minutes	60 Minutes or More
City	21.4	32.0	27.5	13.4	5.6
MSA[1]	23.8	38.7	23.0	8.5	6.1
U.S.	29.4	36.1	19.1	7.4	8.0

Note: Figures are percentages and include workers 16 years old and over; (1) Metropolitan Statistical Area - see Appendix A for areas included
Source: Census 2000, Summary File 3

Travel Time Index

Area	1982	1995	2004	2005
Urban Area[1]	1.07	1.13	1.25	1.23
Average[2]	1.11	1.22	1.29	1.30

Note: Travel Time Index - The ratio of travel time in the peak period to the travel time at free-flow conditions. A value of 1.35 indicates a 20-minute free-flow trip takes 27 minutes in the peak. Free-flow speeds (60 mph on freeways and 35 mph on principal arterials) are used as the comparison threshold; (1) Covers the Charlotte, NC-SC urban area; (2) average of 85 urban areas
Source: Texas Transportation Institute, The 2007 Urban Mobility Report, September 2007

Living Environment

COST OF LIVING

Cost of Living Index

Composite Index	Groceries	Housing	Utilities	Trans- portation	Health Care	Misc. Goods/ Services
90.0	99.2	76.5	83.5	92.4	104.3	96.9

Note: U.S. = 100; Figures cover the Charlotte NC urban area.
Source: The Council for Community and Economic Research (formerly ACCRA), Cost of Living Index, 2007

Grocery Prices

Area[1]	T-Bone Steak ($/pound)	Frying Chicken ($/pound)	Whole Milk ($/half gal.)	Eggs ($/dozen)	Orange Juice ($/64 oz.)	Coffee ($/11.5 oz.)
City[2]	9.41	1.04	2.59	1.65	3.26	2.92
Avg.	8.93	1.12	2.13	1.52	3.26	3.31
Min.	5.88	0.71	1.33	0.83	2.30	2.20
Max.	12.80	2.07	3.43	3.54	5.79	6.20

Note: (1) Values for the local area are compared with the average, minimum and maximum values for all 331 areas in the Cost of Living Index report; (2) Figures cover the Charlotte NC urban area; **T-Bone Steak** *(price per pound);* **Frying Chicken** *(price per pound, whole fryer);* **Whole Milk** *(half gallon carton);* **Eggs** *(price per dozen, Grade A, large);* **Orange Juice** *(64 oz. Tropicana or Florida Natural);* **Coffee** *(11.5 oz. can, vacuum-packed, Maxwell House, Hills Bros, or Folgers).*
Source: The Council for Community and Economic Research (formerly ACCRA), Cost of Living Index, 2007

Housing and Utility Costs

Area[1]	New Home Price ($)	Apartment Rent ($/month)	All Electric ($/month)	Part Electric ($/month)	Other Energy ($/month)	Telephone ($/month)
City[2]	235,835	658	130.06	-	-	23.29
Avg.	309,605	782	146.13	78.67	90.16	26.14
Min.	189,877	n/a	82.03	37.41	33.15	17.08
Max.	1,202,800	3,481	271.14	150.60	257.67	37.45

Note: (1) Values for the local area are compared with the average, minimum and maximum values for all 331 areas in the Cost of Living Index report; (2) Figures cover the Charlotte NC urban area; **New Home Price** *(2,400 sf living area, 8,000 sf lot, in urban area with full utilities);* **Apartment Rent** *(950 sf 2 bedroom/1.5 or 2 bath, unfurnished, excluding all utilities except water);* **All Electric** *(average monthly cost for an all-electric home);* **Part Electric** *(average monthly cost for a part-electric home);* **Other Energy** *(average monthly cost for natural gas, fuel oil, coal, wood, and any other forms of energy except electricity);* **Telephone** *(price includes basic monthly rate for a private residential line plus additional local usage charges incurred by a family of four).*
Source: The Council for Community and Economic Research (formerly ACCRA), Cost of Living Index, 2007

Health Care, Transportation, and Other Costs

Area[1]	Doctor ($/visit)	Dentist ($/visit)	Optometrist ($/visit)	Gasoline ($/gallon)	Beauty Salon ($/visit)	Men's Shirt ($)
City[2]	79.40	81.33	80.65	2.60	24.70	22.39
Avg.	79.48	71.93	79.55	2.64	29.52	25.77
Min.	52.08	44.80	43.95	2.19	15.58	16.19
Max.	148.44	126.27	158.83	3.48	60.62	48.53

Note: (1) Values for the local area are compared with the average, minimum and maximum values for all 331 areas in the Cost of Living Index report; (2) Figures cover the Charlotte NC urban area; **Doctor** *(general practitioners routine exam of an established patient);* **Dentist** *(adult teeth cleaning and periodic oral examination);* **Optometrist** *(full vision eye exam for established adult patient);* **Gasoline** *(one gallon regular unleaded, national brand, including all taxes, cash price at self-service pump if available);* **Beauty Salon** *(woman's shampoo, trim, and blow-dry);* **Men's Shirt** *(cotton/polyester dress shirt, pinpoint weave, long sleeves).*
Source: The Council for Community and Economic Research (formerly ACCRA), Cost of Living Index, 2007

HOUSING

House Price Index (HPI)

Area	National Ranking[2]	Quarterly Change (%)	One-Year Change (%)	Five-Year Change (%)
MSA[1]	23	0.06	6.08	27.81
U.S.[3]	-	0.10	0.84	41.37

Note: The HPI is a weighted repeat sales index. It measures average price changes in repeat sales or refinancings on the same properties. This information is obtained by reviewing repeat mortgage transactions on single-family properties whose mortgages have been purchased or securitized by Fannie Mae or Freddie Mac in January 1975; (1) Metropolitan Statistical Area - see Appendix B for areas included; (2) Rankings are based on annual percentage change for all metro areas containing at least 15,000 transactions over the last 10 years and ranges from 1 to 291; (3) figures based on a weighted average of Census Division estimates; all figures are for the period ending December 31, 2007
Source: Office of Federal Housing Enterprise Oversight, House Price Index, February 26, 2008

House Price Valuations

Area	Q1 2000	Q1 2001	Q1 2002	Q1 2003	Q1 2004	Q1 2005	Q1 2006	Q1 2007	Q1 2008
MSA[1]	-9.3	-9.4	-11.9	-9.6	-12.0	-12.6	-11.8	-10.5	-10.1

Note: Figures show the percentage of over- or under-valuation of single family homes relative to statistically normal house values (e.g. a value of 23.6 indicates that house values are 23.6% overvalued). Statistically normal house values are based on house prices, interest rates, household incomes, population densities, and any historical premiums or discounts metropolitan areas have exhibited over time; (1) Figures cover the Metropolitan Statistical Area - see Appendix B for areas included
Source: Global Insight/National City Corporation, House Prices in America, May 2008

Median Home Prices

Area	2005	2006	2007[r]	Percent Change 2006 to 2007
MSA[1]	180.9	190.6	204.3	7.2
U.S. Average	219.0	221.9	217.9	-1.8

Note: Figures are median sales prices of existing single-family homes in thousands of dollars; (r) revised; n/a not available; (1) Metropolitan Statistical Area - see Appendix B for areas included
Source: National Association of Realtors, Metropolitan Area Prices, 1st Quarter 2008

Housing: Year Structure Built

Area	1990 -2000	1980 -1989	1970 -1979	1960 -1969	1950 -1959	1940 -1949	Before 1940	Median Year
City	39.9	36.8	13.3	6.0	2.3	1.3	0.5	1987
MSA[1]	30.3	19.1	16.3	12.7	10.0	5.5	6.1	1980
U.S.	17.0	15.8	18.5	13.7	12.7	7.3	15.0	1971

Note: Figures are percentages; (1) Metropolitan Statistical Area - see Appendix A for areas included
Source: Census 2000, Summary File 3

HEALTH

Health Risk Data

Category	Area[1] (%)	U.S. (%)
Adults who have been told they have high blood pressure[3]	26.7	25.5
Adults who have been told they have high blood cholesterol[3]	35.2	35.6
Adults who have been told they have diabetes[2]	7.7	7.5
Adults who have been told they have arthritis[3]	25.0	27.0
Adults who have been told they currently have asthma	5.3	8.5
Adults who are current smokers	19.3	20.1
Adults who are heavy drinkers[4]	4.1	4.9
Adults who are overweight (BMI 25.0 - 29.9)	37.5	36.5
Adults who are obese (BMI 30.0 - 99.8)	23.3	25.1

Note: Data as of 2006 unless otherwise noted; (1) Figures cover the Metropolitan Statistical Area - see Appendix B for areas included; (2) Figures do not include pregnancy-related diabetes, pre-diabetes or borderline diabetes; (3) 2005 data; (4) Heavy drinkers are classified as adult men having more than two drinks per day or adult women having more than one drink per day
Source: Centers for Disease Control and Prevention, Behaviorial Risk Factor Surveillance System, SMART: Selected Metropolitan/Micropolitan Area Risk Trends, 2005, 2006

Mortality Rates for the Top 10 Causes of Death in the U.S.

ICD-10[a] Sub-Chapter	ICD-10[a] Code	Age-Adjusted Mortality Rate[1] per 100,000 population	
		County[2]	U.S.
Malignant neoplasms	C00-C97	178.3	186.5
Ischaemic heart diseases	I20-I25	104.7	152.3
Other forms of heart disease	I30-I51	58.7	51.5
Cerebrovascular diseases	I60-I69	55.5	50.0
Chronic lower respiratory diseases	J40-J47	38.3	42.6
Diabetes mellitus	E10-E14	19.9	24.8
Other degenerative diseases of the nervous system	G30-G31	47.2	22.6
Other external causes of accidental injury	W00-X59	19.2	21.4
Influenza and pneumonia	J10-J18	17.5	20.7
Hypertensive diseases	I10-I13	19.0	18.2

Note: (a) ICD-10 = International Classification of Diseases 10th Revision; (1) Mortality rates are a three year average covering 2003-2005; (2) Figures cover Mecklenburg County
Source: Centers for Disease Control and Prevention, National Center for Health Statistics. Compressed Mortality File 1999-2004. CDC WONDER On-line Database, compiled from Compressed Mortality File 1999-2005 Series 20 No. 2K, 2008.

Mortality Rates for Selected Causes of Death

ICD-10[a] Sub-Chapter	ICD-10[a] Code	Age-Adjusted Mortality Rate[1] per 100,000 population	
		County[2]	U.S.
Assault	X85-Y09	9.6	5.9
Human immunodeficiency virus (HIV) disease	B20-B24	10.5	4.5
Intentional self-harm	X60-X84	9.3	10.8
Malnutrition	E40-E46	1.6	1.0
Obesity and other hyperalimentation	E65-E68	1.4	1.4
Organic, including symptomatic, mental disorders	F01-F09	36.6	16.8
Transport accidents	V01-V99	11.2	16.1
Viral hepatitis	B15-B19	1.5	1.8

Note: (a) ICD-10 = International Classification of Diseases 10th Revision; (1) Mortality rates are a three year average covering 2003-2005; (2) Figures cover Mecklenburg County
Source: Centers for Disease Control and Prevention, National Center for Health Statistics. Compressed Mortality File 1999-2004. CDC WONDER On-line Database, compiled from Compressed Mortality File 1999-2005 Series 20 No. 2K, 2008.

Distribution of Physicians[1]

Area	Total	Family/ General Practice	Specialties	
			Medical	Surgical
Mecklenburg County (number)	1,851	389	702	466
Mecklenburg County (rate per 10,000 pop.)	23.2	4.9	8.8	5.9
U.S. (rate per 10,000 pop.)	17.7	4.6	6.9	4.3

Note: Data as of 2005; (1) Includes all non-federal, patient-care, office-based MDs
Source: Area Resource File (ARF). June 2007. U.S. Department of Health and Human Services, Health Resources and Services Administration, Bureau of Health Professions, Rockville, MD.

Hospitals

Matthews has the following hospitals: 1 general medical and surgical.
AHA Guide to the Healthcare Field 2008

According to *U.S. News,* the Charlotte-Gastonia-Concord, NC-SC metro area is home to one of the best hospitals in the U.S.: **Carolinas Medical Center**. *U.S. News Online, "America's Best Hospitals 2007"*

EDUCATION

Public School District Statistics

District Name	Schls	Pupils	Pupil/ Teacher Ratio	Minority Pupils[1] (%)	Free Lunch Eligible[2] (%)	IEP[3] (%)
Charlotte-Mecklenburg Schools	142	124,005	14.4	62.4	39.5	11.6
Union County Public Schools	40	31,584	15.2	28.2	23.8	11.5

Note: Table includes regular local school districts with 2,000 or more students; (1) Percentage of students that are not white, non-Hispanic; (2) Percentage of students that are eligible for the free lunch program; (3) Percentage of students that have an Individualized Education Program.
Source: U.S. Department of Education, National Center for Education Statistics, Common Core of Data, Local Education Agency (School District) Universe Survey: School Year 2005-2006; U.S. Department of Education, National Center for Education Statistics, Common Core of Data, Public Elementary/Secondary School Universe Survey: School Year 2005-2006

Top Public High Schools

High School Name	Index[1]	Rank[1]	Subsidized Lunch (%)[2]	E&E (%)[3]
Butler	2.167	424	17.0	50.7
Weddington	1.283	1,124	4.5	34.6

Note: (1) Public schools are ranked according to a ratio that is the number of Advanced Placement, International Baccalaureate, and/or Cambridge tests taken by all students at a school in 2007 divided by the number of graduating seniors. All of the schools on the list have an index of at least 1.000; they are in the top five percent of public schools measured this way. The rankings range from 1 to 1,422; (2) Percentage of students receiving federally subsidized meals; (3) E & E stands for equity and excellence percentage: the portion of all graduating seniors at a school that had at least one passing grade on one AP or IB test; (**) Gave both IB and AP tests. AP and IB participation are indicators of a school's efforts to get students to excel and prepare for college.
Source: Newsweek Online, "Top High Schools 2008"

Highest Level of Education

Area	Less than H.S.	H.S. Diploma	Some College, No Deg.	Associate Degree	Bachelors Degree	Masters Degree	Profess. School Degree	Doctorate Degree
City	6.9	17.9	24.8	8.3	29.7	9.3	2.3	0.7
MSA[1]	17.9	24.6	21.9	6.9	20.8	5.7	1.6	0.6
U.S.	19.4	28.4	21.2	6.4	15.7	5.9	2.0	1.0

Note: Figures are 2007 estimated percentages and cover persons age 25 and over; (1) Metropolitan Statistical Area - see Appendix B for areas included
Source: Claritas, Inc.

Educational Attainment by Race

Area	High School Graduate (%)					Bachelor's Degree (%)				
	Total	White	Black	Asian	Hisp.[2]	Total	White	Black	Asian	Hisp.[2]
City	93.2	93.5	96.3	85.8	83.7	42.3	42.3	49.9	33.2	42.5
MSA[1]	80.5	83.0	74.7	76.4	48.6	26.5	29.1	16.5	37.8	11.9
U.S.	80.4	83.6	72.3	80.4	52.4	24.4	26.1	14.3	44.1	10.4

Note: Figures shown cover persons 25 years old and over; (1) Metropolitan Statistical Area - see Appendix A for areas included; (2) people of Hispanic origin can be of any race
Source: Census 2000, Summary File 3

School Enrollment by Type

Area	Grades KG to 8				Grades 9 to 12			
	Public		Private		Public		Private	
	Enrollment	%	Enrollment	%	Enrollment	%	Enrollment	%
City	2,930	81.1	681	18.9	1,257	84.4	232	15.6
MSA[1]	176,153	88.3	23,233	11.7	71,217	91.1	6,951	8.9
U.S.	33,526,011	88.7	4,285,121	11.3	14,848,628	90.6	1,532,323	9.4

Note: Figures shown cover persons 3 years old and over; (1) Metropolitan Statistical Area - see Appendix A for areas included
Source: Census 2000, Summary File 3

School Enrollment by Race

Area	Grades KG to 8 (%)				Grades 9 to 12 (%)			
	White	Black	Asian	Hisp.[1]	White	Black	Asian	Hisp.[1]
City	90.5	4.7	3.1	4.0	91.5	5.0	2.1	2.3
MSA[2]	67.2	26.1	1.8	5.0	67.2	27.1	2.2	3.8
U.S.	68.5	15.5	3.3	16.8	68.8	15.5	3.8	15.7

Note: Figures shown cover persons 3 years old and over; (1) people of Hispanic origin can be of any race; (2) Metropolitan Statistical Area - see Appendix A for areas included
Source: Census 2000, Summary File 3

Average Salaries of Public School Classroom Teachers

District	2005-06		2006-07		Percent Change 2005-06 to 2006-07
	Dollars	Rank[1]	Dollars	Rank[1]	
North Carolina	43,922	27	46,410	25	5.66
U.S. Average	49,026	-	50,816	-	3.65

Note: (1) State rank ranges from 1 to 51.
Source: National Education Association, Rankings & Estimates: Rankings of the States 2006 and Estimates of School Statistics 2007, December 2007

Higher Education

Four-Year Colleges			Two-Year Colleges			Medical Schools[1]	Law Schools[2]	Voc/ Tech[3]
Public	Private Non-profit	Private For-profit	Public	Private Non-profit	Private For-profit			
0	0	0	0	0	0	0	0	1

Note: Figures cover institutions located within the city limits; (1) includes schools accredited by the Liaison Committee on Medical Education and the American Osteopathic Association; (2) includes American Bar Association-accredited law schools; (3) includes all schools with programs that are less than 2 years.
Source: National Center for Education Statistics, The Integrated Postsecondary Education System (IPEDS) Peer Analysis System, 2007; www.usnews.com, Law and Medical School Directories, 2009

PRESIDENTIAL ELECTION

2004 Presidential Election Results

Area	Bush	Kerry	Nader	Other
Mecklenburg County	48.0	51.6	0.1	0.3
U.S.	50.7	48.3	0.4	0.6

Note: Results are percentages and may not add to 100% due to rounding
Source: Dave Leip's Atlas of U.S. Presidential Elections, www.uselectionatlas.org

EMPLOYERS

Major Employers

Company Name	Industry	Type of Site
Bank of America	National commercial banks	Headquarters
Carlisle Companies Inc	Asphalt felts and coatings	Headquarters
Carolinas Healthcare System	General medical and surgical hospitals	Headquarters
Caromont Health	General medical and surgical hospitals	Single
Chancellors Office	Colleges and universities	Branch
Chrysler Freight Line	Truck and bus bodies	Branch
Duke Power	Electric services	Headquarters
IBM	Calculating and accounting equipment	Branch
IBM	Office equipment	Branch
Insource Contract Services LLC	Help supply services	Single
M C A	Business consulting, nec	Single
Medcath Incorporated	Specialty hospitals, except psychiatric	Headquarters
Northeast Medical Ctr	General medical and surgical hospitals	Headquarters
PGI Nonwovens	Nonwoven fabrics	Headquarters
Rohr Inc Credit Corporation	Aircraft engines and engine parts	Single
University NC At Chapel Hl	Schools and educational services	Branch
Wachovia	Bank holding companies	Headquarters
Wachovia	Management consulting services	Branch

Note: Companies shown are located within the Charlotte metropolitan area; nec = not elsewhere classified.
Source: www.zapdata.com, May 2008

PUBLIC SAFETY

Crime Rate

Area	All Crimes	Violent Crimes				Property Crimes		
		Murder	Forcible Rape	Robbery	Aggrav. Assault	Burglary	Larceny -Theft	Motor Vehicle Theft
City	4,742.2	3.9	23.2	81.4	124.0	743.9	3,475.3	290.6
Metro[1]	n/a	8.3	36.7	269.5	n/a	1,405.5	3,220.5	622.0
U.S.	3,808.1	5.7	30.9	149.4	287.5	729.4	2,206.8	398.4

Note: Figures are crimes per 100,000 population; (1) Metropolitan Statistical Area - see Appendix B for areas included
Source: FBI Uniform Crime Reports, 2006

Hate Crimes

Area	Number of Quarters Reported	Bias Motivation				
		Race	Religion	Sexual Orientation	Ethnicity	Disability
City	4	3	0	0	0	0

Source: Federal Bureau of Investigation, Hate Crime Statistics 2006

RECREATION

Culture

Dance[1]	Theatre[1]	Instrumental Music[1]	Vocal Music[1]	Series/ Festivals	Museums	Zoos and Aquariums[2]
0	1	0	0	0	0	0

Note: (1) Number of professional perfoming groups; (2) AZA-accredited
Source: The Grey House Performing Arts Directory, 2007; Official Museum Directory, 2008; Association of Zoos & Aquariums, AZA Member Zoos & Aquariums, June 2008

Professional Sports Teams

Team Name	League
Charlotte Bobcats	National Basketball Association (NBA)
Carolina Panthers	National Football League (NFL)

Note: Includes teams located in the Charlotte metro area.
Source: Original research

MEDIA

Newspapers

Name	News Focus	Frequency	Circulation
Matthews News & Record	Local	n/a	n/a
Neighbors of Southern Mecklenburg - The Charlotte Observer	Local	n/a	n/a

Note: Includes newspapers with offices located in the city; n/a not available
Source: MediaContactsPro, March 2008

Television Stations

Name	Ch.	Network(s)	Type	Ownership
WBTV	3	CBS	Commercial	Jefferson-Pilot Communications Company
WSOC	9	ABC	Commercial	Cox Enterprises Inc.
WHKY	14	n/a	Commercial	Long Family Partnership
WCCB	18	Fox	Commercial	Bahakel Communications Inc.
WNSC	30	PBS	Public	South Carolina Educational Television Commission
WCNC	36	NBC	Commercial	Belo Corporation
WTVI	42	PBS	Public	Charlotte-Mecklenburg Public Broadcasting Authority
WJZY	46	UPN	Commercial	Capitol Broadcasting Company Inc.
WWWB	55	WBN	Commercial	Capitol Broadcasting Company Inc.
WAXN	64	n/a	Commercial	Cox Enterprises Inc.

Note: Stations included cover the Charlotte DMA (Designated Market Area); n/a not available
BurrellesLuce, MediaContacts Online, January 2007

Major AM Radio Stations

Call Letters	Freq. (kHz)	Station Type	Target Audience	Station Format	Music Format
WFNZ	610	n/a	General	News/Sports/Talk	n/a
WLWL	770	Commercial	General	Educational/Music/Talk	Oldies
WYFQ	930	n/a	Religious	Music/News/Talk	n/a
WNOW	1030	Commercial	General/Hispanic	Music/News	Latin
WKGX	1080	Commercial	General	Music	Country
WBT	1110	Commercial	General	News/Talk	n/a
WCXN	1170	Commercial	General/Hisp/Rel	Music/News	Latin
WCGC	1270	Commercial	General	Educational/Music/News	Gospel
WHKY	1290	Commercial	General	News/Talk	n/a
WLTC	1370	Commercial	Religious	Music/News	Christian
WMNC	1430	Commercial	General	Music	Country
WGFY	1480	Commercial	Children/General	Ed/Music/News/Sports/Talk	Top 40
WAGL	1560	Commercial	General/Hisp/Rel	Music/Talk	Latin

Note: Stations included cover the Charlotte DMA (Designated Market Area); n/a not available
Source: BurrellesLuce, MediaContacts Online, January 2007

Major FM Radio Stations

Call Letters	Freq. (mHz)	Station Type	Target Audience	Station Format	Music Format
WPIR	88.1	Non-Comm	General/Religious	Educational/Music	Gospel
WGWG	88.3	College	General/Religious	Educational/Music/Talk	Blues
WDAV	89.9	College	General	Music/Talk	Classical
WFAE	90.7	College	General	Educational/Talk	n/a
WMNC	92.1	Commercial	General	Music	Contemp. Country
WNKS	95.1	Commercial	Young Adult	Music/News/Talk	Top 40
WXRC	95.7	Commercial	General	Music	Classic Rock
WKKT	96.9	Commercial	General	Music	Contemp. Country
WPEG	97.9	Commercial	General	Music/News/Talk	Urban Contemp.
WBT	99.3	Commercial	General	News/Sports/Talk	n/a
WRFX	99.7	Commercial	General	Music	Classic Rock
WZJS	100.7	Commercial	General	Music	Country
WBAV	101.9	Commercial	General	Music	Urban Contemp.
WECR	102.3	Commercial	General	Music	Oldies
WLYT	102.9	Commercial	General	Music/News/Talk	Adult Contemp.
WKVS	103.3	Commercial	General	Music	Country
WSOC	103.7	Commercial	General	Music/News/Talk	Country
WSSS	104.7	Commercial	General	Music/Talk	80's
WFMX	105.7	n/a	General	Music/News	n/a
WNMX	106.1	Commercial	General	Music/News/Talk	Adult Standards
WEND	106.5	n/a	General	Music/News/Talk	n/a
WRHM	107.1	Commercial	General	Music/News	Country
WLNK	107.9	Commercial	General	Music/News/Talk	Adult Contemp.

Note: Stations included cover the Charlotte DMA (Designated Market Area); n/a not available
BurrellesLuce, MediaContacts Online, January 2007

CLIMATE

Average and Extreme Temperatures

Temperature	Jan	Feb	Mar	Apr	May	Jun	Jul	Aug	Sep	Oct	Nov	Dec	Yr.
Extreme High (°F)	78	81	86	93	97	103	103	103	104	98	85	77	104
Average High (°F)	51	54	62	72	80	86	89	88	82	72	62	53	71
Average Temp. (°F)	41	44	51	61	69	76	79	78	72	61	51	43	61
Average Low (°F)	31	33	40	48	57	65	69	68	62	50	40	33	50
Extreme Low (°F)	-5	5	4	25	32	45	53	53	39	24	11	2	-5

Note: Figures cover the years 1948-1990
Source: National Climatic Data Center, International Station Meteorological Climate Summary, 9/96

Average Precipitation/Snowfall/Humidity

Precip./Humidity	Jan	Feb	Mar	Apr	May	Jun	Jul	Aug	Sep	Oct	Nov	Dec	Yr.
Avg. Precip. (in.)	3.6	3.8	4.5	3.0	3.7	3.4	3.9	3.9	3.4	3.2	3.1	3.4	42.8
Avg. Snowfall (in.)	2	2	1	Tr	0	0	0	0	0	0	Tr	1	6
Avg. Rel. Hum. 7am (%)	78	77	78	78	82	83	86	89	89	87	83	79	82
Avg. Rel. Hum. 4pm (%)	53	49	46	43	49	51	54	55	54	50	50	54	51

Note: Figures cover the years 1948-1990; Tr = Trace amounts (<0.05 in. of rain; <0.5 in. of snow)
Source: National Climatic Data Center, International Station Meteorological Climate Summary, 9/96

Weather Conditions

Temperature			Daytime Sky			Precipitation		
10°F & below	32°F & below	90°F & above	Clear	Partly cloudy	Cloudy	0.01 inch or more precip.	0.1 inch or more snow/ice	Thunderstorms
1	65	44	98	142	125	113	3	41

Note: Figures are average number of days per year and cover the years 1948-1990
Source: National Climatic Data Center, International Station Meteorological Climate Summary, 9/96

HAZARDOUS WASTE

Superfund Sites

Matthews has no sites on the EPA's Superfund Final National Priorities List.
U.S. Environmental Protection Agency, Final National Priorities List, June 23, 2008

AIR & WATER QUALITY

Air Quality Index

Area	Percent of Days when Air Quality was...[2]				AQI Statistics	
	Good	Moderate	Unhealthy for Sensitive Groups	Unhealthy	Maximum	Median
MSA[1]	40.8	43.8	13.7	1.6	205	55

Note: The Air Quality Index (AQI) is an index for reporting daily air quality. EPA calculates the AQI for five major air pollutants regulated by the Clean Air Act: ground-level ozone, particle pollution (also known as particulate matter), carbon monoxide, sulfur dioxide, and nitrogen dioxide. The AQI runs from 0 to 500. The higher the AQI value, the greater the level of air pollution and the greater the health concern. There are six AQI categories: "Good" The AQI is between 0 and 50. Air quality is considered satisfactory; "Moderate" The AQI is between 51 and 100. Air quality is acceptable; "Unhealthy for Sensitive Groups" When AQI values are between 101 and 150, members of sensitive groups may experience health effects; "Unhealthy" When AQI values are between 151 and 200 everyone may begin to experience health effects; "Very Unhealthy" AQI values between 201 and 300 trigger a health alert; "Hazardous" AQI values over 300 trigger health warnings of emergency conditions; (1) Metropolitan Statistical Area - see Appendix A for areas included; (2) Based on 365 days with AQI data in 2007.
Source: U.S. Environmental Protection Agency, Air Quality Index Report, 2007

Air Quality Index Pollutants

Area	Percent of Days when AQI Pollutant was...[2]					
	Carbon Monoxide	Nitrogen Dioxide	Ozone	Sulfur Dioxide	Particulate Matter 2.5	Particulate Matter 10
MSA[1]	0.0	0.0	59.2	0.0	40.8	0.0

Note: The Air Quality Index (AQI) is an index for reporting daily air quality. EPA calculates the AQI for five major air pollutants regulated by the Clean Air Act: ground-level ozone, particle pollution (also known as particulate matter), carbon monoxide, sulfur dioxide, and nitrogen dioxide. The AQI runs from 0 to 500. The higher the AQI value, the greater the level of air pollution and the greater the health concern; (1) Metropolitan Statistical Area - see Appendix A for areas included; (2) Based on 365 days with AQI data in 2007.
Source: U.S. Environmental Protection Agency, Air Quality Index Report, 2007

Air Quality Index Trends

Area	Trend Sites (11)								All Sites (70)
	1999	2000	2001	2002	2003	2004	2005	2006	2006
MSA[1]	34	22	13	27	4	5	11	8	18

Note: An AQI value greater than 100 indicates that air quality would have been in the unhealthful range on that day. Data from exceptional events are not included. These counts are presented in two ways. First, the counts are based on sites having an adequate record of monitoring data during the trend period (trend sites). These counts represent the relative change in the number of days with AQI values greater than 100. In the last column, the counts are based on all sites with data in the most recent year (because it is possible for a site to have data in the most recent year but not enough data to be a trend site); (1) Metropolitan Statistical Area - see Appendix A for areas included.
Source: U.S. Environmental Protection Agency, Office of Air and Radiation, Air Trends, Factbook and Related Information, Air Pollution Trends in Selected Metropolitan Areas 2006

Maximum Air Pollutant Concentrations

	Particulate Matter 10 (ug/m^3)	Particulate Matter 2.5 (ug/m^3)	Ozone (ppm)	Carbon Monoxide (ppm)	Sulfur Dioxide (ppm)	Nitrogen Dioxide (ppm)	Lead (ug/m^3)
MSA[1] Level	62	32	0.115	2	0.013	0.013	0
NAAQS[2]	150	35	0.125	9	0.140	0.053	1.50
Met NAAQS[2]	Yes	Yes	Yes	Yes	Yes	Yes	Yes

Note: Data from exceptional events are not included; (1) Metropolitan Statistical Area - see Appendix A for areas included; (2) National Ambient Air Quality Standards; n/a not available
Concentrations: Particulate Matter 10 (coarse particulate) - highest second maximum 24-hour concentration; Particulate Matter 2.5 (fine particulate) - highest 98th percentile 24-hour concentration; Ozone - highest second daily maximum 1-hour concentration; Carbon Monoxide - highest second maximum non-overlapping 8-hour concentration; Sulfur Dioxide - highest second maximum 24-hour concentration; Nitrogen Dioxide - highest arithmetic mean concentration; Lead - highest quarterly maximum concentration
Units: ppm = parts per million; ug/m^3 = micrograms per cubic meter
Source: U.S. Environmental Protection Agency, MSA Factbook 2006, Air Quality Statistics by City

Drinking Water

Water System Name	Pop. Served	Primary Water Source Type	Violations[1]	
			Health Based	Monitoring/ Reporting
Charlotte-Mecklenburg Utility	750,000	Surface	0	0

Note: (1) Based on violation data from January 1, 2007 to December 31, 2007 (includes unresolved violations from earlier years)
Source: U.S. Environmental Protection Agency, Office of Ground Water and Drinking Water, Safe Drinking Water Information System (based on data extracted April 15, 2008)

Fargo, North Dakota

Background

Fargo sits on the western bank of the Red River in the Red River Valley in the southeastern part of the state. The city is in Cass County and about 300 miles northwest of Minneapolis.

Fargo was originally a stopping point for steamboats on the Red River in the later part of the 19th century. Founded in 1871, the city was originally named Centralia, but renamed Fargo in honor of the Northern Pacific Railway director Wells Fargo. It began to flourish after the arrival of the railroad and became known as the "Gateway to the West." During the 1880s, Fargo was also known for its unusually lenient divorce laws.

A major fire in 1893 destroyed hundreds of homes and businesses but the city was quickly rebuilt with new brick buildings, new streets and a water system. The North Dakota State Agricultural College was founded in 1890 as the state's land-grant university and was accredited by the North Central Association in 1915. The school eventually became known as North Dakota State University during the 1960s.

Fargo grew rapidly after World War II as the connection of two interstates, I-29 and I-94, revolutionized travel in the region and allowed for further expansion in the southern and western parts of the city. In 1972, the West Acres Shopping Center was constructed near the intersection of thc two interstates and served as a catalyst for retail growth in the area.

Fargo is the crossroads and economic center of eastern North Dakota and western Minnesota. Though the economy of the region has historically be dependent on agriculture, other sectors have become increasingly prevalent in recent years. Today, the city's growing economy is based on food processing, manufacturing, technology, retail trade, higher education, and healthcare. The largest non-government employers in the city are MeritCare Health System, Blue Cross/Blue Shield, US Bank, and Microsoft. The University is the city's largest public sector employer.

A significant landmark in Fargo is the main campus of North Dakota State University, which has a full-time enrollment of nearly 9,000. The city also features a large number of public parks including Percy Godwin Park, Lindenwood Park, Mickelson Field, Island Park, Roosevelt Playground, and Oak Grove Park.

A downtown revitalization project is underway in Fargo, as the city works to energize downtown area. To this end, the Renaissance Zone and Storefront Rehab programs are designed to encourage new business, renovate deteriorating buildings, and increase the availability of housing in the downtown area.

Fargo has a moderate northern climate. Summer temperatures average 65 degrees, while winter averages fall to 10 degrees during December and January. The city averages 2.5 inches of rainfall per month from April to October and 8 inches of snowfall per month from December to March.

Rankings

General Rankings

- Fargo* was ranked #40 out of 375 metro areas in *Cities Ranked & Rated*. Criteria: cost of living; climate; crime; transportation; economy and jobs; education; arts and culture; health and healthcare; leisure; quality of life. *Cities Ranked & Rated, 2nd Edition, 2007*
- Fargo* was ranked #82 out of 379 metro areas in *Places Rated Almanac*. Criteria: health care; education; recreation; transportation; ambience; climate; crime; housing costs; jobs. *Places Rated Almanac, 7th Edition, 2007*
- *Men's Health Living* ranked 100 U.S. cities in terms of quality of life. Fargo was ranked #4 and received a grade of A. Criteria: number of fitness facilities; air quality; number of physicians; male/female ratio; education levels; household income; cost of living. *Men's Health Living, Spring 2008*
- *Expansion Management* rated 362 metro areas to find out which offer the best middle class lifestyle for manufacturing and service companies. The Fargo* metro area was selected as a "5-Star Quality of Life Metro" (a distinction the magazine awards to the top 20 percent of metro areas studied). The annual "Quality of Life Quotient" measures dozens of indicators across nine major categories and compares them among 362 metropolitan statistical areas in the United States. The categories are: affordable housing; good public schools; low crime levels; adult education level; standard of living; traffic and commuting; continuing education opportunities; commercial air access; labor market. *Expansion Management, June 2007*
- Fargo was selected as one of "America's Best Places to Live" by monstermoving.com. The top 10 cities were selected based on the fact that they appear repeatedly on other publications' "Top Cities" lists. *www.monstermoving.com, February 26, 2004*
- Fargo was selected as one of the "2006 Best Places to Live" by *Money* magazine. Places were ranked using 38 quality-of-life indicators and six economic opportunity measures in the following categories: ease of living; health; education; crime; park space; arts and leisure. *CNNMoney.com, "Best Places to Live 2006"*

Business/Finance Rankings

- The Fargo* metro area was selected one of America's "Top 50 Business Opportunity Metros" by *Expansion Management* in their 5th annual Mayor's Challenge ranking of metro areas that have achieved solid ratings across the board in numerous *EM* studies during the past 12 months. The area ranked #9. Criteria: public schools; quality of life; college educated workers; logistics infrastructure; healthcare costs; taxes and government spending; reputation among site consultants. *Expansion Management, August 2007*
- Fargo* was selected as one of the best places to start and grow a company by *Entrepreneur* and the National Policy Research Council. The Fargo* metro area ranked #43 out of 162 small metro areas. Criteria: business formation and growth (firms started four to 14 years ago that still employ at least 5 people and experienced rapid growth over the last four years). *Entrepreneur/National Policy Research Council, "Hot Cities for Entrepreneurs," September 2006*
- Fargo was selected as one of the "100 Best Places to Live and Launch" in the U.S. The city ranked #24. The editors at *Fortune Small Business* ranked 296 Census-designated metro areas by business friendliness (Launching Score, % New Businesses) and lifestyle offerings (Living Score). Then, through reporting, they picked the town within each of the top 100 metro areas that best blends business and pleasure. *Fortune Small Business, "100 Best Places to Live and Launch 2008," April 2008*
- The Fargo* metro area appeared on the Milken Institute "2007 Best Performing Cities" index. Rank: #36 out of 179 small metro areas. Criteria: job growth; wage and salary growth; high-tech output growth. *Milken Institute, "2007 Best Performing Cities"*

- *Forbes* ranked 179 smaller metro areas in the U.S. in terms of the "Best Places for Business and Careers." The Fargo* metro area was ranked #11. Criteria: business costs (labor, energy, tax and office space expenses); living costs (housing, transportation, food and other household expenditures); education levels of the work force; job growth; income growth; migration trends; crime rates; and culture/leisure. *Forbes, "Best Places for Business and Careers," March 19, 2008*

- *Kiplinger's Personal Finance* ranked 101 U.S. cities in terms of their total tax burdens. Fargo ranked #23 (#1 had the lowest overall tax burden). Criteria: state income tax; property tax; sales tax; personal property tax; and gasoline tax. *Kiplinger's Personal Finance, July 2004*

- Fargo appeared on *Kiplinger's Personal Finance* list of the "Top Ten Tax-Friendly Cities." The city was ranked #23. Criteria: income tax; sales tax; real estate and car/personal property tax. *Kiplinger's Personal Finance, May 2007*

Health/Environment Rankings

- *Men's Health* examined the nation's largest 100 cities and identified the cities with the best and worst teeth. Fargo was ranked among the ten best at #9. Criteria: annual dentist visits; canceled appointments; regular flossers; fluoride usage; dental extractions. *Men's Health, April 2008*

- The Fargo* metro area appeared in *Country Home's* "2008 Best Green Places" report. The area ranked #46 out of 379. Criteria: official energy policies; green power; green buildings; availability of fresh, locally grown food. *Country Home, "2008 Best Green Places"*

- The American Podiatric Medical Association and *Prevention* magazine ranked America's 100 most populated cities based on fitness-walker friendliness. The best cities have safe streets, beautiful places to walk, mild weather and good air quality. Fargo ranked #284. *Prevention, "The Best Walking Cities of 2008," April 2008; American Podiatric Medical Association, "2008 Best Fitness-Walking Cities, "April 2008*

- *Men's Health* examined 100 U.S. cities and selected the best and worst cities for men. Fargo was ranked among the ten best at #6. Criteria: dozens of statistical parameters of long life in the categories of health, quality of life, and fitness. *Men's Health, "Best and Worst Cities for Men," January/February 2008*

- *Men's Health* ranked 100 U.S. cities in terms of the quality of their tap water. Fargo was ranked #16 and received a grade of B. Criteria: levels of total coliform bacteria, arsenic, lead, total trihalomethanes (linked to cancer), and halo-acetic acids; number of EPA water-system violations from 1995 to 2005. *Men's Health, March 2007*

- Sperling's BestPlaces ranked 331 metro areas and identified the most and least stressful U.S. cities. The Fargo* metro area ranked #116 out of the 117 smallest metro areas (#1 = most stressful). Criteria: divorce rate; unemployment rate; violent and property crime; suicide rate; commute time; mental health; alcohol consumption; cloudy days. *Sperling's BestPlaces, www.BestPlaces.net, "America's Most (and Least) Stressful Cities," January 9, 2004*

- Fargo* was highlighted as one of the top 25 cleanest metro areas for long-term particle pollution (PM 2.5) in the U.S. The area ranked #19. *American Lung Association, State of the Air: 2007*

- Fargo* was highlighted as one of the cleanest metro areas for ozone air pollution in the U.S. The list represents cities with no monitored ozone air pollution in unhealthful ranges. *American Lung Association, State of the Air: 2007*

Women/Minorities Rankings

- Fargo* was ranked #10 out of 100 metro areas in *SELF Magazine's* ranking of "America's Best Places for Women." A panel of experts came up with more than 50 criteria including death and disease rates, environmental indicators, community resources, and lifestyle habits. *SELF Magazine, "America's Best Places for Women 2007," December 2007*

Seniors/Retirement Rankings

- A.G. Edwards ranked America's 500 top-performing communities based on their residents' personal savings and investing behavior. The Fargo* metro area ranked #391 with an index score of 97.24 (national average = 100.00). A dozen statistical factors were measured including: participation in retirement savings plans; personal debt levels; and home ownership. *A.G. Edwards, "2007 Nest Egg Index", September 12, 2007*

Children/Family Rankings

- Fargo was selected as one of the top 100 best places to raise a family in the U.S. Criteria: demographic characteristics; standard of living; education; lifestyle; health and safety. *Best Place to Raise Your Family: The Top 100 Affordable Communities in the U.S., 1st Edition, 2006*

Safety Rankings

- The National Insurance Crime Bureau ranked 361 metro areas in the U.S. in terms of per capita rates of vehicle theft. The Fargo* metro area ranked #268 (#1 = highest rate). Criteria: number of vehicle theft offenses per 100,000 inhabitants. *National Insurance Crime Bureau, "NICB Vehicle Theft Study," April 22, 2008*

- Farmers Insurance Group of Companies, in partnership with Sperling's BestPlaces, ranked 379 metro areas and identified the "Most Secure U.S. Place to Live." The Fargo* metro area ranked #6 out of 127 in the mid-size city category (150,000 to 500,000 residents). Criteria: crime rates; extreme weather; risk of natural disasters; environmental hazards; terrorism threats; air quality; life expectancy; job loss numbers. *Farmers Insurance Group, "Most Secure U.S. Places to Live 2007"*

Sports/Recreation Rankings

- *Golf Digest* ranked 330 metro areas in the U.S. in terms of golf. The Fargo* metro area was ranked #142. Criteria: access to golf; weather; value of golf; and quality of golf. *Golf Digest, "Metro Golf Rankings," August 2005*

Culture/Performing Arts Rankings

- Fargo was selected as one of America's 10 best large (population 30,000 - 100,000) art towns. The city ranked #1. Criteria: number of art galleries; affordability; natural beauty; local support for the arts; availability of suitable studio and rehearsal space; frequency and impact of art festivals; cohesiveness of the local arts community; diversity of creative statements being made by local visual and performing artists; number of theaters, art schools, art museums, and alternative exhibition and performance venues. *The 100 Best Art Towns in America: A Guide to Galleries, Museums, Festivals, Lodging, and Dining, 4th Edition, 2005*

Fargo is located within the Fargo, ND-MN Metropolitan Statistical Area.

Business Environment

CITY FINANCES

City Government Finances

Component	2004-2005 ($000)	2004-2005 ($ per capita)
Total Revenues	185,465	2,045
Total Expenditures	167,003	1,842
Debt Outstanding	428,515	4,726
Cash and Securities	273,113	3,012

Source: U.S Census Bureau, Government Finances 2004-2005

City Government Revenue by Source

Source	2004-2005 ($000)	2004-2005 ($ per capita)
General Revenue		
From Federal Government	5,586	62
From State Government	41,522	458
From Local Governments	1,302	14
Taxes		
Property	12,988	143
Sales	20,567	227
Personal Income	0	0
License	2,233	25
Charges	30,620	338
Liquor Store	0	0
Utility	14,041	155
Employee Retirement	6,243	69
Other	50,363	555

Source: U.S Census Bureau, Government Finances 2004-2005

City Government Expenditures by Function

Function	2004-2005 ($000)	2004-2005 ($ per capita)	2004-2005 (%)
General Expenditures			
Airports	2,569	28	1.5
Corrections	0	0	0.0
Education	0	0	0.0
Fire Protection	7,611	84	4.6
Governmental Administration	8,471	93	5.1
Health	5,965	66	3.6
Highways	23,486	259	14.1
Hospitals	0	0	0.0
Housing and Community Development	2,885	32	1.7
Interest on General Debt	21,404	236	12.8
Libraries	1,415	16	0.8
Parking	701	8	0.4
Parks and Recreation	16,017	177	9.6
Police Protection	10,062	111	6.0
Public Welfare	614	7	0.4
Sewerage	3,301	36	2.0
Solid Waste Management	6,954	77	4.2
Liquor Store	0	0	0.0
Utility	11,487	127	6.9
Employee Retirement	3,623	40	2.2
Other	40,438	446	24.2

Source: U.S Census Bureau, Government Finances 2004-2005

Municipal Bond Ratings

Area	Moody's
City	Aaa

Source: Mergent Bond Record, January 2008 (unless noted otherwise)

DEMOGRAPHICS

Population Growth

Area	1990 Census	2000 Census	2007 Estimate	2012 Projection	Population Growth (%) 1990-2000	Population Growth (%) 2000-2012
City	74,372	90,599	91,758	93,165	21.8	2.8
MSA[1]	153,296	174,367	187,764	196,539	13.7	12.7
U.S.	248,709,873	281,421,906	301,045,522	314,920,978	13.2	11.9

Note: (1) Metropolitan Statistical Area - see Appendix B for areas included
Source: Claritas, Inc.

Number of Households and Average Household Size

Area	2007 Estimate	2007 Average Household Size
City	41,663	2.20
MSA[1]	78,017	2.41
U.S.	113,668,003	2.65

Note: (1) Metropolitan Statistical Area - see Appendix B for areas included
Source: Claritas, Inc.

Race and Ethnicity

Area	White Alone[2]	Black Alone[2]	Asian Alone[2]	Other Race Alone[2]	Hispanic[3]
City	92.9	1.6	1.6	3.9	1.6
MSA[1]	94.0	1.1	1.1	3.8	2.0
U.S.	73.1	12.4	4.3	10.3	14.9

Note: Figures are 2007 estimates; (1) Metropolitan Statistical Area - see Appendix B for areas included (2) Alone is defined as not being in combination with one or more other races; (3) May be of any race.
Source: Claritas, Inc.

Ancestry

Area	German	Irish[2]	English	American	Italian	Polish	French[3]	Scottish
City	40.6	8.6	5.2	2.0	1.0	2.8	4.7	1.2
MSA[1]	40.6	8.0	5.2	1.8	1.1	2.8	4.6	1.2
U.S.	15.2	10.9	8.7	7.3	5.6	3.2	3.0	1.7

Note: Figures include multiple ancestry (e.g. if a person reported being Irish and Italian, they were included in both columns); (1) Metropolitan Statistical Area - see Appendix A for areas included; (2) Includes Celtic; (3) Includes Alsatian but excludes Basque
Source: Census 2000, Summary File 3

Foreign-Born Population

Area	Percent of Population Born in							
	Any Foreign Country	Europe	Asia	Africa	Oceania[2]	Canada	Mexico	Latin America[3]
City	4.0	1.4	1.3	0.7	0.0	0.4	0.1	0.1
MSA[1]	3.0	0.9	1.0	0.4	0.0	0.3	0.2	0.1
U.S.	11.1	1.7	2.9	0.3	0.1	0.3	3.3	2.5

Note: (1) Metropolitan Statistical Area - see Appendix A for areas included; (2) Includes Australia, New Zealand subregion, Melanesia, Micronesia, Polynesia, and Oceania n.e.c; (3) Includes Central America (excluding Mexico), South America, and the Caribbean.
Source: Census 2000, Summary File 3

Marriage Status

Area	Never Married	Now Married (excluding Separated)	Separated	Widowed	Divorced
City	37.8	47.7	0.8	4.7	9.0
MSA[1]	33.8	52.2	0.8	5.0	8.2
U.S.	27.1	54.4	2.2	6.6	9.7

Note: Figures are percentages and cover the population 15 years of age and older; (1) Metropolitan Statistical Area - see Appendix A for areas included
Source: Census 2000, Summary File 3

Age Distribution

Area	Under Age 5	Age 5 to 17	Age 18 to 34	Age 35 to 49	Age 50 to 64	Age 65 to 79	80 Years and Over
	Percent of Population						
City	6.4	14.8	35.6	21.5	11.6	7.0	3.0
MSA[1]	6.4	17.5	30.6	22.6	12.3	7.5	3.2
U.S.	6.8	18.9	23.7	23.5	14.8	9.2	3.2

Note: (1) Metropolitan Statistical Area - see Appendix A for areas included
Source: Census 2000, Summary File 3

Male/Female Ratio

Area	Males	Females	Males per 100 Females
City	46,143	45,615	101.2
MSA[1]	93,192	94,572	98.5
U.S.	148,320,305	152,725,217	97.1

Note: Figures are 2007 estimates; (1) Metropolitan Statistical Area - see Appendix B for areas included
Source: Claritas, Inc.

Religion

Area	Catholic	Southern Baptist	United Meth-odist	ELCA[1]	LDS[2]	Presby-terian Church USA	Jewish Est.	Muslim Est.
County	14.5	0.2	2.4	27.6	0.3	2.0	0.5	0.5
U.S.	22.0	7.1	3.7	1.8	1.5	1.1	2.2	0.6

Note: Figures are the number of adherents as a percentage of the total population; Adherents are defined as all members, including full members, their children and the estimated number of other participants who are not considered members (e.g. the baptized, those not confirmed, those regularly attending services, etc.); (1) Evangelical Lutheran Church in America; (2) The Church of Jesus Christ of Latter Day Saints
Source: Reprinted with permission from Religious Congregations and Membership in the United States 2000 (Nashville, Glenmary Research Center, 2002) Copyright Association of Statisticians of American Religious Bodies. All rights reserved.

ECONOMY

Gross Metropolitan Product

Area	2002	2003	2004	2005	2005 Rank[2]
MSA[1]	6.3	6.7	7.3	7.8	204

Note: Figures are in billions of dollars; (1) Fargo, ND-MN Metropolitan Statistical Area - see Appendix A for areas included; (2) Rank ranges from 1 to 361
Source: The U.S. Conference of Mayors, "U.S. Metro Economies: GMP - The Engines of America's Growth," January 2007

Economic Growth

Area	1995 GMP	2005 GMP	Average Annual Growth Rate	Growth Rate Rank[2]
MSA[1]	4.3	7.8	6.1	113

Note: Figures are in billions of dollars; GMP = Gross Metropolitan Product; (1) Fargo, ND-MN Metropolitan Statistical Area - see Appendix A for areas included; (2) Rank ranges from 1 to 361
Source: The U.S. Conference of Mayors, "U.S. Metro Economies: GMP - The Engines of America's Growth," January 2007

INCOME

Per Capita/Median/Average Income

Area	Per Capita ($)	Median Household ($)	Average Household ($)
City	26,129	41,346	56,524
MSA[1]	25,033	45,767	59,349
U.S.	25,495	49,280	66,670

Note: Figures are 2007 estimates; (1) Metropolitan Statistical Area - see Appendix B for areas included
Source: Claritas, Inc.

Household Income Distribution

Area	Under $15,000	$15,000 -24,999	$25,000 -34,999	$35,000 -49,999	$50,000 -74,999	$75,000 -99,000	$100,000 -149,999	$150,000 and up
	Percent of Households Earning							
City	14.3	14.0	13.4	17.9	18.7	9.3	8.0	4.2
MSA[1]	12.7	12.3	12.4	17.0	20.9	11.4	9.0	4.2
U.S.	13.1	10.9	11.2	15.6	19.5	11.9	11.3	6.6

Note: Figures are 2007 estimates; (1) Metropolitan Statistical Area - see Appendix B for areas included
Source: Claritas, Inc.

Poverty Rates by Age

Area	All Ages	Under 5 Years Old	5 to 17 Years Old	18 to 64 Years Old	65 Years and Over
City	11.8	1.0	1.4	8.7	0.7
MSA[1]	11.0	1.0	1.7	7.5	0.8
U.S.	12.4	1.2	3.0	6.9	1.2

Note: Figures are percent of population with income in 1999 below poverty level and only include population for whom poverty status is determined; (1) Metropolitan Statistical Area - see Appendix A for areas included
Source: Census 2000, Summary File 3

Personal Bankruptcy Filing Rate

Area	2004	2005	2006
Cass County	3.88	6.32	1.29
U.S.	5.31	6.82	2.00

Note: Numbers are per 1,000 population and include Chapter 7 and Chapter 13 filings
Source: Federal Deposit Insurance Corporation (FDIC), Regional Economic Conditions (RECON), 8/23/2007

EMPLOYMENT

Labor Force and Employment

Area	Civilian Labor Force			Workers Employed		
	Dec. 2006	Dec. 2007	% Chg.	Dec. 2006	Dec. 2007	% Chg.
City	58,778	60,004	2.1	57,372	58,480	1.9
MSA[1]	116,907	118,806	1.6	113,760	115,497	1.5
U.S.	152,571,000	153,705,000	0.7	146,081,000	146,334,000	0.2

Note: Data is not seasonally adjusted and covers workers 16 years of age and older;
(1) Metropolitan Statistical Area - see Appendix B for areas included
Source: Bureau of Labor Statistics, http://stats.bls.gov

Unemployment Rate

Area	2007											
	Jan.	Feb.	Mar.	Apr.	May	Jun.	Jul.	Aug.	Sep.	Oct.	Nov.	Dec.
City	3.1	3.0	3.1	2.8	2.4	2.8	2.4	2.4	2.3	1.9	2.1	2.5
MSA[1]	3.5	3.4	3.5	3.1	2.6	3.2	2.6	2.5	2.4	2.1	2.2	2.8
U.S.	5.0	4.9	4.5	4.3	4.3	4.7	4.9	4.6	4.5	4.4	4.5	4.8

Note: Data is not seasonally adjusted and covers workers 16 years of age and older; All figures are percentages; (1) Metropolitan Statistical Area - see Appendix B for areas included
Source: Bureau of Labor Statistics, http://stats.bls.gov

Employment by Occupation

Occupation Classification	City (%)	MSA[1] (%)	U.S. (%)
Sales and Office	31.2	30.0	26.7
Professional and Related	21.1	19.8	20.2
Service	15.2	15.4	14.9
Production, Transportation, and Material Moving	11.5	12.5	14.6
Management, Business, and Financial	13.0	13.1	13.5
Construction, Extraction, and Maintenance	7.5	8.6	9.4
Farming, Forestry, and Fishing	0.4	0.6	0.7

Note: Figures cover employed civilians 16 years of age and older;
(1) Metropolitan Statistical Area - see Appendix A for areas included
Source: Census 2000, Summary File 3

Employment by Industry

Sector	MSA[1] Number of Employees	MSA[1] Percent of Total	U.S. Percent of Total
Government	17,900	14.9	16.3
Education and Health Services	17,000	14.1	13.4
Professional and Business Services	12,800	10.6	13.1
Retail Trade	15,400	12.8	11.6
Manufacturing	9,300	7.7	9.9
Leisure and Hospitality	11,900	9.9	9.6
Financial Activities	8,900	7.4	5.9
Construction	n/a	n/a	5.3
Wholesale Trade	7,500	6.2	4.4
Other Services	5,000	4.2	3.9
Transportation and Utilities	4,200	3.5	3.7
Information	3,200	2.7	2.2
Natural Resources and Mining	n/a	n/a	0.5

Note: Figures cover non-farm employment as of December 2007 and are not seasonally adjusted; (1) Metropolitan Statistical Area - see Appendix B for areas included; n/a not available
Source: Bureau of Labor Statistics, http://stats.bls.gov

Average Wages

Occupation	$/Hr.	Occupation	$/Hr.
Accountants and Auditors	23.50	Maids and Housekeeping Cleaners	8.41
Automotive Mechanics	17.82	Maintenance and Repair Workers	15.15
Bookkeepers	14.33	Marketing Managers	35.09
Carpenters	15.85	Nuclear Medicine Technologists	n/a
Cashiers	8.06	Nurses, Licensed Practical	16.04
Clerks, General Office	11.48	Nurses, Registered	26.19
Clerks, Receptionists/Information	11.17	Nursing Aides/Orderlies/Attendants	11.19
Clerks, Shipping/Receiving	12.28	Packers and Packagers, Hand	8.14
Computer Programmers	23.09	Physical Therapists	32.04
Computer Support Specialists	n/a	Postal Service Mail Carriers	21.22
Computer Systems Analysts	22.75	Real Estate Brokers	n/a
Cooks, Restaurant	9.94	Retail Salespersons	10.63
Dentists	n/a	Sales Reps., Exc. Tech./Scientific	25.26
Electrical Engineers	32.89	Sales Reps., Tech./Scientific	33.90
Electricians	20.05	Secretaries, Exc. Legal/Med./Exec.	14.59
Financial Managers	42.23	Security Guards	10.01
First-Line Supervisors/Mgrs., Sales	17.45	Surgeons	64.17
Food Preparation Workers	9.81	Teacher Assistants	12.00
General and Operations Managers	46.34	Teachers, Elementary School	19.60
Hairdressers/Cosmetologists	11.14	Teachers, Secondary School	20.80
Internists	n/a	Telemarketers	8.80
Janitors and Cleaners	10.53	Truck Drivers, Heavy/Tractor-Trailer	17.42
Landscaping/Groundskeeping Workers	11.47	Truck Drivers, Light/Delivery Svcs.	15.14
Lawyers	55.90	Waiters and Waitresses	7.92

Note: Wage data covers the Fargo, ND-MN Metropolitan Statistical Area - see Appendix B for areas included. Hourly wages for elementary/secondary school teachers and teacher assistants were calculated by the editors from annual wage data assuming a 40 hour work week; n/a not available.
Source: Bureau of Labor Statistics, May 2007 Metro Area Occupational Employment and Wage Estimates

RESIDENTIAL REAL ESTATE

Building Permits

Area	Single-Family			Multi-Family			Total		
	2006	2007p	Pct. Chg.	2006	2007p	Pct. Chg.	2006	2007p	Pct. Chg.
City	470	447	-4.9	383	537	40.2	853	984	15.4
U.S.	1,378,200	973,300	-29.4	460,700	407,200	-11.6	1,838,900	1,380,500	-24.9

Note: (p) preliminary; figures cover and represent new, privately-owned housing units authorized (unadjusted data); All permit data are based on estimates with imputation; U.S. figures are based on the new 20,000-place series.
Source: U.S. Census Bureau, Manufacturing, Mining, and Construction Statistics

Homeownership and Housing Vacancies

Area	Homeownership Rate[2] (%)			Rental Vacancy Rate[3] (%)			Homeowner Vacancy Rate[4] (%)		
	2005	2006	2007	2005	2006	2007	2005	2006	2007
MSA[1]	n/a	n/a	n/a	n/a	n/a	n/a	n/a	n/a	n/a
U.S.	68.9	68.8	68.1	9.8	9.8	9.7	1.9	2.4	2.7

Note: (1) Metropolitan Statistical Area - see Appendix B for areas included; (2) The proportion of households that are owners; (3) The proportion of the rental inventory that is vacant for rent; (4) The proportion of the homeowner inventory that is vacant for sale; n/a not available
Source: U.S. Census Bureau, Housing Vacancies and Homeownership Annual Statistics: 2007

TAXES

State Corporate Income Tax Rates

State	Rates and Tax Brackets
North Dakota	2.6% > $0; 4.1% > 3K; 5.6% > 8K; 6.4% > 20K; 6.5% > 30K

Note: Tax rates as of January 1, 2008; 7% for financial institutions with a minimum of $50. Corporations making a water's-edge election must pay an additional 3.5% tax.
Source: Tax Foundation, www.taxfoundation.org

State Individual Income Tax Rates

State	Federal Deductibility	Marginal Rates (%)	Standard Deduction ($)		Personal Exemptions ($)[1]	
			Single	Joint	Single	Dependents
North Dakota	No	2.1 - 5.54 (r)(y)	5,350 (s)	10,700 (s)	3,400 (s)	3,400 (s)

Note: Tax rates as of January 1, 2008; Local- and county-level taxes are not included; n/a not applicable; (1) Married joint filers generally receive double the single exemption; (r) State adjusts its bracket levels for inflation at the end of each year before printing tax forms; (s) Deductions and exemptions tied to federal tax system. Federal deductions and exemptions are indexed for inflation; (y) Brackets are not double for married taxpayers.
Source: Tax Foundation, www.taxfoundation.org

Various State and Local Tax Rates

State and Local Sales and Use (%)	State Sales and Use (%)	Gasoline[1,2] ($/gal.)	Cigarette ($/pack)	Spirits ($/gal.)	Table Wine ($/gal.)	Beer ($/gal.)
6.0	5.0	0.23	0.44	2.50	0.50	0.16

Note: Tax rates as of January 1, 2008; (1) In addition to the 18.4 cpg Federal gasoline tax; (2) Rates may include additional state sales taxes, environmental protection and storage fees/taxes, and local taxes. When necessary, the volume-weighted average of all local taxes is used to approximate the typical statewide rate including local tax
Source: Tax Foundation, www.taxfoundation.org; Original research

State Tax Burdens

Area	Combined State and Local Tax Burden		Combined Federal, State and Local Tax Burden	
	Percent	Rank	Percent	Rank
North Dakota	9.9	39	30.2	37
U.S. Average	11.0	-	32.7	-

Note: Figures cover 2007 and measure taxes as a percentage of income
Source: Tax Foundation, www.taxfoundation.org

State Business Tax Climate Index Rankings

State	Overall Rank	Corporate Tax Index Rank	Individual Income Tax Index Rank	Sales Tax Index Rank	Unemployment Insurance Tax Index Rank	Property Tax Index Rank
North Dakota	30	27	36	29	26	6

Note: Rankings range from 1 to 50 where 1 is best. Rankings do not average across to Overall Rank. States without a given tax are given a ranking of 1.
Source: Tax Foundation, State Business Tax Climate Index 2008

TRANSPORTATION

Means of Transportation to Work

Area	Car/Truck/Van		Public Transportation			Bicycle	Walked	Other Means	Worked at Home
	Drove Alone	Car-pooled	Bus	Subway	Railroad				
City	83.6	7.7	0.4	0.0	0.0	0.6	4.4	0.6	2.9
MSA[1]	81.8	8.6	0.4	0.0	0.0	0.5	4.7	0.5	3.5
U.S.	75.7	12.2	2.5	1.5	0.5	0.4	2.9	1.0	3.3

Note: Figures are percentages and cover workers 16 years of age and older;
(1) Metropolitan Statistical Area - see Appendix A for areas included
Source: Census 2000, Summary File 3

Travel Time to Work

Area	Less Than 15 Minutes	15 to 29 Minutes	30 to 44 Minutes	45 to 59 Minutes	60 Minutes or More
City	56.9	36.6	2.8	1.1	2.6
MSA[1]	51.2	37.9	6.1	2.0	2.8
U.S.	29.4	36.1	19.1	7.4	8.0

Note: Figures are percentages and include workers 16 years old and over; (1) Metropolitan Statistical Area - see Appendix A for areas included
Source: Census 2000, Summary File 3

Living Environment

COST OF LIVING

Cost of Living Index

Composite Index	Groceries	Housing	Utilities	Trans-portation	Health Care	Misc. Goods/ Services
95.8	97.5	82.9	123.0	101.9	97.8	95.6

Note: U.S. = 100; Figures cover the Fargo-Moorhead ND-MN urban area.
Source: The Council for Community and Economic Research (formerly ACCRA), Cost of Living Index, 2007

Grocery Prices

Area[1]	T-Bone Steak ($/pound)	Frying Chicken ($/pound)	Whole Milk ($/half gal.)	Eggs ($/dozen)	Orange Juice ($/64 oz.)	Coffee ($/11.5 oz.)
City[2]	8.91	1.35	2.52	1.30	3.11	3.25
Avg.	8.93	1.12	2.13	1.52	3.26	3.31
Min.	5.88	0.71	1.33	0.83	2.30	2.20
Max.	12.80	2.07	3.43	3.54	5.79	6.20

Note: (1) Values for the local area are compared with the average, minimum and maximum values for all 331 areas in the Cost of Living Index report; (2) Figures cover the Fargo-Moorhead ND-MN urban area; **T-Bone Steak** *(price per pound);* **Frying Chicken** *(price per pound, whole fryer);* **Whole Milk** *(half gallon carton);* **Eggs** *(price per dozen, Grade A, large);* **Orange Juice** *(64 oz. Tropicana or Florida Natural);* **Coffee** *(11.5 oz. can, vacuum-packed, Maxwell House, Hills Bros, or Folgers).*
Source: The Council for Community and Economic Research (formerly ACCRA), Cost of Living Index, 2007

Housing and Utility Costs

Area[1]	New Home Price ($)	Apartment Rent ($/month)	All Electric ($/month)	Part Electric ($/month)	Other Energy ($/month)	Telephone ($/month)
City[2]	259,475	658	-	54.21	171.86	25.67
Avg.	309,605	782	146.13	78.67	90.16	26.14
Min.	189,877	n/a	82.03	37.41	33.15	17.08
Max.	1,202,800	3,481	271.14	150.60	257.67	37.45

Note: (1) Values for the local area are compared with the average, minimum and maximum values for all 331 areas in the Cost of Living Index report; (2) Figures cover the Fargo-Moorhead ND-MN urban area; **New Home Price** *(2,400 sf living area, 8,000 sf lot, in urban area with full utilities);* **Apartment Rent** *(950 sf 2 bedroom/1.5 or 2 bath, unfurnished, excluding all utilities except water);* **All Electric** *(average monthly cost for an all-electric home);* **Part Electric** *(average monthly cost for a part-electric home);* **Other Energy** *(average monthly cost for natural gas, fuel oil, coal, wood, and any other forms of energy except electricity);* **Telephone** *(price includes basic monthly rate for a private residential line plus additional local usage charges incurred by a family of four).*
Source: The Council for Community and Economic Research (formerly ACCRA), Cost of Living Index, 2007

Health Care, Transportation, and Other Costs

Area[1]	Doctor ($/visit)	Dentist ($/visit)	Optometrist ($/visit)	Gasoline ($/gallon)	Beauty Salon ($/visit)	Men's Shirt ($)
City[2]	86.50	68.10	55.67	2.69	23.93	22.93
Avg.	79.48	71.93	79.55	2.64	29.52	25.77
Min.	52.08	44.80	43.95	2.19	15.58	16.19
Max.	148.44	126.27	158.83	3.48	60.62	48.53

Note: (1) Values for the local area are compared with the average, minimum and maximum values for all 331 areas in the Cost of Living Index report; (2) Figures cover the Fargo-Moorhead ND-MN urban area; **Doctor** *(general practitioners routine exam of an established patient);* **Dentist** *(adult teeth cleaning and periodic oral examination);* **Optometrist** *(full vision eye exam for established adult patient);* **Gasoline** *(one gallon regular unleaded, national brand, including all taxes, cash price at self-service pump if available);* **Beauty Salon** *(woman's shampoo, trim, and blow-dry);* **Men's Shirt** *(cotton/polyester dress shirt, pinpoint weave, long sleeves).*
Source: The Council for Community and Economic Research (formerly ACCRA), Cost of Living Index, 2007

HOUSING

House Price Index (HPI)

Area	National Ranking[2]	Quarterly Change (%)	One-Year Change (%)	Five-Year Change (%)
MSA[1]	71	1.46	3.80	32.69
U.S.[3]	-	0.10	0.84	41.37

Note: The HPI is a weighted repeat sales index. It measures average price changes in repeat sales or refinancings on the same properties. This information is obtained by reviewing repeat mortgage transactions on single-family properties whose mortgages have been purchased or securitized by Fannie Mae or Freddie Mac in January 1975; (1) Metropolitan Statistical Area - see Appendix B for areas included; (2) Rankings are based on annual percentage change for all metro areas containing at least 15,000 transactions over the last 10 years and ranges from 1 to 291; (3) figures based on a weighted average of Census Division estimates; all figures are for the period ending December 31, 2007
Source: Office of Federal Housing Enterprise Oversight, House Price Index, February 26, 2008

House Price Valuations

Area	Q1 2000	Q1 2001	Q1 2002	Q1 2003	Q1 2004	Q1 2005	Q1 2006	Q1 2007	Q1 2008
MSA[1]	-13.8	-7.1	-10.8	-3.2	-3.9	3.8	7.1	0.1	-1.3

Note: Figures show the percentage of over- or under-valuation of single family homes relative to statistically normal house values (e.g. a value of 23.6 indicates that house values are 23.6% overvalued). Statistically normal house values are based on house prices, interest rates, household incomes, population densities, and any historical premiums or discounts metropolitan areas have exhibited over time; (1) Figures cover the Metropolitan Statistical Area - see Appendix B for areas included
Source: Global Insight/National City Corporation, House Prices in America, May 2008

Median Home Prices

Area	2005	2006	2007[r]	Percent Change 2006 to 2007
MSA[1]	133	137	141	2.9
U.S. Average	219.0	221.9	217.9	-1.8

Note: Figures are median sales prices of existing single-family homes in thousands of dollars; (r) revised; n/a not available; (1) Metropolitan Statistical Area - see Appendix B for areas included
Source: National Association of Realtors, Metropolitan Area Prices, 1st Quarter 2008

Housing: Year Structure Built

Area	1990 -2000	1980 -1989	1970 -1979	1960 -1969	1950 -1959	1940 -1949	Before 1940	Median Year
City	25.9	16.2	21.1	9.3	10.1	4.6	12.8	1976
MSA[1]	21.7	14.3	22.9	11.3	11.4	4.8	13.6	1974
U.S.	17.0	15.8	18.5	13.7	12.7	7.3	15.0	1971

Note: Figures are percentages; (1) Metropolitan Statistical Area - see Appendix A for areas included
Source: Census 2000, Summary File 3

HEALTH

Health Risk Data

Category	Area[1] (%)	U.S. (%)
Adults who have been told they have high blood pressure[3]	16.5	25.5
Adults who have been told they have high blood cholesterol[3]	34.0	35.6
Adults who have been told they have diabetes[2]	4.9	7.5
Adults who have been told they have arthritis[3]	23.2	27.0
Adults who have been told they currently have asthma	5.5	8.5
Adults who are current smokers	23.3	20.1
Adults who are heavy drinkers[4]	6.2	4.9
Adults who are overweight (BMI 25.0 - 29.9)	38.4	36.5
Adults who are obese (BMI 30.0 - 99.8)	21.6	25.1

Note: Data as of 2006 unless otherwise noted; (1) Figures cover the Metropolitan Statistical Area - see Appendix B for areas included; (2) Figures do not include pregnancy-related diabetes, pre-diabetes or borderline diabetes; (3) 2005 data; (4) Heavy drinkers are classified as adult men having more than two drinks per day or adult women having more than one drink per day
Source: Centers for Disease Control and Prevention, Behaviorial Risk Factor Surveillance System, SMART: Selected Metropolitan/Micropolitan Area Risk Trends, 2005, 2006

Mortality Rates for the Top 10 Causes of Death in the U.S.

ICD-10[a] Sub-Chapter	ICD-10[a] Code	Age-Adjusted Mortality Rate[1] per 100,000 population	
		County[2]	U.S.
Malignant neoplasms	C00-C97	183.5	186.5
Ischaemic heart diseases	I20-I25	124.8	152.3
Other forms of heart disease	I30-I51	35.3	51.5
Cerebrovascular diseases	I60-I69	48.6	50.0
Chronic lower respiratory diseases	J40-J47	34.1	42.6
Diabetes mellitus	E10-E14	13.4	24.8
Other degenerative diseases of the nervous system	G30-G31	39.3	22.6
Other external causes of accidental injury	W00-X59	15.5	21.4
Influenza and pneumonia	J10-J18	27.8	20.7
Hypertensive diseases	I10-I13	12.6	18.2

Note: (a) ICD-10 = International Classification of Diseases 10th Revision; (1) Mortality rates are a three year average covering 2003-2005; (2) Figures cover Cass County
Source: Centers for Disease Control and Prevention, National Center for Health Statistics. Compressed Mortality File 1999-2004. CDC WONDER On-line Database, compiled from Compressed Mortality File 1999-2005 Series 20 No. 2K, 2008.

Mortality Rates for Selected Causes of Death

ICD-10[a] Sub-Chapter	ICD-10[a] Code	Age-Adjusted Mortality Rate[1] per 100,000 population	
		County[2]	U.S.
Assault	X85-Y09	*0.8	5.9
Human immunodeficiency virus (HIV) disease	B20-B24	*0.8	4.5
Intentional self-harm	X60-X84	10.1	10.8
Malnutrition	E40-E46	*0.6	1.0
Obesity and other hyperalimentation	E65-E68	*1.1	1.4
Organic, including symptomatic, mental disorders	F01-F09	11.0	16.8
Transport accidents	V01-V99	10.4	16.1
Viral hepatitis	B15-B19	*1.0	1.8

Note: (a) ICD-10 = International Classification of Diseases 10th Revision; (1) Mortality rates are a three year average covering 2003-2005; (2) Figures cover Cass County; (*) Unreliable data as per CDC
Source: Centers for Disease Control and Prevention, National Center for Health Statistics. Compressed Mortality File 1999-2004. CDC WONDER On-line Database, compiled from Compressed Mortality File 1999-2005 Series 20 No. 2K, 2008.

Distribution of Physicians[1]

Area	Total	Family/ General Practice	Specialties	
			Medical	Surgical
Cass County (number)	421	125	158	88
Cass County (rate per 10,000 pop.)	32.1	9.5	12.1	6.7
U.S. (rate per 10,000 pop.)	17.7	4.6	6.9	4.3

Note: Data as of 2005; (1) Includes all non-federal, patient-care, office-based MDs
Source: Area Resource File (ARF). June 2007. U.S. Department of Health and Human Services, Health Resources and Services Administration, Bureau of Health Professions, Rockville, MD.

Hospitals

Fargo has the following hospitals: 3 general medical and surgical; 1 long-term acute care; 1 other specialty.
AHA Guide to the Healthcare Field 2008

According to *U.S. News,* the Fargo, ND-MN metro area is home to one of the best hospitals in the U.S.: **MeritCare Hospital**. *U.S. News Online, "America's Best Hospitals 2007"*

EDUCATION

Public School District Statistics

District Name	Schls	Pupils	Pupil/ Teacher Ratio	Minority Pupils[1] (%)	Free Lunch Eligible[2] (%)	IEP[3] (%)
Fargo 1	22	10,849	15.3	11.1	15.1	12.0

Note: Table includes regular local school districts with 2,000 or more students; (1) Percentage of students that are not white, non-Hispanic; (2) Percentage of students that are eligible for the free lunch program; (3) Percentage of students that have an Individualized Education Program.
Source: U.S. Department of Education, National Center for Education Statistics, Common Core of Data, Local Education Agency (School District) Universe Survey: School Year 2005-2006; U.S. Department of Education, National Center for Education Statistics, Common Core of Data, Public Elementary/Secondary School Universe Survey: School Year 2005-2006

Highest Level of Education

Area	Less than H.S.	H.S. Diploma	Some College, No Deg.	Associate Degree	Bachelors Degree	Masters Degree	Profess. School Degree	Doctorate Degree
City	8.6	21.3	25.7	9.4	25.4	5.6	2.3	1.6
MSA[1]	9.9	24.3	26.6	9.6	21.7	4.8	1.8	1.3
U.S.	19.4	28.4	21.2	6.4	15.7	5.9	2.0	1.0

Note: Figures are 2007 estimated percentages and cover persons age 25 and over; (1) Metropolitan Statistical Area - see Appendix B for areas included
Source: Claritas, Inc.

Educational Attainment by Race

Area	High School Graduate (%)					Bachelor's Degree (%)				
	Total	White	Black	Asian	Hisp.[2]	Total	White	Black	Asian	Hisp.[2]
City	91.0	91.3	94.3	82.6	78.8	34.4	34.7	23.2	61.3	19.4
MSA[1]	89.7	90.2	92.4	82.8	64.2	29.4	29.7	23.8	53.0	11.3
U.S.	80.4	83.6	72.3	80.4	52.4	24.4	26.1	14.3	44.1	10.4

Note: Figures shown cover persons 25 years old and over; (1) Metropolitan Statistical Area - see Appendix A for areas included; (2) people of Hispanic origin can be of any race
Source: Census 2000, Summary File 3

School Enrollment by Type

Area	Grades KG to 8				Grades 9 to 12			
	Public		Private		Public		Private	
	Enrollment	%	Enrollment	%	Enrollment	%	Enrollment	%
City	8,463	90.9	845	9.1	3,834	92.9	294	7.1
MSA[1]	19,637	92.4	1,620	7.6	8,982	94.6	515	5.4
U.S.	33,526,011	88.7	4,285,121	11.3	14,848,628	90.6	1,532,323	9.4

Note: Figures shown cover persons 3 years old and over; (1) Metropolitan Statistical Area - see Appendix A for areas included
Source: Census 2000, Summary File 3

School Enrollment by Race

Area	Grades KG to 8 (%)				Grades 9 to 12 (%)			
	White	Black	Asian	Hisp.[1]	White	Black	Asian	Hisp.[1]
City	89.5	2.9	1.8	1.9	92.8	1.2	1.8	3.2
MSA[2]	90.9	1.5	1.0	3.5	93.4	0.8	1.2	3.6
U.S.	68.5	15.5	3.3	16.8	68.8	15.5	3.8	15.7

Note: Figures shown cover persons 3 years old and over; (1) people of Hispanic origin can be of any race; (2) Metropolitan Statistical Area - see Appendix A for areas included
Source: Census 2000, Summary File 3

Average Salaries of Public School Classroom Teachers

District	2005-06 Dollars	2005-06 Rank[1]	2006-07 Dollars	2006-07 Rank[1]	Percent Change 2005-06 to 2006-07
North Dakota	37,764	50	38,822	50	2.80
U.S. Average	49,026	-	50,816	-	3.65

Note: (1) State rank ranges from 1 to 51.
Source: National Education Association, Rankings & Estimates: Rankings of the States 2006 and Estimates of School Statistics 2007, December 2007

Higher Education

Four-Year Colleges			Two-Year Colleges			Medical Schools[1]	Law Schools[2]	Voc/ Tech[3]
Public	Private Non-profit	Private For-profit	Public	Private Non-profit	Private For-profit			
1	0	1	0	0	2	0	0	1

Note: Figures cover institutions located within the city limits; (1) includes schools accredited by the Liaison Committee on Medical Education and the American Osteopathic Association; (2) includes American Bar Association-accredited law schools; (3) includes all schools with programs that are less than 2 years.
Source: National Center for Education Statistics, The Integrated Postsecondary Education System (IPEDS) Peer Analysis System, 2007; www.usnews.com, Law and Medical School Directories, 2009

PRESIDENTIAL ELECTION

2004 Presidential Election Results

Area	Bush	Kerry	Nader	Other
Cass County	59.4	39.0	1.1	0.5
U.S.	50.7	48.3	0.4	0.6

Note: Results are percentages and may not add to 100% due to rounding
Source: Dave Leip's Atlas of U.S. Presidential Elections, www.uselectionatlas.org

EMPLOYERS

Major Employers

Company Name	Industry	Type of Site
Atlas Intl Fd & Eqp Co Inc	Management services	Headquarters
BLUE CROSS BLUE SHIELD OF NORT	Hospital and medical service plans	Headquarters
Bethany Homes Inc	Nursing and personal care, nec	Headquarters
City Commission Office	General government, nec	Branch
Dakota Clinic Ltd	Offices and clinics of medical doctors	Headquarters
Fargo Dome	Sports clubs, managers, and promoters	Branch
Fargo V A Medical/Reg	Administration of veterans' affairs	Branch
Hornbachers Foods	Grocery stores	Single
Meritcare Childrens Hospital	General medical and surgical hospitals	Headquarters
Microsoft	Prepackaged software	Branch
Noridian ADM Svcs LLC	Insurance agents, brokers, and service	Single
North Dakota State University	Colleges and universities	Headquarters
Park District of The Cy Fargo	Amusement and recreation, nec	Single
Pepsiamericas	Bottled and canned soft drinks	Headquarters
US Bank	National commercial banks	Branch
US Post Office	U.s. postal service	Branch
Upstream LLC	Business services, nec	Single
Wanzek Construction Inc	Heavy construction, nec	Single

Note: Companies shown are located within the Fargo metropolitan area; nec = not elsewhere classified.
Source: www.zapdata.com, May 2008

PUBLIC SAFETY

Crime Rate

Area	All Crimes	Violent Crimes				Property Crimes		
		Murder	Forcible Rape	Robbery	Aggrav. Assault	Burglary	Larceny -Theft	Motor Vehicle Theft
City	3,204.2	2.2	76.0	20.9	155.3	578.1	2,125.1	246.6
Metro[1]	n/a	1.1	n/a	16.2	116.2	442.0	1,732.5	186.4
U.S.	3,808.1	5.7	30.9	149.4	287.5	729.4	2,206.8	398.4

Note: Figures are crimes per 100,000 population; (1) Metropolitan Statistical Area - see Appendix B for areas included
Source: FBI Uniform Crime Reports, 2006

Hate Crimes

Area	Number of Quarters Reported	Bias Motivation				
		Race	Religion	Sexual Orientation	Ethnicity	Disability
City	4	2	0	0	0	0

Source: Federal Bureau of Investigation, Hate Crime Statistics 2006

RECREATION

Culture

Dance[1]	Theatre[1]	Instrumental Music[1]	Vocal Music[1]	Series/ Festivals	Museums	Zoos and Aquariums[2]
0	2	0	1	1	4	1

Note: (1) Number of professional perfoming groups; (2) AZA-accredited
Source: The Grey House Performing Arts Directory, 2007; Official Museum Directory, 2008; Association of Zoos & Aquariums, AZA Member Zoos & Aquariums, June 2008

Professional Sports Teams

Team Name	League
No teams are located in the metro area	

Source: Original research

MEDIA

Newspapers

Name	News Focus	Frequency	Circulation
The Forum	Local	Daily	62,097
New Earth	Regional	Monthly	27,085

Note: Includes newspapers with offices located in the city
Source: MediaContactsPro, March 2008

Television Stations

Name	Ch.	Network(s)	Type	Ownership
KGFE	2	PBS	Public	Prairie Public Broadcasting Inc.
KBME	3	PBS	Public	Prairie Public Broadcasting Inc.
KWSE	4	PBS	Public	Prairie Public Broadcasting Inc.
KXJB	4	CBS	Commercial	Catamount Broadcast Group
KSRE	6	PBS	Public	Prairie Public Broadcasting Inc.
WDAY	6	ABC	Commercial	Forum Communications Company
KJRR	7	Fox	Commercial	Red River Broadcast Corporation
WDAZ	8	ABC	Commercial	n/a
KDSE	9	PBS	Public	Prairie Public Broadcasting Inc.
KBRR	10	Fox	Commercial	Red River Broadcast Corporation
KVLY	11	NBC	Commercial	Sunrise Broadcasting Inc.
KNRR	12	Fox	Commercial	Red River Broadcast Corporation
KFME	13	PBS	Public	Prairie Public Broadcasting Inc.
KVRR	15	Fox	Commercial	Red River Broadcast Corporation
KJRE	19	PBS	Public	Prairie Public Broadcasting Inc.

Note: Stations included cover the Fargo-Valley City DMA (Designated Market Area)
BurrellesLuce, MediaContacts Online, January 2007

Major AM Radio Stations

Call Letters	Freq. (kHz)	Station Type	Target Audience	Station Format	Music Format
KSJB	600	Commercial	General	Music/News/Talk	Country
KFGO	790	Commercial	General	News/Talk	n/a
KQLX	890	Commercial	General	Music/News	Country
WDAY	970	Commercial	General	News/Sports/Talk	n/a
KJJK	1020	Commercial	General	Music	Oldies
KNDK	1080	Commercial	General	Ed/Music/News/Sports/Talk	Country
KFNW	1200	College	General/Religious	Music/Talk	Christian
KDDR	1220	n/a	General	Music/News/Sports	n/a
KTRF	1230	Commercial	General	News/Talk	n/a
KDLR	1240	Commercial	General	Music/News/Sports	Country
KBRF	1250	Commercial	General	News/Sports/Talk	n/a
KROX	1260	Commercial	General	Music/Sports/Talk	Oldies
KVOX	1280	Commercial	General	Sports	n/a
KNOX	1310	Commercial	General	Talk	n/a
KDLM	1340	n/a	General	Music/News	n/a
KXPO	1340	Commercial	General	Music/News	Christian
KQDJ	1400	Commercial	General	Music/Talk	Adult Standards
KRWB	1410	Commercial	General	Music/News	Classic Rock
KKXL	1440	n/a	General	News/Talk	n/a
KBMW	1450	Commercial	General	Music/Talk	Country
KKAQ	1460	Commercial	General	Music/News	Country
KKCQ	1480	Commercial	General	Music/Talk	Oldies
KOVC	1490	n/a	General	Music/News/Sports/Talk	n/a
KMAV	1520	Commercial	General	News/Sports	n/a
KCNN	1590	Commercial	General	News/Sports/Talk	n/a
KDAK	1600	n/a	General	Music/News/Sports	n/a
KQWB	1660	Commercial	General	Music/News	Oldies

Note: Stations included cover the Fargo-Valley City DMA (Designated Market Area); n/a not available
Source: BurrellesLuce, MediaContacts Online, January 2007

Major FM Radio Stations

Call Letters	Freq. (mHz)	Station Type	Target Audience	Station Format	Music Format
KSRQ	90.1	College	General	Educational/Music	Country
KCCD	90.3	College	General	n/a	n/a
KCCM	91.1	Public	General	Music	Classical
KQMN	91.5	College	General	Educational/Music	Classical
KKWQ	92.5	Commercial	General	Music/News/Talk	Country
KSJZ	93.3	n/a	General	Music/News/Sports	n/a
WDAY	93.7	Commercial	General	Music	Modern Rock
KNOX	94.7	Commercial	General	Music/News	Country
KXGT	95.5	Commercial	General	Music	Oldies
KNDK	95.7	Commercial	General	Ed/Music/News/Sports/Talk	Country
KQHT	96.1	Commercial	General	Music	Classic Rock
KJJK	96.5	Commercial	General	Music	Contemp. Country
KYCK	97.1	Commercial	General	Music	Country
KFNW	97.9	College	General/Religious	Music/Talk	Christian
KYNU	98.3	Commercial	General	Music	Contemp. Country
KQWB	98.7	Commercial	General	Music/News	Modern Rock
KKDQ	99.3	Commercial	General	Music	Country
KPRW	99.5	Commercial	General	Music/News/Sports/Talk	Adult Top 40
KVOX	99.9	Commercial	General	Music/News	Country
KSNR	100.3	Commercial	General	Music	Oldies
KRCQ	102.3	Commercial	General	Music/News	Country
KDVL	102.5	Commercial	General	Music/News	Oldies
KNTN	102.7	Public	General	Educational/News/Talk	n/a
KZCR	103.3	Commercial	General	Music	Adult Top 40
KZZY	103.5	Commercial	General	Music/News	Country
KBOT	104.1	Commercial	General	Music	Contemp. Country
KZLT	104.3	Commercial	General/Women	Music	Soft Rock
KLTA	105.1	Commercial	General	Music/News	Soft Rock
KMAV	105.5	Commercial	General	News/Sports	n/a
KQLX	106.1	Commercial	General	Music/News/Sports	Country
KKCQ	107.1	Commercial	Christian/General	Music	Country
KJKJ	107.5	Commercial	General	Music	Modern Rock

Note: Stations included cover the Fargo-Valley City DMA (Designated Market Area); n/a not available
BurrellesLuce, MediaContacts Online, January 2007

CLIMATE

Average and Extreme Temperatures

Temperature	Jan	Feb	Mar	Apr	May	Jun	Jul	Aug	Sep	Oct	Nov	Dec	Yr.
Extreme High (°F)	52	66	78	100	98	100	106	106	102	93	74	57	106
Average High (°F)	15	21	34	54	69	77	83	81	70	57	36	21	52
Average Temp. (°F)	6	12	26	43	56	66	71	69	58	46	28	13	41
Average Low (°F)	-3	3	17	32	44	54	59	57	46	35	19	4	31
Extreme Low (°F)	-36	-34	-34	-7	20	30	36	33	19	5	-24	-32	-36

Note: Figures cover the years 1948-1995
Source: National Climatic Data Center, International Station Meteorological Climate Summary, 9/96

Average Precipitation/Snowfall/Humidity

Precip./Humidity	Jan	Feb	Mar	Apr	May	Jun	Jul	Aug	Sep	Oct	Nov	Dec	Yr.
Avg. Precip. (in.)	0.6	0.5	1.0	1.7	2.3	3.1	3.2	2.4	1.8	1.5	0.8	0.6	19.6
Avg. Snowfall (in.)	9	6	7	3	Tr	0	0	0	Tr	1	6	7	40
Avg. Rel. Hum. 6am (%)	75	77	82	79	77	82	86	86	85	80	81	78	81
Avg. Rel. Hum. 3pm (%)	70	71	67	51	45	50	50	47	49	51	65	73	57

Note: Figures cover the years 1948-1995; Tr = Trace amounts (<0.05 in. of rain; <0.5 in. of snow)
Source: National Climatic Data Center, International Station Meteorological Climate Summary, 9/96

Weather Conditions

Temperature			Daytime Sky			Precipitation		
5°F & below	32°F & below	90°F & above	Clear	Partly cloudy	Cloudy	0.01 inch or more precip.	0.1 inch or more snow/ice	Thunder-storms
65	180	15	81	145	139	100	38	31

Note: Figures are average number of days per year and cover the years 1948-1995
Source: National Climatic Data Center, International Station Meteorological Climate Summary, 9/96

HAZARDOUS WASTE

Superfund Sites

Fargo has no sites on the EPA's Superfund Final National Priorities List.
U.S. Environmental Protection Agency, Final National Priorities List, June 23, 2008

AIR & WATER QUALITY

Air Quality Index

Area	Percent of Days when Air Quality was...[2]				AQI Statistics	
	Good	Moderate	Unhealthy for Sensitive Groups	Unhealthy	Maximum	Median
MSA[1]	95.9	3.3	0.3	0.5	162	29

Note: The Air Quality Index (AQI) is an index for reporting daily air quality. EPA calculates the AQI for five major air pollutants regulated by the Clean Air Act: ground-level ozone, particle pollution (also known as particulate matter), carbon monoxide, sulfur dioxide, and nitrogen dioxide. The AQI runs from 0 to 500. The higher the AQI value, the greater the level of air pollution and the greater the health concern. There are six AQI categories: "Good" The AQI is between 0 and 50. Air quality is considered satisfactory; "Moderate" The AQI is between 51 and 100. Air quality is acceptable; "Unhealthy for Sensitive Groups" When AQI values are between 101 and 150, members of sensitive groups may experience health effects; "Unhealthy" When AQI values are between 151 and 200 everyone may begin to experience health effects; "Very Unhealthy" AQI values between 201 and 300 trigger a health alert; "Hazardous" AQI values over 300 trigger health warnings of emergency conditions; (1) Metropolitan Statistical Area - see Appendix A for areas included; (2) Based on 365 days with AQI data in 2007.
Source: U.S. Environmental Protection Agency, Air Quality Index Report, 2007

Air Quality Index Pollutants

Area	Percent of Days when AQI Pollutant was...[2]					
	Carbon Monoxide	Nitrogen Dioxide	Ozone	Sulfur Dioxide	Particulate Matter 2.5	Particulate Matter 10
MSA[1]	0.0	0.0	78.9	0.0	14.2	6.8

Note: The Air Quality Index (AQI) is an index for reporting daily air quality. EPA calculates the AQI for five major air pollutants regulated by the Clean Air Act: ground-level ozone, particle pollution (also known as particulate matter), carbon monoxide, sulfur dioxide, and nitrogen dioxide. The AQI runs from 0 to 500. The higher the AQI value, the greater the level of air pollution and the greater the health concern; (1) Metropolitan Statistical Area - see Appendix A for areas included; (2) Based on 365 days with AQI data in 2007.
Source: U.S. Environmental Protection Agency, Air Quality Index Report, 2007

Air Quality Index Trends

Area	Trend Sites								All Sites
	1999	2000	2001	2002	2003	2004	2005	2006	2006
MSA[1]	n/a	n/a	n/a	n/a	n/a	n/a	n/a	n/a	n/a

Note: An AQI value greater than 100 indicates that air quality would have been in the unhealthful range on that day. Data from exceptional events are not included. These counts are presented in two ways. First, the counts are based on sites having an adequate record of monitoring data during the trend period (trend sites). These counts represent the relative change in the number of days with AQI values greater than 100. In the last column, the counts are based on all sites with data in the most recent year (because it is possible for a site to have data in the most recent year but not enough data to be a trend site); (1) Metropolitan Statistical Area - see Appendix A for areas included; n/a not available.
Source: U.S. Environmental Protection Agency, Office of Air and Radiation, Air Trends, Factbook and Related Information, Air Pollution Trends in Selected Metropolitan Areas 2006

Maximum Air Pollutant Concentrations

	Particulate Matter 10 (ug/m^3)	Particulate Matter 2.5 (ug/m^3)	Ozone (ppm)	Carbon Monoxide (ppm)	Sulfur Dioxide (ppm)	Nitrogen Dioxide (ppm)	Lead (ug/m^3)
MSA[1] Level	55	19	0.071	n/a	0.002	0.006	n/a
NAAQS[2]	150	35	0.125	9	0.140	0.053	1.50
Met NAAQS[2]	Yes	Yes	Yes	n/a	Yes	Yes	n/a

Note: Data from exceptional events are not included; (1) Metropolitan Statistical Area - see Appendix A for areas included; (2) National Ambient Air Quality Standards; n/a not available
Concentrations: Particulate Matter 10 (coarse particulate) - highest second maximum 24-hour concentration; Particulate Matter 2.5 (fine particulate) - highest 98th percentile 24-hour concentration; Ozone - highest second daily maximum 1-hour concentration; Carbon Monoxide - highest second maximum non-overlapping 8-hour concentration; Sulfur Dioxide - highest second maximum 24-hour concentration; Nitrogen Dioxide - highest arithmetic mean concentration; Lead - highest quarterly maximum concentration
Units: ppm = parts per million; ug/m^3 = micrograms per cubic meter
Source: U.S. Environmental Protection Agency, MSA Factbook 2006, Air Quality Statistics by City

Drinking Water

Water System Name	Pop. Served	Primary Water Source Type	Violations[1]	
			Health Based	Monitoring/ Reporting
City of Fargo	90,599	Surface	0	0

Note: (1) Based on violation data from January 1, 2007 to December 31, 2007 (includes unresolved violations from earlier years)
Source: U.S. Environmental Protection Agency, Office of Ground Water and Drinking Water, Safe Drinking Water Information System (based on data extracted April 15, 2008)

Beavercreek, Ohio

Background

Beavercreek sits in the wooded rolling hills of Ohio on over 27 square miles, 12 miles southeast of Dayton, which influences Beavercreek through its population, attractions and amenities, and politics.

A portion of Beavercreek lies in the Beavercreek Township, all of which is a part of Greene County. The area where Beavercreek currently sits was once a prominent hunting ground of the Shawnee and Miami Indians. In the late 1700s, European settlers arrived in the area, typically along the Little Beaver Creek or Big Beaver Creek. Greene County was formed in the early 1800s with Beavercreek as its county seat. Beavercreek traces its beginnings back to its establishment as a county seat; however, the city itself was not incorporated until 1980, from a portion of the Beavercreek Township. Beavercreek includes the areas known as Apple Valley, Big Beaver Valley, Indian Ripple, Knollwood, New Germany, Spicer, Zimmermanville, and the village of Alpha.

Wright-Patterson Air Force Base has a large influence on Beavercreek, employing over 5,000 military personnel and 8,100 civilians. The air force base has a positive impact on the Beavercreek economy, and the large number of technical and research jobs at the air force base pushed the city's median household income to over $75,000 per year. Furthermore, due to military base realignment, Wright-Patterson AFB is set to have an even larger positive influence on Beavercreek as the jobs available to local residents increase and people move to the area to support the growth of the base.

Education within the city of Beavercreek is provided by the Beavercreek City School District. The city school district is growing rapidly and district officials are actively planning solutions to limit enrollment to ensure quality education for their students. The University of Dayton, a private catholic institution, Wright State University, and several small colleges are available for those seeking higher education.

While Beavercreek's primary attractions include The Mall at Fairfield Common, the abundant bike trails, seasonal concerts, golfing and other outdoor activities, there are many other attractions available in the Dayton metropolitan area a short drive away. The area offers several museums, the Cox Arboretum and Gardens MetroPark, as well as many aviation-related attractions to commemorate the Wright Brothers who were from the area. In addition, there are ample opportunities to participate in the arts and sports.

Beavercreek has a humid continental climate with four distinct seasons. Average winter lows typically dip just below 20 in January and average normal highs reach the mid-80s in July.

Summers are generally humid and hot and winters are dry and cold. Average precipitation ranges from two to four inches a month with the most precipitation in April, May, and June.

Beavercreek's transportation needs are served by the James M. Cox Dayton International Airport that offers non-stop flights to many hubs across the nation including Chicago, Denver, Las Vegas, Miami, and New York.

Rankings

General Rankings

- Dayton* was ranked #84 out of 375 metro areas in *Cities Ranked & Rated*. Criteria: cost of living; climate; crime; transportation; economy and jobs; education; arts and culture; health and healthcare; leisure; quality of life. *Cities Ranked & Rated, 2nd Edition, 2007*
- Dayton* was ranked #74 out of 379 metro areas in *Places Rated Almanac*. Criteria: health care; education; recreation; transportation; ambience; climate; crime; housing costs; jobs. *Places Rated Almanac, 7th Edition, 2007*
- Beavercreek was selected as one of the "2007 Best Places to Live" by *Money* magazine. The city ranked #84 out of 100. Methodology: Places on the list had to have populations above 7,500 and under 50,000. Retirement-oriented communities, places where income is less than 90% or more than 180% of the state median and towns that were more than 95% white were screened out. Towns with low education scores, high crime rates, declines or sharp increases in population, projected job losses or lack of access to airports or teaching hospitals were eliminated. The remaining places were ranked based on job, income and cost-of-living data; housing affordability; school quality; arts and leisure opportunities; ease of living; health-care access; and racial diversity. Finally, the sense of community, vibrancy of town center, natural surroundings, amenities, real estate and congestion were assessed.

  CNNMoney.com, "Best Places to Live 2007"

Business/Finance Rankings

- The nation's 100 largest metro areas were analysed in terms of the percentage of households entering some stage of foreclosure in 2007. The Dayton* metro area ranked #15 out of 100 (#1 = highest foreclosure rate). *RealtyTrac, "Year-End 2007 Metropolitan Foreclosure Report"*
- The Dayton* metro area was identified as one of the least expensive places to rent in the U.S. The area ranked #15 out of 10 markets with an average effective rent of $570 per month. The rental figures cover apartment properties in complexes with 40 or more units (20 or more units in California and Arizona). The figures are blended average rents, which include all unit sizes. Effective rents include free rent incentives and other landlord concessions. *Wall Street Journal Online, January 17, 2008*
- Dayton* was selected as one of the best places to start and grow a company by *Entrepreneur* and the National Policy Research Council. The Dayton* metro area ranked #21 out of 63 mid-size metro areas. Criteria: business formation and growth (firms started four to 14 years ago that still employ at least 5 people and experienced rapid growth over the last four years). *Entrepreneur/National Policy Research Council, "Hot Cities for Entrepreneurs," September 2006*
- Dayton* was cited as one of America's top mid-size metros (population 200,000 to 1 million) for new and expanded facility projects in 2007. The area appeared in the top 10 with 27 projects. *Site Selection, "Top Metropolitan Area Awards," March 2008*
- Intel, in partnership with Sperling's BestPlaces, ranked the 80 "Best Cities for Teleworking" in America. The Dayton* metro area ranked #25 among mid-sized metro areas. The study identifies cities that hold the greatest potential for teleworking based on a host of factors including typical commuting times, fuel prices, availability of broadband Internet access and percentage of the population in telework friendly jobs. The study also factored in extreme climate and natural hazards. *Intel, "Best Cities for Teleworking," March 30, 2006*
- The Dayton* metro area appeared on the Milken Institute "2007 Best Performing Cities" index. Rank: #190 out of 200 large metro areas. Criteria: job growth; wage and salary growth; high-tech output growth. *Milken Institute, "2007 Best Performing Cities"*
- Dayton* was identified as one of the 100 "Most Unwired Cities" in the U.S. The area ranked #70 out of the 100 largest metro areas in the U.S. Criteria: number of public and commercial wireless access points (hotspots); airports with wireless Internet access; broadband availability; local wireless networks; and wireless email devices. *Intel, "Most Unwired Cities Survey," June 7, 2005*

- *Forbes* ranked the 200 most populous metro areas in the U.S. in terms of the "Best Places for Business and Careers." The Dayton* metro area was ranked #144. Criteria: business costs (labor, energy, tax and office space expenses); living costs (housing, transportation, food and other household expenditures); education levels of the work force; job growth; income growth; migration trends; crime rates; and culture/leisure. *Forbes, "Best Places for Business and Careers," March 19, 2008*
- *Fortune* ranked the 100 largest metro areas in the U.S. in terms of projected median home price change in 2007. The Dayton* metro area ranked #49. *Fortune.com, "Hot Spots, Cold Spots"*

Health/Environment Rankings

- 100 of the largest metro areas in the U.S. were analyzed in terms of their current drought severity. The Dayton* metro area ranked #50 (#1 = driest). The rankings were based on statistics such as long-term precipitation trends and patterns and the Palmer drought indices. *Sperling's BestPlaces, www.BestPlaces.net, "America's Drought-Riskiest Cities," November 2007*
- The Dayton* metro area appeared in *Country Home's* "2008 Best Green Places" report. The area ranked #223 out of 379. Criteria: official energy policies; green power; green buildings; availability of fresh, locally grown food. *Country Home, "2008 Best Green Places"*
- Dayton* was identified as a "2008 Asthma Capital." The area ranked #53 out of the nation's 100 largest metropolitan areas. Twelve factors were used to identify the most challenging places to live for people with asthma: estimated prevalence; self-reported prevalence; crude death rate for asthma; annual pollen score; annual air quality; public smoking laws; number of board-certified asthma specialists; school inhaler access laws; rescue medication use; controller medication use; uninsured rate; poverty rate. *Asthma and Allergy Foundation of America, "2008 Asthma Capitals"*
- Dayton* was identified as a "Spring Allergy Capital." The area ranked #57 out of 100. Three groups of factors were used to identify the most severe cities for people with allergies during the spring season: annual pollen levels; medicine utilization; access to board-certified allergists. *Asthma and Allergy Foundation of America, "2007 Spring Allergy Capital Rankings"*
- Dayton* was identified as a "Fall Allergy Capital." The area ranked #77 out of 100. Three groups of factors were used to identify the most severe cities for people with allergies during the fall season: annual pollen levels; medicine utilization; access to board-certified allergists. *Asthma and Allergy Foundation of America, "2007 Fall Allergy Capital Rankings"*
- Ortho-McNeil Neurologics, in partnership with Sperling's BestPlaces, analyzed 110 metro areas and identified those U.S. cities with the highest prevalence of factors that are most commonly associated with migraine headaches. The Dayton* metro area ranked #24. Criteria: number of migraine-related drug prescriptions per capita; lifestyle factors that can contribute to migraines; environmental factors that can trigger migraines; and consumption of migraine-triggering foods. *Ortho-McNeil Neurologics, "America's Migraine Hot Spots," March 14, 2006*
- Sperling's BestPlaces ranked 331 metro areas and identified the most and least stressful U.S. cities. The Dayton* metro area ranked #53 out of the 100 largest metro areas (#1 = most stressful). Criteria: divorce rate; unemployment rate; violent and property crime; suicide rate; commute time; mental health; alcohol consumption; cloudy days. *Sperling's BestPlaces, www.BestPlaces.net, "America's Most (and Least) Stressful Cities," January 9, 2004*

Seniors/Retirement Rankings

- A.G. Edwards ranked America's 500 top-performing communities based on their residents' personal savings and investing behavior. The Dayton* metro area ranked #246 with an index score of 101.51 (national average = 100.00). A dozen statistical factors were measured including: participation in retirement savings plans; personal debt levels; and home ownership. *A.G. Edwards, "2007 Nest Egg Index", September 12, 2007*

Children/Family Rankings

- The Dayton* metro area was selected as one of the "Best Cities for Relocating Families" by Worldwide ERC and Primacy Relocation. The 2007 study placed a special emphasis on the housing market, which has significantly impacted the relocation industry and an employer's ability to transfer employees. The variables which weigh heavily in this category include home price, home affordability index, appreciation rates, and property tax. Other criteria include cost of living, crime rates, education, climate, focus on diversity, physicians per capita, recreation and leisure, arts and culture, air quality, watershed quality, sales tax, unemployment rate, job growth, high school and higher education index, school expenditures per student, students in public school, SAT/ACT percentile, and population growth. *Worldwide ERC and Primacy Relocation, "2007 Best Cities for Relocating Families"*

Safety Rankings

- The National Insurance Crime Bureau ranked 361 metro areas in the U.S. in terms of per capita rates of vehicle theft. The Dayton* metro area ranked #85 (#1 = highest rate). Criteria: number of vehicle theft offenses per 100,000 inhabitants. *National Insurance Crime Bureau, "NICB Vehicle Theft Study," April 22, 2008*

- Farmers Insurance Group of Companies, in partnership with Sperling's BestPlaces, ranked 379 metro areas and identified the "Most Secure U.S. Place to Live." The Dayton* metro area ranked #73 out of 114 in the large metro area category (500,000 or more residents). Criteria: crime rates; extreme weather; risk of natural disasters; environmental hazards; terrorism threats; air quality; life expectancy; job loss numbers. *Farmers Insurance Group, "Most Secure U.S. Places to Live 2007"*

Sports/Recreation Rankings

- The Dayton* metro area appeared on the *Sporting News* list of the "Best Sports Cities 2007". The area ranked #127 out of 150 cities in the U.S. *Sporting News* takes a 12-month snapshot, roughly July to July, of each city's sports, putting a heavy premium on regular-season won-lost records (from the most recently completed season). Other criteria include: playoff berths, bowl appearances and tournament bids; championships; applicable power ratings; quality of competition; overall fan fervor as measured in part by attendance as percentage of venue capacity; abundance of teams (rewarding quality over quantity); stadium and arena quality; ticket availability and prices; franchise ownership; and marquee appeal of athletes. *SportingNews.com, "Best Sports Cities 2007," August 1, 2007*

- *Golf Digest* ranked 330 metro areas in the U.S. in terms of golf. The Dayton* metro area was ranked #91. Criteria: access to golf; weather; value of golf; and quality of golf. *Golf Digest, "Metro Golf Rankings," August 2005*

Dating/Romance Rankings

- The Dayton* metro area was selected as one of the "Best Cities for Relocating Singles" by Worldwide ERC and Primacy Relocation. The area ranked #10 out of the 100 largest metro areas in the U.S. Areas were selected based on the following criteria: a robust cost-of-living index; adventure and outdoor recreation opportunities; violent crime and property crime rates; percentage of the population that is unmarried (ages 25-34); ratio of single men and single women; affordability of quality higher education, including in-state and out-of-state tuition requirements and rates; number of newcomers to the area; commute times; tax rates; fee and occupancy rates for temporary housing and mini-storage; quality and quantity of collegiate and professional sporting events and fun, fan-friendly venues. *Worldwide ERC and Primacy Relocation, "2007 Best Cities for Relocating Singles," October 25, 2007*

- Sperling's BestPlaces in partnership with AXE Deodorant Bodyspray ranked 80 metro areas and identified "America's Best (and Worst) Cities for Dating." The Dayton* metro area ranked #24 (#1 = best). Criteria: percentage of singles ages 18-24; population density; dating venues per capita. *AXE Deodorant Bodyspray, "America's Best (and Worst) Cities for Dating," May 2004*

Miscellaneous Rankings

- Scarborough Research, a leading market research firm, identified the top local markets for grocery coupon use. The Dayton* DMA (Designated Market Area) ranked in the top 25 with 35% of consumers reporting that they use grocery coupons at least once per week.
  Scarborough Research, December 8, 2004

- A study by Sperling's BestPlaces examined which U.S. metro areas were most affected by high fuel prices in 2006. The Dayton* metro area was ranked #51 out of 80 (#1 = most expensive city for driving). Rankings are based on the average dollars spent on gas per year by two driver households. Criteria: cost of regular-grade gasoline; average miles driven per day; average number of gallons each driver uses and wastes in traffic congestion each day.
  Sperling's BestPlaces, www.bestplaces.net, "Pain at the Pump," May 18, 2006

Beavercreek is located within the Dayton, OH Metropolitan Statistical Area.

Business Environment

CITY FINANCES

City Government Finances

Component	2004-2005 ($000)	2004-2005 ($ per capita)
Total Revenues	n/a	n/a
Total Expenditures	n/a	n/a
Debt Outstanding	n/a	n/a
Cash and Securities	n/a	n/a

Source: U.S Census Bureau, Government Finances 2004-2005

City Government Revenue by Source

Source	2004-2005 ($000)	2004-2005 ($ per capita)
General Revenue		
From Federal Government	n/a	n/a
From State Government	n/a	n/a
From Local Governments	n/a	n/a
Taxes		
Property	n/a	n/a
Sales	n/a	n/a
Personal Income	n/a	n/a
License	n/a	n/a
Charges	n/a	n/a
Liquor Store	n/a	n/a
Utility	n/a	n/a
Employee Retirement	n/a	n/a
Other	n/a	n/a

Source: U.S Census Bureau, Government Finances 2004-2005

City Government Expenditures by Function

Function	2004-2005 ($000)	2004-2005 ($ per capita)	2004-2005 (%)
General Expenditures			
Airports	n/a	n/a	n/a
Corrections	n/a	n/a	n/a
Education	n/a	n/a	n/a
Fire Protection	n/a	n/a	n/a
Governmental Administration	n/a	n/a	n/a
Health	n/a	n/a	n/a
Highways	n/a	n/a	n/a
Hospitals	n/a	n/a	n/a
Housing and Community Development	n/a	n/a	n/a
Interest on General Debt	n/a	n/a	n/a
Libraries	n/a	n/a	n/a
Parking	n/a	n/a	n/a
Parks and Recreation	n/a	n/a	n/a
Police Protection	n/a	n/a	n/a
Public Welfare	n/a	n/a	n/a
Sewerage	n/a	n/a	n/a
Solid Waste Management	n/a	n/a	n/a
Liquor Store	n/a	n/a	n/a
Utility	n/a	n/a	n/a
Employee Retirement	n/a	n/a	n/a
Other	n/a	n/a	n/a

Source: U.S Census Bureau, Government Finances 2004-2005

Municipal Bond Ratings

Area	Moody's
City	n/a

Source: Mergent Bond Record, January 2008 (unless noted otherwise)

DEMOGRAPHICS

Population Growth

Area	1990 Census	2000 Census	2007 Estimate	2012 Projection	Population Growth (%) 1990-2000	Population Growth (%) 2000-2012
City	33,946	37,984	39,794	40,817	11.9	7.5
MSA[1]	843,857	848,153	842,572	835,991	0.5	-1.4
U.S.	248,709,873	281,421,906	301,045,522	314,920,978	13.2	11.9

Note: (1) Metropolitan Statistical Area - see Appendix B for areas included
Source: Claritas, Inc.

Number of Households and Average Household Size

Area	2007 Estimate	2007 Average Household Size
City	15,357	2.59
MSA[1]	344,303	2.45
U.S.	113,668,003	2.65

Note: (1) Metropolitan Statistical Area - see Appendix B for areas included
Source: Claritas, Inc.

Race and Ethnicity

Area	White Alone[2]	Black Alone[2]	Asian Alone[2]	Other Race Alone[2]	Hispanic[3]
City	91.6	1.7	4.6	2.1	1.6
MSA[1]	81.1	14.8	1.6	2.6	1.5
U.S.	73.1	12.4	4.3	10.3	14.9

Note: Figures are 2007 estimates; (1) Metropolitan Statistical Area - see Appendix B for areas included (2) Alone is defined as not being in combination with one or more other races; (3) May be of any race.
Source: Claritas, Inc.

Ancestry

Area	German	Irish[2]	English	American	Italian	Polish	French[3]	Scottish
City	30.2	14.4	14.3	10.3	5.1	3.3	2.9	2.3
MSA[1]	23.8	11.5	9.6	10.9	2.9	1.7	2.5	1.8
U.S.	15.2	10.9	8.7	7.3	5.6	3.2	3.0	1.7

Note: Figures include multiple ancestry (e.g. if a person reported being Irish and Italian, they were included in both columns); (1) Metropolitan Statistical Area - see Appendix A for areas included; (2) Includes Celtic; (3) Includes Alsatian but excludes Basque
Source: Census 2000, Summary File 3

Foreign-Born Population

Area	Percent of Population Born in: Any Foreign Country	Europe	Asia	Africa	Oceania[2]	Canada	Mexico	Latin America[3]
City	4.7	1.1	3.1	0.1	0.0	0.2	0.0	0.3
MSA[1]	2.3	0.7	1.1	0.2	0.0	0.1	0.1	0.2
U.S.	11.1	1.7	2.9	0.3	0.1	0.3	3.3	2.5

Note: (1) Metropolitan Statistical Area - see Appendix A for areas included; (2) Includes Australia, New Zealand subregion, Melanesia, Micronesia, Polynesia, and Oceania n.e.c; (3) Includes Central America (excluding Mexico), South America, and the Caribbean.
Source: Census 2000, Summary File 3

Marriage Status

Area	Never Married	Now Married (excluding Separated)	Separated	Widowed	Divorced
City	19.1	68.6	0.7	4.8	6.8
MSA[1]	25.8	54.2	1.6	6.9	11.5
U.S.	27.1	54.4	2.2	6.6	9.7

Note: Figures are percentages and cover the population 15 years of age and older; (1) Metropolitan Statistical Area - see Appendix A for areas included
Source: Census 2000, Summary File 3

Age Distribution

Area	Percent of Population						
	Under Age 5	Age 5 to 17	Age 18 to 34	Age 35 to 49	Age 50 to 64	Age 65 to 79	80 Years and Over
City	5.2	20.0	15.9	26.2	20.6	9.5	2.6
MSA[1]	6.5	18.2	22.9	22.8	16.0	10.2	3.3
U.S.	6.8	18.9	23.7	23.5	14.8	9.2	3.2

Note: (1) Metropolitan Statistical Area - see Appendix A for areas included
Source: Census 2000, Summary File 3

Male/Female Ratio

Area	Males	Females	Males per 100 Females
City	19,755	20,039	98.6
MSA[1]	409,112	433,460	94.4
U.S.	148,320,305	152,725,217	97.1

Note: Figures are 2007 estimates; (1) Metropolitan Statistical Area - see Appendix B for areas included
Source: Claritas, Inc.

Religion

Area	Catholic	Southern Baptist	United Meth-odist	ELCA[1]	LDS[2]	Presby-terian Church USA	Jewish Est.	Muslim Est.
County	9.0	3.8	2.5	1.8	0.9	2.1	0.0	0.4
U.S.	22.0	7.1	3.7	1.8	1.5	1.1	2.2	0.6

Note: Figures are the number of adherents as a percentage of the total population; Adherents are defined as all members, including full members, their children and the estimated number of other participants who are not considered members (e.g. the baptized, those not confirmed, those regularly attending services, etc.); (1) Evangelical Lutheran Church in America; (2) The Church of Jesus Christ of Latter Day Saints
Source: Reprinted with permission from Religious Congregations and Membership in the United States 2000 (Nashville, Glenmary Research Center, 2002) Copyright Association of Statisticians of American Religious Bodies. All rights reserved.

ECONOMY

Gross Metropolitan Product

Area	2002	2003	2004	2005	2005 Rank[2]
MSA[1]	30.4	31.3	32.7	33.7	59

Note: Figures are in billions of dollars; (1) Dayton, OH Metropolitan Statistical Area - see Appendix A for areas included; (2) Rank ranges from 1 to 361
Source: The U.S. Conference of Mayors, "U.S. Metro Economies: GMP - The Engines of America's Growth," January 2007

Economic Growth

Area	1995 GMP	2005 GMP	Average Annual Growth Rate	Growth Rate Rank[2]
MSA[1]	24.2	33.7	3.3	343

Note: Figures are in billions of dollars; GMP = Gross Metropolitan Product; (1) Dayton, OH Metropolitan Statistical Area - see Appendix A for areas included; (2) Rank ranges from 1 to 361
Source: The U.S. Conference of Mayors, "U.S. Metro Economies: GMP - The Engines of America's Growth," January 2007

INCOME

Per Capita/Median/Average Income

Area	Per Capita ($)	Median Household ($)	Average Household ($)
City	36,713	80,790	94,104
MSA[1]	25,401	47,625	61,409
U.S.	25,495	49,280	66,670

Note: Figures are 2007 estimates; (1) Metropolitan Statistical Area - see Appendix B for areas included
Source: Claritas, Inc.

Household Income Distribution

Area	Percent of Households Earning							
	Under $15,000	$15,000 -24,999	$25,000 -34,999	$35,000 -49,999	$50,000 -74,999	$75,000 -99,000	$100,000 -149,999	$150,000 and up
City	3.5	3.9	6.4	10.8	20.9	19.3	23.1	12.1
MSA[1]	12.6	11.2	11.9	16.8	20.3	12.1	10.4	4.7
U.S.	13.1	10.9	11.2	15.6	19.5	11.9	11.3	6.6

Note: Figures are 2007 estimates; (1) Metropolitan Statistical Area - see Appendix B for areas included
Source: Claritas, Inc.

Poverty Rates by Age

Area	All Ages	Under 5 Years Old	5 to 17 Years Old	18 to 64 Years Old	65 Years and Over
City	2.4	0.1	0.4	1.4	0.4
MSA[1]	10.3	1.1	2.4	5.8	1.0
U.S.	12.4	1.2	3.0	6.9	1.2

Note: Figures are percent of population with income in 1999 below poverty level and only include population for whom poverty status is determined; (1) Metropolitan Statistical Area - see Appendix A for areas included
Source: Census 2000, Summary File 3

Personal Bankruptcy Filing Rate

Area	2004	2005	2006
Greene County	5.42	7.81	2.29
U.S.	5.31	6.82	2.00

Note: Numbers are per 1,000 population and include Chapter 7 and Chapter 13 filings
Source: Federal Deposit Insurance Corporation (FDIC), Regional Economic Conditions (RECON), 8/23/2007

EMPLOYMENT

Labor Force and Employment

Area	Civilian Labor Force			Workers Employed		
	Dec. 2006	Dec. 2007	% Chg.	Dec. 2006	Dec. 2007	% Chg.
City	20,972	20,762	-1.0	20,105	19,814	-1.4
MSA[1]	430,746	426,835	-0.9	407,083	401,192	-1.4
U.S.	152,571,000	153,705,000	0.7	146,081,000	146,334,000	0.2

Note: Data is not seasonally adjusted and covers workers 16 years of age and older;
(1) Metropolitan Statistical Area - see Appendix B for areas included
Source: Bureau of Labor Statistics, http://stats.bls.gov

Unemployment Rate

Area	2007											
	Jan.	Feb.	Mar.	Apr.	May	Jun.	Jul.	Aug.	Sep.	Oct.	Nov.	Dec.
City	4.8	4.3	4.2	4.3	4.1	4.9	4.7	4.5	4.7	4.4	4.3	4.6
MSA[1]	7.0	6.0	5.6	5.7	5.5	6.1	6.1	5.8	5.8	5.6	5.6	6.0
U.S.	5.0	4.9	4.5	4.3	4.3	4.7	4.9	4.6	4.5	4.4	4.5	4.8

Note: Data is not seasonally adjusted and covers workers 16 years of age and older; All figures are percentages; (1) Metropolitan Statistical Area - see Appendix B for areas included
Source: Bureau of Labor Statistics, http://stats.bls.gov

Employment by Occupation

Occupation Classification	City (%)	MSA[1] (%)	U.S. (%)
Sales and Office	25.4	26.3	26.7
Professional and Related	32.3	20.3	20.2
Service	8.9	14.6	14.9
Production, Transportation, and Material Moving	9.0	18.1	14.6
Management, Business, and Financial	18.9	12.5	13.5
Construction, Extraction, and Maintenance	5.4	7.9	9.4
Farming, Forestry, and Fishing	0.2	0.2	0.7

Note: Figures cover employed civilians 16 years of age and older;
(1) Metropolitan Statistical Area - see Appendix A for areas included
Source: Census 2000, Summary File 3

Employment by Industry

Sector	MSA[1] Number of Employees	MSA[1] Percent of Total	U.S. Percent of Total
Government	65,300	16.1	16.3
Education and Health Services	67,500	16.6	13.4
Professional and Business Services	52,400	12.9	13.1
Retail Trade	44,300	10.9	11.6
Manufacturing	53,000	13.0	9.9
Leisure and Hospitality	36,900	9.1	9.6
Financial Activities	19,900	4.9	5.9
Construction	n/a	n/a	5.3
Wholesale Trade	14,100	3.5	4.4
Other Services	15,800	3.9	3.9
Transportation and Utilities	11,900	2.9	3.7
Information	10,900	2.7	2.2
Natural Resources and Mining	n/a	n/a	0.5

Note: Figures cover non-farm employment as of December 2007 and are not seasonally adjusted; (1) Metropolitan Statistical Area - see Appendix B for areas included; n/a not available
Source: Bureau of Labor Statistics, http://stats.bls.gov

Average Wages

Occupation	$/Hr.	Occupation	$/Hr.
Accountants and Auditors	31.84	Maids and Housekeeping Cleaners	8.93
Automotive Mechanics	16.33	Maintenance and Repair Workers	15.53
Bookkeepers	15.20	Marketing Managers	49.71
Carpenters	18.82	Nuclear Medicine Technologists	30.58
Cashiers	8.57	Nurses, Licensed Practical	19.21
Clerks, General Office	12.36	Nurses, Registered	27.42
Clerks, Receptionists/Information	11.09	Nursing Aides/Orderlies/Attendants	11.45
Clerks, Shipping/Receiving	13.78	Packers and Packagers, Hand	8.93
Computer Programmers	31.08	Physical Therapists	34.16
Computer Support Specialists	20.08	Postal Service Mail Carriers	21.29
Computer Systems Analysts	34.39	Real Estate Brokers	n/a
Cooks, Restaurant	9.42	Retail Salespersons	11.31
Dentists	n/a	Sales Reps., Exc. Tech./Scientific	27.84
Electrical Engineers	36.90	Sales Reps., Tech./Scientific	32.27
Electricians	23.31	Secretaries, Exc. Legal/Med./Exec.	14.83
Financial Managers	44.83	Security Guards	10.83
First-Line Supervisors/Mgrs., Sales	18.40	Surgeons	89.48
Food Preparation Workers	8.81	Teacher Assistants	12.00
General and Operations Managers	48.84	Teachers, Elementary School	25.00
Hairdressers/Cosmetologists	13.43	Teachers, Secondary School	25.70
Internists	89.34	Telemarketers	10.11
Janitors and Cleaners	12.05	Truck Drivers, Heavy/Tractor-Trailer	18.78
Landscaping/Groundskeeping Workers	11.76	Truck Drivers, Light/Delivery Svcs.	14.53
Lawyers	54.67	Waiters and Waitresses	7.76

Note: Wage data covers the Dayton, OH Metropolitan Statistical Area - see Appendix B for areas included. Hourly wages for elementary/secondary school teachers and teacher assistants were calculated by the editors from annual wage data assuming a 40 hour work week; n/a not available.
Source: Bureau of Labor Statistics, May 2007 Metro Area Occupational Employment and Wage Estimates

RESIDENTIAL REAL ESTATE

Building Permits

Area	Single-Family 2006	Single-Family 2007[p]	Single-Family Pct. Chg.	Multi-Family 2006	Multi-Family 2007[p]	Multi-Family Pct. Chg.	Total 2006	Total 2007[p]	Total Pct. Chg.
City	n/a	n/a	n/a	n/a	n/a	n/a	n/a	n/a	n/a
U.S.	1,378,200	973,300	-29.4	460,700	407,200	-11.6	1,838,900	1,380,500	-24.9

Note: (p) preliminary; figures cover and represent new, privately-owned housing units authorized (unadjusted data); All permit data are based on estimates with imputation; U.S. figures are based on the new 20,000-place series.
Source: U.S. Census Bureau, Manufacturing, Mining, and Construction Statistics

Homeownership and Housing Vacancies

Area	Homeownership Rate[2] (%)			Rental Vacancy Rate[3] (%)			Homeowner Vacancy Rate[4] (%)		
	2005	2006	2007	2005	2006	2007	2005	2006	2007
MSA[1]	66.1	64.6	64.2	14.6	16.4	16.6	3.9	3.1	1.2
U.S.	68.9	68.8	68.1	9.8	9.8	9.7	1.9	2.4	2.7

Note: (1) Metropolitan Statistical Area - see Appendix B for areas included; (2) The proportion of households that are owners; (3) The proportion of the rental inventory that is vacant for rent; (4) The proportion of the homeowner inventory that is vacant for sale; n/a not available
Source: U.S. Census Bureau, Housing Vacancies and Homeownership Annual Statistics: 2007

TAXES

State Corporate Income Tax Rates

State	Rates and Tax Brackets
Ohio	5.1% > $0; 8.5% > 50K

Note: Tax rates as of January 1, 2008; A value added-style tax, the Corporate Activities Tax (CAT) was instituted in 2005. It will be phased in through 2010 while the Corporate Franchise Tax (Ohio's income tax) is phased out. Beginning April 1, 2008 the CAT rate is.208% (80% of.26%). For tax year 2008 companies owe 40% of Corporate Franchise Tax liability.
Source: Tax Foundation, www.taxfoundation.org

State Individual Income Tax Rates

State	Federal Deductibility	Marginal Rates (%)	Standard Deduction ($)		Personal Exemptions ($)[1]	
			Single	Joint	Single	Dependents
Ohio	No	0.649 - 6.555 (y)	n/a	n/a	1,450 (g)(r)	1,450 (g)(r)

Note: Tax rates as of January 1, 2008; Local- and county-level taxes are not included; n/a not applicable; (1) Married joint filers generally receive double the single exemption; (g) Taxpayers receive a $20 tax credit per exemption in addition to the normal exemption amount; (r) State adjusts its bracket levels for inflation at the end of each year before printing tax forms; (y) Brackets are not double for married taxpayers.
Source: Tax Foundation, www.taxfoundation.org

Various State and Local Tax Rates

State and Local Sales and Use (%)	State Sales and Use (%)	Gasoline[1,2] ($/gal.)	Cigarette ($/pack)	Spirits ($/gal.)	Table Wine ($/gal.)	Beer ($/gal.)
7.0	5.5 (h)	0.28	1.25	8.46 (n)	0.32	0.18

Note: Tax rates as of January 1, 2008; (1) In addition to the 18.4 cpg Federal gasoline tax; (2) Rates may include additional state sales taxes, environmental protection and storage fees/taxes, and local taxes. When necessary, the volume-weighted average of all local taxes is used to approximate the typical statewide rate including local tax; (h) Ohio has a GRT that is levied in addition to its 5.5% sales tax. It is called the commercial activity tax (CAT). Firms with receipts over $1 million pay the CAT; firms with receipts between $150K and $1 million pay a minimum tax of $150. The rate i

2008 is 0.156%, and increases are scheduled in law to 0.208% on 4/1/2008 and 0.26% on 4/1/2009. The CAT is being phased in to replace Ohio's Corporate Franchise Tax, which is simultaneously being phased out; (n) The state government controls all sales. The implied excise tax rate is calculated using methodology designed by the Distilled Spirits Council of the United States (DISCUS).
Source: Tax Foundation, www.taxfoundation.org; Original research

State Tax Burdens

Area	Combined State and Local Tax Burden		Combined Federal, State and Local Tax Burden	
	Percent	Rank	Percent	Rank
Ohio	12.4	5	32.4	18
U.S. Average	11.0	-	32.7	-

Note: Figures cover 2007 and measure taxes as a percentage of income
Source: Tax Foundation, www.taxfoundation.org

State Business Tax Climate Index Rankings

State	Overall Rank	Corporate Tax Index Rank	Individual Income Tax Index Rank	Sales Tax Index Rank	Unemployment Insurance Tax Index Rank	Property Tax Index Rank
Ohio	46	37	48	36	11	44

Note: Rankings range from 1 to 50 where 1 is best. Rankings do not average across to Overall Rank. States without a given tax are given a ranking of 1.
Source: Tax Foundation, State Business Tax Climate Index 2008

TRANSPORTATION

Means of Transportation to Work

Area	Car/Truck/Van		Public Transportation			Bicycle	Walked	Other Means	Worked at Home
	Drove Alone	Car-pooled	Bus	Subway	Railroad				
City	90.0	5.8	0.1	0.0	0.0	0.0	0.6	0.3	3.2
MSA[1]	84.0	8.9	1.7	0.0	0.0	0.2	2.4	0.6	2.3
U.S.	75.7	12.2	2.5	1.5	0.5	0.4	2.9	1.0	3.3

Note: Figures are percentages and cover workers 16 years of age and older;
(1) Metropolitan Statistical Area - see Appendix A for areas included
Source: Census 2000, Summary File 3

Travel Time to Work

Area	Less Than 15 Minutes	15 to 29 Minutes	30 to 44 Minutes	45 to 59 Minutes	60 Minutes or More
City	32.1	54.2	9.5	1.7	2.5
MSA[1]	33.3	44.5	14.8	3.7	3.8
U.S.	29.4	36.1	19.1	7.4	8.0

Note: Figures are percentages and include workers 16 years old and over; (1) Metropolitan Statistical Area - see Appendix A for areas included
Source: Census 2000, Summary File 3

Travel Time Index

Area	1982	1995	2004	2005
Urban Area[1]	1.07	1.12	1.11	1.10
Average[2]	1.11	1.22	1.29	1.30

Note: Travel Time Index - The ratio of travel time in the peak period to the travel time at free-flow conditions. A value of 1.35 indicates a 20-minute free-flow trip takes 27 minutes in the peak. Free-flow speeds (60 mph on freeways and 35 mph on principal arterials) are used as the comparison threshold; (1) Covers the Dayton, OH urban area;
(2) average of 85 urban areas
Source: Texas Transportation Institute, The 2007 Urban Mobility Report, September 2007

Living Environment

COST OF LIVING

Cost of Living Index

Composite Index	Groceries	Housing	Utilities	Trans-portation	Health Care	Misc. Goods/ Services
93.9	91.9	81.4	101.1	103.5	93.8	99.8

Note: U.S. = 100; Figures cover the Dayton OH urban area.
Source: The Council for Community and Economic Research (formerly ACCRA), Cost of Living Index, 2007

Grocery Prices

Area[1]	T-Bone Steak ($/pound)	Frying Chicken ($/pound)	Whole Milk ($/half gal.)	Eggs ($/dozen)	Orange Juice ($/64 oz.)	Coffee ($/11.5 oz.)
City[2]	9.08	1.09	1.57	1.34	2.93	3.32
Avg.	8.93	1.12	2.13	1.52	3.26	3.31
Min.	5.88	0.71	1.33	0.83	2.30	2.20
Max.	12.80	2.07	3.43	3.54	5.79	6.20

Note: (1) Values for the local area are compared with the average, minimum and maximum values for all 331 areas in the Cost of Living Index report; (2) Figures cover the Dayton OH urban area; **T-Bone Steak** *(price per pound);* **Frying Chicken** *(price per pound, whole fryer);* **Whole Milk** *(half gallon carton);* **Eggs** *(price per dozen, Grade A, large);* **Orange Juice** *(64 oz. Tropicana or Florida Natural);* **Coffee** *(11.5 oz. can, vacuum-packed, Maxwell House, Hills Bros, or Folgers).*
Source: The Council for Community and Economic Research (formerly ACCRA), Cost of Living Index, 2007

Housing and Utility Costs

Area[1]	New Home Price ($)	Apartment Rent ($/month)	All Electric ($/month)	Part Electric ($/month)	Other Energy ($/month)	Telephone ($/month)
City[2]	248,709	666	-	98.40	85.79	21.55
Avg.	309,605	782	146.13	78.67	90.16	26.14
Min.	189,877	n/a	82.03	37.41	33.15	17.08
Max.	1,202,800	3,481	271.14	150.60	257.67	37.45

Note: (1) Values for the local area are compared with the average, minimum and maximum values for all 331 areas in the Cost of Living Index report; (2) Figures cover the Dayton OH urban area; **New Home Price** *(2,400 sf living area, 8,000 sf lot, in urban area with full utilities);* **Apartment Rent** *(950 sf 2 bedroom/1.5 or 2 bath, unfurnished, excluding all utilities except water);* **All Electric** *(average monthly cost for an all-electric home);* **Part Electric** *(average monthly cost for a part-electric home);* **Other Energy** *(average monthly cost for natural gas, fuel oil, coal, wood, and any other forms of energy except electricity);* **Telephone** *(price includes basic monthly rate for a private residential line plus additional local usage charges incurred by a family of four).*
Source: The Council for Community and Economic Research (formerly ACCRA), Cost of Living Index, 2007

Health Care, Transportation, and Other Costs

Area[1]	Doctor ($/visit)	Dentist ($/visit)	Optometrist ($/visit)	Gasoline ($/gallon)	Beauty Salon ($/visit)	Men's Shirt ($)
City[2]	68.00	64.85	83.48	2.67	30.26	22.74
Avg.	79.48	71.93	79.55	2.64	29.52	25.77
Min.	52.08	44.80	43.95	2.19	15.58	16.19
Max.	148.44	126.27	158.83	3.48	60.62	48.53

Note: (1) Values for the local area are compared with the average, minimum and maximum values for all 331 areas in the Cost of Living Index report; (2) Figures cover the Dayton OH urban area; **Doctor** *(general practitioners routine exam of an established patient);* **Dentist** *(adult teeth cleaning and periodic oral examination);* **Optometrist** *(full vision eye exam for established adult patient);* **Gasoline** *(one gallon regular unleaded, national brand, including all taxes, cash price at self-service pump if available);* **Beauty Salon** *(woman's shampoo, trim, and blow-dry);* **Men's Shirt** *(cotton/polyester dress shirt, pinpoint weave, long sleeves).*
Source: The Council for Community and Economic Research (formerly ACCRA), Cost of Living Index, 2007

HOUSING

House Price Index (HPI)

Area	National Ranking[2]	Quarterly Change (%)	One-Year Change (%)	Five-Year Change (%)
MSA[1]	191	0.50	0.07	11.11
U.S.[3]	-	0.10	0.84	41.37

Note: The HPI is a weighted repeat sales index. It measures average price changes in repeat sales or refinancings on the same properties. This information is obtained by reviewing repeat mortgage transactions on single-family properties whose mortgages have been purchased or securitized by Fannie Mae or Freddie Mac in January 1975; (1) Metropolitan Statistical Area - see Appendix B for areas included; (2) Rankings are based on annual percentage change for all metro areas containing at least 15,000 transactions over the last 10 years and ranges from 1 to 291; (3) figures based on a weighted average of Census Division estimates; all figures are for the period ending December 31, 2007

Source: Office of Federal Housing Enterprise Oversight, House Price Index, February 26, 2008

House Price Valuations

Area	Q1 2000	Q1 2001	Q1 2002	Q1 2003	Q1 2004	Q1 2005	Q1 2006	Q1 2007	Q1 2008
MSA[1]	-2.7	-4.0	-3.4	-5.7	0.0	0.2	-1.5	-5.6	-11.2

Note: Figures show the percentage of over- or under-valuation of single family homes relative to statistically normal house values (e.g. a value of 23.6 indicates that house values are 23.6% overvalued). Statistically normal house values are based on house prices, interest rates, household incomes, population densities, and any historical premiums or discounts metropolitan areas have exhibited over time; (1) Figures cover the Metropolitan Statistical Area - see Appendix B for areas included

Source: Global Insight/National City Corporation, House Prices in America, May 2008

Median Home Prices

Area	2005	2006	2007[r]	Percent Change 2006 to 2007
MSA[1]	119.7	116.7	115.6	-0.9
U.S. Average	219.0	221.9	217.9	-1.8

Note: Figures are median sales prices of existing single-family homes in thousands of dollars; (r) revised; n/a not available; (1) Metropolitan Statistical Area - see Appendix B for areas included

Source: National Association of Realtors, Metropolitan Area Prices, 1st Quarter 2008

Housing: Year Structure Built

Area	1990 -2000	1980 -1989	1970 -1979	1960 -1969	1950 -1959	1940 -1949	Before 1940	Median Year
City	21.7	10.6	24.9	20.2	17.2	3.0	2.4	1973
MSA[1]	9.9	8.3	17.3	18.8	18.4	9.5	17.8	1962
U.S.	17.0	15.8	18.5	13.7	12.7	7.3	15.0	1971

Note: Figures are percentages; (1) Metropolitan Statistical Area - see Appendix A for areas included

Source: Census 2000, Summary File 3

HEALTH

Health Risk Data

Category	Area[1] (%)	U.S. (%)
Adults who have been told they have high blood pressure[3]	n/a	25.5
Adults who have been told they have high blood cholesterol[3]	n/a	35.6
Adults who have been told they have diabetes[2]	7.3	7.5
Adults who have been told they have arthritis[3]	n/a	27.0
Adults who have been told they currently have asthma	8.8	8.5
Adults who are current smokers	20.8	20.1
Adults who are heavy drinkers[4]	3.6	4.9
Adults who are overweight (BMI 25.0 - 29.9)	33.6	36.5
Adults who are obese (BMI 30.0 - 99.8)	28.3	25.1

Note: Data as of 2006 unless otherwise noted; n/a not available; (1) Figures cover the Metropolitan Statistical Area - see Appendix B for areas included; (2) Figures do not include pregnancy-related diabetes, pre-diabetes or borderline diabetes; (3) 2005 data; (4) Heavy drinkers are classified as adult men having more than two drinks per day or adult women having more than one drink per day

Source: Centers for Disease Control and Prevention, Behaviorial Risk Factor Surveillance System, SMART: Selected Metropolitan/Micropolitan Area Risk Trends, 2005, 2006

Mortality Rates for the Top 10 Causes of Death in the U.S.

ICD-10[a] Sub-Chapter	ICD-10[a] Code	Age-Adjusted Mortality Rate[1] per 100,000 population	
		County[2]	U.S.
Malignant neoplasms	C00-C97	183.3	186.5
Ischaemic heart diseases	I20-I25	157.4	152.3
Other forms of heart disease	I30-I51	38.5	51.5
Cerebrovascular diseases	I60-I69	60.0	50.0
Chronic lower respiratory diseases	J40-J47	44.5	42.6
Diabetes mellitus	E10-E14	30.5	24.8
Other degenerative diseases of the nervous system	G30-G31	39.1	22.6
Other external causes of accidental injury	W00-X59	27.6	21.4
Influenza and pneumonia	J10-J18	13.8	20.7
Hypertensive diseases	I10-I13	25.1	18.2

Note: (a) ICD-10 = International Classification of Diseases 10th Revision; (1) Mortality rates are a three year average covering 2003-2005; (2) Figures cover Greene County
Source: Centers for Disease Control and Prevention, National Center for Health Statistics. Compressed Mortality File 1999-2004. CDC WONDER On-line Database, compiled from Compressed Mortality File 1999-2005 Series 20 No. 2K, 2008.

Mortality Rates for Selected Causes of Death

ICD-10[a] Sub-Chapter	ICD-10[a] Code	Age-Adjusted Mortality Rate[1] per 100,000 population	
		County[2]	U.S.
Assault	X85-Y09	*0.9	5.9
Human immunodeficiency virus (HIV) disease	B20-B24	*0.9	4.5
Intentional self-harm	X60-X84	9.9	10.8
Malnutrition	E40-E46	*2.3	1.0
Obesity and other hyperalimentation	E65-E68	*1.4	1.4
Organic, including symptomatic, mental disorders	F01-F09	28.7	16.8
Transport accidents	V01-V99	13.1	16.1
Viral hepatitis	B15-B19	*1.2	1.8

Note: (a) ICD-10 = International Classification of Diseases 10th Revision; (1) Mortality rates are a three year average covering 2003-2005; (2) Figures cover Greene County; (*) Unreliable data as per CDC
Source: Centers for Disease Control and Prevention, National Center for Health Statistics. Compressed Mortality File 1999-2004. CDC WONDER On-line Database, compiled from Compressed Mortality File 1999-2005 Series 20 No. 2K, 2008.

Distribution of Physicians[1]

Area	Total	Family/ General Practice	Specialties	
			Medical	Surgical
Greene County (number)	250	111	79	39
Greene County (rate per 10,000 pop.)	16.4	7.3	5.2	2.6
U.S. (rate per 10,000 pop.)	17.7	4.6	6.9	4.3

Note: Data as of 2005; (1) Includes all non-federal, patient-care, office-based MDs
Source: Area Resource File (ARF). June 2007. U.S. Department of Health and Human Services, Health Resources and Services Administration, Bureau of Health Professions, Rockville, MD.

Hospitals

There were no hospitals listed within the city limits.
AHA Guide to the Healthcare Field 2008

According to *U.S. News,* the Dayton, OH metro area is home to two of the best hospitals in the U.S.: **Kettering Medical Center**; **Miami Valley Hospital**. *U.S. News Online, "America's Best Hospitals 2007"*

EDUCATION

Public School District Statistics

District Name	Schls	Pupils	Pupil/ Teacher Ratio	Minority Pupils[1] (%)	Free Lunch Eligible[2] (%)	IEP[3] (%)
Beavercreek City	8	7,626	19.1	12.4	6.1	13.5

Note: Table includes regular local school districts with 2,000 or more students; (1) Percentage of students that are not white, non-Hispanic; (2) Percentage of students that are eligible for the free lunch program; (3) Percentage of students that have an Individualized Education Program.
Source: U.S. Department of Education, National Center for Education Statistics, Common Core of Data, Local Education Agency (School District) Universe Survey: School Year 2005-2006; U.S. Department of Education, National Center for Education Statistics, Common Core of Data, Public Elementary/Secondary School Universe Survey: School Year 2005-2006

Highest Level of Education

Area	Less than H.S.	H.S. Diploma	Some College, No Deg.	Associate Degree	Bachelors Degree	Masters Degree	Profess. School Degree	Doctorate Degree
City	7.3	21.9	20.7	6.2	22.6	16.4	2.4	2.5
MSA[1]	15.6	32.2	22.1	7.0	14.2	6.5	1.6	0.9
U.S.	19.4	28.4	21.2	6.4	15.7	5.9	2.0	1.0

Note: Figures are 2007 estimated percentages and cover persons age 25 and over; (1) Metropolitan Statistical Area - see Appendix B for areas included
Source: Claritas, Inc.

Educational Attainment by Race

Area	High School Graduate (%)					Bachelor's Degree (%)				
	Total	White	Black	Asian	Hisp.[2]	Total	White	Black	Asian	Hisp.[2]
City	92.4	92.5	98.8	84.2	98.0	42.9	42.0	67.5	62.8	59.0
MSA[1]	83.7	84.6	78.0	86.5	80.2	22.1	22.7	15.5	53.9	28.0
U.S.	80.4	83.6	72.3	80.4	52.4	24.4	26.1	14.3	44.1	10.4

Note: Figures shown cover persons 25 years old and over; (1) Metropolitan Statistical Area - see Appendix A for areas included; (2) people of Hispanic origin can be of any race
Source: Census 2000, Summary File 3

School Enrollment by Type

Area	Grades KG to 8				Grades 9 to 12			
	Public		Private		Public		Private	
	Enrollment	%	Enrollment	%	Enrollment	%	Enrollment	%
City	4,002	77.5	1,165	22.5	2,045	82.3	440	17.7
MSA[1]	106,102	86.2	16,953	13.8	46,603	89.5	5,468	10.5
U.S.	33,526,011	88.7	4,285,121	11.3	14,848,628	90.6	1,532,323	9.4

Note: Figures shown cover persons 3 years old and over; (1) Metropolitan Statistical Area - see Appendix A for areas included
Source: Census 2000, Summary File 3

School Enrollment by Race

Area	Grades KG to 8 (%)				Grades 9 to 12 (%)			
	White	Black	Asian	Hisp.[1]	White	Black	Asian	Hisp.[1]
City	92.6	2.4	2.2	1.8	93.1	1.4	4.0	0.8
MSA[2]	76.7	18.4	1.0	1.3	79.2	17.1	1.1	1.0
U.S.	68.5	15.5	3.3	16.8	68.8	15.5	3.8	15.7

Note: Figures shown cover persons 3 years old and over; (1) people of Hispanic origin can be of any race; (2) Metropolitan Statistical Area - see Appendix A for areas included
Source: Census 2000, Summary File 3

Average Salaries of Public School Classroom Teachers

District	2005-06 Dollars	2005-06 Rank[1]	2006-07 Dollars	2006-07 Rank[1]	Percent Change 2005-06 to 2006-07
Ohio	50,314	14	51,937	14	3.23
U.S. Average	49,026	-	50,816	-	3.65

Note: (1) State rank ranges from 1 to 51.
Source: National Education Association, Rankings & Estimates: Rankings of the States 2006 and Estimates of School Statistics 2007, December 2007

Higher Education

Four-Year Colleges			Two-Year Colleges			Medical Schools[1]	Law Schools[2]	Voc/ Tech[3]
Public	Private Non-profit	Private For-profit	Public	Private Non-profit	Private For-profit			
0	0	0	0	0	0	0	0	0

Note: Figures cover institutions located within the city limits; (1) includes schools accredited by the Liaison Committee on Medical Education and the American Osteopathic Association; (2) includes American Bar Association-accredited law schools; (3) includes all schools with programs that are less than 2 years.
Source: National Center for Education Statistics, The Integrated Postsecondary Education System (IPEDS) Peer Analysis System, 2007; www.usnews.com, Law and Medical School Directories, 2009

PRESIDENTIAL ELECTION

2004 Presidential Election Results

Area	Bush	Kerry	Nader	Other
Greene County	61.0	38.5	0.0	0.5
U.S.	50.7	48.3	0.4	0.6

Note: Results are percentages and may not add to 100% due to rounding
Source: Dave Leip's Atlas of U.S. Presidential Elections, www.uselectionatlas.org

EMPLOYERS

Major Employers

Company Name	Industry	Type of Site
Behr Dayton Thermal Products	Fabricated plate work (boiler shop)	Branch
Dayton Children	Specialty hospitals, except psychiatric	Single
Dayton V A Medical Center	Administration of veterans' affairs	Branch
GE	Business services, nec	Branch
General Motors	Automotive services, nec	Branch
Honorable Michael Tucker	Courts	Branch
Mead Corporation	Paper mills	Single
Mead Timber Company	Timber tracts	Single
Med America Hlth Systems Corp	General medical and surgical hospitals	Headquarters
NATIONAL CITY BANK	Mortgage bankers and correspondents	Headquarters
NCR	Computer terminals	Headquarters
Nasco Services	Management consulting services	Branch
Patterson Air Force	National security	Branch
Samaritan Health Partners	General medical and surgical hospitals	Headquarters
US Post Office	U.S. postal service	Branch
University of Dayton	Colleges and universities	Headquarters
Wright State University	Colleges and universities	Headquarters

Note: Companies shown are located within the Dayton metropolitan area; nec = not elsewhere classified.
Source: www.zapdata.com, May 2008

PUBLIC SAFETY

Crime Rate

Area	All Crimes	Violent Crimes				Property Crimes		
		Murder	Forcible Rape	Robbery	Aggrav. Assault	Burglary	Larceny -Theft	Motor Vehicle Theft
City	3,143.3	0.0	15.1	37.8	55.4	304.8	2,569.1	161.2
Metro[1]	4,069.6	5.3	43.5	136.5	139.9	867.0	2,459.7	417.6
U.S.	3,808.1	5.7	30.9	149.4	287.5	729.4	2,206.8	398.4

Note: Figures are crimes per 100,000 population; (1) Metropolitan Statistical Area - see Appendix B for areas included
Source: FBI Uniform Crime Reports, 2006

Hate Crimes

Area	Number of Quarters Reported	Bias Motivation				
		Race	Religion	Sexual Orientation	Ethnicity	Disability
City	4	0	0	0	0	0

Source: Federal Bureau of Investigation, Hate Crime Statistics 2006

RECREATION

Culture

Dance[1]	Theatre[1]	Instrumental Music[1]	Vocal Music[1]	Series/ Festivals	Museums	Zoos and Aquariums[2]
0	0	0	0	0	0	0

Note: (1) Number of professional perfoming groups; (2) AZA-accredited
Source: The Grey House Performing Arts Directory, 2007; Official Museum Directory, 2008; Association of Zoos & Aquariums, AZA Member Zoos & Aquariums, June 2008

Professional Sports Teams

Team Name	League
No teams are located in the metro area	

Source: Original research

MEDIA

Newspapers

Name	News Focus	Frequency	Circulation
No newspapers have an office in the city			

Note: Includes newspapers with offices located in the city
Source: MediaContactsPro, March 2008

Television Stations

Name	Ch.	Network(s)	Type	Ownership
WDTN	2	ABC	Commercial	Sunrise Television Corp.
WHIO	7	CBS	Commercial	Cox Enterprises Inc.
WPTO	14	PBS	Public	Greater Dayton Public Television
WPTD	16	PBS	Public	Greater Dayton Public Television
WKEF	22	NBC	Commercial	Sinclair Broadcast Group
WBDT	26	WBN	Commercial	Paxson Communications Corporation
WKOI	43	n/a	Non-comm.	TBN
WRGT	45	Fox	Commercial	Sinclair Broadcast Group

Note: Stations included cover the Dayton DMA (Designated Market Area)
BurrellesLuce, MediaContacts Online, January 2007

Major AM Radio Stations

Call Letters	Freq. (kHz)	Station Type	Target Audience	Station Format	Music Format
WHON	930	Commercial	General	News/Talk	n/a
WONE	980	n/a	General	Music	n/a
WGNZ	1110	Commercial	General/Religious	Music/News/Talk	Gospel
WDAO	1210	Commercial	General	Music/Talk	Rhythm & Blues
WHIO	1290	n/a	General	News/Talk	n/a
WCSM	1350	n/a	General	Music	n/a
WIZE	1360	Commercial	General	Music	Adult Contemp.
WBLL	1390	Commercial	General	News/Talk	n/a
WING	1410	n/a	General	News/Sports/Talk	n/a
WKBV	1490	Commercial	General	News/Talk	n/a
WBZI	1500	Commercial	General	Music	Country
WPTW	1570	Commercial	General	Music/News	Adult Contemp.
WULM	1600	Commercial	General	News/Sports/Talk	n/a

Note: Stations included cover the Dayton DMA (Designated Market Area); n/a not available
Source: BurrellesLuce, MediaContacts Online, January 2007

Major FM Radio Stations

Call Letters	Freq. (mHz)	Station Type	Target Audience	Station Format	Music Format
WDPR	88.1	Public	General	Music/Talk	Classical
WDPG	89.9	Public	General	Music	Classical
WCDR	90.3	Public	General/Religious	Educational/Music	Christian
WYSO	91.3	College	General	Educational	n/a
WGTZ	92.9	Commercial	General	Music/News/Talk	Top 40
WFCJ	93.7	Commercial	General/Religious	Educational/Music/Talk	Christian
WDKF	94.5	n/a	General	Music/News/Talk	n/a
WDPT	95.7	n/a	General	Music/News	n/a
WQLK	96.1	n/a	General	Music/News	n/a
WCSM	96.7	Commercial	General	Music/News	Adult Contemp.
WTGR	97.5	Commercial	General	Music	Classic Rock
WPKO	98.3	Commercial	General	Music/News	Adult Contemp.
WHKO	99.1	n/a	General	Music	n/a
WLQT	99.9	n/a	General/Women	Music	n/a
WEEC	100.7	Non-Comm	Christian/General/Hisp	Educational/News	n/a
WFMG	101.3	Commercial	General/Women	Music/News/Talk	Adult Contemp.
WKSW	101.7	n/a	General	Music/News/Talk	n/a
WDHT	102.9	Commercial	General	Music/Talk	Urban Contemp.
WXEG	103.9	Commercial	General	Music	Alternative
WTUE	104.7	Commercial	General	Music	Album Rock
WMVR	105.5	Commercial	General	Music/News	Adult Contemp.
WMMX	107.7	n/a	General	Music	n/a

Note: Stations included cover the Dayton DMA (Designated Market Area); n/a not available
BurrellesLuce, MediaContacts Online, January 2007

CLIMATE

Average and Extreme Temperatures

Temperature	Jan	Feb	Mar	Apr	May	Jun	Jul	Aug	Sep	Oct	Nov	Dec	Yr.
Extreme High (°F)	71	69	82	89	93	102	102	102	101	89	79	72	102
Average High (°F)	35	39	49	62	72	81	85	83	76	65	51	39	62
Average Temp. (°F)	27	31	40	52	62	71	75	73	66	55	43	32	52
Average Low (°F)	19	22	31	41	51	60	65	62	55	44	34	24	42
Extreme Low (°F)	-25	-16	-7	15	26	40	44	40	32	21	-2	-20	-25

Note: Figures cover the years 1948-1995
Source: National Climatic Data Center, International Station Meteorological Climate Summary, 9/96

Average Precipitation/Snowfall/Humidity

Precip./Humidity	Jan	Feb	Mar	Apr	May	Jun	Jul	Aug	Sep	Oct	Nov	Dec	Yr.
Avg. Precip. (in.)	2.8	2.3	3.2	3.7	3.9	3.9	3.7	3.1	2.5	2.4	3.1	2.8	37.4
Avg. Snowfall (in.)	8	6	5	1	Tr	0	0	0	0	Tr	2	5	29
Avg. Rel. Hum. 7am (%)	80	79	79	77	78	80	83	86	87	83	81	81	81
Avg. Rel. Hum. 4pm (%)	68	64	59	53	52	52	53	53	52	52	63	69	57

Note: Figures cover the years 1948-1995; Tr = Trace amounts (<0.05 in. of rain; <0.5 in. of snow)
Source: National Climatic Data Center, International Station Meteorological Climate Summary, 9/96

Weather Conditions

Temperature			Daytime Sky			Precipitation		
10°F & below	32°F & below	90°F & above	Clear	Partly cloudy	Cloudy	0.01 inch or more precip.	0.1 inch or more snow/ice	Thunder-storms
18	117	17	80	121	164	133	28	40

Note: Figures are average number of days per year and cover the years 1948-1995
Source: National Climatic Data Center, International Station Meteorological Climate Summary, 9/96

HAZARDOUS WASTE

Superfund Sites

Beavercreek has one hazardous waste site on the EPA's Superfund Final National Priorities List: **Lammers Barrel Factory**. *U.S. Environmental Protection Agency, Final National Priorities List, June 23, 2008*

AIR & WATER QUALITY

Air Quality Index

Area	Percent of Days when Air Quality was...[2]				AQI Statistics	
	Good	Moderate	Unhealthy for Sensitive Groups	Unhealthy	Maximum	Median
MSA[1]	69.0	26.3	4.4	0.3	151	40

Note: The Air Quality Index (AQI) is an index for reporting daily air quality. EPA calculates the AQI for five major air pollutants regulated by the Clean Air Act: ground-level ozone, particle pollution (also known as particulate matter), carbon monoxide, sulfur dioxide, and nitrogen dioxide. The AQI runs from 0 to 500. The higher the AQI value, the greater the level of air pollution and the greater the health concern. There are six AQI categories: "Good" The AQI is between 0 and 50. Air quality is considered satisfactory; "Moderate" The AQI is between 51 and 100. Air quality is acceptable; "Unhealthy for Sensitive Groups" When AQI values are between 101 and 150, members of sensitive groups may experience health effects; "Unhealthy" When AQI values are between 151 and 200 everyone may begin to experience health effects; "Very Unhealthy" AQI values between 201 and 300 trigger a health alert; "Hazardous" AQI values over 300 trigger health warnings of emergency conditions; (1) Metropolitan Statistical Area - see Appendix A for areas included; (2) Based on 365 days with AQI data in 2007.
Source: U.S. Environmental Protection Agency, Air Quality Index Report, 2007

Air Quality Index Pollutants

Area	Percent of Days when AQI Pollutant was...[2]					
	Carbon Monoxide	Nitrogen Dioxide	Ozone	Sulfur Dioxide	Particulate Matter 2.5	Particulate Matter 10
MSA[1]	21.9	0.0	51.5	4.7	21.9	0.0

Note: The Air Quality Index (AQI) is an index for reporting daily air quality. EPA calculates the AQI for five major air pollutants regulated by the Clean Air Act: ground-level ozone, particle pollution (also known as particulate matter), carbon monoxide, sulfur dioxide, and nitrogen dioxide. The AQI runs from 0 to 500. The higher the AQI value, the greater the level of air pollution and the greater the health concern; (1) Metropolitan Statistical Area - see Appendix A for areas included; (2) Based on 365 days with AQI data in 2007.
Source: U.S. Environmental Protection Agency, Air Quality Index Report, 2007

Air Quality Index Trends

Area	Trend Sites (8)								All Sites (22)
	1999	2000	2001	2002	2003	2004	2005	2006	2006
MSA[1]	17	9	10	25	7	2	9	1	2

Note: An AQI value greater than 100 indicates that air quality would have been in the unhealthful range on that day. Data from exceptional events are not included. These counts are presented in two ways. First, the counts are based on sites having an adequate record of monitoring data during the trend period (trend sites). These counts represent the relative change in the number of days with AQI values greater than 100. In the last column, the counts are based on all sites with data in the most recent year (because it is possible for a site to have data in the most recent year but not enough data to be a trend site); (1) Metropolitan Statistical Area - see Appendix A for areas included.
Source: U.S. Environmental Protection Agency, Office of Air and Radiation, Air Trends, Factbook and Related Information, Air Pollution Trends in Selected Metropolitan Areas 2006

Maximum Air Pollutant Concentrations

	Particulate Matter 10 (ug/m^3)	Particulate Matter 2.5 (ug/m^3)	Ozone (ppm)	Carbon Monoxide (ppm)	Sulfur Dioxide (ppm)	Nitrogen Dioxide (ppm)	Lead (ug/m^3)
MSA[1] Level	45	31	0.097	2	0.013	n/a	n/a
NAAQS[2]	150	35	0.125	9	0.140	0.053	1.50
Met NAAQS[2]	Yes	Yes	Yes	Yes	Yes	n/a	n/a

Note: Data from exceptional events are not included; (1) Metropolitan Statistical Area - see Appendix A for areas included; (2) National Ambient Air Quality Standards; n/a not available
Concentrations: Particulate Matter 10 (coarse particulate) - highest second maximum 24-hour concentration; Particulate Matter 2.5 (fine particulate) - highest 98th percentile 24-hour concentration; Ozone - highest second daily maximum 1-hour concentration; Carbon Monoxide - highest second maximum non-overlapping 8-hour concentration; Sulfur Dioxide - highest second maximum 24-hour concentration; Nitrogen Dioxide - highest arithmetic mean concentration; Lead - highest quarterly maximum concentration
Units: ppm = parts per million; ug/m^3 = micrograms per cubic meter
Source: U.S. Environmental Protection Agency, MSA Factbook 2006, Air Quality Statistics by City

Drinking Water

Water System Name	Pop. Served	Primary Water Source Type	Violations[1]	
			Health Based	Monitoring/ Reporting
Green Co. NW Regional Water	35,450	Ground	0	0

Note: (1) Based on violation data from January 1, 2007 to December 31, 2007 (includes unresolved violations from earlier years)
Source: U.S. Environmental Protection Agency, Office of Ground Water and Drinking Water, Safe Drinking Water Information System (based on data extracted April 15, 2008)

Dublin, Ohio

Background

Dublin, located in the central part of the state, lies on the banks of the Scioto River in Franklin County. The city is a 20-minute drive from Ohio's capital of Columbus. Dublin's phenomenal growth can be attributed to a number of factors, not the least being its energetic corporate climate, attracting family-owned businesses as well as several major corporations.

In short, Dublin has it all. Its stable and diverse economic base, direct regional highway access, top-rated school system, and high-quality city services make it a refreshingly pleasant place to live. In 2001, Dublin City Schools became the country's first school district to reach the highest possible level of accreditation given by the North Central Association, the nation's premier accrediting institution. In addition, Dublin offers indoor and outdoor recreation facilities, entertaining events, and eclectic shopping and dining, as well as varied residential property surrounded by open spaces, parks, bike paths, and a protected natural environment.

The settlement of Franklin County began in 1802 when Peter and Benjamin Sells of Huntington, Pennsylvania, purchased 400 acres of land in the area for their brother, John, who came with his family in 1808 to claim the land. When John Sells and John Shields began surveying lots for the town in 1810, Shields decided to name the new town after his birthplace of Dublin, Ireland. In 1881, Dublin was incorporated as a village. Nearly 90 years later, growth began and continued enough to warrant incorporation as a city in 1987.

More than 90% of Dublin students continue their education after graduating from high school and over 19% of the student population is culturally diverse, representing 65 countries. In 2003, 14 students were named as National Merit semifinalists. The student/teacher ratio is 19:1 district-wide, with more than 65% of teachers holding a master's degree or Ph.D.

Eleven colleges or universities, including Ohio State University, are within a 35-minute commuting distance from Dublin. Columbus State Community College-Dublin Center is the Dublin branch campus of Columbus State Community College. Franklin University offers both MBA and undergraduate courses at its Northwest Campus in Dublin.

The original village of Dublin was located in what is now called Historic Dublin, a lovely district where the streets and sidewalks are brick, the teahouses are Irish, and the shops sell unique Irish imported goods. Brazenhead, a genuine Irish pub named for the oldest watering hole in Dublin, Ireland, offers Guinness, Irish whiskey, and authentic fish and chips. The Annual Dublin Art and Music Festival, showcasing all aspects of Irish culture, draws tens of thousands of people each year. It is sponsored by the Dublin Arts Council, which offers many other events and programs throughout the year.

Other attractions include the Columbus Zoo & Aquarium, featuring 700 species of wildlife and over 400 acres of habitats and recreation areas, including Manatee Coast — one of only three facilities outside Florida to exhibit these endangered animals. Along those lines, the first gorilla born in captivity was born at the Columbus Zoo in 1956.

Listed on the national Register of Historic Places, the Fletcher-Coffman Homestead was built in the early 1860s. The Dublin Historical Society has restored the house to its original period and renovated the barn, which houses the early farm machinery used in the area.

Dublin has the usual four seasons associated with a continental climate. Extremes of high and low temperatures are possible. Summers are pleasant and mild. Though variable from year to year, rainfall is slightly in excess of the national average.

Rankings

General Rankings

- Columbus* was ranked #36 out of 375 metro areas in *Cities Ranked & Rated*. Criteria: cost of living; climate; crime; transportation; economy and jobs; education; arts and culture; health and healthcare; leisure; quality of life. *Cities Ranked & Rated, 2nd Edition, 2007*
- Columbus* was ranked #46 out of 379 metro areas in *Places Rated Almanac*. Criteria: health care; education; recreation; transportation; ambience; climate; crime; housing costs; jobs. *Places Rated Almanac, 7th Edition, 2007*

Business/Finance Rankings

- The nation's 100 largest metro areas were analysed in terms of the percentage of households entering some stage of foreclosure in 2007. The Columbus* metro area ranked #25 out of 100 (#1 = highest foreclosure rate). *RealtyTrac, "Year-End 2007 Metropolitan Foreclosure Report"*
- The Columbus* metro area was selected one of America's "Top 50 Business Opportunity Metros" by *Expansion Management* in their 5th annual Mayor's Challenge ranking of metro areas that have achieved solid ratings across the board in numerous *EM* studies during the past 12 months. The area ranked #44. Criteria: public schools; quality of life; college educated workers; logistics infrastructure; healthcare costs; taxes and government spending; reputation among site consultants. *Expansion Management, August 2007*
- The Columbus* metro area was selected as one of "America's Most Wired Cities" by *Forbes*. The metro area was ranked #21 out of 30. Criteria: percentage of Internet users with high-speed access; the range of service providers within a city; availability of public wireless hot spots. *Forbes, "America's Most Wired Cities," January 10, 2008*
- The Columbus* metro area was identified as one of 10 "Top Up-and-Coming Tech Cities" by *Forbes*. The metro area ranked #1. Criteria: regional innovation trends; important patents. *Forbes.com, "Top Up-and-Coming Tech Cities," March 11, 2008*
- Columbus* was selected as one of the best places to start and grow a company by *Entrepreneur* and the National Policy Research Council. The Columbus* metro area ranked #13 out of 50 large metro areas. Criteria: business formation and growth (firms started four to 14 years ago that still employ at least 5 people and experienced rapid growth over the last four years). *Entrepreneur/National Policy Research Council, "Hot Cities for Entrepreneurs," September 2006*
- The Columbus* metro area was selected as one of "America's 50 Hottest Cities" for business relocations and expansions. Criteria: industry's most prominent site selection consultants were asked to list their top city choices for relocating and expanding manufacturing companies, taking into consideration such factors as the business climate, work force quality, operating costs, incentive programs, and the ease of working with local political and economic development officials. *Expansion Management, January-February 2007*
- The Columbus* metro area was selected as one of the "Top 20 Real Estate Markets" for expanding or relocating companies. The area ranked #10. Criteria: low rental costs; low purchase prices; high vacancy rates of office and warehouse space. *Expansion Management, October 2007*
- Intel, in partnership with Sperling's BestPlaces, ranked the 80 "Best Cities for Teleworking" in America. The Columbus* metro area ranked #7 among large metro areas. The study identifies cities that hold the greatest potential for teleworking based on a host of factors including typical commuting times, fuel prices, availability of broadband Internet access and percentage of the population in telework friendly jobs. The study also factored in extreme climate and natural hazards. *Intel, "Best Cities for Teleworking," March 30, 2006*
- The Columbus* metro area appeared on the Milken Institute "2007 Best Performing Cities" index. Rank: #154 out of 200 large metro areas. Criteria: job growth; wage and salary growth; high-tech output growth. *Milken Institute, "2007 Best Performing Cities"*

- Columbus* was identified as one of the 100 "Most Unwired Cities" in the U.S. The area ranked #16 out of the 100 largest metro areas in the U.S. Criteria: number of public and commercial wireless access points (hotspots); airports with wireless Internet access; broadband availability; local wireless networks; and wireless email devices. *Intel, "Most Unwired Cities Survey," June 7, 2005*

- Columbus* was ranked #30 out of 125 regions worldwide in terms of its "Knowledge Competitiveness Index." The index attempts to measure the knowledge-based development taking place throughout the world and is based on 19 measures of economic performance that indicate a region's ability to translate its knowledge capacity into economic value. *Robert Huggins Associates, World Knowledge Competitiveness Index 2005*

- *Forbes* ranked the 200 most populous metro areas in the U.S. in terms of the "Best Places for Business and Careers." The Columbus* metro area was ranked #80. Criteria: business costs (labor, energy, tax and office space expenses); living costs (housing, transportation, food and other household expenditures); education levels of the work force; job growth; income growth; migration trends; crime rates; and culture/leisure. *Forbes, "Best Places for Business and Careers," March 19, 2008*

- *Fortune* ranked the 100 largest metro areas in the U.S. in terms of projected median home price change in 2007. The Columbus* metro area ranked #34. *Fortune.com, "Hot Spots, Cold Spots"*

Health/Environment Rankings

- 100 of the largest metro areas in the U.S. were analyzed in terms of their current drought severity. The Columbus* metro area ranked #56 (#1 = driest). The rankings were based on statistics such as long-term precipitation trends and patterns and the Palmer drought indices. *Sperling's BestPlaces, www.BestPlaces.net, "America's Drought-Riskiest Cities," November 2007*

- Doctors at the Harvard School of Public Health ranked 40 metropolitan areas based on data from the government-sponsored Hospital Quality Alliance program. The program tracks the performance of individual hospitals in treating patients for three common health problems: heart attacks, congestive heart failure, and pneumonia. The Columbus* metro area ranked #9 in quality of care for heart attacks, #6 for congestive heart failure, and #9 for pneumonia. *New England Journal of Medicine, July 21, 2005*

- Scarborough Research, a leading market research firm, identified the top local markets for diabetes medication purchasers. The Columbus* DMA (Designated Market Area) ranked in the top 13 with 11% of consumers reporting that they purchased medication for diabetes within the past 12 months. *Scarborough Research, March 19, 2007*

- *Reader's Digest* ranked the 50 largest metro areas in the U.S. in terms of how "clean" they are. The Columbus* metro area ranked #4. Criteria: air quality; water quality; toxic industrial pollution; Superfund sites; and sanitation. *Reader's Digest, "The 50 Cleanest (and Dirtiest) Cities in America," July 2005*

- The Columbus* metro area appeared in *Country Home's* "2008 Best Green Places" report. The area ranked #158 out of 379. Criteria: official energy policies; green power; green buildings; availability of fresh, locally grown food. *Country Home, "2008 Best Green Places"*

- Wyeth Consumer Healthcare, in partnership with Sperling's BestPlaces, ranked the nation's 50 most populous metro areas in terms of five key health factors. The Columbus* metro area ranked #45. Criteria: physical activity; health status; nutrition; lifestyle pursuits; and mental wellness. *Wyeth Consumer Healthcare, "Centrum Healthiest Cities Study," April 19, 2005*

- Columbus* was identified as a "2008 Asthma Capital." The area ranked #34 out of the nation's 100 largest metropolitan areas. Twelve factors were used to identify the most challenging places to live for people with asthma: estimated prevalence; self-reported prevalence; crude death rate for asthma; annual pollen score; annual air quality; public smoking laws; number of board-certified asthma specialists; school inhaler access laws; rescue medication use; controller medication use; uninsured rate; poverty rate. *Asthma and Allergy Foundation of America, "2008 Asthma Capitals"*

- Columbus* was identified as a "Spring Allergy Capital." The area ranked #68 out of 100. Three groups of factors were used to identify the most severe cities for people with allergies during the spring season: annual pollen levels; medicine utilization; access to board-certified allergists. *Asthma and Allergy Foundation of America, "2007 Spring Allergy Capital Rankings"*

- Columbus* was identified as a "Fall Allergy Capital." The area ranked #80 out of 100. Three groups of factors were used to identify the most severe cities for people with allergies during the fall season: annual pollen levels; medicine utilization; access to board-certified allergists. *Asthma and Allergy Foundation of America, "2007 Fall Allergy Capital Rankings"*

- Ortho-McNeil Neurologics, in partnership with Sperling's BestPlaces, analyzed 110 metro areas and identified those U.S. cities with the highest prevalence of factors that are most commonly associated with migraine headaches. The Columbus* metro area ranked #13. Criteria: number of migraine-related drug prescriptions per capita; lifestyle factors that can contribute to migraines; environmental factors that can trigger migraines; and consumption of migraine-triggering foods. *Ortho-McNeil Neurologics, "America's Migraine Hot Spots," March 14, 2006*

- Sperling's BestPlaces ranked 331 metro areas and identified the most and least stressful U.S. cities. The Columbus* metro area ranked #82 out of the 100 largest metro areas (#1 = most stressful). Criteria: divorce rate; unemployment rate; violent and property crime; suicide rate; commute time; mental health; alcohol consumption; cloudy days. *Sperling's BestPlaces, www.BestPlaces.net, "America's Most (and Least) Stressful Cities," January 9, 2004*

- An analysis of the "Best & Worst Cities for Sleep" was conducted by Sperling's BestPlaces. The study ranked America's 50 most populated metro areas. The Columbus* metro area ranked #43 (#1 = best city for sleep). Criteria: number of days residents didn't get enough rest or sleep during the past month; average length of daily commute; divorce rate; unemployment rate. *Sperling's BestPlaces, www.BestPlaces.net, "Best & Worst Cities for Sleep," 2006*

- Columbus* was selected as one of "America's Pet Healthiest Cities" by Purina. The city ranked #8 out of 50. Criteria: veterinary services; environment; legislation; preventative care; obesity/body condition. *Purina Pet Institute, "America's Pet Healthiest Cities," May 20, 2003*

Women/Minorities Rankings

- Columbus* was ranked #96 out of 100 metro areas in *SELF Magazine's* ranking of "America's Best Places for Women." A panel of experts came up with more than 50 criteria including death and disease rates, environmental indicators, community resources, and lifestyle habits. *SELF Magazine, "America's Best Places for Women 2007," December 2007*

- Columbus* appeared on *Black Enterprise's* list of the "Ten Best Cities for African Americans." The top picks were culled from more than 2,000 interactive surveys completed on www.blackenterprise.com and by editorial staff evaluation. The editors weighed the following criteria as it pertained to African Americans in each city: median household income; percentage of households earning more than $100,000; percentage of businesses owned; percentage of college graduates; unemployment rates; home loan rejections; and homeownership rates. *Black Enterprise, May 2007*

Seniors/Retirement Rankings

- Sperling's BestPlaces in partnership with Bankers Life & Casualty Company designed a survey to identify the top 50 metro areas in the U.S. that offer the best overall qualities for senior living. The Columbus* metro area ranked #28. The following criteria were statistically weighted to reflect the needs of the senior population: health; disease; economics; social; environment; spiritual; transportation; housing; and crime. *Bankers Life & Casualty Company, "Best Cities for Seniors 2005"*

- A.G. Edwards ranked America's 500 top-performing communities based on their residents' personal savings and investing behavior. The Columbus* metro area ranked #269 with an index score of 100.80 (national average = 100.00). A dozen statistical factors were measured including: participation in retirement savings plans; personal debt levels; and home ownership. *A.G. Edwards, "2007 Nest Egg Index", September 12, 2007*

Children/Family Rankings

- The Columbus* metro area was selected as one of the "Best Cities for Relocating Families" by Worldwide ERC and Primacy Relocation. The 2007 study placed a special emphasis on the housing market, which has significantly impacted the relocation industry and an employer's ability to transfer employees. The variables which weigh heavily in this category include home price, home affordability index, appreciation rates, and property tax. Other criteria include cost of living, crime rates, education, climate, focus on diversity, physicians per capita, recreation and leisure, arts and culture, air quality, watershed quality, sales tax, unemployment rate, job growth, high school and higher education index, school expenditures per student, students in public school, SAT/ACT percentile, and population growth. *Worldwide ERC and Primacy Relocation, "2007 Best Cities for Relocating Families"*

Safety Rankings

- The National Insurance Crime Bureau ranked 361 metro areas in the U.S. in terms of per capita rates of vehicle theft. The Columbus* metro area ranked #87 (#1 = highest rate). Criteria: number of vehicle theft offenses per 100,000 inhabitants. *National Insurance Crime Bureau, "NICB Vehicle Theft Study," April 22, 2008*
- Columbus* appeared on Sperling's BestPlaces list of the "Riskiest Cities for Identity Theft." The area ranked #31 out of the nations 50 largest metro areas. Over 80 criteria were analyzed across four major categories: technology impact; crime; transactions; and risk profile. *Sperling's BestPlaces, www.BestPlaces.net, "Riskiest Cities for Identity Theft," July 2006*
- Farmers Insurance Group of Companies, in partnership with Sperling's BestPlaces, ranked 379 metro areas and identified the "Most Secure U.S. Place to Live." The Columbus* metro area ranked #74 out of 114 in the large metro area category (500,000 or more residents). Criteria: crime rates; extreme weather; risk of natural disasters; environmental hazards; terrorism threats; air quality; life expectancy; job loss numbers. *Farmers Insurance Group, "Most Secure U.S. Places to Live 2007"*
- Columbus* was identified as one of the most dangerous large metro areas for pedestrians in the U.S. The area ranked #41 out of the nations 50 largest metro areas. Criteria: average yearly pedestrian fatalities per capita (for the years 2002 and 2003) adjusted for the number of walkers. *Surface Transportation Policy Project, "Mean Streets 2004"*

Sports/Recreation Rankings

- The Columbus* metro area appeared on the *Sporting News* list of the "Best Sports Cities 2007". The area ranked #39 out of 150 cities in the U.S. *Sporting News* takes a 12-month snapshot, roughly July to July, of each city's sports, putting a heavy premium on regular-season won-lost records (from the most recently completed season). Other criteria include: playoff berths, bowl appearances and tournament bids; championships; applicable power ratings; quality of competition; overall fan fervor as measured in part by attendance as percentage of venue capacity; abundance of teams (rewarding quality over quantity); stadium and arena quality; ticket availability and prices; franchise ownership; and marquee appeal of athletes. *SportingNews.com, "Best Sports Cities 2007," August 1, 2007*
- The Columbus* metro area was selected by *Cranium* as one of the "Top 50 Fun Cities" in America. The area ranked #21. Criteria includes: number of sports teams, restaurants, and dance performances; number of toy stores; city budget spent on recreation. *Cranium, November 4, 2003*
- *Golf Digest* ranked 330 metro areas in the U.S. in terms of golf. The Columbus* metro area was ranked #120. Criteria: access to golf; weather; value of golf; and quality of golf. *Golf Digest, "Metro Golf Rankings," August 2005*

Dating/Romance Rankings

- Eli Lily and Company, in partnership with Sperling's BestPlaces, ranked the nation's 50 largest metro areas in terms of the "Most Romantic Cities for Baby Boomers." The Columbus* metro area ranked #39. Criteria: marriage and divorce rates among "baby boomers" age 45 to 60; great restaurants; dance studios; chocolate, jewelry and flower sales. *Eli Lily and Company, "Most Romantic Cities for Baby Boomers," April 20, 2007*
- The Columbus* metro area was selected as one of the "Best Cities for Relocating Singles" by Worldwide ERC and Primacy Relocation. The area ranked #33 out of the 100 largest metro areas in the U.S. Areas were selected based on the following criteria: a robust cost-of-living index; adventure and outdoor recreation opportunities; violent crime and property crime rates; percentage of the population that is unmarried (ages 25-34); ratio of single men and single women; affordability of quality higher education, including in-state and out-of-state tuition requirements and rates; number of newcomers to the area; commute times; tax rates; fee and occupancy rates for temporary housing and mini-storage; quality and quantity of collegiate and professional sporting events and fun, fan-friendly venues. *Worldwide ERC and Primacy Relocation, "2007 Best Cities for Relocating Singles," October 25, 2007*
- *Forbes* ranked the 40 most populous urbanized areas in the U.S. in terms of the "Best Cities for Singles." The Columbus* metro area ranked #19. Criteria: number of singles; cost of living alone; nightlife; culture; job growth; coolness; and online dating. *Forbes.com, August 21, 2007*
- Sperling's BestPlaces in partnership with AXE Deodorant Bodyspray ranked 80 metro areas and identified "America's Best (and Worst) Cities for Dating." The Columbus* metro area ranked #12 (#1 = best). Criteria: percentage of singles ages 18-24; population density; dating venues per capita. *AXE Deodorant Bodyspray, "America's Best (and Worst) Cities for Dating," May 2004*

Culture/Performing Arts Rankings

- Scarborough Research, a leading market research firm, identified the top local markets for rock concert attendance. The Columbus* DMA (Designated Market Area) ranked in the top 25 with 14% of consumers, 18 years old and over, reporting that they have attended a rock concert during the past year. *Scarborough Research, June 14, 2004*

Miscellaneous Rankings

- Scarborough Research, a leading market research firm, identified the top local markets for bloggers. The Columbus* DMA (Designated Market Area) ranked in the top 13 with 11% of adults reporting that they had read or contributed to a blog within the past 30 days. *Scarborough Research, October 24, 2007*
- The Columbus* metro area appeared on *Forbes* list of "America's Drunkest Cities". The area ranked #3. Criteria: 35 of the largest continental U.S. metro areas were chosen based on availability of data and geographic diversity. Each metro was ranked in five areas: state laws; drinkers; heavy drinkers; binge drinkers; and alcoholism. *Forbes.com, "America's Drunkest Cities," August 22, 2006*
- Sperling's BestPlaces in partnership with Pep Boys ranked 77 metro areas and identified "America's Most Drivable Cities." The Columbus* metro area ranked #36. Criteria: climate; road roughness; urban mobility; gas prices. *Pep Boys, "America's Most Drivable Cities," April 9, 2003*
- State Farm Insurance, in partnership with Sperling's BestPlaces, analyzed several key factors that contribute to overall family preparedness. The Columbus* metro area ranked #21 out of the nation's 50 most populous metro areas. Criteria: quality of life; life insurance coverage; and investments. *State Farm Life Insurance, "Fiscally Fit Cities Report," July 20, 2004*
- Scarborough Research, a leading market research firm, identified the top local markets for reality television. The Columbus* DMA (Designated Market Area) ranked in the top 10 with 26% of consumers reporting that they "typically watch" reality-dating, reality-talent, or reality- adventure television shows. *Scarborough Research, January 11, 2005*

- Scarborough Research, a leading market research firm, identified the top local markets for grocery coupon use. The Columbus* DMA (Designated Market Area) ranked in the top 25 with 36% of consumers reporting that they use grocery coupons at least once per week. *Scarborough Research, December 8, 2004*
- Scarborough Research, a leading market research firm, identified the top local markets for gift card purchasers. The Columbus* DMA (Designated Market Area) ranked in the top 10 with 54% of consumers reporting that they purchased a gift card within the past 12 months. *Scarborough Research, November 15, 2006*
- A study by Sperling's BestPlaces examined which U.S. metro areas were most affected by high fuel prices in 2006. The Columbus* metro area was ranked #41 out of 80 (#1 = most expensive city for driving). Rankings are based on the average dollars spent on gas per year by two driver households. Criteria: cost of regular-grade gasoline; average miles driven per day; average number of gallons each driver uses and wastes in traffic congestion each day. *Sperling's BestPlaces, www.bestplaces.net, "Pain at the Pump," May 18, 2006*

Dublin is located within the Columbus, OH Metropolitan Statistical Area.

Business Environment

CITY FINANCES

City Government Finances

Component	2004-2005 ($000)	2004-2005 ($ per capita)
Total Revenues	84,259	2,410
Total Expenditures	89,286	2,554
Debt Outstanding	72,769	2,081
Cash and Securities	95,935	2,744

Source: U.S Census Bureau, Government Finances 2004-2005

City Government Revenue by Source

Source	2004-2005 ($000)	2004-2005 ($ per capita)
General Revenue		
From Federal Government	0	0
From State Government	3,865	111
From Local Governments	0	0
Taxes		
Property	7,018	201
Sales	1,468	42
Personal Income	53,107	1,519
License	2,953	84
Charges	7,877	225
Liquor Store	0	0
Utility	1,835	52
Employee Retirement	0	0
Other	6,136	175

Source: U.S Census Bureau, Government Finances 2004-2005

City Government Expenditures by Function

Function	2004-2005 ($000)	2004-2005 ($ per capita)	2004-2005 (%)
General Expenditures			
Airports	0	0	0.0
Corrections	0	0	0.0
Education	0	0	0.0
Fire Protection	0	0	0.0
Governmental Administration	13,717	392	15.4
Health	151	4	0.2
Highways	8,915	255	10.0
Hospitals	0	0	0.0
Housing and Community Development	0	0	0.0
Interest on General Debt	4,878	140	5.5
Libraries	0	0	0.0
Parking	23	1	0.0
Parks and Recreation	18,802	538	21.1
Police Protection	8,418	241	9.4
Public Welfare	0	0	0.0
Sewerage	2,288	65	2.6
Solid Waste Management	1,892	54	2.1
Liquor Store	0	0	0.0
Utility	860	25	1.0
Employee Retirement	0	0	0.0
Other	29,342	839	32.9

Source: U.S Census Bureau, Government Finances 2004-2005

Municipal Bond Ratings

Area	Moody's
City	Aaa

Source: Mergent Bond Record, January 2008 (unless noted otherwise)

DEMOGRAPHICS

Population Growth

Area	1990 Census	2000 Census	2007 Estimate	2012 Projection	Population Growth (%) 1990-2000	Population Growth (%) 2000-2012
City	17,231	31,392	35,862	38,751	82.2	23.4
MSA[1]	1,405,176	1,612,694	1,733,942	1,811,223	14.8	12.3
U.S.	248,709,873	281,421,906	301,045,522	314,920,978	13.2	11.9

Note: (1) Metropolitan Statistical Area - see Appendix B for areas included
Source: Claritas, Inc.

Number of Households and Average Household Size

Area	2007 Estimate	2007 Average Household Size
City	13,027	2.75
MSA[1]	691,073	2.51
U.S.	113,668,003	2.65

Note: (1) Metropolitan Statistical Area - see Appendix B for areas included
Source: Claritas, Inc.

Race and Ethnicity

Area	White Alone[2]	Black Alone[2]	Asian Alone[2]	Other Race Alone[2]	Hispanic[3]
City	86.3	2.5	9.4	1.7	1.6
MSA[1]	79.4	14.0	2.8	3.7	2.6
U.S.	73.1	12.4	4.3	10.3	14.9

Note: Figures are 2007 estimates; (1) Metropolitan Statistical Area - see Appendix B for areas included (2) Alone is defined as not being in combination with one or more other races; (3) May be of any race.
Source: Claritas, Inc.

Ancestry

Area	German	Irish[2]	English	American	Italian	Polish	French[3]	Scottish
City	31.3	17.0	12.3	5.5	9.4	3.9	2.7	3.1
MSA[1]	23.4	13.1	10.0	9.3	5.0	2.2	2.2	2.0
U.S.	15.2	10.9	8.7	7.3	5.6	3.2	3.0	1.7

Note: Figures include multiple ancestry (e.g. if a person reported being Irish and Italian, they were included in both columns); (1) Metropolitan Statistical Area - see Appendix A for areas included; (2) Includes Celtic; (3) Includes Alsatian but excludes Basque
Source: Census 2000, Summary File 3

Foreign-Born Population

Area	Percent of Population Born in							
	Any Foreign Country	Europe	Asia	Africa	Oceania[2]	Canada	Mexico	Latin America[3]
City	9.1	1.5	6.6	0.3	0.0	0.5	0.0	0.1
MSA[1]	4.6	0.9	2.1	0.7	0.0	0.2	0.4	0.3
U.S.	11.1	1.7	2.9	0.3	0.1	0.3	3.3	2.5

Note: (1) Metropolitan Statistical Area - see Appendix A for areas included; (2) Includes Australia, New Zealand subregion, Melanesia, Micronesia, Polynesia, and Oceania n.e.c; (3) Includes Central America (excluding Mexico), South America, and the Caribbean.
Source: Census 2000, Summary File 3

Marriage Status

Area	Never Married	Now Married (excluding Separated)	Separated	Widowed	Divorced
City	18.9	71.5	0.7	2.9	6.0
MSA[1]	29.6	52.1	1.7	5.5	11.1
U.S.	27.1	54.4	2.2	6.6	9.7

Note: Figures are percentages and cover the population 15 years of age and older; (1) Metropolitan Statistical Area - see Appendix A for areas included
Source: Census 2000, Summary File 3

Age Distribution

Area	Percent of Population: Under Age 5	Age 5 to 17	Age 18 to 34	Age 35 to 49	Age 50 to 64	Age 65 to 79	80 Years and Over
City	8.7	24.0	16.5	30.9	14.2	4.3	1.3
MSA[1]	7.1	18.3	26.7	23.9	14.0	7.7	2.4
U.S.	6.8	18.9	23.7	23.5	14.8	9.2	3.2

Note: (1) Metropolitan Statistical Area - see Appendix A for areas included
Source: Census 2000, Summary File 3

Male/Female Ratio

Area	Males	Females	Males per 100 Females
City	17,806	18,056	98.6
MSA[1]	854,714	879,228	97.2
U.S.	148,320,305	152,725,217	97.1

Note: Figures are 2007 estimates; (1) Metropolitan Statistical Area - see Appendix B for areas included
Source: Claritas, Inc.

Religion

Area	Catholic	Southern Baptist	United Meth-odist	ELCA[1]	LDS[2]	Presby-terian Church USA	Jewish Est.	Muslim Est.
County	13.7	2.1	4.1	2.8	0.4	1.5	1.5	0.6
U.S.	22.0	7.1	3.7	1.8	1.5	1.1	2.2	0.6

Note: Figures are the number of adherents as a percentage of the total population; Adherents are defined as all members, including full members, their children and the estimated number of other participants who are not considered members (e.g. the baptized, those not confirmed, those regularly attending services, etc.); (1) Evangelical Lutheran Church in America; (2) The Church of Jesus Christ of Latter Day Saints
Source: Reprinted with permission from Religious Congregations and Membership in the United States 2000 (Nashville, Glenmary Research Center, 2002) Copyright Association of Statisticians of American Religious Bodies. All rights reserved.

ECONOMY

Gross Metropolitan Product

Area	2002	2003	2004	2005	2005 Rank[2]
MSA[1]	63.8	66.5	70.2	73.1	34

Note: Figures are in billions of dollars; (1) Columbus, OH Metropolitan Statistical Area - see Appendix A for areas included; (2) Rank ranges from 1 to 361
Source: The U.S. Conference of Mayors, "U.S. Metro Economies: GMP - The Engines of America's Growth," January 2007

Economic Growth

Area	1995 GMP	2005 GMP	Average Annual Growth Rate	Growth Rate Rank[2]
MSA[1]	44.9	73.1	5.0	219

Note: Figures are in billions of dollars; GMP = Gross Metropolitan Product; (1) Columbus, OH Metropolitan Statistical Area - see Appendix A for areas included; (2) Rank ranges from 1 to 361
Source: The U.S. Conference of Mayors, "U.S. Metro Economies: GMP - The Engines of America's Growth," January 2007

INCOME

Per Capita/Median/Average Income

Area	Per Capita ($)	Median Household ($)	Average Household ($)
City	47,352	102,571	130,187
MSA[1]	27,475	52,886	68,386
U.S.	25,495	49,280	66,670

Note: Figures are 2007 estimates; (1) Metropolitan Statistical Area - see Appendix B for areas included
Source: Claritas, Inc.

Household Income Distribution

Area	Percent of Households Earning							
	Under $15,000	$15,000 -24,999	$25,000 -34,999	$35,000 -49,999	$50,000 -74,999	$75,000 -99,000	$100,000 -149,999	$150,000 and up
City	3.5	3.7	4.0	8.3	14.0	15.1	25.0	26.3
MSA[1]	11.0	9.6	10.9	16.0	20.7	13.2	12.4	6.3
U.S.	13.1	10.9	11.2	15.6	19.5	11.9	11.3	6.6

Note: Figures are 2007 estimates; (1) Metropolitan Statistical Area - see Appendix B for areas included
Source: Claritas, Inc.

Poverty Rates by Age

Area	All Ages	Under 5 Years Old	5 to 17 Years Old	18 to 64 Years Old	65 Years and Over
City	2.7	0.3	0.6	1.6	0.2
MSA[1]	10.1	1.1	2.2	6.0	0.8
U.S.	12.4	1.2	3.0	6.9	1.2

Note: Figures are percent of population with income in 1999 below poverty level and only include population for whom poverty status is determined; (1) Metropolitan Statistical Area - see Appendix A for areas included
Source: Census 2000, Summary File 3

Personal Bankruptcy Filing Rate

Area	2004	2005	2006
Franklin County	9.53	13.80	3.56
U.S.	5.31	6.82	2.00

Note: Numbers are per 1,000 population and include Chapter 7 and Chapter 13 filings
Source: Federal Deposit Insurance Corporation (FDIC), Regional Economic Conditions (RECON), 8/23/2007

EMPLOYMENT

Labor Force and Employment

Area	Civilian Labor Force			Workers Employed		
	Dec. 2006	Dec. 2007	% Chg.	Dec. 2006	Dec. 2007	% Chg.
City	19,619	19,829	1.1	18,994	19,136	0.7
MSA[1]	955,896	967,649	1.2	914,318	921,121	0.7
U.S.	152,571,000	153,705,000	0.7	146,081,000	146,334,000	0.2

Note: Data is not seasonally adjusted and covers workers 16 years of age and older;
(1) Metropolitan Statistical Area - see Appendix B for areas included
Source: Bureau of Labor Statistics, http://stats.bls.gov

Unemployment Rate

Area	2007											
	Jan.	Feb.	Mar.	Apr.	May	Jun.	Jul.	Aug.	Sep.	Oct.	Nov.	Dec.
City	3.2	3.2	3.1	3.3	3.3	3.9	3.6	3.8	3.9	3.7	3.6	3.5
MSA[1]	4.9	4.8	4.6	4.7	4.5	5.1	4.8	4.8	4.8	4.6	4.5	4.8
U.S.	5.0	4.9	4.5	4.3	4.3	4.7	4.9	4.6	4.5	4.4	4.5	4.8

Note: Data is not seasonally adjusted and covers workers 16 years of age and older; All figures are percentages; (1) Metropolitan Statistical Area - see Appendix B for areas included
Source: Bureau of Labor Statistics, http://stats.bls.gov

Employment by Occupation

Occupation Classification	City (%)	MSA[1] (%)	U.S. (%)
Sales and Office	28.3	29.2	26.7
Professional and Related	29.9	21.1	20.2
Service	6.5	13.7	14.9
Production, Transportation, and Material Moving	3.3	13.0	14.6
Management, Business, and Financial	29.9	15.3	13.5
Construction, Extraction, and Maintenance	2.0	7.4	9.4
Farming, Forestry, and Fishing	0.1	0.2	0.7

Note: Figures cover employed civilians 16 years of age and older;
(1) Metropolitan Statistical Area - see Appendix A for areas included
Source: Census 2000, Summary File 3

Employment by Industry

Sector	MSA[1] Number of Employees	MSA[1] Percent of Total	U.S. Percent of Total
Government	159,400	16.6	16.3
Education and Health Services	113,000	11.8	13.4
Professional and Business Services	153,800	16.0	13.1
Retail Trade	109,900	11.4	11.6
Manufacturing	76,600	8.0	9.9
Leisure and Hospitality	88,300	9.2	9.6
Financial Activities	74,100	7.7	5.9
Construction	n/a	n/a	5.3
Wholesale Trade	39,500	4.1	4.4
Other Services	37,000	3.9	3.9
Transportation and Utilities	52,700	5.5	3.7
Information	18,600	1.9	2.2
Natural Resources and Mining	n/a	n/a	0.5

Note: Figures cover non-farm employment as of December 2007 and are not seasonally adjusted; (1) Metropolitan Statistical Area - see Appendix B for areas included; n/a not available
Source: Bureau of Labor Statistics, http://stats.bls.gov

Average Wages

Occupation	$/Hr.	Occupation	$/Hr.
Accountants and Auditors	27.73	Maids and Housekeeping Cleaners	9.14
Automotive Mechanics	17.84	Maintenance and Repair Workers	16.76
Bookkeepers	16.13	Marketing Managers	49.33
Carpenters	18.66	Nuclear Medicine Technologists	30.45
Cashiers	8.81	Nurses, Licensed Practical	19.54
Clerks, General Office	12.69	Nurses, Registered	27.23
Clerks, Receptionists/Information	11.56	Nursing Aides/Orderlies/Attendants	11.69
Clerks, Shipping/Receiving	14.07	Packers and Packagers, Hand	10.57
Computer Programmers	32.85	Physical Therapists	33.59
Computer Support Specialists	18.75	Postal Service Mail Carriers	21.25
Computer Systems Analysts	35.78	Real Estate Brokers	38.54
Cooks, Restaurant	10.26	Retail Salespersons	11.54
Dentists	n/a	Sales Reps., Exc. Tech./Scientific	30.67
Electrical Engineers	33.98	Sales Reps., Tech./Scientific	35.02
Electricians	21.76	Secretaries, Exc. Legal/Med./Exec.	15.56
Financial Managers	51.84	Security Guards	12.21
First-Line Supervisors/Mgrs., Sales	19.12	Surgeons	n/a
Food Preparation Workers	9.38	Teacher Assistants	13.30
General and Operations Managers	50.09	Teachers, Elementary School	27.20
Hairdressers/Cosmetologists	12.04	Teachers, Secondary School	26.20
Internists	83.78	Telemarketers	10.27
Janitors and Cleaners	11.24	Truck Drivers, Heavy/Tractor-Trailer	18.23
Landscaping/Groundskeeping Workers	11.53	Truck Drivers, Light/Delivery Svcs.	14.86
Lawyers	43.34	Waiters and Waitresses	8.21

Note: Wage data covers the Columbus, OH Metropolitan Statistical Area - see Appendix B for areas included. Hourly wages for elementary/secondary school teachers and teacher assistants were calculated by the editors from annual wage data assuming a 40 hour work week; n/a not available.
Source: Bureau of Labor Statistics, May 2007 Metro Area Occupational Employment and Wage Estimates

RESIDENTIAL REAL ESTATE

Building Permits

Area	Single-Family			Multi-Family			Total		
	2006	2007p	Pct. Chg.	2006	2007p	Pct. Chg.	2006	2007p	Pct. Chg.
City	253	131	-48.2	153	54	-64.7	406	185	-54.4
U.S.	1,378,200	973,300	-29.4	460,700	407,200	-11.6	1,838,900	1,380,500	-24.9

Note: (p) preliminary; figures cover and represent new, privately-owned housing units authorized (unadjusted data); All permit data are based on estimates with imputation; U.S. figures are based on the new 20,000-place series.
Source: U.S. Census Bureau, Manufacturing, Mining, and Construction Statistics

Homeownership and Housing Vacancies

Area	Homeownership Rate[2] (%)			Rental Vacancy Rate[3] (%)			Homeowner Vacancy Rate[4] (%)		
	2005	2006	2007	2005	2006	2007	2005	2006	2007
MSA[1]	68.9	65.8	66.1	13.8	13.1	13.3	3.0	3.4	2.8
U.S.	68.9	68.8	68.1	9.8	9.8	9.7	1.9	2.4	2.7

Note: (1) Metropolitan Statistical Area - see Appendix B for areas included; (2) The proportion of households that are owners; (3) The proportion of the rental inventory that is vacant for rent; (4) The proportion of the homeowner inventory that is vacant for sale; n/a not available
Source: U.S. Census Bureau, Housing Vacancies and Homeownership Annual Statistics: 2007

TAXES

State Corporate Income Tax Rates

State	Rates and Tax Brackets
Ohio	5.1% > $0; 8.5% > 50K

Note: Tax rates as of January 1, 2008; A value added-style tax, the Corporate Activities Tax (CAT) was instituted in 2005. It will be phased in through 2010 while the Corporate Franchise Tax (Ohio's income tax) is phased out. Beginning April 1, 2008 the CAT rate is.208% (80% of.26%). For tax year 2008 companies owe 40% of Corporate Franchise Tax liability.
Source: Tax Foundation, www.taxfoundation.org

State Individual Income Tax Rates

State	Federal Deductibility	Marginal Rates (%)	Standard Deduction ($)		Personal Exemptions ($)[1]	
			Single	Joint	Single	Dependents
Ohio	No	0.649 - 6.555 (y)	n/a	n/a	1,450 (g)(r)	1,450 (g)(r)

Note: Tax rates as of January 1, 2008; Local- and county-level taxes are not included; n/a not applicable; (1) Married joint filers generally receive double the single exemption; (g) Taxpayers receive a $20 tax credit per exemption in addition to the normal exemption amount; (r) State adjusts its bracket levels for inflation at the end of each year before printing tax forms; (y) Brackets are not double for married taxpayers.
Source: Tax Foundation, www.taxfoundation.org

Various State and Local Tax Rates

State and Local Sales and Use (%)	State Sales and Use (%)	Gasoline[1,2] ($/gal.)	Cigarette ($/pack)	Spirits ($/gal.)	Table Wine ($/gal.)	Beer ($/gal.)
6.75	5.5 (h)	0.28	1.25	8.46 (n)	0.32	0.18

Note: Tax rates as of January 1, 2008; (1) In addition to the 18.4 cpg Federal gasoline tax; (2) Rates may include additional state sales taxes, environmental protection and storage fees/taxes, and local taxes. When necessary, the volume-weighted average of all local taxes is used to approximate the typical statewide rate including local tax; (h) Ohio has a GRT that is levied in addition to its 5.5% sales tax. It is called the commercial activity tax (CAT). Firms with receipts over $1 million pay the CAT; firms with receipts between $150K and $1 million pay a minimum tax of $150. The rate i

2008 is 0.156%, and increases are scheduled in law to 0.208% on 4/1/2008 and 0.26% on 4/1/2009. The CAT is being phased in to replace Ohio's Corporate Franchise Tax, which is simultaneously being phased out; (n) The state government controls all sales. The implied excise tax rate is calculated using methodology designed by the Distilled Spirits Council of the United States (DISCUS).
Source: Tax Foundation, www.taxfoundation.org; Original research

State Tax Burdens

Area	Combined State and Local Tax Burden		Combined Federal, State and Local Tax Burden	
	Percent	Rank	Percent	Rank
Ohio	12.4	5	32.4	18
U.S. Average	11.0	-	32.7	-

Note: Figures cover 2007 and measure taxes as a percentage of income
Source: Tax Foundation, www.taxfoundation.org

State Business Tax Climate Index Rankings

State	Overall Rank	Corporate Tax Index Rank	Individual Income Tax Index Rank	Sales Tax Index Rank	Unemployment Insurance Tax Index Rank	Property Tax Index Rank
Ohio	46	37	48	36	11	44

Note: Rankings range from 1 to 50 where 1 is best. Rankings do not average across to Overall Rank. States without a given tax are given a ranking of 1.
Source: Tax Foundation, State Business Tax Climate Index 2008

TRANSPORTATION

Means of Transportation to Work

Area	Car/Truck/Van		Public Transportation			Bicycle	Walked	Other Means	Worked at Home
	Drove Alone	Car-pooled	Bus	Subway	Railroad				
City	89.4	4.0	0.4	0.0	0.0	0.0	0.5	0.4	5.4
MSA[1]	82.0	9.6	2.2	0.0	0.0	0.2	2.4	0.6	3.0
U.S.	75.7	12.2	2.5	1.5	0.5	0.4	2.9	1.0	3.3

Note: Figures are percentages and cover workers 16 years of age and older;
(1) Metropolitan Statistical Area - see Appendix A for areas included
Source: Census 2000, Summary File 3

Travel Time to Work

Area	Less Than 15 Minutes	15 to 29 Minutes	30 to 44 Minutes	45 to 59 Minutes	60 Minutes or More
City	28.2	37.4	26.3	4.4	3.7
MSA[1]	26.6	44.1	19.6	5.5	4.2
U.S.	29.4	36.1	19.1	7.4	8.0

Note: Figures are percentages and include workers 16 years old and over; (1) Metropolitan Statistical Area - see Appendix A for areas included
Source: Census 2000, Summary File 3

Travel Time Index

Area	1982	1995	2004	2005
Urban Area[1]	1.03	1.15	1.20	1.19
Average[2]	1.11	1.22	1.29	1.30

Note: Travel Time Index - The ratio of travel time in the peak period to the travel time at free-flow conditions. A value of 1.35 indicates a 20-minute free-flow trip takes 27 minutes in the peak. Free-flow speeds (60 mph on freeways and 35 mph on principal arterials) are used as the comparison threshold; (1) Covers the Columbus, OH urban area; (2) average of 85 urban areas
Source: Texas Transportation Institute, The 2007 Urban Mobility Report, September 2007

Living Environment

COST OF LIVING

Cost of Living Index

Composite Index	Groceries	Housing	Utilities	Trans-portation	Health Care	Misc. Goods/ Services
97.7	96.3	97.0	102.7	103.6	104.1	95.0

Note: U.S. = 100; Figures cover the Columbus OH urban area.
Source: The Council for Community and Economic Research (formerly ACCRA), Cost of Living Index, 2007

Grocery Prices

Area[1]	T-Bone Steak ($/pound)	Frying Chicken ($/pound)	Whole Milk ($/half gal.)	Eggs ($/dozen)	Orange Juice ($/64 oz.)	Coffee ($/11.5 oz.)
City[2]	10.75	1.29	1.79	1.27	3.13	3.26
Avg.	8.93	1.12	2.13	1.52	3.26	3.31
Min.	5.88	0.71	1.33	0.83	2.30	2.20
Max.	12.80	2.07	3.43	3.54	5.79	6.20

Note: (1) Values for the local area are compared with the average, minimum and maximum values for all 331 areas in the Cost of Living Index report; (2) Figures cover the Columbus OH urban area; **T-Bone Steak** *(price per pound);* **Frying Chicken** *(price per pound, whole fryer);* **Whole Milk** *(half gallon carton);* **Eggs** *(price per dozen, Grade A, large);* **Orange Juice** *(64 oz. Tropicana or Florida Natural);* **Coffee** *(11.5 oz. can, vacuum-packed, Maxwell House, Hills Bros, or Folgers).*
Source: The Council for Community and Economic Research (formerly ACCRA), Cost of Living Index, 2007

Housing and Utility Costs

Area[1]	New Home Price ($)	Apartment Rent ($/month)	All Electric ($/month)	Part Electric ($/month)	Other Energy ($/month)	Telephone ($/month)
City[2]	303,182	778	-	68.02	97.08	27.36
Avg.	309,605	782	146.13	78.67	90.16	26.14
Min.	189,877	n/a	82.03	37.41	33.15	17.08
Max.	1,202,800	3,481	271.14	150.60	257.67	37.45

Note: (1) Values for the local area are compared with the average, minimum and maximum values for all 331 areas in the Cost of Living Index report; (2) Figures cover the Columbus OH urban area; **New Home Price** *(2,400 sf living area, 8,000 sf lot, in urban area with full utilities);* **Apartment Rent** *(950 sf 2 bedroom/1.5 or 2 bath, unfurnished, excluding all utilities except water);* **All Electric** *(average monthly cost for an all-electric home);* **Part Electric** *(average monthly cost for a part-electric home);* **Other Energy** *(average monthly cost for natural gas, fuel oil, coal, wood, and any other forms of energy except electricity);* **Telephone** *(price includes basic monthly rate for a private residential line plus additional local usage charges incurred by a family of four).*
Source: The Council for Community and Economic Research (formerly ACCRA), Cost of Living Index, 2007

Health Care, Transportation, and Other Costs

Area[1]	Doctor ($/visit)	Dentist ($/visit)	Optometrist ($/visit)	Gasoline ($/gallon)	Beauty Salon ($/visit)	Men's Shirt ($)
City[2]	70.09	85.33	88.04	2.79	33.60	26.22
Avg.	79.48	71.93	79.55	2.64	29.52	25.77
Min.	52.08	44.80	43.95	2.19	15.58	16.19
Max.	148.44	126.27	158.83	3.48	60.62	48.53

Note: (1) Values for the local area are compared with the average, minimum and maximum values for all 331 areas in the Cost of Living Index report; (2) Figures cover the Columbus OH urban area; **Doctor** *(general practitioners routine exam of an established patient);* **Dentist** *(adult teeth cleaning and periodic oral examination);* **Optometrist** *(full vision eye exam for established adult patient);* **Gasoline** *(one gallon regular unleaded, national brand, including all taxes, cash price at self-service pump if available);* **Beauty Salon** *(woman's shampoo, trim, and blow-dry);* **Men's Shirt** *(cotton/polyester dress shirt, pinpoint weave, long sleeves).*
Source: The Council for Community and Economic Research (formerly ACCRA), Cost of Living Index, 2007

HOUSING

House Price Index (HPI)

Area	National Ranking[2]	Quarterly Change (%)	One-Year Change (%)	Five-Year Change (%)
MSA[1]	190	0.33	0.10	13.49
U.S.[3]	-	0.10	0.84	41.37

Note: The HPI is a weighted repeat sales index. It measures average price changes in repeat sales or refinancings on the same properties. This information is obtained by reviewing repeat mortgage transactions on single-family properties whose mortgages have been purchased or securitized by Fannie Mae or Freddie Mac in January 1975; (1) Metropolitan Statistical Area - see Appendix B for areas included; (2) Rankings are based on annual percentage change for all metro areas containing at least 15,000 transactions over the last 10 years and ranges from 1 to 291; (3) figures based on a weighted average of Census Division estimates; all figures are for the period ending December 31, 2007
Source: Office of Federal Housing Enterprise Oversight, House Price Index, February 26, 2008

House Price Valuations

Area	Q1 2000	Q1 2001	Q1 2002	Q1 2003	Q1 2004	Q1 2005	Q1 2006	Q1 2007	Q1 2008
MSA[1]	-5.7	-6.5	-6.4	-6.4	-2.8	-4.1	-3.6	-9.0	-14.6

Note: Figures show the percentage of over- or under-valuation of single family homes relative to statistically normal house values (e.g. a value of 23.6 indicates that house values are 23.6% overvalued). Statistically normal house values are based on house prices, interest rates, household incomes, population densities, and any historical premiums or discounts metropolitan areas have exhibited over time; (1) Figures cover the Metropolitan Statistical Area - see Appendix B for areas included
Source: Global Insight/National City Corporation, House Prices in America, May 2008

Median Home Prices

Area	2005	2006	2007[r]	Percent Change 2006 to 2007
MSA[1]	152.0	148.1	147.4	-0.5
U.S. Average	219.0	221.9	217.9	-1.8

Note: Figures are median sales prices of existing single-family homes in thousands of dollars; (r) revised; n/a not available; (1) Metropolitan Statistical Area - see Appendix B for areas included
Source: National Association of Realtors, Metropolitan Area Prices, 1st Quarter 2008

Housing: Year Structure Built

Area	1990 -2000	1980 -1989	1970 -1979	1960 -1969	1950 -1959	1940 -1949	Before 1940	Median Year
City	54.1	32.6	7.6	2.2	2.1	0.3	1.2	1991
MSA[1]	20.7	13.5	17.5	15.0	12.8	6.3	14.2	1971
U.S.	17.0	15.8	18.5	13.7	12.7	7.3	15.0	1971

Note: Figures are percentages; (1) Metropolitan Statistical Area - see Appendix A for areas included
Source: Census 2000, Summary File 3

HEALTH

Health Risk Data

Category	Area[1] (%)	U.S. (%)
Adults who have been told they have high blood pressure[3]	26.7	25.5
Adults who have been told they have high blood cholesterol[3]	38.2	35.6
Adults who have been told they have diabetes[2]	n/a	7.5
Adults who have been told they have arthritis[3]	27.8	27.0
Adults who have been told they currently have asthma	n/a	8.5
Adults who are current smokers	n/a	20.1
Adults who are heavy drinkers[4]	n/a	4.9
Adults who are overweight (BMI 25.0 - 29.9)	n/a	36.5
Adults who are obese (BMI 30.0 - 99.8)	n/a	25.1

Note: Data as of 2006 unless otherwise noted; n/a not available; (1) Figures cover the Metropolitan Statistical Area - see Appendix B for areas included; (2) Figures do not include pregnancy-related diabetes, pre-diabetes or borderline diabetes; (3) 2005 data; (4) Heavy drinkers are classified as adult men having more than two drinks per day or adult women having more than one drink per day
Source: Centers for Disease Control and Prevention, Behaviorial Risk Factor Surveillance System, SMART: Selected Metropolitan/Micropolitan Area Risk Trends, 2005, 2006

Mortality Rates for the Top 10 Causes of Death in the U.S.

ICD-10[a] Sub-Chapter	ICD-10[a] Code	Age-Adjusted Mortality Rate[1] per 100,000 population	
		County[2]	U.S.
Malignant neoplasms	C00-C97	212.5	186.5
Ischaemic heart diseases	I20-I25	143.4	152.3
Other forms of heart disease	I30-I51	61.9	51.5
Cerebrovascular diseases	I60-I69	57.7	50.0
Chronic lower respiratory diseases	J40-J47	52.6	42.6
Diabetes mellitus	E10-E14	30.5	24.8
Other degenerative diseases of the nervous system	G30-G31	28.5	22.6
Other external causes of accidental injury	W00-X59	23.5	21.4
Influenza and pneumonia	J10-J18	22.1	20.7
Hypertensive diseases	I10-I13	21.4	18.2

Note: (a) ICD-10 = International Classification of Diseases 10th Revision; (1) Mortality rates are a three year average covering 2003-2005; (2) Figures cover Franklin County
Source: Centers for Disease Control and Prevention, National Center for Health Statistics. Compressed Mortality File 1999-2004. CDC WONDER On-line Database, compiled from Compressed Mortality File 1999-2005 Series 20 No. 2K, 2008.

Mortality Rates for Selected Causes of Death

ICD-10[a] Sub-Chapter	ICD-10[a] Code	Age-Adjusted Mortality Rate[1] per 100,000 population	
		County[2]	U.S.
Assault	X85-Y09	9.2	5.9
Human immunodeficiency virus (HIV) disease	B20-B24	3.7	4.5
Intentional self-harm	X60-X84	9.7	10.8
Malnutrition	E40-E46	2.4	1.0
Obesity and other hyperalimentation	E65-E68	1.8	1.4
Organic, including symptomatic, mental disorders	F01-F09	32.1	16.8
Transport accidents	V01-V99	9.4	16.1
Viral hepatitis	B15-B19	0.8	1.8

Note: (a) ICD-10 = International Classification of Diseases 10th Revision; (1) Mortality rates are a three year average covering 2003-2005; (2) Figures cover Franklin County
Source: Centers for Disease Control and Prevention, National Center for Health Statistics. Compressed Mortality File 1999-2004. CDC WONDER On-line Database, compiled from Compressed Mortality File 1999-2005 Series 20 No. 2K, 2008.

Distribution of Physicians[1]

Area	Total	Family/ General Practice	Specialties	
			Medical	Surgical
Franklin County (number)	2,473	657	868	585
Franklin County (rate per 10,000 pop.)	22.7	6.0	8.0	5.4
U.S. (rate per 10,000 pop.)	17.7	4.6	6.9	4.3

Note: Data as of 2005; (1) Includes all non-federal, patient-care, office-based MDs
Source: Area Resource File (ARF). June 2007. U.S. Department of Health and Human Services, Health Resources and Services Administration, Bureau of Health Professions, Rockville, MD.

Hospitals

There were no hospitals listed within the city limits.
AHA Guide to the Healthcare Field 2008

According to *U.S. News,* the Columbus, OH metro area is home to four of the best hospitals in the U.S.: **Columbus Children's Hospital**; **Grant Medical Center-OhioHealth**; **Ohio State University Hospital**; **Riverside Methodist Hospital-Ohio Health**. *U.S. News Online, "America's Best Hospitals 2007"*

EDUCATION

Public School District Statistics

District Name	Schls	Pupils	Pupil/ Teacher Ratio	Minority Pupils[1] (%)	Free Lunch Eligible[2] (%)	IEP[3] (%)
Columbus City	147	58,961	17.3	70.3	50.5	15.3
Dublin City	19	12,939	15.6	22.1	5.0	10.0

Note: Table includes regular local school districts with 2,000 or more students; (1) Percentage of students that are not white, non-Hispanic; (2) Percentage of students that are eligible for the free lunch program; (3) Percentage of students that have an Individualized Education Program.
Source: U.S. Department of Education, National Center for Education Statistics, Common Core of Data, Local Education Agency (School District) Universe Survey: School Year 2005-2006; U.S. Department of Education, National Center for Education Statistics, Common Core of Data, Public Elementary/Secondary School Universe Survey: School Year 2005-2006

Top Public High Schools

High School Name	Index[1]	Rank[1]	Subsidized Lunch (%)[2]	E&E (%)[3]
Dublin Coffman	1.709	712	6.0	30.4
Dublin Jerome	2.485	292	1.0	45.9
Dublin Scioto	1.478	910	16.0	27.2

Note: (1) Public schools are ranked according to a ratio that is the number of Advanced Placement, International Baccalaureate, and/or Cambridge tests taken by all students at a school in 2007 divided by the number of graduating seniors. All of the schools on the list have an index of at least 1.000; they are in the top five percent of public schools measured this way. The rankings range from 1 to 1,422; (2) Percentage of students receiving federally subsidized meals; (3) E & E stands for equity and excellence percentage: the portion of all graduating seniors at a school that had at least one passing grade on one AP or IB test; (**) Gave both IB and AP tests. AP and IB participation are indicators of a school's efforts to get students to excel and prepare for college.
Source: Newsweek Online, "Top High Schools 2008"

Highest Level of Education

Area	Less than H.S.	H.S. Diploma	Some College, No Deg.	Associate Degree	Bachelors Degree	Masters Degree	Profess. School Degree	Doctorate Degree
City	2.8	11.6	16.8	5.3	41.4	15.4	4.9	2.0
MSA[1]	13.7	30.6	21.0	5.8	19.6	6.2	2.1	1.1
U.S.	19.4	28.4	21.2	6.4	15.7	5.9	2.0	1.0

Note: Figures are 2007 estimated percentages and cover persons age 25 and over; (1) Metropolitan Statistical Area - see Appendix B for areas included
Source: Claritas, Inc.

Educational Attainment by Race

Area	High School Graduate (%)					Bachelor's Degree (%)				
	Total	White	Black	Asian	Hisp.[2]	Total	White	Black	Asian	Hisp.[2]
City	97.3	97.6	98.6	94.7	100.0	64.7	64.8	61.0	66.4	70.6
MSA[1]	85.8	87.2	78.1	86.1	67.9	29.1	30.4	15.4	59.7	21.6
U.S.	80.4	83.6	72.3	80.4	52.4	24.4	26.1	14.3	44.1	10.4

Note: Figures shown cover persons 25 years old and over; (1) Metropolitan Statistical Area - see Appendix A for areas included; (2) people of Hispanic origin can be of any race
Source: Census 2000, Summary File 3

School Enrollment by Type

Area	Grades KG to 8				Grades 9 to 12			
	Public		Private		Public		Private	
	Enrollment	%	Enrollment	%	Enrollment	%	Enrollment	%
City	4,591	86.7	707	13.3	1,859	90.4	197	9.6
MSA[1]	178,054	88.0	24,285	12.0	73,403	89.9	8,275	10.1
U.S.	33,526,011	88.7	4,285,121	11.3	14,848,628	90.6	1,532,323	9.4

Note: Figures shown cover persons 3 years old and over; (1) Metropolitan Statistical Area - see Appendix A for areas included
Source: Census 2000, Summary File 3

School Enrollment by Race

Area	Grades KG to 8 (%)				Grades 9 to 12 (%)			
	White	Black	Asian	Hisp.[1]	White	Black	Asian	Hisp.[1]
City	86.7	2.1	8.2	1.1	91.6	0.5	5.1	0.4
MSA[2]	76.5	17.1	2.0	2.1	77.3	16.8	1.9	2.0
U.S.	68.5	15.5	3.3	16.8	68.8	15.5	3.8	15.7

Note: Figures shown cover persons 3 years old and over; (1) people of Hispanic origin can be of any race; (2) Metropolitan Statistical Area - see Appendix A for areas included
Source: Census 2000, Summary File 3

Average Salaries of Public School Classroom Teachers

District	2005-06		2006-07		Percent Change 2005-06 to 2006-07
	Dollars	Rank[1]	Dollars	Rank[1]	
Ohio	50,314	14	51,937	14	3.23
U.S. Average	49,026	-	50,816	-	3.65

Note: (1) State rank ranges from 1 to 51.
Source: National Education Association, Rankings & Estimates: Rankings of the States 2006 and Estimates of School Statistics 2007, December 2007

Higher Education

Four-Year Colleges			Two-Year Colleges			Medical Schools[1]	Law Schools[2]	Voc/ Tech[3]
Public	Private Non-profit	Private For-profit	Public	Private Non-profit	Private For-profit			
0	0	0	0	0	0	0	0	0

Note: Figures cover institutions located within the city limits; (1) includes schools accredited by the Liaison Committee on Medical Education and the American Osteopathic Association; (2) includes American Bar Association-accredited law schools; (3) includes all schools with programs that are less than 2 years.
Source: National Center for Education Statistics, The Integrated Postsecondary Education System (IPEDS) Peer Analysis System, 2007; www.usnews.com, Law and Medical School Directories, 2009

PRESIDENTIAL ELECTION

2004 Presidential Election Results

Area	Bush	Kerry	Nader	Other
Franklin County	45.1	54.4	0.0	0.5
U.S.	50.7	48.3	0.4	0.6

Note: Results are percentages and may not add to 100% due to rounding
Source: Dave Leip's Atlas of U.S. Presidential Elections, www.uselectionatlas.org

EMPLOYERS

Major Employers

Company Name	Industry	Type of Site
Abbott Laboratories	Dry, condensed, evaporated products	Branch
Abbott Laboratories	Pharmaceutical preparations	Branch
America Electric Power Texas	Electric services	Headquarters
Bank One	Business services, nec	Headquarters
Battelle Memorial Institute	Commercial physical research	Headquarters
Chase Manhattan	Mortgage bankers and correspondents	Branch
Columbia Energy	Natural gas transmission	Single
Columbus Childrens Hospital	Specialty hospitals, except psychiatric	Headquarters
DFAS-Columbus Center	Finance, taxation, and monetary policy	Branch
Express Inc	Women's clothing stores	Single
Facilities Operation and Dev	Electric and other services combined	Branch
Fairfield Medical Center	General medical and surgical hospitals	Headquarters
Indiana Michigan Power Company	Electric services	Headquarters
Limited Brands Inc	Women's accessory and specialty stores	Headquarters
Medical Center	Offices and clinics of medical doctors	Branch
Mount Crmel Hlth Sys Fundation	General medical and surgical hospitals	Headquarters
Nationwide	Fire, marine, and casualty insurance	Headquarters
Ohio Department Public Safety	Public order and safety, nec	Branch
Ohio Dept Administrative Svcs	General government, nec	Branch
Safelite Solutions LLC	Management consulting services	Single
State Automobile Mutl Insur Co	Fire, marine, and casualty insurance	Single
State Farm Insurance	Insurance agents, brokers, and service	Branch
The Ohio State University	Colleges and universities	Branch
US Bank	National commercial banks	Branch

Note: Companies shown are located within the Columbus metropolitan area; nec = not elsewhere classified.
Source: www.zapdata.com, May 2008

PUBLIC SAFETY

Crime Rate

Area	All Crimes	Violent Crimes				Property Crimes		
		Murder	Forcible Rape	Robbery	Aggrav. Assault	Burglary	Larceny -Theft	Motor Vehicle Theft
City	2,051.0	0.0	17.1	31.4	2.9	402.8	1,539.7	57.1
Metro[1]	5,125.8	6.6	51.1	246.4	122.2	1,252.1	2,989.9	457.5
U.S.	3,808.1	5.7	30.9	149.4	287.5	729.4	2,206.8	398.4

Note: Figures are crimes per 100,000 population; (1) Metropolitan Statistical Area - see Appendix B for areas included
Source: FBI Uniform Crime Reports, 2006

Hate Crimes

Area	Number of Quarters Reported	Bias Motivation				
		Race	Religion	Sexual Orientation	Ethnicity	Disability
City	n/a	n/a	n/a	n/a	n/a	n/a

Note: n/a not available.
Source: Federal Bureau of Investigation, Hate Crime Statistics 2006

RECREATION

Culture

Dance[1]	Theatre[1]	Instrumental Music[1]	Vocal Music[1]	Series/ Festivals	Museums	Zoos and Aquariums[2]
0	0	0	0	0	0	0

Note: (1) Number of professional perfoming groups; (2) AZA-accredited
Source: The Grey House Performing Arts Directory, 2007; Official Museum Directory, 2008; Association of Zoos & Aquariums, AZA Member Zoos & Aquariums, June 2008

Professional Sports Teams

Team Name	League
Columbus Crew	Major League Soccer (MLS)
Columbus Blue Jackets	National Hockey League (NHL)

Note: Includes teams located in the Columbus metro area.
Source: Original research

MEDIA

Newspapers

Name	News Focus	Frequency	Circulation
No newspapers have an office in the city			

Note: Includes newspapers with offices located in the city
Source: MediaContactsPro, March 2008

Television Stations

Name	Ch.	Network(s)	Type	Ownership
WCMH	4	NBC	Commercial	General Electric Corporation
WSYX	6	Fox/ABC	Commercial	Sinclair Broadcast Group
WBNS	10	CBS	Commercial	Dispatch Broadcast Group
WTTE	28	ABC	Commercial	Sinclair Broadcast Group
WOSU	34	PBS	Public	Ohio State University
WPBO	42	PBS	Public	Ohio State University
WSFJ	51	Pax/NBC	Commercial	Christian Television Network
WWHO	53	WBN/UPN	Commercial	Paramount Stations Group

Note: Stations included cover the Columbus DMA (Designated Market Area)
BurrellesLuce, MediaContacts Online, January 2007

Major AM Radio Stations

Call Letters	Freq. (kHz)	Station Type	Target Audience	Station Format	Music Format
WTVN	610	Commercial	General	Talk	n/a
WXIC	660	Commercial	General/Rel/Senior	Educational/Music/Talk	Gospel
WHTH	790	Commercial	General	Talk	n/a
WOSU	820	College	General	Talk	n/a
WRFD	880	Commercial	General/Men	News/Talk	n/a
WMNI	920	Commercial	General	Music	Adult Standards
WCHO	1250	Commercial	General	Music/News/Sports/Talk	Adult Standards
WILE	1270	n/a	General	News/Talk	n/a
WUCO	1270	Commercial	General	Music	Country
WMVO	1300	Commercial	General	News/Talk	n/a
WLOH	1320	n/a	General	Music/News/Sports	n/a
WCHI	1350	Commercial	General	Music	Adult Standards
WCLT	1430	Commercial	General	News/Sports/Talk	n/a
WBNS	1460	Commercial	General/Men	News/Sports	n/a
WMRN	1490	Commercial	General	Music/News/Sports/Talk	Oldies
WBEX	1490	Commercial	General	News/Sports	n/a
WLGN	1510	Commercial	General	Music/News/Sports	Country
WBCO	1540	Commercial	General	Educational/Music/Talk	Oldies
WTNS	1560	Commercial	General	Music/News	Country
WVKO	1580	Commercial	Black/General/Rel	Music	Rhythm & Blues

Note: Stations included cover the Columbus DMA (Designated Market Area); n/a not available
Source: BurrellesLuce, MediaContacts Online, January 2007

Major FM Radio Stations

Call Letters	Freq. (mHz)	Station Type	Target Audience	Station Format	Music Format
WOSU	89.7	College	General	Music	Classical
WCBE	90.5	Public	General	Educational/Music	Jazz
WOSB	91.1	College	General	Music/News/Talk	Classical
WOSP	91.5	College	General	Music/News/Talk	Classical
WKCO	91.9	College	General	Music/News/Sports	Rhythm & Blues
WCOL	92.3	Commercial	General	Music/News/Talk	Country
WKKJ	93.3	Commercial	General	Music/Sports	Country
WQIO	93.7	Commercial	General	Music/News/Sports	Adult Contemp.
WSNY	94.7	Commercial	General	Music/News	Adult Contemp.
WHOK	95.5	Commercial	General	Music/News	Country
WLVQ	96.3	Commercial	General	Music	Classic Rock
WBNS	97.1	Commercial	General	Music/Sports	Adult Contemp.
WNCI	97.9	Commercial	General	Music/News/Talk	Top 40
WTNS	99.3	Commercial	General	Music/Sports/Talk	Top 40
WBZX	99.7	Commercial	General	Music/News	Modern Rock
WXZQ	100.1	n/a	General	Music	n/a
WCLT	100.3	Commercial	General	Music/News	Country
WWCD	101.1	Commercial	General	Music/Sports	Alternative
WEGE	103.9	Commercial	General	Music	Classic Rock
WJZK	104.3	Commercial	General	Music	Jazz
WCVO	104.9	Non-Comm	General/Religious	Music/Talk	Christian
WWJM	105.9	Commercial	General	Music	Adult Contemp.
WJYD	106.3	Commercial	General/Religious	Music/News	Gospel
WMRN	106.9	Commercial	General	Music/News	Country
WCKX	107.5	Commercial	General	Music/News	Urban Contemp.
WBZW	107.7	Commercial	General	Music	Top 40
WODB	107.9	Commercial	General	Music/News/Talk	Oldies

Note: Stations included cover the Columbus DMA (Designated Market Area); n/a not available
BurrellesLuce, MediaContacts Online, January 2007

CLIMATE

Average and Extreme Temperatures

Temperature	Jan	Feb	Mar	Apr	May	Jun	Jul	Aug	Sep	Oct	Nov	Dec	Yr.
Extreme High (°F)	74	73	82	89	93	101	104	101	100	90	80	76	104
Average High (°F)	36	39	50	62	73	82	85	83	77	65	51	40	62
Average Temp. (°F)	28	31	41	52	62	70	74	73	66	54	43	32	52
Average Low (°F)	20	22	31	40	50	59	63	62	55	43	34	24	42
Extreme Low (°F)	-19	-13	-6	14	25	35	43	39	31	17	-4	-17	-19

Note: Figures cover the years 1948-1990
Source: National Climatic Data Center, International Station Meteorological Climate Summary, 9/96

Average Precipitation/Snowfall/Humidity

Precip./Humidity	Jan	Feb	Mar	Apr	May	Jun	Jul	Aug	Sep	Oct	Nov	Dec	Yr.
Avg. Precip. (in.)	2.8	2.4	3.1	3.3	3.9	4.0	4.3	3.3	2.7	2.1	3.0	2.8	37.9
Avg. Snowfall (in.)	8	6	5	1	Tr	0	0	0	Tr	Tr	2	6	28
Avg. Rel. Hum. 7am (%)	78	78	76	76	79	81	84	87	87	83	80	79	81
Avg. Rel. Hum. 4pm (%)	66	62	55	51	52	53	53	54	53	53	61	68	57

Note: Figures cover the years 1948-1990; Tr = Trace amounts (<0.05 in. of rain; <0.5 in. of snow)
Source: National Climatic Data Center, International Station Meteorological Climate Summary, 9/96

Weather Conditions

Temperature			Daytime Sky			Precipitation		
5°F & below	32°F & below	90°F & above	Clear	Partly cloudy	Cloudy	0.01 inch or more precip.	0.1 inch or more snow/ice	Thunder-storms
10	118	19	72	137	156	136	29	40

Note: Figures are average number of days per year and cover the years 1948-1990
Source: National Climatic Data Center, International Station Meteorological Climate Summary, 9/96

HAZARDOUS WASTE

Superfund Sites

Dublin has no sites on the EPA's Superfund Final National Priorities List.
U.S. Environmental Protection Agency, Final National Priorities List, June 23, 2008

AIR & WATER QUALITY

Air Quality Index

Area	Percent of Days when Air Quality was...[2]				AQI Statistics	
	Good	Moderate	Unhealthy for Sensitive Groups	Unhealthy	Maximum	Median
MSA[1]	64.9	26.8	8.2	0.0	147	42

Note: The Air Quality Index (AQI) is an index for reporting daily air quality. EPA calculates the AQI for five major air pollutants regulated by the Clean Air Act: ground-level ozone, particle pollution (also known as particulate matter), carbon monoxide, sulfur dioxide, and nitrogen dioxide. The AQI runs from 0 to 500. The higher the AQI value, the greater the level of air pollution and the greater the health concern. There are six AQI categories: "Good" The AQI is between 0 and 50. Air quality is considered satisfactory; "Moderate" The AQI is between 51 and 100. Air quality is acceptable; "Unhealthy for Sensitive Groups" When AQI values are between 101 and 150, members of sensitive groups may experience health effects; "Unhealthy" When AQI values are between 151 and 200 everyone may begin to experience health effects; "Very Unhealthy" AQI values between 201 and 300 trigger a health alert; "Hazardous" AQI values over 300 trigger health warnings of emergency conditions; (1) Metropolitan Statistical Area - see Appendix A for areas included; (2) Based on 365 days with AQI data in 2007.
Source: U.S. Environmental Protection Agency, Air Quality Index Report, 2007

Air Quality Index Pollutants

Area	Percent of Days when AQI Pollutant was...[2]					
	Carbon Monoxide	Nitrogen Dioxide	Ozone	Sulfur Dioxide	Particulate Matter 2.5	Particulate Matter 10
MSA[1]	10.7	0.0	52.1	2.7	18.9	15.6

Note: The Air Quality Index (AQI) is an index for reporting daily air quality. EPA calculates the AQI for five major air pollutants regulated by the Clean Air Act: ground-level ozone, particle pollution (also known as particulate matter), carbon monoxide, sulfur dioxide, and nitrogen dioxide. The AQI runs from 0 to 500. The higher the AQI value, the greater the level of air pollution and the greater the health concern; (1) Metropolitan Statistical Area - see Appendix A for areas included; (2) Based on 365 days with AQI data in 2007.
Source: U.S. Environmental Protection Agency, Air Quality Index Report, 2007

Air Quality Index Trends

Area	Trend Sites (7)								All Sites (30)
	1999	2000	2001	2002	2003	2004	2005	2006	2006
MSA[1]	24	12	14	21	9	1	8	1	3

Note: An AQI value greater than 100 indicates that air quality would have been in the unhealthful range on that day. Data from exceptional events are not included. These counts are presented in two ways. First, the counts are based on sites having an adequate record of monitoring data during the trend period (trend sites). These counts represent the relative change in the number of days with AQI values greater than 100. In the last column, the counts are based on all sites with data in the most recent year (because it is possible for a site to have data in the most recent year but not enough data to be a trend site); (1) Metropolitan Statistical Area - see Appendix A for areas included.
Source: U.S. Environmental Protection Agency, Office of Air and Radiation, Air Trends, Factbook and Related Information, Air Pollution Trends in Selected Metropolitan Areas 2006

Maximum Air Pollutant Concentrations

	Particulate Matter 10 (ug/m³)	Particulate Matter 2.5 (ug/m³)	Ozone (ppm)	Carbon Monoxide (ppm)	Sulfur Dioxide (ppm)	Nitrogen Dioxide (ppm)	Lead (ug/m³)
MSA[1] Level	64	34	0.094	2	0.011	n/a	0.01 (a)
NAAQS[2]	150	35	0.125	9	0.140	0.053	1.50
Met NAAQS[2]	Yes	Yes	Yes	Yes	Yes	n/a	Yes

Note: Data from exceptional events are not included; (1) Metropolitan Statistical Area - see Appendix A for areas included; (2) National Ambient Air Quality Standards; n/a not available; (a) Localized impact from an industrial source in Columbus

Concentrations: Particulate Matter 10 (coarse particulate) - highest second maximum 24-hour concentration; Particulate Matter 2.5 (fine particulate) - highest 98th percentile 24-hour concentration; Ozone - highest second daily maximum 1-hour concentration; Carbon Monoxide - highest second maximum non-overlapping 8-hour concentration; Sulfur Dioxide - highest second maximum 24-hour concentration; Nitrogen Dioxide - highest arithmetic mean concentration; Lead - highest quarterly maximum concentration

Units: ppm = parts per million; ug/m³ = micrograms per cubic meter

Source: U.S. Environmental Protection Agency, MSA Factbook 2006, Air Quality Statistics by City

Drinking Water

Water System Name	Pop. Served	Primary Water Source Type	Violations[1]	
			Health Based	Monitoring/ Reporting
Columbus Public Water System	983,264	Surface	1	0

Note: (1) Based on violation data from January 1, 2007 to December 31, 2007 (includes unresolved violations from earlier years)

Source: U.S. Environmental Protection Agency, Office of Ground Water and Drinking Water, Safe Drinking Water Information System (based on data extracted April 15, 2008)

Hilliard, Ohio

Background

Hilliard is located in Franklin County, 11 miles northwest of Columbus. The city borders Upper Arlington and Dublin. Interstate 270 runs through the eastern part of the city.

In 1852, John Reed Hilliard purchased ten acres of farmland that eventually became the city of Hilliard. Because of its proximity to the Indiana Railroad, it was an ideal shipping point for shipping out agricultural products and receiving farming supplies. The area was plated by John Hilliard in 1853 and originally called Hilliard Station until 1854, when a post office was established in the town and the word "station" was dropped. The village was incorporated in 1869 with a population of 280. The first railroad station was built in town in 1886, which stood until 1962 when rail service ceased.

The construction of three large residential subdivisions in the 1950s brought explosive growth to Hilliard and the connection to the Columbus regional sewer and water systems in the 1960s created even more development possibilities. The Village of Hilliard became a city in 1960, with a population of nearly 5,700. The completion of the Interstate 270 in the 1980s brought a second wave of rapid growth. Today, Hilliard looks towards the future by continuing it economic development efforts while striving to retain the charm of its historic roots.

Hilliard's largest employer is the Hilliard City School District. The city's largest private industries are manufacturing, retail, and wholesale trade.

Notable attractions in Hilliard include the Franklin County Fairgrounds, Hilliard Municipal Park, Hamilton Park, and Weaver Park. Additionally, the city hosts the Old Hilliard Street and Art Festival annually on the second Saturday of September.

Some of the city's recent projects to support its rapid growth are the Scioto and Darby Creek Road and the Alton and Darby Creek Road projects. Funded by the Ohio Public Works Commission, the projects widened and expanded three of the citiy's major roads to relieve congestion.

Hilliard has a seasonal climate with hot summers and cold winters. Median summer temperatures average 70 degrees, while winter averages can be as low as 25 degrees during December and January. The city averages 4 inches of rainfall per month from April to October and 7 inches of snowfall per month from December to March.

Rankings

General Rankings

- Columbus* was ranked #36 out of 375 metro areas in *Cities Ranked & Rated*. Criteria: cost of living; climate; crime; transportation; economy and jobs; education; arts and culture; health and healthcare; leisure; quality of life. *Cities Ranked & Rated, 2nd Edition, 2007*

- Columbus* was ranked #46 out of 379 metro areas in *Places Rated Almanac*. Criteria: health care; education; recreation; transportation; ambience; climate; crime; housing costs; jobs. *Places Rated Almanac, 7th Edition, 2007*

Business/Finance Rankings

- The nation's 100 largest metro areas were analysed in terms of the percentage of households entering some stage of foreclosure in 2007. The Columbus* metro area ranked #25 out of 100 (#1 = highest foreclosure rate). *RealtyTrac, "Year-End 2007 Metropolitan Foreclosure Report"*

- The Columbus* metro area was selected one of America's "Top 50 Business Opportunity Metros" by *Expansion Management* in their 5th annual Mayor's Challenge ranking of metro areas that have achieved solid ratings across the board in numerous *EM* studies during the past 12 months. The area ranked #44. Criteria: public schools; quality of life; college educated workers; logistics infrastructure; healthcare costs; taxes and government spending; reputation among site consultants. *Expansion Management, August 2007*

- The Columbus* metro area was selected as one of "America's Most Wired Cities" by *Forbes*. The metro area was ranked #21 out of 30. Criteria: percentage of Internet users with high-speed access; the range of service providers within a city; availability of public wireless hot spots. *Forbes, "America's Most Wired Cities," January 10, 2008*

- The Columbus* metro area was identified as one of 10 "Top Up-and-Coming Tech Cities" by *Forbes*. The metro area ranked #1. Criteria: regional innovation trends; important patents. *Forbes.com, "Top Up-and-Coming Tech Cities," March 11, 2008*

- Columbus* was selected as one of the best places to start and grow a company by *Entrepreneur* and the National Policy Research Council. The Columbus* metro area ranked #13 out of 50 large metro areas. Criteria: business formation and growth (firms started four to 14 years ago that still employ at least 5 people and experienced rapid growth over the last four years). *Entrepreneur/National Policy Research Council, "Hot Cities for Entrepreneurs," September 2006*

- The Columbus* metro area was selected as one of "America's 50 Hottest Cities" for business relocations and expansions. Criteria: industry's most prominent site selection consultants were asked to list their top city choices for relocating and expanding manufacturing companies, taking into consideration such factors as the business climate, work force quality, operating costs, incentive programs, and the ease of working with local political and economic development officials. *Expansion Management, January-February 2007*

- The Columbus* metro area was selected as one of the "Top 20 Real Estate Markets" for expanding or relocating companies. The area ranked #10. Criteria: low rental costs; low purchase prices; high vacancy rates of office and warehouse space. *Expansion Management, October 2007*

- Intel, in partnership with Sperling's BestPlaces, ranked the 80 "Best Cities for Teleworking" in America. The Columbus* metro area ranked #7 among large metro areas. The study identifies cities that hold the greatest potential for teleworking based on a host of factors including typical commuting times, fuel prices, availability of broadband Internet access and percentage of the population in telework friendly jobs. The study also factored in extreme climate and natural hazards. *Intel, "Best Cities for Teleworking," March 30, 2006*

- The Columbus* metro area appeared on the Milken Institute "2007 Best Performing Cities" index. Rank: #154 out of 200 large metro areas. Criteria: job growth; wage and salary growth; high-tech output growth. *Milken Institute, "2007 Best Performing Cities"*

- Columbus* was identified as one of the 100 "Most Unwired Cities" in the U.S. The area ranked #16 out of the 100 largest metro areas in the U.S. Criteria: number of public and commercial wireless access points (hotspots); airports with wireless Internet access; broadband availability; local wireless networks; and wireless email devices. *Intel, "Most Unwired Cities Survey," June 7, 2005*

- Columbus* was ranked #30 out of 125 regions worldwide in terms of its "Knowledge Competitiveness Index." The index attempts to measure the knowledge-based development taking place throughout the world and is based on 19 measures of economic performance that indicate a region's ability to translate its knowledge capacity into economic value. *Robert Huggins Associates, World Knowledge Competitiveness Index 2005*

- *Forbes* ranked the 200 most populous metro areas in the U.S. in terms of the "Best Places for Business and Careers." The Columbus* metro area was ranked #80. Criteria: business costs (labor, energy, tax and office space expenses); living costs (housing, transportation, food and other household expenditures); education levels of the work force; job growth; income growth; migration trends; crime rates; and culture/leisure. *Forbes, "Best Places for Business and Careers," March 19, 2008*

- *Fortune* ranked the 100 largest metro areas in the U.S. in terms of projected median home price change in 2007. The Columbus* metro area ranked #34. *Fortune.com, "Hot Spots, Cold Spots"*

Health/Environment Rankings

- 100 of the largest metro areas in the U.S. were analyzed in terms of their current drought severity. The Columbus* metro area ranked #56 (#1 = driest). The rankings were based on statistics such as long-term precipitation trends and patterns and the Palmer drought indices. *Sperling's BestPlaces, www.BestPlaces.net, "America's Drought-Riskiest Cities," November 2007*

- Doctors at the Harvard School of Public Health ranked 40 metropolitan areas based on data from the government-sponsored Hospital Quality Alliance program. The program tracks the performance of individual hospitals in treating patients for three common health problems: heart attacks, congestive heart failure, and pneumonia. The Columbus* metro area ranked #9 in quality of care for heart attacks, #6 for congestive heart failure, and #9 for pneumonia. *New England Journal of Medicine, July 21, 2005*

- Scarborough Research, a leading market research firm, identified the top local markets for diabetes medication purchasers. The Columbus* DMA (Designated Market Area) ranked in the top 13 with 11% of consumers reporting that they purchased medication for diabetes within the past 12 months. *Scarborough Research, March 19, 2007*

- *Reader's Digest* ranked the 50 largest metro areas in the U.S. in terms of how "clean" they are. The Columbus* metro area ranked #4. Criteria: air quality; water quality; toxic industrial pollution; Superfund sites; and sanitation. *Reader's Digest, "The 50 Cleanest (and Dirtiest) Cities in America," July 2005*

- The Columbus* metro area appeared in *Country Home's* "2008 Best Green Places" report. The area ranked #158 out of 379. Criteria: official energy policies; green power; green buildings; availability of fresh, locally grown food. *Country Home, "2008 Best Green Places"*

- Wyeth Consumer Healthcare, in partnership with Sperling's BestPlaces, ranked the nation's 50 most populous metro areas in terms of five key health factors. The Columbus* metro area ranked #45. Criteria: physical activity; health status; nutrition; lifestyle pursuits; and mental wellness. *Wyeth Consumer Healthcare, "Centrum Healthiest Cities Study," April 19, 2005*

- Columbus* was identified as a "2008 Asthma Capital." The area ranked #34 out of the nation's 100 largest metropolitan areas. Twelve factors were used to identify the most challenging places to live for people with asthma: estimated prevalence; self-reported prevalence; crude death rate for asthma; annual pollen score; annual air quality; public smoking laws; number of board-certified asthma specialists; school inhaler access laws; rescue medication use; controller medication use; uninsured rate; poverty rate. *Asthma and Allergy Foundation of America, "2008 Asthma Capitals"*

- Columbus* was identified as a "Spring Allergy Capital." The area ranked #68 out of 100. Three groups of factors were used to identify the most severe cities for people with allergies during the spring season: annual pollen levels; medicine utilization; access to board-certified allergists. *Asthma and Allergy Foundation of America, "2007 Spring Allergy Capital Rankings"*

- Columbus* was identified as a "Fall Allergy Capital." The area ranked #80 out of 100. Three groups of factors were used to identify the most severe cities for people with allergies during the fall season: annual pollen levels; medicine utilization; access to board-certified allergists. *Asthma and Allergy Foundation of America, "2007 Fall Allergy Capital Rankings"*

- Ortho-McNeil Neurologics, in partnership with Sperling's BestPlaces, analyzed 110 metro areas and identified those U.S. cities with the highest prevalence of factors that are most commonly associated with migraine headaches. The Columbus* metro area ranked #13. Criteria: number of migraine-related drug prescriptions per capita; lifestyle factors that can contribute to migraines; environmental factors that can trigger migraines; and consumption of migraine-triggering foods. *Ortho-McNeil Neurologics, "America's Migraine Hot Spots," March 14, 2006*

- Sperling's BestPlaces ranked 331 metro areas and identified the most and least stressful U.S. cities. The Columbus* metro area ranked #82 out of the 100 largest metro areas (#1 = most stressful). Criteria: divorce rate; unemployment rate; violent and property crime; suicide rate; commute time; mental health; alcohol consumption; cloudy days. *Sperling's BestPlaces, www.BestPlaces.net, "America's Most (and Least) Stressful Cities," January 9, 2004*

- An analysis of the "Best & Worst Cities for Sleep" was conducted by Sperling's BestPlaces. The study ranked America's 50 most populated metro areas. The Columbus* metro area ranked #43 (#1 = best city for sleep). Criteria: number of days residents didn't get enough rest or sleep during the past month; average length of daily commute; divorce rate; unemployment rate. *Sperling's BestPlaces, www.BestPlaces.net, "Best & Worst Cities for Sleep," 2006*

- Columbus* was selected as one of "America's Pet Healthiest Cities" by Purina. The city ranked #8 out of 50. Criteria: veterinary services; environment; legislation; preventative care; obesity/body condition. *Purina Pet Institute, "America's Pet Healthiest Cities," May 20, 2003*

Women/Minorities Rankings

- Columbus* was ranked #96 out of 100 metro areas in *SELF Magazine's* ranking of "America's Best Places for Women." A panel of experts came up with more than 50 criteria including death and disease rates, environmental indicators, community resources, and lifestyle habits. *SELF Magazine, "America's Best Places for Women 2007," December 2007*

- Columbus* appeared on *Black Enterprise's* list of the "Ten Best Cities for African Americans." The top picks were culled from more than 2,000 interactive surveys completed on www.blackenterprise.com and by editorial staff evaluation. The editors weighed the following criteria as it pertained to African Americans in each city: median household income; percentage of households earning more than $100,000; percentage of businesses owned; percentage of college graduates; unemployment rates; home loan rejections; and homeownership rates. *Black Enterprise, May 2007*

Seniors/Retirement Rankings

- Sperling's BestPlaces in partnership with Bankers Life & Casualty Company designed a survey to identify the top 50 metro areas in the U.S. that offer the best overall qualities for senior living. The Columbus* metro area ranked #28. The following criteria were statistically weighted to reflect the needs of the senior population: health; disease; economics; social; environment; spiritual; transportation; housing; and crime. *Bankers Life & Casualty Company, "Best Cities for Seniors 2005"*

- A.G. Edwards ranked America's 500 top-performing communities based on their residents' personal savings and investing behavior. The Columbus* metro area ranked #269 with an index score of 100.80 (national average = 100.00). A dozen statistical factors were measured including: participation in retirement savings plans; personal debt levels; and home ownership. *A.G. Edwards, "2007 Nest Egg Index", September 12, 2007*

Children/Family Rankings

- Hilliard was selected as one of the top 100 best places to raise a family in the U.S. Criteria: demographic characteristics; standard of living; education; lifestyle; health and safety. *Best Place to Raise Your Family: The Top 100 Affordable Communities in the U.S., 1st Edition, 2006*
- The Columbus* metro area was selected as one of the "Best Cities for Relocating Families" by Worldwide ERC and Primacy Relocation. The 2007 study placed a special emphasis on the housing market, which has significantly impacted the relocation industry and an employer's ability to transfer employees. The variables which weigh heavily in this category include home price, home affordability index, appreciation rates, and property tax. Other criteria include cost of living, crime rates, education, climate, focus on diversity, physicians per capita, recreation and leisure, arts and culture, air quality, watershed quality, sales tax, unemployment rate, job growth, high school and higher education index, school expenditures per student, students in public school, SAT/ACT percentile, and population growth. *Worldwide ERC and Primacy Relocation, "2007 Best Cities for Relocating Families"*

Safety Rankings

- The National Insurance Crime Bureau ranked 361 metro areas in the U.S. in terms of per capita rates of vehicle theft. The Columbus* metro area ranked #87 (#1 = highest rate). Criteria: number of vehicle theft offenses per 100,000 inhabitants. *National Insurance Crime Bureau, "NICB Vehicle Theft Study," April 22, 2008*
- Columbus* appeared on Sperling's BestPlaces list of the "Riskiest Cities for Identity Theft." The area ranked #31 out of the nations 50 largest metro areas. Over 80 criteria were analyzed across four major categories: technology impact; crime; transactions; and risk profile. *Sperling's BestPlaces, www.BestPlaces.net, "Riskiest Cities for Identity Theft," July 2006*
- Farmers Insurance Group of Companies, in partnership with Sperling's BestPlaces, ranked 379 metro areas and identified the "Most Secure U.S. Place to Live." The Columbus* metro area ranked #74 out of 114 in the large metro area category (500,000 or more residents). Criteria: crime rates; extreme weather; risk of natural disasters; environmental hazards; terrorism threats; air quality; life expectancy; job loss numbers. *Farmers Insurance Group, "Most Secure U.S. Places to Live 2007"*
- Columbus* was identified as one of the most dangerous large metro areas for pedestrians in the U.S. The area ranked #41 out of the nations 50 largest metro areas. Criteria: average yearly pedestrian fatalities per capita (for the years 2002 and 2003) adjusted for the number of walkers. *Surface Transportation Policy Project, "Mean Streets 2004"*

Sports/Recreation Rankings

- The Columbus* metro area appeared on the *Sporting News* list of the "Best Sports Cities 2007". The area ranked #39 out of 150 cities in the U.S. *Sporting News* takes a 12-month snapshot, roughly July to July, of each city's sports, putting a heavy premium on regular-season won-lost records (from the most recently completed season). Other criteria include: playoff berths, bowl appearances and tournament bids; championships; applicable power ratings; quality of competition; overall fan fervor as measured in part by attendance as percentage of venue capacity; abundance of teams (rewarding quality over quantity); stadium and arena quality; ticket availability and prices; franchise ownership; and marquee appeal of athletes. *SportingNews.com, "Best Sports Cities 2007," August 1, 2007*
- The Columbus* metro area was selected by *Cranium* as one of the "Top 50 Fun Cities" in America. The area ranked #21. Criteria includes: number of sports teams, restaurants, and dance performances; number of toy stores; city budget spent on recreation. *Cranium, November 4, 2003*
- *Golf Digest* ranked 330 metro areas in the U.S. in terms of golf. The Columbus* metro area was ranked #120. Criteria: access to golf; weather; value of golf; and quality of golf. *Golf Digest, "Metro Golf Rankings," August 2005*

Dating/Romance Rankings

- Eli Lily and Company, in partnership with Sperling's BestPlaces, ranked the nation's 50 largest metro areas in terms of the "Most Romantic Cities for Baby Boomers." The Columbus* metro area ranked #39. Criteria: marriage and divorce rates among "baby boomers" age 45 to 60; great restaurants; dance studios; chocolate, jewelry and flower sales. *Eli Lily and Company, "Most Romantic Cities for Baby Boomers," April 20, 2007*
- The Columbus* metro area was selected as one of the "Best Cities for Relocating Singles" by Worldwide ERC and Primacy Relocation. The area ranked #33 out of the 100 largest metro areas in the U.S. Areas were selected based on the following criteria: a robust cost-of-living index; adventure and outdoor recreation opportunities; violent crime and property crime rates; percentage of the population that is unmarried (ages 25-34); ratio of single men and single women; affordability of quality higher education, including in-state and out-of-state tuition requirements and rates; number of newcomers to the area; commute times; tax rates; fee and occupancy rates for temporary housing and mini-storage; quality and quantity of collegiate and professional sporting events and fun, fan-friendly venues. *Worldwide ERC and Primacy Relocation, "2007 Best Cities for Relocating Singles," October 25, 2007*
- *Forbes* ranked the 40 most populous urbanized areas in the U.S. in terms of the "Best Cities for Singles." The Columbus* metro area ranked #19. Criteria: number of singles; cost of living alone; nightlife; culture; job growth; coolness; and online dating. *Forbes.com, August 21, 2007*
- Sperling's BestPlaces in partnership with AXE Deodorant Bodyspray ranked 80 metro areas and identified "America's Best (and Worst) Cities for Dating." The Columbus* metro area ranked #12 (#1 = best). Criteria: percentage of singles ages 18-24; population density; dating venues per capita. *AXE Deodorant Bodyspray, "America's Best (and Worst) Cities for Dating," May 2004*

Culture/Performing Arts Rankings

- Scarborough Research, a leading market research firm, identified the top local markets for rock concert attendance. The Columbus* DMA (Designated Market Area) ranked in the top 25 with 14% of consumers, 18 years old and over, reporting that they have attended a rock concert during the past year. *Scarborough Research, June 14, 2004*

Miscellaneous Rankings

- Hilliard was selected as one of the "50 Best Affordable Suburbs" in the U.S. by *Business Week.*. The 50 suburbs were chosen based on dozens of factors including: median home prices; population growth; crime rates; levels of education; unemployment rate; commute times; and affordability. One suburb from each state was selected. *BusinessWeek, "Where the Affordable Suburbs Are," December 13, 2007*
- Scarborough Research, a leading market research firm, identified the top local markets for bloggers. The Columbus* DMA (Designated Market Area) ranked in the top 13 with 11% of adults reporting that they had read or contributed to a blog within the past 30 days. *Scarborough Research, October 24, 2007*
- The Columbus* metro area appeared on *Forbes* list of "America's Drunkest Cities". The area ranked #3. Criteria: 35 of the largest continental U.S. metro areas were chosen based on availability of data and geographic diversity. Each metro was ranked in five areas: state laws; drinkers; heavy drinkers; binge drinkers; and alcoholism. *Forbes.com, "America's Drunkest Cities," August 22, 2006*
- Sperling's BestPlaces in partnership with Pep Boys ranked 77 metro areas and identified "America's Most Drivable Cities." The Columbus* metro area ranked #36. Criteria: climate; road roughness; urban mobility; gas prices. *Pep Boys, "America's Most Drivable Cities," April 9, 2003*
- State Farm Insurance, in partnership with Sperling's BestPlaces, analyzed several key factors that contribute to overall family preparedness. The Columbus* metro area ranked #21 out of the nation's 50 most populous metro areas. Criteria: quality of life; life insurance coverage; and investments. *State Farm Life Insurance, "Fiscally Fit Cities Report," July 20, 2004*

- Scarborough Research, a leading market research firm, identified the top local markets for reality television. The Columbus* DMA (Designated Market Area) ranked in the top 10 with 26% of consumers reporting that they "typically watch" reality-dating, reality-talent, or reality- adventure television shows. *Scarborough Research, January 11, 2005*

- Scarborough Research, a leading market research firm, identified the top local markets for grocery coupon use. The Columbus* DMA (Designated Market Area) ranked in the top 25 with 36% of consumers reporting that they use grocery coupons at least once per week. *Scarborough Research, December 8, 2004*

- Scarborough Research, a leading market research firm, identified the top local markets for gift card purchasers. The Columbus* DMA (Designated Market Area) ranked in the top 10 with 54% of consumers reporting that they purchased a gift card within the past 12 months. *Scarborough Research, November 15, 2006*

- A study by Sperling's BestPlaces examined which U.S. metro areas were most affected by high fuel prices in 2006. The Columbus* metro area was ranked #41 out of 80 (#1 = most expensive city for driving). Rankings are based on the average dollars spent on gas per year by two driver households. Criteria: cost of regular-grade gasoline; average miles driven per day; average number of gallons each driver uses and wastes in traffic congestion each day. *Sperling's BestPlaces, www.bestplaces.net, "Pain at the Pump," May 18, 2006*

Hilliard is located within the Columbus, OH Metropolitan Statistical Area.

Business Environment

CITY FINANCES

City Government Finances

Component	2004-2005 ($000)	2004-2005 ($ per capita)
Total Revenues	24,200	908
Total Expenditures	20,318	762
Debt Outstanding	32,370	1,214
Cash and Securities	25,600	960

Source: U.S Census Bureau, Government Finances 2004-2005

City Government Revenue by Source

Source	2004-2005 ($000)	2004-2005 ($ per capita)
General Revenue		
From Federal Government	117	4
From State Government	1,340	50
From Local Governments	1,551	58
Taxes		
Property	1,249	47
Sales	204	8
Personal Income	11,914	447
License	1,026	38
Charges	2,543	95
Liquor Store	0	0
Utility	803	30
Employee Retirement	0	0
Other	3,453	130

Source: U.S Census Bureau, Government Finances 2004-2005

City Government Expenditures by Function

Function	2004-2005 ($000)	2004-2005 ($ per capita)	2004-2005 (%)
General Expenditures			
Airports	0	0	0.0
Corrections	0	0	0.0
Education	0	0	0.0
Fire Protection	0	0	0.0
Governmental Administration	2,980	112	14.7
Health	119	4	0.6
Highways	2,972	111	14.6
Hospitals	0	0	0.0
Housing and Community Development	0	0	0.0
Interest on General Debt	793	30	3.9
Libraries	0	0	0.0
Parking	0	0	0.0
Parks and Recreation	2,137	80	10.5
Police Protection	5,203	195	25.6
Public Welfare	0	0	0.0
Sewerage	484	18	2.4
Solid Waste Management	657	25	3.2
Liquor Store	0	0	0.0
Utility	0	0	0.0
Employee Retirement	0	0	0.0
Other	4,973	187	24.5

Source: U.S Census Bureau, Government Finances 2004-2005

Municipal Bond Ratings

Area	Moody's
City	Aaa

Source: Mergent Bond Record, January 2008 (unless noted otherwise)

DEMOGRAPHICS

Population Growth

Area	1990 Census	2000 Census	2007 Estimate	2012 Projection	Population Growth (%) 1990-2000	Population Growth (%) 2000-2012
City	12,516	24,230	27,143	28,913	93.6	19.3
MSA[1]	1,405,176	1,612,694	1,733,942	1,811,223	14.8	12.3
U.S.	248,709,873	281,421,906	301,045,522	314,920,978	13.2	11.9

Note: (1) Metropolitan Statistical Area - see Appendix B for areas included
Source: Claritas, Inc.

Number of Households and Average Household Size

Area	2007 Estimate	2007 Average Household Size
City	9,564	2.84
MSA[1]	691,073	2.51
U.S.	113,668,003	2.65

Note: (1) Metropolitan Statistical Area - see Appendix B for areas included
Source: Claritas, Inc.

Race and Ethnicity

Area	White Alone[2]	Black Alone[2]	Asian Alone[2]	Other Race Alone[2]	Hispanic[3]
City	89.8	2.2	4.8	3.2	2.8
MSA[1]	79.4	14.0	2.8	3.7	2.6
U.S.	73.1	12.4	4.3	10.3	14.9

Note: Figures are 2007 estimates; (1) Metropolitan Statistical Area - see Appendix B for areas included (2) Alone is defined as not being in combination with one or more other races; (3) May be of any race.
Source: Claritas, Inc.

Ancestry

Area	German	Irish[2]	English	American	Italian	Polish	French[3]	Scottish
City	30.1	17.2	12.7	8.3	7.8	3.8	3.6	2.9
MSA[1]	23.4	13.1	10.0	9.3	5.0	2.2	2.2	2.0
U.S.	15.2	10.9	8.7	7.3	5.6	3.2	3.0	1.7

Note: Figures include multiple ancestry (e.g. if a person reported being Irish and Italian, they were included in both columns); (1) Metropolitan Statistical Area - see Appendix A for areas included; (2) Includes Celtic; (3) Includes Alsatian but excludes Basque
Source: Census 2000, Summary File 3

Foreign-Born Population

Area	Percent of Population Born in: Any Foreign Country	Europe	Asia	Africa	Oceania[2]	Canada	Mexico	Latin America[3]
City	4.2	0.6	3.1	0.2	0.0	0.2	0.0	0.3
MSA[1]	4.6	0.9	2.1	0.7	0.0	0.2	0.4	0.3
U.S.	11.1	1.7	2.9	0.3	0.1	0.3	3.3	2.5

Note: (1) Metropolitan Statistical Area - see Appendix A for areas included; (2) Includes Australia, New Zealand subregion, Melanesia, Micronesia, Polynesia, and Oceania n.e.c; (3) Includes Central America (excluding Mexico), South America, and the Caribbean.
Source: Census 2000, Summary File 3

Marriage Status

Area	Never Married	Now Married (excluding Separated)	Separated	Widowed	Divorced
City	19.8	67.7	0.4	3.6	8.4
MSA[1]	29.6	52.1	1.7	5.5	11.1
U.S.	27.1	54.4	2.2	6.6	9.7

Note: Figures are percentages and cover the population 15 years of age and older; (1) Metropolitan Statistical Area - see Appendix A for areas included
Source: Census 2000, Summary File 3

Age Distribution

Area	Percent of Population						
	Under Age 5	Age 5 to 17	Age 18 to 34	Age 35 to 49	Age 50 to 64	Age 65 to 79	80 Years and Over
City	9.3	22.4	21.9	28.8	10.4	5.2	1.9
MSA[1]	7.1	18.3	26.7	23.9	14.0	7.7	2.4
U.S.	6.8	18.9	23.7	23.5	14.8	9.2	3.2

Note: (1) Metropolitan Statistical Area - see Appendix A for areas included
Source: Census 2000, Summary File 3

Male/Female Ratio

Area	Males	Females	Males per 100 Females
City	13,390	13,753	97.4
MSA[1]	854,714	879,228	97.2
U.S.	148,320,305	152,725,217	97.1

Note: Figures are 2007 estimates; (1) Metropolitan Statistical Area - see Appendix B for areas included
Source: Claritas, Inc.

Religion

Area	Catholic	Southern Baptist	United Meth-odist	ELCA[1]	LDS[2]	Presby-terian Church USA	Jewish Est.	Muslim Est.
County	13.7	2.1	4.1	2.8	0.4	1.5	1.5	0.6
U.S.	22.0	7.1	3.7	1.8	1.5	1.1	2.2	0.6

Note: Figures are the number of adherents as a percentage of the total population; Adherents are defined as all members, including full members, their children and the estimated number of other participants who are not considered members (e.g. the baptized, those not confirmed, those regularly attending services, etc.); (1) Evangelical Lutheran Church in America; (2) The Church of Jesus Christ of Latter Day Saints
Source: Reprinted with permission from Religious Congregations and Membership in the United States 2000 (Nashville, Glenmary Research Center, 2002) Copyright Association of Statisticians of American Religious Bodies. All rights reserved.

ECONOMY

Gross Metropolitan Product

Area	2002	2003	2004	2005	2005 Rank[2]
MSA[1]	63.8	66.5	70.2	73.1	34

Note: Figures are in billions of dollars; (1) Columbus, OH Metropolitan Statistical Area - see Appendix A for areas included; (2) Rank ranges from 1 to 361
Source: The U.S. Conference of Mayors, "U.S. Metro Economies: GMP - The Engines of America's Growth," January 2007

Economic Growth

Area	1995 GMP	2005 GMP	Average Annual Growth Rate	Growth Rate Rank[2]
MSA[1]	44.9	73.1	5.0	219

Note: Figures are in billions of dollars; GMP = Gross Metropolitan Product; (1) Columbus, OH Metropolitan Statistical Area - see Appendix A for areas included; (2) Rank ranges from 1 to 361
Source: The U.S. Conference of Mayors, "U.S. Metro Economies: GMP - The Engines of America's Growth," January 2007

INCOME

Per Capita/Median/Average Income

Area	Per Capita ($)	Median Household ($)	Average Household ($)
City	35,419	86,024	100,215
MSA[1]	27,475	52,886	68,386
U.S.	25,495	49,280	66,670

Note: Figures are 2007 estimates; (1) Metropolitan Statistical Area - see Appendix B for areas included
Source: Claritas, Inc.

Household Income Distribution

Area	Percent of Households Earning							
	Under $15,000	$15,000 -24,999	$25,000 -34,999	$35,000 -49,999	$50,000 -74,999	$75,000 -99,000	$100,000 -149,999	$150,000 and up
City	4.3	3.6	4.8	10.3	18.4	19.3	25.0	14.2
MSA[1]	11.0	9.6	10.9	16.0	20.7	13.2	12.4	6.3
U.S.	13.1	10.9	11.2	15.6	19.5	11.9	11.3	6.6

Note: Figures are 2007 estimates; (1) Metropolitan Statistical Area - see Appendix B for areas included
Source: Claritas, Inc.

Poverty Rates by Age

Area	All Ages	Under 5 Years Old	5 to 17 Years Old	18 to 64 Years Old	65 Years and Over
City	2.2	0.1	0.2	1.2	0.5
MSA[1]	10.1	1.1	2.2	6.0	0.8
U.S.	12.4	1.2	3.0	6.9	1.2

Note: Figures are percent of population with income in 1999 below poverty level and only include population for whom poverty status is determined; (1) Metropolitan Statistical Area - see Appendix A for areas included
Source: Census 2000, Summary File 3

Personal Bankruptcy Filing Rate

Area	2004	2005	2006
Franklin County	9.53	13.80	3.56
U.S.	5.31	6.82	2.00

Note: Numbers are per 1,000 population and include Chapter 7 and Chapter 13 filings
Source: Federal Deposit Insurance Corporation (FDIC), Regional Economic Conditions (RECON), 8/23/2007

EMPLOYMENT

Labor Force and Employment

Area	Civilian Labor Force			Workers Employed		
	Dec. 2006	Dec. 2007	% Chg.	Dec. 2006	Dec. 2007	% Chg.
City	15,366	15,548	1.2	14,877	14,988	0.7
MSA[1]	955,896	967,649	1.2	914,318	921,121	0.7
U.S.	152,571,000	153,705,000	0.7	146,081,000	146,334,000	0.2

Note: Data is not seasonally adjusted and covers workers 16 years of age and older;
(1) Metropolitan Statistical Area - see Appendix B for areas included
Source: Bureau of Labor Statistics, http://stats.bls.gov

Unemployment Rate

Area	2007											
	Jan.	Feb.	Mar.	Apr.	May	Jun.	Jul.	Aug.	Sep.	Oct.	Nov.	Dec.
City	3.4	3.4	3.4	3.4	3.3	3.9	3.6	3.8	3.7	3.7	3.6	3.6
MSA[1]	4.9	4.8	4.6	4.7	4.5	5.1	4.8	4.8	4.8	4.6	4.5	4.8
U.S.	5.0	4.9	4.5	4.3	4.3	4.7	4.9	4.6	4.5	4.4	4.5	4.8

Note: Data is not seasonally adjusted and covers workers 16 years of age and older; All figures are percentages; (1) Metropolitan Statistical Area - see Appendix B for areas included
Source: Bureau of Labor Statistics, http://stats.bls.gov

Employment by Occupation

Occupation Classification	City (%)	MSA[1] (%)	U.S. (%)
Sales and Office	27.9	29.2	26.7
Professional and Related	27.3	21.1	20.2
Service	10.9	13.7	14.9
Production, Transportation, and Material Moving	8.4	13.0	14.6
Management, Business, and Financial	19.4	15.3	13.5
Construction, Extraction, and Maintenance	6.1	7.4	9.4
Farming, Forestry, and Fishing	0.0	0.2	0.7

Note: Figures cover employed civilians 16 years of age and older;
(1) Metropolitan Statistical Area - see Appendix A for areas included
Source: Census 2000, Summary File 3

Employment by Industry

Sector	MSA[1] Number of Employees	MSA[1] Percent of Total	U.S. Percent of Total
Government	159,400	16.6	16.3
Education and Health Services	113,000	11.8	13.4
Professional and Business Services	153,800	16.0	13.1
Retail Trade	109,900	11.4	11.6
Manufacturing	76,600	8.0	9.9
Leisure and Hospitality	88,300	9.2	9.6
Financial Activities	74,100	7.7	5.9
Construction	n/a	n/a	5.3
Wholesale Trade	39,500	4.1	4.4
Other Services	37,000	3.9	3.9
Transportation and Utilities	52,700	5.5	3.7
Information	18,600	1.9	2.2
Natural Resources and Mining	n/a	n/a	0.5

Note: Figures cover non-farm employment as of December 2007 and are not seasonally adjusted; (1) Metropolitan Statistical Area - see Appendix B for areas included; n/a not available
Source: Bureau of Labor Statistics, http://stats.bls.gov

Average Wages

Occupation	$/Hr.	Occupation	$/Hr.
Accountants and Auditors	27.73	Maids and Housekeeping Cleaners	9.14
Automotive Mechanics	17.84	Maintenance and Repair Workers	16.76
Bookkeepers	16.13	Marketing Managers	49.33
Carpenters	18.66	Nuclear Medicine Technologists	30.45
Cashiers	8.81	Nurses, Licensed Practical	19.54
Clerks, General Office	12.69	Nurses, Registered	27.23
Clerks, Receptionists/Information	11.56	Nursing Aides/Orderlies/Attendants	11.69
Clerks, Shipping/Receiving	14.07	Packers and Packagers, Hand	10.57
Computer Programmers	32.85	Physical Therapists	33.59
Computer Support Specialists	18.75	Postal Service Mail Carriers	21.25
Computer Systems Analysts	35.78	Real Estate Brokers	38.54
Cooks, Restaurant	10.26	Retail Salespersons	11.54
Dentists	n/a	Sales Reps., Exc. Tech./Scientific	30.67
Electrical Engineers	33.98	Sales Reps., Tech./Scientific	35.02
Electricians	21.76	Secretaries, Exc. Legal/Med./Exec.	15.56
Financial Managers	51.84	Security Guards	12.21
First-Line Supervisors/Mgrs., Sales	19.12	Surgeons	n/a
Food Preparation Workers	9.38	Teacher Assistants	13.30
General and Operations Managers	50.09	Teachers, Elementary School	27.20
Hairdressers/Cosmetologists	12.04	Teachers, Secondary School	26.20
Internists	83.78	Telemarketers	10.27
Janitors and Cleaners	11.24	Truck Drivers, Heavy/Tractor-Trailer	18.23
Landscaping/Groundskeeping Workers	11.53	Truck Drivers, Light/Delivery Svcs.	14.86
Lawyers	43.34	Waiters and Waitresses	8.21

Note: Wage data covers the Columbus, OH Metropolitan Statistical Area - see Appendix B for areas included. Hourly wages for elementary/secondary school teachers and teacher assistants were calculated by the editors from annual wage data assuming a 40 hour work week; n/a not available.
Source: Bureau of Labor Statistics, May 2007 Metro Area Occupational Employment and Wage Estimates

RESIDENTIAL REAL ESTATE

Building Permits

Area	Single-Family 2006	Single-Family 2007p	Single-Family Pct. Chg.	Multi-Family 2006	Multi-Family 2007p	Multi-Family Pct. Chg.	Total 2006	Total 2007p	Total Pct. Chg.
City	65	92	41.5	57	34	-40.4	122	126	3.3
U.S.	1,378,200	973,300	-29.4	460,700	407,200	-11.6	1,838,900	1,380,500	-24.9

Note: (p) preliminary; figures cover and represent new, privately-owned housing units authorized (unadjusted data); All permit data are based on estimates with imputation; U.S. figures are based on the new 20,000-place series.
Source: U.S. Census Bureau, Manufacturing, Mining, and Construction Statistics

Homeownership and Housing Vacancies

Area	Homeownership Rate[2] (%)			Rental Vacancy Rate[3] (%)			Homeowner Vacancy Rate[4] (%)		
	2005	2006	2007	2005	2006	2007	2005	2006	2007
MSA[1]	68.9	65.8	66.1	13.8	13.1	13.3	3.0	3.4	2.8
U.S.	68.9	68.8	68.1	9.8	9.8	9.7	1.9	2.4	2.7

Note: (1) Metropolitan Statistical Area - see Appendix B for areas included; (2) The proportion of households that are owners; (3) The proportion of the rental inventory that is vacant for rent; (4) The proportion of the homeowner inventory that is vacant for sale; n/a not available
Source: U.S. Census Bureau, Housing Vacancies and Homeownership Annual Statistics: 2007

TAXES

State Corporate Income Tax Rates

State	Rates and Tax Brackets
Ohio	5.1% > $0; 8.5% > 50K

Note: Tax rates as of January 1, 2008; A value added-style tax, the Corporate Activities Tax (CAT) was instituted in 2005. It will be phased in through 2010 while the Corporate Franchise Tax (Ohio's income tax) is phased out. Beginning April 1, 2008 the CAT rate is.208% (80% of.26%). For tax year 2008 companies owe 40% of Corporate Franchise Tax liability.
Source: Tax Foundation, www.taxfoundation.org

State Individual Income Tax Rates

State	Federal Deductibility	Marginal Rates (%)	Standard Deduction ($)		Personal Exemptions ($)[1]	
			Single	Joint	Single	Dependents
Ohio	No	0.649 - 6.555 (y)	n/a	n/a	1,450 (g)(r)	1,450 (g)(r)

Note: Tax rates as of January 1, 2008; Local- and county-level taxes are not included; n/a not applicable; (1) Married joint filers generally receive double the single exemption; (g) Taxpayers receive a $20 tax credit per exemption in addition to the normal exemption amount; (r) State adjusts its bracket levels for inflation at the end of each year before printing tax forms; (y) Brackets are not double for married taxpayers.
Source: Tax Foundation, www.taxfoundation.org

Various State and Local Tax Rates

State and Local Sales and Use (%)	State Sales and Use (%)	Gasoline[1,2] ($/gal.)	Cigarette ($/pack)	Spirits ($/gal.)	Table Wine ($/gal.)	Beer ($/gal.)
6.75	5.5 (h)	0.28	1.25	8.46 (n)	0.32	0.18

Note: Tax rates as of January 1, 2008; (1) In addition to the 18.4 cpg Federal gasoline tax; (2) Rates may include additional state sales taxes, environmental protection and storage fees/taxes, and local taxes. When necessary, the volume-weighted average of all local taxes is used to approximate the typical statewide rate including local tax; (h) Ohio has a GRT that is levied in addition to its 5.5% sales tax. It is called the commercial activity tax (CAT). Firms with receipts over $1 million pay the CAT; firms with receipts between $150K and $1 million pay a minimum tax of $150. The rate i

2008 is 0.156%, and increases are scheduled in law to 0.208% on 4/1/2008 and 0.26% on 4/1/2009. The CAT is being phased in to replace Ohio's Corporate Franchise Tax, which is simultaneously being phased out; (n) The state government controls all sales. The implied excise tax rate is calculated using methodology designed by the Distilled Spirits Council of the United States (DISCUS).
Source: Tax Foundation, www.taxfoundation.org; Original research

State Tax Burdens

Area	Combined State and Local Tax Burden		Combined Federal, State and Local Tax Burden	
	Percent	Rank	Percent	Rank
Ohio	12.4	5	32.4	18
U.S. Average	11.0	-	32.7	-

Note: Figures cover 2007 and measure taxes as a percentage of income
Source: Tax Foundation, www.taxfoundation.org

State Business Tax Climate Index Rankings

State	Overall Rank	Corporate Tax Index Rank	Individual Income Tax Index Rank	Sales Tax Index Rank	Unemployment Insurance Tax Index Rank	Property Tax Index Rank
Ohio	46	37	48	36	11	44

Note: Rankings range from 1 to 50 where 1 is best. Rankings do not average across to Overall Rank. States without a given tax are given a ranking of 1.
Source: Tax Foundation, State Business Tax Climate Index 2008

TRANSPORTATION

Means of Transportation to Work

Area	Car/Truck/Van		Public Transportation			Bicycle	Walked	Other Means	Worked at Home
	Drove Alone	Car-pooled	Bus	Subway	Railroad				
City	88.2	5.6	0.7	0.0	0.0	0.0	0.7	0.4	4.4
MSA[1]	82.0	9.6	2.2	0.0	0.0	0.2	2.4	0.6	3.0
U.S.	75.7	12.2	2.5	1.5	0.5	0.4	2.9	1.0	3.3

Note: Figures are percentages and cover workers 16 years of age and older; (1) Metropolitan Statistical Area - see Appendix A for areas included
Source: Census 2000, Summary File 3

Travel Time to Work

Area	Less Than 15 Minutes	15 to 29 Minutes	30 to 44 Minutes	45 to 59 Minutes	60 Minutes or More
City	28.8	43.7	19.4	4.4	3.7
MSA[1]	26.6	44.1	19.6	5.5	4.2
U.S.	29.4	36.1	19.1	7.4	8.0

Note: Figures are percentages and include workers 16 years old and over; (1) Metropolitan Statistical Area - see Appendix A for areas included
Source: Census 2000, Summary File 3

Travel Time Index

Area	1982	1995	2004	2005
Urban Area[1]	1.03	1.15	1.20	1.19
Average[2]	1.11	1.22	1.29	1.30

Note: Travel Time Index - The ratio of travel time in the peak period to the travel time at free-flow conditions. A value of 1.35 indicates a 20-minute free-flow trip takes 27 minutes in the peak. Free-flow speeds (60 mph on freeways and 35 mph on principal arterials) are used as the comparison threshold; (1) Covers the Columbus, OH urban area; (2) average of 85 urban areas
Source: Texas Transportation Institute, The 2007 Urban Mobility Report, September 2007

Living Environment

COST OF LIVING

Cost of Living Index

Composite Index	Groceries	Housing	Utilities	Trans-portation	Health Care	Misc. Goods/ Services
97.7	96.3	97.0	102.7	103.6	104.1	95.0

Note: U.S. = 100; Figures cover the Columbus OH urban area.
Source: The Council for Community and Economic Research (formerly ACCRA), Cost of Living Index, 2007

Grocery Prices

Area[1]	T-Bone Steak ($/pound)	Frying Chicken ($/pound)	Whole Milk ($/half gal.)	Eggs ($/dozen)	Orange Juice ($/64 oz.)	Coffee ($/11.5 oz.)
City[2]	10.75	1.29	1.79	1.27	3.13	3.26
Avg.	8.93	1.12	2.13	1.52	3.26	3.31
Min.	5.88	0.71	1.33	0.83	2.30	2.20
Max.	12.80	2.07	3.43	3.54	5.79	6.20

Note: (1) Values for the local area are compared with the average, minimum and maximum values for all 331 areas in the Cost of Living Index report; (2) Figures cover the Columbus OH urban area; **T-Bone Steak** *(price per pound);* **Frying Chicken** *(price per pound, whole fryer);* **Whole Milk** *(half gallon carton);* **Eggs** *(price per dozen, Grade A, large);* **Orange Juice** *(64 oz. Tropicana or Florida Natural);* **Coffee** *(11.5 oz. can, vacuum-packed, Maxwell House, Hills Bros, or Folgers).*
Source: The Council for Community and Economic Research (formerly ACCRA), Cost of Living Index, 2007

Housing and Utility Costs

Area[1]	New Home Price ($)	Apartment Rent ($/month)	All Electric ($/month)	Part Electric ($/month)	Other Energy ($/month)	Telephone ($/month)
City[2]	303,182	778	-	68.02	97.08	27.36
Avg.	309,605	782	146.13	78.67	90.16	26.14
Min.	189,877	n/a	82.03	37.41	33.15	17.08
Max.	1,202,800	3,481	271.14	150.60	257.67	37.45

Note: (1) Values for the local area are compared with the average, minimum and maximum values for all 331 areas in the Cost of Living Index report; (2) Figures cover the Columbus OH urban area; **New Home Price** *(2,400 sf living area, 8,000 sf lot, in urban area with full utilities);* **Apartment Rent** *(950 sf 2 bedroom/1.5 or 2 bath, unfurnished, excluding all utilities except water);* **All Electric** *(average monthly cost for an all-electric home);* **Part Electric** *(average monthly cost for a part-electric home);* **Other Energy** *(average monthly cost for natural gas, fuel oil, coal, wood, and any other forms of energy except electricity);* **Telephone** *(price includes basic monthly rate for a private residential line plus additional local usage charges incurred by a family of four).*
Source: The Council for Community and Economic Research (formerly ACCRA), Cost of Living Index, 2007

Health Care, Transportation, and Other Costs

Area[1]	Doctor ($/visit)	Dentist ($/visit)	Optometrist ($/visit)	Gasoline ($/gallon)	Beauty Salon ($/visit)	Men's Shirt ($)
City[2]	70.09	85.33	88.04	2.79	33.60	26.22
Avg.	79.48	71.93	79.55	2.64	29.52	25.77
Min.	52.08	44.80	43.95	2.19	15.58	16.19
Max.	148.44	126.27	158.83	3.48	60.62	48.53

Note: (1) Values for the local area are compared with the average, minimum and maximum values for all 331 areas in the Cost of Living Index report; (2) Figures cover the Columbus OH urban area; **Doctor** *(general practitioners routine exam of an established patient);* **Dentist** *(adult teeth cleaning and periodic oral examination);* **Optometrist** *(full vision eye exam for established adult patient);* **Gasoline** *(one gallon regular unleaded, national brand, including all taxes, cash price at self-service pump if available);* **Beauty Salon** *(woman's shampoo, trim, and blow-dry);* **Men's Shirt** *(cotton/polyester dress shirt, pinpoint weave, long sleeves).*
Source: The Council for Community and Economic Research (formerly ACCRA), Cost of Living Index, 2007

HOUSING

House Price Index (HPI)

Area	National Ranking[2]	Quarterly Change (%)	One-Year Change (%)	Five-Year Change (%)
MSA[1]	190	0.33	0.10	13.49
U.S.[3]	-	0.10	0.84	41.37

Note: The HPI is a weighted repeat sales index. It measures average price changes in repeat sales or refinancings on the same properties. This information is obtained by reviewing repeat mortgage transactions on single-family properties whose mortgages have been purchased or securitized by Fannie Mae or Freddie Mac in January 1975; (1) Metropolitan Statistical Area - see Appendix B for areas included; (2) Rankings are based on annual percentage change for all metro areas containing at least 15,000 transactions over the last 10 years and ranges from 1 to 291; (3) figures based on a weighted average of Census Division estimates; all figures are for the period ending December 31, 2007
Source: Office of Federal Housing Enterprise Oversight, House Price Index, February 26, 2008

House Price Valuations

Area	Q1 2000	Q1 2001	Q1 2002	Q1 2003	Q1 2004	Q1 2005	Q1 2006	Q1 2007	Q1 2008
MSA[1]	-5.7	-6.5	-6.4	-6.4	-2.8	-4.1	-3.6	-9.0	-14.6

Note: Figures show the percentage of over- or under-valuation of single family homes relative to statistically normal house values (e.g. a value of 23.6 indicates that house values are 23.6% overvalued). Statistically normal house values are based on house prices, interest rates, household incomes, population densities, and any historical premiums or discounts metropolitan areas have exhibited over time; (1) Figures cover the Metropolitan Statistical Area - see Appendix B for areas included
Source: Global Insight/National City Corporation, House Prices in America, May 2008

Median Home Prices

Area	2005	2006	2007[r]	Percent Change 2006 to 2007
MSA[1]	152.0	148.1	147.4	-0.5
U.S. Average	219.0	221.9	217.9	-1.8

Note: Figures are median sales prices of existing single-family homes in thousands of dollars; (r) revised; n/a not available; (1) Metropolitan Statistical Area - see Appendix B for areas included
Source: National Association of Realtors, Metropolitan Area Prices, 1st Quarter 2008

Housing: Year Structure Built

Area	1990 -2000	1980 -1989	1970 -1979	1960 -1969	1950 -1959	1940 -1949	Before 1940	Median Year
City	53.5	16.0	7.0	5.9	14.5	1.3	1.8	1991
MSA[1]	20.7	13.5	17.5	15.0	12.8	6.3	14.2	1971
U.S.	17.0	15.8	18.5	13.7	12.7	7.3	15.0	1971

Note: Figures are percentages; (1) Metropolitan Statistical Area - see Appendix A for areas included
Source: Census 2000, Summary File 3

HEALTH

Health Risk Data

Category	Area[1] (%)	U.S. (%)
Adults who have been told they have high blood pressure[3]	26.7	25.5
Adults who have been told they have high blood cholesterol[3]	38.2	35.6
Adults who have been told they have diabetes[2]	n/a	7.5
Adults who have been told they have arthritis[3]	27.8	27.0
Adults who have been told they currently have asthma	n/a	8.5
Adults who are current smokers	n/a	20.1
Adults who are heavy drinkers[4]	n/a	4.9
Adults who are overweight (BMI 25.0 - 29.9)	n/a	36.5
Adults who are obese (BMI 30.0 - 99.8)	n/a	25.1

Note: Data as of 2006 unless otherwise noted; n/a not available; (1) Figures cover the Metropolitan Statistical Area - see Appendix B for areas included; (2) Figures do not include pregnancy-related diabetes, pre-diabetes or borderline diabetes; (3) 2005 data; (4) Heavy drinkers are classified as adult men having more than two drinks per day or adult women having more than one drink per day
Source: Centers for Disease Control and Prevention, Behaviorial Risk Factor Surveillance System, SMART: Selected Metropolitan/Micropolitan Area Risk Trends, 2005, 2006

Mortality Rates for the Top 10 Causes of Death in the U.S.

ICD-10[a] Sub-Chapter	ICD-10[a] Code	Age-Adjusted Mortality Rate[1] per 100,000 population	
		County[2]	U.S.
Malignant neoplasms	C00-C97	212.5	186.5
Ischaemic heart diseases	I20-I25	143.4	152.3
Other forms of heart disease	I30-I51	61.9	51.5
Cerebrovascular diseases	I60-I69	57.7	50.0
Chronic lower respiratory diseases	J40-J47	52.6	42.6
Diabetes mellitus	E10-E14	30.5	24.8
Other degenerative diseases of the nervous system	G30-G31	28.5	22.6
Other external causes of accidental injury	W00-X59	23.5	21.4
Influenza and pneumonia	J10-J18	22.1	20.7
Hypertensive diseases	I10-I13	21.4	18.2

Note: (a) ICD-10 = International Classification of Diseases 10th Revision; (1) Mortality rates are a three year average covering 2003-2005; (2) Figures cover Franklin County
Source: Centers for Disease Control and Prevention, National Center for Health Statistics. Compressed Mortality File 1999-2004. CDC WONDER On-line Database, compiled from Compressed Mortality File 1999-2005 Series 20 No. 2K, 2008.

Mortality Rates for Selected Causes of Death

ICD-10[a] Sub-Chapter	ICD-10[a] Code	Age-Adjusted Mortality Rate[1] per 100,000 population	
		County[2]	U.S.
Assault	X85-Y09	9.2	5.9
Human immunodeficiency virus (HIV) disease	B20-B24	3.7	4.5
Intentional self-harm	X60-X84	9.7	10.8
Malnutrition	E40-E46	2.4	1.0
Obesity and other hyperalimentation	E65-E68	1.8	1.4
Organic, including symptomatic, mental disorders	F01-F09	32.1	16.8
Transport accidents	V01-V99	9.4	16.1
Viral hepatitis	B15-B19	0.8	1.8

Note: (a) ICD-10 = International Classification of Diseases 10th Revision; (1) Mortality rates are a three year average covering 2003-2005; (2) Figures cover Franklin County
Source: Centers for Disease Control and Prevention, National Center for Health Statistics. Compressed Mortality File 1999-2004. CDC WONDER On-line Database, compiled from Compressed Mortality File 1999-2005 Series 20 No. 2K, 2008.

Distribution of Physicians[1]

Area	Total	Family/ General Practice	Specialties	
			Medical	Surgical
Franklin County (number)	2,473	657	868	585
Franklin County (rate per 10,000 pop.)	22.7	6.0	8.0	5.4
U.S. (rate per 10,000 pop.)	17.7	4.6	6.9	4.3

Note: Data as of 2005; (1) Includes all non-federal, patient-care, office-based MDs
Source: Area Resource File (ARF). June 2007. U.S. Department of Health and Human Services, Health Resources and Services Administration, Bureau of Health Professions, Rockville, MD.

Hospitals

There were no hospitals listed within the city limits.
AHA Guide to the Healthcare Field 2008

According to *U.S. News,* the Columbus, OH metro area is home to four of the best hospitals in the U.S.: **Columbus Children's Hospital**; **Grant Medical Center-OhioHealth**; **Ohio State University Hospital**; **Riverside Methodist Hospital-Ohio Health**. *U.S. News Online, "America's Best Hospitals 2007"*

EDUCATION

Public School District Statistics

District Name	Schls	Pupils	Pupil/ Teacher Ratio	Minority Pupils[1] (%)	Free Lunch Eligible[2] (%)	IEP[3] (%)
Hilliard City	20	14,851	16.5	17.4	10.4	11.5

Note: Table includes regular local school districts with 2,000 or more students; (1) Percentage of students that are not white, non-Hispanic; (2) Percentage of students that are eligible for the free lunch program; (3) Percentage of students that have an Individualized Education Program.
Source: U.S. Department of Education, National Center for Education Statistics, Common Core of Data, Local Education Agency (School District) Universe Survey: School Year 2005-2006; U.S. Department of Education, National Center for Education Statistics, Common Core of Data, Public Elementary/Secondary School Universe Survey: School Year 2005-2006

Highest Level of Education

Area	Less than H.S.	H.S. Diploma	Some College, No Deg.	Associate Degree	Bachelors Degree	Masters Degree	Profess. School Degree	Doctorate Degree
City	7.5	20.8	19.3	6.5	31.6	9.0	3.3	2.1
MSA[1]	13.7	30.6	21.0	5.8	19.6	6.2	2.1	1.1
U.S.	19.4	28.4	21.2	6.4	15.7	5.9	2.0	1.0

Note: Figures are 2007 estimated percentages and cover persons age 25 and over; (1) Metropolitan Statistical Area - see Appendix B for areas included
Source: Claritas, Inc.

Educational Attainment by Race

Area	High School Graduate (%)					Bachelor's Degree (%)				
	Total	White	Black	Asian	Hisp.[2]	Total	White	Black	Asian	Hisp.[2]
City	92.5	92.6	92.0	95.2	80.4	46.1	45.1	57.2	68.2	50.0
MSA[1]	85.8	87.2	78.1	86.1	67.9	29.1	30.4	15.4	59.7	21.6
U.S.	80.4	83.6	72.3	80.4	52.4	24.4	26.1	14.3	44.1	10.4

Note: Figures shown cover persons 25 years old and over; (1) Metropolitan Statistical Area - see Appendix A for areas included; (2) people of Hispanic origin can be of any race
Source: Census 2000, Summary File 3

School Enrollment by Type

Area	Grades KG to 8				Grades 9 to 12			
	Public		Private		Public		Private	
	Enrollment	%	Enrollment	%	Enrollment	%	Enrollment	%
City	3,467	87.1	515	12.9	1,229	93.7	83	6.3
MSA[1]	178,054	88.0	24,285	12.0	73,403	89.9	8,275	10.1
U.S.	33,526,011	88.7	4,285,121	11.3	14,848,628	90.6	1,532,323	9.4

Note: Figures shown cover persons 3 years old and over; (1) Metropolitan Statistical Area - see Appendix A for areas included
Source: Census 2000, Summary File 3

School Enrollment by Race

Area	Grades KG to 8 (%)				Grades 9 to 12 (%)			
	White	Black	Asian	Hisp.[1]	White	Black	Asian	Hisp.[1]
City	91.9	1.4	4.9	1.4	93.8	0.8	5.5	1.0
MSA[2]	76.5	17.1	2.0	2.1	77.3	16.8	1.9	2.0
U.S.	68.5	15.5	3.3	16.8	68.8	15.5	3.8	15.7

Note: Figures shown cover persons 3 years old and over; (1) people of Hispanic origin can be of any race; (2) Metropolitan Statistical Area - see Appendix A for areas included
Source: Census 2000, Summary File 3

Average Salaries of Public School Classroom Teachers

District	2005-06		2006-07		Percent Change 2005-06 to 2006-07
	Dollars	Rank[1]	Dollars	Rank[1]	
Ohio	50,314	14	51,937	14	3.23
U.S. Average	49,026	-	50,816	-	3.65

Note: (1) State rank ranges from 1 to 51.
Source: National Education Association, Rankings & Estimates: Rankings of the States 2006 and Estimates of School Statistics 2007, December 2007

Higher Education

Four-Year Colleges			Two-Year Colleges			Medical Schools[1]	Law Schools[2]	Voc/ Tech[3]
Public	Private Non-profit	Private For-profit	Public	Private Non-profit	Private For-profit			
0	0	0	0	0	1	0	0	0

Note: Figures cover institutions located within the city limits; (1) includes schools accredited by the Liaison Committee on Medical Education and the American Osteopathic Association; (2) includes American Bar Association-accredited law schools; (3) includes all schools with programs that are less than 2 years.
Source: National Center for Education Statistics, The Integrated Postsecondary Education System (IPEDS) Peer Analysis System, 2007; www.usnews.com, Law and Medical School Directories, 2009

PRESIDENTIAL ELECTION

2004 Presidential Election Results

Area	Bush	Kerry	Nader	Other
Franklin County	45.1	54.4	0.0	0.5
U.S.	50.7	48.3	0.4	0.6

Note: Results are percentages and may not add to 100% due to rounding
Source: Dave Leip's Atlas of U.S. Presidential Elections, www.uselectionatlas.org

EMPLOYERS

Major Employers

Company Name	Industry	Type of Site
Abbott Laboratories	Dry, condensed, evaporated products	Branch
Abbott Laboratories	Pharmaceutical preparations	Branch
America Electric Power Texas	Electric services	Headquarters
Bank One	Business services, nec	Headquarters
Battelle Memorial Institute	Commercial physical research	Headquarters
Chase Manhattan	Mortgage bankers and correspondents	Branch
Columbia Energy	Natural gas transmission	Single
Columbus Childrens Hospital	Specialty hospitals, except psychiatric	Headquarters
DFAS-Columbus Center	Finance, taxation, and monetary policy	Branch
Express Inc	Women's clothing stores	Single
Facilities Operation and Dev	Electric and other services combined	Branch
Fairfield Medical Center	General medical and surgical hospitals	Headquarters
Indiana Michigan Power Company	Electric services	Headquarters
Limited Brands Inc	Women's accessory and specialty stores	Headquarters
Medical Center	Offices and clinics of medical doctors	Branch
Mount Crmel Hlth Sys Fundation	General medical and surgical hospitals	Headquarters
Nationwide	Fire, marine, and casualty insurance	Headquarters
Ohio Department Public Safety	Public order and safety, nec	Branch
Ohio Dept Administrative Svcs	General government, nec	Branch
Safelite Solutions LLC	Management consulting services	Single
State Automobile Mutl Insur Co	Fire, marine, and casualty insurance	Single
State Farm Insurance	Insurance agents, brokers, and service	Branch
The Ohio State University	Colleges and universities	Branch
US Bank	National commercial banks	Branch

Note: Companies shown are located within the Columbus metropolitan area; nec = not elsewhere classified.
Source: www.zapdata.com, May 2008

PUBLIC SAFETY

Crime Rate

Area	All Crimes	Violent Crimes				Property Crimes		
		Murder	Forcible Rape	Robbery	Aggrav. Assault	Burglary	Larceny -Theft	Motor Vehicle Theft
City	3,499.7	0.0	11.2	71.2	30.0	573.3	2,712.8	101.2
Metro[1]	5,125.8	6.6	51.1	246.4	122.2	1,252.1	2,989.9	457.5
U.S.	3,808.1	5.7	30.9	149.4	287.5	729.4	2,206.8	398.4

Note: Figures are crimes per 100,000 population; (1) Metropolitan Statistical Area - see Appendix B for areas included
Source: FBI Uniform Crime Reports, 2006

Hate Crimes

Area	Number of Quarters Reported	Bias Motivation				
		Race	Religion	Sexual Orientation	Ethnicity	Disability
City	4	0	0	0	0	0

Source: Federal Bureau of Investigation, Hate Crime Statistics 2006

RECREATION

Culture

Dance[1]	Theatre[1]	Instrumental Music[1]	Vocal Music[1]	Series/ Festivals	Museums	Zoos and Aquariums[2]
0	0	0	0	0	0	0

Note: (1) Number of professional perfoming groups; (2) AZA-accredited
Source: The Grey House Performing Arts Directory, 2007; Official Museum Directory, 2008; Association of Zoos & Aquariums, AZA Member Zoos & Aquariums, June 2008

Professional Sports Teams

Team Name	League
Columbus Crew	Major League Soccer (MLS)
Columbus Blue Jackets	National Hockey League (NHL)

Note: Includes teams located in the Columbus metro area.
Source: Original research

MEDIA

Newspapers

Name	News Focus	Frequency	Circulation
No newspapers have an office in the city			

Note: Includes newspapers with offices located in the city
Source: MediaContactsPro, March 2008

Television Stations

Name	Ch.	Network(s)	Type	Ownership
WCMH	4	NBC	Commercial	General Electric Corporation
WSYX	6	Fox/ABC	Commercial	Sinclair Broadcast Group
WBNS	10	CBS	Commercial	Dispatch Broadcast Group
WTTE	28	ABC	Commercial	Sinclair Broadcast Group
WOSU	34	PBS	Public	Ohio State University
WPBO	42	PBS	Public	Ohio State University
WSFJ	51	Pax/NBC	Commercial	Christian Television Network
WWHO	53	WBN/UPN	Commercial	Paramount Stations Group

Note: Stations included cover the Columbus DMA (Designated Market Area)
BurrellesLuce, MediaContacts Online, January 2007

Major AM Radio Stations

Call Letters	Freq. (kHz)	Station Type	Target Audience	Station Format	Music Format
WTVN	610	Commercial	General	Talk	n/a
WXIC	660	Commercial	General/Rel/Senior	Educational/Music/Talk	Gospel
WHTH	790	Commercial	General	Talk	n/a
WOSU	820	College	General	Talk	n/a
WRFD	880	Commercial	General/Men	News/Talk	n/a
WMNI	920	Commercial	General	Music	Adult Standards
WCHO	1250	Commercial	General	Music/News/Sports/Talk	Adult Standards
WILE	1270	n/a	General	News/Talk	n/a
WUCO	1270	Commercial	General	Music	Country
WMVO	1300	Commercial	General	News/Talk	n/a
WLOH	1320	n/a	General	Music/News/Sports	n/a
WCHI	1350	Commercial	General	Music	Adult Standards
WCLT	1430	Commercial	General	News/Sports/Talk	n/a
WBNS	1460	Commercial	General/Men	News/Sports	n/a
WMRN	1490	Commercial	General	Music/News/Sports/Talk	Oldies
WBEX	1490	Commercial	General	News/Sports	n/a
WLGN	1510	Commercial	General	Music/News/Sports	Country
WBCO	1540	Commercial	General	Educational/Music/Talk	Oldies
WTNS	1560	Commercial	General	Music/News	Country
WVKO	1580	Commercial	Black/General/Rel	Music	Rhythm & Blues

Note: Stations included cover the Columbus DMA (Designated Market Area); n/a not available
Source: BurrellesLuce, MediaContacts Online, January 2007

Major FM Radio Stations

Call Letters	Freq. (mHz)	Station Type	Target Audience	Station Format	Music Format
WOSU	89.7	College	General	Music	Classical
WCBE	90.5	Public	General	Educational/Music	Jazz
WOSB	91.1	College	General	Music/News/Talk	Classical
WOSP	91.5	College	General	Music/News/Talk	Classical
WKCO	91.9	College	General	Music/News/Sports	Rhythm & Blues
WCOL	92.3	Commercial	General	Music/News/Talk	Country
WKKJ	93.3	Commercial	General	Music/Sports	Country
WQIO	93.7	Commercial	General	Music/News/Sports	Adult Contemp.
WSNY	94.7	Commercial	General	Music/News	Adult Contemp.
WHOK	95.5	Commercial	General	Music/News	Country
WLVQ	96.3	Commercial	General	Music	Classic Rock
WBNS	97.1	Commercial	General	Music/Sports	Adult Contemp.
WNCI	97.9	Commercial	General	Music/News/Talk	Top 40
WTNS	99.3	Commercial	General	Music/Sports/Talk	Top 40
WBZX	99.7	Commercial	General	Music/News	Modern Rock
WXZQ	100.1	n/a	General	Music	n/a
WCLT	100.3	Commercial	General	Music/News	Country
WWCD	101.1	Commercial	General	Music/Sports	Alternative
WEGE	103.9	Commercial	General	Music	Classic Rock
WJZK	104.3	Commercial	General	Music	Jazz
WCVO	104.9	Non-Comm	General/Religious	Music/Talk	Christian
WWJM	105.9	Commercial	General	Music	Adult Contemp.
WJYD	106.3	Commercial	General/Religious	Music/News	Gospel
WMRN	106.9	Commercial	General	Music/News	Country
WCKX	107.5	Commercial	General	Music/News	Urban Contemp.
WBZW	107.7	Commercial	General	Music	Top 40
WODB	107.9	Commercial	General	Music/News/Talk	Oldies

Note: Stations included cover the Columbus DMA (Designated Market Area); n/a not available
BurrellesLuce, MediaContacts Online, January 2007

CLIMATE

Average and Extreme Temperatures

Temperature	Jan	Feb	Mar	Apr	May	Jun	Jul	Aug	Sep	Oct	Nov	Dec	Yr.
Extreme High (°F)	74	73	82	89	93	101	104	101	100	90	80	76	104
Average High (°F)	36	39	50	62	73	82	85	83	77	65	51	40	62
Average Temp. (°F)	28	31	41	52	62	70	74	73	66	54	43	32	52
Average Low (°F)	20	22	31	40	50	59	63	62	55	43	34	24	42
Extreme Low (°F)	-19	-13	-6	14	25	35	43	39	31	17	-4	-17	-19

Note: Figures cover the years 1948-1990
Source: National Climatic Data Center, International Station Meteorological Climate Summary, 9/96

Average Precipitation/Snowfall/Humidity

Precip./Humidity	Jan	Feb	Mar	Apr	May	Jun	Jul	Aug	Sep	Oct	Nov	Dec	Yr.
Avg. Precip. (in.)	2.8	2.4	3.1	3.3	3.9	4.0	4.3	3.3	2.7	2.1	3.0	2.8	37.9
Avg. Snowfall (in.)	8	6	5	1	Tr	0	0	0	Tr	Tr	2	6	28
Avg. Rel. Hum. 7am (%)	78	78	76	76	79	81	84	87	87	83	80	79	81
Avg. Rel. Hum. 4pm (%)	66	62	55	51	52	53	53	54	53	53	61	68	57

Note: Figures cover the years 1948-1990; Tr = Trace amounts (<0.05 in. of rain; <0.5 in. of snow)
Source: National Climatic Data Center, International Station Meteorological Climate Summary, 9/96

Weather Conditions

Temperature			Daytime Sky			Precipitation		
5°F & below	32°F & below	90°F & above	Clear	Partly cloudy	Cloudy	0.01 inch or more precip.	0.1 inch or more snow/ice	Thunder-storms
10	118	19	72	137	156	136	29	40

Note: Figures are average number of days per year and cover the years 1948-1990
Source: National Climatic Data Center, International Station Meteorological Climate Summary, 9/96

HAZARDOUS WASTE

Superfund Sites

Hilliard has no sites on the EPA's Superfund Final National Priorities List.
U.S. Environmental Protection Agency, Final National Priorities List, June 23, 2008

AIR & WATER QUALITY

Air Quality Index

Area	Percent of Days when Air Quality was...[2]				AQI Statistics	
	Good	Moderate	Unhealthy for Sensitive Groups	Unhealthy	Maximum	Median
MSA[1]	64.9	26.8	8.2	0.0	147	42

Note: The Air Quality Index (AQI) is an index for reporting daily air quality. EPA calculates the AQI for five major air pollutants regulated by the Clean Air Act: ground-level ozone, particle pollution (also known as particulate matter), carbon monoxide, sulfur dioxide, and nitrogen dioxide. The AQI runs from 0 to 500. The higher the AQI value, the greater the level of air pollution and the greater the health concern. There are six AQI categories: "Good" The AQI is between 0 and 50. Air quality is considered satisfactory; "Moderate" The AQI is between 51 and 100. Air quality is acceptable; "Unhealthy for Sensitive Groups" When AQI values are between 101 and 150, members of sensitive groups may experience health effects; "Unhealthy" When AQI values are between 151 and 200 everyone may begin to experience health effects; "Very Unhealthy" AQI values between 201 and 300 trigger a health alert; "Hazardous" AQI values over 300 trigger health warnings of emergency conditions; (1) Metropolitan Statistical Area - see Appendix A for areas included; (2) Based on 365 days with AQI data in 2007.
Source: U.S. Environmental Protection Agency, Air Quality Index Report, 2007

Air Quality Index Pollutants

Area	Percent of Days when AQI Pollutant was...[2]					
	Carbon Monoxide	Nitrogen Dioxide	Ozone	Sulfur Dioxide	Particulate Matter 2.5	Particulate Matter 10
MSA[1]	10.7	0.0	52.1	2.7	18.9	15.6

Note: The Air Quality Index (AQI) is an index for reporting daily air quality. EPA calculates the AQI for five major air pollutants regulated by the Clean Air Act: ground-level ozone, particle pollution (also known as particulate matter), carbon monoxide, sulfur dioxide, and nitrogen dioxide. The AQI runs from 0 to 500. The higher the AQI value, the greater the level of air pollution and the greater the health concern; (1) Metropolitan Statistical Area - see Appendix A for areas included; (2) Based on 365 days with AQI data in 2007.
Source: U.S. Environmental Protection Agency, Air Quality Index Report, 2007

Air Quality Index Trends

Area	Trend Sites (7)								All Sites (30)
	1999	2000	2001	2002	2003	2004	2005	2006	2006
MSA[1]	24	12	14	21	9	1	8	1	3

Note: An AQI value greater than 100 indicates that air quality would have been in the unhealthful range on that day. Data from exceptional events are not included. These counts are presented in two ways. First, the counts are based on sites having an adequate record of monitoring data during the trend period (trend sites). These counts represent the relative change in the number of days with AQI values greater than 100. In the last column, the counts are based on all sites with data in the most recent year (because it is possible for a site to have data in the most recent year but not enough data to be a trend site); (1) Metropolitan Statistical Area - see Appendix A for areas included.
Source: U.S. Environmental Protection Agency, Office of Air and Radiation, Air Trends, Factbook and Related Information, Air Pollution Trends in Selected Metropolitan Areas 2006

Maximum Air Pollutant Concentrations

	Particulate Matter 10 (ug/m^3)	Particulate Matter 2.5 (ug/m^3)	Ozone (ppm)	Carbon Monoxide (ppm)	Sulfur Dioxide (ppm)	Nitrogen Dioxide (ppm)	Lead (ug/m^3)
MSA[1] Level	64	34	0.094	2	0.011	n/a	0.01 (a)
NAAQS[2]	150	35	0.125	9	0.140	0.053	1.50
Met NAAQS[2]	Yes	Yes	Yes	Yes	Yes	n/a	Yes

Note: Data from exceptional events are not included; (1) Metropolitan Statistical Area - see Appendix A for areas included; (2) National Ambient Air Quality Standards; n/a not available; (a) Localized impact from an industrial source in Columbus
Concentrations: Particulate Matter 10 (coarse particulate) - highest second maximum 24-hour concentration; Particulate Matter 2.5 (fine particulate) - highest 98th percentile 24-hour concentration; Ozone - highest second daily maximum 1-hour concentration; Carbon Monoxide - highest second maximum non-overlapping 8-hour concentration; Sulfur Dioxide - highest second maximum 24-hour concentration; Nitrogen Dioxide - highest arithmetic mean concentration; Lead - highest quarterly maximum concentration
Units: ppm = parts per million; ug/m^3 = micrograms per cubic meter
Source: U.S. Environmental Protection Agency, MSA Factbook 2006, Air Quality Statistics by City

Drinking Water

Water System Name	Pop. Served	Primary Water Source Type	Violations[1]	
			Health Based	Monitoring/ Reporting
Columbus Public Water System	983,264	Surface	1	0

Note: (1) Based on violation data from January 1, 2007 to December 31, 2007 (includes unresolved violations from earlier years)
Source: U.S. Environmental Protection Agency, Office of Ground Water and Drinking Water, Safe Drinking Water Information System (based on data extracted April 15, 2008)

Stow, Ohio

Background

Stow is located eight miles northeast of Akron and 30 miles southeast of downtown Cleveland. The third-largest city in Summit County, Stow lies between Silver Lake and Sugar Bush Knolls along Highway 91, near Kent State University. The city has grown substantially over the past 30 years, with five parks and many new homes constructed to accommodate the burgeoning populace.

In addition to being the polymer research and development center of the U.S. — giving rise to its moniker "Polymer Valley" — the area is home to many manufacturers in diverse industries such as aerospace, metals, plastics, and chemicals.

Approximately 500 Native Americans lived along the banks of the Cuyahoga River and Silver Lake during the War of 1812, and though their relationship with Stow residents appears to have been peaceful, the Native Americans left to fight with the British, believing that if the British won, they would be able to reclaim their land. The area contributed several soldiers to the war, and many more to the Union Army during the Civil War. Stow was established in 1958 as a village and as a city in 1960.

Stow has large and well-planned areas dedicated to light and heavy manufacturing, and the city is committed to the retention of businesses. The city established an Enterprise Zone under the State of Ohio Enterprise Program to offer real and personal property tax abatements so that businesses can expand. The city has been designated a Business Friendly community by the Greater Akron Chamber and Cleveland Growth Association, the only city in Summit County to receive this distinction.

The top employers include MACTAC, Matco Tools Corporation, National Machine Company, Wrayco Industries Inc., Audio Technica U.S. Inc, Wheeler Boyce Company, Centimark Corporation, Ferry Industries, Esterle Mold & Machine Co., and Wilkinson Hi-Rise.

Transportation facilities are excellent, as Stow is located within seven miles of the Ohio Turnpike. Akron-Canton Airport is located less than 20 miles south of the city, near Akron, and the Cleveland Hopkins International Airport is approximately 30 miles northwest of the city.

Stow-Munroe Falls City School District serves over 6,000 students in nine schools. Reflecting the region's fame as the nation's polymer R&D center, Stow-Munroe Falls City schools offer a Manufacturing & Preengineering Academy that exposes students to four high-skilled technical occupations — electronics, polymers, machining, and computer-aided design; successful participants are guaranteed admission into the Community and Technical College of the University of Akron or Cuyahoga Community College. Other colleges and universities in the area include the University of Akron, Kent State University — and a bit farther away in Cleveland — Cleveland State University, Cleveland Institute of Art, and Cleveland Institute of Music, out of many, many more.

Stow maintains facilities for swimming, tennis, basketball, picnicking, baseball, and boating. Akron is home to Akron Zoological Park, with over 300 animals, birds and reptiles; the Akron Art Museum, featuring regional, national and international art and photography from 1850 to the present; and the Akron Civic Theatre, showing movies, concerts, and live theater. Other attractions in the area are Cedar Point Amusement Park, Cleveland Museum of Art, Hale Farm & Village, the Rock and Roll Hall of Fame, and Six Flags Ohio.

Hospitals and medical centers in the are include Cuyahoga Falls General Hospital and Sempercare Hospital of Akron. Akron General Hospital has recently embarked on the construction of a new Wellness Center in Stow. This 176,000 square feet facility employs 250-300 employees.

The weather in Stow is influenced considerably by Lake Erie, tempering cold air masses during the late fall and early winter, as well as bringing brief and heavy snow squalls. Springs arrive late; summers are moderately warm and humid. Fall is generally pleasant.

Rankings

General Rankings

- Akron* was ranked #298 out of 375 metro areas in *Cities Ranked & Rated*. Criteria: cost of living; climate; crime; transportation; economy and jobs; education; arts and culture; health and healthcare; leisure; quality of life. *Cities Ranked & Rated, 2nd Edition, 2007*
- Akron* was ranked #59 out of 379 metro areas in *Places Rated Almanac*. Criteria: health care; education; recreation; transportation; ambience; climate; crime; housing costs; jobs. *Places Rated Almanac, 7th Edition, 2007*

Business/Finance Rankings

- The nation's 100 largest metro areas were analysed in terms of the percentage of households entering some stage of foreclosure in 2007. The Akron* metro area ranked #12 out of 100 (#1 = highest foreclosure rate). *RealtyTrac, "Year-End 2007 Metropolitan Foreclosure Report"*
- Akron* was selected as one of the best places to start and grow a company by *Entrepreneur* and the National Policy Research Council. The Akron* metro area ranked #23 out of 50 large metro areas. Criteria: business formation and growth (firms started four to 14 years ago that still employ at least 5 people and experienced rapid growth over the last four years). *Entrepreneur/National Policy Research Council, "Hot Cities for Entrepreneurs," September 2006*
- Akron* was cited as one of America's top mid-size metros (population 200,000 to 1 million) for new and expanded facility projects in 2007. The area appeared in the top 10 with 29 projects. *Site Selection, "Top Metropolitan Area Awards," March 2008*
- Intel, in partnership with Sperling's BestPlaces, ranked the 80 "Best Cities for Teleworking" in America. The Akron* metro area ranked #4 among small metro areas. The study identifies cities that hold the greatest potential for teleworking based on a host of factors including typical commuting times, fuel prices, availability of broadband Internet access and percentage of the population in telework friendly jobs. The study also factored in extreme climate and natural hazards. *Intel, "Best Cities for Teleworking," March 30, 2006*
- The Akron* metro area appeared on the Milken Institute "2007 Best Performing Cities" index. Rank: #155 out of 200 large metro areas. Criteria: job growth; wage and salary growth; high-tech output growth. *Milken Institute, "2007 Best Performing Cities"*
- Akron* was identified as one of the 100 "Most Unwired Cities" in the U.S. The area ranked #78 out of the 100 largest metro areas in the U.S. Criteria: number of public and commercial wireless access points (hotspots); airports with wireless Internet access; broadband availability; local wireless networks; and wireless email devices. *Intel, "Most Unwired Cities Survey," June 7, 2005*
- *Forbes* ranked the 200 most populous metro areas in the U.S. in terms of the "Best Places for Business and Careers." The Akron* metro area was ranked #135. Criteria: business costs (labor, energy, tax and office space expenses); living costs (housing, transportation, food and other household expenditures); education levels of the work force; job growth; income growth; migration trends; crime rates; and culture/leisure. *Forbes, "Best Places for Business and Careers," March 19, 2008*
- *Fortune* ranked the 100 largest metro areas in the U.S. in terms of projected median home price change in 2007. The Akron* metro area ranked #25. *Fortune.com, "Hot Spots, Cold Spots"*

Health/Environment Rankings

- 100 of the largest metro areas in the U.S. were analyzed in terms of their current drought severity. The Akron* metro area ranked #79 (#1 = driest). The rankings were based on statistics such as long-term precipitation trends and patterns and the Palmer drought indices. *Sperling's BestPlaces, www.BestPlaces.net, "America's Drought-Riskiest Cities," November 2007*

- The Akron* metro area appeared in *Country Home's* "2008 Best Green Places" report. The area ranked #336 out of 379. Criteria: official energy policies; green power; green buildings; availability of fresh, locally grown food. *Country Home, "2008 Best Green Places"*

- Ortho-McNeil Neurologics, in partnership with Sperling's BestPlaces, analyzed 110 metro areas and identified those U.S. cities with the highest prevalence of factors that are most commonly associated with migraine headaches. The Akron* metro area ranked #43. Criteria: number of migraine-related drug prescriptions per capita; lifestyle factors that can contribute to migraines; environmental factors that can trigger migraines; and consumption of migraine-triggering foods. *Ortho-McNeil Neurologics, "America's Migraine Hot Spots," March 14, 2006*

- Sperling's BestPlaces ranked 331 metro areas and identified the most and least stressful U.S. cities. The Akron* metro area ranked #73 out of the 100 largest metro areas (#1 = most stressful). Criteria: divorce rate; unemployment rate; violent and property crime; suicide rate; commute time; mental health; alcohol consumption; cloudy days. *Sperling's BestPlaces, www.BestPlaces.net, "America's Most (and Least) Stressful Cities," January 9, 2004*

Women/Minorities Rankings

- Akron* was ranked #88 out of 100 metro areas in *SELF Magazine's* ranking of "America's Best Places for Women." A panel of experts came up with more than 50 criteria including death and disease rates, environmental indicators, community resources, and lifestyle habits. *SELF Magazine, "America's Best Places for Women 2007," December 2007*

Seniors/Retirement Rankings

- A.G. Edwards ranked America's 500 top-performing communities based on their residents' personal savings and investing behavior. The Akron* metro area ranked #229 with an index score of 102.15 (national average = 100.00). A dozen statistical factors were measured including: participation in retirement savings plans; personal debt levels; and home ownership. *A.G. Edwards, "2007 Nest Egg Index", September 12, 2007*

Children/Family Rankings

- The Akron* metro area was selected as one of the "Best Cities for Relocating Families" by Worldwide ERC and Primacy Relocation. The 2007 study placed a special emphasis on the housing market, which has significantly impacted the relocation industry and an employer's ability to transfer employees. The variables which weigh heavily in this category include home price, home affordability index, appreciation rates, and property tax. Other criteria include cost of living, crime rates, education, climate, focus on diversity, physicians per capita, recreation and leisure, arts and culture, air quality, watershed quality, sales tax, unemployment rate, job growth, high school and higher education index, school expenditures per student, students in public school, SAT/ACT percentile, and population growth. *Worldwide ERC and Primacy Relocation, "2007 Best Cities for Relocating Families"*

Safety Rankings

- The National Insurance Crime Bureau ranked 361 metro areas in the U.S. in terms of per capita rates of vehicle theft. The Akron* metro area ranked #165 (#1 = highest rate). Criteria: number of vehicle theft offenses per 100,000 inhabitants. *National Insurance Crime Bureau, "NICB Vehicle Theft Study," April 22, 2008*

- Farmers Insurance Group of Companies, in partnership with Sperling's BestPlaces, ranked 379 metro areas and identified the "Most Secure U.S. Place to Live." The Akron* metro area ranked #32 out of 114 in the large metro area category (500,000 or more residents). Criteria: crime rates; extreme weather; risk of natural disasters; environmental hazards; terrorism threats; air quality; life expectancy; job loss numbers. *Farmers Insurance Group, "Most Secure U.S. Places to Live 2007"*

- Akron* was identified as one of the most dangerous large metro areas for pedestrians in the U.S. The area ranked #48 out of the nations 50 largest metro areas. Criteria: average yearly pedestrian fatalities per capita (for the years 2002 and 2003) adjusted for the number of walkers. *Surface Transportation Policy Project, "Mean Streets 2004"*

Sports/Recreation Rankings

- The Akron* metro area appeared on the *Sporting News* list of the "Best Sports Cities 2007". The area ranked #106 out of 150 cities in the U.S. *Sporting News* takes a 12-month snapshot, roughly July to July, of each city's sports, putting a heavy premium on regular-season won-lost records (from the most recently completed season). Other criteria include: playoff berths, bowl appearances and tournament bids; championships; applicable power ratings; quality of competition; overall fan fervor as measured in part by attendance as percentage of venue capacity; abundance of teams (rewarding quality over quantity); stadium and arena quality; ticket availability and prices; franchise ownership; and marquee appeal of athletes. *SportingNews.com, "Best Sports Cities 2007," August 1, 2007*

- *Golf Digest* ranked 330 metro areas in the U.S. in terms of golf. The Akron* metro area was ranked #158. Criteria: access to golf; weather; value of golf; and quality of golf. *Golf Digest, "Metro Golf Rankings," August 2005*

Dating/Romance Rankings

- The Akron* metro area was selected as one of the "Best Cities for Relocating Singles" by Worldwide ERC and Primacy Relocation. The area ranked #58 out of the 100 largest metro areas in the U.S. Areas were selected based on the following criteria: a robust cost-of-living index; adventure and outdoor recreation opportunities; violent crime and property crime rates; percentage of the population that is unmarried (ages 25-34); ratio of single men and single women; affordability of quality higher education, including in-state and out-of-state tuition requirements and rates; number of newcomers to the area; commute times; tax rates; fee and occupancy rates for temporary housing and mini-storage; quality and quantity of collegiate and professional sporting events and fun, fan-friendly venues. *Worldwide ERC and Primacy Relocation, "2007 Best Cities for Relocating Singles," October 25, 2007*

- Sperling's BestPlaces in partnership with AXE Deodorant Bodyspray ranked 80 metro areas and identified "America's Best (and Worst) Cities for Dating." The Akron* metro area ranked #25 (#1 = best). Criteria: percentage of singles ages 18-24; population density; dating venues per capita. *AXE Deodorant Bodyspray, "America's Best (and Worst) Cities for Dating," May 2004*

Miscellaneous Rankings

- Scarborough Research, a leading market research firm, identified the top local markets for grocery coupon use. The Akron* DMA (Designated Market Area) ranked in the top 25 with 40% of consumers reporting that they use grocery coupons at least once per week. *Scarborough Research, December 8, 2004*

- A study by Sperling's BestPlaces examined which U.S. metro areas were most affected by high fuel prices in 2006. The Akron* metro area was ranked #65 out of 80 (#1 = most expensive city for driving). Rankings are based on the average dollars spent on gas per year by two driver households. Criteria: cost of regular-grade gasoline; average miles driven per day; average number of gallons each driver uses and wastes in traffic congestion each day. *Sperling's BestPlaces, www.bestplaces.net, "Pain at the Pump," May 18, 2006*

Stow is located within the Akron, OH Metropolitan Statistical Area.

Business Environment

CITY FINANCES

City Government Finances

Component	2004-2005 ($000)	2004-2005 ($ per capita)
Total Revenues	30,686	892
Total Expenditures	33,980	988
Debt Outstanding	6,100	177
Cash and Securities	14,046	408

Source: U.S Census Bureau, Government Finances 2004-2005

City Government Revenue by Source

Source	2004-2005 ($000)	2004-2005 ($ per capita)
General Revenue		
From Federal Government	111	3
From State Government	5,258	153
From Local Governments	0	0
Taxes		
Property	6,616	192
Sales	0	0
Personal Income	11,353	330
License	818	24
Charges	1,010	29
Liquor Store	0	0
Utility	4,404	128
Employee Retirement	0	0
Other	1,116	32

Source: U.S Census Bureau, Government Finances 2004-2005

City Government Expenditures by Function

Function	2004-2005 ($000)	2004-2005 ($ per capita)	2004-2005 (%)
General Expenditures			
Airports	0	0	0.0
Corrections	0	0	0.0
Education	0	0	0.0
Fire Protection	7,704	224	22.7
Governmental Administration	5,122	149	15.1
Health	1,070	31	3.1
Highways	3,332	97	9.8
Hospitals	0	0	0.0
Housing and Community Development	1,223	36	3.6
Interest on General Debt	222	6	0.7
Libraries	0	0	0.0
Parking	0	0	0.0
Parks and Recreation	1,809	53	5.3
Police Protection	3,202	93	9.4
Public Welfare	0	0	0.0
Sewerage	22	1	0.1
Solid Waste Management	58	2	0.2
Liquor Store	0	0	0.0
Utility	3,485	101	10.3
Employee Retirement	0	0	0.0
Other	6,731	196	19.8

Source: U.S Census Bureau, Government Finances 2004-2005

Municipal Bond Ratings

Area	Moody's
City	Aaa

Source: Mergent Bond Record, January 2008 (unless noted otherwise)

DEMOGRAPHICS

Population Growth

Area	1990 Census	2000 Census	2007 Estimate	2012 Projection	Population Growth (%)	
					1990-2000	2000-2012
City	27,702	32,139	34,687	36,200	16.0	12.6
MSA[1]	657,575	694,960	703,447	706,262	5.7	1.6
U.S.	248,709,873	281,421,906	301,045,522	314,920,978	13.2	11.9

Note: (1) Metropolitan Statistical Area - see Appendix B for areas included
Source: Claritas, Inc.

Number of Households and Average Household Size

Area	2007 Estimate	2007 Average Household Size
City	13,485	2.57
MSA[1]	282,029	2.49
U.S.	113,668,003	2.65

Note: (1) Metropolitan Statistical Area - see Appendix B for areas included
Source: Claritas, Inc.

Race and Ethnicity

Area	White Alone[2]	Black Alone[2]	Asian Alone[2]	Other Race Alone[2]	Hispanic[3]
City	94.1	1.9	2.3	1.7	1.2
MSA[1]	84.5	11.7	1.6	2.2	1.1
U.S.	73.1	12.4	4.3	10.3	14.9

Note: Figures are 2007 estimates; (1) Metropolitan Statistical Area - see Appendix B for areas included (2) Alone is defined as not being in combination with one or more other races; (3) May be of any race.
Source: Claritas, Inc.

Ancestry

Area	German	Irish[2]	English	American	Italian	Polish	French[3]	Scottish
City	29.7	17.7	14.3	4.3	12.0	6.5	3.3	2.8
MSA[1]	24.5	14.3	10.7	6.6	9.0	4.9	2.4	2.1
U.S.	15.2	10.9	8.7	7.3	5.6	3.2	3.0	1.7

Note: Figures include multiple ancestry (e.g. if a person reported being Irish and Italian, they were included in both columns); (1) Metropolitan Statistical Area - see Appendix A for areas included; (2) Includes Celtic; (3) Includes Alsatian but excludes Basque
Source: Census 2000, Summary File 3

Foreign-Born Population

Area	Percent of Population Born in							
	Any Foreign Country	Europe	Asia	Africa	Oceania[2]	Canada	Mexico	Latin America[3]
City	3.7	1.2	1.9	0.1	0.0	0.2	0.1	0.2
MSA[1]	3.0	1.3	1.2	0.1	0.0	0.2	0.1	0.2
U.S.	11.1	1.7	2.9	0.3	0.1	0.3	3.3	2.5

Note: (1) Metropolitan Statistical Area - see Appendix A for areas included; (2) Includes Australia, New Zealand subregion, Melanesia, Micronesia, Polynesia, and Oceania n.e.c; (3) Includes Central America (excluding Mexico), South America, and the Caribbean.
Source: Census 2000, Summary File 3

Marriage Status

Area	Never Married	Now Married (excluding Separated)	Separated	Widowed	Divorced
City	21.8	63.0	0.5	5.5	9.3
MSA[1]	26.8	54.1	1.3	6.9	10.9
U.S.	27.1	54.4	2.2	6.6	9.7

Note: Figures are percentages and cover the population 15 years of age and older; (1) Metropolitan Statistical Area - see Appendix A for areas included
Source: Census 2000, Summary File 3

Age Distribution

Area	Percent of Population						
	Under Age 5	Age 5 to 17	Age 18 to 34	Age 35 to 49	Age 50 to 64	Age 65 to 79	80 Years and Over
City	6.6	19.5	21.0	25.8	15.3	8.5	3.4
MSA[1]	6.5	18.3	22.7	23.8	15.3	10.1	3.3
U.S.	6.8	18.9	23.7	23.5	14.8	9.2	3.2

Note: (1) Metropolitan Statistical Area - see Appendix A for areas included
Source: Census 2000, Summary File 3

Male/Female Ratio

Area	Males	Females	Males per 100 Females
City	16,808	17,879	94.0
MSA[1]	340,261	363,186	93.7
U.S.	148,320,305	152,725,217	97.1

Note: Figures are 2007 estimates; (1) Metropolitan Statistical Area - see Appendix B for areas included
Source: Claritas, Inc.

Religion

Area	Catholic	Southern Baptist	United Meth-odist	ELCA[1]	LDS[2]	Presby-terian Church USA	Jewish Est.	Muslim Est.
County	22.4	0.3	3.9	1.3	0.3	1.1	0.7	0.0
U.S.	22.0	7.1	3.7	1.8	1.5	1.1	2.2	0.6

Note: Figures are the number of adherents as a percentage of the total population; Adherents are defined as all members, including full members, their children and the estimated number of other participants who are not considered members (e.g. the baptized, those not confirmed, those regularly attending services, etc.); (1) Evangelical Lutheran Church in America; (2) The Church of Jesus Christ of Latter Day Saints
Source: Reprinted with permission from Religious Congregations and Membership in the United States 2000 (Nashville, Glenmary Research Center, 2002) Copyright Association of Statisticians of American Religious Bodies. All rights reserved.

ECONOMY

Gross Metropolitan Product

Area	2002	2003	2004	2005	2005 Rank[2]
MSA[1]	22.8	24.1	25.7	27.1	71

Note: Figures are in billions of dollars; (1) Akron, OH Metropolitan Statistical Area - see Appendix A for areas included; (2) Rank ranges from 1 to 361
Source: The U.S. Conference of Mayors, "U.S. Metro Economies: GMP - The Engines of America's Growth," January 2007

Economic Growth

Area	1995 GMP	2005 GMP	Average Annual Growth Rate	Growth Rate Rank[2]
MSA[1]	17.6	27.1	4.4	282

Note: Figures are in billions of dollars; GMP = Gross Metropolitan Product; (1) Akron, OH Metropolitan Statistical Area - see Appendix A for areas included; (2) Rank ranges from 1 to 361
Source: The U.S. Conference of Mayors, "U.S. Metro Economies: GMP - The Engines of America's Growth," January 2007

INCOME

Per Capita/Median/Average Income

Area	Per Capita ($)	Median Household ($)	Average Household ($)
City	29,949	65,252	76,185
MSA[1]	26,172	49,020	64,123
U.S.	25,495	49,280	66,670

Note: Figures are 2007 estimates; (1) Metropolitan Statistical Area - see Appendix B for areas included
Source: Claritas, Inc.

Household Income Distribution

Area	Percent of Households Earning							
	Under $15,000	$15,000 -24,999	$25,000 -34,999	$35,000 -49,999	$50,000 -74,999	$75,000 -99,000	$100,000 -149,999	$150,000 and up
City	7.2	6.4	7.1	14.8	23.7	17.6	16.0	7.2
MSA[1]	12.5	10.9	11.4	16.2	20.6	12.3	10.6	5.5
U.S.	13.1	10.9	11.2	15.6	19.5	11.9	11.3	6.6

Note: Figures are 2007 estimates; (1) Metropolitan Statistical Area - see Appendix B for areas included
Source: Claritas, Inc.

Poverty Rates by Age

Area	All Ages	Under 5 Years Old	5 to 17 Years Old	18 to 64 Years Old	65 Years and Over
City	4.0	0.1	0.9	2.3	0.6
MSA[1]	9.8	1.1	2.3	5.6	0.9
U.S.	12.4	1.2	3.0	6.9	1.2

Note: Figures are percent of population with income in 1999 below poverty level and only include population for whom poverty status is determined; (1) Metropolitan Statistical Area - see Appendix A for areas included
Source: Census 2000, Summary File 3

Personal Bankruptcy Filing Rate

Area	2004	2005	2006
Summit County	8.53	13.63	3.51
U.S.	5.31	6.82	2.00

Note: Numbers are per 1,000 population and include Chapter 7 and Chapter 13 filings
Source: Federal Deposit Insurance Corporation (FDIC), Regional Economic Conditions (RECON), 8/23/2007

EMPLOYMENT

Labor Force and Employment

Area	Civilian Labor Force			Workers Employed		
	Dec. 2006	Dec. 2007	% Chg.	Dec. 2006	Dec. 2007	% Chg.
City	20,074	20,175	0.5	19,271	19,229	-0.2
MSA[1]	389,238	390,380	0.3	369,201	368,396	-0.2
U.S.	152,571,000	153,705,000	0.7	146,081,000	146,334,000	0.2

Note: Data is not seasonally adjusted and covers workers 16 years of age and older;
(1) Metropolitan Statistical Area - see Appendix B for areas included
Source: Bureau of Labor Statistics, http://stats.bls.gov

Unemployment Rate

Area	2007											
	Jan.	Feb.	Mar.	Apr.	May	Jun.	Jul.	Aug.	Sep.	Oct.	Nov.	Dec.
City	4.7	4.5	4.3	4.3	4.2	4.8	4.6	4.4	4.5	4.4	4.2	4.7
MSA[1]	6.0	5.8	5.5	5.5	5.1	5.6	5.3	5.2	5.2	5.0	5.0	5.6
U.S.	5.0	4.9	4.5	4.3	4.3	4.7	4.9	4.6	4.5	4.4	4.5	4.8

Note: Data is not seasonally adjusted and covers workers 16 years of age and older; All figures are percentages; (1) Metropolitan Statistical Area - see Appendix B for areas included
Source: Bureau of Labor Statistics, http://stats.bls.gov

Employment by Occupation

Occupation Classification	City (%)	MSA[1] (%)	U.S. (%)
Sales and Office	27.2	27.8	26.7
Professional and Related	26.5	19.3	20.2
Service	11.9	14.6	14.9
Production, Transportation, and Material Moving	12.5	17.3	14.6
Management, Business, and Financial	15.8	12.7	13.5
Construction, Extraction, and Maintenance	6.1	8.3	9.4
Farming, Forestry, and Fishing	0.0	0.2	0.7

Note: Figures cover employed civilians 16 years of age and older;
(1) Metropolitan Statistical Area - see Appendix A for areas included
Source: Census 2000, Summary File 3

Employment by Industry

Sector	MSA[1] Number of Employees	MSA[1] Percent of Total	U.S. Percent of Total
Government	51,300	14.9	16.3
Education and Health Services	47,700	13.9	13.4
Professional and Business Services	51,300	14.9	13.1
Retail Trade	40,800	11.8	11.6
Manufacturing	46,700	13.6	9.9
Leisure and Hospitality	30,600	8.9	9.6
Financial Activities	13,900	4.0	5.9
Construction	n/a	n/a	5.3
Wholesale Trade	18,400	5.3	4.4
Other Services	13,800	4.0	3.9
Transportation and Utilities	11,000	3.2	3.7
Information	4,500	1.3	2.2
Natural Resources and Mining	n/a	n/a	0.5

Note: Figures cover non-farm employment as of December 2007 and are not seasonally adjusted; (1) Metropolitan Statistical Area - see Appendix B for areas included; n/a not available
Source: Bureau of Labor Statistics, http://stats.bls.gov

Average Wages

Occupation	$/Hr.	Occupation	$/Hr.
Accountants and Auditors	28.21	Maids and Housekeeping Cleaners	8.48
Automotive Mechanics	17.08	Maintenance and Repair Workers	16.84
Bookkeepers	15.07	Marketing Managers	48.33
Carpenters	20.99	Nuclear Medicine Technologists	31.13
Cashiers	8.38	Nurses, Licensed Practical	18.47
Clerks, General Office	11.72	Nurses, Registered	27.23
Clerks, Receptionists/Information	10.79	Nursing Aides/Orderlies/Attendants	11.06
Clerks, Shipping/Receiving	13.13	Packers and Packagers, Hand	10.53
Computer Programmers	30.07	Physical Therapists	34.59
Computer Support Specialists	20.32	Postal Service Mail Carriers	21.47
Computer Systems Analysts	31.58	Real Estate Brokers	24.62
Cooks, Restaurant	9.97	Retail Salespersons	11.54
Dentists	n/a	Sales Reps., Exc. Tech./Scientific	29.35
Electrical Engineers	31.28	Sales Reps., Tech./Scientific	32.23
Electricians	22.70	Secretaries, Exc. Legal/Med./Exec.	13.90
Financial Managers	46.19	Security Guards	11.76
First-Line Supervisors/Mgrs., Sales	18.28	Surgeons	n/a
Food Preparation Workers	9.19	Teacher Assistants	12.60
General and Operations Managers	45.02	Teachers, Elementary School	23.80
Hairdressers/Cosmetologists	10.63	Teachers, Secondary School	26.70
Internists	85.19	Telemarketers	9.74
Janitors and Cleaners	11.94	Truck Drivers, Heavy/Tractor-Trailer	17.98
Landscaping/Groundskeeping Workers	11.04	Truck Drivers, Light/Delivery Svcs.	13.74
Lawyers	49.22	Waiters and Waitresses	8.72

Note: Wage data covers the Akron, OH Metropolitan Statistical Area - see Appendix B for areas included. Hourly wages for elementary/secondary school teachers and teacher assistants were calculated by the editors from annual wage data assuming a 40 hour work week; n/a not available.
Source: Bureau of Labor Statistics, May 2007 Metro Area Occupational Employment and Wage Estimates

RESIDENTIAL REAL ESTATE

Building Permits

Area	Single-Family 2006	Single-Family 2007p	Single-Family Pct. Chg.	Multi-Family 2006	Multi-Family 2007p	Multi-Family Pct. Chg.	Total 2006	Total 2007p	Total Pct. Chg.
City	52	40	-23.1	9	3	-66.7	61	43	-29.5
U.S.	1,378,200	973,300	-29.4	460,700	407,200	-11.6	1,838,900	1,380,500	-24.9

Note: (p) preliminary; figures cover and represent new, privately-owned housing units authorized (unadjusted data); All permit data are based on estimates with imputation; U.S. figures are based on the new 20,000-place series.
Source: U.S. Census Bureau, Manufacturing, Mining, and Construction Statistics

Homeownership and Housing Vacancies

Area	Homeownership Rate[2] (%)			Rental Vacancy Rate[3] (%)			Homeowner Vacancy Rate[4] (%)		
	2005	2006	2007	2005	2006	2007	2005	2006	2007
MSA[1]	78.1	77.1	74.6	9.3	7.7	8.4	2.1	3.2	4.5
U.S.	68.9	68.8	68.1	9.8	9.8	9.7	1.9	2.4	2.7

Note: (1) Metropolitan Statistical Area - see Appendix B for areas included; (2) The proportion of households that are owners; (3) The proportion of the rental inventory that is vacant for rent; (4) The proportion of the homeowner inventory that is vacant for sale; n/a not available
Source: U.S. Census Bureau, Housing Vacancies and Homeownership Annual Statistics: 2007

TAXES

State Corporate Income Tax Rates

State	Rates and Tax Brackets
Ohio	5.1% > $0; 8.5% > 50K

Note: Tax rates as of January 1, 2008; A value added-style tax, the Corporate Activities Tax (CAT) was instituted in 2005. It will be phased in through 2010 while the Corporate Franchise Tax (Ohio's income tax) is phased out. Beginning April 1, 2008 the CAT rate is.208% (80% of.26%). For tax year 2008 companies owe 40% of Corporate Franchise Tax liability.
Source: Tax Foundation, www.taxfoundation.org

State Individual Income Tax Rates

State	Federal Deductibility	Marginal Rates (%)	Standard Deduction ($)		Personal Exemptions ($)[1]	
			Single	Joint	Single	Dependents
Ohio	No	0.649 - 6.555 (y)	n/a	n/a	1,450 (g)(r)	1,450 (g)(r)

Note: Tax rates as of January 1, 2008; Local- and county-level taxes are not included; n/a not applicable; (1) Married joint filers generally receive double the single exemption; (g) Taxpayers receive a $20 tax credit per exemption in addition to the normal exemption amount; (r) State adjusts its bracket levels for inflation at the end of each year before printing tax forms; (y) Brackets are not double for married taxpayers.
Source: Tax Foundation, www.taxfoundation.org

Various State and Local Tax Rates

State and Local Sales and Use (%)	State Sales and Use (%)	Gasoline[1,2] ($/gal.)	Cigarette ($/pack)	Spirits ($/gal.)	Table Wine ($/gal.)	Beer ($/gal.)
6.25	5.5 (h)	0.28	1.25	8.46 (n)	0.32	0.18

Note: Tax rates as of January 1, 2008; (1) In addition to the 18.4 cpg Federal gasoline tax; (2) Rates may include additional state sales taxes, environmental protection and storage fees/taxes, and local taxes. When necessary, the volume-weighted average of all local taxes is used to approximate the typical statewide rate including local tax; (h) Ohio has a GRT that is levied in addition to its 5.5% sales tax. It is called the commercial activity tax (CAT). Firms with receipts over $1 million pay the CAT; firms with receipts between $150K and $1 million pay a minimum tax of $150. The rate i

2008 is 0.156%, and increases are scheduled in law to 0.208% on 4/1/2008 and 0.26% on 4/1/2009. The CAT is being phased in to replace Ohio's Corporate Franchise Tax, which is simultaneously being phased out; (n) The state government controls all sales. The implied excise tax rate is calculated using methodology designed by the Distilled Spirits Council of the United States (DISCUS).
Source: Tax Foundation, www.taxfoundation.org; Original research

State Tax Burdens

Area	Combined State and Local Tax Burden		Combined Federal, State and Local Tax Burden	
	Percent	Rank	Percent	Rank
Ohio	12.4	5	32.4	18
U.S. Average	11.0	-	32.7	-

Note: Figures cover 2007 and measure taxes as a percentage of income
Source: Tax Foundation, www.taxfoundation.org

State Business Tax Climate Index Rankings

State	Overall Rank	Corporate Tax Index Rank	Individual Income Tax Index Rank	Sales Tax Index Rank	Unemployment Insurance Tax Index Rank	Property Tax Index Rank
Ohio	46	37	48	36	11	44

Note: Rankings range from 1 to 50 where 1 is best. Rankings do not average across to Overall Rank. States without a given tax are given a ranking of 1.
Source: Tax Foundation, State Business Tax Climate Index 2008

TRANSPORTATION

Means of Transportation to Work

Area	Car/Truck/Van		Public Transportation			Bicycle	Walked	Other Means	Worked at Home
	Drove Alone	Car-pooled	Bus	Subway	Railroad				
City	89.9	5.6	0.3	0.0	0.0	0.2	0.6	0.5	2.9
MSA[1]	85.4	8.0	1.3	0.0	0.0	0.1	2.0	0.6	2.6
U.S.	75.7	12.2	2.5	1.5	0.5	0.4	2.9	1.0	3.3

Note: Figures are percentages and cover workers 16 years of age and older; (1) Metropolitan Statistical Area - see Appendix A for areas included
Source: Census 2000, Summary File 3

Travel Time to Work

Area	Less Than 15 Minutes	15 to 29 Minutes	30 to 44 Minutes	45 to 59 Minutes	60 Minutes or More
City	27.1	42.0	19.1	7.5	4.3
MSA[1]	30.1	41.0	17.9	6.4	4.6
U.S.	29.4	36.1	19.1	7.4	8.0

Note: Figures are percentages and include workers 16 years old and over; (1) Metropolitan Statistical Area - see Appendix A for areas included
Source: Census 2000, Summary File 3

Travel Time Index

Area	1982	1995	2004	2005
Urban Area[1]	1.02	1.06	1.08	1.07
Average[2]	1.11	1.22	1.29	1.30

Note: Travel Time Index - The ratio of travel time in the peak period to the travel time at free-flow conditions. A value of 1.35 indicates a 20-minute free-flow trip takes 27 minutes in the peak. Free-flow speeds (60 mph on freeways and 35 mph on principal arterials) are used as the comparison threshold; (1) Covers the Akron, OH urban area; (2) average of 85 urban areas
Source: Texas Transportation Institute, The 2007 Urban Mobility Report, September 2007

Living Environment

COST OF LIVING

Cost of Living Index

Composite Index	Groceries	Housing	Utilities	Transportation	Health Care	Misc. Goods/ Services
94.0	98.8	81.7	100.0	101.9	92.4	98.2

Note: U.S. = 100; Figures cover the Akron OH urban area.
Source: The Council for Community and Economic Research (formerly ACCRA), Cost of Living Index, 2007

Grocery Prices

Area[1]	T-Bone Steak ($/pound)	Frying Chicken ($/pound)	Whole Milk ($/half gal.)	Eggs ($/dozen)	Orange Juice ($/64 oz.)	Coffee ($/11.5 oz.)
City[2]	8.89	1.37	1.98	1.13	3.10	3.24
Avg.	8.93	1.12	2.13	1.52	3.26	3.31
Min.	5.88	0.71	1.33	0.83	2.30	2.20
Max.	12.80	2.07	3.43	3.54	5.79	6.20

Note: (1) Values for the local area are compared with the average, minimum and maximum values for all 331 areas in the Cost of Living Index report; (2) Figures cover the Akron OH urban area; **T-Bone Steak** *(price per pound);* **Frying Chicken** *(price per pound, whole fryer);* **Whole Milk** *(half gallon carton);* **Eggs** *(price per dozen, Grade A, large);* **Orange Juice** *(64 oz. Tropicana or Florida Natural);* **Coffee** *(11.5 oz. can, vacuum-packed, Maxwell House, Hills Bros, or Folgers).*
Source: The Council for Community and Economic Research (formerly ACCRA), Cost of Living Index, 2007

Housing and Utility Costs

Area[1]	New Home Price ($)	Apartment Rent ($/month)	All Electric ($/month)	Part Electric ($/month)	Other Energy ($/month)	Telephone ($/month)
City[2]	246,770	699	-	82.72	92.62	22.98
Avg.	309,605	782	146.13	78.67	90.16	26.14
Min.	189,877	n/a	82.03	37.41	33.15	17.08
Max.	1,202,800	3,481	271.14	150.60	257.67	37.45

Note: (1) Values for the local area are compared with the average, minimum and maximum values for all 331 areas in the Cost of Living Index report; (2) Figures cover the Akron OH urban area; **New Home Price** *(2,400 sf living area, 8,000 sf lot, in urban area with full utilities);* **Apartment Rent** *(950 sf 2 bedroom/1.5 or 2 bath, unfurnished, excluding all utilities except water);* **All Electric** *(average monthly cost for an all-electric home);* **Part Electric** *(average monthly cost for a part-electric home);* **Other Energy** *(average monthly cost for natural gas, fuel oil, coal, wood, and any other forms of energy except electricity);* **Telephone** *(price includes basic monthly rate for a private residential line plus additional local usage charges incurred by a family of four).*
Source: The Council for Community and Economic Research (formerly ACCRA), Cost of Living Index, 2007

Health Care, Transportation, and Other Costs

Area[1]	Doctor ($/visit)	Dentist ($/visit)	Optometrist ($/visit)	Gasoline ($/gallon)	Beauty Salon ($/visit)	Men's Shirt ($)
City[2]	64.27	67.39	68.73	2.59	38.52	26.46
Avg.	79.48	71.93	79.55	2.64	29.52	25.77
Min.	52.08	44.80	43.95	2.19	15.58	16.19
Max.	148.44	126.27	158.83	3.48	60.62	48.53

Note: (1) Values for the local area are compared with the average, minimum and maximum values for all 331 areas in the Cost of Living Index report; (2) Figures cover the Akron OH urban area; **Doctor** *(general practitioners routine exam of an established patient);* **Dentist** *(adult teeth cleaning and periodic oral examination);* **Optometrist** *(full vision eye exam for established adult patient);* **Gasoline** *(one gallon regular unleaded, national brand, including all taxes, cash price at self-service pump if available);* **Beauty Salon** *(woman's shampoo, trim, and blow-dry);* **Men's Shirt** *(cotton/polyester dress shirt, pinpoint weave, long sleeves).*
Source: The Council for Community and Economic Research (formerly ACCRA), Cost of Living Index, 2007

HOUSING

House Price Index (HPI)

Area	National Ranking[2]	Quarterly Change (%)	One-Year Change (%)	Five-Year Change (%)
MSA[1]	224	-0.08	-2.16	7.84
U.S.[3]	-	0.10	0.84	41.37

Note: The HPI is a weighted repeat sales index. It measures average price changes in repeat sales or refinancings on the same properties. This information is obtained by reviewing repeat mortgage transactions on single-family properties whose mortgages have been purchased or securitized by Fannie Mae or Freddie Mac in January 1975; (1) Metropolitan Statistical Area - see Appendix B for areas included; (2) Rankings are based on annual percentage change for all metro areas containing at least 15,000 transactions over the last 10 years and ranges from 1 to 291; (3) figures based on a weighted average of Census Division estimates; all figures are for the period ending December 31, 2007
Source: Office of Federal Housing Enterprise Oversight, House Price Index, February 26, 2008

House Price Valuations

Area	Q1 2000	Q1 2001	Q1 2002	Q1 2003	Q1 2004	Q1 2005	Q1 2006	Q1 2007	Q1 2008
MSA[1]	-4.8	-0.2	2.2	-1.5	0.4	-3.3	-1.9	-8.4	-15.7

Note: Figures show the percentage of over- or under-valuation of single family homes relative to statistically normal house values (e.g. a value of 23.6 indicates that house values are 23.6% overvalued). Statistically normal house values are based on house prices, interest rates, household incomes, population densities, and any historical premiums or discounts metropolitan areas have exhibited over time; (1) Figures cover the Metropolitan Statistical Area - see Appendix B for areas included
Source: Global Insight/National City Corporation, House Prices in America, May 2008

Median Home Prices

Area	2005	2006	2007[r]	Percent Change 2006 to 2007
MSA[1]	120.5	114.6	119.3	4.1
U.S. Average	219.0	221.9	217.9	-1.8

Note: Figures are median sales prices of existing single-family homes in thousands of dollars; (r) revised; n/a not available; (1) Metropolitan Statistical Area - see Appendix B for areas included
Source: National Association of Realtors, Metropolitan Area Prices, 1st Quarter 2008

Housing: Year Structure Built

Area	1990 -2000	1980 -1989	1970 -1979	1960 -1969	1950 -1959	1940 -1949	Before 1940	Median Year
City	23.4	15.8	23.0	18.0	10.1	3.7	6.0	1975
MSA[1]	13.6	8.8	14.7	15.3	17.1	9.8	20.7	1962
U.S.	17.0	15.8	18.5	13.7	12.7	7.3	15.0	1971

Note: Figures are percentages; (1) Metropolitan Statistical Area - see Appendix A for areas included
Source: Census 2000, Summary File 3

HEALTH

Health Risk Data

Category	Area[1] (%)	U.S. (%)
Adults who have been told they have high blood pressure[3]	n/a	25.5
Adults who have been told they have high blood cholesterol[3]	n/a	35.6
Adults who have been told they have diabetes[2]	8.0	7.5
Adults who have been told they have arthritis[3]	n/a	27.0
Adults who have been told they currently have asthma	7.4	8.5
Adults who are current smokers	19.8	20.1
Adults who are heavy drinkers[4]	6.0	4.9
Adults who are overweight (BMI 25.0 - 29.9)	33.9	36.5
Adults who are obese (BMI 30.0 - 99.8)	27.8	25.1

Note: Data as of 2006 unless otherwise noted; n/a not available; (1) Figures cover the Metropolitan Statistical Area - see Appendix B for areas included; (2) Figures do not include pregnancy-related diabetes, pre-diabetes or borderline diabetes; (3) 2005 data; (4) Heavy drinkers are classified as adult men having more than two drinks per day or adult women having more than one drink per day
Source: Centers for Disease Control and Prevention, Behaviorial Risk Factor Surveillance System, SMART: Selected Metropolitan/Micropolitan Area Risk Trends, 2005, 2006

Mortality Rates for the Top 10 Causes of Death in the U.S.

ICD-10[a] Sub-Chapter	ICD-10[a] Code	Age-Adjusted Mortality Rate[1] per 100,000 population	
		County[2]	U.S.
Malignant neoplasms	C00-C97	201.0	186.5
Ischaemic heart diseases	I20-I25	134.5	152.3
Other forms of heart disease	I30-I51	62.5	51.5
Cerebrovascular diseases	I60-I69	54.1	50.0
Chronic lower respiratory diseases	J40-J47	54.6	42.6
Diabetes mellitus	E10-E14	24.9	24.8
Other degenerative diseases of the nervous system	G30-G31	22.0	22.6
Other external causes of accidental injury	W00-X59	22.2	21.4
Influenza and pneumonia	J10-J18	23.2	20.7
Hypertensive diseases	I10-I13	30.3	18.2

Note: (a) ICD-10 = International Classification of Diseases 10th Revision; (1) Mortality rates are a three year average covering 2003-2005; (2) Figures cover Summit County
Source: Centers for Disease Control and Prevention, National Center for Health Statistics. Compressed Mortality File 1999-2004. CDC WONDER On-line Database, compiled from Compressed Mortality File 1999-2005 Series 20 No. 2K, 2008.

Mortality Rates for Selected Causes of Death

ICD-10[a] Sub-Chapter	ICD-10[a] Code	Age-Adjusted Mortality Rate[1] per 100,000 population	
		County[2]	U.S.
Assault	X85-Y09	4.3	5.9
Human immunodeficiency virus (HIV) disease	B20-B24	1.9	4.5
Intentional self-harm	X60-X84	10.5	10.8
Malnutrition	E40-E46	1.8	1.0
Obesity and other hyperalimentation	E65-E68	1.6	1.4
Organic, including symptomatic, mental disorders	F01-F09	27.8	16.8
Transport accidents	V01-V99	9.2	16.1
Viral hepatitis	B15-B19	1.3	1.8

Note: (a) ICD-10 = International Classification of Diseases 10th Revision; (1) Mortality rates are a three year average covering 2003-2005; (2) Figures cover Summit County
Source: Centers for Disease Control and Prevention, National Center for Health Statistics. Compressed Mortality File 1999-2004. CDC WONDER On-line Database, compiled from Compressed Mortality File 1999-2005 Series 20 No. 2K, 2008.

Distribution of Physicians[1]

Area	Total	Family/ General Practice	Specialties	
			Medical	Surgical
Summit County (number)	1,060	267	383	242
Summit County (rate per 10,000 pop.)	19.4	4.9	7.0	4.4
U.S. (rate per 10,000 pop.)	17.7	4.6	6.9	4.3

Note: Data as of 2005; (1) Includes all non-federal, patient-care, office-based MDs
Source: Area Resource File (ARF). June 2007. U.S. Department of Health and Human Services, Health Resources and Services Administration, Bureau of Health Professions, Rockville, MD.

Hospitals

There were no hospitals listed within the city limits.
AHA Guide to the Healthcare Field 2008

According to *U.S. News,* the Akron, OH metro area is home to one of the best hospitals in the U.S.: **Summa Health System**. *U.S. News Online, "America's Best Hospitals 2007"*

EDUCATION

Public School District Statistics

District Name	Schls	Pupils	Pupil/ Teacher Ratio	Minority Pupils[1] (%)	Free Lunch Eligible[2] (%)	IEP[3] (%)
Stow-Munroe Falls City	9	5,951	17.5	6.4	5.8	10.9

Note: Table includes regular local school districts with 2,000 or more students; (1) Percentage of students that are not white, non-Hispanic; (2) Percentage of students that are eligible for the free lunch program; (3) Percentage of students that have an Individualized Education Program.
Source: U.S. Department of Education, National Center for Education Statistics, Common Core of Data, Local Education Agency (School District) Universe Survey: School Year 2005-2006; U.S. Department of Education, National Center for Education Statistics, Common Core of Data, Public Elementary/Secondary School Universe Survey: School Year 2005-2006

Highest Level of Education

Area	Less than H.S.	H.S. Diploma	Some College, No Deg.	Associate Degree	Bachelors Degree	Masters Degree	Profess. School Degree	Doctorate Degree
City	6.8	28.2	21.5	6.7	24.2	8.9	2.3	1.4
MSA[1]	14.0	34.6	21.4	5.2	16.4	5.5	1.8	1.0
U.S.	19.4	28.4	21.2	6.4	15.7	5.9	2.0	1.0

Note: Figures are 2007 estimated percentages and cover persons age 25 and over; (1) Metropolitan Statistical Area - see Appendix B for areas included
Source: Claritas, Inc.

Educational Attainment by Race

Area	High School Graduate (%)					Bachelor's Degree (%)				
	Total	White	Black	Asian	Hisp.[2]	Total	White	Black	Asian	Hisp.[2]
City	93.0	93.1	95.7	89.9	85.0	36.2	36.0	30.1	67.1	16.8
MSA[1]	85.7	86.9	75.7	88.7	80.3	24.3	25.2	10.9	64.0	25.7
U.S.	80.4	83.6	72.3	80.4	52.4	24.4	26.1	14.3	44.1	10.4

Note: Figures shown cover persons 25 years old and over; (1) Metropolitan Statistical Area - see Appendix A for areas included; (2) people of Hispanic origin can be of any race
Source: Census 2000, Summary File 3

School Enrollment by Type

Area	Grades KG to 8				Grades 9 to 12			
	Public		Private		Public		Private	
	Enrollment	%	Enrollment	%	Enrollment	%	Enrollment	%
City	3,608	80.2	892	19.8	1,633	88.0	223	12.0
MSA[1]	78,037	86.1	12,558	13.9	34,447	91.1	3,370	8.9
U.S.	33,526,011	88.7	4,285,121	11.3	14,848,628	90.6	1,532,323	9.4

Note: Figures shown cover persons 3 years old and over; (1) Metropolitan Statistical Area - see Appendix A for areas included
Source: Census 2000, Summary File 3

School Enrollment by Race

Area	Grades KG to 8 (%)				Grades 9 to 12 (%)			
	White	Black	Asian	Hisp.[1]	White	Black	Asian	Hisp.[1]
City	92.9	2.8	1.7	0.8	96.0	0.0	1.9	1.2
MSA[2]	80.1	15.1	1.2	1.1	81.6	14.8	1.3	0.8
U.S.	68.5	15.5	3.3	16.8	68.8	15.5	3.8	15.7

Note: Figures shown cover persons 3 years old and over; (1) people of Hispanic origin can be of any race; (2) Metropolitan Statistical Area - see Appendix A for areas included
Source: Census 2000, Summary File 3

Average Salaries of Public School Classroom Teachers

District	2005-06 Dollars	2005-06 Rank[1]	2006-07 Dollars	2006-07 Rank[1]	Percent Change 2005-06 to 2006-07
Ohio	50,314	14	51,937	14	3.23
U.S. Average	49,026	-	50,816	-	3.65

Note: (1) State rank ranges from 1 to 51.
Source: National Education Association, Rankings & Estimates: Rankings of the States 2006 and Estimates of School Statistics 2007, December 2007

Higher Education

Four-Year Colleges			Two-Year Colleges			Medical Schools[1]	Law Schools[2]	Voc/ Tech[3]
Public	Private Non-profit	Private For-profit	Public	Private Non-profit	Private For-profit			
0	0	0	0	0	0	0	0	0

Note: Figures cover institutions located within the city limits; (1) includes schools accredited by the Liaison Committee on Medical Education and the American Osteopathic Association; (2) includes American Bar Association-accredited law schools; (3) includes all schools with programs that are less than 2 years.
Source: National Center for Education Statistics, The Integrated Postsecondary Education System (IPEDS) Peer Analysis System, 2007; www.usnews.com, Law and Medical School Directories, 2009

PRESIDENTIAL ELECTION

2004 Presidential Election Results

Area	Bush	Kerry	Nader	Other
Summit County	42.9	56.7	0.0	0.4
U.S.	50.7	48.3	0.4	0.6

Note: Results are percentages and may not add to 100% due to rounding
Source: Dave Leip's Atlas of U.S. Presidential Elections, www.uselectionatlas.org

EMPLOYERS

Major Employers

Company Name	Industry	Type of Site
Aircraft Braking Systems Corp	Aircraft parts and equipment, nec	Headquarters
Akron Childrens Hospital	Specialty hospitals, except psychiatric	Headquarters
Akron General Health System	General medical and surgical hospitals	Headquarters
Barberton Health Systems LLC	General medical and surgical hospitals	Headquarters
Bekaert Corporation	Steel wire and related products	Headquarters
CVCA	Elementary and secondary schools	Single
Chrysler Twinsburg Stamping	Automotive stampings	Branch
Cuyhoga Falls General Hospital	Elementary and secondary schools	Single
First Energy Nuclear Oper Co	Electric services	Headquarters
Firstenergy	Electric services	Headquarters
Goodyear	Tires and inner tubes	Headquarters
Jo-Ann Fabrics & Crafts	Hobby, toy and game shops	Headquarters
Kent State University	Colleges and universities	Headquarters
Little Tikes Company	Games, toys and children's vehicles	Headquarters
Mature Services Incorporated	Individual and family services	Headquarters
Med Center One	General medical and surgical hospitals	Headquarters
Roadway Express	Trucking, except local	Headquarters
Sterling Jewelers Inc	Jewelry stores	Headquarters
University of Akron	Colleges and universities	Headquarters

Note: Companies shown are located within the Akron metropolitan area; nec = not elsewhere classified.
Source: www.zapdata.com, May 2008

PUBLIC SAFETY

Crime Rate

Area	All Crimes	Violent Crimes				Property Crimes		
		Murder	Forcible Rape	Robbery	Aggrav. Assault	Burglary	Larceny -Theft	Motor Vehicle Theft
City	2,705.7	0.0	26.1	34.8	14.5	325.1	2,264.4	40.6
Metro[1]	n/a	n/a	n/a	n/a	n/a	n/a	n/a	n/a
U.S.	3,808.1	5.7	30.9	149.4	287.5	729.4	2,206.8	398.4

Note: Figures are crimes per 100,000 population; (1) Metropolitan Statistical Area - see Appendix B for areas included; n/a not available
Source: FBI Uniform Crime Reports, 2006

Hate Crimes

Area	Number of Quarters Reported	Bias Motivation				
		Race	Religion	Sexual Orientation	Ethnicity	Disability
City	3	1	0	0	0	0

Source: Federal Bureau of Investigation, Hate Crime Statistics 2006

RECREATION

Culture

Dance[1]	Theatre[1]	Instrumental Music[1]	Vocal Music[1]	Series/ Festivals	Museums	Zoos and Aquariums[2]
2	0	0	0	0	0	0

Note: (1) Number of professional perfoming groups; (2) AZA-accredited
Source: The Grey House Performing Arts Directory, 2007; Official Museum Directory, 2008; Association of Zoos & Aquariums, AZA Member Zoos & Aquariums, June 2008

Professional Sports Teams

Team Name	League
Cleveland Indians	Major League Baseball (MLB)
Cleveland Cavaliers	National Basketball Association (NBA)
Cleveland Browns	National Football League (NFL)

Note: Includes teams located in the Cleveland-Akron metro area.
Source: Original research

MEDIA

Newspapers

Name	News Focus	Frequency	Circulation
Aurora Advocate	Community	Weekly	6,900
Cuyahoga Falls News/Press	Local	Weekly	25,500
Gateway News	Community	Weekly	11,000
Hudson Hub-Times	Local	Twice a week	9,100
News Leader	Community	Weekly	10,000
Record Publishing Company	Local	n/a	n/a
Stow Sentry	Community	Weekly	14,280
Tallmadge Express	Community	Weekly	6,700
Twinsburg Bulletin	Community	Weekly	8,000

Note: Includes newspapers with offices located in the city; n/a not available
Source: MediaContactsPro, March 2008

Television Stations

Name	Ch.	Network(s)	Type	Ownership
WKYC	3	NBC	Commercial	Gannett Broadcasting
WEWS	5	ABC	Commercial	Scripps Howard Broadcasting
WJW	8	Fox	Commercial	Fox Television Stations Inc.
WDLI	17	n/a	Commercial	Trinity Broadcasting Network
WOIO	19	CBS	Commercial	Raycom Media Inc.
WVPX	23	Pax	Commercial	Paxson Communications Corporation
WVIZ	25	PBS	Public	Educational TV Association of Metropolitan Cleveland
WAOH	29	n/a	Commercial	Media-Com Television Inc.
WUAB	43	UPN	Commercial	Raycom Media Inc.
WNEO	45	PBS	Public	Northeastern Educational TV of Ohio
WEAO	49	PBS	Public	Northeastern Educational TV of Ohio
WGGN	52	n/a	Commercial	Christian Faith Broadcasting Inc.
WBNX	55	WBN	Commercial	Winston Broadcasting Network Inc.
WQHS	61	Univision	Commercial	Univision Communications Inc.
WOAC	67	n/a	Commercial	Shop at Home Inc.
WMFD	68	n/a	Commercial	Mid-State Broadcasting Corporation

Note: Stations included cover the Cleveland DMA (Designated Market Area); n/a not available
BurrellesLuce, MediaContacts Online, January 2007

Major AM Radio Stations

Call Letters	Freq. (kHz)	Station Type	Target Audience	Station Format	Music Format
WKNR	850	Commercial	General	Sports/Talk	n/a
WEOL	930	n/a	General	News/Sports/Talk	n/a
WKVX	960	n/a	General	Music/News/Sports	n/a
WFUN	970	Commercial	General	News/Sports/Talk	n/a
WJTB	1040	Commercial	Men/Women	Music/News/Talk	Adult Contemp.
WTAM	1100	n/a	General	News/Sports/Talk	n/a
WCUE	1150	Non-Comm	Religious	Music/Talk	Christian
WHK	1220	n/a	General	Music/News/Talk	n/a
WWMK	1260	Commercial	Child/Gen/Men/Women	Ed/Music/News/Talk	Top 40
WERE	1300	Commercial	General	News/Talk	n/a
WDPN	1310	n/a	General	Music/Sports	n/a
WOBL	1320	Commercial	General	Music/News	Country
WNCO	1340	n/a	General	Music	Middle Road
WTOU	1350	Commercial	General	Sports/Talk	n/a
WWOW	1360	Commercial	General	News/Sports	n/a
WMAN	1400	n/a	General	News/Sports/Talk	n/a
WRMR	1420	n/a	General	Music/Talk	n/a
WRGM	1440	Commercial	General	News/Sports	n/a
WLEC	1450	n/a	General	Music/News	n/a
WJER	1450	Commercial	General	Music/News	Adult Contemp.
WBKC	1460	Commercial	General	Educational/Music/News	Middle Road
WHBC	1480	n/a	General	Music/News	n/a
WJMO	1490	Commercial	General/Religious	Music/News/Talk	Gospel
WINW	1520	n/a	General/Religious	Music/News/Sports	n/a
WJMP	1520	Commercial	General	Music/Talk	Oldies
WABQ	1540	Commercial	Black/General/Rel	Music/News	Christian
WAKR	1590	n/a	General	Music/News/Sports	n/a

Note: Stations included cover the Cleveland DMA (Designated Market Area); n/a not available
Source: BurrellesLuce, MediaContacts Online, January 2007

Major FM Radio Stations

Call Letters	Freq. (mHz)	Station Type	Target Audience	Station Format	Music Format
WCPN	90.3	Public	General	Music/Talk	World Music
WXTM	92.3	Commercial	General	Music	Alternative
WZKL	92.5	Commercial	General	Music/News	Adult Contemp.
WHBC	94.1	n/a	General	Music/News/Sports	n/a
WAKS	96.5	Commercial	General	Music/News/Sports/Talk	Top 40
WREO	97.1	Commercial	General	Music	Adult Contemp.
WKDD	98.1	Commercial	General	Music	Adult Top 40
WGAR	99.5	n/a	General	Music	n/a
WMMS	100.7	Commercial	General	Music/News/Sports	Modern Rock
WNCO	101.3	Commercial	General	Music	Country
WDOK	102.1	n/a	General	Music/News/Talk	n/a
WCPZ	102.7	n/a	General	Music/News/Talk	n/a
WQKT	104.5	n/a	General	Music/News/Sports	n/a
WYHT	105.3	Commercial	General	Music	Adult Top 40
WVNO	106.1	Commercial	General	Music/News	Adult Contemp.
WMVX	106.5	Commercial	General	Music/News/Sports/Talk	Adult Top 40
WNWV	107.3	n/a	General	Music/News/Talk	n/a

Note: Stations included cover the Cleveland DMA (Designated Market Area); n/a not available
BurrellesLuce, MediaContacts Online, January 2007

CLIMATE

Average and Extreme Temperatures

Temperature	Jan	Feb	Mar	Apr	May	Jun	Jul	Aug	Sep	Oct	Nov	Dec	Yr.
Extreme High (°F)	70	68	81	88	92	100	101	98	99	86	80	76	101
Average High (°F)	33	36	46	59	70	79	82	81	74	62	49	37	59
Average Temp. (°F)	26	28	37	49	59	68	72	71	64	53	42	31	50
Average Low (°F)	18	20	28	38	48	57	61	60	53	43	33	23	40
Extreme Low (°F)	-24	-13	-3	10	24	32	43	41	32	20	-1	-16	-24

Note: Figures cover the years 1948-1990
Source: National Climatic Data Center, International Station Meteorological Climate Summary, 9/96

Average Precipitation/Snowfall/Humidity

Precip./Humidity	Jan	Feb	Mar	Apr	May	Jun	Jul	Aug	Sep	Oct	Nov	Dec	Yr.
Avg. Precip. (in.)	2.6	2.3	3.2	3.3	3.7	3.4	4.0	3.2	3.1	2.3	2.8	2.8	36.7
Avg. Snowfall (in.)	11	9	9	3	Tr	0	0	0	0	1	5	10	47
Avg. Rel. Hum. 7am (%)	80	80	79	77	77	80	83	87	87	84	80	80	81
Avg. Rel. Hum. 4pm (%)	68	65	59	53	53	54	54	55	56	56	64	70	59

Note: Figures cover the years 1948-1990; Tr = Trace amounts (<0.05 in. of rain; <0.5 in. of snow)
Source: National Climatic Data Center, International Station Meteorological Climate Summary, 9/96

Weather Conditions

Temperature			Daytime Sky			Precipitation		
5°F & below	32°F & below	90°F & above	Clear	Partly cloudy	Cloudy	0.01 inch or more precip.	0.1 inch or more snow/ice	Thunder-storms
12	129	8	67	134	164	153	48	38

Note: Figures are average number of days per year and cover the years 1948-1990
Source: National Climatic Data Center, International Station Meteorological Climate Summary, 9/96

HAZARDOUS WASTE

Superfund Sites

Stow has no sites on the EPA's Superfund Final National Priorities List.
U.S. Environmental Protection Agency, Final National Priorities List, June 23, 2008

AIR & WATER QUALITY

Air Quality Index

Area	Percent of Days when Air Quality was...[2]				AQI Statistics	
	Good	Moderate	Unhealthy for Sensitive Groups	Unhealthy	Maximum	Median
MSA[1]	73.2	20.8	5.8	0.3	154	39

Note: The Air Quality Index (AQI) is an index for reporting daily air quality. EPA calculates the AQI for five major air pollutants regulated by the Clean Air Act: ground-level ozone, particle pollution (also known as particulate matter), carbon monoxide, sulfur dioxide, and nitrogen dioxide. The AQI runs from 0 to 500. The higher the AQI value, the greater the level of air pollution and the greater the health concern. There are six AQI categories: "Good" The AQI is between 0 and 50. Air quality is considered satisfactory; "Moderate" The AQI is between 51 and 100. Air quality is acceptable; "Unhealthy for Sensitive Groups" When AQI values are between 101 and 150, members of sensitive groups may experience health effects; "Unhealthy" When AQI values are between 151 and 200 everyone may begin to experience health effects; "Very Unhealthy" AQI values between 201 and 300 trigger a health alert; "Hazardous" AQI values over 300 trigger health warnings of emergency conditions; (1) Metropolitan Statistical Area - see Appendix A for areas included; (2) Based on 365 days with AQI data in 2007.
Source: U.S. Environmental Protection Agency, Air Quality Index Report, 2007

Air Quality Index Pollutants

Area	Percent of Days when AQI Pollutant was...[2]					
	Carbon Monoxide	Nitrogen Dioxide	Ozone	Sulfur Dioxide	Particulate Matter 2.5	Particulate Matter 10
MSA[1]	12.6	0.0	50.7	15.1	21.6	0.0

Note: The Air Quality Index (AQI) is an index for reporting daily air quality. EPA calculates the AQI for five major air pollutants regulated by the Clean Air Act: ground-level ozone, particle pollution (also known as particulate matter), carbon monoxide, sulfur dioxide, and nitrogen dioxide. The AQI runs from 0 to 500. The higher the AQI value, the greater the level of air pollution and the greater the health concern; (1) Metropolitan Statistical Area - see Appendix A for areas included; (2) Based on 365 days with AQI data in 2007.
Source: U.S. Environmental Protection Agency, Air Quality Index Report, 2007

Air Quality Index Trends

Area	Trend Sites (7)								All Sites (18)
	1999	2000	2001	2002	2003	2004	2005	2006	2006
MSA[1]	25	9	22	24	6	6	13	0	0

Note: An AQI value greater than 100 indicates that air quality would have been in the unhealthful range on that day. Data from exceptional events are not included. These counts are presented in two ways. First, the counts are based on sites having an adequate record of monitoring data during the trend period (trend sites). These counts represent the relative change in the number of days with AQI values greater than 100. In the last column, the counts are based on all sites with data in the most recent year (because it is possible for a site to have data in the most recent year but not enough data to be a trend site); (1) Metropolitan Statistical Area - see Appendix A for areas included.
Source: U.S. Environmental Protection Agency, Office of Air and Radiation, Air Trends, Factbook and Related Information, Air Pollution Trends in Selected Metropolitan Areas 2006

Maximum Air Pollutant Concentrations

	Particulate Matter 10 (ug/m^3)	Particulate Matter 2.5 (ug/m^3)	Ozone (ppm)	Carbon Monoxide (ppm)	Sulfur Dioxide (ppm)	Nitrogen Dioxide (ppm)	Lead (ug/m^3)
MSA[1] Level	n/a	32	0.09	2	0.038	n/a	n/a
NAAQS[2]	150	35	0.125	9	0.140	0.053	1.50
Met NAAQS[2]	Yes	Yes	Yes	Yes	Yes	n/a	n/a

Note: Data from exceptional events are not included; (1) Metropolitan Statistical Area - see Appendix A for areas included; (2) National Ambient Air Quality Standards; n/a not available
Concentrations: Particulate Matter 10 (coarse particulate) - highest second maximum 24-hour concentration; Particulate Matter 2.5 (fine particulate) - highest 98th percentile 24-hour concentration; Ozone - highest second daily maximum 1-hour concentration; Carbon Monoxide - highest second maximum non-overlapping 8-hour concentration; Sulfur Dioxide - highest second maximum 24-hour concentration; Nitrogen Dioxide - highest arithmetic mean concentration; Lead - highest quarterly maximum concentration
Units: ppm = parts per million; ug/m^3 = micrograms per cubic meter
Source: U.S. Environmental Protection Agency, MSA Factbook 2006, Air Quality Statistics by City

Drinking Water

Water System Name	Pop. Served	Primary Water Source Type	Violations[1]	
			Health Based	Monitoring/ Reporting
Stow Public Water System	34,394	Purchased Surface	0	0

Note: (1) Based on violation data from January 1, 2007 to December 31, 2007 (includes unresolved violations from earlier years)
Source: U.S. Environmental Protection Agency, Office of Ground Water and Drinking Water, Safe Drinking Water Information System (based on data extracted April 15, 2008)

Edmond, Oklahoma

Background

The city of Edmond lies in the central part of the state, 15 miles north of Oklahoma City. It has a city-council-manager form of government. There are four councilmen elected by the people, with the mayor acting as councilman-at-large; a city manager is appointed by the council.

Edmond is a rapidly growing, affluent city. Although Oklahoma's fastest-growing high-tech job base exists in Edmond, an agricultural spirit still permeates the city. Other employers include the University of Central Oklahoma, Edmond Public Schools, Edmond Regional Medical Center, Applied Intelligence Group, PepsiCo Bottling, and Ralston Purina.

The Edmond site was originally explored by Washington Irving in 1832 and described in his publication, *A Tour on the Prairies*. In 1870, the U.S. Government issued a directive to survey the western portion of the Indian Territories. After establishing treaties with the Creek and Seminole Indian nations, and the assignment of other reservations within Indian Territory, it was discovered that a large area in the center of this region — of which Edmond was included — had been left unassigned. The region later became known as Oklahoma. In 1886, a route going through the state was surveyed for the Santa Fe Railroad. Several railroad workers were among the first to stake out claims during the Great Oklahoma Land Run of April 22, 1889, at 12:00 noon. At 12:05 p.m., a crew of surveyors began laying out the town of Edmond.

Two major universities, as well as the most honored public school system in Oklahoma, are located in Edmond. The state's first public college, the University of Central Oklahoma, is now the premier educational institution in the region, with many of the campus buildings dating back to the 1890s. The university offers undergraduate studies in business administration, education, liberal arts, mathematics and science, as well as five master's degree programs.

Edmond's schools are innovative and comprehensive, with gifted programs and special education services. Students maintain an attendance rate of 95.8%. In each of the city's elementary schools, a media center is provided, along with instructional specialists in music, art, physical education, and gifted education. The high schools provide a wide array of subjects beyond the required curriculum, including fine arts, business and vocational education, foreign languages, computer technology, and professional internships.

Edmond Regional Medical Center, a contemporary, 139-bed facility, has expanded to meet the needs of the area's growing population. Over 240 highly skilled physicians in all specialty areas, as well as comprehensive specialized services and facilities, ensure quality medical care for Edmond's residents within their own community.

The city is home to the famous Oak Tree Golf Club, the site of PGA Tour events. There are 10 golf courses in the area, but golf is only part of Edmond's recreational activities. Arcadia Lake offers fishing, skiing, camping, and 17 miles of hiking trails. Historic downtown Edmond features diverse shopping, and the Fine Arts Institute sponsors and hosts art shows. Nearby Oklahoma City Zoo is one of the country's largest and best zoos, while Remington Park offers exciting thoroughbred horseracing.

The award-winning Cross Timbers Municipal Complex, the largest municipal project in Edmond's history, houses the town's Public Service Center, a fire station, fire department administrative and training offices, and an animal welfare facility.

The climate of Edmond is affected mainly by winds from the continental Great Plains, though occasionally moist air comes up from the Gulf Coast. Pronounced changes in temperature, both daily and seasonally, are the rule. Winters are short and mild. Summers are hot, but the heat is mitigated by low humidity.

Rankings

General Rankings

- Oklahoma City* was ranked #185 out of 375 metro areas in *Cities Ranked & Rated*. Criteria: cost of living; climate; crime; transportation; economy and jobs; education; arts and culture; health and healthcare; leisure; quality of life. *Cities Ranked & Rated, 2nd Edition, 2007*
- Oklahoma City* was ranked #78 out of 379 metro areas in *Places Rated Almanac*. Criteria: health care; education; recreation; transportation; ambience; climate; crime; housing costs; jobs. *Places Rated Almanac, 7th Edition, 2007*
- Edmond was selected as one of the "2006 Best Places to Live" by *Money* magazine. Places were ranked using 38 quality-of-life indicators and six economic opportunity measures in the following categories: ease of living; health; education; crime; park space; arts and leisure. *CNNMoney.com, "Best Places to Live 2006"*

Business/Finance Rankings

- The nation's 100 largest metro areas were analysed in terms of the percentage of households entering some stage of foreclosure in 2007. The Oklahoma City* metro area ranked #62 out of 100 (#1 = highest foreclosure rate). *RealtyTrac, "Year-End 2007 Metropolitan Foreclosure Report"*
- The Oklahoma City* metro area was identified as one of the least expensive places to rent in the U.S. The area ranked #62 out of 10 markets with an average effective rent of $490 per month. The rental figures cover apartment properties in complexes with 40 or more units (20 or more units in California and Arizona). The figures are blended average rents, which include all unit sizes. Effective rents include free rent incentives and other landlord concessions. *Wall Street Journal Online, January 17, 2008*
- The Oklahoma City* metro area was selected one of America's "Top 50 Business Opportunity Metros" by *Expansion Management* in their 5th annual Mayor's Challenge ranking of metro areas that have achieved solid ratings across the board in numerous *EM* studies during the past 12 months. The area ranked #33. Criteria: public schools; quality of life; college educated workers; logistics infrastructure; healthcare costs; taxes and government spending; reputation among site consultants. *Expansion Management, August 2007*
- Oklahoma City* was selected as one of the best places to start and grow a company by *Entrepreneur* and the National Policy Research Council. The Oklahoma City* metro area ranked #24 out of 50 large metro areas. Criteria: business formation and growth (firms started four to 14 years ago that still employ at least 5 people and experienced rapid growth over the last four years). *Entrepreneur/National Policy Research Council, "Hot Cities for Entrepreneurs," September 2006*
- The Oklahoma City* metro area was selected as one of "America's 50 Hottest Cities" for business relocations and expansions. Criteria: industry's most prominent site selection consultants were asked to list their top city choices for relocating and expanding manufacturing companies, taking into consideration such factors as the business climate, work force quality, operating costs, incentive programs, and the ease of working with local political and economic development officials. *Expansion Management, January-February 2007*
- The Oklahoma City* metro area was selected as one of the "Top 20 Real Estate Markets" for expanding or relocating companies. The area ranked #4. Criteria: low rental costs; low purchase prices; high vacancy rates of office and warehouse space. *Expansion Management, October 2007*
- Intel, in partnership with Sperling's BestPlaces, ranked the 80 "Best Cities for Teleworking" in America. The Oklahoma City* metro area ranked #26 among mid-sized metro areas. The study identifies cities that hold the greatest potential for teleworking based on a host of factors including typical commuting times, fuel prices, availability of broadband Internet access and percentage of the population in telework friendly jobs. The study also factored in extreme climate and natural hazards. *Intel, "Best Cities for Teleworking," March 30, 2006*

- Edmond was selected as one of the "100 Best Places to Live and Launch" in the U.S. The city ranked #93. The editors at *Fortune Small Business* ranked 296 Census-designated metro areas by business friendliness (Launching Score, % New Businesses) and lifestyle offerings (Living Score). Then, through reporting, they picked the town within each of the top 100 metro areas that best blends business and pleasure. *Fortune Small Business, "100 Best Places to Live and Launch 2008," April 2008*

- The Oklahoma City* metro area was identified as one of the "25 Hottest Housing Markets" in the U.S. The area ranked #93 out of 156 markets with a home price appreciation rate of 8.2%. Criteria: year-over-year change of median sales price of existing single-family homes between the 4th quarter of 2006 and the 4th quarter of 2007. *National Association of Realtors, Median Sales Price of Existing Single-Family Homes for Metropolitan Areas, 4th Quarter 2007*

- The Oklahoma City* metro area appeared on the Milken Institute "2007 Best Performing Cities" index. Rank: #108 out of 200 large metro areas. Criteria: job growth; wage and salary growth; high-tech output growth. *Milken Institute, "2007 Best Performing Cities"*

- Oklahoma City* was identified as one of the 100 "Most Unwired Cities" in the U.S. The area ranked #83 out of the 100 largest metro areas in the U.S. Criteria: number of public and commercial wireless access points (hotspots); airports with wireless Internet access; broadband availability; local wireless networks; and wireless email devices. *Intel, "Most Unwired Cities Survey," June 7, 2005*

- *Forbes* ranked the 200 most populous metro areas in the U.S. in terms of the "Best Places for Business and Careers." The Oklahoma City* metro area was ranked #45. Criteria: business costs (labor, energy, tax and office space expenses); living costs (housing, transportation, food and other household expenditures); education levels of the work force; job growth; income growth; migration trends; crime rates; and culture/leisure. *Forbes, "Best Places for Business and Careers," March 19, 2008*

- *Fortune* ranked the 100 largest metro areas in the U.S. in terms of projected median home price change in 2007. The Oklahoma City* metro area ranked #23. *Fortune.com, "Hot Spots, Cold Spots"*

Health/Environment Rankings

- The Oklahoma City* metro area was identified as one of "America's 20 Most Sedentary Cities" by *Forbes*. The metro area ranked #15. Criteria: percentage of overweight or obese people; percentage of people who had not engaged in any physical activity in the past 30 days; average number of hours of TV watched per week. *Forbes.com, "America's Most Sedentary Cities," October 29, 2007*

- The Oklahoma City* metro area was selected as one of "America's Cleanest Cities" by *Forbes*. The metro area ranked #6 out of 10. Criteria: air quality; water quality; per capita spending on Superfund site cleanup and solid-waste management. *Forbes.com, "America's Cleanest Cities," March 11, 2008*

- 100 of the largest metro areas in the U.S. were analyzed in terms of their current drought severity. The Oklahoma City* metro area ranked #100 (#1 = driest). The rankings were based on statistics such as long-term precipitation trends and patterns and the Palmer drought indices. *Sperling's BestPlaces, www.BestPlaces.net, "America's Drought-Riskiest Cities," November 2007*

- Doctors at the Harvard School of Public Health ranked 40 metropolitan areas based on data from the government-sponsored Hospital Quality Alliance program. The program tracks the performance of individual hospitals in treating patients for three common health problems: heart attacks, congestive heart failure, and pneumonia. The Oklahoma City* metro area ranked #16 in quality of care for heart attacks, #33 for congestive heart failure, and #1 for pneumonia. *New England Journal of Medicine, July 21, 2005*

- *Reader's Digest* ranked the 50 largest metro areas in the U.S. in terms of how "clean" they are. The Oklahoma City* metro area ranked #15. Criteria: air quality; water quality; toxic industrial pollution; Superfund sites; and sanitation. *Reader's Digest, "The 50 Cleanest (and Dirtiest) Cities in America," July 2005*

- The Oklahoma City* metro area was identified as one of "America's Most Obese Cities" by *Forbes*. The magazine analyzed BMI (body mass index) data from the CDC in the 50 most populated metro areas in the U.S. and ranked the top 20. The area ranked #8. *Forbes, "America's Most Obese Cities," November 26, 2007*

- The Oklahoma City* metro area appeared in *Country Home's* "2008 Best Green Places" report. The area ranked #352 out of 379. Criteria: official energy policies; green power; green buildings; availability of fresh, locally grown food. *Country Home, "2008 Best Green Places"*

- The American Podiatric Medical Association and *Prevention* magazine ranked America's 100 most populated cities based on fitness-walker friendliness. The best cities have safe streets, beautiful places to walk, mild weather and good air quality. Edmond ranked #317. *Prevention, "The Best Walking Cities of 2008," April 2008; American Podiatric Medical Association, "2008 Best Fitness-Walking Cities, "April 2008*

- Oklahoma City* was identified as a "2008 Asthma Capital." The area ranked #44 out of the nation's 100 largest metropolitan areas. Twelve factors were used to identify the most challenging places to live for people with asthma: estimated prevalence; self-reported prevalence; crude death rate for asthma; annual pollen score; annual air quality; public smoking laws; number of board-certified asthma specialists; school inhaler access laws; rescue medication use; controller medication use; uninsured rate; poverty rate. *Asthma and Allergy Foundation of America, "2008 Asthma Capitals"*

- Oklahoma City* was identified as a "Spring Allergy Capital." The area ranked #15 out of 100. Three groups of factors were used to identify the most severe cities for people with allergies during the spring season: annual pollen levels; medicine utilization; access to board-certified allergists. *Asthma and Allergy Foundation of America, "2007 Spring Allergy Capital Rankings"*

- Oklahoma City* was identified as a "Fall Allergy Capital." The area ranked #3 out of 100. Three groups of factors were used to identify the most severe cities for people with allergies during the fall season: annual pollen levels; medicine utilization; access to board-certified allergists. *Asthma and Allergy Foundation of America, "2007 Fall Allergy Capital Rankings"*

- Ortho-McNeil Neurologics, in partnership with Sperling's BestPlaces, analyzed 110 metro areas and identified those U.S. cities with the highest prevalence of factors that are most commonly associated with migraine headaches. The Oklahoma City* metro area ranked #30. Criteria: number of migraine-related drug prescriptions per capita; lifestyle factors that can contribute to migraines; environmental factors that can trigger migraines; and consumption of migraine-triggering foods. *Ortho-McNeil Neurologics, "America's Migraine Hot Spots," March 14, 2006*

- Sperling's BestPlaces ranked 331 metro areas and identified the most and least stressful U.S. cities. The Oklahoma City* metro area ranked #61 out of the 100 largest metro areas (#1 = most stressful). Criteria: divorce rate; unemployment rate; violent and property crime; suicide rate; commute time; mental health; alcohol consumption; cloudy days. *Sperling's BestPlaces, www.BestPlaces.net, "America's Most (and Least) Stressful Cities," January 9, 2004*

Women/Minorities Rankings

- Oklahoma City* was ranked #97 out of 100 metro areas in *SELF Magazine's* ranking of "America's Best Places for Women." A panel of experts came up with more than 50 criteria including death and disease rates, environmental indicators, community resources, and lifestyle habits. *SELF Magazine, "America's Best Places for Women 2007," December 2007*

Children/Family Rankings

- The Oklahoma City* metro area was selected as one of the "Best Cities for Relocating Families" by Worldwide ERC and Primacy Relocation. The 2007 study placed a special emphasis on the housing market, which has significantly impacted the relocation industry and an employer's ability to transfer employees. The variables which weigh heavily in this category include home price, home affordability index, appreciation rates, and property tax. Other criteria include cost of living, crime rates, education, climate, focus on diversity, physicians per capita, recreation and leisure, arts and culture, air quality, watershed quality, sales tax, unemployment rate, job growth, high school and higher education index, school expenditures per student, students in public school, SAT/ACT percentile, and population growth. *Worldwide ERC and Primacy Relocation, "2007 Best Cities for Relocating Families"*

Safety Rankings

- The National Insurance Crime Bureau ranked 361 metro areas in the U.S. in terms of per capita rates of vehicle theft. The Oklahoma City* metro area ranked #41 (#1 = highest rate). Criteria: number of vehicle theft offenses per 100,000 inhabitants. *National Insurance Crime Bureau, "NICB Vehicle Theft Study," April 22, 2008*
- Oklahoma City* appeared on Sperling's BestPlaces list of the "Riskiest Cities for Identity Theft." The area ranked #33 out of the nations 50 largest metro areas. Over 80 criteria were analyzed across four major categories: technology impact; crime; transactions; and risk profile. *Sperling's BestPlaces, www.BestPlaces.net, "Riskiest Cities for Identity Theft," July 2006*
- Farmers Insurance Group of Companies, in partnership with Sperling's BestPlaces, ranked 379 metro areas and identified the "Most Secure U.S. Place to Live." The Oklahoma City* metro area ranked #112 out of 114 in the large metro area category (500,000 or more residents). Criteria: crime rates; extreme weather; risk of natural disasters; environmental hazards; terrorism threats; air quality; life expectancy; job loss numbers. *Farmers Insurance Group, "Most Secure U.S. Places to Live 2007"*
- Oklahoma City* was identified as one of the most dangerous large metro areas for pedestrians in the U.S. The area ranked #19 out of the nations 50 largest metro areas. Criteria: average yearly pedestrian fatalities per capita (for the years 2002 and 2003) adjusted for the number of walkers. *Surface Transportation Policy Project, "Mean Streets 2004"*

Sports/Recreation Rankings

- The Oklahoma City* metro area appeared on the *Sporting News* list of the "Best Sports Cities 2007". The area ranked #45 out of 150 cities in the U.S. *Sporting News* takes a 12-month snapshot, roughly July to July, of each city's sports, putting a heavy premium on regular-season won-lost records (from the most recently completed season). Other criteria include: playoff berths, bowl appearances and tournament bids; championships; applicable power ratings; quality of competition; overall fan fervor as measured in part by attendance as percentage of venue capacity; abundance of teams (rewarding quality over quantity); stadium and arena quality; ticket availability and prices; franchise ownership; and marquee appeal of athletes. *SportingNews.com, "Best Sports Cities 2007," August 1, 2007*
- *Golf Digest* ranked 330 metro areas in the U.S. in terms of golf. The Oklahoma City* metro area was ranked #69. Criteria: access to golf; weather; value of golf; and quality of golf. *Golf Digest, "Metro Golf Rankings," August 2005*

Dating/Romance Rankings

- Eli Lily and Company, in partnership with Sperling's BestPlaces, ranked the nation's 50 largest metro areas in terms of the "Most Romantic Cities for Baby Boomers." The Oklahoma City* metro area ranked #26. Criteria: marriage and divorce rates among "baby boomers" age 45 to 60; great restaurants; dance studios; chocolate, jewelry and flower sales. *Eli Lily and Company, "Most Romantic Cities for Baby Boomers," April 20, 2007*

- The Oklahoma City* metro area was selected as one of the "Best Cities for Relocating Singles" by Worldwide ERC and Primacy Relocation. The area ranked #44 out of the 100 largest metro areas in the U.S. Areas were selected based on the following criteria: a robust cost-of-living index; adventure and outdoor recreation opportunities; violent crime and property crime rates; percentage of the population that is unmarried (ages 25-34); ratio of single men and single women; affordability of quality higher education, including in-state and out-of-state tuition requirements and rates; number of newcomers to the area; commute times; tax rates; fee and occupancy rates for temporary housing and mini-storage; quality and quantity of collegiate and professional sporting events and fun, fan-friendly venues. *Worldwide ERC and Primacy Relocation, "2007 Best Cities for Relocating Singles," October 25, 2007*

- Sperling's BestPlaces in partnership with AXE Deodorant Bodyspray ranked 80 metro areas and identified "America's Best (and Worst) Cities for Dating." The Oklahoma City* metro area ranked #45 (#1 = best). Criteria: percentage of singles ages 18-24; population density; dating venues per capita. *AXE Deodorant Bodyspray, "America's Best (and Worst) Cities for Dating," May 2004*

Miscellaneous Rankings

- Sperling's BestPlaces in partnership with Pep Boys ranked 77 metro areas and identified "America's Most Drivable Cities." The Oklahoma City* metro area ranked #6. Criteria: climate; road roughness; urban mobility; gas prices. *Pep Boys, "America's Most Drivable Cities," April 9, 2003*

- Scarborough Research, a leading market research firm, identified the top local markets for reality television. The Oklahoma City* DMA (Designated Market Area) ranked in the top 10 with 28% of consumers reporting that they "typically watch" reality-dating, reality-talent, or reality- adventure television shows. *Scarborough Research, January 11, 2005*

- Scarborough Research, a leading market research firm, identified the top local markets for frequent fast food restaurant patronage. The Oklahoma City* DMA (Designated Market Area) ranked in the top 10 with consumers reporting an average of 6.2 visits within the past 30 days. *Scarborough Research, May 31, 2006*

- A study by Sperling's BestPlaces examined which U.S. metro areas were most affected by high fuel prices in 2006. The Oklahoma City* metro area was ranked #55 out of 80 (#1 = most expensive city for driving). Rankings are based on the average dollars spent on gas per year by two driver households. Criteria: cost of regular-grade gasoline; average miles driven per day; average number of gallons each driver uses and wastes in traffic congestion each day. *Sperling's BestPlaces, www.bestplaces.net, "Pain at the Pump," May 18, 2006*

Edmond is located within the Oklahoma City, OK Metropolitan Statistical Area.

Business Environment

CITY FINANCES

City Government Finances

Component	2004-2005 ($000)	2004-2005 ($ per capita)
Total Revenues	126,440	1,689
Total Expenditures	132,160	1,765
Debt Outstanding	131,719	1,759
Cash and Securities	114,994	1,536

Source: U.S Census Bureau, Government Finances 2004-2005

City Government Revenue by Source

Source	2004-2005 ($000)	2004-2005 ($ per capita)
General Revenue		
From Federal Government	1,140	15
From State Government	1,120	15
From Local Governments	0	0
Taxes		
Property	0	0
Sales	37,162	496
Personal Income	0	0
License	3,374	45
Charges	13,847	185
Liquor Store	0	0
Utility	60,070	802
Employee Retirement	0	0
Other	9,727	130

Source: U.S Census Bureau, Government Finances 2004-2005

City Government Expenditures by Function

Function	2004-2005 ($000)	2004-2005 ($ per capita)	2004-2005 (%)
General Expenditures			
Airports	0	0	0.0
Corrections	0	0	0.0
Education	0	0	0.0
Fire Protection	14,968	200	11.3
Governmental Administration	7,040	94	5.3
Health	0	0	0.0
Highways	11,500	154	8.7
Hospitals	0	0	0.0
Housing and Community Development	1,069	14	0.8
Interest on General Debt	2,967	40	2.2
Libraries	0	0	0.0
Parking	0	0	0.0
Parks and Recreation	7,240	97	5.5
Police Protection	13,504	180	10.2
Public Welfare	1,438	19	1.1
Sewerage	2,633	35	2.0
Solid Waste Management	4,828	64	3.7
Liquor Store	0	0	0.0
Utility	53,154	710	40.2
Employee Retirement	0	0	0.0
Other	11,819	158	8.9

Source: U.S Census Bureau, Government Finances 2004-2005

Municipal Bond Ratings

Area	Moody's
City	n/a

Source: Mergent Bond Record, January 2008 (unless noted otherwise)

DEMOGRAPHICS

Population Growth

Area	1990 Census	2000 Census	2007 Estimate	2012 Projection	Population Growth (%) 1990-2000	Population Growth (%) 2000-2012
City	52,239	68,315	77,125	82,640	30.8	21.0
MSA[1]	971,042	1,095,421	1,175,422	1,230,177	12.8	12.3
U.S.	248,709,873	281,421,906	301,045,522	314,920,978	13.2	11.9

Note: (1) Metropolitan Statistical Area - see Appendix B for areas included
Source: Claritas, Inc.

Number of Households and Average Household Size

Area	2007 Estimate	2007 Average Household Size
City	29,028	2.66
MSA[1]	470,187	2.50
U.S.	113,668,003	2.65

Note: (1) Metropolitan Statistical Area - see Appendix B for areas included
Source: Claritas, Inc.

Race and Ethnicity

Area	White Alone[2]	Black Alone[2]	Asian Alone[2]	Other Race Alone[2]	Hispanic[3]
City	84.7	4.4	3.7	7.2	3.7
MSA[1]	74.2	10.6	2.7	12.5	8.9
U.S.	73.1	12.4	4.3	10.3	14.9

Note: Figures are 2007 estimates; (1) Metropolitan Statistical Area - see Appendix B for areas included (2) Alone is defined as not being in combination with one or more other races; (3) May be of any race.
Source: Claritas, Inc.

Ancestry

Area	German	Irish[2]	English	American	Italian	Polish	French[3]	Scottish
City	19.0	11.9	14.0	9.9	2.5	1.5	3.6	2.8
MSA[1]	13.4	10.3	9.4	10.2	1.6	1.0	2.5	1.8
U.S.	15.2	10.9	8.7	7.3	5.6	3.2	3.0	1.7

Note: Figures include multiple ancestry (e.g. if a person reported being Irish and Italian, they were included in both columns); (1) Metropolitan Statistical Area - see Appendix A for areas included; (2) Includes Celtic; (3) Includes Alsatian but excludes Basque
Source: Census 2000, Summary File 3

Foreign-Born Population

Area	Percent of Population Born in							
	Any Foreign Country	Europe	Asia	Africa	Oceania[2]	Canada	Mexico	Latin America[3]
City	5.2	0.7	3.1	0.4	0.0	0.2	0.5	0.3
MSA[1]	5.7	0.5	2.2	0.3	0.0	0.1	2.2	0.4
U.S.	11.1	1.7	2.9	0.3	0.1	0.3	3.3	2.5

Note: (1) Metropolitan Statistical Area - see Appendix A for areas included; (2) Includes Australia, New Zealand subregion, Melanesia, Micronesia, Polynesia, and Oceania n.e.c; (3) Includes Central America (excluding Mexico), South America, and the Caribbean.
Source: Census 2000, Summary File 3

Marriage Status

Area	Never Married	Now Married (excluding Separated)	Separated	Widowed	Divorced
City	24.5	61.5	0.9	4.8	8.5
MSA[1]	25.2	54.4	1.8	6.2	12.4
U.S.	27.1	54.4	2.2	6.6	9.7

Note: Figures are percentages and cover the population 15 years of age and older; (1) Metropolitan Statistical Area - see Appendix A for areas included
Source: Census 2000, Summary File 3

Age Distribution

Area	Under Age 5	Age 5 to 17	Age 18 to 34	Age 35 to 49	Age 50 to 64	Age 65 to 79	80 Years and Over
	Percent of Population						
City	7.1	20.3	24.1	25.4	14.3	6.3	2.5
MSA[1]	6.9	18.6	25.4	23.1	14.6	8.5	2.8
U.S.	6.8	18.9	23.7	23.5	14.8	9.2	3.2

Note: (1) Metropolitan Statistical Area - see Appendix A for areas included
Source: Census 2000, Summary File 3

Male/Female Ratio

Area	Males	Females	Males per 100 Females
City	37,544	39,581	94.9
MSA[1]	579,468	595,954	97.2
U.S.	148,320,305	152,725,217	97.1

Note: Figures are 2007 estimates; (1) Metropolitan Statistical Area - see Appendix B for areas included
Source: Claritas, Inc.

Religion

Area	Catholic	Southern Baptist	United Meth-odist	ELCA[1]	LDS[2]	Presby-terian Church USA	Jewish Est.	Muslim Est.
County	6.5	26.4	9.4	0.6	0.7	1.3	0.4	0.4
U.S.	22.0	7.1	3.7	1.8	1.5	1.1	2.2	0.6

Note: Figures are the number of adherents as a percentage of the total population; Adherents are defined as all members, including full members, their children and the estimated number of other participants who are not considered members (e.g. the baptized, those not confirmed, those regularly attending services, etc.); (1) Evangelical Lutheran Church in America; (2) The Church of Jesus Christ of Latter Day Saints
Source: Reprinted with permission from Religious Congregations and Membership in the United States 2000 (Nashville, Glenmary Research Center, 2002) Copyright Association of Statisticians of American Religious Bodies. All rights reserved.

ECONOMY

Gross Metropolitan Product

Area	2002	2003	2004	2005	2005 Rank[2]
MSA[1]	34.0	36.4	39.6	43.1	51

Note: Figures are in billions of dollars; (1) Oklahoma City, OK Metropolitan Statistical Area - see Appendix A for areas included; (2) Rank ranges from 1 to 361
Source: The U.S. Conference of Mayors, "U.S. Metro Economies: GMP - The Engines of America's Growth," January 2007

Economic Growth

Area	1995 GMP	2005 GMP	Average Annual Growth Rate	Growth Rate Rank[2]
MSA[1]	23.8	43.1	6.1	114

Note: Figures are in billions of dollars; GMP = Gross Metropolitan Product; (1) Oklahoma City, OK Metropolitan Statistical Area - see Appendix A for areas included; (2) Rank ranges from 1 to 361
Source: The U.S. Conference of Mayors, "U.S. Metro Economies: GMP - The Engines of America's Growth," January 2007

INCOME

Per Capita/Median/Average Income

Area	Per Capita ($)	Median Household ($)	Average Household ($)
City	32,769	65,921	86,535
MSA[1]	23,211	43,244	57,303
U.S.	25,495	49,280	66,670

Note: Figures are 2007 estimates; (1) Metropolitan Statistical Area - see Appendix B for areas included
Source: Claritas, Inc.

Household Income Distribution

Area	Percent of Households Earning							
	Under $15,000	$15,000 -24,999	$25,000 -34,999	$35,000 -49,999	$50,000 -74,999	$75,000 -99,000	$100,000 -149,999	$150,000 and up
City	9.1	6.9	8.3	13.2	19.6	14.8	16.8	11.3
MSA[1]	14.6	12.6	12.9	17.1	19.4	10.5	8.7	4.1
U.S.	13.1	10.9	11.2	15.6	19.5	11.9	11.3	6.6

Note: Figures are 2007 estimates; (1) Metropolitan Statistical Area - see Appendix B for areas included
Source: Claritas, Inc.

Poverty Rates by Age

Area	All Ages	Under 5 Years Old	5 to 17 Years Old	18 to 64 Years Old	65 Years and Over
City	7.2	0.6	1.2	5.0	0.4
MSA[1]	13.5	1.5	3.3	7.8	0.9
U.S.	12.4	1.2	3.0	6.9	1.2

Note: Figures are percent of population with income in 1999 below poverty level and only include population for whom poverty status is determined; (1) Metropolitan Statistical Area - see Appendix A for areas included
Source: Census 2000, Summary File 3

Personal Bankruptcy Filing Rate

Area	2004	2005	2006
Oklahoma County	9.37	14.49	2.54
U.S.	5.31	6.82	2.00

Note: Numbers are per 1,000 population and include Chapter 7 and Chapter 13 filings
Source: Federal Deposit Insurance Corporation (FDIC), Regional Economic Conditions (RECON), 8/23/2007

EMPLOYMENT

Labor Force and Employment

Area	Civilian Labor Force			Workers Employed		
	Dec. 2006	Dec. 2007	% Chg.	Dec. 2006	Dec. 2007	% Chg.
City	36,737	36,677	-0.2	35,919	35,799	-0.3
MSA[1]	572,031	571,342	-0.1	549,042	547,206	-0.3
U.S.	152,571,000	153,705,000	0.7	146,081,000	146,334,000	0.2

Note: Data is not seasonally adjusted and covers workers 16 years of age and older; (1) Metropolitan Statistical Area - see Appendix B for areas included
Source: Bureau of Labor Statistics, http://stats.bls.gov

Unemployment Rate

Area	2007											
	Jan.	Feb.	Mar.	Apr.	May	Jun.	Jul.	Aug.	Sep.	Oct.	Nov.	Dec.
City	2.6	2.7	2.5	2.3	2.5	2.6	2.4	2.4	2.3	2.3	2.3	2.4
MSA[1]	4.7	4.7	4.4	4.0	4.4	4.6	4.3	4.2	4.0	4.1	4.0	4.2
U.S.	5.0	4.9	4.5	4.3	4.3	4.7	4.9	4.6	4.5	4.4	4.5	4.8

Note: Data is not seasonally adjusted and covers workers 16 years of age and older; All figures are percentages; (1) Metropolitan Statistical Area - see Appendix B for areas included
Source: Bureau of Labor Statistics, http://stats.bls.gov

Employment by Occupation

Occupation Classification	City (%)	MSA[1] (%)	U.S. (%)
Sales and Office	30.6	28.8	26.7
Professional and Related	26.5	19.6	20.2
Service	11.6	15.1	14.9
Production, Transportation, and Material Moving	6.1	12.9	14.6
Management, Business, and Financial	19.2	12.8	13.5
Construction, Extraction, and Maintenance	5.9	10.5	9.4
Farming, Forestry, and Fishing	0.2	0.3	0.7

Note: Figures cover employed civilians 16 years of age and older; (1) Metropolitan Statistical Area - see Appendix A for areas included
Source: Census 2000, Summary File 3

Employment by Industry

Sector	MSA[1] Number of Employees	MSA[1] Percent of Total	U.S. Percent of Total
Government	114,500	19.9	16.3
Education and Health Services	73,800	12.8	13.4
Professional and Business Services	75,400	13.1	13.1
Retail Trade	65,300	11.4	11.6
Manufacturing	36,700	6.4	9.9
Leisure and Hospitality	55,800	9.7	9.6
Financial Activities	34,600	6.0	5.9
Construction	28,200	4.9	5.3
Wholesale Trade	23,800	4.1	4.4
Other Services	22,600	3.9	3.9
Transportation and Utilities	17,100	3.0	3.7
Information	12,300	2.1	2.2
Natural Resources and Mining	15,000	2.6	0.5

Note: Figures cover non-farm employment as of December 2007 and are not seasonally adjusted; (1) Metropolitan Statistical Area - see Appendix B for areas included
Source: Bureau of Labor Statistics, http://stats.bls.gov

Average Wages

Occupation	$/Hr.	Occupation	$/Hr.
Accountants and Auditors	24.17	Maids and Housekeeping Cleaners	7.84
Automotive Mechanics	15.77	Maintenance and Repair Workers	15.04
Bookkeepers	14.29	Marketing Managers	32.72
Carpenters	14.92	Nuclear Medicine Technologists	32.14
Cashiers	7.88	Nurses, Licensed Practical	15.82
Clerks, General Office	10.80	Nurses, Registered	24.75
Clerks, Receptionists/Information	10.73	Nursing Aides/Orderlies/Attendants	9.82
Clerks, Shipping/Receiving	12.91	Packers and Packagers, Hand	8.32
Computer Programmers	31.00	Physical Therapists	34.62
Computer Support Specialists	16.71	Postal Service Mail Carriers	21.17
Computer Systems Analysts	30.84	Real Estate Brokers	n/a
Cooks, Restaurant	8.93	Retail Salespersons	10.93
Dentists	n/a	Sales Reps., Exc. Tech./Scientific	25.41
Electrical Engineers	30.21	Sales Reps., Tech./Scientific	27.80
Electricians	17.72	Secretaries, Exc. Legal/Med./Exec.	11.94
Financial Managers	36.41	Security Guards	12.90
First-Line Supervisors/Mgrs., Sales	16.79	Surgeons	n/a
Food Preparation Workers	7.59	Teacher Assistants	7.70
General and Operations Managers	36.91	Teachers, Elementary School	17.10
Hairdressers/Cosmetologists	9.02	Teachers, Secondary School	17.80
Internists	89.51	Telemarketers	9.29
Janitors and Cleaners	9.24	Truck Drivers, Heavy/Tractor-Trailer	17.44
Landscaping/Groundskeeping Workers	9.80	Truck Drivers, Light/Delivery Svcs.	12.61
Lawyers	48.28	Waiters and Waitresses	7.51

Note: Wage data covers the Oklahoma City, OK Metropolitan Statistical Area - see Appendix B for areas included. Hourly wages for elementary/secondary school teachers and teacher assistants were calculated by the editors from annual wage data assuming a 40 hour work week; n/a not available.
Source: Bureau of Labor Statistics, May 2007 Metro Area Occupational Employment and Wage Estimates

RESIDENTIAL REAL ESTATE

Building Permits

Area	Single-Family 2006	Single-Family 2007p	Single-Family Pct. Chg.	Multi-Family 2006	Multi-Family 2007p	Multi-Family Pct. Chg.	Total 2006	Total 2007p	Total Pct. Chg.
City	521	471	-9.6	0	265	-	521	736	41.3
U.S.	1,378,200	973,300	-29.4	460,700	407,200	-11.6	1,838,900	1,380,500	-24.9

Note: (p) preliminary; figures cover and represent new, privately-owned housing units authorized (unadjusted data); All permit data are based on estimates with imputation; U.S. figures are based on the new 20,000-place series.
Source: U.S. Census Bureau, Manufacturing, Mining, and Construction Statistics

Homeownership and Housing Vacancies

Area	Homeownership Rate[2] (%)			Rental Vacancy Rate[3] (%)			Homeowner Vacancy Rate[4] (%)		
	2005	2006	2007	2005	2006	2007	2005	2006	2007
MSA[1]	72.9	71.8	68.2	13.5	10.9	7.4	2.5	2.5	2.5
U.S.	68.9	68.8	68.1	9.8	9.8	9.7	1.9	2.4	2.7

Note: (1) Metropolitan Statistical Area - see Appendix B for areas included; (2) The proportion of households that are owners; (3) The proportion of the rental inventory that is vacant for rent; (4) The proportion of the homeowner inventory that is vacant for sale; n/a not available
Source: U.S. Census Bureau, Housing Vacancies and Homeownership Annual Statistics: 2007

TAXES

State Corporate Income Tax Rates

State	Rates and Tax Brackets
Oklahoma	6.0%

Note: Tax rates as of January 1, 2008; Additional franchise tax of $1.25 for each $1,000 of capital invested or used in Oklahoma.
Source: Tax Foundation, www.taxfoundation.org

State Individual Income Tax Rates

State	Federal Deductibility	Marginal Rates (%)	Standard Deduction ($)		Personal Exemptions ($)[1]	
			Single	Joint	Single	Dependents
Oklahoma	No (d)	0.5 - 5.65 (y)	2,000	3,000	1,000	1,000

Note: Tax rates as of January 1, 2008; Local- and county-level taxes are not included; n/a not applicable; (1) Married joint filers generally receive double the single exemption; (d) Federal deductibility repealed; (y) Brackets are not double for married taxpayers.
Source: Tax Foundation, www.taxfoundation.org

Various State and Local Tax Rates

State and Local Sales and Use (%)	State Sales and Use (%)	Gasoline[1,2] ($/gal.)	Cigarette ($/pack)	Spirits ($/gal.)	Table Wine ($/gal.)	Beer ($/gal.)
7.75	4.5	0.17	1.03	5.56	0.72	0.40

Note: Tax rates as of January 1, 2008; (1) In addition to the 18.4 cpg Federal gasoline tax; (2) Rates may include additional state sales taxes, environmental protection and storage fees/taxes, and local taxes. When necessary, the volume-weighted average of all local taxes is used to approximate the typical statewide rate including local tax
Source: Tax Foundation, www.taxfoundation.org; Original research

State Tax Burdens

Area	Combined State and Local Tax Burden		Combined Federal, State and Local Tax Burden	
	Percent	Rank	Percent	Rank
Oklahoma	9.0	45	27.8	50
U.S. Average	11.0	-	32.7	-

Note: Figures cover 2007 and measure taxes as a percentage of income
Source: Tax Foundation, www.taxfoundation.org

State Business Tax Climate Index Rankings

State	Overall Rank	Corporate Tax Index Rank	Individual Income Tax Index Rank	Sales Tax Index Rank	Unemployment Insurance Tax Index Rank	Property Tax Index Rank
Oklahoma	19	13	22	31	1	24

Note: Rankings range from 1 to 50 where 1 is best. Rankings do not average across to Overall Rank. States without a given tax are given a ranking of 1.
Source: Tax Foundation, State Business Tax Climate Index 2008

TRANSPORTATION

Means of Transportation to Work

Area	Car/Truck/Van		Public Transportation			Bicycle	Walked	Other Means	Worked at Home
	Drove Alone	Car-pooled	Bus	Subway	Railroad				
City	84.7	8.3	0.2	0.0	0.0	0.2	1.9	0.7	4.0
MSA[1]	81.8	12.0	0.5	0.0	0.0	0.2	1.7	1.0	2.8
U.S.	75.7	12.2	2.5	1.5	0.5	0.4	2.9	1.0	3.3

Note: Figures are percentages and cover workers 16 years of age and older;
(1) Metropolitan Statistical Area - see Appendix A for areas included
Source: Census 2000, Summary File 3

Travel Time to Work

Area	Less Than 15 Minutes	15 to 29 Minutes	30 to 44 Minutes	45 to 59 Minutes	60 Minutes or More
City	29.2	44.0	21.0	2.6	3.1
MSA[1]	30.2	43.4	18.3	4.4	3.7
U.S.	29.4	36.1	19.1	7.4	8.0

Note: Figures are percentages and include workers 16 years old and over; (1) Metropolitan Statistical Area - see Appendix A for areas included
Source: Census 2000, Summary File 3

Travel Time Index

Area	1982	1995	2004	2005
Urban Area[1]	1.02	1.07	1.09	1.09
Average[2]	1.11	1.22	1.29	1.30

Note: Travel Time Index - The ratio of travel time in the peak period to the travel time at free-flow conditions. A value of 1.35 indicates a 20-minute free-flow trip takes 27 minutes in the peak. Free-flow speeds (60 mph on freeways and 35 mph on principal arterials) are used as the comparison threshold; (1) Covers the Oklahoma City, OK urban area; (2) average of 85 urban areas
Source: Texas Transportation Institute, The 2007 Urban Mobility Report, September 2007

Living Environment

COST OF LIVING

Cost of Living Index

Composite Index	Groceries	Housing	Utilities	Trans-portation	Health Care	Misc. Goods/Services
90.4	88.6	81.2	90.3	98.6	96.0	95.3

Note: U.S. = 100; Figures cover the Edmond OK urban area.
Source: The Council for Community and Economic Research (formerly ACCRA), Cost of Living Index, 2007

Grocery Prices

Area[1]	T-Bone Steak ($/pound)	Frying Chicken ($/pound)	Whole Milk ($/half gal.)	Eggs ($/dozen)	Orange Juice ($/64 oz.)	Coffee ($/11.5 oz.)
City[2]	8.76	0.91	2.01	1.38	2.97	3.12
Avg.	8.93	1.12	2.13	1.52	3.26	3.31
Min.	5.88	0.71	1.33	0.83	2.30	2.20
Max.	12.80	2.07	3.43	3.54	5.79	6.20

Note: (1) Values for the local area are compared with the average, minimum and maximum values for all 331 areas in the Cost of Living Index report; (2) Figures cover the Edmond OK urban area; **T-Bone Steak** *(price per pound);* **Frying Chicken** *(price per pound, whole fryer);* **Whole Milk** *(half gallon carton);* **Eggs** *(price per dozen, Grade A, large);* **Orange Juice** *(64 oz. Tropicana or Florida Natural);* **Coffee** *(11.5 oz. can, vacuum-packed, Maxwell House, Hills Bros, or Folgers).*
Source: The Council for Community and Economic Research (formerly ACCRA), Cost of Living Index, 2007

Housing and Utility Costs

Area[1]	New Home Price ($)	Apartment Rent ($/month)	All Electric ($/month)	Part Electric ($/month)	Other Energy ($/month)	Telephone ($/month)
City[2]	248,942	670	-	69.74	66.55	26.33
Avg.	309,605	782	146.13	78.67	90.16	26.14
Min.	189,877	n/a	82.03	37.41	33.15	17.08
Max.	1,202,800	3,481	271.14	150.60	257.67	37.45

Note: (1) Values for the local area are compared with the average, minimum and maximum values for all 331 areas in the Cost of Living Index report; (2) Figures cover the Edmond OK urban area; **New Home Price** *(2,400 sf living area, 8,000 sf lot, in urban area with full utilities);* **Apartment Rent** *(950 sf 2 bedroom/1.5 or 2 bath, unfurnished, excluding all utilities except water);* **All Electric** *(average monthly cost for an all-electric home);* **Part Electric** *(average monthly cost for a part-electric home);* **Other Energy** *(average monthly cost for natural gas, fuel oil, coal, wood, and any other forms of energy except electricity);* **Telephone** *(price includes basic monthly rate for a private residential line plus additional local usage charges incurred by a family of four).*
Source: The Council for Community and Economic Research (formerly ACCRA), Cost of Living Index, 2007

Health Care, Transportation, and Other Costs

Area[1]	Doctor ($/visit)	Dentist ($/visit)	Optometrist ($/visit)	Gasoline ($/gallon)	Beauty Salon ($/visit)	Men's Shirt ($)
City[2]	72.01	69.00	81.93	2.54	33.49	26.33
Avg.	79.48	71.93	79.55	2.64	29.52	25.77
Min.	52.08	44.80	43.95	2.19	15.58	16.19
Max.	148.44	126.27	158.83	3.48	60.62	48.53

Note: (1) Values for the local area are compared with the average, minimum and maximum values for all 331 areas in the Cost of Living Index report; (2) Figures cover the Edmond OK urban area; **Doctor** *(general practitioners routine exam of an established patient);* **Dentist** *(adult teeth cleaning and periodic oral examination);* **Optometrist** *(full vision eye exam for established adult patient);* **Gasoline** *(one gallon regular unleaded, national brand, including all taxes, cash price at self-service pump if available);* **Beauty Salon** *(woman's shampoo, trim, and blow-dry);* **Men's Shirt** *(cotton/polyester dress shirt, pinpoint weave, long sleeves).*
Source: The Council for Community and Economic Research (formerly ACCRA), Cost of Living Index, 2007

HOUSING

House Price Index (HPI)

Area	National Ranking[2]	Quarterly Change (%)	One-Year Change (%)	Five-Year Change (%)
MSA[1]	51	0.63	4.59	29.80
U.S.[3]	-	0.10	0.84	41.37

Note: The HPI is a weighted repeat sales index. It measures average price changes in repeat sales or refinancings on the same properties. This information is obtained by reviewing repeat mortgage transactions on single-family properties whose mortgages have been purchased or securitized by Fannie Mae or Freddie Mac in January 1975; (1) Metropolitan Statistical Area - see Appendix B for areas included; (2) Rankings are based on annual percentage change for all metro areas containing at least 15,000 transactions over the last 10 years and ranges from 1 to 291; (3) figures based on a weighted average of Census Division estimates; all figures are for the period ending December 31, 2007
Source: Office of Federal Housing Enterprise Oversight, House Price Index, February 26, 2008

House Price Valuations

Area	Q1 2000	Q1 2001	Q1 2002	Q1 2003	Q1 2004	Q1 2005	Q1 2006	Q1 2007	Q1 2008
MSA[1]	-5.3	-13.7	-10.8	-10.8	-14.3	-16.4	-16.9	-16.4	-21.3

Note: Figures show the percentage of over- or under-valuation of single family homes relative to statistically normal house values (e.g. a value of 23.6 indicates that house values are 23.6% overvalued). Statistically normal house values are based on house prices, interest rates, household incomes, population densities, and any historical premiums or discounts metropolitan areas have exhibited over time; (1) Figures cover the Metropolitan Statistical Area - see Appendix B for areas included
Source: Global Insight/National City Corporation, House Prices in America, May 2008

Median Home Prices

Area	2005	2006	2007[r]	Percent Change 2006 to 2007
MSA[1]	114.7	125.0	134.9	7.9
U.S. Average	219.0	221.9	217.9	-1.8

Note: Figures are median sales prices of existing single-family homes in thousands of dollars; (r) revised; n/a not available; (1) Metropolitan Statistical Area - see Appendix B for areas included
Source: National Association of Realtors, Metropolitan Area Prices, 1st Quarter 2008

Housing: Year Structure Built

Area	1990 -2000	1980 -1989	1970 -1979	1960 -1969	1950 -1959	1940 -1949	Before 1940	Median Year
City	26.1	31.1	25.3	9.2	3.7	1.6	2.9	1982
MSA[1]	13.8	19.8	21.9	16.3	13.4	7.1	7.8	1972
U.S.	17.0	15.8	18.5	13.7	12.7	7.3	15.0	1971

Note: Figures are percentages; (1) Metropolitan Statistical Area - see Appendix A for areas included
Source: Census 2000, Summary File 3

HEALTH

Health Risk Data

Category	Area[1] (%)	U.S. (%)
Adults who have been told they have high blood pressure[3]	26.8	25.5
Adults who have been told they have high blood cholesterol[3]	36.3	35.6
Adults who have been told they have diabetes[2]	9.1	7.5
Adults who have been told they have arthritis[3]	26.8	27.0
Adults who have been told they currently have asthma	9.7	8.5
Adults who are current smokers	23.9	20.1
Adults who are heavy drinkers[4]	4.5	4.9
Adults who are overweight (BMI 25.0 - 29.9)	35.1	36.5
Adults who are obese (BMI 30.0 - 99.8)	27.5	25.1

Note: Data as of 2006 unless otherwise noted; (1) Figures cover the Metropolitan Statistical Area - see Appendix B for areas included; (2) Figures do not include pregnancy-related diabetes, pre-diabetes or borderline diabetes; (3) 2005 data; (4) Heavy drinkers are classified as adult men having more than two drinks per day or adult women having more than one drink per day
Source: Centers for Disease Control and Prevention, Behaviorial Risk Factor Surveillance System, SMART: Selected Metropolitan/Micropolitan Area Risk Trends, 2005, 2006

Mortality Rates for the Top 10 Causes of Death in the U.S.

ICD-10[a] Sub-Chapter	ICD-10[a] Code	Age-Adjusted Mortality Rate[1] per 100,000 population	
		County[2]	U.S.
Malignant neoplasms	C00-C97	192.5	186.5
Ischaemic heart diseases	I20-I25	186.4	152.3
Other forms of heart disease	I30-I51	61.1	51.5
Cerebrovascular diseases	I60-I69	65.9	50.0
Chronic lower respiratory diseases	J40-J47	57.3	42.6
Diabetes mellitus	E10-E14	26.9	24.8
Other degenerative diseases of the nervous system	G30-G31	20.8	22.6
Other external causes of accidental injury	W00-X59	27.3	21.4
Influenza and pneumonia	J10-J18	19.5	20.7
Hypertensive diseases	I10-I13	18.3	18.2

Note: (a) ICD-10 = International Classification of Diseases 10th Revision; (1) Mortality rates are a three year average covering 2003-2005; (2) Figures cover Oklahoma County
Source: Centers for Disease Control and Prevention, National Center for Health Statistics. Compressed Mortality File 1999-2004. CDC WONDER On-line Database, compiled from Compressed Mortality File 1999-2005 Series 20 No. 2K, 2008.

Mortality Rates for Selected Causes of Death

ICD-10[a] Sub-Chapter	ICD-10[a] Code	Age-Adjusted Mortality Rate[1] per 100,000 population	
		County[2]	U.S.
Assault	X85-Y09	8.4	5.9
Human immunodeficiency virus (HIV) disease	B20-B24	4.4	4.5
Intentional self-harm	X60-X84	13.7	10.8
Malnutrition	E40-E46	2.2	1.0
Obesity and other hyperalimentation	E65-E68	1.3	1.4
Organic, including symptomatic, mental disorders	F01-F09	20.1	16.8
Transport accidents	V01-V99	14.6	16.1
Viral hepatitis	B15-B19	4.5	1.8

Note: (a) ICD-10 = International Classification of Diseases 10th Revision; (1) Mortality rates are a three year average covering 2003-2005; (2) Figures cover Oklahoma County
Source: Centers for Disease Control and Prevention, National Center for Health Statistics. Compressed Mortality File 1999-2004. CDC WONDER On-line Database, compiled from Compressed Mortality File 1999-2005 Series 20 No. 2K, 2008.

Distribution of Physicians[1]

Area	Total	Family/ General Practice	Specialties	
			Medical	Surgical
Oklahoma County (number)	1,739	362	583	424
Oklahoma County (rate per 10,000 pop.)	25.4	5.3	8.5	6.2
U.S. (rate per 10,000 pop.)	17.7	4.6	6.9	4.3

Note: Data as of 2005; (1) Includes all non-federal, patient-care, office-based MDs
Source: Area Resource File (ARF). June 2007. U.S. Department of Health and Human Services, Health Resources and Services Administration, Bureau of Health Professions, Rockville, MD.

Hospitals

Edmond has the following hospitals: 1 general medical and surgical; 1 long-term acute care; 1 other specialty.
AHA Guide to the Healthcare Field 2008

EDUCATION

Public School District Statistics

District Name	Schls	Pupils	Pupil/ Teacher Ratio	Minority Pupils[1] (%)	Free Lunch Eligible[2] (%)	IEP[3] (%)
Deer Creek	5	2,569	16.4	14.7	3.3	12.7
Edmond	21	19,178	17.5	22.0	15.4	13.6

Note: Table includes regular local school districts with 2,000 or more students; (1) Percentage of students that are not white, non-Hispanic; (2) Percentage of students that are eligible for the free lunch program; (3) Percentage of students that have an Individualized Education Program.
Source: U.S. Department of Education, National Center for Education Statistics, Common Core of Data, Local Education Agency (School District) Universe Survey: School Year 2005-2006; U.S. Department of Education, National Center for Education Statistics, Common Core of Data, Public Elementary/Secondary School Universe Survey: School Year 2005-2006

Top Public High Schools

High School Name	Index[1]	Rank[1]	Subsidized Lunch (%)[2]	E&E (%)[3]
Edmond Memorial	1.277	1,129	17.0	31.4
Edmond North	2.058	470	15.0	36.8
Edmond Santa Fe	1.211	1,205	18.0	23.0

Note: (1) Public schools are ranked according to a ratio that is the number of Advanced Placement, International Baccalaureate, and/or Cambridge tests taken by all students at a school in 2007 divided by the number of graduating seniors. All of the schools on the list have an index of at least 1.000; they are in the top five percent of public schools measured this way. The rankings range from 1 to 1,422; (2) Percentage of students receiving federally subsidized meals; (3) E & E stands for equity and excellence percentage: the portion of all graduating seniors at a school that had at least one passing grade on one AP or IB test; (**) Gave both IB and AP tests. AP and IB participation are indicators of a school's efforts to get students to excel and prepare for college.
Source: Newsweek Online, "Top High Schools 2008"

Highest Level of Education

Area	Less than H.S.	H.S. Diploma	Some College, No Deg.	Associate Degree	Bachelors Degree	Masters Degree	Profess. School Degree	Doctorate Degree
City	5.5	16.3	25.0	4.2	31.0	11.3	4.8	1.9
MSA[1]	15.9	27.9	26.1	5.3	16.3	5.6	1.9	0.9
U.S.	19.4	28.4	21.2	6.4	15.7	5.9	2.0	1.0

Note: Figures are 2007 estimated percentages and cover persons age 25 and over; (1) Metropolitan Statistical Area - see Appendix B for areas included
Source: Claritas, Inc.

Educational Attainment by Race

Area	High School Graduate (%)					Bachelor's Degree (%)				
	Total	White	Black	Asian	Hisp.[2]	Total	White	Black	Asian	Hisp.[2]
City	94.2	94.6	94.4	94.8	77.2	47.8	48.5	32.2	67.0	26.4
MSA[1]	83.6	85.7	80.7	76.8	50.1	24.4	26.1	15.6	37.3	9.6
U.S.	80.4	83.6	72.3	80.4	52.4	24.4	26.1	14.3	44.1	10.4

Note: Figures shown cover persons 25 years old and over; (1) Metropolitan Statistical Area - see Appendix A for areas included; (2) people of Hispanic origin can be of any race
Source: Census 2000, Summary File 3

School Enrollment by Type

Area	Grades KG to 8				Grades 9 to 12			
	Public		Private		Public		Private	
	Enrollment	%	Enrollment	%	Enrollment	%	Enrollment	%
City	8,602	87.1	1,273	12.9	3,922	91.7	357	8.3
MSA[1]	129,199	91.2	12,443	8.8	57,617	92.5	4,701	7.5
U.S.	33,526,011	88.7	4,285,121	11.3	14,848,628	90.6	1,532,323	9.4

Note: Figures shown cover persons 3 years old and over; (1) Metropolitan Statistical Area - see Appendix A for areas included
Source: Census 2000, Summary File 3

School Enrollment by Race

Area	Grades KG to 8 (%)				Grades 9 to 12 (%)			
	White	Black	Asian	Hisp.[1]	White	Black	Asian	Hisp.[1]
City	86.8	4.9	1.5	3.6	86.9	5.0	0.8	2.8
MSA[2]	67.3	13.6	2.2	9.9	69.2	14.0	2.4	7.6
U.S.	68.5	15.5	3.3	16.8	68.8	15.5	3.8	15.7

Note: Figures shown cover persons 3 years old and over; (1) people of Hispanic origin can be of any race; (2) Metropolitan Statistical Area - see Appendix A for areas included
Source: Census 2000, Summary File 3

Average Salaries of Public School Classroom Teachers

District	2005-06		2006-07		Percent Change 2005-06 to 2006-07
	Dollars	Rank[1]	Dollars	Rank[1]	
Oklahoma	38,772	48	42,379	42	9.30
U.S. Average	49,026	-	50,816	-	3.65

Note: (1) State rank ranges from 1 to 51.
Source: National Education Association, Rankings & Estimates: Rankings of the States 2006 and Estimates of School Statistics 2007, December 2007

Higher Education

Four-Year Colleges			Two-Year Colleges			Medical Schools[1]	Law Schools[2]	Voc/ Tech[3]
Public	Private Non-profit	Private For-profit	Public	Private Non-profit	Private For-profit			
1	1	0	0	0	0	0	0	0

Note: Figures cover institutions located within the city limits; (1) includes schools accredited by the Liaison Committee on Medical Education and the American Osteopathic Association; (2) includes American Bar Association-accredited law schools; (3) includes all schools with programs that are less than 2 years.
Source: National Center for Education Statistics, The Integrated Postsecondary Education System (IPEDS) Peer Analysis System, 2007; www.usnews.com, Law and Medical School Directories, 2009

PRESIDENTIAL ELECTION

2004 Presidential Election Results

Area	Bush	Kerry	Nader	Other
Oklahoma County	64.2	35.8	0.0	0.0
U.S.	50.7	48.3	0.4	0.6

Note: Results are percentages and may not add to 100% due to rounding
Source: Dave Leip's Atlas of U.S. Presidential Elections, www.uselectionatlas.org

EMPLOYERS

Major Employers

Company Name	Industry	Type of Site
Advance Food Company Inc	Sausages and other prepared meats	Branch
CPNI	National commercial banks	Branch
Chesapeake Operating Inc	Crude petroleum and natural gas	Headquarters
City Clerk Office	General government, nec	Single
County of Oklahoma	Executive offices	Headquarters
DOT Federal Aviation Admin	Regulation, administration of transportation	Branch
Health & Science Center	Colleges and universities	Branch
Health Sciences Center	Colleges and universities	Branch
Mercy Health Center Inc	General medical and surgical hospitals	Headquarters
Mike Monroney Aeronautical Ctr	Airports, flying fields, and services	Single
Mike Monroney Aeronautical Ctr	Regulation, administration of transportation	Branch
Oklahoma Dept of Corrections	Correctional institutions	Branch
Oklahoma Medical Center	General medical and surgical hospitals	Branch
Ou Medical Center	General medical and surgical hospitals	Single
Physicians Services	Offices and clinics of medical doctors	Branch
Southwest Medical Center Okla	General medical and surgical hospitals	Headquarters
Terex Roadbuilding	Construction machinery	Headquarters
Tinker Air Force Base	National security	Branch
Tronox LLC	Industrial inorganic chemicals, nec	Single
Universtiy of Oklahoma Press	Colleges and universities	Headquarters

Note: Companies shown are located within the Oklahoma City metropolitan area; nec = not elsewhere classified.
Source: www.zapdata.com, May 2008

PUBLIC SAFETY

Crime Rate

Area	All Crimes	Violent Crimes				Property Crimes		
		Murder	Forcible Rape	Robbery	Aggrav. Assault	Burglary	Larceny -Theft	Motor Vehicle Theft
City	2,716.4	1.3	39.7	18.5	60.9	489.8	1,984.3	121.8
Metro[1]	5,128.7	7.0	46.5	124.4	337.4	1,214.1	2,853.8	545.3
U.S.	3,808.1	5.7	30.9	149.4	287.5	729.4	2,206.8	398.4

Note: Figures are crimes per 100,000 population; (1) Metropolitan Statistical Area - see Appendix B for areas included
Source: FBI Uniform Crime Reports, 2006

Hate Crimes

Area	Number of Quarters Reported	Bias Motivation				
		Race	Religion	Sexual Orientation	Ethnicity	Disability
City	4	3	3	1	0	1

Source: Federal Bureau of Investigation, Hate Crime Statistics 2006

RECREATION

Culture

Dance[1]	Theatre[1]	Instrumental Music[1]	Vocal Music[1]	Series/ Festivals	Museums	Zoos and Aquariums[2]
0	2	0	0	2	1	0

Note: (1) Number of professional perfoming groups; (2) AZA-accredited
Source: The Grey House Performing Arts Directory, 2007; Official Museum Directory, 2008; Association of Zoos & Aquariums, AZA Member Zoos & Aquariums, June 2008

Professional Sports Teams

Team Name	League
No teams are located in the metro area	

Source: Original research

MEDIA

Newspapers

Name	News Focus	Frequency	Circulation
The Edmond Sun	Local	Daily	10,500

Note: Includes newspapers with offices located in the city
Source: MediaContactsPro, March 2008

Television Stations

Name	Ch.	Network(s)	Type	Ownership
KOET	3	PBS	Public	Oklahoma Educational Television Authority
KFOR	4	NBC	Commercial	New York Times Company
KOCO	5	ABC	Commercial	Hearst-Argyle Broadcasting
KWTV	9	CBS	Commercial	Griffin Television Inc.
KWET	12	PBS	Public	Oklahoma Educational Television Authority
KETA	13	PBS	Public	Oklahoma Educational Television Authority
KTBO	14	n/a	Commercial	Trinity Broadcasting Network
KOKH	25	Fox/WBN	Commercial	Sinclair Broadcast Group
KOCB	34	Fox/WBN	Commercial	Sinclair Broadcast Group
KAUT	43	UPN	Commercial	Paramount Stations Group
KSBI	52	n/a	Commercial	Locke Supply Company
KOPX	62	Pax	n/a	Paxson Communications Corporation

Note: Stations included cover the Oklahoma City DMA (Designated Market Area); n/a not available
BurrellesLuce, MediaContacts Online, January 2007

Major AM Radio Stations

Call Letters	Freq. (kHz)	Station Type	Target Audience	Station Format	Music Format
WWLS	640	Commercial	General	Sports	n/a
KQCV	800	Commercial	Religious	Music/News/Talk	Christian
KTLR	890	Commercial	General/Religious	News	n/a
WKY	930	Commercial	General	Talk	n/a
KGWA	960	Commercial	General	News/Talk	n/a
KTOK	1000	Commercial	General	News/Talk	n/a
KVSP	1140	Commercial	Black/General	Music/Talk	Urban Contemp.
WBBZ	1230	Commercial	General	Music	Adult Standards
KWSH	1260	Commercial	General/Native Amer	Music/News	Country
KCLI	1320	n/a	General	Music/News/Sports	n/a
KCRC	1390	Commercial	General	News/Talk	n/a
KREF	1400	Commercial	General	n/a	n/a
KTJS	1420	Commercial	General/Religious	Music/News	Country
KGFF	1450	Commercial	General	Music/Sports	Adult Standards
KSIW	1450	Commercial	General	Music/News	Oldies
KOMA	1520	Commercial	General	News/Talk	n/a
KWCO	1560	Commercial	General	Music/News	Oldies
KOKB	1580	Commercial	General	Sports/Talk	n/a
KWEY	1590	Commercial	General	Music	Country
KUSH	1600	Commercial	General	Music/News/Sports	Contemp. Country

Note: Stations included cover the Oklahoma City DMA (Designated Market Area); n/a not available
Source: BurrellesLuce, MediaContacts Online, January 2007

Major FM Radio Stations

Call Letters	Freq. (mHz)	Station Type	Target Audience	Station Format	Music Format
KLVV	88.7	Non-Comm	General/Religious	Music	Christian
KCSC	90.1	College	General	Music/News	Classical
KOKF	90.9	n/a	General	Music	n/a
KOSU	91.7	College	General	Educational	n/a
KOMA	92.5	n/a	General	Music/News/Sports	n/a
KKNG	93.3	Commercial	General	Music/News/Talk	Country
KSPI	93.7	n/a	General	Music/News/Talk	n/a
KHBZ	94.7	Commercial	General	n/a	n/a
KQMX	95.5	Commercial	General	Music	Top 40
KXLS	95.7	Commercial	General	Music/News/Sports	Adult Contemp.
KXXY	96.1	Commercial	General	Music/News	Country
KECO	96.5	Commercial	General	Music/News	Country
KWEY	97.3	Commercial	General	Music/News	Country
KKWD	97.9	Commercial	General	Music/News/Talk	Urban Contemp.
KYIS	98.9	Commercial	General	Music	Top 40
KNID	99.7	n/a	General	Music	n/a
KATT	100.5	Commercial	General	Music	Alternative
KPNC	100.9	Commercial	General	Music	Country
KWOX	101.1	Commercial	General	Music/News	Country
KTST	101.9	n/a	General	Music	n/a
KJYO	102.7	Commercial	General	Music	Adult Contemp.
KOFM	103.1	Commercial	General	Music/News	Country
KMGL	104.1	Commercial	General	Music	Adult Contemp.
KBLP	105.1	n/a	Religious	Music/News/Sports/Talk	n/a
KOSB	105.1	n/a	General	Music	n/a
KGFY	105.5	Commercial	General	Music/News	Country
KIRC	105.9	n/a	General	Music	n/a
KGOU	106.3	College	General	Music/Talk	Blues
KTUZ	106.7	Commercial	General/Hispanic	Music/News	Top 40
KRXO	107.7	Commercial	General	Music	Classic Rock

Note: Stations included cover the Oklahoma City DMA (Designated Market Area); n/a not available
BurrellesLuce, MediaContacts Online, January 2007

CLIMATE

Average and Extreme Temperatures

Temperature	Jan	Feb	Mar	Apr	May	Jun	Jul	Aug	Sep	Oct	Nov	Dec	Yr.
Extreme High (°F)	80	84	93	100	104	105	109	110	104	96	87	86	110
Average High (°F)	47	52	61	72	79	87	93	92	84	74	60	50	71
Average Temp. (°F)	36	41	50	60	69	77	82	81	73	62	49	40	60
Average Low (°F)	26	30	38	49	58	66	71	70	62	51	38	29	49
Extreme Low (°F)	-4	-3	1	20	32	47	53	51	36	22	11	-8	-8

Note: Figures cover the years 1948-1990
Source: National Climatic Data Center, International Station Meteorological Climate Summary, 9/96

Average Precipitation/Snowfall/Humidity

Precip./Humidity	Jan	Feb	Mar	Apr	May	Jun	Jul	Aug	Sep	Oct	Nov	Dec	Yr.
Avg. Precip. (in.)	1.2	1.5	2.5	2.8	5.6	4.4	2.8	2.5	3.5	3.1	1.6	1.3	32.8
Avg. Snowfall (in.)	3	3	2	Tr	0	0	0	0	0	Tr	1	2	10
Avg. Rel. Hum. 6am (%)	78	78	76	77	84	84	81	81	82	79	78	77	80
Avg. Rel. Hum. 3pm (%)	53	52	47	46	52	51	46	44	47	46	48	52	49

Note: Figures cover the years 1948-1990; Tr = Trace amounts (<0.05 in. of rain; <0.5 in. of snow)
Source: National Climatic Data Center, International Station Meteorological Climate Summary, 9/96

Weather Conditions

Temperature			Daytime Sky			Precipitation		
10°F & below	32°F & below	90°F & above	Clear	Partly cloudy	Cloudy	0.01 inch or more precip.	0.1 inch or more snow/ice	Thunder-storms
5	79	70	124	131	110	80	8	50

Note: Figures are average number of days per year and cover the years 1948-1990
Source: National Climatic Data Center, International Station Meteorological Climate Summary, 9/96

HAZARDOUS WASTE

Superfund Sites

Edmond has no sites on the EPA's Superfund Final National Priorities List.
U.S. Environmental Protection Agency, Final National Priorities List, June 23, 2008

AIR & WATER QUALITY

Air Quality Index

Area	Percent of Days when Air Quality was...[2]				AQI Statistics	
	Good	Moderate	Unhealthy for Sensitive Groups	Unhealthy	Maximum	Median
MSA[1]	72.9	25.5	1.6	0.0	135	41

Note: The Air Quality Index (AQI) is an index for reporting daily air quality. EPA calculates the AQI for five major air pollutants regulated by the Clean Air Act: ground-level ozone, particle pollution (also known as particulate matter), carbon monoxide, sulfur dioxide, and nitrogen dioxide. The AQI runs from 0 to 500. The higher the AQI value, the greater the level of air pollution and the greater the health concern. There are six AQI categories: "Good" The AQI is between 0 and 50. Air quality is considered satisfactory; "Moderate" The AQI is between 51 and 100. Air quality is acceptable; "Unhealthy for Sensitive Groups" When AQI values are between 101 and 150, members of sensitive groups may experience health effects; "Unhealthy" When AQI values are between 151 and 200 everyone may begin to experience health effects; "Very Unhealthy" AQI values between 201 and 300 trigger a health alert; "Hazardous" AQI values over 300 trigger health warnings of emergency conditions; (1) Metropolitan Statistical Area - see Appendix A for areas included; (2) Based on 365 days with AQI data in 2007.
Source: U.S. Environmental Protection Agency, Air Quality Index Report, 2007

Air Quality Index Pollutants

Area	Percent of Days when AQI Pollutant was...[2]					
	Carbon Monoxide	Nitrogen Dioxide	Ozone	Sulfur Dioxide	Particulate Matter 2.5	Particulate Matter 10
MSA[1]	0.0	0.0	58.6	0.0	41.1	0.3

Note: The Air Quality Index (AQI) is an index for reporting daily air quality. EPA calculates the AQI for five major air pollutants regulated by the Clean Air Act: ground-level ozone, particle pollution (also known as particulate matter), carbon monoxide, sulfur dioxide, and nitrogen dioxide. The AQI runs from 0 to 500. The higher the AQI value, the greater the level of air pollution and the greater the health concern; (1) Metropolitan Statistical Area - see Appendix A for areas included; (2) Based on 365 days with AQI data in 2007.
Source: U.S. Environmental Protection Agency, Air Quality Index Report, 2007

Air Quality Index Trends

Area	Trend Sites (9)								All Sites (30)
	1999	2000	2001	2002	2003	2004	2005	2006	2006
MSA[1]	4	7	2	2	2	0	2	11	11

Note: An AQI value greater than 100 indicates that air quality would have been in the unhealthful range on that day. Data from exceptional events are not included. These counts are presented in two ways. First, the counts are based on sites having an adequate record of monitoring data during the trend period (trend sites). These counts represent the relative change in the number of days with AQI values greater than 100. In the last column, the counts are based on all sites with data in the most recent year (because it is possible for a site to have data in the most recent year but not enough data to be a trend site); (1) Metropolitan Statistical Area - see Appendix A for areas included.
Source: U.S. Environmental Protection Agency, Office of Air and Radiation, Air Trends, Factbook and Related Information, Air Pollution Trends in Selected Metropolitan Areas 2006

Maximum Air Pollutant Concentrations

	Particulate Matter 10 (ug/m^3)	Particulate Matter 2.5 (ug/m^3)	Ozone (ppm)	Carbon Monoxide (ppm)	Sulfur Dioxide (ppm)	Nitrogen Dioxide (ppm)	Lead (ug/m^3)
MSA[1] Level	51	22	0.101	2	0.003	0.01	n/a
NAAQS[2]	150	35	0.125	9	0.140	0.053	1.50
Met NAAQS[2]	Yes	Yes	Yes	Yes	Yes	Yes	n/a

Note: Data from exceptional events are not included; (1) Metropolitan Statistical Area - see Appendix A for areas included; (2) National Ambient Air Quality Standards; n/a not available
Concentrations: Particulate Matter 10 (coarse particulate) - highest second maximum 24-hour concentration; Particulate Matter 2.5 (fine particulate) - highest 98th percentile 24-hour concentration; Ozone - highest second daily maximum 1-hour concentration; Carbon Monoxide - highest second maximum non-overlapping 8-hour concentration; Sulfur Dioxide - highest second maximum 24-hour concentration; Nitrogen Dioxide - highest arithmetic mean concentration; Lead - highest quarterly maximum concentration
Units: ppm = parts per million; ug/m^3 = micrograms per cubic meter
Source: U.S. Environmental Protection Agency, MSA Factbook 2006, Air Quality Statistics by City

Drinking Water

Water System Name	Pop. Served	Primary Water Source Type	Violations[1]	
			Health Based	Monitoring/ Reporting
Edmond PWA - Arcadia	73,870	Surface	4	0

Note: (1) Based on violation data from January 1, 2007 to December 31, 2007 (includes unresolved violations from earlier years)
Source: U.S. Environmental Protection Agency, Office of Ground Water and Drinking Water, Safe Drinking Water Information System (based on data extracted April 15, 2008)

Bend, Oregon

Background

Located in the foothills of the Cascade Mountains, Bend is noted for its vibrant downtown area, scenic setting, mild climate, year-round recreation and growing economy. The city covers 32 square miles along the western border of Central Oregon's high desert plateau. Bend is the geological result of dynamic lava flows and volcanic ash that shaped the Deschutes River. Canyon walls still punctuate the area and many wildlife species inhabit Deschutes' corridor.

The first permanent settlement was established in 1870. By 1877 a land claim was filed for the "Farewell Bend" ranch, located at the dramatic 90 degree bend in the Deschutes River just south of the current downtown. A post office was granted in 1886, and the name changed to Bend.

Shortly after the turn of the century, East Coast developers formed the first irrigation companies in the area, and construction was begun on several large canals and dams needed to take water out of the Deschutes River to irrigate the desert. The main canals are still in operation today.

Bend was incorporated in 1905. In 1911 the Oregon Trunk Line Railroad, coming south from the Columbia River, was completed to Bend. Four years later, plans were announced to build large sawmills there. The railroad and lumber mills created an explosion in population, which led to a tremendous growth in commerce and housing that is still evident today. Bend's historic architecture is the direct product of the boom period of the first part of the 20th century.

In the 1970s the economy began to diversify, and the number of jobs in the county increased dramatically during the last quarter of the century. Most of this growth has been in non-manufacturing sectors, as small, innovative niche-product companies began relocating or expanding here to escape skyrocketing costs, electricity shortages and tight labor markets.

The abundance of scenic and recreational amenities is complemented by a diverse cultural climate, which includes performing arts at the Community Theatre of the Cascades and The Central Oregon Community College presentations of the Magic Circle Theatre, Central Oregon Symphony, jazz band, and choir performances. In Drake Park, along the banks of Deschutes River, the Cascade Festival of Music presents classical, pops, and jazz concerts. The Munch & Music evening concerts offer free music, fine food, and spectacular mountain sunsets.

Many families choose Central Oregon because of its quality public schools. In 1991, Oregon passed legislation that offer students in grades 11 and 12 the Certificate of Advanced Mastery (CAM), which signifies that they are workforce ready. The college board is working on expanding Central Oregon Community College into a fully accredited, four -year college.

The Parks and School systems coordinate to complement one another, especially with regard to outdoor programs offered to school-aged children. The Bend Metro Park and Recreation District has dozens of parks, and over 900 acres of park land. The 600 acres of wildlife refuge along Tumolo Creek are used for hiking and picnicking. Butte State Park — a volcanic cinder cone in the center of town with a commanding view of the urban area — is a favorite spot for residents and visitors. Public parks and trails follow the Deschutes River which runs for eight miles through the city's center.

Bend's climate is typical of the high desert plateau, dry with low humidity, cool nights and sunny days. A typical Central Oregon summer is marked with daily temperatures in the 80s and 90s during the day, and the mid 40s and 50s during the night. Hard frosts are not unheard of during summer months. Autumn brings warm days and cooler nights, and "Indian Summer." The winter season provides typical daytime temperatures in the 40s to 50s. Nighttime temperatures range from 22 to 51 degrees.

Rankings

General Rankings

- Bend* was ranked #56 out of 375 metro areas in *Cities Ranked & Rated*. Criteria: cost of living; climate; crime; transportation; economy and jobs; education; arts and culture; health and healthcare; leisure; quality of life. *Cities Ranked & Rated, 2nd Edition, 2007*

- Bend* was ranked #212 out of 379 metro areas in *Places Rated Almanac*. Criteria: health care; education; recreation; transportation; ambience; climate; crime; housing costs; jobs. *Places Rated Almanac, 7th Edition, 2007*

- Bend was selected as one of the "2006 Best Places to Live" by *Money* magazine. Places were ranked using 38 quality-of-life indicators and six economic opportunity measures in the following categories: ease of living; health; education; crime; park space; arts and leisure. *CNNMoney.com, "Best Places to Live 2006"*

Business/Finance Rankings

- Bend was selected as one of the "100 Best Places to Live and Launch" in the U.S. The city ranked #87. The editors at *Fortune Small Business* ranked 296 Census-designated metro areas by business friendliness (Launching Score, % New Businesses) and lifestyle offerings (Living Score). Then, through reporting, they picked the town within each of the top 100 metro areas that best blends business and pleasure. *Fortune Small Business, "100 Best Places to Live and Launch 2008," April 2008*

- The Bend* metro area appeared on the Milken Institute "2007 Best Performing Cities" index. Rank: #1 out of 179 small metro areas. Criteria: job growth; wage and salary growth; high-tech output growth. *Milken Institute, "2007 Best Performing Cities"*

- The Bend* metro area was selected as one of the hottest cities for entrepreneurs in America by *Inc. Magazine.* Criteria: job-growth data for 393 metro was analyzed for current-year employment growth, average annual employment growth over past three years, and employment growth by industry sector. The Bend* metro area ranked #6 among small metro areas and #10 overall. *Inc. Magazine, May 2007*

- *Forbes* ranked 179 smaller metro areas in the U.S. in terms of the "Best Places for Business and Careers." The Bend* metro area was ranked #36. Criteria: business costs (labor, energy, tax and office space expenses); living costs (housing, transportation, food and other household expenditures); education levels of the work force; job growth; income growth; migration trends; crime rates; and culture/leisure. *Forbes, "Best Places for Business and Careers," March 19, 2008*

- *Kiplinger's Personal Finance* ranked 101 U.S. cities in terms of their total tax burdens. Bend ranked #82 (#1 had the lowest overall tax burden). Criteria: state income tax; property tax; sales tax; personal property tax; and gasoline tax. *Kiplinger's Personal Finance, July 2004*

- Bend appeared on *Kiplinger's Personal Finance* list of the "Top Ten Tax-Friendly Cities." The city was ranked #82. Criteria: income tax; sales tax; real estate and car/personal property tax. *Kiplinger's Personal Finance, May 2007*

Health/Environment Rankings

- The Bend* metro area appeared in *Country Home's* "2008 Best Green Places" report. The area ranked #9 out of 379. Criteria: official energy policies; green power; green buildings; availability of fresh, locally grown food. *Country Home, "2008 Best Green Places"*

- The American Podiatric Medical Association and *Prevention* magazine ranked America's 100 most populated cities based on fitness-walker friendliness. The best cities have safe streets, beautiful places to walk, mild weather and good air quality. Bend ranked #269. *Prevention, "The Best Walking Cities of 2008," April 2008; American Podiatric Medical Association, "2008 Best Fitness-Walking Cities, "April 2008*

Seniors/Retirement Rankings

- Bend was profiled in the book *America's 100 Best Places to Retire*. Criteria: comfortable climate; nearby health-care facilities; affordable housing; access to shopping and cultural venues; opportunities for community involvement and continuing education. *America's 100 Best Places to Retire, 4th Edition, 2007*

- Bend was profiled in the book *Where to Retire: America's Best and Most Affordable Places.* Cities were selected based on personal visits by the author and interviews with local residents coupled with statistics from various government agencies. *Where to Retire: America's Best and Most Affordable Places, 2006*

- Bend was profiled in the book *Retire in Style: 60 Outstanding Places Across the USA and Canada.* Criteria: landscape; climate; quality of life; cost of living; transportation; retail services; health care; community services; cultural and educational activities; recreational activities; work and volunteer activities; crime rates and public safety. *Retire in Style: 60 Outstanding Places Across the USA and Canada, 2nd Edition, 2005*

- Bend was identified as one of the best places to retire in *Retirement Places Rated.* Criteria: population above 10,000; attractiveness to older adults; affordability; climate and natural endowments; personal safety. The city was ranked #29 out of 200. *Retirement Places Rated, 7th Edition, 2007*

- A.G. Edwards ranked America's 500 top-performing communities based on their residents' personal savings and investing behavior. The Bend* metro area ranked #191 with an index score of 103.44 (national average = 100.00). A dozen statistical factors were measured including: participation in retirement savings plans; personal debt levels; and home ownership. *A.G. Edwards, "2007 Nest Egg Index", September 12, 2007*

Safety Rankings

- The National Insurance Crime Bureau ranked 361 metro areas in the U.S. in terms of per capita rates of vehicle theft. The Bend* metro area ranked #222 (#1 = highest rate). Criteria: number of vehicle theft offenses per 100,000 inhabitants. *National Insurance Crime Bureau, "NICB Vehicle Theft Study," April 22, 2008*

- Farmers Insurance Group of Companies, in partnership with Sperling's BestPlaces, ranked 379 metro areas and identified the "Most Secure U.S. Place to Live." The Bend* metro area ranked #10 out of 138 in the small town category (fewer than 150,000 residents). Criteria: crime rates; extreme weather; risk of natural disasters; environmental hazards; terrorism threats; air quality; life expectancy; job loss numbers. *Farmers Insurance Group, "Most Secure U.S. Places to Live 2007"*

Sports/Recreation Rankings

- The Bend* metro area appeared on the *Sporting News* list of the "Best Sports Cities 2007". The area ranked #50 out of 150 cities in the U.S. *Sporting News* takes a 12-month snapshot, roughly July to July, of each city's sports, putting a heavy premium on regular-season won-lost records (from the most recently completed season). Other criteria include: playoff berths, bowl appearances and tournament bids; championships; applicable power ratings; quality of competition; overall fan fervor as measured in part by attendance as percentage of venue capacity; abundance of teams (rewarding quality over quantity); stadium and arena quality; ticket availability and prices; franchise ownership; and marquee appeal of athletes. *SportingNews.com, "Best Sports Cities 2007," August 1, 2007*

- Bend was selected as one of the best towns in the U.S. Editors at *Outside Magazine* asked the best adventure athletes in America where they live and why. *Outside Magazine, "Best Towns 2007," August 2007*

Culture/Performing Arts Rankings

- Bend was selected as one of America's 10 best large (population 30,000 - 100,000) art towns. The city ranked #1. Criteria: number of art galleries; affordability; natural beauty; local support for the arts; availability of suitable studio and rehearsal space; frequency and impact of art festivals; cohesiveness of the local arts community; diversity of creative statements being made by local visual and performing artists; number of theaters, art schools, art museums, and alternative exhibition and performance venues. *The 100 Best Art Towns in America: A Guide to Galleries, Museums, Festivals, Lodging, and Dining, 4th Edition, 2005*

Bend is located within the Bend, OR Metropolitan Statistical Area.

Business Environment

CITY FINANCES

City Government Finances

Component	2004-2005 ($000)	2004-2005 ($ per capita)
Total Revenues	76,803	1,144
Total Expenditures	65,450	975
Debt Outstanding	79,178	1,179
Cash and Securities	61,041	909

Source: U.S Census Bureau, Government Finances 2004-2005

City Government Revenue by Source

Source	2004-2005 ($000)	2004-2005 ($ per capita)
General Revenue		
From Federal Government	1,183	18
From State Government	5,863	87
From Local Governments	2,839	42
Taxes		
Property	16,720	249
Sales	7,082	105
Personal Income	0	0
License	17,479	260
Charges	12,571	187
Liquor Store	0	0
Utility	9,024	134
Employee Retirement	0	0
Other	4,042	60

Source: U.S Census Bureau, Government Finances 2004-2005

City Government Expenditures by Function

Function	2004-2005 ($000)	2004-2005 ($ per capita)	2004-2005 (%)
General Expenditures			
Airports	2,161	32	3.3
Corrections	0	0	0.0
Education	0	0	0.0
Fire Protection	8,850	132	13.5
Governmental Administration	4,647	69	7.1
Health	0	0	0.0
Highways	8,092	121	12.4
Hospitals	0	0	0.0
Housing and Community Development	4,681	70	7.2
Interest on General Debt	3,528	53	5.4
Libraries	0	0	0.0
Parking	255	4	0.4
Parks and Recreation	0	0	0.0
Police Protection	11,063	165	16.9
Public Welfare	0	0	0.0
Sewerage	4,729	70	7.2
Solid Waste Management	0	0	0.0
Liquor Store	0	0	0.0
Utility	9,296	138	14.2
Employee Retirement	0	0	0.0
Other	8,148	121	12.4

Source: U.S Census Bureau, Government Finances 2004-2005

Municipal Bond Ratings

Area	Moody's
City	n/a

Source: Mergent Bond Record, January 2008 (unless noted otherwise)

DEMOGRAPHICS

Population Growth

Area	1990 Census	2000 Census	2007 Estimate	2012 Projection	Population Growth (%) 1990-2000	Population Growth (%) 2000-2012
City	34,266	52,029	72,339	86,617	51.8	66.5
MSA[1]	74,958	115,367	150,650	176,024	53.9	52.6
U.S.	248,709,873	281,421,906	301,045,522	314,920,978	13.2	11.9

Note: (1) Metropolitan Statistical Area - see Appendix B for areas included
Source: Claritas, Inc.

Number of Households and Average Household Size

Area	2007 Estimate	2007 Average Household Size
City	30,240	2.39
MSA[1]	61,521	2.45
U.S.	113,668,003	2.65

Note: (1) Metropolitan Statistical Area - see Appendix B for areas included
Source: Claritas, Inc.

Race and Ethnicity

Area	White Alone[2]	Black Alone[2]	Asian Alone[2]	Other Race Alone[2]	Hispanic[3]
City	92.3	0.6	1.2	6.0	6.6
MSA[1]	93.3	0.4	0.9	5.4	5.5
U.S.	73.1	12.4	4.3	10.3	14.9

Note: Figures are 2007 estimates; (1) Metropolitan Statistical Area - see Appendix B for areas included (2) Alone is defined as not being in combination with one or more other races; (3) May be of any race.
Source: Claritas, Inc.

Ancestry

Area	German	Irish[2]	English	American	Italian	Polish	French[3]	Scottish
City	20.9	13.8	14.9	6.8	4.3	2.1	4.2	4.3
MSA[1]	n/a	n/a	n/a	n/a	n/a	n/a	n/a	n/a
U.S.	15.2	10.9	8.7	7.3	5.6	3.2	3.0	1.7

Note: Figures include multiple ancestry (e.g. if a person reported being Irish and Italian, they were included in both columns); (1) Metropolitan Statistical Area - see Appendix A for areas included; (2) Includes Celtic; (3) Includes Alsatian but excludes Basque
Source: Census 2000, Summary File 3

Foreign-Born Population

Area	Percent of Population Born in: Any Foreign Country	Europe	Asia	Africa	Oceania[2]	Canada	Mexico	Latin America[3]
City	3.7	0.8	0.5	0.1	0.1	0.5	1.1	0.6
MSA[1]	n/a	n/a	n/a	n/a	n/a	n/a	n/a	n/a
U.S.	11.1	1.7	2.9	0.3	0.1	0.3	3.3	2.5

Note: (1) Metropolitan Statistical Area - see Appendix A for areas included; (2) Includes Australia, New Zealand subregion, Melanesia, Micronesia, Polynesia, and Oceania n.e.c; (3) Includes Central America (excluding Mexico), South America, and the Caribbean.
Source: Census 2000, Summary File 3

Marriage Status

Area	Never Married	Now Married (excluding Separated)	Separated	Widowed	Divorced
City	23.9	55.8	2.0	5.7	12.5
MSA[1]	n/a	n/a	n/a	n/a	n/a
U.S.	27.1	54.4	2.2	6.6	9.7

Note: Figures are percentages and cover the population 15 years of age and older; (1) Metropolitan Statistical Area - see Appendix A for areas included
Source: Census 2000, Summary File 3

Age Distribution

Area	Percent of Population						
	Under Age 5	Age 5 to 17	Age 18 to 34	Age 35 to 49	Age 50 to 64	Age 65 to 79	80 Years and Over
City	6.8	17.6	25.7	23.4	14.3	8.5	3.7
MSA[1]	n/a	n/a	n/a	n/a	n/a	n/a	n/a
U.S.	6.8	18.9	23.7	23.5	14.8	9.2	3.2

Note: (1) Metropolitan Statistical Area - see Appendix A for areas included
Source: Census 2000, Summary File 3

Male/Female Ratio

Area	Males	Females	Males per 100 Females
City	35,799	36,540	98.0
MSA[1]	74,771	75,879	98.5
U.S.	148,320,305	152,725,217	97.1

Note: Figures are 2007 estimates; (1) Metropolitan Statistical Area - see Appendix B for areas included
Source: Claritas, Inc.

Religion

Area	Catholic	Southern Baptist	United Meth-odist	ELCA[1]	LDS[2]	Presby-terian Church USA	Jewish Est.	Muslim Est.
County	8.6	1.2	0.5	0.9	3.0	1.0	0.2	0.0
U.S.	22.0	7.1	3.7	1.8	1.5	1.1	2.2	0.6

Note: Figures are the number of adherents as a percentage of the total population; Adherents are defined as all members, including full members, their children and the estimated number of other participants who are not considered members (e.g. the baptized, those not confirmed, those regularly attending services, etc.); (1) Evangelical Lutheran Church in America; (2) The Church of Jesus Christ of Latter Day Saints
Source: Reprinted with permission from Religious Congregations and Membership in the United States 2000 (Nashville, Glenmary Research Center, 2002) Copyright Association of Statisticians of American Religious Bodies. All rights reserved.

ECONOMY

Gross Metropolitan Product

Area	2002	2003	2004	2005	2005 Rank[2]
MSA[1]	3.8	4.0	4.7	5.2	270

Note: Figures are in billions of dollars; (1) Bend, OR Metropolitan Statistical Area - see Appendix A for areas included; (2) Rank ranges from 1 to 361
Source: The U.S. Conference of Mayors, "U.S. Metro Economies: GMP - The Engines of America's Growth," January 2007

Economic Growth

Area	1995 GMP	2005 GMP	Average Annual Growth Rate	Growth Rate Rank[2]
MSA[1]	2.1	5.2	9.2	4

Note: Figures are in billions of dollars; GMP = Gross Metropolitan Product; (1) Bend, OR Metropolitan Statistical Area - see Appendix A for areas included; (2) Rank ranges from 1 to 361
Source: The U.S. Conference of Mayors, "U.S. Metro Economies: GMP - The Engines of America's Growth," January 2007

INCOME

Per Capita/Median/Average Income

Area	Per Capita ($)	Median Household ($)	Average Household ($)
City	26,849	48,521	63,681
MSA[1]	27,306	50,110	66,489
U.S.	25,495	49,280	66,670

Note: Figures are 2007 estimates; (1) Metropolitan Statistical Area - see Appendix B for areas included
Source: Claritas, Inc.

Household Income Distribution

Area	Percent of Households Earning							
	Under $15,000	$15,000 -24,999	$25,000 -34,999	$35,000 -49,999	$50,000 -74,999	$75,000 -99,000	$100,000 -149,999	$150,000 and up
City	10.5	10.8	12.2	18.0	20.5	11.9	10.8	5.1
MSA[1]	10.0	10.2	12.0	17.7	21.3	12.1	10.8	5.9
U.S.	13.1	10.9	11.2	15.6	19.5	11.9	11.3	6.6

Note: Figures are 2007 estimates; (1) Metropolitan Statistical Area - see Appendix B for areas included
Source: Claritas, Inc.

Poverty Rates by Age

Area	All Ages	Under 5 Years Old	5 to 17 Years Old	18 to 64 Years Old	65 Years and Over
City	10.5	0.8	2.7	6.4	0.7
MSA[1]	n/a	n/a	n/a	n/a	n/a
U.S.	12.4	1.2	3.0	6.9	1.2

Note: Figures are percent of population with income in 1999 below poverty level and only include population for whom poverty status is determined; (1) Metropolitan Statistical Area - see Appendix A for areas included
Source: Census 2000, Summary File 3

Personal Bankruptcy Filing Rate

Area	2004	2005	2006
Deschutes County	7.03	9.07	1.82
U.S.	5.31	6.82	2.00

Note: Numbers are per 1,000 population and include Chapter 7 and Chapter 13 filings
Source: Federal Deposit Insurance Corporation (FDIC), Regional Economic Conditions (RECON), 8/23/2007

EMPLOYMENT

Labor Force and Employment

Area	Civilian Labor Force			Workers Employed		
	Dec. 2006	Dec. 2007	% Chg.	Dec. 2006	Dec. 2007	% Chg.
City	40,907	41,919	2.5	39,278	39,568	0.7
MSA[1]	80,986	83,025	2.5	77,370	77,942	0.7
U.S.	152,571,000	153,705,000	0.7	146,081,000	146,334,000	0.2

Note: Data is not seasonally adjusted and covers workers 16 years of age and older;
(1) Metropolitan Statistical Area - see Appendix B for areas included
Source: Bureau of Labor Statistics, http://stats.bls.gov

Unemployment Rate

Area	2007											
	Jan.	Feb.	Mar.	Apr.	May	Jun.	Jul.	Aug.	Sep.	Oct.	Nov.	Dec.
City	4.9	5.2	4.7	4.1	3.8	4.0	4.2	4.3	4.2	4.6	5.1	5.6
MSA[1]	5.6	5.7	5.2	4.6	4.3	4.5	4.5	4.6	4.5	4.9	5.4	6.1
U.S.	5.0	4.9	4.5	4.3	4.3	4.7	4.9	4.6	4.5	4.4	4.5	4.8

Note: Data is not seasonally adjusted and covers workers 16 years of age and older; All figures are percentages; (1) Metropolitan Statistical Area - see Appendix B for areas included
Source: Bureau of Labor Statistics, http://stats.bls.gov

Employment by Occupation

Occupation Classification	City (%)	MSA[1] (%)	U.S. (%)
Sales and Office	27.3	n/a	26.7
Professional and Related	19.9	n/a	20.2
Service	14.7	n/a	14.9
Production, Transportation, and Material Moving	11.4	n/a	14.6
Management, Business, and Financial	14.0	n/a	13.5
Construction, Extraction, and Maintenance	12.2	n/a	9.4
Farming, Forestry, and Fishing	0.6	n/a	0.7

Note: Figures cover employed civilians 16 years of age and older;
(1) Metropolitan Statistical Area - see Appendix A for areas included
Source: Census 2000, Summary File 3

Employment by Industry

Sector	MSA[1] Number of Employees	MSA[1] Percent of Total	U.S. Percent of Total
Government	8,300	11.5	16.3
Education and Health Services	9,000	12.5	13.4
Professional and Business Services	7,700	10.7	13.1
Retail Trade	11,000	15.3	11.6
Manufacturing	5,500	7.6	9.9
Leisure and Hospitality	10,000	13.9	9.6
Financial Activities	5,300	7.4	5.9
Construction	n/a	n/a	5.3
Wholesale Trade	1,700	2.4	4.4
Other Services	2,400	3.3	3.9
Transportation and Utilities	1,500	2.1	3.7
Information	1,700	2.4	2.2
Natural Resources and Mining	n/a	n/a	0.5

Note: Figures cover non-farm employment as of December 2007 and are not seasonally adjusted; (1) Metropolitan Statistical Area - see Appendix B for areas included; n/a not available
Source: Bureau of Labor Statistics, http://stats.bls.gov

Average Wages

Occupation	$/Hr.	Occupation	$/Hr.
Accountants and Auditors	34.96	Maids and Housekeeping Cleaners	9.46
Automotive Mechanics	22.16	Maintenance and Repair Workers	16.64
Bookkeepers	15.27	Marketing Managers	42.07
Carpenters	16.34	Nuclear Medicine Technologists	n/a
Cashiers	10.15	Nurses, Licensed Practical	19.35
Clerks, General Office	14.25	Nurses, Registered	33.34
Clerks, Receptionists/Information	11.89	Nursing Aides/Orderlies/Attendants	12.42
Clerks, Shipping/Receiving	14.13	Packers and Packagers, Hand	9.61
Computer Programmers	30.08	Physical Therapists	31.32
Computer Support Specialists	17.51	Postal Service Mail Carriers	22.16
Computer Systems Analysts	32.67	Real Estate Brokers	26.39
Cooks, Restaurant	11.39	Retail Salespersons	13.22
Dentists	n/a	Sales Reps., Exc. Tech./Scientific	23.87
Electrical Engineers	33.07	Sales Reps., Tech./Scientific	46.14
Electricians	27.71	Secretaries, Exc. Legal/Med./Exec.	14.25
Financial Managers	52.79	Security Guards	10.62
First-Line Supervisors/Mgrs., Sales	20.02	Surgeons	n/a
Food Preparation Workers	10.01	Teacher Assistants	13.00
General and Operations Managers	39.58	Teachers, Elementary School	22.10
Hairdressers/Cosmetologists	10.53	Teachers, Secondary School	n/a
Internists	n/a	Telemarketers	13.26
Janitors and Cleaners	13.05	Truck Drivers, Heavy/Tractor-Trailer	17.61
Landscaping/Groundskeeping Workers	12.20	Truck Drivers, Light/Delivery Svcs.	13.64
Lawyers	29.85	Waiters and Waitresses	11.17

Note: Wage data covers the Bend, OR Metropolitan Statistical Area - see Appendix B for areas included. Hourly wages for elementary/secondary school teachers and teacher assistants were calculated by the editors from annual wage data assuming a 40 hour work week; n/a not available.
Source: Bureau of Labor Statistics, May 2007 Metro Area Occupational Employment and Wage Estimates

RESIDENTIAL REAL ESTATE

Building Permits

Area	Single-Family 2006	Single-Family 2007p	Single-Family Pct. Chg.	Multi-Family 2006	Multi-Family 2007p	Multi-Family Pct. Chg.	Total 2006	Total 2007p	Total Pct. Chg.
City	1,517	759	-50.0	162	152	-6.2	1,679	911	-45.7
U.S.	1,378,200	973,300	-29.4	460,700	407,200	-11.6	1,838,900	1,380,500	-24.9

Note: (p) preliminary; figures cover and represent new, privately-owned housing units authorized (unadjusted data); All permit data are based on estimates with imputation; U.S. figures are based on the new 20,000-place series.
Source: U.S. Census Bureau, Manufacturing, Mining, and Construction Statistics

Homeownership and Housing Vacancies

Area	Homeownership Rate[2] (%)			Rental Vacancy Rate[3] (%)			Homeowner Vacancy Rate[4] (%)		
	2005	2006	2007	2005	2006	2007	2005	2006	2007
MSA[1]	n/a	n/a	n/a	n/a	n/a	n/a	n/a	n/a	n/a
U.S.	68.9	68.8	68.1	9.8	9.8	9.7	1.9	2.4	2.7

Note: (1) Metropolitan Statistical Area - see Appendix B for areas included; (2) The proportion of households that are owners; (3) The proportion of the rental inventory that is vacant for rent; (4) The proportion of the homeowner inventory that is vacant for sale; n/a not available
Source: U.S. Census Bureau, Housing Vacancies and Homeownership Annual Statistics: 2007

TAXES

State Corporate Income Tax Rates

State	Rates and Tax Brackets
Oregon	6.6%

Note: Tax rates as of January 1, 2008; Minimum tax $10.
Source: Tax Foundation, www.taxfoundation.org

State Individual Income Tax Rates

State	Federal Deductibility	Marginal Rates (%)	Standard Deduction ($)		Personal Exemptions ($)[1]	
			Single	Joint	Single	Dependents
Oregon	Yes (z)	5.0 - 9.0 (r)	1,850 (r)	3,650 (r)	165 (c)(r)	165 (c)(r)

Note: Tax rates as of January 1, 2008; Local- and county-level taxes are not included; n/a not applicable; (1) Married joint filers generally receive double the single exemption; (c) Tax Credit; (r) State adjusts its bracket levels for inflation at the end of each year before printing tax forms; (z) Deduction limited to no more than $5,000.
Source: Tax Foundation, www.taxfoundation.org

Various State and Local Tax Rates

State and Local Sales and Use (%)	State Sales and Use (%)	Gasoline[1,2] ($/gal.)	Cigarette ($/pack)	Spirits ($/gal.)	Table Wine ($/gal.)	Beer ($/gal.)
None	None	0.25	1.18	19.26 (n)	0.67	0.08

Note: Tax rates as of January 1, 2008; (1) In addition to the 18.4 cpg Federal gasoline tax; (2) Rates may include additional state sales taxes, environmental protection and storage fees/taxes, and local taxes. When necessary, the volume-weighted average of all local taxes is used to approximate the typical statewide rate including local tax; (n) The state government controls all sales. The implied excise tax rate is calculated using methodology designed by the Distilled Spirits Council of the United States (DISCUS).
Source: Tax Foundation, www.taxfoundation.org; Original research

State Tax Burdens

Area	Combined State and Local Tax Burden		Combined Federal, State and Local Tax Burden	
	Percent	Rank	Percent	Rank
Oregon	10.0	37	30.7	31
U.S. Average	11.0	-	32.7	-

Note: Figures cover 2007 and measure taxes as a percentage of income
Source: Tax Foundation, www.taxfoundation.org

State Business Tax Climate Index Rankings

State	Overall Rank	Corporate Tax Index Rank	Individual Income Tax Index Rank	Sales Tax Index Rank	Unemployment Insurance Tax Index Rank	Property Tax Index Rank
Oregon	10	20	35	4	32	14

Note: Rankings range from 1 to 50 where 1 is best. Rankings do not average across to Overall Rank. States without a given tax are given a ranking of 1.
Source: Tax Foundation, State Business Tax Climate Index 2008

TRANSPORTATION

Means of Transportation to Work

Area	Car/Truck/Van		Public Transportation			Bicycle	Walked	Other Means	Worked at Home
	Drove Alone	Car-pooled	Bus	Subway	Railroad				
City	74.6	12.7	1.2	0.0	0.0	1.9	2.8	1.1	5.7
MSA[1]	n/a	n/a	n/a	n/a	n/a	n/a	n/a	n/a	n/a
U.S.	75.7	12.2	2.5	1.5	0.5	0.4	2.9	1.0	3.3

Note: Figures are percentages and cover workers 16 years of age and older; (1) Metropolitan Statistical Area - see Appendix A for areas included
Source: Census 2000, Summary File 3

Travel Time to Work

Area	Less Than 15 Minutes	15 to 29 Minutes	30 to 44 Minutes	45 to 59 Minutes	60 Minutes or More
City	58.6	29.8	7.0	2.0	2.5
MSA[1]	n/a	n/a	n/a	n/a	n/a
U.S.	29.4	36.1	19.1	7.4	8.0

Note: Figures are percentages and include workers 16 years old and over; (1) Metropolitan Statistical Area - see Appendix A for areas included
Source: Census 2000, Summary File 3

Living Environment

COST OF LIVING

Cost of Living Index

Composite Index	Groceries	Housing	Utilities	Trans-portation	Health Care	Misc. Goods/ Services
116.6	122.2	130.8	82.0	115.9	113.9	113.4

Note: U.S. = 100; Figures cover the Bend OR urban area.
Source: The Council for Community and Economic Research (formerly ACCRA), Cost of Living Index, 2007

Grocery Prices

Area[1]	T-Bone Steak ($/pound)	Frying Chicken ($/pound)	Whole Milk ($/half gal.)	Eggs ($/dozen)	Orange Juice ($/64 oz.)	Coffee ($/11.5 oz.)
City[2]	10.42	1.36	1.92	1.95	4.02	4.44
Avg.	8.93	1.12	2.13	1.52	3.26	3.31
Min.	5.88	0.71	1.33	0.83	2.30	2.20
Max.	12.80	2.07	3.43	3.54	5.79	6.20

Note: (1) Values for the local area are compared with the average, minimum and maximum values for all 331 areas in the Cost of Living Index report; (2) Figures cover the Bend OR urban area; **T-Bone Steak** *(price per pound);* **Frying Chicken** *(price per pound, whole fryer);* **Whole Milk** *(half gallon carton);* **Eggs** *(price per dozen, Grade A, large);* **Orange Juice** *(64 oz. Tropicana or Florida Natural);* **Coffee** *(11.5 oz. can, vacuum-packed, Maxwell House, Hills Bros, or Folgers).*
Source: The Council for Community and Economic Research (formerly ACCRA), Cost of Living Index, 2007

Housing and Utility Costs

Area[1]	New Home Price ($)	Apartment Rent ($/month)	All Electric ($/month)	Part Electric ($/month)	Other Energy ($/month)	Telephone ($/month)
City[2]	442,674	603	118.95	-	-	25.00
Avg.	309,605	782	146.13	78.67	90.16	26.14
Min.	189,877	n/a	82.03	37.41	33.15	17.08
Max.	1,202,800	3,481	271.14	150.60	257.67	37.45

Note: (1) Values for the local area are compared with the average, minimum and maximum values for all 331 areas in the Cost of Living Index report; (2) Figures cover the Bend OR urban area; **New Home Price** *(2,400 sf living area, 8,000 sf lot, in urban area with full utilities);* **Apartment Rent** *(950 sf 2 bedroom/1.5 or 2 bath, unfurnished, excluding all utilities except water);* **All Electric** *(average monthly cost for an all-electric home);* **Part Electric** *(average monthly cost for a part-electric home);* **Other Energy** *(average monthly cost for natural gas, fuel oil, coal, wood, and any other forms of energy except electricity);* **Telephone** *(price includes basic monthly rate for a private residential line plus additional local usage charges incurred by a family of four).*
Source: The Council for Community and Economic Research (formerly ACCRA), Cost of Living Index, 2007

Health Care, Transportation, and Other Costs

Area[1]	Doctor ($/visit)	Dentist ($/visit)	Optometrist ($/visit)	Gasoline ($/gallon)	Beauty Salon ($/visit)	Men's Shirt ($)
City[2]	98.90	85.19	99.05	3.04	32.06	33.30
Avg.	79.48	71.93	79.55	2.64	29.52	25.77
Min.	52.08	44.80	43.95	2.19	15.58	16.19
Max.	148.44	126.27	158.83	3.48	60.62	48.53

Note: (1) Values for the local area are compared with the average, minimum and maximum values for all 331 areas in the Cost of Living Index report; (2) Figures cover the Bend OR urban area; **Doctor** *(general practitioners routine exam of an established patient);* **Dentist** *(adult teeth cleaning and periodic oral examination);* **Optometrist** *(full vision eye exam for established adult patient);* **Gasoline** *(one gallon regular unleaded, national brand, including all taxes, cash price at self-service pump if available);* **Beauty Salon** *(woman's shampoo, trim, and blow-dry);* **Men's Shirt** *(cotton/polyester dress shirt, pinpoint weave, long sleeves).*
Source: The Council for Community and Economic Research (formerly ACCRA), Cost of Living Index, 2007

HOUSING

House Price Index (HPI)

Area	National Ranking[2]	Quarterly Change (%)	One-Year Change (%)	Five-Year Change (%)
MSA[1]	236	-1.44	-2.84	84.37
U.S.[3]	-	0.10	0.84	41.37

Note: The HPI is a weighted repeat sales index. It measures average price changes in repeat sales or refinancings on the same properties. This information is obtained by reviewing repeat mortgage transactions on single-family properties whose mortgages have been purchased or securitized by Fannie Mae or Freddie Mac in January 1975; (1) Metropolitan Statistical Area - see Appendix B for areas included; (2) Rankings are based on annual percentage change for all metro areas containing at least 15,000 transactions over the last 10 years and ranges from 1 to 291; (3) figures based on a weighted average of Census Division estimates; all figures are for the period ending December 31, 2007
Source: Office of Federal Housing Enterprise Oversight, House Price Index, February 26, 2008

House Price Valuations

Area	Q1 2000	Q1 2001	Q1 2002	Q1 2003	Q1 2004	Q1 2005	Q1 2006	Q1 2007	Q1 2008
MSA[1]	-3.7	-3.9	2.4	8.3	13.2	20.9	52.2	65.7	49.5

Note: Figures show the percentage of over- or under-valuation of single family homes relative to statistically normal house values (e.g. a value of 23.6 indicates that house values are 23.6% overvalued). Statistically normal house values are based on house prices, interest rates, household incomes, population densities, and any historical premiums or discounts metropolitan areas have exhibited over time; (1) Figures cover the Metropolitan Statistical Area - see Appendix B for areas included
Source: Global Insight/National City Corporation, House Prices in America, May 2008

Median Home Prices

Area	2005	2006	2007[r]	Percent Change 2006 to 2007
MSA[1]	n/a	n/a	n/a	n/a
U.S. Average	219.0	221.9	217.9	-1.8

Note: Figures are median sales prices of existing single-family homes in thousands of dollars; (r) revised; n/a not available; (1) Metropolitan Statistical Area - see Appendix B for areas included
Source: National Association of Realtors, Metropolitan Area Prices, 1st Quarter 2008

Housing: Year Structure Built

Area	1990 -2000	1980 -1989	1970 -1979	1960 -1969	1950 -1959	1940 -1949	Before 1940	Median Year
City	38.3	14.3	23.8	6.8	5.7	3.8	7.2	1982
MSA[1]	0.0	0.0	0.0	0.0	0.0	0.0	0.0	0
U.S.	17.0	15.8	18.5	13.7	12.7	7.3	15.0	1971

Note: Figures are percentages; (1) Metropolitan Statistical Area - see Appendix A for areas included
Source: Census 2000, Summary File 3

HEALTH

Health Risk Data

Category	Area[1] (%)	U.S. (%)
Adults who have been told they have high blood pressure[3]	n/a	25.5
Adults who have been told they have high blood cholesterol[3]	n/a	35.6
Adults who have been told they have diabetes[2]	n/a	7.5
Adults who have been told they have arthritis[3]	n/a	27.0
Adults who have been told they currently have asthma	n/a	8.5
Adults who are current smokers	n/a	20.1
Adults who are heavy drinkers[4]	n/a	4.9
Adults who are overweight (BMI 25.0 - 29.9)	n/a	36.5
Adults who are obese (BMI 30.0 - 99.8)	n/a	25.1

Note: Data as of 2006 unless otherwise noted; n/a not available; (1) Figures cover the Metropolitan Statistical Area - see Appendix B for areas included; (2) Figures do not include pregnancy-related diabetes, pre-diabetes or borderline diabetes; (3) 2005 data; (4) Heavy drinkers are classified as adult men having more than two drinks per day or adult women having more than one drink per day
Source: Centers for Disease Control and Prevention, Behaviorial Risk Factor Surveillance System, SMART: Selected Metropolitan/Micropolitan Area Risk Trends, 2005, 2006

Mortality Rates for the Top 10 Causes of Death in the U.S.

ICD-10[a] Sub-Chapter	ICD-10[a] Code	Age-Adjusted Mortality Rate[1] per 100,000 population	
		County[2]	U.S.
Malignant neoplasms	C00-C97	165.5	186.5
Ischaemic heart diseases	I20-I25	109.0	152.3
Other forms of heart disease	I30-I51	46.6	51.5
Cerebrovascular diseases	I60-I69	54.7	50.0
Chronic lower respiratory diseases	J40-J47	40.3	42.6
Diabetes mellitus	E10-E14	20.9	24.8
Other degenerative diseases of the nervous system	G30-G31	29.1	22.6
Other external causes of accidental injury	W00-X59	22.8	21.4
Influenza and pneumonia	J10-J18	11.0	20.7
Hypertensive diseases	I10-I13	11.6	18.2

Note: (a) ICD-10 = International Classification of Diseases 10th Revision; (1) Mortality rates are a three year average covering 2003-2005; (2) Figures cover Deschutes County
Source: Centers for Disease Control and Prevention, National Center for Health Statistics. Compressed Mortality File 1999-2004. CDC WONDER On-line Database, compiled from Compressed Mortality File 1999-2005 Series 20 No. 2K, 2008.

Mortality Rates for Selected Causes of Death

ICD-10[a] Sub-Chapter	ICD-10[a] Code	Age-Adjusted Mortality Rate[1] per 100,000 population	
		County[2]	U.S.
Assault	X85-Y09	*2.2	5.9
Human immunodeficiency virus (HIV) disease	B20-B24	*1.2	4.5
Intentional self-harm	X60-X84	15.8	10.8
Malnutrition	E40-E46	*0.2	1.0
Obesity and other hyperalimentation	E65-E68	*2.4	1.4
Organic, including symptomatic, mental disorders	F01-F09	31.6	16.8
Transport accidents	V01-V99	20.3	16.1
Viral hepatitis	B15-B19	*1.7	1.8

Note: (a) ICD-10 = International Classification of Diseases 10th Revision; (1) Mortality rates are a three year average covering 2003-2005; (2) Figures cover Deschutes County; (*) Unreliable data as per CDC
Source: Centers for Disease Control and Prevention, National Center for Health Statistics. Compressed Mortality File 1999-2004. CDC WONDER On-line Database, compiled from Compressed Mortality File 1999-2005 Series 20 No. 2K, 2008.

Distribution of Physicians[1]

Area	Total	Family/ General Practice	Specialties	
			Medical	Surgical
Deschutes County (number)	329	105	82	96
Deschutes County (rate per 10,000 pop.)	23.3	7.4	5.8	6.8
U.S. (rate per 10,000 pop.)	17.7	4.6	6.9	4.3

Note: Data as of 2005; (1) Includes all non-federal, patient-care, office-based MDs
Source: Area Resource File (ARF). June 2007. U.S. Department of Health and Human Services, Health Resources and Services Administration, Bureau of Health Professions, Rockville, MD.

Hospitals

Bend has the following hospitals: 1 general medical and surgical.
AHA Guide to the Healthcare Field 2008

EDUCATION

Public School District Statistics

District Name	Schls	Pupils	Pupil/ Teacher Ratio	Minority Pupils[1] (%)	Free Lunch Eligible[2] (%)	IEP[3] (%)
Bend-Lapine Administrative SD 1	26	14,605	21.4	10.8	25.0	15.0
Redmond Sd 2j	10	6,309	21.5	13.0	32.0	14.3

Note: Table includes regular local school districts with 2,000 or more students; (1) Percentage of students that are not white, non-Hispanic; (2) Percentage of students that are eligible for the free lunch program; (3) Percentage of students that have an Individualized Education Program.
Source: U.S. Department of Education, National Center for Education Statistics, Common Core of Data, Local Education Agency (School District) Universe Survey: School Year 2005-2006; U.S. Department of Education, National Center for Education Statistics, Common Core of Data, Public Elementary/Secondary School Universe Survey: School Year 2005-2006

Highest Level of Education

Area	Less than H.S.	H.S. Diploma	Some College, No Deg.	Associate Degree	Bachelors Degree	Masters Degree	Profess. School Degree	Doctorate Degree
City	9.7	23.7	28.4	8.4	20.5	6.0	2.6	0.8
MSA[1]	11.4	27.1	28.4	7.8	17.3	5.2	2.0	0.7
U.S.	19.4	28.4	21.2	6.4	15.7	5.9	2.0	1.0

Note: Figures are 2007 estimated percentages and cover persons age 25 and over; (1) Metropolitan Statistical Area - see Appendix B for areas included
Source: Claritas, Inc.

Educational Attainment by Race

Area	High School Graduate (%)					Bachelor's Degree (%)				
	Total	White	Black	Asian	Hisp.[2]	Total	White	Black	Asian	Hisp.[2]
City	90.2	90.9	48.9	86.7	69.0	29.4	30.0	0.0	44.3	8.2
MSA[1]	n/a	n/a	n/a	n/a	n/a	n/a	n/a	n/a	n/a	n/a
U.S.	80.4	83.6	72.3	80.4	52.4	24.4	26.1	14.3	44.1	10.4

Note: Figures shown cover persons 25 years old and over; (1) Metropolitan Statistical Area - see Appendix A for areas included; (2) people of Hispanic origin can be of any race
Source: Census 2000, Summary File 3

School Enrollment by Type

Area	Grades KG to 8				Grades 9 to 12			
	Public		Private		Public		Private	
	Enrollment	%	Enrollment	%	Enrollment	%	Enrollment	%
City	5,520	88.1	744	11.9	2,710	93.8	180	6.2
MSA[1]	n/a	n/a	n/a	n/a	n/a	n/a	n/a	n/a
U.S.	33,526,011	88.7	4,285,121	11.3	14,848,628	90.6	1,532,323	9.4

Note: Figures shown cover persons 3 years old and over; (1) Metropolitan Statistical Area - see Appendix A for areas included
Source: Census 2000, Summary File 3

School Enrollment by Race

Area	Grades KG to 8 (%)				Grades 9 to 12 (%)			
	White	Black	Asian	Hisp.[1]	White	Black	Asian	Hisp.[1]
City	89.4	0.5	1.2	6.9	90.3	0.9	1.2	7.5
MSA[1]	n/a	n/a	n/a	n/a	n/a	n/a	n/a	n/a
U.S.	68.5	15.5	3.3	16.8	68.8	15.5	3.8	15.7

Note: Figures shown cover persons 3 years old and over; (1) people of Hispanic origin can be of any race; (2) Metropolitan Statistical Area - see Appendix A for areas included
Source: Census 2000, Summary File 3

Average Salaries of Public School Classroom Teachers

District	2005-06 Dollars	2005-06 Rank[1]	2006-07 Dollars	2006-07 Rank[1]	Percent Change 2005-06 to 2006-07
Oregon	50,044	15	50,911	16	1.73
U.S. Average	49,026	-	50,816	-	3.65

Note: (1) State rank ranges from 1 to 51.
Source: National Education Association, Rankings & Estimates: Rankings of the States 2006 and Estimates of School Statistics 2007, December 2007

Higher Education

Four-Year Colleges			Two-Year Colleges			Medical Schools[1]	Law Schools[2]	Voc/ Tech[3]
Public	Private Non-profit	Private For-profit	Public	Private Non-profit	Private For-profit			
1	0	0	1	0	1	0	0	0

Note: Figures cover institutions located within the city limits; (1) includes schools accredited by the Liaison Committee on Medical Education and the American Osteopathic Association; (2) includes American Bar Association-accredited law schools; (3) includes all schools with programs that are less than 2 years.
Source: National Center for Education Statistics, The Integrated Postsecondary Education System (IPEDS) Peer Analysis System, 2007; www.usnews.com, Law and Medical School Directories, 2009

PRESIDENTIAL ELECTION

2004 Presidential Election Results

Area	Bush	Kerry	Nader	Other
Deschutes County	56.4	42.1	0.0	1.5
U.S.	50.7	48.3	0.4	0.6

Note: Results are percentages and may not add to 100% due to rounding
Source: Dave Leip's Atlas of U.S. Presidential Elections, www.uselectionatlas.org

EMPLOYERS

Major Employers

Company Name	Industry	Type of Site
911	Police protection	Branch
Beaver Coaches	Motor vehicles and car bodies	Branch
Bright Wood Corporation	Sawmills and planing mills, general	Branch
Bulletin The	Newspapers	Headquarters
Central Oregon Community Hosp	General medical and surgical hospitals	Single
Cessna Aircraft Company	Aircraft	Branch
City Recorders Office	Business services, nec	Branch
Cocc	Junior colleges	Headquarters
Costco Wholesale	Miscellaneous general merchandise	Branch
Eagle Crest Resort	Subdividers and developers, nec	Headquarters
Fuqua Homes Inc	Mobile homes	Branch
Hooker Creek Companies LLC	Single-family housing construction	Single
Isky Inc (delaware)	Commercial nonphysical research	Branch
Jeld - Wen Inc	Metal doors, sash, and trim	Branch
Kirby Nagelhout Cnstr Co	Nonresidential construction, nec	Single
Pozzi Window	Metal doors, sash, and trim	Single
Redmond Air Center	Land, mineral, and wildlife conservation	Branch
Riverhouse Restaurant & Lounge	Hotels and motels	Single
Saddleback Stables	Hotels and motels	Branch
St Charles Medical Center-Bend	General medical and surgical hospitals	Headquarters
Target	Department stores	Branch
Team Millwork Bright	Millwork	Branch
Wal-Mart	Department stores	Branch

Note: Companies shown are located within the Bend metropolitan area; nec = not elsewhere classified.
Source: www.zapdata.com, May 2008

PUBLIC SAFETY

Crime Rate

Area	All Crimes	Violent Crimes				Property Crimes		
		Murder	Forcible Rape	Robbery	Aggrav. Assault	Burglary	Larceny -Theft	Motor Vehicle Theft
City	4,484.8	1.5	32.2	46.9	137.7	716.5	3,213.0	337.0
Metro[1]	3,774.5	1.4	29.9	33.4	153.1	670.8	2,624.2	261.7
U.S.	3,808.1	5.7	30.9	149.4	287.5	729.4	2,206.8	398.4

Note: Figures are crimes per 100,000 population; (1) Metropolitan Statistical Area - see Appendix B for areas included
Source: FBI Uniform Crime Reports, 2006

Hate Crimes

Area	Number of Quarters Reported	Bias Motivation				
		Race	Religion	Sexual Orientation	Ethnicity	Disability
City	4	4	0	2	0	0

Source: Federal Bureau of Investigation, Hate Crime Statistics 2006

RECREATION

Culture

Dance[1]	Theatre[1]	Instrumental Music[1]	Vocal Music[1]	Series/ Festivals	Museums	Zoos and Aquariums[2]
0	1	0	0	1	3	0

Note: (1) Number of professional perfoming groups; (2) AZA-accredited
Source: The Grey House Performing Arts Directory, 2007; Official Museum Directory, 2008; Association of Zoos & Aquariums, AZA Member Zoos & Aquariums, June 2008

Professional Sports Teams

Team Name	League
No teams are located in the metro area	

Source: Original research

MEDIA

Newspapers

Name	News Focus	Frequency	Circulation
Bend Weekly	Local	n/a	n/a
The Bulletin	Local	Daily	28,479
The Source	Local	Weekly	47,410

Note: Includes newspapers with offices located in the city; n/a not available
Source: MediaContactsPro, March 2008

Television Stations

Name	Ch.	Network(s)	Type	Ownership
KTVZ	21	NBC	Commercial	n/a
KFXO	39	Fox	Commercial	Meredith Communications LLC

Note: Stations included cover the Bend DMA (Designated Market Area)
BurrellesLuce, MediaContacts Online, January 2007

Major AM Radio Stations

Call Letters	Freq. (kHz)	Station Type	Target Audience	Station Format	Music Format
KICE	940	Commercial	General	Sports/Talk	n/a
KBND	1110	Commercial	General	Sports	n/a

Note: Stations included cover the Bend DMA (Designated Market Area); n/a not available
Source: BurrellesLuce, MediaContacts Online, January 2007

Major FM Radio Stations

Call Letters	Freq. (mHz)	Station Type	Target Audience	Station Format	Music Format
KXIX	94.1	Commercial	General	Music	Adult Contemp.
KWLZ	95.1	Commercial	General	Music	Modern Rock
KWPK	96.5	Commercial	General	n/a	n/a
KNLR	97.5	Commercial	General/Religious	Music/Talk	Gospel
KTWS	98.3	Commercial	General	Music/News	Classic Rock
KMGX	100.7	Commercial	General	Music	Adult Contemp.
KLRR	101.7	Commercial	General	Music/News	Adult Contemp.
KSJJ	102.9	Commercial	General	Music	Contemp. Country
KQAK	105.7	Commercial	General	Music	Oldies

Note: Stations included cover the Bend DMA (Designated Market Area); n/a not available
BurrellesLuce, MediaContacts Online, January 2007

CLIMATE

Average and Extreme Temperatures

Temperature	Jan	Feb	Mar	Apr	May	Jun	Jul	Aug	Sep	Oct	Nov	Dec	Yr.
Extreme High (°F)	67	69	77	86	93	102	105	108	103	94	76	68	108
Average High (°F)	46	51	55	61	67	74	82	82	76	64	53	47	63
Average Temp. (°F)	40	44	46	50	55	61	67	67	62	53	46	41	53
Average Low (°F)	33	35	37	39	43	48	51	51	48	42	38	35	42
Extreme Low (°F)	-4	-3	20	27	28	32	39	38	32	19	12	-12	-12

Note: Figures cover the years 1948-1992
Source: National Climatic Data Center, International Station Meteorological Climate Summary, 9/96

Average Precipitation/Snowfall/Humidity

Precip./Humidity	Jan	Feb	Mar	Apr	May	Jun	Jul	Aug	Sep	Oct	Nov	Dec	Yr.
Avg. Precip. (in.)	7.8	5.6	5.3	3.0	2.2	1.4	0.4	0.8	1.4	3.6	7.6	8.2	47.3
Avg. Snowfall (in.)	4	1	1	Tr	Tr	0	0	0	0	Tr	Tr	1	7
Avg. Rel. Hum. 7am (%)	91	92	91	88	84	81	78	82	88	93	93	92	88
Avg. Rel. Hum. 4pm (%)	79	73	64	57	54	49	38	39	44	61	79	84	60

Note: Figures cover the years 1948-1992; Tr = Trace amounts (<0.05 in. of rain; <0.5 in. of snow)
Source: National Climatic Data Center, International Station Meteorological Climate Summary, 9/96

Weather Conditions

Temperature			Daytime Sky			Precipitation		
32°F & below	45°F & below	90°F & above	Clear	Partly cloudy	Cloudy	0.01 inch or more precip.	0.1 inch or more snow/ice	Thunder-storms
54	233	15	75	115	175	136	4	3

Note: Figures are average number of days per year and cover the years 1948-1992
Source: National Climatic Data Center, International Station Meteorological Climate Summary, 9/96

HAZARDOUS WASTE

Superfund Sites

Bend has no sites on the EPA's Superfund Final National Priorities List.
U.S. Environmental Protection Agency, Final National Priorities List, June 23, 2008

AIR & WATER QUALITY

Air Quality Index

Area	Percent of Days when Air Quality was...[2]				AQI Statistics	
	Good	Moderate	Unhealthy for Sensitive Groups	Unhealthy	Maximum	Median
Area[1]	96.7	3.3	0.0	0.0	70	13

Note: The Air Quality Index (AQI) is an index for reporting daily air quality. EPA calculates the AQI for five major air pollutants regulated by the Clean Air Act: ground-level ozone, particle pollution (also known as particulate matter), carbon monoxide, sulfur dioxide, and nitrogen dioxide. The AQI runs from 0 to 500. The higher the AQI value, the greater the level of air pollution and the greater the health concern. There are six AQI categories: "Good" The AQI is between 0 and 50. Air quality is considered satisfactory; "Moderate" The AQI is between 51 and 100. Air quality is acceptable; "Unhealthy for Sensitive Groups" When AQI values are between 101 and 150, members of sensitive groups may experience health effects; "Unhealthy" When AQI values are between 151 and 200 everyone may begin to experience health effects; "Very Unhealthy" AQI values between 201 and 300 trigger a health alert; "Hazardous" AQI values over 300 trigger health warnings of emergency conditions; (1) Data covers Deschutes County; (2) Based on 362 days with AQI data in 2007.
Source: U.S. Environmental Protection Agency, Air Quality Index Report, 2007

Air Quality Index Pollutants

Area	Percent of Days when AQI Pollutant was...[2]					
	Carbon Monoxide	Nitrogen Dioxide	Ozone	Sulfur Dioxide	Particulate Matter 2.5	Particulate Matter 10
Area[1]	0.0	0.0	0.0	0.0	92.3	7.7

Note: The Air Quality Index (AQI) is an index for reporting daily air quality. EPA calculates the AQI for five major air pollutants regulated by the Clean Air Act: ground-level ozone, particle pollution (also known as particulate matter), carbon monoxide, sulfur dioxide, and nitrogen dioxide. The AQI runs from 0 to 500. The higher the AQI value, the greater the level of air pollution and the greater the health concern; (1) Data covers Deschutes County; (2) Based on 362 days with AQI data in 2007.
Source: U.S. Environmental Protection Agency, Air Quality Index Report, 2007

Air Quality Index Trends

Area	Trend Sites								All Sites
	1999	2000	2001	2002	2003	2004	2005	2006	2006
MSA[1]	n/a	n/a	n/a	n/a	n/a	n/a	n/a	n/a	n/a

Note: An AQI value greater than 100 indicates that air quality would have been in the unhealthful range on that day. Data from exceptional events are not included. These counts are presented in two ways. First, the counts are based on sites having an adequate record of monitoring data during the trend period (trend sites). These counts represent the relative change in the number of days with AQI values greater than 100. In the last column, the counts are based on all sites with data in the most recent year (because it is possible for a site to have data in the most recent year but not enough data to be a trend site); (1) Metropolitan Statistical Area - see Appendix A for areas included; n/a not available.
Source: U.S. Environmental Protection Agency, Office of Air and Radiation, Air Trends, Factbook and Related Information, Air Pollution Trends in Selected Metropolitan Areas 2006

Maximum Air Pollutant Concentrations

	Particulate Matter 10 (ug/m^3)	Particulate Matter 2.5 (ug/m^3)	Ozone (ppm)	Carbon Monoxide (ppm)	Sulfur Dioxide (ppm)	Nitrogen Dioxide (ppm)	Lead (ug/m^3)
MSA[1] Level	n/a	n/a	n/a	n/a	n/a	n/a	n/a
NAAQS[2]	150	35	0.125	9	0.140	0.053	1.50
Met NAAQS[2]	Yes	Yes	Yes	Yes	Yes	Yes	Yes

Note: Data from exceptional events are not included; (1) Metropolitan Statistical Area - see Appendix A for areas included; (2) National Ambient Air Quality Standards; n/a not available
Concentrations: Particulate Matter 10 (coarse particulate) - highest second maximum 24-hour concentration; Particulate Matter 2.5 (fine particulate) - highest 98th percentile 24-hour concentration; Ozone - highest second daily maximum 1-hour concentration; Carbon Monoxide - highest second maximum non-overlapping 8-hour concentration; Sulfur Dioxide - highest second maximum 24-hour concentration; Nitrogen Dioxide - highest arithmetic mean concentration; Lead - highest quarterly maximum concentration
Units: ppm = parts per million; ug/m^3 = micrograms per cubic meter
Source: U.S. Environmental Protection Agency, MSA Factbook 2006, Air Quality Statistics by City

Drinking Water

Water System Name	Pop. Served	Primary Water Source Type	Violations[1]	
			Health Based	Monitoring/ Reporting
Bend Water Dept	52,320	Surface	0	2

Note: (1) Based on violation data from January 1, 2007 to December 31, 2007 (includes unresolved violations from earlier years)
Source: U.S. Environmental Protection Agency, Office of Ground Water and Drinking Water, Safe Drinking Water Information System (based on data extracted April 15, 2008)

Tualatin, Oregon

Background

One of the first settlements established along the Tualatin River, this city was first called Bridgeport. In 1856, it was changed to Tualatin when Samuel Galbreath built the first bridge to cross the Tualatin River. Since that time, the city has become a thriving suburb of Portland, just 13 miles away. Many consider the quality of life in Tualatin is unsurpassed, and the community prides itself in its many parks and green spaces, small town atmosphere, family-friendly environment, exceptional school system, upscale shopping, and prime location.

For 30 years after the bridge was built, Tualatin's commerce consisted of a blacksmith, a boarding house, a general store, and a saloon. When the Portland & Willamette Railway Company purchased land along the Tualatin River in 1886 the town began to grow, and soon saw construction of stables, a hotel, saloons, and a sawmill. The community's proximity to Portland also spurred new growth, attracting residents from across the country. In 1913, with the creation of its first official government, the city of Tualatin was incorporated.

Since the 1970s the community has been growing exponentially. Due to the rapid expansion and little cohesive city planning, Tualatin had no city center or historic downtown. In the mid-1990s, plans to build a centerpiece for the city were developed, resulting in Tualatin Commons. The Commons features a three-acre lake, surrounded by wide promenades and plazas that house professional office space, an upscale hotel and restaurant, and urban dwellings. Tualatin residents now consider the Commons to be the heart of their community.

Tualatin strives to be a premier site of business and industry in the Portland metropolitan area. A leading example toward this goal is the upscale retail development, Bridgeport Village, where you will find a wide array of open-air shopping, dining, and entertainment. Its design was inspired by the European al fresco shopping experience. In addition, Bridgeport Village is affiliated with non-retail businesses, hotels and lodging, making it a destination of its own.

The city provides a family-friendly environment that encourages growth and exploration. Children's creativity thrives at Willowbrook Summer Arts Camp in Browns Ferry Park. Teen programs are abundant, and include camps, Henna tattoo workshops, surfing lessons, paintball tournaments, TualaFest Battle of the Bands, and Movies on the Commons. For older residents, the Tualatin/Durham Senior Center is an exemplary facility with a wide variety of programs and opportunities.

The city dedicates over 200 acres to parks, trails, and areas of natural environment. Residents and visitors can canoe or kayak down the Tualatin River, and walk or bike through the nature paths. Self-guided tours through the interconnected trails of the ArtWalk offer exploration of the natural and cultural history of Tualatin, as does the Tualatin Heritage Center. During the summer months, there is a constant stream of activity at the Tualatin Commons, including concerts and reading programs.

Most of Tualatin is served by the Tigard-Tualatin School District which, due to excellence in teaching literacy grades, is used as a model throughout the state. Tualatin is located near several colleges and universities, including Portland State University.

Portland International Airport, an approximate 30-minute drive, conveniently provides air travel from Tualatin.

Rankings

General Rankings

- Portland* was ranked #3 out of 375 metro areas in *Cities Ranked & Rated*. Criteria: cost of living; climate; crime; transportation; economy and jobs; education; arts and culture; health and healthcare; leisure; quality of life. *Cities Ranked & Rated, 2nd Edition, 2007*
- Portland* was ranked #4 out of 379 metro areas in *Places Rated Almanac*. Criteria: health care; education; recreation; transportation; ambience; climate; crime; housing costs; jobs. *Places Rated Almanac, 7th Edition, 2007*

Business/Finance Rankings

- The nation's 100 largest metro areas were analysed in terms of the percentage of households entering some stage of foreclosure in 2007. The Portland* metro area ranked #73 out of 100 (#1 = highest foreclosure rate). *RealtyTrac, "Year-End 2007 Metropolitan Foreclosure Report"*
- The Portland* metro area was selected one of America's "Top 50 Business Opportunity Metros" by *Expansion Management* in their 5th annual Mayor's Challenge ranking of metro areas that have achieved solid ratings across the board in numerous *EM* studies during the past 12 months. The area ranked #19. Criteria: public schools; quality of life; college educated workers; logistics infrastructure; healthcare costs; taxes and government spending; reputation among site consultants. *Expansion Management, August 2007*
- The Portland* metro area was selected as one of "America's Most Wired Cities" by *Forbes*. The metro area was ranked #10 out of 30. Criteria: percentage of Internet users with high-speed access; the range of service providers within a city; availability of public wireless hot spots. *Forbes, "America's Most Wired Cities," January 10, 2008*
- Portland* was selected as one of the best places to start and grow a company by *Entrepreneur* and the National Policy Research Council. The Portland* metro area ranked #36 out of 50 large metro areas. Criteria: business formation and growth (firms started four to 14 years ago that still employ at least 5 people and experienced rapid growth over the last four years). *Entrepreneur/National Policy Research Council, "Hot Cities for Entrepreneurs," September 2006*
- The Portland* metro area was selected as one of "America's 50 Hottest Cities" for business relocations and expansions. Criteria: industry's most prominent site selection consultants were asked to list their top city choices for relocating and expanding manufacturing companies, taking into consideration such factors as the business climate, work force quality, operating costs, incentive programs, and the ease of working with local political and economic development officials. *Expansion Management, January-February 2007*
- Intel, in partnership with Sperling's BestPlaces, ranked the 80 "Best Cities for Teleworking" in America. The Portland* metro area ranked #16 among large metro areas. The study identifies cities that hold the greatest potential for teleworking based on a host of factors including typical commuting times, fuel prices, availability of broadband Internet access and percentage of the population in telework friendly jobs. The study also factored in extreme climate and natural hazards. *Intel, "Best Cities for Teleworking," March 30, 2006*
- The Portland* metro area appeared on the Milken Institute "2007 Best Performing Cities" index. Rank: #38 out of 200 large metro areas. Criteria: job growth; wage and salary growth; high-tech output growth. *Milken Institute, "2007 Best Performing Cities"*
- The Portland* metro area was selected as one of the hottest cities for entrepreneurs in America by *Inc. Magazine*. Criteria: job-growth data for 393 metro was analyzed for current-year employment growth, average annual employment growth over past three years, and employment growth by industry sector. The Portland* metro area ranked #20 among large metro areas and #139 overall. *Inc. Magazine, May 2007*

- Portland* was identified as one of the 100 "Most Unwired Cities" in the U.S. The area ranked #4 out of the 100 largest metro areas in the U.S. Criteria: number of public and commercial wireless access points (hotspots); airports with wireless Internet access; broadband availability; local wireless networks; and wireless email devices. *Intel, "Most Unwired Cities Survey," June 7, 2005*

- Portland* was ranked #18 out of 125 regions worldwide in terms of its "Knowledge Competitiveness Index." The index attempts to measure the knowledge-based development taking place throughout the world and is based on 19 measures of economic performance that indicate a region's ability to translate its knowledge capacity into economic value. *Robert Huggins Associates, World Knowledge Competitiveness Index 2005*

- *Forbes* ranked the 200 most populous metro areas in the U.S. in terms of the "Best Places for Business and Careers." The Portland* metro area was ranked #35. Criteria: business costs (labor, energy, tax and office space expenses); living costs (housing, transportation, food and other household expenditures); education levels of the work force; job growth; income growth; migration trends; crime rates; and culture/leisure. *Forbes, "Best Places for Business and Careers," March 19, 2008*

- *Fortune* ranked the 100 largest metro areas in the U.S. in terms of projected median home price change in 2007. The Portland* metro area ranked #47. *Fortune.com, "Hot Spots, Cold Spots"*

Health/Environment Rankings

- The Portland* metro area was selected as one of "America's Cleanest Cities" by *Forbes*. The metro area ranked #5 out of 10. Criteria: air quality; water quality; per capita spending on Superfund site cleanup and solid-waste management. *Forbes.com, "America's Cleanest Cities," March 11, 2008*

- 100 of the largest metro areas in the U.S. were analyzed in terms of their current drought severity. The Portland* metro area ranked #51 (#1 = driest). The rankings were based on statistics such as long-term precipitation trends and patterns and the Palmer drought indices. *Sperling's BestPlaces, www.BestPlaces.net, "America's Drought-Riskiest Cities," November 2007*

- Tahitian Noni International Hiro™, in partnership with Sperling's BestPlaces, ranked the nation's 50 largest metro areas in terms of the "Most Energetic Cities." The Portland* metro area ranked #8. Criteria: percentage of population that walk or bicycle to work; BMI score; number of food co-ops; number of farmers markets. *Tahitian Noni International Hiro™, "Most Energetic Cities," March 13, 2007*

- Scarborough Research, a leading market research firm, identified the top local markets for organic consumers. The Portland* DMA (Designated Market Area) ranked in the top 15 with 27% of adults reporting that they used any organic food product in their household during the past month. *Scarborough Research, October 10, 2007*

- *Reader's Digest* ranked the 50 largest metro areas in the U.S. in terms of how "clean" they are. The Portland* metro area ranked #1. Criteria: air quality; water quality; toxic industrial pollution; Superfund sites; and sanitation. *Reader's Digest, "The 50 Cleanest (and Dirtiest) Cities in America," July 2005*

- The American Academy of Dermatology ranked 32 U.S. metropolitan regions in terms of their residents knowledge, attitude and behaviors towards tanning and sun protection. The Portland* metro area ranked #13. The results of the study are based on an online national survey of 3,342 respondents. *American Academy of Dermatology, "RAYS: Your Grade," May 7, 2007*

- *Business Week* identified the 15 metro areas that saw the steepest declines in ground-level ozone pollution between 1990 and 2005. The Portland* metro area ranked #10. *Business Week, "America's Most Cleaned-Up Metro Areas," March 23, 2007*

- The Portland* metro area appeared in *Country Home's* "2008 Best Green Places" report. The area ranked #2 out of 379. Criteria: official energy policies; green power; green buildings; availability of fresh, locally grown food. *Country Home, "2008 Best Green Places"*

- Wyeth Consumer Healthcare, in partnership with Sperling's BestPlaces, ranked the nation's 50 most populous metro areas in terms of five key health factors. The Portland* metro area ranked #16. Criteria: physical activity; health status; nutrition; lifestyle pursuits; and mental wellness. *Wyeth Consumer Healthcare, "Centrum Healthiest Cities Study," April 19, 2005*
- Portland* was identified as a "2008 Asthma Capital." The area ranked #77 out of the nation's 100 largest metropolitan areas. Twelve factors were used to identify the most challenging places to live for people with asthma: estimated prevalence; self-reported prevalence; crude death rate for asthma; annual pollen score; annual air quality; public smoking laws; number of board-certified asthma specialists; school inhaler access laws; rescue medication use; controller medication use; uninsured rate; poverty rate. *Asthma and Allergy Foundation of America, "2008 Asthma Capitals"*
- Portland* was identified as a "Spring Allergy Capital." The area ranked #84 out of 100. Three groups of factors were used to identify the most severe cities for people with allergies during the spring season: annual pollen levels; medicine utilization; access to board-certified allergists. *Asthma and Allergy Foundation of America, "2007 Spring Allergy Capital Rankings"*
- Portland* was identified as a "Fall Allergy Capital." The area ranked #97 out of 100. Three groups of factors were used to identify the most severe cities for people with allergies during the fall season: annual pollen levels; medicine utilization; access to board-certified allergists. *Asthma and Allergy Foundation of America, "2007 Fall Allergy Capital Rankings"*
- Ortho-McNeil Neurologics, in partnership with Sperling's BestPlaces, analyzed 110 metro areas and identified those U.S. cities with the highest prevalence of factors that are most commonly associated with migraine headaches. The Portland* metro area ranked #70. Criteria: number of migraine-related drug prescriptions per capita; lifestyle factors that can contribute to migraines; environmental factors that can trigger migraines; and consumption of migraine-triggering foods. *Ortho-McNeil Neurologics, "America's Migraine Hot Spots," March 14, 2006*
- Sperling's BestPlaces ranked 331 metro areas and identified the most and least stressful U.S. cities. The Portland* metro area ranked #6 out of the 100 largest metro areas (#1 = most stressful). Criteria: divorce rate; unemployment rate; violent and property crime; suicide rate; commute time; mental health; alcohol consumption; cloudy days. *Sperling's BestPlaces, www.BestPlaces.net, "America's Most (and Least) Stressful Cities," January 9, 2004*
- An analysis of the "Best & Worst Cities for Sleep" was conducted by Sperling's BestPlaces. The study ranked America's 50 most populated metro areas. The Portland* metro area ranked #27 (#1 = best city for sleep). Criteria: number of days residents didn't get enough rest or sleep during the past month; average length of daily commute; divorce rate; unemployment rate. *Sperling's BestPlaces, www.BestPlaces.net, "Best & Worst Cities for Sleep," 2006*
- Sperling's BestPlaces in partnership with Vistakon ranked the 100 largest metro areas and identified "America's 10 Best Cities for Comfortable Eyes." The Portland* metro area ranked #5. Criteria: altitude; sunny days; wind; extreme temperatures; humidity; pollution; commute time; computer use. *Vistakon, "America's Best and Worst Cities for Comfortable Eyes," June 15, 2004*
- HealthGrades evaluated the performance of America's 25 most populous metropolitan areas by measuring the outcomes of five of the highest volume and most widely studied procedures and diagnoses: coronary artery bypass graft surgery; percutaneus coronary interventions; acute myocardial infarction/heart attack in angioplasty-capable hospitals; congestive heart failure; and community acquired pneumonia. The Portland* metro area ranked #25. *HealthGrades, "HealthGrades Hospital Quality in America Study," October 12, 2004*
- Portland* was highlighted as one of the cleanest metro areas for ozone air pollution in the U.S. The list represents cities with no monitored ozone air pollution in unhealthful ranges. *American Lung Association, State of the Air: 2007*
- Portland* was selected as one of "America's Top 10 Low-Carb Cities" by *LowCarbiz Magazine*. Criteria: abundance of low-carb products; restaurants with low-carb menu items; health practitioners supportive of carb-cutting regimens; local culture generally conducive to exercise and health. *LowCarbiz Magazine, April 2004*

- Portland* was selected as one of "America's Pet Healthiest Cities" by Purina. The city ranked #3 out of 50. Criteria: veterinary services; environment; legislation; preventative care; obesity/body condition. *Purina Pet Institute, "America's Pet Healthiest Cities," May 20, 2003*

Women/Minorities Rankings

- Portland* was ranked #29 out of 100 metro areas in *SELF Magazine's* ranking of "America's Best Places for Women." A panel of experts came up with more than 50 criteria including death and disease rates, environmental indicators, community resources, and lifestyle habits. *SELF Magazine, "America's Best Places for Women 2007," December 2007*

Seniors/Retirement Rankings

- Sperling's BestPlaces in partnership with Bankers Life & Casualty Company designed a survey to identify the top 50 metro areas in the U.S. that offer the best overall qualities for senior living. The Portland* metro area ranked #1. The following criteria were statistically weighted to reflect the needs of the senior population: health; disease; economics; social; environment; spiritual; transportation; housing; and crime. *Bankers Life & Casualty Company, "Best Cities for Seniors 2005"*

- A.G. Edwards ranked America's 500 top-performing communities based on their residents' personal savings and investing behavior. The Portland* metro area ranked #174 with an index score of 103.99 (national average = 100.00). A dozen statistical factors were measured including: participation in retirement savings plans; personal debt levels; and home ownership. *A.G. Edwards, "2007 Nest Egg Index", September 12, 2007*

Children/Family Rankings

- The Portland* metro area was selected as one of the "Best Cities for Relocating Families" by Worldwide ERC and Primacy Relocation. The 2007 study placed a special emphasis on the housing market, which has significantly impacted the relocation industry and an employer's ability to transfer employees. The variables which weigh heavily in this category include home price, home affordability index, appreciation rates, and property tax. Other criteria include cost of living, crime rates, education, climate, focus on diversity, physicians per capita, recreation and leisure, arts and culture, air quality, watershed quality, sales tax, unemployment rate, job growth, high school and higher education index, school expenditures per student, students in public school, SAT/ACT percentile, and population growth. *Worldwide ERC and Primacy Relocation, "2007 Best Cities for Relocating Families"*

Safety Rankings

- The National Insurance Crime Bureau ranked 361 metro areas in the U.S. in terms of per capita rates of vehicle theft. The Portland* metro area ranked #54 (#1 = highest rate). Criteria: number of vehicle theft offenses per 100,000 inhabitants. *National Insurance Crime Bureau, "NICB Vehicle Theft Study," April 22, 2008*

- Portland* appeared on Sperling's BestPlaces list of the "Riskiest Cities for Identity Theft." The area ranked #11 out of the nations 50 largest metro areas. Over 80 criteria were analyzed across four major categories: technology impact; crime; transactions; and risk profile. *Sperling's BestPlaces, www.BestPlaces.net, "Riskiest Cities for Identity Theft," July 2006*

- Farmers Insurance Group of Companies, in partnership with Sperling's BestPlaces, ranked 379 metro areas and identified the "Most Secure U.S. Place to Live." The Portland* metro area ranked #14 out of 114 in the large metro area category (500,000 or more residents). Criteria: crime rates; extreme weather; risk of natural disasters; environmental hazards; terrorism threats; air quality; life expectancy; job loss numbers. *Farmers Insurance Group, "Most Secure U.S. Places to Live 2007"*

- Portland* was identified as one of the most dangerous large metro areas for pedestrians in the U.S. The area ranked #39 out of the nations 50 largest metro areas. Criteria: average yearly pedestrian fatalities per capita (for the years 2002 and 2003) adjusted for the number of walkers. *Surface Transportation Policy Project, "Mean Streets 2004"*

Sports/Recreation Rankings

- The Portland* metro area appeared on the *Sporting News* list of the "Best Sports Cities 2007". The area ranked #56 out of 150 cities in the U.S. *Sporting News* takes a 12-month snapshot, roughly July to July, of each city's sports, putting a heavy premium on regular-season won-lost records (from the most recently completed season). Other criteria include: playoff berths, bowl appearances and tournament bids; championships; applicable power ratings; quality of competition; overall fan fervor as measured in part by attendance as percentage of venue capacity; abundance of teams (rewarding quality over quantity); stadium and arena quality; ticket availability and prices; franchise ownership; and marquee appeal of athletes. *SportingNews.com, "Best Sports Cities 2007," August 1, 2007*
- The Portland* metro area was selected by *Cranium* as one of the "Top 50 Fun Cities" in America. The area ranked #11. Criteria includes: number of sports teams, restaurants, and dance performances; number of toy stores; city budget spent on recreation. *Cranium, November 4, 2003*
- *Golf Digest* ranked 330 metro areas in the U.S. in terms of golf. The Portland* metro area was ranked #302. Criteria: access to golf; weather; value of golf; and quality of golf. *Golf Digest, "Metro Golf Rankings," August 2005*

Dating/Romance Rankings

- Eli Lily and Company, in partnership with Sperling's BestPlaces, ranked the nation's 50 largest metro areas in terms of the "Most Romantic Cities for Baby Boomers." The Portland* metro area ranked #27. Criteria: marriage and divorce rates among "baby boomers" age 45 to 60; great restaurants; dance studios; chocolate, jewelry and flower sales. *Eli Lily and Company, "Most Romantic Cities for Baby Boomers," April 20, 2007*
- The Portland* metro area was selected as one of the "Best Cities for Relocating Singles" by Worldwide ERC and Primacy Relocation. The area ranked #31 out of the 100 largest metro areas in the U.S. Areas were selected based on the following criteria: a robust cost-of-living index; adventure and outdoor recreation opportunities; violent crime and property crime rates; percentage of the population that is unmarried (ages 25-34); ratio of single men and single women; affordability of quality higher education, including in-state and out-of-state tuition requirements and rates; number of newcomers to the area; commute times; tax rates; fee and occupancy rates for temporary housing and mini-storage; quality and quantity of collegiate and professional sporting events and fun, fan-friendly venues. *Worldwide ERC and Primacy Relocation, "2007 Best Cities for Relocating Singles," October 25, 2007*
- *Forbes* ranked the 40 most populous urbanized areas in the U.S. in terms of the "Best Cities for Singles." The Portland* metro area ranked #29. Criteria: number of singles; cost of living alone; nightlife; culture; job growth; coolness; and online dating. *Forbes.com, August 21, 2007*
- Sperling's BestPlaces in partnership with AXE Deodorant Bodyspray ranked 80 metro areas and identified "America's Best (and Worst) Cities for Dating." The Portland* metro area ranked #15 (#1 = best). Criteria: percentage of singles ages 18-24; population density; dating venues per capita. *AXE Deodorant Bodyspray, "America's Best (and Worst) Cities for Dating," May 2004*

Culture/Performing Arts Rankings

- Scarborough Research, a leading market research firm, identified the top local markets for rock concert attendance. The Portland* DMA (Designated Market Area) ranked in the top 25 with 16% of consumers, 18 years old and over, reporting that they have attended a rock concert during the past year. *Scarborough Research, June 14, 2004*

Miscellaneous Rankings

- Scarborough Research, a leading market research firm, identified the top local markets for bloggers. The Portland* DMA (Designated Market Area) ranked in the top 13 with 14% of adults reporting that they had read or contributed to a blog within the past 30 days. *Scarborough Research, October 24, 2007*

- The Portland* metro area appeared on *Forbes* list of "America's Drunkest Cities". The area ranked #19. Criteria: 35 of the largest continental U.S. metro areas were chosen based on availability of data and geographic diversity. Each metro was ranked in five areas: state laws; drinkers; heavy drinkers; binge drinkers; and alcoholism. *Forbes.com, "America's Drunkest Cities," August 22, 2006*

- Sperling's BestPlaces in partnership with Pep Boys ranked 77 metro areas and identified "America's Most Drivable Cities." The Portland* metro area ranked #58. Criteria: climate; road roughness; urban mobility; gas prices. *Pep Boys, "America's Most Drivable Cities," April 9, 2003*

- State Farm Insurance, in partnership with Sperling's BestPlaces, analyzed several key factors that contribute to overall family preparedness. The Portland* metro area ranked #2 out of the nation's 50 most populous metro areas. Criteria: quality of life; life insurance coverage; and investments. *State Farm Life Insurance, "Fiscally Fit Cities Report," July 20, 2004*

- Scarborough Research, a leading market research firm, identified the top local markets for coffee bar patronage. The Portland* DMA (Designated Market Area) ranked in the top 10 with 21% of adults reporting that they have used any coffee house/bar during the past 30 days. *Scarborough Research, October 14, 2004*

- A study by Sperling's BestPlaces examined which U.S. metro areas were most affected by high fuel prices in 2006. The Portland* metro area was ranked #60 out of 80 (#1 = most expensive city for driving). Rankings are based on the average dollars spent on gas per year by two driver households. Criteria: cost of regular-grade gasoline; average miles driven per day; average number of gallons each driver uses and wastes in traffic congestion each day. *Sperling's BestPlaces, www.bestplaces.net, "Pain at the Pump," May 18, 2006*

Tualatin is located within the Portland-Vancouver-Beaverton, OR-WA Metropolitan Statistical Area.

Business Environment

CITY FINANCES

City Government Finances

Component	2004-2005 ($000)	2004-2005 ($ per capita)
Total Revenues	n/a	n/a
Total Expenditures	n/a	n/a
Debt Outstanding	n/a	n/a
Cash and Securities	n/a	n/a

Source: U.S Census Bureau, Government Finances 2004-2005

City Government Revenue by Source

Source	2004-2005 ($000)	2004-2005 ($ per capita)
General Revenue		
From Federal Government	n/a	n/a
From State Government	n/a	n/a
From Local Governments	n/a	n/a
Taxes		
Property	n/a	n/a
Sales	n/a	n/a
Personal Income	n/a	n/a
License	n/a	n/a
Charges	n/a	n/a
Liquor Store	n/a	n/a
Utility	n/a	n/a
Employee Retirement	n/a	n/a
Other	n/a	n/a

Source: U.S Census Bureau, Government Finances 2004-2005

City Government Expenditures by Function

Function	2004-2005 ($000)	2004-2005 ($ per capita)	2004-2005 (%)
General Expenditures			
Airports	n/a	n/a	n/a
Corrections	n/a	n/a	n/a
Education	n/a	n/a	n/a
Fire Protection	n/a	n/a	n/a
Governmental Administration	n/a	n/a	n/a
Health	n/a	n/a	n/a
Highways	n/a	n/a	n/a
Hospitals	n/a	n/a	n/a
Housing and Community Development	n/a	n/a	n/a
Interest on General Debt	n/a	n/a	n/a
Libraries	n/a	n/a	n/a
Parking	n/a	n/a	n/a
Parks and Recreation	n/a	n/a	n/a
Police Protection	n/a	n/a	n/a
Public Welfare	n/a	n/a	n/a
Sewerage	n/a	n/a	n/a
Solid Waste Management	n/a	n/a	n/a
Liquor Store	n/a	n/a	n/a
Utility	n/a	n/a	n/a
Employee Retirement	n/a	n/a	n/a
Other	n/a	n/a	n/a

Source: U.S Census Bureau, Government Finances 2004-2005

Municipal Bond Ratings

Area	Moody's
City	n/a

Source: Mergent Bond Record, January 2008 (unless noted otherwise)

DEMOGRAPHICS

Population Growth

Area	1990 Census	2000 Census	2007 Estimate	2012 Projection	Population Growth (%) 1990-2000	Population Growth (%) 2000-2012
City	15,782	22,791	26,439	28,844	44.4	26.6
MSA[1]	1,523,741	1,927,881	2,138,513	2,283,958	26.5	18.5
U.S.	248,709,873	281,421,906	301,045,522	314,920,978	13.2	11.9

Note: (1) Metropolitan Statistical Area - see Appendix B for areas included
Source: Claritas, Inc.

Number of Households and Average Household Size

Area	2007 Estimate	2007 Average Household Size
City	9,987	2.65
MSA[1]	829,870	2.58
U.S.	113,668,003	2.65

Note: (1) Metropolitan Statistical Area - see Appendix B for areas included
Source: Claritas, Inc.

Race and Ethnicity

Area	White Alone[2]	Black Alone[2]	Asian Alone[2]	Other Race Alone[2]	Hispanic[3]
City	83.5	0.9	4.4	11.2	16.2
MSA[1]	82.1	2.7	5.3	9.9	9.7
U.S.	73.1	12.4	4.3	10.3	14.9

Note: Figures are 2007 estimates; (1) Metropolitan Statistical Area - see Appendix B for areas included (2) Alone is defined as not being in combination with one or more other races; (3) May be of any race.
Source: Claritas, Inc.

Ancestry

Area	German	Irish[2]	English	American	Italian	Polish	French[3]	Scottish
City	20.4	11.5	12.7	5.0	3.6	1.4	4.3	4.0
MSA[1]	20.8	11.8	12.7	5.5	3.5	1.8	3.7	3.1
U.S.	15.2	10.9	8.7	7.3	5.6	3.2	3.0	1.7

Note: Figures include multiple ancestry (e.g. if a person reported being Irish and Italian, they were included in both columns); (1) Metropolitan Statistical Area - see Appendix A for areas included; (2) Includes Celtic; (3) Includes Alsatian but excludes Basque
Source: Census 2000, Summary File 3

Foreign-Born Population

Area	Percent of Population Born in: Any Foreign Country	Europe	Asia	Africa	Oceania[2]	Canada	Mexico	Latin America[3]
City	12.5	1.4	3.2	0.0	0.0	0.8	6.5	0.6
MSA[1]	10.9	2.5	3.6	0.2	0.2	0.6	3.1	0.6
U.S.	11.1	1.7	2.9	0.3	0.1	0.3	3.3	2.5

Note: (1) Metropolitan Statistical Area - see Appendix A for areas included; (2) Includes Australia, New Zealand subregion, Melanesia, Micronesia, Polynesia, and Oceania n.e.c; (3) Includes Central America (excluding Mexico), South America, and the Caribbean.
Source: Census 2000, Summary File 3

Marriage Status

Area	Never Married	Now Married (excluding Separated)	Separated	Widowed	Divorced
City	26.6	57.2	1.9	3.7	10.7
MSA[1]	26.8	54.6	1.7	5.3	11.6
U.S.	27.1	54.4	2.2	6.6	9.7

Note: Figures are percentages and cover the population 15 years of age and older; (1) Metropolitan Statistical Area - see Appendix A for areas included
Source: Census 2000, Summary File 3

Age Distribution

Area	Percent of Population						
	Under Age 5	Age 5 to 17	Age 18 to 34	Age 35 to 49	Age 50 to 64	Age 65 to 79	80 Years and Over
City	7.4	20.6	26.6	27.5	11.9	3.9	2.0
MSA[1]	7.0	18.4	24.8	24.7	14.7	7.4	3.0
U.S.	6.8	18.9	23.7	23.5	14.8	9.2	3.2

Note: (1) Metropolitan Statistical Area - see Appendix A for areas included
Source: Census 2000, Summary File 3

Male/Female Ratio

Area	Males	Females	Males per 100 Females
City	13,203	13,236	99.8
MSA[1]	1,065,621	1,072,892	99.3
U.S.	148,320,305	152,725,217	97.1

Note: Figures are 2007 estimates; (1) Metropolitan Statistical Area - see Appendix B for areas included
Source: Claritas, Inc.

Religion

Area	Catholic	Southern Baptist	United Methodist	ELCA[1]	LDS[2]	Presbyterian Church USA	Jewish Est.	Muslim Est.
County	6.5	0.7	0.9	1.2	3.8	0.7	0.7	0.1
U.S.	22.0	7.1	3.7	1.8	1.5	1.1	2.2	0.6

Note: Figures are the number of adherents as a percentage of the total population; Adherents are defined as all members, including full members, their children and the estimated number of other participants who are not considered members (e.g. the baptized, those not confirmed, those regularly attending services, etc.); (1) Evangelical Lutheran Church in America; (2) The Church of Jesus Christ of Latter Day Saints
Source: Reprinted with permission from Religious Congregations and Membership in the United States 2000 (Nashville, Glenmary Research Center, 2002) Copyright Association of Statisticians of American Religious Bodies. All rights reserved.

ECONOMY

Gross Metropolitan Product

Area	2002	2003	2004	2005	2005 Rank[2]
MSA[1]	70.3	72.1	80.0	85.7	26

Note: Figures are in billions of dollars; (1) Portland-Vancouver-Beaverton, OR-WA Metropolitan Statistical Area - see Appendix A for areas included; (2) Rank ranges from 1 to 361
Source: The U.S. Conference of Mayors, "U.S. Metro Economies: GMP - The Engines of America's Growth," January 2007

Economic Growth

Area	1995 GMP	2005 GMP	Average Annual Growth Rate	Growth Rate Rank[2]
MSA[1]	47.4	85.7	6.1	112

Note: Figures are in billions of dollars; GMP = Gross Metropolitan Product; (1) Portland-Vancouver-Beaverton, OR-WA Metropolitan Statistical Area - see Appendix A for areas included; (2) Rank ranges from 1 to 361
Source: The U.S. Conference of Mayors, "U.S. Metro Economies: GMP - The Engines of America's Growth," January 2007

INCOME

Per Capita/Median/Average Income

Area	Per Capita ($)	Median Household ($)	Average Household ($)
City	30,745	60,212	80,835
MSA[1]	26,987	53,775	68,909
U.S.	25,495	49,280	66,670

Note: Figures are 2007 estimates; (1) Metropolitan Statistical Area - see Appendix B for areas included
Source: Claritas, Inc.

Household Income Distribution

Area	Percent of Households Earning							
	Under $15,000	$15,000 -24,999	$25,000 -34,999	$35,000 -49,999	$50,000 -74,999	$75,000 -99,000	$100,000 -149,999	$150,000 and up
City	6.1	6.9	12.0	15.6	20.3	13.9	15.8	9.5
MSA[1]	9.9	9.4	10.7	16.4	21.6	13.4	12.3	6.3
U.S.	13.1	10.9	11.2	15.6	19.5	11.9	11.3	6.6

Note: Figures are 2007 estimates; (1) Metropolitan Statistical Area - see Appendix B for areas included
Source: Claritas, Inc.

Poverty Rates by Age

Area	All Ages	Under 5 Years Old	5 to 17 Years Old	18 to 64 Years Old	65 Years and Over
City	5.5	0.4	1.0	3.9	0.2
MSA[1]	9.5	0.9	2.0	5.7	0.7
U.S.	12.4	1.2	3.0	6.9	1.2

Note: Figures are percent of population with income in 1999 below poverty level and only include population for whom poverty status is determined; (1) Metropolitan Statistical Area - see Appendix A for areas included
Source: Census 2000, Summary File 3

Personal Bankruptcy Filing Rate

Area	2004	2005	2006
Washington County	6.30	8.43	1.83
U.S.	5.31	6.82	2.00

Note: Numbers are per 1,000 population and include Chapter 7 and Chapter 13 filings
Source: Federal Deposit Insurance Corporation (FDIC), Regional Economic Conditions (RECON), 8/23/2007

EMPLOYMENT

Labor Force and Employment

Area	Civilian Labor Force			Workers Employed		
	Dec. 2006	Dec. 2007	% Chg.	Dec. 2006	Dec. 2007	% Chg.
City	15,125	15,300	1.2	14,611	14,748	0.9
MSA[1]	1,145,573	1,161,260	1.4	1,094,566	1,105,347	1.0
U.S.	152,571,000	153,705,000	0.7	146,081,000	146,334,000	0.2

Note: Data is not seasonally adjusted and covers workers 16 years of age and older; (1) Metropolitan Statistical Area - see Appendix B for areas included
Source: Bureau of Labor Statistics, http://stats.bls.gov

Unemployment Rate

Area	2007											
	Jan.	Feb.	Mar.	Apr.	May	Jun.	Jul.	Aug.	Sep.	Oct.	Nov.	Dec.
City	3.8	3.9	3.8	3.6	3.2	3.8	3.9	3.8	3.7	3.8	3.7	3.6
MSA[1]	5.3	5.4	5.0	4.7	4.5	4.9	5.0	5.0	4.6	4.6	4.7	4.8
U.S.	5.0	4.9	4.5	4.3	4.3	4.7	4.9	4.6	4.5	4.4	4.5	4.8

Note: Data is not seasonally adjusted and covers workers 16 years of age and older; All figures are percentages; (1) Metropolitan Statistical Area - see Appendix B for areas included
Source: Bureau of Labor Statistics, http://stats.bls.gov

Employment by Occupation

Occupation Classification	City (%)	MSA[1] (%)	U.S. (%)
Sales and Office	31.6	27.3	26.7
Professional and Related	18.5	20.7	20.2
Service	11.1	13.6	14.9
Production, Transportation, and Material Moving	11.9	14.3	14.6
Management, Business, and Financial	19.5	14.6	13.5
Construction, Extraction, and Maintenance	7.0	8.8	9.4
Farming, Forestry, and Fishing	0.3	0.7	0.7

Note: Figures cover employed civilians 16 years of age and older; (1) Metropolitan Statistical Area - see Appendix A for areas included
Source: Census 2000, Summary File 3

Employment by Industry

Sector	MSA[1] Number of Employees	MSA[1] Percent of Total	U.S. Percent of Total
Government	147,100	13.9	16.3
Education and Health Services	131,500	12.5	13.4
Professional and Business Services	137,600	13.0	13.1
Retail Trade	117,600	11.1	11.6
Manufacturing	125,900	11.9	9.9
Leisure and Hospitality	99,600	9.4	9.6
Financial Activities	71,000	6.7	5.9
Construction	65,200	6.2	5.3
Wholesale Trade	58,400	5.5	4.4
Other Services	36,800	3.5	3.9
Transportation and Utilities	39,000	3.7	3.7
Information	24,800	2.3	2.2
Natural Resources and Mining	1,600	0.2	0.5

Note: Figures cover non-farm employment as of December 2007 and are not seasonally adjusted; (1) Metropolitan Statistical Area - see Appendix B for areas included
Source: Bureau of Labor Statistics, http://stats.bls.gov

Average Wages

Occupation	$/Hr.	Occupation	$/Hr.
Accountants and Auditors	29.64	Maids and Housekeeping Cleaners	9.80
Automotive Mechanics	17.89	Maintenance and Repair Workers	17.31
Bookkeepers	16.85	Marketing Managers	51.55
Carpenters	19.99	Nuclear Medicine Technologists	34.64
Cashiers	10.54	Nurses, Licensed Practical	22.13
Clerks, General Office	13.95	Nurses, Registered	33.48
Clerks, Receptionists/Information	12.61	Nursing Aides/Orderlies/Attendants	12.60
Clerks, Shipping/Receiving	14.61	Packers and Packagers, Hand	10.04
Computer Programmers	34.48	Physical Therapists	31.83
Computer Support Specialists	21.32	Postal Service Mail Carriers	21.24
Computer Systems Analysts	35.96	Real Estate Brokers	42.80
Cooks, Restaurant	10.94	Retail Salespersons	13.03
Dentists	n/a	Sales Reps., Exc. Tech./Scientific	31.76
Electrical Engineers	40.20	Sales Reps., Tech./Scientific	39.10
Electricians	27.91	Secretaries, Exc. Legal/Med./Exec.	15.08
Financial Managers	51.13	Security Guards	11.51
First-Line Supervisors/Mgrs., Sales	20.11	Surgeons	88.60
Food Preparation Workers	10.45	Teacher Assistants	13.00
General and Operations Managers	52.07	Teachers, Elementary School	24.20
Hairdressers/Cosmetologists	11.12	Teachers, Secondary School	24.40
Internists	86.78	Telemarketers	11.78
Janitors and Cleaners	11.32	Truck Drivers, Heavy/Tractor-Trailer	18.32
Landscaping/Groundskeeping Workers	11.77	Truck Drivers, Light/Delivery Svcs.	14.49
Lawyers	48.06	Waiters and Waitresses	10.53

Note: Wage data covers the Portland-Vancouver-Beaverton, OR-WA Metropolitan Statistical Area - see Appendix B for areas included. Hourly wages for elementary/secondary school teachers and teacher assistants were calculated by the editors from annual wage data assuming a 40 hour work week; n/a not available.
Source: Bureau of Labor Statistics, May 2007 Metro Area Occupational Employment and Wage Estimates

RESIDENTIAL REAL ESTATE

Building Permits

Area	Single-Family			Multi-Family			Total		
	2006	2007p	Pct. Chg.	2006	2007p	Pct. Chg.	2006	2007p	Pct. Chg.
City	101	48	-52.5	0	0	-	101	48	-52.5
U.S.	1,378,200	973,300	-29.4	460,700	407,200	-11.6	1,838,900	1,380,500	-24.9

Note: (p) preliminary; figures cover and represent new, privately-owned housing units authorized (unadjusted data); All permit data are based on estimates with imputation; U.S. figures are based on the new 20,000-place series.
Source: U.S. Census Bureau, Manufacturing, Mining, and Construction Statistics

Homeownership and Housing Vacancies

Area	Homeownership Rate[2] (%)			Rental Vacancy Rate[3] (%)			Homeowner Vacancy Rate[4] (%)		
	2005	2006	2007	2005	2006	2007	2005	2006	2007
MSA[1]	68.3	66.0	61.2	9.7	7.1	4.8	1.6	1.7	2.3
U.S.	68.9	68.8	68.1	9.8	9.8	9.7	1.9	2.4	2.7

Note: (1) Metropolitan Statistical Area - see Appendix B for areas included; (2) The proportion of households that are owners; (3) The proportion of the rental inventory that is vacant for rent; (4) The proportion of the homeowner inventory that is vacant for sale; n/a not available
Source: U.S. Census Bureau, Housing Vacancies and Homeownership Annual Statistics: 2007

TAXES

State Corporate Income Tax Rates

State	Rates and Tax Brackets
Oregon	6.6%

Note: Tax rates as of January 1, 2008; Minimum tax $10.
Source: Tax Foundation, www.taxfoundation.org

State Individual Income Tax Rates

State	Federal Deductibility	Marginal Rates (%)	Standard Deduction ($)		Personal Exemptions ($)[1]	
			Single	Joint	Single	Dependents
Oregon	Yes (z)	5.0 - 9.0 (r)	1,850 (r)	3,650 (r)	165 (c)(r)	165 (c)(r)

Note: Tax rates as of January 1, 2008; Local- and county-level taxes are not included; n/a not applicable; (1) Married joint filers generally receive double the single exemption; (c) Tax Credit; (r) State adjusts its bracket levels for inflation at the end of each year before printing tax forms; (z) Deduction limited to no more than $5,000.
Source: Tax Foundation, www.taxfoundation.org

Various State and Local Tax Rates

State and Local Sales and Use (%)	State Sales and Use (%)	Gasoline[1,2] ($/gal.)	Cigarette ($/pack)	Spirits ($/gal.)	Table Wine ($/gal.)	Beer ($/gal.)
None	None	0.25	1.18	19.26 (n)	0.67	0.08

Note: Tax rates as of January 1, 2008; (1) In addition to the 18.4 cpg Federal gasoline tax; (2) Rates may include additional state sales taxes, environmental protection and storage fees/taxes, and local taxes. When necessary, the volume-weighted average of all local taxes is used to approximate the typical statewide rate including local tax; (n) The state government controls all sales. The implied excise tax rate is calculated using methodology designed by the Distilled Spirits Council of the United States (DISCUS).
Source: Tax Foundation, www.taxfoundation.org; Original research

State Tax Burdens

Area	Combined State and Local Tax Burden		Combined Federal, State and Local Tax Burden	
	Percent	Rank	Percent	Rank
Oregon	10.0	37	30.7	31
U.S. Average	11.0	-	32.7	-

Note: Figures cover 2007 and measure taxes as a percentage of income
Source: Tax Foundation, www.taxfoundation.org

State Business Tax Climate Index Rankings

State	Overall Rank	Corporate Tax Index Rank	Individual Income Tax Index Rank	Sales Tax Index Rank	Unemployment Insurance Tax Index Rank	Property Tax Index Rank
Oregon	10	20	35	4	32	14

Note: Rankings range from 1 to 50 where 1 is best. Rankings do not average across to Overall Rank. States without a given tax are given a ranking of 1.
Source: Tax Foundation, State Business Tax Climate Index 2008

TRANSPORTATION

Means of Transportation to Work

Area	Car/Truck/Van		Public Transportation			Bicycle	Walked	Other Means	Worked at Home
	Drove Alone	Car-pooled	Bus	Subway	Railroad				
City	77.3	10.1	4.4	0.2	0.0	0.9	2.4	0.3	4.6
MSA[1]	73.1	11.5	5.3	0.4	0.2	0.8	3.0	1.1	4.6
U.S.	75.7	12.2	2.5	1.5	0.5	0.4	2.9	1.0	3.3

Note: Figures are percentages and cover workers 16 years of age and older; (1) Metropolitan Statistical Area - see Appendix A for areas included
Source: Census 2000, Summary File 3

Travel Time to Work

Area	Less Than 15 Minutes	15 to 29 Minutes	30 to 44 Minutes	45 to 59 Minutes	60 Minutes or More
City	32.4	36.3	23.8	4.9	2.6
MSA[1]	26.3	40.0	21.1	7.0	5.5
U.S.	29.4	36.1	19.1	7.4	8.0

Note: Figures are percentages and include workers 16 years old and over; (1) Metropolitan Statistical Area - see Appendix A for areas included
Source: Census 2000, Summary File 3

Travel Time Index

Area	1982	1995	2004	2005
Urban Area[1]	1.07	1.20	1.27	1.29
Average[2]	1.11	1.22	1.29	1.30

Note: Travel Time Index - The ratio of travel time in the peak period to the travel time at free-flow conditions. A value of 1.35 indicates a 20-minute free-flow trip takes 27 minutes in the peak. Free-flow speeds (60 mph on freeways and 35 mph on principal arterials) are used as the comparison threshold; (1) Covers the Portland, OR-WA urban area; (2) average of 85 urban areas
Source: Texas Transportation Institute, The 2007 Urban Mobility Report, September 2007

Living Environment

COST OF LIVING

Cost of Living Index

Composite Index	Groceries	Housing	Utilities	Trans-portation	Health Care	Misc. Goods/ Services
121.4	124.3	135.8	104.0	111.1	107.9	118.2

Note: U.S. = 100; Figures cover the Portland OR urban area.
Source: The Council for Community and Economic Research (formerly ACCRA), Cost of Living Index, 2007

Grocery Prices

Area[1]	T-Bone Steak ($/pound)	Frying Chicken ($/pound)	Whole Milk ($/half gal.)	Eggs ($/dozen)	Orange Juice ($/64 oz.)	Coffee ($/11.5 oz.)
City[2]	9.78	1.92	1.95	2.66	3.96	3.98
Avg.	8.93	1.12	2.13	1.52	3.26	3.31
Min.	5.88	0.71	1.33	0.83	2.30	2.20
Max.	12.80	2.07	3.43	3.54	5.79	6.20

Note: (1) Values for the local area are compared with the average, minimum and maximum values for all 331 areas in the Cost of Living Index report; (2) Figures cover the Portland OR urban area; **T-Bone Steak** *(price per pound);* **Frying Chicken** *(price per pound, whole fryer);* **Whole Milk** *(half gallon carton);* **Eggs** *(price per dozen, Grade A, large);* **Orange Juice** *(64 oz. Tropicana or Florida Natural);* **Coffee** *(11.5 oz. can, vacuum-packed, Maxwell House, Hills Bros, or Folgers).*
Source: The Council for Community and Economic Research (formerly ACCRA), Cost of Living Index, 2007

Housing and Utility Costs

Area[1]	New Home Price ($)	Apartment Rent ($/month)	All Electric ($/month)	Part Electric ($/month)	Other Energy ($/month)	Telephone ($/month)
City[2]	434,461	946	-	88.95	85.14	25.99
Avg.	309,605	782	146.13	78.67	90.16	26.14
Min.	189,877	n/a	82.03	37.41	33.15	17.08
Max.	1,202,800	3,481	271.14	150.60	257.67	37.45

Note: (1) Values for the local area are compared with the average, minimum and maximum values for all 331 areas in the Cost of Living Index report; (2) Figures cover the Portland OR urban area; **New Home Price** *(2,400 sf living area, 8,000 sf lot, in urban area with full utilities);* **Apartment Rent** *(950 sf 2 bedroom/1.5 or 2 bath, unfurnished, excluding all utilities except water);* **All Electric** *(average monthly cost for an all-electric home);* **Part Electric** *(average monthly cost for a part-electric home);* **Other Energy** *(average monthly cost for natural gas, fuel oil, coal, wood, and any other forms of energy except electricity);* **Telephone** *(price includes basic monthly rate for a private residential line plus additional local usage charges incurred by a family of four).*
Source: The Council for Community and Economic Research (formerly ACCRA), Cost of Living Index, 2007

Health Care, Transportation, and Other Costs

Area[1]	Doctor ($/visit)	Dentist ($/visit)	Optometrist ($/visit)	Gasoline ($/gallon)	Beauty Salon ($/visit)	Men's Shirt ($)
City[2]	96.67	79.62	90.50	2.92	32.87	40.65
Avg.	79.48	71.93	79.55	2.64	29.52	25.77
Min.	52.08	44.80	43.95	2.19	15.58	16.19
Max.	148.44	126.27	158.83	3.48	60.62	48.53

Note: (1) Values for the local area are compared with the average, minimum and maximum values for all 331 areas in the Cost of Living Index report; (2) Figures cover the Portland OR urban area; **Doctor** *(general practitioners routine exam of an established patient);* **Dentist** *(adult teeth cleaning and periodic oral examination);* **Optometrist** *(full vision eye exam for established adult patient);* **Gasoline** *(one gallon regular unleaded, national brand, including all taxes, cash price at self-service pump if available);* **Beauty Salon** *(woman's shampoo, trim, and blow-dry);* **Men's Shirt** *(cotton/polyester dress shirt, pinpoint weave, long sleeves).*
Source: The Council for Community and Economic Research (formerly ACCRA), Cost of Living Index, 2007

HOUSING

House Price Index (HPI)

Area	National Ranking[2]	Quarterly Change (%)	One-Year Change (%)	Five-Year Change (%)
MSA[1]	61	0.30	4.24	66.54
U.S.[3]	-	0.10	0.84	41.37

Note: The HPI is a weighted repeat sales index. It measures average price changes in repeat sales or refinancings on the same properties. This information is obtained by reviewing repeat mortgage transactions on single-family properties whose mortgages have been purchased or securitized by Fannie Mae or Freddie Mac in January 1975; (1) Metropolitan Statistical Area - see Appendix B for areas included; (2) Rankings are based on annual percentage change for all metro areas containing at least 15,000 transactions over the last 10 years and ranges from 1 to 291; (3) figures based on a weighted average of Census Division estimates; all figures are for the period ending December 31, 2007
Source: Office of Federal Housing Enterprise Oversight, House Price Index, February 26, 2008

House Price Valuations

Area	Q1 2000	Q1 2001	Q1 2002	Q1 2003	Q1 2004	Q1 2005	Q1 2006	Q1 2007	Q1 2008
MSA[1]	-6.2	-6.0	-1.2	3.3	11.3	20.1	37.0	43.8	36.2

Note: Figures show the percentage of over- or under-valuation of single family homes relative to statistically normal house values (e.g. a value of 23.6 indicates that house values are 23.6% overvalued). Statistically normal house values are based on house prices, interest rates, household incomes, population densities, and any historical premiums or discounts metropolitan areas have exhibited over time; (1) Figures cover the Metropolitan Statistical Area - see Appendix B for areas included
Source: Global Insight/National City Corporation, House Prices in America, May 2008

Median Home Prices

Area	2005	2006	2007[r]	Percent Change 2006 to 2007
MSA[1]	244.9	280.8	295.2	5.1
U.S. Average	219.0	221.9	217.9	-1.8

Note: Figures are median sales prices of existing single-family homes in thousands of dollars; (r) revised; n/a not available; (1) Metropolitan Statistical Area - see Appendix B for areas included
Source: National Association of Realtors, Metropolitan Area Prices, 1st Quarter 2008

Housing: Year Structure Built

Area	1990 -2000	1980 -1989	1970 -1979	1960 -1969	1950 -1959	1940 -1949	Before 1940	Median Year
City	41.1	27.4	27.1	2.4	1.0	0.6	0.4	1987
MSA[1]	24.6	13.0	20.9	11.3	9.1	6.5	14.7	1974
U.S.	17.0	15.8	18.5	13.7	12.7	7.3	15.0	1971

Note: Figures are percentages; (1) Metropolitan Statistical Area - see Appendix A for areas included
Source: Census 2000, Summary File 3

HEALTH

Health Risk Data

Category	Area[1] (%)	U.S. (%)
Adults who have been told they have high blood pressure[3]	21.5	25.5
Adults who have been told they have high blood cholesterol[3]	34.2	35.6
Adults who have been told they have diabetes[2]	5.9	7.5
Adults who have been told they have arthritis[3]	24.0	27.0
Adults who have been told they currently have asthma	10.9	8.5
Adults who are current smokers	16.9	20.1
Adults who are heavy drinkers[4]	5.6	4.9
Adults who are overweight (BMI 25.0 - 29.9)	36.9	36.5
Adults who are obese (BMI 30.0 - 99.8)	24.2	25.1

Note: Data as of 2006 unless otherwise noted; (1) Figures cover the Metropolitan Statistical Area - see Appendix B for areas included; (2) Figures do not include pregnancy-related diabetes, pre-diabetes or borderline diabetes; (3) 2005 data; (4) Heavy drinkers are classified as adult men having more than two drinks per day or adult women having more than one drink per day
Source: Centers for Disease Control and Prevention, Behaviorial Risk Factor Surveillance System, SMART: Selected Metropolitan/Micropolitan Area Risk Trends, 2005, 2006

Mortality Rates for the Top 10 Causes of Death in the U.S.

ICD-10[a] Sub-Chapter	ICD-10[a] Code	Age-Adjusted Mortality Rate[1] per 100,000 population	
		County[2]	U.S.
Malignant neoplasms	C00-C97	169.9	186.5
Ischaemic heart diseases	I20-I25	96.8	152.3
Other forms of heart disease	I30-I51	49.8	51.5
Cerebrovascular diseases	I60-I69	58.3	50.0
Chronic lower respiratory diseases	J40-J47	34.9	42.6
Diabetes mellitus	E10-E14	26.4	24.8
Other degenerative diseases of the nervous system	G30-G31	34.7	22.6
Other external causes of accidental injury	W00-X59	18.1	21.4
Influenza and pneumonia	J10-J18	13.2	20.7
Hypertensive diseases	I10-I13	14.7	18.2

Note: (a) ICD-10 = International Classification of Diseases 10th Revision; (1) Mortality rates are a three year average covering 2003-2005; (2) Figures cover Washington County
Source: Centers for Disease Control and Prevention, National Center for Health Statistics. Compressed Mortality File 1999-2004. CDC WONDER On-line Database, compiled from Compressed Mortality File 1999-2005 Series 20 No. 2K, 2008.

Mortality Rates for Selected Causes of Death

ICD-10[a] Sub-Chapter	ICD-10[a] Code	Age-Adjusted Mortality Rate[1] per 100,000 population	
		County[2]	U.S.
Assault	X85-Y09	1.5	5.9
Human immunodeficiency virus (HIV) disease	B20-B24	1.3	4.5
Intentional self-harm	X60-X84	11.7	10.8
Malnutrition	E40-E46	*0.1	1.0
Obesity and other hyperalimentation	E65-E68	*1.2	1.4
Organic, including symptomatic, mental disorders	F01-F09	22.7	16.8
Transport accidents	V01-V99	8.1	16.1
Viral hepatitis	B15-B19	1.5	1.8

Note: (a) ICD-10 = International Classification of Diseases 10th Revision; (1) Mortality rates are a three year average covering 2003-2005; (2) Figures cover Washington County; (*) Unreliable data as per CDC
Source: Centers for Disease Control and Prevention, National Center for Health Statistics. Compressed Mortality File 1999-2004. CDC WONDER On-line Database, compiled from Compressed Mortality File 1999-2005 Series 20 No. 2K, 2008.

Distribution of Physicians[1]

Area	Total	Family/ General Practice	Specialties	
			Medical	Surgical
Washington County (number)	1,052	240	399	241
Washington County (rate per 10,000 pop.)	21.0	4.8	8.0	4.8
U.S. (rate per 10,000 pop.)	17.7	4.6	6.9	4.3

Note: Data as of 2005; (1) Includes all non-federal, patient-care, office-based MDs
Source: Area Resource File (ARF). June 2007. U.S. Department of Health and Human Services, Health Resources and Services Administration, Bureau of Health Professions, Rockville, MD.

Hospitals

Tualatin has the following hospitals: 1 general medical and surgical.
AHA Guide to the Healthcare Field 2008

According to *U.S. News,* the Portland-Vancouver-Beaverton, OR-WA metro area is home to one of the best hospitals in the U.S.: **Oregon Health and Science University Hospital**. *U.S. News Online, "America's Best Hospitals 2007"*

EDUCATION

Public School District Statistics

District Name	Schls	Pupils	Pupil/ Teacher Ratio	Minority Pupils[1] (%)	Free Lunch Eligible[2] (%)	IEP[3] (%)
Tigard-Tualatin SD 23J	15	11,920	19.9	27.6	18.9	11.3

Note: Table includes regular local school districts with 2,000 or more students; (1) Percentage of students that are not white, non-Hispanic; (2) Percentage of students that are eligible for the free lunch program; (3) Percentage of students that have an Individualized Education Program.
Source: U.S. Department of Education, National Center for Education Statistics, Common Core of Data, Local Education Agency (School District) Universe Survey: School Year 2005-2006; U.S. Department of Education, National Center for Education Statistics, Common Core of Data, Public Elementary/Secondary School Universe Survey: School Year 2005-2006

Highest Level of Education

Area	Less than H.S.	H.S. Diploma	Some College, No Deg.	Associate Degree	Bachelors Degree	Masters Degree	Profess. School Degree	Doctorate Degree
City	6.8	18.4	29.6	7.1	27.5	7.3	2.3	1.0
MSA[1]	12.7	23.9	27.7	7.0	19.2	6.5	2.0	0.9
U.S.	19.4	28.4	21.2	6.4	15.7	5.9	2.0	1.0

Note: Figures are 2007 estimated percentages and cover persons age 25 and over; (1) Metropolitan Statistical Area - see Appendix B for areas included
Source: Claritas, Inc.

Educational Attainment by Race

Area	High School Graduate (%)					Bachelor's Degree (%)				
	Total	White	Black	Asian	Hisp.[2]	Total	White	Black	Asian	Hisp.[2]
City	92.9	94.5	100.0	90.7	71.8	37.5	38.9	0.0	45.5	17.5
MSA[1]	87.2	89.4	80.4	79.1	53.7	28.8	29.6	18.0	38.3	11.8
U.S.	80.4	83.6	72.3	80.4	52.4	24.4	26.1	14.3	44.1	10.4

Note: Figures shown cover persons 25 years old and over; (1) Metropolitan Statistical Area - see Appendix A for areas included; (2) people of Hispanic origin can be of any race
Source: Census 2000, Summary File 3

School Enrollment by Type

Area	Grades KG to 8				Grades 9 to 12			
	Public		Private		Public		Private	
	Enrollment	%	Enrollment	%	Enrollment	%	Enrollment	%
City	2,875	92.4	236	7.6	1,394	93.7	93	6.3
MSA[1]	219,761	88.8	27,653	11.2	95,236	91.4	8,906	8.6
U.S.	33,526,011	88.7	4,285,121	11.3	14,848,628	90.6	1,532,323	9.4

Note: Figures shown cover persons 3 years old and over; (1) Metropolitan Statistical Area - see Appendix A for areas included
Source: Census 2000, Summary File 3

School Enrollment by Race

Area	Grades KG to 8 (%)				Grades 9 to 12 (%)			
	White	Black	Asian	Hisp.[1]	White	Black	Asian	Hisp.[1]
City	86.0	0.3	2.9	11.0	83.3	0.0	8.2	12.2
MSA[2]	80.1	3.1	4.4	9.9	81.9	3.4	4.8	7.7
U.S.	68.5	15.5	3.3	16.8	68.8	15.5	3.8	15.7

Note: Figures shown cover persons 3 years old and over; (1) people of Hispanic origin can be of any race; (2) Metropolitan Statistical Area - see Appendix A for areas included
Source: Census 2000, Summary File 3

Average Salaries of Public School Classroom Teachers

District	2005-06 Dollars	2005-06 Rank[1]	2006-07 Dollars	2006-07 Rank[1]	Percent Change 2005-06 to 2006-07
Oregon	50,044	15	50,911	16	1.73
U.S. Average	49,026	-	50,816	-	3.65

Note: (1) State rank ranges from 1 to 51.
Source: National Education Association, Rankings & Estimates: Rankings of the States 2006 and Estimates of School Statistics 2007, December 2007

Higher Education

Four-Year Colleges			Two-Year Colleges			Medical Schools[1]	Law Schools[2]	Voc/ Tech[3]
Public	Private Non-profit	Private For-profit	Public	Private Non-profit	Private For-profit			
0	0	0	0	0	0	0	0	0

Note: Figures cover institutions located within the city limits; (1) includes schools accredited by the Liaison Committee on Medical Education and the American Osteopathic Association; (2) includes American Bar Association-accredited law schools; (3) includes all schools with programs that are less than 2 years.
Source: National Center for Education Statistics, The Integrated Postsecondary Education System (IPEDS) Peer Analysis System, 2007; www.usnews.com, Law and Medical School Directories, 2009

PRESIDENTIAL ELECTION

2004 Presidential Election Results

Area	Bush	Kerry	Nader	Other
Washington County	46.4	52.4	0.0	1.3
U.S.	50.7	48.3	0.4	0.6

Note: Results are percentages and may not add to 100% due to rounding
Source: Dave Leip's Atlas of U.S. Presidential Elections, www.uselectionatlas.org

EMPLOYERS

Major Employers

Company Name	Industry	Type of Site
Blount International Inc	Lawn and garden equipment	Headquarters
Emanual Hospital	General medical and surgical hospitals	Headquarters
HP	Computer peripheral equipment, nec	Branch
Medical Center Campus	General medical and surgical hospitals	Headquarters
Nike	Rubber and plastics footwear	Headquarters
Occuptnal Envmtl Mdcine Clinic	Offices and clinics of medical doctors	Branch
Oregon Health & Science Univ	Colleges and universities	Headquarters
PCC Structurals Inc	Aircraft parts and equipment, nec	Headquarters
Portland Community College	Junior colleges	Headquarters
Portland State University	Colleges and universities	Headquarters
Portland Vamc	Administration of veterans' affairs	Branch
Rebound Physical Therapy	Hospital and medical service plans	Single
Resource Staffing Group	Help supply services	Headquarters
Shilo Inns	Hotels and motels	Single
Stancorp Mrtg Investors LLC	Life insurance	Single
Xerox	Office machines, nec	Branch

Note: Companies shown are located within the Portland metropolitan area; nec = not elsewhere classified.
Source: www.zapdata.com, May 2008

PUBLIC SAFETY

Crime Rate

Area	All Crimes	Violent Crimes				Property Crimes		
		Murder	Forcible Rape	Robbery	Aggrav. Assault	Burglary	Larceny -Theft	Motor Vehicle Theft
City	3,269.3	0.0	7.6	49.4	68.4	463.8	2,395.0	285.1
Metro[1]	3,968.4	2.3	39.7	98.5	183.3	619.1	2,574.8	450.7
U.S.	3,808.1	5.7	30.9	149.4	287.5	729.4	2,206.8	398.4

Note: Figures are crimes per 100,000 population; (1) Metropolitan Statistical Area - see Appendix B for areas included
Source: FBI Uniform Crime Reports, 2006

Hate Crimes

Area	Number of Quarters Reported	Bias Motivation				
		Race	Religion	Sexual Orientation	Ethnicity	Disability
City	4	0	0	0	0	0

Source: Federal Bureau of Investigation, Hate Crime Statistics 2006

RECREATION

Culture

Dance[1]	Theatre[1]	Instrumental Music[1]	Vocal Music[1]	Series/ Festivals	Museums	Zoos and Aquariums[2]
0	0	0	0	0	0	0

Note: (1) Number of professional perfoming groups; (2) AZA-accredited
Source: The Grey House Performing Arts Directory, 2007; Official Museum Directory, 2008; Association of Zoos & Aquariums, AZA Member Zoos & Aquariums, June 2008

Professional Sports Teams

Team Name	League
Portland Trail Blazers	National Basketball Association (NBA)

Note: Includes teams located in the Portland metro area.
Source: Original research

MEDIA

Newspapers

Name	News Focus	Frequency	Circulation
No newspapers have an office in the city			

Note: Includes newspapers with offices located in the city
Source: MediaContactsPro, March 2008

Television Stations

Name	Ch.	Network(s)	Type	Ownership
KATU	2	ABC	Commercial	Fisher Broadcasting Inc.
KOAB	3	PBS	Public	Oregon Public Broadcasting Inc.
KOIN	6	CBS	Commercial	Emmis Communications Corporation
KOAC	7	PBS	Public	Oregon Public Broadcasting Inc.
KGW	8	NBC	Commercial	Belo Corporation
KOPB	10	PBS	Public	Oregon Public Broadcasting Inc.
KPTV	12	Fox/UPN	Commercial	Meredith Communications LLC
KTVR	13	PBS	Public	Oregon Public Broadcasting Inc.
KPXG	22	Pax	Commercial	Paxson Communications Corporation
KNMT	24	n/a	Non-comm.	National Minority Television Inc.
KEPB	28	PBS	Public	Oregon Public Broadcasting Inc.
KWBP	32	WBN	Commercial	Acme Television Holdings
KPDX	49	Fox	Commercial	Meredith Communications LLC

Note: Stations included cover the Portland DMA (Designated Market Area)
BurrellesLuce, MediaContacts Online, January 2007

Major AM Radio Stations

Call Letters	Freq. (kHz)	Station Type	Target Audience	Station Format	Music Format
KTLK	620	Commercial	General	Music/News/Talk	Adult Contemp.
KXL	750	n/a	General	News/Talk	n/a
KPAM	860	n/a	General/Men	News/Talk	n/a
KOTK	910	n/a	General	Talk	n/a
KFXX	910	n/a	General	Sports/Talk	n/a
KWBY	940	Commercial	General/Hispanic	Educational/Music	Latin
KCMD	970	Commercial	General	Comedy	n/a
KEX	1190	Commercial	General/Men/Women	News	n/a
KBAM	1270	n/a	General	Music/News	n/a
KKSL	1290	Commercial	General/Religious	Educational/Music	Gospel
KNPT	1310	n/a	General	News/Sports/Talk	n/a
KKPZ	1330	Commercial	General/Religious	Educational	n/a
KUIK	1360	Commercial	Hispanic	News/Sports/Talk	n/a
KBNP	1410	Commercial	General	n/a	n/a
KYKN	1430	Commercial	General	News/Talk	n/a
KODL	1440	Commercial	General	Music/News	Adult Standards
KKSN	1520	Commercial	General	Music/News/Sports	Adult Standards
KKAD	1550	Commercial	General	News/Talk	n/a
KMBD	1590	Commercial	General	News/Sports/Talk	n/a

Note: Stations included cover the Portland DMA (Designated Market Area); n/a not available
Source: BurrellesLuce, MediaContacts Online, January 2007

Major FM Radio Stations

Call Letters	Freq. (mHz)	Station Type	Target Audience	Station Format	Music Format
KMHD	89.1	College	General	Music	n/a
KBPS	89.9	n/a	General	Music/News	n/a
KBOO	90.7	Non-Comm	Ethnic/General	Music/Sports/Talk	World Music
KOPB	91.5	Public	General	Educational/News	n/a
KGON	92.3	n/a	General/Men	Music/News	n/a
KAST	92.9	Commercial	General	Music	Adult Contemp.
KPDQ	93.7	Commercial	General/Religious	Music/Talk	Gospel
KTIL	94.1	Commercial	General	Music/News	Easy Listening
KUKN	94.5	Commercial	General	Music	Country
KKBC	95.3	Commercial	General	Music	Oldies
KXJM	95.5	n/a	General	Music/News/Talk	n/a
KKSN	97.1	Commercial	General	Music	Oldies
KUPL	98.7	n/a	General	Music/Talk	n/a
KUBQ	98.7	Commercial	General	Music	Top 40
KWJJ	99.5	Commercial	General	Music	Country
KRKT	99.9	Commercial	General	Music/News	Country
KKRZ	100.3	Commercial	General	Music	Top 40
KPPT	100.7	Commercial	General	Music	Classic Rock
KUFO	101.1	n/a	General	Music	n/a
KINK	101.9	Commercial	General	Music/Talk	Alternative
KCRX	102.3	Commercial	General	Music/News/Sports	Classic Rock
KYTE	102.7	n/a	General	Music	n/a
KKCW	103.3	Commercial	General	Music	Adult Contemp.
KXPC	103.7	n/a	General	Music/News	n/a
KVAS	103.9	Commercial	General	Music/News	Country
KMCQ	104.5	Commercial	General	Music/News	Adult Contemp.
KCMB	104.7	Commercial	General	Music/News	Country
KRSK	105.1	Commercial	General	Music	Adult Contemp.
KLOO	106.1	n/a	General	Music/News	n/a
KVMX	107.5	n/a	General	Music	n/a
KHPE	107.9	n/a	General/Religious	Educational/Music/Talk	n/a

Note: Stations included cover the Portland DMA (Designated Market Area); n/a not available
BurrellesLuce, MediaContacts Online, January 2007

CLIMATE

Average and Extreme Temperatures

Temperature	Jan	Feb	Mar	Apr	May	Jun	Jul	Aug	Sep	Oct	Nov	Dec	Yr.
Extreme High (°F)	65	71	83	93	100	102	107	107	105	92	73	64	107
Average High (°F)	45	50	56	61	68	73	80	79	74	64	53	46	62
Average Temp. (°F)	39	43	48	52	58	63	68	68	63	55	46	41	54
Average Low (°F)	34	36	39	42	48	53	57	57	52	46	40	36	45
Extreme Low (°F)	-2	-3	19	29	29	39	43	44	34	26	13	6	-3

Note: Figures cover the years 1926-1992
Source: National Climatic Data Center, International Station Meteorological Climate Summary, 9/96

Average Precipitation/Snowfall/Humidity

Precip./Humidity	Jan	Feb	Mar	Apr	May	Jun	Jul	Aug	Sep	Oct	Nov	Dec	Yr.
Avg. Precip. (in.)	5.5	4.2	3.8	2.4	2.0	1.5	0.5	0.9	1.7	3.0	5.5	6.6	37.5
Avg. Snowfall (in.)	3	1	1	Tr	Tr	0	0	0	0	0	1	2	7
Avg. Rel. Hum. 7am (%)	85	86	86	84	80	78	77	81	87	90	88	87	84
Avg. Rel. Hum. 4pm (%)	75	67	60	55	53	50	45	45	49	61	74	79	59

Note: Figures cover the years 1926-1992; Tr = Trace amounts (<0.05 in. of rain; <0.5 in. of snow)
Source: National Climatic Data Center, International Station Meteorological Climate Summary, 9/96

Weather Conditions

Temperature			Daytime Sky			Precipitation		
5°F & below	32°F & below	90°F & above	Clear	Partly cloudy	Cloudy	0.01 inch or more precip.	0.1 inch or more snow/ice	Thunder-storms
< 1	37	11	67	116	182	152	4	7

Note: Figures are average number of days per year and cover the years 1926-1992
Source: National Climatic Data Center, International Station Meteorological Climate Summary, 9/96

HAZARDOUS WASTE

Superfund Sites

Tualatin has no sites on the EPA's Superfund Final National Priorities List.
U.S. Environmental Protection Agency, Final National Priorities List, June 23, 2008

AIR & WATER QUALITY

Air Quality Index

Area	Percent of Days when Air Quality was...[2]				AQI Statistics	
	Good	Moderate	Unhealthy for Sensitive Groups	Unhealthy	Maximum	Median
MSA[1]	76.4	20.5	3.0	0.0	150	34

Note: The Air Quality Index (AQI) is an index for reporting daily air quality. EPA calculates the AQI for five major air pollutants regulated by the Clean Air Act: ground-level ozone, particle pollution (also known as particulate matter), carbon monoxide, sulfur dioxide, and nitrogen dioxide. The AQI runs from 0 to 500. The higher the AQI value, the greater the level of air pollution and the greater the health concern. There are six AQI categories: "Good" The AQI is between 0 and 50. Air quality is considered satisfactory; "Moderate" The AQI is between 51 and 100. Air quality is acceptable; "Unhealthy for Sensitive Groups" When AQI values are between 101 and 150, members of sensitive groups may experience health effects; "Unhealthy" When AQI values are between 151 and 200 everyone may begin to experience health effects; "Very Unhealthy" AQI values between 201 and 300 trigger a health alert; "Hazardous" AQI values over 300 trigger health warnings of emergency conditions; (1) Metropolitan Statistical Area - see Appendix A for areas included; (2) Based on 365 days with AQI data in 2007.
Source: U.S. Environmental Protection Agency, Air Quality Index Report, 2007

Air Quality Index Pollutants

Area	Percent of Days when AQI Pollutant was...[2]					
	Carbon Monoxide	Nitrogen Dioxide	Ozone	Sulfur Dioxide	Particulate Matter 2.5	Particulate Matter 10
MSA[1]	0.5	0.0	44.1	0.0	55.1	0.3

Note: The Air Quality Index (AQI) is an index for reporting daily air quality. EPA calculates the AQI for five major air pollutants regulated by the Clean Air Act: ground-level ozone, particle pollution (also known as particulate matter), carbon monoxide, sulfur dioxide, and nitrogen dioxide. The AQI runs from 0 to 500. The higher the AQI value, the greater the level of air pollution and the greater the health concern; (1) Metropolitan Statistical Area - see Appendix A for areas included; (2) Based on 365 days with AQI data in 2007.
Source: U.S. Environmental Protection Agency, Air Quality Index Report, 2007

Air Quality Index Trends

Area	Trend Sites (14)								All Sites (67)
	1999	2000	2001	2002	2003	2004	2005	2006	2006
MSA[1]	5	6	2	6	0	3	2	2	7

Note: An AQI value greater than 100 indicates that air quality would have been in the unhealthful range on that day. Data from exceptional events are not included. These counts are presented in two ways. First, the counts are based on sites having an adequate record of monitoring data during the trend period (trend sites). These counts represent the relative change in the number of days with AQI values greater than 100. In the last column, the counts are based on all sites with data in the most recent year (because it is possible for a site to have data in the most recent year but not enough data to be a trend site); (1) Metropolitan Statistical Area - see Appendix A for areas included.
Source: U.S. Environmental Protection Agency, Office of Air and Radiation, Air Trends, Factbook and Related Information, Air Pollution Trends in Selected Metropolitan Areas 2006

Maximum Air Pollutant Concentrations

	Particulate Matter 10 (ug/m^3)	Particulate Matter 2.5 (ug/m^3)	Ozone (ppm)	Carbon Monoxide (ppm)	Sulfur Dioxide (ppm)	Nitrogen Dioxide (ppm)	Lead (ug/m^3)
MSA[1] Level	45	39	0.092	8	0.006	n/a	n/a
NAAQS[2]	150	35	0.125	9	0.140	0.053	1.50
Met NAAQS[2]	Yes	No	Yes	Yes	Yes	n/a	n/a

Note: Data from exceptional events are not included; (1) Metropolitan Statistical Area - see Appendix A for areas included; (2) National Ambient Air Quality Standards; n/a not available
Concentrations: Particulate Matter 10 (coarse particulate) - highest second maximum 24-hour concentration; Particulate Matter 2.5 (fine particulate) - highest 98th percentile 24-hour concentration; Ozone - highest second daily maximum 1-hour concentration; Carbon Monoxide - highest second maximum non-overlapping 8-hour concentration; Sulfur Dioxide - highest second maximum 24-hour concentration; Nitrogen Dioxide - highest arithmetic mean concentration; Lead - highest quarterly maximum concentration
Units: ppm = parts per million; ug/m^3 = micrograms per cubic meter
Source: U.S. Environmental Protection Agency, MSA Factbook 2006, Air Quality Statistics by City

Drinking Water

Water System Name	Pop. Served	Primary Water Source Type	Violations[1]	
			Health Based	Monitoring/ Reporting
City of Tualatin	25,464	Purchased Surface	0	1

Note: (1) Based on violation data from January 1, 2007 to December 31, 2007 (includes unresolved violations from earlier years)
Source: U.S. Environmental Protection Agency, Office of Ground Water and Drinking Water, Safe Drinking Water Information System (based on data extracted April 15, 2008)

West Linn, Oregon

Background

Known as "The City of Hills, Trees, and Rivers," West Linn is a picturesque suburban town, situated between the Willamette and Tualatin Rivers in Oregon. West Linn is located in northwest Clackamas County, and is a prosperous suburb of the Portland metropolitan area. A vibrant and naturally beautiful city, West Linn is reputed to be one of the most desirable places to live in the area.

In the 1840s Robert Moore purchased the land surrounding Willamette Falls from the "Wallamut" Indians, where present-day West Linn is located. Settlement of the area began with Moore's building of flour and lumber mills and the living accommodations for the men that he employed. Over the years, local business expanded with the additions of gristmills, a sawmill, a warehouse, and wharves to dock the boats used for transport. Robert Moore died in 1857, before he could see his vision for West Linn realized. Not long after, a horrific fire devastated the bustling center of industry. The community was all but wiped off the map. The community was able to survive through the operations of the Willamette Transportation Locks Company, the business that provides passage to ships over Willamette Falls. The company is still in business and is credited with giving West Linn an opportunity to rebuild what was lost and the fresh start it needed to become the thriving community it is today.

Today, West Linn is a charming suburban community featuring historic Victorian architecture and dramatic scenic beauty. The city strives to maintain a small-town atmosphere and preserve the surrounding natural environment. The north end of the community is bordered by Mary S. Young State Park, the Willamette River, and Marylhurst University. In southern West Linn, the area where historic downtown is located, the streets are lined with Victorian-era homes. The more recently developed areas of the West Linn are atop the hills edging the city. With apartments, affordable homes, condominiums, and luxury estates, residents can choose from a wide array of dwellings. What is lost in history in these newer-built homes is more than made up for with the spectacular panoramic views. From some places in the city, these vistas include the majestic Cascades and the snow-capped peaks of Mount Hood, Mount Adams and Mount St. Helens.

The parks and recreation system of West Linn has something to offer to every member of the community. Over 400 acres of protected natural area border the city. 180 of these acres are designated as city parkland, making hiking, biking, picnicking, and nature walks a prime source of recreation in the area. The Camassia Natural Area, adjacent to West Linn, is one of the nation's most remarkable and diverse nature sanctuaries. It is accessible only by trail and is home to over 300 plant species. Scenic Mary S. Young State Park, located alongside the Willamette River, is idyllic for hikers and nature-lovers alike. The amenities of the park include group shelters and picnic areas able to be reserved, hiking and bicycle trails, waterways able to be used year-round, a wide variety of flora and fauna, restroom facilities, and handicap accessible trails and facilities.

The parks found within the city of West Linn provide just as many opportunities for amusement. Willamette Park provides access to the Willamette River though a boat ramp and floating dock, allowing visitors and residents to fish, boat, and canoe year-round. The park is also the annual site of the West Linn Old Time Fair, a community-wide celebration of music, food, and entertainment. Throughout the city's parks are hiking trails, wildlife-viewing platforms, playgrounds, river access, picnic tables, and basketball courts. During the summer months, the Parks and Recreation Department offers children's programs that encourage artistic and educational development through projects and area field trips.

West Linn strives to produce students who are among the greatest thinkers in the world. The community is served by the West Linn-Wilsonville School District, where emphasis is placed on academic excellence, personalized, holistic education, and community partnerships. The district serves over 8,000 students with seven primary schools, three middle schools, two high schools, and runs the Center for Research in Environmental Sciences and Technologies (CREST). West Linn is located near several colleges and universities, including Marylhurst University and Portland State University.

Air travel is conveniently provided by Portland International Airport, an approximately 30 minute drive from West Linn.

Rankings

General Rankings

- Portland* was ranked #3 out of 375 metro areas in *Cities Ranked & Rated*. Criteria: cost of living; climate; crime; transportation; economy and jobs; education; arts and culture; health and healthcare; leisure; quality of life. *Cities Ranked & Rated, 2nd Edition, 2007*
- Portland* was ranked #4 out of 379 metro areas in *Places Rated Almanac*. Criteria: health care; education; recreation; transportation; ambience; climate; crime; housing costs; jobs. *Places Rated Almanac, 7th Edition, 2007*

Business/Finance Rankings

- The nation's 100 largest metro areas were analysed in terms of the percentage of households entering some stage of foreclosure in 2007. The Portland* metro area ranked #73 out of 100 (#1 = highest foreclosure rate). *RealtyTrac, "Year-End 2007 Metropolitan Foreclosure Report"*
- The Portland* metro area was selected one of America's "Top 50 Business Opportunity Metros" by *Expansion Management* in their 5th annual Mayor's Challenge ranking of metro areas that have achieved solid ratings across the board in numerous *EM* studies during the past 12 months. The area ranked #19. Criteria: public schools; quality of life; college educated workers; logistics infrastructure; healthcare costs; taxes and government spending; reputation among site consultants. *Expansion Management, August 2007*
- The Portland* metro area was selected as one of "America's Most Wired Cities" by *Forbes*. The metro area was ranked #10 out of 30. Criteria: percentage of Internet users with high-speed access; the range of service providers within a city; availability of public wireless hot spots. *Forbes, "America's Most Wired Cities," January 10, 2008*
- Portland* was selected as one of the best places to start and grow a company by *Entrepreneur* and the National Policy Research Council. The Portland* metro area ranked #36 out of 50 large metro areas. Criteria: business formation and growth (firms started four to 14 years ago that still employ at least 5 people and experienced rapid growth over the last four years). *Entrepreneur/National Policy Research Council, "Hot Cities for Entrepreneurs," September 2006*
- The Portland* metro area was selected as one of "America's 50 Hottest Cities" for business relocations and expansions. Criteria: industry's most prominent site selection consultants were asked to list their top city choices for relocating and expanding manufacturing companies, taking into consideration such factors as the business climate, work force quality, operating costs, incentive programs, and the ease of working with local political and economic development officials. *Expansion Management, January-February 2007*
- Intel, in partnership with Sperling's BestPlaces, ranked the 80 "Best Cities for Teleworking" in America. The Portland* metro area ranked #16 among large metro areas. The study identifies cities that hold the greatest potential for teleworking based on a host of factors including typical commuting times, fuel prices, availability of broadband Internet access and percentage of the population in telework friendly jobs. The study also factored in extreme climate and natural hazards. *Intel, "Best Cities for Teleworking," March 30, 2006*
- The Portland* metro area appeared on the Milken Institute "2007 Best Performing Cities" index. Rank: #38 out of 200 large metro areas. Criteria: job growth; wage and salary growth; high-tech output growth. *Milken Institute, "2007 Best Performing Cities"*
- The Portland* metro area was selected as one of the hottest cities for entrepreneurs in America by *Inc. Magazine*. Criteria: job-growth data for 393 metro was analyzed for current-year employment growth, average annual employment growth over past three years, and employment growth by industry sector. The Portland* metro area ranked #20 among large metro areas and #139 overall. *Inc. Magazine, May 2007*

- Portland* was identified as one of the 100 "Most Unwired Cities" in the U.S. The area ranked #4 out of the 100 largest metro areas in the U.S. Criteria: number of public and commercial wireless access points (hotspots); airports with wireless Internet access; broadband availability; local wireless networks; and wireless email devices. *Intel, "Most Unwired Cities Survey," June 7, 2005*

- Portland* was ranked #18 out of 125 regions worldwide in terms of its "Knowledge Competitiveness Index." The index attempts to measure the knowledge-based development taking place throughout the world and is based on 19 measures of economic performance that indicate a region's ability to translate its knowledge capacity into economic value. *Robert Huggins Associates, World Knowledge Competitiveness Index 2005*

- *Forbes* ranked the 200 most populous metro areas in the U.S. in terms of the "Best Places for Business and Careers." The Portland* metro area was ranked #35. Criteria: business costs (labor, energy, tax and office space expenses); living costs (housing, transportation, food and other household expenditures); education levels of the work force; job growth; income growth; migration trends; crime rates; and culture/leisure. *Forbes, "Best Places for Business and Careers," March 19, 2008*

- *Fortune* ranked the 100 largest metro areas in the U.S. in terms of projected median home price change in 2007. The Portland* metro area ranked #47. *Fortune.com, "Hot Spots, Cold Spots"*

Health/Environment Rankings

- The Portland* metro area was selected as one of "America's Cleanest Cities" by *Forbes*. The metro area ranked #5 out of 10. Criteria: air quality; water quality; per capita spending on Superfund site cleanup and solid-waste management. *Forbes.com, "America's Cleanest Cities," March 11, 2008*

- 100 of the largest metro areas in the U.S. were analyzed in terms of their current drought severity. The Portland* metro area ranked #51 (#1 = driest). The rankings were based on statistics such as long-term precipitation trends and patterns and the Palmer drought indices. *Sperling's BestPlaces, www.BestPlaces.net, "America's Drought-Riskiest Cities," November 2007*

- Tahitian Noni International Hiro™, in partnership with Sperling's BestPlaces, ranked the nation's 50 largest metro areas in terms of the "Most Energetic Cities." The Portland* metro area ranked #8. Criteria: percentage of population that walk or bicycle to work; BMI score; number of food co-ops; number of farmers markets. *Tahitian Noni International Hiro™, "Most Energetic Cities," March 13, 2007*

- Scarborough Research, a leading market research firm, identified the top local markets for organic consumers. The Portland* DMA (Designated Market Area) ranked in the top 15 with 27% of adults reporting that they used any organic food product in their household during the past month. *Scarborough Research, October 10, 2007*

- *Reader's Digest* ranked the 50 largest metro areas in the U.S. in terms of how "clean" they are. The Portland* metro area ranked #1. Criteria: air quality; water quality; toxic industrial pollution; Superfund sites; and sanitation. *Reader's Digest, "The 50 Cleanest (and Dirtiest) Cities in America," July 2005*

- The American Academy of Dermatology ranked 32 U.S. metropolitan regions in terms of their residents knowledge, attitude and behaviors towards tanning and sun protection. The Portland* metro area ranked #13. The results of the study are based on an online national survey of 3,342 respondents. *American Academy of Dermatology, "RAYS: Your Grade," May 7, 2007*

- *Business Week* identified the 15 metro areas that saw the steepest declines in ground-level ozone pollution between 1990 and 2005. The Portland* metro area ranked #10. *Business Week, "America's Most Cleaned-Up Metro Areas," March 23, 2007*

- The Portland* metro area appeared in *Country Home's* "2008 Best Green Places" report. The area ranked #2 out of 379. Criteria: official energy policies; green power; green buildings; availability of fresh, locally grown food. *Country Home, "2008 Best Green Places"*

- Wyeth Consumer Healthcare, in partnership with Sperling's BestPlaces, ranked the nation's 50 most populous metro areas in terms of five key health factors. The Portland* metro area ranked #16. Criteria: physical activity; health status; nutrition; lifestyle pursuits; and mental wellness. *Wyeth Consumer Healthcare, "Centrum Healthiest Cities Study," April 19, 2005*

- Portland* was identified as a "2008 Asthma Capital." The area ranked #77 out of the nation's 100 largest metropolitan areas. Twelve factors were used to identify the most challenging places to live for people with asthma: estimated prevalence; self-reported prevalence; crude death rate for asthma; annual pollen score; annual air quality; public smoking laws; number of board-certified asthma specialists; school inhaler access laws; rescue medication use; controller medication use; uninsured rate; poverty rate. *Asthma and Allergy Foundation of America, "2008 Asthma Capitals"*

- Portland* was identified as a "Spring Allergy Capital." The area ranked #84 out of 100. Three groups of factors were used to identify the most severe cities for people with allergies during the spring season: annual pollen levels; medicine utilization; access to board-certified allergists. *Asthma and Allergy Foundation of America, "2007 Spring Allergy Capital Rankings"*

- Portland* was identified as a "Fall Allergy Capital." The area ranked #97 out of 100. Three groups of factors were used to identify the most severe cities for people with allergies during the fall season: annual pollen levels; medicine utilization; access to board-certified allergists. *Asthma and Allergy Foundation of America, "2007 Fall Allergy Capital Rankings"*

- Ortho-McNeil Neurologics, in partnership with Sperling's BestPlaces, analyzed 110 metro areas and identified those U.S. cities with the highest prevalence of factors that are most commonly associated with migraine headaches. The Portland* metro area ranked #70. Criteria: number of migraine-related drug prescriptions per capita; lifestyle factors that can contribute to migraines; environmental factors that can trigger migraines; and consumption of migraine-triggering foods. *Ortho-McNeil Neurologics, "America's Migraine Hot Spots," March 14, 2006*

- Sperling's BestPlaces ranked 331 metro areas and identified the most and least stressful U.S. cities. The Portland* metro area ranked #6 out of the 100 largest metro areas (#1 = most stressful). Criteria: divorce rate; unemployment rate; violent and property crime; suicide rate; commute time; mental health; alcohol consumption; cloudy days. *Sperling's BestPlaces, www.BestPlaces.net, "America's Most (and Least) Stressful Cities," January 9, 2004*

- An analysis of the "Best & Worst Cities for Sleep" was conducted by Sperling's BestPlaces. The study ranked America's 50 most populated metro areas. The Portland* metro area ranked #27 (#1 = best city for sleep). Criteria: number of days residents didn't get enough rest or sleep during the past month; average length of daily commute; divorce rate; unemployment rate. *Sperling's BestPlaces, www.BestPlaces.net, "Best & Worst Cities for Sleep," 2006*

- Sperling's BestPlaces in partnership with Vistakon ranked the 100 largest metro areas and identified "America's 10 Best Cities for Comfortable Eyes." The Portland* metro area ranked #5. Criteria: altitude; sunny days; wind; extreme temperatures; humidity; pollution; commute time; computer use. *Vistakon, "America's Best and Worst Cities for Comfortable Eyes," June 15, 2004*

- HealthGrades evaluated the performance of America's 25 most populous metropolitan areas by measuring the outcomes of five of the highest volume and most widely studied procedures and diagnoses: coronary artery bypass graft surgery; percutaneous coronary interventions; acute myocardial infarction/heart attack in angioplasty-capable hospitals; congestive heart failure; and community acquired pneumonia. The Portland* metro area ranked #25. *HealthGrades, "HealthGrades Hospital Quality in America Study," October 12, 2004*

- Portland* was highlighted as one of the cleanest metro areas for ozone air pollution in the U.S. The list represents cities with no monitored ozone air pollution in unhealthful ranges. *American Lung Association, State of the Air: 2007*

- Portland* was selected as one of "America's Top 10 Low-Carb Cities" by *LowCarbiz Magazine*. Criteria: abundance of low-carb products; restaurants with low-carb menu items; health practitioners supportive of carb-cutting regimens; local culture generally conducive to exercise and health. *LowCarbiz Magazine, April 2004*

- Portland* was selected as one of "America's Pet Healthiest Cities" by Purina. The city ranked #3 out of 50. Criteria: veterinary services; environment; legislation; preventative care; obesity/body condition. *Purina Pet Institute, "America's Pet Healthiest Cities," May 20, 2003*

Women/Minorities Rankings

- Portland* was ranked #29 out of 100 metro areas in *SELF Magazine's* ranking of "America's Best Places for Women." A panel of experts came up with more than 50 criteria including death and disease rates, environmental indicators, community resources, and lifestyle habits. *SELF Magazine, "America's Best Places for Women 2007," December 2007*

Seniors/Retirement Rankings

- Sperling's BestPlaces in partnership with Bankers Life & Casualty Company designed a survey to identify the top 50 metro areas in the U.S. that offer the best overall qualities for senior living. The Portland* metro area ranked #1. The following criteria were statistically weighted to reflect the needs of the senior population: health; disease; economics; social; environment; spiritual; transportation; housing; and crime. *Bankers Life & Casualty Company, "Best Cities for Seniors 2005"*

- A.G. Edwards ranked America's 500 top-performing communities based on their residents' personal savings and investing behavior. The Portland* metro area ranked #174 with an index score of 103.99 (national average = 100.00). A dozen statistical factors were measured including: participation in retirement savings plans; personal debt levels; and home ownership. *A.G. Edwards, "2007 Nest Egg Index", September 12, 2007*

Children/Family Rankings

- The Portland* metro area was selected as one of the "Best Cities for Relocating Families" by Worldwide ERC and Primacy Relocation. The 2007 study placed a special emphasis on the housing market, which has significantly impacted the relocation industry and an employer's ability to transfer employees. The variables which weigh heavily in this category include home price, home affordability index, appreciation rates, and property tax. Other criteria include cost of living, crime rates, education, climate, focus on diversity, physicians per capita, recreation and leisure, arts and culture, air quality, watershed quality, sales tax, unemployment rate, job growth, high school and higher education index, school expenditures per student, students in public school, SAT/ACT percentile, and population growth. *Worldwide ERC and Primacy Relocation, "2007 Best Cities for Relocating Families"*

Safety Rankings

- The National Insurance Crime Bureau ranked 361 metro areas in the U.S. in terms of per capita rates of vehicle theft. The Portland* metro area ranked #54 (#1 = highest rate). Criteria: number of vehicle theft offenses per 100,000 inhabitants. *National Insurance Crime Bureau, "NICB Vehicle Theft Study," April 22, 2008*

- Portland* appeared on Sperling's BestPlaces list of the "Riskiest Cities for Identity Theft." The area ranked #11 out of the nations 50 largest metro areas. Over 80 criteria were analyzed across four major categories: technology impact; crime; transactions; and risk profile. *Sperling's BestPlaces, www.BestPlaces.net, "Riskiest Cities for Identity Theft," July 2006*

- Farmers Insurance Group of Companies, in partnership with Sperling's BestPlaces, ranked 379 metro areas and identified the "Most Secure U.S. Place to Live." The Portland* metro area ranked #14 out of 114 in the large metro area category (500,000 or more residents). Criteria: crime rates; extreme weather; risk of natural disasters; environmental hazards; terrorism threats; air quality; life expectancy; job loss numbers. *Farmers Insurance Group, "Most Secure U.S. Places to Live 2007"*

- Portland* was identified as one of the most dangerous large metro areas for pedestrians in the U.S. The area ranked #39 out of the nations 50 largest metro areas. Criteria: average yearly pedestrian fatalities per capita (for the years 2002 and 2003) adjusted for the number of walkers. *Surface Transportation Policy Project, "Mean Streets 2004"*

Sports/Recreation Rankings

- The Portland* metro area appeared on the *Sporting News* list of the "Best Sports Cities 2007". The area ranked #56 out of 150 cities in the U.S. *Sporting News* takes a 12-month snapshot, roughly July to July, of each city's sports, putting a heavy premium on regular-season won-lost records (from the most recently completed season). Other criteria include: playoff berths, bowl appearances and tournament bids; championships; applicable power ratings; quality of competition; overall fan fervor as measured in part by attendance as percentage of venue capacity; abundance of teams (rewarding quality over quantity); stadium and arena quality; ticket availability and prices; franchise ownership; and marquee appeal of athletes. *SportingNews.com, "Best Sports Cities 2007," August 1, 2007*
- The Portland* metro area was selected by *Cranium* as one of the "Top 50 Fun Cities" in America. The area ranked #11. Criteria includes: number of sports teams, restaurants, and dance performances; number of toy stores; city budget spent on recreation. *Cranium, November 4, 2003*
- *Golf Digest* ranked 330 metro areas in the U.S. in terms of golf. The Portland* metro area was ranked #302. Criteria: access to golf; weather; value of golf; and quality of golf. *Golf Digest, "Metro Golf Rankings," August 2005*

Dating/Romance Rankings

- Eli Lily and Company, in partnership with Sperling's BestPlaces, ranked the nation's 50 largest metro areas in terms of the "Most Romantic Cities for Baby Boomers." The Portland* metro area ranked #27. Criteria: marriage and divorce rates among "baby boomers" age 45 to 60; great restaurants; dance studios; chocolate, jewelry and flower sales. *Eli Lily and Company, "Most Romantic Cities for Baby Boomers," April 20, 2007*
- The Portland* metro area was selected as one of the "Best Cities for Relocating Singles" by Worldwide ERC and Primacy Relocation. The area ranked #31 out of the 100 largest metro areas in the U.S. Areas were selected based on the following criteria: a robust cost-of-living index; adventure and outdoor recreation opportunities; violent crime and property crime rates; percentage of the population that is unmarried (ages 25-34); ratio of single men and single women; affordability of quality higher education, including in-state and out-of-state tuition requirements and rates; number of newcomers to the area; commute times; tax rates; fee and occupancy rates for temporary housing and mini-storage; quality and quantity of collegiate and professional sporting events and fun, fan-friendly venues. *Worldwide ERC and Primacy Relocation, "2007 Best Cities for Relocating Singles," October 25, 2007*
- *Forbes* ranked the 40 most populous urbanized areas in the U.S. in terms of the "Best Cities for Singles." The Portland* metro area ranked #29. Criteria: number of singles; cost of living alone; nightlife; culture; job growth; coolness; and online dating. *Forbes.com, August 21, 2007*
- Sperling's BestPlaces in partnership with AXE Deodorant Bodyspray ranked 80 metro areas and identified "America's Best (and Worst) Cities for Dating." The Portland* metro area ranked #15 (#1 = best). Criteria: percentage of singles ages 18-24; population density; dating venues per capita. *AXE Deodorant Bodyspray, "America's Best (and Worst) Cities for Dating," May 2004*

Culture/Performing Arts Rankings

- Scarborough Research, a leading market research firm, identified the top local markets for rock concert attendance. The Portland* DMA (Designated Market Area) ranked in the top 25 with 16% of consumers, 18 years old and over, reporting that they have attended a rock concert during the past year. *Scarborough Research, June 14, 2004*

Miscellaneous Rankings

- Scarborough Research, a leading market research firm, identified the top local markets for bloggers. The Portland* DMA (Designated Market Area) ranked in the top 13 with 14% of adults reporting that they had read or contributed to a blog within the past 30 days. *Scarborough Research, October 24, 2007*

- The Portland* metro area appeared on *Forbes* list of "America's Drunkest Cities". The area ranked #19. Criteria: 35 of the largest continental U.S. metro areas were chosen based on availability of data and geographic diversity. Each metro was ranked in five areas: state laws; drinkers; heavy drinkers; binge drinkers; and alcoholism. *Forbes.com, "America's Drunkest Cities," August 22, 2006*

- Sperling's BestPlaces in partnership with Pep Boys ranked 77 metro areas and identified "America's Most Drivable Cities." The Portland* metro area ranked #58. Criteria: climate; road roughness; urban mobility; gas prices. *Pep Boys, "America's Most Drivable Cities," April 9, 2003*

- State Farm Insurance, in partnership with Sperling's BestPlaces, analyzed several key factors that contribute to overall family preparedness. The Portland* metro area ranked #2 out of the nation's 50 most populous metro areas. Criteria: quality of life; life insurance coverage; and investments. *State Farm Life Insurance, "Fiscally Fit Cities Report," July 20, 2004*

- Scarborough Research, a leading market research firm, identified the top local markets for coffee bar patronage. The Portland* DMA (Designated Market Area) ranked in the top 10 with 21% of adults reporting that they have used any coffee house/bar during the past 30 days. *Scarborough Research, October 14, 2004*

- A study by Sperling's BestPlaces examined which U.S. metro areas were most affected by high fuel prices in 2006. The Portland* metro area was ranked #60 out of 80 (#1 = most expensive city for driving). Rankings are based on the average dollars spent on gas per year by two driver households. Criteria: cost of regular-grade gasoline; average miles driven per day; average number of gallons each driver uses and wastes in traffic congestion each day. *Sperling's BestPlaces, www.bestplaces.net, "Pain at the Pump," May 18, 2006*

West Linn is located within the Portland-Vancouver-Beaverton, OR-WA Metropolitan Statistical Area.

Business Environment

CITY FINANCES

City Government Finances

Component	2004-2005 ($000)	2004-2005 ($ per capita)
Total Revenues	n/a	n/a
Total Expenditures	n/a	n/a
Debt Outstanding	n/a	n/a
Cash and Securities	n/a	n/a

Source: U.S Census Bureau, Government Finances 2004-2005

City Government Revenue by Source

Source	2004-2005 ($000)	2004-2005 ($ per capita)
General Revenue		
From Federal Government	n/a	n/a
From State Government	n/a	n/a
From Local Governments	n/a	n/a
Taxes		
Property	n/a	n/a
Sales	n/a	n/a
Personal Income	n/a	n/a
License	n/a	n/a
Charges	n/a	n/a
Liquor Store	n/a	n/a
Utility	n/a	n/a
Employee Retirement	n/a	n/a
Other	n/a	n/a

Source: U.S Census Bureau, Government Finances 2004-2005

City Government Expenditures by Function

Function	2004-2005 ($000)	2004-2005 ($ per capita)	2004-2005 (%)
General Expenditures			
Airports	n/a	n/a	n/a
Corrections	n/a	n/a	n/a
Education	n/a	n/a	n/a
Fire Protection	n/a	n/a	n/a
Governmental Administration	n/a	n/a	n/a
Health	n/a	n/a	n/a
Highways	n/a	n/a	n/a
Hospitals	n/a	n/a	n/a
Housing and Community Development	n/a	n/a	n/a
Interest on General Debt	n/a	n/a	n/a
Libraries	n/a	n/a	n/a
Parking	n/a	n/a	n/a
Parks and Recreation	n/a	n/a	n/a
Police Protection	n/a	n/a	n/a
Public Welfare	n/a	n/a	n/a
Sewerage	n/a	n/a	n/a
Solid Waste Management	n/a	n/a	n/a
Liquor Store	n/a	n/a	n/a
Utility	n/a	n/a	n/a
Employee Retirement	n/a	n/a	n/a
Other	n/a	n/a	n/a

Source: U.S Census Bureau, Government Finances 2004-2005

Municipal Bond Ratings

Area	Moody's
City	n/a

Source: Mergent Bond Record, January 2008 (unless noted otherwise)

DEMOGRAPHICS

Population Growth

Area	1990 Census	2000 Census	2007 Estimate	2012 Projection	Population Growth (%) 1990-2000	Population Growth (%) 2000-2012
City	17,500	22,261	25,429	27,454	27.2	23.3
MSA[1]	1,523,741	1,927,881	2,138,513	2,283,958	26.5	18.5
U.S.	248,709,873	281,421,906	301,045,522	314,920,978	13.2	11.9

Note: (1) Metropolitan Statistical Area - see Appendix B for areas included
Source: Claritas, Inc.

Number of Households and Average Household Size

Area	2007 Estimate	2007 Average Household Size
City	9,496	2.68
MSA[1]	829,870	2.58
U.S.	113,668,003	2.65

Note: (1) Metropolitan Statistical Area - see Appendix B for areas included
Source: Claritas, Inc.

Race and Ethnicity

Area	White Alone[2]	Black Alone[2]	Asian Alone[2]	Other Race Alone[2]	Hispanic[3]
City	91.4	0.6	4.1	3.9	3.9
MSA[1]	82.1	2.7	5.3	9.9	9.7
U.S.	73.1	12.4	4.3	10.3	14.9

Note: Figures are 2007 estimates; (1) Metropolitan Statistical Area - see Appendix B for areas included (2) Alone is defined as not being in combination with one or more other races; (3) May be of any race.
Source: Claritas, Inc.

Ancestry

Area	German	Irish[2]	English	American	Italian	Polish	French[3]	Scottish
City	26.7	13.4	15.7	5.0	5.6	2.0	4.7	4.0
MSA[1]	20.8	11.8	12.7	5.5	3.5	1.8	3.7	3.1
U.S.	15.2	10.9	8.7	7.3	5.6	3.2	3.0	1.7

Note: Figures include multiple ancestry (e.g. if a person reported being Irish and Italian, they were included in both columns); (1) Metropolitan Statistical Area - see Appendix A for areas included; (2) Includes Celtic; (3) Includes Alsatian but excludes Basque
Source: Census 2000, Summary File 3

Foreign-Born Population

Area	Percent of Population Born in							
	Any Foreign Country	Europe	Asia	Africa	Oceania[2]	Canada	Mexico	Latin America[3]
City	5.6	1.4	2.4	0.3	0.2	0.7	0.3	0.3
MSA[1]	10.9	2.5	3.6	0.2	0.2	0.6	3.1	0.6
U.S.	11.1	1.7	2.9	0.3	0.1	0.3	3.3	2.5

Note: (1) Metropolitan Statistical Area - see Appendix A for areas included; (2) Includes Australia, New Zealand subregion, Melanesia, Micronesia, Polynesia, and Oceania n.e.c; (3) Includes Central America (excluding Mexico), South America, and the Caribbean.
Source: Census 2000, Summary File 3

Marriage Status

Area	Never Married	Now Married (excluding Separated)	Separated	Widowed	Divorced
City	20.9	63.4	1.4	3.3	11.1
MSA[1]	26.8	54.6	1.7	5.3	11.6
U.S.	27.1	54.4	2.2	6.6	9.7

Note: Figures are percentages and cover the population 15 years of age and older; (1) Metropolitan Statistical Area - see Appendix A for areas included
Source: Census 2000, Summary File 3

Age Distribution

Area	Percent of Population						
	Under Age 5	Age 5 to 17	Age 18 to 34	Age 35 to 49	Age 50 to 64	Age 65 to 79	80 Years and Over
City	6.9	22.1	16.0	29.7	17.4	6.1	1.8
MSA[1]	7.0	18.4	24.8	24.7	14.7	7.4	3.0
U.S.	6.8	18.9	23.7	23.5	14.8	9.2	3.2

Note: (1) Metropolitan Statistical Area - see Appendix A for areas included
Source: Census 2000, Summary File 3

Male/Female Ratio

Area	Males	Females	Males per 100 Females
City	12,646	12,783	98.9
MSA[1]	1,065,621	1,072,892	99.3
U.S.	148,320,305	152,725,217	97.1

Note: Figures are 2007 estimates; (1) Metropolitan Statistical Area - see Appendix B for areas included
Source: Claritas, Inc.

Religion

Area	Catholic	Southern Baptist	United Meth-odist	ELCA[1]	LDS[2]	Presby-terian Church USA	Jewish Est.	Muslim Est.
County	6.3	0.5	1.0	2.0	3.3	0.9	0.9	0.0
U.S.	22.0	7.1	3.7	1.8	1.5	1.1	2.2	0.6

Note: Figures are the number of adherents as a percentage of the total population; Adherents are defined as all members, including full members, their children and the estimated number of other participants who are not considered members (e.g. the baptized, those not confirmed, those regularly attending services, etc.); (1) Evangelical Lutheran Church in America; (2) The Church of Jesus Christ of Latter Day Saints
Source: Reprinted with permission from Religious Congregations and Membership in the United States 2000 (Nashville, Glenmary Research Center, 2002) Copyright Association of Statisticians of American Religious Bodies. All rights reserved.

ECONOMY

Gross Metropolitan Product

Area	2002	2003	2004	2005	2005 Rank[2]
MSA[1]	70.3	72.1	80.0	85.7	26

Note: Figures are in billions of dollars; (1) Portland-Vancouver-Beaverton, OR-WA Metropolitan Statistical Area - see Appendix A for areas included; (2) Rank ranges from 1 to 361
Source: The U.S. Conference of Mayors, "U.S. Metro Economies: GMP - The Engines of America's Growth," January 2007

Economic Growth

Area	1995 GMP	2005 GMP	Average Annual Growth Rate	Growth Rate Rank[2]
MSA[1]	47.4	85.7	6.1	112

Note: Figures are in billions of dollars; GMP = Gross Metropolitan Product; (1) Portland-Vancouver-Beaverton, OR-WA Metropolitan Statistical Area - see Appendix A for areas included; (2) Rank ranges from 1 to 361
Source: The U.S. Conference of Mayors, "U.S. Metro Economies: GMP - The Engines of America's Growth," January 2007

INCOME

Per Capita/Median/Average Income

Area	Per Capita ($)	Median Household ($)	Average Household ($)
City	41,068	83,695	109,846
MSA[1]	26,987	53,775	68,909
U.S.	25,495	49,280	66,670

Note: Figures are 2007 estimates; (1) Metropolitan Statistical Area - see Appendix B for areas included
Source: Claritas, Inc.

Household Income Distribution

Area	Percent of Households Earning							
	Under $15,000	$15,000 -24,999	$25,000 -34,999	$35,000 -49,999	$50,000 -74,999	$75,000 -99,000	$100,000 -149,999	$150,000 and up
City	3.8	5.7	6.5	11.4	17.7	14.1	22.1	18.8
MSA[1]	9.9	9.4	10.7	16.4	21.6	13.4	12.3	6.3
U.S.	13.1	10.9	11.2	15.6	19.5	11.9	11.3	6.6

Note: Figures are 2007 estimates; (1) Metropolitan Statistical Area - see Appendix B for areas included
Source: Claritas, Inc.

Poverty Rates by Age

Area	All Ages	Under 5 Years Old	5 to 17 Years Old	18 to 64 Years Old	65 Years and Over
City	3.9	0.3	0.8	2.5	0.3
MSA[1]	9.5	0.9	2.0	5.7	0.7
U.S.	12.4	1.2	3.0	6.9	1.2

Note: Figures are percent of population with income in 1999 below poverty level and only include population for whom poverty status is determined; (1) Metropolitan Statistical Area - see Appendix A for areas included
Source: Census 2000, Summary File 3

Personal Bankruptcy Filing Rate

Area	2004	2005	2006
Clackamas County	6.44	8.04	1.96
U.S.	5.31	6.82	2.00

Note: Numbers are per 1,000 population and include Chapter 7 and Chapter 13 filings
Source: Federal Deposit Insurance Corporation (FDIC), Regional Economic Conditions (RECON), 8/23/2007

EMPLOYMENT

Labor Force and Employment

Area	Civilian Labor Force			Workers Employed		
	Dec. 2006	Dec. 2007	% Chg.	Dec. 2006	Dec. 2007	% Chg.
City	13,636	13,808	1.3	13,193	13,317	0.9
MSA[1]	1,145,573	1,161,260	1.4	1,094,566	1,105,347	1.0
U.S.	152,571,000	153,705,000	0.7	146,081,000	146,334,000	0.2

Note: Data is not seasonally adjusted and covers workers 16 years of age and older; (1) Metropolitan Statistical Area - see Appendix B for areas included
Source: Bureau of Labor Statistics, http://stats.bls.gov

Unemployment Rate

Area	2007											
	Jan.	Feb.	Mar.	Apr.	May	Jun.	Jul.	Aug.	Sep.	Oct.	Nov.	Dec.
City	3.9	4.2	4.0	3.4	3.2	3.7	3.9	3.7	3.5	3.7	3.6	3.6
MSA[1]	5.3	5.4	5.0	4.7	4.5	4.9	5.0	5.0	4.6	4.6	4.7	4.8
U.S.	5.0	4.9	4.5	4.3	4.3	4.7	4.9	4.6	4.5	4.4	4.5	4.8

Note: Data is not seasonally adjusted and covers workers 16 years of age and older; All figures are percentages; (1) Metropolitan Statistical Area - see Appendix B for areas included
Source: Bureau of Labor Statistics, http://stats.bls.gov

Employment by Occupation

Occupation Classification	City (%)	MSA[1] (%)	U.S. (%)
Sales and Office	27.8	27.3	26.7
Professional and Related	25.0	20.7	20.2
Service	8.5	13.6	14.9
Production, Transportation, and Material Moving	7.7	14.3	14.6
Management, Business, and Financial	24.7	14.6	13.5
Construction, Extraction, and Maintenance	6.2	8.8	9.4
Farming, Forestry, and Fishing	0.1	0.7	0.7

Note: Figures cover employed civilians 16 years of age and older; (1) Metropolitan Statistical Area - see Appendix A for areas included
Source: Census 2000, Summary File 3

Employment by Industry

Sector	MSA[1] Number of Employees	MSA[1] Percent of Total	U.S. Percent of Total
Government	147,100	13.9	16.3
Education and Health Services	131,500	12.5	13.4
Professional and Business Services	137,600	13.0	13.1
Retail Trade	117,600	11.1	11.6
Manufacturing	125,900	11.9	9.9
Leisure and Hospitality	99,600	9.4	9.6
Financial Activities	71,000	6.7	5.9
Construction	65,200	6.2	5.3
Wholesale Trade	58,400	5.5	4.4
Other Services	36,800	3.5	3.9
Transportation and Utilities	39,000	3.7	3.7
Information	24,800	2.3	2.2
Natural Resources and Mining	1,600	0.2	0.5

Note: Figures cover non-farm employment as of December 2007 and are not seasonally adjusted; (1) Metropolitan Statistical Area - see Appendix B for areas included
Source: Bureau of Labor Statistics, http://stats.bls.gov

Average Wages

Occupation	$/Hr.	Occupation	$/Hr.
Accountants and Auditors	29.64	Maids and Housekeeping Cleaners	9.80
Automotive Mechanics	17.89	Maintenance and Repair Workers	17.31
Bookkeepers	16.85	Marketing Managers	51.55
Carpenters	19.99	Nuclear Medicine Technologists	34.64
Cashiers	10.54	Nurses, Licensed Practical	22.13
Clerks, General Office	13.95	Nurses, Registered	33.48
Clerks, Receptionists/Information	12.61	Nursing Aides/Orderlies/Attendants	12.60
Clerks, Shipping/Receiving	14.61	Packers and Packagers, Hand	10.04
Computer Programmers	34.48	Physical Therapists	31.83
Computer Support Specialists	21.32	Postal Service Mail Carriers	21.24
Computer Systems Analysts	35.96	Real Estate Brokers	42.80
Cooks, Restaurant	10.94	Retail Salespersons	13.03
Dentists	n/a	Sales Reps., Exc. Tech./Scientific	31.76
Electrical Engineers	40.20	Sales Reps., Tech./Scientific	39.10
Electricians	27.91	Secretaries, Exc. Legal/Med./Exec.	15.08
Financial Managers	51.13	Security Guards	11.51
First-Line Supervisors/Mgrs., Sales	20.11	Surgeons	88.60
Food Preparation Workers	10.45	Teacher Assistants	13.00
General and Operations Managers	52.07	Teachers, Elementary School	24.20
Hairdressers/Cosmetologists	11.12	Teachers, Secondary School	24.40
Internists	86.78	Telemarketers	11.78
Janitors and Cleaners	11.32	Truck Drivers, Heavy/Tractor-Trailer	18.32
Landscaping/Groundskeeping Workers	11.77	Truck Drivers, Light/Delivery Svcs.	14.49
Lawyers	48.06	Waiters and Waitresses	10.53

Note: Wage data covers the Portland-Vancouver-Beaverton, OR-WA Metropolitan Statistical Area - see Appendix B for areas included. Hourly wages for elementary/secondary school teachers and teacher assistants were calculated by the editors from annual wage data assuming a 40 hour work week; n/a not available.
Source: Bureau of Labor Statistics, May 2007 Metro Area Occupational Employment and Wage Estimates

RESIDENTIAL REAL ESTATE

Building Permits

Area	Single-Family 2006	Single-Family 2007p	Single-Family Pct. Chg.	Multi-Family 2006	Multi-Family 2007p	Multi-Family Pct. Chg.	Total 2006	Total 2007p	Total Pct. Chg.
City	63	89	41.3	0	0	-	63	89	41.3
U.S.	1,378,200	973,300	-29.4	460,700	407,200	-11.6	1,838,900	1,380,500	-24.9

Note: (p) preliminary; figures cover and represent new, privately-owned housing units authorized (unadjusted data); All permit data are based on estimates with imputation; U.S. figures are based on the new 20,000-place series.
Source: U.S. Census Bureau, Manufacturing, Mining, and Construction Statistics

Homeownership and Housing Vacancies

Area	Homeownership Rate[2] (%)			Rental Vacancy Rate[3] (%)			Homeowner Vacancy Rate[4] (%)		
	2005	2006	2007	2005	2006	2007	2005	2006	2007
MSA[1]	68.3	66.0	61.2	9.7	7.1	4.8	1.6	1.7	2.3
U.S.	68.9	68.8	68.1	9.8	9.8	9.7	1.9	2.4	2.7

Note: (1) Metropolitan Statistical Area - see Appendix B for areas included; (2) The proportion of households that are owners; (3) The proportion of the rental inventory that is vacant for rent; (4) The proportion of the homeowner inventory that is vacant for sale; n/a not available
Source: U.S. Census Bureau, Housing Vacancies and Homeownership Annual Statistics: 2007

TAXES

State Corporate Income Tax Rates

State	Rates and Tax Brackets
Oregon	6.6%

Note: Tax rates as of January 1, 2008; Minimum tax $10.
Source: Tax Foundation, www.taxfoundation.org

State Individual Income Tax Rates

State	Federal Deductibility	Marginal Rates (%)	Standard Deduction ($)		Personal Exemptions ($)[1]	
			Single	Joint	Single	Dependents
Oregon	Yes (z)	5.0 - 9.0 (r)	1,850 (r)	3,650 (r)	165 (c)(r)	165 (c)(r)

Note: Tax rates as of January 1, 2008; Local- and county-level taxes are not included; n/a not applicable; (1) Married joint filers generally receive double the single exemption; (c) Tax Credit; (r) State adjusts its bracket levels for inflation at the end of each year before printing tax forms; (z) Deduction limited to no more than $5,000.
Source: Tax Foundation, www.taxfoundation.org

Various State and Local Tax Rates

State and Local Sales and Use (%)	State Sales and Use (%)	Gasoline[1,2] ($/gal.)	Cigarette ($/pack)	Spirits ($/gal.)	Table Wine ($/gal.)	Beer ($/gal.)
None	None	0.25	1.18	19.26 (n)	0.67	0.08

Note: Tax rates as of January 1, 2008; (1) In addition to the 18.4 cpg Federal gasoline tax; (2) Rates may include additional state sales taxes, environmental protection and storage fees/taxes, and local taxes. When necessary, the volume-weighted average of all local taxes is used to approximate the typical statewide rate including local tax; (n) The state government controls all sales. The implied excise tax rate is calculated using methodology designed by the Distilled Spirits Council of the United States (DISCUS).
Source: Tax Foundation, www.taxfoundation.org; Original research

State Tax Burdens

Area	Combined State and Local Tax Burden		Combined Federal, State and Local Tax Burden	
	Percent	Rank	Percent	Rank
Oregon	10.0	37	30.7	31
U.S. Average	11.0	-	32.7	-

Note: Figures cover 2007 and measure taxes as a percentage of income
Source: Tax Foundation, www.taxfoundation.org

State Business Tax Climate Index Rankings

State	Overall Rank	Corporate Tax Index Rank	Individual Income Tax Index Rank	Sales Tax Index Rank	Unemployment Insurance Tax Index Rank	Property Tax Index Rank
Oregon	10	20	35	4	32	14

Note: Rankings range from 1 to 50 where 1 is best. Rankings do not average across to Overall Rank. States without a given tax are given a ranking of 1.
Source: Tax Foundation, State Business Tax Climate Index 2008

TRANSPORTATION

Means of Transportation to Work

Area	Car/Truck/Van		Public Transportation			Bicycle	Walked	Other Means	Worked at Home
	Drove Alone	Car-pooled	Bus	Subway	Railroad				
City	78.5	8.7	2.6	0.1	0.1	0.2	1.4	0.5	7.9
MSA[1]	73.1	11.5	5.3	0.4	0.2	0.8	3.0	1.1	4.6
U.S.	75.7	12.2	2.5	1.5	0.5	0.4	2.9	1.0	3.3

Note: Figures are percentages and cover workers 16 years of age and older; (1) Metropolitan Statistical Area - see Appendix A for areas included
Source: Census 2000, Summary File 3

Travel Time to Work

Area	Less Than 15 Minutes	15 to 29 Minutes	30 to 44 Minutes	45 to 59 Minutes	60 Minutes or More
City	20.3	46.4	25.0	4.8	3.5
MSA[1]	26.3	40.0	21.1	7.0	5.5
U.S.	29.4	36.1	19.1	7.4	8.0

Note: Figures are percentages and include workers 16 years old and over; (1) Metropolitan Statistical Area - see Appendix A for areas included
Source: Census 2000, Summary File 3

Travel Time Index

Area	1982	1995	2004	2005
Urban Area[1]	1.07	1.20	1.27	1.29
Average[2]	1.11	1.22	1.29	1.30

Note: Travel Time Index - The ratio of travel time in the peak period to the travel time at free-flow conditions. A value of 1.35 indicates a 20-minute free-flow trip takes 27 minutes in the peak. Free-flow speeds (60 mph on freeways and 35 mph on principal arterials) are used as the comparison threshold; (1) Covers the Portland, OR-WA urban area; (2) average of 85 urban areas
Source: Texas Transportation Institute, The 2007 Urban Mobility Report, September 2007

Living Environment

COST OF LIVING

Cost of Living Index

Composite Index	Groceries	Housing	Utilities	Trans-portation	Health Care	Misc. Goods/ Services
121.4	124.3	135.8	104.0	111.1	107.9	118.2

Note: U.S. = 100; Figures cover the Portland OR urban area.
Source: The Council for Community and Economic Research (formerly ACCRA), Cost of Living Index, 2007

Grocery Prices

Area[1]	T-Bone Steak ($/pound)	Frying Chicken ($/pound)	Whole Milk ($/half gal.)	Eggs ($/dozen)	Orange Juice ($/64 oz.)	Coffee ($/11.5 oz.)
City[2]	9.78	1.92	1.95	2.66	3.96	3.98
Avg.	8.93	1.12	2.13	1.52	3.26	3.31
Min.	5.88	0.71	1.33	0.83	2.30	2.20
Max.	12.80	2.07	3.43	3.54	5.79	6.20

Note: (1) Values for the local area are compared with the average, minimum and maximum values for all 331 areas in the Cost of Living Index report; (2) Figures cover the Portland OR urban area; **T-Bone Steak** *(price per pound);* **Frying Chicken** *(price per pound, whole fryer);* **Whole Milk** *(half gallon carton);* **Eggs** *(price per dozen, Grade A, large);* **Orange Juice** *(64 oz. Tropicana or Florida Natural);* **Coffee** *(11.5 oz. can, vacuum-packed, Maxwell House, Hills Bros, or Folgers).*
Source: The Council for Community and Economic Research (formerly ACCRA), Cost of Living Index, 2007

Housing and Utility Costs

Area[1]	New Home Price ($)	Apartment Rent ($/month)	All Electric ($/month)	Part Electric ($/month)	Other Energy ($/month)	Telephone ($/month)
City[2]	434,461	946	-	88.95	85.14	25.99
Avg.	309,605	782	146.13	78.67	90.16	26.14
Min.	189,877	n/a	82.03	37.41	33.15	17.08
Max.	1,202,800	3,481	271.14	150.60	257.67	37.45

Note: (1) Values for the local area are compared with the average, minimum and maximum values for all 331 areas in the Cost of Living Index report; (2) Figures cover the Portland OR urban area; **New Home Price** *(2,400 sf living area, 8,000 sf lot, in urban area with full utilities);* **Apartment Rent** *(950 sf 2 bedroom/1.5 or 2 bath, unfurnished, excluding all utilities except water);* **All Electric** *(average monthly cost for an all-electric home);* **Part Electric** *(average monthly cost for a part-electric home);* **Other Energy** *(average monthly cost for natural gas, fuel oil, coal, wood, and any other forms of energy except electricity);* **Telephone** *(price includes basic monthly rate for a private residential line plus additional local usage charges incurred by a family of four).*
Source: The Council for Community and Economic Research (formerly ACCRA), Cost of Living Index, 2007

Health Care, Transportation, and Other Costs

Area[1]	Doctor ($/visit)	Dentist ($/visit)	Optometrist ($/visit)	Gasoline ($/gallon)	Beauty Salon ($/visit)	Men's Shirt ($)
City[2]	96.67	79.62	90.50	2.92	32.87	40.65
Avg.	79.48	71.93	79.55	2.64	29.52	25.77
Min.	52.08	44.80	43.95	2.19	15.58	16.19
Max.	148.44	126.27	158.83	3.48	60.62	48.53

Note: (1) Values for the local area are compared with the average, minimum and maximum values for all 331 areas in the Cost of Living Index report; (2) Figures cover the Portland OR urban area; **Doctor** *(general practitioners routine exam of an established patient);* **Dentist** *(adult teeth cleaning and periodic oral examination);* **Optometrist** *(full vision eye exam for established adult patient);* **Gasoline** *(one gallon regular unleaded, national brand, including all taxes, cash price at self-service pump if available);* **Beauty Salon** *(woman's shampoo, trim, and blow-dry);* **Men's Shirt** *(cotton/polyester dress shirt, pinpoint weave, long sleeves).*
Source: The Council for Community and Economic Research (formerly ACCRA), Cost of Living Index, 2007

HOUSING

House Price Index (HPI)

Area	National Ranking[2]	Quarterly Change (%)	One-Year Change (%)	Five-Year Change (%)
MSA[1]	61	0.30	4.24	66.54
U.S.[3]	-	0.10	0.84	41.37

Note: The HPI is a weighted repeat sales index. It measures average price changes in repeat sales or refinancings on the same properties. This information is obtained by reviewing repeat mortgage transactions on single-family properties whose mortgages have been purchased or securitized by Fannie Mae or Freddie Mac in January 1975; (1) Metropolitan Statistical Area - see Appendix B for areas included; (2) Rankings are based on annual percentage change for all metro areas containing at least 15,000 transactions over the last 10 years and ranges from 1 to 291; (3) figures based on a weighted average of Census Division estimates; all figures are for the period ending December 31, 2007
Source: Office of Federal Housing Enterprise Oversight, House Price Index, February 26, 2008

House Price Valuations

Area	Q1 2000	Q1 2001	Q1 2002	Q1 2003	Q1 2004	Q1 2005	Q1 2006	Q1 2007	Q1 2008
MSA[1]	-6.2	-6.0	-1.2	3.3	11.3	20.1	37.0	43.8	36.2

Note: Figures show the percentage of over- or under-valuation of single family homes relative to statistically normal house values (e.g. a value of 23.6 indicates that house values are 23.6% overvalued). Statistically normal house values are based on house prices, interest rates, household incomes, population densities, and any historical premiums or discounts metropolitan areas have exhibited over time; (1) Figures cover the Metropolitan Statistical Area - see Appendix B for areas included
Source: Global Insight/National City Corporation, House Prices in America, May 2008

Median Home Prices

Area	2005	2006	2007[r]	Percent Change 2006 to 2007
MSA[1]	244.9	280.8	295.2	5.1
U.S. Average	219.0	221.9	217.9	-1.8

Note: Figures are median sales prices of existing single-family homes in thousands of dollars; (r) revised; n/a not available; (1) Metropolitan Statistical Area - see Appendix B for areas included
Source: National Association of Realtors, Metropolitan Area Prices, 1st Quarter 2008

Housing: Year Structure Built

Area	1990 -2000	1980 -1989	1970 -1979	1960 -1969	1950 -1959	1940 -1949	Before 1940	Median Year
City	33.3	18.8	23.7	8.2	6.3	3.5	6.3	1981
MSA[1]	24.6	13.0	20.9	11.3	9.1	6.5	14.7	1974
U.S.	17.0	15.8	18.5	13.7	12.7	7.3	15.0	1971

Note: Figures are percentages; (1) Metropolitan Statistical Area - see Appendix A for areas included
Source: Census 2000, Summary File 3

HEALTH

Health Risk Data

Category	Area[1] (%)	U.S. (%)
Adults who have been told they have high blood pressure[3]	21.5	25.5
Adults who have been told they have high blood cholesterol[3]	34.2	35.6
Adults who have been told they have diabetes[2]	5.9	7.5
Adults who have been told they have arthritis[3]	24.0	27.0
Adults who have been told they currently have asthma	10.9	8.5
Adults who are current smokers	16.9	20.1
Adults who are heavy drinkers[4]	5.6	4.9
Adults who are overweight (BMI 25.0 - 29.9)	36.9	36.5
Adults who are obese (BMI 30.0 - 99.8)	24.2	25.1

Note: Data as of 2006 unless otherwise noted; (1) Figures cover the Metropolitan Statistical Area - see Appendix B for areas included; (2) Figures do not include pregnancy-related diabetes, pre-diabetes or borderline diabetes; (3) 2005 data; (4) Heavy drinkers are classified as adult men having more than two drinks per day or adult women having more than one drink per day
Source: Centers for Disease Control and Prevention, Behaviorial Risk Factor Surveillance System, SMART: Selected Metropolitan/Micropolitan Area Risk Trends, 2005, 2006

Mortality Rates for the Top 10 Causes of Death in the U.S.

ICD-10[a] Sub-Chapter	ICD-10[a] Code	Age-Adjusted Mortality Rate[1] per 100,000 population	
		County[2]	U.S.
Malignant neoplasms	C00-C97	180.0	186.5
Ischaemic heart diseases	I20-I25	112.2	152.3
Other forms of heart disease	I30-I51	55.7	51.5
Cerebrovascular diseases	I60-I69	63.3	50.0
Chronic lower respiratory diseases	J40-J47	44.2	42.6
Diabetes mellitus	E10-E14	25.5	24.8
Other degenerative diseases of the nervous system	G30-G31	36.7	22.6
Other external causes of accidental injury	W00-X59	21.1	21.4
Influenza and pneumonia	J10-J18	15.3	20.7
Hypertensive diseases	I10-I13	15.2	18.2

Note: (a) ICD-10 = International Classification of Diseases 10th Revision; (1) Mortality rates are a three year average covering 2003-2005; (2) Figures cover Clackamas County
Source: Centers for Disease Control and Prevention, National Center for Health Statistics. Compressed Mortality File 1999-2004. CDC WONDER On-line Database, compiled from Compressed Mortality File 1999-2005 Series 20 No. 2K, 2008.

Mortality Rates for Selected Causes of Death

ICD-10[a] Sub-Chapter	ICD-10[a] Code	Age-Adjusted Mortality Rate[1] per 100,000 population	
		County[2]	U.S.
Assault	X85-Y09	2.0	5.9
Human immunodeficiency virus (HIV) disease	B20-B24	*0.8	4.5
Intentional self-harm	X60-X84	12.8	10.8
Malnutrition	E40-E46	*0.3	1.0
Obesity and other hyperalimentation	E65-E68	*1.0	1.4
Organic, including symptomatic, mental disorders	F01-F09	22.6	16.8
Transport accidents	V01-V99	12.7	16.1
Viral hepatitis	B15-B19	2.1	1.8

Note: (a) ICD-10 = International Classification of Diseases 10th Revision; (1) Mortality rates are a three year average covering 2003-2005; (2) Figures cover Clackamas County; (*) Unreliable data as per CDC
Source: Centers for Disease Control and Prevention, National Center for Health Statistics. Compressed Mortality File 1999-2004. CDC WONDER On-line Database, compiled from Compressed Mortality File 1999-2005 Series 20 No. 2K, 2008.

Distribution of Physicians[1]

Area	Total	Family/ General Practice	Specialties	
			Medical	Surgical
Clackamas County (number)	636	130	211	146
Clackamas County (rate per 10,000 pop.)	17.3	3.5	5.7	4.0
U.S. (rate per 10,000 pop.)	17.7	4.6	6.9	4.3

Note: Data as of 2005; (1) Includes all non-federal, patient-care, office-based MDs
Source: Area Resource File (ARF). June 2007. U.S. Department of Health and Human Services, Health Resources and Services Administration, Bureau of Health Professions, Rockville, MD.

Hospitals

There were no hospitals listed within the city limits.
AHA Guide to the Healthcare Field 2008

According to *U.S. News,* the Portland-Vancouver-Beaverton, OR-WA metro area is home to one of the best hospitals in the U.S.: **Oregon Health and Science University Hospital**. *U.S. News Online, "America's Best Hospitals 2007"*

EDUCATION

Public School District Statistics

District Name	Schls	Pupils	Pupil/ Teacher Ratio	Minority Pupils[1] (%)	Free Lunch Eligible[2] (%)	IEP[3] (%)
West Linn-Wilsonville SD 3J	13	8,039	20.5	12.2	9.8	12.0

Note: Table includes regular local school districts with 2,000 or more students; (1) Percentage of students that are not white, non-Hispanic; (2) Percentage of students that are eligible for the free lunch program; (3) Percentage of students that have an Individualized Education Program.
Source: U.S. Department of Education, National Center for Education Statistics, Common Core of Data, Local Education Agency (School District) Universe Survey: School Year 2005-2006; U.S. Department of Education, National Center for Education Statistics, Common Core of Data, Public Elementary/Secondary School Universe Survey: School Year 2005-2006

Highest Level of Education

Area	Less than H.S.	H.S. Diploma	Some College, No Deg.	Associate Degree	Bachelors Degree	Masters Degree	Profess. School Degree	Doctorate Degree
City	4.6	13.5	26.0	6.9	32.4	11.4	4.0	1.2
MSA[1]	12.7	23.9	27.7	7.0	19.2	6.5	2.0	0.9
U.S.	19.4	28.4	21.2	6.4	15.7	5.9	2.0	1.0

Note: Figures are 2007 estimated percentages and cover persons age 25 and over; (1) Metropolitan Statistical Area - see Appendix B for areas included
Source: Claritas, Inc.

Educational Attainment by Race

Area	High School Graduate (%)					Bachelor's Degree (%)				
	Total	White	Black	Asian	Hisp.[2]	Total	White	Black	Asian	Hisp.[2]
City	95.5	95.7	88.6	97.9	89.1	49.2	49.3	46.2	60.6	38.0
MSA[1]	87.2	89.4	80.4	79.1	53.7	28.8	29.6	18.0	38.3	11.8
U.S.	80.4	83.6	72.3	80.4	52.4	24.4	26.1	14.3	44.1	10.4

Note: Figures shown cover persons 25 years old and over; (1) Metropolitan Statistical Area - see Appendix A for areas included; (2) people of Hispanic origin can be of any race
Source: Census 2000, Summary File 3

School Enrollment by Type

Area	Grades KG to 8				Grades 9 to 12			
	Public		Private		Public		Private	
	Enrollment	%	Enrollment	%	Enrollment	%	Enrollment	%
City	2,821	83.6	554	16.4	1,467	93.9	95	6.1
MSA[1]	219,761	88.8	27,653	11.2	95,236	91.4	8,906	8.6
U.S.	33,526,011	88.7	4,285,121	11.3	14,848,628	90.6	1,532,323	9.4

Note: Figures shown cover persons 3 years old and over; (1) Metropolitan Statistical Area - see Appendix A for areas included
Source: Census 2000, Summary File 3

School Enrollment by Race

Area	Grades KG to 8 (%)				Grades 9 to 12 (%)			
	White	Black	Asian	Hisp.[1]	White	Black	Asian	Hisp.[1]
City	91.0	1.0	2.6	3.5	93.0	0.0	2.9	2.8
MSA[2]	80.1	3.1	4.4	9.9	81.9	3.4	4.8	7.7
U.S.	68.5	15.5	3.3	16.8	68.8	15.5	3.8	15.7

Note: Figures shown cover persons 3 years old and over; (1) people of Hispanic origin can be of any race; (2) Metropolitan Statistical Area - see Appendix A for areas included
Source: Census 2000, Summary File 3

Average Salaries of Public School Classroom Teachers

District	2005-06		2006-07		Percent Change 2005-06 to 2006-07
	Dollars	Rank[1]	Dollars	Rank[1]	
Oregon	50,044	15	50,911	16	1.73
U.S. Average	49,026	-	50,816	-	3.65

Note: (1) State rank ranges from 1 to 51.
Source: National Education Association, Rankings & Estimates: Rankings of the States 2006 and Estimates of School Statistics 2007, December 2007

Higher Education

Four-Year Colleges			Two-Year Colleges			Medical Schools[1]	Law Schools[2]	Voc/ Tech[3]
Public	Private Non-profit	Private For-profit	Public	Private Non-profit	Private For-profit			
0	0	0	0	0	0	0	0	0

Note: Figures cover institutions located within the city limits; (1) includes schools accredited by the Liaison Committee on Medical Education and the American Osteopathic Association; (2) includes American Bar Association-accredited law schools; (3) includes all schools with programs that are less than 2 years.
Source: National Center for Education Statistics, The Integrated Postsecondary Education System (IPEDS) Peer Analysis System, 2007; www.usnews.com, Law and Medical School Directories, 2009

PRESIDENTIAL ELECTION

2004 Presidential Election Results

Area	Bush	Kerry	Nader	Other
Clackamas County	50.1	48.8	0.0	1.1
U.S.	50.7	48.3	0.4	0.6

Note: Results are percentages and may not add to 100% due to rounding
Source: Dave Leip's Atlas of U.S. Presidential Elections, www.uselectionatlas.org

EMPLOYERS

Major Employers

Company Name	Industry	Type of Site
Blount International Inc	Lawn and garden equipment	Headquarters
Emanual Hospital	General medical and surgical hospitals	Headquarters
HP	Computer peripheral equipment, nec	Branch
Medical Center Campus	General medical and surgical hospitals	Headquarters
Nike	Rubber and plastics footwear	Headquarters
Occuptnal Envmtl Mdcine Clinic	Offices and clinics of medical doctors	Branch
Oregon Health & Science Univ	Colleges and universities	Headquarters
PCC Structurals Inc	Aircraft parts and equipment, nec	Headquarters
Portland Community College	Junior colleges	Headquarters
Portland State University	Colleges and universities	Headquarters
Portland Vamc	Administration of veterans' affairs	Branch
Rebound Physical Therapy	Hospital and medical service plans	Single
Resource Staffing Group	Help supply services	Headquarters
Shilo Inns	Hotels and motels	Single
Stancorp Mrtg Investors LLC	Life insurance	Single
Xerox	Office machines, nec	Branch

Note: Companies shown are located within the Portland metropolitan area; nec = not elsewhere classified.
Source: www.zapdata.com, May 2008

PUBLIC SAFETY

Crime Rate

Area	All Crimes	Violent Crimes				Property Crimes		
		Murder	Forcible Rape	Robbery	Aggrav. Assault	Burglary	Larceny -Theft	Motor Vehicle Theft
City	1,270.3	0.0	19.6	19.6	58.8	239.2	886.1	47.0
Metro[1]	3,968.4	2.3	39.7	98.5	183.3	619.1	2,574.8	450.7
U.S.	3,808.1	5.7	30.9	149.4	287.5	729.4	2,206.8	398.4

Note: Figures are crimes per 100,000 population; (1) Metropolitan Statistical Area - see Appendix B for areas included
Source: FBI Uniform Crime Reports, 2006

Hate Crimes

Area	Number of Quarters Reported	Bias Motivation				
		Race	Religion	Sexual Orientation	Ethnicity	Disability
City	4	0	0	0	0	0

Source: Federal Bureau of Investigation, Hate Crime Statistics 2006

RECREATION

Culture

Dance[1]	Theatre[1]	Instrumental Music[1]	Vocal Music[1]	Series/ Festivals	Museums	Zoos and Aquariums[2]
0	0	0	0	0	0	0

Note: (1) Number of professional perfoming groups; (2) AZA-accredited
Source: The Grey House Performing Arts Directory, 2007; Official Museum Directory, 2008; Association of Zoos & Aquariums, AZA Member Zoos & Aquariums, June 2008

Professional Sports Teams

Team Name	League
Portland Trail Blazers	National Basketball Association (NBA)

Note: Includes teams located in the Portland metro area.
Source: Original research

MEDIA

Newspapers

Name	News Focus	Frequency	Circulation
No newspapers have an office in the city			

Note: Includes newspapers with offices located in the city
Source: MediaContactsPro, March 2008

Television Stations

Name	Ch.	Network(s)	Type	Ownership
KATU	2	ABC	Commercial	Fisher Broadcasting Inc.
KOAB	3	PBS	Public	Oregon Public Broadcasting Inc.
KOIN	6	CBS	Commercial	Emmis Communications Corporation
KOAC	7	PBS	Public	Oregon Public Broadcasting Inc.
KGW	8	NBC	Commercial	Belo Corporation
KOPB	10	PBS	Public	Oregon Public Broadcasting Inc.
KPTV	12	Fox/UPN	Commercial	Meredith Communications LLC
KTVR	13	PBS	Public	Oregon Public Broadcasting Inc.
KPXG	22	Pax	Commercial	Paxson Communications Corporation
KNMT	24	n/a	Non-comm.	National Minority Television Inc.
KEPB	28	PBS	Public	Oregon Public Broadcasting Inc.
KWBP	32	WBN	Commercial	Acme Television Holdings
KPDX	49	Fox	Commercial	Meredith Communications LLC

Note: Stations included cover the Portland DMA (Designated Market Area)
BurrellesLuce, MediaContacts Online, January 2007

Major AM Radio Stations

Call Letters	Freq. (kHz)	Station Type	Target Audience	Station Format	Music Format
KTLK	620	Commercial	General	Music/News/Talk	Adult Contemp.
KXL	750	n/a	General	News/Talk	n/a
KPAM	860	n/a	General/Men	News/Talk	n/a
KOTK	910	n/a	General	Talk	n/a
KFXX	910	n/a	General	Sports/Talk	n/a
KWBY	940	Commercial	General/Hispanic	Educational/Music	Latin
KCMD	970	Commercial	General	Comedy	n/a
KEX	1190	Commercial	General/Men/Women	News	n/a
KBAM	1270	n/a	General	Music/News	n/a
KKSL	1290	Commercial	General/Religious	Educational/Music	Gospel
KNPT	1310	n/a	General	News/Sports/Talk	n/a
KKPZ	1330	Commercial	General/Religious	Educational	n/a
KUIK	1360	Commercial	Hispanic	News/Sports/Talk	n/a
KBNP	1410	Commercial	General	n/a	n/a
KYKN	1430	Commercial	General	News/Talk	n/a
KODL	1440	Commercial	General	Music/News	Adult Standards
KKSN	1520	Commercial	General	Music/News/Sports	Adult Standards
KKAD	1550	Commercial	General	News/Talk	n/a
KMBD	1590	Commercial	General	News/Sports/Talk	n/a

Note: Stations included cover the Portland DMA (Designated Market Area); n/a not available
Source: BurrellesLuce, MediaContacts Online, January 2007

Major FM Radio Stations

Call Letters	Freq. (mHz)	Station Type	Target Audience	Station Format	Music Format
KMHD	89.1	College	General	Music	n/a
KBPS	89.9	n/a	General	Music/News	n/a
KBOO	90.7	Non-Comm	Ethnic/General	Music/Sports/Talk	World Music
KOPB	91.5	Public	General	Educational/News	n/a
KGON	92.3	n/a	General/Men	Music/News	n/a
KAST	92.9	Commercial	General	Music	Adult Contemp.
KPDQ	93.7	Commercial	General/Religious	Music/Talk	Gospel
KTIL	94.1	Commercial	General	Music/News	Easy Listening
KUKN	94.5	Commercial	General	Music	Country
KKBC	95.3	Commercial	General	Music	Oldies
KXJM	95.5	n/a	General	Music/News/Talk	n/a
KKSN	97.1	Commercial	General	Music	Oldies
KUPL	98.7	n/a	General	Music/Talk	n/a
KUBQ	98.7	Commercial	General	Music	Top 40
KWJJ	99.5	Commercial	General	Music	Country
KRKT	99.9	Commercial	General	Music/News	Country
KKRZ	100.3	Commercial	General	Music	Top 40
KPPT	100.7	Commercial	General	Music	Classic Rock
KUFO	101.1	n/a	General	Music	n/a
KINK	101.9	Commercial	General	Music/Talk	Alternative
KCRX	102.3	Commercial	General	Music/News/Sports	Classic Rock
KYTE	102.7	n/a	General	Music	n/a
KKCW	103.3	Commercial	General	Music	Adult Contemp.
KXPC	103.7	n/a	General	Music/News	n/a
KVAS	103.9	Commercial	General	Music/News	Country
KMCQ	104.5	Commercial	General	Music/News	Adult Contemp.
KCMB	104.7	Commercial	General	Music/News	Country
KRSK	105.1	Commercial	General	Music	Adult Contemp.
KLOO	106.1	n/a	General	Music/News	n/a
KVMX	107.5	n/a	General	Music	n/a
KHPE	107.9	n/a	General/Religious	Educational/Music/Talk	n/a

Note: Stations included cover the Portland DMA (Designated Market Area); n/a not available
BurrellesLuce, MediaContacts Online, January 2007

CLIMATE

Average and Extreme Temperatures

Temperature	Jan	Feb	Mar	Apr	May	Jun	Jul	Aug	Sep	Oct	Nov	Dec	Yr.
Extreme High (°F)	65	71	83	93	100	102	107	107	105	92	73	64	107
Average High (°F)	45	50	56	61	68	73	80	79	74	64	53	46	62
Average Temp. (°F)	39	43	48	52	58	63	68	68	63	55	46	41	54
Average Low (°F)	34	36	39	42	48	53	57	57	52	46	40	36	45
Extreme Low (°F)	-2	-3	19	29	29	39	43	44	34	26	13	6	-3

Note: Figures cover the years 1926-1992
Source: National Climatic Data Center, International Station Meteorological Climate Summary, 9/96

Average Precipitation/Snowfall/Humidity

Precip./Humidity	Jan	Feb	Mar	Apr	May	Jun	Jul	Aug	Sep	Oct	Nov	Dec	Yr.
Avg. Precip. (in.)	5.5	4.2	3.8	2.4	2.0	1.5	0.5	0.9	1.7	3.0	5.5	6.6	37.5
Avg. Snowfall (in.)	3	1	1	Tr	Tr	0	0	0	0	0	1	2	7
Avg. Rel. Hum. 7am (%)	85	86	86	84	80	78	77	81	87	90	88	87	84
Avg. Rel. Hum. 4pm (%)	75	67	60	55	53	50	45	45	49	61	74	79	59

Note: Figures cover the years 1926-1992; Tr = Trace amounts (<0.05 in. of rain; <0.5 in. of snow)
Source: National Climatic Data Center, International Station Meteorological Climate Summary, 9/96

Weather Conditions

Temperature			Daytime Sky			Precipitation		
5°F & below	32°F & below	90°F & above	Clear	Partly cloudy	Cloudy	0.01 inch or more precip.	0.1 inch or more snow/ice	Thunder-storms
< 1	37	11	67	116	182	152	4	7

Note: Figures are average number of days per year and cover the years 1926-1992
Source: National Climatic Data Center, International Station Meteorological Climate Summary, 9/96

HAZARDOUS WASTE

Superfund Sites

West Linn has no sites on the EPA's Superfund Final National Priorities List.
U.S. Environmental Protection Agency, Final National Priorities List, June 23, 2008

AIR & WATER QUALITY

Air Quality Index

Area	Percent of Days when Air Quality was...[2]				AQI Statistics	
	Good	Moderate	Unhealthy for Sensitive Groups	Unhealthy	Maximum	Median
MSA[1]	76.4	20.5	3.0	0.0	150	34

Note: The Air Quality Index (AQI) is an index for reporting daily air quality. EPA calculates the AQI for five major air pollutants regulated by the Clean Air Act: ground-level ozone, particle pollution (also known as particulate matter), carbon monoxide, sulfur dioxide, and nitrogen dioxide. The AQI runs from 0 to 500. The higher the AQI value, the greater the level of air pollution and the greater the health concern. There are six AQI categories: "Good" The AQI is between 0 and 50. Air quality is considered satisfactory; "Moderate" The AQI is between 51 and 100. Air quality is acceptable; "Unhealthy for Sensitive Groups" When AQI values are between 101 and 150, members of sensitive groups may experience health effects; "Unhealthy" When AQI values are between 151 and 200 everyone may begin to experience health effects; "Very Unhealthy" AQI values between 201 and 300 trigger a health alert; "Hazardous" AQI values over 300 trigger health warnings of emergency conditions; (1) Metropolitan Statistical Area - see Appendix A for areas included; (2) Based on 365 days with AQI data in 2007.
Source: U.S. Environmental Protection Agency, Air Quality Index Report, 2007

Air Quality Index Pollutants

Area	Percent of Days when AQI Pollutant was...[2]					
	Carbon Monoxide	Nitrogen Dioxide	Ozone	Sulfur Dioxide	Particulate Matter 2.5	Particulate Matter 10
MSA[1]	0.5	0.0	44.1	0.0	55.1	0.3

Note: The Air Quality Index (AQI) is an index for reporting daily air quality. EPA calculates the AQI for five major air pollutants regulated by the Clean Air Act: ground-level ozone, particle pollution (also known as particulate matter), carbon monoxide, sulfur dioxide, and nitrogen dioxide. The AQI runs from 0 to 500. The higher the AQI value, the greater the level of air pollution and the greater the health concern; (1) Metropolitan Statistical Area - see Appendix A for areas included; (2) Based on 365 days with AQI data in 2007.
Source: U.S. Environmental Protection Agency, Air Quality Index Report, 2007

Air Quality Index Trends

Area	Trend Sites (14)								All Sites (67)
	1999	2000	2001	2002	2003	2004	2005	2006	2006
MSA[1]	5	6	2	6	0	3	2	2	7

Note: An AQI value greater than 100 indicates that air quality would have been in the unhealthful range on that day. Data from exceptional events are not included. These counts are presented in two ways. First, the counts are based on sites having an adequate record of monitoring data during the trend period (trend sites). These counts represent the relative change in the number of days with AQI values greater than 100. In the last column, the counts are based on all sites with data in the most recent year (because it is possible for a site to have data in the most recent year but not enough data to be a trend site); (1) Metropolitan Statistical Area - see Appendix A for areas included.
Source: U.S. Environmental Protection Agency, Office of Air and Radiation, Air Trends, Factbook and Related Information, Air Pollution Trends in Selected Metropolitan Areas 2006

Maximum Air Pollutant Concentrations

	Particulate Matter 10 (ug/m^3)	Particulate Matter 2.5 (ug/m^3)	Ozone (ppm)	Carbon Monoxide (ppm)	Sulfur Dioxide (ppm)	Nitrogen Dioxide (ppm)	Lead (ug/m^3)
MSA[1] Level	45	39	0.092	8	0.006	n/a	n/a
NAAQS[2]	150	35	0.125	9	0.140	0.053	1.50
Met NAAQS[2]	Yes	No	Yes	Yes	Yes	n/a	n/a

Note: Data from exceptional events are not included; (1) Metropolitan Statistical Area - see Appendix A for areas included; (2) National Ambient Air Quality Standards; n/a not available
Concentrations: Particulate Matter 10 (coarse particulate) - highest second maximum 24-hour concentration; Particulate Matter 2.5 (fine particulate) - highest 98th percentile 24-hour concentration; Ozone - highest second daily maximum 1-hour concentration; Carbon Monoxide - highest second maximum non-overlapping 8-hour concentration; Sulfur Dioxide - highest second maximum 24-hour concentration; Nitrogen Dioxide - highest arithmetic mean concentration; Lead - highest quarterly maximum concentration
Units: ppm = parts per million; ug/m^3 = micrograms per cubic meter
Source: U.S. Environmental Protection Agency, MSA Factbook 2006, Air Quality Statistics by City

Drinking Water

Water System Name	Pop. Served	Primary Water Source Type	Violations[1]	
			Health Based	Monitoring/ Reporting
City of West Linn	24,000	Purchased Surface	0	0

Note: (1) Based on violation data from January 1, 2007 to December 31, 2007 (includes unresolved violations from earlier years)
Source: U.S. Environmental Protection Agency, Office of Ground Water and Drinking Water, Safe Drinking Water Information System (based on data extracted April 15, 2008)

Cranberry, Pennsylvania

Background

Cranberry township is located about 20 miles north of Pittsburg in the southwest corner of Butler County. Incorporated in 1803, it was originally named for the wild cranberries that grew rampant in the area. Cranberry is now a rapidly growing municipality, with a population that has nearly doubled since 1990 to approximately 28,000. Interstate highways facilitate travel to and from the city and nearby Pittsburgh.

Surrounded by rolling wooded hills, Cranberry's landscape includes 250-year-old oak trees, and Brush Creek meanders through a corner of the township and in places its brush-covered banks are reminiscent of when the first settlers arrived in the late 1700s. The original bogs and marshes that were home to cranberries that gave the township its name were drained long ago, but efforts are ongoing to recreate them in city parks.

Oil was discovered in Pennsylvania in 1859 and the oil boom included the township of Cranberry. Historic remnants of the oil drilling can still be seen and, in 1940, there were about 150 registered active wells listed in the city. After World War II, the desire for "black gold" was replaced by the value and desire for surface real estate.

In the early part of the 1900s, Cranberry was often cut off from surrounding areas due to heavily rutted roads and trails that leading in and out of town becoming impassible in wet weather. The Harmony Line railroad helped make the local area accessible to the residents of Cranberry. In 1908, the railway began hourly travels through the township. Used first as a passenger train, the Harmony Line later added freight cars that allowed the farmers in Cranberry to sell their goods in Pittsburg. Harmony Line eventually lost out to the ever-expanding world of Henry Ford's automobile but signs of the railway can still be seen today.

Activities and attractions in Cranberry include a water park, summer camps, sport leagues, golf courses and concerts. Free summer concerts can be enjoyed at the Rotary Amphitheater in Community Park and the Cranberry Municipal Center. Community Days is also celebrated in the summer, including games, food, informational booths, and fireworks.

Business in Cranberry is booming. There are over 3,000 national and international firms ranging from small businesses to major corporations. Westinghouse Electric Inc. has chosen Cranberry as its new headquarters for a nuclear energy complex which, when completed, will employ over 3,000 people. The Cranberry Board of Supervisors adopted a plan to ensure that present development does not hurt future generations. Local leaders are working hard to ensure the present level of development is sustainable.

Institutions of higher learning close to Cranberry are University of Pittsburg, Penn State University, and Slippery Rock University.

The climate of Cranberry is varied, averaging around 165 days of sunshine throughout the year. Precipitation levels include 40 inches of rain in the summer and 41 inches of snow in the winter, both slightly above the national average. Summer highs are around 87 degrees F and lows in the winter are close to 20 degrees F.

Rankings

General Rankings

- Pittsburgh* was ranked #74 out of 375 metro areas in *Cities Ranked & Rated*. Criteria: cost of living; climate; crime; transportation; economy and jobs; education; arts and culture; health and healthcare; leisure; quality of life. *Cities Ranked & Rated, 2nd Edition, 2007*
- Pittsburgh* was ranked #1 out of 379 metro areas in *Places Rated Almanac*. Criteria: health care; education; recreation; transportation; ambience; climate; crime; housing costs; jobs. *Places Rated Almanac, 7th Edition, 2007*
- *Expansion Management* rated 362 metro areas to find out which offer the best middle class lifestyle for manufacturing and service companies. The Pittsburgh* metro area was selected as a "5-Star Quality of Life Metro" (a distinction the magazine awards to the top 20 percent of metro areas studied). The annual "Quality of Life Quotient" measures dozens of indicators across nine major categories and compares them among 362 metropolitan statistical areas in the United States. The categories are: affordable housing; good public schools; low crime levels; adult education level; standard of living; traffic and commuting; continuing education opportunities; commercial air access; labor market. *Expansion Management, June 2007*

Business/Finance Rankings

- The nation's 100 largest metro areas were analysed in terms of the percentage of households entering some stage of foreclosure in 2007. The Pittsburgh* metro area ranked #86 out of 100 (#1 = highest foreclosure rate). *RealtyTrac, "Year-End 2007 Metropolitan Foreclosure Report"*
- The Pittsburgh* metro area was selected one of America's "Top 50 Business Opportunity Metros" by *Expansion Management* in their 5th annual Mayor's Challenge ranking of metro areas that have achieved solid ratings across the board in numerous *EM* studies during the past 12 months. The area ranked #7. Criteria: public schools; quality of life; college educated workers; logistics infrastructure; healthcare costs; taxes and government spending; reputation among site consultants. *Expansion Management, August 2007*
- The Pittsburgh* metro area was selected as one of "America's Most Wired Cities" by *Forbes*. The metro area was ranked #23 out of 30. Criteria: percentage of Internet users with high-speed access; the range of service providers within a city; availability of public wireless hot spots. *Forbes, "America's Most Wired Cities," January 10, 2008*
- The Pittsburgh* metro area was identified as one of 10 "Top Up-and-Coming Tech Cities" by *Forbes*. The metro area ranked #6. Criteria: regional innovation trends; important patents. *Forbes.com, "Top Up-and-Coming Tech Cities," March 11, 2008*
- Pittsburgh* was selected as one of the best places to start and grow a company by *Entrepreneur* and the National Policy Research Council. The Pittsburgh* metro area ranked #48 out of 50 large metro areas. Criteria: business formation and growth (firms started four to 14 years ago that still employ at least 5 people and experienced rapid growth over the last four years). *Entrepreneur/National Policy Research Council, "Hot Cities for Entrepreneurs," September 2006*
- The Pittsburgh* metro area was selected as one of "America's 50 Hottest Cities" for business relocations and expansions. Criteria: industry's most prominent site selection consultants were asked to list their top city choices for relocating and expanding manufacturing companies, taking into consideration such factors as the business climate, work force quality, operating costs, incentive programs, and the ease of working with local political and economic development officials. *Expansion Management, January-February 2007*
- The Pittsburgh* metro area was selected as one of the "Top 20 Real Estate Markets" for expanding or relocating companies. The area ranked #20. Criteria: low rental costs; low purchase prices; high vacancy rates of office and warehouse space. *Expansion Management, October 2007*

- Intel, in partnership with Sperling's BestPlaces, ranked the 80 "Best Cities for Teleworking" in America. The Pittsburgh* metro area ranked #18 among large metro areas. The study identifies cities that hold the greatest potential for teleworking based on a host of factors including typical commuting times, fuel prices, availability of broadband Internet access and percentage of the population in telework friendly jobs. The study also factored in extreme climate and natural hazards. *Intel, "Best Cities for Teleworking," March 30, 2006*
- The Pittsburgh* metro area appeared on the Milken Institute "2007 Best Performing Cities" index. Rank: #176 out of 200 large metro areas. Criteria: job growth; wage and salary growth; high-tech output growth. *Milken Institute, "2007 Best Performing Cities"*
- Pittsburgh* was identified as one of the 100 "Most Unwired Cities" in the U.S. The area ranked #53 out of the 100 largest metro areas in the U.S. Criteria: number of public and commercial wireless access points (hotspots); airports with wireless Internet access; broadband availability; local wireless networks; and wireless email devices. *Intel, "Most Unwired Cities Survey," June 7, 2005*
- Pittsburgh* was ranked #43 out of 125 regions worldwide in terms of its "Knowledge Competitiveness Index." The index attempts to measure the knowledge-based development taking place throughout the world and is based on 19 measures of economic performance that indicate a region's ability to translate its knowledge capacity into economic value. *Robert Huggins Associates, World Knowledge Competitiveness Index 2005*
- *Forbes* ranked the 200 most populous metro areas in the U.S. in terms of the "Best Places for Business and Careers." The Pittsburgh* metro area was ranked #83. Criteria: business costs (labor, energy, tax and office space expenses); living costs (housing, transportation, food and other household expenditures); education levels of the work force; job growth; income growth; migration trends; crime rates; and culture/leisure. *Forbes, "Best Places for Business and Careers," March 19, 2008*
- *Fortune* ranked the 100 largest metro areas in the U.S. in terms of projected median home price change in 2007. The Pittsburgh* metro area ranked #29. *Fortune.com, "Hot Spots, Cold Spots"*

Health/Environment Rankings

- The Pittsburgh* metro area was identified as one of "America's 20 Most Sedentary Cities" by *Forbes*. The metro area ranked #14. Criteria: percentage of overweight or obese people; percentage of people who had not engaged in any physical activity in the past 30 days; average number of hours of TV watched per week. *Forbes.com, "America's Most Sedentary Cities," October 29, 2007*
- 100 of the largest metro areas in the U.S. were analyzed in terms of their current drought severity. The Pittsburgh* metro area ranked #67 (#1 = driest). The rankings were based on statistics such as long-term precipitation trends and patterns and the Palmer drought indices. *Sperling's BestPlaces, www.BestPlaces.net, "America's Drought-Riskiest Cities," November 2007*
- Doctors at the Harvard School of Public Health ranked 40 metropolitan areas based on data from the government-sponsored Hospital Quality Alliance program. The program tracks the performance of individual hospitals in treating patients for three common health problems: heart attacks, congestive heart failure, and pneumonia. The Pittsburgh* metro area ranked #29 in quality of care for heart attacks, #28 for congestive heart failure, and #21 for pneumonia. *New England Journal of Medicine, July 21, 2005*
- *Reader's Digest* ranked the 50 largest metro areas in the U.S. in terms of how "clean" they are. The Pittsburgh* metro area ranked #48. Criteria: air quality; water quality; toxic industrial pollution; Superfund sites; and sanitation. *Reader's Digest, "The 50 Cleanest (and Dirtiest) Cities in America," July 2005*

- The American Academy of Dermatology ranked 32 U.S. metropolitan regions in terms of their residents knowledge, attitude and behaviors towards tanning and sun protection. The Pittsburgh* metro area ranked #30. The results of the study are based on an online national survey of 3,342 respondents. *American Academy of Dermatology, "RAYS: Your Grade," May 7, 2007*

- The Pittsburgh* metro area appeared in *Country Home's* "2008 Best Green Places" report. The area ranked #125 out of 379. Criteria: official energy policies; green power; green buildings; availability of fresh, locally grown food. *Country Home, "2008 Best Green Places"*

- Wyeth Consumer Healthcare, in partnership with Sperling's BestPlaces, ranked the nation's 50 most populous metro areas in terms of five key health factors. The Pittsburgh* metro area ranked #22. Criteria: physical activity; health status; nutrition; lifestyle pursuits; and mental wellness. *Wyeth Consumer Healthcare, "Centrum Healthiest Cities Study," April 19, 2005*

- Pittsburgh* was identified as a "2008 Asthma Capital." The area ranked #19 out of the nation's 100 largest metropolitan areas. Twelve factors were used to identify the most challenging places to live for people with asthma: estimated prevalence; self-reported prevalence; crude death rate for asthma; annual pollen score; annual air quality; public smoking laws; number of board-certified asthma specialists; school inhaler access laws; rescue medication use; controller medication use; uninsured rate; poverty rate. *Asthma and Allergy Foundation of America, "2008 Asthma Capitals"*

- Pittsburgh* was identified as a "Spring Allergy Capital." The area ranked #41 out of 100. Three groups of factors were used to identify the most severe cities for people with allergies during the spring season: annual pollen levels; medicine utilization; access to board-certified allergists. *Asthma and Allergy Foundation of America, "2007 Spring Allergy Capital Rankings"*

- Pittsburgh* was identified as a "Fall Allergy Capital." The area ranked #75 out of 100. Three groups of factors were used to identify the most severe cities for people with allergies during the fall season: annual pollen levels; medicine utilization; access to board-certified allergists. *Asthma and Allergy Foundation of America, "2007 Fall Allergy Capital Rankings"*

- Ortho-McNeil Neurologics, in partnership with Sperling's BestPlaces, analyzed 110 metro areas and identified those U.S. cities with the highest prevalence of factors that are most commonly associated with migraine headaches. The Pittsburgh* metro area ranked #35. Criteria: number of migraine-related drug prescriptions per capita; lifestyle factors that can contribute to migraines; environmental factors that can trigger migraines; and consumption of migraine-triggering foods. *Ortho-McNeil Neurologics, "America's Migraine Hot Spots," March 14, 2006*

- Sperling's BestPlaces ranked 331 metro areas and identified the most and least stressful U.S. cities. The Pittsburgh* metro area ranked #74 out of the 100 largest metro areas (#1 = most stressful). Criteria: divorce rate; unemployment rate; violent and property crime; suicide rate; commute time; mental health; alcohol consumption; cloudy days. *Sperling's BestPlaces, www.BestPlaces.net, "America's Most (and Least) Stressful Cities," January 9, 2004*

- An analysis of the "Best & Worst Cities for Sleep" was conducted by Sperling's BestPlaces. The study ranked America's 50 most populated metro areas. The Pittsburgh* metro area ranked #6 (#1 = best city for sleep). Criteria: number of days residents didn't get enough rest or sleep during the past month; average length of daily commute; divorce rate; unemployment rate. *Sperling's BestPlaces, www.BestPlaces.net, "Best & Worst Cities for Sleep," 2006*

- HealthGrades evaluated the performance of America's 25 most populous metropolitan areas by measuring the outcomes of five of the highest volume and most widely studied procedures and diagnoses: coronary artery bypass graft surgery; percutaneus coronary interventions; acute myocardial infarction/heart attack in angioplasty-capable hospitals; congestive heart failure; and community acquired pneumonia. The Pittsburgh* metro area ranked #16. *HealthGrades, "HealthGrades Hospital Quality in America Study," October 12, 2004*

- Pittsburgh* was highlighted as one of the 25 metro areas most polluted by year-round particle pollution (PM 2.5) in the U.S. The area ranked #2. *American Lung Association, State of the Air: 2007*

- Pittsburgh* was selected as one of "America's Pet Healthiest Cities" by Purina. The city ranked #35 out of 50. Criteria: veterinary services; environment; legislation; preventative care; obesity/body condition. *Purina Pet Institute, "America's Pet Healthiest Cities," May 20, 2003*

Women/Minorities Rankings

- Pittsburgh* was ranked #69 out of 100 metro areas in *SELF Magazine's* ranking of "America's Best Places for Women." A panel of experts came up with more than 50 criteria including death and disease rates, environmental indicators, community resources, and lifestyle habits. *SELF Magazine, "America's Best Places for Women 2007," December 2007*

Seniors/Retirement Rankings

- Sperling's BestPlaces in partnership with Bankers Life & Casualty Company designed a survey to identify the top 50 metro areas in the U.S. that offer the best overall qualities for senior living. The Pittsburgh* metro area ranked #4. The following criteria were statistically weighted to reflect the needs of the senior population: health; disease; economics; social; environment; spiritual; transportation; housing; and crime. *Bankers Life & Casualty Company, "Best Cities for Seniors 2005"*

- A.G. Edwards ranked America's 500 top-performing communities based on their residents' personal savings and investing behavior. The Pittsburgh* metro area ranked #255 with an index score of 101.13 (national average = 100.00). A dozen statistical factors were measured including: participation in retirement savings plans; personal debt levels; and home ownership. *A.G. Edwards, "2007 Nest Egg Index", September 12, 2007*

Children/Family Rankings

- The Pittsburgh* metro area was selected as one of the "Best Cities for Relocating Families" by Worldwide ERC and Primacy Relocation. The 2007 study placed a special emphasis on the housing market, which has significantly impacted the relocation industry and an employer's ability to transfer employees. The variables which weigh heavily in this category include home price, home affordability index, appreciation rates, and property tax. Other criteria include cost of living, crime rates, education, climate, focus on diversity, physicians per capita, recreation and leisure, arts and culture, air quality, watershed quality, sales tax, unemployment rate, job growth, high school and higher education index, school expenditures per student, students in public school, SAT/ACT percentile, and population growth. *Worldwide ERC and Primacy Relocation, "2007 Best Cities for Relocating Families"*

Safety Rankings

- The National Insurance Crime Bureau ranked 361 metro areas in the U.S. in terms of per capita rates of vehicle theft. The Pittsburgh* metro area ranked #257 (#1 = highest rate). Criteria: number of vehicle theft offenses per 100,000 inhabitants. *National Insurance Crime Bureau, "NICB Vehicle Theft Study," April 22, 2008*

- Pittsburgh* appeared on Sperling's BestPlaces list of the "Riskiest Cities for Identity Theft." The area ranked #50 out of the nations 50 largest metro areas. Over 80 criteria were analyzed across four major categories: technology impact; crime; transactions; and risk profile. *Sperling's BestPlaces, www.BestPlaces.net, "Riskiest Cities for Identity Theft," July 2006*

- Farmers Insurance Group of Companies, in partnership with Sperling's BestPlaces, ranked 379 metro areas and identified the "Most Secure U.S. Place to Live." The Pittsburgh* metro area ranked #22 out of 114 in the large metro area category (500,000 or more residents). Criteria: crime rates; extreme weather; risk of natural disasters; environmental hazards; terrorism threats; air quality; life expectancy; job loss numbers. *Farmers Insurance Group, "Most Secure U.S. Places to Live 2007"*

- Pittsburgh* was identified as one of the most dangerous large metro areas for pedestrians in the U.S. The area ranked #49 out of the nations 50 largest metro areas. Criteria: average yearly pedestrian fatalities per capita (for the years 2002 and 2003) adjusted for the number of walkers. *Surface Transportation Policy Project, "Mean Streets 2004"*

Sports/Recreation Rankings

- The Pittsburgh* metro area appeared on the *Sporting News* list of the "Best Sports Cities 2007". The area ranked #21 out of 150 cities in the U.S. *Sporting News* takes a 12-month snapshot, roughly July to July, of each city's sports, putting a heavy premium on regular-season won-lost records (from the most recently completed season). Other criteria include: playoff berths, bowl appearances and tournament bids; championships; applicable power ratings; quality of competition; overall fan fervor as measured in part by attendance as percentage of venue capacity; abundance of teams (rewarding quality over quantity); stadium and arena quality; ticket availability and prices; franchise ownership; and marquee appeal of athletes. *SportingNews.com, "Best Sports Cities 2007," August 1, 2007*

- *Golf Digest* ranked 330 metro areas in the U.S. in terms of golf. The Pittsburgh* metro area was ranked #220. Criteria: access to golf; weather; value of golf; and quality of golf. *Golf Digest, "Metro Golf Rankings," August 2005*

Dating/Romance Rankings

- Eli Lily and Company, in partnership with Sperling's BestPlaces, ranked the nation's 50 largest metro areas in terms of the "Most Romantic Cities for Baby Boomers." The Pittsburgh* metro area ranked #1. Criteria: marriage and divorce rates among "baby boomers" age 45 to 60; great restaurants; dance studios; chocolate, jewelry and flower sales. *Eli Lily and Company, "Most Romantic Cities for Baby Boomers," April 20, 2007*

- The Pittsburgh* metro area was selected as one of the "Best Cities for Relocating Singles" by Worldwide ERC and Primacy Relocation. The area ranked #25 out of the 100 largest metro areas in the U.S. Areas were selected based on the following criteria: a robust cost-of-living index; adventure and outdoor recreation opportunities; violent crime and property crime rates; percentage of the population that is unmarried (ages 25-34); ratio of single men and single women; affordability of quality higher education, including in-state and out-of-state tuition requirements and rates; number of newcomers to the area; commute times; tax rates; fee and occupancy rates for temporary housing and mini-storage; quality and quantity of collegiate and professional sporting events and fun, fan-friendly venues. *Worldwide ERC and Primacy Relocation, "2007 Best Cities for Relocating Singles," October 25, 2007*

- *Forbes* ranked the 40 most populous urbanized areas in the U.S. in terms of the "Best Cities for Singles." The Pittsburgh* metro area ranked #35. Criteria: number of singles; cost of living alone; nightlife; culture; job growth; coolness; and online dating. *Forbes.com, August 21, 2007*

- Sperling's BestPlaces in partnership with AXE Deodorant Bodyspray ranked 80 metro areas and identified "America's Best (and Worst) Cities for Dating." The Pittsburgh* metro area ranked #73 (#1 = best). Criteria: percentage of singles ages 18-24; population density; dating venues per capita. *AXE Deodorant Bodyspray, "America's Best (and Worst) Cities for Dating," May 2004*

Miscellaneous Rankings

- The Pittsburgh* metro area appeared on *Forbes* list of "America's Drunkest Cities". The area ranked #8. Criteria: 35 of the largest continental U.S. metro areas were chosen based on availability of data and geographic diversity. Each metro was ranked in five areas: state laws; drinkers; heavy drinkers; binge drinkers; and alcoholism. *Forbes.com, "America's Drunkest Cities," August 22, 2006*

- Sperling's BestPlaces in partnership with Pep Boys ranked 77 metro areas and identified "America's Most Drivable Cities." The Pittsburgh* metro area ranked #32. Criteria: climate; road roughness; urban mobility; gas prices. *Pep Boys, "America's Most Drivable Cities," April 9, 2003*

- State Farm Insurance, in partnership with Sperling's BestPlaces, analyzed several key factors that contribute to overall family preparedness. The Pittsburgh* metro area ranked #4 out of the nation's 50 most populous metro areas. Criteria: quality of life; life insurance coverage; and investments. *State Farm Life Insurance, "Fiscally Fit Cities Report," July 20, 2004*

- Scarborough Research, a leading market research firm, identified the top local markets for grocery coupon use. The Pittsburgh* DMA (Designated Market Area) ranked in the top 25 with 41% of consumers reporting that they use grocery coupons at least once per week. *Scarborough Research, December 8, 2004*

- A study by Sperling's BestPlaces examined which U.S. metro areas were most affected by high fuel prices in 2006. The Pittsburgh* metro area was ranked #67 out of 80 (#1 = most expensive city for driving). Rankings are based on the average dollars spent on gas per year by two driver households. Criteria: cost of regular-grade gasoline; average miles driven per day; average number of gallons each driver uses and wastes in traffic congestion each day. *Sperling's BestPlaces, www.bestplaces.net, "Pain at the Pump," May 18, 2006*

Cranberry is located within the Pittsburgh, PA Metropolitan Statistical Area.

Business Environment

CITY FINANCES

City Government Finances

Component	2004-2005 ($000)	2004-2005 ($ per capita)
Total Revenues	29,589	1,095
Total Expenditures	34,923	1,292
Debt Outstanding	52,102	1,927
Cash and Securities	17,338	641

Source: U.S Census Bureau, Government Finances 2004-2005

City Government Revenue by Source

Source	2004-2005 ($000)	2004-2005 ($ per capita)
General Revenue		
From Federal Government	64	2
From State Government	1,039	38
From Local Governments	0	0
Taxes		
Property	3,209	119
Sales	0	0
Personal Income	3,784	140
License	3,773	140
Charges	9,677	358
Liquor Store	0	0
Utility	3,289	122
Employee Retirement	0	0
Other	4,754	176

Source: U.S Census Bureau, Government Finances 2004-2005

City Government Expenditures by Function

Function	2004-2005 ($000)	2004-2005 ($ per capita)	2004-2005 (%)
General Expenditures			
Airports	0	0	0.0
Corrections	0	0	0.0
Education	0	0	0.0
Fire Protection	958	35	2.7
Governmental Administration	8,022	297	23.0
Health	225	8	0.6
Highways	5,482	203	15.7
Hospitals	0	0	0.0
Housing and Community Development	559	21	1.6
Interest on General Debt	1,498	55	4.3
Libraries	233	9	0.7
Parking	0	0	0.0
Parks and Recreation	3,642	135	10.4
Police Protection	2,852	106	8.2
Public Welfare	0	0	0.0
Sewerage	5,224	193	15.0
Solid Waste Management	924	34	2.6
Liquor Store	0	0	0.0
Utility	3,683	136	10.5
Employee Retirement	0	0	0.0
Other	1,621	60	4.6

Source: U.S Census Bureau, Government Finances 2004-2005

Municipal Bond Ratings

Area	Moody's
City	n/a

Source: Mergent Bond Record, January 2008 (unless noted otherwise)

DEMOGRAPHICS

Population Growth

Area	1990 Census	2000 Census	2007 Estimate	2012 Projection	Population Growth (%) 1990-2000	Population Growth (%) 2000-2012
City	14,764	23,625	27,640	30,111	60.0	27.5
MSA[1]	2,468,289	2,431,087	2,372,530	2,324,047	-1.5	-4.4
U.S.	248,709,873	281,421,906	301,045,522	314,920,978	13.2	11.9

Note: (1) Metropolitan Statistical Area - see Appendix B for areas included
Source: Claritas, Inc.

Number of Households and Average Household Size

Area	2007 Estimate	2007 Average Household Size
City	9,808	2.82
MSA[1]	991,033	2.39
U.S.	113,668,003	2.65

Note: (1) Metropolitan Statistical Area - see Appendix B for areas included
Source: Claritas, Inc.

Race and Ethnicity

Area	White Alone[2]	Black Alone[2]	Asian Alone[2]	Other Race Alone[2]	Hispanic[3]
City	95.5	1.2	2.2	1.2	1.0
MSA[1]	88.9	8.2	1.4	1.5	0.9
U.S.	73.1	12.4	4.3	10.3	14.9

Note: Figures are 2007 estimates; (1) Metropolitan Statistical Area - see Appendix B for areas included (2) Alone is defined as not being in combination with one or more other races; (3) May be of any race.
Source: Claritas, Inc.

Ancestry

Area	German	Irish[2]	English	American	Italian	Polish	French[3]	Scottish
City	34.3	21.4	10.2	4.7	17.0	8.6	2.2	2.6
MSA[1]	26.5	17.1	8.5	3.8	15.2	8.9	1.8	1.9
U.S.	15.2	10.9	8.7	7.3	5.6	3.2	3.0	1.7

Note: Figures include multiple ancestry (e.g. if a person reported being Irish and Italian, they were included in both columns); (1) Metropolitan Statistical Area - see Appendix A for areas included; (2) Includes Celtic; (3) Includes Alsatian but excludes Basque
Source: Census 2000, Summary File 3

Foreign-Born Population

Area	Percent of Population Born in: Any Foreign Country	Europe	Asia	Africa	Oceania[2]	Canada	Mexico	Latin America[3]
City	3.2	1.1	1.5	0.1	0.1	0.1	0.2	0.0
MSA[1]	2.6	1.3	0.9	0.1	0.0	0.1	0.0	0.2
U.S.	11.1	1.7	2.9	0.3	0.1	0.3	3.3	2.5

Note: (1) Metropolitan Statistical Area - see Appendix A for areas included; (2) Includes Australia, New Zealand subregion, Melanesia, Micronesia, Polynesia, and Oceania n.e.c; (3) Includes Central America (excluding Mexico), South America, and the Caribbean.
Source: Census 2000, Summary File 3

Marriage Status

Area	Never Married	Now Married (excluding Separated)	Separated	Widowed	Divorced
City	18.0	69.9	1.3	4.9	5.9
MSA[1]	26.2	54.5	1.9	9.2	8.3
U.S.	27.1	54.4	2.2	6.6	9.7

Note: Figures are percentages and cover the population 15 years of age and older; (1) Metropolitan Statistical Area - see Appendix A for areas included
Source: Census 2000, Summary File 3

Age Distribution

Area	Percent of Population						
	Under Age 5	Age 5 to 17	Age 18 to 34	Age 35 to 49	Age 50 to 64	Age 65 to 79	80 Years and Over
City	9.3	21.1	20.1	29.3	12.1	5.3	2.8
MSA[1]	5.5	16.7	20.2	23.7	16.1	12.9	4.9
U.S.	6.8	18.9	23.7	23.5	14.8	9.2	3.2

Note: (1) Metropolitan Statistical Area - see Appendix A for areas included
Source: Census 2000, Summary File 3

Male/Female Ratio

Area	Males	Females	Males per 100 Females
City	13,640	14,000	97.4
MSA[1]	1,138,277	1,234,253	92.2
U.S.	148,320,305	152,725,217	97.1

Note: Figures are 2007 estimates; (1) Metropolitan Statistical Area - see Appendix B for areas included
Source: Claritas, Inc.

Religion

Area	Catholic	Southern Baptist	United Meth-odist	ELCA[1]	LDS[2]	Presby-terian Church USA	Jewish Est.	Muslim Est.
County	30.3	0.3	6.5	6.4	0.6	6.5	0.1	0.0
U.S.	22.0	7.1	3.7	1.8	1.5	1.1	2.2	0.6

Note: Figures are the number of adherents as a percentage of the total population; Adherents are defined as all members, including full members, their children and the estimated number of other participants who are not considered members (e.g. the baptized, those not confirmed, those regularly attending services, etc.); (1) Evangelical Lutheran Church in America; (2) The Church of Jesus Christ of Latter Day Saints
Source: Reprinted with permission from Religious Congregations and Membership in the United States 2000 (Nashville, Glenmary Research Center, 2002) Copyright Association of Statisticians of American Religious Bodies. All rights reserved.

ECONOMY

Gross Metropolitan Product

Area	2002	2003	2004	2005	2005 Rank[2]
MSA[1]	84.7	87.6	91.9	96.2	22

Note: Figures are in billions of dollars; (1) Pittsburgh, PA Metropolitan Statistical Area - see Appendix A for areas included; (2) Rank ranges from 1 to 361
Source: The U.S. Conference of Mayors, "U.S. Metro Economies: GMP - The Engines of America's Growth," January 2007

Economic Growth

Area	1995 GMP	2005 GMP	Average Annual Growth Rate	Growth Rate Rank[2]
MSA[1]	64.0	96.2	4.2	301

Note: Figures are in billions of dollars; GMP = Gross Metropolitan Product; (1) Pittsburgh, PA Metropolitan Statistical Area - see Appendix A for areas included; (2) Rank ranges from 1 to 361
Source: The U.S. Conference of Mayors, "U.S. Metro Economies: GMP - The Engines of America's Growth," January 2007

INCOME

Per Capita/Median/Average Income

Area	Per Capita ($)	Median Household ($)	Average Household ($)
City	34,011	82,173	95,426
MSA[1]	25,023	43,657	59,040
U.S.	25,495	49,280	66,670

Note: Figures are 2007 estimates; (1) Metropolitan Statistical Area - see Appendix B for areas included
Source: Claritas, Inc.

Household Income Distribution

Area	Percent of Households Earning							
	Under $15,000	$15,000 -24,999	$25,000 -34,999	$35,000 -49,999	$50,000 -74,999	$75,000 -99,000	$100,000 -149,999	$150,000 and up
City	4.2	4.2	5.5	10.8	20.0	18.3	23.5	13.5
MSA[1]	14.9	13.1	12.4	15.9	18.9	10.7	9.2	4.7
U.S.	13.1	10.9	11.2	15.6	19.5	11.9	11.3	6.6

Note: Figures are 2007 estimates; (1) Metropolitan Statistical Area - see Appendix B for areas included
Source: Claritas, Inc.

Poverty Rates by Age

Area	All Ages	Under 5 Years Old	5 to 17 Years Old	18 to 64 Years Old	65 Years and Over
City	2.9	0.2	0.8	1.4	0.4
MSA[1]	10.8	0.9	2.4	5.9	1.6
U.S.	12.4	1.2	3.0	6.9	1.2

Note: Figures are percent of population with income in 1999 below poverty level and only include population for whom poverty status is determined; (1) Metropolitan Statistical Area - see Appendix A for areas included
Source: Census 2000, Summary File 3

Personal Bankruptcy Filing Rate

Area	2004	2005	2006
Butler County	4.28	5.94	1.90
U.S.	5.31	6.82	2.00

Note: Numbers are per 1,000 population and include Chapter 7 and Chapter 13 filings
Source: Federal Deposit Insurance Corporation (FDIC), Regional Economic Conditions (RECON), 8/23/2007

EMPLOYMENT

Labor Force and Employment

Area	Civilian Labor Force			Workers Employed		
	Dec. 2006	Dec. 2007	% Chg.	Dec. 2006	Dec. 2007	% Chg.
City	15,647	15,597	-0.3	15,279	15,172	-0.7
MSA[1]	1,200,792	1,196,486	-0.4	1,152,140	1,144,059	-0.7
U.S.	152,571,000	153,705,000	0.7	146,081,000	146,334,000	0.2

Note: Data is not seasonally adjusted and covers workers 16 years of age and older;
(1) Metropolitan Statistical Area - see Appendix B for areas included
Source: Bureau of Labor Statistics, http://stats.bls.gov

Unemployment Rate

Area	2007											
	Jan.	Feb.	Mar.	Apr.	May	Jun.	Jul.	Aug.	Sep.	Oct.	Nov.	Dec.
City	3.0	2.7	2.6	2.2	2.6	2.8	2.7	2.8	2.7	2.7	3.2	2.7
MSA[1]	5.1	4.9	4.4	3.8	4.1	4.4	4.6	4.4	3.9	3.9	4.0	4.4
U.S.	5.0	4.9	4.5	4.3	4.3	4.7	4.9	4.6	4.5	4.4	4.5	4.8

Note: Data is not seasonally adjusted and covers workers 16 years of age and older; All figures are percentages; (1) Metropolitan Statistical Area - see Appendix B for areas included
Source: Bureau of Labor Statistics, http://stats.bls.gov

Employment by Occupation

Occupation Classification	City (%)	MSA[1] (%)	U.S. (%)
Sales and Office	30.7	27.7	26.7
Professional and Related	25.0	21.1	20.2
Service	9.7	15.9	14.9
Production, Transportation, and Material Moving	7.9	13.4	14.6
Management, Business, and Financial	21.2	12.8	13.5
Construction, Extraction, and Maintenance	5.4	8.9	9.4
Farming, Forestry, and Fishing	0.1	0.2	0.7

Note: Figures cover employed civilians 16 years of age and older;
(1) Metropolitan Statistical Area - see Appendix A for areas included
Source: Census 2000, Summary File 3

Employment by Industry

Sector	MSA[1] Number of Employees	MSA[1] Percent of Total	U.S. Percent of Total
Government	128,900	11.2	16.3
Education and Health Services	230,800	20.0	13.4
Professional and Business Services	154,900	13.4	13.1
Retail Trade	136,500	11.8	11.6
Manufacturing	100,000	8.7	9.9
Leisure and Hospitality	105,700	9.1	9.6
Financial Activities	68,300	5.9	5.9
Construction	56,700	4.9	5.3
Wholesale Trade	49,400	4.3	4.4
Other Services	52,800	4.6	3.9
Transportation and Utilities	45,500	3.9	3.7
Information	21,600	1.9	2.2
Natural Resources and Mining	4,800	0.4	0.5

Note: Figures cover non-farm employment as of December 2007 and are not seasonally adjusted; (1) Metropolitan Statistical Area - see Appendix B for areas included
Source: Bureau of Labor Statistics, http://stats.bls.gov

Average Wages

Occupation	$/Hr.	Occupation	$/Hr.
Accountants and Auditors	29.18	Maids and Housekeeping Cleaners	9.13
Automotive Mechanics	15.81	Maintenance and Repair Workers	16.19
Bookkeepers	14.37	Marketing Managers	46.08
Carpenters	19.32	Nuclear Medicine Technologists	24.86
Cashiers	8.29	Nurses, Licensed Practical	17.59
Clerks, General Office	12.06	Nurses, Registered	27.02
Clerks, Receptionists/Information	10.81	Nursing Aides/Orderlies/Attendants	11.29
Clerks, Shipping/Receiving	13.36	Packers and Packagers, Hand	10.11
Computer Programmers	30.79	Physical Therapists	31.34
Computer Support Specialists	19.22	Postal Service Mail Carriers	21.40
Computer Systems Analysts	31.81	Real Estate Brokers	n/a
Cooks, Restaurant	10.70	Retail Salespersons	11.18
Dentists	n/a	Sales Reps., Exc. Tech./Scientific	31.68
Electrical Engineers	37.60	Sales Reps., Tech./Scientific	34.95
Electricians	24.24	Secretaries, Exc. Legal/Med./Exec.	13.29
Financial Managers	43.34	Security Guards	11.52
First-Line Supervisors/Mgrs., Sales	20.06	Surgeons	84.47
Food Preparation Workers	9.11	Teacher Assistants	9.80
General and Operations Managers	44.82	Teachers, Elementary School	25.20
Hairdressers/Cosmetologists	9.15	Teachers, Secondary School	25.70
Internists	88.07	Telemarketers	13.31
Janitors and Cleaners	10.92	Truck Drivers, Heavy/Tractor-Trailer	18.09
Landscaping/Groundskeeping Workers	11.75	Truck Drivers, Light/Delivery Svcs.	13.86
Lawyers	50.18	Waiters and Waitresses	7.84

Note: Wage data covers the Pittsburgh, PA Metropolitan Statistical Area - see Appendix B for areas included. Hourly wages for elementary/secondary school teachers and teacher assistants were calculated by the editors from annual wage data assuming a 40 hour work week; n/a not available.
Source: Bureau of Labor Statistics, May 2007 Metro Area Occupational Employment and Wage Estimates

RESIDENTIAL REAL ESTATE

Building Permits

Area	Single-Family 2006	Single-Family 2007p	Single-Family Pct. Chg.	Multi-Family 2006	Multi-Family 2007p	Multi-Family Pct. Chg.	Total 2006	Total 2007p	Total Pct. Chg.
City	87	96	10.3	0	0	-	87	96	10.3
U.S.	1,378,200	973,300	-29.4	460,700	407,200	-11.6	1,838,900	1,380,500	-24.9

Note: (p) preliminary; figures cover and represent new, privately-owned housing units authorized (unadjusted data); All permit data are based on estimates with imputation; U.S. figures are based on the new 20,000-place series.
Source: U.S. Census Bureau, Manufacturing, Mining, and Construction Statistics

Homeownership and Housing Vacancies

Area	Homeownership Rate[2] (%)			Rental Vacancy Rate[3] (%)			Homeowner Vacancy Rate[4] (%)		
	2005	2006	2007	2005	2006	2007	2005	2006	2007
MSA[1]	73.1	72.2	73.6	10.0	13.4	9.3	2.1	2.3	3.0
U.S.	68.9	68.8	68.1	9.8	9.8	9.7	1.9	2.4	2.7

Note: (1) Metropolitan Statistical Area - see Appendix B for areas included; (2) The proportion of households that are owners; (3) The proportion of the rental inventory that is vacant for rent; (4) The proportion of the homeowner inventory that is vacant for sale; n/a not available
Source: U.S. Census Bureau, Housing Vacancies and Homeownership Annual Statistics: 2007

TAXES

State Corporate Income Tax Rates

State	Rates and Tax Brackets
Pennsylvania	9.99%

Note: Tax rates as of January 1, 2008; Imposes a capital stock and foreign franchise tax of 0.289% on taxable income over $125K. Bank and Trust Company Shares Tax is 1.25%.
Source: Tax Foundation, www.taxfoundation.org

State Individual Income Tax Rates

State	Federal Deductibility	Marginal Rates (%)	Standard Deduction ($)		Personal Exemptions ($)[1]	
			Single	Joint	Single	Dependents
Pennsylvania	No	3.07	n/a	n/a	n/a	n/a

Note: Tax rates as of January 1, 2008; Local- and county-level taxes are not included; n/a not applicable; (1) Married joint filers generally receive double the single exemption
Source: Tax Foundation, www.taxfoundation.org

Various State and Local Tax Rates

State and Local Sales and Use (%)	State Sales and Use (%)	Gasoline[1,2] ($/gal.)	Cigarette ($/pack)	Spirits ($/gal.)	Table Wine ($/gal.)	Beer ($/gal.)
6.0	6.0	0.323	1.35	6.59 (n)	(p)	0.08

Note: Tax rates as of January 1, 2008; (1) In addition to the 18.4 cpg Federal gasoline tax; (2) Rates may include additional state sales taxes, environmental protection and storage fees/taxes, and local taxes. When necessary, the volume-weighted average of all local taxes is used to approximate the typical statewide rate including local tax; (n) The state government controls all sales. The implied excise tax rate is calculated using methodology designed by the Distilled Spirits Council of the United States (DISCUS); (p) All wine sales are through state-run stores. Revenue in these states is generated from various taxes, fees and net profits.
Source: Tax Foundation, www.taxfoundation.org; Original research

State Tax Burdens

Area	Combined State and Local Tax Burden		Combined Federal, State and Local Tax Burden	
	Percent	Rank	Percent	Rank
Pennsylvania	10.8	24	31.9	20
U.S. Average	11.0	-	32.7	-

Note: Figures cover 2007 and measure taxes as a percentage of income
Source: Tax Foundation, www.taxfoundation.org

State Business Tax Climate Index Rankings

State	Overall Rank	Corporate Tax Index Rank	Individual Income Tax Index Rank	Sales Tax Index Rank	Unemployment Insurance Tax Index Rank	Property Tax Index Rank
Pennsylvania	27	42	11	26	25	47

Note: Rankings range from 1 to 50 where 1 is best. Rankings do not average across to Overall Rank. States without a given tax are given a ranking of 1.
Source: Tax Foundation, State Business Tax Climate Index 2008

TRANSPORTATION

Means of Transportation to Work

Area	Car/Truck/Van		Public Transportation			Bicycle	Walked	Other Means	Worked at Home
	Drove Alone	Car-pooled	Bus	Subway	Railroad				
City	87.5	7.2	0.4	0.0	0.0	0.1	0.8	0.4	3.7
MSA[1]	77.4	9.7	5.6	0.1	0.0	0.1	3.6	1.0	2.4
U.S.	75.7	12.2	2.5	1.5	0.5	0.4	2.9	1.0	3.3

Note: Figures are percentages and cover workers 16 years of age and older;
(1) Metropolitan Statistical Area - see Appendix A for areas included
Source: Census 2000, Summary File 3

Travel Time to Work

Area	Less Than 15 Minutes	15 to 29 Minutes	30 to 44 Minutes	45 to 59 Minutes	60 Minutes or More
City	27.2	24.3	32.1	11.5	4.9
MSA[1]	28.3	36.4	20.2	8.3	6.9
U.S.	29.4	36.1	19.1	7.4	8.0

Note: Figures are percentages and include workers 16 years old and over; (1) Metropolitan Statistical Area - see Appendix A for areas included
Source: Census 2000, Summary File 3

Travel Time Index

Area	1982	1995	2004	2005
Urban Area[1]	1.06	1.10	1.10	1.09
Average[2]	1.11	1.22	1.29	1.30

Note: Travel Time Index - The ratio of travel time in the peak period to the travel time at free-flow conditions. A value of 1.35 indicates a 20-minute free-flow trip takes 27 minutes in the peak. Free-flow speeds (60 mph on freeways and 35 mph on principal arterials) are used as the comparison threshold; (1) Covers the Pittsburgh, PA urban area; (2) average of 85 urban areas
Source: Texas Transportation Institute, The 2007 Urban Mobility Report, September 2007

Living Environment

COST OF LIVING

Cost of Living Index

Composite Index	Groceries	Housing	Utilities	Trans-portation	Health Care	Misc. Goods/ Services
99.3	98.3	93.7	108.6	105.8	87.3	101.1

Note: U.S. = 100; Figures cover the Pittsburgh PA urban area.
Source: The Council for Community and Economic Research (formerly ACCRA), Cost of Living Index, 2007

Grocery Prices

Area[1]	T-Bone Steak ($/pound)	Frying Chicken ($/pound)	Whole Milk ($/half gal.)	Eggs ($/dozen)	Orange Juice ($/64 oz.)	Coffee ($/11.5 oz.)
City[2]	9.43	1.32	1.80	1.45	3.10	3.30
Avg.	8.93	1.12	2.13	1.52	3.26	3.31
Min.	5.88	0.71	1.33	0.83	2.30	2.20
Max.	12.80	2.07	3.43	3.54	5.79	6.20

Note: (1) Values for the local area are compared with the average, minimum and maximum values for all 331 areas in the Cost of Living Index report; (2) Figures cover the Pittsburgh PA urban area; **T-Bone Steak** *(price per pound);* **Frying Chicken** *(price per pound, whole fryer);* **Whole Milk** *(half gallon carton);* **Eggs** *(price per dozen, Grade A, large);* **Orange Juice** *(64 oz. Tropicana or Florida Natural);* **Coffee** *(11.5 oz. can, vacuum-packed, Maxwell House, Hills Bros, or Folgers).*
Source: The Council for Community and Economic Research (formerly ACCRA), Cost of Living Index, 2007

Housing and Utility Costs

Area[1]	New Home Price ($)	Apartment Rent ($/month)	All Electric ($/month)	Part Electric ($/month)	Other Energy ($/month)	Telephone ($/month)
City[2]	282,911	780	-	69.34	129.37	22.90
Avg.	309,605	782	146.13	78.67	90.16	26.14
Min.	189,877	n/a	82.03	37.41	33.15	17.08
Max.	1,202,800	3,481	271.14	150.60	257.67	37.45

Note: (1) Values for the local area are compared with the average, minimum and maximum values for all 331 areas in the Cost of Living Index report; (2) Figures cover the Pittsburgh PA urban area; **New Home Price** *(2,400 sf living area, 8,000 sf lot, in urban area with full utilities);* **Apartment Rent** *(950 sf 2 bedroom/1.5 or 2 bath, unfurnished, excluding all utilities except water);* **All Electric** *(average monthly cost for an all-electric home);* **Part Electric** *(average monthly cost for a part-electric home);* **Other Energy** *(average monthly cost for natural gas, fuel oil, coal, wood, and any other forms of energy except electricity);* **Telephone** *(price includes basic monthly rate for a private residential line plus additional local usage charges incurred by a family of four).*
Source: The Council for Community and Economic Research (formerly ACCRA), Cost of Living Index, 2007

Health Care, Transportation, and Other Costs

Area[1]	Doctor ($/visit)	Dentist ($/visit)	Optometrist ($/visit)	Gasoline ($/gallon)	Beauty Salon ($/visit)	Men's Shirt ($)
City[2]	64.33	53.95	68.25	2.61	29.93	31.57
Avg.	79.48	71.93	79.55	2.64	29.52	25.77
Min.	52.08	44.80	43.95	2.19	15.58	16.19
Max.	148.44	126.27	158.83	3.48	60.62	48.53

Note: (1) Values for the local area are compared with the average, minimum and maximum values for all 331 areas in the Cost of Living Index report; (2) Figures cover the Pittsburgh PA urban area; **Doctor** *(general practitioners routine exam of an established patient);* **Dentist** *(adult teeth cleaning and periodic oral examination);* **Optometrist** *(full vision eye exam for established adult patient);* **Gasoline** *(one gallon regular unleaded, national brand, including all taxes, cash price at self-service pump if available);* **Beauty Salon** *(woman's shampoo, trim, and blow-dry);* **Men's Shirt** *(cotton/polyester dress shirt, pinpoint weave, long sleeves).*
Source: The Council for Community and Economic Research (formerly ACCRA), Cost of Living Index, 2007

HOUSING

House Price Index (HPI)

Area	National Ranking[2]	Quarterly Change (%)	One-Year Change (%)	Five-Year Change (%)
MSA[1]	105	0.55	2.80	22.52
U.S.[3]	-	0.10	0.84	41.37

Note: The HPI is a weighted repeat sales index. It measures average price changes in repeat sales or refinancings on the same properties. This information is obtained by reviewing repeat mortgage transactions on single-family properties whose mortgages have been purchased or securitized by Fannie Mae or Freddie Mac in January 1975; (1) Metropolitan Statistical Area - see Appendix B for areas included; (2) Rankings are based on annual percentage change for all metro areas containing at least 15,000 transactions over the last 10 years and ranges from 1 to 291; (3) figures based on a weighted average of Census Division estimates; all figures are for the period ending December 31, 2007
Source: Office of Federal Housing Enterprise Oversight, House Price Index, February 26, 2008

House Price Valuations

Area	Q1 2000	Q1 2001	Q1 2002	Q1 2003	Q1 2004	Q1 2005	Q1 2006	Q1 2007	Q1 2008
MSA[1]	-7.5	-8.4	-5.8	-3.3	-1.7	-0.5	-1.5	-5.4	-9.0

Note: Figures show the percentage of over- or under-valuation of single family homes relative to statistically normal house values (e.g. a value of 23.6 indicates that house values are 23.6% overvalued). Statistically normal house values are based on house prices, interest rates, household incomes, population densities, and any historical premiums or discounts metropolitan areas have exhibited over time; (1) Figures cover the Metropolitan Statistical Area - see Appendix B for areas included
Source: Global Insight/National City Corporation, House Prices in America, May 2008

Median Home Prices

Area	2005	2006	2007[r]	Percent Change 2006 to 2007
MSA[1]	116.1	116.1	120.7	4.0
U.S. Average	219.0	221.9	217.9	-1.8

Note: Figures are median sales prices of existing single-family homes in thousands of dollars; (r) revised; n/a not available; (1) Metropolitan Statistical Area - see Appendix B for areas included
Source: National Association of Realtors, Metropolitan Area Prices, 1st Quarter 2008

Housing: Year Structure Built

Area	1990 -2000	1980 -1989	1970 -1979	1960 -1969	1950 -1959	1940 -1949	Before 1940	Median Year
City	40.1	24.6	21.9	5.4	4.9	1.3	1.8	1986
MSA[1]	7.8	7.5	12.7	12.3	17.2	11.9	30.5	1954
U.S.	17.0	15.8	18.5	13.7	12.7	7.3	15.0	1971

Note: Figures are percentages; (1) Metropolitan Statistical Area - see Appendix A for areas included
Source: Census 2000, Summary File 3

HEALTH

Health Risk Data

Category	Area[1] (%)	U.S. (%)
Adults who have been told they have high blood pressure[3]	27.6	25.5
Adults who have been told they have high blood cholesterol[3]	39.3	35.6
Adults who have been told they have diabetes[2]	8.0	7.5
Adults who have been told they have arthritis[3]	34.0	27.0
Adults who have been told they currently have asthma	8.8	8.5
Adults who are current smokers	22.2	20.1
Adults who are heavy drinkers[4]	4.2	4.9
Adults who are overweight (BMI 25.0 - 29.9)	37.5	36.5
Adults who are obese (BMI 30.0 - 99.8)	24.3	25.1

Note: Data as of 2006 unless otherwise noted; (1) Figures cover the Metropolitan Statistical Area - see Appendix B for areas included; (2) Figures do not include pregnancy-related diabetes, pre-diabetes or borderline diabetes; (3) 2005 data; (4) Heavy drinkers are classified as adult men having more than two drinks per day or adult women having more than one drink per day
Source: Centers for Disease Control and Prevention, Behaviorial Risk Factor Surveillance System, SMART: Selected Metropolitan/Micropolitan Area Risk Trends, 2005, 2006

Mortality Rates for the Top 10 Causes of Death in the U.S.

ICD-10[a] Sub-Chapter	ICD-10[a] Code	Age-Adjusted Mortality Rate[1] per 100,000 population	
		County[2]	U.S.
Malignant neoplasms	C00-C97	189.7	186.5
Ischaemic heart diseases	I20-I25	152.6	152.3
Other forms of heart disease	I30-I51	76.6	51.5
Cerebrovascular diseases	I60-I69	49.8	50.0
Chronic lower respiratory diseases	J40-J47	40.9	42.6
Diabetes mellitus	E10-E14	23.8	24.8
Other degenerative diseases of the nervous system	G30-G31	27.0	22.6
Other external causes of accidental injury	W00-X59	21.2	21.4
Influenza and pneumonia	J10-J18	24.3	20.7
Hypertensive diseases	I10-I13	9.3	18.2

Note: (a) ICD-10 = International Classification of Diseases 10th Revision; (1) Mortality rates are a three year average covering 2003-2005; (2) Figures cover Butler County
Source: Centers for Disease Control and Prevention, National Center for Health Statistics. Compressed Mortality File 1999-2004. CDC WONDER On-line Database, compiled from Compressed Mortality File 1999-2005 Series 20 No. 2K, 2008.

Mortality Rates for Selected Causes of Death

ICD-10[a] Sub-Chapter	ICD-10[a] Code	Age-Adjusted Mortality Rate[1] per 100,000 population	
		County[2]	U.S.
Assault	X85-Y09	*0.8	5.9
Human immunodeficiency virus (HIV) disease	B20-B24	*0.3	4.5
Intentional self-harm	X60-X84	10.3	10.8
Malnutrition	E40-E46	*0.4	1.0
Obesity and other hyperalimentation	E65-E68	*1.0	1.4
Organic, including symptomatic, mental disorders	F01-F09	24.1	16.8
Transport accidents	V01-V99	16.8	16.1
Viral hepatitis	B15-B19	*0.8	1.8

Note: (a) ICD-10 = International Classification of Diseases 10th Revision; (1) Mortality rates are a three year average covering 2003-2005; (2) Figures cover Butler County; (*) Unreliable data as per CDC
Source: Centers for Disease Control and Prevention, National Center for Health Statistics. Compressed Mortality File 1999-2004. CDC WONDER On-line Database, compiled from Compressed Mortality File 1999-2005 Series 20 No. 2K, 2008.

Distribution of Physicians[1]

Area	Total	Family/ General Practice	Specialties	
			Medical	Surgical
Butler County (number)	188	43	72	35
Butler County (rate per 10,000 pop.)	10.3	2.4	4.0	1.9
U.S. (rate per 10,000 pop.)	17.7	4.6	6.9	4.3

Note: Data as of 2005; (1) Includes all non-federal, patient-care, office-based MDs
Source: Area Resource File (ARF). June 2007. U.S. Department of Health and Human Services, Health Resources and Services Administration, Bureau of Health Professions, Rockville, MD.

Hospitals

There were no hospitals listed within the city limits.
AHA Guide to the Healthcare Field 2008

According to *U.S. News,* the Pittsburgh, PA metro area is home to three of the best hospitals in the U.S.: **Children's Hospital of Pittsburgh of UPMC**; **Magee-Womens Hospital of UPMC**; **University of Pittsburgh Medical Center**. *U.S. News Online, "America's Best Hospitals 2007"*

EDUCATION

Public School District Statistics

District Name	Schls	Pupils	Pupil/ Teacher Ratio	Minority Pupils[1] (%)	Free Lunch Eligible[2] (%)	IEP[3] (%)
Seneca Valley SD	9	7,644	14.7	3.3	6.6	14.2

Note: Table includes regular local school districts with 2,000 or more students; (1) Percentage of students that are not white, non-Hispanic; (2) Percentage of students that are eligible for the free lunch program; (3) Percentage of students that have an Individualized Education Program.
Source: U.S. Department of Education, National Center for Education Statistics, Common Core of Data, Local Education Agency (School District) Universe Survey: School Year 2005-2006; U.S. Department of Education, National Center for Education Statistics, Common Core of Data, Public Elementary/Secondary School Universe Survey: School Year 2005-2006

Highest Level of Education

Area	Less than H.S.	H.S. Diploma	Some College, No Deg.	Associate Degree	Bachelors Degree	Masters Degree	Profess. School Degree	Doctorate Degree
City	4.9	23.0	17.4	7.4	32.1	11.1	2.8	1.3
MSA[1]	15.0	38.0	16.3	7.0	15.0	5.6	2.0	1.0
U.S.	19.4	28.4	21.2	6.4	15.7	5.9	2.0	1.0

Note: Figures are 2007 estimated percentages and cover persons age 25 and over; (1) Metropolitan Statistical Area - see Appendix B for areas included
Source: Claritas, Inc.

Educational Attainment by Race

Area	High School Graduate (%)					Bachelor's Degree (%)				
	Total	White	Black	Asian	Hisp.[2]	Total	White	Black	Asian	Hisp.[2]
City	95.0	95.0	86.2	95.0	78.0	47.1	46.4	38.5	82.9	50.0
MSA[1]	85.1	85.5	78.2	90.5	80.7	23.8	24.2	12.8	70.8	31.6
U.S.	80.4	83.6	72.3	80.4	52.4	24.4	26.1	14.3	44.1	10.4

Note: Figures shown cover persons 25 years old and over; (1) Metropolitan Statistical Area - see Appendix A for areas included; (2) people of Hispanic origin can be of any race
Source: Census 2000, Summary File 3

School Enrollment by Type

Area	Grades KG to 8				Grades 9 to 12			
	Public		Private		Public		Private	
	Enrollment	%	Enrollment	%	Enrollment	%	Enrollment	%
City	3,285	89.4	389	10.6	1,235	96.0	52	4.0
MSA[1]	237,516	86.3	37,647	13.7	114,399	91.8	10,230	8.2
U.S.	33,526,011	88.7	4,285,121	11.3	14,848,628	90.6	1,532,323	9.4

Note: Figures shown cover persons 3 years old and over; (1) Metropolitan Statistical Area - see Appendix A for areas included
Source: Census 2000, Summary File 3

School Enrollment by Race

Area	Grades KG to 8 (%)				Grades 9 to 12 (%)			
	White	Black	Asian	Hisp.[1]	White	Black	Asian	Hisp.[1]
City	97.1	0.3	0.5	1.7	98.0	0.8	0.0	0.9
MSA[2]	84.8	11.9	1.0	0.9	87.2	9.9	0.9	1.0
U.S.	68.5	15.5	3.3	16.8	68.8	15.5	3.8	15.7

Note: Figures shown cover persons 3 years old and over; (1) people of Hispanic origin can be of any race; (2) Metropolitan Statistical Area - see Appendix A for areas included
Source: Census 2000, Summary File 3

Average Salaries of Public School Classroom Teachers

District	2005-06		2006-07		Percent Change 2005-06 to 2006-07
	Dollars	Rank[1]	Dollars	Rank[1]	
Pennsylvania	54,027	12	54,970	10	1.75
U.S. Average	49,026	-	50,816	-	3.65

Note: (1) State rank ranges from 1 to 51.
Source: National Education Association, Rankings & Estimates: Rankings of the States 2006 and Estimates of School Statistics 2007, December 2007

Higher Education

Four-Year Colleges			Two-Year Colleges			Medical Schools[1]	Law Schools[2]	Voc/ Tech[3]
Public	Private Non-profit	Private For-profit	Public	Private Non-profit	Private For-profit			
0	0	0	0	0	0	0	0	0

Note: Figures cover institutions located within the city limits; (1) includes schools accredited by the Liaison Committee on Medical Education and the American Osteopathic Association; (2) includes American Bar Association-accredited law schools; (3) includes all schools with programs that are less than 2 years.
Source: National Center for Education Statistics, The Integrated Postsecondary Education System (IPEDS) Peer Analysis System, 2007; www.usnews.com, Law and Medical School Directories, 2009

PRESIDENTIAL ELECTION

2004 Presidential Election Results

Area	Bush	Kerry	Nader	Other
Butler County	64.3	35.2	0.0	0.4
U.S.	50.7	48.3	0.4	0.6

Note: Results are percentages and may not add to 100% due to rounding
Source: Dave Leip's Atlas of U.S. Presidential Elections, www.uselectionatlas.org

EMPLOYERS

Major Employers

Company Name	Industry	Type of Site
Allegheny General Hospital	General medical and surgical hospitals	Headquarters
Allegheny General Hospital	Management services	Branch
Continuing Care Center	Skilled nursing care facilities	Branch
Div of Continuing Education	Colleges and universities	Branch
Fedex	Trucking, except local	Headquarters
First Class Staffing Inc	Employment agencies	Single
Magee-Womens Hospital	General medical and surgical hospitals	Headquarters
National Enrgy Tech Lnboratory	Noncommercial research organizations	Branch
PNC	National commercial banks	Branch
PNC Bank Corp	National commercial banks	Single
Pittsburgh Mercy Health System	General medical and surgical hospitals	Headquarters
Sewickley Valley Hospital	Offices and clinics of medical doctors	Single
U S S I	Metals service centers and offices	Single
UPMC Presbyterian Shadyside	General medical and surgical hospitals	Headquarters
University of Pittsburgh	Colleges and universities	Headquarters
V A General Library	Libraries	Branch
VA Medical Center	Administration of veterans' affairs	Branch
Valley Medical Facilities	General medical and surgical hospitals	Branch
Western Pennsylvania Hospital	General medical and surgical hospitals	Headquarters
Westinghouse Electric Co LLC	Engineering services	Headquarters

Note: Companies shown are located within the Pittsburgh metropolitan area; nec = not elsewhere classified.
Source: www.zapdata.com, May 2008

PUBLIC SAFETY

Crime Rate

Area	All Crimes	Violent Crimes				Property Crimes		
		Murder	Forcible Rape	Robbery	Aggrav. Assault	Burglary	Larceny -Theft	Motor Vehicle Theft
City	1,504.2	0.0	0.0	51.7	114.6	85.0	1,219.6	33.3
Metro[1]	2,694.4	4.4	18.9	130.4	206.1	470.7	1,660.3	203.6
U.S.	3,808.1	5.7	30.9	149.4	287.5	729.4	2,206.8	398.4

Note: Figures are crimes per 100,000 population; (1) Metropolitan Statistical Area - see Appendix B for areas included
Source: FBI Uniform Crime Reports, 2006

Hate Crimes

Area	Number of Quarters Reported	Bias Motivation				
		Race	Religion	Sexual Orientation	Ethnicity	Disability
City	4	0	0	0	0	0

Source: Federal Bureau of Investigation, Hate Crime Statistics 2006

RECREATION

Culture

Dance[1]	Theatre[1]	Instrumental Music[1]	Vocal Music[1]	Series/ Festivals	Museums	Zoos and Aquariums[2]
0	0	0	0	0	0	0

Note: (1) Number of professional perfoming groups; (2) AZA-accredited
Source: The Grey House Performing Arts Directory, 2007; Official Museum Directory, 2008; Association of Zoos & Aquariums, AZA Member Zoos & Aquariums, June 2008

Professional Sports Teams

Team Name	League
Pittsburgh Pirates	Major League Baseball (MLB)
Pittsburgh Steelers	National Football League (NFL)
Pittsburgh Penguins	National Hockey League (NHL)

Note: Includes teams located in the Pittsburgh metro area.
Source: Original research

MEDIA

Newspapers

Name	News Focus	Frequency	Circulation
Cranberry Eagle	Local	Weekly	20,000
Hampton-Richland Eagle	Local	n/a	12,000
News Weekly	Community	Weekly	7,647
Sunday Cranberry Eagle	Community	Weekly	n/a

Note: Includes newspapers with offices located in the city; n/a not available
Source: MediaContactsPro, March 2008

Television Stations

Name	Ch.	Network(s)	Type	Ownership
KDKA	2	UPN/CBS	Commercial	CBS
WTAE	4	ABC	Commercial	Hearst-Argyle Broadcasting
WPXI	11	NBC	Commercial	Cox Enterprises Inc.
WQED	13	PBS	Public	WQED
WNPA	19	UPN	Commercial	Viacom International Inc.
WCWB	22	WBN	Commercial	Sinclair Broadcast Group
WNPB	24	PBS	Public	WV Educational Broadcasting Authority
WPCB	40	n/a	Commercial	Cornerstone Television Inc.
WPGH	53	Fox	Commercial	Sinclair Broadcast Group

Note: Stations included cover the Pittsburgh DMA (Designated Market Area)
BurrellesLuce, MediaContacts Online, January 2007

Major AM Radio Stations

Call Letters	Freq. (kHz)	Station Type	Target Audience	Station Format	Music Format
WWCS	540	n/a	General	News/Talk	n/a
WKHB	620	Commercial	General	News/Talk	n/a
WPIT	730	n/a	Religious	n/a	n/a
WAVL	910	n/a	Religious	Music/News/Sports/Talk	n/a
WBGG	970	Commercial	General	Sports/Talk	n/a
KDKA	1020	Commercial	General	News/Talk	n/a
WASP	1130	Commercial	General	Music	Oldies
WCCS	1160	n/a	General	Music/News	n/a
WKST	1200	Commercial	General	Talk	n/a
WEAE	1250	n/a	General	Music/Sports	n/a
WBZY	1280	Commercial	General	Music/News	Oldies
WCLG	1300	n/a	General	Music/News	n/a
WJAS	1320	Commercial	General	Music	Adult Standards
WPTT	1360	Commercial	General	Music/Talk	Album Rock
KQV	1410	n/a	General	Music/News/Talk	n/a
WAJR	1440	Commercial	General	News/Talk	n/a

Note: Stations included cover the Pittsburgh DMA (Designated Market Area); n/a not available
Source: BurrellesLuce, MediaContacts Online, January 2007

Major FM Radio Stations

Call Letters	Freq. (mHz)	Station Type	Target Audience	Station Format	Music Format
WKJL	88.1	n/a	General/Religious	Music/Talk	n/a
WQED	89.3	Public	General	Music	Classical
WLTJ	92.9	n/a	General/Women	Music/News	n/a
WBZZ	93.7	Commercial	General	Music	Top 40
WWSW	94.5	Commercial	General	Music/News	Oldies
WKST	96.1	n/a	General	Music/News/Talk	n/a
WRRK	96.9	n/a	General	Music/News	n/a
WKKW	97.9	n/a	General	Music	n/a
WZPT	100.7	Commercial	General	Music	Adult Contemp.
WVAQ	101.9	n/a	General	n/a	n/a
WDVE	102.5	Commercial	General	Music	Album Rock
WJJJ	104.7	Commercial	General	Music/News/Talk	80's
WXDX	105.9	Commercial	General	Music/Talk	Alternative
WAMO	106.7	Commercial	Black/General	Music	Urban Contemp.
WDSY	107.9	Commercial	General	Music	Country

Note: Stations included cover the Pittsburgh DMA (Designated Market Area); n/a not available
BurrellesLuce, MediaContacts Online, January 2007

CLIMATE

Average and Extreme Temperatures

Temperature	Jan	Feb	Mar	Apr	May	Jun	Jul	Aug	Sep	Oct	Nov	Dec	Yr.
Extreme High (°F)	75	69	83	89	91	98	103	100	97	89	82	74	103
Average High (°F)	35	38	48	61	71	79	83	81	75	63	50	39	60
Average Temp. (°F)	28	30	39	50	60	68	73	71	64	53	42	32	51
Average Low (°F)	20	22	29	39	49	57	62	61	54	43	34	25	41
Extreme Low (°F)	-18	-12	-1	14	26	34	42	39	31	16	-1	-12	-18

Note: Figures cover the years 1948-1990
Source: National Climatic Data Center, International Station Meteorological Climate Summary, 9/96

Average Precipitation/Snowfall/Humidity

Precip./Humidity	Jan	Feb	Mar	Apr	May	Jun	Jul	Aug	Sep	Oct	Nov	Dec	Yr.
Avg. Precip. (in.)	2.8	2.4	3.4	3.3	3.6	3.9	3.8	3.2	2.8	2.4	2.7	2.8	37.1
Avg. Snowfall (in.)	11	9	8	2	Tr	0	0	0	0	Tr	4	8	43
Avg. Rel. Hum. 7am (%)	76	75	75	73	76	79	82	86	85	81	78	77	79
Avg. Rel. Hum. 4pm (%)	64	60	54	49	50	51	53	54	55	53	60	66	56

Note: Figures cover the years 1948-1990; Tr = Trace amounts (<0.05 in. of rain; <0.5 in. of snow)
Source: National Climatic Data Center, International Station Meteorological Climate Summary, 9/96

Weather Conditions

Temperature			Daytime Sky			Precipitation		
5°F & below	32°F & below	90°F & above	Clear	Partly cloudy	Cloudy	0.01 inch or more precip.	0.1 inch or more snow/ice	Thunder-storms
9	121	8	62	137	166	154	42	35

Note: Figures are average number of days per year and cover the years 1948-1990
Source: National Climatic Data Center, International Station Meteorological Climate Summary, 9/96

HAZARDOUS WASTE

Superfund Sites

Cranberry has no sites on the EPA's Superfund Final National Priorities List.
U.S. Environmental Protection Agency, Final National Priorities List, June 23, 2008

AIR & WATER QUALITY

Air Quality Index

Area	Percent of Days when Air Quality was...[2]				AQI Statistics	
	Good	Moderate	Unhealthy for Sensitive Groups	Unhealthy	Maximum	Median
MSA[1]	34.0	50.1	13.7	2.2	159	58

Note: The Air Quality Index (AQI) is an index for reporting daily air quality. EPA calculates the AQI for five major air pollutants regulated by the Clean Air Act: ground-level ozone, particle pollution (also known as particulate matter), carbon monoxide, sulfur dioxide, and nitrogen dioxide. The AQI runs from 0 to 500. The higher the AQI value, the greater the level of air pollution and the greater the health concern. There are six AQI categories: "Good" The AQI is between 0 and 50. Air quality is considered satisfactory; "Moderate" The AQI is between 51 and 100. Air quality is acceptable; "Unhealthy for Sensitive Groups" When AQI values are between 101 and 150, members of sensitive groups may experience health effects; "Unhealthy" When AQI values are between 151 and 200 everyone may begin to experience health effects; "Very Unhealthy" AQI values between 201 and 300 trigger a health alert; "Hazardous" AQI values over 300 trigger health warnings of emergency conditions; (1) Metropolitan Statistical Area - see Appendix A for areas included; (2) Based on 365 days with AQI data in 2007.
Source: U.S. Environmental Protection Agency, Air Quality Index Report, 2007

Air Quality Index Pollutants

Area	Percent of Days when AQI Pollutant was...[2]					
	Carbon Monoxide	Nitrogen Dioxide	Ozone	Sulfur Dioxide	Particulate Matter 2.5	Particulate Matter 10
MSA[1]	0.0	0.0	17.5	0.3	81.1	1.1

Note: The Air Quality Index (AQI) is an index for reporting daily air quality. EPA calculates the AQI for five major air pollutants regulated by the Clean Air Act: ground-level ozone, particle pollution (also known as particulate matter), carbon monoxide, sulfur dioxide, and nitrogen dioxide. The AQI runs from 0 to 500. The higher the AQI value, the greater the level of air pollution and the greater the health concern; (1) Metropolitan Statistical Area - see Appendix A for areas included; (2) Based on 365 days with AQI data in 2007.
Source: U.S. Environmental Protection Agency, Air Quality Index Report, 2007

Air Quality Index Trends

Area	Trend Sites (45)								All Sites (126)
	1999	2000	2001	2002	2003	2004	2005	2006	2006
MSA[1]	40	32	50	50	37	39	48	36	45

Note: An AQI value greater than 100 indicates that air quality would have been in the unhealthful range on that day. Data from exceptional events are not included. These counts are presented in two ways. First, the counts are based on sites having an adequate record of monitoring data during the trend period (trend sites). These counts represent the relative change in the number of days with AQI values greater than 100. In the last column, the counts are based on all sites with data in the most recent year (because it is possible for a site to have data in the most recent year but not enough data to be a trend site); (1) Metropolitan Statistical Area - see Appendix A for areas included.
Source: U.S. Environmental Protection Agency, Office of Air and Radiation, Air Trends, Factbook and Related Information, Air Pollution Trends in Selected Metropolitan Areas 2006

Maximum Air Pollutant Concentrations

	Particulate Matter 10 (ug/m^3)	Particulate Matter 2.5 (ug/m^3)	Ozone (ppm)	Carbon Monoxide (ppm)	Sulfur Dioxide (ppm)	Nitrogen Dioxide (ppm)	Lead (ug/m^3)
MSA[1] Level	128	58	0.103	2	0.054	0.018	0.18
NAAQS[2]	150	35	0.125	9	0.140	0.053	1.50
Met NAAQS[2]	Yes	No	Yes	Yes	Yes	Yes	Yes

Note: Data from exceptional events are not included; (1) Metropolitan Statistical Area - see Appendix A for areas included; (2) National Ambient Air Quality Standards; n/a not available
Concentrations: Particulate Matter 10 (coarse particulate) - highest second maximum 24-hour concentration; Particulate Matter 2.5 (fine particulate) - highest 98th percentile 24-hour concentration; Ozone - highest second daily maximum 1-hour concentration; Carbon Monoxide - highest second maximum non-overlapping 8-hour concentration; Sulfur Dioxide - highest second maximum 24-hour concentration; Nitrogen Dioxide - highest arithmetic mean concentration; Lead - highest quarterly maximum concentration
Units: ppm = parts per million; ug/m^3 = micrograms per cubic meter
Source: U.S. Environmental Protection Agency, MSA Factbook 2006, Air Quality Statistics by City

Drinking Water

Water System Name	Pop. Served	Primary Water Source Type	Violations[1]	
			Health Based	Monitoring/ Reporting
Cranberry Township WTP	28,000	Purchased Surface	0	0

Note: (1) Based on violation data from January 1, 2007 to December 31, 2007 (includes unresolved violations from earlier years)
Source: U.S. Environmental Protection Agency, Office of Ground Water and Drinking Water, Safe Drinking Water Information System (based on data extracted April 15, 2008)

Hampden, Pennsylvania

Background

Hampden is located across the Susquehanna River from Harrisburg, the state capital of Pennsylvania. With multiple bridges spanning the river, Hampden is one of fifteen municipalities in what is now called West Susquehanna, part of the greater Harrisburg-Carlisle metro area, situated in the south central part of the state in the Cumberland Valley.

The name Hampden is of English origin, and the area was originally settled in the 1800s by Scotch-Irish immigrants. In 1845 Hampden became a township. Until the 1970s the area was primarily farm land with small villages and residential pockets. Recent development includes housing in the suburbs of Hampden. Route 11, now Carlisle Turnpike, was originally a roadway to the West for the earliest settlers. Now it is the most commercially developed shopping area of southern Hampden, and distinct from the industrial north, which houses a Medical Technology Park and Cumberland Technology Development.

Hampden's government includes five elected commissioners and 100 employees. Hampden belongs to the West Shore Chamber of Commerce and is part of the Cumberland Valley School District. Nearby educational institutions include Dickens College, Elizabethtown College, Gettysburg College, Harrisburg Community College, and Penn State University campuses in York and Harrisburg.

Hampden employs its own police force and ambulance service, the latter transporting to Milton Hershey Medical Center and Harrisburg hospitals. A highly organized recreation department offers more than 80 acres of parks, and 2 large pools encircled with tennis and ball courts, and outdoor amenities. Hampden's golf course was willed to the township in the 1980s.

The nearby city of Harrisburg offers the Hershey Symphony Orchestra, the Hershey Museum, the National Apple Museum, National Watch and Clock Museum, and the State Museum of Pennsylvania. Eisenhower National Historic Site, Gettysburg National Military Park, and Milton S. Hershey Mansion are also worth the trip. Hampden offers expedient bus transportation to Philadelphia and New York City.

Midway between the eastern seaboard and northeast areas, Hampden's weather spans four seasons. Blizzards are a part of the winter and summer can be very humid. The trees provided by the many wooded areas throughout the region have a positive impact on the weather and air quality.

Rankings

General Rankings

- Harrisburg* was ranked #107 out of 375 metro areas in *Cities Ranked & Rated*. Criteria: cost of living; climate; crime; transportation; economy and jobs; education; arts and culture; health and healthcare; leisure; quality of life. *Cities Ranked & Rated, 2nd Edition, 2007*

- Harrisburg* was ranked #40 out of 379 metro areas in *Places Rated Almanac*. Criteria: health care; education; recreation; transportation; ambience; climate; crime; housing costs; jobs. *Places Rated Almanac, 7th Edition, 2007*

- *Expansion Management* rated 362 metro areas to find out which offer the best middle class lifestyle for manufacturing and service companies. The Harrisburg* metro area was selected as a "5-Star Quality of Life Metro" (a distinction the magazine awards to the top 20 percent of metro areas studied). The annual "Quality of Life Quotient" measures dozens of indicators across nine major categories and compares them among 362 metropolitan statistical areas in the United States. The categories are: affordable housing; good public schools; low crime levels; adult education level; standard of living; traffic and commuting; continuing education opportunities; commercial air access; labor market. *Expansion Management, June 2007*

Business/Finance Rankings

- The Harrisburg* metro area was selected one of America's "Top 50 Business Opportunity Metros" by *Expansion Management* in their 5th annual Mayor's Challenge ranking of metro areas that have achieved solid ratings across the board in numerous *EM* studies during the past 12 months. The area ranked #40. Criteria: public schools; quality of life; college educated workers; logistics infrastructure; healthcare costs; taxes and government spending; reputation among site consultants. *Expansion Management, August 2007*

- Harrisburg* was selected as one of the best places to start and grow a company by *Entrepreneur* and the National Policy Research Council. The Harrisburg* metro area ranked #51 out of 63 mid-size metro areas. Criteria: business formation and growth (firms started four to 14 years ago that still employ at least 5 people and experienced rapid growth over the last four years). *Entrepreneur/National Policy Research Council, "Hot Cities for Entrepreneurs," September 2006*

- The Harrisburg* metro area appeared on the Milken Institute "2007 Best Performing Cities" index. Rank: #99 out of 200 large metro areas. Criteria: job growth; wage and salary growth; high-tech output growth. *Milken Institute, "2007 Best Performing Cities"*

- Harrisburg* was identified as one of the 100 "Most Unwired Cities" in the U.S. The area ranked #47 out of the 100 largest metro areas in the U.S. Criteria: number of public and commercial wireless access points (hotspots); airports with wireless Internet access; broadband availability; local wireless networks; and wireless email devices. *Intel, "Most Unwired Cities Survey," June 7, 2005*

- *Forbes* ranked the 200 most populous metro areas in the U.S. in terms of the "Best Places for Business and Careers." The Harrisburg* metro area was ranked #53. Criteria: business costs (labor, energy, tax and office space expenses); living costs (housing, transportation, food and other household expenditures); education levels of the work force; job growth; income growth; migration trends; crime rates; and culture/leisure. *Forbes, "Best Places for Business and Careers," March 19, 2008*

Health/Environment Rankings

- 100 of the largest metro areas in the U.S. were analyzed in terms of their current drought severity. The Harrisburg* metro area ranked #44 (#1 = driest). The rankings were based on statistics such as long-term precipitation trends and patterns and the Palmer drought indices. *Sperling's BestPlaces, www.BestPlaces.net, "America's Drought-Riskiest Cities," November 2007*

- The Harrisburg* metro area appeared in *Country Home's* "2008 Best Green Places" report. The area ranked #84 out of 379. Criteria: official energy policies; green power; green buildings; availability of fresh, locally grown food. *Country Home, "2008 Best Green Places"*

- Harrisburg* was identified as a "2008 Asthma Capital." The area ranked #14 out of the nation's 100 largest metropolitan areas. Twelve factors were used to identify the most challenging places to live for people with asthma: estimated prevalence; self-reported prevalence; crude death rate for asthma; annual pollen score; annual air quality; public smoking laws; number of board-certified asthma specialists; school inhaler access laws; rescue medication use; controller medication use; uninsured rate; poverty rate. *Asthma and Allergy Foundation of America, "2008 Asthma Capitals"*

- Harrisburg* was identified as a "Spring Allergy Capital." The area ranked #76 out of 100. Three groups of factors were used to identify the most severe cities for people with allergies during the spring season: annual pollen levels; medicine utilization; access to board-certified allergists. *Asthma and Allergy Foundation of America, "2007 Spring Allergy Capital Rankings"*

- Harrisburg* was identified as a "Fall Allergy Capital." The area ranked #88 out of 100. Three groups of factors were used to identify the most severe cities for people with allergies during the fall season: annual pollen levels; medicine utilization; access to board-certified allergists. *Asthma and Allergy Foundation of America, "2007 Fall Allergy Capital Rankings"*

- Ortho-McNeil Neurologics, in partnership with Sperling's BestPlaces, analyzed 110 metro areas and identified those U.S. cities with the highest prevalence of factors that are most commonly associated with migraine headaches. The Harrisburg* metro area ranked #67. Criteria: number of migraine-related drug prescriptions per capita; lifestyle factors that can contribute to migraines; environmental factors that can trigger migraines; and consumption of migraine-triggering foods. *Ortho-McNeil Neurologics, "America's Migraine Hot Spots," March 14, 2006*

- Sperling's BestPlaces ranked 331 metro areas and identified the most and least stressful U.S. cities. The Harrisburg* metro area ranked #99 out of the 100 largest metro areas (#1 = most stressful). Criteria: divorce rate; unemployment rate; violent and property crime; suicide rate; commute time; mental health; alcohol consumption; cloudy days. *Sperling's BestPlaces, www.BestPlaces.net, "America's Most (and Least) Stressful Cities," January 9, 2004*

Seniors/Retirement Rankings

- A.G. Edwards ranked America's 500 top-performing communities based on their residents' personal savings and investing behavior. The Harrisburg* metro area ranked #103 with an index score of 106.54 (national average = 100.00). A dozen statistical factors were measured including: participation in retirement savings plans; personal debt levels; and home ownership. *A.G. Edwards, "2007 Nest Egg Index", September 12, 2007*

Children/Family Rankings

- The Harrisburg* metro area was selected as one of the "Best Cities for Relocating Families" by Worldwide ERC and Primacy Relocation. The 2007 study placed a special emphasis on the housing market, which has significantly impacted the relocation industry and an employer's ability to transfer employees. The variables which weigh heavily in this category include home price, home affordability index, appreciation rates, and property tax. Other criteria include cost of living, crime rates, education, climate, focus on diversity, physicians per capita, recreation and leisure, arts and culture, air quality, watershed quality, sales tax, unemployment rate, job growth, high school and higher education index, school expenditures per student, students in public school, SAT/ACT percentile, and population growth. *Worldwide ERC and Primacy Relocation, "2007 Best Cities for Relocating Families"*

Safety Rankings

- The National Insurance Crime Bureau ranked 361 metro areas in the U.S. in terms of per capita rates of vehicle theft. The Harrisburg* metro area ranked #317 (#1 = highest rate). Criteria: number of vehicle theft offenses per 100,000 inhabitants. *National Insurance Crime Bureau, "NICB Vehicle Theft Study," April 22, 2008*

- Farmers Insurance Group of Companies, in partnership with Sperling's BestPlaces, ranked 379 metro areas and identified the "Most Secure U.S. Place to Live." The Harrisburg* metro area ranked #23 out of 114 in the large metro area category (500,000 or more residents). Criteria: crime rates; extreme weather; risk of natural disasters; environmental hazards; terrorism threats; air quality; life expectancy; job loss numbers. *Farmers Insurance Group, "Most Secure U.S. Places to Live 2007"*

Sports/Recreation Rankings

- *Golf Digest* ranked 330 metro areas in the U.S. in terms of golf. The Harrisburg* metro area was ranked #194. Criteria: access to golf; weather; value of golf; and quality of golf. *Golf Digest, "Metro Golf Rankings," August 2005*

Dating/Romance Rankings

- The Harrisburg* metro area was selected as one of the "Best Cities for Relocating Singles" by Worldwide ERC and Primacy Relocation. The area ranked #6 out of the 100 largest metro areas in the U.S. Areas were selected based on the following criteria: a robust cost-of-living index; adventure and outdoor recreation opportunities; violent crime and property crime rates; percentage of the population that is unmarried (ages 25-34); ratio of single men and single women; affordability of quality higher education, including in-state and out-of-state tuition requirements and rates; number of newcomers to the area; commute times; tax rates; fee and occupancy rates for temporary housing and mini-storage; quality and quantity of collegiate and professional sporting events and fun, fan-friendly venues. *Worldwide ERC and Primacy Relocation, "2007 Best Cities for Relocating Singles," October 25, 2007*

- Sperling's BestPlaces in partnership with AXE Deodorant Bodyspray ranked 80 metro areas and identified "America's Best (and Worst) Cities for Dating." The Harrisburg* metro area ranked #68 (#1 = best). Criteria: percentage of singles ages 18-24; population density; dating venues per capita. *AXE Deodorant Bodyspray, "America's Best (and Worst) Cities for Dating," May 2004*

Miscellaneous Rankings

- Scarborough Research, a leading market research firm, identified the top local markets for grocery coupon use. The Harrisburg* DMA (Designated Market Area) ranked in the top 25 with 40% of consumers reporting that they use grocery coupons at least once per week. *Scarborough Research, December 8, 2004*

- Scarborough Research, a leading market research firm, identified the top local markets for gift card purchasers. The Harrisburg* DMA (Designated Market Area) ranked in the top 10 with 57% of consumers reporting that they purchased a gift card within the past 12 months. *Scarborough Research, November 15, 2006*

Hampden is located within the Harrisburg-Carlisle, PA Metropolitan Statistical Area.

Business Environment

CITY FINANCES

City Government Finances

Component	2004-2005 ($000)	2004-2005 ($ per capita)
Total Revenues	16,047	622
Total Expenditures	21,707	842
Debt Outstanding	5,715	222
Cash and Securities	9,805	380

Source: U.S Census Bureau, Government Finances 2004-2005

City Government Revenue by Source

Source	2004-2005 ($000)	2004-2005 ($ per capita)
General Revenue		
From Federal Government	14	1
From State Government	1,121	43
From Local Governments	155	6
Taxes		
Property	423	16
Sales	0	0
Personal Income	4,284	166
License	849	33
Charges	8,002	310
Liquor Store	0	0
Utility	0	0
Employee Retirement	0	0
Other	1,199	46

Source: U.S Census Bureau, Government Finances 2004-2005

City Government Expenditures by Function

Function	2004-2005 ($000)	2004-2005 ($ per capita)	2004-2005 (%)
General Expenditures			
Airports	0	0	0.0
Corrections	0	0	0.0
Education	0	0	0.0
Fire Protection	467	18	2.2
Governmental Administration	1,679	65	7.7
Health	666	26	3.1
Highways	2,813	109	13.0
Hospitals	0	0	0.0
Housing and Community Development	338	13	1.6
Interest on General Debt	4	< 1	< 0.1
Libraries	0	0	0.0
Parking	0	0	0.0
Parks and Recreation	2,224	86	10.2
Police Protection	1,616	63	7.4
Public Welfare	0	0	0.0
Sewerage	9,700	376	44.7
Solid Waste Management	1,465	57	6.7
Liquor Store	0	0	0.0
Utility	0	0	0.0
Employee Retirement	0	0	0.0
Other	735	29	3.4

Source: U.S Census Bureau, Government Finances 2004-2005

Municipal Bond Ratings

Area	Moody's
City	n/a

Source: Mergent Bond Record, January 2008 (unless noted otherwise)

DEMOGRAPHICS

Population Growth

Area	1990 Census	2000 Census	2007 Estimate	2012 Projection	Population Growth (%) 1990-2000	Population Growth (%) 2000-2012
City	20,384	24,135	26,207	27,557	18.4	14.2
MSA[1]	474,242	509,074	525,711	536,090	7.3	5.3
U.S.	248,709,873	281,421,906	301,045,522	314,920,978	13.2	11.9

Note: (1) Metropolitan Statistical Area - see Appendix B for areas included
Source: Claritas, Inc.

Number of Households and Average Household Size

Area	2007 Estimate	2007 Average Household Size
City	10,666	2.46
MSA[1]	211,758	2.48
U.S.	113,668,003	2.65

Note: (1) Metropolitan Statistical Area - see Appendix B for areas included
Source: Claritas, Inc.

Race and Ethnicity

Area	White Alone[2]	Black Alone[2]	Asian Alone[2]	Other Race Alone[2]	Hispanic[3]
City	92.3	1.2	4.9	1.6	1.6
MSA[1]	84.8	9.7	2.2	3.3	3.4
U.S.	73.1	12.4	4.3	10.3	14.9

Note: Figures are 2007 estimates; (1) Metropolitan Statistical Area - see Appendix B for areas included
(2) Alone is defined as not being in combination with one or more other races; (3) May be of any race.
Source: Claritas, Inc.

Ancestry

Area	German	Irish[2]	English	American	Italian	Polish	French[3]	Scottish
City	35.0	17.5	11.9	6.3	8.4	4.3	2.3	2.2
MSA[1]	34.2	11.4	6.9	7.6	6.2	3.0	1.8	1.5
U.S.	15.2	10.9	8.7	7.3	5.6	3.2	3.0	1.7

Note: Figures include multiple ancestry (e.g. if a person reported being Irish and Italian, they were included in both columns); (1) Metropolitan Statistical Area - see Appendix A for areas included; (2) Includes Celtic; (3) Includes Alsatian but excludes Basque
Source: Census 2000, Summary File 3

Foreign-Born Population

Area	Percent of Population Born in							
	Any Foreign Country	Europe	Asia	Africa	Oceania[2]	Canada	Mexico	Latin America[3]
City	4.6	1.1	2.8	0.3	0.1	0.1	0.0	0.2
MSA[1]	3.3	1.0	1.3	0.2	0.0	0.1	0.2	0.4
U.S.	11.1	1.7	2.9	0.3	0.1	0.3	3.3	2.5

Note: (1) Metropolitan Statistical Area - see Appendix A for areas included; (2) Includes Australia, New Zealand subregion, Melanesia, Micronesia, Polynesia, and Oceania n.e.c; (3) Includes Central America (excluding Mexico), South America, and the Caribbean.
Source: Census 2000, Summary File 3

Marriage Status

Area	Never Married	Now Married (excluding Separated)	Separated	Widowed	Divorced
City	20.3	64.6	1.8	6.0	7.4
MSA[1]	25.3	56.5	2.0	7.3	8.8
U.S.	27.1	54.4	2.2	6.6	9.7

Note: Figures are percentages and cover the population 15 years of age and older;
(1) Metropolitan Statistical Area - see Appendix A for areas included
Source: Census 2000, Summary File 3

Age Distribution

Area	Under Age 5	Age 5 to 17	Age 18 to 34	Age 35 to 49	Age 50 to 64	Age 65 to 79	80 Years and Over
	Percent of Population						
City	5.6	18.7	17.4	25.8	19.3	9.5	3.7
MSA[1]	5.8	17.6	21.6	24.1	16.1	10.8	3.9
U.S.	6.8	18.9	23.7	23.5	14.8	9.2	3.2

Note: (1) Metropolitan Statistical Area - see Appendix A for areas included
Source: Census 2000, Summary File 3

Male/Female Ratio

Area	Males	Females	Males per 100 Females
City	12,740	13,467	94.6
MSA[1]	255,654	270,057	94.7
U.S.	148,320,305	152,725,217	97.1

Note: Figures are 2007 estimates; (1) Metropolitan Statistical Area - see Appendix B for areas included
Source: Claritas, Inc.

Religion

Area	Catholic	Southern Baptist	United Meth-odist	ELCA[1]	LDS[2]	Presby-terian Church USA	Jewish Est.	Muslim Est.
County	16.5	0.6	10.1	8.3	0.4	3.7	0.9	0.0
U.S.	22.0	7.1	3.7	1.8	1.5	1.1	2.2	0.6

Note: Figures are the number of adherents as a percentage of the total population; Adherents are defined as all members, including full members, their children and the estimated number of other participants who are not considered members (e.g. the baptized, those not confirmed, those regularly attending services, etc.); (1) Evangelical Lutheran Church in America; (2) The Church of Jesus Christ of Latter Day Saints
Source: Reprinted with permission from Religious Congregations and Membership in the United States 2000 (Nashville, Glenmary Research Center, 2002) Copyright Association of Statisticians of American Religious Bodies. All rights reserved.

ECONOMY

Gross Metropolitan Product

Area	2002	2003	2004	2005	2005 Rank[2]
MSA[1]	23.7	24.6	25.9	27.2	70

Note: Figures are in billions of dollars; (1) Harrisburg-Carlisle, PA Metropolitan Statistical Area - see Appendix A for areas included; (2) Rank ranges from 1 to 361
Source: The U.S. Conference of Mayors, "U.S. Metro Economies: GMP - The Engines of America's Growth," January 2007

Economic Growth

Area	1995 GMP	2005 GMP	Average Annual Growth Rate	Growth Rate Rank[2]
MSA[1]	17.7	27.2	4.4	281

Note: Figures are in billions of dollars; GMP = Gross Metropolitan Product; (1) Harrisburg-Carlisle, PA Metropolitan Statistical Area - see Appendix A for areas included; (2) Rank ranges from 1 to 361
Source: The U.S. Conference of Mayors, "U.S. Metro Economies: GMP - The Engines of America's Growth," January 2007

INCOME

Per Capita/Median/Average Income

Area	Per Capita ($)	Median Household ($)	Average Household ($)
City	36,255	71,273	88,217
MSA[1]	27,040	51,772	65,721
U.S.	25,495	49,280	66,670

Note: Figures are 2007 estimates; (1) Metropolitan Statistical Area - see Appendix B for areas included
Source: Claritas, Inc.

Household Income Distribution

Area	Percent of Households Earning							
	Under $15,000	$15,000 -24,999	$25,000 -34,999	$35,000 -49,999	$50,000 -74,999	$75,000 -99,000	$100,000 -149,999	$150,000 and up
City	4.2	6.7	8.9	12.6	20.6	15.6	19.5	11.9
MSA[1]	10.0	10.3	11.5	16.4	21.6	13.2	11.9	5.1
U.S.	13.1	10.9	11.2	15.6	19.5	11.9	11.3	6.6

Note: Figures are 2007 estimates; (1) Metropolitan Statistical Area - see Appendix B for areas included
Source: Claritas, Inc.

Poverty Rates by Age

Area	All Ages	Under 5 Years Old	5 to 17 Years Old	18 to 64 Years Old	65 Years and Over
City	2.8	0.2	0.6	1.6	0.5
MSA[1]	8.1	0.8	1.9	4.4	1.0
U.S.	12.4	1.2	3.0	6.9	1.2

Note: Figures are percent of population with income in 1999 below poverty level and only include population for whom poverty status is determined; (1) Metropolitan Statistical Area - see Appendix A for areas included
Source: Census 2000, Summary File 3

Personal Bankruptcy Filing Rate

Area	2004	2005	2006
Cumberland County	4.03	5.21	1.95
U.S.	5.31	6.82	2.00

Note: Numbers are per 1,000 population and include Chapter 7 and Chapter 13 filings
Source: Federal Deposit Insurance Corporation (FDIC), Regional Economic Conditions (RECON), 8/23/2007

EMPLOYMENT

Labor Force and Employment

Area	Civilian Labor Force			Workers Employed		
	Dec. 2006	Dec. 2007	% Chg.	Dec. 2006	Dec. 2007	% Chg.
City	14,846	14,752	-0.6	14,517	14,386	-0.9
MSA[1]	282,110	280,672	-0.5	273,090	270,634	-0.9
U.S.	152,571,000	153,705,000	0.7	146,081,000	146,334,000	0.2

Note: Data is not seasonally adjusted and covers workers 16 years of age and older;
(1) Metropolitan Statistical Area - see Appendix B for areas included
Source: Bureau of Labor Statistics, http://stats.bls.gov

Unemployment Rate

Area	2007											
	Jan.	Feb.	Mar.	Apr.	May	Jun.	Jul.	Aug.	Sep.	Oct.	Nov.	Dec.
City	2.7	2.4	2.5	2.1	2.4	2.8	2.8	2.6	2.4	2.5	2.5	2.5
MSA[1]	4.0	3.9	3.7	3.2	3.4	3.7	3.7	3.6	3.3	3.4	3.4	3.6
U.S.	5.0	4.9	4.5	4.3	4.3	4.7	4.9	4.6	4.5	4.4	4.5	4.8

Note: Data is not seasonally adjusted and covers workers 16 years of age and older; All figures are percentages; (1) Metropolitan Statistical Area - see Appendix B for areas included
Source: Bureau of Labor Statistics, http://stats.bls.gov

Employment by Occupation

Occupation Classification	City (%)	MSA[1] (%)	U.S. (%)
Sales and Office	32.3	28.1	26.7
Professional and Related	27.8	19.3	20.2
Service	8.5	14.1	14.9
Production, Transportation, and Material Moving	8.7	16.5	14.6
Management, Business, and Financial	18.5	12.9	13.5
Construction, Extraction, and Maintenance	4.1	8.5	9.4
Farming, Forestry, and Fishing	0.1	0.6	0.7

Note: Figures cover employed civilians 16 years of age and older;
(1) Metropolitan Statistical Area - see Appendix A for areas included
Source: Census 2000, Summary File 3

Employment by Industry

Sector	MSA[1] Number of Employees	MSA[1] Percent of Total	U.S. Percent of Total
Government	62,300	18.7	16.3
Education and Health Services	46,300	13.9	13.4
Professional and Business Services	39,600	11.9	13.1
Retail Trade	35,800	10.7	11.6
Manufacturing	23,900	7.2	9.9
Leisure and Hospitality	28,000	8.4	9.6
Financial Activities	24,500	7.4	5.9
Construction	n/a	n/a	5.3
Wholesale Trade	14,200	4.3	4.4
Other Services	16,500	5.0	3.9
Transportation and Utilities	22,800	6.8	3.7
Information	6,500	2.0	2.2
Natural Resources and Mining	n/a	n/a	0.5

Note: Figures cover non-farm employment as of December 2007 and are not seasonally adjusted; (1) Metropolitan Statistical Area - see Appendix B for areas included; n/a not available
Source: Bureau of Labor Statistics, http://stats.bls.gov

Average Wages

Occupation	$/Hr.	Occupation	$/Hr.
Accountants and Auditors	29.42	Maids and Housekeeping Cleaners	9.03
Automotive Mechanics	17.03	Maintenance and Repair Workers	16.76
Bookkeepers	15.55	Marketing Managers	43.78
Carpenters	19.13	Nuclear Medicine Technologists	n/a
Cashiers	8.35	Nurses, Licensed Practical	18.91
Clerks, General Office	13.47	Nurses, Registered	n/a
Clerks, Receptionists/Information	11.45	Nursing Aides/Orderlies/Attendants	12.08
Clerks, Shipping/Receiving	14.25	Packers and Packagers, Hand	9.31
Computer Programmers	33.41	Physical Therapists	38.30
Computer Support Specialists	19.07	Postal Service Mail Carriers	21.49
Computer Systems Analysts	33.02	Real Estate Brokers	42.99
Cooks, Restaurant	11.13	Retail Salespersons	11.12
Dentists	n/a	Sales Reps., Exc. Tech./Scientific	34.06
Electrical Engineers	34.15	Sales Reps., Tech./Scientific	31.84
Electricians	22.89	Secretaries, Exc. Legal/Med./Exec.	14.65
Financial Managers	42.17	Security Guards	11.38
First-Line Supervisors/Mgrs., Sales	19.09	Surgeons	87.58
Food Preparation Workers	8.94	Teacher Assistants	9.90
General and Operations Managers	43.52	Teachers, Elementary School	24.10
Hairdressers/Cosmetologists	9.47	Teachers, Secondary School	24.00
Internists	75.95	Telemarketers	n/a
Janitors and Cleaners	11.38	Truck Drivers, Heavy/Tractor-Trailer	21.05
Landscaping/Groundskeeping Workers	12.18	Truck Drivers, Light/Delivery Svcs.	14.08
Lawyers	48.22	Waiters and Waitresses	8.06

Note: Wage data covers the Harrisburg-Carlisle, PA Metropolitan Statistical Area - see Appendix B for areas included. Hourly wages for elementary/secondary school teachers and teacher assistants were calculated by the editors from annual wage data assuming a 40 hour work week; n/a not available.
Source: Bureau of Labor Statistics, May 2007 Metro Area Occupational Employment and Wage Estimates

RESIDENTIAL REAL ESTATE

Building Permits

Area	Single-Family 2006	Single-Family 2007p	Single-Family Pct. Chg.	Multi-Family 2006	Multi-Family 2007p	Multi-Family Pct. Chg.	Total 2006	Total 2007p	Total Pct. Chg.
City	188	240	27.7	5	0	-100.0	193	240	24.4
U.S.	1,378,200	973,300	-29.4	460,700	407,200	-11.6	1,838,900	1,380,500	-24.9

Note: (p) preliminary; figures cover and represent new, privately-owned housing units authorized (unadjusted data); All permit data are based on estimates with imputation; U.S. figures are based on the new 20,000-place series.
Source: U.S. Census Bureau, Manufacturing, Mining, and Construction Statistics

Homeownership and Housing Vacancies

Area	Homeownership Rate[2] (%)			Rental Vacancy Rate[3] (%)			Homeowner Vacancy Rate[4] (%)		
	2005	2006	2007	2005	2006	2007	2005	2006	2007
MSA[1]	n/a	n/a	n/a	n/a	n/a	n/a	n/a	n/a	n/a
U.S.	68.9	68.8	68.1	9.8	9.8	9.7	1.9	2.4	2.7

Note: (1) Metropolitan Statistical Area - see Appendix B for areas included; (2) The proportion of households that are owners; (3) The proportion of the rental inventory that is vacant for rent; (4) The proportion of the homeowner inventory that is vacant for sale; n/a not available
Source: U.S. Census Bureau, Housing Vacancies and Homeownership Annual Statistics: 2007

TAXES

State Corporate Income Tax Rates

State	Rates and Tax Brackets
Pennsylvania	9.99%

Note: Tax rates as of January 1, 2008; Imposes a capital stock and foreign franchise tax of 0.289% on taxable income over $125K. Bank and Trust Company Shares Tax is 1.25%.
Source: Tax Foundation, www.taxfoundation.org

State Individual Income Tax Rates

State	Federal Deductibility	Marginal Rates (%)	Standard Deduction ($)		Personal Exemptions ($)[1]	
			Single	Joint	Single	Dependents
Pennsylvania	No	3.07	n/a	n/a	n/a	n/a

Note: Tax rates as of January 1, 2008; Local- and county-level taxes are not included; n/a not applicable; (1) Married joint filers generally receive double the single exemption
Source: Tax Foundation, www.taxfoundation.org

Various State and Local Tax Rates

State and Local Sales and Use (%)	State Sales and Use (%)	Gasoline[1,2] ($/gal.)	Cigarette ($/pack)	Spirits ($/gal.)	Table Wine ($/gal.)	Beer ($/gal.)
6.0	6.0	0.323	1.35	6.59 (n)	(p)	0.08

Note: Tax rates as of January 1, 2008; (1) In addition to the 18.4 cpg Federal gasoline tax; (2) Rates may include additional state sales taxes, environmental protection and storage fees/taxes, and local taxes. When necessary, the volume-weighted average of all local taxes is used to approximate the typical statewide rate including local tax; (n) The state government controls all sales. The implied excise tax rate is calculated using methodology designed by the Distilled Spirits Council of the United States (DISCUS); (p) All wine sales are through state-run stores. Revenue in these states is generated from various taxes, fees and net profits.
Source: Tax Foundation, www.taxfoundation.org; Original research

State Tax Burdens

Area	Combined State and Local Tax Burden		Combined Federal, State and Local Tax Burden	
	Percent	Rank	Percent	Rank
Pennsylvania	10.8	24	31.9	20
U.S. Average	11.0	-	32.7	-

Note: Figures cover 2007 and measure taxes as a percentage of income
Source: Tax Foundation, www.taxfoundation.org

State Business Tax Climate Index Rankings

State	Overall Rank	Corporate Tax Index Rank	Individual Income Tax Index Rank	Sales Tax Index Rank	Unemployment Insurance Tax Index Rank	Property Tax Index Rank
Pennsylvania	27	42	11	26	25	47

Note: Rankings range from 1 to 50 where 1 is best. Rankings do not average across to Overall Rank. States without a given tax are given a ranking of 1.
Source: Tax Foundation, State Business Tax Climate Index 2008

TRANSPORTATION

Means of Transportation to Work

Area	Car/Truck/Van		Public Transportation			Bicycle	Walked	Other Means	Worked at Home
	Drove Alone	Car-pooled	Bus	Subway	Railroad				
City	88.1	6.8	0.2	0.0	0.0	0.2	1.4	0.3	3.0
MSA[1]	80.2	11.0	1.0	0.0	0.0	0.2	3.6	0.8	3.1
U.S.	75.7	12.2	2.5	1.5	0.5	0.4	2.9	1.0	3.3

Note: Figures are percentages and cover workers 16 years of age and older; (1) Metropolitan Statistical Area - see Appendix A for areas included
Source: Census 2000, Summary File 3

Travel Time to Work

Area	Less Than 15 Minutes	15 to 29 Minutes	30 to 44 Minutes	45 to 59 Minutes	60 Minutes or More
City	30.2	54.1	11.1	2.2	2.4
MSA[1]	32.7	41.3	15.7	5.9	4.4
U.S.	29.4	36.1	19.1	7.4	8.0

Note: Figures are percentages and include workers 16 years old and over; (1) Metropolitan Statistical Area - see Appendix A for areas included
Source: Census 2000, Summary File 3

Living Environment

COST OF LIVING

Cost of Living Index

Composite Index	Groceries	Housing	Utilities	Trans-portation	Health Care	Misc. Goods/ Services
n/a	n/a	n/a	n/a	n/a	n/a	n/a

Note: U.S. = 100; n/a not available
Source: The Council for Community and Economic Research (formerly ACCRA), Cost of Living Index, 2007

Grocery Prices

Area[1]	T-Bone Steak ($/pound)	Frying Chicken ($/pound)	Whole Milk ($/half gal.)	Eggs ($/dozen)	Orange Juice ($/64 oz.)	Coffee ($/11.5 oz.)
City[2]	n/a	n/a	n/a	n/a	n/a	n/a
Avg.	8.93	1.12	2.13	1.52	3.26	3.31
Min.	5.88	0.71	1.33	0.83	2.30	2.20
Max.	12.80	2.07	3.43	3.54	5.79	6.20

Note: (1) Values for the local area are compared with the average, minimum and maximum values for all 331 areas in the Cost of Living Index report; n/a not available; (2) Figures cover the Hampden PA urban area; **T-Bone Steak** *(price per pound);* **Frying Chicken** *(price per pound, whole fryer);* **Whole Milk** *(half gallon carton);* **Eggs** *(price per dozen, Grade A, large);* **Orange Juice** *(64 oz. Tropicana or Florida Natural);* **Coffee** *(11.5 oz. can, vacuum-packed, Maxwell House, Hills Bros, or Folgers).*
Source: The Council for Community and Economic Research (formerly ACCRA), Cost of Living Index, 2007

Housing and Utility Costs

Area[1]	New Home Price ($)	Apartment Rent ($/month)	All Electric ($/month)	Part Electric ($/month)	Other Energy ($/month)	Telephone ($/month)
City[2]	n/a	n/a	n/a	n/a	n/a	n/a
Avg.	309,605	782	146.13	78.67	90.16	26.14
Min.	189,877	n/a	82.03	37.41	33.15	17.08
Max.	1,202,800	3,481	271.14	150.60	257.67	37.45

Note: (1) Values for the local area are compared with the average, minimum and maximum values for all 331 areas in the Cost of Living Index report; n/a not available; (2) Figures cover the Hampden PA urban area; **New Home Price** *(2,400 sf living area, 8,000 sf lot, in urban area with full utilities);* **Apartment Rent** *(950 sf 2 bedroom/1.5 or 2 bath, unfurnished, excluding all utilities except water);* **All Electric** *(average monthly cost for an all-electric home);* **Part Electric** *(average monthly cost for a part-electric home);* **Other Energy** *(average monthly cost for natural gas, fuel oil, coal, wood, and any other forms of energy except electricity);* **Telephone** *(price includes basic monthly rate for a private residential line plus additional local usage charges incurred by a family of four).*
Source: The Council for Community and Economic Research (formerly ACCRA), Cost of Living Index, 2007

Health Care, Transportation, and Other Costs

Area[1]	Doctor ($/visit)	Dentist ($/visit)	Optometrist ($/visit)	Gasoline ($/gallon)	Beauty Salon ($/visit)	Men's Shirt ($)
City[2]	n/a	n/a	n/a	n/a	n/a	n/a
Avg.	79.48	71.93	79.55	2.64	29.52	25.77
Min.	52.08	44.80	43.95	2.19	15.58	16.19
Max.	148.44	126.27	158.83	3.48	60.62	48.53

Note: (1) Values for the local area are compared with the average, minimum and maximum values for all 331 areas in the Cost of Living Index report; n/a not available; (2) Figures cover the Hampden PA urban area; **Doctor** *(general practitioners routine exam of an established patient);* **Dentist** *(adult teeth cleaning and periodic oral examination);* **Optometrist** *(full vision eye exam for established adult patient);* **Gasoline** *(one gallon regular unleaded, national brand, including all taxes, cash price at self-service pump if available);* **Beauty Salon** *(woman's shampoo, trim, and blow-dry);* **Men's Shirt** *(cotton/polyester dress shirt, pinpoint weave, long sleeves).*
Source: The Council for Community and Economic Research (formerly ACCRA), Cost of Living Index, 2007

HOUSING

House Price Index (HPI)

Area	National Ranking[2]	Quarterly Change (%)	One-Year Change (%)	Five-Year Change (%)
MSA[1]	42	1.61	4.94	41.91
U.S.[3]	-	0.10	0.84	41.37

Note: The HPI is a weighted repeat sales index. It measures average price changes in repeat sales or refinancings on the same properties. This information is obtained by reviewing repeat mortgage transactions on single-family properties whose mortgages have been purchased or securitized by Fannie Mae or Freddie Mac in January 1975; (1) Metropolitan Statistical Area - see Appendix B for areas included; (2) Rankings are based on annual percentage change for all metro areas containing at least 15,000 transactions over the last 10 years and ranges from 1 to 291; (3) figures based on a weighted average of Census Division estimates; all figures are for the period ending December 31, 2007
Source: Office of Federal Housing Enterprise Oversight, House Price Index, February 26, 2008

House Price Valuations

Area	Q1 2000	Q1 2001	Q1 2002	Q1 2003	Q1 2004	Q1 2005	Q1 2006	Q1 2007	Q1 2008
MSA[1]	-5.0	-8.4	-8.9	-7.4	-3.8	-1.1	6.7	10.3	6.8

Note: Figures show the percentage of over- or under-valuation of single family homes relative to statistically normal house values (e.g. a value of 23.6 indicates that house values are 23.6% overvalued). Statistically normal house values are based on house prices, interest rates, household incomes, population densities, and any historical premiums or discounts metropolitan areas have exhibited over time; (1) Figures cover the Metropolitan Statistical Area - see Appendix B for areas included
Source: Global Insight/National City Corporation, House Prices in America, May 2008

Median Home Prices

Area	2005	2006	2007[r]	Percent Change 2006 to 2007
MSA[1]	n/a	n/a	n/a	n/a
U.S. Average	219.0	221.9	217.9	-1.8

Note: Figures are median sales prices of existing single-family homes in thousands of dollars; (r) revised; n/a not available; (1) Metropolitan Statistical Area - see Appendix B for areas included
Source: National Association of Realtors, Metropolitan Area Prices, 1st Quarter 2008

Housing: Year Structure Built

Area	1990 -2000	1980 -1989	1970 -1979	1960 -1969	1950 -1959	1940 -1949	Before 1940	Median Year
City	26.8	19.0	24.3	14.1	11.2	2.5	2.0	1978
MSA[1]	13.8	13.0	16.6	11.9	13.5	8.1	23.1	1965
U.S.	17.0	15.8	18.5	13.7	12.7	7.3	15.0	1971

Note: Figures are percentages; (1) Metropolitan Statistical Area - see Appendix A for areas included
Source: Census 2000, Summary File 3

HEALTH

Health Risk Data

Category	Area[1] (%)	U.S. (%)
Adults who have been told they have high blood pressure[3]	n/a	25.5
Adults who have been told they have high blood cholesterol[3]	n/a	35.6
Adults who have been told they have diabetes[2]	n/a	7.5
Adults who have been told they have arthritis[3]	n/a	27.0
Adults who have been told they currently have asthma	n/a	8.5
Adults who are current smokers	n/a	20.1
Adults who are heavy drinkers[4]	n/a	4.9
Adults who are overweight (BMI 25.0 - 29.9)	n/a	36.5
Adults who are obese (BMI 30.0 - 99.8)	n/a	25.1

Note: Data as of 2006 unless otherwise noted; n/a not available; (1) Figures cover the Metropolitan Statistical Area - see Appendix B for areas included; (2) Figures do not include pregnancy-related diabetes, pre-diabetes or borderline diabetes; (3) 2005 data; (4) Heavy drinkers are classified as adult men having more than two drinks per day or adult women having more than one drink per day
Source: Centers for Disease Control and Prevention, Behaviorial Risk Factor Surveillance System, SMART: Selected Metropolitan/Micropolitan Area Risk Trends, 2005, 2006

Mortality Rates for the Top 10 Causes of Death in the U.S.

ICD-10[a] Sub-Chapter	ICD-10[a] Code	Age-Adjusted Mortality Rate[1] per 100,000 population	
		County[2]	U.S.
Malignant neoplasms	C00-C97	164.1	186.5
Ischaemic heart diseases	I20-I25	146.5	152.3
Other forms of heart disease	I30-I51	57.5	51.5
Cerebrovascular diseases	I60-I69	50.3	50.0
Chronic lower respiratory diseases	J40-J47	44.9	42.6
Diabetes mellitus	E10-E14	14.4	24.8
Other degenerative diseases of the nervous system	G30-G31	18.6	22.6
Other external causes of accidental injury	W00-X59	15.9	21.4
Influenza and pneumonia	J10-J18	20.5	20.7
Hypertensive diseases	I10-I13	10.9	18.2

Note: (a) ICD-10 = International Classification of Diseases 10th Revision; (1) Mortality rates are a three year average covering 2003-2005; (2) Figures cover Cumberland County
Source: Centers for Disease Control and Prevention, National Center for Health Statistics. Compressed Mortality File 1999-2004. CDC WONDER On-line Database, compiled from Compressed Mortality File 1999-2005 Series 20 No. 2K, 2008.

Mortality Rates for Selected Causes of Death

ICD-10[a] Sub-Chapter	ICD-10[a] Code	Age-Adjusted Mortality Rate[1] per 100,000 population	
		County[2]	U.S.
Assault	X85-Y09	*1.0	5.9
Human immunodeficiency virus (HIV) disease	B20-B24	*1.8	4.5
Intentional self-harm	X60-X84	9.2	10.8
Malnutrition	E40-E46	*0.3	1.0
Obesity and other hyperalimentation	E65-E68	*0.8	1.4
Organic, including symptomatic, mental disorders	F01-F09	13.8	16.8
Transport accidents	V01-V99	13.0	16.1
Viral hepatitis	B15-B19	*0.9	1.8

Note: (a) ICD-10 = International Classification of Diseases 10th Revision; (1) Mortality rates are a three year average covering 2003-2005; (2) Figures cover Cumberland County; (*) Unreliable data as per CDC
Source: Centers for Disease Control and Prevention, National Center for Health Statistics. Compressed Mortality File 1999-2004. CDC WONDER On-line Database, compiled from Compressed Mortality File 1999-2005 Series 20 No. 2K, 2008.

Distribution of Physicians[1]

Area	Total	Family/ General Practice	Specialties	
			Medical	Surgical
Cumberland County (number)	455	125	147	126
Cumberland County (rate per 10,000 pop.)	20.4	5.6	6.6	5.6
U.S. (rate per 10,000 pop.)	17.7	4.6	6.9	4.3

Note: Data as of 2005; (1) Includes all non-federal, patient-care, office-based MDs
Source: Area Resource File (ARF). June 2007. U.S. Department of Health and Human Services, Health Resources and Services Administration, Bureau of Health Professions, Rockville, MD.

Hospitals

There were no hospitals listed within the city limits.
AHA Guide to the Healthcare Field 2008

According to *U.S. News,* the Harrisburg-Carlisle, PA metro area is home to one of the best hospitals in the U.S.: **Pinnacle Health System**. *U.S. News Online, "America's Best Hospitals 2007"*

EDUCATION

Public School District Statistics

District Name	Schls	Pupils	Pupil/ Teacher Ratio	Minority Pupils[1] (%)	Free Lunch Eligible[2] (%)	IEP[3] (%)
Cumberland Valley SD	10	7,772	15.7	9.9	5.0	13.0

Note: Table includes regular local school districts with 2,000 or more students; (1) Percentage of students that are not white, non-Hispanic; (2) Percentage of students that are eligible for the free lunch program; (3) Percentage of students that have an Individualized Education Program.
Source: U.S. Department of Education, National Center for Education Statistics, Common Core of Data, Local Education Agency (School District) Universe Survey: School Year 2005-2006; U.S. Department of Education, National Center for Education Statistics, Common Core of Data, Public Elementary/Secondary School Universe Survey: School Year 2005-2006

Highest Level of Education

Area	Less than H.S.	H.S. Diploma	Some College, No Deg.	Associate Degree	Bachelors Degree	Masters Degree	Profess. School Degree	Doctorate Degree
City	6.8	26.6	17.6	6.8	27.2	9.9	3.9	1.2
MSA[1]	15.6	37.6	16.0	6.2	15.7	5.8	2.4	0.7
U.S.	19.4	28.4	21.2	6.4	15.7	5.9	2.0	1.0

Note: Figures are 2007 estimated percentages and cover persons age 25 and over; (1) Metropolitan Statistical Area - see Appendix B for areas included
Source: Claritas, Inc.

Educational Attainment by Race

Area	High School Graduate (%)					Bachelor's Degree (%)				
	Total	White	Black	Asian	Hisp.[2]	Total	White	Black	Asian	Hisp.[2]
City	93.1	93.7	87.9	80.3	82.5	41.7	41.7	21.0	50.5	22.7
MSA[1]	83.1	84.1	75.2	77.3	60.5	22.6	23.2	12.8	41.7	8.8
U.S.	80.4	83.6	72.3	80.4	52.4	24.4	26.1	14.3	44.1	10.4

Note: Figures shown cover persons 25 years old and over; (1) Metropolitan Statistical Area - see Appendix A for areas included; (2) people of Hispanic origin can be of any race
Source: Census 2000, Summary File 3

School Enrollment by Type

Area	Grades KG to 8				Grades 9 to 12			
	Public		Private		Public		Private	
	Enrollment	%	Enrollment	%	Enrollment	%	Enrollment	%
City	2,644	84.9	471	15.1	1,299	82.7	272	17.3
MSA[1]	68,133	87.0	10,192	13.0	29,993	89.6	3,475	10.4
U.S.	33,526,011	88.7	4,285,121	11.3	14,848,628	90.6	1,532,323	9.4

Note: Figures shown cover persons 3 years old and over; (1) Metropolitan Statistical Area - see Appendix A for areas included
Source: Census 2000, Summary File 3

School Enrollment by Race

Area	Grades KG to 8 (%)				Grades 9 to 12 (%)			
	White	Black	Asian	Hisp.[1]	White	Black	Asian	Hisp.[1]
City	92.9	1.0	3.7	1.5	88.6	3.8	6.1	0.4
MSA[2]	81.8	10.8	1.7	5.2	83.7	9.6	2.3	4.5
U.S.	68.5	15.5	3.3	16.8	68.8	15.5	3.8	15.7

Note: Figures shown cover persons 3 years old and over; (1) people of Hispanic origin can be of any race; (2) Metropolitan Statistical Area - see Appendix A for areas included
Source: Census 2000, Summary File 3

Average Salaries of Public School Classroom Teachers

District	2005-06		2006-07		Percent Change 2005-06 to 2006-07
	Dollars	Rank[1]	Dollars	Rank[1]	
Pennsylvania	54,027	12	54,970	10	1.75
U.S. Average	49,026	-	50,816	-	3.65

Note: (1) State rank ranges from 1 to 51.
Source: National Education Association, Rankings & Estimates: Rankings of the States 2006 and Estimates of School Statistics 2007, December 2007

Higher Education

Four-Year Colleges			Two-Year Colleges			Medical Schools[1]	Law Schools[2]	Voc/ Tech[3]
Public	Private Non-profit	Private For-profit	Public	Private Non-profit	Private For-profit			
0	0	0	0	0	0	0	0	0

Note: Figures cover institutions located within the city limits; (1) includes schools accredited by the Liaison Committee on Medical Education and the American Osteopathic Association; (2) includes American Bar Association-accredited law schools; (3) includes all schools with programs that are less than 2 years.
Source: National Center for Education Statistics, The Integrated Postsecondary Education System (IPEDS) Peer Analysis System, 2007; www.usnews.com, Law and Medical School Directories, 2009

PRESIDENTIAL ELECTION

2004 Presidential Election Results

Area	Bush	Kerry	Nader	Other
Cumberland County	63.8	35.8	0.0	0.5
U.S.	50.7	48.3	0.4	0.6

Note: Results are percentages and may not add to 100% due to rounding
Source: Dave Leip's Atlas of U.S. Presidential Elections, www.uselectionatlas.org

EMPLOYERS

Major Employers

Company Name	Industry	Type of Site
Capital Blue Cross	Accident and health insurance	Headquarters
Chief of Staff	National security	Branch
County of Dauphin	Executive offices	Headquarters
Ddre	General warehousing and storage	Branch
Diakon Lutheran Social Miniatr	Individual and family services	Branch
Harrisburg Hospital	General medical and surgical hospitals	Branch
Hersey Milton S Medical Ctr	Offices and clinics of medical doctors	Branch
Hershey Lodge & Convention Ctr	Amusement parks	Head
Hershey Medical Center	Colleges and universities	Branch
Higher Edcatn Asstnce Agcy PA	General credit unions	Headquarters
House Representatives PA	Legislative bodies	Headquarters
Legislative Off Comm of PA	Legislative bodies	Headquarters
Medical Center of Harrisburg	General medical and surgical hospitals	Branch
Naval Inventory Control Point	National security,	
PA Dept Public Welfare	Administration of social and manpower programs,	
PA Dept Transportation	Regulation, administration of transportation	Headquarters
US Post Office	U.s. postal service	Branch
VA Medical Center	General medical and surgical hospitals	Single

Note: Companies shown are located within the Harrisburg metropolitan area; nec = not elsewhere classified.
Source: www.zapdata.com, May 2008

PUBLIC SAFETY

Crime Rate

Area	All Crimes	Violent Crimes				Property Crimes		
		Murder	Forcible Rape	Robbery	Aggrav. Assault	Burglary	Larceny -Theft	Motor Vehicle Theft
City	1,392.9	0.0	11.9	11.9	7.9	119.0	1,206.3	35.7
Metro[1]	2,604.3	2.9	31.4	115.4	156.8	411.8	1,771.7	114.4
U.S.	3,977.3	5.5	32.4	136.7	288.6	730.3	2,362.3	421.5

Note: Figures are crimes per 100,000 population; (1) Metropolitan Statistical Area - see Appendix B for areas included
Source: FBI Uniform Crime Reports, 2004

Hate Crimes

Area	Number of Quarters Reported	Bias Motivation				
		Race	Religion	Sexual Orientation	Ethnicity	Disability
City	4	0	0	0	0	0

Source: Federal Bureau of Investigation, Hate Crime Statistics 2006

RECREATION

Culture

Dance[1]	Theatre[1]	Instrumental Music[1]	Vocal Music[1]	Series/ Festivals	Museums	Zoos and Aquariums[2]
0	0	0	0	0	0	0

Note: (1) Number of professional perfoming groups; (2) AZA-accredited
Source: The Grey House Performing Arts Directory, 2007; Official Museum Directory, 2008; Association of Zoos & Aquariums, AZA Member Zoos & Aquariums, June 2008

Professional Sports Teams

Team Name	League
No teams are located in the metro area	

Source: Original research

MEDIA

Newspapers

Name	News Focus	Frequency	Circulation
No newspapers have an office in the city			

Note: Includes newspapers with offices located in the city
Source: MediaContactsPro, March 2008

Television Stations

Name	Ch.	Network(s)	Type	Ownership
WGAL	8	NBC	Commercial	Hearst-Argyle Broadcasting
WLYH	15	UPN	Commercial	Clear Channel Communications Inc.
WHP	21	CBS	Commercial	Clear Channel Communications Inc.
WHTM	27	ABC	Commercial	Allbritton Communications Company
WITF	33	PBS	Public	WITF Inc.
WPMT	43	Fox	Commercial	Tribune Broadcasting Company
WGCB	49	n/a	Commercial	John H. Norris

Note: Stations included cover the Harrisburg-Lancaster-Lebanon-York DMA (Designated Market Area); n/a not available
BurrellesLuce, MediaContacts Online, January 2007

Major AM Radio Stations

Call Letters	Freq. (kHz)	Station Type	Target Audience	Station Format	Music Format
WHP	580	Commercial	General	News/Talk	n/a
WIEZ	670	Commercial	General	Music/News/Talk	Oldies
WWII	720	Commercial	General/Hisp/Rel	Music/News	Christian
WSBA	910	Commercial	General	News/Talk	n/a
WKVA	920	Commercial	General	Music	Oldies
WADV	940	Commercial	Religious	Music/Talk	Gospel
WHYL	960	Commercial	General	Music/News/Talk	Oldies
WIOO	1000	Commercial	General	Music	Country
WJUN	1220	Commercial	General/Religious	News/Sports	n/a
WKBO	1230	Commercial	General/Religious	Music	Christian
WIOV	1240	Commercial	General/Hispanic	News/Talk	n/a
WLBR	1270	Commercial	General	Music/News/Sports/Talk	Adult Contemp.
WHVR	1280	Commercial	General	Music/Talk	Country
WGET	1320	Commercial	General	Music/News	Oldies
WOYK	1350	Commercial	Men	Music/Sports/Talk	Soft Rock
WLAN	1390	Commercial	General	Sports/Talk	Adult Standards
WTCY	1400	Commercial	Black/General	Music/News	Urban Contemp.
WTHM	1440	Non-Comm	General/Religious	Educational/Talk	n/a
WTKT	1460	n/a	General	Music/Sports/Talk	Classic Rock
WLPA	1490	n/a	General	News	n/a
WWSM	1510	Commercial	General	Educational/Music/News	Gospel
WPDC	1600	Commercial	Hispanic	Music/Talk	Latin

Note: Stations included cover the Harrisburg-Lancaster-Lebanon-York DMA (Designated Market Area); n/a not available
Source: BurrellesLuce, MediaContacts Online, January 2007

Major FM Radio Stations

Call Letters	Freq. (mHz)	Station Type	Target Audience	Station Format	Music Format
WITF	89.5	Public	General	Music/News	Classical
WJTL	90.3	Public	General/Religious	Music/News	Christian
WJUN	92.5	Commercial	General	Music/News	Country
WTPA	93.5	n/a	General	Music/News/Sports	n/a
WDAC	94.5	Commercial	General/Religious	Music/Talk	Christian
WRBT	94.9	Commercial	General	Music	Country
WMRF	95.9	Commercial	General	Music/News	Adult Contemp.
WSOX	96.1	n/a	General	Music/News	n/a
WLAN	96.9	Commercial	General	Music/News/Talk	Album Rock
WRVV	97.3	Commercial	General	Music	Modern Rock
WYCR	98.5	Commercial	General	Music/News	Top 40
WQLV	98.9	Commercial	General	Music/News	Soft Rock
WHKF	99.3	Commercial	General	Music/News/Talk	Urban Contemp.
WROZ	101.3	Commercial	General/Women	Music/News	Urban Contemp.
WARM	103.3	n/a	General	News	n/a
WLAK	103.5	Commercial	General	Music/News	Adult Contemp.
WNNK	104.1	Commercial	General	n/a	n/a
WIOV	105.1	Commercial	General	Music	Country
WQXA	105.7	Commercial	General	Music	Modern Rock
WCAT	106.7	Commercial	General	Music/News	Country
WGTY	107.7	Commercial	General	Music/News	Contemp. Country

Note: Stations included cover the Harrisburg-Lancaster-Lebanon-York DMA (Designated Market Area); n/a not available
BurrellesLuce, MediaContacts Online, January 2007

CLIMATE

Average and Extreme Temperatures

Temperature	Jan	Feb	Mar	Apr	May	Jun	Jul	Aug	Sep	Oct	Nov	Dec	Yr.
Extreme High (°F)	73	75	84	93	95	100	107	100	102	90	84	75	107
Average High (°F)	37	40	50	62	73	81	86	84	76	65	53	41	62
Average Temp. (°F)	30	32	41	52	62	71	76	74	67	55	44	34	53
Average Low (°F)	23	24	32	42	51	61	66	64	56	45	36	26	44
Extreme Low (°F)	-9	-5	5	19	31	40	50	45	30	23	13	-8	-9

Note: Figures cover the years 1948-1991
Source: National Climatic Data Center, International Station Meteorological Climate Summary, 9/96

Average Precipitation/Snowfall/Humidity

Precip./Humidity	Jan	Feb	Mar	Apr	May	Jun	Jul	Aug	Sep	Oct	Nov	Dec	Yr.
Avg. Precip. (in.)	2.8	2.8	3.3	3.2	4.1	3.5	3.5	3.3	3.2	2.8	3.3	3.2	39.0
Avg. Snowfall (in.)	9	10	6	1	Tr	0	0	0	0	Tr	2	7	35
Avg. Rel. Hum. 7am (%)	71	71	70	71	75	77	79	83	85	82	77	72	76
Avg. Rel. Hum. 4pm (%)	56	53	49	47	51	51	52	54	55	53	56	58	53

Note: Figures cover the years 1948-1991; Tr = Trace amounts (<0.05 in. of rain; <0.5 in. of snow)
Source: National Climatic Data Center, International Station Meteorological Climate Summary, 9/96

Weather Conditions

Temperature			Daytime Sky			Precipitation		
5°F & below	32°F & below	90°F & above	Clear	Partly cloudy	Cloudy	0.01 inch or more precip.	0.1 inch or more snow/ice	Thunder-storms
3	106	22	83	134	148	124	20	31

Note: Figures are average number of days per year and cover the years 1948-1991
Source: National Climatic Data Center, International Station Meteorological Climate Summary, 9/96

HAZARDOUS WASTE

Superfund Sites

Hampden has no sites on the EPA's Superfund Final National Priorities List.
U.S. Environmental Protection Agency, Final National Priorities List, June 23, 2008

AIR & WATER QUALITY

Air Quality Index

Area	Percent of Days when Air Quality was...[2]				AQI Statistics	
	Good	Moderate	Unhealthy for Sensitive Groups	Unhealthy	Maximum	Median
MSA[1]	57.3	37.5	5.2	0.0	127	46

Note: The Air Quality Index (AQI) is an index for reporting daily air quality. EPA calculates the AQI for five major air pollutants regulated by the Clean Air Act: ground-level ozone, particle pollution (also known as particulate matter), carbon monoxide, sulfur dioxide, and nitrogen dioxide. The AQI runs from 0 to 500. The higher the AQI value, the greater the level of air pollution and the greater the health concern. There are six AQI categories: "Good" The AQI is between 0 and 50. Air quality is considered satisfactory; "Moderate" The AQI is between 51 and 100. Air quality is acceptable; "Unhealthy for Sensitive Groups" When AQI values are between 101 and 150, members of sensitive groups may experience health effects; "Unhealthy" When AQI values are between 151 and 200 everyone may begin to experience health effects; "Very Unhealthy" AQI values between 201 and 300 trigger a health alert; "Hazardous" AQI values over 300 trigger health warnings of emergency conditions; (1) Metropolitan Statistical Area - see Appendix A for areas included; (2) Based on 365 days with AQI data in 2007.
Source: U.S. Environmental Protection Agency, Air Quality Index Report, 2007

Air Quality Index Pollutants

Area	Percent of Days when AQI Pollutant was...[2]					
	Carbon Monoxide	Nitrogen Dioxide	Ozone	Sulfur Dioxide	Particulate Matter 2.5	Particulate Matter 10
MSA[1]	0.0	0.0	37.5	0.5	59.5	2.5

Note: The Air Quality Index (AQI) is an index for reporting daily air quality. EPA calculates the AQI for five major air pollutants regulated by the Clean Air Act: ground-level ozone, particle pollution (also known as particulate matter), carbon monoxide, sulfur dioxide, and nitrogen dioxide. The AQI runs from 0 to 500. The higher the AQI value, the greater the level of air pollution and the greater the health concern; (1) Metropolitan Statistical Area - see Appendix A for areas included; (2) Based on 365 days with AQI data in 2007.
Source: U.S. Environmental Protection Agency, Air Quality Index Report, 2007

Air Quality Index Trends

Area	Trend Sites (9)								All Sites (16)
	1999	2000	2001	2002	2003	2004	2005	2006	2006
MSA[1]	19	16	22	20	9	5	11	7	7

Note: An AQI value greater than 100 indicates that air quality would have been in the unhealthful range on that day. Data from exceptional events are not included. These counts are presented in two ways. First, the counts are based on sites having an adequate record of monitoring data during the trend period (trend sites). These counts represent the relative change in the number of days with AQI values greater than 100. In the last column, the counts are based on all sites with data in the most recent year (because it is possible for a site to have data in the most recent year but not enough data to be a trend site); (1) Metropolitan Statistical Area - see Appendix A for areas included.
Source: U.S. Environmental Protection Agency, Office of Air and Radiation, Air Trends, Factbook and Related Information, Air Pollution Trends in Selected Metropolitan Areas 2006

Maximum Air Pollutant Concentrations

	Particulate Matter 10 (ug/m^3)	Particulate Matter 2.5 (ug/m^3)	Ozone (ppm)	Carbon Monoxide (ppm)	Sulfur Dioxide (ppm)	Nitrogen Dioxide (ppm)	Lead (ug/m^3)
MSA[1] Level	53	37	0.096	1	0.014	0.013	n/a
NAAQS[2]	150	35	0.125	9	0.140	0.053	1.50
Met NAAQS[2]	Yes	No	Yes	Yes	Yes	Yes	n/a

Note: Data from exceptional events are not included; (1) Metropolitan Statistical Area - see Appendix A for areas included; (2) National Ambient Air Quality Standards; n/a not available
Concentrations: Particulate Matter 10 (coarse particulate) - highest second maximum 24-hour concentration; Particulate Matter 2.5 (fine particulate) - highest 98th percentile 24-hour concentration; Ozone - highest second daily maximum 1-hour concentration; Carbon Monoxide - highest second maximum non-overlapping 8-hour concentration; Sulfur Dioxide - highest second maximum 24-hour concentration; Nitrogen Dioxide - highest arithmetic mean concentration; Lead - highest quarterly maximum concentration
Units: ppm = parts per million; ug/m^3 = micrograms per cubic meter
Source: U.S. Environmental Protection Agency, MSA Factbook 2006, Air Quality Statistics by City

Drinking Water

Water System Name	Pop. Served	Primary Water Source Type	Violations[1]	
			Health Based	Monitoring/ Reporting
United Water Mechanicsburg	25,850	Surface	0	0

Note: (1) Based on violation data from January 1, 2007 to December 31, 2007 (includes unresolved violations from earlier years)
Source: U.S. Environmental Protection Agency, Office of Ground Water and Drinking Water, Safe Drinking Water Information System (based on data extracted April 15, 2008)

Lower Providence, Pennsylvania

Background

Lower Providence, a township of approximately 15 square miles, is located in Montgomery County just seventeen miles outside of Philadelphia. Lower Providence includes Audubon, Eagleville, Evansburg, and Trooper villages. Lower Providence has grown significantly (an estimated 14 percent) since the 2000 Census.

In 1805 Greater Providence split, forming Lower Providence, where agriculture dominated the economy. In the last century, the economy has transitioned away from agriculture to commercial businesses and industry. Valley Forge Industrial Park and Corporate Center, one of Montgomery County's largest industrial parks, is located in Lower Providence.

This progressive township has made an effort to be environmentally conscious adopting new initiatives to "go green" including the use of solar power, storm water basin retrofits, recycling, efficient lighting, the purchase of earth friendly products, and the use of hybrid vehicles in the municipal fleet.

Within its limits, Lower Providence offers residents and visitors many attractions replete with historical significance, including the homestead of Henry Muhlenberg (considered the founder of the Lutheran faith), Washington Memorial Chapel, Peter Wentz Farmstead (celebrated example of German heritage and General George Washington's headquarters in 1777), and one of the country's oldest bridges. Another popular attraction is the wildlife refuge and museum in Mill Grove, which was also home to environmentalist John James Audubon.

Lower Providence's proximity to Philadelphia makes a wide range of activities easily accessible, including shopping at Reading Terminal Market (America's oldest farmers' market), visiting Independence Hall or the Philadelphia Museum of Art, and attending a Philadelphia Eagles football game. Known for the "Philly cheesesteak" sandwich, Philadelphia offers a variety of dining choices all within minutes of Lower Providence.

There are 12 parks that provide residents of Lower Providence many choices for outdoor recreation. The annual Easter Egg Hunt, Fourth of July celebration, Fall Festival, and Turkey "Fowl" Shooting Contest all have large turnouts. Valley Forge National Historical Park offers biking, hiking, and fishing, and Once Upon a Nation Storytelling Benches. Evansburg State Park combines historic 18th and 19th century buildings with baseball fields, mountain biking trails, and a premier golf course.

During the summer months, Lower Providence Parks and Recreation Department sponsors a recreational day camp for children, as well as exercise programs, guitar lessons, and a drama camp for all ages. The city also supports a Summer Concert Series at Eagleville Park Amphitheatre. Shopping options nearby includes King of Prussia Mall, the largest on the East Coast, plus a large variety of upscale shopping centers.

Serving Lower Providence is the Methacton School District, which boasts a lower than average student/teacher ratio and a high percentage of students performing higher than average in both mathematics and reading.

Mercy Suburban Hospital, on of two hospitals that serve Lower Providence, recently received two prestigious accreditations-one for their Cancer Program and one for its Radiology Department.

Rankings

General Rankings

- Philadelphia* was ranked #153 out of 375 metro areas in *Cities Ranked & Rated*. Criteria: cost of living; climate; crime; transportation; economy and jobs; education; arts and culture; health and healthcare; leisure; quality of life. *Cities Ranked & Rated, 2nd Edition, 2007*
- Philadelphia* was ranked #5 out of 379 metro areas in *Places Rated Almanac*. Criteria: health care; education; recreation; transportation; ambience; climate; crime; housing costs; jobs. *Places Rated Almanac, 7th Edition, 2007*

Business/Finance Rankings

- The nation's 100 largest metro areas were analysed in terms of the percentage of households entering some stage of foreclosure in 2007. The Philadelphia* metro area ranked #79 out of 100 (#1 = highest foreclosure rate). *RealtyTrac, "Year-End 2007 Metropolitan Foreclosure Report"*
- The Philadelphia* metro area was selected one of America's "Top 50 Business Opportunity Metros" by *Expansion Management* in their 5th annual Mayor's Challenge ranking of metro areas that have achieved solid ratings across the board in numerous *EM* studies during the past 12 months. The area ranked #28. Criteria: public schools; quality of life; college educated workers; logistics infrastructure; healthcare costs; taxes and government spending; reputation among site consultants. *Expansion Management, August 2007*
- The Philadelphia* metro area was selected as one of "America's Most Wired Cities" by *Forbes*. The metro area was ranked #26 out of 30. Criteria: percentage of Internet users with high-speed access; the range of service providers within a city; availability of public wireless hot spots. *Forbes, "America's Most Wired Cities," January 10, 2008*
- Philadelphia* was selected as one of the best places to start and grow a company by *Entrepreneur* and the National Policy Research Council. The Philadelphia* metro area ranked #45 out of 50 large metro areas. Criteria: business formation and growth (firms started four to 14 years ago that still employ at least 5 people and experienced rapid growth over the last four years). *Entrepreneur/National Policy Research Council, "Hot Cities for Entrepreneurs," September 2006*
- The Philadelphia* metro area was selected as one of "America's 50 Hottest Cities" for business relocations and expansions. Criteria: industry's most prominent site selection consultants were asked to list their top city choices for relocating and expanding manufacturing companies, taking into consideration such factors as the business climate, work force quality, operating costs, incentive programs, and the ease of working with local political and economic development officials. *Expansion Management, January-February 2007*
- Intel, in partnership with Sperling's BestPlaces, ranked the 80 "Best Cities for Teleworking" in America. The Philadelphia* metro area ranked #7 among extra large metro areas. The study identifies cities that hold the greatest potential for teleworking based on a host of factors including typical commuting times, fuel prices, availability of broadband Internet access and percentage of the population in telework friendly jobs. The study also factored in extreme climate and natural hazards. *Intel, "Best Cities for Teleworking," March 30, 2006*
- The Philadelphia* metro area appeared on the Milken Institute "2007 Best Performing Cities" index. Rank: #142 out of 200 large metro areas. Criteria: job growth; wage and salary growth; high-tech output growth. *Milken Institute, "2007 Best Performing Cities"*
- The Philadelphia* metro area was selected as one of "The Top 20 Boom Towns in America." *Business 2.0* magazine and econometric research firm Global Insight compared 319 metropolitan areas in the U.S. and ranked the 61 with populations over 1 million. Criteria: a weighted formula that includes forecast growth rates in sectors that contain the economy's 10 most skilled occupational clusters; the prevalence of college degrees in the local workforce; median salary. The area ranked #20 among large metro areas. *Business 2.0 Magazine, March 2004*

- Philadelphia* was identified as one of the 100 "Most Unwired Cities" in the U.S. The area ranked #50 out of the 100 largest metro areas in the U.S. Criteria: number of public and commercial wireless access points (hotspots); airports with wireless Internet access; broadband availability; local wireless networks; and wireless email devices. *Intel, "Most Unwired Cities Survey," June 7, 2005*

- Philadelphia* was ranked #17 out of 125 regions worldwide in terms of its "Knowledge Competitiveness Index." The index attempts to measure the knowledge-based development taking place throughout the world and is based on 19 measures of economic performance that indicate a region's ability to translate its knowledge capacity into economic value. *Robert Huggins Associates, World Knowledge Competitiveness Index 2005*

- *Forbes* ranked the 200 most populous metro areas in the U.S. in terms of the "Best Places for Business and Careers." The Philadelphia* metro area was ranked #132. Criteria: business costs (labor, energy, tax and office space expenses); living costs (housing, transportation, food and other household expenditures); education levels of the work force; job growth; income growth; migration trends; crime rates; and culture/leisure. *Forbes, "Best Places for Business and Careers," March 19, 2008*

- *Fortune* ranked the 100 largest metro areas in the U.S. in terms of projected median home price change in 2007. The Philadelphia* metro area ranked #61. *Fortune.com, "Hot Spots, Cold Spots"*

Health/Environment Rankings

- The Philadelphia* metro area was identified as one of "America's 20 Most Sedentary Cities" by *Forbes*. The metro area ranked #20. Criteria: percentage of overweight or obese people; percentage of people who had not engaged in any physical activity in the past 30 days; average number of hours of TV watched per week. *Forbes.com, "America's Most Sedentary Cities," October 29, 2007*

- 100 of the largest metro areas in the U.S. were analyzed in terms of their current drought severity. The Philadelphia* metro area ranked #57 (#1 = driest). The rankings were based on statistics such as long-term precipitation trends and patterns and the Palmer drought indices. *Sperling's BestPlaces, www.BestPlaces.net, "America's Drought-Riskiest Cities," November 2007*

- Doctors at the Harvard School of Public Health ranked 40 metropolitan areas based on data from the government-sponsored Hospital Quality Alliance program. The program tracks the performance of individual hospitals in treating patients for three common health problems: heart attacks, congestive heart failure, and pneumonia. The Philadelphia* metro area ranked #11 in quality of care for heart attacks, #20 for congestive heart failure, and #35 for pneumonia. *New England Journal of Medicine, July 21, 2005*

- *Reader's Digest* ranked the 50 largest metro areas in the U.S. in terms of how "clean" they are. The Philadelphia* metro area ranked #44. Criteria: air quality; water quality; toxic industrial pollution; Superfund sites; and sanitation. *Reader's Digest, "The 50 Cleanest (and Dirtiest) Cities in America," July 2005*

- The American Academy of Dermatology ranked 32 U.S. metropolitan regions in terms of their residents knowledge, attitude and behaviors towards tanning and sun protection. The Philadelphia* metro area ranked #9. The results of the study are based on an online national survey of 3,342 respondents. *American Academy of Dermatology, "RAYS: Your Grade," May 7, 2007*

- The Philadelphia* metro area appeared in *Country Home's* "2008 Best Green Places" report. The area ranked #87 out of 379. Criteria: official energy policies; green power; green buildings; availability of fresh, locally grown food. *Country Home, "2008 Best Green Places"*

- Wyeth Consumer Healthcare, in partnership with Sperling's BestPlaces, ranked the nation's 50 most populous metro areas in terms of five key health factors. The Philadelphia* metro area ranked #24. Criteria: physical activity; health status; nutrition; lifestyle pursuits; and mental wellness. *Wyeth Consumer Healthcare, "Centrum Healthiest Cities Study," April 19, 2005*

- HealthGrades surveyed over 41,000 individuals on doctor satisfaction and ranked the 20 largest metro areas based on the highest "definitely yes" responses to the question "Do you trust the physician to make decisions/recommendations that are in your best interest?" The Philadelphia* metro area ranked #5. *HealthGrades.com, "Top Cities in Doctor-Trust," September 7, 2006*

- Philadelphia* was identified as a "2008 Asthma Capital." The area ranked #12 out of the nation's 100 largest metropolitan areas. Twelve factors were used to identify the most challenging places to live for people with asthma: estimated prevalence; self-reported prevalence; crude death rate for asthma; annual pollen score; annual air quality; public smoking laws; number of board-certified asthma specialists; school inhaler access laws; rescue medication use; controller medication use; uninsured rate; poverty rate. *Asthma and Allergy Foundation of America, "2008 Asthma Capitals"*

- Philadelphia* was identified as a "Spring Allergy Capital." The area ranked #33 out of 100. Three groups of factors were used to identify the most severe cities for people with allergies during the spring season: annual pollen levels; medicine utilization; access to board-certified allergists. *Asthma and Allergy Foundation of America, "2007 Spring Allergy Capital Rankings"*

- Philadelphia* was identified as a "Fall Allergy Capital." The area ranked #58 out of 100. Three groups of factors were used to identify the most severe cities for people with allergies during the fall season: annual pollen levels; medicine utilization; access to board-certified allergists. *Asthma and Allergy Foundation of America, "2007 Fall Allergy Capital Rankings"*

- Ortho-McNeil Neurologics, in partnership with Sperling's BestPlaces, analyzed 110 metro areas and identified those U.S. cities with the highest prevalence of factors that are most commonly associated with migraine headaches. The Philadelphia* metro area ranked #88. Criteria: number of migraine-related drug prescriptions per capita; lifestyle factors that can contribute to migraines; environmental factors that can trigger migraines; and consumption of migraine-triggering foods. *Ortho-McNeil Neurologics, "America's Migraine Hot Spots," March 14, 2006*

- Sperling's BestPlaces ranked 331 metro areas and identified the most and least stressful U.S. cities. The Philadelphia* metro area ranked #49 out of the 100 largest metro areas (#1 = most stressful). Criteria: divorce rate; unemployment rate; violent and property crime; suicide rate; commute time; mental health; alcohol consumption; cloudy days. *Sperling's BestPlaces, www.BestPlaces.net, "America's Most (and Least) Stressful Cities," January 9, 2004*

- An analysis of the "Best & Worst Cities for Sleep" was conducted by Sperling's BestPlaces. The study ranked America's 50 most populated metro areas. The Philadelphia* metro area ranked #32 (#1 = best city for sleep). Criteria: number of days residents didn't get enough rest or sleep during the past month; average length of daily commute; divorce rate; unemployment rate. *Sperling's BestPlaces, www.BestPlaces.net, "Best & Worst Cities for Sleep," 2006*

- HealthGrades evaluated the performance of America's 25 most populous metropolitan areas by measuring the outcomes of five of the highest volume and most widely studied procedures and diagnoses: coronary artery bypass graft surgery; percutaneus coronary interventions; acute myocardial infarction/heart attack in angioplasty-capable hospitals; congestive heart failure; and community acquired pneumonia. The Philadelphia* metro area ranked #23. *HealthGrades, "HealthGrades Hospital Quality in America Study," October 12, 2004*

- Philadelphia* was highlighted as one of the 25 metro areas most polluted by year-round particle pollution (PM 2.5) in the U.S. The area ranked #24. *American Lung Association, State of the Air: 2007*

- Philadelphia* was highlighted as one of the 25 most ozone-polluted metro areas in the U.S. The area ranked #12. *American Lung Association, State of the Air: 2007*

- Philadelphia* was selected as one of "America's Pet Healthiest Cities" by Purina. The city ranked #9 out of 50. Criteria: veterinary services; environment; legislation; preventative care; obesity/body condition. *Purina Pet Institute, "America's Pet Healthiest Cities," May 20, 2003*

Women/Minorities Rankings

- Philadelphia* was ranked #81 out of 100 metro areas in *SELF Magazine's* ranking of "America's Best Places for Women." A panel of experts came up with more than 50 criteria including death and disease rates, environmental indicators, community resources, and lifestyle habits. *SELF Magazine, "America's Best Places for Women 2007," December 2007*

Seniors/Retirement Rankings

- Sperling's BestPlaces in partnership with Bankers Life & Casualty Company designed a survey to identify the top 50 metro areas in the U.S. that offer the best overall qualities for senior living. The Philadelphia* metro area ranked #6. The following criteria were statistically weighted to reflect the needs of the senior population: health; disease; economics; social; environment; spiritual; transportation; housing; and crime. *Bankers Life & Casualty Company, "Best Cities for Seniors 2005"*

- A.G. Edwards ranked America's 500 top-performing communities based on their residents' personal savings and investing behavior. The Philadelphia* metro area ranked #73 with an index score of 107.82 (national average = 100.00). A dozen statistical factors were measured including: participation in retirement savings plans; personal debt levels; and home ownership. *A.G. Edwards, "2007 Nest Egg Index", September 12, 2007*

Children/Family Rankings

- The Philadelphia* metro area was selected as one of the "Best Cities for Relocating Families" by Worldwide ERC and Primacy Relocation. The 2007 study placed a special emphasis on the housing market, which has significantly impacted the relocation industry and an employer's ability to transfer employees. The variables which weigh heavily in this category include home price, home affordability index, appreciation rates, and property tax. Other criteria include cost of living, crime rates, education, climate, focus on diversity, physicians per capita, recreation and leisure, arts and culture, air quality, watershed quality, sales tax, unemployment rate, job growth, high school and higher education index, school expenditures per student, students in public school, SAT/ACT percentile, and population growth. *Worldwide ERC and Primacy Relocation, "2007 Best Cities for Relocating Families"*

Safety Rankings

- The National Insurance Crime Bureau ranked 361 metro areas in the U.S. in terms of per capita rates of vehicle theft. The Philadelphia* metro area ranked #110 (#1 = highest rate). Criteria: number of vehicle theft offenses per 100,000 inhabitants. *National Insurance Crime Bureau, "NICB Vehicle Theft Study," April 22, 2008*

- Philadelphia* appeared on Sperling's BestPlaces list of the "Riskiest Cities for Identity Theft." The area ranked #30 out of the nations 50 largest metro areas. Over 80 criteria were analyzed across four major categories: technology impact; crime; transactions; and risk profile. *Sperling's BestPlaces, www.BestPlaces.net, "Riskiest Cities for Identity Theft," July 2006*

- Farmers Insurance Group of Companies, in partnership with Sperling's BestPlaces, ranked 379 metro areas and identified the "Most Secure U.S. Place to Live." The Philadelphia* metro area ranked #86 out of 114 in the large metro area category (500,000 or more residents). Criteria: crime rates; extreme weather; risk of natural disasters; environmental hazards; terrorism threats; air quality; life expectancy; job loss numbers. *Farmers Insurance Group, "Most Secure U.S. Places to Live 2007"*

- Philadelphia* was identified as one of the most dangerous large metro areas for pedestrians in the U.S. The area ranked #38 out of the nations 50 largest metro areas. Criteria: average yearly pedestrian fatalities per capita (for the years 2002 and 2003) adjusted for the number of walkers. *Surface Transportation Policy Project, "Mean Streets 2004"*

Sports/Recreation Rankings

- The Philadelphia* metro area appeared on the *Sporting News* list of the "Best Sports Cities 2007". The area ranked #9 out of 150 cities in the U.S. *Sporting News* takes a 12-month snapshot, roughly July to July, of each city's sports, putting a heavy premium on regular-season won-lost records (from the most recently completed season). Other criteria include: playoff berths, bowl appearances and tournament bids; championships; applicable power ratings; quality of competition; overall fan fervor as measured in part by attendance as percentage of venue capacity; abundance of teams (rewarding quality over quantity); stadium and arena quality; ticket availability and prices; franchise ownership; and marquee appeal of athletes. *SportingNews.com, "Best Sports Cities 2007," August 1, 2007*
- The Philadelphia* metro area was selected by *Cranium* as one of the "Top 50 Fun Cities" in America. The area ranked #22. Criteria includes: number of sports teams, restaurants, and dance performances; number of toy stores; city budget spent on recreation. *Cranium, November 4, 2003*
- *Golf Digest* ranked 330 metro areas in the U.S. in terms of golf. The Philadelphia* metro area was ranked #322. Criteria: access to golf; weather; value of golf; and quality of golf. *Golf Digest, "Metro Golf Rankings," August 2005*

Dating/Romance Rankings

- Eli Lily and Company, in partnership with Sperling's BestPlaces, ranked the nation's 50 largest metro areas in terms of the "Most Romantic Cities for Baby Boomers." The Philadelphia* metro area ranked #14. Criteria: marriage and divorce rates among "baby boomers" age 45 to 60; great restaurants; dance studios; chocolate, jewelry and flower sales. *Eli Lily and Company, "Most Romantic Cities for Baby Boomers," April 20, 2007*
- The Philadelphia* metro area was selected as one of the "Top Ten U.S. Cities for Finding a Rich, Single Woman" by Teasley, a Manhattan-based marketing consulting firm. The area ranked #6. Criteria: high single-female to single-male ratio; higher income to cost-of-living ratio; percentage of population that is single. *Teasley, "Where to Find a Rich, Single Woman in the United States," 2005*
- The Philadelphia* metro area was selected as one of the "Best Cities for Relocating Singles" by Worldwide ERC and Primacy Relocation. The area ranked #13 out of the 100 largest metro areas in the U.S. Areas were selected based on the following criteria: a robust cost-of-living index; adventure and outdoor recreation opportunities; violent crime and property crime rates; percentage of the population that is unmarried (ages 25-34); ratio of single men and single women; affordability of quality higher education, including in-state and out-of-state tuition requirements and rates; number of newcomers to the area; commute times; tax rates; fee and occupancy rates for temporary housing and mini-storage; quality and quantity of collegiate and professional sporting events and fun, fan-friendly venues. *Worldwide ERC and Primacy Relocation, "2007 Best Cities for Relocating Singles," October 25, 2007*
- *Forbes* ranked the 40 most populous urbanized areas in the U.S. in terms of the "Best Cities for Singles." The Philadelphia* metro area ranked #10. Criteria: number of singles; cost of living alone; nightlife; culture; job growth; coolness; and online dating. *Forbes.com, August 21, 2007*
- Sperling's BestPlaces in partnership with AXE Deodorant Bodyspray ranked 80 metro areas and identified "America's Best (and Worst) Cities for Dating." The Philadelphia* metro area ranked #64 (#1 = best). Criteria: percentage of singles ages 18-24; population density; dating venues per capita. *AXE Deodorant Bodyspray, "America's Best (and Worst) Cities for Dating," May 2004*

Culture/Perfoming Arts Rankings

- Scarborough Research, a leading market research firm, identified the top local markets for rock concert attendance. The Philadelphia* DMA (Designated Market Area) ranked in the top 25 with 16% of consumers, 18 years old and over, reporting that they have attended a rock concert during the past year. *Scarborough Research, June 14, 2004*

Miscellaneous Rankings

- The Philadelphia* metro area was identified as one of "The 10 Worst Commuter Cities" in the U.S. by the *U.S. News and World Report*. The mean travel time to work is 32 minutes. *U.S. News and World Report, May 7, 2007*
- The Philadelphia* metro area appeared on *Forbes* list of "America's Drunkest Cities". The area ranked #9. Criteria: 35 of the largest continental U.S. metro areas were chosen based on availability of data and geographic diversity. Each metro was ranked in five areas: state laws; drinkers; heavy drinkers; binge drinkers; and alcoholism. *Forbes.com, "America's Drunkest Cities," August 22, 2006*
- Sperling's BestPlaces in partnership with Pep Boys ranked 77 metro areas and identified "America's Most Drivable Cities." The Philadelphia* metro area ranked #44. Criteria: climate; road roughness; urban mobility; gas prices. *Pep Boys, "America's Most Drivable Cities," April 9, 2003*
- State Farm Insurance, in partnership with Sperling's BestPlaces, analyzed several key factors that contribute to overall family preparedness. The Philadelphia* metro area ranked #16 out of the nation's 50 most populous metro areas. Criteria: quality of life; life insurance coverage; and investments. *State Farm Life Insurance, "Fiscally Fit Cities Report," July 20, 2004*
- Scarborough Research, a leading market research firm, identified the top local markets for grocery coupon use. The Philadelphia* DMA (Designated Market Area) ranked in the top 25 with 42% of consumers reporting that they use grocery coupons at least once per week. *Scarborough Research, December 8, 2004*
- A study by Sperling's BestPlaces examined which U.S. metro areas were most affected by high fuel prices in 2006. The Philadelphia* metro area was ranked #72 out of 80 (#1 = most expensive city for driving). Rankings are based on the average dollars spent on gas per year by two driver households. Criteria: cost of regular-grade gasoline; average miles driven per day; average number of gallons each driver uses and wastes in traffic congestion each day. *Sperling's BestPlaces, www.bestplaces.net, "Pain at the Pump," May 18, 2006*

Lower Providence is located within the Philadelphia-Camden-Wilmington, PA-NJ-DE-MD Metropolitan Statistical Area and Philadelphia, PA Metropolitan Division.

Business Environment

CITY FINANCES

City Government Finances

Component	2004-2005 ($000)	2004-2005 ($ per capita)
Total Revenues	12,893	517
Total Expenditures	12,230	490
Debt Outstanding	7,865	315
Cash and Securities	5,020	201

Source: U.S Census Bureau, Government Finances 2004-2005

City Government Revenue by Source

Source	2004-2005 ($000)	2004-2005 ($ per capita)
General Revenue		
From Federal Government	165	7
From State Government	953	38
From Local Governments	118	5
Taxes		
Property	2,207	89
Sales	3	0
Personal Income	3,379	136
License	293	12
Charges	3,858	155
Liquor Store	0	0
Utility	0	0
Employee Retirement	0	0
Other	1,917	77

Source: U.S Census Bureau, Government Finances 2004-2005

City Government Expenditures by Function

Function	2004-2005 ($000)	2004-2005 ($ per capita)	2004-2005 (%)
General Expenditures			
Airports	0	0	0.0
Corrections	0	0	0.0
Education	0	0	0.0
Fire Protection	410	16	3.4
Governmental Administration	1,256	50	10.3
Health	70	3	0.6
Highways	1,802	72	14.7
Hospitals	0	0	0.0
Housing and Community Development	371	15	3.0
Interest on General Debt	378	15	3.1
Libraries	377	15	3.1
Parking	0	0	0.0
Parks and Recreation	1,241	50	10.1
Police Protection	2,413	97	19.7
Public Welfare	0	0	0.0
Sewerage	0	0	0.0
Solid Waste Management	1,585	64	13.0
Liquor Store	0	0	0.0
Utility	0	0	0.0
Employee Retirement	0	0	0.0
Other	2,327	93	19.0

Source: U.S Census Bureau, Government Finances 2004-2005

Municipal Bond Ratings

Area	Moody's
City	n/a

Source: Mergent Bond Record, January 2008 (unless noted otherwise)

DEMOGRAPHICS

Population Growth

Area	1990 Census	2000 Census	2007 Estimate	2012 Projection	Population Growth (%) 1990-2000	Population Growth (%) 2000-2012
City	19,351	22,390	25,805	27,844	15.7	24.4
MSA[1]	5,435,470	5,687,147	5,862,653	5,970,852	4.6	5.0
U.S.	248,709,873	281,421,906	301,045,522	314,920,978	13.2	11.9

Note: (1) Metropolitan Statistical Area - see Appendix B for areas included
Source: Claritas, Inc.

Number of Households and Average Household Size

Area	2007 Estimate	2007 Average Household Size
City	8,603	3.00
MSA[1]	2,221,104	2.64
U.S.	113,668,003	2.65

Note: (1) Metropolitan Statistical Area - see Appendix B for areas included
Source: Claritas, Inc.

Race and Ethnicity

Area	White Alone[2]	Black Alone[2]	Asian Alone[2]	Other Race Alone[2]	Hispanic[3]
City	83.2	7.9	6.6	2.3	2.9
MSA[1]	70.2	20.5	4.1	5.2	6.2
U.S.	73.1	12.4	4.3	10.3	14.9

Note: Figures are 2007 estimates; (1) Metropolitan Statistical Area - see Appendix B for areas included (2) Alone is defined as not being in combination with one or more other races; (3) May be of any race.
Source: Claritas, Inc.

Ancestry

Area	German	Irish[2]	English	American	Italian	Polish	French[3]	Scottish
City	20.3	24.4	11.0	2.7	20.7	8.2	2.5	1.6
MSA[1]	17.1	20.6	8.3	3.2	14.4	5.7	1.6	1.4
U.S.	15.2	10.9	8.7	7.3	5.6	3.2	3.0	1.7

Note: Figures include multiple ancestry (e.g. if a person reported being Irish and Italian, they were included in both columns); (1) Metropolitan Statistical Area - see Appendix A for areas included; (2) Includes Celtic; (3) Includes Alsatian but excludes Basque
Source: Census 2000, Summary File 3

Foreign-Born Population

Area	Percent of Population Born in							
	Any Foreign Country	Europe	Asia	Africa	Oceania[2]	Canada	Mexico	Latin America[3]
City	6.4	1.9	3.6	0.5	0.0	0.1	0.0	0.3
MSA[1]	7.0	2.3	2.8	0.4	0.0	0.2	0.3	1.1
U.S.	11.1	1.7	2.9	0.3	0.1	0.3	3.3	2.5

Note: (1) Metropolitan Statistical Area - see Appendix A for areas included; (2) Includes Australia, New Zealand subregion, Melanesia, Micronesia, Polynesia, and Oceania n.e.c; (3) Includes Central America (excluding Mexico), South America, and the Caribbean.
Source: Census 2000, Summary File 3

Marriage Status

Area	Never Married	Now Married (excluding Separated)	Separated	Widowed	Divorced
City	21.7	65.2	1.5	5.4	6.2
MSA[1]	30.6	51.3	2.7	7.6	7.8
U.S.	27.1	54.4	2.2	6.6	9.7

Note: Figures are percentages and cover the population 15 years of age and older; (1) Metropolitan Statistical Area - see Appendix A for areas included
Source: Census 2000, Summary File 3

Age Distribution

Area	Under Age 5	Age 5 to 17	Age 18 to 34	Age 35 to 49	Age 50 to 64	Age 65 to 79	80 Years and Over
	Percent of Population						
City	6.5	19.4	21.0	27.5	15.4	8.6	1.6
MSA[1]	6.4	18.9	22.2	23.9	14.9	10.0	3.6
U.S.	6.8	18.9	23.7	23.5	14.8	9.2	3.2

Note: (1) Metropolitan Statistical Area - see Appendix A for areas included
Source: Census 2000, Summary File 3

Male/Female Ratio

Area	Males	Females	Males per 100 Females
City	13,611	12,194	111.6
MSA[1]	2,831,289	3,031,364	93.4
U.S.	148,320,305	152,725,217	97.1

Note: Figures are 2007 estimates; (1) Metropolitan Statistical Area - see Appendix B for areas included
Source: Claritas, Inc.

Religion

Area	Catholic	Southern Baptist	United Meth-odist	ELCA[1]	LDS[2]	Presby-terian Church USA	Jewish Est.	Muslim Est.
County	35.1	0.2	2.2	5.8	0.1	2.3	7.9	0.0
U.S.	22.0	7.1	3.7	1.8	1.5	1.1	2.2	0.6

Note: Figures are the number of adherents as a percentage of the total population; Adherents are defined as all members, including full members, their children and the estimated number of other participants who are not considered members (e.g. the baptized, those not confirmed, those regularly attending services, etc.); (1) Evangelical Lutheran Church in America; (2) The Church of Jesus Christ of Latter Day Saints
Source: Reprinted with permission from Religious Congregations and Membership in the United States 2000 (Nashville, Glenmary Research Center, 2002) Copyright Association of Statisticians of American Religious Bodies. All rights reserved.

ECONOMY

Gross Metropolitan Product

Area	2002	2003	2004	2005	2005 Rank[2]
MSA[1]	227.1	236.5	250.3	264.8	6

Note: Figures are in billions of dollars; (1) Philadelphia-Camden-Wilmington, PA-NJ-DE-MD Metropolitan Statistical Area - see Appendix A for areas included; (2) Rank ranges from 1 to 361
Source: The U.S. Conference of Mayors, "U.S. Metro Economies: GMP - The Engines of America's Growth," January 2007

Economic Growth

Area	1995 GMP	2005 GMP	Average Annual Growth Rate	Growth Rate Rank[2]
MSA[1]	164.1	264.8	4.9	230

Note: Figures are in billions of dollars; GMP = Gross Metropolitan Product; (1) Philadelphia-Camden-Wilmington, PA-NJ-DE-MD Metropolitan Statistical Area - see Appendix A for areas included; (2) Rank ranges from 1 to 361
Source: The U.S. Conference of Mayors, "U.S. Metro Economies: GMP - The Engines of America's Growth," January 2007

INCOME

Per Capita/Median/Average Income

Area	Per Capita ($)	Median Household ($)	Average Household ($)
City	33,095	83,415	95,833
MSA[1]	29,121	57,357	75,797
U.S.	25,495	49,280	66,670

Note: Figures are 2007 estimates; (1) Metropolitan Statistical Area - see Appendix B for areas included
Source: Claritas, Inc.

Household Income Distribution

Area	Percent of Households Earning							
	Under $15,000	$15,000 -24,999	$25,000 -34,999	$35,000 -49,999	$50,000 -74,999	$75,000 -99,000	$100,000 -149,999	$150,000 and up
City	4.5	5.1	6.7	12.0	15.6	18.3	23.4	14.4
MSA[1]	11.8	8.9	9.4	13.9	19.0	13.4	14.6	8.9
U.S.	13.1	10.9	11.2	15.6	19.5	11.9	11.3	6.6

Note: Figures are 2007 estimates; (1) Metropolitan Statistical Area - see Appendix B for areas included
Source: Claritas, Inc.

Poverty Rates by Age

Area	All Ages	Under 5 Years Old	5 to 17 Years Old	18 to 64 Years Old	65 Years and Over
City	4.4	0.6	0.8	2.7	0.4
MSA[1]	11.1	1.0	2.8	6.1	1.3
U.S.	12.4	1.2	3.0	6.9	1.2

Note: Figures are percent of population with income in 1999 below poverty level and only include population for whom poverty status is determined; (1) Metropolitan Statistical Area - see Appendix A for areas included
Source: Census 2000, Summary File 3

Personal Bankruptcy Filing Rate

Area	2004	2005	2006
Montgomery County	3.09	3.58	0.97
U.S.	5.31	6.82	2.00

Note: Numbers are per 1,000 population and include Chapter 7 and Chapter 13 filings
Source: Federal Deposit Insurance Corporation (FDIC), Regional Economic Conditions (RECON), 8/23/2007

EMPLOYMENT

Labor Force and Employment

Area	Civilian Labor Force			Workers Employed		
	Dec. 2006	Dec. 2007	% Chg.	Dec. 2006	Dec. 2007	% Chg.
City	13,408	13,361	-0.4	13,027	12,959	-0.5
MD[1]	1,938,477	1,934,718	-0.2	1,862,759	1,853,023	-0.5
U.S.	152,571,000	153,705,000	0.7	146,081,000	146,334,000	0.2

Note: Data is not seasonally adjusted and covers workers 16 years of age and older;
(1) Metropolitan Division - see Appendix B for areas included
Source: Bureau of Labor Statistics, http://stats.bls.gov

Unemployment Rate

Area	2007											
	Jan.	Feb.	Mar.	Apr.	May	Jun.	Jul.	Aug.	Sep.	Oct.	Nov.	Dec.
City	3.5	3.4	3.2	2.9	3.2	3.3	3.1	3.1	2.9	2.9	3.0	3.0
MD[1]	4.7	4.5	4.3	3.9	4.3	4.5	4.6	4.5	4.3	4.3	4.2	4.2
U.S.	5.0	4.9	4.5	4.3	4.3	4.7	4.9	4.6	4.5	4.4	4.5	4.8

Note: Data is not seasonally adjusted and covers workers 16 years of age and older; All figures are percentages; (1) Metropolitan Division - see Appendix B for areas included
Source: Bureau of Labor Statistics, http://stats.bls.gov

Employment by Occupation

Occupation Classification	City (%)	MSA[1] (%)	U.S. (%)
Sales and Office	29.8	28.9	26.7
Professional and Related	27.1	23.2	20.2
Service	9.9	13.9	14.9
Production, Transportation, and Material Moving	8.3	11.5	14.6
Management, Business, and Financial	17.9	14.6	13.5
Construction, Extraction, and Maintenance	6.8	7.7	9.4
Farming, Forestry, and Fishing	0.1	0.2	0.7

Note: Figures cover employed civilians 16 years of age and older;
(1) Metropolitan Statistical Area - see Appendix A for areas included
Source: Census 2000, Summary File 3

Employment by Industry

Sector	MSA[1] Number of Employees	MSA[1] Percent of Total	U.S. Percent of Total
Government	218,900	11.3	16.3
Education and Health Services	405,600	20.9	13.4
Professional and Business Services	306,400	15.8	13.1
Retail Trade	209,600	10.8	11.6
Manufacturing	150,000	7.7	9.9
Leisure and Hospitality	151,400	7.8	9.6
Financial Activities	144,800	7.4	5.9
Construction	n/a	n/a	5.3
Wholesale Trade	86,000	4.4	4.4
Other Services	84,800	4.4	3.9
Transportation and Utilities	62,400	3.2	3.7
Information	42,500	2.2	2.2
Natural Resources and Mining	n/a	n/a	0.5

Note: Figures cover non-farm employment as of December 2007 and are not seasonally adjusted; (1) Metropolitan Statistical Area - see Appendix B for areas included; n/a not available
Source: Bureau of Labor Statistics, http://stats.bls.gov

Average Wages

Occupation	$/Hr.	Occupation	$/Hr.
Accountants and Auditors	34.90	Maids and Housekeeping Cleaners	10.25
Automotive Mechanics	18.52	Maintenance and Repair Workers	17.61
Bookkeepers	16.93	Marketing Managers	54.59
Carpenters	22.94	Nuclear Medicine Technologists	31.96
Cashiers	8.79	Nurses, Licensed Practical	22.50
Clerks, General Office	13.93	Nurses, Registered	32.05
Clerks, Receptionists/Information	12.36	Nursing Aides/Orderlies/Attendants	12.59
Clerks, Shipping/Receiving	15.30	Packers and Packagers, Hand	10.09
Computer Programmers	39.03	Physical Therapists	34.98
Computer Support Specialists	20.89	Postal Service Mail Carriers	21.45
Computer Systems Analysts	37.81	Real Estate Brokers	n/a
Cooks, Restaurant	12.91	Retail Salespersons	12.34
Dentists	n/a	Sales Reps., Exc. Tech./Scientific	32.29
Electrical Engineers	40.50	Sales Reps., Tech./Scientific	42.06
Electricians	31.80	Secretaries, Exc. Legal/Med./Exec.	14.99
Financial Managers	55.12	Security Guards	10.80
First-Line Supervisors/Mgrs., Sales	22.15	Surgeons	78.71
Food Preparation Workers	9.82	Teacher Assistants	10.60
General and Operations Managers	55.09	Teachers, Elementary School	24.30
Hairdressers/Cosmetologists	11.88	Teachers, Secondary School	26.70
Internists	63.10	Telemarketers	14.41
Janitors and Cleaners	11.68	Truck Drivers, Heavy/Tractor-Trailer	19.38
Landscaping/Groundskeeping Workers	13.33	Truck Drivers, Light/Delivery Svcs.	14.97
Lawyers	56.01	Waiters and Waitresses	8.78

Note: Wage data covers the Philadelphia, PA Metropolitan Division - see Appendix B for areas included. Hourly wages for elementary/secondary school teachers and teacher assistants were calculated by the editors from annual wage data assuming a 40 hour work week; n/a not available.
Source: Bureau of Labor Statistics, May 2007 Metro Area Occupational Employment and Wage Estimates

RESIDENTIAL REAL ESTATE

Building Permits

Area	Single-Family			Multi-Family			Total		
	2006	2007p	Pct. Chg.	2006	2007p	Pct. Chg.	2006	2007p	Pct. Chg.
City	21	17	-19.0	183	13	-92.9	204	30	-85.3
U.S.	1,378,200	973,300	-29.4	460,700	407,200	-11.6	1,838,900	1,380,500	-24.9

Note: (p) preliminary; figures cover and represent new, privately-owned housing units authorized (unadjusted data); All permit data are based on estimates with imputation; U.S. figures are based on the new 20,000-place series.
Source: U.S. Census Bureau, Manufacturing, Mining, and Construction Statistics

Homeownership and Housing Vacancies

Area	Homeownership Rate[2] (%)			Rental Vacancy Rate[3] (%)			Homeowner Vacancy Rate[4] (%)		
	2005	2006	2007	2005	2006	2007	2005	2006	2007
MSA[1]	73.5	73.1	73.1	11.6	11.6	12.6	1.7	1.7	1.9
U.S.	68.9	68.8	68.1	9.8	9.8	9.7	1.9	2.4	2.7

Note: (1) Metropolitan Statistical Area - see Appendix B for areas included; (2) The proportion of households that are owners; (3) The proportion of the rental inventory that is vacant for rent; (4) The proportion of the homeowner inventory that is vacant for sale; n/a not available
Source: U.S. Census Bureau, Housing Vacancies and Homeownership Annual Statistics: 2007

TAXES

State Corporate Income Tax Rates

State	Rates and Tax Brackets
Pennsylvania	9.99%

Note: Tax rates as of January 1, 2008; Imposes a capital stock and foreign franchise tax of 0.289% on taxable income over $125K. Bank and Trust Company Shares Tax is 1.25%.
Source: Tax Foundation, www.taxfoundation.org

State Individual Income Tax Rates

State	Federal Deductibility	Marginal Rates (%)	Standard Deduction ($)		Personal Exemptions ($)[1]	
			Single	Joint	Single	Dependents
Pennsylvania	No	3.07	n/a	n/a	n/a	n/a

Note: Tax rates as of January 1, 2008; Local- and county-level taxes are not included; n/a not applicable; (1) Married joint filers generally receive double the single exemption
Source: Tax Foundation, www.taxfoundation.org

Various State and Local Tax Rates

State and Local Sales and Use (%)	State Sales and Use (%)	Gasoline[1,2] ($/gal.)	Cigarette ($/pack)	Spirits ($/gal.)	Table Wine ($/gal.)	Beer ($/gal.)
6.0	6.0	0.323	1.35	6.59 (n)	(p)	0.08

Note: Tax rates as of January 1, 2008; (1) In addition to the 18.4 cpg Federal gasoline tax; (2) Rates may include additional state sales taxes, environmental protection and storage fees/taxes, and local taxes. When necessary, the volume-weighted average of all local taxes is used to approximate the typical statewide rate including local tax; (n) The state government controls all sales. The implied excise tax rate is calculated using methodology designed by the Distilled Spirits Council of the United States (DISCUS); (p) All wine sales are through state-run stores. Revenue in these states is generated from various taxes, fees and net profits.
Source: Tax Foundation, www.taxfoundation.org; Original research

State Tax Burdens

Area	Combined State and Local Tax Burden		Combined Federal, State and Local Tax Burden	
	Percent	Rank	Percent	Rank
Pennsylvania	10.8	24	31.9	20
U.S. Average	11.0	-	32.7	-

Note: Figures cover 2007 and measure taxes as a percentage of income
Source: Tax Foundation, www.taxfoundation.org

State Business Tax Climate Index Rankings

State	Overall Rank	Corporate Tax Index Rank	Individual Income Tax Index Rank	Sales Tax Index Rank	Unemployment Insurance Tax Index Rank	Property Tax Index Rank
Pennsylvania	27	42	11	26	25	47

Note: Rankings range from 1 to 50 where 1 is best. Rankings do not average across to Overall Rank. States without a given tax are given a ranking of 1.
Source: Tax Foundation, State Business Tax Climate Index 2008

TRANSPORTATION

Means of Transportation to Work

Area	Car/Truck/Van		Public Transportation			Bicycle	Walked	Other Means	Worked at Home
	Drove Alone	Car-pooled	Bus	Subway	Railroad				
City	86.3	6.6	0.4	0.0	0.9	0.1	1.0	0.2	4.5
MSA[1]	72.3	10.1	5.5	1.8	2.1	0.3	4.1	0.9	2.9
U.S.	75.7	12.2	2.5	1.5	0.5	0.4	2.9	1.0	3.3

Note: Figures are percentages and cover workers 16 years of age and older; (1) Metropolitan Statistical Area - see Appendix A for areas included
Source: Census 2000, Summary File 3

Travel Time to Work

Area	Less Than 15 Minutes	15 to 29 Minutes	30 to 44 Minutes	45 to 59 Minutes	60 Minutes or More
City	22.3	35.7	23.7	9.5	8.8
MSA[1]	23.7	33.2	22.6	10.4	10.0
U.S.	29.4	36.1	19.1	7.4	8.0

Note: Figures are percentages and include workers 16 years old and over; (1) Metropolitan Statistical Area - see Appendix A for areas included
Source: Census 2000, Summary File 3

Travel Time Index

Area	1982	1995	2004	2005
Urban Area[1]	1.12	1.18	1.27	1.28
Average[2]	1.11	1.22	1.29	1.30

Note: Travel Time Index - The ratio of travel time in the peak period to the travel time at free-flow conditions. A value of 1.35 indicates a 20-minute free-flow trip takes 27 minutes in the peak. Free-flow speeds (60 mph on freeways and 35 mph on principal arterials) are used as the comparison threshold; (1) Covers the Philadelphia, PA-NJ-DE-MD urban area; (2) average of 85 urban areas
Source: Texas Transportation Institute, The 2007 Urban Mobility Report, September 2007

Living Environment

COST OF LIVING

Cost of Living Index

Composite Index	Groceries	Housing	Utilities	Trans-portation	Health Care	Misc. Goods/ Services
124.1	124.4	146.1	116.5	105.9	110.9	115.3

Note: U.S. = 100; Figures cover the Philadelphia PA urban area.
Source: The Council for Community and Economic Research (formerly ACCRA), Cost of Living Index, 2007

Grocery Prices

Area[1]	T-Bone Steak ($/pound)	Frying Chicken ($/pound)	Whole Milk ($/half gal.)	Eggs ($/dozen)	Orange Juice ($/64 oz.)	Coffee ($/11.5 oz.)
City[2]	9.62	1.53	2.16	1.94	4.33	3.81
Avg.	8.93	1.12	2.13	1.52	3.26	3.31
Min.	5.88	0.71	1.33	0.83	2.30	2.20
Max.	12.80	2.07	3.43	3.54	5.79	6.20

Note: (1) Values for the local area are compared with the average, minimum and maximum values for all 331 areas in the Cost of Living Index report; (2) Figures cover the Philadelphia PA urban area; **T-Bone Steak** *(price per pound);* **Frying Chicken** *(price per pound, whole fryer);* **Whole Milk** *(half gallon carton);* **Eggs** *(price per dozen, Grade A, large);* **Orange Juice** *(64 oz. Tropicana or Florida Natural);* **Coffee** *(11.5 oz. can, vacuum-packed, Maxwell House, Hills Bros, or Folgers).*
Source: The Council for Community and Economic Research (formerly ACCRA), Cost of Living Index, 2007

Housing and Utility Costs

Area[1]	New Home Price ($)	Apartment Rent ($/month)	All Electric ($/month)	Part Electric ($/month)	Other Energy ($/month)	Telephone ($/month)
City[2]	424,647	1,385	-	55.44	112.57	35.89
Avg.	309,605	782	146.13	78.67	90.16	26.14
Min.	189,877	n/a	82.03	37.41	33.15	17.08
Max.	1,202,800	3,481	271.14	150.60	257.67	37.45

Note: (1) Values for the local area are compared with the average, minimum and maximum values for all 331 areas in the Cost of Living Index report; (2) Figures cover the Philadelphia PA urban area; **New Home Price** *(2,400 sf living area, 8,000 sf lot, in urban area with full utilities);* **Apartment Rent** *(950 sf 2 bedroom/1.5 or 2 bath, unfurnished, excluding all utilities except water);* **All Electric** *(average monthly cost for an all-electric home);* **Part Electric** *(average monthly cost for a part-electric home);* **Other Energy** *(average monthly cost for natural gas, fuel oil, coal, wood, and any other forms of energy except electricity);* **Telephone** *(price includes basic monthly rate for a private residential line plus additional local usage charges incurred by a family of four).*
Source: The Council for Community and Economic Research (formerly ACCRA), Cost of Living Index, 2007

Health Care, Transportation, and Other Costs

Area[1]	Doctor ($/visit)	Dentist ($/visit)	Optometrist ($/visit)	Gasoline ($/gallon)	Beauty Salon ($/visit)	Men's Shirt ($)
City[2]	100.28	80.89	94.67	2.70	54.67	37.35
Avg.	79.48	71.93	79.55	2.64	29.52	25.77
Min.	52.08	44.80	43.95	2.19	15.58	16.19
Max.	148.44	126.27	158.83	3.48	60.62	48.53

Note: (1) Values for the local area are compared with the average, minimum and maximum values for all 331 areas in the Cost of Living Index report; (2) Figures cover the Philadelphia PA urban area; **Doctor** *(general practitioners routine exam of an established patient);* **Dentist** *(adult teeth cleaning and periodic oral examination);* **Optometrist** *(full vision eye exam for established adult patient);* **Gasoline** *(one gallon regular unleaded, national brand, including all taxes, cash price at self-service pump if available);* **Beauty Salon** *(woman's shampoo, trim, and blow-dry);* **Men's Shirt** *(cotton/polyester dress shirt, pinpoint weave, long sleeves).*
Source: The Council for Community and Economic Research (formerly ACCRA), Cost of Living Index, 2007

HOUSING

House Price Index (HPI)

Area	National Ranking[2]	Quarterly Change (%)	One-Year Change (%)	Five-Year Change (%)
MD[1]	130	0.22	2.04	57.85
U.S.[3]	-	0.10	0.84	41.37

Note: The HPI is a weighted repeat sales index. It measures average price changes in repeat sales or refinancings on the same properties. This information is obtained by reviewing repeat mortgage transactions on single-family properties whose mortgages have been purchased or securitized by Fannie Mae or Freddie Mac in January 1975; (1) Metropolitan Division - see Appendix B for areas included; (2) Rankings are based on annual percentage change for all metro areas containing at least 15,000 transactions over the last 10 years and ranges from 1 to 291; (3) figures based on a weighted average of Census Division estimates; all figures are for the period ending December 31, 2007

Source: Office of Federal Housing Enterprise Oversight, House Price Index, February 26, 2008

House Price Valuations

Area	Q1 2000	Q1 2001	Q1 2002	Q1 2003	Q1 2004	Q1 2005	Q1 2006	Q1 2007	Q1 2008
MD[1]	-20.0	-19.0	-15.6	-9.7	-3.2	4.6	12.7	10.0	4.1

Note: Figures show the percentage of over- or under-valuation of single family homes relative to statistically normal house values (e.g. a value of 23.6 indicates that house values are 23.6% overvalued). Statistically normal house values are based on house prices, interest rates, household incomes, population densities, and any historical premiums or discounts metropolitan areas have exhibited over time; (1) Figures cover the Metropolitan Division - see Appendix B for areas included

Source: Global Insight/National City Corporation, House Prices in America, May 2008

Median Home Prices

Area	2005	2006	2007[r]	Percent Change 2006 to 2007
MSA[1]	215.3	230.2	234.9	2.0
U.S. Average	219.0	221.9	217.9	-1.8

Note: Figures are median sales prices of existing single-family homes in thousands of dollars; (r) revised; n/a not available; (1) Metropolitan Statistical Area - see Appendix B for areas included

Source: National Association of Realtors, Metropolitan Area Prices, 1st Quarter 2008

Housing: Year Structure Built

Area	1990 -2000	1980 -1989	1970 -1979	1960 -1969	1950 -1959	1940 -1949	Before 1940	Median Year
City	18.1	6.5	23.9	20.9	15.0	6.5	9.1	1969
MSA[1]	9.4	10.0	13.0	13.9	17.3	11.1	25.3	1958
U.S.	17.0	15.8	18.5	13.7	12.7	7.3	15.0	1971

Note: Figures are percentages; (1) Metropolitan Statistical Area - see Appendix A for areas included

Source: Census 2000, Summary File 3

HEALTH

Health Risk Data

Category	Area[1] (%)	U.S. (%)
Adults who have been told they have high blood pressure[3]	28.5	25.5
Adults who have been told they have high blood cholesterol[3]	35.0	35.6
Adults who have been told they have diabetes[2]	7.2	7.5
Adults who have been told they have arthritis[3]	28.0	27.0
Adults who have been told they currently have asthma	10.5	8.5
Adults who are current smokers	20.0	20.1
Adults who are heavy drinkers[4]	3.8	4.9
Adults who are overweight (BMI 25.0 - 29.9)	34.6	36.5
Adults who are obese (BMI 30.0 - 99.8)	22.0	25.1

Note: Data as of 2006 unless otherwise noted; (1) Figures cover the Metropolitan Division - see Appendix B for areas included; (2) Figures do not include pregnancy-related diabetes, pre-diabetes or borderline diabetes; (3) 2005 data; (4) Heavy drinkers are classified as adult men having more than two drinks per day or adult women having more than one drink per day

Source: Centers for Disease Control and Prevention, Behaviorial Risk Factor Surveillance System, SMART: Selected Metropolitan/Micropolitan Area Risk Trends, 2005, 2006

Mortality Rates for the Top 10 Causes of Death in the U.S.

ICD-10[a] Sub-Chapter	ICD-10[a] Code	Age-Adjusted Mortality Rate[1] per 100,000 population	
		County[2]	U.S.
Malignant neoplasms	C00-C97	181.7	186.5
Ischaemic heart diseases	I20-I25	120.9	152.3
Other forms of heart disease	I30-I51	55.7	51.5
Cerebrovascular diseases	I60-I69	53.3	50.0
Chronic lower respiratory diseases	J40-J47	35.0	42.6
Diabetes mellitus	E10-E14	14.9	24.8
Other degenerative diseases of the nervous system	G30-G31	20.2	22.6
Other external causes of accidental injury	W00-X59	22.5	21.4
Influenza and pneumonia	J10-J18	19.4	20.7
Hypertensive diseases	I10-I13	9.8	18.2

Note: (a) ICD-10 = International Classification of Diseases 10th Revision; (1) Mortality rates are a three year average covering 2003-2005; (2) Figures cover Montgomery County
Source: Centers for Disease Control and Prevention, National Center for Health Statistics. Compressed Mortality File 1999-2004. CDC WONDER On-line Database, compiled from Compressed Mortality File 1999-2005 Series 20 No. 2K, 2008.

Mortality Rates for Selected Causes of Death

ICD-10[a] Sub-Chapter	ICD-10[a] Code	Age-Adjusted Mortality Rate[1] per 100,000 population	
		County[2]	U.S.
Assault	X85-Y09	2.6	5.9
Human immunodeficiency virus (HIV) disease	B20-B24	1.9	4.5
Intentional self-harm	X60-X84	8.3	10.8
Malnutrition	E40-E46	0.7	1.0
Obesity and other hyperalimentation	E65-E68	0.9	1.4
Organic, including symptomatic, mental disorders	F01-F09	22.0	16.8
Transport accidents	V01-V99	9.9	16.1
Viral hepatitis	B15-B19	1.8	1.8

Note: (a) ICD-10 = International Classification of Diseases 10th Revision; (1) Mortality rates are a three year average covering 2003-2005; (2) Figures cover Montgomery County
Source: Centers for Disease Control and Prevention, National Center for Health Statistics. Compressed Mortality File 1999-2004. CDC WONDER On-line Database, compiled from Compressed Mortality File 1999-2005 Series 20 No. 2K, 2008.

Distribution of Physicians[1]

Area	Total	Family/ General Practice	Specialties	
			Medical	Surgical
Montgomery County (number)	2,989	419	1,167	604
Montgomery County (rate per 10,000 pop.)	38.5	5.4	15.0	7.8
U.S. (rate per 10,000 pop.)	17.7	4.6	6.9	4.3

Note: Data as of 2005; (1) Includes all non-federal, patient-care, office-based MDs
Source: Area Resource File (ARF). June 2007. U.S. Department of Health and Human Services, Health Resources and Services Administration, Bureau of Health Professions, Rockville, MD.

Hospitals

There were no hospitals listed within the city limits.
AHA Guide to the Healthcare Field 2008

According to *U.S. News,* the Philadelphia-Camden-Wilmington, PA-NJ-DE-MD metro area is home to 10 of the best hospitals in the U.S.: **Children's Hospital of Philadelphia**; **Christiana Care Health System**; **Fox Chase Cancer Center**; **Hahnemann University Hospital**; **Hospital of the University of Pennsylvania**; **Magee Rehabilitation Hospital**; **Moss Rehab**; **Pennsylvania Hospital**; **Thomas Jefferson University Hospital**; **Wills Eye Hospital**. *U.S. News Online, "America's Best Hospitals 2007"*

EDUCATION

Public School District Statistics

District Name	Schls	Pupils	Pupil/ Teacher Ratio	Minority Pupils[1] (%)	Free Lunch Eligible[2] (%)	IEP[3] (%)
Methacton SD	7	5,413	15.0	16.9	1.8	11.7

Note: Table includes regular local school districts with 2,000 or more students; (1) Percentage of students that are not white, non-Hispanic; (2) Percentage of students that are eligible for the free lunch program; (3) Percentage of students that have an Individualized Education Program.
Source: U.S. Department of Education, National Center for Education Statistics, Common Core of Data, Local Education Agency (School District) Universe Survey: School Year 2005-2006; U.S. Department of Education, National Center for Education Statistics, Common Core of Data, Public Elementary/Secondary School Universe Survey: School Year 2005-2006

Highest Level of Education

Area	Less than H.S.	H.S. Diploma	Some College, No Deg.	Associate Degree	Bachelors Degree	Masters Degree	Profess. School Degree	Doctorate Degree
City	12.2	29.8	16.3	6.6	23.9	7.6	1.1	2.5
MSA[1]	17.3	31.4	17.5	5.8	17.4	6.8	2.5	1.3
U.S.	19.4	28.4	21.2	6.4	15.7	5.9	2.0	1.0

Note: Figures are 2007 estimated percentages and cover persons age 25 and over; (1) Metropolitan Statistical Area - see Appendix B for areas included
Source: Claritas, Inc.

Educational Attainment by Race

Area	High School Graduate (%)					Bachelor's Degree (%)				
	Total	White	Black	Asian	Hisp.[2]	Total	White	Black	Asian	Hisp.[2]
City	87.5	90.5	54.0	94.8	62.4	34.8	34.0	16.2	80.2	37.1
MSA[1]	82.2	85.7	71.9	77.2	55.5	27.7	31.1	12.8	46.7	12.8
U.S.	80.4	83.6	72.3	80.4	52.4	24.4	26.1	14.3	44.1	10.4

Note: Figures shown cover persons 25 years old and over; (1) Metropolitan Statistical Area - see Appendix A for areas included; (2) people of Hispanic origin can be of any race
Source: Census 2000, Summary File 3

School Enrollment by Type

Area	Grades KG to 8				Grades 9 to 12			
	Public		Private		Public		Private	
	Enrollment	%	Enrollment	%	Enrollment	%	Enrollment	%
City	2,661	87.2	390	12.8	1,168	79.5	301	20.5
MSA[1]	544,674	79.7	138,763	20.3	248,356	81.5	56,489	18.5
U.S.	33,526,011	88.7	4,285,121	11.3	14,848,628	90.6	1,532,323	9.4

Note: Figures shown cover persons 3 years old and over; (1) Metropolitan Statistical Area - see Appendix A for areas included
Source: Census 2000, Summary File 3

School Enrollment by Race

Area	Grades KG to 8 (%)				Grades 9 to 12 (%)			
	White	Black	Asian	Hisp.[1]	White	Black	Asian	Hisp.[1]
City	91.1	2.0	3.1	0.9	76.2	16.5	3.7	4.6
MSA[2]	65.6	24.9	3.1	7.0	64.8	25.6	3.7	6.4
U.S.	68.5	15.5	3.3	16.8	68.8	15.5	3.8	15.7

Note: Figures shown cover persons 3 years old and over; (1) people of Hispanic origin can be of any race; (2) Metropolitan Statistical Area - see Appendix A for areas included
Source: Census 2000, Summary File 3

Average Salaries of Public School Classroom Teachers

District	2005-06 Dollars	2005-06 Rank[1]	2006-07 Dollars	2006-07 Rank[1]	Percent Change 2005-06 to 2006-07
Pennsylvania	54,027	12	54,970	10	1.75
U.S. Average	49,026	-	50,816	-	3.65

Note: (1) State rank ranges from 1 to 51.
Source: National Education Association, Rankings & Estimates: Rankings of the States 2006 and Estimates of School Statistics 2007, December 2007

Higher Education

Four-Year Colleges			Two-Year Colleges			Medical Schools[1]	Law Schools[2]	Voc/ Tech[3]
Public	Private Non-profit	Private For-profit	Public	Private Non-profit	Private For-profit			
0	0	0	0	0	0	0	0	0

Note: Figures cover institutions located within the city limits; (1) includes schools accredited by the Liaison Committee on Medical Education and the American Osteopathic Association; (2) includes American Bar Association-accredited law schools; (3) includes all schools with programs that are less than 2 years.
Source: National Center for Education Statistics, The Integrated Postsecondary Education System (IPEDS) Peer Analysis System, 2007; www.usnews.com, Law and Medical School Directories, 2009

PRESIDENTIAL ELECTION

2004 Presidential Election Results

Area	Bush	Kerry	Nader	Other
Montgomery County	44.0	55.6	0.0	0.5
U.S.	50.7	48.3	0.4	0.6

Note: Results are percentages and may not add to 100% due to rounding
Source: Dave Leip's Atlas of U.S. Presidential Elections, www.uselectionatlas.org

EMPLOYERS

Major Employers

Company Name	Industry	Type of Site
Abington Memorial Hospital	General medical and surgical hospitals	Headquarters
Childrens Hosp of Philadelphia	Specialty hospitals, except psychiatric	Headquarters
Clinical Practices of Univ PA	Colleges and universities	Headquarters
Comcast Holdings Corporation	Cable and other pay television services	Headquarters
Glaxosmithkline	Commercial physical research	Branch
Lockheed Martin	Search and navigation equipment	Branch
Lockheed Martin	Transportation services, nec	Headquarters
Lockheed Martin Integrated TEC	Management services	Single
Mercy Hlth Corp Sutheastern PA	Management services	Headquarters
Navy Aviation Supply Office	National security	Branch
Our Lady of Lourdes Health	Management services	Single
Police Dept	Police protection	Branch
Temple University Hospital	General medical and surgical hospitals	Single
The Vanguard Group Inc	Management investment, open-ended	Headquarters
Thomas Jefferson Univ Hosp	General medical and surgical hospitals	Headquarters
Toll Bros Inc	Residential construction, nec	Single
Tyco Electronics Corporation	Electronic connectors	Headquarters
University of Pennsylvania	General medical and surgical hospitals	Branch

Note: Companies shown are located within the Philadelphia metropolitan area; nec = not elsewhere classified.
Source: www.zapdata.com, May 2008

PUBLIC SAFETY

Crime Rate

Area	All Crimes	Violent Crimes: Murder	Violent Crimes: Forcible Rape	Violent Crimes: Robbery	Violent Crimes: Aggrav. Assault	Property Crimes: Burglary	Property Crimes: Larceny -Theft	Property Crimes: Motor Vehicle Theft
City	1,230.0	4.0	8.0	16.0	16.0	208.3	925.5	52.1
Metro[1]	3,647.7	11.8	35.0	332.8	377.0	486.7	2,008.3	396.1
U.S.	3,808.1	5.7	30.9	149.4	287.5	729.4	2,206.8	398.4

Note: Figures are crimes per 100,000 population; (1) Metropolitan Division - see Appendix B for areas included
Source: FBI Uniform Crime Reports, 2006

Hate Crimes

Area	Number of Quarters Reported	Bias Motivation				
		Race	Religion	Sexual Orientation	Ethnicity	Disability
City	4	0	0	0	0	0

Source: Federal Bureau of Investigation, Hate Crime Statistics 2006

RECREATION

Culture

Dance[1]	Theatre[1]	Instrumental Music[1]	Vocal Music[1]	Series/ Festivals	Museums	Zoos and Aquariums[2]
0	0	0	0	0	0	0

Note: (1) Number of professional perfoming groups; (2) AZA-accredited
Source: The Grey House Performing Arts Directory, 2007; Official Museum Directory, 2008; Association of Zoos & Aquariums, AZA Member Zoos & Aquariums, June 2008

Professional Sports Teams

Team Name	League
Philadelphia Phillies	Major League Baseball (MLB)
Unnamed Expansion Team (2010)	Major League Soccer (MLS)
Philadelphia 76ers	National Basketball Association (NBA)
Philadelphia Eagles	National Football League (NFL)
Philadelphia Flyers	National Hockey League (NHL)

Note: Includes teams located in the Philadelphia metro area.
Source: Original research

MEDIA

Newspapers

Name	News Focus	Frequency	Circulation
No newspapers have an office in the city			

Note: Includes newspapers with offices located in the city
Source: MediaContactsPro, March 2008

Television Stations

Name	Ch.	Network(s)	Type	Ownership
KYW	3	CBS	Commercial	CBS
WPVI	6	ABC	Commercial	ABC Inc.
WCAU	10	NBC	Commercial	General Electric Corporation
WHYY	12	PBS	Public	WHYY Inc.
WPHL	17	WBN	Commercial	Tribune Broadcasting Company
WNJS	23	PBS	Public	New Jersey Public Broadcasting Authority
WZBN	25	n/a	Public	n/a
WTXF	29	Fox	Commercial	Fox Television Stations Inc.
WYBE	35	PBS	Public	Independence Public Media of Philadelphia Inc.
WLVT	39	PBS	Public	Lehigh Valley Public Telecommunications
WMGM	40	NBC	Commercial	The Greene Group
WGTW	48	n/a	Commercial	Brunson Communications
WNJN	50	PBS	Public	New Jersey Public Broadcasting Authority
WTVE	51	n/a	Commercial	Reading Broadcasting Inc.
WNJT	52	PBS	Public	New Jersey Public Broadcasting Authority
WMCN	53	n/a	Commercial	WWAC
WPSG	57	UPN	Commercial	Paramount Communications Inc.
WNJB	58	n/a	Public	New Jersey Public Broadcasting Authority
WBPH	60	n/a	Commercial	Sonshine Family Television Inc.
WPPX	61	Pax	Commercial	Paxson Communications Corporation
WWSI	62	Telemundo	Commercial	Hispanic Broadcasters of Philadelphia
WUVP	65	n/a	Commercial	Univision Inc.
WFMZ	69	n/a	Commercial	Maranatha Broadcasting

Note: Stations included cover the Philadelphia DMA (Designated Market Area); n/a not available
BurrellesLuce, MediaContacts Online, January 2007

Major AM Radio Stations

Call Letters	Freq. (kHz)	Station Type	Target Audience	Station Format	Music Format
WFIL	560	n/a	General	Ed/Music/News/Talk	Easy Listening
WIP	610	Commercial	General	Sports/Talk	n/a
WTMR	800	n/a	General/Religious	Music	n/a
WPEN	950	Commercial	General	Music/Talk	Big Band
WJHR	1040	Commercial	General	News/Talk	n/a
KYW	1060	n/a	General	Music/News	n/a
WDEL	1150	Commercial	General	Sports/Talk	n/a
WPHT	1210	Commercial	General	Talk	n/a
WBUD	1260	n/a	General	Music/News/Talk	n/a
WMIZ	1270	n/a	General/Hispanic	Music/News	n/a
WIMG	1300	n/a	Black/General	Music/News/Talk	n/a
WTKZ	1320	Commercial	Hispanic	Music	Latin
WHWH	1350	n/a	General	News/Sports/Talk	n/a
WDOV	1410	Commercial	General	News/Talk	n/a
WCOJ	1420	n/a	General	Music/News/Talk	n/a
WIFI	1460	Commercial	General/Religious	Music/News/Talk	Christian
WKAP	1470	n/a	General	Music	n/a
WDAS	1480	n/a	Black/Gen/Rel/Women	Sports	n/a
WNWR	1540	n/a	General/Religious	Music/News/Sports	n/a
WISP	1570	n/a	Catholic/General	Educational/Talk	n/a
WHOL	1600	n/a	General/Hisp/Rel	Music/News/Sports	n/a

Note: Stations included cover the Philadelphia DMA (Designated Market Area); n/a not available
Source: BurrellesLuce, MediaContacts Online, January 2007

Major FM Radio Stations

Call Letters	Freq. (mHz)	Station Type	Target Audience	Station Format	Music Format
WXPH	88.1	College	General	Music/News/Sports/Talk	Adult Contemp.
WXTU	92.5	n/a	General	Music	n/a
WSTW	93.7	Commercial	General	Music/News	Adult Top 40
WRDX	94.7	Commercial	General	Music	Alternative
WAYV	95.1	Commercial	General	Music/Talk	Top 40
WCTO	96.1	n/a	General	Music	n/a
WFPG	96.9	n/a	General	News/Talk	n/a
WPST	97.5	n/a	General	Music	n/a
WJBR	99.5	Commercial	General	Music/News/Sports/Talk	Adult Contemp.
WODE	99.9	n/a	General	Music	n/a
WLEV	100.7	Commercial	General/Women	Music	Soft Rock
WBEB	101.1	Commercial	General	Music	Soft Rock
WKXW	101.5	n/a	General	Music/News/Sports/Talk	n/a
WMGM	103.7	Commercial	General	Music/Talk	Classic Rock
WAEB	104.1	n/a	General	Music	n/a
WBYN	107.5	n/a	General/Religious	Ed/Music/News/Talk	n/a

Note: Stations included cover the Philadelphia DMA (Designated Market Area); n/a not available
BurrellesLuce, MediaContacts Online, January 2007

CLIMATE

Average and Extreme Temperatures

Temperature	Jan	Feb	Mar	Apr	May	Jun	Jul	Aug	Sep	Oct	Nov	Dec	Yr.
Extreme High (°F)	74	74	85	94	96	100	104	101	100	89	84	72	104
Average High (°F)	39	42	51	63	73	82	86	85	78	67	55	43	64
Average Temp. (°F)	32	34	42	53	63	72	77	76	68	57	47	36	55
Average Low (°F)	24	26	33	43	53	62	67	66	59	47	38	28	45
Extreme Low (°F)	-7	-4	7	19	28	44	51	44	35	25	15	1	-7

Note: Figures cover the years 1948-1990
Source: National Climatic Data Center, International Station Meteorological Climate Summary, 9/96

Average Precipitation/Snowfall/Humidity

Precip./Humidity	Jan	Feb	Mar	Apr	May	Jun	Jul	Aug	Sep	Oct	Nov	Dec	Yr.
Avg. Precip. (in.)	3.2	2.8	3.7	3.5	3.7	3.6	4.1	4.0	3.3	2.7	3.4	3.3	41.4
Avg. Snowfall (in.)	7	7	4	Tr	Tr	0	0	0	0	Tr	1	4	22
Avg. Rel. Hum. 7am (%)	74	73	73	72	75	77	80	82	84	83	79	75	77
Avg. Rel. Hum. 4pm (%)	60	55	51	48	51	52	54	55	55	54	57	60	54

Note: Figures cover the years 1948-1990; Tr = Trace amounts (<0.05 in. of rain; <0.5 in. of snow)
Source: National Climatic Data Center, International Station Meteorological Climate Summary, 9/96

Weather Conditions

Temperature			Daytime Sky			Precipitation		
10°F & below	32°F & below	90°F & above	Clear	Partly cloudy	Cloudy	0.01 inch or more precip.	0.1 inch or more snow/ice	Thunder-storms
5	94	23	81	146	138	117	14	27

Note: Figures are average number of days per year and cover the years 1948-1990
Source: National Climatic Data Center, International Station Meteorological Climate Summary, 9/96

HAZARDOUS WASTE

Superfund Sites

Lower Providence has one hazardous waste site on the EPA's Superfund Final National Priorities List: **Commodore Semiconductor Group**. *U.S. Environmental Protection Agency, Final National Priorities List, June 23, 2008*

AIR & WATER QUALITY

Air Quality Index

Area	Percent of Days when Air Quality was...[2]				AQI Statistics	
	Good	Moderate	Unhealthy for Sensitive Groups	Unhealthy	Maximum	Median
MSA[1]	44.9	44.1	9.0	1.9	203	54

Note: The Air Quality Index (AQI) is an index for reporting daily air quality. EPA calculates the AQI for five major air pollutants regulated by the Clean Air Act: ground-level ozone, particle pollution (also known as particulate matter), carbon monoxide, sulfur dioxide, and nitrogen dioxide. The AQI runs from 0 to 500. The higher the AQI value, the greater the level of air pollution and the greater the health concern. There are six AQI categories: "Good" The AQI is between 0 and 50. Air quality is considered satisfactory; "Moderate" The AQI is between 51 and 100. Air quality is acceptable; "Unhealthy for Sensitive Groups" When AQI values are between 101 and 150, members of sensitive groups may experience health effects; "Unhealthy" When AQI values are between 151 and 200 everyone may begin to experience health effects; "Very Unhealthy" AQI values between 201 and 300 trigger a health alert; "Hazardous" AQI values over 300 trigger health warnings of emergency conditions; (1) Metropolitan Statistical Area - see Appendix A for areas included; (2) Based on 365 days with AQI data in 2007.
Source: U.S. Environmental Protection Agency, Air Quality Index Report, 2007

Air Quality Index Pollutants

Area	Percent of Days when AQI Pollutant was...[2]					
	Carbon Monoxide	Nitrogen Dioxide	Ozone	Sulfur Dioxide	Particulate Matter 2.5	Particulate Matter 10
MSA[1]	0.8	0.0	47.7	0.0	50.4	1.1

Note: The Air Quality Index (AQI) is an index for reporting daily air quality. EPA calculates the AQI for five major air pollutants regulated by the Clean Air Act: ground-level ozone, particle pollution (also known as particulate matter), carbon monoxide, sulfur dioxide, and nitrogen dioxide. The AQI runs from 0 to 500. The higher the AQI value, the greater the level of air pollution and the greater the health concern; (1) Metropolitan Statistical Area - see Appendix A for areas included; (2) Based on 365 days with AQI data in 2007.
Source: U.S. Environmental Protection Agency, Air Quality Index Report, 2007

Air Quality Index Trends

Area	Trend Sites (45)								All Sites (98)
	1999	2000	2001	2002	2003	2004	2005	2006	2006
MSA[1]	33	21	34	35	19	9	21	18	20

Note: An AQI value greater than 100 indicates that air quality would have been in the unhealthful range on that day. Data from exceptional events are not included. These counts are presented in two ways. First, the counts are based on sites having an adequate record of monitoring data during the trend period (trend sites). These counts represent the relative change in the number of days with AQI values greater than 100. In the last column, the counts are based on all sites with data in the most recent year (because it is possible for a site to have data in the most recent year but not enough data to be a trend site); (1) Metropolitan Statistical Area - see Appendix A for areas included.
Source: U.S. Environmental Protection Agency, Office of Air and Radiation, Air Trends, Factbook and Related Information, Air Pollution Trends in Selected Metropolitan Areas 2006

Maximum Air Pollutant Concentrations

	Particulate Matter 10 (ug/m^3)	Particulate Matter 2.5 (ug/m^3)	Ozone (ppm)	Carbon Monoxide (ppm)	Sulfur Dioxide (ppm)	Nitrogen Dioxide (ppm)	Lead (ug/m^3)
MSA[1] Level	159	39	0.124	3	0.024	0.021	0.05
NAAQS[2]	150	35	0.125	9	0.140	0.053	1.50
Met NAAQS[2]	No	No	Yes	Yes	Yes	Yes	Yes

Note: Data from exceptional events are not included; (1) Metropolitan Statistical Area - see Appendix A for areas included; (2) National Ambient Air Quality Standards; n/a not available
Concentrations: Particulate Matter 10 (coarse particulate) - highest second maximum 24-hour concentration; Particulate Matter 2.5 (fine particulate) - highest 98th percentile 24-hour concentration; Ozone - highest second daily maximum 1-hour concentration; Carbon Monoxide - highest second maximum non-overlapping 8-hour concentration; Sulfur Dioxide - highest second maximum 24-hour concentration; Nitrogen Dioxide - highest arithmetic mean concentration; Lead - highest quarterly maximum concentration
Units: ppm = parts per million; ug/m^3 = micrograms per cubic meter
Source: U.S. Environmental Protection Agency, MSA Factbook 2006, Air Quality Statistics by City

Drinking Water

Water System Name	Pop. Served	Primary Water Source Type	Violations[1]	
			Health Based	Monitoring/ Reporting
Audubon Water Company	8,800	Purchased Surface	0	270

Note: (1) Based on violation data from January 1, 2007 to December 31, 2007 (includes unresolved violations from earlier years)
Source: U.S. Environmental Protection Agency, Office of Ground Water and Drinking Water, Safe Drinking Water Information System (based on data extracted April 15, 2008)

Northampton, Pennsylvania

Background

Northampton Township in Bucks County, Pennsylvania is a growing suburb located 12 miles northeast of Philadelphia. The community of nearly 40,000 residents encompasses 26 square miles. Most of the township is residential, but also includes small businesses, light manufacturing industrial parks, and business parks.

The Northampton Township Historical Society describes Bucks County as "one of America's most historic counties," and for good reason, given the large number of historic sites in the area. English Friends, who came to North America with William Penn in the late 1600s, originally settled the Northampton Township. They named the township after Northampton, a small village near London in Northamptonshire, England. The township was incorporated in 1722. Dutch farmers joined the English immigrants, and the settlement was born.

Various regions in Northampton include: Richboro, the oldest, called "The Black Bear" after the sign on its tavern; Churchville, named Smoketown in the mid-1700s because many of its Dutch settlers smoked long stemmed pipes; and Holland, originally called Finney's Mill for the family who operated the grist mill, whish was changed to Rocksville for its rocky creek banks and finally to Holland, in 1870, in honor of its Dutch settlers.

Northampton offers a wide variety of recreational opportunities, including the 54-acre Churchville Nature Center located on the Churchville Reservoir (or Springfield Lake). The Center consists of woodlands, meadows, and two miles of developed trails. The wheelchair accessible Center offers faculties for picnics, bird watching, nature walks, and nature-related educational programs. Other facilities include a replica of a Lenape Indian Village, an Environmental Center, and an Old Farmhouse. Tyler State Park, located west of the Neshaminy Creek, is also in Northampton Township, offering picnic areas, walking and bicycling trails, and facilities for water sports and horse riding.

Hampton Hill in Richboro is comprised of houses built by the Benet family who migrated to the area from New York in the early 1700s. According to legend, the Delaware Indians traded with settlers here in the 1700s, and the cellars under the houses may have been used to hide runaway slaves on the Underground Railway.

The Northampton Township Parks and Recreation Department works with local groups to provide recreational activities in nearly two dozen sites throughout the township, including golf, basketball, baseball, football, soccer, driver's education, day camps, Tai Chi, music, and science, sewing, magician camps.

Among the many employers located in Northampton's many industrial parks are Durphy Packaging Co., Neshaminy Valley Natural Foods Distributor, Ltd., CRC Industries, and Tetratec PTFE Technologies, a division of Donaldson Company, Inc. Shopping is available at the Holland Shopping Center and the Holland Village Shopping Center.

Northampton is close to many Bucks County attractions, including 10 vineyards and wineries, many of which offer tours and wine tasting, a long list of museums and famous places, such as Mercer Museum, Fonthill Museum, Grundy Mansion, and Washington Crossing Historic Park, and over a dozen covered bridges. The Naval Air Development Center, located in nearby Warminster, develops and tests many of the U.S. Navy's aircraft systems. Bucks County Community College, offering a variety of Associates Degree programs, has three campuses in the county.

Northampton receives about 45 inches of rain and 24 inches of snowfall per year. The average high temperature in July high is around 86 degrees F and the average low temperature in January is around 21 degrees F.

Rankings

General Rankings

- Philadelphia* was ranked #153 out of 375 metro areas in *Cities Ranked & Rated.* Criteria: cost of living; climate; crime; transportation; economy and jobs; education; arts and culture; health and healthcare; leisure; quality of life. *Cities Ranked & Rated, 2nd Edition, 2007*
- Philadelphia* was ranked #5 out of 379 metro areas in *Places Rated Almanac.* Criteria: health care; education; recreation; transportation; ambience; climate; crime; housing costs; jobs. *Places Rated Almanac, 7th Edition, 2007*

Business/Finance Rankings

- The nation's 100 largest metro areas were analysed in terms of the percentage of households entering some stage of foreclosure in 2007. The Philadelphia* metro area ranked #79 out of 100 (#1 = highest foreclosure rate). *RealtyTrac, "Year-End 2007 Metropolitan Foreclosure Report"*
- The Philadelphia* metro area was selected one of America's "Top 50 Business Opportunity Metros" by *Expansion Management* in their 5th annual Mayor's Challenge ranking of metro areas that have achieved solid ratings across the board in numerous *EM* studies during the past 12 months. The area ranked #28. Criteria: public schools; quality of life; college educated workers; logistics infrastructure; healthcare costs; taxes and government spending; reputation among site consultants. *Expansion Management, August 2007*
- The Philadelphia* metro area was selected as one of "America's Most Wired Cities" by *Forbes.* The metro area was ranked #26 out of 30. Criteria: percentage of Internet users with high-speed access; the range of service providers within a city; availability of public wireless hot spots. *Forbes, "America's Most Wired Cities," January 10, 2008*
- Philadelphia* was selected as one of the best places to start and grow a company by *Entrepreneur* and the National Policy Research Council. The Philadelphia* metro area ranked #45 out of 50 large metro areas. Criteria: business formation and growth (firms started four to 14 years ago that still employ at least 5 people and experienced rapid growth over the last four years). *Entrepreneur/National Policy Research Council, "Hot Cities for Entrepreneurs," September 2006*
- The Philadelphia* metro area was selected as one of "America's 50 Hottest Cities" for business relocations and expansions. Criteria: industry's most prominent site selection consultants were asked to list their top city choices for relocating and expanding manufacturing companies, taking into consideration such factors as the business climate, work force quality, operating costs, incentive programs, and the ease of working with local political and economic development officials. *Expansion Management, January-February 2007*
- Intel, in partnership with Sperling's BestPlaces, ranked the 80 "Best Cities for Teleworking" in America. The Philadelphia* metro area ranked #7 among extra large metro areas. The study identifies cities that hold the greatest potential for teleworking based on a host of factors including typical commuting times, fuel prices, availability of broadband Internet access and percentage of the population in telework friendly jobs. The study also factored in extreme climate and natural hazards. *Intel, "Best Cities for Teleworking," March 30, 2006*
- The Philadelphia* metro area appeared on the Milken Institute "2007 Best Performing Cities" index. Rank: #142 out of 200 large metro areas. Criteria: job growth; wage and salary growth; high-tech output growth. *Milken Institute, "2007 Best Performing Cities"*
- The Philadelphia* metro area was selected as one of "The Top 20 Boom Towns in America." *Business 2.0* magazine and econometric research firm Global Insight compared 319 metropolitan areas in the U.S. and ranked the 61 with populations over 1 million. Criteria: a weighted formula that includes forecast growth rates in sectors that contain the economy's 10 most skilled occupational clusters; the prevalence of college degrees in the local workforce; median salary. The area ranked #20 among large metro areas. *Business 2.0 Magazine, March 2004*

- Philadelphia* was identified as one of the 100 "Most Unwired Cities" in the U.S. The area ranked #50 out of the 100 largest metro areas in the U.S. Criteria: number of public and commercial wireless access points (hotspots); airports with wireless Internet access; broadband availability; local wireless networks; and wireless email devices. *Intel, "Most Unwired Cities Survey," June 7, 2005*

- Philadelphia* was ranked #17 out of 125 regions worldwide in terms of its "Knowledge Competitiveness Index." The index attempts to measure the knowledge-based development taking place throughout the world and is based on 19 measures of economic performance that indicate a region's ability to translate its knowledge capacity into economic value. *Robert Huggins Associates, World Knowledge Competitiveness Index 2005*

- *Forbes* ranked the 200 most populous metro areas in the U.S. in terms of the "Best Places for Business and Careers." The Philadelphia* metro area was ranked #132. Criteria: business costs (labor, energy, tax and office space expenses); living costs (housing, transportation, food and other household expenditures); education levels of the work force; job growth; income growth; migration trends; crime rates; and culture/leisure. *Forbes, "Best Places for Business and Careers," March 19, 2008*

- *Fortune* ranked the 100 largest metro areas in the U.S. in terms of projected median home price change in 2007. The Philadelphia* metro area ranked #61. *Fortune.com, "Hot Spots, Cold Spots"*

Health/Environment Rankings

- The Philadelphia* metro area was identified as one of "America's 20 Most Sedentary Cities" by *Forbes*. The metro area ranked #20. Criteria: percentage of overweight or obese people; percentage of people who had not engaged in any physical activity in the past 30 days; average number of hours of TV watched per week. *Forbes.com, "America's Most Sedentary Cities," October 29, 2007*

- 100 of the largest metro areas in the U.S. were analyzed in terms of their current drought severity. The Philadelphia* metro area ranked #57 (#1 = driest). The rankings were based on statistics such as long-term precipitation trends and patterns and the Palmer drought indices. *Sperling's BestPlaces, www.BestPlaces.net, "America's Drought-Riskiest Cities," November 2007*

- Doctors at the Harvard School of Public Health ranked 40 metropolitan areas based on data from the government-sponsored Hospital Quality Alliance program. The program tracks the performance of individual hospitals in treating patients for three common health problems: heart attacks, congestive heart failure, and pneumonia. The Philadelphia* metro area ranked #11 in quality of care for heart attacks, #20 for congestive heart failure, and #35 for pneumonia. *New England Journal of Medicine, July 21, 2005*

- *Reader's Digest* ranked the 50 largest metro areas in the U.S. in terms of how "clean" they are. The Philadelphia* metro area ranked #44. Criteria: air quality; water quality; toxic industrial pollution; Superfund sites; and sanitation. *Reader's Digest, "The 50 Cleanest (and Dirtiest) Cities in America," July 2005*

- The American Academy of Dermatology ranked 32 U.S. metropolitan regions in terms of their residents knowledge, attitude and behaviors towards tanning and sun protection. The Philadelphia* metro area ranked #9. The results of the study are based on an online national survey of 3,342 respondents. *American Academy of Dermatology, "RAYS: Your Grade," May 7, 2007*

- The Philadelphia* metro area appeared in *Country Home's* "2008 Best Green Places" report. The area ranked #87 out of 379. Criteria: official energy policies; green power; green buildings; availability of fresh, locally grown food. *Country Home, "2008 Best Green Places"*

- Wyeth Consumer Healthcare, in partnership with Sperling's BestPlaces, ranked the nation's 50 most populous metro areas in terms of five key health factors. The Philadelphia* metro area ranked #24. Criteria: physical activity; health status; nutrition; lifestyle pursuits; and mental wellness. *Wyeth Consumer Healthcare, "Centrum Healthiest Cities Study," April 19, 2005*

- HealthGrades surveyed over 41,000 individuals on doctor satisfaction and ranked the 20 largest metro areas based on the highest "definitely yes" responses to the question "Do you trust the physician to make decisions/recommendations that are in your best interest?" The Philadelphia* metro area ranked #5. *HealthGrades.com, "Top Cities in Doctor-Trust," September 7, 2006*

- Philadelphia* was identified as a "2008 Asthma Capital." The area ranked #12 out of the nation's 100 largest metropolitan areas. Twelve factors were used to identify the most challenging places to live for people with asthma: estimated prevalence; self-reported prevalence; crude death rate for asthma; annual pollen score; annual air quality; public smoking laws; number of board-certified asthma specialists; school inhaler access laws; rescue medication use; controller medication use; uninsured rate; poverty rate. *Asthma and Allergy Foundation of America, "2008 Asthma Capitals"*

- Philadelphia* was identified as a "Spring Allergy Capital." The area ranked #33 out of 100. Three groups of factors were used to identify the most severe cities for people with allergies during the spring season: annual pollen levels; medicine utilization; access to board-certified allergists. *Asthma and Allergy Foundation of America, "2007 Spring Allergy Capital Rankings"*

- Philadelphia* was identified as a "Fall Allergy Capital." The area ranked #58 out of 100. Three groups of factors were used to identify the most severe cities for people with allergies during the fall season: annual pollen levels; medicine utilization; access to board-certified allergists. *Asthma and Allergy Foundation of America, "2007 Fall Allergy Capital Rankings"*

- Ortho-McNeil Neurologics, in partnership with Sperling's BestPlaces, analyzed 110 metro areas and identified those U.S. cities with the highest prevalence of factors that are most commonly associated with migraine headaches. The Philadelphia* metro area ranked #88. Criteria: number of migraine-related drug prescriptions per capita; lifestyle factors that can contribute to migraines; environmental factors that can trigger migraines; and consumption of migraine-triggering foods. *Ortho-McNeil Neurologics, "America's Migraine Hot Spots," March 14, 2006*

- Sperling's BestPlaces ranked 331 metro areas and identified the most and least stressful U.S. cities. The Philadelphia* metro area ranked #49 out of the 100 largest metro areas (#1 = most stressful). Criteria: divorce rate; unemployment rate; violent and property crime; suicide rate; commute time; mental health; alcohol consumption; cloudy days. *Sperling's BestPlaces, www.BestPlaces.net, "America's Most (and Least) Stressful Cities," January 9, 2004*

- An analysis of the "Best & Worst Cities for Sleep" was conducted by Sperling's BestPlaces. The study ranked America's 50 most populated metro areas. The Philadelphia* metro area ranked #32 (#1 = best city for sleep). Criteria: number of days residents didn't get enough rest or sleep during the past month; average length of daily commute; divorce rate; unemployment rate. *Sperling's BestPlaces, www.BestPlaces.net, "Best & Worst Cities for Sleep," 2006*

- HealthGrades evaluated the performance of America's 25 most populous metropolitan areas by measuring the outcomes of five of the highest volume and most widely studied procedures and diagnoses: coronary artery bypass graft surgery; percutaneus coronary interventions; acute myocardial infarction/heart attack in angioplasty-capable hospitals; congestive heart failure; and community acquired pneumonia. The Philadelphia* metro area ranked #23. *HealthGrades, "HealthGrades Hospital Quality in America Study," October 12, 2004*

- Philadelphia* was highlighted as one of the 25 metro areas most polluted by year-round particle pollution (PM 2.5) in the U.S. The area ranked #24. *American Lung Association, State of the Air: 2007*

- Philadelphia* was highlighted as one of the 25 most ozone-polluted metro areas in the U.S. The area ranked #12. *American Lung Association, State of the Air: 2007*

- Philadelphia* was selected as one of "America's Pet Healthiest Cities" by Purina. The city ranked #9 out of 50. Criteria: veterinary services; environment; legislation; preventative care; obesity/body condition. *Purina Pet Institute, "America's Pet Healthiest Cities," May 20, 2003*

Women/Minorities Rankings

- Philadelphia* was ranked #81 out of 100 metro areas in *SELF Magazine's* ranking of "America's Best Places for Women." A panel of experts came up with more than 50 criteria including death and disease rates, environmental indicators, community resources, and lifestyle habits. *SELF Magazine, "America's Best Places for Women 2007," December 2007*

Seniors/Retirement Rankings

- Sperling's BestPlaces in partnership with Bankers Life & Casualty Company designed a survey to identify the top 50 metro areas in the U.S. that offer the best overall qualities for senior living. The Philadelphia* metro area ranked #6. The following criteria were statistically weighted to reflect the needs of the senior population: health; disease; economics; social; environment; spiritual; transportation; housing; and crime. *Bankers Life & Casualty Company, "Best Cities for Seniors 2005"*

- A.G. Edwards ranked America's 500 top-performing communities based on their residents' personal savings and investing behavior. The Philadelphia* metro area ranked #73 with an index score of 107.82 (national average = 100.00). A dozen statistical factors were measured including: participation in retirement savings plans; personal debt levels; and home ownership. *A.G. Edwards, "2007 Nest Egg Index", September 12, 2007*

Children/Family Rankings

- The Philadelphia* metro area was selected as one of the "Best Cities for Relocating Families" by Worldwide ERC and Primacy Relocation. The 2007 study placed a special emphasis on the housing market, which has significantly impacted the relocation industry and an employer's ability to transfer employees. The variables which weigh heavily in this category include home price, home affordability index, appreciation rates, and property tax. Other criteria include cost of living, crime rates, education, climate, focus on diversity, physicians per capita, recreation and leisure, arts and culture, air quality, watershed quality, sales tax, unemployment rate, job growth, high school and higher education index, school expenditures per student, students in public school, SAT/ACT percentile, and population growth. *Worldwide ERC and Primacy Relocation, "2007 Best Cities for Relocating Families"*

Safety Rankings

- The National Insurance Crime Bureau ranked 361 metro areas in the U.S. in terms of per capita rates of vehicle theft. The Philadelphia* metro area ranked #110 (#1 = highest rate). Criteria: number of vehicle theft offenses per 100,000 inhabitants. *National Insurance Crime Bureau, "NICB Vehicle Theft Study," April 22, 2008*

- Philadelphia* appeared on Sperling's BestPlaces list of the "Riskiest Cities for Identity Theft." The area ranked #30 out of the nations 50 largest metro areas. Over 80 criteria were analyzed across four major categories: technology impact; crime; transactions; and risk profile. *Sperling's BestPlaces, www.BestPlaces.net, "Riskiest Cities for Identity Theft," July 2006*

- Farmers Insurance Group of Companies, in partnership with Sperling's BestPlaces, ranked 379 metro areas and identified the "Most Secure U.S. Place to Live." The Philadelphia* metro area ranked #86 out of 114 in the large metro area category (500,000 or more residents). Criteria: crime rates; extreme weather; risk of natural disasters; environmental hazards; terrorism threats; air quality; life expectancy; job loss numbers. *Farmers Insurance Group, "Most Secure U.S. Places to Live 2007"*

- Philadelphia* was identified as one of the most dangerous large metro areas for pedestrians in the U.S. The area ranked #38 out of the nations 50 largest metro areas. Criteria: average yearly pedestrian fatalities per capita (for the years 2002 and 2003) adjusted for the number of walkers. *Surface Transportation Policy Project, "Mean Streets 2004"*

Sports/Recreation Rankings

- The Philadelphia* metro area appeared on the *Sporting News* list of the "Best Sports Cities 2007". The area ranked #9 out of 150 cities in the U.S. *Sporting News* takes a 12-month snapshot, roughly July to July, of each city's sports, putting a heavy premium on regular-season won-lost records (from the most recently completed season). Other criteria include: playoff berths, bowl appearances and tournament bids; championships; applicable power ratings; quality of competition; overall fan fervor as measured in part by attendance as percentage of venue capacity; abundance of teams (rewarding quality over quantity); stadium and arena quality; ticket availability and prices; franchise ownership; and marquee appeal of athletes. *SportingNews.com, "Best Sports Cities 2007," August 1, 2007*
- The Philadelphia* metro area was selected by *Cranium* as one of the "Top 50 Fun Cities" in America. The area ranked #22. Criteria includes: number of sports teams, restaurants, and dance performances; number of toy stores; city budget spent on recreation. *Cranium, November 4, 2003*
- *Golf Digest* ranked 330 metro areas in the U.S. in terms of golf. The Philadelphia* metro area was ranked #322. Criteria: access to golf; weather; value of golf; and quality of golf. *Golf Digest, "Metro Golf Rankings," August 2005*

Dating/Romance Rankings

- Eli Lily and Company, in partnership with Sperling's BestPlaces, ranked the nation's 50 largest metro areas in terms of the "Most Romantic Cities for Baby Boomers." The Philadelphia* metro area ranked #14. Criteria: marriage and divorce rates among "baby boomers" age 45 to 60; great restaurants; dance studios; chocolate, jewelry and flower sales. *Eli Lily and Company, "Most Romantic Cities for Baby Boomers," April 20, 2007*
- The Philadelphia* metro area was selected as one of the "Top Ten U.S. Cities for Finding a Rich, Single Woman" by Teasley, a Manhattan-based marketing consulting firm. The area ranked #6. Criteria: high single-female to single-male ratio; higher income to cost-of-living ratio; percentage of population that is single. *Teasley, "Where to Find a Rich, Single Woman in the United States," 2005*
- The Philadelphia* metro area was selected as one of the "Best Cities for Relocating Singles" by Worldwide ERC and Primacy Relocation. The area ranked #13 out of the 100 largest metro areas in the U.S. Areas were selected based on the following criteria: a robust cost-of-living index; adventure and outdoor recreation opportunities; violent crime and property crime rates; percentage of the population that is unmarried (ages 25-34); ratio of single men and single women; affordability of quality higher education, including in-state and out-of-state tuition requirements and rates; number of newcomers to the area; commute times; tax rates; fee and occupancy rates for temporary housing and mini-storage; quality and quantity of collegiate and professional sporting events and fun, fan-friendly venues. *Worldwide ERC and Primacy Relocation, "2007 Best Cities for Relocating Singles," October 25, 2007*
- *Forbes* ranked the 40 most populous urbanized areas in the U.S. in terms of the "Best Cities for Singles." The Philadelphia* metro area ranked #10. Criteria: number of singles; cost of living alone; nightlife; culture; job growth; coolness; and online dating. *Forbes.com, August 21, 2007*
- Sperling's BestPlaces in partnership with AXE Deodorant Bodyspray ranked 80 metro areas and identified "America's Best (and Worst) Cities for Dating." The Philadelphia* metro area ranked #64 (#1 = best). Criteria: percentage of singles ages 18-24; population density; dating venues per capita. *AXE Deodorant Bodyspray, "America's Best (and Worst) Cities for Dating," May 2004*

Culture/Performing Arts Rankings

- Scarborough Research, a leading market research firm, identified the top local markets for rock concert attendance. The Philadelphia* DMA (Designated Market Area) ranked in the top 25 with 16% of consumers, 18 years old and over, reporting that they have attended a rock concert during the past year. *Scarborough Research, June 14, 2004*

Miscellaneous Rankings

- The Philadelphia* metro area was identified as one of "The 10 Worst Commuter Cities" in the U.S. by the *U.S. News and World Report*. The mean travel time to work is 32 minutes. *U.S. News and World Report, May 7, 2007*

- The Philadelphia* metro area appeared on *Forbes* list of "America's Drunkest Cities". The area ranked #9. Criteria: 35 of the largest continental U.S. metro areas were chosen based on availability of data and geographic diversity. Each metro was ranked in five areas: state laws; drinkers; heavy drinkers; binge drinkers; and alcoholism. *Forbes.com, "America's Drunkest Cities," August 22, 2006*

- Sperling's BestPlaces in partnership with Pep Boys ranked 77 metro areas and identified "America's Most Drivable Cities." The Philadelphia* metro area ranked #44. Criteria: climate; road roughness; urban mobility; gas prices. *Pep Boys, "America's Most Drivable Cities," April 9, 2003*

- State Farm Insurance, in partnership with Sperling's BestPlaces, analyzed several key factors that contribute to overall family preparedness. The Philadelphia* metro area ranked #16 out of the nation's 50 most populous metro areas. Criteria: quality of life; life insurance coverage; and investments. *State Farm Life Insurance, "Fiscally Fit Cities Report," July 20, 2004*

- Scarborough Research, a leading market research firm, identified the top local markets for grocery coupon use. The Philadelphia* DMA (Designated Market Area) ranked in the top 25 with 42% of consumers reporting that they use grocery coupons at least once per week. *Scarborough Research, December 8, 2004*

- A study by Sperling's BestPlaces examined which U.S. metro areas were most affected by high fuel prices in 2006. The Philadelphia* metro area was ranked #72 out of 80 (#1 = most expensive city for driving). Rankings are based on the average dollars spent on gas per year by two driver households. Criteria: cost of regular-grade gasoline; average miles driven per day; average number of gallons each driver uses and wastes in traffic congestion each day. *Sperling's BestPlaces, www.bestplaces.net, "Pain at the Pump," May 18, 2006*

Northampton is located within the Philadelphia-Camden-Wilmington, PA-NJ-DE-MD Metropolitan Statistical Area and Philadelphia, PA Metropolitan Division.

Business Environment

CITY FINANCES

City Government Finances

Component	2004-2005 ($000)	2004-2005 ($ per capita)
Total Revenues	19,028	464
Total Expenditures	26,188	638
Debt Outstanding	0	0
Cash and Securities	6,983	170

Source: U.S Census Bureau, Government Finances 2004-2005

City Government Revenue by Source

Source	2004-2005 ($000)	2004-2005 ($ per capita)
General Revenue		
From Federal Government	0	0
From State Government	1,732	42
From Local Governments	124	3
Taxes		
Property	2,654	65
Sales	0	0
Personal Income	6,323	154
License	486	12
Charges	5,170	126
Liquor Store	0	0
Utility	0	0
Employee Retirement	0	0
Other	2,539	62

Source: U.S Census Bureau, Government Finances 2004-2005

City Government Expenditures by Function

Function	2004-2005 ($000)	2004-2005 ($ per capita)	2004-2005 (%)
General Expenditures			
Airports	0	0	0.0
Corrections	0	0	0.0
Education	0	0	0.0
Fire Protection	1,113	27	4.3
Governmental Administration	1,291	31	4.9
Health	65	2	0.2
Highways	2,267	55	8.7
Hospitals	0	0	0.0
Housing and Community Development	417	10	1.6
Interest on General Debt	1,523	37	5.8
Libraries	1,021	25	3.9
Parking	0	0	0.0
Parks and Recreation	4,847	118	18.5
Police Protection	3,795	93	14.5
Public Welfare	0	0	0.0
Sewerage	0	0	0.0
Solid Waste Management	3,224	79	12.3
Liquor Store	0	0	0.0
Utility	0	0	0.0
Employee Retirement	0	0	0.0
Other	6,625	162	25.3

Source: U.S Census Bureau, Government Finances 2004-2005

Municipal Bond Ratings

Area	Moody's
City	n/a

Source: Mergent Bond Record, January 2008 (unless noted otherwise)

DEMOGRAPHICS

Population Growth

Area	1990 Census	2000 Census	2007 Estimate	2012 Projection	Population Growth (%) 1990-2000	Population Growth (%) 2000-2012
City	35,406	39,384	41,326	42,596	11.2	8.2
MSA[1]	5,435,470	5,687,147	5,862,653	5,970,852	4.6	5.0
U.S.	248,709,873	281,421,906	301,045,522	314,920,978	13.2	11.9

Note: (1) Metropolitan Statistical Area - see Appendix B for areas included
Source: Claritas, Inc.

Number of Households and Average Household Size

Area	2007 Estimate	2007 Average Household Size
City	13,861	2.98
MSA[1]	2,221,104	2.64
U.S.	113,668,003	2.65

Note: (1) Metropolitan Statistical Area - see Appendix B for areas included
Source: Claritas, Inc.

Race and Ethnicity

Area	White Alone[2]	Black Alone[2]	Asian Alone[2]	Other Race Alone[2]	Hispanic[3]
City	96.2	0.4	2.4	1.0	1.1
MSA[1]	70.2	20.5	4.1	5.2	6.2
U.S.	73.1	12.4	4.3	10.3	14.9

Note: Figures are 2007 estimates; (1) Metropolitan Statistical Area - see Appendix B for areas included (2) Alone is defined as not being in combination with one or more other races; (3) May be of any race.
Source: Claritas, Inc.

Ancestry

Area	German	Irish[2]	English	American	Italian	Polish	French[3]	Scottish
City	23.1	27.0	9.1	5.2	16.5	7.6	1.4	1.7
MSA[1]	17.1	20.6	8.3	3.2	14.4	5.7	1.6	1.4
U.S.	15.2	10.9	8.7	7.3	5.6	3.2	3.0	1.7

Note: Figures include multiple ancestry (e.g. if a person reported being Irish and Italian, they were included in both columns); (1) Metropolitan Statistical Area - see Appendix A for areas included; (2) Includes Celtic; (3) Includes Alsatian but excludes Basque
Source: Census 2000, Summary File 3

Foreign-Born Population

Area	Percent of Population Born in							
	Any Foreign Country	Europe	Asia	Africa	Oceania[2]	Canada	Mexico	Latin America[3]
City	9.5	7.2	1.7	0.1	0.0	0.2	0.0	0.2
MSA[1]	7.0	2.3	2.8	0.4	0.0	0.2	0.3	1.1
U.S.	11.1	1.7	2.9	0.3	0.1	0.3	3.3	2.5

Note: (1) Metropolitan Statistical Area - see Appendix A for areas included; (2) Includes Australia, New Zealand subregion, Melanesia, Micronesia, Polynesia, and Oceania n.e.c; (3) Includes Central America (excluding Mexico), South America, and the Caribbean.
Source: Census 2000, Summary File 3

Marriage Status

Area	Never Married	Now Married (excluding Separated)	Separated	Widowed	Divorced
City	21.9	67.6	1.4	4.4	4.8
MSA[1]	30.6	51.3	2.7	7.6	7.8
U.S.	27.1	54.4	2.2	6.6	9.7

Note: Figures are percentages and cover the population 15 years of age and older; (1) Metropolitan Statistical Area - see Appendix A for areas included
Source: Census 2000, Summary File 3

Age Distribution

Area	Percent of Population						
	Under Age 5	Age 5 to 17	Age 18 to 34	Age 35 to 49	Age 50 to 64	Age 65 to 79	80 Years and Over
City	5.8	22.3	15.5	27.1	19.4	7.2	2.6
MSA[1]	6.4	18.9	22.2	23.9	14.9	10.0	3.6
U.S.	6.8	18.9	23.7	23.5	14.8	9.2	3.2

Note: (1) Metropolitan Statistical Area - see Appendix A for areas included
Source: Census 2000, Summary File 3

Male/Female Ratio

Area	Males	Females	Males per 100 Females
City	20,176	21,150	95.4
MSA[1]	2,831,289	3,031,364	93.4
U.S.	148,320,305	152,725,217	97.1

Note: Figures are 2007 estimates; (1) Metropolitan Statistical Area - see Appendix B for areas included
Source: Claritas, Inc.

Religion

Area	Catholic	Southern Baptist	United Meth-odist	ELCA[1]	LDS[2]	Presby-terian Church USA	Jewish Est.	Muslim Est.
County	43.8	0.1	2.7	4.0	0.1	2.3	5.8	0.3
U.S.	22.0	7.1	3.7	1.8	1.5	1.1	2.2	0.6

Note: Figures are the number of adherents as a percentage of the total population; Adherents are defined as all members, including full members, their children and the estimated number of other participants who are not considered members (e.g. the baptized, those not confirmed, those regularly attending services, etc.); (1) Evangelical Lutheran Church in America; (2) The Church of Jesus Christ of Latter Day Saints
Source: Reprinted with permission from Religious Congregations and Membership in the United States 2000 (Nashville, Glenmary Research Center, 2002) Copyright Association of Statisticians of American Religious Bodies. All rights reserved.

ECONOMY

Gross Metropolitan Product

Area	2002	2003	2004	2005	2005 Rank[2]
MSA[1]	227.1	236.5	250.3	264.8	6

Note: Figures are in billions of dollars; (1) Philadelphia-Camden-Wilmington, PA-NJ-DE-MD Metropolitan Statistical Area - see Appendix A for areas included; (2) Rank ranges from 1 to 361
Source: The U.S. Conference of Mayors, "U.S. Metro Economies: GMP - The Engines of America's Growth," January 2007

Economic Growth

Area	1995 GMP	2005 GMP	Average Annual Growth Rate	Growth Rate Rank[2]
MSA[1]	164.1	264.8	4.9	230

Note: Figures are in billions of dollars; GMP = Gross Metropolitan Product; (1) Philadelphia-Camden-Wilmington, PA-NJ-DE-MD Metropolitan Statistical Area - see Appendix A for areas included; (2) Rank ranges from 1 to 361
Source: The U.S. Conference of Mayors, "U.S. Metro Economies: GMP - The Engines of America's Growth," January 2007

INCOME

Per Capita/Median/Average Income

Area	Per Capita ($)	Median Household ($)	Average Household ($)
City	40,164	96,608	119,232
MSA[1]	29,121	57,357	75,797
U.S.	25,495	49,280	66,670

Note: Figures are 2007 estimates; (1) Metropolitan Statistical Area - see Appendix B for areas included
Source: Claritas, Inc.

Household Income Distribution

Area	Percent of Households Earning							
	Under $15,000	$15,000 -24,999	$25,000 -34,999	$35,000 -49,999	$50,000 -74,999	$75,000 -99,000	$100,000 -149,999	$150,000 and up
City	2.6	4.2	5.0	9.7	15.3	15.3	24.8	23.1
MSA[1]	11.8	8.9	9.4	13.9	19.0	13.4	14.6	8.9
U.S.	13.1	10.9	11.2	15.6	19.5	11.9	11.3	6.6

Note: Figures are 2007 estimates; (1) Metropolitan Statistical Area - see Appendix B for areas included
Source: Claritas, Inc.

Poverty Rates by Age

Area	All Ages	Under 5 Years Old	5 to 17 Years Old	18 to 64 Years Old	65 Years and Over
City	1.8	0.1	0.4	0.9	0.3
MSA[1]	11.1	1.0	2.8	6.1	1.3
U.S.	12.4	1.2	3.0	6.9	1.2

Note: Figures are percent of population with income in 1999 below poverty level and only include population for whom poverty status is determined; (1) Metropolitan Statistical Area - see Appendix A for areas included
Source: Census 2000, Summary File 3

Personal Bankruptcy Filing Rate

Area	2004	2005	2006
Bucks County	3.67	4.64	1.23
U.S.	5.31	6.82	2.00

Note: Numbers are per 1,000 population and include Chapter 7 and Chapter 13 filings
Source: Federal Deposit Insurance Corporation (FDIC), Regional Economic Conditions (RECON), 8/23/2007

EMPLOYMENT

Labor Force and Employment

Area	Civilian Labor Force			Workers Employed		
	Dec. 2006	Dec. 2007	% Chg.	Dec. 2006	Dec. 2007	% Chg.
City	22,865	22,846	-0.1	22,243	22,127	-0.5
MD[1]	1,938,477	1,934,718	-0.2	1,862,759	1,853,023	-0.5
U.S.	152,571,000	153,705,000	0.7	146,081,000	146,334,000	0.2

Note: Data is not seasonally adjusted and covers workers 16 years of age and older;
(1) Metropolitan Division - see Appendix B for areas included
Source: Bureau of Labor Statistics, http://stats.bls.gov

Unemployment Rate

Area	2007											
	Jan.	Feb.	Mar.	Apr.	May	Jun.	Jul.	Aug.	Sep.	Oct.	Nov.	Dec.
City	3.3	3.1	3.0	2.6	3.0	3.3	3.6	3.5	3.0	3.2	3.3	3.1
MD[1]	4.7	4.5	4.3	3.9	4.3	4.5	4.6	4.5	4.3	4.3	4.2	4.2
U.S.	5.0	4.9	4.5	4.3	4.3	4.7	4.9	4.6	4.5	4.4	4.5	4.8

Note: Data is not seasonally adjusted and covers workers 16 years of age and older; All figures are percentages; (1) Metropolitan Division - see Appendix B for areas included
Source: Bureau of Labor Statistics, http://stats.bls.gov

Employment by Occupation

Occupation Classification	City (%)	MSA[1] (%)	U.S. (%)
Sales and Office	31.6	28.9	26.7
Professional and Related	26.7	23.2	20.2
Service	8.5	13.9	14.9
Production, Transportation, and Material Moving	7.0	11.5	14.6
Management, Business, and Financial	20.2	14.6	13.5
Construction, Extraction, and Maintenance	5.8	7.7	9.4
Farming, Forestry, and Fishing	0.1	0.2	0.7

Note: Figures cover employed civilians 16 years of age and older;
(1) Metropolitan Statistical Area - see Appendix A for areas included
Source: Census 2000, Summary File 3

Employment by Industry

Sector	MSA[1] Number of Employees	MSA[1] Percent of Total	U.S. Percent of Total
Government	218,900	11.3	16.3
Education and Health Services	405,600	20.9	13.4
Professional and Business Services	306,400	15.8	13.1
Retail Trade	209,600	10.8	11.6
Manufacturing	150,000	7.7	9.9
Leisure and Hospitality	151,400	7.8	9.6
Financial Activities	144,800	7.4	5.9
Construction	n/a	n/a	5.3
Wholesale Trade	86,000	4.4	4.4
Other Services	84,800	4.4	3.9
Transportation and Utilities	62,400	3.2	3.7
Information	42,500	2.2	2.2
Natural Resources and Mining	n/a	n/a	0.5

Note: Figures cover non-farm employment as of December 2007 and are not seasonally adjusted; (1) Metropolitan Statistical Area - see Appendix B for areas included; n/a not available
Source: Bureau of Labor Statistics, http://stats.bls.gov

Average Wages

Occupation	$/Hr.	Occupation	$/Hr.
Accountants and Auditors	34.90	Maids and Housekeeping Cleaners	10.25
Automotive Mechanics	18.52	Maintenance and Repair Workers	17.61
Bookkeepers	16.93	Marketing Managers	54.59
Carpenters	22.94	Nuclear Medicine Technologists	31.96
Cashiers	8.79	Nurses, Licensed Practical	22.50
Clerks, General Office	13.93	Nurses, Registered	32.05
Clerks, Receptionists/Information	12.36	Nursing Aides/Orderlies/Attendants	12.59
Clerks, Shipping/Receiving	15.30	Packers and Packagers, Hand	10.09
Computer Programmers	39.03	Physical Therapists	34.98
Computer Support Specialists	20.89	Postal Service Mail Carriers	21.45
Computer Systems Analysts	37.81	Real Estate Brokers	n/a
Cooks, Restaurant	12.91	Retail Salespersons	12.34
Dentists	n/a	Sales Reps., Exc. Tech./Scientific	32.29
Electrical Engineers	40.50	Sales Reps., Tech./Scientific	42.06
Electricians	31.80	Secretaries, Exc. Legal/Med./Exec.	14.99
Financial Managers	55.12	Security Guards	10.80
First-Line Supervisors/Mgrs., Sales	22.15	Surgeons	78.71
Food Preparation Workers	9.82	Teacher Assistants	10.60
General and Operations Managers	55.09	Teachers, Elementary School	24.30
Hairdressers/Cosmetologists	11.88	Teachers, Secondary School	26.70
Internists	63.10	Telemarketers	14.41
Janitors and Cleaners	11.68	Truck Drivers, Heavy/Tractor-Trailer	19.38
Landscaping/Groundskeeping Workers	13.33	Truck Drivers, Light/Delivery Svcs.	14.97
Lawyers	56.01	Waiters and Waitresses	8.78

Note: Wage data covers the Philadelphia, PA Metropolitan Division - see Appendix B for areas included. Hourly wages for elementary/secondary school teachers and teacher assistants were calculated by the editors from annual wage data assuming a 40 hour work week; n/a not available.
Source: Bureau of Labor Statistics, May 2007 Metro Area Occupational Employment and Wage Estimates

RESIDENTIAL REAL ESTATE

Building Permits

Area	Single-Family			Multi-Family			Total		
	2006	2007p	Pct. Chg.	2006	2007p	Pct. Chg.	2006	2007p	Pct. Chg.
City	46	10	-78.3	0	0	-	46	10	-78.3
U.S.	1,378,200	973,300	-29.4	460,700	407,200	-11.6	1,838,900	1,380,500	-24.9

Note: (p) preliminary; figures cover and represent new, privately-owned housing units authorized (unadjusted data); All permit data are based on estimates with imputation; U.S. figures are based on the new 20,000-place series.
Source: U.S. Census Bureau, Manufacturing, Mining, and Construction Statistics

Homeownership and Housing Vacancies

Area	Homeownership Rate[2] (%)			Rental Vacancy Rate[3] (%)			Homeowner Vacancy Rate[4] (%)		
	2005	2006	2007	2005	2006	2007	2005	2006	2007
MSA[1]	73.5	73.1	73.1	11.6	11.6	12.6	1.7	1.7	1.9
U.S.	68.9	68.8	68.1	9.8	9.8	9.7	1.9	2.4	2.7

Note: (1) Metropolitan Statistical Area - see Appendix B for areas included; (2) The proportion of households that are owners; (3) The proportion of the rental inventory that is vacant for rent; (4) The proportion of the homeowner inventory that is vacant for sale; n/a not available
Source: U.S. Census Bureau, Housing Vacancies and Homeownership Annual Statistics: 2007

TAXES

State Corporate Income Tax Rates

State	Rates and Tax Brackets
Pennsylvania	9.99%

Note: Tax rates as of January 1, 2008; Imposes a capital stock and foreign franchise tax of 0.289% on taxable income over $125K. Bank and Trust Company Shares Tax is 1.25%.
Source: Tax Foundation, www.taxfoundation.org

State Individual Income Tax Rates

State	Federal Deductibility	Marginal Rates (%)	Standard Deduction ($)		Personal Exemptions ($)[1]	
			Single	Joint	Single	Dependents
Pennsylvania	No	3.07	n/a	n/a	n/a	n/a

Note: Tax rates as of January 1, 2008; Local- and county-level taxes are not included; n/a not applicable; (1) Married joint filers generally receive double the single exemption
Source: Tax Foundation, www.taxfoundation.org

Various State and Local Tax Rates

State and Local Sales and Use (%)	State Sales and Use (%)	Gasoline[1,2] ($/gal.)	Cigarette ($/pack)	Spirits ($/gal.)	Table Wine ($/gal.)	Beer ($/gal.)
6.0	6.0	0.323	1.35	6.59 (n)	(p)	0.08

Note: Tax rates as of January 1, 2008; (1) In addition to the 18.4 cpg Federal gasoline tax; (2) Rates may include additional state sales taxes, environmental protection and storage fees/taxes, and local taxes. When necessary, the volume-weighted average of all local taxes is used to approximate the typical statewide rate including local tax; (n) The state government controls all sales. The implied excise tax rate is calculated using methodology designed by the Distilled Spirits Council of the United States (DISCUS); (p) All wine sales are through state-run stores. Revenue in these states is generated from various taxes, fees and net profits.
Source: Tax Foundation, www.taxfoundation.org; Original research

State Tax Burdens

Area	Combined State and Local Tax Burden		Combined Federal, State and Local Tax Burden	
	Percent	Rank	Percent	Rank
Pennsylvania	10.8	24	31.9	20
U.S. Average	11.0	-	32.7	-

Note: Figures cover 2007 and measure taxes as a percentage of income
Source: Tax Foundation, www.taxfoundation.org

State Business Tax Climate Index Rankings

State	Overall Rank	Corporate Tax Index Rank	Individual Income Tax Index Rank	Sales Tax Index Rank	Unemployment Insurance Tax Index Rank	Property Tax Index Rank
Pennsylvania	27	42	11	26	25	47

Note: Rankings range from 1 to 50 where 1 is best. Rankings do not average across to Overall Rank. States without a given tax are given a ranking of 1.
Source: Tax Foundation, State Business Tax Climate Index 2008

TRANSPORTATION

Means of Transportation to Work

Area	Car/Truck/Van		Public Transportation			Bicycle	Walked	Other Means	Worked at Home
	Drove Alone	Car-pooled	Bus	Subway	Railroad				
City	85.2	6.6	0.0	0.1	3.0	0.0	0.6	0.5	4.0
MSA[1]	72.3	10.1	5.5	1.8	2.1	0.3	4.1	0.9	2.9
U.S.	75.7	12.2	2.5	1.5	0.5	0.4	2.9	1.0	3.3

Note: Figures are percentages and cover workers 16 years of age and older; (1) Metropolitan Statistical Area - see Appendix A for areas included
Source: Census 2000, Summary File 3

Travel Time to Work

Area	Less Than 15 Minutes	15 to 29 Minutes	30 to 44 Minutes	45 to 59 Minutes	60 Minutes or More
City	19.6	32.7	21.8	11.1	14.8
MSA[1]	23.7	33.2	22.6	10.4	10.0
U.S.	29.4	36.1	19.1	7.4	8.0

Note: Figures are percentages and include workers 16 years old and over; (1) Metropolitan Statistical Area - see Appendix A for areas included
Source: Census 2000, Summary File 3

Travel Time Index

Area	1982	1995	2004	2005
Urban Area[1]	1.12	1.18	1.27	1.28
Average[2]	1.11	1.22	1.29	1.30

Note: Travel Time Index - The ratio of travel time in the peak period to the travel time at free-flow conditions. A value of 1.35 indicates a 20-minute free-flow trip takes 27 minutes in the peak. Free-flow speeds (60 mph on freeways and 35 mph on principal arterials) are used as the comparison threshold; (1) Covers the Philadelphia, PA-NJ-DE-MD urban area; (2) average of 85 urban areas
Source: Texas Transportation Institute, The 2007 Urban Mobility Report, September 2007

Living Environment

COST OF LIVING

Cost of Living Index

Composite Index	Groceries	Housing	Utilities	Trans-portation	Health Care	Misc. Goods/ Services
124.1	124.4	146.1	116.5	105.9	110.9	115.3

Note: U.S. = 100; Figures cover the Philadelphia PA urban area.
Source: The Council for Community and Economic Research (formerly ACCRA), Cost of Living Index, 2007

Grocery Prices

Area[1]	T-Bone Steak ($/pound)	Frying Chicken ($/pound)	Whole Milk ($/half gal.)	Eggs ($/dozen)	Orange Juice ($/64 oz.)	Coffee ($/11.5 oz.)
City[2]	9.62	1.53	2.16	1.94	4.33	3.81
Avg.	8.93	1.12	2.13	1.52	3.26	3.31
Min.	5.88	0.71	1.33	0.83	2.30	2.20
Max.	12.80	2.07	3.43	3.54	5.79	6.20

Note: (1) Values for the local area are compared with the average, minimum and maximum values for all 331 areas in the Cost of Living Index report; (2) Figures cover the Philadelphia PA urban area; **T-Bone Steak** *(price per pound);* **Frying Chicken** *(price per pound, whole fryer);* **Whole Milk** *(half gallon carton);* **Eggs** *(price per dozen, Grade A, large);* **Orange Juice** *(64 oz. Tropicana or Florida Natural);* **Coffee** *(11.5 oz. can, vacuum-packed, Maxwell House, Hills Bros, or Folgers).*
Source: The Council for Community and Economic Research (formerly ACCRA), Cost of Living Index, 2007

Housing and Utility Costs

Area[1]	New Home Price ($)	Apartment Rent ($/month)	All Electric ($/month)	Part Electric ($/month)	Other Energy ($/month)	Telephone ($/month)
City[2]	424,647	1,385	-	55.44	112.57	35.89
Avg.	309,605	782	146.13	78.67	90.16	26.14
Min.	189,877	n/a	82.03	37.41	33.15	17.08
Max.	1,202,800	3,481	271.14	150.60	257.67	37.45

Note: (1) Values for the local area are compared with the average, minimum and maximum values for all 331 areas in the Cost of Living Index report; (2) Figures cover the Philadelphia PA urban area; **New Home Price** *(2,400 sf living area, 8,000 sf lot, in urban area with full utilities);* **Apartment Rent** *(950 sf 2 bedroom/1.5 or 2 bath, unfurnished, excluding all utilities except water);* **All Electric** *(average monthly cost for an all-electric home);* **Part Electric** *(average monthly cost for a part-electric home);* **Other Energy** *(average monthly cost for natural gas, fuel oil, coal, wood, and any other forms of energy except electricity);* **Telephone** *(price includes basic monthly rate for a private residential line plus additional local usage charges incurred by a family of four).*
Source: The Council for Community and Economic Research (formerly ACCRA), Cost of Living Index, 2007

Health Care, Transportation, and Other Costs

Area[1]	Doctor ($/visit)	Dentist ($/visit)	Optometrist ($/visit)	Gasoline ($/gallon)	Beauty Salon ($/visit)	Men's Shirt ($)
City[2]	100.28	80.89	94.67	2.70	54.67	37.35
Avg.	79.48	71.93	79.55	2.64	29.52	25.77
Min.	52.08	44.80	43.95	2.19	15.58	16.19
Max.	148.44	126.27	158.83	3.48	60.62	48.53

Note: (1) Values for the local area are compared with the average, minimum and maximum values for all 331 areas in the Cost of Living Index report; (2) Figures cover the Philadelphia PA urban area; **Doctor** *(general practitioners routine exam of an established patient);* **Dentist** *(adult teeth cleaning and periodic oral examination);* **Optometrist** *(full vision eye exam for established adult patient);* **Gasoline** *(one gallon regular unleaded, national brand, including all taxes, cash price at self-service pump if available);* **Beauty Salon** *(woman's shampoo, trim, and blow-dry);* **Men's Shirt** *(cotton/polyester dress shirt, pinpoint weave, long sleeves).*
Source: The Council for Community and Economic Research (formerly ACCRA), Cost of Living Index, 2007

HOUSING

House Price Index (HPI)

Area	National Ranking[2]	Quarterly Change (%)	One-Year Change (%)	Five-Year Change (%)
MD[1]	130	0.22	2.04	57.85
U.S.[3]	-	0.10	0.84	41.37

Note: The HPI is a weighted repeat sales index. It measures average price changes in repeat sales or refinancings on the same properties. This information is obtained by reviewing repeat mortgage transactions on single-family properties whose mortgages have been purchased or securitized by Fannie Mae or Freddie Mac in January 1975; (1) Metropolitan Division - see Appendix B for areas included; (2) Rankings are based on annual percentage change for all metro areas containing at least 15,000 transactions over the last 10 years and ranges from 1 to 291; (3) figures based on a weighted average of Census Division estimates; all figures are for the period ending December 31, 2007
Source: Office of Federal Housing Enterprise Oversight, House Price Index, February 26, 2008

House Price Valuations

Area	Q1 2000	Q1 2001	Q1 2002	Q1 2003	Q1 2004	Q1 2005	Q1 2006	Q1 2007	Q1 2008
MD[1]	-20.0	-19.0	-15.6	-9.7	-3.2	4.6	12.7	10.0	4.1

Note: Figures show the percentage of over- or under-valuation of single family homes relative to statistically normal house values (e.g. a value of 23.6 indicates that house values are 23.6% overvalued). Statistically normal house values are based on house prices, interest rates, household incomes, population densities, and any historical premiums or discounts metropolitan areas have exhibited over time; (1) Figures cover the Metropolitan Division - see Appendix B for areas included
Source: Global Insight/National City Corporation, House Prices in America, May 2008

Median Home Prices

Area	2005	2006	2007[r]	Percent Change 2006 to 2007
MSA[1]	215.3	230.2	234.9	2.0
U.S. Average	219.0	221.9	217.9	-1.8

Note: Figures are median sales prices of existing single-family homes in thousands of dollars; (r) revised; n/a not available; (1) Metropolitan Statistical Area - see Appendix B for areas included
Source: National Association of Realtors, Metropolitan Area Prices, 1st Quarter 2008

Housing: Year Structure Built

Area	1990 -2000	1980 -1989	1970 -1979	1960 -1969	1950 -1959	1940 -1949	Before 1940	Median Year
City	16.8	28.9	27.6	14.6	7.0	1.2	3.9	1978
MSA[1]	9.4	10.0	13.0	13.9	17.3	11.1	25.3	1958
U.S.	17.0	15.8	18.5	13.7	12.7	7.3	15.0	1971

Note: Figures are percentages; (1) Metropolitan Statistical Area - see Appendix A for areas included
Source: Census 2000, Summary File 3

HEALTH

Health Risk Data

Category	Area[1] (%)	U.S. (%)
Adults who have been told they have high blood pressure[3]	28.5	25.5
Adults who have been told they have high blood cholesterol[3]	35.0	35.6
Adults who have been told they have diabetes[2]	7.2	7.5
Adults who have been told they have arthritis[3]	28.0	27.0
Adults who have been told they currently have asthma	10.5	8.5
Adults who are current smokers	20.0	20.1
Adults who are heavy drinkers[4]	3.8	4.9
Adults who are overweight (BMI 25.0 - 29.9)	34.6	36.5
Adults who are obese (BMI 30.0 - 99.8)	22.0	25.1

Note: Data as of 2006 unless otherwise noted; (1) Figures cover the Metropolitan Division - see Appendix B for areas included; (2) Figures do not include pregnancy-related diabetes, pre-diabetes or borderline diabetes; (3) 2005 data; (4) Heavy drinkers are classified as adult men having more than two drinks per day or adult women having more than one drink per day
Source: Centers for Disease Control and Prevention, Behaviorial Risk Factor Surveillance System, SMART: Selected Metropolitan/Micropolitan Area Risk Trends, 2005, 2006

Mortality Rates for the Top 10 Causes of Death in the U.S.

ICD-10[a] Sub-Chapter	ICD-10[a] Code	Age-Adjusted Mortality Rate[1] per 100,000 population	
		County[2]	U.S.
Malignant neoplasms	C00-C97	192.9	186.5
Ischaemic heart diseases	I20-I25	125.7	152.3
Other forms of heart disease	I30-I51	65.8	51.5
Cerebrovascular diseases	I60-I69	54.2	50.0
Chronic lower respiratory diseases	J40-J47	44.3	42.6
Diabetes mellitus	E10-E14	18.4	24.8
Other degenerative diseases of the nervous system	G30-G31	18.0	22.6
Other external causes of accidental injury	W00-X59	22.0	21.4
Influenza and pneumonia	J10-J18	15.6	20.7
Hypertensive diseases	I10-I13	11.9	18.2

Note: (a) ICD-10 = International Classification of Diseases 10th Revision; (1) Mortality rates are a three year average covering 2003-2005; (2) Figures cover Bucks County
Source: Centers for Disease Control and Prevention, National Center for Health Statistics. Compressed Mortality File 1999-2004. CDC WONDER On-line Database, compiled from Compressed Mortality File 1999-2005 Series 20 No. 2K, 2008.

Mortality Rates for Selected Causes of Death

ICD-10[a] Sub-Chapter	ICD-10[a] Code	Age-Adjusted Mortality Rate[1] per 100,000 population	
		County[2]	U.S.
Assault	X85-Y09	1.8	5.9
Human immunodeficiency virus (HIV) disease	B20-B24	1.1	4.5
Intentional self-harm	X60-X84	11.6	10.8
Malnutrition	E40-E46	*0.5	1.0
Obesity and other hyperalimentation	E65-E68	1.8	1.4
Organic, including symptomatic, mental disorders	F01-F09	28.2	16.8
Transport accidents	V01-V99	13.0	16.1
Viral hepatitis	B15-B19	1.2	1.8

Note: (a) ICD-10 = International Classification of Diseases 10th Revision; (1) Mortality rates are a three year average covering 2003-2005; (2) Figures cover Bucks County; (*) Unreliable data as per CDC
Source: Centers for Disease Control and Prevention, National Center for Health Statistics. Compressed Mortality File 1999-2004. CDC WONDER On-line Database, compiled from Compressed Mortality File 1999-2005 Series 20 No. 2K, 2008.

Distribution of Physicians[1]

Area	Total	Family/ General Practice	Specialties	
			Medical	Surgical
Bucks County (number)	1,077	225	440	237
Bucks County (rate per 10,000 pop.)	17.3	3.6	7.1	3.8
U.S. (rate per 10,000 pop.)	17.7	4.6	6.9	4.3

Note: Data as of 2005; (1) Includes all non-federal, patient-care, office-based MDs
Source: Area Resource File (ARF). June 2007. U.S. Department of Health and Human Services, Health Resources and Services Administration, Bureau of Health Professions, Rockville, MD.

Hospitals

There were no hospitals listed within the city limits.
AHA Guide to the Healthcare Field 2008

According to *U.S. News,* the Philadelphia-Camden-Wilmington, PA-NJ-DE-MD metro area is home to 10 of the best hospitals in the U.S.: **Children's Hospital of Philadelphia**; **Christiana Care Health System**; **Fox Chase Cancer Center**; **Hahnemann University Hospital**; **Hospital of the University of Pennsylvania**; **Magee Rehabilitation Hospital**; **Moss Rehab**; **Pennsylvania Hospital**; **Thomas Jefferson University Hospital**; **Wills Eye Hospital**. *U.S. News Online, "America's Best Hospitals 2007"*

EDUCATION

Public School District Statistics

District Name	Schls	Pupils	Pupil/ Teacher Ratio	Minority Pupils[1] (%)	Free Lunch Eligible[2] (%)	IEP[3] (%)
Northampton Area SD	6	5,835	16.5	5.3	8.4	15.7

Note: Table includes regular local school districts with 2,000 or more students; (1) Percentage of students that are not white, non-Hispanic; (2) Percentage of students that are eligible for the free lunch program; (3) Percentage of students that have an Individualized Education Program.
Source: U.S. Department of Education, National Center for Education Statistics, Common Core of Data, Local Education Agency (School District) Universe Survey: School Year 2005-2006; U.S. Department of Education, National Center for Education Statistics, Common Core of Data, Public Elementary/Secondary School Universe Survey: School Year 2005-2006

Highest Level of Education

Area	Less than H.S.	H.S. Diploma	Some College, No Deg.	Associate Degree	Bachelors Degree	Masters Degree	Profess. School Degree	Doctorate Degree
City	5.3	26.7	18.4	6.2	26.4	11.4	3.9	1.6
MSA[1]	17.3	31.4	17.5	5.8	17.4	6.8	2.5	1.3
U.S.	19.4	28.4	21.2	6.4	15.7	5.9	2.0	1.0

Note: Figures are 2007 estimated percentages and cover persons age 25 and over; (1) Metropolitan Statistical Area - see Appendix B for areas included
Source: Claritas, Inc.

Educational Attainment by Race

Area	High School Graduate (%)					Bachelor's Degree (%)				
	Total	White	Black	Asian	Hisp.[2]	Total	White	Black	Asian	Hisp.[2]
City	94.7	94.8	88.1	92.1	79.5	43.2	42.6	40.7	76.9	22.7
MSA[1]	82.2	85.7	71.9	77.2	55.5	27.7	31.1	12.8	46.7	12.8
U.S.	80.4	83.6	72.3	80.4	52.4	24.4	26.1	14.3	44.1	10.4

Note: Figures shown cover persons 25 years old and over; (1) Metropolitan Statistical Area - see Appendix A for areas included; (2) people of Hispanic origin can be of any race
Source: Census 2000, Summary File 3

School Enrollment by Type

Area	Grades KG to 8				Grades 9 to 12			
	Public		Private		Public		Private	
	Enrollment	%	Enrollment	%	Enrollment	%	Enrollment	%
City	5,107	85.2	890	14.8	2,277	81.6	514	18.4
MSA[1]	544,674	79.7	138,763	20.3	248,356	81.5	56,489	18.5
U.S.	33,526,011	88.7	4,285,121	11.3	14,848,628	90.6	1,532,323	9.4

Note: Figures shown cover persons 3 years old and over; (1) Metropolitan Statistical Area - see Appendix A for areas included
Source: Census 2000, Summary File 3

School Enrollment by Race

Area	Grades KG to 8 (%)				Grades 9 to 12 (%)			
	White	Black	Asian	Hisp.[1]	White	Black	Asian	Hisp.[1]
City	96.9	0.3	2.3	0.2	96.4	0.0	3.6	0.5
MSA[2]	65.6	24.9	3.1	7.0	64.8	25.6	3.7	6.4
U.S.	68.5	15.5	3.3	16.8	68.8	15.5	3.8	15.7

Note: Figures shown cover persons 3 years old and over; (1) people of Hispanic origin can be of any race; (2) Metropolitan Statistical Area - see Appendix A for areas included
Source: Census 2000, Summary File 3

Average Salaries of Public School Classroom Teachers

District	2005-06 Dollars	2005-06 Rank[1]	2006-07 Dollars	2006-07 Rank[1]	Percent Change 2005-06 to 2006-07
Pennsylvania	54,027	12	54,970	10	1.75
U.S. Average	49,026	-	50,816	-	3.65

Note: (1) State rank ranges from 1 to 51.
Source: National Education Association, Rankings & Estimates: Rankings of the States 2006 and Estimates of School Statistics 2007, December 2007

Higher Education

Four-Year Colleges			Two-Year Colleges			Medical Schools[1]	Law Schools[2]	Voc/ Tech[3]
Public	Private Non-profit	Private For-profit	Public	Private Non-profit	Private For-profit			
0	0	0	0	0	0	0	0	0

Note: Figures cover institutions located within the city limits; (1) includes schools accredited by the Liaison Committee on Medical Education and the American Osteopathic Association; (2) includes American Bar Association-accredited law schools; (3) includes all schools with programs that are less than 2 years.
Source: National Center for Education Statistics, The Integrated Postsecondary Education System (IPEDS) Peer Analysis System, 2007; www.usnews.com, Law and Medical School Directories, 2009

PRESIDENTIAL ELECTION

2004 Presidential Election Results

Area	Bush	Kerry	Nader	Other
Bucks County	48.3	51.1	0.0	0.6
U.S.	50.7	48.3	0.4	0.6

Note: Results are percentages and may not add to 100% due to rounding
Source: Dave Leip's Atlas of U.S. Presidential Elections, www.uselectionatlas.org

EMPLOYERS

Major Employers

Company Name	Industry	Type of Site
Abington Memorial Hospital	General medical and surgical hospitals	Headquarters
Childrens Hosp of Philadelphia	Specialty hospitals, except psychiatric	Headquarters
Clinical Practices of Univ PA	Colleges and universities	Headquarters
Comcast Holdings Corporation	Cable and other pay television services	Headquarters
Glaxosmithkline	Commercial physical research	Branch
Lockheed Martin	Search and navigation equipment	Branch
Lockheed Martin	Transportation services, nec	Headquarters
Lockheed Martin Integrated TEC	Management services	Single
Mercy Hlth Corp Sutheastern PA	Management services	Headquarters
Navy Aviation Supply Office	National security	Branch
Our Lady of Lourdes Health	Management services	Single
Police Dept	Police protection	Branch
Temple University Hospital	General medical and surgical hospitals	Single
The Vanguard Group Inc	Management investment, open-ended	Headquarters
Thomas Jefferson Univ Hosp	General medical and surgical hospitals	Headquarters
Toll Bros Inc	Residential construction, nec	Single
Tyco Electronics Corporation	Electronic connectors	Headquarters
University of Pennsylvania	General medical and surgical hospitals	Branch

Note: Companies shown are located within the Philadelphia metropolitan area; nec = not elsewhere classified.
Source: www.zapdata.com, May 2008

PUBLIC SAFETY

Crime Rate

Area	All Crimes	Violent Crimes: Murder	Violent Crimes: Forcible Rape	Violent Crimes: Robbery	Violent Crimes: Aggrav. Assault	Property Crimes: Burglary	Property Crimes: Larceny -Theft	Property Crimes: Motor Vehicle Theft
City	988.9	0.0	4.9	17.1	17.1	192.4	721.0	36.5
Metro[1]	3,647.7	11.8	35.0	332.8	377.0	486.7	2,008.3	396.1
U.S.	3,808.1	5.7	30.9	149.4	287.5	729.4	2,206.8	398.4

Note: Figures are crimes per 100,000 population; (1) Metropolitan Division - see Appendix B for areas included
Source: FBI Uniform Crime Reports, 2006

Hate Crimes

Area	Number of Quarters Reported	Bias Motivation				
		Race	Religion	Sexual Orientation	Ethnicity	Disability
City	4	0	0	0	0	0

Source: Federal Bureau of Investigation, Hate Crime Statistics 2006

RECREATION

Culture

Dance[1]	Theatre[1]	Instrumental Music[1]	Vocal Music[1]	Series/ Festivals	Museums	Zoos and Aquariums[2]
0	0	0	0	0	0	0

Note: (1) Number of professional perfoming groups; (2) AZA-accredited
Source: The Grey House Performing Arts Directory, 2007; Official Museum Directory, 2008; Association of Zoos & Aquariums, AZA Member Zoos & Aquariums, June 2008

Professional Sports Teams

Team Name	League
Philadelphia Phillies	Major League Baseball (MLB)
Unnamed Expansion Team (2010)	Major League Soccer (MLS)
Philadelphia 76ers	National Basketball Association (NBA)
Philadelphia Eagles	National Football League (NFL)
Philadelphia Flyers	National Hockey League (NHL)

Note: Includes teams located in the Philadelphia metro area.
Source: Original research

MEDIA

Newspapers

Name	News Focus	Frequency	Circulation
No newspapers have an office in the city			

Note: Includes newspapers with offices located in the city
Source: MediaContactsPro, March 2008

Television Stations

Name	Ch.	Network(s)	Type	Ownership
KYW	3	CBS	Commercial	CBS
WPVI	6	ABC	Commercial	ABC Inc.
WCAU	10	NBC	Commercial	General Electric Corporation
WHYY	12	PBS	Public	WHYY Inc.
WPHL	17	WBN	Commercial	Tribune Broadcasting Company
WNJS	23	PBS	Public	New Jersey Public Broadcasting Authority
WZBN	25	n/a	Public	n/a
WTXF	29	Fox	Commercial	Fox Television Stations Inc.
WYBE	35	PBS	Public	Independence Public Media of Philadelphia Inc.
WLVT	39	PBS	Public	Lehigh Valley Public Telecommunications
WMGM	40	NBC	Commercial	The Greene Group
WGTW	48	n/a	Commercial	Brunson Communications
WNJN	50	PBS	Public	New Jersey Public Broadcasting Authority
WTVE	51	n/a	Commercial	Reading Broadcasting Inc.
WNJT	52	PBS	Public	New Jersey Public Broadcasting Authority
WMCN	53	n/a	Commercial	WWAC
WPSG	57	UPN	Commercial	Paramount Communications Inc.
WNJB	58	n/a	Public	New Jersey Public Broadcasting Authority
WBPH	60	n/a	Commercial	Sonshine Family Television Inc.
WPPX	61	Pax	Commercial	Paxson Communications Corporation
WWSI	62	Telemundo	Commercial	Hispanic Broadcasters of Philadelphia
WUVP	65	n/a	Commercial	Univision Inc.
WFMZ	69	n/a	Commercial	Maranatha Broadcasting

Note: Stations included cover the Philadelphia DMA (Designated Market Area); n/a not available
BurrellesLuce, MediaContacts Online, January 2007

Major AM Radio Stations

Call Letters	Freq. (kHz)	Station Type	Target Audience	Station Format	Music Format
WFIL	560	n/a	General	Ed/Music/News/Talk	Easy Listening
WIP	610	Commercial	General	Sports/Talk	n/a
WTMR	800	n/a	General/Religious	Music	n/a
WPEN	950	Commercial	General	Music/Talk	Big Band
WJHR	1040	Commercial	General	News/Talk	n/a
KYW	1060	n/a	General	Music/News	n/a
WDEL	1150	Commercial	General	Sports/Talk	n/a
WPHT	1210	Commercial	General	Talk	n/a
WBUD	1260	n/a	General	Music/News/Talk	n/a
WMIZ	1270	n/a	General/Hispanic	Music/News	n/a
WIMG	1300	n/a	Black/General	Music/News/Talk	n/a
WTKZ	1320	Commercial	Hispanic	Music	Latin
WHWH	1350	n/a	General	News/Sports/Talk	n/a
WDOV	1410	Commercial	General	News/Talk	n/a
WCOJ	1420	n/a	General	Music/News/Talk	n/a
WIFI	1460	Commercial	General/Religious	Music/News/Talk	Christian
WKAP	1470	n/a	General	Music	n/a
WDAS	1480	n/a	Black/Gen/Rel/Women	Sports	n/a
WNWR	1540	n/a	General/Religious	Music/News/Sports	n/a
WISP	1570	n/a	Catholic/General	Educational/Talk	n/a
WHOL	1600	n/a	General/Hisp/Rel	Music/News/Sports	n/a

Note: Stations included cover the Philadelphia DMA (Designated Market Area); n/a not available
Source: BurrellesLuce, MediaContacts Online, January 2007

Major FM Radio Stations

Call Letters	Freq. (mHz)	Station Type	Target Audience	Station Format	Music Format
WXPH	88.1	College	General	Music/News/Sports/Talk	Adult Contemp.
WXTU	92.5	n/a	General	Music	n/a
WSTW	93.7	Commercial	General	Music/News	Adult Top 40
WRDX	94.7	Commercial	General	Music	Alternative
WAYV	95.1	Commercial	General	Music/Talk	Top 40
WCTO	96.1	n/a	General	Music	n/a
WFPG	96.9	n/a	General	News/Talk	n/a
WPST	97.5	n/a	General	Music	n/a
WJBR	99.5	Commercial	General	Music/News/Sports/Talk	Adult Contemp.
WODE	99.9	n/a	General	Music	n/a
WLEV	100.7	Commercial	General/Women	Music	Soft Rock
WBEB	101.1	Commercial	General	Music	Soft Rock
WKXW	101.5	n/a	General	Music/News/Sports/Talk	n/a
WMGM	103.7	Commercial	General	Music/Talk	Classic Rock
WAEB	104.1	n/a	General	Music	n/a
WBYN	107.5	n/a	General/Religious	Ed/Music/News/Talk	n/a

Note: Stations included cover the Philadelphia DMA (Designated Market Area); n/a not available
BurrellesLuce, MediaContacts Online, January 2007

CLIMATE

Average and Extreme Temperatures

Temperature	Jan	Feb	Mar	Apr	May	Jun	Jul	Aug	Sep	Oct	Nov	Dec	Yr.
Extreme High (°F)	74	74	85	94	96	100	104	101	100	89	84	72	104
Average High (°F)	39	42	51	63	73	82	86	85	78	67	55	43	64
Average Temp. (°F)	32	34	42	53	63	72	77	76	68	57	47	36	55
Average Low (°F)	24	26	33	43	53	62	67	66	59	47	38	28	45
Extreme Low (°F)	-7	-4	7	19	28	44	51	44	35	25	15	1	-7

Note: Figures cover the years 1948-1990
Source: National Climatic Data Center, International Station Meteorological Climate Summary, 9/96

Average Precipitation/Snowfall/Humidity

Precip./Humidity	Jan	Feb	Mar	Apr	May	Jun	Jul	Aug	Sep	Oct	Nov	Dec	Yr.
Avg. Precip. (in.)	3.2	2.8	3.7	3.5	3.7	3.6	4.1	4.0	3.3	2.7	3.4	3.3	41.4
Avg. Snowfall (in.)	7	7	4	Tr	Tr	0	0	0	0	Tr	1	4	22
Avg. Rel. Hum. 7am (%)	74	73	73	72	75	77	80	82	84	83	79	75	77
Avg. Rel. Hum. 4pm (%)	60	55	51	48	51	52	54	55	55	54	57	60	54

Note: Figures cover the years 1948-1990; Tr = Trace amounts (<0.05 in. of rain; <0.5 in. of snow)
Source: National Climatic Data Center, International Station Meteorological Climate Summary, 9/96

Weather Conditions

Temperature			Daytime Sky			Precipitation		
10°F & below	32°F & below	90°F & above	Clear	Partly cloudy	Cloudy	0.01 inch or more precip.	0.1 inch or more snow/ice	Thunder-storms
5	94	23	81	146	138	117	14	27

Note: Figures are average number of days per year and cover the years 1948-1990
Source: National Climatic Data Center, International Station Meteorological Climate Summary, 9/96

HAZARDOUS WASTE

Superfund Sites

Northampton has no sites on the EPA's Superfund Final National Priorities List.
U.S. Environmental Protection Agency, Final National Priorities List, June 23, 2008

AIR & WATER QUALITY

Air Quality Index

Area	Percent of Days when Air Quality was...[2]				AQI Statistics	
	Good	Moderate	Unhealthy for Sensitive Groups	Unhealthy	Maximum	Median
MSA[1]	44.9	44.1	9.0	1.9	203	54

Note: The Air Quality Index (AQI) is an index for reporting daily air quality. EPA calculates the AQI for five major air pollutants regulated by the Clean Air Act: ground-level ozone, particle pollution (also known as particulate matter), carbon monoxide, sulfur dioxide, and nitrogen dioxide. The AQI runs from 0 to 500. The higher the AQI value, the greater the level of air pollution and the greater the health concern. There are six AQI categories: "Good" The AQI is between 0 and 50. Air quality is considered satisfactory; "Moderate" The AQI is between 51 and 100. Air quality is acceptable; "Unhealthy for Sensitive Groups" When AQI values are between 101 and 150, members of sensitive groups may experience health effects; "Unhealthy" When AQI values are between 151 and 200 everyone may begin to experience health effects; "Very Unhealthy" AQI values between 201 and 300 trigger a health alert; "Hazardous" AQI values over 300 trigger health warnings of emergency conditions; (1) Metropolitan Statistical Area - see Appendix A for areas included; (2) Based on 365 days with AQI data in 2007.
Source: U.S. Environmental Protection Agency, Air Quality Index Report, 2007

Air Quality Index Pollutants

Area	Percent of Days when AQI Pollutant was...[2]					
	Carbon Monoxide	Nitrogen Dioxide	Ozone	Sulfur Dioxide	Particulate Matter 2.5	Particulate Matter 10
MSA[1]	0.8	0.0	47.7	0.0	50.4	1.1

Note: The Air Quality Index (AQI) is an index for reporting daily air quality. EPA calculates the AQI for five major air pollutants regulated by the Clean Air Act: ground-level ozone, particle pollution (also known as particulate matter), carbon monoxide, sulfur dioxide, and nitrogen dioxide. The AQI runs from 0 to 500. The higher the AQI value, the greater the level of air pollution and the greater the health concern; (1) Metropolitan Statistical Area - see Appendix A for areas included; (2) Based on 365 days with AQI data in 2007.
Source: U.S. Environmental Protection Agency, Air Quality Index Report, 2007

Air Quality Index Trends

Area	Trend Sites (45)								All Sites (98)
	1999	2000	2001	2002	2003	2004	2005	2006	2006
MSA[1]	33	21	34	35	19	9	21	18	20

Note: An AQI value greater than 100 indicates that air quality would have been in the unhealthful range on that day. Data from exceptional events are not included. These counts are presented in two ways. First, the counts are based on sites having an adequate record of monitoring data during the trend period (trend sites). These counts represent the relative change in the number of days with AQI values greater than 100. In the last column, the counts are based on all sites with data in the most recent year (because it is possible for a site to have data in the most recent year but not enough data to be a trend site); (1) Metropolitan Statistical Area - see Appendix A for areas included.
Source: U.S. Environmental Protection Agency, Office of Air and Radiation, Air Trends, Factbook and Related Information, Air Pollution Trends in Selected Metropolitan Areas 2006

Maximum Air Pollutant Concentrations

	Particulate Matter 10 (ug/m^3)	Particulate Matter 2.5 (ug/m^3)	Ozone (ppm)	Carbon Monoxide (ppm)	Sulfur Dioxide (ppm)	Nitrogen Dioxide (ppm)	Lead (ug/m^3)
MSA[1] Level	159	39	0.124	3	0.024	0.021	0.05
NAAQS[2]	150	35	0.125	9	0.140	0.053	1.50
Met NAAQS[2]	No	No	Yes	Yes	Yes	Yes	Yes

Note: Data from exceptional events are not included; (1) Metropolitan Statistical Area - see Appendix A for areas included; (2) National Ambient Air Quality Standards; n/a not available
Concentrations: Particulate Matter 10 (coarse particulate) - highest second maximum 24-hour concentration; Particulate Matter 2.5 (fine particulate) - highest 98th percentile 24-hour concentration; Ozone - highest second daily maximum 1-hour concentration; Carbon Monoxide - highest second maximum non-overlapping 8-hour concentration; Sulfur Dioxide - highest second maximum 24-hour concentration; Nitrogen Dioxide - highest arithmetic mean concentration; Lead - highest quarterly maximum concentration
Units: ppm = parts per million; ug/m^3 = micrograms per cubic meter
Source: U.S. Environmental Protection Agency, MSA Factbook 2006, Air Quality Statistics by City

Drinking Water

Water System Name	Pop. Served	Primary Water Source Type	Violations[1]	
			Health Based	Monitoring/ Reporting
Northampton Bucks Co. Muni. Auth.	37,700	Purchased Surface	0	19

Note: (1) Based on violation data from January 1, 2007 to December 31, 2007 (includes unresolved violations from earlier years)
Source: U.S. Environmental Protection Agency, Office of Ground Water and Drinking Water, Safe Drinking Water Information System (based on data extracted April 15, 2008)

South Kingstown, Rhode Island

Background

South Kingstown lies in southern Rhode Island, adjacent to the town of Narragansett, on the west side of Narragansett Bay. Its history properly begins in 1674 with the formation of "Kings Towne," which then encompassed both North Kingstown and South Kingstown. The two were separated and incorporated as separate towns in 1723. Today South Kingstown is a combination of beautiful rural spaces and picturesque villages.

South Kingstown is the county seat for Washington County. Like other New England townships, it includes a number of villages. Wakefield, the primary commercial center, is also blessed with a number of fine buildings of eighteenth- and nineteenth-century architecture. Kingston, two miles northwest, is home of the University of Rhode Island. Other villages include West Kingston, Peace Dale, Green Hill, Matunuck, Usquepaugh, Middlebridge, Rocky Brook, Indian Lake Shores, Perryville, Tuckertown, Curtis Corner, and Snug Harbor. South Kingstown as a whole is governed by a town council and town manager, occupying a historic town hall in Wakefield.

Wakefield was the birthplace of Oliver Hazard Perry (1785-1819), the naval hero of the War of 1812 whose famous words "We have met the enemy and he is ours" signaled his victory over the British in the Battle of Lake Erie (1813). His birthplace is now a museum. In 1804, Rowland Hazard arrived here from Charleston, South Carolina, and gave Peace Dale its name. In 1847, the Hazard family founded the textile-manufacturing firm that was to be the dominant industry in town for four generations. Later Hazzards built the Peace Dale Public Library, designed in the Richardsonian Romanesque style, and commissioned a bronze relief, The Weaver, sculpted by Daniel Chester French, who is best known for the massive seated figure of Lincoln in the Lincoln Memorial in Washington.

South Kingston likewise has a distinguished library building. First built as a court house in 1775 and used as one of five rotating state houses for the Rhode Island General Assembly in 1776-1791, the library was remodeled in the Victorian style in 1876 and is now on the National Register of Historic Places. The city's University of Rhode Island is home to over 13,000 students and innumerable cultural and recreational opportunities, including a full schedule of concerts and theatrical performances.

The next township east, Narragansett, also offers opportunities for culture and recreation. The South County Museum celebrates Rhode Island's heritage. And from Narragansett, one can go fishing, swimming, sailing, whale-watching, or hop a ferry to Block Island. Also from Narragansett, it is but a short trip across the bridge to Newport, with its bustling streets, glittering mansions, and historic houses.

With its shoreline on Block Island Sound and its proximity to Narragansett Bay, South Kingstown enjoys a four-season climate that is moderated by the sea. Precipitation occurs evenly throughout the year. In winter, snow is generally light and mixed with rain, though occasionally storms do sweep up the Atlantic coast, to collide with cold air from interior New England and drop large amounts of snow along the shore. Spring is pleasant and early, though the warmest days of spring can be cooler here than farther inland. Summer is high season, with comfortable temperatures for all outdoor activities.

Rankings

General Rankings

- Providence* was ranked #266 out of 375 metro areas in *Cities Ranked & Rated*. Criteria: cost of living; climate; crime; transportation; economy and jobs; education; arts and culture; health and healthcare; leisure; quality of life. *Cities Ranked & Rated, 2nd Edition, 2007*

- Providence* was ranked #26 out of 379 metro areas in *Places Rated Almanac*. Criteria: health care; education; recreation; transportation; ambience; climate; crime; housing costs; jobs. *Places Rated Almanac, 7th Edition, 2007*

Business/Finance Rankings

- The nation's 100 largest metro areas were analysed in terms of the percentage of households entering some stage of foreclosure in 2007. The Providence* metro area ranked #83 out of 100 (#1 = highest foreclosure rate). *RealtyTrac, "Year-End 2007 Metropolitan Foreclosure Report"*

- Providence* was selected as one of the best places to start and grow a company by *Entrepreneur* and the National Policy Research Council. The Providence* metro area ranked #39 out of 50 large metro areas. Criteria: business formation and growth (firms started four to 14 years ago that still employ at least 5 people and experienced rapid growth over the last four years). *Entrepreneur/National Policy Research Council, "Hot Cities for Entrepreneurs," September 2006*

- Intel, in partnership with Sperling's BestPlaces, ranked the 80 "Best Cities for Teleworking" in America. The Providence* metro area ranked #12 among large metro areas. The study identifies cities that hold the greatest potential for teleworking based on a host of factors including typical commuting times, fuel prices, availability of broadband Internet access and percentage of the population in telework friendly jobs. The study also factored in extreme climate and natural hazards. *Intel, "Best Cities for Teleworking," March 30, 2006*

- The Providence* metro area appeared on the Milken Institute "2007 Best Performing Cities" index. Rank: #150 out of 200 large metro areas. Criteria: job growth; wage and salary growth; high-tech output growth. *Milken Institute, "2007 Best Performing Cities"*

- Providence* was identified as one of the 100 "Most Unwired Cities" in the U.S. The area ranked #57 out of the 100 largest metro areas in the U.S. Criteria: number of public and commercial wireless access points (hotspots); airports with wireless Internet access; broadband availability; local wireless networks; and wireless email devices. *Intel, "Most Unwired Cities Survey," June 7, 2005*

- *Forbes* ranked the 200 most populous metro areas in the U.S. in terms of the "Best Places for Business and Careers." The Providence* metro area was ranked #118. Criteria: business costs (labor, energy, tax and office space expenses); living costs (housing, transportation, food and other household expenditures); education levels of the work force; job growth; income growth; migration trends; crime rates; and culture/leisure. *Forbes, "Best Places for Business and Careers," March 19, 2008*

- *Fortune* ranked the 100 largest metro areas in the U.S. in terms of projected median home price change in 2007. The Providence* metro area ranked #78. *Fortune.com, "Hot Spots, Cold Spots"*

Health/Environment Rankings

- 100 of the largest metro areas in the U.S. were analyzed in terms of their current drought severity. The Providence* metro area ranked #74 (#1 = driest). The rankings were based on statistics such as long-term precipitation trends and patterns and the Palmer drought indices. *Sperling's BestPlaces, www.BestPlaces.net, "America's Drought-Riskiest Cities," November 2007*

- *Reader's Digest* ranked the 50 largest metro areas in the U.S. in terms of how "clean" they are. The Providence* metro area ranked #33. Criteria: air quality; water quality; toxic industrial pollution; Superfund sites; and sanitation. *Reader's Digest, "The 50 Cleanest (and Dirtiest) Cities in America," July 2005*

- The American Academy of Dermatology ranked 32 U.S. metropolitan regions in terms of their residents knowledge, attitude and behaviors towards tanning and sun protection. The Providence* metro area ranked #15. The results of the study are based on an online national survey of 3,342 respondents. *American Academy of Dermatology, "RAYS: Your Grade," May 7, 2007*

- The Providence* metro area appeared in *Country Home's* "2008 Best Green Places" report. The area ranked #85 out of 379. Criteria: official energy policies; green power; green buildings; availability of fresh, locally grown food. *Country Home, "2008 Best Green Places"*

- Wyeth Consumer Healthcare, in partnership with Sperling's BestPlaces, ranked the nation's 50 most populous metro areas in terms of five key health factors. The Providence* metro area ranked #38. Criteria: physical activity; health status; nutrition; lifestyle pursuits; and mental wellness. *Wyeth Consumer Healthcare, "Centrum Healthiest Cities Study," April 19, 2005*

- Providence* was identified as a "2008 Asthma Capital." The area ranked #33 out of the nation's 100 largest metropolitan areas. Twelve factors were used to identify the most challenging places to live for people with asthma: estimated prevalence; self-reported prevalence; crude death rate for asthma; annual pollen score; annual air quality; public smoking laws; number of board-certified asthma specialists; school inhaler access laws; rescue medication use; controller medication use; uninsured rate; poverty rate. *Asthma and Allergy Foundation of America, "2008 Asthma Capitals"*

- Providence* was identified as a "Spring Allergy Capital." The area ranked #82 out of 100. Three groups of factors were used to identify the most severe cities for people with allergies during the spring season: annual pollen levels; medicine utilization; access to board-certified allergists. *Asthma and Allergy Foundation of America, "2007 Spring Allergy Capital Rankings"*

- Providence* was identified as a "Fall Allergy Capital." The area ranked #95 out of 100. Three groups of factors were used to identify the most severe cities for people with allergies during the fall season: annual pollen levels; medicine utilization; access to board-certified allergists. *Asthma and Allergy Foundation of America, "2007 Fall Allergy Capital Rankings"*

- Ortho-McNeil Neurologics, in partnership with Sperling's BestPlaces, analyzed 110 metro areas and identified those U.S. cities with the highest prevalence of factors that are most commonly associated with migraine headaches. The Providence* metro area ranked #86. Criteria: number of migraine-related drug prescriptions per capita; lifestyle factors that can contribute to migraines; environmental factors that can trigger migraines; and consumption of migraine-triggering foods. *Ortho-McNeil Neurologics, "America's Migraine Hot Spots," March 14, 2006*

- Sperling's BestPlaces ranked 331 metro areas and identified the most and least stressful U.S. cities. The Providence* metro area ranked #85 out of the 100 largest metro areas (#1 = most stressful). Criteria: divorce rate; unemployment rate; violent and property crime; suicide rate; commute time; mental health; alcohol consumption; cloudy days. *Sperling's BestPlaces, www.BestPlaces.net, "America's Most (and Least) Stressful Cities," January 9, 2004*

- Providence* was selected as one of "America's Pet Healthiest Cities" by Purina. The city ranked #31 out of 50. Criteria: veterinary services; environment; legislation; preventative care; obesity/body condition. *Purina Pet Institute, "America's Pet Healthiest Cities," May 20, 2003*

Women/Minorities Rankings

- Providence* was ranked #60 out of 100 metro areas in *SELF Magazine's* ranking of "America's Best Places for Women." A panel of experts came up with more than 50 criteria including death and disease rates, environmental indicators, community resources, and lifestyle habits. *SELF Magazine, "America's Best Places for Women 2007," December 2007*

Seniors/Retirement Rankings

- Sperling's BestPlaces in partnership with Bankers Life & Casualty Company designed a survey to identify the top 50 metro areas in the U.S. that offer the best overall qualities for senior living. The Providence* metro area ranked #23. The following criteria were statistically weighted to reflect the needs of the senior population: health; disease; economics; social; environment; spiritual; transportation; housing; and crime. *Bankers Life & Casualty Company, "Best Cities for Seniors 2005"*
- A.G. Edwards ranked America's 500 top-performing communities based on their residents' personal savings and investing behavior. The Providence* metro area ranked #172 with an index score of 104.15 (national average = 100.00). A dozen statistical factors were measured including: participation in retirement savings plans; personal debt levels; and home ownership. *A.G. Edwards, "2007 Nest Egg Index", September 12, 2007*

Children/Family Rankings

- The Providence* metro area was selected as one of the "Best Cities for Relocating Families" by Worldwide ERC and Primacy Relocation. The 2007 study placed a special emphasis on the housing market, which has significantly impacted the relocation industry and an employer's ability to transfer employees. The variables which weigh heavily in this category include home price, home affordability index, appreciation rates, and property tax. Other criteria include cost of living, crime rates, education, climate, focus on diversity, physicians per capita, recreation and leisure, arts and culture, air quality, watershed quality, sales tax, unemployment rate, job growth, high school and higher education index, school expenditures per student, students in public school, SAT/ACT percentile, and population growth. *Worldwide ERC and Primacy Relocation, "2007 Best Cities for Relocating Families"*

Safety Rankings

- The National Insurance Crime Bureau ranked 361 metro areas in the U.S. in terms of per capita rates of vehicle theft. The Providence* metro area ranked #140 (#1 = highest rate). Criteria: number of vehicle theft offenses per 100,000 inhabitants. *National Insurance Crime Bureau, "NICB Vehicle Theft Study," April 22, 2008*
- Providence* appeared on Sperling's BestPlaces list of the "Riskiest Cities for Identity Theft." The area ranked #42 out of the nations 50 largest metro areas. Over 80 criteria were analyzed across four major categories: technology impact; crime; transactions; and risk profile. *Sperling's BestPlaces, www.BestPlaces.net, "Riskiest Cities for Identity Theft," July 2006*
- Farmers Insurance Group of Companies, in partnership with Sperling's BestPlaces, ranked 379 metro areas and identified the "Most Secure U.S. Place to Live." The Providence* metro area ranked #28 out of 114 in the large metro area category (500,000 or more residents). Criteria: crime rates; extreme weather; risk of natural disasters; environmental hazards; terrorism threats; air quality; life expectancy; job loss numbers. *Farmers Insurance Group, "Most Secure U.S. Places to Live 2007"*

Sports/Recreation Rankings

- *Golf Digest* ranked 330 metro areas in the U.S. in terms of golf. The Providence* metro area was ranked #323. Criteria: access to golf; weather; value of golf; and quality of golf. *Golf Digest, "Metro Golf Rankings," August 2005*

Dating/Romance Rankings

- Eli Lily and Company, in partnership with Sperling's BestPlaces, ranked the nation's 50 largest metro areas in terms of the "Most Romantic Cities for Baby Boomers." The Providence* metro area ranked #4. Criteria: marriage and divorce rates among "baby boomers" age 45 to 60; great restaurants; dance studios; chocolate, jewelry and flower sales. *Eli Lily and Company, "Most Romantic Cities for Baby Boomers," April 20, 2007*

- The Providence* metro area was selected as one of the "Best Cities for Relocating Singles" by Worldwide ERC and Primacy Relocation. The area ranked #22 out of the 100 largest metro areas in the U.S. Areas were selected based on the following criteria: a robust cost-of-living index; adventure and outdoor recreation opportunities; violent crime and property crime rates; percentage of the population that is unmarried (ages 25-34); ratio of single men and single women; affordability of quality higher education, including in-state and out-of-state tuition requirements and rates; number of newcomers to the area; commute times; tax rates; fee and occupancy rates for temporary housing and mini-storage; quality and quantity of collegiate and professional sporting events and fun, fan-friendly venues. *Worldwide ERC and Primacy Relocation, "2007 Best Cities for Relocating Singles," October 25, 2007*

- *Forbes* ranked the 40 most populous urbanized areas in the U.S. in terms of the "Best Cities for Singles." The Providence* metro area ranked #40. Criteria: number of singles; cost of living alone; nightlife; culture; job growth; coolness; and online dating. *Forbes.com, August 21, 2007*

- Sperling's BestPlaces in partnership with AXE Deodorant Bodyspray ranked 80 metro areas and identified "America's Best (and Worst) Cities for Dating." The Providence* metro area ranked #20 (#1 = best). Criteria: percentage of singles ages 18-24; population density; dating venues per capita. *AXE Deodorant Bodyspray, "America's Best (and Worst) Cities for Dating," May 2004*

Culture/Performing Arts Rankings

- Scarborough Research, a leading market research firm, identified the top local markets for rock concert attendance. The Providence* DMA (Designated Market Area) ranked in the top 25 with 15% of consumers, 18 years old and over, reporting that they have attended a rock concert during the past year. *Scarborough Research, June 14, 2004*

Miscellaneous Rankings

- Avis Rent-A-Car and Motorola, in partnership with Sperling's BestPlaces, ranked the nation's 75 most populous metro areas in terms of how difficult they are to navigate. The Providence* metro area ranked #9 with #1 being the most challenging. Criteria: street layouts; overall design and layout; travel time index; percent of congested freeway and street lane miles; bodies of water; complexity of directions needed to travel from major airports to city center; annual delay per person; days of snow exceeding 1.5 inches; and days of rain exceeding 0.5 inch. *Avis Rent-A-Car and Motorola, "America's Most Challenging Cities to Navigate," August 3, 2004*

- The Providence* metro area appeared on *Forbes* list of "America's Drunkest Cities". The area ranked #10. Criteria: 35 of the largest continental U.S. metro areas were chosen based on availability of data and geographic diversity. Each metro was ranked in five areas: state laws; drinkers; heavy drinkers; binge drinkers; and alcoholism. *Forbes.com, "America's Drunkest Cities," August 22, 2006*

- Sperling's BestPlaces in partnership with Pep Boys ranked 77 metro areas and identified "America's Most Drivable Cities." The Providence* metro area ranked #56. Criteria: climate; road roughness; urban mobility; gas prices. *Pep Boys, "America's Most Drivable Cities," April 9, 2003*

- Scarborough Research, a leading market research firm, identified the top local markets for reality television. The Providence* DMA (Designated Market Area) ranked in the top 10 with 30% of consumers reporting that they "typically watch" reality-dating, reality-talent, or reality- adventure television shows. *Scarborough Research, January 11, 2005*

- Scarborough Research, a leading market research firm, identified the top local markets for grocery coupon use. The Providence* DMA (Designated Market Area) ranked in the top 25 with 46% of consumers reporting that they use grocery coupons at least once per week. *Scarborough Research, December 8, 2004*

- A study by Sperling's BestPlaces examined which U.S. metro areas were most affected by high fuel prices in 2006. The Providence* metro area was ranked #63 out of 80 (#1 = most expensive city for driving). Rankings are based on the average dollars spent on gas per year by two driver households. Criteria: cost of regular-grade gasoline; average miles driven per day; average number of gallons each driver uses and wastes in traffic congestion each day. *Sperling's BestPlaces, www.bestplaces.net, "Pain at the Pump," May 18, 2006*

South Kingstown is located within the Providence-New Bedford-Fall River, RI-MA Metropolitan Statistical Area.

Business Environment

CITY FINANCES

City Government Finances

Component	2004-2005 ($000)	2004-2005 ($ per capita)
Total Revenues	81,433	2,777
Total Expenditures	79,252	2,702
Debt Outstanding	39,667	1,353
Cash and Securities	27,576	940

Source: U.S Census Bureau, Government Finances 2004-2005

City Government Revenue by Source

Source	2004-2005 ($000)	2004-2005 ($ per capita)
General Revenue		
From Federal Government	0	0
From State Government	17,476	596
From Local Governments	0	0
Taxes		
Property	51,575	1,759
Sales	471	16
Personal Income	0	0
License	1,159	40
Charges	6,986	238
Liquor Store	0	0
Utility	782	27
Employee Retirement	0	0
Other	2,984	102

Source: U.S Census Bureau, Government Finances 2004-2005

City Government Expenditures by Function

Function	2004-2005 ($000)	2004-2005 ($ per capita)	2004-2005 (%)
General Expenditures			
Airports	0	0	0.0
Corrections	0	0	0.0
Education	51,915	1,770	65.5
Fire Protection	4	< 1	< 0.1
Governmental Administration	2,018	69	2.5
Health	1,198	41	1.5
Highways	3,449	118	4.4
Hospitals	0	0	0.0
Housing and Community Development	129	4	0.2
Interest on General Debt	1,675	57	2.1
Libraries	886	30	1.1
Parking	0	0	0.0
Parks and Recreation	2,019	69	2.5
Police Protection	4,318	147	5.4
Public Welfare	850	29	1.1
Sewerage	3,014	103	3.8
Solid Waste Management	1,263	43	1.6
Liquor Store	0	0	0.0
Utility	1,209	41	1.5
Employee Retirement	0	0	0.0
Other	5,305	181	6.7

Source: U.S Census Bureau, Government Finances 2004-2005

Municipal Bond Ratings

Area	Moody's
City	n/a

Source: Mergent Bond Record, January 2008 (unless noted otherwise)

DEMOGRAPHICS

Population Growth

Area	1990 Census	2000 Census	2007 Estimate	2012 Projection	Population Growth (%) 1990-2000	Population Growth (%) 2000-2012
City	24,631	27,921	29,693	30,646	13.4	9.8
MSA[1]	1,509,789	1,582,997	1,626,234	1,642,634	4.8	3.8
U.S.	248,709,873	281,421,906	301,045,522	314,920,978	13.2	11.9

Note: (1) Metropolitan Statistical Area - see Appendix B for areas included
Source: Claritas, Inc.

Number of Households and Average Household Size

Area	2007 Estimate	2007 Average Household Size
City	10,176	2.92
MSA[1]	637,423	2.55
U.S.	113,668,003	2.65

Note: (1) Metropolitan Statistical Area - see Appendix B for areas included
Source: Claritas, Inc.

Race and Ethnicity

Area	White Alone[2]	Black Alone[2]	Asian Alone[2]	Other Race Alone[2]	Hispanic[3]
City	90.4	1.8	3.7	4.1	2.2
MSA[1]	84.4	4.3	2.3	9.0	9.0
U.S.	73.1	12.4	4.3	10.3	14.9

Note: Figures are 2007 estimates; (1) Metropolitan Statistical Area - see Appendix B for areas included (2) Alone is defined as not being in combination with one or more other races; (3) May be of any race.
Source: Claritas, Inc.

Ancestry

Area	German	Irish[2]	English	American	Italian	Polish	French[3]	Scottish
City	8.5	23.9	18.6	3.5	16.5	4.9	9.1	3.3
MSA[1]	4.6	17.6	11.7	3.0	16.9	4.1	11.9	1.8
U.S.	15.2	10.9	8.7	7.3	5.6	3.2	3.0	1.7

Note: Figures include multiple ancestry (e.g. if a person reported being Irish and Italian, they were included in both columns); (1) Metropolitan Statistical Area - see Appendix A for areas included; (2) Includes Celtic; (3) Includes Alsatian but excludes Basque
Source: Census 2000, Summary File 3

Foreign-Born Population

Area	Percent of Population Born in: Any Foreign Country	Europe	Asia	Africa	Oceania[2]	Canada	Mexico	Latin America[3]
City	5.8	1.8	2.9	0.2	0.0	0.3	0.1	0.5
MSA[1]	12.0	4.8	1.9	1.0	0.0	0.4	0.2	3.6
U.S.	11.1	1.7	2.9	0.3	0.1	0.3	3.3	2.5

Note: (1) Metropolitan Statistical Area - see Appendix A for areas included; (2) Includes Australia, New Zealand subregion, Melanesia, Micronesia, Polynesia, and Oceania n.e.c; (3) Includes Central America (excluding Mexico), South America, and the Caribbean.
Source: Census 2000, Summary File 3

Marriage Status

Area	Never Married	Now Married (excluding Separated)	Separated	Widowed	Divorced
City	33.0	52.4	0.9	5.5	8.3
MSA[1]	29.2	52.0	1.9	7.7	9.2
U.S.	27.1	54.4	2.2	6.6	9.7

Note: Figures are percentages and cover the population 15 years of age and older; (1) Metropolitan Statistical Area - see Appendix A for areas included
Source: Census 2000, Summary File 3

Age Distribution

Area	Under Age 5	Age 5 to 17	Age 18 to 34	Age 35 to 49	Age 50 to 64	Age 65 to 79	80 Years and Over
	Percent of Population						
City	5.3	16.9	29.7	22.5	13.8	8.4	3.4
MSA[1]	6.0	17.8	23.2	23.5	14.9	10.4	4.3
U.S.	6.8	18.9	23.7	23.5	14.8	9.2	3.2

Note: (1) Metropolitan Statistical Area - see Appendix A for areas included
Source: Census 2000, Summary File 3

Male/Female Ratio

Area	Males	Females	Males per 100 Females
City	14,213	15,480	91.8
MSA[1]	785,710	840,524	93.5
U.S.	148,320,305	152,725,217	97.1

Note: Figures are 2007 estimates; (1) Metropolitan Statistical Area - see Appendix B for areas included
Source: Claritas, Inc.

Religion

Area	Catholic	Southern Baptist	United Meth-odist	ELCA[1]	LDS[2]	Presby-terian Church USA	Jewish Est.	Muslim Est.
County	47.5	0.5	0.6	0.6	0.0	0.5	1.0	0.0
U.S.	22.0	7.1	3.7	1.8	1.5	1.1	2.2	0.6

Note: Figures are the number of adherents as a percentage of the total population; Adherents are defined as all members, including full members, their children and the estimated number of other participants who are not considered members (e.g. the baptized, those not confirmed, those regularly attending services, etc.); (1) Evangelical Lutheran Church in America; (2) The Church of Jesus Christ of Latter Day Saints
Source: Reprinted with permission from Religious Congregations and Membership in the United States 2000 (Nashville, Glenmary Research Center, 2002) Copyright Association of Statisticians of American Religious Bodies. All rights reserved.

ECONOMY

Gross Metropolitan Product

Area	2002	2003	2004	2005	2005 Rank[2]
MSA[1]	56.4	60.0	63.8	66.6	37

Note: Figures are in billions of dollars; (1) Providence-New Bedford-Fall River, RI-MA Metropolitan Statistical Area - see Appendix A for areas included; (2) Rank ranges from 1 to 361
Source: The U.S. Conference of Mayors, "U.S. Metro Economies: GMP - The Engines of America's Growth," January 2007

Economic Growth

Area	1995 GMP	2005 GMP	Average Annual Growth Rate	Growth Rate Rank[2]
MSA[1]	39.2	66.6	5.4	172

Note: Figures are in billions of dollars; GMP = Gross Metropolitan Product; (1) Providence-New Bedford-Fall River, RI-MA Metropolitan Statistical Area - see Appendix A for areas included; (2) Rank ranges from 1 to 361
Source: The U.S. Conference of Mayors, "U.S. Metro Economies: GMP - The Engines of America's Growth," January 2007

INCOME

Per Capita/Median/Average Income

Area	Per Capita ($)	Median Household ($)	Average Household ($)
City	31,012	71,010	88,720
MSA[1]	26,302	51,397	66,195
U.S.	25,495	49,280	66,670

Note: Figures are 2007 estimates; (1) Metropolitan Statistical Area - see Appendix B for areas included
Source: Claritas, Inc.

Household Income Distribution

Area	Percent of Households Earning							
	Under $15,000	$15,000 -24,999	$25,000 -34,999	$35,000 -49,999	$50,000 -74,999	$75,000 -99,000	$100,000 -149,999	$150,000 and up
City	6.8	6.5	7.2	12.5	20.0	16.3	18.4	12.3
MSA[1]	14.2	10.8	9.8	14.0	19.4	13.0	12.7	6.0
U.S.	13.1	10.9	11.2	15.6	19.5	11.9	11.3	6.6

Note: Figures are 2007 estimates; (1) Metropolitan Statistical Area - see Appendix B for areas included
Source: Claritas, Inc.

Poverty Rates by Age

Area	All Ages	Under 5 Years Old	5 to 17 Years Old	18 to 64 Years Old	65 Years and Over
City	5.3	0.3	1.1	3.3	0.6
MSA[1]	11.8	1.1	2.9	6.2	1.6
U.S.	12.4	1.2	3.0	6.9	1.2

Note: Figures are percent of population with income in 1999 below poverty level and only include population for whom poverty status is determined; (1) Metropolitan Statistical Area - see Appendix A for areas included
Source: Census 2000, Summary File 3

Personal Bankruptcy Filing Rate

Area	2004	2005	2006
Washington County	2.67	3.25	1.00
U.S.	5.31	6.82	2.00

Note: Numbers are per 1,000 population and include Chapter 7 and Chapter 13 filings
Source: Federal Deposit Insurance Corporation (FDIC), Regional Economic Conditions (RECON), 8/23/2007

EMPLOYMENT

Labor Force and Employment

Area	Civilian Labor Force			Workers Employed		
	Dec. 2006	Dec. 2007	% Chg.	Dec. 2006	Dec. 2007	% Chg.
City	16,278	16,166	-0.7	15,637	15,488	-1.0
NECTA[1]	717,880	712,660	-0.7	682,575	674,551	-1.2
U.S.	152,571,000	153,705,000	0.7	146,081,000	146,334,000	0.2

Note: Data is not seasonally adjusted and covers workers 16 years of age and older;
(1) New England City and Town Area - see Appendix B for areas included
Source: Bureau of Labor Statistics, http://stats.bls.gov

Unemployment Rate

Area	2007											
	Jan.	Feb.	Mar.	Apr.	May	Jun.	Jul.	Aug.	Sep.	Oct.	Nov.	Dec.
City	5.5	5.1	4.5	4.2	3.9	4.0	4.7	4.2	3.5	3.4	4.0	4.2
NECTA[1]	6.1	5.8	5.5	5.2	4.8	4.9	5.7	5.3	4.8	4.6	4.7	5.3
U.S.	5.0	4.9	4.5	4.3	4.3	4.7	4.9	4.6	4.5	4.4	4.5	4.8

Note: Data is not seasonally adjusted and covers workers 16 years of age and older; All figures are percentages; (1) New England City and Town Area - see Appendix B for areas included
Source: Bureau of Labor Statistics, http://stats.bls.gov

Employment by Occupation

Occupation Classification	City (%)	MSA[1] (%)	U.S. (%)
Sales and Office	22.5	27.1	26.7
Professional and Related	29.8	20.8	20.2
Service	18.1	15.3	14.9
Production, Transportation, and Material Moving	7.8	16.3	14.6
Management, Business, and Financial	14.7	12.1	13.5
Construction, Extraction, and Maintenance	5.7	8.0	9.4
Farming, Forestry, and Fishing	1.4	0.3	0.7

Note: Figures cover employed civilians 16 years of age and older;
(1) Metropolitan Statistical Area - see Appendix A for areas included
Source: Census 2000, Summary File 3

Employment by Industry

Sector	NECTA[1] Number of Employees	NECTA[1] Percent of Total	U.S. Percent of Total
Government	75,100	12.8	16.3
Education and Health Services	116,100	19.8	13.4
Professional and Business Services	63,600	10.8	13.1
Retail Trade	70,800	12.1	11.6
Manufacturing	64,700	11.0	9.9
Leisure and Hospitality	58,700	10.0	9.6
Financial Activities	37,500	6.4	5.9
Construction	27,200	4.6	5.3
Wholesale Trade	21,200	3.6	4.4
Other Services	26,200	4.5	3.9
Transportation and Utilities	13,200	2.3	3.7
Information	11,600	2.0	2.2
Natural Resources and Mining	300	0.1	0.5

Note: Figures cover non-farm employment as of December 2007 and are not seasonally adjusted; (1) New England City and Town Area - see Appendix B for areas included
Source: Bureau of Labor Statistics, http://stats.bls.gov

Average Wages

Occupation	$/Hr.	Occupation	$/Hr.
Accountants and Auditors	30.86	Maids and Housekeeping Cleaners	10.96
Automotive Mechanics	17.76	Maintenance and Repair Workers	17.05
Bookkeepers	16.96	Marketing Managers	44.47
Carpenters	21.25	Nuclear Medicine Technologists	35.70
Cashiers	9.24	Nurses, Licensed Practical	22.50
Clerks, General Office	12.54	Nurses, Registered	31.20
Clerks, Receptionists/Information	12.34	Nursing Aides/Orderlies/Attendants	13.02
Clerks, Shipping/Receiving	13.98	Packers and Packagers, Hand	9.73
Computer Programmers	32.40	Physical Therapists	36.50
Computer Support Specialists	20.47	Postal Service Mail Carriers	21.38
Computer Systems Analysts	39.49	Real Estate Brokers	n/a
Cooks, Restaurant	12.00	Retail Salespersons	11.84
Dentists	n/a	Sales Reps., Exc. Tech./Scientific	29.18
Electrical Engineers	39.84	Sales Reps., Tech./Scientific	35.68
Electricians	24.17	Secretaries, Exc. Legal/Med./Exec.	16.01
Financial Managers	49.18	Security Guards	12.34
First-Line Supervisors/Mgrs., Sales	19.46	Surgeons	n/a
Food Preparation Workers	9.85	Teacher Assistants	12.20
General and Operations Managers	53.03	Teachers, Elementary School	29.10
Hairdressers/Cosmetologists	12.72	Teachers, Secondary School	29.00
Internists	83.10	Telemarketers	11.33
Janitors and Cleaners	12.47	Truck Drivers, Heavy/Tractor-Trailer	18.75
Landscaping/Groundskeeping Workers	12.87	Truck Drivers, Light/Delivery Svcs.	14.46
Lawyers	48.82	Waiters and Waitresses	9.52

Note: Wage data covers the Providence-Fall River-Warwick, RI-MA Metropolitan NECTA - see Appendix B for areas included. Hourly wages for elementary/secondary school teachers and teacher assistants were calculated by the editors from annual wage data assuming a 40 hour work week; n/a not available.
Source: Bureau of Labor Statistics, May 2007 Metro Area Occupational Employment and Wage Estimates

RESIDENTIAL REAL ESTATE

Building Permits

Area	Single-Family 2006	Single-Family 2007[p]	Single-Family Pct. Chg.	Multi-Family 2006	Multi-Family 2007[p]	Multi-Family Pct. Chg.	Total 2006	Total 2007[p]	Total Pct. Chg.
City	95	57	-40.0	0	28	-	95	85	-10.5
U.S.	1,378,200	973,300	-29.4	460,700	407,200	-11.6	1,838,900	1,380,500	-24.9

Note: (p) preliminary; figures cover and represent new, privately-owned housing units authorized (unadjusted data); All permit data are based on estimates with imputation; U.S. figures are based on the new 20,000-place series.
Source: U.S. Census Bureau, Manufacturing, Mining, and Construction Statistics

Homeownership and Housing Vacancies

Area	Homeownership Rate[2] (%)			Rental Vacancy Rate[3] (%)			Homeowner Vacancy Rate[4] (%)		
	2005	2006	2007	2005	2006	2007	2005	2006	2007
MSA[1]	63.1	65.5	64.1	7.0	8.6	9.2	1.4	1.8	1.6
U.S.	68.9	68.8	68.1	9.8	9.8	9.7	1.9	2.4	2.7

Note: (1) Metropolitan Statistical Area - see Appendix B for areas included; (2) The proportion of households that are owners; (3) The proportion of the rental inventory that is vacant for rent; (4) The proportion of the homeowner inventory that is vacant for sale; n/a not available
Source: U.S. Census Bureau, Housing Vacancies and Homeownership Annual Statistics: 2007

TAXES

State Corporate Income Tax Rates

State	Rates and Tax Brackets
Rhode Island	9.0%

Note: Tax rates as of January 1, 2008; Greater of 9% of net income apportioned to Rhode Island, or a franchise tax on authorized capital stock at the rate of $2.50 for each $10,000.00 or fractional part thereof (minimum of $500).
Source: Tax Foundation, www.taxfoundation.org

State Individual Income Tax Rates

State	Federal Deductibility	Marginal Rates (%)	Standard Deduction ($)		Personal Exemptions ($)[1]	
			Single	Joint	Single	Dependents
Rhode Island	No	3.75 - 9.9 (y)(aa)	5,350 (s)	10,700 (s)	3,400 (s)	3,400 (s)

Note: Tax rates as of January 1, 2008; Local- and county-level taxes are not included; n/a not applicable; (1) Married joint filers generally receive double the single exemption; (s) Deductions and exemptions tied to federal tax system. Federal deductions and exemptions are indexed for inflation; (y) Brackets are not double for married taxpayers; (aa) Taxpayers calculate tax under a flat tax system and pay the lesser of the liability. The flat tax applies to all types of income with no exemptions or deductions and treats capital income as wages. The flat tax rates are 8.0 percent for 2006; 7.5

cent for 2007; 7 percent for 2008; 6.5 percent for 2009; 6 percent for 2010; and 5.5 percent for 2011 and beyond.
Source: Tax Foundation, www.taxfoundation.org

Various State and Local Tax Rates

State and Local Sales and Use (%)	State Sales and Use (%)	Gasoline[1,2] ($/gal.)	Cigarette ($/pack)	Spirits ($/gal.)	Table Wine ($/gal.)	Beer ($/gal.)
7.0	7.0	0.31	2.46	3.75	0.60	0.10

Note: Tax rates as of January 1, 2008; (1) In addition to the 18.4 cpg Federal gasoline tax; (2) Rates may include additional state sales taxes, environmental protection and storage fees/taxes, and local taxes. When necessary, the volume-weighted average of all local taxes is used to approximate the typical statewide rate including local tax
Source: Tax Foundation, www.taxfoundation.org; Original research

State Tax Burdens

Area	Combined State and Local Tax Burden		Combined Federal, State and Local Tax Burden	
	Percent	Rank	Percent	Rank
Rhode Island	12.7	4	35.1	6
U.S. Average	11.0	-	32.7	-

Note: Figures cover 2007 and measure taxes as a percentage of income
Source: Tax Foundation, www.taxfoundation.org

State Business Tax Climate Index Rankings

State	Overall Rank	Corporate Tax Index Rank	Individual Income Tax Index Rank	Sales Tax Index Rank	Unemployment Insurance Tax Index Rank	Property Tax Index Rank
Rhode Island	50	34	47	33	50	48

Note: Rankings range from 1 to 50 where 1 is best. Rankings do not average across to Overall Rank. States without a given tax are given a ranking of 1.
Source: Tax Foundation, State Business Tax Climate Index 2008

TRANSPORTATION

Means of Transportation to Work

Area	Car/Truck/Van		Public Transportation			Bicycle	Walked	Other Means	Worked at Home
	Drove Alone	Car-pooled	Bus	Subway	Railroad				
City	76.0	8.0	0.5	0.0	0.1	0.1	10.2	0.5	4.6
MSA[1]	80.7	10.6	1.7	0.0	0.6	0.2	3.3	0.8	2.1
U.S.	75.7	12.2	2.5	1.5	0.5	0.4	2.9	1.0	3.3

Note: Figures are percentages and cover workers 16 years of age and older; (1) Metropolitan Statistical Area - see Appendix A for areas included
Source: Census 2000, Summary File 3

Travel Time to Work

Area	Less Than 15 Minutes	15 to 29 Minutes	30 to 44 Minutes	45 to 59 Minutes	60 Minutes or More
City	41.0	27.0	18.1	8.3	5.5
MSA[1]	32.2	39.9	16.3	5.4	6.2
U.S.	29.4	36.1	19.1	7.4	8.0

Note: Figures are percentages and include workers 16 years old and over; (1) Metropolitan Statistical Area - see Appendix A for areas included
Source: Census 2000, Summary File 3

Travel Time Index

Area	1982	1995	2004	2005
Urban Area[1]	1.03	1.08	1.17	1.16
Average[2]	1.11	1.22	1.29	1.30

Note: Travel Time Index - The ratio of travel time in the peak period to the travel time at free-flow conditions. A value of 1.35 indicates a 20-minute free-flow trip takes 27 minutes in the peak. Free-flow speeds (60 mph on freeways and 35 mph on principal arterials) are used as the comparison threshold; (1) Covers the Providence, RI-MA urban area; (2) average of 85 urban areas
Source: Texas Transportation Institute, The 2007 Urban Mobility Report, September 2007

Living Environment

COST OF LIVING

Cost of Living Index

Composite Index	Groceries	Housing	Utilities	Trans-portation	Health Care	Misc. Goods/ Services
121.1	116.5	136.3	119.4	101.2	115.7	117.4

Note: U.S. = 100; Figures cover the Providence RI urban area.
Source: The Council for Community and Economic Research (formerly ACCRA), Cost of Living Index, 2007

Grocery Prices

Area[1]	T-Bone Steak ($/pound)	Frying Chicken ($/pound)	Whole Milk ($/half gal.)	Eggs ($/dozen)	Orange Juice ($/64 oz.)	Coffee ($/11.5 oz.)
City[2]	10.08	1.42	2.22	2.05	3.12	3.27
Avg.	8.93	1.12	2.13	1.52	3.26	3.31
Min.	5.88	0.71	1.33	0.83	2.30	2.20
Max.	12.80	2.07	3.43	3.54	5.79	6.20

Note: (1) Values for the local area are compared with the average, minimum and maximum values for all 331 areas in the Cost of Living Index report; (2) Figures cover the Providence RI urban area; **T-Bone Steak** *(price per pound);* **Frying Chicken** *(price per pound, whole fryer);* **Whole Milk** *(half gallon carton);* **Eggs** *(price per dozen, Grade A, large);* **Orange Juice** *(64 oz. Tropicana or Florida Natural);* **Coffee** *(11.5 oz. can, vacuum-packed, Maxwell House, Hills Bros, or Folgers).*
Source: The Council for Community and Economic Research (formerly ACCRA), Cost of Living Index, 2007

Housing and Utility Costs

Area[1]	New Home Price ($)	Apartment Rent ($/month)	All Electric ($/month)	Part Electric ($/month)	Other Energy ($/month)	Telephone ($/month)
City[2]	409,494	1,155	-	80.37	101.22	34.45
Avg.	309,605	782	146.13	78.67	90.16	26.14
Min.	189,877	n/a	82.03	37.41	33.15	17.08
Max.	1,202,800	3,481	271.14	150.60	257.67	37.45

Note: (1) Values for the local area are compared with the average, minimum and maximum values for all 331 areas in the Cost of Living Index report; (2) Figures cover the Providence RI urban area; **New Home Price** *(2,400 sf living area, 8,000 sf lot, in urban area with full utilities);* **Apartment Rent** *(950 sf 2 bedroom/1.5 or 2 bath, unfurnished, excluding all utilities except water);* **All Electric** *(average monthly cost for an all-electric home);* **Part Electric** *(average monthly cost for a part-electric home);* **Other Energy** *(average monthly cost for natural gas, fuel oil, coal, wood, and any other forms of energy except electricity);* **Telephone** *(price includes basic monthly rate for a private residential line plus additional local usage charges incurred by a family of four).*
Source: The Council for Community and Economic Research (formerly ACCRA), Cost of Living Index, 2007

Health Care, Transportation, and Other Costs

Area[1]	Doctor ($/visit)	Dentist ($/visit)	Optometrist ($/visit)	Gasoline ($/gallon)	Beauty Salon ($/visit)	Men's Shirt ($)
City[2]	110.33	82.47	79.17	2.56	42.67	35.34
Avg.	79.48	71.93	79.55	2.64	29.52	25.77
Min.	52.08	44.80	43.95	2.19	15.58	16.19
Max.	148.44	126.27	158.83	3.48	60.62	48.53

Note: (1) Values for the local area are compared with the average, minimum and maximum values for all 331 areas in the Cost of Living Index report; (2) Figures cover the Providence RI urban area; **Doctor** *(general practitioners routine exam of an established patient);* **Dentist** *(adult teeth cleaning and periodic oral examination);* **Optometrist** *(full vision eye exam for established adult patient);* **Gasoline** *(one gallon regular unleaded, national brand, including all taxes, cash price at self-service pump if available);* **Beauty Salon** *(woman's shampoo, trim, and blow-dry);* **Men's Shirt** *(cotton/polyester dress shirt, pinpoint weave, long sleeves).*
Source: The Council for Community and Economic Research (formerly ACCRA), Cost of Living Index, 2007

HOUSING

House Price Index (HPI)

Area	National Ranking[2]	Quarterly Change (%)	One-Year Change (%)	Five-Year Change (%)
MSA[1]	232	0.14	-2.57	46.05
U.S.[3]	-	0.10	0.84	41.37

Note: The HPI is a weighted repeat sales index. It measures average price changes in repeat sales or refinancings on the same properties. This information is obtained by reviewing repeat mortgage transactions on single-family properties whose mortgages have been purchased or securitized by Fannie Mae or Freddie Mac in January 1975; (1) Metropolitan Statistical Area - see Appendix B for areas included; (2) Rankings are based on annual percentage change for all metro areas containing at least 15,000 transactions over the last 10 years and ranges from 1 to 291; (3) figures based on a weighted average of Census Division estimates; all figures are for the period ending December 31, 2007
Source: Office of Federal Housing Enterprise Oversight, House Price Index, February 26, 2008

House Price Valuations

Area	Q1 2000	Q1 2001	Q1 2002	Q1 2003	Q1 2004	Q1 2005	Q1 2006	Q1 2007	Q1 2008
MSA[1]	-19.5	-16.3	-5.3	6.0	18.9	31.0	28.8	17.4	11.6

Note: Figures show the percentage of over- or under-valuation of single family homes relative to statistically normal house values (e.g. a value of 23.6 indicates that house values are 23.6% overvalued). Statistically normal house values are based on house prices, interest rates, household incomes, population densities, and any historical premiums or discounts metropolitan areas have exhibited over time; (1) Figures cover the Metropolitan Statistical Area - see Appendix B for areas included
Source: Global Insight/National City Corporation, House Prices in America, May 2008

Median Home Prices

Area	2005	2006	2007[r]	Percent Change 2006 to 2007
MSA[1]	293.4	289.6	286.5	-1.1
U.S. Average	219.0	221.9	217.9	-1.8

Note: Figures are median sales prices of existing single-family homes in thousands of dollars; (r) revised; n/a not available; (1) Metropolitan Statistical Area - see Appendix B for areas included
Source: National Association of Realtors, Metropolitan Area Prices, 1st Quarter 2008

Housing: Year Structure Built

Area	1990 -2000	1980 -1989	1970 -1979	1960 -1969	1950 -1959	1940 -1949	Before 1940	Median Year
City	18.2	17.5	16.8	10.4	11.9	5.6	19.5	1971
MSA[1]	8.7	11.1	13.3	12.7	13.7	9.8	30.7	1957
U.S.	17.0	15.8	18.5	13.7	12.7	7.3	15.0	1971

Note: Figures are percentages; (1) Metropolitan Statistical Area - see Appendix A for areas included
Source: Census 2000, Summary File 3

HEALTH

Health Risk Data

Category	Area[1] (%)	U.S. (%)
Adults who have been told they have high blood pressure[3]	26.5	25.5
Adults who have been told they have high blood cholesterol[3]	35.8	35.6
Adults who have been told they have diabetes[2]	7.4	7.5
Adults who have been told they have arthritis[3]	28.0	27.0
Adults who have been told they currently have asthma	10.5	8.5
Adults who are current smokers	20.2	20.1
Adults who are heavy drinkers[4]	6.0	4.9
Adults who are overweight (BMI 25.0 - 29.9)	38.5	36.5
Adults who are obese (BMI 30.0 - 99.8)	22.3	25.1

Note: Data as of 2006 unless otherwise noted; (1) Figures cover the Metropolitan Statistical Area - see Appendix B for areas included; (2) Figures do not include pregnancy-related diabetes, pre-diabetes or borderline diabetes; (3) 2005 data; (4) Heavy drinkers are classified as adult men having more than two drinks per day or adult women having more than one drink per day
Source: Centers for Disease Control and Prevention, Behaviorial Risk Factor Surveillance System, SMART: Selected Metropolitan/Micropolitan Area Risk Trends, 2005, 2006

Mortality Rates for the Top 10 Causes of Death in the U.S.

ICD-10[a] Sub-Chapter	ICD-10[a] Code	Age-Adjusted Mortality Rate[1] per 100,000 population	
		County[2]	U.S.
Malignant neoplasms	C00-C97	182.7	186.5
Ischaemic heart diseases	I20-I25	171.4	152.3
Other forms of heart disease	I30-I51	26.2	51.5
Cerebrovascular diseases	I60-I69	37.1	50.0
Chronic lower respiratory diseases	J40-J47	38.2	42.6
Diabetes mellitus	E10-E14	16.8	24.8
Other degenerative diseases of the nervous system	G30-G31	19.5	22.6
Other external causes of accidental injury	W00-X59	17.8	21.4
Influenza and pneumonia	J10-J18	12.5	20.7
Hypertensive diseases	I10-I13	10.1	18.2

Note: (a) ICD-10 = International Classification of Diseases 10th Revision; (1) Mortality rates are a three year average covering 2003-2005; (2) Figures cover Washington County
Source: Centers for Disease Control and Prevention, National Center for Health Statistics. Compressed Mortality File 1999-2004. CDC WONDER On-line Database, compiled from Compressed Mortality File 1999-2005 Series 20 No. 2K, 2008.

Mortality Rates for Selected Causes of Death

ICD-10[a] Sub-Chapter	ICD-10[a] Code	Age-Adjusted Mortality Rate[1] per 100,000 population	
		County[2]	U.S.
Assault	X85-Y09	*0.4	5.9
Human immunodeficiency virus (HIV) disease	B20-B24	*0.5	4.5
Intentional self-harm	X60-X84	6.2	10.8
Malnutrition	E40-E46	*0.9	1.0
Obesity and other hyperalimentation	E65-E68	*1.0	1.4
Organic, including symptomatic, mental disorders	F01-F09	16.7	16.8
Transport accidents	V01-V99	11.1	16.1
Viral hepatitis	B15-B19	*0.7	1.8

Note: (a) ICD-10 = International Classification of Diseases 10th Revision; (1) Mortality rates are a three year average covering 2003-2005; (2) Figures cover Washington County; (*) Unreliable data as per CDC
Source: Centers for Disease Control and Prevention, National Center for Health Statistics. Compressed Mortality File 1999-2004. CDC WONDER On-line Database, compiled from Compressed Mortality File 1999-2005 Series 20 No. 2K, 2008.

Distribution of Physicians[1]

Area	Total	Family/ General Practice	Specialties	
			Medical	Surgical
Washington County (number)	265	46	118	57
Washington County (rate per 10,000 pop.)	20.6	3.6	9.2	4.4
U.S. (rate per 10,000 pop.)	17.7	4.6	6.9	4.3

Note: Data as of 2005; (1) Includes all non-federal, patient-care, office-based MDs
Source: Area Resource File (ARF). June 2007. U.S. Department of Health and Human Services, Health Resources and Services Administration, Bureau of Health Professions, Rockville, MD.

Hospitals

There were no hospitals listed within the city limits.
AHA Guide to the Healthcare Field 2008

EDUCATION

Public School District Statistics

District Name	Schls	Pupils	Pupil/ Teacher Ratio	Minority Pupils[1] (%)	Free Lunch Eligible[2] (%)	IEP[3] (%)
South Kingstown	9	3,912	9.9	11.8	9.2	19.2

Note: Table includes regular local school districts with 2,000 or more students; (1) Percentage of students that are not white, non-Hispanic; (2) Percentage of students that are eligible for the free lunch program; (3) Percentage of students that have an Individualized Education Program.
Source: U.S. Department of Education, National Center for Education Statistics, Common Core of Data, Local Education Agency (School District) Universe Survey: School Year 2005-2006; U.S. Department of Education, National Center for Education Statistics, Common Core of Data, Public Elementary/Secondary School Universe Survey: School Year 2005-2006

Highest Level of Education

Area	Less than H.S.	H.S. Diploma	Some College, No Deg.	Associate Degree	Bachelors Degree	Masters Degree	Profess. School Degree	Doctorate Degree
City	8.5	20.6	17.8	6.0	27.1	13.0	2.6	4.4
MSA[1]	23.8	28.4	17.1	7.1	15.0	6.0	1.7	0.8
U.S.	19.4	28.4	21.2	6.4	15.7	5.9	2.0	1.0

Note: Figures are 2007 estimated percentages and cover persons age 25 and over; (1) Metropolitan Statistical Area - see Appendix B for areas included
Source: Claritas, Inc.

Educational Attainment by Race

Area	High School Graduate (%)					Bachelor's Degree (%)				
	Total	White	Black	Asian	Hisp.[2]	Total	White	Black	Asian	Hisp.[2]
City	91.3	92.1	87.7	89.3	83.3	46.8	47.3	19.2	70.7	37.3
MSA[1]	76.0	77.8	70.5	68.3	50.2	23.6	24.5	16.8	35.4	8.5
U.S.	80.4	83.6	72.3	80.4	52.4	24.4	26.1	14.3	44.1	10.4

Note: Figures shown cover persons 25 years old and over; (1) Metropolitan Statistical Area - see Appendix A for areas included; (2) people of Hispanic origin can be of any race
Source: Census 2000, Summary File 3

School Enrollment by Type

Area	Grades KG to 8				Grades 9 to 12			
	Public		Private		Public		Private	
	Enrollment	%	Enrollment	%	Enrollment	%	Enrollment	%
City	3,218	93.3	231	6.7	1,363	94.3	82	5.7
MSA[1]	131,803	87.2	19,325	12.8	57,810	87.9	7,987	12.1
U.S.	33,526,011	88.7	4,285,121	11.3	14,848,628	90.6	1,532,323	9.4

Note: Figures shown cover persons 3 years old and over; (1) Metropolitan Statistical Area - see Appendix A for areas included
Source: Census 2000, Summary File 3

School Enrollment by Race

Area	Grades KG to 8 (%)				Grades 9 to 12 (%)			
	White	Black	Asian	Hisp.[1]	White	Black	Asian	Hisp.[1]
City	91.3	0.7	2.6	2.0	86.4	1.7	5.5	2.0
MSA[2]	79.3	5.8	2.7	12.8	79.8	5.6	3.6	11.5
U.S.	68.5	15.5	3.3	16.8	68.8	15.5	3.8	15.7

Note: Figures shown cover persons 3 years old and over; (1) people of Hispanic origin can be of any race; (2) Metropolitan Statistical Area - see Appendix A for areas included
Source: Census 2000, Summary File 3

Average Salaries of Public School Classroom Teachers

District	2005-06 Dollars	2005-06 Rank[1]	2006-07 Dollars	2006-07 Rank[1]	Percent Change 2005-06 to 2006-07
Rhode Island	54,730	9	55,956	9	2.24
U.S. Average	49,026	-	50,816	-	3.65

Note: (1) State rank ranges from 1 to 51.
Source: National Education Association, Rankings & Estimates: Rankings of the States 2006 and Estimates of School Statistics 2007, December 2007

Higher Education

Four-Year Colleges			Two-Year Colleges			Medical Schools[1]	Law Schools[2]	Voc/ Tech[3]
Public	Private Non-profit	Private For-profit	Public	Private Non-profit	Private For-profit			
0	0	0	0	0	0	0	0	0

Note: Figures cover institutions located within the city limits; (1) includes schools accredited by the Liaison Committee on Medical Education and the American Osteopathic Association; (2) includes American Bar Association-accredited law schools; (3) includes all schools with programs that are less than 2 years.
Source: National Center for Education Statistics, The Integrated Postsecondary Education System (IPEDS) Peer Analysis System, 2007; www.usnews.com, Law and Medical School Directories, 2009

PRESIDENTIAL ELECTION

2004 Presidential Election Results

Area	Bush	Kerry	Nader	Other
Washington County	42.4	55.4	1.3	1.0
U.S.	50.7	48.3	0.4	0.6

Note: Results are percentages and may not add to 100% due to rounding
Source: Dave Leip's Atlas of U.S. Presidential Elections, www.uselectionatlas.org

EMPLOYERS

Major Employers

Company Name	Industry	Type of Site
Brown University	Colleges and universities	Headquarters
CVS	Drug stores and proprietary stores	Headquarters
Charlton Memorial Hospital	General medical and surgical hospitals	Branch
City of Providence	General government, nec	Branch
Dean of Medicine	Colleges and universities	Branch
Fall River Public School Dst	Elementary and secondary schools	Branch
Kent Hospital	General medical and surgical hospitals	Headquarters
Memorial Hospital of RI	General medical and surgical hospitals	Headquarters
Playskool & Playskool Baby	Games, toys, and children's vehicles	Headquarters
Providence School Department	Elementary and secondary schools	Headquarters
Rhode Island Hospital	General medical and surgical hospitals	Headquarters
St Vincent Home	Religious organizations	Headquarters
University of Rhode Island	Colleges and universities	Branch
Women & Infants Hospital RI	Specialty outpatient clinics, nec	Headquarters

Note: Companies shown are located within the Providence metropolitan area; nec = not elsewhere classified.
Source: www.zapdata.com, May 2008

PUBLIC SAFETY

Crime Rate

Area	All Crimes	Violent Crimes				Property Crimes		
		Murder	Forcible Rape	Robbery	Aggrav. Assault	Burglary	Larceny -Theft	Motor Vehicle Theft
City	1,196.2	0.0	17.2	10.3	41.2	189.0	900.6	37.8
Metro[1]	n/a	n/a	n/a	n/a	n/a	n/a	n/a	n/a
U.S.	3,808.1	5.7	30.9	149.4	287.5	729.4	2,206.8	398.4

Note: Figures are crimes per 100,000 population; (1) Metropolitan Statistical Area - see Appendix B for areas included; n/a not available
Source: FBI Uniform Crime Reports, 2006

Hate Crimes

Area	Number of Quarters Reported	Bias Motivation				
		Race	Religion	Sexual Orientation	Ethnicity	Disability
City	4	1	0	0	0	0

Source: Federal Bureau of Investigation, Hate Crime Statistics 2006

RECREATION

Culture

Dance[1]	Theatre[1]	Instrumental Music[1]	Vocal Music[1]	Series/ Festivals	Museums	Zoos and Aquariums[2]
0	0	0	0	0	0	0

Note: (1) Number of professional perfoming groups; (2) AZA-accredited
Source: The Grey House Performing Arts Directory, 2007; Official Museum Directory, 2008; Association of Zoos & Aquariums, AZA Member Zoos & Aquariums, June 2008

Professional Sports Teams

Team Name	League
No teams are located in the metro area	

Source: Original research

MEDIA

Newspapers

Name	News Focus	Frequency	Circulation
No newspapers have an office in the city			

Note: Includes newspapers with offices located in the city
Source: MediaContactsPro, March 2008

Television Stations

Name	Ch.	Network(s)	Type	Ownership
WLNE	6	ABC	Commercial	Freedom Communications Inc.
WJAR	10	NBC	Commercial	n/a
WPRI	12	CBS	Commercial	Sunrise Television Corp.
WRRW	23	n/a	Commercial	n/a
WLWC	28	UPN	Commercial	Straight Line Communications Inc.
WSBE	36	PBS	Public	Rhode Island Public Telecommunication Authority
WNAC	64	Fox	Commercial	Sunrise Television Corp.
WPXQ	69	n/a	Commercial	Paxson Communications Corporation

Note: Stations included cover the Providence DMA (Designated Market Area); n/a not available
BurrellesLuce, MediaContacts Online, January 2007

Major AM Radio Stations

Call Letters	Freq. (kHz)	Station Type	Target Audience	Station Format	Music Format
WDDZ	550	Commercial	Children/General	Music/Talk	Top 40
WLKW	550	n/a	General	News/Sports/Talk	n/a
WPRO	630	n/a	General	News/Sports/Talk	n/a
WSKO	790	n/a	General	Sports	n/a
WHJJ	920	Commercial	General	News/Talk	n/a
WALE	990	Commercial	General	Music/News	Latin
WPMZ	1110	Commercial	General/Hispanic	Music/Sports	Reggae
WRIB	1220	n/a	General/Hisp/Rel	Music/Talk	n/a
WXNI	1230	College	General	News/Talk	n/a
WOON	1240	n/a	General	Music/Sports	n/a
WRNI	1290	College	General	News/Talk	n/a
WNBH	1340	n/a	General	Music/News/Sports	n/a
WNRI	1380	Commercial	General	News/Talk	n/a
WHTB	1400	Commercial	Ethnic	Music/Talk	International
WBSM	1420	Commercial	General	Talk	n/a
WSAR	1480	Commercial	General	News/Talk	n/a
WADK	1540	Commercial	General	News/Talk	n/a
WPEP	1570	Commercial	General	News/Talk	n/a
WARV	1590	Commercial	General/Religious	Music/News/Talk	Christian

Note: Stations included cover the Providence DMA (Designated Market Area); n/a not available
Source: BurrellesLuce, MediaContacts Online, January 2007

Major FM Radio Stations

Call Letters	Freq. (mHz)	Station Type	Target Audience	Station Format	Music Format
WRIU	90.3	College	General	Music/News/Sports	World Music
WPRO	92.3	Commercial	General	Music	Top 40
WSNE	93.3	Commercial	General	Music/News/Talk	Adult Contemp.
WHJY	94.1	Commercial	General	Music	Modern Rock
WBRU	95.5	Commercial	General	Music/Talk	Alternative
WCRI	95.9	Commercial	General	Music	Classical
WJFD	97.3	n/a	General/Hispanic	Music/Sports	n/a
WCTK	98.1	Commercial	General	Music/Sports/Talk	Country
WADK	99.3	Commercial	General	Music	Jazz
WWBB	101.5	Commercial	General	Music/News/Talk	Oldies
WWRX	103.7	Commercial	General	Music/News	Modern Rock
WWLI	105.1	n/a	General	Music	n/a
WWKX	106.3	Commercial	General	Music	Urban Contemp.
WFHN	107.1	n/a	General	Music	n/a

Note: Stations included cover the Providence DMA (Designated Market Area); n/a not available
BurrellesLuce, MediaContacts Online, January 2007

CLIMATE

Average and Extreme Temperatures

Temperature	Jan	Feb	Mar	Apr	May	Jun	Jul	Aug	Sep	Oct	Nov	Dec	Yr.
Extreme High (°F)	66	72	80	98	94	97	102	104	100	88	81	70	104
Average High (°F)	37	39	46	58	68	77	82	80	73	63	52	41	60
Average Temp. (°F)	29	30	38	48	58	67	73	71	64	54	44	33	51
Average Low (°F)	20	22	29	39	48	57	63	62	54	43	35	25	42
Extreme Low (°F)	-13	-7	1	14	29	41	48	40	32	20	6	-10	-13

Note: Figures cover the years 1948-1992
Source: National Climatic Data Center, International Station Meteorological Climate Summary, 9/96

Average Precipitation/Snowfall/Humidity

Precip./Humidity	Jan	Feb	Mar	Apr	May	Jun	Jul	Aug	Sep	Oct	Nov	Dec	Yr.
Avg. Precip. (in.)	3.9	3.6	4.2	4.1	3.7	2.9	3.2	4.0	3.5	3.6	4.5	4.3	45.3
Avg. Snowfall (in.)	10	10	7	1	Tr	0	0	0	0	Tr	1	7	35
Avg. Rel. Hum. 7am (%)	71	71	71	70	73	75	78	81	83	81	78	74	75
Avg. Rel. Hum. 4pm (%)	58	56	54	51	55	58	58	60	60	58	60	60	57

Note: Figures cover the years 1948-1992; Tr = Trace amounts (<0.05 in. of rain; <0.5 in. of snow)
Source: National Climatic Data Center, International Station Meteorological Climate Summary, 9/96

Weather Conditions

Temperature			Daytime Sky			Precipitation		
5°F & below	32°F & below	90°F & above	Clear	Partly cloudy	Cloudy	0.01 inch or more precip.	0.1 inch or more snow/ice	Thunder-storms
6	117	9	85	134	146	123	21	21

Note: Figures are average number of days per year and cover the years 1948-1992
Source: National Climatic Data Center, International Station Meteorological Climate Summary, 9/96

HAZARDOUS WASTE

Superfund Sites

South Kingstown has two hazardous waste sites on the EPA's Superfund Final National Priorities List: **West Kingston Town Dump/URI Disposal Area**; **Rose Hill Regional Landfill**. *U.S. Environmental Protection Agency, Final National Priorities List, June 23, 2008*

AIR & WATER QUALITY

Air Quality Index

Area	Percent of Days when Air Quality was...[2]				AQI Statistics	
	Good	Moderate	Unhealthy for Sensitive Groups	Unhealthy	Maximum	Median
MSA[1]	72.1	22.7	4.9	0.3	161	39

Note: The Air Quality Index (AQI) is an index for reporting daily air quality. EPA calculates the AQI for five major air pollutants regulated by the Clean Air Act: ground-level ozone, particle pollution (also known as particulate matter), carbon monoxide, sulfur dioxide, and nitrogen dioxide. The AQI runs from 0 to 500. The higher the AQI value, the greater the level of air pollution and the greater the health concern. There are six AQI categories: "Good" The AQI is between 0 and 50. Air quality is considered satisfactory; "Moderate" The AQI is between 51 and 100. Air quality is acceptable; "Unhealthy for Sensitive Groups" When AQI values are between 101 and 150, members of sensitive groups may experience health effects; "Unhealthy" When AQI values are between 151 and 200 everyone may begin to experience health effects; "Very Unhealthy" AQI values between 201 and 300 trigger a health alert; "Hazardous" AQI values over 300 trigger health warnings of emergency conditions; (1) Metropolitan Statistical Area - see Appendix A for areas included; (2) Based on 365 days with AQI data in 2007.
Source: U.S. Environmental Protection Agency, Air Quality Index Report, 2007

Air Quality Index Pollutants

Area	Percent of Days when AQI Pollutant was...[2]					
	Carbon Monoxide	Nitrogen Dioxide	Ozone	Sulfur Dioxide	Particulate Matter 2.5	Particulate Matter 10
MSA[1]	0.3	0.0	40.3	4.4	55.1	0.0

Note: The Air Quality Index (AQI) is an index for reporting daily air quality. EPA calculates the AQI for five major air pollutants regulated by the Clean Air Act: ground-level ozone, particle pollution (also known as particulate matter), carbon monoxide, sulfur dioxide, and nitrogen dioxide. The AQI runs from 0 to 500. The higher the AQI value, the greater the level of air pollution and the greater the health concern; (1) Metropolitan Statistical Area - see Appendix A for areas included; (2) Based on 365 days with AQI data in 2007.
Source: U.S. Environmental Protection Agency, Air Quality Index Report, 2007

Air Quality Index Trends

Area	Trend Sites (8)								All Sites (55)
	1999	2000	2001	2002	2003	2004	2005	2006	2006
MSA[1]	8	5	14	13	3	2	6	2	4

Note: An AQI value greater than 100 indicates that air quality would have been in the unhealthful range on that day. Data from exceptional events are not included. These counts are presented in two ways. First, the counts are based on sites having an adequate record of monitoring data during the trend period (trend sites). These counts represent the relative change in the number of days with AQI values greater than 100. In the last column, the counts are based on all sites with data in the most recent year (because it is possible for a site to have data in the most recent year but not enough data to be a trend site); (1) Metropolitan Statistical Area - see Appendix A for areas included.
Source: U.S. Environmental Protection Agency, Office of Air and Radiation, Air Trends, Factbook and Related Information, Air Pollution Trends in Selected Metropolitan Areas 2006

Maximum Air Pollutant Concentrations

	Particulate Matter 10 (ug/m^3)	Particulate Matter 2.5 (ug/m^3)	Ozone (ppm)	Carbon Monoxide (ppm)	Sulfur Dioxide (ppm)	Nitrogen Dioxide (ppm)	Lead (ug/m^3)
MSA[1] Level	50	30	0.123	3	0.02	0.015	n/a
NAAQS[2]	150	35	0.125	9	0.140	0.053	1.50
Met NAAQS[2]	Yes	Yes	Yes	Yes	Yes	Yes	n/a

Note: Data from exceptional events are not included; (1) Metropolitan Statistical Area - see Appendix A for areas included; (2) National Ambient Air Quality Standards; n/a not available
Concentrations: Particulate Matter 10 (coarse particulate) - highest second maximum 24-hour concentration; Particulate Matter 2.5 (fine particulate) - highest 98th percentile 24-hour concentration; Ozone - highest second daily maximum 1-hour concentration; Carbon Monoxide - highest second maximum non-overlapping 8-hour concentration; Sulfur Dioxide - highest second maximum 24-hour concentration; Nitrogen Dioxide - highest arithmetic mean concentration; Lead - highest quarterly maximum concentration
Units: ppm = parts per million; ug/m^3 = micrograms per cubic meter
Source: U.S. Environmental Protection Agency, MSA Factbook 2006, Air Quality Statistics by City

Drinking Water

Water System Name	Pop. Served	Primary Water Source Type	Violations[1]	
			Health Based	Monitoring/ Reporting
United Water Rhode Island	17,500	Ground	0	2

Note: (1) Based on violation data from January 1, 2007 to December 31, 2007 (includes unresolved violations from earlier years)
Source: U.S. Environmental Protection Agency, Office of Ground Water and Drinking Water, Safe Drinking Water Information System (based on data extracted April 15, 2008)

Mount Pleasant, South Carolina

Background

Mount Pleasant is located along the eastern coast of South Carolina, part of the Charleston metro area. It lies northeast of the Cooper River in Charleston County, across the harbor from the City of Charleston, bordered on the west by the Wando River and on the east by the Inter Coastal Waterway, Sullivan's Island and the Isle of Palms. A mild climate, excellent public schools, low crime rates, abundant housing, ample opportunities for employment, and access to artistic and cultural amenities are fueling the region's rapid growth

Originally occupied by the Sewee Indians, Mount Pleasant's first white settlers arrived from England in 1680 under the leadership of Captain Florentia O'Sullivan, who was granted acreage which included not only the island that bears his name, but also the land that was to become Mount Pleasant. A greater part of the area was also called Shipyard Plantation because its deep water and abundance of good timber made it ideal for a prosperous shipbuilding enterprise.

Mount Pleasant played a leading role in the first major military engagement - and victory - of the Revolutionary War. When Charleston finally fell to the British on November 12, 1775, Cornwallis crossed the Cooper River with 2,500 troops and took possession of Haddrell's Point. The British headquarters is said to have been the home of Jacob Motte, later known as Hibben House.

Mount Pleasant was incorporated as a city in 1837. In 1860, a public meeting was held in Mount Pleasant that produced the first secession resolution of the state. The secession convention met in Charleston December 20, 1860 and seven southern states formed the Confederate States of America.

Twenty years after the Civil War, Mount Pleasant was populated by 783 residents. Four miles of street were laid with shells and the town was known as a pleasure and health resort. Truck farming was a major occupation and Mount Pleasant was the site of a sawmill and brick factory. A steam ferry provided transportation between Charleston and Mount Pleasant until the first Cooper River Bridge was built in 1929.

Today, Mount Pleasant is proven an outstanding location for business, offering a highly desirable lifestyle to attract and retain key employees, while providing a highly skilled regional workforce. A wide range of sites and facilities exist for offices, research and development companies and information/technology intensive operations. The community has an impressive list of companies that have benefited from the mix of essential factors for corporate growth, including the headquarters of Motley Rice P.A., Automated Trading Desk, Inc., Benetfitfocus.com; and Hubner GmbH Manufacturing Corporation.

With an integrated highway system, a growing international airport and the second busiest container port along the Atlantic and Gulf coasts, businesses located in the Charleston region benefit from highly efficient access to their markets.

Mount Pleasant offers bountiful facilities and natural settings perfect for golfing, tennis, boating, kayaking, nature tours, and deep-sea fishing. Practically an island for its expansive waterfront, Mount Pleasant offers quick access to the beaches of Isle of Palms and Sullivan's Island.

Mount Pleasant is home to the most comprehensive collections of naval aircraft and is a tour departure point to Fort Sumter National Monument, and home of the Congressional Medal of Honor Museum. Boone Hall Plantation is one of the few surviving working plantations in the nation and Charles Pinckney National Historic Site is the former residence of one of the framers of the U.S. Constitution.

Mount Pleasant's mild year-round climate is greatly affected by its close proximity to the Atlantic Ocean and the Intercoastal Waterway.

Rankings

General Rankings

- Charleston* was ranked #174 out of 375 metro areas in *Cities Ranked & Rated*. Criteria: cost of living; climate; crime; transportation; economy and jobs; education; arts and culture; health and healthcare; leisure; quality of life. *Cities Ranked & Rated, 2nd Edition, 2007*
- Charleston* was ranked #76 out of 379 metro areas in *Places Rated Almanac*. Criteria: health care; education; recreation; transportation; ambience; climate; crime; housing costs; jobs. *Places Rated Almanac, 7th Edition, 2007*
- Mount Pleasant was selected as one of the "2006 Best Places to Live" by *Money* magazine. Places were ranked using 38 quality-of-life indicators and six economic opportunity measures in the following categories: ease of living; health; education; crime; park space; arts and leisure. *CNNMoney.com, "Best Places to Live 2006"*

Business/Finance Rankings

- The nation's 100 largest metro areas were analysed in terms of the percentage of households entering some stage of foreclosure in 2007. The Charleston* metro area ranked #89 out of 100 (#1 = highest foreclosure rate). *RealtyTrac, "Year-End 2007 Metropolitan Foreclosure Report"*
- Charleston* was selected as one of the best places to start and grow a company by *Entrepreneur* and the National Policy Research Council. The Charleston* metro area ranked #2 out of 63 mid-size metro areas. Criteria: business formation and growth (firms started four to 14 years ago that still employ at least 5 people and experienced rapid growth over the last four years). *Entrepreneur/National Policy Research Council, "Hot Cities for Entrepreneurs," September 2006*
- The Charleston* metro area was selected as one of "America's 50 Hottest Cities" for business relocations and expansions. Criteria: industry's most prominent site selection consultants were asked to list their top city choices for relocating and expanding manufacturing companies, taking into consideration such factors as the business climate, work force quality, operating costs, incentive programs, and the ease of working with local political and economic development officials. *Expansion Management, January-February 2007*
- The Charleston* metro area was selected as one of the "Top 20 Real Estate Markets" for expanding or relocating companies. The area ranked #13. Criteria: low rental costs; low purchase prices; high vacancy rates of office and warehouse space. *Expansion Management, October 2007*
- Intel, in partnership with Sperling's BestPlaces, ranked the 80 "Best Cities for Teleworking" in America. The Charleston* metro area ranked #10 among small metro areas. The study identifies cities that hold the greatest potential for teleworking based on a host of factors including typical commuting times, fuel prices, availability of broadband Internet access and percentage of the population in telework friendly jobs. The study also factored in extreme climate and natural hazards. *Intel, "Best Cities for Teleworking," March 30, 2006*
- The Charleston* metro area appeared on the Milken Institute "2007 Best Performing Cities" index. Rank: #12 out of 200 large metro areas. Criteria: job growth; wage and salary growth; high-tech output growth. *Milken Institute, "2007 Best Performing Cities"*
- The Charleston* metro area was selected as one of the hottest cities for entrepreneurs in America by *Inc. Magazine*. Criteria: job-growth data for 393 metro was analyzed for current-year employment growth, average annual employment growth over past three years, and employment growth by industry sector. The Charleston* metro area ranked #15 among mid-sized metro areas and #61 overall. *Inc. Magazine, May 2007*
- Charleston* was identified as one of the 100 "Most Unwired Cities" in the U.S. The area ranked #32 out of the 100 largest metro areas in the U.S. Criteria: number of public and commercial wireless access points (hotspots); airports with wireless Internet access; broadband availability; local wireless networks; and wireless email devices. *Intel, "Most Unwired Cities Survey," June 7, 2005*

- *Forbes* ranked the 200 most populous metro areas in the U.S. in terms of the "Best Places for Business and Careers." The Charleston* metro area was ranked #89. Criteria: business costs (labor, energy, tax and office space expenses); living costs (housing, transportation, food and other household expenditures); education levels of the work force; job growth; income growth; migration trends; crime rates; and culture/leisure. *Forbes, "Best Places for Business and Careers," March 19, 2008*

Health/Environment Rankings

- 100 of the largest metro areas in the U.S. were analyzed in terms of their current drought severity. The Charleston* metro area ranked #36 (#1 = driest). The rankings were based on statistics such as long-term precipitation trends and patterns and the Palmer drought indices. *Sperling's BestPlaces, www.BestPlaces.net, "America's Drought-Riskiest Cities," November 2007*
- The Charleston* metro area appeared in *Country Home's* "2008 Best Green Places" report. The area ranked #146 out of 379. Criteria: official energy policies; green power; green buildings; availability of fresh, locally grown food. *Country Home, "2008 Best Green Places"*
- The American Podiatric Medical Association and *Prevention* magazine ranked America's 100 most populated cities based on fitness-walker friendliness. The best cities have safe streets, beautiful places to walk, mild weather and good air quality. Mount Pleasant ranked #497. *Prevention, "The Best Walking Cities of 2008," April 2008; American Podiatric Medical Association, "2008 Best Fitness-Walking Cities, "April 2008*
- Charleston* was identified as a "2008 Asthma Capital." The area ranked #66 out of the nation's 100 largest metropolitan areas. Twelve factors were used to identify the most challenging places to live for people with asthma: estimated prevalence; self-reported prevalence; crude death rate for asthma; annual pollen score; annual air quality; public smoking laws; number of board-certified asthma specialists; school inhaler access laws; rescue medication use; controller medication use; uninsured rate; poverty rate. *Asthma and Allergy Foundation of America, "2008 Asthma Capitals"*
- Charleston* was identified as a "Spring Allergy Capital." The area ranked #31 out of 100. Three groups of factors were used to identify the most severe cities for people with allergies during the spring season: annual pollen levels; medicine utilization; access to board-certified allergists. *Asthma and Allergy Foundation of America, "2007 Spring Allergy Capital Rankings"*
- Charleston* was identified as a "Fall Allergy Capital." The area ranked #35 out of 100. Three groups of factors were used to identify the most severe cities for people with allergies during the fall season: annual pollen levels; medicine utilization; access to board-certified allergists. *Asthma and Allergy Foundation of America, "2007 Fall Allergy Capital Rankings"*
- Ortho-McNeil Neurologics, in partnership with Sperling's BestPlaces, analyzed 110 metro areas and identified those U.S. cities with the highest prevalence of factors that are most commonly associated with migraine headaches. The Charleston* metro area ranked #56. Criteria: number of migraine-related drug prescriptions per capita; lifestyle factors that can contribute to migraines; environmental factors that can trigger migraines; and consumption of migraine-triggering foods. *Ortho-McNeil Neurologics, "America's Migraine Hot Spots," March 14, 2006*
- Sperling's BestPlaces ranked 331 metro areas and identified the most and least stressful U.S. cities. The Charleston* metro area ranked #71 out of the 100 largest metro areas (#1 = most stressful). Criteria: divorce rate; unemployment rate; violent and property crime; suicide rate; commute time; mental health; alcohol consumption; cloudy days. *Sperling's BestPlaces, www.BestPlaces.net, "America's Most (and Least) Stressful Cities," January 9, 2004*
- Sperling's BestPlaces in partnership with Vistakon ranked the 100 largest metro areas and identified "America's 10 Best Cities for Comfortable Eyes." The Charleston* metro area ranked #1. Criteria: altitude; sunny days; wind; extreme temperatures; humidity; pollution; commute time; computer use. *Vistakon, "America's Best and Worst Cities for Comfortable Eyes," June 15, 2004*

Seniors/Retirement Rankings

- A.G. Edwards ranked America's 500 top-performing communities based on their residents' personal savings and investing behavior. The Charleston* metro area ranked #424 with an index score of 96.25 (national average = 100.00). A dozen statistical factors were measured including: participation in retirement savings plans; personal debt levels; and home ownership. *A.G. Edwards, "2007 Nest Egg Index", September 12, 2007*

Children/Family Rankings

- The Charleston* metro area was selected as one of the "Best Cities for Relocating Families" by Worldwide ERC and Primacy Relocation. The 2007 study placed a special emphasis on the housing market, which has significantly impacted the relocation industry and an employer's ability to transfer employees. The variables which weigh heavily in this category include home price, home affordability index, appreciation rates, and property tax. Other criteria include cost of living, crime rates, education, climate, focus on diversity, physicians per capita, recreation and leisure, arts and culture, air quality, watershed quality, sales tax, unemployment rate, job growth, high school and higher education index, school expenditures per student, students in public school, SAT/ACT percentile, and population growth. *Worldwide ERC and Primacy Relocation, "2007 Best Cities for Relocating Families"*

Safety Rankings

- The National Insurance Crime Bureau ranked 361 metro areas in the U.S. in terms of per capita rates of vehicle theft. The Charleston* metro area ranked #132 (#1 = highest rate). Criteria: number of vehicle theft offenses per 100,000 inhabitants. *National Insurance Crime Bureau, "NICB Vehicle Theft Study," April 22, 2008*
- Farmers Insurance Group of Companies, in partnership with Sperling's BestPlaces, ranked 379 metro areas and identified the "Most Secure U.S. Place to Live." The Charleston* metro area ranked #103 out of 114 in the large metro area category (500,000 or more residents). Criteria: crime rates; extreme weather; risk of natural disasters; environmental hazards; terrorism threats; air quality; life expectancy; job loss numbers. *Farmers Insurance Group, "Most Secure U.S. Places to Live 2007"*

Sports/Recreation Rankings

- *Golf Digest* ranked 330 metro areas in the U.S. in terms of golf. The Charleston* metro area was ranked #109. Criteria: access to golf; weather; value of golf; and quality of golf. *Golf Digest, "Metro Golf Rankings," August 2005*

Dating/Romance Rankings

- The Charleston* metro area was selected as one of the "Best Cities for Relocating Singles" by Worldwide ERC and Primacy Relocation. The area ranked #18 out of the 100 largest metro areas in the U.S. Areas were selected based on the following criteria: a robust cost-of-living index; adventure and outdoor recreation opportunities; violent crime and property crime rates; percentage of the population that is unmarried (ages 25-34); ratio of single men and single women; affordability of quality higher education, including in-state and out-of-state tuition requirements and rates; number of newcomers to the area; commute times; tax rates; fee and occupancy rates for temporary housing and mini-storage; quality and quantity of collegiate and professional sporting events and fun, fan-friendly venues. *Worldwide ERC and Primacy Relocation, "2007 Best Cities for Relocating Singles," October 25, 2007*
- Sperling's BestPlaces in partnership with AXE Deodorant Bodyspray ranked 80 metro areas and identified "America's Best (and Worst) Cities for Dating." The Charleston* metro area ranked #6 (#1 = best). Criteria: percentage of singles ages 18-24; population density; dating venues per capita. *AXE Deodorant Bodyspray, "America's Best (and Worst) Cities for Dating," May 2004*

Miscellaneous Rankings

- Mount Pleasant was selected as one of the "50 Best Affordable Suburbs" in the U.S. by *Business Week*.. The 50 suburbs were chosen based on dozens of factors including: median home prices; population growth; crime rates; levels of education; unemployment rate; commute times; and affordability. One suburb from each state was selected. *BusinessWeek, "Where the Affordable Suburbs Are," December 13, 2007*

- Sperling's BestPlaces in partnership with Pep Boys ranked 77 metro areas and identified "America's Most Drivable Cities." The Charleston* metro area ranked #15. Criteria: climate; road roughness; urban mobility; gas prices. *Pep Boys, "America's Most Drivable Cities," April 9, 2003*

- A study by Sperling's BestPlaces examined which U.S. metro areas were most affected by high fuel prices in 2006. The Charleston* metro area was ranked #76 out of 80 (#1 = most expensive city for driving). Rankings are based on the average dollars spent on gas per year by two driver households. Criteria: cost of regular-grade gasoline; average miles driven per day; average number of gallons each driver uses and wastes in traffic congestion each day. *Sperling's BestPlaces, www.bestplaces.net, "Pain at the Pump," May 18, 2006*

Mount Pleasant is located within the Charleston-North Charleston, SC Metropolitan Statistical Area.

Business Environment

CITY FINANCES

City Government Finances

Component	2004-2005 ($000)	2004-2005 ($ per capita)
Total Revenues	73,675	1,272
Total Expenditures	64,473	1,113
Debt Outstanding	74,089	1,279
Cash and Securities	73,039	1,261

Source: U.S Census Bureau, Government Finances 2004-2005

City Government Revenue by Source

Source	2004-2005 ($000)	2004-2005 ($ per capita)
General Revenue		
From Federal Government	1,266	22
From State Government	3,252	56
From Local Governments	5,780	100
Taxes		
Property	15,106	261
Sales	6,158	106
Personal Income	0	0
License	10,641	184
Charges	14,961	258
Liquor Store	0	0
Utility	10,598	183
Employee Retirement	0	0
Other	5,913	102

Source: U.S Census Bureau, Government Finances 2004-2005

City Government Expenditures by Function

Function	2004-2005 ($000)	2004-2005 ($ per capita)	2004-2005 (%)
General Expenditures			
Airports	0	0	0.0
Corrections	0	0	0.0
Education	0	0	0.0
Fire Protection	4,471	77	6.9
Governmental Administration	7,818	135	12.1
Health	0	0	0.0
Highways	2,002	35	3.1
Hospitals	0	0	0.0
Housing and Community Development	0	0	0.0
Interest on General Debt	1,232	21	1.9
Libraries	0	0	0.0
Parking	0	0	0.0
Parks and Recreation	4,047	70	6.3
Police Protection	8,168	141	12.7
Public Welfare	0	0	0.0
Sewerage	8,077	139	12.5
Solid Waste Management	4,667	81	7.2
Liquor Store	0	0	0.0
Utility	8,040	139	12.5
Employee Retirement	0	0	0.0
Other	15,951	275	24.7

Source: U.S Census Bureau, Government Finances 2004-2005

Municipal Bond Ratings

Area	Moody's
City	n/a

Source: Mergent Bond Record, January 2008 (unless noted otherwise)

DEMOGRAPHICS

Population Growth

Area	1990 Census	2000 Census	2007 Estimate	2012 Projection	Population Growth (%) 1990-2000	Population Growth (%) 2000-2012
City	33,294	47,609	58,507	65,691	43.0	38.0
MSA[1]	506,875	549,033	610,328	655,197	8.3	19.3
U.S.	248,709,873	281,421,906	301,045,522	314,920,978	13.2	11.9

Note: (1) Metropolitan Statistical Area - see Appendix B for areas included
Source: Claritas, Inc.

Number of Households and Average Household Size

Area	2007 Estimate	2007 Average Household Size
City	24,036	2.43
MSA[1]	239,842	2.54
U.S.	113,668,003	2.65

Note: (1) Metropolitan Statistical Area - see Appendix B for areas included
Source: Claritas, Inc.

Race and Ethnicity

Area	White Alone[2]	Black Alone[2]	Asian Alone[2]	Other Race Alone[2]	Hispanic[3]
City	92.7	4.1	1.5	1.7	1.7
MSA[1]	65.4	29.7	1.5	3.4	3.1
U.S.	73.1	12.4	4.3	10.3	14.9

Note: Figures are 2007 estimates; (1) Metropolitan Statistical Area - see Appendix B for areas included (2) Alone is defined as not being in combination with one or more other races; (3) May be of any race.
Source: Claritas, Inc.

Ancestry

Area	German	Irish[2]	English	American	Italian	Polish	French[3]	Scottish
City	16.6	13.7	17.1	9.2	5.4	2.2	4.0	4.5
MSA[1]	10.7	9.0	9.5	9.4	3.1	1.3	2.7	2.4
U.S.	15.2	10.9	8.7	7.3	5.6	3.2	3.0	1.7

Note: Figures include multiple ancestry (e.g. if a person reported being Irish and Italian, they were included in both columns); (1) Metropolitan Statistical Area - see Appendix A for areas included; (2) Includes Celtic; (3) Includes Alsatian but excludes Basque
Source: Census 2000, Summary File 3

Foreign-Born Population

Area	Percent of Population Born in: Any Foreign Country	Europe	Asia	Africa	Oceania[2]	Canada	Mexico	Latin America[3]
City	4.3	2.0	0.9	0.1	0.3	0.3	0.2	0.7
MSA[1]	3.3	1.0	1.0	0.1	0.1	0.2	0.6	0.4
U.S.	11.1	1.7	2.9	0.3	0.1	0.3	3.3	2.5

Note: (1) Metropolitan Statistical Area - see Appendix A for areas included; (2) Includes Australia, New Zealand subregion, Melanesia, Micronesia, Polynesia, and Oceania n.e.c; (3) Includes Central America (excluding Mexico), South America, and the Caribbean.
Source: Census 2000, Summary File 3

Marriage Status

Area	Never Married	Now Married (excluding Separated)	Separated	Widowed	Divorced
City	22.1	61.6	1.4	5.6	9.2
MSA[1]	29.5	51.6	3.3	6.3	9.3
U.S.	27.1	54.4	2.2	6.6	9.7

Note: Figures are percentages and cover the population 15 years of age and older; (1) Metropolitan Statistical Area - see Appendix A for areas included
Source: Census 2000, Summary File 3

Age Distribution

Area	Percent of Population						
	Under Age 5	Age 5 to 17	Age 18 to 34	Age 35 to 49	Age 50 to 64	Age 65 to 79	80 Years and Over
City	7.7	17.3	22.9	26.9	15.1	7.5	2.6
MSA[1]	6.7	19.0	25.6	23.6	14.8	8.0	2.4
U.S.	6.8	18.9	23.7	23.5	14.8	9.2	3.2

Note: (1) Metropolitan Statistical Area - see Appendix A for areas included
Source: Census 2000, Summary File 3

Male/Female Ratio

Area	Males	Females	Males per 100 Females
City	28,142	30,365	92.7
MSA[1]	299,081	311,247	96.1
U.S.	148,320,305	152,725,217	97.1

Note: Figures are 2007 estimates; (1) Metropolitan Statistical Area - see Appendix B for areas included
Source: Claritas, Inc.

Religion

Area	Catholic	Southern Baptist	United Meth-odist	ELCA[1]	LDS[2]	Presby-terian Church USA	Jewish Est.	Muslim Est.
County	7.7	11.6	5.7	1.9	0.5	3.9	1.6	0.7
U.S.	22.0	7.1	3.7	1.8	1.5	1.1	2.2	0.6

Note: Figures are the number of adherents as a percentage of the total population; Adherents are defined as all members, including full members, their children and the estimated number of other participants who are not considered members (e.g. the baptized, those not confirmed, those regularly attending services, etc.); (1) Evangelical Lutheran Church in America; (2) The Church of Jesus Christ of Latter Day Saints
Source: Reprinted with permission from Religious Congregations and Membership in the United States 2000 (Nashville, Glenmary Research Center, 2002) Copyright Association of Statisticians of American Religious Bodies. All rights reserved.

ECONOMY

Gross Metropolitan Product

Area	2002	2003	2004	2005	2005 Rank[2]
MSA[1]	17.0	17.9	19.1	20.6	90

Note: Figures are in billions of dollars; (1) Charleston-North Charleston, SC Metropolitan Statistical Area - see Appendix A for areas included; (2) Rank ranges from 1 to 361
Source: The U.S. Conference of Mayors, "U.S. Metro Economies: GMP - The Engines of America's Growth," January 2007

Economic Growth

Area	1995 GMP	2005 GMP	Average Annual Growth Rate	Growth Rate Rank[2]
MSA[1]	11.3	20.6	6.2	103

Note: Figures are in billions of dollars; GMP = Gross Metropolitan Product; (1) Charleston-North Charleston, SC Metropolitan Statistical Area - see Appendix A for areas included; (2) Rank ranges from 1 to 361
Source: The U.S. Conference of Mayors, "U.S. Metro Economies: GMP - The Engines of America's Growth," January 2007

INCOME

Per Capita/Median/Average Income

Area	Per Capita ($)	Median Household ($)	Average Household ($)
City	40,488	76,073	98,366
MSA[1]	24,660	47,122	61,957
U.S.	25,495	49,280	66,670

Note: Figures are 2007 estimates; (1) Metropolitan Statistical Area - see Appendix B for areas included
Source: Claritas, Inc.

Household Income Distribution

Area	Percent of Households Earning							
	Under $15,000	$15,000 -24,999	$25,000 -34,999	$35,000 -49,999	$50,000 -74,999	$75,000 -99,000	$100,000 -149,999	$150,000 and up
City	4.7	4.7	7.4	12.1	20.4	17.7	18.7	14.3
MSA[1]	14.2	11.0	11.7	16.2	20.0	11.7	10.3	5.0
U.S.	13.1	10.9	11.2	15.6	19.5	11.9	11.3	6.6

Note: Figures are 2007 estimates; (1) Metropolitan Statistical Area - see Appendix B for areas included
Source: Claritas, Inc.

Poverty Rates by Age

Area	All Ages	Under 5 Years Old	5 to 17 Years Old	18 to 64 Years Old	65 Years and Over
City	5.0	0.4	1.0	3.0	0.6
MSA[1]	14.0	1.4	3.6	7.7	1.3
U.S.	12.4	1.2	3.0	6.9	1.2

Note: Figures are percent of population with income in 1999 below poverty level and only include population for whom poverty status is determined; (1) Metropolitan Statistical Area - see Appendix A for areas included
Source: Census 2000, Summary File 3

Personal Bankruptcy Filing Rate

Area	2004	2005	2006
Charleston County	2.86	2.70	0.88
U.S.	5.31	6.82	2.00

Note: Numbers are per 1,000 population and include Chapter 7 and Chapter 13 filings
Source: Federal Deposit Insurance Corporation (FDIC), Regional Economic Conditions (RECON), 8/23/2007

EMPLOYMENT

Labor Force and Employment

Area	Civilian Labor Force			Workers Employed		
	Dec. 2006	Dec. 2007	% Chg.	Dec. 2006	Dec. 2007	% Chg.
City	34,022	34,405	1.1	33,048	33,246	0.6
MSA[1]	307,693	311,261	1.2	294,016	295,777	0.6
U.S.	152,571,000	153,705,000	0.7	146,081,000	146,334,000	0.2

Note: Data is not seasonally adjusted and covers workers 16 years of age and older; (1) Metropolitan Statistical Area - see Appendix B for areas included
Source: Bureau of Labor Statistics, http://stats.bls.gov

Unemployment Rate

Area	2007											
	Jan.	Feb.	Mar.	Apr.	May	Jun.	Jul.	Aug.	Sep.	Oct.	Nov.	Dec.
City	3.1	3.2	2.8	2.6	2.5	3.2	3.2	3.4	3.4	3.5	3.2	3.4
MSA[1]	4.8	4.8	4.2	3.9	3.8	4.6	4.7	4.8	4.8	4.8	4.6	5.0
U.S.	5.0	4.9	4.5	4.3	4.3	4.7	4.9	4.6	4.5	4.4	4.5	4.8

Note: Data is not seasonally adjusted and covers workers 16 years of age and older; All figures are percentages; (1) Metropolitan Statistical Area - see Appendix B for areas included
Source: Bureau of Labor Statistics, http://stats.bls.gov

Employment by Occupation

Occupation Classification	City (%)	MSA[1] (%)	U.S. (%)
Sales and Office	25.9	26.3	26.7
Professional and Related	31.3	20.4	20.2
Service	11.8	16.2	14.9
Production, Transportation, and Material Moving	5.5	13.1	14.6
Management, Business, and Financial	19.7	12.1	13.5
Construction, Extraction, and Maintenance	5.6	11.5	9.4
Farming, Forestry, and Fishing	0.3	0.5	0.7

Note: Figures cover employed civilians 16 years of age and older; (1) Metropolitan Statistical Area - see Appendix A for areas included
Source: Census 2000, Summary File 3

Employment by Industry

Sector	MSA[1] Number of Employees	MSA[1] Percent of Total	U.S. Percent of Total
Government	56,700	18.9	16.3
Education and Health Services	30,600	10.2	13.4
Professional and Business Services	41,300	13.8	13.1
Retail Trade	38,900	13.0	11.6
Manufacturing	22,400	7.5	9.9
Leisure and Hospitality	35,200	11.7	9.6
Financial Activities	14,600	4.9	5.9
Construction	n/a	n/a	5.3
Wholesale Trade	8,900	3.0	4.4
Other Services	11,800	3.9	3.9
Transportation and Utilities	12,900	4.3	3.7
Information	5,100	1.7	2.2
Natural Resources and Mining	n/a	n/a	0.5

Note: Figures cover non-farm employment as of December 2007 and are not seasonally adjusted; (1) Metropolitan Statistical Area - see Appendix B for areas included; n/a not available
Source: Bureau of Labor Statistics, http://stats.bls.gov

Average Wages

Occupation	$/Hr.	Occupation	$/Hr.
Accountants and Auditors	29.42	Maids and Housekeeping Cleaners	8.37
Automotive Mechanics	15.95	Maintenance and Repair Workers	15.73
Bookkeepers	14.53	Marketing Managers	40.72
Carpenters	16.55	Nuclear Medicine Technologists	27.17
Cashiers	7.59	Nurses, Licensed Practical	18.16
Clerks, General Office	11.06	Nurses, Registered	26.87
Clerks, Receptionists/Information	11.12	Nursing Aides/Orderlies/Attendants	9.83
Clerks, Shipping/Receiving	14.71	Packers and Packagers, Hand	8.24
Computer Programmers	25.14	Physical Therapists	30.53
Computer Support Specialists	20.61	Postal Service Mail Carriers	21.06
Computer Systems Analysts	30.05	Real Estate Brokers	55.68
Cooks, Restaurant	10.35	Retail Salespersons	11.14
Dentists	n/a	Sales Reps., Exc. Tech./Scientific	25.85
Electrical Engineers	37.01	Sales Reps., Tech./Scientific	28.77
Electricians	18.29	Secretaries, Exc. Legal/Med./Exec.	14.11
Financial Managers	40.17	Security Guards	10.39
First-Line Supervisors/Mgrs., Sales	18.45	Surgeons	96.67
Food Preparation Workers	7.90	Teacher Assistants	9.90
General and Operations Managers	41.26	Teachers, Elementary School	20.40
Hairdressers/Cosmetologists	15.02	Teachers, Secondary School	21.80
Internists	101.73	Telemarketers	10.74
Janitors and Cleaners	8.19	Truck Drivers, Heavy/Tractor-Trailer	16.35
Landscaping/Groundskeeping Workers	10.04	Truck Drivers, Light/Delivery Svcs.	12.40
Lawyers	49.30	Waiters and Waitresses	7.84

Note: Wage data covers the Charleston-North Charleston, SC Metropolitan Statistical Area - see Appendix B for areas included. Hourly wages for elementary/secondary school teachers and teacher assistants were calculated by the editors from annual wage data assuming a 40 hour work week; n/a not available.
Source: Bureau of Labor Statistics, May 2007 Metro Area Occupational Employment and Wage Estimates

RESIDENTIAL REAL ESTATE

Building Permits

Area	Single-Family 2006	Single-Family 2007p	Single-Family Pct. Chg.	Multi-Family 2006	Multi-Family 2007p	Multi-Family Pct. Chg.	Total 2006	Total 2007p	Total Pct. Chg.
City	829	361	-56.5	253	0	-100.0	1,082	361	-66.6
U.S.	1,378,200	973,300	-29.4	460,700	407,200	-11.6	1,838,900	1,380,500	-24.9

Note: (p) preliminary; figures cover and represent new, privately-owned housing units authorized (unadjusted data); All permit data are based on estimates with imputation; U.S. figures are based on the new 20,000-place series.
Source: U.S. Census Bureau, Manufacturing, Mining, and Construction Statistics

Homeownership and Housing Vacancies

Area	Homeownership Rate² (%)			Rental Vacancy Rate³ (%)			Homeowner Vacancy Rate⁴ (%)		
	2005	2006	2007	2005	2006	2007	2005	2006	2007
MSA[1]	n/a	n/a	n/a	n/a	n/a	n/a	n/a	n/a	n/a
U.S.	68.9	68.8	68.1	9.8	9.8	9.7	1.9	2.4	2.7

Note: (1) Metropolitan Statistical Area - see Appendix B for areas included; (2) The proportion of households that are owners; (3) The proportion of the rental inventory that is vacant for rent; (4) The proportion of the homeowner inventory that is vacant for sale; n/a not available
Source: U.S. Census Bureau, Housing Vacancies and Homeownership Annual Statistics: 2007

TAXES

State Corporate Income Tax Rates

State	Rates and Tax Brackets
South Carolina	5.0%

Note: Tax rates as of January 1, 2008; 4.5% for banks; 6% for savings and loans.
Source: Tax Foundation, www.taxfoundation.org

State Individual Income Tax Rates

State	Federal Deductibility	Marginal Rates (%)	Standard Deduction ($)		Personal Exemptions ($)[1]	
			Single	Joint	Single	Dependents
South Carolina	No	2.5 - 7.0 (r)(y)	5,350 (s)	10,700 (s)	3,400 (s)	3,400 (s)

Note: Tax rates as of January 1, 2008; Local- and county-level taxes are not included; n/a not applicable; (1) Married joint filers generally receive double the single exemption; (r) State adjusts its bracket levels for inflation at the end of each year before printing tax forms; (s) Deductions and exemptions tied to federal tax system. Federal deductions and exemptions are indexed for inflation; (y) Brackets are not double for married taxpayers.
Source: Tax Foundation, www.taxfoundation.org

Various State and Local Tax Rates

State and Local Sales and Use (%)	State Sales and Use (%)	Gasoline[1,2] ($/gal.)	Cigarette ($/pack)	Spirits ($/gal.)	Table Wine ($/gal.)	Beer ($/gal.)
7.5	6.0	0.168	0.07	2.72	1.08	0.77

Note: Tax rates as of January 1, 2008; (1) In addition to the 18.4 cpg Federal gasoline tax; (2) Rates may include additional state sales taxes, environmental protection and storage fees/taxes, and local taxes. When necessary, the volume-weighted average of all local taxes is used to approximate the typical statewide rate including local tax
Source: Tax Foundation, www.taxfoundation.org; Original research

State Tax Burdens

Area	Combined State and Local Tax Burden		Combined Federal, State and Local Tax Burden	
	Percent	Rank	Percent	Rank
South Carolina	10.7	26	30.3	35
U.S. Average	11.0	-	32.7	-

Note: Figures cover 2007 and measure taxes as a percentage of income
Source: Tax Foundation, www.taxfoundation.org

State Business Tax Climate Index Rankings

State	Overall Rank	Corporate Tax Index Rank	Individual Income Tax Index Rank	Sales Tax Index Rank	Unemployment Insurance Tax Index Rank	Property Tax Index Rank
South Carolina	26	11	27	18	43	29

Note: Rankings range from 1 to 50 where 1 is best. Rankings do not average across to Overall Rank. States without a given tax are given a ranking of 1.
Source: Tax Foundation, State Business Tax Climate Index 2008

TRANSPORTATION

Means of Transportation to Work

Area	Car/Truck/Van: Drove Alone	Car/Truck/Van: Car-pooled	Public Transportation: Bus	Public Transportation: Subway	Public Transportation: Railroad	Bicycle	Walked	Other Means	Worked at Home
City	85.6	7.6	0.1	0.0	0.0	0.1	0.9	1.5	4.3
MSA[1]	78.1	13.0	1.1	0.0	0.0	0.5	3.5	1.6	2.2
U.S.	75.7	12.2	2.5	1.5	0.5	0.4	2.9	1.0	3.3

Note: Figures are percentages and cover workers 16 years of age and older;
(1) Metropolitan Statistical Area - see Appendix A for areas included
Source: Census 2000, Summary File 3

Travel Time to Work

Area	Less Than 15 Minutes	15 to 29 Minutes	30 to 44 Minutes	45 to 59 Minutes	60 Minutes or More
City	29.1	46.4	17.9	2.5	4.1
MSA[1]	26.7	39.6	21.5	6.9	5.2
U.S.	29.4	36.1	19.1	7.4	8.0

Note: Figures are percentages and include workers 16 years old and over; (1) Metropolitan Statistical Area - see Appendix A for areas included
Source: Census 2000, Summary File 3

Travel Time Index

Area	1982	1995	2004	2005
Urban Area[1]	1.08	1.14	1.18	1.17
Average[2]	1.11	1.22	1.29	1.30

Note: Travel Time Index - The ratio of travel time in the peak period to the travel time at free-flow conditions. A value of 1.35 indicates a 20-minute free-flow trip takes 27 minutes in the peak. Free-flow speeds (60 mph on freeways and 35 mph on principal arterials) are used as the comparison threshold; (1) Covers the Charleston-North Charleston, SC urban area; (2) average of 85 urban areas
Source: Texas Transportation Institute, The 2007 Urban Mobility Report, September 2007

Living Environment

COST OF LIVING

Cost of Living Index

Composite Index	Groceries	Housing	Utilities	Trans-portation	Health Care	Misc. Goods/ Services
98.1	100.5	91.4	102.3	97.9	110.3	100.2

Note: U.S. = 100; Figures cover the Charleston-N Charleston SC urban area.
Source: The Council for Community and Economic Research (formerly ACCRA), Cost of Living Index, 2007

Grocery Prices

Area[1]	T-Bone Steak ($/pound)	Frying Chicken ($/pound)	Whole Milk ($/half gal.)	Eggs ($/dozen)	Orange Juice ($/64 oz.)	Coffee ($/11.5 oz.)
City[2]	10.31	1.08	2.52	1.55	3.39	2.73
Avg.	8.93	1.12	2.13	1.52	3.26	3.31
Min.	5.88	0.71	1.33	0.83	2.30	2.20
Max.	12.80	2.07	3.43	3.54	5.79	6.20

Note: (1) Values for the local area are compared with the average, minimum and maximum values for all 331 areas in the Cost of Living Index report; (2) Figures cover the Charleston-N Charleston SC urban area; **T-Bone Steak** *(price per pound);* **Frying Chicken** *(price per pound, whole fryer);* **Whole Milk** *(half gallon carton);* **Eggs** *(price per dozen, Grade A, large);* **Orange Juice** *(64 oz. Tropicana or Florida Natural);* **Coffee** *(11.5 oz. can, vacuum-packed, Maxwell House, Hills Bros, or Folgers).*
Source: The Council for Community and Economic Research (formerly ACCRA), Cost of Living Index, 2007

Housing and Utility Costs

Area[1]	New Home Price ($)	Apartment Rent ($/month)	All Electric ($/month)	Part Electric ($/month)	Other Energy ($/month)	Telephone ($/month)
City[2]	272,635	902	182.59	-	-	22.75
Avg.	309,605	782	146.13	78.67	90.16	26.14
Min.	189,877	n/a	82.03	37.41	33.15	17.08
Max.	1,202,800	3,481	271.14	150.60	257.67	37.45

Note: (1) Values for the local area are compared with the average, minimum and maximum values for all 331 areas in the Cost of Living Index report; (2) Figures cover the Charleston-N Charleston SC urban area; **New Home Price** *(2,400 sf living area, 8,000 sf lot, in urban area with full utilities);* **Apartment Rent** *(950 sf 2 bedroom/1.5 or 2 bath, unfurnished, excluding all utilities except water);* **All Electric** *(average monthly cost for an all-electric home);* **Part Electric** *(average monthly cost for a part-electric home);* **Other Energy** *(average monthly cost for natural gas, fuel oil, coal, wood, and any other forms of energy except electricity);* **Telephone** *(price includes basic monthly rate for a private residential line plus additional local usage charges incurred by a family of four).*
Source: The Council for Community and Economic Research (formerly ACCRA), Cost of Living Index, 2007

Health Care, Transportation, and Other Costs

Area[1]	Doctor ($/visit)	Dentist ($/visit)	Optometrist ($/visit)	Gasoline ($/gallon)	Beauty Salon ($/visit)	Men's Shirt ($)
City[2]	76.00	92.42	84.50	2.48	42.73	27.11
Avg.	79.48	71.93	79.55	2.64	29.52	25.77
Min.	52.08	44.80	43.95	2.19	15.58	16.19
Max.	148.44	126.27	158.83	3.48	60.62	48.53

Note: (1) Values for the local area are compared with the average, minimum and maximum values for all 331 areas in the Cost of Living Index report; (2) Figures cover the Charleston-N Charleston SC urban area; **Doctor** *(general practitioners routine exam of an established patient);* **Dentist** *(adult teeth cleaning and periodic oral examination);* **Optometrist** *(full vision eye exam for established adult patient);* **Gasoline** *(one gallon regular unleaded, national brand, including all taxes, cash price at self-service pump if available);* **Beauty Salon** *(woman's shampoo, trim, and blow-dry);* **Men's Shirt** *(cotton/polyester dress shirt, pinpoint weave, long sleeves).*
Source: The Council for Community and Economic Research (formerly ACCRA), Cost of Living Index, 2007

HOUSING

House Price Index (HPI)

Area	National Ranking[2]	Quarterly Change (%)	One-Year Change (%)	Five-Year Change (%)
MSA[1]	132	-0.03	1.99	55.55
U.S.[3]	-	0.10	0.84	41.37

Note: The HPI is a weighted repeat sales index. It measures average price changes in repeat sales or refinancings on the same properties. This information is obtained by reviewing repeat mortgage transactions on single-family properties whose mortgages have been purchased or securitized by Fannie Mae or Freddie Mac in January 1975; (1) Metropolitan Statistical Area - see Appendix B for areas included; (2) Rankings are based on annual percentage change for all metro areas containing at least 15,000 transactions over the last 10 years and ranges from 1 to 291; (3) figures based on a weighted average of Census Division estimates; all figures are for the period ending December 31, 2007

Source: Office of Federal Housing Enterprise Oversight, House Price Index, February 26, 2008

House Price Valuations

Area	Q1 2000	Q1 2001	Q1 2002	Q1 2003	Q1 2004	Q1 2005	Q1 2006	Q1 2007	Q1 2008
MSA[1]	0.7	0.4	1.7	0.7	4.4	6.2	17.3	22.3	16.9

Note: Figures show the percentage of over- or under-valuation of single family homes relative to statistically normal house values (e.g. a value of 23.6 indicates that house values are 23.6% overvalued). Statistically normal house values are based on house prices, interest rates, household incomes, population densities, and any historical premiums or discounts metropolitan areas have exhibited over time; (1) Figures cover the Metropolitan Statistical Area - see Appendix B for areas included

Source: Global Insight/National City Corporation, House Prices in America, May 2008

Median Home Prices

Area	2005	2006	2007[r]	Percent Change 2006 to 2007
MSA[1]	197.0	212.4	215.4	1.4
U.S. Average	219.0	221.9	217.9	-1.8

Note: Figures are median sales prices of existing single-family homes in thousands of dollars; (r) revised; n/a not available; (1) Metropolitan Statistical Area - see Appendix B for areas included

Source: National Association of Realtors, Metropolitan Area Prices, 1st Quarter 2008

Housing: Year Structure Built

Area	1990 -2000	1980 -1989	1970 -1979	1960 -1969	1950 -1959	1940 -1949	Before 1940	Median Year
City	39.1	28.8	16.7	6.9	5.0	1.5	2.0	1986
MSA[1]	22.0	23.9	21.3	14.0	8.4	4.7	5.9	1978
U.S.	17.0	15.8	18.5	13.7	12.7	7.3	15.0	1971

Note: Figures are percentages; (1) Metropolitan Statistical Area - see Appendix A for areas included

Source: Census 2000, Summary File 3

HEALTH

Health Risk Data

Category	Area[1] (%)	U.S. (%)
Adults who have been told they have high blood pressure[3]	26.0	25.5
Adults who have been told they have high blood cholesterol[3]	36.6	35.6
Adults who have been told they have diabetes[2]	7.8	7.5
Adults who have been told they have arthritis[3]	26.7	27.0
Adults who have been told they currently have asthma	7.3	8.5
Adults who are current smokers	21.3	20.1
Adults who are heavy drinkers[4]	7.0	4.9
Adults who are overweight (BMI 25.0 - 29.9)	34.0	36.5
Adults who are obese (BMI 30.0 - 99.8)	28.8	25.1

Note: Data as of 2006 unless otherwise noted; (1) Figures cover the Metropolitan Statistical Area - see Appendix B for areas included; (2) Figures do not include pregnancy-related diabetes, pre-diabetes or borderline diabetes; (3) 2005 data; (4) Heavy drinkers are classified as adult men having more than two drinks per day or adult women having more than one drink per day

Source: Centers for Disease Control and Prevention, Behaviorial Risk Factor Surveillance System, SMART: Selected Metropolitan/Micropolitan Area Risk Trends, 2005, 2006

Mortality Rates for the Top 10 Causes of Death in the U.S.

ICD-10[a] Sub-Chapter	ICD-10[a] Code	Age-Adjusted Mortality Rate[1] per 100,000 population	
		County[2]	U.S.
Malignant neoplasms	C00-C97	186.0	186.5
Ischaemic heart diseases	I20-I25	116.2	152.3
Other forms of heart disease	I30-I51	59.9	51.5
Cerebrovascular diseases	I60-I69	73.0	50.0
Chronic lower respiratory diseases	J40-J47	44.2	42.6
Diabetes mellitus	E10-E14	30.1	24.8
Other degenerative diseases of the nervous system	G30-G31	38.4	22.6
Other external causes of accidental injury	W00-X59	22.6	21.4
Influenza and pneumonia	J10-J18	15.6	20.7
Hypertensive diseases	I10-I13	18.0	18.2

Note: (a) ICD-10 = International Classification of Diseases 10th Revision; (1) Mortality rates are a three year average covering 2003-2005; (2) Figures cover Charleston County
Source: Centers for Disease Control and Prevention, National Center for Health Statistics. Compressed Mortality File 1999-2004. CDC WONDER On-line Database, compiled from Compressed Mortality File 1999-2005 Series 20 No. 2K, 2008.

Mortality Rates for Selected Causes of Death

ICD-10[a] Sub-Chapter	ICD-10[a] Code	Age-Adjusted Mortality Rate[1] per 100,000 population	
		County[2]	U.S.
Assault	X85-Y09	9.0	5.9
Human immunodeficiency virus (HIV) disease	B20-B24	8.5	4.5
Intentional self-harm	X60-X84	12.0	10.8
Malnutrition	E40-E46	*1.0	1.0
Obesity and other hyperalimentation	E65-E68	*0.9	1.4
Organic, including symptomatic, mental disorders	F01-F09	19.5	16.8
Transport accidents	V01-V99	16.4	16.1
Viral hepatitis	B15-B19	*1.6	1.8

Note: (a) ICD-10 = International Classification of Diseases 10th Revision; (1) Mortality rates are a three year average covering 2003-2005; (2) Figures cover Charleston County; (*) Unreliable data as per CDC
Source: Centers for Disease Control and Prevention, National Center for Health Statistics. Compressed Mortality File 1999-2004. CDC WONDER On-line Database, compiled from Compressed Mortality File 1999-2005 Series 20 No. 2K, 2008.

Distribution of Physicians[1]

Area	Total	Family/ General Practice	Specialties	
			Medical	Surgical
Charleston County (number)	1,433	249	481	354
Charleston County (rate per 10,000 pop.)	43.4	7.5	14.6	10.7
U.S. (rate per 10,000 pop.)	17.7	4.6	6.9	4.3

Note: Data as of 2005; (1) Includes all non-federal, patient-care, office-based MDs
Source: Area Resource File (ARF). June 2007. U.S. Department of Health and Human Services, Health Resources and Services Administration, Bureau of Health Professions, Rockville, MD.

Hospitals

Mount Pleasant has the following hospitals: 1 general medical and surgical.
AHA Guide to the Healthcare Field 2008

According to *U.S. News,* the Charleston-North Charleston, SC metro area is home to one of the best hospitals in the U.S.: **Medical University of South Carolina**. *U.S. News Online, "America's Best Hospitals 2007"*

EDUCATION

Public School District Statistics

District Name	Schls	Pupils	Pupil/ Teacher Ratio	Minority Pupils[1] (%)	Free Lunch Eligible[2] (%)	IEP[3] (%)
Charleston County School District	80	42,970	13.4	59.2	43.8	13.3

Note: Table includes regular local school districts with 2,000 or more students; (1) Percentage of students that are not white, non-Hispanic; (2) Percentage of students that are eligible for the free lunch program; (3) Percentage of students that have an Individualized Education Program.
Source: U.S. Department of Education, National Center for Education Statistics, Common Core of Data, Local Education Agency (School District) Universe Survey: School Year 2005-2006; U.S. Department of Education, National Center for Education Statistics, Common Core of Data, Public Elementary/Secondary School Universe Survey: School Year 2005-2006

Highest Level of Education

Area	Less than H.S.	H.S. Diploma	Some College, No Deg.	Associate Degree	Bachelors Degree	Masters Degree	Profess. School Degree	Doctorate Degree
City	5.4	13.6	19.2	7.9	34.8	11.4	5.5	2.3
MSA[1]	18.3	26.8	22.4	7.1	16.6	5.8	2.1	0.9
U.S.	19.4	28.4	21.2	6.4	15.7	5.9	2.0	1.0

Note: Figures are 2007 estimated percentages and cover persons age 25 and over; (1) Metropolitan Statistical Area - see Appendix B for areas included
Source: Claritas, Inc.

Educational Attainment by Race

Area	High School Graduate (%)					Bachelor's Degree (%)				
	Total	White	Black	Asian	Hisp.[2]	Total	White	Black	Asian	Hisp.[2]
City	94.0	95.8	72.6	90.3	75.1	52.6	54.9	18.3	74.5	37.2
MSA[1]	81.3	87.4	67.3	79.3	67.5	25.0	30.9	10.7	38.0	16.5
U.S.	80.4	83.6	72.3	80.4	52.4	24.4	26.1	14.3	44.1	10.4

Note: Figures shown cover persons 25 years old and over; (1) Metropolitan Statistical Area - see Appendix A for areas included; (2) people of Hispanic origin can be of any race
Source: Census 2000, Summary File 3

School Enrollment by Type

Area	Grades KG to 8				Grades 9 to 12			
	Public		Private		Public		Private	
	Enrollment	%	Enrollment	%	Enrollment	%	Enrollment	%
City	4,504	74.4	1,546	25.6	1,867	77.8	534	22.2
MSA[1]	65,879	86.6	10,174	13.4	27,841	87.9	3,845	12.1
U.S.	33,526,011	88.7	4,285,121	11.3	14,848,628	90.6	1,532,323	9.4

Note: Figures shown cover persons 3 years old and over; (1) Metropolitan Statistical Area - see Appendix A for areas included
Source: Census 2000, Summary File 3

School Enrollment by Race

Area	Grades KG to 8 (%)				Grades 9 to 12 (%)			
	White	Black	Asian	Hisp.[1]	White	Black	Asian	Hisp.[1]
City	89.3	7.0	1.3	0.8	86.0	10.2	0.3	4.1
MSA[2]	54.5	40.7	1.0	2.6	53.4	42.0	1.5	2.5
U.S.	68.5	15.5	3.3	16.8	68.8	15.5	3.8	15.7

Note: Figures shown cover persons 3 years old and over; (1) people of Hispanic origin can be of any race; (2) Metropolitan Statistical Area - see Appendix A for areas included
Source: Census 2000, Summary File 3

Average Salaries of Public School Classroom Teachers

District	2005-06 Dollars	2005-06 Rank[1]	2006-07 Dollars	2006-07 Rank[1]	Percent Change 2005-06 to 2006-07
South Carolina	43,011	31	44,133	33	2.61
U.S. Average	49,026	-	50,816	-	3.65

Note: (1) State rank ranges from 1 to 51.
Source: National Education Association, Rankings & Estimates: Rankings of the States 2006 and Estimates of School Statistics 2007, December 2007

Higher Education

Four-Year Colleges			Two-Year Colleges			Medical Schools[1]	Law Schools[2]	Voc/ Tech[3]
Public	Private Non-profit	Private For-profit	Public	Private Non-profit	Private For-profit			
0	0	0	0	0	0	0	0	0

Note: Figures cover institutions located within the city limits; (1) includes schools accredited by the Liaison Committee on Medical Education and the American Osteopathic Association; (2) includes American Bar Association-accredited law schools; (3) includes all schools with programs that are less than 2 years.
Source: National Center for Education Statistics, The Integrated Postsecondary Education System (IPEDS) Peer Analysis System, 2007; www.usnews.com, Law and Medical School Directories, 2009

PRESIDENTIAL ELECTION

2004 Presidential Election Results

Area	Bush	Kerry	Nader	Other
Charleston County	51.6	46.8	0.4	1.2
U.S.	50.7	48.3	0.4	0.6

Note: Results are percentages and may not add to 100% due to rounding
Source: Dave Leip's Atlas of U.S. Presidential Elections, www.uselectionatlas.org

EMPLOYERS

Major Employers

Company Name	Industry	Type of Site
Abel Leasing	Help supply services	Single
Charleston County Sheriffs Off	Police protection	Branch
Cummins	Internal combustion engines, nec	Branch
Kiawah Island Golf Tnnis Rsort	Hotels and motels	Headquarters
Medical Center	Special warehousing and storage, nec	Branch
Medical University Hosp Auth	General medical and surgical hospitals	Single
Medical University SC	Colleges and universities	Headquarters
Medical University SC	Hospital and medical service plans	Branch
Naval Nclear Pwr Training Unit	National security	Branch
Pediatric Plmnlgy Allrgy	General medical and surgical hospitals	Branch
ROPER ST FRANCIS HEALTHCARE	General medical and surgical hospitals	Headquarters
Ralph H Johnson V A Med Ctr	Administration of veterans' affairs	Branch
Trident Medical Center LLC	General medical and surgical hospitals	Headquarters
University of Charleston	Colleges and universities	Headquarters
Verizon Wireless	Radiotelephone communication	Branch

Note: Companies shown are located within the Charleston metropolitan area; nec = not elsewhere classified.
Source: www.zapdata.com, May 2008

PUBLIC SAFETY

Crime Rate

Area	All Crimes	Violent Crimes				Property Crimes		
		Murder	Forcible Rape	Robbery	Aggrav. Assault	Burglary	Larceny -Theft	Motor Vehicle Theft
City	2,459.5	0.0	18.7	37.4	283.9	324.6	1,692.9	102.0
Metro[1]	5,177.5	12.6	48.2	202.9	566.7	892.2	2,931.9	523.0
U.S.	3,808.1	5.7	30.9	149.4	287.5	729.4	2,206.8	398.4

Note: Figures are crimes per 100,000 population; (1) Metropolitan Statistical Area - see Appendix B for areas included
Source: FBI Uniform Crime Reports, 2006

Hate Crimes

Area	Number of Quarters Reported	Bias Motivation				
		Race	Religion	Sexual Orientation	Ethnicity	Disability
City	4	0	0	0	0	0

Source: Federal Bureau of Investigation, Hate Crime Statistics 2006

RECREATION

Culture

Dance[1]	Theatre[1]	Instrumental Music[1]	Vocal Music[1]	Series/ Festivals	Museums	Zoos and Aquariums[2]
0	0	0	0	0	2	0

Note: (1) Number of professional perfoming groups; (2) AZA-accredited
Source: The Grey House Performing Arts Directory, 2007; Official Museum Directory, 2008; Association of Zoos & Aquariums, AZA Member Zoos & Aquariums, June 2008

Professional Sports Teams

Team Name	League
No teams are located in the metro area	

Source: Original research

MEDIA

Newspapers

Name	News Focus	Frequency	Circulation
The Catalyst	Regional	Weekly	5,400
The Charleston Navy Shoreline Weekly	Local	Weekly	7,000
The James Island Journal	Regional	Weekly	n/a
The Journal	Community	Weekly	4,000
Moultrie News	Community	Weekly	27,800

Note: Includes newspapers with offices located in the city; n/a not available
Source: MediaContactsPro, March 2008

Television Stations

Name	Ch.	Network(s)	Type	Ownership
WCBD	2	NBC	Commercial	Media General Inc.
WCIV	4	ABC	Commercial	Allbritton Communications Company
WCSC	5	CBS	Commercial	Jefferson-Pilot Communications Company
WTAT	24	Fox	Commercial	Sinclair Broadcast Group
WMMP	36	UPN	Commercial	Sinclair Broadcast Group

Note: Stations included cover the Charleston DMA (Designated Market Area)
BurrellesLuce, MediaContacts Online, January 2007

Major AM Radio Stations

Call Letters	Freq. (kHz)	Station Type	Target Audience	Station Format	Music Format
WTMA	1250	Commercial	General	Talk	n/a
WDKD	1310	Commercial	General	Sports	n/a
WQSC	1340	Commercial	General	Sports	n/a
WGTN	1400	n/a	General	Music/News/Talk	n/a
WQNT	1450	Commercial	General	News/Talk	n/a

Note: Stations included cover the Charleston DMA (Designated Market Area); n/a not available
Source: BurrellesLuce, MediaContacts Online, January 2007

Major FM Radio Stations

Call Letters	Freq. (mHz)	Station Type	Target Audience	Station Format	Music Format
WYFH	90.7	Public	Religious	Music/Talk	Christian
WLGI	90.9	Non-Comm	General	Educational/Music/Talk	Jazz
WKCL	91.5	n/a	General/Religious	Music/News/Sports/Talk	n/a
WALI	93.7	Commercial	General/Religious	Music/News	Country
WSSP	94.3	Commercial	General	Music	Urban Contemp.
WAVF	96.1	n/a	General	Music/News/Talk	n/a
WYBB	98.1	n/a	General	Music/News	n/a
WWKT	99.3	Commercial	General	Music	Urban Contemp.
WALC	100.5	n/a	General	News	n/a
WXLY	102.5	Commercial	General	Music/News/Talk	Oldies
WEZL	103.5	Commercial	General	Music/News/Talk	Contemp. Country
WRFQ	104.5	Commercial	General	Music/News/Talk	Classic Rock
WCOO	105.3	Commercial	General	News/Talk	n/a

Note: Stations included cover the Charleston DMA (Designated Market Area); n/a not available
BurrellesLuce, MediaContacts Online, January 2007

CLIMATE

Average and Extreme Temperatures

Temperature	Jan	Feb	Mar	Apr	May	Jun	Jul	Aug	Sep	Oct	Nov	Dec	Yr.
Extreme High (°F)	83	87	90	94	98	101	104	102	97	94	88	83	104
Average High (°F)	59	62	68	76	83	88	90	89	85	77	69	61	76
Average Temp. (°F)	49	51	57	65	73	78	81	81	76	67	58	51	66
Average Low (°F)	38	40	46	53	62	69	72	72	67	56	46	39	55
Extreme Low (°F)	6	12	15	30	36	50	58	56	42	27	15	8	6

Note: Figures cover the years 1945-1995
Source: National Climatic Data Center, International Station Meteorological Climate Summary, 9/96

Average Precipitation/Snowfall/Humidity

Precip./Humidity	Jan	Feb	Mar	Apr	May	Jun	Jul	Aug	Sep	Oct	Nov	Dec	Yr.
Avg. Precip. (in.)	3.5	3.1	4.4	2.8	4.1	6.0	7.2	6.9	5.6	3.1	2.5	3.1	52.1
Avg. Snowfall (in.)	Tr	Tr	Tr	0	0	0	0	0	0	0	Tr	Tr	1
Avg. Rel. Hum. 7am (%)	83	81	83	84	85	86	88	90	91	89	86	83	86
Avg. Rel. Hum. 4pm (%)	55	52	51	51	56	62	66	66	65	58	56	55	58

Note: Figures cover the years 1945-1995; Tr = Trace amounts (<0.05 in. of rain; <0.5 in. of snow)
Source: National Climatic Data Center, International Station Meteorological Climate Summary, 9/96

Weather Conditions

Temperature			Daytime Sky			Precipitation		
10°F & below	32°F & below	90°F & above	Clear	Partly cloudy	Cloudy	0.01 inch or more precip.	0.1 inch or more snow/ice	Thunder-storms
< 1	33	53	89	162	114	114	1	59

Note: Figures are average number of days per year and cover the years 1945-1995
Source: National Climatic Data Center, International Station Meteorological Climate Summary, 9/96

HAZARDOUS WASTE

Superfund Sites

Mount Pleasant has no sites on the EPA's Superfund Final National Priorities List.
U.S. Environmental Protection Agency, Final National Priorities List, June 23, 2008

AIR & WATER QUALITY

Air Quality Index

Area	Percent of Days when Air Quality was...[2]				AQI Statistics	
	Good	Moderate	Unhealthy for Sensitive Groups	Unhealthy	Maximum	Median
MSA[1]	74.5	24.1	1.1	0.3	154	41

Note: The Air Quality Index (AQI) is an index for reporting daily air quality. EPA calculates the AQI for five major air pollutants regulated by the Clean Air Act: ground-level ozone, particle pollution (also known as particulate matter), carbon monoxide, sulfur dioxide, and nitrogen dioxide. The AQI runs from 0 to 500. The higher the AQI value, the greater the level of air pollution and the greater the health concern. There are six AQI categories: "Good" The AQI is between 0 and 50. Air quality is considered satisfactory; "Moderate" The AQI is between 51 and 100. Air quality is acceptable; "Unhealthy for Sensitive Groups" When AQI values are between 101 and 150, members of sensitive groups may experience health effects; "Unhealthy" When AQI values are between 151 and 200 everyone may begin to experience health effects; "Very Unhealthy" AQI values between 201 and 300 trigger a health alert; "Hazardous" AQI values over 300 trigger health warnings of emergency conditions; (1) Metropolitan Statistical Area - see Appendix A for areas included; (2) Based on 365 days with AQI data in 2007.
Source: U.S. Environmental Protection Agency, Air Quality Index Report, 2007

Air Quality Index Pollutants

Area	Percent of Days when AQI Pollutant was...[2]					
	Carbon Monoxide	Nitrogen Dioxide	Ozone	Sulfur Dioxide	Particulate Matter 2.5	Particulate Matter 10
MSA[1]	0.0	0.0	57.8	0.0	42.2	0.0

Note: The Air Quality Index (AQI) is an index for reporting daily air quality. EPA calculates the AQI for five major air pollutants regulated by the Clean Air Act: ground-level ozone, particle pollution (also known as particulate matter), carbon monoxide, sulfur dioxide, and nitrogen dioxide. The AQI runs from 0 to 500. The higher the AQI value, the greater the level of air pollution and the greater the health concern; (1) Metropolitan Statistical Area - see Appendix A for areas included; (2) Based on 365 days with AQI data in 2007.
Source: U.S. Environmental Protection Agency, Air Quality Index Report, 2007

Air Quality Index Trends

Area	Trend Sites (12)								All Sites (21)
	1999	2000	2001	2002	2003	2004	2005	2006	2006
MSA[1]	5	7	0	3	0	1	4	1	1

Note: An AQI value greater than 100 indicates that air quality would have been in the unhealthful range on that day. Data from exceptional events are not included. These counts are presented in two ways. First, the counts are based on sites having an adequate record of monitoring data during the trend period (trend sites). These counts represent the relative change in the number of days with AQI values greater than 100. In the last column, the counts are based on all sites with data in the most recent year (because it is possible for a site to have data in the most recent year but not enough data to be a trend site); (1) Metropolitan Statistical Area - see Appendix A for areas included.
Source: U.S. Environmental Protection Agency, Office of Air and Radiation, Air Trends, Factbook and Related Information, Air Pollution Trends in Selected Metropolitan Areas 2006

Maximum Air Pollutant Concentrations

	Particulate Matter 10 (ug/m^3)	Particulate Matter 2.5 (ug/m^3)	Ozone (ppm)	Carbon Monoxide (ppm)	Sulfur Dioxide (ppm)	Nitrogen Dioxide (ppm)	Lead (ug/m^3)
MSA[1] Level	37	25	0.099	0	0.009	0.009	0
NAAQS[2]	150	35	0.125	9	0.140	0.053	1.50
Met NAAQS[2]	Yes	Yes	Yes	Yes	Yes	Yes	Yes

Note: Data from exceptional events are not included; (1) Metropolitan Statistical Area - see Appendix A for areas included; (2) National Ambient Air Quality Standards; n/a not available
Concentrations: Particulate Matter 10 (coarse particulate) - highest second maximum 24-hour concentration; Particulate Matter 2.5 (fine particulate) - highest 98th percentile 24-hour concentration; Ozone - highest second daily maximum 1-hour concentration; Carbon Monoxide - highest second maximum non-overlapping 8-hour concentration; Sulfur Dioxide - highest second maximum 24-hour concentration; Nitrogen Dioxide - highest arithmetic mean concentration; Lead - highest quarterly maximum concentration
Units: ppm = parts per million; ug/m^3 = micrograms per cubic meter
Source: U.S. Environmental Protection Agency, MSA Factbook 2006, Air Quality Statistics by City

Drinking Water

Water System Name	Pop. Served	Primary Water Source Type	Violations[1]	
			Health Based	Monitoring/ Reporting
Mount Pleasant Water Works	67,652	Purchased Surface	0	0

Note: (1) Based on violation data from January 1, 2007 to December 31, 2007 (includes unresolved violations from earlier years)

Source: U.S. Environmental Protection Agency, Office of Ground Water and Drinking Water, Safe Drinking Water Information System (based on data extracted April 15, 2008)

Rapid City, South Dakota

Background

Located in western South Dakota, in the foothills of the Black Hills, Rapid City was founded in 1876 by a group of disenchanted prospectors who had failed to find gold. The town was incorporated in 1882. It is governed today by a mayor and a city council.

From the beginning, Rapid City enjoyed a diverse economy as a center of commerce and transportation on the high plains and a gateway to the mountain states. Lumbering, ranching, and mining have always been important. The area is rich in history, with many famous names connected with the region — Jim Bridger, General George Armstrong Custer, and Wild Bill Hickok, as well as the Sioux leaders Sitting Bull, Crazy Horse, and Red Cloud.

In recent decades, Ellsworth Air Force Base, seven miles east of town, has been a major factor in Rapid City life. During the Cold War it was known as "the showplace of Strategic Air Command," as it maintained facilities for both strategic bombardment and ICBMs. The missile silos were dismantled during the 1990s, and today the base is home to the B-1B Lancer bomber.

Rapid City enjoys proximity to many natural and man-made attractions, including the Black Forest National Park and Mount Rushmore National Memorial, the Crazy Horse Memorial, Custer State Park, the Badlands National Monument, the Devil's Tower National Monument, and Wind Caves National Park. There is also the famed old mining town of Deadwood and the Journey Museum in downtown Rapid City.

The city provides ample opportunity for biking, hiking, camping, fishing, water sports, and golfing. Mountain climbing is among the best in the world, with many short, steep ascents suitable for face climbing.

Family attractions include The Reptile Gardens, touted as having one of the world's largest collections of snakes, lizards, crocodiles, exotic birds, and other animals; the Sky Dome, the nation's first walk-through jungle, features not only animals but stunning orchids. Giant tortoises are a favorite here: Methuselah, a 600-pound Galapagos tortoise born in 1881, is South Dakota's oldest resident. Since the Galapagos tortoise is an endangered species, Reptile Gardens has been working with the Charles Darwin Research Station in the Galapagos to ensure their survival.

The Black Hills Symphony Orchestra has performed concerts in Rapid City for more than 70 years. They have a regular season of concerts in the Civic Center and offer special seasonal performances such as The Nutcracker at Christmastime.

The climate in Rapid City is semi-arid continental, and it displays extremes of temperature, but the Black Hills to the west form a partial barrier to the strongest winds. At times during the winter, cold air from Canada bypasses Rapid City, flowing farther to the east. This fact, along with warm Chinook winds, can make Rapid City the warmest place in the state on some occasions. Summers are warm and dry.

Rankings

General Rankings

- Rapid City* was ranked #157 out of 375 metro areas in *Cities Ranked & Rated.* Criteria: cost of living; climate; crime; transportation; economy and jobs; education; arts and culture; health and healthcare; leisure; quality of life. *Cities Ranked & Rated, 2nd Edition, 2007*
- Rapid City* was ranked #166 out of 379 metro areas in *Places Rated Almanac.* Criteria: health care; education; recreation; transportation; ambience; climate; crime; housing costs; jobs. *Places Rated Almanac, 7th Edition, 2007*
- *Expansion Management* rated 362 metro areas to find out which offer the best middle class lifestyle for manufacturing and service companies. The Rapid City* metro area was selected as a "5-Star Quality of Life Metro" (a distinction the magazine awards to the top 20 percent of metro areas studied). The annual "Quality of Life Quotient" measures dozens of indicators across nine major categories and compares them among 362 metropolitan statistical areas in the United States. The categories are: affordable housing; good public schools; low crime levels; adult education level; standard of living; traffic and commuting; continuing education opportunities; commercial air access; labor market. *Expansion Management, June 2007*

Business/Finance Rankings

- Rapid City* was selected as one of the best places to start and grow a company by *Entrepreneur* and the National Policy Research Council. The Rapid City* metro area ranked #12 out of 162 small metro areas. Criteria: business formation and growth (firms started four to 14 years ago that still employ at least 5 people and experienced rapid growth over the last four years). *Entrepreneur/National Policy Research Council, "Hot Cities for Entrepreneurs," September 2006*
- The Rapid City* metro area appeared on the Milken Institute "2007 Best Performing Cities" index. Rank: #92 out of 179 small metro areas. Criteria: job growth; wage and salary growth; high-tech output growth. *Milken Institute, "2007 Best Performing Cities"*
- *Forbes* ranked 179 smaller metro areas in the U.S. in terms of the "Best Places for Business and Careers." The Rapid City* metro area was ranked #7. Criteria: business costs (labor, energy, tax and office space expenses); living costs (housing, transportation, food and other household expenditures); education levels of the work force; job growth; income growth; migration trends; crime rates; and culture/leisure. *Forbes, "Best Places for Business and Careers," March 19, 2008*
- *Kiplinger's Personal Finance* ranked 101 U.S. cities in terms of their total tax burdens. Rapid City ranked #11 (#1 had the lowest overall tax burden). Criteria: state income tax; property tax; sales tax; personal property tax; and gasoline tax. *Kiplinger's Personal Finance, July 2004*
- Rapid City appeared on *Kiplinger's Personal Finance* list of the "Top Ten Tax-Friendly Cities." The city was ranked #11. Criteria: income tax; sales tax; real estate and car/personal property tax. *Kiplinger's Personal Finance, May 2007*

Health/Environment Rankings

- The Rapid City* metro area appeared in *Country Home's* "2008 Best Green Places" report. The area ranked #145 out of 379. Criteria: official energy policies; green power; green buildings; availability of fresh, locally grown food. *Country Home, "2008 Best Green Places"*
- Sperling's BestPlaces ranked 331 metro areas and identified the most and least stressful U.S. cities. The Rapid City* metro area ranked #100 out of the 117 smallest metro areas (#1 = most stressful). Criteria: divorce rate; unemployment rate; violent and property crime; suicide rate; commute time; mental health; alcohol consumption; cloudy days. *Sperling's BestPlaces, www.BestPlaces.net, "America's Most (and Least) Stressful Cities," January 9, 2004*
- Rapid City* was highlighted as one of the top 25 cleanest metro areas for long-term particle pollution (PM 2.5) in the U.S. The area ranked #14. *American Lung Association, State of the Air: 2007*

- Rapid City* was highlighted as one of the cleanest metro areas for ozone air pollution in the U.S. The list represents cities with no monitored ozone air pollution in unhealthful ranges. *American Lung Association, State of the Air: 2007*

Seniors/Retirement Rankings

- A.G. Edwards ranked America's 500 top-performing communities based on their residents' personal savings and investing behavior. The Rapid City* metro area ranked #330 with an index score of 98.91 (national average = 100.00). A dozen statistical factors were measured including: participation in retirement savings plans; personal debt levels; and home ownership. *A.G. Edwards, "2007 Nest Egg Index", September 12, 2007*

Children/Family Rankings

- Rapid City was selected as one of the top 100 best places to raise a family in the U.S. Criteria: demographic characteristics; standard of living; education; lifestyle; health and safety. *Best Place to Raise Your Family: The Top 100 Affordable Communities in the U.S., 1st Edition, 2006*

Safety Rankings

- The National Insurance Crime Bureau ranked 361 metro areas in the U.S. in terms of per capita rates of vehicle theft. The Rapid City* metro area ranked #306 (#1 = highest rate). Criteria: number of vehicle theft offenses per 100,000 inhabitants. *National Insurance Crime Bureau, "NICB Vehicle Theft Study," April 22, 2008*
- Farmers Insurance Group of Companies, in partnership with Sperling's BestPlaces, ranked 379 metro areas and identified the "Most Secure U.S. Place to Live." The Rapid City* metro area ranked #51 out of 138 in the small town category (fewer than 150,000 residents). Criteria: crime rates; extreme weather; risk of natural disasters; environmental hazards; terrorism threats; air quality; life expectancy; job loss numbers. *Farmers Insurance Group, "Most Secure U.S. Places to Live 2007"*

Sports/Recreation Rankings

- *Golf Digest* ranked 330 metro areas in the U.S. in terms of golf. The Rapid City* metro area was ranked #107. Criteria: access to golf; weather; value of golf; and quality of golf. *Golf Digest, "Metro Golf Rankings," August 2005*

Rapid City is located within the Rapid City, SD Metropolitan Statistical Area.

Business Environment

CITY FINANCES

City Government Finances

Component	2004-2005 ($000)	2004-2005 ($ per capita)
Total Revenues	89,399	1,438
Total Expenditures	89,177	1,434
Debt Outstanding	61,527	990
Cash and Securities	60,744	977

Source: U.S Census Bureau, Government Finances 2004-2005

City Government Revenue by Source

Source	2004-2005 ($000)	2004-2005 ($ per capita)
General Revenue		
From Federal Government	5,005	81
From State Government	1,018	16
From Local Governments	241	4
Taxes		
Property	9,622	155
Sales	35,101	565
Personal Income	0	0
License	2,064	33
Charges	22,292	359
Liquor Store	0	0
Utility	8,393	135
Employee Retirement	0	0
Other	5,663	91

Source: U.S Census Bureau, Government Finances 2004-2005

City Government Expenditures by Function

Function	2004-2005 ($000)	2004-2005 ($ per capita)	2004-2005 (%)
General Expenditures			
Airports	9,177	148	10.3
Corrections	20	< 1	< 0.1
Education	0	0	0.0
Fire Protection	6,384	103	7.2
Governmental Administration	2,091	34	2.3
Health	2,274	37	2.5
Highways	10,953	176	12.3
Hospitals	0	0	0.0
Housing and Community Development	682	11	0.8
Interest on General Debt	1,983	32	2.2
Libraries	2,464	40	2.8
Parking	311	5	0.3
Parks and Recreation	10,391	167	11.7
Police Protection	9,644	155	10.8
Public Welfare	0	0	0.0
Sewerage	6,024	97	6.8
Solid Waste Management	4,680	75	5.2
Liquor Store	0	0	0.0
Utility	10,889	175	12.2
Employee Retirement	0	0	0.0
Other	11,210	180	12.6

Source: U.S Census Bureau, Government Finances 2004-2005

Municipal Bond Ratings

Area	Moody's
City	MIG 1

Source: Mergent Bond Record, January 2008 (unless noted otherwise)

DEMOGRAPHICS

Population Growth

Area	1990 Census	2000 Census	2007 Estimate	2012 Projection	Population Growth (%) 1990-2000	Population Growth (%) 2000-2012
City	55,829	59,607	61,942	63,478	6.8	6.5
MSA[1]	103,221	112,818	119,619	123,962	9.3	9.9
U.S.	248,709,873	281,421,906	301,045,522	314,920,978	13.2	11.9

Note: (1) Metropolitan Statistical Area - see Appendix B for areas included
Source: Claritas, Inc.

Number of Households and Average Household Size

Area	2007 Estimate	2007 Average Household Size
City	25,659	2.41
MSA[1]	47,603	2.51
U.S.	113,668,003	2.65

Note: (1) Metropolitan Statistical Area - see Appendix B for areas included
Source: Claritas, Inc.

Race and Ethnicity

Area	White Alone[2]	Black Alone[2]	Asian Alone[2]	Other Race Alone[2]	Hispanic[3]
City	83.3	1.2	0.8	14.7	3.4
MSA[1]	87.2	1.1	0.7	11.0	3.4
U.S.	73.1	12.4	4.3	10.3	14.9

Note: Figures are 2007 estimates; (1) Metropolitan Statistical Area - see Appendix B for areas included (2) Alone is defined as not being in combination with one or more other races; (3) May be of any race.
Source: Claritas, Inc.

Ancestry

Area	German	Irish[2]	English	American	Italian	Polish	French[3]	Scottish
City	33.8	13.8	9.9	4.5	2.3	1.5	3.3	1.6
MSA[1]	35.4	13.8	9.9	4.8	2.1	1.6	3.7	1.5
U.S.	15.2	10.9	8.7	7.3	5.6	3.2	3.0	1.7

Note: Figures include multiple ancestry (e.g. if a person reported being Irish and Italian, they were included in both columns); (1) Metropolitan Statistical Area - see Appendix A for areas included; (2) Includes Celtic; (3) Includes Alsatian but excludes Basque
Source: Census 2000, Summary File 3

Foreign-Born Population

Area	Percent of Population Born in: Any Foreign Country	Europe	Asia	Africa	Oceania[2]	Canada	Mexico	Latin America[3]
City	2.4	1.0	0.9	0.1	0.0	0.2	0.2	0.1
MSA[1]	2.1	0.8	0.7	0.1	0.0	0.2	0.2	0.1
U.S.	11.1	1.7	2.9	0.3	0.1	0.3	3.3	2.5

Note: (1) Metropolitan Statistical Area - see Appendix A for areas included; (2) Includes Australia, New Zealand subregion, Melanesia, Micronesia, Polynesia, and Oceania n.e.c; (3) Includes Central America (excluding Mexico), South America, and the Caribbean.
Source: Census 2000, Summary File 3

Marriage Status

Area	Never Married	Now Married (excluding Separated)	Separated	Widowed	Divorced
City	27.3	52.5	1.6	6.5	12.1
MSA[1]	25.5	55.8	1.5	5.7	11.6
U.S.	27.1	54.4	2.2	6.6	9.7

Note: Figures are percentages and cover the population 15 years of age and older; (1) Metropolitan Statistical Area - see Appendix A for areas included
Source: Census 2000, Summary File 3

Age Distribution

Area	Under Age 5	Age 5 to 17	Age 18 to 34	Age 35 to 49	Age 50 to 64	Age 65 to 79	80 Years and Over
	Percent of Population						
City	6.9	18.1	24.8	23.1	13.8	9.4	3.8
MSA[1]	7.1	19.5	23.2	24.2	14.2	8.7	3.1
U.S.	6.8	18.9	23.7	23.5	14.8	9.2	3.2

Note: (1) Metropolitan Statistical Area - see Appendix A for areas included
Source: Census 2000, Summary File 3

Male/Female Ratio

Area	Males	Females	Males per 100 Females
City	30,416	31,526	96.5
MSA[1]	59,460	60,159	98.8
U.S.	148,320,305	152,725,217	97.1

Note: Figures are 2007 estimates; (1) Metropolitan Statistical Area - see Appendix B for areas included
Source: Claritas, Inc.

Religion

Area	Catholic	Southern Baptist	United Methodist	ELCA[1]	LDS[2]	Presbyterian Church USA	Jewish Est.	Muslim Est.
County	27.9	3.3	3.0	8.4	1.5	2.0	0.1	0.0
U.S.	22.0	7.1	3.7	1.8	1.5	1.1	2.2	0.6

Note: Figures are the number of adherents as a percentage of the total population; Adherents are defined as all members, including full members, their children and the estimated number of other participants who are not considered members (e.g. the baptized, those not confirmed, those regularly attending services, etc.); (1) Evangelical Lutheran Church in America; (2) The Church of Jesus Christ of Latter Day Saints
Source: Reprinted with permission from Religious Congregations and Membership in the United States 2000 (Nashville, Glenmary Research Center, 2002) Copyright Association of Statisticians of American Religious Bodies. All rights reserved.

ECONOMY

Gross Metropolitan Product

Area	2002	2003	2004	2005	2005 Rank[2]
MSA[1]	3.9	4.0	4.4	4.6	293

Note: Figures are in billions of dollars; (1) Rapid City, SD Metropolitan Statistical Area - see Appendix A for areas included; (2) Rank ranges from 1 to 361
Source: The U.S. Conference of Mayors, "U.S. Metro Economies: GMP - The Engines of America's Growth," January 2007

Economic Growth

Area	1995 GMP	2005 GMP	Average Annual Growth Rate	Growth Rate Rank[2]
MSA[1]	2.7	4.6	5.5	156

Note: Figures are in billions of dollars; GMP = Gross Metropolitan Product; (1) Rapid City, SD Metropolitan Statistical Area - see Appendix A for areas included; (2) Rank ranges from 1 to 361
Source: The U.S. Conference of Mayors, "U.S. Metro Economies: GMP - The Engines of America's Growth," January 2007

INCOME

Per Capita/Median/Average Income

Area	Per Capita ($)	Median Household ($)	Average Household ($)
City	23,223	41,561	55,227
MSA[1]	23,184	44,723	57,449
U.S.	25,495	49,280	66,670

Note: Figures are 2007 estimates; (1) Metropolitan Statistical Area - see Appendix B for areas included
Source: Claritas, Inc.

Household Income Distribution

Area	Under $15,000	$15,000 -24,999	$25,000 -34,999	$35,000 -49,999	$50,000 -74,999	$75,000 -99,000	$100,000 -149,999	$150,000 and up
	Percent of Households Earning							
City	13.6	13.5	14.9	17.6	19.7	9.5	7.4	3.7
MSA[1]	11.5	12.3	13.9	18.8	21.8	9.9	7.9	3.9
U.S.	13.1	10.9	11.2	15.6	19.5	11.9	11.3	6.6

Note: Figures are 2007 estimates; (1) Metropolitan Statistical Area - see Appendix B for areas included
Source: Claritas, Inc.

Poverty Rates by Age

Area	All Ages	Under 5 Years Old	5 to 17 Years Old	18 to 64 Years Old	65 Years and Over
City	12.7	1.6	3.0	7.2	0.9
MSA[1]	11.5	1.5	2.8	6.4	0.7
U.S.	12.4	1.2	3.0	6.9	1.2

Note: Figures are percent of population with income in 1999 below poverty level and only include population for whom poverty status is determined; (1) Metropolitan Statistical Area - see Appendix A for areas included
Source: Census 2000, Summary File 3

Personal Bankruptcy Filing Rate

Area	2004	2005	2006
Pennington County	4.28	5.41	1.66
U.S.	5.31	6.82	2.00

Note: Numbers are per 1,000 population and include Chapter 7 and Chapter 13 filings
Source: Federal Deposit Insurance Corporation (FDIC), Regional Economic Conditions (RECON), 8/23/2007

EMPLOYMENT

Labor Force and Employment

Area	Civilian Labor Force			Workers Employed		
	Dec. 2006	Dec. 2007	% Chg.	Dec. 2006	Dec. 2007	% Chg.
City	34,617	34,984	1.1	33,536	33,835	0.9
MSA[1]	64,961	65,608	1.0	63,070	63,632	0.9
U.S.	152,571,000	153,705,000	0.7	146,081,000	146,334,000	0.2

Note: Data is not seasonally adjusted and covers workers 16 years of age and older; (1) Metropolitan Statistical Area - see Appendix B for areas included
Source: Bureau of Labor Statistics, http://stats.bls.gov

Unemployment Rate

Area	Jan.	Feb.	Mar.	Apr.	May	Jun.	Jul.	Aug.	Sep.	Oct.	Nov.	Dec.
	2007											
City	4.0	3.7	3.5	2.9	3.0	2.9	2.8	2.7	2.9	2.8	3.0	3.3
MSA[1]	3.6	3.4	3.2	2.7	2.8	2.6	2.6	2.5	2.7	2.6	2.7	3.0
U.S.	5.0	4.9	4.5	4.3	4.3	4.7	4.9	4.6	4.5	4.4	4.5	4.8

Note: Data is not seasonally adjusted and covers workers 16 years of age and older; All figures are percentages; (1) Metropolitan Statistical Area - see Appendix B for areas included
Source: Bureau of Labor Statistics, http://stats.bls.gov

Employment by Occupation

Occupation Classification	City (%)	MSA[1] (%)	U.S. (%)
Sales and Office	29.5	28.6	26.7
Professional and Related	20.7	19.6	20.2
Service	17.1	16.8	14.9
Production, Transportation, and Material Moving	11.5	12.1	14.6
Management, Business, and Financial	12.2	12.2	13.5
Construction, Extraction, and Maintenance	8.6	9.9	9.4
Farming, Forestry, and Fishing	0.4	0.9	0.7

Note: Figures cover employed civilians 16 years of age and older; (1) Metropolitan Statistical Area - see Appendix A for areas included
Source: Census 2000, Summary File 3

Employment by Industry

Sector	MSA[1] Number of Employees	MSA[1] Percent of Total	U.S. Percent of Total
Government	10,200	17.0	16.3
Education and Health Services	9,300	15.5	13.4
Professional and Business Services	4,400	7.3	13.1
Retail Trade	9,000	15.0	11.6
Manufacturing	3,400	5.7	9.9
Leisure and Hospitality	7,400	12.3	9.6
Financial Activities	3,700	6.2	5.9
Construction	n/a	n/a	5.3
Wholesale Trade	2,100	3.5	4.4
Other Services	2,700	4.5	3.9
Transportation and Utilities	2,000	3.3	3.7
Information	1,100	1.8	2.2
Natural Resources and Mining	n/a	n/a	0.5

Note: Figures cover non-farm employment as of December 2007 and are not seasonally adjusted; (1) Metropolitan Statistical Area - see Appendix B for areas included; n/a not available
Source: Bureau of Labor Statistics, http://stats.bls.gov

Average Wages

Occupation	$/Hr.	Occupation	$/Hr.
Accountants and Auditors	24.46	Maids and Housekeeping Cleaners	7.98
Automotive Mechanics	16.11	Maintenance and Repair Workers	13.61
Bookkeepers	12.03	Marketing Managers	n/a
Carpenters	14.28	Nuclear Medicine Technologists	n/a
Cashiers	7.98	Nurses, Licensed Practical	15.86
Clerks, General Office	9.68	Nurses, Registered	26.78
Clerks, Receptionists/Information	9.96	Nursing Aides/Orderlies/Attendants	10.59
Clerks, Shipping/Receiving	12.07	Packers and Packagers, Hand	8.15
Computer Programmers	22.53	Physical Therapists	28.45
Computer Support Specialists	15.20	Postal Service Mail Carriers	21.46
Computer Systems Analysts	28.02	Real Estate Brokers	n/a
Cooks, Restaurant	9.57	Retail Salespersons	10.77
Dentists	n/a	Sales Reps., Exc. Tech./Scientific	21.49
Electrical Engineers	31.71	Sales Reps., Tech./Scientific	29.42
Electricians	19.10	Secretaries, Exc. Legal/Med./Exec.	11.06
Financial Managers	44.49	Security Guards	10.12
First-Line Supervisors/Mgrs., Sales	19.42	Surgeons	n/a
Food Preparation Workers	7.73	Teacher Assistants	10.80
General and Operations Managers	46.54	Teachers, Elementary School	19.60
Hairdressers/Cosmetologists	12.24	Teachers, Secondary School	21.30
Internists	n/a	Telemarketers	11.03
Janitors and Cleaners	9.75	Truck Drivers, Heavy/Tractor-Trailer	15.60
Landscaping/Groundskeeping Workers	9.63	Truck Drivers, Light/Delivery Svcs.	11.90
Lawyers	33.88	Waiters and Waitresses	6.91

Note: Wage data covers the Rapid City, SD Metropolitan Statistical Area - see Appendix B for areas included. Hourly wages for elementary/secondary school teachers and teacher assistants were calculated by the editors from annual wage data assuming a 40 hour work week; n/a not available.
Source: Bureau of Labor Statistics, May 2007 Metro Area Occupational Employment and Wage Estimates

RESIDENTIAL REAL ESTATE

Building Permits

Area	Single-Family			Multi-Family			Total		
	2006	2007p	Pct. Chg.	2006	2007p	Pct. Chg.	2006	2007p	Pct. Chg.
City	320	253	-20.9	240	324	35.0	560	577	3.0
U.S.	1,378,200	973,300	-29.4	460,700	407,200	-11.6	1,838,900	1,380,500	-24.9

Note: (p) preliminary; figures cover and represent new, privately-owned housing units authorized (unadjusted data); All permit data are based on estimates with imputation; U.S. figures are based on the new 20,000-place series.
Source: U.S. Census Bureau, Manufacturing, Mining, and Construction Statistics

Homeownership and Housing Vacancies

Area	Homeownership Rate[2] (%)			Rental Vacancy Rate[3] (%)			Homeowner Vacancy Rate[4] (%)		
	2005	2006	2007	2005	2006	2007	2005	2006	2007
MSA[1]	n/a	n/a	n/a	n/a	n/a	n/a	n/a	n/a	n/a
U.S.	68.9	68.8	68.1	9.8	9.8	9.7	1.9	2.4	2.7

Note: (1) Metropolitan Statistical Area - see Appendix B for areas included; (2) The proportion of households that are owners; (3) The proportion of the rental inventory that is vacant for rent; (4) The proportion of the homeowner inventory that is vacant for sale; n/a not available
Source: U.S. Census Bureau, Housing Vacancies and Homeownership Annual Statistics: 2007

TAXES

State Corporate Income Tax Rates

State	Rates and Tax Brackets
South Dakota	None

Note: Tax rates as of January 1, 2008; 6% on a bank's net income. Minimum tax is $200 per location (banks).
Source: Tax Foundation, www.taxfoundation.org

State Individual Income Tax Rates

State	Federal Deductibility	Marginal Rates (%)	Standard Deduction ($)		Personal Exemptions ($)[1]	
			Single	Joint	Single	Dependents
South Dakota	No	None	n/a	n/a	n/a	n/a

Note: Tax rates as of January 1, 2008; Local- and county-level taxes are not included; n/a not applicable; (1) Married joint filers generally receive double the single exemption
Source: Tax Foundation, www.taxfoundation.org

Various State and Local Tax Rates

State and Local Sales and Use (%)	State Sales and Use (%)	Gasoline[1,2] ($/gal.)	Cigarette ($/pack)	Spirits ($/gal.)	Table Wine ($/gal.)	Beer ($/gal.)
6.0	4.0	0.24	1.53	3.93 (s)	0.93 (s)	0.27

Note: Tax rates as of January 1, 2008; (1) In addition to the 18.4 cpg Federal gasoline tax; (2) Rates may include additional state sales taxes, environmental protection and storage fees/taxes, and local taxes. When necessary, the volume-weighted average of all local taxes is used to approximate the typical statewide rate including local tax; (s) There is an additional 2% wholesale tax on wine and spirits.
Source: Tax Foundation, www.taxfoundation.org; Original research

State Tax Burdens

Area	Combined State and Local Tax Burden		Combined Federal, State and Local Tax Burden	
	Percent	Rank	Percent	Rank
South Dakota	9.0	44	29.3	43
U.S. Average	11.0	-	32.7	-

Note: Figures cover 2007 and measure taxes as a percentage of income
Source: Tax Foundation, www.taxfoundation.org

State Business Tax Climate Index Rankings

State	Overall Rank	Corporate Tax Index Rank	Individual Income Tax Index Rank	Sales Tax Index Rank	Unemployment Insurance Tax Index Rank	Property Tax Index Rank
South Dakota	2	1	1	38	33	11

Note: Rankings range from 1 to 50 where 1 is best. Rankings do not average across to Overall Rank. States without a given tax are given a ranking of 1.
Source: Tax Foundation, State Business Tax Climate Index 2008

TRANSPORTATION

Means of Transportation to Work

Area	Car/Truck/Van		Public Transportation			Bicycle	Walked	Other Means	Worked at Home
	Drove Alone	Car-pooled	Bus	Subway	Railroad				
City	84.1	9.9	0.7	0.0	0.0	0.2	2.1	0.6	2.4
MSA[1]	82.9	10.4	0.5	0.0	0.0	0.1	2.3	0.6	3.1
U.S.	75.7	12.2	2.5	1.5	0.5	0.4	2.9	1.0	3.3

Note: Figures are percentages and cover workers 16 years of age and older;
(1) Metropolitan Statistical Area - see Appendix A for areas included
Source: Census 2000, Summary File 3

Travel Time to Work

Area	Less Than 15 Minutes	15 to 29 Minutes	30 to 44 Minutes	45 to 59 Minutes	60 Minutes or More
City	53.1	38.2	4.9	1.1	2.6
MSA[1]	45.8	42.5	6.9	1.7	3.0
U.S.	29.4	36.1	19.1	7.4	8.0

Note: Figures are percentages and include workers 16 years old and over; (1) Metropolitan Statistical Area - see Appendix A for areas included
Source: Census 2000, Summary File 3

Living Environment

COST OF LIVING

Cost of Living Index

Composite Index	Groceries	Housing	Utilities	Trans-portation	Health Care	Misc. Goods/ Services
n/a	n/a	n/a	n/a	n/a	n/a	n/a

Note: U.S. = 100; n/a not available
Source: The Council for Community and Economic Research (formerly ACCRA), Cost of Living Index, 2007

Grocery Prices

Area[1]	T-Bone Steak ($/pound)	Frying Chicken ($/pound)	Whole Milk ($/half gal.)	Eggs ($/dozen)	Orange Juice ($/64 oz.)	Coffee ($/11.5 oz.)
City[2]	n/a	n/a	n/a	n/a	n/a	n/a
Avg.	8.93	1.12	2.13	1.52	3.26	3.31
Min.	5.88	0.71	1.33	0.83	2.30	2.20
Max.	12.80	2.07	3.43	3.54	5.79	6.20

Note: (1) Values for the local area are compared with the average, minimum and maximum values for all 331 areas in the Cost of Living Index report; n/a not available; (2) Figures cover the Rapid City SD urban area; **T-Bone Steak** *(price per pound);* **Frying Chicken** *(price per pound, whole fryer);* **Whole Milk** *(half gallon carton);* **Eggs** *(price per dozen, Grade A, large);* **Orange Juice** *(64 oz. Tropicana or Florida Natural);* **Coffee** *(11.5 oz. can, vacuum-packed, Maxwell House, Hills Bros, or Folgers).*
Source: The Council for Community and Economic Research (formerly ACCRA), Cost of Living Index, 2007

Housing and Utility Costs

Area[1]	New Home Price ($)	Apartment Rent ($/month)	All Electric ($/month)	Part Electric ($/month)	Other Energy ($/month)	Telephone ($/month)
City[2]	n/a	n/a	n/a	n/a	n/a	n/a
Avg.	309,605	782	146.13	78.67	90.16	26.14
Min.	189,877	n/a	82.03	37.41	33.15	17.08
Max.	1,202,800	3,481	271.14	150.60	257.67	37.45

Note: (1) Values for the local area are compared with the average, minimum and maximum values for all 331 areas in the Cost of Living Index report; n/a not available; (2) Figures cover the Rapid City SD urban area; **New Home Price** *(2,400 sf living area, 8,000 sf lot, in urban area with full utilities);* **Apartment Rent** *(950 sf 2 bedroom/1.5 or 2 bath, unfurnished, excluding all utilities except water);* **All Electric** *(average monthly cost for an all-electric home);* **Part Electric** *(average monthly cost for a part-electric home);* **Other Energy** *(average monthly cost for natural gas, fuel oil, coal, wood, and any other forms of energy except electricity);* **Telephone** *(price includes basic monthly rate for a private residential line plus additional local usage charges incurred by a family of four).*
Source: The Council for Community and Economic Research (formerly ACCRA), Cost of Living Index, 2007

Health Care, Transportation, and Other Costs

Area[1]	Doctor ($/visit)	Dentist ($/visit)	Optometrist ($/visit)	Gasoline ($/gallon)	Beauty Salon ($/visit)	Men's Shirt ($)
City[2]	n/a	n/a	n/a	n/a	n/a	n/a
Avg.	79.48	71.93	79.55	2.64	29.52	25.77
Min.	52.08	44.80	43.95	2.19	15.58	16.19
Max.	148.44	126.27	158.83	3.48	60.62	48.53

Note: (1) Values for the local area are compared with the average, minimum and maximum values for all 331 areas in the Cost of Living Index report; n/a not available; (2) Figures cover the Rapid City SD urban area; **Doctor** *(general practitioners routine exam of an established patient);* **Dentist** *(adult teeth cleaning and periodic oral examination);* **Optometrist** *(full vision eye exam for established adult patient);* **Gasoline** *(one gallon regular unleaded, national brand, including all taxes, cash price at self-service pump if available);* **Beauty Salon** *(woman's shampoo, trim, and blow-dry);* **Men's Shirt** *(cotton/polyester dress shirt, pinpoint weave, long sleeves).*
Source: The Council for Community and Economic Research (formerly ACCRA), Cost of Living Index, 2007

HOUSING

House Price Index (HPI)

Area	National Ranking[2]	Quarterly Change (%)	One-Year Change (%)	Five-Year Change (%)
MSA[1]	136	1.75	1.92	32.08
U.S.[3]	-	0.10	0.84	41.37

Note: The HPI is a weighted repeat sales index. It measures average price changes in repeat sales or refinancings on the same properties. This information is obtained by reviewing repeat mortgage transactions on single-family properties whose mortgages have been purchased or securitized by Fannie Mae or Freddie Mac in January 1975; (1) Metropolitan Statistical Area - see Appendix B for areas included; (2) Rankings are based on annual percentage change for all metro areas containing at least 15,000 transactions over the last 10 years and ranges from 1 to 291; (3) figures based on a weighted average of Census Division estimates; all figures are for the period ending December 31, 2007
Source: Office of Federal Housing Enterprise Oversight, House Price Index, February 26, 2008

House Price Valuations

Area	Q1 2000	Q1 2001	Q1 2002	Q1 2003	Q1 2004	Q1 2005	Q1 2006	Q1 2007	Q1 2008
MSA[1]	n/a	n/a	n/a	n/a	n/a	n/a	n/a	n/a	n/a

Note: Figures show the percentage of over- or under-valuation of single family homes relative to statistically normal house values (e.g. a value of 23.6 indicates that house values are 23.6% overvalued). Statistically normal house values are based on house prices, interest rates, household incomes, population densities, and any historical premiums or discounts metropolitan areas have exhibited over time; (1) Figures cover the Metropolitan Statistical Area - see Appendix B for areas included; n/a not available
Source: Global Insight/National City Corporation, House Prices in America, May 2008

Median Home Prices

Area	2005	2006	2007[r]	Percent Change 2006 to 2007
MSA[1]	n/a	n/a	n/a	n/a
U.S. Average	219.0	221.9	217.9	-1.8

Note: Figures are median sales prices of existing single-family homes in thousands of dollars; (r) revised; n/a not available; (1) Metropolitan Statistical Area - see Appendix B for areas included
Source: National Association of Realtors, Metropolitan Area Prices, 1st Quarter 2008

Housing: Year Structure Built

Area	1990 -2000	1980 -1989	1970 -1979	1960 -1969	1950 -1959	1940 -1949	Before 1940	Median Year
City	14.1	13.9	23.6	13.6	20.5	6.4	7.9	1971
MSA[1]	17.1	15.6	25.8	12.1	15.9	5.7	7.8	1973
U.S.	17.0	15.8	18.5	13.7	12.7	7.3	15.0	1971

Note: Figures are percentages; (1) Metropolitan Statistical Area - see Appendix A for areas included
Source: Census 2000, Summary File 3

HEALTH

Health Risk Data

Category	Area[1] (%)	U.S. (%)
Adults who have been told they have high blood pressure[3]	22.5	25.5
Adults who have been told they have high blood cholesterol[3]	33.3	35.6
Adults who have been told they have diabetes[2]	5.4	7.5
Adults who have been told they have arthritis[3]	28.0	27.0
Adults who have been told they currently have asthma	8.9	8.5
Adults who are current smokers	20.7	20.1
Adults who are heavy drinkers[4]	3.9	4.9
Adults who are overweight (BMI 25.0 - 29.9)	40.6	36.5
Adults who are obese (BMI 30.0 - 99.8)	22.6	25.1

Note: Data as of 2006 unless otherwise noted; (1) Figures cover the Metropolitan Statistical Area - see Appendix B for areas included; (2) Figures do not include pregnancy-related diabetes, pre-diabetes or borderline diabetes; (3) 2005 data; (4) Heavy drinkers are classified as adult men having more than two drinks per day or adult women having more than one drink per day
Source: Centers for Disease Control and Prevention, Behaviorial Risk Factor Surveillance System, SMART: Selected Metropolitan/Micropolitan Area Risk Trends, 2005, 2006

Mortality Rates for the Top 10 Causes of Death in the U.S.

ICD-10[a] Sub-Chapter	ICD-10[a] Code	Age-Adjusted Mortality Rate[1] per 100,000 population	
		County[2]	U.S.
Malignant neoplasms	C00-C97	188.5	186.5
Ischaemic heart diseases	I20-I25	135.1	152.3
Other forms of heart disease	I30-I51	36.4	51.5
Cerebrovascular diseases	I60-I69	33.7	50.0
Chronic lower respiratory diseases	J40-J47	49.6	42.6
Diabetes mellitus	E10-E14	27.7	24.8
Other degenerative diseases of the nervous system	G30-G31	31.2	22.6
Other external causes of accidental injury	W00-X59	18.8	21.4
Influenza and pneumonia	J10-J18	14.9	20.7
Hypertensive diseases	I10-I13	9.1	18.2

Note: (a) ICD-10 = International Classification of Diseases 10th Revision; (1) Mortality rates are a three year average covering 2003-2005; (2) Figures cover Pennington County
Source: Centers for Disease Control and Prevention, National Center for Health Statistics. Compressed Mortality File 1999-2004. CDC WONDER On-line Database, compiled from Compressed Mortality File 1999-2005 Series 20 No. 2K, 2008.

Mortality Rates for Selected Causes of Death

ICD-10[a] Sub-Chapter	ICD-10[a] Code	Age-Adjusted Mortality Rate[1] per 100,000 population	
		County[2]	U.S.
Assault	X85-Y09	*0.8	5.9
Human immunodeficiency virus (HIV) disease	B20-B24	*1.2	4.5
Intentional self-harm	X60-X84	13.1	10.8
Malnutrition	E40-E46	*0.0	1.0
Obesity and other hyperalimentation	E65-E68	*0.7	1.4
Organic, including symptomatic, mental disorders	F01-F09	9.9	16.8
Transport accidents	V01-V99	15.3	16.1
Viral hepatitis	B15-B19	*1.1	1.8

Note: (a) ICD-10 = International Classification of Diseases 10th Revision; (1) Mortality rates are a three year average covering 2003-2005; (2) Figures cover Pennington County; (*) Unreliable data as per CDC
Source: Centers for Disease Control and Prevention, National Center for Health Statistics. Compressed Mortality File 1999-2004. CDC WONDER On-line Database, compiled from Compressed Mortality File 1999-2005 Series 20 No. 2K, 2008.

Distribution of Physicians[1]

Area	Total	Family/ General Practice	Specialties	
			Medical	Surgical
Pennington County (number)	236	66	76	61
Pennington County (rate per 10,000 pop.)	25.2	7.1	8.1	6.5
U.S. (rate per 10,000 pop.)	17.7	4.6	6.9	4.3

Note: Data as of 2005; (1) Includes all non-federal, patient-care, office-based MDs
Source: Area Resource File (ARF). June 2007. U.S. Department of Health and Human Services, Health Resources and Services Administration, Bureau of Health Professions, Rockville, MD.

Hospitals

Rapid City has the following hospitals: 3 general medical and surgical; 1 surgical.
AHA Guide to the Healthcare Field 2008

EDUCATION

Public School District Statistics

District Name	Schls	Pupils	Pupil/ Teacher Ratio	Minority Pupils[1] (%)	Free Lunch Eligible[2] (%)	IEP[3] (%)
Rapid City Area SD 51-4	24	12,900	16.1	20.6	23.8	13.9

Note: Table includes regular local school districts with 2,000 or more students; (1) Percentage of students that are not white, non-Hispanic; (2) Percentage of students that are eligible for the free lunch program; (3) Percentage of students that have an Individualized Education Program.
Source: U.S. Department of Education, National Center for Education Statistics, Common Core of Data, Local Education Agency (School District) Universe Survey: School Year 2005-2006; U.S. Department of Education, National Center for Education Statistics, Common Core of Data, Public Elementary/Secondary School Universe Survey: School Year 2005-2006

Highest Level of Education

Area	Less than H.S.	H.S. Diploma	Some College, No Deg.	Associate Degree	Bachelors Degree	Masters Degree	Profess. School Degree	Doctorate Degree
City	12.9	27.4	25.6	7.7	17.8	5.6	2.2	0.9
MSA[1]	12.3	30.4	26.3	7.9	15.8	4.9	1.7	0.7
U.S.	19.4	28.4	21.2	6.4	15.7	5.9	2.0	1.0

Note: Figures are 2007 estimated percentages and cover persons age 25 and over; (1) Metropolitan Statistical Area - see Appendix B for areas included
Source: Claritas, Inc.

Educational Attainment by Race

Area	High School Graduate (%)					Bachelor's Degree (%)				
	Total	White	Black	Asian	Hisp.[2]	Total	White	Black	Asian	Hisp.[2]
City	87.3	89.1	86.6	76.7	72.1	26.7	28.5	7.4	38.0	8.1
MSA[1]	87.8	89.3	86.9	79.2	74.3	25.0	26.3	10.5	30.7	8.8
U.S.	80.4	83.6	72.3	80.4	52.4	24.4	26.1	14.3	44.1	10.4

Note: Figures shown cover persons 25 years old and over; (1) Metropolitan Statistical Area - see Appendix A for areas included; (2) people of Hispanic origin can be of any race
Source: Census 2000, Summary File 3

School Enrollment by Type

Area	Grades KG to 8				Grades 9 to 12			
	Public		Private		Public		Private	
	Enrollment	%	Enrollment	%	Enrollment	%	Enrollment	%
City	6,832	92.7	538	7.3	3,137	90.6	324	9.4
MSA[1]	11,127	92.5	903	7.5	4,868	91.5	454	8.5
U.S.	33,526,011	88.7	4,285,121	11.3	14,848,628	90.6	1,532,323	9.4

Note: Figures shown cover persons 3 years old and over; (1) Metropolitan Statistical Area - see Appendix A for areas included
Source: Census 2000, Summary File 3

School Enrollment by Race

Area	Grades KG to 8 (%)				Grades 9 to 12 (%)			
	White	Black	Asian	Hisp.[1]	White	Black	Asian	Hisp.[1]
City	74.2	0.7	1.4	4.3	82.5	0.9	1.4	4.1
MSA[2]	78.9	0.9	1.2	4.2	85.3	1.2	1.1	3.2
U.S.	68.5	15.5	3.3	16.8	68.8	15.5	3.8	15.7

Note: Figures shown cover persons 3 years old and over; (1) people of Hispanic origin can be of any race; (2) Metropolitan Statistical Area - see Appendix A for areas included
Source: Census 2000, Summary File 3

Average Salaries of Public School Classroom Teachers

District	2005-06		2006-07		Percent Change 2005-06 to 2006-07
	Dollars	Rank[1]	Dollars	Rank[1]	
South Dakota	34,709	51	35,378	51	1.93
U.S. Average	49,026	-	50,816	-	3.65

Note: (1) State rank ranges from 1 to 51.
Source: National Education Association, Rankings & Estimates: Rankings of the States 2006 and Estimates of School Statistics 2007, December 2007

Higher Education

Four-Year Colleges			Two-Year Colleges			Medical Schools[1]	Law Schools[2]	Voc/ Tech[3]
Public	Private Non-profit	Private For-profit	Public	Private Non-profit	Private For-profit			
1	0	1	1	0	2	0	0	0

Note: Figures cover institutions located within the city limits; (1) includes schools accredited by the Liaison Committee on Medical Education and the American Osteopathic Association; (2) includes American Bar Association-accredited law schools; (3) includes all schools with programs that are less than 2 years.
Source: National Center for Education Statistics, The Integrated Postsecondary Education System (IPEDS) Peer Analysis System, 2007; www.usnews.com, Law and Medical School Directories, 2009

PRESIDENTIAL ELECTION

2004 Presidential Election Results

Area	Bush	Kerry	Nader	Other
Pennington County	66.7	31.6	1.2	0.5
U.S.	50.7	48.3	0.4	0.6

Note: Results are percentages and may not add to 100% due to rounding
Source: Dave Leip's Atlas of U.S. Presidential Elections, www.uselectionatlas.org

EMPLOYERS

Major Employers

Company Name	Industry	Type of Site
Bhw Residential Services	Highway and street construction	Branch
Black Hills Corporation	Passenger transportation arrangement	Branch
Business Name	Lumber and other building materials	Branch
Central High School	Watches, clocks, watchcases, and parts	Headquarters
Dacotah Cement	Highway and street construction	Headquarters
Excavating Specialists	Administration of public health programs	Branch
FAIRWAY HILLS	Telephone communication, except radio	Branch
Heavy Constructors Inc	Elementary and secondary schools	Branch
Herbergers	Grocery stores	Branch
Hills Materials Company	Personal credit institutions	Branch
Indian Health Service	Business consulting, nec	Branch
Lowes	Newspapers	Headquarters
Lucent	Elementary and secondary schools	Branch
Mileage Plus	Offices and clinics of medical doctors	Headquarters
Mt Rushmore Black Hills Gold	General medical and surgical hospitals	Headquarters
New Albertsons Inc	Engineering services	Single
Northern Hills Advertiser	Colleges and universities	Headquarters
Onegci Inc	Department stores	Branch
Prairiewave Communications Inc	Vocational schools, nec	Single
Rapid City Medical Center LLP	Building maintenance services, nec	Single
Rapid City Regional Hosp Inc	Department stores	Branch
South Dakota Schl Minds & Tech	Civic and social associations	Headquarters
South Dakota Schl Mines & Tech	Residential care	Single
Stevens High School	Telephone communication, except radio	Headquarters
Total Quality Maintenance	Cement, hydraulic	Headquarters
Wal-Mart	Nonresidential construction, nec	Headquarters
YMCA	Colleges and universities	Headquarters

Note: Companies shown are located within the Rapid City metropolitan area; nec = not elsewhere classified.
Source: www.zapdata.com, May 2008

PUBLIC SAFETY

Crime Rate

Area	All Crimes	Violent Crimes				Property Crimes		
		Murder	Forcible Rape	Robbery	Aggrav. Assault	Burglary	Larceny -Theft	Motor Vehicle Theft
City	3,866.1	0.0	89.4	60.7	220.3	649.7	2,680.1	166.0
Metro[1]	2,708.3	0.0	80.6	31.9	157.0	495.3	1,820.1	123.4
U.S.	3,808.1	5.7	30.9	149.4	287.5	729.4	2,206.8	398.4

Note: Figures are crimes per 100,000 population; (1) Metropolitan Statistical Area - see Appendix B for areas included
Source: FBI Uniform Crime Reports, 2006

Hate Crimes

Area	Number of Quarters Reported	Bias Motivation				
		Race	Religion	Sexual Orientation	Ethnicity	Disability
City	4	42	0	0	0	0

Source: Federal Bureau of Investigation, Hate Crime Statistics 2006

RECREATION

Culture

Dance[1]	Theatre[1]	Instrumental Music[1]	Vocal Music[1]	Series/ Festivals	Museums	Zoos and Aquariums[2]
0	1	1	0	0	7	0

Note: (1) Number of professional perfoming groups; (2) AZA-accredited
Source: The Grey House Performing Arts Directory, 2007; Official Museum Directory, 2008; Association of Zoos & Aquariums, AZA Member Zoos & Aquariums, June 2008

Professional Sports Teams

Team Name	League
No teams are located in the metro area	

Source: Original research

MEDIA

Newspapers

Name	News Focus	Frequency	Circulation
Rapid City Journal	Local	Daily	31,826
West River Catholic	Regional	Monthly	13,000

Note: Includes newspapers with offices located in the city
Source: MediaContactsPro, March 2008

Television Stations

Name	Ch.	Network(s)	Type	Ownership
KOTA	3	ABC	Commercial	Duhamal Broadcasting Enterprises
KIVV	5	Fox	Commercial	Missions Broadcasting
KEVN	7	Fox	Commercial	Missions Broadcasting
KHSD	11	ABC	Commercial	Duhamal Broadcasting Enterprises
KSGW	12	n/a	Commercial	Duhamal Broadcasting Enterprises
KCLO	15	CBS	Commercial	Young Broadcasting Inc.

Note: Stations included cover the Rapid City DMA (Designated Market Area)
BurrellesLuce, MediaContacts Online, January 2007

Major AM Radio Stations

Call Letters	Freq. (kHz)	Station Type	Target Audience	Station Format	Music Format
KZMX	580	n/a	General	Music/News/Sports	n/a
KBHB	810	Commercial	General	Educational/News/Talk	n/a
KKLS	920	Commercial	General	Music/News	Oldies
KROE	930	Commercial	General	Music/Talk	Oldies
KDSJ	980	Commercial	General	Music/Sports	Oldies
KIMM	1150	Commercial	General	Music/News	Country
KASL	1240	Commercial	General	Music/News	Oldies
KTOQ	1340	Commercial	General	News/Talk	n/a
KOTA	1380	n/a	General	News/Talk	n/a
KBJM	1400	Commercial	General	Music/News	Country
KWYO	1410	Commercial	General	Music/Talk	Adult Standards
KBFS	1450	Commercial	General	Music/News/Sports	Country
KFCR	1490	n/a	General	Music/News/Sports	n/a

Note: Stations included cover the Rapid City DMA (Designated Market Area); n/a not available
Source: BurrellesLuce, MediaContacts Online, January 2007

Major FM Radio Stations

Call Letters	Freq. (mHz)	Station Type	Target Audience	Station Format	Music Format
KBHE	89.3	n/a	General	Music/News/Talk	n/a
KILI	90.1	n/a	Native American	Music/News/Sports	Urban Contemp.
KRCS	93.1	n/a	General	Music	n/a
KYTI	93.7	n/a	General	Music/News	n/a
KKMK	93.9	n/a	General	Music	n/a
KZWY	94.9	Commercial	General	Music/News	Classic Rock
KSQY	95.1	Commercial	General/Men	News	n/a
KSDZ	95.5	Commercial	General	Music	Oldies
KZZI	95.9	Commercial	General/Religious	Music	Country
KZMX	96.7	Commercial	General	Music/News	Country
KLMP	97.9	n/a	General/Religious	Educational/Music	n/a
KOUT	98.7	n/a	General	Music/News	n/a
KFXS	100.3	Commercial	General	Music/News	Classic Rock
KDDX	101.1	Commercial	General	n/a	n/a
KYDT	103.1	Commercial	General	News/Sports/Talk	n/a
KIQK	104.1	Commercial	General	Music/News	Country
KAWK	105.1	Commercial	General	Music	Oldies
KSLT	107.3	n/a	General/Religious	Music/Talk	n/a

Note: Stations included cover the Rapid City DMA (Designated Market Area); n/a not available
BurrellesLuce, MediaContacts Online, January 2007

CLIMATE

Average and Extreme Temperatures

Temperature	Jan	Feb	Mar	Apr	May	Jun	Jul	Aug	Sep	Oct	Nov	Dec	Yr.
Extreme High (°F)	76	75	82	93	98	106	110	106	104	94	78	75	110
Average High (°F)	34	38	45	58	68	78	86	86	75	63	47	37	60
Average Temp. (°F)	22	27	34	45	56	65	73	72	61	49	35	26	47
Average Low (°F)	10	15	22	32	43	52	58	57	46	36	23	14	34
Extreme Low (°F)	-27	-25	-17	1	18	31	39	38	18	-2	-19	-30	-30

Note: Figures cover the years 1949-1995
Source: National Climatic Data Center, International Station Meteorological Climate Summary, 9/96

Average Precipitation/Snowfall/Humidity

Precip./Humidity	Jan	Feb	Mar	Apr	May	Jun	Jul	Aug	Sep	Oct	Nov	Dec	Yr.
Avg. Precip. (in.)	0.4	0.5	1.0	1.8	2.7	3.0	2.0	1.5	1.1	1.0	0.6	0.4	16.1
Avg. Snowfall (in.)	5	7	9	7	1	Tr	0	0	Tr	2	5	5	40
Avg. Rel. Hum. 6am (%)	69	73	76	72	73	74	70	69	69	68	71	70	71
Avg. Rel. Hum. 3pm (%)	54	53	49	42	45	47	38	33	35	38	49	56	45

Note: Figures cover the years 1949-1995; Tr = Trace amounts (<0.05 in. of rain; <0.5 in. of snow)
Source: National Climatic Data Center, International Station Meteorological Climate Summary, 9/96

Weather Conditions

Temperature			Daytime Sky			Precipitation		
5°F & below	32°F & below	90°F & above	Clear	Partly cloudy	Cloudy	0.01 inch or more precip.	0.1 inch or more snow/ice	Thunder-storms
30	169	31	89	168	108	98	37	40

Note: Figures are average number of days per year and cover the years 1949-1995
Source: National Climatic Data Center, International Station Meteorological Climate Summary, 9/96

HAZARDOUS WASTE

Superfund Sites

Rapid City has no sites on the EPA's Superfund Final National Priorities List.
U.S. Environmental Protection Agency, Final National Priorities List, June 23, 2008

AIR & WATER QUALITY

Air Quality Index

Area	Percent of Days when Air Quality was...[2]				AQI Statistics	
	Good	Moderate	Unhealthy for Sensitive Groups	Unhealthy	Maximum	Median
MSA[1]	80.4	19.6	0.0	0.0	78	31

Note: The Air Quality Index (AQI) is an index for reporting daily air quality. EPA calculates the AQI for five major air pollutants regulated by the Clean Air Act: ground-level ozone, particle pollution (also known as particulate matter), carbon monoxide, sulfur dioxide, and nitrogen dioxide. The AQI runs from 0 to 500. The higher the AQI value, the greater the level of air pollution and the greater the health concern. There are six AQI categories: "Good" The AQI is between 0 and 50. Air quality is considered satisfactory; "Moderate" The AQI is between 51 and 100. Air quality is acceptable; "Unhealthy for Sensitive Groups" When AQI values are between 101 and 150, members of sensitive groups may experience health effects; "Unhealthy" When AQI values are between 151 and 200 everyone may begin to experience health effects; "Very Unhealthy" AQI values between 201 and 300 trigger a health alert; "Hazardous" AQI values over 300 trigger health warnings of emergency conditions; (1) Metropolitan Statistical Area - see Appendix A for areas included; (2) Based on 362 days with AQI data in 2007.
Source: U.S. Environmental Protection Agency, Air Quality Index Report, 2007

Air Quality Index Pollutants

Area	Percent of Days when AQI Pollutant was...[2]					
	Carbon Monoxide	Nitrogen Dioxide	Ozone	Sulfur Dioxide	Particulate Matter 2.5	Particulate Matter 10
MSA[1]	0.0	0.0	0.0	0.0	11.0	89.0

Note: The Air Quality Index (AQI) is an index for reporting daily air quality. EPA calculates the AQI for five major air pollutants regulated by the Clean Air Act: ground-level ozone, particle pollution (also known as particulate matter), carbon monoxide, sulfur dioxide, and nitrogen dioxide. The AQI runs from 0 to 500. The higher the AQI value, the greater the level of air pollution and the greater the health concern; (1) Metropolitan Statistical Area - see Appendix A for areas included; (2) Based on 362 days with AQI data in 2007.
Source: U.S. Environmental Protection Agency, Air Quality Index Report, 2007

Air Quality Index Trends

Area	Trend Sites								All Sites
	1999	2000	2001	2002	2003	2004	2005	2006	2006
MSA[1]	n/a	n/a	n/a	n/a	n/a	n/a	n/a	n/a	n/a

Note: An AQI value greater than 100 indicates that air quality would have been in the unhealthful range on that day. Data from exceptional events are not included. These counts are presented in two ways. First, the counts are based on sites having an adequate record of monitoring data during the trend period (trend sites). These counts represent the relative change in the number of days with AQI values greater than 100. In the last column, the counts are based on all sites with data in the most recent year (because it is possible for a site to have data in the most recent year but not enough data to be a trend site); (1) Metropolitan Statistical Area - see Appendix A for areas included; n/a not available.
Source: U.S. Environmental Protection Agency, Office of Air and Radiation, Air Trends, Factbook and Related Information, Air Pollution Trends in Selected Metropolitan Areas 2006

Maximum Air Pollutant Concentrations

	Particulate Matter 10 (ug/m^3)	Particulate Matter 2.5 (ug/m^3)	Ozone (ppm)	Carbon Monoxide (ppm)	Sulfur Dioxide (ppm)	Nitrogen Dioxide (ppm)	Lead (ug/m^3)
MSA[1] Level	125	20	0.069	n/a	n/a	n/a	n/a
NAAQS[2]	150	35	0.125	9	0.140	0.053	1.50
Met NAAQS[2]	Yes	Yes	Yes	n/a	n/a	n/a	n/a

Note: Data from exceptional events are not included; (1) Metropolitan Statistical Area - see Appendix A for areas included; (2) National Ambient Air Quality Standards; n/a not available
Concentrations: Particulate Matter 10 (coarse particulate) - highest second maximum 24-hour concentration; Particulate Matter 2.5 (fine particulate) - highest 98th percentile 24-hour concentration; Ozone - highest second daily maximum 1-hour concentration; Carbon Monoxide - highest second maximum non-overlapping 8-hour concentration; Sulfur Dioxide - highest second maximum 24-hour concentration; Nitrogen Dioxide - highest arithmetic mean concentration; Lead - highest quarterly maximum concentration
Units: ppm = parts per million; ug/m^3 = micrograms per cubic meter
Source: U.S. Environmental Protection Agency, MSA Factbook 2006, Air Quality Statistics by City

Drinking Water

Water System Name	Pop. Served	Primary Water Source Type	Violations[1]	
			Health Based	Monitoring/ Reporting
Rapid City	57,983	Surface	0	0

Note: (1) Based on violation data from January 1, 2007 to December 31, 2007 (includes unresolved violations from earlier years)
Source: U.S. Environmental Protection Agency, Office of Ground Water and Drinking Water, Safe Drinking Water Information System (based on data extracted April 15, 2008)

Brentwood, Tennessee

Background

Located 10 miles south of Nashville, in Williamson County, Brentwood is an attractive suburban community that has grown, in part, to major nearby transportation improvements.

According to the city's historian, the Brentwood area first was settled in the late 1700s as Revolutionary War soldiers, granted property by the state of North Carolina, moved into the area. Plantations and beautiful homes flourished by the time of the Civil War, signs of prosperity amid fertile farmland. During the war, both sides of the conflict used these dwellings. However, like much of the South, the war left the town with a broken economy. Improvement came gradually, and as the twentieth century progressed, the city's homes were restored. Starting in the 1960s, the interstate highways arrived.

Today, Brentwood is primarily a residential community with most of its land zoned residential with a minimum one-acre density, and less than 10% zoned for commercial use. Brentwood's largest employers are Comdata Network and Service Merchandise. The Cool Springs area, situated in Brentwood and nearby Franklin, is home to the Cool Springs Galleria, a shopping center that fills 1.3 million square feet.

The city's students attend the Williamson County School System or the many private schools in the area. Upon graduation, they can attend 16 institutions of higher education within easy driving distance, including notable Vanderbilt University in nearby Nashville.

To relax, Brentwood residents can head out to the Deerwood Arboretum and Natural Area. In addition to a nature center with an observation deck and small amphitheater, the area's facilities include nature trails, the Little Harpeth River, and man-made lakes. Brentwood is also home to Crockett Park, more than 159 acres with tennis courts, ball fields, bikeway/jogging trails, an amphitheater, two historic homes, and more. Also in town is the Williamson County Indoor Sports Complex, a facility with tennis courts, and a 50 + meter indoor training pool, fitness equipment and more.

Nearby Nashville offers a multitude of activities befitting "Music City USA," including the fabled Grand Ole Opry, the Carol Van Vechten Gallery at Fisk University, featuring the Alfred Steiglitz Collection.

Brentwood has much the same climate as nearby Nashville. The average relative humidity is moderate, as are temperatures. The city is not in the most common path of storms that cross the country, but it is in a zone of moderate frequency for thunderstorms.

Rankings

General Rankings

- Nashville* was ranked #281 out of 375 metro areas in *Cities Ranked & Rated*. Criteria: cost of living; climate; crime; transportation; economy and jobs; education; arts and culture; health and healthcare; leisure; quality of life. *Cities Ranked & Rated, 2nd Edition, 2007*

- Nashville* was ranked #58 out of 379 metro areas in *Places Rated Almanac*. Criteria: health care; education; recreation; transportation; ambience; climate; crime; housing costs; jobs. *Places Rated Almanac, 7th Edition, 2007*

Business/Finance Rankings

- The nation's 100 largest metro areas were analysed in terms of the percentage of households entering some stage of foreclosure in 2007. The Nashville* metro area ranked #59 out of 100 (#1 = highest foreclosure rate). *RealtyTrac, "Year-End 2007 Metropolitan Foreclosure Report"*

- The Nashville* metro area was selected one of America's "Top 50 Business Opportunity Metros" by *Expansion Management* in their 5th annual Mayor's Challenge ranking of metro areas that have achieved solid ratings across the board in numerous *EM* studies during the past 12 months. The area ranked #18. Criteria: public schools; quality of life; college educated workers; logistics infrastructure; healthcare costs; taxes and government spending; reputation among site consultants. *Expansion Management, August 2007*

- The Nashville* metro area was selected as one of "America's Most Wired Cities" by *Forbes*. The metro area was ranked #25 out of 30. Criteria: percentage of Internet users with high-speed access; the range of service providers within a city; availability of public wireless hot spots. *Forbes, "America's Most Wired Cities," January 10, 2008*

- Nashville* was selected as one of the best places to start and grow a company by *Entrepreneur* and the National Policy Research Council. The Nashville* metro area ranked #8 out of 50 large metro areas. Criteria: business formation and growth (firms started four to 14 years ago that still employ at least 5 people and experienced rapid growth over the last four years). *Entrepreneur/National Policy Research Council, "Hot Cities for Entrepreneurs," September 2006*

- The Nashville* metro area was selected as one of "America's 50 Hottest Cities" for business relocations and expansions. Criteria: industry's most prominent site selection consultants were asked to list their top city choices for relocating and expanding manufacturing companies, taking into consideration such factors as the business climate, work force quality, operating costs, incentive programs, and the ease of working with local political and economic development officials. *Expansion Management, January-February 2007*

- Nashville* was cited as one of America's top large metros (population over 1 million) for new and expanded facility projects in 2007. The area appeared in the top 10 with 73 projects. *Site Selection, "Top Metropolitan Area Awards," March 2008*

- Intel, in partnership with Sperling's BestPlaces, ranked the 80 "Best Cities for Teleworking" in America. The Nashville* metro area ranked #11 among mid-sized metro areas. The study identifies cities that hold the greatest potential for teleworking based on a host of factors including typical commuting times, fuel prices, availability of broadband Internet access and percentage of the population in telework friendly jobs. The study also factored in extreme climate and natural hazards. *Intel, "Best Cities for Teleworking," March 30, 2006*

- The Nashville* metro area appeared on the Milken Institute "2007 Best Performing Cities" index. Rank: #61 out of 200 large metro areas. Criteria: job growth; wage and salary growth; high-tech output growth. *Milken Institute, "2007 Best Performing Cities"*

- The Nashville* metro area was selected as one of the hottest cities for entrepreneurs in America by *Inc. Magazine*. Criteria: job-growth data for 393 metro was analyzed for current-year employment growth, average annual employment growth over past three years, and employment growth by industry sector. The Nashville* metro area ranked #14 among large metro areas and #102 overall. *Inc. Magazine, May 2007*

- Nashville* was identified as one of the 100 "Most Unwired Cities" in the U.S. The area ranked #27 out of the 100 largest metro areas in the U.S. Criteria: number of public and commercial wireless access points (hotspots); airports with wireless Internet access; broadband availability; local wireless networks; and wireless email devices. *Intel, "Most Unwired Cities Survey," June 7, 2005*

- Nashville* was ranked #59 out of 125 regions worldwide in terms of its "Knowledge Competitiveness Index." The index attempts to measure the knowledge-based development taking place throughout the world and is based on 19 measures of economic performance that indicate a region's ability to translate its knowledge capacity into economic value. *Robert Huggins Associates, World Knowledge Competitiveness Index 2005*

- *Forbes* ranked the 200 most populous metro areas in the U.S. in terms of the "Best Places for Business and Careers." The Nashville* metro area was ranked #15. Criteria: business costs (labor, energy, tax and office space expenses); living costs (housing, transportation, food and other household expenditures); education levels of the work force; job growth; income growth; migration trends; crime rates; and culture/leisure. *Forbes, "Best Places for Business and Careers," March 19, 2008*

- *Fortune* ranked the 100 largest metro areas in the U.S. in terms of projected median home price change in 2007. The Nashville* metro area ranked #19. *Fortune.com, "Hot Spots, Cold Spots"*

Health/Environment Rankings

- The Nashville* metro area was identified as one of "America's 20 Most Sedentary Cities" by *Forbes*. The metro area ranked #9. Criteria: percentage of overweight or obese people; percentage of people who had not engaged in any physical activity in the past 30 days; average number of hours of TV watched per week. *Forbes.com, "America's Most Sedentary Cities," October 29, 2007*

- 100 of the largest metro areas in the U.S. were analyzed in terms of their current drought severity. The Nashville* metro area ranked #6 (#1 = driest). The rankings were based on statistics such as long-term precipitation trends and patterns and the Palmer drought indices. *Sperling's BestPlaces, www.BestPlaces.net, "America's Drought-Riskiest Cities," November 2007*

- Doctors at the Harvard School of Public Health ranked 40 metropolitan areas based on data from the government-sponsored Hospital Quality Alliance program. The program tracks the performance of individual hospitals in treating patients for three common health problems: heart attacks, congestive heart failure, and pneumonia. The Nashville* metro area ranked #20 in quality of care for heart attacks, #37 for congestive heart failure, and #6 for pneumonia. *New England Journal of Medicine, July 21, 2005*

- *Reader's Digest* ranked the 50 largest metro areas in the U.S. in terms of how "clean" they are. The Nashville* metro area ranked #23. Criteria: air quality; water quality; toxic industrial pollution; Superfund sites; and sanitation. *Reader's Digest, "The 50 Cleanest (and Dirtiest) Cities in America," July 2005*

- The Nashville* metro area was identified as one of "America's Most Obese Cities" by *Forbes*. The magazine analyzed BMI (body mass index) data from the CDC in the 50 most populated metro areas in the U.S. and ranked the top 20. The area ranked #7. *Forbes, "America's Most Obese Cities," November 26, 2007*

- The Nashville* metro area appeared in *Country Home's* "2008 Best Green Places" report. The area ranked #216 out of 379. Criteria: official energy policies; green power; green buildings; availability of fresh, locally grown food. *Country Home, "2008 Best Green Places"*

- Wyeth Consumer Healthcare, in partnership with Sperling's BestPlaces, ranked the nation's 50 most populous metro areas in terms of five key health factors. The Nashville* metro area ranked #18. Criteria: physical activity; health status; nutrition; lifestyle pursuits; and mental wellness. *Wyeth Consumer Healthcare, "Centrum Healthiest Cities Study," April 19, 2005*

- Nashville* was identified as a "2008 Asthma Capital." The area ranked #29 out of the nation's 100 largest metropolitan areas. Twelve factors were used to identify the most challenging places to live for people with asthma: estimated prevalence; self-reported prevalence; crude death rate for asthma; annual pollen score; annual air quality; public smoking laws; number of board-certified asthma specialists; school inhaler access laws; rescue medication use; controller medication use; uninsured rate; poverty rate. *Asthma and Allergy Foundation of America, "2008 Asthma Capitals"*

- Nashville* was identified as a "Spring Allergy Capital." The area ranked #65 out of 100. Three groups of factors were used to identify the most severe cities for people with allergies during the spring season: annual pollen levels; medicine utilization; access to board-certified allergists. *Asthma and Allergy Foundation of America, "2007 Spring Allergy Capital Rankings"*

- Nashville* was identified as a "Fall Allergy Capital." The area ranked #60 out of 100. Three groups of factors were used to identify the most severe cities for people with allergies during the fall season: annual pollen levels; medicine utilization; access to board-certified allergists. *Asthma and Allergy Foundation of America, "2007 Fall Allergy Capital Rankings"*

- Ortho-McNeil Neurologics, in partnership with Sperling's BestPlaces, analyzed 110 metro areas and identified those U.S. cities with the highest prevalence of factors that are most commonly associated with migraine headaches. The Nashville* metro area ranked #6. Criteria: number of migraine-related drug prescriptions per capita; lifestyle factors that can contribute to migraines; environmental factors that can trigger migraines; and consumption of migraine-triggering foods. *Ortho-McNeil Neurologics, "America's Migraine Hot Spots," March 14, 2006*

- Sperling's BestPlaces ranked 331 metro areas and identified the most and least stressful U.S. cities. The Nashville* metro area ranked #39 out of the 100 largest metro areas (#1 = most stressful). Criteria: divorce rate; unemployment rate; violent and property crime; suicide rate; commute time; mental health; alcohol consumption; cloudy days. *Sperling's BestPlaces, www.BestPlaces.net, "America's Most (and Least) Stressful Cities," January 9, 2004*

- An analysis of the "Best & Worst Cities for Sleep" was conducted by Sperling's BestPlaces. The study ranked America's 50 most populated metro areas. The Nashville* metro area ranked #49 (#1 = best city for sleep). Criteria: number of days residents didn't get enough rest or sleep during the past month; average length of daily commute; divorce rate; unemployment rate. *Sperling's BestPlaces, www.BestPlaces.net, "Best & Worst Cities for Sleep," 2006*

- Nashville* was selected as one of "America's Pet Healthiest Cities" by Purina. The city ranked #29 out of 50. Criteria: veterinary services; environment; legislation; preventative care; obesity/body condition. *Purina Pet Institute, "America's Pet Healthiest Cities," May 20, 2003*

Women/Minorities Rankings

- Nashville* was ranked #56 out of 100 metro areas in *SELF Magazine's* ranking of "America's Best Places for Women." A panel of experts came up with more than 50 criteria including death and disease rates, environmental indicators, community resources, and lifestyle habits. *SELF Magazine, "America's Best Places for Women 2007," December 2007*

- Nashville* appeared on *Black Enterprise's* list of the "Ten Best Cities for African Americans." The top picks were culled from more than 2,000 interactive surveys completed on www.blackenterprise.com and by editorial staff evaluation. The editors weighed the following criteria as it pertained to African Americans in each city: median household income; percentage of households earning more than $100,000; percentage of businesses owned; percentage of college graduates; unemployment rates; home loan rejections; and homeownership rates. *Black Enterprise, May 2007*

Seniors/Retirement Rankings

- Sperling's BestPlaces in partnership with Bankers Life & Casualty Company designed a survey to identify the top 50 metro areas in the U.S. that offer the best overall qualities for senior living. The Nashville* metro area ranked #22. The following criteria were statistically weighted to reflect the needs of the senior population: health; disease; economics; social; environment; spiritual; transportation; housing; and crime. *Bankers Life & Casualty Company, "Best Cities for Seniors 2005"*
- A.G. Edwards ranked America's 500 top-performing communities based on their residents' personal savings and investing behavior. The Nashville* metro area ranked #294 with an index score of 100.05 (national average = 100.00). A dozen statistical factors were measured including: participation in retirement savings plans; personal debt levels; and home ownership. *A.G. Edwards, "2007 Nest Egg Index", September 12, 2007*

Children/Family Rankings

- The Nashville* metro area was selected as one of the "Best Cities for Relocating Families" by Worldwide ERC and Primacy Relocation. The 2007 study placed a special emphasis on the housing market, which has significantly impacted the relocation industry and an employer's ability to transfer employees. The variables which weigh heavily in this category include home price, home affordability index, appreciation rates, and property tax. Other criteria include cost of living, crime rates, education, climate, focus on diversity, physicians per capita, recreation and leisure, arts and culture, air quality, watershed quality, sales tax, unemployment rate, job growth, high school and higher education index, school expenditures per student, students in public school, SAT/ACT percentile, and population growth. *Worldwide ERC and Primacy Relocation, "2007 Best Cities for Relocating Families"*

Safety Rankings

- The National Insurance Crime Bureau ranked 361 metro areas in the U.S. in terms of per capita rates of vehicle theft. The Nashville* metro area ranked #145 (#1 = highest rate). Criteria: number of vehicle theft offenses per 100,000 inhabitants. *National Insurance Crime Bureau, "NICB Vehicle Theft Study," April 22, 2008*
- Nashville* appeared on Sperling's BestPlaces list of the "Riskiest Cities for Identity Theft." The area ranked #40 out of the nations 50 largest metro areas. Over 80 criteria were analyzed across four major categories: technology impact; crime; transactions; and risk profile. *Sperling's BestPlaces, www.BestPlaces.net, "Riskiest Cities for Identity Theft," July 2006*
- Farmers Insurance Group of Companies, in partnership with Sperling's BestPlaces, ranked 379 metro areas and identified the "Most Secure U.S. Place to Live." The Nashville* metro area ranked #89 out of 114 in the large metro area category (500,000 or more residents). Criteria: crime rates; extreme weather; risk of natural disasters; environmental hazards; terrorism threats; air quality; life expectancy; job loss numbers. *Farmers Insurance Group, "Most Secure U.S. Places to Live 2007"*
- Nashville* was identified as one of the most dangerous large metro areas for pedestrians in the U.S. The area ranked #18 out of the nations 50 largest metro areas. Criteria: average yearly pedestrian fatalities per capita (for the years 2002 and 2003) adjusted for the number of walkers. *Surface Transportation Policy Project, "Mean Streets 2004"*

Sports/Recreation Rankings

- The Nashville* metro area appeared on the *Sporting News* list of the "Best Sports Cities 2007". The area ranked #16 out of 150 cities in the U.S. *Sporting News* takes a 12-month snapshot, roughly July to July, of each city's sports, putting a heavy premium on regular-season won-lost records (from the most recently completed season). Other criteria include: playoff berths, bowl appearances and tournament bids; championships; applicable power ratings; quality of competition; overall fan fervor as measured in part by attendance as percentage of venue capacity; abundance of teams (rewarding quality over quantity); stadium and arena quality; ticket availability and prices; franchise ownership; and marquee appeal of athletes. *SportingNews.com, "Best Sports Cities 2007," August 1, 2007*

- The Nashville* metro area was selected by *Cranium* as one of the "Top 50 Fun Cities" in America. The area ranked #24. Criteria includes: number of sports teams, restaurants, and dance performances; number of toy stores; city budget spent on recreation. *Cranium, November 4, 2003*

- *Golf Digest* ranked 330 metro areas in the U.S. in terms of golf. The Nashville* metro area was ranked #188. Criteria: access to golf; weather; value of golf; and quality of golf. *Golf Digest, "Metro Golf Rankings," August 2005*

Dating/Romance Rankings

- Eli Lily and Company, in partnership with Sperling's BestPlaces, ranked the nation's 50 largest metro areas in terms of the "Most Romantic Cities for Baby Boomers." The Nashville* metro area ranked #17. Criteria: marriage and divorce rates among "baby boomers" age 45 to 60; great restaurants; dance studios; chocolate, jewelry and flower sales. *Eli Lily and Company, "Most Romantic Cities for Baby Boomers," April 20, 2007*

- The Nashville* metro area was selected as one of the "Best Cities for Relocating Singles" by Worldwide ERC and Primacy Relocation. The area ranked #43 out of the 100 largest metro areas in the U.S. Areas were selected based on the following criteria: a robust cost-of-living index; adventure and outdoor recreation opportunities; violent crime and property crime rates; percentage of the population that is unmarried (ages 25-34); ratio of single men and single women; affordability of quality higher education, including in-state and out-of-state tuition requirements and rates; number of newcomers to the area; commute times; tax rates; fee and occupancy rates for temporary housing and mini-storage; quality and quantity of collegiate and professional sporting events and fun, fan-friendly venues. *Worldwide ERC and Primacy Relocation, "2007 Best Cities for Relocating Singles," October 25, 2007*

- Sperling's BestPlaces in partnership with AXE Deodorant Bodyspray ranked 80 metro areas and identified "America's Best (and Worst) Cities for Dating." The Nashville* metro area ranked #42 (#1 = best). Criteria: percentage of singles ages 18-24; population density; dating venues per capita. *AXE Deodorant Bodyspray, "America's Best (and Worst) Cities for Dating," May 2004*

Culture/Performing Arts Rankings

- The Nashville* metro area was selected as one of the "Best Places for Artists in America" by *BusinessWeek.com.* Criteria: percentage of young people age 25 to 34; population diversity; concentration of museums, philharmonic orchestras, dance companies, theater troupes, library resources, and college arts programs. *BusinessWeek.com, "Best Places for Artists in America," February 26, 2007*

Miscellaneous Rankings

- Scarborough Research, a leading market research firm, identified the top local markets for bloggers. The Nashville* DMA (Designated Market Area) ranked in the top 13 with 11% of adults reporting that they had read or contributed to a blog within the past 30 days. *Scarborough Research, October 24, 2007*

- The Nashville* metro area appeared on *Forbes* list of "America's Drunkest Cities". The area ranked #35. Criteria: 35 of the largest continental U.S. metro areas were chosen based on availability of data and geographic diversity. Each metro was ranked in five areas: state laws; drinkers; heavy drinkers; binge drinkers; and alcoholism. *Forbes.com, "America's Drunkest Cities," August 22, 2006*

- Sperling's BestPlaces in partnership with Pep Boys ranked 77 metro areas and identified "America's Most Drivable Cities." The Nashville* metro area ranked #16. Criteria: climate; road roughness; urban mobility; gas prices. *Pep Boys, "America's Most Drivable Cities," April 9, 2003*

- State Farm Insurance, in partnership with Sperling's BestPlaces, analyzed several key factors that contribute to overall family preparedness. The Nashville* metro area ranked #25 out of the nation's 50 most populous metro areas. Criteria: quality of life; life insurance coverage; and investments. *State Farm Life Insurance, "Fiscally Fit Cities Report," July 20, 2004*

- Scarborough Research, a leading market research firm, identified the top local markets for frequent fast food restaurant patronage. The Nashville* DMA (Designated Market Area) ranked in the top 10 with consumers reporting an average of 6.1 visits within the past 30 days. *Scarborough Research, May 31, 2006*

- A study by Sperling's BestPlaces examined which U.S. metro areas were most affected by high fuel prices in 2006. The Nashville* metro area was ranked #7 out of 80 (#1 = most expensive city for driving). Rankings are based on the average dollars spent on gas per year by two driver households. Criteria: cost of regular-grade gasoline; average miles driven per day; average number of gallons each driver uses and wastes in traffic congestion each day. *Sperling's BestPlaces, www.bestplaces.net, "Pain at the Pump," May 18, 2006*

Brentwood is located within the Nashville-Davidson—Murfreesboro, TN Metropolitan Statistical Area.

Business Environment

CITY FINANCES

City Government Finances

Component	2004-2005 ($000)	2004-2005 ($ per capita)
Total Revenues	40,322	1,244
Total Expenditures	36,343	1,121
Debt Outstanding	35,002	1,079
Cash and Securities	34,419	1,061

Source: U.S Census Bureau, Government Finances 2004-2005

City Government Revenue by Source

Source	2004-2005 ($000)	2004-2005 ($ per capita)
General Revenue		
From Federal Government	0	0
From State Government	4,472	138
From Local Governments	8,692	268
Taxes		
Property	8,473	261
Sales	1,773	55
Personal Income	0	0
License	2,831	87
Charges	5,863	181
Liquor Store	0	0
Utility	6,452	199
Employee Retirement	0	0
Other	1,766	54

Source: U.S Census Bureau, Government Finances 2004-2005

City Government Expenditures by Function

Function	2004-2005 ($000)	2004-2005 ($ per capita)	2004-2005 (%)
General Expenditures			
Airports	0	0	0.0
Corrections	0	0	0.0
Education	200	6	0.6
Fire Protection	4,270	132	11.7
Governmental Administration	1,348	42	3.7
Health	72	2	0.2
Highways	1,835	57	5.0
Hospitals	0	0	0.0
Housing and Community Development	0	0	0.0
Interest on General Debt	1,568	48	4.3
Libraries	1,518	47	4.2
Parking	0	0	0.0
Parks and Recreation	1,125	35	3.1
Police Protection	4,545	140	12.5
Public Welfare	0	0	0.0
Sewerage	2,379	73	6.5
Solid Waste Management	0	0	0.0
Liquor Store	0	0	0.0
Utility	7,396	228	20.4
Employee Retirement	0	0	0.0
Other	10,087	311	27.8

Source: U.S Census Bureau, Government Finances 2004-2005

Municipal Bond Ratings

Area	Moody's
City	n/a

Source: Mergent Bond Record, January 2008 (unless noted otherwise)

DEMOGRAPHICS

Population Growth

Area	1990 Census	2000 Census	2007 Estimate	2012 Projection	Population Growth (%) 1990-2000	Population Growth (%) 2000-2012
City	17,287	23,445	29,886	34,424	35.6	46.8
MSA[1]	1,048,218	1,311,789	1,458,115	1,561,775	25.1	19.1
U.S.	248,709,873	281,421,906	301,045,522	314,920,978	13.2	11.9

Note: (1) Metropolitan Statistical Area - see Appendix B for areas included
Source: Claritas, Inc.

Number of Households and Average Household Size

Area	2007 Estimate	2007 Average Household Size
City	9,931	3.01
MSA[1]	575,173	2.54
U.S.	113,668,003	2.65

Note: (1) Metropolitan Statistical Area - see Appendix B for areas included
Source: Claritas, Inc.

Race and Ethnicity

Area	White Alone[2]	Black Alone[2]	Asian Alone[2]	Other Race Alone[2]	Hispanic[3]
City	92.9	1.9	3.9	1.2	1.5
MSA[1]	78.4	15.2	1.9	4.5	5.0
U.S.	73.1	12.4	4.3	10.3	14.9

Note: Figures are 2007 estimates; (1) Metropolitan Statistical Area - see Appendix B for areas included (2) Alone is defined as not being in combination with one or more other races; (3) May be of any race.
Source: Claritas, Inc.

Ancestry

Area	German	Irish[2]	English	American	Italian	Polish	French[3]	Scottish
City	16.7	11.6	21.3	11.0	2.9	2.9	4.1	4.2
MSA[1]	9.8	10.2	10.4	15.4	2.1	1.1	2.1	2.2
U.S.	15.2	10.9	8.7	7.3	5.6	3.2	3.0	1.7

Note: Figures include multiple ancestry (e.g. if a person reported being Irish and Italian, they were included in both columns); (1) Metropolitan Statistical Area - see Appendix A for areas included; (2) Includes Celtic; (3) Includes Alsatian but excludes Basque
Source: Census 2000, Summary File 3

Foreign-Born Population

Area	Percent of Population Born in							
	Any Foreign Country	Europe	Asia	Africa	Oceania[2]	Canada	Mexico	Latin America[3]
City	4.5	0.9	2.7	0.3	0.1	0.3	0.1	0.1
MSA[1]	4.7	0.7	1.5	0.4	0.0	0.2	1.3	0.6
U.S.	11.1	1.7	2.9	0.3	0.1	0.3	3.3	2.5

Note: (1) Metropolitan Statistical Area - see Appendix A for areas included; (2) Includes Australia, New Zealand subregion, Melanesia, Micronesia, Polynesia, and Oceania n.e.c; (3) Includes Central America (excluding Mexico), South America, and the Caribbean.
Source: Census 2000, Summary File 3

Marriage Status

Area	Never Married	Now Married (excluding Separated)	Separated	Widowed	Divorced
City	17.5	74.3	0.7	3.3	4.2
MSA[1]	26.3	54.8	1.8	5.6	11.5
U.S.	27.1	54.4	2.2	6.6	9.7

Note: Figures are percentages and cover the population 15 years of age and older; (1) Metropolitan Statistical Area - see Appendix A for areas included
Source: Census 2000, Summary File 3

Age Distribution

Area	Percent of Population						
	Under Age 5	Age 5 to 17	Age 18 to 34	Age 35 to 49	Age 50 to 64	Age 65 to 79	80 Years and Over
City	6.2	25.7	9.8	29.7	21.0	6.4	1.2
MSA[1]	6.9	17.9	25.9	24.8	14.5	7.6	2.5
U.S.	6.8	18.9	23.7	23.5	14.8	9.2	3.2

Note: (1) Metropolitan Statistical Area - see Appendix A for areas included
Source: Census 2000, Summary File 3

Male/Female Ratio

Area	Males	Females	Males per 100 Females
City	14,739	15,147	97.3
MSA[1]	719,926	738,189	97.5
U.S.	148,320,305	152,725,217	97.1

Note: Figures are 2007 estimates; (1) Metropolitan Statistical Area - see Appendix B for areas included
Source: Claritas, Inc.

Religion

Area	Catholic	Southern Baptist	United Meth-odist	ELCA[1]	LDS[2]	Presby-terian Church USA	Jewish Est.	Muslim Est.
County	11.3	14.2	11.0	0.6	1.4	1.9	0.0	0.0
U.S.	22.0	7.1	3.7	1.8	1.5	1.1	2.2	0.6

Note: Figures are the number of adherents as a percentage of the total population; Adherents are defined as all members, including full members, their children and the estimated number of other participants who are not considered members (e.g. the baptized, those not confirmed, those regularly attending services, etc.); (1) Evangelical Lutheran Church in America; (2) The Church of Jesus Christ of Latter Day Saints
Source: Reprinted with permission from Religious Congregations and Membership in the United States 2000 (Nashville, Glenmary Research Center, 2002) Copyright Association of Statisticians of American Religious Bodies. All rights reserved.

ECONOMY

Gross Metropolitan Product

Area	2002	2003	2004	2005	2005 Rank[2]
MSA[1]	48.8	51.8	56.3	60.3	40

Note: Figures are in billions of dollars; (1) Nashville-Davidson—Murfreesboro, TN Metropolitan Statistical Area - see Appendix A for areas included; (2) Rank ranges from 1 to 361
Source: The U.S. Conference of Mayors, "U.S. Metro Economies: GMP - The Engines of America's Growth," January 2007

Economic Growth

Area	1995 GMP	2005 GMP	Average Annual Growth Rate	Growth Rate Rank[2]
MSA[1]	33.4	60.3	6.1	111

Note: Figures are in billions of dollars; GMP = Gross Metropolitan Product; (1) Nashville-Davidson—Murfreesboro, TN Metropolitan Statistical Area - see Appendix A for areas included; (2) Rank ranges from 1 to 361
Source: The U.S. Conference of Mayors, "U.S. Metro Economies: GMP - The Engines of America's Growth," January 2007

INCOME

Per Capita/Median/Average Income

Area	Per Capita ($)	Median Household ($)	Average Household ($)
City	56,834	132,495	170,704
MSA[1]	26,706	50,679	67,062
U.S.	25,495	49,280	66,670

Note: Figures are 2007 estimates; (1) Metropolitan Statistical Area - see Appendix B for areas included
Source: Claritas, Inc.

Household Income Distribution

Area	Percent of Households Earning							
	Under $15,000	$15,000 -24,999	$25,000 -34,999	$35,000 -49,999	$50,000 -74,999	$75,000 -99,000	$100,000 -149,999	$150,000 and up
City	3.1	1.9	2.7	5.4	10.5	11.0	23.3	42.2
MSA[1]	11.8	10.0	11.2	16.3	21.0	12.3	11.1	6.3
U.S.	13.1	10.9	11.2	15.6	19.5	11.9	11.3	6.6

Note: Figures are 2007 estimates; (1) Metropolitan Statistical Area - see Appendix B for areas included
Source: Claritas, Inc.

Poverty Rates by Age

Area	All Ages	Under 5 Years Old	5 to 17 Years Old	18 to 64 Years Old	65 Years and Over
City	2.0	0.1	0.8	0.8	0.3
MSA[1]	10.1	1.1	2.3	5.7	1.0
U.S.	12.4	1.2	3.0	6.9	1.2

Note: Figures are percent of population with income in 1999 below poverty level and only include population for whom poverty status is determined; (1) Metropolitan Statistical Area - see Appendix A for areas included
Source: Census 2000, Summary File 3

Personal Bankruptcy Filing Rate

Area	2004	2005	2006
Williamson County	3.44	3.92	1.60
U.S.	5.31	6.82	2.00

Note: Numbers are per 1,000 population and include Chapter 7 and Chapter 13 filings
Source: Federal Deposit Insurance Corporation (FDIC), Regional Economic Conditions (RECON), 8/23/2007

EMPLOYMENT

Labor Force and Employment

Area	Civilian Labor Force			Workers Employed		
	Dec. 2006	Dec. 2007	% Chg.	Dec. 2006	Dec. 2007	% Chg.
City	17,168	17,445	1.6	16,691	16,858	1.0
MSA[1]	786,226	799,308	1.7	758,387	765,980	1.0
U.S.	152,571,000	153,705,000	0.7	146,081,000	146,334,000	0.2

Note: Data is not seasonally adjusted and covers workers 16 years of age and older; (1) Metropolitan Statistical Area - see Appendix B for areas included
Source: Bureau of Labor Statistics, http://stats.bls.gov

Unemployment Rate

Area	2007											
	Jan.	Feb.	Mar.	Apr.	May	Jun.	Jul.	Aug.	Sep.	Oct.	Nov.	Dec.
City	2.9	2.8	2.5	2.5	2.9	3.2	2.9	3.5	3.6	3.5	3.5	3.4
MSA[1]	4.1	4.0	3.8	3.5	3.5	3.9	3.8	4.0	4.0	4.0	4.3	4.2
U.S.	5.0	4.9	4.5	4.3	4.3	4.7	4.9	4.6	4.5	4.4	4.5	4.8

Note: Data is not seasonally adjusted and covers workers 16 years of age and older; All figures are percentages; (1) Metropolitan Statistical Area - see Appendix B for areas included
Source: Bureau of Labor Statistics, http://stats.bls.gov

Employment by Occupation

Occupation Classification	City (%)	MSA[1] (%)	U.S. (%)
Sales and Office	26.3	28.3	26.7
Professional and Related	28.8	19.8	20.2
Service	6.3	12.7	14.9
Production, Transportation, and Material Moving	3.4	14.4	14.6
Management, Business, and Financial	32.7	14.8	13.5
Construction, Extraction, and Maintenance	2.2	9.6	9.4
Farming, Forestry, and Fishing	0.2	0.3	0.7

Note: Figures cover employed civilians 16 years of age and older; (1) Metropolitan Statistical Area - see Appendix A for areas included
Source: Census 2000, Summary File 3

Employment by Industry

Sector	MSA[1] Number of Employees	MSA[1] Percent of Total	U.S. Percent of Total
Government	101,300	13.1	16.3
Education and Health Services	110,600	14.3	13.4
Professional and Business Services	103,600	13.4	13.1
Retail Trade	92,300	11.9	11.6
Manufacturing	78,000	10.1	9.9
Leisure and Hospitality	81,200	10.5	9.6
Financial Activities	46,600	6.0	5.9
Construction	n/a	n/a	5.3
Wholesale Trade	37,400	4.8	4.4
Other Services	30,100	3.9	3.9
Transportation and Utilities	31,300	4.0	3.7
Information	19,700	2.5	2.2
Natural Resources and Mining	n/a	n/a	0.5

Note: Figures cover non-farm employment as of December 2007 and are not seasonally adjusted; (1) Metropolitan Statistical Area - see Appendix B for areas included; n/a not available
Source: Bureau of Labor Statistics, http://stats.bls.gov

Average Wages

Occupation	$/Hr.	Occupation	$/Hr.
Accountants and Auditors	27.01	Maids and Housekeeping Cleaners	8.69
Automotive Mechanics	16.48	Maintenance and Repair Workers	16.26
Bookkeepers	15.40	Marketing Managers	39.16
Carpenters	15.07	Nuclear Medicine Technologists	31.29
Cashiers	8.35	Nurses, Licensed Practical	17.89
Clerks, General Office	13.38	Nurses, Registered	27.94
Clerks, Receptionists/Information	12.23	Nursing Aides/Orderlies/Attendants	11.30
Clerks, Shipping/Receiving	12.76	Packers and Packagers, Hand	9.60
Computer Programmers	28.69	Physical Therapists	34.28
Computer Support Specialists	21.74	Postal Service Mail Carriers	21.34
Computer Systems Analysts	29.52	Real Estate Brokers	27.53
Cooks, Restaurant	9.98	Retail Salespersons	11.48
Dentists	n/a	Sales Reps., Exc. Tech./Scientific	29.65
Electrical Engineers	37.31	Sales Reps., Tech./Scientific	34.46
Electricians	17.73	Secretaries, Exc. Legal/Med./Exec.	13.47
Financial Managers	38.73	Security Guards	11.58
First-Line Supervisors/Mgrs., Sales	18.42	Surgeons	n/a
Food Preparation Workers	9.15	Teacher Assistants	9.70
General and Operations Managers	44.34	Teachers, Elementary School	21.60
Hairdressers/Cosmetologists	17.11	Teachers, Secondary School	21.80
Internists	77.72	Telemarketers	12.77
Janitors and Cleaners	10.34	Truck Drivers, Heavy/Tractor-Trailer	18.90
Landscaping/Groundskeeping Workers	11.42	Truck Drivers, Light/Delivery Svcs.	14.68
Lawyers	48.83	Waiters and Waitresses	7.74

Note: Wage data covers the Nashville-Davidson—Murfreesboro, TN Metropolitan Statistical Area - see Appendix B for areas included. Hourly wages for elementary/secondary school teachers and teacher assistants were calculated by the editors from annual wage data assuming a 40 hour work week; n/a not available.
Source: Bureau of Labor Statistics, May 2007 Metro Area Occupational Employment and Wage Estimates

RESIDENTIAL REAL ESTATE

Building Permits

Area	Single-Family 2006	Single-Family 2007p	Single-Family Pct. Chg.	Multi-Family 2006	Multi-Family 2007p	Multi-Family Pct. Chg.	Total 2006	Total 2007p	Total Pct. Chg.
City	502	294	-41.4	0	0	-	502	294	-41.4
U.S.	1,378,200	973,300	-29.4	460,700	407,200	-11.6	1,838,900	1,380,500	-24.9

Note: (p) preliminary; figures cover and represent new, privately-owned housing units authorized (unadjusted data); All permit data are based on estimates with imputation; U.S. figures are based on the new 20,000-place series.
Source: U.S. Census Bureau, Manufacturing, Mining, and Construction Statistics

Homeownership and Housing Vacancies

Area	Homeownership Rate[2] (%)			Rental Vacancy Rate[3] (%)			Homeowner Vacancy Rate[4] (%)		
	2005	2006	2007	2005	2006	2007	2005	2006	2007
MSA[1]	73.0	72.4	70.0	14.6	10.5	7.6	1.9	1.5	2.4
U.S.	68.9	68.8	68.1	9.8	9.8	9.7	1.9	2.4	2.7

Note: (1) Metropolitan Statistical Area - see Appendix B for areas included; (2) The proportion of households that are owners; (3) The proportion of the rental inventory that is vacant for rent; (4) The proportion of the homeowner inventory that is vacant for sale; n/a not available
Source: U.S. Census Bureau, Housing Vacancies and Homeownership Annual Statistics: 2007

TAXES

State Corporate Income Tax Rates

State	Rates and Tax Brackets
Tennessee	6.5%

Note: Tax rates as of January 1, 2008; Franchise tax of.25% of the greater of net worth or real and tangible property (minimum $100)
Source: Tax Foundation, www.taxfoundation.org

State Individual Income Tax Rates

State	Federal Deductibility	Marginal Rates (%)	Standard Deduction ($)		Personal Exemptions ($)[1]	
			Single	Joint	Single	Dependents
Tennessee	No	6 (h)	n/a	n/a	1,250	n/a

Note: Tax rates as of January 1, 2008; Local- and county-level taxes are not included; n/a not applicable; (1) Married joint filers generally receive double the single exemption; (h) Applies to interest and dividend income only.
Source: Tax Foundation, www.taxfoundation.org

Various State and Local Tax Rates

State and Local Sales and Use (%)	State Sales and Use (%)	Gasoline[1,2] ($/gal.)	Cigarette ($/pack)	Spirits ($/gal.)	Table Wine ($/gal.)	Beer ($/gal.)
9.25	7.0	0.214	0.62	4.40	1.21	0.14 (r)

Note: Tax rates as of January 1, 2008; (1) In addition to the 18.4 cpg Federal gasoline tax; (2) Rates may include additional state sales taxes, environmental protection and storage fees/taxes, and local taxes. When necessary, the volume-weighted average of all local taxes is used to approximate the typical statewide rate including local tax; (r) There is an additional 17% wholesale tax on beer.
Source: Tax Foundation, www.taxfoundation.org; Original research

State Tax Burdens

Area	Combined State and Local Tax Burden		Combined Federal, State and Local Tax Burden	
	Percent	Rank	Percent	Rank
Tennessee	8.5	48	28.8	46
U.S. Average	11.0	-	32.7	-

Note: Figures cover 2007 and measure taxes as a percentage of income
Source: Tax Foundation, www.taxfoundation.org

State Business Tax Climate Index Rankings

State	Overall Rank	Corporate Tax Index Rank	Individual Income Tax Index Rank	Sales Tax Index Rank	Unemployment Insurance Tax Index Rank	Property Tax Index Rank
Tennessee	16	12	8	48	31	35

Note: Rankings range from 1 to 50 where 1 is best. Rankings do not average across to Overall Rank. States without a given tax are given a ranking of 1.
Source: Tax Foundation, State Business Tax Climate Index 2008

TRANSPORTATION

Means of Transportation to Work

Area	Car/Truck/Van		Public Transportation			Bicycle	Walked	Other Means	Worked at Home
	Drove Alone	Car-pooled	Bus	Subway	Railroad				
City	85.4	5.9	0.3	0.1	0.0	0.0	0.7	0.8	6.7
MSA[1]	80.7	12.8	0.9	0.0	0.0	0.1	1.5	0.8	3.2
U.S.	75.7	12.2	2.5	1.5	0.5	0.4	2.9	1.0	3.3

Note: Figures are percentages and cover workers 16 years of age and older; (1) Metropolitan Statistical Area - see Appendix A for areas included
Source: Census 2000, Summary File 3

Travel Time to Work

Area	Less Than 15 Minutes	15 to 29 Minutes	30 to 44 Minutes	45 to 59 Minutes	60 Minutes or More
City	23.8	51.3	18.8	2.2	3.9
MSA[1]	23.9	38.6	23.0	8.8	5.7
U.S.	29.4	36.1	19.1	7.4	8.0

Note: Figures are percentages and include workers 16 years old and over; (1) Metropolitan Statistical Area - see Appendix A for areas included
Source: Census 2000, Summary File 3

Travel Time Index

Area	1982	1995	2004	2005
Urban Area[1]	1.09	1.13	1.17	1.17
Average[2]	1.11	1.22	1.29	1.30

Note: Travel Time Index - The ratio of travel time in the peak period to the travel time at free-flow conditions. A value of 1.35 indicates a 20-minute free-flow trip takes 27 minutes in the peak. Free-flow speeds (60 mph on freeways and 35 mph on principal arterials) are used as the comparison threshold; (1) Covers the Nashville-Davidson, TN urban area; (2) average of 85 urban areas
Source: Texas Transportation Institute, The 2007 Urban Mobility Report, September 2007

Living Environment

COST OF LIVING

Cost of Living Index

Composite Index	Groceries	Housing	Utilities	Trans-portation	Health Care	Misc. Goods/ Services
88.2	90.4	78.6	87.9	94.3	85.4	93.8

Note: U.S. = 100; Figures cover the Nashville-Franklin TN urban area.
Source: The Council for Community and Economic Research (formerly ACCRA), Cost of Living Index, 2007

Grocery Prices

Area[1]	T-Bone Steak ($/pound)	Frying Chicken ($/pound)	Whole Milk ($/half gal.)	Eggs ($/dozen)	Orange Juice ($/64 oz.)	Coffee ($/11.5 oz.)
City[2]	8.50	0.91	1.72	1.22	3.07	3.04
Avg.	8.93	1.12	2.13	1.52	3.26	3.31
Min.	5.88	0.71	1.33	0.83	2.30	2.20
Max.	12.80	2.07	3.43	3.54	5.79	6.20

Note: (1) Values for the local area are compared with the average, minimum and maximum values for all 331 areas in the Cost of Living Index report; (2) Figures cover the Nashville-Franklin TN urban area; **T-Bone Steak** *(price per pound);* **Frying Chicken** *(price per pound, whole fryer);* **Whole Milk** *(half gallon carton);* **Eggs** *(price per dozen, Grade A, large);* **Orange Juice** *(64 oz. Tropicana or Florida Natural);* **Coffee** *(11.5 oz. can, vacuum-packed, Maxwell House, Hills Bros, or Folgers).*
Source: The Council for Community and Economic Research (formerly ACCRA), Cost of Living Index, 2007

Housing and Utility Costs

Area[1]	New Home Price ($)	Apartment Rent ($/month)	All Electric ($/month)	Part Electric ($/month)	Other Energy ($/month)	Telephone ($/month)
City[2]	238,782	687	-	67.29	76.50	23.08
Avg.	309,605	782	146.13	78.67	90.16	26.14
Min.	189,877	n/a	82.03	37.41	33.15	17.08
Max.	1,202,800	3,481	271.14	150.60	257.67	37.45

Note: (1) Values for the local area are compared with the average, minimum and maximum values for all 331 areas in the Cost of Living Index report; (2) Figures cover the Nashville-Franklin TN urban area; **New Home Price** *(2,400 sf living area, 8,000 sf lot, in urban area with full utilities);* **Apartment Rent** *(950 sf 2 bedroom/1.5 or 2 bath, unfurnished, excluding all utilities except water);* **All Electric** *(average monthly cost for an all-electric home);* **Part Electric** *(average monthly cost for a part-electric home);* **Other Energy** *(average monthly cost for natural gas, fuel oil, coal, wood, and any other forms of energy except electricity);* **Telephone** *(price includes basic monthly rate for a private residential line plus additional local usage charges incurred by a family of four).*
Source: The Council for Community and Economic Research (formerly ACCRA), Cost of Living Index, 2007

Health Care, Transportation, and Other Costs

Area[1]	Doctor ($/visit)	Dentist ($/visit)	Optometrist ($/visit)	Gasoline ($/gallon)	Beauty Salon ($/visit)	Men's Shirt ($)
City[2]	65.55	58.81	64.80	2.56	26.11	18.26
Avg.	79.48	71.93	79.55	2.64	29.52	25.77
Min.	52.08	44.80	43.95	2.19	15.58	16.19
Max.	148.44	126.27	158.83	3.48	60.62	48.53

Note: (1) Values for the local area are compared with the average, minimum and maximum values for all 331 areas in the Cost of Living Index report; (2) Figures cover the Nashville-Franklin TN urban area; **Doctor** *(general practitioners routine exam of an established patient);* **Dentist** *(adult teeth cleaning and periodic oral examination);* **Optometrist** *(full vision eye exam for established adult patient);* **Gasoline** *(one gallon regular unleaded, national brand, including all taxes, cash price at self-service pump if available);* **Beauty Salon** *(woman's shampoo, trim, and blow-dry);* **Men's Shirt** *(cotton/polyester dress shirt, pinpoint weave, long sleeves).*
Source: The Council for Community and Economic Research (formerly ACCRA), Cost of Living Index, 2007

HOUSING

House Price Index (HPI)

Area	National Ranking[2]	Quarterly Change (%)	One-Year Change (%)	Five-Year Change (%)
MSA[1]	54	0.19	4.57	34.80
U.S.[3]	-	0.10	0.84	41.37

Note: The HPI is a weighted repeat sales index. It measures average price changes in repeat sales or refinancings on the same properties. This information is obtained by reviewing repeat mortgage transactions on single-family properties whose mortgages have been purchased or securitized by Fannie Mae or Freddie Mac in January 1975; (1) Metropolitan Statistical Area - see Appendix B for areas included; (2) Rankings are based on annual percentage change for all metro areas containing at least 15,000 transactions over the last 10 years and ranges from 1 to 291; (3) figures based on a weighted average of Census Division estimates; all figures are for the period ending December 31, 2007
Source: Office of Federal Housing Enterprise Oversight, House Price Index, February 26, 2008

House Price Valuations

Area	Q1 2000	Q1 2001	Q1 2002	Q1 2003	Q1 2004	Q1 2005	Q1 2006	Q1 2007	Q1 2008
MSA[1]	-5.0	-7.1	-7.3	-8.9	-9.0	-8.0	-3.7	-1.9	-4.3

Note: Figures show the percentage of over- or under-valuation of single family homes relative to statistically normal house values (e.g. a value of 23.6 indicates that house values are 23.6% overvalued). Statistically normal house values are based on house prices, interest rates, household incomes, population densities, and any historical premiums or discounts metropolitan areas have exhibited over time; (1) Figures cover the Metropolitan Statistical Area - see Appendix B for areas included
Source: Global Insight/National City Corporation, House Prices in America, May 2008

Median Home Prices

Area	2005	2006	2007[r]	Percent Change 2006 to 2007
MSA[1]	161.8	n/a	n/a	n/a
U.S. Average	219.0	221.9	217.9	-1.8

Note: Figures are median sales prices of existing single-family homes in thousands of dollars; (r) revised; n/a not available; (1) Metropolitan Statistical Area - see Appendix B for areas included
Source: National Association of Realtors, Metropolitan Area Prices, 1st Quarter 2008

Housing: Year Structure Built

Area	1990 -2000	1980 -1989	1970 -1979	1960 -1969	1950 -1959	1940 -1949	Before 1940	Median Year
City	32.5	27.2	26.6	11.1	0.5	0.9	1.2	1984
MSA[1]	25.8	20.1	19.1	13.8	9.8	4.9	6.6	1978
U.S.	17.0	15.8	18.5	13.7	12.7	7.3	15.0	1971

Note: Figures are percentages; (1) Metropolitan Statistical Area - see Appendix A for areas included
Source: Census 2000, Summary File 3

HEALTH

Health Risk Data

Category	Area[1] (%)	U.S. (%)
Adults who have been told they have high blood pressure[3]	27.0	25.5
Adults who have been told they have high blood cholesterol[3]	32.8	35.6
Adults who have been told they have diabetes[2]	9.6	7.5
Adults who have been told they have arthritis[3]	26.0	27.0
Adults who have been told they currently have asthma	6.8	8.5
Adults who are current smokers	21.4	20.1
Adults who are heavy drinkers[4]	3.5	4.9
Adults who are overweight (BMI 25.0 - 29.9)	39.0	36.5
Adults who are obese (BMI 30.0 - 99.8)	28.8	25.1

Note: Data as of 2006 unless otherwise noted; (1) Figures cover the Metropolitan Statistical Area - see Appendix B for areas included; (2) Figures do not include pregnancy-related diabetes, pre-diabetes or borderline diabetes; (3) 2005 data; (4) Heavy drinkers are classified as adult men having more than two drinks per day or adult women having more than one drink per day
Source: Centers for Disease Control and Prevention, Behaviorial Risk Factor Surveillance System, SMART: Selected Metropolitan/Micropolitan Area Risk Trends, 2005, 2006

Mortality Rates for the Top 10 Causes of Death in the U.S.

ICD-10[a] Sub-Chapter	ICD-10[a] Code	Age-Adjusted Mortality Rate[1] per 100,000 population	
		County[2]	U.S.
Malignant neoplasms	C00-C97	180.5	186.5
Ischaemic heart diseases	I20-I25	124.3	152.3
Other forms of heart disease	I30-I51	36.2	51.5
Cerebrovascular diseases	I60-I69	65.8	50.0
Chronic lower respiratory diseases	J40-J47	48.5	42.6
Diabetes mellitus	E10-E14	21.4	24.8
Other degenerative diseases of the nervous system	G30-G31	34.1	22.6
Other external causes of accidental injury	W00-X59	24.4	21.4
Influenza and pneumonia	J10-J18	16.4	20.7
Hypertensive diseases	I10-I13	18.3	18.2

Note: (a) ICD-10 = International Classification of Diseases 10th Revision; (1) Mortality rates are a three year average covering 2003-2005; (2) Figures cover Williamson County
Source: Centers for Disease Control and Prevention, National Center for Health Statistics. Compressed Mortality File 1999-2004. CDC WONDER On-line Database, compiled from Compressed Mortality File 1999-2005 Series 20 No. 2K, 2008.

Mortality Rates for Selected Causes of Death

ICD-10[a] Sub-Chapter	ICD-10[a] Code	Age-Adjusted Mortality Rate[1] per 100,000 population	
		County[2]	U.S.
Assault	X85-Y09	*2.1	5.9
Human immunodeficiency virus (HIV) disease	B20-B24	*0.7	4.5
Intentional self-harm	X60-X84	8.2	10.8
Malnutrition	E40-E46	*0.0	1.0
Obesity and other hyperalimentation	E65-E68	*0.9	1.4
Organic, including symptomatic, mental disorders	F01-F09	29.8	16.8
Transport accidents	V01-V99	11.5	16.1
Viral hepatitis	B15-B19	*0.8	1.8

Note: (a) ICD-10 = International Classification of Diseases 10th Revision; (1) Mortality rates are a three year average covering 2003-2005; (2) Figures cover Williamson County; (*) Unreliable data as per CDC
Source: Centers for Disease Control and Prevention, National Center for Health Statistics. Compressed Mortality File 1999-2004. CDC WONDER On-line Database, compiled from Compressed Mortality File 1999-2005 Series 20 No. 2K, 2008.

Distribution of Physicians[1]

Area	Total	Family/ General Practice	Specialties	
			Medical	Surgical
Williamson County (number)	662	104	236	123
Williamson County (rate per 10,000 pop.)	43.1	6.8	15.4	8.0
U.S. (rate per 10,000 pop.)	17.7	4.6	6.9	4.3

Note: Data as of 2005; (1) Includes all non-federal, patient-care, office-based MDs
Source: Area Resource File (ARF). June 2007. U.S. Department of Health and Human Services, Health Resources and Services Administration, Bureau of Health Professions, Rockville, MD.

Hospitals

There were no hospitals listed within the city limits.
AHA Guide to the Healthcare Field 2008

According to *U.S. News,* the Nashville-Davidson-Murfreesboro-Franklin, TN metro area is home to one of the best hospitals in the U.S.: **Vanderbilt University Medical Center**. *U.S. News Online, "America's Best Hospitals 2007"*

EDUCATION

Public School District Statistics

District Name	Schls	Pupils	Pupil/ Teacher Ratio	Minority Pupils[1] (%)	Free Lunch Eligible[2] (%)	IEP[3] (%)
Nashville-Davidson County School District	132	72,713	14.7	63.0	n/a	12.5
Williamson County School District	36	25,791	16.8	10.2	n/a	9.8

Note: Table includes regular local school districts with 2,000 or more students; (1) Percentage of students that are not white, non-Hispanic; (2) Percentage of students that are eligible for the free lunch program; (3) Percentage of students that have an Individualized Education Program.
Source: U.S. Department of Education, National Center for Education Statistics, Common Core of Data, Local Education Agency (School District) Universe Survey: School Year 2005-2006; U.S. Department of Education, National Center for Education Statistics, Common Core of Data, Public Elementary/Secondary School Universe Survey: School Year 2005-2006

Top Public High Schools

High School Name	Index[1]	Rank[1]	Subsidized Lunch (%)[2]	E&E (%)[3]
Brentwood	2.852	192	3.0	97.1
Ravenwood	2.053	473	2.0	30.6

Note: (1) Public schools are ranked according to a ratio that is the number of Advanced Placement, International Baccalaureate, and/or Cambridge tests taken by all students at a school in 2007 divided by the number of graduating seniors. All of the schools on the list have an index of at least 1.000; they are in the top five percent of public schools measured this way. The rankings range from 1 to 1,422; (2) Percentage of students receiving federally subsidized meals; (3) E & E stands for equity and excellence percentage: the portion of all graduating seniors at a school that had at least one passing grade on one AP or IB test; (**) Gave both IB and AP tests. AP and IB participation are indicators of a school's efforts to get students to excel and prepare for college.
Source: Newsweek Online, "Top High Schools 2008"

Highest Level of Education

Area	Less than H.S.	H.S. Diploma	Some College, No Deg.	Associate Degree	Bachelors Degree	Masters Degree	Profess. School Degree	Doctorate Degree
City	2.6	9.9	17.9	4.8	39.0	16.9	6.7	2.3
MSA[1]	19.1	28.7	21.1	5.1	17.8	5.5	1.9	0.9
U.S.	19.4	28.4	21.2	6.4	15.7	5.9	2.0	1.0

Note: Figures are 2007 estimated percentages and cover persons age 25 and over; (1) Metropolitan Statistical Area - see Appendix B for areas included
Source: Claritas, Inc.

Educational Attainment by Race

Area	High School Graduate (%)					Bachelor's Degree (%)				
	Total	White	Black	Asian	Hisp.[2]	Total	White	Black	Asian	Hisp.[2]
City	97.4	97.5	100.0	92.4	95.1	64.7	64.7	77.1	58.6	65.7
MSA[1]	81.4	83.2	74.4	81.1	54.5	26.9	28.2	18.9	46.1	14.2
U.S.	80.4	83.6	72.3	80.4	52.4	24.4	26.1	14.3	44.1	10.4

Note: Figures shown cover persons 25 years old and over; (1) Metropolitan Statistical Area - see Appendix A for areas included; (2) people of Hispanic origin can be of any race
Source: Census 2000, Summary File 3

School Enrollment by Type

Area	Grades KG to 8				Grades 9 to 12			
	Public		Private		Public		Private	
	Enrollment	%	Enrollment	%	Enrollment	%	Enrollment	%
City	3,230	79.5	835	20.5	1,531	74.3	530	25.7
MSA[1]	136,243	86.5	21,347	13.5	56,641	85.6	9,515	14.4
U.S.	33,526,011	88.7	4,285,121	11.3	14,848,628	90.6	1,532,323	9.4

Note: Figures shown cover persons 3 years old and over; (1) Metropolitan Statistical Area - see Appendix A for areas included
Source: Census 2000, Summary File 3

School Enrollment by Race

Area	Grades KG to 8 (%)				Grades 9 to 12 (%)			
	White	Black	Asian	Hisp.[1]	White	Black	Asian	Hisp.[1]
City	94.2	2.3	3.0	1.0	88.9	5.5	4.2	0.4
MSA[2]	74.7	19.8	1.4	3.3	74.4	20.7	1.5	2.6
U.S.	68.5	15.5	3.3	16.8	68.8	15.5	3.8	15.7

Note: Figures shown cover persons 3 years old and over; (1) people of Hispanic origin can be of any race; (2) Metropolitan Statistical Area - see Appendix A for areas included
Source: Census 2000, Summary File 3

Average Salaries of Public School Classroom Teachers

District	2005-06		2006-07		Percent Change 2005-06 to 2006-07
	Dollars	Rank[1]	Dollars	Rank[1]	
Tennessee	42,537	34	43,816	34	3.01
U.S. Average	49,026	-	50,816	-	3.65

Note: (1) State rank ranges from 1 to 51.
Source: National Education Association, Rankings & Estimates: Rankings of the States 2006 and Estimates of School Statistics 2007, December 2007

Higher Education

Four-Year Colleges			Two-Year Colleges			Medical Schools[1]	Law Schools[2]	Voc/ Tech[3]
Public	Private Non-profit	Private For-profit	Public	Private Non-profit	Private For-profit			
0	0	0	0	0	0	0	0	0

Note: Figures cover institutions located within the city limits; (1) includes schools accredited by the Liaison Committee on Medical Education and the American Osteopathic Association; (2) includes American Bar Association-accredited law schools; (3) includes all schools with programs that are less than 2 years.
Source: National Center for Education Statistics, The Integrated Postsecondary Education System (IPEDS) Peer Analysis System, 2007; www.usnews.com, Law and Medical School Directories, 2009

PRESIDENTIAL ELECTION

2004 Presidential Election Results

Area	Bush	Kerry	Nader	Other
Williamson County	72.1	27.3	0.3	0.3
U.S.	50.7	48.3	0.4	0.6

Note: Results are percentages and may not add to 100% due to rounding
Source: Dave Leip's Atlas of U.S. Presidential Elections, www.uselectionatlas.org

EMPLOYERS

Major Employers

Company Name	Industry	Type of Site
Aim Healthcare Services Inc	Management services	Single
American Home Patients	Home health care services	Single
Asurion Corporation	Automotive services, nec	Headquarters
Baptist Hospital	General medical and surgical hospitals	Headquarters
Bell South	Telephone communication, except radio	Single
County of Sumner	Executive offices	Headquarters
Firestone	Auto and home supply stores	Branch
Gaylord Entertainment Company	Hotels and motels	Headquarters
Grand Ole Opry	Amusement parks	Headquarters
ITS	Security systems services	Single
Ingram Book Group Inc	Books, periodicals, and newspapers	Headquarters
Lifeway Christian Store	Book stores	Headquarters
Mazda America Credit	Personal credit institutions	Headquarters
Middle Tennessee State Univ	Colleges and universities	Headquarters
Nissan	Automobiles and other motor vehicles	Headquarters
Psychiatric Solutions Inc	Offices and clinics of medical doctors	Headquarters
State Industries Inc	Household appliances, nec	Headquarters
UPS	Courier services, except by air	Branch
Vanderbilt University Med Ctr	Colleges and universities	Headquarters
Yates Services LLC	Building maintenance services, nec	Single

Note: Companies shown are located within the Nashville metropolitan area; nec = not elsewhere classified.
Source: www.zapdata.com, May 2008

PUBLIC SAFETY

Crime Rate

Area	All Crimes	Violent Crimes				Property Crimes		
		Murder	Forcible Rape	Robbery	Aggrav. Assault	Burglary	Larceny -Theft	Motor Vehicle Theft
City	1,793.7	0.0	9.1	15.2	60.9	268.0	1,403.9	36.5
Metro[1]	4,699.8	7.2	41.2	204.6	604.8	792.2	2,717.1	332.8
U.S.	3,808.1	5.7	30.9	149.4	287.5	729.4	2,206.8	398.4

Note: Figures are crimes per 100,000 population; (1) Metropolitan Statistical Area - see Appendix B for areas included
Source: FBI Uniform Crime Reports, 2006

Hate Crimes

Area	Number of Quarters Reported	Bias Motivation				
		Race	Religion	Sexual Orientation	Ethnicity	Disability
City	4	0	0	0	0	0

Source: Federal Bureau of Investigation, Hate Crime Statistics 2006

RECREATION

Culture

Dance[1]	Theatre[1]	Instrumental Music[1]	Vocal Music[1]	Series/ Festivals	Museums	Zoos and Aquariums[2]
0	0	0	0	0	0	0

Note: (1) Number of professional perfoming groups; (2) AZA-accredited
Source: The Grey House Performing Arts Directory, 2007; Official Museum Directory, 2008; Association of Zoos & Aquariums, AZA Member Zoos & Aquariums, June 2008

Professional Sports Teams

Team Name	League
Tennessee Titans	National Football League (NFL)
Nashville Predators	National Hockey League (NHL)

Note: Includes teams located in the Nashville metro area.
Source: Original research

MEDIA

Newspapers

Name	News Focus	Frequency	Circulation
Charlotte Medical News	Local	n/a	n/a
Memphis Medical News	Local	Monthly	9,050
Mississippi Medical News	Regional	Monthly	12,000
Nashville Medical News	Local	Monthly	10,250

Note: Includes newspapers with offices located in the city; n/a not available
Source: MediaContactsPro, March 2008

Television Stations

Name	Ch.	Network(s)	Type	Ownership
WKRN	2	ABC	Commercial	Young Broadcasting Inc.
WSMV	4	NBC	Commercial	Meredith Communications LLC
WTVF	5	CBS	Commercial	Landmark Television of Tennessee Inc.
WNPT	8	PBS	Public	n/a
WZTV	17	Fox	Commercial	Sinclair Broadcast Group
WCTE	22	PBS	Public	Upper Cumberland Broadcast Council
WNPX	28	Pax	Commercial	Paxson Communications Corporation
WUXP	30	UPN	Commercial	Sinclair Broadcast Group
WHTN	39	CTN	Non-comm.	Christian Television Network
WPGD	50	n/a	Non-comm.	All American Network
WNAB	58	WBN	Commercial	Lambert Television
WJFB	66	n/a	Commercial	n/a

Note: Stations included cover the Nashville DMA (Designated Market Area); n/a not available
BurrellesLuce, MediaContacts Online, January 2007

Major AM Radio Stations

Call Letters	Freq. (kHz)	Station Type	Target Audience	Station Format	Music Format
WSM	650	Commercial	General	Music/News	Country
WAKM	950	Commercial	General	Music/News	Country
WYFN	980	n/a	General/Religious	Educational/Music	n/a
WMUF	1000	n/a	General	Music/Sports	n/a
WHIN	1010	Commercial	General	Music/Talk	Country
WAMB	1160	n/a	General	Music	n/a
WDKN	1260	Commercial	General	Music/News/Sports	Country
WMCP	1280	Commercial	General	Music/News	Gospel
WNQM	1300	Commercial	General/Hisp/Rel	News/Sports/Talk	n/a
WMSR	1320	Commercial	General	Music/Sports	Oldies
WNAH	1360	Commercial	Religious	Music/News/Sports/Talk	Gospel
WKSR	1420	Commercial	General	Music/News	Oldies
WKDA	1430	Commercial	General	Music/News	Latin
WZYX	1440	n/a	General	Music/News/Sports/Talk	n/a
WGNS	1450	Commercial	General	News/Talk	n/a
WVOL	1470	Commercial	General	Music/News	Rhythm & Blues
WLAC	1510	Commercial	General	Talk	n/a
WNKX	1570	Commercial	General	Music	Contemp. Country
WLIJ	1580	Commercial	General	Music/News	Folk

Note: Stations included cover the Nashville DMA (Designated Market Area); n/a not available
Source: BurrellesLuce, MediaContacts Online, January 2007

Major FM Radio Stations

Call Letters	Freq. (mHz)	Station Type	Target Audience	Station Format	Music Format
WFSK	88.1	College	Black/Religious	Ed/Music/News/Talk	World Music
WMOT	89.5	College	General	Music/News/Sports	Jazz
WPLN	90.3	n/a	General	Music/News	n/a
WJXA	92.9	Commercial	General	Music/News	Adult Contemp.
WFGZ	94.5	Commercial	General	Music/News	Country
WGSQ	94.7	Commercial	General	Music/Talk	Country
WSM	95.5	Commercial	General	Music/News/Talk	Country
WMAK	96.3	Commercial	General	Music/News	Oldies
WSIX	97.9	Commercial	General	Music	Country
WGIC	98.5	Commercial	General	Talk	n/a
WHOP	98.7	Commercial	General	Music	Adult Contemp.
WWTN	99.7	Commercial	Men	Music/News/Sports/Talk	Jazz
WVVR	100.3	n/a	General	Music	n/a
WUBT	101.1	Commercial	General	Music/News/Talk	Urban Contemp.
WTPR	101.5	Commercial	General	Music	Oldies
WQZQ	102.5	n/a	General	Music	n/a
WBUZ	102.9	Commercial	General	Music/News/Talk	Modern Rock
WKDF	103.3	Commercial	General	Music	Contemp. Country
WGFX	104.5	Commercial	General	News/Sports/Talk	n/a
WVRY	105.1	n/a	Christian/General	Music/News/Sports	n/a
WNRQ	105.9	Commercial	General	Music	Classic Rock
WKXD	106.9	Commercial	General	Music	Adult Contemp.
WRVW	107.5	Commercial	General	Music	Top 40
WCVQ	107.9	n/a	General/Women	Music	n/a

Note: Stations included cover the Nashville DMA (Designated Market Area); n/a not available
BurrellesLuce, MediaContacts Online, January 2007

CLIMATE

Average and Extreme Temperatures

Temperature	Jan	Feb	Mar	Apr	May	Jun	Jul	Aug	Sep	Oct	Nov	Dec	Yr.
Extreme High (°F)	78	84	86	91	95	106	107	104	105	94	84	79	107
Average High (°F)	47	51	60	71	79	87	90	89	83	72	60	50	70
Average Temp. (°F)	38	41	50	60	68	76	80	79	72	61	49	41	60
Average Low (°F)	28	31	39	48	57	65	69	68	61	48	39	31	49
Extreme Low (°F)	-17	-13	2	23	34	42	54	49	36	26	-1	-10	-17

Note: Figures cover the years 1948-1990
Source: National Climatic Data Center, International Station Meteorological Climate Summary, 9/96

Average Precipitation/Snowfall/Humidity

Precip./Humidity	Jan	Feb	Mar	Apr	May	Jun	Jul	Aug	Sep	Oct	Nov	Dec	Yr.
Avg. Precip. (in.)	4.4	4.2	5.0	4.1	4.6	3.7	3.8	3.3	3.2	2.6	3.9	4.6	47.4
Avg. Snowfall (in.)	4	3	1	Tr	0	0	0	0	0	Tr	1	1	11
Avg. Rel. Hum. 6am (%)	81	81	80	81	86	86	88	90	90	87	83	82	85
Avg. Rel. Hum. 3pm (%)	61	57	51	48	52	52	54	53	52	49	55	59	54

Note: Figures cover the years 1948-1990; Tr = Trace amounts (<0.05 in. of rain; <0.5 in. of snow)
Source: National Climatic Data Center, International Station Meteorological Climate Summary, 9/96

Weather Conditions

Temperature			Daytime Sky			Precipitation		
10°F & below	32°F & below	90°F & above	Clear	Partly cloudy	Cloudy	0.01 inch or more precip.	0.1 inch or more snow/ice	Thunder-storms
5	76	51	98	135	132	119	8	54

Note: Figures are average number of days per year and cover the years 1948-1990
Source: National Climatic Data Center, International Station Meteorological Climate Summary, 9/96

HAZARDOUS WASTE

Superfund Sites

Brentwood has no sites on the EPA's Superfund Final National Priorities List.
U.S. Environmental Protection Agency, Final National Priorities List, June 23, 2008

AIR & WATER QUALITY

Air Quality Index

Area	Percent of Days when Air Quality was...[2]				AQI Statistics	
	Good	Moderate	Unhealthy for Sensitive Groups	Unhealthy	Maximum	Median
MSA[1]	49.6	40.0	9.9	0.5	172	51

Note: The Air Quality Index (AQI) is an index for reporting daily air quality. EPA calculates the AQI for five major air pollutants regulated by the Clean Air Act: ground-level ozone, particle pollution (also known as particulate matter), carbon monoxide, sulfur dioxide, and nitrogen dioxide. The AQI runs from 0 to 500. The higher the AQI value, the greater the level of air pollution and the greater the health concern. There are six AQI categories: "Good" The AQI is between 0 and 50. Air quality is considered satisfactory; "Moderate" The AQI is between 51 and 100. Air quality is acceptable; "Unhealthy for Sensitive Groups" When AQI values are between 101 and 150, members of sensitive groups may experience health effects; "Unhealthy" When AQI values are between 151 and 200 everyone may begin to experience health effects; "Very Unhealthy" AQI values between 201 and 300 trigger a health alert; "Hazardous" AQI values over 300 trigger health warnings of emergency conditions; (1) Metropolitan Statistical Area - see Appendix A for areas included; (2) Based on 365 days with AQI data in 2007.
Source: U.S. Environmental Protection Agency, Air Quality Index Report, 2007

Air Quality Index Pollutants

Area	Percent of Days when AQI Pollutant was...[2]					
	Carbon Monoxide	Nitrogen Dioxide	Ozone	Sulfur Dioxide	Particulate Matter 2.5	Particulate Matter 10
MSA[1]	0.0	0.0	46.0	0.0	54.0	0.0

Note: The Air Quality Index (AQI) is an index for reporting daily air quality. EPA calculates the AQI for five major air pollutants regulated by the Clean Air Act: ground-level ozone, particle pollution (also known as particulate matter), carbon monoxide, sulfur dioxide, and nitrogen dioxide. The AQI runs from 0 to 500. The higher the AQI value, the greater the level of air pollution and the greater the health concern; (1) Metropolitan Statistical Area - see Appendix A for areas included; (2) Based on 365 days with AQI data in 2007.
Source: U.S. Environmental Protection Agency, Air Quality Index Report, 2007

Air Quality Index Trends

Area	Trend Sites (19)								All Sites (50)
	1999	2000	2001	2002	2003	2004	2005	2006	2006
MSA[1]	37	20	7	16	7	1	10	6	7

Note: An AQI value greater than 100 indicates that air quality would have been in the unhealthful range on that day. Data from exceptional events are not included. These counts are presented in two ways. First, the counts are based on sites having an adequate record of monitoring data during the trend period (trend sites). These counts represent the relative change in the number of days with AQI values greater than 100. In the last column, the counts are based on all sites with data in the most recent year (because it is possible for a site to have data in the most recent year but not enough data to be a trend site); (1) Metropolitan Statistical Area - see Appendix A for areas included.
Source: U.S. Environmental Protection Agency, Office of Air and Radiation, Air Trends, Factbook and Related Information, Air Pollution Trends in Selected Metropolitan Areas 2006

Maximum Air Pollutant Concentrations

	Particulate Matter 10 (ug/m^3)	Particulate Matter 2.5 (ug/m^3)	Ozone (ppm)	Carbon Monoxide (ppm)	Sulfur Dioxide (ppm)	Nitrogen Dioxide (ppm)	Lead (ug/m^3)
MSA[1] Level	50	32	0.104	3	0.009	0.017	n/a
NAAQS[2]	150	35	0.125	9	0.140	0.053	1.50
Met NAAQS[2]	Yes	Yes	Yes	Yes	Yes	Yes	n/a

Note: Data from exceptional events are not included; (1) Metropolitan Statistical Area - see Appendix A for areas included; (2) National Ambient Air Quality Standards; n/a not available

Concentrations: Particulate Matter 10 (coarse particulate) - highest second maximum 24-hour concentration; Particulate Matter 2.5 (fine particulate) - highest 98th percentile 24-hour concentration; Ozone - highest second daily maximum 1-hour concentration; Carbon Monoxide - highest second maximum non-overlapping 8-hour concentration; Sulfur Dioxide - highest second maximum 24-hour concentration; Nitrogen Dioxide - highest arithmetic mean concentration; Lead - highest quarterly maximum concentration

Units: ppm = parts per million; ug/m^3 = micrograms per cubic meter

Source: U.S. Environmental Protection Agency, MSA Factbook 2006, Air Quality Statistics by City

Drinking Water

Water System Name	Pop. Served	Primary Water Source Type	Violations[1]	
			Health Based	Monitoring/ Reporting
Brentwood Water Dept.	22,606	Purchased Surface	0	0

Note: (1) Based on violation data from January 1, 2007 to December 31, 2007 (includes unresolved violations from earlier years)

Source: U.S. Environmental Protection Agency, Office of Ground Water and Drinking Water, Safe Drinking Water Information System (based on data extracted April 15, 2008)

Collierville, Tennessee

Background

One of Tennessee's fastest growing cities, Collierville in Shelby County is located southeast of Memphis near the Mississippi state line, and only 30 minutes from Memphis International Airport.

Although the city's residential and commercial development has boomed in recent years, Collierville still manages to maintain its small-town charm.

Named after a pioneer family, Collierville began to develop around 1840. It was incorporated as a town in 1850, and became the site of four minor battles during the Civil War. The town experienced rapid growth in the late nineteenth century, finally becoming incorporated as a city in 1903.

Still showing signs of growth, the 18,357-acre city maintains a reserve area to expand to 32,505 acres total.

Federal Express's World Tech Center in Collierville is one of the town's largest non-manufacturing employers, with a work-force of 2,900. The Carrier Corporation is one of the largest manufacturers, with 1,600 employees in Collierville facilities.

The negative factors that often accompany growth have not affected Collierville, which remains a healthy, stable place to raise a family. The crime rate is low, while Collierville's public school system is well regarded. The city offers 11 regional and neighborhood parks with approximately 300 acres of parkland, 25 athletic fields, and over six miles of Greenbelt trails.

Collierville's historic Town Square is the hub of the city's community and social activities. Donated in 1870, it hosts the Mulberry Fine Arts Festival, the Fair on the Square, and Dickens on the Square, which features Victorian-costumed characters, horse-drawn carriage rides, and live music. Situated in the square is an old train depot, along with antique and crafts shops, and Southern-style restaurants. The summertime Sunset on the Square concert series features a variety of music styles from bluegrass to pop.

Outdoor recreation in Collierville is encouraged by Shelby Forest State Recreational Park, bordering the Mississippi River. Comprising two lakes and many miles of hiking and bridle trails, it offers a 50-site campground, fishing, boating, picnicking, hiking, and horseback riding.

Collierville generally experiences mild winters and hot summers. Rainfall is well distributed throughout the year. The town is not in the normal path of winds from the Gulf of Mexico or from Canada, but such winds are occasionally a factor, producing rapid shifts in temperature. Humidity is generally high, but temperatures are seldom extremely high or low.

Rankings

General Rankings

- Memphis* was ranked #278 out of 375 metro areas in *Cities Ranked & Rated*. Criteria: cost of living; climate; crime; transportation; economy and jobs; education; arts and culture; health and healthcare; leisure; quality of life. *Cities Ranked & Rated, 2nd Edition, 2007*
- Memphis* was ranked #99 out of 379 metro areas in *Places Rated Almanac*. Criteria: health care; education; recreation; transportation; ambience; climate; crime; housing costs; jobs. *Places Rated Almanac, 7th Edition, 2007*

Business/Finance Rankings

- The nation's 100 largest metro areas were analysed in terms of the percentage of households entering some stage of foreclosure in 2007. The Memphis* metro area ranked #13 out of 100 (#1 = highest foreclosure rate). *RealtyTrac, "Year-End 2007 Metropolitan Foreclosure Report"*
- Memphis* was selected as one of the best places to start and grow a company by *Entrepreneur* and the National Policy Research Council. The Memphis* metro area ranked #7 out of 50 large metro areas. Criteria: business formation and growth (firms started four to 14 years ago that still employ at least 5 people and experienced rapid growth over the last four years). *Entrepreneur/National Policy Research Council, "Hot Cities for Entrepreneurs," September 2006*
- The Memphis* metro area was selected as one of "America's 50 Hottest Cities" for business relocations and expansions. Criteria: industry's most prominent site selection consultants were asked to list their top city choices for relocating and expanding manufacturing companies, taking into consideration such factors as the business climate, work force quality, operating costs, incentive programs, and the ease of working with local political and economic development officials. *Expansion Management, January-February 2007*
- Intel, in partnership with Sperling's BestPlaces, ranked the 80 "Best Cities for Teleworking" in America. The Memphis* metro area ranked #20 among mid-sized metro areas. The study identifies cities that hold the greatest potential for teleworking based on a host of factors including typical commuting times, fuel prices, availability of broadband Internet access and percentage of the population in telework friendly jobs. The study also factored in extreme climate and natural hazards. *Intel, "Best Cities for Teleworking," March 30, 2006*
- The Memphis* metro area appeared on the Milken Institute "2007 Best Performing Cities" index. Rank: #141 out of 200 large metro areas. Criteria: job growth; wage and salary growth; high-tech output growth. *Milken Institute, "2007 Best Performing Cities"*
- Memphis* was identified as one of the 100 "Most Unwired Cities" in the U.S. The area ranked #68 out of the 100 largest metro areas in the U.S. Criteria: number of public and commercial wireless access points (hotspots); airports with wireless Internet access; broadband availability; local wireless networks; and wireless email devices. *Intel, "Most Unwired Cities Survey," June 7, 2005*
- Memphis* was ranked #61 out of 125 regions worldwide in terms of its "Knowledge Competitiveness Index." The index attempts to measure the knowledge-based development taking place throughout the world and is based on 19 measures of economic performance that indicate a region's ability to translate its knowledge capacity into economic value. *Robert Huggins Associates, World Knowledge Competitiveness Index 2005*
- *Forbes* ranked the 200 most populous metro areas in the U.S. in terms of the "Best Places for Business and Careers." The Memphis* metro area was ranked #152. Criteria: business costs (labor, energy, tax and office space expenses); living costs (housing, transportation, food and other household expenditures); education levels of the work force; job growth; income growth; migration trends; crime rates; and culture/leisure. *Forbes, "Best Places for Business and Careers," March 19, 2008*
- *Fortune* ranked the 100 largest metro areas in the U.S. in terms of projected median home price change in 2007. The Memphis* metro area ranked #26. *Fortune.com, "Hot Spots, Cold Spots"*

Health/Environment Rankings

- The Memphis* metro area was identified as one of "America's 20 Most Sedentary Cities" by *Forbes*. The metro area ranked #1. Criteria: percentage of overweight or obese people; percentage of people who had not engaged in any physical activity in the past 30 days; average number of hours of TV watched per week. *Forbes.com, "America's Most Sedentary Cities," October 29, 2007*

- 100 of the largest metro areas in the U.S. were analyzed in terms of their current drought severity. The Memphis* metro area ranked #33 (#1 = driest). The rankings were based on statistics such as long-term precipitation trends and patterns and the Palmer drought indices. *Sperling's BestPlaces, www.BestPlaces.net, "America's Drought-Riskiest Cities," November 2007*

- Doctors at the Harvard School of Public Health ranked 40 metropolitan areas based on data from the government-sponsored Hospital Quality Alliance program. The program tracks the performance of individual hospitals in treating patients for three common health problems: heart attacks, congestive heart failure, and pneumonia. The Memphis* metro area ranked #39 in quality of care for heart attacks, #35 for congestive heart failure, and #33 for pneumonia. *New England Journal of Medicine, July 21, 2005*

- Scarborough Research, a leading market research firm, identified the top local markets for diabetes medication purchasers. The Memphis* DMA (Designated Market Area) ranked in the top 13 with 11% of consumers reporting that they purchased medication for diabetes within the past 12 months. *Scarborough Research, March 19, 2007*

- *Reader's Digest* ranked the 50 largest metro areas in the U.S. in terms of how "clean" they are. The Memphis* metro area ranked #32. Criteria: air quality; water quality; toxic industrial pollution; Superfund sites; and sanitation. *Reader's Digest, "The 50 Cleanest (and Dirtiest) Cities in America," July 2005*

- The Memphis* metro area was identified as one of "America's Most Obese Cities" by *Forbes*. The magazine analyzed BMI (body mass index) data from the CDC in the 50 most populated metro areas in the U.S. and ranked the top 20. The area ranked #1. *Forbes, "America's Most Obese Cities," November 26, 2007*

- The Memphis* metro area appeared in *Country Home's* "2008 Best Green Places" report. The area ranked #285 out of 379. Criteria: official energy policies; green power; green buildings; availability of fresh, locally grown food. *Country Home, "2008 Best Green Places"*

- Memphis* was identified as a "Spring Allergy Capital." The area ranked #26 out of 100. Three groups of factors were used to identify the most severe cities for people with allergies during the spring season: annual pollen levels; medicine utilization; access to board-certified allergists. *Asthma and Allergy Foundation of America, "2007 Spring Allergy Capital Rankings"*

- Memphis* was identified as a "Fall Allergy Capital." The area ranked #31 out of 100. Three groups of factors were used to identify the most severe cities for people with allergies during the fall season: annual pollen levels; medicine utilization; access to board-certified allergists. *Asthma and Allergy Foundation of America, "2007 Fall Allergy Capital Rankings"*

- Ortho-McNeil Neurologics, in partnership with Sperling's BestPlaces, analyzed 110 metro areas and identified those U.S. cities with the highest prevalence of factors that are most commonly associated with migraine headaches. The Memphis* metro area ranked #51. Criteria: number of migraine-related drug prescriptions per capita; lifestyle factors that can contribute to migraines; environmental factors that can trigger migraines; and consumption of migraine-triggering foods. *Ortho-McNeil Neurologics, "America's Migraine Hot Spots," March 14, 2006*

- Sperling's BestPlaces ranked 331 metro areas and identified the most and least stressful U.S. cities. The Memphis* metro area ranked #38 out of the 100 largest metro areas (#1 = most stressful). Criteria: divorce rate; unemployment rate; violent and property crime; suicide rate; commute time; mental health; alcohol consumption; cloudy days. *Sperling's BestPlaces, www.BestPlaces.net, "America's Most (and Least) Stressful Cities," January 9, 2004*

Children/Family Rankings

- The Memphis* metro area was selected as one of the "Best Cities for Relocating Families" by Worldwide ERC and Primacy Relocation. The 2007 study placed a special emphasis on the housing market, which has significantly impacted the relocation industry and an employer's ability to transfer employees. The variables which weigh heavily in this category include home price, home affordability index, appreciation rates, and property tax. Other criteria include cost of living, crime rates, education, climate, focus on diversity, physicians per capita, recreation and leisure, arts and culture, air quality, watershed quality, sales tax, unemployment rate, job growth, high school and higher education index, school expenditures per student, students in public school, SAT/ACT percentile, and population growth. *Worldwide ERC and Primacy Relocation, "2007 Best Cities for Relocating Families"*

Safety Rankings

- The National Insurance Crime Bureau ranked 361 metro areas in the U.S. in terms of per capita rates of vehicle theft. The Memphis* metro area ranked #39 (#1 = highest rate). Criteria: number of vehicle theft offenses per 100,000 inhabitants. *National Insurance Crime Bureau, "NICB Vehicle Theft Study," April 22, 2008*

- Memphis* appeared on Sperling's BestPlaces list of the "Riskiest Cities for Identity Theft." The area ranked #39 out of the nations 50 largest metro areas. Over 80 criteria were analyzed across four major categories: technology impact; crime; transactions; and risk profile. *Sperling's BestPlaces, www.BestPlaces.net, "Riskiest Cities for Identity Theft," July 2006*

- Farmers Insurance Group of Companies, in partnership with Sperling's BestPlaces, ranked 379 metro areas and identified the "Most Secure U.S. Place to Live." The Memphis* metro area ranked #114 out of 114 in the large metro area category (500,000 or more residents). Criteria: crime rates; extreme weather; risk of natural disasters; environmental hazards; terrorism threats; air quality; life expectancy; job loss numbers. *Farmers Insurance Group, "Most Secure U.S. Places to Live 2007"*

- Memphis* was identified as one of the most dangerous large metro areas for pedestrians in the U.S. The area ranked #5 out of the nations 50 largest metro areas. Criteria: average yearly pedestrian fatalities per capita (for the years 2002 and 2003) adjusted for the number of walkers. *Surface Transportation Policy Project, "Mean Streets 2004"*

- Memphis* was identified as one of the least safe places in the U.S. in terms of its vulnerability to natural disasters and weather extremes. The city ranked #9 out of 10. Sperling's BestPlaces analyzed data to show a metro areas' relative tendency to experience natural disasters (hail, tornados, high winds, hurricanes, earthquakes, and brush fires) or extreme weather (abundant rain or snowfall or days that are below freezing or above 90 degrees Fahrenheit). *Forbes, "Safest and Least Safe Places in the U.S.," August 30, 2005*

Sports/Recreation Rankings

- The Memphis* metro area appeared on the *Sporting News* list of the "Best Sports Cities 2007". The area ranked #53 out of 150 cities in the U.S. *Sporting News* takes a 12-month snapshot, roughly July to July, of each city's sports, putting a heavy premium on regular-season won-lost records (from the most recently completed season). Other criteria include: playoff berths, bowl appearances and tournament bids; championships; applicable power ratings; quality of competition; overall fan fervor as measured in part by attendance as percentage of venue capacity; abundance of teams (rewarding quality over quantity); stadium and arena quality; ticket availability and prices; franchise ownership; and marquee appeal of athletes. *SportingNews.com, "Best Sports Cities 2007," August 1, 2007*

- Scarborough Research, a leading market research firm, identified the top local markets for avid NBA fans. The Memphis* DMA (Designated Market Area) ranked in the top 10 with 17% of consumers 18 years and over reporting that they are "very interested in the NBA". *Scarborough Research, April 24, 2006*

- The Memphis* metro area was selected by *Cranium* as one of the "Top 50 Fun Cities" in America. The area ranked #35. Criteria includes: number of sports teams, restaurants, and dance performances; number of toy stores; city budget spent on recreation. *Cranium, November 4, 2003*

- *Golf Digest* ranked 330 metro areas in the U.S. in terms of golf. The Memphis* metro area was ranked #272. Criteria: access to golf; weather; value of golf; and quality of golf. *Golf Digest, "Metro Golf Rankings," August 2005*

Dating/Romance Rankings

- Eli Lily and Company, in partnership with Sperling's BestPlaces, ranked the nation's 50 largest metro areas in terms of the "Most Romantic Cities for Baby Boomers." The Memphis* metro area ranked #50. Criteria: marriage and divorce rates among "baby boomers" age 45 to 60; great restaurants; dance studios; chocolate, jewelry and flower sales. *Eli Lily and Company, "Most Romantic Cities for Baby Boomers," April 20, 2007*

- The Memphis* metro area was selected as one of the "Best Cities for Relocating Singles" by Worldwide ERC and Primacy Relocation. The area ranked #69 out of the 100 largest metro areas in the U.S. Areas were selected based on the following criteria: a robust cost-of-living index; adventure and outdoor recreation opportunities; violent crime and property crime rates; percentage of the population that is unmarried (ages 25-34); ratio of single men and single women; affordability of quality higher education, including in-state and out-of-state tuition requirements and rates; number of newcomers to the area; commute times; tax rates; fee and occupancy rates for temporary housing and mini-storage; quality and quantity of collegiate and professional sporting events and fun, fan-friendly venues. *Worldwide ERC and Primacy Relocation, "2007 Best Cities for Relocating Singles," October 25, 2007*

- *Forbes* ranked the 40 most populous urbanized areas in the U.S. in terms of the "Best Cities for Singles." The Memphis* metro area ranked #23. Criteria: number of singles; cost of living alone; nightlife; culture; job growth; coolness; and online dating. *Forbes.com, August 21, 2007*

- Sperling's BestPlaces in partnership with AXE Deodorant Bodyspray ranked 80 metro areas and identified "America's Best (and Worst) Cities for Dating." The Memphis* metro area ranked #66 (#1 = best). Criteria: percentage of singles ages 18-24; population density; dating venues per capita. *AXE Deodorant Bodyspray, "America's Best (and Worst) Cities for Dating," May 2004*

Miscellaneous Rankings

- Sperling's BestPlaces in partnership with Pep Boys ranked 77 metro areas and identified "America's Most Drivable Cities." The Memphis* metro area ranked #9. Criteria: climate; road roughness; urban mobility; gas prices. *Pep Boys, "America's Most Drivable Cities," April 9, 2003*

- Scarborough Research, a leading market research firm, identified the top local markets for frequent fast food restaurant patronage. The Memphis* DMA (Designated Market Area) ranked in the top 10 with consumers reporting an average of 6.3 visits within the past 30 days. *Scarborough Research, May 31, 2006*

- A study by Sperling's BestPlaces examined which U.S. metro areas were most affected by high fuel prices in 2006. The Memphis* metro area was ranked #34 out of 80 (#1 = most expensive city for driving). Rankings are based on the average dollars spent on gas per year by two driver households. Criteria: cost of regular-grade gasoline; average miles driven per day; average number of gallons each driver uses and wastes in traffic congestion each day. *Sperling's BestPlaces, www.bestplaces.net, "Pain at the Pump," May 18, 2006*

Collierville is located within the Memphis, TN-MS-AR Metropolitan Statistical Area.

Business Environment

CITY FINANCES

City Government Finances

Component	2004-2005 ($000)	2004-2005 ($ per capita)
Total Revenues	46,390	1,235
Total Expenditures	43,721	1,164
Debt Outstanding	41,705	1,110
Cash and Securities	28,707	764

Source: U.S Census Bureau, Government Finances 2004-2005

City Government Revenue by Source

Source	2004-2005 ($000)	2004-2005 ($ per capita)
General Revenue		
From Federal Government	163	4
From State Government	4,194	112
From Local Governments	5,627	150
Taxes		
Property	13,575	361
Sales	1,821	48
Personal Income	0	0
License	3,389	90
Charges	7,372	196
Liquor Store	0	0
Utility	2,927	78
Employee Retirement	0	0
Other	7,322	195

Source: U.S Census Bureau, Government Finances 2004-2005

City Government Expenditures by Function

Function	2004-2005 ($000)	2004-2005 ($ per capita)	2004-2005 (%)
General Expenditures			
Airports	0	0	0.0
Corrections	0	0	0.0
Education	0	0	0.0
Fire Protection	5,851	156	13.4
Governmental Administration	3,095	82	7.1
Health	310	8	0.7
Highways	5,908	157	13.5
Hospitals	0	0	0.0
Housing and Community Development	0	0	0.0
Interest on General Debt	1,135	30	2.6
Libraries	866	23	2.0
Parking	0	0	0.0
Parks and Recreation	5,739	153	13.1
Police Protection	7,034	187	16.1
Public Welfare	0	0	0.0
Sewerage	2,450	65	5.6
Solid Waste Management	2,063	55	4.7
Liquor Store	0	0	0.0
Utility	3,792	101	8.7
Employee Retirement	0	0	0.0
Other	5,478	146	12.5

Source: U.S Census Bureau, Government Finances 2004-2005

Municipal Bond Ratings

Area	Moody's
City	MIG 1

Source: Mergent Bond Record, January 2008 (unless noted otherwise)

DEMOGRAPHICS

Population Growth

Area	1990 Census	2000 Census	2007 Estimate	2012 Projection	Population Growth (%) 1990-2000	Population Growth (%) 2000-2012
City	15,439	31,872	37,957	41,675	106.4	30.8
MSA[1]	1,067,263	1,205,204	1,280,575	1,329,939	12.9	10.3
U.S.	248,709,873	281,421,906	301,045,522	314,920,978	13.2	11.9

Note: (1) Metropolitan Statistical Area - see Appendix B for areas included
Source: Claritas, Inc.

Number of Households and Average Household Size

Area	2007 Estimate	2007 Average Household Size
City	12,577	3.02
MSA[1]	482,754	2.65
U.S.	113,668,003	2.65

Note: (1) Metropolitan Statistical Area - see Appendix B for areas included
Source: Claritas, Inc.

Race and Ethnicity

Area	White Alone[2]	Black Alone[2]	Asian Alone[2]	Other Race Alone[2]	Hispanic[3]
City	86.4	8.8	2.6	2.2	2.2
MSA[1]	50.0	45.4	1.7	3.0	3.3
U.S.	73.1	12.4	4.3	10.3	14.9

Note: Figures are 2007 estimates; (1) Metropolitan Statistical Area - see Appendix B for areas included (2) Alone is defined as not being in combination with one or more other races; (3) May be of any race.
Source: Claritas, Inc.

Ancestry

Area	German	Irish[2]	English	American	Italian	Polish	French[3]	Scottish
City	12.9	12.3	14.2	14.4	4.6	1.7	2.9	3.4
MSA[1]	6.3	7.5	7.2	8.6	2.2	0.7	1.6	1.5
U.S.	15.2	10.9	8.7	7.3	5.6	3.2	3.0	1.7

Note: Figures include multiple ancestry (e.g. if a person reported being Irish and Italian, they were included in both columns); (1) Metropolitan Statistical Area - see Appendix A for areas included; (2) Includes Celtic; (3) Includes Alsatian but excludes Basque
Source: Census 2000, Summary File 3

Foreign-Born Population

Area	Percent of Population Born in							
	Any Foreign Country	Europe	Asia	Africa	Oceania[2]	Canada	Mexico	Latin America[3]
City	2.8	0.5	1.1	0.3	0.0	0.4	0.2	0.3
MSA[1]	3.3	0.5	1.2	0.2	0.0	0.1	1.0	0.3
U.S.	11.1	1.7	2.9	0.3	0.1	0.3	3.3	2.5

Note: (1) Metropolitan Statistical Area - see Appendix A for areas included; (2) Includes Australia, New Zealand subregion, Melanesia, Micronesia, Polynesia, and Oceania n.e.c; (3) Includes Central America (excluding Mexico), South America, and the Caribbean.
Source: Census 2000, Summary File 3

Marriage Status

Area	Never Married	Now Married (excluding Separated)	Separated	Widowed	Divorced
City	19.1	71.1	0.9	3.2	5.7
MSA[1]	29.8	49.1	3.6	6.7	10.7
U.S.	27.1	54.4	2.2	6.6	9.7

Note: Figures are percentages and cover the population 15 years of age and older; (1) Metropolitan Statistical Area - see Appendix A for areas included
Source: Census 2000, Summary File 3

Age Distribution

Area	Percent of Population						
	Under Age 5	Age 5 to 17	Age 18 to 34	Age 35 to 49	Age 50 to 64	Age 65 to 79	80 Years and Over
City	7.7	25.7	16.0	31.6	13.0	4.9	1.1
MSA[1]	7.6	20.7	24.1	23.7	13.9	7.6	2.4
U.S.	6.8	18.9	23.7	23.5	14.8	9.2	3.2

Note: (1) Metropolitan Statistical Area - see Appendix A for areas included
Source: Census 2000, Summary File 3

Male/Female Ratio

Area	Males	Females	Males per 100 Females
City	18,710	19,247	97.2
MSA[1]	619,790	660,785	93.8
U.S.	148,320,305	152,725,217	97.1

Note: Figures are 2007 estimates; (1) Metropolitan Statistical Area - see Appendix B for areas included
Source: Claritas, Inc.

Religion

Area	Catholic	Southern Baptist	United Meth-odist	ELCA[1]	LDS[2]	Presby-terian Church USA	Jewish Est.	Muslim Est.
County	5.7	16.9	5.4	0.2	0.3	1.2	1.0	0.4
U.S.	22.0	7.1	3.7	1.8	1.5	1.1	2.2	0.6

Note: Figures are the number of adherents as a percentage of the total population; Adherents are defined as all members, including full members, their children and the estimated number of other participants who are not considered members (e.g. the baptized, those not confirmed, those regularly attending services, etc.); (1) Evangelical Lutheran Church in America; (2) The Church of Jesus Christ of Latter Day Saints
Source: Reprinted with permission from Religious Congregations and Membership in the United States 2000 (Nashville, Glenmary Research Center, 2002) Copyright Association of Statisticians of American Religious Bodies. All rights reserved.

ECONOMY

Gross Metropolitan Product

Area	2002	2003	2004	2005	2005 Rank[2]
MSA[1]	42.5	45.0	47.5	50.3	46

Note: Figures are in billions of dollars; (1) Memphis, TN-MS-AR Metropolitan Statistical Area - see Appendix A for areas included; (2) Rank ranges from 1 to 361
Source: The U.S. Conference of Mayors, "U.S. Metro Economies: GMP - The Engines of America's Growth," January 2007

Economic Growth

Area	1995 GMP	2005 GMP	Average Annual Growth Rate	Growth Rate Rank[2]
MSA[1]	30.1	50.3	5.3	191

Note: Figures are in billions of dollars; GMP = Gross Metropolitan Product; (1) Memphis, TN-MS-AR Metropolitan Statistical Area - see Appendix A for areas included; (2) Rank ranges from 1 to 361
Source: The U.S. Conference of Mayors, "U.S. Metro Economies: GMP - The Engines of America's Growth," January 2007

INCOME

Per Capita/Median/Average Income

Area	Per Capita ($)	Median Household ($)	Average Household ($)
City	38,765	96,045	116,893
MSA[1]	23,459	45,624	61,677
U.S.	25,495	49,280	66,670

Note: Figures are 2007 estimates; (1) Metropolitan Statistical Area - see Appendix B for areas included
Source: Claritas, Inc.

Household Income Distribution

Area	Percent of Households Earning							
	Under $15,000	$15,000 -24,999	$25,000 -34,999	$35,000 -49,999	$50,000 -74,999	$75,000 -99,000	$100,000 -149,999	$150,000 and up
City	2.9	3.7	5.4	7.4	15.9	17.4	26.2	21.1
MSA[1]	15.6	11.2	11.6	15.9	19.1	11.3	9.8	5.4
U.S.	13.1	10.9	11.2	15.6	19.5	11.9	11.3	6.6

Note: Figures are 2007 estimates; (1) Metropolitan Statistical Area - see Appendix B for areas included
Source: Claritas, Inc.

Poverty Rates by Age

Area	All Ages	Under 5 Years Old	5 to 17 Years Old	18 to 64 Years Old	65 Years and Over
City	2.4	0.2	0.8	1.2	0.2
MSA[1]	15.3	1.9	4.3	7.7	1.3
U.S.	12.4	1.2	3.0	6.9	1.2

Note: Figures are percent of population with income in 1999 below poverty level and only include population for whom poverty status is determined; (1) Metropolitan Statistical Area - see Appendix A for areas included
Source: Census 2000, Summary File 3

Personal Bankruptcy Filing Rate

Area	2004	2005	2006
Shelby County	19.73	21.75	11.58
U.S.	5.31	6.82	2.00

Note: Numbers are per 1,000 population and include Chapter 7 and Chapter 13 filings
Source: Federal Deposit Insurance Corporation (FDIC), Regional Economic Conditions (RECON), 8/23/2007

EMPLOYMENT

Labor Force and Employment

Area	Civilian Labor Force			Workers Employed		
	Dec. 2006	Dec. 2007	% Chg.	Dec. 2006	Dec. 2007	% Chg.
City	20,546	20,685	0.7	19,711	19,859	0.8
MSA[1]	622,864	629,858	1.1	591,733	595,007	0.6
U.S.	152,571,000	153,705,000	0.7	146,081,000	146,334,000	0.2

Note: Data is not seasonally adjusted and covers workers 16 years of age and older;
(1) Metropolitan Statistical Area - see Appendix B for areas included
Source: Bureau of Labor Statistics, http://stats.bls.gov

Unemployment Rate

Area	2007											
	Jan.	Feb.	Mar.	Apr.	May	Jun.	Jul.	Aug.	Sep.	Oct.	Nov.	Dec.
City	4.7	3.8	3.4	3.1	3.0	3.4	3.3	3.6	3.7	3.9	4.1	4.0
MSA[1]	5.8	5.3	5.1	4.6	4.6	5.3	5.2	5.1	5.2	5.2	5.3	5.5
U.S.	5.0	4.9	4.5	4.3	4.3	4.7	4.9	4.6	4.5	4.4	4.5	4.8

Note: Data is not seasonally adjusted and covers workers 16 years of age and older; All figures are percentages; (1) Metropolitan Statistical Area - see Appendix B for areas included
Source: Bureau of Labor Statistics, http://stats.bls.gov

Employment by Occupation

Occupation Classification	City (%)	MSA[1] (%)	U.S. (%)
Sales and Office	31.1	29.7	26.7
Professional and Related	20.6	18.5	20.2
Service	9.7	14.1	14.9
Production, Transportation, and Material Moving	10.2	15.4	14.6
Management, Business, and Financial	23.2	13.2	13.5
Construction, Extraction, and Maintenance	5.3	8.9	9.4
Farming, Forestry, and Fishing	0.0	0.2	0.7

Note: Figures cover employed civilians 16 years of age and older;
(1) Metropolitan Statistical Area - see Appendix A for areas included
Source: Census 2000, Summary File 3

Employment by Industry

Sector	MSA[1] Number of Employees	MSA[1] Percent of Total	U.S. Percent of Total
Government	90,700	13.9	16.3
Education and Health Services	78,100	11.9	13.4
Professional and Business Services	89,700	13.7	13.1
Retail Trade	76,000	11.6	11.6
Manufacturing	51,100	7.8	9.9
Leisure and Hospitality	72,400	11.1	9.6
Financial Activities	33,500	5.1	5.9
Construction	n/a	n/a	5.3
Wholesale Trade	37,600	5.7	4.4
Other Services	24,700	3.8	3.9
Transportation and Utilities	66,900	10.2	3.7
Information	7,500	1.1	2.2
Natural Resources and Mining	n/a	n/a	0.5

Note: Figures cover non-farm employment as of December 2007 and are not seasonally adjusted; (1) Metropolitan Statistical Area - see Appendix B for areas included; n/a not available
Source: Bureau of Labor Statistics, http://stats.bls.gov

Average Wages

Occupation	$/Hr.	Occupation	$/Hr.
Accountants and Auditors	27.92	Maids and Housekeeping Cleaners	8.00
Automotive Mechanics	17.48	Maintenance and Repair Workers	16.62
Bookkeepers	15.81	Marketing Managers	45.35
Carpenters	15.78	Nuclear Medicine Technologists	29.44
Cashiers	8.28	Nurses, Licensed Practical	18.93
Clerks, General Office	12.60	Nurses, Registered	28.58
Clerks, Receptionists/Information	11.16	Nursing Aides/Orderlies/Attendants	10.42
Clerks, Shipping/Receiving	13.19	Packers and Packagers, Hand	9.68
Computer Programmers	33.09	Physical Therapists	36.53
Computer Support Specialists	22.63	Postal Service Mail Carriers	21.29
Computer Systems Analysts	30.71	Real Estate Brokers	n/a
Cooks, Restaurant	9.83	Retail Salespersons	11.39
Dentists	n/a	Sales Reps., Exc. Tech./Scientific	28.51
Electrical Engineers	34.55	Sales Reps., Tech./Scientific	35.16
Electricians	20.05	Secretaries, Exc. Legal/Med./Exec.	13.05
Financial Managers	39.37	Security Guards	9.74
First-Line Supervisors/Mgrs., Sales	18.40	Surgeons	68.72
Food Preparation Workers	8.88	Teacher Assistants	9.30
General and Operations Managers	44.61	Teachers, Elementary School	19.60
Hairdressers/Cosmetologists	15.87	Teachers, Secondary School	20.60
Internists	81.16	Telemarketers	12.04
Janitors and Cleaners	9.98	Truck Drivers, Heavy/Tractor-Trailer	19.75
Landscaping/Groundskeeping Workers	10.91	Truck Drivers, Light/Delivery Svcs.	13.85
Lawyers	54.48	Waiters and Waitresses	8.00

Note: Wage data covers the Memphis, TN-MS-AR Metropolitan Statistical Area - see Appendix B for areas included. Hourly wages for elementary/secondary school teachers and teacher assistants were calculated by the editors from annual wage data assuming a 40 hour work week; n/a not available.
Source: Bureau of Labor Statistics, May 2007 Metro Area Occupational Employment and Wage Estimates

RESIDENTIAL REAL ESTATE

Building Permits

Area	Single-Family 2006	Single-Family 2007p	Single-Family Pct. Chg.	Multi-Family 2006	Multi-Family 2007p	Multi-Family Pct. Chg.	Total 2006	Total 2007p	Total Pct. Chg.
City	378	226	-40.2	0	0	-	378	226	-40.2
U.S.	1,378,200	973,300	-29.4	460,700	407,200	-11.6	1,838,900	1,380,500	-24.9

Note: (p) preliminary; figures cover and represent new, privately-owned housing units authorized (unadjusted data); All permit data are based on estimates with imputation; U.S. figures are based on the new 20,000-place series.
Source: U.S. Census Bureau, Manufacturing, Mining, and Construction Statistics

Homeownership and Housing Vacancies

Area	Homeownership Rate[2] (%)			Rental Vacancy Rate[3] (%)			Homeowner Vacancy Rate[4] (%)		
	2005	2006	2007	2005	2006	2007	2005	2006	2007
MSA[1]	64.8	61.6	60.6	10.2	9.5	12.8	1.9	1.9	2.8
U.S.	68.9	68.8	68.1	9.8	9.8	9.7	1.9	2.4	2.7

Note: (1) Metropolitan Statistical Area - see Appendix B for areas included; (2) The proportion of households that are owners; (3) The proportion of the rental inventory that is vacant for rent; (4) The proportion of the homeowner inventory that is vacant for sale; n/a not available
Source: U.S. Census Bureau, Housing Vacancies and Homeownership Annual Statistics: 2007

TAXES

State Corporate Income Tax Rates

State	Rates and Tax Brackets
Tennessee	6.5%

Note: Tax rates as of January 1, 2008; Franchise tax of.25% of the greater of net worth or real and tangible property (minimum $100)
Source: Tax Foundation, www.taxfoundation.org

State Individual Income Tax Rates

State	Federal Deductibility	Marginal Rates (%)	Standard Deduction ($)		Personal Exemptions ($)[1]	
			Single	Joint	Single	Dependents
Tennessee	No	6 (h)	n/a	n/a	1,250	n/a

Note: Tax rates as of January 1, 2008; Local- and county-level taxes are not included; n/a not applicable; (1) Married joint filers generally receive double the single exemption; (h) Applies to interest and dividend income only.
Source: Tax Foundation, www.taxfoundation.org

Various State and Local Tax Rates

State and Local Sales and Use (%)	State Sales and Use (%)	Gasoline[1,2] ($/gal.)	Cigarette ($/pack)	Spirits ($/gal.)	Table Wine ($/gal.)	Beer ($/gal.)
9.25	7.0	0.214	0.62	4.40	1.21	0.14 (r)

Note: Tax rates as of January 1, 2008; (1) In addition to the 18.4 cpg Federal gasoline tax; (2) Rates may include additional state sales taxes, environmental protection and storage fees/taxes, and local taxes. When necessary, the volume-weighted average of all local taxes is used to approximate the typical statewide rate including local tax; (r) There is an additional 17% wholesale tax on beer.
Source: Tax Foundation, www.taxfoundation.org; Original research

State Tax Burdens

Area	Combined State and Local Tax Burden		Combined Federal, State and Local Tax Burden	
	Percent	Rank	Percent	Rank
Tennessee	8.5	48	28.8	46
U.S. Average	11.0	-	32.7	-

Note: Figures cover 2007 and measure taxes as a percentage of income
Source: Tax Foundation, www.taxfoundation.org

State Business Tax Climate Index Rankings

State	Overall Rank	Corporate Tax Index Rank	Individual Income Tax Index Rank	Sales Tax Index Rank	Unemployment Insurance Tax Index Rank	Property Tax Index Rank
Tennessee	16	12	8	48	31	35

Note: Rankings range from 1 to 50 where 1 is best. Rankings do not average across to Overall Rank. States without a given tax are given a ranking of 1.
Source: Tax Foundation, State Business Tax Climate Index 2008

TRANSPORTATION

Means of Transportation to Work

Area	Car/Truck/Van		Public Transportation			Bicycle	Walked	Other Means	Worked at Home
	Drove Alone	Car-pooled	Bus	Subway	Railroad				
City	88.4	6.6	0.0	0.1	0.0	0.0	0.3	0.8	3.7
MSA[1]	80.9	13.0	1.6	0.0	0.0	0.1	1.3	0.9	2.2
U.S.	75.7	12.2	2.5	1.5	0.5	0.4	2.9	1.0	3.3

Note: Figures are percentages and cover workers 16 years of age and older;
(1) Metropolitan Statistical Area - see Appendix A for areas included
Source: Census 2000, Summary File 3

Travel Time to Work

Area	Less Than 15 Minutes	15 to 29 Minutes	30 to 44 Minutes	45 to 59 Minutes	60 Minutes or More
City	23.4	31.3	31.5	10.4	3.4
MSA[1]	22.9	43.4	23.2	6.1	4.4
U.S.	29.4	36.1	19.1	7.4	8.0

Note: Figures are percentages and include workers 16 years old and over; (1) Metropolitan Statistical Area - see Appendix A for areas included
Source: Census 2000, Summary File 3

Travel Time Index

Area	1982	1995	2004	2005
Urban Area[1]	1.04	1.11	1.14	1.13
Average[2]	1.11	1.22	1.29	1.30

Note: Travel Time Index - The ratio of travel time in the peak period to the travel time at free-flow conditions. A value of 1.35 indicates a 20-minute free-flow trip takes 27 minutes in the peak. Free-flow speeds (60 mph on freeways and 35 mph on principal arterials) are used as the comparison threshold; (1) Covers the Memphis TN-MS-AR urban area; (2) average of 85 urban areas
Source: Texas Transportation Institute, The 2007 Urban Mobility Report, September 2007

Living Environment

COST OF LIVING

Cost of Living Index

Composite Index	Groceries	Housing	Utilities	Trans-portation	Health Care	Misc. Goods/ Services
89.7	90.5	77.4	84.1	92.3	97.1	99.1

Note: U.S. = 100; Figures cover the Memphis TN urban area.
Source: The Council for Community and Economic Research (formerly ACCRA), Cost of Living Index, 2007

Grocery Prices

Area[1]	T-Bone Steak ($/pound)	Frying Chicken ($/pound)	Whole Milk ($/half gal.)	Eggs ($/dozen)	Orange Juice ($/64 oz.)	Coffee ($/11.5 oz.)
City[2]	9.96	0.85	2.07	1.33	2.93	3.13
Avg.	8.93	1.12	2.13	1.52	3.26	3.31
Min.	5.88	0.71	1.33	0.83	2.30	2.20
Max.	12.80	2.07	3.43	3.54	5.79	6.20

Note: (1) Values for the local area are compared with the average, minimum and maximum values for all 331 areas in the Cost of Living Index report; (2) Figures cover the Memphis TN urban area; **T-Bone Steak** *(price per pound);* **Frying Chicken** *(price per pound, whole fryer);* **Whole Milk** *(half gallon carton);* **Eggs** *(price per dozen, Grade A, large);* **Orange Juice** *(64 oz. Tropicana or Florida Natural);* **Coffee** *(11.5 oz. can, vacuum-packed, Maxwell House, Hills Bros, or Folgers).*
Source: The Council for Community and Economic Research (formerly ACCRA), Cost of Living Index, 2007

Housing and Utility Costs

Area[1]	New Home Price ($)	Apartment Rent ($/month)	All Electric ($/month)	Part Electric ($/month)	Other Energy ($/month)	Telephone ($/month)
City[2]	226,932	750	-	67.56	62.99	23.57
Avg.	309,605	782	146.13	78.67	90.16	26.14
Min.	189,877	n/a	82.03	37.41	33.15	17.08
Max.	1,202,800	3,481	271.14	150.60	257.67	37.45

Note: (1) Values for the local area are compared with the average, minimum and maximum values for all 331 areas in the Cost of Living Index report; (2) Figures cover the Memphis TN urban area; **New Home Price** *(2,400 sf living area, 8,000 sf lot, in urban area with full utilities);* **Apartment Rent** *(950 sf 2 bedroom/1.5 or 2 bath, unfurnished, excluding all utilities except water);* **All Electric** *(average monthly cost for an all-electric home);* **Part Electric** *(average monthly cost for a part-electric home);* **Other Energy** *(average monthly cost for natural gas, fuel oil, coal, wood, and any other forms of energy except electricity);* **Telephone** *(price includes basic monthly rate for a private residential line plus additional local usage charges incurred by a family of four).*
Source: The Council for Community and Economic Research (formerly ACCRA), Cost of Living Index, 2007

Health Care, Transportation, and Other Costs

Area[1]	Doctor ($/visit)	Dentist ($/visit)	Optometrist ($/visit)	Gasoline ($/gallon)	Beauty Salon ($/visit)	Men's Shirt ($)
City[2]	68.14	68.95	79.93	2.54	31.67	24.94
Avg.	79.48	71.93	79.55	2.64	29.52	25.77
Min.	52.08	44.80	43.95	2.19	15.58	16.19
Max.	148.44	126.27	158.83	3.48	60.62	48.53

Note: (1) Values for the local area are compared with the average, minimum and maximum values for all 331 areas in the Cost of Living Index report; (2) Figures cover the Memphis TN urban area; **Doctor** *(general practitioners routine exam of an established patient);* **Dentist** *(adult teeth cleaning and periodic oral examination);* **Optometrist** *(full vision eye exam for established adult patient);* **Gasoline** *(one gallon regular unleaded, national brand, including all taxes, cash price at self-service pump if available);* **Beauty Salon** *(woman's shampoo, trim, and blow-dry);* **Men's Shirt** *(cotton/polyester dress shirt, pinpoint weave, long sleeves).*
Source: The Council for Community and Economic Research (formerly ACCRA), Cost of Living Index, 2007

HOUSING

House Price Index (HPI)

Area	National Ranking[2]	Quarterly Change (%)	One-Year Change (%)	Five-Year Change (%)
MSA[1]	159	0.80	1.36	18.47
U.S.[3]	-	0.10	0.84	41.37

Note: The HPI is a weighted repeat sales index. It measures average price changes in repeat sales or refinancings on the same properties. This information is obtained by reviewing repeat mortgage transactions on single-family properties whose mortgages have been purchased or securitized by Fannie Mae or Freddie Mac in January 1975; (1) Metropolitan Statistical Area - see Appendix B for areas included; (2) Rankings are based on annual percentage change for all metro areas containing at least 15,000 transactions over the last 10 years and ranges from 1 to 291; (3) figures based on a weighted average of Census Division estimates; all figures are for the period ending December 31, 2007
Source: Office of Federal Housing Enterprise Oversight, House Price Index, February 26, 2008

House Price Valuations

Area	Q1 2000	Q1 2001	Q1 2002	Q1 2003	Q1 2004	Q1 2005	Q1 2006	Q1 2007	Q1 2008
MSA[1]	-4.6	-10.7	-12.6	-13.2	-15.2	-12.9	-10.4	-12.1	-16.4

Note: Figures show the percentage of over- or under-valuation of single family homes relative to statistically normal house values (e.g. a value of 23.6 indicates that house values are 23.6% overvalued). Statistically normal house values are based on house prices, interest rates, household incomes, population densities, and any historical premiums or discounts metropolitan areas have exhibited over time; (1) Figures cover the Metropolitan Statistical Area - see Appendix B for areas included
Source: Global Insight/National City Corporation, House Prices in America, May 2008

Median Home Prices

Area	2005	2006	2007[r]	Percent Change 2006 to 2007
MSA[1]	141.2	142.3	137.2	-3.6
U.S. Average	219.0	221.9	217.9	-1.8

Note: Figures are median sales prices of existing single-family homes in thousands of dollars; (r) revised; n/a not available; (1) Metropolitan Statistical Area - see Appendix B for areas included
Source: National Association of Realtors, Metropolitan Area Prices, 1st Quarter 2008

Housing: Year Structure Built

Area	1990 -2000	1980 -1989	1970 -1979	1960 -1969	1950 -1959	1940 -1949	Before 1940	Median Year
City	59.4	19.8	11.7	4.2	1.7	1.3	1.9	1992
MSA[1]	21.3	16.3	20.1	16.1	13.2	6.6	6.4	1974
U.S.	17.0	15.8	18.5	13.7	12.7	7.3	15.0	1971

Note: Figures are percentages; (1) Metropolitan Statistical Area - see Appendix A for areas included
Source: Census 2000, Summary File 3

HEALTH

Health Risk Data

Category	Area[1] (%)	U.S. (%)
Adults who have been told they have high blood pressure[3]	32.5	25.5
Adults who have been told they have high blood cholesterol[3]	29.0	35.6
Adults who have been told they have diabetes[2]	9.3	7.5
Adults who have been told they have arthritis[3]	27.0	27.0
Adults who have been told they currently have asthma	7.8	8.5
Adults who are current smokers	22.0	20.1
Adults who are heavy drinkers[4]	5.2	4.9
Adults who are overweight (BMI 25.0 - 29.9)	30.5	36.5
Adults who are obese (BMI 30.0 - 99.8)	34.0	25.1

Note: Data as of 2006 unless otherwise noted; (1) Figures cover the Metropolitan Statistical Area - see Appendix B for areas included; (2) Figures do not include pregnancy-related diabetes, pre-diabetes or borderline diabetes; (3) 2005 data; (4) Heavy drinkers are classified as adult men having more than two drinks per day or adult women having more than one drink per day
Source: Centers for Disease Control and Prevention, Behaviorial Risk Factor Surveillance System, SMART: Selected Metropolitan/Micropolitan Area Risk Trends, 2005, 2006

Mortality Rates for the Top 10 Causes of Death in the U.S.

ICD-10[a] Sub-Chapter	ICD-10[a] Code	Age-Adjusted Mortality Rate[1] per 100,000 population	
		County[2]	U.S.
Malignant neoplasms	C00-C97	215.8	186.5
Ischaemic heart diseases	I20-I25	195.0	152.3
Other forms of heart disease	I30-I51	55.1	51.5
Cerebrovascular diseases	I60-I69	72.9	50.0
Chronic lower respiratory diseases	J40-J47	42.1	42.6
Diabetes mellitus	E10-E14	33.0	24.8
Other degenerative diseases of the nervous system	G30-G31	30.6	22.6
Other external causes of accidental injury	W00-X59	22.5	21.4
Influenza and pneumonia	J10-J18	24.3	20.7
Hypertensive diseases	I10-I13	50.3	18.2

Note: (a) ICD-10 = International Classification of Diseases 10th Revision; (1) Mortality rates are a three year average covering 2003-2005; (2) Figures cover Shelby County
Source: Centers for Disease Control and Prevention, National Center for Health Statistics. Compressed Mortality File 1999-2004. CDC WONDER On-line Database, compiled from Compressed Mortality File 1999-2005 Series 20 No. 2K, 2008.

Mortality Rates for Selected Causes of Death

ICD-10[a] Sub-Chapter	ICD-10[a] Code	Age-Adjusted Mortality Rate[1] per 100,000 population	
		County[2]	U.S.
Assault	X85-Y09	15.9	5.9
Human immunodeficiency virus (HIV) disease	B20-B24	13.1	4.5
Intentional self-harm	X60-X84	10.4	10.8
Malnutrition	E40-E46	1.8	1.0
Obesity and other hyperalimentation	E65-E68	1.9	1.4
Organic, including symptomatic, mental disorders	F01-F09	13.7	16.8
Transport accidents	V01-V99	17.1	16.1
Viral hepatitis	B15-B19	3.6	1.8

Note: (a) ICD-10 = International Classification of Diseases 10th Revision; (1) Mortality rates are a three year average covering 2003-2005; (2) Figures cover Shelby County
Source: Centers for Disease Control and Prevention, National Center for Health Statistics. Compressed Mortality File 1999-2004. CDC WONDER On-line Database, compiled from Compressed Mortality File 1999-2005 Series 20 No. 2K, 2008.

Distribution of Physicians[1]

Area	Total	Family/ General Practice	Specialties	
			Medical	Surgical
Shelby County (number)	2,249	385	939	527
Shelby County (rate per 10,000 pop.)	24.7	4.2	10.3	5.8
U.S. (rate per 10,000 pop.)	17.7	4.6	6.9	4.3

Note: Data as of 2005; (1) Includes all non-federal, patient-care, office-based MDs
Source: Area Resource File (ARF). June 2007. U.S. Department of Health and Human Services, Health Resources and Services Administration, Bureau of Health Professions, Rockville, MD.

Hospitals

Collierville has the following hospitals: 1 general medical and surgical.
AHA Guide to the Healthcare Field 2008

According to *U.S. News,* the Memphis, TN-MS-AR metro area is home to one of the best hospitals in the U.S.: **Saint Jude Children's Research Hospital**. *U.S. News Online, "America's Best Hospitals 2007"*

EDUCATION

Public School District Statistics

District Name	Schls	Pupils	Pupil/ Teacher Ratio	Minority Pupils[1] (%)	Free Lunch Eligible[2] (%)	IEP[3] (%)
Shelby County School District	48	45,922	17.4	39.4	n/a	18.9

Note: Table includes regular local school districts with 2,000 or more students; (1) Percentage of students that are not white, non-Hispanic; (2) Percentage of students that are eligible for the free lunch program; (3) Percentage of students that have an Individualized Education Program.
Source: U.S. Department of Education, National Center for Education Statistics, Common Core of Data, Local Education Agency (School District) Universe Survey: School Year 2005-2006; U.S. Department of Education, National Center for Education Statistics, Common Core of Data, Public Elementary/Secondary School Universe Survey: School Year 2005-2006

Top Public High Schools

High School Name	Index[1]	Rank[1]	Subsidized Lunch (%)[2]	E&E (%)[3]
Collierville	1.409	992	9.0	24.0

Note: (1) Public schools are ranked according to a ratio that is the number of Advanced Placement, International Baccalaureate, and/or Cambridge tests taken by all students at a school in 2007 divided by the number of graduating seniors. All of the schools on the list have an index of at least 1.000; they are in the top five percent of public schools measured this way. The rankings range from 1 to 1,422; (2) Percentage of students receiving federally subsidized meals; (3) E & E stands for equity and excellence percentage: the portion of all graduating seniors at a school that had at least one passing grade on one AP or IB test; (**) Gave both IB and AP tests. AP and IB participation are indicators of a school's efforts to get students to excel and prepare for college.
Source: Newsweek Online, "Top High Schools 2008"

Highest Level of Education

Area	Less than H.S.	H.S. Diploma	Some College, No Deg.	Associate Degree	Bachelors Degree	Masters Degree	Profess. School Degree	Doctorate Degree
City	5.9	18.2	26.9	6.3	30.6	9.1	1.9	1.0
MSA[1]	20.2	28.0	23.9	5.3	14.9	5.1	1.9	0.8
U.S.	19.4	28.4	21.2	6.4	15.7	5.9	2.0	1.0

Note: Figures are 2007 estimated percentages and cover persons age 25 and over; (1) Metropolitan Statistical Area - see Appendix B for areas included
Source: Claritas, Inc.

Educational Attainment by Race

Area	High School Graduate (%)					Bachelor's Degree (%)				
	Total	White	Black	Asian	Hisp.[2]	Total	White	Black	Asian	Hisp.[2]
City	93.2	95.3	70.4	82.5	72.7	41.2	43.0	20.4	41.4	26.7
MSA[1]	79.8	87.1	69.6	78.7	52.4	22.7	29.2	12.1	48.4	14.1
U.S.	80.4	83.6	72.3	80.4	52.4	24.4	26.1	14.3	44.1	10.4

Note: Figures shown cover persons 25 years old and over; (1) Metropolitan Statistical Area - see Appendix A for areas included; (2) people of Hispanic origin can be of any race
Source: Census 2000, Summary File 3

School Enrollment by Type

Area	Grades KG to 8				Grades 9 to 12			
	Public		Private		Public		Private	
	Enrollment	%	Enrollment	%	Enrollment	%	Enrollment	%
City	5,357	91.2	514	8.8	2,072	89.7	238	10.3
MSA[1]	149,569	88.4	19,693	11.6	61,138	87.4	8,828	12.6
U.S.	33,526,011	88.7	4,285,121	11.3	14,848,628	90.6	1,532,323	9.4

Note: Figures shown cover persons 3 years old and over; (1) Metropolitan Statistical Area - see Appendix A for areas included
Source: Census 2000, Summary File 3

School Enrollment by Race

Area	Grades KG to 8 (%)				Grades 9 to 12 (%)			
	White	Black	Asian	Hisp.[1]	White	Black	Asian	Hisp.[1]
City	88.5	7.4	1.4	1.4	91.6	5.9	0.3	0.9
MSA[2]	43.1	53.1	1.2	2.2	44.0	52.4	1.3	1.9
U.S.	68.5	15.5	3.3	16.8	68.8	15.5	3.8	15.7

Note: Figures shown cover persons 3 years old and over; (1) people of Hispanic origin can be of any race; (2) Metropolitan Statistical Area - see Appendix A for areas included
Source: Census 2000, Summary File 3

Average Salaries of Public School Classroom Teachers

District	2005-06		2006-07		Percent Change 2005-06 to 2006-07
	Dollars	Rank[1]	Dollars	Rank[1]	
Tennessee	42,537	34	43,816	34	3.01
U.S. Average	49,026	-	50,816	-	3.65

Note: (1) State rank ranges from 1 to 51.
Source: National Education Association, Rankings & Estimates: Rankings of the States 2006 and Estimates of School Statistics 2007, December 2007

Higher Education

Four-Year Colleges			Two-Year Colleges			Medical Schools[1]	Law Schools[2]	Voc/ Tech[3]
Public	Private Non-profit	Private For-profit	Public	Private Non-profit	Private For-profit			
0	0	0	0	0	0	0	0	0

Note: Figures cover institutions located within the city limits; (1) includes schools accredited by the Liaison Committee on Medical Education and the American Osteopathic Association; (2) includes American Bar Association-accredited law schools; (3) includes all schools with programs that are less than 2 years.
Source: National Center for Education Statistics, The Integrated Postsecondary Education System (IPEDS) Peer Analysis System, 2007; www.usnews.com, Law and Medical School Directories, 2009

PRESIDENTIAL ELECTION

2004 Presidential Election Results

Area	Bush	Kerry	Nader	Other
Shelby County	41.9	57.5	0.3	0.3
U.S.	50.7	48.3	0.4	0.6

Note: Results are percentages and may not add to 100% due to rounding
Source: Dave Leip's Atlas of U.S. Presidential Elections, www.uselectionatlas.org

EMPLOYERS

Major Employers

Company Name	Industry	Type of Site
American Residential Services	Lawn and garden services	Headquarters
American Rsdntal Inv Holdg LLC	Hotels and motels	Single
Baptist Mem Hospital-Memphis	Air courier services	Headquarters
Brother Industries (USA) Inc	Medical laboratories	Branch
Brother International Corp	Household audio and video equipment	Branch
Davidson Hotel Company LLC	Office machines, nec	Single
Department Cmparative Medicine	Elevators and moving stairways	Headquarters
FEDEX	Household appliances, nec	Branch
FEDEX	Prefabricated metal buildings	Headquarters
FREDS XPRESS	Plumbing, heating, air-conditioning	Headquarters
Fedex	General medical and surgical hospitals	Headquarters
Flextronics Logistics USA Inc	Paper mills	Headquarters
Perkins Mrie Cllnders Hldg Inc	General medical and surgical hospitals	Headquarters
Pinnacle Airlines Corp	Packing and crating	Single
ServiceMaster Company	Air transportation, scheduled	Headquarters
St Francis Hospital	Air courier services	Headquarters
UPS	Holding companies, nec	Single
US Post Office	Air transportation, scheduled	Branch
Varco Pruden Builidngs Inc	U.s. postal service	Branch

Note: Companies shown are located within the Memphis metropolitan area; nec = not elsewhere classified.
Source: www.zapdata.com, May 2008

PUBLIC SAFETY

Crime Rate

Area	All Crimes	Violent Crimes				Property Crimes		
		Murder	Forcible Rape	Robbery	Aggrav. Assault	Burglary	Larceny -Theft	Motor Vehicle Theft
City	2,255.4	0.0	10.5	57.8	89.4	291.8	1,648.2	157.7
Metro[1]	7,275.5	13.7	46.3	458.5	744.2	1,700.3	3,647.3	665.1
U.S.	3,808.1	5.7	30.9	149.4	287.5	729.4	2,206.8	398.4

Note: Figures are crimes per 100,000 population; (1) Metropolitan Statistical Area - see Appendix B for areas included
Source: FBI Uniform Crime Reports, 2006

Hate Crimes

Area	Number of Quarters Reported	Bias Motivation				
		Race	Religion	Sexual Orientation	Ethnicity	Disability
City	4	0	0	0	0	0

Source: Federal Bureau of Investigation, Hate Crime Statistics 2006

RECREATION

Culture

Dance[1]	Theatre[1]	Instrumental Music[1]	Vocal Music[1]	Series/ Festivals	Museums	Zoos and Aquariums[2]
0	0	0	0	0	1	0

Note: (1) Number of professional perfoming groups; (2) AZA-accredited
Source: The Grey House Performing Arts Directory, 2007; Official Museum Directory, 2008; Association of Zoos & Aquariums, AZA Member Zoos & Aquariums, June 2008

Professional Sports Teams

Team Name	League
Memphis Grizzlies	National Basketball Association (NBA)

Note: Includes teams located in the Memphis metro area.
Source: Original research

MEDIA

Newspapers

Name	News Focus	Frequency	Circulation
Collierville Herald	Community	Weekly	7,200
Independent	Local	Daily	12,600

Note: Includes newspapers with offices located in the city
Source: MediaContactsPro, March 2008

Television Stations

Name	Ch.	Network(s)	Type	Ownership
WREG	3	CBS	Commercial	New York Times Company
WMC	5	NBC	Commercial	Raycom Media Inc.
WKNO	10	PBS	Public	n/a
WHBQ	13	Fox	Commercial	Fox Television Stations Inc.
WPTY	24	ABC	Commercial	Clear Channel Communications Inc.
WLMT	30	UPN	Commercial	Clear Channel Communications Inc.
WBUY	40	n/a	Non-comm.	Trinity Broadcasting Network
WPXX	50	Pax	Commercial	Paxson Communications Corporation

Note: Stations included cover the Memphis DMA (Designated Market Area)
BurrellesLuce, MediaContacts Online, January 2007

Major AM Radio Stations

Call Letters	Freq. (kHz)	Station Type	Target Audience	Station Format	Music Format
WHBQ	560	n/a	General	Sports/Talk	n/a
WREC	600	Commercial	General	News	n/a
WCRV	640	n/a	General/Religious	News	n/a
WJCE	680	Commercial	General	Music	Easy Listening
WMC	790	Commercial	General	News/Sports/Talk	n/a
WLRC	850	Commercial	General/Religious	Music/News/Sports/Talk	Gospel
KOSE	860	Commercial	General/Religious	Music	Gospel
KLCN	910	Commercial	General	Music	Country
KXJK	950	Commercial	General	Music/News	Modern Rock
KWAM	990	n/a	General	Music/News	n/a
WGSF	1030	Commercial	Christian/Gen/Hisp	Music	Latin
WDIA	1070	Commercial	Black/General	Music/Talk	Adult Contemp.
WKRA	1110	Commercial	General	Ed/Music/News/Sports/Talk	Gospel
WSAO	1140	Commercial	General	Educational/Music/Talk	Gospel
WKBL	1250	Commercial	General/Religious	Music/News	Country
WJBI	1290	Commercial	Christian/General	Music	Urban Contemp.
WLOK	1340	Commercial	General	Music/News	Gospel
WKCU	1350	Commercial	General/Religious	Music	Gospel
KFFA	1360	Commercial	General	Music/News	Christian
KWYN	1400	Commercial	General	Music/News	Country
WTRO	1450	Commercial	General	Music/News	Oldies
WBBP	1480	n/a	General/Religious	Music/News/Sports	n/a
WTRB	1570	Commercial	General	Music/Sports/Talk	Gospel

Note: Stations included cover the Memphis DMA (Designated Market Area); n/a not available
Source: BurrellesLuce, MediaContacts Online, January 2007

Major FM Radio Stations

Call Letters	Freq. (mHz)	Station Type	Target Audience	Station Format	Music Format
WKNA	88.9	Public	General	Ed/Music/News/Talk	n/a
WEVL	89.9	n/a	General	Educational/Music	Oldies
WKNP	90.1	Public	General	Music/Talk	Classical
WKNQ	90.7	Public	General	News/Talk	n/a
WKNO	91.1	Public	General	Music/Talk	Classical
WUMR	91.7	College	General	Ed/Music/News/Sports/Talk	Jazz
KWYN	92.5	n/a	General	Music/News	n/a
WMFS	92.9	n/a	General	Music/Talk	n/a
KBFC	93.5	Commercial	General	Music	Country
WKBQ	93.5	Commercial	General	Music/News	Adult Contemp.
WQLJ	93.7	Commercial	General/Religious	Music/News	Adult Contemp.
WTKB	93.7	Commercial	General/Religious	Music/News	Oldies
WMBZ	94.1	Commercial	General	Music	Alternative
WLSQ	94.3	Commercial	General	Music/News/Sports/Talk	Alternative
WXRZ	94.3	Commercial	General	Talk	n/a
KJIW	94.5	Commercial	General/Religious	Educational/Music/News	Christian
WHAL	95.7	n/a	General/Women	Music/News/Talk	n/a
KHLS	96.3	Commercial	General	Music	Contemp. Country
WHRK	97.1	Commercial	General	Music	Urban Contemp.
WTNE	97.5	Commercial	General	Music/News	Country
WSRR	98.1	Commercial	General	Music	Top 40
WMC	99.7	Commercial	General	Music/News	Top 40
WASL	100.1	Commercial	General	Music	Adult Contemp.
WBLE	100.5	Commercial	General	Music/News/Sports	Contemp. Country
KJMS	101.1	Commercial	General	n/a	n/a
WEGR	102.7	n/a	General	Music/News	n/a
KFFA	103.1	n/a	General	Music/News/Sports	n/a
WRVR	104.5	Commercial	General	Music	Soft Rock
KAKJ	105.3	Commercial	General	Music/News	Urban Contemp.
WLSZ	105.3	Commercial	General	Music/News/Sports/Talk	Album Rock
WGKX	105.9	n/a	General	Music	n/a
WHKL	106.9	Commercial	General	Music	Oldies
KXHT	107.1	Commercial	Black/Gen/Young Adult	Music	Urban Contemp.
WMPS	107.5	Commercial	General	n/a	n/a

Note: Stations included cover the Memphis DMA (Designated Market Area); n/a not available
BurrellesLuce, MediaContacts Online, January 2007

CLIMATE

Average and Extreme Temperatures

Temperature	Jan	Feb	Mar	Apr	May	Jun	Jul	Aug	Sep	Oct	Nov	Dec	Yr.
Extreme High (°F)	83	85	90	95	99	104	107	104	105	97	86	82	107
Average High (°F)	57	62	69	78	84	90	92	92	87	78	68	60	77
Average Temp. (°F)	46	50	57	65	72	79	81	81	76	65	55	48	65
Average Low (°F)	34	37	44	51	59	67	70	69	64	51	42	36	52
Extreme Low (°F)	0	8	15	28	38	42	55	53	34	24	16	2	0

Note: Figures cover the years 1948-1990
Source: National Climatic Data Center, International Station Meteorological Climate Summary, 9/96

Average Precipitation/Snowfall/Humidity

Precip./Humidity	Jan	Feb	Mar	Apr	May	Jun	Jul	Aug	Sep	Oct	Nov	Dec	Yr.
Avg. Precip. (in.)	4.9	5.1	6.6	5.2	4.3	3.7	5.3	3.5	3.6	2.7	4.2	5.6	54.8
Avg. Snowfall (in.)	1	Tr	Tr	Tr	0	0	0	0	0	0	Tr	Tr	1
Avg. Rel. Hum. 6am (%)	87	86	87	90	91	91	93	93	92	91	88	87	90
Avg. Rel. Hum. 3pm (%)	56	51	47	46	50	52	57	54	54	48	49	54	51

Note: Figures cover the years 1948-1990; Tr = Trace amounts (<0.05 in. of rain; <0.5 in. of snow)
Source: National Climatic Data Center, International Station Meteorological Climate Summary, 9/96

Weather Conditions

Temperature			Daytime Sky			Precipitation		
10°F & below	32°F & below	90°F & above	Clear	Partly cloudy	Cloudy	0.01 inch or more precip.	0.1 inch or more snow/ice	Thunder-storms
1	53	86	101	152	112	104	2	59

Note: Figures are average number of days per year and cover the years 1948-1990
Source: National Climatic Data Center, International Station Meteorological Climate Summary, 9/96

HAZARDOUS WASTE

Superfund Sites

Collierville has two hazardous waste sites on the EPA's Superfund Final National Priorities List: **Smalley-Piper**; **Carrier Air Conditioning Co.**. *U.S. Environmental Protection Agency, Final National Priorities List, June 23, 2008*

AIR & WATER QUALITY

Air Quality Index

Area	Percent of Days when Air Quality was...[2]				AQI Statistics	
	Good	Moderate	Unhealthy for Sensitive Groups	Unhealthy	Maximum	Median
MSA[1]	47.9	41.6	9.9	0.5	182	52

Note: The Air Quality Index (AQI) is an index for reporting daily air quality. EPA calculates the AQI for five major air pollutants regulated by the Clean Air Act: ground-level ozone, particle pollution (also known as particulate matter), carbon monoxide, sulfur dioxide, and nitrogen dioxide. The AQI runs from 0 to 500. The higher the AQI value, the greater the level of air pollution and the greater the health concern. There are six AQI categories: "Good" The AQI is between 0 and 50. Air quality is considered satisfactory; "Moderate" The AQI is between 51 and 100. Air quality is acceptable; "Unhealthy for Sensitive Groups" When AQI values are between 101 and 150, members of sensitive groups may experience health effects; "Unhealthy" When AQI values are between 151 and 200 everyone may begin to experience health effects; "Very Unhealthy" AQI values between 201 and 300 trigger a health alert; "Hazardous" AQI values over 300 trigger health warnings of emergency conditions; (1) Metropolitan Statistical Area - see Appendix A for areas included; (2) Based on 365 days with AQI data in 2007.
Source: U.S. Environmental Protection Agency, Air Quality Index Report, 2007

Air Quality Index Pollutants

Area	Percent of Days when AQI Pollutant was...[2]					
	Carbon Monoxide	Nitrogen Dioxide	Ozone	Sulfur Dioxide	Particulate Matter 2.5	Particulate Matter 10
MSA[1]	0.0	0.0	42.5	0.3	57.3	0.0

Note: The Air Quality Index (AQI) is an index for reporting daily air quality. EPA calculates the AQI for five major air pollutants regulated by the Clean Air Act: ground-level ozone, particle pollution (also known as particulate matter), carbon monoxide, sulfur dioxide, and nitrogen dioxide. The AQI runs from 0 to 500. The higher the AQI value, the greater the level of air pollution and the greater the health concern; (1) Metropolitan Statistical Area - see Appendix A for areas included; (2) Based on 365 days with AQI data in 2007.
Source: U.S. Environmental Protection Agency, Air Quality Index Report, 2007

Air Quality Index Trends

Area	Trend Sites (14)								All Sites (42)
	1999	2000	2001	2002	2003	2004	2005	2006	2006
MSA[1]	35	28	15	17	9	2	12	9	9

Note: An AQI value greater than 100 indicates that air quality would have been in the unhealthful range on that day. Data from exceptional events are not included. These counts are presented in two ways. First, the counts are based on sites having an adequate record of monitoring data during the trend period (trend sites). These counts represent the relative change in the number of days with AQI values greater than 100. In the last column, the counts are based on all sites with data in the most recent year (because it is possible for a site to have data in the most recent year but not enough data to be a trend site); (1) Metropolitan Statistical Area - see Appendix A for areas included.
Source: U.S. Environmental Protection Agency, Office of Air and Radiation, Air Trends, Factbook and Related Information, Air Pollution Trends in Selected Metropolitan Areas 2006

Maximum Air Pollutant Concentrations

	Particulate Matter 10 (ug/m^3)	Particulate Matter 2.5 (ug/m^3)	Ozone (ppm)	Carbon Monoxide (ppm)	Sulfur Dioxide (ppm)	Nitrogen Dioxide (ppm)	Lead (ug/m^3)
MSA[1] Level	67	31	0.125	3	0.035	0.012	n/a
NAAQS[2]	150	35	0.125	9	0.140	0.053	1.50
Met NAAQS[2]	Yes	Yes	Yes	Yes	Yes	Yes	n/a

Note: Data from exceptional events are not included; (1) Metropolitan Statistical Area - see Appendix A for areas included; (2) National Ambient Air Quality Standards; n/a not available
Concentrations: Particulate Matter 10 (coarse particulate) - highest second maximum 24-hour concentration; Particulate Matter 2.5 (fine particulate) - highest 98th percentile 24-hour concentration; Ozone - highest second daily maximum 1-hour concentration; Carbon Monoxide - highest second maximum non-overlapping 8-hour concentration; Sulfur Dioxide - highest second maximum 24-hour concentration; Nitrogen Dioxide - highest arithmetic mean concentration; Lead - highest quarterly maximum concentration
Units: ppm = parts per million; ug/m^3 = micrograms per cubic meter
Source: U.S. Environmental Protection Agency, MSA Factbook 2006, Air Quality Statistics by City

Drinking Water

Water System Name	Pop. Served	Primary Water Source Type	Violations[1]	
			Health Based	Monitoring/ Reporting
Collierville Water Dept.	41,277	Ground	0	0

Note: (1) Based on violation data from January 1, 2007 to December 31, 2007 (includes unresolved violations from earlier years)
Source: U.S. Environmental Protection Agency, Office of Ground Water and Drinking Water, Safe Drinking Water Information System (based on data extracted April 15, 2008)

Allen, Texas

Background

Settlers arrived in the area now known as Allen in the early 1840s in search of free land, traveling the Texas Road and the Central National Road, constructed by the Republic of Texas. The town, located just north of Dallas in northwestern Texas, was officially founded in 1870 as a railroad stop for the Houston Texas railroad, connecting the railway to nearby farms. The town was named after former Texas attorney general and railroad promoter Ebenezer Allen.

It is believed that the first train robbery in Texas took place in Allen on February 22, 1878, when Sam Bass and his associates attacked and stole from a train. The Allen stop was only a short ride from the Bass gang's hideouts in the Elm Trinity brush lands.

The Allen train station closed in 1948 after ownership of the tracks changed several hands, and a devastating fire destroyed most of the business district. When the tracks closed, the population of Allen declined to 400 in a matter of two years. It was only the construction of the US highway 75 that finally boosted the city's population. In the 1980s two companies, Developmental Learning Materials and InteCom, Inc. relocated to Allen, leading the way to a healthy and developing corporate environment. Allen continues to attract telecommunications and technology-related companies, with AT&T and Fiber Systems International among the top employers in the area.

The Allen Independent School District has 13 elementary schools, 3 middle schools, 1 freshman center, 1 alternate school, and one high school, serving almost all of Allen. The Allen High School was named 2001-2002 Blue Ribbon School by the U.S. Department of Education, a recognition only given to 172 across the nation. In addition to the independent school system, Allen also hosts a campus of the Collin Community College District, located inside Allen High School.

Allen boasts "an activity for everyone." The city has planned parks and recreational areas for the outdoorsman, premium retail outlets for the shopper, and a Civic Ballet and Philharmonic Symphony for the arts enthusiast. Bookworms can visit Allen's public library, which has over 125,000 volumes in its 54,000 square foot facility that includes an auditorium, meeting rooms and an art gallery.

The Presbyterian Hospital of Allen operates a 56-bed hospital. The hospital provides top-notch ambulatory and surgical services, diagnostic services and emergency care. The hospital also has two, 60,000 square foot Medical Office Buildings that include a state-of-the-art breast care and sleep disorders center.

Colin County Airport, Dallas/Fortworth Airport and Dallas Love Field Airport all serve the Allen and Dallas area.

Rankings

General Rankings

- Dallas* was ranked #132 out of 375 metro areas in *Cities Ranked & Rated*. Criteria: cost of living; climate; crime; transportation; economy and jobs; education; arts and culture; health and healthcare; leisure; quality of life. *Cities Ranked & Rated, 2nd Edition, 2007*
- Dallas* was ranked #43 out of 379 metro areas in *Places Rated Almanac*. Criteria: health care; education; recreation; transportation; ambience; climate; crime; housing costs; jobs. *Places Rated Almanac, 7th Edition, 2007*

Business/Finance Rankings

- The nation's 100 largest metro areas were analysed in terms of the percentage of households entering some stage of foreclosure in 2007. The Dallas* metro area ranked #28 out of 100 (#1 = highest foreclosure rate). *RealtyTrac, "Year-End 2007 Metropolitan Foreclosure Report"*
- The Dallas* metro area was selected one of America's "Top 50 Business Opportunity Metros" by *Expansion Management* in their 5th annual Mayor's Challenge ranking of metro areas that have achieved solid ratings across the board in numerous *EM* studies during the past 12 months. The area ranked #13. Criteria: public schools; quality of life; college educated workers; logistics infrastructure; healthcare costs; taxes and government spending; reputation among site consultants. *Expansion Management, August 2007*
- The Dallas* metro area was selected as one of "America's Most Wired Cities" by *Forbes*. The metro area was ranked #19 out of 30. Criteria: percentage of Internet users with high-speed access; the range of service providers within a city; availability of public wireless hot spots. *Forbes, "America's Most Wired Cities," January 10, 2008*
- Dallas* was selected as one of the best places to start and grow a company by *Entrepreneur* and the National Policy Research Council. The Dallas* metro area ranked #17 out of 50 large metro areas. Criteria: business formation and growth (firms started four to 14 years ago that still employ at least 5 people and experienced rapid growth over the last four years). *Entrepreneur/National Policy Research Council, "Hot Cities for Entrepreneurs," September 2006*
- The Dallas* metro area was selected as one of "America's Greediest Cities" by *Forbes*. The area was ranked #7 out of 10. Criteria: number of Forbes 400 (*Forbes* annual list of the richest Americans) members per capita. *Forbes, "America's Greediest Cities," December 7, 2007*
- The Dallas* metro area was selected as one of "America's 50 Hottest Cities" for business relocations and expansions. Criteria: industry's most prominent site selection consultants were asked to list their top city choices for relocating and expanding manufacturing companies, taking into consideration such factors as the business climate, work force quality, operating costs, incentive programs, and the ease of working with local political and economic development officials. *Expansion Management, January-February 2007*
- Dallas* was cited as one of America's top large metros (population over 1 million) for new and expanded facility projects in 2007. The area appeared in the top 10 with 73 projects. *Site Selection, "Top Metropolitan Area Awards," March 2008*
- The Dallas* metro area was selected as one of the "Top 20 Real Estate Markets" for expanding or relocating companies. The area ranked #7. Criteria: low rental costs; low purchase prices; high vacancy rates of office and warehouse space. *Expansion Management, October 2007*
- Intel, in partnership with Sperling's BestPlaces, ranked the 80 "Best Cities for Teleworking" in America. The Dallas* metro area ranked #8 among extra large metro areas. The study identifies cities that hold the greatest potential for teleworking based on a host of factors including typical commuting times, fuel prices, availability of broadband Internet access and percentage of the population in telework friendly jobs. The study also factored in extreme climate and natural hazards. *Intel, "Best Cities for Teleworking," March 30, 2006*

- The Dallas* metro area appeared on the Milken Institute "2007 Best Performing Cities" index. Rank: #59 out of 200 large metro areas. Criteria: job growth; wage and salary growth; high-tech output growth. *Milken Institute, "2007 Best Performing Cities"*

- The Dallas* metro area was selected as one of "The Top 20 Boom Towns in America." *Business 2.0* magazine and econometric research firm Global Insight compared 319 metropolitan areas in the U.S. and ranked the 61 with populations over 1 million. Criteria: a weighted formula that includes forecast growth rates in sectors that contain the economy's 10 most skilled occupational clusters; the prevalence of college degrees in the local workforce; median salary. The area ranked #18 among large metro areas. *Business 2.0 Magazine, March 2004*

- Dallas* was identified as one of the 100 "Most Unwired Cities" in the U.S. The area ranked #23 out of the 100 largest metro areas in the U.S. Criteria: number of public and commercial wireless access points (hotspots); airports with wireless Internet access; broadband availability; local wireless networks; and wireless email devices. *Intel, "Most Unwired Cities Survey," June 7, 2005*

- Dallas* was ranked #21 out of 125 regions worldwide in terms of its "Knowledge Competitiveness Index." The index attempts to measure the knowledge-based development taking place throughout the world and is based on 19 measures of economic performance that indicate a region's ability to translate its knowledge capacity into economic value. *Robert Huggins Associates, World Knowledge Competitiveness Index 2005*

- *Forbes* ranked the 200 most populous metro areas in the U.S. in terms of the "Best Places for Business and Careers." The Dallas* metro area was ranked #93. Criteria: business costs (labor, energy, tax and office space expenses); living costs (housing, transportation, food and other household expenditures); education levels of the work force; job growth; income growth; migration trends; crime rates; and culture/leisure. *Forbes, "Best Places for Business and Careers," March 19, 2008*

- *Fortune* ranked the 100 largest metro areas in the U.S. in terms of projected median home price change in 2007. The Dallas* metro area ranked #13. *Fortune.com, "Hot Spots, Cold Spots"*

Health/Environment Rankings

- 100 of the largest metro areas in the U.S. were analyzed in terms of their current drought severity. The Dallas* metro area ranked #97 (#1 = driest). The rankings were based on statistics such as long-term precipitation trends and patterns and the Palmer drought indices. *Sperling's BestPlaces, www.BestPlaces.net, "America's Drought-Riskiest Cities," November 2007*

- Doctors at the Harvard School of Public Health ranked 40 metropolitan areas based on data from the government-sponsored Hospital Quality Alliance program. The program tracks the performance of individual hospitals in treating patients for three common health problems: heart attacks, congestive heart failure, and pneumonia. The Dallas* metro area ranked #22 in quality of care for heart attacks, #25 for congestive heart failure, and #7 for pneumonia. *New England Journal of Medicine, July 21, 2005*

- *Reader's Digest* ranked the 50 largest metro areas in the U.S. in terms of how "clean" they are. The Dallas* metro area ranked #30. Criteria: air quality; water quality; toxic industrial pollution; Superfund sites; and sanitation. *Reader's Digest, "The 50 Cleanest (and Dirtiest) Cities in America," July 2005*

- The American Academy of Dermatology ranked 32 U.S. metropolitan regions in terms of their residents knowledge, attitude and behaviors towards tanning and sun protection. The Dallas* metro area ranked #6. The results of the study are based on an online national survey of 3,342 respondents. *American Academy of Dermatology, "RAYS: Your Grade," May 7, 2007*

- The Dallas* metro area appeared in *Country Home's* "2008 Best Green Places" report. The area ranked #94 out of 379. Criteria: official energy policies; green power; green buildings; availability of fresh, locally grown food. *Country Home, "2008 Best Green Places"*

- Wyeth Consumer Healthcare, in partnership with Sperling's BestPlaces, ranked the nation's 50 most populous metro areas in terms of five key health factors. The Dallas* metro area ranked #35. Criteria: physical activity; health status; nutrition; lifestyle pursuits; and mental wellness. *Wyeth Consumer Healthcare, "Centrum Healthiest Cities Study," April 19, 2005*

- HealthGrades surveyed over 41,000 individuals on doctor satisfaction and ranked the 20 largest metro areas based on the highest "definitely yes" responses to the question "Do you trust the physician to make decisions/recommendations that are in your best interest?" The Dallas* metro area ranked #2. *HealthGrades.com, "Top Cities in Doctor-Trust," September 7, 2006*

- Dallas* was identified as a "2008 Asthma Capital." The area ranked #23 out of the nation's 100 largest metropolitan areas. Twelve factors were used to identify the most challenging places to live for people with asthma: estimated prevalence; self-reported prevalence; crude death rate for asthma; annual pollen score; annual air quality; public smoking laws; number of board-certified asthma specialists; school inhaler access laws; rescue medication use; controller medication use; uninsured rate; poverty rate. *Asthma and Allergy Foundation of America, "2008 Asthma Capitals"*

- Dallas* was identified as a "Spring Allergy Capital." The area ranked #2 out of 100. Three groups of factors were used to identify the most severe cities for people with allergies during the spring season: annual pollen levels; medicine utilization; access to board-certified allergists. *Asthma and Allergy Foundation of America, "2007 Spring Allergy Capital Rankings"*

- Dallas* was identified as a "Fall Allergy Capital." The area ranked #21 out of 100. Three groups of factors were used to identify the most severe cities for people with allergies during the fall season: annual pollen levels; medicine utilization; access to board-certified allergists. *Asthma and Allergy Foundation of America, "2007 Fall Allergy Capital Rankings"*

- Ortho-McNeil Neurologics, in partnership with Sperling's BestPlaces, analyzed 110 metro areas and identified those U.S. cities with the highest prevalence of factors that are most commonly associated with migraine headaches. The Dallas* metro area ranked #82. Criteria: number of migraine-related drug prescriptions per capita; lifestyle factors that can contribute to migraines; environmental factors that can trigger migraines; and consumption of migraine-triggering foods. *Ortho-McNeil Neurologics, "America's Migraine Hot Spots," March 14, 2006*

- Sperling's BestPlaces ranked 331 metro areas and identified the most and least stressful U.S. cities. The Dallas* metro area ranked #10 out of the 100 largest metro areas (#1 = most stressful). Criteria: divorce rate; unemployment rate; violent and property crime; suicide rate; commute time; mental health; alcohol consumption; cloudy days. *Sperling's BestPlaces, www.BestPlaces.net, "America's Most (and Least) Stressful Cities," January 9, 2004*

- An analysis of the "Best & Worst Cities for Sleep" was conducted by Sperling's BestPlaces. The study ranked America's 50 most populated metro areas. The Dallas* metro area ranked #21 (#1 = best city for sleep). Criteria: number of days residents didn't get enough rest or sleep during the past month; average length of daily commute; divorce rate; unemployment rate. *Sperling's BestPlaces, www.BestPlaces.net, "Best & Worst Cities for Sleep," 2006*

- HealthGrades evaluated the performance of America's 25 most populous metropolitan areas by measuring the outcomes of five of the highest volume and most widely studied procedures and diagnoses: coronary artery bypass graft surgery; percutaneus coronary interventions; acute myocardial infarction/heart attack in angioplasty-capable hospitals; congestive heart failure; and community acquired pneumonia. The Dallas* metro area ranked #21. *HealthGrades, "HealthGrades Hospital Quality in America Study," October 12, 2004*

- Dallas* was highlighted as one of the 25 most ozone-polluted metro areas in the U.S. The area ranked #7. *American Lung Association, State of the Air: 2007*

- Dallas* was selected as one of "America's Top 10 Low-Carb Cities" by *LowCarbiz Magazine.* Criteria: abundance of low-carb products; restaurants with low-carb menu items; health practitioners supportive of carb-cutting regimens; local culture generally conducive to exercise and health. *LowCarbiz Magazine, April 2004*

- Dallas* was selected as one of "America's Pet Healthiest Cities" by Purina. The city ranked #40 out of 50. Criteria: veterinary services; environment; legislation; preventative care; obesity/body condition. *Purina Pet Institute, "America's Pet Healthiest Cities," May 20, 2003*

Women/Minorities Rankings

- Dallas* was ranked #84 out of 100 metro areas in *SELF Magazine's* ranking of "America's Best Places for Women." A panel of experts came up with more than 50 criteria including death and disease rates, environmental indicators, community resources, and lifestyle habits. *SELF Magazine, "America's Best Places for Women 2007," December 2007*
- Dallas* appeared on *Black Enterprise's* list of the "Ten Best Cities for African Americans." The top picks were culled from more than 2,000 interactive surveys completed on www.blackenterprise.com and by editorial staff evaluation. The editors weighed the following criteria as it pertained to African Americans in each city: median household income; percentage of households earning more than $100,000; percentage of businesses owned; percentage of college graduates; unemployment rates; home loan rejections; and homeownership rates. *Black Enterprise, May 2007*

Seniors/Retirement Rankings

- Sperling's BestPlaces in partnership with Bankers Life & Casualty Company designed a survey to identify the top 50 metro areas in the U.S. that offer the best overall qualities for senior living. The Dallas* metro area ranked #44. The following criteria were statistically weighted to reflect the needs of the senior population: health; disease; economics; social; environment; spiritual; transportation; housing; and crime. *Bankers Life & Casualty Company, "Best Cities for Seniors 2005"*

Children/Family Rankings

- The Dallas* metro area was selected as one of the "Best Cities for Relocating Families" by Worldwide ERC and Primacy Relocation. The 2007 study placed a special emphasis on the housing market, which has significantly impacted the relocation industry and an employer's ability to transfer employees. The variables which weigh heavily in this category include home price, home affordability index, appreciation rates, and property tax. Other criteria include cost of living, crime rates, education, climate, focus on diversity, physicians per capita, recreation and leisure, arts and culture, air quality, watershed quality, sales tax, unemployment rate, job growth, high school and higher education index, school expenditures per student, students in public school, SAT/ACT percentile, and population growth. *Worldwide ERC and Primacy Relocation, "2007 Best Cities for Relocating Families"*

Safety Rankings

- The National Insurance Crime Bureau ranked 361 metro areas in the U.S. in terms of per capita rates of vehicle theft. The Dallas* metro area ranked #50 (#1 = highest rate). Criteria: number of vehicle theft offenses per 100,000 inhabitants. *National Insurance Crime Bureau, "NICB Vehicle Theft Study," April 22, 2008*
- Dallas* appeared on Sperling's BestPlaces list of the "Riskiest Cities for Identity Theft." The area ranked #13 out of the nations 50 largest metro areas. Over 80 criteria were analyzed across four major categories: technology impact; crime; transactions; and risk profile. *Sperling's BestPlaces, www.BestPlaces.net, "Riskiest Cities for Identity Theft," July 2006*
- Farmers Insurance Group of Companies, in partnership with Sperling's BestPlaces, ranked 379 metro areas and identified the "Most Secure U.S. Place to Live." The Dallas* metro area ranked #91 out of 114 in the large metro area category (500,000 or more residents). Criteria: crime rates; extreme weather; risk of natural disasters; environmental hazards; terrorism threats; air quality; life expectancy; job loss numbers. *Farmers Insurance Group, "Most Secure U.S. Places to Live 2007"*

- Dallas* was identified as one of the most dangerous large metro areas for pedestrians in the U.S. The area ranked #14 out of the nations 50 largest metro areas. Criteria: average yearly pedestrian fatalities per capita (for the years 2002 and 2003) adjusted for the number of walkers. *Surface Transportation Policy Project, "Mean Streets 2004"*

- Dallas* was identified as one of the least safe places in the U.S. in terms of its vulnerability to natural disasters and weather extremes. The city ranked #2 out of 10. Sperling's BestPlaces analyzed data to show a metro areas' relative tendency to experience natural disasters (hail, tornados, high winds, hurricanes, earthquakes, and brush fires) or extreme weather (abundant rain or snowfall or days that are below freezing or above 90 degrees Fahrenheit). *Forbes, "Safest and Least Safe Places in the U.S.," August 30, 2005*

Sports/Recreation Rankings

- The Dallas* metro area appeared on the *Sporting News* list of the "Best Sports Cities 2007". The area ranked #3 out of 150 cities in the U.S. *Sporting News* takes a 12-month snapshot, roughly July to July, of each city's sports, putting a heavy premium on regular-season won-lost records (from the most recently completed season). Other criteria include: playoff berths, bowl appearances and tournament bids; championships; applicable power ratings; quality of competition; overall fan fervor as measured in part by attendance as percentage of venue capacity; abundance of teams (rewarding quality over quantity); stadium and arena quality; ticket availability and prices; franchise ownership; and marquee appeal of athletes. *SportingNews.com, "Best Sports Cities 2007," August 1, 2007*

- Scarborough Research, a leading market research firm, identified the top local markets for avid NBA fans. The Dallas* DMA (Designated Market Area) ranked in the top 10 with 13% of consumers 18 years and over reporting that they are "very interested in the NBA". *Scarborough Research, April 24, 2006*

- The Dallas* metro area was selected by *Cranium* as one of the "Top 50 Fun Cities" in America. The area ranked #34. Criteria includes: number of sports teams, restaurants, and dance performances; number of toy stores; city budget spent on recreation. *Cranium, November 4, 2003*

- *Golf Digest* ranked 330 metro areas in the U.S. in terms of golf. The Dallas* metro area was ranked #256. Criteria: access to golf; weather; value of golf; and quality of golf. *Golf Digest, "Metro Golf Rankings," August 2005*

Dating/Romance Rankings

- Eli Lily and Company, in partnership with Sperling's BestPlaces, ranked the nation's 50 largest metro areas in terms of the "Most Romantic Cities for Baby Boomers." The Dallas* metro area ranked #9. Criteria: marriage and divorce rates among "baby boomers" age 45 to 60; great restaurants; dance studios; chocolate, jewelry and flower sales. *Eli Lily and Company, "Most Romantic Cities for Baby Boomers," April 20, 2007*

- The Dallas* metro area was selected as one of the "Top Ten U.S. Cities for Finding a Rich, Single Man" by Teasley, a Manhattan-based marketing consulting firm. The area ranked #10. Criteria: high single-male to single-female ratios; higher income to cost-of-living ratios. *Teasley, "Top Ten U.S. Cities for Finding a Rich, Single Man," February 10, 2004*

- The Dallas* metro area was selected as one of the "Best Cities for Relocating Singles" by Worldwide ERC and Primacy Relocation. The area ranked #52 out of the 100 largest metro areas in the U.S. Areas were selected based on the following criteria: a robust cost-of-living index; adventure and outdoor recreation opportunities; violent crime and property crime rates; percentage of the population that is unmarried (ages 25-34); ratio of single men and single women; affordability of quality higher education, including in-state and out-of-state tuition requirements and rates; number of newcomers to the area; commute times; tax rates; fee and occupancy rates for temporary housing and mini-storage; quality and quantity of collegiate and professional sporting events and fun, fan-friendly venues. *Worldwide ERC and Primacy Relocation, "2007 Best Cities for Relocating Singles," October 25, 2007*

- *Forbes* ranked the 40 most populous urbanized areas in the U.S. in terms of the "Best Cities for Singles." The Dallas* metro area ranked #9. Criteria: number of singles; cost of living alone; nightlife; culture; job growth; coolness; and online dating. *Forbes.com, August 21, 2007*

- Sperling's BestPlaces in partnership with AXE Deodorant Bodyspray ranked 80 metro areas and identified "America's Best (and Worst) Cities for Dating." The Dallas* metro area ranked #51 (#1 = best). Criteria: percentage of singles ages 18-24; population density; dating venues per capita. *AXE Deodorant Bodyspray, "America's Best (and Worst) Cities for Dating," May 2004*

Miscellaneous Rankings

- The Dallas* metro area was identified as one of 10 "Worst Cities for Commuters" by *Forbes*. The metro area ranked #5. Criteria: traffic delays; travel times; how efficiently commuters use existing infrastructure. *Forbes.com, "Worst Cities for Commuters," April 29, 2008*

- Scarborough Research, a leading market research firm, identified the top local markets for bloggers. The Dallas* DMA (Designated Market Area) ranked in the top 13 with 11% of adults reporting that they had read or contributed to a blog within the past 30 days. *Scarborough Research, October 24, 2007*

- Allen was identified as one of the 100 fastest-growing suburbs in America by "Forbes." The city ranked #33. Criteria: suburban cities, townships and villages with more than 10,000 people in 2000 were ranked by their population growth from 2000 to 2006. *Forbes.com, "America's Fastest-Growing Suburbs," July 16, 2007*

- The Dallas* metro area was selected as one of the "Top 10 Most Independent Cities for Homesellers". The area ranked #9. The cities listed had more consumers choosing to sell their homes without the help of a real-estate agent than anywhere else. Data was based on geographical information for listings posted on ForSaleByOwner.com from January 1, 2007 through June 30, 2007. *ForSaleByOwner.com, October 1, 2007*

- The Dallas* metro area appeared on *Forbes* list of "America's Drunkest Cities". The area ranked #27. Criteria: 35 of the largest continental U.S. metro areas were chosen based on availability of data and geographic diversity. Each metro was ranked in five areas: state laws; drinkers; heavy drinkers; binge drinkers; and alcoholism. *Forbes.com, "America's Drunkest Cities," August 22, 2006*

- Sperling's BestPlaces in partnership with Pep Boys ranked 77 metro areas and identified "America's Most Drivable Cities." The Dallas* metro area ranked #40. Criteria: climate; road roughness; urban mobility; gas prices. *Pep Boys, "America's Most Drivable Cities," April 9, 2003*

- State Farm Insurance, in partnership with Sperling's BestPlaces, analyzed several key factors that contribute to overall family preparedness. The Dallas* metro area ranked #28 out of the nation's 50 most populous metro areas. Criteria: quality of life; life insurance coverage; and investments. *State Farm Life Insurance, "Fiscally Fit Cities Report," July 20, 2004*

- A study by Sperling's BestPlaces examined which U.S. metro areas were most affected by high fuel prices in 2006. The Dallas* metro area was ranked #37 out of 80 (#1 = most expensive city for driving). Rankings are based on the average dollars spent on gas per year by two driver households. Criteria: cost of regular-grade gasoline; average miles driven per day; average number of gallons each driver uses and wastes in traffic congestion each day. *Sperling's BestPlaces, www.bestplaces.net, "Pain at the Pump," May 18, 2006*

Allen is located within the Dallas-Fort Worth-Arlington, TX Metropolitan Statistical Area and Dallas-Plano-Irving, TX Metropolitan Division.

Business Environment

CITY FINANCES

City Government Finances

Component	2004-2005 ($000)	2004-2005 ($ per capita)
Total Revenues	n/a	n/a
Total Expenditures	n/a	n/a
Debt Outstanding	n/a	n/a
Cash and Securities	n/a	n/a

Source: U.S Census Bureau, Government Finances 2004-2005

City Government Revenue by Source

Source	2004-2005 ($000)	2004-2005 ($ per capita)
General Revenue		
From Federal Government	n/a	n/a
From State Government	n/a	n/a
From Local Governments	n/a	n/a
Taxes		
Property	n/a	n/a
Sales	n/a	n/a
Personal Income	n/a	n/a
License	n/a	n/a
Charges	n/a	n/a
Liquor Store	n/a	n/a
Utility	n/a	n/a
Employee Retirement	n/a	n/a
Other	n/a	n/a

Source: U.S Census Bureau, Government Finances 2004-2005

City Government Expenditures by Function

Function	2004-2005 ($000)	2004-2005 ($ per capita)	2004-2005 (%)
General Expenditures			
Airports	n/a	n/a	n/a
Corrections	n/a	n/a	n/a
Education	n/a	n/a	n/a
Fire Protection	n/a	n/a	n/a
Governmental Administration	n/a	n/a	n/a
Health	n/a	n/a	n/a
Highways	n/a	n/a	n/a
Hospitals	n/a	n/a	n/a
Housing and Community Development	n/a	n/a	n/a
Interest on General Debt	n/a	n/a	n/a
Libraries	n/a	n/a	n/a
Parking	n/a	n/a	n/a
Parks and Recreation	n/a	n/a	n/a
Police Protection	n/a	n/a	n/a
Public Welfare	n/a	n/a	n/a
Sewerage	n/a	n/a	n/a
Solid Waste Management	n/a	n/a	n/a
Liquor Store	n/a	n/a	n/a
Utility	n/a	n/a	n/a
Employee Retirement	n/a	n/a	n/a
Other	n/a	n/a	n/a

Source: U.S Census Bureau, Government Finances 2004-2005

Municipal Bond Ratings

Area	Moody's
City	Aaa

Source: Mergent Bond Record, January 2008 (unless noted otherwise)

DEMOGRAPHICS

Population Growth

Area	1990 Census	2000 Census	2007 Estimate	2012 Projection	Population Growth (%) 1990-2000	Population Growth (%) 2000-2012
City	19,208	43,554	73,030	92,773	126.7	113.0
MSA[1]	3,989,294	5,161,544	6,007,731	6,587,538	29.4	27.6
U.S.	248,709,873	281,421,906	301,045,522	314,920,978	13.2	11.9

Note: (1) Metropolitan Statistical Area - see Appendix B for areas included
Source: Claritas, Inc.

Number of Households and Average Household Size

Area	2007 Estimate	2007 Average Household Size
City	23,954	3.05
MSA[1]	2,171,092	2.77
U.S.	113,668,003	2.65

Note: (1) Metropolitan Statistical Area - see Appendix B for areas included
Source: Claritas, Inc.

Race and Ethnicity

Area	White Alone[2]	Black Alone[2]	Asian Alone[2]	Other Race Alone[2]	Hispanic[3]
City	79.8	6.9	6.8	6.5	9.3
MSA[1]	65.6	14.0	4.6	15.8	26.4
U.S.	73.1	12.4	4.3	10.3	14.9

Note: Figures are 2007 estimates; (1) Metropolitan Statistical Area - see Appendix B for areas included (2) Alone is defined as not being in combination with one or more other races; (3) May be of any race.
Source: Claritas, Inc.

Ancestry

Area	German	Irish[2]	English	American	Italian	Polish	French[3]	Scottish
City	18.1	14.3	12.7	10.2	4.6	2.1	3.7	3.0
MSA[1]	10.0	8.1	8.2	7.8	2.1	1.2	2.1	1.7
U.S.	15.2	10.9	8.7	7.3	5.6	3.2	3.0	1.7

Note: Figures include multiple ancestry (e.g. if a person reported being Irish and Italian, they were included in both columns); (1) Metropolitan Statistical Area - see Appendix A for areas included; (2) Includes Celtic; (3) Includes Alsatian but excludes Basque
Source: Census 2000, Summary File 3

Foreign-Born Population

Area	Percent of Population Born in: Any Foreign Country	Europe	Asia	Africa	Oceania[2]	Canada	Mexico	Latin America[3]
City	7.3	1.3	2.6	0.6	0.1	0.9	1.1	0.8
MSA[1]	16.8	0.9	3.4	0.6	0.0	0.3	9.8	1.8
U.S.	11.1	1.7	2.9	0.3	0.1	0.3	3.3	2.5

Note: (1) Metropolitan Statistical Area - see Appendix A for areas included; (2) Includes Australia, New Zealand subregion, Melanesia, Micronesia, Polynesia, and Oceania n.e.c; (3) Includes Central America (excluding Mexico), South America, and the Caribbean.
Source: Census 2000, Summary File 3

Marriage Status

Area	Never Married	Now Married (excluding Separated)	Separated	Widowed	Divorced
City	18.0	72.2	0.9	1.6	7.4
MSA[1]	27.2	55.6	2.5	4.6	10.1
U.S.	27.1	54.4	2.2	6.6	9.7

Note: Figures are percentages and cover the population 15 years of age and older; (1) Metropolitan Statistical Area - see Appendix A for areas included
Source: Census 2000, Summary File 3

Age Distribution

Area	Percent of Population						
	Under Age 5	Age 5 to 17	Age 18 to 34	Age 35 to 49	Age 50 to 64	Age 65 to 79	80 Years and Over
City	10.6	24.1	23.0	30.5	8.9	2.3	0.5
MSA[1]	8.1	19.9	27.3	24.4	12.7	5.8	1.8
U.S.	6.8	18.9	23.7	23.5	14.8	9.2	3.2

Note: (1) Metropolitan Statistical Area - see Appendix A for areas included
Source: Census 2000, Summary File 3

Male/Female Ratio

Area	Males	Females	Males per 100 Females
City	36,601	36,429	100.5
MSA[1]	3,012,647	2,995,084	100.6
U.S.	148,320,305	152,725,217	97.1

Note: Figures are 2007 estimates; (1) Metropolitan Statistical Area - see Appendix B for areas included
Source: Claritas, Inc.

Religion

Area	Catholic	Southern Baptist	United Meth-odist	ELCA[1]	LDS[2]	Presby-terian Church USA	Jewish Est.	Muslim Est.
County	18.3	16.0	6.1	0.6	1.3	0.7	1.4	1.2
U.S.	22.0	7.1	3.7	1.8	1.5	1.1	2.2	0.6

Note: Figures are the number of adherents as a percentage of the total population; Adherents are defined as all members, including full members, their children and the estimated number of other participants who are not considered members (e.g. the baptized, those not confirmed, those regularly attending services, etc.); (1) Evangelical Lutheran Church in America; (2) The Church of Jesus Christ of Latter Day Saints
Source: Reprinted with permission from Religious Congregations and Membership in the United States 2000 (Nashville, Glenmary Research Center, 2002) Copyright Association of Statisticians of American Religious Bodies. All rights reserved.

ECONOMY

Gross Metropolitan Product

Area	2002	2003	2004	2005	2005 Rank[2]
MSA[1]	229.2	238.6	260.0	284.5	5

Note: Figures are in billions of dollars; (1) Dallas-Fort Worth-Arlington, TX Metropolitan Statistical Area - see Appendix A for areas included; (2) Rank ranges from 1 to 361
Source: The U.S. Conference of Mayors, "U.S. Metro Economies: GMP - The Engines of America's Growth," January 2007

Economic Growth

Area	1995 GMP	2005 GMP	Average Annual Growth Rate	Growth Rate Rank[2]
MSA[1]	143.0	284.5	7.1	35

Note: Figures are in billions of dollars; GMP = Gross Metropolitan Product; (1) Dallas-Fort Worth-Arlington, TX Metropolitan Statistical Area - see Appendix A for areas included; (2) Rank ranges from 1 to 361
Source: The U.S. Conference of Mayors, "U.S. Metro Economies: GMP - The Engines of America's Growth," January 2007

INCOME

Per Capita/Median/Average Income

Area	Per Capita ($)	Median Household ($)	Average Household ($)
City	34,198	90,467	104,107
MSA[1]	27,089	55,079	74,352
U.S.	25,495	49,280	66,670

Note: Figures are 2007 estimates; (1) Metropolitan Statistical Area - see Appendix B for areas included
Source: Claritas, Inc.

Household Income Distribution

Area	Percent of Households Earning							
	Under $15,000	$15,000 -24,999	$25,000 -34,999	$35,000 -49,999	$50,000 -74,999	$75,000 -99,000	$100,000 -149,999	$150,000 and up
City	2.2	3.3	4.9	8.9	18.3	19.9	27.1	15.3
MSA[1]	10.0	9.1	10.7	15.8	19.8	13.0	13.2	8.5
U.S.	13.1	10.9	11.2	15.6	19.5	11.9	11.3	6.6

Note: Figures are 2007 estimates; (1) Metropolitan Statistical Area - see Appendix B for areas included
Source: Claritas, Inc.

Poverty Rates by Age

Area	All Ages	Under 5 Years Old	5 to 17 Years Old	18 to 64 Years Old	65 Years and Over
City	3.0	0.3	0.9	1.8	0.1
MSA[1]	11.1	1.3	2.8	6.3	0.7
U.S.	12.4	1.2	3.0	6.9	1.2

Note: Figures are percent of population with income in 1999 below poverty level and only include population for whom poverty status is determined; (1) Metropolitan Statistical Area - see Appendix A for areas included
Source: Census 2000, Summary File 3

Personal Bankruptcy Filing Rate

Area	2004	2005	2006
Collin County	5.58	7.92	1.76
U.S.	5.31	6.82	2.00

Note: Numbers are per 1,000 population and include Chapter 7 and Chapter 13 filings
Source: Federal Deposit Insurance Corporation (FDIC), Regional Economic Conditions (RECON), 8/23/2007

EMPLOYMENT

Labor Force and Employment

Area	Civilian Labor Force			Workers Employed		
	Dec. 2006	Dec. 2007	% Chg.	Dec. 2006	Dec. 2007	% Chg.
City	39,657	40,015	0.9	38,247	38,503	0.7
MD[1]	2,068,085	2,086,426	0.9	1,984,055	1,997,359	0.7
U.S.	152,571,000	153,705,000	0.7	146,081,000	146,334,000	0.2

Note: Data is not seasonally adjusted and covers workers 16 years of age and older; (1) Metropolitan Division - see Appendix B for areas included
Source: Bureau of Labor Statistics, http://stats.bls.gov

Unemployment Rate

Area	2007											
	Jan.	Feb.	Mar.	Apr.	May	Jun.	Jul.	Aug.	Sep.	Oct.	Nov.	Dec.
City	3.9	3.9	3.6	3.5	3.6	3.9	3.9	3.7	3.7	3.6	3.7	3.8
MD[1]	4.7	4.5	4.1	4.0	4.0	4.6	4.6	4.3	4.4	4.1	4.2	4.3
U.S.	5.0	4.9	4.5	4.3	4.3	4.7	4.9	4.6	4.5	4.4	4.5	4.8

Note: Data is not seasonally adjusted and covers workers 16 years of age and older; All figures are percentages; (1) Metropolitan Division - see Appendix B for areas included
Source: Bureau of Labor Statistics, http://stats.bls.gov

Employment by Occupation

Occupation Classification	City (%)	MSA[1] (%)	U.S. (%)
Sales and Office	27.3	28.7	26.7
Professional and Related	28.8	20.4	20.2
Service	8.0	12.3	14.9
Production, Transportation, and Material Moving	4.8	11.8	14.6
Management, Business, and Financial	25.6	16.8	13.5
Construction, Extraction, and Maintenance	5.3	9.9	9.4
Farming, Forestry, and Fishing	0.1	0.2	0.7

Note: Figures cover employed civilians 16 years of age and older; (1) Metropolitan Statistical Area - see Appendix A for areas included
Source: Census 2000, Summary File 3

Employment by Industry

Sector	MSA[1] Number of Employees	MSA[1] Percent of Total	U.S. Percent of Total
Government	261,800	12.4	16.3
Education and Health Services	225,600	10.7	13.4
Professional and Business Services	339,800	16.1	13.1
Retail Trade	221,000	10.5	11.6
Manufacturing	198,400	9.4	9.9
Leisure and Hospitality	193,100	9.2	9.6
Financial Activities	186,000	8.8	5.9
Construction	n/a	n/a	5.3
Wholesale Trade	130,600	6.2	4.4
Other Services	75,400	3.6	3.9
Transportation and Utilities	78,100	3.7	3.7
Information	72,600	3.4	2.2
Natural Resources and Mining	n/a	n/a	0.5

Note: Figures cover non-farm employment as of December 2007 and are not seasonally adjusted; (1) Metropolitan Statistical Area - see Appendix B for areas included; n/a not available
Source: Bureau of Labor Statistics, http://stats.bls.gov

Average Wages

Occupation	$/Hr.	Occupation	$/Hr.
Accountants and Auditors	31.56	Maids and Housekeeping Cleaners	8.23
Automotive Mechanics	17.72	Maintenance and Repair Workers	15.14
Bookkeepers	16.06	Marketing Managers	60.78
Carpenters	16.08	Nuclear Medicine Technologists	30.51
Cashiers	8.45	Nurses, Licensed Practical	19.58
Clerks, General Office	11.71	Nurses, Registered	30.37
Clerks, Receptionists/Information	12.41	Nursing Aides/Orderlies/Attendants	11.11
Clerks, Shipping/Receiving	12.87	Packers and Packagers, Hand	9.24
Computer Programmers	38.32	Physical Therapists	39.04
Computer Support Specialists	22.07	Postal Service Mail Carriers	21.40
Computer Systems Analysts	39.12	Real Estate Brokers	45.42
Cooks, Restaurant	10.19	Retail Salespersons	11.71
Dentists	n/a	Sales Reps., Exc. Tech./Scientific	29.44
Electrical Engineers	44.17	Sales Reps., Tech./Scientific	35.60
Electricians	19.29	Secretaries, Exc. Legal/Med./Exec.	13.40
Financial Managers	55.42	Security Guards	12.88
First-Line Supervisors/Mgrs., Sales	19.02	Surgeons	n/a
Food Preparation Workers	8.57	Teacher Assistants	9.40
General and Operations Managers	56.15	Teachers, Elementary School	22.00
Hairdressers/Cosmetologists	10.95	Teachers, Secondary School	21.40
Internists	90.82	Telemarketers	13.10
Janitors and Cleaners	9.02	Truck Drivers, Heavy/Tractor-Trailer	19.27
Landscaping/Groundskeeping Workers	10.25	Truck Drivers, Light/Delivery Svcs.	14.20
Lawyers	65.73	Waiters and Waitresses	8.06

Note: Wage data covers the Dallas-Plano-Irving, TX Metropolitan Division - see Appendix B for areas included. Hourly wages for elementary/secondary school teachers and teacher assistants were calculated by the editors from annual wage data assuming a 40 hour work week; n/a not available.
Source: Bureau of Labor Statistics, May 2007 Metro Area Occupational Employment and Wage Estimates

RESIDENTIAL REAL ESTATE

Building Permits

Area	Single-Family 2006	Single-Family 2007p	Single-Family Pct. Chg.	Multi-Family 2006	Multi-Family 2007p	Multi-Family Pct. Chg.	Total 2006	Total 2007p	Total Pct. Chg.
City	1,248	879	-29.6	348	184	-47.1	1,596	1,063	-33.4
U.S.	1,378,200	973,300	-29.4	460,700	407,200	-11.6	1,838,900	1,380,500	-24.9

Note: (p) preliminary; figures cover and represent new, privately-owned housing units authorized (unadjusted data); All permit data are based on estimates with imputation; U.S. figures are based on the new 20,000-place series.
Source: U.S. Census Bureau, Manufacturing, Mining, and Construction Statistics

Homeownership and Housing Vacancies

Area	Homeownership Rate[2] (%)			Rental Vacancy Rate[3] (%)			Homeowner Vacancy Rate[4] (%)		
	2005	2006	2007	2005	2006	2007	2005	2006	2007
MSA[1]	62.3	60.7	60.9	13.6	11.7	11.0	2.2	2.3	2.5
U.S.	68.9	68.8	68.1	9.8	9.8	9.7	1.9	2.4	2.7

Note: (1) Metropolitan Statistical Area - see Appendix B for areas included; (2) The proportion of households that are owners; (3) The proportion of the rental inventory that is vacant for rent; (4) The proportion of the homeowner inventory that is vacant for sale; n/a not available
Source: U.S. Census Bureau, Housing Vacancies and Homeownership Annual Statistics: 2007

TAXES

State Corporate Income Tax Rates

State	Rates and Tax Brackets
Texas	1.0%

Note: Tax rates as of January 1, 2008; Texas's 1% franchise tax is a gross receipts tax paid by most taxable entities. Retailers pay 0.5%.
Source: Tax Foundation, www.taxfoundation.org

State Individual Income Tax Rates

State	Federal Deductibility	Marginal Rates (%)	Standard Deduction ($)		Personal Exemptions ($)[1]	
			Single	Joint	Single	Dependents
Texas	No	None	n/a	n/a	n/a	n/a

Note: Tax rates as of January 1, 2008; Local- and county-level taxes are not included; n/a not applicable; (1) Married joint filers generally receive double the single exemption
Source: Tax Foundation, www.taxfoundation.org

Various State and Local Tax Rates

State and Local Sales and Use (%)	State Sales and Use (%)	Gasoline[1,2] ($/gal.)	Cigarette ($/pack)	Spirits ($/gal.)	Table Wine ($/gal.)	Beer ($/gal.)
8.25	6.25 (i)	0.20	1.41	2.40	0.204	0.19

Note: Tax rates as of January 1, 2008; (1) In addition to the 18.4 cpg Federal gasoline tax; (2) Rates may include additional state sales taxes, environmental protection and storage fees/taxes, and local taxes. When necessary, the volume-weighted average of all local taxes is used to approximate the typical statewide rate including local tax; (i) Texas has a GRT that is levied in addition to its 6.25% sales tax. It is called the franchise tax and the rate is 1% (.5% for retailers).
Source: Tax Foundation, www.taxfoundation.org; Original research

State Tax Burdens

Area	Combined State and Local Tax Burden		Combined Federal, State and Local Tax Burden	
	Percent	Rank	Percent	Rank
Texas	9.3	43	29.8	41
U.S. Average	11.0	-	32.7	-

Note: Figures cover 2007 and measure taxes as a percentage of income
Source: Tax Foundation, www.taxfoundation.org

State Business Tax Climate Index Rankings

State	Overall Rank	Corporate Tax Index Rank	Individual Income Tax Index Rank	Sales Tax Index Rank	Unemployment Insurance Tax Index Rank	Property Tax Index Rank
Texas	8	47	7	28	14	27

Note: Rankings range from 1 to 50 where 1 is best. Rankings do not average across to Overall Rank. States without a given tax are given a ranking of 1.
Source: Tax Foundation, State Business Tax Climate Index 2008

TRANSPORTATION

Means of Transportation to Work

Area	Car/Truck/Van		Public Transportation			Bicycle	Walked	Other Means	Worked at Home
	Drove Alone	Car-pooled	Bus	Subway	Railroad				
City	86.1	7.7	1.0	0.0	0.0	0.0	0.5	0.3	4.3
MSA[1]	77.6	14.3	2.1	0.1	0.1	0.1	1.5	1.0	3.1
U.S.	75.7	12.2	2.5	1.5	0.5	0.4	2.9	1.0	3.3

Note: Figures are percentages and cover workers 16 years of age and older;
(1) Metropolitan Statistical Area - see Appendix A for areas included
Source: Census 2000, Summary File 3

Travel Time to Work

Area	Less Than 15 Minutes	15 to 29 Minutes	30 to 44 Minutes	45 to 59 Minutes	60 Minutes or More
City	19.8	32.0	25.1	13.3	9.8
MSA[1]	22.0	35.0	24.7	10.4	7.9
U.S.	29.4	36.1	19.1	7.4	8.0

Note: Figures are percentages and include workers 16 years old and over; (1) Metropolitan Statistical Area - see Appendix A for areas included
Source: Census 2000, Summary File 3

Travel Time Index

Area	1982	1995	2004	2005
Urban Area[1]	1.05	1.16	1.31	1.35
Average[2]	1.11	1.22	1.29	1.30

Note: Travel Time Index - The ratio of travel time in the peak period to the travel time at free-flow conditions. A value of 1.35 indicates a 20-minute free-flow trip takes 27 minutes in the peak. Free-flow speeds (60 mph on freeways and 35 mph on principal arterials) are used as the comparison threshold; (1) Covers the Dallas-Fort Worth-Arlington, TX urban area; (2) average of 85 urban areas
Source: Texas Transportation Institute, The 2007 Urban Mobility Report, September 2007

Living Environment

COST OF LIVING

Cost of Living Index

Composite Index	Groceries	Housing	Utilities	Trans-portation	Health Care	Misc. Goods/ Services
91.5	99.0	72.3	98.9	103.5	101.6	97.5

Note: U.S. = 100; Figures cover the Dallas TX urban area.
Source: The Council for Community and Economic Research (formerly ACCRA), Cost of Living Index, 2007

Grocery Prices

Area[1]	T-Bone Steak ($/pound)	Frying Chicken ($/pound)	Whole Milk ($/half gal.)	Eggs ($/dozen)	Orange Juice ($/64 oz.)	Coffee ($/11.5 oz.)
City[2]	8.81	1.24	2.26	1.40	3.17	3.43
Avg.	8.93	1.12	2.13	1.52	3.26	3.31
Min.	5.88	0.71	1.33	0.83	2.30	2.20
Max.	12.80	2.07	3.43	3.54	5.79	6.20

Note: (1) Values for the local area are compared with the average, minimum and maximum values for all 331 areas in the Cost of Living Index report; (2) Figures cover the Dallas TX urban area; **T-Bone Steak** *(price per pound);* **Frying Chicken** *(price per pound, whole fryer);* **Whole Milk** *(half gallon carton);* **Eggs** *(price per dozen, Grade A, large);* **Orange Juice** *(64 oz. Tropicana or Florida Natural);* **Coffee** *(11.5 oz. can, vacuum-packed, Maxwell House, Hills Bros, or Folgers).*
Source: The Council for Community and Economic Research (formerly ACCRA), Cost of Living Index, 2007

Housing and Utility Costs

Area[1]	New Home Price ($)	Apartment Rent ($/month)	All Electric ($/month)	Part Electric ($/month)	Other Energy ($/month)	Telephone ($/month)
City[2]	213,140	715	-	107.07	50.72	26.67
Avg.	309,605	782	146.13	78.67	90.16	26.14
Min.	189,877	n/a	82.03	37.41	33.15	17.08
Max.	1,202,800	3,481	271.14	150.60	257.67	37.45

Note: (1) Values for the local area are compared with the average, minimum and maximum values for all 331 areas in the Cost of Living Index report; (2) Figures cover the Dallas TX urban area; **New Home Price** *(2,400 sf living area, 8,000 sf lot, in urban area with full utilities);* **Apartment Rent** *(950 sf 2 bedroom/1.5 or 2 bath, unfurnished, excluding all utilities except water);* **All Electric** *(average monthly cost for an all-electric home);* **Part Electric** *(average monthly cost for a part-electric home);* **Other Energy** *(average monthly cost for natural gas, fuel oil, coal, wood, and any other forms of energy except electricity);* **Telephone** *(price includes basic monthly rate for a private residential line plus additional local usage charges incurred by a family of four).*
Source: The Council for Community and Economic Research (formerly ACCRA), Cost of Living Index, 2007

Health Care, Transportation, and Other Costs

Area[1]	Doctor ($/visit)	Dentist ($/visit)	Optometrist ($/visit)	Gasoline ($/gallon)	Beauty Salon ($/visit)	Men's Shirt ($)
City[2]	74.44	77.38	77.68	2.52	26.77	22.20
Avg.	79.48	71.93	79.55	2.64	29.52	25.77
Min.	52.08	44.80	43.95	2.19	15.58	16.19
Max.	148.44	126.27	158.83	3.48	60.62	48.53

Note: (1) Values for the local area are compared with the average, minimum and maximum values for all 331 areas in the Cost of Living Index report; (2) Figures cover the Dallas TX urban area; **Doctor** *(general practitioners routine exam of an established patient);* **Dentist** *(adult teeth cleaning and periodic oral examination);* **Optometrist** *(full vision eye exam for established adult patient);* **Gasoline** *(one gallon regular unleaded, national brand, including all taxes, cash price at self-service pump if available);* **Beauty Salon** *(woman's shampoo, trim, and blow-dry);* **Men's Shirt** *(cotton/polyester dress shirt, pinpoint weave, long sleeves).*
Source: The Council for Community and Economic Research (formerly ACCRA), Cost of Living Index, 2007

HOUSING

House Price Index (HPI)

Area	National Ranking[2]	Quarterly Change (%)	One-Year Change (%)	Five-Year Change (%)
MD[1]	97	0.16	2.95	15.82
U.S.[3]	-	0.10	0.84	41.37

Note: The HPI is a weighted repeat sales index. It measures average price changes in repeat sales or refinancings on the same properties. This information is obtained by reviewing repeat mortgage transactions on single-family properties whose mortgages have been purchased or securitized by Fannie Mae or Freddie Mac in January 1975; (1) Metropolitan Division - see Appendix B for areas included; (2) Rankings are based on annual percentage change for all metro areas containing at least 15,000 transactions over the last 10 years and ranges from 1 to 291; (3) figures based on a weighted average of Census Division estimates; all figures are for the period ending December 31, 2007
Source: Office of Federal Housing Enterprise Oversight, House Price Index, February 26, 2008

House Price Valuations

Area	Q1 2000	Q1 2001	Q1 2002	Q1 2003	Q1 2004	Q1 2005	Q1 2006	Q1 2007	Q1 2008
MD[1]	-22.2	-21.3	-17.8	-16.4	-19.3	-23.0	-23.6	-26.9	-30.6

Note: Figures show the percentage of over- or under-valuation of single family homes relative to statistically normal house values (e.g. a value of 23.6 indicates that house values are 23.6% overvalued). Statistically normal house values are based on house prices, interest rates, household incomes, population densities, and any historical premiums or discounts metropolitan areas have exhibited over time; (1) Figures cover the Metropolitan Division - see Appendix B for areas included
Source: Global Insight/National City Corporation, House Prices in America, May 2008

Median Home Prices

Area	2005	2006	2007[r]	Percent Change 2006 to 2007
MSA[1]	147.6	149.5	150.9	0.9
U.S. Average	219.0	221.9	217.9	-1.8

Note: Figures are median sales prices of existing single-family homes in thousands of dollars; (r) revised; n/a not available; (1) Metropolitan Statistical Area - see Appendix B for areas included
Source: National Association of Realtors, Metropolitan Area Prices, 1st Quarter 2008

Housing: Year Structure Built

Area	1990 -2000	1980 -1989	1970 -1979	1960 -1969	1950 -1959	1940 -1949	Before 1940	Median Year
City	58.3	24.0	14.0	2.5	0.9	0.2	0.0	1993
MSA[1]	23.9	24.7	20.2	13.7	9.8	4.0	3.7	1979
U.S.	17.0	15.8	18.5	13.7	12.7	7.3	15.0	1971

Note: Figures are percentages; (1) Metropolitan Statistical Area - see Appendix A for areas included
Source: Census 2000, Summary File 3

HEALTH

Health Risk Data

Category	Area[1] (%)	U.S. (%)
Adults who have been told they have high blood pressure[3]	22.2	25.5
Adults who have been told they have high blood cholesterol[3]	37.6	35.6
Adults who have been told they have diabetes[2]	5.3	7.5
Adults who have been told they have arthritis[3]	19.5	27.0
Adults who have been told they currently have asthma	4.5	8.5
Adults who are current smokers	11.5	20.1
Adults who are heavy drinkers[4]	5.3	4.9
Adults who are overweight (BMI 25.0 - 29.9)	35.7	36.5
Adults who are obese (BMI 30.0 - 99.8)	21.4	25.1

Note: Data as of 2006 unless otherwise noted; (1) Figures cover the Metropolitan Division - see Appendix B for areas included; (2) Figures do not include pregnancy-related diabetes, pre-diabetes or borderline diabetes; (3) 2005 data; (4) Heavy drinkers are classified as adult men having more than two drinks per day or adult women having more than one drink per day
Source: Centers for Disease Control and Prevention, Behaviorial Risk Factor Surveillance System, SMART: Selected Metropolitan/Micropolitan Area Risk Trends, 2005, 2006

Mortality Rates for the Top 10 Causes of Death in the U.S.

ICD-10[a] Sub-Chapter	ICD-10[a] Code	Age-Adjusted Mortality Rate[1] per 100,000 population	
		County[2]	U.S.
Malignant neoplasms	C00-C97	153.6	186.5
Ischaemic heart diseases	I20-I25	124.5	152.3
Other forms of heart disease	I30-I51	36.4	51.5
Cerebrovascular diseases	I60-I69	42.0	50.0
Chronic lower respiratory diseases	J40-J47	33.6	42.6
Diabetes mellitus	E10-E14	15.8	24.8
Other degenerative diseases of the nervous system	G30-G31	38.8	22.6
Other external causes of accidental injury	W00-X59	21.7	21.4
Influenza and pneumonia	J10-J18	19.1	20.7
Hypertensive diseases	I10-I13	14.6	18.2

Note: (a) ICD-10 = International Classification of Diseases 10th Revision; (1) Mortality rates are a three year average covering 2003-2005; (2) Figures cover Collin County
Source: Centers for Disease Control and Prevention, National Center for Health Statistics. Compressed Mortality File 1999-2004. CDC WONDER On-line Database, compiled from Compressed Mortality File 1999-2005 Series 20 No. 2K, 2008.

Mortality Rates for Selected Causes of Death

ICD-10[a] Sub-Chapter	ICD-10[a] Code	Age-Adjusted Mortality Rate[1] per 100,000 population	
		County[2]	U.S.
Assault	X85-Y09	2.6	5.9
Human immunodeficiency virus (HIV) disease	B20-B24	*0.9	4.5
Intentional self-harm	X60-X84	8.6	10.8
Malnutrition	E40-E46	*1.3	1.0
Obesity and other hyperalimentation	E65-E68	*0.6	1.4
Organic, including symptomatic, mental disorders	F01-F09	28.1	16.8
Transport accidents	V01-V99	10.3	16.1
Viral hepatitis	B15-B19	*1.0	1.8

Note: (a) ICD-10 = International Classification of Diseases 10th Revision; (1) Mortality rates are a three year average covering 2003-2005; (2) Figures cover Collin County; (*) Unreliable data as per CDC
Source: Centers for Disease Control and Prevention, National Center for Health Statistics. Compressed Mortality File 1999-2004. CDC WONDER On-line Database, compiled from Compressed Mortality File 1999-2005 Series 20 No. 2K, 2008.

Distribution of Physicians[1]

Area	Total	Family/ General Practice	Specialties	
			Medical	Surgical
Collin County (number)	1,264	321	471	269
Collin County (rate per 10,000 pop.)	19.2	4.9	7.1	4.1
U.S. (rate per 10,000 pop.)	17.7	4.6	6.9	4.3

Note: Data as of 2005; (1) Includes all non-federal, patient-care, office-based MDs
Source: Area Resource File (ARF). June 2007. U.S. Department of Health and Human Services, Health Resources and Services Administration, Bureau of Health Professions, Rockville, MD.

Hospitals

Allen has the following hospitals: 1 general medical and surgical.
AHA Guide to the Healthcare Field 2008

According to *U.S. News,* the Dallas-Fort Worth-Arlington, TX metro area is home to six of the best hospitals in the U.S.: **Baylor Institute for Rehabilitation**; **Baylor University Medical Center**; **Children's Medical Center Dallas**; **Parkland Memorial Hospital**; **Presbyterian Hospital**; **University of Texas Southwestern Medical Center**. *U.S. News Online, "America's Best Hospitals 2007"*

EDUCATION

Public School District Statistics

District Name	Schls	Pupils	Pupil/ Teacher Ratio	Minority Pupils[1] (%)	Free Lunch Eligible[2] (%)	IEP[3] (%)
Allen ISD	20	15,961	15.6	29.5	9.3	11.3
Anna ISD	5	1,533	14.4	27.3	23.0	11.9
Lovejoy ISD	6	1,316	15.9	13.0	2.1	7.1
Plano ISD	82	53,238	14.0	43.2	16.0	11.6

Note: Table includes regular local school districts with 2,000 or more students; (1) Percentage of students that are not white, non-Hispanic; (2) Percentage of students that are eligible for the free lunch program; (3) Percentage of students that have an Individualized Education Program.
Source: U.S. Department of Education, National Center for Education Statistics, Common Core of Data, Local Education Agency (School District) Universe Survey: School Year 2005-2006; U.S. Department of Education, National Center for Education Statistics, Common Core of Data, Public Elementary/Secondary School Universe Survey: School Year 2005-2006

Top Public High Schools

High School Name	Index[1]	Rank[1]	Subsidized Lunch (%)[2]	E&E (%)[3]
Allen **	1.420	983	9.0	23.5

Note: (1) Public schools are ranked according to a ratio that is the number of Advanced Placement, International Baccalaureate, and/or Cambridge tests taken by all students at a school in 2007 divided by the number of graduating seniors. All of the schools on the list have an index of at least 1.000; they are in the top five percent of public schools measured this way. The rankings range from 1 to 1,422; (2) Percentage of students receiving federally subsidized meals; (3) E & E stands for equity and excellence percentage: the portion of all graduating seniors at a school that had at least one passing grade on one AP or IB test; (**) Gave both IB and AP tests. AP and IB participation are indicators of a school's efforts to get students to excel and prepare for college.
Source: Newsweek Online, "Top High Schools 2008"

Highest Level of Education

Area	Less than H.S.	H.S. Diploma	Some College, No Deg.	Associate Degree	Bachelors Degree	Masters Degree	Profess. School Degree	Doctorate Degree
City	3.9	13.3	24.5	7.7	38.0	10.5	1.2	0.9
MSA[1]	19.2	22.3	23.5	5.7	20.3	6.4	1.7	0.8
U.S.	19.4	28.4	21.2	6.4	15.7	5.9	2.0	1.0

Note: Figures are 2007 estimated percentages and cover persons age 25 and over; (1) Metropolitan Statistical Area - see Appendix B for areas included
Source: Claritas, Inc.

Educational Attainment by Race

Area	High School Graduate (%)					Bachelor's Degree (%)				
	Total	White	Black	Asian	Hisp.[2]	Total	White	Black	Asian	Hisp.[2]
City	95.6	96.4	94.6	90.7	80.2	47.5	47.3	50.9	59.8	32.3
MSA[1]	79.4	84.4	78.9	83.4	41.5	30.0	34.0	18.5	52.2	8.7
U.S.	80.4	83.6	72.3	80.4	52.4	24.4	26.1	14.3	44.1	10.4

Note: Figures shown cover persons 25 years old and over; (1) Metropolitan Statistical Area - see Appendix A for areas included; (2) people of Hispanic origin can be of any race
Source: Census 2000, Summary File 3

School Enrollment by Type

Area	Grades KG to 8				Grades 9 to 12			
	Public		Private		Public		Private	
	Enrollment	%	Enrollment	%	Enrollment	%	Enrollment	%
City	7,056	93.4	498	6.6	2,736	96.6	95	3.4
MSA[1]	456,971	90.7	46,953	9.3	181,249	92.2	15,405	7.8
U.S.	33,526,011	88.7	4,285,121	11.3	14,848,628	90.6	1,532,323	9.4

Note: Figures shown cover persons 3 years old and over; (1) Metropolitan Statistical Area - see Appendix A for areas included
Source: Census 2000, Summary File 3

School Enrollment by Race

Area	Grades KG to 8 (%)				Grades 9 to 12 (%)			
	White	Black	Asian	Hisp.[1]	White	Black	Asian	Hisp.[1]
City	86.8	3.9	3.0	8.3	86.1	7.1	1.1	7.3
MSA[2]	60.7	18.0	3.6	28.9	61.2	18.7	4.0	25.8
U.S.	68.5	15.5	3.3	16.8	68.8	15.5	3.8	15.7

Note: Figures shown cover persons 3 years old and over; (1) people of Hispanic origin can be of any race; (2) Metropolitan Statistical Area - see Appendix A for areas included
Source: Census 2000, Summary File 3

Average Salaries of Public School Classroom Teachers

District	2005-06		2006-07		Percent Change 2005-06 to 2006-07
	Dollars	Rank[1]	Dollars	Rank[1]	
Texas	41,744	35	44,897	30	7.55
U.S. Average	49,026	-	50,816	-	3.65

Note: (1) State rank ranges from 1 to 51.
Source: National Education Association, Rankings & Estimates: Rankings of the States 2006 and Estimates of School Statistics 2007, December 2007

Higher Education

Four-Year Colleges			Two-Year Colleges			Medical Schools[1]	Law Schools[2]	Voc/ Tech[3]
Public	Private Non-profit	Private For-profit	Public	Private Non-profit	Private For-profit			
0	0	0	0	0	0	0	0	0

Note: Figures cover institutions located within the city limits; (1) includes schools accredited by the Liaison Committee on Medical Education and the American Osteopathic Association; (2) includes American Bar Association-accredited law schools; (3) includes all schools with programs that are less than 2 years.
Source: National Center for Education Statistics, The Integrated Postsecondary Education System (IPEDS) Peer Analysis System, 2007; www.usnews.com, Law and Medical School Directories, 2009

PRESIDENTIAL ELECTION

2004 Presidential Election Results

Area	Bush	Kerry	Nader	Other
Collin County	71.2	28.1	0.1	0.6
U.S.	50.7	48.3	0.4	0.6

Note: Results are percentages and may not add to 100% due to rounding
Source: Dave Leip's Atlas of U.S. Presidential Elections, www.uselectionatlas.org

EMPLOYERS

Major Employers

Company Name	Industry	Type of Site
Associates Corp North America	Personal credit institutions	Headquarters
Associates First Capital Corp	Mortgage bankers and correspondents	Headquarters
Baylor University Medical Ctr	General medical and surgical hospitals	Headquarters
Dallas Cnty Commissioners Crt	Executive offices	Branch
EDS	Data processing and preparation	Headquarters
JC Penney	Department stores	Headquarters
Lockheed Martin	Aircraft	Branch
MCI	Telephone communication, except radio	Branch
National Elec Contrs Assn	Insurance agents, brokers, and service	Single
Odyssey Healthcare Inc	Skilled nursing care facilities	Headquarters
Parkland Health & Hospital Sys	General medical and surgical hospitals	Headquarters
Raytheon	Radio and t.v. communications equipment	Single
Romanos Macaroni Grill	Eating places	Single
SFG Management Ltd Lblty Co	Fluid milk	Single
Southwestern Medical School	Accident and health insurance	Headquarters
Teaching Assistance Office	Colleges and universities	Branch
Texas Instruments	Semiconductors and related devices	Headquarters
UPS	Courier services, except by air	Branch
Verizon	Business consulting, nec	Branch
Verizon	Telephone communication, except radio	Branch

Note: Companies shown are located within the Dallas metropolitan area; nec = not elsewhere classified.
Source: www.zapdata.com, May 2008

PUBLIC SAFETY

Crime Rate

Area	All Crimes	Violent Crimes				Property Crimes		
		Murder	Forcible Rape	Robbery	Aggrav. Assault	Burglary	Larceny -Theft	Motor Vehicle Theft
City	2,712.7	0.0	9.8	22.5	50.6	467.8	2,062.3	99.7
Metro[1]	4,891.4	4.6	25.7	78.1	270.1	850.6	3,288.2	374.1
U.S.	3,808.1	5.7	30.9	149.4	287.5	729.4	2,206.8	398.4

Note: Figures are crimes per 100,000 population; (1) Metropolitan Statistical Area - see Appendix B for areas included
Source: FBI Uniform Crime Reports, 2006

Hate Crimes

Area	Number of Quarters Reported	Bias Motivation				
		Race	Religion	Sexual Orientation	Ethnicity	Disability
City	4	0	0	0	0	0

Source: Federal Bureau of Investigation, Hate Crime Statistics 2006

RECREATION

Culture

Dance[1]	Theatre[1]	Instrumental Music[1]	Vocal Music[1]	Series/ Festivals	Museums	Zoos and Aquariums[2]
0	0	0	0	0	0	0

Note: (1) Number of professional perfoming groups; (2) AZA-accredited
Source: The Grey House Performing Arts Directory, 2007; Official Museum Directory, 2008; Association of Zoos & Aquariums, AZA Member Zoos & Aquariums, June 2008

Professional Sports Teams

Team Name	League
Texas Rangers	Major League Baseball (MLB)
FC Dallas	Major League Soccer (MLS)
Dallas Mavericks	National Basketball Association (NBA)
Dallas Cowboys	National Football League (NFL)
Dallas Stars	National Hockey League (NHL)

Note: Includes teams located in the Dallas-Fort Worth metro area.
Source: Original research

MEDIA

Newspapers

Name	News Focus	Frequency	Circulation
Allen American	Community	Twice a week	5,200

Note: Includes newspapers with offices located in the city
Source: MediaContactsPro, March 2008

Television Stations

Name	Ch.	Network(s)	Type	Ownership
KDTN	2	PBS	Public	North Texas Public Broadcasting Inc.
KDFW	4	Fox	Commercial	Fox Television Stations Inc.
KXAS	5	NBC	Commercial	General Electric Corporation
WFAA	8	ABC	Commercial	Belo Corporation
KTVT	11	CBS	Commercial	CBS
KERA	13	PBS	Public	North Texas Public Broadcasting Inc.
KSST	18	n/a	Commercial	Hopkins County Broadcasting Inc.
KTXA	21	UPN	Commercial	CBS
KUVN	23	Univision	Commercial	Perenchio Television Inc.
KDFI	27	Fox	Commercial	Fox Television Stations Inc.
KMPX	29	n/a	Non-comm.	n/a
KDAF	33	WBN	Commercial	Tribune Broadcasting Company
KXTX	39	Telemundo	Commercial	Telemundo Group Inc.
KTAQ	47	n/a	Commercial	Michael Simons
KSTR	49	Univision	Commercial	Univision Television Group
KFWD	52	n/a	Commercial	n/a
KDTX	58	n/a	Non-comm.	Trinity Broadcasting Network
KPXD	68	Pax	Commercial	Paxson Communications Corporation

Note: Stations included cover the Dallas-Fort Worth DMA (Designated Market Area)
BurrellesLuce, MediaContacts Online, January 2007

Major AM Radio Stations

Call Letters	Freq. (kHz)	Station Type	Target Audience	Station Format	Music Format
KLIF	570	Commercial	General/Men	News/Talk	n/a
KMKI	620	n/a	General	Music	n/a
KSKY	660	n/a	General/Hisp/Rel	Music/Sports/Talk	n/a
KKDA	730	Commercial	General	Music/News	Rhythm & Blues
KAAM	770	Commercial	General	Music	Adult Standards
WBAP	820	Commercial	General	Educational/News/Talk	n/a
KFJZ	870	Commercial	General/Hispanic	Music/News/Sports/Talk	Latin
KKLF	950	n/a	General	News/Talk	n/a
KHVN	970	n/a	Christian/General	Music	n/a
KGGR	1040	n/a	Black/General/Rel	Talk	n/a
KRLD	1080	n/a	General	n/a	n/a
KBIS	1150	n/a	General/Hispanic	Music/News/Talk	n/a
KSST	1230	n/a	General	Music/News	Easy Listening
KPJC	1250	College	General	Music/News	Jazz
KTCK	1310	Commercial	General	Talk	n/a
KAND	1340	Commercial	General	Music/News	Country
KAHZ	1360	n/a	General/Hispanic	Ed/News/Sports/Talk	n/a
KBEC	1390	Commercial	General	Music	Country
KGVL	1400	n/a	General	Music/News/Sports	n/a
KLVQ	1410	n/a	General/Religious	Music	n/a
KFYN	1420	n/a	General	Music/News/Sports	n/a
KTNO	1440	Commercial	Hispanic/Religious	Music/Talk	Gospel
KNET	1450	n/a	General	Music	n/a
KTFW	1460	Commercial	General/Hispanic	n/a	n/a
KPLT	1490	Commercial	General	Music/News/Sports/Talk	Gospel
KSTV	1510	Commercial	General/Hispanic	Music	Top 40
KZMP	1540	n/a	General/Hispanic	Music	n/a
KCOM	1550	Commercial	General/Hispanic	Music	Country
KTBK	1700	Commercial	General	Sports/Talk	n/a

Note: Stations included cover the Dallas-Fort Worth DMA (Designated Market Area); n/a not available
Source: BurrellesLuce, MediaContacts Online, January 2007

Major FM Radio Stations

Call Letters	Freq. (mHz)	Station Type	Target Audience	Station Format	Music Format
KNTU	88.1	College	General	Educational/Music/News	n/a
KEOM	88.5	n/a	General	Ed/Music/News/Sports	n/a
KETR	88.9	College	General	Music/Sports	n/a
KNON	89.3	Non-Comm	Black/Hispanic	Ed/Music/News/Talk	Album Rock
KERA	90.1	Public	General	Music/Talk	Folk
KCBI	90.9	n/a	General/Religious	Music/News	n/a
KVTT	91.7	n/a	General/Religious	Educational/Talk	n/a
KZPS	92.5	n/a	General	Music/News/Talk	n/a
KSTV	93.1	Commercial	General	Music/News	Country
KDBN	93.3	Commercial	General	Music/Talk	Classic Rock
KLNO	94.1	Commercial	General/Hispanic	Music	Latin
KLTY	94.9	Commercial	General/Religious	Music/News/Talk	Christian
KZZA	95.1	Commercial	General	Music	Latin
KSCS	96.3	Commercial	General	Music/News/Talk	Country
KEGL	97.1	Commercial	General	Music/News/Sports	Modern Rock
KBFB	97.9	Commercial	General	Music	Urban Contemp.
KYYK	98.3	n/a	General	Music	n/a
KLUV	98.7	Commercial	General	Music/News/Talk	Oldies
KHCK	99.1	Commercial	General/Hispanic	Music	Latin
KPLX	99.5	Commercial	General	Music	Country
WRR	101.1	Commercial	General	Music/News/Talk	Classical
KZMP	101.7	n/a	General/Hispanic	Music	n/a
KBUS	101.9	Commercial	General	Music/News	Classic Rock
KDGE	102.1	Commercial	Young Adult	Music/News/Talk	Alternative
KDMX	102.9	Commercial	General/Women	Music/News/Talk	Adult Top 40
KVIL	103.7	n/a	General	Music	n/a
KKDA	104.5	n/a	Black/General	Music	n/a
KRNB	105.7	n/a	General	Music/News/Sports	n/a
KHKS	106.1	Commercial	General	Music/News/Talk	Top 40
KOAI	107.5	n/a	General	Music/Talk	n/a
KPLT	107.7	n/a	General	Music/News	Top 40
KDXX	107.9	Commercial	General/Hispanic	Music/News/Talk	Adult Contemp.

Note: Stations included cover the Dallas-Fort Worth DMA (Designated Market Area); n/a not available
BurrellesLuce, MediaContacts Online, January 2007

CLIMATE

Average and Extreme Temperatures

Temperature	Jan	Feb	Mar	Apr	May	Jun	Jul	Aug	Sep	Oct	Nov	Dec	Yr.
Extreme High (°F)	85	90	100	100	101	112	111	109	107	101	91	87	112
Average High (°F)	55	60	68	76	84	92	96	96	89	79	67	58	77
Average Temp. (°F)	45	50	57	66	74	82	86	86	79	68	56	48	67
Average Low (°F)	35	39	47	56	64	72	76	75	68	57	46	38	56
Extreme Low (°F)	-2	9	12	30	39	53	58	58	42	24	16	0	-2

Note: Figures cover the years 1945-1993
Source: National Climatic Data Center, International Station Meteorological Climate Summary, 9/96

Average Precipitation/Snowfall/Humidity

Precip./Humidity	Jan	Feb	Mar	Apr	May	Jun	Jul	Aug	Sep	Oct	Nov	Dec	Yr.
Avg. Precip. (in.)	1.9	2.3	2.6	3.8	4.9	3.4	2.1	2.3	2.9	3.3	2.3	2.1	33.9
Avg. Snowfall (in.)	1	1	Tr	Tr	0	0	0	0	0	Tr	Tr	Tr	3
Avg. Rel. Hum. 6am (%)	78	77	75	77	82	81	77	76	80	79	78	77	78
Avg. Rel. Hum. 3pm (%)	53	51	47	49	51	48	43	41	46	46	48	51	48

Note: Figures cover the years 1945-1993; Tr = Trace amounts (<0.05 in. of rain; <0.5 in. of snow)
Source: National Climatic Data Center, International Station Meteorological Climate Summary, 9/96

Weather Conditions

Temperature			Daytime Sky			Precipitation		
10°F & below	32°F & below	90°F & above	Clear	Partly cloudy	Cloudy	0.01 inch or more precip.	0.1 inch or more snow/ice	Thunder-storms
1	34	102	108	160	97	78	2	49

Note: Figures are average number of days per year and cover the years 1945-1993
Source: National Climatic Data Center, International Station Meteorological Climate Summary, 9/96

HAZARDOUS WASTE

Superfund Sites

Allen has no sites on the EPA's Superfund Final National Priorities List.
U.S. Environmental Protection Agency, Final National Priorities List, June 23, 2008

AIR & WATER QUALITY

Air Quality Index

Area	Percent of Days when Air Quality was...[2]				AQI Statistics	
	Good	Moderate	Unhealthy for Sensitive Groups	Unhealthy	Maximum	Median
MSA[1]	67.1	27.7	4.4	0.8	177	44

Note: The Air Quality Index (AQI) is an index for reporting daily air quality. EPA calculates the AQI for five major air pollutants regulated by the Clean Air Act: ground-level ozone, particle pollution (also known as particulate matter), carbon monoxide, sulfur dioxide, and nitrogen dioxide. The AQI runs from 0 to 500. The higher the AQI value, the greater the level of air pollution and the greater the health concern. There are six AQI categories: "Good" The AQI is between 0 and 50. Air quality is considered satisfactory; "Moderate" The AQI is between 51 and 100. Air quality is acceptable; "Unhealthy for Sensitive Groups" When AQI values are between 101 and 150, members of sensitive groups may experience health effects; "Unhealthy" When AQI values are between 151 and 200 everyone may begin to experience health effects; "Very Unhealthy" AQI values between 201 and 300 trigger a health alert; "Hazardous" AQI values over 300 trigger health warnings of emergency conditions; (1) Metropolitan Statistical Area - see Appendix A for areas included; (2) Based on 365 days with AQI data in 2007.
Source: U.S. Environmental Protection Agency, Air Quality Index Report, 2007

Air Quality Index Pollutants

Area	Percent of Days when AQI Pollutant was...[2]					
	Carbon Monoxide	Nitrogen Dioxide	Ozone	Sulfur Dioxide	Particulate Matter 2.5	Particulate Matter 10
MSA[1]	0.0	0.0	61.6	0.3	38.1	0.0

Note: The Air Quality Index (AQI) is an index for reporting daily air quality. EPA calculates the AQI for five major air pollutants regulated by the Clean Air Act: ground-level ozone, particle pollution (also known as particulate matter), carbon monoxide, sulfur dioxide, and nitrogen dioxide. The AQI runs from 0 to 500. The higher the AQI value, the greater the level of air pollution and the greater the health concern; (1) Metropolitan Statistical Area - see Appendix A for areas included; (2) Based on 365 days with AQI data in 2007.
Source: U.S. Environmental Protection Agency, Air Quality Index Report, 2007

Air Quality Index Trends

Area	Trend Sites (7)								All Sites (83)
	1999	2000	2001	2002	2003	2004	2005	2006	2006
MSA[1]	16	20	14	7	5	9	10	13	26

Note: An AQI value greater than 100 indicates that air quality would have been in the unhealthful range on that day. Data from exceptional events are not included. These counts are presented in two ways. First, the counts are based on sites having an adequate record of monitoring data during the trend period (trend sites). These counts represent the relative change in the number of days with AQI values greater than 100. In the last column, the counts are based on all sites with data in the most recent year (because it is possible for a site to have data in the most recent year but not enough data to be a trend site); (1) Metropolitan Statistical Area - see Appendix A for areas included.
Source: U.S. Environmental Protection Agency, Office of Air and Radiation, Air Trends, Factbook and Related Information, Air Pollution Trends in Selected Metropolitan Areas 2006

Maximum Air Pollutant Concentrations

	Particulate Matter 10 (ug/m³)	Particulate Matter 2.5 (ug/m³)	Ozone (ppm)	Carbon Monoxide (ppm)	Sulfur Dioxide (ppm)	Nitrogen Dioxide (ppm)	Lead (ug/m³)
MSA[1] Level	56	23	0.115	2	0.02	0.016	0.77 (a)
NAAQS[2]	150	35	0.125	9	0.140	0.053	1.50
Met NAAQS[2]	Yes	Yes	Yes	Yes	Yes	Ycs	Yes

Note: Data from exceptional events are not included; (1) Metropolitan Statistical Area - see Appendix A for areas included; (2) National Ambient Air Quality Standards; n/a not available; (a) Localized impact from an industrial source in Dallas. Concentration from highest nonpoint source site is 0.14 ug/m³ in Collin County
Concentrations: Particulate Matter 10 (coarse particulate) - highest second maximum 24-hour concentration; Particulate Matter 2.5 (fine particulate) - highest 98th percentile 24-hour concentration; Ozone - highest second daily maximum 1-hour concentration; Carbon Monoxide - highest second maximum non-overlapping 8-hour concentration; Sulfur Dioxide - highest second maximum 24-hour concentration; Nitrogen Dioxide - highest arithmetic mean concentration; Lead - highest quarterly maximum concentration
Units: ppm = parts per million; ug/m³ = micrograms per cubic meter
Source: U.S. Environmental Protection Agency, MSA Factbook 2006, Air Quality Statistics by City

Drinking Water

Water System Name	Pop. Served	Primary Water Source Type	Violations[1]	
			Health Based	Monitoring/ Reporting
City of Allen	69,708	Purchased Surface	0	0

Note: (1) Based on violation data from January 1, 2007 to December 31, 2007 (includes unresolved violations from earlier years)
Source: U.S. Environmental Protection Agency, Office of Ground Water and Drinking Water, Safe Drinking Water Information System (based on data extracted April 15, 2008)

Flower Mound, Texas

Background

Situated at the southern edge of Denton County, Flower Mound is 23 miles northwest of Dallas and five miles north of DFW International Airport. The city is a rapidly growing community of highly educated, affluent residents.

A prime location for business development, Flower Mound has good schools, a low tax rate, and significant recreational attractions. Its proximity to Dallas and Fort Worth offers cultural activities, dining, and shopping, as well as several excellent colleges and universities.

Located on the shore of Grapevine Lake, Flower Mound was established soon after Sam Houston settled a tribal dispute in 1844, leading to the cessation of Indian raids in the area. Permanent settlers arrived, attracted by the quality of the soil, which was suitable for raising cotton, corn, and wheat. The town was named for a 50-foot-high mound covered with Indian paintbrush and blue stem grasses. Historians believe the mound was once used by the Wichita Indians as a sacred ceremonial ground dating back to the early 1800s. During the first half of the twentieth century, Flower Mound was a substantial farming and cattle-raising community. In the mid-1950s the town really began to grow, thanks to construction by the United States Corps of Engineers of Grapevine Lake, which stimulated the town's economy and attracted workers who preferred to live outside the central Dallas area. Flower Mound was incorporated as a city in February 1961.

The Flower Mound school system, part of the Lewisville Independent School District, has received several awards, including the Texas Successful Schools and the National Blue Ribbon Schools of Excellence awards. The city's schools all have been rated "exemplary" by the Texas Education Agency. Area universities include the Southern Methodist University, University of Dallas, University of North Texas, and Texas Women's University.

Located only minutes from Flower Mound are two hospitals — Medical Center of Lewisville and Baylor Medical Center at Grapevine. In addition, Trinity Medical Center in Flower Mound offers an urgent and extended primary care clinic, physical therapy, and radiology and diagnostic imaging.

Unsurpassed recreational facilities thrive in Flower Mound, with its heavily wooded hills, panoramic views, and the creeks and shorelines provided by Lake Grapevine and Lewisville Lake. The city maintains baseball and softball fields, soccer fields, public tennis courts, and some 550 acres of parkland, with more than 30 miles of multi-purpose trail linking parks, neighborhoods, schools, and businesses. The parks host a range of facilities, including playgrounds, picnic kiosks and grills, and basketball play pads. Two notable golf courses, Tour 18 and Bridlewood, are open to the public.

Nearby Grapevine Mills Mall houses over 250 outlet stores, an ice rink, and a 30-screen theater, while the Dallas Metroplex offers the Texas Motor Speedway, Six Flags and Hurricane Harbor, and Texas Stadium, as well as the symphony halls and art museums of Dallas and Fort Worth.

Flower Mound is a four-season city, with mild winters, and hot, humid summers. The town's location on the shores of Lake Grapevine provides welcome respite during the summer. Look for bluebonnets in spring.

Rankings

General Rankings

- Dallas* was ranked #132 out of 375 metro areas in *Cities Ranked & Rated*. Criteria: cost of living; climate; crime; transportation; economy and jobs; education; arts and culture; health and healthcare; leisure; quality of life. *Cities Ranked & Rated, 2nd Edition, 2007*
- Dallas* was ranked #43 out of 379 metro areas in *Places Rated Almanac*. Criteria: health care; education; recreation; transportation; ambience; climate; crime; housing costs; jobs. *Places Rated Almanac, 7th Edition, 2007*

Business/Finance Rankings

- The nation's 100 largest metro areas were analysed in terms of the percentage of households entering some stage of foreclosure in 2007. The Dallas* metro area ranked #28 out of 100 (#1 = highest foreclosure rate). *RealtyTrac, "Year-End 2007 Metropolitan Foreclosure Report"*
- The Dallas* metro area was selected one of America's "Top 50 Business Opportunity Metros" by *Expansion Management* in their 5th annual Mayor's Challenge ranking of metro areas that have achieved solid ratings across the board in numerous *EM* studies during the past 12 months. The area ranked #13. Criteria: public schools; quality of life; college educated workers; logistics infrastructure; healthcare costs; taxes and government spending; reputation among site consultants. *Expansion Management, August 2007*
- The Dallas* metro area was selected as one of "America's Most Wired Cities" by *Forbes*. The metro area was ranked #19 out of 30. Criteria: percentage of Internet users with high-speed access; the range of service providers within a city; availability of public wireless hot spots. *Forbes, "America's Most Wired Cities," January 10, 2008*
- Dallas* was selected as one of the best places to start and grow a company by *Entrepreneur* and the National Policy Research Council. The Dallas* metro area ranked #17 out of 50 large metro areas. Criteria: business formation and growth (firms started four to 14 years ago that still employ at least 5 people and experienced rapid growth over the last four years). *Entrepreneur/National Policy Research Council, "Hot Cities for Entrepreneurs," September 2006*
- The Dallas* metro area was selected as one of "America's Greediest Cities" by *Forbes*. The area was ranked #7 out of 10. Criteria: number of Forbes 400 (*Forbes* annual list of the richest Americans) members per capita. *Forbes, "America's Greediest Cities," December 7, 2007*
- The Dallas* metro area was selected as one of "America's 50 Hottest Cities" for business relocations and expansions. Criteria: industry's most prominent site selection consultants were asked to list their top city choices for relocating and expanding manufacturing companies, taking into consideration such factors as the business climate, work force quality, operating costs, incentive programs, and the ease of working with local political and economic development officials. *Expansion Management, January-February 2007*
- Dallas* was cited as one of America's top large metros (population over 1 million) for new and expanded facility projects in 2007. The area appeared in the top 10 with 73 projects. *Site Selection, "Top Metropolitan Area Awards," March 2008*
- The Dallas* metro area was selected as one of the "Top 20 Real Estate Markets" for expanding or relocating companies. The area ranked #7. Criteria: low rental costs; low purchase prices; high vacancy rates of office and warehouse space. *Expansion Management, October 2007*
- Intel, in partnership with Sperling's BestPlaces, ranked the 80 "Best Cities for Teleworking" in America. The Dallas* metro area ranked #8 among extra large metro areas. The study identifies cities that hold the greatest potential for teleworking based on a host of factors including typical commuting times, fuel prices, availability of broadband Internet access and percentage of the population in telework friendly jobs. The study also factored in extreme climate and natural hazards. *Intel, "Best Cities for Teleworking," March 30, 2006*

- The Dallas* metro area appeared on the Milken Institute "2007 Best Performing Cities" index. Rank: #59 out of 200 large metro areas. Criteria: job growth; wage and salary growth; high-tech output growth. *Milken Institute, "2007 Best Performing Cities"*

- The Dallas* metro area was selected as one of "The Top 20 Boom Towns in America." *Business 2.0* magazine and econometric research firm Global Insight compared 319 metropolitan areas in the U.S. and ranked the 61 with populations over 1 million. Criteria: a weighted formula that includes forecast growth rates in sectors that contain the economy's 10 most skilled occupational clusters; the prevalence of college degrees in the local workforce; median salary. The area ranked #18 among large metro areas. *Business 2.0 Magazine, March 2004*

- Dallas* was identified as one of the 100 "Most Unwired Cities" in the U.S. The area ranked #23 out of the 100 largest metro areas in the U.S. Criteria: number of public and commercial wireless access points (hotspots); airports with wireless Internet access; broadband availability; local wireless networks; and wireless email devices. *Intel, "Most Unwired Cities Survey," June 7, 2005*

- Dallas* was ranked #21 out of 125 regions worldwide in terms of its "Knowledge Competitiveness Index." The index attempts to measure the knowledge-based development taking place throughout the world and is based on 19 measures of economic performance that indicate a region's ability to translate its knowledge capacity into economic value. *Robert Huggins Associates, World Knowledge Competitiveness Index 2005*

- *Forbes* ranked the 200 most populous metro areas in the U.S. in terms of the "Best Places for Business and Careers." The Dallas* metro area was ranked #93. Criteria: business costs (labor, energy, tax and office space expenses); living costs (housing, transportation, food and other household expenditures); education levels of the work force; job growth; income growth; migration trends; crime rates; and culture/leisure. *Forbes, "Best Places for Business and Careers," March 19, 2008*

- Flower Mound was selected as a 2007 Digital Cities Survey winner. The city ranked #9 in the very small city (30,000 to 74,999 population) category. The survey examined and assessed how city governments are utilizing information technology to operate and deliver quality service to their customers and citizens. Survey questions focused on implementation and adoption of online service delivery; planning and governance; and the infrastructure and architecture that make the transformation to digital government possible. *Center for Digital Government, "2007 Digital Cities Survey"*

- *Fortune* ranked the 100 largest metro areas in the U.S. in terms of projected median home price change in 2007. The Dallas* metro area ranked #13. *Fortune.com, "Hot Spots, Cold Spots"*

Health/Environment Rankings

- 100 of the largest metro areas in the U.S. were analyzed in terms of their current drought severity. The Dallas* metro area ranked #97 (#1 = driest). The rankings were based on statistics such as long-term precipitation trends and patterns and the Palmer drought indices. *Sperling's BestPlaces, www.BestPlaces.net, "America's Drought-Riskiest Cities," November 2007*

- Doctors at the Harvard School of Public Health ranked 40 metropolitan areas based on data from the government-sponsored Hospital Quality Alliance program. The program tracks the performance of individual hospitals in treating patients for three common health problems: heart attacks, congestive heart failure, and pneumonia. The Dallas* metro area ranked #22 in quality of care for heart attacks, #25 for congestive heart failure, and #7 for pneumonia. *New England Journal of Medicine, July 21, 2005*

- *Reader's Digest* ranked the 50 largest metro areas in the U.S. in terms of how "clean" they are. The Dallas* metro area ranked #30. Criteria: air quality; water quality; toxic industrial pollution; Superfund sites; and sanitation. *Reader's Digest, "The 50 Cleanest (and Dirtiest) Cities in America," July 2005*

- The American Academy of Dermatology ranked 32 U.S. metropolitan regions in terms of their residents knowledge, attitude and behaviors towards tanning and sun protection. The Dallas* metro area ranked #6. The results of the study are based on an online national survey of 3,342 respondents. *American Academy of Dermatology, "RAYS: Your Grade," May 7, 2007*

- The Dallas* metro area appeared in *Country Home's* "2008 Best Green Places" report. The area ranked #94 out of 379. Criteria: official energy policies; green power; green buildings; availability of fresh, locally grown food. *Country Home, "2008 Best Green Places"*

- Wyeth Consumer Healthcare, in partnership with Sperling's BestPlaces, ranked the nation's 50 most populous metro areas in terms of five key health factors. The Dallas* metro area ranked #35. Criteria: physical activity; health status; nutrition; lifestyle pursuits; and mental wellness. *Wyeth Consumer Healthcare, "Centrum Healthiest Cities Study," April 19, 2005*

- HealthGrades surveyed over 41,000 individuals on doctor satisfaction and ranked the 20 largest metro areas based on the highest "definitely yes" responses to the question "Do you trust the physician to make decisions/recommendations that are in your best interest?" The Dallas* metro area ranked #2. *HealthGrades.com, "Top Cities in Doctor-Trust," September 7, 2006*

- Dallas* was identified as a "2008 Asthma Capital." The area ranked #23 out of the nation's 100 largest metropolitan areas. Twelve factors were used to identify the most challenging places to live for people with asthma: estimated prevalence; self-reported prevalence; crude death rate for asthma; annual pollen score; annual air quality; public smoking laws; number of board-certified asthma specialists; school inhaler access laws; rescue medication use; controller medication use; uninsured rate; poverty rate. *Asthma and Allergy Foundation of America, "2008 Asthma Capitals"*

- Dallas* was identified as a "Spring Allergy Capital." The area ranked #2 out of 100. Three groups of factors were used to identify the most severe cities for people with allergies during the spring season: annual pollen levels; medicine utilization; access to board-certified allergists. *Asthma and Allergy Foundation of America, "2007 Spring Allergy Capital Rankings"*

- Dallas* was identified as a "Fall Allergy Capital." The area ranked #21 out of 100. Three groups of factors were used to identify the most severe cities for people with allergies during the fall season: annual pollen levels; medicine utilization; access to board-certified allergists. *Asthma and Allergy Foundation of America, "2007 Fall Allergy Capital Rankings"*

- Ortho-McNeil Neurologics, in partnership with Sperling's BestPlaces, analyzed 110 metro areas and identified those U.S. cities with the highest prevalence of factors that are most commonly associated with migraine headaches. The Dallas* metro area ranked #82. Criteria: number of migraine-related drug prescriptions per capita; lifestyle factors that can contribute to migraines; environmental factors that can trigger migraines; and consumption of migraine-triggering foods. *Ortho-McNeil Neurologics, "America's Migraine Hot Spots," March 14, 2006*

- Sperling's BestPlaces ranked 331 metro areas and identified the most and least stressful U.S. cities. The Dallas* metro area ranked #10 out of the 100 largest metro areas (#1 = most stressful). Criteria: divorce rate; unemployment rate; violent and property crime; suicide rate; commute time; mental health; alcohol consumption; cloudy days. *Sperling's BestPlaces, www.BestPlaces.net, "America's Most (and Least) Stressful Cities," January 9, 2004*

- An analysis of the "Best & Worst Cities for Sleep" was conducted by Sperling's BestPlaces. The study ranked America's 50 most populated metro areas. The Dallas* metro area ranked #21 (#1 = best city for sleep). Criteria: number of days residents didn't get enough rest or sleep during the past month; average length of daily commute; divorce rate; unemployment rate. *Sperling's BestPlaces, www.BestPlaces.net, "Best & Worst Cities for Sleep," 2006*

- HealthGrades evaluated the performance of America's 25 most populous metropolitan areas by measuring the outcomes of five of the highest volume and most widely studied procedures and diagnoses: coronary artery bypass graft surgery; percutaneous coronary interventions; acute myocardial infarction/heart attack in angioplasty-capable hospitals; congestive heart failure; and community acquired pneumonia. The Dallas* metro area ranked #21. *HealthGrades, "HealthGrades Hospital Quality in America Study," October 12, 2004*

- Dallas* was highlighted as one of the 25 most ozone-polluted metro areas in the U.S. The area ranked #7. *American Lung Association, State of the Air: 2007*
- Dallas* was selected as one of "America's Top 10 Low-Carb Cities" by *LowCarbiz Magazine*. Criteria: abundance of low-carb products; restaurants with low-carb menu items; health practitioners supportive of carb-cutting regimens; local culture generally conducive to exercise and health. *LowCarbiz Magazine, April 2004*
- Dallas* was selected as one of "America's Pet Healthiest Cities" by Purina. The city ranked #40 out of 50. Criteria: veterinary services; environment; legislation; preventative care; obesity/body condition. *Purina Pet Institute, "America's Pet Healthiest Cities," May 20, 2003*

Women/Minorities Rankings

- Dallas* was ranked #84 out of 100 metro areas in *SELF Magazine's* ranking of "America's Best Places for Women." A panel of experts came up with more than 50 criteria including death and disease rates, environmental indicators, community resources, and lifestyle habits. *SELF Magazine, "America's Best Places for Women 2007," December 2007*
- Dallas* appeared on *Black Enterprise's* list of the "Ten Best Cities for African Americans." The top picks were culled from more than 2,000 interactive surveys completed on www.blackenterprise.com and by editorial staff evaluation. The editors weighed the following criteria as it pertained to African Americans in each city: median household income; percentage of households earning more than $100,000; percentage of businesses owned; percentage of college graduates; unemployment rates; home loan rejections; and homeownership rates. *Black Enterprise, May 2007*

Seniors/Retirement Rankings

- Sperling's BestPlaces in partnership with Bankers Life & Casualty Company designed a survey to identify the top 50 metro areas in the U.S. that offer the best overall qualities for senior living. The Dallas* metro area ranked #44. The following criteria were statistically weighted to reflect the needs of the senior population: health; disease; economics; social; environment; spiritual; transportation; housing; and crime. *Bankers Life & Casualty Company, "Best Cities for Seniors 2005"*

Children/Family Rankings

- Flower Mound was selected as one of the ten "Best of the Best" places to raise a family in the U.S. The city was ranked #5.Criteria: demographic characteristics; standard of living; education; lifestyle; health and safety. *Best Place to Raise Your Family: The Top 100 Affordable Communities in the U.S., 1st Edition, 2006*
- The Dallas* metro area was selected as one of the "Best Cities for Relocating Families" by Worldwide ERC and Primacy Relocation. The 2007 study placed a special emphasis on the housing market, which has significantly impacted the relocation industry and an employer's ability to transfer employees. The variables which weigh heavily in this category include home price, home affordability index, appreciation rates, and property tax. Other criteria include cost of living, crime rates, education, climate, focus on diversity, physicians per capita, recreation and leisure, arts and culture, air quality, watershed quality, sales tax, unemployment rate, job growth, high school and higher education index, school expenditures per student, students in public school, SAT/ACT percentile, and population growth. *Worldwide ERC and Primacy Relocation, "2007 Best Cities for Relocating Families"*

Safety Rankings

- The National Insurance Crime Bureau ranked 361 metro areas in the U.S. in terms of per capita rates of vehicle theft. The Dallas* metro area ranked #50 (#1 = highest rate). Criteria: number of vehicle theft offenses per 100,000 inhabitants. *National Insurance Crime Bureau, "NICB Vehicle Theft Study," April 22, 2008*

- Dallas* appeared on Sperling's BestPlaces list of the "Riskiest Cities for Identity Theft." The area ranked #13 out of the nations 50 largest metro areas. Over 80 criteria were analyzed across four major categories: technology impact; crime; transactions; and risk profile. *Sperling's BestPlaces, www.BestPlaces.net, "Riskiest Cities for Identity Theft," July 2006*

- Farmers Insurance Group of Companies, in partnership with Sperling's BestPlaces, ranked 379 metro areas and identified the "Most Secure U.S. Place to Live." The Dallas* metro area ranked #91 out of 114 in the large metro area category (500,000 or more residents). Criteria: crime rates; extreme weather; risk of natural disasters; environmental hazards; terrorism threats; air quality; life expectancy; job loss numbers. *Farmers Insurance Group, "Most Secure U.S. Places to Live 2007"*

- Dallas* was identified as one of the most dangerous large metro areas for pedestrians in the U.S. The area ranked #14 out of the nations 50 largest metro areas. Criteria: average yearly pedestrian fatalities per capita (for the years 2002 and 2003) adjusted for the number of walkers. *Surface Transportation Policy Project, "Mean Streets 2004"*

- Dallas* was identified as one of the least safe places in the U.S. in terms of its vulnerability to natural disasters and weather extremes. The city ranked #2 out of 10. Sperling's BestPlaces analyzed data to show a metro areas' relative tendency to experience natural disasters (hail, tornados, high winds, hurricanes, earthquakes, and brush fires) or extreme weather (abundant rain or snowfall or days that are below freezing or above 90 degrees Fahrenheit). *Forbes, "Safest and Least Safe Places in the U.S.," August 30, 2005*

Sports/Recreation Rankings

- The Dallas* metro area appeared on the *Sporting News* list of the "Best Sports Cities 2007". The area ranked #3 out of 150 cities in the U.S. *Sporting News* takes a 12-month snapshot, roughly July to July, of each city's sports, putting a heavy premium on regular-season won-lost records (from the most recently completed season). Other criteria include: playoff berths, bowl appearances and tournament bids; championships; applicable power ratings; quality of competition; overall fan fervor as measured in part by attendance as percentage of venue capacity; abundance of teams (rewarding quality over quantity); stadium and arena quality; ticket availability and prices; franchise ownership; and marquee appeal of athletes. *SportingNews.com, "Best Sports Cities 2007," August 1, 2007*

- Scarborough Research, a leading market research firm, identified the top local markets for avid NBA fans. The Dallas* DMA (Designated Market Area) ranked in the top 10 with 13% of consumers 18 years and over reporting that they are "very interested in the NBA". *Scarborough Research, April 24, 2006*

- The Dallas* metro area was selected by *Cranium* as one of the "Top 50 Fun Cities" in America. The area ranked #34. Criteria includes: number of sports teams, restaurants, and dance performances; number of toy stores; city budget spent on recreation. *Cranium, November 4, 2003*

- *Golf Digest* ranked 330 metro areas in the U.S. in terms of golf. The Dallas* metro area was ranked #256. Criteria: access to golf; weather; value of golf; and quality of golf. *Golf Digest, "Metro Golf Rankings," August 2005*

Dating/Romance Rankings

- Eli Lily and Company, in partnership with Sperling's BestPlaces, ranked the nation's 50 largest metro areas in terms of the "Most Romantic Cities for Baby Boomers." The Dallas* metro area ranked #9. Criteria: marriage and divorce rates among "baby boomers" age 45 to 60; great restaurants; dance studios; chocolate, jewelry and flower sales. *Eli Lily and Company, "Most Romantic Cities for Baby Boomers," April 20, 2007*

- The Dallas* metro area was selected as one of the "Top Ten U.S. Cities for Finding a Rich, Single Man" by Teasley, a Manhattan-based marketing consulting firm. The area ranked #10. Criteria: high single-male to single-female ratios; higher income to cost-of-living ratios. *Teasley, "Top Ten U.S. Cities for Finding a Rich, Single Man," February 10, 2004*

- The Dallas* metro area was selected as one of the "Best Cities for Relocating Singles" by Worldwide ERC and Primacy Relocation. The area ranked #52 out of the 100 largest metro areas in the U.S. Areas were selected based on the following criteria: a robust cost-of-living index; adventure and outdoor recreation opportunities; violent crime and property crime rates; percentage of the population that is unmarried (ages 25-34); ratio of single men and single women; affordability of quality higher education, including in-state and out-of-state tuition requirements and rates; number of newcomers to the area; commute times; tax rates; fee and occupancy rates for temporary housing and mini-storage; quality and quantity of collegiate and professional sporting events and fun, fan-friendly venues. *Worldwide ERC and Primacy Relocation, "2007 Best Cities for Relocating Singles," October 25, 2007*

- *Forbes* ranked the 40 most populous urbanized areas in the U.S. in terms of the "Best Cities for Singles." The Dallas* metro area ranked #9. Criteria: number of singles; cost of living alone; nightlife; culture; job growth; coolness; and online dating. *Forbes.com, August 21, 2007*

- Sperling's BestPlaces in partnership with AXE Deodorant Bodyspray ranked 80 metro areas and identified "America's Best (and Worst) Cities for Dating." The Dallas* metro area ranked #51 (#1 = best). Criteria: percentage of singles ages 18-24; population density; dating venues per capita. *AXE Deodorant Bodyspray, "America's Best (and Worst) Cities for Dating," May 2004*

Miscellaneous Rankings

- The Dallas* metro area was identified as one of 10 "Worst Cities for Commuters" by *Forbes*. The metro area ranked #5. Criteria: traffic delays; travel times; how efficiently commuters use existing infrastructure. *Forbes.com, "Worst Cities for Commuters," April 29, 2008*

- Scarborough Research, a leading market research firm, identified the top local markets for bloggers. The Dallas* DMA (Designated Market Area) ranked in the top 13 with 11% of adults reporting that they had read or contributed to a blog within the past 30 days. *Scarborough Research, October 24, 2007*

- The Dallas* metro area was selected as one of the "Top 10 Most Independent Cities for Homesellers". The area ranked #9. The cities listed had more consumers choosing to sell their homes without the help of a real-estate agent than anywhere else. Data was based on geographical information for listings posted on ForSaleByOwner.com from January 1, 2007 through June 30, 2007. *ForSaleByOwner.com, October 1, 2007*

- The Dallas* metro area appeared on *Forbes* list of "America's Drunkest Cities". The area ranked #27. Criteria: 35 of the largest continental U.S. metro areas were chosen based on availability of data and geographic diversity. Each metro was ranked in five areas: state laws; drinkers; heavy drinkers; binge drinkers; and alcoholism. *Forbes.com, "America's Drunkest Cities," August 22, 2006*

- Sperling's BestPlaces in partnership with Pep Boys ranked 77 metro areas and identified "America's Most Drivable Cities." The Dallas* metro area ranked #40. Criteria: climate; road roughness; urban mobility; gas prices. *Pep Boys, "America's Most Drivable Cities," April 9, 2003*

- State Farm Insurance, in partnership with Sperling's BestPlaces, analyzed several key factors that contribute to overall family preparedness. The Dallas* metro area ranked #28 out of the nation's 50 most populous metro areas. Criteria: quality of life; life insurance coverage; and investments. *State Farm Life Insurance, "Fiscally Fit Cities Report," July 20, 2004*

- A study by Sperling's BestPlaces examined which U.S. metro areas were most affected by high fuel prices in 2006. The Dallas* metro area was ranked #37 out of 80 (#1 = most expensive city for driving). Rankings are based on the average dollars spent on gas per year by two driver households. Criteria: cost of regular-grade gasoline; average miles driven per day; average number of gallons each driver uses and wastes in traffic congestion each day. *Sperling's BestPlaces, www.bestplaces.net, "Pain at the Pump," May 18, 2006*

Flower Mound is located within the Dallas-Fort Worth-Arlington, TX Metropolitan Statistical Area and Dallas-Plano-Irving, TX Metropolitan Division.

Business Environment

CITY FINANCES

City Government Finances

Component	2004-2005 ($000)	2004-2005 ($ per capita)
Total Revenues	n/a	n/a
Total Expenditures	n/a	n/a
Debt Outstanding	n/a	n/a
Cash and Securities	n/a	n/a

Source: U.S Census Bureau, Government Finances 2004-2005

City Government Revenue by Source

Source	2004-2005 ($000)	2004-2005 ($ per capita)
General Revenue		
From Federal Government	n/a	n/a
From State Government	n/a	n/a
From Local Governments	n/a	n/a
Taxes		
Property	n/a	n/a
Sales	n/a	n/a
Personal Income	n/a	n/a
License	n/a	n/a
Charges	n/a	n/a
Liquor Store	n/a	n/a
Utility	n/a	n/a
Employee Retirement	n/a	n/a
Other	n/a	n/a

Source: U.S Census Bureau, Government Finances 2004-2005

City Government Expenditures by Function

Function	2004-2005 ($000)	2004-2005 ($ per capita)	2004-2005 (%)
General Expenditures			
Airports	n/a	n/a	n/a
Corrections	n/a	n/a	n/a
Education	n/a	n/a	n/a
Fire Protection	n/a	n/a	n/a
Governmental Administration	n/a	n/a	n/a
Health	n/a	n/a	n/a
Highways	n/a	n/a	n/a
Hospitals	n/a	n/a	n/a
Housing and Community Development	n/a	n/a	n/a
Interest on General Debt	n/a	n/a	n/a
Libraries	n/a	n/a	n/a
Parking	n/a	n/a	n/a
Parks and Recreation	n/a	n/a	n/a
Police Protection	n/a	n/a	n/a
Public Welfare	n/a	n/a	n/a
Sewerage	n/a	n/a	n/a
Solid Waste Management	n/a	n/a	n/a
Liquor Store	n/a	n/a	n/a
Utility	n/a	n/a	n/a
Employee Retirement	n/a	n/a	n/a
Other	n/a	n/a	n/a

Source: U.S Census Bureau, Government Finances 2004-2005

Municipal Bond Ratings

Area	Moody's
City	Aaa

Source: Mergent Bond Record, January 2008 (unless noted otherwise)

DEMOGRAPHICS

Population Growth

Area	1990 Census	2000 Census	2007 Estimate	2012 Projection	Population Growth (%) 1990-2000	Population Growth (%) 2000-2012
City	15,788	50,702	65,576	76,168	221.1	50.2
MSA[1]	3,989,294	5,161,544	6,007,731	6,587,538	29.4	27.6
U.S.	248,709,873	281,421,906	301,045,522	314,920,978	13.2	11.9

Note: (1) Metropolitan Statistical Area - see Appendix B for areas included
Source: Claritas, Inc.

Number of Households and Average Household Size

Area	2007 Estimate	2007 Average Household Size
City	20,691	3.17
MSA[1]	2,171,092	2.77
U.S.	113,668,003	2.65

Note: (1) Metropolitan Statistical Area - see Appendix B for areas included
Source: Claritas, Inc.

Race and Ethnicity

Area	White Alone[2]	Black Alone[2]	Asian Alone[2]	Other Race Alone[2]	Hispanic[3]
City	86.2	4.2	5.1	4.5	6.8
MSA[1]	65.6	14.0	4.6	15.8	26.4
U.S.	73.1	12.4	4.3	10.3	14.9

Note: Figures are 2007 estimates; (1) Metropolitan Statistical Area - see Appendix B for areas included (2) Alone is defined as not being in combination with one or more other races; (3) May be of any race.
Source: Claritas, Inc.

Ancestry

Area	German	Irish[2]	English	American	Italian	Polish	French[3]	Scottish
City	20.7	15.2	15.1	8.7	4.4	3.1	3.3	3.4
MSA[1]	10.0	8.1	8.2	7.8	2.1	1.2	2.1	1.7
U.S.	15.2	10.9	8.7	7.3	5.6	3.2	3.0	1.7

Note: Figures include multiple ancestry (e.g. if a person reported being Irish and Italian, they were included in both columns); (1) Metropolitan Statistical Area - see Appendix A for areas included; (2) Includes Celtic; (3) Includes Alsatian but excludes Basque
Source: Census 2000, Summary File 3

Foreign-Born Population

Area	Percent of Population Born in: Any Foreign Country	Europe	Asia	Africa	Oceania[2]	Canada	Mexico	Latin America[3]
City	5.4	1.2	2.3	0.2	0.0	0.4	0.5	0.7
MSA[1]	16.8	0.9	3.4	0.6	0.0	0.3	9.8	1.8
U.S.	11.1	1.7	2.9	0.3	0.1	0.3	3.3	2.5

Note: (1) Metropolitan Statistical Area - see Appendix A for areas included; (2) Includes Australia, New Zealand subregion, Melanesia, Micronesia, Polynesia, and Oceania n.e.c; (3) Includes Central America (excluding Mexico), South America, and the Caribbean.
Source: Census 2000, Summary File 3

Marriage Status

Area	Never Married	Now Married (excluding Separated)	Separated	Widowed	Divorced
City	16.1	75.2	0.8	2.1	5.8
MSA[1]	27.2	55.6	2.5	4.6	10.1
U.S.	27.1	54.4	2.2	6.6	9.7

Note: Figures are percentages and cover the population 15 years of age and older; (1) Metropolitan Statistical Area - see Appendix A for areas included
Source: Census 2000, Summary File 3

Age Distribution

Area	Percent of Population						
	Under Age 5	Age 5 to 17	Age 18 to 34	Age 35 to 49	Age 50 to 64	Age 65 to 79	80 Years and Over
City	10.4	24.1	19.4	32.3	11.1	1.9	0.6
MSA[1]	8.1	19.9	27.3	24.4	12.7	5.8	1.8
U.S.	6.8	18.9	23.7	23.5	14.8	9.2	3.2

Note: (1) Metropolitan Statistical Area - see Appendix A for areas included
Source: Census 2000, Summary File 3

Male/Female Ratio

Area	Males	Females	Males per 100 Females
City	32,595	32,981	98.8
MSA[1]	3,012,647	2,995,084	100.6
U.S.	148,320,305	152,725,217	97.1

Note: Figures are 2007 estimates; (1) Metropolitan Statistical Area - see Appendix B for areas included
Source: Claritas, Inc.

Religion

Area	Catholic	Southern Baptist	United Meth-odist	ELCA[1]	LDS[2]	Presby-terian Church USA	Jewish Est.	Muslim Est.
County	6.4	12.4	4.6	0.6	1.5	0.5	0.0	1.3
U.S.	22.0	7.1	3.7	1.8	1.5	1.1	2.2	0.6

Note: Figures are the number of adherents as a percentage of the total population; Adherents are defined as all members, including full members, their children and the estimated number of other participants who are not considered members (e.g. the baptized, those not confirmed, those regularly attending services, etc.); (1) Evangelical Lutheran Church in America; (2) The Church of Jesus Christ of Latter Day Saints
Source: Reprinted with permission from Religious Congregations and Membership in the United States 2000 (Nashville, Glenmary Research Center, 2002) Copyright Association of Statisticians of American Religious Bodies. All rights reserved.

ECONOMY

Gross Metropolitan Product

Area	2002	2003	2004	2005	2005 Rank[2]
MSA[1]	229.2	238.6	260.0	284.5	5

Note: Figures are in billions of dollars; (1) Dallas-Fort Worth-Arlington, TX Metropolitan Statistical Area - see Appendix A for areas included; (2) Rank ranges from 1 to 361
Source: The U.S. Conference of Mayors, "U.S. Metro Economies: GMP - The Engines of America's Growth," January 2007

Economic Growth

Area	1995 GMP	2005 GMP	Average Annual Growth Rate	Growth Rate Rank[2]
MSA[1]	143.0	284.5	7.1	35

Note: Figures are in billions of dollars; GMP = Gross Metropolitan Product; (1) Dallas-Fort Worth-Arlington, TX Metropolitan Statistical Area - see Appendix A for areas included; (2) Rank ranges from 1 to 361
Source: The U.S. Conference of Mayors, "U.S. Metro Economies: GMP - The Engines of America's Growth," January 2007

INCOME

Per Capita/Median/Average Income

Area	Per Capita ($)	Median Household ($)	Average Household ($)
City	42,669	114,441	134,905
MSA[1]	27,089	55,079	74,352
U.S.	25,495	49,280	66,670

Note: Figures are 2007 estimates; (1) Metropolitan Statistical Area - see Appendix B for areas included
Source: Claritas, Inc.

Household Income Distribution

Area	Percent of Households Earning							
	Under $15,000	$15,000 -24,999	$25,000 -34,999	$35,000 -49,999	$50,000 -74,999	$75,000 -99,000	$100,000 -149,999	$150,000 and up
City	1.8	1.8	1.9	5.8	12.3	16.8	30.8	28.9
MSA[1]	10.0	9.1	10.7	15.8	19.8	13.0	13.2	8.5
U.S.	13.1	10.9	11.2	15.6	19.5	11.9	11.3	6.6

Note: Figures are 2007 estimates; (1) Metropolitan Statistical Area - see Appendix B for areas included
Source: Claritas, Inc.

Poverty Rates by Age

Area	All Ages	Under 5 Years Old	5 to 17 Years Old	18 to 64 Years Old	65 Years and Over
City	2.5	0.2	0.7	1.5	0.0
MSA[1]	11.1	1.3	2.8	6.3	0.7
U.S.	12.4	1.2	3.0	6.9	1.2

Note: Figures are percent of population with income in 1999 below poverty level and only include population for whom poverty status is determined; (1) Metropolitan Statistical Area - see Appendix A for areas included
Source: Census 2000, Summary File 3

Personal Bankruptcy Filing Rate

Area	2004	2005	2006
Denton County	4.24	6.09	1.45
U.S.	5.31	6.82	2.00

Note: Numbers are per 1,000 population and include Chapter 7 and Chapter 13 filings
Source: Federal Deposit Insurance Corporation (FDIC), Regional Economic Conditions (RECON), 8/23/2007

EMPLOYMENT

Labor Force and Employment

Area	Civilian Labor Force			Workers Employed		
	Dec. 2006	Dec. 2007	% Chg.	Dec. 2006	Dec. 2007	% Chg.
City	35,456	35,772	0.9	34,283	34,513	0.7
MD[1]	2,068,085	2,086,426	0.9	1,984,055	1,997,359	0.7
U.S.	152,571,000	153,705,000	0.7	146,081,000	146,334,000	0.2

Note: Data is not seasonally adjusted and covers workers 16 years of age and older;
(1) Metropolitan Division - see Appendix B for areas included
Source: Bureau of Labor Statistics, http://stats.bls.gov

Unemployment Rate

Area	2007											
	Jan.	Feb.	Mar.	Apr.	May	Jun.	Jul.	Aug.	Sep.	Oct.	Nov.	Dec.
City	3.7	3.6	3.3	3.1	3.1	3.7	3.7	3.4	3.4	3.3	3.5	3.5
MD[1]	4.7	4.5	4.1	4.0	4.0	4.6	4.6	4.3	4.4	4.1	4.2	4.3
U.S.	5.0	4.9	4.5	4.3	4.3	4.7	4.9	4.6	4.5	4.4	4.5	4.8

Note: Data is not seasonally adjusted and covers workers 16 years of age and older; All figures are percentages; (1) Metropolitan Division - see Appendix B for areas included
Source: Bureau of Labor Statistics, http://stats.bls.gov

Employment by Occupation

Occupation Classification	City (%)	MSA[1] (%)	U.S. (%)
Sales and Office	28.0	28.7	26.7
Professional and Related	25.4	20.4	20.2
Service	7.9	12.3	14.9
Production, Transportation, and Material Moving	5.3	11.8	14.6
Management, Business, and Financial	29.1	16.8	13.5
Construction, Extraction, and Maintenance	4.3	9.9	9.4
Farming, Forestry, and Fishing	0.0	0.2	0.7

Note: Figures cover employed civilians 16 years of age and older;
(1) Metropolitan Statistical Area - see Appendix A for areas included
Source: Census 2000, Summary File 3

Employment by Industry

Sector	MSA[1] Number of Employees	MSA[1] Percent of Total	U.S. Percent of Total
Government	261,800	12.4	16.3
Education and Health Services	225,600	10.7	13.4
Professional and Business Services	339,800	16.1	13.1
Retail Trade	221,000	10.5	11.6
Manufacturing	198,400	9.4	9.9
Leisure and Hospitality	193,100	9.2	9.6
Financial Activities	186,000	8.8	5.9
Construction	n/a	n/a	5.3
Wholesale Trade	130,600	6.2	4.4
Other Services	75,400	3.6	3.9
Transportation and Utilities	78,100	3.7	3.7
Information	72,600	3.4	2.2
Natural Resources and Mining	n/a	n/a	0.5

Note: Figures cover non-farm employment as of December 2007 and are not seasonally adjusted; (1) Metropolitan Statistical Area - see Appendix B for areas included; n/a not available
Source: Bureau of Labor Statistics, http://stats.bls.gov

Average Wages

Occupation	$/Hr.	Occupation	$/Hr.
Accountants and Auditors	31.56	Maids and Housekeeping Cleaners	8.23
Automotive Mechanics	17.72	Maintenance and Repair Workers	15.14
Bookkeepers	16.06	Marketing Managers	60.78
Carpenters	16.08	Nuclear Medicine Technologists	30.51
Cashiers	8.45	Nurses, Licensed Practical	19.58
Clerks, General Office	11.71	Nurses, Registered	30.37
Clerks, Receptionists/Information	12.41	Nursing Aides/Orderlies/Attendants	11.11
Clerks, Shipping/Receiving	12.87	Packers and Packagers, Hand	9.24
Computer Programmers	38.32	Physical Therapists	39.04
Computer Support Specialists	22.07	Postal Service Mail Carriers	21.40
Computer Systems Analysts	39.12	Real Estate Brokers	45.42
Cooks, Restaurant	10.19	Retail Salespersons	11.71
Dentists	n/a	Sales Reps., Exc. Tech./Scientific	29.44
Electrical Engineers	44.17	Sales Reps., Tech./Scientific	35.60
Electricians	19.29	Secretaries, Exc. Legal/Med./Exec.	13.40
Financial Managers	55.42	Security Guards	12.88
First-Line Supervisors/Mgrs., Sales	19.02	Surgeons	n/a
Food Preparation Workers	8.57	Teacher Assistants	9.40
General and Operations Managers	56.15	Teachers, Elementary School	22.00
Hairdressers/Cosmetologists	10.95	Teachers, Secondary School	21.40
Internists	90.82	Telemarketers	13.10
Janitors and Cleaners	9.02	Truck Drivers, Heavy/Tractor-Trailer	19.27
Landscaping/Groundskeeping Workers	10.25	Truck Drivers, Light/Delivery Svcs.	14.20
Lawyers	65.73	Waiters and Waitresses	8.06

Note: Wage data covers the Dallas-Plano-Irving, TX Metropolitan Division - see Appendix B for areas included. Hourly wages for elementary/secondary school teachers and teacher assistants were calculated by the editors from annual wage data assuming a 40 hour work week; n/a not available.
Source: Bureau of Labor Statistics, May 2007 Metro Area Occupational Employment and Wage Estimates

RESIDENTIAL REAL ESTATE

Building Permits

Area	Single-Family 2006	Single-Family 2007p	Single-Family Pct. Chg.	Multi-Family 2006	Multi-Family 2007p	Multi-Family Pct. Chg.	Total 2006	Total 2007p	Total Pct. Chg.
City	174	87	-50.0	0	0	-	174	87	-50.0
U.S.	1,378,200	973,300	-29.4	460,700	407,200	-11.6	1,838,900	1,380,500	-24.9

Note: (p) preliminary; figures cover and represent new, privately-owned housing units authorized (unadjusted data); All permit data are based on estimates with imputation; U.S. figures are based on the new 20,000-place series.
Source: U.S. Census Bureau, Manufacturing, Mining, and Construction Statistics

Homeownership and Housing Vacancies

Area	Homeownership Rate² (%)			Rental Vacancy Rate³ (%)			Homeowner Vacancy Rate⁴ (%)		
	2005	2006	2007	2005	2006	2007	2005	2006	2007
MSA[1]	62.3	60.7	60.9	13.6	11.7	11.0	2.2	2.3	2.5
U.S.	68.9	68.8	68.1	9.8	9.8	9.7	1.9	2.4	2.7

Note: (1) Metropolitan Statistical Area - see Appendix B for areas included; (2) The proportion of households that are owners; (3) The proportion of the rental inventory that is vacant for rent; (4) The proportion of the homeowner inventory that is vacant for sale; n/a not available
Source: U.S. Census Bureau, Housing Vacancies and Homeownership Annual Statistics: 2007

TAXES

State Corporate Income Tax Rates

State	Rates and Tax Brackets
Texas	1.0%

Note: Tax rates as of January 1, 2008; Texas's 1% franchise tax is a gross receipts tax paid by most taxable entities. Retailers pay 0.5%.
Source: Tax Foundation, www.taxfoundation.org

State Individual Income Tax Rates

State	Federal Deductibility	Marginal Rates (%)	Standard Deduction ($)		Personal Exemptions ($)[1]	
			Single	Joint	Single	Dependents
Texas	No	None	n/a	n/a	n/a	n/a

Note: Tax rates as of January 1, 2008; Local- and county-level taxes are not included; n/a not applicable; (1) Married joint filers generally receive double the single exemption
Source: Tax Foundation, www.taxfoundation.org

Various State and Local Tax Rates

State and Local Sales and Use (%)	State Sales and Use (%)	Gasoline[1,2] ($/gal.)	Cigarette ($/pack)	Spirits ($/gal.)	Table Wine ($/gal.)	Beer ($/gal.)
7.25	6.25 (i)	0.20	1.41	2.40	0.204	0.19

Note: Tax rates as of January 1, 2008; (1) In addition to the 18.4 cpg Federal gasoline tax; (2) Rates may include additional state sales taxes, environmental protection and storage fees/taxes, and local taxes. When necessary, the volume-weighted average of all local taxes is used to approximate the typical statewide rate including local tax; (i) Texas has a GRT that is levied in addition to its 6.25% sales tax. It is called the franchise tax and the rate is 1% (.5% for retailers).
Source: Tax Foundation, www.taxfoundation.org; Original research

State Tax Burdens

Area	Combined State and Local Tax Burden		Combined Federal, State and Local Tax Burden	
	Percent	Rank	Percent	Rank
Texas	9.3	43	29.8	41
U.S. Average	11.0	-	32.7	-

Note: Figures cover 2007 and measure taxes as a percentage of income
Source: Tax Foundation, www.taxfoundation.org

State Business Tax Climate Index Rankings

State	Overall Rank	Corporate Tax Index Rank	Individual Income Tax Index Rank	Sales Tax Index Rank	Unemployment Insurance Tax Index Rank	Property Tax Index Rank
Texas	8	47	7	28	14	27

Note: Rankings range from 1 to 50 where 1 is best. Rankings do not average across to Overall Rank. States without a given tax are given a ranking of 1.
Source: Tax Foundation, State Business Tax Climate Index 2008

TRANSPORTATION

Means of Transportation to Work

Area	Car/Truck/Van		Public Transportation			Bicycle	Walked	Other Means	Worked at Home
	Drove Alone	Car-pooled	Bus	Subway	Railroad				
City	84.1	7.3	0.3	0.0	0.0	0.1	0.5	1.4	6.4
MSA[1]	77.6	14.3	2.1	0.1	0.1	0.1	1.5	1.0	3.1
U.S.	75.7	12.2	2.5	1.5	0.5	0.4	2.9	1.0	3.3

Note: Figures are percentages and cover workers 16 years of age and older; (1) Metropolitan Statistical Area - see Appendix A for areas included
Source: Census 2000, Summary File 3

Travel Time to Work

Area	Less Than 15 Minutes	15 to 29 Minutes	30 to 44 Minutes	45 to 59 Minutes	60 Minutes or More
City	15.8	28.8	30.6	17.7	7.1
MSA[1]	22.0	35.0	24.7	10.4	7.9
U.S.	29.4	36.1	19.1	7.4	8.0

Note: Figures are percentages and include workers 16 years old and over; (1) Metropolitan Statistical Area - see Appendix A for areas included
Source: Census 2000, Summary File 3

Travel Time Index

Area	1982	1995	2004	2005
Urban Area[1]	1.05	1.16	1.31	1.35
Average[2]	1.11	1.22	1.29	1.30

Note: Travel Time Index - The ratio of travel time in the peak period to the travel time at free-flow conditions. A value of 1.35 indicates a 20-minute free-flow trip takes 27 minutes in the peak. Free-flow speeds (60 mph on freeways and 35 mph on principal arterials) are used as the comparison threshold; (1) Covers the Dallas-Fort Worth-Arlington, TX urban area; (2) average of 85 urban areas
Source: Texas Transportation Institute, The 2007 Urban Mobility Report, September 2007

Living Environment

COST OF LIVING

Cost of Living Index

Composite Index	Groceries	Housing	Utilities	Trans-portation	Health Care	Misc. Goods/ Services
88.5	95.3	74.9	98.3	97.7	90.1	91.2

Note: U.S. = 100; Figures cover the Fort Worth TX urban area.
Source: The Council for Community and Economic Research (formerly ACCRA), Cost of Living Index, 2007

Grocery Prices

Area[1]	T-Bone Steak ($/pound)	Frying Chicken ($/pound)	Whole Milk ($/half gal.)	Eggs ($/dozen)	Orange Juice ($/64 oz.)	Coffee ($/11.5 oz.)
City[2]	9.03	0.96	2.28	1.50	3.11	3.04
Avg.	8.93	1.12	2.13	1.52	3.26	3.31
Min.	5.88	0.71	1.33	0.83	2.30	2.20
Max.	12.80	2.07	3.43	3.54	5.79	6.20

Note: (1) Values for the local area are compared with the average, minimum and maximum values for all 331 areas in the Cost of Living Index report; (2) Figures cover the Fort Worth TX urban area; **T-Bone Steak** *(price per pound);* **Frying Chicken** *(price per pound, whole fryer);* **Whole Milk** *(half gallon carton);* **Eggs** *(price per dozen, Grade A, large);* **Orange Juice** *(64 oz. Tropicana or Florida Natural);* **Coffee** *(11.5 oz. can, vacuum-packed, Maxwell House, Hills Bros, or Folgers).*
Source: The Council for Community and Economic Research (formerly ACCRA), Cost of Living Index, 2007

Housing and Utility Costs

Area[1]	New Home Price ($)	Apartment Rent ($/month)	All Electric ($/month)	Part Electric ($/month)	Other Energy ($/month)	Telephone ($/month)
City[2]	213,267	815	-	112.12	50.83	24.95
Avg.	309,605	782	146.13	78.67	90.16	26.14
Min.	189,877	n/a	82.03	37.41	33.15	17.08
Max.	1,202,800	3,481	271.14	150.60	257.67	37.45

Note: (1) Values for the local area are compared with the average, minimum and maximum values for all 331 areas in the Cost of Living Index report; (2) Figures cover the Fort Worth TX urban area; **New Home Price** *(2,400 sf living area, 8,000 sf lot, in urban area with full utilities);* **Apartment Rent** *(950 sf 2 bedroom/1.5 or 2 bath, unfurnished, excluding all utilities except water);* **All Electric** *(average monthly cost for an all-electric home);* **Part Electric** *(average monthly cost for a part-electric home);* **Other Energy** *(average monthly cost for natural gas, fuel oil, coal, wood, and any other forms of energy except electricity);* **Telephone** *(price includes basic monthly rate for a private residential line plus additional local usage charges incurred by a family of four).*
Source: The Council for Community and Economic Research (formerly ACCRA), Cost of Living Index, 2007

Health Care, Transportation, and Other Costs

Area[1]	Doctor ($/visit)	Dentist ($/visit)	Optometrist ($/visit)	Gasoline ($/gallon)	Beauty Salon ($/visit)	Men's Shirt ($)
City[2]	61.32	67.49	47.44	2.46	30.46	21.38
Avg.	79.48	71.93	79.55	2.64	29.52	25.77
Min.	52.08	44.80	43.95	2.19	15.58	16.19
Max.	148.44	126.27	158.83	3.48	60.62	48.53

Note: (1) Values for the local area are compared with the average, minimum and maximum values for all 331 areas in the Cost of Living Index report; (2) Figures cover the Fort Worth TX urban area; **Doctor** *(general practitioners routine exam of an established patient);* **Dentist** *(adult teeth cleaning and periodic oral examination);* **Optometrist** *(full vision eye exam for established adult patient);* **Gasoline** *(one gallon regular unleaded, national brand, including all taxes, cash price at self-service pump if available);* **Beauty Salon** *(woman's shampoo, trim, and blow-dry);* **Men's Shirt** *(cotton/polyester dress shirt, pinpoint weave, long sleeves).*
Source: The Council for Community and Economic Research (formerly ACCRA), Cost of Living Index, 2007

HOUSING

House Price Index (HPI)

Area	National Ranking[2]	Quarterly Change (%)	One-Year Change (%)	Five-Year Change (%)
MD[1]	97	0.16	2.95	15.82
U.S.[3]	-	0.10	0.84	41.37

Note: The HPI is a weighted repeat sales index. It measures average price changes in repeat sales or refinancings on the same properties. This information is obtained by reviewing repeat mortgage transactions on single-family properties whose mortgages have been purchased or securitized by Fannie Mae or Freddie Mac in January 1975; (1) Metropolitan Division - see Appendix B for areas included; (2) Rankings are based on annual percentage change for all metro areas containing at least 15,000 transactions over the last 10 years and ranges from 1 to 291; (3) figures based on a weighted average of Census Division estimates; all figures are for the period ending December 31, 2007
Source: Office of Federal Housing Enterprise Oversight, House Price Index, February 26, 2008

House Price Valuations

Area	Q1 2000	Q1 2001	Q1 2002	Q1 2003	Q1 2004	Q1 2005	Q1 2006	Q1 2007	Q1 2008
MD[1]	-22.2	-21.3	-17.8	-16.4	-19.3	-23.0	-23.6	-26.9	-30.6

Note: Figures show the percentage of over- or under-valuation of single family homes relative to statistically normal house values (e.g. a value of 23.6 indicates that house values are 23.6% overvalued). Statistically normal house values are based on house prices, interest rates, household incomes, population densities, and any historical premiums or discounts metropolitan areas have exhibited over time; (1) Figures cover the Metropolitan Division - see Appendix B for areas included
Source: Global Insight/National City Corporation, House Prices in America, May 2008

Median Home Prices

Area	2005	2006	2007[r]	Percent Change 2006 to 2007
MSA[1]	147.6	149.5	150.9	0.9
U.S. Average	219.0	221.9	217.9	-1.8

Note: Figures are median sales prices of existing single-family homes in thousands of dollars; (r) revised; n/a not available; (1) Metropolitan Statistical Area - see Appendix B for areas included
Source: National Association of Realtors, Metropolitan Area Prices, 1st Quarter 2008

Housing: Year Structure Built

Area	1990 -2000	1980 -1989	1970 -1979	1960 -1969	1950 -1959	1940 -1949	Before 1940	Median Year
City	69.6	21.3	6.6	1.3	0.7	0.2	0.3	1994
MSA[1]	23.9	24.7	20.2	13.7	9.8	4.0	3.7	1979
U.S.	17.0	15.8	18.5	13.7	12.7	7.3	15.0	1971

Note: Figures are percentages; (1) Metropolitan Statistical Area - see Appendix A for areas included
Source: Census 2000, Summary File 3

HEALTH

Health Risk Data

Category	Area[1] (%)	U.S. (%)
Adults who have been told they have high blood pressure[3]	22.2	25.5
Adults who have been told they have high blood cholesterol[3]	37.6	35.6
Adults who have been told they have diabetes[2]	5.3	7.5
Adults who have been told they have arthritis[3]	19.5	27.0
Adults who have been told they currently have asthma	4.5	8.5
Adults who are current smokers	11.5	20.1
Adults who are heavy drinkers[4]	5.3	4.9
Adults who are overweight (BMI 25.0 - 29.9)	35.7	36.5
Adults who are obese (BMI 30.0 - 99.8)	21.4	25.1

Note: Data as of 2006 unless otherwise noted; (1) Figures cover the Metropolitan Division - see Appendix B for areas included; (2) Figures do not include pregnancy-related diabetes, pre-diabetes or borderline diabetes; (3) 2005 data; (4) Heavy drinkers are classified as adult men having more than two drinks per day or adult women having more than one drink per day
Source: Centers for Disease Control and Prevention, Behaviorial Risk Factor Surveillance System, SMART: Selected Metropolitan/Micropolitan Area Risk Trends, 2005, 2006

Mortality Rates for the Top 10 Causes of Death in the U.S.

ICD-10[a] Sub-Chapter	ICD-10[a] Code	Age-Adjusted Mortality Rate[1] per 100,000 population	
		County[2]	U.S.
Malignant neoplasms	C00-C97	169.4	186.5
Ischaemic heart diseases	I20-I25	128.7	152.3
Other forms of heart disease	I30-I51	55.1	51.5
Cerebrovascular diseases	I60-I69	47.0	50.0
Chronic lower respiratory diseases	J40-J47	58.8	42.6
Diabetes mellitus	E10-E14	26.9	24.8
Other degenerative diseases of the nervous system	G30-G31	28.4	22.6
Other external causes of accidental injury	W00-X59	15.4	21.4
Influenza and pneumonia	J10-J18	28.1	20.7
Hypertensive diseases	I10-I13	16.2	18.2

Note: (a) ICD-10 = International Classification of Diseases 10th Revision; (1) Mortality rates are a three year average covering 2003-2005; (2) Figures cover Denton County
Source: Centers for Disease Control and Prevention, National Center for Health Statistics. Compressed Mortality File 1999-2004. CDC WONDER On-line Database, compiled from Compressed Mortality File 1999-2005 Series 20 No. 2K, 2008.

Mortality Rates for Selected Causes of Death

ICD-10[a] Sub-Chapter	ICD-10[a] Code	Age-Adjusted Mortality Rate[1] per 100,000 population	
		County[2]	U.S.
Assault	X85-Y09	2.9	5.9
Human immunodeficiency virus (HIV) disease	B20-B24	1.6	4.5
Intentional self-harm	X60-X84	9.3	10.8
Malnutrition	E40-E46	*1.0	1.0
Obesity and other hyperalimentation	E65-E68	*1.2	1.4
Organic, including symptomatic, mental disorders	F01-F09	29.4	16.8
Transport accidents	V01-V99	13.5	16.1
Viral hepatitis	B15-B19	*1.2	1.8

Note: (a) ICD-10 = International Classification of Diseases 10th Revision; (1) Mortality rates are a three year average covering 2003-2005; (2) Figures cover Denton County; (*) Unreliable data as per CDC
Source: Centers for Disease Control and Prevention, National Center for Health Statistics. Compressed Mortality File 1999-2004. CDC WONDER On-line Database, compiled from Compressed Mortality File 1999-2005 Series 20 No. 2K, 2008.

Distribution of Physicians[1]

Area	Total	Family/ General Practice	Specialties	
			Medical	Surgical
Denton County (number)	682	226	247	158
Denton County (rate per 10,000 pop.)	12.3	4.1	4.5	2.8
U.S. (rate per 10,000 pop.)	17.7	4.6	6.9	4.3

Note: Data as of 2005; (1) Includes all non-federal, patient-care, office-based MDs
Source: Area Resource File (ARF). June 2007. U.S. Department of Health and Human Services, Health Resources and Services Administration, Bureau of Health Professions, Rockville, MD.

Hospitals

There were no hospitals listed within the city limits.
AHA Guide to the Healthcare Field 2008

According to *U.S. News,* the Dallas-Fort Worth-Arlington, TX metro area is home to six of the best hospitals in the U.S.: **Baylor Institute for Rehabilitation**; **Baylor University Medical Center**; **Children's Medical Center Dallas**; **Parkland Memorial Hospital**; **Presbyterian Hospital**; **University of Texas Southwestern Medical Center**. *U.S. News Online, "America's Best Hospitals 2007"*

EDUCATION

Public School District Statistics

District Name	Schls	Pupils	Pupil/ Teacher Ratio	Minority Pupils[1] (%)	Free Lunch Eligible[2] (%)	IEP[3] (%)
Lewisville ISD	65	47,497	14.0	35.7	15.3	11.3

Note: Table includes regular local school districts with 2,000 or more students; (1) Percentage of students that are not white, non-Hispanic; (2) Percentage of students that are eligible for the free lunch program; (3) Percentage of students that have an Individualized Education Program.
Source: U.S. Department of Education, National Center for Education Statistics, Common Core of Data, Local Education Agency (School District) Universe Survey: School Year 2005-2006; U.S. Department of Education, National Center for Education Statistics, Common Core of Data, Public Elementary/Secondary School Universe Survey: School Year 2005-2006

Top Public High Schools

High School Name	Index[1]	Rank[1]	Subsidized Lunch (%)[2]	E&E (%)[3]
Flower Mound	1.620	782	2.0	39.8

Note: (1) Public schools are ranked according to a ratio that is the number of Advanced Placement, International Baccalaureate, and/or Cambridge tests taken by all students at a school in 2007 divided by the number of graduating seniors. All of the schools on the list have an index of at least 1.000; they are in the top five percent of public schools measured this way. The rankings range from 1 to 1,422; (2) Percentage of students receiving federally subsidized meals; (3) E & E stands for equity and excellence percentage: the portion of all graduating seniors at a school that had at least one passing grade on one AP or IB test; (**) Gave both IB and AP tests. AP and IB participation are indicators of a school's efforts to get students to excel and prepare for college.
Source: Newsweek Online, "Top High Schools 2008"

Highest Level of Education

Area	Less than H.S.	H.S. Diploma	Some College, No Deg.	Associate Degree	Bachelors Degree	Masters Degree	Profess. School Degree	Doctorate Degree
City	2.7	11.9	24.2	7.7	40.3	11.0	1.5	0.7
MSA[1]	19.2	22.3	23.5	5.7	20.3	6.4	1.7	0.8
U.S.	19.4	28.4	21.2	6.4	15.7	5.9	2.0	1.0

Note: Figures are 2007 estimated percentages and cover persons age 25 and over; (1) Metropolitan Statistical Area - see Appendix B for areas included
Source: Claritas, Inc.

Educational Attainment by Race

Area	High School Graduate (%)					Bachelor's Degree (%)				
	Total	White	Black	Asian	Hisp.[2]	Total	White	Black	Asian	Hisp.[2]
City	97.4	97.6	99.2	92.9	94.6	53.1	53.1	57.5	69.2	46.7
MSA[1]	79.4	84.4	78.9	83.4	41.5	30.0	34.0	18.5	52.2	8.7
U.S.	80.4	83.6	72.3	80.4	52.4	24.4	26.1	14.3	44.1	10.4

Note: Figures shown cover persons 25 years old and over; (1) Metropolitan Statistical Area - see Appendix A for areas included; (2) people of Hispanic origin can be of any race
Source: Census 2000, Summary File 3

School Enrollment by Type

Area	Grades KG to 8				Grades 9 to 12			
	Public		Private		Public		Private	
	Enrollment	%	Enrollment	%	Enrollment	%	Enrollment	%
City	8,124	92.4	664	7.6	2,937	95.4	143	4.6
MSA[1]	456,971	90.7	46,953	9.3	181,249	92.2	15,405	7.8
U.S.	33,526,011	88.7	4,285,121	11.3	14,848,628	90.6	1,532,323	9.4

Note: Figures shown cover persons 3 years old and over; (1) Metropolitan Statistical Area - see Appendix A for areas included
Source: Census 2000, Summary File 3

School Enrollment by Race

Area	Grades KG to 8 (%)				Grades 9 to 12 (%)			
	White	Black	Asian	Hisp.[1]	White	Black	Asian	Hisp.[1]
City	90.5	2.2	1.8	6.6	88.0	3.1	2.1	7.3
MSA[2]	60.7	18.0	3.6	28.9	61.2	18.7	4.0	25.8
U.S.	68.5	15.5	3.3	16.8	68.8	15.5	3.8	15.7

Note: Figures shown cover persons 3 years old and over; (1) people of Hispanic origin can be of any race; (2) Metropolitan Statistical Area - see Appendix A for areas included
Source: Census 2000, Summary File 3

Average Salaries of Public School Classroom Teachers

District	2005-06		2006-07		Percent Change 2005-06 to 2006-07
	Dollars	Rank[1]	Dollars	Rank[1]	
Texas	41,744	35	44,897	30	7.55
U.S. Average	49,026	-	50,816	-	3.65

Note: (1) State rank ranges from 1 to 51.
Source: National Education Association, Rankings & Estimates: Rankings of the States 2006 and Estimates of School Statistics 2007, December 2007

Higher Education

Four-Year Colleges			Two-Year Colleges			Medical Schools[1]	Law Schools[2]	Voc/ Tech[3]
Public	Private Non-profit	Private For-profit	Public	Private Non-profit	Private For-profit			
0	0	0	0	0	0	0	0	0

Note: Figures cover institutions located within the city limits; (1) includes schools accredited by the Liaison Committee on Medical Education and the American Osteopathic Association; (2) includes American Bar Association-accredited law schools; (3) includes all schools with programs that are less than 2 years.
Source: National Center for Education Statistics, The Integrated Postsecondary Education System (IPEDS) Peer Analysis System, 2007; www.usnews.com, Law and Medical School Directories, 2009

PRESIDENTIAL ELECTION

2004 Presidential Election Results

Area	Bush	Kerry	Nader	Other
Denton County	70.0	29.5	0.0	0.5
U.S.	50.7	48.3	0.4	0.6

Note: Results are percentages and may not add to 100% due to rounding
Source: Dave Leip's Atlas of U.S. Presidential Elections, www.uselectionatlas.org

EMPLOYERS

Major Employers

Company Name	Industry	Type of Site
Associates Corp North America	Personal credit institutions	Headquarters
Associates First Capital Corp	Mortgage bankers and correspondents	Headquarters
Baylor University Medical Ctr	General medical and surgical hospitals	Headquarters
Dallas Cnty Commissioners Crt	Executive offices	Branch
EDS	Data processing and preparation	Headquarters
JC Penney	Department stores	Headquarters
Lockheed Martin	Aircraft	Branch
MCI	Telephone communication, except radio	Branch
National Elec Contrs Assn	Insurance agents, brokers, and service	Single
Odyssey Healthcare Inc	Skilled nursing care facilities	Headquarters
Parkland Health & Hospital Sys	General medical and surgical hospitals	Headquarters
Raytheon	Radio and t.v. communications equipment	Single
Romanos Macaroni Grill	Eating places	Single
SFG Management Ltd Lblty Co	Fluid milk	Single
Southwestern Medical School	Accident and health insurance	Headquarters
Teaching Assistance Office	Colleges and universities	Branch
Texas Instruments	Semiconductors and related devices	Headquarters
UPS	Courier services, except by air	Branch
Verizon	Business consulting, nec	Branch
Verizon	Telephone communication, except radio	Branch

Note: Companies shown are located within the Dallas metropolitan area; nec = not elsewhere classified.
Source: www.zapdata.com, May 2008

PUBLIC SAFETY

Crime Rate

Area	All Crimes	Violent Crimes				Property Crimes		
		Murder	Forcible Rape	Robbery	Aggrav. Assault	Burglary	Larceny -Theft	Motor Vehicle Theft
City	1,258.3	3.1	12.2	6.1	36.7	206.7	943.0	50.5
Metro[1]	4,972.8	6.4	32.8	219.6	300.8	1,025.0	2,827.7	560.5
U.S.	3,808.1	5.7	30.9	149.4	287.5	729.4	2,206.8	398.4

Note: Figures are crimes per 100,000 population; (1) Metropolitan Division - see Appendix B for areas included
Source: FBI Uniform Crime Reports, 2006

Hate Crimes

Area	Number of Quarters Reported	Bias Motivation				
		Race	Religion	Sexual Orientation	Ethnicity	Disability
City	4	0	0	0	0	0

Source: Federal Bureau of Investigation, Hate Crime Statistics 2006

RECREATION

Culture

Dance[1]	Theatre[1]	Instrumental Music[1]	Vocal Music[1]	Series/ Festivals	Museums	Zoos and Aquariums[2]
0	0	0	0	0	0	0

Note: (1) Number of professional perfoming groups; (2) AZA-accredited
Source: The Grey House Performing Arts Directory, 2007; Official Museum Directory, 2008; Association of Zoos & Aquariums, AZA Member Zoos & Aquariums, June 2008

Professional Sports Teams

Team Name	League
Texas Rangers	Major League Baseball (MLB)
FC Dallas	Major League Soccer (MLS)
Dallas Mavericks	National Basketball Association (NBA)
Dallas Cowboys	National Football League (NFL)
Dallas Stars	National Hockey League (NHL)

Note: Includes teams located in the Dallas-Fort Worth metro area.
Source: Original research

MEDIA

Newspapers

Name	News Focus	Frequency	Circulation
The Flower Mound Messenger	Local	Weekly	40,000

Note: Includes newspapers with offices located in the city
Source: MediaContactsPro, March 2008

Television Stations

Name	Ch.	Network(s)	Type	Ownership
KDTN	2	PBS	Public	North Texas Public Broadcasting Inc.
KDFW	4	Fox	Commercial	Fox Television Stations Inc.
KXAS	5	NBC	Commercial	General Electric Corporation
WFAA	8	ABC	Commercial	Belo Corporation
KTVT	11	CBS	Commercial	CBS
KERA	13	PBS	Public	North Texas Public Broadcasting Inc.
KSST	18	n/a	Commercial	Hopkins County Broadcasting Inc.
KTXA	21	UPN	Commercial	CBS
KUVN	23	Univision	Commercial	Perenchio Television Inc.
KDFI	27	Fox	Commercial	Fox Television Stations Inc.
KMPX	29	n/a	Non-comm.	n/a
KDAF	33	WBN	Commercial	Tribune Broadcasting Company
KXTX	39	Telemundo	Commercial	Telemundo Group Inc.
KTAQ	47	n/a	Commercial	Michael Simons
KSTR	49	Univision	Commercial	Univision Television Group
KFWD	52	n/a	Commercial	n/a
KDTX	58	n/a	Non-comm.	Trinity Broadcasting Network
KPXD	68	Pax	Commercial	Paxson Communications Corporation

Note: Stations included cover the Dallas-Fort Worth DMA (Designated Market Area)
BurrellesLuce, MediaContacts Online, January 2007

Major AM Radio Stations

Call Letters	Freq. (kHz)	Station Type	Target Audience	Station Format	Music Format
KLIF	570	Commercial	General/Men	News/Talk	n/a
KMKI	620	n/a	General	Music	n/a
KSKY	660	n/a	General/Hisp/Rel	Music/Sports/Talk	n/a
KKDA	730	Commercial	General	Music/News	Rhythm & Blues
KAAM	770	Commercial	General	Music	Adult Standards
WBAP	820	Commercial	General	Educational/News/Talk	n/a
KFJZ	870	Commercial	General/Hispanic	Music/News/Sports/Talk	Latin
KKLF	950	n/a	General	News/Talk	n/a
KHVN	970	n/a	Christian/General	Music	n/a
KGGR	1040	n/a	Black/General/Rel	Talk	n/a
KRLD	1080	n/a	General	n/a	n/a
KBIS	1150	n/a	General/Hispanic	Music/News/Talk	n/a
KSST	1230	n/a	General	Music/News	Easy Listening
KPJC	1250	College	General	Music/News	Jazz
KTCK	1310	Commercial	General	Talk	n/a
KAND	1340	Commercial	General	Music/News	Country
KAHZ	1360	n/a	General/Hispanic	Ed/News/Sports/Talk	n/a
KBEC	1390	Commercial	General	Music	Country
KGVL	1400	n/a	General	Music/News/Sports	n/a
KLVQ	1410	n/a	General/Religious	Music	n/a
KFYN	1420	n/a	General	Music/News/Sports	n/a
KTNO	1440	Commercial	Hispanic/Religious	Music/Talk	Gospel
KNET	1450	n/a	General	Music	n/a
KTFW	1460	Commercial	General/Hispanic	n/a	n/a
KPLT	1490	Commercial	General	Music/News/Sports/Talk	Gospel
KSTV	1510	Commercial	General/Hispanic	Music	Top 40
KZMP	1540	n/a	General/Hispanic	Music	n/a
KCOM	1550	Commercial	General/Hispanic	Music	Country
KTBK	1700	Commercial	General	Sports/Talk	n/a

Note: Stations included cover the Dallas-Fort Worth DMA (Designated Market Area); n/a not available
Source: BurrellesLuce, MediaContacts Online, January 2007

Major FM Radio Stations

Call Letters	Freq. (mHz)	Station Type	Target Audience	Station Format	Music Format
KNTU	88.1	College	General	Educational/Music/News	n/a
KEOM	88.5	n/a	General	Ed/Music/News/Sports	n/a
KETR	88.9	College	General	Music/Sports	n/a
KNON	89.3	Non-Comm	Black/Hispanic	Ed/Music/News/Talk	Album Rock
KERA	90.1	Public	General	Music/Talk	Folk
KCBI	90.9	n/a	General/Religious	Music/News	n/a
KVTT	91.7	n/a	General/Religious	Educational/Talk	n/a
KZPS	92.5	n/a	General	Music/News/Talk	n/a
KSTV	93.1	Commercial	General	Music/News	Country
KDBN	93.3	Commercial	General	Music/Talk	Classic Rock
KLNO	94.1	Commercial	General/Hispanic	Music	Latin
KLTY	94.9	Commercial	General/Religious	Music/News/Talk	Christian
KZZA	95.1	Commercial	General	Music	Latin
KSCS	96.3	Commercial	General	Music/News/Talk	Country
KEGL	97.1	Commercial	General	Music/News/Sports	Modern Rock
KBFB	97.9	Commercial	General	Music	Urban Contemp.
KYYK	98.3	n/a	General	Music	n/a
KLUV	98.7	Commercial	General	Music/News/Talk	Oldies
KHCK	99.1	Commercial	General/Hispanic	Music	Latin
KPLX	99.5	Commercial	General	Music	Country
WRR	101.1	Commercial	General	Music/News/Talk	Classical
KZMP	101.7	n/a	General/Hispanic	Music	n/a
KBUS	101.9	Commercial	General	Music/News	Classic Rock
KDGE	102.1	Commercial	Young Adult	Music/News/Talk	Alternative
KDMX	102.9	Commercial	General/Women	Music/News/Talk	Adult Top 40
KVIL	103.7	n/a	General	Music	n/a
KKDA	104.5	n/a	Black/General	Music	n/a
KRNB	105.7	n/a	General	Music/News/Sports	n/a
KHKS	106.1	Commercial	General	Music/News/Talk	Top 40
KOAI	107.5	n/a	General	Music/Talk	n/a
KPLT	107.7	n/a	General	Music/News	Top 40
KDXX	107.9	Commercial	General/Hispanic	Music/News/Talk	Adult Contemp.

Note: Stations included cover the Dallas-Fort Worth DMA (Designated Market Area); n/a not available
BurrellesLuce, MediaContacts Online, January 2007

CLIMATE

Average and Extreme Temperatures

Temperature	Jan	Feb	Mar	Apr	May	Jun	Jul	Aug	Sep	Oct	Nov	Dec	Yr.
Extreme High (°F)	85	90	100	100	101	112	111	109	107	101	91	87	112
Average High (°F)	55	60	68	76	84	92	96	96	89	79	67	58	77
Average Temp. (°F)	45	50	57	66	74	82	86	86	79	68	56	48	67
Average Low (°F)	35	39	47	56	64	72	76	75	68	57	46	38	56
Extreme Low (°F)	-2	9	12	30	39	53	58	58	42	24	16	0	-2

Note: Figures cover the years 1945-1993
Source: National Climatic Data Center, International Station Meteorological Climate Summary, 9/96

Average Precipitation/Snowfall/Humidity

Precip./Humidity	Jan	Feb	Mar	Apr	May	Jun	Jul	Aug	Sep	Oct	Nov	Dec	Yr.
Avg. Precip. (in.)	1.9	2.3	2.6	3.8	4.9	3.4	2.1	2.3	2.9	3.3	2.3	2.1	33.9
Avg. Snowfall (in.)	1	1	Tr	Tr	0	0	0	0	0	Tr	Tr	Tr	3
Avg. Rel. Hum. 6am (%)	78	77	75	77	82	81	77	76	80	79	78	77	78
Avg. Rel. Hum. 3pm (%)	53	51	47	49	51	48	43	41	46	46	48	51	48

Note: Figures cover the years 1945-1993; Tr = Trace amounts (<0.05 in. of rain; <0.5 in. of snow)
Source: National Climatic Data Center, International Station Meteorological Climate Summary, 9/96

Weather Conditions

Temperature			Daytime Sky			Precipitation		
10°F & below	32°F & below	90°F & above	Clear	Partly cloudy	Cloudy	0.01 inch or more precip.	0.1 inch or more snow/ice	Thunder-storms
1	34	102	108	160	97	78	2	49

Note: Figures are average number of days per year and cover the years 1945-1993
Source: National Climatic Data Center, International Station Meteorological Climate Summary, 9/96

HAZARDOUS WASTE

Superfund Sites

Flower Mound has no sites on the EPA's Superfund Final National Priorities List.
U.S. Environmental Protection Agency, Final National Priorities List, June 23, 2008

AIR & WATER QUALITY

Air Quality Index

Area	Percent of Days when Air Quality was...[2]				AQI Statistics	
	Good	Moderate	Unhealthy for Sensitive Groups	Unhealthy	Maximum	Median
MSA[1]	67.1	27.7	4.4	0.8	177	44

Note: The Air Quality Index (AQI) is an index for reporting daily air quality. EPA calculates the AQI for five major air pollutants regulated by the Clean Air Act: ground-level ozone, particle pollution (also known as particulate matter), carbon monoxide, sulfur dioxide, and nitrogen dioxide. The AQI runs from 0 to 500. The higher the AQI value, the greater the level of air pollution and the greater the health concern. There are six AQI categories: "Good" The AQI is between 0 and 50. Air quality is considered satisfactory; "Moderate" The AQI is between 51 and 100. Air quality is acceptable; "Unhealthy for Sensitive Groups" When AQI values are between 101 and 150, members of sensitive groups may experience health effects; "Unhealthy" When AQI values are between 151 and 200 everyone may begin to experience health effects; "Very Unhealthy" AQI values between 201 and 300 trigger a health alert; "Hazardous" AQI values over 300 trigger health warnings of emergency conditions; (1) Metropolitan Statistical Area - see Appendix A for areas included; (2) Based on 365 days with AQI data in 2007.
Source: U.S. Environmental Protection Agency, Air Quality Index Report, 2007

Air Quality Index Pollutants

Area	Percent of Days when AQI Pollutant was...[2]					
	Carbon Monoxide	Nitrogen Dioxide	Ozone	Sulfur Dioxide	Particulate Matter 2.5	Particulate Matter 10
MSA[1]	0.0	0.0	61.6	0.3	38.1	0.0

Note: The Air Quality Index (AQI) is an index for reporting daily air quality. EPA calculates the AQI for five major air pollutants regulated by the Clean Air Act: ground-level ozone, particle pollution (also known as particulate matter), carbon monoxide, sulfur dioxide, and nitrogen dioxide. The AQI runs from 0 to 500. The higher the AQI value, the greater the level of air pollution and the greater the health concern; (1) Metropolitan Statistical Area - see Appendix A for areas included; (2) Based on 365 days with AQI data in 2007.
Source: U.S. Environmental Protection Agency, Air Quality Index Report, 2007

Air Quality Index Trends

Area	Trend Sites (7)								All Sites (83)
	1999	2000	2001	2002	2003	2004	2005	2006	2006
MSA[1]	16	20	14	7	5	9	10	13	26

Note: An AQI value greater than 100 indicates that air quality would have been in the unhealthful range on that day. Data from exceptional events are not included. These counts are presented in two ways. First, the counts are based on sites having an adequate record of monitoring data during the trend period (trend sites). These counts represent the relative change in the number of days with AQI values greater than 100. In the last column, the counts are based on all sites with data in the most recent year (because it is possible for a site to have data in the most recent year but not enough data to be a trend site); (1) Metropolitan Statistical Area - see Appendix A for areas included.
Source: U.S. Environmental Protection Agency, Office of Air and Radiation, Air Trends, Factbook and Related Information, Air Pollution Trends in Selected Metropolitan Areas 2006

Maximum Air Pollutant Concentrations

	Particulate Matter 10 (ug/m^3)	Particulate Matter 2.5 (ug/m^3)	Ozone (ppm)	Carbon Monoxide (ppm)	Sulfur Dioxide (ppm)	Nitrogen Dioxide (ppm)	Lead (ug/m^3)
MSA[1] Level	56	23	0.115	2	0.02	0.016	0.77 (a)
NAAQS[2]	150	35	0.125	9	0.140	0.053	1.50
Met NAAQS[2]	Yes	Yes	Yes	Yes	Yes	Yes	Yes

Note: Data from exceptional events are not included; (1) Metropolitan Statistical Area - see Appendix A for areas included; (2) National Ambient Air Quality Standards; n/a not available; (a) Localized impact from an industrial source in Dallas. Concentration from highest nonpoint source site is 0.14 ug/m^3 in Collin County
Concentrations: Particulate Matter 10 (coarse particulate) - highest second maximum 24-hour concentration; Particulate Matter 2.5 (fine particulate) - highest 98th percentile 24-hour concentration; Ozone - highest second daily maximum 1-hour concentration; Carbon Monoxide - highest second maximum non-overlapping 8-hour concentration; Sulfur Dioxide - highest second maximum 24-hour concentration; Nitrogen Dioxide - highest arithmetic mean concentration; Lead - highest quarterly maximum concentration
Units: ppm = parts per million; ug/m^3 = micrograms per cubic meter
Source: U.S. Environmental Protection Agency, MSA Factbook 2006, Air Quality Statistics by City

Drinking Water

Water System Name	Pop. Served	Primary Water Source Type	Violations[1]	
			Health Based	Monitoring/ Reporting
Town of Flower Mound	60,000	Purchased Surface	0	0

Note: (1) Based on violation data from January 1, 2007 to December 31, 2007 (includes unresolved violations from earlier years)
Source: U.S. Environmental Protection Agency, Office of Ground Water and Drinking Water, Safe Drinking Water Information System (based on data extracted April 15, 2008)

Frisco, Texas

Background

Frisco is located in northwestern Texas and straddles the line between Collins and Denton Counties. A suburb of Dallas, it sits at an elevation of 696 feet on the rich black farmland that covers the region. Frisco is fast becoming a desirable community for suburban Dallas residents.

European immigrants journeying by wagon on the Shawnee Trail north of Austin, used to drive cattle to seasonal grazing grounds, were the first to pass through the area. Lebanon, just east of Frisco, was settled first along the St. Louis-San Francisco Railway line, but its location did not allow it to be a "watering hole" to refill steam engines. Thus, Frisco was settled four miles to the west where lower ground sits and a lake provided water for the railway.

Frisco was formally established in 1902 when the land owned by the Frisco Railroad was divided into lots and auctioned off to settlers. The settlement was originally named Emerson, but the U.S. Postal Service rejected the name since it was similar to another Texas town Frisco was chosen to honor the St. Louis-San Francisco Railway that ran through the community.

Frisco soon became a thriving trading hub for the surrounding farming communities. By 1910, there were 332 residents. Within the next ten years the population doubled, but it was not until the 1960s that the population surpassed 1,000. In the early 1990s Frisco's population exploded to over 20,000 people. Currently, with population of over 80,000, it's considered one of the fastest growing suburbs in the country. This is due in part to efforts of the Frisco Economic Development Corporation that focus on improving the quality of life in the thriving community, and developing strong industry that includes tourism.

This motivated community developed a strong education system. Frisco is also home to the Preston Ridge campus of the Collin County Community College system, Amberton University, and a regional academic center of the Dallas Baptist University.

Frisco offers many forms of recreation ranging from cultural and fine arts to sports and leisure. The city is home to the Texas sculpture garden, the largest private collection of Texas contemporary sculptures available for public viewing. Frisco is also home to both the Dr. Pepper/7-up Ballpark and the Frisco Recreation Center. Frisco's Pizza Hut Soccer Park boasts seven fields and is surrounded by shopping and restaurants. Additional shopping is available at Stonebriar Center featuring over 160 shops, an ice rink, numerous restaurants, a carousel, and a 24-screen movie theater. The community has an extensive system of 27 public parks and trails, and is a 30-minute drive from Collin County Ballet Theater and the Courtyard Theater in Plano.

Frisco is known for its many sports teams, including RoughRiders, a minor league baseball team, Dallas Stars, of the National Hockey League, Texas Tornado, a North American Hockey League team, Frisco Thunder, of the Intense Football League, and the FC Dallas, a Major League Soccer team.

The yearly average temperature in Frisco is 40 degrees F in January to just over 80 degrees F in July.

Rankings

General Rankings

- Dallas* was ranked #132 out of 375 metro areas in *Cities Ranked & Rated*. Criteria: cost of living; climate; crime; transportation; economy and jobs; education; arts and culture; health and healthcare; leisure; quality of life. *Cities Ranked & Rated, 2nd Edition, 2007*
- Dallas* was ranked #43 out of 379 metro areas in *Places Rated Almanac*. Criteria: health care; education; recreation; transportation; ambience; climate; crime; housing costs; jobs. *Places Rated Almanac, 7th Edition, 2007*

Business/Finance Rankings

- The nation's 100 largest metro areas were analysed in terms of the percentage of households entering some stage of foreclosure in 2007. The Dallas* metro area ranked #28 out of 100 (#1 = highest foreclosure rate). *RealtyTrac, "Year-End 2007 Metropolitan Foreclosure Report"*
- The Dallas* metro area was selected one of America's "Top 50 Business Opportunity Metros" by *Expansion Management* in their 5th annual Mayor's Challenge ranking of metro areas that have achieved solid ratings across the board in numerous *EM* studies during the past 12 months. The area ranked #13. Criteria: public schools; quality of life; college educated workers; logistics infrastructure; healthcare costs; taxes and government spending; reputation among site consultants. *Expansion Management, August 2007*
- The Dallas* metro area was selected as one of "America's Most Wired Cities" by *Forbes*. The metro area was ranked #19 out of 30. Criteria: percentage of Internet users with high-speed access; the range of service providers within a city; availability of public wireless hot spots. *Forbes, "America's Most Wired Cities," January 10, 2008*
- Dallas* was selected as one of the best places to start and grow a company by *Entrepreneur* and the National Policy Research Council. The Dallas* metro area ranked #17 out of 50 large metro areas. Criteria: business formation and growth (firms started four to 14 years ago that still employ at least 5 people and experienced rapid growth over the last four years). *Entrepreneur/National Policy Research Council, "Hot Cities for Entrepreneurs," September 2006*
- The Dallas* metro area was selected as one of "America's Greediest Cities" by *Forbes*. The area was ranked #7 out of 10. Criteria: number of Forbes 400 (*Forbes* annual list of the richest Americans) members per capita. *Forbes, "America's Greediest Cities," December 7, 2007*
- The Dallas* metro area was selected as one of "America's 50 Hottest Cities" for business relocations and expansions. Criteria: industry's most prominent site selection consultants were asked to list their top city choices for relocating and expanding manufacturing companies, taking into consideration such factors as the business climate, work force quality, operating costs, incentive programs, and the ease of working with local political and economic development officials. *Expansion Management, January-February 2007*
- Dallas* was cited as one of America's top large metros (population over 1 million) for new and expanded facility projects in 2007. The area appeared in the top 10 with 73 projects. *Site Selection, "Top Metropolitan Area Awards," March 2008*
- The Dallas* metro area was selected as one of the "Top 20 Real Estate Markets" for expanding or relocating companies. The area ranked #7. Criteria: low rental costs; low purchase prices; high vacancy rates of office and warehouse space. *Expansion Management, October 2007*
- Intel, in partnership with Sperling's BestPlaces, ranked the 80 "Best Cities for Teleworking" in America. The Dallas* metro area ranked #8 among extra large metro areas. The study identifies cities that hold the greatest potential for teleworking based on a host of factors including typical commuting times, fuel prices, availability of broadband Internet access and percentage of the population in telework friendly jobs. The study also factored in extreme climate and natural hazards. *Intel, "Best Cities for Teleworking," March 30, 2006*

- The Dallas* metro area appeared on the Milken Institute "2007 Best Performing Cities" index. Rank: #59 out of 200 large metro areas. Criteria: job growth; wage and salary growth; high-tech output growth. *Milken Institute, "2007 Best Performing Cities"*

- The Dallas* metro area was selected as one of "The Top 20 Boom Towns in America." *Business 2.0* magazine and econometric research firm Global Insight compared 319 metropolitan areas in the U.S. and ranked the 61 with populations over 1 million. Criteria: a weighted formula that includes forecast growth rates in sectors that contain the economy's 10 most skilled occupational clusters; the prevalence of college degrees in the local workforce; median salary. The area ranked #18 among large metro areas. *Business 2.0 Magazine, March 2004*

- Dallas* was identified as one of the 100 "Most Unwired Cities" in the U.S. The area ranked #23 out of the 100 largest metro areas in the U.S. Criteria: number of public and commercial wireless access points (hotspots); airports with wireless Internet access; broadband availability; local wireless networks; and wireless email devices. *Intel, "Most Unwired Cities Survey," June 7, 2005*

- Dallas* was ranked #21 out of 125 regions worldwide in terms of its "Knowledge Competitiveness Index." The index attempts to measure the knowledge-based development taking place throughout the world and is based on 19 measures of economic performance that indicate a region's ability to translate its knowledge capacity into economic value. *Robert Huggins Associates, World Knowledge Competitiveness Index 2005*

- *Forbes* ranked the 200 most populous metro areas in the U.S. in terms of the "Best Places for Business and Careers." The Dallas* metro area was ranked #93. Criteria: business costs (labor, energy, tax and office space expenses); living costs (housing, transportation, food and other household expenditures); education levels of the work force; job growth; income growth; migration trends; crime rates; and culture/leisure. *Forbes, "Best Places for Business and Careers," March 19, 2008*

- *Fortune* ranked the 100 largest metro areas in the U.S. in terms of projected median home price change in 2007. The Dallas* metro area ranked #13. *Fortune.com, "Hot Spots, Cold Spots"*

Health/Environment Rankings

- 100 of the largest metro areas in the U.S. were analyzed in terms of their current drought severity. The Dallas* metro area ranked #97 (#1 = driest). The rankings were based on statistics such as long-term precipitation trends and patterns and the Palmer drought indices. *Sperling's BestPlaces, www.BestPlaces.net, "America's Drought-Riskiest Cities," November 2007*

- Doctors at the Harvard School of Public Health ranked 40 metropolitan areas based on data from the government-sponsored Hospital Quality Alliance program. The program tracks the performance of individual hospitals in treating patients for three common health problems: heart attacks, congestive heart failure, and pneumonia. The Dallas* metro area ranked #22 in quality of care for heart attacks, #25 for congestive heart failure, and #7 for pneumonia. *New England Journal of Medicine, July 21, 2005*

- *Reader's Digest* ranked the 50 largest metro areas in the U.S. in terms of how "clean" they are. The Dallas* metro area ranked #30. Criteria: air quality; water quality; toxic industrial pollution; Superfund sites; and sanitation. *Reader's Digest, "The 50 Cleanest (and Dirtiest) Cities in America," July 2005*

- The American Academy of Dermatology ranked 32 U.S. metropolitan regions in terms of their residents knowledge, attitude and behaviors towards tanning and sun protection. The Dallas* metro area ranked #6. The results of the study are based on an online national survey of 3,342 respondents. *American Academy of Dermatology, "RAYS: Your Grade," May 7, 2007*

- The Dallas* metro area appeared in *Country Home's* "2008 Best Green Places" report. The area ranked #94 out of 379. Criteria: official energy policies; green power; green buildings; availability of fresh, locally grown food. *Country Home, "2008 Best Green Places"*

- Wyeth Consumer Healthcare, in partnership with Sperling's BestPlaces, ranked the nation's 50 most populous metro areas in terms of five key health factors. The Dallas* metro area ranked #35. Criteria: physical activity; health status; nutrition; lifestyle pursuits; and mental wellness. *Wyeth Consumer Healthcare, "Centrum Healthiest Cities Study," April 19, 2005*

- HealthGrades surveyed over 41,000 individuals on doctor satisfaction and ranked the 20 largest metro areas based on the highest "definitely yes" responses to the question "Do you trust the physician to make decisions/recommendations that are in your best interest?" The Dallas* metro area ranked #2. *HealthGrades.com, "Top Cities in Doctor-Trust," September 7, 2006*

- Dallas* was identified as a "2008 Asthma Capital." The area ranked #23 out of the nation's 100 largest metropolitan areas. Twelve factors were used to identify the most challenging places to live for people with asthma: estimated prevalence; self-reported prevalence; crude death rate for asthma; annual pollen score; annual air quality; public smoking laws; number of board-certified asthma specialists; school inhaler access laws; rescue medication use; controller medication use; uninsured rate; poverty rate. *Asthma and Allergy Foundation of America, "2008 Asthma Capitals"*

- Dallas* was identified as a "Spring Allergy Capital." The area ranked #2 out of 100. Three groups of factors were used to identify the most severe cities for people with allergies during the spring season: annual pollen levels; medicine utilization; access to board-certified allergists. *Asthma and Allergy Foundation of America, "2007 Spring Allergy Capital Rankings"*

- Dallas* was identified as a "Fall Allergy Capital." The area ranked #21 out of 100. Three groups of factors were used to identify the most severe cities for people with allergies during the fall season: annual pollen levels; medicine utilization; access to board-certified allergists. *Asthma and Allergy Foundation of America, "2007 Fall Allergy Capital Rankings"*

- Ortho-McNeil Neurologics, in partnership with Sperling's BestPlaces, analyzed 110 metro areas and identified those U.S. cities with the highest prevalence of factors that are most commonly associated with migraine headaches. The Dallas* metro area ranked #82. Criteria: number of migraine-related drug prescriptions per capita; lifestyle factors that can contribute to migraines; environmental factors that can trigger migraines; and consumption of migraine-triggering foods. *Ortho-McNeil Neurologics, "America's Migraine Hot Spots," March 14, 2006*

- Sperling's BestPlaces ranked 331 metro areas and identified the most and least stressful U.S. cities. The Dallas* metro area ranked #10 out of the 100 largest metro areas (#1 = most stressful). Criteria: divorce rate; unemployment rate; violent and property crime; suicide rate; commute time; mental health; alcohol consumption; cloudy days. *Sperling's BestPlaces, www.BestPlaces.net, "America's Most (and Least) Stressful Cities," January 9, 2004*

- An analysis of the "Best & Worst Cities for Sleep" was conducted by Sperling's BestPlaces. The study ranked America's 50 most populated metro areas. The Dallas* metro area ranked #21 (#1 = best city for sleep). Criteria: number of days residents didn't get enough rest or sleep during the past month; average length of daily commute; divorce rate; unemployment rate. *Sperling's BestPlaces, www.BestPlaces.net, "Best & Worst Cities for Sleep," 2006*

- HealthGrades evaluated the performance of America's 25 most populous metropolitan areas by measuring the outcomes of five of the highest volume and most widely studied procedures and diagnoses: coronary artery bypass graft surgery; percutaneus coronary interventions; acute myocardial infarction/heart attack in angioplasty-capable hospitals; congestive heart failure; and community acquired pneumonia. The Dallas* metro area ranked #21. *HealthGrades, "HealthGrades Hospital Quality in America Study," October 12, 2004*

- Dallas* was highlighted as one of the 25 most ozone-polluted metro areas in the U.S. The area ranked #7. *American Lung Association, State of the Air: 2007*

- Dallas* was selected as one of "America's Top 10 Low-Carb Cities" by *LowCarbiz Magazine*. Criteria: abundance of low-carb products; restaurants with low-carb menu items; health practitioners supportive of carb-cutting regimens; local culture generally conducive to exercise and health. *LowCarbiz Magazine, April 2004*

- Dallas* was selected as one of "America's Pet Healthiest Cities" by Purina. The city ranked #40 out of 50. Criteria: veterinary services; environment; legislation; preventative care; obesity/body condition. *Purina Pet Institute, "America's Pet Healthiest Cities," May 20, 2003*

Women/Minorities Rankings

- Dallas* was ranked #84 out of 100 metro areas in *SELF Magazine's* ranking of "America's Best Places for Women." A panel of experts came up with more than 50 criteria including death and disease rates, environmental indicators, community resources, and lifestyle habits. *SELF Magazine, "America's Best Places for Women 2007," December 2007*

- Dallas* appeared on *Black Enterprise's* list of the "Ten Best Cities for African Americans." The top picks were culled from more than 2,000 interactive surveys completed on www.blackenterprise.com and by editorial staff evaluation. The editors weighed the following criteria as it pertained to African Americans in each city: median household income; percentage of households earning more than $100,000; percentage of businesses owned; percentage of college graduates; unemployment rates; home loan rejections; and homeownership rates. *Black Enterprise, May 2007*

Seniors/Retirement Rankings

- Frisco was identified as one of the "100 Most Popular Places to Retire" by *Where to Retire* magazine. The city ranked #67. Criteria: net retirees received from 1995-2000 (derived by subtracting all outbound retirees from inbound retirees for the county or county group - includes interstate moves only). *Where to Retire, "100 Most Popular Places to Retire," January/February 2007*

- Sperling's BestPlaces in partnership with Bankers Life & Casualty Company designed a survey to identify the top 50 metro areas in the U.S. that offer the best overall qualities for senior living. The Dallas* metro area ranked #44. The following criteria were statistically weighted to reflect the needs of the senior population: health; disease; economics; social; environment; spiritual; transportation; housing; and crime. *Bankers Life & Casualty Company, "Best Cities for Seniors 2005"*

Children/Family Rankings

- The Dallas* metro area was selected as one of the "Best Cities for Relocating Families" by Worldwide ERC and Primacy Relocation. The 2007 study placed a special emphasis on the housing market, which has significantly impacted the relocation industry and an employer's ability to transfer employees. The variables which weigh heavily in this category include home price, home affordability index, appreciation rates, and property tax. Other criteria include cost of living, crime rates, education, climate, focus on diversity, physicians per capita, recreation and leisure, arts and culture, air quality, watershed quality, sales tax, unemployment rate, job growth, high school and higher education index, school expenditures per student, students in public school, SAT/ACT percentile, and population growth. *Worldwide ERC and Primacy Relocation, "2007 Best Cities for Relocating Families"*

Safety Rankings

- The National Insurance Crime Bureau ranked 361 metro areas in the U.S. in terms of per capita rates of vehicle theft. The Dallas* metro area ranked #50 (#1 = highest rate). Criteria: number of vehicle theft offenses per 100,000 inhabitants. *National Insurance Crime Bureau, "NICB Vehicle Theft Study," April 22, 2008*

- Dallas* appeared on Sperling's BestPlaces list of the "Riskiest Cities for Identity Theft." The area ranked #13 out of the nations 50 largest metro areas. Over 80 criteria were analyzed across four major categories: technology impact; crime; transactions; and risk profile. *Sperling's BestPlaces, www.BestPlaces.net, "Riskiest Cities for Identity Theft," July 2006*

- Farmers Insurance Group of Companies, in partnership with Sperling's BestPlaces, ranked 379 metro areas and identified the "Most Secure U.S. Place to Live." The Dallas* metro area ranked #91 out of 114 in the large metro area category (500,000 or more residents). Criteria: crime rates; extreme weather; risk of natural disasters; environmental hazards; terrorism threats; air quality; life expectancy; job loss numbers. *Farmers Insurance Group, "Most Secure U.S. Places to Live 2007"*

- Dallas* was identified as one of the most dangerous large metro areas for pedestrians in the U.S. The area ranked #14 out of the nations 50 largest metro areas. Criteria: average yearly pedestrian fatalities per capita (for the years 2002 and 2003) adjusted for the number of walkers. *Surface Transportation Policy Project, "Mean Streets 2004"*

- Dallas* was identified as one of the least safe places in the U.S. in terms of its vulnerability to natural disasters and weather extremes. The city ranked #2 out of 10. Sperling's BestPlaces analyzed data to show a metro areas' relative tendency to experience natural disasters (hail, tornados, high winds, hurricanes, earthquakes, and brush fires) or extreme weather (abundant rain or snowfall or days that are below freezing or above 90 degrees Fahrenheit). *Forbes, "Safest and Least Safe Places in the U.S.," August 30, 2005*

Sports/Recreation Rankings

- The Dallas* metro area appeared on the *Sporting News* list of the "Best Sports Cities 2007". The area ranked #3 out of 150 cities in the U.S. *Sporting News* takes a 12-month snapshot, roughly July to July, of each city's sports, putting a heavy premium on regular-season won-lost records (from the most recently completed season). Other criteria include: playoff berths, bowl appearances and tournament bids; championships; applicable power ratings; quality of competition; overall fan fervor as measured in part by attendance as percentage of venue capacity; abundance of teams (rewarding quality over quantity); stadium and arena quality; ticket availability and prices; franchise ownership; and marquee appeal of athletes. *SportingNews.com, "Best Sports Cities 2007," August 1, 2007*

- Scarborough Research, a leading market research firm, identified the top local markets for avid NBA fans. The Dallas* DMA (Designated Market Area) ranked in the top 10 with 13% of consumers 18 years and over reporting that they are "very interested in the NBA". *Scarborough Research, April 24, 2006*

- The Dallas* metro area was selected by *Cranium* as one of the "Top 50 Fun Cities" in America. The area ranked #34. Criteria includes: number of sports teams, restaurants, and dance performances; number of toy stores; city budget spent on recreation. *Cranium, November 4, 2003*

- *Golf Digest* ranked 330 metro areas in the U.S. in terms of golf. The Dallas* metro area was ranked #256. Criteria: access to golf; weather; value of golf; and quality of golf. *Golf Digest, "Metro Golf Rankings," August 2005*

Dating/Romance Rankings

- Eli Lily and Company, in partnership with Sperling's BestPlaces, ranked the nation's 50 largest metro areas in terms of the "Most Romantic Cities for Baby Boomers." The Dallas* metro area ranked #9. Criteria: marriage and divorce rates among "baby boomers" age 45 to 60; great restaurants; dance studios; chocolate, jewelry and flower sales. *Eli Lily and Company, "Most Romantic Cities for Baby Boomers," April 20, 2007*

- The Dallas* metro area was selected as one of the "Top Ten U.S. Cities for Finding a Rich, Single Man" by Teasley, a Manhattan-based marketing consulting firm. The area ranked #10. Criteria: high single-male to single-female ratios; higher income to cost-of-living ratios. *Teasley, "Top Ten U.S. Cities for Finding a Rich, Single Man," February 10, 2004*

- The Dallas* metro area was selected as one of the "Best Cities for Relocating Singles" by Worldwide ERC and Primacy Relocation. The area ranked #52 out of the 100 largest metro areas in the U.S. Areas were selected based on the following criteria: a robust cost-of-living index; adventure and outdoor recreation opportunities; violent crime and property crime rates; percentage of the population that is unmarried (ages 25-34); ratio of single men and single women; affordability of quality higher education, including in-state and out-of-state tuition requirements and rates; number of newcomers to the area; commute times; tax rates; fee and occupancy rates for temporary housing and mini-storage; quality and quantity of collegiate and professional sporting events and fun, fan-friendly venues. *Worldwide ERC and Primacy Relocation, "2007 Best Cities for Relocating Singles," October 25, 2007*
- *Forbes* ranked the 40 most populous urbanized areas in the U.S. in terms of the "Best Cities for Singles." The Dallas* metro area ranked #9. Criteria: number of singles; cost of living alone; nightlife; culture; job growth; coolness; and online dating. *Forbes.com, August 21, 2007*
- Sperling's BestPlaces in partnership with AXE Deodorant Bodyspray ranked 80 metro areas and identified "America's Best (and Worst) Cities for Dating." The Dallas* metro area ranked #51 (#1 = best). Criteria: percentage of singles ages 18-24; population density; dating venues per capita. *AXE Deodorant Bodyspray, "America's Best (and Worst) Cities for Dating," May 2004*

Miscellaneous Rankings

- The Dallas* metro area was identified as one of 10 "Worst Cities for Commuters" by *Forbes*. The metro area ranked #5. Criteria: traffic delays; travel times; how efficiently commuters use existing infrastructure. *Forbes.com, "Worst Cities for Commuters," April 29, 2008*
- Scarborough Research, a leading market research firm, identified the top local markets for bloggers. The Dallas* DMA (Designated Market Area) ranked in the top 13 with 11% of adults reporting that they had read or contributed to a blog within the past 30 days. *Scarborough Research, October 24, 2007*
- Frisco was identified as one of the 100 fastest-growing suburbs in America by "Forbes." The city ranked #7. Criteria: suburban cities, townships and villages with more than 10,000 people in 2000 were ranked by their population growth from 2000 to 2006. *Forbes.com, "America's Fastest-Growing Suburbs," July 16, 2007*
- The Dallas* metro area was selected as one of the "Top 10 Most Independent Cities for Homesellers". The area ranked #9. The cities listed had more consumers choosing to sell their homes without the help of a real-estate agent than anywhere else. Data was based on geographical information for listings posted on ForSaleByOwner.com from January 1, 2007 through June 30, 2007. *ForSaleByOwner.com, October 1, 2007*
- The Dallas* metro area appeared on *Forbes* list of "America's Drunkest Cities". The area ranked #27. Criteria: 35 of the largest continental U.S. metro areas were chosen based on availability of data and geographic diversity. Each metro was ranked in five areas: state laws; drinkers; heavy drinkers; binge drinkers; and alcoholism. *Forbes.com, "America's Drunkest Cities," August 22, 2006*
- Sperling's BestPlaces in partnership with Pep Boys ranked 77 metro areas and identified "America's Most Drivable Cities." The Dallas* metro area ranked #40. Criteria: climate; road roughness; urban mobility; gas prices. *Pep Boys, "America's Most Drivable Cities," April 9, 2003*
- State Farm Insurance, in partnership with Sperling's BestPlaces, analyzed several key factors that contribute to overall family preparedness. The Dallas* metro area ranked #28 out of the nation's 50 most populous metro areas. Criteria: quality of life; life insurance coverage; and investments. *State Farm Life Insurance, "Fiscally Fit Cities Report," July 20, 2004*

- A study by Sperling's BestPlaces examined which U.S. metro areas were most affected by high fuel prices in 2006. The Dallas* metro area was ranked #37 out of 80 (#1 = most expensive city for driving). Rankings are based on the average dollars spent on gas per year by two driver households. Criteria: cost of regular-grade gasoline; average miles driven per day; average number of gallons each driver uses and wastes in traffic congestion each day. *Sperling's BestPlaces, www.bestplaces.net, "Pain at the Pump," May 18, 2006*

Frisco is located within the Dallas-Fort Worth-Arlington, TX Metropolitan Statistical Area and Dallas-Plano-Irving, TX Metropolitan Division.

Business Environment

CITY FINANCES

City Government Finances

Component	2004-2005 ($000)	2004-2005 ($ per capita)
Total Revenues	130,676	1,846
Total Expenditures	166,741	2,355
Debt Outstanding	436,017	6,159
Cash and Securities	269,757	3,811

Source: U.S Census Bureau, Government Finances 2004-2005

City Government Revenue by Source

Source	2004-2005 ($000)	2004-2005 ($ per capita)
General Revenue		
From Federal Government	0	0
From State Government	1,506	21
From Local Governments	9,134	129
Taxes		
Property	28,655	405
Sales	31,615	447
Personal Income	0	0
License	10,520	149
Charges	11,924	168
Liquor Store	0	0
Utility	16,537	234
Employee Retirement	0	0
Other	20,785	294

Source: U.S Census Bureau, Government Finances 2004-2005

City Government Expenditures by Function

Function	2004-2005 ($000)	2004-2005 ($ per capita)	2004-2005 (%)
General Expenditures			
Airports	0	0	0.0
Corrections	0	0	0.0
Education	6,434	91	3.9
Fire Protection	7,978	113	4.8
Governmental Administration	6,057	86	3.6
Health	0	0	0.0
Highways	53,236	752	31.9
Hospitals	0	0	0.0
Housing and Community Development	0	0	0.0
Interest on General Debt	18,417	260	11.0
Libraries	720	10	0.4
Parking	0	0	0.0
Parks and Recreation	5,270	74	3.2
Police Protection	7,647	108	4.6
Public Welfare	0	0	0.0
Sewerage	8,659	122	5.2
Solid Waste Management	4,953	70	3.0
Liquor Store	0	0	0.0
Utility	22,710	321	13.6
Employee Retirement	0	0	0.0
Other	24,660	348	14.8

Source: U.S Census Bureau, Government Finances 2004-2005

Municipal Bond Ratings

Area	Moody's
City	Aaa

Source: Mergent Bond Record, January 2008 (unless noted otherwise)

DEMOGRAPHICS

Population Growth

Area	1990 Census	2000 Census	2007 Estimate	2012 Projection	Population Growth (%) 1990-2000	Population Growth (%) 2000-2012
City	6,767	33,714	80,107	110,533	398.2	227.9
MSA[1]	3,989,294	5,161,544	6,007,731	6,587,538	29.4	27.6
U.S.	248,709,873	281,421,906	301,045,522	314,920,978	13.2	11.9

Note: (1) Metropolitan Statistical Area - see Appendix B for areas included
Source: Claritas, Inc.

Number of Households and Average Household Size

Area	2007 Estimate	2007 Average Household Size
City	29,268	2.74
MSA[1]	2,171,092	2.77
U.S.	113,668,003	2.65

Note: (1) Metropolitan Statistical Area - see Appendix B for areas included
Source: Claritas, Inc.

Race and Ethnicity

Area	White Alone[2]	Black Alone[2]	Asian Alone[2]	Other Race Alone[2]	Hispanic[3]
City	81.8	7.2	4.2	6.9	11.7
MSA[1]	65.6	14.0	4.6	15.8	26.4
U.S.	73.1	12.4	4.3	10.3	14.9

Note: Figures are 2007 estimates; (1) Metropolitan Statistical Area - see Appendix B for areas included (2) Alone is defined as not being in combination with one or more other races; (3) May be of any race.
Source: Claritas, Inc.

Ancestry

Area	German	Irish[2]	English	American	Italian	Polish	French[3]	Scottish
City	18.5	11.6	11.7	8.7	4.5	2.4	3.0	2.5
MSA[1]	10.0	8.1	8.2	7.8	2.1	1.2	2.1	1.7
U.S.	15.2	10.9	8.7	7.3	5.6	3.2	3.0	1.7

Note: Figures include multiple ancestry (e.g. if a person reported being Irish and Italian, they were included in both columns); (1) Metropolitan Statistical Area - see Appendix A for areas included; (2) Includes Celtic; (3) Includes Alsatian but excludes Basque
Source: Census 2000, Summary File 3

Foreign-Born Population

Area	Percent of Population Born in: Any Foreign Country	Europe	Asia	Africa	Oceania[2]	Canada	Mexico	Latin America[3]
City	7.8	1.2	1.8	0.3	0.0	0.6	3.2	0.7
MSA[1]	16.8	0.9	3.4	0.6	0.0	0.3	9.8	1.8
U.S.	11.1	1.7	2.9	0.3	0.1	0.3	3.3	2.5

Note: (1) Metropolitan Statistical Area - see Appendix A for areas included; (2) Includes Australia, New Zealand subregion, Melanesia, Micronesia, Polynesia, and Oceania n.e.c; (3) Includes Central America (excluding Mexico), South America, and the Caribbean.
Source: Census 2000, Summary File 3

Marriage Status

Area	Never Married	Now Married (excluding Separated)	Separated	Widowed	Divorced
City	15.0	74.0	1.0	1.9	8.0
MSA[1]	27.2	55.6	2.5	4.6	10.1
U.S.	27.1	54.4	2.2	6.6	9.7

Note: Figures are percentages and cover the population 15 years of age and older; (1) Metropolitan Statistical Area - see Appendix A for areas included
Source: Census 2000, Summary File 3

Age Distribution

Area	Percent of Population						
	Under Age 5	Age 5 to 17	Age 18 to 34	Age 35 to 49	Age 50 to 64	Age 65 to 79	80 Years and Over
City	12.9	17.9	30.5	26.0	9.4	2.7	0.6
MSA[1]	8.1	19.9	27.3	24.4	12.7	5.8	1.8
U.S.	6.8	18.9	23.7	23.5	14.8	9.2	3.2

Note: (1) Metropolitan Statistical Area - see Appendix A for areas included
Source: Census 2000, Summary File 3

Male/Female Ratio

Area	Males	Females	Males per 100 Females
City	39,914	40,193	99.3
MSA[1]	3,012,647	2,995,084	100.6
U.S.	148,320,305	152,725,217	97.1

Note: Figures are 2007 estimates; (1) Metropolitan Statistical Area - see Appendix B for areas included
Source: Claritas, Inc.

Religion

Area	Catholic	Southern Baptist	United Meth-odist	ELCA[1]	LDS[2]	Presby-terian Church USA	Jewish Est.	Muslim Est.
County	18.3	16.0	6.1	0.6	1.3	0.7	1.4	1.2
U.S.	22.0	7.1	3.7	1.8	1.5	1.1	2.2	0.6

Note: Figures are the number of adherents as a percentage of the total population; Adherents are defined as all members, including full members, their children and the estimated number of other participants who are not considered members (e.g. the baptized, those not confirmed, those regularly attending services, etc.);
(1) Evangelical Lutheran Church in America; (2) The Church of Jesus Christ of Latter Day Saints
Source: Reprinted with permission from Religious Congregations and Membership in the United States 2000 (Nashville, Glenmary Research Center, 2002) Copyright Association of Statisticians of American Religious Bodies. All rights reserved.

ECONOMY

Gross Metropolitan Product

Area	2002	2003	2004	2005	2005 Rank[2]
MSA[1]	229.2	238.6	260.0	284.5	5

Note: Figures are in billions of dollars; (1) Dallas-Fort Worth-Arlington, TX Metropolitan Statistical Area - see Appendix A for areas included; (2) Rank ranges from 1 to 361
Source: The U.S. Conference of Mayors, "U.S. Metro Economies: GMP - The Engines of America's Growth," January 2007

Economic Growth

Area	1995 GMP	2005 GMP	Average Annual Growth Rate	Growth Rate Rank[2]
MSA[1]	143.0	284.5	7.1	35

Note: Figures are in billions of dollars; GMP = Gross Metropolitan Product; (1) Dallas-Fort Worth-Arlington, TX Metropolitan Statistical Area - see Appendix A for areas included; (2) Rank ranges from 1 to 361
Source: The U.S. Conference of Mayors, "U.S. Metro Economies: GMP - The Engines of America's Growth," January 2007

INCOME

Per Capita/Median/Average Income

Area	Per Capita ($)	Median Household ($)	Average Household ($)
City	40,658	91,779	111,213
MSA[1]	27,089	55,079	74,352
U.S.	25,495	49,280	66,670

Note: Figures are 2007 estimates; (1) Metropolitan Statistical Area - see Appendix B for areas included
Source: Claritas, Inc.

Household Income Distribution

Area	Percent of Households Earning							
	Under $15,000	$15,000 -24,999	$25,000 -34,999	$35,000 -49,999	$50,000 -74,999	$75,000 -99,000	$100,000 -149,999	$150,000 and up
City	3.4	3.0	4.4	8.2	17.2	20.6	25.5	17.8
MSA[1]	10.0	9.1	10.7	15.8	19.8	13.0	13.2	8.5
U.S.	13.1	10.9	11.2	15.6	19.5	11.9	11.3	6.6

Note: Figures are 2007 estimates; (1) Metropolitan Statistical Area - see Appendix B for areas included
Source: Claritas, Inc.

Poverty Rates by Age

Area	All Ages	Under 5 Years Old	5 to 17 Years Old	18 to 64 Years Old	65 Years and Over
City	3.4	0.4	0.7	2.2	0.1
MSA[1]	11.1	1.3	2.8	6.3	0.7
U.S.	12.4	1.2	3.0	6.9	1.2

Note: Figures are percent of population with income in 1999 below poverty level and only include population for whom poverty status is determined; (1) Metropolitan Statistical Area - see Appendix A for areas included
Source: Census 2000, Summary File 3

Personal Bankruptcy Filing Rate

Area	2004	2005	2006
Collin County	5.58	7.92	1.76
U.S.	5.31	6.82	2.00

Note: Numbers are per 1,000 population and include Chapter 7 and Chapter 13 filings
Source: Federal Deposit Insurance Corporation (FDIC), Regional Economic Conditions (RECON), 8/23/2007

EMPLOYMENT

Labor Force and Employment

Area	Civilian Labor Force			Workers Employed		
	Dec. 2006	Dec. 2007	% Chg.	Dec. 2006	Dec. 2007	% Chg.
City	44,667	45,258	1.3	43,173	43,462	0.7
MD[1]	2,068,085	2,086,426	0.9	1,984,055	1,997,359	0.7
U.S.	152,571,000	153,705,000	0.7	146,081,000	146,334,000	0.2

Note: Data is not seasonally adjusted and covers workers 16 years of age and older;
(1) Metropolitan Division - see Appendix B for areas included
Source: Bureau of Labor Statistics, http://stats.bls.gov

Unemployment Rate

Area	2007											
	Jan.	Feb.	Mar.	Apr.	May	Jun.	Jul.	Aug.	Sep.	Oct.	Nov.	Dec.
City	4.0	3.8	3.6	3.3	3.4	3.7	3.7	3.5	3.7	3.7	3.9	4.0
MD[1]	4.7	4.5	4.1	4.0	4.0	4.6	4.6	4.3	4.4	4.1	4.2	4.3
U.S.	5.0	4.9	4.5	4.3	4.3	4.7	4.9	4.6	4.5	4.4	4.5	4.8

Note: Data is not seasonally adjusted and covers workers 16 years of age and older; All figures are percentages; (1) Metropolitan Division - see Appendix B for areas included
Source: Bureau of Labor Statistics, http://stats.bls.gov

Employment by Occupation

Occupation Classification	City (%)	MSA[1] (%)	U.S. (%)
Sales and Office	27.9	28.7	26.7
Professional and Related	27.1	20.4	20.2
Service	7.3	12.3	14.9
Production, Transportation, and Material Moving	5.0	11.8	14.6
Management, Business, and Financial	27.5	16.8	13.5
Construction, Extraction, and Maintenance	5.2	9.9	9.4
Farming, Forestry, and Fishing	0.2	0.2	0.7

Note: Figures cover employed civilians 16 years of age and older;
(1) Metropolitan Statistical Area - see Appendix A for areas included
Source: Census 2000, Summary File 3

Employment by Industry

Sector	MSA[1] Number of Employees	MSA[1] Percent of Total	U.S. Percent of Total
Government	261,800	12.4	16.3
Education and Health Services	225,600	10.7	13.4
Professional and Business Services	339,800	16.1	13.1
Retail Trade	221,000	10.5	11.6
Manufacturing	198,400	9.4	9.9
Leisure and Hospitality	193,100	9.2	9.6
Financial Activities	186,000	8.8	5.9
Construction	n/a	n/a	5.3
Wholesale Trade	130,600	6.2	4.4
Other Services	75,400	3.6	3.9
Transportation and Utilities	78,100	3.7	3.7
Information	72,600	3.4	2.2
Natural Resources and Mining	n/a	n/a	0.5

Note: Figures cover non-farm employment as of December 2007 and are not seasonally adjusted; (1) Metropolitan Statistical Area - see Appendix B for areas included; n/a not available
Source: Bureau of Labor Statistics, http://stats.bls.gov

Average Wages

Occupation	$/Hr.	Occupation	$/Hr.
Accountants and Auditors	31.56	Maids and Housekeeping Cleaners	8.23
Automotive Mechanics	17.72	Maintenance and Repair Workers	15.14
Bookkeepers	16.06	Marketing Managers	60.78
Carpenters	16.08	Nuclear Medicine Technologists	30.51
Cashiers	8.45	Nurses, Licensed Practical	19.58
Clerks, General Office	11.71	Nurses, Registered	30.37
Clerks, Receptionists/Information	12.41	Nursing Aides/Orderlies/Attendants	11.11
Clerks, Shipping/Receiving	12.87	Packers and Packagers, Hand	9.24
Computer Programmers	38.32	Physical Therapists	39.04
Computer Support Specialists	22.07	Postal Service Mail Carriers	21.40
Computer Systems Analysts	39.12	Real Estate Brokers	45.42
Cooks, Restaurant	10.19	Retail Salespersons	11.71
Dentists	n/a	Sales Reps., Exc. Tech./Scientific	29.44
Electrical Engineers	44.17	Sales Reps., Tech./Scientific	35.60
Electricians	19.29	Secretaries, Exc. Legal/Med./Exec.	13.40
Financial Managers	55.42	Security Guards	12.88
First-Line Supervisors/Mgrs., Sales	19.02	Surgeons	n/a
Food Preparation Workers	8.57	Teacher Assistants	9.40
General and Operations Managers	56.15	Teachers, Elementary School	22.00
Hairdressers/Cosmetologists	10.95	Teachers, Secondary School	21.40
Internists	90.82	Telemarketers	13.10
Janitors and Cleaners	9.02	Truck Drivers, Heavy/Tractor-Trailer	19.27
Landscaping/Groundskeeping Workers	10.25	Truck Drivers, Light/Delivery Svcs.	14.20
Lawyers	65.73	Waiters and Waitresses	8.06

Note: Wage data covers the Dallas-Plano-Irving, TX Metropolitan Division - see Appendix B for areas included. Hourly wages for elementary/secondary school teachers and teacher assistants were calculated by the editors from annual wage data assuming a 40 hour work week; n/a not available.
Source: Bureau of Labor Statistics, May 2007 Metro Area Occupational Employment and Wage Estimates

RESIDENTIAL REAL ESTATE

Building Permits

Area	Single-Family			Multi-Family			Total		
	2006	2007p	Pct. Chg.	2006	2007p	Pct. Chg.	2006	2007p	Pct. Chg.
City	3,414	1,719	-49.6	0	1,198	-	3,414	2,917	-14.6
U.S.	1,378,200	973,300	-29.4	460,700	407,200	-11.6	1,838,900	1,380,500	-24.9

Note: (p) preliminary; figures cover and represent new, privately-owned housing units authorized (unadjusted data); All permit data are based on estimates with imputation; U.S. figures are based on the new 20,000-place series.
Source: U.S. Census Bureau, Manufacturing, Mining, and Construction Statistics

Homeownership and Housing Vacancies

Area	Homeownership Rate[2] (%)			Rental Vacancy Rate[3] (%)			Homeowner Vacancy Rate[4] (%)		
	2005	2006	2007	2005	2006	2007	2005	2006	2007
MSA[1]	62.3	60.7	60.9	13.6	11.7	11.0	2.2	2.3	2.5
U.S.	68.9	68.8	68.1	9.8	9.8	9.7	1.9	2.4	2.7

Note: (1) Metropolitan Statistical Area - see Appendix B for areas included; (2) The proportion of households that are owners; (3) The proportion of the rental inventory that is vacant for rent; (4) The proportion of the homeowner inventory that is vacant for sale; n/a not available
Source: U.S. Census Bureau, Housing Vacancies and Homeownership Annual Statistics: 2007

TAXES

State Corporate Income Tax Rates

State	Rates and Tax Brackets
Texas	1.0%

Note: Tax rates as of January 1, 2008; Texas's 1% franchise tax is a gross receipts tax paid by most taxable entities. Retailers pay 0.5%.
Source: Tax Foundation, www.taxfoundation.org

State Individual Income Tax Rates

State	Federal Deductibility	Marginal Rates (%)	Standard Deduction ($)		Personal Exemptions ($)[1]	
			Single	Joint	Single	Dependents
Texas	No	None	n/a	n/a	n/a	n/a

Note: Tax rates as of January 1, 2008; Local- and county-level taxes are not included; n/a not applicable; (1) Married joint filers generally receive double the single exemption
Source: Tax Foundation, www.taxfoundation.org

Various State and Local Tax Rates

State and Local Sales and Use (%)	State Sales and Use (%)	Gasoline[1,2] ($/gal.)	Cigarette ($/pack)	Spirits ($/gal.)	Table Wine ($/gal.)	Beer ($/gal.)
8.25	6.25 (i)	0.20	1.41	2.40	0.204	0.19

Note: Tax rates as of January 1, 2008; (1) In addition to the 18.4 cpg Federal gasoline tax; (2) Rates may include additional state sales taxes, environmental protection and storage fees/taxes, and local taxes. When necessary, the volume-weighted average of all local taxes is used to approximate the typical statewide rate including local tax; (i) Texas has a GRT that is levied in addition to its 6.25% sales tax. It is called the franchise tax and the rate is 1% (.5% for retailers).
Source: Tax Foundation, www.taxfoundation.org; Original research

State Tax Burdens

Area	Combined State and Local Tax Burden		Combined Federal, State and Local Tax Burden	
	Percent	Rank	Percent	Rank
Texas	9.3	43	29.8	41
U.S. Average	11.0	-	32.7	-

Note: Figures cover 2007 and measure taxes as a percentage of income
Source: Tax Foundation, www.taxfoundation.org

State Business Tax Climate Index Rankings

State	Overall Rank	Corporate Tax Index Rank	Individual Income Tax Index Rank	Sales Tax Index Rank	Unemployment Insurance Tax Index Rank	Property Tax Index Rank
Texas	8	47	7	28	14	27

Note: Rankings range from 1 to 50 where 1 is best. Rankings do not average across to Overall Rank. States without a given tax are given a ranking of 1.
Source: Tax Foundation, State Business Tax Climate Index 2008

TRANSPORTATION

Means of Transportation to Work

Area	Car/Truck/Van		Public Transportation			Bicycle	Walked	Other Means	Worked at Home
	Drove Alone	Car-pooled	Bus	Subway	Railroad				
City	85.0	8.9	0.1	0.0	0.0	0.1	0.6	0.9	4.3
MSA[1]	77.6	14.3	2.1	0.1	0.1	0.1	1.5	1.0	3.1
U.S.	75.7	12.2	2.5	1.5	0.5	0.4	2.9	1.0	3.3

Note: Figures are percentages and cover workers 16 years of age and older; (1) Metropolitan Statistical Area - see Appendix A for areas included
Source: Census 2000, Summary File 3

Travel Time to Work

Area	Less Than 15 Minutes	15 to 29 Minutes	30 to 44 Minutes	45 to 59 Minutes	60 Minutes or More
City	16.7	27.8	28.9	17.7	8.9
MSA[1]	22.0	35.0	24.7	10.4	7.9
U.S.	29.4	36.1	19.1	7.4	8.0

Note: Figures are percentages and include workers 16 years old and over; (1) Metropolitan Statistical Area - see Appendix A for areas included
Source: Census 2000, Summary File 3

Travel Time Index

Area	1982	1995	2004	2005
Urban Area[1]	1.05	1.16	1.31	1.35
Average[2]	1.11	1.22	1.29	1.30

Note: Travel Time Index - The ratio of travel time in the peak period to the travel time at free-flow conditions. A value of 1.35 indicates a 20-minute free-flow trip takes 27 minutes in the peak. Free-flow speeds (60 mph on freeways and 35 mph on principal arterials) are used as the comparison threshold; (1) Covers the Dallas-Fort Worth-Arlington, TX urban area; (2) average of 85 urban areas
Source: Texas Transportation Institute, The 2007 Urban Mobility Report, September 2007

Living Environment

COST OF LIVING

Cost of Living Index

Composite Index	Groceries	Housing	Utilities	Transportation	Health Care	Misc. Goods/ Services
91.5	99.0	72.3	98.9	103.5	101.6	97.5

Note: U.S. = 100; Figures cover the Dallas TX urban area.
Source: The Council for Community and Economic Research (formerly ACCRA), Cost of Living Index, 2007

Grocery Prices

Area[1]	T-Bone Steak ($/pound)	Frying Chicken ($/pound)	Whole Milk ($/half gal.)	Eggs ($/dozen)	Orange Juice ($/64 oz.)	Coffee ($/11.5 oz.)
City[2]	8.81	1.24	2.26	1.40	3.17	3.43
Avg.	8.93	1.12	2.13	1.52	3.26	3.31
Min.	5.88	0.71	1.33	0.83	2.30	2.20
Max.	12.80	2.07	3.43	3.54	5.79	6.20

Note: (1) Values for the local area are compared with the average, minimum and maximum values for all 331 areas in the Cost of Living Index report; (2) Figures cover the Dallas TX urban area; **T-Bone Steak** *(price per pound);* **Frying Chicken** *(price per pound, whole fryer);* **Whole Milk** *(half gallon carton);* **Eggs** *(price per dozen, Grade A, large);* **Orange Juice** *(64 oz. Tropicana or Florida Natural);* **Coffee** *(11.5 oz. can, vacuum-packed, Maxwell House, Hills Bros, or Folgers).*
Source: The Council for Community and Economic Research (formerly ACCRA), Cost of Living Index, 2007

Housing and Utility Costs

Area[1]	New Home Price ($)	Apartment Rent ($/month)	All Electric ($/month)	Part Electric ($/month)	Other Energy ($/month)	Telephone ($/month)
City[2]	213,140	715	-	107.07	50.72	26.67
Avg.	309,605	782	146.13	78.67	90.16	26.14
Min.	189,877	n/a	82.03	37.41	33.15	17.08
Max.	1,202,800	3,481	271.14	150.60	257.67	37.45

Note: (1) Values for the local area are compared with the average, minimum and maximum values for all 331 areas in the Cost of Living Index report; (2) Figures cover the Dallas TX urban area; **New Home Price** *(2,400 sf living area, 8,000 sf lot, in urban area with full utilities);* **Apartment Rent** *(950 sf 2 bedroom/1.5 or 2 bath, unfurnished, excluding all utilities except water);* **All Electric** *(average monthly cost for an all-electric home);* **Part Electric** *(average monthly cost for a part-electric home);* **Other Energy** *(average monthly cost for natural gas, fuel oil, coal, wood, and any other forms of energy except electricity);* **Telephone** *(price includes basic monthly rate for a private residential line plus additional local usage charges incurred by a family of four).*
Source: The Council for Community and Economic Research (formerly ACCRA), Cost of Living Index, 2007

Health Care, Transportation, and Other Costs

Area[1]	Doctor ($/visit)	Dentist ($/visit)	Optometrist ($/visit)	Gasoline ($/gallon)	Beauty Salon ($/visit)	Men's Shirt ($)
City[2]	74.44	77.38	77.68	2.52	26.77	22.20
Avg.	79.48	71.93	79.55	2.64	29.52	25.77
Min.	52.08	44.80	43.95	2.19	15.58	16.19
Max.	148.44	126.27	158.83	3.48	60.62	48.53

Note: (1) Values for the local area are compared with the average, minimum and maximum values for all 331 areas in the Cost of Living Index report; (2) Figures cover the Dallas TX urban area; **Doctor** *(general practitioners routine exam of an established patient);* **Dentist** *(adult teeth cleaning and periodic oral examination);* **Optometrist** *(full vision eye exam for established adult patient);* **Gasoline** *(one gallon regular unleaded, national brand, including all taxes, cash price at self-service pump if available);* **Beauty Salon** *(woman's shampoo, trim, and blow-dry);* **Men's Shirt** *(cotton/polyester dress shirt, pinpoint weave, long sleeves).*
Source: The Council for Community and Economic Research (formerly ACCRA), Cost of Living Index, 2007

HOUSING

House Price Index (HPI)

Area	National Ranking[2]	Quarterly Change (%)	One-Year Change (%)	Five-Year Change (%)
MD[1]	97	0.16	2.95	15.82
U.S.[3]	-	0.10	0.84	41.37

Note: The HPI is a weighted repeat sales index. It measures average price changes in repeat sales or refinancings on the same properties. This information is obtained by reviewing repeat mortgage transactions on single-family properties whose mortgages have been purchased or securitized by Fannie Mae or Freddie Mac in January 1975; (1) Metropolitan Division - see Appendix B for areas included; (2) Rankings are based on annual percentage change for all metro areas containing at least 15,000 transactions over the last 10 years and ranges from 1 to 291; (3) figures based on a weighted average of Census Division estimates; all figures are for the period ending December 31, 2007

Source: Office of Federal Housing Enterprise Oversight, House Price Index, February 26, 2008

House Price Valuations

Area	Q1 2000	Q1 2001	Q1 2002	Q1 2003	Q1 2004	Q1 2005	Q1 2006	Q1 2007	Q1 2008
MD[1]	-22.2	-21.3	-17.8	-16.4	-19.3	-23.0	-23.6	-26.9	-30.6

Note: Figures show the percentage of over- or under-valuation of single family homes relative to statistically normal house values (e.g. a value of 23.6 indicates that house values are 23.6% overvalued). Statistically normal house values are based on house prices, interest rates, household incomes, population densities, and any historical premiums or discounts metropolitan areas have exhibited over time; (1) Figures cover the Metropolitan Division - see Appendix B for areas included

Source: Global Insight/National City Corporation, House Prices in America, May 2008

Median Home Prices

Area	2005	2006	2007[r]	Percent Change 2006 to 2007
MSA[1]	147.6	149.5	150.9	0.9
U.S. Average	219.0	221.9	217.9	-1.8

Note: Figures are median sales prices of existing single-family homes in thousands of dollars; (r) revised; n/a not available; (1) Metropolitan Statistical Area - see Appendix B for areas included

Source: National Association of Realtors, Metropolitan Area Prices, 1st Quarter 2008

Housing: Year Structure Built

Area	1990 -2000	1980 -1989	1970 -1979	1960 -1969	1950 -1959	1940 -1949	Before 1940	Median Year
City	83.0	10.2	3.4	1.7	0.8	0.3	0.6	1997
MSA[1]	23.9	24.7	20.2	13.7	9.8	4.0	3.7	1979
U.S.	17.0	15.8	18.5	13.7	12.7	7.3	15.0	1971

Note: Figures are percentages; (1) Metropolitan Statistical Area - see Appendix A for areas included

Source: Census 2000, Summary File 3

HEALTH

Health Risk Data

Category	Area[1] (%)	U.S. (%)
Adults who have been told they have high blood pressure[3]	22.2	25.5
Adults who have been told they have high blood cholesterol[3]	37.6	35.6
Adults who have been told they have diabetes[2]	5.3	7.5
Adults who have been told they have arthritis[3]	19.5	27.0
Adults who have been told they currently have asthma	4.5	8.5
Adults who are current smokers	11.5	20.1
Adults who are heavy drinkers[4]	5.3	4.9
Adults who are overweight (BMI 25.0 - 29.9)	35.7	36.5
Adults who are obese (BMI 30.0 - 99.8)	21.4	25.1

Note: Data as of 2006 unless otherwise noted; (1) Figures cover the Metropolitan Division - see Appendix B for areas included; (2) Figures do not include pregnancy-related diabetes, pre-diabetes or borderline diabetes; (3) 2005 data; (4) Heavy drinkers are classified as adult men having more than two drinks per day or adult women having more than one drink per day

Source: Centers for Disease Control and Prevention, Behaviorial Risk Factor Surveillance System, SMART: Selected Metropolitan/Micropolitan Area Risk Trends, 2005, 2006

Mortality Rates for the Top 10 Causes of Death in the U.S.

ICD-10[a] Sub-Chapter	ICD-10[a] Code	Age-Adjusted Mortality Rate[1] per 100,000 population	
		County[2]	U.S.
Malignant neoplasms	C00-C97	153.6	186.5
Ischaemic heart diseases	I20-I25	124.5	152.3
Other forms of heart disease	I30-I51	36.4	51.5
Cerebrovascular diseases	I60-I69	42.0	50.0
Chronic lower respiratory diseases	J40-J47	33.6	42.6
Diabetes mellitus	E10-E14	15.8	24.8
Other degenerative diseases of the nervous system	G30-G31	38.8	22.6
Other external causes of accidental injury	W00-X59	21.7	21.4
Influenza and pneumonia	J10-J18	19.1	20.7
Hypertensive diseases	I10-I13	14.6	18.2

Note: (a) ICD-10 = International Classification of Diseases 10th Revision; (1) Mortality rates are a three year average covering 2003-2005; (2) Figures cover Collin County
Source: Centers for Disease Control and Prevention, National Center for Health Statistics. Compressed Mortality File 1999-2004. CDC WONDER On-line Database, compiled from Compressed Mortality File 1999-2005 Series 20 No. 2K, 2008.

Mortality Rates for Selected Causes of Death

ICD-10[a] Sub-Chapter	ICD-10[a] Code	Age-Adjusted Mortality Rate[1] per 100,000 population	
		County[2]	U.S.
Assault	X85-Y09	2.6	5.9
Human immunodeficiency virus (HIV) disease	B20-B24	*0.9	4.5
Intentional self-harm	X60-X84	8.6	10.8
Malnutrition	E40-E46	*1.3	1.0
Obesity and other hyperalimentation	E65-E68	*0.6	1.4
Organic, including symptomatic, mental disorders	F01-F09	28.1	16.8
Transport accidents	V01-V99	10.3	16.1
Viral hepatitis	B15-B19	*1.0	1.8

Note: (a) ICD-10 = International Classification of Diseases 10th Revision; (1) Mortality rates are a three year average covering 2003-2005; (2) Figures cover Collin County; (*) Unreliable data as per CDC
Source: Centers for Disease Control and Prevention, National Center for Health Statistics. Compressed Mortality File 1999-2004. CDC WONDER On-line Database, compiled from Compressed Mortality File 1999-2005 Series 20 No. 2K, 2008.

Distribution of Physicians[1]

Area	Total	Family/ General Practice	Specialties	
			Medical	Surgical
Collin County (number)	1,264	321	471	269
Collin County (rate per 10,000 pop.)	19.2	4.9	7.1	4.1
U.S. (rate per 10,000 pop.)	17.7	4.6	6.9	4.3

Note: Data as of 2005; (1) Includes all non-federal, patient-care, office-based MDs
Source: Area Resource File (ARF). June 2007. U.S. Department of Health and Human Services, Health Resources and Services Administration, Bureau of Health Professions, Rockville, MD.

Hospitals

Frisco has the following hospitals: 2 general medical and surgical.
AHA Guide to the Healthcare Field 2008

According to *U.S. News,* the Dallas-Fort Worth-Arlington, TX metro area is home to six of the best hospitals in the U.S.: **Baylor Institute for Rehabilitation**; **Baylor University Medical Center**; **Children's Medical Center Dallas**; **Parkland Memorial Hospital**; **Presbyterian Hospital**; **University of Texas Southwestern Medical Center**. *U.S. News Online, "America's Best Hospitals 2007"*

EDUCATION

Public School District Statistics

District Name	Schls	Pupils	Pupil/ Teacher Ratio	Minority Pupils[1] (%)	Free Lunch Eligible[2] (%)	IEP[3] (%)
Frisco ISD	35	19,881	14.8	33.3	8.1	8.8
Lewisville ISD	65	47,497	14.0	35.7	15.3	11.3
Little Elm Isd	10	4,657	14.9	48.6	28.1	12.0

Note: Table includes regular local school districts with 2,000 or more students; (1) Percentage of students that are not white, non-Hispanic; (2) Percentage of students that are eligible for the free lunch program; (3) Percentage of students that have an Individualized Education Program.
Source: U.S. Department of Education, National Center for Education Statistics, Common Core of Data, Local Education Agency (School District) Universe Survey: School Year 2005-2006; U.S. Department of Education, National Center for Education Statistics, Common Core of Data, Public Elementary/Secondary School Universe Survey: School Year 2005-2006

Top Public High Schools

High School Name	Index[1]	Rank[1]	Subsidized Lunch (%)[2]	E&E (%)[3]
Centennial	1.098	1,323		25.6

Note: (1) Public schools are ranked according to a ratio that is the number of Advanced Placement, International Baccalaureate, and/or Cambridge tests taken by all students at a school in 2007 divided by the number of graduating seniors. All of the schools on the list have an index of at least 1.000; they are in the top five percent of public schools measured this way. The rankings range from 1 to 1,422; (2) Percentage of students receiving federally subsidized meals; (3) E & E stands for equity and excellence percentage: the portion of all graduating seniors at a school that had at least one passing grade on one AP or IB test; (**) Gave both IB and AP tests. AP and IB participation are indicators of a school's efforts to get students to excel and prepare for college.
Source: Newsweek Online, "Top High Schools 2008"

Highest Level of Education

Area	Less than H.S.	H.S. Diploma	Some College, No Deg.	Associate Degree	Bachelors Degree	Masters Degree	Profess. School Degree	Doctorate Degree
City	5.4	12.9	24.1	7.2	37.7	9.4	2.1	1.2
MSA[1]	19.2	22.3	23.5	5.7	20.3	6.4	1.7	0.8
U.S.	19.4	28.4	21.2	6.4	15.7	5.9	2.0	1.0

Note: Figures are 2007 estimated percentages and cover persons age 25 and over; (1) Metropolitan Statistical Area - see Appendix B for areas included
Source: Claritas, Inc.

Educational Attainment by Race

Area	High School Graduate (%)					Bachelor's Degree (%)				
	Total	White	Black	Asian	Hisp.[2]	Total	White	Black	Asian	Hisp.[2]
City	94.5	96.1	96.2	98.7	66.5	49.8	50.8	47.0	75.9	25.5
MSA[1]	79.4	84.4	78.9	83.4	41.5	30.0	34.0	18.5	52.2	8.7
U.S.	80.4	83.6	72.3	80.4	52.4	24.4	26.1	14.3	44.1	10.4

Note: Figures shown cover persons 25 years old and over; (1) Metropolitan Statistical Area - see Appendix A for areas included; (2) people of Hispanic origin can be of any race
Source: Census 2000, Summary File 3

School Enrollment by Type

Area	Grades KG to 8				Grades 9 to 12			
	Public		Private		Public		Private	
	Enrollment	%	Enrollment	%	Enrollment	%	Enrollment	%
City	3,964	90.7	405	9.3	1,258	92.5	102	7.5
MSA[1]	456,971	90.7	46,953	9.3	181,249	92.2	15,405	7.8
U.S.	33,526,011	88.7	4,285,121	11.3	14,848,628	90.6	1,532,323	9.4

Note: Figures shown cover persons 3 years old and over; (1) Metropolitan Statistical Area - see Appendix A for areas included
Source: Census 2000, Summary File 3

PRESIDENTIAL ELECTION

School Enrollment by Race

Area	Grades KG to 8 (%)				Grades 9 to 12 (%)			
	White	Black	Asian	Hisp.[1]	White	Black	Asian	Hisp.[1]
City	85.4	4.9	1.5	15.8	84.2	1.3	1.0	17.8
MSA[2]	60.7	18.0	3.6	28.9	61.2	18.7	4.0	25.8
U.S.	68.5	15.5	3.3	16.8	68.8	15.5	3.8	15.7

Note: Figures shown cover persons 3 years old and over; (1) people of Hispanic origin can be of any race; (2) Metropolitan Statistical Area - see Appendix A for areas included
Source: Census 2000, Summary File 3

Average Salaries of Public School Classroom Teachers

District	2005-06		2006-07		Percent Change 2005-06 to 2006-07
	Dollars	Rank[1]	Dollars	Rank[1]	
Texas	41,744	35	44,897	30	7.55
U.S. Average	49,026	-	50,816	-	3.65

Note: (1) State rank ranges from 1 to 51.
Source: National Education Association, Rankings & Estimates: Rankings of the States 2006 and Estimates of School Statistics 2007, December 2007

Higher Education

Four-Year Colleges			Two-Year Colleges			Medical Schools[1]	Law Schools[2]	Voc/ Tech[3]
Public	Private Non-profit	Private For-profit	Public	Private Non-profit	Private For-profit			
0	0	0	0	0	0	0	0	0

Note: Figures cover institutions located within the city limits; (1) includes schools accredited by the Liaison Committee on Medical Education and the American Osteopathic Association; (2) includes American Bar Association-accredited law schools; (3) includes all schools with programs that are less than 2 years.
Source: National Center for Education Statistics, The Integrated Postsecondary Education System (IPEDS) Peer Analysis System, 2007; www.usnews.com, Law and Medical School Directories, 2009

2004 Presidential Election Results

Area	Bush	Kerry	Nader	Other
Collin County	71.2	28.1	0.1	0.6
U.S.	50.7	48.3	0.4	0.6

Note: Results are percentages and may not add to 100% due to rounding
Source: Dave Leip's Atlas of U.S. Presidential Elections, www.uselectionatlas.org

EMPLOYERS

Major Employers

Company Name	Industry	Type of Site
Associates Corp North America	Personal credit institutions	Headquarters
Associates First Capital Corp	Mortgage bankers and correspondents	Headquarters
Baylor University Medical Ctr	General medical and surgical hospitals	Headquarters
Dallas Cnty Commissioners Crt	Executive offices	Branch
EDS	Data processing and preparation	Headquarters
JC Penney	Department stores	Headquarters
Lockheed Martin	Aircraft	Branch
MCI	Telephone communication, except radio	Branch
National Elec Contrs Assn	Insurance agents, brokers, and service	Single
Odyssey Healthcare Inc	Skilled nursing care facilities	Headquarters
Parkland Health & Hospital Sys	General medical and surgical hospitals	Headquarters
Raytheon	Radio and t.v. communications equipment	Single
Romanos Macaroni Grill	Eating places	Single
SFG Management Ltd Lblty Co	Fluid milk	Single
Southwestern Medical School	Accident and health insurance	Headquarters
Teaching Assistance Office	Colleges and universities	Branch
Texas Instruments	Semiconductors and related devices	Headquarters
UPS	Courier services, except by air	Branch
Verizon	Business consulting, nec	Branch
Verizon	Telephone communication, except radio	Branch

Note: Companies shown are located within the Dallas metropolitan area; nec = not elsewhere classified.
Source: www.zapdata.com, May 2008

PUBLIC SAFETY

Crime Rate

Area	All Crimes	Violent Crimes				Property Crimes		
		Murder	Forcible Rape	Robbery	Aggrav. Assault	Burglary	Larceny -Theft	Motor Vehicle Theft
City	4,508.3	1.4	15.1	19.2	98.9	1,006.9	3,267.9	98.9
Metro[1]	4,972.8	6.4	32.8	219.6	300.8	1,025.0	2,827.7	560.5
U.S.	3,808.1	5.7	30.9	149.4	287.5	729.4	2,206.8	398.4

Note: Figures are crimes per 100,000 population; (1) Metropolitan Division - see Appendix B for areas included
Source: FBI Uniform Crime Reports, 2006

Hate Crimes

Area	Number of Quarters Reported	Bias Motivation				
		Race	Religion	Sexual Orientation	Ethnicity	Disability
City	4	0	0	0	0	0

Source: Federal Bureau of Investigation, Hate Crime Statistics 2006

RECREATION

Culture

Dance[1]	Theatre[1]	Instrumental Music[1]	Vocal Music[1]	Series/ Festivals	Museums	Zoos and Aquariums[2]
0	0	0	0	0	0	0

Note: (1) Number of professional perfoming groups; (2) AZA-accredited
Source: The Grey House Performing Arts Directory, 2007; Official Museum Directory, 2008; Association of Zoos & Aquariums, AZA Member Zoos & Aquariums, June 2008

Professional Sports Teams

Team Name	League
Texas Rangers	Major League Baseball (MLB)
FC Dallas	Major League Soccer (MLS)
Dallas Mavericks	National Basketball Association (NBA)
Dallas Cowboys	National Football League (NFL)
Dallas Stars	National Hockey League (NHL)

Note: Includes teams located in the Dallas-Fort Worth metro area.
Source: Original research

MEDIA

Newspapers

Name	News Focus	Frequency	Circulation
All About Frisco Monthly	Local	Monthly	13,500
Frisco Enterprise	Local	Twice a week	4,500

Note: Includes newspapers with offices located in the city
Source: MediaContactsPro, March 2008

Television Stations

Name	Ch.	Network(s)	Type	Ownership
KDTN	2	PBS	Public	North Texas Public Broadcasting Inc.
KDFW	4	Fox	Commercial	Fox Television Stations Inc.
KXAS	5	NBC	Commercial	General Electric Corporation
WFAA	8	ABC	Commercial	Belo Corporation
KTVT	11	CBS	Commercial	CBS
KERA	13	PBS	Public	North Texas Public Broadcasting Inc.
KSST	18	n/a	Commercial	Hopkins County Broadcasting Inc.
KTXA	21	UPN	Commercial	CBS
KUVN	23	Univision	Commercial	Perenchio Television Inc.
KDFI	27	Fox	Commercial	Fox Television Stations Inc.
KMPX	29	n/a	Non-comm.	n/a
KDAF	33	WBN	Commercial	Tribune Broadcasting Company
KXTX	39	Telemundo	Commercial	Telemundo Group Inc.
KTAQ	47	n/a	Commercial	Michael Simons
KSTR	49	Univision	Commercial	Univision Television Group
KFWD	52	n/a	Commercial	n/a
KDTX	58	n/a	Non-comm.	Trinity Broadcasting Network
KPXD	68	Pax	Commercial	Paxson Communications Corporation

Note: Stations included cover the Dallas-Fort Worth DMA (Designated Market Area)
BurrellesLuce, MediaContacts Online, January 2007

Major AM Radio Stations

Call Letters	Freq. (kHz)	Station Type	Target Audience	Station Format	Music Format
KLIF	570	Commercial	General/Men	News/Talk	n/a
KMKI	620	n/a	General	Music	n/a
KSKY	660	n/a	General/Hisp/Rel	Music/Sports/Talk	n/a
KKDA	730	Commercial	General	Music/News	Rhythm & Blues
KAAM	770	Commercial	General	Music	Adult Standards
WBAP	820	Commercial	General	Educational/News/Talk	n/a
KFJZ	870	Commercial	General/Hispanic	Music/News/Sports/Talk	Latin
KKLF	950	n/a	General	News/Talk	n/a
KHVN	970	n/a	Christian/General	Music	n/a
KGGR	1040	n/a	Black/General/Rel	Talk	n/a
KRLD	1080	n/a	General	n/a	n/a
KBIS	1150	n/a	General/Hispanic	Music/News/Talk	n/a
KSST	1230	n/a	General	Music/News	Easy Listening
KPJC	1250	College	General	Music/News	Jazz
KTCK	1310	Commercial	General	Talk	n/a
KAND	1340	Commercial	General	Music/News	Country
KAHZ	1360	n/a	General/Hispanic	Ed/News/Sports/Talk	n/a
KBEC	1390	Commercial	General	Music	Country
KGVL	1400	n/a	General	Music/News/Sports	n/a
KLVQ	1410	n/a	General/Religious	Music	n/a
KFYN	1420	n/a	General	Music/News/Sports	n/a
KTNO	1440	Commercial	Hispanic/Religious	Music/Talk	Gospel
KNET	1450	n/a	General	Music	n/a
KTFW	1460	Commercial	General/Hispanic	n/a	n/a
KPLT	1490	Commercial	General	Music/News/Sports/Talk	Gospel
KSTV	1510	Commercial	General/Hispanic	Music	Top 40
KZMP	1540	n/a	General/Hispanic	Music	n/a
KCOM	1550	Commercial	General/Hispanic	Music	Country
KTBK	1700	Commercial	General	Sports/Talk	n/a

Note: Stations included cover the Dallas-Fort Worth DMA (Designated Market Area); n/a not available
Source: BurrellesLuce, MediaContacts Online, January 2007

Major FM Radio Stations

Call Letters	Freq. (mHz)	Station Type	Target Audience	Station Format	Music Format
KNTU	88.1	College	General	Educational/Music/News	n/a
KEOM	88.5	n/a	General	Ed/Music/News/Sports	n/a
KETR	88.9	College	General	Music/Sports	n/a
KNON	89.3	Non-Comm	Black/Hispanic	Ed/Music/News/Talk	Album Rock
KERA	90.1	Public	General	Music/Talk	Folk
KCBI	90.9	n/a	General/Religious	Music/News	n/a
KVTT	91.7	n/a	General/Religious	Educational/Talk	n/a
KZPS	92.5	n/a	General	Music/News/Talk	n/a
KSTV	93.1	Commercial	General	Music/News	Country
KDBN	93.3	Commercial	General	Music/Talk	Classic Rock
KLNO	94.1	Commercial	General/Hispanic	Music	Latin
KLTY	94.9	Commercial	General/Religious	Music/News/Talk	Christian
KZZA	95.1	Commercial	General	Music	Latin
KSCS	96.3	Commercial	General	Music/News/Talk	Country
KEGL	97.1	Commercial	General	Music/News/Sports	Modern Rock
KBFB	97.9	Commercial	General	Music	Urban Contemp.
KYYK	98.3	n/a	General	Music	n/a
KLUV	98.7	Commercial	General	Music/News/Talk	Oldies
KHCK	99.1	Commercial	General/Hispanic	Music	Latin
KPLX	99.5	Commercial	General	Music	Country
WRR	101.1	Commercial	General	Music/News/Talk	Classical
KZMP	101.7	n/a	General/Hispanic	Music	n/a
KBUS	101.9	Commercial	General	Music/News	Classic Rock
KDGE	102.1	Commercial	Young Adult	Music/News/Talk	Alternative
KDMX	102.9	Commercial	General/Women	Music/News/Talk	Adult Top 40
KVIL	103.7	n/a	General	Music	n/a
KKDA	104.5	n/a	Black/General	Music	n/a
KRNB	105.7	n/a	General	Music/News/Sports	n/a
KHKS	106.1	Commercial	General	Music/News/Talk	Top 40
KOAI	107.5	n/a	General	Music/Talk	n/a
KPLT	107.7	n/a	General	Music/News	Top 40
KDXX	107.9	Commercial	General/Hispanic	Music/News/Talk	Adult Contemp.

Note: Stations included cover the Dallas-Fort Worth DMA (Designated Market Area); n/a not available
BurrellesLuce, MediaContacts Online, January 2007

CLIMATE

Average and Extreme Temperatures

Temperature	Jan	Feb	Mar	Apr	May	Jun	Jul	Aug	Sep	Oct	Nov	Dec	Yr.
Extreme High (°F)	85	90	100	100	101	112	111	109	107	101	91	87	112
Average High (°F)	55	60	68	76	84	92	96	96	89	79	67	58	77
Average Temp. (°F)	45	50	57	66	74	82	86	86	79	68	56	48	67
Average Low (°F)	35	39	47	56	64	72	76	75	68	57	46	38	56
Extreme Low (°F)	-2	9	12	30	39	53	58	58	42	24	16	0	-2

Note: Figures cover the years 1945-1993
Source: National Climatic Data Center, International Station Meteorological Climate Summary, 9/96

Average Precipitation/Snowfall/Humidity

Precip./Humidity	Jan	Feb	Mar	Apr	May	Jun	Jul	Aug	Sep	Oct	Nov	Dec	Yr.
Avg. Precip. (in.)	1.9	2.3	2.6	3.8	4.9	3.4	2.1	2.3	2.9	3.3	2.3	2.1	33.9
Avg. Snowfall (in.)	1	1	Tr	Tr	0	0	0	0	0	Tr	Tr	Tr	3
Avg. Rel. Hum. 6am (%)	78	77	75	77	82	81	77	76	80	79	78	77	78
Avg. Rel. Hum. 3pm (%)	53	51	47	49	51	48	43	41	46	46	48	51	48

Note: Figures cover the years 1945-1993; Tr = Trace amounts (<0.05 in. of rain; <0.5 in. of snow)
Source: National Climatic Data Center, International Station Meteorological Climate Summary, 9/96

Weather Conditions

Temperature			Daytime Sky			Precipitation		
10°F & below	32°F & below	90°F & above	Clear	Partly cloudy	Cloudy	0.01 inch or more precip.	0.1 inch or more snow/ice	Thunder-storms
1	34	102	108	160	97	78	2	49

Note: Figures are average number of days per year and cover the years 1945-1993
Source: National Climatic Data Center, International Station Meteorological Climate Summary, 9/96

HAZARDOUS WASTE

Superfund Sites

Frisco has no sites on the EPA's Superfund Final National Priorities List.
U.S. Environmental Protection Agency, Final National Priorities List, June 23, 2008

AIR & WATER QUALITY

Air Quality Index

Area	Percent of Days when Air Quality was...[2]				AQI Statistics	
	Good	Moderate	Unhealthy for Sensitive Groups	Unhealthy	Maximum	Median
MSA[1]	67.1	27.7	4.4	0.8	177	44

Note: The Air Quality Index (AQI) is an index for reporting daily air quality. EPA calculates the AQI for five major air pollutants regulated by the Clean Air Act: ground-level ozone, particle pollution (also known as particulate matter), carbon monoxide, sulfur dioxide, and nitrogen dioxide. The AQI runs from 0 to 500. The higher the AQI value, the greater the level of air pollution and the greater the health concern. There are six AQI categories: "Good" The AQI is between 0 and 50. Air quality is considered satisfactory; "Moderate" The AQI is between 51 and 100. Air quality is acceptable; "Unhealthy for Sensitive Groups" When AQI values are between 101 and 150, members of sensitive groups may experience health effects; "Unhealthy" When AQI values are between 151 and 200 everyone may begin to experience health effects; "Very Unhealthy" AQI values between 201 and 300 trigger a health alert; "Hazardous" AQI values over 300 trigger health warnings of emergency conditions; (1) Metropolitan Statistical Area - see Appendix A for areas included; (2) Based on 365 days with AQI data in 2007.
Source: U.S. Environmental Protection Agency, Air Quality Index Report, 2007

Air Quality Index Pollutants

Area	Percent of Days when AQI Pollutant was...[2]					
	Carbon Monoxide	Nitrogen Dioxide	Ozone	Sulfur Dioxide	Particulate Matter 2.5	Particulate Matter 10
MSA[1]	0.0	0.0	61.6	0.3	38.1	0.0

Note: The Air Quality Index (AQI) is an index for reporting daily air quality. EPA calculates the AQI for five major air pollutants regulated by the Clean Air Act: ground-level ozone, particle pollution (also known as particulate matter), carbon monoxide, sulfur dioxide, and nitrogen dioxide. The AQI runs from 0 to 500. The higher the AQI value, the greater the level of air pollution and the greater the health concern; (1) Metropolitan Statistical Area - see Appendix A for areas included; (2) Based on 365 days with AQI data in 2007.
Source: U.S. Environmental Protection Agency, Air Quality Index Report, 2007

Air Quality Index Trends

Area	Trend Sites (7)								All Sites (83)
	1999	2000	2001	2002	2003	2004	2005	2006	2006
MSA[1]	16	20	14	7	5	9	10	13	26

Note: An AQI value greater than 100 indicates that air quality would have been in the unhealthful range on that day. Data from exceptional events are not included. These counts are presented in two ways. First, the counts are based on sites having an adequate record of monitoring data during the trend period (trend sites). These counts represent the relative change in the number of days with AQI values greater than 100. In the last column, the counts are based on all sites with data in the most recent year (because it is possible for a site to have data in the most recent year but not enough data to be a trend site); (1) Metropolitan Statistical Area - see Appendix A for areas included.
Source: U.S. Environmental Protection Agency, Office of Air and Radiation, Air Trends, Factbook and Related Information, Air Pollution Trends in Selected Metropolitan Areas 2006

Maximum Air Pollutant Concentrations

	Particulate Matter 10 (ug/m³)	Particulate Matter 2.5 (ug/m³)	Ozone (ppm)	Carbon Monoxide (ppm)	Sulfur Dioxide (ppm)	Nitrogen Dioxide (ppm)	Lead (ug/m³)
MSA[1] Level	56	23	0.115	2	0.02	0.016	0.77 (a)
NAAQS[2]	150	35	0.125	9	0.140	0.053	1.50
Met NAAQS[2]	Yes	Yes	Yes	Yes	Yes	Yes	Yes

Note: Data from exceptional events are not included; (1) Metropolitan Statistical Area - see Appendix A for areas included; (2) National Ambient Air Quality Standards; n/a not available; (a) Localized impact from an industrial source in Dallas. Concentration from highest nonpoint source site is 0.14 ug/m³ in Collin County
Concentrations: Particulate Matter 10 (coarse particulate) - highest second maximum 24-hour concentration; Particulate Matter 2.5 (fine particulate) - highest 98th percentile 24-hour concentration; Ozone - highest second daily maximum 1-hour concentration; Carbon Monoxide - highest second maximum non-overlapping 8-hour concentration; Sulfur Dioxide - highest second maximum 24-hour concentration; Nitrogen Dioxide - highest arithmetic mean concentration; Lead - highest quarterly maximum concentration
Units: ppm = parts per million; ug/m³ = micrograms per cubic meter
Source: U.S. Environmental Protection Agency, MSA Factbook 2006, Air Quality Statistics by City

Drinking Water

Water System Name	Pop. Served	Primary Water Source Type	Violations[1]	
			Health Based	Monitoring/ Reporting
City of Frisco	82,000	Purchased Surface	0	0

Note: (1) Based on violation data from January 1, 2007 to December 31, 2007 (includes unresolved violations from earlier years)
Source: U.S. Environmental Protection Agency, Office of Ground Water and Drinking Water, Safe Drinking Water Information System (based on data extracted April 15, 2008)

Keller, Texas

Background

Located in north Central Texas, Keller retains its country feel while located only a short commute from both Dallas and Fort Worth. The town was established in 1881 during the rapid development of the railroad service through the area, and was named after John C. Keller, a foreman on the railroad.

While Keller's residents were originally farmers, the arrival of the railroad helped develop the city into a successful trade center where a number of businesses flourished. Many of the buildings housing those original businesses still stand today in the Old Town Keller area of the city. The city has improved the historic area with pedestrian walkways, landscaping, lighting areas, and renovated facades. The renovations continue to attract local business such as tea rooms, specialty shops, and cafes, creating a vibrant historic district.

In addition to Old Town, there is the Keller Town Center, which is located in a park-like setting of lakes, walking paths, and open green land. The Town Center's infrastructure was created through a public-private partnership between the City of Keller and TriWest Enterprises. Through the partnership, the Keller Town Hall, Town Hall Plaza and Keller Independent School District's Natatorium are incorporated with private businesses and homes in the form of detached villas, luxury rental housing, ground floor retail with office lofts above, restaurants, and entertainment venue, all combining to create a bustling downtown.

The forward-looking city is also going high-tech. Keller was the first city in the country to receive Verizon's new Fiber to the Premises (FTTP) technology which was made available to individual homeowners and businesses through the community. The FTTP wiring, in its most basic form, is three-times faster than the fastest broadband technology offered today.

The newest technology is not only found in the businesses and the homes of the residents of Keller, but also in the Keller Public Library, where there is wireless Internet access for patrons throughout the 12,000-foot facility.

If residents are looking to enjoy the warm Texas climate, with summer temperatures hovering in the late 80s, they can visit any number of the seven parks and 13 miles of hike and bike trails that meander throughout the city. The city's Keller Point is an aquatic and recreation center, with indoor and outdoor pools, fitness facilities, and meeting rooms.

The city is part of the Keller Independent School District, which encompasses six cities with campus including: three high schools, four intermediate schools, four middle schools and fifteen elementary schools, which serve more than 25,000 students. Due to its proximity to two major Texas cities, Keller is also close to some of top universities in the state, including Southern Methodist University, Texas Christian University, University of North Texas and University of Texas at Dallas.

The city is served by the Dallas/Fort Worth airport, which is about 15 miles away.

Rankings

General Rankings

- Fort Worth* was ranked #133 out of 375 metro areas in *Cities Ranked & Rated*. Criteria: cost of living; climate; crime; transportation; economy and jobs; education; arts and culture; health and healthcare; leisure; quality of life. *Cities Ranked & Rated, 2nd Edition, 2007*
- Fort Worth* was ranked #92 out of 379 metro areas in *Places Rated Almanac*. Criteria: health care; education; recreation; transportation; ambience; climate; crime; housing costs; jobs. *Places Rated Almanac, 7th Edition, 2007*
- Keller was selected as one of the "2007 Best Places to Live" by *Money* magazine. The city ranked #50 out of 100. Methodology: Places on the list had to have populations above 7,500 and under 50,000. Retirement-oriented communities, places where income is less than 90% or more than 180% of the state median and towns that were more than 95% white were screened out. Towns with low education scores, high crime rates, declines or sharp increases in population, projected job losses or lack of access to airports or teaching hospitals were eliminated. The remaining places were ranked based on job, income and cost-of-living data; housing affordability; school quality; arts and leisure opportunities; ease of living; health-care access; and racial diversity. Finally, the sense of community, vibrancy of town center, natural surroundings, amenities, real estate and congestion were assessed. *CNNMoney.com, "Best Places to Live 2007"*

Business/Finance Rankings

- The nation's 100 largest metro areas were analysed in terms of the percentage of households entering some stage of foreclosure in 2007. The Fort Worth* metro area ranked #29 out of 100 (#1 = highest foreclosure rate). *RealtyTrac, "Year-End 2007 Metropolitan Foreclosure Report"*
- The Fort Worth* metro area was identified as one of the "10 Best Cities for Jobs in 2008" by *Forbes*. The metro area ranked #5. Criteria: state unemployment rate; job growth; income growth; median household income; cost of living. *Forbes.com, "Best Cities for Jobs in 2008," January 10, 2008*
- The Fort Worth* metro area was selected one of America's "Top 50 Business Opportunity Metros" by *Expansion Management* in their 5th annual Mayor's Challenge ranking of metro areas that have achieved solid ratings across the board in numerous *EM* studies during the past 12 months. The area ranked #13. Criteria: public schools; quality of life; college educated workers; logistics infrastructure; healthcare costs; taxes and government spending; reputation among site consultants. *Expansion Management, August 2007*
- The Dallas* metro area was selected as one of "America's Most Wired Cities" by *Forbes*. The metro area was ranked #19 out of 30. Criteria: percentage of Internet users with high-speed access; the range of service providers within a city; availability of public wireless hot spots. *Forbes, "America's Most Wired Cities," January 10, 2008*
- Fort Worth* was selected as one of the best places to start and grow a company by *Entrepreneur* and the National Policy Research Council. The Fort Worth* metro area ranked #17 out of 50 large metro areas. Criteria: business formation and growth (firms started four to 14 years ago that still employ at least 5 people and experienced rapid growth over the last four years). *Entrepreneur/National Policy Research Council, "Hot Cities for Entrepreneurs," September 2006*
- The Dallas* metro area was selected as one of "America's Greediest Cities" by *Forbes*. The area was ranked #7 out of 10. Criteria: number of Forbes 400 (*Forbes* annual list of the richest Americans) members per capita. *Forbes, "America's Greediest Cities," December 7, 2007*
- The Fort Worth* metro area was selected as one of "America's 50 Hottest Cities" for business relocations and expansions. Criteria: industry's most prominent site selection consultants were asked to list their top city choices for relocating and expanding manufacturing companies, taking into consideration such factors as the business climate, work force quality, operating costs, incentive programs, and the ease of working with local political and economic development officials. *Expansion Management, January-February 2007*

- Dallas* was cited as one of America's top large metros (population over 1 million) for new and expanded facility projects in 2007. The area appeared in the top 10 with 73 projects. *Site Selection, "Top Metropolitan Area Awards," March 2008*

- The Fort Worth* metro area was selected as one of the "Top 20 Real Estate Markets" for expanding or relocating companies. The area ranked #7. Criteria: low rental costs; low purchase prices; high vacancy rates of office and warehouse space. *Expansion Management, October 2007*

- Intel, in partnership with Sperling's BestPlaces, ranked the 80 "Best Cities for Teleworking" in America. The Fort Worth* metro area ranked #8 among extra large metro areas. The study identifies cities that hold the greatest potential for teleworking based on a host of factors including typical commuting times, fuel prices, availability of broadband Internet access and percentage of the population in telework friendly jobs. The study also factored in extreme climate and natural hazards. *Intel, "Best Cities for Teleworking," March 30, 2006*

- The Fort Worth* metro area appeared on the Milken Institute "2007 Best Performing Cities" index. Rank: #60 out of 200 large metro areas. Criteria: job growth; wage and salary growth; high-tech output growth. *Milken Institute, "2007 Best Performing Cities"*

- The Dallas* metro area was selected as one of "The Top 20 Boom Towns in America." *Business 2.0* magazine and econometric research firm Global Insight compared 319 metropolitan areas in the U.S. and ranked the 61 with populations over 1 million. Criteria: a weighted formula that includes forecast growth rates in sectors that contain the economy's 10 most skilled occupational clusters; the prevalence of college degrees in the local workforce; median salary. The area ranked #18 among large metro areas. *Business 2.0 Magazine, March 2004*

- Fort Worth* was identified as one of the 100 "Most Unwired Cities" in the U.S. The area ranked #23 out of the 100 largest metro areas in the U.S. Criteria: number of public and commercial wireless access points (hotspots); airports with wireless Internet access; broadband availability; local wireless networks; and wireless email devices. *Intel, "Most Unwired Cities Survey," June 7, 2005*

- Dallas* was ranked #21 out of 125 regions worldwide in terms of its "Knowledge Competitiveness Index." The index attempts to measure the knowledge-based development taking place throughout the world and is based on 19 measures of economic performance that indicate a region's ability to translate its knowledge capacity into economic value. *Robert Huggins Associates, World Knowledge Competitiveness Index 2005*

- *Forbes* ranked the 200 most populous metro areas in the U.S. in terms of the "Best Places for Business and Careers." The Fort Worth* metro area was ranked #63. Criteria: business costs (labor, energy, tax and office space expenses); living costs (housing, transportation, food and other household expenditures); education levels of the work force; job growth; income growth; migration trends; crime rates; and culture/leisure. *Forbes, "Best Places for Business and Careers," March 19, 2008*

- *Fortune* ranked the 100 largest metro areas in the U.S. in terms of projected median home price change in 2007. The Fort Worth* metro area ranked #9. *Fortune.com, "Hot Spots, Cold Spots"*

Health/Environment Rankings

- 100 of the largest metro areas in the U.S. were analyzed in terms of their current drought severity. The Fort Worth* metro area ranked #97 (#1 = driest). The rankings were based on statistics such as long-term precipitation trends and patterns and the Palmer drought indices. *Sperling's BestPlaces, www.BestPlaces.net, "America's Drought-Riskiest Cities," November 2007*

- Doctors at the Harvard School of Public Health ranked 40 metropolitan areas based on data from the government-sponsored Hospital Quality Alliance program. The program tracks the performance of individual hospitals in treating patients for three common health problems: heart attacks, congestive heart failure, and pneumonia. The Dallas* metro area ranked #22 in quality of care for heart attacks, #25 for congestive heart failure, and #7 for pneumonia. *New England Journal of Medicine, July 21, 2005*

- *Reader's Digest* ranked the 50 largest metro areas in the U.S. in terms of how "clean" they are. The Dallas* metro area ranked #30. Criteria: air quality; water quality; toxic industrial pollution; Superfund sites; and sanitation. *Reader's Digest, "The 50 Cleanest (and Dirtiest) Cities in America," July 2005*

- The American Academy of Dermatology ranked 32 U.S. metropolitan regions in terms of their residents knowledge, attitude and behaviors towards tanning and sun protection. The Dallas* metro area ranked #6. The results of the study are based on an online national survey of 3,342 respondents. *American Academy of Dermatology, "RAYS: Your Grade," May 7, 2007*

- The Fort Worth* metro area appeared in *Country Home's* "2008 Best Green Places" report. The area ranked #171 out of 379. Criteria: official energy policies; green power; green buildings; availability of fresh, locally grown food. *Country Home, "2008 Best Green Places"*

- Wyeth Consumer Healthcare, in partnership with Sperling's BestPlaces, ranked the nation's 50 most populous metro areas in terms of five key health factors. The Fort Worth* metro area ranked #37. Criteria: physical activity; health status; nutrition; lifestyle pursuits; and mental wellness. *Wyeth Consumer Healthcare, "Centrum Healthiest Cities Study," April 19, 2005*

- HealthGrades surveyed over 41,000 individuals on doctor satisfaction and ranked the 20 largest metro areas based on the highest "definitely yes" responses to the question "Do you trust the physician to make decisions/recommendations that are in your best interest?" The Fort Worth* metro area ranked #2. *HealthGrades.com, "Top Cities in Doctor-Trust," September 7, 2006*

- Fort Worth* was identified as a "2008 Asthma Capital." The area ranked #23 out of the nation's 100 largest metropolitan areas. Twelve factors were used to identify the most challenging places to live for people with asthma: estimated prevalence; self-reported prevalence; crude death rate for asthma; annual pollen score; annual air quality; public smoking laws; number of board-certified asthma specialists; school inhaler access laws; rescue medication use; controller medication use; uninsured rate; poverty rate. *Asthma and Allergy Foundation of America, "2008 Asthma Capitals"*

- Fort Worth* was identified as a "Spring Allergy Capital." The area ranked #2 out of 100. Three groups of factors were used to identify the most severe cities for people with allergies during the spring season: annual pollen levels; medicine utilization; access to board-certified allergists. *Asthma and Allergy Foundation of America, "2007 Spring Allergy Capital Rankings"*

- Fort Worth* was identified as a "Fall Allergy Capital." The area ranked #21 out of 100. Three groups of factors were used to identify the most severe cities for people with allergies during the fall season: annual pollen levels; medicine utilization; access to board-certified allergists. *Asthma and Allergy Foundation of America, "2007 Fall Allergy Capital Rankings"*

- Ortho-McNeil Neurologics, in partnership with Sperling's BestPlaces, analyzed 110 metro areas and identified those U.S. cities with the highest prevalence of factors that are most commonly associated with migraine headaches. The Fort Worth* metro area ranked #82. Criteria: number of migraine-related drug prescriptions per capita; lifestyle factors that can contribute to migraines; environmental factors that can trigger migraines; and consumption of migraine-triggering foods. *Ortho-McNeil Neurologics, "America's Migraine Hot Spots," March 14, 2006*

- Sperling's BestPlaces ranked 331 metro areas and identified the most and least stressful U.S. cities. The Fort Worth* metro area ranked #23 out of the 100 largest metro areas (#1 = most stressful). Criteria: divorce rate; unemployment rate; violent and property crime; suicide rate; commute time; mental health; alcohol consumption; cloudy days. *Sperling's BestPlaces, www.BestPlaces.net, "America's Most (and Least) Stressful Cities," January 9, 2004*

- An analysis of the "Best & Worst Cities for Sleep" was conducted by Sperling's BestPlaces. The study ranked America's 50 most populated metro areas. The Fort Worth* metro area ranked #40 (#1 = best city for sleep). Criteria: number of days residents didn't get enough rest or sleep during the past month; average length of daily commute; divorce rate; unemployment rate. *Sperling's BestPlaces, www.BestPlaces.net, "Best & Worst Cities for Sleep," 2006*

- HealthGrades evaluated the performance of America's 25 most populous metropolitan areas by measuring the outcomes of five of the highest volume and most widely studied procedures and diagnoses: coronary artery bypass graft surgery; percutaneus coronary interventions; acute myocardial infarction/heart attack in angioplasty-capable hospitals; congestive heart failure; and community acquired pneumonia. The Dallas* metro area ranked #21. *HealthGrades, "HealthGrades Hospital Quality in America Study," October 12, 2004*

- Fort Worth* was highlighted as one of the 25 most ozone-polluted metro areas in the U.S. The area ranked #7. *American Lung Association, State of the Air: 2007*

- Fort Worth* was selected as one of "America's Top 10 Low-Carb Cities" by *LowCarbiz Magazine*. Criteria: abundance of low-carb products; restaurants with low-carb menu items; health practitioners supportive of carb-cutting regimens; local culture generally conducive to exercise and health. *LowCarbiz Magazine, April 2004*

- Fort Worth* was selected as one of "America's Pet Healthiest Cities" by Purina. The city ranked #36 out of 50. Criteria: veterinary services; environment; legislation; preventative care; obesity/body condition. *Purina Pet Institute, "America's Pet Healthiest Cities," May 20, 2003*

Women/Minorities Rankings

- Fort Worth* was ranked #80 out of 100 metro areas in *SELF Magazine's* ranking of "America's Best Places for Women." A panel of experts came up with more than 50 criteria including death and disease rates, environmental indicators, community resources, and lifestyle habits. *SELF Magazine, "America's Best Places for Women 2007," December 2007*

- Dallas* appeared on *Black Enterprise's* list of the "Ten Best Cities for African Americans." The top picks were culled from more than 2,000 interactive surveys completed on www.blackenterprise.com and by editorial staff evaluation. The editors weighed the following criteria as it pertained to African Americans in each city: median household income; percentage of households earning more than $100,000; percentage of businesses owned; percentage of college graduates; unemployment rates; home loan rejections; and homeownership rates. *Black Enterprise, May 2007*

Seniors/Retirement Rankings

- The Fort Worth* metro area was selected as one of "Best Places for Retirees" by *Forbes*. The area was ranked #2 out of 10. Criteria: cost and availability of health care; sales, property and income-tax rates; arts and leisure activities; cost of living; retirement job market; inter-metro migration patterns of people between the ages of 55 and 65. *Forbes, "Best Places for Retirees," January 18, 2007*

- Sperling's BestPlaces in partnership with Bankers Life & Casualty Company designed a survey to identify the top 50 metro areas in the U.S. that offer the best overall qualities for senior living. The Fort Worth* metro area ranked #38. The following criteria were statistically weighted to reflect the needs of the senior population: health; disease; economics; social; environment; spiritual; transportation; housing; and crime. *Bankers Life & Casualty Company, "Best Cities for Seniors 2005"*

- A.G. Edwards ranked America's 500 top-performing communities based on their residents' personal savings and investing behavior. The Fort Worth* metro area ranked #353 with an index score of 98.36 (national average = 100.00). A dozen statistical factors were measured including: participation in retirement savings plans; personal debt levels; and home ownership. *A.G. Edwards, "2007 Nest Egg Index", September 12, 2007*

Children/Family Rankings

- The Fort Worth* metro area was selected as one of the "Best Cities for Relocating Families" by Worldwide ERC and Primacy Relocation. The 2007 study placed a special emphasis on the housing market, which has significantly impacted the relocation industry and an employer's ability to transfer employees. The variables which weigh heavily in this category include home price, home affordability index, appreciation rates, and property tax. Other criteria include cost of living, crime rates, education, climate, focus on diversity, physicians per capita, recreation and leisure, arts and culture, air quality, watershed quality, sales tax, unemployment rate, job growth, high school and higher education index, school expenditures per student, students in public school, SAT/ACT percentile, and population growth. *Worldwide ERC and Primacy Relocation, "2007 Best Cities for Relocating Families"*

Safety Rankings

- The National Insurance Crime Bureau ranked 361 metro areas in the U.S. in terms of per capita rates of vehicle theft. The Fort Worth* metro area ranked #50 (#1 = highest rate). Criteria: number of vehicle theft offenses per 100,000 inhabitants. *National Insurance Crime Bureau, "NICB Vehicle Theft Study," April 22, 2008*

- Fort Worth* appeared on Sperling's BestPlaces list of the "Riskiest Cities for Identity Theft." The area ranked #13 out of the nations 50 largest metro areas. Over 80 criteria were analyzed across four major categories: technology impact; crime; transactions; and risk profile. *Sperling's BestPlaces, www.BestPlaces.net, "Riskiest Cities for Identity Theft," July 2006*

- Farmers Insurance Group of Companies, in partnership with Sperling's BestPlaces, ranked 379 metro areas and identified the "Most Secure U.S. Place to Live." The Fort Worth* metro area ranked #94 out of 114 in the large metro area category (500,000 or more residents). Criteria: crime rates; extreme weather; risk of natural disasters; environmental hazards; terrorism threats; air quality; life expectancy; job loss numbers. *Farmers Insurance Group, "Most Secure U.S. Places to Live 2007"*

- Fort Worth* was identified as one of the most dangerous large metro areas for pedestrians in the U.S. The area ranked #14 out of the nations 50 largest metro areas. Criteria: average yearly pedestrian fatalities per capita (for the years 2002 and 2003) adjusted for the number of walkers. *Surface Transportation Policy Project, "Mean Streets 2004"*

- Dallas* was identified as one of the least safe places in the U.S. in terms of its vulnerability to natural disasters and weather extremes. The city ranked #2 out of 10. Sperling's BestPlaces analyzed data to show a metro areas' relative tendency to experience natural disasters (hail, tornados, high winds, hurricanes, earthquakes, and brush fires) or extreme weather (abundant rain or snowfall or days that are below freezing or above 90 degrees Fahrenheit). *Forbes, "Safest and Least Safe Places in the U.S.," August 30, 2005*

Sports/Recreation Rankings

- The Fort Worth* metro area appeared on the *Sporting News* list of the "Best Sports Cities 2007". The area ranked #3 out of 150 cities in the U.S. *Sporting News* takes a 12-month snapshot, roughly July to July, of each city's sports, putting a heavy premium on regular-season won-lost records (from the most recently completed season). Other criteria include: playoff berths, bowl appearances and tournament bids; championships; applicable power ratings; quality of competition; overall fan fervor as measured in part by attendance as percentage of venue capacity; abundance of teams (rewarding quality over quantity); stadium and arena quality; ticket availability and prices; franchise ownership; and marquee appeal of athletes. *SportingNews.com, "Best Sports Cities 2007," August 1, 2007*

- Scarborough Research, a leading market research firm, identified the top local markets for avid NBA fans. The Fort Worth* DMA (Designated Market Area) ranked in the top 10 with 13% of consumers 18 years and over reporting that they are "very interested in the NBA". *Scarborough Research, April 24, 2006*

- The Fort Worth* metro area was selected by *Cranium* as one of the "Top 50 Fun Cities" in America. The area ranked #38. Criteria includes: number of sports teams, restaurants, and dance performances; number of toy stores; city budget spent on recreation. *Cranium, November 4, 2003*

- *Golf Digest* ranked 330 metro areas in the U.S. in terms of golf. The Fort Worth* metro area was ranked #243. Criteria: access to golf; weather; value of golf; and quality of golf. *Golf Digest, "Metro Golf Rankings," August 2005*

Dating/Romance Rankings

- Eli Lily and Company, in partnership with Sperling's BestPlaces, ranked the nation's 50 largest metro areas in terms of the "Most Romantic Cities for Baby Boomers." The Dallas* metro area ranked #9. Criteria: marriage and divorce rates among "baby boomers" age 45 to 60; great restaurants; dance studios; chocolate, jewelry and flower sales. *Eli Lily and Company, "Most Romantic Cities for Baby Boomers," April 20, 2007*

- The Dallas* metro area was selected as one of the "Top Ten U.S. Cities for Finding a Rich, Single Man" by Teasley, a Manhattan-based marketing consulting firm. The area ranked #10. Criteria: high single-male to single-female ratios; higher income to cost-of-living ratios. *Teasley, "Top Ten U.S. Cities for Finding a Rich, Single Man," February 10, 2004*

- The Fort Worth* metro area was selected as one of the "Best Cities for Relocating Singles" by Worldwide ERC and Primacy Relocation. The area ranked #49 out of the 100 largest metro areas in the U.S. Areas were selected based on the following criteria: a robust cost-of-living index; adventure and outdoor recreation opportunities; violent crime and property crime rates; percentage of the population that is unmarried (ages 25-34); ratio of single men and single women; affordability of quality higher education, including in-state and out-of-state tuition requirements and rates; number of newcomers to the area; commute times; tax rates; fee and occupancy rates for temporary housing and mini-storage; quality and quantity of collegiate and professional sporting events and fun, fan-friendly venues. *Worldwide ERC and Primacy Relocation, "2007 Best Cities for Relocating Singles," October 25, 2007*

- *Forbes* ranked the 40 most populous urbanized areas in the U.S. in terms of the "Best Cities for Singles." The Dallas* metro area ranked #9. Criteria: number of singles; cost of living alone; nightlife; culture; job growth; coolness; and online dating. *Forbes.com, August 21, 2007*

- Sperling's BestPlaces in partnership with AXE Deodorant Bodyspray ranked 80 metro areas and identified "America's Best (and Worst) Cities for Dating." The Fort Worth* metro area ranked #30 (#1 = best). Criteria: percentage of singles ages 18-24; population density; dating venues per capita. *AXE Deodorant Bodyspray, "America's Best (and Worst) Cities for Dating," May 2004*

Miscellaneous Rankings

- The Dallas* metro area was identified as one of 10 "Worst Cities for Commuters" by *Forbes*. The metro area ranked #5. Criteria: traffic delays; travel times; how efficiently commuters use existing infrastructure. *Forbes.com, "Worst Cities for Commuters," April 29, 2008*

- Scarborough Research, a leading market research firm, identified the top local markets for bloggers. The Fort Worth* DMA (Designated Market Area) ranked in the top 13 with 11% of adults reporting that they had read or contributed to a blog within the past 30 days. *Scarborough Research, October 24, 2007*

- The Dallas* metro area was selected as one of the "Top 10 Most Independent Cities for Homesellers". The area ranked #9. The cities listed had more consumers choosing to sell their homes without the help of a real-estate agent than anywhere else. Data was based on geographical information for listings posted on ForSaleByOwner.com from January 1, 2007 through June 30, 2007. *ForSaleByOwner.com, October 1, 2007*

- The Fort Worth* metro area appeared on *Forbes* list of "America's Drunkest Cities". The area ranked #27. Criteria: 35 of the largest continental U.S. metro areas were chosen based on availability of data and geographic diversity. Each metro was ranked in five areas: state laws; drinkers; heavy drinkers; binge drinkers; and alcoholism. *Forbes.com, "America's Drunkest Cities," August 22, 2006*

- Sperling's BestPlaces in partnership with Pep Boys ranked 77 metro areas and identified "America's Most Drivable Cities." The Fort Worth* metro area ranked #35. Criteria: climate; road roughness; urban mobility; gas prices. *Pep Boys, "America's Most Drivable Cities," April 9, 2003*

- State Farm Insurance, in partnership with Sperling's BestPlaces, analyzed several key factors that contribute to overall family preparedness. The Fort Worth* metro area ranked #11 out of the nation's 50 most populous metro areas. Criteria: quality of life; life insurance coverage; and investments. *State Farm Life Insurance, "Fiscally Fit Cities Report," July 20, 2004*

- A study by Sperling's BestPlaces examined which U.S. metro areas were most affected by high fuel prices in 2006. The Dallas* metro area was ranked #37 out of 80 (#1 = most expensive city for driving). Rankings are based on the average dollars spent on gas per year by two driver households. Criteria: cost of regular-grade gasoline; average miles driven per day; average number of gallons each driver uses and wastes in traffic congestion each day. *Sperling's BestPlaces, www.bestplaces.net, "Pain at the Pump," May 18, 2006*

Keller is located within the Dallas-Fort Worth-Arlington, TX Metropolitan Statistical Area and Fort Worth-Arlington, TX Metropolitan Division.

Business Environment

CITY FINANCES

City Government Finances

Component	2004-2005 ($000)	2004-2005 ($ per capita)
Total Revenues	n/a	n/a
Total Expenditures	n/a	n/a
Debt Outstanding	n/a	n/a
Cash and Securities	n/a	n/a

Source: U.S Census Bureau, Government Finances 2004-2005

City Government Revenue by Source

Source	2004-2005 ($000)	2004-2005 ($ per capita)
General Revenue		
From Federal Government	n/a	n/a
From State Government	n/a	n/a
From Local Governments	n/a	n/a
Taxes		
Property	n/a	n/a
Sales	n/a	n/a
Personal Income	n/a	n/a
License	n/a	n/a
Charges	n/a	n/a
Liquor Store	n/a	n/a
Utility	n/a	n/a
Employee Retirement	n/a	n/a
Other	n/a	n/a

Source: U.S Census Bureau, Government Finances 2004-2005

City Government Expenditures by Function

Function	2004-2005 ($000)	2004-2005 ($ per capita)	2004-2005 (%)
General Expenditures			
Airports	n/a	n/a	n/a
Corrections	n/a	n/a	n/a
Education	n/a	n/a	n/a
Fire Protection	n/a	n/a	n/a
Governmental Administration	n/a	n/a	n/a
Health	n/a	n/a	n/a
Highways	n/a	n/a	n/a
Hospitals	n/a	n/a	n/a
Housing and Community Development	n/a	n/a	n/a
Interest on General Debt	n/a	n/a	n/a
Libraries	n/a	n/a	n/a
Parking	n/a	n/a	n/a
Parks and Recreation	n/a	n/a	n/a
Police Protection	n/a	n/a	n/a
Public Welfare	n/a	n/a	n/a
Sewerage	n/a	n/a	n/a
Solid Waste Management	n/a	n/a	n/a
Liquor Store	n/a	n/a	n/a
Utility	n/a	n/a	n/a
Employee Retirement	n/a	n/a	n/a
Other	n/a	n/a	n/a

Source: U.S Census Bureau, Government Finances 2004-2005

Municipal Bond Ratings

Area	Moody's
City	n/a

Source: Mergent Bond Record, January 2008 (unless noted otherwise)

DEMOGRAPHICS

Population Growth

Area	1990 Census	2000 Census	2007 Estimate	2012 Projection	Population Growth (%) 1990-2000	Population Growth (%) 2000-2012
City	13,683	27,345	38,275	45,313	99.8	65.7
MSA[1]	3,989,294	5,161,544	6,007,731	6,587,538	29.4	27.6
U.S.	248,709,873	281,421,906	301,045,522	314,920,978	13.2	11.9

Note: (1) Metropolitan Statistical Area - see Appendix B for areas included
Source: Claritas, Inc.

Number of Households and Average Household Size

Area	2007 Estimate	2007 Average Household Size
City	12,057	3.17
MSA[1]	2,171,092	2.77
U.S.	113,668,003	2.65

Note: (1) Metropolitan Statistical Area - see Appendix B for areas included
Source: Claritas, Inc.

Race and Ethnicity

Area	White Alone[2]	Black Alone[2]	Asian Alone[2]	Other Race Alone[2]	Hispanic[3]
City	91.8	1.9	2.1	4.1	6.1
MSA[1]	65.6	14.0	4.6	15.8	26.4
U.S.	73.1	12.4	4.3	10.3	14.9

Note: Figures are 2007 estimates; (1) Metropolitan Statistical Area - see Appendix B for areas included (2) Alone is defined as not being in combination with one or more other races; (3) May be of any race.
Source: Claritas, Inc.

Ancestry

Area	German	Irish[2]	English	American	Italian	Polish	French[3]	Scottish
City	18.5	15.1	15.3	10.5	4.0	2.1	2.9	3.0
MSA[1]	11.4	9.2	9.1	9.7	2.0	1.2	2.4	1.9
U.S.	15.2	10.9	8.7	7.3	5.6	3.2	3.0	1.7

Note: Figures include multiple ancestry (e.g. if a person reported being Irish and Italian, they were included in both columns); (1) Metropolitan Statistical Area - see Appendix A for areas included; (2) Includes Celtic; (3) Includes Alsatian but excludes Basque
Source: Census 2000, Summary File 3

Foreign-Born Population

Area	Percent of Population Born in: Any Foreign Country	Europe	Asia	Africa	Oceania[2]	Canada	Mexico	Latin America[3]
City	5.2	1.9	1.8	0.0	0.0	0.7	0.3	0.6
MSA[1]	11.4	0.8	2.6	0.4	0.1	0.2	6.5	0.8
U.S.	11.1	1.7	2.9	0.3	0.1	0.3	3.3	2.5

Note: (1) Metropolitan Statistical Area - see Appendix A for areas included; (2) Includes Australia, New Zealand subregion, Melanesia, Micronesia, Polynesia, and Oceania n.e.c; (3) Includes Central America (excluding Mexico), South America, and the Caribbean.
Source: Census 2000, Summary File 3

Marriage Status

Area	Never Married	Now Married (excluding Separated)	Separated	Widowed	Divorced
City	15.1	77.0	0.5	2.1	5.3
MSA[1]	24.3	57.5	2.3	4.9	11.0
U.S.	27.1	54.4	2.2	6.6	9.7

Note: Figures are percentages and cover the population 15 years of age and older; (1) Metropolitan Statistical Area - see Appendix A for areas included
Source: Census 2000, Summary File 3

Age Distribution

Area	Percent of Population						
	Under Age 5	Age 5 to 17	Age 18 to 34	Age 35 to 49	Age 50 to 64	Age 65 to 79	80 Years and Over
City	8.4	25.8	16.3	31.4	14.0	3.5	0.6
MSA[1]	7.7	20.2	25.2	24.6	13.5	6.7	2.0
U.S.	6.8	18.9	23.7	23.5	14.8	9.2	3.2

Note: (1) Metropolitan Statistical Area - see Appendix A for areas included
Source: Census 2000, Summary File 3

Male/Female Ratio

Area	Males	Females	Males per 100 Females
City	19,084	19,191	99.4
MSA[1]	3,012,647	2,995,084	100.6
U.S.	148,320,305	152,725,217	97.1

Note: Figures are 2007 estimates; (1) Metropolitan Statistical Area - see Appendix B for areas included
Source: Claritas, Inc.

Religion

Area	Catholic	Southern Baptist	United Meth-odist	ELCA[1]	LDS[2]	Presby-terian Church USA	Jewish Est.	Muslim Est.
County	11.5	18.7	6.8	0.6	0.8	0.8	0.4	1.0
U.S.	22.0	7.1	3.7	1.8	1.5	1.1	2.2	0.6

Note: Figures are the number of adherents as a percentage of the total population; Adherents are defined as all members, including full members, their children and the estimated number of other participants who are not considered members (e.g. the baptized, those not confirmed, those regularly attending services, etc.); (1) Evangelical Lutheran Church in America; (2) The Church of Jesus Christ of Latter Day Saints
Source: Reprinted with permission from Religious Congregations and Membership in the United States 2000 (Nashville, Glenmary Research Center, 2002) Copyright Association of Statisticians of American Religious Bodies. All rights reserved.

ECONOMY

Gross Metropolitan Product

Area	2002	2003	2004	2005	2005 Rank[2]
MSA[1]	229.2	238.6	260.0	284.5	5

Note: Figures are in billions of dollars; (1) Dallas-Fort Worth-Arlington, TX Metropolitan Statistical Area - see Appendix A for areas included; (2) Rank ranges from 1 to 361
Source: The U.S. Conference of Mayors, "U.S. Metro Economies: GMP - The Engines of America's Growth," January 2007

Economic Growth

Area	1995 GMP	2005 GMP	Average Annual Growth Rate	Growth Rate Rank[2]
MSA[1]	143.0	284.5	7.1	35

Note: Figures are in billions of dollars; GMP = Gross Metropolitan Product; (1) Dallas-Fort Worth-Arlington, TX Metropolitan Statistical Area - see Appendix A for areas included; (2) Rank ranges from 1 to 361
Source: The U.S. Conference of Mayors, "U.S. Metro Economies: GMP - The Engines of America's Growth," January 2007

INCOME

Per Capita/Median/Average Income

Area	Per Capita ($)	Median Household ($)	Average Household ($)
City	37,653	103,011	119,511
MSA[1]	27,089	55,079	74,352
U.S.	25,495	49,280	66,670

Note: Figures are 2007 estimates; (1) Metropolitan Statistical Area - see Appendix B for areas included
Source: Claritas, Inc.

Household Income Distribution

Area	Percent of Households Earning							
	Under $15,000	$15,000 -24,999	$25,000 -34,999	$35,000 -49,999	$50,000 -74,999	$75,000 -99,000	$100,000 -149,999	$150,000 and up
City	1.3	2.7	3.8	5.4	15.0	19.5	31.3	20.9
MSA[1]	10.0	9.1	10.7	15.8	19.8	13.0	13.2	8.5
U.S.	13.1	10.9	11.2	15.6	19.5	11.9	11.3	6.6

Note: Figures are 2007 estimates; (1) Metropolitan Statistical Area - see Appendix B for areas included
Source: Claritas, Inc.

Poverty Rates by Age

Area	All Ages	Under 5 Years Old	5 to 17 Years Old	18 to 64 Years Old	65 Years and Over
City	1.4	0.1	0.4	0.8	0.1
MSA[1]	10.3	1.2	2.6	5.7	0.8
U.S.	12.4	1.2	3.0	6.9	1.2

Note: Figures are percent of population with income in 1999 below poverty level and only include population for whom poverty status is determined; (1) Metropolitan Statistical Area - see Appendix A for areas included
Source: Census 2000, Summary File 3

Personal Bankruptcy Filing Rate

Area	2004	2005	2006
Tarrant County	6.46	8.04	2.34
U.S.	5.31	6.82	2.00

Note: Numbers are per 1,000 population and include Chapter 7 and Chapter 13 filings
Source: Federal Deposit Insurance Corporation (FDIC), Regional Economic Conditions (RECON), 8/23/2007

EMPLOYMENT

Labor Force and Employment

Area	Civilian Labor Force			Workers Employed		
	Dec. 2006	Dec. 2007	% Chg.	Dec. 2006	Dec. 2007	% Chg.
City	19,617	19,725	0.6	18,993	19,077	0.4
MD[1]	1,026,983	1,032,143	0.5	985,677	990,075	0.4
U.S.	152,571,000	153,705,000	0.7	146,081,000	146,334,000	0.2

Note: Data is not seasonally adjusted and covers workers 16 years of age and older;
(1) Metropolitan Division - see Appendix B for areas included
Source: Bureau of Labor Statistics, http://stats.bls.gov

Unemployment Rate

Area	2007											
	Jan.	Feb.	Mar.	Apr.	May	Jun.	Jul.	Aug.	Sep.	Oct.	Nov.	Dec.
City	3.6	3.5	3.2	3.1	3.1	3.8	3.8	3.4	3.6	3.3	3.4	3.3
MD[1]	4.9	4.5	4.1	3.9	4.0	4.6	4.6	4.2	4.2	3.9	4.0	4.1
U.S.	5.0	4.9	4.5	4.3	4.3	4.7	4.9	4.6	4.5	4.4	4.5	4.8

Note: Data is not seasonally adjusted and covers workers 16 years of age and older; All figures are percentages; (1) Metropolitan Division - see Appendix B for areas included
Source: Bureau of Labor Statistics, http://stats.bls.gov

Employment by Occupation

Occupation Classification	City (%)	MSA[1] (%)	U.S. (%)
Sales and Office	27.9	29.3	26.7
Professional and Related	24.4	19.0	20.2
Service	10.1	12.8	14.9
Production, Transportation, and Material Moving	7.6	13.8	14.6
Management, Business, and Financial	23.9	14.6	13.5
Construction, Extraction, and Maintenance	6.2	10.3	9.4
Farming, Forestry, and Fishing	0.0	0.1	0.7

Note: Figures cover employed civilians 16 years of age and older;
(1) Metropolitan Statistical Area - see Appendix A for areas included
Source: Census 2000, Summary File 3

Employment by Industry

Sector	MSA[1] Number of Employees	MSA[1] Percent of Total	U.S. Percent of Total
Government	118,300	13.4	16.3
Education and Health Services	99,200	11.2	13.4
Professional and Business Services	104,600	11.9	13.1
Retail Trade	107,100	12.1	11.6
Manufacturing	99,300	11.3	9.9
Leisure and Hospitality	85,600	9.7	9.6
Financial Activities	48,500	5.5	5.9
Construction	n/a	n/a	5.3
Wholesale Trade	42,400	4.8	4.4
Other Services	32,700	3.7	3.9
Transportation and Utilities	64,700	7.3	3.7
Information	16,600	1.9	2.2
Natural Resources and Mining	n/a	n/a	0.5

Note: Figures cover non-farm employment as of December 2007 and are not seasonally adjusted; (1) Metropolitan Statistical Area - see Appendix B for areas included; n/a not available
Source: Bureau of Labor Statistics, http://stats.bls.gov

Average Wages

Occupation	$/Hr.	Occupation	$/Hr.
Accountants and Auditors	29.28	Maids and Housekeeping Cleaners	7.99
Automotive Mechanics	16.59	Maintenance and Repair Workers	14.88
Bookkeepers	15.17	Marketing Managers	50.62
Carpenters	13.98	Nuclear Medicine Technologists	32.29
Cashiers	8.48	Nurses, Licensed Practical	19.07
Clerks, General Office	10.99	Nurses, Registered	28.31
Clerks, Receptionists/Information	11.62	Nursing Aides/Orderlies/Attendants	10.32
Clerks, Shipping/Receiving	13.23	Packers and Packagers, Hand	9.27
Computer Programmers	37.02	Physical Therapists	35.73
Computer Support Specialists	19.60	Postal Service Mail Carriers	21.42
Computer Systems Analysts	34.67	Real Estate Brokers	60.65
Cooks, Restaurant	9.77	Retail Salespersons	11.37
Dentists	n/a	Sales Reps., Exc. Tech./Scientific	28.58
Electrical Engineers	37.06	Sales Reps., Tech./Scientific	35.67
Electricians	19.68	Secretaries, Exc. Legal/Med./Exec.	12.96
Financial Managers	51.18	Security Guards	12.69
First-Line Supervisors/Mgrs., Sales	18.36	Surgeons	89.84
Food Preparation Workers	8.34	Teacher Assistants	8.00
General and Operations Managers	49.14	Teachers, Elementary School	22.40
Hairdressers/Cosmetologists	11.26	Teachers, Secondary School	23.80
Internists	71.55	Telemarketers	9.61
Janitors and Cleaners	9.36	Truck Drivers, Heavy/Tractor-Trailer	17.47
Landscaping/Groundskeeping Workers	10.75	Truck Drivers, Light/Delivery Svcs.	13.97
Lawyers	51.71	Waiters and Waitresses	7.67

Note: Wage data covers the Fort Worth-Arlington, TX Metropolitan Division - see Appendix B for areas included. Hourly wages for elementary/secondary school teachers and teacher assistants were calculated by the editors from annual wage data assuming a 40 hour work week; n/a not available.
Source: Bureau of Labor Statistics, May 2007 Metro Area Occupational Employment and Wage Estimates

RESIDENTIAL REAL ESTATE

Building Permits

Area	Single-Family 2006	Single-Family 2007[p]	Single-Family Pct. Chg.	Multi-Family 2006	Multi-Family 2007[p]	Multi-Family Pct. Chg.	Total 2006	Total 2007[p]	Total Pct. Chg.
City	369	254	-31.2	0	0	-	369	254	-31.2
U.S.	1,378,200	973,300	-29.4	460,700	407,200	-11.6	1,838,900	1,380,500	-24.9

Note: (p) preliminary; figures cover and represent new, privately-owned housing units authorized (unadjusted data); All permit data are based on estimates with imputation; U.S. figures are based on the new 20,000-place series.
Source: U.S. Census Bureau, Manufacturing, Mining, and Construction Statistics

Homeownership and Housing Vacancies

Area	Homeownership Rate[2] (%)			Rental Vacancy Rate[3] (%)			Homeowner Vacancy Rate[4] (%)		
	2005	2006	2007	2005	2006	2007	2005	2006	2007
MSA[1]	62.3	60.7	60.9	13.6	11.7	11.0	2.2	2.3	2.5
U.S.	68.9	68.8	68.1	9.8	9.8	9.7	1.9	2.4	2.7

Note: (1) Metropolitan Statistical Area - see Appendix B for areas included; (2) The proportion of households that are owners; (3) The proportion of the rental inventory that is vacant for rent; (4) The proportion of the homeowner inventory that is vacant for sale; n/a not available
Source: U.S. Census Bureau, Housing Vacancies and Homeownership Annual Statistics: 2007

TAXES

State Corporate Income Tax Rates

State	Rates and Tax Brackets
Texas	1.0%

Note: Tax rates as of January 1, 2008; Texas's 1% franchise tax is a gross receipts tax paid by most taxable entities. Retailers pay 0.5%.
Source: Tax Foundation, www.taxfoundation.org

State Individual Income Tax Rates

State	Federal Deductibility	Marginal Rates (%)	Standard Deduction ($)		Personal Exemptions ($)[1]	
			Single	Joint	Single	Dependents
Texas	No	None	n/a	n/a	n/a	n/a

Note: Tax rates as of January 1, 2008; Local- and county-level taxes are not included; n/a not applicable; (1) Married joint filers generally receive double the single exemption
Source: Tax Foundation, www.taxfoundation.org

Various State and Local Tax Rates

State and Local Sales and Use (%)	State Sales and Use (%)	Gasoline[1,2] ($/gal.)	Cigarette ($/pack)	Spirits ($/gal.)	Table Wine ($/gal.)	Beer ($/gal.)
8.25	6.25 (i)	0.20	1.41	2.40	0.204	0.19

Note: Tax rates as of January 1, 2008; (1) In addition to the 18.4 cpg Federal gasoline tax; (2) Rates may include additional state sales taxes, environmental protection and storage fees/taxes, and local taxes. When necessary, the volume-weighted average of all local taxes is used to approximate the typical statewide rate including local tax; (i) Texas has a GRT that is levied in addition to its 6.25% sales tax. It is called the franchise tax and the rate is 1% (.5% for retailers).
Source: Tax Foundation, www.taxfoundation.org; Original research

State Tax Burdens

Area	Combined State and Local Tax Burden		Combined Federal, State and Local Tax Burden	
	Percent	Rank	Percent	Rank
Texas	9.3	43	29.8	41
U.S. Average	11.0	-	32.7	-

Note: Figures cover 2007 and measure taxes as a percentage of income
Source: Tax Foundation, www.taxfoundation.org

State Business Tax Climate Index Rankings

State	Overall Rank	Corporate Tax Index Rank	Individual Income Tax Index Rank	Sales Tax Index Rank	Unemployment Insurance Tax Index Rank	Property Tax Index Rank
Texas	8	47	7	28	14	27

Note: Rankings range from 1 to 50 where 1 is best. Rankings do not average across to Overall Rank. States without a given tax are given a ranking of 1.
Source: Tax Foundation, State Business Tax Climate Index 2008

TRANSPORTATION

Means of Transportation to Work

Area	Car/Truck/Van		Public Transportation			Bicycle	Walked	Other Means	Worked at Home
	Drove Alone	Car-pooled	Bus	Subway	Railroad				
City	85.2	6.9	0.0	0.1	0.0	0.0	1.0	0.7	6.2
MSA[1]	81.2	13.3	0.4	0.0	0.0	0.1	1.4	0.9	2.7
U.S.	75.7	12.2	2.5	1.5	0.5	0.4	2.9	1.0	3.3

Note: Figures are percentages and cover workers 16 years of age and older; (1) Metropolitan Statistical Area - see Appendix A for areas included
Source: Census 2000, Summary File 3

Travel Time to Work

Area	Less Than 15 Minutes	15 to 29 Minutes	30 to 44 Minutes	45 to 59 Minutes	60 Minutes or More
City	15.6	32.4	30.0	14.1	7.9
MSA[1]	23.4	37.8	22.6	8.8	7.5
U.S.	29.4	36.1	19.1	7.4	8.0

Note: Figures are percentages and include workers 16 years old and over; (1) Metropolitan Statistical Area - see Appendix A for areas included
Source: Census 2000, Summary File 3

Travel Time Index

Area	1982	1995	2004	2005
Urban Area[1]	1.05	1.16	1.31	1.35
Average[2]	1.11	1.22	1.29	1.30

Note: Travel Time Index - The ratio of travel time in the peak period to the travel time at free-flow conditions. A value of 1.35 indicates a 20-minute free-flow trip takes 27 minutes in the peak. Free-flow speeds (60 mph on freeways and 35 mph on principal arterials) are used as the comparison threshold; (1) Covers the Dallas-Fort Worth-Arlington, TX urban area; (2) average of 85 urban areas
Source: Texas Transportation Institute, The 2007 Urban Mobility Report, September 2007

Living Environment

COST OF LIVING

Cost of Living Index

Composite Index	Groceries	Housing	Utilities	Trans-portation	Health Care	Misc. Goods/ Services
88.5	95.3	74.9	98.3	97.7	90.1	91.2

Note: U.S. = 100; Figures cover the Fort Worth TX urban area.
Source: The Council for Community and Economic Research (formerly ACCRA), Cost of Living Index, 2007

Grocery Prices

Area[1]	T-Bone Steak ($/pound)	Frying Chicken ($/pound)	Whole Milk ($/half gal.)	Eggs ($/dozen)	Orange Juice ($/64 oz.)	Coffee ($/11.5 oz.)
City[2]	9.03	0.96	2.28	1.50	3.11	3.04
Avg.	8.93	1.12	2.13	1.52	3.26	3.31
Min.	5.88	0.71	1.33	0.83	2.30	2.20
Max.	12.80	2.07	3.43	3.54	5.79	6.20

Note: (1) Values for the local area are compared with the average, minimum and maximum values for all 331 areas in the Cost of Living Index report; (2) Figures cover the Fort Worth TX urban area; **T-Bone Steak** *(price per pound);* **Frying Chicken** *(price per pound, whole fryer);* **Whole Milk** *(half gallon carton);* **Eggs** *(price per dozen, Grade A, large);* **Orange Juice** *(64 oz. Tropicana or Florida Natural);* **Coffee** *(11.5 oz. can, vacuum-packed, Maxwell House, Hills Bros, or Folgers).*
Source: The Council for Community and Economic Research (formerly ACCRA), Cost of Living Index, 2007

Housing and Utility Costs

Area[1]	New Home Price ($)	Apartment Rent ($/month)	All Electric ($/month)	Part Electric ($/month)	Other Energy ($/month)	Telephone ($/month)
City[2]	213,267	815	-	112.12	50.83	24.95
Avg.	309,605	782	146.13	78.67	90.16	26.14
Min.	189,877	n/a	82.03	37.41	33.15	17.08
Max.	1,202,800	3,481	271.14	150.60	257.67	37.45

Note: (1) Values for the local area are compared with the average, minimum and maximum values for all 331 areas in the Cost of Living Index report; (2) Figures cover the Fort Worth TX urban area; **New Home Price** *(2,400 sf living area, 8,000 sf lot, in urban area with full utilities);* **Apartment Rent** *(950 sf 2 bedroom/1.5 or 2 bath, unfurnished, excluding all utilities except water);* **All Electric** *(average monthly cost for an all-electric home);* **Part Electric** *(average monthly cost for a part-electric home);* **Other Energy** *(average monthly cost for natural gas, fuel oil, coal, wood, and any other forms of energy except electricity);* **Telephone** *(price includes basic monthly rate for a private residential line plus additional local usage charges incurred by a family of four).*
Source: The Council for Community and Economic Research (formerly ACCRA), Cost of Living Index, 2007

Health Care, Transportation, and Other Costs

Area[1]	Doctor ($/visit)	Dentist ($/visit)	Optometrist ($/visit)	Gasoline ($/gallon)	Beauty Salon ($/visit)	Men's Shirt ($)
City[2]	61.32	67.49	47.44	2.46	30.46	21.38
Avg.	79.48	71.93	79.55	2.64	29.52	25.77
Min.	52.08	44.80	43.95	2.19	15.58	16.19
Max.	148.44	126.27	158.83	3.48	60.62	48.53

Note: (1) Values for the local area are compared with the average, minimum and maximum values for all 331 areas in the Cost of Living Index report; (2) Figures cover the Fort Worth TX urban area; **Doctor** *(general practitioners routine exam of an established patient);* **Dentist** *(adult teeth cleaning and periodic oral examination);* **Optometrist** *(full vision eye exam for established adult patient);* **Gasoline** *(one gallon regular unleaded, national brand, including all taxes, cash price at self-service pump if available);* **Beauty Salon** *(woman's shampoo, trim, and blow-dry);* **Men's Shirt** *(cotton/polyester dress shirt, pinpoint weave, long sleeves).*
Source: The Council for Community and Economic Research (formerly ACCRA), Cost of Living Index, 2007

HOUSING

House Price Index (HPI)

Area	National Ranking[2]	Quarterly Change (%)	One-Year Change (%)	Five-Year Change (%)
MD[1]	101	0.50	2.89	17.43
U.S.[3]	-	0.10	0.84	41.37

Note: The HPI is a weighted repeat sales index. It measures average price changes in repeat sales or refinancings on the same properties. This information is obtained by reviewing repeat mortgage transactions on single-family properties whose mortgages have been purchased or securitized by Fannie Mae or Freddie Mac in January 1975; (1) Metropolitan Division - see Appendix B for areas included; (2) Rankings are based on annual percentage change for all metro areas containing at least 15,000 transactions over the last 10 years and ranges from 1 to 291; (3) figures based on a weighted average of Census Division estimates; all figures are for the period ending December 31, 2007
Source: Office of Federal Housing Enterprise Oversight, House Price Index, February 26, 2008

House Price Valuations

Area	Q1 2000	Q1 2001	Q1 2002	Q1 2003	Q1 2004	Q1 2005	Q1 2006	Q1 2007	Q1 2008
MD[1]	-14.6	-20.0	-17.5	-16.8	-19.8	-20.4	-21.9	-24.8	-28.8

Note: Figures show the percentage of over- or under-valuation of single family homes relative to statistically normal house values (e.g. a value of 23.6 indicates that house values are 23.6% overvalued). Statistically normal house values are based on house prices, interest rates, household incomes, population densities, and any historical premiums or discounts metropolitan areas have exhibited over time; (1) Figures cover the Metropolitan Division - see Appendix B for areas included
Source: Global Insight/National City Corporation, House Prices in America, May 2008

Median Home Prices

Area	2005	2006	2007[r]	Percent Change 2006 to 2007
MSA[1]	147.6	149.5	150.9	0.9
U.S. Average	219.0	221.9	217.9	-1.8

Note: Figures are median sales prices of existing single-family homes in thousands of dollars; (r) revised; n/a not available; (1) Metropolitan Statistical Area - see Appendix B for areas included
Source: National Association of Realtors, Metropolitan Area Prices, 1st Quarter 2008

Housing: Year Structure Built

Area	1990 -2000	1980 -1989	1970 -1979	1960 -1969	1950 -1959	1940 -1949	Before 1940	Median Year
City	52.2	26.9	14.2	2.7	1.4	1.9	0.6	1991
MSA[1]	21.4	26.8	19.2	12.5	11.1	4.9	4.1	1979
U.S.	17.0	15.8	18.5	13.7	12.7	7.3	15.0	1971

Note: Figures are percentages; (1) Metropolitan Statistical Area - see Appendix A for areas included
Source: Census 2000, Summary File 3

HEALTH

Health Risk Data

Category	Area[1] (%)	U.S. (%)
Adults who have been told they have high blood pressure[3]	22.8	25.5
Adults who have been told they have high blood cholesterol[3]	31.8	35.6
Adults who have been told they have diabetes[2]	8.2	7.5
Adults who have been told they have arthritis[3]	20.0	27.0
Adults who have been told they currently have asthma	7.5	8.5
Adults who are current smokers	19.9	20.1
Adults who are heavy drinkers[4]	3.8	4.9
Adults who are overweight (BMI 25.0 - 29.9)	43.2	36.5
Adults who are obese (BMI 30.0 - 99.8)	23.9	25.1

Note: Data as of 2006 unless otherwise noted; (1) Figures cover the Metropolitan Division - see Appendix B for areas included; (2) Figures do not include pregnancy-related diabetes, pre-diabetes or borderline diabetes; (3) 2005 data; (4) Heavy drinkers are classified as adult men having more than two drinks per day or adult women having more than one drink per day
Source: Centers for Disease Control and Prevention, Behaviorial Risk Factor Surveillance System, SMART: Selected Metropolitan/Micropolitan Area Risk Trends, 2005, 2006

Mortality Rates for the Top 10 Causes of Death in the U.S.

ICD-10[a] Sub-Chapter	ICD-10[a] Code	Age-Adjusted Mortality Rate[1] per 100,000 population	
		County[2]	U.S.
Malignant neoplasms	C00-C97	182.1	186.5
Ischaemic heart diseases	I20-I25	159.9	152.3
Other forms of heart disease	I30-I51	47.7	51.5
Cerebrovascular diseases	I60-I69	64.5	50.0
Chronic lower respiratory diseases	J40-J47	49.3	42.6
Diabetes mellitus	E10-E14	26.0	24.8
Other degenerative diseases of the nervous system	G30-G31	28.3	22.6
Other external causes of accidental injury	W00-X59	18.0	21.4
Influenza and pneumonia	J10-J18	14.4	20.7
Hypertensive diseases	I10-I13	27.7	18.2

Note: (a) ICD-10 = International Classification of Diseases 10th Revision; (1) Mortality rates are a three year average covering 2003-2005; (2) Figures cover Tarrant County
Source: Centers for Disease Control and Prevention, National Center for Health Statistics. Compressed Mortality File 1999-2004. CDC WONDER On-line Database, compiled from Compressed Mortality File 1999-2005 Series 20 No. 2K, 2008.

Mortality Rates for Selected Causes of Death

ICD-10[a] Sub-Chapter	ICD-10[a] Code	Age-Adjusted Mortality Rate[1] per 100,000 population	
		County[2]	U.S.
Assault	X85-Y09	5.6	5.9
Human immunodeficiency virus (HIV) disease	B20-B24	4.2	4.5
Intentional self-harm	X60-X84	10.9	10.8
Malnutrition	E40-E46	1.3	1.0
Obesity and other hyperalimentation	E65-E68	1.3	1.4
Organic, including symptomatic, mental disorders	F01-F09	26.5	16.8
Transport accidents	V01-V99	13.1	16.1
Viral hepatitis	B15-B19	2.1	1.8

Note: (a) ICD-10 = International Classification of Diseases 10th Revision; (1) Mortality rates are a three year average covering 2003-2005; (2) Figures cover Tarrant County
Source: Centers for Disease Control and Prevention, National Center for Health Statistics. Compressed Mortality File 1999-2004. CDC WONDER On-line Database, compiled from Compressed Mortality File 1999-2005 Series 20 No. 2K, 2008.

Distribution of Physicians[1]

Area	Total	Family/ General Practice	Specialties	
			Medical	Surgical
Tarrant County (number)	2,255	578	750	598
Tarrant County (rate per 10,000 pop.)	13.9	3.6	4.6	3.7
U.S. (rate per 10,000 pop.)	17.7	4.6	6.9	4.3

Note: Data as of 2005; (1) Includes all non-federal, patient-care, office-based MDs
Source: Area Resource File (ARF). June 2007. U.S. Department of Health and Human Services, Health Resources and Services Administration, Bureau of Health Professions, Rockville, MD.

Hospitals

There were no hospitals listed within the city limits.
AHA Guide to the Healthcare Field 2008

According to *U.S. News,* the Dallas-Fort Worth-Arlington, TX metro area is home to six of the best hospitals in the U.S.: **Baylor Institute for Rehabilitation**; **Baylor University Medical Center**; **Children's Medical Center Dallas**; **Parkland Memorial Hospital**; **Presbyterian Hospital**; **University of Texas Southwestern Medical Center**. *U.S. News Online, "America's Best Hospitals 2007"*

EDUCATION

Public School District Statistics

District Name	Schls	Pupils	Pupil/ Teacher Ratio	Minority Pupils[1] (%)	Free Lunch Eligible[2] (%)	IEP[3] (%)
Keller ISD	33	25,873	17.3	26.9	7.6	8.0

Note: Table includes regular local school districts with 2,000 or more students; (1) Percentage of students that are not white, non-Hispanic; (2) Percentage of students that are eligible for the free lunch program; (3) Percentage of students that have an Individualized Education Program.

Source: U.S. Department of Education, National Center for Education Statistics, Common Core of Data, Local Education Agency (School District) Universe Survey: School Year 2005-2006; U.S. Department of Education, National Center for Education Statistics, Common Core of Data, Public Elementary/Secondary School Universe Survey: School Year 2005-2006

Highest Level of Education

Area	Less than H.S.	H.S. Diploma	Some College, No Deg.	Associate Degree	Bachelors Degree	Masters Degree	Profess. School Degree	Doctorate Degree
City	4.1	15.9	27.5	8.7	32.9	8.8	1.1	1.0
MSA[1]	19.2	22.3	23.5	5.7	20.3	6.4	1.7	0.8
U.S.	19.4	28.4	21.2	6.4	15.7	5.9	2.0	1.0

Note: Figures are 2007 estimated percentages and cover persons age 25 and over; (1) Metropolitan Statistical Area - see Appendix B for areas included

Source: Claritas, Inc.

Educational Attainment by Race

Area	High School Graduate (%)					Bachelor's Degree (%)				
	Total	White	Black	Asian	Hisp.[2]	Total	White	Black	Asian	Hisp.[2]
City	95.6	95.7	100.0	94.8	88.4	44.6	44.5	36.7	62.1	29.3
MSA[1]	81.0	84.9	80.2	72.4	46.6	25.1	27.3	16.8	36.3	9.2
U.S.	80.4	83.6	72.3	80.4	52.4	24.4	26.1	14.3	44.1	10.4

Note: Figures shown cover persons 25 years old and over; (1) Metropolitan Statistical Area - see Appendix A for areas included; (2) people of Hispanic origin can be of any race

Source: Census 2000, Summary File 3

School Enrollment by Type

Area	Grades KG to 8				Grades 9 to 12			
	Public		Private		Public		Private	
	Enrollment	%	Enrollment	%	Enrollment	%	Enrollment	%
City	4,451	89.4	530	10.6	1,627	91.4	153	8.6
MSA[1]	224,258	91.0	22,110	9.0	91,305	92.3	7,600	7.7
U.S.	33,526,011	88.7	4,285,121	11.3	14,848,628	90.6	1,532,323	9.4

Note: Figures shown cover persons 3 years old and over; (1) Metropolitan Statistical Area - see Appendix A for areas included

Source: Census 2000, Summary File 3

School Enrollment by Race

Area	Grades KG to 8 (%)				Grades 9 to 12 (%)			
	White	Black	Asian	Hisp.[1]	White	Black	Asian	Hisp.[1]
City	90.4	1.5	1.7	7.0	93.7	0.8	0.6	5.8
MSA[2]	69.1	12.9	2.8	23.7	69.0	14.1	3.6	19.9
U.S.	68.5	15.5	3.3	16.8	68.8	15.5	3.8	15.7

Note: Figures shown cover persons 3 years old and over; (1) people of Hispanic origin can be of any race; (2) Metropolitan Statistical Area - see Appendix A for areas included

Source: Census 2000, Summary File 3

Average Salaries of Public School Classroom Teachers

District	2005-06		2006-07		Percent Change 2005-06 to 2006-07
	Dollars	Rank[1]	Dollars	Rank[1]	
Texas	41,744	35	44,897	30	7.55
U.S. Average	49,026	-	50,816	-	3.65

Note: (1) State rank ranges from 1 to 51.
Source: National Education Association, Rankings & Estimates: Rankings of the States 2006 and Estimates of School Statistics 2007, December 2007

Higher Education

Four-Year Colleges			Two-Year Colleges			Medical Schools[1]	Law Schools[2]	Voc/ Tech[3]
Public	Private Non-profit	Private For-profit	Public	Private Non-profit	Private For-profit			
0	0	0	0	0	0	0	0	0

Note: Figures cover institutions located within the city limits; (1) includes schools accredited by the Liaison Committee on Medical Education and the American Osteopathic Association; (2) includes American Bar Association-accredited law schools; (3) includes all schools with programs that are less than 2 years.
Source: National Center for Education Statistics, The Integrated Postsecondary Education System (IPEDS) Peer Analysis System, 2007; www.usnews.com, Law and Medical School Directories, 2009

PRESIDENTIAL ELECTION

2004 Presidential Election Results

Area	Bush	Kerry	Nader	Other
Tarrant County	62.4	37.0	0.1	0.5
U.S.	50.7	48.3	0.4	0.6

Note: Results are percentages and may not add to 100% due to rounding
Source: Dave Leip's Atlas of U.S. Presidential Elections, www.uselectionatlas.org

EMPLOYERS

Major Employers

Company Name	Industry	Type of Site
A M R Corporation	Air transportation, scheduled	Headquarters
Alcon Holdings Inc	Pharmaceutical preparations	Headquarters
Archer-Western Contractors	Nonresidential construction, nec	Single
BNSF Railway Company	Railroads, line-haul operating	Branch
Bell Helicopter Textron Inc	Aircraft	Headquarters
Bimbo Bakeries Usa Inc	Bread, cake, and related products	Headquarters
Federal Aviation ADM	Regulation, administration of transportation	Branch
Gamestop	Catalog and mail-order houses	Headquarters
General Motors	Motor vehicles and car bodies	Branch
General Motors	New and used car dealers	Branch
John Peter Smith Hospital	General medical and surgical hospitals	Headquarters
Mrs Bairds Bakeries Bus Tr	Bread, cake, and related products	Headquarters
Psychological/Deaf Svcs Dept	Elementary and secondary schools	Branch
Radio Shack	Radio, television, and electronic stores	Branch
Sabre Travel Info Network	Travel agencies	Headquarters
Tpg Capital - New York Inc	Investors, nec	Headquarters

Note: Companies shown are located within the Fort Worth metropolitan area; nec = not elsewhere classified.
Source: www.zapdata.com, May 2008

PUBLIC SAFETY

Crime Rate

Area	All Crimes	Violent Crimes				Property Crimes		
		Murder	Forcible Rape	Robbery	Aggrav. Assault	Burglary	Larceny -Theft	Motor Vehicle Theft
City	1,566.0	5.4	19.1	10.9	32.7	269.6	1,173.8	54.5
Metro[1]	4,914.1	4.1	36.5	143.0	299.9	984.4	3,066.3	379.9
U.S.	3,808.1	5.7	30.9	149.4	287.5	729.4	2,206.8	398.4

Note: Figures are crimes per 100,000 population; (1) Metropolitan Division - see Appendix B for areas included
Source: FBI Uniform Crime Reports, 2006

Hate Crimes

Area	Number of Quarters Reported	Bias Motivation				
		Race	Religion	Sexual Orientation	Ethnicity	Disability
City	4	0	0	0	0	0

Source: Federal Bureau of Investigation, Hate Crime Statistics 2006

RECREATION

Culture

Dance[1]	Theatre[1]	Instrumental Music[1]	Vocal Music[1]	Series/ Festivals	Museums	Zoos and Aquariums[2]
0	0	0	0	0	0	0

Note: (1) Number of professional perfoming groups; (2) AZA-accredited
Source: The Grey House Performing Arts Directory, 2007; Official Museum Directory, 2008; Association of Zoos & Aquariums, AZA Member Zoos & Aquariums, June 2008

Professional Sports Teams

Team Name	League
Texas Rangers	Major League Baseball (MLB)
FC Dallas	Major League Soccer (MLS)
Dallas Mavericks	National Basketball Association (NBA)
Dallas Cowboys	National Football League (NFL)
Dallas Stars	National Hockey League (NHL)

Note: Includes teams located in the Dallas-Fort Worth metro area.
Source: Original research

MEDIA

Newspapers

Name	News Focus	Frequency	Circulation
Keller Citizen	Community	Weekly	36,000

Note: Includes newspapers with offices located in the city
Source: MediaContactsPro, March 2008

Television Stations

Name	Ch.	Network(s)	Type	Ownership
KDTN	2	PBS	Public	North Texas Public Broadcasting Inc.
KDFW	4	Fox	Commercial	Fox Television Stations Inc.
KXAS	5	NBC	Commercial	General Electric Corporation
WFAA	8	ABC	Commercial	Belo Corporation
KTVT	11	CBS	Commercial	CBS
KERA	13	PBS	Public	North Texas Public Broadcasting Inc.
KSST	18	n/a	Commercial	Hopkins County Broadcasting Inc.
KTXA	21	UPN	Commercial	CBS
KUVN	23	Univision	Commercial	Perenchio Television Inc.
KDFI	27	Fox	Commercial	Fox Television Stations Inc.
KMPX	29	n/a	Non-comm.	n/a
KDAF	33	WBN	Commercial	Tribune Broadcasting Company
KXTX	39	Telemundo	Commercial	Telemundo Group Inc.
KTAQ	47	n/a	Commercial	Michael Simons
KSTR	49	Univision	Commercial	Univision Television Group
KFWD	52	n/a	Commercial	n/a
KDTX	58	n/a	Non-comm.	Trinity Broadcasting Network
KPXD	68	Pax	Commercial	Paxson Communications Corporation

Note: Stations included cover the Dallas-Fort Worth DMA (Designated Market Area)
BurrellesLuce, MediaContacts Online, January 2007

Major AM Radio Stations

Call Letters	Freq. (kHz)	Station Type	Target Audience	Station Format	Music Format
KLIF	570	Commercial	General/Men	News/Talk	n/a
KMKI	620	n/a	General	Music	n/a
KSKY	660	n/a	General/Hisp/Rel	Music/Sports/Talk	n/a
KKDA	730	Commercial	General	Music/News	Rhythm & Blues
KAAM	770	Commercial	General	Music	Adult Standards
WBAP	820	Commercial	General	Educational/News/Talk	n/a
KFJZ	870	Commercial	General/Hispanic	Music/News/Sports/Talk	Latin
KKLF	950	n/a	General	News/Talk	n/a
KHVN	970	n/a	Christian/General	Music	n/a
KGGR	1040	n/a	Black/General/Rel	Talk	n/a
KRLD	1080	n/a	General	n/a	n/a
KBIS	1150	n/a	General/Hispanic	Music/News/Talk	n/a
KSST	1230	n/a	General	Music/News	Easy Listening
KPJC	1250	College	General	Music/News	Jazz
KTCK	1310	Commercial	General	Talk	n/a
KAND	1340	Commercial	General	Music/News	Country
KAHZ	1360	n/a	General/Hispanic	Ed/News/Sports/Talk	n/a
KBEC	1390	Commercial	General	Music	Country
KGVL	1400	n/a	General	Music/News/Sports	n/a
KLVQ	1410	n/a	General/Religious	Music	n/a
KFYN	1420	n/a	General	Music/News/Sports	n/a
KTNO	1440	Commercial	Hispanic/Religious	Music/Talk	Gospel
KNET	1450	n/a	General	Music	n/a
KTFW	1460	Commercial	General/Hispanic	n/a	n/a
KPLT	1490	Commercial	General	Music/News/Sports/Talk	Gospel
KSTV	1510	Commercial	General/Hispanic	Music	Top 40
KZMP	1540	n/a	General/Hispanic	Music	n/a
KCOM	1550	Commercial	General/Hispanic	Music	Country
KTBK	1700	Commercial	General	Sports/Talk	n/a

Note: Stations included cover the Dallas-Fort Worth DMA (Designated Market Area); n/a not available
Source: BurrellesLuce, MediaContacts Online, January 2007

Major FM Radio Stations

Call Letters	Freq. (mHz)	Station Type	Target Audience	Station Format	Music Format
KNTU	88.1	College	General	Educational/Music/News	n/a
KEOM	88.5	n/a	General	Ed/Music/News/Sports	n/a
KETR	88.9	College	General	Music/Sports	n/a
KNON	89.3	Non-Comm	Black/Hispanic	Ed/Music/News/Talk	Album Rock
KERA	90.1	Public	General	Music/Talk	Folk
KCBI	90.9	n/a	General/Religious	Music/News	n/a
KVTT	91.7	n/a	General/Religious	Educational/Talk	n/a
KZPS	92.5	n/a	General	Music/News/Talk	n/a
KSTV	93.1	Commercial	General	Music/News	Country
KDBN	93.3	Commercial	General	Music/Talk	Classic Rock
KLNO	94.1	Commercial	General/Hispanic	Music	Latin
KLTY	94.9	Commercial	General/Religious	Music/News/Talk	Christian
KZZA	95.1	Commercial	General	Music	Latin
KSCS	96.3	Commercial	General	Music/News/Talk	Country
KEGL	97.1	Commercial	General	Music/News/Sports	Modern Rock
KBFB	97.9	Commercial	General	Music	Urban Contemp.
KYYK	98.3	n/a	General	Music	n/a
KLUV	98.7	Commercial	General	Music/News/Talk	Oldies
KHCK	99.1	Commercial	General/Hispanic	Music	Latin
KPLX	99.5	Commercial	General	Music	Country
WRR	101.1	Commercial	General	Music/News/Talk	Classical
KZMP	101.7	n/a	General/Hispanic	Music	n/a
KBUS	101.9	Commercial	General	Music/News	Classic Rock
KDGE	102.1	Commercial	Young Adult	Music/News/Talk	Alternative
KDMX	102.9	Commercial	General/Women	Music/News/Talk	Adult Top 40
KVIL	103.7	n/a	General	Music	n/a
KKDA	104.5	n/a	Black/General	Music	n/a
KRNB	105.7	n/a	General	Music/News/Sports	n/a
KHKS	106.1	Commercial	General	Music/News/Talk	Top 40
KOAI	107.5	n/a	General	Music/Talk	n/a
KPLT	107.7	n/a	General	Music/News	Top 40
KDXX	107.9	Commercial	General/Hispanic	Music/News/Talk	Adult Contemp.

Note: Stations included cover the Dallas-Fort Worth DMA (Designated Market Area); n/a not available
BurrellesLuce, MediaContacts Online, January 2007

CLIMATE

Average and Extreme Temperatures

Temperature	Jan	Feb	Mar	Apr	May	Jun	Jul	Aug	Sep	Oct	Nov	Dec	Yr.
Extreme High (°F)	88	88	96	98	103	113	110	108	107	106	89	90	113
Average High (°F)	54	59	67	76	83	92	96	96	88	79	67	58	76
Average Temp. (°F)	44	49	57	66	73	81	85	85	78	68	56	47	66
Average Low (°F)	33	38	45	54	63	71	75	74	67	56	45	37	55
Extreme Low (°F)	4	6	11	29	41	51	59	56	43	29	19	-1	-1

Note: Figures cover the years 1953-1990
Source: National Climatic Data Center, International Station Meteorological Climate Summary, 9/96

Average Precipitation/Snowfall/Humidity

Precip./Humidity	Jan	Feb	Mar	Apr	May	Jun	Jul	Aug	Sep	Oct	Nov	Dec	Yr.
Avg. Precip. (in.)	1.8	2.2	2.6	3.7	4.9	2.8	2.1	1.9	3.0	3.3	2.1	1.7	32.3
Avg. Snowfall (in.)	1	1	Tr	0	0	0	0	0	0	0	Tr	Tr	3
Avg. Rel. Hum. 6am (%)	79	79	79	81	86	85	80	79	83	82	80	79	81
Avg. Rel. Hum. 3pm (%)	52	51	48	50	53	47	42	41	46	47	49	51	48

Note: Figures cover the years 1953-1990; Tr = Trace amounts (<0.05 in. of rain; <0.5 in. of snow)
Source: National Climatic Data Center, International Station Meteorological Climate Summary, 9/96

Weather Conditions

Temperature			Daytime Sky			Precipitation		
10°F & below	32°F & below	90°F & above	Clear	Partly cloudy	Cloudy	0.01 inch or more precip.	0.1 inch or more snow/ice	Thunder-storms
1	40	100	123	136	106	79	3	47

Note: Figures are average number of days per year and cover the years 1953-1990
Source: National Climatic Data Center, International Station Meteorological Climate Summary, 9/96

HAZARDOUS WASTE

Superfund Sites

Keller has no sites on the EPA's Superfund Final National Priorities List.
U.S. Environmental Protection Agency, Final National Priorities List, June 23, 2008

AIR & WATER QUALITY

Air Quality Index

Area	Percent of Days when Air Quality was...[2]				AQI Statistics	
	Good	Moderate	Unhealthy for Sensitive Groups	Unhealthy	Maximum	Median
MSA[1]	65.2	29.0	5.2	0.5	203	43

Note: The Air Quality Index (AQI) is an index for reporting daily air quality. EPA calculates the AQI for five major air pollutants regulated by the Clean Air Act: ground-level ozone, particle pollution (also known as particulate matter), carbon monoxide, sulfur dioxide, and nitrogen dioxide. The AQI runs from 0 to 500. The higher the AQI value, the greater the level of air pollution and the greater the health concern. There are six AQI categories: "Good" The AQI is between 0 and 50. Air quality is considered satisfactory; "Moderate" The AQI is between 51 and 100. Air quality is acceptable; "Unhealthy for Sensitive Groups" When AQI values are between 101 and 150, members of sensitive groups may experience health effects; "Unhealthy" When AQI values are between 151 and 200 everyone may begin to experience health effects; "Very Unhealthy" AQI values between 201 and 300 trigger a health alert; "Hazardous" AQI values over 300 trigger health warnings of emergency conditions; (1) Metropolitan Statistical Area - see Appendix A for areas included; (2) Based on 365 days with AQI data in 2007.
Source: U.S. Environmental Protection Agency, Air Quality Index Report, 2007

Air Quality Index Pollutants

Area	Percent of Days when AQI Pollutant was...[2]					
	Carbon Monoxide	Nitrogen Dioxide	Ozone	Sulfur Dioxide	Particulate Matter 2.5	Particulate Matter 10
MSA[1]	0.0	0.0	59.2	0.0	40.8	0.0

Note: The Air Quality Index (AQI) is an index for reporting daily air quality. EPA calculates the AQI for five major air pollutants regulated by the Clean Air Act: ground-level ozone, particle pollution (also known as particulate matter), carbon monoxide, sulfur dioxide, and nitrogen dioxide. The AQI runs from 0 to 500. The higher the AQI value, the greater the level of air pollution and the greater the health concern; (1) Metropolitan Statistical Area - see Appendix A for areas included; (2) Based on 365 days with AQI data in 2007.
Source: U.S. Environmental Protection Agency, Air Quality Index Report, 2007

Air Quality Index Trends

Area	Trend Sites (7)								All Sites (33)
	1999	2000	2001	2002	2003	2004	2005	2006	2006
MSA[1]	19	17	17	23	25	11	22	19	23

Note: An AQI value greater than 100 indicates that air quality would have been in the unhealthful range on that day. Data from exceptional events are not included. These counts are presented in two ways. First, the counts are based on sites having an adequate record of monitoring data during the trend period (trend sites). These counts represent the relative change in the number of days with AQI values greater than 100. In the last column, the counts are based on all sites with data in the most recent year (because it is possible for a site to have data in the most recent year but not enough data to be a trend site); (1) Metropolitan Statistical Area - see Appendix A for areas included.
Source: U.S. Environmental Protection Agency, Office of Air and Radiation, Air Trends, Factbook and Related Information, Air Pollution Trends in Selected Metropolitan Areas 2006

Maximum Air Pollutant Concentrations

	Particulate Matter 10 (ug/m^3)	Particulate Matter 2.5 (ug/m^3)	Ozone (ppm)	Carbon Monoxide (ppm)	Sulfur Dioxide (ppm)	Nitrogen Dioxide (ppm)	Lead (ug/m^3)
MSA[1] Level	34	23	0.114	1	n/a	0.014	n/a
NAAQS[2]	150	35	0.125	9	0.140	0.053	1.50
Met NAAQS[2]	Yes	Yes	Yes	Yes	n/a	Yes	n/a

Note: Data from exceptional events are not included; (1) Metropolitan Statistical Area - see Appendix A for areas included; (2) National Ambient Air Quality Standards; n/a not available
Concentrations: Particulate Matter 10 (coarse particulate) - highest second maximum 24-hour concentration; Particulate Matter 2.5 (fine particulate) - highest 98th percentile 24-hour concentration; Ozone - highest second daily maximum 1-hour concentration; Carbon Monoxide - highest second maximum non-overlapping 8-hour concentration; Sulfur Dioxide - highest second maximum 24-hour concentration; Nitrogen Dioxide - highest arithmetic mean concentration; Lead - highest quarterly maximum concentration
Units: ppm = parts per million; ug/m^3 = micrograms per cubic meter
Source: U.S. Environmental Protection Agency, MSA Factbook 2006, Air Quality Statistics by City

Drinking Water

Water System Name	Pop. Served	Primary Water Source Type	Violations[1]	
			Health Based	Monitoring/ Reporting
City of Keller	38,400	Purchased Surface	0	0

Note: (1) Based on violation data from January 1, 2007 to December 31, 2007 (includes unresolved violations from earlier years)
Source: U.S. Environmental Protection Agency, Office of Ground Water and Drinking Water, Safe Drinking Water Information System (based on data extracted April 15, 2008)

League City, Texas

Background

League City is located about 20 miles southeast of Houston, on the south shore of Clear Lake, which feeds into Galveston Bay. Lying within the greater Houston-Galveston area, it enjoys the benefits of both these great cities. Occupying 55 square miles, the city lies in both Galveston and Harris Counties.

The indigenous people of the area were the Karakawas, Coco, Tonkawas, and Akokisa Indians. Europeans began arriving in 1825, when Stephen F. Austin first settled the area. The G. W. Butler family was an important ranching family, originators of Bevo, the famous Texas Longhorn bull, whose fine pedigree is the source of much of today's remarkable stock. J. C. League began acquiring land from the Butler family in the 1890s, and in 1892 League City was established. It was formally incorporated as a Texas Home Rule City in 1962.

A blend of high-tech aerospace industries and petrochemical industries, along with a quaint, tree-lined historic district characterize League City. NASA's Johnson Space Center, the Texas Medical Center in Houston, and the Bayport Industrial Complex (home to 65 specialty chemical and petrochemical plants) are the main sources of employment. They ensure that the population of League City is young, technically trained, and generally prosperous. Tourism is also an important business; the city fronts Clear Lake, which connects directly to Galveston Bay and all its boating attractions.

The city is served by two school districts, The Clear Creek Independent School District and Dickinson Independent School District. Nearly 80% of high school graduates enter college. There are two private schools, Bay Area Christian School and St. Mary's Elementary School.

Excellent medical services are offered locally by Clear Lake Regional Medical Center. Christus-St. John Hospital is an acute care facility, and Devereux Hospital and Neurobehavorial Institute is one of a nationwide network of treatment facilities specializing in treating children and adolescents in a wide range of emotional, psychological, and chemical-dependency disorders,

The Butler Longhorn Museum displays life in the early days - the hardships of the settlers and the rugged cattle-ranchers. The museum is located in a 10.5-acre Heritage Park, which also includes the Ghirardi home, the original homestead of a family who was prominent among the early farming community of League City. The park's new Big League Dreams Sports Park draws thousands of new visitors to the area.

Due to its proximity to the Gulf of Mexico, League City has a marine climate, with winter temperatures moderated by the Gulf of Mexico. Summers are hot and humid. Cloud cover is relatively abundant from December through May, and partly cloudy days are the norm from June to September. Destructive wind storms are fairly infrequent, but both thunder-squalls and tropical storms occasionally occur.

Rankings

General Rankings

- Houston* was ranked #256 out of 375 metro areas in *Cities Ranked & Rated*. Criteria: cost of living; climate; crime; transportation; economy and jobs; education; arts and culture; health and healthcare; leisure; quality of life. *Cities Ranked & Rated, 2nd Edition, 2007*
- Houston* was ranked #48 out of 379 metro areas in *Places Rated Almanac*. Criteria: health care; education; recreation; transportation; ambience; climate; crime; housing costs; jobs. *Places Rated Almanac, 7th Edition, 2007*
- The Houston* metro area was selected one of America's "Best Cities to Live, Work and Play" by *Kiplinger Personal Finance*. Criteria: population growth; percentage of workforce in the creative class (scientists, engineers, educators, writers, artists, entertainers, etc.); job quality; income growth; cost of living. *Kiplinger Personal Finance, "Best Cities to Live, Work and Play," July 2008*
- League City was selected as one of the "2006 Best Places to Live" by *Money* magazine. Places were ranked using 38 quality-of-life indicators and six economic opportunity measures in the following categories: ease of living; health; education; crime; park space; arts and leisure. *CNNMoney.com, "Best Places to Live 2006"*

Business/Finance Rankings

- The nation's 100 largest metro areas were analysed in terms of the percentage of households entering some stage of foreclosure in 2007. The Houston* metro area ranked #39 out of 100 (#1 = highest foreclosure rate). *RealtyTrac, "Year-End 2007 Metropolitan Foreclosure Report"*
- The Houston* metro area was identified as one of the "10 Best Cities for Jobs in 2008" by *Forbes*. The metro area ranked #7. Criteria: state unemployment rate; job growth; income growth; median household income; cost of living. *Forbes.com, "Best Cities for Jobs in 2008," January 10, 2008*
- The Houston* metro area was identified as one of the "Top 12 Nano Metros" in the U.S. by the Woodrow Wilson International Center for Scholars. The metro area is home to 18 companies, universities, government laboratories and/or organizations working in nanotechnology. *Woodrow Wilson International Center for Scholars, May 17, 2007*
- The Houston* metro area was selected one of America's "Top 50 Business Opportunity Metros" by *Expansion Management* in their 5th annual Mayor's Challenge ranking of metro areas that have achieved solid ratings across the board in numerous *EM* studies during the past 12 months. The area ranked #16. Criteria: public schools; quality of life; college educated workers; logistics infrastructure; healthcare costs; taxes and government spending; reputation among site consultants. *Expansion Management, August 2007*
- The Houston* metro area was identified as one of 10 "Top Up-and-Coming Tech Cities" by *Forbes*. The metro area ranked #4. Criteria: regional innovation trends; important patents. *Forbes.com, "Top Up-and-Coming Tech Cities," March 11, 2008*
- Galveston* was selected as one of the best places to start and grow a company by *Entrepreneur* and the National Policy Research Council. The Galveston* metro area ranked #14 out of 50 large metro areas. Criteria: business formation and growth (firms started four to 14 years ago that still employ at least 5 people and experienced rapid growth over the last four years). *Entrepreneur/National Policy Research Council, "Hot Cities for Entrepreneurs," September 2006*
- The Houston* metro area was selected as one of "America's 50 Hottest Cities" for business relocations and expansions. Criteria: industry's most prominent site selection consultants were asked to list their top city choices for relocating and expanding manufacturing companies, taking into consideration such factors as the business climate, work force quality, operating costs, incentive programs, and the ease of working with local political and economic development officials. *Expansion Management, January-February 2007*

- Houston* was cited as one of America's top large metros (population over 1 million) for new and expanded facility projects in 2007. The area appeared in the top 10 with 75 projects. *Site Selection, "Top Metropolitan Area Awards," March 2008*

- Intel, in partnership with Sperling's BestPlaces, ranked the 80 "Best Cities for Teleworking" in America. The Houston* metro area ranked #11 among extra large metro areas. The study identifies cities that hold the greatest potential for teleworking based on a host of factors including typical commuting times, fuel prices, availability of broadband Internet access and percentage of the population in telework friendly jobs. The study also factored in extreme climate and natural hazards. *Intel, "Best Cities for Teleworking," March 30, 2006*

- The Houston* metro area appeared on the Milken Institute "2007 Best Performing Cities" index. Rank: #32 out of 200 large metro areas. Criteria: job growth; wage and salary growth; high-tech output growth. *Milken Institute, "2007 Best Performing Cities"*

- The Houston* metro area was selected as one of the hottest cities for entrepreneurs in America by *Inc. Magazine.* Criteria: job-growth data for 393 metro was analyzed for current-year employment growth, average annual employment growth over past three years, and employment growth by industry sector. The Houston* metro area ranked #17 among large metro areas and #120 overall. *Inc. Magazine, May 2007*

- Houston* was identified as one of the 100 "Most Unwired Cities" in the U.S. The area ranked #28 out of the 100 largest metro areas in the U.S. Criteria: number of public and commercial wireless access points (hotspots); airports with wireless Internet access; broadband availability; local wireless networks; and wireless email devices. *Intel, "Most Unwired Cities Survey," June 7, 2005*

- Houston* was ranked #26 out of 125 regions worldwide in terms of its "Knowledge Competitiveness Index." The index attempts to measure the knowledge-based development taking place throughout the world and is based on 19 measures of economic performance that indicate a region's ability to translate its knowledge capacity into economic value. *Robert Huggins Associates, World Knowledge Competitiveness Index 2005*

- *Forbes* ranked the 200 most populous metro areas in the U.S. in terms of the "Best Places for Business and Careers." The Houston* metro area was ranked #33. Criteria: business costs (labor, energy, tax and office space expenses); living costs (housing, transportation, food and other household expenditures); education levels of the work force; job growth; income growth; migration trends; crime rates; and culture/leisure. *Forbes, "Best Places for Business and Careers," March 19, 2008*

- *Fortune* ranked the 100 largest metro areas in the U.S. in terms of projected median home price change in 2007. The Houston* metro area ranked #11. *Fortune.com, "Hot Spots, Cold Spots"*

Health/Environment Rankings

- The Houston* metro area was identified as one of "America's 20 Most Sedentary Cities" by *Forbes*. The metro area ranked #11. Criteria: percentage of overweight or obese people; percentage of people who had not engaged in any physical activity in the past 30 days; average number of hours of TV watched per week. *Forbes.com, "America's Most Sedentary Cities," October 29, 2007*

- 100 of the largest metro areas in the U.S. were analyzed in terms of their current drought severity. The Houston* metro area ranked #96 (#1 = driest). The rankings were based on statistics such as long-term precipitation trends and patterns and the Palmer drought indices. *Sperling's BestPlaces, www.BestPlaces.net, "America's Drought-Riskiest Cities," November 2007*

- Doctors at the Harvard School of Public Health ranked 40 metropolitan areas based on data from the government-sponsored Hospital Quality Alliance program. The program tracks the performance of individual hospitals in treating patients for three common health problems: heart attacks, congestive heart failure, and pneumonia. The Houston* metro area ranked #33 in quality of care for heart attacks, #27 for congestive heart failure, and #32 for pneumonia. *New England Journal of Medicine, July 21, 2005*

- *Reader's Digest* ranked the 50 largest metro areas in the U.S. in terms of how "clean" they are. The Houston* metro area ranked #41. Criteria: air quality; water quality; toxic industrial pollution; Superfund sites; and sanitation. *Reader's Digest, "The 50 Cleanest (and Dirtiest) Cities in America," July 2005*

- The American Academy of Dermatology ranked 32 U.S. metropolitan regions in terms of their residents knowledge, attitude and behaviors towards tanning and sun protection. The Houston* metro area ranked #20. The results of the study are based on an online national survey of 3,342 respondents. *American Academy of Dermatology, "RAYS: Your Grade," May 7, 2007*

- *Business Week* identified the 15 metro areas that saw the steepest declines in ground-level ozone pollution between 1990 and 2005. The Houston* metro area ranked #4. *Business Week, "America's Most Cleaned-Up Metro Areas," March 23, 2007*

- The Houston* metro area appeared in *Country Home's* "2008 Best Green Places" report. The area ranked #122 out of 379. Criteria: official energy policies; green power; green buildings; availability of fresh, locally grown food. *Country Home, "2008 Best Green Places"*

- Wyeth Consumer Healthcare, in partnership with Sperling's BestPlaces, ranked the nation's 50 most populous metro areas in terms of five key health factors. The Houston* metro area ranked #36. Criteria: physical activity; health status; nutrition; lifestyle pursuits; and mental wellness. *Wyeth Consumer Healthcare, "Centrum Healthiest Cities Study," April 19, 2005*

- HealthGrades surveyed over 41,000 individuals on doctor satisfaction and ranked the 20 largest metro areas based on the highest "definitely yes" responses to the question "Do you trust the physician to make decisions/recommendations that are in your best interest?" The Houston* metro area ranked #1. *HealthGrades.com, "Top Cities in Doctor-Trust," September 7, 2006*

- Houston* was identified as a "2008 Asthma Capital." The area ranked #72 out of the nation's 100 largest metropolitan areas. Twelve factors were used to identify the most challenging places to live for people with asthma: estimated prevalence; self-reported prevalence; crude death rate for asthma; annual pollen score; annual air quality; public smoking laws; number of board-certified asthma specialists; school inhaler access laws; rescue medication use; controller medication use; uninsured rate; poverty rate. *Asthma and Allergy Foundation of America, "2008 Asthma Capitals"*

- Houston* was identified as a "Spring Allergy Capital." The area ranked #28 out of 100. Three groups of factors were used to identify the most severe cities for people with allergies during the spring season: annual pollen levels; medicine utilization; access to board-certified allergists. *Asthma and Allergy Foundation of America, "2007 Spring Allergy Capital Rankings"*

- Houston* was identified as a "Fall Allergy Capital." The area ranked #17 out of 100. Three groups of factors were used to identify the most severe cities for people with allergies during the fall season: annual pollen levels; medicine utilization; access to board-certified allergists. *Asthma and Allergy Foundation of America, "2007 Fall Allergy Capital Rankings"*

- Ortho-McNeil Neurologics, in partnership with Sperling's BestPlaces, analyzed 110 metro areas and identified those U.S. cities with the highest prevalence of factors that are most commonly associated with migraine headaches. The Galveston* metro area ranked #95. Criteria: number of migraine-related drug prescriptions per capita; lifestyle factors that can contribute to migraines; environmental factors that can trigger migraines; and consumption of migraine-triggering foods. *Ortho-McNeil Neurologics, "America's Migraine Hot Spots," March 14, 2006*

- Sperling's BestPlaces ranked 331 metro areas and identified the most and least stressful U.S. cities. The Galveston* metro area ranked #1 out of 114 mid-size metro areas (#1 = most stressful). Criteria: divorce rate; unemployment rate; violent and property crime; suicide rate; commute time; mental health; alcohol consumption; cloudy days. *Sperling's BestPlaces, www.BestPlaces.net, "America's Most (and Least) Stressful Cities," January 9, 2004*

- An analysis of the "Best & Worst Cities for Sleep" was conducted by Sperling's BestPlaces. The study ranked America's 50 most populated metro areas. The Houston* metro area ranked #48 (#1 = best city for sleep). Criteria: number of days residents didn't get enough rest or sleep during the past month; average length of daily commute; divorce rate; unemployment rate. *Sperling's BestPlaces, www.BestPlaces.net, "Best & Worst Cities for Sleep," 2006*

- HealthGrades evaluated the performance of America's 25 most populous metropolitan areas by measuring the outcomes of five of the highest volume and most widely studied procedures and diagnoses: coronary artery bypass graft surgery; percutaneus coronary interventions; acute myocardial infarction/heart attack in angioplasty-capable hospitals; congestive heart failure; and community acquired pneumonia. The Houston* metro area ranked #15. *HealthGrades, "HealthGrades Hospital Quality in America Study," October 12, 2004*

- Houston* was highlighted as one of the 25 most ozone-polluted metro areas in the U.S. The area ranked #5. *American Lung Association, State of the Air: 2007*

- Houston* was selected as one of "America's Pet Healthiest Cities" by Purina. The city ranked #32 out of 50. Criteria: veterinary services; environment; legislation; preventative care; obesity/body condition. *Purina Pet Institute, "America's Pet Healthiest Cities," May 20, 2003*

Women/Minorities Rankings

- Houston* was ranked #89 out of 100 metro areas in *SELF Magazine's* ranking of "America's Best Places for Women." A panel of experts came up with more than 50 criteria including death and disease rates, environmental indicators, community resources, and lifestyle habits. *SELF Magazine, "America's Best Places for Women 2007," December 2007*

- Houston* appeared on *Black Enterprise's* list of the "Ten Best Cities for African Americans." The top picks were culled from more than 2,000 interactive surveys completed on www.blackenterprise.com and by editorial staff evaluation. The editors weighed the following criteria as it pertained to African Americans in each city: median household income; percentage of households earning more than $100,000; percentage of businesses owned; percentage of college graduates; unemployment rates; home loan rejections; and homeownership rates. *Black Enterprise, May 2007*

Seniors/Retirement Rankings

- The Houston* metro area was selected as one of "Best Places for Retirees" by *Forbes*. The area was ranked #5 out of 10. Criteria: cost and availability of health care; sales, property and income-tax rates; arts and leisure activities; cost of living; retirement job market; inter-metro migration patterns of people between the ages of 55 and 65. *Forbes, "Best Places for Retirees," January 18, 2007*

- Sperling's BestPlaces in partnership with Bankers Life & Casualty Company designed a survey to identify the top 50 metro areas in the U.S. that offer the best overall qualities for senior living. The Houston* metro area ranked #24. The following criteria were statistically weighted to reflect the needs of the senior population: health; disease; economics; social; environment; spiritual; transportation; housing; and crime. *Bankers Life & Casualty Company, "Best Cities for Seniors 2005"*

- A.G. Edwards ranked America's 500 top-performing communities based on their residents' personal savings and investing behavior. The Houston* metro area ranked #440 with an index score of 95.95 (national average = 100.00). A dozen statistical factors were measured including: participation in retirement savings plans; personal debt levels; and home ownership. *A.G. Edwards, "2007 Nest Egg Index", September 12, 2007*

Children/Family Rankings

- The Houston* metro area was selected as one of the "Best Cities for Relocating Families" by Worldwide ERC and Primacy Relocation. The 2007 study placed a special emphasis on the housing market, which has significantly impacted the relocation industry and an employer's ability to transfer employees. The variables which weigh heavily in this category include home price, home affordability index, appreciation rates, and property tax. Other criteria include cost of living, crime rates, education, climate, focus on diversity, physicians per capita, recreation and leisure, arts and culture, air quality, watershed quality, sales tax, unemployment rate, job growth, high school and higher education index, school expenditures per student, students in public school, SAT/ACT percentile, and population growth. *Worldwide ERC and Primacy Relocation, "2007 Best Cities for Relocating Families"*

Safety Rankings

- The National Insurance Crime Bureau ranked 361 metro areas in the U.S. in terms of per capita rates of vehicle theft. The Houston* metro area ranked #31 (#1 = highest rate). Criteria: number of vehicle theft offenses per 100,000 inhabitants. *National Insurance Crime Bureau, "NICB Vehicle Theft Study," April 22, 2008*
- Houston* appeared on Sperling's BestPlaces list of the "Riskiest Cities for Identity Theft." The area ranked #22 out of the nations 50 largest metro areas. Over 80 criteria were analyzed across four major categories: technology impact; crime; transactions; and risk profile. *Sperling's BestPlaces, www.BestPlaces.net, "Riskiest Cities for Identity Theft," July 2006*
- Farmers Insurance Group of Companies, in partnership with Sperling's BestPlaces, ranked 379 metro areas and identified the "Most Secure U.S. Place to Live." The Houston* metro area ranked #70 out of 114 in the large metro area category (500,000 or more residents). Criteria: crime rates; extreme weather; risk of natural disasters; environmental hazards; terrorism threats; air quality; life expectancy; job loss numbers. *Farmers Insurance Group, "Most Secure U.S. Places to Live 2007"*
- Galveston* was identified as one of the most dangerous large metro areas for pedestrians in the U.S. The area ranked #8 out of the nations 50 largest metro areas. Criteria: average yearly pedestrian fatalities per capita (for the years 2002 and 2003) adjusted for the number of walkers. *Surface Transportation Policy Project, "Mean Streets 2004"*
- Sperling's BestPlaces analyzed the tracks of tropical storms for the past 100 years and ranked which areas are most likely to be hit by a major hurricane. The Galveston* metro area ranked #6 out of 10. *Sperlings BestPlaces, www.bestplaces.net, February 2, 2006*

Sports/Recreation Rankings

- The Houston* metro area appeared on the *Sporting News* list of the "Best Sports Cities 2007". The area ranked #11 out of 150 cities in the U.S. *Sporting News* takes a 12-month snapshot, roughly July to July, of each city's sports, putting a heavy premium on regular-season won-lost records (from the most recently completed season). Other criteria include: playoff berths, bowl appearances and tournament bids; championships; applicable power ratings; quality of competition; overall fan fervor as measured in part by attendance as percentage of venue capacity; abundance of teams (rewarding quality over quantity); stadium and arena quality; ticket availability and prices; franchise ownership; and marquee appeal of athletes. *SportingNews.com, "Best Sports Cities 2007," August 1, 2007*
- Scarborough Research, a leading market research firm, identified the top local markets for avid NBA fans. The Houston* DMA (Designated Market Area) ranked in the top 10 with 14% of consumers 18 years and over reporting that they are "very interested in the NBA". *Scarborough Research, April 24, 2006*
- The Houston* metro area was selected by *Cranium* as one of the "Top 50 Fun Cities" in America. The area ranked #32. Criteria includes: number of sports teams, restaurants, and dance performances; number of toy stores; city budget spent on recreation. *Cranium, November 4, 2003*

- *Golf Digest* ranked 330 metro areas in the U.S. in terms of golf. The Galveston* metro area was ranked #160. Criteria: access to golf; weather; value of golf; and quality of golf. *Golf Digest, "Metro Golf Rankings," August 2005*

Dating/Romance Rankings

- Eli Lily and Company, in partnership with Sperling's BestPlaces, ranked the nation's 50 largest metro areas in terms of the "Most Romantic Cities for Baby Boomers." The Houston* metro area ranked #10. Criteria: marriage and divorce rates among "baby boomers" age 45 to 60; great restaurants; dance studios; chocolate, jewelry and flower sales. *Eli Lily and Company, "Most Romantic Cities for Baby Boomers," April 20, 2007*

- The Houston* metro area was selected as one of the "Best Cities for Relocating Singles" by Worldwide ERC and Primacy Relocation. The area ranked #53 out of the 100 largest metro areas in the U.S. Areas were selected based on the following criteria: a robust cost-of-living index; adventure and outdoor recreation opportunities; violent crime and property crime rates; percentage of the population that is unmarried (ages 25-34); ratio of single men and single women; affordability of quality higher education, including in-state and out-of-state tuition requirements and rates; number of newcomers to the area; commute times; tax rates; fee and occupancy rates for temporary housing and mini-storage; quality and quantity of collegiate and professional sporting events and fun, fan-friendly venues. *Worldwide ERC and Primacy Relocation, "2007 Best Cities for Relocating Singles," October 25, 2007*

- *Forbes* ranked the 40 most populous urbanized areas in the U.S. in terms of the "Best Cities for Singles." The Houston* metro area ranked #14. Criteria: number of singles; cost of living alone; nightlife; culture; job growth; coolness; and online dating. *Forbes.com, August 21, 2007*

- Sperling's BestPlaces in partnership with AXE Deodorant Bodyspray ranked 80 metro areas and identified "America's Best (and Worst) Cities for Dating." The Houston* metro area ranked #72 (#1 = best). Criteria: percentage of singles ages 18-24; population density; dating venues per capita. *AXE Deodorant Bodyspray, "America's Best (and Worst) Cities for Dating," May 2004*

Miscellaneous Rankings

- The Houston* metro area was identified as one of 10 "Worst Cities for Commuters" by *Forbes*. The metro area ranked #8. Criteria: traffic delays; travel times; how efficiently commuters use existing infrastructure. *Forbes.com, "Worst Cities for Commuters," April 29, 2008*

- League City was identified as one of the 100 fastest-growing suburbs in America by "Forbes." The city ranked #65. Criteria: suburban cities, townships and villages with more than 10,000 people in 2000 were ranked by their population growth from 2000 to 2006. *Forbes.com, "America's Fastest-Growing Suburbs," July 16, 2007*

- The Houston* metro area appeared on *Forbes* list of "America's Drunkest Cities". The area ranked #18. Criteria: 35 of the largest continental U.S. metro areas were chosen based on availability of data and geographic diversity. Each metro was ranked in five areas: state laws; drinkers; heavy drinkers; binge drinkers; and alcoholism. *Forbes.com, "America's Drunkest Cities," August 22, 2006*

- Sperling's BestPlaces in partnership with Pep Boys ranked 77 metro areas and identified "America's Most Drivable Cities." The Houston* metro area ranked #34. Criteria: climate; road roughness; urban mobility; gas prices. *Pep Boys, "America's Most Drivable Cities," April 9, 2003*

- State Farm Insurance, in partnership with Sperling's BestPlaces, analyzed several key factors that contribute to overall family preparedness. The Houston* metro area ranked #36 out of the nation's 50 most populous metro areas. Criteria: quality of life; life insurance coverage; and investments. *State Farm Life Insurance, "Fiscally Fit Cities Report," July 20, 2004*

- Scarborough Research, a leading market research firm, identified the top local markets for frequent sit-down restaurant patronage. The Houston* DMA (Designated Market Area) ranked in the top 10 with consumers reporting an average of 4.0 visits within the past 30 days.
  Scarborough Research, May 31, 2006

- A study by Sperling's BestPlaces examined which U.S. metro areas were most affected by high fuel prices in 2006. The Houston* metro area was ranked #27 out of 80 (#1 = most expensive city for driving). Rankings are based on the average dollars spent on gas per year by two driver households. Criteria: cost of regular-grade gasoline; average miles driven per day; average number of gallons each driver uses and wastes in traffic congestion each day.
  Sperling's BestPlaces, www.bestplaces.net, "Pain at the Pump," May 18, 2006

League City is located within the Houston-Sugar Land-Baytown, TX Metropolitan Statistical Area and.

Business Environment

CITY FINANCES

City Government Finances

Component	2004-2005 ($000)	2004-2005 ($ per capita)
Total Revenues	53,899	877
Total Expenditures	65,199	1,060
Debt Outstanding	102,731	1,671
Cash and Securities	54,633	888

Source: U.S Census Bureau, Government Finances 2004-2005

City Government Revenue by Source

Source	2004-2005 ($000)	2004-2005 ($ per capita)
General Revenue		
From Federal Government	0	0
From State Government	2,135	35
From Local Governments	0	0
Taxes		
Property	18,384	299
Sales	7,618	124
Personal Income	0	0
License	2,722	44
Charges	9,835	160
Liquor Store	0	0
Utility	11,073	180
Employee Retirement	0	0
Other	2,132	35

Source: U.S Census Bureau, Government Finances 2004-2005

City Government Expenditures by Function

Function	2004-2005 ($000)	2004-2005 ($ per capita)	2004-2005 (%)
General Expenditures			
Airports	0	0	0.0
Corrections	0	0	0.0
Education	0	0	0.0
Fire Protection	3,581	58	5.5
Governmental Administration	5,441	88	8.3
Health	1,091	18	1.7
Highways	5,192	84	8.0
Hospitals	0	0	0.0
Housing and Community Development	0	0	0.0
Interest on General Debt	4,372	71	6.7
Libraries	1,483	24	2.3
Parking	0	0	0.0
Parks and Recreation	12,877	209	19.8
Police Protection	8,164	133	12.5
Public Welfare	0	0	0.0
Sewerage	5,882	96	9.0
Solid Waste Management	0	0	0.0
Liquor Store	0	0	0.0
Utility	9,686	158	14.9
Employee Retirement	0	0	0.0
Other	7,430	121	11.4

Source: U.S Census Bureau, Government Finances 2004-2005

Municipal Bond Ratings

Area	Moody's
City	Aaa

Source: Mergent Bond Record, January 2008 (unless noted otherwise)

DEMOGRAPHICS

Population Growth

Area	1990 Census	2000 Census	2007 Estimate	2012 Projection	Population Growth (%) 1990-2000	Population Growth (%) 2000-2012
City	30,247	45,444	65,374	77,497	50.2	70.5
MSA[1]	3,767,335	4,715,407	5,489,519	5,965,317	25.2	26.5
U.S.	248,709,873	281,421,906	301,045,522	314,920,978	13.2	11.9

Note: (1) Metropolitan Statistical Area - see Appendix B for areas included
Source: Claritas, Inc.

Number of Households and Average Household Size

Area	2007 Estimate	2007 Average Household Size
City	23,502	2.78
MSA[1]	1,914,046	2.87
U.S.	113,668,003	2.65

Note: (1) Metropolitan Statistical Area - see Appendix B for areas included
Source: Claritas, Inc.

Race and Ethnicity

Area	White Alone[2]	Black Alone[2]	Asian Alone[2]	Other Race Alone[2]	Hispanic[3]
City	82.0	5.2	4.0	8.8	15.0
MSA[1]	60.2	16.4	5.6	17.8	33.0
U.S.	73.1	12.4	4.3	10.3	14.9

Note: Figures are 2007 estimates; (1) Metropolitan Statistical Area - see Appendix B for areas included (2) Alone is defined as not being in combination with one or more other races; (3) May be of any race.
Source: Claritas, Inc.

Ancestry

Area	German	Irish[2]	English	American	Italian	Polish	French[3]	Scottish
City	17.8	11.3	10.8	9.0	4.5	2.1	4.2	2.2
MSA[1]	12.3	9.2	8.3	7.7	3.8	1.3	3.7	1.5
U.S.	15.2	10.9	8.7	7.3	5.6	3.2	3.0	1.7

Note: Figures include multiple ancestry (e.g. if a person reported being Irish and Italian, they were included in both columns); (1) Metropolitan Statistical Area - see Appendix A for areas included; (2) Includes Celtic; (3) Includes Alsatian but excludes Basque
Source: Census 2000, Summary File 3

Foreign-Born Population

Area	Percent of Population Born in: Any Foreign Country	Europe	Asia	Africa	Oceania[2]	Canada	Mexico	Latin America[3]
City	8.9	1.3	2.6	0.2	0.1	0.5	2.9	1.4
MSA[1]	8.3	0.8	1.8	0.1	0.0	0.3	4.2	1.1
U.S.	11.1	1.7	2.9	0.3	0.1	0.3	3.3	2.5

Note: (1) Metropolitan Statistical Area - see Appendix A for areas included; (2) Includes Australia, New Zealand subregion, Melanesia, Micronesia, Polynesia, and Oceania n.e.c; (3) Includes Central America (excluding Mexico), South America, and the Caribbean.
Source: Census 2000, Summary File 3

Marriage Status

Area	Never Married	Now Married (excluding Separated)	Separated	Widowed	Divorced
City	19.3	66.6	1.4	3.5	9.2
MSA[1]	23.6	55.9	2.6	6.3	11.6
U.S.	27.1	54.4	2.2	6.6	9.7

Note: Figures are percentages and cover the population 15 years of age and older; (1) Metropolitan Statistical Area - see Appendix A for areas included
Source: Census 2000, Summary File 3

Age Distribution

Area	Percent of Population						
	Under Age 5	Age 5 to 17	Age 18 to 34	Age 35 to 49	Age 50 to 64	Age 65 to 79	80 Years and Over
City	8.1	21.1	21.7	29.4	13.7	4.5	1.5
MSA[1]	6.9	19.7	21.8	25.2	15.4	8.4	2.6
U.S.	6.8	18.9	23.7	23.5	14.8	9.2	3.2

Note: (1) Metropolitan Statistical Area - see Appendix A for areas included
Source: Census 2000, Summary File 3

Male/Female Ratio

Area	Males	Females	Males per 100 Females
City	32,458	32,916	98.6
MSA[1]	2,742,445	2,747,074	99.8
U.S.	148,320,305	152,725,217	97.1

Note: Figures are 2007 estimates; (1) Metropolitan Statistical Area - see Appendix B for areas included
Source: Claritas, Inc.

Religion

Area	Catholic	Southern Baptist	United Meth-odist	ELCA[1]	LDS[2]	Presby-terian Church USA	Jewish Est.	Muslim Est.
County	16.9	13.3	5.3	1.3	0.9	0.5	0.8	0.0
U.S.	22.0	7.1	3.7	1.8	1.5	1.1	2.2	0.6

Note: Figures are the number of adherents as a percentage of the total population; Adherents are defined as all members, including full members, their children and the estimated number of other participants who are not considered members (e.g. the baptized, those not confirmed, those regularly attending services, etc.); (1) Evangelical Lutheran Church in America; (2) The Church of Jesus Christ of Latter Day Saints
Source: Reprinted with permission from Religious Congregations and Membership in the United States 2000 (Nashville, Glenmary Research Center, 2002) Copyright Association of Statisticians of American Religious Bodies. All rights reserved.

ECONOMY

Gross Metropolitan Product

Area	2002	2003	2004	2005	2005 Rank[2]
MSA[1]	191.9	204.0	221.2	244.4	7

Note: Figures are in billions of dollars; (1) Houston-Sugar Land-Baytown, TX Metropolitan Statistical Area - see Appendix A for areas included; (2) Rank ranges from 1 to 361
Source: The U.S. Conference of Mayors, "U.S. Metro Economies: GMP - The Engines of America's Growth," January 2007

Economic Growth

Area	1995 GMP	2005 GMP	Average Annual Growth Rate	Growth Rate Rank[2]
MSA[1]	121.8	244.4	7.2	31

Note: Figures are in billions of dollars; GMP = Gross Metropolitan Product; (1) Houston-Sugar Land-Baytown, TX Metropolitan Statistical Area - see Appendix A for areas included; (2) Rank ranges from 1 to 361
Source: The U.S. Conference of Mayors, "U.S. Metro Economies: GMP - The Engines of America's Growth," January 2007

INCOME

Per Capita/Median/Average Income

Area	Per Capita ($)	Median Household ($)	Average Household ($)
City	32,106	77,025	89,026
MSA[1]	25,018	51,630	71,229
U.S.	25,495	49,280	66,670

Note: Figures are 2007 estimates; (1) Metropolitan Statistical Area - see Appendix B for areas included
Source: Claritas, Inc.

Household Income Distribution

Area	Percent of Households Earning							
	Under $15,000	$15,000 -24,999	$25,000 -34,999	$35,000 -49,999	$50,000 -74,999	$75,000 -99,000	$100,000 -149,999	$150,000 and up
City	4.4	4.7	5.8	12.0	21.5	19.5	22.5	9.6
MSA[1]	12.2	10.1	11.0	15.4	18.5	12.0	12.7	8.1
U.S.	13.1	10.9	11.2	15.6	19.5	11.9	11.3	6.6

Note: Figures are 2007 estimates; (1) Metropolitan Statistical Area - see Appendix B for areas included
Source: Claritas, Inc.

Poverty Rates by Age

Area	All Ages	Under 5 Years Old	5 to 17 Years Old	18 to 64 Years Old	65 Years and Over
City	4.8	0.5	1.0	2.9	0.3
MSA[1]	13.2	1.4	3.4	7.3	1.1
U.S.	12.4	1.2	3.0	6.9	1.2

Note: Figures are percent of population with income in 1999 below poverty level and only include population for whom poverty status is determined; (1) Metropolitan Statistical Area - see Appendix A for areas included
Source: Census 2000, Summary File 3

Personal Bankruptcy Filing Rate

Area	2004	2005	2006
Galveston County	4.26	5.38	1.43
U.S.	5.31	6.82	2.00

Note: Numbers are per 1,000 population and include Chapter 7 and Chapter 13 filings
Source: Federal Deposit Insurance Corporation (FDIC), Regional Economic Conditions (RECON), 8/23/2007

EMPLOYMENT

Labor Force and Employment

Area	Civilian Labor Force			Workers Employed		
	Dec. 2006	Dec. 2007	% Chg.	Dec. 2006	Dec. 2007	% Chg.
City	35,670	36,403	2.1	34,483	35,123	1.9
MSA[1]	2,713,998	2,767,131	2.0	2,603,369	2,651,639	1.9
U.S.	152,571,000	153,705,000	0.7	146,081,000	146,334,000	0.2

Note: Data is not seasonally adjusted and covers workers 16 years of age and older; (1) Metropolitan Statistical Area - see Appendix B for areas included
Source: Bureau of Labor Statistics, http://stats.bls.gov

Unemployment Rate

Area	2007											
	Jan.	Feb.	Mar.	Apr.	May	Jun.	Jul.	Aug.	Sep.	Oct.	Nov.	Dec.
City	3.9	3.8	3.4	3.2	3.3	3.9	4.0	3.7	3.7	3.4	3.5	3.5
MSA[1]	4.7	4.5	4.1	3.9	3.9	4.6	4.6	4.3	4.3	4.0	4.1	4.2
U.S.	5.0	4.9	4.5	4.3	4.3	4.7	4.9	4.6	4.5	4.4	4.5	4.8

Note: Data is not seasonally adjusted and covers workers 16 years of age and older; All figures are percentages; (1) Metropolitan Statistical Area - see Appendix B for areas included
Source: Bureau of Labor Statistics, http://stats.bls.gov

Employment by Occupation

Occupation Classification	City (%)	MSA[1] (%)	U.S. (%)
Sales and Office	24.0	25.4	26.7
Professional and Related	30.2	22.9	20.2
Service	10.0	15.8	14.9
Production, Transportation, and Material Moving	9.6	11.3	14.6
Management, Business, and Financial	17.7	12.9	13.5
Construction, Extraction, and Maintenance	8.2	11.2	9.4
Farming, Forestry, and Fishing	0.3	0.4	0.7

Note: Figures cover employed civilians 16 years of age and older; (1) Metropolitan Statistical Area - see Appendix A for areas included
Source: Census 2000, Summary File 3

Employment by Industry

Sector	MSA[1] Number of Employees	MSA[1] Percent of Total	U.S. Percent of Total
Government	357,000	13.7	16.3
Education and Health Services	289,300	11.1	13.4
Professional and Business Services	390,000	14.9	13.1
Retail Trade	276,700	10.6	11.6
Manufacturing	236,700	9.1	9.9
Leisure and Hospitality	229,000	8.8	9.6
Financial Activities	146,500	5.6	5.9
Construction	203,800	7.8	5.3
Wholesale Trade	136,800	5.2	4.4
Other Services	94,500	3.6	3.9
Transportation and Utilities	128,000	4.9	3.7
Information	37,200	1.4	2.2
Natural Resources and Mining	87,300	3.3	0.5

Note: Figures cover non-farm employment as of December 2007 and are not seasonally adjusted; (1) Metropolitan Statistical Area - see Appendix B for areas included
Source: Bureau of Labor Statistics, http://stats.bls.gov

Average Wages

Occupation	$/Hr.	Occupation	$/Hr.
Accountants and Auditors	30.78	Maids and Housekeeping Cleaners	7.73
Automotive Mechanics	17.99	Maintenance and Repair Workers	14.25
Bookkeepers	15.84	Marketing Managers	57.18
Carpenters	15.28	Nuclear Medicine Technologists	35.31
Cashiers	8.21	Nurses, Licensed Practical	19.09
Clerks, General Office	11.43	Nurses, Registered	30.66
Clerks, Receptionists/Information	11.25	Nursing Aides/Orderlies/Attendants	10.82
Clerks, Shipping/Receiving	13.07	Packers and Packagers, Hand	8.43
Computer Programmers	38.89	Physical Therapists	36.73
Computer Support Specialists	22.23	Postal Service Mail Carriers	21.44
Computer Systems Analysts	36.57	Real Estate Brokers	41.88
Cooks, Restaurant	9.19	Retail Salespersons	11.51
Dentists	n/a	Sales Reps., Exc. Tech./Scientific	29.31
Electrical Engineers	44.72	Sales Reps., Tech./Scientific	38.96
Electricians	19.91	Secretaries, Exc. Legal/Med./Exec.	13.16
Financial Managers	56.30	Security Guards	11.34
First-Line Supervisors/Mgrs., Sales	19.68	Surgeons	86.19
Food Preparation Workers	8.22	Teacher Assistants	8.50
General and Operations Managers	53.98	Teachers, Elementary School	22.00
Hairdressers/Cosmetologists	10.96	Teachers, Secondary School	23.30
Internists	71.46	Telemarketers	10.47
Janitors and Cleaners	8.74	Truck Drivers, Heavy/Tractor-Trailer	16.73
Landscaping/Groundskeeping Workers	9.47	Truck Drivers, Light/Delivery Svcs.	13.11
Lawyers	62.17	Waiters and Waitresses	7.74

Note: Wage data covers the Houston-Sugar Land-Baytown, TX Metropolitan Statistical Area - see Appendix B for areas included. Hourly wages for elementary/secondary school teachers and teacher assistants were calculated by the editors from annual wage data assuming a 40 hour work week; n/a not available.
Source: Bureau of Labor Statistics, May 2007 Metro Area Occupational Employment and Wage Estimates

RESIDENTIAL REAL ESTATE

Building Permits

Area	Single-Family 2006	Single-Family 2007p	Single-Family Pct. Chg.	Multi-Family 2006	Multi-Family 2007p	Multi-Family Pct. Chg.	Total 2006	Total 2007p	Total Pct. Chg.
City	1,510	1,345	-10.9	244	100	-59.0	1,754	1,445	-17.6
U.S.	1,378,200	973,300	-29.4	460,700	407,200	-11.6	1,838,900	1,380,500	-24.9

Note: (p) preliminary; figures cover and represent new, privately-owned housing units authorized (unadjusted data); All permit data are based on estimates with imputation; U.S. figures are based on the new 20,000-place series.
Source: U.S. Census Bureau, Manufacturing, Mining, and Construction Statistics

Homeownership and Housing Vacancies

Area	Homeownership Rate[2] (%)			Rental Vacancy Rate[3] (%)			Homeowner Vacancy Rate[4] (%)		
	2005	2006	2007	2005	2006	2007	2005	2006	2007
MSA[1]	61.7	63.5	64.5	15.4	16.8	17.3	3.5	2.8	3.1
U.S.	68.9	68.8	68.1	9.8	9.8	9.7	1.9	2.4	2.7

Note: (1) Metropolitan Statistical Area - see Appendix B for areas included; (2) The proportion of households that are owners; (3) The proportion of the rental inventory that is vacant for rent; (4) The proportion of the homeowner inventory that is vacant for sale; n/a not available
Source: U.S. Census Bureau, Housing Vacancies and Homeownership Annual Statistics: 2007

TAXES

State Corporate Income Tax Rates

State	Rates and Tax Brackets
Texas	1.0%

Note: Tax rates as of January 1, 2008; Texas's 1% franchise tax is a gross receipts tax paid by most taxable entities. Retailers pay 0.5%.
Source: Tax Foundation, www.taxfoundation.org

State Individual Income Tax Rates

State	Federal Deductibility	Marginal Rates (%)	Standard Deduction ($)		Personal Exemptions ($)[1]	
			Single	Joint	Single	Dependents
Texas	No	None	n/a	n/a	n/a	n/a

Note: Tax rates as of January 1, 2008; Local- and county-level taxes are not included; n/a not applicable; (1) Married joint filers generally receive double the single exemption
Source: Tax Foundation, www.taxfoundation.org

Various State and Local Tax Rates

State and Local Sales and Use (%)	State Sales and Use (%)	Gasoline[1,2] ($/gal.)	Cigarette ($/pack)	Spirits ($/gal.)	Table Wine ($/gal.)	Beer ($/gal.)
8.0	6.25 (i)	0.20	1.41	2.40	0.204	0.19

Note: Tax rates as of January 1, 2008; (1) In addition to the 18.4 cpg Federal gasoline tax; (2) Rates may include additional state sales taxes, environmental protection and storage fees/taxes, and local taxes. When necessary, the volume-weighted average of all local taxes is used to approximate the typical statewide rate including local tax; (i) Texas has a GRT that is levied in addition to its 6.25% sales tax. It is called the franchise tax and the rate is 1% (.5% for retailers).
Source: Tax Foundation, www.taxfoundation.org; Original research

State Tax Burdens

Area	Combined State and Local Tax Burden		Combined Federal, State and Local Tax Burden	
	Percent	Rank	Percent	Rank
Texas	9.3	43	29.8	41
U.S. Average	11.0	-	32.7	-

Note: Figures cover 2007 and measure taxes as a percentage of income
Source: Tax Foundation, www.taxfoundation.org

State Business Tax Climate Index Rankings

State	Overall Rank	Corporate Tax Index Rank	Individual Income Tax Index Rank	Sales Tax Index Rank	Unemployment Insurance Tax Index Rank	Property Tax Index Rank
Texas	8	47	7	28	14	27

Note: Rankings range from 1 to 50 where 1 is best. Rankings do not average across to Overall Rank. States without a given tax are given a ranking of 1.
Source: Tax Foundation, State Business Tax Climate Index 2008

TRANSPORTATION

Means of Transportation to Work

Area	Car/Truck/Van		Public Transportation			Bicycle	Walked	Other Means	Worked at Home
	Drove Alone	Car-pooled	Bus	Subway	Railroad				
City	83.7	10.2	1.0	0.0	0.0	0.2	0.8	1.1	3.0
MSA[1]	78.2	13.6	1.0	0.0	0.0	0.7	2.3	1.6	2.5
U.S.	75.7	12.2	2.5	1.5	0.5	0.4	2.9	1.0	3.3

Note: Figures are percentages and cover workers 16 years of age and older; (1) Metropolitan Statistical Area - see Appendix A for areas included
Source: Census 2000, Summary File 3

Travel Time to Work

Area	Less Than 15 Minutes	15 to 29 Minutes	30 to 44 Minutes	45 to 59 Minutes	60 Minutes or More
City	18.6	37.4	23.4	11.8	8.8
MSA[1]	28.7	34.5	19.7	8.7	8.3
U.S.	29.4	36.1	19.1	7.4	8.0

Note: Figures are percentages and include workers 16 years old and over; (1) Metropolitan Statistical Area - see Appendix A for areas included
Source: Census 2000, Summary File 3

Travel Time Index

Area	1982	1995	2004	2005
Urban Area[1]	1.19	1.19	1.32	1.36
Average[2]	1.11	1.22	1.29	1.30

Note: Travel Time Index - The ratio of travel time in the peak period to the travel time at free-flow conditions. A value of 1.35 indicates a 20-minute free-flow trip takes 27 minutes in the peak. Free-flow speeds (60 mph on freeways and 35 mph on principal arterials) are used as the comparison threshold; (1) Covers the Houston, TX urban area; (2) average of 85 urban areas
Source: Texas Transportation Institute, The 2007 Urban Mobility Report, September 2007

Living Environment

COST OF LIVING

Cost of Living Index

Composite Index	Groceries	Housing	Utilities	Trans-portation	Health Care	Misc. Goods/ Services
88.0	83.1	74.4	101.0	96.2	101.2	93.1

Note: U.S. = 100; Figures cover the Houston TX urban area.
Source: The Council for Community and Economic Research (formerly ACCRA), Cost of Living Index, 2007

Grocery Prices

Area[1]	T-Bone Steak ($/pound)	Frying Chicken ($/pound)	Whole Milk ($/half gal.)	Eggs ($/dozen)	Orange Juice ($/64 oz.)	Coffee ($/11.5 oz.)
City[2]	6.49	0.96	2.13	1.33	2.90	2.90
Avg.	8.93	1.12	2.13	1.52	3.26	3.31
Min.	5.88	0.71	1.33	0.83	2.30	2.20
Max.	12.80	2.07	3.43	3.54	5.79	6.20

Note: (1) Values for the local area are compared with the average, minimum and maximum values for all 331 areas in the Cost of Living Index report; (2) Figures cover the Houston TX urban area; **T-Bone Steak** *(price per pound);* **Frying Chicken** *(price per pound, whole fryer);* **Whole Milk** *(half gallon carton);* **Eggs** *(price per dozen, Grade A, large);* **Orange Juice** *(64 oz. Tropicana or Florida Natural);* **Coffee** *(11.5 oz. can, vacuum-packed, Maxwell House, Hills Bros, or Folgers).*
Source: The Council for Community and Economic Research (formerly ACCRA), Cost of Living Index, 2007

Housing and Utility Costs

Area[1]	New Home Price ($)	Apartment Rent ($/month)	All Electric ($/month)	Part Electric ($/month)	Other Energy ($/month)	Telephone ($/month)
City[2]	214,931	812	-	130.96	44.20	23.71
Avg.	309,605	782	146.13	78.67	90.16	26.14
Min.	189,877	n/a	82.03	37.41	33.15	17.08
Max.	1,202,800	3,481	271.14	150.60	257.67	37.45

Note: (1) Values for the local area are compared with the average, minimum and maximum values for all 331 areas in the Cost of Living Index report; (2) Figures cover the Houston TX urban area; **New Home Price** *(2,400 sf living area, 8,000 sf lot, in urban area with full utilities);* **Apartment Rent** *(950 sf 2 bedroom/1.5 or 2 bath, unfurnished, excluding all utilities except water);* **All Electric** *(average monthly cost for an all-electric home);* **Part Electric** *(average monthly cost for a part-electric home);* **Other Energy** *(average monthly cost for natural gas, fuel oil, coal, wood, and any other forms of energy except electricity);* **Telephone** *(price includes basic monthly rate for a private residential line plus additional local usage charges incurred by a family of four).*
Source: The Council for Community and Economic Research (formerly ACCRA), Cost of Living Index, 2007

Health Care, Transportation, and Other Costs

Area[1]	Doctor ($/visit)	Dentist ($/visit)	Optometrist ($/visit)	Gasoline ($/gallon)	Beauty Salon ($/visit)	Men's Shirt ($)
City[2]	81.72	76.13	82.50	2.51	31.37	23.16
Avg.	79.48	71.93	79.55	2.64	29.52	25.77
Min.	52.08	44.80	43.95	2.19	15.58	16.19
Max.	148.44	126.27	158.83	3.48	60.62	48.53

Note: (1) Values for the local area are compared with the average, minimum and maximum values for all 331 areas in the Cost of Living Index report; (2) Figures cover the Houston TX urban area; **Doctor** *(general practitioners routine exam of an established patient);* **Dentist** *(adult teeth cleaning and periodic oral examination);* **Optometrist** *(full vision eye exam for established adult patient);* **Gasoline** *(one gallon regular unleaded, national brand, including all taxes, cash price at self-service pump if available);* **Beauty Salon** *(woman's shampoo, trim, and blow-dry);* **Men's Shirt** *(cotton/polyester dress shirt, pinpoint weave, long sleeves).*
Source: The Council for Community and Economic Research (formerly ACCRA), Cost of Living Index, 2007

HOUSING

House Price Index (HPI)

Area	National Ranking[2]	Quarterly Change (%)	One-Year Change (%)	Five-Year Change (%)
MSA[1]	44	1.38	4.79	25.12
U.S.[3]	-	0.10	0.84	41.37

Note: The HPI is a weighted repeat sales index. It measures average price changes in repeat sales or refinancings on the same properties. This information is obtained by reviewing repeat mortgage transactions on single-family properties whose mortgages have been purchased or securitized by Fannie Mae or Freddie Mac in January 1975; (1) Metropolitan Statistical Area - see Appendix B for areas included; (2) Rankings are based on annual percentage change for all metro areas containing at least 15,000 transactions over the last 10 years and ranges from 1 to 291; (3) figures based on a weighted average of Census Division estimates; all figures are for the period ending December 31, 2007

Source: Office of Federal Housing Enterprise Oversight, House Price Index, February 26, 2008

House Price Valuations

Area	Q1 2000	Q1 2001	Q1 2002	Q1 2003	Q1 2004	Q1 2005	Q1 2006	Q1 2007	Q1 2008
MSA[1]	-16.2	-23.5	-17.0	-17.1	-21.3	-26.3	-26.6	-29.5	-33.1

Note: Figures show the percentage of over- or under-valuation of single family homes relative to statistically normal house values (e.g. a value of 23.6 indicates that house values are 23.6% overvalued). Statistically normal house values are based on house prices, interest rates, household incomes, population densities, and any historical premiums or discounts metropolitan areas have exhibited over time; (1) Figures cover the Metropolitan Statistical Area - see Appendix B for areas included

Source: Global Insight/National City Corporation, House Prices in America, May 2008

Median Home Prices

Area	2005	2006	2007[r]	Percent Change 2006 to 2007
MSA[1]	143.0	149.1	152.5	2.3
U.S. Average	219.0	221.9	217.9	-1.8

Note: Figures are median sales prices of existing single-family homes in thousands of dollars; (r) revised; n/a not available; (1) Metropolitan Statistical Area - see Appendix B for areas included

Source: National Association of Realtors, Metropolitan Area Prices, 1st Quarter 2008

Housing: Year Structure Built

Area	1990 -2000	1980 -1989	1970 -1979	1960 -1969	1950 -1959	1940 -1949	Before 1940	Median Year
City	37.6	33.3	16.0	7.9	2.8	1.4	1.1	1986
MSA[1]	17.4	20.9	20.9	14.7	11.7	6.7	7.7	1974
U.S.	17.0	15.8	18.5	13.7	12.7	7.3	15.0	1971

Note: Figures are percentages; (1) Metropolitan Statistical Area - see Appendix A for areas included

Source: Census 2000, Summary File 3

HEALTH

Health Risk Data

Category	Area[1] (%)	U.S. (%)
Adults who have been told they have high blood pressure[3]	23.2	25.5
Adults who have been told they have high blood cholesterol[3]	32.8	35.6
Adults who have been told they have diabetes[2]	5.8	7.5
Adults who have been told they have arthritis[3]	21.1	27.0
Adults who have been told they currently have asthma	8.7	8.5
Adults who are current smokers	14.4	20.1
Adults who are heavy drinkers[4]	4.2	4.9
Adults who are overweight (BMI 25.0 - 29.9)	36.4	36.5
Adults who are obese (BMI 30.0 - 99.8)	22.5	25.1

Note: Data as of 2006 unless otherwise noted; (1) Figures cover the Metropolitan Statistical Area - see Appendix B for areas included; (2) Figures do not include pregnancy-related diabetes, pre-diabetes or borderline diabetes; (3) 2005 data; (4) Heavy drinkers are classified as adult men having more than two drinks per day or adult women having more than one drink per day

Source: Centers for Disease Control and Prevention, Behaviorial Risk Factor Surveillance System, SMART: Selected Metropolitan/Micropolitan Area Risk Trends, 2005, 2006

Mortality Rates for the Top 10 Causes of Death in the U.S.

ICD-10[a] Sub-Chapter	ICD-10[a] Code	Age-Adjusted Mortality Rate[1] per 100,000 population	
		County[2]	U.S.
Malignant neoplasms	C00-C97	220.2	186.5
Ischaemic heart diseases	I20-I25	160.0	152.3
Other forms of heart disease	I30-I51	49.3	51.5
Cerebrovascular diseases	I60-I69	57.5	50.0
Chronic lower respiratory diseases	J40-J47	44.3	42.6
Diabetes mellitus	E10-E14	28.6	24.8
Other degenerative diseases of the nervous system	G30-G31	30.2	22.6
Other external causes of accidental injury	W00-X59	28.4	21.4
Influenza and pneumonia	J10-J18	14.1	20.7
Hypertensive diseases	I10-I13	31.0	18.2

Note: (a) ICD-10 = International Classification of Diseases 10th Revision; (1) Mortality rates are a three year average covering 2003-2005; (2) Figures cover Galveston County
Source: Centers for Disease Control and Prevention, National Center for Health Statistics. Compressed Mortality File 1999-2004. CDC WONDER On-line Database, compiled from Compressed Mortality File 1999-2005 Series 20 No. 2K, 2008.

Mortality Rates for Selected Causes of Death

ICD-10[a] Sub-Chapter	ICD-10[a] Code	Age-Adjusted Mortality Rate[1] per 100,000 population	
		County[2]	U.S.
Assault	X85-Y09	7.1	5.9
Human immunodeficiency virus (HIV) disease	B20-B24	8.7	4.5
Intentional self-harm	X60-X84	11.5	10.8
Malnutrition	E40-E46	*1.7	1.0
Obesity and other hyperalimentation	E65-E68	2.7	1.4
Organic, including symptomatic, mental disorders	F01-F09	27.5	16.8
Transport accidents	V01-V99	16.7	16.1
Viral hepatitis	B15-B19	6.0	1.8

Note: (a) ICD-10 = International Classification of Diseases 10th Revision; (1) Mortality rates are a three year average covering 2003-2005; (2) Figures cover Galveston County; (*) Unreliable data as per CDC
Source: Centers for Disease Control and Prevention, National Center for Health Statistics. Compressed Mortality File 1999-2004. CDC WONDER On-line Database, compiled from Compressed Mortality File 1999-2005 Series 20 No. 2K, 2008.

Distribution of Physicians[1]

Area	Total	Family/ General Practice	Specialties	
			Medical	Surgical
Galveston County (number)	611	134	198	128
Galveston County (rate per 10,000 pop.)	22.0	4.8	7.1	4.6
U.S. (rate per 10,000 pop.)	17.7	4.6	6.9	4.3

Note: Data as of 2005; (1) Includes all non-federal, patient-care, office-based MDs
Source: Area Resource File (ARF). June 2007. U.S. Department of Health and Human Services, Health Resources and Services Administration, Bureau of Health Professions, Rockville, MD.

Hospitals

League City has the following hospitals: 1 children's psychiatric.
AHA Guide to the Healthcare Field 2008

According to *U.S. News,* the Houston-Sugar Land-Baytown, TX metro area is home to seven of the best hospitals in the U.S.: **Memorial Hermann TIRR**; **Menninger Clinic**; **Methodist Hospital**; **Saint Luke's Episcopal Hospital**; **Texas Children's Hospital**; **University of Texas M.D. Anderson Cancer Center**; **Woman's Hospital of Texas**. *U.S. News Online, "America's Best Hospitals 2007"*

EDUCATION

Public School District Statistics

District Name	Schls	Pupils	Pupil/ Teacher Ratio	Minority Pupils[1] (%)	Free Lunch Eligible[2] (%)	IEP[3] (%)
Clear Creek ISD	39	35,232	17.1	36.9	13.8	9.9
Whitewright ISD	4	805	12.6	14.8	30.6	19.1

Note: Table includes regular local school districts with 2,000 or more students; (1) Percentage of students that are not white, non-Hispanic; (2) Percentage of students that are eligible for the free lunch program; (3) Percentage of students that have an Individualized Education Program.
Source: U.S. Department of Education, National Center for Education Statistics, Common Core of Data, Local Education Agency (School District) Universe Survey: School Year 2005-2006; U.S. Department of Education, National Center for Education Statistics, Common Core of Data, Public Elementary/Secondary School Universe Survey: School Year 2005-2006

Highest Level of Education

Area	Less than H.S.	H.S. Diploma	Some College, No Deg.	Associate Degree	Bachelors Degree	Masters Degree	Profess. School Degree	Doctorate Degree
City	9.1	19.7	27.2	8.5	24.0	7.9	1.7	1.9
MSA[1]	22.8	22.8	22.3	5.2	18.2	5.8	2.0	1.0
U.S.	19.4	28.4	21.2	6.4	15.7	5.9	2.0	1.0

Note: Figures are 2007 estimated percentages and cover persons age 25 and over; (1) Metropolitan Statistical Area - see Appendix B for areas included
Source: Claritas, Inc.

Educational Attainment by Race

Area	High School Graduate (%)					Bachelor's Degree (%)				
	Total	White	Black	Asian	Hisp.[2]	Total	White	Black	Asian	Hisp.[2]
City	90.9	92.8	92.3	77.4	70.7	35.5	36.6	41.9	36.3	19.2
MSA[1]	80.9	85.1	71.3	76.9	58.0	22.7	25.4	10.7	48.1	10.1
U.S.	80.4	83.6	72.3	80.4	52.4	24.4	26.1	14.3	44.1	10.4

Note: Figures shown cover persons 25 years old and over; (1) Metropolitan Statistical Area - see Appendix A for areas included; (2) people of Hispanic origin can be of any race
Source: Census 2000, Summary File 3

School Enrollment by Type

Area	Grades KG to 8				Grades 9 to 12			
	Public		Private		Public		Private	
	Enrollment	%	Enrollment	%	Enrollment	%	Enrollment	%
City	6,226	90.1	686	9.9	2,355	90.5	248	9.5
MSA[1]	32,155	91.5	3,001	8.5	14,281	94.5	830	5.5
U.S.	33,526,011	88.7	4,285,121	11.3	14,848,628	90.6	1,532,323	9.4

Note: Figures shown cover persons 3 years old and over; (1) Metropolitan Statistical Area - see Appendix A for areas included
Source: Census 2000, Summary File 3

School Enrollment by Race

Area	Grades KG to 8 (%)				Grades 9 to 12 (%)			
	White	Black	Asian	Hisp.[1]	White	Black	Asian	Hisp.[1]
City	83.1	6.4	3.3	15.3	82.6	5.9	2.3	18.9
MSA[2]	67.0	17.8	2.1	22.4	66.0	19.7	1.7	22.0
U.S.	68.5	15.5	3.3	16.8	68.8	15.5	3.8	15.7

Note: Figures shown cover persons 3 years old and over; (1) people of Hispanic origin can be of any race; (2) Metropolitan Statistical Area - see Appendix A for areas included
Source: Census 2000, Summary File 3

Average Salaries of Public School Classroom Teachers

District	2005-06		2006-07		Percent Change 2005-06 to 2006-07
	Dollars	Rank[1]	Dollars	Rank[1]	
Texas	41,744	35	44,897	30	7.55
U.S. Average	49,026	-	50,816	-	3.65

Note: (1) State rank ranges from 1 to 51.
Source: National Education Association, Rankings & Estimates: Rankings of the States 2006 and Estimates of School Statistics 2007, December 2007

Higher Education

Four-Year Colleges			Two-Year Colleges			Medical Schools[1]	Law Schools[2]	Voc/ Tech[3]
Public	Private Non-profit	Private For-profit	Public	Private Non-profit	Private For-profit			
0	0	0	0	0	0	0	0	0

Note: Figures cover institutions located within the city limits; (1) includes schools accredited by the Liaison Committee on Medical Education and the American Osteopathic Association; (2) includes American Bar Association-accredited law schools; (3) includes all schools with programs that are less than 2 years.
Source: National Center for Education Statistics, The Integrated Postsecondary Education System (IPEDS) Peer Analysis System, 2007; www.usnews.com, Law and Medical School Directories, 2009

PRESIDENTIAL ELECTION

2004 Presidential Election Results

Area	Bush	Kerry	Nader	Other
Galveston County	57.8	41.4	0.2	0.5
U.S.	50.7	48.3	0.4	0.6

Note: Results are percentages and may not add to 100% due to rounding
Source: Dave Leip's Atlas of U.S. Presidential Elections, www.uselectionatlas.org

EMPLOYERS

Major Employers

Company Name	Industry	Type of Site
A Med Medical Inc	Home health care services	Headquarters
Anico	Life insurance	Headquarters
Ant Unit Galveston	Regulation, administration of transportation	Branch
B P Amoco Chemical Company	Petroleum refining	Branch
City of Texas City	Executive offices	Branch
College of Mainland Foundation	Junior colleges	Single
County Sheriff Department	Police protection	Branch
County of Galveston	Executive offices	Headquarters
Dillards 779	Department stores	Branch
Extended Hours Lab	Medical laboratories	Branch
Fiscal Office	Accounting, auditing, and bookkeeping	Branch
Gaidos Seafood Restaurant	Eating places	Single
Garden Restraunt	Amusement and recreation, nec	Single
Gulf Greyhound Park	Racing, including track operation	Single
Hosp/Galveston	Correctional institutions	Branch
I B E W Local Union 527	Labor organizations	Single
IHOP	Hotels and motels	Headquarters
Mainland Medical Center	General medical and surgical hospitals	Single
Massey Gale	Management investment, open-ended	Single
Sears Roebuck and Co	Department stores	Branch
Shriners Hospital For Children	Specialty hospitals, except psychiatric	Branch
Texas City Secretary Office	Executive offices	Branch
Texas City Sun The	Newspapers	Single
Texas Home Health	Skilled nursing care facilities	Branch
U Texas Med BR Pathology Dept	Colleges and universities	Single
University Texas Medical BR	General medical and surgical hospitals	Branch
University of Houston	Colleges and universities	Branch
University of TX Med Brnch Gal	Colleges and universities	Branch
University of Texas Medical BR	Accident and health insurance	Headquarters
Utmb Pediatrics	General medical and surgical hospitals	Branch
Valero	Petroleum refining	Branch
Wal-Mart	Department stores	Branch

Note: Companies shown are located within the Galveston metropolitan area; nec = not elsewhere classified.
Source: www.zapdata.com, May 2008

PUBLIC SAFETY

Crime Rate

Area	All Crimes	Violent Crimes				Property Crimes		
		Murder	Forcible Rape	Robbery	Aggrav. Assault	Burglary	Larceny -Theft	Motor Vehicle Theft
City	2,784.9	0.0	28.5	38.0	64.8	540.9	1,975.2	137.6
Metro[1]	4,829.8	9.6	34.6	279.6	383.4	964.9	2,570.8	586.9
U.S.	3,808.1	5.7	30.9	149.4	287.5	729.4	2,206.8	398.4

Note: Figures are crimes per 100,000 population; (1) Metropolitan Statistical Area - see Appendix B for areas included
Source: FBI Uniform Crime Reports, 2006

Hate Crimes

Area	Number of Quarters Reported	Bias Motivation				
		Race	Religion	Sexual Orientation	Ethnicity	Disability
City	4	0	0	0	0	0

Source: Federal Bureau of Investigation, Hate Crime Statistics 2006

RECREATION

Culture

Dance[1]	Theatre[1]	Instrumental Music[1]	Vocal Music[1]	Series/ Festivals	Museums	Zoos and Aquariums[2]
0	0	0	0	0	1	0

Note: (1) Number of professional perfoming groups; (2) AZA-accredited
Source: The Grey House Performing Arts Directory, 2007; Official Museum Directory, 2008; Association of Zoos & Aquariums, AZA Member Zoos & Aquariums, June 2008

Professional Sports Teams

Team Name	League
Houston Astros	Major League Baseball (MLB)
Houston Dynamo	Major League Soccer (MLS)
Houston Rockets	National Basketball Association (NBA)
Houston Texans	National Football League (NFL)

Note: Includes teams located in the Houston metro area.
Source: Original research

MEDIA

Newspapers

Name	News Focus	Frequency	Circulation
Bay Area Advertiser	Community	Weekly	21,000
Galveston County Advertiser	Local	n/a	14,000

Note: Includes newspapers with offices located in the city; n/a not available
Source: MediaContactsPro, March 2008

Television Stations

Name	Ch.	Network(s)	Type	Ownership
KPRC	2	NBC	Commercial	Post-Newsweek Business Information Inc.
KUHT	8	PBS	Public	University of Houston
KHOU	11	CBS	Commercial	Belo Corporation
KTRK	13	ABC	Commercial	ABC Inc.
KTXH	20	Fox	Commercial	United Paramount Network
KRIV	26	Fox	Commercial	Fox Television Stations Inc.
KHWB	39	WBN	Commercial	Tribune Broadcasting Company
KXLN	45	Univision	Commercial	Univision Television Group
KTMD	48	Telemundo	Commercial	Telemundo Group Inc.
KPXB	49	Pax	Commercial	Paxson Communications Corporation
KNWS	51	n/a	Commercial	Johnson Broadcasting Corporation
KTBU	55	n/a	Commercial	n/a
KZJL	61	n/a	Commercial	Liberman Broadcasting

Note: Stations included cover the Houston DMA (Designated Market Area); n/a not available
BurrellesLuce, MediaContacts Online, January 2007

Major AM Radio Stations

Call Letters	Freq. (kHz)	Station Type	Target Audience	Station Format	Music Format
KILT	610	n/a	General	Sports/Talk	n/a
KSEV	700	Commercial	General	News/Talk	n/a
KTRH	740	Commercial	General	Sports	n/a
KBME	790	Commercial	General	Music/News	Adult Standards
KYST	920	Commercial	General/Hispanic	Music/Sports/Talk	Latin
KPRC	950	n/a	General	Music/Talk	n/a
KRTX	980	n/a	General	Music	Latin
KLAT	1010	n/a	General/Hispanic	Music	n/a
KKHT	1070	Commercial	General/Religious	Talk	n/a
KTEK	1110	Commercial	Ethnic/General	Music/Talk	Christian
KYOK	1140	Commercial	General/Religious	Music/News	Gospel
KGOL	1180	Commercial	General	Ed/Music/News/Talk	World Music
KWHI	1280	n/a	General	Music/Sports	n/a
KXYZ	1320	n/a	Hispanic	n/a	n/a
KHCB	1400	n/a	General/Hisp/Rel	Educational/Music/Talk	n/a
KHCH	1400	Non-Comm	General/Religious	Music/News/Talk	Gospel
KCOH	1430	Commercial	Black/General	Ed/Music/News/Talk	Urban Contemp.
KHVL	1490	n/a	General/Religious	Music/News	n/a
KYND	1520	Commercial	General/Hispanic	Educational/News/Talk	n/a
KGBC	1540	Commercial	General	Music/News/Sports	Oldies

Note: Stations included cover the Houston DMA (Designated Market Area); n/a not available
Source: BurrellesLuce, MediaContacts Online, January 2007

Major FM Radio Stations

Call Letters	Freq. (mHz)	Station Type	Target Audience	Station Format	Music Format
KUHF	88.7	College	General	Music/News	n/a
KSBJ	89.3	Non-Comm	General/Religious	Educational/Music/Talk	Christian
KETX	92.3	n/a	General	Music	n/a
KKRW	93.7	n/a	General	Music	n/a
KTBZ	94.5	Commercial	General	Music/News/Talk	Alternative
KHMX	96.5	n/a	General	Music/News/Sports	n/a
KTHT	97.1	n/a	General	Music/Talk	n/a
KBXX	97.9	Commercial	Black/General/Hisp/Men	Music/News/Talk	Urban Contemp.
KTJM	98.5	Commercial	General	Music/News/Talk	Latin
KODA	99.1	n/a	General	Music	n/a
KILT	100.3	n/a	General	Music/News/Talk	n/a
KRTX	100.7	n/a	General/Hispanic	Music	n/a
KMJQ	102.1	n/a	General	Music	n/a
KMKS	102.5	Commercial	General	Music/News	Country
KLTN	102.9	n/a	General/Hispanic	Music	n/a
KRBE	104.1	n/a	General	Music/News/Talk	n/a
KHCB	105.7	n/a	General/Religious	Music/Talk	n/a
KTTX	106.1	n/a	General/Young Adult	Music	n/a
KHPT	106.9	Commercial	General	Music/News/Talk	80's
KLDE	107.5	n/a	General	Music	n/a

Note: Stations included cover the Houston DMA (Designated Market Area); n/a not available
BurrellesLuce, MediaContacts Online, January 2007

CLIMATE

Average and Extreme Temperatures

Temperature	Jan	Feb	Mar	Apr	May	Jun	Jul	Aug	Sep	Oct	Nov	Dec	Yr.
Extreme High (°F)	84	91	91	95	97	103	104	107	102	94	89	83	107
Average High (°F)	61	65	73	79	85	91	93	93	89	81	72	65	79
Average Temp. (°F)	51	54	62	69	75	81	83	83	79	70	61	54	69
Average Low (°F)	41	43	51	58	65	71	73	73	68	58	50	43	58
Extreme Low (°F)	12	20	22	31	44	52	62	62	48	32	19	7	7

Note: Figures cover the years 1969-1990
Source: National Climatic Data Center, International Station Meteorological Climate Summary, 9/96

Average Precipitation/Snowfall/Humidity

Precip./Humidity	Jan	Feb	Mar	Apr	May	Jun	Jul	Aug	Sep	Oct	Nov	Dec	Yr.
Avg. Precip. (in.)	3.3	2.7	3.3	3.3	5.6	4.9	3.7	3.7	4.8	4.7	3.7	3.3	46.9
Avg. Snowfall (in.)	Tr	Tr	0	0	0	0	0	0	0	0	Tr	Tr	Tr
Avg. Rel. Hum. 6am (%)	85	86	87	89	91	92	93	93	93	91	89	86	90
Avg. Rel. Hum. 3pm (%)	58	55	54	54	57	56	55	55	57	53	55	57	55

Note: Figures cover the years 1969-1990; Tr = Trace amounts (<0.05 in. of rain; <0.5 in. of snow)
Source: National Climatic Data Center, International Station Meteorological Climate Summary, 9/96

Weather Conditions

Temperature			Daytime Sky			Precipitation		
32°F & below	45°F & below	90°F & above	Clear	Partly cloudy	Cloudy	0.01 inch or more precip.	0.1 inch or more snow/ice	Thunder-storms
21	87	96	83	168	114	101	1	62

Note: Figures are average number of days per year and cover the years 1969-1990
Source: National Climatic Data Center, International Station Meteorological Climate Summary, 9/96

HAZARDOUS WASTE

Superfund Sites

League City has no sites on the EPA's Superfund Final National Priorities List.
U.S. Environmental Protection Agency, Final National Priorities List, June 23, 2008

AIR & WATER QUALITY

Air Quality Index

Area	Percent of Days when Air Quality was...[2]				AQI Statistics	
	Good	Moderate	Unhealthy for Sensitive Groups	Unhealthy	Maximum	Median
MSA[1]	77.5	19.7	2.2	0.5	156	37

Note: The Air Quality Index (AQI) is an index for reporting daily air quality. EPA calculates the AQI for five major air pollutants regulated by the Clean Air Act: ground-level ozone, particle pollution (also known as particulate matter), carbon monoxide, sulfur dioxide, and nitrogen dioxide. The AQI runs from 0 to 500. The higher the AQI value, the greater the level of air pollution and the greater the health concern. There are six AQI categories: "Good" The AQI is between 0 and 50. Air quality is considered satisfactory; "Moderate" The AQI is between 51 and 100. Air quality is acceptable; "Unhealthy for Sensitive Groups" When AQI values are between 101 and 150, members of sensitive groups may experience health effects; "Unhealthy" When AQI values are between 151 and 200 everyone may begin to experience health effects; "Very Unhealthy" AQI values between 201 and 300 trigger a health alert; "Hazardous" AQI values over 300 trigger health warnings of emergency conditions; (1) Metropolitan Statistical Area - see Appendix A for areas included; (2) Based on 365 days with AQI data in 2007.
Source: U.S. Environmental Protection Agency, Air Quality Index Report, 2007

Air Quality Index Pollutants

Area	Percent of Days when AQI Pollutant was...[2]					
	Carbon Monoxide	Nitrogen Dioxide	Ozone	Sulfur Dioxide	Particulate Matter 2.5	Particulate Matter 10
MSA[1]	0.0	0.0	63.0	0.0	35.9	1.1

Note: The Air Quality Index (AQI) is an index for reporting daily air quality. EPA calculates the AQI for five major air pollutants regulated by the Clean Air Act: ground-level ozone, particle pollution (also known as particulate matter), carbon monoxide, sulfur dioxide, and nitrogen dioxide. The AQI runs from 0 to 500. The higher the AQI value, the greater the level of air pollution and the greater the health concern; (1) Metropolitan Statistical Area - see Appendix A for areas included; (2) Based on 365 days with AQI data in 2007.
Source: U.S. Environmental Protection Agency, Air Quality Index Report, 2007

Air Quality Index Trends

Area	Trend Sites (24)								All Sites (94)
	1999	2000	2001	2002	2003	2004	2005	2006	2006
MSA[1]	51	42	28	21	31	22	28	18	30

Note: An AQI value greater than 100 indicates that air quality would have been in the unhealthful range on that day. Data from exceptional events are not included. These counts are presented in two ways. First, the counts are based on sites having an adequate record of monitoring data during the trend period (trend sites). These counts represent the relative change in the number of days with AQI values greater than 100. In the last column, the counts are based on all sites with data in the most recent year (because it is possible for a site to have data in the most recent year but not enough data to be a trend site); (1) Metropolitan Statistical Area - see Appendix A for areas included.

Source: U.S. Environmental Protection Agency, Office of Air and Radiation, Air Trends, Factbook and Related Information, Air Pollution Trends in Selected Metropolitan Areas 2006

Maximum Air Pollutant Concentrations

	Particulate Matter 10 (ug/m^3)	Particulate Matter 2.5 (ug/m^3)	Ozone (ppm)	Carbon Monoxide (ppm)	Sulfur Dioxide (ppm)	Nitrogen Dioxide (ppm)	Lead (ug/m^3)
MSA[1] Level	173	32	0.15	3	0.023	0.016	0.01
NAAQS[2]	150	35	0.125	9	0.140	0.053	1.50
Met NAAQS[2]	No	Yes	No	Yes	Yes	Yes	Yes

Note: Data from exceptional events are not included; (1) Metropolitan Statistical Area - see Appendix A for areas included; (2) National Ambient Air Quality Standards; n/a not available

Concentrations: Particulate Matter 10 (coarse particulate) - highest second maximum 24-hour concentration; Particulate Matter 2.5 (fine particulate) - highest 98th percentile 24-hour concentration; Ozone - highest second daily maximum 1-hour concentration; Carbon Monoxide - highest second maximum non-overlapping 8-hour concentration; Sulfur Dioxide - highest second maximum 24-hour concentration; Nitrogen Dioxide - highest arithmetic mean concentration; Lead - highest quarterly maximum concentration

Units: ppm = parts per million; ug/m^3 = micrograms per cubic meter

Source: U.S. Environmental Protection Agency, MSA Factbook 2006, Air Quality Statistics by City

Drinking Water

Water System Name	Pop. Served	Primary Water Source Type	Violations[1]	
			Health Based	Monitoring/ Reporting
City of League City	66,819	Purchased Surface	0	1

Note: (1) Based on violation data from January 1, 2007 to December 31, 2007 (includes unresolved violations from earlier years)

Source: U.S. Environmental Protection Agency, Office of Ground Water and Drinking Water, Safe Drinking Water Information System (based on data extracted April 15, 2008)

Pflugerville, Texas

Background

Pflugerville is located in Traverse County in west-central Texas. It's situated about 15 miles north of the Colorado River on the blackland prairies, and only 15 minutes northeast of the urban center of Austin. The community covers an area of 11.3 square miles, including the man-made reservoir Lake Pflugerville, which serves as both the community's water source and a city park.

The area that is now Pflugerville was first settled by the Henry Pfluger family in 1849, who left Germany during the Prussian War. In Texas, they lived in a five-room log cabin and raised corn, wheat, sugar cane, and cattle. In 1860, William Bohls established a general store and post office in his home and named the community Pflugerville in honor of its founding resident. In 1904, two noteworthy events that started a period of great growth in Pflugerville. The first was the construction of a rail line by the Missouri-Kansas-Texas railroad, the first railroad track through the community. The second was the building of the community's first cotton gin by Otto Pfluger, one of Henry Pfluger's eight sons. In 1909, a second cotton gin added, and Pfluger constructed an ice factory. In 1913, Pfluger brought the entertainment industry to the emerging community by building the Sky Dome Theater, which showed motion pictures on Friday and Saturday nights.

The population of Pflugerville varied overtime. During the mid-1890s the community had a population of 250 residents, which doubled by 1914. The ensuing Great Depression caused the community's population to sharply decline when citizens began moving to more developed areas to find work; by the end of World War II, the population of Pflugerville had dropped to 380. The community experienced another period of growth during the 1960s and was incorporated in 1965. By 1980, the population of Pflugerville rose to 662 residents. During the next eight years, the rapid development in Pflugerville made it the fastest growing community in Texas. Currently, it's home to just under 30,000.

The rapid growth of Pflugerville in the early 1990s spawned the creation of the Pflugerville Community Development Corporation (PCDC). The PCDC strives to continue economic growth in the community and to increase the quality of life of the residents. The Pflugerville Independent School District is a source of pride among its residents. The strong education system that Pflugerville has constructed is evident with an average student SAT score of 1,021 out of 1600. Students seeking higher education have their choice of six universities, all 20 minutes away.

Pflugerville also has a thriving economic base constructed from its many hometown retail establishments, plus national retail chains such as Wal-Mart, Home Depot, and Starbucks. According to the Pflugerville Community Development Corporation, currently over one million square feet of retail shopping is currently being developed.

Pflugerville contains many cultural and recreational sites. The community has nearly 20 public parks including the Green Red Barn Park, whose event shelter is equipped with photovoltaic cells that convert sunlight into electricity. Lake Pflugerville is a 180-acre reservoir open to the public for fishing, swimming, canoeing and kayaking. Pflugerville also houses the Heritage House Museum whose mission is to promote, preserve and protect the history of Pflugerville and to educate those who visit. Notably, the community is home to sets used in the NBC television show Friday Night Lights, i.e. Pflugerville's High School stadium was used to film the show's football games.

Pflugerville is served by the Austin-Bergstrom International Airport and several other regional airports.

The average temperature in Pflugerville ranges from a very tolerable 58 degrees to a very pleasant 79 degrees.

Rankings

General Rankings

- Austin* was ranked #103 out of 375 metro areas in *Cities Ranked & Rated*. Criteria: cost of living; climate; crime; transportation; economy and jobs; education; arts and culture; health and healthcare; leisure; quality of life. *Cities Ranked & Rated, 2nd Edition, 2007*

- Austin* was ranked #35 out of 379 metro areas in *Places Rated Almanac*. Criteria: health care; education; recreation; transportation; ambience; climate; crime; housing costs; jobs. *Places Rated Almanac, 7th Edition, 2007*

- The Austin* metro area was selected one of America's "Best Cities to Live, Work and Play" by *Kiplinger Personal Finance*. Criteria: population growth; percentage of workforce in the creative class (scientists, engineers, educators, writers, artists, entertainers, etc.); job quality; income growth; cost of living. *Kiplinger Personal Finance, "Best Cities to Live, Work and Play," July 2008*

- *Expansion Management* rated 362 metro areas to find out which offer the best middle class lifestyle for manufacturing and service companies. The Austin* metro area was selected as a "5-Star Quality of Life Metro" (a distinction the magazine awards to the top 20 percent of metro areas studied). The annual "Quality of Life Quotient" measures dozens of indicators across nine major categories and compares them among 362 metropolitan statistical areas in the United States. The categories are: affordable housing; good public schools; low crime levels; adult education level; standard of living; traffic and commuting; continuing education opportunities; commercial air access; labor market. *Expansion Management, June 2007*

Business/Finance Rankings

- The nation's 100 largest metro areas were analysed in terms of the percentage of households entering some stage of foreclosure in 2007. The Austin* metro area ranked #58 out of 100 (#1 = highest foreclosure rate). *RealtyTrac, "Year-End 2007 Metropolitan Foreclosure Report"*

- The Austin* metro area was identified as one of the "10 Best Cities for Jobs in 2008" by *Forbes*. The metro area ranked #3. Criteria: state unemployment rate; job growth; income growth; median household income; cost of living. *Forbes.com, "Best Cities for Jobs in 2008," January 10, 2008*

- The Austin* metro area was identified as one of the "Top 12 Nano Metros" in the U.S. by the Woodrow Wilson International Center for Scholars. The metro area is home to 18 companies, universities, government laboratories and/or organizations working in nanotechnology. *Woodrow Wilson International Center for Scholars, May 17, 2007*

- The Austin* metro area was selected one of America's "Top 50 Business Opportunity Metros" by *Expansion Management* in their 5th annual Mayor's Challenge ranking of metro areas that have achieved solid ratings across the board in numerous *EM* studies during the past 12 months. The area ranked #1. Criteria: public schools; quality of life; college educated workers; logistics infrastructure; healthcare costs; taxes and government spending; reputation among site consultants. *Expansion Management, August 2007*

- Austin* was selected as one of the best places to start and grow a company by *Entrepreneur* and the National Policy Research Council. The Austin* metro area ranked #5 out of 50 large metro areas. Criteria: business formation and growth (firms started four to 14 years ago that still employ at least 5 people and experienced rapid growth over the last four years). *Entrepreneur/National Policy Research Council, "Hot Cities for Entrepreneurs," September 2006*

- The Austin* metro area was selected as one of "America's 50 Hottest Cities" for business relocations and expansions. Criteria: industry's most prominent site selection consultants were asked to list their top city choices for relocating and expanding manufacturing companies, taking into consideration such factors as the business climate, work force quality, operating costs, incentive programs, and the ease of working with local political and economic development officials. *Expansion Management, January-February 2007*

- Intel, in partnership with Sperling's BestPlaces, ranked the 80 "Best Cities for Teleworking" in America. The Austin* metro area ranked #4 among mid-sized metro areas. The study identifies cities that hold the greatest potential for teleworking based on a host of factors including typical commuting times, fuel prices, availability of broadband Internet access and percentage of the population in telework friendly jobs. The study also factored in extreme climate and natural hazards. *Intel, "Best Cities for Teleworking," March 30, 2006*

- The Austin* metro area was identified as one of the "25 Hottest Housing Markets" in the U.S. The area ranked #4 out of 156 markets with a home price appreciation rate of 6.4%. Criteria: year-over-year change of median sales price of existing single-family homes between the 4th quarter of 2006 and the 4th quarter of 2007. *National Association of Realtors, Median Sales Price of Existing Single-Family Homes for Metropolitan Areas, 4th Quarter 2007*

- The Austin* metro area appeared on the Milken Institute "2007 Best Performing Cities" index. Rank: #20 out of 200 large metro areas. Criteria: job growth; wage and salary growth; high-tech output growth. *Milken Institute, "2007 Best Performing Cities"*

- The Austin* metro area was selected as one of the hottest cities for entrepreneurs in America by *Inc. Magazine.* Criteria: job-growth data for 393 metro was analyzed for current-year employment growth, average annual employment growth over past three years, and employment growth by industry sector. The Austin* metro area ranked #16 among large metro areas and #110 overall. *Inc. Magazine, May 2007*

- The Austin* metro area was selected as one of "The Top 20 Boom Towns in America." *Business 2.0* magazine and econometric research firm Global Insight compared 319 metropolitan areas in the U.S. and ranked the 61 with populations over 1 million. Criteria: a weighted formula that includes forecast growth rates in sectors that contain the economy's 10 most skilled occupational clusters; the prevalence of college degrees in the local workforce; median salary. The area ranked #4 among large metro areas. *Business 2.0 Magazine, March 2004*

- Austin* was identified as one of the 100 "Most Unwired Cities" in the U.S. The area ranked #3 out of the 100 largest metro areas in the U.S. Criteria: number of public and commercial wireless access points (hotspots); airports with wireless Internet access; broadband availability; local wireless networks; and wireless email devices. *Intel, "Most Unwired Cities Survey," June 7, 2005*

- Austin* was ranked #19 out of 125 regions worldwide in terms of its "Knowledge Competitiveness Index." The index attempts to measure the knowledge-based development taking place throughout the world and is based on 19 measures of economic performance that indicate a region's ability to translate its knowledge capacity into economic value. *Robert Huggins Associates, World Knowledge Competitiveness Index 2005*

- *Forbes* ranked the 200 most populous metro areas in the U.S. in terms of the "Best Places for Business and Careers." The Austin* metro area was ranked #47. Criteria: business costs (labor, energy, tax and office space expenses); living costs (housing, transportation, food and other household expenditures); education levels of the work force; job growth; income growth; migration trends; crime rates; and culture/leisure. *Forbes, "Best Places for Business and Careers," March 19, 2008*

- Austin* was identified as one of the top 20 metro areas with the highest rate of house price appreciation in 2007. The area ranked #11 with a one-year price appreciation of 8.0% through the 4th quarter 2007. *Office of Federal Housing Enterprise Oversight, House Price Index, 4th Quarter 2007*

- *Fortune* ranked the 100 largest metro areas in the U.S. in terms of projected median home price change in 2007. The Austin* metro area ranked #12. *Fortune.com, "Hot Spots, Cold Spots"*

Health/Environment Rankings

- 100 of the largest metro areas in the U.S. were analyzed in terms of their current drought severity. The Austin* metro area ranked #98 (#1 = driest). The rankings were based on statistics such as long-term precipitation trends and patterns and the Palmer drought indices. *Sperling's BestPlaces, www.BestPlaces.net, "America's Drought-Riskiest Cities," November 2007*

- Scarborough Research, a leading market research firm, identified the top local markets for organic consumers. The Austin* DMA (Designated Market Area) ranked in the top 15 with 23% of adults reporting that they used any organic food product in their household during the past month. *Scarborough Research, October 10, 2007*

- *Reader's Digest* ranked the 50 largest metro areas in the U.S. in terms of how "clean" they are. The Austin* metro area ranked #8. Criteria: air quality; water quality; toxic industrial pollution; Superfund sites; and sanitation. *Reader's Digest, "The 50 Cleanest (and Dirtiest) Cities in America," July 2005*

- The Austin* metro area was identified as one of "America's Most Obese Cities" by *Forbes*. The magazine analyzed BMI (body mass index) data from the CDC in the 50 most populated metro areas in the U.S. and ranked the top 20. The area ranked #18. *Forbes, "America's Most Obese Cities," November 26, 2007*

- The Austin* metro area appeared in *Country Home's* "2008 Best Green Places" report. The area ranked #33 out of 379. Criteria: official energy policies; green power; green buildings; availability of fresh, locally grown food. *Country Home, "2008 Best Green Places"*

- Wyeth Consumer Healthcare, in partnership with Sperling's BestPlaces, ranked the nation's 50 most populous metro areas in terms of five key health factors. The Austin* metro area ranked #10. Criteria: physical activity; health status; nutrition; lifestyle pursuits; and mental wellness. *Wyeth Consumer Healthcare, "Centrum Healthiest Cities Study," April 19, 2005*

- Austin* was identified as a "2008 Asthma Capital." The area ranked #67 out of the nation's 100 largest metropolitan areas. Twelve factors were used to identify the most challenging places to live for people with asthma: estimated prevalence; self-reported prevalence; crude death rate for asthma; annual pollen score; annual air quality; public smoking laws; number of board-certified asthma specialists; school inhaler access laws; rescue medication use; controller medication use; uninsured rate; poverty rate. *Asthma and Allergy Foundation of America, "2008 Asthma Capitals"*

- Austin* was identified as a "Spring Allergy Capital." The area ranked #24 out of 100. Three groups of factors were used to identify the most severe cities for people with allergies during the spring season: annual pollen levels; medicine utilization; access to board-certified allergists. *Asthma and Allergy Foundation of America, "2007 Spring Allergy Capital Rankings"*

- Austin* was identified as a "Fall Allergy Capital." The area ranked #1 out of 100. Three groups of factors were used to identify the most severe cities for people with allergies during the fall season: annual pollen levels; medicine utilization; access to board-certified allergists. *Asthma and Allergy Foundation of America, "2007 Fall Allergy Capital Rankings"*

- Ortho-McNeil Neurologics, in partnership with Sperling's BestPlaces, analyzed 110 metro areas and identified those U.S. cities with the highest prevalence of factors that are most commonly associated with migraine headaches. The Austin* metro area ranked #65. Criteria: number of migraine-related drug prescriptions per capita; lifestyle factors that can contribute to migraines; environmental factors that can trigger migraines; and consumption of migraine-triggering foods. *Ortho-McNeil Neurologics, "America's Migraine Hot Spots," March 14, 2006*

- Sperling's BestPlaces ranked 331 metro areas and identified the most and least stressful U.S. cities. The Austin* metro area ranked #60 out of the 100 largest metro areas (#1 = most stressful). Criteria: divorce rate; unemployment rate; violent and property crime; suicide rate; commute time; mental health; alcohol consumption; cloudy days. *Sperling's BestPlaces, www.BestPlaces.net, "America's Most (and Least) Stressful Cities," January 9, 2004*

- An analysis of the "Best & Worst Cities for Sleep" was conducted by Sperling's BestPlaces. The study ranked America's 50 most populated metro areas. The Austin* metro area ranked #14 (#1 = best city for sleep). Criteria: number of days residents didn't get enough rest or sleep during the past month; average length of daily commute; divorce rate; unemployment rate. *Sperling's BestPlaces, www.BestPlaces.net, "Best & Worst Cities for Sleep," 2006*

Women/Minorities Rankings

- Austin* was ranked #48 out of 100 metro areas in *SELF Magazine's* ranking of "America's Best Places for Women." A panel of experts came up with more than 50 criteria including death and disease rates, environmental indicators, community resources, and lifestyle habits. *SELF Magazine, "America's Best Places for Women 2007," December 2007*
- Austin* appeared on a list of the top 10 metro areas with the highest concentration of same-sex households. The area ranked #5. *Urban Institute Press, The Gay and Lesbian Atlas, May 2004*

Seniors/Retirement Rankings

- Sperling's BestPlaces in partnership with Bankers Life & Casualty Company designed a survey to identify the top 50 metro areas in the U.S. that offer the best overall qualities for senior living. The Austin* metro area ranked #27. The following criteria were statistically weighted to reflect the needs of the senior population: health; disease; economics; social; environment; spiritual; transportation; housing; and crime. *Bankers Life & Casualty Company, "Best Cities for Seniors 2005"*
- A.G. Edwards ranked America's 500 top-performing communities based on their residents' personal savings and investing behavior. The Austin* metro area ranked #395 with an index score of 97.15 (national average = 100.00). A dozen statistical factors were measured including: participation in retirement savings plans; personal debt levels; and home ownership. *A.G. Edwards, "2007 Nest Egg Index", September 12, 2007*

Children/Family Rankings

- The Austin* metro area was selected as one of the "Best Cities for Relocating Families" by Worldwide ERC and Primacy Relocation. The 2007 study placed a special emphasis on the housing market, which has significantly impacted the relocation industry and an employer's ability to transfer employees. The variables which weigh heavily in this category include home price, home affordability index, appreciation rates, and property tax. Other criteria include cost of living, crime rates, education, climate, focus on diversity, physicians per capita, recreation and leisure, arts and culture, air quality, watershed quality, sales tax, unemployment rate, job growth, high school and higher education index, school expenditures per student, students in public school, SAT/ACT percentile, and population growth. *Worldwide ERC and Primacy Relocation, "2007 Best Cities for Relocating Families"*

Safety Rankings

- The National Insurance Crime Bureau ranked 361 metro areas in the U.S. in terms of per capita rates of vehicle theft. The Austin* metro area ranked #161 (#1 = highest rate). Criteria: number of vehicle theft offenses per 100,000 inhabitants. *National Insurance Crime Bureau, "NICB Vehicle Theft Study," April 22, 2008*
- Austin* appeared on Sperling's BestPlaces list of the "Riskiest Cities for Identity Theft." The area ranked #18 out of the nations 50 largest metro areas. Over 80 criteria were analyzed across four major categories: technology impact; crime; transactions; and risk profile. *Sperling's BestPlaces, www.BestPlaces.net, "Riskiest Cities for Identity Theft," July 2006*
- Farmers Insurance Group of Companies, in partnership with Sperling's BestPlaces, ranked 379 metro areas and identified the "Most Secure U.S. Place to Live." The Austin* metro area ranked #31 out of 114 in the large metro area category (500,000 or more residents). Criteria: crime rates; extreme weather; risk of natural disasters; environmental hazards; terrorism threats; air quality; life expectancy; job loss numbers. *Farmers Insurance Group, "Most Secure U.S. Places to Live 2007"*

- Austin* was identified as one of the most dangerous large metro areas for pedestrians in the U.S. The area ranked #30 out of the nations 50 largest metro areas. Criteria: average yearly pedestrian fatalities per capita (for the years 2002 and 2003) adjusted for the number of walkers. *Surface Transportation Policy Project, "Mean Streets 2004"*

Sports/Recreation Rankings

- The Austin* metro area appeared on the *Sporting News* list of the "Best Sports Cities 2007". The area ranked #57 out of 150 cities in the U.S. *Sporting News* takes a 12-month snapshot, roughly July to July, of each city's sports, putting a heavy premium on regular-season won-lost records (from the most recently completed season). Other criteria include: playoff berths, bowl appearances and tournament bids; championships; applicable power ratings; quality of competition; overall fan fervor as measured in part by attendance as percentage of venue capacity; abundance of teams (rewarding quality over quantity); stadium and arena quality; ticket availability and prices; franchise ownership; and marquee appeal of athletes. *SportingNews.com, "Best Sports Cities 2007," August 1, 2007*

- The Austin* metro area was selected by *Cranium* as one of the "Top 50 Fun Cities" in America. The area ranked #44. Criteria includes: number of sports teams, restaurants, and dance performances; number of toy stores; city budget spent on recreation. *Cranium, November 4, 2003*

- *Golf Digest* ranked 330 metro areas in the U.S. in terms of golf. The Austin* metro area was ranked #241. Criteria: access to golf; weather; value of golf; and quality of golf. *Golf Digest, "Metro Golf Rankings," August 2005*

Dating/Romance Rankings

- Eli Lily and Company, in partnership with Sperling's BestPlaces, ranked the nation's 50 largest metro areas in terms of the "Most Romantic Cities for Baby Boomers." The Austin* metro area ranked #32. Criteria: marriage and divorce rates among "baby boomers" age 45 to 60; great restaurants; dance studios; chocolate, jewelry and flower sales. *Eli Lily and Company, "Most Romantic Cities for Baby Boomers," April 20, 2007*

- The Austin* metro area was selected as one of the "Best Cities for Relocating Singles" by Worldwide ERC and Primacy Relocation. The area ranked #8 out of the 100 largest metro areas in the U.S. Areas were selected based on the following criteria: a robust cost-of-living index; adventure and outdoor recreation opportunities; violent crime and property crime rates; percentage of the population that is unmarried (ages 25-34); ratio of single men and single women; affordability of quality higher education, including in-state and out-of-state tuition requirements and rates; number of newcomers to the area; commute times; tax rates; fee and occupancy rates for temporary housing and mini-storage; quality and quantity of collegiate and professional sporting events and fun, fan-friendly venues. *Worldwide ERC and Primacy Relocation, "2007 Best Cities for Relocating Singles," October 25, 2007*

- *Forbes* ranked the 40 most populous urbanized areas in the U.S. in terms of the "Best Cities for Singles." The Austin* metro area ranked #12. Criteria: number of singles; cost of living alone; nightlife; culture; job growth; coolness; and online dating. *Forbes.com, August 21, 2007*

- Sperling's BestPlaces in partnership with AXE Deodorant Bodyspray ranked 80 metro areas and identified "America's Best (and Worst) Cities for Dating." The Austin* metro area ranked #1 (#1 = best). Criteria: percentage of singles ages 18-24; population density; dating venues per capita. *AXE Deodorant Bodyspray, "America's Best (and Worst) Cities for Dating," May 2004*

Culture/Performing Arts Rankings

- Scarborough Research, a leading market research firm, identified the top local markets for rock concert attendance. The Austin* DMA (Designated Market Area) ranked in the top 25 with 18% of consumers, 18 years old and over, reporting that they have attended a rock concert during the past year. *Scarborough Research, June 14, 2004*

Miscellaneous Rankings

- Scarborough Research, a leading market research firm, identified the top local markets for bloggers. The Austin* DMA (Designated Market Area) ranked in the top 13 with 15% of adults reporting that they had read or contributed to a blog within the past 30 days. *Scarborough Research, October 24, 2007*
- Pflugerville was identified as one of the 100 fastest-growing suburbs in America by "Forbes." The city ranked #23. Criteria: suburban cities, townships and villages with more than 10,000 people in 2000 were ranked by their population growth from 2000 to 2006. *Forbes.com, "America's Fastest-Growing Suburbs," July 16, 2007*
- The Austin* metro area appeared on *Forbes* list of "America's Drunkest Cities". The area ranked #5. Criteria: 35 of the largest continental U.S. metro areas were chosen based on availability of data and geographic diversity. Each metro was ranked in five areas: state laws; drinkers; heavy drinkers; binge drinkers; and alcoholism. *Forbes.com, "America's Drunkest Cities," August 22, 2006*
- Sperling's BestPlaces in partnership with Pep Boys ranked 77 metro areas and identified "America's Most Drivable Cities." The Austin* metro area ranked #25. Criteria: climate; road roughness; urban mobility; gas prices. *Pep Boys, "America's Most Drivable Cities," April 9, 2003*
- State Farm Insurance, in partnership with Sperling's BestPlaces, analyzed several key factors that contribute to overall family preparedness. The Austin* metro area ranked #32 out of the nation's 50 most populous metro areas. Criteria: quality of life; life insurance coverage; and investments. *State Farm Life Insurance, "Fiscally Fit Cities Report," July 20, 2004*
- Scarborough Research, a leading market research firm, identified the top local markets for gift card purchasers. The Austin* DMA (Designated Market Area) ranked in the top 10 with 54% of consumers reporting that they purchased a gift card within the past 12 months. *Scarborough Research, November 15, 2006*
- Scarborough Research, a leading market research firm, identified the top local markets for frequent fast food restaurant patronage. The Austin* DMA (Designated Market Area) ranked in the top 10 with consumers reporting an average of 6.3 visits within the past 30 days. *Scarborough Research, May 31, 2006*
- Scarborough Research, a leading market research firm, identified the top local markets for frequent sit-down restaurant patronage. The Austin* DMA (Designated Market Area) ranked in the top 10 with consumers reporting an average of 4.0 visits within the past 30 days. *Scarborough Research, May 31, 2006*
- A study by Sperling's BestPlaces examined which U.S. metro areas were most affected by high fuel prices in 2006. The Austin* metro area was ranked #38 out of 80 (#1 = most expensive city for driving). Rankings are based on the average dollars spent on gas per year by two driver households. Criteria: cost of regular-grade gasoline; average miles driven per day; average number of gallons each driver uses and wastes in traffic congestion each day. *Sperling's BestPlaces, www.bestplaces.net, "Pain at the Pump," May 18, 2006*

Pflugerville is located within the Austin-Round Rock, TX Metropolitan Statistical Area.

Business Environment

CITY FINANCES

City Government Finances

Component	2004-2005 ($000)	2004-2005 ($ per capita)
Total Revenues	n/a	n/a
Total Expenditures	n/a	n/a
Debt Outstanding	n/a	n/a
Cash and Securities	n/a	n/a

Source: U.S Census Bureau, Government Finances 2004-2005

City Government Revenue by Source

Source	2004-2005 ($000)	2004-2005 ($ per capita)
General Revenue		
From Federal Government	n/a	n/a
From State Government	n/a	n/a
From Local Governments	n/a	n/a
Taxes		
Property	n/a	n/a
Sales	n/a	n/a
Personal Income	n/a	n/a
License	n/a	n/a
Charges	n/a	n/a
Liquor Store	n/a	n/a
Utility	n/a	n/a
Employee Retirement	n/a	n/a
Other	n/a	n/a

Source: U.S Census Bureau, Government Finances 2004-2005

City Government Expenditures by Function

Function	2004-2005 ($000)	2004-2005 ($ per capita)	2004-2005 (%)
General Expenditures			
Airports	n/a	n/a	n/a
Corrections	n/a	n/a	n/a
Education	n/a	n/a	n/a
Fire Protection	n/a	n/a	n/a
Governmental Administration	n/a	n/a	n/a
Health	n/a	n/a	n/a
Highways	n/a	n/a	n/a
Hospitals	n/a	n/a	n/a
Housing and Community Development	n/a	n/a	n/a
Interest on General Debt	n/a	n/a	n/a
Libraries	n/a	n/a	n/a
Parking	n/a	n/a	n/a
Parks and Recreation	n/a	n/a	n/a
Police Protection	n/a	n/a	n/a
Public Welfare	n/a	n/a	n/a
Sewerage	n/a	n/a	n/a
Solid Waste Management	n/a	n/a	n/a
Liquor Store	n/a	n/a	n/a
Utility	n/a	n/a	n/a
Employee Retirement	n/a	n/a	n/a
Other	n/a	n/a	n/a

Source: U.S Census Bureau, Government Finances 2004-2005

Municipal Bond Ratings

Area	Moody's
City	n/a

Source: Mergent Bond Record, January 2008 (unless noted otherwise)

DEMOGRAPHICS

Population Growth

Area	1990 Census	2000 Census	2007 Estimate	2012 Projection	Population Growth (%) 1990-2000	Population Growth (%) 2000-2012
City	5,830	16,335	27,258	34,128	180.2	108.9
MSA[1]	846,217	1,249,763	1,503,872	1,677,632	47.7	34.2
U.S.	248,709,873	281,421,906	301,045,522	314,920,978	13.2	11.9

Note: (1) Metropolitan Statistical Area - see Appendix B for areas included
Source: Claritas, Inc.

Number of Households and Average Household Size

Area	2007 Estimate	2007 Average Household Size
City	8,574	3.18
MSA[1]	568,544	2.65
U.S.	113,668,003	2.65

Note: (1) Metropolitan Statistical Area - see Appendix B for areas included
Source: Claritas, Inc.

Race and Ethnicity

Area	White Alone[2]	Black Alone[2]	Asian Alone[2]	Other Race Alone[2]	Hispanic[3]
City	72.4	11.8	5.7	10.1	21.2
MSA[1]	70.2	7.4	4.3	18.1	29.6
U.S.	73.1	12.4	4.3	10.3	14.9

Note: Figures are 2007 estimates; (1) Metropolitan Statistical Area - see Appendix B for areas included (2) Alone is defined as not being in combination with one or more other races; (3) May be of any race.
Source: Claritas, Inc.

Ancestry

Area	German	Irish[2]	English	American	Italian	Polish	French[3]	Scottish
City	21.7	11.7	10.0	5.5	3.2	1.7	4.0	2.5
MSA[1]	15.3	9.3	9.7	5.3	2.5	1.5	2.9	2.4
U.S.	15.2	10.9	8.7	7.3	5.6	3.2	3.0	1.7

Note: Figures include multiple ancestry (e.g. if a person reported being Irish and Italian, they were included in both columns); (1) Metropolitan Statistical Area - see Appendix A for areas included; (2) Includes Celtic; (3) Includes Alsatian but excludes Basque
Source: Census 2000, Summary File 3

Foreign-Born Population

Area	Percent of Population Born in: Any Foreign Country	Europe	Asia	Africa	Oceania[2]	Canada	Mexico	Latin America[3]
City	6.4	0.7	3.5	0.8	0.0	0.1	0.9	0.5
MSA[1]	12.2	1.0	2.9	0.3	0.0	0.2	6.7	1.1
U.S.	11.1	1.7	2.9	0.3	0.1	0.3	3.3	2.5

Note: (1) Metropolitan Statistical Area - see Appendix A for areas included; (2) Includes Australia, New Zealand subregion, Melanesia, Micronesia, Polynesia, and Oceania n.e.c; (3) Includes Central America (excluding Mexico), South America, and the Caribbean.
Source: Census 2000, Summary File 3

Marriage Status

Area	Never Married	Now Married (excluding Separated)	Separated	Widowed	Divorced
City	20.6	66.5	0.8	2.8	9.3
MSA[1]	32.2	51.7	1.8	3.8	10.4
U.S.	27.1	54.4	2.2	6.6	9.7

Note: Figures are percentages and cover the population 15 years of age and older; (1) Metropolitan Statistical Area - see Appendix A for areas included
Source: Census 2000, Summary File 3

Age Distribution

Area	Percent of Population						
	Under Age 5	Age 5 to 17	Age 18 to 34	Age 35 to 49	Age 50 to 64	Age 65 to 79	80 Years and Over
City	8.8	25.3	23.3	30.1	8.6	2.8	1.0
MSA[1]	7.4	17.9	31.5	24.4	11.7	5.4	1.8
U.S.	6.8	18.9	23.7	23.5	14.8	9.2	3.2

Note: (1) Metropolitan Statistical Area - see Appendix A for areas included
Source: Census 2000, Summary File 3

Male/Female Ratio

Area	Males	Females	Males per 100 Females
City	13,516	13,742	98.4
MSA[1]	762,780	741,092	102.9
U.S.	148,320,305	152,725,217	97.1

Note: Figures are 2007 estimates; (1) Metropolitan Statistical Area - see Appendix B for areas included
Source: Claritas, Inc.

Religion

Area	Catholic	Southern Baptist	United Meth-odist	ELCA[1]	LDS[2]	Presby-terian Church USA	Jewish Est.	Muslim Est.
County	20.4	9.5	2.7	1.5	0.6	1.3	1.7	0.4
U.S.	22.0	7.1	3.7	1.8	1.5	1.1	2.2	0.6

Note: Figures are the number of adherents as a percentage of the total population; Adherents are defined as all members, including full members, their children and the estimated number of other participants who are not considered members (e.g. the baptized, those not confirmed, those regularly attending services, etc.); (1) Evangelical Lutheran Church in America; (2) The Church of Jesus Christ of Latter Day Saints
Source: Reprinted with permission from Religious Congregations and Membership in the United States 2000 (Nashville, Glenmary Research Center, 2002) Copyright Association of Statisticians of American Religious Bodies. All rights reserved.

ECONOMY

Gross Metropolitan Product

Area	2002	2003	2004	2005	2005 Rank[2]
MSA[1]	52.0	54.3	59.7	66.2	38

Note: Figures are in billions of dollars; (1) Austin-Round Rock, TX Metropolitan Statistical Area - see Appendix A for areas included; (2) Rank ranges from 1 to 361
Source: The U.S. Conference of Mayors, "U.S. Metro Economies: GMP - The Engines of America's Growth," January 2007

Economic Growth

Area	1995 GMP	2005 GMP	Average Annual Growth Rate	Growth Rate Rank[2]
MSA[1]	30.2	66.2	8.2	11

Note: Figures are in billions of dollars; GMP = Gross Metropolitan Product; (1) Austin-Round Rock, TX Metropolitan Statistical Area - see Appendix A for areas included; (2) Rank ranges from 1 to 361
Source: The U.S. Conference of Mayors, "U.S. Metro Economies: GMP - The Engines of America's Growth," January 2007

INCOME

Per Capita/Median/Average Income

Area	Per Capita ($)	Median Household ($)	Average Household ($)
City	29,046	79,339	92,087
MSA[1]	27,754	55,339	72,712
U.S.	25,495	49,280	66,670

Note: Figures are 2007 estimates; (1) Metropolitan Statistical Area - see Appendix B for areas included
Source: Claritas, Inc.

Household Income Distribution

Area	Percent of Households Earning							
	Under $15,000	$15,000 -24,999	$25,000 -34,999	$35,000 -49,999	$50,000 -74,999	$75,000 -99,000	$100,000 -149,999	$150,000 and up
City	2.0	3.2	5.0	11.1	24.8	22.8	22.0	9.2
MSA[1]	10.7	8.9	10.4	15.4	20.3	13.4	13.0	8.0
U.S.	13.1	10.9	11.2	15.6	19.5	11.9	11.3	6.6

Note: Figures are 2007 estimates; (1) Metropolitan Statistical Area - see Appendix B for areas included
Source: Claritas, Inc.

Poverty Rates by Age

Area	All Ages	Under 5 Years Old	5 to 17 Years Old	18 to 64 Years Old	65 Years and Over
City	1.7	0.3	0.5	0.9	0.0
MSA[1]	11.1	1.0	2.1	7.4	0.6
U.S.	12.4	1.2	3.0	6.9	1.2

Note: Figures are percent of population with income in 1999 below poverty level and only include population for whom poverty status is determined; (1) Metropolitan Statistical Area - see Appendix A for areas included
Source: Census 2000, Summary File 3

Personal Bankruptcy Filing Rate

Area	2004	2005	2006
Travis County	3.70	5.32	1.17
U.S.	5.31	6.82	2.00

Note: Numbers are per 1,000 population and include Chapter 7 and Chapter 13 filings
Source: Federal Deposit Insurance Corporation (FDIC), Regional Economic Conditions (RECON), 8/23/2007

EMPLOYMENT

Labor Force and Employment

Area	Civilian Labor Force			Workers Employed		
	Dec. 2006	Dec. 2007	% Chg.	Dec. 2006	Dec. 2007	% Chg.
City	17,247	17,526	1.6	16,755	16,982	1.4
MSA[1]	841,139	854,956	1.6	813,117	824,154	1.4
U.S.	152,571,000	153,705,000	0.7	146,081,000	146,334,000	0.2

Note: Data is not seasonally adjusted and covers workers 16 years of age and older; (1) Metropolitan Statistical Area - see Appendix B for areas included
Source: Bureau of Labor Statistics, http://stats.bls.gov

Unemployment Rate

Area	2007											
	Jan.	Feb.	Mar.	Apr.	May	Jun.	Jul.	Aug.	Sep.	Oct.	Nov.	Dec.
City	3.3	3.1	3.2	2.8	2.8	3.6	3.6	3.2	3.3	3.2	3.1	3.1
MSA[1]	3.9	3.8	3.5	3.2	3.3	3.9	4.0	3.7	3.7	3.5	3.5	3.6
U.S.	5.0	4.9	4.5	4.3	4.3	4.7	4.9	4.6	4.5	4.4	4.5	4.8

Note: Data is not seasonally adjusted and covers workers 16 years of age and older; All figures are percentages; (1) Metropolitan Statistical Area - see Appendix B for areas included
Source: Bureau of Labor Statistics, http://stats.bls.gov

Employment by Occupation

Occupation Classification	City (%)	MSA[1] (%)	U.S. (%)
Sales and Office	28.0	26.7	26.7
Professional and Related	28.9	25.7	20.2
Service	10.9	12.4	14.9
Production, Transportation, and Material Moving	8.3	9.3	14.6
Management, Business, and Financial	17.1	16.2	13.5
Construction, Extraction, and Maintenance	6.5	9.5	9.4
Farming, Forestry, and Fishing	0.2	0.2	0.7

Note: Figures cover employed civilians 16 years of age and older; (1) Metropolitan Statistical Area - see Appendix A for areas included
Source: Census 2000, Summary File 3

Employment by Industry

Sector	MSA[1] Number of Employees	MSA[1] Percent of Total	U.S. Percent of Total
Government	157,200	20.4	16.3
Education and Health Services	78,600	10.2	13.4
Professional and Business Services	109,900	14.2	13.1
Retail Trade	86,100	11.2	11.6
Manufacturing	60,500	7.8	9.9
Leisure and Hospitality	79,100	10.3	9.6
Financial Activities	45,600	5.9	5.9
Construction	n/a	n/a	5.3
Wholesale Trade	41,100	5.3	4.4
Other Services	28,300	3.7	3.9
Transportation and Utilities	13,800	1.8	3.7
Information	21,800	2.8	2.2
Natural Resources and Mining	n/a	n/a	0.5

Note: Figures cover non-farm employment as of December 2007 and are not seasonally adjusted; (1) Metropolitan Statistical Area - see Appendix B for areas included; n/a not available
Source: Bureau of Labor Statistics, http://stats.bls.gov

Average Wages

Occupation	$/Hr.	Occupation	$/Hr.
Accountants and Auditors	30.35	Maids and Housekeeping Cleaners	8.27
Automotive Mechanics	19.58	Maintenance and Repair Workers	14.38
Bookkeepers	14.97	Marketing Managers	59.62
Carpenters	16.33	Nuclear Medicine Technologists	30.52
Cashiers	8.78	Nurses, Licensed Practical	19.01
Clerks, General Office	11.34	Nurses, Registered	28.89
Clerks, Receptionists/Information	12.26	Nursing Aides/Orderlies/Attendants	10.81
Clerks, Shipping/Receiving	12.66	Packers and Packagers, Hand	8.27
Computer Programmers	35.04	Physical Therapists	30.35
Computer Support Specialists	20.59	Postal Service Mail Carriers	21.56
Computer Systems Analysts	35.01	Real Estate Brokers	34.56
Cooks, Restaurant	9.37	Retail Salespersons	11.25
Dentists	n/a	Sales Reps., Exc. Tech./Scientific	25.70
Electrical Engineers	44.77	Sales Reps., Tech./Scientific	41.47
Electricians	17.49	Secretaries, Exc. Legal/Med./Exec.	13.04
Financial Managers	51.75	Security Guards	11.55
First-Line Supervisors/Mgrs., Sales	19.76	Surgeons	92.76
Food Preparation Workers	9.59	Teacher Assistants	10.40
General and Operations Managers	50.80	Teachers, Elementary School	20.40
Hairdressers/Cosmetologists	12.26	Teachers, Secondary School	21.60
Internists	67.24	Telemarketers	10.37
Janitors and Cleaners	9.41	Truck Drivers, Heavy/Tractor-Trailer	15.67
Landscaping/Groundskeeping Workers	9.80	Truck Drivers, Light/Delivery Svcs.	14.09
Lawyers	50.25	Waiters and Waitresses	7.58

Note: Wage data covers the Austin-Round Rock, TX Metropolitan Statistical Area - see Appendix B for areas included. Hourly wages for elementary/secondary school teachers and teacher assistants were calculated by the editors from annual wage data assuming a 40 hour work week; n/a not available.
Source: Bureau of Labor Statistics, May 2007 Metro Area Occupational Employment and Wage Estimates

RESIDENTIAL REAL ESTATE

Building Permits

Area	Single-Family 2006	Single-Family 2007p	Single-Family Pct. Chg.	Multi-Family 2006	Multi-Family 2007p	Multi-Family Pct. Chg.	Total 2006	Total 2007p	Total Pct. Chg.
City	781	469	-39.9	560	42	-92.5	1,341	511	-61.9
U.S.	1,378,200	973,300	-29.4	460,700	407,200	-11.6	1,838,900	1,380,500	-24.9

Note: (p) preliminary; figures cover and represent new, privately-owned housing units authorized (unadjusted data); All permit data are based on estimates with imputation; U.S. figures are based on the new 20,000-place series.
Source: U.S. Census Bureau, Manufacturing, Mining, and Construction Statistics

Homeownership and Housing Vacancies

Area	Homeownership Rate² (%)			Rental Vacancy Rate³ (%)			Homeowner Vacancy Rate⁴ (%)		
	2005	2006	2007	2005	2006	2007	2005	2006	2007
MSA[1]	63.9	66.7	66.4	9.4	7.2	6.8	2.4	1.5	1.5
U.S.	68.9	68.8	68.1	9.8	9.8	9.7	1.9	2.4	2.7

Note: (1) Metropolitan Statistical Area - see Appendix B for areas included; (2) The proportion of households that are owners; (3) The proportion of the rental inventory that is vacant for rent; (4) The proportion of the homeowner inventory that is vacant for sale; n/a not available
Source: U.S. Census Bureau, Housing Vacancies and Homeownership Annual Statistics: 2007

TAXES

State Corporate Income Tax Rates

State	Rates and Tax Brackets
Texas	1.0%

Note: Tax rates as of January 1, 2008; Texas's 1% franchise tax is a gross receipts tax paid by most taxable entities. Retailers pay 0.5%.
Source: Tax Foundation, www.taxfoundation.org

State Individual Income Tax Rates

State	Federal Deductibility	Marginal Rates (%)	Standard Deduction ($)		Personal Exemptions ($)[1]	
			Single	Joint	Single	Dependents
Texas	No	None	n/a	n/a	n/a	n/a

Note: Tax rates as of January 1, 2008; Local- and county-level taxes are not included; n/a not applicable; (1) Married joint filers generally receive double the single exemption
Source: Tax Foundation, www.taxfoundation.org

Various State and Local Tax Rates

State and Local Sales and Use (%)	State Sales and Use (%)	Gasoline[1,2] ($/gal.)	Cigarette ($/pack)	Spirits ($/gal.)	Table Wine ($/gal.)	Beer ($/gal.)
8.0	6.25 (i)	0.20	1.41	2.40	0.204	0.19

Note: Tax rates as of January 1, 2008; (1) In addition to the 18.4 cpg Federal gasoline tax; (2) Rates may include additional state sales taxes, environmental protection and storage fees/taxes, and local taxes. When necessary, the volume-weighted average of all local taxes is used to approximate the typical statewide rate including local tax; (i) Texas has a GRT that is levied in addition to its 6.25% sales tax. It is called the franchise tax and the rate is 1% (.5% for retailers).
Source: Tax Foundation, www.taxfoundation.org; Original research

State Tax Burdens

Area	Combined State and Local Tax Burden		Combined Federal, State and Local Tax Burden	
	Percent	Rank	Percent	Rank
Texas	9.3	43	29.8	41
U.S. Average	11.0	-	32.7	-

Note: Figures cover 2007 and measure taxes as a percentage of income
Source: Tax Foundation, www.taxfoundation.org

State Business Tax Climate Index Rankings

State	Overall Rank	Corporate Tax Index Rank	Individual Income Tax Index Rank	Sales Tax Index Rank	Unemployment Insurance Tax Index Rank	Property Tax Index Rank
Texas	8	47	7	28	14	27

Note: Rankings range from 1 to 50 where 1 is best. Rankings do not average across to Overall Rank. States without a given tax are given a ranking of 1.
Source: Tax Foundation, State Business Tax Climate Index 2008

TRANSPORTATION

Means of Transportation to Work

Area	Car/Truck/Van		Public Transportation			Bicycle	Walked	Other Means	Worked at Home
	Drove Alone	Car-pooled	Bus	Subway	Railroad				
City	85.9	9.6	0.1	0.1	0.0	0.0	0.5	0.8	3.0
MSA[1]	76.5	13.7	2.5	0.0	0.0	0.6	2.1	1.1	3.6
U.S.	75.7	12.2	2.5	1.5	0.5	0.4	2.9	1.0	3.3

Note: Figures are percentages and cover workers 16 years of age and older; (1) Metropolitan Statistical Area - see Appendix A for areas included
Source: Census 2000, Summary File 3

Travel Time to Work

Area	Less Than 15 Minutes	15 to 29 Minutes	30 to 44 Minutes	45 to 59 Minutes	60 Minutes or More
City	19.2	41.6	27.7	6.0	5.6
MSA[1]	24.5	38.6	22.5	8.3	6.1
U.S.	29.4	36.1	19.1	7.4	8.0

Note: Figures are percentages and include workers 16 years old and over; (1) Metropolitan Statistical Area - see Appendix A for areas included
Source: Census 2000, Summary File 3

Travel Time Index

Area	1982	1995	2004	2005
Urban Area[1]	1.07	1.18	1.29	1.31
Average[2]	1.11	1.22	1.29	1.30

Note: Travel Time Index - The ratio of travel time in the peak period to the travel time at free-flow conditions. A value of 1.35 indicates a 20-minute free-flow trip takes 27 minutes in the peak. Free-flow speeds (60 mph on freeways and 35 mph on principal arterials) are used as the comparison threshold; (1) Covers the Austin, TX urban area; (2) average of 85 urban areas
Source: Texas Transportation Institute, The 2007 Urban Mobility Report, September 2007

Living Environment

COST OF LIVING

Cost of Living Index

Composite Index	Groceries	Housing	Utilities	Trans-portation	Health Care	Misc. Goods/ Services
94.8	89.9	81.8	95.0	99.3	98.0	105.4

Note: U.S. = 100; Figures cover the Austin TX urban area.
Source: The Council for Community and Economic Research (formerly ACCRA), Cost of Living Index, 2007

Grocery Prices

Area[1]	T-Bone Steak ($/pound)	Frying Chicken ($/pound)	Whole Milk ($/half gal.)	Eggs ($/dozen)	Orange Juice ($/64 oz.)	Coffee ($/11.5 oz.)
City[2]	8.24	1.02	2.09	1.94	3.19	3.22
Avg.	8.93	1.12	2.13	1.52	3.26	3.31
Min.	5.88	0.71	1.33	0.83	2.30	2.20
Max.	12.80	2.07	3.43	3.54	5.79	6.20

Note: (1) Values for the local area are compared with the average, minimum and maximum values for all 331 areas in the Cost of Living Index report; (2) Figures cover the Austin TX urban area; **T-Bone Steak** *(price per pound);* **Frying Chicken** *(price per pound, whole fryer);* **Whole Milk** *(half gallon carton);* **Eggs** *(price per dozen, Grade A, large);* **Orange Juice** *(64 oz. Tropicana or Florida Natural);* **Coffee** *(11.5 oz. can, vacuum-packed, Maxwell House, Hills Bros, or Folgers).*
Source: The Council for Community and Economic Research (formerly ACCRA), Cost of Living Index, 2007

Housing and Utility Costs

Area[1]	New Home Price ($)	Apartment Rent ($/month)	All Electric ($/month)	Part Electric ($/month)	Other Energy ($/month)	Telephone ($/month)
City[2]	228,613	946	-	94.41	54.62	26.29
Avg.	309,605	782	146.13	78.67	90.16	26.14
Min.	189,877	n/a	82.03	37.41	33.15	17.08
Max.	1,202,800	3,481	271.14	150.60	257.67	37.45

Note: (1) Values for the local area are compared with the average, minimum and maximum values for all 331 areas in the Cost of Living Index report; (2) Figures cover the Austin TX urban area; **New Home Price** *(2,400 sf living area, 8,000 sf lot, in urban area with full utilities);* **Apartment Rent** *(950 sf 2 bedroom/1.5 or 2 bath, unfurnished, excluding all utilities except water);* **All Electric** *(average monthly cost for an all-electric home);* **Part Electric** *(average monthly cost for a part-electric home);* **Other Energy** *(average monthly cost for natural gas, fuel oil, coal, wood, and any other forms of energy except electricity);* **Telephone** *(price includes basic monthly rate for a private residential line plus additional local usage charges incurred by a family of four).*
Source: The Council for Community and Economic Research (formerly ACCRA), Cost of Living Index, 2007

Health Care, Transportation, and Other Costs

Area[1]	Doctor ($/visit)	Dentist ($/visit)	Optometrist ($/visit)	Gasoline ($/gallon)	Beauty Salon ($/visit)	Men's Shirt ($)
City[2]	68.27	74.11	78.25	2.59	55.00	25.94
Avg.	79.48	71.93	79.55	2.64	29.52	25.77
Min.	52.08	44.80	43.95	2.19	15.58	16.19
Max.	148.44	126.27	158.83	3.48	60.62	48.53

Note: (1) Values for the local area are compared with the average, minimum and maximum values for all 331 areas in the Cost of Living Index report; (2) Figures cover the Austin TX urban area; **Doctor** *(general practitioners routine exam of an established patient);* **Dentist** *(adult teeth cleaning and periodic oral examination);* **Optometrist** *(full vision eye exam for established adult patient);* **Gasoline** *(one gallon regular unleaded, national brand, including all taxes, cash price at self-service pump if available);* **Beauty Salon** *(woman's shampoo, trim, and blow-dry);* **Men's Shirt** *(cotton/polyester dress shirt, pinpoint weave, long sleeves).*
Source: The Council for Community and Economic Research (formerly ACCRA), Cost of Living Index, 2007

HOUSING

House Price Index (HPI)

Area	National Ranking[2]	Quarterly Change (%)	One-Year Change (%)	Five-Year Change (%)
MSA[1]	11	0.33	7.95	28.88
U.S.[3]	-	0.10	0.84	41.37

Note: The HPI is a weighted repeat sales index. It measures average price changes in repeat sales or refinancings on the same properties. This information is obtained by reviewing repeat mortgage transactions on single-family properties whose mortgages have been purchased or securitized by Fannie Mae or Freddie Mac in January 1975; (1) Metropolitan Statistical Area - see Appendix B for areas included; (2) Rankings are based on annual percentage change for all metro areas containing at least 15,000 transactions over the last 10 years and ranges from 1 to 291; (3) figures based on a weighted average of Census Division estimates; all figures are for the period ending December 31, 2007

Source: Office of Federal Housing Enterprise Oversight, House Price Index, February 26, 2008

House Price Valuations

Area	Q1 2000	Q1 2001	Q1 2002	Q1 2003	Q1 2004	Q1 2005	Q1 2006	Q1 2007	Q1 2008
MSA[1]	-20.3	-13.8	-7.0	-6.9	-10.0	-14.7	-13.1	-10.2	-10.9

Note: Figures show the percentage of over- or under-valuation of single family homes relative to statistically normal house values (e.g. a value of 23.6 indicates that house values are 23.6% overvalued). Statistically normal house values are based on house prices, interest rates, household incomes, population densities, and any historical premiums or discounts metropolitan areas have exhibited over time; (1) Figures cover the Metropolitan Statistical Area - see Appendix B for areas included

Source: Global Insight/National City Corporation, House Prices in America, May 2008

Median Home Prices

Area	2005	2006	2007[r]	Percent Change 2006 to 2007
MSA[1]	163.8	173.7	183.7	5.8
U.S. Average	219.0	221.9	217.9	-1.8

Note: Figures are median sales prices of existing single-family homes in thousands of dollars; (r) revised; n/a not available; (1) Metropolitan Statistical Area - see Appendix B for areas included

Source: National Association of Realtors, Metropolitan Area Prices, 1st Quarter 2008

Housing: Year Structure Built

Area	1990 -2000	1980 -1989	1970 -1979	1960 -1969	1950 -1959	1940 -1949	Before 1940	Median Year
City	63.1	27.7	5.4	2.1	0.2	0.7	0.8	1993
MSA[1]	30.2	27.4	20.2	8.8	6.2	3.3	3.9	1983
U.S.	17.0	15.8	18.5	13.7	12.7	7.3	15.0	1971

Note: Figures are percentages; (1) Metropolitan Statistical Area - see Appendix A for areas included

Source: Census 2000, Summary File 3

HEALTH

Health Risk Data

Category	Area[1] (%)	U.S. (%)
Adults who have been told they have high blood pressure[3]	14.7	25.5
Adults who have been told they have high blood cholesterol[3]	30.7	35.6
Adults who have been told they have diabetes[2]	6.7	7.5
Adults who have been told they have arthritis[3]	15.1	27.0
Adults who have been told they currently have asthma	7.1	8.5
Adults who are current smokers	19.2	20.1
Adults who are heavy drinkers[4]	5.2	4.9
Adults who are overweight (BMI 25.0 - 29.9)	35.1	36.5
Adults who are obese (BMI 30.0 - 99.8)	24.9	25.1

Note: Data as of 2006 unless otherwise noted; (1) Figures cover the Metropolitan Statistical Area - see Appendix B for areas included; (2) Figures do not include pregnancy-related diabetes, pre-diabetes or borderline diabetes; (3) 2005 data; (4) Heavy drinkers are classified as adult men having more than two drinks per day or adult women having more than one drink per day

Source: Centers for Disease Control and Prevention, Behaviorial Risk Factor Surveillance System, SMART: Selected Metropolitan/Micropolitan Area Risk Trends, 2005, 2006

Mortality Rates for the Top 10 Causes of Death in the U.S.

ICD-10[a] Sub-Chapter	ICD-10[a] Code	Age-Adjusted Mortality Rate[1] per 100,000 population	
		County[2]	U.S.
Malignant neoplasms	C00-C97	165.7	186.5
Ischaemic heart diseases	I20-I25	119.7	152.3
Other forms of heart disease	I30-I51	40.0	51.5
Cerebrovascular diseases	I60-I69	53.4	50.0
Chronic lower respiratory diseases	J40-J47	35.7	42.6
Diabetes mellitus	E10-E14	23.3	24.8
Other degenerative diseases of the nervous system	G30-G31	24.3	22.6
Other external causes of accidental injury	W00-X59	20.6	21.4
Influenza and pneumonia	J10-J18	12.9	20.7
Hypertensive diseases	I10-I13	16.3	18.2

Note: (a) ICD-10 = International Classification of Diseases 10th Revision; (1) Mortality rates are a three year average covering 2003-2005; (2) Figures cover Travis County
Source: Centers for Disease Control and Prevention, National Center for Health Statistics. Compressed Mortality File 1999-2004. CDC WONDER On-line Database, compiled from Compressed Mortality File 1999-2005 Series 20 No. 2K, 2008.

Mortality Rates for Selected Causes of Death

ICD-10[a] Sub-Chapter	ICD-10[a] Code	Age-Adjusted Mortality Rate[1] per 100,000 population	
		County[2]	U.S.
Assault	X85-Y09	3.2	5.9
Human immunodeficiency virus (HIV) disease	B20-B24	4.7	4.5
Intentional self-harm	X60-X84	12.0	10.8
Malnutrition	E40-E46	1.3	1.0
Obesity and other hyperalimentation	E65-E68	1.1	1.4
Organic, including symptomatic, mental disorders	F01-F09	31.6	16.8
Transport accidents	V01-V99	12.3	16.1
Viral hepatitis	B15-B19	1.7	1.8

Note: (a) ICD-10 = International Classification of Diseases 10th Revision; (1) Mortality rates are a three year average covering 2003-2005; (2) Figures cover Travis County
Source: Centers for Disease Control and Prevention, National Center for Health Statistics. Compressed Mortality File 1999-2004. CDC WONDER On-line Database, compiled from Compressed Mortality File 1999-2005 Series 20 No. 2K, 2008.

Distribution of Physicians[1]

Area	Total	Family/ General Practice	Specialties	
			Medical	Surgical
Travis County (number)	2,115	531	686	499
Travis County (rate per 10,000 pop.)	23.8	6.0	7.7	5.6
U.S. (rate per 10,000 pop.)	17.7	4.6	6.9	4.3

Note: Data as of 2005; (1) Includes all non-federal, patient-care, office-based MDs
Source: Area Resource File (ARF). June 2007. U.S. Department of Health and Human Services, Health Resources and Services Administration, Bureau of Health Professions, Rockville, MD.

Hospitals

There were no hospitals listed within the city limits.
AHA Guide to the Healthcare Field 2008

EDUCATION

Public School District Statistics

District Name	Schls	Pupils	Pupil/ Teacher Ratio	Minority Pupils[1] (%)	Free Lunch Eligible[2] (%)	IEP[3] (%)
Pflugerville Isd	27	18,761	16.0	64.9	29.1	10.4

Note: Table includes regular local school districts with 2,000 or more students; (1) Percentage of students that are not white, non-Hispanic; (2) Percentage of students that are eligible for the free lunch program; (3) Percentage of students that have an Individualized Education Program.
Source: U.S. Department of Education, National Center for Education Statistics, Common Core of Data, Local Education Agency (School District) Universe Survey: School Year 2005-2006; U.S. Department of Education, National Center for Education Statistics, Common Core of Data, Public Elementary/Secondary School Universe Survey: School Year 2005-2006

Highest Level of Education

Area	Less than H.S.	H.S. Diploma	Some College, No Deg.	Associate Degree	Bachelors Degree	Masters Degree	Profess. School Degree	Doctorate Degree
City	5.5	17.5	29.7	8.7	27.7	8.0	1.9	0.9
MSA[1]	14.9	20.1	23.0	5.6	24.3	8.2	2.1	1.7
U.S.	19.4	28.4	21.2	6.4	15.7	5.9	2.0	1.0

Note: Figures are 2007 estimated percentages and cover persons age 25 and over; (1) Metropolitan Statistical Area - see Appendix B for areas included
Source: Claritas, Inc.

Educational Attainment by Race

Area	High School Graduate (%)					Bachelor's Degree (%)				
	Total	White	Black	Asian	Hisp.[2]	Total	White	Black	Asian	Hisp.[2]
City	94.7	95.8	98.2	80.7	87.4	38.3	39.0	42.7	36.1	24.5
MSA[1]	84.8	89.7	80.0	88.5	58.6	36.7	41.1	20.1	62.2	14.7
U.S.	80.4	83.6	72.3	80.4	52.4	24.4	26.1	14.3	44.1	10.4

Note: Figures shown cover persons 25 years old and over; (1) Metropolitan Statistical Area - see Appendix A for areas included; (2) people of Hispanic origin can be of any race
Source: Census 2000, Summary File 3

School Enrollment by Type

Area	Grades KG to 8				Grades 9 to 12			
	Public		Private		Public		Private	
	Enrollment	%	Enrollment	%	Enrollment	%	Enrollment	%
City	2,990	93.8	196	6.2	946	99.3	7	0.7
MSA[1]	147,604	92.3	12,299	7.7	60,104	94.4	3,576	5.6
U.S.	33,526,011	88.7	4,285,121	11.3	14,848,628	90.6	1,532,323	9.4

Note: Figures shown cover persons 3 years old and over; (1) Metropolitan Statistical Area - see Appendix A for areas included
Source: Census 2000, Summary File 3

School Enrollment by Race

Area	Grades KG to 8 (%)				Grades 9 to 12 (%)			
	White	Black	Asian	Hisp.[1]	White	Black	Asian	Hisp.[1]
City	78.5	8.5	3.8	18.1	74.5	8.8	2.1	23.3
MSA[2]	66.6	9.5	2.7	34.2	67.3	10.3	2.5	31.0
U.S.	68.5	15.5	3.3	16.8	68.8	15.5	3.8	15.7

Note: Figures shown cover persons 3 years old and over; (1) people of Hispanic origin can be of any race; (2) Metropolitan Statistical Area - see Appendix A for areas included
Source: Census 2000, Summary File 3

Average Salaries of Public School Classroom Teachers

District	2005-06		2006-07		Percent Change 2005-06 to 2006-07
	Dollars	Rank[1]	Dollars	Rank[1]	
Texas	41,744	35	44,897	30	7.55
U.S. Average	49,026	-	50,816	-	3.65

Note: (1) State rank ranges from 1 to 51.
Source: National Education Association, Rankings & Estimates: Rankings of the States 2006 and Estimates of School Statistics 2007, December 2007

Higher Education

Four-Year Colleges			Two-Year Colleges			Medical Schools[1]	Law Schools[2]	Voc/ Tech[3]
Public	Private Non-profit	Private For-profit	Public	Private Non-profit	Private For-profit			
0	0	0	0	0	0	0	0	0

Note: Figures cover institutions located within the city limits; (1) includes schools accredited by the Liaison Committee on Medical Education and the American Osteopathic Association; (2) includes American Bar Association-accredited law schools; (3) includes all schools with programs that are less than 2 years.
Source: National Center for Education Statistics, The Integrated Postsecondary Education System (IPEDS) Peer Analysis System, 2007; www.usnews.com, Law and Medical School Directories, 2009

PRESIDENTIAL ELECTION

2004 Presidential Election Results

Area	Bush	Kerry	Nader	Other
Travis County	42.0	56.0	0.4	1.6
U.S.	50.7	48.3	0.4	0.6

Note: Results are percentages and may not add to 100% due to rounding
Source: Dave Leip's Atlas of U.S. Presidential Elections, www.uselectionatlas.org

EMPLOYERS

Major Employers

Company Name	Industry	Type of Site
3M	Paper; coated and laminated, nec	Branch
American Achievement Corp	Jewelry, precious metal	Headquarters
Attorney General Texas	General government, nec	Branch
Attorney General Texas	Legal counsel and prosecution	Branch
Austin Community College Dst	Junior colleges	Headquarters
Carter & Burgess Inc	Engineering services	Branch
Dell Inc	Electronic computers	Headquarters
Department Mechanical Engrg	Colleges and universities	Branch
Eltech	Electric lamps	Single
Environmental and Occupational	General government, nec	Branch
Gracywoods Nursing Center	Nursing and personal care, nec	Single
HR Trust LLC	Employment agencies	Single
Hospital Housekeeping Systems	Building maintenance services, nec	Single
IBM	Business services, nec	Branch
Long Term Care Regulatory Off	Administration of social & manpower programs	Branch
Motorola	Telephone and telegraph apparatus	Branch
Nextel	Radiotelephone communication	Single
Office of The Attorney General	Legal counsel and prosecution	Branch
State Farm Insurance	Fire, marine, and casualty insurance	Branch
TCEQ	Air, water, and solid waste management	Branch
TX Dept of Public Safety	Police protection	Headquarters
Texas Comm On Envmtl Qulty	Air, water, and solid waste management	Headquarters
Texas Highway Patrol	Police protection	Branch
Texas Lgislative Off The State	Legislative bodies	Headquarters
Texas State Unvrsty-San Marcos	Colleges and universities	Headquarters
Texas Workforce Commission	Regulation, miscellaneous commercial sectors	Headquarters
Workforce Commission Texas	Regulation, miscellaneous commercial sectors	Headquarters

Note: Companies shown are located within the Austin metropolitan area; nec = not elsewhere classified.
Source: www.zapdata.com, May 2008

PUBLIC SAFETY

Crime Rate

Area	All Crimes	Violent Crimes				Property Crimes		
		Murder	Forcible Rape	Robbery	Aggrav. Assault	Burglary	Larceny -Theft	Motor Vehicle Theft
City	2,409.0	0.0	49.5	31.8	67.1	480.4	1,706.1	74.2
Metro[1]	4,288.0	1.9	35.0	104.8	203.5	765.2	2,951.7	225.9
U.S.	3,808.1	5.7	30.9	149.4	287.5	729.4	2,206.8	398.4

Note: Figures are crimes per 100,000 population; (1) Metropolitan Statistical Area - see Appendix B for areas included
Source: FBI Uniform Crime Reports, 2006

Hate Crimes

Area	Number of Quarters Reported	Bias Motivation				
		Race	Religion	Sexual Orientation	Ethnicity	Disability
City	4	0	0	0	0	0

Source: Federal Bureau of Investigation, Hate Crime Statistics 2006

RECREATION

Culture

Dance[1]	Theatre[1]	Instrumental Music[1]	Vocal Music[1]	Series/ Festivals	Museums	Zoos and Aquariums[2]
0	0	0	0	0	0	0

Note: (1) Number of professional perfoming groups; (2) AZA-accredited
Source: The Grey House Performing Arts Directory, 2007; Official Museum Directory, 2008; Association of Zoos & Aquariums, AZA Member Zoos & Aquariums, June 2008

Professional Sports Teams

Team Name	League
No teams are located in the metro area	

Source: Original research

MEDIA

Newspapers

Name	News Focus	Frequency	Circulation
Pflugerville Pflag	Community	Weekly	4,000

Note: Includes newspapers with offices located in the city
Source: MediaContactsPro, March 2008

Television Stations

Name	Ch.	Network(s)	Type	Ownership
KTBC	7	Fox	Commercial	Fox Television Stations Inc.
KXAM	14	NBC	Commercial	n/a
KLRU	18	PBS	Public	Capital of Texas Public Telecommunications
KVUE	24	ABC	Commercial	Belo Corporation
KXAN	36	NBC	Commercial	Lin Broadcasting
KEYE	42	CBS	Commercial	CBS Broadcasting Company
KNVA	54	WBN	Commercial	54 Broadcasting Inc.

Note: Stations included cover the Austin DMA (Designated Market Area)
BurrellesLuce, MediaContacts Online, January 2007

Major AM Radio Stations

Call Letters	Freq. (kHz)	Station Type	Target Audience	Station Format	Music Format
KLBJ	590	n/a	General	News/Sports/Talk	n/a
KNAF	910	Commercial	General	Music/News	Country
KIXL	970	n/a	General/Religious	Talk	n/a
KFIT	1060	Commercial	Black/General/Hisp	Educational/Music	Gospel
KVET	1300	Commercial	General	Music	Country
KHLB	1340	Commercial	General	Music/News/Sports/Talk	Country
KJCE	1370	Commercial	General	News/Sports/Talk	n/a
KFON	1490	Commercial	General	Music	Latin
KQQA	1530	Commercial	General/Hispanic	Music	Latin
KTXZ	1560	Commercial	General/Hispanic	Music/News/Sports	Latin
KVLG	1570	Commercial	General	Music/News	Latin

Note: Stations included cover the Austin DMA (Designated Market Area); n/a not available
Source: BurrellesLuce, MediaContacts Online, January 2007

Major FM Radio Stations

Call Letters	Freq. (mHz)	Station Type	Target Audience	Station Format	Music Format
KNLE	88.1	Non-Comm	General	Music	Christian
KMFA	89.5	Non-Comm	General	Music	Classical
KUTX	90.1	College	General	Ed/Music/News/Talk	Top 40
KUT	90.5	College	General	Educational/Music/News	Top 40
KKLB	92.5	Commercial	General/Hispanic	Music	Latin
KLBJ	93.7	Commercial	General	Music/News/Sports	Album Rock
KAMX	94.7	n/a	General	n/a	n/a
KKMJ	95.5	n/a	General	Music	n/a
KHFI	96.7	Commercial	General	Music/News/Talk	Top 40
KVET	98.1	Commercial	General	Music/News	Country
KHHL	98.9	Commercial	Hispanic	Music	Latin
KASE	100.7	Commercial	General	Music/News/Talk	Contemp. Country
KROX	101.5	n/a	General/Young Adult	Music/Talk	n/a
KPEZ	102.3	Commercial	General	Music/News	Classic Rock
KEYI	103.5	Commercial	General	Music/News	Oldies
KQBT	104.3	Commercial	General	Music/News/Sports/Talk	Urban Contemp.
KHLB	106.9	Commercial	General	Music/News	Country
KGSR	107.1	n/a	General	Music	n/a
KFAN	107.9	Commercial	General	Music/News	Folk

Note: Stations included cover the Austin DMA (Designated Market Area); n/a not available
BurrellesLuce, MediaContacts Online, January 2007

CLIMATE

Average and Extreme Temperatures

Temperature	Jan	Feb	Mar	Apr	May	Jun	Jul	Aug	Sep	Oct	Nov	Dec	Yr.
Extreme High (°F)	90	97	98	98	100	105	109	106	104	98	91	90	109
Average High (°F)	60	64	72	79	85	91	95	96	90	81	70	63	79
Average Temp. (°F)	50	53	61	69	75	82	85	85	80	70	60	52	69
Average Low (°F)	39	43	50	58	65	72	74	74	69	59	49	41	58
Extreme Low (°F)	-2	7	18	35	43	53	64	61	47	32	20	4	-2

Note: Figures cover the years 1948-1990
Source: National Climatic Data Center, International Station Meteorological Climate Summary, 9/96

Average Precipitation/Snowfall/Humidity

Precip./Humidity	Jan	Feb	Mar	Apr	May	Jun	Jul	Aug	Sep	Oct	Nov	Dec	Yr.
Avg. Precip. (in.)	1.6	2.3	1.8	2.9	4.3	3.5	1.9	1.9	3.3	3.5	2.1	1.9	31.1
Avg. Snowfall (in.)	1	Tr	Tr	0	0	0	0	0	0	0	Tr	Tr	1
Avg. Rel. Hum. 6am (%)	79	80	79	83	88	89	88	87	86	84	81	79	84
Avg. Rel. Hum. 3pm (%)	53	51	47	50	53	49	43	42	47	47	49	51	48

Note: Figures cover the years 1948-1990; Tr = Trace amounts (<0.05 in. of rain; <0.5 in. of snow)
Source: National Climatic Data Center, International Station Meteorological Climate Summary, 9/96

Weather Conditions

Temperature			Daytime Sky			Precipitation		
10°F & below	32°F & below	90°F & above	Clear	Partly cloudy	Cloudy	0.01 inch or more precip.	0.1 inch or more snow/ice	Thunder-storms
< 1	20	111	105	148	112	83	1	41

Note: Figures are average number of days per year and cover the years 1948-1990
Source: National Climatic Data Center, International Station Meteorological Climate Summary, 9/96

HAZARDOUS WASTE

Superfund Sites

Pflugerville has no sites on the EPA's Superfund Final National Priorities List.
U.S. Environmental Protection Agency, Final National Priorities List, June 23, 2008

AIR & WATER QUALITY

Air Quality Index

Area	Percent of Days when Air Quality was...[2]				AQI Statistics	
	Good	Moderate	Unhealthy for Sensitive Groups	Unhealthy	Maximum	Median
MSA[1]	81.1	17.8	1.1	0.0	145	36

Note: The Air Quality Index (AQI) is an index for reporting daily air quality. EPA calculates the AQI for five major air pollutants regulated by the Clean Air Act: ground-level ozone, particle pollution (also known as particulate matter), carbon monoxide, sulfur dioxide, and nitrogen dioxide. The AQI runs from 0 to 500. The higher the AQI value, the greater the level of air pollution and the greater the health concern. There are six AQI categories: "Good" The AQI is between 0 and 50. Air quality is considered satisfactory; "Moderate" The AQI is between 51 and 100. Air quality is acceptable; "Unhealthy for Sensitive Groups" When AQI values are between 101 and 150, members of sensitive groups may experience health effects; "Unhealthy" When AQI values are between 151 and 200 everyone may begin to experience health effects; "Very Unhealthy" AQI values between 201 and 300 trigger a health alert; "Hazardous" AQI values over 300 trigger health warnings of emergency conditions; (1) Metropolitan Statistical Area - see Appendix A for areas included; (2) Based on 365 days with AQI data in 2007.
Source: U.S. Environmental Protection Agency, Air Quality Index Report, 2007

Air Quality Index Pollutants

Area	Percent of Days when AQI Pollutant was...[2]					
	Carbon Monoxide	Nitrogen Dioxide	Ozone	Sulfur Dioxide	Particulate Matter 2.5	Particulate Matter 10
MSA[1]	0.0	0.0	63.6	0.0	36.2	0.3

Note: The Air Quality Index (AQI) is an index for reporting daily air quality. EPA calculates the AQI for five major air pollutants regulated by the Clean Air Act: ground-level ozone, particle pollution (also known as particulate matter), carbon monoxide, sulfur dioxide, and nitrogen dioxide. The AQI runs from 0 to 500. The higher the AQI value, the greater the level of air pollution and the greater the health concern; (1) Metropolitan Statistical Area - see Appendix A for areas included; (2) Based on 365 days with AQI data in 2007.
Source: U.S. Environmental Protection Agency, Air Quality Index Report, 2007

Air Quality Index Trends

Area	Trend Sites (1)								All Sites (21)
	1999	2000	2001	2002	2003	2004	2005	2006	2006
MSA[1]	8	6	0	5	3	2	1	3	4

Note: An AQI value greater than 100 indicates that air quality would have been in the unhealthful range on that day. Data from exceptional events are not included. These counts are presented in two ways. First, the counts are based on sites having an adequate record of monitoring data during the trend period (trend sites). These counts represent the relative change in the number of days with AQI values greater than 100. In the last column, the counts are based on all sites with data in the most recent year (because it is possible for a site to have data in the most recent year but not enough data to be a trend site); (1) Metropolitan Statistical Area - see Appendix A for areas included.
Source: U.S. Environmental Protection Agency, Office of Air and Radiation, Air Trends, Factbook and Related Information, Air Pollution Trends in Selected Metropolitan Areas 2006

Maximum Air Pollutant Concentrations

	Particulate Matter 10 (ug/m^3)	Particulate Matter 2.5 (ug/m^3)	Ozone (ppm)	Carbon Monoxide (ppm)	Sulfur Dioxide (ppm)	Nitrogen Dioxide (ppm)	Lead (ug/m^3)
MSA[1] Level	32	n/a	0.099	1	n/a	0.004	n/a
NAAQS[2]	150	35	0.125	9	0.140	0.053	1.50
Met NAAQS[2]	Yes	Yes	Yes	Yes	n/a	Yes	n/a

Note: Data from exceptional events are not included; (1) Metropolitan Statistical Area - see Appendix A for areas included; (2) National Ambient Air Quality Standards; n/a not available
Concentrations: Particulate Matter 10 (coarse particulate) - highest second maximum 24-hour concentration; Particulate Matter 2.5 (fine particulate) - highest 98th percentile 24-hour concentration; Ozone - highest second daily maximum 1-hour concentration; Carbon Monoxide - highest second maximum non-overlapping 8-hour concentration; Sulfur Dioxide - highest second maximum 24-hour concentration; Nitrogen Dioxide - highest arithmetic mean concentration; Lead - highest quarterly maximum concentration
Units: ppm = parts per million; ug/m^3 = micrograms per cubic meter
Source: U.S. Environmental Protection Agency, MSA Factbook 2006, Air Quality Statistics by City

Drinking Water

Water System Name	Pop. Served	Primary Water Source Type	Violations[1]	
			Health Based	Monitoring/ Reporting
City of Pflugerville	14,460	Surface	0	2

Note: (1) Based on violation data from January 1, 2007 to December 31, 2007 (includes unresolved violations from earlier years)
Source: U.S. Environmental Protection Agency, Office of Ground Water and Drinking Water, Safe Drinking Water Information System (based on data extracted April 15, 2008)

Round Rock, Texas

Background

The city of Round Rock is located in Travis and Williamson counties, 15 miles north of Austin on Interstate 35. Round Rock offers excellent employment opportunities, easy access to local colleges and universities, and Blue Ribbon public schools. High-profile companies that call the city home include Dell, Inc., TECO/Westinghouse, and DuPont Photomasks.

The earliest residents of the Round Rock area were the Tonkawa Indians, who were eventually driven to extinction by both the Comanches and the white settlers moving west. In 1850, newcomers from the East seeking land established a settlement called Brushy, located near the banks of Brushy Creek at the natural fording area created by the large, "round rock" in the creek bed. The settlement flourished until 1876, when the International and Great Northern Railroad forced the commercial area of Round Rock, as it was now known, to move to the east. The original settlement of Brushy, still part of Round Rock, came to be known as Old Town.

As "New Town" developed, it became the predominant section until recently, when the city began reinvesting in Old Town. New Town, however, has remained a viable business district, and its Old West flavor has contributed to its designation as a commercial historic district.

There are three major historical sections in Round Rock. Historic Downtown is a two-block area with restored buildings dating back to the 1880s. The Chisholm Trail includes the old stagecoach stop, an old cantina and other historic buildings, and wagon wheel ruts imbedded in the limestone surrounding Brushy Creek. The third historic site is Palm Valley Church, which marks an early Swedish settlement.

The Round Rock Independent School District is highly rated. Many of the town's schools have been recognized as National Blue Ribbon schools and/or Texas Blue Ribbon schools, and the district as a whole was recently recognized as one of the top mid-sized metropolitan districts in the country.

Higher learning in the Austin metropolitan area is represented by seven colleges and universities, including the University of Texas at Austin, the largest public university in the United States, with almost 50,000 students; Southwestern University; Concordia University; and Austin Community College, focusing on high-tech job training.

For entertainment, Palm Valley Park offers monthly festivals and sports activities. For boating and swimming, Round Rock residents are within 15 minutes of Lake Austin, Lake Georgetown, and Lake Granger. Other attractions include a roller rink, an ice-skating rink, and a golf course in the city, with six other golf courses within a 20-mile radius.

The climate of Round Rock is subtropical with hot summers. Winters are mild, with below-freezing temperatures occurring on an average of 25 days a year. Cold spells are short, seldom lasting more than two days. Daytime temperatures in summer are hot, while summer nights are usually pleasant.

Rankings

General Rankings

- Austin* was ranked #103 out of 375 metro areas in *Cities Ranked & Rated*. Criteria: cost of living; climate; crime; transportation; economy and jobs; education; arts and culture; health and healthcare; leisure; quality of life. *Cities Ranked & Rated, 2nd Edition, 2007*
- Austin* was ranked #35 out of 379 metro areas in *Places Rated Almanac*. Criteria: health care; education; recreation; transportation; ambience; climate; crime; housing costs; jobs. *Places Rated Almanac, 7th Edition, 2007*
- The Austin* metro area was selected one of America's "Best Cities to Live, Work and Play" by *Kiplinger Personal Finance*. Criteria: population growth; percentage of workforce in the creative class (scientists, engineers, educators, writers, artists, entertainers, etc.); job quality; income growth; cost of living. *Kiplinger Personal Finance, "Best Cities to Live, Work and Play," July 2008*
- *Expansion Management* rated 362 metro areas to find out which offer the best middle class lifestyle for manufacturing and service companies. The Austin* metro area was selected as a "5-Star Quality of Life Metro" (a distinction the magazine awards to the top 20 percent of metro areas studied). The annual "Quality of Life Quotient" measures dozens of indicators across nine major categories and compares them among 362 metropolitan statistical areas in the United States. The categories are: affordable housing; good public schools; low crime levels; adult education level; standard of living; traffic and commuting; continuing education opportunities; commercial air access; labor market. *Expansion Management, June 2007*
- Round Rock was selected as one of the "2006 Best Places to Live" by *Money* magazine. Places were ranked using 38 quality-of-life indicators and six economic opportunity measures in the following categories: ease of living; health; education; crime; park space; arts and leisure. *CNNMoney.com, "Best Places to Live 2006"*

Business/Finance Rankings

- The nation's 100 largest metro areas were analysed in terms of the percentage of households entering some stage of foreclosure in 2007. The Austin* metro area ranked #58 out of 100 (#1 = highest foreclosure rate). *RealtyTrac, "Year-End 2007 Metropolitan Foreclosure Report"*
- The Austin* metro area was identified as one of the "10 Best Cities for Jobs in 2008" by *Forbes*. The metro area ranked #3. Criteria: state unemployment rate; job growth; income growth; median household income; cost of living. *Forbes.com, "Best Cities for Jobs in 2008," January 10, 2008*
- The Austin* metro area was identified as one of the "Top 12 Nano Metros" in the U.S. by the Woodrow Wilson International Center for Scholars. The metro area is home to 18 companies, universities, government laboratories and/or organizations working in nanotechnology. *Woodrow Wilson International Center for Scholars, May 17, 2007*
- The Austin* metro area was selected one of America's "Top 50 Business Opportunity Metros" by *Expansion Management* in their 5th annual Mayor's Challenge ranking of metro areas that have achieved solid ratings across the board in numerous *EM* studies during the past 12 months. The area ranked #1. Criteria: public schools; quality of life; college educated workers; logistics infrastructure; healthcare costs; taxes and government spending; reputation among site consultants. *Expansion Management, August 2007*
- Austin* was selected as one of the best places to start and grow a company by *Entrepreneur* and the National Policy Research Council. The Austin* metro area ranked #5 out of 50 large metro areas. Criteria: business formation and growth (firms started four to 14 years ago that still employ at least 5 people and experienced rapid growth over the last four years). *Entrepreneur/National Policy Research Council, "Hot Cities for Entrepreneurs," September 2006*

- The Austin* metro area was selected as one of "America's 50 Hottest Cities" for business relocations and expansions. Criteria: industry's most prominent site selection consultants were asked to list their top city choices for relocating and expanding manufacturing companies, taking into consideration such factors as the business climate, work force quality, operating costs, incentive programs, and the ease of working with local political and economic development officials. *Expansion Management, January-February 2007*

- Intel, in partnership with Sperling's BestPlaces, ranked the 80 "Best Cities for Teleworking" in America. The Austin* metro area ranked #4 among mid-sized metro areas. The study identifies cities that hold the greatest potential for teleworking based on a host of factors including typical commuting times, fuel prices, availability of broadband Internet access and percentage of the population in telework friendly jobs. The study also factored in extreme climate and natural hazards. *Intel, "Best Cities for Teleworking," March 30, 2006*

- The Austin* metro area was identified as one of the "25 Hottest Housing Markets" in the U.S. The area ranked #4 out of 156 markets with a home price appreciation rate of 6.4%. Criteria: year-over-year change of median sales price of existing single-family homes between the 4th quarter of 2006 and the 4th quarter of 2007. *National Association of Realtors, Median Sales Price of Existing Single-Family Homes for Metropolitan Areas, 4th Quarter 2007*

- The Austin* metro area appeared on the Milken Institute "2007 Best Performing Cities" index. Rank: #20 out of 200 large metro areas. Criteria: job growth; wage and salary growth; high-tech output growth. *Milken Institute, "2007 Best Performing Cities"*

- The Austin* metro area was selected as one of the hottest cities for entrepreneurs in America by *Inc. Magazine.* Criteria: job-growth data for 393 metro was analyzed for current-year employment growth, average annual employment growth over past three years, and employment growth by industry sector. The Austin* metro area ranked #16 among large metro areas and #110 overall. *Inc. Magazine, May 2007*

- The Austin* metro area was selected as one of "The Top 20 Boom Towns in America." *Business 2.0* magazine and econometric research firm Global Insight compared 319 metropolitan areas in the U.S. and ranked the 61 with populations over 1 million. Criteria: a weighted formula that includes forecast growth rates in sectors that contain the economy's 10 most skilled occupational clusters; the prevalence of college degrees in the local workforce; median salary. The area ranked #4 among large metro areas. *Business 2.0 Magazine, March 2004*

- Austin* was identified as one of the 100 "Most Unwired Cities" in the U.S. The area ranked #3 out of the 100 largest metro areas in the U.S. Criteria: number of public and commercial wireless access points (hotspots); airports with wireless Internet access; broadband availability; local wireless networks; and wireless email devices. *Intel, "Most Unwired Cities Survey," June 7, 2005*

- Austin* was ranked #19 out of 125 regions worldwide in terms of its "Knowledge Competitiveness Index." The index attempts to measure the knowledge-based development taking place throughout the world and is based on 19 measures of economic performance that indicate a region's ability to translate its knowledge capacity into economic value. *Robert Huggins Associates, World Knowledge Competitiveness Index 2005*

- *Forbes* ranked the 200 most populous metro areas in the U.S. in terms of the "Best Places for Business and Careers." The Austin* metro area was ranked #47. Criteria: business costs (labor, energy, tax and office space expenses); living costs (housing, transportation, food and other household expenditures); education levels of the work force; job growth; income growth; migration trends; crime rates; and culture/leisure. *Forbes, "Best Places for Business and Careers," March 19, 2008*

- Austin* was identified as one of the top 20 metro areas with the highest rate of house price appreciation in 2007. The area ranked #11 with a one-year price appreciation of 8.0% through the 4th quarter 2007. *Office of Federal Housing Enterprise Oversight, House Price Index, 4th Quarter 2007*

- *Fortune* ranked the 100 largest metro areas in the U.S. in terms of projected median home price change in 2007. The Austin* metro area ranked #12. *Fortune.com, "Hot Spots, Cold Spots"*

Health/Environment Rankings

- 100 of the largest metro areas in the U.S. were analyzed in terms of their current drought severity. The Austin* metro area ranked #98 (#1 = driest). The rankings were based on statistics such as long-term precipitation trends and patterns and the Palmer drought indices. *Sperling's BestPlaces, www.BestPlaces.net, "America's Drought-Riskiest Cities," November 2007*

- Scarborough Research, a leading market research firm, identified the top local markets for organic consumers. The Austin* DMA (Designated Market Area) ranked in the top 15 with 23% of adults reporting that they used any organic food product in their household during the past month. *Scarborough Research, October 10, 2007*

- *Reader's Digest* ranked the 50 largest metro areas in the U.S. in terms of how "clean" they are. The Austin* metro area ranked #8. Criteria: air quality; water quality; toxic industrial pollution; Superfund sites; and sanitation. *Reader's Digest, "The 50 Cleanest (and Dirtiest) Cities in America," July 2005*

- The Austin* metro area was identified as one of "America's Most Obese Cities" by *Forbes*. The magazine analyzed BMI (body mass index) data from the CDC in the 50 most populated metro areas in the U.S. and ranked the top 20. The area ranked #18. *Forbes, "America's Most Obese Cities," November 26, 2007*

- The Austin* metro area appeared in *Country Home's* "2008 Best Green Places" report. The area ranked #33 out of 379. Criteria: official energy policies; green power; green buildings; availability of fresh, locally grown food. *Country Home, "2008 Best Green Places"*

- Wyeth Consumer Healthcare, in partnership with Sperling's BestPlaces, ranked the nation's 50 most populous metro areas in terms of five key health factors. The Austin* metro area ranked #10. Criteria: physical activity; health status; nutrition; lifestyle pursuits; and mental wellness. *Wyeth Consumer Healthcare, "Centrum Healthiest Cities Study," April 19, 2005*

- Austin* was identified as a "2008 Asthma Capital." The area ranked #67 out of the nation's 100 largest metropolitan areas. Twelve factors were used to identify the most challenging places to live for people with asthma: estimated prevalence; self-reported prevalence; crude death rate for asthma; annual pollen score; annual air quality; public smoking laws; number of board-certified asthma specialists; school inhaler access laws; rescue medication use; controller medication use; uninsured rate; poverty rate. *Asthma and Allergy Foundation of America, "2008 Asthma Capitals"*

- Austin* was identified as a "Spring Allergy Capital." The area ranked #24 out of 100. Three groups of factors were used to identify the most severe cities for people with allergies during the spring season: annual pollen levels; medicine utilization; access to board-certified allergists. *Asthma and Allergy Foundation of America, "2007 Spring Allergy Capital Rankings"*

- Austin* was identified as a "Fall Allergy Capital." The area ranked #1 out of 100. Three groups of factors were used to identify the most severe cities for people with allergies during the fall season: annual pollen levels; medicine utilization; access to board-certified allergists. *Asthma and Allergy Foundation of America, "2007 Fall Allergy Capital Rankings"*

- Ortho-McNeil Neurologics, in partnership with Sperling's BestPlaces, analyzed 110 metro areas and identified those U.S. cities with the highest prevalence of factors that are most commonly associated with migraine headaches. The Austin* metro area ranked #65. Criteria: number of migraine-related drug prescriptions per capita; lifestyle factors that can contribute to migraines; environmental factors that can trigger migraines; and consumption of migraine-triggering foods. *Ortho-McNeil Neurologics, "America's Migraine Hot Spots," March 14, 2006*

- Sperling's BestPlaces ranked 331 metro areas and identified the most and least stressful U.S. cities. The Austin* metro area ranked #60 out of the 100 largest metro areas (#1 = most stressful). Criteria: divorce rate; unemployment rate; violent and property crime; suicide rate; commute time; mental health; alcohol consumption; cloudy days. *Sperling's BestPlaces, www.BestPlaces.net, "America's Most (and Least) Stressful Cities," January 9, 2004*

- An analysis of the "Best & Worst Cities for Sleep" was conducted by Sperling's BestPlaces. The study ranked America's 50 most populated metro areas. The Austin* metro area ranked #14 (#1 = best city for sleep). Criteria: number of days residents didn't get enough rest or sleep during the past month; average length of daily commute; divorce rate; unemployment rate. *Sperling's BestPlaces, www.BestPlaces.net, "Best & Worst Cities for Sleep," 2006*

Women/Minorities Rankings

- Austin* was ranked #48 out of 100 metro areas in *SELF Magazine's* ranking of "America's Best Places for Women." A panel of experts came up with more than 50 criteria including death and disease rates, environmental indicators, community resources, and lifestyle habits. *SELF Magazine, "America's Best Places for Women 2007," December 2007*

- Austin* appeared on a list of the top 10 metro areas with the highest concentration of same-sex households. The area ranked #5. *Urban Institute Press, The Gay and Lesbian Atlas, May 2004*

Seniors/Retirement Rankings

- Sperling's BestPlaces in partnership with Bankers Life & Casualty Company designed a survey to identify the top 50 metro areas in the U.S. that offer the best overall qualities for senior living. The Austin* metro area ranked #27. The following criteria were statistically weighted to reflect the needs of the senior population: health; disease; economics; social; environment; spiritual; transportation; housing; and crime. *Bankers Life & Casualty Company, "Best Cities for Seniors 2005"*

- A.G. Edwards ranked America's 500 top-performing communities based on their residents' personal savings and investing behavior. The Austin* metro area ranked #395 with an index score of 97.15 (national average = 100.00). A dozen statistical factors were measured including: participation in retirement savings plans; personal debt levels; and home ownership. *A.G. Edwards, "2007 Nest Egg Index", September 12, 2007*

Children/Family Rankings

- The Austin* metro area was selected as one of the "Best Cities for Relocating Families" by Worldwide ERC and Primacy Relocation. The 2007 study placed a special emphasis on the housing market, which has significantly impacted the relocation industry and an employer's ability to transfer employees. The variables which weigh heavily in this category include home price, home affordability index, appreciation rates, and property tax. Other criteria include cost of living, crime rates, education, climate, focus on diversity, physicians per capita, recreation and leisure, arts and culture, air quality, watershed quality, sales tax, unemployment rate, job growth, high school and higher education index, school expenditures per student, students in public school, SAT/ACT percentile, and population growth. *Worldwide ERC and Primacy Relocation, "2007 Best Cities for Relocating Families"*

Safety Rankings

- The National Insurance Crime Bureau ranked 361 metro areas in the U.S. in terms of per capita rates of vehicle theft. The Austin* metro area ranked #161 (#1 = highest rate). Criteria: number of vehicle theft offenses per 100,000 inhabitants. *National Insurance Crime Bureau, "NICB Vehicle Theft Study," April 22, 2008*

- Austin* appeared on Sperling's BestPlaces list of the "Riskiest Cities for Identity Theft." The area ranked #18 out of the nations 50 largest metro areas. Over 80 criteria were analyzed across four major categories: technology impact; crime; transactions; and risk profile. *Sperling's BestPlaces, www.BestPlaces.net, "Riskiest Cities for Identity Theft," July 2006*

- Farmers Insurance Group of Companies, in partnership with Sperling's BestPlaces, ranked 379 metro areas and identified the "Most Secure U.S. Place to Live." The Austin* metro area ranked #31 out of 114 in the large metro area category (500,000 or more residents). Criteria: crime rates; extreme weather; risk of natural disasters; environmental hazards; terrorism threats; air quality; life expectancy; job loss numbers. *Farmers Insurance Group, "Most Secure U.S. Places to Live 2007"*

- Austin* was identified as one of the most dangerous large metro areas for pedestrians in the U.S. The area ranked #30 out of the nations 50 largest metro areas. Criteria: average yearly pedestrian fatalities per capita (for the years 2002 and 2003) adjusted for the number of walkers. *Surface Transportation Policy Project, "Mean Streets 2004"*
- Round Rock was identified as one of the safest cities in America by Morgan Quitno. All 371 cities with populations over 75,000 that reported crime rates in 2006 for murder, rape, robbery, aggravated assault, burglary, and motor vehicle thefts were ranked. The city ranked #13 out of the top 25. *www.morganquitno.com, 14th Annual America's Safest (and Most Dangerous) Cities Awards*
- Round Rock was identified as one of the safest smaller cities in America by Morgan Quitno. All 129 cities with populations of 75,000 to 99,999 that reported crime rates in 2006 for murder, rape, robbery, aggravated assault, burglary, and motor vehicle thefts were ranked. The city ranked #10 out of the top 10. *www.morganquitno.com, 14th Annual America's Safest (and Most Dangerous) Cities Awards*

Sports/Recreation Rankings

- The Austin* metro area appeared on the *Sporting News* list of the "Best Sports Cities 2007". The area ranked #57 out of 150 cities in the U.S. *Sporting News* takes a 12-month snapshot, roughly July to July, of each city's sports, putting a heavy premium on regular-season won-lost records (from the most recently completed season). Other criteria include: playoff berths, bowl appearances and tournament bids; championships; applicable power ratings; quality of competition; overall fan fervor as measured in part by attendance as percentage of venue capacity; abundance of teams (rewarding quality over quantity); stadium and arena quality; ticket availability and prices; franchise ownership; and marquee appeal of athletes. *SportingNews.com, "Best Sports Cities 2007," August 1, 2007*
- The Austin* metro area was selected by *Cranium* as one of the "Top 50 Fun Cities" in America. The area ranked #44. Criteria includes: number of sports teams, restaurants, and dance performances; number of toy stores; city budget spent on recreation. *Cranium, November 4, 2003*
- *Golf Digest* ranked 330 metro areas in the U.S. in terms of golf. The Austin* metro area was ranked #241. Criteria: access to golf; weather; value of golf; and quality of golf. *Golf Digest, "Metro Golf Rankings," August 2005*

Dating/Romance Rankings

- Eli Lily and Company, in partnership with Sperling's BestPlaces, ranked the nation's 50 largest metro areas in terms of the "Most Romantic Cities for Baby Boomers." The Austin* metro area ranked #32. Criteria: marriage and divorce rates among "baby boomers" age 45 to 60; great restaurants; dance studios; chocolate, jewelry and flower sales. *Eli Lily and Company, "Most Romantic Cities for Baby Boomers," April 20, 2007*
- The Austin* metro area was selected as one of the "Best Cities for Relocating Singles" by Worldwide ERC and Primacy Relocation. The area ranked #8 out of the 100 largest metro areas in the U.S. Areas were selected based on the following criteria: a robust cost-of-living index; adventure and outdoor recreation opportunities; violent crime and property crime rates; percentage of the population that is unmarried (ages 25-34); ratio of single men and single women; affordability of quality higher education, including in-state and out-of-state tuition requirements and rates; number of newcomers to the area; commute times; tax rates; fee and occupancy rates for temporary housing and mini-storage; quality and quantity of collegiate and professional sporting events and fun, fan-friendly venues. *Worldwide ERC and Primacy Relocation, "2007 Best Cities for Relocating Singles," October 25, 2007*
- *Forbes* ranked the 40 most populous urbanized areas in the U.S. in terms of the "Best Cities for Singles." The Austin* metro area ranked #12. Criteria: number of singles; cost of living alone; nightlife; culture; job growth; coolness; and online dating. *Forbes.com, August 21, 2007*

- Sperling's BestPlaces in partnership with AXE Deodorant Bodyspray ranked 80 metro areas and identified "America's Best (and Worst) Cities for Dating." The Austin* metro area ranked #1 (#1 = best). Criteria: percentage of singles ages 18-24; population density; dating venues per capita. *AXE Deodorant Bodyspray, "America's Best (and Worst) Cities for Dating," May 2004*

Culture/Performing Arts Rankings

- Scarborough Research, a leading market research firm, identified the top local markets for rock concert attendance. The Austin* DMA (Designated Market Area) ranked in the top 25 with 18% of consumers, 18 years old and over, reporting that they have attended a rock concert during the past year. *Scarborough Research, June 14, 2004*

Miscellaneous Rankings

- Scarborough Research, a leading market research firm, identified the top local markets for bloggers. The Austin* DMA (Designated Market Area) ranked in the top 13 with 15% of adults reporting that they had read or contributed to a blog within the past 30 days. *Scarborough Research, October 24, 2007*
- Round Rock was identified as one of the 100 fastest-growing suburbs in America by "Forbes." The city ranked #49. Criteria: suburban cities, townships and villages with more than 10,000 people in 2000 were ranked by their population growth from 2000 to 2006. *Forbes.com, "America's Fastest-Growing Suburbs," July 16, 2007*
- The Austin* metro area appeared on *Forbes* list of "America's Drunkest Cities". The area ranked #5. Criteria: 35 of the largest continental U.S. metro areas were chosen based on availability of data and geographic diversity. Each metro was ranked in five areas: state laws; drinkers; heavy drinkers; binge drinkers; and alcoholism. *Forbes.com, "America's Drunkest Cities," August 22, 2006*
- Sperling's BestPlaces in partnership with Pep Boys ranked 77 metro areas and identified "America's Most Drivable Cities." The Austin* metro area ranked #25. Criteria: climate; road roughness; urban mobility; gas prices. *Pep Boys, "America's Most Drivable Cities," April 9, 2003*
- State Farm Insurance, in partnership with Sperling's BestPlaces, analyzed several key factors that contribute to overall family preparedness. The Austin* metro area ranked #32 out of the nation's 50 most populous metro areas. Criteria: quality of life; life insurance coverage; and investments. *State Farm Life Insurance, "Fiscally Fit Cities Report," July 20, 2004*
- Scarborough Research, a leading market research firm, identified the top local markets for gift card purchasers. The Austin* DMA (Designated Market Area) ranked in the top 10 with 54% of consumers reporting that they purchased a gift card within the past 12 months. *Scarborough Research, November 15, 2006*
- Scarborough Research, a leading market research firm, identified the top local markets for frequent fast food restaurant patronage. The Austin* DMA (Designated Market Area) ranked in the top 10 with consumers reporting an average of 6.3 visits within the past 30 days. *Scarborough Research, May 31, 2006*
- Scarborough Research, a leading market research firm, identified the top local markets for frequent sit-down restaurant patronage. The Austin* DMA (Designated Market Area) ranked in the top 10 with consumers reporting an average of 4.0 visits within the past 30 days. *Scarborough Research, May 31, 2006*
- A study by Sperling's BestPlaces examined which U.S. metro areas were most affected by high fuel prices in 2006. The Austin* metro area was ranked #38 out of 80 (#1 = most expensive city for driving). Rankings are based on the average dollars spent on gas per year by two driver households. Criteria: cost of regular-grade gasoline; average miles driven per day; average number of gallons each driver uses and wastes in traffic congestion each day. *Sperling's BestPlaces, www.bestplaces.net, "Pain at the Pump," May 18, 2006*

Round Rock is located within the Austin-Round Rock, TX Metropolitan Statistical Area.

Business Environment

CITY FINANCES

City Government Finances

Component	2004-2005 ($000)	2004-2005 ($ per capita)
Total Revenues	n/a	n/a
Total Expenditures	n/a	n/a
Debt Outstanding	n/a	n/a
Cash and Securities	n/a	n/a

Source: U.S Census Bureau, Government Finances 2004-2005

City Government Revenue by Source

Source	2004-2005 ($000)	2004-2005 ($ per capita)
General Revenue		
From Federal Government	n/a	n/a
From State Government	n/a	n/a
From Local Governments	n/a	n/a
Taxes		
Property	n/a	n/a
Sales	n/a	n/a
Personal Income	n/a	n/a
License	n/a	n/a
Charges	n/a	n/a
Liquor Store	n/a	n/a
Utility	n/a	n/a
Employee Retirement	n/a	n/a
Other	n/a	n/a

Source: U.S Census Bureau, Government Finances 2004-2005

City Government Expenditures by Function

Function	2004-2005 ($000)	2004-2005 ($ per capita)	2004-2005 (%)
General Expenditures			
Airports	n/a	n/a	n/a
Corrections	n/a	n/a	n/a
Education	n/a	n/a	n/a
Fire Protection	n/a	n/a	n/a
Governmental Administration	n/a	n/a	n/a
Health	n/a	n/a	n/a
Highways	n/a	n/a	n/a
Hospitals	n/a	n/a	n/a
Housing and Community Development	n/a	n/a	n/a
Interest on General Debt	n/a	n/a	n/a
Libraries	n/a	n/a	n/a
Parking	n/a	n/a	n/a
Parks and Recreation	n/a	n/a	n/a
Police Protection	n/a	n/a	n/a
Public Welfare	n/a	n/a	n/a
Sewerage	n/a	n/a	n/a
Solid Waste Management	n/a	n/a	n/a
Liquor Store	n/a	n/a	n/a
Utility	n/a	n/a	n/a
Employee Retirement	n/a	n/a	n/a
Other	n/a	n/a	n/a

Source: U.S Census Bureau, Government Finances 2004-2005

Municipal Bond Ratings

Area	Moody's
City	Aaa

Source: Mergent Bond Record, January 2008 (unless noted otherwise)

DEMOGRAPHICS

Population Growth

Area	1990 Census	2000 Census	2007 Estimate	2012 Projection	Population Growth (%) 1990-2000	Population Growth (%) 2000-2012
City	32,854	61,136	85,275	101,318	86.1	65.7
MSA[1]	846,217	1,249,763	1,503,872	1,677,632	47.7	34.2
U.S.	248,709,873	281,421,906	301,045,522	314,920,978	13.2	11.9

Note: (1) Metropolitan Statistical Area - see Appendix B for areas included
Source: Claritas, Inc.

Number of Households and Average Household Size

Area	2007 Estimate	2007 Average Household Size
City	29,688	2.87
MSA[1]	568,544	2.65
U.S.	113,668,003	2.65

Note: (1) Metropolitan Statistical Area - see Appendix B for areas included
Source: Claritas, Inc.

Race and Ethnicity

Area	White Alone[2]	Black Alone[2]	Asian Alone[2]	Other Race Alone[2]	Hispanic[3]
City	69.3	10.7	4.8	15.1	25.5
MSA[1]	70.2	7.4	4.3	18.1	29.6
U.S.	73.1	12.4	4.3	10.3	14.9

Note: Figures are 2007 estimates; (1) Metropolitan Statistical Area - see Appendix B for areas included (2) Alone is defined as not being in combination with one or more other races; (3) May be of any race.
Source: Claritas, Inc.

Ancestry

Area	German	Irish[2]	English	American	Italian	Polish	French[3]	Scottish
City	18.0	10.8	9.8	5.3	3.5	1.6	3.3	2.4
MSA[1]	15.3	9.3	9.7	5.3	2.5	1.5	2.9	2.4
U.S.	15.2	10.9	8.7	7.3	5.6	3.2	3.0	1.7

Note: Figures include multiple ancestry (e.g. if a person reported being Irish and Italian, they were included in both columns); (1) Metropolitan Statistical Area - see Appendix A for areas included; (2) Includes Celtic; (3) Includes Alsatian but excludes Basque
Source: Census 2000, Summary File 3

Foreign-Born Population

Area	Percent of Population Born in							
	Any Foreign Country	Europe	Asia	Africa	Oceania[2]	Canada	Mexico	Latin America[3]
City	9.2	0.8	2.3	0.4	0.0	0.3	4.6	0.8
MSA[1]	12.2	1.0	2.9	0.3	0.0	0.2	6.7	1.1
U.S.	11.1	1.7	2.9	0.3	0.1	0.3	3.3	2.5

Note: (1) Metropolitan Statistical Area - see Appendix A for areas included; (2) Includes Australia, New Zealand subregion, Melanesia, Micronesia, Polynesia, and Oceania n.e.c; (3) Includes Central America (excluding Mexico), South America, and the Caribbean.
Source: Census 2000, Summary File 3

Marriage Status

Area	Never Married	Now Married (excluding Separated)	Separated	Widowed	Divorced
City	23.3	62.7	1.8	3.1	9.1
MSA[1]	32.2	51.7	1.8	3.8	10.4
U.S.	27.1	54.4	2.2	6.6	9.7

Note: Figures are percentages and cover the population 15 years of age and older; (1) Metropolitan Statistical Area - see Appendix A for areas included
Source: Census 2000, Summary File 3

Age Distribution

Area	Under Age 5	Age 5 to 17	Age 18 to 34	Age 35 to 49	Age 50 to 64	Age 65 to 79	80 Years and Over
	Percent of Population						
City	9.8	22.1	27.6	26.1	9.8	3.0	1.5
MSA[1]	7.4	17.9	31.5	24.4	11.7	5.4	1.8
U.S.	6.8	18.9	23.7	23.5	14.8	9.2	3.2

Note: (1) Metropolitan Statistical Area - see Appendix A for areas included
Source: Census 2000, Summary File 3

Male/Female Ratio

Area	Males	Females	Males per 100 Females
City	42,678	42,597	100.2
MSA[1]	762,780	741,092	102.9
U.S.	148,320,305	152,725,217	97.1

Note: Figures are 2007 estimates; (1) Metropolitan Statistical Area - see Appendix B for areas included
Source: Claritas, Inc.

Religion

Area	Catholic	Southern Baptist	United Meth-odist	ELCA[1]	LDS[2]	Presby-terian Church USA	Jewish Est.	Muslim Est.
County	12.4	10.2	5.7	1.8	1.5	0.6	0.0	0.0
U.S.	22.0	7.1	3.7	1.8	1.5	1.1	2.2	0.6

Note: Figures are the number of adherents as a percentage of the total population; Adherents are defined as all members, including full members, their children and the estimated number of other participants who are not considered members (e.g. the baptized, those not confirmed, those regularly attending services, etc.); (1) Evangelical Lutheran Church in America; (2) The Church of Jesus Christ of Latter Day Saints
Source: Reprinted with permission from Religious Congregations and Membership in the United States 2000 (Nashville, Glenmary Research Center, 2002) Copyright Association of Statisticians of American Religious Bodies. All rights reserved.

ECONOMY

Gross Metropolitan Product

Area	2002	2003	2004	2005	2005 Rank[2]
MSA[1]	52.0	54.3	59.7	66.2	38

Note: Figures are in billions of dollars; (1) Austin-Round Rock, TX Metropolitan Statistical Area - see Appendix A for areas included; (2) Rank ranges from 1 to 361
Source: The U.S. Conference of Mayors, "U.S. Metro Economies: GMP - The Engines of America's Growth," January 2007

Economic Growth

Area	1995 GMP	2005 GMP	Average Annual Growth Rate	Growth Rate Rank[2]
MSA[1]	30.2	66.2	8.2	11

Note: Figures are in billions of dollars; GMP = Gross Metropolitan Product; (1) Austin-Round Rock, TX Metropolitan Statistical Area - see Appendix A for areas included; (2) Rank ranges from 1 to 361
Source: The U.S. Conference of Mayors, "U.S. Metro Economies: GMP - The Engines of America's Growth," January 2007

INCOME

Per Capita/Median/Average Income

Area	Per Capita ($)	Median Household ($)	Average Household ($)
City	28,157	66,571	80,468
MSA[1]	27,754	55,339	72,712
U.S.	25,495	49,280	66,670

Note: Figures are 2007 estimates; (1) Metropolitan Statistical Area - see Appendix B for areas included
Source: Claritas, Inc.

Household Income Distribution

Area	Percent of Households Earning							
	Under $15,000	$15,000 -24,999	$25,000 -34,999	$35,000 -49,999	$50,000 -74,999	$75,000 -99,000	$100,000 -149,999	$150,000 and up
City	4.8	5.6	7.7	15.3	25.0	17.8	15.4	8.6
MSA[1]	10.7	8.9	10.4	15.4	20.3	13.4	13.0	8.0
U.S.	13.1	10.9	11.2	15.6	19.5	11.9	11.3	6.6

Note: Figures are 2007 estimates; (1) Metropolitan Statistical Area - see Appendix B for areas included
Source: Claritas, Inc.

Poverty Rates by Age

Area	All Ages	Under 5 Years Old	5 to 17 Years Old	18 to 64 Years Old	65 Years and Over
City	4.0	0.4	1.0	2.2	0.3
MSA[1]	11.1	1.0	2.1	7.4	0.6
U.S.	12.4	1.2	3.0	6.9	1.2

Note: Figures are percent of population with income in 1999 below poverty level and only include population for whom poverty status is determined; (1) Metropolitan Statistical Area - see Appendix A for areas included
Source: Census 2000, Summary File 3

Personal Bankruptcy Filing Rate

Area	2004	2005	2006
Williamson County	5.28	6.94	1.53
U.S.	5.31	6.82	2.00

Note: Numbers are per 1,000 population and include Chapter 7 and Chapter 13 filings
Source: Federal Deposit Insurance Corporation (FDIC), Regional Economic Conditions (RECON), 8/23/2007

EMPLOYMENT

Labor Force and Employment

Area	Civilian Labor Force			Workers Employed		
	Dec. 2006	Dec. 2007	% Chg.	Dec. 2006	Dec. 2007	% Chg.
City	50,970	51,755	1.5	49,344	50,014	1.4
MSA[1]	841,139	854,956	1.6	813,117	824,154	1.4
U.S.	152,571,000	153,705,000	0.7	146,081,000	146,334,000	0.2

Note: Data is not seasonally adjusted and covers workers 16 years of age and older; (1) Metropolitan Statistical Area - see Appendix B for areas included
Source: Bureau of Labor Statistics, http://stats.bls.gov

Unemployment Rate

Area	2007											
	Jan.	Feb.	Mar.	Apr.	May	Jun.	Jul.	Aug.	Sep.	Oct.	Nov.	Dec.
City	3.7	3.7	3.3	3.0	3.1	3.6	3.4	3.2	3.4	3.2	3.3	3.4
MSA[1]	3.9	3.8	3.5	3.2	3.3	3.9	4.0	3.7	3.7	3.5	3.5	3.6
U.S.	5.0	4.9	4.5	4.3	4.3	4.7	4.9	4.6	4.5	4.4	4.5	4.8

Note: Data is not seasonally adjusted and covers workers 16 years of age and older; All figures are percentages; (1) Metropolitan Statistical Area - see Appendix B for areas included
Source: Bureau of Labor Statistics, http://stats.bls.gov

Employment by Occupation

Occupation Classification	City (%)	MSA[1] (%)	U.S. (%)
Sales and Office	29.2	26.7	26.7
Professional and Related	23.7	25.7	20.2
Service	10.0	12.4	14.9
Production, Transportation, and Material Moving	10.2	9.3	14.6
Management, Business, and Financial	18.2	16.2	13.5
Construction, Extraction, and Maintenance	8.6	9.5	9.4
Farming, Forestry, and Fishing	0.3	0.2	0.7

Note: Figures cover employed civilians 16 years of age and older; (1) Metropolitan Statistical Area - see Appendix A for areas included
Source: Census 2000, Summary File 3

Employment by Industry

Sector	MSA[1] Number of Employees	MSA[1] Percent of Total	U.S. Percent of Total
Government	157,200	20.4	16.3
Education and Health Services	78,600	10.2	13.4
Professional and Business Services	109,900	14.2	13.1
Retail Trade	86,100	11.2	11.6
Manufacturing	60,500	7.8	9.9
Leisure and Hospitality	79,100	10.3	9.6
Financial Activities	45,600	5.9	5.9
Construction	n/a	n/a	5.3
Wholesale Trade	41,100	5.3	4.4
Other Services	28,300	3.7	3.9
Transportation and Utilities	13,800	1.8	3.7
Information	21,800	2.8	2.2
Natural Resources and Mining	n/a	n/a	0.5

Note: Figures cover non-farm employment as of December 2007 and are not seasonally adjusted; (1) Metropolitan Statistical Area - see Appendix B for areas included; n/a not available
Source: Bureau of Labor Statistics, http://stats.bls.gov

Average Wages

Occupation	$/Hr.	Occupation	$/Hr.
Accountants and Auditors	30.35	Maids and Housekeeping Cleaners	8.27
Automotive Mechanics	19.58	Maintenance and Repair Workers	14.38
Bookkeepers	14.97	Marketing Managers	59.62
Carpenters	16.33	Nuclear Medicine Technologists	30.52
Cashiers	8.78	Nurses, Licensed Practical	19.01
Clerks, General Office	11.34	Nurses, Registered	28.89
Clerks, Receptionists/Information	12.26	Nursing Aides/Orderlies/Attendants	10.81
Clerks, Shipping/Receiving	12.66	Packers and Packagers, Hand	8.27
Computer Programmers	35.04	Physical Therapists	30.35
Computer Support Specialists	20.59	Postal Service Mail Carriers	21.56
Computer Systems Analysts	35.01	Real Estate Brokers	34.56
Cooks, Restaurant	9.37	Retail Salespersons	11.25
Dentists	n/a	Sales Reps., Exc. Tech./Scientific	25.70
Electrical Engineers	44.77	Sales Reps., Tech./Scientific	41.47
Electricians	17.49	Secretaries, Exc. Legal/Med./Exec.	13.04
Financial Managers	51.75	Security Guards	11.55
First-Line Supervisors/Mgrs., Sales	19.76	Surgeons	92.76
Food Preparation Workers	9.59	Teacher Assistants	10.40
General and Operations Managers	50.80	Teachers, Elementary School	20.40
Hairdressers/Cosmetologists	12.26	Teachers, Secondary School	21.60
Internists	67.24	Telemarketers	10.37
Janitors and Cleaners	9.41	Truck Drivers, Heavy/Tractor-Trailer	15.67
Landscaping/Groundskeeping Workers	9.80	Truck Drivers, Light/Delivery Svcs.	14.09
Lawyers	50.25	Waiters and Waitresses	7.58

Note: Wage data covers the Austin-Round Rock, TX Metropolitan Statistical Area - see Appendix B for areas included. Hourly wages for elementary/secondary school teachers and teacher assistants were calculated by the editors from annual wage data assuming a 40 hour work week; n/a not available.
Source: Bureau of Labor Statistics, May 2007 Metro Area Occupational Employment and Wage Estimates

RESIDENTIAL REAL ESTATE

Building Permits

Area	Single-Family 2006	Single-Family 2007p	Single-Family Pct. Chg.	Multi-Family 2006	Multi-Family 2007p	Multi-Family Pct. Chg.	Total 2006	Total 2007p	Total Pct. Chg.
City	1,307	796	-39.1	320	1,480	362.5	1,627	2,276	39.9
U.S.	1,378,200	973,300	-29.4	460,700	407,200	-11.6	1,838,900	1,380,500	-24.9

Note: (p) preliminary; figures cover and represent new, privately-owned housing units authorized (unadjusted data); All permit data are based on estimates with imputation; U.S. figures are based on the new 20,000-place series.
Source: U.S. Census Bureau, Manufacturing, Mining, and Construction Statistics

Homeownership and Housing Vacancies

Area	Homeownership Rate[2] (%)			Rental Vacancy Rate[3] (%)			Homeowner Vacancy Rate[4] (%)		
	2005	2006	2007	2005	2006	2007	2005	2006	2007
MSA[1]	63.9	66.7	66.4	9.4	7.2	6.8	2.4	1.5	1.5
U.S.	68.9	68.8	68.1	9.8	9.8	9.7	1.9	2.4	2.7

Note: (1) Metropolitan Statistical Area - see Appendix B for areas included; (2) The proportion of households that are owners; (3) The proportion of the rental inventory that is vacant for rent; (4) The proportion of the homeowner inventory that is vacant for sale; n/a not available
Source: U.S. Census Bureau, Housing Vacancies and Homeownership Annual Statistics: 2007

TAXES

State Corporate Income Tax Rates

State	Rates and Tax Brackets
Texas	1.0%

Note: Tax rates as of January 1, 2008; Texas's 1% franchise tax is a gross receipts tax paid by most taxable entities. Retailers pay 0.5%.
Source: Tax Foundation, www.taxfoundation.org

State Individual Income Tax Rates

State	Federal Deductibility	Marginal Rates (%)	Standard Deduction ($)		Personal Exemptions ($)[1]	
			Single	Joint	Single	Dependents
Texas	No	None	n/a	n/a	n/a	n/a

Note: Tax rates as of January 1, 2008; Local- and county-level taxes are not included; n/a not applicable; (1) Married joint filers generally receive double the single exemption
Source: Tax Foundation, www.taxfoundation.org

Various State and Local Tax Rates

State and Local Sales and Use (%)	State Sales and Use (%)	Gasoline[1,2] ($/gal.)	Cigarette ($/pack)	Spirits ($/gal.)	Table Wine ($/gal.)	Beer ($/gal.)
8.25	6.25 (i)	0.20	1.41	2.40	0.204	0.19

Note: Tax rates as of January 1, 2008; (1) In addition to the 18.4 cpg Federal gasoline tax; (2) Rates may include additional state sales taxes, environmental protection and storage fees/taxes, and local taxes. When necessary, the volume-weighted average of all local taxes is used to approximate the typical statewide rate including local tax; (i) Texas has a GRT that is levied in addition to its 6.25% sales tax. It is called the franchise tax and the rate is 1% (.5% for retailers).
Source: Tax Foundation, www.taxfoundation.org; Original research

State Tax Burdens

Area	Combined State and Local Tax Burden		Combined Federal, State and Local Tax Burden	
	Percent	Rank	Percent	Rank
Texas	9.3	43	29.8	41
U.S. Average	11.0	-	32.7	-

Note: Figures cover 2007 and measure taxes as a percentage of income
Source: Tax Foundation, www.taxfoundation.org

State Business Tax Climate Index Rankings

State	Overall Rank	Corporate Tax Index Rank	Individual Income Tax Index Rank	Sales Tax Index Rank	Unemployment Insurance Tax Index Rank	Property Tax Index Rank
Texas	8	47	7	28	14	27

Note: Rankings range from 1 to 50 where 1 is best. Rankings do not average across to Overall Rank. States without a given tax are given a ranking of 1.
Source: Tax Foundation, State Business Tax Climate Index 2008

TRANSPORTATION

Means of Transportation to Work

Area	Car/Truck/Van		Public Transportation			Bicycle	Walked	Other Means	Worked at Home
	Drove Alone	Car-pooled	Bus	Subway	Railroad				
City	82.9	12.8	0.1	0.0	0.0	0.4	0.5	0.7	2.7
MSA[1]	76.5	13.7	2.5	0.0	0.0	0.6	2.1	1.1	3.6
U.S.	75.7	12.2	2.5	1.5	0.5	0.4	2.9	1.0	3.3

Note: Figures are percentages and cover workers 16 years of age and older; (1) Metropolitan Statistical Area - see Appendix A for areas included
Source: Census 2000, Summary File 3

Travel Time to Work

Area	Less Than 15 Minutes	15 to 29 Minutes	30 to 44 Minutes	45 to 59 Minutes	60 Minutes or More
City	24.0	33.1	27.1	10.6	5.2
MSA[1]	24.5	38.6	22.5	8.3	6.1
U.S.	29.4	36.1	19.1	7.4	8.0

Note: Figures are percentages and include workers 16 years old and over; (1) Metropolitan Statistical Area - see Appendix A for areas included
Source: Census 2000, Summary File 3

Travel Time Index

Area	1982	1995	2004	2005
Urban Area[1]	1.07	1.18	1.29	1.31
Average[2]	1.11	1.22	1.29	1.30

Note: Travel Time Index - The ratio of travel time in the peak period to the travel time at free-flow conditions. A value of 1.35 indicates a 20-minute free-flow trip takes 27 minutes in the peak. Free-flow speeds (60 mph on freeways and 35 mph on principal arterials) are used as the comparison threshold; (1) Covers the Austin, TX urban area; (2) average of 85 urban areas
Source: Texas Transportation Institute, The 2007 Urban Mobility Report, September 2007

Living Environment

COST OF LIVING

Cost of Living Index

Composite Index	Groceries	Housing	Utilities	Trans-portation	Health Care	Misc. Goods/ Services
92.4	85.0	76.4	108.7	95.3	106.3	100.9

Note: U.S. = 100; Figures cover the Round Rock TX urban area.
Source: The Council for Community and Economic Research (formerly ACCRA), Cost of Living Index, 2007

Grocery Prices

Area[1]	T-Bone Steak ($/pound)	Frying Chicken ($/pound)	Whole Milk ($/half gal.)	Eggs ($/dozen)	Orange Juice ($/64 oz.)	Coffee ($/11.5 oz.)
City[2]	7.08	0.84	2.35	1.02	2.56	3.22
Avg.	8.93	1.12	2.13	1.52	3.26	3.31
Min.	5.88	0.71	1.33	0.83	2.30	2.20
Max.	12.80	2.07	3.43	3.54	5.79	6.20

Note: (1) Values for the local area are compared with the average, minimum and maximum values for all 331 areas in the Cost of Living Index report; (2) Figures cover the Round Rock TX urban area; **T-Bone Steak** *(price per pound);* **Frying Chicken** *(price per pound, whole fryer);* **Whole Milk** *(half gallon carton);* **Eggs** *(price per dozen, Grade A, large);* **Orange Juice** *(64 oz. Tropicana or Florida Natural);* **Coffee** *(11.5 oz. can, vacuum-packed, Maxwell House, Hills Bros, or Folgers).*
Source: The Council for Community and Economic Research (formerly ACCRA), Cost of Living Index, 2007

Housing and Utility Costs

Area[1]	New Home Price ($)	Apartment Rent ($/month)	All Electric ($/month)	Part Electric ($/month)	Other Energy ($/month)	Telephone ($/month)
City[2]	219,990	803	-	138.72	50.24	25.43
Avg.	309,605	782	146.13	78.67	90.16	26.14
Min.	189,877	n/a	82.03	37.41	33.15	17.08
Max.	1,202,800	3,481	271.14	150.60	257.67	37.45

Note: (1) Values for the local area are compared with the average, minimum and maximum values for all 331 areas in the Cost of Living Index report; (2) Figures cover the Round Rock TX urban area; **New Home Price** *(2,400 sf living area, 8,000 sf lot, in urban area with full utilities);* **Apartment Rent** *(950 sf 2 bedroom/1.5 or 2 bath, unfurnished, excluding all utilities except water);* **All Electric** *(average monthly cost for an all-electric home);* **Part Electric** *(average monthly cost for a part-electric home);* **Other Energy** *(average monthly cost for natural gas, fuel oil, coal, wood, and any other forms of energy except electricity);* **Telephone** *(price includes basic monthly rate for a private residential line plus additional local usage charges incurred by a family of four).*
Source: The Council for Community and Economic Research (formerly ACCRA), Cost of Living Index, 2007

Health Care, Transportation, and Other Costs

Area[1]	Doctor ($/visit)	Dentist ($/visit)	Optometrist ($/visit)	Gasoline ($/gallon)	Beauty Salon ($/visit)	Men's Shirt ($)
City[2]	79.44	89.00	88.00	2.58	30.83	29.94
Avg.	79.48	71.93	79.55	2.64	29.52	25.77
Min.	52.08	44.80	43.95	2.19	15.58	16.19
Max.	148.44	126.27	158.83	3.48	60.62	48.53

Note: (1) Values for the local area are compared with the average, minimum and maximum values for all 331 areas in the Cost of Living Index report; (2) Figures cover the Round Rock TX urban area; **Doctor** *(general practitioners routine exam of an established patient);* **Dentist** *(adult teeth cleaning and periodic oral examination);* **Optometrist** *(full vision eye exam for established adult patient);* **Gasoline** *(one gallon regular unleaded, national brand, including all taxes, cash price at self-service pump if available);* **Beauty Salon** *(woman's shampoo, trim, and blow-dry);* **Men's Shirt** *(cotton/polyester dress shirt, pinpoint weave, long sleeves).*
Source: The Council for Community and Economic Research (formerly ACCRA), Cost of Living Index, 2007

HOUSING

House Price Index (HPI)

Area	National Ranking[2]	Quarterly Change (%)	One-Year Change (%)	Five-Year Change (%)
MSA[1]	11	0.33	7.95	28.88
U.S.[3]	-	0.10	0.84	41.37

Note: The HPI is a weighted repeat sales index. It measures average price changes in repeat sales or refinancings on the same properties. This information is obtained by reviewing repeat mortgage transactions on single-family properties whose mortgages have been purchased or securitized by Fannie Mae or Freddie Mac in January 1975; (1) Metropolitan Statistical Area - see Appendix B for areas included; (2) Rankings are based on annual percentage change for all metro areas containing at least 15,000 transactions over the last 10 years and ranges from 1 to 291; (3) figures based on a weighted average of Census Division estimates; all figures are for the period ending December 31, 2007
Source: Office of Federal Housing Enterprise Oversight, House Price Index, February 26, 2008

House Price Valuations

Area	Q1 2000	Q1 2001	Q1 2002	Q1 2003	Q1 2004	Q1 2005	Q1 2006	Q1 2007	Q1 2008
MSA[1]	-20.3	-13.8	-7.0	-6.9	-10.0	-14.7	-13.1	-10.2	-10.9

Note: Figures show the percentage of over- or under-valuation of single family homes relative to statistically normal house values (e.g. a value of 23.6 indicates that house values are 23.6% overvalued). Statistically normal house values are based on house prices, interest rates, household incomes, population densities, and any historical premiums or discounts metropolitan areas have exhibited over time; (1) Figures cover the Metropolitan Statistical Area - see Appendix B for areas included
Source: Global Insight/National City Corporation, House Prices in America, May 2008

Median Home Prices

Area	2005	2006	2007[r]	Percent Change 2006 to 2007
MSA[1]	163.8	173.7	183.7	5.8
U.S. Average	219.0	221.9	217.9	-1.8

Note: Figures are median sales prices of existing single-family homes in thousands of dollars; (r) revised; n/a not available; (1) Metropolitan Statistical Area - see Appendix B for areas included
Source: National Association of Realtors, Metropolitan Area Prices, 1st Quarter 2008

Housing: Year Structure Built

Area	1990 -2000	1980 -1989	1970 -1979	1960 -1969	1950 -1959	1940 -1949	Before 1940	Median Year
City	48.1	32.3	15.7	1.6	0.9	0.5	1.0	1989
MSA[1]	30.2	27.4	20.2	8.8	6.2	3.3	3.9	1983
U.S.	17.0	15.8	18.5	13.7	12.7	7.3	15.0	1971

Note: Figures are percentages; (1) Metropolitan Statistical Area - see Appendix A for areas included
Source: Census 2000, Summary File 3

HEALTH

Health Risk Data

Category	Area[1] (%)	U.S. (%)
Adults who have been told they have high blood pressure[3]	14.7	25.5
Adults who have been told they have high blood cholesterol[3]	30.7	35.6
Adults who have been told they have diabetes[2]	6.7	7.5
Adults who have been told they have arthritis[3]	15.1	27.0
Adults who have been told they currently have asthma	7.1	8.5
Adults who are current smokers	19.2	20.1
Adults who are heavy drinkers[4]	5.2	4.9
Adults who are overweight (BMI 25.0 - 29.9)	35.1	36.5
Adults who are obese (BMI 30.0 - 99.8)	24.9	25.1

Note: Data as of 2006 unless otherwise noted; (1) Figures cover the Metropolitan Statistical Area - see Appendix B for areas included; (2) Figures do not include pregnancy-related diabetes, pre-diabetes or borderline diabetes; (3) 2005 data; (4) Heavy drinkers are classified as adult men having more than two drinks per day or adult women having more than one drink per day
Source: Centers for Disease Control and Prevention, Behaviorial Risk Factor Surveillance System, SMART: Selected Metropolitan/Micropolitan Area Risk Trends, 2005, 2006

Mortality Rates for the Top 10 Causes of Death in the U.S.

ICD-10[a] Sub-Chapter	ICD-10[a] Code	Age-Adjusted Mortality Rate[1] per 100,000 population	
		County[2]	U.S.
Malignant neoplasms	C00-C97	149.7	186.5
Ischaemic heart diseases	I20-I25	105.1	152.3
Other forms of heart disease	I30-I51	36.8	51.5
Cerebrovascular diseases	I60-I69	46.4	50.0
Chronic lower respiratory diseases	J40-J47	36.8	42.6
Diabetes mellitus	E10-E14	18.0	24.8
Other degenerative diseases of the nervous system	G30-G31	33.8	22.6
Other external causes of accidental injury	W00-X59	15.1	21.4
Influenza and pneumonia	J10-J18	18.6	20.7
Hypertensive diseases	I10-I13	9.9	18.2

Note: (a) ICD-10 = International Classification of Diseases 10th Revision; (1) Mortality rates are a three year average covering 2003-2005; (2) Figures cover Williamson County
Source: Centers for Disease Control and Prevention, National Center for Health Statistics. Compressed Mortality File 1999-2004. CDC WONDER On-line Database, compiled from Compressed Mortality File 1999-2005 Series 20 No. 2K, 2008.

Mortality Rates for Selected Causes of Death

ICD-10[a] Sub-Chapter	ICD-10[a] Code	Age-Adjusted Mortality Rate[1] per 100,000 population	
		County[2]	U.S.
Assault	X85-Y09	*1.9	5.9
Human immunodeficiency virus (HIV) disease	B20-B24	*1.3	4.5
Intentional self-harm	X60-X84	7.6	10.8
Malnutrition	E40-E46	*0.8	1.0
Obesity and other hyperalimentation	E65-E68	*0.8	1.4
Organic, including symptomatic, mental disorders	F01-F09	22.5	16.8
Transport accidents	V01-V99	13.9	16.1
Viral hepatitis	B15-B19	*0.7	1.8

Note: (a) ICD-10 = International Classification of Diseases 10th Revision; (1) Mortality rates are a three year average covering 2003-2005; (2) Figures cover Williamson County; (*) Unreliable data as per CDC
Source: Centers for Disease Control and Prevention, National Center for Health Statistics. Compressed Mortality File 1999-2004. CDC WONDER On-line Database, compiled from Compressed Mortality File 1999-2005 Series 20 No. 2K, 2008.

Distribution of Physicians[1]

Area	Total	Family/ General Practice	Specialties	
			Medical	Surgical
Williamson County (number)	329	178	99	68
Williamson County (rate per 10,000 pop.)	9.9	5.3	3.0	2.0
U.S. (rate per 10,000 pop.)	17.7	4.6	6.9	4.3

Note: Data as of 2005; (1) Includes all non-federal, patient-care, office-based MDs
Source: Area Resource File (ARF). June 2007. U.S. Department of Health and Human Services, Health Resources and Services Administration, Bureau of Health Professions, Rockville, MD.

Hospitals

Round Rock has the following hospitals: 1 general medical and surgical.
AHA Guide to the Healthcare Field 2008

EDUCATION

Public School District Statistics

District Name	Schls	Pupils	Pupil/ Teacher Ratio	Minority Pupils[1] (%)	Free Lunch Eligible[2] (%)	IEP[3] (%)
Pflugerville Isd	27	18,761	16.0	64.9	29.1	10.4
Round Rock ISD	58	37,847	15.0	43.9	18.4	9.2

Note: Table includes regular local school districts with 2,000 or more students; (1) Percentage of students that are not white, non-Hispanic; (2) Percentage of students that are eligible for the free lunch program; (3) Percentage of students that have an Individualized Education Program.
Source: U.S. Department of Education, National Center for Education Statistics, Common Core of Data, Local Education Agency (School District) Universe Survey: School Year 2005-2006; U.S. Department of Education, National Center for Education Statistics, Common Core of Data, Public Elementary/Secondary School Universe Survey: School Year 2005-2006

Top Public High Schools

High School Name	Index[1]	Rank[1]	Subsidized Lunch (%)[2]	E&E (%)[3]
Round Rock	1.572	827	23.9	60.7

Note: (1) Public schools are ranked according to a ratio that is the number of Advanced Placement, International Baccalaureate, and/or Cambridge tests taken by all students at a school in 2007 divided by the number of graduating seniors. All of the schools on the list have an index of at least 1.000; they are in the top five percent of public schools measured this way. The rankings range from 1 to 1,422; (2) Percentage of students receiving federally subsidized meals; (3) E & E stands for equity and excellence percentage: the portion of all graduating seniors at a school that had at least one passing grade on one AP or IB test; (**) Gave both IB and AP tests. AP and IB participation are indicators of a school's efforts to get students to excel and prepare for college.
Source: Newsweek Online, "Top High Schools 2008"

Highest Level of Education

Area	Less than H.S.	H.S. Diploma	Some College, No Deg.	Associate Degree	Bachelors Degree	Masters Degree	Profess. School Degree	Doctorate Degree
City	9.3	21.1	27.9	7.8	24.7	6.9	1.3	1.0
MSA[1]	14.9	20.1	23.0	5.6	24.3	8.2	2.1	1.7
U.S.	19.4	28.4	21.2	6.4	15.7	5.9	2.0	1.0

Note: Figures are 2007 estimated percentages and cover persons age 25 and over; (1) Metropolitan Statistical Area - see Appendix B for areas included
Source: Claritas, Inc.

Educational Attainment by Race

Area	High School Graduate (%)					Bachelor's Degree (%)				
	Total	White	Black	Asian	Hisp.[2]	Total	White	Black	Asian	Hisp.[2]
City	89.6	92.1	95.5	82.2	70.1	32.9	35.6	27.3	51.4	15.9
MSA[1]	84.8	89.7	80.0	88.5	58.6	36.7	41.1	20.1	62.2	14.7
U.S.	80.4	83.6	72.3	80.4	52.4	24.4	26.1	14.3	44.1	10.4

Note: Figures shown cover persons 25 years old and over; (1) Metropolitan Statistical Area - see Appendix A for areas included; (2) people of Hispanic origin can be of any race
Source: Census 2000, Summary File 3

School Enrollment by Type

Area	Grades KG to 8				Grades 9 to 12			
	Public		Private		Public		Private	
	Enrollment	%	Enrollment	%	Enrollment	%	Enrollment	%
City	9,001	92.2	763	7.8	3,272	95.1	169	4.9
MSA[1]	147,604	92.3	12,299	7.7	60,104	94.4	3,576	5.6
U.S.	33,526,011	88.7	4,285,121	11.3	14,848,628	90.6	1,532,323	9.4

Note: Figures shown cover persons 3 years old and over; (1) Metropolitan Statistical Area - see Appendix A for areas included
Source: Census 2000, Summary File 3

School Enrollment by Race

Area	Grades KG to 8 (%)				Grades 9 to 12 (%)			
	White	Black	Asian	Hisp.[1]	White	Black	Asian	Hisp.[1]
City	72.8	9.6	2.1	27.1	75.1	8.7	3.6	23.9
MSA[2]	66.6	9.5	2.7	34.2	67.3	10.3	2.5	31.0
U.S.	68.5	15.5	3.3	16.8	68.8	15.5	3.8	15.7

Note: Figures shown cover persons 3 years old and over; (1) people of Hispanic origin can be of any race; (2) Metropolitan Statistical Area - see Appendix A for areas included
Source: Census 2000, Summary File 3

Average Salaries of Public School Classroom Teachers

District	2005-06		2006-07		Percent Change 2005-06 to 2006-07
	Dollars	Rank[1]	Dollars	Rank[1]	
Texas	41,744	35	44,897	30	7.55
U.S. Average	49,026	-	50,816	-	3.65

Note: (1) State rank ranges from 1 to 51.
Source: National Education Association, Rankings & Estimates: Rankings of the States 2006 and Estimates of School Statistics 2007, December 2007

Higher Education

Four-Year Colleges			Two-Year Colleges			Medical Schools[1]	Law Schools[2]	Voc/ Tech[3]
Public	Private Non-profit	Private For-profit	Public	Private Non-profit	Private For-profit			
0	0	0	0	0	0	0	0	1

Note: Figures cover institutions located within the city limits; (1) includes schools accredited by the Liaison Committee on Medical Education and the American Osteopathic Association; (2) includes American Bar Association-accredited law schools; (3) includes all schools with programs that are less than 2 years.
Source: National Center for Education Statistics, The Integrated Postsecondary Education System (IPEDS) Peer Analysis System, 2007; www.usnews.com, Law and Medical School Directories, 2009

PRESIDENTIAL ELECTION

2004 Presidential Election Results

Area	Bush	Kerry	Nader	Other
Williamson County	65.0	33.6	0.2	1.2
U.S.	50.7	48.3	0.4	0.6

Note: Results are percentages and may not add to 100% due to rounding
Source: Dave Leip's Atlas of U.S. Presidential Elections, www.uselectionatlas.org

EMPLOYERS

Major Employers

Company Name	Industry	Type of Site
3M	Paper; coated and laminated, nec	Branch
American Achievement Corp	Jewelry, precious metal	Headquarters
Attorney General Texas	General government, nec	Branch
Attorney General Texas	Legal counsel and prosecution	Branch
Austin Community College Dst	Junior colleges	Headquarters
Carter & Burgess Inc	Engineering services	Branch
Dell Inc	Electronic computers	Headquarters
Department Mechanical Engrg	Colleges and universities	Branch
Eltech	Electric lamps	Single
Environmental and Occupational	General government, nec	Branch
Gracywoods Nursing Center	Nursing and personal care, nec	Single
HR Trust LLC	Employment agencies	Single
Hospital Housekeeping Systems	Building maintenance services, nec	Single
IBM	Business services, nec	Branch
Long Term Care Regulatory Off	Administration of social & manpower programs	Branch
Motorola	Telephone and telegraph apparatus	Branch
Nextel	Radiotelephone communication	Single
Office of The Attorney General	Legal counsel and prosecution	Branch
State Farm Insurance	Fire, marine, and casualty insurance	Branch
TCEQ	Air, water, and solid waste management	Branch
TX Dept of Public Safety	Police protection	Headquarters
Texas Comm On Envmtl Qulty	Air, water, and solid waste management	Headquarters
Texas Highway Patrol	Police protection	Branch
Texas Lgislative Off The State	Legislative bodies	Headquarters
Texas State Unvrsty-San Marcos	Colleges and universities	Headquarters
Texas Workforce Commission	Regulation, miscellaneous commercial sectors	Headquarters
Workforce Commission Texas	Regulation, miscellaneous commercial sectors	Headquarters

Note: Companies shown are located within the Austin metropolitan area; nec = not elsewhere classified.
Source: www.zapdata.com, May 2008

PUBLIC SAFETY

Crime Rate

Area	All Crimes	Violent Crimes				Property Crimes		
		Murder	Forcible Rape	Robbery	Aggrav. Assault	Burglary	Larceny -Theft	Motor Vehicle Theft
City	2,334.3	0.0	25.9	34.9	56.3	312.1	1,849.9	55.2
Metro[1]	4,288.0	1.9	35.0	104.8	203.5	765.2	2,951.7	225.9
U.S.	3,808.1	5.7	30.9	149.4	287.5	729.4	2,206.8	398.4

Note: Figures are crimes per 100,000 population; (1) Metropolitan Statistical Area - see Appendix B for areas included
Source: FBI Uniform Crime Reports, 2006

Hate Crimes

Area	Number of Quarters Reported	Bias Motivation				
		Race	Religion	Sexual Orientation	Ethnicity	Disability
City	4	1	0	0	0	0

Source: Federal Bureau of Investigation, Hate Crime Statistics 2006

RECREATION

Culture

Dance[1]	Theatre[1]	Instrumental Music[1]	Vocal Music[1]	Series/ Festivals	Museums	Zoos and Aquariums[2]
0	0	0	0	0	0	0

Note: (1) Number of professional perfoming groups; (2) AZA-accredited
Source: The Grey House Performing Arts Directory, 2007; Official Museum Directory, 2008; Association of Zoos & Aquariums, AZA Member Zoos & Aquariums, June 2008

Professional Sports Teams

Team Name	League
No teams are located in the metro area	

Source: Original research

MEDIA

Newspapers

Name	News Focus	Frequency	Circulation
Round Rock Leader	Local	Daily	7,000
Texas Capital News	n/a	Monthly	n/a

Note: Includes newspapers with offices located in the city; n/a not available
Source: MediaContactsPro, March 2008

Television Stations

Name	Ch.	Network(s)	Type	Ownership
KTBC	7	Fox	Commercial	Fox Television Stations Inc.
KXAM	14	NBC	Commercial	n/a
KLRU	18	PBS	Public	Capital of Texas Public Telecommunications
KVUE	24	ABC	Commercial	Belo Corporation
KXAN	36	NBC	Commercial	Lin Broadcasting
KEYE	42	CBS	Commercial	CBS Broadcasting Company
KNVA	54	WBN	Commercial	54 Broadcasting Inc.

Note: Stations included cover the Austin DMA (Designated Market Area)
BurrellesLuce, MediaContacts Online, January 2007

Major AM Radio Stations

Call Letters	Freq. (kHz)	Station Type	Target Audience	Station Format	Music Format
KLBJ	590	n/a	General	News/Sports/Talk	n/a
KNAF	910	Commercial	General	Music/News	Country
KIXL	970	n/a	General/Religious	Talk	n/a
KFIT	1060	Commercial	Black/General/Hisp	Educational/Music	Gospel
KVET	1300	Commercial	General	Music	Country
KHLB	1340	Commercial	General	Music/News/Sports/Talk	Country
KJCE	1370	Commercial	General	News/Sports/Talk	n/a
KFON	1490	Commercial	General	Music	Latin
KQQA	1530	Commercial	General/Hispanic	Music	Latin
KTXZ	1560	Commercial	General/Hispanic	Music/News/Sports	Latin
KVLG	1570	Commercial	General	Music/News	Latin

Note: Stations included cover the Austin DMA (Designated Market Area); n/a not available
Source: BurrellesLuce, MediaContacts Online, January 2007

Major FM Radio Stations

Call Letters	Freq. (mHz)	Station Type	Target Audience	Station Format	Music Format
KNLE	88.1	Non-Comm	General	Music	Christian
KMFA	89.5	Non-Comm	General	Music	Classical
KUTX	90.1	College	General	Ed/Music/News/Talk	Top 40
KUT	90.5	College	General	Educational/Music/News	Top 40
KKLB	92.5	Commercial	General/Hispanic	Music	Latin
KLBJ	93.7	Commercial	General	Music/News/Sports	Album Rock
KAMX	94.7	n/a	General	n/a	n/a
KKMJ	95.5	n/a	General	Music	n/a
KHFI	96.7	Commercial	General	Music/News/Talk	Top 40
KVET	98.1	Commercial	General	Music/News	Country
KHHL	98.9	Commercial	Hispanic	Music	Latin
KASE	100.7	Commercial	General	Music/News/Talk	Contemp. Country
KROX	101.5	n/a	General/Young Adult	Music/Talk	n/a
KPEZ	102.3	Commercial	General	Music/News	Classic Rock
KEYI	103.5	Commercial	General	Music/News	Oldies
KQBT	104.3	Commercial	General	Music/News/Sports/Talk	Urban Contemp.
KHLB	106.9	Commercial	General	Music/News	Country
KGSR	107.1	n/a	General	Music	n/a
KFAN	107.9	Commercial	General	Music/News	Folk

Note: Stations included cover the Austin DMA (Designated Market Area); n/a not available
BurrellesLuce, MediaContacts Online, January 2007

CLIMATE

Average and Extreme Temperatures

Temperature	Jan	Feb	Mar	Apr	May	Jun	Jul	Aug	Sep	Oct	Nov	Dec	Yr.
Extreme High (°F)	90	97	98	98	100	105	109	106	104	98	91	90	109
Average High (°F)	60	64	72	79	85	91	95	96	90	81	70	63	79
Average Temp. (°F)	50	53	61	69	75	82	85	85	80	70	60	52	69
Average Low (°F)	39	43	50	58	65	72	74	74	69	59	49	41	58
Extreme Low (°F)	-2	7	18	35	43	53	64	61	47	32	20	4	-2

Note: Figures cover the years 1948-1990
Source: National Climatic Data Center, International Station Meteorological Climate Summary, 9/96

Average Precipitation/Snowfall/Humidity

Precip./Humidity	Jan	Feb	Mar	Apr	May	Jun	Jul	Aug	Sep	Oct	Nov	Dec	Yr.
Avg. Precip. (in.)	1.6	2.3	1.8	2.9	4.3	3.5	1.9	1.9	3.3	3.5	2.1	1.9	31.1
Avg. Snowfall (in.)	1	Tr	Tr	0	0	0	0	0	0	0	Tr	Tr	1
Avg. Rel. Hum. 6am (%)	79	80	79	83	88	89	88	87	86	84	81	79	84
Avg. Rel. Hum. 3pm (%)	53	51	47	50	53	49	43	42	47	47	49	51	48

Note: Figures cover the years 1948-1990; Tr = Trace amounts (<0.05 in. of rain; <0.5 in. of snow)
Source: National Climatic Data Center, International Station Meteorological Climate Summary, 9/96

Weather Conditions

Temperature			Daytime Sky			Precipitation		
10°F & below	32°F & below	90°F & above	Clear	Partly cloudy	Cloudy	0.01 inch or more precip.	0.1 inch or more snow/ice	Thunder-storms
< 1	20	111	105	148	112	83	1	41

Note: Figures are average number of days per year and cover the years 1948-1990
Source: National Climatic Data Center, International Station Meteorological Climate Summary, 9/96

HAZARDOUS WASTE

Superfund Sites

Round Rock has no sites on the EPA's Superfund Final National Priorities List.
U.S. Environmental Protection Agency, Final National Priorities List, June 23, 2008

AIR & WATER QUALITY

Air Quality Index

Area	Percent of Days when Air Quality was...[2]				AQI Statistics	
	Good	Moderate	Unhealthy for Sensitive Groups	Unhealthy	Maximum	Median
MSA[1]	81.1	17.8	1.1	0.0	145	36

Note: The Air Quality Index (AQI) is an index for reporting daily air quality. EPA calculates the AQI for five major air pollutants regulated by the Clean Air Act: ground-level ozone, particle pollution (also known as particulate matter), carbon monoxide, sulfur dioxide, and nitrogen dioxide. The AQI runs from 0 to 500. The higher the AQI value, the greater the level of air pollution and the greater the health concern. There are six AQI categories: "Good" The AQI is between 0 and 50. Air quality is considered satisfactory; "Moderate" The AQI is between 51 and 100. Air quality is acceptable; "Unhealthy for Sensitive Groups" When AQI values are between 101 and 150, members of sensitive groups may experience health effects; "Unhealthy" When AQI values are between 151 and 200 everyone may begin to experience health effects; "Very Unhealthy" AQI values between 201 and 300 trigger a health alert; "Hazardous" AQI values over 300 trigger health warnings of emergency conditions; (1) Metropolitan Statistical Area - see Appendix A for areas included; (2) Based on 365 days with AQI data in 2007.
Source: U.S. Environmental Protection Agency, Air Quality Index Report, 2007

Air Quality Index Pollutants

Area	Percent of Days when AQI Pollutant was...[2]					
	Carbon Monoxide	Nitrogen Dioxide	Ozone	Sulfur Dioxide	Particulate Matter 2.5	Particulate Matter 10
MSA[1]	0.0	0.0	63.6	0.0	36.2	0.3

Note: The Air Quality Index (AQI) is an index for reporting daily air quality. EPA calculates the AQI for five major air pollutants regulated by the Clean Air Act: ground-level ozone, particle pollution (also known as particulate matter), carbon monoxide, sulfur dioxide, and nitrogen dioxide. The AQI runs from 0 to 500. The higher the AQI value, the greater the level of air pollution and the greater the health concern; (1) Metropolitan Statistical Area - see Appendix A for areas included; (2) Based on 365 days with AQI data in 2007.
Source: U.S. Environmental Protection Agency, Air Quality Index Report, 2007

Air Quality Index Trends

Area	Trend Sites (1)								All Sites (21)
	1999	2000	2001	2002	2003	2004	2005	2006	2006
MSA[1]	8	6	0	5	3	2	1	3	4

Note: An AQI value greater than 100 indicates that air quality would have been in the unhealthful range on that day. Data from exceptional events are not included. These counts are presented in two ways. First, the counts are based on sites having an adequate record of monitoring data during the trend period (trend sites). These counts represent the relative change in the number of days with AQI values greater than 100. In the last column, the counts are based on all sites with data in the most recent year (because it is possible for a site to have data in the most recent year but not enough data to be a trend site); (1) Metropolitan Statistical Area - see Appendix A for areas included.
Source: U.S. Environmental Protection Agency, Office of Air and Radiation, Air Trends, Factbook and Related Information, Air Pollution Trends in Selected Metropolitan Areas 2006

Maximum Air Pollutant Concentrations

	Particulate Matter 10 (ug/m^3)	Particulate Matter 2.5 (ug/m^3)	Ozone (ppm)	Carbon Monoxide (ppm)	Sulfur Dioxide (ppm)	Nitrogen Dioxide (ppm)	Lead (ug/m^3)
MSA[1] Level	32	n/a	0.099	1	n/a	0.004	n/a
NAAQS[2]	150	35	0.125	9	0.140	0.053	1.50
Met NAAQS[2]	Yes	Yes	Yes	Yes	n/a	Yes	n/a

Note: Data from exceptional events are not included; (1) Metropolitan Statistical Area - see Appendix A for areas included; (2) National Ambient Air Quality Standards; n/a not available
Concentrations: Particulate Matter 10 (coarse particulate) - highest second maximum 24-hour concentration; Particulate Matter 2.5 (fine particulate) - highest 98th percentile 24-hour concentration; Ozone - highest second daily maximum 1-hour concentration; Carbon Monoxide - highest second maximum non-overlapping 8-hour concentration; Sulfur Dioxide - highest second maximum 24-hour concentration; Nitrogen Dioxide - highest arithmetic mean concentration; Lead - highest quarterly maximum concentration
Units: ppm = parts per million; ug/m^3 = micrograms per cubic meter
Source: U.S. Environmental Protection Agency, MSA Factbook 2006, Air Quality Statistics by City

Drinking Water

Water System Name	Pop. Served	Primary Water Source Type	Violations[1]	
			Health Based	Monitoring/ Reporting
City of Round Rock	91,151	Surface	0	0

Note: (1) Based on violation data from January 1, 2007 to December 31, 2007 (includes unresolved violations from earlier years)
Source: U.S. Environmental Protection Agency, Office of Ground Water and Drinking Water, Safe Drinking Water Information System (based on data extracted April 15, 2008)

Southlake, Texas

Background

Southlake is a suburb of Dallas/Fort Worth, located in northern Texas in Northeast Tarrant County. It has been described as "Perfect City, USA" and boasts of a comfortable suburban community lifestyle and a welcoming hospitality that is unrivaled, making Southlake a leading place to live, work, and play.

Southlake did not exist before 1952. That year, U.S. Army Corp of Engineers built a reservoir to supply water to the growing population of northeast Texas. The reservoir in northeast Tarrant County was later named Lake Grapevine; the community of farmers that made their living south of the lake aptly named their settlement Southlake. Since then, Southlake has been growing exponentially and today has over 25,000 residents.

Southlake's Town Square, located at the heart of the city on Main Street, is the hub of activity in community and the surrounding area. Reflective of an earlier era, nostalgic for a more traditional time, Town Square incorporates ideals about living, playing and working in the community into a place where these activities are all done in chorus. By providing amenities such as shopping, dining, lodging, and entertainment alongside professional and government services and private residences, Southlake's Town Square aims to create a sense of small-town community within the context of a larger, suburban area.

Southlake's commitment to community is further demonstrated by the its use of technology and social organizations. One example is the Southlake Program for the Involvement of Neighborhoods, or SPIN. Comprised of City Council-appointed volunteers, each represents a geographic area of the city, with the goal of providing an on-line medium by which information can be passed from the city staff to the residents. In addition, Southlake has its own neighborhood-oriented website that allows neighbors to meet each other, discuss neighborhood topics, exchange goods and services, and post area events and happenings.

The city's park system contains nearly 700 acres designated for recreational use. There are 45 practice and game fields, lighted tennis courts and inline hockey facilities, miles of park trails for walking, biking, or inline skating, beautiful ponds, concessions and restrooms, and eleven pavilions for open-air entertainment. Living in Southlake makes it easy to enjoy the outdoors.

Students served by Southlake's Carroll Independent School District are awarded millions of dollars in scholarships each year, a testament to the district's commitment to quality education and athletic excellence. The Dragons, Southlake High School's athletic team, have an unbeatable reputation in football, basketball, lacrosse, cross-country, baseball, and swim team and represent an important source of community pride. Additionally, Southlake is located near several intuitions of higher education, including The University of North Texas, the University of Texas at Arlington, and Tarrant County College Northeast.

Several medical facilities serve the residents of Southlake. Local hospitals include: Harris Methodist Southlake Center for Diagnostics and Surgery, Baylor Regional Medical Centers at Grapevine and at Trophy Club, Cook Children's Health Care Center (internationally renowned in pediatrics), and Parkland Memorial Hospital System. Additionally, there are over 40 hospitals in the Dallas/Fort Worth metropolitan area.

Air travel is conveniently provided by two local facilities, only minutes away from Southlake: the Dallas/Fort Worth International Airport and Alliance Airport.

Rankings

General Rankings

- Fort Worth* was ranked #133 out of 375 metro areas in *Cities Ranked & Rated*. Criteria: cost of living; climate; crime; transportation; economy and jobs; education; arts and culture; health and healthcare; leisure; quality of life. *Cities Ranked & Rated, 2nd Edition, 2007*
- Fort Worth* was ranked #92 out of 379 metro areas in *Places Rated Almanac*. Criteria: health care; education; recreation; transportation; ambience; climate; crime; housing costs; jobs. *Places Rated Almanac, 7th Edition, 2007*

Business/Finance Rankings

- The nation's 100 largest metro areas were analysed in terms of the percentage of households entering some stage of foreclosure in 2007. The Fort Worth* metro area ranked #29 out of 100 (#1 = highest foreclosure rate). *RealtyTrac, "Year-End 2007 Metropolitan Foreclosure Report"*
- The Fort Worth* metro area was identified as one of the "10 Best Cities for Jobs in 2008" by *Forbes*. The metro area ranked #5. Criteria: state unemployment rate; job growth; income growth; median household income; cost of living. *Forbes.com, "Best Cities for Jobs in 2008," January 10, 2008*
- The Fort Worth* metro area was selected one of America's "Top 50 Business Opportunity Metros" by *Expansion Management* in their 5th annual Mayor's Challenge ranking of metro areas that have achieved solid ratings across the board in numerous *EM* studies during the past 12 months. The area ranked #13. Criteria: public schools; quality of life; college educated workers; logistics infrastructure; healthcare costs; taxes and government spending; reputation among site consultants. *Expansion Management, August 2007*
- The Dallas* metro area was selected as one of "America's Most Wired Cities" by *Forbes*. The metro area was ranked #19 out of 30. Criteria: percentage of Internet users with high-speed access; the range of service providers within a city; availability of public wireless hot spots. *Forbes, "America's Most Wired Cities," January 10, 2008*
- Fort Worth* was selected as one of the best places to start and grow a company by *Entrepreneur* and the National Policy Research Council. The Fort Worth* metro area ranked #17 out of 50 large metro areas. Criteria: business formation and growth (firms started four to 14 years ago that still employ at least 5 people and experienced rapid growth over the last four years). *Entrepreneur/National Policy Research Council, "Hot Cities for Entrepreneurs," September 2006*
- The Dallas* metro area was selected as one of "America's Greediest Cities" by *Forbes*. The area was ranked #7 out of 10. Criteria: number of Forbes 400 (*Forbes* annual list of the richest Americans) members per capita. *Forbes, "America's Greediest Cities," December 7, 2007*
- The Fort Worth* metro area was selected as one of "America's 50 Hottest Cities" for business relocations and expansions. Criteria: industry's most prominent site selection consultants were asked to list their top city choices for relocating and expanding manufacturing companies, taking into consideration such factors as the business climate, work force quality, operating costs, incentive programs, and the ease of working with local political and economic development officials. *Expansion Management, January-February 2007*
- Dallas* was cited as one of America's top large metros (population over 1 million) for new and expanded facility projects in 2007. The area appeared in the top 10 with 73 projects. *Site Selection, "Top Metropolitan Area Awards," March 2008*
- The Fort Worth* metro area was selected as one of the "Top 20 Real Estate Markets" for expanding or relocating companies. The area ranked #7. Criteria: low rental costs; low purchase prices; high vacancy rates of office and warehouse space. *Expansion Management, October 2007*

- Intel, in partnership with Sperling's BestPlaces, ranked the 80 "Best Cities for Teleworking" in America. The Fort Worth* metro area ranked #8 among extra large metro areas. The study identifies cities that hold the greatest potential for teleworking based on a host of factors including typical commuting times, fuel prices, availability of broadband Internet access and percentage of the population in telework friendly jobs. The study also factored in extreme climate and natural hazards. *Intel, "Best Cities for Teleworking," March 30, 2006*

- The Fort Worth* metro area appeared on the Milken Institute "2007 Best Performing Cities" index. Rank: #60 out of 200 large metro areas. Criteria: job growth; wage and salary growth; high-tech output growth. *Milken Institute, "2007 Best Performing Cities"*

- The Dallas* metro area was selected as one of "The Top 20 Boom Towns in America." *Business 2.0* magazine and econometric research firm Global Insight compared 319 metropolitan areas in the U.S. and ranked the 61 with populations over 1 million. Criteria: a weighted formula that includes forecast growth rates in sectors that contain the economy's 10 most skilled occupational clusters; the prevalence of college degrees in the local workforce; median salary. The area ranked #18 among large metro areas. *Business 2.0 Magazine, March 2004*

- Fort Worth* was identified as one of the 100 "Most Unwired Cities" in the U.S. The area ranked #23 out of the 100 largest metro areas in the U.S. Criteria: number of public and commercial wireless access points (hotspots); airports with wireless Internet access; broadband availability; local wireless networks; and wireless email devices. *Intel, "Most Unwired Cities Survey," June 7, 2005*

- Dallas* was ranked #21 out of 125 regions worldwide in terms of its "Knowledge Competitiveness Index." The index attempts to measure the knowledge-based development taking place throughout the world and is based on 19 measures of economic performance that indicate a region's ability to translate its knowledge capacity into economic value. *Robert Huggins Associates, World Knowledge Competitiveness Index 2005*

- *Forbes* ranked the 200 most populous metro areas in the U.S. in terms of the "Best Places for Business and Careers." The Fort Worth* metro area was ranked #63. Criteria: business costs (labor, energy, tax and office space expenses); living costs (housing, transportation, food and other household expenditures); education levels of the work force; job growth; income growth; migration trends; crime rates; and culture/leisure. *Forbes, "Best Places for Business and Careers," March 19, 2008*

- *Fortune* ranked the 100 largest metro areas in the U.S. in terms of projected median home price change in 2007. The Fort Worth* metro area ranked #9. *Fortune.com, "Hot Spots, Cold Spots"*

Health/Environment Rankings

- 100 of the largest metro areas in the U.S. were analyzed in terms of their current drought severity. The Fort Worth* metro area ranked #97 (#1 = driest). The rankings were based on statistics such as long-term precipitation trends and patterns and the Palmer drought indices. *Sperling's BestPlaces, www.BestPlaces.net, "America's Drought-Riskiest Cities," November 2007*

- Doctors at the Harvard School of Public Health ranked 40 metropolitan areas based on data from the government-sponsored Hospital Quality Alliance program. The program tracks the performance of individual hospitals in treating patients for three common health problems: heart attacks, congestive heart failure, and pneumonia. The Dallas* metro area ranked #22 in quality of care for heart attacks, #25 for congestive heart failure, and #7 for pneumonia. *New England Journal of Medicine, July 21, 2005*

- *Reader's Digest* ranked the 50 largest metro areas in the U.S. in terms of how "clean" they are. The Dallas* metro area ranked #30. Criteria: air quality; water quality; toxic industrial pollution; Superfund sites; and sanitation. *Reader's Digest, "The 50 Cleanest (and Dirtiest) Cities in America," July 2005*

- The American Academy of Dermatology ranked 32 U.S. metropolitan regions in terms of their residents knowledge, attitude and behaviors towards tanning and sun protection. The Dallas* metro area ranked #6. The results of the study are based on an online national survey of 3,342 respondents. *American Academy of Dermatology, "RAYS: Your Grade," May 7, 2007*

- The Fort Worth* metro area appeared in *Country Home's* "2008 Best Green Places" report. The area ranked #171 out of 379. Criteria: official energy policies; green power; green buildings; availability of fresh, locally grown food. *Country Home, "2008 Best Green Places"*

- Wyeth Consumer Healthcare, in partnership with Sperling's BestPlaces, ranked the nation's 50 most populous metro areas in terms of five key health factors. The Fort Worth* metro area ranked #37. Criteria: physical activity; health status; nutrition; lifestyle pursuits; and mental wellness. *Wyeth Consumer Healthcare, "Centrum Healthiest Cities Study," April 19, 2005*

- HealthGrades surveyed over 41,000 individuals on doctor satisfaction and ranked the 20 largest metro areas based on the highest "definitely yes" responses to the question "Do you trust the physician to make decisions/recommendations that are in your best interest?" The Fort Worth* metro area ranked #2. *HealthGrades.com, "Top Cities in Doctor-Trust," September 7, 2006*

- Fort Worth* was identified as a "2008 Asthma Capital." The area ranked #23 out of the nation's 100 largest metropolitan areas. Twelve factors were used to identify the most challenging places to live for people with asthma: estimated prevalence; self-reported prevalence; crude death rate for asthma; annual pollen score; annual air quality; public smoking laws; number of board-certified asthma specialists; school inhaler access laws; rescue medication use; controller medication use; uninsured rate; poverty rate. *Asthma and Allergy Foundation of America, "2008 Asthma Capitals"*

- Fort Worth* was identified as a "Spring Allergy Capital." The area ranked #2 out of 100. Three groups of factors were used to identify the most severe cities for people with allergies during the spring season: annual pollen levels; medicine utilization; access to board-certified allergists. *Asthma and Allergy Foundation of America, "2007 Spring Allergy Capital Rankings"*

- Fort Worth* was identified as a "Fall Allergy Capital." The area ranked #21 out of 100. Three groups of factors were used to identify the most severe cities for people with allergies during the fall season: annual pollen levels; medicine utilization; access to board-certified allergists. *Asthma and Allergy Foundation of America, "2007 Fall Allergy Capital Rankings"*

- Ortho-McNeil Neurologics, in partnership with Sperling's BestPlaces, analyzed 110 metro areas and identified those U.S. cities with the highest prevalence of factors that are most commonly associated with migraine headaches. The Fort Worth* metro area ranked #82. Criteria: number of migraine-related drug prescriptions per capita; lifestyle factors that can contribute to migraines; environmental factors that can trigger migraines; and consumption of migraine-triggering foods. *Ortho-McNeil Neurologics, "America's Migraine Hot Spots," March 14, 2006*

- Sperling's BestPlaces ranked 331 metro areas and identified the most and least stressful U.S. cities. The Fort Worth* metro area ranked #23 out of the 100 largest metro areas (#1 = most stressful). Criteria: divorce rate; unemployment rate; violent and property crime; suicide rate; commute time; mental health; alcohol consumption; cloudy days. *Sperling's BestPlaces, www.BestPlaces.net, "America's Most (and Least) Stressful Cities," January 9, 2004*

- An analysis of the "Best & Worst Cities for Sleep" was conducted by Sperling's BestPlaces. The study ranked America's 50 most populated metro areas. The Fort Worth* metro area ranked #40 (#1 = best city for sleep). Criteria: number of days residents didn't get enough rest or sleep during the past month; average length of daily commute; divorce rate; unemployment rate. *Sperling's BestPlaces, www.BestPlaces.net, "Best & Worst Cities for Sleep," 2006*

- HealthGrades evaluated the performance of America's 25 most populous metropolitan areas by measuring the outcomes of five of the highest volume and most widely studied procedures and diagnoses: coronary artery bypass graft surgery; percutaneous coronary interventions; acute myocardial infarction/heart attack in angioplasty-capable hospitals; congestive heart failure; and community acquired pneumonia. The Dallas* metro area ranked #21. *HealthGrades, "HealthGrades Hospital Quality in America Study," October 12, 2004*

- Fort Worth* was highlighted as one of the 25 most ozone-polluted metro areas in the U.S. The area ranked #7. *American Lung Association, State of the Air: 2007*
- Fort Worth* was selected as one of "America's Top 10 Low-Carb Cities" by *LowCarbiz Magazine*. Criteria: abundance of low-carb products; restaurants with low-carb menu items; health practitioners supportive of carb-cutting regimens; local culture generally conducive to exercise and health. *LowCarbiz Magazine, April 2004*
- Fort Worth* was selected as one of "America's Pet Healthiest Cities" by Purina. The city ranked #36 out of 50. Criteria: veterinary services; environment; legislation; preventative care; obesity/body condition. *Purina Pet Institute, "America's Pet Healthiest Cities," May 20, 2003*

Women/Minorities Rankings

- Fort Worth* was ranked #80 out of 100 metro areas in *SELF Magazine's* ranking of "America's Best Places for Women." A panel of experts came up with more than 50 criteria including death and disease rates, environmental indicators, community resources, and lifestyle habits. *SELF Magazine, "America's Best Places for Women 2007," December 2007*
- Dallas* appeared on *Black Enterprise's* list of the "Ten Best Cities for African Americans." The top picks were culled from more than 2,000 interactive surveys completed on www.blackenterprise.com and by editorial staff evaluation. The editors weighed the following criteria as it pertained to African Americans in each city: median household income; percentage of households earning more than $100,000; percentage of businesses owned; percentage of college graduates; unemployment rates; home loan rejections; and homeownership rates. *Black Enterprise, May 2007*

Seniors/Retirement Rankings

- The Fort Worth* metro area was selected as one of "Best Places for Retirees" by *Forbes*. The area was ranked #2 out of 10. Criteria: cost and availability of health care; sales, property and income-tax rates; arts and leisure activities; cost of living; retirement job market; inter-metro migration patterns of people between the ages of 55 and 65. *Forbes, "Best Places for Retirees," January 18, 2007*
- Sperling's BestPlaces in partnership with Bankers Life & Casualty Company designed a survey to identify the top 50 metro areas in the U.S. that offer the best overall qualities for senior living. The Fort Worth* metro area ranked #38. The following criteria were statistically weighted to reflect the needs of the senior population: health; disease; economics; social; environment; spiritual; transportation; housing; and crime. *Bankers Life & Casualty Company, "Best Cities for Seniors 2005"*
- A.G. Edwards ranked America's 500 top-performing communities based on their residents' personal savings and investing behavior. The Fort Worth* metro area ranked #353 with an index score of 98.36 (national average = 100.00). A dozen statistical factors were measured including: participation in retirement savings plans; personal debt levels; and home ownership. *A.G. Edwards, "2007 Nest Egg Index", September 12, 2007*

Children/Family Rankings

- The Fort Worth* metro area was selected as one of the "Best Cities for Relocating Families" by Worldwide ERC and Primacy Relocation. The 2007 study placed a special emphasis on the housing market, which has significantly impacted the relocation industry and an employer's ability to transfer employees. The variables which weigh heavily in this category include home price, home affordability index, appreciation rates, and property tax. Other criteria include cost of living, crime rates, education, climate, focus on diversity, physicians per capita, recreation and leisure, arts and culture, air quality, watershed quality, sales tax, unemployment rate, job growth, high school and higher education index, school expenditures per student, students in public school, SAT/ACT percentile, and population growth. *Worldwide ERC and Primacy Relocation, "2007 Best Cities for Relocating Families"*

Safety Rankings

- The National Insurance Crime Bureau ranked 361 metro areas in the U.S. in terms of per capita rates of vehicle theft. The Fort Worth* metro area ranked #50 (#1 = highest rate). Criteria: number of vehicle theft offenses per 100,000 inhabitants. *National Insurance Crime Bureau, "NICB Vehicle Theft Study," April 22, 2008*
- Fort Worth* appeared on Sperling's BestPlaces list of the "Riskiest Cities for Identity Theft." The area ranked #13 out of the nations 50 largest metro areas. Over 80 criteria were analyzed across four major categories: technology impact; crime; transactions; and risk profile. *Sperling's BestPlaces, www.BestPlaces.net, "Riskiest Cities for Identity Theft," July 2006*
- Farmers Insurance Group of Companies, in partnership with Sperling's BestPlaces, ranked 379 metro areas and identified the "Most Secure U.S. Place to Live." The Fort Worth* metro area ranked #94 out of 114 in the large metro area category (500,000 or more residents). Criteria: crime rates; extreme weather; risk of natural disasters; environmental hazards; terrorism threats; air quality; life expectancy; job loss numbers. *Farmers Insurance Group, "Most Secure U.S. Places to Live 2007"*
- Fort Worth* was identified as one of the most dangerous large metro areas for pedestrians in the U.S. The area ranked #14 out of the nations 50 largest metro areas. Criteria: average yearly pedestrian fatalities per capita (for the years 2002 and 2003) adjusted for the number of walkers. *Surface Transportation Policy Project, "Mean Streets 2004"*
- Dallas* was identified as one of the least safe places in the U.S. in terms of its vulnerability to natural disasters and weather extremes. The city ranked #2 out of 10. Sperling's BestPlaces analyzed data to show a metro areas' relative tendency to experience natural disasters (hail, tornados, high winds, hurricanes, earthquakes, and brush fires) or extreme weather (abundant rain or snowfall or days that are below freezing or above 90 degrees Fahrenheit). *Forbes, "Safest and Least Safe Places in the U.S.," August 30, 2005*

Sports/Recreation Rankings

- The Fort Worth* metro area appeared on the *Sporting News* list of the "Best Sports Cities 2007". The area ranked #3 out of 150 cities in the U.S. *Sporting News* takes a 12-month snapshot, roughly July to July, of each city's sports, putting a heavy premium on regular-season won-lost records (from the most recently completed season). Other criteria include: playoff berths, bowl appearances and tournament bids; championships; applicable power ratings; quality of competition; overall fan fervor as measured in part by attendance as percentage of venue capacity; abundance of teams (rewarding quality over quantity); stadium and arena quality; ticket availability and prices; franchise ownership; and marquee appeal of athletes. *SportingNews.com, "Best Sports Cities 2007," August 1, 2007*
- Scarborough Research, a leading market research firm, identified the top local markets for avid NBA fans. The Fort Worth* DMA (Designated Market Area) ranked in the top 10 with 13% of consumers 18 years and over reporting that they are "very interested in the NBA". *Scarborough Research, April 24, 2006*
- The Fort Worth* metro area was selected by *Cranium* as one of the "Top 50 Fun Cities" in America. The area ranked #38. Criteria includes: number of sports teams, restaurants, and dance performances; number of toy stores; city budget spent on recreation. *Cranium, November 4, 2003*
- *Golf Digest* ranked 330 metro areas in the U.S. in terms of golf. The Fort Worth* metro area was ranked #243. Criteria: access to golf; weather; value of golf; and quality of golf. *Golf Digest, "Metro Golf Rankings," August 2005*

Dating/Romance Rankings

- Eli Lily and Company, in partnership with Sperling's BestPlaces, ranked the nation's 50 largest metro areas in terms of the "Most Romantic Cities for Baby Boomers." The Dallas* metro area ranked #9. Criteria: marriage and divorce rates among "baby boomers" age 45 to 60; great restaurants; dance studios; chocolate, jewelry and flower sales. *Eli Lily and Company, "Most Romantic Cities for Baby Boomers," April 20, 2007*

- The Dallas* metro area was selected as one of the "Top Ten U.S. Cities for Finding a Rich, Single Man" by Teasley, a Manhattan-based marketing consulting firm. The area ranked #10. Criteria: high single-male to single-female ratios; higher income to cost-of-living ratios. *Teasley, "Top Ten U.S. Cities for Finding a Rich, Single Man," February 10, 2004*

- The Fort Worth* metro area was selected as one of the "Best Cities for Relocating Singles" by Worldwide ERC and Primacy Relocation. The area ranked #49 out of the 100 largest metro areas in the U.S. Areas were selected based on the following criteria: a robust cost-of-living index; adventure and outdoor recreation opportunities; violent crime and property crime rates; percentage of the population that is unmarried (ages 25-34); ratio of single men and single women; affordability of quality higher education, including in-state and out-of-state tuition requirements and rates; number of newcomers to the area; commute times; tax rates; fee and occupancy rates for temporary housing and mini-storage; quality and quantity of collegiate and professional sporting events and fun, fan-friendly venues. *Worldwide ERC and Primacy Relocation, "2007 Best Cities for Relocating Singles," October 25, 2007*

- *Forbes* ranked the 40 most populous urbanized areas in the U.S. in terms of the "Best Cities for Singles." The Dallas* metro area ranked #9. Criteria: number of singles; cost of living alone; nightlife; culture; job growth; coolness; and online dating. *Forbes.com, August 21, 2007*

- Sperling's BestPlaces in partnership with AXE Deodorant Bodyspray ranked 80 metro areas and identified "America's Best (and Worst) Cities for Dating." The Fort Worth* metro area ranked #30 (#1 = best). Criteria: percentage of singles ages 18-24; population density; dating venues per capita. *AXE Deodorant Bodyspray, "America's Best (and Worst) Cities for Dating," May 2004*

Miscellaneous Rankings

- The Dallas* metro area was identified as one of 10 "Worst Cities for Commuters" by *Forbes*. The metro area ranked #5. Criteria: traffic delays; travel times; how efficiently commuters use existing infrastructure. *Forbes.com, "Worst Cities for Commuters," April 29, 2008*

- Scarborough Research, a leading market research firm, identified the top local markets for bloggers. The Fort Worth* DMA (Designated Market Area) ranked in the top 13 with 11% of adults reporting that they had read or contributed to a blog within the past 30 days. *Scarborough Research, October 24, 2007*

- The Dallas* metro area was selected as one of the "Top 10 Most Independent Cities for Homesellers". The area ranked #9. The cities listed had more consumers choosing to sell their homes without the help of a real-estate agent than anywhere else. Data was based on geographical information for listings posted on ForSaleByOwner.com from January 1, 2007 through June 30, 2007. *ForSaleByOwner.com, October 1, 2007*

- The Fort Worth* metro area appeared on *Forbes* list of "America's Drunkest Cities". The area ranked #27. Criteria: 35 of the largest continental U.S. metro areas were chosen based on availability of data and geographic diversity. Each metro was ranked in five areas: state laws; drinkers; heavy drinkers; binge drinkers; and alcoholism. *Forbes.com, "America's Drunkest Cities," August 22, 2006*

- Sperling's BestPlaces in partnership with Pep Boys ranked 77 metro areas and identified "America's Most Drivable Cities." The Fort Worth* metro area ranked #35. Criteria: climate; road roughness; urban mobility; gas prices. *Pep Boys, "America's Most Drivable Cities," April 9, 2003*

- State Farm Insurance, in partnership with Sperling's BestPlaces, analyzed several key factors that contribute to overall family preparedness. The Fort Worth* metro area ranked #11 out of the nation's 50 most populous metro areas. Criteria: quality of life; life insurance coverage; and investments. *State Farm Life Insurance, "Fiscally Fit Cities Report," July 20, 2004*

- A study by Sperling's BestPlaces examined which U.S. metro areas were most affected by high fuel prices in 2006. The Dallas* metro area was ranked #37 out of 80 (#1 = most expensive city for driving). Rankings are based on the average dollars spent on gas per year by two driver households. Criteria: cost of regular-grade gasoline; average miles driven per day; average number of gallons each driver uses and wastes in traffic congestion each day. *Sperling's BestPlaces, www.bestplaces.net, "Pain at the Pump," May 18, 2006*

***Southlake is located within the Dallas-Fort Worth-Arlington, TX Metropolitan Statistical Area and Fort Worth-Arlington, TX Metropolitan Division.**

Business Environment

CITY FINANCES

City Government Finances

Component	2004-2005 ($000)	2004-2005 ($ per capita)
Total Revenues	51,795	2,080
Total Expenditures	48,922	1,965
Debt Outstanding	159,144	6,391
Cash and Securities	62,926	2,527

Source: U.S Census Bureau, Government Finances 2004-2005

City Government Revenue by Source

Source	2004-2005 ($000)	2004-2005 ($ per capita)
General Revenue		
From Federal Government	100	4
From State Government	35	1
From Local Governments	18	1
Taxes		
Property	18,694	751
Sales	12,706	510
Personal Income	0	0
License	1,438	58
Charges	4,983	200
Liquor Store	0	0
Utility	9,593	385
Employee Retirement	0	0
Other	4,228	170

Source: U.S Census Bureau, Government Finances 2004-2005

City Government Expenditures by Function

Function	2004-2005 ($000)	2004-2005 ($ per capita)	2004-2005 (%)
General Expenditures			
Airports	0	0	0.0
Corrections	0	0	0.0
Education	0	0	0.0
Fire Protection	3,140	126	6.4
Governmental Administration	3,340	134	6.8
Health	0	0	0.0
Highways	6,438	259	13.2
Hospitals	0	0	0.0
Housing and Community Development	0	0	0.0
Interest on General Debt	4,363	175	8.9
Libraries	387	16	0.8
Parking	0	0	0.0
Parks and Recreation	4,710	189	9.6
Police Protection	5,265	211	10.8
Public Welfare	0	0	0.0
Sewerage	1,634	66	3.3
Solid Waste Management	706	28	1.4
Liquor Store	0	0	0.0
Utility	12,649	508	25.9
Employee Retirement	0	0	0.0
Other	6,290	253	12.9

Source: U.S Census Bureau, Government Finances 2004-2005

Municipal Bond Ratings

Area	Moody's
City	n/a

Source: Mergent Bond Record, January 2008 (unless noted otherwise)

DEMOGRAPHICS

Population Growth

Area	1990 Census	2000 Census	2007 Estimate	2012 Projection	Population Growth (%) 1990-2000	Population Growth (%) 2000-2012
City	7,155	21,519	25,609	28,381	200.8	31.9
MSA[1]	3,989,294	5,161,544	6,007,731	6,587,538	29.4	27.6
U.S.	248,709,873	281,421,906	301,045,522	314,920,978	13.2	11.9

Note: (1) Metropolitan Statistical Area - see Appendix B for areas included
Source: Claritas, Inc.

Number of Households and Average Household Size

Area	2007 Estimate	2007 Average Household Size
City	7,492	3.42
MSA[1]	2,171,092	2.77
U.S.	113,668,003	2.65

Note: (1) Metropolitan Statistical Area - see Appendix B for areas included
Source: Claritas, Inc.

Race and Ethnicity

Area	White Alone[2]	Black Alone[2]	Asian Alone[2]	Other Race Alone[2]	Hispanic[3]
City	92.4	2.1	2.5	3.0	4.7
MSA[1]	65.6	14.0	4.6	15.8	26.4
U.S.	73.1	12.4	4.3	10.3	14.9

Note: Figures are 2007 estimates; (1) Metropolitan Statistical Area - see Appendix B for areas included (2) Alone is defined as not being in combination with one or more other races; (3) May be of any race.
Source: Claritas, Inc.

Ancestry

Area	German	Irish[2]	English	American	Italian	Polish	French[3]	Scottish
City	21.5	13.9	17.5	8.8	5.1	2.6	3.0	3.9
MSA[1]	11.4	9.2	9.1	9.7	2.0	1.2	2.4	1.9
U.S.	15.2	10.9	8.7	7.3	5.6	3.2	3.0	1.7

Note: Figures include multiple ancestry (e.g. if a person reported being Irish and Italian, they were included in both columns); (1) Metropolitan Statistical Area - see Appendix A for areas included; (2) Includes Celtic; (3) Includes Alsatian but excludes Basque
Source: Census 2000, Summary File 3

Foreign-Born Population

Area	Percent of Population Born in: Any Foreign Country	Europe	Asia	Africa	Oceania[2]	Canada	Mexico	Latin America[3]
City	5.1	1.8	1.7	0.1	0.0	0.5	0.4	0.7
MSA[1]	11.4	0.8	2.6	0.4	0.1	0.2	6.5	0.8
U.S.	11.1	1.7	2.9	0.3	0.1	0.3	3.3	2.5

Note: (1) Metropolitan Statistical Area - see Appendix A for areas included; (2) Includes Australia, New Zealand subregion, Melanesia, Micronesia, Polynesia, and Oceania n.e.c; (3) Includes Central America (excluding Mexico), South America, and the Caribbean.
Source: Census 2000, Summary File 3

Marriage Status

Area	Never Married	Now Married (excluding Separated)	Separated	Widowed	Divorced
City	16.7	78.4	0.3	1.3	3.3
MSA[1]	24.3	57.5	2.3	4.9	11.0
U.S.	27.1	54.4	2.2	6.6	9.7

Note: Figures are percentages and cover the population 15 years of age and older; (1) Metropolitan Statistical Area - see Appendix A for areas included
Source: Census 2000, Summary File 3

Age Distribution

Area	Percent of Population						
	Under Age 5	Age 5 to 17	Age 18 to 34	Age 35 to 49	Age 50 to 64	Age 65 to 79	80 Years and Over
City	7.9	29.1	9.6	35.8	14.5	2.6	0.5
MSA[1]	7.7	20.2	25.2	24.6	13.5	6.7	2.0
U.S.	6.8	18.9	23.7	23.5	14.8	9.2	3.2

Note: (1) Metropolitan Statistical Area - see Appendix A for areas included
Source: Census 2000, Summary File 3

Male/Female Ratio

Area	Males	Females	Males per 100 Females
City	12,810	12,799	100.1
MSA[1]	3,012,647	2,995,084	100.6
U.S.	148,320,305	152,725,217	97.1

Note: Figures are 2007 estimates; (1) Metropolitan Statistical Area - see Appendix B for areas included
Source: Claritas, Inc.

Religion

Area	Catholic	Southern Baptist	United Meth-odist	ELCA[1]	LDS[2]	Presby-terian Church USA	Jewish Est.	Muslim Est.
County	11.5	18.7	6.8	0.6	0.8	0.8	0.4	1.0
U.S.	22.0	7.1	3.7	1.8	1.5	1.1	2.2	0.6

Note: Figures are the number of adherents as a percentage of the total population; Adherents are defined as all members, including full members, their children and the estimated number of other participants who are not considered members (e.g. the baptized, those not confirmed, those regularly attending services, etc.); (1) Evangelical Lutheran Church in America; (2) The Church of Jesus Christ of Latter Day Saints
Source: Reprinted with permission from Religious Congregations and Membership in the United States 2000 (Nashville, Glenmary Research Center, 2002) Copyright Association of Statisticians of American Religious Bodies. All rights reserved.

ECONOMY

Gross Metropolitan Product

Area	2002	2003	2004	2005	2005 Rank[2]
MSA[1]	229.2	238.6	260.0	284.5	5

Note: Figures are in billions of dollars; (1) Dallas-Fort Worth-Arlington, TX Metropolitan Statistical Area - see Appendix A for areas included; (2) Rank ranges from 1 to 361
Source: The U.S. Conference of Mayors, "U.S. Metro Economies: GMP - The Engines of America's Growth," January 2007

Economic Growth

Area	1995 GMP	2005 GMP	Average Annual Growth Rate	Growth Rate Rank[2]
MSA[1]	143.0	284.5	7.1	35

Note: Figures are in billions of dollars; GMP = Gross Metropolitan Product; (1) Dallas-Fort Worth-Arlington, TX Metropolitan Statistical Area - see Appendix A for areas included; (2) Rank ranges from 1 to 361
Source: The U.S. Conference of Mayors, "U.S. Metro Economies: GMP - The Engines of America's Growth," January 2007

INCOME

Per Capita/Median/Average Income

Area	Per Capita ($)	Median Household ($)	Average Household ($)
City	58,034	160,217	198,336
MSA[1]	27,089	55,079	74,352
U.S.	25,495	49,280	66,670

Note: Figures are 2007 estimates; (1) Metropolitan Statistical Area - see Appendix B for areas included
Source: Claritas, Inc.

Household Income Distribution

Area	Percent of Households Earning							
	Under $15,000	$15,000 -24,999	$25,000 -34,999	$35,000 -49,999	$50,000 -74,999	$75,000 -99,000	$100,000 -149,999	$150,000 and up
City	2.0	1.7	2.7	3.1	8.0	7.8	21.2	53.6
MSA[1]	10.0	9.1	10.7	15.8	19.8	13.0	13.2	8.5
U.S.	13.1	10.9	11.2	15.6	19.5	11.9	11.3	6.6

Note: Figures are 2007 estimates; (1) Metropolitan Statistical Area - see Appendix B for areas included
Source: Claritas, Inc.

Poverty Rates by Age

Area	All Ages	Under 5 Years Old	5 to 17 Years Old	18 to 64 Years Old	65 Years and Over
City	1.8	0.0	0.7	1.0	0.1
MSA[1]	10.3	1.2	2.6	5.7	0.8
U.S.	12.4	1.2	3.0	6.9	1.2

Note: Figures are percent of population with income in 1999 below poverty level and only include population for whom poverty status is determined; (1) Metropolitan Statistical Area - see Appendix A for areas included
Source: Census 2000, Summary File 3

Personal Bankruptcy Filing Rate

Area	2004	2005	2006
Tarrant County	6.46	8.04	2.34
U.S.	5.31	6.82	2.00

Note: Numbers are per 1,000 population and include Chapter 7 and Chapter 13 filings
Source: Federal Deposit Insurance Corporation (FDIC), Regional Economic Conditions (RECON), 8/23/2007

EMPLOYMENT

Labor Force and Employment

Area	Civilian Labor Force			Workers Employed		
	Dec. 2006	Dec. 2007	% Chg.	Dec. 2006	Dec. 2007	% Chg.
City	12,242	12,307	0.5	11,825	11,879	0.5
MD[1]	1,026,983	1,032,143	0.5	985,677	990,075	0.4
U.S.	152,571,000	153,705,000	0.7	146,081,000	146,334,000	0.2

Note: Data is not seasonally adjusted and covers workers 16 years of age and older;
(1) Metropolitan Division - see Appendix B for areas included
Source: Bureau of Labor Statistics, http://stats.bls.gov

Unemployment Rate

Area	2007											
	Jan.	Feb.	Mar.	Apr.	May	Jun.	Jul.	Aug.	Sep.	Oct.	Nov.	Dec.
City	4.0	3.9	3.5	3.3	3.4	4.1	4.0	3.6	3.6	3.5	3.6	3.5
MD[1]	4.9	4.5	4.1	3.9	4.0	4.6	4.6	4.2	4.2	3.9	4.0	4.1
U.S.	5.0	4.9	4.5	4.3	4.3	4.7	4.9	4.6	4.5	4.4	4.5	4.8

Note: Data is not seasonally adjusted and covers workers 16 years of age and older; All figures are percentages; (1) Metropolitan Division - see Appendix B for areas included
Source: Bureau of Labor Statistics, http://stats.bls.gov

Employment by Occupation

Occupation Classification	City (%)	MSA[1] (%)	U.S. (%)
Sales and Office	26.6	29.3	26.7
Professional and Related	20.2	19.0	20.2
Service	7.0	12.8	14.9
Production, Transportation, and Material Moving	7.6	13.8	14.6
Management, Business, and Financial	34.8	14.6	13.5
Construction, Extraction, and Maintenance	3.7	10.3	9.4
Farming, Forestry, and Fishing	0.1	0.1	0.7

Note: Figures cover employed civilians 16 years of age and older;
(1) Metropolitan Statistical Area - see Appendix A for areas included
Source: Census 2000, Summary File 3

Employment by Industry

Sector	MSA[1] Number of Employees	MSA[1] Percent of Total	U.S. Percent of Total
Government	118,300	13.4	16.3
Education and Health Services	99,200	11.2	13.4
Professional and Business Services	104,600	11.9	13.1
Retail Trade	107,100	12.1	11.6
Manufacturing	99,300	11.3	9.9
Leisure and Hospitality	85,600	9.7	9.6
Financial Activities	48,500	5.5	5.9
Construction	n/a	n/a	5.3
Wholesale Trade	42,400	4.8	4.4
Other Services	32,700	3.7	3.9
Transportation and Utilities	64,700	7.3	3.7
Information	16,600	1.9	2.2
Natural Resources and Mining	n/a	n/a	0.5

Note: Figures cover non-farm employment as of December 2007 and are not seasonally adjusted; (1) Metropolitan Statistical Area - see Appendix B for areas included; n/a not available
Source: Bureau of Labor Statistics, http://stats.bls.gov

Average Wages

Occupation	$/Hr.	Occupation	$/Hr.
Accountants and Auditors	29.28	Maids and Housekeeping Cleaners	7.99
Automotive Mechanics	16.59	Maintenance and Repair Workers	14.88
Bookkeepers	15.17	Marketing Managers	50.62
Carpenters	13.98	Nuclear Medicine Technologists	32.29
Cashiers	8.48	Nurses, Licensed Practical	19.07
Clerks, General Office	10.99	Nurses, Registered	28.31
Clerks, Receptionists/Information	11.62	Nursing Aides/Orderlies/Attendants	10.32
Clerks, Shipping/Receiving	13.23	Packers and Packagers, Hand	9.27
Computer Programmers	37.02	Physical Therapists	35.73
Computer Support Specialists	19.60	Postal Service Mail Carriers	21.42
Computer Systems Analysts	34.67	Real Estate Brokers	60.65
Cooks, Restaurant	9.77	Retail Salespersons	11.37
Dentists	n/a	Sales Reps., Exc. Tech./Scientific	28.58
Electrical Engineers	37.06	Sales Reps., Tech./Scientific	35.67
Electricians	19.68	Secretaries, Exc. Legal/Med./Exec.	12.96
Financial Managers	51.18	Security Guards	12.69
First-Line Supervisors/Mgrs., Sales	18.36	Surgeons	89.84
Food Preparation Workers	8.34	Teacher Assistants	8.00
General and Operations Managers	49.14	Teachers, Elementary School	22.40
Hairdressers/Cosmetologists	11.26	Teachers, Secondary School	23.80
Internists	71.55	Telemarketers	9.61
Janitors and Cleaners	9.36	Truck Drivers, Heavy/Tractor-Trailer	17.47
Landscaping/Groundskeeping Workers	10.75	Truck Drivers, Light/Delivery Svcs.	13.97
Lawyers	51.71	Waiters and Waitresses	7.67

Note: Wage data covers the Fort Worth-Arlington, TX Metropolitan Division - see Appendix B for areas included. Hourly wages for elementary/secondary school teachers and teacher assistants were calculated by the editors from annual wage data assuming a 40 hour work week; n/a not available.
Source: Bureau of Labor Statistics, May 2007 Metro Area Occupational Employment and Wage Estimates

RESIDENTIAL REAL ESTATE

Building Permits

Area	Single-Family 2006	Single-Family 2007p	Single-Family Pct. Chg.	Multi-Family 2006	Multi-Family 2007p	Multi-Family Pct. Chg.	Total 2006	Total 2007p	Total Pct. Chg.
City	129	96	-25.6	0	0	-	129	96	-25.6
U.S.	1,378,200	973,300	-29.4	460,700	407,200	-11.6	1,838,900	1,380,500	-24.9

Note: (p) preliminary; figures cover and represent new, privately-owned housing units authorized (unadjusted data); All permit data are based on estimates with imputation; U.S. figures are based on the new 20,000-place series.
Source: U.S. Census Bureau, Manufacturing, Mining, and Construction Statistics

Homeownership and Housing Vacancies

Area	Homeownership Rate[2] (%)			Rental Vacancy Rate[3] (%)			Homeowner Vacancy Rate[4] (%)		
	2005	2006	2007	2005	2006	2007	2005	2006	2007
MSA[1]	62.3	60.7	60.9	13.6	11.7	11.0	2.2	2.3	2.5
U.S.	68.9	68.8	68.1	9.8	9.8	9.7	1.9	2.4	2.7

Note: (1) Metropolitan Statistical Area - see Appendix B for areas included; (2) The proportion of households that are owners; (3) The proportion of the rental inventory that is vacant for rent; (4) The proportion of the homeowner inventory that is vacant for sale; n/a not available
Source: U.S. Census Bureau, Housing Vacancies and Homeownership Annual Statistics: 2007

TAXES

State Corporate Income Tax Rates

State	Rates and Tax Brackets
Texas	1.0%

Note: Tax rates as of January 1, 2008; Texas's 1% franchise tax is a gross receipts tax paid by most taxable entities. Retailers pay 0.5%.
Source: Tax Foundation, www.taxfoundation.org

State Individual Income Tax Rates

State	Federal Deductibility	Marginal Rates (%)	Standard Deduction ($)		Personal Exemptions ($)[1]	
			Single	Joint	Single	Dependents
Texas	No	None	n/a	n/a	n/a	n/a

Note: Tax rates as of January 1, 2008; Local- and county-level taxes are not included; n/a not applicable; (1) Married joint filers generally receive double the single exemption
Source: Tax Foundation, www.taxfoundation.org

Various State and Local Tax Rates

State and Local Sales and Use (%)	State Sales and Use (%)	Gasoline[1,2] ($/gal.)	Cigarette ($/pack)	Spirits ($/gal.)	Table Wine ($/gal.)	Beer ($/gal.)
8.25	6.25 (i)	0.20	1.41	2.40	0.204	0.19

Note: Tax rates as of January 1, 2008; (1) In addition to the 18.4 cpg Federal gasoline tax; (2) Rates may include additional state sales taxes, environmental protection and storage fees/taxes, and local taxes. When necessary, the volume-weighted average of all local taxes is used to approximate the typical statewide rate including local tax; (i) Texas has a GRT that is levied in addition to its 6.25% sales tax. It is called the franchise tax and the rate is 1% (.5% for retailers).
Source: Tax Foundation, www.taxfoundation.org; Original research

State Tax Burdens

Area	Combined State and Local Tax Burden		Combined Federal, State and Local Tax Burden	
	Percent	Rank	Percent	Rank
Texas	9.3	43	29.8	41
U.S. Average	11.0	-	32.7	-

Note: Figures cover 2007 and measure taxes as a percentage of income
Source: Tax Foundation, www.taxfoundation.org

State Business Tax Climate Index Rankings

State	Overall Rank	Corporate Tax Index Rank	Individual Income Tax Index Rank	Sales Tax Index Rank	Unemployment Insurance Tax Index Rank	Property Tax Index Rank
Texas	8	47	7	28	14	27

Note: Rankings range from 1 to 50 where 1 is best. Rankings do not average across to Overall Rank. States without a given tax are given a ranking of 1.
Source: Tax Foundation, State Business Tax Climate Index 2008

TRANSPORTATION

Means of Transportation to Work

Area	Car/Truck/Van		Public Transportation			Bicycle	Walked	Other Means	Worked at Home
	Drove Alone	Car-pooled	Bus	Subway	Railroad				
City	84.8	6.1	0.0	0.0	0.0	0.1	0.7	1.7	6.6
MSA[1]	81.2	13.3	0.4	0.0	0.0	0.1	1.4	0.9	2.7
U.S.	75.7	12.2	2.5	1.5	0.5	0.4	2.9	1.0	3.3

Note: Figures are percentages and cover workers 16 years of age and older; (1) Metropolitan Statistical Area - see Appendix A for areas included
Source: Census 2000, Summary File 3

Travel Time to Work

Area	Less Than 15 Minutes	15 to 29 Minutes	30 to 44 Minutes	45 to 59 Minutes	60 Minutes or More
City	18.3	29.9	33.1	12.6	6.1
MSA[1]	23.4	37.8	22.6	8.8	7.5
U.S.	29.4	36.1	19.1	7.4	8.0

Note: Figures are percentages and include workers 16 years old and over; (1) Metropolitan Statistical Area - see Appendix A for areas included
Source: Census 2000, Summary File 3

Travel Time Index

Area	1982	1995	2004	2005
Urban Area[1]	1.05	1.16	1.31	1.35
Average[2]	1.11	1.22	1.29	1.30

Note: Travel Time Index - The ratio of travel time in the peak period to the travel time at free-flow conditions. A value of 1.35 indicates a 20-minute free-flow trip takes 27 minutes in the peak. Free-flow speeds (60 mph on freeways and 35 mph on principal arterials) are used as the comparison threshold; (1) Covers the Dallas-Fort Worth-Arlington, TX urban area; (2) average of 85 urban areas
Source: Texas Transportation Institute, The 2007 Urban Mobility Report, September 2007

Living Environment

COST OF LIVING

Cost of Living Index

Composite Index	Groceries	Housing	Utilities	Trans-portation	Health Care	Misc. Goods/ Services
88.5	95.3	74.9	98.3	97.7	90.1	91.2

Note: U.S. = 100; Figures cover the Fort Worth TX urban area.
Source: The Council for Community and Economic Research (formerly ACCRA), Cost of Living Index, 2007

Grocery Prices

Area[1]	T-Bone Steak ($/pound)	Frying Chicken ($/pound)	Whole Milk ($/half gal.)	Eggs ($/dozen)	Orange Juice ($/64 oz.)	Coffee ($/11.5 oz.)
City[2]	9.03	0.96	2.28	1.50	3.11	3.04
Avg.	8.93	1.12	2.13	1.52	3.26	3.31
Min.	5.88	0.71	1.33	0.83	2.30	2.20
Max.	12.80	2.07	3.43	3.54	5.79	6.20

Note: (1) Values for the local area are compared with the average, minimum and maximum values for all 331 areas in the Cost of Living Index report; (2) Figures cover the Fort Worth TX urban area; **T-Bone Steak** *(price per pound);* **Frying Chicken** *(price per pound, whole fryer);* **Whole Milk** *(half gallon carton);* **Eggs** *(price per dozen, Grade A, large);* **Orange Juice** *(64 oz. Tropicana or Florida Natural);* **Coffee** *(11.5 oz. can, vacuum-packed, Maxwell House, Hills Bros, or Folgers).*
Source: The Council for Community and Economic Research (formerly ACCRA), Cost of Living Index, 2007

Housing and Utility Costs

Area[1]	New Home Price ($)	Apartment Rent ($/month)	All Electric ($/month)	Part Electric ($/month)	Other Energy ($/month)	Telephone ($/month)
City[2]	213,267	815	-	112.12	50.83	24.95
Avg.	309,605	782	146.13	78.67	90.16	26.14
Min.	189,877	n/a	82.03	37.41	33.15	17.08
Max.	1,202,800	3,481	271.14	150.60	257.67	37.45

Note: (1) Values for the local area are compared with the average, minimum and maximum values for all 331 areas in the Cost of Living Index report; (2) Figures cover the Fort Worth TX urban area; **New Home Price** *(2,400 sf living area, 8,000 sf lot, in urban area with full utilities);* **Apartment Rent** *(950 sf 2 bedroom/1.5 or 2 bath, unfurnished, excluding all utilities except water);* **All Electric** *(average monthly cost for an all-electric home);* **Part Electric** *(average monthly cost for a part-electric home);* **Other Energy** *(average monthly cost for natural gas, fuel oil, coal, wood, and any other forms of energy except electricity);* **Telephone** *(price includes basic monthly rate for a private residential line plus additional local usage charges incurred by a family of four).*
Source: The Council for Community and Economic Research (formerly ACCRA), Cost of Living Index, 2007

Health Care, Transportation, and Other Costs

Area[1]	Doctor ($/visit)	Dentist ($/visit)	Optometrist ($/visit)	Gasoline ($/gallon)	Beauty Salon ($/visit)	Men's Shirt ($)
City[2]	61.32	67.49	47.44	2.46	30.46	21.38
Avg.	79.48	71.93	79.55	2.64	29.52	25.77
Min.	52.08	44.80	43.95	2.19	15.58	16.19
Max.	148.44	126.27	158.83	3.48	60.62	48.53

Note: (1) Values for the local area are compared with the average, minimum and maximum values for all 331 areas in the Cost of Living Index report; (2) Figures cover the Fort Worth TX urban area; **Doctor** *(general practitioners routine exam of an established patient);* **Dentist** *(adult teeth cleaning and periodic oral examination);* **Optometrist** *(full vision eye exam for established adult patient);* **Gasoline** *(one gallon regular unleaded, national brand, including all taxes, cash price at self-service pump if available);* **Beauty Salon** *(woman's shampoo, trim, and blow-dry);* **Men's Shirt** *(cotton/polyester dress shirt, pinpoint weave, long sleeves).*
Source: The Council for Community and Economic Research (formerly ACCRA), Cost of Living Index, 2007

HOUSING

House Price Index (HPI)

Area	National Ranking[2]	Quarterly Change (%)	One-Year Change (%)	Five-Year Change (%)
MD[1]	101	0.50	2.89	17.43
U.S.[3]	-	0.10	0.84	41.37

Note: The HPI is a weighted repeat sales index. It measures average price changes in repeat sales or refinancings on the same properties. This information is obtained by reviewing repeat mortgage transactions on single-family properties whose mortgages have been purchased or securitized by Fannie Mae or Freddie Mac in January 1975; (1) Metropolitan Division - see Appendix B for areas included; (2) Rankings are based on annual percentage change for all metro areas containing at least 15,000 transactions over the last 10 years and ranges from 1 to 291; (3) figures based on a weighted average of Census Division estimates; all figures are for the period ending December 31, 2007
Source: Office of Federal Housing Enterprise Oversight, House Price Index, February 26, 2008

House Price Valuations

Area	Q1 2000	Q1 2001	Q1 2002	Q1 2003	Q1 2004	Q1 2005	Q1 2006	Q1 2007	Q1 2008
MD[1]	-14.6	-20.0	-17.5	-16.8	-19.8	-20.4	-21.9	-24.8	-28.8

Note: Figures show the percentage of over- or under-valuation of single family homes relative to statistically normal house values (e.g. a value of 23.6 indicates that house values are 23.6% overvalued). Statistically normal house values are based on house prices, interest rates, household incomes, population densities, and any historical premiums or discounts metropolitan areas have exhibited over time; (1) Figures cover the Metropolitan Division - see Appendix B for areas included
Source: Global Insight/National City Corporation, House Prices in America, May 2008

Median Home Prices

Area	2005	2006	2007[r]	Percent Change 2006 to 2007
MSA[1]	147.6	149.5	150.9	0.9
U.S. Average	219.0	221.9	217.9	-1.8

Note: Figures are median sales prices of existing single-family homes in thousands of dollars; (r) revised; n/a not available; (1) Metropolitan Statistical Area - see Appendix B for areas included
Source: National Association of Realtors, Metropolitan Area Prices, 1st Quarter 2008

Housing: Year Structure Built

Area	1990 -2000	1980 -1989	1970 -1979	1960 -1969	1950 -1959	1940 -1949	Before 1940	Median Year
City	67.5	19.3	6.8	3.3	1.9	0.8	0.5	1994
MSA[1]	21.4	26.8	19.2	12.5	11.1	4.9	4.1	1979
U.S.	17.0	15.8	18.5	13.7	12.7	7.3	15.0	1971

Note: Figures are percentages; (1) Metropolitan Statistical Area - see Appendix A for areas included
Source: Census 2000, Summary File 3

HEALTH

Health Risk Data

Category	Area[1] (%)	U.S. (%)
Adults who have been told they have high blood pressure[3]	22.8	25.5
Adults who have been told they have high blood cholesterol[3]	31.8	35.6
Adults who have been told they have diabetes[2]	8.2	7.5
Adults who have been told they have arthritis[3]	20.0	27.0
Adults who have been told they currently have asthma	7.5	8.5
Adults who are current smokers	19.9	20.1
Adults who are heavy drinkers[4]	3.8	4.9
Adults who are overweight (BMI 25.0 - 29.9)	43.2	36.5
Adults who are obese (BMI 30.0 - 99.8)	23.9	25.1

Note: Data as of 2006 unless otherwise noted; (1) Figures cover the Metropolitan Division - see Appendix B for areas included; (2) Figures do not include pregnancy-related diabetes, pre-diabetes or borderline diabetes; (3) 2005 data; (4) Heavy drinkers are classified as adult men having more than two drinks per day or adult women having more than one drink per day
Source: Centers for Disease Control and Prevention, Behaviorial Risk Factor Surveillance System, SMART: Selected Metropolitan/Micropolitan Area Risk Trends, 2005, 2006

Mortality Rates for the Top 10 Causes of Death in the U.S.

ICD-10[a] Sub-Chapter	ICD-10[a] Code	Age-Adjusted Mortality Rate[1] per 100,000 population	
		County[2]	U.S.
Malignant neoplasms	C00-C97	182.1	186.5
Ischaemic heart diseases	I20-I25	159.9	152.3
Other forms of heart disease	I30-I51	47.7	51.5
Cerebrovascular diseases	I60-I69	64.5	50.0
Chronic lower respiratory diseases	J40-J47	49.3	42.6
Diabetes mellitus	E10-E14	26.0	24.8
Other degenerative diseases of the nervous system	G30-G31	28.3	22.6
Other external causes of accidental injury	W00-X59	18.0	21.4
Influenza and pneumonia	J10-J18	14.4	20.7
Hypertensive diseases	I10-I13	27.7	18.2

Note: (a) ICD-10 = International Classification of Diseases 10th Revision; (1) Mortality rates are a three year average covering 2003-2005; (2) Figures cover Tarrant County
Source: Centers for Disease Control and Prevention, National Center for Health Statistics. Compressed Mortality File 1999-2004. CDC WONDER On-line Database, compiled from Compressed Mortality File 1999-2005 Series 20 No. 2K, 2008.

Mortality Rates for Selected Causes of Death

ICD-10[a] Sub-Chapter	ICD-10[a] Code	Age-Adjusted Mortality Rate[1] per 100,000 population	
		County[2]	U.S.
Assault	X85-Y09	5.6	5.9
Human immunodeficiency virus (HIV) disease	B20-B24	4.2	4.5
Intentional self-harm	X60-X84	10.9	10.8
Malnutrition	E40-E46	1.3	1.0
Obesity and other hyperalimentation	E65-E68	1.3	1.4
Organic, including symptomatic, mental disorders	F01-F09	26.5	16.8
Transport accidents	V01-V99	13.1	16.1
Viral hepatitis	B15-B19	2.1	1.8

Note: (a) ICD-10 = International Classification of Diseases 10th Revision; (1) Mortality rates are a three year average covering 2003-2005; (2) Figures cover Tarrant County
Source: Centers for Disease Control and Prevention, National Center for Health Statistics. Compressed Mortality File 1999-2004. CDC WONDER On-line Database, compiled from Compressed Mortality File 1999-2005 Series 20 No. 2K, 2008.

Distribution of Physicians[1]

Area	Total	Family/ General Practice	Specialties	
			Medical	Surgical
Tarrant County (number)	2,255	578	750	598
Tarrant County (rate per 10,000 pop.)	13.9	3.6	4.6	3.7
U.S. (rate per 10,000 pop.)	17.7	4.6	6.9	4.3

Note: Data as of 2005; (1) Includes all non-federal, patient-care, office-based MDs
Source: Area Resource File (ARF). June 2007. U.S. Department of Health and Human Services, Health Resources and Services Administration, Bureau of Health Professions, Rockville, MD.

Hospitals

There were no hospitals listed within the city limits.
AHA Guide to the Healthcare Field 2008

According to *U.S. News,* the Dallas-Fort Worth-Arlington, TX metro area is home to six of the best hospitals in the U.S.: **Baylor Institute for Rehabilitation**; **Baylor University Medical Center**; **Children's Medical Center Dallas**; **Parkland Memorial Hospital**; **Presbyterian Hospital**; **University of Texas Southwestern Medical Center**. *U.S. News Online, "America's Best Hospitals 2007"*

EDUCATION

Public School District Statistics

District Name	Schls	Pupils	Pupil/ Teacher Ratio	Minority Pupils[1] (%)	Free Lunch Eligible[2] (%)	IEP[3] (%)
Carroll ISD	12	7,559	15.6	11.7	1.3	10.8
Keller ISD	33	25,873	17.3	26.9	7.6	8.0

Note: Table includes regular local school districts with 2,000 or more students; (1) Percentage of students that are not white, non-Hispanic; (2) Percentage of students that are eligible for the free lunch program; (3) Percentage of students that have an Individualized Education Program.
Source: U.S. Department of Education, National Center for Education Statistics, Common Core of Data, Local Education Agency (School District) Universe Survey: School Year 2005-2006; U.S. Department of Education, National Center for Education Statistics, Common Core of Data, Public Elementary/Secondary School Universe Survey: School Year 2005-2006

Highest Level of Education

Area	Less than H.S.	H.S. Diploma	Some College, No Deg.	Associate Degree	Bachelors Degree	Masters Degree	Profess. School Degree	Doctorate Degree
City	3.5	12.2	20.1	5.3	39.7	14.6	3.4	1.1
MSA[1]	19.2	22.3	23.5	5.7	20.3	6.4	1.7	0.8
U.S.	19.4	28.4	21.2	6.4	15.7	5.9	2.0	1.0

Note: Figures are 2007 estimated percentages and cover persons age 25 and over; (1) Metropolitan Statistical Area - see Appendix B for areas included
Source: Claritas, Inc.

Educational Attainment by Race

Area	High School Graduate (%)					Bachelor's Degree (%)				
	Total	White	Black	Asian	Hisp.[2]	Total	White	Black	Asian	Hisp.[2]
City	96.6	96.9	94.5	90.1	87.1	59.2	59.5	48.6	69.3	49.5
MSA[1]	81.0	84.9	80.2	72.4	46.6	25.1	27.3	16.8	36.3	9.2
U.S.	80.4	83.6	72.3	80.4	52.4	24.4	26.1	14.3	44.1	10.4

Note: Figures shown cover persons 25 years old and over; (1) Metropolitan Statistical Area - see Appendix A for areas included; (2) people of Hispanic origin can be of any race
Source: Census 2000, Summary File 3

School Enrollment by Type

Area	Grades KG to 8				Grades 9 to 12			
	Public		Private		Public		Private	
	Enrollment	%	Enrollment	%	Enrollment	%	Enrollment	%
City	4,093	92.0	355	8.0	1,749	96.1	71	3.9
MSA[1]	224,258	91.0	22,110	9.0	91,305	92.3	7,600	7.7
U.S.	33,526,011	88.7	4,285,121	11.3	14,848,628	90.6	1,532,323	9.4

Note: Figures shown cover persons 3 years old and over; (1) Metropolitan Statistical Area - see Appendix A for areas included
Source: Census 2000, Summary File 3

School Enrollment by Race

Area	Grades KG to 8 (%)				Grades 9 to 12 (%)			
	White	Black	Asian	Hisp.[1]	White	Black	Asian	Hisp.[1]
City	94.8	1.4	1.1	3.9	93.8	1.1	2.7	4.0
MSA[2]	69.1	12.9	2.8	23.7	69.0	14.1	3.6	19.9
U.S.	68.5	15.5	3.3	16.8	68.8	15.5	3.8	15.7

Note: Figures shown cover persons 3 years old and over; (1) people of Hispanic origin can be of any race; (2) Metropolitan Statistical Area - see Appendix A for areas included
Source: Census 2000, Summary File 3

Average Salaries of Public School Classroom Teachers

District	2005-06		2006-07		Percent Change
	Dollars	Rank[1]	Dollars	Rank[1]	2005-06 to 2006-07
Texas	41,744	35	44,897	30	7.55
U.S. Average	49,026	-	50,816	-	3.65

Note: (1) State rank ranges from 1 to 51.
Source: National Education Association, Rankings & Estimates: Rankings of the States 2006 and Estimates of School Statistics 2007, December 2007

Higher Education

Four-Year Colleges			Two-Year Colleges			Medical Schools[1]	Law Schools[2]	Voc/ Tech[3]
Public	Private Non-profit	Private For-profit	Public	Private Non-profit	Private For-profit			
0	0	0	0	0	0	0	0	0

Note: Figures cover institutions located within the city limits; (1) includes schools accredited by the Liaison Committee on Medical Education and the American Osteopathic Association; (2) includes American Bar Association-accredited law schools; (3) includes all schools with programs that are less than 2 years.
Source: National Center for Education Statistics, The Integrated Postsecondary Education System (IPEDS) Peer Analysis System, 2007; www.usnews.com, Law and Medical School Directories, 2009

PRESIDENTIAL ELECTION

2004 Presidential Election Results

Area	Bush	Kerry	Nader	Other
Tarrant County	62.4	37.0	0.1	0.5
U.S.	50.7	48.3	0.4	0.6

Note: Results are percentages and may not add to 100% due to rounding
Source: Dave Leip's Atlas of U.S. Presidential Elections, www.uselectionatlas.org

EMPLOYERS

Major Employers

Company Name	Industry	Type of Site
A M R Corporation	Air transportation, scheduled	Headquarters
Alcon Holdings Inc	Pharmaceutical preparations	Headquarters
Archer-Western Contractors	Nonresidential construction, nec	Single
BNSF Railway Company	Railroads, line-haul operating	Branch
Bell Helicopter Textron Inc	Aircraft	Headquarters
Bimbo Bakeries Usa Inc	Bread, cake, and related products	Headquarters
Federal Aviation ADM	Regulation, administration of transportation	Branch
Gamestop	Catalog and mail-order houses	Headquarters
General Motors	Motor vehicles and car bodies	Branch
General Motors	New and used car dealers	Branch
John Peter Smith Hospital	General medical and surgical hospitals	Headquarters
Mrs Bairds Bakeries Bus Tr	Bread, cake, and related products	Headquarters
Psychological/Deaf Svcs Dept	Elementary and secondary schools	Branch
Radio Shack	Radio, television, and electronic stores	Branch
Sabre Travel Info Network	Travel agencies	Headquarters
Tpg Capital - New York Inc	Investors, nec	Headquarters

Note: Companies shown are located within the Fort Worth metropolitan area; nec = not elsewhere classified.
Source: www.zapdata.com, May 2008

PUBLIC SAFETY

Crime Rate

Area	All Crimes	Violent Crimes				Property Crimes		
		Murder	Forcible Rape	Robbery	Aggrav. Assault	Burglary	Larceny -Theft	Motor Vehicle Theft
City	2,323.5	0.0	0.0	11.7	39.1	413.9	1,776.8	82.0
Metro[1]	4,914.1	4.1	36.5	143.0	299.9	984.4	3,066.3	379.9
U.S.	3,808.1	5.7	30.9	149.4	287.5	729.4	2,206.8	398.4

Note: Figures are crimes per 100,000 population; (1) Metropolitan Division - see Appendix B for areas included
Source: FBI Uniform Crime Reports, 2006

Hate Crimes

Area	Number of Quarters Reported	Bias Motivation				
		Race	Religion	Sexual Orientation	Ethnicity	Disability
City	4	0	0	0	0	0

Source: Federal Bureau of Investigation, Hate Crime Statistics 2006

RECREATION

Culture

Dance[1]	Theatre[1]	Instrumental Music[1]	Vocal Music[1]	Series/ Festivals	Museums	Zoos and Aquariums[2]
0	0	0	0	0	0	0

Note: (1) Number of professional perfoming groups; (2) AZA-accredited
Source: The Grey House Performing Arts Directory, 2007; Official Museum Directory, 2008; Association of Zoos & Aquariums, AZA Member Zoos & Aquariums, June 2008

Professional Sports Teams

Team Name	League
Texas Rangers	Major League Baseball (MLB)
FC Dallas	Major League Soccer (MLS)
Dallas Mavericks	National Basketball Association (NBA)
Dallas Cowboys	National Football League (NFL)
Dallas Stars	National Hockey League (NHL)

Note: Includes teams located in the Dallas-Fort Worth metro area.
Source: Original research

MEDIA

Newspapers

Name	News Focus	Frequency	Circulation
Southlake Journal	Community	Weekly	n/a

Note: Includes newspapers with offices located in the city; n/a not available
Source: MediaContactsPro, March 2008

Television Stations

Name	Ch.	Network(s)	Type	Ownership
KDTN	2	PBS	Public	North Texas Public Broadcasting Inc.
KDFW	4	Fox	Commercial	Fox Television Stations Inc.
KXAS	5	NBC	Commercial	General Electric Corporation
WFAA	8	ABC	Commercial	Belo Corporation
KTVT	11	CBS	Commercial	CBS
KERA	13	PBS	Public	North Texas Public Broadcasting Inc.
KSST	18	n/a	Commercial	Hopkins County Broadcasting Inc.
KTXA	21	UPN	Commercial	CBS
KUVN	23	Univision	Commercial	Perenchio Television Inc.
KDFI	27	Fox	Commercial	Fox Television Stations Inc.
KMPX	29	n/a	Non-comm.	n/a
KDAF	33	WBN	Commercial	Tribune Broadcasting Company
KXTX	39	Telemundo	Commercial	Telemundo Group Inc.
KTAQ	47	n/a	Commercial	Michael Simons
KSTR	49	Univision	Commercial	Univision Television Group
KFWD	52	n/a	Commercial	n/a
KDTX	58	n/a	Non-comm.	Trinity Broadcasting Network
KPXD	68	Pax	Commercial	Paxson Communications Corporation

Note: Stations included cover the Dallas-Fort Worth DMA (Designated Market Area)
BurrellesLuce, MediaContacts Online, January 2007

Major AM Radio Stations

Call Letters	Freq. (kHz)	Station Type	Target Audience	Station Format	Music Format
KLIF	570	Commercial	General/Men	News/Talk	n/a
KMKI	620	n/a	General	Music	n/a
KSKY	660	n/a	General/Hisp/Rel	Music/Sports/Talk	n/a
KKDA	730	Commercial	General	Music/News	Rhythm & Blues
KAAM	770	Commercial	General	Music	Adult Standards
WBAP	820	Commercial	General	Educational/News/Talk	n/a
KFJZ	870	Commercial	General/Hispanic	Music/News/Sports/Talk	Latin
KKLF	950	n/a	General	News/Talk	n/a
KHVN	970	n/a	Christian/General	Music	n/a
KGGR	1040	n/a	Black/General/Rel	Talk	n/a
KRLD	1080	n/a	General	n/a	n/a
KBIS	1150	n/a	General/Hispanic	Music/News/Talk	n/a
KSST	1230	n/a	General	Music/News	Easy Listening
KPJC	1250	College	General	Music/News	Jazz
KTCK	1310	Commercial	General	Talk	n/a
KAND	1340	Commercial	General	Music/News	Country
KAHZ	1360	n/a	General/Hispanic	Ed/News/Sports/Talk	n/a
KBEC	1390	Commercial	General	Music	Country
KGVL	1400	n/a	General	Music/News/Sports	n/a
KLVQ	1410	n/a	General/Religious	Music	n/a
KFYN	1420	n/a	General	Music/News/Sports	n/a
KTNO	1440	Commercial	Hispanic/Religious	Music/Talk	Gospel
KNET	1450	n/a	General	Music	n/a
KTFW	1460	Commercial	General/Hispanic	n/a	n/a
KPLT	1490	Commercial	General	Music/News/Sports/Talk	Gospel
KSTV	1510	Commercial	General/Hispanic	Music	Top 40
KZMP	1540	n/a	General/Hispanic	Music	n/a
KCOM	1550	Commercial	General/Hispanic	Music	Country
KTBK	1700	Commercial	General	Sports/Talk	n/a

Note: Stations included cover the Dallas-Fort Worth DMA (Designated Market Area); n/a not available
Source: BurrellesLuce, MediaContacts Online, January 2007

Major FM Radio Stations

Call Letters	Freq. (mHz)	Station Type	Target Audience	Station Format	Music Format
KNTU	88.1	College	General	Educational/Music/News	n/a
KEOM	88.5	n/a	General	Ed/Music/News/Sports	n/a
KETR	88.9	College	General	Music/Sports	n/a
KNON	89.3	Non-Comm	Black/Hispanic	Ed/Music/News/Talk	Album Rock
KERA	90.1	Public	General	Music/Talk	Folk
KCBI	90.9	n/a	General/Religious	Music/News	n/a
KVTT	91.7	n/a	General/Religious	Educational/Talk	n/a
KZPS	92.5	n/a	General	Music/News/Talk	n/a
KSTV	93.1	Commercial	General	Music/News	Country
KDBN	93.3	Commercial	General	Music/Talk	Classic Rock
KLNO	94.1	Commercial	General/Hispanic	Music	Latin
KLTY	94.9	Commercial	General/Religious	Music/News/Talk	Christian
KZZA	95.1	Commercial	General	Music	Latin
KSCS	96.3	Commercial	General	Music/News/Talk	Country
KEGL	97.1	Commercial	General	Music/News/Sports	Modern Rock
KBFB	97.9	Commercial	General	Music	Urban Contemp.
KYYK	98.3	n/a	General	Music	n/a
KLUV	98.7	Commercial	General	Music/News/Talk	Oldies
KHCK	99.1	Commercial	General/Hispanic	Music	Latin
KPLX	99.5	Commercial	General	Music	Country
WRR	101.1	Commercial	General	Music/News/Talk	Classical
KZMP	101.7	n/a	General/Hispanic	Music	n/a
KBUS	101.9	Commercial	General	Music/News	Classic Rock
KDGE	102.1	Commercial	Young Adult	Music/News/Talk	Alternative
KDMX	102.9	Commercial	General/Women	Music/News/Talk	Adult Top 40
KVIL	103.7	n/a	General	Music	n/a
KKDA	104.5	n/a	Black/General	Music	n/a
KRNB	105.7	n/a	General	Music/News/Sports	n/a
KHKS	106.1	Commercial	General	Music/News/Talk	Top 40
KOAI	107.5	n/a	General	Music/Talk	n/a
KPLT	107.7	n/a	General	Music/News	Top 40
KDXX	107.9	Commercial	General/Hispanic	Music/News/Talk	Adult Contemp.

Note: Stations included cover the Dallas-Fort Worth DMA (Designated Market Area); n/a not available
BurrellesLuce, MediaContacts Online, January 2007

CLIMATE

Average and Extreme Temperatures

Temperature	Jan	Feb	Mar	Apr	May	Jun	Jul	Aug	Sep	Oct	Nov	Dec	Yr.
Extreme High (°F)	88	88	96	98	103	113	110	108	107	106	89	90	113
Average High (°F)	54	59	67	76	83	92	96	96	88	79	67	58	76
Average Temp. (°F)	44	49	57	66	73	81	85	85	78	68	56	47	66
Average Low (°F)	33	38	45	54	63	71	75	74	67	56	45	37	55
Extreme Low (°F)	4	6	11	29	41	51	59	56	43	29	19	-1	-1

Note: Figures cover the years 1953-1990
Source: National Climatic Data Center, International Station Meteorological Climate Summary, 9/96

Average Precipitation/Snowfall/Humidity

Precip./Humidity	Jan	Feb	Mar	Apr	May	Jun	Jul	Aug	Sep	Oct	Nov	Dec	Yr.
Avg. Precip. (in.)	1.8	2.2	2.6	3.7	4.9	2.8	2.1	1.9	3.0	3.3	2.1	1.7	32.3
Avg. Snowfall (in.)	1	1	Tr	0	0	0	0	0	0	0	Tr	Tr	3
Avg. Rel. Hum. 6am (%)	79	79	79	81	86	85	80	79	83	82	80	79	81
Avg. Rel. Hum. 3pm (%)	52	51	48	50	53	47	42	41	46	47	49	51	48

Note: Figures cover the years 1953-1990; Tr = Trace amounts (<0.05 in. of rain; <0.5 in. of snow)
Source: National Climatic Data Center, International Station Meteorological Climate Summary, 9/96

Weather Conditions

Temperature			Daytime Sky			Precipitation		
10°F & below	32°F & below	90°F & above	Clear	Partly cloudy	Cloudy	0.01 inch or more precip.	0.1 inch or more snow/ice	Thunder-storms
1	40	100	123	136	106	79	3	47

Note: Figures are average number of days per year and cover the years 1953-1990
Source: National Climatic Data Center, International Station Meteorological Climate Summary, 9/96

HAZARDOUS WASTE

Superfund Sites

Southlake has no sites on the EPA's Superfund Final National Priorities List.
U.S. Environmental Protection Agency, Final National Priorities List, June 23, 2008

AIR & WATER QUALITY

Air Quality Index

Area	Percent of Days when Air Quality was...[2]				AQI Statistics	
	Good	Moderate	Unhealthy for Sensitive Groups	Unhealthy	Maximum	Median
MSA[1]	65.2	29.0	5.2	0.5	203	43

Note: The Air Quality Index (AQI) is an index for reporting daily air quality. EPA calculates the AQI for five major air pollutants regulated by the Clean Air Act: ground-level ozone, particle pollution (also known as particulate matter), carbon monoxide, sulfur dioxide, and nitrogen dioxide. The AQI runs from 0 to 500. The higher the AQI value, the greater the level of air pollution and the greater the health concern. There are six AQI categories: "Good" The AQI is between 0 and 50. Air quality is considered satisfactory; "Moderate" The AQI is between 51 and 100. Air quality is acceptable; "Unhealthy for Sensitive Groups" When AQI values are between 101 and 150, members of sensitive groups may experience health effects; "Unhealthy" When AQI values are between 151 and 200 everyone may begin to experience health effects; "Very Unhealthy" AQI values between 201 and 300 trigger a health alert; "Hazardous" AQI values over 300 trigger health warnings of emergency conditions; (1) Metropolitan Statistical Area - see Appendix A for areas included; (2) Based on 365 days with AQI data in 2007.
Source: U.S. Environmental Protection Agency, Air Quality Index Report, 2007

Air Quality Index Pollutants

Area	Percent of Days when AQI Pollutant was...[2]					
	Carbon Monoxide	Nitrogen Dioxide	Ozone	Sulfur Dioxide	Particulate Matter 2.5	Particulate Matter 10
MSA[1]	0.0	0.0	59.2	0.0	40.8	0.0

Note: The Air Quality Index (AQI) is an index for reporting daily air quality. EPA calculates the AQI for five major air pollutants regulated by the Clean Air Act: ground-level ozone, particle pollution (also known as particulate matter), carbon monoxide, sulfur dioxide, and nitrogen dioxide. The AQI runs from 0 to 500. The higher the AQI value, the greater the level of air pollution and the greater the health concern; (1) Metropolitan Statistical Area - see Appendix A for areas included; (2) Based on 365 days with AQI data in 2007.
Source: U.S. Environmental Protection Agency, Air Quality Index Report, 2007

Air Quality Index Trends

Area	Trend Sites (7)								All Sites (33)
	1999	2000	2001	2002	2003	2004	2005	2006	2006
MSA[1]	19	17	17	23	25	11	22	19	23

Note: An AQI value greater than 100 indicates that air quality would have been in the unhealthful range on that day. Data from exceptional events are not included. These counts are presented in two ways. First, the counts are based on sites having an adequate record of monitoring data during the trend period (trend sites). These counts represent the relative change in the number of days with AQI values greater than 100. In the last column, the counts are based on all sites with data in the most recent year (because it is possible for a site to have data in the most recent year but not enough data to be a trend site); (1) Metropolitan Statistical Area - see Appendix A for areas included.
Source: U.S. Environmental Protection Agency, Office of Air and Radiation, Air Trends, Factbook and Related Information, Air Pollution Trends in Selected Metropolitan Areas 2006

Maximum Air Pollutant Concentrations

	Particulate Matter 10 (ug/m^3)	Particulate Matter 2.5 (ug/m^3)	Ozone (ppm)	Carbon Monoxide (ppm)	Sulfur Dioxide (ppm)	Nitrogen Dioxide (ppm)	Lead (ug/m^3)
MSA[1] Level	34	23	0.114	1	n/a	0.014	n/a
NAAQS[2]	150	35	0.125	9	0.140	0.053	1.50
Met NAAQS[2]	Yes	Yes	Yes	Yes	n/a	Yes	n/a

Note: Data from exceptional events are not included; (1) Metropolitan Statistical Area - see Appendix A for areas included; (2) National Ambient Air Quality Standards; n/a not available
Concentrations: Particulate Matter 10 (coarse particulate) - highest second maximum 24-hour concentration; Particulate Matter 2.5 (fine particulate) - highest 98th percentile 24-hour concentration; Ozone - highest second daily maximum 1-hour concentration; Carbon Monoxide - highest second maximum non-overlapping 8-hour concentration; Sulfur Dioxide - highest second maximum 24-hour concentration; Nitrogen Dioxide - highest arithmetic mean concentration; Lead - highest quarterly maximum concentration
Units: ppm = parts per million; ug/m^3 = micrograms per cubic meter
Source: U.S. Environmental Protection Agency, MSA Factbook 2006, Air Quality Statistics by City

Drinking Water

Water System Name	Pop. Served	Primary Water Source Type	Violations[1]	
			Health Based	Monitoring/ Reporting
City of Southlake	25,700	Purchased Surface	0	0

Note: (1) Based on violation data from January 1, 2007 to December 31, 2007 (includes unresolved violations from earlier years)
Source: U.S. Environmental Protection Agency, Office of Ground Water and Drinking Water, Safe Drinking Water Information System (based on data extracted April 15, 2008)

Sugar Land, Texas

Background

Sugar Land is located in northeast Fort Bend County, 25 miles southwest of Houston, along the Gulf Coast of Texas. The Brazos River and Oyster Creek run through the city. Sugar Land also has many natural and man-made lakes.

Sugar Land's history dates back to the original Mexican land grant to Stephen F. Austin. Early settler Samuel M. Williams, called it Oakland Plantation because of the different oak varieties - Willow, Post , Water, Southern Red, and Live - that survived there. Williams' brother, Nathaniel, purchased the land in 1838 and together they grew cotton, corn, and sugarcane. In 1853, Benjamin Terry and William J. Kyle purchased the Oakland Plantation from the Williams family. Terry is known for organizing Terry's Texas Rangers during the Civil War, and is believed to have introduced the name Sugar Land. Shortly after the war, Colonel E. H. Cunningham bought the land and developed a town around his sugar refining plant.

In 1906, Isaac H. Kempner and William T. Eldridge purchased nearby Ellis Plantation and, in 1908, purchased the Cunningham Plantation with its raw sugar mill and cane-sugar refinery — Imperial Sugar Company was born. The oldest railroad in Texas went right through the middle of the town, by the sugar refinery. Until 1959, Sugar Land was virtually self-contained. Imperial Sugar Company provided housing, a school, a hospital, and businesses to meet the workers' needs. Many of the original homes built by Imperial remain today.

In the 1950s, Imperial Sugar expanded the town with the creation of Venetian Estates, featuring waterfront home sites. In the early 1960s Covington Woods was built. In 1968, the 1,200-acre Imperial Cattle Ranch became Sugar Creek, introducing country club living, golf courses, swimming pools, and security. Sugar Land annexed Sugar Creek in 1986, First Colony (another small independent nearby community) in 1997, with 5 more annexations completed in 2004.

The city is still home to Imperial Sugar headquarters although Sugar Land today is considered more an affluent Houston suburb than the blue-collar, agriculture-dependent town it was a generation ago. It has become the largest economic center of Fort Bend County, supplying a large percentage of the labor for Houston's renowned energy industry.

Corporate presence in Sugar Land includes Nalco/Exxon, Western Airways, Fluor Daniel, Schlumberger, and Unocal. Sugar Land Town Square is a pedestrian-oriented business district, walking distance of stores, services, mid-rise office buildings, restaurants, entertainment and Marriott Hotel/Conference Center. The area boasts a wide range of recreational activities including golf courses, country clubs and the Sugar Land Ice & Sports Center, the home practice facility for the Houston Aeros.

Sugar Lands School District includes a Technical Education Center, the M. R. Wood Alternative Education Center, and the Progressive High School, serving a variety of vocational interests as well as special learning needs. Individual high schools have garnered exemplary awards. In 2002, the University of Houston System at Fort Bend relocated to what became the University of Houston System at Sugar Land.

The climate is humid subtropical. Prevailing winds, from the south/southeast, bring heat from the deserts of Mexico and moisture from the Gulf of Mexico nearly year round. High temperatures dominate throughout much of July and August, with extremely high humidity. Summer thunderstorms sometimes bring tornadoes to the area. Afternoon rains are not uncommon. Winters are cool and temperate. The coldest period is usually in January, when north winds bring winter rains. Snow is almost unheard of.

Rankings

General Rankings

- Houston* was ranked #256 out of 375 metro areas in *Cities Ranked & Rated*. Criteria: cost of living; climate; crime; transportation; economy and jobs; education; arts and culture; health and healthcare; leisure; quality of life. *Cities Ranked & Rated, 2nd Edition, 2007*
- Houston* was ranked #48 out of 379 metro areas in *Places Rated Almanac*. Criteria: health care; education; recreation; transportation; ambience; climate; crime; housing costs; jobs. *Places Rated Almanac, 7th Edition, 2007*
- The Houston* metro area was selected one of America's "Best Cities to Live, Work and Play" by *Kiplinger Personal Finance*. Criteria: population growth; percentage of workforce in the creative class (scientists, engineers, educators, writers, artists, entertainers, etc.); job quality; income growth; cost of living. *Kiplinger Personal Finance, "Best Cities to Live, Work and Play," July 2008*
- Sugar Land was selected as one of the "2006 Best Places to Live" by *Money* magazine. Places were ranked using 38 quality-of-life indicators and six economic opportunity measures in the following categories: ease of living; health; education; crime; park space; arts and leisure. *CNNMoney.com, "Best Places to Live 2006"*
- The U.S. Conference of Mayors and Waste Management sponsor the City Livability Awards Program. The awards recognize and honor mayors for exemplary leadership in developing and implementing programs that improve the quality of life in America's cities. Sugar Land received an Outstanding Achievement Award in the small cities category. *U.S Conference of Mayors, "2007 City Livability Awards"*

Business/Finance Rankings

- The nation's 100 largest metro areas were analysed in terms of the percentage of households entering some stage of foreclosure in 2007. The Houston* metro area ranked #39 out of 100 (#1 = highest foreclosure rate). *RealtyTrac, "Year-End 2007 Metropolitan Foreclosure Report"*
- The Houston* metro area was identified as one of the "10 Best Cities for Jobs in 2008" by *Forbes*. The metro area ranked #7. Criteria: state unemployment rate; job growth; income growth; median household income; cost of living. *Forbes.com, "Best Cities for Jobs in 2008," January 10, 2008*
- The Houston* metro area was identified as one of the "Top 12 Nano Metros" in the U.S. by the Woodrow Wilson International Center for Scholars. The metro area is home to 18 companies, universities, government laboratories and/or organizations working in nanotechnology. *Woodrow Wilson International Center for Scholars, May 17, 2007*
- The Houston* metro area was selected one of America's "Top 50 Business Opportunity Metros" by *Expansion Management* in their 5th annual Mayor's Challenge ranking of metro areas that have achieved solid ratings across the board in numerous *EM* studies during the past 12 months. The area ranked #16. Criteria: public schools; quality of life; college educated workers; logistics infrastructure; healthcare costs; taxes and government spending; reputation among site consultants. *Expansion Management, August 2007*
- The Houston* metro area was identified as one of 10 "Top Up-and-Coming Tech Cities" by *Forbes*. The metro area ranked #4. Criteria: regional innovation trends; important patents. *Forbes.com, "Top Up-and-Coming Tech Cities," March 11, 2008*
- Houston* was selected as one of the best places to start and grow a company by *Entrepreneur* and the National Policy Research Council. The Houston* metro area ranked #14 out of 50 large metro areas. Criteria: business formation and growth (firms started four to 14 years ago that still employ at least 5 people and experienced rapid growth over the last four years). *Entrepreneur/National Policy Research Council, "Hot Cities for Entrepreneurs," September 2006*

- The Houston* metro area was selected as one of "America's 50 Hottest Cities" for business relocations and expansions. Criteria: industry's most prominent site selection consultants were asked to list their top city choices for relocating and expanding manufacturing companies, taking into consideration such factors as the business climate, work force quality, operating costs, incentive programs, and the ease of working with local political and economic development officials. *Expansion Management, January-February 2007*

- Houston* was cited as one of America's top large metros (population over 1 million) for new and expanded facility projects in 2007. The area appeared in the top 10 with 75 projects. *Site Selection, "Top Metropolitan Area Awards," March 2008*

- Intel, in partnership with Sperling's BestPlaces, ranked the 80 "Best Cities for Teleworking" in America. The Houston* metro area ranked #11 among extra large metro areas. The study identifies cities that hold the greatest potential for teleworking based on a host of factors including typical commuting times, fuel prices, availability of broadband Internet access and percentage of the population in telework friendly jobs. The study also factored in extreme climate and natural hazards. *Intel, "Best Cities for Teleworking," March 30, 2006*

- The Houston* metro area appeared on the Milken Institute "2007 Best Performing Cities" index. Rank: #32 out of 200 large metro areas. Criteria: job growth; wage and salary growth; high-tech output growth. *Milken Institute, "2007 Best Performing Cities"*

- The Houston* metro area was selected as one of the hottest cities for entrepreneurs in America by *Inc. Magazine.* Criteria: job-growth data for 393 metro was analyzed for current-year employment growth, average annual employment growth over past three years, and employment growth by industry sector. The Houston* metro area ranked #17 among large metro areas and #120 overall. *Inc. Magazine, May 2007*

- Houston* was identified as one of the 100 "Most Unwired Cities" in the U.S. The area ranked #28 out of the 100 largest metro areas in the U.S. Criteria: number of public and commercial wireless access points (hotspots); airports with wireless Internet access; broadband availability; local wireless networks; and wireless email devices. *Intel, "Most Unwired Cities Survey," June 7, 2005*

- Houston* was ranked #26 out of 125 regions worldwide in terms of its "Knowledge Competitiveness Index." The index attempts to measure the knowledge-based development taking place throughout the world and is based on 19 measures of economic performance that indicate a region's ability to translate its knowledge capacity into economic value. *Robert Huggins Associates, World Knowledge Competitiveness Index 2005*

- *Forbes* ranked the 200 most populous metro areas in the U.S. in terms of the "Best Places for Business and Careers." The Houston* metro area was ranked #33. Criteria: business costs (labor, energy, tax and office space expenses); living costs (housing, transportation, food and other household expenditures); education levels of the work force; job growth; income growth; migration trends; crime rates; and culture/leisure. *Forbes, "Best Places for Business and Careers," March 19, 2008*

- *Fortune* ranked the 100 largest metro areas in the U.S. in terms of projected median home price change in 2007. The Houston* metro area ranked #11. *Fortune.com, "Hot Spots, Cold Spots"*

Health/Environment Rankings

- The Houston* metro area was identified as one of "America's 20 Most Sedentary Cities" by *Forbes*. The metro area ranked #11. Criteria: percentage of overweight or obese people; percentage of people who had not engaged in any physical activity in the past 30 days; average number of hours of TV watched per week. *Forbes.com, "America's Most Sedentary Cities," October 29, 2007*

- 100 of the largest metro areas in the U.S. were analyzed in terms of their current drought severity. The Houston* metro area ranked #96 (#1 = driest). The rankings were based on statistics such as long-term precipitation trends and patterns and the Palmer drought indices. *Sperling's BestPlaces, www.BestPlaces.net, "America's Drought-Riskiest Cities," November 2007*

- Doctors at the Harvard School of Public Health ranked 40 metropolitan areas based on data from the government-sponsored Hospital Quality Alliance program. The program tracks the performance of individual hospitals in treating patients for three common health problems: heart attacks, congestive heart failure, and pneumonia. The Houston* metro area ranked #33 in quality of care for heart attacks, #27 for congestive heart failure, and #32 for pneumonia. *New England Journal of Medicine, July 21, 2005*

- *Reader's Digest* ranked the 50 largest metro areas in the U.S. in terms of how "clean" they are. The Houston* metro area ranked #41. Criteria: air quality; water quality; toxic industrial pollution; Superfund sites; and sanitation. *Reader's Digest, "The 50 Cleanest (and Dirtiest) Cities in America," July 2005*

- The American Academy of Dermatology ranked 32 U.S. metropolitan regions in terms of their residents knowledge, attitude and behaviors towards tanning and sun protection. The Houston* metro area ranked #20. The results of the study are based on an online national survey of 3,342 respondents. *American Academy of Dermatology, "RAYS: Your Grade," May 7, 2007*

- *Business Week* identified the 15 metro areas that saw the steepest declines in ground-level ozone pollution between 1990 and 2005. The Houston* metro area ranked #4. *Business Week, "America's Most Cleaned-Up Metro Areas," March 23, 2007*

- The Houston* metro area appeared in *Country Home's* "2008 Best Green Places" report. The area ranked #122 out of 379. Criteria: official energy policies; green power; green buildings; availability of fresh, locally grown food. *Country Home, "2008 Best Green Places"*

- Wyeth Consumer Healthcare, in partnership with Sperling's BestPlaces, ranked the nation's 50 most populous metro areas in terms of five key health factors. The Houston* metro area ranked #36. Criteria: physical activity; health status; nutrition; lifestyle pursuits; and mental wellness. *Wyeth Consumer Healthcare, "Centrum Healthiest Cities Study," April 19, 2005*

- HealthGrades surveyed over 41,000 individuals on doctor satisfaction and ranked the 20 largest metro areas based on the highest "definitely yes" responses to the question "Do you trust the physician to make decisions/recommendations that are in your best interest?" The Houston* metro area ranked #1. *HealthGrades.com, "Top Cities in Doctor-Trust," September 7, 2006*

- Houston* was identified as a "2008 Asthma Capital." The area ranked #72 out of the nation's 100 largest metropolitan areas. Twelve factors were used to identify the most challenging places to live for people with asthma: estimated prevalence; self-reported prevalence; crude death rate for asthma; annual pollen score; annual air quality; public smoking laws; number of board-certified asthma specialists; school inhaler access laws; rescue medication use; controller medication use; uninsured rate; poverty rate. *Asthma and Allergy Foundation of America, "2008 Asthma Capitals"*

- Houston* was identified as a "Spring Allergy Capital." The area ranked #28 out of 100. Three groups of factors were used to identify the most severe cities for people with allergies during the spring season: annual pollen levels; medicine utilization; access to board-certified allergists. *Asthma and Allergy Foundation of America, "2007 Spring Allergy Capital Rankings"*

- Houston* was identified as a "Fall Allergy Capital." The area ranked #17 out of 100. Three groups of factors were used to identify the most severe cities for people with allergies during the fall season: annual pollen levels; medicine utilization; access to board-certified allergists. *Asthma and Allergy Foundation of America, "2007 Fall Allergy Capital Rankings"*

- Ortho-McNeil Neurologics, in partnership with Sperling's BestPlaces, analyzed 110 metro areas and identified those U.S. cities with the highest prevalence of factors that are most commonly associated with migraine headaches. The Houston* metro area ranked #95. Criteria: number of migraine-related drug prescriptions per capita; lifestyle factors that can contribute to migraines; environmental factors that can trigger migraines; and consumption of migraine-triggering foods. *Ortho-McNeil Neurologics, "America's Migraine Hot Spots," March 14, 2006*

- Sperling's BestPlaces ranked 331 metro areas and identified the most and least stressful U.S. cities. The Houston* metro area ranked #13 out of the 100 largest metro areas (#1 = most stressful). Criteria: divorce rate; unemployment rate; violent and property crime; suicide rate; commute time; mental health; alcohol consumption; cloudy days. *Sperling's BestPlaces, www.BestPlaces.net, "America's Most (and Least) Stressful Cities," January 9, 2004*

- An analysis of the "Best & Worst Cities for Sleep" was conducted by Sperling's BestPlaces. The study ranked America's 50 most populated metro areas. The Houston* metro area ranked #48 (#1 = best city for sleep). Criteria: number of days residents didn't get enough rest or sleep during the past month; average length of daily commute; divorce rate; unemployment rate. *Sperling's BestPlaces, www.BestPlaces.net, "Best & Worst Cities for Sleep," 2006*

- HealthGrades evaluated the performance of America's 25 most populous metropolitan areas by measuring the outcomes of five of the highest volume and most widely studied procedures and diagnoses: coronary artery bypass graft surgery; percutaneus coronary interventions; acute myocardial infarction/heart attack in angioplasty-capable hospitals; congestive heart failure; and community acquired pneumonia. The Houston* metro area ranked #15. *HealthGrades, "HealthGrades Hospital Quality in America Study," October 12, 2004*

- Houston* was highlighted as one of the 25 most ozone-polluted metro areas in the U.S. The area ranked #5. *American Lung Association, State of the Air: 2007*

- Houston* was selected as one of "America's Pet Healthiest Cities" by Purina. The city ranked #32 out of 50. Criteria: veterinary services; environment; legislation; preventative care; obesity/body condition. *Purina Pet Institute, "America's Pet Healthiest Cities," May 20, 2003*

Women/Minorities Rankings

- Houston* was ranked #89 out of 100 metro areas in *SELF Magazine's* ranking of "America's Best Places for Women." A panel of experts came up with more than 50 criteria including death and disease rates, environmental indicators, community resources, and lifestyle habits. *SELF Magazine, "America's Best Places for Women 2007," December 2007*

- Houston* appeared on *Black Enterprise's* list of the "Ten Best Cities for African Americans." The top picks were culled from more than 2,000 interactive surveys completed on www.blackenterprise.com and by editorial staff evaluation. The editors weighed the following criteria as it pertained to African Americans in each city: median household income; percentage of households earning more than $100,000; percentage of businesses owned; percentage of college graduates; unemployment rates; home loan rejections; and homeownership rates. *Black Enterprise, May 2007*

Seniors/Retirement Rankings

- The Houston* metro area was selected as one of "Best Places for Retirees" by *Forbes*. The area was ranked #5 out of 10. Criteria: cost and availability of health care; sales, property and income-tax rates; arts and leisure activities; cost of living; retirement job market; inter-metro migration patterns of people between the ages of 55 and 65. *Forbes, "Best Places for Retirees," January 18, 2007*

- Sperling's BestPlaces in partnership with Bankers Life & Casualty Company designed a survey to identify the top 50 metro areas in the U.S. that offer the best overall qualities for senior living. The Houston* metro area ranked #24. The following criteria were statistically weighted to reflect the needs of the senior population: health; disease; economics; social; environment; spiritual; transportation; housing; and crime. *Bankers Life & Casualty Company, "Best Cities for Seniors 2005"*

- A.G. Edwards ranked America's 500 top-performing communities based on their residents' personal savings and investing behavior. The Houston* metro area ranked #440 with an index score of 95.95 (national average = 100.00). A dozen statistical factors were measured including: participation in retirement savings plans; personal debt levels; and home ownership. *A.G. Edwards, "2007 Nest Egg Index", September 12, 2007*

Children/Family Rankings

- Sugar Land was selected as one of the ten "Best of the Best" places to raise a family in the U.S. The city was ranked #8.Criteria: demographic characteristics; standard of living; education; lifestyle; health and safety. *Best Place to Raise Your Family: The Top 100 Affordable Communities in the U.S., 1st Edition, 2006*

- The Houston* metro area was selected as one of the "Best Cities for Relocating Families" by Worldwide ERC and Primacy Relocation. The 2007 study placed a special emphasis on the housing market, which has significantly impacted the relocation industry and an employer's ability to transfer employees. The variables which weigh heavily in this category include home price, home affordability index, appreciation rates, and property tax. Other criteria include cost of living, crime rates, education, climate, focus on diversity, physicians per capita, recreation and leisure, arts and culture, air quality, watershed quality, sales tax, unemployment rate, job growth, high school and higher education index, school expenditures per student, students in public school, SAT/ACT percentile, and population growth. *Worldwide ERC and Primacy Relocation, "2007 Best Cities for Relocating Families"*

Safety Rankings

- The National Insurance Crime Bureau ranked 361 metro areas in the U.S. in terms of per capita rates of vehicle theft. The Houston* metro area ranked #31 (#1 = highest rate). Criteria: number of vehicle theft offenses per 100,000 inhabitants. *National Insurance Crime Bureau, "NICB Vehicle Theft Study," April 22, 2008*

- Houston* appeared on Sperling's BestPlaces list of the "Riskiest Cities for Identity Theft." The area ranked #22 out of the nations 50 largest metro areas. Over 80 criteria were analyzed across four major categories: technology impact; crime; transactions; and risk profile. *Sperling's BestPlaces, www.BestPlaces.net, "Riskiest Cities for Identity Theft," July 2006*

- Farmers Insurance Group of Companies, in partnership with Sperling's BestPlaces, ranked 379 metro areas and identified the "Most Secure U.S. Place to Live." The Houston* metro area ranked #70 out of 114 in the large metro area category (500,000 or more residents). Criteria: crime rates; extreme weather; risk of natural disasters; environmental hazards; terrorism threats; air quality; life expectancy; job loss numbers. *Farmers Insurance Group, "Most Secure U.S. Places to Live 2007"*

- Houston* was identified as one of the most dangerous large metro areas for pedestrians in the U.S. The area ranked #8 out of the nations 50 largest metro areas. Criteria: average yearly pedestrian fatalities per capita (for the years 2002 and 2003) adjusted for the number of walkers. *Surface Transportation Policy Project, "Mean Streets 2004"*

- Sugar Land was identified as one of the safest cities in America by Morgan Quitno. All 371 cities with populations over 75,000 that reported crime rates in 2006 for murder, rape, robbery, aggravated assault, burglary, and motor vehicle thefts were ranked. The city ranked #5 out of the top 25. *www.morganquitno.com, 14th Annual America's Safest (and Most Dangerous) Cities Awards*

- Sugar Land was identified as one of the safest smaller cities in America by Morgan Quitno. All 129 cities with populations of 75,000 to 99,999 that reported crime rates in 2006 for murder, rape, robbery, aggravated assault, burglary, and motor vehicle thefts were ranked. The city ranked #4 out of the top 10. *www.morganquitno.com, 14th Annual America's Safest (and Most Dangerous) Cities Awards*

Sports/Recreation Rankings

- The Houston* metro area appeared on the *Sporting News* list of the "Best Sports Cities 2007". The area ranked #11 out of 150 cities in the U.S. *Sporting News* takes a 12-month snapshot, roughly July to July, of each city's sports, putting a heavy premium on regular-season won-lost records (from the most recently completed season). Other criteria include: playoff berths, bowl appearances and tournament bids; championships; applicable power ratings; quality of competition; overall fan fervor as measured in part by attendance as percentage of venue capacity; abundance of teams (rewarding quality over quantity); stadium and arena quality; ticket availability and prices; franchise ownership; and marquee appeal of athletes. *SportingNews.com, "Best Sports Cities 2007," August 1, 2007*

- Scarborough Research, a leading market research firm, identified the top local markets for avid NBA fans. The Houston* DMA (Designated Market Area) ranked in the top 10 with 14% of consumers 18 years and over reporting that they are "very interested in the NBA". *Scarborough Research, April 24, 2006*

- The Houston* metro area was selected by *Cranium* as one of the "Top 50 Fun Cities" in America. The area ranked #32. Criteria includes: number of sports teams, restaurants, and dance performances; number of toy stores; city budget spent on recreation. *Cranium, November 4, 2003*

- *Golf Digest* ranked 330 metro areas in the U.S. in terms of golf. The Houston* metro area was ranked #263. Criteria: access to golf; weather; value of golf; and quality of golf. *Golf Digest, "Metro Golf Rankings," August 2005*

Dating/Romance Rankings

- Eli Lily and Company, in partnership with Sperling's BestPlaces, ranked the nation's 50 largest metro areas in terms of the "Most Romantic Cities for Baby Boomers." The Houston* metro area ranked #10. Criteria: marriage and divorce rates among "baby boomers" age 45 to 60; great restaurants; dance studios; chocolate, jewelry and flower sales. *Eli Lily and Company, "Most Romantic Cities for Baby Boomers," April 20, 2007*

- The Houston* metro area was selected as one of the "Best Cities for Relocating Singles" by Worldwide ERC and Primacy Relocation. The area ranked #53 out of the 100 largest metro areas in the U.S. Areas were selected based on the following criteria: a robust cost-of-living index; adventure and outdoor recreation opportunities; violent crime and property crime rates; percentage of the population that is unmarried (ages 25-34); ratio of single men and single women; affordability of quality higher education, including in-state and out-of-state tuition requirements and rates; number of newcomers to the area; commute times; tax rates; fee and occupancy rates for temporary housing and mini-storage; quality and quantity of collegiate and professional sporting events and fun, fan-friendly venues. *Worldwide ERC and Primacy Relocation, "2007 Best Cities for Relocating Singles," October 25, 2007*

- *Forbes* ranked the 40 most populous urbanized areas in the U.S. in terms of the "Best Cities for Singles." The Houston* metro area ranked #14. Criteria: number of singles; cost of living alone; nightlife; culture; job growth; coolness; and online dating. *Forbes.com, August 21, 2007*

- Sperling's BestPlaces in partnership with AXE Deodorant Bodyspray ranked 80 metro areas and identified "America's Best (and Worst) Cities for Dating." The Houston* metro area ranked #72 (#1 = best). Criteria: percentage of singles ages 18-24; population density; dating venues per capita. *AXE Deodorant Bodyspray, "America's Best (and Worst) Cities for Dating," May 2004*

Miscellaneous Rankings

- The Houston* metro area was identified as one of 10 "Worst Cities for Commuters" by *Forbes*. The metro area ranked #8. Criteria: traffic delays; travel times; how efficiently commuters use existing infrastructure. *Forbes.com, "Worst Cities for Commuters," April 29, 2008*

- The Houston* metro area appeared on *Forbes* list of "America's Drunkest Cities". The area ranked #18. Criteria: 35 of the largest continental U.S. metro areas were chosen based on availability of data and geographic diversity. Each metro was ranked in five areas: state laws; drinkers; heavy drinkers; binge drinkers; and alcoholism. *Forbes.com, "America's Drunkest Cities," August 22, 2006*

- Sperling's BestPlaces in partnership with Pep Boys ranked 77 metro areas and identified "America's Most Drivable Cities." The Houston* metro area ranked #34. Criteria: climate; road roughness; urban mobility; gas prices. *Pep Boys, "America's Most Drivable Cities," April 9, 2003*

- State Farm Insurance, in partnership with Sperling's BestPlaces, analyzed several key factors that contribute to overall family preparedness. The Houston* metro area ranked #36 out of the nation's 50 most populous metro areas. Criteria: quality of life; life insurance coverage; and investments. *State Farm Life Insurance, "Fiscally Fit Cities Report," July 20, 2004*

- Scarborough Research, a leading market research firm, identified the top local markets for frequent sit-down restaurant patronage. The Houston* DMA (Designated Market Area) ranked in the top 10 with consumers reporting an average of 4.0 visits within the past 30 days. *Scarborough Research, May 31, 2006*

- A study by Sperling's BestPlaces examined which U.S. metro areas were most affected by high fuel prices in 2006. The Houston* metro area was ranked #27 out of 80 (#1 = most expensive city for driving). Rankings are based on the average dollars spent on gas per year by two driver households. Criteria: cost of regular-grade gasoline; average miles driven per day; average number of gallons each driver uses and wastes in traffic congestion each day. *Sperling's BestPlaces, www.bestplaces.net, "Pain at the Pump," May 18, 2006*

Sugar Land is located within the Houston-Sugar Land-Baytown, TX Metropolitan Statistical Area and.

Business Environment

CITY FINANCES

City Government Finances

Component	2004-2005 ($000)	2004-2005 ($ per capita)
Total Revenues	90,654	1,197
Total Expenditures	103,270	1,363
Debt Outstanding	154,149	2,035
Cash and Securities	50,288	664

Source: U.S Census Bureau, Government Finances 2004-2005

City Government Revenue by Source

Source	2004-2005 ($000)	2004-2005 ($ per capita)
General Revenue		
From Federal Government	1,670	22
From State Government	1,807	24
From Local Governments	3,890	51
Taxes		
Property	18,927	250
Sales	33,960	448
Personal Income	0	0
License	1,086	14
Charges	19,416	256
Liquor Store	0	0
Utility	7,432	98
Employee Retirement	0	0
Other	2,466	33

Source: U.S Census Bureau, Government Finances 2004-2005

City Government Expenditures by Function

Function	2004-2005 ($000)	2004-2005 ($ per capita)	2004-2005 (%)
General Expenditures			
Airports	7,933	105	7.7
Corrections	0	0	0.0
Education	0	0	0.0
Fire Protection	7,060	93	6.8
Governmental Administration	9,190	121	8.9
Health	572	8	0.6
Highways	4,231	56	4.1
Hospitals	0	0	0.0
Housing and Community Development	223	3	0.2
Interest on General Debt	7,170	95	6.9
Libraries	0	0	0.0
Parking	0	0	0.0
Parks and Recreation	1,969	26	1.9
Police Protection	9,444	125	9.1
Public Welfare	0	0	0.0
Sewerage	9,364	124	9.1
Solid Waste Management	2,668	35	2.6
Liquor Store	0	0	0.0
Utility	9,515	126	9.2
Employee Retirement	0	0	0.0
Other	33,931	448	32.9

Source: U.S Census Bureau, Government Finances 2004-2005

Municipal Bond Ratings

Area	Moody's
City	n/a

Source: Mergent Bond Record, January 2008 (unless noted otherwise)

DEMOGRAPHICS

Population Growth

Area	1990 Census	2000 Census	2007 Estimate	2012 Projection	Population Growth (%) 1990-2000	Population Growth (%) 2000-2012
City	44,150	63,328	78,549	88,074	43.4	39.1
MSA[1]	3,767,335	4,715,407	5,489,519	5,965,317	25.2	26.5
U.S.	248,709,873	281,421,906	301,045,522	314,920,978	13.2	11.9

Note: (1) Metropolitan Statistical Area - see Appendix B for areas included
Source: Claritas, Inc.

Number of Households and Average Household Size

Area	2007 Estimate	2007 Average Household Size
City	25,597	3.07
MSA[1]	1,914,046	2.87
U.S.	113,668,003	2.65

Note: (1) Metropolitan Statistical Area - see Appendix B for areas included
Source: Claritas, Inc.

Race and Ethnicity

Area	White Alone[2]	Black Alone[2]	Asian Alone[2]	Other Race Alone[2]	Hispanic[3]
City	54.8	6.4	32.2	6.6	9.6
MSA[1]	60.2	16.4	5.6	17.8	33.0
U.S.	73.1	12.4	4.3	10.3	14.9

Note: Figures are 2007 estimates; (1) Metropolitan Statistical Area - see Appendix B for areas included (2) Alone is defined as not being in combination with one or more other races; (3) May be of any race.
Source: Claritas, Inc.

Ancestry

Area	German	Irish[2]	English	American	Italian	Polish	French[3]	Scottish
City	14.6	9.3	10.9	5.3	3.1	2.2	3.5	2.0
MSA[1]	9.2	6.6	6.6	5.9	2.2	1.4	2.6	1.3
U.S.	15.2	10.9	8.7	7.3	5.6	3.2	3.0	1.7

Note: Figures include multiple ancestry (e.g. if a person reported being Irish and Italian, they were included in both columns); (1) Metropolitan Statistical Area - see Appendix A for areas included; (2) Includes Celtic; (3) Includes Alsatian but excludes Basque
Source: Census 2000, Summary File 3

Foreign-Born Population

Area	Percent of Population Born in: Any Foreign Country	Europe	Asia	Africa	Oceania[2]	Canada	Mexico	Latin America[3]
City	23.5	1.9	17.6	1.1	0.0	0.6	0.8	1.5
MSA[1]	20.5	1.1	4.3	0.6	0.0	0.2	10.4	3.8
U.S.	11.1	1.7	2.9	0.3	0.1	0.3	3.3	2.5

Note: (1) Metropolitan Statistical Area - see Appendix A for areas included; (2) Includes Australia, New Zealand subregion, Melanesia, Micronesia, Polynesia, and Oceania n.e.c; (3) Includes Central America (excluding Mexico), South America, and the Caribbean.
Source: Census 2000, Summary File 3

Marriage Status

Area	Never Married	Now Married (excluding Separated)	Separated	Widowed	Divorced
City	20.9	68.1	0.9	3.7	6.3
MSA[1]	27.4	55.6	2.8	4.8	9.5
U.S.	27.1	54.4	2.2	6.6	9.7

Note: Figures are percentages and cover the population 15 years of age and older; (1) Metropolitan Statistical Area - see Appendix A for areas included
Source: Census 2000, Summary File 3

Age Distribution

Area	Under Age 5	Age 5 to 17	Age 18 to 34	Age 35 to 49	Age 50 to 64	Age 65 to 79	80 Years and Over
	Percent of Population						
City	6.1	25.1	15.0	31.4	15.7	5.0	1.8
MSA[1]	8.1	21.1	26.0	24.6	12.9	5.8	1.6
U.S.	6.8	18.9	23.7	23.5	14.8	9.2	3.2

Note: (1) Metropolitan Statistical Area - see Appendix A for areas included
Source: Census 2000, Summary File 3

Male/Female Ratio

Area	Males	Females	Males per 100 Females
City	38,366	40,183	95.5
MSA[1]	2,742,445	2,747,074	99.8
U.S.	148,320,305	152,725,217	97.1

Note: Figures are 2007 estimates; (1) Metropolitan Statistical Area - see Appendix B for areas included
Source: Claritas, Inc.

Religion

Area	Catholic	Southern Baptist	United Meth-odist	ELCA[1]	LDS[2]	Presby-terian Church USA	Jewish Est.	Muslim Est.
County	24.8	8.7	4.4	0.6	0.8	0.5	0.5	0.7
U.S.	22.0	7.1	3.7	1.8	1.5	1.1	2.2	0.6

Note: Figures are the number of adherents as a percentage of the total population; Adherents are defined as all members, including full members, their children and the estimated number of other participants who are not considered members (e.g. the baptized, those not confirmed, those regularly attending services, etc.); (1) Evangelical Lutheran Church in America; (2) The Church of Jesus Christ of Latter Day Saints
Source: Reprinted with permission from Religious Congregations and Membership in the United States 2000 (Nashville, Glenmary Research Center, 2002) Copyright Association of Statisticians of American Religious Bodies. All rights reserved.

ECONOMY

Gross Metropolitan Product

Area	2002	2003	2004	2005	2005 Rank[2]
MSA[1]	191.9	204.0	221.2	244.4	7

Note: Figures are in billions of dollars; (1) Houston-Sugar Land-Baytown, TX Metropolitan Statistical Area - see Appendix A for areas included; (2) Rank ranges from 1 to 361
Source: The U.S. Conference of Mayors, "U.S. Metro Economies: GMP - The Engines of America's Growth," January 2007

Economic Growth

Area	1995 GMP	2005 GMP	Average Annual Growth Rate	Growth Rate Rank[2]
MSA[1]	121.8	244.4	7.2	31

Note: Figures are in billions of dollars; GMP = Gross Metropolitan Product; (1) Houston-Sugar Land-Baytown, TX Metropolitan Statistical Area - see Appendix A for areas included; (2) Rank ranges from 1 to 361
Source: The U.S. Conference of Mayors, "U.S. Metro Economies: GMP - The Engines of America's Growth," January 2007

INCOME

Per Capita/Median/Average Income

Area	Per Capita ($)	Median Household ($)	Average Household ($)
City	36,831	88,452	112,590
MSA[1]	25,018	51,630	71,229
U.S.	25,495	49,280	66,670

Note: Figures are 2007 estimates; (1) Metropolitan Statistical Area - see Appendix B for areas included
Source: Claritas, Inc.

Household Income Distribution

Area	Percent of Households Earning							
	Under $15,000	$15,000 -24,999	$25,000 -34,999	$35,000 -49,999	$50,000 -74,999	$75,000 -99,000	$100,000 -149,999	$150,000 and up
City	4.4	4.4	4.8	10.7	17.6	15.2	22.7	20.3
MSA[1]	12.2	10.1	11.0	15.4	18.5	12.0	12.7	8.1
U.S.	13.1	10.9	11.2	15.6	19.5	11.9	11.3	6.6

Note: Figures are 2007 estimates; (1) Metropolitan Statistical Area - see Appendix B for areas included
Source: Claritas, Inc.

Poverty Rates by Age

Area	All Ages	Under 5 Years Old	5 to 17 Years Old	18 to 64 Years Old	65 Years and Over
City	3.8	0.2	0.9	2.1	0.6
MSA[1]	13.9	1.6	3.7	7.7	0.9
U.S.	12.4	1.2	3.0	6.9	1.2

Note: Figures are percent of population with income in 1999 below poverty level and only include population for whom poverty status is determined; (1) Metropolitan Statistical Area - see Appendix A for areas included
Source: Census 2000, Summary File 3

Personal Bankruptcy Filing Rate

Area	2004	2005	2006
Fort Bend County	4.41	5.28	1.63
U.S.	5.31	6.82	2.00

Note: Numbers are per 1,000 population and include Chapter 7 and Chapter 13 filings
Source: Federal Deposit Insurance Corporation (FDIC), Regional Economic Conditions (RECON), 8/23/2007

EMPLOYMENT

Labor Force and Employment

Area	Civilian Labor Force			Workers Employed		
	Dec. 2006	Dec. 2007	% Chg.	Dec. 2006	Dec. 2007	% Chg.
City	41,536	42,328	1.9	40,232	40,978	1.9
MSA[1]	2,713,998	2,767,131	2.0	2,603,369	2,651,639	1.9
U.S.	152,571,000	153,705,000	0.7	146,081,000	146,334,000	0.2

Note: Data is not seasonally adjusted and covers workers 16 years of age and older; (1) Metropolitan Statistical Area - see Appendix B for areas included
Source: Bureau of Labor Statistics, http://stats.bls.gov

Unemployment Rate

Area	2007											
	Jan.	Feb.	Mar.	Apr.	May	Jun.	Jul.	Aug.	Sep.	Oct.	Nov.	Dec.
City	3.8	3.8	3.5	3.2	3.2	3.9	3.7	3.4	3.4	3.1	3.2	3.2
MSA[1]	4.7	4.5	4.1	3.9	3.9	4.6	4.6	4.3	4.3	4.0	4.1	4.2
U.S.	5.0	4.9	4.5	4.3	4.3	4.7	4.9	4.6	4.5	4.4	4.5	4.8

Note: Data is not seasonally adjusted and covers workers 16 years of age and older; All figures are percentages; (1) Metropolitan Statistical Area - see Appendix B for areas included
Source: Bureau of Labor Statistics, http://stats.bls.gov

Employment by Occupation

Occupation Classification	City (%)	MSA[1] (%)	U.S. (%)
Sales and Office	27.1	27.6	26.7
Professional and Related	32.2	20.5	20.2
Service	7.4	13.6	14.9
Production, Transportation, and Material Moving	5.0	12.5	14.6
Management, Business, and Financial	24.6	14.8	13.5
Construction, Extraction, and Maintenance	3.5	10.9	9.4
Farming, Forestry, and Fishing	0.2	0.2	0.7

Note: Figures cover employed civilians 16 years of age and older; (1) Metropolitan Statistical Area - see Appendix A for areas included
Source: Census 2000, Summary File 3

Employment by Industry

Sector	MSA[1] Number of Employees	MSA[1] Percent of Total	U.S. Percent of Total
Government	357,000	13.7	16.3
Education and Health Services	289,300	11.1	13.4
Professional and Business Services	390,000	14.9	13.1
Retail Trade	276,700	10.6	11.6
Manufacturing	236,700	9.1	9.9
Leisure and Hospitality	229,000	8.8	9.6
Financial Activities	146,500	5.6	5.9
Construction	203,800	7.8	5.3
Wholesale Trade	136,800	5.2	4.4
Other Services	94,500	3.6	3.9
Transportation and Utilities	128,000	4.9	3.7
Information	37,200	1.4	2.2
Natural Resources and Mining	87,300	3.3	0.5

Note: Figures cover non-farm employment as of December 2007 and are not seasonally adjusted; (1) Metropolitan Statistical Area - see Appendix B for areas included
Source: Bureau of Labor Statistics, http://stats.bls.gov

Average Wages

Occupation	$/Hr.	Occupation	$/Hr.
Accountants and Auditors	30.78	Maids and Housekeeping Cleaners	7.73
Automotive Mechanics	17.99	Maintenance and Repair Workers	14.25
Bookkeepers	15.84	Marketing Managers	57.18
Carpenters	15.28	Nuclear Medicine Technologists	35.31
Cashiers	8.21	Nurses, Licensed Practical	19.09
Clerks, General Office	11.43	Nurses, Registered	30.66
Clerks, Receptionists/Information	11.25	Nursing Aides/Orderlies/Attendants	10.82
Clerks, Shipping/Receiving	13.07	Packers and Packagers, Hand	8.43
Computer Programmers	38.89	Physical Therapists	36.73
Computer Support Specialists	22.23	Postal Service Mail Carriers	21.44
Computer Systems Analysts	36.57	Real Estate Brokers	41.88
Cooks, Restaurant	9.19	Retail Salespersons	11.51
Dentists	n/a	Sales Reps., Exc. Tech./Scientific	29.31
Electrical Engineers	44.72	Sales Reps., Tech./Scientific	38.96
Electricians	19.91	Secretaries, Exc. Legal/Med./Exec.	13.16
Financial Managers	56.30	Security Guards	11.34
First-Line Supervisors/Mgrs., Sales	19.68	Surgeons	86.19
Food Preparation Workers	8.22	Teacher Assistants	8.50
General and Operations Managers	53.98	Teachers, Elementary School	22.00
Hairdressers/Cosmetologists	10.96	Teachers, Secondary School	23.30
Internists	71.46	Telemarketers	10.47
Janitors and Cleaners	8.74	Truck Drivers, Heavy/Tractor-Trailer	16.73
Landscaping/Groundskeeping Workers	9.47	Truck Drivers, Light/Delivery Svcs.	13.11
Lawyers	62.17	Waiters and Waitresses	7.74

Note: Wage data covers the Houston-Sugar Land-Baytown, TX Metropolitan Statistical Area - see Appendix B for areas included. Hourly wages for elementary/secondary school teachers and teacher assistants were calculated by the editors from annual wage data assuming a 40 hour work week; n/a not available.
Source: Bureau of Labor Statistics, May 2007 Metro Area Occupational Employment and Wage Estimates

RESIDENTIAL REAL ESTATE

Building Permits

Area	Single-Family 2006	Single-Family 2007p	Single-Family Pct. Chg.	Multi-Family 2006	Multi-Family 2007p	Multi-Family Pct. Chg.	Total 2006	Total 2007p	Total Pct. Chg.
City	502	500	-0.4	32	4	-87.5	534	504	-5.6
U.S.	1,378,200	973,300	-29.4	460,700	407,200	-11.6	1,838,900	1,380,500	-24.9

Note: (p) preliminary; figures cover and represent new, privately-owned housing units authorized (unadjusted data); All permit data are based on estimates with imputation; U.S. figures are based on the new 20,000-place series.
Source: U.S. Census Bureau, Manufacturing, Mining, and Construction Statistics

Homeownership and Housing Vacancies

Area	Homeownership Rate[2] (%)			Rental Vacancy Rate[3] (%)			Homeowner Vacancy Rate[4] (%)		
	2005	2006	2007	2005	2006	2007	2005	2006	2007
MSA[1]	61.7	63.5	64.5	15.4	16.8	17.3	3.5	2.8	3.1
U.S.	68.9	68.8	68.1	9.8	9.8	9.7	1.9	2.4	2.7

Note: (1) Metropolitan Statistical Area - see Appendix B for areas included; (2) The proportion of households that are owners; (3) The proportion of the rental inventory that is vacant for rent; (4) The proportion of the homeowner inventory that is vacant for sale; n/a not available
Source: U.S. Census Bureau, Housing Vacancies and Homeownership Annual Statistics: 2007

TAXES

State Corporate Income Tax Rates

State	Rates and Tax Brackets
Texas	1.0%

Note: Tax rates as of January 1, 2008; Texas's 1% franchise tax is a gross receipts tax paid by most taxable entities. Retailers pay 0.5%.
Source: Tax Foundation, www.taxfoundation.org

State Individual Income Tax Rates

State	Federal Deductibility	Marginal Rates (%)	Standard Deduction ($)		Personal Exemptions ($)[1]	
			Single	Joint	Single	Dependents
Texas	No	None	n/a	n/a	n/a	n/a

Note: Tax rates as of January 1, 2008; Local- and county-level taxes are not included; n/a not applicable; (1) Married joint filers generally receive double the single exemption
Source: Tax Foundation, www.taxfoundation.org

Various State and Local Tax Rates

State and Local Sales and Use (%)	State Sales and Use (%)	Gasoline[1,2] ($/gal.)	Cigarette ($/pack)	Spirits ($/gal.)	Table Wine ($/gal.)	Beer ($/gal.)
8.25	6.25 (i)	0.20	1.41	2.40	0.204	0.19

Note: Tax rates as of January 1, 2008; (1) In addition to the 18.4 cpg Federal gasoline tax; (2) Rates may include additional state sales taxes, environmental protection and storage fees/taxes, and local taxes. When necessary, the volume-weighted average of all local taxes is used to approximate the typical statewide rate including local tax; (i) Texas has a GRT that is levied in addition to its 6.25% sales tax. It is called the franchise tax and the rate is 1% (.5% for retailers).
Source: Tax Foundation, www.taxfoundation.org; Original research

State Tax Burdens

Area	Combined State and Local Tax Burden		Combined Federal, State and Local Tax Burden	
	Percent	Rank	Percent	Rank
Texas	9.3	43	29.8	41
U.S. Average	11.0	-	32.7	-

Note: Figures cover 2007 and measure taxes as a percentage of income
Source: Tax Foundation, www.taxfoundation.org

State Business Tax Climate Index Rankings

State	Overall Rank	Corporate Tax Index Rank	Individual Income Tax Index Rank	Sales Tax Index Rank	Unemployment Insurance Tax Index Rank	Property Tax Index Rank
Texas	8	47	7	28	14	27

Note: Rankings range from 1 to 50 where 1 is best. Rankings do not average across to Overall Rank. States without a given tax are given a ranking of 1.
Source: Tax Foundation, State Business Tax Climate Index 2008

TRANSPORTATION

Means of Transportation to Work

Area	Car/Truck/Van		Public Transportation			Bicycle	Walked	Other Means	Worked at Home
	Drove Alone	Car-pooled	Bus	Subway	Railroad				
City	84.3	9.3	1.4	0.0	0.0	0.2	0.2	0.4	4.1
MSA[1]	76.6	14.4	3.4	0.0	0.0	0.3	1.6	1.2	2.5
U.S.	75.7	12.2	2.5	1.5	0.5	0.4	2.9	1.0	3.3

Note: Figures are percentages and cover workers 16 years of age and older; (1) Metropolitan Statistical Area - see Appendix A for areas included
Source: Census 2000, Summary File 3

Travel Time to Work

Area	Less Than 15 Minutes	15 to 29 Minutes	30 to 44 Minutes	45 to 59 Minutes	60 Minutes or More
City	18.9	29.5	29.4	15.2	7.0
MSA[1]	20.3	33.8	25.5	11.1	9.3
U.S.	29.4	36.1	19.1	7.4	8.0

Note: Figures are percentages and include workers 16 years old and over; (1) Metropolitan Statistical Area - see Appendix A for areas included
Source: Census 2000, Summary File 3

Travel Time Index

Area	1982	1995	2004	2005
Urban Area[1]	1.19	1.19	1.32	1.36
Average[2]	1.11	1.22	1.29	1.30

Note: Travel Time Index - The ratio of travel time in the peak period to the travel time at free-flow conditions. A value of 1.35 indicates a 20-minute free-flow trip takes 27 minutes in the peak. Free-flow speeds (60 mph on freeways and 35 mph on principal arterials) are used as the comparison threshold; (1) Covers the Houston, TX urban area; (2) average of 85 urban areas
Source: Texas Transportation Institute, The 2007 Urban Mobility Report, September 2007

Living Environment

COST OF LIVING

Cost of Living Index

Composite Index	Groceries	Housing	Utilities	Trans-portation	Health Care	Misc. Goods/ Services
88.0	83.1	74.4	101.0	96.2	101.2	93.1

Note: U.S. = 100; Figures cover the Houston TX urban area.
Source: The Council for Community and Economic Research (formerly ACCRA), Cost of Living Index, 2007

Grocery Prices

Area[1]	T-Bone Steak ($/pound)	Frying Chicken ($/pound)	Whole Milk ($/half gal.)	Eggs ($/dozen)	Orange Juice ($/64 oz.)	Coffee ($/11.5 oz.)
City[2]	6.49	0.96	2.13	1.33	2.90	2.90
Avg.	8.93	1.12	2.13	1.52	3.26	3.31
Min.	5.88	0.71	1.33	0.83	2.30	2.20
Max.	12.80	2.07	3.43	3.54	5.79	6.20

Note: (1) Values for the local area are compared with the average, minimum and maximum values for all 331 areas in the Cost of Living Index report; (2) Figures cover the Houston TX urban area; **T-Bone Steak** *(price per pound);* **Frying Chicken** *(price per pound, whole fryer);* **Whole Milk** *(half gallon carton);* **Eggs** *(price per dozen, Grade A, large);* **Orange Juice** *(64 oz. Tropicana or Florida Natural);* **Coffee** *(11.5 oz. can, vacuum-packed, Maxwell House, Hills Bros, or Folgers).*
Source: The Council for Community and Economic Research (formerly ACCRA), Cost of Living Index, 2007

Housing and Utility Costs

Area[1]	New Home Price ($)	Apartment Rent ($/month)	All Electric ($/month)	Part Electric ($/month)	Other Energy ($/month)	Telephone ($/month)
City[2]	214,931	812	-	130.96	44.20	23.71
Avg.	309,605	782	146.13	78.67	90.16	26.14
Min.	189,877	n/a	82.03	37.41	33.15	17.08
Max.	1,202,800	3,481	271.14	150.60	257.67	37.45

Note: (1) Values for the local area are compared with the average, minimum and maximum values for all 331 areas in the Cost of Living Index report; (2) Figures cover the Houston TX urban area; **New Home Price** *(2,400 sf living area, 8,000 sf lot, in urban area with full utilities);* **Apartment Rent** *(950 sf 2 bedroom/1.5 or 2 bath, unfurnished, excluding all utilities except water);* **All Electric** *(average monthly cost for an all-electric home);* **Part Electric** *(average monthly cost for a part-electric home);* **Other Energy** *(average monthly cost for natural gas, fuel oil, coal, wood, and any other forms of energy except electricity);* **Telephone** *(price includes basic monthly rate for a private residential line plus additional local usage charges incurred by a family of four).*
Source: The Council for Community and Economic Research (formerly ACCRA), Cost of Living Index, 2007

Health Care, Transportation, and Other Costs

Area[1]	Doctor ($/visit)	Dentist ($/visit)	Optometrist ($/visit)	Gasoline ($/gallon)	Beauty Salon ($/visit)	Men's Shirt ($)
City[2]	81.72	76.13	82.50	2.51	31.37	23.16
Avg.	79.48	71.93	79.55	2.64	29.52	25.77
Min.	52.08	44.80	43.95	2.19	15.58	16.19
Max.	148.44	126.27	158.83	3.48	60.62	48.53

Note: (1) Values for the local area are compared with the average, minimum and maximum values for all 331 areas in the Cost of Living Index report; (2) Figures cover the Houston TX urban area; **Doctor** *(general practitioners routine exam of an established patient);* **Dentist** *(adult teeth cleaning and periodic oral examination);* **Optometrist** *(full vision eye exam for established adult patient);* **Gasoline** *(one gallon regular unleaded, national brand, including all taxes, cash price at self-service pump if available);* **Beauty Salon** *(woman's shampoo, trim, and blow-dry);* **Men's Shirt** *(cotton/polyester dress shirt, pinpoint weave, long sleeves).*
Source: The Council for Community and Economic Research (formerly ACCRA), Cost of Living Index, 2007

HOUSING

House Price Index (HPI)

Area	National Ranking[2]	Quarterly Change (%)	One-Year Change (%)	Five-Year Change (%)
MSA[1]	44	1.38	4.79	25.12
U.S.[3]	-	0.10	0.84	41.37

Note: The HPI is a weighted repeat sales index. It measures average price changes in repeat sales or refinancings on the same properties. This information is obtained by reviewing repeat mortgage transactions on single-family properties whose mortgages have been purchased or securitized by Fannie Mae or Freddie Mac in January 1975; (1) Metropolitan Statistical Area - see Appendix B for areas included; (2) Rankings are based on annual percentage change for all metro areas containing at least 15,000 transactions over the last 10 years and ranges from 1 to 291; (3) figures based on a weighted average of Census Division estimates; all figures are for the period ending December 31, 2007
Source: Office of Federal Housing Enterprise Oversight, House Price Index, February 26, 2008

House Price Valuations

Area	Q1 2000	Q1 2001	Q1 2002	Q1 2003	Q1 2004	Q1 2005	Q1 2006	Q1 2007	Q1 2008
MSA[1]	-16.2	-23.5	-17.0	-17.1	-21.3	-26.3	-26.6	-29.5	-33.1

Note: Figures show the percentage of over- or under-valuation of single family homes relative to statistically normal house values (e.g. a value of 23.6 indicates that house values are 23.6% overvalued). Statistically normal house values are based on house prices, interest rates, household incomes, population densities, and any historical premiums or discounts metropolitan areas have exhibited over time; (1) Figures cover the Metropolitan Statistical Area - see Appendix B for areas included
Source: Global Insight/National City Corporation, House Prices in America, May 2008

Median Home Prices

Area	2005	2006	2007[r]	Percent Change 2006 to 2007
MSA[1]	143.0	149.1	152.5	2.3
U.S. Average	219.0	221.9	217.9	-1.8

Note: Figures are median sales prices of existing single-family homes in thousands of dollars; (r) revised; n/a not available; (1) Metropolitan Statistical Area - see Appendix B for areas included
Source: National Association of Realtors, Metropolitan Area Prices, 1st Quarter 2008

Housing: Year Structure Built

Area	1990 -2000	1980 -1989	1970 -1979	1960 -1969	1950 -1959	1940 -1949	Before 1940	Median Year
City	32.3	44.1	18.0	2.4	1.7	0.5	1.0	1986
MSA[1]	19.8	23.0	26.6	13.6	9.4	4.3	3.4	1977
U.S.	17.0	15.8	18.5	13.7	12.7	7.3	15.0	1971

Note: Figures are percentages; (1) Metropolitan Statistical Area - see Appendix A for areas included
Source: Census 2000, Summary File 3

HEALTH

Health Risk Data

Category	Area[1] (%)	U.S. (%)
Adults who have been told they have high blood pressure[3]	23.2	25.5
Adults who have been told they have high blood cholesterol[3]	32.8	35.6
Adults who have been told they have diabetes[2]	5.8	7.5
Adults who have been told they have arthritis[3]	21.1	27.0
Adults who have been told they currently have asthma	8.7	8.5
Adults who are current smokers	14.4	20.1
Adults who are heavy drinkers[4]	4.2	4.9
Adults who are overweight (BMI 25.0 - 29.9)	36.4	36.5
Adults who are obese (BMI 30.0 - 99.8)	22.5	25.1

Note: Data as of 2006 unless otherwise noted; (1) Figures cover the Metropolitan Statistical Area - see Appendix B for areas included; (2) Figures do not include pregnancy-related diabetes, pre-diabetes or borderline diabetes; (3) 2005 data; (4) Heavy drinkers are classified as adult men having more than two drinks per day or adult women having more than one drink per day
Source: Centers for Disease Control and Prevention, Behaviorial Risk Factor Surveillance System, SMART: Selected Metropolitan/Micropolitan Area Risk Trends, 2005, 2006

Mortality Rates for the Top 10 Causes of Death in the U.S.

ICD-10[a] Sub-Chapter	ICD-10[a] Code	Age-Adjusted Mortality Rate[1] per 100,000 population	
		County[2]	U.S.
Malignant neoplasms	C00-C97	153.0	186.5
Ischaemic heart diseases	I20-I25	126.7	152.3
Other forms of heart disease	I30-I51	46.4	51.5
Cerebrovascular diseases	I60-I69	48.7	50.0
Chronic lower respiratory diseases	J40-J47	26.4	42.6
Diabetes mellitus	E10-E14	24.4	24.8
Other degenerative diseases of the nervous system	G30-G31	29.2	22.6
Other external causes of accidental injury	W00-X59	12.7	21.4
Influenza and pneumonia	J10-J18	17.9	20.7
Hypertensive diseases	I10-I13	21.1	18.2

Note: (a) ICD-10 = International Classification of Diseases 10th Revision; (1) Mortality rates are a three year average covering 2003-2005; (2) Figures cover Fort Bend County
Source: Centers for Disease Control and Prevention, National Center for Health Statistics. Compressed Mortality File 1999-2004. CDC WONDER On-line Database, compiled from Compressed Mortality File 1999-2005 Series 20 No. 2K, 2008.

Mortality Rates for Selected Causes of Death

ICD-10[a] Sub-Chapter	ICD-10[a] Code	Age-Adjusted Mortality Rate[1] per 100,000 population	
		County[2]	U.S.
Assault	X85-Y09	4.2	5.9
Human immunodeficiency virus (HIV) disease	B20-B24	2.6	4.5
Intentional self-harm	X60-X84	8.6	10.8
Malnutrition	E40-E46	4.0	1.0
Obesity and other hyperalimentation	E65-E68	*1.0	1.4
Organic, including symptomatic, mental disorders	F01-F09	21.4	16.8
Transport accidents	V01-V99	13.0	16.1
Viral hepatitis	B15-B19	2.0	1.8

Note: (a) ICD-10 = International Classification of Diseases 10th Revision; (1) Mortality rates are a three year average covering 2003-2005; (2) Figures cover Fort Bend County; (*) Unreliable data as per CDC
Source: Centers for Disease Control and Prevention, National Center for Health Statistics. Compressed Mortality File 1999-2004. CDC WONDER On-line Database, compiled from Compressed Mortality File 1999-2005 Series 20 No. 2K, 2008.

Distribution of Physicians[1]

Area	Total	Family/ General Practice	Specialties	
			Medical	Surgical
Fort Bend County (number)	717	250	260	126
Fort Bend County (rate per 10,000 pop.)	15.5	5.4	5.6	2.7
U.S. (rate per 10,000 pop.)	17.7	4.6	6.9	4.3

Note: Data as of 2005; (1) Includes all non-federal, patient-care, office-based MDs
Source: Area Resource File (ARF). June 2007. U.S. Department of Health and Human Services, Health Resources and Services Administration, Bureau of Health Professions, Rockville, MD.

Hospitals

Sugar Land has the following hospitals: 2 general medical and surgical; 1 surgical; 1 long-term acute care.
AHA Guide to the Healthcare Field 2008

According to *U.S. News,* the Houston-Sugar Land-Baytown, TX metro area is home to seven of the best hospitals in the U.S.: **Memorial Hermann TIRR**; **Menninger Clinic**; **Methodist Hospital**; **Saint Luke's Episcopal Hospital**; **Texas Children's Hospital**; **University of Texas M.D. Anderson Cancer Center**; **Woman's Hospital of Texas**. *U.S. News Online, "America's Best Hospitals 2007"*

EDUCATION

Public School District Statistics

District Name	Schls	Pupils	Pupil/ Teacher Ratio	Minority Pupils[1] (%)	Free Lunch Eligible[2] (%)	IEP[3] (%)
Fort Bend ISD	69	66,104	17.2	72.8	24.8	9.5
Lamar CISD	30	19,662	15.9	66.4	37.7	11.4

Note: Table includes regular local school districts with 2,000 or more students; (1) Percentage of students that are not white, non-Hispanic; (2) Percentage of students that are eligible for the free lunch program; (3) Percentage of students that have an Individualized Education Program.
Source: U.S. Department of Education, National Center for Education Statistics, Common Core of Data, Local Education Agency (School District) Universe Survey: School Year 2005-2006; U.S. Department of Education, National Center for Education Statistics, Common Core of Data, Public Elementary/Secondary School Universe Survey: School Year 2005-2006

Top Public High Schools

High School Name	Index[1]	Rank[1]	Subsidized Lunch (%)[2]	E&E (%)[3]
Clements	2.287	366	2.6	46.2

Note: (1) Public schools are ranked according to a ratio that is the number of Advanced Placement, International Baccalaureate, and/or Cambridge tests taken by all students at a school in 2007 divided by the number of graduating seniors. All of the schools on the list have an index of at least 1.000; they are in the top five percent of public schools measured this way. The rankings range from 1 to 1,422; (2) Percentage of students receiving federally subsidized meals; (3) E & E stands for equity and excellence percentage: the portion of all graduating seniors at a school that had at least one passing grade on one AP or IB test; (**) Gave both IB and AP tests. AP and IB participation are indicators of a school's efforts to get students to excel and prepare for college.
Source: Newsweek Online, "Top High Schools 2008"

Highest Level of Education

Area	Less than H.S.	H.S. Diploma	Some College, No Deg.	Associate Degree	Bachelors Degree	Masters Degree	Profess. School Degree	Doctorate Degree
City	6.7	13.4	19.7	6.4	34.3	13.1	4.1	2.2
MSA[1]	22.8	22.8	22.3	5.2	18.2	5.8	2.0	1.0
U.S.	19.4	28.4	21.2	6.4	15.7	5.9	2.0	1.0

Note: Figures are 2007 estimated percentages and cover persons age 25 and over; (1) Metropolitan Statistical Area - see Appendix B for areas included
Source: Claritas, Inc.

Educational Attainment by Race

Area	High School Graduate (%)					Bachelor's Degree (%)				
	Total	White	Black	Asian	Hisp.[2]	Total	White	Black	Asian	Hisp.[2]
City	93.4	95.8	93.7	87.9	83.7	53.7	52.7	51.2	60.7	33.0
MSA[1]	75.9	81.4	77.5	80.1	43.6	27.2	31.4	18.4	47.7	8.5
U.S.	80.4	83.6	72.3	80.4	52.4	24.4	26.1	14.3	44.1	10.4

Note: Figures shown cover persons 25 years old and over; (1) Metropolitan Statistical Area - see Appendix A for areas included; (2) people of Hispanic origin can be of any race
Source: Census 2000, Summary File 3

School Enrollment by Type

Area	Grades KG to 8				Grades 9 to 12			
	Public		Private		Public		Private	
	Enrollment	%	Enrollment	%	Enrollment	%	Enrollment	%
City	9,478	85.9	1,559	14.1	4,778	90.1	525	9.9
MSA[1]	589,699	92.3	49,169	7.7	244,239	93.2	17,795	6.8
U.S.	33,526,011	88.7	4,285,121	11.3	14,848,628	90.6	1,532,323	9.4

Note: Figures shown cover persons 3 years old and over; (1) Metropolitan Statistical Area - see Appendix A for areas included
Source: Census 2000, Summary File 3

School Enrollment by Race

Area	Grades KG to 8 (%)				Grades 9 to 12 (%)			
	White	Black	Asian	Hisp.[1]	White	Black	Asian	Hisp.[1]
City	66.2	5.7	21.8	9.9	63.5	5.1	26.0	6.5
MSA[2]	56.0	19.6	4.3	36.5	56.0	19.8	5.4	32.8
U.S.	68.5	15.5	3.3	16.8	68.8	15.5	3.8	15.7

Note: Figures shown cover persons 3 years old and over; (1) people of Hispanic origin can be of any race; (2) Metropolitan Statistical Area - see Appendix A for areas included
Source: Census 2000, Summary File 3

Average Salaries of Public School Classroom Teachers

District	2005-06		2006-07		Percent Change 2005-06 to 2006-07
	Dollars	Rank[1]	Dollars	Rank[1]	
Texas	41,744	35	44,897	30	7.55
U.S. Average	49,026	-	50,816	-	3.65

Note: (1) State rank ranges from 1 to 51.
Source: National Education Association, Rankings & Estimates: Rankings of the States 2006 and Estimates of School Statistics 2007, December 2007

Higher Education

Four-Year Colleges			Two-Year Colleges			Medical Schools[1]	Law Schools[2]	Voc/ Tech[3]
Public	Private Non-profit	Private For-profit	Public	Private Non-profit	Private For-profit			
0	0	0	0	0	0	0	0	0

Note: Figures cover institutions located within the city limits; (1) includes schools accredited by the Liaison Committee on Medical Education and the American Osteopathic Association; (2) includes American Bar Association-accredited law schools; (3) includes all schools with programs that are less than 2 years.
Source: National Center for Education Statistics, The Integrated Postsecondary Education System (IPEDS) Peer Analysis System, 2007; www.usnews.com, Law and Medical School Directories, 2009

PRESIDENTIAL ELECTION

2004 Presidential Election Results

Area	Bush	Kerry	Nader	Other
Fort Bend County	57.4	42.1	0.1	0.4
U.S.	50.7	48.3	0.4	0.6

Note: Results are percentages and may not add to 100% due to rounding
Source: Dave Leip's Atlas of U.S. Presidential Elections, www.uselectionatlas.org

EMPLOYERS

Major Employers

Company Name	Industry	Type of Site
AEI Services LLC	Electric services	Single
American Residential Svcs LLC	Plumbing, heating, air-conditioning	Single
Brown & Root Inc	Heavy construction, nec	Headquarters
F Charles Brunicardi MD	Professional organizations	Single
HP	Electronic computers	Branch
Halliburton Energy Services	Oil and gas field services, nec	Headquarters
Hanover Compression Ltd Partnr	Heavy construction equipment rental	Single
Houston V A Medical Center	Administration of veterans' affairs	Branch
M D Anderson Cancer Centre	Specialty hospitals, except psychiatric	Headquarters
Methodist Hospital	General medical and surgical hospitals	Headquarters
Philip Industrial Services USA	Business consulting, nec	Single
Quaker State Corporation	Lubricating oils and greases	Single
St Lukes Episcopal Health Sys	General medical and surgical hospitals	Headquarters
Star Enterprise	Petroleum refining	Single
University of Houston System	Colleges and universities	Branch

Note: Companies shown are located within the Houston metropolitan area; nec = not elsewhere classified.
Source: www.zapdata.com, May 2008

PUBLIC SAFETY

Crime Rate

Area	All Crimes	Violent Crimes: Murder	Violent Crimes: Forcible Rape	Violent Crimes: Robbery	Violent Crimes: Aggrav. Assault	Property Crimes: Burglary	Property Crimes: Larceny -Theft	Property Crimes: Motor Vehicle Theft
City	2,195.1	0.0	7.7	57.8	64.2	272.1	1,697.0	96.3
Metro[1]	4,829.8	9.6	34.6	279.6	383.4	964.9	2,570.8	586.9
U.S.	3,808.1	5.7	30.9	149.4	287.5	729.4	2,206.8	398.4

Note: Figures are crimes per 100,000 population; (1) Metropolitan Statistical Area - see Appendix B for areas included
Source: FBI Uniform Crime Reports, 2006

Hate Crimes

Area	Number of Quarters Reported	Bias Motivation: Race	Religion	Sexual Orientation	Ethnicity	Disability
City	4	0	0	0	0	0

Source: Federal Bureau of Investigation, Hate Crime Statistics 2006

RECREATION

Culture

Dance[1]	Theatre[1]	Instrumental Music[1]	Vocal Music[1]	Series/ Festivals	Museums	Zoos and Aquariums[2]
0	0	1	0	0	1	0

Note: (1) Number of professional perfoming groups; (2) AZA-accredited
Source: The Grey House Performing Arts Directory, 2007; Official Museum Directory, 2008; Association of Zoos & Aquariums, AZA Member Zoos & Aquariums, June 2008

Professional Sports Teams

Team Name	League
Houston Astros	Major League Baseball (MLB)
Houston Dynamo	Major League Soccer (MLS)
Houston Rockets	National Basketball Association (NBA)
Houston Texans	National Football League (NFL)

Note: Includes teams located in the Houston metro area.
Source: Original research

MEDIA

Newspapers

Name	News Focus	Frequency	Circulation
First Colony Monthly	Community	Monthly	40,000
Fort Bend/Southwest Sun	Community	Weekly	30,000

Note: Includes newspapers with offices located in the city
Source: MediaContactsPro, March 2008

Television Stations

Name	Ch.	Network(s)	Type	Ownership
KPRC	2	NBC	Commercial	Post-Newsweek Business Information Inc.
KUHT	8	PBS	Public	University of Houston
KHOU	11	CBS	Commercial	Belo Corporation
KTRK	13	ABC	Commercial	ABC Inc.
KTXH	20	Fox	Commercial	United Paramount Network
KRIV	26	Fox	Commercial	Fox Television Stations Inc.
KHWB	39	WBN	Commercial	Tribune Broadcasting Company
KXLN	45	Univision	Commercial	Univision Television Group
KTMD	48	Telemundo	Commercial	Telemundo Group Inc.
KPXB	49	Pax	Commercial	Paxson Communications Corporation
KNWS	51	n/a	Commercial	Johnson Broadcasting Corporation
KTBU	55	n/a	Commercial	n/a
KZJL	61	n/a	Commercial	Liberman Broadcasting

Note: Stations included cover the Houston DMA (Designated Market Area); n/a not available
BurrellesLuce, MediaContacts Online, January 2007

Major AM Radio Stations

Call Letters	Freq. (kHz)	Station Type	Target Audience	Station Format	Music Format
KILT	610	n/a	General	Sports/Talk	n/a
KSEV	700	Commercial	General	News/Talk	n/a
KTRH	740	Commercial	General	Sports	n/a
KBME	790	Commercial	General	Music/News	Adult Standards
KYST	920	Commercial	General/Hispanic	Music/Sports/Talk	Latin
KPRC	950	n/a	General	Music/Talk	n/a
KRTX	980	n/a	General	Music	Latin
KLAT	1010	n/a	General/Hispanic	Music	n/a
KKHT	1070	Commercial	General/Religious	Talk	n/a
KTEK	1110	Commercial	Ethnic/General	Music/Talk	Christian
KYOK	1140	Commercial	General/Religious	Music/News	Gospel
KGOL	1180	Commercial	General	Ed/Music/News/Talk	World Music
KWHI	1280	n/a	General	Music/Sports	n/a
KXYZ	1320	n/a	Hispanic	n/a	n/a
KHCB	1400	n/a	General/Hisp/Rel	Educational/Music/Talk	n/a
KHCH	1400	Non-Comm	General/Religious	Music/News/Talk	Gospel
KCOH	1430	Commercial	Black/General	Ed/Music/News/Talk	Urban Contemp.
KHVL	1490	n/a	General/Religious	Music/News	n/a
KYND	1520	Commercial	General/Hispanic	Educational/News/Talk	n/a
KGBC	1540	Commercial	General	Music/News/Sports	Oldies

Note: Stations included cover the Houston DMA (Designated Market Area); n/a not available
Source: BurrellesLuce, MediaContacts Online, January 2007

Major FM Radio Stations

Call Letters	Freq. (mHz)	Station Type	Target Audience	Station Format	Music Format
KUHF	88.7	College	General	Music/News	n/a
KSBJ	89.3	Non-Comm	General/Religious	Educational/Music/Talk	Christian
KETX	92.3	n/a	General	Music	n/a
KKRW	93.7	n/a	General	Music	n/a
KTBZ	94.5	Commercial	General	Music/News/Talk	Alternative
KHMX	96.5	n/a	General	Music/News/Sports	n/a
KTHT	97.1	n/a	General	Music/Talk	n/a
KBXX	97.9	Commercial	Black/General/Hisp/Men	Music/News/Talk	Urban Contemp.
KTJM	98.5	Commercial	General	Music/News/Talk	Latin
KODA	99.1	n/a	General	Music	n/a
KILT	100.3	n/a	General	Music/News/Talk	n/a
KRTX	100.7	n/a	General/Hispanic	Music	n/a
KMJQ	102.1	n/a	General	Music	n/a
KMKS	102.5	Commercial	General	Music/News	Country
KLTN	102.9	n/a	General/Hispanic	Music	n/a
KRBE	104.1	n/a	General	Music/News/Talk	n/a
KHCB	105.7	n/a	General/Religious	Music/Talk	n/a
KTTX	106.1	n/a	General/Young Adult	Music	n/a
KHPT	106.9	Commercial	General	Music/News/Talk	80's
KLDE	107.5	n/a	General	Music	n/a

Note: Stations included cover the Houston DMA (Designated Market Area); n/a not available
BurrellesLuce, MediaContacts Online, January 2007

CLIMATE

Average and Extreme Temperatures

Temperature	Jan	Feb	Mar	Apr	May	Jun	Jul	Aug	Sep	Oct	Nov	Dec	Yr.
Extreme High (°F)	84	91	91	95	97	103	104	107	102	94	89	83	107
Average High (°F)	61	65	73	79	85	91	93	93	89	81	72	65	79
Average Temp. (°F)	51	54	62	69	75	81	83	83	79	70	61	54	69
Average Low (°F)	41	43	51	58	65	71	73	73	68	58	50	43	58
Extreme Low (°F)	12	20	22	31	44	52	62	62	48	32	19	7	7

Note: Figures cover the years 1969-1990
Source: National Climatic Data Center, International Station Meteorological Climate Summary, 9/96

Average Precipitation/Snowfall/Humidity

Precip./Humidity	Jan	Feb	Mar	Apr	May	Jun	Jul	Aug	Sep	Oct	Nov	Dec	Yr.
Avg. Precip. (in.)	3.3	2.7	3.3	3.3	5.6	4.9	3.7	3.7	4.8	4.7	3.7	3.3	46.9
Avg. Snowfall (in.)	Tr	Tr	0	0	0	0	0	0	0	0	Tr	Tr	Tr
Avg. Rel. Hum. 6am (%)	85	86	87	89	91	92	93	93	93	91	89	86	90
Avg. Rel. Hum. 3pm (%)	58	55	54	54	57	56	55	55	57	53	55	57	55

Note: Figures cover the years 1969-1990; Tr = Trace amounts (<0.05 in. of rain; <0.5 in. of snow)
Source: National Climatic Data Center, International Station Meteorological Climate Summary, 9/96

Weather Conditions

Temperature			Daytime Sky			Precipitation		
32°F & below	45°F & below	90°F & above	Clear	Partly cloudy	Cloudy	0.01 inch or more precip.	0.1 inch or more snow/ice	Thunder-storms
21	87	96	83	168	114	101	1	62

Note: Figures are average number of days per year and cover the years 1969-1990
Source: National Climatic Data Center, International Station Meteorological Climate Summary, 9/96

HAZARDOUS WASTE

Superfund Sites

Sugar Land has no sites on the EPA's Superfund Final National Priorities List.
U.S. Environmental Protection Agency, Final National Priorities List, June 23, 2008

AIR & WATER QUALITY

Air Quality Index

Area	Percent of Days when Air Quality was...[2]				AQI Statistics	
	Good	Moderate	Unhealthy for Sensitive Groups	Unhealthy	Maximum	Median
MSA[1]	40.0	49.3	9.9	0.8	174	56

Note: The Air Quality Index (AQI) is an index for reporting daily air quality. EPA calculates the AQI for five major air pollutants regulated by the Clean Air Act: ground-level ozone, particle pollution (also known as particulate matter), carbon monoxide, sulfur dioxide, and nitrogen dioxide. The AQI runs from 0 to 500. The higher the AQI value, the greater the level of air pollution and the greater the health concern. There are six AQI categories: "Good" The AQI is between 0 and 50. Air quality is considered satisfactory; "Moderate" The AQI is between 51 and 100. Air quality is acceptable; "Unhealthy for Sensitive Groups" When AQI values are between 101 and 150, members of sensitive groups may experience health effects; "Unhealthy" When AQI values are between 151 and 200 everyone may begin to experience health effects; "Very Unhealthy" AQI values between 201 and 300 trigger a health alert; "Hazardous" AQI values over 300 trigger health warnings of emergency conditions; (1) Metropolitan Statistical Area - see Appendix A for areas included; (2) Based on 365 days with AQI data in 2007.
Source: U.S. Environmental Protection Agency, Air Quality Index Report, 2007

Air Quality Index Pollutants

Area	Percent of Days when AQI Pollutant was...[2]					
	Carbon Monoxide	Nitrogen Dioxide	Ozone	Sulfur Dioxide	Particulate Matter 2.5	Particulate Matter 10
MSA[1]	0.0	0.0	30.1	0.0	58.6	11.2

Note: The Air Quality Index (AQI) is an index for reporting daily air quality. EPA calculates the AQI for five major air pollutants regulated by the Clean Air Act: ground-level ozone, particle pollution (also known as particulate matter), carbon monoxide, sulfur dioxide, and nitrogen dioxide. The AQI runs from 0 to 500. The higher the AQI value, the greater the level of air pollution and the greater the health concern; (1) Metropolitan Statistical Area - see Appendix A for areas included; (2) Based on 365 days with AQI data in 2007.
Source: U.S. Environmental Protection Agency, Air Quality Index Report, 2007

Air Quality Index Trends

Area	Trend Sites (24)								All Sites (94)
	1999	2000	2001	2002	2003	2004	2005	2006	2006
MSA[1]	51	42	28	21	31	22	28	18	30

Note: An AQI value greater than 100 indicates that air quality would have been in the unhealthful range on that day. Data from exceptional events are not included. These counts are presented in two ways. First, the counts are based on sites having an adequate record of monitoring data during the trend period (trend sites). These counts represent the relative change in the number of days with AQI values greater than 100. In the last column, the counts are based on all sites with data in the most recent year (because it is possible for a site to have data in the most recent year but not enough data to be a trend site); (1) Metropolitan Statistical Area - see Appendix A for areas included.

Source: U.S. Environmental Protection Agency, Office of Air and Radiation, Air Trends, Factbook and Related Information, Air Pollution Trends in Selected Metropolitan Areas 2006

Maximum Air Pollutant Concentrations

	Particulate Matter 10 (ug/m^3)	Particulate Matter 2.5 (ug/m^3)	Ozone (ppm)	Carbon Monoxide (ppm)	Sulfur Dioxide (ppm)	Nitrogen Dioxide (ppm)	Lead (ug/m^3)
MSA[1] Level	173	32	0.15	3	0.023	0.016	0.01
NAAQS[2]	150	35	0.125	9	0.140	0.053	1.50
Met NAAQS[2]	No	Yes	No	Yes	Yes	Yes	Yes

Note: Data from exceptional events are not included; (1) Metropolitan Statistical Area - see Appendix A for areas included; (2) National Ambient Air Quality Standards; n/a not available

Concentrations: Particulate Matter 10 (coarse particulate) - highest second maximum 24-hour concentration; Particulate Matter 2.5 (fine particulate) - highest 98th percentile 24-hour concentration; Ozone - highest second daily maximum 1-hour concentration; Carbon Monoxide - highest second maximum non-overlapping 8-hour concentration; Sulfur Dioxide - highest second maximum 24-hour concentration; Nitrogen Dioxide - highest arithmetic mean concentration; Lead - highest quarterly maximum concentration

Units: ppm = parts per million; ug/m^3 = micrograms per cubic meter

Source: U.S. Environmental Protection Agency, MSA Factbook 2006, Air Quality Statistics by City

Drinking Water

Water System Name	Pop. Served	Primary Water Source Type	Violations[1]	
			Health Based	Monitoring/ Reporting
City of Sugar Land	73,362	Ground	0	0

Note: (1) Based on violation data from January 1, 2007 to December 31, 2007 (includes unresolved violations from earlier years)

Source: U.S. Environmental Protection Agency, Office of Ground Water and Drinking Water, Safe Drinking Water Information System (based on data extracted April 15, 2008)

Draper, Utah

Background

Surrounded by Rocky Mountain peaks, Draper lies 25 miles south of Salt Lake City and about 5,000 feet above sea level. The town possesses the benefits of a quiet country village with a sophisticated population. Farmers and factory workers, doctors and lawyers, musicians and teachers, entertainers and business people combine to create a diverse mix of old timers and newcomers drawn to this town by the common desire to achieve a safe haven for their families, away from urban sprawl.

Draper is home to many small businesses, including farming, health care, and a cluster of high-tech industries. The city has its own Arts Council and symphony, and a wide variety of cultural and sports venues, including amenities, including NBA Jazz Basketball, Utah Symphony, Ballet West, and many other cultural and entertainment possibilities.

Nearby are two major universities and the Salt Lake City International Airport.

Draper was first called South Willow Creek. Ebenezer Brown, his wife, and their five children are acknowledged as the first settlers of Draper in 1849. They farmed the land and raised cattle to sell to emigrants going to the gold fields out west. The name of their home was Draper Fort. When a post office was established there about 1854, the name was changed to Draperville Post Office, then to just Draperville later. The name was for William Draper, who was the first Presiding Elder of the Mormon Church at that time. The city was incorporated in 1978.

Draper is served by the Jordan School District, which is the largest of Utah's 40 school districts and covers approximately 250 square miles in the southern half of Salt Lake County.

A 20-minute drive from Draper will place you in the Rocky Mountains, which offer world class skiing and trails for hiking, horses, RV's, and bikes. Nearby ski resorts include Snowbird, Alta, Solitude, and Brighton. In addition, Draper is home to one of the best hang gliding sites in the United States and to the largest hang gliding school in the nation at Point of the Mountain.

Rankings

General Rankings

- Salt Lake City* was ranked #27 out of 375 metro areas in *Cities Ranked & Rated.* Criteria: cost of living; climate; crime; transportation; economy and jobs; education; arts and culture; health and healthcare; leisure; quality of life. *Cities Ranked & Rated, 2nd Edition, 2007*
- Salt Lake City* was ranked #56 out of 379 metro areas in *Places Rated Almanac.* Criteria: health care; education; recreation; transportation; ambience; climate; crime; housing costs; jobs. *Places Rated Almanac, 7th Edition, 2007*

Business/Finance Rankings

- The nation's 100 largest metro areas were analysed in terms of the percentage of households entering some stage of foreclosure in 2007. The Salt Lake City* metro area ranked #52 out of 100 (#1 = highest foreclosure rate). *RealtyTrac, "Year-End 2007 Metropolitan Foreclosure Report"*
- The Salt Lake City* metro area was identified as one of the "10 Best Cities for Jobs in 2008" by *Forbes.* The metro area ranked #1. Criteria: state unemployment rate; job growth; income growth; median household income; cost of living. *Forbes.com, "Best Cities for Jobs in 2008," January 10, 2008*
- The Salt Lake City* metro area was selected one of America's "Top 50 Business Opportunity Metros" by *Expansion Management* in their 5th annual Mayor's Challenge ranking of metro areas that have achieved solid ratings across the board in numerous *EM* studies during the past 12 months. The area ranked #24. Criteria: public schools; quality of life; college educated workers; logistics infrastructure; healthcare costs; taxes and government spending; reputation among site consultants. *Expansion Management, August 2007*
- Salt Lake City* was selected as one of the best places to start and grow a company by *Entrepreneur* and the National Policy Research Council. The Salt Lake City* metro area ranked #42 out of 50 large metro areas. Criteria: business formation and growth (firms started four to 14 years ago that still employ at least 5 people and experienced rapid growth over the last four years). *Entrepreneur/National Policy Research Council, "Hot Cities for Entrepreneurs," September 2006*
- Intel, in partnership with Sperling's BestPlaces, ranked the 80 "Best Cities for Teleworking" in America. The Salt Lake City* metro area ranked #16 among mid-sized metro areas. The study identifies cities that hold the greatest potential for teleworking based on a host of factors including typical commuting times, fuel prices, availability of broadband Internet access and percentage of the population in telework friendly jobs. The study also factored in extreme climate and natural hazards. *Intel, "Best Cities for Teleworking," March 30, 2006*
- The Salt Lake City* metro area appeared on the Milken Institute "2007 Best Performing Cities" index. Rank: #18 out of 200 large metro areas. Criteria: job growth; wage and salary growth; high-tech output growth. *Milken Institute, "2007 Best Performing Cities"*
- The Salt Lake City* metro area was selected as one of the hottest cities for entrepreneurs in America by *Inc. Magazine.* Criteria: job-growth data for 393 metro was analyzed for current-year employment growth, average annual employment growth over past three years, and employment growth by industry sector. The Salt Lake City* metro area ranked #10 among large metro areas and #68 overall. *Inc. Magazine, May 2007*
- Salt Lake City* was identified as one of the 100 "Most Unwired Cities" in the U.S. The area ranked #33 out of the 100 largest metro areas in the U.S. Criteria: number of public and commercial wireless access points (hotspots); airports with wireless Internet access; broadband availability; local wireless networks; and wireless email devices. *Intel, "Most Unwired Cities Survey," June 7, 2005*

- Salt Lake City* was ranked #34 out of 125 regions worldwide in terms of its "Knowledge Competitiveness Index." The index attempts to measure the knowledge-based development taking place throughout the world and is based on 19 measures of economic performance that indicate a region's ability to translate its knowledge capacity into economic value. *Robert Huggins Associates, World Knowledge Competitiveness Index 2005*

- *Forbes* ranked the 200 most populous metro areas in the U.S. in terms of the "Best Places for Business and Careers." The Salt Lake City* metro area was ranked #82. Criteria: business costs (labor, energy, tax and office space expenses); living costs (housing, transportation, food and other household expenditures); education levels of the work force; job growth; income growth; migration trends; crime rates; and culture/leisure. *Forbes, "Best Places for Business and Careers," March 19, 2008*

- Salt Lake City* was identified as one of the top 20 metro areas with the highest rate of house price appreciation in 2007. The area ranked #7 with a one-year price appreciation of 9.7% through the 4th quarter 2007. *Office of Federal Housing Enterprise Oversight, House Price Index, 4th Quarter 2007*

- *Fortune* ranked the 100 largest metro areas in the U.S. in terms of projected median home price change in 2007. The Salt Lake City* metro area ranked #4. *Fortune.com, "Hot Spots, Cold Spots"*

Health/Environment Rankings

- 100 of the largest metro areas in the U.S. were analyzed in terms of their current drought severity. The Salt Lake City* metro area ranked #5 (#1 = driest). The rankings were based on statistics such as long-term precipitation trends and patterns and the Palmer drought indices. *Sperling's BestPlaces, www.BestPlaces.net, "America's Drought-Riskiest Cities," November 2007*

- *Reader's Digest* ranked the 50 largest metro areas in the U.S. in terms of how "clean" they are. The Salt Lake City* metro area ranked #18. Criteria: air quality; water quality; toxic industrial pollution; Superfund sites; and sanitation. *Reader's Digest, "The 50 Cleanest (and Dirtiest) Cities in America," July 2005*

- The American Academy of Dermatology ranked 32 U.S. metropolitan regions in terms of their residents knowledge, attitude and behaviors towards tanning and sun protection. The Salt Lake City* metro area ranked #7. The results of the study are based on an online national survey of 3,342 respondents. *American Academy of Dermatology, "RAYS: Your Grade," May 7, 2007*

- The Salt Lake City* metro area appeared in *Country Home's* "2008 Best Green Places" report. The area ranked #133 out of 379. Criteria: official energy policies; green power; green buildings; availability of fresh, locally grown food. *Country Home, "2008 Best Green Places"*

- Wyeth Consumer Healthcare, in partnership with Sperling's BestPlaces, ranked the nation's 50 most populous metro areas in terms of five key health factors. The Salt Lake City* metro area ranked #5. Criteria: physical activity; health status; nutrition; lifestyle pursuits; and mental wellness. *Wyeth Consumer Healthcare, "Centrum Healthiest Cities Study," April 19, 2005*

- Salt Lake City* was identified as a "2008 Asthma Capital." The area ranked #58 out of the nation's 100 largest metropolitan areas. Twelve factors were used to identify the most challenging places to live for people with asthma: estimated prevalence; self-reported prevalence; crude death rate for asthma; annual pollen score; annual air quality; public smoking laws; number of board-certified asthma specialists; school inhaler access laws; rescue medication use; controller medication use; uninsured rate; poverty rate. *Asthma and Allergy Foundation of America, "2008 Asthma Capitals"*

- Salt Lake City* was identified as a "Spring Allergy Capital." The area ranked #60 out of 100. Three groups of factors were used to identify the most severe cities for people with allergies during the spring season: annual pollen levels; medicine utilization; access to board-certified allergists. *Asthma and Allergy Foundation of America, "2007 Spring Allergy Capital Rankings"*

- Salt Lake City* was identified as a "Fall Allergy Capital." The area ranked #63 out of 100. Three groups of factors were used to identify the most severe cities for people with allergies during the fall season: annual pollen levels; medicine utilization; access to board-certified allergists. *Asthma and Allergy Foundation of America, "2007 Fall Allergy Capital Rankings"*

- Ortho-McNeil Neurologics, in partnership with Sperling's BestPlaces, analyzed 110 metro areas and identified those U.S. cities with the highest prevalence of factors that are most commonly associated with migraine headaches. The Salt Lake City* metro area ranked #21. Criteria: number of migraine-related drug prescriptions per capita; lifestyle factors that can contribute to migraines; environmental factors that can trigger migraines; and consumption of migraine-triggering foods. *Ortho-McNeil Neurologics, "America's Migraine Hot Spots," March 14, 2006*

- Sperling's BestPlaces ranked 331 metro areas and identified the most and least stressful U.S. cities. The Salt Lake City* metro area ranked #64 out of the 100 largest metro areas (#1 = most stressful). Criteria: divorce rate; unemployment rate; violent and property crime; suicide rate; commute time; mental health; alcohol consumption; cloudy days. *Sperling's BestPlaces, www.BestPlaces.net, "America's Most (and Least) Stressful Cities," January 9, 2004*

- An analysis of the "Best & Worst Cities for Sleep" was conducted by Sperling's BestPlaces. The study ranked America's 50 most populated metro areas. The Salt Lake City* metro area ranked #31 (#1 = best city for sleep). Criteria: number of days residents didn't get enough rest or sleep during the past month; average length of daily commute; divorce rate; unemployment rate. *Sperling's BestPlaces, www.BestPlaces.net, "Best & Worst Cities for Sleep," 2006*

- Sperling's BestPlaces in partnership with Vistakon ranked the 100 largest metro areas and identified "America's 10 Worst Cities for Comfortable Eyes." The Salt Lake City* metro area ranked #3. Criteria: altitude; sunny days; wind; extreme temperatures; humidity; pollution; commute time; computer use. *Vistakon, "America's Best and Worst Cities for Comfortable Eyes," June 15, 2004*

- Salt Lake City* was selected as one of "America's Pet Healthiest Cities" by Purina. The city ranked #10 out of 50. Criteria: veterinary services; environment; legislation; preventative care; obesity/body condition. *Purina Pet Institute, "America's Pet Healthiest Cities," May 20, 2003*

Women/Minorities Rankings

- Salt Lake City* was ranked #30 out of 100 metro areas in *SELF Magazine's* ranking of "America's Best Places for Women." A panel of experts came up with more than 50 criteria including death and disease rates, environmental indicators, community resources, and lifestyle habits. *SELF Magazine, "America's Best Places for Women 2007," December 2007*

Seniors/Retirement Rankings

- Sperling's BestPlaces in partnership with Bankers Life & Casualty Company designed a survey to identify the top 50 metro areas in the U.S. that offer the best overall qualities for senior living. The Salt Lake City* metro area ranked #12. The following criteria were statistically weighted to reflect the needs of the senior population: health; disease; economics; social; environment; spiritual; transportation; housing; and crime. *Bankers Life & Casualty Company, "Best Cities for Seniors 2005"*

- A.G. Edwards ranked America's 500 top-performing communities based on their residents' personal savings and investing behavior. The Salt Lake City* metro area ranked #100 with an index score of 106.66 (national average = 100.00). A dozen statistical factors were measured including: participation in retirement savings plans; personal debt levels; and home ownership. *A.G. Edwards, "2007 Nest Egg Index", September 12, 2007*

Children/Family Rankings

- The Salt Lake City* metro area was selected as one of the "Best Cities for Relocating Families" by Worldwide ERC and Primacy Relocation. The 2007 study placed a special emphasis on the housing market, which has significantly impacted the relocation industry and an employer's ability to transfer employees. The variables which weigh heavily in this category include home price, home affordability index, appreciation rates, and property tax. Other criteria include cost of living, crime rates, education, climate, focus on diversity, physicians per capita, recreation and leisure, arts and culture, air quality, watershed quality, sales tax, unemployment rate, job growth, high school and higher education index, school expenditures per student, students in public school, SAT/ACT percentile, and population growth. *Worldwide ERC and Primacy Relocation, "2007 Best Cities for Relocating Families"*

Safety Rankings

- The National Insurance Crime Bureau ranked 361 metro areas in the U.S. in terms of per capita rates of vehicle theft. The Salt Lake City* metro area ranked #34 (#1 = highest rate). Criteria: number of vehicle theft offenses per 100,000 inhabitants. *National Insurance Crime Bureau, "NICB Vehicle Theft Study," April 22, 2008*

- Salt Lake City* appeared on Sperling's BestPlaces list of the "Riskiest Cities for Identity Theft." The area ranked #7 out of the nations 50 largest metro areas. Over 80 criteria were analyzed across four major categories: technology impact; crime; transactions; and risk profile. *Sperling's BestPlaces, www.BestPlaces.net, "Riskiest Cities for Identity Theft," July 2006*

- Farmers Insurance Group of Companies, in partnership with Sperling's BestPlaces, ranked 379 metro areas and identified the "Most Secure U.S. Place to Live." The Salt Lake City* metro area ranked #64 out of 114 in the large metro area category (500,000 or more residents). Criteria: crime rates; extreme weather; risk of natural disasters; environmental hazards; terrorism threats; air quality; life expectancy; job loss numbers. *Farmers Insurance Group, "Most Secure U.S. Places to Live 2007"*

- Salt Lake City* was identified as one of the most dangerous large metro areas for pedestrians in the U.S. The area ranked #31 out of the nations 50 largest metro areas. Criteria: average yearly pedestrian fatalities per capita (for the years 2002 and 2003) adjusted for the number of walkers. *Surface Transportation Policy Project, "Mean Streets 2004"*

Sports/Recreation Rankings

- The Salt Lake City* metro area appeared on the *Sporting News* list of the "Best Sports Cities 2007". The area ranked #22 out of 150 cities in the U.S. *Sporting News* takes a 12-month snapshot, roughly July to July, of each city's sports, putting a heavy premium on regular-season won-lost records (from the most recently completed season). Other criteria include: playoff berths, bowl appearances and tournament bids; championships; applicable power ratings; quality of competition; overall fan fervor as measured in part by attendance as percentage of venue capacity; abundance of teams (rewarding quality over quantity); stadium and arena quality; ticket availability and prices; franchise ownership; and marquee appeal of athletes. *SportingNews.com, "Best Sports Cities 2007," August 1, 2007*

- Scarborough Research, a leading market research firm, identified the top local markets for video gaming households. The Salt Lake City* DMA (Designated Market Area) ranked in the top 10 with 32% of households reporting that they own a video game system. *Scarborough Research, March 14, 2007*

- Scarborough Research, a leading market research firm, identified the top local markets for avid NBA fans. The Salt Lake City* DMA (Designated Market Area) ranked in the top 10 with 13% of consumers 18 years and over reporting that they are "very interested in the NBA". *Scarborough Research, April 24, 2006*

- The Salt Lake City* metro area was selected by *Cranium* as one of the "Top 50 Fun Cities" in America. The area ranked #9. Criteria includes: number of sports teams, restaurants, and dance performances; number of toy stores; city budget spent on recreation. *Cranium, November 4, 2003*

- *Golf Digest* ranked 330 metro areas in the U.S. in terms of golf. The Salt Lake City* metro area was ranked #210. Criteria: access to golf; weather; value of golf; and quality of golf. *Golf Digest, "Metro Golf Rankings," August 2005*

Dating/Romance Rankings

- Eli Lily and Company, in partnership with Sperling's BestPlaces, ranked the nation's 50 largest metro areas in terms of the "Most Romantic Cities for Baby Boomers." The Salt Lake City* metro area ranked #2. Criteria: marriage and divorce rates among "baby boomers" age 45 to 60; great restaurants; dance studios; chocolate, jewelry and flower sales. *Eli Lily and Company, "Most Romantic Cities for Baby Boomers," April 20, 2007*

- The Salt Lake City* metro area was selected as one of the "Best Cities for Relocating Singles" by Worldwide ERC and Primacy Relocation. The area ranked #65 out of the 100 largest metro areas in the U.S. Areas were selected based on the following criteria: a robust cost-of-living index; adventure and outdoor recreation opportunities; violent crime and property crime rates; percentage of the population that is unmarried (ages 25-34); ratio of single men and single women; affordability of quality higher education, including in-state and out-of-state tuition requirements and rates; number of newcomers to the area; commute times; tax rates; fee and occupancy rates for temporary housing and mini-storage; quality and quantity of collegiate and professional sporting events and fun, fan-friendly venues. *Worldwide ERC and Primacy Relocation, "2007 Best Cities for Relocating Singles," October 25, 2007*

- *Forbes* ranked the 40 most populous urbanized areas in the U.S. in terms of the "Best Cities for Singles." The Salt Lake City* metro area ranked #36. Criteria: number of singles; cost of living alone; nightlife; culture; job growth; coolness; and online dating. *Forbes.com, August 21, 2007*

- Sperling's BestPlaces in partnership with AXE Deodorant Bodyspray ranked 80 metro areas and identified "America's Best (and Worst) Cities for Dating." The Salt Lake City* metro area ranked #41 (#1 = best). Criteria: percentage of singles ages 18-24; population density; dating venues per capita. *AXE Deodorant Bodyspray, "America's Best (and Worst) Cities for Dating," May 2004*

Culture/Performing Arts Rankings

- Scarborough Research, a leading market research firm, identified the top local markets for rock concert attendance. The Salt Lake City* DMA (Designated Market Area) ranked in the top 25 with 14% of consumers, 18 years old and over, reporting that they have attended a rock concert during the past year. *Scarborough Research, June 14, 2004*

Miscellaneous Rankings

- Draper was identified as one of the 100 fastest-growing suburbs in America by "Forbes." The city ranked #59. Criteria: suburban cities, townships and villages with more than 10,000 people in 2000 were ranked by their population growth from 2000 to 2006. *Forbes.com, "America's Fastest-Growing Suburbs," July 16, 2007*

- The Salt Lake City* metro area was selected as one of the "Top 10 Most Independent Cities for Homesellers". The area ranked #8. The cities listed had more consumers choosing to sell their homes without the help of a real-estate agent than anywhere else. Data was based on geographical information for listings posted on ForSaleByOwner.com from January 1, 2007 through June 30, 2007. *ForSaleByOwner.com, October 1, 2007*

- Sperling's BestPlaces in partnership with Pep Boys ranked 77 metro areas and identified "America's Most Drivable Cities." The Salt Lake City* metro area ranked #51. Criteria: climate; road roughness; urban mobility; gas prices. *Pep Boys, "America's Most Drivable Cities," April 9, 2003*

- State Farm Insurance, in partnership with Sperling's BestPlaces, analyzed several key factors that contribute to overall family preparedness. The Salt Lake City* metro area ranked #1 out of the nation's 50 most populous metro areas. Criteria: quality of life; life insurance coverage; and investments. *State Farm Life Insurance, "Fiscally Fit Cities Report," July 20, 2004*

- A study by Sperling's BestPlaces examined which U.S. metro areas were most affected by high fuel prices in 2006. The Salt Lake City* metro area was ranked #35 out of 80 (#1 = most expensive city for driving). Rankings are based on the average dollars spent on gas per year by two driver households. Criteria: cost of regular-grade gasoline; average miles driven per day; average number of gallons each driver uses and wastes in traffic congestion each day. *Sperling's BestPlaces, www.bestplaces.net, "Pain at the Pump," May 18, 2006*

***Draper is located within the Salt Lake City, UT Metropolitan Statistical Area.**

Business Environment

CITY FINANCES

City Government Finances

Component	2004-2005 ($000)	2004-2005 ($ per capita)
Total Revenues	25,119	715
Total Expenditures	24,807	706
Debt Outstanding	20,352	580
Cash and Securities	38,124	1,086

Source: U.S Census Bureau, Government Finances 2004-2005

City Government Revenue by Source

Source	2004-2005 ($000)	2004-2005 ($ per capita)
General Revenue		
From Federal Government	188	5
From State Government	1,107	32
From Local Governments	0	0
Taxes		
Property	4,371	124
Sales	7,366	210
Personal Income	0	0
License	252	7
Charges	8,078	230
Liquor Store	0	0
Utility	1,688	48
Employee Retirement	0	0
Other	2,069	59

Source: U.S Census Bureau, Government Finances 2004-2005

City Government Expenditures by Function

Function	2004-2005 ($000)	2004-2005 ($ per capita)	2004-2005 (%)
General Expenditures			
Airports	0	0	0.0
Corrections	0	0	0.0
Education	0	0	0.0
Fire Protection	2,547	73	10.3
Governmental Administration	4,509	128	18.2
Health	68	2	0.3
Highways	6,029	172	24.3
Hospitals	0	0	0.0
Housing and Community Development	2,144	61	8.6
Interest on General Debt	537	15	2.2
Libraries	0	0	0.0
Parking	0	0	0.0
Parks and Recreation	1,152	33	4.6
Police Protection	2,517	72	10.1
Public Welfare	0	0	0.0
Sewerage	604	17	2.4
Solid Waste Management	1,173	33	4.7
Liquor Store	0	0	0.0
Utility	2,458	70	9.9
Employee Retirement	0	0	0.0
Other	1,069	30	4.3

Source: U.S Census Bureau, Government Finances 2004-2005

Municipal Bond Ratings

Area	Moody's
City	Aaa

Source: Mergent Bond Record, January 2008 (unless noted otherwise)

DEMOGRAPHICS

Population Growth

Area	1990 Census	2000 Census	2007 Estimate	2012 Projection	Population Growth (%) 1990-2000	Population Growth (%) 2000-2012
City	7,250	25,220	36,803	44,006	247.9	74.5
MSA[1]	768,075	968,858	1,055,059	1,116,816	26.1	15.3
U.S.	248,709,873	281,421,906	301,045,522	314,920,978	13.2	11.9

Note: (1) Metropolitan Statistical Area - see Appendix B for areas included
Source: Claritas, Inc.

Number of Households and Average Household Size

Area	2007 Estimate	2007 Average Household Size
City	9,754	3.77
MSA[1]	345,652	3.05
U.S.	113,668,003	2.65

Note: (1) Metropolitan Statistical Area - see Appendix B for areas included
Source: Claritas, Inc.

Race and Ethnicity

Area	White Alone[2]	Black Alone[2]	Asian Alone[2]	Other Race Alone[2]	Hispanic[3]
City	91.2	1.3	1.5	6.0	6.5
MSA[1]	84.4	1.2	2.7	11.7	14.9
U.S.	73.1	12.4	4.3	10.3	14.9

Note: Figures are 2007 estimates; (1) Metropolitan Statistical Area - see Appendix B for areas included (2) Alone is defined as not being in combination with one or more other races; (3) May be of any race.
Source: Claritas, Inc.

Ancestry

Area	German	Irish[2]	English	American	Italian	Polish	French[3]	Scottish
City	12.4	6.5	28.3	6.3	3.3	0.9	3.3	4.2
MSA[1]	12.0	6.2	27.4	6.4	2.8	0.8	2.3	4.3
U.S.	15.2	10.9	8.7	7.3	5.6	3.2	3.0	1.7

Note: Figures include multiple ancestry (e.g. if a person reported being Irish and Italian, they were included in both columns); (1) Metropolitan Statistical Area - see Appendix A for areas included; (2) Includes Celtic; (3) Includes Alsatian but excludes Basque
Source: Census 2000, Summary File 3

Foreign-Born Population

Area	Percent of Population Born in: Any Foreign Country	Europe	Asia	Africa	Oceania[2]	Canada	Mexico	Latin America[3]
City	3.7	1.2	0.9	0.0	0.2	0.5	0.7	0.2
MSA[1]	8.6	1.5	1.7	0.2	0.4	0.3	3.5	1.1
U.S.	11.1	1.7	2.9	0.3	0.1	0.3	3.3	2.5

Note: (1) Metropolitan Statistical Area - see Appendix A for areas included; (2) Includes Australia, New Zealand subregion, Melanesia, Micronesia, Polynesia, and Oceania n.e.c; (3) Includes Central America (excluding Mexico), South America, and the Caribbean.
Source: Census 2000, Summary File 3

Marriage Status

Area	Never Married	Now Married (excluding Separated)	Separated	Widowed	Divorced
City	25.5	60.4	1.5	2.3	10.2
MSA[1]	27.6	57.6	1.4	4.1	9.3
U.S.	27.1	54.4	2.2	6.6	9.7

Note: Figures are percentages and cover the population 15 years of age and older; (1) Metropolitan Statistical Area - see Appendix A for areas included
Source: Census 2000, Summary File 3

Age Distribution

Area	Under Age 5	Age 5 to 17	Age 18 to 34	Age 35 to 49	Age 50 to 64	Age 65 to 79	80 Years and Over
	Percent of Population						
City	10.2	21.2	32.2	23.6	9.4	2.7	0.7
MSA[1]	9.1	22.2	28.1	20.9	11.4	6.2	2.1
U.S.	6.8	18.9	23.7	23.5	14.8	9.2	3.2

Note: (1) Metropolitan Statistical Area - see Appendix A for areas included
Source: Census 2000, Summary File 3

Male/Female Ratio

Area	Males	Females	Males per 100 Females
City	20,294	16,509	122.9
MSA[1]	533,785	521,274	102.4
U.S.	148,320,305	152,725,217	97.1

Note: Figures are 2007 estimates; (1) Metropolitan Statistical Area - see Appendix B for areas included
Source: Claritas, Inc.

Religion

Area	Catholic	Southern Baptist	United Meth-odist	ELCA[1]	LDS[2]	Presby-terian Church USA	Jewish Est.	Muslim Est.
County	6.0	0.6	0.5	0.4	56.0	0.4	0.5	0.4
U.S.	22.0	7.1	3.7	1.8	1.5	1.1	2.2	0.6

Note: Figures are the number of adherents as a percentage of the total population; Adherents are defined as all members, including full members, their children and the estimated number of other participants who are not considered members (e.g. the baptized, those not confirmed, those regularly attending services, etc.); (1) Evangelical Lutheran Church in America; (2) The Church of Jesus Christ of Latter Day Saints
Source: Reprinted with permission from Religious Congregations and Membership in the United States 2000 (Nashville, Glenmary Research Center, 2002) Copyright Association of Statisticians of American Religious Bodies. All rights reserved.

ECONOMY

Gross Metropolitan Product

Area	2002	2003	2004	2005	2005 Rank[2]
MSA[1]	38.2	39.5	42.2	46.4	48

Note: Figures are in billions of dollars; (1) Salt Lake City, UT Metropolitan Statistical Area - see Appendix A for areas included; (2) Rank ranges from 1 to 361
Source: The U.S. Conference of Mayors, "U.S. Metro Economies: GMP - The Engines of America's Growth," January 2007

Economic Growth

Area	1995 GMP	2005 GMP	Average Annual Growth Rate	Growth Rate Rank[2]
MSA[1]	25.1	46.4	6.4	88

Note: Figures are in billions of dollars; GMP = Gross Metropolitan Product; (1) Salt Lake City, UT Metropolitan Statistical Area - see Appendix A for areas included; (2) Rank ranges from 1 to 361
Source: The U.S. Conference of Mayors, "U.S. Metro Economies: GMP - The Engines of America's Growth," January 2007

INCOME

Per Capita/Median/Average Income

Area	Per Capita ($)	Median Household ($)	Average Household ($)
City	29,513	90,650	107,497
MSA[1]	23,629	55,931	71,457
U.S.	25,495	49,280	66,670

Note: Figures are 2007 estimates; (1) Metropolitan Statistical Area - see Appendix B for areas included
Source: Claritas, Inc.

Household Income Distribution

Area	Percent of Households Earning							
	Under $15,000	$15,000 -24,999	$25,000 -34,999	$35,000 -49,999	$50,000 -74,999	$75,000 -99,000	$100,000 -149,999	$150,000 and up
City	2.3	3.0	4.7	10.9	17.7	18.1	26.5	16.8
MSA[1]	8.2	8.8	10.4	16.7	22.7	13.9	12.8	6.6
U.S.	13.1	10.9	11.2	15.6	19.5	11.9	11.3	6.6

Note: Figures are 2007 estimates; (1) Metropolitan Statistical Area - see Appendix B for areas included
Source: Claritas, Inc.

Poverty Rates by Age

Area	All Ages	Under 5 Years Old	5 to 17 Years Old	18 to 64 Years Old	65 Years and Over
City	2.7	0.4	0.7	1.6	0.0
MSA[1]	7.7	1.0	1.9	4.4	0.4
U.S.	12.4	1.2	3.0	6.9	1.2

Note: Figures are percent of population with income in 1999 below poverty level and only include population for whom poverty status is determined; (1) Metropolitan Statistical Area - see Appendix A for areas included
Source: Census 2000, Summary File 3

Personal Bankruptcy Filing Rate

Area	2004	2005	2006
Salt Lake County	10.59	10.75	2.57
U.S.	5.31	6.82	2.00

Note: Numbers are per 1,000 population and include Chapter 7 and Chapter 13 filings
Source: Federal Deposit Insurance Corporation (FDIC), Regional Economic Conditions (RECON), 8/23/2007

EMPLOYMENT

Labor Force and Employment

Area	Civilian Labor Force			Workers Employed		
	Dec. 2006	Dec. 2007	% Chg.	Dec. 2006	Dec. 2007	% Chg.
City	13,255	13,604	2.6	13,155	13,475	2.4
MSA[1]	596,424	614,462	3.0	583,449	597,668	2.4
U.S.	152,571,000	153,705,000	0.7	146,081,000	146,334,000	0.2

Note: Data is not seasonally adjusted and covers workers 16 years of age and older; (1) Metropolitan Statistical Area - see Appendix B for areas included
Source: Bureau of Labor Statistics, http://stats.bls.gov

Unemployment Rate

Area	2007											
	Jan.	Feb.	Mar.	Apr.	May	Jun.	Jul.	Aug.	Sep.	Oct.	Nov.	Dec.
City	0.9	0.9	0.8	0.8	0.8	1.0	0.9	1.0	0.9	0.9	0.9	0.9
MSA[1]	2.7	2.6	2.4	2.3	2.3	2.7	2.7	2.9	2.6	2.6	2.6	2.7
U.S.	5.0	4.9	4.5	4.3	4.3	4.7	4.9	4.6	4.5	4.4	4.5	4.8

Note: Data is not seasonally adjusted and covers workers 16 years of age and older; All figures are percentages; (1) Metropolitan Statistical Area - see Appendix B for areas included
Source: Bureau of Labor Statistics, http://stats.bls.gov

Employment by Occupation

Occupation Classification	City (%)	MSA[1] (%)	U.S. (%)
Sales and Office	31.0	30.8	26.7
Professional and Related	21.4	19.1	20.2
Service	10.2	13.0	14.9
Production, Transportation, and Material Moving	6.2	13.3	14.6
Management, Business, and Financial	22.2	13.6	13.5
Construction, Extraction, and Maintenance	8.6	10.0	9.4
Farming, Forestry, and Fishing	0.3	0.2	0.7

Note: Figures cover employed civilians 16 years of age and older; (1) Metropolitan Statistical Area - see Appendix A for areas included
Source: Census 2000, Summary File 3

Employment by Industry

Sector	MSA[1] Number of Employees	MSA[1] Percent of Total	U.S. Percent of Total
Government	93,600	14.3	16.3
Education and Health Services	61,500	9.4	13.4
Professional and Business Services	101,900	15.5	13.1
Retail Trade	75,600	11.5	11.6
Manufacturing	58,800	9.0	9.9
Leisure and Hospitality	60,800	9.3	9.6
Financial Activities	52,700	8.0	5.9
Construction	n/a	n/a	5.3
Wholesale Trade	31,500	4.8	4.4
Other Services	19,800	3.0	3.9
Transportation and Utilities	31,600	4.8	3.7
Information	19,100	2.9	2.2
Natural Resources and Mining	n/a	n/a	0.5

Note: Figures cover non-farm employment as of December 2007 and are not seasonally adjusted; (1) Metropolitan Statistical Area - see Appendix B for areas included; n/a not available
Source: Bureau of Labor Statistics, http://stats.bls.gov

Average Wages

Occupation	$/Hr.	Occupation	$/Hr.
Accountants and Auditors	29.12	Maids and Housekeeping Cleaners	8.69
Automotive Mechanics	18.64	Maintenance and Repair Workers	16.60
Bookkeepers	14.43	Marketing Managers	43.33
Carpenters	16.74	Nuclear Medicine Technologists	27.43
Cashiers	8.84	Nurses, Licensed Practical	18.41
Clerks, General Office	11.85	Nurses, Registered	28.07
Clerks, Receptionists/Information	10.45	Nursing Aides/Orderlies/Attendants	10.39
Clerks, Shipping/Receiving	12.84	Packers and Packagers, Hand	9.74
Computer Programmers	38.00	Physical Therapists	34.31
Computer Support Specialists	20.31	Postal Service Mail Carriers	21.30
Computer Systems Analysts	33.25	Real Estate Brokers	33.09
Cooks, Restaurant	10.53	Retail Salespersons	11.99
Dentists	n/a	Sales Reps., Exc. Tech./Scientific	27.93
Electrical Engineers	39.78	Sales Reps., Tech./Scientific	35.34
Electricians	20.21	Secretaries, Exc. Legal/Med./Exec.	13.29
Financial Managers	45.48	Security Guards	12.44
First-Line Supervisors/Mgrs., Sales	18.97	Surgeons	n/a
Food Preparation Workers	8.40	Teacher Assistants	10.00
General and Operations Managers	45.74	Teachers, Elementary School	22.00
Hairdressers/Cosmetologists	9.07	Teachers, Secondary School	24.90
Internists	n/a	Telemarketers	10.80
Janitors and Cleaners	10.00	Truck Drivers, Heavy/Tractor-Trailer	18.36
Landscaping/Groundskeeping Workers	10.87	Truck Drivers, Light/Delivery Svcs.	11.70
Lawyers	58.49	Waiters and Waitresses	9.43

Note: Wage data covers the Salt Lake City, UT Metropolitan Statistical Area - see Appendix B for areas included. Hourly wages for elementary/secondary school teachers and teacher assistants were calculated by the editors from annual wage data assuming a 40 hour work week; n/a not available.
Source: Bureau of Labor Statistics, May 2007 Metro Area Occupational Employment and Wage Estimates

RESIDENTIAL REAL ESTATE

Building Permits

Area	Single-Family 2006	Single-Family 2007p	Single-Family Pct. Chg.	Multi-Family 2006	Multi-Family 2007p	Multi-Family Pct. Chg.	Total 2006	Total 2007p	Total Pct. Chg.
City	456	304	-33.3	156	140	-10.3	612	444	-27.5
U.S.	1,378,200	973,300	-29.4	460,700	407,200	-11.6	1,838,900	1,380,500	-24.9

Note: (p) preliminary; figures cover and represent new, privately-owned housing units authorized (unadjusted data); All permit data are based on estimates with imputation; U.S. figures are based on the new 20,000-place series.
Source: U.S. Census Bureau, Manufacturing, Mining, and Construction Statistics

Homeownership and Housing Vacancies

Area	Homeownership Rate[2] (%)			Rental Vacancy Rate[3] (%)			Homeowner Vacancy Rate[4] (%)		
	2005	2006	2007	2005	2006	2007	2005	2006	2007
MSA[1]	68.8	69.6	71.8	7.0	4.7	5.3	1.5	2.7	2.2
U.S.	68.9	68.8	68.1	9.8	9.8	9.7	1.9	2.4	2.7

Note: (1) Metropolitan Statistical Area - see Appendix B for areas included; (2) The proportion of households that are owners; (3) The proportion of the rental inventory that is vacant for rent; (4) The proportion of the homeowner inventory that is vacant for sale; n/a not available
Source: U.S. Census Bureau, Housing Vacancies and Homeownership Annual Statistics: 2007

TAXES

State Corporate Income Tax Rates

State	Rates and Tax Brackets
Utah	5.0%

Note: Tax rates as of January 1, 2008; Minimum tax $100.
Source: Tax Foundation, www.taxfoundation.org

State Individual Income Tax Rates

State	Federal Deductibility	Marginal Rates (%)	Standard Deduction ($)		Personal Exemptions ($)[1]	
			Single	Joint	Single	Dependents
Utah	Yes (bb)	2.3 - 6.98 (cc)	5,150 (s)	10,300 (s)	2,475 (q)	2,475 (q)

Note: Tax rates as of January 1, 2008; Local- and county-level taxes are not included; n/a not applicable; (1) Married joint filers generally receive double the single exemption; (q) Three fourths federal exemption; (s) Deductions and exemptions tied to federal tax system. Federal deductions and exemptions are indexed for inflation; (bb) Half of federal income tax deductible; (cc) An optional 5.35% flat tax will be available.
Source: Tax Foundation, www.taxfoundation.org

Various State and Local Tax Rates

State and Local Sales and Use (%)	State Sales and Use (%)	Gasoline[1,2] ($/gal.)	Cigarette ($/pack)	Spirits ($/gal.)	Table Wine ($/gal.)	Beer ($/gal.)
6.8	4.65	0.245	0.695	10.13 (n)	(p)	0.41

Note: Tax rates as of January 1, 2008; (1) In addition to the 18.4 cpg Federal gasoline tax; (2) Rates may include additional state sales taxes, environmental protection and storage fees/taxes, and local taxes. When necessary, the volume-weighted average of all local taxes is used to approximate the typical statewide rate including local tax; (n) The state government controls all sales. The implied excise tax rate is calculated using methodology designed by the Distilled Spirits Council of the United States (DISCUS); (p) All wine sales are through state-run stores. Revenue in these states is generated from various taxes, fees and net profits.
Source: Tax Foundation, www.taxfoundation.org; Original research

State Tax Burdens

Area	Combined State and Local Tax Burden		Combined Federal, State and Local Tax Burden	
	Percent	Rank	Percent	Rank
Utah	10.7	27	30.3	36
U.S. Average	11.0	-	32.7	-

Note: Figures cover 2007 and measure taxes as a percentage of income
Source: Tax Foundation, www.taxfoundation.org

State Business Tax Climate Index Rankings

State	Overall Rank	Corporate Tax Index Rank	Individual Income Tax Index Rank	Sales Tax Index Rank	Unemployment Insurance Tax Index Rank	Property Tax Index Rank
Utah	17	5	30	27	28	3

Note: Rankings range from 1 to 50 where 1 is best. Rankings do not average across to Overall Rank. States without a given tax are given a ranking of 1.
Source: Tax Foundation, State Business Tax Climate Index 2008

TRANSPORTATION

Means of Transportation to Work

Area	Car/Truck/Van		Public Transportation			Bicycle	Walked	Other Means	Worked at Home
	Drove Alone	Car-pooled	Bus	Subway	Railroad				
City	81.6	8.9	0.5	0.3	0.8	0.1	0.7	0.8	6.4
MSA[1]	77.2	13.1	2.5	0.1	0.2	0.4	1.8	0.9	3.8
U.S.	75.7	12.2	2.5	1.5	0.5	0.4	2.9	1.0	3.3

Note: Figures are percentages and cover workers 16 years of age and older;
(1) Metropolitan Statistical Area - see Appendix A for areas included
Source: Census 2000, Summary File 3

Travel Time to Work

Area	Less Than 15 Minutes	15 to 29 Minutes	30 to 44 Minutes	45 to 59 Minutes	60 Minutes or More
City	24.8	35.8	28.5	6.1	4.8
MSA[1]	29.2	43.6	18.0	4.8	4.4
U.S.	29.4	36.1	19.1	7.4	8.0

Note: Figures are percentages and include workers 16 years old and over; (1) Metropolitan Statistical Area - see Appendix A for areas included
Source: Census 2000, Summary File 3

Travel Time Index

Area	1982	1995	2004	2005
Urban Area[1]	1.05	1.19	1.21	1.19
Average[2]	1.11	1.22	1.29	1.30

Note: Travel Time Index - The ratio of travel time in the peak period to the travel time at free-flow conditions. A value of 1.35 indicates a 20-minute free-flow trip takes 27 minutes in the peak. Free-flow speeds (60 mph on freeways and 35 mph on principal arterials) are used as the comparison threshold; (1) Covers the Salt Lake City, UT urban area;
(2) average of 85 urban areas
Source: Texas Transportation Institute, The 2007 Urban Mobility Report, September 2007

Living Environment

COST OF LIVING

Cost of Living Index

Composite Index	Groceries	Housing	Utilities	Trans-portation	Health Care	Misc. Goods/ Services
101.1	102.3	99.2	87.7	103.6	99.2	105.5

Note: U.S. = 100; Figures cover the Salt Lake City UT urban area.
Source: The Council for Community and Economic Research (formerly ACCRA), Cost of Living Index, 2007

Grocery Prices

Area[1]	T-Bone Steak ($/pound)	Frying Chicken ($/pound)	Whole Milk ($/half gal.)	Eggs ($/dozen)	Orange Juice ($/64 oz.)	Coffee ($/11.5 oz.)
City[2]	9.29	1.29	1.89	1.46	3.19	3.56
Avg.	8.93	1.12	2.13	1.52	3.26	3.31
Min.	5.88	0.71	1.33	0.83	2.30	2.20
Max.	12.80	2.07	3.43	3.54	5.79	6.20

Note: (1) Values for the local area are compared with the average, minimum and maximum values for all 331 areas in the Cost of Living Index report; (2) Figures cover the Salt Lake City UT urban area; **T-Bone Steak** *(price per pound);* **Frying Chicken** *(price per pound, whole fryer);* **Whole Milk** *(half gallon carton);* **Eggs** *(price per dozen, Grade A, large);* **Orange Juice** *(64 oz. Tropicana or Florida Natural);* **Coffee** *(11.5 oz. can, vacuum-packed, Maxwell House, Hills Bros, or Folgers).*
Source: The Council for Community and Economic Research (formerly ACCRA), Cost of Living Index, 2007

Housing and Utility Costs

Area[1]	New Home Price ($)	Apartment Rent ($/month)	All Electric ($/month)	Part Electric ($/month)	Other Energy ($/month)	Telephone ($/month)
City[2]	307,604	777	-	53.08	73.82	26.91
Avg.	309,605	782	146.13	78.67	90.16	26.14
Min.	189,877	n/a	82.03	37.41	33.15	17.08
Max.	1,202,800	3,481	271.14	150.60	257.67	37.45

Note: (1) Values for the local area are compared with the average, minimum and maximum values for all 331 areas in the Cost of Living Index report; (2) Figures cover the Salt Lake City UT urban area; **New Home Price** *(2,400 sf living area, 8,000 sf lot, in urban area with full utilities);* **Apartment Rent** *(950 sf 2 bedroom/1.5 or 2 bath, unfurnished, excluding all utilities except water);* **All Electric** *(average monthly cost for an all-electric home);* **Part Electric** *(average monthly cost for a part-electric home);* **Other Energy** *(average monthly cost for natural gas, fuel oil, coal, wood, and any other forms of energy except electricity);* **Telephone** *(price includes basic monthly rate for a private residential line plus additional local usage charges incurred by a family of four).*
Source: The Council for Community and Economic Research (formerly ACCRA), Cost of Living Index, 2007

Health Care, Transportation, and Other Costs

Area[1]	Doctor ($/visit)	Dentist ($/visit)	Optometrist ($/visit)	Gasoline ($/gallon)	Beauty Salon ($/visit)	Men's Shirt ($)
City[2]	77.80	72.35	75.47	2.62	32.00	27.88
Avg.	79.48	71.93	79.55	2.64	29.52	25.77
Min.	52.08	44.80	43.95	2.19	15.58	16.19
Max.	148.44	126.27	158.83	3.48	60.62	48.53

Note: (1) Values for the local area are compared with the average, minimum and maximum values for all 331 areas in the Cost of Living Index report; (2) Figures cover the Salt Lake City UT urban area; **Doctor** *(general practitioners routine exam of an established patient);* **Dentist** *(adult teeth cleaning and periodic oral examination);* **Optometrist** *(full vision eye exam for established adult patient);* **Gasoline** *(one gallon regular unleaded, national brand, including all taxes, cash price at self-service pump if available);* **Beauty Salon** *(woman's shampoo, trim, and blow-dry);* **Men's Shirt** *(cotton/polyester dress shirt, pinpoint weave, long sleeves).*
Source: The Council for Community and Economic Research (formerly ACCRA), Cost of Living Index, 2007

HOUSING

House Price Index (HPI)

Area	National Ranking[2]	Quarterly Change (%)	One-Year Change (%)	Five-Year Change (%)
MSA[1]	7	0.49	9.68	59.84
U.S.[3]	-	0.10	0.84	41.37

Note: The HPI is a weighted repeat sales index. It measures average price changes in repeat sales or refinancings on the same properties. This information is obtained by reviewing repeat mortgage transactions on single-family properties whose mortgages have been purchased or securitized by Fannie Mae or Freddie Mac in January 1975; (1) Metropolitan Statistical Area - see Appendix B for areas included; (2) Rankings are based on annual percentage change for all metro areas containing at least 15,000 transactions over the last 10 years and ranges from 1 to 291; (3) figures based on a weighted average of Census Division estimates; all figures are for the period ending December 31, 2007
Source: Office of Federal Housing Enterprise Oversight, House Price Index, February 26, 2008

House Price Valuations

Area	Q1 2000	Q1 2001	Q1 2002	Q1 2003	Q1 2004	Q1 2005	Q1 2006	Q1 2007	Q1 2008
MSA[1]	-0.8	-5.6	-6.7	-2.6	-2.4	-3.2	8.0	19.1	16.1

Note: Figures show the percentage of over- or under-valuation of single family homes relative to statistically normal house values (e.g. a value of 23.6 indicates that house values are 23.6% overvalued). Statistically normal house values are based on house prices, interest rates, household incomes, population densities, and any historical premiums or discounts metropolitan areas have exhibited over time; (1) Figures cover the Metropolitan Statistical Area - see Appendix B for areas included
Source: Global Insight/National City Corporation, House Prices in America, May 2008

Median Home Prices

Area	2005	2006	2007[r]	Percent Change 2006 to 2007
MSA[1]	173.9	203.0	232.0	14.3
U.S. Average	219.0	221.9	217.9	-1.8

Note: Figures are median sales prices of existing single-family homes in thousands of dollars; (r) revised; n/a not available; (1) Metropolitan Statistical Area - see Appendix B for areas included
Source: National Association of Realtors, Metropolitan Area Prices, 1st Quarter 2008

Housing: Year Structure Built

Area	1990 -2000	1980 -1989	1970 -1979	1960 -1969	1950 -1959	1940 -1949	Before 1940	Median Year
City	80.5	4.7	4.7	3.0	2.4	1.3	3.4	1996
MSA[1]	22.0	16.4	22.5	11.9	11.7	6.0	9.4	1975
U.S.	17.0	15.8	18.5	13.7	12.7	7.3	15.0	1971

Note: Figures are percentages; (1) Metropolitan Statistical Area - see Appendix A for areas included
Source: Census 2000, Summary File 3

HEALTH

Health Risk Data

Category	Area[1] (%)	U.S. (%)
Adults who have been told they have high blood pressure[3]	19.2	25.5
Adults who have been told they have high blood cholesterol[3]	33.0	35.6
Adults who have been told they have diabetes[2]	6.3	7.5
Adults who have been told they have arthritis[3]	21.8	27.0
Adults who have been told they currently have asthma	9.8	8.5
Adults who are current smokers	11.1	20.1
Adults who are heavy drinkers[4]	3.1	4.9
Adults who are overweight (BMI 25.0 - 29.9)	33.2	36.5
Adults who are obese (BMI 30.0 - 99.8)	21.2	25.1

Note: Data as of 2006 unless otherwise noted; (1) Figures cover the Metropolitan Statistical Area - see Appendix B for areas included; (2) Figures do not include pregnancy-related diabetes, pre-diabetes or borderline diabetes; (3) 2005 data; (4) Heavy drinkers are classified as adult men having more than two drinks per day or adult women having more than one drink per day
Source: Centers for Disease Control and Prevention, Behaviorial Risk Factor Surveillance System, SMART: Selected Metropolitan/Micropolitan Area Risk Trends, 2005, 2006

Mortality Rates for the Top 10 Causes of Death in the U.S.

ICD-10[a] Sub-Chapter	ICD-10[a] Code	Age-Adjusted Mortality Rate[1] per 100,000 population	
		County[2]	U.S.
Malignant neoplasms	C00-C97	143.7	186.5
Ischaemic heart diseases	I20-I25	84.6	152.3
Other forms of heart disease	I30-I51	66.4	51.5
Cerebrovascular diseases	I60-I69	47.2	50.0
Chronic lower respiratory diseases	J40-J47	36.7	42.6
Diabetes mellitus	E10-E14	29.4	24.8
Other degenerative diseases of the nervous system	G30-G31	16.7	22.6
Other external causes of accidental injury	W00-X59	18.8	21.4
Influenza and pneumonia	J10-J18	23.3	20.7
Hypertensive diseases	I10-I13	11.5	18.2

Note: (a) ICD-10 = International Classification of Diseases 10th Revision; (1) Mortality rates are a three year average covering 2003-2005; (2) Figures cover Salt Lake County
Source: Centers for Disease Control and Prevention, National Center for Health Statistics. Compressed Mortality File 1999-2004. CDC WONDER On-line Database, compiled from Compressed Mortality File 1999-2005 Series 20 No. 2K, 2008.

Mortality Rates for Selected Causes of Death

ICD-10[a] Sub-Chapter	ICD-10[a] Code	Age-Adjusted Mortality Rate[1] per 100,000 population	
		County[2]	U.S.
Assault	X85-Y09	3.3	5.9
Human immunodeficiency virus (HIV) disease	B20-B24	1.7	4.5
Intentional self-harm	X60-X84	16.3	10.8
Malnutrition	E40-E46	*0.9	1.0
Obesity and other hyperalimentation	E65-E68	1.6	1.4
Organic, including symptomatic, mental disorders	F01-F09	39.4	16.8
Transport accidents	V01-V99	13.5	16.1
Viral hepatitis	B15-B19	0.9	1.8

Note: (a) ICD-10 = International Classification of Diseases 10th Revision; (1) Mortality rates are a three year average covering 2003-2005; (2) Figures cover Salt Lake County; (*) Unreliable data as per CDC
Source: Centers for Disease Control and Prevention, National Center for Health Statistics. Compressed Mortality File 1999-2004. CDC WONDER On-line Database, compiled from Compressed Mortality File 1999-2005 Series 20 No. 2K, 2008.

Distribution of Physicians[1]

Area	Total	Family/ General Practice	Specialties	
			Medical	Surgical
Salt Lake County (number)	2,119	430	750	496
Salt Lake County (rate per 10,000 pop.)	22.3	4.5	7.9	5.2
U.S. (rate per 10,000 pop.)	17.7	4.6	6.9	4.3

Note: Data as of 2005; (1) Includes all non-federal, patient-care, office-based MDs
Source: Area Resource File (ARF). June 2007. U.S. Department of Health and Human Services, Health Resources and Services Administration, Bureau of Health Professions, Rockville, MD.

Hospitals

There were no hospitals listed within the city limits.
AHA Guide to the Healthcare Field 2008

According to *U.S. News,* the Salt Lake City, UT metro area is home to three of the best hospitals in the U.S.: **LDS Hospital**; **Primary Children's Medical Center**; **University of Utah Hospitals and Clinics**. *U.S. News Online, "America's Best Hospitals 2007"*

EDUCATION

Public School District Statistics

District Name	Schls	Pupils	Pupil/ Teacher Ratio	Minority Pupils[1] (%)	Free Lunch Eligible[2] (%)	IEP[3] (%)
American Preparatory Academy	1	520	21.5	5.4	n/a	9.0
Jordan District	92	77,110	24.7	11.8	14.7	13.0
Summit Academy	1	536	26.8	5.6	n/a	8.8

Note: Table includes regular local school districts with 2,000 or more students; (1) Percentage of students that are not white, non-Hispanic; (2) Percentage of students that are eligible for the free lunch program; (3) Percentage of students that have an Individualized Education Program.
Source: U.S. Department of Education, National Center for Education Statistics, Common Core of Data, Local Education Agency (School District) Universe Survey: School Year 2005-2006; U.S. Department of Education, National Center for Education Statistics, Common Core of Data, Public Elementary/Secondary School Universe Survey: School Year 2005-2006

Highest Level of Education

Area	Less than H.S.	H.S. Diploma	Some College, No Deg.	Associate Degree	Bachelors Degree	Masters Degree	Profess. School Degree	Doctorate Degree
City	7.9	16.9	31.5	8.2	25.2	7.3	2.0	1.1
MSA[1]	12.6	24.1	28.1	7.6	18.6	5.7	2.1	1.1
U.S.	19.4	28.4	21.2	6.4	15.7	5.9	2.0	1.0

Note: Figures are 2007 estimated percentages and cover persons age 25 and over; (1) Metropolitan Statistical Area - see Appendix B for areas included
Source: Claritas, Inc.

Educational Attainment by Race

Area	High School Graduate (%)					Bachelor's Degree (%)				
	Total	White	Black	Asian	Hisp.[2]	Total	White	Black	Asian	Hisp.[2]
City	91.1	93.1	83.0	97.3	65.4	33.5	35.6	15.6	53.7	9.9
MSA[1]	87.5	89.9	83.0	78.2	56.5	26.5	27.6	19.5	34.8	9.4
U.S.	80.4	83.6	72.3	80.4	52.4	24.4	26.1	14.3	44.1	10.4

Note: Figures shown cover persons 25 years old and over; (1) Metropolitan Statistical Area - see Appendix A for areas included; (2) people of Hispanic origin can be of any race
Source: Census 2000, Summary File 3

School Enrollment by Type

Area	Grades KG to 8				Grades 9 to 12			
	Public		Private		Public		Private	
	Enrollment	%	Enrollment	%	Enrollment	%	Enrollment	%
City	3,409	89.4	404	10.6	1,702	92.4	140	7.6
MSA[1]	189,691	94.4	11,196	5.6	93,135	95.6	4,302	4.4
U.S.	33,526,011	88.7	4,285,121	11.3	14,848,628	90.6	1,532,323	9.4

Note: Figures shown cover persons 3 years old and over; (1) Metropolitan Statistical Area - see Appendix A for areas included
Source: Census 2000, Summary File 3

School Enrollment by Race

Area	Grades KG to 8 (%)				Grades 9 to 12 (%)			
	White	Black	Asian	Hisp.[1]	White	Black	Asian	Hisp.[1]
City	95.5	0.7	1.0	3.6	88.1	0.8	0.9	7.4
MSA[2]	85.4	1.1	1.7	12.7	87.1	1.0	2.1	10.6
U.S.	68.5	15.5	3.3	16.8	68.8	15.5	3.8	15.7

Note: Figures shown cover persons 3 years old and over; (1) people of Hispanic origin can be of any race; (2) Metropolitan Statistical Area - see Appendix A for areas included
Source: Census 2000, Summary File 3

Average Salaries of Public School Classroom Teachers

District	2005-06		2006-07		Percent Change 2005-06 to 2006-07
	Dollars	Rank[1]	Dollars	Rank[1]	
Utah	40,007	46	40,566	47	1.40
U.S. Average	49,026	-	50,816	-	3.65

Note: (1) State rank ranges from 1 to 51.
Source: National Education Association, Rankings & Estimates: Rankings of the States 2006 and Estimates of School Statistics 2007, December 2007

Higher Education

Four-Year Colleges			Two-Year Colleges			Medical Schools[1]	Law Schools[2]	Voc/ Tech[3]
Public	Private Non-profit	Private For-profit	Public	Private Non-profit	Private For-profit			
0	0	1	0	0	1	0	0	0

Note: Figures cover institutions located within the city limits; (1) includes schools accredited by the Liaison Committee on Medical Education and the American Osteopathic Association; (2) includes American Bar Association-accredited law schools; (3) includes all schools with programs that are less than 2 years.
Source: National Center for Education Statistics, The Integrated Postsecondary Education System (IPEDS) Peer Analysis System, 2007; www.usnews.com, Law and Medical School Directories, 2009

PRESIDENTIAL ELECTION

2004 Presidential Election Results

Area	Bush	Kerry	Nader	Other
Salt Lake County	59.6	37.5	1.7	1.2
U.S.	50.7	48.3	0.4	0.6

Note: Results are percentages and may not add to 100% due to rounding
Source: Dave Leip's Atlas of U.S. Presidential Elections, www.uselectionatlas.org

EMPLOYERS

Major Employers

Company Name	Industry	Type of Site
American Express	Short-term business credit	Branch
Arup Laboratories	Medical laboratories	Single
Cottonwood Hospital	General medical and surgical hospitals	Single
Discover Financial Services	Short-term business credit	Branch
Edo Electro Ceramic Products	Search and navigation equipment	Single
Kennecott Corporation	Gold ores	Headquarters
LDS Church	Religious organizations	Branch
Marketstar Corporation	Management consulting services	Single
Mormon Church	Religious organizations	Headquarters
National Guard Utah	National security	Headquarters
Service Center	Finance, taxation, and monetary policy	Branch
Sportsmans Warehouse	Sporting goods and bicycle shops	Single
US Post Office	U.S. postal service	Branch
Unibase Technologies	Data processing and preparation	Headquarters
University Utah Hsptals Clnics	General medical and surgical hospitals	Headquarters

Note: Companies shown are located within the Salt Lake City metropolitan area; nec = not elsewhere classified.
Source: www.zapdata.com, May 2008

PUBLIC SAFETY

Crime Rate

Area	All Crimes	Violent Crimes				Property Crimes		
		Murder	Forcible Rape	Robbery	Aggrav. Assault	Burglary	Larceny -Theft	Motor Vehicle Theft
City	3,058.2	0.0	16.5	19.3	35.8	581.9	2,197.8	206.8
Metro[1]	5,195.3	2.2	44.3	88.4	210.6	743.9	3,535.6	570.4
U.S.	3,808.1	5.7	30.9	149.4	287.5	729.4	2,206.8	398.4

Note: Figures are crimes per 100,000 population; (1) Metropolitan Statistical Area - see Appendix B for areas included
Source: FBI Uniform Crime Reports, 2006

Hate Crimes

Area	Number of Quarters Reported	Bias Motivation				
		Race	Religion	Sexual Orientation	Ethnicity	Disability
City	4	0	0	0	0	0

Source: Federal Bureau of Investigation, Hate Crime Statistics 2006

RECREATION

Culture

Dance[1]	Theatre[1]	Instrumental Music[1]	Vocal Music[1]	Series/ Festivals	Museums	Zoos and Aquariums[2]
0	0	0	0	0	0	0

Note: (1) Number of professional perfoming groups; (2) AZA-accredited
Source: The Grey House Performing Arts Directory, 2007; Official Museum Directory, 2008; Association of Zoos & Aquariums, AZA Member Zoos & Aquariums, June 2008

Professional Sports Teams

Team Name	League
Real Salt Lake	Major League Soccer (MLS)
Utah Jazz	National Basketball Association (NBA)

Note: Includes teams located in the Salt Lake City metro area.
Source: Original research

MEDIA

Newspapers

Name	News Focus	Frequency	Circulation
No newspapers have an office in the city			

Note: Includes newspapers with offices located in the city
Source: MediaContactsPro, March 2008

Television Stations

Name	Ch.	Network(s)	Type	Ownership
KUTV	2	CBS	Commercial	CBS
KCSG	4	Pax	Commercial	n/a
KTVX	4	ABC	Commercial	n/a
KSL	5	NBC	Commercial	Bonneville International Corporation
KUED	7	PBS	Public	University of Utah
KUEN	9	n/a	Public	Utah State Board of Regents
KENV	10	NBC	Commercial	Sunbelt Broadcasting Company
KBYU	11	PBS	Public	Brigham Young University
KDLQ	13	Fox/ABC	Commercial	n/a
KSTU	13	Fox	Commercial	Fox Television Stations Inc.
KJZZ	14	n/a	Commercial	Larry H. Miller Communications
KUPX	16	Pax	Commercial	Paxson Communications Corporation
KUEW	18	PBS	n/a	University of Utah
KUWB	30	WBN	Commercial	Acme Television Holdings

Note: Stations included cover the Salt Lake City DMA (Designated Market Area)
BurrellesLuce, MediaContacts Online, January 2007

Major AM Radio Stations

Call Letters	Freq. (kHz)	Station Type	Target Audience	Station Format	Music Format
KNRS	570	Commercial	General	News/Talk	n/a
KSUB	590	n/a	General	News/Sports/Talk	n/a
KVNU	610	Commercial	General	News/Talk	n/a
KMTI	650	Commercial	General	Music/News/Sports/Talk	Country
KOAL	750	n/a	General	News/Sports/Talk	n/a
KBEE	860	Commercial	General	Music/Talk	Country
KDXU	890	Commercial	General	News/Talk	n/a
KALL	910	Commercial	General	News	n/a
KMER	950	Commercial	General	News	n/a
KOVO	960	Commercial	General	Sports/Talk	n/a
KSVC	980	Commercial	General	News/Sports/Talk	n/a
KKDS	1060	Commercial	General	Music/News	Adult Contemp.
KAFL	1080	Commercial	General	Music	Country
KANN	1120	Non-Comm	Religious	Educational/Music/News	Christian
KSL	1160	Commercial	General	News/Talk	n/a
KUNF	1210	Commercial	General	Music/News	Easy Listening
KRSV	1210	Commercial	General	Music/News/Sports	Country
KEVA	1240	Commercial	General	News	n/a
KNEU	1250	Commercial	General	Music/News	Country
KZNS	1280	Commercial	General	News/Sports/Talk	n/a
KFNZ	1320	n/a	General/Men	Music/Sports	n/a
KRKK	1360	n/a	General	Music/News	n/a
KSOP	1370	Commercial	General	Music/News	Country
KLGN	1390	Commercial	General	Music/News/Sports/Talk	Adult Standards
KLO	1430	Commercial	General	Music/News/Sports/Talk	n/a
KXOL	1660	n/a	General	Music	n/a

Note: Stations included cover the Salt Lake City DMA (Designated Market Area); n/a not available
Source: BurrellesLuce, MediaContacts Online, January 2007

Major FM Radio Stations

Call Letters	Freq. (mHz)	Station Type	Target Audience	Station Format	Music Format
KBYU	89.1	College	General	Music/News	Classical
KUER	90.1	College	General	Music/News	Jazz
KUSU	91.5	College	General	Educational/Music/News	Classic Rock
KBLQ	92.9	Commercial	General	Music/News/Sports	Soft Rock
KCYQ	93.7	Commercial	General	Music	Country
KODJ	94.1	Commercial	General	Music	Oldies
KVFX	94.5	Commercial	General	Music	Adult Contemp.
KZHT	94.9	Commercial	General/Women	Music	Top 40
KXBN	94.9	Commercial	General	Music	Top 40
KYCS	95.1	Commercial	General	Music/News	Adult Contemp.
KYFO	95.5	Non-Comm	General	Music/Talk	Christian
KFNN	95.7	Commercial	General	Music/News	Adult Contemp.
KXRK	96.3	n/a	Gay/Lesbian	Music	n/a
KQSW	96.5	Commercial	General	Music/News	Country
KISN	97.1	Commercial	General	Music	Adult Contemp.
KREC	98.1	Commercial	General	Educational/Music/News	Adult Contemp.
KBEE	98.7	n/a	General	Music/News/Sports	n/a
KURR	99.5	Commercial	General/Native Amer	Music/Talk	Classic Rock
KONY	101.1	Commercial	General	Music	Contemp. Country
KXFF	102.9	n/a	n/a	n/a	n/a
KUDD	103.9	Commercial	General/Women	Music	Top 40
KSIT	104.5	Commercial	General	Music/News	Classic Rock
KNFL	104.9	n/a	General	Music	Oldies
KENZ	107.5	n/a	General	Music	n/a

Note: Stations included cover the Salt Lake City DMA (Designated Market Area); n/a not available
BurrellesLuce, MediaContacts Online, January 2007

CLIMATE

Average and Extreme Temperatures

Temperature	Jan	Feb	Mar	Apr	May	Jun	Jul	Aug	Sep	Oct	Nov	Dec	Yr.
Extreme High (°F)	62	69	78	85	93	104	107	104	100	89	75	67	107
Average High (°F)	37	43	52	62	72	83	93	90	80	66	50	38	64
Average Temp. (°F)	28	34	41	50	59	69	78	76	65	53	40	30	52
Average Low (°F)	19	24	31	38	46	54	62	61	51	40	30	22	40
Extreme Low (°F)	-22	-14	2	15	25	35	40	37	27	16	-14	-15	-22

Note: Figures cover the years 1948-1990
Source: National Climatic Data Center, International Station Meteorological Climate Summary, 9/96

Average Precipitation/Snowfall/Humidity

Precip./Humidity	Jan	Feb	Mar	Apr	May	Jun	Jul	Aug	Sep	Oct	Nov	Dec	Yr.
Avg. Precip. (in.)	1.3	1.2	1.8	2.0	1.7	0.9	0.8	0.9	1.1	1.3	1.3	1.4	15.6
Avg. Snowfall (in.)	13	10	11	6	1	Tr	0	0	Tr	2	6	13	63
Avg. Rel. Hum. 5am (%)	79	77	71	67	66	60	53	54	60	68	75	79	67
Avg. Rel. Hum. 5pm (%)	69	59	47	38	33	26	22	23	28	40	59	71	43

Note: Figures cover the years 1948-1990; Tr = Trace amounts (<0.05 in. of rain; <0.5 in. of snow)
Source: National Climatic Data Center, International Station Meteorological Climate Summary, 9/96

Weather Conditions

Temperature			Daytime Sky			Precipitation		
5°F & below	32°F & below	90°F & above	Clear	Partly cloudy	Cloudy	0.01 inch or more precip.	0.1 inch or more snow/ice	Thunder-storms
7	128	56	94	152	119	92	38	38

Note: Figures are average number of days per year and cover the years 1948-1990
Source: National Climatic Data Center, International Station Meteorological Climate Summary, 9/96

HAZARDOUS WASTE

Superfund Sites

Draper has no sites on the EPA's Superfund Final National Priorities List.
U.S. Environmental Protection Agency, Final National Priorities List, June 23, 2008

AIR & WATER QUALITY

Air Quality Index

Area	Percent of Days when Air Quality was...[2]				AQI Statistics	
	Good	Moderate	Unhealthy for Sensitive Groups	Unhealthy	Maximum	Median
MSA[1]	41.6	45.5	10.4	2.5	166	55

Note: The Air Quality Index (AQI) is an index for reporting daily air quality. EPA calculates the AQI for five major air pollutants regulated by the Clean Air Act: ground-level ozone, particle pollution (also known as particulate matter), carbon monoxide, sulfur dioxide, and nitrogen dioxide. The AQI runs from 0 to 500. The higher the AQI value, the greater the level of air pollution and the greater the health concern. There are six AQI categories: "Good" The AQI is between 0 and 50. Air quality is considered satisfactory; "Moderate" The AQI is between 51 and 100. Air quality is acceptable; "Unhealthy for Sensitive Groups" When AQI values are between 101 and 150, members of sensitive groups may experience health effects; "Unhealthy" When AQI values are between 151 and 200 everyone may begin to experience health effects; "Very Unhealthy" AQI values between 201 and 300 trigger a health alert; "Hazardous" AQI values over 300 trigger health warnings of emergency conditions; (1) Metropolitan Statistical Area - see Appendix A for areas included; (2) Based on 365 days with AQI data in 2007.
Source: U.S. Environmental Protection Agency, Air Quality Index Report, 2007

Air Quality Index Pollutants

Area	Percent of Days when AQI Pollutant was...[2]					
	Carbon Monoxide	Nitrogen Dioxide	Ozone	Sulfur Dioxide	Particulate Matter 2.5	Particulate Matter 10
MSA[1]	1.6	0.0	42.7	0.0	37.0	18.6

Note: The Air Quality Index (AQI) is an index for reporting daily air quality. EPA calculates the AQI for five major air pollutants regulated by the Clean Air Act: ground-level ozone, particle pollution (also known as particulate matter), carbon monoxide, sulfur dioxide, and nitrogen dioxide. The AQI runs from 0 to 500. The higher the AQI value, the greater the level of air pollution and the greater the health concern; (1) Metropolitan Statistical Area - see Appendix A for areas included; (2) Based on 365 days with AQI data in 2007.
Source: U.S. Environmental Protection Agency, Air Quality Index Report, 2007

Air Quality Index Trends

Area	Trend Sites (13)								All Sites (72)
	1999	2000	2001	2002	2003	2004	2005	2006	2006
MSA[1]	12	19	25	27	10	37	24	11	16

Note: An AQI value greater than 100 indicates that air quality would have been in the unhealthful range on that day. Data from exceptional events are not included. These counts are presented in two ways. First, the counts are based on sites having an adequate record of monitoring data during the trend period (trend sites). These counts represent the relative change in the number of days with AQI values greater than 100. In the last column, the counts are based on all sites with data in the most recent year (because it is possible for a site to have data in the most recent year but not enough data to be a trend site); (1) Metropolitan Statistical Area - see Appendix A for areas included.
Source: U.S. Environmental Protection Agency, Office of Air and Radiation, Air Trends, Factbook and Related Information, Air Pollution Trends in Selected Metropolitan Areas 2006

Maximum Air Pollutant Concentrations

	Particulate Matter 10 (ug/m^3)	Particulate Matter 2.5 (ug/m^3)	Ozone (ppm)	Carbon Monoxide (ppm)	Sulfur Dioxide (ppm)	Nitrogen Dioxide (ppm)	Lead (ug/m^3)
MSA[1] Level	164	40	0.104	3	0.007	0.022	n/a
NAAQS[2]	150	35	0.125	9	0.140	0.053	1.50
Met NAAQS[2]	No	No	Yes	Yes	Yes	Yes	n/a

Note: Data from exceptional events are not included; (1) Metropolitan Statistical Area - see Appendix A for areas included; (2) National Ambient Air Quality Standards; n/a not available
Concentrations: Particulate Matter 10 (coarse particulate) - highest second maximum 24-hour concentration; Particulate Matter 2.5 (fine particulate) - highest 98th percentile 24-hour concentration; Ozone - highest second daily maximum 1-hour concentration; Carbon Monoxide - highest second maximum non-overlapping 8-hour concentration; Sulfur Dioxide - highest second maximum 24-hour concentration; Nitrogen Dioxide - highest arithmetic mean concentration; Lead - highest quarterly maximum concentration
Units: ppm = parts per million; ug/m^3 = micrograms per cubic meter
Source: U.S. Environmental Protection Agency, MSA Factbook 2006, Air Quality Statistics by City

Drinking Water

Water System Name	Pop. Served	Primary Water Source Type	Violations[1]	
			Health Based	Monitoring/ Reporting
Draper City Water System	15,000	Purchased Ground	0	1
Draper Irrigation Company	28,000	Surface	0	0

Note: (1) Based on violation data from January 1, 2007 to December 31, 2007 (includes unresolved violations from earlier years)
Source: U.S. Environmental Protection Agency, Office of Ground Water and Drinking Water, Safe Drinking Water Information System (based on data extracted April 15, 2008)

Lehi, Utah

Background

Lehi occupies 21 square miles in the northern part of Utah County. Part of the Provo-Orem metropolitan area, the city proudly proclaims its slogan, "Pioneers Past and Present." First settled by Mormon pioneers in 1850, the area of Lehi was known as Sulphur Springs, Dry Creek, and Evansville before finally being named after a prophet from the Book of Mormon. In 1852, Lehi received its current name and was incorporated, making the city one of the oldest cities in Utah.

The Overland Stage Coach Route, the Pony Express Trail, and the Transcontinental Telegraph Line impacted the city's early development. Lehi's early economy was driven primarily by industry related to agriculture and animals. Currently the city's economic growth rate is strong and driven by its largest businesses including Cabela's, Costco Wholesale, IM Flash Technologies, Jack B. Parsons, Lehi Block, and others.

This historically small city has grown more than 86 percent since the 2000 Census. Despite its recent growth spurt, the city remains a welcoming place for families due to its low crime rate, high employment rate, and low cost of living. The city's school system, attractions, temperate climate, and available services are just a few additional reasons Lehi is a great place to live.

In keeping with the high literacy and high school graduation rates in the state of Utah, Lehi schools boast more than a 90 percent high school graduation rate. Brigham Young University, Utah Valley State College, and the University of Utah are just a few of the institutions of higher education within 30 miles of Lehi.

Outdoor attractions abound in the Lehi area, including more than twenty parks, a scenic paved path along the Jordan River, Utah Lake and the Wasatch Mountains. The Saratoga Hot Springs in Lehi offer a way for people to simultaneously enjoy nature and relax.

Nature is not the only thing that attracts residents and visitors to Lehi. Thanksgiving Point, a more than 700-acre area housing a golf course, restaurant, gardens, shops, and more, features a popular open-air Farmer's Market in the summer, where residents shop for fresh local produce, snack at the food vendors, and purchase local crafts. For more fun in the summer, Lehi's annual festival, known as the Lehi Roundup rodeo, is celebrated every in June.

The John Hutchings Museum of Natural History, Railroad Depot Museum, Legacy Center, Roller Mill, the city sports complex, and local movie theaters and stores offer opportunities for entertainment. Also notable is that Lehi 's flourmill was featured in the 1984 movie "Footloose."

Provo, Utah, made famous by Butch Cassidy and the Sundance Kid, offers many additional opportunities for employment and entertainment for Lehi residents. Bridal Veil Falls, Sundance Ski Resort, and the McCurdy Doll Museum are a few examples of Provo's attractions. In addition, Lehi's proximity to Salt Lake City opens up another world of opportunity.

The mild weather in Lehi is one of its most attractive features. The mountains surrounding the city keep the air dry. While the weather varies, as one would expect with the changing seasons, the city does not experience the extreme heat, cold, or precipitation associated with other parts of the country. Average rainfall is around 15 inches while the average annual snowfall is less than 27 inches.

Travel in and out of Lehi is facilitated by two conveniently located airports. Provo Airport is 17 miles away and Salt Lake City International Airport is 28 miles away.

Rankings

General Rankings

- Provo* was ranked #13 out of 375 metro areas in *Cities Ranked & Rated*. Criteria: cost of living; climate; crime; transportation; economy and jobs; education; arts and culture; health and healthcare; leisure; quality of life. *Cities Ranked & Rated, 2nd Edition, 2007*
- Provo* was ranked #217 out of 379 metro areas in *Places Rated Almanac*. Criteria: health care; education; recreation; transportation; ambience; climate; crime; housing costs; jobs. *Places Rated Almanac, 7th Edition, 2007*
- The Provo* metro area was selected one of America's "Best Cities to Live, Work and Play" by *Kiplinger Personal Finance*. Criteria: population growth; percentage of workforce in the creative class (scientists, engineers, educators, writers, artists, entertainers, etc.); job quality; income growth; cost of living. *Kiplinger Personal Finance, "Best Cities to Live, Work and Play," July 2008*

Business/Finance Rankings

- Provo* was selected as one of the best places to start and grow a company by *Entrepreneur* and the National Policy Research Council. The Provo* metro area ranked #32 out of 63 mid-size metro areas. Criteria: business formation and growth (firms started four to 14 years ago that still employ at least 5 people and experienced rapid growth over the last four years). *Entrepreneur/National Policy Research Council, "Hot Cities for Entrepreneurs," September 2006*
- The Provo* metro area appeared on the Milken Institute "2007 Best Performing Cities" index. Rank: #8 out of 200 large metro areas. Criteria: job growth; wage and salary growth; high-tech output growth. *Milken Institute, "2007 Best Performing Cities"*
- The Provo* metro area was selected as one of the hottest cities for entrepreneurs in America by *Inc. Magazine*. Criteria: job-growth data for 393 metro was analyzed for current-year employment growth, average annual employment growth over past three years, and employment growth by industry sector. The Provo* metro area ranked #7 among mid-sized metro areas and #31 overall. *Inc. Magazine, May 2007*
- *Forbes* ranked the 200 most populous metro areas in the U.S. in terms of the "Best Places for Business and Careers." The Provo* metro area was ranked #11. Criteria: business costs (labor, energy, tax and office space expenses); living costs (housing, transportation, food and other household expenditures); education levels of the work force; job growth; income growth; migration trends; crime rates; and culture/leisure. *Forbes, "Best Places for Business and Careers," March 19, 2008*
- Provo* was identified as one of the top 20 metro areas with the highest rate of house price appreciation in 2007. The area ranked #6 with a one-year price appreciation of 10.5% through the 4th quarter 2007. *Office of Federal Housing Enterprise Oversight, House Price Index, 4th Quarter 2007*

Health/Environment Rankings

- The Provo* metro area appeared in *Country Home's* "2008 Best Green Places" report. The area ranked #155 out of 379. Criteria: official energy policies; green power; green buildings; availability of fresh, locally grown food. *Country Home, "2008 Best Green Places"*
- Ortho-McNeil Neurologics, in partnership with Sperling's BestPlaces, analyzed 110 metro areas and identified those U.S. cities with the highest prevalence of factors that are most commonly associated with migraine headaches. The Provo* metro area ranked #85. Criteria: number of migraine-related drug prescriptions per capita; lifestyle factors that can contribute to migraines; environmental factors that can trigger migraines; and consumption of migraine-triggering foods. *Ortho-McNeil Neurologics, "America's Migraine Hot Spots," March 14, 2006*

- Sperling's BestPlaces ranked 331 metro areas and identified the most and least stressful U.S. cities. The Provo* metro area ranked #114 out of 114 mid-size metro areas (#1 = most stressful). Criteria: divorce rate; unemployment rate; violent and property crime; suicide rate; commute time; mental health; alcohol consumption; cloudy days. *Sperling's BestPlaces, www.BestPlaces.net, "America's Most (and Least) Stressful Cities," January 9, 2004*

Seniors/Retirement Rankings

- A.G. Edwards ranked America's 500 top-performing communities based on their residents' personal savings and investing behavior. The Provo* metro area ranked #206 with an index score of 102.84 (national average = 100.00). A dozen statistical factors were measured including: participation in retirement savings plans; personal debt levels; and home ownership. *A.G. Edwards, "2007 Nest Egg Index", September 12, 2007*

Children/Family Rankings

- The Provo* metro area was selected as one of the "Best Cities for Relocating Families" by Worldwide ERC and Primacy Relocation. The 2007 study placed a special emphasis on the housing market, which has significantly impacted the relocation industry and an employer's ability to transfer employees. The variables which weigh heavily in this category include home price, home affordability index, appreciation rates, and property tax. Other criteria include cost of living, crime rates, education, climate, focus on diversity, physicians per capita, recreation and leisure, arts and culture, air quality, watershed quality, sales tax, unemployment rate, job growth, high school and higher education index, school expenditures per student, students in public school, SAT/ACT percentile, and population growth. *Worldwide ERC and Primacy Relocation, "2007 Best Cities for Relocating Families"*

Safety Rankings

- The National Insurance Crime Bureau ranked 361 metro areas in the U.S. in terms of per capita rates of vehicle theft. The Provo* metro area ranked #296 (#1 = highest rate). Criteria: number of vehicle theft offenses per 100,000 inhabitants. *National Insurance Crime Bureau, "NICB Vehicle Theft Study," April 22, 2008*
- Farmers Insurance Group of Companies, in partnership with Sperling's BestPlaces, ranked 379 metro areas and identified the "Most Secure U.S. Place to Live." The Provo* metro area ranked #24 out of 127 in the mid-size city category (150,000 to 500,000 residents). Criteria: crime rates; extreme weather; risk of natural disasters; environmental hazards; terrorism threats; air quality; life expectancy; job loss numbers. *Farmers Insurance Group, "Most Secure U.S. Places to Live 2007"*

Sports/Recreation Rankings

- The Provo* metro area appeared on the *Sporting News* list of the "Best Sports Cities 2007". The area ranked #22 out of 150 cities in the U.S. *Sporting News* takes a 12-month snapshot, roughly July to July, of each city's sports, putting a heavy premium on regular-season won-lost records (from the most recently completed season). Other criteria include: playoff berths, bowl appearances and tournament bids; championships; applicable power ratings; quality of competition; overall fan fervor as measured in part by attendance as percentage of venue capacity; abundance of teams (rewarding quality over quantity); stadium and arena quality; ticket availability and prices; franchise ownership; and marquee appeal of athletes. *SportingNews.com, "Best Sports Cities 2007," August 1, 2007*
- *Golf Digest* ranked 330 metro areas in the U.S. in terms of golf. The Provo* metro area was ranked #232. Criteria: access to golf; weather; value of golf; and quality of golf. *Golf Digest, "Metro Golf Rankings," August 2005*

Lehi is located within the Provo-Orem, UT Metropolitan Statistical Area.

Business Environment

CITY FINANCES

City Government Finances

Component	2004-2005 ($000)	2004-2005 ($ per capita)
Total Revenues	48,840	1,539
Total Expenditures	63,200	1,992
Debt Outstanding	91,817	2,894
Cash and Securities	27,249	859

Source: U.S Census Bureau, Government Finances 2004-2005

City Government Revenue by Source

Source	2004-2005 ($000)	2004-2005 ($ per capita)
General Revenue		
From Federal Government	0	0
From State Government	792	25
From Local Governments	57	2
Taxes		
Property	4,892	154
Sales	4,553	143
Personal Income	0	0
License	1,632	51
Charges	14,387	453
Liquor Store	0	0
Utility	16,871	532
Employee Retirement	0	0
Other	5,656	178

Source: U.S Census Bureau, Government Finances 2004-2005

City Government Expenditures by Function

Function	2004-2005 ($000)	2004-2005 ($ per capita)	2004-2005 (%)
General Expenditures			
Airports	0	0	0.0
Corrections	0	0	0.0
Education	0	0	0.0
Fire Protection	412	13	0.7
Governmental Administration	2,724	86	4.3
Health	420	13	0.7
Highways	8,253	260	13.1
Hospitals	0	0	0.0
Housing and Community Development	223	7	0.4
Interest on General Debt	3,523	111	5.6
Libraries	711	22	1.1
Parking	0	0	0.0
Parks and Recreation	8,621	272	13.6
Police Protection	3,570	113	5.6
Public Welfare	0	0	0.0
Sewerage	6,520	205	10.3
Solid Waste Management	1,257	40	2.0
Liquor Store	0	0	0.0
Utility	25,491	803	40.3
Employee Retirement	0	0	0.0
Other	1,475	46	2.3

Source: U.S Census Bureau, Government Finances 2004-2005

Municipal Bond Ratings

Area	Moody's
City	n/a

Source: Mergent Bond Record, January 2008 (unless noted otherwise)

DEMOGRAPHICS

Population Growth

Area	1990 Census	2000 Census	2007 Estimate	2012 Projection	Population Growth (%) 1990-2000	Population Growth (%) 2000-2012
City	9,766	19,028	30,371	37,831	94.8	98.8
MSA[1]	269,407	376,774	470,487	536,515	39.9	42.4
U.S.	248,709,873	281,421,906	301,045,522	314,920,978	13.2	11.9

Note: (1) Metropolitan Statistical Area - see Appendix B for areas included
Source: Claritas, Inc.

Number of Households and Average Household Size

Area	2007 Estimate	2007 Average Household Size
City	8,175	3.72
MSA[1]	129,123	3.64
U.S.	113,668,003	2.65

Note: (1) Metropolitan Statistical Area - see Appendix B for areas included
Source: Claritas, Inc.

Race and Ethnicity

Area	White Alone[2]	Black Alone[2]	Asian Alone[2]	Other Race Alone[2]	Hispanic[3]
City	93.9	0.3	0.6	5.2	4.4
MSA[1]	91.2	0.3	1.1	7.3	8.6
U.S.	73.1	12.4	4.3	10.3	14.9

Note: Figures are 2007 estimates; (1) Metropolitan Statistical Area - see Appendix B for areas included (2) Alone is defined as not being in combination with one or more other races; (3) May be of any race.
Source: Claritas, Inc.

Ancestry

Area	German	Irish[2]	English	American	Italian	Polish	French[3]	Scottish
City	9.5	4.2	34.4	9.0	1.2	0.2	2.8	4.7
MSA[1]	10.8	4.7	33.5	6.9	2.1	0.5	2.2	4.8
U.S.	15.2	10.9	8.7	7.3	5.6	3.2	3.0	1.7

Note: Figures include multiple ancestry (e.g. if a person reported being Irish and Italian, they were included in both columns); (1) Metropolitan Statistical Area - see Appendix A for areas included; (2) Includes Celtic; (3) Includes Alsatian but excludes Basque
Source: Census 2000, Summary File 3

Foreign-Born Population

Area	Percent of Population Born in: Any Foreign Country	Europe	Asia	Africa	Oceania[2]	Canada	Mexico	Latin America[3]
City	3.1	0.3	0.4	0.2	0.0	0.7	1.0	0.4
MSA[1]	6.3	0.7	0.9	0.1	0.2	0.6	2.5	1.4
U.S.	11.1	1.7	2.9	0.3	0.1	0.3	3.3	2.5

Note: (1) Metropolitan Statistical Area - see Appendix A for areas included; (2) Includes Australia, New Zealand subregion, Melanesia, Micronesia, Polynesia, and Oceania n.e.c; (3) Includes Central America (excluding Mexico), South America, and the Caribbean.
Source: Census 2000, Summary File 3

Marriage Status

Area	Never Married	Now Married (excluding Separated)	Separated	Widowed	Divorced
City	18.4	72.9	1.0	2.4	5.3
MSA[1]	32.6	58.6	0.8	3.0	4.9
U.S.	27.1	54.4	2.2	6.6	9.7

Note: Figures are percentages and cover the population 15 years of age and older; (1) Metropolitan Statistical Area - see Appendix A for areas included
Source: Census 2000, Summary File 3

Age Distribution

Area	Percent of Population						
	Under Age 5	Age 5 to 17	Age 18 to 34	Age 35 to 49	Age 50 to 64	Age 65 to 79	80 Years and Over
City	15.5	25.4	30.4	16.6	6.7	3.9	1.3
MSA[1]	10.9	23.0	36.0	15.4	8.2	4.8	1.7
U.S.	6.8	18.9	23.7	23.5	14.8	9.2	3.2

Note: (1) Metropolitan Statistical Area - see Appendix A for areas included
Source: Census 2000, Summary File 3

Male/Female Ratio

Area	Males	Females	Males per 100 Females
City	15,158	15,213	99.6
MSA[1]	233,386	237,101	98.4
U.S.	148,320,305	152,725,217	97.1

Note: Figures are 2007 estimates; (1) Metropolitan Statistical Area - see Appendix B for areas included
Source: Claritas, Inc.

Religion

Area	Catholic	Southern Baptist	United Meth-odist	ELCA[1]	LDS[2]	Presby-terian Church USA	Jewish Est.	Muslim Est.
County	1.0	0.1	0.0	0.0	88.1	0.1	0.0	0.0
U.S.	22.0	7.1	3.7	1.8	1.5	1.1	2.2	0.6

Note: Figures are the number of adherents as a percentage of the total population; Adherents are defined as all members, including full members, their children and the estimated number of other participants who are not considered members (e.g. the baptized, those not confirmed, those regularly attending services, etc.); (1) Evangelical Lutheran Church in America; (2) The Church of Jesus Christ of Latter Day Saints
Source: Reprinted with permission from Religious Congregations and Membership in the United States 2000 (Nashville, Glenmary Research Center, 2002) Copyright Association of Statisticians of American Religious Bodies. All rights reserved.

ECONOMY

Gross Metropolitan Product

Area	2002	2003	2004	2005	2005 Rank[2]
MSA[1]	9.9	10.5	11.6	12.9	146

Note: Figures are in billions of dollars; (1) Provo-Orem, UT Metropolitan Statistical Area - see Appendix A for areas included; (2) Rank ranges from 1 to 361
Source: The U.S. Conference of Mayors, "U.S. Metro Economies: GMP - The Engines of America's Growth," January 2007

Economic Growth

Area	1995 GMP	2005 GMP	Average Annual Growth Rate	Growth Rate Rank[2]
MSA[1]	6.5	12.9	7.0	41

Note: Figures are in billions of dollars; GMP = Gross Metropolitan Product; (1) Provo-Orem, UT Metropolitan Statistical Area - see Appendix A for areas included; (2) Rank ranges from 1 to 361
Source: The U.S. Conference of Mayors, "U.S. Metro Economies: GMP - The Engines of America's Growth," January 2007

INCOME

Per Capita/Median/Average Income

Area	Per Capita ($)	Median Household ($)	Average Household ($)
City	18,036	58,449	66,846
MSA[1]	17,896	51,529	64,693
U.S.	25,495	49,280	66,670

Note: Figures are 2007 estimates; (1) Metropolitan Statistical Area - see Appendix B for areas included
Source: Claritas, Inc.

Household Income Distribution

Area	Percent of Households Earning							
	Under $15,000	$15,000 -24,999	$25,000 -34,999	$35,000 -49,999	$50,000 -74,999	$75,000 -99,000	$100,000 -149,999	$150,000 and up
City	5.4	7.3	7.8	19.3	28.0	16.2	12.3	3.6
MSA[1]	8.4	10.3	11.5	18.2	22.7	12.8	11.1	4.9
U.S.	13.1	10.9	11.2	15.6	19.5	11.9	11.3	6.6

Note: Figures are 2007 estimates; (1) Metropolitan Statistical Area - see Appendix B for areas included
Source: Claritas, Inc.

Poverty Rates by Age

Area	All Ages	Under 5 Years Old	5 to 17 Years Old	18 to 64 Years Old	65 Years and Over
City	5.5	1.2	1.8	2.3	0.2
MSA[1]	12.0	1.1	1.9	8.6	0.3
U.S.	12.4	1.2	3.0	6.9	1.2

Note: Figures are percent of population with income in 1999 below poverty level and only include population for whom poverty status is determined; (1) Metropolitan Statistical Area - see Appendix A for areas included
Source: Census 2000, Summary File 3

Personal Bankruptcy Filing Rate

Area	2004	2005	2006
Utah County	5.98	6.23	1.46
U.S.	5.31	6.82	2.00

Note: Numbers are per 1,000 population and include Chapter 7 and Chapter 13 filings
Source: Federal Deposit Insurance Corporation (FDIC), Regional Economic Conditions (RECON), 8/23/2007

EMPLOYMENT

Labor Force and Employment

Area	Civilian Labor Force			Workers Employed		
	Dec. 2006	Dec. 2007	% Chg.	Dec. 2006	Dec. 2007	% Chg.
City	11,110	11,432	2.9	10,955	11,233	2.5
MSA[1]	225,624	232,573	3.1	221,015	226,628	2.5
U.S.	152,571,000	153,705,000	0.7	146,081,000	146,334,000	0.2

Note: Data is not seasonally adjusted and covers workers 16 years of age and older;
(1) Metropolitan Statistical Area - see Appendix B for areas included
Source: Bureau of Labor Statistics, http://stats.bls.gov

Unemployment Rate

Area	2007											
	Jan.	Feb.	Mar.	Apr.	May	Jun.	Jul.	Aug.	Sep.	Oct.	Nov.	Dec.
City	1.8	1.7	1.6	1.5	1.5	1.9	1.9	1.9	1.6	1.7	1.6	1.7
MSA[1]	2.6	2.5	2.4	2.2	2.2	2.8	2.8	2.8	2.4	2.5	2.4	2.6
U.S.	5.0	4.9	4.5	4.3	4.3	4.7	4.9	4.6	4.5	4.4	4.5	4.8

Note: Data is not seasonally adjusted and covers workers 16 years of age and older; All figures are percentages; (1) Metropolitan Statistical Area - see Appendix B for areas included
Source: Bureau of Labor Statistics, http://stats.bls.gov

Employment by Occupation

Occupation Classification	City (%)	MSA[1] (%)	U.S. (%)
Sales and Office	29.0	27.7	26.7
Professional and Related	19.1	24.3	20.2
Service	12.3	14.0	14.9
Production, Transportation, and Material Moving	12.2	11.4	14.6
Management, Business, and Financial	14.0	12.2	13.5
Construction, Extraction, and Maintenance	13.1	10.1	9.4
Farming, Forestry, and Fishing	0.3	0.3	0.7

Note: Figures cover employed civilians 16 years of age and older;
(1) Metropolitan Statistical Area - see Appendix A for areas included
Source: Census 2000, Summary File 3

Employment by Industry

Sector	MSA[1] Number of Employees	MSA[1] Percent of Total	U.S. Percent of Total
Government	26,100	13.3	16.3
Education and Health Services	40,800	20.9	13.4
Professional and Business Services	23,500	12.0	13.1
Retail Trade	25,200	12.9	11.6
Manufacturing	20,100	10.3	9.9
Leisure and Hospitality	14,000	7.2	9.6
Financial Activities	6,800	3.5	5.9
Construction	n/a	n/a	5.3
Wholesale Trade	5,400	2.8	4.4
Other Services	4,300	2.2	3.9
Transportation and Utilities	2,400	1.2	3.7
Information	8,100	4.1	2.2
Natural Resources and Mining	n/a	n/a	0.5

Note: Figures cover non-farm employment as of December 2007 and are not seasonally adjusted; (1) Metropolitan Statistical Area - see Appendix B for areas included; n/a not available
Source: Bureau of Labor Statistics, http://stats.bls.gov

Average Wages

Occupation	$/Hr.	Occupation	$/Hr.
Accountants and Auditors	31.16	Maids and Housekeeping Cleaners	8.88
Automotive Mechanics	16.54	Maintenance and Repair Workers	12.97
Bookkeepers	12.79	Marketing Managers	43.94
Carpenters	17.10	Nuclear Medicine Technologists	n/a
Cashiers	8.39	Nurses, Licensed Practical	15.71
Clerks, General Office	10.23	Nurses, Registered	26.37
Clerks, Receptionists/Information	10.56	Nursing Aides/Orderlies/Attendants	9.69
Clerks, Shipping/Receiving	11.56	Packers and Packagers, Hand	8.48
Computer Programmers	30.38	Physical Therapists	30.49
Computer Support Specialists	17.10	Postal Service Mail Carriers	21.14
Computer Systems Analysts	33.42	Real Estate Brokers	n/a
Cooks, Restaurant	10.71	Retail Salespersons	10.60
Dentists	n/a	Sales Reps., Exc. Tech./Scientific	22.78
Electrical Engineers	n/a	Sales Reps., Tech./Scientific	28.98
Electricians	23.41	Secretaries, Exc. Legal/Med./Exec.	12.95
Financial Managers	38.14	Security Guards	13.32
First-Line Supervisors/Mgrs., Sales	16.55	Surgeons	n/a
Food Preparation Workers	8.03	Teacher Assistants	9.70
General and Operations Managers	38.97	Teachers, Elementary School	21.10
Hairdressers/Cosmetologists	10.20	Teachers, Secondary School	23.30
Internists	n/a	Telemarketers	11.47
Janitors and Cleaners	9.07	Truck Drivers, Heavy/Tractor-Trailer	18.39
Landscaping/Groundskeeping Workers	9.31	Truck Drivers, Light/Delivery Svcs.	10.60
Lawyers	45.25	Waiters and Waitresses	7.93

Note: Wage data covers the Provo-Orem, UT Metropolitan Statistical Area - see Appendix B for areas included. Hourly wages for elementary/secondary school teachers and teacher assistants were calculated by the editors from annual wage data assuming a 40 hour work week; n/a not available.
Source: Bureau of Labor Statistics, May 2007 Metro Area Occupational Employment and Wage Estimates

RESIDENTIAL REAL ESTATE

Building Permits

Area	Single-Family 2006	Single-Family 2007p	Single-Family Pct. Chg.	Multi-Family 2006	Multi-Family 2007p	Multi-Family Pct. Chg.	Total 2006	Total 2007p	Total Pct. Chg.
City	1,629	849	-47.9	0	33	-	1,629	882	-45.9
U.S.	1,378,200	973,300	-29.4	460,700	407,200	-11.6	1,838,900	1,380,500	-24.9

Note: (p) preliminary; figures cover and represent new, privately-owned housing units authorized (unadjusted data); All permit data are based on estimates with imputation; U.S. figures are based on the new 20,000-place series.
Source: U.S. Census Bureau, Manufacturing, Mining, and Construction Statistics

Homeownership and Housing Vacancies

Area	Homeownership Rate[2] (%)			Rental Vacancy Rate[3] (%)			Homeowner Vacancy Rate[4] (%)		
	2005	2006	2007	2005	2006	2007	2005	2006	2007
MSA[1]	n/a	n/a	n/a	n/a	n/a	n/a	n/a	n/a	n/a
U.S.	68.9	68.8	68.1	9.8	9.8	9.7	1.9	2.4	2.7

Note: (1) Metropolitan Statistical Area - see Appendix B for areas included; (2) The proportion of households that are owners; (3) The proportion of the rental inventory that is vacant for rent; (4) The proportion of the homeowner inventory that is vacant for sale; n/a not available
Source: U.S. Census Bureau, Housing Vacancies and Homeownership Annual Statistics: 2007

TAXES

State Corporate Income Tax Rates

State	Rates and Tax Brackets
Utah	5.0%

Note: Tax rates as of January 1, 2008; Minimum tax $100.
Source: Tax Foundation, www.taxfoundation.org

State Individual Income Tax Rates

State	Federal Deductibility	Marginal Rates (%)	Standard Deduction ($)		Personal Exemptions ($)[1]	
			Single	Joint	Single	Dependents
Utah	Yes (bb)	2.3 - 6.98 (cc)	5,150 (s)	10,300 (s)	2,475 (q)	2,475 (q)

Note: Tax rates as of January 1, 2008; Local- and county-level taxes are not included; n/a not applicable; (1) Married joint filers generally receive double the single exemption; (q) Three fourths federal exemption; (s) Deductions and exemptions tied to federal tax system. Federal deductions and exemptions are indexed for inflation; (bb) Half of federal income tax deductible; (cc) An optional 5.35% flat tax will be available.
Source: Tax Foundation, www.taxfoundation.org

Various State and Local Tax Rates

State and Local Sales and Use (%)	State Sales and Use (%)	Gasoline[1,2] ($/gal.)	Cigarette ($/pack)	Spirits ($/gal.)	Table Wine ($/gal.)	Beer ($/gal.)
6.45	4.65	0.245	0.695	10.13 (n)	(p)	0.41

Note: Tax rates as of January 1, 2008; (1) In addition to the 18.4 cpg Federal gasoline tax; (2) Rates may include additional state sales taxes, environmental protection and storage fees/taxes, and local taxes. When necessary, the volume-weighted average of all local taxes is used to approximate the typical statewide rate including local tax; (n) The state government controls all sales. The implied excise tax rate is calculated using methodology designed by the Distilled Spirits Council of the United States (DISCUS); (p) All wine sales are through state-run stores. Revenue in these states is generated from various taxes, fees and net profits.
Source: Tax Foundation, www.taxfoundation.org; Original research

State Tax Burdens

Area	Combined State and Local Tax Burden		Combined Federal, State and Local Tax Burden	
	Percent	Rank	Percent	Rank
Utah	10.7	27	30.3	36
U.S. Average	11.0	-	32.7	-

Note: Figures cover 2007 and measure taxes as a percentage of income
Source: Tax Foundation, www.taxfoundation.org

State Business Tax Climate Index Rankings

State	Overall Rank	Corporate Tax Index Rank	Individual Income Tax Index Rank	Sales Tax Index Rank	Unemployment Insurance Tax Index Rank	Property Tax Index Rank
Utah	17	5	30	27	28	3

Note: Rankings range from 1 to 50 where 1 is best. Rankings do not average across to Overall Rank. States without a given tax are given a ranking of 1.
Source: Tax Foundation, State Business Tax Climate Index 2008

TRANSPORTATION

Means of Transportation to Work

Area	Car/Truck/Van		Public Transportation			Bicycle	Walked	Other Means	Worked at Home
	Drove Alone	Car-pooled	Bus	Subway	Railroad				
City	76.2	14.6	1.5	0.2	0.1	0.3	0.8	0.8	5.6
MSA[1]	72.5	14.9	1.3	0.0	0.0	0.8	4.9	0.5	5.0
U.S.	75.7	12.2	2.5	1.5	0.5	0.4	2.9	1.0	3.3

Note: Figures are percentages and cover workers 16 years of age and older; (1) Metropolitan Statistical Area - see Appendix A for areas included
Source: Census 2000, Summary File 3

Travel Time to Work

Area	Less Than 15 Minutes	15 to 29 Minutes	30 to 44 Minutes	45 to 59 Minutes	60 Minutes or More
City	30.2	39.0	19.8	6.7	4.3
MSA[1]	45.0	35.9	10.7	4.2	4.2
U.S.	29.4	36.1	19.1	7.4	8.0

Note: Figures are percentages and include workers 16 years old and over; (1) Metropolitan Statistical Area - see Appendix A for areas included
Source: Census 2000, Summary File 3

Living Environment

COST OF LIVING

Cost of Living Index

Composite Index	Groceries	Housing	Utilities	Trans-portation	Health Care	Misc. Goods/ Services
n/a	n/a	n/a	n/a	n/a	n/a	n/a

Note: U.S. = 100; n/a not available
Source: The Council for Community and Economic Research (formerly ACCRA), Cost of Living Index, 2007

Grocery Prices

Area[1]	T-Bone Steak ($/pound)	Frying Chicken ($/pound)	Whole Milk ($/half gal.)	Eggs ($/dozen)	Orange Juice ($/64 oz.)	Coffee ($/11.5 oz.)
City[2]	n/a	n/a	n/a	n/a	n/a	n/a
Avg.	8.93	1.12	2.13	1.52	3.26	3.31
Min.	5.88	0.71	1.33	0.83	2.30	2.20
Max.	12.80	2.07	3.43	3.54	5.79	6.20

Note: (1) Values for the local area are compared with the average, minimum and maximum values for all 331 areas in the Cost of Living Index report; n/a not available; (2) Figures cover the Lehi UT urban area; **T-Bone Steak** *(price per pound);* **Frying Chicken** *(price per pound, whole fryer);* **Whole Milk** *(half gallon carton);* **Eggs** *(price per dozen, Grade A, large);* **Orange Juice** *(64 oz. Tropicana or Florida Natural);* **Coffee** *(11.5 oz. can, vacuum-packed, Maxwell House, Hills Bros, or Folgers).*
Source: The Council for Community and Economic Research (formerly ACCRA), Cost of Living Index, 2007

Housing and Utility Costs

Area[1]	New Home Price ($)	Apartment Rent ($/month)	All Electric ($/month)	Part Electric ($/month)	Other Energy ($/month)	Telephone ($/month)
City[2]	n/a	n/a	n/a	n/a	n/a	n/a
Avg.	309,605	782	146.13	78.67	90.16	26.14
Min.	189,877	n/a	82.03	37.41	33.15	17.08
Max.	1,202,800	3,481	271.14	150.60	257.67	37.45

Note: (1) Values for the local area are compared with the average, minimum and maximum values for all 331 areas in the Cost of Living Index report; n/a not available; (2) Figures cover the Lehi UT urban area; **New Home Price** *(2,400 sf living area, 8,000 sf lot, in urban area with full utilities);* **Apartment Rent** *(950 sf 2 bedroom/1.5 or 2 bath, unfurnished, excluding all utilities except water);* **All Electric** *(average monthly cost for an all-electric home);* **Part Electric** *(average monthly cost for a part-electric home);* **Other Energy** *(average monthly cost for natural gas, fuel oil, coal, wood, and any other forms of energy except electricity);* **Telephone** *(price includes basic monthly rate for a private residential line plus additional local usage charges incurred by a family of four).*
Source: The Council for Community and Economic Research (formerly ACCRA), Cost of Living Index, 2007

Health Care, Transportation, and Other Costs

Area[1]	Doctor ($/visit)	Dentist ($/visit)	Optometrist ($/visit)	Gasoline ($/gallon)	Beauty Salon ($/visit)	Men's Shirt ($)
City[2]	n/a	n/a	n/a	n/a	n/a	n/a
Avg.	79.48	71.93	79.55	2.64	29.52	25.77
Min.	52.08	44.80	43.95	2.19	15.58	16.19
Max.	148.44	126.27	158.83	3.48	60.62	48.53

Note: (1) Values for the local area are compared with the average, minimum and maximum values for all 331 areas in the Cost of Living Index report; n/a not available; (2) Figures cover the Lehi UT urban area; **Doctor** *(general practitioners routine exam of an established patient);* **Dentist** *(adult teeth cleaning and periodic oral examination);* **Optometrist** *(full vision eye exam for established adult patient);* **Gasoline** *(one gallon regular unleaded, national brand, including all taxes, cash price at self-service pump if available);* **Beauty Salon** *(woman's shampoo, trim, and blow-dry);* **Men's Shirt** *(cotton/polyester dress shirt, pinpoint weave, long sleeves).*
Source: The Council for Community and Economic Research (formerly ACCRA), Cost of Living Index, 2007

HOUSING

House Price Index (HPI)

Area	National Ranking[2]	Quarterly Change (%)	One-Year Change (%)	Five-Year Change (%)
MSA[1]	6	0.77	10.46	51.51
U.S.[3]	-	0.10	0.84	41.37

Note: The HPI is a weighted repeat sales index. It measures average price changes in repeat sales or refinancings on the same properties. This information is obtained by reviewing repeat mortgage transactions on single-family properties whose mortgages have been purchased or securitized by Fannie Mae or Freddie Mac in January 1975; (1) Metropolitan Statistical Area - see Appendix B for areas included; (2) Rankings are based on annual percentage change for all metro areas containing at least 15,000 transactions over the last 10 years and ranges from 1 to 291; (3) figures based on a weighted average of Census Division estimates; all figures are for the period ending December 31, 2007
Source: Office of Federal Housing Enterprise Oversight, House Price Index, February 26, 2008

House Price Valuations

Area	Q1 2000	Q1 2001	Q1 2002	Q1 2003	Q1 2004	Q1 2005	Q1 2006	Q1 2007	Q1 2008
MSA[1]	-2.6	-1.8	0.8	3.0	9.9	6.8	14.4	25.8	25.7

Note: Figures show the percentage of over- or under-valuation of single family homes relative to statistically normal house values (e.g. a value of 23.6 indicates that house values are 23.6% overvalued). Statistically normal house values are based on house prices, interest rates, household incomes, population densities, and any historical premiums or discounts metropolitan areas have exhibited over time; (1) Figures cover the Metropolitan Statistical Area - see Appendix B for areas included
Source: Global Insight/National City Corporation, House Prices in America, May 2008

Median Home Prices

Area	2005	2006	2007[r]	Percent Change 2006 to 2007
MSA[1]	n/a	n/a	n/a	n/a
U.S. Average	219.0	221.9	217.9	-1.8

Note: Figures are median sales prices of existing single-family homes in thousands of dollars; (r) revised; n/a not available; (1) Metropolitan Statistical Area - see Appendix B for areas included
Source: National Association of Realtors, Metropolitan Area Prices, 1st Quarter 2008

Housing: Year Structure Built

Area	1990 -2000	1980 -1989	1970 -1979	1960 -1969	1950 -1959	1940 -1949	Before 1940	Median Year
City	53.6	8.7	13.3	3.3	8.2	3.4	9.5	1991
MSA[1]	33.9	12.7	22.8	9.1	8.4	5.4	7.8	1978
U.S.	17.0	15.8	18.5	13.7	12.7	7.3	15.0	1971

Note: Figures are percentages; (1) Metropolitan Statistical Area - see Appendix A for areas included
Source: Census 2000, Summary File 3

HEALTH

Health Risk Data

Category	Area[1] (%)	U.S. (%)
Adults who have been told they have high blood pressure[3]	13.1	25.5
Adults who have been told they have high blood cholesterol[3]	29.2	35.6
Adults who have been told they have diabetes[2]	3.9	7.5
Adults who have been told they have arthritis[3]	17.5	27.0
Adults who have been told they currently have asthma	8.6	8.5
Adults who are current smokers	5.9	20.1
Adults who are heavy drinkers[4]	1.0	4.9
Adults who are overweight (BMI 25.0 - 29.9)	33.0	36.5
Adults who are obese (BMI 30.0 - 99.8)	21.3	25.1

Note: Data as of 2006 unless otherwise noted; (1) Figures cover the Metropolitan Statistical Area - see Appendix B for areas included; (2) Figures do not include pregnancy-related diabetes, pre-diabetes or borderline diabetes; (3) 2005 data; (4) Heavy drinkers are classified as adult men having more than two drinks per day or adult women having more than one drink per day
Source: Centers for Disease Control and Prevention, Behaviorial Risk Factor Surveillance System, SMART: Selected Metropolitan/Micropolitan Area Risk Trends, 2005, 2006

Mortality Rates for the Top 10 Causes of Death in the U.S.

ICD-10[a] Sub-Chapter	ICD-10[a] Code	Age-Adjusted Mortality Rate[1] per 100,000 population	
		County[2]	U.S.
Malignant neoplasms	C00-C97	126.8	186.5
Ischaemic heart diseases	I20-I25	86.9	152.3
Other forms of heart disease	I30-I51	73.2	51.5
Cerebrovascular diseases	I60-I69	53.3	50.0
Chronic lower respiratory diseases	J40-J47	24.4	42.6
Diabetes mellitus	E10-E14	31.3	24.8
Other degenerative diseases of the nervous system	G30-G31	25.5	22.6
Other external causes of accidental injury	W00-X59	17.3	21.4
Influenza and pneumonia	J10-J18	18.2	20.7
Hypertensive diseases	I10-I13	14.8	18.2

Note: (a) ICD-10 = International Classification of Diseases 10th Revision; (1) Mortality rates are a three year average covering 2003-2005; (2) Figures cover Utah County
Source: Centers for Disease Control and Prevention, National Center for Health Statistics. Compressed Mortality File 1999-2004. CDC WONDER On-line Database, compiled from Compressed Mortality File 1999-2005 Series 20 No. 2K, 2008.

Mortality Rates for Selected Causes of Death

ICD-10[a] Sub-Chapter	ICD-10[a] Code	Age-Adjusted Mortality Rate[1] per 100,000 population	
		County[2]	U.S.
Assault	X85-Y09	*1.0	5.9
Human immunodeficiency virus (HIV) disease	B20-B24	*0.2	4.5
Intentional self-harm	X60-X84	12.9	10.8
Malnutrition	E40-E46	*1.1	1.0
Obesity and other hyperalimentation	E65-E68	2.6	1.4
Organic, including symptomatic, mental disorders	F01-F09	25.8	16.8
Transport accidents	V01-V99	12.2	16.1
Viral hepatitis	B15-B19	*1.0	1.8

Note: (a) ICD-10 = International Classification of Diseases 10th Revision; (1) Mortality rates are a three year average covering 2003-2005; (2) Figures cover Utah County; (*) Unreliable data as per CDC
Source: Centers for Disease Control and Prevention, National Center for Health Statistics. Compressed Mortality File 1999-2004. CDC WONDER On-line Database, compiled from Compressed Mortality File 1999-2005 Series 20 No. 2K, 2008.

Distribution of Physicians[1]

Area	Total	Family/ General Practice	Specialties	
			Medical	Surgical
Utah County (number)	470	196	127	124
Utah County (rate per 10,000 pop.)	10.6	4.4	2.9	2.8
U.S. (rate per 10,000 pop.)	17.7	4.6	6.9	4.3

Note: Data as of 2005; (1) Includes all non-federal, patient-care, office-based MDs
Source: Area Resource File (ARF). June 2007. U.S. Department of Health and Human Services, Health Resources and Services Administration, Bureau of Health Professions, Rockville, MD.

Hospitals

There were no hospitals listed within the city limits.
AHA Guide to the Healthcare Field 2008

EDUCATION

Public School District Statistics

District Name	Schls	Pupils	Pupil/ Teacher Ratio	Minority Pupils[1] (%)	Free Lunch Eligible[2] (%)	IEP[3] (%)
Alpine District	72	55,383	24.8	10.6	16.4	11.4

Note: Table includes regular local school districts with 2,000 or more students; (1) Percentage of students that are not white, non-Hispanic; (2) Percentage of students that are eligible for the free lunch program; (3) Percentage of students that have an Individualized Education Program.
Source: U.S. Department of Education, National Center for Education Statistics, Common Core of Data, Local Education Agency (School District) Universe Survey: School Year 2005-2006; U.S. Department of Education, National Center for Education Statistics, Common Core of Data, Public Elementary/Secondary School Universe Survey: School Year 2005-2006

Highest Level of Education

Area	Less than H.S.	H.S. Diploma	Some College, No Deg.	Associate Degree	Bachelors Degree	Masters Degree	Profess. School Degree	Doctorate Degree
City	8.3	25.6	30.1	9.1	19.9	5.3	1.0	0.7
MSA[1]	8.8	19.6	30.8	9.8	21.5	6.3	1.6	1.8
U.S.	19.4	28.4	21.2	6.4	15.7	5.9	2.0	1.0

Note: Figures are 2007 estimated percentages and cover persons age 25 and over; (1) Metropolitan Statistical Area - see Appendix B for areas included
Source: Claritas, Inc.

Educational Attainment by Race

Area	High School Graduate (%)					Bachelor's Degree (%)				
	Total	White	Black	Asian	Hisp.[2]	Total	White	Black	Asian	Hisp.[2]
City	91.5	91.5	0.0	92.8	75.4	26.1	25.8	0.0	41.2	27.2
MSA[1]	90.9	92.2	78.7	91.5	62.8	31.5	32.1	25.7	48.7	16.2
U.S.	80.4	83.6	72.3	80.4	52.4	24.4	26.1	14.3	44.1	10.4

Note: Figures shown cover persons 25 years old and over; (1) Metropolitan Statistical Area - see Appendix A for areas included; (2) people of Hispanic origin can be of any race
Source: Census 2000, Summary File 3

School Enrollment by Type

Area	Grades KG to 8				Grades 9 to 12			
	Public		Private		Public		Private	
	Enrollment	%	Enrollment	%	Enrollment	%	Enrollment	%
City	3,327	96.8	110	3.2	1,206	94.3	73	5.7
MSA[1]	56,391	96.9	1,786	3.1	24,610	96.2	976	3.8
U.S.	33,526,011	88.7	4,285,121	11.3	14,848,628	90.6	1,532,323	9.4

Note: Figures shown cover persons 3 years old and over; (1) Metropolitan Statistical Area - see Appendix A for areas included
Source: Census 2000, Summary File 3

School Enrollment by Race

Area	Grades KG to 8 (%)				Grades 9 to 12 (%)			
	White	Black	Asian	Hisp.[1]	White	Black	Asian	Hisp.[1]
City	92.5	0.3	1.1	2.6	98.0	0.0	0.0	2.7
MSA[2]	91.8	0.5	0.6	7.5	93.6	0.2	0.6	6.1
U.S.	68.5	15.5	3.3	16.8	68.8	15.5	3.8	15.7

Note: Figures shown cover persons 3 years old and over; (1) people of Hispanic origin can be of any race; (2) Metropolitan Statistical Area - see Appendix A for areas included
Source: Census 2000, Summary File 3

Average Salaries of Public School Classroom Teachers

District	2005-06		2006-07		Percent Change 2005-06 to 2006-07
	Dollars	Rank[1]	Dollars	Rank[1]	
Utah	40,007	46	40,566	47	1.40
U.S. Average	49,026	-	50,816	-	3.65

Note: (1) State rank ranges from 1 to 51.
Source: National Education Association, Rankings & Estimates: Rankings of the States 2006 and Estimates of School Statistics 2007, December 2007

Higher Education

Four-Year Colleges			Two-Year Colleges			Medical Schools[1]	Law Schools[2]	Voc/ Tech[3]
Public	Private Non-profit	Private For-profit	Public	Private Non-profit	Private For-profit			
0	0	0	0	0	0	0	0	0

Note: Figures cover institutions located within the city limits; (1) includes schools accredited by the Liaison Committee on Medical Education and the American Osteopathic Association; (2) includes American Bar Association-accredited law schools; (3) includes all schools with programs that are less than 2 years.
Source: National Center for Education Statistics, The Integrated Postsecondary Education System (IPEDS) Peer Analysis System, 2007; www.usnews.com, Law and Medical School Directories, 2009

PRESIDENTIAL ELECTION

2004 Presidential Election Results

Area	Bush	Kerry	Nader	Other
Utah County	86.0	11.6	0.9	1.5
U.S.	50.7	48.3	0.4	0.6

Note: Results are percentages and may not add to 100% due to rounding
Source: Dave Leip's Atlas of U.S. Presidential Elections, www.uselectionatlas.org

EMPLOYERS

Major Employers

Company Name	Industry	Type of Site
Brigham Young University	Colleges and universities	Headquarters
City of Provo	Executive offices	Headquarters
Geneva Steel	Blast furnaces and steel mills	Headquarters
Missionary Training Center	Religious organizations	Branch
Natures Sunshine	Medicinals and botanicals	Branch
Natures Sunshine Products	Pharmaceutical preparations	Headquarters
Nu Skin Enterprises Inc	Toilet preparations	Headquarters
Nu Skin Enterprises US Inc	Drugs, proprietaries, and sundries	Headquarters
Nu Skin United States Inc	Drugs, proprietaries, and sundries	Branch
Phone Directories Company	Miscellaneous publishing	Headquarters
Tahitian Noni International	Groceries and related products, nec	Headquarters
Timpangos Strytelling Festival	Membership organizations, nec	Single
Utah State Development Center	Elementary and secondary schools	Branch
Utah State Hospital	Psychiatric hospitals	Branch
Utah Valley State College	Colleges and universities	Headquarters
Western Wats	Business services, nec	Single
Xango LLC	Catalog and mail-order houses	Single

Note: Companies shown are located within the Provo metropolitan area; nec = not elsewhere classified.
Source: www.zapdata.com, May 2008

PUBLIC SAFETY

Crime Rate

Area	All Crimes	Violent Crimes				Property Crimes		
		Murder	Forcible Rape	Robbery	Aggrav. Assault	Burglary	Larceny -Theft	Motor Vehicle Theft
City	2,109.0	0.0	18.3	6.1	54.9	653.2	1,254.4	122.1
Metro[1]	2,591.3	0.6	23.3	13.5	56.0	465.1	1,896.2	136.4
U.S.	3,808.1	5.7	30.9	149.4	287.5	729.4	2,206.8	398.4

Note: Figures are crimes per 100,000 population; (1) Metropolitan Statistical Area - see Appendix B for areas included
Source: FBI Uniform Crime Reports, 2006

Hate Crimes

Area	Number of Quarters Reported	Bias Motivation				
		Race	Religion	Sexual Orientation	Ethnicity	Disability
City	4	0	0	0	0	0

Source: Federal Bureau of Investigation, Hate Crime Statistics 2006

RECREATION

Culture

Dance[1]	Theatre[1]	Instrumental Music[1]	Vocal Music[1]	Series/ Festivals	Museums	Zoos and Aquariums[2]
0	0	0	0	0	1	0

Note: (1) Number of professional perfoming groups; (2) AZA-accredited
Source: The Grey House Performing Arts Directory, 2007; Official Museum Directory, 2008; Association of Zoos & Aquariums, AZA Member Zoos & Aquariums, June 2008

Professional Sports Teams

Team Name	League
No teams are located in the metro area	

Source: Original research

MEDIA

Newspapers

Name	News Focus	Frequency	Circulation
No newspapers have an office in the city			

Note: Includes newspapers with offices located in the city
Source: MediaContactsPro, March 2008

Television Stations

Name	Ch.	Network(s)	Type	Ownership
KUTV	2	CBS	Commercial	CBS
KCSG	4	Pax	Commercial	n/a
KTVX	4	ABC	Commercial	n/a
KSL	5	NBC	Commercial	Bonneville International Corporation
KUED	7	PBS	Public	University of Utah
KUEN	9	n/a	Public	Utah State Board of Regents
KENV	10	NBC	Commercial	Sunbelt Broadcasting Company
KBYU	11	PBS	Public	Brigham Young University
KDLQ	13	Fox/ABC	Commercial	n/a
KSTU	13	Fox	Commercial	Fox Television Stations Inc.
KJZZ	14	n/a	Commercial	Larry H. Miller Communications
KUPX	16	Pax	Commercial	Paxson Communications Corporation
KUEW	18	PBS	n/a	University of Utah
KUWB	30	WBN	Commercial	Acme Television Holdings

Note: Stations included cover the Salt Lake City DMA (Designated Market Area)
BurrellesLuce, MediaContacts Online, January 2007

Major AM Radio Stations

Call Letters	Freq. (kHz)	Station Type	Target Audience	Station Format	Music Format
KNRS	570	Commercial	General	News/Talk	n/a
KSUB	590	n/a	General	News/Sports/Talk	n/a
KVNU	610	Commercial	General	News/Talk	n/a
KMTI	650	Commercial	General	Music/News/Sports/Talk	Country
KOAL	750	n/a	General	News/Sports/Talk	n/a
KBEE	860	Commercial	General	Music/Talk	Country
KDXU	890	Commercial	General	News/Talk	n/a
KALL	910	Commercial	General	News	n/a
KMER	950	Commercial	General	News	n/a
KOVO	960	Commercial	General	Sports/Talk	n/a
KSVC	980	Commercial	General	News/Sports/Talk	n/a
KKDS	1060	Commercial	General	Music/News	Adult Contemp.
KAFL	1080	Commercial	General	Music	Country
KANN	1120	Non-Comm	Religious	Educational/Music/News	Christian
KSL	1160	Commercial	General	News/Talk	n/a
KUNF	1210	Commercial	General	Music/News	Easy Listening
KRSV	1210	Commercial	General	Music/News/Sports	Country
KEVA	1240	Commercial	General	News	n/a
KNEU	1250	Commercial	General	Music/News	Country
KZNS	1280	Commercial	General	News/Sports/Talk	n/a
KFNZ	1320	n/a	General/Men	Music/Sports	n/a
KRKK	1360	n/a	General	Music/News	n/a
KSOP	1370	Commercial	General	Music/News	Country
KLGN	1390	Commercial	General	Music/News/Sports/Talk	Adult Standards
KLO	1430	Commercial	General	Music/News/Sports/Talk	n/a
KXOL	1660	n/a	General	Music	n/a

Note: Stations included cover the Salt Lake City DMA (Designated Market Area); n/a not available
Source: BurrellesLuce, MediaContacts Online, January 2007

Major FM Radio Stations

Call Letters	Freq. (mHz)	Station Type	Target Audience	Station Format	Music Format
KBYU	89.1	College	General	Music/News	Classical
KUER	90.1	College	General	Music/News	Jazz
KUSU	91.5	College	General	Educational/Music/News	Classic Rock
KBLQ	92.9	Commercial	General	Music/News/Sports	Soft Rock
KCYQ	93.7	Commercial	General	Music	Country
KODJ	94.1	Commercial	General	Music	Oldies
KVFX	94.5	Commercial	General	Music	Adult Contemp.
KZHT	94.9	Commercial	General/Women	Music	Top 40
KXBN	94.9	Commercial	General	Music	Top 40
KYCS	95.1	Commercial	General	Music/News	Adult Contemp.
KYFO	95.5	Non-Comm	General	Music/Talk	Christian
KFNN	95.7	Commercial	General	Music/News	Adult Contemp.
KXRK	96.3	n/a	Gay/Lesbian	Music	n/a
KQSW	96.5	Commercial	General	Music/News	Country
KISN	97.1	Commercial	General	Music	Adult Contemp.
KREC	98.1	Commercial	General	Educational/Music/News	Adult Contemp.
KBEE	98.7	n/a	General	Music/News/Sports	n/a
KURR	99.5	Commercial	General/Native Amer	Music/Talk	Classic Rock
KONY	101.1	Commercial	General	Music	Contemp. Country
KXFF	102.9	n/a	n/a	n/a	n/a
KUDD	103.9	Commercial	General/Women	Music	Top 40
KSIT	104.5	Commercial	General	Music/News	Classic Rock
KNFL	104.9	n/a	General	Music	Oldies
KENZ	107.5	n/a	General	Music	n/a

Note: Stations included cover the Salt Lake City DMA (Designated Market Area); n/a not available
BurrellesLuce, MediaContacts Online, January 2007

CLIMATE

Average and Extreme Temperatures

Temperature	Jan	Feb	Mar	Apr	May	Jun	Jul	Aug	Sep	Oct	Nov	Dec	Yr.
Extreme High (°F)	62	69	78	85	93	104	107	104	100	89	75	67	107
Average High (°F)	37	43	52	62	72	83	93	90	80	66	50	38	64
Average Temp. (°F)	28	34	41	50	59	69	78	76	65	53	40	30	52
Average Low (°F)	19	24	31	38	46	54	62	61	51	40	30	22	40
Extreme Low (°F)	-22	-14	2	15	25	35	40	37	27	16	-14	-15	-22

Note: Figures cover the years 1948-1990
Source: National Climatic Data Center, International Station Meteorological Climate Summary, 9/96

Average Precipitation/Snowfall/Humidity

Precip./Humidity	Jan	Feb	Mar	Apr	May	Jun	Jul	Aug	Sep	Oct	Nov	Dec	Yr.
Avg. Precip. (in.)	1.3	1.2	1.8	2.0	1.7	0.9	0.8	0.9	1.1	1.3	1.3	1.4	15.6
Avg. Snowfall (in.)	13	10	11	6	1	Tr	0	0	Tr	2	6	13	63
Avg. Rel. Hum. 5am (%)	79	77	71	67	66	60	53	54	60	68	75	79	67
Avg. Rel. Hum. 5pm (%)	69	59	47	38	33	26	22	23	28	40	59	71	43

Note: Figures cover the years 1948-1990; Tr = Trace amounts (<0.05 in. of rain; <0.5 in. of snow)
Source: National Climatic Data Center, International Station Meteorological Climate Summary, 9/96

Weather Conditions

Temperature			Daytime Sky			Precipitation		
5°F & below	32°F & below	90°F & above	Clear	Partly cloudy	Cloudy	0.01 inch or more precip.	0.1 inch or more snow/ice	Thunder-storms
7	128	56	94	152	119	92	38	38

Note: Figures are average number of days per year and cover the years 1948-1990
Source: National Climatic Data Center, International Station Meteorological Climate Summary, 9/96

HAZARDOUS WASTE

Superfund Sites

Lehi has no sites on the EPA's Superfund Final National Priorities List.
U.S. Environmental Protection Agency, Final National Priorities List, June 23, 2008

AIR & WATER QUALITY

Air Quality Index

Area	Percent of Days when Air Quality was...[2]				AQI Statistics	
	Good	Moderate	Unhealthy for Sensitive Groups	Unhealthy	Maximum	Median
MSA[1]	57.5	35.6	5.2	1.6	156	46

Note: The Air Quality Index (AQI) is an index for reporting daily air quality. EPA calculates the AQI for five major air pollutants regulated by the Clean Air Act: ground-level ozone, particle pollution (also known as particulate matter), carbon monoxide, sulfur dioxide, and nitrogen dioxide. The AQI runs from 0 to 500. The higher the AQI value, the greater the level of air pollution and the greater the health concern. There are six AQI categories: "Good" The AQI is between 0 and 50. Air quality is considered satisfactory; "Moderate" The AQI is between 51 and 100. Air quality is acceptable; "Unhealthy for Sensitive Groups" When AQI values are between 101 and 150, members of sensitive groups may experience health effects; "Unhealthy" When AQI values are between 151 and 200 everyone may begin to experience health effects; "Very Unhealthy" AQI values between 201 and 300 trigger a health alert; "Hazardous" AQI values over 300 trigger health warnings of emergency conditions; (1) Metropolitan Statistical Area - see Appendix A for areas included; (2) Based on 365 days with AQI data in 2007.
Source: U.S. Environmental Protection Agency, Air Quality Index Report, 2007

Air Quality Index Pollutants

Area	Percent of Days when AQI Pollutant was...[2]					
	Carbon Monoxide	Nitrogen Dioxide	Ozone	Sulfur Dioxide	Particulate Matter 2.5	Particulate Matter 10
MSA[1]	0.8	0.0	38.1	0.0	54.0	7.1

Note: The Air Quality Index (AQI) is an index for reporting daily air quality. EPA calculates the AQI for five major air pollutants regulated by the Clean Air Act: ground-level ozone, particle pollution (also known as particulate matter), carbon monoxide, sulfur dioxide, and nitrogen dioxide. The AQI runs from 0 to 500. The higher the AQI value, the greater the level of air pollution and the greater the health concern; (1) Metropolitan Statistical Area - see Appendix A for areas included; (2) Based on 365 days with AQI data in 2007.
Source: U.S. Environmental Protection Agency, Air Quality Index Report, 2007

Air Quality Index Trends

Area	Trend Sites								All Sites
	1999	2000	2001	2002	2003	2004	2005	2006	2006
MSA[1]	n/a	n/a	n/a	n/a	n/a	n/a	n/a	n/a	n/a

Note: An AQI value greater than 100 indicates that air quality would have been in the unhealthful range on that day. Data from exceptional events are not included. These counts are presented in two ways. First, the counts are based on sites having an adequate record of monitoring data during the trend period (trend sites). These counts represent the relative change in the number of days with AQI values greater than 100. In the last column, the counts are based on all sites with data in the most recent year (because it is possible for a site to have data in the most recent year but not enough data to be a trend site); (1) Metropolitan Statistical Area - see Appendix A for areas included; n/a not available.
Source: U.S. Environmental Protection Agency, Office of Air and Radiation, Air Trends, Factbook and Related Information, Air Pollution Trends in Selected Metropolitan Areas 2006

Maximum Air Pollutant Concentrations

	Particulate Matter 10 (ug/m^3)	Particulate Matter 2.5 (ug/m^3)	Ozone (ppm)	Carbon Monoxide (ppm)	Sulfur Dioxide (ppm)	Nitrogen Dioxide (ppm)	Lead (ug/m^3)
MSA[1] Level	90	32	0.101	3	n/a	0.029	n/a
NAAQS[2]	150	35	0.125	9	0.140	0.053	1.50
Met NAAQS[2]	Yes	Yes	Yes	Yes	n/a	Yes	n/a

Note: Data from exceptional events are not included; (1) Metropolitan Statistical Area - see Appendix A for areas included; (2) National Ambient Air Quality Standards; n/a not available
Concentrations: Particulate Matter 10 (coarse particulate) - highest second maximum 24-hour concentration; Particulate Matter 2.5 (fine particulate) - highest 98th percentile 24-hour concentration; Ozone - highest second daily maximum 1-hour concentration; Carbon Monoxide - highest second maximum non-overlapping 8-hour concentration; Sulfur Dioxide - highest second maximum 24-hour concentration; Nitrogen Dioxide - highest arithmetic mean concentration; Lead - highest quarterly maximum concentration
Units: ppm = parts per million; ug/m^3 = micrograms per cubic meter
Source: U.S. Environmental Protection Agency, MSA Factbook 2006, Air Quality Statistics by City

Drinking Water

Water System Name	Pop. Served	Primary Water Source Type	Violations[1]	
			Health Based	Monitoring/ Reporting
Lehi	39,900	Ground	0	0

Note: (1) Based on violation data from January 1, 2007 to December 31, 2007 (includes unresolved violations from earlier years)
Source: U.S. Environmental Protection Agency, Office of Ground Water and Drinking Water, Safe Drinking Water Information System (based on data extracted April 15, 2008)

South Jordan, Utah

Background

South Jordan, in southern Salt Lake County, is located 15 miles from Salt Lake City. The city adjoins West Jordan to the north, Sandy to the east, and Riverton to the south. Still in the first stages of growth, South Jordan is carefully planning for controlled future development in order to preserve the unique quality of life enjoyed by its citizens.

The state of Utah experienced a tremendous growth spurt during the 1990s, upon which South Jordan is capitalizing as it clears and zones substantial tracts of land for business development. Close proximity to Salt Lake City International Airport also favorably positions South Jordan for growth.

The region's first inhabitants were the Ute Indians. Mormon pioneers began immigrating to the area in July 1847, and within two years, several communities emerged throughout the valley. A small number of settlers traveled across the Jordan River to establish homes and farms, raise livestock, and grow grain and alfalfa. South Jordan itself was settled in 1857 by Alexander and Catherine Lince Beckstead. After digging their first home out of a cave in the riverbank, the Beckstead family built the "Beckstead Ditch," bringing water from the Jordan River to irrigate crops.

South Jordan was primarily a rural farming community in its earliest years. During most of the twentieth century, the area's major crop was sugar beets, but today, only grain and hay are grown to feed horses and cattle. South Jordan was incorporated in 1935.

The city has six elementary schools, two middle schools and one high school. In Salt Lake City, higher learning is represented by the University of Utah, Westminster College, L.D.S. Business College, and Salt Lake Community College, among others.

South Jordan lies in an extraordinarily beautiful region. The Bingham open-pit copper mine and the Oquirrh Mountains are visible several miles to the west. Over 233 acres of land are either already developed or have been set aside for parklands, and there are over 10 golf courses in the area, including a private golf course within the city, as well as a county-operated equestrian complex and racetrack. The ski resorts closest to South Jordan have an average annual snowfall of nearly 42 feet covering a wide variety of terrain from gentle runs and winding cross-country trails to helicopter-accessed peaks.

A wealth of cultural and recreational attractions can be pursued in nearby Salt Lake City, including the Utah Museum of Fine Arts, the Hansen Planetarium, Red Butte Botanical Gardens, the Tracy Aviary, the Utah Museum of Natural History, and the Hogle Zoo, among numerous others.

The climate of South Jordan, like that of Salt Lake City and other nearby communities, is semi-arid and continental, with some moderating of temperatures by the Great Salt Lake. Summers are generally hot and dry; winters are cold but not severe. Mountains act as a barrier to frequent invasions of cold air. Temperature inversions can occur in winter, when heavy fog at ground level is held down by warmer air aloft.

Rankings

General Rankings

- Salt Lake City* was ranked #27 out of 375 metro areas in *Cities Ranked & Rated*. Criteria: cost of living; climate; crime; transportation; economy and jobs; education; arts and culture; health and healthcare; leisure; quality of life. *Cities Ranked & Rated, 2nd Edition, 2007*
- Salt Lake City* was ranked #56 out of 379 metro areas in *Places Rated Almanac*. Criteria: health care; education; recreation; transportation; ambience; climate; crime; housing costs; jobs. *Places Rated Almanac, 7th Edition, 2007*

Business/Finance Rankings

- The nation's 100 largest metro areas were analysed in terms of the percentage of households entering some stage of foreclosure in 2007. The Salt Lake City* metro area ranked #52 out of 100 (#1 = highest foreclosure rate). *RealtyTrac, "Year-End 2007 Metropolitan Foreclosure Report"*
- The Salt Lake City* metro area was identified as one of the "10 Best Cities for Jobs in 2008" by *Forbes*. The metro area ranked #1. Criteria: state unemployment rate; job growth; income growth; median household income; cost of living. *Forbes.com, "Best Cities for Jobs in 2008," January 10, 2008*
- The Salt Lake City* metro area was selected one of America's "Top 50 Business Opportunity Metros" by *Expansion Management* in their 5th annual Mayor's Challenge ranking of metro areas that have achieved solid ratings across the board in numerous *EM* studies during the past 12 months. The area ranked #24. Criteria: public schools; quality of life; college educated workers; logistics infrastructure; healthcare costs; taxes and government spending; reputation among site consultants. *Expansion Management, August 2007*
- Salt Lake City* was selected as one of the best places to start and grow a company by *Entrepreneur* and the National Policy Research Council. The Salt Lake City* metro area ranked #42 out of 50 large metro areas. Criteria: business formation and growth (firms started four to 14 years ago that still employ at least 5 people and experienced rapid growth over the last four years). *Entrepreneur/National Policy Research Council, "Hot Cities for Entrepreneurs," September 2006*
- Intel, in partnership with Sperling's BestPlaces, ranked the 80 "Best Cities for Teleworking" in America. The Salt Lake City* metro area ranked #16 among mid-sized metro areas. The study identifies cities that hold the greatest potential for teleworking based on a host of factors including typical commuting times, fuel prices, availability of broadband Internet access and percentage of the population in telework friendly jobs. The study also factored in extreme climate and natural hazards. *Intel, "Best Cities for Teleworking," March 30, 2006*
- The Salt Lake City* metro area appeared on the Milken Institute "2007 Best Performing Cities" index. Rank: #18 out of 200 large metro areas. Criteria: job growth; wage and salary growth; high-tech output growth. *Milken Institute, "2007 Best Performing Cities"*
- The Salt Lake City* metro area was selected as one of the hottest cities for entrepreneurs in America by *Inc. Magazine.* Criteria: job-growth data for 393 metro was analyzed for current-year employment growth, average annual employment growth over past three years, and employment growth by industry sector. The Salt Lake City* metro area ranked #10 among large metro areas and #68 overall. *Inc. Magazine, May 2007*
- Salt Lake City* was identified as one of the 100 "Most Unwired Cities" in the U.S. The area ranked #33 out of the 100 largest metro areas in the U.S. Criteria: number of public and commercial wireless access points (hotspots); airports with wireless Internet access; broadband availability; local wireless networks; and wireless email devices. *Intel, "Most Unwired Cities Survey," June 7, 2005*

- Salt Lake City* was ranked #34 out of 125 regions worldwide in terms of its "Knowledge Competitiveness Index." The index attempts to measure the knowledge-based development taking place throughout the world and is based on 19 measures of economic performance that indicate a region's ability to translate its knowledge capacity into economic value. *Robert Huggins Associates, World Knowledge Competitiveness Index 2005*

- *Forbes* ranked the 200 most populous metro areas in the U.S. in terms of the "Best Places for Business and Careers." The Salt Lake City* metro area was ranked #82. Criteria: business costs (labor, energy, tax and office space expenses); living costs (housing, transportation, food and other household expenditures); education levels of the work force; job growth; income growth; migration trends; crime rates; and culture/leisure. *Forbes, "Best Places for Business and Careers," March 19, 2008*

- Salt Lake City* was identified as one of the top 20 metro areas with the highest rate of house price appreciation in 2007. The area ranked #7 with a one-year price appreciation of 9.7% through the 4th quarter 2007. *Office of Federal Housing Enterprise Oversight, House Price Index, 4th Quarter 2007*

- *Fortune* ranked the 100 largest metro areas in the U.S. in terms of projected median home price change in 2007. The Salt Lake City* metro area ranked #4. *Fortune.com, "Hot Spots, Cold Spots"*

Health/Environment Rankings

- 100 of the largest metro areas in the U.S. were analyzed in terms of their current drought severity. The Salt Lake City* metro area ranked #5 (#1 = driest). The rankings were based on statistics such as long-term precipitation trends and patterns and the Palmer drought indices. *Sperling's BestPlaces, www.BestPlaces.net, "America's Drought-Riskiest Cities," November 2007*

- *Reader's Digest* ranked the 50 largest metro areas in the U.S. in terms of how "clean" they are. The Salt Lake City* metro area ranked #18. Criteria: air quality; water quality; toxic industrial pollution; Superfund sites; and sanitation. *Reader's Digest, "The 50 Cleanest (and Dirtiest) Cities in America," July 2005*

- The American Academy of Dermatology ranked 32 U.S. metropolitan regions in terms of their residents knowledge, attitude and behaviors towards tanning and sun protection. The Salt Lake City* metro area ranked #7. The results of the study are based on an online national survey of 3,342 respondents. *American Academy of Dermatology, "RAYS: Your Grade," May 7, 2007*

- The Salt Lake City* metro area appeared in *Country Home's* "2008 Best Green Places" report. The area ranked #133 out of 379. Criteria: official energy policies; green power; green buildings; availability of fresh, locally grown food. *Country Home, "2008 Best Green Places"*

- Wyeth Consumer Healthcare, in partnership with Sperling's BestPlaces, ranked the nation's 50 most populous metro areas in terms of five key health factors. The Salt Lake City* metro area ranked #5. Criteria: physical activity; health status; nutrition; lifestyle pursuits; and mental wellness. *Wyeth Consumer Healthcare, "Centrum Healthiest Cities Study," April 19, 2005*

- Salt Lake City* was identified as a "2008 Asthma Capital." The area ranked #58 out of the nation's 100 largest metropolitan areas. Twelve factors were used to identify the most challenging places to live for people with asthma: estimated prevalence; self-reported prevalence; crude death rate for asthma; annual pollen score; annual air quality; public smoking laws; number of board-certified asthma specialists; school inhaler access laws; rescue medication use; controller medication use; uninsured rate; poverty rate. *Asthma and Allergy Foundation of America, "2008 Asthma Capitals"*

- Salt Lake City* was identified as a "Spring Allergy Capital." The area ranked #60 out of 100. Three groups of factors were used to identify the most severe cities for people with allergies during the spring season: annual pollen levels; medicine utilization; access to board-certified allergists. *Asthma and Allergy Foundation of America, "2007 Spring Allergy Capital Rankings"*

- Salt Lake City* was identified as a "Fall Allergy Capital." The area ranked #63 out of 100. Three groups of factors were used to identify the most severe cities for people with allergies during the fall season: annual pollen levels; medicine utilization; access to board-certified allergists. *Asthma and Allergy Foundation of America, "2007 Fall Allergy Capital Rankings"*

- Ortho-McNeil Neurologics, in partnership with Sperling's BestPlaces, analyzed 110 metro areas and identified those U.S. cities with the highest prevalence of factors that are most commonly associated with migraine headaches. The Salt Lake City* metro area ranked #21. Criteria: number of migraine-related drug prescriptions per capita; lifestyle factors that can contribute to migraines; environmental factors that can trigger migraines; and consumption of migraine-triggering foods. *Ortho-McNeil Neurologics, "America's Migraine Hot Spots," March 14, 2006*

- Sperling's BestPlaces ranked 331 metro areas and identified the most and least stressful U.S. cities. The Salt Lake City* metro area ranked #64 out of the 100 largest metro areas (#1 = most stressful). Criteria: divorce rate; unemployment rate; violent and property crime; suicide rate; commute time; mental health; alcohol consumption; cloudy days. *Sperling's BestPlaces, www.BestPlaces.net, "America's Most (and Least) Stressful Cities," January 9, 2004*

- An analysis of the "Best & Worst Cities for Sleep" was conducted by Sperling's BestPlaces. The study ranked America's 50 most populated metro areas. The Salt Lake City* metro area ranked #31 (#1 = best city for sleep). Criteria: number of days residents didn't get enough rest or sleep during the past month; average length of daily commute; divorce rate; unemployment rate. *Sperling's BestPlaces, www.BestPlaces.net, "Best & Worst Cities for Sleep," 2006*

- Sperling's BestPlaces in partnership with Vistakon ranked the 100 largest metro areas and identified "America's 10 Worst Cities for Comfortable Eyes." The Salt Lake City* metro area ranked #3. Criteria: altitude; sunny days; wind; extreme temperatures; humidity; pollution; commute time; computer use. *Vistakon, "America's Best and Worst Cities for Comfortable Eyes," June 15, 2004*

- Salt Lake City* was selected as one of "America's Pet Healthiest Cities" by Purina. The city ranked #10 out of 50. Criteria: veterinary services; environment; legislation; preventative care; obesity/body condition. *Purina Pet Institute, "America's Pet Healthiest Cities," May 20, 2003*

Women/Minorities Rankings

- Salt Lake City* was ranked #30 out of 100 metro areas in *SELF Magazine's* ranking of "America's Best Places for Women." A panel of experts came up with more than 50 criteria including death and disease rates, environmental indicators, community resources, and lifestyle habits. *SELF Magazine, "America's Best Places for Women 2007," December 2007*

Seniors/Retirement Rankings

- Sperling's BestPlaces in partnership with Bankers Life & Casualty Company designed a survey to identify the top 50 metro areas in the U.S. that offer the best overall qualities for senior living. The Salt Lake City* metro area ranked #12. The following criteria were statistically weighted to reflect the needs of the senior population: health; disease; economics; social; environment; spiritual; transportation; housing; and crime. *Bankers Life & Casualty Company, "Best Cities for Seniors 2005"*

- A.G. Edwards ranked America's 500 top-performing communities based on their residents' personal savings and investing behavior. The Salt Lake City* metro area ranked #100 with an index score of 106.66 (national average = 100.00). A dozen statistical factors were measured including: participation in retirement savings plans; personal debt levels; and home ownership. *A.G. Edwards, "2007 Nest Egg Index", September 12, 2007*

Children/Family Rankings

- The Salt Lake City* metro area was selected as one of the "Best Cities for Relocating Families" by Worldwide ERC and Primacy Relocation. The 2007 study placed a special emphasis on the housing market, which has significantly impacted the relocation industry and an employer's ability to transfer employees. The variables which weigh heavily in this category include home price, home affordability index, appreciation rates, and property tax. Other criteria include cost of living, crime rates, education, climate, focus on diversity, physicians per capita, recreation and leisure, arts and culture, air quality, watershed quality, sales tax, unemployment rate, job growth, high school and higher education index, school expenditures per student, students in public school, SAT/ACT percentile, and population growth. *Worldwide ERC and Primacy Relocation, "2007 Best Cities for Relocating Families"*

Safety Rankings

- The National Insurance Crime Bureau ranked 361 metro areas in the U.S. in terms of per capita rates of vehicle theft. The Salt Lake City* metro area ranked #34 (#1 = highest rate). Criteria: number of vehicle theft offenses per 100,000 inhabitants. *National Insurance Crime Bureau, "NICB Vehicle Theft Study," April 22, 2008*

- Salt Lake City* appeared on Sperling's BestPlaces list of the "Riskiest Cities for Identity Theft." The area ranked #7 out of the nations 50 largest metro areas. Over 80 criteria were analyzed across four major categories: technology impact; crime; transactions; and risk profile. *Sperling's BestPlaces, www.BestPlaces.net, "Riskiest Cities for Identity Theft," July 2006*

- Farmers Insurance Group of Companies, in partnership with Sperling's BestPlaces, ranked 379 metro areas and identified the "Most Secure U.S. Place to Live." The Salt Lake City* metro area ranked #64 out of 114 in the large metro area category (500,000 or more residents). Criteria: crime rates; extreme weather; risk of natural disasters; environmental hazards; terrorism threats; air quality; life expectancy; job loss numbers. *Farmers Insurance Group, "Most Secure U.S. Places to Live 2007"*

- Salt Lake City* was identified as one of the most dangerous large metro areas for pedestrians in the U.S. The area ranked #31 out of the nations 50 largest metro areas. Criteria: average yearly pedestrian fatalities per capita (for the years 2002 and 2003) adjusted for the number of walkers. *Surface Transportation Policy Project, "Mean Streets 2004"*

Sports/Recreation Rankings

- The Salt Lake City* metro area appeared on the *Sporting News* list of the "Best Sports Cities 2007". The area ranked #22 out of 150 cities in the U.S. *Sporting News* takes a 12-month snapshot, roughly July to July, of each city's sports, putting a heavy premium on regular-season won-lost records (from the most recently completed season). Other criteria include: playoff berths, bowl appearances and tournament bids; championships; applicable power ratings; quality of competition; overall fan fervor as measured in part by attendance as percentage of venue capacity; abundance of teams (rewarding quality over quantity); stadium and arena quality; ticket availability and prices; franchise ownership; and marquee appeal of athletes. *SportingNews.com, "Best Sports Cities 2007," August 1, 2007*

- Scarborough Research, a leading market research firm, identified the top local markets for video gaming households. The Salt Lake City* DMA (Designated Market Area) ranked in the top 10 with 32% of households reporting that they own a video game system. *Scarborough Research, March 14, 2007*

- Scarborough Research, a leading market research firm, identified the top local markets for avid NBA fans. The Salt Lake City* DMA (Designated Market Area) ranked in the top 10 with 13% of consumers 18 years and over reporting that they are "very interested in the NBA". *Scarborough Research, April 24, 2006*

- The Salt Lake City* metro area was selected by *Cranium* as one of the "Top 50 Fun Cities" in America. The area ranked #9. Criteria includes: number of sports teams, restaurants, and dance performances; number of toy stores; city budget spent on recreation. *Cranium, November 4, 2003*

- *Golf Digest* ranked 330 metro areas in the U.S. in terms of golf. The Salt Lake City* metro area was ranked #210. Criteria: access to golf; weather; value of golf; and quality of golf. *Golf Digest, "Metro Golf Rankings," August 2005*

Dating/Romance Rankings

- Eli Lily and Company, in partnership with Sperling's BestPlaces, ranked the nation's 50 largest metro areas in terms of the "Most Romantic Cities for Baby Boomers." The Salt Lake City* metro area ranked #2. Criteria: marriage and divorce rates among "baby boomers" age 45 to 60; great restaurants; dance studios; chocolate, jewelry and flower sales. *Eli Lily and Company, "Most Romantic Cities for Baby Boomers," April 20, 2007*

- The Salt Lake City* metro area was selected as one of the "Best Cities for Relocating Singles" by Worldwide ERC and Primacy Relocation. The area ranked #65 out of the 100 largest metro areas in the U.S. Areas were selected based on the following criteria: a robust cost-of-living index; adventure and outdoor recreation opportunities; violent crime and property crime rates; percentage of the population that is unmarried (ages 25-34); ratio of single men and single women; affordability of quality higher education, including in-state and out-of-state tuition requirements and rates; number of newcomers to the area; commute times; tax rates; fee and occupancy rates for temporary housing and mini-storage; quality and quantity of collegiate and professional sporting events and fun, fan-friendly venues. *Worldwide ERC and Primacy Relocation, "2007 Best Cities for Relocating Singles," October 25, 2007*

- *Forbes* ranked the 40 most populous urbanized areas in the U.S. in terms of the "Best Cities for Singles." The Salt Lake City* metro area ranked #36. Criteria: number of singles; cost of living alone; nightlife; culture; job growth; coolness; and online dating. *Forbes.com, August 21, 2007*

- Sperling's BestPlaces in partnership with AXE Deodorant Bodyspray ranked 80 metro areas and identified "America's Best (and Worst) Cities for Dating." The Salt Lake City* metro area ranked #41 (#1 = best). Criteria: percentage of singles ages 18-24; population density; dating venues per capita. *AXE Deodorant Bodyspray, "America's Best (and Worst) Cities for Dating," May 2004*

Culture/Performing Arts Rankings

- Scarborough Research, a leading market research firm, identified the top local markets for rock concert attendance. The Salt Lake City* DMA (Designated Market Area) ranked in the top 25 with 14% of consumers, 18 years old and over, reporting that they have attended a rock concert during the past year. *Scarborough Research, June 14, 2004*

Miscellaneous Rankings

- South Jordan was identified as one of the 100 fastest-growing suburbs in America by "Forbes." The city ranked #48. Criteria: suburban cities, townships and villages with more than 10,000 people in 2000 were ranked by their population growth from 2000 to 2006. *Forbes.com, "America's Fastest-Growing Suburbs," July 16, 2007*

- The Salt Lake City* metro area was selected as one of the "Top 10 Most Independent Cities for Homesellers". The area ranked #8. The cities listed had more consumers choosing to sell their homes without the help of a real-estate agent than anywhere else. Data was based on geographical information for listings posted on ForSaleByOwner.com from January 1, 2007 through June 30, 2007. *ForSaleByOwner.com, October 1, 2007*

- Sperling's BestPlaces in partnership with Pep Boys ranked 77 metro areas and identified "America's Most Drivable Cities." The Salt Lake City* metro area ranked #51. Criteria: climate; road roughness; urban mobility; gas prices. *Pep Boys, "America's Most Drivable Cities," April 9, 2003*

- State Farm Insurance, in partnership with Sperling's BestPlaces, analyzed several key factors that contribute to overall family preparedness. The Salt Lake City* metro area ranked #1 out of the nation's 50 most populous metro areas. Criteria: quality of life; life insurance coverage; and investments. *State Farm Life Insurance, "Fiscally Fit Cities Report," July 20, 2004*

- A study by Sperling's BestPlaces examined which U.S. metro areas were most affected by high fuel prices in 2006. The Salt Lake City* metro area was ranked #35 out of 80 (#1 = most expensive city for driving). Rankings are based on the average dollars spent on gas per year by two driver households. Criteria: cost of regular-grade gasoline; average miles driven per day; average number of gallons each driver uses and wastes in traffic congestion each day. *Sperling's BestPlaces, www.bestplaces.net, "Pain at the Pump," May 18, 2006*

South Jordan is located within the Salt Lake City, UT Metropolitan Statistical Area.

Business Environment

CITY FINANCES

City Government Finances

Component	2004-2005 ($000)	2004-2005 ($ per capita)
Total Revenues	38,710	963
Total Expenditures	30,968	770
Debt Outstanding	69,743	1,735
Cash and Securities	38,254	951

Source: U.S Census Bureau, Government Finances 2004-2005

City Government Revenue by Source

Source	2004-2005 ($000)	2004-2005 ($ per capita)
General Revenue		
From Federal Government	359	9
From State Government	1,805	45
From Local Governments	0	0
Taxes		
Property	5,593	139
Sales	6,029	150
Personal Income	0	0
License	2,949	73
Charges	7,579	188
Liquor Store	0	0
Utility	7,504	187
Employee Retirement	0	0
Other	6,892	171

Source: U.S Census Bureau, Government Finances 2004-2005

City Government Expenditures by Function

Function	2004-2005 ($000)	2004-2005 ($ per capita)	2004-2005 (%)
General Expenditures			
Airports	0	0	0.0
Corrections	0	0	0.0
Education	0	0	0.0
Fire Protection	2,444	61	7.9
Governmental Administration	6,338	158	20.5
Health	0	0	0.0
Highways	1,907	47	6.2
Hospitals	0	0	0.0
Housing and Community Development	3,765	94	12.2
Interest on General Debt	3,040	76	9.8
Libraries	0	0	0.0
Parking	0	0	0.0
Parks and Recreation	1,298	32	4.2
Police Protection	2,857	71	9.2
Public Welfare	0	0	0.0
Sewerage	0	0	0.0
Solid Waste Management	1,227	31	4.0
Liquor Store	0	0	0.0
Utility	4,613	115	14.9
Employee Retirement	0	0	0.0
Other	3,479	87	11.2

Source: U.S Census Bureau, Government Finances 2004-2005

Municipal Bond Ratings

Area	Moody's
City	Aaa

Source: Mergent Bond Record, January 2008 (unless noted otherwise)

DEMOGRAPHICS

Population Growth

Area	1990 Census	2000 Census	2007 Estimate	2012 Projection	Population Growth (%) 1990-2000	Population Growth (%) 2000-2012
City	12,183	29,437	44,224	53,721	141.6	82.5
MSA[1]	768,075	968,858	1,055,059	1,116,816	26.1	15.3
U.S.	248,709,873	281,421,906	301,045,522	314,920,978	13.2	11.9

Note: (1) Metropolitan Statistical Area - see Appendix B for areas included
Source: Claritas, Inc.

Number of Households and Average Household Size

Area	2007 Estimate	2007 Average Household Size
City	11,498	3.85
MSA[1]	345,652	3.05
U.S.	113,668,003	2.65

Note: (1) Metropolitan Statistical Area - see Appendix B for areas included
Source: Claritas, Inc.

Race and Ethnicity

Area	White Alone[2]	Black Alone[2]	Asian Alone[2]	Other Race Alone[2]	Hispanic[3]
City	94.3	0.4	1.2	4.0	4.3
MSA[1]	84.4	1.2	2.7	11.7	14.9
U.S.	73.1	12.4	4.3	10.3	14.9

Note: Figures are 2007 estimates; (1) Metropolitan Statistical Area - see Appendix B for areas included (2) Alone is defined as not being in combination with one or more other races; (3) May be of any race.
Source: Claritas, Inc.

Ancestry

Area	German	Irish[2]	English	American	Italian	Polish	French[3]	Scottish
City	12.4	6.0	36.6	6.4	1.8	0.5	2.7	5.4
MSA[1]	12.0	6.2	27.4	6.4	2.8	0.8	2.3	4.3
U.S.	15.2	10.9	8.7	7.3	5.6	3.2	3.0	1.7

Note: Figures include multiple ancestry (e.g. if a person reported being Irish and Italian, they were included in both columns); (1) Metropolitan Statistical Area - see Appendix A for areas included; (2) Includes Celtic; (3) Includes Alsatian but excludes Basque
Source: Census 2000, Summary File 3

Foreign-Born Population

Area	Percent of Population Born in							
	Any Foreign Country	Europe	Asia	Africa	Oceania[2]	Canada	Mexico	Latin America[3]
City	3.1	1.0	0.8	0.0	0.2	0.4	0.3	0.3
MSA[1]	8.6	1.5	1.7	0.2	0.4	0.3	3.5	1.1
U.S.	11.1	1.7	2.9	0.3	0.1	0.3	3.3	2.5

Note: (1) Metropolitan Statistical Area - see Appendix A for areas included; (2) Includes Australia, New Zealand subregion, Melanesia, Micronesia, Polynesia, and Oceania n.e.c; (3) Includes Central America (excluding Mexico), South America, and the Caribbean.
Source: Census 2000, Summary File 3

Marriage Status

Area	Never Married	Now Married (excluding Separated)	Separated	Widowed	Divorced
City	27.3	65.3	0.7	2.5	4.2
MSA[1]	27.6	57.6	1.4	4.1	9.3
U.S.	27.1	54.4	2.2	6.6	9.7

Note: Figures are percentages and cover the population 15 years of age and older; (1) Metropolitan Statistical Area - see Appendix A for areas included
Source: Census 2000, Summary File 3

Age Distribution

Area	Percent of Population						
	Under Age 5	Age 5 to 17	Age 18 to 34	Age 35 to 49	Age 50 to 64	Age 65 to 79	80 Years and Over
City	8.8	30.5	20.5	24.3	11.4	3.1	1.4
MSA[1]	9.1	22.2	28.1	20.9	11.4	6.2	2.1
U.S.	6.8	18.9	23.7	23.5	14.8	9.2	3.2

Note: (1) Metropolitan Statistical Area - see Appendix A for areas included
Source: Census 2000, Summary File 3

Male/Female Ratio

Area	Males	Females	Males per 100 Females
City	22,207	22,017	100.9
MSA[1]	533,785	521,274	102.4
U.S.	148,320,305	152,725,217	97.1

Note: Figures are 2007 estimates; (1) Metropolitan Statistical Area - see Appendix B for areas included
Source: Claritas, Inc.

Religion

Area	Catholic	Southern Baptist	United Meth-odist	ELCA[1]	LDS[2]	Presby-terian Church USA	Jewish Est.	Muslim Est.
County	6.0	0.6	0.5	0.4	56.0	0.4	0.5	0.4
U.S.	22.0	7.1	3.7	1.8	1.5	1.1	2.2	0.6

Note: Figures are the number of adherents as a percentage of the total population; Adherents are defined as all members, including full members, their children and the estimated number of other participants who are not considered members (e.g. the baptized, those not confirmed, those regularly attending services, etc.); (1) Evangelical Lutheran Church in America; (2) The Church of Jesus Christ of Latter Day Saints
Source: Reprinted with permission from Religious Congregations and Membership in the United States 2000 (Nashville, Glenmary Research Center, 2002) Copyright Association of Statisticians of American Religious Bodies. All rights reserved.

ECONOMY

Gross Metropolitan Product

Area	2002	2003	2004	2005	2005 Rank[2]
MSA[1]	38.2	39.5	42.2	46.4	48

Note: Figures are in billions of dollars; (1) Salt Lake City, UT Metropolitan Statistical Area - see Appendix A for areas included; (2) Rank ranges from 1 to 361
Source: The U.S. Conference of Mayors, "U.S. Metro Economies: GMP - The Engines of America's Growth," January 2007

Economic Growth

Area	1995 GMP	2005 GMP	Average Annual Growth Rate	Growth Rate Rank[2]
MSA[1]	25.1	46.4	6.4	88

Note: Figures are in billions of dollars; GMP = Gross Metropolitan Product; (1) Salt Lake City, UT Metropolitan Statistical Area - see Appendix A for areas included; (2) Rank ranges from 1 to 361
Source: The U.S. Conference of Mayors, "U.S. Metro Economies: GMP - The Engines of America's Growth," January 2007

INCOME

Per Capita/Median/Average Income

Area	Per Capita ($)	Median Household ($)	Average Household ($)
City	25,627	88,398	98,428
MSA[1]	23,629	55,931	71,457
U.S.	25,495	49,280	66,670

Note: Figures are 2007 estimates; (1) Metropolitan Statistical Area - see Appendix B for areas included
Source: Claritas, Inc.

Household Income Distribution

Area	Percent of Households Earning							
	Under $15,000	$15,000 -24,999	$25,000 -34,999	$35,000 -49,999	$50,000 -74,999	$75,000 -99,000	$100,000 -149,999	$150,000 and up
City	2.1	3.2	3.5	8.1	21.1	22.3	29.2	10.5
MSA[1]	8.2	8.8	10.4	16.7	22.7	13.9	12.8	6.6
U.S.	13.1	10.9	11.2	15.6	19.5	11.9	11.3	6.6

Note: Figures are 2007 estimates; (1) Metropolitan Statistical Area - see Appendix B for areas included
Source: Claritas, Inc.

Poverty Rates by Age

Area	All Ages	Under 5 Years Old	5 to 17 Years Old	18 to 64 Years Old	65 Years and Over
City	1.7	0.2	0.7	0.7	0.1
MSA[1]	7.7	1.0	1.9	4.4	0.4
U.S.	12.4	1.2	3.0	6.9	1.2

Note: Figures are percent of population with income in 1999 below poverty level and only include population for whom poverty status is determined; (1) Metropolitan Statistical Area - see Appendix A for areas included
Source: Census 2000, Summary File 3

Personal Bankruptcy Filing Rate

Area	2004	2005	2006
Salt Lake County	10.59	10.75	2.57
U.S.	5.31	6.82	2.00

Note: Numbers are per 1,000 population and include Chapter 7 and Chapter 13 filings
Source: Federal Deposit Insurance Corporation (FDIC), Regional Economic Conditions (RECON), 8/23/2007

EMPLOYMENT

Labor Force and Employment

Area	Civilian Labor Force			Workers Employed		
	Dec. 2006	Dec. 2007	% Chg.	Dec. 2006	Dec. 2007	% Chg.
City	16,802	17,273	2.8	16,573	16,977	2.4
MSA[1]	596,424	614,462	3.0	583,449	597,668	2.4
U.S.	152,571,000	153,705,000	0.7	146,081,000	146,334,000	0.2

Note: Data is not seasonally adjusted and covers workers 16 years of age and older;
(1) Metropolitan Statistical Area - see Appendix B for areas included
Source: Bureau of Labor Statistics, http://stats.bls.gov

Unemployment Rate

Area	2007											
	Jan.	Feb.	Mar.	Apr.	May	Jun.	Jul.	Aug.	Sep.	Oct.	Nov.	Dec.
City	1.7	1.6	1.5	1.5	1.4	1.7	1.7	1.8	1.6	1.6	1.6	1.7
MSA[1]	2.7	2.6	2.4	2.3	2.3	2.7	2.7	2.9	2.6	2.6	2.6	2.7
U.S.	5.0	4.9	4.5	4.3	4.3	4.7	4.9	4.6	4.5	4.4	4.5	4.8

Note: Data is not seasonally adjusted and covers workers 16 years of age and older; All figures are percentages; (1) Metropolitan Statistical Area - see Appendix B for areas included
Source: Bureau of Labor Statistics, http://stats.bls.gov

Employment by Occupation

Occupation Classification	City (%)	MSA[1] (%)	U.S. (%)
Sales and Office	32.7	30.8	26.7
Professional and Related	18.7	19.1	20.2
Service	10.6	13.0	14.9
Production, Transportation, and Material Moving	10.2	13.3	14.6
Management, Business, and Financial	18.8	13.6	13.5
Construction, Extraction, and Maintenance	9.0	10.0	9.4
Farming, Forestry, and Fishing	0.1	0.2	0.7

Note: Figures cover employed civilians 16 years of age and older;
(1) Metropolitan Statistical Area - see Appendix A for areas included
Source: Census 2000, Summary File 3

Employment by Industry

Sector	MSA[1] Number of Employees	MSA[1] Percent of Total	U.S. Percent of Total
Government	93,600	14.3	16.3
Education and Health Services	61,500	9.4	13.4
Professional and Business Services	101,900	15.5	13.1
Retail Trade	75,600	11.5	11.6
Manufacturing	58,800	9.0	9.9
Leisure and Hospitality	60,800	9.3	9.6
Financial Activities	52,700	8.0	5.9
Construction	n/a	n/a	5.3
Wholesale Trade	31,500	4.8	4.4
Other Services	19,800	3.0	3.9
Transportation and Utilities	31,600	4.8	3.7
Information	19,100	2.9	2.2
Natural Resources and Mining	n/a	n/a	0.5

Note: Figures cover non-farm employment as of December 2007 and are not seasonally adjusted; (1) Metropolitan Statistical Area - see Appendix B for areas included; n/a not available
Source: Bureau of Labor Statistics, http://stats.bls.gov

Average Wages

Occupation	$/Hr.	Occupation	$/Hr.
Accountants and Auditors	29.12	Maids and Housekeeping Cleaners	8.69
Automotive Mechanics	18.64	Maintenance and Repair Workers	16.60
Bookkeepers	14.43	Marketing Managers	43.33
Carpenters	16.74	Nuclear Medicine Technologists	27.43
Cashiers	8.84	Nurses, Licensed Practical	18.41
Clerks, General Office	11.85	Nurses, Registered	28.07
Clerks, Receptionists/Information	10.45	Nursing Aides/Orderlies/Attendants	10.39
Clerks, Shipping/Receiving	12.84	Packers and Packagers, Hand	9.74
Computer Programmers	38.00	Physical Therapists	34.31
Computer Support Specialists	20.31	Postal Service Mail Carriers	21.30
Computer Systems Analysts	33.25	Real Estate Brokers	33.09
Cooks, Restaurant	10.53	Retail Salespersons	11.99
Dentists	n/a	Sales Reps., Exc. Tech./Scientific	27.93
Electrical Engineers	39.78	Sales Reps., Tech./Scientific	35.34
Electricians	20.21	Secretaries, Exc. Legal/Med./Exec.	13.29
Financial Managers	45.48	Security Guards	12.44
First-Line Supervisors/Mgrs., Sales	18.97	Surgeons	n/a
Food Preparation Workers	8.40	Teacher Assistants	10.00
General and Operations Managers	45.74	Teachers, Elementary School	22.00
Hairdressers/Cosmetologists	9.07	Teachers, Secondary School	24.90
Internists	n/a	Telemarketers	10.80
Janitors and Cleaners	10.00	Truck Drivers, Heavy/Tractor-Trailer	18.36
Landscaping/Groundskeeping Workers	10.87	Truck Drivers, Light/Delivery Svcs.	11.70
Lawyers	58.49	Waiters and Waitresses	9.43

Note: Wage data covers the Salt Lake City, UT Metropolitan Statistical Area - see Appendix B for areas included. Hourly wages for elementary/secondary school teachers and teacher assistants were calculated by the editors from annual wage data assuming a 40 hour work week; n/a not available.
Source: Bureau of Labor Statistics, May 2007 Metro Area Occupational Employment and Wage Estimates

RESIDENTIAL REAL ESTATE

Building Permits

Area	Single-Family			Multi-Family			Total		
	2006	2007p	Pct. Chg.	2006	2007p	Pct. Chg.	2006	2007p	Pct. Chg.
City	1,088	798	-26.7	0	36	-	1,088	834	-23.3
U.S.	1,378,200	973,300	-29.4	460,700	407,200	-11.6	1,838,900	1,380,500	-24.9

Note: (p) preliminary; figures cover and represent new, privately-owned housing units authorized (unadjusted data); All permit data are based on estimates with imputation; U.S. figures are based on the new 20,000-place series.
Source: U.S. Census Bureau, Manufacturing, Mining, and Construction Statistics

Homeownership and Housing Vacancies

Area	Homeownership Rate[2] (%)			Rental Vacancy Rate[3] (%)			Homeowner Vacancy Rate[4] (%)		
	2005	2006	2007	2005	2006	2007	2005	2006	2007
MSA[1]	68.8	69.6	71.8	7.0	4.7	5.3	1.5	2.7	2.2
U.S.	68.9	68.8	68.1	9.8	9.8	9.7	1.9	2.4	2.7

Note: (1) Metropolitan Statistical Area - see Appendix B for areas included; (2) The proportion of households that are owners; (3) The proportion of the rental inventory that is vacant for rent; (4) The proportion of the homeowner inventory that is vacant for sale; n/a not available
Source: U.S. Census Bureau, Housing Vacancies and Homeownership Annual Statistics: 2007

TAXES

State Corporate Income Tax Rates

State	Rates and Tax Brackets
Utah	5.0%

Note: Tax rates as of January 1, 2008; Minimum tax $100.
Source: Tax Foundation, www.taxfoundation.org

State Individual Income Tax Rates

State	Federal Deductibility	Marginal Rates (%)	Standard Deduction ($)		Personal Exemptions ($)[1]	
			Single	Joint	Single	Dependents
Utah	Yes (bb)	2.3 - 6.98 (cc)	5,150 (s)	10,300 (s)	2,475 (q)	2,475 (q)

Note: Tax rates as of January 1, 2008; Local- and county-level taxes are not included; n/a not applicable; (1) Married joint filers generally receive double the single exemption; (q) Three fourths federal exemption; (s) Deductions and exemptions tied to federal tax system. Federal deductions and exemptions are indexed for inflation; (bb) Half of federal income tax deductible; (cc) An optional 5.35% flat tax will be available.
Source: Tax Foundation, www.taxfoundation.org

Various State and Local Tax Rates

State and Local Sales and Use (%)	State Sales and Use (%)	Gasoline[1,2] ($/gal.)	Cigarette ($/pack)	Spirits ($/gal.)	Table Wine ($/gal.)	Beer ($/gal.)
6.8	4.65	0.245	0.695	10.13 (n)	(p)	0.41

Note: Tax rates as of January 1, 2008; (1) In addition to the 18.4 cpg Federal gasoline tax; (2) Rates may include additional state sales taxes, environmental protection and storage fees/taxes, and local taxes. When necessary, the volume-weighted average of all local taxes is used to approximate the typical statewide rate including local tax; (n) The state government controls all sales. The implied excise tax rate is calculated using methodology designed by the Distilled Spirits Council of the United States (DISCUS); (p) All wine sales are through state-run stores. Revenue in these states is generated from various taxes, fees and net profits.
Source: Tax Foundation, www.taxfoundation.org; Original research

State Tax Burdens

Area	Combined State and Local Tax Burden		Combined Federal, State and Local Tax Burden	
	Percent	Rank	Percent	Rank
Utah	10.7	27	30.3	36
U.S. Average	11.0	-	32.7	-

Note: Figures cover 2007 and measure taxes as a percentage of income
Source: Tax Foundation, www.taxfoundation.org

State Business Tax Climate Index Rankings

State	Overall Rank	Corporate Tax Index Rank	Individual Income Tax Index Rank	Sales Tax Index Rank	Unemployment Insurance Tax Index Rank	Property Tax Index Rank
Utah	17	5	30	27	28	3

Note: Rankings range from 1 to 50 where 1 is best. Rankings do not average across to Overall Rank. States without a given tax are given a ranking of 1.
Source: Tax Foundation, State Business Tax Climate Index 2008

TRANSPORTATION

Means of Transportation to Work

Area	Car/Truck/Van		Public Transportation			Bicycle	Walked	Other Means	Worked at Home
	Drove Alone	Car-pooled	Bus	Subway	Railroad				
City	81.8	9.3	1.1	0.2	0.4	0.1	0.4	0.8	6.0
MSA[1]	77.2	13.1	2.5	0.1	0.2	0.4	1.8	0.9	3.8
U.S.	75.7	12.2	2.5	1.5	0.5	0.4	2.9	1.0	3.3

Note: Figures are percentages and cover workers 16 years of age and older; (1) Metropolitan Statistical Area - see Appendix A for areas included
Source: Census 2000, Summary File 3

Travel Time to Work

Area	Less Than 15 Minutes	15 to 29 Minutes	30 to 44 Minutes	45 to 59 Minutes	60 Minutes or More
City	20.4	38.9	28.6	6.9	5.2
MSA[1]	29.2	43.6	18.0	4.8	4.4
U.S.	29.4	36.1	19.1	7.4	8.0

Note: Figures are percentages and include workers 16 years old and over; (1) Metropolitan Statistical Area - see Appendix A for areas included
Source: Census 2000, Summary File 3

Travel Time Index

Area	1982	1995	2004	2005
Urban Area[1]	1.05	1.19	1.21	1.19
Average[2]	1.11	1.22	1.29	1.30

Note: Travel Time Index - The ratio of travel time in the peak period to the travel time at free-flow conditions. A value of 1.35 indicates a 20-minute free-flow trip takes 27 minutes in the peak. Free-flow speeds (60 mph on freeways and 35 mph on principal arterials) are used as the comparison threshold; (1) Covers the Salt Lake City, UT urban area; (2) average of 85 urban areas
Source: Texas Transportation Institute, The 2007 Urban Mobility Report, September 2007

Living Environment

COST OF LIVING

Cost of Living Index

Composite Index	Groceries	Housing	Utilities	Trans-portation	Health Care	Misc. Goods/ Services
101.1	102.3	99.2	87.7	103.6	99.2	105.5

Note: U.S. = 100; Figures cover the Salt Lake City UT urban area.
Source: The Council for Community and Economic Research (formerly ACCRA), Cost of Living Index, 2007

Grocery Prices

Area[1]	T-Bone Steak ($/pound)	Frying Chicken ($/pound)	Whole Milk ($/half gal.)	Eggs ($/dozen)	Orange Juice ($/64 oz.)	Coffee ($/11.5 oz.)
City[2]	9.29	1.29	1.89	1.46	3.19	3.56
Avg.	8.93	1.12	2.13	1.52	3.26	3.31
Min.	5.88	0.71	1.33	0.83	2.30	2.20
Max.	12.80	2.07	3.43	3.54	5.79	6.20

Note: (1) Values for the local area are compared with the average, minimum and maximum values for all 331 areas in the Cost of Living Index report; (2) Figures cover the Salt Lake City UT urban area; **T-Bone Steak** *(price per pound);* **Frying Chicken** *(price per pound, whole fryer);* **Whole Milk** *(half gallon carton);* **Eggs** *(price per dozen, Grade A, large);* **Orange Juice** *(64 oz. Tropicana or Florida Natural);* **Coffee** *(11.5 oz. can, vacuum-packed, Maxwell House, Hills Bros, or Folgers).*
Source: The Council for Community and Economic Research (formerly ACCRA), Cost of Living Index, 2007

Housing and Utility Costs

Area[1]	New Home Price ($)	Apartment Rent ($/month)	All Electric ($/month)	Part Electric ($/month)	Other Energy ($/month)	Telephone ($/month)
City[2]	307,604	777	-	53.08	73.82	26.91
Avg.	309,605	782	146.13	78.67	90.16	26.14
Min.	189,877	n/a	82.03	37.41	33.15	17.08
Max.	1,202,800	3,481	271.14	150.60	257.67	37.45

Note: (1) Values for the local area are compared with the average, minimum and maximum values for all 331 areas in the Cost of Living Index report; (2) Figures cover the Salt Lake City UT urban area; **New Home Price** *(2,400 sf living area, 8,000 sf lot, in urban area with full utilities);* **Apartment Rent** *(950 sf 2 bedroom/1.5 or 2 bath, unfurnished, excluding all utilities except water);* **All Electric** *(average monthly cost for an all-electric home);* **Part Electric** *(average monthly cost for a part-electric home);* **Other Energy** *(average monthly cost for natural gas, fuel oil, coal, wood, and any other forms of energy except electricity);* **Telephone** *(price includes basic monthly rate for a private residential line plus additional local usage charges incurred by a family of four).*
Source: The Council for Community and Economic Research (formerly ACCRA), Cost of Living Index, 2007

Health Care, Transportation, and Other Costs

Area[1]	Doctor ($/visit)	Dentist ($/visit)	Optometrist ($/visit)	Gasoline ($/gallon)	Beauty Salon ($/visit)	Men's Shirt ($)
City[2]	77.80	72.35	75.47	2.62	32.00	27.88
Avg.	79.48	71.93	79.55	2.64	29.52	25.77
Min.	52.08	44.80	43.95	2.19	15.58	16.19
Max.	148.44	126.27	158.83	3.48	60.62	48.53

Note: (1) Values for the local area are compared with the average, minimum and maximum values for all 331 areas in the Cost of Living Index report; (2) Figures cover the Salt Lake City UT urban area; **Doctor** *(general practitioners routine exam of an established patient);* **Dentist** *(adult teeth cleaning and periodic oral examination);* **Optometrist** *(full vision eye exam for established adult patient);* **Gasoline** *(one gallon regular unleaded, national brand, including all taxes, cash price at self-service pump if available);* **Beauty Salon** *(woman's shampoo, trim, and blow-dry);* **Men's Shirt** *(cotton/polyester dress shirt, pinpoint weave, long sleeves).*
Source: The Council for Community and Economic Research (formerly ACCRA), Cost of Living Index, 2007

HOUSING

House Price Index (HPI)

Area	National Ranking[2]	Quarterly Change (%)	One-Year Change (%)	Five-Year Change (%)
MSA[1]	7	0.49	9.68	59.84
U.S.[3]	-	0.10	0.84	41.37

Note: The HPI is a weighted repeat sales index. It measures average price changes in repeat sales or refinancings on the same properties. This information is obtained by reviewing repeat mortgage transactions on single-family properties whose mortgages have been purchased or securitized by Fannie Mae or Freddie Mac in January 1975; (1) Metropolitan Statistical Area - see Appendix B for areas included; (2) Rankings are based on annual percentage change for all metro areas containing at least 15,000 transactions over the last 10 years and ranges from 1 to 291; (3) figures based on a weighted average of Census Division estimates; all figures are for the period ending December 31, 2007
Source: Office of Federal Housing Enterprise Oversight, House Price Index, February 26, 2008

House Price Valuations

Area	Q1 2000	Q1 2001	Q1 2002	Q1 2003	Q1 2004	Q1 2005	Q1 2006	Q1 2007	Q1 2008
MSA[1]	-0.8	-5.6	-6.7	-2.6	-2.4	-3.2	8.0	19.1	16.1

Note: Figures show the percentage of over- or under-valuation of single family homes relative to statistically normal house values (e.g. a value of 23.6 indicates that house values are 23.6% overvalued). Statistically normal house values are based on house prices, interest rates, household incomes, population densities, and any historical premiums or discounts metropolitan areas have exhibited over time; (1) Figures cover the Metropolitan Statistical Area - see Appendix B for areas included
Source: Global Insight/National City Corporation, House Prices in America, May 2008

Median Home Prices

Area	2005	2006	2007[r]	Percent Change 2006 to 2007
MSA[1]	173.9	203.0	232.0	14.3
U.S. Average	219.0	221.9	217.9	-1.8

Note: Figures are median sales prices of existing single-family homes in thousands of dollars; (r) revised; n/a not available; (1) Metropolitan Statistical Area - see Appendix B for areas included
Source: National Association of Realtors, Metropolitan Area Prices, 1st Quarter 2008

Housing: Year Structure Built

Area	1990 -2000	1980 -1989	1970 -1979	1960 -1969	1950 -1959	1940 -1949	Before 1940	Median Year
City	62.2	17.0	13.3	3.6	1.4	0.7	1.8	1992
MSA[1]	22.0	16.4	22.5	11.9	11.7	6.0	9.4	1975
U.S.	17.0	15.8	18.5	13.7	12.7	7.3	15.0	1971

Note: Figures are percentages; (1) Metropolitan Statistical Area - see Appendix A for areas included
Source: Census 2000, Summary File 3

HEALTH

Health Risk Data

Category	Area[1] (%)	U.S. (%)
Adults who have been told they have high blood pressure[3]	19.2	25.5
Adults who have been told they have high blood cholesterol[3]	33.0	35.6
Adults who have been told they have diabetes[2]	6.3	7.5
Adults who have been told they have arthritis[3]	21.8	27.0
Adults who have been told they currently have asthma	9.8	8.5
Adults who are current smokers	11.1	20.1
Adults who are heavy drinkers[4]	3.1	4.9
Adults who are overweight (BMI 25.0 - 29.9)	33.2	36.5
Adults who are obese (BMI 30.0 - 99.8)	21.2	25.1

Note: Data as of 2006 unless otherwise noted; (1) Figures cover the Metropolitan Statistical Area - see Appendix B for areas included; (2) Figures do not include pregnancy-related diabetes, pre-diabetes or borderline diabetes; (3) 2005 data; (4) Heavy drinkers are classified as adult men having more than two drinks per day or adult women having more than one drink per day
Source: Centers for Disease Control and Prevention, Behaviorial Risk Factor Surveillance System, SMART: Selected Metropolitan/Micropolitan Area Risk Trends, 2005, 2006

Mortality Rates for the Top 10 Causes of Death in the U.S.

ICD-10[a] Sub-Chapter	ICD-10[a] Code	Age-Adjusted Mortality Rate[1] per 100,000 population	
		County[2]	U.S.
Malignant neoplasms	C00-C97	143.7	186.5
Ischaemic heart diseases	I20-I25	84.6	152.3
Other forms of heart disease	I30-I51	66.4	51.5
Cerebrovascular diseases	I60-I69	47.2	50.0
Chronic lower respiratory diseases	J40-J47	36.7	42.6
Diabetes mellitus	E10-E14	29.4	24.8
Other degenerative diseases of the nervous system	G30-G31	16.7	22.6
Other external causes of accidental injury	W00-X59	18.8	21.4
Influenza and pneumonia	J10-J18	23.3	20.7
Hypertensive diseases	I10-I13	11.5	18.2

Note: (a) ICD-10 = International Classification of Diseases 10th Revision; (1) Mortality rates are a three year average covering 2003-2005; (2) Figures cover Salt Lake County
Source: Centers for Disease Control and Prevention, National Center for Health Statistics. Compressed Mortality File 1999-2004. CDC WONDER On-line Database, compiled from Compressed Mortality File 1999-2005 Series 20 No. 2K, 2008.

Mortality Rates for Selected Causes of Death

ICD-10[a] Sub-Chapter	ICD-10[a] Code	Age-Adjusted Mortality Rate[1] per 100,000 population	
		County[2]	U.S.
Assault	X85-Y09	3.3	5.9
Human immunodeficiency virus (HIV) disease	B20-B24	1.7	4.5
Intentional self-harm	X60-X84	16.3	10.8
Malnutrition	E40-E46	*0.9	1.0
Obesity and other hyperalimentation	E65-E68	1.6	1.4
Organic, including symptomatic, mental disorders	F01-F09	39.4	16.8
Transport accidents	V01-V99	13.5	16.1
Viral hepatitis	B15-B19	0.9	1.8

Note: (a) ICD-10 = International Classification of Diseases 10th Revision; (1) Mortality rates are a three year average covering 2003-2005; (2) Figures cover Salt Lake County; (*) Unreliable data as per CDC
Source: Centers for Disease Control and Prevention, National Center for Health Statistics. Compressed Mortality File 1999-2004. CDC WONDER On-line Database, compiled from Compressed Mortality File 1999-2005 Series 20 No. 2K, 2008.

Distribution of Physicians[1]

Area	Total	Family/ General Practice	Specialties	
			Medical	Surgical
Salt Lake County (number)	2,119	430	750	496
Salt Lake County (rate per 10,000 pop.)	22.3	4.5	7.9	5.2
U.S. (rate per 10,000 pop.)	17.7	4.6	6.9	4.3

Note: Data as of 2005; (1) Includes all non-federal, patient-care, office-based MDs
Source: Area Resource File (ARF). June 2007. U.S. Department of Health and Human Services, Health Resources and Services Administration, Bureau of Health Professions, Rockville, MD.

Hospitals

There were no hospitals listed within the city limits.
AHA Guide to the Healthcare Field 2008

According to *U.S. News,* the Salt Lake City, UT metro area is home to three of the best hospitals in the U.S.: **LDS Hospital**; **Primary Children's Medical Center**; **University of Utah Hospitals and Clinics**. *U.S. News Online, "America's Best Hospitals 2007"*

EDUCATION

Public School District Statistics

District Name	Schls	Pupils	Pupil/ Teacher Ratio	Minority Pupils[1] (%)	Free Lunch Eligible[2] (%)	IEP[3] (%)
Jordan District	92	77,110	24.7	11.8	14.7	13.0

Note: Table includes regular local school districts with 2,000 or more students; (1) Percentage of students that are not white, non-Hispanic; (2) Percentage of students that are eligible for the free lunch program; (3) Percentage of students that have an Individualized Education Program.
Source: U.S. Department of Education, National Center for Education Statistics, Common Core of Data, Local Education Agency (School District) Universe Survey: School Year 2005-2006; U.S. Department of Education, National Center for Education Statistics, Common Core of Data, Public Elementary/Secondary School Universe Survey: School Year 2005-2006

Highest Level of Education

Area	Less than H.S.	H.S. Diploma	Some College, No Deg.	Associate Degree	Bachelors Degree	Masters Degree	Profess. School Degree	Doctorate Degree
City	4.3	22.6	33.3	9.2	22.5	6.6	1.0	0.4
MSA[1]	12.6	24.1	28.1	7.6	18.6	5.7	2.1	1.1
U.S.	19.4	28.4	21.2	6.4	15.7	5.9	2.0	1.0

Note: Figures are 2007 estimated percentages and cover persons age 25 and over; (1) Metropolitan Statistical Area - see Appendix B for areas included
Source: Claritas, Inc.

Educational Attainment by Race

Area	High School Graduate (%)					Bachelor's Degree (%)				
	Total	White	Black	Asian	Hisp.[2]	Total	White	Black	Asian	Hisp.[2]
City	95.8	96.3	80.9	89.9	84.1	30.9	31.1	29.8	46.8	15.2
MSA[1]	87.5	89.9	83.0	78.2	56.5	26.5	27.6	19.5	34.8	9.4
U.S.	80.4	83.6	72.3	80.4	52.4	24.4	26.1	14.3	44.1	10.4

Note: Figures shown cover persons 25 years old and over; (1) Metropolitan Statistical Area - see Appendix A for areas included; (2) people of Hispanic origin can be of any race
Source: Census 2000, Summary File 3

School Enrollment by Type

Area	Grades KG to 8				Grades 9 to 12			
	Public		Private		Public		Private	
	Enrollment	%	Enrollment	%	Enrollment	%	Enrollment	%
City	5,718	96.3	220	3.7	3,230	97.2	93	2.8
MSA[1]	189,691	94.4	11,196	5.6	93,135	95.6	4,302	4.4
U.S.	33,526,011	88.7	4,285,121	11.3	14,848,628	90.6	1,532,323	9.4

Note: Figures shown cover persons 3 years old and over; (1) Metropolitan Statistical Area - see Appendix A for areas included
Source: Census 2000, Summary File 3

School Enrollment by Race

Area	Grades KG to 8 (%)				Grades 9 to 12 (%)			
	White	Black	Asian	Hisp.[1]	White	Black	Asian	Hisp.[1]
City	95.5	0.3	0.5	4.2	95.0	0.5	1.0	2.0
MSA[2]	85.4	1.1	1.7	12.7	87.1	1.0	2.1	10.6
U.S.	68.5	15.5	3.3	16.8	68.8	15.5	3.8	15.7

Note: Figures shown cover persons 3 years old and over; (1) people of Hispanic origin can be of any race; (2) Metropolitan Statistical Area - see Appendix A for areas included
Source: Census 2000, Summary File 3

Average Salaries of Public School Classroom Teachers

District	2005-06 Dollars	2005-06 Rank[1]	2006-07 Dollars	2006-07 Rank[1]	Percent Change 2005-06 to 2006-07
Utah	40,007	46	40,566	47	1.40
U.S. Average	49,026	-	50,816	-	3.65

Note: (1) State rank ranges from 1 to 51.
Source: National Education Association, Rankings & Estimates: Rankings of the States 2006 and Estimates of School Statistics 2007, December 2007

Higher Education

Four-Year Colleges			Two-Year Colleges			Medical Schools[1]	Law Schools[2]	Voc/ Tech[3]
Public	Private Non-profit	Private For-profit	Public	Private Non-profit	Private For-profit			
0	0	1	0	0	0	0	0	0

Note: Figures cover institutions located within the city limits; (1) includes schools accredited by the Liaison Committee on Medical Education and the American Osteopathic Association; (2) includes American Bar Association-accredited law schools; (3) includes all schools with programs that are less than 2 years.
Source: National Center for Education Statistics, The Integrated Postsecondary Education System (IPEDS) Peer Analysis System, 2007; www.usnews.com, Law and Medical School Directories, 2009

PRESIDENTIAL ELECTION

2004 Presidential Election Results

Area	Bush	Kerry	Nader	Other
Salt Lake County	59.6	37.5	1.7	1.2
U.S.	50.7	48.3	0.4	0.6

Note: Results are percentages and may not add to 100% due to rounding
Source: Dave Leip's Atlas of U.S. Presidential Elections, www.uselectionatlas.org

EMPLOYERS

Major Employers

Company Name	Industry	Type of Site
American Express	Short-term business credit	Branch
Arup Laboratories	Medical laboratories	Single
Cottonwood Hospital	General medical and surgical hospitals	Single
Discover Financial Services	Short-term business credit	Branch
Edo Electro Ceramic Products	Search and navigation equipment	Single
Kennecott Corporation	Gold ores	Headquarters
LDS Church	Religious organizations	Branch
Marketstar Corporation	Management consulting services	Single
Mormon Church	Religious organizations	Headquarters
National Guard Utah	National security	Headquarters
Service Center	Finance, taxation, and monetary policy	Branch
Sportsmans Warehouse	Sporting goods and bicycle shops	Single
US Post Office	U.S. postal service	Branch
Unibase Technologies	Data processing and preparation	Headquarters
University Utah Hsptals Clnics	General medical and surgical hospitals	Headquarters

Note: Companies shown are located within the Salt Lake City metropolitan area; nec = not elsewhere classified.
Source: www.zapdata.com, May 2008

PUBLIC SAFETY

Crime Rate

Area	All Crimes	Violent Crimes				Property Crimes		
		Murder	Forcible Rape	Robbery	Aggrav. Assault	Burglary	Larceny -Theft	Motor Vehicle Theft
City	2,194.2	0.0	16.9	14.5	53.0	315.5	1,620.9	173.4
Metro[1]	5,195.3	2.2	44.3	88.4	210.6	743.9	3,535.6	570.4
U.S.	3,808.1	5.7	30.9	149.4	287.5	729.4	2,206.8	398.4

Note: Figures are crimes per 100,000 population; (1) Metropolitan Statistical Area - see Appendix B for areas included
Source: FBI Uniform Crime Reports, 2006

Hate Crimes

Area	Number of Quarters Reported	Bias Motivation				
		Race	Religion	Sexual Orientation	Ethnicity	Disability
City	4	2	0	2	0	0

Source: Federal Bureau of Investigation, Hate Crime Statistics 2006

RECREATION

Culture

Dance[1]	Theatre[1]	Instrumental Music[1]	Vocal Music[1]	Series/ Festivals	Museums	Zoos and Aquariums[2]
0	0	0	0	0	0	0

Note: (1) Number of professional perfoming groups; (2) AZA-accredited
Source: The Grey House Performing Arts Directory, 2007; Official Museum Directory, 2008; Association of Zoos & Aquariums, AZA Member Zoos & Aquariums, June 2008

Professional Sports Teams

Team Name	League
Real Salt Lake	Major League Soccer (MLS)
Utah Jazz	National Basketball Association (NBA)

Note: Includes teams located in the Salt Lake City metro area.
Source: Original research

MEDIA

Newspapers

Name	News Focus	Frequency	Circulation
No newspapers have an office in the city			

Note: Includes newspapers with offices located in the city
Source: MediaContactsPro, March 2008

Television Stations

Name	Ch.	Network(s)	Type	Ownership
KUTV	2	CBS	Commercial	CBS
KCSG	4	Pax	Commercial	n/a
KTVX	4	ABC	Commercial	n/a
KSL	5	NBC	Commercial	Bonneville International Corporation
KUED	7	PBS	Public	University of Utah
KUEN	9	n/a	Public	Utah State Board of Regents
KENV	10	NBC	Commercial	Sunbelt Broadcasting Company
KBYU	11	PBS	Public	Brigham Young University
KDLQ	13	Fox/ABC	Commercial	n/a
KSTU	13	Fox	Commercial	Fox Television Stations Inc.
KJZZ	14	n/a	Commercial	Larry H. Miller Communications
KUPX	16	Pax	Commercial	Paxson Communications Corporation
KUEW	18	PBS	n/a	University of Utah
KUWB	30	WBN	Commercial	Acme Television Holdings

Note: Stations included cover the Salt Lake City DMA (Designated Market Area)
BurrellesLuce, MediaContacts Online, January 2007

Major AM Radio Stations

Call Letters	Freq. (kHz)	Station Type	Target Audience	Station Format	Music Format
KNRS	570	Commercial	General	News/Talk	n/a
KSUB	590	n/a	General	News/Sports/Talk	n/a
KVNU	610	Commercial	General	News/Talk	n/a
KMTI	650	Commercial	General	Music/News/Sports/Talk	Country
KOAL	750	n/a	General	News/Sports/Talk	n/a
KBEE	860	Commercial	General	Music/Talk	Country
KDXU	890	Commercial	General	News/Talk	n/a
KALL	910	Commercial	General	News	n/a
KMER	950	Commercial	General	News	n/a
KOVO	960	Commercial	General	Sports/Talk	n/a
KSVC	980	Commercial	General	News/Sports/Talk	n/a
KKDS	1060	Commercial	General	Music/News	Adult Contemp.
KAFL	1080	Commercial	General	Music	Country
KANN	1120	Non-Comm	Religious	Educational/Music/News	Christian
KSL	1160	Commercial	General	News/Talk	n/a
KUNF	1210	Commercial	General	Music/News	Easy Listening
KRSV	1210	Commercial	General	Music/News/Sports	Country
KEVA	1240	Commercial	General	News	n/a
KNEU	1250	Commercial	General	Music/News	Country
KZNS	1280	Commercial	General	News/Sports/Talk	n/a
KFNZ	1320	n/a	General/Men	Music/Sports	n/a
KRKK	1360	n/a	General	Music/News	n/a
KSOP	1370	Commercial	General	Music/News	Country
KLGN	1390	Commercial	General	Music/News/Sports/Talk	Adult Standards
KLO	1430	Commercial	General	Music/News/Sports/Talk	n/a
KXOL	1660	n/a	General	Music	n/a

Note: Stations included cover the Salt Lake City DMA (Designated Market Area); n/a not available
Source: BurrellesLuce, MediaContacts Online, January 2007

Major FM Radio Stations

Call Letters	Freq. (mHz)	Station Type	Target Audience	Station Format	Music Format
KBYU	89.1	College	General	Music/News	Classical
KUER	90.1	College	General	Music/News	Jazz
KUSU	91.5	College	General	Educational/Music/News	Classic Rock
KBLQ	92.9	Commercial	General	Music/News/Sports	Soft Rock
KCYQ	93.7	Commercial	General	Music	Country
KODJ	94.1	Commercial	General	Music	Oldies
KVFX	94.5	Commercial	General	Music	Adult Contemp.
KZHT	94.9	Commercial	General/Women	Music	Top 40
KXBN	94.9	Commercial	General	Music	Top 40
KYCS	95.1	Commercial	General	Music/News	Adult Contemp.
KYFO	95.5	Non-Comm	General	Music/Talk	Christian
KFNN	95.7	Commercial	General	Music/News	Adult Contemp.
KXRK	96.3	n/a	Gay/Lesbian	Music	n/a
KQSW	96.5	Commercial	General	Music/News	Country
KISN	97.1	Commercial	General	Music	Adult Contemp.
KREC	98.1	Commercial	General	Educational/Music/News	Adult Contemp.
KBEE	98.7	n/a	General	Music/News/Sports	n/a
KURR	99.5	Commercial	General/Native Amer	Music/Talk	Classic Rock
KONY	101.1	Commercial	General	Music	Contemp. Country
KXFF	102.9	n/a	n/a	n/a	n/a
KUDD	103.9	Commercial	General/Women	Music	Top 40
KSIT	104.5	Commercial	General	Music/News	Classic Rock
KNFL	104.9	n/a	General	Music	Oldies
KENZ	107.5	n/a	General	Music	n/a

Note: Stations included cover the Salt Lake City DMA (Designated Market Area); n/a not available
BurrellesLuce, MediaContacts Online, January 2007

CLIMATE

Average and Extreme Temperatures

Temperature	Jan	Feb	Mar	Apr	May	Jun	Jul	Aug	Sep	Oct	Nov	Dec	Yr.
Extreme High (°F)	62	69	78	85	93	104	107	104	100	89	75	67	107
Average High (°F)	37	43	52	62	72	83	93	90	80	66	50	38	64
Average Temp. (°F)	28	34	41	50	59	69	78	76	65	53	40	30	52
Average Low (°F)	19	24	31	38	46	54	62	61	51	40	30	22	40
Extreme Low (°F)	-22	-14	2	15	25	35	40	37	27	16	-14	-15	-22

Note: Figures cover the years 1948-1990
Source: National Climatic Data Center, International Station Meteorological Climate Summary, 9/96

Average Precipitation/Snowfall/Humidity

Precip./Humidity	Jan	Feb	Mar	Apr	May	Jun	Jul	Aug	Sep	Oct	Nov	Dec	Yr.
Avg. Precip. (in.)	1.3	1.2	1.8	2.0	1.7	0.9	0.8	0.9	1.1	1.3	1.3	1.4	15.6
Avg. Snowfall (in.)	13	10	11	6	1	Tr	0	0	Tr	2	6	13	63
Avg. Rel. Hum. 5am (%)	79	77	71	67	66	60	53	54	60	68	75	79	67
Avg. Rel. Hum. 5pm (%)	69	59	47	38	33	26	22	23	28	40	59	71	43

Note: Figures cover the years 1948-1990; Tr = Trace amounts (<0.05 in. of rain; <0.5 in. of snow)
Source: National Climatic Data Center, International Station Meteorological Climate Summary, 9/96

Weather Conditions

Temperature			Daytime Sky			Precipitation		
5°F & below	32°F & below	90°F & above	Clear	Partly cloudy	Cloudy	0.01 inch or more precip.	0.1 inch or more snow/ice	Thunder-storms
7	128	56	94	152	119	92	38	38

Note: Figures are average number of days per year and cover the years 1948-1990
Source: National Climatic Data Center, International Station Meteorological Climate Summary, 9/96

HAZARDOUS WASTE

Superfund Sites

South Jordan has no sites on the EPA's Superfund Final National Priorities List.
U.S. Environmental Protection Agency, Final National Priorities List, June 23, 2008

AIR & WATER QUALITY

Air Quality Index

Area	Percent of Days when Air Quality was...[2]				AQI Statistics	
	Good	Moderate	Unhealthy for Sensitive Groups	Unhealthy	Maximum	Median
MSA[1]	41.6	45.5	10.4	2.5	166	55

Note: The Air Quality Index (AQI) is an index for reporting daily air quality. EPA calculates the AQI for five major air pollutants regulated by the Clean Air Act: ground-level ozone, particle pollution (also known as particulate matter), carbon monoxide, sulfur dioxide, and nitrogen dioxide. The AQI runs from 0 to 500. The higher the AQI value, the greater the level of air pollution and the greater the health concern. There are six AQI categories: "Good" The AQI is between 0 and 50. Air quality is considered satisfactory; "Moderate" The AQI is between 51 and 100. Air quality is acceptable; "Unhealthy for Sensitive Groups" When AQI values are between 101 and 150, members of sensitive groups may experience health effects; "Unhealthy" When AQI values are between 151 and 200 everyone may begin to experience health effects; "Very Unhealthy" AQI values between 201 and 300 trigger a health alert; "Hazardous" AQI values over 300 trigger health warnings of emergency conditions; (1) Metropolitan Statistical Area - see Appendix A for areas included; (2) Based on 365 days with AQI data in 2007.
Source: U.S. Environmental Protection Agency, Air Quality Index Report, 2007

Air Quality Index Pollutants

Area	Percent of Days when AQI Pollutant was...[2]					
	Carbon Monoxide	Nitrogen Dioxide	Ozone	Sulfur Dioxide	Particulate Matter 2.5	Particulate Matter 10
MSA[1]	1.6	0.0	42.7	0.0	37.0	18.6

Note: The Air Quality Index (AQI) is an index for reporting daily air quality. EPA calculates the AQI for five major air pollutants regulated by the Clean Air Act: ground-level ozone, particle pollution (also known as particulate matter), carbon monoxide, sulfur dioxide, and nitrogen dioxide. The AQI runs from 0 to 500. The higher the AQI value, the greater the level of air pollution and the greater the health concern; (1) Metropolitan Statistical Area - see Appendix A for areas included; (2) Based on 365 days with AQI data in 2007.
Source: U.S. Environmental Protection Agency, Air Quality Index Report, 2007

Air Quality Index Trends

Area	Trend Sites (13)								All Sites (72)
	1999	2000	2001	2002	2003	2004	2005	2006	2006
MSA[1]	12	19	25	27	10	37	24	11	16

Note: An AQI value greater than 100 indicates that air quality would have been in the unhealthful range on that day. Data from exceptional events are not included. These counts are presented in two ways. First, the counts are based on sites having an adequate record of monitoring data during the trend period (trend sites). These counts represent the relative change in the number of days with AQI values greater than 100. In the last column, the counts are based on all sites with data in the most recent year (because it is possible for a site to have data in the most recent year but not enough data to be a trend site); (1) Metropolitan Statistical Area - see Appendix A for areas included.
Source: U.S. Environmental Protection Agency, Office of Air and Radiation, Air Trends, Factbook and Related Information, Air Pollution Trends in Selected Metropolitan Areas 2006

Maximum Air Pollutant Concentrations

	Particulate Matter 10 (ug/m^3)	Particulate Matter 2.5 (ug/m^3)	Ozone (ppm)	Carbon Monoxide (ppm)	Sulfur Dioxide (ppm)	Nitrogen Dioxide (ppm)	Lead (ug/m^3)
MSA[1] Level	164	40	0.104	3	0.007	0.022	n/a
NAAQS[2]	150	35	0.125	9	0.140	0.053	1.50
Met NAAQS[2]	No	No	Yes	Yes	Yes	Yes	n/a

Note: Data from exceptional events are not included; (1) Metropolitan Statistical Area - see Appendix A for areas included; (2) National Ambient Air Quality Standards; n/a not available
Concentrations: Particulate Matter 10 (coarse particulate) - highest second maximum 24-hour concentration; Particulate Matter 2.5 (fine particulate) - highest 98th percentile 24-hour concentration; Ozone - highest second daily maximum 1-hour concentration; Carbon Monoxide - highest second maximum non-overlapping 8-hour concentration; Sulfur Dioxide - highest second maximum 24-hour concentration; Nitrogen Dioxide - highest arithmetic mean concentration; Lead - highest quarterly maximum concentration
Units: ppm = parts per million; ug/m^3 = micrograms per cubic meter
Source: U.S. Environmental Protection Agency, MSA Factbook 2006, Air Quality Statistics by City

Drinking Water

Water System Name	Pop. Served	Primary Water Source Type	Violations[1]	
			Health Based	Monitoring/ Reporting
South Jordan City	40,000	Purchased Ground	0	0

Note: (1) Based on violation data from January 1, 2007 to December 31, 2007 (includes unresolved violations from earlier years)
Source: U.S. Environmental Protection Agency, Office of Ground Water and Drinking Water, Safe Drinking Water Information System (based on data extracted April 15, 2008)

Spanish Fork, Utah

Background

Located in central Utah, Spanish Fork is situated between beautiful Utah Lake to the northwest and picturesque Wasatch Mountains to the southeast. The community is part of the Provo-Orem metropolitan area in south central Utah County. With an emphasis on quality of life, the city of Spanish Fork is an ideal location for living and working.

Explorers Silvestre Valez de Escalante and Francisco Atanasio de Dominguez originally passed through the Spanish Fork Canyon in 1776 as they searched for a direct route from Santa Fe, New Mexico to Monterey, California. Before its settlement, Spanish Fork was populated primarily by the Ute Indian tribe. In 1850, Enoch Reece built Spanish Fork's first homestead. Soon after Reece's arrival, Charles Ferguson and George Sevey brought cattle to the area, and used their livestock to establish Spanish Fork's first business enterprise. The settlement grew to over 1,000 residents, and in 1855, Spanish Fork was recognized as its own municipality. Since then, the city has grown to over 26,000 residents and is not expected to slow down anytime soon.

Spanish Fork is well-suited for recreation, with over 50 play and practice fields, more than 20 public parks and playgrounds, indoor and outdoor tennis courts, miles of bike paths, covered pavilions for open-air entertainment, a golf course, a water park, and a RV park. The city is ideally located just minutes southeast of scenic Utah Lake State Park, allowing residents to fish, boat, canoe, kayak, and camp year round. Alternatively, it's about an hour southwest of stunning Wasatch Mountain State Park. During the warmer months, visitors to the park can camp, picnic, hike, or go horseback riding. When snow is on the ground, Wasatch Mountains State Park offers snowmobiling and cross-country skiing.

Spanish Fork is a business-friendly community that promotes new commerce which, in turn, increases the community's tax base and enhances the quality of life. There is considerable diversity of industry within the community, with major employers being the Nebo School District, Mountain Country Foods, Provo Craft, Alcoa, Longview Fiber, and Nature Sunshine. Other leading employers in the community include Banta, Casalle Inc., Ensign-Bickford Klune Industries, PDM Steel, Rocky Mountain Composites, and J.C. Penny's.

Most of Spanish Fork is served by the Nebo School District, which has grown significantly since the 1980s, with plans to open one new elementary school, two new junior high schools, and two new high schools over the next couple of years. Currently, the Nebo School District is the 5th largest employer in Utah County. In addition to several private schools located in Spanish Fork, the American Heritage School and the American Leadership Academy, institutions of higher education in area include Brigham Young University, Utah State University, Utah Valley State College and Provo College.

The climate of Spanish Fork varies from season to season. Throughout the summer, Spanish Fork tends to be hot and arid. Autumn brings rain and comfortable temperatures. The cold and often snowy winter months are followed by spring rains that often lead to flooding in the surrounding area. The city is situated on a plateau 60 feet above the Spanish Fork River floodplain. Because of the canyon breezes that blow year-round, the air in Spanish Fork is relatively pollution free.

Air travel is provided by the Salt Lake City International Airport, roughly an hour away from Spanish Fork.

Rankings

General Rankings

- Provo* was ranked #13 out of 375 metro areas in *Cities Ranked & Rated*. Criteria: cost of living; climate; crime; transportation; economy and jobs; education; arts and culture; health and healthcare; leisure; quality of life. *Cities Ranked & Rated, 2nd Edition, 2007*
- Provo* was ranked #217 out of 379 metro areas in *Places Rated Almanac*. Criteria: health care; education; recreation; transportation; ambience; climate; crime; housing costs; jobs. *Places Rated Almanac, 7th Edition, 2007*
- The Provo* metro area was selected one of America's "Best Cities to Live, Work and Play" by *Kiplinger Personal Finance*. Criteria: population growth; percentage of workforce in the creative class (scientists, engineers, educators, writers, artists, entertainers, etc.); job quality; income growth; cost of living. *Kiplinger Personal Finance, "Best Cities to Live, Work and Play," July 2008*

Business/Finance Rankings

- Provo* was selected as one of the best places to start and grow a company by *Entrepreneur* and the National Policy Research Council. The Provo* metro area ranked #32 out of 63 mid-size metro areas. Criteria: business formation and growth (firms started four to 14 years ago that still employ at least 5 people and experienced rapid growth over the last four years). *Entrepreneur/National Policy Research Council, "Hot Cities for Entrepreneurs," September 2006*
- The Provo* metro area appeared on the Milken Institute "2007 Best Performing Cities" index. Rank: #8 out of 200 large metro areas. Criteria: job growth; wage and salary growth; high-tech output growth. *Milken Institute, "2007 Best Performing Cities"*
- The Provo* metro area was selected as one of the hottest cities for entrepreneurs in America by *Inc. Magazine*. Criteria: job-growth data for 393 metro was analyzed for current-year employment growth, average annual employment growth over past three years, and employment growth by industry sector. The Provo* metro area ranked #7 among mid-sized metro areas and #31 overall. *Inc. Magazine, May 2007*
- *Forbes* ranked the 200 most populous metro areas in the U.S. in terms of the "Best Places for Business and Careers." The Provo* metro area was ranked #11. Criteria: business costs (labor, energy, tax and office space expenses); living costs (housing, transportation, food and other household expenditures); education levels of the work force; job growth; income growth; migration trends; crime rates; and culture/leisure. *Forbes, "Best Places for Business and Careers," March 19, 2008*
- Provo* was identified as one of the top 20 metro areas with the highest rate of house price appreciation in 2007. The area ranked #6 with a one-year price appreciation of 10.5% through the 4th quarter 2007. *Office of Federal Housing Enterprise Oversight, House Price Index, 4th Quarter 2007*

Health/Environment Rankings

- The Provo* metro area appeared in *Country Home's* "2008 Best Green Places" report. The area ranked #155 out of 379. Criteria: official energy policies; green power; green buildings; availability of fresh, locally grown food. *Country Home, "2008 Best Green Places"*
- Ortho-McNeil Neurologics, in partnership with Sperling's BestPlaces, analyzed 110 metro areas and identified those U.S. cities with the highest prevalence of factors that are most commonly associated with migraine headaches. The Provo* metro area ranked #85. Criteria: number of migraine-related drug prescriptions per capita; lifestyle factors that can contribute to migraines; environmental factors that can trigger migraines; and consumption of migraine-triggering foods. *Ortho-McNeil Neurologics, "America's Migraine Hot Spots," March 14, 2006*

- Sperling's BestPlaces ranked 331 metro areas and identified the most and least stressful U.S. cities. The Provo* metro area ranked #114 out of 114 mid-size metro areas (#1 = most stressful). Criteria: divorce rate; unemployment rate; violent and property crime; suicide rate; commute time; mental health; alcohol consumption; cloudy days. *Sperling's BestPlaces, www.BestPlaces.net, "America's Most (and Least) Stressful Cities," January 9, 2004*

Seniors/Retirement Rankings

- A.G. Edwards ranked America's 500 top-performing communities based on their residents' personal savings and investing behavior. The Provo* metro area ranked #206 with an index score of 102.84 (national average = 100.00). A dozen statistical factors were measured including: participation in retirement savings plans; personal debt levels; and home ownership. *A.G. Edwards, "2007 Nest Egg Index", September 12, 2007*

Children/Family Rankings

- The Provo* metro area was selected as one of the "Best Cities for Relocating Families" by Worldwide ERC and Primacy Relocation. The 2007 study placed a special emphasis on the housing market, which has significantly impacted the relocation industry and an employer's ability to transfer employees. The variables which weigh heavily in this category include home price, home affordability index, appreciation rates, and property tax. Other criteria include cost of living, crime rates, education, climate, focus on diversity, physicians per capita, recreation and leisure, arts and culture, air quality, watershed quality, sales tax, unemployment rate, job growth, high school and higher education index, school expenditures per student, students in public school, SAT/ACT percentile, and population growth. *Worldwide ERC and Primacy Relocation, "2007 Best Cities for Relocating Families"*

Safety Rankings

- The National Insurance Crime Bureau ranked 361 metro areas in the U.S. in terms of per capita rates of vehicle theft. The Provo* metro area ranked #296 (#1 = highest rate). Criteria: number of vehicle theft offenses per 100,000 inhabitants. *National Insurance Crime Bureau, "NICB Vehicle Theft Study," April 22, 2008*
- Farmers Insurance Group of Companies, in partnership with Sperling's BestPlaces, ranked 379 metro areas and identified the "Most Secure U.S. Place to Live." The Provo* metro area ranked #24 out of 127 in the mid-size city category (150,000 to 500,000 residents). Criteria: crime rates; extreme weather; risk of natural disasters; environmental hazards; terrorism threats; air quality; life expectancy; job loss numbers. *Farmers Insurance Group, "Most Secure U.S. Places to Live 2007"*

Sports/Recreation Rankings

- The Provo* metro area appeared on the *Sporting News* list of the "Best Sports Cities 2007". The area ranked #22 out of 150 cities in the U.S. *Sporting News* takes a 12-month snapshot, roughly July to July, of each city's sports, putting a heavy premium on regular-season won-lost records (from the most recently completed season). Other criteria include: playoff berths, bowl appearances and tournament bids; championships; applicable power ratings; quality of competition; overall fan fervor as measured in part by attendance as percentage of venue capacity; abundance of teams (rewarding quality over quantity); stadium and arena quality; ticket availability and prices; franchise ownership; and marquee appeal of athletes. *SportingNews.com, "Best Sports Cities 2007," August 1, 2007*
- *Golf Digest* ranked 330 metro areas in the U.S. in terms of golf. The Provo* metro area was ranked #232. Criteria: access to golf; weather; value of golf; and quality of golf. *Golf Digest, "Metro Golf Rankings," August 2005*

Spanish Fork is located within the Provo-Orem, UT Metropolitan Statistical Area.

Business Environment

CITY FINANCES

City Government Finances

Component	2004-2005 ($000)	2004-2005 ($ per capita)
Total Revenues	40,936	1,539
Total Expenditures	32,130	1,208
Debt Outstanding	20,257	761
Cash and Securities	30,479	1,146

Source: U.S Census Bureau, Government Finances 2004-2005

City Government Revenue by Source

Source	2004-2005 ($000)	2004-2005 ($ per capita)
General Revenue		
From Federal Government	241	9
From State Government	747	28
From Local Governments	1,459	55
Taxes		
Property	1,637	62
Sales	4,399	165
Personal Income	0	0
License	706	27
Charges	7,694	289
Liquor Store	0	0
Utility	21,751	818
Employee Retirement	0	0
Other	2,302	87

Source: U.S Census Bureau, Government Finances 2004-2005

City Government Expenditures by Function

Function	2004-2005 ($000)	2004-2005 ($ per capita)	2004-2005 (%)
General Expenditures			
Airports	0	0	0.0
Corrections	0	0	0.0
Education	0	0	0.0
Fire Protection	349	13	1.1
Governmental Administration	2,690	101	8.4
Health	284	11	0.9
Highways	2,204	83	6.9
Hospitals	0	0	0.0
Housing and Community Development	0	0	0.0
Interest on General Debt	61	2	0.2
Libraries	421	16	1.3
Parking	0	0	0.0
Parks and Recreation	4,078	153	12.7
Police Protection	2,779	104	8.6
Public Welfare	0	0	0.0
Sewerage	1,625	61	5.1
Solid Waste Management	654	25	2.0
Liquor Store	0	0	0.0
Utility	15,880	597	49.4
Employee Retirement	0	0	0.0
Other	1,105	42	3.4

Source: U.S Census Bureau, Government Finances 2004-2005

Municipal Bond Ratings

Area	Moody's
City	Aaa

Source: Mergent Bond Record, January 2008 (unless noted otherwise)

DEMOGRAPHICS

Population Growth

Area	1990 Census	2000 Census	2007 Estimate	2012 Projection	Population Growth (%) 1990-2000	Population Growth (%) 2000-2012
City	12,183	20,246	27,926	33,194	66.2	64.0
MSA[1]	269,407	376,774	470,487	536,515	39.9	42.4
U.S.	248,709,873	281,421,906	301,045,522	314,920,978	13.2	11.9

Note: (1) Metropolitan Statistical Area - see Appendix B for areas included
Source: Claritas, Inc.

Number of Households and Average Household Size

Area	2007 Estimate	2007 Average Household Size
City	7,592	3.68
MSA[1]	129,123	3.64
U.S.	113,668,003	2.65

Note: (1) Metropolitan Statistical Area - see Appendix B for areas included
Source: Claritas, Inc.

Race and Ethnicity

Area	White Alone[2]	Black Alone[2]	Asian Alone[2]	Other Race Alone[2]	Hispanic[3]
City	93.9	0.2	0.4	5.5	5.6
MSA[1]	91.2	0.3	1.1	7.3	8.6
U.S.	73.1	12.4	4.3	10.3	14.9

Note: Figures are 2007 estimates; (1) Metropolitan Statistical Area - see Appendix B for areas included (2) Alone is defined as not being in combination with one or more other races; (3) May be of any race.
Source: Claritas, Inc.

Ancestry

Area	German	Irish[2]	English	American	Italian	Polish	French[3]	Scottish
City	9.7	4.7	32.7	8.6	1.5	0.5	2.4	4.3
MSA[1]	10.8	4.7	33.5	6.9	2.1	0.5	2.2	4.8
U.S.	15.2	10.9	8.7	7.3	5.6	3.2	3.0	1.7

Note: Figures include multiple ancestry (e.g. if a person reported being Irish and Italian, they were included in both columns); (1) Metropolitan Statistical Area - see Appendix A for areas included; (2) Includes Celtic; (3) Includes Alsatian but excludes Basque
Source: Census 2000, Summary File 3

Foreign-Born Population

Area	Percent of Population Born in: Any Foreign Country	Europe	Asia	Africa	Oceania[2]	Canada	Mexico	Latin America[3]
City	3.1	0.1	0.1	0.1	0.2	0.2	1.5	0.9
MSA[1]	6.3	0.7	0.9	0.1	0.2	0.6	2.5	1.4
U.S.	11.1	1.7	2.9	0.3	0.1	0.3	3.3	2.5

Note: (1) Metropolitan Statistical Area - see Appendix A for areas included; (2) Includes Australia, New Zealand subregion, Melanesia, Micronesia, Polynesia, and Oceania n.e.c; (3) Includes Central America (excluding Mexico), South America, and the Caribbean.
Source: Census 2000, Summary File 3

Marriage Status

Area	Never Married	Now Married (excluding Separated)	Separated	Widowed	Divorced
City	22.4	66.4	1.3	3.8	6.2
MSA[1]	32.6	58.6	0.8	3.0	4.9
U.S.	27.1	54.4	2.2	6.6	9.7

Note: Figures are percentages and cover the population 15 years of age and older; (1) Metropolitan Statistical Area - see Appendix A for areas included
Source: Census 2000, Summary File 3

ECONOMY

INCOME

Age Distribution

Area	Percent of Population						
	Under Age 5	Age 5 to 17	Age 18 to 34	Age 35 to 49	Age 50 to 64	Age 65 to 79	80 Years and Over
City	13.4	25.9	29.1	17.2	8.2	4.5	1.6
MSA[1]	10.9	23.0	36.0	15.4	8.2	4.8	1.7
U.S.	6.8	18.9	23.7	23.5	14.8	9.2	3.2

Note: (1) Metropolitan Statistical Area - see Appendix A for areas included
Source: Census 2000, Summary File 3

Male/Female Ratio

Area	Males	Females	Males per 100 Females
City	14,060	13,866	101.4
MSA[1]	233,386	237,101	98.4
U.S.	148,320,305	152,725,217	97.1

Note: Figures are 2007 estimates; (1) Metropolitan Statistical Area - see Appendix B for areas included
Source: Claritas, Inc.

Religion

Area	Catholic	Southern Baptist	United Meth-odist	ELCA[1]	LDS[2]	Presby-terian Church USA	Jewish Est.	Muslim Est.
County	1.0	0.1	0.0	0.0	88.1	0.1	0.0	0.0
U.S.	22.0	7.1	3.7	1.8	1.5	1.1	2.2	0.6

Note: Figures are the number of adherents as a percentage of the total population; Adherents are defined as all members, including full members, their children and the estimated number of other participants who are not considered members (e.g. the baptized, those not confirmed, those regularly attending services, etc.); (1) Evangelical Lutheran Church in America; (2) The Church of Jesus Christ of Latter Day Saints
Source: Reprinted with permission from Religious Congregations and Membership in the United States 2000 (Nashville, Glenmary Research Center, 2002) Copyright Association of Statisticians of American Religious Bodies. All rights reserved.

Gross Metropolitan Product

Area	2002	2003	2004	2005	2005 Rank[2]
MSA[1]	9.9	10.5	11.6	12.9	146

Note: Figures are in billions of dollars; (1) Provo-Orem, UT Metropolitan Statistical Area - see Appendix A for areas included; (2) Rank ranges from 1 to 361
Source: The U.S. Conference of Mayors, "U.S. Metro Economies: GMP - The Engines of America's Growth," January 2007

Economic Growth

Area	1995 GMP	2005 GMP	Average Annual Growth Rate	Growth Rate Rank[2]
MSA[1]	6.5	12.9	7.0	41

Note: Figures are in billions of dollars; GMP = Gross Metropolitan Product; (1) Provo-Orem, UT Metropolitan Statistical Area - see Appendix A for areas included; (2) Rank ranges from 1 to 361
Source: The U.S. Conference of Mayors, "U.S. Metro Economies: GMP - The Engines of America's Growth," January 2007

Per Capita/Median/Average Income

Area	Per Capita ($)	Median Household ($)	Average Household ($)
City	17,508	54,761	63,950
MSA[1]	17,896	51,529	64,693
U.S.	25,495	49,280	66,670

Note: Figures are 2007 estimates; (1) Metropolitan Statistical Area - see Appendix B for areas included
Source: Claritas, Inc.

Household Income Distribution

Area	Percent of Households Earning							
	Under $15,000	$15,000 -24,999	$25,000 -34,999	$35,000 -49,999	$50,000 -74,999	$75,000 -99,000	$100,000 -149,999	$150,000 and up
City	5.0	8.6	9.0	21.7	28.7	14.8	8.6	3.6
MSA[1]	8.4	10.3	11.5	18.2	22.7	12.8	11.1	4.9
U.S.	13.1	10.9	11.2	15.6	19.5	11.9	11.3	6.6

Note: Figures are 2007 estimates; (1) Metropolitan Statistical Area - see Appendix B for areas included
Source: Claritas, Inc.

Poverty Rates by Age

Area	All Ages	Under 5 Years Old	5 to 17 Years Old	18 to 64 Years Old	65 Years and Over
City	4.5	0.8	1.3	2.2	0.3
MSA[1]	12.0	1.1	1.9	8.6	0.3
U.S.	12.4	1.2	3.0	6.9	1.2

Note: Figures are percent of population with income in 1999 below poverty level and only include population for whom poverty status is determined; (1) Metropolitan Statistical Area - see Appendix A for areas included
Source: Census 2000, Summary File 3

Personal Bankruptcy Filing Rate

Area	2004	2005	2006
Utah County	5.98	6.23	1.46
U.S.	5.31	6.82	2.00

Note: Numbers are per 1,000 population and include Chapter 7 and Chapter 13 filings
Source: Federal Deposit Insurance Corporation (FDIC), Regional Economic Conditions (RECON), 8/23/2007

EMPLOYMENT

Labor Force and Employment

Area	Civilian Labor Force			Workers Employed		
	Dec. 2006	Dec. 2007	% Chg.	Dec. 2006	Dec. 2007	% Chg.
City	11,938	12,297	3.0	11,721	12,018	2.5
MSA[1]	225,624	232,573	3.1	221,015	226,628	2.5
U.S.	152,571,000	153,705,000	0.7	146,081,000	146,334,000	0.2

Note: Data is not seasonally adjusted and covers workers 16 years of age and older;
(1) Metropolitan Statistical Area - see Appendix B for areas included
Source: Bureau of Labor Statistics, http://stats.bls.gov

Unemployment Rate

Area	2007											
	Jan.	Feb.	Mar.	Apr.	May	Jun.	Jul.	Aug.	Sep.	Oct.	Nov.	Dec.
City	2.3	2.2	2.1	2.0	2.0	2.5	2.5	2.5	2.1	2.2	2.1	2.3
MSA[1]	2.6	2.5	2.4	2.2	2.2	2.8	2.8	2.8	2.4	2.5	2.4	2.6
U.S.	5.0	4.9	4.5	4.3	4.3	4.7	4.9	4.6	4.5	4.4	4.5	4.8

Note: Data is not seasonally adjusted and covers workers 16 years of age and older; All figures are percentages; (1) Metropolitan Statistical Area - see Appendix B for areas included
Source: Bureau of Labor Statistics, http://stats.bls.gov

Employment by Occupation

Occupation Classification	City (%)	MSA[1] (%)	U.S. (%)
Sales and Office	26.7	27.7	26.7
Professional and Related	18.4	24.3	20.2
Service	13.2	14.0	14.9
Production, Transportation, and Material Moving	16.1	11.4	14.6
Management, Business, and Financial	12.7	12.2	13.5
Construction, Extraction, and Maintenance	12.4	10.1	9.4
Farming, Forestry, and Fishing	0.4	0.3	0.7

Note: Figures cover employed civilians 16 years of age and older;
(1) Metropolitan Statistical Area - see Appendix A for areas included
Source: Census 2000, Summary File 3

Employment by Industry

Sector	MSA[1] Number of Employees	MSA[1] Percent of Total	U.S. Percent of Total
Government	26,100	13.3	16.3
Education and Health Services	40,800	20.9	13.4
Professional and Business Services	23,500	12.0	13.1
Retail Trade	25,200	12.9	11.6
Manufacturing	20,100	10.3	9.9
Leisure and Hospitality	14,000	7.2	9.6
Financial Activities	6,800	3.5	5.9
Construction	n/a	n/a	5.3
Wholesale Trade	5,400	2.8	4.4
Other Services	4,300	2.2	3.9
Transportation and Utilities	2,400	1.2	3.7
Information	8,100	4.1	2.2
Natural Resources and Mining	n/a	n/a	0.5

Note: Figures cover non-farm employment as of December 2007 and are not seasonally adjusted; (1) Metropolitan Statistical Area - see Appendix B for areas included; n/a not available
Source: Bureau of Labor Statistics, http://stats.bls.gov

Average Wages

Occupation	$/Hr.	Occupation	$/Hr.
Accountants and Auditors	31.16	Maids and Housekeeping Cleaners	8.88
Automotive Mechanics	16.54	Maintenance and Repair Workers	12.97
Bookkeepers	12.79	Marketing Managers	43.94
Carpenters	17.10	Nuclear Medicine Technologists	n/a
Cashiers	8.39	Nurses, Licensed Practical	15.71
Clerks, General Office	10.23	Nurses, Registered	26.37
Clerks, Receptionists/Information	10.56	Nursing Aides/Orderlies/Attendants	9.69
Clerks, Shipping/Receiving	11.56	Packers and Packagers, Hand	8.48
Computer Programmers	30.38	Physical Therapists	30.49
Computer Support Specialists	17.10	Postal Service Mail Carriers	21.14
Computer Systems Analysts	33.42	Real Estate Brokers	n/a
Cooks, Restaurant	10.71	Retail Salespersons	10.60
Dentists	n/a	Sales Reps., Exc. Tech./Scientific	22.78
Electrical Engineers	n/a	Sales Reps., Tech./Scientific	28.98
Electricians	23.41	Secretaries, Exc. Legal/Med./Exec.	12.95
Financial Managers	38.14	Security Guards	13.32
First-Line Supervisors/Mgrs., Sales	16.55	Surgeons	n/a
Food Preparation Workers	8.03	Teacher Assistants	9.70
General and Operations Managers	38.97	Teachers, Elementary School	21.10
Hairdressers/Cosmetologists	10.20	Teachers, Secondary School	23.30
Internists	n/a	Telemarketers	11.47
Janitors and Cleaners	9.07	Truck Drivers, Heavy/Tractor-Trailer	18.39
Landscaping/Groundskeeping Workers	9.31	Truck Drivers, Light/Delivery Svcs.	10.60
Lawyers	45.25	Waiters and Waitresses	7.93

Note: Wage data covers the Provo-Orem, UT Metropolitan Statistical Area - see Appendix B for areas included. Hourly wages for elementary/secondary school teachers and teacher assistants were calculated by the editors from annual wage data assuming a 40 hour work week; n/a not available.
Source: Bureau of Labor Statistics, May 2007 Metro Area Occupational Employment and Wage Estimates

RESIDENTIAL REAL ESTATE

Building Permits

Area	Single-Family 2006	Single-Family 2007p	Single-Family Pct. Chg.	Multi-Family 2006	Multi-Family 2007p	Multi-Family Pct. Chg.	Total 2006	Total 2007p	Total Pct. Chg.
City	652	415	-36.3	10	12	20.0	662	427	-35.5
U.S.	1,378,200	973,300	-29.4	460,700	407,200	-11.6	1,838,900	1,380,500	-24.9

Note: (p) preliminary; figures cover and represent new, privately-owned housing units authorized (unadjusted data); All permit data are based on estimates with imputation; U.S. figures are based on the new 20,000-place series.
Source: U.S. Census Bureau, Manufacturing, Mining, and Construction Statistics

Homeownership and Housing Vacancies

Area	Homeownership Rate[2] (%)			Rental Vacancy Rate[3] (%)			Homeowner Vacancy Rate[4] (%)		
	2005	2006	2007	2005	2006	2007	2005	2006	2007
MSA[1]	n/a	n/a	n/a	n/a	n/a	n/a	n/a	n/a	n/a
U.S.	68.9	68.8	68.1	9.8	9.8	9.7	1.9	2.4	2.7

Note: (1) Metropolitan Statistical Area - see Appendix B for areas included; (2) The proportion of households that are owners; (3) The proportion of the rental inventory that is vacant for rent; (4) The proportion of the homeowner inventory that is vacant for sale; n/a not available
Source: U.S. Census Bureau, Housing Vacancies and Homeownership Annual Statistics: 2007

TAXES

State Corporate Income Tax Rates

State	Rates and Tax Brackets
Utah	5.0%

Note: Tax rates as of January 1, 2008; Minimum tax $100.
Source: Tax Foundation, www.taxfoundation.org

State Individual Income Tax Rates

State	Federal Deductibility	Marginal Rates (%)	Standard Deduction ($)		Personal Exemptions ($)[1]	
			Single	Joint	Single	Dependents
Utah	Yes (bb)	2.3 - 6.98 (cc)	5,150 (s)	10,300 (s)	2,475 (q)	2,475 (q)

Note: Tax rates as of January 1, 2008; Local- and county-level taxes are not included; n/a not applicable; (1) Married joint filers generally receive double the single exemption; (q) Three fourths federal exemption; (s) Deductions and exemptions tied to federal tax system. Federal deductions and exemptions are indexed for inflation; (bb) Half of federal income tax deductible; (cc) An optional 5.35% flat tax will be available.
Source: Tax Foundation, www.taxfoundation.org

Various State and Local Tax Rates

State and Local Sales and Use (%)	State Sales and Use (%)	Gasoline[1,2] ($/gal.)	Cigarette ($/pack)	Spirits ($/gal.)	Table Wine ($/gal.)	Beer ($/gal.)
6.45	4.65	0.245	0.695	10.13 (n)	(p)	0.41

Note: Tax rates as of January 1, 2008; (1) In addition to the 18.4 cpg Federal gasoline tax; (2) Rates may include additional state sales taxes, environmental protection and storage fees/taxes, and local taxes. When necessary, the volume-weighted average of all local taxes is used to approximate the typical statewide rate including local tax; (n) The state government controls all sales. The implied excise tax rate is calculated using methodology designed by the Distilled Spirits Council of the United States (DISCUS); (p) All wine sales are through state-run stores. Revenue in these states is generated from various taxes, fees and net profits.
Source: Tax Foundation, www.taxfoundation.org; Original research

State Tax Burdens

Area	Combined State and Local Tax Burden		Combined Federal, State and Local Tax Burden	
	Percent	Rank	Percent	Rank
Utah	10.7	27	30.3	36
U.S. Average	11.0	-	32.7	-

Note: Figures cover 2007 and measure taxes as a percentage of income
Source: Tax Foundation, www.taxfoundation.org

State Business Tax Climate Index Rankings

State	Overall Rank	Corporate Tax Index Rank	Individual Income Tax Index Rank	Sales Tax Index Rank	Unemployment Insurance Tax Index Rank	Property Tax Index Rank
Utah	17	5	30	27	28	3

Note: Rankings range from 1 to 50 where 1 is best. Rankings do not average across to Overall Rank. States without a given tax are given a ranking of 1.
Source: Tax Foundation, State Business Tax Climate Index 2008

TRANSPORTATION

Means of Transportation to Work

Area	Car/Truck/Van		Public Transportation			Bicycle	Walked	Other Means	Worked at Home
	Drove Alone	Car-pooled	Bus	Subway	Railroad				
City	77.5	14.8	1.2	0.0	0.0	0.1	1.5	0.7	4.2
MSA[1]	72.5	14.9	1.3	0.0	0.0	0.8	4.9	0.5	5.0
U.S.	75.7	12.2	2.5	1.5	0.5	0.4	2.9	1.0	3.3

Note: Figures are percentages and cover workers 16 years of age and older;
(1) Metropolitan Statistical Area - see Appendix A for areas included
Source: Census 2000, Summary File 3

Travel Time to Work

Area	Less Than 15 Minutes	15 to 29 Minutes	30 to 44 Minutes	45 to 59 Minutes	60 Minutes or More
City	42.2	41.0	8.1	3.7	5.0
MSA[1]	45.0	35.9	10.7	4.2	4.2
U.S.	29.4	36.1	19.1	7.4	8.0

Note: Figures are percentages and include workers 16 years old and over; (1) Metropolitan Statistical Area - see Appendix A for areas included
Source: Census 2000, Summary File 3

Living Environment

COST OF LIVING

Cost of Living Index

Composite Index	Groceries	Housing	Utilities	Trans-portation	Health Care	Misc. Goods/ Services
n/a	n/a	n/a	n/a	n/a	n/a	n/a

Note: U.S. = 100; n/a not available
Source: The Council for Community and Economic Research (formerly ACCRA), Cost of Living Index, 2007

Grocery Prices

Area[1]	T-Bone Steak ($/pound)	Frying Chicken ($/pound)	Whole Milk ($/half gal.)	Eggs ($/dozen)	Orange Juice ($/64 oz.)	Coffee ($/11.5 oz.)
City[2]	n/a	n/a	n/a	n/a	n/a	n/a
Avg.	8.93	1.12	2.13	1.52	3.26	3.31
Min.	5.88	0.71	1.33	0.83	2.30	2.20
Max.	12.80	2.07	3.43	3.54	5.79	6.20

Note: (1) Values for the local area are compared with the average, minimum and maximum values for all 331 areas in the Cost of Living Index report; n/a not available; (2) Figures cover the Spanish Fork UT urban area; **T-Bone Steak** *(price per pound);* **Frying Chicken** *(price per pound, whole fryer);* **Whole Milk** *(half gallon carton);* **Eggs** *(price per dozen, Grade A, large);* **Orange Juice** *(64 oz. Tropicana or Florida Natural);* **Coffee** *(11.5 oz. can, vacuum-packed, Maxwell House, Hills Bros, or Folgers).*
Source: The Council for Community and Economic Research (formerly ACCRA), Cost of Living Index, 2007

Housing and Utility Costs

Area[1]	New Home Price ($)	Apartment Rent ($/month)	All Electric ($/month)	Part Electric ($/month)	Other Energy ($/month)	Telephone ($/month)
City[2]	n/a	n/a	n/a	n/a	n/a	n/a
Avg.	309,605	782	146.13	78.67	90.16	26.14
Min.	189,877	n/a	82.03	37.41	33.15	17.08
Max.	1,202,800	3,481	271.14	150.60	257.67	37.45

Note: (1) Values for the local area are compared with the average, minimum and maximum values for all 331 areas in the Cost of Living Index report; n/a not available; (2) Figures cover the Spanish Fork UT urban area; **New Home Price** *(2,400 sf living area, 8,000 sf lot, in urban area with full utilities);* **Apartment Rent** *(950 sf 2 bedroom/1.5 or 2 bath, unfurnished, excluding all utilities except water);* **All Electric** *(average monthly cost for an all-electric home);* **Part Electric** *(average monthly cost for a part-electric home);* **Other Energy** *(average monthly cost for natural gas, fuel oil, coal, wood, and any other forms of energy except electricity);* **Telephone** *(price includes basic monthly rate for a private residential line plus additional local usage charges incurred by a family of four).*
Source: The Council for Community and Economic Research (formerly ACCRA), Cost of Living Index, 2007

Health Care, Transportation, and Other Costs

Area[1]	Doctor ($/visit)	Dentist ($/visit)	Optometrist ($/visit)	Gasoline ($/gallon)	Beauty Salon ($/visit)	Men's Shirt ($)
City[2]	n/a	n/a	n/a	n/a	n/a	n/a
Avg.	79.48	71.93	79.55	2.64	29.52	25.77
Min.	52.08	44.80	43.95	2.19	15.58	16.19
Max.	148.44	126.27	158.83	3.48	60.62	48.53

Note: (1) Values for the local area are compared with the average, minimum and maximum values for all 331 areas in the Cost of Living Index report; n/a not available; (2) Figures cover the Spanish Fork UT urban area; **Doctor** *(general practitioners routine exam of an established patient);* **Dentist** *(adult teeth cleaning and periodic oral examination);* **Optometrist** *(full vision eye exam for established adult patient);* **Gasoline** *(one gallon regular unleaded, national brand, including all taxes, cash price at self-service pump if available);* **Beauty Salon** *(woman's shampoo, trim, and blow-dry);* **Men's Shirt** *(cotton/polyester dress shirt, pinpoint weave, long sleeves).*
Source: The Council for Community and Economic Research (formerly ACCRA), Cost of Living Index, 2007

HOUSING

House Price Index (HPI)

Area	National Ranking[2]	Quarterly Change (%)	One-Year Change (%)	Five-Year Change (%)
MSA[1]	6	0.77	10.46	51.51
U.S.[3]	-	0.10	0.84	41.37

Note: The HPI is a weighted repeat sales index. It measures average price changes in repeat sales or refinancings on the same properties. This information is obtained by reviewing repeat mortgage transactions on single-family properties whose mortgages have been purchased or securitized by Fannie Mae or Freddie Mac in January 1975; (1) Metropolitan Statistical Area - see Appendix B for areas included; (2) Rankings are based on annual percentage change for all metro areas containing at least 15,000 transactions over the last 10 years and ranges from 1 to 291; (3) figures based on a weighted average of Census Division estimates; all figures are for the period ending December 31, 2007
Source: Office of Federal Housing Enterprise Oversight, House Price Index, February 26, 2008

House Price Valuations

Area	Q1 2000	Q1 2001	Q1 2002	Q1 2003	Q1 2004	Q1 2005	Q1 2006	Q1 2007	Q1 2008
MSA[1]	-2.6	-1.8	0.8	3.0	9.9	6.8	14.4	25.8	25.7

Note: Figures show the percentage of over- or under-valuation of single family homes relative to statistically normal house values (e.g. a value of 23.6 indicates that house values are 23.6% overvalued). Statistically normal house values are based on house prices, interest rates, household incomes, population densities, and any historical premiums or discounts metropolitan areas have exhibited over time; (1) Figures cover the Metropolitan Statistical Area - see Appendix B for areas included
Source: Global Insight/National City Corporation, House Prices in America, May 2008

Median Home Prices

Area	2005	2006	2007[r]	Percent Change 2006 to 2007
MSA[1]	n/a	n/a	n/a	n/a
U.S. Average	219.0	221.9	217.9	-1.8

Note: Figures are median sales prices of existing single-family homes in thousands of dollars; (r) revised; n/a not available; (1) Metropolitan Statistical Area - see Appendix B for areas included
Source: National Association of Realtors, Metropolitan Area Prices, 1st Quarter 2008

Housing: Year Structure Built

Area	1990 -2000	1980 -1989	1970 -1979	1960 -1969	1950 -1959	1940 -1949	Before 1940	Median Year
City	41.1	5.9	18.3	6.9	9.0	6.3	12.5	1978
MSA[1]	33.9	12.7	22.8	9.1	8.4	5.4	7.8	1978
U.S.	17.0	15.8	18.5	13.7	12.7	7.3	15.0	1971

Note: Figures are percentages; (1) Metropolitan Statistical Area - see Appendix A for areas included
Source: Census 2000, Summary File 3

HEALTH

Health Risk Data

Category	Area[1] (%)	U.S. (%)
Adults who have been told they have high blood pressure[3]	13.1	25.5
Adults who have been told they have high blood cholesterol[3]	29.2	35.6
Adults who have been told they have diabetes[2]	3.9	7.5
Adults who have been told they have arthritis[3]	17.5	27.0
Adults who have been told they currently have asthma	8.6	8.5
Adults who are current smokers	5.9	20.1
Adults who are heavy drinkers[4]	1.0	4.9
Adults who are overweight (BMI 25.0 - 29.9)	33.0	36.5
Adults who are obese (BMI 30.0 - 99.8)	21.3	25.1

Note: Data as of 2006 unless otherwise noted; (1) Figures cover the Metropolitan Statistical Area - see Appendix B for areas included; (2) Figures do not include pregnancy-related diabetes, pre-diabetes or borderline diabetes; (3) 2005 data; (4) Heavy drinkers are classified as adult men having more than two drinks per day or adult women having more than one drink per day
Source: Centers for Disease Control and Prevention, Behaviorial Risk Factor Surveillance System, SMART: Selected Metropolitan/Micropolitan Area Risk Trends, 2005, 2006

Mortality Rates for the Top 10 Causes of Death in the U.S.

ICD-10[a] Sub-Chapter	ICD-10[a] Code	Age-Adjusted Mortality Rate[1] per 100,000 population	
		County[2]	U.S.
Malignant neoplasms	C00-C97	126.8	186.5
Ischaemic heart diseases	I20-I25	86.9	152.3
Other forms of heart disease	I30-I51	73.2	51.5
Cerebrovascular diseases	I60-I69	53.3	50.0
Chronic lower respiratory diseases	J40-J47	24.4	42.6
Diabetes mellitus	E10-E14	31.3	24.8
Other degenerative diseases of the nervous system	G30-G31	25.5	22.6
Other external causes of accidental injury	W00-X59	17.3	21.4
Influenza and pneumonia	J10-J18	18.2	20.7
Hypertensive diseases	I10-I13	14.8	18.2

Note: (a) ICD-10 = International Classification of Diseases 10th Revision; (1) Mortality rates are a three year average covering 2003-2005; (2) Figures cover Utah County
Source: Centers for Disease Control and Prevention, National Center for Health Statistics. Compressed Mortality File 1999-2004. CDC WONDER On-line Database, compiled from Compressed Mortality File 1999-2005 Series 20 No. 2K, 2008.

Mortality Rates for Selected Causes of Death

ICD-10[a] Sub-Chapter	ICD-10[a] Code	Age-Adjusted Mortality Rate[1] per 100,000 population	
		County[2]	U.S.
Assault	X85-Y09	*1.0	5.9
Human immunodeficiency virus (HIV) disease	B20-B24	*0.2	4.5
Intentional self-harm	X60-X84	12.9	10.8
Malnutrition	E40-E46	*1.1	1.0
Obesity and other hyperalimentation	E65-E68	2.6	1.4
Organic, including symptomatic, mental disorders	F01-F09	25.8	16.8
Transport accidents	V01-V99	12.2	16.1
Viral hepatitis	B15-B19	*1.0	1.8

Note: (a) ICD-10 = International Classification of Diseases 10th Revision; (1) Mortality rates are a three year average covering 2003-2005; (2) Figures cover Utah County; (*) Unreliable data as per CDC
Source: Centers for Disease Control and Prevention, National Center for Health Statistics. Compressed Mortality File 1999-2004. CDC WONDER On-line Database, compiled from Compressed Mortality File 1999-2005 Series 20 No. 2K, 2008.

Distribution of Physicians[1]

Area	Total	Family/ General Practice	Specialties	
			Medical	Surgical
Utah County (number)	470	196	127	124
Utah County (rate per 10,000 pop.)	10.6	4.4	2.9	2.8
U.S. (rate per 10,000 pop.)	17.7	4.6	6.9	4.3

Note: Data as of 2005; (1) Includes all non-federal, patient-care, office-based MDs
Source: Area Resource File (ARF). June 2007. U.S. Department of Health and Human Services, Health Resources and Services Administration, Bureau of Health Professions, Rockville, MD.

Hospitals

There were no hospitals listed within the city limits.
AHA Guide to the Healthcare Field 2008

EDUCATION

Public School District Statistics

District Name	Schls	Pupils	Pupil/ Teacher Ratio	Minority Pupils[1] (%)	Free Lunch Eligible[2] (%)	IEP[3] (%)
American Leadership Academy	1	1,196	26.1	5.3	n/a	11.5
Nebo District	47	24,098	23.1	9.9	20.3	15.4

Note: Table includes regular local school districts with 2,000 or more students; (1) Percentage of students that are not white, non-Hispanic; (2) Percentage of students that are eligible for the free lunch program; (3) Percentage of students that have an Individualized Education Program.
Source: U.S. Department of Education, National Center for Education Statistics, Common Core of Data, Local Education Agency (School District) Universe Survey: School Year 2005-2006; U.S. Department of Education, National Center for Education Statistics, Common Core of Data, Public Elementary/Secondary School Universe Survey: School Year 2005-2006

Highest Level of Education

Area	Less than H.S.	H.S. Diploma	Some College, No Deg.	Associate Degree	Bachelors Degree	Masters Degree	Profess. School Degree	Doctorate Degree
City	7.9	24.7	32.7	11.2	17.2	4.5	1.5	0.4
MSA[1]	8.8	19.6	30.8	9.8	21.5	6.3	1.6	1.8
U.S.	19.4	28.4	21.2	6.4	15.7	5.9	2.0	1.0

Note: Figures are 2007 estimated percentages and cover persons age 25 and over; (1) Metropolitan Statistical Area - see Appendix B for areas included
Source: Claritas, Inc.

Educational Attainment by Race

Area	High School Graduate (%)					Bachelor's Degree (%)				
	Total	White	Black	Asian	Hisp.[2]	Total	White	Black	Asian	Hisp.[2]
City	91.2	92.2	36.4	100.0	64.3	21.9	22.5	0.0	31.3	18.3
MSA[1]	90.9	92.2	78.7	91.5	62.8	31.5	32.1	25.7	48.7	16.2
U.S.	80.4	83.6	72.3	80.4	52.4	24.4	26.1	14.3	44.1	10.4

Note: Figures shown cover persons 25 years old and over; (1) Metropolitan Statistical Area - see Appendix A for areas included; (2) people of Hispanic origin can be of any race
Source: Census 2000, Summary File 3

School Enrollment by Type

Area	Grades KG to 8				Grades 9 to 12			
	Public		Private		Public		Private	
	Enrollment	%	Enrollment	%	Enrollment	%	Enrollment	%
City	3,717	98.6	53	1.4	1,341	96.1	55	3.9
MSA[1]	56,391	96.9	1,786	3.1	24,610	96.2	976	3.8
U.S.	33,526,011	88.7	4,285,121	11.3	14,848,628	90.6	1,532,323	9.4

Note: Figures shown cover persons 3 years old and over; (1) Metropolitan Statistical Area - see Appendix A for areas included
Source: Census 2000, Summary File 3

School Enrollment by Race

Area	Grades KG to 8 (%)				Grades 9 to 12 (%)			
	White	Black	Asian	Hisp.[1]	White	Black	Asian	Hisp.[1]
City	93.7	0.0	0.2	4.9	94.1	0.0	1.0	3.2
MSA[2]	91.8	0.5	0.6	7.5	93.6	0.2	0.6	6.1
U.S.	68.5	15.5	3.3	16.8	68.8	15.5	3.8	15.7

Note: Figures shown cover persons 3 years old and over; (1) people of Hispanic origin can be of any race; (2) Metropolitan Statistical Area - see Appendix A for areas included
Source: Census 2000, Summary File 3

Average Salaries of Public School Classroom Teachers

District	2005-06 Dollars	2005-06 Rank[1]	2006-07 Dollars	2006-07 Rank[1]	Percent Change 2005-06 to 2006-07
Utah	40,007	46	40,566	47	1.40
U.S. Average	49,026	-	50,816	-	3.65

Note: (1) State rank ranges from 1 to 51.
Source: National Education Association, Rankings & Estimates: Rankings of the States 2006 and Estimates of School Statistics 2007, December 2007

Higher Education

Four-Year Colleges			Two-Year Colleges			Medical Schools[1]	Law Schools[2]	Voc/ Tech[3]
Public	Private Non-profit	Private For-profit	Public	Private Non-profit	Private For-profit			
0	0	0	0	0	1	0	0	0

Note: Figures cover institutions located within the city limits; (1) includes schools accredited by the Liaison Committee on Medical Education and the American Osteopathic Association; (2) includes American Bar Association-accredited law schools; (3) includes all schools with programs that are less than 2 years.
Source: National Center for Education Statistics, The Integrated Postsecondary Education System (IPEDS) Peer Analysis System, 2007; www.usnews.com, Law and Medical School Directories, 2009

PRESIDENTIAL ELECTION

2004 Presidential Election Results

Area	Bush	Kerry	Nader	Other
Utah County	86.0	11.6	0.9	1.5
U.S.	50.7	48.3	0.4	0.6

Note: Results are percentages and may not add to 100% due to rounding
Source: Dave Leip's Atlas of U.S. Presidential Elections, www.uselectionatlas.org

EMPLOYERS

Major Employers

Company Name	Industry	Type of Site
Brigham Young University	Colleges and universities	Headquarters
City of Provo	Executive offices	Headquarters
Geneva Steel	Blast furnaces and steel mills	Headquarters
Missionary Training Center	Religious organizations	Branch
Natures Sunshine	Medicinals and botanicals	Branch
Natures Sunshine Products	Pharmaceutical preparations	Headquarters
Nu Skin Enterprises Inc	Toilet preparations	Headquarters
Nu Skin Enterprises US Inc	Drugs, proprietaries, and sundries	Headquarters
Nu Skin United States Inc	Drugs, proprietaries, and sundries	Branch
Phone Directories Company	Miscellaneous publishing	Headquarters
Tahitian Noni International	Groceries and related products, nec	Headquarters
Timpangos Strytelling Festival	Membership organizations, nec	Single
Utah State Development Center	Elementary and secondary schools	Branch
Utah State Hospital	Psychiatric hospitals	Branch
Utah Valley State College	Colleges and universities	Headquarters
Western Wats	Business services, nec	Single
Xango LLC	Catalog and mail-order houses	Single

Note: Companies shown are located within the Provo metropolitan area; nec = not elsewhere classified.
Source: www.zapdata.com, May 2008

PUBLIC SAFETY

Crime Rate

Area	All Crimes	Violent Crimes: Murder	Violent Crimes: Forcible Rape	Violent Crimes: Robbery	Violent Crimes: Aggrav. Assault	Property Crimes: Burglary	Property Crimes: Larceny -Theft	Property Crimes: Motor Vehicle Theft
City	2,507.9	0.0	29.1	3.6	40.0	458.6	1,900.0	76.4
Metro[1]	2,591.3	0.6	23.3	13.5	56.0	465.1	1,896.2	136.4
U.S.	3,808.1	5.7	30.9	149.4	287.5	729.4	2,206.8	398.4

Note: Figures are crimes per 100,000 population; (1) Metropolitan Statistical Area - see Appendix B for areas included
Source: FBI Uniform Crime Reports, 2006

Hate Crimes

Area	Number of Quarters Reported	Bias Motivation				
		Race	Religion	Sexual Orientation	Ethnicity	Disability
City	4	0	0	0	0	0

Source: Federal Bureau of Investigation, Hate Crime Statistics 2006

RECREATION

Culture

Dance[1]	Theatre[1]	Instrumental Music[1]	Vocal Music[1]	Series/ Festivals	Museums	Zoos and Aquariums[2]
0	0	0	0	0	0	0

Note: (1) Number of professional perfoming groups; (2) AZA-accredited
Source: The Grey House Performing Arts Directory, 2007; Official Museum Directory, 2008; Association of Zoos & Aquariums, AZA Member Zoos & Aquariums, June 2008

Professional Sports Teams

Team Name	League
No teams are located in the metro area	

Source: Original research

MEDIA

Newspapers

Name	News Focus	Frequency	Circulation
Press	Local	n/a	3,000

Note: Includes newspapers with offices located in the city; n/a not available
Source: MediaContactsPro, March 2008

Television Stations

Name	Ch.	Network(s)	Type	Ownership
KUTV	2	CBS	Commercial	CBS
KCSG	4	Pax	Commercial	n/a
KTVX	4	ABC	Commercial	n/a
KSL	5	NBC	Commercial	Bonneville International Corporation
KUED	7	PBS	Public	University of Utah
KUEN	9	n/a	Public	Utah State Board of Regents
KENV	10	NBC	Commercial	Sunbelt Broadcasting Company
KBYU	11	PBS	Public	Brigham Young University
KDLQ	13	Fox/ABC	Commercial	n/a
KSTU	13	Fox	Commercial	Fox Television Stations Inc.
KJZZ	14	n/a	Commercial	Larry H. Miller Communications
KUPX	16	Pax	Commercial	Paxson Communications Corporation
KUEW	18	PBS	n/a	University of Utah
KUWB	30	WBN	Commercial	Acme Television Holdings

Note: Stations included cover the Salt Lake City DMA (Designated Market Area)
BurrellesLuce, MediaContacts Online, January 2007

Major AM Radio Stations

Call Letters	Freq. (kHz)	Station Type	Target Audience	Station Format	Music Format
KNRS	570	Commercial	General	News/Talk	n/a
KSUB	590	n/a	General	News/Sports/Talk	n/a
KVNU	610	Commercial	General	News/Talk	n/a
KMTI	650	Commercial	General	Music/News/Sports/Talk	Country
KOAL	750	n/a	General	News/Sports/Talk	n/a
KBEE	860	Commercial	General	Music/Talk	Country
KDXU	890	Commercial	General	News/Talk	n/a
KALL	910	Commercial	General	News	n/a
KMER	950	Commercial	General	News	n/a
KOVO	960	Commercial	General	Sports/Talk	n/a
KSVC	980	Commercial	General	News/Sports/Talk	n/a
KKDS	1060	Commercial	General	Music/News	Adult Contemp.
KAFL	1080	Commercial	General	Music	Country
KANN	1120	Non-Comm	Religious	Educational/Music/News	Christian
KSL	1160	Commercial	General	News/Talk	n/a
KUNF	1210	Commercial	General	Music/News	Easy Listening
KRSV	1210	Commercial	General	Music/News/Sports	Country
KEVA	1240	Commercial	General	News	n/a
KNEU	1250	Commercial	General	Music/News	Country
KZNS	1280	Commercial	General	News/Sports/Talk	n/a
KFNZ	1320	n/a	General/Men	Music/Sports	n/a
KRKK	1360	n/a	General	Music/News	n/a
KSOP	1370	Commercial	General	Music/News	Country
KLGN	1390	Commercial	General	Music/News/Sports/Talk	Adult Standards
KLO	1430	Commercial	General	Music/News/Sports/Talk	n/a
KXOL	1660	n/a	General	Music	n/a

Note: Stations included cover the Salt Lake City DMA (Designated Market Area); n/a not available
Source: BurrellesLuce, MediaContacts Online, January 2007

Major FM Radio Stations

Call Letters	Freq. (mHz)	Station Type	Target Audience	Station Format	Music Format
KBYU	89.1	College	General	Music/News	Classical
KUER	90.1	College	General	Music/News	Jazz
KUSU	91.5	College	General	Educational/Music/News	Classic Rock
KBLQ	92.9	Commercial	General	Music/News/Sports	Soft Rock
KCYQ	93.7	Commercial	General	Music	Country
KODJ	94.1	Commercial	General	Music	Oldies
KVFX	94.5	Commercial	General	Music	Adult Contemp.
KZHT	94.9	Commercial	General/Women	Music	Top 40
KXBN	94.9	Commercial	General	Music	Top 40
KYCS	95.1	Commercial	General	Music/News	Adult Contemp.
KYFO	95.5	Non-Comm	General	Music/Talk	Christian
KFNN	95.7	Commercial	General	Music/News	Adult Contemp.
KXRK	96.3	n/a	Gay/Lesbian	Music	n/a
KQSW	96.5	Commercial	General	Music/News	Country
KISN	97.1	Commercial	General	Music	Adult Contemp.
KREC	98.1	Commercial	General	Educational/Music/News	Adult Contemp.
KBEE	98.7	n/a	General	Music/News/Sports	n/a
KURR	99.5	Commercial	General/Native Amer	Music/Talk	Classic Rock
KONY	101.1	Commercial	General	Music	Contemp. Country
KXFF	102.9	n/a	n/a	n/a	n/a
KUDD	103.9	Commercial	General/Women	Music	Top 40
KSIT	104.5	Commercial	General	Music/News	Classic Rock
KNFL	104.9	n/a	General	Music	Oldies
KENZ	107.5	n/a	General	Music	n/a

Note: Stations included cover the Salt Lake City DMA (Designated Market Area); n/a not available
BurrellesLuce, MediaContacts Online, January 2007

CLIMATE

Average and Extreme Temperatures

Temperature	Jan	Feb	Mar	Apr	May	Jun	Jul	Aug	Sep	Oct	Nov	Dec	Yr.
Extreme High (°F)	62	69	78	85	93	104	107	104	100	89	75	67	107
Average High (°F)	37	43	52	62	72	83	93	90	80	66	50	38	64
Average Temp. (°F)	28	34	41	50	59	69	78	76	65	53	40	30	52
Average Low (°F)	19	24	31	38	46	54	62	61	51	40	30	22	40
Extreme Low (°F)	-22	-14	2	15	25	35	40	37	27	16	-14	-15	-22

Note: Figures cover the years 1948-1990
Source: National Climatic Data Center, International Station Meteorological Climate Summary, 9/96

Average Precipitation/Snowfall/Humidity

Precip./Humidity	Jan	Feb	Mar	Apr	May	Jun	Jul	Aug	Sep	Oct	Nov	Dec	Yr.
Avg. Precip. (in.)	1.3	1.2	1.8	2.0	1.7	0.9	0.8	0.9	1.1	1.3	1.3	1.4	15.6
Avg. Snowfall (in.)	13	10	11	6	1	Tr	0	0	Tr	2	6	13	63
Avg. Rel. Hum. 5am (%)	79	77	71	67	66	60	53	54	60	68	75	79	67
Avg. Rel. Hum. 5pm (%)	69	59	47	38	33	26	22	23	28	40	59	71	43

Note: Figures cover the years 1948-1990; Tr = Trace amounts (<0.05 in. of rain; <0.5 in. of snow)
Source: National Climatic Data Center, International Station Meteorological Climate Summary, 9/96

Weather Conditions

Temperature			Daytime Sky			Precipitation		
5°F & below	32°F & below	90°F & above	Clear	Partly cloudy	Cloudy	0.01 inch or more precip.	0.1 inch or more snow/ice	Thunder-storms
7	128	56	94	152	119	92	38	38

Note: Figures are average number of days per year and cover the years 1948-1990
Source: National Climatic Data Center, International Station Meteorological Climate Summary, 9/96

HAZARDOUS WASTE

Superfund Sites

Spanish Fork has no sites on the EPA's Superfund Final National Priorities List.
U.S. Environmental Protection Agency, Final National Priorities List, June 23, 2008

AIR & WATER QUALITY

Air Quality Index

Area	Percent of Days when Air Quality was...[2]				AQI Statistics	
	Good	Moderate	Unhealthy for Sensitive Groups	Unhealthy	Maximum	Median
MSA[1]	57.5	35.6	5.2	1.6	156	46

Note: The Air Quality Index (AQI) is an index for reporting daily air quality. EPA calculates the AQI for five major air pollutants regulated by the Clean Air Act: ground-level ozone, particle pollution (also known as particulate matter), carbon monoxide, sulfur dioxide, and nitrogen dioxide. The AQI runs from 0 to 500. The higher the AQI value, the greater the level of air pollution and the greater the health concern. There are six AQI categories: "Good" The AQI is between 0 and 50. Air quality is considered satisfactory; "Moderate" The AQI is between 51 and 100. Air quality is acceptable; "Unhealthy for Sensitive Groups" When AQI values are between 101 and 150, members of sensitive groups may experience health effects; "Unhealthy" When AQI values are between 151 and 200 everyone may begin to experience health effects; "Very Unhealthy" AQI values between 201 and 300 trigger a health alert; "Hazardous" AQI values over 300 trigger health warnings of emergency conditions; (1) Metropolitan Statistical Area - see Appendix A for areas included; (2) Based on 365 days with AQI data in 2007.
Source: U.S. Environmental Protection Agency, Air Quality Index Report, 2007

Air Quality Index Pollutants

Area	Percent of Days when AQI Pollutant was...[2]					
	Carbon Monoxide	Nitrogen Dioxide	Ozone	Sulfur Dioxide	Particulate Matter 2.5	Particulate Matter 10
MSA[1]	0.8	0.0	38.1	0.0	54.0	7.1

Note: The Air Quality Index (AQI) is an index for reporting daily air quality. EPA calculates the AQI for five major air pollutants regulated by the Clean Air Act: ground-level ozone, particle pollution (also known as particulate matter), carbon monoxide, sulfur dioxide, and nitrogen dioxide. The AQI runs from 0 to 500. The higher the AQI value, the greater the level of air pollution and the greater the health concern; (1) Metropolitan Statistical Area - see Appendix A for areas included; (2) Based on 365 days with AQI data in 2007.
Source: U.S. Environmental Protection Agency, Air Quality Index Report, 2007

Air Quality Index Trends

Area	Trend Sites								All Sites
	1999	2000	2001	2002	2003	2004	2005	2006	2006
MSA[1]	n/a	n/a	n/a	n/a	n/a	n/a	n/a	n/a	n/a

Note: An AQI value greater than 100 indicates that air quality would have been in the unhealthful range on that day. Data from exceptional events are not included. These counts are presented in two ways. First, the counts are based on sites having an adequate record of monitoring data during the trend period (trend sites). These counts represent the relative change in the number of days with AQI values greater than 100. In the last column, the counts are based on all sites with data in the most recent year (because it is possible for a site to have data in the most recent year but not enough data to be a trend site); (1) Metropolitan Statistical Area - see Appendix A for areas included; n/a not available.
Source: U.S. Environmental Protection Agency, Office of Air and Radiation, Air Trends, Factbook and Related Information, Air Pollution Trends in Selected Metropolitan Areas 2006

Maximum Air Pollutant Concentrations

	Particulate Matter 10 (ug/m^3)	Particulate Matter 2.5 (ug/m^3)	Ozone (ppm)	Carbon Monoxide (ppm)	Sulfur Dioxide (ppm)	Nitrogen Dioxide (ppm)	Lead (ug/m^3)
MSA[1] Level	90	32	0.101	3	n/a	0.029	n/a
NAAQS[2]	150	35	0.125	9	0.140	0.053	1.50
Met NAAQS[2]	Yes	Yes	Yes	Yes	n/a	Yes	n/a

Note: Data from exceptional events are not included; (1) Metropolitan Statistical Area - see Appendix A for areas included; (2) National Ambient Air Quality Standards; n/a not available
Concentrations: Particulate Matter 10 (coarse particulate) - highest second maximum 24-hour concentration; Particulate Matter 2.5 (fine particulate) - highest 98th percentile 24-hour concentration; Ozone - highest second daily maximum 1-hour concentration; Carbon Monoxide - highest second maximum non-overlapping 8-hour concentration; Sulfur Dioxide - highest second maximum 24-hour concentration; Nitrogen Dioxide - highest arithmetic mean concentration; Lead - highest quarterly maximum concentration
Units: ppm = parts per million; ug/m^3 = micrograms per cubic meter
Source: U.S. Environmental Protection Agency, MSA Factbook 2006, Air Quality Statistics by City

Drinking Water

Water System Name	Pop. Served	Primary Water Source Type	Violations[1]	
			Health Based	Monitoring/ Reporting
Spanish Fork	21,941	Ground	0	0

Note: (1) Based on violation data from January 1, 2007 to December 31, 2007 (includes unresolved violations from earlier years)
Source: U.S. Environmental Protection Agency, Office of Ground Water and Drinking Water, Safe Drinking Water Information System (based on data extracted April 15, 2008)

Burlington, Vermont

Background

Situated on Lake Champlain's eastern shore, between the Adirondack Mountains and Green Mountains, Burlington is one of the nation's most livable smaller cities. During the last decades of the twentieth century, it enjoyed robust growth in many spheres - population, economics, and quality of life, to name three. The city has become the most diverse and advanced in the state of Vermont. The greater Burlington area, which embraces surrounding communities such as Colchester, Winooski, Essex Junction, South Burlington, and Shelburne, is consistently cited in "the best of" surveys of every kind.

The record for civic improvements is outstanding. Burlington was one of the first cities to create a downtown pedestrian shopping mall, and it has completely restored its waterfront.

The city is highly favorable for business, with a well-educated work force in many types of industry - electronic circuitry, software, printing, complex instruments large machine tools, chemicals, and food products, among others. Top employers include IBM, Fletcher Allen Health Care, Chittenden Corporation, Verizon, Banknorth, IDX Corporation, and Ben & Jerry's Homemade, Inc.

The school system is forward-looking. There is an active school-to-work program. In 2003 a new nonprofit organization, Linking Learning to Life, Inc. (LLC), was formed to manage and support all school-to-work activities in the region. The Greater Burlington Chamber of Commerce is a strong partner in this endeavor. Finally, the Learn to Earn education initiative encourages students toward higher-level math, science, and technology courses, making them better prepared for the high-tech and specialized manufacturing jobs of the future.

Burlington is equally well endowed as to higher education. The University of Vermont (UVM), founded in 1791, offers seven undergraduate schools and colleges, more than 90 academic programs, five pre-professional programs, and a fine medical school, which is affiliated with Fletcher Allen Health Care, a major teaching hospital.

Champlain College, founded in 1878, offers four-year and two-year degrees that are highly attuned to the needs of the marketplace; there is an active internship program. The Community College of Vermont has one of its 12 statewide centers in downtown Burlington, offering associate degrees and career-oriented programs. Burlington College focuses on a progressive liberal-arts program. Middlebury College, one of the nation's finest liberal arts colleges, is nearby.

The cultural offerings of the Burlington area are in keeping with the interests of its diverse and broadly educated population. The Shelburne Museum in Shelburne, Vermont, has an eclectic collection of art, Americana, architecture, and artifacts, housed in 37 buildings on a 45-acre campus. Exhibits are truly unusual, including an exhibit of children's pedal cars from 1907 to 1970. The Fleming Museum, affiliated with the University of Vermont, houses the state's most comprehensive collection of art and archaeology and serves as a vital teaching center. And at Middlebury College there is Henry Sheldon Museum of Early Vermont History.

Notable musical festivals take place each summer, including the Vermont Mozart Festival, held at Shelburne Museum and other venues, and the Champlain Valley Folk Festival in nearby Ferrisburgh.

Burlington has a generally continental climate with prevailing westerly winds and four distinct seasons. However, Lake Champlain does much to reduce extremes of temperature, prompting the description "banana belt." Winters are milder, and spring comes a little earlier here than elsewhere in the state, and the lake effect prolongs summery weather well into the fall.

Rankings

General Rankings

- Burlington* was ranked #307 out of 375 metro areas in *Cities Ranked & Rated*. Criteria: cost of living; climate; crime; transportation; economy and jobs; education; arts and culture; health and healthcare; leisure; quality of life. *Cities Ranked & Rated, 2nd Edition, 2007*

- Burlington* was ranked #55 out of 379 metro areas in *Places Rated Almanac*. Criteria: health care; education; recreation; transportation; ambience; climate; crime; housing costs; jobs. *Places Rated Almanac, 7th Edition, 2007*

- *Men's Health Living* ranked 100 U.S. cities in terms of quality of life. Burlington was ranked #2 and received a grade of A+. Criteria: number of fitness facilities; air quality; number of physicians; male/female ratio; education levels; household income; cost of living. *Men's Health Living, Spring 2008*

- *Expansion Management* rated 362 metro areas to find out which offer the best middle class lifestyle for manufacturing and service companies. The Burlington* metro area was selected as a "5-Star Quality of Life Metro" (a distinction the magazine awards to the top 20 percent of metro areas studied). The annual "Quality of Life Quotient" measures dozens of indicators across nine major categories and compares them among 362 metropolitan statistical areas in the United States. The categories are: affordable housing; good public schools; low crime levels; adult education level; standard of living; traffic and commuting; continuing education opportunities; commercial air access; labor market. *Expansion Management, June 2007*

- Burlington was selected as one of "America's Best Places to Live" by monstermoving.com. The top 10 cities were selected based on the fact that they appear repeatedly on other publications' "Top Cities" lists. *www.monstermoving.com, February 26, 2004*

Business/Finance Rankings

- The Burlington* metro area was selected one of America's "Top 50 Business Opportunity Metros" by *Expansion Management* in their 5th annual Mayor's Challenge ranking of metro areas that have achieved solid ratings across the board in numerous *EM* studies during the past 12 months. The area ranked #38. Criteria: public schools; quality of life; college educated workers; logistics infrastructure; healthcare costs; taxes and government spending; reputation among site consultants. *Expansion Management, August 2007*

- Burlington* was selected as one of the best places to start and grow a company by *Entrepreneur* and the National Policy Research Council. The Burlington* metro area ranked #131 out of 162 small metro areas. Criteria: business formation and growth (firms started four to 14 years ago that still employ at least 5 people and experienced rapid growth over the last four years). *Entrepreneur/National Policy Research Council, "Hot Cities for Entrepreneurs," September 2006*

- Burlington was selected as one of 20 cities in North America that is doing its part to host green conventions by providing renewable energy, intelligent recycling programs, transportation that minimizes usage of fossil fuels, and plenty of parkland. The city was ranked #18. *Meetings and Conventions, "Natural Choices," August 2006*

- The Burlington* metro area appeared on the Milken Institute "2007 Best Performing Cities" index. Rank: #125 out of 179 small metro areas. Criteria: job growth; wage and salary growth; high-tech output growth. *Milken Institute, "2007 Best Performing Cities"*

- *Forbes* ranked 179 smaller metro areas in the U.S. in terms of the "Best Places for Business and Careers." The Burlington* metro area was ranked #86. Criteria: business costs (labor, energy, tax and office space expenses); living costs (housing, transportation, food and other household expenditures); education levels of the work force; job growth; income growth; migration trends; crime rates; and culture/leisure. *Forbes, "Best Places for Business and Careers," March 19, 2008*

- *Kiplinger's Personal Finance* ranked 101 U.S. cities in terms of their total tax burdens. Burlington ranked #37 (#1 had the lowest overall tax burden). Criteria: state income tax; property tax; sales tax; personal property tax; and gasoline tax. *Kiplinger's Personal Finance, July 2004*

- Burlington appeared on *Kiplinger's Personal Finance* list of the "Top Ten Tax-Friendly Cities." The city was ranked #37. Criteria: income tax; sales tax; real estate and car/personal property tax. *Kiplinger's Personal Finance, May 2007*

Health/Environment Rankings

- The American Academy of Dermatology ranked 32 U.S. metropolitan regions in terms of their residents knowledge, attitude and behaviors towards tanning and sun protection. The Burlington* metro area ranked #14. The results of the study are based on an online national survey of 3,342 respondents. *American Academy of Dermatology, "RAYS: Your Grade," May 7, 2007*

- The Burlington* metro area appeared in *Country Home's* "2008 Best Green Places" report. The area ranked #36 out of 379. Criteria: official energy policies; green power; green buildings; availability of fresh, locally grown food. *Country Home, "2008 Best Green Places"*

- The American Podiatric Medical Association and *Prevention* magazine ranked America's 100 most populated cities based on fitness-walker friendliness. The best cities have safe streets, beautiful places to walk, mild weather and good air quality. Burlington ranked #42. *Prevention, "The Best Walking Cities of 2008," April 2008; American Podiatric Medical Association, "2008 Best Fitness-Walking Cities, "April 2008*

- Burlington was selected as one of "The Top Ten Greenest Cities" in the U.S. Criteria: cities that are obsessed with clean air and clean water, renewable energy, reliable city buses, trams, streetcars and subways, a growing number of parks, greenbelts, farmer's markets, and opportunities for community involvement. *Move.com, "The Top Ten Greenest Cities," May 18, 2007*

- *Men's Health* ranked 100 U.S. cities in terms of the quality of their tap water. Burlington was ranked #84 and received a grade of D. Criteria: levels of total coliform bacteria, arsenic, lead, total trihalomethanes (linked to cancer), and halo-acetic acids; number of EPA water-system violations from 1995 to 2005. *Men's Health, March 2007*

- Sperling's BestPlaces ranked 331 metro areas and identified the most and least stressful U.S. cities. The Burlington* metro area ranked #95 out of the 117 smallest metro areas (#1 = most stressful). Criteria: divorce rate; unemployment rate; violent and property crime; suicide rate; commute time; mental health; alcohol consumption; cloudy days. *Sperling's BestPlaces, www.BestPlaces.net, "America's Most (and Least) Stressful Cities," January 9, 2004*

- Burlington* was highlighted as one of the cleanest metro areas for ozone air pollution in the U.S. The list represents cities with no monitored ozone air pollution in unhealthful ranges. *American Lung Association, State of the Air: 2007*

Women/Minorities Rankings

- Burlington* was ranked #5 out of 100 metro areas in *SELF Magazine's* ranking of "America's Best Places for Women." A panel of experts came up with more than 50 criteria including death and disease rates, environmental indicators, community resources, and lifestyle habits. *SELF Magazine, "America's Best Places for Women 2007," December 2007*

- Burlington was profiled in the book *50 Fabulous Gay-Friendly Places to Live.* Criteria: an active gay community; positive gay health programs; youth outreach; gay-friendly politics; gay-owned and gay-friendly businesses; employment opportunities; fun nightlife; cultural opportunities; recreational opportunities; housing options. *50 Fabulous Gay-Friendly Places to Live, 2005*

- Burlington* appeared on a list of the top 10 metro areas with the highest concentration of lesbian couples. The area ranked #6. *Urban Institute Press, The Gay and Lesbian Atlas, May 2004*

Seniors/Retirement Rankings

- Burlington was profiled in the book *Where to Retire: America's Best and Most Affordable Places.* Cities were selected based on personal visits by the author and interviews with local residents coupled with statistics from various government agencies. *Where to Retire: America's Best and Most Affordable Places, 2006*
- Burlington was identified as one of the 50 best places to retire in America. Criteria: climate; taxes; cost of living; jobs; medical care; services for seniors; continuing education; crime and safety; transportation; culture and recreation. *50 Fabulous Places to Retire in America, 3rd Edition, 2006*
- Burlington was profiled in the book *Retire in Style: 60 Outstanding Places Across the USA and Canada.* Criteria: landscape; climate; quality of life; cost of living; transportation; retail services; health care; community services; cultural and educational activities; recreational activities; work and volunteer activities; crime rates and public safety. *Retire in Style: 60 Outstanding Places Across the USA and Canada, 2nd Edition, 2005*
- Burlington was identified as one of the best places to retire in *Retirement Places Rated.* Criteria: population above 10,000; attractiveness to older adults; affordability; climate and natural endowments; personal safety. The city was ranked #62 out of 200. *Retirement Places Rated, 7th Edition, 2007*
- A.G. Edwards ranked America's 500 top-performing communities based on their residents' personal savings and investing behavior. The Burlington* metro area ranked #77 with an index score of 107.35 (national average = 100.00). A dozen statistical factors were measured including: participation in retirement savings plans; personal debt levels; and home ownership. *A.G. Edwards, "2007 Nest Egg Index", September 12, 2007*

Safety Rankings

- The National Insurance Crime Bureau ranked 361 metro areas in the U.S. in terms of per capita rates of vehicle theft. The Burlington* metro area ranked #328 (#1 = highest rate). Criteria: number of vehicle theft offenses per 100,000 inhabitants. *National Insurance Crime Bureau, "NICB Vehicle Theft Study," April 22, 2008*
- Farmers Insurance Group of Companies, in partnership with Sperling's BestPlaces, ranked 379 metro areas and identified the "Most Secure U.S. Place to Live." The Burlington* metro area ranked #13 out of 127 in the mid-size city category (150,000 to 500,000 residents). Criteria: crime rates; extreme weather; risk of natural disasters; environmental hazards; terrorism threats; air quality; life expectancy; job loss numbers. *Farmers Insurance Group, "Most Secure U.S. Places to Live 2007"*

Sports/Recreation Rankings

- Burlington was chosen as one of "The 10 Best Cities for Mountain Bikers." The city was ranked #10. Criteria: great trails within or very close to the city; the city had to be a place where people could actually live—with good jobs, decent schools, affordable housing, arts and sports, and a sense of community. *Mountain Bike, June 2001*
- Burlington was selected as one of the best towns in the U.S. Editors at *Outside Magazine* asked the best adventure athletes in America where they live and why. *Outside Magazine, "Best Towns 2007," August 2007*
- *Golf Digest* ranked 330 metro areas in the U.S. in terms of golf. The Burlington* metro area was ranked #270. Criteria: access to golf; weather; value of golf; and quality of golf. *Golf Digest, "Metro Golf Rankings," August 2005*

Culture/Performing Arts Rankings

- Burlington was selected as one of America's 10 best large (population 30,000 - 100,000) art towns. The city ranked #1. Criteria: number of art galleries; affordability; natural beauty; local support for the arts; availability of suitable studio and rehearsal space; frequency and impact of art festivals; cohesiveness of the local arts community; diversity of creative statements being made by local visual and performing artists; number of theaters, art schools, art museums, and alternative exhibition and performance venues. *The 100 Best Art Towns in America: A Guide to Galleries, Museums, Festivals, Lodging, and Dining, 4th Edition, 2005*

- Burlington was selected as one of "America's Top 25 Arts Destinations." The city ranked #17 in the small city (population under 100,000) category. Criteria: readers' top choices for arts travel destinations based on the richness and variety of visual arts sites, activities and events. *American Style, June 2007*

Miscellaneous Rankings

- Burlington appeared on Procter & Gamble's list of the "Top 100 Sweatiest Cities". The city was ranked #93. The ranking was based on computer simulations of the amount of sweat a person of average height and weight would produce walking around for an hour in the average high temperatures during June, July and August of 2006 for each city. *Procter & Gamble, Old Spice, June 18, 2007*

  Burlington is located within the Burlington-South Burlington, VT Metropolitan Statistical Area.

Business Environment

CITY FINANCES

City Government Finances

Component	2004-2005 ($000)	2004-2005 ($ per capita)
Total Revenues	129,686	3,366
Total Expenditures	135,325	3,512
Debt Outstanding	194,005	5,035
Cash and Securities	49,875	1,294

Source: U.S Census Bureau, Government Finances 2004-2005

City Government Revenue by Source

Source	2004-2005 ($000)	2004-2005 ($ per capita)
General Revenue		
From Federal Government	7,319	190
From State Government	797	21
From Local Governments	1,232	32
Taxes		
Property	21,692	563
Sales	3,388	88
Personal Income	0	0
License	1,764	46
Charges	28,106	729
Liquor Store	0	0
Utility	47,965	1,245
Employee Retirement	8,301	215
Other	9,122	237

Source: U.S Census Bureau, Government Finances 2004-2005

City Government Expenditures by Function

Function	2004-2005 ($000)	2004-2005 ($ per capita)	2004-2005 (%)
General Expenditures			
Airports	15,998	415	11.8
Corrections	0	0	0.0
Education	0	0	0.0
Fire Protection	5,035	131	3.7
Governmental Administration	8,407	218	6.2
Health	0	0	0.0
Highways	5,711	148	4.2
Hospitals	0	0	0.0
Housing and Community Development	6,768	176	5.0
Interest on General Debt	3,038	79	2.2
Libraries	1,638	43	1.2
Parking	3,510	91	2.6
Parks and Recreation	4,269	111	3.2
Police Protection	8,893	231	6.6
Public Welfare	0	0	0.0
Sewerage	5,443	141	4.0
Solid Waste Management	1,026	27	0.8
Liquor Store	0	0	0.0
Utility	47,137	1,223	34.8
Employee Retirement	7,454	193	5.5
Other	10,998	285	8.1

Source: U.S Census Bureau, Government Finances 2004-2005

Municipal Bond Ratings

Area	Moody's
City	Aa3

Source: Mergent Bond Record, January 2008 (unless noted otherwise)

DEMOGRAPHICS

Population Growth

Area	1990 Census	2000 Census	2007 Estimate	2012 Projection	Population Growth (%) 1990-2000	Population Growth (%) 2000-2012
City	39,127	38,889	37,232	36,069	-0.6	-7.3
MSA[1]	177,059	198,889	206,666	211,157	12.3	6.2
U.S.	248,709,873	281,421,906	301,045,522	314,920,978	13.2	11.9

Note: (1) Metropolitan Statistical Area - see Appendix B for areas included
Source: Claritas, Inc.

Number of Households and Average Household Size

Area	2007 Estimate	2007 Average Household Size
City	15,530	2.40
MSA[1]	80,431	2.57
U.S.	113,668,003	2.65

Note: (1) Metropolitan Statistical Area - see Appendix B for areas included
Source: Claritas, Inc.

Race and Ethnicity

Area	White Alone[2]	Black Alone[2]	Asian Alone[2]	Other Race Alone[2]	Hispanic[3]
City	90.6	2.2	3.1	4.2	1.6
MSA[1]	94.8	0.9	1.7	2.6	1.1
U.S.	73.1	12.4	4.3	10.3	14.9

Note: Figures are 2007 estimates; (1) Metropolitan Statistical Area - see Appendix B for areas included (2) Alone is defined as not being in combination with one or more other races; (3) May be of any race.
Source: Claritas, Inc.

Ancestry

Area	German	Irish[2]	English	American	Italian	Polish	French[3]	Scottish
City	10.2	17.8	13.6	4.7	7.1	3.6	12.7	3.7
MSA[1]	9.9	17.8	15.8	6.7	6.5	3.3	14.7	3.8
U.S.	15.2	10.9	8.7	7.3	5.6	3.2	3.0	1.7

Note: Figures include multiple ancestry (e.g. if a person reported being Irish and Italian, they were included in both columns); (1) Metropolitan Statistical Area - see Appendix A for areas included; (2) Includes Celtic; (3) Includes Alsatian but excludes Basque
Source: Census 2000, Summary File 3

Foreign-Born Population

Area	Percent of Population Born in: Any Foreign Country	Europe	Asia	Africa	Oceania[2]	Canada	Mexico	Latin America[3]
City	8.1	4.0	2.5	0.2	0.0	1.0	0.0	0.3
MSA[1]	5.7	2.1	1.5	0.1	0.0	1.7	0.0	0.2
U.S.	11.1	1.7	2.9	0.3	0.1	0.3	3.3	2.5

Note: (1) Metropolitan Statistical Area - see Appendix A for areas included; (2) Includes Australia, New Zealand subregion, Melanesia, Micronesia, Polynesia, and Oceania n.e.c; (3) Includes Central America (excluding Mexico), South America, and the Caribbean.
Source: Census 2000, Summary File 3

Marriage Status

Area	Never Married	Now Married (excluding Separated)	Separated	Widowed	Divorced
City	50.5	34.1	1.1	5.0	9.2
MSA[1]	31.6	52.9	1.2	5.0	9.5
U.S.	27.1	54.4	2.2	6.6	9.7

Note: Figures are percentages and cover the population 15 years of age and older; (1) Metropolitan Statistical Area - see Appendix A for areas included
Source: Census 2000, Summary File 3

Age Distribution

Area	Under Age 5	Age 5 to 17	Age 18 to 34	Age 35 to 49	Age 50 to 64	Age 65 to 79	80 Years and Over
	Percent of Population						
City	4.3	12.0	42.9	19.0	11.3	7.3	3.3
MSA[1]	6.0	18.0	26.8	25.2	14.2	7.3	2.6
U.S.	6.8	18.9	23.7	23.5	14.8	9.2	3.2

Note: (1) Metropolitan Statistical Area - see Appendix A for areas included
Source: Census 2000, Summary File 3

Male/Female Ratio

Area	Males	Females	Males per 100 Females
City	18,091	19,141	94.5
MSA[1]	101,581	105,085	96.7
U.S.	148,320,305	152,725,217	97.1

Note: Figures are 2007 estimates; (1) Metropolitan Statistical Area - see Appendix B for areas included
Source: Claritas, Inc.

Religion

Area	Catholic	Southern Baptist	United Meth-odist	ELCA[1]	LDS[2]	Presby-terian Church USA	Jewish Est.	Muslim Est.
County	25.3	0.0	2.3	0.4	0.5	0.1	2.1	0.1
U.S.	22.0	7.1	3.7	1.8	1.5	1.1	2.2	0.6

Note: Figures are the number of adherents as a percentage of the total population; Adherents are defined as all members, including full members, their children and the estimated number of other participants who are not considered members (e.g. the baptized, those not confirmed, those regularly attending services, etc.); (1) Evangelical Lutheran Church in America; (2) The Church of Jesus Christ of Latter Day Saints
Source: Reprinted with permission from Religious Congregations and Membership in the United States 2000 (Nashville, Glenmary Research Center, 2002) Copyright Association of Statisticians of American Religious Bodies. All rights reserved.

ECONOMY

Gross Metropolitan Product

Area	2002	2003	2004	2005	2005 Rank[2]
MSA[1]	7.4	7.8	8.4	8.7	188

Note: Figures are in billions of dollars; (1) Burlington-South Burlington, VT Metropolitan Statistical Area - see Appendix A for areas included; (2) Rank ranges from 1 to 361
Source: The U.S. Conference of Mayors, "U.S. Metro Economies: GMP - The Engines of America's Growth," January 2007

Economic Growth

Area	1995 GMP	2005 GMP	Average Annual Growth Rate	Growth Rate Rank[2]
MSA[1]	5.0	8.7	5.8	137

Note: Figures are in billions of dollars; GMP = Gross Metropolitan Product; (1) Burlington-South Burlington, VT Metropolitan Statistical Area - see Appendix A for areas included; (2) Rank ranges from 1 to 361
Source: The U.S. Conference of Mayors, "U.S. Metro Economies: GMP - The Engines of America's Growth," January 2007

INCOME

Per Capita/Median/Average Income

Area	Per Capita ($)	Median Household ($)	Average Household ($)
City	23,140	39,360	53,276
MSA[1]	27,214	55,036	69,063
U.S.	25,495	49,280	66,670

Note: Figures are 2007 estimates; (1) Metropolitan Statistical Area - see Appendix B for areas included
Source: Claritas, Inc.

Household Income Distribution

Area	Percent of Households Earning							
	Under $15,000	$15,000 -24,999	$25,000 -34,999	$35,000 -49,999	$50,000 -74,999	$75,000 -99,000	$100,000 -149,999	$150,000 and up
City	17.0	13.4	13.8	17.8	17.3	9.3	7.8	3.6
MSA[1]	9.3	9.3	10.2	16.2	21.9	14.3	13.0	5.8
U.S.	13.1	10.9	11.2	15.6	19.5	11.9	11.3	6.6

Note: Figures are 2007 estimates; (1) Metropolitan Statistical Area - see Appendix B for areas included
Source: Claritas, Inc.

Poverty Rates by Age

Area	All Ages	Under 5 Years Old	5 to 17 Years Old	18 to 64 Years Old	65 Years and Over
City	20.0	0.9	2.7	15.4	1.1
MSA[1]	8.6	0.6	1.5	5.7	0.8
U.S.	12.4	1.2	3.0	6.9	1.2

Note: Figures are percent of population with income in 1999 below poverty level and only include population for whom poverty status is determined; (1) Metropolitan Statistical Area - see Appendix A for areas included
Source: Census 2000, Summary File 3

Personal Bankruptcy Filing Rate

Area	2004	2005	2006
Chittenden County	2.26	3.67	0.96
U.S.	5.31	6.82	2.00

Note: Numbers are per 1,000 population and include Chapter 7 and Chapter 13 filings
Source: Federal Deposit Insurance Corporation (FDIC), Regional Economic Conditions (RECON), 8/23/2007

EMPLOYMENT

Labor Force and Employment

Area	Civilian Labor Force			Workers Employed		
	Dec. 2006	Dec. 2007	% Chg.	Dec. 2006	Dec. 2007	% Chg.
City	22,381	22,026	-1.6	21,795	21,451	-1.6
NECTA[1]	112,948	111,157	-1.6	109,438	107,711	-1.6
U.S.	152,571,000	153,705,000	0.7	146,081,000	146,334,000	0.2

Note: Data is not seasonally adjusted and covers workers 16 years of age and older;
(1) New England City and Town Area - see Appendix B for areas included
Source: Bureau of Labor Statistics, http://stats.bls.gov

Unemployment Rate

Area	2007											
	Jan.	Feb.	Mar.	Apr.	May	Jun.	Jul.	Aug.	Sep.	Oct.	Nov.	Dec.
City	3.3	3.0	2.9	3.0	2.7	3.5	3.2	2.9	3.2	3.1	2.8	2.6
NECTA[1]	4.0	3.8	3.6	3.6	3.0	3.5	3.3	3.0	3.3	3.1	3.0	3.1
U.S.	5.0	4.9	4.5	4.3	4.3	4.7	4.9	4.6	4.5	4.4	4.5	4.8

Note: Data is not seasonally adjusted and covers workers 16 years of age and older; All figures are percentages; (1) New England City and Town Area - see Appendix B for areas included
Source: Bureau of Labor Statistics, http://stats.bls.gov

Employment by Occupation

Occupation Classification	City (%)	MSA[1] (%)	U.S. (%)
Sales and Office	28.6	26.0	26.7
Professional and Related	27.6	27.0	20.2
Service	16.4	13.0	14.9
Production, Transportation, and Material Moving	10.4	11.7	14.6
Management, Business, and Financial	11.7	14.5	13.5
Construction, Extraction, and Maintenance	5.2	7.3	9.4
Farming, Forestry, and Fishing	0.2	0.5	0.7

Note: Figures cover employed civilians 16 years of age and older;
(1) Metropolitan Statistical Area - see Appendix A for areas included
Source: Census 2000, Summary File 3

Employment by Industry

Sector	NECTA[1] Number of Employees	NECTA[1] Percent of Total	U.S. Percent of Total
Government	20,800	17.9	16.3
Education and Health Services	19,100	16.5	13.4
Professional and Business Services	10,500	9.1	13.1
Retail Trade	15,900	13.7	11.6
Manufacturing	14,900	12.9	9.9
Leisure and Hospitality	10,300	8.9	9.6
Financial Activities	5,200	4.5	5.9
Construction	n/a	n/a	5.3
Wholesale Trade	4,000	3.5	4.4
Other Services	3,500	3.0	3.9
Transportation and Utilities	3,000	2.6	3.7
Information	2,900	2.5	2.2
Natural Resources and Mining	n/a	n/a	0.5

Note: Figures cover non-farm employment as of December 2007 and are not seasonally adjusted; (1) New England City and Town Area - see Appendix B for areas included; n/a not available
Source: Bureau of Labor Statistics, http://stats.bls.gov

Average Wages

Occupation	$/Hr.	Occupation	$/Hr.
Accountants and Auditors	29.76	Maids and Housekeeping Cleaners	10.01
Automotive Mechanics	17.08	Maintenance and Repair Workers	15.71
Bookkeepers	16.16	Marketing Managers	47.88
Carpenters	19.20	Nuclear Medicine Technologists	n/a
Cashiers	9.33	Nurses, Licensed Practical	19.82
Clerks, General Office	12.69	Nurses, Registered	31.18
Clerks, Receptionists/Information	12.42	Nursing Aides/Orderlies/Attendants	12.56
Clerks, Shipping/Receiving	14.55	Packers and Packagers, Hand	11.68
Computer Programmers	35.40	Physical Therapists	27.94
Computer Support Specialists	20.11	Postal Service Mail Carriers	21.21
Computer Systems Analysts	36.45	Real Estate Brokers	16.70
Cooks, Restaurant	11.94	Retail Salespersons	12.46
Dentists	n/a	Sales Reps., Exc. Tech./Scientific	25.50
Electrical Engineers	36.47	Sales Reps., Tech./Scientific	26.45
Electricians	20.05	Secretaries, Exc. Legal/Med./Exec.	14.05
Financial Managers	52.94	Security Guards	12.67
First-Line Supervisors/Mgrs., Sales	21.97	Surgeons	n/a
Food Preparation Workers	9.98	Teacher Assistants	11.20
General and Operations Managers	51.69	Teachers, Elementary School	24.30
Hairdressers/Cosmetologists	16.81	Teachers, Secondary School	24.10
Internists	n/a	Telemarketers	13.61
Janitors and Cleaners	11.58	Truck Drivers, Heavy/Tractor-Trailer	17.62
Landscaping/Groundskeeping Workers	11.96	Truck Drivers, Light/Delivery Svcs.	16.15
Lawyers	51.01	Waiters and Waitresses	11.87

Note: Wage data covers the Burlington-South Burlington, VT Metropolitan NECTA - see Appendix B for areas included. Hourly wages for elementary/secondary school teachers and teacher assistants were calculated by the editors from annual wage data assuming a 40 hour work week; n/a not available.
Source: Bureau of Labor Statistics, May 2007 Metro Area Occupational Employment and Wage Estimates

RESIDENTIAL REAL ESTATE

Building Permits

Area	Single-Family 2006	Single-Family 2007p	Single-Family Pct. Chg.	Multi-Family 2006	Multi-Family 2007p	Multi-Family Pct. Chg.	Total 2006	Total 2007p	Total Pct. Chg.
City	10	8	-20.0	0	0	-	10	8	-20.0
U.S.	1,378,200	973,300	-29.4	460,700	407,200	-11.6	1,838,900	1,380,500	-24.9

Note: (p) preliminary; figures cover and represent new, privately-owned housing units authorized (unadjusted data); All permit data are based on estimates with imputation; U.S. figures are based on the new 20,000-place series.
Source: U.S. Census Bureau, Manufacturing, Mining, and Construction Statistics

Homeownership and Housing Vacancies

Area	Homeownership Rate[2] (%)			Rental Vacancy Rate[3] (%)			Homeowner Vacancy Rate[4] (%)		
	2005	2006	2007	2005	2006	2007	2005	2006	2007
MSA[1]	n/a	n/a	n/a	n/a	n/a	n/a	n/a	n/a	n/a
U.S.	68.9	68.8	68.1	9.8	9.8	9.7	1.9	2.4	2.7

Note: (1) Metropolitan Statistical Area - see Appendix B for areas included; (2) The proportion of households that are owners; (3) The proportion of the rental inventory that is vacant for rent; (4) The proportion of the homeowner inventory that is vacant for sale; n/a not available
Source: U.S. Census Bureau, Housing Vacancies and Homeownership Annual Statistics: 2007

TAXES

State Corporate Income Tax Rates

State	Rates and Tax Brackets
Vermont	6.0% > $0; 7.0% > 10k; 8.5% > 25k

Note: Tax rates as of January 1, 2008; Minimum tax $250.
Source: Tax Foundation, www.taxfoundation.org

State Individual Income Tax Rates

State	Federal Deductibility	Marginal Rates (%)	Standard Deduction ($)		Personal Exemptions ($)[1]	
			Single	Joint	Single	Dependents
Vermont	No	3.6 - 9.5 (r)(y)	5,350 (s)	10,700 (s)	3,400 (s)	3,400 (s)

Note: Tax rates as of January 1, 2008; Local- and county-level taxes are not included; n/a not applicable; (1) Married joint filers generally receive double the single exemption; (r) State adjusts its bracket levels for inflation at the end of each year before printing tax forms; (s) Deductions and exemptions tied to federal tax system. Federal deductions and exemptions are indexed for inflation; (y) Brackets are not double for married taxpayers.
Source: Tax Foundation, www.taxfoundation.org

Various State and Local Tax Rates

State and Local Sales and Use (%)	State Sales and Use (%)	Gasoline[1,2] ($/gal.)	Cigarette ($/pack)	Spirits ($/gal.)	Table Wine ($/gal.)	Beer ($/gal.)
7.0	6.0	0.20	1.79	(q)	0.55	0.265

Note: Tax rates as of January 1, 2008; (1) In addition to the 18.4 cpg Federal gasoline tax; (2) Rates may include additional state sales taxes, environmental protection and storage fees/taxes, and local taxes. When necessary, the volume-weighted average of all local taxes is used to approximate the typical statewide rate including local tax; (q) Control state where the implied excise tax rate as calculated by DISCUS is less then zero.
Source: Tax Foundation, www.taxfoundation.org; Original research

State Tax Burdens

Area	Combined State and Local Tax Burden		Combined Federal, State and Local Tax Burden	
	Percent	Rank	Percent	Rank
Vermont	14.1	1	35.1	5
U.S. Average	11.0	-	32.7	-

Note: Figures cover 2007 and measure taxes as a percentage of income
Source: Tax Foundation, www.taxfoundation.org

State Business Tax Climate Index Rankings

State	Overall Rank	Corporate Tax Index Rank	Individual Income Tax Index Rank	Sales Tax Index Rank	Unemployment Insurance Tax Index Rank	Property Tax Index Rank
Vermont	44	32	46	15	16	46

Note: Rankings range from 1 to 50 where 1 is best. Rankings do not average across to Overall Rank. States without a given tax are given a ranking of 1.
Source: Tax Foundation, State Business Tax Climate Index 2008

TRANSPORTATION

Means of Transportation to Work

Area	Car/Truck/Van		Public Transportation			Bicycle	Walked	Other Means	Worked at Home
	Drove Alone	Car-pooled	Bus	Subway	Railroad				
City	62.4	12.0	3.2	0.1	0.0	1.2	16.8	1.2	3.1
MSA[1]	75.7	11.8	1.1	0.0	0.0	0.5	6.1	0.7	4.1
U.S.	75.7	12.2	2.5	1.5	0.5	0.4	2.9	1.0	3.3

Note: Figures are percentages and cover workers 16 years of age and older; (1) Metropolitan Statistical Area - see Appendix A for areas included
Source: Census 2000, Summary File 3

Travel Time to Work

Area	Less Than 15 Minutes	15 to 29 Minutes	30 to 44 Minutes	45 to 59 Minutes	60 Minutes or More
City	46.3	39.0	10.0	2.7	2.1
MSA[1]	36.8	40.9	15.9	3.6	2.9
U.S.	29.4	36.1	19.1	7.4	8.0

Note: Figures are percentages and include workers 16 years old and over; (1) Metropolitan Statistical Area - see Appendix A for areas included
Source: Census 2000, Summary File 3

Living Environment

COST OF LIVING

Cost of Living Index

Composite Index	Groceries	Housing	Utilities	Trans-portation	Health Care	Misc. Goods/ Services
116.8	110.5	132.2	124.9	106.3	104.7	108.8

Note: U.S. = 100; Figures cover the Burlington-Chittenden County VT urban area.
Source: The Council for Community and Economic Research (formerly ACCRA), Cost of Living Index, 2007

Grocery Prices

Area[1]	T-Bone Steak ($/pound)	Frying Chicken ($/pound)	Whole Milk ($/half gal.)	Eggs ($/dozen)	Orange Juice ($/64 oz.)	Coffee ($/11.5 oz.)
City[2]	7.97	1.32	2.38	1.78	3.36	3.04
Avg.	8.93	1.12	2.13	1.52	3.26	3.31
Min.	5.88	0.71	1.33	0.83	2.30	2.20
Max.	12.80	2.07	3.43	3.54	5.79	6.20

Note: (1) Values for the local area are compared with the average, minimum and maximum values for all 331 areas in the Cost of Living Index report; (2) Figures cover the Burlington-Chittenden County VT urban area; **T-Bone Steak** *(price per pound);* **Frying Chicken** *(price per pound, whole fryer);* **Whole Milk** *(half gallon carton);* **Eggs** *(price per dozen, Grade A, large);* **Orange Juice** *(64 oz. Tropicana or Florida Natural);* **Coffee** *(11.5 oz. can, vacuum-packed, Maxwell House, Hills Bros, or Folgers).*
Source: The Council for Community and Economic Research (formerly ACCRA), Cost of Living Index, 2007

Housing and Utility Costs

Area[1]	New Home Price ($)	Apartment Rent ($/month)	All Electric ($/month)	Part Electric ($/month)	Other Energy ($/month)	Telephone ($/month)
City[2]	395,295	1,083	-	85.71	147.39	25.21
Avg.	309,605	782	146.13	78.67	90.16	26.14
Min.	189,877	n/a	82.03	37.41	33.15	17.08
Max.	1,202,800	3,481	271.14	150.60	257.67	37.45

Note: (1) Values for the local area are compared with the average, minimum and maximum values for all 331 areas in the Cost of Living Index report; (2) Figures cover the Burlington-Chittenden County VT urban area; **New Home Price** *(2,400 sf living area, 8,000 sf lot, in urban area with full utilities);* **Apartment Rent** *(950 sf 2 bedroom/1.5 or 2 bath, unfurnished, excluding all utilities except water);* **All Electric** *(average monthly cost for an all-electric home);* **Part Electric** *(average monthly cost for a part-electric home);* **Other Energy** *(average monthly cost for natural gas, fuel oil, coal, wood, and any other forms of energy except electricity);* **Telephone** *(price includes basic monthly rate for a private residential line plus additional local usage charges incurred by a family of four).*
Source: The Council for Community and Economic Research (formerly ACCRA), Cost of Living Index, 2007

Health Care, Transportation, and Other Costs

Area[1]	Doctor ($/visit)	Dentist ($/visit)	Optometrist ($/visit)	Gasoline ($/gallon)	Beauty Salon ($/visit)	Men's Shirt ($)
City[2]	92.72	69.03	86.33	2.72	30.11	34.30
Avg.	79.48	71.93	79.55	2.64	29.52	25.77
Min.	52.08	44.80	43.95	2.19	15.58	16.19
Max.	148.44	126.27	158.83	3.48	60.62	48.53

Note: (1) Values for the local area are compared with the average, minimum and maximum values for all 331 areas in the Cost of Living Index report; (2) Figures cover the Burlington-Chittenden County VT urban area; **Doctor** *(general practitioners routine exam of an established patient);* **Dentist** *(adult teeth cleaning and periodic oral examination);* **Optometrist** *(full vision eye exam for established adult patient);* **Gasoline** *(one gallon regular unleaded, national brand, including all taxes, cash price at self-service pump if available);* **Beauty Salon** *(woman's shampoo, trim, and blow-dry);* **Men's Shirt** *(cotton/polyester dress shirt, pinpoint weave, long sleeves).*
Source: The Council for Community and Economic Research (formerly ACCRA), Cost of Living Index, 2007

HOUSING

House Price Index (HPI)

Area	National Ranking[2]	Quarterly Change (%)	One-Year Change (%)	Five-Year Change (%)
MSA[1]	155	-0.03	1.54	51.67
U.S.[3]	-	0.10	0.84	41.37

Note: The HPI is a weighted repeat sales index. It measures average price changes in repeat sales or refinancings on the same properties. This information is obtained by reviewing repeat mortgage transactions on single-family properties whose mortgages have been purchased or securitized by Fannie Mae or Freddie Mac in January 1975; (1) Metropolitan Statistical Area - see Appendix B for areas included; (2) Rankings are based on annual percentage change for all metro areas containing at least 15,000 transactions over the last 10 years and ranges from 1 to 291; (3) figures based on a weighted average of Census Division estimates; all figures are for the period ending December 31, 2007

Source: Office of Federal Housing Enterprise Oversight, House Price Index, February 26, 2008

House Price Valuations

Area	Q1 2000	Q1 2001	Q1 2002	Q1 2003	Q1 2004	Q1 2005	Q1 2006	Q1 2007	Q1 2008
MSA[1]	-13.9	-13.2	-7.7	-7.4	0.8	11.3	14.4	15.4	13.6

Note: Figures show the percentage of over- or under-valuation of single family homes relative to statistically normal house values (e.g. a value of 23.6 indicates that house values are 23.6% overvalued). Statistically normal house values are based on house prices, interest rates, household incomes, population densities, and any historical premiums or discounts metropolitan areas have exhibited over time; (1) Figures cover the Metropolitan Statistical Area - see Appendix B for areas included

Source: Global Insight/National City Corporation, House Prices in America, May 2008

Median Home Prices

Area	2005	2006	2007[r]	Percent Change 2006 to 2007
MSA[1]	n/a	n/a	n/a	n/a
U.S. Average	219.0	221.9	217.9	-1.8

Note: Figures are median sales prices of existing single-family homes in thousands of dollars; (r) revised; n/a not available; (1) Metropolitan Statistical Area - see Appendix B for areas included

Source: National Association of Realtors, Metropolitan Area Prices, 1st Quarter 2008

Housing: Year Structure Built

Area	1990 -2000	1980 -1989	1970 -1979	1960 -1969	1950 -1959	1940 -1949	Before 1940	Median Year
City	7.9	10.3	10.0	11.0	13.2	8.8	38.8	1952
MSA[1]	16.3	17.7	18.0	11.5	9.1	4.8	22.6	1971
U.S.	17.0	15.8	18.5	13.7	12.7	7.3	15.0	1971

Note: Figures are percentages; (1) Metropolitan Statistical Area - see Appendix A for areas included

Source: Census 2000, Summary File 3

HEALTH

Health Risk Data

Category	Area[1] (%)	U.S. (%)
Adults who have been told they have high blood pressure[3]	22.0	25.5
Adults who have been told they have high blood cholesterol[3]	29.6	35.6
Adults who have been told they have diabetes[2]	4.5	7.5
Adults who have been told they have arthritis[3]	22.6	27.0
Adults who have been told they currently have asthma	8.5	8.5
Adults who are current smokers	15.4	20.1
Adults who are heavy drinkers[4]	7.5	4.9
Adults who are overweight (BMI 25.0 - 29.9)	35.1	36.5
Adults who are obese (BMI 30.0 - 99.8)	18.9	25.1

Note: Data as of 2006 unless otherwise noted; (1) Figures cover the Metropolitan Statistical Area - see Appendix B for areas included; (2) Figures do not include pregnancy-related diabetes, pre-diabetes or borderline diabetes; (3) 2005 data; (4) Heavy drinkers are classified as adult men having more than two drinks per day or adult women having more than one drink per day

Source: Centers for Disease Control and Prevention, Behaviorial Risk Factor Surveillance System, SMART: Selected Metropolitan/Micropolitan Area Risk Trends, 2005, 2006

Mortality Rates for the Top 10 Causes of Death in the U.S.

ICD-10[a] Sub-Chapter	ICD-10[a] Code	Age-Adjusted Mortality Rate[1] per 100,000 population	
		County[2]	U.S.
Malignant neoplasms	C00-C97	188.2	186.5
Ischaemic heart diseases	I20-I25	128.4	152.3
Other forms of heart disease	I30-I51	38.6	51.5
Cerebrovascular diseases	I60-I69	36.3	50.0
Chronic lower respiratory diseases	J40-J47	49.2	42.6
Diabetes mellitus	E10-E14	25.2	24.8
Other degenerative diseases of the nervous system	G30-G31	33.5	22.6
Other external causes of accidental injury	W00-X59	25.9	21.4
Influenza and pneumonia	J10-J18	12.2	20.7
Hypertensive diseases	I10-I13	23.1	18.2

Note: (a) ICD-10 = International Classification of Diseases 10th Revision; (1) Mortality rates are a three year average covering 2003-2005; (2) Figures cover Chittenden County
Source: Centers for Disease Control and Prevention, National Center for Health Statistics. Compressed Mortality File 1999-2004. CDC WONDER On-line Database, compiled from Compressed Mortality File 1999-2005 Series 20 No. 2K, 2008.

Mortality Rates for Selected Causes of Death

ICD-10[a] Sub-Chapter	ICD-10[a] Code	Age-Adjusted Mortality Rate[1] per 100,000 population	
		County[2]	U.S.
Assault	X85-Y09	*1.5	5.9
Human immunodeficiency virus (HIV) disease	B20-B24	*1.9	4.5
Intentional self-harm	X60-X84	11.6	10.8
Malnutrition	E40-E46	*0.5	1.0
Obesity and other hyperalimentation	E65-E68	*1.1	1.4
Organic, including symptomatic, mental disorders	F01-F09	22.3	16.8
Transport accidents	V01-V99	8.6	16.1
Viral hepatitis	B15-B19	*1.1	1.8

Note: (a) ICD-10 = International Classification of Diseases 10th Revision; (1) Mortality rates are a three year average covering 2003-2005; (2) Figures cover Chittenden County; (*) Unreliable data as per CDC
Source: Centers for Disease Control and Prevention, National Center for Health Statistics. Compressed Mortality File 1999-2004. CDC WONDER On-line Database, compiled from Compressed Mortality File 1999-2005 Series 20 No. 2K, 2008.

Distribution of Physicians[1]

Area	Total	Family/ General Practice	Specialties	
			Medical	Surgical
Chittenden County (number)	610	151	215	128
Chittenden County (rate per 10,000 pop.)	40.8	10.1	14.4	8.6
U.S. (rate per 10,000 pop.)	17.7	4.6	6.9	4.3

Note: Data as of 2005; (1) Includes all non-federal, patient-care, office-based MDs
Source: Area Resource File (ARF). June 2007. U.S. Department of Health and Human Services, Health Resources and Services Administration, Bureau of Health Professions, Rockville, MD.

Hospitals

Burlington has the following hospitals: 1 general medical and surgical.
AHA Guide to the Healthcare Field 2008

EDUCATION

Public School District Statistics

District Name	Schls	Pupils	Pupil/ Teacher Ratio	Minority Pupils[1] (%)	Free Lunch Eligible[2] (%)	IEP[3] (%)
Burlington School District	12	3,607	10.8	19.1	39.5	14.2

Note: Table includes regular local school districts with 2,000 or more students; (1) Percentage of students that are not white, non-Hispanic; (2) Percentage of students that are eligible for the free lunch program; (3) Percentage of students that have an Individualized Education Program.

Source: U.S. Department of Education, National Center for Education Statistics, Common Core of Data, Local Education Agency (School District) Universe Survey: School Year 2005-2006; U.S. Department of Education, National Center for Education Statistics, Common Core of Data, Public Elementary/Secondary School Universe Survey: School Year 2005-2006

Highest Level of Education

Area	Less than H.S.	H.S. Diploma	Some College, No Deg.	Associate Degree	Bachelors Degree	Masters Degree	Profess. School Degree	Doctorate Degree
City	12.2	22.2	16.7	6.3	26.9	9.9	3.3	2.5
MSA[1]	11.5	27.9	16.8	8.9	21.7	9.0	2.6	1.7
U.S.	19.4	28.4	21.2	6.4	15.7	5.9	2.0	1.0

Note: Figures are 2007 estimated percentages and cover persons age 25 and over; (1) Metropolitan Statistical Area - see Appendix B for areas included

Source: Claritas, Inc.

Educational Attainment by Race

Area	High School Graduate (%)					Bachelor's Degree (%)				
	Total	White	Black	Asian	Hisp.[2]	Total	White	Black	Asian	Hisp.[2]
City	87.7	88.7	76.2	61.9	87.9	42.0	42.7	33.6	35.2	43.8
MSA[1]	89.5	89.9	84.0	76.7	88.2	37.2	37.2	37.3	46.5	45.1
U.S.	80.4	83.6	72.3	80.4	52.4	24.4	26.1	14.3	44.1	10.4

Note: Figures shown cover persons 25 years old and over; (1) Metropolitan Statistical Area - see Appendix A for areas included; (2) people of Hispanic origin can be of any race

Source: Census 2000, Summary File 3

School Enrollment by Type

Area	Grades KG to 8				Grades 9 to 12			
	Public		Private		Public		Private	
	Enrollment	%	Enrollment	%	Enrollment	%	Enrollment	%
City	2,896	89.9	325	10.1	1,355	89.3	162	10.7
MSA[1]	19,471	91.8	1,745	8.2	8,141	89.3	975	10.7
U.S.	33,526,011	88.7	4,285,121	11.3	14,848,628	90.6	1,532,323	9.4

Note: Figures shown cover persons 3 years old and over; (1) Metropolitan Statistical Area - see Appendix A for areas included

Source: Census 2000, Summary File 3

School Enrollment by Race

Area	Grades KG to 8 (%)				Grades 9 to 12 (%)			
	White	Black	Asian	Hisp.[1]	White	Black	Asian	Hisp.[1]
City	87.6	4.7	4.1	1.3	83.3	7.0	6.3	3.2
MSA[2]	94.4	1.2	1.7	0.8	93.3	1.5	2.2	1.8
U.S.	68.5	15.5	3.3	16.8	68.8	15.5	3.8	15.7

Note: Figures shown cover persons 3 years old and over; (1) people of Hispanic origin can be of any race; (2) Metropolitan Statistical Area - see Appendix A for areas included

Source: Census 2000, Summary File 3

Average Salaries of Public School Classroom Teachers

District	2005-06		2006-07		Percent Change
	Dollars	Rank[1]	Dollars	Rank[1]	2005-06 to 2006-07
Vermont	46,622	20	48,370	20	3.75
U.S. Average	49,026	-	50,816	-	3.65

Note: (1) State rank ranges from 1 to 51.
Source: National Education Association, Rankings & Estimates: Rankings of the States 2006 and Estimates of School Statistics 2007, December 2007

Higher Education

Four-Year Colleges			Two-Year Colleges			Medical Schools[1]	Law Schools[2]	Voc/ Tech[3]
Public	Private Non-profit	Private For-profit	Public	Private Non-profit	Private For-profit			
1	2	0	0	0	0	1	0	1

Note: Figures cover institutions located within the city limits; (1) includes schools accredited by the Liaison Committee on Medical Education and the American Osteopathic Association; (2) includes American Bar Association-accredited law schools; (3) includes all schools with programs that are less than 2 years.
Source: National Center for Education Statistics, The Integrated Postsecondary Education System (IPEDS) Peer Analysis System, 2007; www.usnews.com, Law and Medical School Directories, 2009

According to *U.S. News & World Report,* Burlington is home to one of the top 130 colleges and universities in the U.S.: **University of Vermont** (#96). The rankings are based on quantitative measurements such as peer assessment, retention, faculty resources, student selectivity, financial resources, graduation rate, and alumni giving rate. *U.S. News & World Report, "America's Best Colleges 2008"*

PRESIDENTIAL ELECTION

2004 Presidential Election Results

Area	Bush	Kerry	Nader	Other
Chittenden County	34.0	63.5	1.7	0.8
U.S.	50.7	48.3	0.4	0.6

Note: Results are percentages and may not add to 100% due to rounding
Source: Dave Leip's Atlas of U.S. Presidential Elections, www.uselectionatlas.org

EMPLOYERS

Major Employers

Company Name	Industry	Type of Site
Administrative Services	Administration of public health programs	Branch
Air National Guard	National security	Branch
Burton Snowboards	Sporting and athletic goods, nec	Headquarters
Chittenden Bank	State commercial banks	Headquarters
Community College of Vermont	Colleges and universities	Branch
Fletcher Allen Health Care	General medical and surgical hospitals	Headquarters
GE	Custom computer programming services	Headquarters
General Dynamics Armament	Aircraft parts and equipment, nec	Headquarters
Husky Injection Molding	Special industry machinery, nec	Branch
IBM	Semiconductors and related devices	Branch
Itech US Inc	Prepackaged software	Single
Lane Press Inc	Commercial printing, nec	Single
National Guard	National security	Branch
Northwestern Medical Center	General medical and surgical hospitals	Headquarters
Nynex	Telephone communication, except radio	Branch
South Burlington High School	Elementary and secondary schools	Branch
South Burlington School Dst	Elementary and secondary schools	Headquarters
St Michaels College	Colleges and universities	Headquarters
St Stephen R C Church	Religious organizations	Branch
State Police	Police protection	Branch
University of Vermont	Colleges and universities	Branch
Vermont Department Corrections	Correctional institutions	Branch
Vermont Service Center	International affairs	Branch
Vermont State Colleges	Colleges and universities	Branch
Vermont Student Assistance	Schools and educational services	Single
Vermont Student Assistant Corp	Federal and federally sponsored credit	Single
Visiting Nurse Association	Home health care services	Single

Note: Companies shown are located within the Burlington metropolitan area; nec = not elsewhere classified.
Source: www.zapdata.com, May 2008

PUBLIC SAFETY

Crime Rate

Area	All Crimes	Violent Crimes				Property Crimes		
		Murder	Forcible Rape	Robbery	Aggrav. Assault	Burglary	Larceny -Theft	Motor Vehicle Theft
City	4,455.2	2.6	59.6	41.5	298.1	673.9	3,265.6	114.0
Metro[1]	n/a	n/a	n/a	n/a	n/a	n/a	n/a	n/a
U.S.	3,808.1	5.7	30.9	149.4	287.5	729.4	2,206.8	398.4

Note: Figures are crimes per 100,000 population; (1) Metropolitan Statistical Area - see Appendix B for areas included; n/a not available
Source: FBI Uniform Crime Reports, 2006

Hate Crimes

Area	Number of Quarters Reported	Bias Motivation				
		Race	Religion	Sexual Orientation	Ethnicity	Disability
City	4	4	0	3	0	0

Source: Federal Bureau of Investigation, Hate Crime Statistics 2006

RECREATION

Culture

Dance[1]	Theatre[1]	Instrumental Music[1]	Vocal Music[1]	Series/ Festivals	Museums	Zoos and Aquariums[2]
1	1	3	0	3	3	0

Note: (1) Number of professional perfoming groups; (2) AZA-accredited
Source: The Grey House Performing Arts Directory, 2007; Official Museum Directory, 2008; Association of Zoos & Aquariums, AZA Member Zoos & Aquariums, June 2008

Professional Sports Teams

Team Name	League
No teams are located in the metro area	

Source: Original research

MEDIA

Newspapers

Name	News Focus	Frequency	Circulation
Burlington Free Press	Regional	Daily	50,575
North Avenue News	n/a	n/a	n/a
The Vermont Catholic Tribune	Regional	Twice a month	17,874

Note: Includes newspapers with offices located in the city; n/a not available
Source: MediaContactsPro, March 2008

Television Stations

Name	Ch.	Network(s)	Type	Ownership
WCAX	3	CBS	Commercial	Mount Mansfield Television Inc.
WPTZ	5	NBC	Commercial	Hearst-Argyle Broadcasting
WVTB	20	PBS	Public	Vermont Public Television
WVNY	22	ABC	Commercial	Straight Line Communications Inc.
WWBI	27	n/a	Commercial	WWBI TV Inc.
WVER	28	PBS	Public	Vermont Public Television
WNNE	31	NBC	Commercial	Hearst-Argyle Broadcasting
WETK	33	PBS	Public	Vermont Public Television
WVTA	41	PBS	Public	Vermont Public Television
WFFF	44	Fox/WBN	Commercial	Smith Broadcasting Corporation
WCFE	57	PBS	Public	Mountain Lake Public Telecommunications Council

Note: Stations included cover the Burlington DMA (Designated Market Area)
BurrellesLuce, MediaContacts Online, January 2007

Major AM Radio Stations

Call Letters	Freq. (kHz)	Station Type	Target Audience	Station Format	Music Format
WDEV	550	Commercial	General	Music/Talk	Easy Listening
WVMT	620	Commercial	General	News/Talk	n/a
WCHP	760	Commercial	French/General/Rel	Educational/Music	Christian
WNHV	910	Commercial	General	News/Talk	n/a
WEAV	960	Commercial	General	Talk	n/a
WTWN	1100	n/a	General	Music/Talk	n/a
WTSV	1230	Commercial	General	News/Sports	n/a
WJOY	1230	Commercial	General	Music/News	Easy Listening
WNBZ	1240	Commercial	General/Women	Music/News	Adult Standards
WSKI	1240	Commercial	General	Music/News/Talk	Big Band
WWWT	1320	n/a	General	Talk	n/a
WDCR	1340	College	General	Ed/Music/News/Sports/Talk	Urban Contemp.
WIRY	1340	Commercial	General	Music/News/Sports	Oldies
WVNR	1340	Commercial	General	Music/News	Oldies
WSTJ	1340	n/a	General	Music	n/a
WSYB	1380	Commercial	General	News/Sports	n/a
WLTN	1400	n/a	General	News/Sports	n/a
WTSL	1400	Commercial	General	News/Talk	n/a
WRSA	1420	Commercial	General	Music/Talk	Soft Rock
WSNO	1450	n/a	General	News/Sports/Talk	n/a
WFAD	1490	Commercial	General	Music/News/Sports/Talk	Oldies
WICY	1490	Commercial	General	Music/News	Oldies
WIKE	1490	Commercial	General	Music/News/Sports	Contemp. Country

Note: Stations included cover the Burlington DMA (Designated Market Area); n/a not available
Source: BurrellesLuce, MediaContacts Online, January 2007

Major FM Radio Stations

Call Letters	Freq. (mHz)	Station Type	Target Audience	Station Format	Music Format
WVPR	89.5	Public	General	Music/News	Jazz
WEZF	92.9	Commercial	General	Music	Adult Contemp.
WZRT	97.1	n/a	General	Music	n/a
WJJR	98.1	Commercial	General	Music	Soft Rock
WOKO	98.9	Commercial	General	Music/Talk	Country
WNCS	104.7	Commercial	General	Music	Reggae
WHDQ	106.1	Commercial	General	Music	Classic Rock
WIZN	106.7	Commercial	General	Music	Classic Rock
WVPS	107.9	Public	General	Music/News	Jazz

Note: Stations included cover the Burlington DMA (Designated Market Area); n/a not available
BurrellesLuce, MediaContacts Online, January 2007

CLIMATE

Average and Extreme Temperatures

Temperature	Jan	Feb	Mar	Apr	May	Jun	Jul	Aug	Sep	Oct	Nov	Dec	Yr.
Extreme High (°F)	66	62	80	91	93	100	100	99	92	85	75	65	100
Average High (°F)	26	28	38	53	67	76	81	78	69	57	44	31	54
Average Temp. (°F)	18	19	30	44	56	65	70	68	59	48	37	24	45
Average Low (°F)	8	10	21	33	44	54	59	57	49	39	30	16	35
Extreme Low (°F)	-30	-30	-20	2	24	33	39	35	25	15	-2	-26	-30

Note: Figures cover the years 1948-1995
Source: National Climatic Data Center, International Station Meteorological Climate Summary, 9/96

Average Precipitation/Snowfall/Humidity

Precip./Humidity	Jan	Feb	Mar	Apr	May	Jun	Jul	Aug	Sep	Oct	Nov	Dec	Yr.
Avg. Precip. (in.)	1.8	1.7	2.2	2.8	3.0	3.3	3.6	4.0	3.3	3.0	3.0	2.3	34.0
Avg. Snowfall (in.)	19	17	13	4	Tr	0	0	0	Tr	Tr	7	19	79
Avg. Rel. Hum. 7am (%)	73	74	75	74	73	76	78	83	85	82	78	76	77
Avg. Rel. Hum. 4pm (%)	65	61	58	52	51	54	53	56	60	61	67	69	59

Note: Figures cover the years 1948-1995; Tr = Trace amounts (<0.05 in. of rain; <0.5 in. of snow)
Source: National Climatic Data Center, International Station Meteorological Climate Summary, 9/96

Weather Conditions

Temperature			Daytime Sky			Precipitation		
5°F & below	32°F & below	90°F & above	Clear	Partly cloudy	Cloudy	0.01 inch or more precip.	0.1 inch or more snow/ice	Thunder-storms
36	156	7	49	146	170	154	55	22

Note: Figures are average number of days per year and cover the years 1948-1995
Source: National Climatic Data Center, International Station Meteorological Climate Summary, 9/96

HAZARDOUS WASTE

Superfund Sites

Burlington has one hazardous waste site on the EPA's Superfund Final National Priorities List: **Pine Street Canal**. *U.S. Environmental Protection Agency, Final National Priorities List, June 23, 2008*

AIR & WATER QUALITY

Air Quality Index

Area	Percent of Days when Air Quality was...[2]				AQI Statistics	
	Good	Moderate	Unhealthy for Sensitive Groups	Unhealthy	Maximum	Median
MSA[1]	94.5	5.5	0.0	0.0	86	8

Note: The Air Quality Index (AQI) is an index for reporting daily air quality. EPA calculates the AQI for five major air pollutants regulated by the Clean Air Act: ground-level ozone, particle pollution (also known as particulate matter), carbon monoxide, sulfur dioxide, and nitrogen dioxide. The AQI runs from 0 to 500. The higher the AQI value, the greater the level of air pollution and the greater the health concern. There are six AQI categories: "Good" The AQI is between 0 and 50. Air quality is considered satisfactory; "Moderate" The AQI is between 51 and 100. Air quality is acceptable; "Unhealthy for Sensitive Groups" When AQI values are between 101 and 150, members of sensitive groups may experience health effects; "Unhealthy" When AQI values are between 151 and 200 everyone may begin to experience health effects; "Very Unhealthy" AQI values between 201 and 300 trigger a health alert; "Hazardous" AQI values over 300 trigger health warnings of emergency conditions; (1) Metropolitan Statistical Area - see Appendix A for areas included; (2) Based on 361 days with AQI data in 2007.
Source: U.S. Environmental Protection Agency, Air Quality Index Report, 2007

Air Quality Index Pollutants

Area	Percent of Days when AQI Pollutant was...[2]					
	Carbon Monoxide	Nitrogen Dioxide	Ozone	Sulfur Dioxide	Particulate Matter 2.5	Particulate Matter 10
MSA[1]	66.2	0.0	0.0	0.0	33.5	0.3

Note: The Air Quality Index (AQI) is an index for reporting daily air quality. EPA calculates the AQI for five major air pollutants regulated by the Clean Air Act: ground-level ozone, particle pollution (also known as particulate matter), carbon monoxide, sulfur dioxide, and nitrogen dioxide. The AQI runs from 0 to 500. The higher the AQI value, the greater the level of air pollution and the greater the health concern; (1) Metropolitan Statistical Area - see Appendix A for areas included; (2) Based on 361 days with AQI data in 2007.
Source: U.S. Environmental Protection Agency, Air Quality Index Report, 2007

Air Quality Index Trends

Area	Trend Sites								All Sites
	1999	2000	2001	2002	2003	2004	2005	2006	2006
MSA[1]	n/a	n/a	n/a	n/a	n/a	n/a	n/a	n/a	n/a

Note: An AQI value greater than 100 indicates that air quality would have been in the unhealthful range on that day. Data from exceptional events are not included. These counts are presented in two ways. First, the counts are based on sites having an adequate record of monitoring data during the trend period (trend sites). These counts represent the relative change in the number of days with AQI values greater than 100. In the last column, the counts are based on all sites with data in the most recent year (because it is possible for a site to have data in the most recent year but not enough data to be a trend site); (1) Metropolitan Statistical Area - see Appendix A for areas included; n/a not available.
Source: U.S. Environmental Protection Agency, Office of Air and Radiation, Air Trends, Factbook and Related Information, Air Pollution Trends in Selected Metropolitan Areas 2006

Maximum Air Pollutant Concentrations

	Particulate Matter 10 (ug/m^3)	Particulate Matter 2.5 (ug/m^3)	Ozone (ppm)	Carbon Monoxide (ppm)	Sulfur Dioxide (ppm)	Nitrogen Dioxide (ppm)	Lead (ug/m^3)
MSA[1] Level	45	28	n/a	1	n/a	0.011	n/a
NAAQS[2]	150	35	0.125	9	0.140	0.053	1.50
Met NAAQS[2]	Yes	Yes	n/a	Yes	n/a	Yes	n/a

Note: Data from exceptional events are not included; (1) Metropolitan Statistical Area - see Appendix A for areas included; (2) National Ambient Air Quality Standards; n/a not available
Concentrations: Particulate Matter 10 (coarse particulate) - highest second maximum 24-hour concentration; Particulate Matter 2.5 (fine particulate) - highest 98th percentile 24-hour concentration; Ozone - highest second daily maximum 1-hour concentration; Carbon Monoxide - highest second maximum non-overlapping 8-hour concentration; Sulfur Dioxide - highest second maximum 24-hour concentration; Nitrogen Dioxide - highest arithmetic mean concentration; Lead - highest quarterly maximum concentration
Units: ppm = parts per million; ug/m^3 = micrograms per cubic meter
Source: U.S. Environmental Protection Agency, MSA Factbook 2006, Air Quality Statistics by City

Drinking Water

Water System Name	Pop. Served	Primary Water Source Type	Violations[1]	
			Health Based	Monitoring/ Reporting
Burlington Dept of Public Works	47,600	Surface	0	0

Note: (1) Based on violation data from January 1, 2007 to December 31, 2007 (includes unresolved violations from earlier years)

Source: U.S. Environmental Protection Agency, Office of Ground Water and Drinking Water, Safe Drinking Water Information System (based on data extracted April 15, 2008)

Leesburg, Virginia

Background

Leesburg, located 35 miles northwest of Washington, D.C., was established in 1758, and is the government seat of Loudon County. Home to Leesburg Executive Airport (Godrey Field), it is also within 15 miles of Washington Dulles International Airport. Set in Virginia's Piedmont Region, between the Potomac River and the Blue Ridge Mountain foothills, the original Leesburg settlement was named George Town, to honor Britain's George II. It was later renamed for the area's prominent Lee family, in particular Thomas Lee, who served as Virginia's governor in 1749.

Leesburg played a role in both the French and Indian War and the Revolutionary War. It served as temporary capital of the nation during the War of 1812, and it was the site of the Battle of Ball's Bluff during the Civil War. The town's historic district has been placed on the National Register of Historic Places as one of Virginia's most picturesque downtown areas. Visitors can explore the town's rich history at The Loudon Museum or Thomas Balch Library and visit the national cemetery at the Ball's Bluff Battlefield.

In recent years, growth in the city has been rapid, in part due to the Dulles Greenway Toll Road, which has cut down traveling time to the District of Columbia and Dulles Airport. Major employers in Loudon County include America Online and the Federal Aviation Administration.

Nearby Washington, D.C. offers a multitude of attractions, most notably the White House, Capitol Building, Washington Monument, the National Gallery of Art, and the Smithsonian Institute museums, which include the National Air & Space Museum and the Steven F. Udvar-Hazy Center at Dulles International Airport that showcases the history of aviation and space flight. Activities available in Leesburg include the Leesburg Flower & Garden Festival, the Potomac Celtic Festival, August Court Days, the Bluemont Concert Series, Leesburg Hauntings and Halloween Parade, the Waterford Homes Tour & Crafts Festival and the Leesburg Holiday Parade & Crafts Show.

The Leesburg Parks and Recreation Department operates 13 public parks with more than 250 acres of land. The largest is Ida Lee Park, with a full service recreation center including an indoor pool, spa, gym, weight room and child care center.

The Leesburg area hosts the George Washington University's Virginia campus, Marymount University's Loudon Center, Northern Virginia Community College, the School of Islamic and Social Sciences, Shenandoah University's Loudon campus and Strayer University.

The weather in Leesburg is typical of northern Virginia: moderately cold winters, pleasant springs, and long summers. Temperatures average about freezing in January; snowfall is moderate and large snowstorms are rare. The long summer shades gradually into fall, with summer-like weather lasting well into October.

Rankings

General Rankings

- Washington* was ranked #130 out of 375 metro areas in *Cities Ranked & Rated*. Criteria: cost of living; climate; crime; transportation; economy and jobs; education; arts and culture; health and healthcare; leisure; quality of life. *Cities Ranked & Rated, 2nd Edition, 2007*
- Washington* was ranked #7 out of 379 metro areas in *Places Rated Almanac*. Criteria: health care; education; recreation; transportation; ambience; climate; crime; housing costs; jobs. *Places Rated Almanac, 7th Edition, 2007*

Business/Finance Rankings

- The nation's 100 largest metro areas were analysed in terms of the percentage of households entering some stage of foreclosure in 2007. The Washington* metro area ranked #41 out of 100 (#1 = highest foreclosure rate). *RealtyTrac, "Year-End 2007 Metropolitan Foreclosure Report"*
- The Washington* metro area was selected one of America's "Top 50 Business Opportunity Metros" by *Expansion Management* in their 5th annual Mayor's Challenge ranking of metro areas that have achieved solid ratings across the board in numerous *EM* studies during the past 12 months. The area ranked #4. Criteria: public schools; quality of life; college educated workers; logistics infrastructure; healthcare costs; taxes and government spending; reputation among site consultants. *Expansion Management, August 2007*
- The Washington* metro area was selected as one of "America's Most Wired Cities" by *Forbes*. The metro area was ranked #11 out of 30. Criteria: percentage of Internet users with high-speed access; the range of service providers within a city; availability of public wireless hot spots. *Forbes, "America's Most Wired Cities," January 10, 2008*
- Northern Virginia* was selected as one of the best places to start and grow a company by *Entrepreneur* and the National Policy Research Council. The Northern Virginia* metro area ranked #6 out of 50 large metro areas. Criteria: business formation and growth (firms started four to 14 years ago that still employ at least 5 people and experienced rapid growth over the last four years). *Entrepreneur/National Policy Research Council, "Hot Cities for Entrepreneurs," September 2006*
- The Washington* metro area was selected as one of "America's Greediest Cities" by *Forbes*. The area was ranked #9 out of 10. Criteria: number of Forbes 400 (*Forbes* annual list of the richest Americans) members per capita. *Forbes, "America's Greediest Cities," December 7, 2007*
- The Washington* metro area was selected one of America's "Top 10 Knowledge Worker Metros." The area ranked #2. Criteria: degree holders (bachelors, masters, professional, and Ph.D.) as a percent of the workforce; science and engineering workers as a percent of the workforce; number of patents issued; number and type of colleges in each metro area. *Expansion Management, April 2007*
- Intel, in partnership with Sperling's BestPlaces, ranked the 80 "Best Cities for Teleworking" in America. The Washington* metro area ranked #1 among extra large metro areas. The study identifies cities that hold the greatest potential for teleworking based on a host of factors including typical commuting times, fuel prices, availability of broadband Internet access and percentage of the population in telework friendly jobs. The study also factored in extreme climate and natural hazards. *Intel, "Best Cities for Teleworking," March 30, 2006*
- Leesburg was selected as one of the "100 Best Places to Live and Launch" in the U.S. The city ranked #31. The editors at *Fortune Small Business* ranked 296 Census-designated metro areas by business friendliness (Launching Score, % New Businesses) and lifestyle offerings (Living Score). Then, through reporting, they picked the town within each of the top 100 metro areas that best blends business and pleasure. *Fortune Small Business, "100 Best Places to Live and Launch 2008," April 2008*

- The Washington* metro area appeared on the Milken Institute "2007 Best Performing Cities" index. Rank: #37 out of 200 large metro areas. Criteria: job growth; wage and salary growth; high-tech output growth. *Milken Institute, "2007 Best Performing Cities"*

- The Northern Virginia* metro area was selected as one of the hottest cities for entrepreneurs in America by *Inc. Magazine.* Criteria: job-growth data for 393 metro was analyzed for current-year employment growth, average annual employment growth over past three years, and employment growth by industry sector. The Northern Virginia* metro area ranked #9 among large metro areas and #66 overall. *Inc. Magazine, May 2007*

- The Washington* metro area was selected as one of "The Top 20 Boom Towns in America." *Business 2.0* magazine and econometric research firm Global Insight compared 319 metropolitan areas in the U.S. and ranked the 61 with populations over 1 million. Criteria: a weighted formula that includes forecast growth rates in sectors that contain the economy's 10 most skilled occupational clusters; the prevalence of college degrees in the local workforce; median salary. The area ranked #3 among large metro areas. *Business 2.0 Magazine, March 2004*

- Washington* was identified as one of the 100 "Most Unwired Cities" in the U.S. The area ranked #14 out of the 100 largest metro areas in the U.S. Criteria: number of public and commercial wireless access points (hotspots); airports with wireless Internet access; broadband availability; local wireless networks; and wireless email devices. *Intel, "Most Unwired Cities Survey," June 7, 2005*

- Washington* was ranked #23 out of 125 regions worldwide in terms of its "Knowledge Competitiveness Index." The index attempts to measure the knowledge-based development taking place throughout the world and is based on 19 measures of economic performance that indicate a region's ability to translate its knowledge capacity into economic value. *Robert Huggins Associates, World Knowledge Competitiveness Index 2005*

- *Forbes* ranked the 200 most populous metro areas in the U.S. in terms of the "Best Places for Business and Careers." The Washington* metro area was ranked #25. Criteria: business costs (labor, energy, tax and office space expenses); living costs (housing, transportation, food and other household expenditures); education levels of the work force; job growth; income growth; migration trends; crime rates; and culture/leisure. *Forbes, "Best Places for Business and Careers," March 19, 2008*

- *Fortune* ranked the 100 largest metro areas in the U.S. in terms of projected median home price change in 2007. The Washington* metro area ranked #89. *Fortune.com, "Hot Spots, Cold Spots"*

- The Washington* metro area was identified as one of "America's Most Overpriced Real Estate Markets." The area ranked #5 out of 10. Criteria: housing "P/E" ratio (a market's median home price divided by annual rents minus taxes and insurance); housing affordability. *Forbes.com, "America's Most Overpriced Real Estate Markets," May 11, 2007*

Health/Environment Rankings

- 100 of the largest metro areas in the U.S. were analyzed in terms of their current drought severity. The Washington* metro area ranked #18 (#1 = driest). The rankings were based on statistics such as long-term precipitation trends and patterns and the Palmer drought indices. *Sperling's BestPlaces, www.BestPlaces.net, "America's Drought-Riskiest Cities," November 2007*

- Tahitian Noni International Hiro™, in partnership with Sperling's BestPlaces, ranked the nation's 50 largest metro areas in terms of the "Most Energetic Cities." The Washington* metro area ranked #10. Criteria: percentage of population that walk or bicycle to work; BMI score; number of food co-ops; number of farmers markets. *Tahitian Noni International Hiro™, "Most Energetic Cities," March 13, 2007*

- Scarborough Research, a leading market research firm, identified the top local markets for organic consumers. The Washington* DMA (Designated Market Area) ranked in the top 15 with 26% of adults reporting that they used any organic food product in their household during the past month. *Scarborough Research, October 10, 2007*

- *Reader's Digest* ranked the 50 largest metro areas in the U.S. in terms of how "clean" they are. The Washington* metro area ranked #35. Criteria: air quality; water quality; toxic industrial pollution; Superfund sites; and sanitation. *Reader's Digest, "The 50 Cleanest (and Dirtiest) Cities in America," July 2005*
- The American Academy of Dermatology ranked 32 U.S. metropolitan regions in terms of their residents knowledge, attitude and behaviors towards tanning and sun protection. The Washington* metro area ranked #1. The results of the study are based on an online national survey of 3,342 respondents. *American Academy of Dermatology, "RAYS: Your Grade," May 7, 2007*
- The Washington* metro area appeared in *Country Home's* "2008 Best Green Places" report. The area ranked #67 out of 379. Criteria: official energy policies; green power; green buildings; availability of fresh, locally grown food. *Country Home, "2008 Best Green Places"*
- Wyeth Consumer Healthcare, in partnership with Sperling's BestPlaces, ranked the nation's 50 most populous metro areas in terms of five key health factors. The Washington* metro area ranked #2. Criteria: physical activity; health status; nutrition; lifestyle pursuits; and mental wellness. *Wyeth Consumer Healthcare, "Centrum Healthiest Cities Study," April 19, 2005*
- HealthGrades surveyed over 41,000 individuals on doctor satisfaction and ranked the 20 largest metro areas based on the highest "definitely yes" responses to the question "Do you trust the physician to make decisions/recommendations that are in your best interest?" The Washington* metro area ranked #8. *HealthGrades.com, "Top Cities in Doctor-Trust," September 7, 2006*
- Washington* was identified as a "2008 Asthma Capital." The area ranked #60 out of the nation's 100 largest metropolitan areas. Twelve factors were used to identify the most challenging places to live for people with asthma: estimated prevalence; self-reported prevalence; crude death rate for asthma; annual pollen score; annual air quality; public smoking laws; number of board-certified asthma specialists; school inhaler access laws; rescue medication use; controller medication use; uninsured rate; poverty rate. *Asthma and Allergy Foundation of America, "2008 Asthma Capitals"*
- Washington* was identified as a "Spring Allergy Capital." The area ranked #71 out of 100. Three groups of factors were used to identify the most severe cities for people with allergies during the spring season: annual pollen levels; medicine utilization; access to board-certified allergists. *Asthma and Allergy Foundation of America, "2007 Spring Allergy Capital Rankings"*
- Washington* was identified as a "Fall Allergy Capital." The area ranked #70 out of 100. Three groups of factors were used to identify the most severe cities for people with allergies during the fall season: annual pollen levels; medicine utilization; access to board-certified allergists. *Asthma and Allergy Foundation of America, "2007 Fall Allergy Capital Rankings"*
- Ortho-McNeil Neurologics, in partnership with Sperling's BestPlaces, analyzed 110 metro areas and identified those U.S. cities with the highest prevalence of factors that are most commonly associated with migraine headaches. The Washington* metro area ranked #75. Criteria: number of migraine-related drug prescriptions per capita; lifestyle factors that can contribute to migraines; environmental factors that can trigger migraines; and consumption of migraine-triggering foods. *Ortho-McNeil Neurologics, "America's Migraine Hot Spots," March 14, 2006*
- Sperling's BestPlaces ranked 331 metro areas and identified the most and least stressful U.S. cities. The Washington* metro area ranked #83 out of the 100 largest metro areas (#1 = most stressful). Criteria: divorce rate; unemployment rate; violent and property crime; suicide rate; commute time; mental health; alcohol consumption; cloudy days. *Sperling's BestPlaces, www.BestPlaces.net, "America's Most (and Least) Stressful Cities," January 9, 2004*
- An analysis of the "Best & Worst Cities for Sleep" was conducted by Sperling's BestPlaces. The study ranked America's 50 most populated metro areas. The Washington* metro area ranked #18 (#1 = best city for sleep). Criteria: number of days residents didn't get enough rest or sleep during the past month; average length of daily commute; divorce rate; unemployment rate. *Sperling's BestPlaces, www.BestPlaces.net, "Best & Worst Cities for Sleep," 2006*

- HealthGrades evaluated the performance of America's 25 most populous metropolitan areas by measuring the outcomes of five of the highest volume and most widely studied procedures and diagnoses: coronary artery bypass graft surgery; percutaneus coronary interventions; acute myocardial infarction/heart attack in angioplasty-capable hospitals; congestive heart failure; and community acquired pneumonia. The Washington* metro area ranked #12. *HealthGrades, "HealthGrades Hospital Quality in America Study," October 12, 2004*

- Northern Virginia* was highlighted as one of the 25 metro areas most polluted by year-round particle pollution (PM 2.5) in the U.S. The area ranked #20. *American Lung Association, State of the Air: 2007*

- Northern Virginia* was highlighted as one of the 25 most ozone-polluted metro areas in the U.S. The area ranked #11. *American Lung Association, State of the Air: 2007*

- Washington* was selected as one of "America's Pet Healthiest Cities" by Purina. The city ranked #6 out of 50. Criteria: veterinary services; environment; legislation; preventative care; obesity/body condition. *Purina Pet Institute, "America's Pet Healthiest Cities," May 20, 2003*

Women/Minorities Rankings

- Washington* was ranked #21 out of 100 metro areas in *SELF Magazine's* ranking of "America's Best Places for Women." A panel of experts came up with more than 50 criteria including death and disease rates, environmental indicators, community resources, and lifestyle habits. *SELF Magazine, "America's Best Places for Women 2007," December 2007*

- Washington* appeared on *Black Enterprise's* list of the "Ten Best Cities for African Americans." The top picks were culled from more than 2,000 interactive surveys completed on www.blackenterprise.com and by editorial staff evaluation. The editors weighed the following criteria as it pertained to African Americans in each city: median household income; percentage of households earning more than $100,000; percentage of businesses owned; percentage of college graduates; unemployment rates; home loan rejections; and homeownership rates. *Black Enterprise, May 2007*

Seniors/Retirement Rankings

- The Washington* metro area was selected as one of "Best Places for Retirees" by *Forbes*. The area was ranked #9 out of 10. Criteria: cost and availability of health care; sales, property and income-tax rates; arts and leisure activities; cost of living; retirement job market; inter-metro migration patterns of people between the ages of 55 and 65. *Forbes, "Best Places for Retirees," January 18, 2007*

- Sperling's BestPlaces in partnership with Bankers Life & Casualty Company designed a survey to identify the top 50 metro areas in the U.S. that offer the best overall qualities for senior living. The Washington* metro area ranked #25. The following criteria were statistically weighted to reflect the needs of the senior population: health; disease; economics; social; environment; spiritual; transportation; housing; and crime. *Bankers Life & Casualty Company, "Best Cities for Seniors 2005"*

- A.G. Edwards ranked America's 500 top-performing communities based on their residents' personal savings and investing behavior. The Washington* metro area ranked #11 with an index score of 116.23 (national average = 100.00). A dozen statistical factors were measured including: participation in retirement savings plans; personal debt levels; and home ownership. *A.G. Edwards, "2007 Nest Egg Index", September 12, 2007*

Children/Family Rankings

- The Washington* metro area was selected as one of the "Best Cities for Relocating Families" by Worldwide ERC and Primacy Relocation. The 2007 study placed a special emphasis on the housing market, which has significantly impacted the relocation industry and an employer's ability to transfer employees. The variables which weigh heavily in this category include home price, home affordability index, appreciation rates, and property tax. Other criteria include cost of living, crime rates, education, climate, focus on diversity, physicians per capita, recreation and leisure, arts and culture, air quality, watershed quality, sales tax, unemployment rate, job growth, high school and higher education index, school expenditures per student, students in public school, SAT/ACT percentile, and population growth. *Worldwide ERC and Primacy Relocation, "2007 Best Cities for Relocating Families"*

Safety Rankings

- The National Insurance Crime Bureau ranked 361 metro areas in the U.S. in terms of per capita rates of vehicle theft. The Washington* metro area ranked #56 (#1 = highest rate). Criteria: number of vehicle theft offenses per 100,000 inhabitants. *National Insurance Crime Bureau, "NICB Vehicle Theft Study," April 22, 2008*

- Washington* appeared on Sperling's BestPlaces list of the "Riskiest Cities for Identity Theft." The area ranked #12 out of the nations 50 largest metro areas. Over 80 criteria were analyzed across four major categories: technology impact; crime; transactions; and risk profile. *Sperling's BestPlaces, www.BestPlaces.net, "Riskiest Cities for Identity Theft," July 2006*

- Farmers Insurance Group of Companies, in partnership with Sperling's BestPlaces, ranked 379 metro areas and identified the "Most Secure U.S. Place to Live." The Washington* metro area ranked #40 out of 114 in the large metro area category (500,000 or more residents). Criteria: crime rates; extreme weather; risk of natural disasters; environmental hazards; terrorism threats; air quality; life expectancy; job loss numbers. *Farmers Insurance Group, "Most Secure U.S. Places to Live 2007"*

- Washington* was identified as one of the most dangerous large metro areas for pedestrians in the U.S. The area ranked #32 out of the nations 50 largest metro areas. Criteria: average yearly pedestrian fatalities per capita (for the years 2002 and 2003) adjusted for the number of walkers. *Surface Transportation Policy Project, "Mean Streets 2004"*

Sports/Recreation Rankings

- The Washington* metro area appeared on the *Sporting News* list of the "Best Sports Cities 2007". The area ranked #24 out of 150 cities in the U.S. *Sporting News* takes a 12-month snapshot, roughly July to July, of each city's sports, putting a heavy premium on regular-season won-lost records (from the most recently completed season). Other criteria include: playoff berths, bowl appearances and tournament bids; championships; applicable power ratings; quality of competition; overall fan fervor as measured in part by attendance as percentage of venue capacity; abundance of teams (rewarding quality over quantity); stadium and arena quality; ticket availability and prices; franchise ownership; and marquee appeal of athletes. *SportingNews.com, "Best Sports Cities 2007," August 1, 2007*

- The Washington* metro area was selected by *Cranium* as one of the "Top 50 Fun Cities" in America. The area ranked #7. Criteria includes: number of sports teams, restaurants, and dance performances; number of toy stores; city budget spent on recreation. *Cranium, November 4, 2003*

- *Golf Digest* ranked 330 metro areas in the U.S. in terms of golf. The Washington* metro area was ranked #304. Criteria: access to golf; weather; value of golf; and quality of golf. *Golf Digest, "Metro Golf Rankings," August 2005*

Dating/Romance Rankings

- Eli Lily and Company, in partnership with Sperling's BestPlaces, ranked the nation's 50 largest metro areas in terms of the "Most Romantic Cities for Baby Boomers." The Washington* metro area ranked #29. Criteria: marriage and divorce rates among "baby boomers" age 45 to 60; great restaurants; dance studios; chocolate, jewelry and flower sales. *Eli Lily and Company, "Most Romantic Cities for Baby Boomers," April 20, 2007*
- The Washington* metro area was selected as one of the "Top Ten U.S. Cities for Finding a Rich, Single Man" by Teasley, a Manhattan-based marketing consulting firm. The area ranked #3. Criteria: high single-male to single-female ratios; higher income to cost-of-living ratios. *Teasley, "Top Ten U.S. Cities for Finding a Rich, Single Man," February 10, 2004*
- The Washington* metro area was selected as one of the "Top Ten U.S. Cities for Finding a Rich, Single Woman" by Teasley, a Manhattan-based marketing consulting firm. The area ranked #1. Criteria: high single-female to single-male ratio; higher income to cost-of-living ratio; percentage of population that is single. *Teasley, "Where to Find a Rich, Single Woman in the United States," 2005*
- The Washington* metro area was selected as one of the "Best Cities for Relocating Singles" by Worldwide ERC and Primacy Relocation. The area ranked #72 out of the 100 largest metro areas in the U.S. Areas were selected based on the following criteria: a robust cost-of-living index; adventure and outdoor recreation opportunities; violent crime and property crime rates; percentage of the population that is unmarried (ages 25-34); ratio of single men and single women; affordability of quality higher education, including in-state and out-of-state tuition requirements and rates; number of newcomers to the area; commute times; tax rates; fee and occupancy rates for temporary housing and mini-storage; quality and quantity of collegiate and professional sporting events and fun, fan-friendly venues. *Worldwide ERC and Primacy Relocation, "2007 Best Cities for Relocating Singles," October 25, 2007*
- *Forbes* ranked the 40 most populous urbanized areas in the U.S. in terms of the "Best Cities for Singles." The Washington* metro area ranked #6. Criteria: number of singles; cost of living alone; nightlife; culture; job growth; coolness; and online dating. *Forbes.com, August 21, 2007*
- Sperling's BestPlaces in partnership with AXE Deodorant Bodyspray ranked 80 metro areas and identified "America's Best (and Worst) Cities for Dating." The Washington* metro area ranked #46 (#1 = best). Criteria: percentage of singles ages 18-24; population density; dating venues per capita. *AXE Deodorant Bodyspray, "America's Best (and Worst) Cities for Dating," May 2004*

Miscellaneous Rankings

- The Washington* metro area was identified as one of 10 "Worst Cities for Commuters" by *Forbes*. The metro area ranked #7. Criteria: traffic delays; travel times; how efficiently commuters use existing infrastructure. *Forbes.com, "Worst Cities for Commuters," April 29, 2008*
- The Washington* metro area was identified as one of "The 10 Worst Commuter Cities" in the U.S. by the *U.S. News and World Report*. The mean travel time to work is 29 minutes. *U.S. News and World Report, May 7, 2007*
- Scarborough Research, a leading market research firm, identified the top local markets for bloggers. The Washington* DMA (Designated Market Area) ranked in the top 13 with 11% of adults reporting that they had read or contributed to a blog within the past 30 days. *Scarborough Research, October 24, 2007*
- The Washington* metro area was selected as one of the "Top 10 Most Independent Cities for Homesellers". The area ranked #3. The cities listed had more consumers choosing to sell their homes without the help of a real-estate agent than anywhere else. Data was based on geographical information for listings posted on ForSaleByOwner.com from January 1, 2007 through June 30, 2007. *ForSaleByOwner.com, October 1, 2007*

- The Washington* metro area appeared on *Forbes* list of "America's Drunkest Cities". The area ranked #20. Criteria: 35 of the largest continental U.S. metro areas were chosen based on availability of data and geographic diversity. Each metro was ranked in five areas: state laws; drinkers; heavy drinkers; binge drinkers; and alcoholism. *Forbes.com, "America's Drunkest Cities," August 22, 2006*
- Sperling's BestPlaces in partnership with Pep Boys ranked 77 metro areas and identified "America's Most Drivable Cities." The Washington* metro area ranked #68. Criteria: climate; road roughness; urban mobility; gas prices. *Pep Boys, "America's Most Drivable Cities," April 9, 2003*
- State Farm Insurance, in partnership with Sperling's BestPlaces, analyzed several key factors that contribute to overall family preparedness. The Washington* metro area ranked #26 out of the nation's 50 most populous metro areas. Criteria: quality of life; life insurance coverage; and investments. *State Farm Life Insurance, "Fiscally Fit Cities Report," July 20, 2004*
- A study by Sperling's BestPlaces examined which U.S. metro areas were most affected by high fuel prices in 2006. The Washington* metro area was ranked #24 out of 80 (#1 = most expensive city for driving). Rankings are based on the average dollars spent on gas per year by two driver households. Criteria: cost of regular-grade gasoline; average miles driven per day; average number of gallons each driver uses and wastes in traffic congestion each day. *Sperling's BestPlaces, www.bestplaces.net, "Pain at the Pump," May 18, 2006*

Leesburg is located within the Washington-Arlington-Alexandria, DC-VA-MD-WV Metropolitan Statistical Area and Washington-Arlington-Alexandria, DC-VA-MD-WV Metropolitan Division.

Business Environment

CITY FINANCES

City Government Finances

Component	2004-2005 ($000)	2004-2005 ($ per capita)
Total Revenues	56,598	1,561
Total Expenditures	47,060	1,298
Debt Outstanding	52,169	1,438
Cash and Securities	80,385	2,216

Source: U.S Census Bureau, Government Finances 2004-2005

City Government Revenue by Source

Source	2004-2005 ($000)	2004-2005 ($ per capita)
General Revenue		
From Federal Government	1,523	42
From State Government	4,334	119
From Local Governments	3,781	104
Taxes		
Property	11,283	311
Sales	6,555	181
Personal Income	0	0
License	3,688	102
Charges	13,459	371
Liquor Store	0	0
Utility	7,093	196
Employee Retirement	0	0
Other	4,882	135

Source: U.S Census Bureau, Government Finances 2004-2005

City Government Expenditures by Function

Function	2004-2005 ($000)	2004-2005 ($ per capita)	2004-2005 (%)
General Expenditures			
Airports	594	16	1.3
Corrections	0	0	0.0
Education	0	0	0.0
Fire Protection	0	0	0.0
Governmental Administration	5,614	155	11.9
Health	0	0	0.0
Highways	5,166	142	11.0
Hospitals	0	0	0.0
Housing and Community Development	0	0	0.0
Interest on General Debt	1,930	53	4.1
Libraries	457	13	1.0
Parking	62	2	0.1
Parks and Recreation	4,820	133	10.2
Police Protection	7,263	200	15.4
Public Welfare	0	0	0.0
Sewerage	7,891	218	16.8
Solid Waste Management	2,122	59	4.5
Liquor Store	0	0	0.0
Utility	7,043	194	15.0
Employee Retirement	0	0	0.0
Other	4,098	113	8.7

Source: U.S Census Bureau, Government Finances 2004-2005

Municipal Bond Ratings

Area	Moody's
City	n/a

Source: Mergent Bond Record, January 2008 (unless noted otherwise)

DEMOGRAPHICS

Population Growth

Area	1990 Census	2000 Census	2007 Estimate	2012 Projection	Population Growth (%) 1990-2000	Population Growth (%) 2000-2012
City	16,240	28,311	38,030	45,147	74.3	59.5
MSA[1]	4,122,914	4,796,183	5,367,465	5,753,170	16.3	20.0
U.S.	248,709,873	281,421,906	301,045,522	314,920,978	13.2	11.9

Note: (1) Metropolitan Statistical Area - see Appendix B for areas included
Source: Claritas, Inc.

Number of Households and Average Household Size

Area	2007 Estimate	2007 Average Household Size
City	13,392	2.84
MSA[1]	2,029,059	2.65
U.S.	113,668,003	2.65

Note: (1) Metropolitan Statistical Area - see Appendix B for areas included
Source: Claritas, Inc.

Race and Ethnicity

Area	White Alone[2]	Black Alone[2]	Asian Alone[2]	Other Race Alone[2]	Hispanic[3]
City	74.1	9.7	6.8	9.5	11.8
MSA[1]	56.8	26.0	8.2	9.0	11.6
U.S.	73.1	12.4	4.3	10.3	14.9

Note: Figures are 2007 estimates; (1) Metropolitan Statistical Area - see Appendix B for areas included (2) Alone is defined as not being in combination with one or more other races; (3) May be of any race.
Source: Claritas, Inc.

Ancestry

Area	German	Irish[2]	English	American	Italian	Polish	French[3]	Scottish
City	21.5	15.6	13.5	7.4	6.3	3.6	2.2	3.6
MSA[1]	12.0	10.5	9.2	5.4	4.4	2.4	2.0	2.0
U.S.	15.2	10.9	8.7	7.3	5.6	3.2	3.0	1.7

Note: Figures include multiple ancestry (e.g. if a person reported being Irish and Italian, they were included in both columns); (1) Metropolitan Statistical Area - see Appendix A for areas included; (2) Includes Celtic; (3) Includes Alsatian but excludes Basque
Source: Census 2000, Summary File 3

Foreign-Born Population

Area	Percent of Population Born in							
	Any Foreign Country	Europe	Asia	Africa	Oceania[2]	Canada	Mexico	Latin America[3]
City	8.6	2.1	2.6	0.3	0.1	0.3	0.3	3.0
MSA[1]	16.9	2.1	6.1	1.9	0.1	0.2	0.7	5.9
U.S.	11.1	1.7	2.9	0.3	0.1	0.3	3.3	2.5

Note: (1) Metropolitan Statistical Area - see Appendix A for areas included; (2) Includes Australia, New Zealand subregion, Melanesia, Micronesia, Polynesia, and Oceania n.e.c; (3) Includes Central America (excluding Mexico), South America, and the Caribbean.
Source: Census 2000, Summary File 3

Marriage Status

Area	Never Married	Now Married (excluding Separated)	Separated	Widowed	Divorced
City	22.3	59.5	3.0	4.4	10.8
MSA[1]	30.9	52.7	2.8	5.1	8.5
U.S.	27.1	54.4	2.2	6.6	9.7

Note: Figures are percentages and cover the population 15 years of age and older; (1) Metropolitan Statistical Area - see Appendix A for areas included
Source: Census 2000, Summary File 3

Age Distribution

Area	Percent of Population						
	Under Age 5	Age 5 to 17	Age 18 to 34	Age 35 to 49	Age 50 to 64	Age 65 to 79	80 Years and Over
City	9.6	19.6	24.8	28.0	12.1	4.3	1.6
MSA[1]	6.9	18.3	24.6	25.8	15.3	6.8	2.2
U.S.	6.8	18.9	23.7	23.5	14.8	9.2	3.2

Note: (1) Metropolitan Statistical Area - see Appendix A for areas included
Source: Census 2000, Summary File 3

Male/Female Ratio

Area	Males	Females	Males per 100 Females
City	18,846	19,184	98.2
MSA[1]	2,624,053	2,743,412	95.6
U.S.	148,320,305	152,725,217	97.1

Note: Figures are 2007 estimates; (1) Metropolitan Statistical Area - see Appendix B for areas included
Source: Claritas, Inc.

Religion

Area	Catholic	Southern Baptist	United Meth-odist	ELCA[1]	LDS[2]	Presby-terian Church USA	Jewish Est.	Muslim Est.
County	17.7	3.3	5.4	1.2	1.6	1.0	2.1	1.1
U.S.	22.0	7.1	3.7	1.8	1.5	1.1	2.2	0.6

Note: Figures are the number of adherents as a percentage of the total population; Adherents are defined as all members, including full members, their children and the estimated number of other participants who are not considered members (e.g. the baptized, those not confirmed, those regularly attending services, etc.); (1) Evangelical Lutheran Church in America; (2) The Church of Jesus Christ of Latter Day Saints
Source: Reprinted with permission from Religious Congregations and Membership in the United States 2000 (Nashville, Glenmary Research Center, 2002) Copyright Association of Statisticians of American Religious Bodies. All rights reserved.

ECONOMY

Gross Metropolitan Product

Area	2002	2003	2004	2005	2005 Rank[2]
MSA[1]	238.6	256.3	280.1	300.4	4

Note: Figures are in billions of dollars; (1) Washington-Arlington-Alexandria, DC-VA-MD-WV Metropolitan Statistical Area - see Appendix A for areas included; (2) Rank ranges from 1 to 361
Source: The U.S. Conference of Mayors, "U.S. Metro Economies: GMP - The Engines of America's Growth," January 2007

Economic Growth

Area	1995 GMP	2005 GMP	Average Annual Growth Rate	Growth Rate Rank[2]
MSA[1]	151.9	300.4	7.1	38

Note: Figures are in billions of dollars; GMP = Gross Metropolitan Product; (1) Washington-Arlington-Alexandria, DC-VA-MD-WV Metropolitan Statistical Area - see Appendix A for areas included; (2) Rank ranges from 1 to 361
Source: The U.S. Conference of Mayors, "U.S. Metro Economies: GMP - The Engines of America's Growth," January 2007

INCOME

Per Capita/Median/Average Income

Area	Per Capita ($)	Median Household ($)	Average Household ($)
City	35,052	85,215	99,084
MSA[1]	37,288	76,534	97,910
U.S.	25,495	49,280	66,670

Note: Figures are 2007 estimates; (1) Metropolitan Statistical Area - see Appendix B for areas included
Source: Claritas, Inc.

Household Income Distribution

Area	Under $15,000	$15,000 -24,999	$25,000 -34,999	$35,000 -49,999	$50,000 -74,999	$75,000 -99,000	$100,000 -149,999	$150,000 and up
	Percent of Households Earning							
City	4.5	3.8	6.3	9.1	18.3	19.8	23.3	15.0
MSA[1]	6.7	5.2	6.7	11.9	18.7	15.4	19.8	15.7
U.S.	13.1	10.9	11.2	15.6	19.5	11.9	11.3	6.6

Note: Figures are 2007 estimates; (1) Metropolitan Statistical Area - see Appendix B for areas included
Source: Claritas, Inc.

Poverty Rates by Age

Area	All Ages	Under 5 Years Old	5 to 17 Years Old	18 to 64 Years Old	65 Years and Over
City	3.6	0.3	0.8	2.1	0.4
MSA[1]	7.4	0.7	1.7	4.4	0.7
U.S.	12.4	1.2	3.0	6.9	1.2

Note: Figures are percent of population with income in 1999 below poverty level and only include population for whom poverty status is determined; (1) Metropolitan Statistical Area - see Appendix A for areas included
Source: Census 2000, Summary File 3

Personal Bankruptcy Filing Rate

Area	2004	2005	2006
Loudoun County	1.87	2.13	0.84
U.S.	5.31	6.82	2.00

Note: Numbers are per 1,000 population and include Chapter 7 and Chapter 13 filings
Source: Federal Deposit Insurance Corporation (FDIC), Regional Economic Conditions (RECON), 8/23/2007

EMPLOYMENT

Labor Force and Employment

Area	Civilian Labor Force			Workers Employed		
	Dec. 2006	Dec. 2007	% Chg.	Dec. 2006	Dec. 2007	% Chg.
City	22,117	22,303	0.8	21,727	21,835	0.5
MD[1]	2,328,726	2,347,351	0.8	2,260,232	2,273,004	0.6
U.S.	152,571,000	153,705,000	0.7	146,081,000	146,334,000	0.2

Note: Data is not seasonally adjusted and covers workers 16 years of age and older;
(1) Metropolitan Division - see Appendix B for areas included
Source: Bureau of Labor Statistics, http://stats.bls.gov

Unemployment Rate

Area	Jan.	Feb.	Mar.	Apr.	May	Jun.	Jul.	Aug.	Sep.	Oct.	Nov.	Dec.
	2007											
City	2.0	1.9	1.8	1.8	1.8	2.1	2.0	2.1	2.1	2.0	2.0	2.1
MD[1]	3.3	3.2	3.0	2.8	2.9	3.3	3.3	3.2	3.1	3.0	3.1	3.2
U.S.	5.0	4.9	4.5	4.3	4.3	4.7	4.9	4.6	4.5	4.4	4.5	4.8

Note: Data is not seasonally adjusted and covers workers 16 years of age and older; All figures are percentages; (1) Metropolitan Division - see Appendix B for areas included
Source: Bureau of Labor Statistics, http://stats.bls.gov

Employment by Occupation

Occupation Classification	City (%)	MSA[1] (%)	U.S. (%)
Sales and Office	25.6	24.3	26.7
Professional and Related	26.5	28.9	20.2
Service	12.6	13.0	14.9
Production, Transportation, and Material Moving	6.6	6.7	14.6
Management, Business, and Financial	21.9	19.6	13.5
Construction, Extraction, and Maintenance	6.6	7.4	9.4
Farming, Forestry, and Fishing	0.1	0.2	0.7

Note: Figures cover employed civilians 16 years of age and older;
(1) Metropolitan Statistical Area - see Appendix A for areas included
Source: Census 2000, Summary File 3

Employment by Industry

Sector	MSA[1] Number of Employees	MSA[1] Percent of Total	U.S. Percent of Total
Government	560,500	22.9	16.3
Education and Health Services	264,300	10.8	13.4
Professional and Business Services	559,400	22.9	13.1
Retail Trade	220,900	9.0	11.6
Manufacturing	41,700	1.7	9.9
Leisure and Hospitality	204,800	8.4	9.6
Financial Activities	112,900	4.6	5.9
Construction	n/a	n/a	5.3
Wholesale Trade	55,100	2.3	4.4
Other Services	150,300	6.2	3.9
Transportation and Utilities	57,900	2.4	3.7
Information	76,200	3.1	2.2
Natural Resources and Mining	n/a	n/a	0.5

Note: Figures cover non-farm employment as of December 2007 and are not seasonally adjusted; (1) Metropolitan Statistical Area - see Appendix B for areas included; n/a not available
Source: Bureau of Labor Statistics, http://stats.bls.gov

Average Wages

Occupation	$/Hr.	Occupation	$/Hr.
Accountants and Auditors	34.57	Maids and Housekeeping Cleaners	11.09
Automotive Mechanics	20.52	Maintenance and Repair Workers	20.39
Bookkeepers	18.94	Marketing Managers	58.72
Carpenters	20.83	Nuclear Medicine Technologists	31.27
Cashiers	9.82	Nurses, Licensed Practical	21.92
Clerks, General Office	15.51	Nurses, Registered	33.65
Clerks, Receptionists/Information	13.48	Nursing Aides/Orderlies/Attendants	12.75
Clerks, Shipping/Receiving	14.76	Packers and Packagers, Hand	10.01
Computer Programmers	39.31	Physical Therapists	34.88
Computer Support Specialists	25.22	Postal Service Mail Carriers	21.22
Computer Systems Analysts	41.55	Real Estate Brokers	34.60
Cooks, Restaurant	12.09	Retail Salespersons	12.11
Dentists	n/a	Sales Reps., Exc. Tech./Scientific	33.00
Electrical Engineers	43.07	Sales Reps., Tech./Scientific	43.12
Electricians	24.94	Secretaries, Exc. Legal/Med./Exec.	19.64
Financial Managers	55.04	Security Guards	14.54
First-Line Supervisors/Mgrs., Sales	21.30	Surgeons	72.31
Food Preparation Workers	10.11	Teacher Assistants	13.00
General and Operations Managers	60.48	Teachers, Elementary School	29.20
Hairdressers/Cosmetologists	17.52	Teachers, Secondary School	30.90
Internists	74.90	Telemarketers	13.27
Janitors and Cleaners	10.88	Truck Drivers, Heavy/Tractor-Trailer	18.31
Landscaping/Groundskeeping Workers	11.76	Truck Drivers, Light/Delivery Svcs.	14.58
Lawyers	66.79	Waiters and Waitresses	9.91

Note: Wage data covers the Washington-Arlington-Alexandria, DC-VA-MD-WV Metropolitan Division - see Appendix B for areas included. Hourly wages for elementary/secondary school teachers and teacher assistants were calculated by the editors from annual wage data assuming a 40 hour work week; n/a not available.
Source: Bureau of Labor Statistics, May 2007 Metro Area Occupational Employment and Wage Estimates

RESIDENTIAL REAL ESTATE

Building Permits

Area	Single-Family 2006	Single-Family 2007p	Single-Family Pct. Chg.	Multi-Family 2006	Multi-Family 2007p	Multi-Family Pct. Chg.	Total 2006	Total 2007p	Total Pct. Chg.
City	n/a	n/a	n/a	n/a	n/a	n/a	n/a	n/a	n/a
U.S.	1,378,200	973,300	-29.4	460,700	407,200	-11.6	1,838,900	1,380,500	-24.9

Note: (p) preliminary; figures cover and represent new, privately-owned housing units authorized (unadjusted data); All permit data are based on estimates with imputation; U.S. figures are based on the new 20,000-place series.
Source: U.S. Census Bureau, Manufacturing, Mining, and Construction Statistics

Homeownership and Housing Vacancies

Area	Homeownership Rate[2] (%)			Rental Vacancy Rate[3] (%)			Homeowner Vacancy Rate[4] (%)		
	2005	2006	2007	2005	2006	2007	2005	2006	2007
MSA[1]	68.4	68.9	69.2	7.1	8.4	10.4	1.3	2.1	2.4
U.S.	68.9	68.8	68.1	9.8	9.8	9.7	1.9	2.4	2.7

Note: (1) Metropolitan Statistical Area - see Appendix B for areas included; (2) The proportion of households that are owners; (3) The proportion of the rental inventory that is vacant for rent; (4) The proportion of the homeowner inventory that is vacant for sale; n/a not available
Source: U.S. Census Bureau, Housing Vacancies and Homeownership Annual Statistics: 2007

TAXES

State Corporate Income Tax Rates

State	Rates and Tax Brackets
Virginia	6.0%

Note: Tax rates as of January 1, 2008; Bank franchise tax is 1.0%.
Source: Tax Foundation, www.taxfoundation.org

State Individual Income Tax Rates

State	Federal Deductibility	Marginal Rates (%)	Standard Deduction ($)		Personal Exemptions ($)[1]	
			Single	Joint	Single	Dependents
Virginia	No	2.0 - 5.75 (y)	3,000	6,000	900	900

Note: Tax rates as of January 1, 2008; Local- and county-level taxes are not included; n/a not applicable; (1) Married joint filers generally receive double the single exemption; (y) Brackets are not double for married taxpayers.
Source: Tax Foundation, www.taxfoundation.org

Various State and Local Tax Rates

State and Local Sales and Use (%)	State Sales and Use (%)	Gasoline[1,2] ($/gal.)	Cigarette ($/pack)	Spirits ($/gal.)	Table Wine ($/gal.)	Beer ($/gal.)
5.0	5.0	0.196	0.30	14.54 (n)	1.51	0.256

Note: Tax rates as of January 1, 2008; (1) In addition to the 18.4 cpg Federal gasoline tax; (2) Rates may include additional state sales taxes, environmental protection and storage fees/taxes, and local taxes. When necessary, the volume-weighted average of all local taxes is used to approximate the typical statewide rate including local tax; (n) The state government controls all sales. The implied excise tax rate is calculated using methodology designed by the Distilled Spirits Council of the United States (DISCUS).
Source: Tax Foundation, www.taxfoundation.org; Original research

State Tax Burdens

Area	Combined State and Local Tax Burden		Combined Federal, State and Local Tax Burden	
	Percent	Rank	Percent	Rank
Virginia	10.2	33	32.9	17
U.S. Average	11.0	-	32.7	-

Note: Figures cover 2007 and measure taxes as a percentage of income
Source: Tax Foundation, www.taxfoundation.org

State Business Tax Climate Index Rankings

State	Overall Rank	Corporate Tax Index Rank	Individual Income Tax Index Rank	Sales Tax Index Rank	Unemployment Insurance Tax Index Rank	Property Tax Index Rank
Virginia	14	4	21	6	29	23

Note: Rankings range from 1 to 50 where 1 is best. Rankings do not average across to Overall Rank. States without a given tax are given a ranking of 1.
Source: Tax Foundation, State Business Tax Climate Index 2008

TRANSPORTATION

Means of Transportation to Work

Area	Car/Truck/Van		Public Transportation			Bicycle	Walked	Other Means	Worked at Home
	Drove Alone	Car-pooled	Bus	Subway	Railroad				
City	82.4	10.0	0.5	0.0	0.1	0.1	1.6	0.6	4.6
MSA[1]	67.8	13.4	4.0	6.5	0.4	0.3	3.0	0.9	3.7
U.S.	75.7	12.2	2.5	1.5	0.5	0.4	2.9	1.0	3.3

Note: Figures are percentages and cover workers 16 years of age and older; (1) Metropolitan Statistical Area - see Appendix A for areas included
Source: Census 2000, Summary File 3

Travel Time to Work

Area	Less Than 15 Minutes	15 to 29 Minutes	30 to 44 Minutes	45 to 59 Minutes	60 Minutes or More
City	27.5	28.0	21.7	12.8	10.0
MSA[1]	16.3	30.3	25.7	13.7	14.0
U.S.	29.4	36.1	19.1	7.4	8.0

Note: Figures are percentages and include workers 16 years old and over; (1) Metropolitan Statistical Area - see Appendix A for areas included
Source: Census 2000, Summary File 3

Travel Time Index

Area	1982	1995	2004	2005
Urban Area[1]	1.12	1.32	1.37	1.37
Average[2]	1.11	1.22	1.29	1.30

Note: Travel Time Index - The ratio of travel time in the peak period to the travel time at free-flow conditions. A value of 1.35 indicates a 20-minute free-flow trip takes 27 minutes in the peak. Free-flow speeds (60 mph on freeways and 35 mph on principal arterials) are used as the comparison threshold; (1) Covers the Washington, DC-VA-MD urban area; (2) average of 85 urban areas
Source: Texas Transportation Institute, The 2007 Urban Mobility Report, September 2007

Living Environment

COST OF LIVING

Cost of Living Index

Composite Index	Groceries	Housing	Utilities	Trans-portation	Health Care	Misc. Goods/ Services
137.2	106.6	213.0	111.8	109.9	110.0	106.1

Note: U.S. = 100; Figures cover the Washington-Arlington-Alexandria DC-VA urban area.
Source: The Council for Community and Economic Research (formerly ACCRA), Cost of Living Index, 2007

Grocery Prices

Area[1]	T-Bone Steak ($/pound)	Frying Chicken ($/pound)	Whole Milk ($/half gal.)	Eggs ($/dozen)	Orange Juice ($/64 oz.)	Coffee ($/11.5 oz.)
City[2]	10.62	1.39	2.16	1.75	3.08	3.58
Avg.	8.93	1.12	2.13	1.52	3.26	3.31
Min.	5.88	0.71	1.33	0.83	2.30	2.20
Max.	12.80	2.07	3.43	3.54	5.79	6.20

Note: (1) Values for the local area are compared with the average, minimum and maximum values for all 331 areas in the Cost of Living Index report; (2) Figures cover the Washington-Arlington-Alexandria DC-VA urban area; **T-Bone Steak** *(price per pound);* **Frying Chicken** *(price per pound, whole fryer);* **Whole Milk** *(half gallon carton);* **Eggs** *(price per dozen, Grade A, large);* **Orange Juice** *(64 oz. Tropicana or Florida Natural);* **Coffee** *(11.5 oz. can, vacuum-packed, Maxwell House, Hills Bros, or Folgers).*
Source: The Council for Community and Economic Research (formerly ACCRA), Cost of Living Index, 2007

Housing and Utility Costs

Area[1]	New Home Price ($)	Apartment Rent ($/month)	All Electric ($/month)	Part Electric ($/month)	Other Energy ($/month)	Telephone ($/month)
City[2]	650,190	1,773	-	67.37	133.18	24.59
Avg.	309,605	782	146.13	78.67	90.16	26.14
Min.	189,877	n/a	82.03	37.41	33.15	17.08
Max.	1,202,800	3,481	271.14	150.60	257.67	37.45

Note: (1) Values for the local area are compared with the average, minimum and maximum values for all 331 areas in the Cost of Living Index report; (2) Figures cover the Washington-Arlington-Alexandria DC-VA urban area; **New Home Price** *(2,400 sf living area, 8,000 sf lot, in urban area with full utilities);* **Apartment Rent** *(950 sf 2 bedroom/1.5 or 2 bath, unfurnished, excluding all utilities except water);* **All Electric** *(average monthly cost for an all-electric home);* **Part Electric** *(average monthly cost for a part-electric home);* **Other Energy** *(average monthly cost for natural gas, fuel oil, coal, wood, and any other forms of energy except electricity);* **Telephone** *(price includes basic monthly rate for a private residential line plus additional local usage charges incurred by a family of four).*
Source: The Council for Community and Economic Research (formerly ACCRA), Cost of Living Index, 2007

Health Care, Transportation, and Other Costs

Area[1]	Doctor ($/visit)	Dentist ($/visit)	Optometrist ($/visit)	Gasoline ($/gallon)	Beauty Salon ($/visit)	Men's Shirt ($)
City[2]	91.47	86.20	75.13	2.64	49.27	30.72
Avg.	79.48	71.93	79.55	2.64	29.52	25.77
Min.	52.08	44.80	43.95	2.19	15.58	16.19
Max.	148.44	126.27	158.83	3.48	60.62	48.53

Note: (1) Values for the local area are compared with the average, minimum and maximum values for all 331 areas in the Cost of Living Index report; (2) Figures cover the Washington-Arlington-Alexandria DC-VA urban area; **Doctor** *(general practitioners routine exam of an established patient);* **Dentist** *(adult teeth cleaning and periodic oral examination);* **Optometrist** *(full vision eye exam for established adult patient);* **Gasoline** *(one gallon regular unleaded, national brand, including all taxes, cash price at self-service pump if available);* **Beauty Salon** *(woman's shampoo, trim, and blow-dry);* **Men's Shirt** *(cotton/polyester dress shirt, pinpoint weave, long sleeves).*
Source: The Council for Community and Economic Research (formerly ACCRA), Cost of Living Index, 2007

HOUSING

House Price Index (HPI)

Area	National Ranking[2]	Quarterly Change (%)	One-Year Change (%)	Five-Year Change (%)
MD[1]	237	-1.91	-2.87	76.21
U.S.[3]	-	0.10	0.84	41.37

Note: The HPI is a weighted repeat sales index. It measures average price changes in repeat sales or refinancings on the same properties. This information is obtained by reviewing repeat mortgage transactions on single-family properties whose mortgages have been purchased or securitized by Fannie Mae or Freddie Mac in January 1975; (1) Metropolitan Division - see Appendix B for areas included; (2) Rankings are based on annual percentage change for all metro areas containing at least 15,000 transactions over the last 10 years and ranges from 1 to 291; (3) figures based on a weighted average of Census Division estimates; all figures are for the period ending December 31, 2007

Source: Office of Federal Housing Enterprise Oversight, House Price Index, February 26, 2008

House Price Valuations

Area	Q1 2000	Q1 2001	Q1 2002	Q1 2003	Q1 2004	Q1 2005	Q1 2006	Q1 2007	Q1 2008
MD[1]	-20.3	-17.3	-8.7	-2.9	15.4	22.3	35.6	38.4	24.6

Note: Figures show the percentage of over- or under-valuation of single family homes relative to statistically normal house values (e.g. a value of 23.6 indicates that house values are 23.6% overvalued). Statistically normal house values are based on house prices, interest rates, household incomes, population densities, and any historical premiums or discounts metropolitan areas have exhibited over time; (1) Figures cover the Metropolitan Division - see Appendix B for areas included

Source: Global Insight/National City Corporation, House Prices in America, May 2008

Median Home Prices

Area	2005	2006	2007[r]	Percent Change 2006 to 2007
MSA[1]	425.8	431.0	430.8	0.0
U.S. Average	219.0	221.9	217.9	-1.8

Note: Figures are median sales prices of existing single-family homes in thousands of dollars; (r) revised; n/a not available; (1) Metropolitan Statistical Area - see Appendix B for areas included

Source: National Association of Realtors, Metropolitan Area Prices, 1st Quarter 2008

Housing: Year Structure Built

Area	1990 -2000	1980 -1989	1970 -1979	1960 -1969	1950 -1959	1940 -1949	Before 1940	Median Year
City	42.5	27.5	17.1	6.1	2.8	0.7	3.4	1987
MSA[1]	18.2	18.9	18.1	16.1	11.9	7.2	9.6	1973
U.S.	17.0	15.8	18.5	13.7	12.7	7.3	15.0	1971

Note: Figures are percentages; (1) Metropolitan Statistical Area - see Appendix A for areas included

Source: Census 2000, Summary File 3

HEALTH

Health Risk Data

Category	Area[1] (%)	U.S. (%)
Adults who have been told they have high blood pressure[3]	22.7	25.5
Adults who have been told they have high blood cholesterol[3]	33.2	35.6
Adults who have been told they have diabetes[2]	8.4	7.5
Adults who have been told they have arthritis[3]	22.7	27.0
Adults who have been told they currently have asthma	7.7	8.5
Adults who are current smokers	17.3	20.1
Adults who are heavy drinkers[4]	4.1	4.9
Adults who are overweight (BMI 25.0 - 29.9)	36.1	36.5
Adults who are obese (BMI 30.0 - 99.8)	23.1	25.1

Note: Data as of 2006 unless otherwise noted; (1) Figures cover the Metropolitan Division - see Appendix B for areas included; (2) Figures do not include pregnancy-related diabetes, pre-diabetes or borderline diabetes; (3) 2005 data; (4) Heavy drinkers are classified as adult men having more than two drinks per day or adult women having more than one drink per day

Source: Centers for Disease Control and Prevention, Behaviorial Risk Factor Surveillance System, SMART: Selected Metropolitan/Micropolitan Area Risk Trends, 2005, 2006

Mortality Rates for the Top 10 Causes of Death in the U.S.

ICD-10[a] Sub-Chapter	ICD-10[a] Code	Age-Adjusted Mortality Rate[1] per 100,000 population	
		County[2]	U.S.
Malignant neoplasms	C00-C97	166.2	186.5
Ischaemic heart diseases	I20-I25	97.7	152.3
Other forms of heart disease	I30-I51	59.4	51.5
Cerebrovascular diseases	I60-I69	46.7	50.0
Chronic lower respiratory diseases	J40-J47	35.7	42.6
Diabetes mellitus	E10-E14	12.9	24.8
Other degenerative diseases of the nervous system	G30-G31	22.5	22.6
Other external causes of accidental injury	W00-X59	16.8	21.4
Influenza and pneumonia	J10-J18	12.8	20.7
Hypertensive diseases	I10-I13	9.8	18.2

Note: (a) ICD-10 = International Classification of Diseases 10th Revision; (1) Mortality rates are a three year average covering 2003-2005; (2) Figures cover Loudoun County
Source: Centers for Disease Control and Prevention, National Center for Health Statistics. Compressed Mortality File 1999-2004. CDC WONDER On-line Database, compiled from Compressed Mortality File 1999-2005 Series 20 No. 2K, 2008.

Mortality Rates for Selected Causes of Death

ICD-10[a] Sub-Chapter	ICD-10[a] Code	Age-Adjusted Mortality Rate[1] per 100,000 population	
		County[2]	U.S.
Assault	X85-Y09	*1.5	5.9
Human immunodeficiency virus (HIV) disease	B20-B24	*1.0	4.5
Intentional self-harm	X60-X84	9.1	10.8
Malnutrition	E40-E46	*0.4	1.0
Obesity and other hyperalimentation	E65-E68	*0.6	1.4
Organic, including symptomatic, mental disorders	F01-F09	25.5	16.8
Transport accidents	V01-V99	13.9	16.1
Viral hepatitis	B15-B19	*1.5	1.8

Note: (a) ICD-10 = International Classification of Diseases 10th Revision; (1) Mortality rates are a three year average covering 2003-2005; (2) Figures cover Loudoun County; (*) Unreliable data as per CDC
Source: Centers for Disease Control and Prevention, National Center for Health Statistics. Compressed Mortality File 1999-2004. CDC WONDER On-line Database, compiled from Compressed Mortality File 1999-2005 Series 20 No. 2K, 2008.

Distribution of Physicians[1]

Area	Total	Family/ General Practice	Specialties	
			Medical	Surgical
Loudoun County (number)	353	104	138	78
Loudoun County (rate per 10,000 pop.)	13.8	4.1	5.4	3.1
U.S. (rate per 10,000 pop.)	17.7	4.6	6.9	4.3

Note: Data as of 2005; (1) Includes all non-federal, patient-care, office-based MDs
Source: Area Resource File (ARF). June 2007. U.S. Department of Health and Human Services, Health Resources and Services Administration, Bureau of Health Professions, Rockville, MD.

Hospitals

Leesburg has the following hospitals: 1 general medical and surgical; 1 psychiatric.
AHA Guide to the Healthcare Field 2008

According to *U.S. News,* the Washington-Arlington-Alexandria, DC-VA-MD-WV metro area is home to five of the best hospitals in the U.S.: **Children's National Medical Center**; **Georgetown University Hospital**; **Inova Fairfax Hospital**; **National Rehabilitation Hospital**; **Washington Hospital Center**. *U.S. News Online, "America's Best Hospitals 2007"*

EDUCATION

Public School District Statistics

District Name	Schls	Pupils	Pupil/ Teacher Ratio	Minority Pupils[1] (%)	Free Lunch Eligible[2] (%)	IEP[3] (%)
Loudoun County Public Schools	68	47,306	13.0	32.7	8.0	10.0

Note: Table includes regular local school districts with 2,000 or more students; (1) Percentage of students that are not white, non-Hispanic; (2) Percentage of students that are eligible for the free lunch program; (3) Percentage of students that have an Individualized Education Program.
Source: U.S. Department of Education, National Center for Education Statistics, Common Core of Data, Local Education Agency (School District) Universe Survey: School Year 2005-2006; U.S. Department of Education, National Center for Education Statistics, Common Core of Data, Public Elementary/Secondary School Universe Survey: School Year 2005-2006

Top Public High Schools

High School Name	Index[1]	Rank[1]	Subsidized Lunch (%)[2]	E&E (%)[3]
Heritage	2.108	448	17.0	33.6
Loudoun County	2.596	255	10.0	40.5

Note: (1) Public schools are ranked according to a ratio that is the number of Advanced Placement, International Baccalaureate, and/or Cambridge tests taken by all students at a school in 2007 divided by the number of graduating seniors. All of the schools on the list have an index of at least 1.000; they are in the top five percent of public schools measured this way. The rankings range from 1 to 1,422; (2) Percentage of students receiving federally subsidized meals; (3) E & E stands for equity and excellence percentage: the portion of all graduating seniors at a school that had at least one passing grade on one AP or IB test; (**) Gave both IB and AP tests. AP and IB participation are indicators of a school's efforts to get students to excel and prepare for college.
Source: Newsweek Online, "Top High Schools 2008"

Highest Level of Education

Area	Less than H.S.	H.S. Diploma	Some College, No Deg.	Associate Degree	Bachelors Degree	Masters Degree	Profess. School Degree	Doctorate Degree
City	9.7	19.2	22.8	7.3	27.9	10.7	1.5	0.9
MSA[1]	12.9	20.4	19.4	5.1	23.5	12.4	3.9	2.4
U.S.	19.4	28.4	21.2	6.4	15.7	5.9	2.0	1.0

Note: Figures are 2007 estimated percentages and cover persons age 25 and over; (1) Metropolitan Statistical Area - see Appendix B for areas included
Source: Claritas, Inc.

Educational Attainment by Race

Area	High School Graduate (%)					Bachelor's Degree (%)				
	Total	White	Black	Asian	Hisp.[2]	Total	White	Black	Asian	Hisp.[2]
City	89.8	92.1	80.6	74.7	63.8	41.3	44.8	16.3	40.7	19.9
MSA[1]	86.7	91.1	81.3	85.4	57.7	41.8	49.2	24.1	53.9	21.0
U.S.	80.4	83.6	72.3	80.4	52.4	24.4	26.1	14.3	44.1	10.4

Note: Figures shown cover persons 25 years old and over; (1) Metropolitan Statistical Area - see Appendix A for areas included; (2) people of Hispanic origin can be of any race
Source: Census 2000, Summary File 3

School Enrollment by Type

Area	Grades KG to 8				Grades 9 to 12			
	Public		Private		Public		Private	
	Enrollment	%	Enrollment	%	Enrollment	%	Enrollment	%
City	3,695	90.1	405	9.9	1,163	92.9	89	7.1
MSA[1]	556,504	85.7	92,990	14.3	239,684	88.0	32,576	12.0
U.S.	33,526,011	88.7	4,285,121	11.3	14,848,628	90.6	1,532,323	9.4

Note: Figures shown cover persons 3 years old and over; (1) Metropolitan Statistical Area - see Appendix A for areas included
Source: Census 2000, Summary File 3

School Enrollment by Race

Area	Grades KG to 8 (%)				Grades 9 to 12 (%)			
	White	Black	Asian	Hisp.[1]	White	Black	Asian	Hisp.[1]
City	79.9	10.4	2.8	6.2	81.7	12.3	1.5	5.1
MSA[2]	54.3	30.4	5.8	9.9	53.1	30.9	6.6	10.2
U.S.	68.5	15.5	3.3	16.8	68.8	15.5	3.8	15.7

Note: Figures shown cover persons 3 years old and over; (1) people of Hispanic origin can be of any race; (2) Metropolitan Statistical Area - see Appendix A for areas included
Source: Census 2000, Summary File 3

Average Salaries of Public School Classroom Teachers

District	2005-06		2006-07		Percent Change 2005-06 to 2006-07
	Dollars	Rank[1]	Dollars	Rank[1]	
Virginia	43,823	28	44,727	31	2.06
U.S. Average	49,026	-	50,816	-	3.65

Note: (1) State rank ranges from 1 to 51.
Source: National Education Association, Rankings & Estimates: Rankings of the States 2006 and Estimates of School Statistics 2007, December 2007

Higher Education

Four-Year Colleges			Two-Year Colleges			Medical Schools[1]	Law Schools[2]	Voc/ Tech[3]
Public	Private Non-profit	Private For-profit	Public	Private Non-profit	Private For-profit			
0	0	0	0	0	0	0	0	0

Note: Figures cover institutions located within the city limits; (1) includes schools accredited by the Liaison Committee on Medical Education and the American Osteopathic Association; (2) includes American Bar Association-accredited law schools; (3) includes all schools with programs that are less than 2 years.
Source: National Center for Education Statistics, The Integrated Postsecondary Education System (IPEDS) Peer Analysis System, 2007; www.usnews.com, Law and Medical School Directories, 2009

PRESIDENTIAL ELECTION

2004 Presidential Election Results

Area	Bush	Kerry	Nader	Other
Loudoun County	55.7	43.6	0.0	0.7
U.S.	50.7	48.3	0.4	0.6

Note: Results are percentages and may not add to 100% due to rounding
Source: Dave Leip's Atlas of U.S. Presidential Elections, www.uselectionatlas.org

EMPLOYERS

Major Employers

Company Name	Industry	Type of Site
DOD	National security	Headquarters
Environmental Protection Agcy	Air, water, and solid waste management	Headquarters
FBI	Police protection	Headquarters
Geico	Fire, marine, and casualty insurance	Headquarters
MCI	Telephone communication, except radio	Single
Morale Welfare & Recreation	National security	Branch
National Institutes of Health	Administration of public health programs	Headquarters
Office of Inspector General	Administration of general economic programs	Branch
U S D A	Regulation of agricultural marketing	Headquarters
US Army Garrison	National security	Branch
US DOC	Administration of general economic programs	Headquarters
US Dept Transportation	Regulation, administration of transportation	Branch
US Dept of Transportation	Regulation, administration of transportation	Headquarters
United States Department Labor	Regulation, miscellaneous commercial sectors	Headquarters
United States Dept of Army	National security	Headquarters
United States Dept of Navy	National security	Headquarters
WHUR-FM	Colleges and universities	Headquarters
World Bank Office of Publisher	Foreign trade and international banks	Headquarters

Note: Companies shown are located within the Washington metropolitan area; nec = not elsewhere classified.
Source: www.zapdata.com, May 2008

PUBLIC SAFETY

Crime Rate

Area	All Crimes	Violent Crimes				Property Crimes		
		Murder	Forcible Rape	Robbery	Aggrav. Assault	Burglary	Larceny -Theft	Motor Vehicle Theft
City	2,336.9	0.0	32.8	51.9	114.7	182.9	1,823.6	131.0
Metro[1]	3,553.3	8.8	20.0	233.7	275.2	411.1	2,001.8	602.8
U.S.	3,808.1	5.7	30.9	149.4	287.5	729.4	2,206.8	398.4

Note: Figures are crimes per 100,000 population; (1) Metropolitan Division - see Appendix B for areas included
Source: FBI Uniform Crime Reports, 2006

Hate Crimes

Area	Number of Quarters Reported	Bias Motivation				
		Race	Religion	Sexual Orientation	Ethnicity	Disability
City	4	1	0	0	0	0

Source: Federal Bureau of Investigation, Hate Crime Statistics 2006

RECREATION

Culture

Dance[1]	Theatre[1]	Instrumental Music[1]	Vocal Music[1]	Series/ Festivals	Museums	Zoos and Aquariums[2]
1	0	0	0	1	3	0

Note: (1) Number of professional perfoming groups; (2) AZA-accredited
Source: The Grey House Performing Arts Directory, 2007; Official Museum Directory, 2008; Association of Zoos & Aquariums, AZA Member Zoos & Aquariums, June 2008

Professional Sports Teams

Team Name	League
Washington Nationals	Major League Baseball (MLB)
D.C. United	Major League Soccer (MLS)
Washington Wizards	National Basketball Association (NBA)
Washington Redskins	National Football League (NFL)
Washington Capitals	National Hockey League (NHL)

Note: Includes teams located in the Washington metro area.
Source: Original research

MEDIA

Newspapers

Name	News Focus	Frequency	Circulation
Leesburg Today	Community	Weekly	38,000
Loudoun Business	Local	Weekly	n/a
Loudoun Times-Mirror	Community	Weekly	17,000
The New Federalist	National	Weekly	n/a

Note: Includes newspapers with offices located in the city; n/a not available
Source: MediaContactsPro, March 2008

Television Stations

Name	Ch.	Network(s)	Type	Ownership
WRC	4	NBC	Commercial	General Electric Corporation
WTTG	5	Fox	Commercial	Fox Television Stations Inc.
WJLA	7	ABC	Commercial	Allbritton Communications Company
WUSA	9	CBS	Commercial	Gannett Broadcasting
WAZT	10	n/a	Commercial	Ruarch Associates LLC.
WDCA	20	Fox	Commercial	Fox Television Stations Inc.
WHAG	25	NBC	Commercial	Quorum Broadcasting
WETA	26	PBS	Public	Greater Washington Education & Telecommunications Association
WMDO	30	Univision	Commercial	Entravision Communications
WHUT	32	PBS	Public	Howard University
WBDC	50	WBN	Commercial	Tribune Broadcasting Company
WNVT	53	n/a	Public	Commonwealth Broadcasting Corporation
WNVC	56	n/a	Public	Commonwealth Broadcasting Corporation
WWPX	60	Pax	Commercial	Paxson Communications Corporation
WPXW	66	Pax/NBC	Commercial	Paxson Communications Corporation
WJAL	68	n/a	Commercial	Entravision Communications

Note: Stations included cover the Washington DMA (Designated Market Area); n/a not available
BurrellesLuce, MediaContacts Online, January 2007

Major AM Radio Stations

Call Letters	Freq. (kHz)	Station Type	Target Audience	Station Format	Music Format
WFRB	560	n/a	General	Music/Talk	n/a
WWRC	570	n/a	General	News	n/a
WMAL	630	Commercial	Senior Citizen	Music/News/Talk	Country
WABS	780	n/a	General/Religious	Music/Talk	n/a
WXTR	820	Commercial	General	n/a	n/a
WFMD	930	n/a	General	News/Sports/Talk	n/a
WTEM	980	Commercial	General/Men	Sports/Talk	n/a
WUST	1120	Commercial	French/Gen/Hisp/Rel	Educational/Music/Sports	Christian
WAGE	1200	Commercial	General	Music/News/Talk	Oldies
WFAX	1220	n/a	General/Religious	Talk	n/a
WPRZ	1250	n/a	Christian/Religious	Music/News/Sports	n/a
WCBC	1270	n/a	General	n/a	n/a
WDCT	1310	Commercial	Christian/General	Music/News/Talk	Christian
WKCW	1420	Commercial	General	Music/News/Talk	Country
WTOP	1500	n/a	General	News	n/a
WACA	1540	n/a	Hispanic	News/Sports/Talk	n/a
WMRE	1550	n/a	General	n/a	n/a
WPGC	1580	n/a	Black/General/Rel	Music/Talk	n/a
WCBG	1590	Commercial	General	News/Sports	n/a

Note: Stations included cover the Washington DMA (Designated Market Area); n/a not available
Source: BurrellesLuce, MediaContacts Online, January 2007

Major FM Radio Stations

Call Letters	Freq. (mHz)	Station Type	Target Audience	Station Format	Music Format
WAMU	88.5	College	General	Music/Talk	n/a
WPFW	89.3	Public	General	Educational/Music/Talk	Latin
WCSP	90.1	Non-Comm	General	News/Talk	n/a
WETA	90.9	n/a	General	Music/News	n/a
WTRM	91.3	n/a	Religious	Ed/Music/News/Talk	n/a
WFLS	93.3	n/a	General	Music/News	n/a
WKYS	93.9	Commercial	Black/General/Women	Music	Urban Contemp.
WQZK	94.1	Commercial	General	Music	Classic Rock
WIKZ	95.1	n/a	General	Music/News	n/a
WPGC	95.5	Commercial	Black/General	Music/News/Talk	Rhythm & Blues
WHUR	96.3	College	General	Music	n/a
WASH	97.1	Commercial	General	Music/News/Talk	Adult Contemp.
WLTF	97.5	n/a	General	Music	n/a
WMZQ	98.7	Commercial	General	Music/News/Talk	Country
WBIG	100.3	n/a	General	Music	n/a
WWMD	101.5	Commercial	General	Music	Top 40
WBQB	101.5	n/a	General	n/a	n/a
WMMJ	102.3	n/a	Black/General	Music/News	n/a
WUSQ	102.5	n/a	General	Music/News/Sports	n/a
WROG	102.9	Commercial	General	Music	Country
WGMS	103.5	n/a	General	Music	n/a
WWZZ	104.1	Commercial	General	Music/News/Talk	Adult Top 40
WAYZ	104.7	n/a	General	Music/News/Sports	n/a
WAVA	105.1	Commercial	General/Religious	Music/News/Talk	Christian
WARX	106.9	n/a	General	Music/News	n/a
WRQX	107.3	Commercial	General	Music/News/Talk	Adult Top 40

Note: Stations included cover the Washington DMA (Designated Market Area); n/a not available
BurrellesLuce, MediaContacts Online, January 2007

CLIMATE

Average and Extreme Temperatures

Temperature	Jan	Feb	Mar	Apr	May	Jun	Jul	Aug	Sep	Oct	Nov	Dec	Yr.
Extreme High (°F)	75	79	89	92	97	100	104	104	99	90	84	78	104
Average High (°F)	41	44	55	66	75	83	87	86	79	68	57	45	65
Average Temp. (°F)	31	34	44	53	63	71	76	75	67	55	46	36	54
Average Low (°F)	22	23	32	41	50	59	65	63	55	42	34	26	43
Extreme Low (°F)	-18	-14	-1	17	28	36	41	38	30	15	9	-4	-18

Note: Figures cover the years 1962-1995
Source: National Climatic Data Center, International Station Meteorological Climate Summary, 9/96

Average Precipitation/Snowfall/Humidity

Precip./Humidity	Jan	Feb	Mar	Apr	May	Jun	Jul	Aug	Sep	Oct	Nov	Dec	Yr.
Avg. Precip. (in.)	2.8	2.7	3.4	3.0	3.9	3.6	3.6	3.8	3.5	3.2	3.4	3.3	40.3
Avg. Snowfall (in.)	7	7	3	Tr	Tr	0	0	0	0	Tr	1	4	23
Avg. Rel. Hum. 4am (%)	77	77	78	77	82	84	86	89	89	88	82	78	82
Avg. Rel. Hum. 4pm (%)	57	52	49	46	53	54	54	55	55	52	54	57	53

Note: Figures cover the years 1962-1995; Tr = Trace amounts (<0.05 in. of rain; <0.5 in. of snow)
Source: National Climatic Data Center, International Station Meteorological Climate Summary, 9/96

Weather Conditions

Temperature			Daytime Sky			Precipitation		
10°F & below	32°F & below	90°F & above	Clear	Partly cloudy	Cloudy	0.01 inch or more precip.	0.1 inch or more snow/ice	Thunder-storms
9	115	30	79	141	145	117	12	28

Note: Figures are average number of days per year and cover the years 1962-1995
Source: National Climatic Data Center, International Station Meteorological Climate Summary, 9/96

HAZARDOUS WASTE

Superfund Sites

Leesburg has no sites on the EPA's Superfund Final National Priorities List.
U.S. Environmental Protection Agency, Final National Priorities List, June 23, 2008

AIR & WATER QUALITY

Air Quality Index

Area	Percent of Days when Air Quality was...[2]				AQI Statistics	
	Good	Moderate	Unhealthy for Sensitive Groups	Unhealthy	Maximum	Median
MSA[1]	49.6	38.4	11.2	0.8	187	51

Note: The Air Quality Index (AQI) is an index for reporting daily air quality. EPA calculates the AQI for five major air pollutants regulated by the Clean Air Act: ground-level ozone, particle pollution (also known as particulate matter), carbon monoxide, sulfur dioxide, and nitrogen dioxide. The AQI runs from 0 to 500. The higher the AQI value, the greater the level of air pollution and the greater the health concern. There are six AQI categories: "Good" The AQI is between 0 and 50. Air quality is considered satisfactory; "Moderate" The AQI is between 51 and 100. Air quality is acceptable; "Unhealthy for Sensitive Groups" When AQI values are between 101 and 150, members of sensitive groups may experience health effects; "Unhealthy" When AQI values are between 151 and 200 everyone may begin to experience health effects; "Very Unhealthy" AQI values between 201 and 300 trigger a health alert; "Hazardous" AQI values over 300 trigger health warnings of emergency conditions; (1) Metropolitan Statistical Area - see Appendix A for areas included; (2) Based on 365 days with AQI data in 2007.
Source: U.S. Environmental Protection Agency, Air Quality Index Report, 2007

Air Quality Index Pollutants

Area	Percent of Days when AQI Pollutant was...[2]					
	Carbon Monoxide	Nitrogen Dioxide	Ozone	Sulfur Dioxide	Particulate Matter 2.5	Particulate Matter 10
MSA[1]	0.0	0.0	60.0	0.0	39.7	0.3

Note: The Air Quality Index (AQI) is an index for reporting daily air quality. EPA calculates the AQI for five major air pollutants regulated by the Clean Air Act: ground-level ozone, particle pollution (also known as particulate matter), carbon monoxide, sulfur dioxide, and nitrogen dioxide. The AQI runs from 0 to 500. The higher the AQI value, the greater the level of air pollution and the greater the health concern; (1) Metropolitan Statistical Area - see Appendix A for areas included; (2) Based on 365 days with AQI data in 2007.
Source: U.S. Environmental Protection Agency, Air Quality Index Report, 2007

Air Quality Index Trends

Area	Trend Sites (41)								All Sites (123)
	1999	2000	2001	2002	2003	2004	2005	2006	2006
MSA[1]	41	20	27	33	12	10	18	18	24

Note: An AQI value greater than 100 indicates that air quality would have been in the unhealthful range on that day. Data from exceptional events are not included. These counts are presented in two ways. First, the counts are based on sites having an adequate record of monitoring data during the trend period (trend sites). These counts represent the relative change in the number of days with AQI values greater than 100. In the last column, the counts are based on all sites with data in the most recent year (because it is possible for a site to have data in the most recent year but not enough data to be a trend site); (1) Metropolitan Statistical Area - see Appendix A for areas included.
Source: U.S. Environmental Protection Agency, Office of Air and Radiation, Air Trends, Factbook and Related Information, Air Pollution Trends in Selected Metropolitan Areas 2006

Maximum Air Pollutant Concentrations

	Particulate Matter 10 (ug/m^3)	Particulate Matter 2.5 (ug/m^3)	Ozone (ppm)	Carbon Monoxide (ppm)	Sulfur Dioxide (ppm)	Nitrogen Dioxide (ppm)	Lead (ug/m^3)
MSA[1] Level	61	34	0.142	3	0.017	0.02	n/a
NAAQS[2]	150	35	0.125	9	0.140	0.053	1.50
Met NAAQS[2]	Yes	Yes	No	Yes	Yes	Yes	n/a

Note: Data from exceptional events are not included; (1) Metropolitan Statistical Area - see Appendix A for areas included; (2) National Ambient Air Quality Standards; n/a not available
Concentrations: Particulate Matter 10 (coarse particulate) - highest second maximum 24-hour concentration; Particulate Matter 2.5 (fine particulate) - highest 98th percentile 24-hour concentration; Ozone - highest second daily maximum 1-hour concentration; Carbon Monoxide - highest second maximum non-overlapping 8-hour concentration; Sulfur Dioxide - highest second maximum 24-hour concentration; Nitrogen Dioxide - highest arithmetic mean concentration; Lead - highest quarterly maximum concentration
Units: ppm = parts per million; ug/m^3 = micrograms per cubic meter
Source: U.S. Environmental Protection Agency, MSA Factbook 2006, Air Quality Statistics by City

Drinking Water

Water System Name	Pop. Served	Primary Water Source Type	Violations[1]	
			Health Based	Monitoring/ Reporting
Town of Leesburg	37,000	Surface	0	0

Note: (1) Based on violation data from January 1, 2007 to December 31, 2007 (includes unresolved violations from earlier years)
Source: U.S. Environmental Protection Agency, Office of Ground Water and Drinking Water, Safe Drinking Water Information System (based on data extracted April 15, 2008)

Redmond, Washington

Background

Redmond is located in King County, Washington, on the eastern edge of Seattle. It sits on the north end of Lake Sammamish, with the Sammamish River running through its center, in a fertile basin created by ancient glaciers that once covered much of King County. Surrounded by towering evergreen forests between the Cascade Mountain Range and sparkling Puget Sound, Redmond is known for its natural beauty.

The greatest challenge for early homesteaders was clearing the vast tracts of towering trees. During the 1880s, loggers built lumber and shingle mills. Their substantial payrolls created a demand for products and services. In 1888, the Seattle Lake Shore and Eastern Railway reached the town, and with it, the marketability of the area's timber was insured.

In its logging heyday, Redmond had a stagecoach office, saloons and hotels, blacksmiths and eateries. In 1912, needing a modern waterworks system and a way to tax its thriving saloons, Redmond incorporated. Soon many new buildings rose in the downtown area, automobiles became a frequent sight on Main Street, the first doctor took up residence in town, and a two-story brick schoolhouse was built.

As virgin forests were exhausted in the 1920s, local logging faded. Prohibition forced saloons to close, cutting off a large portion of the city's tax base. In the following decades, agriculture became the mainstay of Redmond's economy. Dairy, chicken and truck farms carried Redmond through the Depression. The town's population grew very little during this period, with many young adults seeking jobs elsewhere.

After World War II, Redmond grew over thirty times larger in area through annexations between 1951 and 1967. In 1963, the Evergreen Point floating bridge was completed, connecting Redmond to Seattle and initiating vigorous residential development. This was followed by commercial growth, fueled by a number of high-tech and service industries that began modestly in the 1970s.

Today, Redmond enjoys a diverse and growing economic base. The community is home to some of the major high-tech firms in the country, including Microsoft, Nintendo of America, Honeywell, General Dynamics Airborne Electronic Systems, and Medtronics Emergency Response Systems. Its strong retail sector is enhanced by Redmond Town Center, a 1.4 million square foot mixed use development that includes retail stores, restaurants, and commercial offices.

Performing arts in Redmond include the Eastside Symphony, the SecondStory Repertory theater company, and the Washington Academy of Performing Arts. Redmond has an extensive collection of high quality outdoor sculptures throughout its streets and parks, a good number of which are part of a rotating sculpture exhibition.

Redmond's 23 developed public parks total over a thousand acres, featuring a climbing rock, a model airplane flying field, a large off-leash dog park, an outdoor theater, and a velodrome. The city also offers 17 miles of developed trails for hiking, bicycling, and horseback riding. Redmond Derby Days, an annual community festival in July, began in 1939 as a race around Lake Sammamish called the Redmond Bicycle Derby, and has since become a multi-day event including a bicycle parade, carnival, and entertainment.

Redmond's climate is mostly damp and cool, with overcast skies. Summers are warm, dry, and sunny, with long days and cool nights. Warm, mild weather often continues into fall, with cooler temperatures at night. The rainy season officially begins October 1, and rain in Redmond is usually a fine mist. Winter is the wettest season and although spring is mild and green, it's often very wet.

Rankings

General Rankings

- Seattle* was ranked #129 out of 375 metro areas in *Cities Ranked & Rated*. Criteria: cost of living; climate; crime; transportation; economy and jobs; education; arts and culture; health and healthcare; leisure; quality of life. *Cities Ranked & Rated, 2nd Edition, 2007*
- Seattle* was ranked #3 out of 379 metro areas in *Places Rated Almanac*. Criteria: health care; education; recreation; transportation; ambience; climate; crime; housing costs; jobs. *Places Rated Almanac, 7th Edition, 2007*

Business/Finance Rankings

- The nation's 100 largest metro areas were analysed in terms of the percentage of households entering some stage of foreclosure in 2007. The Seattle* metro area ranked #81 out of 100 (#1 = highest foreclosure rate). *RealtyTrac, "Year-End 2007 Metropolitan Foreclosure Report"*
- The Seattle* metro area was identified as one of the "10 Best Cities for Jobs in 2008" by *Forbes*. The metro area ranked #10. Criteria: state unemployment rate; job growth; income growth; median household income; cost of living. *Forbes.com, "Best Cities for Jobs in 2008," January 10, 2008*
- The Seattle* metro area was identified as one of the "Top 12 Nano Metros" in the U.S. by the Woodrow Wilson International Center for Scholars. The metro area is home to 15 companies, universities, government laboratories and/or organizations working in nanotechnology. *Woodrow Wilson International Center for Scholars, May 17, 2007*
- The Seattle* metro area was selected one of America's "Top 50 Business Opportunity Metros" by *Expansion Management* in their 5th annual Mayor's Challenge ranking of metro areas that have achieved solid ratings across the board in numerous *EM* studies during the past 12 months. The area ranked #10. Criteria: public schools; quality of life; college educated workers; logistics infrastructure; healthcare costs; taxes and government spending; reputation among site consultants. *Expansion Management, August 2007*
- The Seattle* metro area was selected as one of "America's Most Wired Cities" by *Forbes*. The metro area was ranked #2 out of 30. Criteria: percentage of Internet users with high-speed access; the range of service providers within a city; availability of public wireless hot spots. *Forbes, "America's Most Wired Cities," January 10, 2008*
- Seattle* was selected as one of the best places to start and grow a company by *Entrepreneur* and the National Policy Research Council. The Seattle* metro area ranked #31 out of 50 large metro areas. Criteria: business formation and growth (firms started four to 14 years ago that still employ at least 5 people and experienced rapid growth over the last four years). *Entrepreneur/National Policy Research Council, "Hot Cities for Entrepreneurs," September 2006*
- The Seattle* metro area was selected as one of "America's Greediest Cities" by *Forbes*. The area was ranked #3 out of 10. Criteria: number of Forbes 400 (*Forbes* annual list of the richest Americans) members per capita. *Forbes, "America's Greediest Cities," December 7, 2007*
- The Seattle* metro area was selected as one of "America's 50 Hottest Cities" for business relocations and expansions. Criteria: industry's most prominent site selection consultants were asked to list their top city choices for relocating and expanding manufacturing companies, taking into consideration such factors as the business climate, work force quality, operating costs, incentive programs, and the ease of working with local political and economic development officials. *Expansion Management, January-February 2007*
- The Seattle* metro area was selected one of America's "Top 10 Knowledge Worker Metros." The area ranked #10. Criteria: degree holders (bachelors, masters, professional, and Ph.D.) as a percent of the workforce; science and engineering workers as a percent of the workforce; number of patents issued; number and type of colleges in each metro area. *Expansion Management, April 2007*

- Intel, in partnership with Sperling's BestPlaces, ranked the 80 "Best Cities for Teleworking" in America. The Seattle* metro area ranked #10 among extra large metro areas. The study identifies cities that hold the greatest potential for teleworking based on a host of factors including typical commuting times, fuel prices, availability of broadband Internet access and percentage of the population in telework friendly jobs. The study also factored in extreme climate and natural hazards. *Intel, "Best Cities for Teleworking," March 30, 2006*

- The Seattle* metro area appeared on the Milken Institute "2007 Best Performing Cities" index. Rank: #77 out of 200 large metro areas. Criteria: job growth; wage and salary growth; high-tech output growth. *Milken Institute, "2007 Best Performing Cities"*

- The Seattle* metro area was selected as one of the hottest cities for entrepreneurs in America by *Inc. Magazine.* Criteria: job-growth data for 393 metro was analyzed for current-year employment growth, average annual employment growth over past three years, and employment growth by industry sector. The Seattle* metro area ranked #18 among large metro areas and #122 overall. *Inc. Magazine, May 2007*

- The Seattle* metro area was selected as one of "The Top 20 Boom Towns in America." *Business 2.0* magazine and econometric research firm Global Insight compared 319 metropolitan areas in the U.S. and ranked the 61 with populations over 1 million. Criteria: a weighted formula that includes forecast growth rates in sectors that contain the economy's 10 most skilled occupational clusters; the prevalence of college degrees in the local workforce; median salary. The area ranked #9 among large metro areas. *Business 2.0 Magazine, March 2004*

- Seattle* was identified as one of the 100 "Most Unwired Cities" in the U.S. The area ranked #1 out of the 100 largest metro areas in the U.S. Criteria: number of public and commercial wireless access points (hotspots); airports with wireless Internet access; broadband availability; local wireless networks; and wireless email devices. *Intel, "Most Unwired Cities Survey," June 7, 2005*

- Seattle* was ranked #5 out of 125 regions worldwide in terms of its "Knowledge Competitiveness Index." The index attempts to measure the knowledge-based development taking place throughout the world and is based on 19 measures of economic performance that indicate a region's ability to translate its knowledge capacity into economic value. *Robert Huggins Associates, World Knowledge Competitiveness Index 2005*

- *Forbes* ranked the 200 most populous metro areas in the U.S. in terms of the "Best Places for Business and Careers." The Seattle* metro area was ranked #20. Criteria: business costs (labor, energy, tax and office space expenses); living costs (housing, transportation, food and other household expenditures); education levels of the work force; job growth; income growth; migration trends; crime rates; and culture/leisure. *Forbes, "Best Places for Business and Careers," March 19, 2008*

- *Fortune* ranked the 100 largest metro areas in the U.S. in terms of projected median home price change in 2007. The Seattle* metro area ranked #37. *Fortune.com, "Hot Spots, Cold Spots"*

Health/Environment Rankings

- The Seattle* metro area was selected as one of "America's Cleanest Cities" by *Forbes*. The metro area ranked #2 out of 10. Criteria: air quality; water quality; per capita spending on Superfund site cleanup and solid-waste management. *Forbes.com, "America's Cleanest Cities," March 11, 2008*

- 100 of the largest metro areas in the U.S. were analyzed in terms of their current drought severity. The Seattle* metro area ranked #66 (#1 = driest). The rankings were based on statistics such as long-term precipitation trends and patterns and the Palmer drought indices. *Sperling's BestPlaces, www.BestPlaces.net, "America's Drought-Riskiest Cities," November 2007*

- Tahitian Noni International Hiro™, in partnership with Sperling's BestPlaces, ranked the nation's 50 largest metro areas in terms of the "Most Energetic Cities." The Seattle* metro area ranked #7. Criteria: percentage of population that walk or bicycle to work; BMI score; number of food co-ops; number of farmers markets. *Tahitian Noni International Hiro™, "Most Energetic Cities," March 13, 2007*

- Scarborough Research, a leading market research firm, identified the top local markets for organic consumers. The Seattle* DMA (Designated Market Area) ranked in the top 15 with 32% of adults reporting that they used any organic food product in their household during the past month. *Scarborough Research, October 10, 2007*

- *Reader's Digest* ranked the 50 largest metro areas in the U.S. in terms of how "clean" they are. The Seattle* metro area ranked #27. Criteria: air quality; water quality; toxic industrial pollution; Superfund sites; and sanitation. *Reader's Digest, "The 50 Cleanest (and Dirtiest) Cities in America," July 2005*

- The American Academy of Dermatology ranked 32 U.S. metropolitan regions in terms of their residents knowledge, attitude and behaviors towards tanning and sun protection. The Seattle* metro area ranked #29. The results of the study are based on an online national survey of 3,342 respondents. *American Academy of Dermatology, "RAYS: Your Grade," May 7, 2007*

- *Business Week* identified the 15 metro areas that saw the steepest declines in ground-level ozone pollution between 1990 and 2005. The Seattle* metro area ranked #2. *Business Week, "America's Most Cleaned-Up Metro Areas," March 23, 2007*

- The Seattle* metro area appeared in *Country Home's* "2008 Best Green Places" report. The area ranked #13 out of 379. Criteria: official energy policies; green power; green buildings; availability of fresh, locally grown food. *Country Home, "2008 Best Green Places"*

- Wyeth Consumer Healthcare, in partnership with Sperling's BestPlaces, ranked the nation's 50 most populous metro areas in terms of five key health factors. The Seattle* metro area ranked #4. Criteria: physical activity; health status; nutrition; lifestyle pursuits; and mental wellness. *Wyeth Consumer Healthcare, "Centrum Healthiest Cities Study," April 19, 2005*

- HealthGrades surveyed over 41,000 individuals on doctor satisfaction and ranked the 20 largest metro areas based on the highest "definitely yes" responses to the question "Do you trust the physician to make decisions/recommendations that are in your best interest?" The Seattle* metro area ranked #9. *HealthGrades.com, "Top Cities in Doctor-Trust," September 7, 2006*

- Seattle* was identified as a "2008 Asthma Capital." The area ranked #92 out of the nation's 100 largest metropolitan areas. Twelve factors were used to identify the most challenging places to live for people with asthma: estimated prevalence; self-reported prevalence; crude death rate for asthma; annual pollen score; annual air quality; public smoking laws; number of board-certified asthma specialists; school inhaler access laws; rescue medication use; controller medication use; uninsured rate; poverty rate. *Asthma and Allergy Foundation of America, "2008 Asthma Capitals"*

- Seattle* was identified as a "Spring Allergy Capital." The area ranked #96 out of 100. Three groups of factors were used to identify the most severe cities for people with allergies during the spring season: annual pollen levels; medicine utilization; access to board-certified allergists. *Asthma and Allergy Foundation of America, "2007 Spring Allergy Capital Rankings"*

- Seattle* was identified as a "Fall Allergy Capital." The area ranked #100 out of 100. Three groups of factors were used to identify the most severe cities for people with allergies during the fall season: annual pollen levels; medicine utilization; access to board-certified allergists. *Asthma and Allergy Foundation of America, "2007 Fall Allergy Capital Rankings"*

- Ortho-McNeil Neurologics, in partnership with Sperling's BestPlaces, analyzed 110 metro areas and identified those U.S. cities with the highest prevalence of factors that are most commonly associated with migraine headaches. The Seattle* metro area ranked #59. Criteria: number of migraine-related drug prescriptions per capita; lifestyle factors that can contribute to migraines; environmental factors that can trigger migraines; and consumption of migraine-triggering foods. *Ortho-McNeil Neurologics, "America's Migraine Hot Spots," March 14, 2006*

- Sperling's BestPlaces ranked 331 metro areas and identified the most and least stressful U.S. cities. The Seattle* metro area ranked #11 out of the 100 largest metro areas (#1 = most stressful). Criteria: divorce rate; unemployment rate; violent and property crime; suicide rate; commute time; mental health; alcohol consumption; cloudy days. *Sperling's BestPlaces, www.BestPlaces.net, "America's Most (and Least) Stressful Cities," January 9, 2004*

- An analysis of the "Best & Worst Cities for Sleep" was conducted by Sperling's BestPlaces. The study ranked America's 50 most populated metro areas. The Seattle* metro area ranked #44 (#1 = best city for sleep). Criteria: number of days residents didn't get enough rest or sleep during the past month; average length of daily commute; divorce rate; unemployment rate. *Sperling's BestPlaces, www.BestPlaces.net, "Best & Worst Cities for Sleep," 2006*

- Sperling's BestPlaces in partnership with Vistakon ranked the 100 largest metro areas and identified "America's 10 Best Cities for Comfortable Eyes." The Seattle* metro area ranked #10. Criteria: altitude; sunny days; wind; extreme temperatures; humidity; pollution; commute time; computer use. *Vistakon, "America's Best and Worst Cities for Comfortable Eyes," June 15, 2004*

- HealthGrades evaluated the performance of America's 25 most populous metropolitan areas by measuring the outcomes of five of the highest volume and most widely studied procedures and diagnoses: coronary artery bypass graft surgery; percutaneus coronary interventions; acute myocardial infarction/heart attack in angioplasty-capable hospitals; congestive heart failure; and community acquired pneumonia. The Seattle* metro area ranked #24. *HealthGrades, "HealthGrades Hospital Quality in America Study," October 12, 2004*

- Seattle* was selected as one of "America's Top 10 Low-Carb Cities" by *LowCarbiz Magazine*. Criteria: abundance of low-carb products; restaurants with low-carb menu items; health practitioners supportive of carb-cutting regimens; local culture generally conducive to exercise and health. *LowCarbiz Magazine, April 2004*

- Seattle* was selected as one of "America's Pet Healthiest Cities" by Purina. The city ranked #11 out of 50. Criteria: veterinary services; environment; legislation; preventative care; obesity/body condition. *Purina Pet Institute, "America's Pet Healthiest Cities," May 20, 2003*

Women/Minorities Rankings

- Seattle* was ranked #14 out of 100 metro areas in *SELF Magazine's* ranking of "America's Best Places for Women." A panel of experts came up with more than 50 criteria including death and disease rates, environmental indicators, community resources, and lifestyle habits. *SELF Magazine, "America's Best Places for Women 2007," December 2007*

- Seattle* appeared on a list of the top 10 metro areas with the highest concentration of same-sex households. The area ranked #3. *Urban Institute Press, The Gay and Lesbian Atlas, May 2004*

- Seattle* appeared on a list of the top 10 metro areas with the highest concentration of gay male couples. The area ranked #4. *Urban Institute Press, The Gay and Lesbian Atlas, May 2004*

- Seattle* appeared on a list of the top 10 metro areas with the highest concentration of African-American same-sex couples among all African-American households. The area ranked #6. *Urban Institute Press, The Gay and Lesbian Atlas, May 2004*

- Seattle* appeared on a list of the top 10 metro areas with the highest concentration of Hispanic same-sex couples among all Hispanic households. The area ranked #5. *Urban Institute Press, The Gay and Lesbian Atlas, May 2004*

Seniors/Retirement Rankings

- Sperling's BestPlaces in partnership with Bankers Life & Casualty Company designed a survey to identify the top 50 metro areas in the U.S. that offer the best overall qualities for senior living. The Seattle* metro area ranked #2. The following criteria were statistically weighted to reflect the needs of the senior population: health; disease; economics; social; environment; spiritual; transportation; housing; and crime. *Bankers Life & Casualty Company, "Best Cities for Seniors 2005"*

- A.G. Edwards ranked America's 500 top-performing communities based on their residents' personal savings and investing behavior. The Seattle* metro area ranked #69 with an index score of 107.96 (national average = 100.00). A dozen statistical factors were measured including: participation in retirement savings plans; personal debt levels; and home ownership. *A.G. Edwards, "2007 Nest Egg Index", September 12, 2007*

Children/Family Rankings

- The Seattle* metro area was selected as one of the "Best Cities for Relocating Families" by Worldwide ERC and Primacy Relocation. The 2007 study placed a special emphasis on the housing market, which has significantly impacted the relocation industry and an employer's ability to transfer employees. The variables which weigh heavily in this category include home price, home affordability index, appreciation rates, and property tax. Other criteria include cost of living, crime rates, education, climate, focus on diversity, physicians per capita, recreation and leisure, arts and culture, air quality, watershed quality, sales tax, unemployment rate, job growth, high school and higher education index, school expenditures per student, students in public school, SAT/ACT percentile, and population growth. *Worldwide ERC and Primacy Relocation, "2007 Best Cities for Relocating Families"*

Safety Rankings

- The National Insurance Crime Bureau ranked 361 metro areas in the U.S. in terms of per capita rates of vehicle theft. The Seattle* metro area ranked #16 (#1 = highest rate). Criteria: number of vehicle theft offenses per 100,000 inhabitants. *National Insurance Crime Bureau, "NICB Vehicle Theft Study," April 22, 2008*

- Seattle* appeared on Sperling's BestPlaces list of the "Riskiest Cities for Identity Theft." The area ranked #2 out of the nations 50 largest metro areas. Over 80 criteria were analyzed across four major categories: technology impact; crime; transactions; and risk profile. *Sperling's BestPlaces, www.BestPlaces.net, "Riskiest Cities for Identity Theft," July 2006*

- Farmers Insurance Group of Companies, in partnership with Sperling's BestPlaces, ranked 379 metro areas and identified the "Most Secure U.S. Place to Live." The Seattle* metro area ranked #17 out of 114 in the large metro area category (500,000 or more residents). Criteria: crime rates; extreme weather; risk of natural disasters; environmental hazards; terrorism threats; air quality; life expectancy; job loss numbers. *Farmers Insurance Group, "Most Secure U.S. Places to Live 2007"*

- Seattle* was identified as one of the most dangerous large metro areas for pedestrians in the U.S. The area ranked #40 out of the nations 50 largest metro areas. Criteria: average yearly pedestrian fatalities per capita (for the years 2002 and 2003) adjusted for the number of walkers. *Surface Transportation Policy Project, "Mean Streets 2004"*

Sports/Recreation Rankings

- The Seattle* metro area appeared on the *Sporting News* list of the "Best Sports Cities 2007". The area ranked #28 out of 150 cities in the U.S. *Sporting News* takes a 12-month snapshot, roughly July to July, of each city's sports, putting a heavy premium on regular-season won-lost records (from the most recently completed season). Other criteria include: playoff berths, bowl appearances and tournament bids; championships; applicable power ratings; quality of competition; overall fan fervor as measured in part by attendance as percentage of venue capacity; abundance of teams (rewarding quality over quantity); stadium and arena quality; ticket availability and prices; franchise ownership; and marquee appeal of athletes. *SportingNews.com, "Best Sports Cities 2007," August 1, 2007*

- The Seattle* metro area was selected by *Cranium* as one of the "Top 50 Fun Cities" in America. The area ranked #10. Criteria includes: number of sports teams, restaurants, and dance performances; number of toy stores; city budget spent on recreation. *Cranium, November 4, 2003*

- *Golf Digest* ranked 330 metro areas in the U.S. in terms of golf. The Seattle* metro area was ranked #315. Criteria: access to golf; weather; value of golf; and quality of golf. *Golf Digest, "Metro Golf Rankings," August 2005*

Dating/Romance Rankings

- Eli Lily and Company, in partnership with Sperling's BestPlaces, ranked the nation's 50 largest metro areas in terms of the "Most Romantic Cities for Baby Boomers." The Seattle* metro area ranked #30. Criteria: marriage and divorce rates among "baby boomers" age 45 to 60; great restaurants; dance studios; chocolate, jewelry and flower sales. *Eli Lily and Company, "Most Romantic Cities for Baby Boomers," April 20, 2007*

- The Seattle* metro area was selected as one of the "Best Cities for Relocating Singles" by Worldwide ERC and Primacy Relocation. The area ranked #9 out of the 100 largest metro areas in the U.S. Areas were selected based on the following criteria: a robust cost-of-living index; adventure and outdoor recreation opportunities; violent crime and property crime rates; percentage of the population that is unmarried (ages 25-34); ratio of single men and single women; affordability of quality higher education, including in-state and out-of-state tuition requirements and rates; number of newcomers to the area; commute times; tax rates; fee and occupancy rates for temporary housing and mini-storage; quality and quantity of collegiate and professional sporting events and fun, fan-friendly venues. *Worldwide ERC and Primacy Relocation, "2007 Best Cities for Relocating Singles," October 25, 2007*

- *Forbes* ranked the 40 most populous urbanized areas in the U.S. in terms of the "Best Cities for Singles." The Seattle* metro area ranked #8. Criteria: number of singles; cost of living alone; nightlife; culture; job growth; coolness; and online dating. *Forbes.com, August 21, 2007*

- Sperling's BestPlaces in partnership with AXE Deodorant Bodyspray ranked 80 metro areas and identified "America's Best (and Worst) Cities for Dating." The Seattle* metro area ranked #5 (#1 = best). Criteria: percentage of singles ages 18-24; population density; dating venues per capita. *AXE Deodorant Bodyspray, "America's Best (and Worst) Cities for Dating," May 2004*

Culture/Performing Arts Rankings

- Scarborough Research, a leading market research firm, identified the top local markets for rock concert attendance. The Seattle* DMA (Designated Market Area) ranked in the top 25 with 14% of consumers, 18 years old and over, reporting that they have attended a rock concert during the past year. *Scarborough Research, June 14, 2004*

Miscellaneous Rankings

- Scarborough Research, a leading market research firm, identified the top local markets for bloggers. The Seattle* DMA (Designated Market Area) ranked in the top 13 with 13% of adults reporting that they had read or contributed to a blog within the past 30 days. *Scarborough Research, October 24, 2007*

- Avis Rent-A-Car and Motorola, in partnership with Sperling's BestPlaces, ranked the nation's 75 most populous metro areas in terms of how difficult they are to navigate. The Seattle* metro area ranked #8 with #1 being the most challenging. Criteria: street layouts; overall design and layout; travel time index; percent of congested freeway and street lane miles; bodies of water; complexity of directions needed to travel from major airports to city center; annual delay per person; days of snow exceeding 1.5 inches; and days of rain exceeding 0.5 inch. *Avis Rent-A-Car and Motorola, "America's Most Challenging Cities to Navigate," August 3, 2004*

- The Seattle* metro area appeared on *Forbes* list of "America's Drunkest Cities". The area ranked #12. Criteria: 35 of the largest continental U.S. metro areas were chosen based on availability of data and geographic diversity. Each metro was ranked in five areas: state laws; drinkers; heavy drinkers; binge drinkers; and alcoholism. *Forbes.com, "America's Drunkest Cities," August 22, 2006*

- Sperling's BestPlaces in partnership with Pep Boys ranked 77 metro areas and identified "America's Most Drivable Cities." The Seattle* metro area ranked #69. Criteria: climate; road roughness; urban mobility; gas prices. *Pep Boys, "America's Most Drivable Cities," April 9, 2003*

- State Farm Insurance, in partnership with Sperling's BestPlaces, analyzed several key factors that contribute to overall family preparedness. The Seattle* metro area ranked #8 out of the nation's 50 most populous metro areas. Criteria: quality of life; life insurance coverage; and investments. *State Farm Life Insurance, "Fiscally Fit Cities Report," July 20, 2004*

- Scarborough Research, a leading market research firm, identified the top local markets for coffee bar patronage. The Seattle* DMA (Designated Market Area) ranked in the top 10 with 23% of adults reporting that they have used any coffee house/bar during the past 30 days. *Scarborough Research, October 14, 2004*

- A study by Sperling's BestPlaces examined which U.S. metro areas were most affected by high fuel prices in 2006. The Seattle* metro area was ranked #26 out of 80 (#1 = most expensive city for driving). Rankings are based on the average dollars spent on gas per year by two driver households. Criteria: cost of regular-grade gasoline; average miles driven per day; average number of gallons each driver uses and wastes in traffic congestion each day. *Sperling's BestPlaces, www.bestplaces.net, "Pain at the Pump," May 18, 2006*

Redmond is located within the Seattle-Tacoma-Bellevue, WA Metropolitan Statistical Area.

Business Environment

CITY FINANCES

City Government Finances

Component	2004-2005 ($000)	2004-2005 ($ per capita)
Total Revenues	110,034	2,313
Total Expenditures	92,894	1,952
Debt Outstanding	9,237	194
Cash and Securities	96,004	2,018

Source: U.S Census Bureau, Government Finances 2004-2005

City Government Revenue by Source

Source	2004-2005 ($000)	2004-2005 ($ per capita)
General Revenue		
From Federal Government	67	1
From State Government	4,202	88
From Local Governments	9,538	200
Taxes		
Property	13,813	290
Sales	27,978	588
Personal Income	0	0
License	10,941	230
Charges	21,286	447
Liquor Store	0	0
Utility	11,863	249
Employee Retirement	0	0
Other	10,346	217

Source: U.S Census Bureau, Government Finances 2004-2005

City Government Expenditures by Function

Function	2004-2005 ($000)	2004-2005 ($ per capita)	2004-2005 (%)
General Expenditures			
Airports	0	0	0.0
Corrections	0	0	0.0
Education	0	0	0.0
Fire Protection	9,133	192	9.8
Governmental Administration	7,749	163	8.3
Health	5,834	123	6.3
Highways	21,625	455	23.3
Hospitals	0	0	0.0
Housing and Community Development	1,174	25	1.3
Interest on General Debt	329	7	0.4
Libraries	0	0	0.0
Parking	0	0	0.0
Parks and Recreation	7,145	150	7.7
Police Protection	7,585	159	8.2
Public Welfare	0	0	0.0
Sewerage	10,649	224	11.5
Solid Waste Management	152	3	0.2
Liquor Store	0	0	0.0
Utility	6,642	140	7.2
Employee Retirement	0	0	0.0
Other	14,877	313	16.0

Source: U.S Census Bureau, Government Finances 2004-2005

Municipal Bond Ratings

Area	Moody's
City	n/a

Source: Mergent Bond Record, January 2008 (unless noted otherwise)

DEMOGRAPHICS

Population Growth

Area	1990 Census	2000 Census	2007 Estimate	2012 Projection	Population Growth (%) 1990-2000	Population Growth (%) 2000-2012
City	36,936	45,256	48,554	50,963	22.5	12.6
MSA[1]	2,559,164	3,043,878	3,270,362	3,439,521	18.9	13.0
U.S.	248,709,873	281,421,906	301,045,522	314,920,978	13.2	11.9

Note: (1) Metropolitan Statistical Area - see Appendix B for areas included
Source: Claritas, Inc.

Number of Households and Average Household Size

Area	2007 Estimate	2007 Average Household Size
City	21,120	2.30
MSA[1]	1,302,483	2.51
U.S.	113,668,003	2.65

Note: (1) Metropolitan Statistical Area - see Appendix B for areas included
Source: Claritas, Inc.

Race and Ethnicity

Area	White Alone[2]	Black Alone[2]	Asian Alone[2]	Other Race Alone[2]	Hispanic[3]
City	73.0	1.7	17.3	7.9	8.0
MSA[1]	75.0	5.2	10.1	9.6	6.9
U.S.	73.1	12.4	4.3	10.3	14.9

Note: Figures are 2007 estimates; (1) Metropolitan Statistical Area - see Appendix B for areas included (2) Alone is defined as not being in combination with one or more other races; (3) May be of any race.
Source: Claritas, Inc.

Ancestry

Area	German	Irish[2]	English	American	Italian	Polish	French[3]	Scottish
City	17.4	10.2	14.1	4.3	3.9	2.2	4.2	3.8
MSA[1]	17.6	11.5	12.3	4.3	3.6	2.0	3.6	3.3
U.S.	15.2	10.9	8.7	7.3	5.6	3.2	3.0	1.7

Note: Figures include multiple ancestry (e.g. if a person reported being Irish and Italian, they were included in both columns); (1) Metropolitan Statistical Area - see Appendix A for areas included; (2) Includes Celtic; (3) Includes Alsatian but excludes Basque
Source: Census 2000, Summary File 3

Foreign-Born Population

Area	Percent of Population Born in: Any Foreign Country	Europe	Asia	Africa	Oceania[2]	Canada	Mexico	Latin America[3]
City	20.6	4.3	10.9	0.4	0.2	1.5	2.4	0.9
MSA[1]	13.8	2.8	6.9	0.7	0.2	1.0	1.5	0.6
U.S.	11.1	1.7	2.9	0.3	0.1	0.3	3.3	2.5

Note: (1) Metropolitan Statistical Area - see Appendix A for areas included; (2) Includes Australia, New Zealand subregion, Melanesia, Micronesia, Polynesia, and Oceania n.e.c; (3) Includes Central America (excluding Mexico), South America, and the Caribbean.
Source: Census 2000, Summary File 3

Marriage Status

Area	Never Married	Now Married (excluding Separated)	Separated	Widowed	Divorced
City	28.1	55.2	1.4	4.4	10.9
MSA[1]	29.2	53.2	1.5	4.8	11.3
U.S.	27.1	54.4	2.2	6.6	9.7

Note: Figures are percentages and cover the population 15 years of age and older; (1) Metropolitan Statistical Area - see Appendix A for areas included
Source: Census 2000, Summary File 3

Age Distribution

Area	Percent of Population						
	Under Age 5	Age 5 to 17	Age 18 to 34	Age 35 to 49	Age 50 to 64	Age 65 to 79	80 Years and Over
City	6.1	15.3	30.0	24.6	14.7	5.3	4.0
MSA[1]	6.3	17.4	25.2	26.1	14.7	7.4	2.9
U.S.	6.8	18.9	23.7	23.5	14.8	9.2	3.2

Note: (1) Metropolitan Statistical Area - see Appendix A for areas included
Source: Census 2000, Summary File 3

Male/Female Ratio

Area	Males	Females	Males per 100 Females
City	24,418	24,136	101.2
MSA[1]	1,633,417	1,636,945	99.8
U.S.	148,320,305	152,725,217	97.1

Note: Figures are 2007 estimates; (1) Metropolitan Statistical Area - see Appendix B for areas included
Source: Claritas, Inc.

Religion

Area	Catholic	Southern Baptist	United Meth-odist	ELCA[1]	LDS[2]	Presby-terian Church USA	Jewish Est.	Muslim Est.
County	16.2	0.7	1.1	2.0	2.3	1.6	1.9	0.5
U.S.	22.0	7.1	3.7	1.8	1.5	1.1	2.2	0.6

Note: Figures are the number of adherents as a percentage of the total population; Adherents are defined as all members, including full members, their children and the estimated number of other participants who are not considered members (e.g. the baptized, those not confirmed, those regularly attending services, etc.); (1) Evangelical Lutheran Church in America; (2) The Church of Jesus Christ of Latter Day Saints
Source: Reprinted with permission from Religious Congregations and Membership in the United States 2000 (Nashville, Glenmary Research Center, 2002) Copyright Association of Statisticians of American Religious Bodies. All rights reserved.

ECONOMY

Gross Metropolitan Product

Area	2002	2003	2004	2005	2005 Rank[2]
MSA[1]	138.9	142.3	149.0	158.0	13

Note: Figures are in billions of dollars; (1) Seattle-Tacoma-Bellevue, WA Metropolitan Statistical Area - see Appendix A for areas included; (2) Rank ranges from 1 to 361
Source: The U.S. Conference of Mayors, "U.S. Metro Economies: GMP - The Engines of America's Growth," January 2007

Economic Growth

Area	1995 GMP	2005 GMP	Average Annual Growth Rate	Growth Rate Rank[2]
MSA[1]	90.9	158.0	5.7	144

Note: Figures are in billions of dollars; GMP = Gross Metropolitan Product; (1) Seattle-Tacoma-Bellevue, WA Metropolitan Statistical Area - see Appendix A for areas included; (2) Rank ranges from 1 to 361
Source: The U.S. Conference of Mayors, "U.S. Metro Economies: GMP - The Engines of America's Growth," January 2007

INCOME

Per Capita/Median/Average Income

Area	Per Capita ($)	Median Household ($)	Average Household ($)
City	41,714	76,315	95,190
MSA[1]	30,164	58,271	74,853
U.S.	25,495	49,280	66,670

Note: Figures are 2007 estimates; (1) Metropolitan Statistical Area - see Appendix B for areas included
Source: Claritas, Inc.

Household Income Distribution

Area	Percent of Households Earning							
	Under $15,000	$15,000 -24,999	$25,000 -34,999	$35,000 -49,999	$50,000 -74,999	$75,000 -99,000	$100,000 -149,999	$150,000 and up
City	5.0	4.6	7.6	11.8	20.1	17.4	19.3	14.2
MSA[1]	9.2	8.3	9.8	15.2	21.0	14.5	14.1	7.8
U.S.	13.1	10.9	11.2	15.6	19.5	11.9	11.3	6.6

Note: Figures are 2007 estimates; (1) Metropolitan Statistical Area - see Appendix B for areas included
Source: Claritas, Inc.

Poverty Rates by Age

Area	All Ages	Under 5 Years Old	5 to 17 Years Old	18 to 64 Years Old	65 Years and Over
City	5.3	0.5	0.8	3.3	0.6
MSA[1]	7.9	0.6	1.6	5.0	0.7
U.S.	12.4	1.2	3.0	6.9	1.2

Note: Figures are percent of population with income in 1999 below poverty level and only include population for whom poverty status is determined; (1) Metropolitan Statistical Area - see Appendix A for areas included
Source: Census 2000, Summary File 3

Personal Bankruptcy Filing Rate

Area	2004	2005	2006
King County	4.69	6.11	1.37
U.S.	5.31	6.82	2.00

Note: Numbers are per 1,000 population and include Chapter 7 and Chapter 13 filings
Source: Federal Deposit Insurance Corporation (FDIC), Regional Economic Conditions (RECON), 8/23/2007

EMPLOYMENT

Labor Force and Employment

Area	Civilian Labor Force			Workers Employed		
	Dec. 2006	Dec. 2007	% Chg.	Dec. 2006	Dec. 2007	% Chg.
City	30,232	30,990	2.5	29,317	30,133	2.8
MD[1]	1,422,350	1,458,732	2.6	1,366,226	1,404,277	2.8
U.S.	152,571,000	153,705,000	0.7	146,081,000	146,334,000	0.2

Note: Data is not seasonally adjusted and covers workers 16 years of age and older;
(1) Metropolitan Division - see Appendix B for areas included
Source: Bureau of Labor Statistics, http://stats.bls.gov

Unemployment Rate

Area	2007											
	Jan.	Feb.	Mar.	Apr.	May	Jun.	Jul.	Aug.	Sep.	Oct.	Nov.	Dec.
City	3.3	3.4	3.2	2.7	3.0	3.1	2.8	2.8	3.1	3.0	2.9	2.8
MD[1]	4.2	4.3	4.0	3.4	3.7	3.8	3.5	3.4	3.8	3.7	3.7	3.7
U.S.	5.0	4.9	4.5	4.3	4.3	4.7	4.9	4.6	4.5	4.4	4.5	4.8

Note: Data is not seasonally adjusted and covers workers 16 years of age and older; All figures are percentages; (1) Metropolitan Division - see Appendix B for areas included
Source: Bureau of Labor Statistics, http://stats.bls.gov

Employment by Occupation

Occupation Classification	City (%)	MSA[1] (%)	U.S. (%)
Sales and Office	23.8	26.4	26.7
Professional and Related	36.0	24.3	20.2
Service	8.5	13.1	14.9
Production, Transportation, and Material Moving	6.9	10.9	14.6
Management, Business, and Financial	20.7	16.6	13.5
Construction, Extraction, and Maintenance	4.1	8.3	9.4
Farming, Forestry, and Fishing	0.0	0.3	0.7

Note: Figures cover employed civilians 16 years of age and older;
(1) Metropolitan Statistical Area - see Appendix A for areas included
Source: Census 2000, Summary File 3

Employment by Industry

Sector	MSA[1] Number of Employees	MSA[1] Percent of Total	U.S. Percent of Total
Government	202,300	13.7	16.3
Education and Health Services	153,800	10.4	13.4
Professional and Business Services	216,800	14.7	13.1
Retail Trade	153,000	10.3	11.6
Manufacturing	170,000	11.5	9.9
Leisure and Hospitality	137,000	9.3	9.6
Financial Activities	89,400	6.0	5.9
Construction	98,600	6.7	5.3
Wholesale Trade	72,700	4.9	4.4
Other Services	49,300	3.3	3.9
Transportation and Utilities	53,200	3.6	3.7
Information	82,000	5.5	2.2
Natural Resources and Mining	1,100	0.1	0.5

Note: Figures cover non-farm employment as of December 2007 and are not seasonally adjusted; (1) Metropolitan Statistical Area - see Appendix B for areas included
Source: Bureau of Labor Statistics, http://stats.bls.gov

Average Wages

Occupation	$/Hr.	Occupation	$/Hr.
Accountants and Auditors	31.35	Maids and Housekeeping Cleaners	11.18
Automotive Mechanics	21.38	Maintenance and Repair Workers	19.22
Bookkeepers	17.84	Marketing Managers	61.63
Carpenters	24.42	Nuclear Medicine Technologists	37.17
Cashiers	12.05	Nurses, Licensed Practical	22.15
Clerks, General Office	14.59	Nurses, Registered	34.79
Clerks, Receptionists/Information	13.02	Nursing Aides/Orderlies/Attendants	13.26
Clerks, Shipping/Receiving	16.08	Packers and Packagers, Hand	10.80
Computer Programmers	41.77	Physical Therapists	33.99
Computer Support Specialists	24.97	Postal Service Mail Carriers	21.09
Computer Systems Analysts	38.87	Real Estate Brokers	47.61
Cooks, Restaurant	11.86	Retail Salespersons	14.03
Dentists	n/a	Sales Reps., Exc. Tech./Scientific	29.85
Electrical Engineers	38.33	Sales Reps., Tech./Scientific	38.80
Electricians	26.80	Secretaries, Exc. Legal/Med./Exec.	17.07
Financial Managers	55.55	Security Guards	14.57
First-Line Supervisors/Mgrs., Sales	24.17	Surgeons	96.01
Food Preparation Workers	11.38	Teacher Assistants	14.10
General and Operations Managers	66.79	Teachers, Elementary School	25.20
Hairdressers/Cosmetologists	15.06	Teachers, Secondary School	26.80
Internists	76.35	Telemarketers	13.54
Janitors and Cleaners	12.93	Truck Drivers, Heavy/Tractor-Trailer	19.80
Landscaping/Groundskeeping Workers	13.94	Truck Drivers, Light/Delivery Svcs.	14.65
Lawyers	n/a	Waiters and Waitresses	13.39

Note: Wage data covers the Seattle-Bellevue-Everett, WA Metropolitan Division - see Appendix B for areas included. Hourly wages for elementary/secondary school teachers and teacher assistants were calculated by the editors from annual wage data assuming a 40 hour work week; n/a not available.
Source: Bureau of Labor Statistics, May 2007 Metro Area Occupational Employment and Wage Estimates

RESIDENTIAL REAL ESTATE

Building Permits

Area	Single-Family			Multi-Family			Total		
	2006	2007p	Pct. Chg.	2006	2007p	Pct. Chg.	2006	2007p	Pct. Chg.
City	206	237	15.0	87	135	55.2	293	372	27.0
U.S.	1,378,200	973,300	-29.4	460,700	407,200	-11.6	1,838,900	1,380,500	-24.9

Note: (p) preliminary; figures cover and represent new, privately-owned housing units authorized (unadjusted data); All permit data are based on estimates with imputation; U.S. figures are based on the new 20,000-place series.
Source: U.S. Census Bureau, Manufacturing, Mining, and Construction Statistics

Homeownership and Housing Vacancies

Area	Homeownership Rate[2] (%)			Rental Vacancy Rate[3] (%)			Homeowner Vacancy Rate[4] (%)		
	2005	2006	2007	2005	2006	2007	2005	2006	2007
MSA[1]	64.5	63.7	62.8	6.9	5.6	4.9	1.0	0.9	1.8
U.S.	68.9	68.8	68.1	9.8	9.8	9.7	1.9	2.4	2.7

Note: (1) Metropolitan Statistical Area - see Appendix B for areas included; (2) The proportion of households that are owners; (3) The proportion of the rental inventory that is vacant for rent; (4) The proportion of the homeowner inventory that is vacant for sale; n/a not available
Source: U.S. Census Bureau, Housing Vacancies and Homeownership Annual Statistics: 2007

TAXES

State Corporate Income Tax Rates

State	Rates and Tax Brackets
Washington	Rate Varies

Note: Tax rates as of January 1, 2008; Washington has no income tax but has a gross receipts tax called the Business & Occupation (B&O) Tax which is levied at various rates. The major rates are 0.471% for retail sales, 0.484% for wholesale and manufacturing, and 1.5% for service and other activities.
Source: Tax Foundation, www.taxfoundation.org

State Individual Income Tax Rates

State	Federal Deductibility	Marginal Rates (%)	Standard Deduction ($)		Personal Exemptions ($)[1]	
			Single	Joint	Single	Dependents
Washington	No	None	n/a	n/a	n/a	n/a

Note: Tax rates as of January 1, 2008; Local- and county-level taxes are not included; n/a not applicable; (1) Married joint filers generally receive double the single exemption
Source: Tax Foundation, www.taxfoundation.org

Various State and Local Tax Rates

State and Local Sales and Use (%)	State Sales and Use (%)	Gasoline[1,2] ($/gal.)	Cigarette ($/pack)	Spirits ($/gal.)	Table Wine ($/gal.)	Beer ($/gal.)
9.0	6.5 (j)	0.36	2.025	19.43 (n)	0.87	0.26

Note: Tax rates as of January 1, 2008; (1) In addition to the 18.4 cpg Federal gasoline tax; (2) Rates may include additional state sales taxes, environmental protection and storage fees/taxes, and local taxes. When necessary, the volume-weighted average of all local taxes is used to approximate the typical statewide rate including local tax; (j) Washington has a GRT in addition to its 6.5% sales tax. It is called the business and occupation tax and is levied at various rates. The major rates are 0.471% for retail sales, 0.484% for wholesale and manufacturing, and 1.5% for service and other

ctivities; (n) The state government controls all sales. The implied excise tax rate is calculated using methodology designed by the Distilled Spirits Council of the United States (DISCUS). Source: Tax Foundation, www.taxfoundation.org; Original research

State Tax Burdens

Area	Combined State and Local Tax Burden		Combined Federal, State and Local Tax Burden	
	Percent	Rank	Percent	Rank
Washington	11.1	16	34.0	9
U.S. Average	11.0	-	32.7	-

Note: Figures cover 2007 and measure taxes as a percentage of income
Source: Tax Foundation, www.taxfoundation.org

State Business Tax Climate Index Rankings

State	Overall Rank	Corporate Tax Index Rank	Individual Income Tax Index Rank	Sales Tax Index Rank	Unemployment Insurance Tax Index Rank	Property Tax Index Rank
Washington	11	31	1	50	36	28

Note: Rankings range from 1 to 50 where 1 is best. Rankings do not average across to Overall Rank. States without a given tax are given a ranking of 1.
Source: Tax Foundation, State Business Tax Climate Index 2008

TRANSPORTATION

Means of Transportation to Work

Area	Car/Truck/Van		Public Transportation			Bicycle	Walked	Other Means	Worked at Home
	Drove Alone	Car-pooled	Bus	Subway	Railroad				
City	76.1	11.3	4.2	0.0	0.0	0.8	2.8	0.5	4.3
MSA[1]	70.4	12.6	7.8	0.0	0.0	0.7	3.2	0.9	4.4
U.S.	75.7	12.2	2.5	1.5	0.5	0.4	2.9	1.0	3.3

Note: Figures are percentages and cover workers 16 years of age and older; (1) Metropolitan Statistical Area - see Appendix A for areas included
Source: Census 2000, Summary File 3

Travel Time to Work

Area	Less Than 15 Minutes	15 to 29 Minutes	30 to 44 Minutes	45 to 59 Minutes	60 Minutes or More
City	34.9	39.8	17.4	4.4	3.5
MSA[1]	22.1	36.9	23.9	9.2	7.9
U.S.	29.4	36.1	19.1	7.4	8.0

Note: Figures are percentages and include workers 16 years old and over; (1) Metropolitan Statistical Area - see Appendix A for areas included
Source: Census 2000, Summary File 3

Travel Time Index

Area	1982	1995	2004	2005
Urban Area[1]	1.07	1.30	1.28	1.30
Average[2]	1.11	1.22	1.29	1.30

Note: Travel Time Index - The ratio of travel time in the peak period to the travel time at free-flow conditions. A value of 1.35 indicates a 20-minute free-flow trip takes 27 minutes in the peak. Free-flow speeds (60 mph on freeways and 35 mph on principal arterials) are used as the comparison threshold; (1) Covers the Seattle, WA urban area; (2) average of 85 urban areas
Source: Texas Transportation Institute, The 2007 Urban Mobility Report, September 2007

Living Environment

COST OF LIVING

Cost of Living Index

Composite Index	Groceries	Housing	Utilities	Trans-portation	Health Care	Misc. Goods/ Services
121.5	113.0	155.0	94.9	106.2	124.0	109.7

Note: U.S. = 100; Figures cover the Seattle WA urban area.
Source: The Council for Community and Economic Research (formerly ACCRA), Cost of Living Index, 2007

Grocery Prices

Area[1]	T-Bone Steak ($/pound)	Frying Chicken ($/pound)	Whole Milk ($/half gal.)	Eggs ($/dozen)	Orange Juice ($/64 oz.)	Coffee ($/11.5 oz.)
City[2]	9.50	1.47	2.33	2.00	3.47	4.32
Avg.	8.93	1.12	2.13	1.52	3.26	3.31
Min.	5.88	0.71	1.33	0.83	2.30	2.20
Max.	12.80	2.07	3.43	3.54	5.79	6.20

Note: (1) Values for the local area are compared with the average, minimum and maximum values for all 331 areas in the Cost of Living Index report; (2) Figures cover the Seattle WA urban area; **T-Bone Steak** *(price per pound);* **Frying Chicken** *(price per pound, whole fryer);* **Whole Milk** *(half gallon carton);* **Eggs** *(price per dozen, Grade A, large);* **Orange Juice** *(64 oz. Tropicana or Florida Natural);* **Coffee** *(11.5 oz. can, vacuum-packed, Maxwell House, Hills Bros, or Folgers).*
Source: The Council for Community and Economic Research (formerly ACCRA), Cost of Living Index, 2007

Housing and Utility Costs

Area[1]	New Home Price ($)	Apartment Rent ($/month)	All Electric ($/month)	Part Electric ($/month)	Other Energy ($/month)	Telephone ($/month)
City[2]	454,300	1,434	142.92	-	-	27.27
Avg.	309,605	782	146.13	78.67	90.16	26.14
Min.	189,877	n/a	82.03	37.41	33.15	17.08
Max.	1,202,800	3,481	271.14	150.60	257.67	37.45

Note: (1) Values for the local area are compared with the average, minimum and maximum values for all 331 areas in the Cost of Living Index report; (2) Figures cover the Seattle WA urban area; **New Home Price** *(2,400 sf living area, 8,000 sf lot, in urban area with full utilities);* **Apartment Rent** *(950 sf 2 bedroom/1.5 or 2 bath, unfurnished, excluding all utilities except water);* **All Electric** *(average monthly cost for an all-electric home);* **Part Electric** *(average monthly cost for a part-electric home);* **Other Energy** *(average monthly cost for natural gas, fuel oil, coal, wood, and any other forms of energy except electricity);* **Telephone** *(price includes basic monthly rate for a private residential line plus additional local usage charges incurred by a family of four).*
Source: The Council for Community and Economic Research (formerly ACCRA), Cost of Living Index, 2007

Health Care, Transportation, and Other Costs

Area[1]	Doctor ($/visit)	Dentist ($/visit)	Optometrist ($/visit)	Gasoline ($/gallon)	Beauty Salon ($/visit)	Men's Shirt ($)
City[2]	99.96	100.52	105.07	2.94	28.75	24.28
Avg.	79.48	71.93	79.55	2.64	29.52	25.77
Min.	52.08	44.80	43.95	2.19	15.58	16.19
Max.	148.44	126.27	158.83	3.48	60.62	48.53

Note: (1) Values for the local area are compared with the average, minimum and maximum values for all 331 areas in the Cost of Living Index report; (2) Figures cover the Seattle WA urban area; **Doctor** *(general practitioners routine exam of an established patient);* **Dentist** *(adult teeth cleaning and periodic oral examination);* **Optometrist** *(full vision eye exam for established adult patient);* **Gasoline** *(one gallon regular unleaded, national brand, including all taxes, cash price at self-service pump if available);* **Beauty Salon** *(woman's shampoo, trim, and blow-dry);* **Men's Shirt** *(cotton/polyester dress shirt, pinpoint weave, long sleeves).*
Source: The Council for Community and Economic Research (formerly ACCRA), Cost of Living Index, 2007

HOUSING

House Price Index (HPI)

Area	National Ranking[2]	Quarterly Change (%)	One-Year Change (%)	Five-Year Change (%)
MD[1]	28	-0.03	5.87	66.13
U.S.[3]	-	0.10	0.84	41.37

Note: The HPI is a weighted repeat sales index. It measures average price changes in repeat sales or refinancings on the same properties. This information is obtained by reviewing repeat mortgage transactions on single-family properties whose mortgages have been purchased or securitized by Fannie Mae or Freddie Mac in January 1975; (1) Metropolitan Division - see Appendix B for areas included; (2) Rankings are based on annual percentage change for all metro areas containing at least 15,000 transactions over the last 10 years and ranges from 1 to 291; (3) figures based on a weighted average of Census Division estimates; all figures are for the period ending December 31, 2007
Source: Office of Federal Housing Enterprise Oversight, House Price Index, February 26, 2008

House Price Valuations

Area	Q1 2000	Q1 2001	Q1 2002	Q1 2003	Q1 2004	Q1 2005	Q1 2006	Q1 2007	Q1 2008
MD[1]	-13.0	-4.4	-1.9	5.2	6.4	15.5	25.3	30.2	22.8

Note: Figures show the percentage of over- or under-valuation of single family homes relative to statistically normal house values (e.g. a value of 23.6 indicates that house values are 23.6% overvalued). Statistically normal house values are based on house prices, interest rates, household incomes, population densities, and any historical premiums or discounts metropolitan areas have exhibited over time; (1) Figures cover the Metropolitan Division - see Appendix B for areas included
Source: Global Insight/National City Corporation, House Prices in America, May 2008

Median Home Prices

Area	2005	2006	2007[r]	Percent Change 2006 to 2007
MSA[1]	316.8	361.2	386.9	7.1
U.S. Average	219.0	221.9	217.9	-1.8

Note: Figures are median sales prices of existing single-family homes in thousands of dollars; (r) revised; n/a not available; (1) Metropolitan Statistical Area - see Appendix B for areas included
Source: National Association of Realtors, Metropolitan Area Prices, 1st Quarter 2008

Housing: Year Structure Built

Area	1990 -2000	1980 -1989	1970 -1979	1960 -1969	1950 -1959	1940 -1949	Before 1940	Median Year
City	29.3	27.6	28.0	11.7	1.8	0.6	1.0	1982
MSA[1]	19.8	18.4	17.7	14.7	10.3	6.4	12.5	1973
U.S.	17.0	15.8	18.5	13.7	12.7	7.3	15.0	1971

Note: Figures are percentages; (1) Metropolitan Statistical Area - see Appendix A for areas included
Source: Census 2000, Summary File 3

HEALTH

Health Risk Data

Category	Area[1] (%)	U.S. (%)
Adults who have been told they have high blood pressure[3]	22.3	25.5
Adults who have been told they have high blood cholesterol[3]	35.5	35.6
Adults who have been told they have diabetes[2]	6.8	7.5
Adults who have been told they have arthritis[3]	23.3	27.0
Adults who have been told they currently have asthma	7.9	8.5
Adults who are current smokers	13.8	20.1
Adults who are heavy drinkers[4]	5.1	4.9
Adults who are overweight (BMI 25.0 - 29.9)	36.0	36.5
Adults who are obese (BMI 30.0 - 99.8)	21.2	25.1

Note: Data as of 2006 unless otherwise noted; (1) Figures cover the Metropolitan Division - see Appendix B for areas included; (2) Figures do not include pregnancy-related diabetes, pre-diabetes or borderline diabetes; (3) 2005 data; (4) Heavy drinkers are classified as adult men having more than two drinks per day or adult women having more than one drink per day
Source: Centers for Disease Control and Prevention, Behaviorial Risk Factor Surveillance System, SMART: Selected Metropolitan/Micropolitan Area Risk Trends, 2005, 2006

Mortality Rates for the Top 10 Causes of Death in the U.S.

ICD-10[a] Sub-Chapter	ICD-10[a] Code	Age-Adjusted Mortality Rate[1] per 100,000 population	
		County[2]	U.S.
Malignant neoplasms	C00-C97	168.6	186.5
Ischaemic heart diseases	I20-I25	112.7	152.3
Other forms of heart disease	I30-I51	31.3	51.5
Cerebrovascular diseases	I60-I69	49.9	50.0
Chronic lower respiratory diseases	J40-J47	33.3	42.6
Diabetes mellitus	E10-E14	21.0	24.8
Other degenerative diseases of the nervous system	G30-G31	36.9	22.6
Other external causes of accidental injury	W00-X59	21.5	21.4
Influenza and pneumonia	J10-J18	15.3	20.7
Hypertensive diseases	I10-I13	15.1	18.2

Note: (a) ICD-10 = International Classification of Diseases 10th Revision; (1) Mortality rates are a three year average covering 2003-2005; (2) Figures cover King County
Source: Centers for Disease Control and Prevention, National Center for Health Statistics. Compressed Mortality File 1999-2004. CDC WONDER On-line Database, compiled from Compressed Mortality File 1999-2005 Series 20 No. 2K, 2008.

Mortality Rates for Selected Causes of Death

ICD-10[a] Sub-Chapter	ICD-10[a] Code	Age-Adjusted Mortality Rate[1] per 100,000 population	
		County[2]	U.S.
Assault	X85-Y09	3.7	5.9
Human immunodeficiency virus (HIV) disease	B20-B24	3.6	4.5
Intentional self-harm	X60-X84	11.6	10.8
Malnutrition	E40-E46	1.1	1.0
Obesity and other hyperalimentation	E65-E68	1.0	1.4
Organic, including symptomatic, mental disorders	F01-F09	8.6	16.8
Transport accidents	V01-V99	9.2	16.1
Viral hepatitis	B15-B19	2.2	1.8

Note: (a) ICD-10 = International Classification of Diseases 10th Revision; (1) Mortality rates are a three year average covering 2003-2005; (2) Figures cover King County
Source: Centers for Disease Control and Prevention, National Center for Health Statistics. Compressed Mortality File 1999-2004. CDC WONDER On-line Database, compiled from Compressed Mortality File 1999-2005 Series 20 No. 2K, 2008.

Distribution of Physicians[1]

Area	Total	Family/ General Practice	Specialties	
			Medical	Surgical
King County (number)	5,520	1,645	1,873	1,110
King County (rate per 10,000 pop.)	30.8	9.2	10.4	6.2
U.S. (rate per 10,000 pop.)	17.7	4.6	6.9	4.3

Note: Data as of 2005; (1) Includes all non-federal, patient-care, office-based MDs
Source: Area Resource File (ARF). June 2007. U.S. Department of Health and Human Services, Health Resources and Services Administration, Bureau of Health Professions, Rockville, MD.

Hospitals

Redmond has the following hospitals: 1 general medical and surgical.
AHA Guide to the Healthcare Field 2008

According to *U.S. News,* the Seattle-Tacoma-Bellevue, WA metro area is home to five of the best hospitals in the U.S.: **Children's Hospital and Regional Medical Center**; **Harborview Medical Center**; **Swedish Health Services**; **University of Washington Medical Center**; **Virginia Mason Medical Center**. *U.S. News Online, "America's Best Hospitals 2007"*

EDUCATION

Public School District Statistics

District Name	Schls	Pupils	Pupil/ Teacher Ratio	Minority Pupils[1] (%)	Free Lunch Eligible[2] (%)	IEP[3] (%)
Lake Washington Sch Dist 414	51	24,332	20.1	24.8	8.7	9.4
Northshore Sch Dist 417	35	20,720	20.6	21.9	8.4	12.6

Note: Table includes regular local school districts with 2,000 or more students; (1) Percentage of students that are not white, non-Hispanic; (2) Percentage of students that are eligible for the free lunch program; (3) Percentage of students that have an Individualized Education Program.
Source: U.S. Department of Education, National Center for Education Statistics, Common Core of Data, Local Education Agency (School District) Universe Survey: School Year 2005-2006; U.S. Department of Education, National Center for Education Statistics, Common Core of Data, Public Elementary/Secondary School Universe Survey: School Year 2005-2006

Highest Level of Education

Area	Less than H.S.	H.S. Diploma	Some College, No Deg.	Associate Degree	Bachelors Degree	Masters Degree	Profess. School Degree	Doctorate Degree
City	5.6	11.6	22.3	7.7	35.9	12.7	2.2	1.9
MSA[1]	10.7	22.9	25.9	8.0	21.9	7.1	2.3	1.2
U.S.	19.4	28.4	21.2	6.4	15.7	5.9	2.0	1.0

Note: Figures are 2007 estimated percentages and cover persons age 25 and over; (1) Metropolitan Statistical Area - see Appendix B for areas included
Source: Claritas, Inc.

Educational Attainment by Race

Area	High School Graduate (%)					Bachelor's Degree (%)				
	Total	White	Black	Asian	Hisp.[2]	Total	White	Black	Asian	Hisp.[2]
City	94.5	95.6	94.4	93.5	69.3	52.9	51.8	48.8	66.9	24.9
MSA[1]	90.1	92.3	82.4	82.2	67.8	35.9	37.0	21.1	40.9	19.0
U.S.	80.4	83.6	72.3	80.4	52.4	24.4	26.1	14.3	44.1	10.4

Note: Figures shown cover persons 25 years old and over; (1) Metropolitan Statistical Area - see Appendix A for areas included; (2) people of Hispanic origin can be of any race
Source: Census 2000, Summary File 3

School Enrollment by Type

Area	Grades KG to 8				Grades 9 to 12			
	Public		Private		Public		Private	
	Enrollment	%	Enrollment	%	Enrollment	%	Enrollment	%
City	4,342	90.6	453	9.4	2,170	95.5	102	4.5
MSA[1]	260,622	88.3	34,672	11.7	116,866	91.1	11,446	8.9
U.S.	33,526,011	88.7	4,285,121	11.3	14,848,628	90.6	1,532,323	9.4

Note: Figures shown cover persons 3 years old and over; (1) Metropolitan Statistical Area - see Appendix A for areas included
Source: Census 2000, Summary File 3

School Enrollment by Race

Area	Grades KG to 8 (%)				Grades 9 to 12 (%)			
	White	Black	Asian	Hisp.[1]	White	Black	Asian	Hisp.[1]
City	74.3	2.6	12.6	8.6	83.5	0.0	9.8	7.3
MSA[2]	73.2	5.5	9.2	6.6	73.1	5.4	10.5	5.8
U.S.	68.5	15.5	3.3	16.8	68.8	15.5	3.8	15.7

Note: Figures shown cover persons 3 years old and over; (1) people of Hispanic origin can be of any race; (2) Metropolitan Statistical Area - see Appendix A for areas included
Source: Census 2000, Summary File 3

Average Salaries of Public School Classroom Teachers

District	2005-06 Dollars	2005-06 Rank[1]	2006-07 Dollars	2006-07 Rank[1]	Percent Change 2005-06 to 2006-07
Washington	46,326	22	47,882	22	3.36
U.S. Average	49,026	-	50,816	-	3.65

Note: (1) State rank ranges from 1 to 51.
Source: National Education Association, Rankings & Estimates: Rankings of the States 2006 and Estimates of School Statistics 2007, December 2007

Higher Education

Four-Year Colleges			Two-Year Colleges			Medical Schools[1]	Law Schools[2]	Voc/ Tech[3]
Public	Private Non-profit	Private For-profit	Public	Private Non-profit	Private For-profit			
0	0	1	0	0	0	0	0	0

Note: Figures cover institutions located within the city limits; (1) includes schools accredited by the Liaison Committee on Medical Education and the American Osteopathic Association; (2) includes American Bar Association-accredited law schools; (3) includes all schools with programs that are less than 2 years.
Source: National Center for Education Statistics, The Integrated Postsecondary Education System (IPEDS) Peer Analysis System, 2007; www.usnews.com, Law and Medical School Directories, 2009

PRESIDENTIAL ELECTION

2004 Presidential Election Results

Area	Bush	Kerry	Nader	Other
King County	33.6	64.9	0.7	0.8
U.S.	50.7	48.3	0.4	0.6

Note: Results are percentages and may not add to 100% due to rounding
Source: Dave Leip's Atlas of U.S. Presidential Elections, www.uselectionatlas.org

EMPLOYERS

Major Employers

Company Name	Industry	Type of Site
Bailey-Boushay House	Offices and clinics of medical doctors	Headquarters
Boeing	Aircraft	Branch
Childrens Health Care System	Specialty hospitals, except psychiatric	Single
Harborview Medical Center	General medical and surgical hospitals	Single
King County Pub Hosp Dst No 2	Management consulting services	Single
Microsoft	Prepackaged software	Headquarters
Neurological Surgery	Offices and clinics of medical doctors	Branch
Rui One Corp	Eating places	Single
SNC Lavalin Thermal Power	Heavy construction, nec	Headquarters
Swedish Med Center/First Hl	General medical and surgical hospitals	Headquarters
University of Washington	Colleges and universities	Branch
University of Washington Press	Colleges and universities	Headquarters
Virginia Mason Hospital	General medical and surgical hospitals	Branch

Note: Companies shown are located within the Seattle metropolitan area; nec = not elsewhere classified.
Source: www.zapdata.com, May 2008

PUBLIC SAFETY

Crime Rate

Area	All Crimes	Violent Crimes: Murder	Forcible Rape	Robbery	Aggrav. Assault	Property Crimes: Burglary	Larceny -Theft	Motor Vehicle Theft
City	3,723.4	0.0	24.8	41.3	66.1	429.8	2,752.2	409.1
Metro[1]	5,424.5	3.6	39.4	143.9	229.0	972.1	3,026.7	1,009.7
U.S.	3,808.1	5.7	30.9	149.4	287.5	729.4	2,206.8	398.4

Note: Figures are crimes per 100,000 population; (1) Metropolitan Statistical Area - see Appendix B for areas included
Source: FBI Uniform Crime Reports, 2006

Hate Crimes

Area	Number of Quarters Reported	Bias Motivation				
		Race	Religion	Sexual Orientation	Ethnicity	Disability
City	4	0	2	1	0	0

Source: Federal Bureau of Investigation, Hate Crime Statistics 2006

RECREATION

Culture

Dance[1]	Theatre[1]	Instrumental Music[1]	Vocal Music[1]	Series/ Festivals	Museums	Zoos and Aquariums[2]
0	0	0	1	0	0	0

Note: (1) Number of professional perfoming groups; (2) AZA-accredited
Source: The Grey House Performing Arts Directory, 2007; Official Museum Directory, 2008; Association of Zoos & Aquariums, AZA Member Zoos & Aquariums, June 2008

Professional Sports Teams

Team Name	League
Seattle Mariners	Major League Baseball (MLB)
Seattle Sounders FC (2009)	Major League Soccer (MLS)
Seattle Supersonics	National Basketball Association (NBA)
Seattle Seahawks	National Football League (NFL)

Note: Includes teams located in the Seattle metro area.
Source: Original research

MEDIA

Newspapers

Name	News Focus	Frequency	Circulation
No newspapers have an office in the city			

Note: Includes newspapers with offices located in the city
Source: MediaContactsPro, March 2008

Television Stations

Name	Ch.	Network(s)	Type	Ownership
KOMO	4	ABC	Commercial	Fisher Broadcasting Inc.
KING	5	NBC	Commercial	Belo Corporation
KIRO	7	CBS	Commercial	Cox Enterprises Inc.
KCTS	9	PBS	Public	KCTS
KSTW	11	UPN	Commercial	Paramount Communications Inc.
KBTC	12	PBS	Public	State Board for Community and Technical Colleges
KVOS	12	n/a	Commercial	Clear Channel Communications Inc.
KCPQ	13	Fox	Commercial	Tribune Broadcasting Company
KONG	16	n/a	Commercial	Zeus Corporation
KTBW	20	n/a	Non-comm.	Trinity Broadcasting Network
KTWB	22	WBN	Commercial	Dudley Broadcast Management
KBCB	24	n/a	Commercial	World Television of Washington
KCKA	28	PBS	Public	State Board for Community and Technical Colleges
KWPX	33	Pax	Commercial	Paxson Communications Corporation

Note: Stations included cover the Seattle-Tacoma DMA (Designated Market Area)
BurrellesLuce, MediaContacts Online, January 2007

Major AM Radio Stations

Call Letters	Freq. (kHz)	Station Type	Target Audience	Station Format	Music Format
KARI	550	n/a	Religious	News/Sports/Talk	n/a
KPQ	560	Commercial	General	News/Talk	n/a
KVI	570	Commercial	General	Talk	n/a
KAPS	660	n/a	General	Music/News	n/a
KIRO	710	Commercial	General	News/Talk	n/a
KNWX	770	n/a	General	News/Talk	n/a
KGMI	790	Commercial	General	News/Talk	n/a
KGNW	820	Commercial	General/Religious	News/Talk	n/a
KMTT	850	Commercial	General	Music	Album Rock
KHHO	850	n/a	General/Men	Music/News/Sports/Talk	n/a
KIXI	880	n/a	General	Music/News	n/a
KJR	950	n/a	General	Music/Sports/Talk	n/a
KOMO	1000	Commercial	General	News/Talk	n/a
KMAS	1030	Commercial	General	Music/News	Adult Contemp.
KYCW	1090	n/a	General	Music	n/a
KKNW	1150	n/a	General	News/Sports	n/a
KPUG	1170	Commercial	General	Sports/Talk	n/a
KLAY	1180	Commercial	General	News/Sports/Talk	n/a
KBSG	1210	Commercial	General	Music	Oldies
KKDZ	1250	n/a	Children	Music	n/a
KKOL	1300	Commercial	General	News/Talk	n/a
KMPS	1300	Commercial	General	Music/News/Sports	Country
KXRO	1320	Commercial	General	Talk	n/a
KKMO	1360	Commercial	General/Hispanic	Music/Talk	Latin
KRKO	1380	n/a	General	News/Sports/Talk	n/a
KITI	1420	Commercial	General	Music/News	Oldies
KBRC	1430	n/a	General	Music/News	n/a
KELA	1470	Commercial	General	News/Sports/Talk	n/a
KXPA	1540	n/a	Ethnic/Hispanic	Ed/Music/News/Talk	n/a
KRPI	1550	n/a	Religious	Educational/Music/News	n/a
KZIZ	1560	Commercial	General	Music	Urban Contemp.
KLFE	1590	Commercial	General/Religious	Music/Talk	Gospel
KYIZ	1620	Commercial	General	Music	Urban Contemp.

Note: Stations included cover the Seattle-Tacoma DMA (Designated Market Area); n/a not available
Source: BurrellesLuce, MediaContacts Online, January 2007

Major FM Radio Stations

Call Letters	Freq. (mHz)	Station Type	Target Audience	Station Format	Music Format
KPLU	88.5	College	General	Music/News	n/a
KVTI	90.9	College	Young Adult	Music/News/Sports	n/a
KLSY	92.5	n/a	General	Music/News	n/a
KISM	92.9	Commercial	General	Music/News	Classic Rock
KUBE	93.3	n/a	General	Music/Talk	n/a
KMPS	94.1	n/a	General	Music	n/a
KUOW	94.9	College	General	Educational/News	n/a
KJR	95.7	n/a	General	n/a	n/a
KXXO	96.1	n/a	General	Music/News	n/a
KBSG	97.3	n/a	General	Music/News	n/a
KING	98.1	Commercial	General	Music	Classical
KISW	99.9	Commercial	General	Music/News/Talk	Classic Rock
KQBZ	100.7	Commercial	General	Talk	n/a
KPLZ	101.5	n/a	General	Music/News	n/a
KMNT	102.9	Commercial	General	Music/News/Sports	Country
KMTT	103.7	n/a	General	Music	n/a
KAFE	104.3	Commercial	General	Music/News	Soft Rock
KCMS	105.3	Commercial	General/Religious	Music	Christian
KBKS	106.1	n/a	General/Women	Music/News/Talk	n/a
KWPZ	106.5	n/a	Religious	Music/Talk	n/a
KRWM	106.9	n/a	General	Music	n/a
KNDD	107.7	Commercial	General	Music/News/Talk	Modern Rock

Note: Stations included cover the Seattle-Tacoma DMA (Designated Market Area); n/a not available
BurrellesLuce, MediaContacts Online, January 2007

CLIMATE

Average and Extreme Temperatures

Temperature	Jan	Feb	Mar	Apr	May	Jun	Jul	Aug	Sep	Oct	Nov	Dec	Yr.
Extreme High (°F)	64	70	75	85	93	96	98	99	98	89	74	63	99
Average High (°F)	44	48	52	57	64	69	75	74	69	59	50	45	59
Average Temp. (°F)	39	43	45	49	55	61	65	65	60	52	45	41	52
Average Low (°F)	34	36	38	41	46	51	54	55	51	45	39	36	44
Extreme Low (°F)	0	1	11	29	28	38	43	44	35	28	6	6	0

Note: Figures cover the years 1948-1990
Source: National Climatic Data Center, International Station Meteorological Climate Summary, 9/96

Average Precipitation/Snowfall/Humidity

Precip./Humidity	Jan	Feb	Mar	Apr	May	Jun	Jul	Aug	Sep	Oct	Nov	Dec	Yr.
Avg. Precip. (in.)	5.7	4.2	3.7	2.4	1.7	1.4	0.8	1.1	1.9	3.5	5.9	5.9	38.4
Avg. Snowfall (in.)	5	2	1	Tr	Tr	0	0	0	0	Tr	1	3	13
Avg. Rel. Hum. 7am (%)	83	83	84	83	80	79	79	84	87	88	85	85	83
Avg. Rel. Hum. 4pm (%)	76	69	63	57	54	54	49	51	57	68	76	79	63

Note: Figures cover the years 1948-1990; Tr = Trace amounts (<0.05 in. of rain; <0.5 in. of snow)
Source: National Climatic Data Center, International Station Meteorological Climate Summary, 9/96

Weather Conditions

Temperature			Daytime Sky			Precipitation		
5°F & below	32°F & below	90°F & above	Clear	Partly cloudy	Cloudy	0.01 inch or more precip.	0.1 inch or more snow/ice	Thunder-storms
< 1	38	3	57	121	187	157	8	8

Note: Figures are average number of days per year and cover the years 1948-1990
Source: National Climatic Data Center, International Station Meteorological Climate Summary, 9/96

HAZARDOUS WASTE

Superfund Sites

Redmond has no sites on the EPA's Superfund Final National Priorities List.
U.S. Environmental Protection Agency, Final National Priorities List, June 23, 2008

AIR & WATER QUALITY

Air Quality Index

Area	Percent of Days when Air Quality was...[2]				AQI Statistics	
	Good	Moderate	Unhealthy for Sensitive Groups	Unhealthy	Maximum	Median
MSA[1]	76.7	20.5	2.5	0.3	155	36

Note: The Air Quality Index (AQI) is an index for reporting daily air quality. EPA calculates the AQI for five major air pollutants regulated by the Clean Air Act: ground-level ozone, particle pollution (also known as particulate matter), carbon monoxide, sulfur dioxide, and nitrogen dioxide. The AQI runs from 0 to 500. The higher the AQI value, the greater the level of air pollution and the greater the health concern. There are six AQI categories: "Good" The AQI is between 0 and 50. Air quality is considered satisfactory; "Moderate" The AQI is between 51 and 100. Air quality is acceptable; "Unhealthy for Sensitive Groups" When AQI values are between 101 and 150, members of sensitive groups may experience health effects; "Unhealthy" When AQI values are between 151 and 200 everyone may begin to experience health effects; "Very Unhealthy" AQI values between 201 and 300 trigger a health alert; "Hazardous" AQI values over 300 trigger health warnings of emergency conditions; (1) Metropolitan Statistical Area - see Appendix A for areas included; (2) Based on 365 days with AQI data in 2007.
Source: U.S. Environmental Protection Agency, Air Quality Index Report, 2007

Air Quality Index Pollutants

Area	Percent of Days when AQI Pollutant was...[2]					
	Carbon Monoxide	Nitrogen Dioxide	Ozone	Sulfur Dioxide	Particulate Matter 2.5	Particulate Matter 10
MSA[1]	0.0	0.0	44.4	0.0	54.8	0.8

Note: The Air Quality Index (AQI) is an index for reporting daily air quality. EPA calculates the AQI for five major air pollutants regulated by the Clean Air Act: ground-level ozone, particle pollution (also known as particulate matter), carbon monoxide, sulfur dioxide, and nitrogen dioxide. The AQI runs from 0 to 500. The higher the AQI value, the greater the level of air pollution and the greater the health concern; (1) Metropolitan Statistical Area - see Appendix A for areas included; (2) Based on 365 days with AQI data in 2007.
Source: U.S. Environmental Protection Agency, Air Quality Index Report, 2007

Air Quality Index Trends

Area	Trend Sites (17)								All Sites (109)
	1999	2000	2001	2002	2003	2004	2005	2006	2006
MSA[1]	6	8	6	7	2	1	3	5	12

Note: An AQI value greater than 100 indicates that air quality would have been in the unhealthful range on that day. Data from exceptional events are not included. These counts are presented in two ways. First, the counts are based on sites having an adequate record of monitoring data during the trend period (trend sites). These counts represent the relative change in the number of days with AQI values greater than 100. In the last column, the counts are based on all sites with data in the most recent year (because it is possible for a site to have data in the most recent year but not enough data to be a trend site); (1) Metropolitan Statistical Area - see Appendix A for areas included.
Source: U.S. Environmental Protection Agency, Office of Air and Radiation, Air Trends, Factbook and Related Information, Air Pollution Trends in Selected Metropolitan Areas 2006

Maximum Air Pollutant Concentrations

	Particulate Matter 10 (ug/m^3)	Particulate Matter 2.5 (ug/m^3)	Ozone (ppm)	Carbon Monoxide (ppm)	Sulfur Dioxide (ppm)	Nitrogen Dioxide (ppm)	Lead (ug/m^3)
MSA[1] Level	63	37	0.129	3	n/a	n/a	n/a
NAAQS[2]	150	35	0.125	9	0.140	0.053	1.50
Met NAAQS[2]	Yes	No	No	Yes	n/a	n/a	n/a

Note: Data from exceptional events are not included; (1) Metropolitan Statistical Area - see Appendix A for areas included; (2) National Ambient Air Quality Standards; n/a not available
Concentrations: Particulate Matter 10 (coarse particulate) - highest second maximum 24-hour concentration; Particulate Matter 2.5 (fine particulate) - highest 98th percentile 24-hour concentration; Ozone - highest second daily maximum 1-hour concentration; Carbon Monoxide - highest second maximum non-overlapping 8-hour concentration; Sulfur Dioxide - highest second maximum 24-hour concentration; Nitrogen Dioxide - highest arithmetic mean concentration; Lead - highest quarterly maximum concentration
Units: ppm = parts per million; ug/m^3 = micrograms per cubic meter
Source: U.S. Environmental Protection Agency, MSA Factbook 2006, Air Quality Statistics by City

Drinking Water

Water System Name	Pop. Served	Primary Water Source Type	Violations[1]	
			Health Based	Monitoring/ Reporting
City of Redmond Water System	56,113	Purchased Surface	0	0

Note: (1) Based on violation data from January 1, 2007 to December 31, 2007 (includes unresolved violations from earlier years)

Source: U.S. Environmental Protection Agency, Office of Ground Water and Drinking Water, Safe Drinking Water Information System (based on data extracted April 15, 2008)

Richland, Washington

Background

Richland is situated in southeastern Washington, in a region of irrigated farms and vineyards. It is one part of the rapidly growing Tri-Cities Metropolitan Area consisting of Richland and Kennewick in Benton County, and Pasco in Franklin County. The Tri-Cities serve as the service and retail center of an eight-county area including southeastern Washington and northeastern Oregon.

Although superimposed over the footprint of a small, riverside, agricultural community incorporated in 1910, modern-day Richland dates from 1943 when the U.S. Army acquired 156 miles, including the Richland town site, as the location of the Hanford Works, a primary component of the World War II project to develop the atomic bomb. Today, most work at the site involves a gigantic cleanup effort, currently funded at more than $2 billion a year, to restore most of the site to a near-original state. The centerpiece of this effort is the $6.5 billion Waste Treatment Plant, designed to transform and stabilize various types of nuclear waste into glass logs for long-term storage.

Another legacy of the work at Hanford is the Pacific Northwest National Laboratory, operated by the Battelle Memorial Foundation. One of a number of national laboratories located around the nation, PNNL is unique in that it undertakes private sector research as well as serving a wide range of government clients. The laboratory currently has 3,800 scientists, researchers and other employees and is expected to grow on its 600-acre campus long into the future. As nuclear work at Hanford declines, it is expected that PNNL will become the community's primary economic driver.

Richland is also home to Kadlec Medical Center, one of the most highy-rated hospital in eastern Washington. The medical center is part of a developing medical district, including a Columbia Basin College Medical Training Center, near the Kadlec facility.

Strategically located at the confluence of the Columbia, Snake and Yakima rivers, with outstanding soil conditions and climate, Richland and the Tri-Cities enjoy an excellent quality of life. Located in the center of Washington's expanding wine country, the area offers extensive golf, recreation and river-oriented activities as well as more than 100 high quality wineries within an hour's drive of the city's downtown. Several of Richland's numerous parks front on the Columbia and Yakima Rivers, which offer boating, water skiing, fishing, kayaking and water fowl hunting. Snow skiing and hiking 1-2 hours away. The city annually designates monies from the Park Reserve Fund to provide matching fund grants to community groups toward making capital improvements to city parks, trails, open space and recreational facilities. Three local professional sports teams are the Tri-City Americans WHL ice hockey team, the Tri-City Dust Devils Single-A baseball team, and the Tri-Cities Fever indoor football team

Richland's population is highly educated and enjoys the second highest per capita income level in the state of Washington. Its K-12 school system is highly rated and, in addition to PNNL, Richland is home to the Tri-Cities campus of Washington State University and the Richland campus of Columbia Basin College.

As a desert region, Richland enjoys a relatively mild climate with an abundance of sunny days each year. Average annual precipitation is less than seven inches. Thanks to winter temperatures hovering at 44 degrees and with little to no snowfall, golf courses are open year-round. Summer temperatures average a pleasant 88 degrees, with river breezes contributing to cool evenings and balmy days.

Rankings

General Rankings

- Kennewick* was ranked #207 out of 375 metro areas in *Cities Ranked & Rated*. Criteria: cost of living; climate; crime; transportation; economy and jobs; education; arts and culture; health and healthcare; leisure; quality of life. *Cities Ranked & Rated, 2nd Edition, 2007*
- Kennewick* was ranked #218 out of 379 metro areas in *Places Rated Almanac*. Criteria: health care; education; recreation; transportation; ambience; climate; crime; housing costs; jobs. *Places Rated Almanac, 7th Edition, 2007*

Business/Finance Rankings

- Kennewick* was selected as one of the best places to start and grow a company by *Entrepreneur* and the National Policy Research Council. The Kennewick* metro area ranked #11 out of 162 small metro areas. Criteria: business formation and growth (firms started four to 14 years ago that still employ at least 5 people and experienced rapid growth over the last four years). *Entrepreneur/National Policy Research Council, "Hot Cities for Entrepreneurs," September 2006*
- The Kennewick* metro area was identified as one of the "25 Hottest Housing Markets" in the U.S. The area ranked #11 out of 156 markets with a home price appreciation rate of 14.0%. Criteria: year-over-year change of median sales price of existing single-family homes between the 4th quarter of 2006 and the 4th quarter of 2007. *National Association of Realtors, Median Sales Price of Existing Single-Family Homes for Metropolitan Areas, 4th Quarter 2007*
- The Kennewick* metro area appeared on the Milken Institute "2007 Best Performing Cities" index. Rank: #69 out of 179 small metro areas. Criteria: job growth; wage and salary growth; high-tech output growth. *Milken Institute, "2007 Best Performing Cities"*
- *Forbes* ranked 179 smaller metro areas in the U.S. in terms of the "Best Places for Business and Careers." The Kennewick* metro area was ranked #69. Criteria: business costs (labor, energy, tax and office space expenses); living costs (housing, transportation, food and other household expenditures); education levels of the work force; job growth; income growth; migration trends; crime rates; and culture/leisure. *Forbes, "Best Places for Business and Careers," March 19, 2008*

Health/Environment Rankings

- The Kennewick* metro area appeared in *Country Home's* "2008 Best Green Places" report. The area ranked #108 out of 379. Criteria: official energy policies; green power; green buildings; availability of fresh, locally grown food. *Country Home, "2008 Best Green Places"*
- Sperling's BestPlaces ranked 331 metro areas and identified the most and least stressful U.S. cities. The Kennewick* metro area ranked #37 out of 114 mid-size metro areas (#1 = most stressful). Criteria: divorce rate; unemployment rate; violent and property crime; suicide rate; commute time; mental health; alcohol consumption; cloudy days. *Sperling's BestPlaces, www.BestPlaces.net, "America's Most (and Least) Stressful Cities," January 9, 2004*

Seniors/Retirement Rankings

- A.G. Edwards ranked America's 500 top-performing communities based on their residents' personal savings and investing behavior. The Kennewick* metro area ranked #210 with an index score of 102.74 (national average = 100.00). A dozen statistical factors were measured including: participation in retirement savings plans; personal debt levels; and home ownership. *A.G. Edwards, "2007 Nest Egg Index", September 12, 2007*

Safety Rankings

- The National Insurance Crime Bureau ranked 361 metro areas in the U.S. in terms of per capita rates of vehicle theft. The Kennewick* metro area ranked #166 (#1 = highest rate). Criteria: number of vehicle theft offenses per 100,000 inhabitants. *National Insurance Crime Bureau, "NICB Vehicle Theft Study," April 22, 2008*

- Farmers Insurance Group of Companies, in partnership with Sperling's BestPlaces, ranked 379 metro areas and identified the "Most Secure U.S. Place to Live." The Kennewick* metro area ranked #44 out of 127 in the mid-size city category (150,000 to 500,000 residents). Criteria: crime rates; extreme weather; risk of natural disasters; environmental hazards; terrorism threats; air quality; life expectancy; job loss numbers. *Farmers Insurance Group, "Most Secure U.S. Places to Live 2007"*

- Kennewick* was identified as one of the safest places in the U.S. in terms of its vulnerability to natural disasters and weather extremes. The city ranked #6 out of 10. Sperling's BestPlaces analyzed data to show a metro areas' relative tendency to experience natural disasters (hail, tornados, high winds, hurricanes, earthquakes, and brush fires) or extreme weather (abundant rain or snowfall or days that are below freezing or above 90 degrees Fahrenheit). *Forbes, "Safest and Least Safe Places in the U.S.," August 30, 2005*

Sports/Recreation Rankings

- *Golf Digest* ranked 330 metro areas in the U.S. in terms of golf. The Kennewick* metro area was ranked #189. Criteria: access to golf; weather; value of golf; and quality of golf. *Golf Digest, "Metro Golf Rankings," August 2005*

Richland is located within the Kennewick-Richland-Pasco, WA Metropolitan Statistical Area.

Business Environment

CITY FINANCES

City Government Finances

Component	2004-2005 ($000)	2004-2005 ($ per capita)
Total Revenues	97,989	2,211
Total Expenditures	106,167	2,396
Debt Outstanding	125,065	2,822
Cash and Securities	39,423	890

Source: U.S Census Bureau, Government Finances 2004-2005

City Government Revenue by Source

Source	2004-2005 ($000)	2004-2005 ($ per capita)
General Revenue		
From Federal Government	1,351	30
From State Government	2,131	48
From Local Governments	232	5
Taxes		
Property	9,763	220
Sales	10,779	243
Personal Income	0	0
License	1,757	40
Charges	18,189	410
Liquor Store	0	0
Utility	48,047	1,084
Employee Retirement	0	0
Other	5,740	130

Source: U.S Census Bureau, Government Finances 2004-2005

City Government Expenditures by Function

Function	2004-2005 ($000)	2004-2005 ($ per capita)	2004-2005 (%)
General Expenditures			
Airports	0	0	0.0
Corrections	0	0	0.0
Education	86	2	0.1
Fire Protection	5,214	118	4.9
Governmental Administration	4,852	109	4.6
Health	1,031	23	1.0
Highways	3,212	72	3.0
Hospitals	0	0	0.0
Housing and Community Development	3,554	80	3.3
Interest on General Debt	2,865	65	2.7
Libraries	1,945	44	1.8
Parking	0	0	0.0
Parks and Recreation	6,029	136	5.7
Police Protection	6,024	136	5.7
Public Welfare	0	0	0.0
Sewerage	4,949	112	4.7
Solid Waste Management	2,632	59	2.5
Liquor Store	0	0	0.0
Utility	57,489	1,297	54.1
Employee Retirement	0	0	0.0
Other	6,285	142	5.9

Source: U.S Census Bureau, Government Finances 2004-2005

Municipal Bond Ratings

Area	Moody's
City	Aaa

Source: Mergent Bond Record, January 2008 (unless noted otherwise)

DEMOGRAPHICS

Population Growth

Area	1990 Census	2000 Census	2007 Estimate	2012 Projection	Population Growth (%) 1990-2000	Population Growth (%) 2000-2012
City	33,058	38,708	46,221	51,524	17.1	33.1
MSA[1]	150,033	191,822	228,828	254,534	27.9	32.7
U.S.	248,709,873	281,421,906	301,045,522	314,920,978	13.2	11.9

Note: (1) Metropolitan Statistical Area - see Appendix B for areas included
Source: Claritas, Inc.

Number of Households and Average Household Size

Area	2007 Estimate	2007 Average Household Size
City	18,441	2.51
MSA[1]	79,651	2.87
U.S.	113,668,003	2.65

Note: (1) Metropolitan Statistical Area - see Appendix B for areas included
Source: Claritas, Inc.

Race and Ethnicity

Area	White Alone[2]	Black Alone[2]	Asian Alone[2]	Other Race Alone[2]	Hispanic[3]
City	88.0	1.6	4.7	5.7	5.7
MSA[1]	77.5	1.4	2.2	19.0	24.7
U.S.	73.1	12.4	4.3	10.3	14.9

Note: Figures are 2007 estimates; (1) Metropolitan Statistical Area - see Appendix B for areas included (2) Alone is defined as not being in combination with one or more other races; (3) May be of any race.
Source: Claritas, Inc.

Ancestry

Area	German	Irish[2]	English	American	Italian	Polish	French[3]	Scottish
City	19.6	10.9	15.5	6.9	3.5	1.9	3.7	3.5
MSA[1]	17.7	9.8	11.5	6.8	2.4	1.2	3.2	2.2
U.S.	15.2	10.9	8.7	7.3	5.6	3.2	3.0	1.7

Note: Figures include multiple ancestry (e.g. if a person reported being Irish and Italian, they were included in both columns); (1) Metropolitan Statistical Area - see Appendix A for areas included; (2) Includes Celtic; (3) Includes Alsatian but excludes Basque
Source: Census 2000, Summary File 3

Foreign-Born Population

Area	Percent of Population Born in							
	Any Foreign Country	Europe	Asia	Africa	Oceania[2]	Canada	Mexico	Latin America[3]
City	7.2	2.7	2.9	0.1	0.1	0.5	0.5	0.5
MSA[1]	12.8	1.3	1.5	0.1	0.0	0.4	8.8	0.5
U.S.	11.1	1.7	2.9	0.3	0.1	0.3	3.3	2.5

Note: (1) Metropolitan Statistical Area - see Appendix A for areas included; (2) Includes Australia, New Zealand subregion, Melanesia, Micronesia, Polynesia, and Oceania n.e.c; (3) Includes Central America (excluding Mexico), South America, and the Caribbean.
Source: Census 2000, Summary File 3

Marriage Status

Area	Never Married	Now Married (excluding Separated)	Separated	Widowed	Divorced
City	22.2	60.6	1.0	5.5	10.7
MSA[1]	24.0	59.2	1.7	4.9	10.1
U.S.	27.1	54.4	2.2	6.6	9.7

Note: Figures are percentages and cover the population 15 years of age and older; (1) Metropolitan Statistical Area - see Appendix A for areas included
Source: Census 2000, Summary File 3

Age Distribution

Area	Percent of Population						
	Under Age 5	Age 5 to 17	Age 18 to 34	Age 35 to 49	Age 50 to 64	Age 65 to 79	80 Years and Over
City	6.5	20.8	18.7	23.9	17.0	10.2	2.9
MSA[1]	8.1	22.9	21.9	23.2	14.2	7.6	2.3
U.S.	6.8	18.9	23.7	23.5	14.8	9.2	3.2

Note: (1) Metropolitan Statistical Area - see Appendix A for areas included
Source: Census 2000, Summary File 3

Male/Female Ratio

Area	Males	Females	Males per 100 Females
City	22,736	23,485	96.8
MSA[1]	115,828	113,000	102.5
U.S.	148,320,305	152,725,217	97.1

Note: Figures are 2007 estimates; (1) Metropolitan Statistical Area - see Appendix B for areas included
Source: Claritas, Inc.

Religion

Area	Catholic	Southern Baptist	United Meth-odist	ELCA[1]	LDS[2]	Presby-terian Church USA	Jewish Est.	Muslim Est.
County	12.7	2.2	3.4	2.2	7.3	1.7	0.2	0.2
U.S.	22.0	7.1	3.7	1.8	1.5	1.1	2.2	0.6

Note: Figures are the number of adherents as a percentage of the total population; Adherents are defined as all members, including full members, their children and the estimated number of other participants who are not considered members (e.g. the baptized, those not confirmed, those regularly attending services, etc.); (1) Evangelical Lutheran Church in America; (2) The Church of Jesus Christ of Latter Day Saints
Source: Reprinted with permission from Religious Congregations and Membership in the United States 2000 (Nashville, Glenmary Research Center, 2002) Copyright Association of Statisticians of American Religious Bodies. All rights reserved.

ECONOMY

Gross Metropolitan Product

Area	2002	2003	2004	2005	2005 Rank[2]
MSA[1]	6.7	7.2	7.7	8.0	198

Note: Figures are in billions of dollars; (1) Kennewick-Richland-Pasco, WA Metropolitan Statistical Area - see Appendix A for areas included; (2) Rank ranges from 1 to 361
Source: The U.S. Conference of Mayors, "U.S. Metro Economies: GMP - The Engines of America's Growth," January 2007

Economic Growth

Area	1995 GMP	2005 GMP	Average Annual Growth Rate	Growth Rate Rank[2]
MSA[1]	4.7	8.0	5.4	180

Note: Figures are in billions of dollars; GMP = Gross Metropolitan Product; (1) Kennewick-Richland-Pasco, WA Metropolitan Statistical Area - see Appendix A for areas included; (2) Rank ranges from 1 to 361
Source: The U.S. Conference of Mayors, "U.S. Metro Economies: GMP - The Engines of America's Growth," January 2007

INCOME

Per Capita/Median/Average Income

Area	Per Capita ($)	Median Household ($)	Average Household ($)
City	30,248	62,081	75,619
MSA[1]	22,982	53,002	65,657
U.S.	25,495	49,280	66,670

Note: Figures are 2007 estimates; (1) Metropolitan Statistical Area - see Appendix B for areas included
Source: Claritas, Inc.

Household Income Distribution

Area	Percent of Households Earning							
	Under $15,000	$15,000 -24,999	$25,000 -34,999	$35,000 -49,999	$50,000 -74,999	$75,000 -99,000	$100,000 -149,999	$150,000 and up
City	9.0	8.3	8.5	14.4	19.9	15.5	16.9	7.5
MSA[1]	10.5	10.6	10.2	16.1	20.5	13.8	13.5	4.9
U.S.	13.1	10.9	11.2	15.6	19.5	11.9	11.3	6.6

Note: Figures are 2007 estimates; (1) Metropolitan Statistical Area - see Appendix B for areas included
Source: Claritas, Inc.

Poverty Rates by Age

Area	All Ages	Under 5 Years Old	5 to 17 Years Old	18 to 64 Years Old	65 Years and Over
City	8.2	0.7	2.3	4.4	0.7
MSA[1]	12.6	1.9	3.7	6.3	0.7
U.S.	12.4	1.2	3.0	6.9	1.2

Note: Figures are percent of population with income in 1999 below poverty level and only include population for whom poverty status is determined; (1) Metropolitan Statistical Area - see Appendix A for areas included
Source: Census 2000, Summary File 3

Personal Bankruptcy Filing Rate

Area	2004	2005	2006
Benton County	7.28	9.55	2.08
U.S.	5.31	6.82	2.00

Note: Numbers are per 1,000 population and include Chapter 7 and Chapter 13 filings
Source: Federal Deposit Insurance Corporation (FDIC), Regional Economic Conditions (RECON), 8/23/2007

EMPLOYMENT

Labor Force and Employment

Area	Civilian Labor Force			Workers Employed		
	Dec. 2006	Dec. 2007	% Chg.	Dec. 2006	Dec. 2007	% Chg.
City	23,081	24,395	5.7	22,121	23,396	5.8
MSA[1]	112,578	118,091	4.9	105,058	111,114	5.8
U.S.	152,571,000	153,705,000	0.7	146,081,000	146,334,000	0.2

Note: Data is not seasonally adjusted and covers workers 16 years of age and older;
(1) Metropolitan Statistical Area - see Appendix B for areas included
Source: Bureau of Labor Statistics, http://stats.bls.gov

Unemployment Rate

Area	2007											
	Jan.	Feb.	Mar.	Apr.	May	Jun.	Jul.	Aug.	Sep.	Oct.	Nov.	Dec.
City	4.8	4.7	4.1	4.0	3.9	4.0	4.6	4.2	3.8	3.7	3.9	4.1
MSA[1]	7.4	6.6	5.4	5.1	4.5	4.6	5.3	4.6	4.3	4.1	5.4	5.9
U.S.	5.0	4.9	4.5	4.3	4.3	4.7	4.9	4.6	4.5	4.4	4.5	4.8

Note: Data is not seasonally adjusted and covers workers 16 years of age and older; All figures are percentages; (1) Metropolitan Statistical Area - see Appendix B for areas included
Source: Bureau of Labor Statistics, http://stats.bls.gov

Employment by Occupation

Occupation Classification	City (%)	MSA[1] (%)	U.S. (%)
Sales and Office	21.5	23.1	26.7
Professional and Related	33.8	21.9	20.2
Service	12.5	14.5	14.9
Production, Transportation, and Material Moving	8.4	12.9	14.6
Management, Business, and Financial	17.0	13.0	13.5
Construction, Extraction, and Maintenance	6.2	9.9	9.4
Farming, Forestry, and Fishing	0.6	4.7	0.7

Note: Figures cover employed civilians 16 years of age and older;
(1) Metropolitan Statistical Area - see Appendix A for areas included
Source: Census 2000, Summary File 3

Employment by Industry

Sector	MSA[1] Number of Employees	MSA[1] Percent of Total	U.S. Percent of Total
Government	16,700	17.8	16.3
Education and Health Services	9,700	10.4	13.4
Professional and Business Services	20,100	21.5	13.1
Retail Trade	12,100	12.9	11.6
Manufacturing	6,900	7.4	9.9
Leisure and Hospitality	8,100	8.7	9.6
Financial Activities	3,600	3.8	5.9
Construction	n/a	n/a	5.3
Wholesale Trade	n/a	n/a	4.4
Other Services	n/a	n/a	3.9
Transportation and Utilities	n/a	n/a	3.7
Information	n/a	n/a	2.2
Natural Resources and Mining	n/a	n/a	0.5

Note: Figures cover non-farm employment as of December 2007 and are not seasonally adjusted; (1) Metropolitan Statistical Area - see Appendix B for areas included; n/a not available
Source: Bureau of Labor Statistics, http://stats.bls.gov

Average Wages

Occupation	$/Hr.	Occupation	$/Hr.
Accountants and Auditors	29.61	Maids and Housekeeping Cleaners	9.88
Automotive Mechanics	18.12	Maintenance and Repair Workers	16.99
Bookkeepers	15.26	Marketing Managers	n/a
Carpenters	21.44	Nuclear Medicine Technologists	n/a
Cashiers	10.27	Nurses, Licensed Practical	19.22
Clerks, General Office	13.79	Nurses, Registered	29.51
Clerks, Receptionists/Information	11.67	Nursing Aides/Orderlies/Attendants	11.31
Clerks, Shipping/Receiving	12.68	Packers and Packagers, Hand	10.44
Computer Programmers	23.88	Physical Therapists	31.41
Computer Support Specialists	21.71	Postal Service Mail Carriers	21.03
Computer Systems Analysts	35.66	Real Estate Brokers	n/a
Cooks, Restaurant	10.67	Retail Salespersons	14.60
Dentists	n/a	Sales Reps., Exc. Tech./Scientific	21.59
Electrical Engineers	41.98	Sales Reps., Tech./Scientific	33.85
Electricians	24.65	Secretaries, Exc. Legal/Med./Exec.	16.30
Financial Managers	41.54	Security Guards	n/a
First-Line Supervisors/Mgrs., Sales	19.69	Surgeons	n/a
Food Preparation Workers	9.82	Teacher Assistants	12.30
General and Operations Managers	59.31	Teachers, Elementary School	24.30
Hairdressers/Cosmetologists	11.61	Teachers, Secondary School	26.50
Internists	n/a	Telemarketers	n/a
Janitors and Cleaners	11.58	Truck Drivers, Heavy/Tractor-Trailer	19.74
Landscaping/Groundskeeping Workers	12.76	Truck Drivers, Light/Delivery Svcs.	12.01
Lawyers	42.87	Waiters and Waitresses	12.54

Note: Wage data covers the Kennewick-Richland-Pasco, WA Metropolitan Statistical Area - see Appendix B for areas included. Hourly wages for elementary/secondary school teachers and teacher assistants were calculated by the editors from annual wage data assuming a 40 hour work week; n/a not available.
Source: Bureau of Labor Statistics, May 2007 Metro Area Occupational Employment and Wage Estimates

RESIDENTIAL REAL ESTATE

Building Permits

Area	Single-Family			Multi-Family			Total		
	2006	2007[p]	Pct. Chg.	2006	2007[p]	Pct. Chg.	2006	2007[p]	Pct. Chg.
City	318	296	-6.9	0	176	-	318	472	48.4
U.S.	1,378,200	973,300	-29.4	460,700	407,200	-11.6	1,838,900	1,380,500	-24.9

Note: (p) preliminary; figures cover and represent new, privately-owned housing units authorized (unadjusted data); All permit data are based on estimates with imputation; U.S. figures are based on the new 20,000-place series.
Source: U.S. Census Bureau, Manufacturing, Mining, and Construction Statistics

Homeownership and Housing Vacancies

Area	Homeownership Rate[2] (%)			Rental Vacancy Rate[3] (%)			Homeowner Vacancy Rate[4] (%)		
	2005	2006	2007	2005	2006	2007	2005	2006	2007
MSA[1]	n/a	n/a	n/a	n/a	n/a	n/a	n/a	n/a	n/a
U.S.	68.9	68.8	68.1	9.8	9.8	9.7	1.9	2.4	2.7

Note: (1) Metropolitan Statistical Area - see Appendix B for areas included; (2) The proportion of households that are owners; (3) The proportion of the rental inventory that is vacant for rent; (4) The proportion of the homeowner inventory that is vacant for sale; n/a not available
Source: U.S. Census Bureau, Housing Vacancies and Homeownership Annual Statistics: 2007

TAXES

State Corporate Income Tax Rates

State	Rates and Tax Brackets
Washington	Rate Varies

Note: Tax rates as of January 1, 2008; Washington has no income tax but has a gross receipts tax called the Business & Occupation (B&O) Tax which is levied at various rates. The major rates are 0.471% for retail sales, 0.484% for wholesale and manufacturing, and 1.5% for service and other activities.
Source: Tax Foundation, www.taxfoundation.org

State Individual Income Tax Rates

State	Federal Deductibility	Marginal Rates (%)	Standard Deduction ($)		Personal Exemptions ($)[1]	
			Single	Joint	Single	Dependents
Washington	No	None	n/a	n/a	n/a	n/a

Note: Tax rates as of January 1, 2008; Local- and county-level taxes are not included; n/a not applicable; (1) Married joint filers generally receive double the single exemption
Source: Tax Foundation, www.taxfoundation.org

Various State and Local Tax Rates

State and Local Sales and Use (%)	State Sales and Use (%)	Gasoline[1,2] ($/gal.)	Cigarette ($/pack)	Spirits ($/gal.)	Table Wine ($/gal.)	Beer ($/gal.)
8.3	6.5 (j)	0.36	2.025	19.43 (n)	0.87	0.26

Note: Tax rates as of January 1, 2008; (1) In addition to the 18.4 cpg Federal gasoline tax; (2) Rates may include additional state sales taxes, environmental protection and storage fees/taxes, and local taxes. When necessary, the volume-weighted average of all local taxes is used to approximate the typical statewide rate including local tax; (j) Washington has a GRT in addition to its 6.5% sales tax. It is called the business and occupation tax and is levied at various rates. The major rates are 0.471% for retail sales, 0.484% for wholesale and manufacturing, and 1.5% for service and other

ctivities; (n) The state government controls all sales. The implied excise tax rate is calculated using methodology designed by the Distilled Spirits Council of the United States (DISCUS). Source: Tax Foundation, www.taxfoundation.org; Original research

State Tax Burdens

Area	Combined State and Local Tax Burden		Combined Federal, State and Local Tax Burden	
	Percent	Rank	Percent	Rank
Washington	11.1	16	34.0	9
U.S. Average	11.0	-	32.7	-

Note: Figures cover 2007 and measure taxes as a percentage of income
Source: Tax Foundation, www.taxfoundation.org

State Business Tax Climate Index Rankings

State	Overall Rank	Corporate Tax Index Rank	Individual Income Tax Index Rank	Sales Tax Index Rank	Unemployment Insurance Tax Index Rank	Property Tax Index Rank
Washington	11	31	1	50	36	28

Note: Rankings range from 1 to 50 where 1 is best. Rankings do not average across to Overall Rank. States without a given tax are given a ranking of 1.
Source: Tax Foundation, State Business Tax Climate Index 2008

TRANSPORTATION

Means of Transportation to Work

Area	Car/Truck/Van		Public Transportation			Bicycle	Walked	Other Means	Worked at Home
	Drove Alone	Car-pooled	Bus	Subway	Railroad				
City	80.5	11.8	1.1	0.0	0.0	0.6	2.0	0.9	3.1
MSA[1]	77.8	14.5	1.0	0.0	0.0	0.3	1.7	1.0	3.8
U.S.	75.7	12.2	2.5	1.5	0.5	0.4	2.9	1.0	3.3

Note: Figures are percentages and cover workers 16 years of age and older;
(1) Metropolitan Statistical Area - see Appendix A for areas included
Source: Census 2000, Summary File 3

Travel Time to Work

Area	Less Than 15 Minutes	15 to 29 Minutes	30 to 44 Minutes	45 to 59 Minutes	60 Minutes or More
City	45.6	36.0	11.3	4.6	2.5
MSA[1]	37.3	38.3	13.8	6.0	4.7
U.S.	29.4	36.1	19.1	7.4	8.0

Note: Figures are percentages and include workers 16 years old and over; (1) Metropolitan Statistical Area - see Appendix A for areas included
Source: Census 2000, Summary File 3

Living Environment

COST OF LIVING

Cost of Living Index

Composite Index	Groceries	Housing	Utilities	Trans-portation	Health Care	Misc. Goods/ Services
94.2	94.1	85.3	89.6	106.5	116.4	96.5

Note: U.S. = 100; Figures cover the Kennewick-Richland-Pasco WA urban area.
Source: The Council for Community and Economic Research (formerly ACCRA), Cost of Living Index, 2007

Grocery Prices

Area[1]	T-Bone Steak ($/pound)	Frying Chicken ($/pound)	Whole Milk ($/half gal.)	Eggs ($/dozen)	Orange Juice ($/64 oz.)	Coffee ($/11.5 oz.)
City[2]	8.93	1.08	1.92	1.70	2.93	3.15
Avg.	8.93	1.12	2.13	1.52	3.26	3.31
Min.	5.88	0.71	1.33	0.83	2.30	2.20
Max.	12.80	2.07	3.43	3.54	5.79	6.20

Note: (1) Values for the local area are compared with the average, minimum and maximum values for all 331 areas in the Cost of Living Index report; (2) Figures cover the Kennewick-Richland-Pasco WA urban area; **T-Bone Steak** *(price per pound);* **Frying Chicken** *(price per pound, whole fryer);* **Whole Milk** *(half gallon carton);* **Eggs** *(price per dozen, Grade A, large);* **Orange Juice** *(64 oz. Tropicana or Florida Natural);* **Coffee** *(11.5 oz. can, vacuum-packed, Maxwell House, Hills Bros, or Folgers).*
Source: The Council for Community and Economic Research (formerly ACCRA), Cost of Living Index, 2007

Housing and Utility Costs

Area[1]	New Home Price ($)	Apartment Rent ($/month)	All Electric ($/month)	Part Electric ($/month)	Other Energy ($/month)	Telephone ($/month)
City[2]	263,727	701	137.79	-	-	25.49
Avg.	309,605	782	146.13	78.67	90.16	26.14
Min.	189,877	n/a	82.03	37.41	33.15	17.08
Max.	1,202,800	3,481	271.14	150.60	257.67	37.45

Note: (1) Values for the local area are compared with the average, minimum and maximum values for all 331 areas in the Cost of Living Index report; (2) Figures cover the Kennewick-Richland-Pasco WA urban area; **New Home Price** *(2,400 sf living area, 8,000 sf lot, in urban area with full utilities);* **Apartment Rent** *(950 sf 2 bedroom/1.5 or 2 bath, unfurnished, excluding all utilities except water);* **All Electric** *(average monthly cost for an all-electric home);* **Part Electric** *(average monthly cost for a part-electric home);* **Other Energy** *(average monthly cost for natural gas, fuel oil, coal, wood, and any other forms of energy except electricity);* **Telephone** *(price includes basic monthly rate for a private residential line plus additional local usage charges incurred by a family of four).*
Source: The Council for Community and Economic Research (formerly ACCRA), Cost of Living Index, 2007

Health Care, Transportation, and Other Costs

Area[1]	Doctor ($/visit)	Dentist ($/visit)	Optometrist ($/visit)	Gasoline ($/gallon)	Beauty Salon ($/visit)	Men's Shirt ($)
City[2]	85.27	91.73	141.00	2.83	33.93	20.75
Avg.	79.48	71.93	79.55	2.64	29.52	25.77
Min.	52.08	44.80	43.95	2.19	15.58	16.19
Max.	148.44	126.27	158.83	3.48	60.62	48.53

Note: (1) Values for the local area are compared with the average, minimum and maximum values for all 331 areas in the Cost of Living Index report; (2) Figures cover the Kennewick-Richland-Pasco WA urban area; **Doctor** *(general practitioners routine exam of an established patient);* **Dentist** *(adult teeth cleaning and periodic oral examination);* **Optometrist** *(full vision eye exam for established adult patient);* **Gasoline** *(one gallon regular unleaded, national brand, including all taxes, cash price at self-service pump if available);* **Beauty Salon** *(woman's shampoo, trim, and blow-dry);* **Men's Shirt** *(cotton/polyester dress shirt, pinpoint weave, long sleeves).*
Source: The Council for Community and Economic Research (formerly ACCRA), Cost of Living Index, 2007

HOUSING

House Price Index (HPI)

Area	National Ranking[2]	Quarterly Change (%)	One-Year Change (%)	Five-Year Change (%)
MSA[1]	112	3.55	2.69	21.32
U.S.[3]	-	0.10	0.84	41.37

Note: The HPI is a weighted repeat sales index. It measures average price changes in repeat sales or refinancings on the same properties. This information is obtained by reviewing repeat mortgage transactions on single-family properties whose mortgages have been purchased or securitized by Fannie Mae or Freddie Mac in January 1975; (1) Metropolitan Statistical Area - see Appendix B for areas included; (2) Rankings are based on annual percentage change for all metro areas containing at least 15,000 transactions over the last 10 years and ranges from 1 to 291; (3) figures based on a weighted average of Census Division estimates; all figures are for the period ending December 31, 2007

Source: Office of Federal Housing Enterprise Oversight, House Price Index, February 26, 2008

House Price Valuations

Area	Q1 2000	Q1 2001	Q1 2002	Q1 2003	Q1 2004	Q1 2005	Q1 2006	Q1 2007	Q1 2008
MSA[1]	-3.5	-6.6	-4.3	-2.3	6.7	3.6	10.2	13.4	6.1

Note: Figures show the percentage of over- or under-valuation of single family homes relative to statistically normal house values (e.g. a value of 23.6 indicates that house values are 23.6% overvalued). Statistically normal house values are based on house prices, interest rates, household incomes, population densities, and any historical premiums or discounts metropolitan areas have exhibited over time; (1) Figures cover the Metropolitan Statistical Area - see Appendix B for areas included

Source: Global Insight/National City Corporation, House Prices in America, May 2008

Median Home Prices

Area	2005	2006	2007[r]	Percent Change 2006 to 2007
MSA[1]	154.1	156.1	169.2	8.4
U.S. Average	219.0	221.9	217.9	-1.8

Note: Figures are median sales prices of existing single-family homes in thousands of dollars; (r) revised; n/a not available; (1) Metropolitan Statistical Area - see Appendix B for areas included

Source: National Association of Realtors, Metropolitan Area Prices, 1st Quarter 2008

Housing: Year Structure Built

Area	1990 -2000	1980 -1989	1970 -1979	1960 -1969	1950 -1959	1940 -1949	Before 1940	Median Year
City	16.4	7.1	27.4	9.5	14.3	24.4	0.8	1970
MSA[1]	21.4	10.0	31.4	10.5	13.3	10.2	3.2	1974
U.S.	17.0	15.8	18.5	13.7	12.7	7.3	15.0	1971

Note: Figures are percentages; (1) Metropolitan Statistical Area - see Appendix A for areas included

Source: Census 2000, Summary File 3

HEALTH

Health Risk Data

Category	Area[1] (%)	U.S. (%)
Adults who have been told they have high blood pressure[3]	23.6	25.5
Adults who have been told they have high blood cholesterol[3]	38.0	35.6
Adults who have been told they have diabetes[2]	7.3	7.5
Adults who have been told they have arthritis[3]	21.6	27.0
Adults who have been told they currently have asthma	6.8	8.5
Adults who are current smokers	16.3	20.1
Adults who are heavy drinkers[4]	2.8	4.9
Adults who are overweight (BMI 25.0 - 29.9)	36.2	36.5
Adults who are obese (BMI 30.0 - 99.8)	26.3	25.1

Note: Data as of 2006 unless otherwise noted; (1) Figures cover the Metropolitan Statistical Area - see Appendix B for areas included; (2) Figures do not include pregnancy-related diabetes, pre-diabetes or borderline diabetes; (3) 2005 data; (4) Heavy drinkers are classified as adult men having more than two drinks per day or adult women having more than one drink per day

Source: Centers for Disease Control and Prevention, Behaviorial Risk Factor Surveillance System, SMART: Selected Metropolitan/Micropolitan Area Risk Trends, 2005, 2006

Mortality Rates for the Top 10 Causes of Death in the U.S.

ICD-10[a] Sub-Chapter	ICD-10[a] Code	Age-Adjusted Mortality Rate[1] per 100,000 population	
		County[2]	U.S.
Malignant neoplasms	C00-C97	186.8	186.5
Ischaemic heart diseases	I20-I25	141.3	152.3
Other forms of heart disease	I30-I51	41.0	51.5
Cerebrovascular diseases	I60-I69	53.3	50.0
Chronic lower respiratory diseases	J40-J47	48.6	42.6
Diabetes mellitus	E10-E14	26.2	24.8
Other degenerative diseases of the nervous system	G30-G31	29.9	22.6
Other external causes of accidental injury	W00-X59	19.4	21.4
Influenza and pneumonia	J10-J18	11.4	20.7
Hypertensive diseases	I10-I13	17.8	18.2

Note: (a) ICD-10 = International Classification of Diseases 10th Revision; (1) Mortality rates are a three year average covering 2003-2005; (2) Figures cover Benton County
Source: Centers for Disease Control and Prevention, National Center for Health Statistics. Compressed Mortality File 1999-2004. CDC WONDER On-line Database, compiled from Compressed Mortality File 1999-2005 Series 20 No. 2K, 2008.

Mortality Rates for Selected Causes of Death

ICD-10[a] Sub-Chapter	ICD-10[a] Code	Age-Adjusted Mortality Rate[1] per 100,000 population	
		County[2]	U.S.
Assault	X85-Y09	*4.0	5.9
Human immunodeficiency virus (HIV) disease	B20-B24	*0.7	4.5
Intentional self-harm	X60-X84	12.4	10.8
Malnutrition	E40-E46	*2.1	1.0
Obesity and other hyperalimentation	E65-E68	*1.4	1.4
Organic, including symptomatic, mental disorders	F01-F09	*4.5	16.8
Transport accidents	V01-V99	13.5	16.1
Viral hepatitis	B15-B19	*1.5	1.8

Note: (a) ICD-10 = International Classification of Diseases 10th Revision; (1) Mortality rates are a three year average covering 2003-2005; (2) Figures cover Benton County; (*) Unreliable data as per CDC
Source: Centers for Disease Control and Prevention, National Center for Health Statistics. Compressed Mortality File 1999-2004. CDC WONDER On-line Database, compiled from Compressed Mortality File 1999-2005 Series 20 No. 2K, 2008.

Distribution of Physicians[1]

Area	Total	Family/ General Practice	Specialties	
			Medical	Surgical
Benton County (number)	259	83	90	62
Benton County (rate per 10,000 pop.)	16.4	5.3	5.7	3.9
U.S. (rate per 10,000 pop.)	17.7	4.6	6.9	4.3

Note: Data as of 2005; (1) Includes all non-federal, patient-care, office-based MDs
Source: Area Resource File (ARF). June 2007. U.S. Department of Health and Human Services, Health Resources and Services Administration, Bureau of Health Professions, Rockville, MD.

Hospitals

Richland has the following hospitals: 1 general medical and surgical; 1 psychiatric.
AHA Guide to the Healthcare Field 2008

EDUCATION

Public School District Statistics

District Name	Schls	Pupils	Pupil/ Teacher Ratio	Minority Pupils[1] (%)	Free Lunch Eligible[2] (%)	IEP[3] (%)
Pasco School Dist 001	17	11,993	19.0	73.3	57.0	10.7
Richland School Dist 400	16	10,203	20.7	15.6	19.0	11.9

Note: Table includes regular local school districts with 2,000 or more students; (1) Percentage of students that are not white, non-Hispanic; (2) Percentage of students that are eligible for the free lunch program; (3) Percentage of students that have an Individualized Education Program.
Source: U.S. Department of Education, National Center for Education Statistics, Common Core of Data, Local Education Agency (School District) Universe Survey: School Year 2005-2006; U.S. Department of Education, National Center for Education Statistics, Common Core of Data, Public Elementary/Secondary School Universe Survey: School Year 2005-2006

Top Public High Schools

High School Name	Index[1]	Rank[1]	Subsidized Lunch (%)[2]	E&E (%)[3]
Hanford	1.060	1,364	16.0	22.2

Note: (1) Public schools are ranked according to a ratio that is the number of Advanced Placement, International Baccalaureate, and/or Cambridge tests taken by all students at a school in 2007 divided by the number of graduating seniors. All of the schools on the list have an index of at least 1.000; they are in the top five percent of public schools measured this way. The rankings range from 1 to 1,422; (2) Percentage of students receiving federally subsidized meals; (3) E & E stands for equity and excellence percentage: the portion of all graduating seniors at a school that had at least one passing grade on one AP or IB test; (**) Gave both IB and AP tests. AP and IB participation are indicators of a school's efforts to get students to excel and prepare for college.
Source: Newsweek Online, "Top High Schools 2008"

Highest Level of Education

Area	Less than H.S.	H.S. Diploma	Some College, No Deg.	Associate Degree	Bachelors Degree	Masters Degree	Profess. School Degree	Doctorate Degree
City	7.2	19.3	24.5	9.2	22.7	11.5	1.8	3.9
MSA[1]	20.2	23.2	24.0	8.7	15.1	6.2	1.1	1.6
U.S.	19.4	28.4	21.2	6.4	15.7	5.9	2.0	1.0

Note: Figures are 2007 estimated percentages and cover persons age 25 and over; (1) Metropolitan Statistical Area - see Appendix B for areas included
Source: Claritas, Inc.

Educational Attainment by Race

Area	High School Graduate (%)					Bachelor's Degree (%)				
	Total	White	Black	Asian	Hisp.[2]	Total	White	Black	Asian	Hisp.[2]
City	92.6	93.3	90.6	92.4	74.1	38.9	38.3	30.7	62.8	20.7
MSA[1]	80.1	86.0	73.0	78.4	32.8	23.3	25.1	17.7	45.1	4.7
U.S.	80.4	83.6	72.3	80.4	52.4	24.4	26.1	14.3	44.1	10.4

Note: Figures shown cover persons 25 years old and over; (1) Metropolitan Statistical Area - see Appendix A for areas included; (2) people of Hispanic origin can be of any race
Source: Census 2000, Summary File 3

School Enrollment by Type

Area	Grades KG to 8				Grades 9 to 12			
	Public		Private		Public		Private	
	Enrollment	%	Enrollment	%	Enrollment	%	Enrollment	%
City	4,874	87.7	685	12.3	2,475	95.7	110	4.3
MSA[1]	28,254	92.9	2,157	7.1	13,361	96.8	438	3.2
U.S.	33,526,011	88.7	4,285,121	11.3	14,848,628	90.6	1,532,323	9.4

Note: Figures shown cover persons 3 years old and over; (1) Metropolitan Statistical Area - see Appendix A for areas included
Source: Census 2000, Summary File 3

School Enrollment by Race

Area	Grades KG to 8 (%)				Grades 9 to 12 (%)			
	White	Black	Asian	Hisp.[1]	White	Black	Asian	Hisp.[1]
City	85.4	2.0	3.6	9.3	87.5	0.0	3.8	4.4
MSA[2]	73.9	1.5	1.5	30.9	75.8	1.1	2.6	26.1
U.S.	68.5	15.5	3.3	16.8	68.8	15.5	3.8	15.7

Note: Figures shown cover persons 3 years old and over; (1) people of Hispanic origin can be of any race; (2) Metropolitan Statistical Area - see Appendix A for areas included
Source: Census 2000, Summary File 3

Average Salaries of Public School Classroom Teachers

District	2005-06		2006-07		Percent Change 2005-06 to 2006-07
	Dollars	Rank[1]	Dollars	Rank[1]	
Washington	46,326	22	47,882	22	3.36
U.S. Average	49,026	-	50,816	-	3.65

Note: (1) State rank ranges from 1 to 51.
Source: National Education Association, Rankings & Estimates: Rankings of the States 2006 and Estimates of School Statistics 2007, December 2007

Higher Education

Four-Year Colleges			Two-Year Colleges			Medical Schools[1]	Law Schools[2]	Voc/ Tech[3]
Public	Private Non-profit	Private For-profit	Public	Private Non-profit	Private For-profit			
0	0	0	0	0	0	0	0	0

Note: Figures cover institutions located within the city limits; (1) includes schools accredited by the Liaison Committee on Medical Education and the American Osteopathic Association; (2) includes American Bar Association-accredited law schools; (3) includes all schools with programs that are less than 2 years.
Source: National Center for Education Statistics, The Integrated Postsecondary Education System (IPEDS) Peer Analysis System, 2007; www.usnews.com, Law and Medical School Directories, 2009

PRESIDENTIAL ELECTION

2004 Presidential Election Results

Area	Bush	Kerry	Nader	Other
Benton County	66.3	32.2	0.6	0.9
U.S.	50.7	48.3	0.4	0.6

Note: Results are percentages and may not add to 100% due to rounding
Source: Dave Leip's Atlas of U.S. Presidential Elections, www.uselectionatlas.org

EMPLOYERS

Major Employers

Company Name	Industry	Type of Site
American Bldg Maint Co-West	Building maintenance services, nec	Branch
Areda	Process control instruments	Branch
Battelle Memorial Institute	Administration of general economic programs	Branch
Bechtel Hanford Inc	Engineering services	Single
Ch2m Hill Hanford Group Inc	Engineering services	Single
City of Kennewick	Executive offices	Branch
City of Richland	Executive offices	Headquarters
Energy Northwest	Electric services	Headquarters
Kadlec Medical Center	General medical and surgical hospitals	Headquarters
Kaiser Engineer Hanford Co	Business consulting, nec	Branch
Kennewick General Hospital	General medical and surgical hospitals	Headquarters
Lockheed Martin	Commercial physical research	Branch
Lourdes Health Network	General medical and surgical hospitals	Headquarters
Mission Support Alliance LLC	Computer integrated systems design	Single
Prosser High School	Elementary and secondary schools	Branch
Twin City Foods Inc	Frozen fruits and vegetables	Branch

Note: Companies shown are located within the Kennewick metropolitan area; nec = not elsewhere classified.
Source: www.zapdata.com, May 2008

PUBLIC SAFETY

Crime Rate

Area	All Crimes	Violent Crimes				Property Crimes		
		Murder	Forcible Rape	Robbery	Aggrav. Assault	Burglary	Larceny -Theft	Motor Vehicle Theft
City	3,411.9	0.0	22.2	31.1	168.6	625.6	2,371.4	193.0
Metro[1]	3,516.7	2.7	30.7	39.6	216.7	662.9	2,318.5	245.6
U.S.	3,808.1	5.7	30.9	149.4	287.5	729.4	2,206.8	398.4

Note: Figures are crimes per 100,000 population; (1) Metropolitan Statistical Area - see Appendix B for areas included
Source: FBI Uniform Crime Reports, 2006

Hate Crimes

Area	Number of Quarters Reported	Bias Motivation				
		Race	Religion	Sexual Orientation	Ethnicity	Disability
City	4	0	0	0	0	0

Source: Federal Bureau of Investigation, Hate Crime Statistics 2006

RECREATION

Culture

Dance[1]	Theatre[1]	Instrumental Music[1]	Vocal Music[1]	Series/ Festivals	Museums	Zoos and Aquariums[2]
0	0	1	0	0	1	0

Note: (1) Number of professional perfoming groups; (2) AZA-accredited
Source: The Grey House Performing Arts Directory, 2007; Official Museum Directory, 2008; Association of Zoos & Aquariums, AZA Member Zoos & Aquariums, June 2008

Professional Sports Teams

Team Name	League
No teams are located in the metro area	

Source: Original research

MEDIA

Newspapers

Name	News Focus	Frequency	Circulation
No newspapers have an office in the city			

Note: Includes newspapers with offices located in the city
Source: MediaContactsPro, March 2008

Television Stations

Name	Ch.	Network(s)	Type	Ownership
KEPR	19	CBS	Commercial	Fisher Broadcasting Inc.
KNDO	23	NBC	Commercial	n/a
KNDU	25	NBC	Commercial	n/a
KIMA	29	CBS	Commercial	Fisher Broadcasting Inc.
KAPP	35	ABC	Commercial	Apple Valley Broadcasting Inc.
KVEW	42	ABC	Commercial	Apple Valley Broadcasting Inc.
KYVE	47	PBS	Public	KCTS
KFFX	66	n/a	Commercial	Northwest Broadcasting Inc.
KCYU	68	Fox	Commercial	Northwest Broadcasting Inc.

Note: Stations included cover the Yakima-Pasco-Richland-Kennewick DMA (Designated Market Area)
BurrellesLuce, MediaContacts Online, January 2007

Major AM Radio Stations

Call Letters	Freq. (kHz)	Station Type	Target Audience	Station Format	Music Format
KONA	610	Commercial	General	News/Sports	n/a
KFLD	870	Commercial	General	Talk	n/a
KYAK	930	n/a	Hispanic/Religious	Music/Talk	n/a
KALE	960	Commercial	General	Sports	n/a
KJOX	980	Commercial	General	News/Sports/Talk	n/a
KYXE	1020	Commercial	General/Hispanic	Music	Latin
KLWJ	1090	Commercial	General/Religious	Music/News/Talk	Gospel
KZTS	1210	Commercial	General/Hispanic	Music/News	Latin
KTIX	1240	Commercial	General	News/Sports	n/a
KXLE	1240	Commercial	General	News/Talk	n/a
KIT	1280	Commercial	General	Talk	n/a
KUMA	1290	Commercial	General	Talk	n/a
KZXR	1310	n/a	General	News/Sports/Talk	n/a
KGDC	1320	n/a	Hispanic	Music/News/Sports	Latin
KTCR	1340	Commercial	General	Talk	n/a
KOHU	1360	Commercial	General	Music/News	Country
KBBO	1390	Commercial	General/Religious	n/a	n/a
KUJ	1420	Commercial	General	Music	n/a
KUTI	1460	Commercial	General	Music	Country
KTEL	1490	Commercial	General	Music/News/Talk	Oldies
KYNR	1490	Non-Comm	General/Hisp/Nat Amer	Ed/Music/News/Talk	International

Note: Stations included cover the Yakima-Pasco-Richland-Kennewick DMA (Designated Market Area); n/a not available
Source: BurrellesLuce, MediaContacts Online, January 2007

Major FM Radio Stations

Call Letters	Freq. (mHz)	Station Type	Target Audience	Station Format	Music Format
KCWU	88.1	College	General	Ed/Music/News/Sports/Talk	Modern Rock
KYVT	88.5	n/a	General	Music	Album Rock
KOLU	90.1	n/a	Religious	Educational/Music/Talk	n/a
KGTS	91.3	College	Religious	Music/Talk	n/a
KDNA	91.9	n/a	Hispanic	Educational/Talk	n/a
KZHR	92.5	Commercial	General/Hispanic	Music	Latin
KQSN	92.9	n/a	General	Music/News	n/a
KATS	94.5	Commercial	General	Music	Album Rock
KIOK	94.9	Commercial	General	Music	Contemp. Country
KNLT	95.7	Commercial	General	Music	Oldies
KZTB	96.7	Commercial	General/Hispanic	Music	Latin
KXRX	97.1	Commercial	General	Music/News	Modern Rock
KEYW	98.3	Commercial	General	Music/News	Adult Contemp.
KHHK	99.7	n/a	General	Music/News	n/a
KQFM	100.5	Commercial	General	Music/News	Modern Rock
KARY	100.9	Commercial	General	Music/News/Sports/Talk	Oldies
KMNA	101.7	n/a	General	Music	n/a
KORD	102.7	Commercial	General	Music/News	Country
KQBE	103.1	Commercial	General	Music/News	Adult Contemp.
KWHT	103.5	Commercial	General	Music	Country
KXDD	104.1	n/a	General	Music	n/a
KONA	105.3	Commercial	General	Music	Soft Rock
KRSE	105.7	Commercial	General	Music	Soft Rock
KEGX	106.5	Commercial	General	Music/News	Classic Rock
KFFM	107.3	Commercial	General	n/a	n/a
KUMA	107.7	Commercial	General	Music	Adult Contemp.

Note: Stations included cover the Yakima-Pasco-Richland-Kennewick DMA (Designated Market Area); n/a not available
BurrellesLuce, MediaContacts Online, January 2007

CLIMATE

Average and Extreme Temperatures

Temperature	Jan	Feb	Mar	Apr	May	Jun	Jul	Aug	Sep	Oct	Nov	Dec	Yr.
Extreme High (°F)	68	68	80	92	102	105	108	110	100	88	73	67	110
Average High (°F)	37	46	55	64	73	80	87	86	78	64	48	38	63
Average Temp. (°F)	29	36	43	50	58	65	70	69	61	50	38	31	50
Average Low (°F)	20	26	30	35	42	49	53	52	44	35	28	22	36
Extreme Low (°F)	-21	-25	-1	20	25	30	34	35	24	11	-13	-17	-25

Note: Figures cover the years 1948-1995
Source: National Climatic Data Center, International Station Meteorological Climate Summary, 9/96

Average Precipitation/Snowfall/Humidity

Precip./Humidity	Jan	Feb	Mar	Apr	May	Jun	Jul	Aug	Sep	Oct	Nov	Dec	Yr.
Avg. Precip. (in.)	1.3	0.8	0.7	0.5	0.5	0.7	0.2	0.3	0.4	0.5	1.0	1.3	8.2
Avg. Snowfall (in.)	8	4	2	Tr	Tr	0	0	0	0	Tr	2	8	24
Avg. Rel. Hum. 7am (%)	84	83	77	64	56	54	54	61	72	81	85	85	71
Avg. Rel. Hum. 4pm (%)	72	59	41	33	30	30	26	28	32	43	63	75	44

Note: Figures cover the years 1948-1995; Tr = Trace amounts (<0.05 in. of rain; <0.5 in. of snow)
Source: National Climatic Data Center, International Station Meteorological Climate Summary, 9/96

Weather Conditions

Temperature			Daytime Sky			Precipitation		
5°F & below	32°F & below	90°F & above	Clear	Partly cloudy	Cloudy	0.01 inch or more precip.	0.1 inch or more snow/ice	Thunder-storms
7	149	32	102	133	130	70	18	6

Note: Figures are average number of days per year and cover the years 1948-1995
Source: National Climatic Data Center, International Station Meteorological Climate Summary, 9/96

HAZARDOUS WASTE

Superfund Sites

Richland has no sites on the EPA's Superfund Final National Priorities List.
U.S. Environmental Protection Agency, Final National Priorities List, June 23, 2008

AIR & WATER QUALITY

Air Quality Index

Area	Percent of Days when Air Quality was...[2]				AQI Statistics	
	Good	Moderate	Unhealthy for Sensitive Groups	Unhealthy	Maximum	Median
MSA[1]	88.5	11.2	0.3	0.0	119	21

Note: The Air Quality Index (AQI) is an index for reporting daily air quality. EPA calculates the AQI for five major air pollutants regulated by the Clean Air Act: ground-level ozone, particle pollution (also known as particulate matter), carbon monoxide, sulfur dioxide, and nitrogen dioxide. The AQI runs from 0 to 500. The higher the AQI value, the greater the level of air pollution and the greater the health concern. There are six AQI categories: "Good" The AQI is between 0 and 50. Air quality is considered satisfactory; "Moderate" The AQI is between 51 and 100. Air quality is acceptable; "Unhealthy for Sensitive Groups" When AQI values are between 101 and 150, members of sensitive groups may experience health effects; "Unhealthy" When AQI values are between 151 and 200 everyone may begin to experience health effects; "Very Unhealthy" AQI values between 201 and 300 trigger a health alert; "Hazardous" AQI values over 300 trigger health warnings of emergency conditions; (1) Metropolitan Statistical Area - see Appendix A for areas included; (2) Based on 365 days with AQI data in 2007.
Source: U.S. Environmental Protection Agency, Air Quality Index Report, 2007

Air Quality Index Pollutants

Area	Percent of Days when AQI Pollutant was...[2]					
	Carbon Monoxide	Nitrogen Dioxide	Ozone	Sulfur Dioxide	Particulate Matter 2.5	Particulate Matter 10
MSA[1]	0.0	0.0	0.0	0.0	63.3	36.7

Note: The Air Quality Index (AQI) is an index for reporting daily air quality. EPA calculates the AQI for five major air pollutants regulated by the Clean Air Act: ground-level ozone, particle pollution (also known as particulate matter), carbon monoxide, sulfur dioxide, and nitrogen dioxide. The AQI runs from 0 to 500. The higher the AQI value, the greater the level of air pollution and the greater the health concern; (1) Metropolitan Statistical Area - see Appendix A for areas included; (2) Based on 365 days with AQI data in 2007.
Source: U.S. Environmental Protection Agency, Air Quality Index Report, 2007

Air Quality Index Trends

Area	Trend Sites								All Sites
	1999	2000	2001	2002	2003	2004	2005	2006	2006
MSA[1]	n/a	n/a	n/a	n/a	n/a	n/a	n/a	n/a	n/a

Note: An AQI value greater than 100 indicates that air quality would have been in the unhealthful range on that day. Data from exceptional events are not included. These counts are presented in two ways. First, the counts are based on sites having an adequate record of monitoring data during the trend period (trend sites). These counts represent the relative change in the number of days with AQI values greater than 100. In the last column, the counts are based on all sites with data in the most recent year (because it is possible for a site to have data in the most recent year but not enough data to be a trend site); (1) Metropolitan Statistical Area - see Appendix A for areas included; n/a not available.
Source: U.S. Environmental Protection Agency, Office of Air and Radiation, Air Trends, Factbook and Related Information, Air Pollution Trends in Selected Metropolitan Areas 2006

Maximum Air Pollutant Concentrations

	Particulate Matter 10 (ug/m^3)	Particulate Matter 2.5 (ug/m^3)	Ozone (ppm)	Carbon Monoxide (ppm)	Sulfur Dioxide (ppm)	Nitrogen Dioxide (ppm)	Lead (ug/m^3)
MSA[1] Level	85	n/a	n/a	n/a	n/a	n/a	n/a
NAAQS[2]	150	35	0.125	9	0.140	0.053	1.50
Met NAAQS[2]	Yes	Yes	n/a	n/a	n/a	n/a	n/a

Note: Data from exceptional events are not included; (1) Metropolitan Statistical Area - see Appendix A for areas included; (2) National Ambient Air Quality Standards; n/a not available
Concentrations: Particulate Matter 10 (coarse particulate) - highest second maximum 24-hour concentration; Particulate Matter 2.5 (fine particulate) - highest 98th percentile 24-hour concentration; Ozone - highest second daily maximum 1-hour concentration; Carbon Monoxide - highest second maximum non-overlapping 8-hour concentration; Sulfur Dioxide - highest second maximum 24-hour concentration; Nitrogen Dioxide - highest arithmetic mean concentration; Lead - highest quarterly maximum concentration
Units: ppm = parts per million; ug/m^3 = micrograms per cubic meter
Source: U.S. Environmental Protection Agency, MSA Factbook 2006, Air Quality Statistics by City

Drinking Water

Water System Name	Pop. Served	Primary Water Source Type	Violations[1]	
			Health Based	Monitoring/ Reporting
City of Richland	45,070	Surface	0	1

Note: (1) Based on violation data from January 1, 2007 to December 31, 2007 (includes unresolved violations from earlier years)
Source: U.S. Environmental Protection Agency, Office of Ground Water and Drinking Water, Safe Drinking Water Information System (based on data extracted April 15, 2008)

Sammamish, Washington

Background

Sammamish is a young city — incorporated in 1999 — situated in Washington state's famously beautiful Olympic Mountains, with the Seattle skyline to its west, and the Cascade range to its east. Less than ten miles away from the larger city of Bellevue, and twenty miles from Seattle, Sammamish is intent on retaining the best of its small town atmosphere and rural character, embarking on new plans to develop and modernize the city while maintaining its rich natural resources.

Generally recognized as one of the most desirable residential communities in the Puget Sound region, median household income in Sammamish is well above the state average, and more than a fifth of its residents hold either graduate or professional degrees.

The name Sammamish is derived from two Native American words: Samena, which means "hunter," and mish, which means "people," and this area, not surprisingly, was inhabited by Native American hunter-gatherers for centuries prior to the arrival of white settlers. The town was originally named Monohon, after Martin Monohon, who arrived in 1877. Shortly thereafter, the first of several lumber industry firms was established and, by the early 1900s, the town hosted a major shingle company. Economic growth was strong enough to support a school (K - 8), churches, various craft businesses dependent on lumber, such as a boat and canoe company, and a wood-turning shop.

There are a number of homes and artifacts remaining from the earlier era in the town's history, including the Reard/Freed House, considered the best remaining example of a frontier farmhouse in the area. Such sites, and the natural environment, are considered prime resources for the town and are carefully preserved and protected.

The Puget Sound area is widely noted for its natural beauty and recreational opportunities, and the town itself owns and operates nearly forty acres of Puget Sound parkland. Sammamish has embarked on an ambitious twenty-year plan to further enhance its already extensive system of trails, and is particularly interested in establishing new non-motorized trail systems to encourage pedestrian and bicycle alternatives to automobiles.

Medical facilities convenient to Sammamish include three hospitals in nearby Redmond, Bellevue or Kirkland, all less than a half-hour away. Sammamish is about twenty miles away from two major international airports, Boeing Field/King County International, and Seattle-Tacoma International.

Schools in Sammamish are in the highly-rated Issaquah School District. The town is also convenient to many institutions of higher learning, including Bellevue Community College, City University, Renton Technical College, Lake Washington Technical College, Seattle University, the University of Washington at Seattle, and Seattle Community College-Central Campus.

Sammamish is governed by a seven member City Council, including a mayor and deputy-mayor. Day to day administrative details are overseen by a city manager, who is selected by the City Council.

Rankings

General Rankings

- Seattle* was ranked #129 out of 375 metro areas in *Cities Ranked & Rated*. Criteria: cost of living; climate; crime; transportation; economy and jobs; education; arts and culture; health and healthcare; leisure; quality of life. *Cities Ranked & Rated, 2nd Edition, 2007*
- Seattle* was ranked #3 out of 379 metro areas in *Places Rated Almanac*. Criteria: health care; education; recreation; transportation; ambience; climate; crime; housing costs; jobs. *Places Rated Almanac, 7th Edition, 2007*
- Sammamish was selected as one of the "2007 Best Places to Live" by *Money* magazine. The city ranked #11 out of 100. Methodology: Places on the list had to have populations above 7,500 and under 50,000. Retirement-oriented communities, places where income is less than 90% or more than 180% of the state median and towns that were more than 95% white were screened out. Towns with low education scores, high crime rates, declines or sharp increases in population, projected job losses or lack of access to airports or teaching hospitals were eliminated. The remaining places were ranked based on job, income and cost-of-living data; housing affordability; school quality; arts and leisure opportunities; ease of living; health-care access; and racial diversity. Finally, the sense of community, vibrancy of town center, natural surroundings, amenities, real estate and congestion were assessed. *CNNMoney.com, "Best Places to Live 2007"*

Business/Finance Rankings

- The nation's 100 largest metro areas were analysed in terms of the percentage of households entering some stage of foreclosure in 2007. The Seattle* metro area ranked #81 out of 100 (#1 = highest foreclosure rate). *RealtyTrac, "Year-End 2007 Metropolitan Foreclosure Report"*
- The Seattle* metro area was identified as one of the "10 Best Cities for Jobs in 2008" by *Forbes*. The metro area ranked #10. Criteria: state unemployment rate; job growth; income growth; median household income; cost of living. *Forbes.com, "Best Cities for Jobs in 2008," January 10, 2008*
- The Seattle* metro area was identified as one of the "Top 12 Nano Metros" in the U.S. by the Woodrow Wilson International Center for Scholars. The metro area is home to 15 companies, universities, government laboratories and/or organizations working in nanotechnology. *Woodrow Wilson International Center for Scholars, May 17, 2007*
- The Seattle* metro area was selected one of America's "Top 50 Business Opportunity Metros" by *Expansion Management* in their 5th annual Mayor's Challenge ranking of metro areas that have achieved solid ratings across the board in numerous *EM* studies during the past 12 months. The area ranked #10. Criteria: public schools; quality of life; college educated workers; logistics infrastructure; healthcare costs; taxes and government spending; reputation among site consultants. *Expansion Management, August 2007*
- The Seattle* metro area was selected as one of "America's Most Wired Cities" by *Forbes*. The metro area was ranked #2 out of 30. Criteria: percentage of Internet users with high-speed access; the range of service providers within a city; availability of public wireless hot spots. *Forbes, "America's Most Wired Cities," January 10, 2008*
- Seattle* was selected as one of the best places to start and grow a company by *Entrepreneur* and the National Policy Research Council. The Seattle* metro area ranked #31 out of 50 large metro areas. Criteria: business formation and growth (firms started four to 14 years ago that still employ at least 5 people and experienced rapid growth over the last four years). *Entrepreneur/National Policy Research Council, "Hot Cities for Entrepreneurs," September 2006*
- The Seattle* metro area was selected as one of "America's Greediest Cities" by *Forbes*. The area was ranked #3 out of 10. Criteria: number of Forbes 400 (*Forbes* annual list of the richest Americans) members per capita. *Forbes, "America's Greediest Cities," December 7, 2007*

- The Seattle* metro area was selected as one of "America's 50 Hottest Cities" for business relocations and expansions. Criteria: industry's most prominent site selection consultants were asked to list their top city choices for relocating and expanding manufacturing companies, taking into consideration such factors as the business climate, work force quality, operating costs, incentive programs, and the ease of working with local political and economic development officials. *Expansion Management, January-February 2007*

- The Seattle* metro area was selected one of America's "Top 10 Knowledge Worker Metros." The area ranked #10. Criteria: degree holders (bachelors, masters, professional, and Ph.D.) as a percent of the workforce; science and engineering workers as a percent of the workforce; number of patents issued; number and type of colleges in each metro area. *Expansion Management, April 2007*

- Intel, in partnership with Sperling's BestPlaces, ranked the 80 "Best Cities for Teleworking" in America. The Seattle* metro area ranked #10 among extra large metro areas. The study identifies cities that hold the greatest potential for teleworking based on a host of factors including typical commuting times, fuel prices, availability of broadband Internet access and percentage of the population in telework friendly jobs. The study also factored in extreme climate and natural hazards. *Intel, "Best Cities for Teleworking," March 30, 2006*

- The Seattle* metro area appeared on the Milken Institute "2007 Best Performing Cities" index. Rank: #77 out of 200 large metro areas. Criteria: job growth; wage and salary growth; high-tech output growth. *Milken Institute, "2007 Best Performing Cities"*

- The Seattle* metro area was selected as one of the hottest cities for entrepreneurs in America by *Inc. Magazine.* Criteria: job-growth data for 393 metro was analyzed for current-year employment growth, average annual employment growth over past three years, and employment growth by industry sector. The Seattle* metro area ranked #18 among large metro areas and #122 overall. *Inc. Magazine, May 2007*

- The Seattle* metro area was selected as one of "The Top 20 Boom Towns in America." *Business 2.0* magazine and econometric research firm Global Insight compared 319 metropolitan areas in the U.S. and ranked the 61 with populations over 1 million. Criteria: a weighted formula that includes forecast growth rates in sectors that contain the economy's 10 most skilled occupational clusters; the prevalence of college degrees in the local workforce; median salary. The area ranked #9 among large metro areas. *Business 2.0 Magazine, March 2004*

- Seattle* was identified as one of the 100 "Most Unwired Cities" in the U.S. The area ranked #1 out of the 100 largest metro areas in the U.S. Criteria: number of public and commercial wireless access points (hotspots); airports with wireless Internet access; broadband availability; local wireless networks; and wireless email devices. *Intel, "Most Unwired Cities Survey," June 7, 2005*

- Seattle* was ranked #5 out of 125 regions worldwide in terms of its "Knowledge Competitiveness Index." The index attempts to measure the knowledge-based development taking place throughout the world and is based on 19 measures of economic performance that indicate a region's ability to translate its knowledge capacity into economic value. *Robert Huggins Associates, World Knowledge Competitiveness Index 2005*

- *Forbes* ranked the 200 most populous metro areas in the U.S. in terms of the "Best Places for Business and Careers." The Seattle* metro area was ranked #20. Criteria: business costs (labor, energy, tax and office space expenses); living costs (housing, transportation, food and other household expenditures); education levels of the work force; job growth; income growth; migration trends; crime rates; and culture/leisure. *Forbes, "Best Places for Business and Careers," March 19, 2008*

- *Fortune* ranked the 100 largest metro areas in the U.S. in terms of projected median home price change in 2007. The Seattle* metro area ranked #37. *Fortune.com, "Hot Spots, Cold Spots"*

Health/Environment Rankings

- The Seattle* metro area was selected as one of "America's Cleanest Cities" by *Forbes*. The metro area ranked #2 out of 10. Criteria: air quality; water quality; per capita spending on Superfund site cleanup and solid-waste management. *Forbes.com, "America's Cleanest Cities," March 11, 2008*

- 100 of the largest metro areas in the U.S. were analyzed in terms of their current drought severity. The Seattle* metro area ranked #66 (#1 = driest). The rankings were based on statistics such as long-term precipitation trends and patterns and the Palmer drought indices. *Sperling's BestPlaces, www.BestPlaces.net, "America's Drought-Riskiest Cities," November 2007*

- Tahitian Noni International Hiro^{TM}, in partnership with Sperling's BestPlaces, ranked the nation's 50 largest metro areas in terms of the "Most Energetic Cities." The Seattle* metro area ranked #7. Criteria: percentage of population that walk or bicycle to work; BMI score; number of food co-ops; number of farmers markets. *Tahitian Noni International Hiro^{TM}, "Most Energetic Cities," March 13, 2007*

- Scarborough Research, a leading market research firm, identified the top local markets for organic consumers. The Seattle* DMA (Designated Market Area) ranked in the top 15 with 32% of adults reporting that they used any organic food product in their household during the past month. *Scarborough Research, October 10, 2007*

- *Reader's Digest* ranked the 50 largest metro areas in the U.S. in terms of how "clean" they are. The Seattle* metro area ranked #27. Criteria: air quality; water quality; toxic industrial pollution; Superfund sites; and sanitation. *Reader's Digest, "The 50 Cleanest (and Dirtiest) Cities in America," July 2005*

- The American Academy of Dermatology ranked 32 U.S. metropolitan regions in terms of their residents knowledge, attitude and behaviors towards tanning and sun protection. The Seattle* metro area ranked #29. The results of the study are based on an online national survey of 3,342 respondents. *American Academy of Dermatology, "RAYS: Your Grade," May 7, 2007*

- *Business Week* identified the 15 metro areas that saw the steepest declines in ground-level ozone pollution between 1990 and 2005. The Seattle* metro area ranked #2. *Business Week, "America's Most Cleaned-Up Metro Areas," March 23, 2007*

- The Seattle* metro area appeared in *Country Home's* "2008 Best Green Places" report. The area ranked #13 out of 379. Criteria: official energy policies; green power; green buildings; availability of fresh, locally grown food. *Country Home, "2008 Best Green Places"*

- Wyeth Consumer Healthcare, in partnership with Sperling's BestPlaces, ranked the nation's 50 most populous metro areas in terms of five key health factors. The Seattle* metro area ranked #4. Criteria: physical activity; health status; nutrition; lifestyle pursuits; and mental wellness. *Wyeth Consumer Healthcare, "Centrum Healthiest Cities Study," April 19, 2005*

- HealthGrades surveyed over 41,000 individuals on doctor satisfaction and ranked the 20 largest metro areas based on the highest "definitely yes" responses to the question "Do you trust the physician to make decisions/recommendations that are in your best interest?" The Seattle* metro area ranked #9. *HealthGrades.com, "Top Cities in Doctor-Trust," September 7, 2006*

- Seattle* was identified as a "2008 Asthma Capital." The area ranked #92 out of the nation's 100 largest metropolitan areas. Twelve factors were used to identify the most challenging places to live for people with asthma: estimated prevalence; self-reported prevalence; crude death rate for asthma; annual pollen score; annual air quality; public smoking laws; number of board-certified asthma specialists; school inhaler access laws; rescue medication use; controller medication use; uninsured rate; poverty rate. *Asthma and Allergy Foundation of America, "2008 Asthma Capitals"*

- Seattle* was identified as a "Spring Allergy Capital." The area ranked #96 out of 100. Three groups of factors were used to identify the most severe cities for people with allergies during the spring season: annual pollen levels; medicine utilization; access to board-certified allergists. *Asthma and Allergy Foundation of America, "2007 Spring Allergy Capital Rankings"*

- Seattle* was identified as a "Fall Allergy Capital." The area ranked #100 out of 100. Three groups of factors were used to identify the most severe cities for people with allergies during the fall season: annual pollen levels; medicine utilization; access to board-certified allergists. *Asthma and Allergy Foundation of America, "2007 Fall Allergy Capital Rankings"*

- Ortho-McNeil Neurologics, in partnership with Sperling's BestPlaces, analyzed 110 metro areas and identified those U.S. cities with the highest prevalence of factors that are most commonly associated with migraine headaches. The Seattle* metro area ranked #59. Criteria: number of migraine-related drug prescriptions per capita; lifestyle factors that can contribute to migraines; environmental factors that can trigger migraines; and consumption of migraine-triggering foods. *Ortho-McNeil Neurologics, "America's Migraine Hot Spots," March 14, 2006*

- Sperling's BestPlaces ranked 331 metro areas and identified the most and least stressful U.S. cities. The Seattle* metro area ranked #11 out of the 100 largest metro areas (#1 = most stressful). Criteria: divorce rate; unemployment rate; violent and property crime; suicide rate; commute time; mental health; alcohol consumption; cloudy days. *Sperling's BestPlaces, www.BestPlaces.net, "America's Most (and Least) Stressful Cities," January 9, 2004*

- An analysis of the "Best & Worst Cities for Sleep" was conducted by Sperling's BestPlaces. The study ranked America's 50 most populated metro areas. The Seattle* metro area ranked #44 (#1 = best city for sleep). Criteria: number of days residents didn't get enough rest or sleep during the past month; average length of daily commute; divorce rate; unemployment rate. *Sperling's BestPlaces, www.BestPlaces.net, "Best & Worst Cities for Sleep," 2006*

- Sperling's BestPlaces in partnership with Vistakon ranked the 100 largest metro areas and identified "America's 10 Best Cities for Comfortable Eyes." The Seattle* metro area ranked #10. Criteria: altitude; sunny days; wind; extreme temperatures; humidity; pollution; commute time; computer use. *Vistakon, "America's Best and Worst Cities for Comfortable Eyes," June 15, 2004*

- HealthGrades evaluated the performance of America's 25 most populous metropolitan areas by measuring the outcomes of five of the highest volume and most widely studied procedures and diagnoses: coronary artery bypass graft surgery; percutaneus coronary interventions; acute myocardial infarction/heart attack in angioplasty-capable hospitals; congestive heart failure; and community acquired pneumonia. The Seattle* metro area ranked #24. *HealthGrades, "HealthGrades Hospital Quality in America Study," October 12, 2004*

- Seattle* was selected as one of "America's Top 10 Low-Carb Cities" by *LowCarbiz Magazine*. Criteria: abundance of low-carb products; restaurants with low-carb menu items; health practitioners supportive of carb-cutting regimens; local culture generally conducive to exercise and health. *LowCarbiz Magazine, April 2004*

- Seattle* was selected as one of "America's Pet Healthiest Cities" by Purina. The city ranked #11 out of 50. Criteria: veterinary services; environment; legislation; preventative care; obesity/body condition. *Purina Pet Institute, "America's Pet Healthiest Cities," May 20, 2003*

Women/Minorities Rankings

- Seattle* was ranked #14 out of 100 metro areas in *SELF Magazine's* ranking of "America's Best Places for Women." A panel of experts came up with more than 50 criteria including death and disease rates, environmental indicators, community resources, and lifestyle habits. *SELF Magazine, "America's Best Places for Women 2007," December 2007*

- Seattle* appeared on a list of the top 10 metro areas with the highest concentration of same-sex households. The area ranked #3. *Urban Institute Press, The Gay and Lesbian Atlas, May 2004*

- Seattle* appeared on a list of the top 10 metro areas with the highest concentration of gay male couples. The area ranked #4. *Urban Institute Press, The Gay and Lesbian Atlas, May 2004*

- Seattle* appeared on a list of the top 10 metro areas with the highest concentration of African-American same-sex couples among all African-American households. The area ranked #6. *Urban Institute Press, The Gay and Lesbian Atlas, May 2004*

- Seattle* appeared on a list of the top 10 metro areas with the highest concentration of Hispanic same-sex couples among all Hispanic households. The area ranked #5. *Urban Institute Press, The Gay and Lesbian Atlas, May 2004*

Seniors/Retirement Rankings

- Sperling's BestPlaces in partnership with Bankers Life & Casualty Company designed a survey to identify the top 50 metro areas in the U.S. that offer the best overall qualities for senior living. The Seattle* metro area ranked #2. The following criteria were statistically weighted to reflect the needs of the senior population: health; disease; economics; social; environment; spiritual; transportation; housing; and crime. *Bankers Life & Casualty Company, "Best Cities for Seniors 2005"*

- A.G. Edwards ranked America's 500 top-performing communities based on their residents' personal savings and investing behavior. The Seattle* metro area ranked #69 with an index score of 107.96 (national average = 100.00). A dozen statistical factors were measured including: participation in retirement savings plans; personal debt levels; and home ownership. *A.G. Edwards, "2007 Nest Egg Index", September 12, 2007*

Children/Family Rankings

- The Seattle* metro area was selected as one of the "Best Cities for Relocating Families" by Worldwide ERC and Primacy Relocation. The 2007 study placed a special emphasis on the housing market, which has significantly impacted the relocation industry and an employer's ability to transfer employees. The variables which weigh heavily in this category include home price, home affordability index, appreciation rates, and property tax. Other criteria include cost of living, crime rates, education, climate, focus on diversity, physicians per capita, recreation and leisure, arts and culture, air quality, watershed quality, sales tax, unemployment rate, job growth, high school and higher education index, school expenditures per student, students in public school, SAT/ACT percentile, and population growth. *Worldwide ERC and Primacy Relocation, "2007 Best Cities for Relocating Families"*

Safety Rankings

- The National Insurance Crime Bureau ranked 361 metro areas in the U.S. in terms of per capita rates of vehicle theft. The Seattle* metro area ranked #16 (#1 = highest rate). Criteria: number of vehicle theft offenses per 100,000 inhabitants. *National Insurance Crime Bureau, "NICB Vehicle Theft Study," April 22, 2008*

- Seattle* appeared on Sperling's BestPlaces list of the "Riskiest Cities for Identity Theft." The area ranked #2 out of the nations 50 largest metro areas. Over 80 criteria were analyzed across four major categories: technology impact; crime; transactions; and risk profile. *Sperling's BestPlaces, www.BestPlaces.net, "Riskiest Cities for Identity Theft," July 2006*

- Farmers Insurance Group of Companies, in partnership with Sperling's BestPlaces, ranked 379 metro areas and identified the "Most Secure U.S. Place to Live." The Seattle* metro area ranked #17 out of 114 in the large metro area category (500,000 or more residents). Criteria: crime rates; extreme weather; risk of natural disasters; environmental hazards; terrorism threats; air quality; life expectancy; job loss numbers. *Farmers Insurance Group, "Most Secure U.S. Places to Live 2007"*

- Seattle* was identified as one of the most dangerous large metro areas for pedestrians in the U.S. The area ranked #40 out of the nations 50 largest metro areas. Criteria: average yearly pedestrian fatalities per capita (for the years 2002 and 2003) adjusted for the number of walkers. *Surface Transportation Policy Project, "Mean Streets 2004"*

Sports/Recreation Rankings

- The Seattle* metro area appeared on the *Sporting News* list of the "Best Sports Cities 2007". The area ranked #28 out of 150 cities in the U.S. *Sporting News* takes a 12-month snapshot, roughly July to July, of each city's sports, putting a heavy premium on regular-season won-lost records (from the most recently completed season). Other criteria include: playoff berths, bowl appearances and tournament bids; championships; applicable power ratings; quality of competition; overall fan fervor as measured in part by attendance as percentage of venue capacity; abundance of teams (rewarding quality over quantity); stadium and arena quality; ticket availability and prices; franchise ownership; and marquee appeal of athletes. *SportingNews.com, "Best Sports Cities 2007," August 1, 2007*
- The Seattle* metro area was selected by *Cranium* as one of the "Top 50 Fun Cities" in America. The area ranked #10. Criteria includes: number of sports teams, restaurants, and dance performances; number of toy stores; city budget spent on recreation. *Cranium, November 4, 2003*
- *Golf Digest* ranked 330 metro areas in the U.S. in terms of golf. The Seattle* metro area was ranked #315. Criteria: access to golf; weather; value of golf; and quality of golf. *Golf Digest, "Metro Golf Rankings," August 2005*

Dating/Romance Rankings

- Eli Lily and Company, in partnership with Sperling's BestPlaces, ranked the nation's 50 largest metro areas in terms of the "Most Romantic Cities for Baby Boomers." The Seattle* metro area ranked #30. Criteria: marriage and divorce rates among "baby boomers" age 45 to 60; great restaurants; dance studios; chocolate, jewelry and flower sales. *Eli Lily and Company, "Most Romantic Cities for Baby Boomers," April 20, 2007*
- The Seattle* metro area was selected as one of the "Best Cities for Relocating Singles" by Worldwide ERC and Primacy Relocation. The area ranked #9 out of the 100 largest metro areas in the U.S. Areas were selected based on the following criteria: a robust cost-of-living index; adventure and outdoor recreation opportunities; violent crime and property crime rates; percentage of the population that is unmarried (ages 25-34); ratio of single men and single women; affordability of quality higher education, including in-state and out-of-state tuition requirements and rates; number of newcomers to the area; commute times; tax rates; fee and occupancy rates for temporary housing and mini-storage; quality and quantity of collegiate and professional sporting events and fun, fan-friendly venues. *Worldwide ERC and Primacy Relocation, "2007 Best Cities for Relocating Singles," October 25, 2007*
- *Forbes* ranked the 40 most populous urbanized areas in the U.S. in terms of the "Best Cities for Singles." The Seattle* metro area ranked #8. Criteria: number of singles; cost of living alone; nightlife; culture; job growth; coolness; and online dating. *Forbes.com, August 21, 2007*
- Sperling's BestPlaces in partnership with AXE Deodorant Bodyspray ranked 80 metro areas and identified "America's Best (and Worst) Cities for Dating." The Seattle* metro area ranked #5 (#1 = best). Criteria: percentage of singles ages 18-24; population density; dating venues per capita. *AXE Deodorant Bodyspray, "America's Best (and Worst) Cities for Dating," May 2004*

Culture/Performing Arts Rankings

- Scarborough Research, a leading market research firm, identified the top local markets for rock concert attendance. The Seattle* DMA (Designated Market Area) ranked in the top 25 with 14% of consumers, 18 years old and over, reporting that they have attended a rock concert during the past year. *Scarborough Research, June 14, 2004*

Miscellaneous Rankings

- Scarborough Research, a leading market research firm, identified the top local markets for bloggers. The Seattle* DMA (Designated Market Area) ranked in the top 13 with 13% of adults reporting that they had read or contributed to a blog within the past 30 days. *Scarborough Research, October 24, 2007*

- Avis Rent-A-Car and Motorola, in partnership with Sperling's BestPlaces, ranked the nation's 75 most populous metro areas in terms of how difficult they are to navigate. The Seattle* metro area ranked #8 with #1 being the most challenging. Criteria: street layouts; overall design and layout; travel time index; percent of congested freeway and street lane miles; bodies of water; complexity of directions needed to travel from major airports to city center; annual delay per person; days of snow exceeding 1.5 inches; and days of rain exceeding 0.5 inch. *Avis Rent-A-Car and Motorola, "America's Most Challenging Cities to Navigate," August 3, 2004*

- The Seattle* metro area appeared on *Forbes* list of "America's Drunkest Cities". The area ranked #12. Criteria: 35 of the largest continental U.S. metro areas were chosen based on availability of data and geographic diversity. Each metro was ranked in five areas: state laws; drinkers; heavy drinkers; binge drinkers; and alcoholism. *Forbes.com, "America's Drunkest Cities," August 22, 2006*

- Sperling's BestPlaces in partnership with Pep Boys ranked 77 metro areas and identified "America's Most Drivable Cities." The Seattle* metro area ranked #69. Criteria: climate; road roughness; urban mobility; gas prices. *Pep Boys, "America's Most Drivable Cities," April 9, 2003*

- State Farm Insurance, in partnership with Sperling's BestPlaces, analyzed several key factors that contribute to overall family preparedness. The Seattle* metro area ranked #8 out of the nation's 50 most populous metro areas. Criteria: quality of life; life insurance coverage; and investments. *State Farm Life Insurance, "Fiscally Fit Cities Report," July 20, 2004*

- Scarborough Research, a leading market research firm, identified the top local markets for coffee bar patronage. The Seattle* DMA (Designated Market Area) ranked in the top 10 with 23% of adults reporting that they have used any coffee house/bar during the past 30 days. *Scarborough Research, October 14, 2004*

- A study by Sperling's BestPlaces examined which U.S. metro areas were most affected by high fuel prices in 2006. The Seattle* metro area was ranked #26 out of 80 (#1 = most expensive city for driving). Rankings are based on the average dollars spent on gas per year by two driver households. Criteria: cost of regular-grade gasoline; average miles driven per day; average number of gallons each driver uses and wastes in traffic congestion each day. *Sperling's BestPlaces, www.bestplaces.net, "Pain at the Pump," May 18, 2006*

Sammamish is located within the Seattle-Tacoma-Bellevue, WA Metropolitan Statistical Area.

Business Environment

CITY FINANCES

City Government Finances

Component	2004-2005 ($000)	2004-2005 ($ per capita)
Total Revenues	33,137	964
Total Expenditures	23,723	690
Debt Outstanding	12,135	353
Cash and Securities	55,370	1,611

Source: U.S Census Bureau, Government Finances 2004-2005

City Government Revenue by Source

Source	2004-2005 ($000)	2004-2005 ($ per capita)
General Revenue		
From Federal Government	277	8
From State Government	2,025	59
From Local Governments	214	6
Taxes		
Property	15,498	451
Sales	3,315	96
Personal Income	0	0
License	1,584	46
Charges	3,252	95
Liquor Store	0	0
Utility	0	0
Employee Retirement	0	0
Other	6,972	203

Source: U.S Census Bureau, Government Finances 2004-2005

City Government Expenditures by Function

Function	2004-2005 ($000)	2004-2005 ($ per capita)	2004-2005 (%)
General Expenditures			
Airports	0	0	0.0
Corrections	0	0	0.0
Education	0	0	0.0
Fire Protection	4,895	142	20.6
Governmental Administration	3,370	98	14.2
Health	0	0	0.0
Highways	6,223	181	26.2
Hospitals	0	0	0.0
Housing and Community Development	985	29	4.2
Interest on General Debt	514	15	2.2
Libraries	0	0	0.0
Parking	0	0	0.0
Parks and Recreation	2,991	87	12.6
Police Protection	3,329	97	14.0
Public Welfare	0	0	0.0
Sewerage	733	21	3.1
Solid Waste Management	0	0	0.0
Liquor Store	0	0	0.0
Utility	0	0	0.0
Employee Retirement	0	0	0.0
Other	683	20	2.9

Source: U.S Census Bureau, Government Finances 2004-2005

Municipal Bond Ratings

Area	Moody's
City	n/a

Source: Mergent Bond Record, January 2008 (unless noted otherwise)

DEMOGRAPHICS

Population Growth

Area	1990 Census	2000 Census	2007 Estimate	2012 Projection	Population Growth (%) 1990-2000	Population Growth (%) 2000-2012
City	23,254	34,104	35,507	36,662	46.7	7.5
MSA[1]	2,559,164	3,043,878	3,270,362	3,439,521	18.9	13.0
U.S.	248,709,873	281,421,906	301,045,522	314,920,978	13.2	11.9

Note: (1) Metropolitan Statistical Area - see Appendix B for areas included
Source: Claritas, Inc.

Number of Households and Average Household Size

Area	2007 Estimate	2007 Average Household Size
City	11,620	3.06
MSA[1]	1,302,483	2.51
U.S.	113,668,003	2.65

Note: (1) Metropolitan Statistical Area - see Appendix B for areas included
Source: Claritas, Inc.

Race and Ethnicity

Area	White Alone[2]	Black Alone[2]	Asian Alone[2]	Other Race Alone[2]	Hispanic[3]
City	83.1	1.1	11.6	4.2	3.0
MSA[1]	75.0	5.2	10.1	9.6	6.9
U.S.	73.1	12.4	4.3	10.3	14.9

Note: Figures are 2007 estimates; (1) Metropolitan Statistical Area - see Appendix B for areas included (2) Alone is defined as not being in combination with one or more other races; (3) May be of any race.
Source: Claritas, Inc.

Ancestry

Area	German	Irish[2]	English	American	Italian	Polish	French[3]	Scottish
City	22.5	13.1	17.5	4.1	5.0	2.6	3.9	4.1
MSA[1]	17.6	11.5	12.3	4.3	3.6	2.0	3.6	3.3
U.S.	15.2	10.9	8.7	7.3	5.6	3.2	3.0	1.7

Note: Figures include multiple ancestry (e.g. if a person reported being Irish and Italian, they were included in both columns); (1) Metropolitan Statistical Area - see Appendix A for areas included; (2) Includes Celtic; (3) Includes Alsatian but excludes Basque
Source: Census 2000, Summary File 3

Foreign-Born Population

Area	Percent of Population Born in: Any Foreign Country	Europe	Asia	Africa	Oceania[2]	Canada	Mexico	Latin America[3]
City	9.9	1.9	5.3	0.3	0.2	1.8	0.1	0.3
MSA[1]	13.8	2.8	6.9	0.7	0.2	1.0	1.5	0.6
U.S.	11.1	1.7	2.9	0.3	0.1	0.3	3.3	2.5

Note: (1) Metropolitan Statistical Area - see Appendix A for areas included; (2) Includes Australia, New Zealand subregion, Melanesia, Micronesia, Polynesia, and Oceania n.e.c; (3) Includes Central America (excluding Mexico), South America, and the Caribbean.
Source: Census 2000, Summary File 3

Marriage Status

Area	Never Married	Now Married (excluding Separated)	Separated	Widowed	Divorced
City	18.4	74.2	0.8	1.5	5.2
MSA[1]	29.2	53.2	1.5	4.8	11.3
U.S.	27.1	54.4	2.2	6.6	9.7

Note: Figures are percentages and cover the population 15 years of age and older; (1) Metropolitan Statistical Area - see Appendix A for areas included
Source: Census 2000, Summary File 3

Age Distribution

Area	Percent of Population						
	Under Age 5	Age 5 to 17	Age 18 to 34	Age 35 to 49	Age 50 to 64	Age 65 to 79	80 Years and Over
City	7.8	25.3	15.8	33.3	14.2	3.2	0.4
MSA[1]	6.3	17.4	25.2	26.1	14.7	7.4	2.9
U.S.	6.8	18.9	23.7	23.5	14.8	9.2	3.2

Note: (1) Metropolitan Statistical Area - see Appendix A for areas included
Source: Census 2000, Summary File 3

Male/Female Ratio

Area	Males	Females	Males per 100 Females
City	17,856	17,651	101.2
MSA[1]	1,633,417	1,636,945	99.8
U.S.	148,320,305	152,725,217	97.1

Note: Figures are 2007 estimates; (1) Metropolitan Statistical Area - see Appendix B for areas included
Source: Claritas, Inc.

Religion

Area	Catholic	Southern Baptist	United Meth-odist	ELCA[1]	LDS[2]	Presby-terian Church USA	Jewish Est.	Muslim Est.
County	16.2	0.7	1.1	2.0	2.3	1.6	1.9	0.5
U.S.	22.0	7.1	3.7	1.8	1.5	1.1	2.2	0.6

Note: Figures are the number of adherents as a percentage of the total population; Adherents are defined as all members, including full members, their children and the estimated number of other participants who are not considered members (e.g. the baptized, those not confirmed, those regularly attending services, etc.); (1) Evangelical Lutheran Church in America; (2) The Church of Jesus Christ of Latter Day Saints
Source: Reprinted with permission from Religious Congregations and Membership in the United States 2000 (Nashville, Glenmary Research Center, 2002) Copyright Association of Statisticians of American Religious Bodies. All rights reserved.

ECONOMY

Gross Metropolitan Product

Area	2002	2003	2004	2005	2005 Rank[2]
MSA[1]	138.9	142.3	149.0	158.0	13

Note: Figures are in billions of dollars; (1) Seattle-Tacoma-Bellevue, WA Metropolitan Statistical Area - see Appendix A for areas included; (2) Rank ranges from 1 to 361
Source: The U.S. Conference of Mayors, "U.S. Metro Economies: GMP - The Engines of America's Growth," January 2007

Economic Growth

Area	1995 GMP	2005 GMP	Average Annual Growth Rate	Growth Rate Rank[2]
MSA[1]	90.9	158.0	5.7	144

Note: Figures are in billions of dollars; GMP = Gross Metropolitan Product; (1) Seattle-Tacoma-Bellevue, WA Metropolitan Statistical Area - see Appendix A for areas included; (2) Rank ranges from 1 to 361
Source: The U.S. Conference of Mayors, "U.S. Metro Economies: GMP - The Engines of America's Growth," January 2007

INCOME

Per Capita/Median/Average Income

Area	Per Capita ($)	Median Household ($)	Average Household ($)
City	49,345	121,154	150,782
MSA[1]	30,164	58,271	74,853
U.S.	25,495	49,280	66,670

Note: Figures are 2007 estimates; (1) Metropolitan Statistical Area - see Appendix B for areas included
Source: Claritas, Inc.

Household Income Distribution

Area	Percent of Households Earning							
	Under $15,000	$15,000 -24,999	$25,000 -34,999	$35,000 -49,999	$50,000 -74,999	$75,000 -99,000	$100,000 -149,999	$150,000 and up
City	1.9	1.6	2.5	5.8	11.5	14.2	27.8	34.8
MSA[1]	9.2	8.3	9.8	15.2	21.0	14.5	14.1	7.8
U.S.	13.1	10.9	11.2	15.6	19.5	11.9	11.3	6.6

Note: Figures are 2007 estimates; (1) Metropolitan Statistical Area - see Appendix B for areas included
Source: Claritas, Inc.

Poverty Rates by Age

Area	All Ages	Under 5 Years Old	5 to 17 Years Old	18 to 64 Years Old	65 Years and Over
City	2.0	0.2	0.5	1.2	0.1
MSA[1]	7.9	0.6	1.6	5.0	0.7
U.S.	12.4	1.2	3.0	6.9	1.2

Note: Figures are percent of population with income in 1999 below poverty level and only include population for whom poverty status is determined; (1) Metropolitan Statistical Area - see Appendix A for areas included
Source: Census 2000, Summary File 3

Personal Bankruptcy Filing Rate

Area	2004	2005	2006
King County	4.69	6.11	1.37
U.S.	5.31	6.82	2.00

Note: Numbers are per 1,000 population and include Chapter 7 and Chapter 13 filings
Source: Federal Deposit Insurance Corporation (FDIC), Regional Economic Conditions (RECON), 8/23/2007

EMPLOYMENT

Labor Force and Employment

Area	Civilian Labor Force			Workers Employed		
	Dec. 2006	Dec. 2007	% Chg.	Dec. 2006	Dec. 2007	% Chg.
City	19,320	19,816	2.6	18,744	19,266	2.8
MD[1]	1,422,350	1,458,732	2.6	1,366,226	1,404,277	2.8
U.S.	152,571,000	153,705,000	0.7	146,081,000	146,334,000	0.2

Note: Data is not seasonally adjusted and covers workers 16 years of age and older;
(1) Metropolitan Division - see Appendix B for areas included
Source: Bureau of Labor Statistics, http://stats.bls.gov

Unemployment Rate

Area	2007											
	Jan.	Feb.	Mar.	Apr.	May	Jun.	Jul.	Aug.	Sep.	Oct.	Nov.	Dec.
City	3.1	3.3	3.2	2.6	2.9	3.2	3.0	2.7	3.0	3.0	3.0	2.8
MD[1]	4.2	4.3	4.0	3.4	3.7	3.8	3.5	3.4	3.8	3.7	3.7	3.7
U.S.	5.0	4.9	4.5	4.3	4.3	4.7	4.9	4.6	4.5	4.4	4.5	4.8

Note: Data is not seasonally adjusted and covers workers 16 years of age and older; All figures are percentages; (1) Metropolitan Division - see Appendix B for areas included
Source: Bureau of Labor Statistics, http://stats.bls.gov

Employment by Occupation

Occupation Classification	City (%)	MSA[1] (%)	U.S. (%)
Sales and Office	24.9	26.4	26.7
Professional and Related	30.9	24.3	20.2
Service	6.6	13.1	14.9
Production, Transportation, and Material Moving	5.2	10.9	14.6
Management, Business, and Financial	28.0	16.6	13.5
Construction, Extraction, and Maintenance	4.1	8.3	9.4
Farming, Forestry, and Fishing	0.3	0.3	0.7

Note: Figures cover employed civilians 16 years of age and older;
(1) Metropolitan Statistical Area - see Appendix A for areas included
Source: Census 2000, Summary File 3

Employment by Industry

Sector	MSA[1] Number of Employees	MSA[1] Percent of Total	U.S. Percent of Total
Government	202,300	13.7	16.3
Education and Health Services	153,800	10.4	13.4
Professional and Business Services	216,800	14.7	13.1
Retail Trade	153,000	10.3	11.6
Manufacturing	170,000	11.5	9.9
Leisure and Hospitality	137,000	9.3	9.6
Financial Activities	89,400	6.0	5.9
Construction	98,600	6.7	5.3
Wholesale Trade	72,700	4.9	4.4
Other Services	49,300	3.3	3.9
Transportation and Utilities	53,200	3.6	3.7
Information	82,000	5.5	2.2
Natural Resources and Mining	1,100	0.1	0.5

Note: Figures cover non-farm employment as of December 2007 and are not seasonally adjusted; (1) Metropolitan Statistical Area - see Appendix B for areas included
Source: Bureau of Labor Statistics, http://stats.bls.gov

Average Wages

Occupation	$/Hr.	Occupation	$/Hr.
Accountants and Auditors	31.35	Maids and Housekeeping Cleaners	11.18
Automotive Mechanics	21.38	Maintenance and Repair Workers	19.22
Bookkeepers	17.84	Marketing Managers	61.63
Carpenters	24.42	Nuclear Medicine Technologists	37.17
Cashiers	12.05	Nurses, Licensed Practical	22.15
Clerks, General Office	14.59	Nurses, Registered	34.79
Clerks, Receptionists/Information	13.02	Nursing Aides/Orderlies/Attendants	13.26
Clerks, Shipping/Receiving	16.08	Packers and Packagers, Hand	10.80
Computer Programmers	41.77	Physical Therapists	33.99
Computer Support Specialists	24.97	Postal Service Mail Carriers	21.09
Computer Systems Analysts	38.87	Real Estate Brokers	47.61
Cooks, Restaurant	11.86	Retail Salespersons	14.03
Dentists	n/a	Sales Reps., Exc. Tech./Scientific	29.85
Electrical Engineers	38.33	Sales Reps., Tech./Scientific	38.80
Electricians	26.80	Secretaries, Exc. Legal/Med./Exec.	17.07
Financial Managers	55.55	Security Guards	14.57
First-Line Supervisors/Mgrs., Sales	24.17	Surgeons	96.01
Food Preparation Workers	11.38	Teacher Assistants	14.10
General and Operations Managers	66.79	Teachers, Elementary School	25.20
Hairdressers/Cosmetologists	15.06	Teachers, Secondary School	26.80
Internists	76.35	Telemarketers	13.54
Janitors and Cleaners	12.93	Truck Drivers, Heavy/Tractor-Trailer	19.80
Landscaping/Groundskeeping Workers	13.94	Truck Drivers, Light/Delivery Svcs.	14.65
Lawyers	n/a	Waiters and Waitresses	13.39

Note: Wage data covers the Seattle-Bellevue-Everett, WA Metropolitan Division - see Appendix B for areas included. Hourly wages for elementary/secondary school teachers and teacher assistants were calculated by the editors from annual wage data assuming a 40 hour work week; n/a not available.
Source: Bureau of Labor Statistics, May 2007 Metro Area Occupational Employment and Wage Estimates

RESIDENTIAL REAL ESTATE

Building Permits

Area	Single-Family			Multi-Family			Total		
	2006	2007p	Pct. Chg.	2006	2007p	Pct. Chg.	2006	2007p	Pct. Chg.
City	0	0	-	0	0	-	0	0	-
U.S.	1,378,200	973,300	-29.4	460,700	407,200	-11.6	1,838,900	1,380,500	-24.9

Note: (p) preliminary; figures cover and represent new, privately-owned housing units authorized (unadjusted data); All permit data are based on estimates with imputation; U.S. figures are based on the new 20,000-place series.
Source: U.S. Census Bureau, Manufacturing, Mining, and Construction Statistics

Homeownership and Housing Vacancies

Area	Homeownership Rate[2] (%)			Rental Vacancy Rate[3] (%)			Homeowner Vacancy Rate[4] (%)		
	2005	2006	2007	2005	2006	2007	2005	2006	2007
MSA[1]	64.5	63.7	62.8	6.9	5.6	4.9	1.0	0.9	1.8
U.S.	68.9	68.8	68.1	9.8	9.8	9.7	1.9	2.4	2.7

Note: (1) Metropolitan Statistical Area - see Appendix B for areas included; (2) The proportion of households that are owners; (3) The proportion of the rental inventory that is vacant for rent; (4) The proportion of the homeowner inventory that is vacant for sale; n/a not available
Source: U.S. Census Bureau, Housing Vacancies and Homeownership Annual Statistics: 2007

TAXES

State Corporate Income Tax Rates

State	Rates and Tax Brackets
Washington	Rate Varies

Note: Tax rates as of January 1, 2008; Washington has no income tax but has a gross receipts tax called the Business & Occupation (B&O) Tax which is levied at various rates. The major rates are 0.471% for retail sales, 0.484% for wholesale and manufacturing, and 1.5% for service and other activities.
Source: Tax Foundation, www.taxfoundation.org

State Individual Income Tax Rates

State	Federal Deductibility	Marginal Rates (%)	Standard Deduction ($)		Personal Exemptions ($)[1]	
			Single	Joint	Single	Dependents
Washington	No	None	n/a	n/a	n/a	n/a

Note: Tax rates as of January 1, 2008; Local- and county-level taxes are not included; n/a not applicable; (1) Married joint filers generally receive double the single exemption
Source: Tax Foundation, www.taxfoundation.org

Various State and Local Tax Rates

State and Local Sales and Use (%)	State Sales and Use (%)	Gasoline[1,2] ($/gal.)	Cigarette ($/pack)	Spirits ($/gal.)	Table Wine ($/gal.)	Beer ($/gal.)
9.0	6.5 (j)	0.36	2.025	19.43 (n)	0.87	0.26

Note: Tax rates as of January 1, 2008; (1) In addition to the 18.4 cpg Federal gasoline tax; (2) Rates may include additional state sales taxes, environmental protection and storage fees/taxes, and local taxes. When necessary, the volume-weighted average of all local taxes is used to approximate the typical statewide rate including local tax; (j) Washington has a GRT in addition to its 6.5% sales tax. It is called the business and occupation tax and is levied at various rates. The major rates are 0.471% for retail sales, 0.484% for wholesale and manufacturing, and 1.5% for service and other

ctivities; (n) The state government controls all sales. The implied excise tax rate is calculated using methodology designed by the Distilled Spirits Council of the United States (DISCUS).
Source: Tax Foundation, www.taxfoundation.org; Original research

State Tax Burdens

Area	Combined State and Local Tax Burden		Combined Federal, State and Local Tax Burden	
	Percent	Rank	Percent	Rank
Washington	11.1	16	34.0	9
U.S. Average	11.0	-	32.7	-

Note: Figures cover 2007 and measure taxes as a percentage of income
Source: Tax Foundation, www.taxfoundation.org

State Business Tax Climate Index Rankings

State	Overall Rank	Corporate Tax Index Rank	Individual Income Tax Index Rank	Sales Tax Index Rank	Unemployment Insurance Tax Index Rank	Property Tax Index Rank
Washington	11	31	1	50	36	28

Note: Rankings range from 1 to 50 where 1 is best. Rankings do not average across to Overall Rank. States without a given tax are given a ranking of 1.
Source: Tax Foundation, State Business Tax Climate Index 2008

TRANSPORTATION

Means of Transportation to Work

Area	Car/Truck/Van		Public Transportation			Bicycle	Walked	Other Means	Worked at Home
	Drove Alone	Car-pooled	Bus	Subway	Railroad				
City	79.7	8.6	2.1	0.0	0.0	0.2	0.9	1.0	7.6
MSA[1]	70.4	12.6	7.8	0.0	0.0	0.7	3.2	0.9	4.4
U.S.	75.7	12.2	2.5	1.5	0.5	0.4	2.9	1.0	3.3

Note: Figures are percentages and cover workers 16 years of age and older; (1) Metropolitan Statistical Area - see Appendix A for areas included
Source: Census 2000, Summary File 3

Travel Time to Work

Area	Less Than 15 Minutes	15 to 29 Minutes	30 to 44 Minutes	45 to 59 Minutes	60 Minutes or More
City	11.3	33.1	38.4	12.2	4.9
MSA[1]	22.1	36.9	23.9	9.2	7.9
U.S.	29.4	36.1	19.1	7.4	8.0

Note: Figures are percentages and include workers 16 years old and over; (1) Metropolitan Statistical Area - see Appendix A for areas included
Source: Census 2000, Summary File 3

Travel Time Index

Area	1982	1995	2004	2005
Urban Area[1]	1.07	1.30	1.28	1.30
Average[2]	1.11	1.22	1.29	1.30

Note: Travel Time Index - The ratio of travel time in the peak period to the travel time at free-flow conditions. A value of 1.35 indicates a 20-minute free-flow trip takes 27 minutes in the peak. Free-flow speeds (60 mph on freeways and 35 mph on principal arterials) are used as the comparison threshold; (1) Covers the Seattle, WA urban area; (2) average of 85 urban areas
Source: Texas Transportation Institute, The 2007 Urban Mobility Report, September 2007

Living Environment

COST OF LIVING

Cost of Living Index

Composite Index	Groceries	Housing	Utilities	Trans-portation	Health Care	Misc. Goods/ Services
121.5	113.0	155.0	94.9	106.2	124.0	109.7

Note: U.S. = 100; Figures cover the Seattle WA urban area.
Source: The Council for Community and Economic Research (formerly ACCRA), Cost of Living Index, 2007

Grocery Prices

Area[1]	T-Bone Steak ($/pound)	Frying Chicken ($/pound)	Whole Milk ($/half gal.)	Eggs ($/dozen)	Orange Juice ($/64 oz.)	Coffee ($/11.5 oz.)
City[2]	9.50	1.47	2.33	2.00	3.47	4.32
Avg.	8.93	1.12	2.13	1.52	3.26	3.31
Min.	5.88	0.71	1.33	0.83	2.30	2.20
Max.	12.80	2.07	3.43	3.54	5.79	6.20

Note: (1) Values for the local area are compared with the average, minimum and maximum values for all 331 areas in the Cost of Living Index report; (2) Figures cover the Seattle WA urban area; **T-Bone Steak** *(price per pound);* **Frying Chicken** *(price per pound, whole fryer);* **Whole Milk** *(half gallon carton);* **Eggs** *(price per dozen, Grade A, large);* **Orange Juice** *(64 oz. Tropicana or Florida Natural);* **Coffee** *(11.5 oz. can, vacuum-packed, Maxwell House, Hills Bros, or Folgers).*
Source: The Council for Community and Economic Research (formerly ACCRA), Cost of Living Index, 2007

Housing and Utility Costs

Area[1]	New Home Price ($)	Apartment Rent ($/month)	All Electric ($/month)	Part Electric ($/month)	Other Energy ($/month)	Telephone ($/month)
City[2]	454,300	1,434	142.92	-	-	27.27
Avg.	309,605	782	146.13	78.67	90.16	26.14
Min.	189,877	n/a	82.03	37.41	33.15	17.08
Max.	1,202,800	3,481	271.14	150.60	257.67	37.45

Note: (1) Values for the local area are compared with the average, minimum and maximum values for all 331 areas in the Cost of Living Index report; (2) Figures cover the Seattle WA urban area; **New Home Price** *(2,400 sf living area, 8,000 sf lot, in urban area with full utilities);* **Apartment Rent** *(950 sf 2 bedroom/1.5 or 2 bath, unfurnished, excluding all utilities except water);* **All Electric** *(average monthly cost for an all-electric home);* **Part Electric** *(average monthly cost for a part-electric home);* **Other Energy** *(average monthly cost for natural gas, fuel oil, coal, wood, and any other forms of energy except electricity);* **Telephone** *(price includes basic monthly rate for a private residential line plus additional local usage charges incurred by a family of four).*
Source: The Council for Community and Economic Research (formerly ACCRA), Cost of Living Index, 2007

Health Care, Transportation, and Other Costs

Area[1]	Doctor ($/visit)	Dentist ($/visit)	Optometrist ($/visit)	Gasoline ($/gallon)	Beauty Salon ($/visit)	Men's Shirt ($)
City[2]	99.96	100.52	105.07	2.94	28.75	24.28
Avg.	79.48	71.93	79.55	2.64	29.52	25.77
Min.	52.08	44.80	43.95	2.19	15.58	16.19
Max.	148.44	126.27	158.83	3.48	60.62	48.53

Note: (1) Values for the local area are compared with the average, minimum and maximum values for all 331 areas in the Cost of Living Index report; (2) Figures cover the Seattle WA urban area; **Doctor** *(general practitioners routine exam of an established patient);* **Dentist** *(adult teeth cleaning and periodic oral examination);* **Optometrist** *(full vision eye exam for established adult patient);* **Gasoline** *(one gallon regular unleaded, national brand, including all taxes, cash price at self-service pump if available);* **Beauty Salon** *(woman's shampoo, trim, and blow-dry);* **Men's Shirt** *(cotton/polyester dress shirt, pinpoint weave, long sleeves).*
Source: The Council for Community and Economic Research (formerly ACCRA), Cost of Living Index, 2007

HOUSING

House Price Index (HPI)

Area	National Ranking[2]	Quarterly Change (%)	One-Year Change (%)	Five-Year Change (%)
MD[1]	28	-0.03	5.87	66.13
U.S.[3]	-	0.10	0.84	41.37

Note: The HPI is a weighted repeat sales index. It measures average price changes in repeat sales or refinancings on the same properties. This information is obtained by reviewing repeat mortgage transactions on single-family properties whose mortgages have been purchased or securitized by Fannie Mae or Freddie Mac in January 1975; (1) Metropolitan Division - see Appendix B for areas included; (2) Rankings are based on annual percentage change for all metro areas containing at least 15,000 transactions over the last 10 years and ranges from 1 to 291; (3) figures based on a weighted average of Census Division estimates; all figures are for the period ending December 31, 2007
Source: Office of Federal Housing Enterprise Oversight, House Price Index, February 26, 2008

House Price Valuations

Area	Q1 2000	Q1 2001	Q1 2002	Q1 2003	Q1 2004	Q1 2005	Q1 2006	Q1 2007	Q1 2008
MD[1]	-13.0	-4.4	-1.9	5.2	6.4	15.5	25.3	30.2	22.8

Note: Figures show the percentage of over- or under-valuation of single family homes relative to statistically normal house values (e.g. a value of 23.6 indicates that house values are 23.6% overvalued). Statistically normal house values are based on house prices, interest rates, household incomes, population densities, and any historical premiums or discounts metropolitan areas have exhibited over time; (1) Figures cover the Metropolitan Division - see Appendix B for areas included
Source: Global Insight/National City Corporation, House Prices in America, May 2008

Median Home Prices

Area	2005	2006	2007[r]	Percent Change 2006 to 2007
MSA[1]	316.8	361.2	386.9	7.1
U.S. Average	219.0	221.9	217.9	-1.8

Note: Figures are median sales prices of existing single-family homes in thousands of dollars; (r) revised; n/a not available; (1) Metropolitan Statistical Area - see Appendix B for areas included
Source: National Association of Realtors, Metropolitan Area Prices, 1st Quarter 2008

Housing: Year Structure Built

Area	1990 -2000	1980 -1989	1970 -1979	1960 -1969	1950 -1959	1940 -1949	Before 1940	Median Year
City	38.6	34.3	17.4	4.5	1.9	1.4	2.0	1987
MSA[1]	19.8	18.4	17.7	14.7	10.3	6.4	12.5	1973
U.S.	17.0	15.8	18.5	13.7	12.7	7.3	15.0	1971

Note: Figures are percentages; (1) Metropolitan Statistical Area - see Appendix A for areas included
Source: Census 2000, Summary File 3

HEALTH

Health Risk Data

Category	Area[1] (%)	U.S. (%)
Adults who have been told they have high blood pressure[3]	22.3	25.5
Adults who have been told they have high blood cholesterol[3]	35.5	35.6
Adults who have been told they have diabetes[2]	6.8	7.5
Adults who have been told they have arthritis[3]	23.3	27.0
Adults who have been told they currently have asthma	7.9	8.5
Adults who are current smokers	13.8	20.1
Adults who are heavy drinkers[4]	5.1	4.9
Adults who are overweight (BMI 25.0 - 29.9)	36.0	36.5
Adults who are obese (BMI 30.0 - 99.8)	21.2	25.1

Note: Data as of 2006 unless otherwise noted; (1) Figures cover the Metropolitan Division - see Appendix B for areas included; (2) Figures do not include pregnancy-related diabetes, pre-diabetes or borderline diabetes; (3) 2005 data; (4) Heavy drinkers are classified as adult men having more than two drinks per day or adult women having more than one drink per day
Source: Centers for Disease Control and Prevention, Behaviorial Risk Factor Surveillance System, SMART: Selected Metropolitan/Micropolitan Area Risk Trends, 2005, 2006

Mortality Rates for the Top 10 Causes of Death in the U.S.

ICD-10[a] Sub-Chapter	ICD-10[a] Code	Age-Adjusted Mortality Rate[1] per 100,000 population	
		County[2]	U.S.
Malignant neoplasms	C00-C97	168.6	186.5
Ischaemic heart diseases	I20-I25	112.7	152.3
Other forms of heart disease	I30-I51	31.3	51.5
Cerebrovascular diseases	I60-I69	49.9	50.0
Chronic lower respiratory diseases	J40-J47	33.3	42.6
Diabetes mellitus	E10-E14	21.0	24.8
Other degenerative diseases of the nervous system	G30-G31	36.9	22.6
Other external causes of accidental injury	W00-X59	21.5	21.4
Influenza and pneumonia	J10-J18	15.3	20.7
Hypertensive diseases	I10-I13	15.1	18.2

Note: (a) ICD-10 = International Classification of Diseases 10th Revision; (1) Mortality rates are a three year average covering 2003-2005; (2) Figures cover King County
Source: Centers for Disease Control and Prevention, National Center for Health Statistics. Compressed Mortality File 1999-2004. CDC WONDER On-line Database, compiled from Compressed Mortality File 1999-2005 Series 20 No. 2K, 2008.

Mortality Rates for Selected Causes of Death

ICD-10[a] Sub-Chapter	ICD-10[a] Code	Age-Adjusted Mortality Rate[1] per 100,000 population	
		County[2]	U.S.
Assault	X85-Y09	3.7	5.9
Human immunodeficiency virus (HIV) disease	B20-B24	3.6	4.5
Intentional self-harm	X60-X84	11.6	10.8
Malnutrition	E40-E46	1.1	1.0
Obesity and other hyperalimentation	E65-E68	1.0	1.4
Organic, including symptomatic, mental disorders	F01-F09	8.6	16.8
Transport accidents	V01-V99	9.2	16.1
Viral hepatitis	B15-B19	2.2	1.8

Note: (a) ICD-10 = International Classification of Diseases 10th Revision; (1) Mortality rates are a three year average covering 2003-2005; (2) Figures cover King County
Source: Centers for Disease Control and Prevention, National Center for Health Statistics. Compressed Mortality File 1999-2004. CDC WONDER On-line Database, compiled from Compressed Mortality File 1999-2005 Series 20 No. 2K, 2008.

Distribution of Physicians[1]

Area	Total	Family/ General Practice	Specialties	
			Medical	Surgical
King County (number)	5,520	1,645	1,873	1,110
King County (rate per 10,000 pop.)	30.8	9.2	10.4	6.2
U.S. (rate per 10,000 pop.)	17.7	4.6	6.9	4.3

Note: Data as of 2005; (1) Includes all non-federal, patient-care, office-based MDs
Source: Area Resource File (ARF). June 2007. U.S. Department of Health and Human Services, Health Resources and Services Administration, Bureau of Health Professions, Rockville, MD.

Hospitals

There were no hospitals listed within the city limits.
AHA Guide to the Healthcare Field 2008

According to *U.S. News,* the Seattle-Tacoma-Bellevue, WA metro area is home to five of the best hospitals in the U.S.: **Children's Hospital and Regional Medical Center**; **Harborview Medical Center**; **Swedish Health Services**; **University of Washington Medical Center**; **Virginia Mason Medical Center**. *U.S. News Online, "America's Best Hospitals 2007"*

EDUCATION

Public School District Statistics

District Name	Schls	Pupils	Pupil/ Teacher Ratio	Minority Pupils[1] (%)	Free Lunch Eligible[2] (%)	IEP[3] (%)
Issaquah Sch Dist 411	25	16,036	20.4	24.5	4.7	10.5
Lake Washington Sch Dist 414	51	24,332	20.1	24.8	8.7	9.4

Note: Table includes regular local school districts with 2,000 or more students; (1) Percentage of students that are not white, non-Hispanic; (2) Percentage of students that are eligible for the free lunch program; (3) Percentage of students that have an Individualized Education Program.
Source: U.S. Department of Education, National Center for Education Statistics, Common Core of Data, Local Education Agency (School District) Universe Survey: School Year 2005-2006; U.S. Department of Education, National Center for Education Statistics, Common Core of Data, Public Elementary/Secondary School Universe Survey: School Year 2005-2006

Highest Level of Education

Area	Less than H.S.	H.S. Diploma	Some College, No Deg.	Associate Degree	Bachelors Degree	Masters Degree	Profess. School Degree	Doctorate Degree
City	1.6	9.3	18.9	8.0	41.1	16.0	3.3	1.9
MSA[1]	10.7	22.9	25.9	8.0	21.9	7.1	2.3	1.2
U.S.	19.4	28.4	21.2	6.4	15.7	5.9	2.0	1.0

Note: Figures are 2007 estimated percentages and cover persons age 25 and over; (1) Metropolitan Statistical Area - see Appendix B for areas included
Source: Claritas, Inc.

Educational Attainment by Race

Area	High School Graduate (%)					Bachelor's Degree (%)				
	Total	White	Black	Asian	Hisp.[2]	Total	White	Black	Asian	Hisp.[2]
City	98.3	98.5	100.0	98.7	96.5	61.5	60.3	43.1	78.3	47.5
MSA[1]	90.1	92.3	82.4	82.2	67.8	35.9	37.0	21.1	40.9	19.0
U.S.	80.4	83.6	72.3	80.4	52.4	24.4	26.1	14.3	44.1	10.4

Note: Figures shown cover persons 25 years old and over; (1) Metropolitan Statistical Area - see Appendix A for areas included; (2) people of Hispanic origin can be of any race
Source: Census 2000, Summary File 3

School Enrollment by Type

Area	Grades KG to 8				Grades 9 to 12			
	Public		Private		Public		Private	
	Enrollment	%	Enrollment	%	Enrollment	%	Enrollment	%
City	5,474	89.5	641	10.5	2,321	95.1	119	4.9
MSA[1]	260,622	88.3	34,672	11.7	116,866	91.1	11,446	8.9
U.S.	33,526,011	88.7	4,285,121	11.3	14,848,628	90.6	1,532,323	9.4

Note: Figures shown cover persons 3 years old and over; (1) Metropolitan Statistical Area - see Appendix A for areas included
Source: Census 2000, Summary File 3

School Enrollment by Race

Area	Grades KG to 8 (%)				Grades 9 to 12 (%)			
	White	Black	Asian	Hisp.[1]	White	Black	Asian	Hisp.[1]
City	86.7	1.0	5.4	4.0	89.3	0.2	6.9	3.3
MSA[2]	73.2	5.5	9.2	6.6	73.1	5.4	10.5	5.8
U.S.	68.5	15.5	3.3	16.8	68.8	15.5	3.8	15.7

Note: Figures shown cover persons 3 years old and over; (1) people of Hispanic origin can be of any race; (2) Metropolitan Statistical Area - see Appendix A for areas included
Source: Census 2000, Summary File 3

Average Salaries of Public School Classroom Teachers

District	2005-06 Dollars	2005-06 Rank[1]	2006-07 Dollars	2006-07 Rank[1]	Percent Change 2005-06 to 2006-07
Washington	46,326	22	47,882	22	3.36
U.S. Average	49,026	-	50,816	-	3.65

Note: (1) State rank ranges from 1 to 51.
Source: National Education Association, Rankings & Estimates: Rankings of the States 2006 and Estimates of School Statistics 2007, December 2007

Higher Education

Four-Year Colleges			Two-Year Colleges			Medical Schools[1]	Law Schools[2]	Voc/ Tech[3]
Public	Private Non-profit	Private For-profit	Public	Private Non-profit	Private For-profit			
0	0	0	0	0	0	0	0	0

Note: Figures cover institutions located within the city limits; (1) includes schools accredited by the Liaison Committee on Medical Education and the American Osteopathic Association; (2) includes American Bar Association-accredited law schools; (3) includes all schools with programs that are less than 2 years.
Source: National Center for Education Statistics, The Integrated Postsecondary Education System (IPEDS) Peer Analysis System, 2007; www.usnews.com, Law and Medical School Directories, 2009

PRESIDENTIAL ELECTION

2004 Presidential Election Results

Area	Bush	Kerry	Nader	Other
King County	33.6	64.9	0.7	0.8
U.S.	50.7	48.3	0.4	0.6

Note: Results are percentages and may not add to 100% due to rounding
Source: Dave Leip's Atlas of U.S. Presidential Elections, www.uselectionatlas.org

EMPLOYERS

Major Employers

Company Name	Industry	Type of Site
Bailey-Boushay House	Offices and clinics of medical doctors	Headquarters
Boeing	Aircraft	Branch
Childrens Health Care System	Specialty hospitals, except psychiatric	Single
Harborview Medical Center	General medical and surgical hospitals	Single
King County Pub Hosp Dst No 2	Management consulting services	Single
Microsoft	Prepackaged software	Headquarters
Neurological Surgery	Offices and clinics of medical doctors	Branch
Rui One Corp	Eating places	Single
SNC Lavalin Thermal Power	Heavy construction, nec	Headquarters
Swedish Med Center/First Hl	General medical and surgical hospitals	Headquarters
University of Washington	Colleges and universities	Branch
University of Washington Press	Colleges and universities	Headquarters
Virginia Mason Hospital	General medical and surgical hospitals	Branch

Note: Companies shown are located within the Seattle metropolitan area; nec = not elsewhere classified.
Source: www.zapdata.com, May 2008

PUBLIC SAFETY

Crime Rate

Area	All Crimes	Violent Crimes: Murder	Forcible Rape	Robbery	Aggrav. Assault	Property Crimes: Burglary	Larceny -Theft	Motor Vehicle Theft
City	1,338.9	0.0	14.3	2.9	14.3	283.2	941.2	83.0
Metro[1]	5,365.3	3.3	37.4	141.0	193.3	933.0	3,021.9	1,035.4
U.S.	3,808.1	5.7	30.9	149.4	287.5	729.4	2,206.8	398.4

Note: Figures are crimes per 100,000 population; (1) Metropolitan Division - see Appendix B for areas included
Source: FBI Uniform Crime Reports, 2006

Hate Crimes

Area	Number of Quarters Reported	Bias Motivation				
		Race	Religion	Sexual Orientation	Ethnicity	Disability
City	4	1	1	0	0	0

Source: Federal Bureau of Investigation, Hate Crime Statistics 2006

RECREATION

Culture

Dance[1]	Theatre[1]	Instrumental Music[1]	Vocal Music[1]	Series/ Festivals	Museums	Zoos and Aquariums[2]
0	0	0	0	0	0	0

Note: (1) Number of professional perfoming groups; (2) AZA-accredited
Source: The Grey House Performing Arts Directory, 2007; Official Museum Directory, 2008; Association of Zoos & Aquariums, AZA Member Zoos & Aquariums, June 2008

Professional Sports Teams

Team Name	League
Seattle Mariners	Major League Baseball (MLB)
Seattle Sounders FC (2009)	Major League Soccer (MLS)
Seattle Supersonics	National Basketball Association (NBA)
Seattle Seahawks	National Football League (NFL)

Note: Includes teams located in the Seattle metro area.
Source: Original research

MEDIA

Newspapers

Name	News Focus	Frequency	Circulation
No newspapers have an office in the city			

Note: Includes newspapers with offices located in the city
Source: MediaContactsPro, March 2008

Television Stations

Name	Ch.	Network(s)	Type	Ownership
KOMO	4	ABC	Commercial	Fisher Broadcasting Inc.
KING	5	NBC	Commercial	Belo Corporation
KIRO	7	CBS	Commercial	Cox Enterprises Inc.
KCTS	9	PBS	Public	KCTS
KSTW	11	UPN	Commercial	Paramount Communications Inc.
KBTC	12	PBS	Public	State Board for Community and Technical Colleges
KVOS	12	n/a	Commercial	Clear Channel Communications Inc.
KCPQ	13	Fox	Commercial	Tribune Broadcasting Company
KONG	16	n/a	Commercial	Zeus Corporation
KTBW	20	n/a	Non-comm.	Trinity Broadcasting Network
KTWB	22	WBN	Commercial	Dudley Broadcast Management
KBCB	24	n/a	Commercial	World Television of Washington
KCKA	28	PBS	Public	State Board for Community and Technical Colleges
KWPX	33	Pax	Commercial	Paxson Communications Corporation

Note: Stations included cover the Seattle-Tacoma DMA (Designated Market Area)
BurrellesLuce, MediaContacts Online, January 2007

Major AM Radio Stations

Call Letters	Freq. (kHz)	Station Type	Target Audience	Station Format	Music Format
KARI	550	n/a	Religious	News/Sports/Talk	n/a
KPQ	560	Commercial	General	News/Talk	n/a
KVI	570	Commercial	General	Talk	n/a
KAPS	660	n/a	General	Music/News	n/a
KIRO	710	Commercial	General	News/Talk	n/a
KNWX	770	n/a	General	News/Talk	n/a
KGMI	790	Commercial	General	News/Talk	n/a
KGNW	820	Commercial	General/Religious	News/Talk	n/a
KMTT	850	Commercial	General	Music	Album Rock
KHHO	850	n/a	General/Men	Music/News/Sports/Talk	n/a
KIXI	880	n/a	General	Music/News	n/a
KJR	950	n/a	General	Music/Sports/Talk	n/a
KOMO	1000	Commercial	General	News/Talk	n/a
KMAS	1030	Commercial	General	Music/News	Adult Contemp.
KYCW	1090	n/a	General	Music	n/a
KKNW	1150	n/a	General	News/Sports	n/a
KPUG	1170	Commercial	General	Sports/Talk	n/a
KLAY	1180	Commercial	General	News/Sports/Talk	n/a
KBSG	1210	Commercial	General	Music	Oldies
KKDZ	1250	n/a	Children	Music	n/a
KKOL	1300	Commercial	General	News/Talk	n/a
KMPS	1300	Commercial	General	Music/News/Sports	Country
KXRO	1320	Commercial	General	Talk	n/a
KKMO	1360	Commercial	General/Hispanic	Music/Talk	Latin
KRKO	1380	n/a	General	News/Sports/Talk	n/a
KITI	1420	Commercial	General	Music/News	Oldies
KBRC	1430	n/a	General	Music/News	n/a
KELA	1470	Commercial	General	News/Sports/Talk	n/a
KXPA	1540	n/a	Ethnic/Hispanic	Ed/Music/News/Talk	n/a
KRPI	1550	n/a	Religious	Educational/Music/News	n/a
KZIZ	1560	Commercial	General	Music	Urban Contemp.
KLFE	1590	Commercial	General/Religious	Music/Talk	Gospel
KYIZ	1620	Commercial	General	Music	Urban Contemp.

Note: Stations included cover the Seattle-Tacoma DMA (Designated Market Area); n/a not available
Source: BurrellesLuce, MediaContacts Online, January 2007

Major FM Radio Stations

Call Letters	Freq. (mHz)	Station Type	Target Audience	Station Format	Music Format
KPLU	88.5	College	General	Music/News	n/a
KVTI	90.9	College	Young Adult	Music/News/Sports	n/a
KLSY	92.5	n/a	General	Music/News	n/a
KISM	92.9	Commercial	General	Music/News	Classic Rock
KUBE	93.3	n/a	General	Music/Talk	n/a
KMPS	94.1	n/a	General	Music	n/a
KUOW	94.9	College	General	Educational/News	n/a
KJR	95.7	n/a	General	n/a	n/a
KXXO	96.1	n/a	General	Music/News	n/a
KBSG	97.3	n/a	General	Music/News	n/a
KING	98.1	Commercial	General	Music	Classical
KISW	99.9	Commercial	General	Music/News/Talk	Classic Rock
KQBZ	100.7	Commercial	General	Talk	n/a
KPLZ	101.5	n/a	General	Music/News	n/a
KMNT	102.9	Commercial	General	Music/News/Sports	Country
KMTT	103.7	n/a	General	Music	n/a
KAFE	104.3	Commercial	General	Music/News	Soft Rock
KCMS	105.3	Commercial	General/Religious	Music	Christian
KBKS	106.1	n/a	General/Women	Music/News/Talk	n/a
KWPZ	106.5	n/a	Religious	Music/Talk	n/a
KRWM	106.9	n/a	General	Music	n/a
KNDD	107.7	Commercial	General	Music/News/Talk	Modern Rock

Note: Stations included cover the Seattle-Tacoma DMA (Designated Market Area); n/a not available
BurrellesLuce, MediaContacts Online, January 2007

CLIMATE

Average and Extreme Temperatures

Temperature	Jan	Feb	Mar	Apr	May	Jun	Jul	Aug	Sep	Oct	Nov	Dec	Yr.
Extreme High (°F)	64	70	75	85	93	96	98	99	98	89	74	63	99
Average High (°F)	44	48	52	57	64	69	75	74	69	59	50	45	59
Average Temp. (°F)	39	43	45	49	55	61	65	65	60	52	45	41	52
Average Low (°F)	34	36	38	41	46	51	54	55	51	45	39	36	44
Extreme Low (°F)	0	1	11	29	28	38	43	44	35	28	6	6	0

Note: Figures cover the years 1948-1990
Source: National Climatic Data Center, International Station Meteorological Climate Summary, 9/96

Average Precipitation/Snowfall/Humidity

Precip./Humidity	Jan	Feb	Mar	Apr	May	Jun	Jul	Aug	Sep	Oct	Nov	Dec	Yr.
Avg. Precip. (in.)	5.7	4.2	3.7	2.4	1.7	1.4	0.8	1.1	1.9	3.5	5.9	5.9	38.4
Avg. Snowfall (in.)	5	2	1	Tr	Tr	0	0	0	0	Tr	1	3	13
Avg. Rel. Hum. 7am (%)	83	83	84	83	80	79	79	84	87	88	85	85	83
Avg. Rel. Hum. 4pm (%)	76	69	63	57	54	54	49	51	57	68	76	79	63

Note: Figures cover the years 1948-1990; Tr = Trace amounts (<0.05 in. of rain; <0.5 in. of snow)
Source: National Climatic Data Center, International Station Meteorological Climate Summary, 9/96

Weather Conditions

Temperature			Daytime Sky			Precipitation		
5°F & below	32°F & below	90°F & above	Clear	Partly cloudy	Cloudy	0.01 inch or more precip.	0.1 inch or more snow/ice	Thunder-storms
< 1	38	3	57	121	187	157	8	8

Note: Figures are average number of days per year and cover the years 1948-1990
Source: National Climatic Data Center, International Station Meteorological Climate Summary, 9/96

HAZARDOUS WASTE

Superfund Sites

Sammamish has no sites on the EPA's Superfund Final National Priorities List.
U.S. Environmental Protection Agency, Final National Priorities List, June 23, 2008

AIR & WATER QUALITY

Air Quality Index

Area	Percent of Days when Air Quality was...[2]				AQI Statistics	
	Good	Moderate	Unhealthy for Sensitive Groups	Unhealthy	Maximum	Median
MSA[1]	76.7	20.5	2.5	0.3	155	36

Note: The Air Quality Index (AQI) is an index for reporting daily air quality. EPA calculates the AQI for five major air pollutants regulated by the Clean Air Act: ground-level ozone, particle pollution (also known as particulate matter), carbon monoxide, sulfur dioxide, and nitrogen dioxide. The AQI runs from 0 to 500. The higher the AQI value, the greater the level of air pollution and the greater the health concern. There are six AQI categories: "Good" The AQI is between 0 and 50. Air quality is considered satisfactory; "Moderate" The AQI is between 51 and 100. Air quality is acceptable; "Unhealthy for Sensitive Groups" When AQI values are between 101 and 150, members of sensitive groups may experience health effects; "Unhealthy" When AQI values are between 151 and 200 everyone may begin to experience health effects; "Very Unhealthy" AQI values between 201 and 300 trigger a health alert; "Hazardous" AQI values over 300 trigger health warnings of emergency conditions; (1) Metropolitan Statistical Area - see Appendix A for areas included; (2) Based on 365 days with AQI data in 2007.
Source: U.S. Environmental Protection Agency, Air Quality Index Report, 2007

Air Quality Index Pollutants

Area	Percent of Days when AQI Pollutant was...[2]					
	Carbon Monoxide	Nitrogen Dioxide	Ozone	Sulfur Dioxide	Particulate Matter 2.5	Particulate Matter 10
MSA[1]	0.0	0.0	44.4	0.0	54.8	0.8

Note: The Air Quality Index (AQI) is an index for reporting daily air quality. EPA calculates the AQI for five major air pollutants regulated by the Clean Air Act: ground-level ozone, particle pollution (also known as particulate matter), carbon monoxide, sulfur dioxide, and nitrogen dioxide. The AQI runs from 0 to 500. The higher the AQI value, the greater the level of air pollution and the greater the health concern; (1) Metropolitan Statistical Area - see Appendix A for areas included; (2) Based on 365 days with AQI data in 2007.
Source: U.S. Environmental Protection Agency, Air Quality Index Report, 2007

Air Quality Index Trends

Area	Trend Sites (17)								All Sites (109)
	1999	2000	2001	2002	2003	2004	2005	2006	2006
MSA[1]	6	8	6	7	2	1	3	5	12

Note: An AQI value greater than 100 indicates that air quality would have been in the unhealthful range on that day. Data from exceptional events are not included. These counts are presented in two ways. First, the counts are based on sites having an adequate record of monitoring data during the trend period (trend sites). These counts represent the relative change in the number of days with AQI values greater than 100. In the last column, the counts are based on all sites with data in the most recent year (because it is possible for a site to have data in the most recent year but not enough data to be a trend site); (1) Metropolitan Statistical Area - see Appendix A for areas included.
Source: U.S. Environmental Protection Agency, Office of Air and Radiation, Air Trends, Factbook and Related Information, Air Pollution Trends in Selected Metropolitan Areas 2006

Maximum Air Pollutant Concentrations

	Particulate Matter 10 (ug/m^3)	Particulate Matter 2.5 (ug/m^3)	Ozone (ppm)	Carbon Monoxide (ppm)	Sulfur Dioxide (ppm)	Nitrogen Dioxide (ppm)	Lead (ug/m^3)
MSA[1] Level	63	37	0.129	3	n/a	n/a	n/a
NAAQS[2]	150	35	0.125	9	0.140	0.053	1.50
Met NAAQS[2]	Yes	No	No	Yes	n/a	n/a	n/a

Note: Data from exceptional events are not included; (1) Metropolitan Statistical Area - see Appendix A for areas included; (2) National Ambient Air Quality Standards; n/a not available
Concentrations: Particulate Matter 10 (coarse particulate) - highest second maximum 24-hour concentration; Particulate Matter 2.5 (fine particulate) - highest 98th percentile 24-hour concentration; Ozone - highest second daily maximum 1-hour concentration; Carbon Monoxide - highest second maximum non-overlapping 8-hour concentration; Sulfur Dioxide - highest second maximum 24-hour concentration; Nitrogen Dioxide - highest arithmetic mean concentration; Lead - highest quarterly maximum concentration
Units: ppm = parts per million; ug/m^3 = micrograms per cubic meter
Source: U.S. Environmental Protection Agency, MSA Factbook 2006, Air Quality Statistics by City

Drinking Water

Water System Name	Pop. Served	Primary Water Source Type	Violations[1]	
			Health Based	Monitoring/ Reporting
Sammamish Plateau Water & Sewer	61,495	Ground	0	0

Note: (1) Based on violation data from January 1, 2007 to December 31, 2007 (includes unresolved violations from earlier years)
Source: U.S. Environmental Protection Agency, Office of Ground Water and Drinking Water, Safe Drinking Water Information System (based on data extracted April 15, 2008)

Morgantown, West Virginia

Background

Morgantown is the County seat of Monongalia County, located along the Pennsylvania border in the north central part of West Virginia. Until the Treaty of Paris in 1763, what is now known as Morgantown was greatly contested among French and English settlers and native Indians. In 1772 Morgantown was settled by Zaquill Morgan and the Virginia Assembly chartered the territory in 1785. The direct result of the Virginia Charter is the present city of Morgantown.

Through most of the nineteenth century, Morgantown was a quiet place with one and two-story houses and stores on tree-lined High Street and its connecting streets down to the river. When the railroad came in 1886 and gas and oil production began nearby, industries sprang up in the outlying areas and Morgantown experienced an economic and population boom. From 1890 to 1900, the population more than doubled and, while more people lived in the industrial areas of Seneca and Sabraton, downtown was booming as a commercial district.

Architecturally, Morgantown's builders preferred traditional forms to high style. This gives High Street the eclectic charm characteristic of Main Street, U.S.A. Elmer F. Jacobs who came to Morgantown by way of Pittsburgh in 1894, renovated High Street and its environs, replacing the modest buildings of an earlier era with Romanesque and Queen Anne Revival structures. By the early 1900s he had designed over 400 buildings, many of which may still be seen in the downtown area.

Downtown Morgantown is a mixture of small retail businesses, professional services, restaurants, and residential units, and boasts an award winning Mainstreet Organization.

In the Wharf District, next to the Monongahela River, unused warehouses were revitalized into commercial and residential use. Public and private investments have combined to include street improvements, restaurants, retail, professional offices, and high-end loft apartments in the Wharf District, with a 16-story Radisson Hotel the newest building. Future projects include a Public Theater and Public Piers.

Morgantown is well known for sporting events at Mountaineer Field and the Coliseum, performing arts at the Creative Arts Center (CAC), and an excellent parks system, including the newly developed Pedestrian Walking and Recreational Trails System. Two main trails traverse Morgantown: The Caperton Trail and the Decker's Creek Trail that, together, provide nearly 10 miles of paved fun and connect into an additional 17 miles of packed sand ways. Just north of Caperton Trail is the Historic B&O Train Depot and the Riverfront Amphitheater which hosts the Wheeling Symphony Orchestra and the Arts and River Festival. Cooper's Rock State Forest provides a popular area for hiking, biking, camping, skiing and white-water rafting.

Morgantown is home to West Virginia University, the largest institution of higher education in the State. WV University's medical center and school of medicine draw a high number of doctors and health care professionals to the city, where the ratio of medical specialists is nearly 3 times the national average.

Along with the University, other major employers in the area include the National Institute of Occupational Safety and Health (NIOSH), Mylan Pharmaceuticals and two large health-care systems serving parts of West Virginia and Pennsylvania.

Rankings

General Rankings

- Morgantown* was ranked #288 out of 375 metro areas in *Cities Ranked & Rated*. Criteria: cost of living; climate; crime; transportation; economy and jobs; education; arts and culture; health and healthcare; leisure; quality of life. *Cities Ranked & Rated, 2nd Edition, 2007*

- Morgantown* was ranked #149 out of 379 metro areas in *Places Rated Almanac*. Criteria: health care; education; recreation; transportation; ambience; climate; crime; housing costs; jobs. *Places Rated Almanac, 7th Edition, 2007*

- *Expansion Management* rated 362 metro areas to find out which offer the best middle class lifestyle for manufacturing and service companies. The Morgantown* metro area was selected as a "5-Star Quality of Life Metro" (a distinction the magazine awards to the top 20 percent of metro areas studied). The annual "Quality of Life Quotient" measures dozens of indicators across nine major categories and compares them among 362 metropolitan statistical areas in the United States. The categories are: affordable housing; good public schools; low crime levels; adult education level; standard of living; traffic and commuting; continuing education opportunities; commercial air access; labor market. *Expansion Management, June 2007*

Business/Finance Rankings

- The Morgantown* metro area appeared on the Milken Institute "2007 Best Performing Cities" index. Rank: #24 out of 179 small metro areas. Criteria: job growth; wage and salary growth; high-tech output growth. *Milken Institute, "2007 Best Performing Cities"*

- The Morgantown* metro area was selected as one of the hottest cities for entrepreneurs in America by *Inc. Magazine*. Criteria: job-growth data for 393 metro was analyzed for current-year employment growth, average annual employment growth over past three years, and employment growth by industry sector. The Morgantown* metro area ranked #5 among small metro areas and #9 overall. *Inc. Magazine, May 2007*

- *Forbes* ranked 179 smaller metro areas in the U.S. in terms of the "Best Places for Business and Careers." The Morgantown* metro area was ranked #6. Criteria: business costs (labor, energy, tax and office space expenses); living costs (housing, transportation, food and other household expenditures); education levels of the work force; job growth; income growth; migration trends; crime rates; and culture/leisure. *Forbes, "Best Places for Business and Careers," March 19, 2008*

- *Kiplinger's Personal Finance* ranked 101 U.S. cities in terms of their total tax burdens. Morgantown ranked #40 (#1 had the lowest overall tax burden). Criteria: state income tax; property tax; sales tax; personal property tax; and gasoline tax. *Kiplinger's Personal Finance, July 2004*

- Morgantown appeared on *Kiplinger's Personal Finance* list of the "Top Ten Tax-Friendly Cities." The city was ranked #40. Criteria: income tax; sales tax; real estate and car/personal property tax. *Kiplinger's Personal Finance, May 2007*

Health/Environment Rankings

- The Morgantown* metro area appeared in *Country Home's* "2008 Best Green Places" report. The area ranked #200 out of 379. Criteria: official energy policies; green power; green buildings; availability of fresh, locally grown food. *Country Home, "2008 Best Green Places"*

- The American Podiatric Medical Association and *Prevention* magazine ranked America's 100 most populated cities based on fitness-walker friendliness. The best cities have safe streets, beautiful places to walk, mild weather and good air quality. Morgantown ranked #34. *Prevention, "The Best Walking Cities of 2008," April 2008; American Podiatric Medical Association, "2008 Best Fitness-Walking Cities, "April 2008*

Safety Rankings

- The National Insurance Crime Bureau ranked 361 metro areas in the U.S. in terms of per capita rates of vehicle theft. The Morgantown* metro area ranked #343 (#1 = highest rate). Criteria: number of vehicle theft offenses per 100,000 inhabitants. *National Insurance Crime Bureau, "NICB Vehicle Theft Study," April 22, 2008*

- Farmers Insurance Group of Companies, in partnership with Sperling's BestPlaces, ranked 379 metro areas and identified the "Most Secure U.S. Place to Live." The Morgantown* metro area ranked #14 out of 138 in the small town category (fewer than 150,000 residents). Criteria: crime rates; extreme weather; risk of natural disasters; environmental hazards; terrorism threats; air quality; life expectancy; job loss numbers. *Farmers Insurance Group, "Most Secure U.S. Places to Live 2007"*

Sports/Recreation Rankings

- The Morgantown* metro area appeared on the *Sporting News* list of the "Best Sports Cities 2007". The area ranked #58 out of 150 cities in the U.S. *Sporting News* takes a 12-month snapshot, roughly July to July, of each city's sports, putting a heavy premium on regular-season won-lost records (from the most recently completed season). Other criteria include: playoff berths, bowl appearances and tournament bids; championships; applicable power ratings; quality of competition; overall fan fervor as measured in part by attendance as percentage of venue capacity; abundance of teams (rewarding quality over quantity); stadium and arena quality; ticket availability and prices; franchise ownership; and marquee appeal of athletes. *SportingNews.com, "Best Sports Cities 2007," August 1, 2007*

Miscellaneous Rankings

- Morgantown was selected as one of 12 "Dozen Distinctive Destinations" for 2007, an annual list of unique and lovingly preserved communities in the U.S. Each year the National Trust for Historic Preservation selects 12 communities where residents have taken forceful action to protect their town's character and sense of place. *National Trust for Historic Preservation, "Dozen Distinctive Destinations 2007"*

Morgantown is located within the Morgantown, WV Metropolitan Statistical Area.

Business Environment

CITY FINANCES

City Government Finances

Component	2004-2005 ($000)	2004-2005 ($ per capita)
Total Revenues	52,307	1,849
Total Expenditures	53,446	1,889
Debt Outstanding	36,605	1,294
Cash and Securities	38,390	1,357

Source: U.S Census Bureau, Government Finances 2004-2005

City Government Revenue by Source

Source	2004-2005 ($000)	2004-2005 ($ per capita)
General Revenue		
From Federal Government	1,429	51
From State Government	6,430	227
From Local Governments	108	4
Taxes		
Property	2,748	97
Sales	1,180	42
Personal Income	0	0
License	235	8
Charges	14,533	514
Liquor Store	0	0
Utility	4,180	148
Employee Retirement	3,548	125
Other	17,916	633

Source: U.S Census Bureau, Government Finances 2004-2005

City Government Expenditures by Function

Function	2004-2005 ($000)	2004-2005 ($ per capita)	2004-2005 (%)
General Expenditures			
Airports	4,352	154	8.1
Corrections	0	0	0.0
Education	0	0	0.0
Fire Protection	3,032	107	5.7
Governmental Administration	3,317	117	6.2
Health	0	0	0.0
Highways	3,138	111	5.9
Hospitals	0	0	0.0
Housing and Community Development	2,783	98	5.2
Interest on General Debt	791	28	1.5
Libraries	1,082	38	2.0
Parking	1,564	55	2.9
Parks and Recreation	2,762	98	5.2
Police Protection	4,563	161	8.5
Public Welfare	0	0	0.0
Sewerage	7,222	255	13.5
Solid Waste Management	0	0	0.0
Liquor Store	0	0	0.0
Utility	6,928	245	13.0
Employee Retirement	3,502	124	6.6
Other	8,410	297	15.7

Source: U.S Census Bureau, Government Finances 2004-2005

Municipal Bond Ratings

Area	Moody's
City	n/a

Source: Mergent Bond Record, January 2008 (unless noted otherwise)

DEMOGRAPHICS

Population Growth

Area	1990 Census	2000 Census	2007 Estimate	2012 Projection	Population Growth (%) 1990-2000	Population Growth (%) 2000-2012
City	26,814	26,809	28,962	30,123	0.0	12.4
MSA[1]	104,546	111,200	115,435	118,038	6.4	6.1
U.S.	248,709,873	281,421,906	301,045,522	314,920,978	13.2	11.9

Note: (1) Metropolitan Statistical Area - see Appendix B for areas included
Source: Claritas, Inc.

Number of Households and Average Household Size

Area	2007 Estimate	2007 Average Household Size
City	11,298	2.56
MSA[1]	47,326	2.44
U.S.	113,668,003	2.65

Note: (1) Metropolitan Statistical Area - see Appendix B for areas included
Source: Claritas, Inc.

Race and Ethnicity

Area	White Alone[2]	Black Alone[2]	Asian Alone[2]	Other Race Alone[2]	Hispanic[3]
City	90.4	3.9	3.2	2.5	1.8
MSA[1]	94.0	2.6	1.6	1.9	1.1
U.S.	73.1	12.4	4.3	10.3	14.9

Note: Figures are 2007 estimates; (1) Metropolitan Statistical Area - see Appendix B for areas included (2) Alone is defined as not being in combination with one or more other races; (3) May be of any race.
Source: Claritas, Inc.

Ancestry

Area	German	Irish[2]	English	American	Italian	Polish	French[3]	Scottish
City	20.7	15.5	11.8	5.5	11.5	4.8	2.3	3.0
MSA[1]	n/a	n/a	n/a	n/a	n/a	n/a	n/a	n/a
U.S.	15.2	10.9	8.7	7.3	5.6	3.2	3.0	1.7

Note: Figures include multiple ancestry (e.g. if a person reported being Irish and Italian, they were included in both columns); (1) Metropolitan Statistical Area - see Appendix A for areas included; (2) Includes Celtic; (3) Includes Alsatian but excludes Basque
Source: Census 2000, Summary File 3

Foreign-Born Population

Area	Percent of Population Born in: Any Foreign Country	Europe	Asia	Africa	Oceania[2]	Canada	Mexico	Latin America[3]
City	5.9	1.5	3.0	0.4	0.1	0.2	0.2	0.5
MSA[1]	n/a	n/a	n/a	n/a	n/a	n/a	n/a	n/a
U.S.	11.1	1.7	2.9	0.3	0.1	0.3	3.3	2.5

Note: (1) Metropolitan Statistical Area - see Appendix A for areas included; (2) Includes Australia, New Zealand subregion, Melanesia, Micronesia, Polynesia, and Oceania n.e.c; (3) Includes Central America (excluding Mexico), South America, and the Caribbean.
Source: Census 2000, Summary File 3

Marriage Status

Area	Never Married	Now Married (excluding Separated)	Separated	Widowed	Divorced
City	58.0	30.3	0.8	5.1	5.7
MSA[1]	n/a	n/a	n/a	n/a	n/a
U.S.	27.1	54.4	2.2	6.6	9.7

Note: Figures are percentages and cover the population 15 years of age and older; (1) Metropolitan Statistical Area - see Appendix A for areas included
Source: Census 2000, Summary File 3

Age Distribution

Area	Percent of Population						
	Under Age 5	Age 5 to 17	Age 18 to 34	Age 35 to 49	Age 50 to 64	Age 65 to 79	80 Years and Over
City	2.9	7.9	56.9	12.6	9.3	7.3	3.1
MSA[1]	n/a	n/a	n/a	n/a	n/a	n/a	n/a
U.S.	6.8	18.9	23.7	23.5	14.8	9.2	3.2

Note: (1) Metropolitan Statistical Area - see Appendix A for areas included
Source: Census 2000, Summary File 3

Male/Female Ratio

Area	Males	Females	Males per 100 Females
City	14,941	14,021	106.6
MSA[1]	58,327	57,108	102.1
U.S.	148,320,305	152,725,217	97.1

Note: Figures are 2007 estimates; (1) Metropolitan Statistical Area - see Appendix B for areas included
Source: Claritas, Inc.

Religion

Area	Catholic	Southern Baptist	United Meth-odist	ELCA[1]	LDS[2]	Presby-terian Church USA	Jewish Est.	Muslim Est.
County	8.8	0.4	7.6	0.7	1.2	0.9	0.2	0.4
U.S.	22.0	7.1	3.7	1.8	1.5	1.1	2.2	0.6

Note: Figures are the number of adherents as a percentage of the total population; Adherents are defined as all members, including full members, their children and the estimated number of other participants who are not considered members (e.g. the baptized, those not confirmed, those regularly attending services, etc.); (1) Evangelical Lutheran Church in America; (2) The Church of Jesus Christ of Latter Day Saints
Source: Reprinted with permission from Religious Congregations and Membership in the United States 2000 (Nashville, Glenmary Research Center, 2002) Copyright Association of Statisticians of American Religious Bodies. All rights reserved.

ECONOMY

Gross Metropolitan Product

Area	2002	2003	2004	2005	2005 Rank[2]
MSA[1]	3.1	3.3	3.6	3.8	321

Note: Figures are in billions of dollars; (1) Morgantown, WV Metropolitan Statistical Area - see Appendix A for areas included; (2) Rank ranges from 1 to 361
Source: The U.S. Conference of Mayors, "U.S. Metro Economies: GMP - The Engines of America's Growth," January 2007

Economic Growth

Area	1995 GMP	2005 GMP	Average Annual Growth Rate	Growth Rate Rank[2]
MSA[1]	2.3	3.8	5.2	197

Note: Figures are in billions of dollars; GMP = Gross Metropolitan Product; (1) Morgantown, WV Metropolitan Statistical Area - see Appendix A for areas included; (2) Rank ranges from 1 to 361
Source: The U.S. Conference of Mayors, "U.S. Metro Economies: GMP - The Engines of America's Growth," January 2007

INCOME

Per Capita/Median/Average Income

Area	Per Capita ($)	Median Household ($)	Average Household ($)
City	16,489	24,121	40,296
MSA[1]	20,239	34,493	48,421
U.S.	25,495	49,280	66,670

Note: Figures are 2007 estimates; (1) Metropolitan Statistical Area - see Appendix B for areas included
Source: Claritas, Inc.

Household Income Distribution

Area	Percent of Households Earning							
	Under $15,000	$15,000 -24,999	$25,000 -34,999	$35,000 -49,999	$50,000 -74,999	$75,000 -99,000	$100,000 -149,999	$150,000 and up
City	36.5	14.6	10.4	12.3	11.7	5.8	6.2	2.5
MSA[1]	23.3	14.8	12.5	15.1	16.5	7.7	7.1	3.0
U.S.	13.1	10.9	11.2	15.6	19.5	11.9	11.3	6.6

Note: Figures are 2007 estimates; (1) Metropolitan Statistical Area - see Appendix B for areas included
Source: Claritas, Inc.

Poverty Rates by Age

Area	All Ages	Under 5 Years Old	5 to 17 Years Old	18 to 64 Years Old	65 Years and Over
City	38.4	0.9	2.1	34.4	1.0
MSA[1]	n/a	n/a	n/a	n/a	n/a
U.S.	12.4	1.2	3.0	6.9	1.2

Note: Figures are percent of population with income in 1999 below poverty level and only include population for whom poverty status is determined; (1) Metropolitan Statistical Area - see Appendix A for areas included
Source: Census 2000, Summary File 3

Personal Bankruptcy Filing Rate

Area	2004	2005	2006
Monongalia County	3.25	5.66	0.92
U.S.	5.31	6.82	2.00

Note: Numbers are per 1,000 population and include Chapter 7 and Chapter 13 filings
Source: Federal Deposit Insurance Corporation (FDIC), Regional Economic Conditions (RECON), 8/23/2007

EMPLOYMENT

Labor Force and Employment

Area	Civilian Labor Force			Workers Employed		
	Dec. 2006	Dec. 2007	% Chg.	Dec. 2006	Dec. 2007	% Chg.
City	16,000	16,212	1.3	15,510	15,698	1.2
MSA[1]	62,174	63,089	1.5	60,500	61,237	1.2
U.S.	152,571,000	153,705,000	0.7	146,081,000	146,334,000	0.2

Note: Data is not seasonally adjusted and covers workers 16 years of age and older;
(1) Metropolitan Statistical Area - see Appendix B for areas included
Source: Bureau of Labor Statistics, http://stats.bls.gov

Unemployment Rate

Area	2007											
	Jan.	Feb.	Mar.	Apr.	May	Jun.	Jul.	Aug.	Sep.	Oct.	Nov.	Dec.
City	3.5	4.1	4.6	3.6	4.0	4.1	3.9	4.5	4.1	3.9	3.7	3.2
MSA[1]	3.3	4.0	3.8	3.2	3.2	3.5	3.4	3.6	3.1	3.1	2.9	2.9
U.S.	5.0	4.9	4.5	4.3	4.3	4.7	4.9	4.6	4.5	4.4	4.5	4.8

Note: Data is not seasonally adjusted and covers workers 16 years of age and older; All figures are percentages; (1) Metropolitan Statistical Area - see Appendix B for areas included
Source: Bureau of Labor Statistics, http://stats.bls.gov

Employment by Occupation

Occupation Classification	City (%)	MSA[1] (%)	U.S. (%)
Sales and Office	26.4	n/a	26.7
Professional and Related	33.9	n/a	20.2
Service	20.2	n/a	14.9
Production, Transportation, and Material Moving	5.6	n/a	14.6
Management, Business, and Financial	8.7	n/a	13.5
Construction, Extraction, and Maintenance	4.9	n/a	9.4
Farming, Forestry, and Fishing	0.3	n/a	0.7

Note: Figures cover employed civilians 16 years of age and older;
(1) Metropolitan Statistical Area - see Appendix A for areas included
Source: Census 2000, Summary File 3

Employment by Industry

Sector	MSA[1] Number of Employees	MSA[1] Percent of Total	U.S. Percent of Total
Government	17,800	28.1	16.3
Education and Health Services	12,100	19.1	13.4
Professional and Business Services	4,300	6.8	13.1
Retail Trade	7,500	11.8	11.6
Manufacturing	4,100	6.5	9.9
Leisure and Hospitality	6,000	9.5	9.6
Financial Activities	n/a	n/a	5.9
Construction	n/a	n/a	5.3
Wholesale Trade	n/a	n/a	4.4
Other Services	n/a	n/a	3.9
Transportation and Utilities	n/a	n/a	3.7
Information	n/a	n/a	2.2
Natural Resources and Mining	n/a	n/a	0.5

Note: Figures cover non-farm employment as of December 2007 and are not seasonally adjusted; (1) Metropolitan Statistical Area - see Appendix B for areas included; n/a not available
Source: Bureau of Labor Statistics, http://stats.bls.gov

Average Wages

Occupation	$/Hr.	Occupation	$/Hr.
Accountants and Auditors	24.51	Maids and Housekeeping Cleaners	8.20
Automotive Mechanics	13.46	Maintenance and Repair Workers	13.91
Bookkeepers	14.32	Marketing Managers	n/a
Carpenters	15.18	Nuclear Medicine Technologists	n/a
Cashiers	7.22	Nurses, Licensed Practical	14.80
Clerks, General Office	11.50	Nurses, Registered	n/a
Clerks, Receptionists/Information	9.24	Nursing Aides/Orderlies/Attendants	9.70
Clerks, Shipping/Receiving	14.72	Packers and Packagers, Hand	8.12
Computer Programmers	24.62	Physical Therapists	38.81
Computer Support Specialists	21.87	Postal Service Mail Carriers	20.85
Computer Systems Analysts	25.29	Real Estate Brokers	n/a
Cooks, Restaurant	8.85	Retail Salespersons	9.68
Dentists	n/a	Sales Reps., Exc. Tech./Scientific	25.64
Electrical Engineers	34.75	Sales Reps., Tech./Scientific	28.97
Electricians	16.39	Secretaries, Exc. Legal/Med./Exec.	11.81
Financial Managers	31.80	Security Guards	9.55
First-Line Supervisors/Mgrs., Sales	14.20	Surgeons	n/a
Food Preparation Workers	8.80	Teacher Assistants	10.10
General and Operations Managers	34.97	Teachers, Elementary School	18.90
Hairdressers/Cosmetologists	10.92	Teachers, Secondary School	20.10
Internists	n/a	Telemarketers	8.23
Janitors and Cleaners	9.34	Truck Drivers, Heavy/Tractor-Trailer	15.45
Landscaping/Groundskeeping Workers	8.93	Truck Drivers, Light/Delivery Svcs.	10.76
Lawyers	39.43	Waiters and Waitresses	7.95

Note: Wage data covers the Morgantown, WV Metropolitan Statistical Area - see Appendix B for areas included. Hourly wages for elementary/secondary school teachers and teacher assistants were calculated by the editors from annual wage data assuming a 40 hour work week; n/a not available.
Source: Bureau of Labor Statistics, May 2007 Metro Area Occupational Employment and Wage Estimates

RESIDENTIAL REAL ESTATE

Building Permits

Area	Single-Family 2006	Single-Family 2007p	Single-Family Pct. Chg.	Multi-Family 2006	Multi-Family 2007p	Multi-Family Pct. Chg.	Total 2006	Total 2007p	Total Pct. Chg.
City	32	24	-25.0	6	70	1,066.7	38	94	147.4
U.S.	1,378,200	973,300	-29.4	460,700	407,200	-11.6	1,838,900	1,380,500	-24.9

Note: (p) preliminary; figures cover and represent new, privately-owned housing units authorized (unadjusted data); All permit data are based on estimates with imputation; U.S. figures are based on the new 20,000-place series.
Source: U.S. Census Bureau, Manufacturing, Mining, and Construction Statistics

Homeownership and Housing Vacancies

Area	Homeownership Rate[2] (%)			Rental Vacancy Rate[3] (%)			Homeowner Vacancy Rate[4] (%)		
	2005	2006	2007	2005	2006	2007	2005	2006	2007
MSA[1]	n/a	n/a	n/a	n/a	n/a	n/a	n/a	n/a	n/a
U.S.	68.9	68.8	68.1	9.8	9.8	9.7	1.9	2.4	2.7

Note: (1) Metropolitan Statistical Area - see Appendix B for areas included; (2) The proportion of households that are owners; (3) The proportion of the rental inventory that is vacant for rent; (4) The proportion of the homeowner inventory that is vacant for sale; n/a not available
Source: U.S. Census Bureau, Housing Vacancies and Homeownership Annual Statistics: 2007

TAXES

State Corporate Income Tax Rates

State	Rates and Tax Brackets
West Virginia	8.75%

Note: Tax rates as of January 1, 2008; Business franchise tax of.55% of taxable capital, or a minimum of $50.
Source: Tax Foundation, www.taxfoundation.org

State Individual Income Tax Rates

State	Federal Deductibility	Marginal Rates (%)	Standard Deduction ($)		Personal Exemptions ($)[1]	
			Single	Joint	Single	Dependents
West Virginia	No	3.0 - 6.5 (y)	n/a	n/a	2,000	2,000

Note: Tax rates as of January 1, 2008; Local- and county-level taxes are not included; n/a not applicable; (1) Married joint filers generally receive double the single exemption; (y) Brackets are not double for married taxpayers.
Source: Tax Foundation, www.taxfoundation.org

Various State and Local Tax Rates

State and Local Sales and Use (%)	State Sales and Use (%)	Gasoline[1,2] ($/gal.)	Cigarette ($/pack)	Spirits ($/gal.)	Table Wine ($/gal.)	Beer ($/gal.)
6.0	6.0	0.315	0.55	1.87 (n)	1.00	0.18

Note: Tax rates as of January 1, 2008; (1) In addition to the 18.4 cpg Federal gasoline tax; (2) Rates may include additional state sales taxes, environmental protection and storage fees/taxes, and local taxes. When necessary, the volume-weighted average of all local taxes is used to approximate the typical statewide rate including local tax; (n) The state government controls all sales. The implied excise tax rate is calculated using methodology designed by the Distilled Spirits Council of the United States (DISCUS).
Source: Tax Foundation, www.taxfoundation.org; Original research

State Tax Burdens

Area	Combined State and Local Tax Burden		Combined Federal, State and Local Tax Burden	
	Percent	Rank	Percent	Rank
West Virginia	10.9	21	29.8	40
U.S. Average	11.0	-	32.7	-

Note: Figures cover 2007 and measure taxes as a percentage of income
Source: Tax Foundation, www.taxfoundation.org

State Business Tax Climate Index Rankings

State	Overall Rank	Corporate Tax Index Rank	Individual Income Tax Index Rank	Sales Tax Index Rank	Unemployment Insurance Tax Index Rank	Property Tax Index Rank
West Virginia	37	28	40	21	35	26

Note: Rankings range from 1 to 50 where 1 is best. Rankings do not average across to Overall Rank. States without a given tax are given a ranking of 1.
Source: Tax Foundation, State Business Tax Climate Index 2008

TRANSPORTATION

Means of Transportation to Work

Area	Car/Truck/Van		Public Transportation			Bicycle	Walked	Other Means	Worked at Home
	Drove Alone	Car-pooled	Bus	Subway	Railroad				
City	64.5	9.9	0.6	0.4	0.0	1.0	16.8	3.0	3.7
MSA[1]	n/a	n/a	n/a	n/a	n/a	n/a	n/a	n/a	n/a
U.S.	75.7	12.2	2.5	1.5	0.5	0.4	2.9	1.0	3.3

Note: Figures are percentages and cover workers 16 years of age and older; (1) Metropolitan Statistical Area - see Appendix A for areas included
Source: Census 2000, Summary File 3

Travel Time to Work

Area	Less Than 15 Minutes	15 to 29 Minutes	30 to 44 Minutes	45 to 59 Minutes	60 Minutes or More
City	56.5	31.8	5.8	2.6	3.3
MSA[1]	n/a	n/a	n/a	n/a	n/a
U.S.	29.4	36.1	19.1	7.4	8.0

Note: Figures are percentages and include workers 16 years old and over; (1) Metropolitan Statistical Area - see Appendix A for areas included
Source: Census 2000, Summary File 3

Living Environment

COST OF LIVING

Cost of Living Index

Composite Index	Groceries	Housing	Utilities	Trans-portation	Health Care	Misc. Goods/ Services
100.5	95.3	107.8	107.4	99.1	103.9	94.7

Note: U.S. = 100; Figures cover the Morgantown WV urban area.
Source: The Council for Community and Economic Research (formerly ACCRA), Cost of Living Index, 2007

Grocery Prices

Area[1]	T-Bone Steak ($/pound)	Frying Chicken ($/pound)	Whole Milk ($/half gal.)	Eggs ($/dozen)	Orange Juice ($/64 oz.)	Coffee ($/11.5 oz.)
City[2]	7.98	1.24	2.05	1.45	2.98	3.39
Avg.	8.93	1.12	2.13	1.52	3.26	3.31
Min.	5.88	0.71	1.33	0.83	2.30	2.20
Max.	12.80	2.07	3.43	3.54	5.79	6.20

Note: (1) Values for the local area are compared with the average, minimum and maximum values for all 331 areas in the Cost of Living Index report; (2) Figures cover the Morgantown WV urban area; **T-Bone Steak** *(price per pound);* **Frying Chicken** *(price per pound, whole fryer);* **Whole Milk** *(half gallon carton);* **Eggs** *(price per dozen, Grade A, large);* **Orange Juice** *(64 oz. Tropicana or Florida Natural);* **Coffee** *(11.5 oz. can, vacuum-packed, Maxwell House, Hills Bros, or Folgers).*
Source: The Council for Community and Economic Research (formerly ACCRA), Cost of Living Index, 2007

Housing and Utility Costs

Area[1]	New Home Price ($)	Apartment Rent ($/month)	All Electric ($/month)	Part Electric ($/month)	Other Energy ($/month)	Telephone ($/month)
City[2]	336,973	782	-	46.48	124.66	29.01
Avg.	309,605	782	146.13	78.67	90.16	26.14
Min.	189,877	n/a	82.03	37.41	33.15	17.08
Max.	1,202,800	3,481	271.14	150.60	257.67	37.45

Note: (1) Values for the local area are compared with the average, minimum and maximum values for all 331 areas in the Cost of Living Index report; (2) Figures cover the Morgantown WV urban area; **New Home Price** *(2,400 sf living area, 8,000 sf lot, in urban area with full utilities);* **Apartment Rent** *(950 sf 2 bedroom/1.5 or 2 bath, unfurnished, excluding all utilities except water);* **All Electric** *(average monthly cost for an all-electric home);* **Part Electric** *(average monthly cost for a part-electric home);* **Other Energy** *(average monthly cost for natural gas, fuel oil, coal, wood, and any other forms of energy except electricity);* **Telephone** *(price includes basic monthly rate for a private residential line plus additional local usage charges incurred by a family of four).*
Source: The Council for Community and Economic Research (formerly ACCRA), Cost of Living Index, 2007

Health Care, Transportation, and Other Costs

Area[1]	Doctor ($/visit)	Dentist ($/visit)	Optometrist ($/visit)	Gasoline ($/gallon)	Beauty Salon ($/visit)	Men's Shirt ($)
City[2]	72.93	86.20	59.93	2.66	30.80	24.50
Avg.	79.48	71.93	79.55	2.64	29.52	25.77
Min.	52.08	44.80	43.95	2.19	15.58	16.19
Max.	148.44	126.27	158.83	3.48	60.62	48.53

Note: (1) Values for the local area are compared with the average, minimum and maximum values for all 331 areas in the Cost of Living Index report; (2) Figures cover the Morgantown WV urban area; **Doctor** *(general practitioners routine exam of an established patient);* **Dentist** *(adult teeth cleaning and periodic oral examination);* **Optometrist** *(full vision eye exam for established adult patient);* **Gasoline** *(one gallon regular unleaded, national brand, including all taxes, cash price at self-service pump if available);* **Beauty Salon** *(woman's shampoo, trim, and blow-dry);* **Men's Shirt** *(cotton/polyester dress shirt, pinpoint weave, long sleeves).*
Source: The Council for Community and Economic Research (formerly ACCRA), Cost of Living Index, 2007

HOUSING

House Price Index (HPI)

Area	National Ranking[2]	Quarterly Change (%)	One-Year Change (%)	Five-Year Change (%)
MSA[1]	(a)	n/a	4.85	50.18
U.S.[3]	-	0.10	0.84	41.37

Note: The HPI is a weighted repeat sales index. It measures average price changes in repeat sales or refinancings on the same properties. This information is obtained by reviewing repeat mortgage transactions on single-family properties whose mortgages have been purchased or securitized by Fannie Mae or Freddie Mac in January 1975; (1) Metropolitan Statistical Area - see Appendix B for areas included; (2) Rankings are based on annual percentage change for all metro areas containing at least 15,000 transactions over the last 10 years and ranges from 1 to 291; (3) figures based on a weighted average of Census Division estimates; all figures are for the period ending December 31, 2007; n/a not available; (a) Not ranked because of increased index variability due to smaller sample size
Source: Office of Federal Housing Enterprise Oversight, House Price Index, February 26, 2008

House Price Valuations

Area	Q1 2000	Q1 2001	Q1 2002	Q1 2003	Q1 2004	Q1 2005	Q1 2006	Q1 2007	Q1 2008
MSA[1]	n/a	n/a	n/a	n/a	n/a	n/a	n/a	n/a	n/a

Note: Figures show the percentage of over- or under-valuation of single family homes relative to statistically normal house values (e.g. a value of 23.6 indicates that house values are 23.6% overvalued). Statistically normal house values are based on house prices, interest rates, household incomes, population densities, and any historical premiums or discounts metropolitan areas have exhibited over time; (1) Figures cover the Metropolitan Statistical Area - see Appendix B for areas included; n/a not available
Source: Global Insight/National City Corporation, House Prices in America, May 2008

Median Home Prices

Area	2005	2006	2007[r]	Percent Change 2006 to 2007
MSA[1]	n/a	n/a	n/a	n/a
U.S. Average	219.0	221.9	217.9	-1.8

Note: Figures are median sales prices of existing single-family homes in thousands of dollars; (r) revised; n/a not available; (1) Metropolitan Statistical Area - see Appendix B for areas included
Source: National Association of Realtors, Metropolitan Area Prices, 1st Quarter 2008

Housing: Year Structure Built

Area	1990 -2000	1980 -1989	1970 -1979	1960 -1969	1950 -1959	1940 -1949	Before 1940	Median Year
City	9.0	6.4	13.6	13.7	15.9	12.6	28.9	1955
MSA[1]	0.0	0.0	0.0	0.0	0.0	0.0	0.0	0
U.S.	17.0	15.8	18.5	13.7	12.7	7.3	15.0	1971

Note: Figures are percentages; (1) Metropolitan Statistical Area - see Appendix A for areas included
Source: Census 2000, Summary File 3

HEALTH

Health Risk Data

Category	Area[1] (%)	U.S. (%)
Adults who have been told they have high blood pressure[3]	n/a	25.5
Adults who have been told they have high blood cholesterol[3]	n/a	35.6
Adults who have been told they have diabetes[2]	n/a	7.5
Adults who have been told they have arthritis[3]	n/a	27.0
Adults who have been told they currently have asthma	n/a	8.5
Adults who are current smokers	n/a	20.1
Adults who are heavy drinkers[4]	n/a	4.9
Adults who are overweight (BMI 25.0 - 29.9)	n/a	36.5
Adults who are obese (BMI 30.0 - 99.8)	n/a	25.1

Note: Data as of 2006 unless otherwise noted; n/a not available; (1) Figures cover the Metropolitan Statistical Area - see Appendix B for areas included; (2) Figures do not include pregnancy-related diabetes, pre-diabetes or borderline diabetes; (3) 2005 data; (4) Heavy drinkers are classified as adult men having more than two drinks per day or adult women having more than one drink per day
Source: Centers for Disease Control and Prevention, Behaviorial Risk Factor Surveillance System, SMART: Selected Metropolitan/Micropolitan Area Risk Trends, 2005, 2006

Mortality Rates for the Top 10 Causes of Death in the U.S.

ICD-10[a] Sub-Chapter	ICD-10[a] Code	Age-Adjusted Mortality Rate[1] per 100,000 population	
		County[2]	U.S.
Malignant neoplasms	C00-C97	171.5	186.5
Ischaemic heart diseases	I20-I25	163.1	152.3
Other forms of heart disease	I30-I51	69.5	51.5
Cerebrovascular diseases	I60-I69	46.3	50.0
Chronic lower respiratory diseases	J40-J47	44.3	42.6
Diabetes mellitus	E10-E14	29.2	24.8
Other degenerative diseases of the nervous system	G30-G31	30.2	22.6
Other external causes of accidental injury	W00-X59	18.5	21.4
Influenza and pneumonia	J10-J18	17.0	20.7
Hypertensive diseases	I10-I13	15.6	18.2

Note: (a) ICD-10 = International Classification of Diseases 10th Revision; (1) Mortality rates are a three year average covering 2003-2005; (2) Figures cover Monongalia County
Source: Centers for Disease Control and Prevention, National Center for Health Statistics. Compressed Mortality File 1999-2004. CDC WONDER On-line Database, compiled from Compressed Mortality File 1999-2005 Series 20 No. 2K, 2008.

Mortality Rates for Selected Causes of Death

ICD-10[a] Sub-Chapter	ICD-10[a] Code	Age-Adjusted Mortality Rate[1] per 100,000 population	
		County[2]	U.S.
Assault	X85-Y09	*1.9	5.9
Human immunodeficiency virus (HIV) disease	B20-B24	*2.5	4.5
Intentional self-harm	X60-X84	9.2	10.8
Malnutrition	E40-E46	*0.5	1.0
Obesity and other hyperalimentation	E65-E68	*0.9	1.4
Organic, including symptomatic, mental disorders	F01-F09	12.0	16.8
Transport accidents	V01-V99	11.1	16.1
Viral hepatitis	B15-B19	*1.8	1.8

Note: (a) ICD-10 = International Classification of Diseases 10th Revision; (1) Mortality rates are a three year average covering 2003-2005; (2) Figures cover Monongalia County; (*) Unreliable data as per CDC
Source: Centers for Disease Control and Prevention, National Center for Health Statistics. Compressed Mortality File 1999-2004. CDC WONDER On-line Database, compiled from Compressed Mortality File 1999-2005 Series 20 No. 2K, 2008.

Distribution of Physicians[1]

Area	Total	Family/ General Practice	Specialties	
			Medical	Surgical
Monongalia County (number)	389	72	119	105
Monongalia County (rate per 10,000 pop.)	46.1	8.5	14.1	12.4
U.S. (rate per 10,000 pop.)	17.7	4.6	6.9	4.3

Note: Data as of 2005; (1) Includes all non-federal, patient-care, office-based MDs
Source: Area Resource File (ARF). June 2007. U.S. Department of Health and Human Services, Health Resources and Services Administration, Bureau of Health Professions, Rockville, MD.

Hospitals

Morgantown has the following hospitals: 2 general medical and surgical; 1 rehabilitation.
AHA Guide to the Healthcare Field 2008

EDUCATION

Public School District Statistics

District Name	Schls	Pupils	Pupil/ Teacher Ratio	Minority Pupils[1] (%)	Free Lunch Eligible[2] (%)	IEP[3] (%)
Monongalia School District	27	10,024	14.4	9.8	30.0	15.3

Note: Table includes regular local school districts with 2,000 or more students; (1) Percentage of students that are not white, non-Hispanic; (2) Percentage of students that are eligible for the free lunch program; (3) Percentage of students that have an Individualized Education Program.
Source: U.S. Department of Education, National Center for Education Statistics, Common Core of Data, Local Education Agency (School District) Universe Survey: School Year 2005-2006; U.S. Department of Education, National Center for Education Statistics, Common Core of Data, Public Elementary/Secondary School Universe Survey: School Year 2005-2006

Top Public High Schools

High School Name	Index[1]	Rank[1]	Subsidized Lunch (%)[2]	E&E (%)[3]
Morgantown	1.172	1,242	27.0	20.8

Note: (1) Public schools are ranked according to a ratio that is the number of Advanced Placement, International Baccalaureate, and/or Cambridge tests taken by all students at a school in 2007 divided by the number of graduating seniors. All of the schools on the list have an index of at least 1.000; they are in the top five percent of public schools measured this way. The rankings range from 1 to 1,422; (2) Percentage of students receiving federally subsidized meals; (3) E & E stands for equity and excellence percentage: the portion of all graduating seniors at a school that had at least one passing grade on one AP or IB test; (**) Gave both IB and AP tests. AP and IB participation are indicators of a school's efforts to get students to excel and prepare for college.
Source: Newsweek Online, "Top High Schools 2008"

Highest Level of Education

Area	Less than H.S.	H.S. Diploma	Some College, No Deg.	Associate Degree	Bachelors Degree	Masters Degree	Profess. School Degree	Doctorate Degree
City	11.0	19.7	18.5	3.0	21.5	14.5	5.2	6.6
MSA[1]	19.0	34.9	16.0	3.5	12.8	8.0	2.8	3.0
U.S.	19.4	28.4	21.2	6.4	15.7	5.9	2.0	1.0

Note: Figures are 2007 estimated percentages and cover persons age 25 and over; (1) Metropolitan Statistical Area - see Appendix B for areas included
Source: Claritas, Inc.

Educational Attainment by Race

Area	High School Graduate (%)					Bachelor's Degree (%)				
	Total	White	Black	Asian	Hisp.[2]	Total	White	Black	Asian	Hisp.[2]
City	89.2	89.3	82.0	100.0	77.0	47.8	47.2	25.3	83.8	39.0
MSA[1]	n/a	n/a	n/a	n/a	n/a	n/a	n/a	n/a	n/a	n/a
U.S.	80.4	83.6	72.3	80.4	52.4	24.4	26.1	14.3	44.1	10.4

Note: Figures shown cover persons 25 years old and over; (1) Metropolitan Statistical Area - see Appendix A for areas included; (2) people of Hispanic origin can be of any race
Source: Census 2000, Summary File 3

School Enrollment by Type

Area	Grades KG to 8				Grades 9 to 12			
	Public		Private		Public		Private	
	Enrollment	%	Enrollment	%	Enrollment	%	Enrollment	%
City	1,274	86.4	201	13.6	637	95.9	27	4.1
MSA[1]	n/a	n/a	n/a	n/a	n/a	n/a	n/a	n/a
U.S.	33,526,011	88.7	4,285,121	11.3	14,848,628	90.6	1,532,323	9.4

Note: Figures shown cover persons 3 years old and over; (1) Metropolitan Statistical Area - see Appendix A for areas included
Source: Census 2000, Summary File 3

School Enrollment by Race

Area	Grades KG to 8 (%)				Grades 9 to 12 (%)			
	White	Black	Asian	Hisp.[1]	White	Black	Asian	Hisp.[1]
City	85.2	8.0	2.2	2.2	92.9	2.3	2.3	1.8
MSA[1]	n/a	n/a	n/a	n/a	n/a	n/a	n/a	n/a
U.S.	68.5	15.5	3.3	16.8	68.8	15.5	3.8	15.7

Note: Figures shown cover persons 3 years old and over; (1) people of Hispanic origin can be of any race; (2) Metropolitan Statistical Area - see Appendix A for areas included
Source: Census 2000, Summary File 3

Average Salaries of Public School Classroom Teachers

District	2005-06		2006-07		Percent Change 2005-06 to 2006-07
	Dollars	Rank[1]	Dollars	Rank[1]	
West Virginia	38,284	49	40,531	48	5.87
U.S. Average	49,026	-	50,816	-	3.65

Note: (1) State rank ranges from 1 to 51.
Source: National Education Association, Rankings & Estimates: Rankings of the States 2006 and Estimates of School Statistics 2007, December 2007

Higher Education

Four-Year Colleges			Two-Year Colleges			Medical Schools[1]	Law Schools[2]	Voc/ Tech[3]
Public	Private Non-profit	Private For-profit	Public	Private Non-profit	Private For-profit			
1	1	0	0	0	2	1	1	1

Note: Figures cover institutions located within the city limits; (1) includes schools accredited by the Liaison Committee on Medical Education and the American Osteopathic Association; (2) includes American Bar Association-accredited law schools; (3) includes all schools with programs that are less than 2 years.
Source: National Center for Education Statistics, The Integrated Postsecondary Education System (IPEDS) Peer Analysis System, 2007; www.usnews.com, Law and Medical School Directories, 2009

PRESIDENTIAL ELECTION

2004 Presidential Election Results

Area	Bush	Kerry	Nader	Other
Monongalia County	51.5	47.6	0.6	0.3
U.S.	50.7	48.3	0.4	0.6

Note: Results are percentages and may not add to 100% due to rounding
Source: Dave Leip's Atlas of U.S. Presidential Elections, www.uselectionatlas.org

EMPLOYERS

Major Employers

Company Name	Industry	Type of Site
Alosh Niosh Procurement	Administration of public health programs	Branch
Chemtura Corporation	Chemical preparations, nec	Branch
Cisco Academy Training Center	Schools and educational services	Branch
City Hall	Executive offices	Branch
College Engrg Mneral Resources	Colleges and universities	Branch
Cooperative Extension Service	Regulation of agricultural marketing	Branch
Coordnting Cncil For Ind Lving	Home health care services	Single
Gabriel Brothers Inc	Family clothing stores	Headquarters
Healthsth Mntnvw Regnl Rehab	Residential care	Single
Hopemont Hosptial	General medical and surgical hospitals	Branch
Kingwood Mining Company LLC	Coal and other minerals and ores	Single
Lakeview Golf Resort & Spa	Hotels and motels	Single
Lakeview Pro Shop	Sporting goods and bicycle shops	Single
Lakeview Scanticon Resort	Hotels and motels	Single
Lowes	Lumber and other building materials	Branch
March-Westin Company Inc	Nonresidential construction, nec	Single
Market Facts	Commercial nonphysical research	Branch
Matthews Bronze	Copper foundries	Branch
Monongalia County	Executive offices	Headquarters
Monongalia General Hospital	General medical and surgical hospitals	Headquarters
Moore John Michael Trauma Ctr	General medical and surgical hospitals	Headquarters
National Institue of Occptnal	Administration of public health programs	Branch
Preston Memorial Hospital Corp	General medical and surgical hospitals	Single
Target	Department stores	Branch
US Department of Energy	Administration of general economic programs	Single
W V U	Building maintenance services, nec	Branch
Wal-Mart	Department stores	Branch
West Virginia University	Colleges and universities	Headquarters

Note: Companies shown are located within the Morgantown metropolitan area; nec = not elsewhere classified.
Source: www.zapdata.com, May 2008

PUBLIC SAFETY

Crime Rate

Area	All Crimes	Violent Crimes				Property Crimes		
		Murder	Forcible Rape	Robbery	Aggrav. Assault	Burglary	Larceny -Theft	Motor Vehicle Theft
City	3,976.4	3.5	91.8	102.4	201.3	822.8	2,609.7	144.8
Metro[1]	2,668.3	3.5	36.6	48.9	151.0	601.2	1,656.2	171.0
U.S.	3,808.1	5.7	30.9	149.4	287.5	729.4	2,206.8	398.4

Note: Figures are crimes per 100,000 population; (1) Metropolitan Statistical Area - see Appendix B for areas included
Source: FBI Uniform Crime Reports, 2006

Hate Crimes

Area	Number of Quarters Reported	Bias Motivation				
		Race	Religion	Sexual Orientation	Ethnicity	Disability
City	4	1	0	0	1	0

Source: Federal Bureau of Investigation, Hate Crime Statistics 2006

RECREATION

Culture

Dance[1]	Theatre[1]	Instrumental Music[1]	Vocal Music[1]	Series/ Festivals	Museums	Zoos and Aquariums[2]
0	2	0	0	2	2	0

Note: (1) Number of professional perfoming groups; (2) AZA-accredited
Source: The Grey House Performing Arts Directory, 2007; Official Museum Directory, 2008; Association of Zoos & Aquariums, AZA Member Zoos & Aquariums, June 2008

Professional Sports Teams

Team Name	League
No teams are located in the metro area	

Source: Original research

MEDIA

Newspapers

Name	News Focus	Frequency	Circulation
The Dominion Post	Local	Daily	25,287

Note: Includes newspapers with offices located in the city
Source: MediaContactsPro, March 2008

Television Stations

Name	Ch.	Network(s)	Type	Ownership
KDKA	2	UPN/CBS	Commercial	CBS
WTAE	4	ABC	Commercial	Hearst-Argyle Broadcasting
WPXI	11	NBC	Commercial	Cox Enterprises Inc.
WQED	13	PBS	Public	WQED
WNPA	19	UPN	Commercial	Viacom International Inc.
WCWB	22	WBN	Commercial	Sinclair Broadcast Group
WNPB	24	PBS	Public	WV Educational Broadcasting Authority
WPCB	40	n/a	Commercial	Cornerstone Television Inc.
WPGH	53	Fox	Commercial	Sinclair Broadcast Group

Note: Stations included cover the Pittsburgh DMA (Designated Market Area)
BurrellesLuce, MediaContacts Online, January 2007

Major AM Radio Stations

Call Letters	Freq. (kHz)	Station Type	Target Audience	Station Format	Music Format
WWCS	540	n/a	General	News/Talk	n/a
WKHB	620	Commercial	General	News/Talk	n/a
WPIT	730	n/a	Religious	n/a	n/a
WAVL	910	n/a	Religious	Music/News/Sports/Talk	n/a
WBGG	970	Commercial	General	Sports/Talk	n/a
KDKA	1020	Commercial	General	News/Talk	n/a
WASP	1130	Commercial	General	Music	Oldies
WCCS	1160	n/a	General	Music/News	n/a
WKST	1200	Commercial	General	Talk	n/a
WEAE	1250	n/a	General	Music/Sports	n/a
WBZY	1280	Commercial	General	Music/News	Oldies
WCLG	1300	n/a	General	Music/News	n/a
WJAS	1320	Commercial	General	Music	Adult Standards
WPTT	1360	Commercial	General	Music/Talk	Album Rock
KQV	1410	n/a	General	Music/News/Talk	n/a
WAJR	1440	Commercial	General	News/Talk	n/a

Note: Stations included cover the Pittsburgh DMA (Designated Market Area); n/a not available
Source: BurrellesLuce, MediaContacts Online, January 2007

Major FM Radio Stations

Call Letters	Freq. (mHz)	Station Type	Target Audience	Station Format	Music Format
WKJL	88.1	n/a	General/Religious	Music/Talk	n/a
WQED	89.3	Public	General	Music	Classical
WLTJ	92.9	n/a	General/Women	Music/News	n/a
WBZZ	93.7	Commercial	General	Music	Top 40
WWSW	94.5	Commercial	General	Music/News	Oldies
WKST	96.1	n/a	General	Music/News/Talk	n/a
WRRK	96.9	n/a	General	Music/News	n/a
WKKW	97.9	n/a	General	Music	n/a
WZPT	100.7	Commercial	General	Music	Adult Contemp.
WVAQ	101.9	n/a	General	n/a	n/a
WDVE	102.5	Commercial	General	Music	Album Rock
WJJJ	104.7	Commercial	General	Music/News/Talk	80's
WXDX	105.9	Commercial	General	Music/Talk	Alternative
WAMO	106.7	Commercial	Black/General	Music	Urban Contemp.
WDSY	107.9	Commercial	General	Music	Country

Note: Stations included cover the Pittsburgh DMA (Designated Market Area); n/a not available
BurrellesLuce, MediaContacts Online, January 2007

CLIMATE

Average and Extreme Temperatures

Temperature	Jan	Feb	Mar	Apr	May	Jun	Jul	Aug	Sep	Oct	Nov	Dec	Yr.
Extreme High (°F)	76	72	84	89	90	93	99	95	97	86	79	76	99
Average High (°F)	40	42	52	62	71	78	81	80	74	64	53	43	62
Average Temp. (°F)	29	31	40	49	58	66	70	68	62	51	41	33	50
Average Low (°F)	18	19	27	36	45	53	58	56	49	37	29	22	38
Extreme Low (°F)	-24	-22	-15	3	20	25	32	34	27	11	2	-24	-24

Note: Figures cover the years 1948-1995
Source: National Climatic Data Center, International Station Meteorological Climate Summary, 9/96

Average Precipitation/Snowfall/Humidity

Precip./Humidity	Jan	Feb	Mar	Apr	May	Jun	Jul	Aug	Sep	Oct	Nov	Dec	Yr.
Avg. Precip. (in.)	3.4	3.0	4.0	3.7	4.1	4.4	4.7	4.1	3.5	2.7	3.3	3.6	44.4
Avg. Snowfall (in.)	20	16	11	4	Tr	0	0	0	0	1	7	14	73
Avg. Rel. Hum. 7am (%)	81	81	82	83	87	92	94	96	95	90	83	82	87
Avg. Rel. Hum. 4pm (%)	64	60	55	50	54	58	61	62	61	54	58	64	58

Note: Figures cover the years 1948-1995; Tr = Trace amounts (<0.05 in. of rain; <0.5 in. of snow)
Source: National Climatic Data Center, International Station Meteorological Climate Summary, 9/96

Weather Conditions

Temperature			Daytime Sky			Precipitation		
10°F & below	32°F & below	90°F & above	Clear	Partly cloudy	Cloudy	0.01 inch or more precip.	0.1 inch or more snow/ice	Thunder-storms
23	144	3	48	133	184	174	49	42

Note: Figures are average number of days per year and cover the years 1948-1995
Source: National Climatic Data Center, International Station Meteorological Climate Summary, 9/96

HAZARDOUS WASTE

Superfund Sites

Morgantown has one hazardous waste site on the EPA's Superfund Final National Priorities List: **Ordnance Works Disposal Areas**. *U.S. Environmental Protection Agency, Final National Priorities List, June 23, 2008*

AIR & WATER QUALITY

Air Quality Index

Area	Percent of Days when Air Quality was...[2]				AQI Statistics	
	Good	Moderate	Unhealthy for Sensitive Groups	Unhealthy	Maximum	Median
Area[1]	79.7	18.4	1.9	0.0	116	36

Note: The Air Quality Index (AQI) is an index for reporting daily air quality. EPA calculates the AQI for five major air pollutants regulated by the Clean Air Act: ground-level ozone, particle pollution (also known as particulate matter), carbon monoxide, sulfur dioxide, and nitrogen dioxide. The AQI runs from 0 to 500. The higher the AQI value, the greater the level of air pollution and the greater the health concern. There are six AQI categories: "Good" The AQI is between 0 and 50. Air quality is considered satisfactory; "Moderate" The AQI is between 51 and 100. Air quality is acceptable; "Unhealthy for Sensitive Groups" When AQI values are between 101 and 150, members of sensitive groups may experience health effects; "Unhealthy" When AQI values are between 151 and 200 everyone may begin to experience health effects; "Very Unhealthy" AQI values between 201 and 300 trigger a health alert; "Hazardous" AQI values over 300 trigger health warnings of emergency conditions; (1) Data covers Monongalia County; (2) Based on 365 days with AQI data in 2007.
Source: U.S. Environmental Protection Agency, Air Quality Index Report, 2007

Air Quality Index Pollutants

Area	Percent of Days when AQI Pollutant was...[2]					
	Carbon Monoxide	Nitrogen Dioxide	Ozone	Sulfur Dioxide	Particulate Matter 2.5	Particulate Matter 10
Area[1]	0.0	0.0	46.0	29.3	24.7	0.0

Note: The Air Quality Index (AQI) is an index for reporting daily air quality. EPA calculates the AQI for five major air pollutants regulated by the Clean Air Act: ground-level ozone, particle pollution (also known as particulate matter), carbon monoxide, sulfur dioxide, and nitrogen dioxide. The AQI runs from 0 to 500. The higher the AQI value, the greater the level of air pollution and the greater the health concern; (1) Data covers Monongalia County; (2) Based on 365 days with AQI data in 2007.
Source: U.S. Environmental Protection Agency, Air Quality Index Report, 2007

Air Quality Index Trends

Area	Trend Sites								All Sites
	1999	2000	2001	2002	2003	2004	2005	2006	2006
MSA[1]	n/a	n/a	n/a	n/a	n/a	n/a	n/a	n/a	n/a

Note: An AQI value greater than 100 indicates that air quality would have been in the unhealthful range on that day. Data from exceptional events are not included. These counts are presented in two ways. First, the counts are based on sites having an adequate record of monitoring data during the trend period (trend sites). These counts represent the relative change in the number of days with AQI values greater than 100. In the last column, the counts are based on all sites with data in the most recent year (because it is possible for a site to have data in the most recent year but not enough data to be a trend site); (1) Metropolitan Statistical Area - see Appendix A for areas included; n/a not available.
Source: U.S. Environmental Protection Agency, Office of Air and Radiation, Air Trends, Factbook and Related Information, Air Pollution Trends in Selected Metropolitan Areas 2006

Maximum Air Pollutant Concentrations

	Particulate Matter 10 (ug/m^3)	Particulate Matter 2.5 (ug/m^3)	Ozone (ppm)	Carbon Monoxide (ppm)	Sulfur Dioxide (ppm)	Nitrogen Dioxide (ppm)	Lead (ug/m^3)
MSA[1] Level	n/a	n/a	n/a	n/a	n/a	n/a	n/a
NAAQS[2]	150	35	0.125	9	0.140	0.053	1.50
Met NAAQS[2]	Yes	Yes	Yes	Yes	Yes	Yes	Yes

Note: Data from exceptional events are not included; (1) Metropolitan Statistical Area - see Appendix A for areas included; (2) National Ambient Air Quality Standards; n/a not available
Concentrations: Particulate Matter 10 (coarse particulate) - highest second maximum 24-hour concentration; Particulate Matter 2.5 (fine particulate) - highest 98th percentile 24-hour concentration; Ozone - highest second daily maximum 1-hour concentration; Carbon Monoxide - highest second maximum non-overlapping 8-hour concentration; Sulfur Dioxide - highest second maximum 24-hour concentration; Nitrogen Dioxide - highest arithmetic mean concentration; Lead - highest quarterly maximum concentration
Units: ppm = parts per million; ug/m^3 = micrograms per cubic meter
Source: U.S. Environmental Protection Agency, MSA Factbook 2006, Air Quality Statistics by City

Drinking Water

Water System Name	Pop. Served	Primary Water Source Type	Violations[1]	
			Health Based	Monitoring/ Reporting
Morgantown Utility Board	53,935	Surface	0	2

Note: (1) Based on violation data from January 1, 2007 to December 31, 2007 (includes unresolved violations from earlier years)
Source: U.S. Environmental Protection Agency, Office of Ground Water and Drinking Water, Safe Drinking Water Information System (based on data extracted April 15, 2008)

Brookfield, Wisconsin

Background

Brookfield is minutes from Milwaukee in Waukesha County. It's a suburb within the Milwaukee/Racine/Waukesha metropolitan area and 90 minutes from Chicago. Brookfield traces its beginnings back to 1820 when William Howe received a presidential land grant. In 1839 the town of Brookfield was established on 36 square miles, which included Elm Grove. Brookfield began to grow around a depot that was situated at the junction of two major rail lines, one from Milwaukee to Waukesha and the other from Milwaukee to La Crosse. Despite the heavy influence of the railroad on the community, Brookfield remained largely an agricultural community.

In 1954, Brookfield became its own city with 7,000 people and, the following year, Elm Grove became its own town. With the surge of automobile ownership, Brookfield developed into a bedroom community for Milwaukee. Over the next four years, the city experienced a population boom more than doubling the population to 15,000, attributed to post-war growth and the influence of the automobile market on suburban areas. Growth in the city began to spread out, causing challenges for city planners years later. Brookfield is now the fourth largest city in the state. Its daytime population is nearly double that of the community's official population, due 9 to 5 employees. Brookfield has developed a master plan for the next 12 years to ensure sustainable future growth and development.

Despite all that Milwaukee has to offer, Brookfield has many attractions of its own. Residents enjoy festivals, a substantial parks and recreation department and a center for the arts. The bigger city is home to several museums, performing arts venues, professional sports, and many outdoor activities, largely based around Lake Michigan. Additionally, the city of Milwaukee is known for its festivals. It's still often referred to as Brew City, its historical nickname referencing a time when Milwaukee was considered the beer capital of the world, as most of the world's beer was once produced there. While Milwaukee's beer production is nowhere near the level it once was, there are still artifacts and attractions that relate to this history.

Brookfield is served primarily by the Elmbrook School District. The city has one university, Ottawa University - Wisconsin. Milwaukee has several more higher education institutions, including Marquette University and University of Wisconsin-Milwaukee; the latter enrolls nearly 30,000 students. A 2000 study from McGill University ranked Milwaukee sixth in a list of North American cities with the highest number of college students per 100 residents.

Brookfield is most directly served by General Mitchell International Airport which offers daily flights to nearly 90 cities including international locations such as Mexico, the Dominican Republic, and Jamaica. Brookfield is also served less directly by airports in Chicago, namely O'Hare.

Brookfield sits in a humid continental climate zone whose weather is often greatly affected by Lake Michigan. Temperatures range from average lows in the teens in January to average highs in the lower 80s in July. Average precipitation ranges from under two inches in a month during January and February to around four inches in August and is, again affected by the lake. Though not extremely common due to wind direction and distance, Brookfield may be affected by lake effect snow during the winter season.

Rankings

General Rankings

- Milwaukee* was ranked #280 out of 375 metro areas in *Cities Ranked & Rated*. Criteria: cost of living; climate; crime; transportation; economy and jobs; education; arts and culture; health and healthcare; leisure; quality of life. *Cities Ranked & Rated, 2nd Edition, 2007*

- Milwaukee* was ranked #33 out of 379 metro areas in *Places Rated Almanac*. Criteria: health care; education; recreation; transportation; ambience; climate; crime; housing costs; jobs. *Places Rated Almanac, 7th Edition, 2007*

Business/Finance Rankings

- The nation's 100 largest metro areas were analysed in terms of the percentage of households entering some stage of foreclosure in 2007. The Milwaukee* metro area ranked #49 out of 100 (#1 = highest foreclosure rate). *RealtyTrac, "Year-End 2007 Metropolitan Foreclosure Report"*

- The Milwaukee* metro area was selected one of America's "Top 50 Business Opportunity Metros" by *Expansion Management* in their 5th annual Mayor's Challenge ranking of metro areas that have achieved solid ratings across the board in numerous *EM* studies during the past 12 months. The area ranked #43. Criteria: public schools; quality of life; college educated workers; logistics infrastructure; healthcare costs; taxes and government spending; reputation among site consultants. *Expansion Management, August 2007*

- The Milwaukee* metro area was selected as one of "America's Most Wired Cities" by *Forbes*. The metro area was ranked #28 out of 30. Criteria: percentage of Internet users with high-speed access; the range of service providers within a city; availability of public wireless hot spots. *Forbes, "America's Most Wired Cities," January 10, 2008*

- The Milwaukee* metro area was identified as one of 10 "Top Up-and-Coming Tech Cities" by *Forbes*. The metro area ranked #5. Criteria: regional innovation trends; important patents. *Forbes.com, "Top Up-and-Coming Tech Cities," March 11, 2008*

- Milwaukee* was selected as one of the best places to start and grow a company by *Entrepreneur* and the National Policy Research Council. The Milwaukee* metro area ranked #18 out of 50 large metro areas. Criteria: business formation and growth (firms started four to 14 years ago that still employ at least 5 people and experienced rapid growth over the last four years). *Entrepreneur/National Policy Research Council, "Hot Cities for Entrepreneurs," September 2006*

- Intel, in partnership with Sperling's BestPlaces, ranked the 80 "Best Cities for Teleworking" in America. The Milwaukee* metro area ranked #13 among large metro areas. The study identifies cities that hold the greatest potential for teleworking based on a host of factors including typical commuting times, fuel prices, availability of broadband Internet access and percentage of the population in telework friendly jobs. The study also factored in extreme climate and natural hazards. *Intel, "Best Cities for Teleworking," March 30, 2006*

- Brookfield was selected as one of the "100 Best Places to Live and Launch" in the U.S. The city ranked #72. The editors at *Fortune Small Business* ranked 296 Census-designated metro areas by business friendliness (Launching Score, % New Businesses) and lifestyle offerings (Living Score). Then, through reporting, they picked the town within each of the top 100 metro areas that best blends business and pleasure. *Fortune Small Business, "100 Best Places to Live and Launch 2008," April 2008*

- The Milwaukee* metro area appeared on the Milken Institute "2007 Best Performing Cities" index. Rank: #162 out of 200 large metro areas. Criteria: job growth; wage and salary growth; high-tech output growth. *Milken Institute, "2007 Best Performing Cities"*

- Milwaukee* was identified as one of the 100 "Most Unwired Cities" in the U.S. The area ranked #26 out of the 100 largest metro areas in the U.S. Criteria: number of public and commercial wireless access points (hotspots); airports with wireless Internet access; broadband availability; local wireless networks; and wireless email devices. *Intel, "Most Unwired Cities Survey," June 7, 2005*

- Milwaukee* was ranked #24 out of 125 regions worldwide in terms of its "Knowledge Competitiveness Index." The index attempts to measure the knowledge-based development taking place throughout the world and is based on 19 measures of economic performance that indicate a region's ability to translate its knowledge capacity into economic value. *Robert Huggins Associates, World Knowledge Competitiveness Index 2005*

- *Forbes* ranked the 200 most populous metro areas in the U.S. in terms of the "Best Places for Business and Careers." The Milwaukee* metro area was ranked #113. Criteria: business costs (labor, energy, tax and office space expenses); living costs (housing, transportation, food and other household expenditures); education levels of the work force; job growth; income growth; migration trends; crime rates; and culture/leisure. *Forbes, "Best Places for Business and Careers," March 19, 2008*

- *Fortune* ranked the 100 largest metro areas in the U.S. in terms of projected median home price change in 2007. The Milwaukee* metro area ranked #59. *Fortune.com, "Hot Spots, Cold Spots"*

Health/Environment Rankings

- 100 of the largest metro areas in the U.S. were analyzed in terms of their current drought severity. The Milwaukee* metro area ranked #82 (#1 = driest). The rankings were based on statistics such as long-term precipitation trends and patterns and the Palmer drought indices. *Sperling's BestPlaces, www.BestPlaces.net, "America's Drought-Riskiest Cities," November 2007*

- Doctors at the Harvard School of Public Health ranked 40 metropolitan areas based on data from the government-sponsored Hospital Quality Alliance program. The program tracks the performance of individual hospitals in treating patients for three common health problems: heart attacks, congestive heart failure, and pneumonia. The Milwaukee* metro area ranked #26 in quality of care for heart attacks, #23 for congestive heart failure, and #14 for pneumonia. *New England Journal of Medicine, July 21, 2005*

- *Reader's Digest* ranked the 50 largest metro areas in the U.S. in terms of how "clean" they are. The Milwaukee* metro area ranked #26. Criteria: air quality; water quality; toxic industrial pollution; Superfund sites; and sanitation. *Reader's Digest, "The 50 Cleanest (and Dirtiest) Cities in America," July 2005*

- The Milwaukee* metro area was identified as one of "America's Most Obese Cities" by *Forbes*. The magazine analyzed BMI (body mass index) data from the CDC in the 50 most populated metro areas in the U.S. and ranked the top 20. The area ranked #17. *Forbes, "America's Most Obese Cities," November 26, 2007*

- The Milwaukee* metro area appeared in *Country Home's* "2008 Best Green Places" report. The area ranked #63 out of 379. Criteria: official energy policies; green power; green buildings; availability of fresh, locally grown food. *Country Home, "2008 Best Green Places"*

- Wyeth Consumer Healthcare, in partnership with Sperling's BestPlaces, ranked the nation's 50 most populous metro areas in terms of five key health factors. The Milwaukee* metro area ranked #27. Criteria: physical activity; health status; nutrition; lifestyle pursuits; and mental wellness. *Wyeth Consumer Healthcare, "Centrum Healthiest Cities Study," April 19, 2005*

- Milwaukee* was identified as a "2008 Asthma Capital." The area ranked #3 out of the nation's 100 largest metropolitan areas. Twelve factors were used to identify the most challenging places to live for people with asthma: estimated prevalence; self-reported prevalence; crude death rate for asthma; annual pollen score; annual air quality; public smoking laws; number of board-certified asthma specialists; school inhaler access laws; rescue medication use; controller medication use; uninsured rate; poverty rate. *Asthma and Allergy Foundation of America, "2008 Asthma Capitals"*

- Milwaukee* was identified as a "Spring Allergy Capital." The area ranked #42 out of 100. Three groups of factors were used to identify the most severe cities for people with allergies during the spring season: annual pollen levels; medicine utilization; access to board-certified allergists. *Asthma and Allergy Foundation of America, "2007 Spring Allergy Capital Rankings"*

- Milwaukee* was identified as a "Fall Allergy Capital." The area ranked #66 out of 100. Three groups of factors were used to identify the most severe cities for people with allergies during the fall season: annual pollen levels; medicine utilization; access to board-certified allergists. *Asthma and Allergy Foundation of America, "2007 Fall Allergy Capital Rankings"*

- Ortho-McNeil Neurologics, in partnership with Sperling's BestPlaces, analyzed 110 metro areas and identified those U.S. cities with the highest prevalence of factors that are most commonly associated with migraine headaches. The Milwaukee* metro area ranked #18. Criteria: number of migraine-related drug prescriptions per capita; lifestyle factors that can contribute to migraines; environmental factors that can trigger migraines; and consumption of migraine-triggering foods. *Ortho-McNeil Neurologics, "America's Migraine Hot Spots," March 14, 2006*

- Sperling's BestPlaces ranked 331 metro areas and identified the most and least stressful U.S. cities. The Milwaukee* metro area ranked #46 out of the 100 largest metro areas (#1 = most stressful). Criteria: divorce rate; unemployment rate; violent and property crime; suicide rate; commute time; mental health; alcohol consumption; cloudy days. *Sperling's BestPlaces, www.BestPlaces.net, "America's Most (and Least) Stressful Cities," January 9, 2004*

- An analysis of the "Best & Worst Cities for Sleep" was conducted by Sperling's BestPlaces. The study ranked America's 50 most populated metro areas. The Milwaukee* metro area ranked #20 (#1 = best city for sleep). Criteria: number of days residents didn't get enough rest or sleep during the past month; average length of daily commute; divorce rate; unemployment rate. *Sperling's BestPlaces, www.BestPlaces.net, "Best & Worst Cities for Sleep," 2006*

- Milwaukee* was highlighted as one of the 25 most ozone-polluted metro areas in the U.S. The area ranked #17. *American Lung Association, State of the Air: 2007*

- Milwaukee* was selected as one of "America's Pet Healthiest Cities" by Purina. The city ranked #22 out of 50. Criteria: veterinary services; environment; legislation; preventative care; obesity/body condition. *Purina Pet Institute, "America's Pet Healthiest Cities," May 20, 2003*

Women/Minorities Rankings

- Milwaukee* was ranked #68 out of 100 metro areas in *SELF Magazine's* ranking of "America's Best Places for Women." A panel of experts came up with more than 50 criteria including death and disease rates, environmental indicators, community resources, and lifestyle habits. *SELF Magazine, "America's Best Places for Women 2007," December 2007*

Seniors/Retirement Rankings

- Sperling's BestPlaces in partnership with Bankers Life & Casualty Company designed a survey to identify the top 50 metro areas in the U.S. that offer the best overall qualities for senior living. The Milwaukee* metro area ranked #5. The following criteria were statistically weighted to reflect the needs of the senior population: health; disease; economics; social; environment; spiritual; transportation; housing; and crime. *Bankers Life & Casualty Company, "Best Cities for Seniors 2005"*

- A.G. Edwards ranked America's 500 top-performing communities based on their residents' personal savings and investing behavior. The Milwaukee* metro area ranked #92 with an index score of 106.93 (national average = 100.00). A dozen statistical factors were measured including: participation in retirement savings plans; personal debt levels; and home ownership. *A.G. Edwards, "2007 Nest Egg Index", September 12, 2007*

Children/Family Rankings

- The Milwaukee* metro area was selected as one of the "Best Cities for Relocating Families" by Worldwide ERC and Primacy Relocation. The 2007 study placed a special emphasis on the housing market, which has significantly impacted the relocation industry and an employer's ability to transfer employees. The variables which weigh heavily in this category include home price, home affordability index, appreciation rates, and property tax. Other criteria include cost of living, crime rates, education, climate, focus on diversity, physicians per capita, recreation and leisure, arts and culture, air quality, watershed quality, sales tax, unemployment rate, job growth, high school and higher education index, school expenditures per student, students in public school, SAT/ACT percentile, and population growth. *Worldwide ERC and Primacy Relocation, "2007 Best Cities for Relocating Families"*

Safety Rankings

- The National Insurance Crime Bureau ranked 361 metro areas in the U.S. in terms of per capita rates of vehicle theft. The Milwaukee* metro area ranked #45 (#1 = highest rate). Criteria: number of vehicle theft offenses per 100,000 inhabitants. *National Insurance Crime Bureau, "NICB Vehicle Theft Study," April 22, 2008*
- Milwaukee* appeared on Sperling's BestPlaces list of the "Riskiest Cities for Identity Theft." The area ranked #36 out of the nations 50 largest metro areas. Over 80 criteria were analyzed across four major categories: technology impact; crime; transactions; and risk profile. *Sperling's BestPlaces, www.BestPlaces.net, "Riskiest Cities for Identity Theft," July 2006*
- Farmers Insurance Group of Companies, in partnership with Sperling's BestPlaces, ranked 379 metro areas and identified the "Most Secure U.S. Place to Live." The Milwaukee* metro area ranked #62 out of 114 in the large metro area category (500,000 or more residents). Criteria: crime rates; extreme weather; risk of natural disasters; environmental hazards; terrorism threats; air quality; life expectancy; job loss numbers. *Farmers Insurance Group, "Most Secure U.S. Places to Live 2007"*
- Milwaukee* was identified as one of the most dangerous large metro areas for pedestrians in the U.S. The area ranked #44 out of the nations 50 largest metro areas. Criteria: average yearly pedestrian fatalities per capita (for the years 2002 and 2003) adjusted for the number of walkers. *Surface Transportation Policy Project, "Mean Streets 2004"*

Sports/Recreation Rankings

- The Milwaukee* metro area appeared on the *Sporting News* list of the "Best Sports Cities 2007". The area ranked #47 out of 150 cities in the U.S. *Sporting News* takes a 12-month snapshot, roughly July to July, of each city's sports, putting a heavy premium on regular-season won-lost records (from the most recently completed season). Other criteria include: playoff berths, bowl appearances and tournament bids; championships; applicable power ratings; quality of competition; overall fan fervor as measured in part by attendance as percentage of venue capacity; abundance of teams (rewarding quality over quantity); stadium and arena quality; ticket availability and prices; franchise ownership; and marquee appeal of athletes. *SportingNews.com, "Best Sports Cities 2007," August 1, 2007*
- The Milwaukee* metro area was selected by *Cranium* as one of the "Top 50 Fun Cities" in America. The area ranked #14. Criteria includes: number of sports teams, restaurants, and dance performances; number of toy stores; city budget spent on recreation. *Cranium, November 4, 2003*
- *Golf Digest* ranked 330 metro areas in the U.S. in terms of golf. The Milwaukee* metro area was ranked #308. Criteria: access to golf; weather; value of golf; and quality of golf. *Golf Digest, "Metro Golf Rankings," August 2005*

Dating/Romance Rankings

- Eli Lily and Company, in partnership with Sperling's BestPlaces, ranked the nation's 50 largest metro areas in terms of the "Most Romantic Cities for Baby Boomers." The Milwaukee* metro area ranked #23. Criteria: marriage and divorce rates among "baby boomers" age 45 to 60; great restaurants; dance studios; chocolate, jewelry and flower sales. *Eli Lily and Company, "Most Romantic Cities for Baby Boomers," April 20, 2007*

- The Milwaukee* metro area was selected as one of the "Top Ten U.S. Cities for Finding a Rich, Single Woman" by Teasley, a Manhattan-based marketing consulting firm. The area ranked #10. Criteria: high single-female to single-male ratio; higher income to cost-of-living ratio; percentage of population that is single. *Teasley, "Where to Find a Rich, Single Woman in the United States," 2005*

- The Milwaukee* metro area was selected as one of the "Best Cities for Relocating Singles" by Worldwide ERC and Primacy Relocation. The area ranked #57 out of the 100 largest metro areas in the U.S. Areas were selected based on the following criteria: a robust cost-of-living index; adventure and outdoor recreation opportunities; violent crime and property crime rates; percentage of the population that is unmarried (ages 25-34); ratio of single men and single women; affordability of quality higher education, including in-state and out-of-state tuition requirements and rates; number of newcomers to the area; commute times; tax rates; fee and occupancy rates for temporary housing and mini-storage; quality and quantity of collegiate and professional sporting events and fun, fan-friendly venues. *Worldwide ERC and Primacy Relocation, "2007 Best Cities for Relocating Singles," October 25, 2007*

- *Forbes* ranked the 40 most populous urbanized areas in the U.S. in terms of the "Best Cities for Singles." The Milwaukee* metro area ranked #24. Criteria: number of singles; cost of living alone; nightlife; culture; job growth; coolness; and online dating. *Forbes.com, August 21, 2007*

- Sperling's BestPlaces in partnership with AXE Deodorant Bodyspray ranked 80 metro areas and identified "America's Best (and Worst) Cities for Dating." The Milwaukee* metro area ranked #43 (#1 = best). Criteria: percentage of singles ages 18-24; population density; dating venues per capita. *AXE Deodorant Bodyspray, "America's Best (and Worst) Cities for Dating," May 2004*

Culture/Performing Arts Rankings

- Scarborough Research, a leading market research firm, identified the top local markets for rock concert attendance. The Milwaukee* DMA (Designated Market Area) ranked in the top 25 with 17% of consumers, 18 years old and over, reporting that they have attended a rock concert during the past year. *Scarborough Research, June 14, 2004*

Miscellaneous Rankings

- The Milwaukee* metro area appeared on *Forbes* list of "America's Drunkest Cities". The area ranked #1. Criteria: 35 of the largest continental U.S. metro areas were chosen based on availability of data and geographic diversity. Each metro was ranked in five areas: state laws; drinkers; heavy drinkers; binge drinkers; and alcoholism. *Forbes.com, "America's Drunkest Cities," August 22, 2006*

- Sperling's BestPlaces in partnership with Pep Boys ranked 77 metro areas and identified "America's Most Drivable Cities." The Milwaukee* metro area ranked #62. Criteria: climate; road roughness; urban mobility; gas prices. *Pep Boys, "America's Most Drivable Cities," April 9, 2003*

- State Farm Insurance, in partnership with Sperling's BestPlaces, analyzed several key factors that contribute to overall family preparedness. The Milwaukee* metro area ranked #46 out of the nation's 50 most populous metro areas. Criteria: quality of life; life insurance coverage; and investments. *State Farm Life Insurance, "Fiscally Fit Cities Report," July 20, 2004*

- Scarborough Research, a leading market research firm, identified the top local markets for grocery coupon use. The Milwaukee* DMA (Designated Market Area) ranked in the top 25 with 45% of consumers reporting that they use grocery coupons at least once per week. *Scarborough Research, December 8, 2004*

- A study by Sperling's BestPlaces examined which U.S. metro areas were most affected by high fuel prices in 2006. The Milwaukee* metro area was ranked #47 out of 80 (#1 = most expensive city for driving). Rankings are based on the average dollars spent on gas per year by two driver households. Criteria: cost of regular-grade gasoline; average miles driven per day; average number of gallons each driver uses and wastes in traffic congestion each day. *Sperling's BestPlaces, www.bestplaces.net, "Pain at the Pump," May 18, 2006*

Brookfield is located within the Milwaukee-Waukesha-West Allis, WI Metropolitan Statistical Area.

Business Environment

CITY FINANCES

City Government Finances

Component	2004-2005 ($000)	2004-2005 ($ per capita)
Total Revenues	56,866	1,434
Total Expenditures	54,227	1,367
Debt Outstanding	116,935	2,949
Cash and Securities	27,398	691

Source: U.S Census Bureau, Government Finances 2004-2005

City Government Revenue by Source

Source	2004-2005 ($000)	2004-2005 ($ per capita)
General Revenue		
From Federal Government	0	0
From State Government	6,620	167
From Local Governments	2,182	55
Taxes		
Property	27,691	698
Sales	2,025	51
Personal Income	0	0
License	1,166	29
Charges	11,341	286
Liquor Store	0	0
Utility	3,457	87
Employee Retirement	0	0
Other	2,384	60

Source: U.S Census Bureau, Government Finances 2004-2005

City Government Expenditures by Function

Function	2004-2005 ($000)	2004-2005 ($ per capita)	2004-2005 (%)
General Expenditures			
Airports	0	0	0.0
Corrections	0	0	0.0
Education	0	0	0.0
Fire Protection	5,024	127	9.3
Governmental Administration	3,729	94	6.9
Health	2,427	61	4.5
Highways	7,678	194	14.2
Hospitals	0	0	0.0
Housing and Community Development	0	0	0.0
Interest on General Debt	3,950	100	7.3
Libraries	2,241	57	4.1
Parking	0	0	0.0
Parks and Recreation	2,499	63	4.6
Police Protection	7,690	194	14.2
Public Welfare	0	0	0.0
Sewerage	12,151	306	22.4
Solid Waste Management	2,142	54	4.0
Liquor Store	0	0	0.0
Utility	2,881	73	5.3
Employee Retirement	0	0	0.0
Other	1,815	46	3.3

Source: U.S Census Bureau, Government Finances 2004-2005

Municipal Bond Ratings

Area	Moody's
City	Aaa

Source: Mergent Bond Record, January 2008 (unless noted otherwise)

DEMOGRAPHICS

Population Growth

Area	1990 Census	2000 Census	2007 Estimate	2012 Projection	Population Growth (%)	
					1990-2000	2000-2012
City	35,183	38,649	39,357	39,738	9.9	2.8
MSA[1]	1,432,149	1,500,741	1,515,804	1,523,297	4.8	1.5
U.S.	248,709,873	281,421,906	301,045,522	314,920,978	13.2	11.9

Note: (1) Metropolitan Statistical Area - see Appendix B for areas included
Source: Claritas, Inc.

Number of Households and Average Household Size

Area	2007 Estimate	2007 Average Household Size
City	14,755	2.67
MSA[1]	610,139	2.48
U.S.	113,668,003	2.65

Note: (1) Metropolitan Statistical Area - see Appendix B for areas included
Source: Claritas, Inc.

Race and Ethnicity

Area	White Alone[2]	Black Alone[2]	Asian Alone[2]	Other Race Alone[2]	Hispanic[3]
City	91.5	1.3	5.8	1.5	1.4
MSA[1]	74.7	16.4	2.5	6.4	7.8
U.S.	73.1	12.4	4.3	10.3	14.9

Note: Figures are 2007 estimates; (1) Metropolitan Statistical Area - see Appendix B for areas included (2) Alone is defined as not being in combination with one or more other races; (3) May be of any race.
Source: Claritas, Inc.

Ancestry

Area	German	Irish[2]	English	American	Italian	Polish	French[3]	Scottish
City	46.1	14.7	7.3	3.4	7.7	11.3	3.3	1.5
MSA[1]	37.7	10.0	5.1	2.7	4.4	12.7	3.1	0.9
U.S.	15.2	10.9	8.7	7.3	5.6	3.2	3.0	1.7

Note: Figures include multiple ancestry (e.g. if a person reported being Irish and Italian, they were included in both columns); (1) Metropolitan Statistical Area - see Appendix A for areas included; (2) Includes Celtic; (3) Includes Alsatian but excludes Basque
Source: Census 2000, Summary File 3

Foreign-Born Population

Area	Percent of Population Born in							
	Any Foreign Country	Europe	Asia	Africa	Oceania[2]	Canada	Mexico	Latin America[3]
City	6.3	3.1	2.4	0.1	0.1	0.3	0.2	0.2
MSA[1]	5.4	1.6	1.5	0.2	0.0	0.1	1.6	0.4
U.S.	11.1	1.7	2.9	0.3	0.1	0.3	3.3	2.5

Note: (1) Metropolitan Statistical Area - see Appendix A for areas included; (2) Includes Australia, New Zealand subregion, Melanesia, Micronesia, Polynesia, and Oceania n.e.c; (3) Includes Central America (excluding Mexico), South America, and the Caribbean.
Source: Census 2000, Summary File 3

Marriage Status

Area	Never Married	Now Married (excluding Separated)	Separated	Widowed	Divorced
City	18.6	69.9	0.5	6.3	4.8
MSA[1]	30.4	52.3	1.5	6.5	9.3
U.S.	27.1	54.4	2.2	6.6	9.7

Note: Figures are percentages and cover the population 15 years of age and older; (1) Metropolitan Statistical Area - see Appendix A for areas included
Source: Census 2000, Summary File 3

Age Distribution

Area	Percent of Population						
	Under Age 5	Age 5 to 17	Age 18 to 34	Age 35 to 49	Age 50 to 64	Age 65 to 79	80 Years and Over
City	5.6	21.0	11.2	25.8	18.7	13.6	4.1
MSA[1]	6.9	19.5	22.8	23.9	14.3	9.1	3.4
U.S.	6.8	18.9	23.7	23.5	14.8	9.2	3.2

Note: (1) Metropolitan Statistical Area - see Appendix A for areas included
Source: Census 2000, Summary File 3

Male/Female Ratio

Area	Males	Females	Males per 100 Females
City	19,082	20,275	94.1
MSA[1]	738,059	777,745	94.9
U.S.	148,320,305	152,725,217	97.1

Note: Figures are 2007 estimates; (1) Metropolitan Statistical Area - see Appendix B for areas included
Source: Claritas, Inc.

Religion

Area	Catholic	Southern Baptist	United Meth-odist	ELCA[1]	LDS[2]	Presby-terian Church USA	Jewish Est.	Muslim Est.
County	37.3	0.1	2.0	7.6	0.3	0.9	0.6	0.0
U.S.	22.0	7.1	3.7	1.8	1.5	1.1	2.2	0.6

Note: Figures are the number of adherents as a percentage of the total population; Adherents are defined as all members, including full members, their children and the estimated number of other participants who are not considered members (e.g. the baptized, those not confirmed, those regularly attending services, etc.);
(1) Evangelical Lutheran Church in America; (2) The Church of Jesus Christ of Latter Day Saints
Source: Reprinted with permission from Religious Congregations and Membership in the United States 2000 (Nashville, Glenmary Research Center, 2002) Copyright Association of Statisticians of American Religious Bodies. All rights reserved.

ECONOMY

Gross Metropolitan Product

Area	2002	2003	2004	2005	2005 Rank[2]
MSA[1]	56.9	58.6	61.3	63.7	39

Note: Figures are in billions of dollars; (1) Milwaukee-Waukesha-West Allis, WI Metropolitan Statistical Area - see Appendix A for areas included; (2) Rank ranges from 1 to 361
Source: The U.S. Conference of Mayors, "U.S. Metro Economies: GMP - The Engines of America's Growth," January 2007

Economic Growth

Area	1995 GMP	2005 GMP	Average Annual Growth Rate	Growth Rate Rank[2]
MSA[1]	43.3	63.7	3.9	322

Note: Figures are in billions of dollars; GMP = Gross Metropolitan Product; (1) Milwaukee-Waukesha-West Allis, WI Metropolitan Statistical Area - see Appendix A for areas included; (2) Rank ranges from 1 to 361
Source: The U.S. Conference of Mayors, "U.S. Metro Economies: GMP - The Engines of America's Growth," January 2007

INCOME

Per Capita/Median/Average Income

Area	Per Capita ($)	Median Household ($)	Average Household ($)
City	42,903	83,387	113,622
MSA[1]	27,789	53,034	68,386
U.S.	25,495	49,280	66,670

Note: Figures are 2007 estimates; (1) Metropolitan Statistical Area - see Appendix B for areas included
Source: Claritas, Inc.

Household Income Distribution

Area	Percent of Households Earning							
	Under $15,000	$15,000 -24,999	$25,000 -34,999	$35,000 -49,999	$50,000 -74,999	$75,000 -99,000	$100,000 -149,999	$150,000 and up
City	3.3	4.6	6.2	10.9	19.0	17.4	19.6	18.8
MSA[1]	11.1	10.0	10.6	15.5	20.6	13.5	12.4	6.2
U.S.	13.1	10.9	11.2	15.6	19.5	11.9	11.3	6.6

Note: Figures are 2007 estimates; (1) Metropolitan Statistical Area - see Appendix B for areas included
Source: Claritas, Inc.

Poverty Rates by Age

Area	All Ages	Under 5 Years Old	5 to 17 Years Old	18 to 64 Years Old	65 Years and Over
City	2.2	0.1	0.5	1.0	0.6
MSA[1]	10.6	1.3	3.0	5.5	0.8
U.S.	12.4	1.2	3.0	6.9	1.2

Note: Figures are percent of population with income in 1999 below poverty level and only include population for whom poverty status is determined; (1) Metropolitan Statistical Area - see Appendix A for areas included
Source: Census 2000, Summary File 3

Personal Bankruptcy Filing Rate

Area	2004	2005	2006
Waukesha County	2.99	4.39	1.35
U.S.	5.31	6.82	2.00

Note: Numbers are per 1,000 population and include Chapter 7 and Chapter 13 filings
Source: Federal Deposit Insurance Corporation (FDIC), Regional Economic Conditions (RECON), 8/23/2007

EMPLOYMENT

Labor Force and Employment

Area	Civilian Labor Force			Workers Employed		
	Dec. 2006	Dec. 2007	% Chg.	Dec. 2006	Dec. 2007	% Chg.
City	20,496	20,184	-1.5	19,875	19,571	-1.5
MSA[1]	807,173	797,111	-1.2	771,560	759,766	-1.5
U.S.	152,571,000	153,705,000	0.7	146,081,000	146,334,000	0.2

Note: Data is not seasonally adjusted and covers workers 16 years of age and older;
(1) Metropolitan Statistical Area - see Appendix B for areas included
Source: Bureau of Labor Statistics, http://stats.bls.gov

Unemployment Rate

Area	2007											
	Jan.	Feb.	Mar.	Apr.	May	Jun.	Jul.	Aug.	Sep.	Oct.	Nov.	Dec.
City	3.4	3.6	3.7	3.7	3.7	4.0	3.7	3.6	3.6	3.2	3.3	3.0
MSA[1]	5.1	5.4	5.2	5.3	5.0	5.5	5.4	5.2	4.9	4.6	4.7	4.7
U.S.	5.0	4.9	4.5	4.3	4.3	4.7	4.9	4.6	4.5	4.4	4.5	4.8

Note: Data is not seasonally adjusted and covers workers 16 years of age and older; All figures are percentages; (1) Metropolitan Statistical Area - see Appendix B for areas included
Source: Bureau of Labor Statistics, http://stats.bls.gov

Employment by Occupation

Occupation Classification	City (%)	MSA[1] (%)	U.S. (%)
Sales and Office	28.1	27.3	26.7
Professional and Related	29.3	21.2	20.2
Service	7.5	13.4	14.9
Production, Transportation, and Material Moving	9.0	17.0	14.6
Management, Business, and Financial	21.9	13.9	13.5
Construction, Extraction, and Maintenance	4.0	7.1	9.4
Farming, Forestry, and Fishing	0.0	0.2	0.7

Note: Figures cover employed civilians 16 years of age and older;
(1) Metropolitan Statistical Area - see Appendix A for areas included
Source: Census 2000, Summary File 3

Employment by Industry

Sector	MSA[1] Number of Employees	MSA[1] Percent of Total	U.S. Percent of Total
Government	94,700	11.0	16.3
Education and Health Services	141,600	16.4	13.4
Professional and Business Services	112,900	13.1	13.1
Retail Trade	84,600	9.8	11.6
Manufacturing	132,200	15.4	9.9
Leisure and Hospitality	71,700	8.3	9.6
Financial Activities	57,700	6.7	5.9
Construction	33,900	3.9	5.3
Wholesale Trade	41,100	4.8	4.4
Other Services	42,200	4.9	3.9
Transportation and Utilities	30,500	3.5	3.7
Information	17,600	2.0	2.2
Natural Resources and Mining	500	0.1	0.5

Note: Figures cover non-farm employment as of December 2007 and are not seasonally adjusted; (1) Metropolitan Statistical Area - see Appendix B for areas included
Source: Bureau of Labor Statistics, http://stats.bls.gov

Average Wages

Occupation	$/Hr.	Occupation	$/Hr.
Accountants and Auditors	31.40	Maids and Housekeeping Cleaners	9.63
Automotive Mechanics	18.54	Maintenance and Repair Workers	17.88
Bookkeepers	15.76	Marketing Managers	53.15
Carpenters	22.98	Nuclear Medicine Technologists	33.06
Cashiers	8.67	Nurses, Licensed Practical	21.17
Clerks, General Office	12.69	Nurses, Registered	29.28
Clerks, Receptionists/Information	12.39	Nursing Aides/Orderlies/Attendants	12.11
Clerks, Shipping/Receiving	14.32	Packers and Packagers, Hand	11.45
Computer Programmers	31.44	Physical Therapists	32.24
Computer Support Specialists	21.28	Postal Service Mail Carriers	21.37
Computer Systems Analysts	32.67	Real Estate Brokers	n/a
Cooks, Restaurant	10.50	Retail Salespersons	11.85
Dentists	n/a	Sales Reps., Exc. Tech./Scientific	30.49
Electrical Engineers	43.48	Sales Reps., Tech./Scientific	39.37
Electricians	25.78	Secretaries, Exc. Legal/Med./Exec.	14.89
Financial Managers	50.47	Security Guards	12.17
First-Line Supervisors/Mgrs., Sales	19.44	Surgeons	96.65
Food Preparation Workers	9.40	Teacher Assistants	13.20
General and Operations Managers	54.26	Teachers, Elementary School	27.50
Hairdressers/Cosmetologists	11.67	Teachers, Secondary School	26.70
Internists	91.80	Telemarketers	10.89
Janitors and Cleaners	11.18	Truck Drivers, Heavy/Tractor-Trailer	18.43
Landscaping/Groundskeeping Workers	12.74	Truck Drivers, Light/Delivery Svcs.	14.35
Lawyers	51.41	Waiters and Waitresses	8.37

Note: Wage data covers the Milwaukee-Waukesha-West Allis, WI Metropolitan Statistical Area - see Appendix B for areas included. Hourly wages for elementary/secondary school teachers and teacher assistants were calculated by the editors from annual wage data assuming a 40 hour work week; n/a not available.
Source: Bureau of Labor Statistics, May 2007 Metro Area Occupational Employment and Wage Estimates

RESIDENTIAL REAL ESTATE

Building Permits

Area	Single-Family 2006	Single-Family 2007p	Single-Family Pct. Chg.	Multi-Family 2006	Multi-Family 2007p	Multi-Family Pct. Chg.	Total 2006	Total 2007p	Total Pct. Chg.
City	39	33	-15.4	0	0	-	39	33	-15.4
U.S.	1,378,200	973,300	-29.4	460,700	407,200	-11.6	1,838,900	1,380,500	-24.9

Note: (p) preliminary; figures cover and represent new, privately-owned housing units authorized (unadjusted data); All permit data are based on estimates with imputation; U.S. figures are based on the new 20,000-place series.
Source: U.S. Census Bureau, Manufacturing, Mining, and Construction Statistics

Homeownership and Housing Vacancies

Area	Homeownership Rate[2] (%)			Rental Vacancy Rate[3] (%)			Homeowner Vacancy Rate[4] (%)		
	2005	2006	2007	2005	2006	2007	2005	2006	2007
MSA[1]	65.7	65.2	64.8	11.6	7.8	8.3	1.3	1.1	1.4
U.S.	68.9	68.8	68.1	9.8	9.8	9.7	1.9	2.4	2.7

Note: (1) Metropolitan Statistical Area - see Appendix B for areas included; (2) The proportion of households that are owners; (3) The proportion of the rental inventory that is vacant for rent; (4) The proportion of the homeowner inventory that is vacant for sale; n/a not available
Source: U.S. Census Bureau, Housing Vacancies and Homeownership Annual Statistics: 2007

TAXES

State Corporate Income Tax Rates

State	Rates and Tax Brackets
Wisconsin	7.9%

Note: Tax rates as of January 1, 2008
Source: Tax Foundation, www.taxfoundation.org

State Individual Income Tax Rates

State	Federal Deductibility	Marginal Rates (%)	Standard Deduction ($)		Personal Exemptions ($)[1]	
			Single	Joint	Single	Dependents
Wisconsin	No	4.60 - 6.75 (r)(y)	8,790 (j)	15,830 (j)	700	700

Note: Tax rates as of January 1, 2008; Local- and county-level taxes are not included; n/a not applicable; (1) Married joint filers generally receive double the single exemption; (j) Deduction phases out to zero for single filers at $82,500 and joint filers at $94,175; (r) State adjusts its bracket levels for inflation at the end of each year before printing tax forms; (y) Brackets are not double for married taxpayers.
Source: Tax Foundation, www.taxfoundation.org

Various State and Local Tax Rates

State and Local Sales and Use (%)	State Sales and Use (%)	Gasoline[1,2] ($/gal.)	Cigarette ($/pack)	Spirits ($/gal.)	Table Wine ($/gal.)	Beer ($/gal.)
5.1	5.0	0.329	1.77	3.36	0.25	0.06

Note: Tax rates as of January 1, 2008; (1) In addition to the 18.4 cpg Federal gasoline tax; (2) Rates may include additional state sales taxes, environmental protection and storage fees/taxes, and local taxes. When necessary, the volume-weighted average of all local taxes is used to approximate the typical statewide rate including local tax
Source: Tax Foundation, www.taxfoundation.org; Original research

State Tax Burdens

Area	Combined State and Local Tax Burden		Combined Federal, State and Local Tax Burden	
	Percent	Rank	Percent	Rank
Wisconsin	12.3	7	33.3	13
U.S. Average	11.0	-	32.7	-

Note: Figures cover 2007 and measure taxes as a percentage of income
Source: Tax Foundation, www.taxfoundation.org

State Business Tax Climate Index Rankings

State	Overall Rank	Corporate Tax Index Rank	Individual Income Tax Index Rank	Sales Tax Index Rank	Unemployment Insurance Tax Index Rank	Property Tax Index Rank
Wisconsin	39	30	42	23	27	37

Note: Rankings range from 1 to 50 where 1 is best. Rankings do not average across to Overall Rank. States without a given tax are given a ranking of 1.
Source: Tax Foundation, State Business Tax Climate Index 2008

TRANSPORTATION

Means of Transportation to Work

Area	Car/Truck/Van		Public Transportation			Bicycle	Walked	Other Means	Worked at Home
	Drove Alone	Car-pooled	Bus	Subway	Railroad				
City	89.4	5.4	0.5	0.0	0.0	0.1	0.4	0.3	3.8
MSA[1]	79.7	9.9	4.1	0.0	0.0	0.2	2.9	0.6	2.6
U.S.	75.7	12.2	2.5	1.5	0.5	0.4	2.9	1.0	3.3

Note: Figures are percentages and cover workers 16 years of age and older; (1) Metropolitan Statistical Area - see Appendix A for areas included
Source: Census 2000, Summary File 3

Travel Time to Work

Area	Less Than 15 Minutes	15 to 29 Minutes	30 to 44 Minutes	45 to 59 Minutes	60 Minutes or More
City	32.3	49.7	13.6	2.5	1.9
MSA[1]	29.7	43.7	18.3	4.6	3.7
U.S.	29.4	36.1	19.1	7.4	8.0

Note: Figures are percentages and include workers 16 years old and over; (1) Metropolitan Statistical Area - see Appendix A for areas included
Source: Census 2000, Summary File 3

Travel Time Index

Area	1982	1995	2004	2005
Urban Area[1]	1.05	1.13	1.13	1.13
Average[2]	1.11	1.22	1.29	1.30

Note: Travel Time Index - The ratio of travel time in the peak period to the travel time at free-flow conditions. A value of 1.35 indicates a 20-minute free-flow trip takes 27 minutes in the peak. Free-flow speeds (60 mph on freeways and 35 mph on principal arterials) are used as the comparison threshold; (1) Covers the Milwaukee, WI urban area; (2) average of 85 urban areas
Source: Texas Transportation Institute, The 2007 Urban Mobility Report, September 2007

Living Environment

COST OF LIVING

Cost of Living Index

Composite Index	Groceries	Housing	Utilities	Trans-portation	Health Care	Misc. Goods/ Services
100.3	95.3	106.4	96.5	100.2	111.1	97.2

Note: U.S. = 100; Figures cover the Milwaukee-Waukesha WI urban area.
Source: The Council for Community and Economic Research (formerly ACCRA), Cost of Living Index, 2007

Grocery Prices

Area[1]	T-Bone Steak ($/pound)	Frying Chicken ($/pound)	Whole Milk ($/half gal.)	Eggs ($/dozen)	Orange Juice ($/64 oz.)	Coffee ($/11.5 oz.)
City[2]	8.52	1.00	2.11	1.19	3.18	3.23
Avg.	8.93	1.12	2.13	1.52	3.26	3.31
Min.	5.88	0.71	1.33	0.83	2.30	2.20
Max.	12.80	2.07	3.43	3.54	5.79	6.20

Note: (1) Values for the local area are compared with the average, minimum and maximum values for all 331 areas in the Cost of Living Index report; (2) Figures cover the Milwaukee-Waukesha WI urban area; **T-Bone Steak** *(price per pound);* **Frying Chicken** *(price per pound, whole fryer);* **Whole Milk** *(half gallon carton);* **Eggs** *(price per dozen, Grade A, large);* **Orange Juice** *(64 oz. Tropicana or Florida Natural);* **Coffee** *(11.5 oz. can, vacuum-packed, Maxwell House, Hills Bros, or Folgers).*
Source: The Council for Community and Economic Research (formerly ACCRA), Cost of Living Index, 2007

Housing and Utility Costs

Area[1]	New Home Price ($)	Apartment Rent ($/month)	All Electric ($/month)	Part Electric ($/month)	Other Energy ($/month)	Telephone ($/month)
City[2]	332,179	773	-	72.78	93.32	23.01
Avg.	309,605	782	146.13	78.67	90.16	26.14
Min.	189,877	n/a	82.03	37.41	33.15	17.08
Max.	1,202,800	3,481	271.14	150.60	257.67	37.45

Note: (1) Values for the local area are compared with the average, minimum and maximum values for all 331 areas in the Cost of Living Index report; (2) Figures cover the Milwaukee-Waukesha WI urban area; **New Home Price** *(2,400 sf living area, 8,000 sf lot, in urban area with full utilities);* **Apartment Rent** *(950 sf 2 bedroom/1.5 or 2 bath, unfurnished, excluding all utilities except water);* **All Electric** *(average monthly cost for an all-electric home);* **Part Electric** *(average monthly cost for a part-electric home);* **Other Energy** *(average monthly cost for natural gas, fuel oil, coal, wood, and any other forms of energy except electricity);* **Telephone** *(price includes basic monthly rate for a private residential line plus additional local usage charges incurred by a family of four).*
Source: The Council for Community and Economic Research (formerly ACCRA), Cost of Living Index, 2007

Health Care, Transportation, and Other Costs

Area[1]	Doctor ($/visit)	Dentist ($/visit)	Optometrist ($/visit)	Gasoline ($/gallon)	Beauty Salon ($/visit)	Men's Shirt ($)
City[2]	96.11	92.91	43.95	2.68	26.87	22.55
Avg.	79.48	71.93	79.55	2.64	29.52	25.77
Min.	52.08	44.80	43.95	2.19	15.58	16.19
Max.	148.44	126.27	158.83	3.48	60.62	48.53

Note: (1) Values for the local area are compared with the average, minimum and maximum values for all 331 areas in the Cost of Living Index report; (2) Figures cover the Milwaukee-Waukesha WI urban area; **Doctor** *(general practitioners routine exam of an established patient);* **Dentist** *(adult teeth cleaning and periodic oral examination);* **Optometrist** *(full vision eye exam for established adult patient);* **Gasoline** *(one gallon regular unleaded, national brand, including all taxes, cash price at self-service pump if available);* **Beauty Salon** *(woman's shampoo, trim, and blow-dry);* **Men's Shirt** *(cotton/polyester dress shirt, pinpoint weave, long sleeves).*
Source: The Council for Community and Economic Research (formerly ACCRA), Cost of Living Index, 2007

HOUSING

House Price Index (HPI)

Area	National Ranking[2]	Quarterly Change (%)	One-Year Change (%)	Five-Year Change (%)
MSA[1]	156	0.72	1.44	35.71
U.S.[3]	-	0.10	0.84	41.37

Note: The HPI is a weighted repeat sales index. It measures average price changes in repeat sales or refinancings on the same properties. This information is obtained by reviewing repeat mortgage transactions on single-family properties whose mortgages have been purchased or securitized by Fannie Mae or Freddie Mac in January 1975; (1) Metropolitan Statistical Area - see Appendix B for areas included; (2) Rankings are based on annual percentage change for all metro areas containing at least 15,000 transactions over the last 10 years and ranges from 1 to 291; (3) figures based on a weighted average of Census Division estimates; all figures are for the period ending December 31, 2007
Source: Office of Federal Housing Enterprise Oversight, House Price Index, February 26, 2008

House Price Valuations

Area	Q1 2000	Q1 2001	Q1 2002	Q1 2003	Q1 2004	Q1 2005	Q1 2006	Q1 2007	Q1 2008
MSA[1]	-6.7	-7.4	-4.2	0.6	6.0	9.3	10.9	6.0	2.7

Note: Figures show the percentage of over- or under-valuation of single family homes relative to statistically normal house values (e.g. a value of 23.6 indicates that house values are 23.6% overvalued). Statistically normal house values are based on house prices, interest rates, household incomes, population densities, and any historical premiums or discounts metropolitan areas have exhibited over time; (1) Figures cover the Metropolitan Statistical Area - see Appendix B for areas included
Source: Global Insight/National City Corporation, House Prices in America, May 2008

Median Home Prices

Area	2005	2006	2007[r]	Percent Change 2006 to 2007
MSA[1]	215.7	220.9	223.4	1.1
U.S. Average	219.0	221.9	217.9	-1.8

Note: Figures are median sales prices of existing single-family homes in thousands of dollars; (r) revised; n/a not available; (1) Metropolitan Statistical Area - see Appendix B for areas included
Source: National Association of Realtors, Metropolitan Area Prices, 1st Quarter 2008

Housing: Year Structure Built

Area	1990 -2000	1980 -1989	1970 -1979	1960 -1969	1950 -1959	1940 -1949	Before 1940	Median Year
City	15.9	12.4	16.1	22.6	25.4	5.0	2.6	1968
MSA[1]	12.6	8.2	14.8	13.7	18.6	9.2	22.9	1960
U.S.	17.0	15.8	18.5	13.7	12.7	7.3	15.0	1971

Note: Figures are percentages; (1) Metropolitan Statistical Area - see Appendix A for areas included
Source: Census 2000, Summary File 3

HEALTH

Health Risk Data

Category	Area[1] (%)	U.S. (%)
Adults who have been told they have high blood pressure[3]	24.0	25.5
Adults who have been told they have high blood cholesterol[3]	35.5	35.6
Adults who have been told they have diabetes[2]	4.6	7.5
Adults who have been told they have arthritis[3]	29.5	27.0
Adults who have been told they currently have asthma	8.8	8.5
Adults who are current smokers	19.1	20.1
Adults who are heavy drinkers[4]	6.9	4.9
Adults who are overweight (BMI 25.0 - 29.9)	37.1	36.5
Adults who are obese (BMI 30.0 - 99.8)	25.4	25.1

Note: Data as of 2006 unless otherwise noted; (1) Figures cover the Metropolitan Statistical Area - see Appendix B for areas included; (2) Figures do not include pregnancy-related diabetes, pre-diabetes or borderline diabetes; (3) 2005 data; (4) Heavy drinkers are classified as adult men having more than two drinks per day or adult women having more than one drink per day
Source: Centers for Disease Control and Prevention, Behaviorial Risk Factor Surveillance System, SMART: Selected Metropolitan/Micropolitan Area Risk Trends, 2005, 2006

Mortality Rates for the Top 10 Causes of Death in the U.S.

ICD-10[a] Sub-Chapter	ICD-10[a] Code	Age-Adjusted Mortality Rate[1] per 100,000 population	
		County[2]	U.S.
Malignant neoplasms	C00-C97	175.8	186.5
Ischaemic heart diseases	I20-I25	121.6	152.3
Other forms of heart disease	I30-I51	50.6	51.5
Cerebrovascular diseases	I60-I69	46.5	50.0
Chronic lower respiratory diseases	J40-J47	35.6	42.6
Diabetes mellitus	E10-E14	18.3	24.8
Other degenerative diseases of the nervous system	G30-G31	20.2	22.6
Other external causes of accidental injury	W00-X59	30.3	21.4
Influenza and pneumonia	J10-J18	17.5	20.7
Hypertensive diseases	I10-I13	14.1	18.2

Note: (a) ICD-10 = International Classification of Diseases 10th Revision; (1) Mortality rates are a three year average covering 2003-2005; (2) Figures cover Waukesha County
Source: Centers for Disease Control and Prevention, National Center for Health Statistics. Compressed Mortality File 1999-2004. CDC WONDER On-line Database, compiled from Compressed Mortality File 1999-2005 Series 20 No. 2K, 2008.

Mortality Rates for Selected Causes of Death

ICD-10[a] Sub-Chapter	ICD-10[a] Code	Age-Adjusted Mortality Rate[1] per 100,000 population	
		County[2]	U.S.
Assault	X85-Y09	*1.1	5.9
Human immunodeficiency virus (HIV) disease	B20-B24	*0.5	4.5
Intentional self-harm	X60-X84	8.2	10.8
Malnutrition	E40-E46	*0.4	1.0
Obesity and other hyperalimentation	E65-E68	*0.7	1.4
Organic, including symptomatic, mental disorders	F01-F09	38.3	16.8
Transport accidents	V01-V99	10.5	16.1
Viral hepatitis	B15-B19	*0.3	1.8

Note: (a) ICD-10 = International Classification of Diseases 10th Revision; (1) Mortality rates are a three year average covering 2003-2005; (2) Figures cover Waukesha County; (*) Unreliable data as per CDC
Source: Centers for Disease Control and Prevention, National Center for Health Statistics. Compressed Mortality File 1999-2004. CDC WONDER On-line Database, compiled from Compressed Mortality File 1999-2005 Series 20 No. 2K, 2008.

Distribution of Physicians[1]

Area	Total	Family/ General Practice	Specialties	
			Medical	Surgical
Waukesha County (number)	1,235	291	437	215
Waukesha County (rate per 10,000 pop.)	32.6	7.7	11.5	5.7
U.S. (rate per 10,000 pop.)	17.7	4.6	6.9	4.3

Note: Data as of 2005; (1) Includes all non-federal, patient-care, office-based MDs
Source: Area Resource File (ARF). June 2007. U.S. Department of Health and Human Services, Health Resources and Services Administration, Bureau of Health Professions, Rockville, MD.

Hospitals

Brookfield has the following hospitals: 1 general medical and surgical.
AHA Guide to the Healthcare Field 2008

According to *U.S. News,* the Milwaukee-Waukesha-West Allis, WI metro area is home to three of the best hospitals in the U.S.: **Aurora Saint Luke's Medical Center**; **Children's Hospital of Wisconsin**; **Froedtert Hospital**. *U.S. News Online, "America's Best Hospitals 2007"*

EDUCATION

Public School District Statistics

District Name	Schls	Pupils	Pupil/ Teacher Ratio	Minority Pupils[1] (%)	Free Lunch Eligible[2] (%)	IEP[3] (%)
Elmbrook	11	7,656	14.8	14.7	n/a	11.5
Waukesha	27	13,611	15.3	19.2	n/a	13.4

Note: Table includes regular local school districts with 2,000 or more students; (1) Percentage of students that are not white, non-Hispanic; (2) Percentage of students that are eligible for the free lunch program; (3) Percentage of students that have an Individualized Education Program.
Source: U.S. Department of Education, National Center for Education Statistics, Common Core of Data, Local Education Agency (School District) Universe Survey: School Year 2005-2006; U.S. Department of Education, National Center for Education Statistics, Common Core of Data, Public Elementary/Secondary School Universe Survey: School Year 2005-2006

Top Public High Schools

High School Name	Index[1]	Rank[1]	Subsidized Lunch (%)[2]	E&E (%)[3]
Brookfield Central	1.725	699	5.5	48.0
Brookfield East	1.632	770	7.0	43.5

Note: (1) Public schools are ranked according to a ratio that is the number of Advanced Placement, International Baccalaureate, and/or Cambridge tests taken by all students at a school in 2007 divided by the number of graduating seniors. All of the schools on the list have an index of at least 1.000; they are in the top five percent of public schools measured this way. The rankings range from 1 to 1,422; (2) Percentage of students receiving federally subsidized meals; (3) E & E stands for equity and excellence percentage: the portion of all graduating seniors at a school that had at least one passing grade on one AP or IB test; (**) Gave both IB and AP tests. AP and IB participation are indicators of a school's efforts to get students to excel and prepare for college.
Source: Newsweek Online, "Top High Schools 2008"

Highest Level of Education

Area	Less than H.S.	H.S. Diploma	Some College, No Deg.	Associate Degree	Bachelors Degree	Masters Degree	Profess. School Degree	Doctorate Degree
City	5.9	19.0	19.8	6.3	31.3	10.7	5.3	1.7
MSA[1]	15.2	29.1	21.7	6.9	18.4	5.9	2.0	0.8
U.S.	19.4	28.4	21.2	6.4	15.7	5.9	2.0	1.0

Note: Figures are 2007 estimated percentages and cover persons age 25 and over; (1) Metropolitan Statistical Area - see Appendix B for areas included
Source: Claritas, Inc.

Educational Attainment by Race

Area	High School Graduate (%)					Bachelor's Degree (%)				
	Total	White	Black	Asian	Hisp.[2]	Total	White	Black	Asian	Hisp.[2]
City	94.0	94.1	75.2	96.1	94.7	49.0	48.3	35.7	79.6	43.2
MSA[1]	84.5	88.2	68.3	77.2	52.4	27.0	29.7	10.3	46.6	10.7
U.S.	80.4	83.6	72.3	80.4	52.4	24.4	26.1	14.3	44.1	10.4

Note: Figures shown cover persons 25 years old and over; (1) Metropolitan Statistical Area - see Appendix A for areas included; (2) people of Hispanic origin can be of any race
Source: Census 2000, Summary File 3

School Enrollment by Type

Area	Grades KG to 8				Grades 9 to 12			
	Public		Private		Public		Private	
	Enrollment	%	Enrollment	%	Enrollment	%	Enrollment	%
City	3,885	68.9	1,751	31.1	2,168	79.8	549	20.2
MSA[1]	168,628	79.3	43,942	20.7	79,263	87.0	11,852	13.0
U.S.	33,526,011	88.7	4,285,121	11.3	14,848,628	90.6	1,532,323	9.4

Note: Figures shown cover persons 3 years old and over; (1) Metropolitan Statistical Area - see Appendix A for areas included
Source: Census 2000, Summary File 3

School Enrollment by Race

Area	Grades KG to 8 (%)				Grades 9 to 12 (%)			
	White	Black	Asian	Hisp.[1]	White	Black	Asian	Hisp.[1]
City	94.6	0.3	3.1	0.8	91.3	0.8	6.7	0.3
MSA[2]	64.7	24.8	2.4	8.9	68.9	21.5	2.4	7.6
U.S.	68.5	15.5	3.3	16.8	68.8	15.5	3.8	15.7

Note: Figures shown cover persons 3 years old and over; (1) people of Hispanic origin can be of any race; (2) Metropolitan Statistical Area - see Appendix A for areas included
Source: Census 2000, Summary File 3

Average Salaries of Public School Classroom Teachers

District	2005-06		2006-07		Percent Change 2005-06 to 2006-07
	Dollars	Rank[1]	Dollars	Rank[1]	
Wisconsin	46,390	21	47,901	21	3.26
U.S. Average	49,026	-	50,816	-	3.65

Note: (1) State rank ranges from 1 to 51.
Source: National Education Association, Rankings & Estimates: Rankings of the States 2006 and Estimates of School Statistics 2007, December 2007

Higher Education

Four-Year Colleges			Two-Year Colleges			Medical Schools[1]	Law Schools[2]	Voc/ Tech[3]
Public	Private Non-profit	Private For-profit	Public	Private Non-profit	Private For-profit			
0	1	1	0	0	1	0	0	0

Note: Figures cover institutions located within the city limits; (1) includes schools accredited by the Liaison Committee on Medical Education and the American Osteopathic Association; (2) includes American Bar Association-accredited law schools; (3) includes all schools with programs that are less than 2 years.
Source: National Center for Education Statistics, The Integrated Postsecondary Education System (IPEDS) Peer Analysis System, 2007; www.usnews.com, Law and Medical School Directories, 2009

PRESIDENTIAL ELECTION

2004 Presidential Election Results

Area	Bush	Kerry	Nader	Other
Waukesha County	67.3	32.0	0.4	0.4
U.S.	50.7	48.3	0.4	0.6

Note: Results are percentages and may not add to 100% due to rounding
Source: Dave Leip's Atlas of U.S. Presidential Elections, www.uselectionatlas.org

EMPLOYERS

Major Employers

Company Name	Industry	Type of Site
Ameritech Wisconsin	Telephone communication, except radio	Single
Baymont Inn & Suites	Hotels and motels	Headquarters
Briggs & Stratton	Internal combustion engines, nec	Headquarters
CSM	General medical and surgical hospitals	Headquarters
Cathedral Square Pharmacy	Drug stores and proprietary stores	Single
Childrens Hosp & Hlth Sys Inc	Specialty hospitals, except psychiatric	Headquarters
Clement J Zablocki Vamc 695	Administration of veterans' affairs	Branch
Froedtert Memorial Lutheran	General medical and surgical hospitals	Headquarters
Metavante Corporation	Data processing and preparation	Headquarters
Midwest Air Group Inc	Air transportation, scheduled	Headquarters
Miller Breweries East Inc	Malt beverages	Single
Office of Continuing Education	Colleges and universities	Headquarters
Prohealth Care Inc	Offices and clinics of medical doctors	Headquarters
Rexnord Corporation	Ball and roller bearings	Single
St Lukes Medical Center Inc	General medical and surgical hospitals	Headquarters
Waukesha Memorial Hospital	General medical and surgical hospitals	Headquarters
West Allis Memorial Hospital	General medical and surgical hospitals	Single
Western Power Products Inc	Noncurrent-carrying wiring devices	Headquarters
Wisconsin Energy Corporation	Electric services	Headquarters

Note: Companies shown are located within the Milwaukee metropolitan area; nec = not elsewhere classified.
Source: www.zapdata.com, May 2008

PUBLIC SAFETY

Crime Rate

Area	All Crimes	Violent Crimes				Property Crimes		
		Murder	Forcible Rape	Robbery	Aggrav. Assault	Burglary	Larceny -Theft	Motor Vehicle Theft
City	2,869.3	0.0	0.0	15.1	5.0	316.6	2,469.8	62.8
Metro[1]	4,506.0	7.4	14.2	266.9	291.1	583.2	2,723.9	619.3
U.S.	3,808.1	5.7	30.9	149.4	287.5	729.4	2,206.8	398.4

Note: Figures are crimes per 100,000 population; (1) Metropolitan Statistical Area - see Appendix B for areas included
Source: FBI Uniform Crime Reports, 2006

Hate Crimes

Area	Number of Quarters Reported	Bias Motivation				
		Race	Religion	Sexual Orientation	Ethnicity	Disability
City	4	0	0	0	0	0

Source: Federal Bureau of Investigation, Hate Crime Statistics 2006

RECREATION

Culture

Dance[1]	Theatre[1]	Instrumental Music[1]	Vocal Music[1]	Series/ Festivals	Museums	Zoos and Aquariums[2]
0	0	0	0	0	0	0

Note: (1) Number of professional perfoming groups; (2) AZA-accredited
Source: The Grey House Performing Arts Directory, 2007; Official Museum Directory, 2008; Association of Zoos & Aquariums, AZA Member Zoos & Aquariums, June 2008

Professional Sports Teams

Team Name	League
Milwaukee Brewers	Major League Baseball (MLB)
Milwaukee Bucks	National Basketball Association (NBA)

Note: Includes teams located in the Milwaukee metro area.
Source: Original research

MEDIA

Newspapers

Name	News Focus	Frequency	Circulation
No newspapers have an office in the city			

Note: Includes newspapers with offices located in the city
Source: MediaContactsPro, March 2008

Television Stations

Name	Ch.	Network(s)	Type	Ownership
WTMJ	4	NBC	Commercial	Journal Communications
WITI	6	Fox	Commercial	Fox Television Stations Inc.
WMVS	10	PBS	Public	Milwaukee Area Technical College
WISN	12	ABC	Commercial	Hearst-Argyle Broadcasting
WVTV	18	WBN	Commercial	Sinclair Broadcast Group
WCGV	24	UPN	Commercial	Sinclair Broadcast Group
WVCY	30	n/a	Non-comm.	VCY America Inc.
WMVT	36	PBS	Public	Milwaukee Area Technical College
WJJA	49	n/a	Commercial	TV 49 Inc.
WPXE	55	Pax	Commercial	Paxson Communications Corporation
WDJT	58	CBS	Commercial	Weigel Broadcasting Company

Note: Stations included cover the Milwaukee DMA (Designated Market Area)
BurrellesLuce, MediaContacts Online, January 2007

Major AM Radio Stations

Call Letters	Freq. (kHz)	Station Type	Target Audience	Station Format	Music Format
WTMJ	620	Commercial	General	News/Talk	n/a
WOKY	920	Commercial	General	Music/News/Talk	Adult Standards
WISN	1130	Commercial	General/Men	News/Talk	n/a
WFDL	1170	Commercial	General	News/Talk	Adult Standards
WSSP	1250	Commercial	General	Music/Talk	Gospel
WMCS	1290	Commercial	General	Music/News/Talk	Urban Contemp.
WHBL	1330	Commercial	General/Men	News/Talk	n/a
WJYI	1340	Commercial	General/Religious	Music	Christian
WRJN	1400	Commercial	General	News/Talk	n/a
WBEV	1430	Commercial	General	Music/News	Adult Contemp.
WBKV	1470	Commercial	General	Music/News	Country
WAUK	1510	Commercial	General	News/Talk	n/a
WTTN	1580	Commercial	General	Music/News	Oldies

Note: Stations included cover the Milwaukee DMA (Designated Market Area); n/a not available
Source: BurrellesLuce, MediaContacts Online, January 2007

Major FM Radio Stations

Call Letters	Freq. (mHz)	Station Type	Target Audience	Station Format	Music Format
WUWM	89.7	Public	General	News/Talk	n/a
WHAD	90.7	n/a	General	News	n/a
WEZY	92.1	n/a	General	Music	n/a
WBWI	92.5	Commercial	General	Music/News	Contemp. Country
WJZI	93.3	Commercial	General	Music	Jazz
WBFM	93.7	Commercial	General/Men	Music/News	Country
WKTI	94.5	n/a	General	Music/News	n/a
WIIL	95.1	Commercial	General	Music/News	Modern Rock
WXRO	95.3	Commercial	General	Music/News	Country
WRIT	95.7	Commercial	General	Music/News/Sports/Talk	Classic Rock
WLKG	96.1	Commercial	General	Music	Adult Contemp.
WKLH	96.5	Commercial	General	Music	Classic Rock
WLTQ	97.3	Commercial	General	Music/News/Talk	Soft Rock
WJMR	98.3	Commercial	General	Music	Classical
WMDC	98.7	n/a	General	Music	n/a
WVCX	98.9	Non-Comm	General/Religious	Educational/Music/Talk	Christian
WMYX	99.1	Commercial	General	Music	Adult Contemp.
WGLB	100.1	n/a	General	Music	n/a
WTLX	100.5	Commercial	General	Sports/Talk	n/a
WKKV	100.7	Commercial	General	Music/News	Urban Contemp.
KVCX	101.5	Non-Comm	General/Religious	Educational/News/Talk	n/a
WIPZ	101.7	College	General	Music/Talk	Album Rock
WLUM	102.1	Commercial	General	Music	Alternative
WLZR	102.9	Commercial	General	Music/Talk	Modern Rock
WXSS	103.7	Commercial	General	Music	Top 40
WXER	104.5	n/a	General	Music/News	n/a
WMIL	106.1	Commercial	General	Music	Country
WHBZ	106.5	Commercial	General/Men	Music/News	Modern Rock
WFMR	106.9	Commercial	General	Music/Talk	Classical
WSJY	107.3	Commercial	General	Music	Adult Contemp.
WVCY	107.7	Non-Comm	General/Religious	Ed/Music/News/Talk	Christian

Note: Stations included cover the Milwaukee DMA (Designated Market Area); n/a not available
BurrellesLuce, MediaContacts Online, January 2007

CLIMATE

Average and Extreme Temperatures

Temperature	Jan	Feb	Mar	Apr	May	Jun	Jul	Aug	Sep	Oct	Nov	Dec	Yr.
Extreme High (°F)	60	65	82	91	92	101	101	103	98	89	77	63	103
Average High (°F)	27	31	40	54	65	76	80	79	71	60	45	32	55
Average Temp. (°F)	20	24	33	45	55	66	71	70	62	51	38	25	47
Average Low (°F)	12	16	26	36	45	55	62	61	53	42	30	18	38
Extreme Low (°F)	-26	-19	-10	12	21	36	40	44	28	18	-5	-20	-26

Note: Figures cover the years 1948-1990
Source: National Climatic Data Center, International Station Meteorological Climate Summary, 9/96

Average Precipitation/Snowfall/Humidity

Precip./Humidity	Jan	Feb	Mar	Apr	May	Jun	Jul	Aug	Sep	Oct	Nov	Dec	Yr.
Avg. Precip. (in.)	1.6	1.4	2.6	3.3	2.9	3.4	3.6	3.4	2.9	2.3	2.3	2.2	32.0
Avg. Snowfall (in.)	13	10	9	2	Tr	0	0	0	0	Tr	3	11	49
Avg. Rel. Hum. 6am (%)	76	77	78	78	77	79	82	86	86	82	80	80	80
Avg. Rel. Hum. 3pm (%)	68	66	64	58	58	58	59	62	61	61	66	70	63

Note: Figures cover the years 1948-1990; Tr = Trace amounts (<0.05 in. of rain; <0.5 in. of snow)
Source: National Climatic Data Center, International Station Meteorological Climate Summary, 9/96

Weather Conditions

Temperature			Daytime Sky			Precipitation		
5°F & below	32°F & below	90°F & above	Clear	Partly cloudy	Cloudy	0.01 inch or more precip.	0.1 inch or more snow/ice	Thunder-storms
22	141	10	90	118	157	126	38	35

Note: Figures are average number of days per year and cover the years 1948-1990
Source: National Climatic Data Center, International Station Meteorological Climate Summary, 9/96

HAZARDOUS WASTE

Superfund Sites

Brookfield has two hazardous waste sites on the EPA's Superfund Final National Priorities List: **Master Disposal Service Landfill**; **Waste Management Of Wisconsin, Inc. (Brookfield Sanitary Landfill)**. *U.S. Environmental Protection Agency, Final National Priorities List, June 23, 2008*

AIR & WATER QUALITY

Air Quality Index

Area	Percent of Days when Air Quality was...[2]				AQI Statistics	
	Good	Moderate	Unhealthy for Sensitive Groups	Unhealthy	Maximum	Median
MSA[1]	74.5	21.6	3.8	0.0	142	38

Note: The Air Quality Index (AQI) is an index for reporting daily air quality. EPA calculates the AQI for five major air pollutants regulated by the Clean Air Act: ground-level ozone, particle pollution (also known as particulate matter), carbon monoxide, sulfur dioxide, and nitrogen dioxide. The AQI runs from 0 to 500. The higher the AQI value, the greater the level of air pollution and the greater the health concern. There are six AQI categories: "Good" The AQI is between 0 and 50. Air quality is considered satisfactory; "Moderate" The AQI is between 51 and 100. Air quality is acceptable; "Unhealthy for Sensitive Groups" When AQI values are between 101 and 150, members of sensitive groups may experience health effects; "Unhealthy" When AQI values are between 151 and 200 everyone may begin to experience health effects; "Very Unhealthy" AQI values between 201 and 300 trigger a health alert; "Hazardous" AQI values over 300 trigger health warnings of emergency conditions; (1) Metropolitan Statistical Area - see Appendix A for areas included; (2) Based on 365 days with AQI data in 2007.
Source: U.S. Environmental Protection Agency, Air Quality Index Report, 2007

Air Quality Index Pollutants

Area	Percent of Days when AQI Pollutant was...[2]					
	Carbon Monoxide	Nitrogen Dioxide	Ozone	Sulfur Dioxide	Particulate Matter 2.5	Particulate Matter 10
MSA[1]	0.0	0.0	64.1	0.0	24.9	11.0

Note: The Air Quality Index (AQI) is an index for reporting daily air quality. EPA calculates the AQI for five major air pollutants regulated by the Clean Air Act: ground-level ozone, particle pollution (also known as particulate matter), carbon monoxide, sulfur dioxide, and nitrogen dioxide. The AQI runs from 0 to 500. The higher the AQI value, the greater the level of air pollution and the greater the health concern; (1) Metropolitan Statistical Area - see Appendix A for areas included; (2) Based on 365 days with AQI data in 2007.
Source: U.S. Environmental Protection Agency, Air Quality Index Report, 2007

Air Quality Index Trends

Area	Trend Sites (16)								All Sites (54)
	1999	2000	2001	2002	2003	2004	2005	2006	2006
MSA[1]	18	5	20	10	9	6	16	4	5

Note: An AQI value greater than 100 indicates that air quality would have been in the unhealthful range on that day. Data from exceptional events are not included. These counts are presented in two ways. First, the counts are based on sites having an adequate record of monitoring data during the trend period (trend sites). These counts represent the relative change in the number of days with AQI values greater than 100. In the last column, the counts are based on all sites with data in the most recent year (because it is possible for a site to have data in the most recent year but not enough data to be a trend site); (1) Metropolitan Statistical Area - see Appendix A for areas included.
Source: U.S. Environmental Protection Agency, Office of Air and Radiation, Air Trends, Factbook and Related Information, Air Pollution Trends in Selected Metropolitan Areas 2006

Maximum Air Pollutant Concentrations

	Particulate Matter 10 (ug/m^3)	Particulate Matter 2.5 (ug/m^3)	Ozone (ppm)	Carbon Monoxide (ppm)	Sulfur Dioxide (ppm)	Nitrogen Dioxide (ppm)	Lead (ug/m^3)
MSA[1] Level	54	44	0.1	2	0.008	0.015	0
NAAQS[2]	150	35	0.125	9	0.140	0.053	1.50
Met NAAQS[2]	Yes	No	Yes	Yes	Yes	Yes	Yes

Note: Data from exceptional events are not included; (1) Metropolitan Statistical Area - see Appendix A for areas included; (2) National Ambient Air Quality Standards; n/a not available
Concentrations: Particulate Matter 10 (coarse particulate) - highest second maximum 24-hour concentration; Particulate Matter 2.5 (fine particulate) - highest 98th percentile 24-hour concentration; Ozone - highest second daily maximum 1-hour concentration; Carbon Monoxide - highest second maximum non-overlapping 8-hour concentration; Sulfur Dioxide - highest second maximum 24-hour concentration; Nitrogen Dioxide - highest arithmetic mean concentration; Lead - highest quarterly maximum concentration
Units: ppm = parts per million; ug/m^3 = micrograms per cubic meter
Source: U.S. Environmental Protection Agency, MSA Factbook 2006, Air Quality Statistics by City

Drinking Water

Water System Name	Pop. Served	Primary Water Source Type	Violations[1]	
			Health Based	Monitoring/ Reporting
Brookfield Water Utility	21,900	Ground	0	0

Note: (1) Based on violation data from January 1, 2007 to December 31, 2007 (includes unresolved violations from earlier years)
Source: U.S. Environmental Protection Agency, Office of Ground Water and Drinking Water, Safe Drinking Water Information System (based on data extracted April 15, 2008)

Sun Prairie, Wisconsin

Background

Sun Prairie prides itself on being a small town with big city advantages. The community attributes this slogan to its attractive location: outside of Madison far enough to still have a rural community feel but close enough to still take advantage of all the amenities the city has to offer. However, as one of the fastest growing cities in the state of Wisconsin, Sun Prairie won't be able to call itself a "small town" for much longer.

The name "Sun Prairie" predates its actual settlement. In May of1837 President Van Buren commissioned a company of over forty men to build a state capitol building in Madison, Wisconsin. Before reaching their destination, the group traveled for days in the pouring rain. Finally, on the 9th of June, as the clouds dissipated, the men came upon an open prairie with rays of sun shining up from the horizon. At this, one of the men carved the words "sun prairie" into a tree. It was not until years later that Charles Bird returned to the land and began its settlement.

Today, visitors and residents alike will find much to do and see in Sun Prairie. Angell Park Speedway offers midget auto racing. From spring through fall the city hosts a bustling farmers market. Sun Prairie Public Library and Sun Prairie Historical Museum both offer a stimulating educational experience. The streets of historic downtown are lined with specialty shopping boutiques and unique dining experiences. Sun Prairie is also the birthplace of world-renowned artist, Georgia O'Keeffe. The farmstead on which she was raised is open to the public for tours.

The Sun Prairie park system consists of more than 30 parks, a 13-diamond baseball complex, four soccer fields, 11 skating rinks, two sledding hills, a public golf course, and a YMCA. In addition, Sun Prairie has a fantastic family aquatic facility that features waterslides, a sandy play area, and a zero depth pool for swimming. Patrick Marsh, a natural wetland area on the northeast side of Sun Prairie, provides the opportunity for a scenic nature walk and offers a tranquil escape from busy city life. There are several attractions in the area, just a short drive from Sun Prairie. These include House on the Rock, the Wisconsin Dells, and the recreation sites of Lake Mendota and Lake Monona.

The city's claim to fame is that the quality of life its residents experience is unparalleled in excellence. To start, Sun Prairie offers residents a small town atmosphere without depriving them of any of the amenities and conveniences of a larger metropolis. The array of housing opportunities range from reasonably priced, affordable starter homes to more expensive, luxury houses built for executives and professionals. The city is also known for its exceptional educational system, comprised of schools that consistently perform well above that state average. The nearness to the University of Wisconsin-Madison is an added educational bonus. Access to quality health care is provided by two clinics in Sun Prairie and is served by three regional hospitals. Finding qualified child care providers is easy with over 40 licensed daycare facilities in the area. As a community, Sun Prairie has made a commitment to providing superior care to its senior citizens and is home to 13 senior living facilities.

The Sun Prairie Area School District serves nearly 6,000 students annually. Their vision is that by working together to provide high quality education for all students, they will build a community of life-long learners, prepared for both higher education and their roles as citizens. The district is comprised of six elementary schools, two middle schools, one senior high school, an alternative high school, and four parochial schools. Nearby is world-class University of Wisconsin-Madison, internationally acclaimed for its academic excellence.

As Sun Prairie continues to expand, the city has placed emphasis on diversification of its economic resources. By balancing the rate at which commercial, residential, and industrial development takes place, the city ensures that the quality of life that it's residents experience only increases. Sun Prairie relies on its location, exponential growth, unparalleled transportation access, affordable utilities, and access to a skilled labor force to attract new business to the area. Additionally, Sun Prairie is engaged in a downtown revitalization plan that will not only rejuvenate the community but will add approximately 29,000 square feet of commercial floor space in two brand new buildings, 44 residential units to house a growing population, a new street to improve the flow of traffic, and three new city parking lots to accommodate new downtown businesses.

Sun Prairie is located only minutes away from Dane County Regional Airport.

Rankings

General Rankings

- Madison* was ranked #78 out of 375 metro areas in *Cities Ranked & Rated*. Criteria: cost of living; climate; crime; transportation; economy and jobs; education; arts and culture; health and healthcare; leisure; quality of life. *Cities Ranked & Rated, 2nd Edition, 2007*
- Madison* was ranked #10 out of 379 metro areas in *Places Rated Almanac*. Criteria: health care; education; recreation; transportation; ambience; climate; crime; housing costs; jobs. *Places Rated Almanac, 7th Edition, 2007*
- *Expansion Management* rated 362 metro areas to find out which offer the best middle class lifestyle for manufacturing and service companies. The Madison* metro area was selected as a "5-Star Quality of Life Metro" (a distinction the magazine awards to the top 20 percent of metro areas studied). The annual "Quality of Life Quotient" measures dozens of indicators across nine major categories and compares them among 362 metropolitan statistical areas in the United States. The categories are: affordable housing; good public schools; low crime levels; adult education level; standard of living; traffic and commuting; continuing education opportunities; commercial air access; labor market. *Expansion Management, June 2007*

Business/Finance Rankings

- The Madison* metro area was selected one of America's "Top 50 Business Opportunity Metros" by *Expansion Management* in their 5th annual Mayor's Challenge ranking of metro areas that have achieved solid ratings across the board in numerous *EM* studies during the past 12 months. The area ranked #14. Criteria: public schools; quality of life; college educated workers; logistics infrastructure; healthcare costs; taxes and government spending; reputation among site consultants. *Expansion Management, August 2007*
- Madison* was selected as one of the best places to start and grow a company by *Entrepreneur* and the National Policy Research Council. The Madison* metro area ranked #6 out of 63 mid-size metro areas. Criteria: business formation and growth (firms started four to 14 years ago that still employ at least 5 people and experienced rapid growth over the last four years). *Entrepreneur/National Policy Research Council, "Hot Cities for Entrepreneurs," September 2006*
- The Madison* metro area was selected one of America's "Top 10 Knowledge Worker Metros." The area ranked #8. Criteria: degree holders (bachelors, masters, professional, and Ph.D.) as a percent of the workforce; science and engineering workers as a percent of the workforce; number of patents issued; number and type of colleges in each metro area. *Expansion Management, April 2007*
- The Madison* metro area appeared on the Milken Institute "2007 Best Performing Cities" index. Rank: #95 out of 200 large metro areas. Criteria: job growth; wage and salary growth; high-tech output growth. *Milken Institute, "2007 Best Performing Cities"*
- *Forbes* ranked the 200 most populous metro areas in the U.S. in terms of the "Best Places for Business and Careers." The Madison* metro area was ranked #29. Criteria: business costs (labor, energy, tax and office space expenses); living costs (housing, transportation, food and other household expenditures); education levels of the work force; job growth; income growth; migration trends; crime rates; and culture/leisure. *Forbes, "Best Places for Business and Careers," March 19, 2008*

Health/Environment Rankings

- 100 of the largest metro areas in the U.S. were analyzed in terms of their current drought severity. The Madison* metro area ranked #87 (#1 = driest). The rankings were based on statistics such as long-term precipitation trends and patterns and the Palmer drought indices. *Sperling's BestPlaces, www.BestPlaces.net, "America's Drought-Riskiest Cities," November 2007*

- The Madison* metro area appeared in *Country Home's* "2008 Best Green Places" report. The area ranked #17 out of 379. Criteria: official energy policies; green power; green buildings; availability of fresh, locally grown food. *Country Home, "2008 Best Green Places"*

- Madison* was identified as a "2008 Asthma Capital." The area ranked #74 out of the nation's 100 largest metropolitan areas. Twelve factors were used to identify the most challenging places to live for people with asthma: estimated prevalence; self-reported prevalence; crude death rate for asthma; annual pollen score; annual air quality; public smoking laws; number of board-certified asthma specialists; school inhaler access laws; rescue medication use; controller medication use; uninsured rate; poverty rate. *Asthma and Allergy Foundation of America, "2008 Asthma Capitals"*

- Madison* was identified as a "Spring Allergy Capital." The area ranked #39 out of 100. Three groups of factors were used to identify the most severe cities for people with allergies during the spring season: annual pollen levels; medicine utilization; access to board-certified allergists. *Asthma and Allergy Foundation of America, "2007 Spring Allergy Capital Rankings"*

- Madison* was identified as a "Fall Allergy Capital." The area ranked #57 out of 100. Three groups of factors were used to identify the most severe cities for people with allergies during the fall season: annual pollen levels; medicine utilization; access to board-certified allergists. *Asthma and Allergy Foundation of America, "2007 Fall Allergy Capital Rankings"*

- Ortho-McNeil Neurologics, in partnership with Sperling's BestPlaces, analyzed 110 metro areas and identified those U.S. cities with the highest prevalence of factors that are most commonly associated with migraine headaches. The Madison* metro area ranked #2. Criteria: number of migraine-related drug prescriptions per capita; lifestyle factors that can contribute to migraines; environmental factors that can trigger migraines; and consumption of migraine-triggering foods. *Ortho-McNeil Neurologics, "America's Migraine Hot Spots," March 14, 2006*

- Sperling's BestPlaces ranked 331 metro areas and identified the most and least stressful U.S. cities. The Madison* metro area ranked #111 out of 114 mid-size metro areas (#1 = most stressful). Criteria: divorce rate; unemployment rate; violent and property crime; suicide rate; commute time; mental health; alcohol consumption; cloudy days. *Sperling's BestPlaces, www.BestPlaces.net, "America's Most (and Least) Stressful Cities," January 9, 2004*

Women/Minorities Rankings

- Madison* appeared on a list of the top 10 metro areas with the highest concentration of lesbian couples. The area ranked #10. *Urban Institute Press, The Gay and Lesbian Atlas, May 2004*

- Madison* appeared on a list of the top 10 metro areas with the highest concentration of Hispanic same-sex couples among all Hispanic households. The area ranked #2. *Urban Institute Press, The Gay and Lesbian Atlas, May 2004*

Seniors/Retirement Rankings

- A.G. Edwards ranked America's 500 top-performing communities based on their residents' personal savings and investing behavior. The Madison* metro area ranked #57 with an index score of 109.04 (national average = 100.00). A dozen statistical factors were measured including: participation in retirement savings plans; personal debt levels; and home ownership. *A.G. Edwards, "2007 Nest Egg Index", September 12, 2007*

Children/Family Rankings

- The Madison* metro area was selected as one of the "Best Cities for Relocating Families" by Worldwide ERC and Primacy Relocation. The 2007 study placed a special emphasis on the housing market, which has significantly impacted the relocation industry and an employer's ability to transfer employees. The variables which weigh heavily in this category include home price, home affordability index, appreciation rates, and property tax. Other criteria include cost of living, crime rates, education, climate, focus on diversity, physicians per capita, recreation and leisure, arts and culture, air quality, watershed quality, sales tax, unemployment rate, job growth, high school and higher education index, school expenditures per student, students in public school, SAT/ACT percentile, and population growth. *Worldwide ERC and Primacy Relocation, "2007 Best Cities for Relocating Families"*

Safety Rankings

- The National Insurance Crime Bureau ranked 361 metro areas in the U.S. in terms of per capita rates of vehicle theft. The Madison* metro area ranked #353 (#1 = highest rate). Criteria: number of vehicle theft offenses per 100,000 inhabitants. *National Insurance Crime Bureau, "NICB Vehicle Theft Study," April 22, 2008*
- Farmers Insurance Group of Companies, in partnership with Sperling's BestPlaces, ranked 379 metro areas and identified the "Most Secure U.S. Place to Live." The Madison* metro area ranked #16 out of 114 in the large metro area category (500,000 or more residents). Criteria: crime rates; extreme weather; risk of natural disasters; environmental hazards; terrorism threats; air quality; life expectancy; job loss numbers. *Farmers Insurance Group, "Most Secure U.S. Places to Live 2007"*

Sports/Recreation Rankings

- The Madison* metro area appeared on the *Sporting News* list of the "Best Sports Cities 2007". The area ranked #40 out of 150 cities in the U.S. *Sporting News* takes a 12-month snapshot, roughly July to July, of each city's sports, putting a heavy premium on regular-season won-lost records (from the most recently completed season). Other criteria include: playoff berths, bowl appearances and tournament bids; championships; applicable power ratings; quality of competition; overall fan fervor as measured in part by attendance as percentage of venue capacity; abundance of teams (rewarding quality over quantity); stadium and arena quality; ticket availability and prices; franchise ownership; and marquee appeal of athletes. *SportingNews.com, "Best Sports Cities 2007," August 1, 2007*
- *Golf Digest* ranked 330 metro areas in the U.S. in terms of golf. The Madison* metro area was ranked #280. Criteria: access to golf; weather; value of golf; and quality of golf. *Golf Digest, "Metro Golf Rankings," August 2005*

Dating/Romance Rankings

- The Madison* metro area was selected as one of the "Best Cities for Relocating Singles" by Worldwide ERC and Primacy Relocation. The area ranked #3 out of the 100 largest metro areas in the U.S. Areas were selected based on the following criteria: a robust cost-of-living index; adventure and outdoor recreation opportunities; violent crime and property crime rates; percentage of the population that is unmarried (ages 25-34); ratio of single men and single women; affordability of quality higher education, including in-state and out-of-state tuition requirements and rates; number of newcomers to the area; commute times; tax rates; fee and occupancy rates for temporary housing and mini-storage; quality and quantity of collegiate and professional sporting events and fun, fan-friendly venues. *Worldwide ERC and Primacy Relocation, "2007 Best Cities for Relocating Singles," October 25, 2007*

Miscellaneous Rankings

- Sun Prairie was selected as one of the "50 Best Affordable Suburbs" in the U.S. by *Business Week.*. The 50 suburbs were chosen based on dozens of factors including: median home prices; population growth; crime rates; levels of education; unemployment rate; commute times; and affordability. One suburb from each state was selected. *BusinessWeek, "Where the Affordable Suburbs Are," December 13, 2007*

Sun Prairie is located within the Madison, WI Metropolitan Statistical Area.

Business Environment

CITY FINANCES

City Government Finances

Component	2004-2005 ($000)	2004-2005 ($ per capita)
Total Revenues	n/a	n/a
Total Expenditures	n/a	n/a
Debt Outstanding	n/a	n/a
Cash and Securities	n/a	n/a

Source: U.S Census Bureau, Government Finances 2004-2005

City Government Revenue by Source

Source	2004-2005 ($000)	2004-2005 ($ per capita)
General Revenue		
From Federal Government	n/a	n/a
From State Government	n/a	n/a
From Local Governments	n/a	n/a
Taxes		
Property	n/a	n/a
Sales	n/a	n/a
Personal Income	n/a	n/a
License	n/a	n/a
Charges	n/a	n/a
Liquor Store	n/a	n/a
Utility	n/a	n/a
Employee Retirement	n/a	n/a
Other	n/a	n/a

Source: U.S Census Bureau, Government Finances 2004-2005

City Government Expenditures by Function

Function	2004-2005 ($000)	2004-2005 ($ per capita)	2004-2005 (%)
General Expenditures			
Airports	n/a	n/a	n/a
Corrections	n/a	n/a	n/a
Education	n/a	n/a	n/a
Fire Protection	n/a	n/a	n/a
Governmental Administration	n/a	n/a	n/a
Health	n/a	n/a	n/a
Highways	n/a	n/a	n/a
Hospitals	n/a	n/a	n/a
Housing and Community Development	n/a	n/a	n/a
Interest on General Debt	n/a	n/a	n/a
Libraries	n/a	n/a	n/a
Parking	n/a	n/a	n/a
Parks and Recreation	n/a	n/a	n/a
Police Protection	n/a	n/a	n/a
Public Welfare	n/a	n/a	n/a
Sewerage	n/a	n/a	n/a
Solid Waste Management	n/a	n/a	n/a
Liquor Store	n/a	n/a	n/a
Utility	n/a	n/a	n/a
Employee Retirement	n/a	n/a	n/a
Other	n/a	n/a	n/a

Source: U.S Census Bureau, Government Finances 2004-2005

Municipal Bond Ratings

Area	Moody's
City	Aaa

Source: Mergent Bond Record, January 2008 (unless noted otherwise)

DEMOGRAPHICS

Population Growth

Area	1990 Census	2000 Census	2007 Estimate	2012 Projection	Population Growth (%) 1990-2000	Population Growth (%) 2000-2012
City	15,836	20,369	25,940	29,449	28.6	44.6
MSA[1]	432,323	501,774	544,682	572,776	16.1	14.2
U.S.	248,709,873	281,421,906	301,045,522	314,920,978	13.2	11.9

Note: (1) Metropolitan Statistical Area - see Appendix B for areas included
Source: Claritas, Inc.

Number of Households and Average Household Size

Area	2007 Estimate	2007 Average Household Size
City	10,242	2.53
MSA[1]	225,458	2.42
U.S.	113,668,003	2.65

Note: (1) Metropolitan Statistical Area - see Appendix B for areas included
Source: Claritas, Inc.

Race and Ethnicity

Area	White Alone[2]	Black Alone[2]	Asian Alone[2]	Other Race Alone[2]	Hispanic[3]
City	90.1	3.9	2.0	4.0	3.8
MSA[1]	88.1	3.7	3.9	4.3	4.1
U.S.	73.1	12.4	4.3	10.3	14.9

Note: Figures are 2007 estimates; (1) Metropolitan Statistical Area - see Appendix B for areas included (2) Alone is defined as not being in combination with one or more other races; (3) May be of any race.
Source: Claritas, Inc.

Ancestry

Area	German	Irish[2]	English	American	Italian	Polish	French[3]	Scottish
City	46.0	13.5	8.4	4.4	3.8	5.7	5.0	1.4
MSA[1]	40.4	14.3	9.7	3.1	3.3	5.0	3.3	1.7
U.S.	15.2	10.9	8.7	7.3	5.6	3.2	3.0	1.7

Note: Figures include multiple ancestry (e.g. if a person reported being Irish and Italian, they were included in both columns); (1) Metropolitan Statistical Area - see Appendix A for areas included; (2) Includes Celtic; (3) Includes Alsatian but excludes Basque
Source: Census 2000, Summary File 3

Foreign-Born Population

Area	Percent of Population Born in: Any Foreign Country	Europe	Asia	Africa	Oceania[2]	Canada	Mexico	Latin America[3]
City	3.7	0.5	0.6	0.3	0.0	0.1	1.7	0.4
MSA[1]	6.3	1.1	2.8	0.3	0.0	0.3	1.2	0.6
U.S.	11.1	1.7	2.9	0.3	0.1	0.3	3.3	2.5

Note: (1) Metropolitan Statistical Area - see Appendix A for areas included; (2) Includes Australia, New Zealand subregion, Melanesia, Micronesia, Polynesia, and Oceania n.e.c; (3) Includes Central America (excluding Mexico), South America, and the Caribbean.
Source: Census 2000, Summary File 3

Marriage Status

Area	Never Married	Now Married (excluding Separated)	Separated	Widowed	Divorced
City	26.1	58.3	1.6	4.8	9.2
MSA[1]	34.8	51.0	1.1	4.0	9.1
U.S.	27.1	54.4	2.2	6.6	9.7

Note: Figures are percentages and cover the population 15 years of age and older; (1) Metropolitan Statistical Area - see Appendix A for areas included
Source: Census 2000, Summary File 3

Age Distribution

Area	Percent of Population						
	Under Age 5	Age 5 to 17	Age 18 to 34	Age 35 to 49	Age 50 to 64	Age 65 to 79	80 Years and Over
City	7.8	21.0	24.5	25.2	12.5	6.2	2.8
MSA[1]	6.0	16.5	30.3	24.3	13.6	6.7	2.7
U.S.	6.8	18.9	23.7	23.5	14.8	9.2	3.2

Note: (1) Metropolitan Statistical Area - see Appendix A for areas included
Source: Census 2000, Summary File 3

Male/Female Ratio

Area	Males	Females	Males per 100 Females
City	12,560	13,380	93.9
MSA[1]	270,366	274,316	98.6
U.S.	148,320,305	152,725,217	97.1

Note: Figures are 2007 estimates; (1) Metropolitan Statistical Area - see Appendix B for areas included
Source: Claritas, Inc.

Religion

Area	Catholic	Southern Baptist	United Meth-odist	ELCA[1]	LDS[2]	Presby-terian Church USA	Jewish Est.	Muslim Est.
County	28.0	0.1	2.0	11.6	0.3	1.0	1.1	0.3
U.S.	22.0	7.1	3.7	1.8	1.5	1.1	2.2	0.6

Note: Figures are the number of adherents as a percentage of the total population; Adherents are defined as all members, including full members, their children and the estimated number of other participants who are not considered members (e.g. the baptized, those not confirmed, those regularly attending services, etc.); (1) Evangelical Lutheran Church in America; (2) The Church of Jesus Christ of Latter Day Saints
Source: Reprinted with permission from Religious Congregations and Membership in the United States 2000 (Nashville, Glenmary Research Center, 2002) Copyright Association of Statisticians of American Religious Bodies. All rights reserved.

ECONOMY

Gross Metropolitan Product

Area	2002	2003	2004	2005	2005 Rank[2]
MSA[1]	20.9	21.9	23.5	24.9	80

Note: Figures are in billions of dollars; (1) Madison, WI Metropolitan Statistical Area - see Appendix A for areas included; (2) Rank ranges from 1 to 361
Source: The U.S. Conference of Mayors, "U.S. Metro Economies: GMP - The Engines of America's Growth," January 2007

Economic Growth

Area	1995 GMP	2005 GMP	Average Annual Growth Rate	Growth Rate Rank[2]
MSA[1]	14.3	24.9	5.7	138

Note: Figures are in billions of dollars; GMP = Gross Metropolitan Product; (1) Madison, WI Metropolitan Statistical Area - see Appendix A for areas included; (2) Rank ranges from 1 to 361
Source: The U.S. Conference of Mayors, "U.S. Metro Economies: GMP - The Engines of America's Growth," January 2007

INCOME

Per Capita/Median/Average Income

Area	Per Capita ($)	Median Household ($)	Average Household ($)
City	29,646	63,838	74,576
MSA[1]	30,052	57,745	71,744
U.S.	25,495	49,280	66,670

Note: Figures are 2007 estimates; (1) Metropolitan Statistical Area - see Appendix B for areas included
Source: Claritas, Inc.

Household Income Distribution

Area	Percent of Households Earning							
	Under $15,000	$15,000 -24,999	$25,000 -34,999	$35,000 -49,999	$50,000 -74,999	$75,000 -99,000	$100,000 -149,999	$150,000 and up
City	5.0	6.9	9.8	15.8	22.4	17.2	16.7	6.2
MSA[1]	9.1	8.4	9.8	15.5	22.1	15.0	13.8	6.4
U.S.	13.1	10.9	11.2	15.6	19.5	11.9	11.3	6.6

Note: Figures are 2007 estimates; (1) Metropolitan Statistical Area - see Appendix B for areas included
Source: Claritas, Inc.

Poverty Rates by Age

Area	All Ages	Under 5 Years Old	5 to 17 Years Old	18 to 64 Years Old	65 Years and Over
City	4.4	0.4	1.5	2.1	0.4
MSA[1]	9.4	0.5	1.2	7.3	0.4
U.S.	12.4	1.2	3.0	6.9	1.2

Note: Figures are percent of population with income in 1999 below poverty level and only include population for whom poverty status is determined; (1) Metropolitan Statistical Area - see Appendix A for areas included
Source: Census 2000, Summary File 3

Personal Bankruptcy Filing Rate

Area	2004	2005	2006
Dane County	3.45	4.80	1.50
U.S.	5.31	6.82	2.00

Note: Numbers are per 1,000 population and include Chapter 7 and Chapter 13 filings
Source: Federal Deposit Insurance Corporation (FDIC), Regional Economic Conditions (RECON), 8/23/2007

EMPLOYMENT

Labor Force and Employment

Area	Civilian Labor Force			Workers Employed		
	Dec. 2006	Dec. 2007	% Chg.	Dec. 2006	Dec. 2007	% Chg.
City	16,025	15,938	-0.5	15,428	15,296	-0.9
MSA[1]	339,368	336,874	-0.7	328,368	325,551	-0.9
U.S.	152,571,000	153,705,000	0.7	146,081,000	146,334,000	0.2

Note: Data is not seasonally adjusted and covers workers 16 years of age and older;
(1) Metropolitan Statistical Area - see Appendix B for areas included
Source: Bureau of Labor Statistics, http://stats.bls.gov

Unemployment Rate

Area	2007											
	Jan.	Feb.	Mar.	Apr.	May	Jun.	Jul.	Aug.	Sep.	Oct.	Nov.	Dec.
City	4.7	5.1	4.9	4.4	4.1	4.3	4.1	4.1	3.9	3.8	3.8	4.0
MSA[1]	3.9	4.2	4.1	3.7	3.6	4.0	3.6	3.5	3.4	3.2	3.3	3.4
U.S.	5.0	4.9	4.5	4.3	4.3	4.7	4.9	4.6	4.5	4.4	4.5	4.8

Note: Data is not seasonally adjusted and covers workers 16 years of age and older; All figures are percentages; (1) Metropolitan Statistical Area - see Appendix B for areas included
Source: Bureau of Labor Statistics, http://stats.bls.gov

Employment by Occupation

Occupation Classification	City (%)	MSA[1] (%)	U.S. (%)
Sales and Office	29.8	26.5	26.7
Professional and Related	22.5	28.4	20.2
Service	10.1	12.7	14.9
Production, Transportation, and Material Moving	12.9	10.1	14.6
Management, Business, and Financial	17.4	15.2	13.5
Construction, Extraction, and Maintenance	7.2	6.7	9.4
Farming, Forestry, and Fishing	0.2	0.4	0.7

Note: Figures cover employed civilians 16 years of age and older;
(1) Metropolitan Statistical Area - see Appendix A for areas included
Source: Census 2000, Summary File 3

Employment by Industry

Sector	MSA[1] Number of Employees	MSA[1] Percent of Total	U.S. Percent of Total
Government	82,300	23.4	16.3
Education and Health Services	35,700	10.1	13.4
Professional and Business Services	37,700	10.7	13.1
Retail Trade	41,800	11.9	11.6
Manufacturing	32,500	9.2	9.9
Leisure and Hospitality	29,600	8.4	9.6
Financial Activities	26,900	7.6	5.9
Construction	n/a	n/a	5.3
Wholesale Trade	12,700	3.6	4.4
Other Services	17,600	5.0	3.9
Transportation and Utilities	8,800	2.5	3.7
Information	9,600	2.7	2.2
Natural Resources and Mining	n/a	n/a	0.5

Note: Figures cover non-farm employment as of December 2007 and are not seasonally adjusted; (1) Metropolitan Statistical Area - see Appendix B for areas included; n/a not available
Source: Bureau of Labor Statistics, http://stats.bls.gov

Average Wages

Occupation	\$/Hr.	Occupation	\$/Hr.
Accountants and Auditors	27.82	Maids and Housekeeping Cleaners	9.55
Automotive Mechanics	17.54	Maintenance and Repair Workers	17.23
Bookkeepers	15.63	Marketing Managers	47.40
Carpenters	21.51	Nuclear Medicine Technologists	n/a
Cashiers	9.38	Nurses, Licensed Practical	18.99
Clerks, General Office	12.87	Nurses, Registered	30.26
Clerks, Receptionists/Information	12.49	Nursing Aides/Orderlies/Attendants	13.08
Clerks, Shipping/Receiving	13.80	Packers and Packagers, Hand	13.33
Computer Programmers	27.08	Physical Therapists	31.14
Computer Support Specialists	20.74	Postal Service Mail Carriers	21.08
Computer Systems Analysts	30.54	Real Estate Brokers	37.97
Cooks, Restaurant	10.44	Retail Salespersons	11.80
Dentists	n/a	Sales Reps., Exc. Tech./Scientific	28.53
Electrical Engineers	32.30	Sales Reps., Tech./Scientific	36.73
Electricians	24.15	Secretaries, Exc. Legal/Med./Exec.	15.02
Financial Managers	46.91	Security Guards	12.44
First-Line Supervisors/Mgrs., Sales	20.11	Surgeons	n/a
Food Preparation Workers	9.03	Teacher Assistants	12.50
General and Operations Managers	47.26	Teachers, Elementary School	22.70
Hairdressers/Cosmetologists	12.47	Teachers, Secondary School	23.10
Internists	98.91	Telemarketers	11.70
Janitors and Cleaners	11.38	Truck Drivers, Heavy/Tractor-Trailer	19.40
Landscaping/Groundskeeping Workers	13.20	Truck Drivers, Light/Delivery Svcs.	15.61
Lawyers	50.47	Waiters and Waitresses	7.99

Note: Wage data covers the Madison, WI Metropolitan Statistical Area - see Appendix B for areas included. Hourly wages for elementary/secondary school teachers and teacher assistants were calculated by the editors from annual wage data assuming a 40 hour work week; n/a not available.
Source: Bureau of Labor Statistics, May 2007 Metro Area Occupational Employment and Wage Estimates

RESIDENTIAL REAL ESTATE

Building Permits

Area	Single-Family 2006	Single-Family 2007p	Single-Family Pct. Chg.	Multi-Family 2006	Multi-Family 2007p	Multi-Family Pct. Chg.	Total 2006	Total 2007p	Total Pct. Chg.
City	167	71	-57.5	325	117	-64.0	492	188	-61.8
U.S.	1,378,200	973,300	-29.4	460,700	407,200	-11.6	1,838,900	1,380,500	-24.9

Note: (p) preliminary; figures cover and represent new, privately-owned housing units authorized (unadjusted data); All permit data are based on estimates with imputation; U.S. figures are based on the new 20,000-place series.
Source: U.S. Census Bureau, Manufacturing, Mining, and Construction Statistics

Homeownership and Housing Vacancies

Area	Homeownership Rate[2] (%)			Rental Vacancy Rate[3] (%)			Homeowner Vacancy Rate[4] (%)		
	2005	2006	2007	2005	2006	2007	2005	2006	2007
MSA[1]	n/a	n/a	n/a	n/a	n/a	n/a	n/a	n/a	n/a
U.S.	68.9	68.8	68.1	9.8	9.8	9.7	1.9	2.4	2.7

Note: (1) Metropolitan Statistical Area - see Appendix B for areas included; (2) The proportion of households that are owners; (3) The proportion of the rental inventory that is vacant for rent; (4) The proportion of the homeowner inventory that is vacant for sale; n/a not available
Source: U.S. Census Bureau, Housing Vacancies and Homeownership Annual Statistics: 2007

TAXES

State Corporate Income Tax Rates

State	Rates and Tax Brackets
Wisconsin	7.9%

Note: Tax rates as of January 1, 2008
Source: Tax Foundation, www.taxfoundation.org

State Individual Income Tax Rates

State	Federal Deductibility	Marginal Rates (%)	Standard Deduction ($)		Personal Exemptions ($)[1]	
			Single	Joint	Single	Dependents
Wisconsin	No	4.60 - 6.75 (r)(y)	8,790 (j)	15,830 (j)	700	700

Note: Tax rates as of January 1, 2008; Local- and county-level taxes are not included; n/a not applicable; (1) Married joint filers generally receive double the single exemption; (j) Deduction phases out to zero for single filers at $82,500 and joint filers at $94,175; (r) State adjusts its bracket levels for inflation at the end of each year before printing tax forms; (y) Brackets are not double for married taxpayers.
Source: Tax Foundation, www.taxfoundation.org

Various State and Local Tax Rates

State and Local Sales and Use (%)	State Sales and Use (%)	Gasoline[1,2] ($/gal.)	Cigarette ($/pack)	Spirits ($/gal.)	Table Wine ($/gal.)	Beer ($/gal.)
5.5	5.0	0.329	1.77	3.36	0.25	0.06

Note: Tax rates as of January 1, 2008; (1) In addition to the 18.4 cpg Federal gasoline tax; (2) Rates may include additional state sales taxes, environmental protection and storage fees/taxes, and local taxes. When necessary, the volume-weighted average of all local taxes is used to approximate the typical statewide rate including local tax
Source: Tax Foundation, www.taxfoundation.org; Original research

State Tax Burdens

Area	Combined State and Local Tax Burden		Combined Federal, State and Local Tax Burden	
	Percent	Rank	Percent	Rank
Wisconsin	12.3	7	33.3	13
U.S. Average	11.0	-	32.7	-

Note: Figures cover 2007 and measure taxes as a percentage of income
Source: Tax Foundation, www.taxfoundation.org

State Business Tax Climate Index Rankings

State	Overall Rank	Corporate Tax Index Rank	Individual Income Tax Index Rank	Sales Tax Index Rank	Unemployment Insurance Tax Index Rank	Property Tax Index Rank
Wisconsin	39	30	42	23	27	37

Note: Rankings range from 1 to 50 where 1 is best. Rankings do not average across to Overall Rank. States without a given tax are given a ranking of 1.
Source: Tax Foundation, State Business Tax Climate Index 2008

TRANSPORTATION

Means of Transportation to Work

Area	Car/Truck/Van		Public Transportation			Bicycle	Walked	Other Means	Worked at Home
	Drove Alone	Car-pooled	Bus	Subway	Railroad				
City	86.9	8.3	0.1	0.0	0.0	0.1	1.4	0.4	2.7
MSA[1]	74.1	9.5	4.0	0.0	0.0	1.7	6.2	0.6	3.8
U.S.	75.7	12.2	2.5	1.5	0.5	0.4	2.9	1.0	3.3

Note: Figures are percentages and cover workers 16 years of age and older;
(1) Metropolitan Statistical Area - see Appendix A for areas included
Source: Census 2000, Summary File 3

Travel Time to Work

Area	Less Than 15 Minutes	15 to 29 Minutes	30 to 44 Minutes	45 to 59 Minutes	60 Minutes or More
City	38.0	36.3	18.5	3.9	3.3
MSA[1]	35.1	45.2	14.0	2.7	3.0
U.S.	29.4	36.1	19.1	7.4	8.0

Note: Figures are percentages and include workers 16 years old and over; (1) Metropolitan Statistical Area - see Appendix A for areas included
Source: Census 2000, Summary File 3

Living Environment

COST OF LIVING

Cost of Living Index

Composite Index	Groceries	Housing	Utilities	Trans-portation	Health Care	Misc. Goods/ Services
n/a	n/a	n/a	n/a	n/a	n/a	n/a

Note: U.S. = 100; n/a not available
Source: The Council for Community and Economic Research (formerly ACCRA), Cost of Living Index, 2007

Grocery Prices

Area[1]	T-Bone Steak ($/pound)	Frying Chicken ($/pound)	Whole Milk ($/half gal.)	Eggs ($/dozen)	Orange Juice ($/64 oz.)	Coffee ($/11.5 oz.)
City[2]	n/a	n/a	n/a	n/a	n/a	n/a
Avg.	8.93	1.12	2.13	1.52	3.26	3.31
Min.	5.88	0.71	1.33	0.83	2.30	2.20
Max.	12.80	2.07	3.43	3.54	5.79	6.20

Note: (1) Values for the local area are compared with the average, minimum and maximum values for all 331 areas in the Cost of Living Index report; n/a not available; (2) Figures cover the Sun Prairie WI urban area; **T-Bone Steak** *(price per pound);* **Frying Chicken** *(price per pound, whole fryer);* **Whole Milk** *(half gallon carton);* **Eggs** *(price per dozen, Grade A, large);* **Orange Juice** *(64 oz. Tropicana or Florida Natural);* **Coffee** *(11.5 oz. can, vacuum-packed, Maxwell House, Hills Bros, or Folgers).*
Source: The Council for Community and Economic Research (formerly ACCRA), Cost of Living Index, 2007

Housing and Utility Costs

Area[1]	New Home Price ($)	Apartment Rent ($/month)	All Electric ($/month)	Part Electric ($/month)	Other Energy ($/month)	Telephone ($/month)
City[2]	n/a	n/a	n/a	n/a	n/a	n/a
Avg.	309,605	782	146.13	78.67	90.16	26.14
Min.	189,877	n/a	82.03	37.41	33.15	17.08
Max.	1,202,800	3,481	271.14	150.60	257.67	37.45

Note: (1) Values for the local area are compared with the average, minimum and maximum values for all 331 areas in the Cost of Living Index report; n/a not available; (2) Figures cover the Sun Prairie WI urban area; **New Home Price** *(2,400 sf living area, 8,000 sf lot, in urban area with full utilities);* **Apartment Rent** *(950 sf 2 bedroom/1.5 or 2 bath, unfurnished, excluding all utilities except water);* **All Electric** *(average monthly cost for an all-electric home);* **Part Electric** *(average monthly cost for a part-electric home);* **Other Energy** *(average monthly cost for natural gas, fuel oil, coal, wood, and any other forms of energy except electricity);* **Telephone** *(price includes basic monthly rate for a private residential line plus additional local usage charges incurred by a family of four).*
Source: The Council for Community and Economic Research (formerly ACCRA), Cost of Living Index, 2007

Health Care, Transportation, and Other Costs

Area[1]	Doctor ($/visit)	Dentist ($/visit)	Optometrist ($/visit)	Gasoline ($/gallon)	Beauty Salon ($/visit)	Men's Shirt ($)
City[2]	n/a	n/a	n/a	n/a	n/a	n/a
Avg.	79.48	71.93	79.55	2.64	29.52	25.77
Min.	52.08	44.80	43.95	2.19	15.58	16.19
Max.	148.44	126.27	158.83	3.48	60.62	48.53

Note: (1) Values for the local area are compared with the average, minimum and maximum values for all 331 areas in the Cost of Living Index report; n/a not available; (2) Figures cover the Sun Prairie WI urban area; **Doctor** *(general practitioners routine exam of an established patient);* **Dentist** *(adult teeth cleaning and periodic oral examination);* **Optometrist** *(full vision eye exam for established adult patient);* **Gasoline** *(one gallon regular unleaded, national brand, including all taxes, cash price at self-service pump if available);* **Beauty Salon** *(woman's shampoo, trim, and blow-dry);* **Men's Shirt** *(cotton/polyester dress shirt, pinpoint weave, long sleeves).*
Source: The Council for Community and Economic Research (formerly ACCRA), Cost of Living Index, 2007

HOUSING

House Price Index (HPI)

Area	National Ranking[2]	Quarterly Change (%)	One-Year Change (%)	Five-Year Change (%)
MSA[1]	126	0.76	2.15	33.23
U.S.[3]	-	0.10	0.84	41.37

Note: The HPI is a weighted repeat sales index. It measures average price changes in repeat sales or refinancings on the same properties. This information is obtained by reviewing repeat mortgage transactions on single-family properties whose mortgages have been purchased or securitized by Fannie Mae or Freddie Mac in January 1975; (1) Metropolitan Statistical Area - see Appendix B for areas included; (2) Rankings are based on annual percentage change for all metro areas containing at least 15,000 transactions over the last 10 years and ranges from 1 to 291; (3) figures based on a weighted average of Census Division estimates; all figures are for the period ending December 31, 2007

Source: Office of Federal Housing Enterprise Oversight, House Price Index, February 26, 2008

House Price Valuations

Area	Q1 2000	Q1 2001	Q1 2002	Q1 2003	Q1 2004	Q1 2005	Q1 2006	Q1 2007	Q1 2008
MSA[1]	-0.8	-3.5	-1.3	2.4	7.3	9.6	11.8	8.8	5.7

Note: Figures show the percentage of over- or under-valuation of single family homes relative to statistically normal house values (e.g. a value of 23.6 indicates that house values are 23.6% overvalued). Statistically normal house values are based on house prices, interest rates, household incomes, population densities, and any historical premiums or discounts metropolitan areas have exhibited over time; (1) Figures cover the Metropolitan Statistical Area - see Appendix B for areas included

Source: Global Insight/National City Corporation, House Prices in America, May 2008

Median Home Prices

Area	2005	2006	2007[r]	Percent Change 2006 to 2007
MSA[1]	218.3	223.2	226.5	1.5
U.S. Average	219.0	221.9	217.9	-1.8

Note: Figures are median sales prices of existing single-family homes in thousands of dollars; (r) revised; n/a not available; (1) Metropolitan Statistical Area - see Appendix B for areas included

Source: National Association of Realtors, Metropolitan Area Prices, 1st Quarter 2008

Housing: Year Structure Built

Area	1990 -2000	1980 -1989	1970 -1979	1960 -1969	1950 -1959	1940 -1949	Before 1940	Median Year
City	32.1	14.9	21.5	16.4	7.8	2.5	4.7	1979
MSA[1]	21.1	13.1	20.0	14.6	10.6	5.6	15.1	1972
U.S.	17.0	15.8	18.5	13.7	12.7	7.3	15.0	1971

Note: Figures are percentages; (1) Metropolitan Statistical Area - see Appendix A for areas included

Source: Census 2000, Summary File 3

HEALTH

Health Risk Data

Category	Area[1] (%)	U.S. (%)
Adults who have been told they have high blood pressure[3]	n/a	25.5
Adults who have been told they have high blood cholesterol[3]	n/a	35.6
Adults who have been told they have diabetes[2]	n/a	7.5
Adults who have been told they have arthritis[3]	n/a	27.0
Adults who have been told they currently have asthma	n/a	8.5
Adults who are current smokers	n/a	20.1
Adults who are heavy drinkers[4]	n/a	4.9
Adults who are overweight (BMI 25.0 - 29.9)	n/a	36.5
Adults who are obese (BMI 30.0 - 99.8)	n/a	25.1

Note: Data as of 2006 unless otherwise noted; n/a not available; (1) Figures cover the Metropolitan Statistical Area - see Appendix B for areas included; (2) Figures do not include pregnancy-related diabetes, pre-diabetes or borderline diabetes; (3) 2005 data; (4) Heavy drinkers are classified as adult men having more than two drinks per day or adult women having more than one drink per day

Source: Centers for Disease Control and Prevention, Behaviorial Risk Factor Surveillance System, SMART: Selected Metropolitan/Micropolitan Area Risk Trends, 2005, 2006

Mortality Rates for the Top 10 Causes of Death in the U.S.

ICD-10[a] Sub-Chapter	ICD-10[a] Code	Age-Adjusted Mortality Rate[1] per 100,000 population	
		County[2]	U.S.
Malignant neoplasms	C00-C97	168.2	186.5
Ischaemic heart diseases	I20-I25	97.7	152.3
Other forms of heart disease	I30-I51	57.1	51.5
Cerebrovascular diseases	I60-I69	49.7	50.0
Chronic lower respiratory diseases	J40-J47	39.0	42.6
Diabetes mellitus	E10-E14	16.6	24.8
Other degenerative diseases of the nervous system	G30-G31	26.8	22.6
Other external causes of accidental injury	W00-X59	17.9	21.4
Influenza and pneumonia	J10-J18	23.0	20.7
Hypertensive diseases	I10-I13	10.8	18.2

Note: (a) ICD-10 = International Classification of Diseases 10th Revision; (1) Mortality rates are a three year average covering 2003-2005; (2) Figures cover Dane County
Source: Centers for Disease Control and Prevention, National Center for Health Statistics. Compressed Mortality File 1999-2004. CDC WONDER On-line Database, compiled from Compressed Mortality File 1999-2005 Series 20 No. 2K, 2008.

Mortality Rates for Selected Causes of Death

ICD-10[a] Sub-Chapter	ICD-10[a] Code	Age-Adjusted Mortality Rate[1] per 100,000 population	
		County[2]	U.S.
Assault	X85-Y09	1.4	5.9
Human immunodeficiency virus (HIV) disease	B20-B24	*1.1	4.5
Intentional self-harm	X60-X84	10.2	10.8
Malnutrition	E40-E46	*0.4	1.0
Obesity and other hyperalimentation	E65-E68	*0.9	1.4
Organic, including symptomatic, mental disorders	F01-F09	22.2	16.8
Transport accidents	V01-V99	11.4	16.1
Viral hepatitis	B15-B19	*0.7	1.8

Note: (a) ICD-10 = International Classification of Diseases 10th Revision; (1) Mortality rates are a three year average covering 2003-2005; (2) Figures cover Dane County; (*) Unreliable data as per CDC
Source: Centers for Disease Control and Prevention, National Center for Health Statistics. Compressed Mortality File 1999-2004. CDC WONDER On-line Database, compiled from Compressed Mortality File 1999-2005 Series 20 No. 2K, 2008.

Distribution of Physicians[1]

Area	Total	Family/ General Practice	Specialties	
			Medical	Surgical
Dane County (number)	1,496	449	496	306
Dane County (rate per 10,000 pop.)	32.7	9.8	10.8	6.7
U.S. (rate per 10,000 pop.)	17.7	4.6	6.9	4.3

Note: Data as of 2005; (1) Includes all non-federal, patient-care, office-based MDs
Source: Area Resource File (ARF). June 2007. U.S. Department of Health and Human Services, Health Resources and Services Administration, Bureau of Health Professions, Rockville, MD.

Hospitals

There were no hospitals listed within the city limits.
AHA Guide to the Healthcare Field 2008

According to *U.S. News,* the Madison, WI metro area is home to one of the best hospitals in the U.S.: **University of Wisconsin Hospital and Clinics**. *U.S. News Online, "America's Best Hospitals 2007"*

EDUCATION

Public School District Statistics

District Name	Schls	Pupils	Pupil/ Teacher Ratio	Minority Pupils[1] (%)	Free Lunch Eligible[2] (%)	IEP[3] (%)
Sun Prairie Area	10	5,691	13.1	19.6	n/a	14.7

Note: Table includes regular local school districts with 2,000 or more students; (1) Percentage of students that are not white, non-Hispanic; (2) Percentage of students that are eligible for the free lunch program; (3) Percentage of students that have an Individualized Education Program.
Source: U.S. Department of Education, National Center for Education Statistics, Common Core of Data, Local Education Agency (School District) Universe Survey: School Year 2005-2006; U.S. Department of Education, National Center for Education Statistics, Common Core of Data, Public Elementary/Secondary School Universe Survey: School Year 2005-2006

Highest Level of Education

Area	Less than H.S.	H.S. Diploma	Some College, No Deg.	Associate Degree	Bachelors Degree	Masters Degree	Profess. School Degree	Doctorate Degree
City	9.2	21.2	22.5	11.6	27.9	5.7	1.6	0.4
MSA[1]	8.5	24.7	20.5	8.8	23.3	9.0	2.7	2.5
U.S.	19.4	28.4	21.2	6.4	15.7	5.9	2.0	1.0

Note: Figures are 2007 estimated percentages and cover persons age 25 and over; (1) Metropolitan Statistical Area - see Appendix B for areas included
Source: Claritas, Inc.

Educational Attainment by Race

Area	High School Graduate (%)					Bachelor's Degree (%)				
	Total	White	Black	Asian	Hisp.[2]	Total	White	Black	Asian	Hisp.[2]
City	90.9	92.1	84.3	81.4	46.5	34.4	34.6	26.4	49.2	15.2
MSA[1]	92.2	93.3	77.6	87.0	67.8	40.6	41.0	19.2	65.5	27.2
U.S.	80.4	83.6	72.3	80.4	52.4	24.4	26.1	14.3	44.1	10.4

Note: Figures shown cover persons 25 years old and over; (1) Metropolitan Statistical Area - see Appendix A for areas included; (2) people of Hispanic origin can be of any race
Source: Census 2000, Summary File 3

School Enrollment by Type

Area	Grades KG to 8				Grades 9 to 12			
	Public		Private		Public		Private	
	Enrollment	%	Enrollment	%	Enrollment	%	Enrollment	%
City	2,614	89.2	316	10.8	1,256	95.4	60	4.6
MSA[1]	44,489	89.8	5,034	10.2	20,659	94.4	1,235	5.6
U.S.	33,526,011	88.7	4,285,121	11.3	14,848,628	90.6	1,532,323	9.4

Note: Figures shown cover persons 3 years old and over; (1) Metropolitan Statistical Area - see Appendix A for areas included
Source: Census 2000, Summary File 3

School Enrollment by Race

Area	Grades KG to 8 (%)				Grades 9 to 12 (%)			
	White	Black	Asian	Hisp.[1]	White	Black	Asian	Hisp.[1]
City	86.6	5.0	2.8	6.2	94.1	2.5	1.8	1.1
MSA[2]	84.2	6.6	3.5	4.3	85.2	6.2	3.7	3.5
U.S.	68.5	15.5	3.3	16.8	68.8	15.5	3.8	15.7

Note: Figures shown cover persons 3 years old and over; (1) people of Hispanic origin can be of any race; (2) Metropolitan Statistical Area - see Appendix A for areas included
Source: Census 2000, Summary File 3

Average Salaries of Public School Classroom Teachers

District	2005-06		2006-07		Percent Change 2005-06 to 2006-07
	Dollars	Rank[1]	Dollars	Rank[1]	
Wisconsin	46,390	21	47,901	21	3.26
U.S. Average	49,026	-	50,816	-	3.65

Note: (1) State rank ranges from 1 to 51.
Source: National Education Association, Rankings & Estimates: Rankings of the States 2006 and Estimates of School Statistics 2007, December 2007

Higher Education

Four-Year Colleges			Two-Year Colleges			Medical Schools[1]	Law Schools[2]	Voc/ Tech[3]
Public	Private Non-profit	Private For-profit	Public	Private Non-profit	Private For-profit			
0	0	0	0	0	0	0	0	0

Note: Figures cover institutions located within the city limits; (1) includes schools accredited by the Liaison Committee on Medical Education and the American Osteopathic Association; (2) includes American Bar Association-accredited law schools; (3) includes all schools with programs that are less than 2 years.
Source: National Center for Education Statistics, The Integrated Postsecondary Education System (IPEDS) Peer Analysis System, 2007; www.usnews.com, Law and Medical School Directories, 2009

PRESIDENTIAL ELECTION

2004 Presidential Election Results

Area	Bush	Kerry	Nader	Other
Dane County	33.0	66.0	0.5	0.5
U.S.	50.7	48.3	0.4	0.6

Note: Results are percentages and may not add to 100% due to rounding
Source: Dave Leip's Atlas of U.S. Presidential Elections, www.uselectionatlas.org

EMPLOYERS

Major Employers

Company Name	Industry	Type of Site
American Family Mutl Insur Co	Fire, marine, and casualty insurance	Headquarters
CUNA Mutual Group	Accident and health insurance	Headquarters
City of Madison	Executive offices	Branch
Community Living Alliance	Individual and family services	Single
Comptrollers Office	Finance, taxation, and monetary policy	Branch
Covance Laboratories Inc	Animal specialties, nec	Headquarters
Division Facilities and Land	Land, mineral, and wildlife conservation	Branch
Doit	Colleges and universities	Branch
Government Agency	Administration of public health programs	Branch
Governors Office	Regulation, administration of transportation	Headquarters
Kraft Foods	Sausages and other prepared meats	Branch
Materials Management	General medical and surgical hospitals	Branch
St Marys Hospital Medical Ctr	General medical and surgical hospitals	Single
Univ of Wisconsin-Madison	Business and secretarial schools	Branch
University Wscnsin Hosp Clnics	General medical and surgical hospitals	Headquarters
University Wscnsin Hosp Clnics	Offices and clinics of medical doctors	Branch
W P S Insurance	Accident and health insurance	Branch
Wisconsin Dept Administration	Administration of general economic programs	Headquarters
Wisconsin Dept Natural Rsurces	Land, mineral, and wildlife conservation	Headquarters
Wisconsin Dept Transportation	Regulation, administration of transportation	Branch
Wisconsin Medical School	Vocational schools, nec	Branch
Wm S Middleton Mem V A Hosp	Administration of veterans' affairs	Branch
Workforce Dev Wisconsin Dept	Regulation, miscellaneous commercial sectors	Headquarters

Note: Companies shown are located within the Madison metropolitan area; nec = not elsewhere classified.
Source: www.zapdata.com, May 2008

PUBLIC SAFETY

Crime Rate

Area	All Crimes	Violent Crimes				Property Crimes		
		Murder	Forcible Rape	Robbery	Aggrav. Assault	Burglary	Larceny -Theft	Motor Vehicle Theft
City	1,824.6	0.0	23.5	19.6	78.5	153.0	1,467.5	82.4
Metro[1]	3,097.2	0.7	25.8	100.6	134.7	510.8	2,173.8	150.8
U.S.	3,808.1	5.7	30.9	149.4	287.5	729.4	2,206.8	398.4

Note: Figures are crimes per 100,000 population; (1) Metropolitan Statistical Area - see Appendix B for areas included
Source: FBI Uniform Crime Reports, 2006

Hate Crimes

Area	Number of Quarters Reported	Bias Motivation				
		Race	Religion	Sexual Orientation	Ethnicity	Disability
City	4	0	0	0	0	0

Source: Federal Bureau of Investigation, Hate Crime Statistics 2006

RECREATION

Culture

Dance[1]	Theatre[1]	Instrumental Music[1]	Vocal Music[1]	Series/ Festivals	Museums	Zoos and Aquariums[2]
0	0	0	0	0	1	0

Note: (1) Number of professional perfoming groups; (2) AZA-accredited
Source: The Grey House Performing Arts Directory, 2007; Official Museum Directory, 2008; Association of Zoos & Aquariums, AZA Member Zoos & Aquariums, June 2008

Professional Sports Teams

Team Name	League
No teams are located in the metro area	

Source: Original research

MEDIA

Newspapers

Name	News Focus	Frequency	Circulation
The Advertiser	Local	Twice a week	21,400
Star	Community	Weekly	2,100

Note: Includes newspapers with offices located in the city
Source: MediaContactsPro, March 2008

Television Stations

Name	Ch.	Network(s)	Type	Ownership
WISC	3	CBS	Commercial	Evening Telegram Company
WMTV	15	NBC	Commercial	Benedek Broadcasting Corporation
WHRM	20	PBS	Public	State of Wisconsin Educational Communications Board
WHA	21	PBS	Public	State of Wisconsin Educational Communications Board
WKOW	27	ABC	Commercial	Quincy Newspapers Inc.
WHWC	28	PBS	Public	State of Wisconsin Educational Communications Board
WHLA	31	PBS	Public	State of Wisconsin Educational Communications Board
WLEF	36	PBS	Public	State of Wisconsin Educational Communications Board
WPNE	38	PBS	Public	State of Wisconsin Educational Communications Board
WMSN	47	Fox	Commercial	Sinclair Broadcast Group
WHPN	57	WBN	Commercial	Acme Broadcasting Inc.

Note: Stations included cover the Madison DMA (Designated Market Area)
BurrellesLuce, MediaContacts Online, January 2007

Major AM Radio Stations

Call Letters	Freq. (kHz)	Station Type	Target Audience	Station Format	Music Format
WRPQ	740	n/a	General	Music/News/Talk	n/a
WDMP	810	n/a	General	Music/News	n/a
WLBL	930	College	General	Educational/Talk	n/a
WHA	970	College	General	Talk	n/a
WTSO	1070	Commercial	General	News/Sports/Talk	n/a
WNWC	1190	College	General/Religious	News/Talk	n/a
WCLO	1230	Commercial	General	News/Sports/Talk	n/a
WEKZ	1260	Commercial	General	Music/News	Country
WRJC	1270	Commercial	General	Music/News	Adult Standards
WGLR	1280	Commercial	General	Music/News	Country
WIBA	1310	Commercial	General	Talk	n/a
WPDR	1350	Commercial	General	News/Talk	n/a
WTJK	1380	n/a	General	News/Sports/Talk	n/a
WRDB	1400	Commercial	General	Sports	n/a
WRCO	1450	Commercial	General	Music/News	Adult Standards
WGEZ	1490	Commercial	General	Music/News	Modern Rock
WPVL	1590	Commercial	General	Music/News	Oldies
WTDY	1670	Commercial	General	News/Talk	n/a

Note: Stations included cover the Madison DMA (Designated Market Area); n/a not available
Source: BurrellesLuce, MediaContacts Online, January 2007

Major FM Radio Stations

Call Letters	Freq. (mHz)	Station Type	Target Audience	Station Format	Music Format
WJTY	88.1	Public	Black/General/Rel	Educational/Music	Gospel
WERN	88.7	College	General	n/a	n/a
WHBM	90.3	College	General	News/Talk	n/a
WHHI	91.3	College	General	n/a	n/a
WMAD	92.1	Commercial	General	Music/Talk	Adult Contemp.
WEKZ	93.7	Commercial	General	Music/News	Adult Contemp.
WJJO	94.1	n/a	General	Music/News/Sports	n/a
WOLX	94.9	Commercial	General	Music/News	Oldies
WMAD	96.3	n/a	General/Men	Music/News/Sports	n/a
WGLR	97.7	Commercial	General	Music/News/Talk	Country
WMGN	98.1	n/a	General	Music	n/a
WDMP	99.3	Commercial	General	Music/News	Country
WJVL	99.9	Commercial	General	Music/News/Sports	Country
WDDC	100.1	Commercial	General	Music/News	Country
WRCO	100.9	Commercial	General	Music/News	Oldies
WIBA	101.5	Commercial	General	Music	Classic Rock
WNWC	102.5	College	General/Religious	Music/News/Talk	Christian
WBDL	102.9	Commercial	General	Music/News	Adult Standards
WZEE	104.1	Commercial	General	Music/News	Top 40
WNFM	104.9	Commercial	General	Music	Country
WBZU	105.1	Commercial	General	Music	80's
WMMM	105.5	Commercial	General	Music	Alternative
WWQM	106.3	n/a	General	Music	n/a
WPVL	107.1	Commercial	General	Music/News	Oldies

Note: Stations included cover the Madison DMA (Designated Market Area); n/a not available
BurrellesLuce, MediaContacts Online, January 2007

CLIMATE

Average and Extreme Temperatures

Temperature	Jan	Feb	Mar	Apr	May	Jun	Jul	Aug	Sep	Oct	Nov	Dec	Yr.
Extreme High (°F)	56	61	82	94	93	101	104	102	99	90	76	62	104
Average High (°F)	26	30	42	58	70	79	84	81	72	61	44	30	57
Average Temp. (°F)	17	21	32	46	57	67	72	69	61	50	36	23	46
Average Low (°F)	8	12	22	35	45	54	59	57	49	38	27	14	35
Extreme Low (°F)	-37	-28	-29	0	19	31	36	35	25	13	-8	-25	-37

Note: Figures cover the years 1948-1990
Source: National Climatic Data Center, International Station Meteorological Climate Summary, 9/96

Average Precipitation/Snowfall/Humidity

Precip./Humidity	Jan	Feb	Mar	Apr	May	Jun	Jul	Aug	Sep	Oct	Nov	Dec	Yr.
Avg. Precip. (in.)	1.1	1.1	2.1	2.9	3.2	3.8	3.9	3.9	3.0	2.3	2.0	1.7	31.1
Avg. Snowfall (in.)	10	7	9	2	Tr	0	0	0	Tr	Tr	4	11	42
Avg. Rel. Hum. 6am (%)	78	80	81	80	79	81	85	89	90	85	84	82	83
Avg. Rel. Hum. 3pm (%)	66	63	59	50	50	51	53	55	55	54	64	69	57

Note: Figures cover the years 1948-1990; Tr = Trace amounts (<0.05 in. of rain; <0.5 in. of snow)
Source: National Climatic Data Center, International Station Meteorological Climate Summary, 9/96

Weather Conditions

Temperature			Daytime Sky			Precipitation		
5°F & below	32°F & below	90°F & above	Clear	Partly cloudy	Cloudy	0.01 inch or more precip.	0.1 inch or more snow/ice	Thunder-storms
35	161	14	88	119	158	118	38	40

Note: Figures are average number of days per year and cover the years 1948-1990
Source: National Climatic Data Center, International Station Meteorological Climate Summary, 9/96

HAZARDOUS WASTE

Superfund Sites

Sun Prairie has no sites on the EPA's Superfund Final National Priorities List.
U.S. Environmental Protection Agency, Final National Priorities List, June 23, 2008

AIR & WATER QUALITY

Air Quality Index

Area	Percent of Days when Air Quality was...[2]				AQI Statistics	
	Good	Moderate	Unhealthy for Sensitive Groups	Unhealthy	Maximum	Median
MSA[1]	69.9	27.7	2.5	0.0	143	40

Note: The Air Quality Index (AQI) is an index for reporting daily air quality. EPA calculates the AQI for five major air pollutants regulated by the Clean Air Act: ground-level ozone, particle pollution (also known as particulate matter), carbon monoxide, sulfur dioxide, and nitrogen dioxide. The AQI runs from 0 to 500. The higher the AQI value, the greater the level of air pollution and the greater the health concern. There are six AQI categories: "Good" The AQI is between 0 and 50. Air quality is considered satisfactory; "Moderate" The AQI is between 51 and 100. Air quality is acceptable; "Unhealthy for Sensitive Groups" When AQI values are between 101 and 150, members of sensitive groups may experience health effects; "Unhealthy" When AQI values are between 151 and 200 everyone may begin to experience health effects; "Very Unhealthy" AQI values between 201 and 300 trigger a health alert; "Hazardous" AQI values over 300 trigger health warnings of emergency conditions; (1) Metropolitan Statistical Area - see Appendix A for areas included; (2) Based on 365 days with AQI data in 2007.
Source: U.S. Environmental Protection Agency, Air Quality Index Report, 2007

Air Quality Index Pollutants

Area	Percent of Days when AQI Pollutant was...[2]					
	Carbon Monoxide	Nitrogen Dioxide	Ozone	Sulfur Dioxide	Particulate Matter 2.5	Particulate Matter 10
MSA[1]	0.0	0.0	48.2	0.0	51.8	0.0

Note: The Air Quality Index (AQI) is an index for reporting daily air quality. EPA calculates the AQI for five major air pollutants regulated by the Clean Air Act: ground-level ozone, particle pollution (also known as particulate matter), carbon monoxide, sulfur dioxide, and nitrogen dioxide. The AQI runs from 0 to 500. The higher the AQI value, the greater the level of air pollution and the greater the health concern; (1) Metropolitan Statistical Area - see Appendix A for areas included; (2) Based on 365 days with AQI data in 2007.
Source: U.S. Environmental Protection Agency, Air Quality Index Report, 2007

Air Quality Index Trends

Area	Trend Sites								All Sites
	1999	2000	2001	2002	2003	2004	2005	2006	2006
MSA[1]	n/a	n/a	n/a	n/a	n/a	n/a	n/a	n/a	n/a

Note: An AQI value greater than 100 indicates that air quality would have been in the unhealthful range on that day. Data from exceptional events are not included. These counts are presented in two ways. First, the counts are based on sites having an adequate record of monitoring data during the trend period (trend sites). These counts represent the relative change in the number of days with AQI values greater than 100. In the last column, the counts are based on all sites with data in the most recent year (because it is possible for a site to have data in the most recent year but not enough data to be a trend site); (1) Metropolitan Statistical Area - see Appendix A for areas included; n/a not available.
Source: U.S. Environmental Protection Agency, Office of Air and Radiation, Air Trends, Factbook and Related Information, Air Pollution Trends in Selected Metropolitan Areas 2006

Maximum Air Pollutant Concentrations

	Particulate Matter 10 (ug/m^3)	Particulate Matter 2.5 (ug/m^3)	Ozone (ppm)	Carbon Monoxide (ppm)	Sulfur Dioxide (ppm)	Nitrogen Dioxide (ppm)	Lead (ug/m^3)
MSA[1] Level	n/a	33	0.076	n/a	n/a	n/a	n/a
NAAQS[2]	150	35	0.125	9	0.140	0.053	1.50
Met NAAQS[2]	Yes	Yes	Yes	n/a	n/a	n/a	n/a

Note: Data from exceptional events are not included; (1) Metropolitan Statistical Area - see Appendix A for areas included; (2) National Ambient Air Quality Standards; n/a not available
Concentrations: Particulate Matter 10 (coarse particulate) - highest second maximum 24-hour concentration; Particulate Matter 2.5 (fine particulate) - highest 98th percentile 24-hour concentration; Ozone - highest second daily maximum 1-hour concentration; Carbon Monoxide - highest second maximum non-overlapping 8-hour concentration; Sulfur Dioxide - highest second maximum 24-hour concentration; Nitrogen Dioxide - highest arithmetic mean concentration; Lead - highest quarterly maximum concentration
Units: ppm = parts per million; ug/m^3 = micrograms per cubic meter
Source: U.S. Environmental Protection Agency, MSA Factbook 2006, Air Quality Statistics by City

Drinking Water

Water System Name	Pop. Served	Primary Water Source Type	Violations[1]	
			Health Based	Monitoring/ Reporting
Sun Prairie Waterworks	24,000	Ground	0	0

Note: (1) Based on violation data from January 1, 2007 to December 31, 2007 (includes unresolved violations from earlier years)
Source: U.S. Environmental Protection Agency, Office of Ground Water and Drinking Water, Safe Drinking Water Information System (based on data extracted April 15, 2008)

Casper, Wyoming

Background

Casper is situated in central Wyoming in the North Platte River Valley of Natrona County. The Casper Mountains rise 3,000 feet above the city. The name is derived from Fort Caspar, built in 1861, named for Lieutenant Caspar Collins, killed in 1865. A clerk's error created its present name as incorporated in 1917.

Settled in the late 1800s, Casper is the point of convergence for all major westward trails - Oregon Trail, Mormon Trail, Bridger Trail, Bozeman Trail, and Pony Express Trail - and developed as a crossroads to the West and North West. The first white man's cabin in Wyoming was built near Bessemer Bend, where a ferry was established in 1847, and a bridge constructed in 1859. When Pathfinder Reservoir was completed in 1909, it was the largest manmade reservoir in the U.S.

Casper is a petroleum-producing and refining center and a vast cattle and sheep ranching area. The first oil well was drilled in 1883, and the first refinery was erected in 1895. The Teapot Dome oil field north of the city gave its name to a major corruption scandal 1922 of the Warren G. Harding presidential administration. In 1924 more oil was shipped by rail from Casper than any other place in the world.

Recognized for providing a low cost of doing business, Casper is connected to I-25, and served by five commercial airlines at the Natrona County International Airport. The second-largest city in Wyoming, Casper was named an All-America City Finalist in 2002. The city is the site of Casper College 1945, a branch of the University of Wyoming and a community college. Vice President Richard Cheney and his wife Lynne were reared in Casper, attending Natrona County High School and Casper College. Dean Conger, photo chief for National Geographic Magazine, began his photo journalism career in Casper.

Casper's vigorous historic downtown has a vibrant entertainment district of restaurants, coffee shops, theaters and a diverse blend of shopping, boasting the largest mall in central Wyoming. The Casper Events Center hosts, among others, the Wyoming Symphony Orchestra. Local festivals include the Bear Trap Summer Festival and the Central Wyoming Fair & Rodeo.

Regardless of the season there is always a diversity of terrain to view, wildlife to see and attractions to enjoy. Casper is central to Wyoming and the Rocky Mountains and within driving distance of numerous national parks and monuments including Devil's Tower National Monument, Grand Teton National Park and Yellowstone. Casper's National Historic Trails Interpretive Center is one of Wyoming's finest museums. Featuring state-of-the-art technology, the center allows a visitor to experience what pioneer life was like. Reconstructed Fort Caspar includes an1865 frontier army fort, 1859 Guinard bridge, and 1847 Mormon ferry. Fort Caspar Museum offers exhibits featuring the social and natural history of central Wyoming from prehistoric occupation through recent regional development.

Casper offers four golf courses, 258 acres of parks, and downhill skiing at the Hogadon Resort on Casper Mountain. The North Platte River provides world-class fly-fishing, rafting, kayaking, or boating at Alcova Reservoir. Hunting, birding, hiking, biking and jogging trails abound.

The city is home to the Casper Rockies baseball team, the Wyoming Cavalry indoor football team, and the College National Finals Rodeo. Cincinnati Reds pitcher Tom Browning received his early experience in youth baseball here and pro ball player Mike Lansing lived, attended school and played baseball in Casper. Joe Alexander studied rodeo at Casper College and went on to become the PRCA bareback bronco champion. He is recognized in the PRCA Rodeo Hall of Fame, Colorado Springs, Colorado.

Located in sometimes mile-high altitude, Casper sits on wind-swept prairies. Mountains to the west act as a moisture barrier, lending to the city's semi-arid climate and prairie winds create unpredictable weather variations. Relative humidity is rarely above 30 percent. With bright, full sun in all four seasons, the city experiences 13 inches of rain and 52 inches of annual snowfall, which quickly melts away. Summers are hot but not humid and summer evenings will be cool.

Rankings

General Rankings

- Casper* was ranked #112 out of 375 metro areas in *Cities Ranked & Rated*. Criteria: cost of living; climate; crime; transportation; economy and jobs; education; arts and culture; health and healthcare; leisure; quality of life. *Cities Ranked & Rated, 2nd Edition, 2007*
- Casper* was ranked #356 out of 379 metro areas in *Places Rated Almanac*. Criteria: health care; education; recreation; transportation; ambience; climate; crime; housing costs; jobs. *Places Rated Almanac, 7th Edition, 2007*

Business/Finance Rankings

- Casper* was selected as one of the best places to start and grow a company by *Entrepreneur* and the National Policy Research Council. The Casper* metro area ranked #6 out of 162 small metro areas. Criteria: business formation and growth (firms started four to 14 years ago that still employ at least 5 people and experienced rapid growth over the last four years). *Entrepreneur/National Policy Research Council, "Hot Cities for Entrepreneurs," September 2006*
- The Casper* metro area appeared on the Milken Institute "2007 Best Performing Cities" index. Rank: #22 out of 179 small metro areas. Criteria: job growth; wage and salary growth; high-tech output growth. *Milken Institute, "2007 Best Performing Cities"*
- The Casper* metro area was selected as one of the hottest cities for entrepreneurs in America by *Inc. Magazine.* Criteria: job-growth data for 393 metro was analyzed for current-year employment growth, average annual employment growth over past three years, and employment growth by industry sector. The Casper* metro area ranked #11 among small metro areas and #17 overall. *Inc. Magazine, May 2007*
- *Forbes* ranked 179 smaller metro areas in the U.S. in terms of the "Best Places for Business and Careers." The Casper* metro area was ranked #97. Criteria: business costs (labor, energy, tax and office space expenses); living costs (housing, transportation, food and other household expenditures); education levels of the work force; job growth; income growth; migration trends; crime rates; and culture/leisure. *Forbes, "Best Places for Business and Careers," March 19, 2008*
- *Kiplinger's Personal Finance* ranked 101 U.S. cities in terms of their total tax burdens. Casper ranked #1 (#1 had the lowest overall tax burden). Criteria: state income tax; property tax; sales tax; personal property tax; and gasoline tax. *Kiplinger's Personal Finance, July 2004*
- Casper appeared on *Kiplinger's Personal Finance* list of the "Top Ten Tax-Friendly Cities." The city was ranked #1. Criteria: income tax; sales tax; real estate and car/personal property tax. *Kiplinger's Personal Finance, May 2007*

Health/Environment Rankings

- The Casper* metro area appeared in *Country Home's* "2008 Best Green Places" report. The area ranked #349 out of 379. Criteria: official energy policies; green power; green buildings; availability of fresh, locally grown food. *Country Home, "2008 Best Green Places"*
- The American Podiatric Medical Association and *Prevention* magazine ranked America's 100 most populated cities based on fitness-walker friendliness. The best cities have safe streets, beautiful places to walk, mild weather and good air quality. Casper ranked #437. *Prevention, "The Best Walking Cities of 2008," April 2008; American Podiatric Medical Association, "2008 Best Fitness-Walking Cities, "April 2008*
- Sperling's BestPlaces ranked 331 metro areas and identified the most and least stressful U.S. cities. The Casper* metro area ranked #62 out of the 117 smallest metro areas (#1 = most stressful). Criteria: divorce rate; unemployment rate; violent and property crime; suicide rate; commute time; mental health; alcohol consumption; cloudy days. *Sperling's BestPlaces, www.BestPlaces.net, "America's Most (and Least) Stressful Cities," January 9, 2004*

Seniors/Retirement Rankings

- A.G. Edwards ranked America's 500 top-performing communities based on their residents' personal savings and investing behavior. The Casper* metro area ranked #465 with an index score of 95.37 (national average = 100.00). A dozen statistical factors were measured including: participation in retirement savings plans; personal debt levels; and home ownership. *A.G. Edwards, "2007 Nest Egg Index", September 12, 2007*

Safety Rankings

- The National Insurance Crime Bureau ranked 361 metro areas in the U.S. in terms of per capita rates of vehicle theft. The Casper* metro area ranked #223 (#1 = highest rate). Criteria: number of vehicle theft offenses per 100,000 inhabitants. *National Insurance Crime Bureau, "NICB Vehicle Theft Study," April 22, 2008*

- Farmers Insurance Group of Companies, in partnership with Sperling's BestPlaces, ranked 379 metro areas and identified the "Most Secure U.S. Place to Live." The Casper* metro area ranked #86 out of 138 in the small town category (fewer than 150,000 residents). Criteria: crime rates; extreme weather; risk of natural disasters; environmental hazards; terrorism threats; air quality; life expectancy; job loss numbers. *Farmers Insurance Group, "Most Secure U.S. Places to Live 2007"*

Sports/Recreation Rankings

- *Golf Digest* ranked 330 metro areas in the U.S. in terms of golf. The Casper* metro area was ranked #206. Criteria: access to golf; weather; value of golf; and quality of golf. *Golf Digest, "Metro Golf Rankings," August 2005*

Casper is located within the Casper, WY Metropolitan Statistical Area.

Business Environment

CITY FINANCES

City Government Finances

Component	2004-2005 ($000)	2004-2005 ($ per capita)
Total Revenues	80,561	1,557
Total Expenditures	93,473	1,807
Debt Outstanding	5,159	100
Cash and Securities	96,489	1,865

Source: U.S Census Bureau, Government Finances 2004-2005

City Government Revenue by Source

Source	2004-2005 ($000)	2004-2005 ($ per capita)
General Revenue		
From Federal Government	4,066	79
From State Government	25,949	502
From Local Governments	13,826	267
Taxes		
Property	2,275	44
Sales	2,323	45
Personal Income	0	0
License	1,196	23
Charges	16,795	325
Liquor Store	0	0
Utility	8,625	167
Employee Retirement	0	0
Other	5,506	106

Source: U.S Census Bureau, Government Finances 2004-2005

City Government Expenditures by Function

Function	2004-2005 ($000)	2004-2005 ($ per capita)	2004-2005 (%)
General Expenditures			
Airports	0	0	0.0
Corrections	0	0	0.0
Education	0	0	0.0
Fire Protection	5,852	113	6.3
Governmental Administration	9,973	193	10.7
Health	958	19	1.0
Highways	9,242	179	9.9
Hospitals	0	0	0.0
Housing and Community Development	967	19	1.0
Interest on General Debt	41	1	0.0
Libraries	0	0	0.0
Parking	51	1	0.1
Parks and Recreation	12,022	232	12.9
Police Protection	7,969	154	8.5
Public Welfare	2,354	45	2.5
Sewerage	6,098	118	6.5
Solid Waste Management	2,725	53	2.9
Liquor Store	0	0	0.0
Utility	9,814	190	10.5
Employee Retirement	0	0	0.0
Other	25,407	491	27.2

Source: U.S Census Bureau, Government Finances 2004-2005

Municipal Bond Ratings

Area	Moody's
City	n/a

Source: Mergent Bond Record, January 2008 (unless noted otherwise)

DEMOGRAPHICS

Population Growth

Area	1990 Census	2000 Census	2007 Estimate	2012 Projection	Population Growth (%)	
					1990-2000	2000-2012
City	46,781	49,644	52,416	54,352	6.1	9.5
MSA[1]	61,226	66,533	70,888	73,963	8.7	11.2
U.S.	248,709,873	281,421,906	301,045,522	314,920,978	13.2	11.9

Note: (1) Metropolitan Statistical Area - see Appendix B for areas included
Source: Claritas, Inc.

Number of Households and Average Household Size

Area	2007 Estimate	2007 Average Household Size
City	21,888	2.39
MSA[1]	29,176	2.43
U.S.	113,668,003	2.65

Note: (1) Metropolitan Statistical Area - see Appendix B for areas included
Source: Claritas, Inc.

Race and Ethnicity

Area	White Alone[2]	Black Alone[2]	Asian Alone[2]	Other Race Alone[2]	Hispanic[3]
City	93.7	1.1	0.4	4.8	5.5
MSA[1]	93.7	1.0	0.4	4.9	5.0
U.S.	73.1	12.4	4.3	10.3	14.9

Note: Figures are 2007 estimates; (1) Metropolitan Statistical Area - see Appendix B for areas included (2) Alone is defined as not being in combination with one or more other races; (3) May be of any race.
Source: Claritas, Inc.

Ancestry

Area	German	Irish[2]	English	American	Italian	Polish	French[3]	Scottish
City	24.8	14.8	13.6	7.8	3.7	1.9	4.1	2.5
MSA[1]	25.3	14.7	13.4	8.6	3.2	1.9	3.8	2.6
U.S.	15.2	10.9	8.7	7.3	5.6	3.2	3.0	1.7

Note: Figures include multiple ancestry (e.g. if a person reported being Irish and Italian, they were included in both columns); (1) Metropolitan Statistical Area - see Appendix A for areas included; (2) Includes Celtic; (3) Includes Alsatian but excludes Basque
Source: Census 2000, Summary File 3

Foreign-Born Population

Area	Percent of Population Born in							
	Any Foreign Country	Europe	Asia	Africa	Oceania[2]	Canada	Mexico	Latin America[3]
City	2.0	0.7	0.4	0.0	0.0	0.2	0.6	0.1
MSA[1]	1.8	0.6	0.4	0.0	0.0	0.2	0.5	0.1
U.S.	11.1	1.7	2.9	0.3	0.1	0.3	3.3	2.5

Note: (1) Metropolitan Statistical Area - see Appendix A for areas included; (2) Includes Australia, New Zealand subregion, Melanesia, Micronesia, Polynesia, and Oceania n.e.c; (3) Includes Central America (excluding Mexico), South America, and the Caribbean.
Source: Census 2000, Summary File 3

Marriage Status

Area	Never Married	Now Married (excluding Separated)	Separated	Widowed	Divorced
City	23.9	54.7	1.3	6.8	13.4
MSA[1]	23.2	55.9	1.3	6.1	13.5
U.S.	27.1	54.4	2.2	6.6	9.7

Note: Figures are percentages and cover the population 15 years of age and older; (1) Metropolitan Statistical Area - see Appendix A for areas included
Source: Census 2000, Summary File 3

Age Distribution

Area	Percent of Population						
	Under Age 5	Age 5 to 17	Age 18 to 34	Age 35 to 49	Age 50 to 64	Age 65 to 79	80 Years and Over
City	6.4	19.3	22.0	23.7	14.9	10.5	3.1
MSA[1]	6.4	19.5	21.6	24.5	15.4	9.9	2.7
U.S.	6.8	18.9	23.7	23.5	14.8	9.2	3.2

Note: (1) Metropolitan Statistical Area - see Appendix A for areas included
Source: Census 2000, Summary File 3

Male/Female Ratio

Area	Males	Females	Males per 100 Females
City	25,619	26,797	95.6
MSA[1]	35,077	35,811	98.0
U.S.	148,320,305	152,725,217	97.1

Note: Figures are 2007 estimates; (1) Metropolitan Statistical Area - see Appendix B for areas included
Source: Claritas, Inc.

Religion

Area	Catholic	Southern Baptist	United Meth-odist	ELCA[1]	LDS[2]	Presby-terian Church USA	Jewish Est.	Muslim Est.
County	15.0	5.0	3.1	2.8	4.7	1.3	0.2	0.0
U.S.	22.0	7.1	3.7	1.8	1.5	1.1	2.2	0.6

Note: Figures are the number of adherents as a percentage of the total population; Adherents are defined as all members, including full members, their children and the estimated number of other participants who are not considered members (e.g. the baptized, those not confirmed, those regularly attending services, etc.); (1) Evangelical Lutheran Church in America; (2) The Church of Jesus Christ of Latter Day Saints
Source: Reprinted with permission from Religious Congregations and Membership in the United States 2000 (Nashville, Glenmary Research Center, 2002) Copyright Association of Statisticians of American Religious Bodies. All rights reserved.

ECONOMY

Gross Metropolitan Product

Area	2002	2003	2004	2005	2005 Rank[2]
MSA[1]	2.6	2.9	3.4	3.8	323

Note: Figures are in billions of dollars; (1) Casper, WY Metropolitan Statistical Area - see Appendix A for areas included; (2) Rank ranges from 1 to 361
Source: The U.S. Conference of Mayors, "U.S. Metro Economies: GMP - The Engines of America's Growth," January 2007

Economic Growth

Area	1995 GMP	2005 GMP	Average Annual Growth Rate	Growth Rate Rank[2]
MSA[1]	1.8	3.8	8.0	12

Note: Figures are in billions of dollars; GMP = Gross Metropolitan Product; (1) Casper, WY Metropolitan Statistical Area - see Appendix A for areas included; (2) Rank ranges from 1 to 361
Source: The U.S. Conference of Mayors, "U.S. Metro Economies: GMP - The Engines of America's Growth," January 2007

INCOME

Per Capita/Median/Average Income

Area	Per Capita ($)	Median Household ($)	Average Household ($)
City	25,068	46,048	59,377
MSA[1]	24,676	46,421	59,372
U.S.	25,495	49,280	66,670

Note: Figures are 2007 estimates; (1) Metropolitan Statistical Area - see Appendix B for areas included
Source: Claritas, Inc.

Household Income Distribution

Area	Percent of Households Earning							
	Under $15,000	$15,000 -24,999	$25,000 -34,999	$35,000 -49,999	$50,000 -74,999	$75,000 -99,000	$100,000 -149,999	$150,000 and up
City	11.8	12.5	12.2	17.4	20.5	12.2	9.5	3.9
MSA[1]	11.8	12.5	12.0	17.5	20.6	12.3	9.4	3.9
U.S.	13.1	10.9	11.2	15.6	19.5	11.9	11.3	6.6

Note: Figures are 2007 estimates; (1) Metropolitan Statistical Area - see Appendix B for areas included
Source: Claritas, Inc.

Poverty Rates by Age

Area	All Ages	Under 5 Years Old	5 to 17 Years Old	18 to 64 Years Old	65 Years and Over
City	11.4	1.5	2.6	6.3	1.0
MSA[1]	11.8	1.5	2.9	6.6	0.9
U.S.	12.4	1.2	3.0	6.9	1.2

Note: Figures are percent of population with income in 1999 below poverty level and only include population for whom poverty status is determined; (1) Metropolitan Statistical Area - see Appendix A for areas included
Source: Census 2000, Summary File 3

Personal Bankruptcy Filing Rate

Area	2004	2005	2006
Natrona County	5.60	7.94	1.58
U.S.	5.31	6.82	2.00

Note: Numbers are per 1,000 population and include Chapter 7 and Chapter 13 filings
Source: Federal Deposit Insurance Corporation (FDIC), Regional Economic Conditions (RECON), 8/23/2007

EMPLOYMENT

Labor Force and Employment

Area	Civilian Labor Force			Workers Employed		
	Dec. 2006	Dec. 2007	% Chg.	Dec. 2006	Dec. 2007	% Chg.
City	30,392	30,334	-0.2	29,535	29,419	-0.4
MSA[1]	40,541	40,469	-0.2	39,340	39,186	-0.4
U.S.	152,571,000	153,705,000	0.7	146,081,000	146,334,000	0.2

Note: Data is not seasonally adjusted and covers workers 16 years of age and older;
(1) Metropolitan Statistical Area - see Appendix B for areas included
Source: Bureau of Labor Statistics, http://stats.bls.gov

Unemployment Rate

Area	2007											
	Jan.	Feb.	Mar.	Apr.	May	Jun.	Jul.	Aug.	Sep.	Oct.	Nov.	Dec.
City	3.5	3.0	2.9	2.6	2.6	2.5	2.5	2.2	2.1	2.1	2.5	3.0
MSA[1]	3.7	3.1	3.0	2.8	2.8	2.6	2.7	2.3	2.2	2.2	2.6	3.2
U.S.	5.0	4.9	4.5	4.3	4.3	4.7	4.9	4.6	4.5	4.4	4.5	4.8

Note: Data is not seasonally adjusted and covers workers 16 years of age and older; All figures are percentages; (1) Metropolitan Statistical Area - see Appendix B for areas included
Source: Bureau of Labor Statistics, http://stats.bls.gov

Employment by Occupation

Occupation Classification	City (%)	MSA[1] (%)	U.S. (%)
Sales and Office	30.6	29.9	26.7
Professional and Related	18.7	17.6	20.2
Service	16.1	15.8	14.9
Production, Transportation, and Material Moving	10.7	12.0	14.6
Management, Business, and Financial	10.9	10.9	13.5
Construction, Extraction, and Maintenance	12.8	13.5	9.4
Farming, Forestry, and Fishing	0.2	0.4	0.7

Note: Figures cover employed civilians 16 years of age and older;
(1) Metropolitan Statistical Area - see Appendix A for areas included
Source: Census 2000, Summary File 3

Employment by Industry

Sector	MSA[1] Number of Employees	MSA[1] Percent of Total	U.S. Percent of Total
Government	n/a	n/a	16.3
Education and Health Services	n/a	n/a	13.4
Professional and Business Services	n/a	n/a	13.1
Retail Trade	n/a	n/a	11.6
Manufacturing	n/a	n/a	9.9
Leisure and Hospitality	n/a	n/a	9.6
Financial Activities	n/a	n/a	5.9
Construction	n/a	n/a	5.3
Wholesale Trade	n/a	n/a	4.4
Other Services	n/a	n/a	3.9
Transportation and Utilities	n/a	n/a	3.7
Information	n/a	n/a	2.2
Natural Resources and Mining	n/a	n/a	0.5

Note: Figures cover non-farm employment as of December 2007 and are not seasonally adjusted; (1) Metropolitan Statistical Area - see Appendix B for areas included; n/a not available
Source: Bureau of Labor Statistics, http://stats.bls.gov

Average Wages

Occupation	$/Hr.	Occupation	$/Hr.
Accountants and Auditors	28.60	Maids and Housekeeping Cleaners	8.20
Automotive Mechanics	15.11	Maintenance and Repair Workers	12.93
Bookkeepers	15.03	Marketing Managers	n/a
Carpenters	15.09	Nuclear Medicine Technologists	n/a
Cashiers	8.47	Nurses, Licensed Practical	17.12
Clerks, General Office	11.15	Nurses, Registered	25.83
Clerks, Receptionists/Information	10.54	Nursing Aides/Orderlies/Attendants	10.79
Clerks, Shipping/Receiving	13.42	Packers and Packagers, Hand	7.87
Computer Programmers	n/a	Physical Therapists	n/a
Computer Support Specialists	17.25	Postal Service Mail Carriers	21.64
Computer Systems Analysts	23.65	Real Estate Brokers	n/a
Cooks, Restaurant	9.85	Retail Salespersons	10.94
Dentists	n/a	Sales Reps., Exc. Tech./Scientific	20.49
Electrical Engineers	n/a	Sales Reps., Tech./Scientific	32.75
Electricians	21.06	Secretaries, Exc. Legal/Med./Exec.	12.08
Financial Managers	36.80	Security Guards	12.00
First-Line Supervisors/Mgrs., Sales	17.04	Surgeons	n/a
Food Preparation Workers	9.00	Teacher Assistants	12.30
General and Operations Managers	38.10	Teachers, Elementary School	n/a
Hairdressers/Cosmetologists	11.77	Teachers, Secondary School	n/a
Internists	n/a	Telemarketers	n/a
Janitors and Cleaners	10.81	Truck Drivers, Heavy/Tractor-Trailer	19.99
Landscaping/Groundskeeping Workers	12.89	Truck Drivers, Light/Delivery Svcs.	13.20
Lawyers	55.51	Waiters and Waitresses	6.99

Note: Wage data covers the Casper, WY Metropolitan Statistical Area - see Appendix B for areas included. Hourly wages for elementary/secondary school teachers and teacher assistants were calculated by the editors from annual wage data assuming a 40 hour work week; n/a not available.
Source: Bureau of Labor Statistics, May 2007 Metro Area Occupational Employment and Wage Estimates

RESIDENTIAL REAL ESTATE

Building Permits

Area	Single-Family			Multi-Family			Total		
	2006	2007p	Pct. Chg.	2006	2007p	Pct. Chg.	2006	2007p	Pct. Chg.
City	292	315	7.9	0	0	-	292	315	7.9
U.S.	1,378,200	973,300	-29.4	460,700	407,200	-11.6	1,838,900	1,380,500	-24.9

Note: (p) preliminary; figures cover and represent new, privately-owned housing units authorized (unadjusted data); All permit data are based on estimates with imputation; U.S. figures are based on the new 20,000-place series.
Source: U.S. Census Bureau, Manufacturing, Mining, and Construction Statistics

Homeownership and Housing Vacancies

Area	Homeownership Rate[2] (%)			Rental Vacancy Rate[3] (%)			Homeowner Vacancy Rate[4] (%)		
	2005	2006	2007	2005	2006	2007	2005	2006	2007
MSA[1]	n/a	n/a	n/a	n/a	n/a	n/a	n/a	n/a	n/a
U.S.	68.9	68.8	68.1	9.8	9.8	9.7	1.9	2.4	2.7

Note: (1) Metropolitan Statistical Area - see Appendix B for areas included; (2) The proportion of households that are owners; (3) The proportion of the rental inventory that is vacant for rent; (4) The proportion of the homeowner inventory that is vacant for sale; n/a not available
Source: U.S. Census Bureau, Housing Vacancies and Homeownership Annual Statistics: 2007

TAXES

State Corporate Income Tax Rates

State	Rates and Tax Brackets
Wyoming	None

Note: Tax rates as of January 1, 2008
Source: Tax Foundation, www.taxfoundation.org

State Individual Income Tax Rates

State	Federal Deductibility	Marginal Rates (%)	Standard Deduction ($)		Personal Exemptions ($)[1]	
			Single	Joint	Single	Dependents
Wyoming	No	None	n/a	n/a	n/a	n/a

Note: Tax rates as of January 1, 2008; Local- and county-level taxes are not included; n/a not applicable; (1) Married joint filers generally receive double the single exemption
Source: Tax Foundation, www.taxfoundation.org

Various State and Local Tax Rates

State and Local Sales and Use (%)	State Sales and Use (%)	Gasoline[1,2] ($/gal.)	Cigarette ($/pack)	Spirits ($/gal.)	Table Wine ($/gal.)	Beer ($/gal.)
5.0	4.0	0.14	0.60	(q)	(p)	0.019

Note: Tax rates as of January 1, 2008; (1) In addition to the 18.4 cpg Federal gasoline tax; (2) Rates may include additional state sales taxes, environmental protection and storage fees/taxes, and local taxes. When necessary, the volume-weighted average of all local taxes is used to approximate the typical statewide rate including local tax; (p) All wine sales are through state-run stores. Revenue in these states is generated from various taxes, fees and net profits; (q) Control state where the implied excise tax rate as calculated by DISCUS is less then zero.
Source: Tax Foundation, www.taxfoundation.org; Original research

State Tax Burdens

Area	Combined State and Local Tax Burden		Combined Federal, State and Local Tax Burden	
	Percent	Rank	Percent	Rank
Wyoming	9.5	42	32.1	19
U.S. Average	11.0	-	32.7	-

Note: Figures cover 2007 and measure taxes as a percentage of income
Source: Tax Foundation, www.taxfoundation.org

State Business Tax Climate Index Rankings

State	Overall Rank	Corporate Tax Index Rank	Individual Income Tax Index Rank	Sales Tax Index Rank	Unemployment Insurance Tax Index Rank	Property Tax Index Rank
Wyoming	1	1	1	9	34	30

Note: Rankings range from 1 to 50 where 1 is best. Rankings do not average across to Overall Rank. States without a given tax are given a ranking of 1.
Source: Tax Foundation, State Business Tax Climate Index 2008

TRANSPORTATION

Means of Transportation to Work

Area	Car/Truck/Van		Public Transportation			Bicycle	Walked	Other Means	Worked at Home
	Drove Alone	Car-pooled	Bus	Subway	Railroad				
City	83.0	11.2	0.5	0.0	0.0	0.1	1.6	0.9	2.7
MSA[1]	82.7	11.3	0.4	0.0	0.0	0.1	1.4	0.8	3.3
U.S.	75.7	12.2	2.5	1.5	0.5	0.4	2.9	1.0	3.3

Note: Figures are percentages and cover workers 16 years of age and older;
(1) Metropolitan Statistical Area - see Appendix A for areas included
Source: Census 2000, Summary File 3

Travel Time to Work

Area	Less Than 15 Minutes	15 to 29 Minutes	30 to 44 Minutes	45 to 59 Minutes	60 Minutes or More
City	58.2	33.7	3.4	1.3	3.5
MSA[1]	53.7	36.5	4.6	1.4	3.8
U.S.	29.4	36.1	19.1	7.4	8.0

Note: Figures are percentages and include workers 16 years old and over; (1) Metropolitan Statistical Area - see Appendix A for areas included
Source: Census 2000, Summary File 3

Living Environment

COST OF LIVING

Cost of Living Index

Composite Index	Groceries	Housing	Utilities	Trans-portation	Health Care	Misc. Goods/ Services
n/a	n/a	n/a	n/a	n/a	n/a	n/a

Note: U.S. = 100; n/a not available
Source: The Council for Community and Economic Research (formerly ACCRA), Cost of Living Index, 2007

Grocery Prices

Area[1]	T-Bone Steak ($/pound)	Frying Chicken ($/pound)	Whole Milk ($/half gal.)	Eggs ($/dozen)	Orange Juice ($/64 oz.)	Coffee ($/11.5 oz.)
City[2]	n/a	n/a	n/a	n/a	n/a	n/a
Avg.	8.93	1.12	2.13	1.52	3.26	3.31
Min.	5.88	0.71	1.33	0.83	2.30	2.20
Max.	12.80	2.07	3.43	3.54	5.79	6.20

Note: (1) Values for the local area are compared with the average, minimum and maximum values for all 331 areas in the Cost of Living Index report; n/a not available; (2) Figures cover the Casper WY urban area; **T-Bone Steak** *(price per pound);* **Frying Chicken** *(price per pound, whole fryer);* **Whole Milk** *(half gallon carton);* **Eggs** *(price per dozen, Grade A, large);* **Orange Juice** *(64 oz. Tropicana or Florida Natural);* **Coffee** *(11.5 oz. can, vacuum-packed, Maxwell House, Hills Bros, or Folgers).*
Source: The Council for Community and Economic Research (formerly ACCRA), Cost of Living Index, 2007

Housing and Utility Costs

Area[1]	New Home Price ($)	Apartment Rent ($/month)	All Electric ($/month)	Part Electric ($/month)	Other Energy ($/month)	Telephone ($/month)
City[2]	n/a	n/a	n/a	n/a	n/a	n/a
Avg.	309,605	782	146.13	78.67	90.16	26.14
Min.	189,877	n/a	82.03	37.41	33.15	17.08
Max.	1,202,800	3,481	271.14	150.60	257.67	37.45

Note: (1) Values for the local area are compared with the average, minimum and maximum values for all 331 areas in the Cost of Living Index report; n/a not available; (2) Figures cover the Casper WY urban area; **New Home Price** *(2,400 sf living area, 8,000 sf lot, in urban area with full utilities);* **Apartment Rent** *(950 sf 2 bedroom/1.5 or 2 bath, unfurnished, excluding all utilities except water);* **All Electric** *(average monthly cost for an all-electric home);* **Part Electric** *(average monthly cost for a part-electric home);* **Other Energy** *(average monthly cost for natural gas, fuel oil, coal, wood, and any other forms of energy except electricity);* **Telephone** *(price includes basic monthly rate for a private residential line plus additional local usage charges incurred by a family of four).*
Source: The Council for Community and Economic Research (formerly ACCRA), Cost of Living Index, 2007

Health Care, Transportation, and Other Costs

Area[1]	Doctor ($/visit)	Dentist ($/visit)	Optometrist ($/visit)	Gasoline ($/gallon)	Beauty Salon ($/visit)	Men's Shirt ($)
City[2]	n/a	n/a	n/a	n/a	n/a	n/a
Avg.	79.48	71.93	79.55	2.64	29.52	25.77
Min.	52.08	44.80	43.95	2.19	15.58	16.19
Max.	148.44	126.27	158.83	3.48	60.62	48.53

Note: (1) Values for the local area are compared with the average, minimum and maximum values for all 331 areas in the Cost of Living Index report; n/a not available; (2) Figures cover the Casper WY urban area; **Doctor** *(general practitioners routine exam of an established patient);* **Dentist** *(adult teeth cleaning and periodic oral examination);* **Optometrist** *(full vision eye exam for established adult patient);* **Gasoline** *(one gallon regular unleaded, national brand, including all taxes, cash price at self-service pump if available);* **Beauty Salon** *(woman's shampoo, trim, and blow-dry);* **Men's Shirt** *(cotton/polyester dress shirt, pinpoint weave, long sleeves).*
Source: The Council for Community and Economic Research (formerly ACCRA), Cost of Living Index, 2007

HOUSING

House Price Index (HPI)

Area	National Ranking[2]	Quarterly Change (%)	One-Year Change (%)	Five-Year Change (%)
MSA[1]	(a)	n/a	7.63	75.09
U.S.[3]	-	0.10	0.84	41.37

Note: The HPI is a weighted repeat sales index. It measures average price changes in repeat sales or refinancings on the same properties. This information is obtained by reviewing repeat mortgage transactions on single-family properties whose mortgages have been purchased or securitized by Fannie Mae or Freddie Mac in January 1975; (1) Metropolitan Statistical Area - see Appendix B for areas included; (2) Rankings are based on annual percentage change for all metro areas containing at least 15,000 transactions over the last 10 years and ranges from 1 to 291; (3) figures based on a weighted average of Census Division estimates; all figures are for the period ending December 31, 2007; n/a not available; (a) Not ranked because of increased index variability due to smaller sample size

Source: Office of Federal Housing Enterprise Oversight, House Price Index, February 26, 2008

House Price Valuations

Area	Q1 2000	Q1 2001	Q1 2002	Q1 2003	Q1 2004	Q1 2005	Q1 2006	Q1 2007	Q1 2008
MSA[1]	-17.2	-8.9	-1.0	-1.4	3.8	13.4	20.9	17.7	20.3

Note: Figures show the percentage of over- or under-valuation of single family homes relative to statistically normal house values (e.g. a value of 23.6 indicates that house values are 23.6% overvalued). Statistically normal house values are based on house prices, interest rates, household incomes, population densities, and any historical premiums or discounts metropolitan areas have exhibited over time; (1) Figures cover the Metropolitan Statistical Area - see Appendix B for areas included

Source: Global Insight/National City Corporation, House Prices in America, May 2008

Median Home Prices

Area	2005	2006	2007[r]	Percent Change 2006 to 2007
MSA[1]	n/a	n/a	n/a	n/a
U.S. Average	219.0	221.9	217.9	-1.8

Note: Figures are median sales prices of existing single-family homes in thousands of dollars; (r) revised; n/a not available; (1) Metropolitan Statistical Area - see Appendix B for areas included

Source: National Association of Realtors, Metropolitan Area Prices, 1st Quarter 2008

Housing: Year Structure Built

Area	1990 -2000	1980 -1989	1970 -1979	1960 -1969	1950 -1959	1940 -1949	Before 1940	Median Year
City	4.5	13.7	27.8	11.9	22.8	6.8	12.5	1967
MSA[1]	6.8	14.1	31.4	11.4	18.9	6.3	11.1	1971
U.S.	17.0	15.8	18.5	13.7	12.7	7.3	15.0	1971

Note: Figures are percentages; (1) Metropolitan Statistical Area - see Appendix A for areas included

Source: Census 2000, Summary File 3

HEALTH

Health Risk Data

Category	Area[1] (%)	U.S. (%)
Adults who have been told they have high blood pressure[3]	24.7	25.5
Adults who have been told they have high blood cholesterol[3]	35.1	35.6
Adults who have been told they have diabetes[2]	7.6	7.5
Adults who have been told they have arthritis[3]	29.0	27.0
Adults who have been told they currently have asthma	8.6	8.5
Adults who are current smokers	31.2	20.1
Adults who are heavy drinkers[4]	6.6	4.9
Adults who are overweight (BMI 25.0 - 29.9)	38.7	36.5
Adults who are obese (BMI 30.0 - 99.8)	23.8	25.1

Note: Data as of 2006 unless otherwise noted; (1) Figures cover the Metropolitan Statistical Area - see Appendix B for areas included; (2) Figures do not include pregnancy-related diabetes, pre-diabetes or borderline diabetes; (3) 2005 data; (4) Heavy drinkers are classified as adult men having more than two drinks per day or adult women having more than one drink per day

Source: Centers for Disease Control and Prevention, Behaviorial Risk Factor Surveillance System, SMART: Selected Metropolitan/Micropolitan Area Risk Trends, 2005, 2006

Mortality Rates for the Top 10 Causes of Death in the U.S.

ICD-10[a] Sub-Chapter	ICD-10[a] Code	Age-Adjusted Mortality Rate[1] per 100,000 population	
		County[2]	U.S.
Malignant neoplasms	C00-C97	178.2	186.5
Ischaemic heart diseases	I20-I25	111.4	152.3
Other forms of heart disease	I30-I51	49.9	51.5
Cerebrovascular diseases	I60-I69	40.7	50.0
Chronic lower respiratory diseases	J40-J47	71.6	42.6
Diabetes mellitus	E10-E14	26.8	24.8
Other degenerative diseases of the nervous system	G30-G31	24.6	22.6
Other external causes of accidental injury	W00-X59	22.9	21.4
Influenza and pneumonia	J10-J18	23.7	20.7
Hypertensive diseases	I10-I13	11.8	18.2

Note: (a) ICD-10 = International Classification of Diseases 10th Revision; (1) Mortality rates are a three year average covering 2003-2005; (2) Figures cover Natrona County
Source: Centers for Disease Control and Prevention, National Center for Health Statistics. Compressed Mortality File 1999-2004. CDC WONDER On-line Database, compiled from Compressed Mortality File 1999-2005 Series 20 No. 2K, 2008.

Mortality Rates for Selected Causes of Death

ICD-10[a] Sub-Chapter	ICD-10[a] Code	Age-Adjusted Mortality Rate[1] per 100,000 population	
		County[2]	U.S.
Assault	X85-Y09	*2.9	5.9
Human immunodeficiency virus (HIV) disease	B20-B24	*2.4	4.5
Intentional self-harm	X60-X84	21.7	10.8
Malnutrition	E40-E46	*1.6	1.0
Obesity and other hyperalimentation	E65-E68	*5.0	1.4
Organic, including symptomatic, mental disorders	F01-F09	*9.4	16.8
Transport accidents	V01-V99	20.9	16.1
Viral hepatitis	B15-B19	*3.3	1.8

Note: (a) ICD-10 = International Classification of Diseases 10th Revision; (1) Mortality rates are a three year average covering 2003-2005; (2) Figures cover Natrona County; (*) Unreliable data as per CDC
Source: Centers for Disease Control and Prevention, National Center for Health Statistics. Compressed Mortality File 1999-2004. CDC WONDER On-line Database, compiled from Compressed Mortality File 1999-2005 Series 20 No. 2K, 2008.

Distribution of Physicians[1]

Area	Total	Family/ General Practice	Specialties	
			Medical	Surgical
Natrona County (number)	138	49	36	38
Natrona County (rate per 10,000 pop.)	19.8	7.0	5.2	5.4
U.S. (rate per 10,000 pop.)	17.7	4.6	6.9	4.3

Note: Data as of 2005; (1) Includes all non-federal, patient-care, office-based MDs
Source: Area Resource File (ARF). June 2007. U.S. Department of Health and Human Services, Health Resources and Services Administration, Bureau of Health Professions, Rockville, MD.

Hospitals

Casper has the following hospitals: 1 general medical and surgical; 1 psychiatric.
AHA Guide to the Healthcare Field 2008

EDUCATION

Public School District Statistics

District Name	Schls	Pupils	Pupil/ Teacher Ratio	Minority Pupils[1] (%)	Free Lunch Eligible[2] (%)	IEP[3] (%)
Natrona County School District #1	35	11,890	15.0	10.4	23.4	12.9

Note: Table includes regular local school districts with 2,000 or more students; (1) Percentage of students that are not white, non-Hispanic; (2) Percentage of students that are eligible for the free lunch program; (3) Percentage of students that have an Individualized Education Program.
Source: U.S. Department of Education, National Center for Education Statistics, Common Core of Data, Local Education Agency (School District) Universe Survey: School Year 2005-2006; U.S. Department of Education, National Center for Education Statistics, Common Core of Data, Public Elementary/Secondary School Universe Survey: School Year 2005-2006

Highest Level of Education

Area	Less than H.S.	H.S. Diploma	Some College, No Deg.	Associate Degree	Bachelors Degree	Masters Degree	Profess. School Degree	Doctorate Degree
City	10.8	29.0	28.8	9.2	14.9	4.8	2.2	0.4
MSA[1]	11.7	30.5	28.7	9.1	13.4	4.3	1.9	0.4
U.S.	19.4	28.4	21.2	6.4	15.7	5.9	2.0	1.0

Note: Figures are 2007 estimated percentages and cover persons age 25 and over; (1) Metropolitan Statistical Area - see Appendix B for areas included
Source: Claritas, Inc.

Educational Attainment by Race

Area	High School Graduate (%)					Bachelor's Degree (%)				
	Total	White	Black	Asian	Hisp.[2]	Total	White	Black	Asian	Hisp.[2]
City	89.1	89.9	74.9	73.4	72.3	22.1	22.7	23.4	38.0	6.7
MSA[1]	88.3	89.0	77.4	75.5	70.3	20.0	20.5	23.7	36.6	7.0
U.S.	80.4	83.6	72.3	80.4	52.4	24.4	26.1	14.3	44.1	10.4

Note: Figures shown cover persons 25 years old and over; (1) Metropolitan Statistical Area - see Appendix A for areas included; (2) people of Hispanic origin can be of any race
Source: Census 2000, Summary File 3

School Enrollment by Type

Area	Grades KG to 8				Grades 9 to 12			
	Public		Private		Public		Private	
	Enrollment	%	Enrollment	%	Enrollment	%	Enrollment	%
City	6,305	97.0	192	3.0	2,969	98.8	36	1.2
MSA[1]	8,473	96.0	356	4.0	3,988	98.8	47	1.2
U.S.	33,526,011	88.7	4,285,121	11.3	14,848,628	90.6	1,532,323	9.4

Note: Figures shown cover persons 3 years old and over; (1) Metropolitan Statistical Area - see Appendix A for areas included
Source: Census 2000, Summary File 3

School Enrollment by Race

Area	Grades KG to 8 (%)				Grades 9 to 12 (%)			
	White	Black	Asian	Hisp.[1]	White	Black	Asian	Hisp.[1]
City	92.4	0.4	1.3	7.7	90.8	1.3	1.3	7.2
MSA[2]	92.0	0.5	1.0	6.9	92.0	1.0	1.0	6.2
U.S.	68.5	15.5	3.3	16.8	68.8	15.5	3.8	15.7

Note: Figures shown cover persons 3 years old and over; (1) people of Hispanic origin can be of any race; (2) Metropolitan Statistical Area - see Appendix A for areas included
Source: Census 2000, Summary File 3

Average Salaries of Public School Classroom Teachers

District	2005-06 Dollars	2005-06 Rank[1]	2006-07 Dollars	2006-07 Rank[1]	Percent Change 2005-06 to 2006-07
Wyoming	43,255	30	50,692	17	17.19
U.S. Average	49,026	-	50,816	-	3.65

Note: (1) State rank ranges from 1 to 51.
Source: National Education Association, Rankings & Estimates: Rankings of the States 2006 and Estimates of School Statistics 2007, December 2007

Higher Education

Four-Year Colleges			Two-Year Colleges			Medical Schools[1]	Law Schools[2]	Voc/ Tech[3]
Public	Private Non-profit	Private For-profit	Public	Private Non-profit	Private For-profit			
0	0	0	1	0	0	0	0	0

Note: Figures cover institutions located within the city limits; (1) includes schools accredited by the Liaison Committee on Medical Education and the American Osteopathic Association; (2) includes American Bar Association-accredited law schools; (3) includes all schools with programs that are less than 2 years.
Source: National Center for Education Statistics, The Integrated Postsecondary Education System (IPEDS) Peer Analysis System, 2007; www.usnews.com, Law and Medical School Directories, 2009

PRESIDENTIAL ELECTION

2004 Presidential Election Results

Area	Bush	Kerry	Nader	Other
Natrona County	67.1	30.8	1.0	1.1
U.S.	50.7	48.3	0.4	0.6

Note: Results are percentages and may not add to 100% due to rounding
Source: Dave Leip's Atlas of U.S. Presidential Elections, www.uselectionatlas.org

EMPLOYERS

Major Employers

Company Name	Industry	Type of Site
Casper Community College Dst	Colleges and universities	Single
Casper Events Center	Amusement and recreation, nec	Branch
Department of Employment	General government, nec	Headquarters
Kelly Walsh High School	Elementary and secondary schools	Branch
Kmart	Department stores	Branch
Mini Mart	Grocery stores	Single
Nabors Drilling USA LP	Drilling oil and gas wells	Branch
Natgrona County District 1	Elementary and secondary schools	Headquarters
New Patriot Drilling Inc	Drilling oil and gas wells	Single
Parkway Plaza Hotel	Hotels and motels	Single
Sehpherd of Valley Care Center	Nursing and personal care, nec	Single
Teton Homes Corporation	Transportation equipment, nec	Single
US Post Office	U.s. postal service	Branch
Unemployment Insur Emplyer Svcs	Administration of social and manpower programs	Branch
Unit Drilling Company	Crude petroleum and natural gas	Branch
Wal-Mart	Department stores	Branch
Wyoming Machinery Company	Construction and mining machinery	Headquarters
Wyoming Medical Center In	General medical and surgical hospitals	Headquarters

Note: Companies shown are located within the Casper metropolitan area; nec = not elsewhere classified.
Source: www.zapdata.com, May 2008

PUBLIC SAFETY

Crime Rate

Area	All Crimes	Violent Crimes				Property Crimes		
		Murder	Forcible Rape	Robbery	Aggrav. Assault	Burglary	Larceny -Theft	Motor Vehicle Theft
City	5,181.8	0.0	38.2	22.9	187.3	842.9	3,866.7	223.6
Metro[1]	4,753.3	2.8	29.8	22.7	184.2	838.7	3,472.6	202.6
U.S.	3,808.1	5.7	30.9	149.4	287.5	729.4	2,206.8	398.4

Note: Figures are crimes per 100,000 population; (1) Metropolitan Statistical Area - see Appendix B for areas included
Source: FBI Uniform Crime Reports, 2006

Hate Crimes

Area	Number of Quarters Reported	Bias Motivation				
		Race	Religion	Sexual Orientation	Ethnicity	Disability
City	4	0	0	1	0	0

Source: Federal Bureau of Investigation, Hate Crime Statistics 2006

RECREATION

Culture

Dance[1]	Theatre[1]	Instrumental Music[1]	Vocal Music[1]	Series/ Festivals	Museums	Zoos and Aquariums[2]
0	0	1	0	1	4	0

Note: (1) Number of professional perfoming groups; (2) AZA-accredited
Source: The Grey House Performing Arts Directory, 2007; Official Museum Directory, 2008; Association of Zoos & Aquariums, AZA Member Zoos & Aquariums, June 2008

Professional Sports Teams

Team Name	League
No teams are located in the metro area	

Source: Original research

MEDIA

Newspapers

Name	News Focus	Frequency	Circulation
Casper Journal	Community	Weekly	5,250
Casper Star-Tribune	Local	Daily	33,700

Note: Includes newspapers with offices located in the city
Source: MediaContactsPro, March 2008

Television Stations

Name	Ch.	Network(s)	Type	Ownership
KTWO	2	NBC	Commercial	Equity Broadcasting
KCWC	4	PBS	Public	Central Wyoming College
KGWL	5	CBS	Commercial	Benedek Broadcasting Corporation
KFNE	10	CBS	Commercial	Wyomedia Corporation
KFNR	11	Pax/CBS	Commercial	Wyomedia Corporation
KGWR	13	CBS	Commercial	Benedek Broadcasting Corporation
KGWC	14	CBS	Commercial	Benedek Broadcasting Corporation
KFNB	20	CBS	Commercial	Wyomedia Corporation
KLWY	27	CBS	Commercial	Wyomedia Corporation

Note: Stations included cover the Casper-Riverton DMA (Designated Market Area)
BurrellesLuce, MediaContacts Online, January 2007

Major AM Radio Stations

Call Letters	Freq. (kHz)	Station Type	Target Audience	Station Format	Music Format
KUYO	830	Commercial	General/Religious	Educational/Music	Gospel
KTWO	1030	Commercial	General	Music	Country
KTHE	1240	Commercial	General	Ed/Music/News/Sports/Talk	Top 40
KOVE	1330	Commercial	General	Music/News/Sports	Country
KWOR	1340	Commercial	General	Music/News/Sports/Talk	Oldies
KVOW	1450	Commercial	General	Music/News	Oldies
KKTY	1470	n/a	General	Music/News	n/a

Note: Stations included cover the Casper-Riverton DMA (Designated Market Area); n/a not available
Source: BurrellesLuce, MediaContacts Online, January 2007

Major FM Radio Stations

Call Letters	Freq. (mHz)	Station Type	Target Audience	Station Format	Music Format
KCWC	88.1	College	General	Music	n/a
KCSP	90.3	Non-Comm	General/Religious	Educational/Music/News	Christian
KTRZ	93.1	Commercial	General	Music/News	Christian
KTAK	93.9	Commercial	General	Music/Sports	Country
KMGW	94.5	Commercial	General	Music/News	Adult Contemp.
KTRS	95.5	Commercial	General	Music/News/Sports	Adult Contemp.
KKLX	96.1	Commercial	General	Ed/Music/News/Sports/Talk	80's
KDLY	97.5	Commercial	General	News	n/a
KKTY	99.3	Commercial	General	Music/News	Oldies
KHOC	102.5	Commercial	General	Music/News	Adult Contemp.
KQLT	103.7	Commercial	General	Music	Country
KASS	106.9	Commercial	General	News	n/a

Note: Stations included cover the Casper-Riverton DMA (Designated Market Area); n/a not available
BurrellesLuce, MediaContacts Online, January 2007

CLIMATE

Average and Extreme Temperatures

Temperature	Jan	Feb	Mar	Apr	May	Jun	Jul	Aug	Sep	Oct	Nov	Dec	Yr.
Extreme High (°F)	60	68	74	84	92	102	104	102	97	87	71	63	104
Average High (°F)	33	38	45	56	67	78	87	86	74	61	44	35	59
Average Temp. (°F)	23	27	34	43	53	63	71	69	59	47	33	26	46
Average Low (°F)	12	16	22	30	39	48	54	53	43	33	22	15	32
Extreme Low (°F)	-40	-29	-21	-4	16	28	30	33	16	-3	-21	-41	-41

Note: Figures cover the years 1949-1995
Source: National Climatic Data Center, International Station Meteorological Climate Summary, 9/96

Average Precipitation/Snowfall/Humidity

Precip./Humidity	Jan	Feb	Mar	Apr	May	Jun	Jul	Aug	Sep	Oct	Nov	Dec	Yr.
Avg. Precip. (in.)	0.5	0.6	0.9	1.4	2.2	1.4	1.2	0.6	0.9	1.0	0.8	0.6	12.2
Avg. Snowfall (in.)	11	10	14	13	4	Tr	0	0	1	6	11	11	80
Avg. Rel. Hum. 6am (%)	67	71	74	74	74	68	63	63	65	66	69	68	68
Avg. Rel. Hum. 3pm (%)	54	52	45	38	36	29	23	22	28	34	48	54	38

Note: Figures cover the years 1949-1995; Tr = Trace amounts (<0.05 in. of rain; <0.5 in. of snow)
Source: National Climatic Data Center, International Station Meteorological Climate Summary, 9/96

Weather Conditions

Temperature			Daytime Sky			Precipitation		
5°F & below	32°F & below	90°F & above	Clear	Partly cloudy	Cloudy	0.01 inch or more precip.	0.1 inch or more snow/ice	Thunder-storms
27	179	28	103	141	121	97	53	34

Note: Figures are average number of days per year and cover the years 1949-1995
Source: National Climatic Data Center, International Station Meteorological Climate Summary, 9/96

HAZARDOUS WASTE

Superfund Sites

Casper has no sites on the EPA's Superfund Final National Priorities List.
U.S. Environmental Protection Agency, Final National Priorities List, June 23, 2008

AIR & WATER QUALITY

Air Quality Index

Area	Percent of Days when Air Quality was...[2]				AQI Statistics	
	Good	Moderate	Unhealthy for Sensitive Groups	Unhealthy	Maximum	Median
MSA[1]	100.0	0.0	0.0	0.0	42	18

Note: The Air Quality Index (AQI) is an index for reporting daily air quality. EPA calculates the AQI for five major air pollutants regulated by the Clean Air Act: ground-level ozone, particle pollution (also known as particulate matter), carbon monoxide, sulfur dioxide, and nitrogen dioxide. The AQI runs from 0 to 500. The higher the AQI value, the greater the level of air pollution and the greater the health concern. There are six AQI categories: "Good" The AQI is between 0 and 50. Air quality is considered satisfactory; "Moderate" The AQI is between 51 and 100. Air quality is acceptable; "Unhealthy for Sensitive Groups" When AQI values are between 101 and 150, members of sensitive groups may experience health effects; "Unhealthy" When AQI values are between 151 and 200 everyone may begin to experience health effects; "Very Unhealthy" AQI values between 201 and 300 trigger a health alert; "Hazardous" AQI values over 300 trigger health warnings of emergency conditions; (1) Metropolitan Statistical Area - see Appendix A for areas included; (2) Based on 115 days with AQI data in 2007.
Source: U.S. Environmental Protection Agency, Air Quality Index Report, 2007

Air Quality Index Pollutants

Area	Percent of Days when AQI Pollutant was...[2]					
	Carbon Monoxide	Nitrogen Dioxide	Ozone	Sulfur Dioxide	Particulate Matter 2.5	Particulate Matter 10
MSA[1]	0.0	0.0	0.0	0.0	0.0	100.0

Note: The Air Quality Index (AQI) is an index for reporting daily air quality. EPA calculates the AQI for five major air pollutants regulated by the Clean Air Act: ground-level ozone, particle pollution (also known as particulate matter), carbon monoxide, sulfur dioxide, and nitrogen dioxide. The AQI runs from 0 to 500. The higher the AQI value, the greater the level of air pollution and the greater the health concern; (1) Metropolitan Statistical Area - see Appendix A for areas included; (2) Based on 115 days with AQI data in 2007.
Source: U.S. Environmental Protection Agency, Air Quality Index Report, 2007

Air Quality Index Trends

Area	Trend Sites								All Sites
	1999	2000	2001	2002	2003	2004	2005	2006	2006
MSA[1]	n/a	n/a	n/a	n/a	n/a	n/a	n/a	n/a	n/a

Note: An AQI value greater than 100 indicates that air quality would have been in the unhealthful range on that day. Data from exceptional events are not included. These counts are presented in two ways. First, the counts are based on sites having an adequate record of monitoring data during the trend period (trend sites). These counts represent the relative change in the number of days with AQI values greater than 100. In the last column, the counts are based on all sites with data in the most recent year (because it is possible for a site to have data in the most recent year but not enough data to be a trend site); (1) Metropolitan Statistical Area - see Appendix A for areas included; n/a not available.
Source: U.S. Environmental Protection Agency, Office of Air and Radiation, Air Trends, Factbook and Related Information, Air Pollution Trends in Selected Metropolitan Areas 2006

Maximum Air Pollutant Concentrations

	Particulate Matter 10 (ug/m³)	Particulate Matter 2.5 (ug/m³)	Ozone (ppm)	Carbon Monoxide (ppm)	Sulfur Dioxide (ppm)	Nitrogen Dioxide (ppm)	Lead (ug/m³)
MSA[1] Level	70	n/a	n/a	n/a	n/a	n/a	n/a
NAAQS[2]	150	35	0.125	9	0.140	0.053	1.50
Met NAAQS[2]	Yes	Yes	n/a	n/a	n/a	n/a	n/a

Note: Data from exceptional events are not included; (1) Metropolitan Statistical Area - see Appendix A for areas included; (2) National Ambient Air Quality Standards; n/a not available
Concentrations: Particulate Matter 10 (coarse particulate) - highest second maximum 24-hour concentration; Particulate Matter 2.5 (fine particulate) - highest 98th percentile 24-hour concentration; Ozone - highest second daily maximum 1-hour concentration; Carbon Monoxide - highest second maximum non-overlapping 8-hour concentration; Sulfur Dioxide - highest second maximum 24-hour concentration; Nitrogen Dioxide - highest arithmetic mean concentration; Lead - highest quarterly maximum concentration
Units: ppm = parts per million; ug/m³ = micrograms per cubic meter
Source: U.S. Environmental Protection Agency, MSA Factbook 2006, Air Quality Statistics by City

Drinking Water

Water System Name	Pop. Served	Primary Water Source Type	Violations[1]	
			Health Based	Monitoring/ Reporting
Casper Board of Public Utilities	54,500	Purchased Surface	0	0

Note: (1) Based on violation data from January 1, 2007 to December 31, 2007 (includes unresolved violations from earlier years)
Source: U.S. Environmental Protection Agency, Office of Ground Water and Drinking Water, Safe Drinking Water Information System (based on data extracted April 15, 2008)

Appendix A: Historical Metropolitan Area Definitions

Metropolitan Statistical Areas (MSA), Primary Metropolitan Statistical Areas (PMSA), Consolidated Metropolitan Statistical Areas (CMSA) and New England County Metropolitan Areas (NECMA)

These historical metropolitan area definitions were in effect from June 30, 1993 to June 5, 2003

Akron, OH PMSA
Portage and Summit Counties

Albany-Schenectady-Troy, NY MSA
Albany, Montgomery, Rensselaer, Saratoga, Schenectady, Schoharie Counties

Albuquerque, NM MSA
Bernalillo, Sandoval, and Valencia Counties

Allen, TX
See Dallas, TX MSA and Dallas-Fort Worth, TX CMSA

Ankeny, IA
See Des Moines, IA MSA

Apex, NC
See Raleigh-Durham-Chapel Hill, NC MSA

Atlanta, GA MSA
Barrow, Bartow, Carroll, Cherokee, Clayton, Cobb, Coweta, DeKalb, Douglas, Fayette, Forsyth, Fulton, Gwinnett, Henry, Newton, Paulding, Pickens, Rockdale, Spalding, and Walton Counties

Austin-San Marcos, TX MSA
Bastrop, Caldwell, Hays, Travis and Williamson Counties

Baltimore, MD
Baltimore City; Anne Arundel, Baltimore, Carroll, Harford, Howard, and Queen Anne's Counties

Bangor, ME
See Bangor, ME MSA and Bangor, ME NECMA

Bangor, ME MSA
Parts of Penobscot and Waldo Counties

Bangor, ME NECMA
Penobscot County

Beavercreek, OH
See Dayton-Springfield, OH MSA

Bellevue, NE
See Omaha, NE MSA

Bend, OR
Not located within a metropolitan area.

Bernards, NJ
See Middlesex-Somerset-Hunterdon, NJ PMSA and New York-Northern New Jersey-Long Island, NY-NJ-CT-PA CMSA

Bethlehem, NY
See Albany, NY MSA

Birmingham, AL MSA
Blount, Jefferson, St. Clair, and Shelby Counties

Boise City, ID MSA
Ada and Canyon Counties

Boston, MA-NH PMSA
Parts of Bristol, Essex, Middlesex, Norfolk, Plymouth, and Worcester Counties, MA; and all of Suffolk County, MA; part of Rockingham County, NH

Boston-Worcester-Lawrence, MA-NH-ME-CT CMSA
Parts of Bristol, Essex, Hampden, Middlesex, Norfolk, Plymouth, Suffolk, and Worcester Counties, MA; Parts of Hillsborough, Merrimack, Rockingham, and Strafford Counties, NH; Part of York County, ME; Part of Windham County, CT

Boston-Worcester-Lawrence-Lowell-Brockton, MA-NH NECMA
Bristol, Essex, Middlesex, Norfolk, Plymouth, Suffolk, and Worcester Counties, MA; Hillsborough, Rockingham, and Strafford Counties, NH

Boulder-Longmont, CO MSA
Boulder County

Bozeman, MT
Not located within a metropolitan area.

Brentwood, TN
See Nashville, TN MSA

Bridgeport, CT PMSA
Parts of Fairfield and New Haven Counties

New Haven-Bridgeport-Stamford-Waterbury-Danbury, CT NECMA
Fairfield and New Haven Counties

Brookfield, WI
See Milwaukee, WI MSA

Broomfield, CO
Not located within a metropolitan area.

Burlington, VT
See Burlington, VT MSA and Burlington, VT NECMA

Burlington, VT MSA
Parts of Chittenden, Franklin and Grand Isle Counties

Burlington, VT NECMA
Chittenden, Franklin, and Grand Isle Counties

Carmel, IN
See Indianapolis, IN MSA

Cary, NC
See Raleigh-Durham-Chapel Hill, NC MSA

Casper, WY
See Casper, WY MSA

Casper, WY MSA
Natrona County

Cedar Rapids, IA MSA
Linn County

Charleston-North Charleston, SC MSA
Berkeley, Charleston and Dorchester Counties

Charlotte-Gastonia-Rock Hill, NC-SC MSA
Cabarrus, Gaston, Lincoln, Mecklenburg, Rowan, and Union Counties, NC; York County, SC

Cheshire, CT
See New Haven-Meriden, CT PMSA and New Haven-Bridgeport-Stamford-Waterbury-Danbury, CT NECMA

Chicago, IL PMSA
Cook, DeKalb, DuPage, Grundy, Kane, Kendall, Lake, McHenry and Will Counties

Chicago-Gary-Kenosha, IL-IN-WI CMSA
Cook, DeKalb, DuPage, Grundy, Kankakee, Kane, Kendall, Lake, McHenry, and Will Counties, IL; Lake and Porter Counties, IN; Kenosha County, WI

Chino Hills, CA
See Riverside, CA MSA

Cleveland-Lorain-Elyria, OH PMSA
Ashtabula, Cuyahoga, Geauga, Lake, Lorain and Medina Counties

Cleveland-Akron, OH CMSA
Ashtabula, Cuyahoga, Geauga, Lake, Lorain, Medina, Portage, and Summit Counties

Collierville, TN
See Memphis, TN MSA

Columbus, OH MSA
Delaware, Fairfield, Franklin, Licking, Madison, and Pickaway Counties

Conway, AR
See Little Rock, AR MSA

Coronado, CA
See San Diego, CA MSA

Cranberry, PA
See Pittsburgh, PA MSA

Dallas, TX PMSA
Collin, Dallas, Denton, Ellis, Henderson, Hunt, Kaufman and Rockwall Counties

Dallas-Fort Worth, TX CMSA
Collin, Dallas, Denton, Ellis, Henderson, Hood, Hunt, Johnson, Kaufman, Parker, Rockwall, and Tarrant Counties

Danbury, CT MSA
Parts of Fairfield County (Bethel town, Brookfield town, Danbury city, New Fairfield town, Newtown town, Redding town, Ridgefield town, Sherman town)

Dayton-Springfield, OH MSA
Clark, Greene, Miami, and Montgomery Counties

Denver, CO PMSA
Adams, Arapahoe, Denver, Douglas, and Jefferson Counties

Denver-Boulder-Greeley, CO CMSA
Adams, Arapahoe, Boulder, Denver, Douglas, Jefferson, and Weld Counties

Des Moines, IA MSA
Dallas, Polk, and Warren Counties

Detroit, MI PMSA
Lapeer, Macomb, Monroe, Oakland, St. Clair, and Wayne Counties

Detroit-Ann Arbor-Flint, MI CMSA
Genesee, Lapeer, Lenawee, Livingston, Macomb, Monroe, Oakland, St. Clair, Washtenaw, and Wayne Counties

Dover, DE MSA
Kent County

Draper, UT
See Salt Lake City, UT MSA

Dublin, OH
See Columbus, OH MSA

Dutchess, NY MSA
Dutchess County

Edmond, OK
See Oklahoma City, OK MSA

Evesham, NJ
See Philadelphia, PA-NJ PMSA and Philadelphia-Wilmington-Atlantic City, PA-NJ-DE-MD CMSA

Fargo-Moorhead, ND-MN MSA
Clay County, MN; Cass County, ND

Farmington, CT
See Hartford, CT MSA and Hartford, CT NECMA

Fayetteville-Springdale-Rogers, AR MSA
Benton and Washington Counties

Fishers, IN
See Indianapolis, IN MSA

Flint, MI PMSA
Genesee County

Flower Mound, TX
See Dallas, TX MSA and Dallas-Fort Worth, TX CMSA

Fort Lauderdale, FL PMSA
Broward County

Fort Worth-Arlington, TX PMSA
Hood, Johnson, Parker and Tarrant Counties

Franklin, MA
See Boston, MA-NH PMSA, Boston-Worcester-Lawrence, MA-NH-ME-CT CMSA and Boston-Worcester-Lawrence-Lowell- Brockton, MA-NH NECMA

Frederick, MD
See Washington, DC-MD-VA-WV PMSA and Washington-Baltimore, DC-MD-VA-WV CMSA

Frisco, TX
See Dallas, TX MSA and Dallas-Fort Worth, TX CMSA

Galveston-Texas City, TX MSA
Galveston County

Gary, IN PMSA
Lake and Porter Counties

Goodyear, AZ
See Phoenix, AZ MSA

Grand Blanc, MI
See Flint, MI PMSA

Greenburgh, NY
See New York, NY PMSA and New York-Northern New Jersey-Long Island, NY-NJ-CT-PA CMSA

Greenwich, CT
See Stamford-Norwalk, CT MSA and New Haven-Bridgeport-Stamford- Waterbury-Danbury, CT NECMA

Hampden, PA
See Harrisburg, PA MSA

Harrisburg-Lebanon-Carlisle, PA MSA
Cumberland, Dauphin, Lebanon and Perry Counties

Hartford, CT MSA
Parts of Hartford, Litchfield, Middlesex, New London, Tolland, and Windham Counties

Hartford, CT NECMA
Hartford, Middlesex, and Tolland Counties

Hendersonville, TN
See Nashville, TN MSA

Hilliard, OH
See Columbus, OH MSA

Honolulu, HI MSA
Honolulu County

Hoover, AL
See Birmingham , AL MSA

Houston, TX PMSA
Chambers, Fort Bend, Harris, Liberty, Montgomery and Waller Counties

Houston-Galveston-Brazoria, TX CMSA
Brazoria, Chambers, Fort Bend, Galveston, Harris, Liberty, Montgomery, and Waller Counties

Huntersville, NC
See Charlotte-Gastonia-Rock Hill, NC-SC MSA

Huntsville, AL MSA
Limestone and Madison Counties

Indianapolis, IN MSA
Boone, Hamilton, Hancock, Hendricks, Johnson, Madison, Marion, Morgan, and Shelby Counties

Juneau, AK
Not located within a metropolitan area.

Kansas City, KS-MO MSA
Cass, Clay, Clinton, Jackson, Lafayette, Platte, and Ray Counties, MO; Johnson, Leavenworth, Miami, and Wyandotte Counties, KS

Keller, TX
See Fort Worth-Arlington, TX PMSA and Dallas-Fort Worth, TX CMSA

Kenner, LA
See New Orleans, LA MSA

Kennesaw, GA
See Atlanta, GA MSA

Lawrence, MA-NH MSA
Essex County, MA; Rockingham County, NH

League City, TX
See Galveston, TX MSA

Leawood, KS
See Kansas City, MO-KS MSA

Lee's Summit, MO
See Kansas City, MO-KS MSA

Leesburg, VA
See Washington, DC-MD-VA-WV PMSA and Washington-Baltimore, DC-MD-VA-WV CMSA

Lehi, UT
See Provo-Orem, UT MSA

Little Rock-North Little Rock, AR MSA
Faulkner, Lonoke, Pulaski and Saline Counties

Los Angeles-Long Beach, CA PMSA
Los Angeles County

Los Angeles-Riverside-Orange, CA CMSA
Los Angeles, Orange, Riverside, San Bernardino, and Ventura Counties

Louisville, KY-IN
Bullitt, Jefferson, and Oldham Counties, KY; Clark, Floyd, Harrison, and Scott Counties, IN

Loveland, CO
See Fort Collins, CO MSA

Lower Providence, PA
See Philadelphia, PA-NJ PMSA and Philadelphia-Wilmington-Atlantic City, PA-NJ-DE-MD CMSA

Madison, AL
See Huntsville, AL MSA

Madison, WI MSA
Dane County

Manchester, NH PMSA
Parts of Hillsborough, Merrimack and Rockingham County, NH

Manhattan Beach, CA
See Los Angeles-Long Beach, CA PMSA and Los Angeles-Riverside-Orange, CA CMSA

Maple Grove, MN
See Minnepolis-St. Paul, MN MSA

Marion, IA
See Cedar Rapids, IA MSA

Marlboro, NJ
See Monmouth-Ocean, NJ PMSA and New York-Northern New Jersey-Long Island, NY-NJ-CT-PA CMSA

Matthews, NC
See Charlotte-Gastonia-Rock Hill, NC-SC MSA

Memphis, TN-AR-MS MSA
Fayette, Shelby, and Tipton Counties, TN; Crittenden County, AR; DeSoto County, MS

Meridian, ID
See Boise City, ID MSA

Merrimack, NH
See Boston- Worcester-Lawrence, MA-NH-ME-CT CMSA and Boston-Worcester-Lawrence-Lowell- Brockton, MA-NH NECMA

Miami-Fort Lauderdale, FL CMSA
Broward and Miami-Dade Counties

Middlesex-Somerset-Hunterdon, NJ PMSA
Hunterdon, Middlesex, and Somerset Counties

Milwaukee-Waukesha, WI PMSA
Milwaukee, Ozaukee, Washington, and Waukesha Counties

Milwaukee-Racine, WI CMSA
Milwaukee, Ozaukee, Washington, Waukesha, and Racine Counties

Minneapolis-St. Paul, MN-WI MSA
Anoka, Carver, Chisago, Dakota, Hennepin, Isanti, Ramsey, Scott, Sherburne, Washington, Wright and Pierce Counties, MN; St. Croix County, WI

Monmouth-Ocean, NJ PMSA
Monmouth and Ocean Counties

Morgantown, WV
Not located within a metropolitan area.

Mount Pleasant, SC
See Charleston-North Charleston, SC MSA

Nashua, NH MSA
Parts of Hillsborough County

Nashville, TN MSA
Cheatham, Davidson, Dickson, Robertson, Rutherford, Sumner, Williamson and Wilson Counties

Nassau-Suffolk, NY MSA
Nassau and Suffolk Counties

New Haven-Meriden, CT PMSA
Parts of New Haven and Middlesex Counties

New Haven-Bridgeport-Stamford-Waterbury-Danbury, CT NECMA
Fairfield and New Haven Counties

New Orleans, LA MSA
Jefferson, Orleans, Plaquemines, St. Bernard, St. Charles, St. James, St. John the Baptist, and St. Tammany Parishes

New York, NY PMSA
Bronx, Kings, New York, Putnam, Queens, Richmond, Rockland, and Westchester Counties

New York-Northern New Jersey-Long Island, NY-NJ-CT-PA CMSA
Bergen, Essex, Hudson, Hunterdon, Mercer, Middlesex, Monmouth, Morris, Ocean, Passaic, Somerset, Sussex, Union, Warren Counties, NJ; Parts of Fairfield, Litchfield, Middlesex, and New Haven Counties, CT; Dutchess, Nassau, Suffolk, Bronx, Kings, New York, Putnam, Queens, Richmond, Rockland, Westchester, and Orange Counties, NY; Pike County, PA

Newark, NJ PMSA
Essex, Morris, Sussex, Union, and Warren Counties

Northampton, PA
See Philadelphia, PA-NJ PMSA and Philadelphia-Wilmington-Atlantic City, PA-NJ-DE-MD CMSA

Northville, MI
See Detroit, MI PMSA and Detroit-Ann Arbor-Flint, MI CMSA

Novi, MI
See Detroit, MI PMSA and Detroit-Ann Arbor-Flint, MI CMSA

O'Fallon, MO
See Saint Louis, MO MSA

Oakland, CA PMSA
Alameda and Contra Costa Counties

Oklahoma City, OK MSA
Canadian, Cleveland, Logan, McClain, Oklahoma and Pottawatomie Counties

Omaha, NE-IA MSA
Cass, Douglas, Sarpy, and Washington Counties, NE; Pottawattamie County, IA

Orange County, CA PMSA
Orange County

Orlando, FL MSA
Lake, Orange, Osceola and Seminole Counties

Oro Valley, AZ
See Tucson, AZ MSA

Oviedo, FL
See Orlando, FL MSA

Palm Beach Gardens, FL
See West Palm Beach-Boca Raton, FL MSA

Parker, CO
See Denver, CO MSA

Peachtree City, GA
See Atlanta, GA MSA

Pflugerville, TX
See Austin-San Marcos, TX MSA

Philadelphia, PA-NJ PMSA
Bucks, Chester, Delaware, Montgomery and Philadelphia Counties, PA; Burlington, Camden, Gloucester and Salem Counties, NJ

Philadelphia-Wilmington-Atlantic City, PA-NJ-DE-MD CMSA
Bucks, Chester, Delaware, Montgomery, and Philadelphia Counties, PA; Atlantic, Burlington, Camden, Cape May, Cumberland, Gloucester, and Salem Counties, NJ; New Castle County, DE; Cecil County, MD

Phoenix-Mesa, AZ MSA
Maricopa and Pinal Counties

Pittsburgh, PA
Allegheny, Beaver, Butler, Fayette, Washington and Westmoreland Counties

Pleasanton, CA
See Oakland, CA PMSA and San Francisco-Oakland-San Jose, CA CMSA

Portland-Vancouver, OR-WA PMSA
Clackamas, Columbia, Multnomah, Washington, and Yamhill Counties, OR; Clark County, WA

Portland-Salem, OR-WA CMSA
Clackamas, Columbia, Marion, Multnomah, Polk, Washington, and Yamhill Counties, OR; Clark County, WA

Providence-Fall River-Warwick, RI-MA MSA
Parts of Newport and Washington Counties, RI; all of Bristol, Kent, and Providence Counties, RI; part of Bristol County, MA

Providence-Warwick-Pawtucket, RI NECMA
Bristol, Kent, Providence, and Washington Counties

Provo-Orem, UT MSA
Utah County

Raleigh-Durham-Chapel Hill, NC MSA
Chatham, Durham, Franklin, Johnston, Orange, and Wake Counties

Rapid City, SD
See Rapid City, SD MSA

Rapid City, SD MSA
Pennington County

Redmond, WA
See Seattle-Bellevue-Everett, WA PMSA and Seattle-Tacoma-Bremerton, WA CMSA

Reno, NV MSA
Washoe County

Richland, WA
See Richland-Kennewick-Pasco, WA MSA

Richland-Kennewick-Pasco, WA MSA
Benton and Franklin Counties

Richmond, KY
Not located within a metropolitan area.

Rio Rancho, NM
See Albuquerque, NM MSA

Riverside-San Bernardino, CA MSA
Riverside and San Bernardino Counties

Rochester, MN
See Rochester, MN MSA

Rochester, MN MSA
Olmsted County

Rockaway, NJ
See Newark, NJ PMSA and New York-Northern New Jersey-Long Island, NY-NJ-CT-PA CMSA

Rocklin, CA
See Sacramento, CA MSA

Rogers, AR
See Fayetteville-Springdale-Rogers, AR MSA

Round Rock, TX
See Austin, TX MSA

Sacramento, CA MSA
El Dorado, Placer, and Sacramento Counties

Saint Louis, MO-IL MSA
St. Louis and Sullivan Cities; Crawford (part), Franklin, Jefferson, Lincoln, St. Charles, St. Louis and Warren Counties, MO; Clinton, Jersey, Madison, Monroe, and St. Clair Counties, IL

Salt Lake City-Ogden, UT MSA
Davis, Salt Lake, and Weber Counties

Sammamish, WA
See Seattle-Bellevue-Everett, WA PMSA and Seattle-Tacoma-Bremerton, WA CMSA

San Diego, CA MSA
San Diego County

San Francisco, CA PMSA
Marin, San Francisco and San Mateo Counties

San Francisco-Oakland-San Jose, CA CMSA
Alameda, Contra Costa, Marin, Napa, San Francisco, San Mateo, Santa Clara, Santa Cruz, Solano, and Sonoma Counties

San Jose, CA PMSA
Santa Clara County

San Ramon, CA
See Oakland, CA PMSA and San Francisco-Oakland-San Jose, CA CMSA

Santa Fe, NM
See Santa Fe, NM MSA

Santa Fe, NM MSA
Los Alamos and Santa Fe Counties

Saratoga, CA
See San Jose, CA PMSA

Savage, MN
See Minneapolis-St. Paul, MN MSA

Schererville, IN
See Gary, IN PMSA and Chicago-Gary-Kenosha, IL-IN-WI CMSA

Seattle-Bellevue-Everett, WA PMSA
Island, King and Snohomish Counties

Seattle-Tacoma-Bremerton, WA CMSA
Island, King, Kitsap, Pierce, Snohomish, and Thurston Counties

Shawnee, KS
See Kansas City, MO-KS MSA

Shrewsbury, MA
See Boston, MA-NH PMSA, Boston-Worcester-Lawrence, MA-NH-ME-CT CMSA and Boston-Worcester-Lawrence-Lowell- Brockton, MA-NH NECMA

South Brunswick, NJ
See Middlesex-Somerset-Hunterdon, NJ PMSA and New York-Northern New Jersey-Long Island, NY-NJ-CT-PA CMSA

South Jordan, UT
See Salt Lake City, UT MSA

South Kingstown, RI
See Providence-Fall River-Warwick, RI-MA MSA and Providence-Warwick-Pawtucket, RI NECMA

Southaven, MS
See Memphis, MS MSA

Southlake, TX
See Fort Worth-Arlington, TX PMSA and Dallas-Fort Worth, TX CMSA

Spanish Fork, UT
See Provo-Orem, UT MSA

Sparks, NV
See Reno, NV MSA

Stamford-Norwalk, CT MSA
Parts of Fairfield County

Stow, OH
See Akron, OH MSA

Sugarland, TX
See Houston, TX MSA

Sun Prairie, WI
See Madison, WI MSA

Trenton, NJ PMSA
Mercer County

Tualatin, OR
See Portland-Vancouver, OR-WA PMSA and Portland-Salem, OR-WA CMSA

Tulsa, OK MSA
Creek, Osage, Rogers, Tulsa, and Wagoner Counties

Tucson, AZ
Pima County

Waimalu, HI
See Honolulu, HI MSA

Washington, DC-MD-VA-WV PMSA
District of Columbia; Calvert, Charles, Frederick, Montgomery and Prince George Counties, MD; Alexandria, Fairfax, Falls Church, Fredericksburg, Manassas and Manassas Park Cities, and Arlington, Clarke, Culpeper, Fairfax, Fauquier, King George, Loudoun, Prince William, Spotsylvania, Stafford and Warren Counties, VA; Berkeley and Jefferson Counties, WV

Washington-Baltimore, DC-MD-VA-WV CMSA
District of Columbia; Anne Arundel, Baltimore, Baltimore City, Calvert, Carroll, Charles, Frederick, Harford, Howard, Montgomery, Prince George's, Queen Anne's, and Washington Counties, MD; Alexandria City, Arlington, Clarke, Culpeper, Fairfax, Fairfax City, Falls Church City, Fauquier, Fredericksburg City, King George, Loudoun, Manassas City, Manassas Park City, Prince William, Spotsylvania, Stafford, and Warren Counties, VA; Berkeley and Jefferson County, WV

Wellington, FL
See West Palm Beach-Boca Raton, FL MSA

West Des Moines, IA
See Des Moines, IA MSA

West Linn, OR
See Portland-Vancouver, OR-WA PMSA and Portland-Salem, OR-WA CMSA

West Windsor, NJ
See Trenton, NJ PMSA and New York-Northern New Jersey-Long Island, NY-NJ-CT-PA CMSA

West Palm Beach-Boca Raton, FL MSA
Palm Beach County

Weston, FL
See Fort Lauderdale, FL PMSA and Miami-Fort Lauderdale, FL CMSA

Wilmington-Newark, DE-MD MSA
New Castle County, DE; Cecil County, MD

Woodbury, MN
See Minneapolis-St. Paul, MN-WI MSA

Woodridge, IL
See Chicago, IL PMSA and Chicago-Gary-Kenosha, IL-IN-WI CMSA

Worcester, MA-CT PMSA
Parts of Hampden and Worcester Counties, MA; Part of Wyndham County, CT

Yorba Linda, CA
See Orange County, CA PMSA and Los Angeles-Riverside-Orange, CA CMSA

Appendix B: Current Metropolitan Area Definitions

Metropolitan Statistical Areas (MSA), Micropolitan Statistical Areas, Metropolitan Divisions (MD), New England City and Town Areas (NECTA), and New England City and Town Area Divisions (NECTA Division)

These metropolitan area definitions went into effect June 2003 and are current as of November 2007.

Akron, OH MSA
Portage and Summit Counties

Albany-Schenectady-Troy, NY MSA
Albany, Rensselaer, Saratoga, Schenectady, and Schoharie Counties

Albuquerque, NM MSA
Bernalillo, Sandoval, Torrance, and Valencia Counties

Allen, TX
See Dallas-Fort Worth-Arlington, TX MSA and Dallas-Plano-Irving, TX MD

Ankeny, IA
See Des Moines-West Des Moines, IA MSA

Apex, NC
See Raleigh-Cary, NC MSA

Atlanta-Sandy Springs-Marietta, GA MSA
Barrow, Bartow, Butts, Carroll, Cherokee, Clayton, Cobb, Coweta, Dawson, DeKalb, Douglas, Fayette, Forsyth, Fulton, Gwinnett, Haralson, Heard, Henry, Jasper, Lamar, Meriwether, Newton, Paulding, Pickens, Pike, Rockdale, Spalding, and Walton Counties

Austin-Round Rock, TX MSA
Bastrop, Caldwell, Hays, Travis, and Williamson Counties

Bangor, ME
See Bangor, ME MSA and Bangor, ME NECTA

Bangor, ME MSA
Penobscot County

Bangor, ME NECTA
Includes 46 cities, towns, reservations and unorganized territories in Maine.

Beavercreek, OH
See Dayton, OH MSA

Bellevue, NE
See Omaha-Council Bluffs, NE-IA MSA

Bend, OR MSA
Deschutes County

Bernards, NJ
See New York-Northern New Jersey-Long Island, NY-NJ-PA MSA and Edison-New Brunswick, NJ MD

Bethesda-Frederick-Gaithersburg, MD MD
Frederick and Montgomery Counties

Bethlehem, NY
See Albany-Schenectady-Troy, NY MSA

Birmingham-Hoover, AL MSA
Bibb, Blount, Chilton, Jefferson, Shelby, St. Clair, and Walker Counties

Boise City-Nampa, ID MSA
Ada, Boise, Canyon, Gem, and Owyhee Counties

Boston-Cambridge-Quincy, MA-NH MSA
Essex, Middlesex, Norfolk, Plymouth, and Suffolk Counties, MA; Rockingham and Strafford Counties, NH

Boston-Quincy, MA MD
Norfolk, Plymouth, and Suffolk Counties

Boston-Cambridge-Quincy, MA-NH NECTA
Includes 155 cities and towns in Massachusetts and 38 cities and towns in New Hampshire

Boston-Cambridge-Quincy, MA NECTA Division
Includes 97 cities and towns in Massachusetts

Bozeman, MT
See Bozeman, MT Micropolitan Statistical Area

Bozeman, MT Micropolitan Statistical Area
Gallatin County

Brentwood, TN
See Nashville-Davidson—Murfreesboro, TN MSA

Bridgeport-Stamford-Norwalk, CT MSA
Fairfield County

Bridgeport-Stamford-Norwalk, CT NECTA
Includes 25 cities and towns in Connecticut

Brookfield, WI
See Milwaukee-Waukesha-West Allis, WI MSA

Broomfield, CO
See Denver-Aurora, CO MSA

Burlington, VT
See Burlington-South Burlington, VT MSA and Burlington-South Burlington, VT NECTA

Burlington-South Burlington, VT MSA
Chittenden, Franklin, and Grand Isle Counties

Burlington-South Burlington, VT NECTA
Includes 33 cities and towns in Vermont

Camden, NJ MD
Burlington, Camden, and Gloucester Counties

Carmel, IN
See Indianapolis, IN MSA

Cary, NC
See Raleigh-Cary, NC MSA

Casper, WY
See Casper, WY MSA

Casper, WY MSA
Natrona County

Cedar Rapids, IA MSA
Benton, Jones, and Linn Counties

Charleston-North Charleston, SC MSA
Berkeley, Charleston, and Dorchester Counties

Charlotte-Gastonia-Concord, NC-SC MSA
Anson, Cabarrus, Gaston, Mecklenburg, Union, and York Counties

Cheshire, CT
See New Haven-Milford, CT MSA and New Haven, CT NECTA

Chicago-Naperville-Joliet, IL-IN-WI MSA
Cook, DeKalb, DuPage, Grundy, Kane, Kendall, Lake, McHenry, and Will Counties, IL; Jasper, Lake, Newton, and Porter Counties, IN; Kenosha County, WI

Chicago-Naperville-Joliet, IL MD
Cook, DeKalb, DuPage, Grundy, Kane, Kendall, McHenry, and Will Counties

Chino Hills, CA
See Riverside-San Bernardino-Ontario, CA MSA

Collierville, TN
See Memphis, TN-MS-AR MSA

Columbus, OH MSA
Delaware, Fairfield, Franklin, Licking, Madison, Morrow, Pickaway, and Union Counties

Conway, AR
See Little Rock-North Little Rock, AR MSA

Coronado, CA
See San Diego-Carlsbad-San Marcos, CA MSA

Cranberry, PA
See Pittsburgh, PA MSA

Dallas-Fort Worth-Arlington, TX MSA
Collin, Dallas, Delta, Denton, Ellis, Hunt, Johnson, Kaufman, Parker, Rockwall, Tarrant, and Wise Counties

Dallas-Plano-Irving, TX MD
Collin, Dallas, Delta, Denton, Ellis, Hunt, Kaufman, and Rockwall Counties

Dayton, OH MSA
Greene, Miami, Montgomery, and Preble Counties

Denver-Aurora, CO MSA
Adams, Arapahoe, Broomfield, Clear Creek, Denver, Douglas, Elbert, Gilpin, Jefferson, and Park Counties

Des Moines-West Des Moines, IA MSA
Dallas, Guthrie, Madison, Polk, and Warren Counties

Detroit-Warren-Livonia, MI MSA
Lapeer, Livingston, Macomb, Oakland, St. Clair, and Wayne Counties

Detroit-Livonia-Dearborn, MI MD
Wayne County

Dover, DE MSA
Kent County

Draper, UT
See Salt Lake City, UT MSA

Dublin, OH
See Columbus, OH MSA

Edison-New Brunswick, NJ MD
Middlesex, Monmouth, Ocean, and Somerset Counties

Edmond, OK
See Oklahoma City, OK MSA

Evesham, NJ
See Philadelphia-Camden-Wilmington, PA-NJ-DE-MD MSA

Fargo, ND-MN MSA
Cass County, ND; Clay County, MN

Farmington, CT
See Hartford-West Hartford-East Hartford, CT MSA and Hartford-West Hartford-East Hartford, CT NECTA

Fayetteville-Springdale-Rogers, AR-MO MSA
Benton, Madison, and Washington Counties, AR; McDonald County, MO

Fishers, IN
See Indianapolis, IN MSA

Flint, MI MSA
Genesee County

Flower Mound, TX
See Dallas-Fort Worth-Arlington, TX MSA and Dallas-Plano-Irving, TX MD

Fort Lauderdale-Pompano Beach-Deerfield Beach, FL MD
Broward County

Fort Worth-Arlington, TX MD
Collin, Dallas, Delta, Denton, Ellis, Hunt, Johnson, Kaufman, Parker, Rockwall, Tarrant, and Wise Counties

Franklin, MA
See Boston-Cambridge-Quincy, MA-NH MSA, Boston-Quincy, MA MD, Boston-Cambridge-Quincy, MA-NH NECTA, and Boston-Cambridge-Quincy, MA NECTA Division

Frederick, MD
See Washington-Arlington-Alexandria, DC-VA-MD-WV MSA and Bethesda-Frederick-Gaithersburg, MD MD

Frisco, TX
See Dallas-Fort Worth-Arlington, TX MSA and Dallas-Plano-Irving, TX MD

Gary, IN MD
Jasper, Lake, Newton, and Porter Counties

Goodyear, AZ
See Phoenix-Mesa-Scottsdale, AZ MSA

Grand Blanc, MI
See Flint, MI MSA

Greenburgh, NY
See New York-Northern New Jersey-Long Island, NY-NJ-PA MSA and New York-White Plains-Wayne, NY-NJ MD

Greenwich, CT
See Bridgeport-Stamford-Norwalk, CT MSA and Bridgeport-Stamford-Norwalk, CT NECTA

Hampden, PA
See Harrisburg-Carlisle, PA MSA

Harrisburg-Carlisle, PA MSA
Cumberland, Dauphin, and Perry Counties

Hartford-West Hartford-East Hartford, CT MSA
Hartford, Middlesex, and Tolland Counties

Hartford-West Hartford-East Hartford, CT NECTA
Includes 52 cities and towns in Connecticut

Hilliard, OH
See Columbus, OH MSA

Honolulu, HI MSA
Honolulu County

Hoover, AL
See Birmingham-Hoover, AL MSA

Houston-Baytown-Sugar Land, TX MSA
Austin, Brazoria, Chambers, Fort Bend, Galveston, Harris, Liberty, Montgomery, San Jacinto, and Waller Counties

Huntersville, NC
See Charlotte-Gastonia-Concord, NC-SC MSA

Huntsville, AL MSA
Limestone and Madison Counties

Indianapolis, IN MSA
Boone, Brown, Hamilton, Hancock, Hendricks, Johnson, Marion, Morgan, Putnam, and Shelby Counties

Juneau, AK
See Juneau, AK Micropolitan Statistical Area

Juneau, AK Micropolitan Statistical Area
Juneau City and Borough

Kansas City, MO-KS MSA
Bates, Caldwell, Cass, Clay, Clinton, Jackson, Lafayette, Platte, and Ray Counties, MO; Franklin, Johnson, Leavenworth, Linn, Miami, and Wyandotte Counties, KS

Keller, TX
See Dallas-Fort Worth-Arlington, TX MSA and Fort Worth-Arlington, TX MD

Kenner, LA
See New Orleans-Metairie-Kenner, LA MSA

Kennesaw, GA
See Atlanta-Sandy Springs-Marietta, GA MSA

Kennewick-Richland-Pasco, WA MSA
Benton and Franklin Counties

League City, TX
See Houston-Baytown-Sugar Land, TX MSA

Leawood, KS
See Kansas City, MO-KS MSA

Lee's Summit, MO
See Kansas City, MO-KS MSA

Leesburg, VA
See Washington-Arlington-Alexandria, DC-VA-MD-WV MSA and Washington-Arlington-Alexandria, DC-VA-MD-WV MD

Lehi, UT
See Provo-Orem, UT MSA

Little Rock-North Little Rock, AR MSA
Faulkner, Grant, Lonoke, Perry, Pulaski, and Saline Counties

Los Angeles-Long Beach-Santa Ana, CA MSA
Los Angeles and Orange Counties

Los Angeles-Long Beach-Glendale, CA MD
Los Angeles County

Louisville, KY-IN MSA
Clark, Floyd, Harrison, and Washington Counties, IN; Bullitt, Henry, Jefferson, Meade, Nelson, Oldham, Shelby, Spencer, and Trimble Counties, KY

Lower Providence, PA
See Philadelphia-Camden-Wilmington, PA-NJ-DE-MD MSA and Philadelphia, PA MD

Madison, AL
See Huntsville, AL MSA

Madison, WI MSA
Columbia, Dane, and Iowa Counties

Manchester-Nashua, NH MSA
Hillsborough County

Manhattan Beach, CA
See Los Angeles-Long Beach-Santa Ana, CA MSA and Los Angeles-Long Beach-Glendale, CA MD

Maple Grove, MN
See Minneapolis-St. Paul-Bloomington, MN-WI MSA

Marion, IA
See Cedar Rapids, IA MSA

Marlboro, NJ
See New York-Northern New Jersey-Long Island, NY-NJ-PA MSA and Edison-New Brunswick, NJ MD

Matthews, NC
See Charlotte-Gastonia-Concord, NC-SC MSA

Memphis, TN-MS-AR MSA
Crittenden County, AR; DeSoto, Marshall, Tate, and Tunica Counties, MS; Fayette, Shelby, and Tipton Counties, TN

Meridian, ID
See Boise City-Nampa, ID MSA

Merrimack, NH
See Manchester-Nashua, NH MSA, Boston-Cambridge-Quincy, MA-NH NECTA, and Nashua, NH-MA NECTA Division

Miami-Fort Lauderdale-Pompano Beach, FL MSA
Broward, Miami-Dade, and Palm Beach Counties

Miami-Miami Beach-Kendall, FL MD
Miami-Dade County

Milwaukee-Waukesha-West Allis, WI MSA
Milwaukee, Ozaukee, Washington, and Waukesha Counties

Minneapolis-St. Paul-Bloomington, MN-WI MSA
Anoka, Carver, Chisago, Dakota, Hennepin, Isanti, Ramsey, Scott, Sherburne, Washington, and Wright Counties, MN; Pierce and St. Croix Counties, WI

Morgantown, WV
See Morgantown, WV MSA

Morgantown, WV MSA
Monongalia and Preston Counties

Mount Pleasant, SC
See Charleston-North Charleston, SC MSA

Nashua, NH-MA NECTA Division
Includes 2 cities and towns in Massachusetts and 19 cities and towns in New Hampshire

Nashville-Davidson—Murfreesboro, TN MSA
Cannon, Cheatham, Davidson, Dickson, Hickman, Macon, Robertson, Rutherford, Smith, Sumner, Trousdale, Williamson, and Wilson Counties

New Haven-Milford, CT MSA
New Haven County

New Haven, CT NECTA
Includes 22 cities and towns in Connecticut

New Orleans-Metairie-Kenner, LA MSA
Jefferson, Orleans, Plaquemines, St. Bernard, St. Charles, St. John the Baptist, and St. Tammany Parishes

New York-Northern New Jersey-Long Island, NY-NJ-PA MSA
Bergen, Essex, Hudson, Hunterdon, Middlesex, Monmouth, Morris, Ocean, Passaic, Somerset, Sussex, and Union Counties, NJ; Bronx, Kings, Nassau, New York, Putnam, Queens, Richmond, Rockland, Suffolk, and Westchester Counties, NY; Pike County, PA

New York-Wayne-White Plains, NY-NJ MD
Bergen, Hudson, and Passaic Counties, NJ; Bronx, Kings, New York, Putnam, Queens, Richmond, Rockland, and Westchester Counties, NY

Newark-Union, NJ-PA MD
Essex, Hunterdon, Morris, Sussex, and Union Counties, NJ; Pike County, PA

Northampton
See Philadelphia-Camden-Wilmington, PA-NJ-DE-MD MSA and Philadelphia, PA MD

Northville, MI
See Detroit-Warren-Livonia, MI MSA and Detroit-Livonia-Dearborn, MI MD

Novi, MI
See Detroit-Warren-Livonia, MI MSA and Warren-Farmington Hills, MI MD

O'Fallon, MO
See St. Louis, MO-IL MSA

Oakland-Fremont-Hayward, CA MD
Alameda and Contra Costa Counties

Oklahoma City, OK MSA
Canadian, Cleveland, Grady, Lincoln, Logan, McClain, and Oklahoma Counties

Omaha-Council Bluffs, NE-IA MSA
Harrison, Mills, and Pottawattamie Counties, IA; Cass, Douglas, Sarpy, Saunders, and Washington Counties, NE

Orlando, FL MSA
Lake, Orange, Osceola, and Seminole Counties

Oro Valley, AZ
See Tucson, AZ MSA

Oviedo, FL
See Orlando, FL MSA

Palm Beach Gardens, FL
See Miami-Fort Lauderdale-Pompano Beach, FL MSA and West Palm Beach-Boca Raton-Boynton Beach, FL MD

Parker, CO
See Denver-Aurora, CO MSA

Peachtree City, GA
See Atlanta-Sandy Springs-Marietta, GA MSA

Pflugerville, TX
See Austin-Round Rock, TX MSA

Philadelphia-Camden-Wilmington, PA-NJ-DE-MD MSA
New Castle County, DE; Cecil County, MD; Burlington, Camden, Gloucester, and Salem Counties, NJ; Bucks, Chester, Delaware, Montgomery, and Philadelphia Counties, PA

Philadelphia, PA MD
Bucks, Chester, Delaware, Montgomery, and Philadelphia Counties

Phoenix-Mesa-Scottsdale, AZ MSA
Maricopa and Pinal Counties

Pleasanton, CA
See San Francisco-Oakland-Fremont, CA MSA and Oakland-Fremont-Hayward, CA MD

Portland-Vancouver-Beaverton, OR-WA MSA
Clackamas, Columbia, Multnomah, Washington, and Yamhill Counties, OR; Clark and Skamania Counties, WA

Poughkeepsie-Newburgh-Middletown, NY MSA
Dutchess and Orange Counties

Providence-New Bedford-Fall River, RI-MA MSA
Bristol County, MA; Bristol, Kent, Newport, Providence, and Washington Counties, RI

Providence-Fall River-Warwick, RI-MA NECTA
Includes 12 cities and towns in Massachusetts and 37 cities and towns in Rhode Island

Provo-Orem, UT MSA
Juab and Utah Counties

Raleigh-Cary, NC MSA
Franklin, Johnston, and Wake Counties

Rapid City, SD
See Rapid City, SD MSA

Rapid City, SD MSA
Meade and Pennington Counties

Redmond, WA
See Seattle-Tacoma-Bellevue, WA MSA and Seattle-Bellevue-Everett, WA MD

Reno-Sparks, NV MSA
Storey and Washoe Counties

Richland, WA
See Kennewick-Richland-Pasco, WA MSA

Richmond, KY
See Richmond-Berea, KY Micropolitan Statistical Area

Richmond-Berea, KY Micropolitan Statistical Area
Madison and Rockcastle Counties

Rio Rancho, NM
See Albuquerque, NM MSA

Riverside-San Bernardino-Ontario, CA MSA
Riverside and San Bernardino Counties

Rockaway, NJ
See New York-Northern New Jersey-Long Island, NY-NJ-PA MSA and Newark-Union, NJ-PA MD

Rocklin, CA
See Sacramento—Arden-Arcade—Roseville, CA MSA

Rogers, AR
See Fayetteville-Springdale-Rogers, AR-MO MSA

Round Rock, TX
See Austin-Round Rock, TX MSA

Sacramento—Arden-Arcade—Roseville, CA MSA
El Dorado, Placer, Sacramento, and Yolo Counties

Saint Louis, MO-IL MSA
Bond, Calhoun, Clinton, Jersey, Macoupin, Madison, Monroe, and St. Clair Counties, IL; St. Louis city; Franklin, Jefferson, Lincoln, St. Charles, St. Louis, Warren, and Washington Counties, MO

Salt Lake City, UT MSA
Salt Lake, Summit, and Tooele Counties

Sammamish, WA
See Seattle-Tacoma-Bellevue, WA MSA and Seattle-Bellevue-Everett, WA MD

San Diego-Carlsbad-San Marcos, CA MSA
San Diego County

San Francisco-Oakland-Fremont, CA MSA
Alameda, Contra Costa, Marin, San Francisco, and San Mateo Counties

San Francisco-San Mateo-Redwood City, CA MD
Marin, San Francisco, and San Mateo Counties

San Jose-Sunnyvale-Santa Clara, CA MSA
San Benito and Santa Clara Counties

San Ramon, CA
See San Francisco-Oakland-Fremont, CA MSA and Oakland-Fremont-Hayward, CA MD

Santa Ana-Anaheim-Irvine, CA MD
Orange County

Santa Fe, NM
See Santa Fe, NM MSA

Santa Fe, NM MSA
Santa Fe County

Saratoga, CA
See San Jose-Sunnyvale-Santa Clara, CA MSA

Savage, MN
See Minneapolis-St. Paul-Bloomington, MN-WI MSA

Schererville, IL
See Chicago-Naperville-Joliet, IL-IN-WI MSA and Gary, IN MD

Seattle-Bellevue-Everett, WA MD
King and Snohomish Counties

Seattle-Tacoma-Bellevue, WA MSA
King, Pierce, and Snohomish Counties

Shawnee, KS
See Kansas City, MO-KS MSA

Shrewsbury, MA
See Worcester, MA MSA and Worcester, MA-CT NECTA

South Brunswick, NJ
See New York-Northern New Jersey-Long Island, NY-NJ-PA MSA and Edison-New Brunswick, NJ MD

South Jordan, UT
See Salt Lake City, UT MSA

South Kingstown, RI
See Providence-New Bedford-Fall River, RI-MA MSA and Providence-Fall River-Warwick, RI-MA NECTA

Southaven, MS
See Memphis, TN-MS-AR MSA

Southlake, TX
See Dallas-Fort Worth-Arlington, TX MSA and Fort Worth-Arlington, TX MD

Spanish Fork, UT
See Provo-Orem, UT MSA

Sparks, NV
See Reno-Sparks, NV MSA

Stow, OH
See Akron, OH MSA

Sugar Land, TX
See Houston-Baytown-Sugar Land, TX MSA

Sun Prairie, WI
See Madison, WI MSA

Trenton-Ewing, NJ MSA
Mercer County

Tualatin, OR
See Portland-Vancouver-Beaverton, OR-WA MSA

Tucson, AZ MSA
Pima County

Waimalu, HI
See Honolulu, HI MSA

Warren-Farmington Hills, MI MD
Lapeer, Livingston, Macomb, Oakland, and St. Clair Counties.

Washington-Arlington-Alexandria, DC-VA-MD-WV MSA
District of Columbia; Calvert, Charles, Frederick, Montgomery, and Prince George's Counties, MD; Alexandria, Fairfax, Falls Church, Fredericksburg, Manassas Park, and Manassas cities, VA; Arlington, Clarke, Fairfax, Fauquier, Loudoun, Prince William, Spotsylvania, Stafford, and Warren Counties, VA; Jefferson County, WV

Washington-Arlington-Alexandria, DC-VA-MD-WV MD
District of Columbia; Calvert, Charles, and Prince George's Counties, MD; Alexandria, Fairfax, Falls Church, Fredericksburg, Manassas Park, and Manassas cities, VA; Arlington, Clarke, Fairfax, Fauquier, Loudoun, Prince William, Spotsylvania, Stafford, and Warren Counties, VA; Jefferson County, WV

Wellington, FL
See Miami-Fort Lauderdale-Pompano Beach, FL MSA and West Palm Beach-Boca Raton-Boynton Beach, FL MD

West Des Moines, IA
See Des Moines, IA MSA

West Linn, OR
See Portland-Vancouver-Beaverton, OR-WA MSA

West Windsor, NJ
See Trenton-Ewing, NJ MSA

Weston, FL
See Miami-Fort Lauderdale-Miami Beach, FL MSA and Fort Lauderdale-Pompano Beach-Deerfield Beach, FL MD

Wilmington, DE-MD-NJ MD
New Castle County, DE; Cecil County, MD; Salem County, NJ

Woodbury, MN
See Minneapolis-St. Paul-Bloomington, MN-WI MSA

Woodridge, IL
See Chicago-Naperville-Joliet, IL-IN-WI MSA and Chicago-Naperville-Joliet, IL MD

Worcester, MA MSA
Worcester County

Worcester, MA-CT NECTA
Includes 37 cities and towns in Massachusetts and 3 cities and towns in Connecticut

Yorba Linda, CA
See Los Angeles-Long Beach-Santa Ana, CA MSA and Santa Ana-Anaheim-Irvine, CA MD

Appendix C: Counties

Allen, TX
Collin County

Ankeny, IA
Polk County

Apex, NC
Wake County

Bangor, ME
Penobscot County

Beavercreek, OH
Greene County

Bellevue, NE
Sarpy County

Bend, OR
Deschutes County

Bernards, NJ
Somerset County

Bethlehem, NY
Albany County

Bozeman, MT
Gallatin County

Brentwood, TN
Williamson County

Brookfield, WI
Waukesha County

Broomfield, CO
Broomfield County

Burlington, VT
Chittenden County

Carmel, IN
Hamilton County

Cary, NC
Wake County

Casper, WY
Natrona County

Cheshire, CT
New Haven County

Chino Hills, CA
San Bernardino County

Collierville, TN
Shelby County

Conway, AR
Faulkner County

Coronado, CA
San Diego County

Cranberry, PA
Butler County

Dover, DE
Kent County

Draper, UT
Salt Lake County

Dublin, OH
Franklin County

Edmond, OK
Oklahoma County

Evesham, NJ
Burlington County

Fargo, ND
Cass County

Farmington, CT
Hartford County

Fishers, IN
Hamilton County

Flower Mound, TX
Denton County

Franklin, MA
Norfolk County

Frederick, MD
Frederick County

Frisco, TX
Collin County

Goodyear, AZ
Maricopa County

Grand Blanc, MI
Genesee County

Greenburgh, NY
Westchester County

Greenwich, CT
Fairfield County

Hampden, PA
Cumberland County

Hilliard, OH
Franklin County

Hoover, AL
Jefferson County

Huntersville, NC
Mecklenburg County

Juneau, AK
Juneau City and Borough

Keller, TX
Tarrant County

Kenner, LA
Jefferson Parish

Kennesaw, GA
Cobb County

League City, TX
Galveston County

Leawood, KS
Johnson County

Lee's Summit, MO
Jackson County

Leesburg, VA
Loudoun County

Lehi, UT
Utah County

Lower Providence, PA
Montgomery County

Madison, AL
Madison County

Manhattan Beach, CA
Los Angeles County

Maple Grove, MN
Hennepin County

Marion, IA
Linn County

Marlboro, NJ
Monmouth County

Matthews, NC
Mecklenburg County

Meridian, ID
Ada County

Merrimack, NH
Hillsborough County

Morgantown, WV
Monongalia County

Mount Pleasant, SC
Charleston County

Northampton, PA
Bucks County

Northville, MI
Wayne County

Novi, MI
Oakland County

O'Fallon, MO
St. Charles County

Oro Valley, AZ
Pima County

Oviedo, FL
Seminole County

Palm Beach Gardens, FL
Palm Beach County

Parker, CO
Douglas County

Peachtree City, GA
Fayette County

Pflugerville, TX
Travis County

Pleasanton, CA
Alameda County

Rapid City, SD
Pennington County

Redmond, WA
King County

Richland, WA
Benton County

Richmond, KY
Madison County

Rio Rancho, NM
Sandoval County

Rockaway, NJ
Morris County

Rocklin, CA
Placer County

Rogers, AR
Benton County

Round Rock, TX
Williamson County

Sammamish, WA
King County

San Ramon, CA
Contra Costa County

Santa Fe, NM
Santa Fe County

Saratoga, CA
Santa Clara County

Savage, MN
Scott County

Schererville, IN
Lake County

Shawnee, KS
Johnson County

Shrewsbury, MA
Worcester County

South Brunswick, NJ
Middlesex County

South Jordan, UT
Salt Lake County

South Kingstown, RI
Washington County

Southaven, MS
DeSoto County

Southlake, TX
Tarrant County

Spanish Fork, UT
Utah County

Sparks, NV
Washoe County

Stow, OH
Summit County

Sugar Land, TX
Fort Bend County

Sun Prairie, WI
Dane County

Tualatin, OR
Washington County

Waimalu, HI
Honolulu County

Wellington, FL
Palm Beach County

West Des Moines, IA
Polk County

West Linn, OR
Clackamas County

West Windsor, NJ
Mercer County

Weston, FL
Broward County

Woodbury, MN
Washington County

Woodridge, IL
DuPage County

Yorba Linda, CA
Orange County

Note: *In cases where a city's population is split over multiple counties (except New York), data in this book reflects the county where the majority of the population resides.*

Appendix D: Chambers of Commerce

Allen, TX

Allen Chamber of Commerce
210 West McDermott Drive
Allen, TX 75013
Phone: 972-727-5585
Fax: 972-727-9000
Web: www.allenchamber.com

Ankeny, IA

Ankeny Area Chamber of Commerce
210 South Ankeny Blvd.
PO Box 488
Ankeny, IA 50023
Phone: 515-964-0685
Fax: 515-964-0487
Web: www.ankeny.org

Apex, NC

Apex Chamber of Commerce
220 North Salem Street
Apex, NC 27502
Phone: 919-362-6456
Fax: 919-362-9050
Web: www.apexchamber.com

Bangor, ME

Bangor Region Chamber of Commerce
519 Main Street
Bangor, ME 04401
Phone: 207-947-0307
Fax: 207-990-1427
Web: www.bangorregion.com

Beavercreek, OH

Beavercreek Chamber of Commerce
3299 Kemp Road
Beavercreek, OH 45431-2550
Phone: 937-426-2202
Fax: 937-426-2204
Web: www.beavercreekchamber.org

Bellevue, NE

Bellevue Chamber of Commerce
1102 Gavin Road South
Bellevue, NE 68005
Phone: 402-898-3000
Fax: 402-291-8729
Web: www.bellevuenebraska.com

Bend, OR

Bend Chamber of Commerce
777 Northwest Wall Street
Suite 200
Bend, OR 97701
Phone: 541-382-3221
Fax: 541-385-9929
Web: www.bendchamber.com

Bernards, NJ

Bernards Township Chamber of Commerce
PO Box 11
Basking Ridge, NJ 07920
Phone: 908-766-6755
Fax: 908-766-6755
Web: www.bernardstownshipchamber.org

Bethlehem, NY

Bethlehem Chamber of Commerce
318 Delaware Avenue
Main Square
Delmar, NY 12054
Phone: 518-439-0512
Fax: 518-475-0910
Web: www.bethlehemchamber.com

Bozeman, MT

Bozeman Chamber of Commerce
2000 Commerce Way
Bozeman, MT 59715
Phone: 406-586-5421
Fax: 406-586-8286
Web: www.bozemanchamber.com

Brentwood, TN

Brentwood Cool Springs Chamber of Commerce
5211 Maryland Way
Suite 1080
Brentwood, TN 37027
Phone: 615-373-1595
Fax: 615-373-8810
Web: www.brentwood.org

Brookfield, WI

The Greater Brookfield Chamber of Commerce
1305 N. Barker Rd.
Suite 5
Brookfield, WI 53045
Phone: 262-786-1886
Fax: 262-786-1959
Web: www.brookfieldchamber.com

Broomfield, CO

The Broomfield Chamber of Commerce
350 Interlocken Blvd.
Suite 250
Broomfield, CO 80021
Phone: 303-466-1775
Fax: 303-466-4481
Web: www.broomfieldchamber.org

Burlington, VT

Lake Champlain Regional Chamber of Commerce
60 Main Street
Suite 100
Burlington, VT 05401
Phone: 802-863-3489
Fax: 802-863-1538
Web: www.vermont.org

Carmel, IN

Carmel Chamber of Commerce
37 East Main Street
Suite 300
Carmel, IN 46032
Phone: 317-846-1049
Fax: 317-844-6843
Web: www.carmelchamber.com

Cary, NC

Cary Chamber of Commerce
307 North Academ Street
Cary, NC 27513
Phone: 919-467-1016
Fax: 919-469-2375
Web: www.carychamber.com

Casper, WY

Casper Chamber of Commerce
500 North Center Street
Casper, WY 82601
Phone: 307-234-5311
Fax: 307-265-2643
Web: www.casperwyoming.org

Cheshire, CT

Cheshire Chamber of Commerce
195 South Main Street
Cheshire, CT 06410
Phone: 203-272-2345
Fax: 203-271-3044
Web: www.cheshirechamber.com

Chino Hills, CA

Chino Valley Chamber of Commerce
2001 Grand Avenue
Chino Hills, CA 91709
Phone: 909-364-2600
Fax: 909-364-2695
Web: www.chinohills.org

Collierville, TN

Collierville Chamber of Commerce
485 Halle Park Drive
Collierville, TN 38017
Phone: 901-853-1949
Fax: 901-853-2399
Web: www.colliervillechamber.com

Conway, AR

Conway Chamber of Commerce
900 Oak Street
Conway, AR 72032
Phone: 501-327-7788
Fax: 501-327-7790
Web: www.conwayarkcc.org

Coronado, CA

Coronado Chamber of Commerce
875 Orange Avenue
Suite 102
Coronado, CA 92118
Phone: 619-435-9260
Fax: 619-522-6577
Web: www.coronadochamber.com

Cranberry, PA

Cranberry Area Chamber of Commerce
2525 Rochester Road
Suite 200
Cranberry, PA 16066
Phone: 724-776-4949
Fax: 724-776-5344
Web: www.cranberrychamber.com

Dover, DE

Central Delaware Chamber of Commerce
435 North Dupont Highway
Dover, DE 19901
Phone: 302-678-0892
Fax: 302-678-0189
Web: www.cdcc.net

Draper, UT

Draper Area Chamber of Commerce
12441 South 900 East Draper
PO Box 1002
Draper, UT 84020
Phone: 801-553-0928
Fax: 801-816-0478
Web: www.draperchamber.com

Dublin, OH

Dublin Chamber of Commerce
129 South High Street
Dublin, OH 43017
Phone: 614-889-2001
Fax: 614-889-2888
Web: www.dublinchamber.org

Edmond, OK

Edmond Area Chamber of Commerce
825 East 2nd Street
Suite 100
Edmond, OK 73003
Phone: 405-341-2808
Fax: 405-340-5512
Web: www.edmondchamber.com

Evesham, NJ

Burlington County Chamber of Commerce
100 Technology Way
Suite 110
Mount Laurel, NJ 08054
Phone: 856-439-2520
Fax: 856-439-2523
Web: www.bccoc.com

Fargo, ND

Fargo Moorhead Chamber of Commerce
202 First Avenue North
Moorhead, MN 56560
Phone: 218-233-1100
Fax: 218-233-1200
Web: www.fmchamber.com

Farmington, CT

Farmington Chamber of Commerce
827 Farmington Avenue
Farmington, CT 06032
Phone: 860-676-8490
Fax: 860-677-8332
Web: www.farmingtonchamber.com

Fishers, IN

Fishers Chamber of Commerece
11601 Municipal Drive
PO Box 353
Fishers, IN 46038
Phone: 317-578-0700
Fax: 317-578-1097
Web: www.fisherschamber.com

Flower Mound, TX

Flower Mound Chamber of Commerce
700 Parker Square
Suite 100
Flower Mound, TX 75028
Phone: 972-539-0500
Fax: 972-539-4307
Web: www.flowermoundchamber.com

Franklin, MA

Franklin United Chamber of Commerce
620 Old West Central Street
Suite 202
Franklin, MA 02038
Phone: 508-528-2800
Fax: 508-520-7864
Web: www.unitedchamber.org

Frederick, MD

Frederick County Chamber of Commerce
8420-B Gas House Pike
Frederick, MD 21701
Phone: 301-662-4164
Fax: 301-846-4427
Web: www.frederickchamber.org

Frisco, TX

Frisco Chamber of Commerce
6843 Main Street
Frisco, TX 75034
Phone: 972-335-9522
Web: www.friscochamber.com

Goodyear, AZ

Southwest Valley Chamber of Commerce
289 North Litchfield Road
Goodyear, AZ 85338
Phone: 623-932-2260
Fax: 623-932-9057
Web: www.southwestvalleychamber.org

Grand Blanc, MI

Grand Blanc Chamber of Commerce
512 E. Grand Blanc Rd.
Grand Blanc, MI 48439
Phone: 810-695-4222
Web: www.grandblancchamber.com

Greenburgh, NY

Westchester County Chamber of Commerce
108 Corporate Park Drive
Suite 101
White Plains, NY 10604
Phone: 914-948-2110
Fax: 914-948-0122
Web: www.westchesterny.org

Greenwich, CT

Greenwich Chamber of Commerce
45 East Putnam Avenue
Suite 121
Greenwich, CT 06830
Phone: 203-869-3500
Fax: 860-869-3502
Web: www.greenwichchamber.com

Hampden, PA

West Shore Chamber of Commerce
4211 Trindle Road
Camp Hill, PA 17011
Phone: 717-761-0702
Fax: 717-761-4315
Web: www.wschamber.org

Hilliard, OH

Hilliard Chamber of Commerce
4081 Main Street
Hilliard, OH 43026
Phone: 614-876-7666
Fax: 614-876-3113
Web: www.hilliardchamber.org

Hoover, AL

Hoover Chamber of Commerce
1694 Montgomery Highway
Suite 108
Hoover, AL 35216
Phone: 205-988-5672
Fax: 205-988-8383
Web: www.hooverchamber.org

Huntersville, NC

Lake Norman NC Chamber of Commerce
19900 West Catawba Avenue
Suite 100
Cornelius, NC 28031
Phone: 704-892-1922
Fax: 704-892-5313
Web: www.lakenormanchamber.org

Juneau, AK

Juneau Chamber of Commerce
3100 Channel Drive
Suite 300
Juneau, AK 99801
Phone: 907-463-3488
Fax: 907-463-3489
Web: www.juneauchamber.com

Keller, TX

Keller Chamber of Commerce
200 South Main Street
PO Box 761
Keller, TX 76248
Phone: 817-431-2169
Fax: 817-431-3789
Web: www.kellerchamber.com

Kenner, LA

Kenner Chamber of Commerce
3501 Chateau Blvd
Kenner, LA 70065
Phone: 504-461-0177
Web:

Kennesaw, GA

Cobb County Chamber of Commerce
PO Box 671868
Marietta, GA 30006
Phone: 770-980-2000
Fax: 770-980-9510
Web: www.cobbchamber.org

League City, TX

League City Chamber of Commerce and Business Assoc.
260 Park Avenue
PO Box 977
League City, TX 77573
Phone: 281-338-7339
Fax: 281-554-8103
Web: www.leaguecitychamber.com

Leawood, KS

Leawood Chamber of Commerce
4707 W 135 Street
Suite 270
Leawood, KS 66224
Phone: 913-498-1514
Fax: 913-491-0134
Web: www.leawoodchamber.org

Lee's Summit, MO

Lee's Summit Chamber of Commerce
220 Southeast Main Street
Lee's Summit, MO 64063-2332
Phone: 816-524-2424
Fax: 816-524-5246
Web: www.lschamber.com

Leesburg, VA

Loudoun County Chamber of Commerce
100 Blue Seal Drive
Suite 100
Leesburg, VA 20175
Phone: 703-777-2176
Fax: 703-777-1392
Web: www.loudounchamber.org

Lehi, UT

Lehi Area Chamber of Commerce
235 East State St.
Lehi, UT 84043
Phone: 801-766-9657
Fax: 801-766-8599
Web: www.lehiareachamber.org

Lower Providence, PA

Lower Providence Township
100 Parklane Drive
Eagleville, PA 19403
Phone: 610-539-8020
Fax: 610-539-6347
Web: www.lowerprovidence.org

Madison, AL

Madison Chamber of Commerce
190 Lime Quarry Road
Suite 105
Madison, AL 35758
Phone: 256-325-8317
Fax: 256-461-0840
Web: www.madisonalchamber.com

Manhattan Beach, CA

Manhattan Beach Chamber of Commerce
425 Fifteenth Street
Manhattan Beach, CA 90266
Phone: 310-545-5313
Fax: 310-545-7203
Web: www.manhattanbeachchamber.net

Maple Grove, MN

North Hennepin Area Chamber of Commerce
229 1st Avenue Northeast
Osseo, MN 55369
Phone: 763-424-6744
Fax: 763-424-6927
Web: www.nhachamber.com

Marion, IA

Cedar Rapids Area Chamber of Commerce
424 First Avenue NE
Cedar Rapids, IA 52401-1196
Phone: 319-398-5317
Fax: 319-398-5228
Web: www.cedarrapids.org

Marlboro, NJ

Western Monmouth Chamber of Commerce
17 Broad Street
Freehold, NJ 07728
Phone: 732-462-3030
Fax: 732-462-2123
Web: www.wmchamber.com

Matthews, NC

Matthews Chamber of Commerce
210 Matthews Stations St
Matthews, NC 28105
Phone: 704-847-3649
Web: www.matthewschamber.com

Meridian, ID

Meridan Chamber of Commerce
215 East Franklin Road
PO Box 7
Meridian, ID 83680
Phone: 208-888-2817
Fax: 208-888-2682
Web: www.meridianchamber.org

Merrimack, NH

Merrimack Chamber of Commerce
301 Daniel Webster Highway
PO Box 254
Merrimack, NH 03054
Phone: 603-424-3669
Fax: 603-429-4325
Web: www.merrimackchamber.org

Morgantown, WV

Morgantown Chamber of Commerce
1009 University Avenue
Morgantown, WV 26505
Phone: 304-292-3311
Fax: 304-296-6619
Web: www.mgnchamber.org

Mount Pleasant, SC

Mount Pleasant Office of Economic Development
Municipal Complex
100 Ann Edwards Lane
Mount Pleasant, SC 29465
Phone: 843-856-2504
Fax: 843-856-2180
Web: www.townofmountpleasant.com

Northampton, PA

Northampton Area Chamber of Commerce
PO Box 355
Northampton, PA 18067
Phone: 610-262-8669
Fax: 610-262-6250
Web: www.northamptonpa.com

Northville, MI

Northville Chamber of Commerce
195 S. Main Street
Northville, MI 48167
Phone: 248-349-7640
Fax: 248-349-8730
Web: www.northville.org

Novi, MI

Novi Chamber of Commerce
41875 W 11 Mile Road
Suite 201
Novi, MI 48374
Phone: 248-349-3743
Fax: 248-349-4523
Web: www.novichamber.com

O'Fallon, MO

O'Fallon Chamber of Commerce
1299 Bryan Road
O'Fallon, MO 63366
Phone: 636-240-1818
Fax: 636-281-8288
Web: www.ofallonchamber.org

Oro Valley, AZ

Oro Valley Community Development Dept.
11000 N La Canada Drive
Oro Valley, AZ 85737
Phone: 520-229-4700
Fax: 520-297-0428
Web: www.ci.oro-valley.az.us

Oviedo, FL

Oviedo Winter Springs Regional Chamber of Commerce
200 West Broadway Street
Oviedo, FL 32765
Phone: 407-365-6500
Fax: 407-365-6587
Web: www.oviedochamber.org

Palm Beach Gardens, FL

Northern Palm Beach County Chamber of Commerce
800 North US Highway One
Jupiter, FL 33477
Phone: 561-694-2300
Fax: 561-694-0126
Web: www.npbchamber.com

Parker, CO

Parker Chamber of Commerce
19751 E Mainstreet
R12
Parker, CO 80138
Phone: 303-841-4268
Fax: 303-841-8061
Web: www.parkerchamber.com

Peachtree City, GA

Fayette County Chamber of Commerce
200 Courthouse Square
Fayetteville, GA 30214
Phone: 770-461-9983
Fax: 770-461-9622
Web: www.fayettechamber.org

Pflugerville, TX

Pflugerville Chamber of Commerce
101 S. Third St.
Pflugerville, TX 78660
Phone: 512-251-7799
Fax: 512-251-7802
Web: www.pfchamber.com

Pleasanton, CA

Pleasanton Chamber of Commerce
777 Peters Avenue
Pleasanton, CA 94566
Phone: 925-846-5858
Fax: 925-846-9697
Web: www.pleasanton.org

Rapid City, SD

Rapid City Area Chamber of Commerce
444 Mt Rushmore Road North
PO Box 747
Rapid City, SD 57701
Phone: 605-343-1744
Fax: 605-343-6550
Web: www.rapidcitychamber.com

Redmond, WA

Greater Redmond Chamber of Commerce
16210 NE 80th Street
PO Box 628
Redmond, WA 98073-0625
Phone: 425-885-4014
Fax: 425-882-0996
Web: www.redmondchamber.org

Richland, WA

Richland Chamber of Commerce
505 Swift Blvd.
Richland, WA 99352
Phone: 509-924-7390
Web: www.ci.richland.wa.us

Richmond, KY

Richmond Chamber of Commerce
201 East Main Street
Richmond, KY 40475
Phone: 859-623-1720
Fax: 859-623-0839
Web: www.richmondchamber.com

Rio Rancho, NM

Rio Rancho Chamber of Commerce
4001 Southern Boulevard Southe
Rio Rancho, NM 87144
Phone: 505-892-1533
Fax: 505-892-6157
Web: www.rrchamber.org

Rockaway, NJ

Tri-County Chamber of Commerce
2055 Hamburg Turnpike
Wayne, NJ 07470
Phone: 973-831-7788
Fax: 973-831-9112
Web: www.tricounty.org

Rocklin, CA

Rocklin Chamber of Commerce
3700 Rocklin Road
Rocklin, CA 95677
Phone: 916-624-2548
Fax: 916-624-5743
Web: www.rocklinchamber.com

Rogers, AR

Rogers Chamber of Commerce
317 West Walnut Street
Rogers, AR 72756
Phone: 479-636-1240
Fax: 479-636-5485
Web: www.rogerslowell.com

Round Rock, TX

Round Rock Chamber of Commerce
212 East Main Street
Round Rock, TX 78664
Phone: 512-255-5805
Fax: 512-255-3345
Web: www.roundrockchamber.org

Sammamish, WA

Sammamish Chamber of Commerce
704 228th Avenue Northeast
#123
Sammamish, WA 98074
Phone: 425-681-4910
Fax: 425-484-6266
Web: www.sammamishchamber.org

San Ramon, CA

San Ramon Chamber of Commerce
12667 Alcosta Blvd.
Suite 160
San Ramon, CA 94583
Phone: 925-242-0600
Fax: 925-242-0603
Web: www.sanramon.org

Santa Fe, NM

Santa Fe Chamber of Commerce
8380 Cerrillos Road
#302
Santa Fe, NM 87507
Phone: 505-988-3279
Fax: 949-984-2205
Web: www.santafechamber.com

Saratoga, CA

Saratoga Chamber of Commerce
14485 Big Basin Way
Saratoga, CA 95070
Phone: 408-867-0753
Web: www.saratogachamber.org

Savage, MN

Savage Chamber of Commerce
14141 Glendale Road
Suite 210
Savage, MN 55378
Phone: 952-894-8876
Fax: 952-894-9906
Web: www.savagechamber.com

Schererville, IN

Schererville Chamber of Commerce
13 West Joliet Street
Schererville, IN 46375
Phone: 219-322-5412
Web: www.46375.org

Shawnee, KS

Shawnee Chamber of Commerce
15100 West 67th Street
Suite 202
Shawnee, KS 66218
Phone: 913-631-6545
Fax: 913-631-9628
Web: www.shawneekschamber.com

Shrewsbury, MA

Corridor Nine Area Chamber of Commerce
30 Lyman Street
Westborough, MA 01581
Phone: 508-836-4444
Fax: 508-836-2652
Web: www.corridornine.org

South Brunswick, NJ

South Brunswick Chamber of Commerce
PO Box 670
Monmouth Jnctn, NJ 08852
Phone: 732-297-2051
Fax: 732-297-1049
Web: www.sbchamber.com

South Jordan, UT

South Jordan Chamber of Commerce
1615 West Town Center Drive
South Jordan, UT 84095
Phone: 801-253-5200
Fax: 801-253-5201
Web: www.southjordanchamber.com

South Kingstown, RI

South Kingstown Chamber of Commerce
230 Old Tower Hill Road
Wakefield, RI 02879
Phone: 401-783-2801
Fax: 401-789-3120
Web: www.skchamber.com

Southaven, MS

Southaven Chamber of Commerce
8700 Northwest Drive
PO Box 211
Southaven, MS 38671
Phone: 662-342-6114
Fax: 662-342-6365
Web: www.southavenchamber.com

Southlake, TX

Southlake Chamber of Commerce
1501 Corporate Circle
Suite 100
Southlake, TX 76092
Phone: 817-481-8200
Web: www.southlakechamber.org

Spanish Fork, UT

Spanish Fork Area Chamber of Commerce
57 East 300 North
Spanish Fork, UT 84660
Phone: 801-798-8352
Web: www.spanishforkchamber.com

Sparks, NV

Sparks Chamber of Commerce
634 Pyramid Way
Sparks, NV 89431
Phone: 775-358-1976
Fax: 775-358-1992
Web: www.sparkschamber.org

Stow, OH

Stow-Munroe Falls Chamber of Commerce
4381 Hudson Drive
Suite K2
Stow, OH 44224
Phone: 330-688-1579
Fax: 330-688-6234
Web: www.smfcc.com

Sugar Land, TX

Fort Bend Chamber of Commerce
445 Commerce Green Boulevard
Sugar Land, TX 77478
Phone: 281-491-0800
Fax: 281-491-0112
Web: www.fortbendchamber.org

Sun Prairie, WI

Sun Prairie Chamber Of Commerce
109 East Main Street
Sun Prairie, WI 53590
Phone: 608-837-4547
Fax: 608-837-8765
Web: www.sunprairiechamber.com

Tualatin, OR

Tualatin Chamber of Commerce
18791 S.W. Martinazzi Ave.
Tualatin, OR 97062
Phone: 503-692-0780
Fax: 503-692-6955
Web: www.tualatinchamber.com

Waimalu, HI

Chamber of Commerce Hawaii
1132 Bishop Street
Suite 402
Honolulu, HI 96813
Phone: 808-545-4300
Fax: 808-545-4369
Web: www.cochawaii.com

Wellington, FL

Wellington Chamber of Commerce
12230 Forest Hill Boulevard
Suite 183
Wellington, FL 33414
Phone: 561-792-6525
Fax: 561-792-6200
Web: www.wellingtonchamber.com

West Des Moines, IA

West Des Moines Chamber of Commerce
4200 Mills Civic Parkway
PO Box 65320
West Des Moines, IA 50265
Phone: 515-225-6009
Fax: 515-225-7129
Web: www.wdmchamber.org

West Linn, OR

West Linn Chamber of Commerce
21420 Willamette Drive
West Linn, OR 97068
Phone: 503-655-6744
Web: www.westlinnchamber.com

West Windsor, NJ

Mercer Regional Chamber of Commerce
1A Quakerbridge Plaza Drive
Mercerville, NJ 08619
Phone: 609-689-9960
Fax: 609-586-9989
Web: www.mercerchamber.org

Weston, FL

Weston Chamber of Commerce
1290 Weston Road
Suite 200
Weston, FL 33326
Phone: 954-389-0600
Fax: 954-384-6133
Web: www.westonchamber.com

Woodbury, MN

Woodbury Chamber of Commerce
7650 Currell Boulevard
Suite 340
Woodbury, MN 55125
Phone: 651-578-0722
Fax: 651-578-7276
Web: www.woodburychamber.org

Woodridge, IL

Woodridge Area Chamber of Commerce
5 Plaza Drive
Suite 212
Woodridge, IL 60517
Phone: 630-960-7080
Fax: 630-852-2316
Web: www.woodridgechamber.org

Yorba Linda, CA

Yorba Linda Chamber of Commerce
17670 Yorba Linda Boulevard
Yorba Linda, CA 92886
Phone: 714-993-9537
Web: www.yorbalindachamber.org

Appendix E: State Departments of Labor

Alabama

Jim Bennett, Commissioner
Alabama Department of Labor
P.O. Box 303500
Montgomery, AL 36130-3500
Phone: (334) 242-3072
www.Alalabor.state.al.us

Alaska

Clark Bishop, Commissioner
Dept of Labor and Workforce Devel.
P.O. Box 11149
Juneau, AK 99822-2249
Phone: (907) 465-2700
www.labor.state.AK.us

Arizona

Brian C. Delfs, Director
Arizona Industrial Commission
800 West Washington Street
Phoenix, AZ 85007
Phone: (602) 542-4515
www.ica.state.AZ.us

Arkansas

James Salkeld, Director
Department of Labor
10421 West Markham
Little Rock, AR 72205
Phone: (501) 682-4500
www.Arkansas.gov/labor

California

Victoria Bradshaw, Director
Labor and Workforce Development
445 Golden Gate Ave., 10th Floor
San Francisco, CA 94102
Phone: (916) 263-1811
www.labor.CA.gov

Colorado

Donald J. Mares, Executive Director
Dept of Labor and Employment
633 17th St., 2nd Floor
Denver, CO 80202-3660
Phone: (888) 390-7936
www.COworkforce.com

Connecticut

Patricia H. Mayfield, Commissioner
Department of Labor
200 Folly Brook Blvd.
Wethersfield, CT 06109-1114
Phone: (860) 263-6000
www.CT.gov/dol

Delaware

Thomas B. Sharp, Secretary of Labor
Department of Labor
4425 N. Market St., 4th Floor
Wilmington, DE 19802
Phone: (302) 451-3423
www.Delawareworks.com

District of Columbia

Ms. Summer Spencer, Director
Employment Services Department
614 New York Ave., NE, Suite 300
Washington, DC 20002
Phone: (202) 671-1900
www.DOES.DC.gov

Florida

Monesia T. Brown, Director
Agency for Workforce Innovation
The Caldwell Building
107 East Madison St. Suite 100
Tallahassee, FL 32399-4120
Phone: (800) 342-3450
www.Floridajobs.org

Georgia

Michael Thurmond, Commissioner
Department of Labor
Sussex Place, Room 600
148 Andrew Young Intl Blvd., NE
Atlanta, GA 30303
Phone: (404) 656-3011
www.dol.state.GA.us

Hawaii

Director
Dept of Labor & Industrial Relations
830 Punchbowl Street
Honolulu, HI 96813
Phone: (808) 586-8842
wwwHawaii.gov/labor

Idaho

Robert B. Madsen, Director
Department of Labor
317 W. Main St.
Boise, ID 83735-0001
Phone: (208) 332-3579
www.labor.Idaho.gov

Illinois

Catherine M. Shannon, Director
Department of Labor
160 N. LaSalle Street, 13th Floor
Suite C-1300
Chicago, IL 60601
Phone: (312) 793-2800
www.state.IL.us/agency/idol

Indiana

Lori Torres, Dept of Labor
Indiana Government Center South
402 W. Washington Street
Room W195
Indianapolis, IN 46204
Phone: (317) 232-2655
www.IN.gov/labor

Iowa

David Neil, Labor Commissioner
Iowa Workforce Development
1000 East Grand Avenue
Des Moines, IA 50319-0209
Phone: (515) 242-5870
www.Iowaworkforce.org/labor

Kansas

Jim Garner, Secretary
Department of Labor
401 S.W. Topeka Blvd.
Topeka, KS 66603-3182
Phone: (785) 296-5000
www.dol.KS.gov

Kentucky

Philip Anderson, Commissioner
Department of Labor
1047 U.S. Hwy 127 South, Suite 4
Frankfort, KY 40601-4381
Phone: (502) 564-3070
www.labor.KY.gov

Louisiana

John Warner Smith, Secretary
Department of Labor
P.O. Box 94094
Baton Rouge, LA 70804-9094
Phone: (225) 342-3111
www.LAworks.net

Maine

Laura Fortman, Commissioner
Department of Labor
45 Commerce Street
Augusta, ME 04330
Phone: (207) 623-7900
www.state.ME.us/labor

Maryland

Tom Perez, Secretary
Department of Labor and Industry
500 N. Calvert Street
Suite 401
Baltimore, MD 21202
Phone: (410) 767-2357
www.dllr.state.MD.us

Massachusetts

Greg Noel, Secretary
Dept of Labor & Work Force Devel.
One Ashburton Place
Room 2112
Boston, MA 02108
Phone: (617) 626-7100
www.Mass.gov/eolwd

Michigan

Keith Cooley, Director
Dept of Labor & Economic Growth
P.O. Box 30004
Lansing, MI 48909
Phone: (517) 335-0400
www.Michigan.gov/cis

Minnesota

Steven A. Sviggum, Commissioner
Dept of Labor and Industry
443 Lafayette Road North
Saint Paul, MN 55155
Phone: (651) 284-5070
www.doli.state.MN.us

Mississippi

Tommye Dale Favre, Executive Director
Dept of Employment Security
P.O. Box 1699
Jackson, MS 39215-1699
Phone: (601) 321-6000
www.mdes.MS.gov

Missouri

Todd Smith, Director
Labor and Industrial Relations
P.O. Box 599
3315 W. Truman Boulevard
Jefferson City, MO 65102-0599
Phone: (573) 751-7500
www.dolir.MO.gov/lirc

Montana

Keith Kelly, Commissioner
Dept of Labor and Industry
P.O. Box 1728
Helena, MT 59624-1728
Phone: (406) 444-9091
www.dli.MT.gov

Nebraska

Fernando Lecuona, Commissioner
Department of Labor
550 South 16th Street
Box 94600
Lincoln, NE 68509-4600
Phone: (402) 471-9000
www.Nebraskaworkforce.com

Nevada

Michael Tanchek, Commissioner
Dept of Business and Industry
555 E. Washington Ave.
Suite 4100
Las Vegas, NV 89101-1050
Phone: (702) 486-2650
www.laborcommissioner.com

New Hampshire

George N. Copadis, Commissioner
Department of Labor
State Office Park South
95 Pleasant Street
Concord, NH 03301
Phone: (603) 271-3176
www.labor.state.NH.us

New Jersey

David Socolow, Commissioner
Department of Labor
John Fitch Plaza, 13th Floor
Suite D
Trenton, NJ 08625-0110
Phone: (609) 777-3200
lwd.dol.state.nj.us/labor

New Mexico

Betty D. Sparrow, Secretary
Department of Labor
401 Broadway, NE
Albuquerque, NM 87103-1928
Phone: (505) 841-8450
www.dol.state.NM.us

New York

M. Patricia Smith, Commissioner
Department of Labor
State Office Bldg. # 12
W.A. Harriman Campus
Albany, NY 12240
Phone: (518) 457-5519
www.labor.state.NY.us

North Carolina

Cherie K. Berry, Commissioner
Department of Labor
4 West Edenton Street
Raleigh, NC 27601-1092
Phone: (919) 733-7166
www.nclabor.com

North Dakota

Lisa Fair McEvers, Commissioner
Department of Labor
State Capitol Building
600 East Boulevard, Dept 406
Bismark, ND 58505-0340
Phone: (701) 328-2660
www.nd.gov/labor

Ohio

Kimberly A. Zurz, Director
Department of Commerce
77 South High Street, 22nd Floor
Columbus, OH 43215
Phone: (614) 644-2239
www.com.state.OH.us

Oklahoma

Lloyd Fields, Commissioner
Department of Labor
4001 N. Lincoln Blvd.
Oklahoma City, OK 73105-5212
Phone: (405) 528-1500
www.state.OK.us/~okdol

Oregon

Dan Gardner, Commissioner
Bureau of Labor and Industries
800 NE Oregon St., #32
Portland, OR 97232
Phone: (971) 673-0761
www.Oregon.gov/boli

Pennsylvania

Stephen M. Schmerin, Secretary
Dept of Labor and Industry
1700 Labor and Industry Bldg
7th and Forster Streets
Harrisburg, PA 17120
Phone: (717) 787-5279
www.dli.state.PA.us

Rhode Island

Adelita S. Orefice, Director
Department of Labor and Training
1511 Pontiac Avenue
Cranston, RI 02920
Phone: (401) 462-8000
www.dlt.state.RI.us

South Carolina

Adrienne R. Youmans, Director
Dept of Labor, Licensing & Regulations
P.O. Box 11329
Columbia, SC 29211-1329
Phone: (803) 896-4300
www.llr.state.SC.us

South Dakota

Pamela S. Roberts, Secretary
Department of Labor
700 Governors Drive
Pierre, SD 57501-2291
Phone: (605) 773-3682
www.state.SD.us

Tennessee

James G. Neeley, Commissioner
Dept of Labor & Workforce Development
Andrew Johnson Tower
710 James Robertson Pkwy
Nashville, TN 37243-0655
Phone: (615) 741-6642
www.state.TN.us/labor-wfd

Texas

Ronald Congleton, Labor Commissioner
Texas Workforce Commission
101 East 15th St.
Austin, TX 78778
Phone: (512) 475-2670
www.twc.state.TX.us

Utah

Sherrie Hayashi, Commissioner
Utah Labor Commission
P.O. Box 146610
Salt Lake City, UT 84114-6610
Phone: (801) 530-6800
Laborcommission.Utah.gov

Vermont

Patricia Moulton Pow, Commissioner
Department of Labor
5 Green Mountain Drive
P.O. Box 488
Montpelier, VT 05601-0488
Phone: (802) 828-4000
www.labor.verMont.gov

Virginia

C. Ray Davenport, Commissioner
Dept of Labor and Industry
Powers-Taylor Building
13 S. 13th Street
Richmond, VA 23219
Phone: (804) 371-2327
www.doli.Virginia.gov

Washington

Judy Schurke, Acting Director
Dept of Labor and Industries
P.O. Box 44001
Olympia, WA 98504-4001
Phone: (360) 902-4200
www.lni.WA.gov

West Virginia

David Mullens, Commissioner
Division of Labor
State Capitol Complex, Building #6
1900 Kanawha Blvd.
Charleston, WV 25305
Phone: (304) 558-7890
www.labor.state.WV.us

Wisconsin

Roberta Gassman, Secretary
Dept of Workforce Development
201 E. Washington Ave., #A400
P.O. Box 7946
Madison, WI 53707-7946
Phone: (608) 266-6861
www.dwd.state.WI.us

Wyoming

Cynthia Pomeroy, Director
Department of Employment
1510 East Pershing Blvd.
Cheyenne, WY 82002
Phone: (307) 777-7261
www.doe.state.WY.us

Source: *U.S. Department of Labor*
http://www.dol.gov/esa/contacts/state_of.htm

Appendix F: Comparative Statistics

Population Growth: City

City	1990 Census	2000 Census	2007 Estimate	2012 Projection	Population Growth (%) 1990-2000	Population Growth (%) 2000-2012
Allen, TX	19,208	43,554	73,030	92,773	126.7	113.0
Ankeny, IA	19,065	27,117	36,664	42,734	42.2	57.6
Apex, NC	7,092	20,212	28,400	34,004	185.0	68.2
Bangor, ME	33,181	31,473	30,824	30,347	-5.1	-3.6
Beavercreek, OH	33,946	37,984	39,794	40,817	11.9	7.5
Bellevue, NE	43,698	44,382	46,425	48,202	1.6	8.6
Bend, OR	34,266	52,029	72,339	86,617	51.8	66.5
Bernards, NJ	17,199	24,575	27,401	29,222	42.9	18.9
Bethlehem, NY	27,552	31,304	33,063	34,057	13.6	8.8
Bozeman, MT	23,499	27,509	33,712	38,073	17.1	38.4
Brentwood, TN	17,287	23,445	29,886	34,424	35.6	46.8
Brookfield, WI	35,183	38,649	39,357	39,738	9.9	2.8
Broomfield, CO	24,789	38,272	44,601	49,265	54.4	28.7
Burlington, VT	39,127	38,889	37,232	36,069	-0.6	-7.3
Carmel, IN	27,705	37,733	47,001	53,598	36.2	42.0
Cary, NC	49,835	94,536	109,793	121,357	89.7	28.4
Casper, WY	46,781	49,644	52,416	54,352	6.1	9.5
Cheshire, CT	25,684	28,543	29,299	29,717	11.1	4.1
Chino Hills, CA	38,388	66,787	76,056	82,933	74.0	24.2
Collierville, TN	15,439	31,872	37,957	41,675	106.4	30.8
Conway, AR	28,997	43,167	53,767	60,953	48.9	41.2
Coronado, CA	26,386	24,100	28,556	31,238	-8.7	29.6
Cranberry, PA	14,764	23,625	27,640	30,111	60.0	27.5
Dover, DE	28,449	32,135	35,435	38,142	13.0	18.7
Draper, UT	7,250	25,220	36,803	44,006	247.9	74.5
Dublin, OH	17,231	31,392	35,862	38,751	82.2	23.4
Edmond, OK	52,239	68,315	77,125	82,640	30.8	21.0
Evesham, NJ	35,309	42,275	47,843	51,265	19.7	21.3
Fargo, ND	74,372	90,599	91,758	93,165	21.8	2.8
Farmington, CT	20,619	23,641	25,270	26,276	14.7	11.1
Fishers, IN	12,437	37,835	60,775	76,023	204.2	100.9
Flower Mound, TX	15,788	50,702	65,576	76,168	221.1	50.2
Franklin, MA	22,095	29,560	31,449	32,523	33.8	10.0
Frederick, MD	41,381	52,767	59,273	63,478	27.5	20.3
Frisco, TX	6,767	33,714	80,107	110,533	398.2	227.9
Goodyear, AZ	6,328	18,911	45,059	61,403	198.8	224.7
Grand Blanc, MI	25,180	29,827	36,288	40,197	18.5	34.8
Greenburgh, NY	83,816	86,764	89,457	90,770	3.5	4.6
Greenwich, CT	58,397	61,101	62,437	63,137	4.6	3.3
Hampden, PA	20,384	24,135	26,207	27,557	18.4	14.2
Hilliard, OH	12,516	24,230	27,143	28,913	93.6	19.3
Hoover, AL	43,995	62,742	69,893	74,416	42.6	18.6
Huntersville, NC	9,131	24,960	38,378	47,223	173.4	89.2
Juneau, AK	26,751	30,711	31,197	31,587	14.8	2.9
Keller, TX	13,683	27,345	38,275	45,313	99.8	65.7
Kenner, LA	72,033	70,517	67,340	70,030	-2.1	-0.7
Kennesaw, GA	10,794	21,675	31,253	37,285	100.8	72.0
League City, TX	30,247	45,444	65,374	77,497	50.2	70.5
Leawood, KS	19,683	27,656	30,342	32,155	40.5	16.3
Lee's Summit, MO	46,585	70,700	82,759	90,189	51.8	27.6
Leesburg, VA	16,240	28,311	38,030	45,147	74.3	59.5
Lehi, UT	9,766	19,028	30,371	37,831	94.8	98.8
Lwr Providence, PA	19,351	22,390	25,805	27,844	15.7	24.4
Madison, AL	16,813	29,329	36,805	41,510	74.4	41.5
Manhattan Bch, CA	32,063	33,852	37,595	40,569	5.6	19.8
Maple Grove, MN	38,868	50,365	61,718	68,875	29.6	36.8
Marion, IA	21,274	26,294	30,869	33,805	23.6	28.6
Marlboro, NJ	27,974	36,398	40,193	42,410	30.1	16.5
Matthews, NC	14,681	22,127	25,128	27,369	50.7	23.7

City	1990 Census	2000 Census	2007 Estimate	2012 Projection	Population Growth (%) 1990-2000	2000-2012
Meridian, ID	12,266	34,919	55,012	68,394	184.7	95.9
Merrimack, NH	22,156	25,119	26,837	27,933	13.4	11.2
Morgantown, WV	26,814	26,809	28,962	30,123	0.0	12.4
Mt Pleasant, SC	33,294	47,609	58,507	65,691	43.0	38.0
Northampton, PA	35,406	39,384	41,326	42,596	11.2	8.2
Northville, MI	17,300	21,036	26,517	29,705	21.6	41.2
Novi, MI	33,103	47,386	54,858	59,356	43.1	25.3
O'Fallon, MO	21,851	46,169	66,824	80,344	111.3	74.0
Oro Valley, AZ	9,492	29,700	37,528	43,304	212.9	45.8
Oviedo, FL	11,588	26,316	32,172	36,509	127.1	38.7
Palm Bch Grdns, FL	24,518	35,058	49,851	59,560	43.0	69.9
Parker, CO	5,562	23,558	39,763	50,807	323.6	115.7
Peachtree City, GA	18,908	31,580	35,383	38,242	67.0	21.1
Pflugerville, TX	5,830	16,335	27,258	34,128	180.2	108.9
Pleasanton, CA	51,592	63,654	67,343	70,765	23.4	11.2
Rapid City, SD	55,829	59,607	61,942	63,478	6.8	6.5
Redmond, WA	36,936	45,256	48,554	50,963	22.5	12.6
Richland, WA	33,058	38,708	46,221	51,524	17.1	33.1
Richmond, KY	22,343	27,152	30,633	33,077	21.5	21.8
Rio Rancho, NM	32,674	51,765	71,284	84,681	58.4	63.6
Rockaway, NJ	19,668	22,930	26,073	27,966	16.6	22.0
Rocklin, CA	19,464	36,330	64,899	83,743	86.7	130.5
Rogers, AR	25,705	38,829	48,762	55,905	51.1	44.0
Round Rock, TX	32,854	61,136	85,275	101,318	86.1	65.7
Sammamish, WA	23,254	34,104	35,507	36,662	46.7	7.5
San Ramon, CA	35,463	44,722	51,565	56,413	26.1	26.1
Santa Fe, NM	56,919	62,203	70,863	76,629	9.3	23.2
Saratoga, CA	28,177	29,843	30,179	30,859	5.9	3.4
Savage, MN	9,906	21,115	27,522	31,936	113.2	51.2
Schererville, IN	19,752	24,851	29,231	32,089	25.8	29.1
Shawnee, KS	37,970	47,996	59,874	67,658	26.4	41.0
Shrewsbury, MA	24,146	31,640	33,390	34,397	31.0	8.7
S Brunswick, NJ	25,792	37,734	41,168	43,268	46.3	14.7
S. Jordan, UT	12,183	29,437	44,224	53,721	141.6	82.5
S Kingstown, RI	24,631	27,921	29,693	30,646	13.4	9.8
Southaven, MS	21,238	28,977	41,310	49,728	36.4	71.6
Southlake, TX	7,155	21,519	25,609	28,381	200.8	31.9
Spanish Fork, UT	12,183	20,246	27,926	33,194	66.2	64.0
Sparks, NV	54,716	66,346	86,298	100,168	21.3	51.0
Stow, OH	27,702	32,139	34,687	36,200	16.0	12.6
Sugar Land, TX	44,150	63,328	78,549	88,074	43.4	39.1
Sun Prairie, WI	15,836	20,369	25,940	29,449	28.6	44.6
Tualatin, OR	15,782	22,791	26,439	28,844	44.4	26.6
Waimalu, HI	29,967	29,371	30,244	30,889	-2.0	5.2
Wellington, FL	22,555	38,216	56,529	68,431	69.4	79.1
W Des Moines, IA	32,549	46,403	54,627	60,179	42.6	29.7
West Linn, OR	17,500	22,261	25,429	27,454	27.2	23.3
West Windsor, NJ	16,021	21,907	27,392	30,743	36.7	40.3
Weston, FL	10,099	49,286	67,538	78,734	388.0	59.7
Woodbury, MN	20,075	46,463	54,403	59,438	131.4	27.9
Woodridge, IL	27,524	30,934	34,123	36,006	12.4	16.4
Yorba Linda, CA	52,827	58,918	66,655	72,596	11.5	23.2
U.S.	248,709,873	281,421,906	301,045,522	314,920,978	13.2	11.9

Source: Claritas, Inc.

Population Growth: Metro Area

Metro Area	1990 Census	2000 Census	2007 Estimate	2012 Projection	Population Growth (%) 1990-2000	Population Growth (%) 2000-2012
Allen, TX	3,989,294	5,161,544	6,007,731	6,587,538	29.4	27.6
Ankeny, IA	416,346	481,394	535,121	572,357	15.6	18.9
Apex, NC	541,081	797,071	994,403	1,134,243	47.3	42.3
Bangor, ME	146,601	144,919	147,514	148,798	-1.1	2.7
Beavercreek, OH	843,857	848,153	842,572	835,991	0.5	-1.4
Bellevue, NE	685,797	767,041	827,708	869,447	11.8	13.4
Bend, OR	74,958	115,367	150,650	176,024	53.9	52.6
Bernards, NJ	16,845,992	18,323,002	18,887,605	19,111,248	8.8	4.3
Bethlehem, NY	809,443	825,875	855,337	872,264	2.0	5.6
Bozeman, MT	50,491	67,831	81,533	91,352	34.3	34.7
Brentwood, TN	1,048,218	1,311,789	1,458,115	1,561,775	25.1	19.1
Brookfield, WI	1,432,149	1,500,741	1,515,804	1,523,297	4.8	1.5
Broomfield, CO	1,666,935	2,179,296	2,409,380	2,564,246	30.7	17.7
Burlington, VT	177,059	198,889	206,666	211,157	12.3	6.2
Carmel, IN	1,294,217	1,525,104	1,672,360	1,771,434	17.8	16.2
Cary, NC	541,081	797,071	994,403	1,134,243	47.3	42.3
Casper, WY	61,226	66,533	70,888	73,963	8.7	11.2
Cheshire, CT	804,219	824,008	852,147	868,281	2.5	5.4
Chino Hills, CA	2,588,793	3,254,821	4,070,565	4,644,528	25.7	42.7
Collierville, TN	1,067,263	1,205,204	1,280,575	1,329,939	12.9	10.3
Conway, AR	535,034	610,518	654,175	684,190	14.1	12.1
Coronado, CA	2,498,016	2,813,833	3,021,921	3,217,765	12.6	14.4
Cranberry, PA	2,468,289	2,431,087	2,372,530	2,324,047	-1.5	-4.4
Dover, DE	110,993	126,697	150,020	167,394	14.1	32.1
Draper, UT	768,075	968,858	1,055,059	1,116,816	26.1	15.3
Dublin, OH	1,405,176	1,612,694	1,733,942	1,811,223	14.8	12.3
Edmond, OK	971,042	1,095,421	1,175,422	1,230,177	12.8	12.3
Evesham, NJ	5,435,470	5,687,147	5,862,653	5,970,852	4.6	5.0
Fargo, ND	153,296	174,367	187,764	196,539	13.7	12.7
Farmington, CT	1,123,706	1,148,618	1,197,603	1,226,581	2.2	6.8
Fishers, IN	1,294,217	1,525,104	1,672,360	1,771,434	17.8	16.2
Flower Mound, TX	3,989,294	5,161,544	6,007,731	6,587,538	29.4	27.6
Franklin, MA	4,133,895	4,391,344	4,405,560	4,387,315	6.2	-0.1
Frederick, MD	4,122,914	4,796,183	5,367,465	5,753,170	16.3	20.0
Frisco, TX	3,989,294	5,161,544	6,007,731	6,587,538	29.4	27.6
Goodyear, AZ	2,238,480	3,251,876	4,033,881	4,601,608	45.3	41.5
Grand Blanc, MI	430,459	436,141	445,377	449,692	1.3	3.1
Greenburgh, NY	16,845,992	18,323,002	18,887,605	19,111,248	8.8	4.3
Greenwich, CT	827,645	882,567	906,582	918,955	6.6	4.1
Hampden, PA	474,242	509,074	525,711	536,090	7.3	5.3
Hilliard, OH	1,405,176	1,612,694	1,733,942	1,811,223	14.8	12.3
Hoover, AL	956,894	1,052,238	1,103,474	1,136,522	10.0	8.0
Huntersville, NC	1,024,331	1,330,448	1,580,079	1,758,436	29.9	32.2
Juneau, AK	26,751	30,711	31,197	31,587	14.8	2.9
Keller, TX	3,989,294	5,161,544	6,007,731	6,587,538	29.4	27.6
Kenner, LA	1,264,391	1,316,510	1,054,044	1,254,608	4.1	-4.7
Kennesaw, GA	3,069,411	4,247,981	5,122,861	5,709,771	38.4	34.4
League City, TX	3,767,335	4,715,407	5,489,519	5,965,317	25.2	26.5
Leawood, KS	1,636,528	1,836,038	1,977,557	2,069,914	12.2	12.7
Lee's Summit, MO	1,636,528	1,836,038	1,977,557	2,069,914	12.2	12.7
Leesburg, VA	4,122,914	4,796,183	5,367,465	5,753,170	16.3	20.0
Lehi, UT	269,407	376,774	470,487	536,515	39.9	42.4
Lwr Providence, PA	5,435,470	5,687,147	5,862,653	5,970,852	4.6	5.0
Madison, AL	293,047	342,376	376,738	399,698	16.8	16.7
Manhattan Bch, CA	11,273,720	12,365,627	13,215,817	13,962,135	9.7	12.9
Maple Grove, MN	2,538,834	2,968,806	3,195,712	3,350,113	16.9	12.8
Marion, IA	210,640	237,230	249,061	256,804	12.6	8.3
Marlboro, NJ	16,845,992	18,323,002	18,887,605	19,111,248	8.8	4.3
Matthews, NC	1,024,331	1,330,448	1,580,079	1,758,436	29.9	32.2

Metro Area	1990 Census	2000 Census	2007 Estimate	2012 Projection	Population Growth (%)	
					1990-2000	2000-2012
Meridian, ID	319,596	464,840	568,090	642,974	45.4	38.3
Merrimack, NH	336,073	380,841	406,243	422,426	13.3	10.9
Morgantown, WV	104,546	111,200	115,435	118,038	6.4	6.1
Mt Pleasant, SC	506,875	549,033	610,328	655,197	8.3	19.3
Northampton, PA	5,435,470	5,687,147	5,862,653	5,970,852	4.6	5.0
Northville, MI	4,248,699	4,452,557	4,493,336	4,501,808	4.8	1.1
Novi, MI	4,248,699	4,452,557	4,493,336	4,501,808	4.8	1.1
O'Fallon, MO	2,582,013	2,700,011	2,811,262	2,881,180	4.6	6.7
Oro Valley, AZ	666,880	843,746	962,051	1,059,425	26.5	25.6
Oviedo, FL	1,224,852	1,644,561	2,028,962	2,309,299	34.3	40.4
Palm Bch Grdns, FL	4,056,100	5,007,564	5,522,069	5,896,545	23.5	17.8
Parker, CO	1,666,935	2,179,296	2,409,380	2,564,246	30.7	17.7
Peachtree City, GA	3,069,411	4,247,981	5,122,861	5,709,771	38.4	34.4
Pflugerville, TX	846,217	1,249,763	1,503,872	1,677,632	47.7	34.2
Pleasanton, CA	3,686,592	4,123,740	4,228,399	4,358,197	11.9	5.7
Rapid City, SD	103,221	112,818	119,619	123,962	9.3	9.9
Redmond, WA	2,559,164	3,043,878	3,270,362	3,439,521	18.9	13.0
Richland, WA	150,033	191,822	228,828	254,534	27.9	32.7
Richmond, KY	72,311	87,454	96,649	103,092	20.9	17.9
Rio Rancho, NM	599,416	729,649	819,948	885,373	21.7	21.3
Rockaway, NJ	16,845,992	18,323,002	18,887,605	19,111,248	8.8	4.3
Rocklin, CA	1,481,126	1,796,857	2,102,212	2,327,104	21.3	29.5
Rogers, AR	239,474	347,045	423,381	478,039	44.9	37.7
Round Rock, TX	846,217	1,249,763	1,503,872	1,677,632	47.7	34.2
Sammamish, WA	2,559,164	3,043,878	3,270,362	3,439,521	18.9	13.0
San Ramon, CA	3,686,592	4,123,740	4,228,399	4,358,197	11.9	5.7
Santa Fe, NM	98,928	129,292	143,831	153,765	30.7	18.9
Saratoga, CA	1,534,280	1,735,819	1,795,315	1,858,798	13.1	7.1
Savage, MN	2,538,834	2,968,806	3,195,712	3,350,113	16.9	12.8
Schererville, IN	8,182,076	9,098,316	9,528,166	9,790,431	11.2	7.6
Shawnee, KS	1,636,528	1,836,038	1,977,557	2,069,914	12.2	12.7
Shrewsbury, MA	709,728	750,963	790,359	813,336	5.8	8.3
S Brunswick, NJ	16,845,992	18,323,002	18,887,605	19,111,248	8.8	4.3
S. Jordan, UT	768,075	968,858	1,055,059	1,116,816	26.1	15.3
S Kingstown, RI	1,509,789	1,582,997	1,626,234	1,642,634	4.8	3.8
Southaven, MS	1,067,263	1,205,204	1,280,575	1,329,939	12.9	10.3
Southlake, TX	3,989,294	5,161,544	6,007,731	6,587,538	29.4	27.6
Spanish Fork, UT	269,407	376,774	470,487	536,515	39.9	42.4
Sparks, NV	257,193	342,885	408,722	456,898	33.3	33.3
Stow, OH	657,575	694,960	703,447	706,262	5.7	1.6
Sugar Land, TX	3,767,335	4,715,407	5,489,519	5,965,317	25.2	26.5
Sun Prairie, WI	432,323	501,774	544,682	572,776	16.1	14.2
Tualatin, OR	1,523,741	1,927,881	2,138,513	2,283,958	26.5	18.5
Waimalu, HI	836,231	876,156	914,561	941,510	4.8	7.5
Wellington, FL	4,056,100	5,007,564	5,522,069	5,896,545	23.5	17.8
W Des Moines, IA	416,346	481,394	535,121	572,357	15.6	18.9
West Linn, OR	1,523,741	1,927,881	2,138,513	2,283,958	26.5	18.5
West Windsor, NJ	325,804	350,761	370,167	382,207	7.7	9.0
Weston, FL	4,056,100	5,007,564	5,522,069	5,896,545	23.5	17.8
Woodbury, MN	2,538,834	2,968,806	3,195,712	3,350,113	16.9	12.8
Woodridge, IL	8,182,076	9,098,316	9,528,166	9,790,431	11.2	7.6
Yorba Linda, CA	11,273,720	12,365,627	13,215,817	13,962,135	9.7	12.9
U.S.	248,709,873	281,421,906	301,045,522	314,920,978	13.2	11.9

Note: Figures cover the Metropolitan Statistical Area (MSA) - see Appendix B for areas included
Source: Claritas, Inc.

Number of Households and Average Household Size: City

City	2007 Estimate	2007 Average Household Size
Allen, TX	23,954	3.05
Ankeny, IA	14,413	2.54
Apex, NC	10,460	2.72
Bangor, ME	13,992	2.20
Beavercreek, OH	15,357	2.59
Bellevue, NE	18,227	2.55
Bend, OR	30,240	2.39
Bernards, NJ	10,105	2.71
Bethlehem, NY	12,996	2.54
Bozeman, MT	13,611	2.48
Brentwood, TN	9,931	3.01
Brookfield, WI	14,755	2.67
Broomfield, CO	16,282	2.74
Burlington, VT	15,530	2.40
Carmel, IN	17,059	2.76
Cary, NC	40,117	2.74
Casper, WY	21,888	2.39
Cheshire, CT	9,678	3.03
Chino Hills, CA	22,198	3.43
Collierville, TN	12,577	3.02
Conway, AR	19,702	2.73
Coronado, CA	8,976	3.18
Cranberry, PA	9,808	2.82
Dover, DE	13,973	2.54
Draper, UT	9,754	3.77
Dublin, OH	13,027	2.75
Edmond, OK	29,028	2.66
Evesham, NJ	18,026	2.65
Fargo, ND	41,663	2.20
Farmington, CT	10,141	2.49
Fishers, IN	22,612	2.69
Flower Mound, TX	20,691	3.17
Franklin, MA	10,749	2.93
Frederick, MD	23,699	2.50
Frisco, TX	29,268	2.74
Goodyear, AZ	15,541	2.90
Grand Blanc, MI	14,526	2.50
Greenburgh, NY	34,116	2.62
Greenwich, CT	23,594	2.65
Hampden, PA	10,666	2.46
Hilliard, OH	9,564	2.84
Hoover, AL	28,331	2.47
Huntersville, NC	14,446	2.66
Juneau, AK	11,865	2.63
Keller, TX	12,057	3.17
Kenner, LA	25,142	2.68
Kennesaw, GA	11,748	2.66
League City, TX	23,502	2.78
Leawood, KS	10,939	2.77
Lee's Summit, MO	30,701	2.70
Leesburg, VA	13,392	2.84
Lehi, UT	8,175	3.72
Lwr Providence, PA	8,603	3.00
Madison, AL	14,017	2.63
Manhattan Bch, CA	15,819	2.38
Maple Grove, MN	21,815	2.83
Marion, IA	12,739	2.42
Marlboro, NJ	12,711	3.16
Matthews, NC	9,149	2.75

City	2007 Estimate	2007 Average Household Size
Meridian, ID	19,026	2.89
Merrimack, NH	9,639	2.78
Morgantown, WV	11,298	2.56
Mt Pleasant, SC	24,036	2.43
Northampton, PA	13,861	2.98
Northville, MI	10,302	2.57
Novi, MI	21,904	2.50
O'Fallon, MO	22,667	2.95
Oro Valley, AZ	15,576	2.41
Oviedo, FL	10,343	3.11
Palm Bch Grdns, FL	22,425	2.22
Parker, CO	13,601	2.92
Peachtree City, GA	12,380	2.86
Pflugerville, TX	8,574	3.18
Pleasanton, CA	24,418	2.76
Rapid City, SD	25,659	2.41
Redmond, WA	21,120	2.30
Richland, WA	18,441	2.51
Richmond, KY	12,750	2.40
Rio Rancho, NM	26,500	2.69
Rockaway, NJ	9,320	2.80
Rocklin, CA	23,461	2.77
Rogers, AR	17,178	2.84
Round Rock, TX	29,688	2.87
Sammamish, WA	11,620	3.06
San Ramon, CA	19,743	2.61
Santa Fe, NM	31,770	2.23
Saratoga, CA	10,346	2.92
Savage, MN	8,749	3.15
Schererville, IN	11,521	2.54
Shawnee, KS	23,167	2.58
Shrewsbury, MA	13,136	2.54
S Brunswick, NJ	14,352	2.87
S. Jordan, UT	11,498	3.85
S Kingstown, RI	10,176	2.92
Southaven, MS	16,217	2.55
Southlake, TX	7,492	3.42
Spanish Fork, UT	7,592	3.68
Sparks, NV	31,178	2.77
Stow, OH	13,485	2.57
Sugar Land, TX	25,597	3.07
Sun Prairie, WI	10,242	2.53
Tualatin, OR	9,987	2.65
Waimalu, HI	11,071	2.73
Wellington, FL	19,312	2.93
W Des Moines, IA	23,815	2.29
West Linn, OR	9,496	2.68
West Windsor, NJ	8,955	3.06
Weston, FL	22,032	3.07
Woodbury, MN	19,882	2.74
Woodridge, IL	12,724	2.68
Yorba Linda, CA	21,728	3.07
U.S.	113,668,003	2.65

Source: Claritas, Inc.

Number of Households and Average Household Size: Metro Area

City	2007 Estimate	2007 Average Household Size
Allen, TX	2,171,092	2.77
Ankeny, IA	214,222	2.50
Apex, NC	384,764	2.58
Bangor, ME	61,282	2.41
Beavercreek, OH	344,303	2.45
Bellevue, NE	322,040	2.57
Bend, OR	61,521	2.45
Bernards, NJ	6,870,593	2.75
Bethlehem, NY	348,278	2.46
Bozeman, MT	32,166	2.53
Brentwood, TN	575,173	2.54
Brookfield, WI	610,139	2.48
Broomfield, CO	939,573	2.56
Burlington, VT	80,431	2.57
Carmel, IN	658,480	2.54
Cary, NC	384,764	2.58
Casper, WY	29,176	2.43
Cheshire, CT	332,237	2.56
Chino Hills, CA	1,272,937	3.20
Collierville, TN	482,754	2.65
Conway, AR	263,287	2.48
Coronado, CA	1,072,228	2.82
Cranberry, PA	991,033	2.39
Dover, DE	56,867	2.64
Draper, UT	345,652	3.05
Dublin, OH	691,073	2.51
Edmond, OK	470,187	2.50
Evesham, NJ	2,221,104	2.64
Fargo, ND	78,017	2.41
Farmington, CT	467,253	2.56
Fishers, IN	658,480	2.54
Flower Mound, TX	2,171,092	2.77
Franklin, MA	1,705,968	2.58
Frederick, MD	2,029,059	2.65
Frisco, TX	2,171,092	2.77
Goodyear, AZ	1,468,904	2.75
Grand Blanc, MI	176,414	2.52
Greenburgh, NY	6,870,593	2.75
Greenwich, CT	332,643	2.73
Hampden, PA	211,758	2.48
Hilliard, OH	691,073	2.51
Hoover, AL	440,039	2.51
Huntersville, NC	614,864	2.57
Juneau, AK	11,865	2.63
Keller, TX	2,171,092	2.77
Kenner, LA	401,314	2.63
Kennesaw, GA	1,865,741	2.75
League City, TX	1,914,046	2.87
Leawood, KS	779,422	2.54
Lee's Summit, MO	779,422	2.54
Leesburg, VA	2,029,059	2.65
Lehi, UT	129,123	3.64
Lwr Providence, PA	2,221,104	2.64
Madison, AL	152,044	2.48
Manhattan Bch, CA	4,301,513	3.07
Maple Grove, MN	1,237,926	2.58
Marion, IA	101,304	2.46
Marlboro, NJ	6,870,593	2.75
Matthews, NC	614,864	2.57

City	2007 Estimate	2007 Average Household Size
Meridian, ID	210,196	2.70
Merrimack, NH	155,658	2.61
Morgantown, WV	47,326	2.44
Mt Pleasant, SC	239,842	2.54
Northampton, PA	2,221,104	2.64
Northville, MI	1,738,130	2.59
Novi, MI	1,738,130	2.59
O'Fallon, MO	1,110,162	2.53
Oro Valley, AZ	383,384	2.51
Oviedo, FL	778,178	2.61
Palm Bch Grdns, FL	2,079,180	2.66
Parker, CO	939,573	2.56
Peachtree City, GA	1,865,741	2.75
Pflugerville, TX	568,544	2.65
Pleasanton, CA	1,571,191	2.69
Rapid City, SD	47,603	2.51
Redmond, WA	1,302,483	2.51
Richland, WA	79,651	2.87
Richmond, KY	38,620	2.50
Rio Rancho, NM	324,089	2.53
Rockaway, NJ	6,870,593	2.75
Rocklin, CA	777,373	2.70
Rogers, AR	160,797	2.63
Round Rock, TX	568,544	2.65
Sammamish, WA	1,302,483	2.51
San Ramon, CA	1,571,191	2.69
Santa Fe, NM	59,497	2.42
Saratoga, CA	593,262	3.03
Savage, MN	1,237,926	2.58
Schererville, IN	3,431,388	2.78
Shawnee, KS	779,422	2.54
Shrewsbury, MA	303,536	2.60
S Brunswick, NJ	6,870,593	2.75
S. Jordan, UT	345,652	3.05
S Kingstown, RI	637,423	2.55
Southaven, MS	482,754	2.65
Southlake, TX	2,171,092	2.77
Spanish Fork, UT	129,123	3.64
Sparks, NV	157,092	2.60
Stow, OH	282,029	2.49
Sugar Land, TX	1,914,046	2.87
Sun Prairie, WI	225,458	2.42
Tualatin, OR	829,870	2.58
Waimalu, HI	304,505	3.00
Wellington, FL	2,079,180	2.66
W Des Moines, IA	214,222	2.50
West Linn, OR	829,870	2.58
West Windsor, NJ	133,646	2.77
Weston, FL	2,079,180	2.66
Woodbury, MN	1,237,926	2.58
Woodridge, IL	3,431,388	2.78
Yorba Linda, CA	4,301,513	3.07
U.S.	113,668,003	2.65

Note: Figures cover the Metropolitan Statistical Area (MSA) - see Appendix B for areas included
Source: Claritas, Inc.

Race and Ethnicity: City

City	White alone[2]	Black alone[2]	Asian alone[2]	Other Race alone[2]	Hispanic[3]
Allen, TX	79.8	6.9	6.8	6.5	.9.3
Ankeny, IA	95.8	1.0	1.2	2.0	1.6
Apex, NC	84.8	4.9	6.2	4.0	4.4
Bangor, ME	94.3	1.2	1.4	3.1	1.6
Beavercreek, OH	91.6	1.7	4.6	2.1	1.6
Bellevue, NE	84.6	5.7	2.2	7.5	8.0
Bend, OR	92.3	0.6	1.2	6.0	6.6
Bernards, NJ	83.6	1.7	12.9	1.9	3.4
Bethlehem, NY	93.7	2.5	2.2	1.6	2.2
Bozeman, MT	94.2	0.5	1.3	4.0	2.4
Brentwood, TN	92.9	1.9	3.9	1.2	1.5
Brookfield, WI	91.5	1.3	5.8	1.5	1.4
Broomfield, CO	87.2	1.2	4.5	7.1	10.7
Burlington, VT	90.6	2.2	3.1	4.2	1.6
Carmel, IN	87.6	3.2	6.7	2.4	2.8
Cary, NC	77.6	6.4	11.3	4.7	5.6
Casper, WY	93.7	1.1	0.4	4.8	5.5
Cheshire, CT	87.5	5.0	3.4	4.1	4.4
Chino Hills, CA	47.7	6.1	28.6	17.6	29.4
Collierville, TN	86.4	8.8	2.6	2.2	2.2
Conway, AR	82.1	13.4	1.3	3.2	3.5
Coronado, CA	82.7	4.8	4.4	8.1	11.5
Cranberry, PA	95.5	1.2	2.2	1.2	1.0
Dover, DE	49.2	41.8	3.7	5.3	5.1
Draper, UT	91.2	1.3	1.5	6.0	6.5
Dublin, OH	86.3	2.5	9.4	1.7	1.6
Edmond, OK	84.7	4.4	3.7	7.2	3.7
Evesham, NJ	88.9	3.5	5.6	2.0	2.6
Fargo, ND	92.9	1.6	1.6	3.9	1.6
Farmington, CT	91.0	1.5	5.2	2.3	2.7
Fishers, IN	86.1	6.3	4.9	2.7	3.3
Flower Mound, TX	86.2	4.2	5.1	4.5	6.8
Franklin, MA	94.4	1.6	2.3	1.6	1.6
Frederick, MD	67.5	18.1	5.7	8.7	9.9
Frisco, TX	81.8	7.2	4.2	6.9	11.7
Goodyear, AZ	77.1	5.3	2.4	15.2	20.6
Grand Blanc, MI	87.4	6.9	2.8	2.9	2.2
Greenburgh, NY	70.0	12.8	10.4	6.9	11.0
Greenwich, CT	88.6	1.4	6.3	3.7	7.8
Hampden, PA	92.3	1.2	4.9	1.6	1.6
Hilliard, OH	89.8	2.2	4.8	3.2	2.8
Hoover, AL	82.4	10.1	3.7	3.8	5.9
Huntersville, NC	86.2	7.7	1.9	4.2	7.3
Juneau, AK	73.4	1.1	5.2	20.3	4.0
Keller, TX	91.8	1.9	2.1	4.1	6.1
Kenner, LA	64.8	23.7	3.7	7.9	15.6
Kennesaw, GA	74.7	13.4	4.1	7.7	10.1
League City, TX	82.0	5.2	4.0	8.8	15.0
Leawood, KS	93.9	2.2	2.3	1.6	1.9
Lee's Summit, MO	91.6	4.5	1.1	2.8	2.7
Leesburg, VA	74.1	9.7	6.8	9.5	11.8
Lehi, UT	93.9	0.3	0.6	5.2	4.4
Lwr Providence, PA	83.2	7.9	6.6	2.3	2.9
Madison, AL	78.0	14.1	4.0	4.0	2.8
Manhattan Bch, CA	88.0	0.6	7.0	4.3	4.9
Maple Grove, MN	93.6	1.2	3.0	2.2	1.4
Marion, IA	96.3	0.8	1.0	1.9	1.2
Marlboro, NJ	79.3	1.7	17.2	1.8	3.6
Matthews, NC	85.7	7.9	3.2	3.3	4.4
Meridian, ID	92.9	0.6	1.5	5.0	4.7
Merrimack, NH	95.6	0.7	2.2	1.5	1.4

City	White alone[2]	Black alone[2]	Asian alone[2]	Other Race alone[2]	Hispanic[3]
Morgantown, WV	90.4	3.9	3.2	2.5	1.8
Mt Pleasant, SC	92.7	4.1	1.5	1.7	1.7
Northampton, PA	96.2	0.4	2.4	1.0	1.1
Northville, MI	88.7	3.7	5.2	2.4	2.4
Novi, MI	81.3	3.0	12.9	2.7	2.2
O'Fallon, MO	92.7	3.3	1.6	2.4	1.8
Oro Valley, AZ	91.9	1.3	2.4	4.4	8.5
Oviedo, FL	81.9	8.3	3.2	6.6	16.5
Palm Bch Grdns, FL	92.2	3.1	2.6	2.1	8.1
Parker, CO	89.5	1.6	2.6	6.3	7.8
Peachtree City, GA	82.2	9.5	4.9	3.4	5.1
Pflugerville, TX	72.4	11.8	5.7	10.1	21.2
Pleasanton, CA	75.1	1.4	15.9	7.5	8.4
Rapid City, SD	83.3	1.2	0.8	14.7	3.4
Redmond, WA	73.0	1.7	17.3	7.9	8.0
Richland, WA	88.0	1.6	4.7	5.7	5.7
Richmond, KY	88.3	7.4	1.5	2.8	1.5
Rio Rancho, NM	75.8	2.6	1.4	20.3	32.0
Rockaway, NJ	85.0	3.4	7.6	4.0	8.8
Rocklin, CA	82.9	1.5	7.3	8.3	8.6
Rogers, AR	78.8	1.1	2.0	18.1	30.0
Round Rock, TX	69.3	10.7	4.8	15.1	25.5
Sammamish, WA	83.1	1.1	11.6	4.2	3.0
San Ramon, CA	70.5	1.9	20.0	7.7	8.7
Santa Fe, NM	76.1	1.0	1.5	21.3	48.7
Saratoga, CA	58.4	0.4	37.8	3.4	3.2
Savage, MN	80.5	3.0	13.2	3.3	2.1
Schererville, IN	88.2	3.2	3.3	5.4	8.4
Shawnee, KS	87.0	4.3	3.4	5.2	5.7
Shrewsbury, MA	84.8	1.8	11.1	2.2	1.7
S Brunswick, NJ	60.7	8.9	25.7	4.8	6.6
S. Jordan, UT	94.3	0.4	1.2	4.0	4.3
S Kingstown, RI	90.4	1.8	3.7	4.1	2.2
Southaven, MS	81.6	13.9	1.2	3.3	3.4
Southlake, TX	92.4	2.1	2.5	3.0	4.7
Spanish Fork, UT	93.9	0.2	0.4	5.5	5.6
Sparks, NV	75.1	2.6	5.5	16.9	24.3
Stow, OH	94.1	1.9	2.3	1.7	1.2
Sugar Land, TX	54.8	6.4	32.2	6.6	9.6
Sun Prairie, WI	90.1	3.9	2.0	4.0	3.8
Tualatin, OR	83.5	0.9	4.4	11.2	16.2
Waimalu, HI	16.1	3.4	55.5	25.0	6.5
Wellington, FL	84.6	7.5	2.4	5.5	16.8
W Des Moines, IA	90.6	2.3	3.6	3.6	3.8
West Linn, OR	91.4	0.6	4.1	3.9	3.9
West Windsor, NJ	60.7	2.6	33.2	3.5	4.9
Weston, FL	83.9	5.2	4.1	6.8	38.4
Woodbury, MN	82.0	4.3	10.2	3.5	2.9
Woodridge, IL	67.7	10.4	14.8	7.1	12.2
Yorba Linda, CA	80.5	1.2	11.9	6.4	11.1
U.S.	73.1	12.4	4.3	10.3	14.9

Note: Figures are 2007 estimates; (2) Alone is defined as not being in combination with one or more other races; (3) May be of any race
Source: Claritas, Inc.

Race and Ethnicity: Metro Area

Metro Area	White alone[2]	Black alone[2]	Asian alone[2]	Other Race alone[2]	Hispanic[3]
Allen, TX	65.6	14.0	4.6	15.8	26.4
Ankeny, IA	88.8	3.8	2.5	4.9	5.4
Apex, NC	69.7	20.2	3.6	6.5	8.2
Bangor, ME	96.3	0.6	0.8	2.3	0.9
Beavercreek, OH	81.1	14.8	1.6	2.6	1.5
Bellevue, NE	84.5	7.7	1.8	6.0	7.2
Bend, OR	93.3	0.4	0.9	5.4	5.5
Bernards, NJ	59.5	17.6	8.8	14.1	21.2
Bethlehem, NY	87.0	7.1	2.8	3.1	3.0
Bozeman, MT	95.5	0.3	0.8	3.4	2.4
Brentwood, TN	78.4	15.2	1.9	4.5	5.0
Brookfield, WI	74.7	16.4	2.5	6.4	7.8
Broomfield, CO	77.3	5.4	3.4	14.0	22.3
Burlington, VT	94.8	0.9	1.7	2.6	1.1
Carmel, IN	79.8	14.5	1.6	4.0	4.3
Cary, NC	69.7	20.2	3.6	6.5	8.2
Casper, WY	93.7	1.0	0.4	4.9	5.0
Cheshire, CT	76.2	12.0	3.2	8.5	12.4
Chino Hills, CA	57.5	7.6	5.1	29.9	44.0
Collierville, TN	50.0	45.4	1.7	3.0	3.3
Conway, AR	73.5	22.0	1.2	3.3	2.9
Coronado, CA	63.8	5.0	10.1	21.1	30.0
Cranberry, PA	88.9	8.2	1.4	1.5	0.9
Dover, DE	71.7	21.8	1.9	4.6	3.9
Draper, UT	84.4	1.2	2.7	11.7	14.9
Dublin, OH	79.4	14.0	2.8	3.7	2.6
Edmond, OK	74.2	10.6	2.7	12.5	8.9
Evesham, NJ	70.2	20.5	4.1	5.2	6.2
Fargo, ND	94.0	1.1	1.1	3.8	2.0
Farmington, CT	78.4	10.1	3.0	8.5	10.6
Fishers, IN	79.8	14.5	1.6	4.0	4.3
Flower Mound, TX	65.6	14.0	4.6	15.8	26.4
Franklin, MA	80.7	6.3	5.8	7.2	7.7
Frederick, MD	56.8	26.0	8.2	9.0	11.6
Frisco, TX	65.6	14.0	4.6	15.8	26.4
Goodyear, AZ	73.2	4.0	2.5	20.3	29.9
Grand Blanc, MI	75.5	19.8	0.9	3.8	2.5
Greenburgh, NY	59.5	17.6	8.8	14.1	21.2
Greenwich, CT	77.1	10.0	4.0	8.8	14.5
Hampden, PA	84.8	9.7	2.2	3.3	3.4
Hilliard, OH	79.4	14.0	2.8	3.7	2.6
Hoover, AL	68.5	28.3	0.9	2.3	2.7
Huntersville, NC	68.3	23.5	2.6	5.7	8.0
Juneau, AK	73.4	1.1	5.2	20.3	4.0
Keller, TX	65.6	14.0	4.6	15.8	26.4
Kenner, LA	63.2	30.3	2.7	3.9	5.5
Kennesaw, GA	59.0	30.7	4.0	6.2	9.1
League City, TX	60.2	16.4	5.6	17.8	33.0
Leawood, KS	80.1	12.1	1.9	5.8	6.7
Lee's Summit, MO	80.1	12.1	1.9	5.8	6.7
Leesburg, VA	56.8	26.0	8.2	9.0	11.6
Lehi, UT	91.2	0.3	1.1	7.3	8.6
Lwr Providence, PA	70.2	20.5	4.1	5.2	6.2
Madison, AL	73.1	21.5	1.7	3.7	2.5
Manhattan Bch, CA	50.2	7.4	13.6	28.8	44.0
Maple Grove, MN	83.4	6.2	4.9	5.5	4.4
Marion, IA	93.8	2.6	1.3	2.4	1.5
Marlboro, NJ	59.5	17.6	8.8	14.1	21.2
Matthews, NC	68.3	23.5	2.6	5.7	8.0

Metro Area	White alone[2]	Black alone[2]	Asian alone[2]	Other Race alone[2]	Hispanic[3]
Meridian, ID	88.3	0.6	1.4	9.6	10.6
Merrimack, NH	91.8	1.5	3.0	3.7	4.4
Morgantown, WV	94.0	2.6	1.6	1.9	1.1
Mt Pleasant, SC	65.4	29.7	1.5	3.4	3.1
Northampton, PA	70.2	20.5	4.1	5.2	6.2
Northville, MI	69.8	22.9	3.1	4.2	3.5
Novi, MI	69.8	22.9	3.1	4.2	3.5
O'Fallon, MO	77.6	18.3	1.8	2.4	1.9
Oro Valley, AZ	72.8	3.1	2.3	21.8	32.5
Oviedo, FL	70.5	15.0	3.4	11.0	22.0
Palm Bch Grdns, FL	69.7	19.8	2.0	8.5	38.4
Parker, CO	77.3	5.4	3.4	14.0	22.3
Peachtree City, GA	59.0	30.7	4.0	6.2	9.1
Pflugerville, TX	70.2	7.4	4.3	18.1	29.6
Pleasanton, CA	53.6	8.7	21.9	15.9	19.7
Rapid City, SD	87.2	1.1	0.7	11.0	3.4
Redmond, WA	75.0	5.2	10.1	9.6	6.9
Richland, WA	77.5	1.4	2.2	19.0	24.7
Richmond, KY	93.8	3.4	0.8	1.9	1.1
Rio Rancho, NM	67.8	2.6	1.7	27.9	43.5
Rockaway, NJ	59.5	17.6	8.8	14.1	21.2
Rocklin, CA	65.8	7.2	10.8	16.2	17.9
Rogers, AR	85.9	1.7	1.7	10.7	13.2
Round Rock, TX	70.2	7.4	4.3	18.1	29.6
Sammamish, WA	75.0	5.2	10.1	9.6	6.9
San Ramon, CA	53.6	8.7	21.9	15.9	19.7
Santa Fe, NM	72.7	1.0	1.0	25.3	49.4
Saratoga, CA	48.6	2.5	29.7	19.2	25.9
Savage, MN	83.4	6.2	4.9	5.5	4.4
Schererville, IN	65.1	18.0	5.0	11.9	19.3
Shawnee, KS	80.1	12.1	1.9	5.8	6.7
Shrewsbury, MA	86.9	3.5	3.7	6.0	8.0
S Brunswick, NJ	59.5	17.6	8.8	14.1	21.2
S. Jordan, UT	84.4	1.2	2.7	11.7	14.9
S Kingstown, RI	84.4	4.3	2.3	9.0	9.0
Southaven, MS	50.0	45.4	1.7	3.0	3.3
Southlake, TX	65.6	14.0	4.6	15.8	26.4
Spanish Fork, UT	91.2	0.3	1.1	7.3	8.6
Sparks, NV	77.2	2.2	4.9	15.8	20.5
Stow, OH	84.5	11.7	1.6	2.2	1.1
Sugar Land, TX	60.2	16.4	5.6	17.8	33.0
Sun Prairie, WI	88.1	3.7	3.9	4.3	4.1
Tualatin, OR	82.1	2.7	5.3	9.9	9.7
Waimalu, HI	20.6	2.9	46.3	30.2	7.2
Wellington, FL	69.7	19.8	2.0	8.5	38.4
W Des Moines, IA	88.8	3.8	2.5	4.9	5.4
West Linn, OR	82.1	2.7	5.3	9.9	9.7
West Windsor, NJ	63.6	19.9	7.9	8.6	12.3
Weston, FL	69.7	19.8	2.0	8.5	38.4
Woodbury, MN	83.4	6.2	4.9	5.5	4.4
Woodridge, IL	65.1	18.0	5.0	11.9	19.3
Yorba Linda, CA	50.2	7.4	13.6	28.8	44.0
U.S.	73.1	12.4	4.3	10.3	14.9

Note: Figures are 2007 estimates and cover the Metropolitan Statistical Area (MSA) - see Appendix B for areas included
(2) Alone is defined as not being in combination with one or more other races; (3) May be of any race
Source: Claritas, Inc.

Age Distribution: City

Area	Percent of Population						
	Under Age 5	Age 5 to 17	Age 18 to 34	Age 35 to 49	Age 50 to 64	Age 65 to 79	80 Years and Over
Allen, TX	10.6	24.1	23.0	30.5	8.9	2.3	0.5
Ankeny, IA	8.2	19.0	28.4	23.6	12.9	5.6	2.3
Apex, NC	10.2	20.4	28.2	28.5	8.5	3.1	1.1
Bangor, ME	5.6	15.5	27.1	22.9	14.8	9.9	4.2
Beavercreek, OH	5.2	20.0	15.9	26.2	20.6	9.5	2.6
Bellevue, NE	7.0	20.2	24.9	23.2	15.3	7.8	1.5
Bend, OR	6.8	17.6	25.7	23.4	14.3	8.5	3.7
Bernards, NJ	8.0	19.7	13.0	30.5	16.4	9.0	3.4
Bethlehem, NY	6.4	21.0	15.0	26.1	17.1	9.6	4.7
Bozeman, MT	5.0	11.4	49.8	17.3	8.8	4.8	3.0
Brentwood, TN	6.2	25.7	9.8	29.7	21.0	6.4	1.2
Brookfield, WI	5.6	21.0	11.2	25.8	18.7	13.6	4.1
Broomfield, CO	7.7	21.6	23.0	28.4	12.7	5.4	1.2
Burlington, VT	4.3	12.0	42.9	19.0	11.3	7.3	3.3
Carmel, IN	7.9	22.4	15.7	27.8	16.4	6.8	3.0
Cary, NC	8.1	21.0	23.3	29.9	12.3	4.1	1.2
Casper, WY	6.4	19.3	22.0	23.7	14.9	10.5	3.1
Cheshire, CT	5.5	19.4	19.4	26.7	16.3	8.0	4.5
Chino Hills, CA	8.4	24.4	21.3	30.4	11.5	3.3	0.7
Collierville, TN	7.7	25.7	16.0	31.6	13.0	4.9	1.1
Conway, AR	6.7	16.6	37.8	19.7	10.4	6.1	2.6
Coronado, CA	4.1	12.0	35.7	20.0	12.8	10.3	5.1
Cranberry, PA	9.3	21.1	20.1	29.3	12.1	5.3	2.8
Dover, DE	6.8	16.7	29.1	20.6	13.4	9.3	4.1
Draper, UT	10.2	21.2	32.2	23.6	9.4	2.7	0.7
Dublin, OH	8.7	24.0	16.5	30.9	14.2	4.3	1.3
Edmond, OK	7.1	20.3	24.1	25.4	14.3	6.3	2.5
Evesham, NJ	7.2	19.5	20.7	28.0	15.7	6.9	2.0
Fargo, ND	6.4	14.8	35.6	21.5	11.6	7.0	3.0
Farmington, CT	5.7	18.6	16.7	26.4	17.0	10.7	4.9
Fishers, IN	11.9	20.2	28.4	27.9	8.4	2.7	0.6
Flower Mound, TX	10.4	24.1	19.4	32.3	11.1	1.9	0.6
Franklin, MA	9.6	20.8	19.9	29.4	11.8	6.3	2.1
Frederick, MD	7.6	17.6	26.9	24.4	12.3	7.8	3.5
Frisco, TX	12.9	17.9	30.5	26.0	9.4	2.7	0.6
Goodyear, AZ	6.8	16.0	25.6	24.2	17.7	8.8	0.9
Grand Blanc, MI	6.9	18.7	23.5	25.0	15.5	7.9	2.6
Greenburgh, NY	6.4	17.3	18.0	26.2	17.7	10.8	3.7
Greenwich, CT	6.9	18.4	15.0	26.0	17.8	11.3	4.5
Hampden, PA	5.6	18.7	17.4	25.8	19.3	9.5	3.7
Hilliard, OH	9.3	22.4	21.9	28.8	10.4	5.2	1.9
Hoover, AL	6.7	17.8	23.7	25.7	15.5	7.8	2.8
Huntersville, NC	9.7	18.6	26.2	27.8	11.5	4.0	2.3
Juneau, AK	6.5	21.0	21.9	28.9	15.5	4.8	1.4
Keller, TX	8.4	25.8	16.3	31.4	14.0	3.5	0.6
Kenner, LA	6.9	20.4	23.2	24.6	16.0	7.3	1.5
Kennesaw, GA	9.7	18.2	29.5	26.3	10.8	4.0	1.5
League City, TX	8.1	21.1	21.7	29.4	13.7	4.5	1.5
Leawood, KS	6.5	23.9	9.7	28.5	19.1	9.9	2.4
Lee's Summit, MO	8.1	21.2	20.4	26.6	13.7	6.3	3.8
Leesburg, VA	9.6	19.6	24.8	28.0	12.1	4.3	1.6
Lehi, UT	15.5	25.4	30.4	16.6	6.7	3.9	1.3
Lwr Providence, PA	6.5	19.4	21.0	27.5	15.4	8.6	1.6
Madison, AL	7.8	21.6	21.1	30.0	14.0	3.9	1.5
Manhattan Bch, CA	6.5	15.7	22.4	27.9	17.3	8.1	2.1
Maple Grove, MN	7.5	23.1	20.2	31.0	14.1	3.5	0.5
Marion, IA	7.3	19.1	23.7	23.9	14.8	8.0	3.2
Marlboro, NJ	7.3	22.8	14.7	28.7	17.5	7.3	1.7

Area	Percent of Population						
	Under Age 5	Age 5 to 17	Age 18 to 34	Age 35 to 49	Age 50 to 64	Age 65 to 79	80 Years and Over
Matthews, NC	7.0	21.9	17.7	28.8	15.3	6.5	2.7
Meridian, ID	11.5	22.5	26.9	22.9	9.9	4.6	1.7
Merrimack, NH	6.8	22.2	19.0	29.0	17.1	4.5	1.4
Morgantown, WV	2.9	7.9	56.9	12.6	9.3	7.3	3.1
Mt Pleasant, SC	7.7	17.3	22.9	26.9	15.1	7.5	2.6
Northampton, PA	5.8	22.3	15.5	27.1	19.4	7.2	2.6
Northville, MI	4.7	16.5	18.3	26.1	20.4	10.5	3.5
Novi, MI	7.3	20.1	22.3	28.6	13.5	6.3	1.9
O'Fallon, MO	10.4	23.0	25.1	25.1	9.8	5.3	1.2
Oro Valley, AZ	4.6	16.5	12.8	23.0	20.5	19.3	3.3
Oviedo, FL	8.2	23.9	22.9	28.3	11.3	4.2	1.2
Palm Bch Grdns, FL	4.3	14.6	15.3	24.1	21.0	15.5	5.3
Parker, CO	11.4	21.8	27.5	28.6	7.7	2.3	0.6
Peachtree City, GA	6.2	25.1	14.1	30.1	16.8	6.0	1.8
Pflugerville, TX	8.8	25.3	23.3	30.1	8.6	2.8	1.0
Pleasanton, CA	6.8	21.1	18.0	30.3	16.2	5.6	1.8
Rapid City, SD	6.9	18.1	24.8	23.1	13.8	9.4	3.8
Redmond, WA	6.1	15.3	30.0	24.6	14.7	5.3	4.0
Richland, WA	6.5	20.8	18.7	23.9	17.0	10.2	2.9
Richmond, KY	6.1	11.3	48.5	15.6	9.4	6.3	2.9
Rio Rancho, NM	7.4	21.9	20.1	26.3	12.6	8.6	3.0
Rockaway, NJ	7.6	19.4	18.4	28.5	16.5	7.8	1.9
Rocklin, CA	7.8	22.3	20.7	27.6	13.4	6.9	1.5
Rogers, AR	8.8	20.6	25.0	21.8	12.0	8.7	3.2
Round Rock, TX	9.8	22.1	27.6	26.1	9.8	3.0	1.5
Sammamish, WA	7.8	25.3	15.8	33.3	14.2	3.2	0.4
San Ramon, CA	7.2	18.9	19.6	31.5	16.5	4.5	1.8
Santa Fe, NM	5.4	14.7	22.1	24.5	19.1	10.5	3.7
Saratoga, CA	5.3	20.7	9.2	27.9	20.3	13.0	3.6
Savage, MN	11.9	23.7	23.4	30.5	7.9	2.4	0.3
Schererville, IN	6.3	18.3	21.1	26.7	17.2	8.5	1.9
Shawnee, KS	7.7	18.9	23.3	26.5	15.2	6.6	1.9
Shrewsbury, MA	7.8	17.8	19.2	26.7	14.9	9.4	4.1
S Brunswick, NJ	7.6	20.8	21.2	29.6	13.4	5.9	1.5
S. Jordan, UT	8.8	30.5	20.5	24.3	11.4	3.1	1.4
S Kingstown, RI	5.3	16.9	29.7	22.5	13.8	8.4	3.4
Southaven, MS	7.7	19.4	25.7	22.4	16.5	6.5	1.9
Southlake, TX	7.9	29.1	9.6	35.8	14.5	2.6	0.5
Spanish Fork, UT	13.4	25.9	29.1	17.2	8.2	4.5	1.6
Sparks, NV	7.2	19.4	23.8	25.0	14.3	8.1	2.2
Stow, OH	6.6	19.5	21.0	25.8	15.3	8.5	3.4
Sugar Land, TX	6.1	25.1	15.0	31.4	15.7	5.0	1.8
Sun Prairie, WI	7.8	21.0	24.5	25.2	12.5	6.2	2.8
Tualatin, OR	7.4	20.6	26.6	27.5	11.9	3.9	2.0
Waimalu, HI	5.6	15.9	23.9	25.8	18.9	8.6	1.3
Wellington, FL	6.6	24.2	16.3	28.9	15.1	7.1	1.9
W Des Moines, IA	7.7	17.2	28.6	23.3	13.6	7.3	2.3
West Linn, OR	6.9	22.1	16.0	29.7	17.4	6.1	1.8
West Windsor, NJ	6.7	24.9	14.3	31.9	16.0	5.1	1.2
Weston, FL	8.8	23.7	19.0	29.8	11.8	5.7	1.2
Woodbury, MN	9.6	21.2	22.4	27.8	13.1	4.7	1.3
Woodridge, IL	7.2	19.5	26.3	26.8	14.3	4.8	1.0
Yorba Linda, CA	5.8	23.3	16.7	29.1	17.6	5.9	1.7
U.S.	6.8	18.9	23.7	23.5	14.8	9.2	3.2

Source: Census 2000, Summary File 3

Age Distribution: Metro Area

Metro Area	Percent of Population						
	Under Age 5	Age 5 to 17	Age 18 to 34	Age 35 to 49	Age 50 to 64	Age 65 to 79	80 Years and Over
Allen, TX	8.1	19.9	27.3	24.4	12.7	5.8	1.8
Ankeny, IA	7.5	18.4	24.6	23.9	14.4	8.1	3.0
Apex, NC	6.9	17.3	29.0	24.9	13.3	6.5	2.1
Bangor, ME	5.2	16.6	26.6	23.7	15.2	9.5	3.1
Beavercreek, OH	6.5	18.2	22.9	22.8	16.0	10.2	3.3
Bellevue, NE	7.3	19.8	24.6	23.7	13.9	7.9	2.8
Bend, OR	n/a	n/a	n/a	n/a	n/a	n/a	n/a
Bernards, NJ	6.7	17.6	22.8	26.1	15.0	8.9	2.9
Bethlehem, NY	6.0	17.8	22.4	23.8	15.7	10.2	4.1
Bozeman, MT	n/a	n/a	n/a	n/a	n/a	n/a	n/a
Brentwood, TN	6.9	17.9	25.9	24.8	14.5	7.6	2.5
Brookfield, WI	6.9	19.5	22.8	23.9	14.3	9.1	3.4
Broomfield, CO	7.1	18.6	25.6	25.6	14.1	6.8	2.2
Burlington, VT	6.0	18.0	26.8	25.2	14.2	7.3	2.6
Carmel, IN	7.4	19.1	24.0	24.3	14.2	8.1	2.8
Cary, NC	6.9	17.3	29.0	24.9	13.3	6.5	2.1
Casper, WY	6.4	19.5	21.6	24.5	15.4	9.9	2.7
Cheshire, CT	6.2	18.0	22.9	23.5	15.4	9.8	4.3
Chino Hills, CA	8.0	23.3	23.2	22.8	12.2	8.0	2.5
Collierville, TN	7.6	20.7	24.1	23.7	13.9	7.6	2.4
Conway, AR	7.0	18.6	24.6	23.6	14.9	8.3	2.9
Coronado, CA	7.0	18.6	26.9	23.5	12.8	8.3	2.9
Cranberry, PA	5.5	16.7	20.2	23.7	16.1	12.9	4.9
Dover, DE	7.2	20.0	23.4	23.3	14.5	8.9	2.7
Draper, UT	9.1	22.2	28.1	20.9	11.4	6.2	2.1
Dublin, OH	7.1	18.3	26.7	23.9	14.0	7.7	2.4
Edmond, OK	6.9	18.6	25.4	23.1	14.6	8.5	2.8
Evesham, NJ	6.4	18.9	22.2	23.9	14.9	10.0	3.6
Fargo, ND	6.4	17.5	30.6	22.6	12.3	7.5	3.2
Farmington, CT	6.3	18.0	21.7	24.7	15.7	9.7	4.0
Fishers, IN	7.4	19.1	24.0	24.3	14.2	8.1	2.8
Flower Mound, TX	8.1	19.9	27.3	24.4	12.7	5.8	1.8
Franklin, MA	6.2	16.2	25.2	24.4	14.9	9.4	3.7
Frederick, MD	6.9	18.3	24.6	25.8	15.3	6.8	2.2
Frisco, TX	8.1	19.9	27.3	24.4	12.7	5.8	1.8
Goodyear, AZ	7.7	19.0	25.8	22.0	13.5	9.0	3.0
Grand Blanc, MI	7.2	20.1	22.5	23.4	15.1	8.9	2.7
Greenburgh, NY	6.7	17.6	25.9	23.2	14.7	8.8	3.2
Greenwich, CT	7.2	17.7	19.1	26.0	16.3	10.0	3.7
Hampden, PA	5.8	17.6	21.6	24.1	16.1	10.8	3.9
Hilliard, OH	7.1	18.3	26.7	23.9	14.0	7.7	2.4
Hoover, AL	6.7	18.4	23.5	23.7	15.0	9.5	3.2
Huntersville, NC	7.1	18.3	25.7	24.4	14.5	7.8	2.4
Juneau, AK	n/a	n/a	n/a	n/a	n/a	n/a	n/a
Keller, TX	7.7	20.2	25.2	24.6	13.5	6.7	2.0
Kenner, LA	6.8	19.9	23.3	23.8	14.8	8.7	2.7
Kennesaw, GA	7.5	19.1	27.0	25.4	13.5	5.8	1.8
League City, TX	6.9	19.7	21.8	25.2	15.4	8.4	2.6
Leawood, KS	7.2	19.3	23.0	24.5	14.6	8.4	3.0
Lee's Summit, MO	7.2	19.3	23.0	24.5	14.6	8.4	3.0
Leesburg, VA	6.9	18.3	24.6	25.8	15.3	6.8	2.2
Lehi, UT	10.9	23.0	36.0	15.4	8.2	4.8	1.7
Lwr Providence, PA	6.4	18.9	22.2	23.9	14.9	10.0	3.6
Madison, AL	6.8	18.6	23.1	25.0	15.6	8.6	2.3
Manhattan Bch, CA	7.7	20.3	26.7	23.0	12.6	7.3	2.4
Maple Grove, MN	7.1	19.6	24.5	25.5	13.7	6.9	2.7
Marion, IA	6.9	18.3	24.3	23.3	14.9	8.8	3.4
Marlboro, NJ	6.6	18.2	18.3	24.1	15.8	12.2	4.8

Metro Area	Percent of Population						
	Under Age 5	Age 5 to 17	Age 18 to 34	Age 35 to 49	Age 50 to 64	Age 65 to 79	80 Years and Over
Matthews, NC	7.1	18.3	25.7	24.4	14.5	7.8	2.4
Meridian, ID	8.1	20.2	25.8	23.1	13.1	6.9	2.8
Merrimack, NH	6.9	20.4	20.8	27.2	15.5	6.9	2.4
Morgantown, WV	n/a	n/a	n/a	n/a	n/a	n/a	n/a
Mt Pleasant, SC	6.7	19.0	25.6	23.6	14.8	8.0	2.4
Northampton, PA	6.4	18.9	22.2	23.9	14.9	10.0	3.6
Northville, MI	7.0	19.5	22.6	24.1	14.8	9.0	3.1
Novi, MI	7.0	19.5	22.6	24.1	14.8	9.0	3.1
O'Fallon, MO	6.7	19.6	22.0	24.2	14.7	9.5	3.4
Oro Valley, AZ	6.5	18.0	24.2	22.3	14.8	10.6	3.6
Oviedo, FL	6.5	18.2	24.4	24.2	14.4	9.5	2.9
Palm Bch Grdns, FL	5.5	15.7	18.2	22.1	15.3	16.2	7.0
Parker, CO	7.1	18.6	25.6	25.6	14.1	6.8	2.2
Peachtree City, GA	7.5	19.1	27.0	25.4	13.5	5.8	1.8
Pflugerville, TX	7.4	17.9	31.5	24.4	11.7	5.4	1.8
Pleasanton, CA	6.8	18.5	23.9	25.3	14.8	7.8	2.9
Rapid City, SD	7.1	19.5	23.2	24.2	14.2	8.7	3.1
Redmond, WA	6.3	17.4	25.2	26.1	14.7	7.4	2.9
Richland, WA	8.1	22.9	21.9	23.2	14.2	7.6	2.3
Richmond, KY	6.4	16.3	29.7	23.3	14.2	7.6	2.6
Rio Rancho, NM	7.0	19.2	23.6	24.3	14.6	8.4	2.8
Rockaway, NJ	7.0	18.5	22.0	24.9	15.5	8.9	3.3
Rocklin, CA	6.9	20.3	22.4	24.4	14.4	8.7	2.9
Rogers, AR	7.5	18.3	26.8	21.4	13.9	9.4	2.7
Round Rock, TX	7.4	17.9	31.5	24.4	11.7	5.4	1.8
Sammamish, WA	6.3	17.4	25.2	26.1	14.7	7.4	2.9
San Ramon, CA	6.8	18.5	23.9	25.3	14.8	7.8	2.9
Santa Fe, NM	6.0	18.2	20.1	26.2	18.6	8.5	2.4
Saratoga, CA	7.0	17.7	26.9	25.0	13.9	7.2	2.3
Savage, MN	7.1	19.6	24.5	25.5	13.7	6.9	2.7
Schererville, IN	7.0	19.5	21.8	23.8	15.4	9.5	3.0
Shawnee, KS	7.2	19.3	23.0	24.5	14.6	8.4	3.0
Shrewsbury, MA	6.5	18.7	22.7	24.5	14.3	9.2	4.1
S Brunswick, NJ	6.7	17.6	22.8	26.1	15.0	8.9	2.9
S. Jordan, UT	9.1	22.2	28.1	20.9	11.4	6.2	2.1
S Kingstown, RI	6.0	17.8	23.2	23.5	14.9	10.4	4.3
Southaven, MS	7.6	20.7	24.1	23.7	13.9	7.6	2.4
Southlake, TX	7.7	20.2	25.2	24.6	13.5	6.7	2.0
Spanish Fork, UT	10.9	23.0	36.0	15.4	8.2	4.8	1.7
Sparks, NV	6.8	18.0	24.1	24.8	15.9	8.3	2.3
Stow, OH	6.5	18.3	22.7	23.8	15.3	10.1	3.3
Sugar Land, TX	8.1	21.1	26.0	24.6	12.9	5.8	1.6
Sun Prairie, WI	6.0	16.5	30.3	24.3	13.6	6.7	2.7
Tualatin, OR	7.0	18.4	24.8	24.7	14.7	7.4	3.0
Waimalu, HI	6.4	17.3	24.8	23.1	14.9	10.2	3.3
Wellington, FL	5.5	15.7	18.2	22.1	15.3	16.2	7.0
W Des Moines, IA	7.5	18.4	24.6	23.9	14.4	8.1	3.0
West Linn, OR	7.0	18.4	24.8	24.7	14.7	7.4	3.0
West Windsor, NJ	6.3	17.5	24.2	24.5	14.9	9.1	3.4
Weston, FL	6.3	17.2	21.3	24.8	14.4	10.7	5.4
Woodbury, MN	7.1	19.6	24.5	25.5	13.7	6.9	2.7
Woodridge, IL	7.4	19.4	24.9	23.6	13.9	7.9	2.8
Yorba Linda, CA	7.5	19.4	25.6	24.0	13.7	7.3	2.5
U.S.	6.8	18.9	23.7	23.5	14.8	9.2	3.2

Note: Figures cover the Metropolitan Statistical Area (MSA) - see Appendix A for areas included
Source: Census 2000, Summary File 3

Religion

City	County	Catholic	Southern Baptist	United Methodist	ELCA[1]	LDS[2]	Presbyterian Church USA	Jewish Est.	Muslim Est.
Allen, TX	Collin	18.3	16.0	6.1	0.6	1.3	0.7	1.4	1.2
Ankeny, IA	Polk	15.5	0.2	5.3	6.3	0.5	1.9	0.6	0.3
Apex, NC	Wake	9.5	12.6	7.4	0.9	0.6	2.7	1.0	0.5
Bangor, ME	Penobscot	19.4	0.0	3.3	0.2	0.5	0.0	0.7	0.1
Beavercreek, OH	Greene	9.0	3.8	2.5	1.8	0.9	2.1	0.0	0.4
Bellevue, NE	Sarpy	17.2	2.6	2.8	4.2	1.2	1.5	0.0	0.0
Bend, OR	Deschutes	8.6	1.2	0.5	0.9	3.0	1.0	0.2	0.0
Bernards, NJ	Somerset	39.9	0.3	1.5	0.6	0.2	2.1	3.7	0.6
Bethlehem, NY	Albany	47.0	0.1	2.6	1.1	0.2	1.1	4.1	0.2
Bozeman, MT	Gallatin	11.7	1.6	1.4	2.2	3.5	1.3	0.1	0.2
Brentwood, TN	Williamson	11.3	14.2	11.0	0.6	1.4	1.9	0.0	0.0
Brookfield, WI	Waukesha	37.3	0.1	2.0	7.6	0.3	0.9	0.6	0.0
Broomfield, CO	Broomfield	20.2	1.0	1.8	3.0	1.6	1.8	4.5	1.4
Burlington, VT	Chittenden	25.3	0.0	2.3	0.4	0.5	0.1	2.1	0.1
Carmel, IN	Hamilton	20.1	0.5	4.9	2.1	0.6	0.5	0.0	0.0
Cary, NC	Wake	9.5	12.6	7.4	0.9	0.6	2.7	1.0	0.5
Casper, WY	Natrona	15.0	5.0	3.1	2.8	4.7	1.3	0.2	0.0
Cheshire, CT	New Haven	38.8	0.0	1.2	0.6	0.2	0.1	3.5	1.4
Chino Hills, CA	San Bernardino	26.1	3.0	0.4	0.3	2.2	0.4	0.2	0.8
Collierville, TN	Shelby	5.7	16.9	5.4	0.2	0.3	1.2	1.0	0.4
Conway, AR	Faulkner	9.2	20.7	5.8	0.2	1.0	0.7	0.0	0.0
Coronado, CA	San Diego	29.5	1.0	0.7	0.6	1.6	0.9	2.5	0.3
Cranberry, PA	Butler	30.3	0.3	6.5	6.4	0.6	6.5	0.1	0.0
Dover, DE	Kent	10.2	0.8	8.3	0.4	0.5	1.5	1.3	0.0
Draper, UT	Salt Lake	6.0	0.6	0.5	0.4	56.0	0.4	0.5	0.4
Dublin, OH	Franklin	13.7	2.1	4.1	2.8	0.4	1.5	1.5	0.6
Edmond, OK	Oklahoma	6.5	26.4	9.4	0.6	0.7	1.3	0.4	0.4
Evesham, NJ	Burlington	31.0	0.2	2.4	1.7	0.3	1.4	3.1	2.0
Fargo, ND	Cass	14.5	0.2	2.4	27.6	0.3	2.0	0.5	0.5
Farmington, CT	Hartford	38.4	0.1	1.6	1.5	0.3	0.2	3.5	0.4
Fishers, IN	Hamilton	20.1	0.5	4.9	2.1	0.6	0.5	0.0	0.0
Flower Mound, TX	Denton	6.4	12.4	4.6	0.6	1.5	0.5	0.0	1.3
Franklin, MA	Norfolk	58.6	0.0	0.7	0.3	0.2	0.2	5.9	0.6
Frederick, MD	Frederick	18.0	2.2	7.8	7.3	0.8	0.4	0.6	0.0
Frisco, TX	Collin	18.3	16.0	6.1	0.6	1.3	0.7	1.4	1.2
Goodyear, AZ	Maricopa	17.3	2.5	1.1	1.7	5.0	0.6	2.0	0.3
Grand Blanc, MI	Genesee	15.0	2.2	2.6	0.4	0.2	1.4	0.3	0.5
Greenburgh, NY	Westchester	50.9	0.1	1.2	0.6	0.2	1.2	10.2	0.6
Greenwich, CT	Fairfield	49.2	0.2	1.7	0.8	0.3	0.7	4.4	1.7
Hampden, PA	Cumberland	16.5	0.6	10.1	8.3	0.4	3.7	0.9	0.0
Hilliard, OH	Franklin	13.7	2.1	4.1	2.8	0.4	1.5	1.5	0.6
Hoover, AL	Jefferson	6.7	29.7	8.0	0.2	0.3	1.5	0.8	0.3
Huntersville, NC	Mecklenburg	8.5	10.8	6.7	1.2	0.5	6.0	1.2	1.1
Juneau, AK	Juneau	7.2	2.4	1.5	2.1	3.3	2.7	0.9	0.0
Keller, TX	Tarrant	11.5	18.7	6.8	0.6	0.8	0.8	0.4	1.0
Kenner, LA	Jefferson	41.5	6.8	1.2	0.2	0.4	0.4	0.6	0.6
Kennesaw, GA	Cobb	9.8	18.5	6.8	0.7	0.7	1.5	1.7	0.1
League City, TX	Galveston	16.9	13.3	5.3	1.3	0.9	0.5	0.8	0.0
Leawood, KS	Johnson	21.3	3.1	4.5	1.8	0.8	3.5	2.7	0.0
Lee's Summit, MO	Jackson	15.5	11.5	4.2	0.4	0.9	1.8	1.1	1.0
Leesburg, VA	Loudoun	17.7	3.3	5.4	1.2	1.6	1.0	2.1	1.1
Lehi, UT	Utah	1.0	0.1	0.0	0.0	88.1	0.1	0.0	0.0
Lwr Providence, PA	Montgomery	35.1	0.2	2.2	5.8	0.1	2.3	7.9	0.0
Madison, AL	Madison	5.8	22.4	7.7	0.7	0.8	1.6	0.3	0.4
Manhattan Bch, CA	Los Angeles	40.0	1.2	0.6	0.3	1.0	0.6	5.9	1.0
Maple Grove, MN	Hennepin	23.4	0.2	2.1	13.7	0.4	1.6	2.8	0.7
Marion, IA	Linn	23.3	0.6	7.5	5.7	0.7	2.9	0.2	1.2
Marlboro, NJ	Monmouth	47.0	0.2	2.1	1.3	0.2	1.3	10.6	1.5

City	County	Catholic	Southern Baptist	United Meth-odist	ELCA[1]	LDS[2]	Presby-terian Church USA	Jewish Est.	Muslim Est.
Matthews, NC	Mecklenburg	8.5	10.8	6.7	1.2	0.5	6.0	1.2	1.1
Meridian, ID	Ada	12.3	1.0	2.0	1.0	15.2	0.7	0.3	0.1
Merrimack, NH	Hillsborough	45.5	0.2	1.0	0.4	0.5	0.4	1.6	0.0
Morgantown, WV	Monongalia	8.8	0.4	7.6	0.7	1.2	0.9	0.2	0.4
Mt Pleasant, SC	Charleston	7.7	11.6	5.7	1.9	0.5	3.9	1.6	0.7
Northampton, PA	Bucks	43.8	0.1	2.7	4.0	0.1	2.3	5.8	0.3
Northville, MI	Wayne	21.9	0.5	1.0	1.0	0.2	1.0	0.4	2.3
Novi, MI	Oakland	25.3	0.6	2.4	1.2	0.3	1.5	6.5	1.1
O'Fallon, MO	St. Charles	27.9	7.2	2.3	0.7	0.8	1.0	0.8	0.0
Oro Valley, AZ	Pima	26.7	2.7	1.1	1.3	2.0	1.1	2.4	0.1
Oviedo, FL	Seminole	16.5	5.3	2.6	0.6	0.5	1.2	1.0	0.0
Palm Bch Grdns, FL	Palm Beach	26.6	3.7	1.7	0.6	0.3	0.6	14.8	0.1
Parker, CO	Douglas	9.6	1.3	1.8	1.9	3.9	0.3	0.0	0.0
Peachtree City, GA	Fayette	13.5	31.1	9.9	3.1	1.1	1.7	2.7	0.0
Pflugerville, TX	Travis	20.4	9.5	2.7	1.5	0.6	1.3	1.7	0.4
Pleasanton, CA	Alameda	21.2	1.6	0.7	0.5	1.2	0.7	2.3	1.6
Rapid City, SD	Pennington	27.9	3.3	3.0	8.4	1.5	2.0	0.1	0.0
Redmond, WA	King	16.2	0.7	1.1	2.0	2.3	1.6	1.9	0.5
Richland, WA	Benton	12.7	2.2	3.4	2.2	7.3	1.7	0.2	0.2
Richmond, KY	Madison	3.3	22.7	2.9	0.2	0.0	0.8	0.0	0.9
Rio Rancho, NM	Sandoval	37.5	2.2	0.4	0.0	2.5	0.7	0.0	0.0
Rockaway, NJ	Morris	38.1	0.1	2.0	0.9	0.3	2.5	7.1	0.5
Rocklin, CA	Placer	15.8	1.9	0.9	1.1	4.1	0.7	0.9	0.0
Rogers, AR	Benton	5.9	19.3	5.2	1.3	1.4	1.3	0.0	0.0
Round Rock, TX	Williamson	12.4	10.2	5.7	1.8	1.5	0.6	0.0	0.0
Sammamish, WA	King	16.2	0.7	1.1	2.0	2.3	1.6	1.9	0.5
San Ramon, CA	Contra Costa	21.5	0.8	0.8	0.7	2.0	1.2	2.3	0.7
Santa Fe, NM	Santa Fe	39.2	2.2	1.2	0.3	1.0	0.6	1.3	0.0
Saratoga, CA	Santa Clara	28.7	1.0	0.9	0.6	1.2	0.6	3.2	1.1
Savage, MN	Scott	24.8	0.0	1.6	9.7	0.4	0.5	0.0	0.0
Schererville, IN	Lake	26.5	2.2	1.6	0.9	0.2	0.8	0.4	0.5
Shawnee, KS	Johnson	21.3	3.1	4.5	1.8	0.8	3.5	2.7	0.0
Shrewsbury, MA	Worcester	41.2	0.2	1.2	1.1	0.3	0.1	2.6	0.8
S Brunswick, NJ	Middlesex	45.7	0.1	0.8	0.6	0.2	1.0	6.0	0.9
S. Jordan, UT	Salt Lake	6.0	0.6	0.5	0.4	56.0	0.4	0.5	0.4
S Kingstown, RI	Washington	47.5	0.5	0.6	0.6	0.0	0.5	1.0	0.0
Southaven, MS	DeSoto	2.7	39.3	6.0	0.0	0.5	0.7	0.0	0.0
Southlake, TX	Tarrant	11.5	18.7	6.8	0.6	0.8	0.8	0.4	1.0
Spanish Fork, UT	Utah	1.0	0.1	0.0	0.0	88.1	0.1	0.0	0.0
Sparks, NV	Washoe	16.2	1.1	0.8	0.6	3.5	0.5	0.6	0.2
Stow, OH	Summit	22.4	0.3	3.9	1.3	0.3	1.1	0.7	0.0
Sugar Land, TX	Fort Bend	24.8	8.7	4.4	0.6	0.8	0.5	0.5	0.7
Sun Prairie, WI	Dane	28.0	0.1	2.0	11.6	0.3	1.0	1.1	0.3
Tualatin, OR	Washington	6.5	0.7	0.9	1.2	3.8	0.7	0.7	0.1
Waimalu, HI	Honolulu	17.6	1.9	0.8	0.3	3.3	0.0	0.7	0.1
Wellington, FL	Palm Beach	26.6	3.7	1.7	0.6	0.3	0.6	14.8	0.1
W Des Moines, IA	Polk	15.5	0.2	5.3	6.3	0.5	1.9	0.6	0.3
West Linn, OR	Clackamas	6.3	0.5	1.0	2.0	3.3	0.9	0.9	0.0
West Windsor, NJ	Mercer	31.2	0.0	1.6	1.2	0.2	2.8	2.6	3.3
Weston, FL	Broward	21.1	3.6	1.2	0.3	0.3	0.4	13.1	0.4
Woodbury, MN	Washington	28.9	0.1	1.8	19.2	0.5	1.0	0.0	0.0
Woodridge, IL	DuPage	38.7	0.2	2.2	3.0	0.3	1.1	0.2	1.7
Yorba Linda, CA	Orange	27.4	1.2	0.6	0.8	1.7	0.9	2.1	1.4
U.S.		22.0	7.1	3.7	1.8	1.5	1.1	2.2	0.6

Note: Figures shown are the number of adherents as a percentage of the total population; Adherents are defined as all members, including full members, their children and the estimated number of other participants who are not considered members (e.g. the baptized, those not confirmed, those not eligible for communion, those regularly attending services, etc.); (1) Evangelical Lutheran Church in America; (2) The Church of Jesus Christ of Latter Day Saints

Source: Reprinted with permission from Religious Congregations and Membership in the United States 2000 (Nashville, Glenmary Research Center, 2002)

Ancestry: City

Area	German	Irish[1]	English	American	Italian	Polish	French[2]	Scottish
Allen, TX	18.1	14.3	12.7	10.2	4.6	2.1	3.7	3.0
Ankeny, IA	35.0	14.6	11.8	6.3	2.5	1.5	3.2	1.2
Apex, NC	17.7	13.5	15.0	8.3	9.0	3.7	2.8	3.2
Bangor, ME	6.2	17.6	18.7	11.0	4.1	1.6	12.5	4.2
Beavercreek, OH	30.2	14.4	14.3	10.3	5.1	3.3	2.9	2.3
Bellevue, NE	28.6	15.5	10.8	5.2	5.0	5.9	3.2	1.7
Bend, OR	20.9	13.8	14.9	6.8	4.3	2.1	4.2	4.3
Bernards, NJ	18.7	23.6	11.0	3.3	19.1	7.1	1.9	3.2
Bethlehem, NY	21.5	24.3	13.7	4.1	16.0	6.2	5.0	2.4
Bozeman, MT	26.0	15.2	11.4	4.0	3.9	2.4	3.7	3.9
Brentwood, TN	16.7	11.6	21.3	11.0	2.9	2.9	4.1	4.2
Brookfield, WI	46.1	14.7	7.3	3.4	7.7	11.3	3.3	1.5
Broomfield, CO	28.8	14.6	13.5	3.3	6.1	3.4	4.4	3.3
Burlington, VT	10.2	17.8	13.6	4.7	7.1	3.6	12.7	3.7
Carmel, IN	28.1	15.1	15.0	7.7	4.4	3.9	2.7	2.8
Cary, NC	17.3	12.3	14.3	7.4	6.5	3.6	3.0	3.2
Casper, WY	24.8	14.8	13.6	7.8	3.7	1.9	4.1	2.5
Cheshire, CT	12.6	22.0	11.8	2.1	26.1	7.6	4.8	2.3
Chino Hills, CA	11.3	8.4	7.6	3.2	4.8	1.5	2.6	1.4
Collierville, TN	12.9	12.3	14.2	14.4	4.6	1.7	2.9	3.4
Conway, AR	13.3	10.3	9.9	12.7	2.0	0.6	2.3	2.0
Coronado, CA	17.7	16.2	13.7	4.4	7.7	2.4	3.8	4.1
Cranberry, PA	34.3	21.4	10.2	4.7	17.0	8.6	2.2	2.6
Dover, DE	13.0	10.5	9.2	3.9	5.6	2.4	2.4	1.5
Draper, UT	12.4	6.5	28.3	6.3	3.3	0.9	3.3	4.2
Dublin, OH	31.3	17.0	12.3	5.5	9.4	3.9	2.7	3.1
Edmond, OK	19.0	11.9	14.0	9.9	2.5	1.5	3.6	2.8
Evesham, NJ	20.4	27.8	9.9	3.1	26.6	9.2	2.2	1.8
Fargo, ND	40.6	8.6	5.2	2.0	1.0	2.8	4.7	1.2
Farmington, CT	11.6	21.3	13.3	2.5	18.8	14.3	6.0	2.1
Fishers, IN	29.2	13.4	13.3	7.2	5.0	4.0	3.6	3.1
Flower Mound, TX	20.7	15.2	15.1	8.7	4.4	3.1	3.3	3.4
Franklin, MA	9.1	32.2	14.6	3.5	24.8	4.4	6.6	3.1
Frederick, MD	21.5	13.5	9.8	8.7	4.6	3.1	2.2	2.0
Frisco, TX	18.5	11.6	11.7	8.7	4.5	2.4	3.0	2.5
Goodyear, AZ	16.5	9.9	8.5	4.4	4.9	2.7	2.9	1.4
Grand Blanc, MI	22.5	14.3	14.6	8.0	3.0	6.9	5.7	2.6
Greenburgh, NY	7.7	13.6	4.6	3.3	17.9	5.4	1.1	1.1
Greenwich, CT	12.0	16.6	13.6	4.5	18.4	5.6	2.6	3.3
Hampden, PA	35.0	17.5	11.9	6.3	8.4	4.3	2.3	2.2
Hilliard, OH	30.1	17.2	12.7	8.3	7.8	3.8	3.6	2.9
Hoover, AL	10.4	10.8	15.3	12.1	3.8	1.4	2.5	3.5
Huntersville, NC	18.0	14.0	13.5	8.6	6.1	2.7	3.4	2.9
Juneau, AK	18.9	13.0	13.1	4.5	3.3	1.5	3.8	3.7
Keller, TX	18.5	15.1	15.3	10.5	4.0	2.1	2.9	3.0
Kenner, LA	12.1	10.4	4.8	5.1	12.8	0.6	15.7	0.7
Kennesaw, GA	12.6	14.1	10.4	10.0	5.4	3.2	3.3	2.5
League City, TX	17.8	11.3	10.8	9.0	4.5	2.1	4.2	2.2
Leawood, KS	29.2	18.9	18.0	4.7	4.8	2.8	3.2	3.1
Lee's Summit, MO	27.9	15.0	14.4	9.0	4.7	1.8	3.6	2.7
Leesburg, VA	21.5	15.6	13.5	7.4	6.3	3.6	2.2	3.6
Lehi, UT	9.5	4.2	34.4	9.0	1.2	0.2	2.8	4.7
Lwr Providence, PA	20.3	24.4	11.0	2.7	20.7	8.2	2.5	1.6
Madison, AL	14.0	11.8	13.4	11.5	3.0	1.7	2.8	2.6
Manhattan Bch, CA	19.7	13.9	14.4	4.6	7.9	3.6	4.1	3.5
Maple Grove, MN	39.7	12.3	8.0	3.2	2.6	6.0	4.0	1.3
Marion, IA	39.7	16.6	11.3	5.5	1.8	1.3	3.3	2.0
Marlboro, NJ	6.7	10.6	2.9	6.4	20.1	10.6	0.7	0.6
Matthews, NC	17.8	12.2	15.4	10.4	5.0	3.2	2.6	2.9
Meridian, ID	21.3	11.4	15.5	9.3	4.0	0.9	3.3	3.4

Area	German	Irish[1]	English	American	Italian	Polish	French[2]	Scottish
Merrimack, NH	11.5	19.8	16.3	4.2	11.4	5.3	13.9	4.7
Morgantown, WV	20.7	15.5	11.8	5.5	11.5	4.8	2.3	3.0
Mt Pleasant, SC	16.6	13.7	17.1	9.2	5.4	2.2	4.0	4.5
Northampton, PA	23.1	27.0	9.1	5.2	16.5	7.6	1.4	1.7
Northville, MI	22.3	16.3	13.8	3.2	8.2	14.4	4.1	4.3
Novi, MI	22.7	14.8	12.9	4.0	9.0	12.5	4.3	3.3
O'Fallon, MO	37.1	18.2	8.9	8.1	5.8	4.4	5.7	1.5
Oro Valley, AZ	24.4	14.9	17.8	4.3	7.6	3.9	3.9	4.1
Oviedo, FL	18.1	13.5	11.7	5.8	11.6	4.6	2.9	2.4
Palm Bch Grdns, FL	17.2	15.3	13.3	6.2	12.9	5.7	4.2	2.3
Parker, CO	29.2	16.6	11.3	7.2	7.8	3.7	3.7	2.5
Peachtree City, GA	16.8	14.6	14.5	9.0	5.9	3.0	4.7	3.9
Pflugerville, TX	21.7	11.7	10.0	5.5	3.2	1.7	4.0	2.5
Pleasanton, CA	17.5	14.2	12.3	3.6	9.4	2.5	3.5	2.8
Rapid City, SD	33.8	13.8	9.9	4.5	2.3	1.5	3.3	1.6
Redmond, WA	17.4	10.2	14.1	4.3	3.9	2.2	4.2	3.8
Richland, WA	19.6	10.9	15.5	6.9	3.5	1.9	3.7	3.5
Richmond, KY	10.9	10.9	11.7	18.1	1.9	0.7	1.9	1.9
Rio Rancho, NM	16.4	11.2	10.5	5.7	6.6	2.7	3.5	2.3
Rockaway, NJ	15.2	19.3	7.9	3.9	23.4	10.0	1.7	1.6
Rocklin, CA	21.0	15.0	14.4	5.5	8.9	2.1	4.5	3.0
Rogers, AR	14.9	10.9	9.8	13.3	2.5	0.9	2.5	1.3
Round Rock, TX	18.0	10.8	9.8	5.3	3.5	1.6	3.3	2.4
Sammamish, WA	22.5	13.1	17.5	4.1	5.0	2.6	3.9	4.1
San Ramon, CA	16.8	13.5	12.1	2.9	9.1	2.5	3.4	2.2
Santa Fe, NM	10.7	8.8	10.2	4.0	2.8	1.9	2.7	2.5
Saratoga, CA	13.2	10.0	13.4	2.8	6.4	2.2	2.8	3.6
Savage, MN	40.9	15.2	7.6	2.0	2.6	4.3	3.7	2.3
Schererville, IN	22.9	15.1	6.8	4.1	6.3	17.3	2.3	1.1
Shawnee, KS	28.9	15.3	12.9	6.5	2.6	2.1	3.2	2.7
Shrewsbury, MA	7.1	23.4	11.8	6.4	18.7	5.1	8.8	2.7
S Brunswick, NJ	13.4	14.1	5.8	2.6	19.2	8.1	1.5	2.0
S. Jordan, UT	12.4	6.0	36.6	6.4	1.8	0.5	2.7	5.4
S Kingstown, RI	8.5	23.9	18.6	3.5	16.5	4.9	9.1	3.3
Southaven, MS	8.2	14.5	9.1	18.3	3.7	0.6	1.9	1.7
Southlake, TX	21.5	13.9	17.5	8.8	5.1	2.6	3.0	3.9
Spanish Fork, UT	9.7	4.7	32.7	8.6	1.5	0.5	2.4	4.3
Sparks, NV	16.5	13.8	12.6	3.7	7.3	1.9	4.0	2.1
Stow, OH	29.7	17.7	14.3	4.3	12.0	6.5	3.3	2.8
Sugar Land, TX	14.6	9.3	10.9	5.3	3.1	2.2	3.5	2.0
Sun Prairie, WI	46.0	13.5	8.4	4.4	3.8	5.7	5.0	1.4
Tualatin, OR	20.4	11.5	12.7	5.0	3.6	1.4	4.3	4.0
Waimalu, HI	5.3	3.3	3.3	1.1	0.9	0.9	1.5	0.6
Wellington, FL	13.6	15.1	11.2	6.8	14.6	4.7	3.6	1.9
W Des Moines, IA	33.2	15.4	11.6	5.5	3.0	2.1	2.5	2.0
West Linn, OR	26.7	13.4	15.7	5.0	5.6	2.0	4.7	4.0
West Windsor, NJ	12.8	15.3	10.0	2.4	14.5	5.5	2.1	1.7
Weston, FL	9.2	7.9	6.1	6.8	9.8	4.8	2.4	1.4
Woodbury, MN	37.6	15.8	7.4	2.8	4.9	5.9	4.1	1.3
Woodridge, IL	21.6	17.4	6.4	1.8	10.0	12.0	2.3	0.9
Yorba Linda, CA	19.2	12.9	13.8	4.3	7.7	2.8	4.1	2.5
U.S.	15.2	10.9	8.7	7.3	5.6	3.2	3.0	1.7

Note: Figures include multiple ancestry (e.g. if a person reported being Irish and Italian, they were included in both columns); (1) Includes Celtic; (2) Includes Alsatian but excludes Basque
Source: Census 2000, Summary File 3

Ancestry: Metro Area

Metro Area	German	Irish[1]	English	American	Italian	Polish	French[2]	Scottish
Allen, TX	10.0	8.1	8.2	7.8	2.1	1.2	2.1	1.7
Ankeny, IA	27.5	13.7	11.0	7.0	3.2	1.2	2.6	1.8
Apex, NC	10.4	8.6	11.8	9.9	3.5	1.8	2.1	2.7
Bangor, ME	6.7	16.2	19.0	10.8	3.7	1.6	13.7	4.6
Beavercreek, OH	23.8	11.5	9.6	10.9	2.9	1.7	2.5	1.8
Bellevue, NE	32.3	16.3	9.6	4.2	4.5	4.5	2.8	1.4
Bend, OR	n/a	n/a	n/a	n/a	n/a	n/a	n/a	n/a
Bernards, NJ	12.8	15.0	5.7	2.9	17.2	9.8	1.5	1.3
Bethlehem, NY	16.9	22.6	10.7	4.2	16.9	7.5	7.6	2.1
Bozeman, MT	n/a	n/a	n/a	n/a	n/a	n/a	n/a	n/a
Brentwood, TN	9.8	10.2	10.4	15.4	2.1	1.1	2.1	2.2
Brookfield, WI	37.7	10.0	5.1	2.7	4.4	12.7	3.1	0.9
Broomfield, CO	21.3	12.5	11.5	4.5	4.9	2.5	3.4	2.5
Burlington, VT	9.9	17.8	15.8	6.7	6.5	3.3	14.7	3.8
Carmel, IN	20.0	11.2	9.8	12.1	2.2	1.6	2.2	2.0
Cary, NC	10.4	8.6	11.8	9.9	3.5	1.8	2.1	2.7
Casper, WY	25.3	14.7	13.4	8.6	3.2	1.9	3.8	2.6
Cheshire, CT	9.2	16.2	8.8	2.7	24.2	7.2	3.8	1.6
Chino Hills, CA	10.9	8.0	7.8	4.1	3.8	1.4	2.6	1.5
Collierville, TN	6.3	7.5	7.2	8.6	2.2	0.7	1.6	1.5
Conway, AR	10.4	9.4	8.8	13.3	1.6	1.0	2.2	1.7
Coronado, CA	12.6	9.6	9.0	3.8	4.7	2.0	2.8	2.0
Cranberry, PA	26.5	17.1	8.5	3.8	15.2	8.9	1.8	1.9
Dover, DE	14.9	13.0	10.9	8.8	5.4	3.0	2.3	1.8
Draper, UT	12.0	6.2	27.4	6.4	2.8	0.8	2.3	4.3
Dublin, OH	23.4	13.1	10.0	9.3	5.0	2.2	2.2	2.0
Edmond, OK	13.4	10.3	9.4	10.2	1.6	1.0	2.5	1.8
Evesham, NJ	17.1	20.6	8.3	3.2	14.4	5.7	1.6	1.4
Fargo, ND	40.6	8.0	5.2	1.8	1.1	2.8	4.6	1.2
Farmington, CT	9.3	16.0	10.4	3.1	16.2	10.6	8.5	1.9
Fishers, IN	20.0	11.2	9.8	12.1	2.2	1.6	2.2	2.0
Flower Mound, TX	10.0	8.1	8.2	7.8	2.1	1.2	2.1	1.7
Franklin, MA	5.9	24.3	10.9	3.9	15.4	3.5	4.7	2.6
Frederick, MD	12.0	10.5	9.2	5.4	4.4	2.4	2.0	2.0
Frisco, TX	10.0	8.1	8.2	7.8	2.1	1.2	2.1	1.7
Goodyear, AZ	16.2	10.5	10.3	4.6	4.9	2.7	2.9	1.9
Grand Blanc, MI	16.7	11.0	10.7	7.0	2.5	5.2	5.1	2.1
Greenburgh, NY	3.9	6.7	2.0	3.1	10.4	2.9	0.8	0.5
Greenwich, CT	10.1	15.4	10.4	3.9	17.3	5.3	2.5	2.3
Hampden, PA	34.2	11.4	6.9	7.6	6.2	3.0	1.8	1.5
Hilliard, OH	23.4	13.1	10.0	9.3	5.0	2.2	2.2	2.0
Hoover, AL	6.0	7.7	9.0	12.8	1.9	0.6	1.5	2.0
Huntersville, NC	11.7	8.1	8.4	12.4	2.7	1.3	1.7	2.2
Juneau, AK	n/a	n/a	n/a	n/a	n/a	n/a	n/a	n/a
Keller, TX	11.4	9.2	9.1	9.7	2.0	1.2	2.4	1.9
Kenner, LA	10.4	8.2	4.9	4.9	8.2	0.6	14.3	0.9
Kennesaw, GA	8.3	8.5	8.8	10.4	2.7	1.4	1.8	2.0
League City, TX	12.3	9.2	8.3	7.7	3.8	1.3	3.7	1.5
Leawood, KS	21.8	13.2	11.2	8.1	3.2	1.7	2.8	2.0
Lee's Summit, MO	21.8	13.2	11.2	8.1	3.2	1.7	2.8	2.0
Leesburg, VA	12.0	10.5	9.2	5.4	4.4	2.4	2.0	2.0
Lehi, UT	10.8	4.7	33.5	6.9	2.1	0.5	2.2	4.8
Lwr Providence, PA	17.1	20.6	8.3	3.2	14.4	5.7	1.6	1.4
Madison, AL	9.0	9.3	10.1	15.8	1.7	1.0	1.9	2.0
Manhattan Bch, CA	5.8	4.6	4.4	2.5	2.8	1.3	1.5	1.0
Maple Grove, MN	34.4	12.8	6.8	2.7	2.8	5.0	4.4	1.4
Marion, IA	36.8	16.7	10.1	5.8	1.8	1.4	2.9	1.8
Marlboro, NJ	16.1	23.3	7.7	3.4	24.1	8.1	2.0	1.8
Matthews, NC	11.7	8.1	8.4	12.4	2.7	1.3	1.7	2.2
Meridian, ID	19.3	11.1	16.0	7.7	2.8	1.2	3.1	3.4

Metro Area	German	Irish[1]	English	American	Italian	Polish	French[2]	Scottish
Merrimack, NH	9.4	21.0	15.3	5.0	9.4	4.5	13.6	3.6
Morgantown, WV	n/a	n/a	n/a	n/a	n/a	n/a	n/a	n/a
Mt Pleasant, SC	10.7	9.0	9.5	9.4	3.1	1.3	2.7	2.4
Northampton, PA	17.1	20.6	8.3	3.2	14.4	5.7	1.6	1.4
Northville, MI	17.0	10.4	8.0	3.8	6.4	10.8	4.4	2.3
Novi, MI	17.0	10.4	8.0	3.8	6.4	10.8	4.4	2.3
O'Fallon, MO	29.6	13.9	8.5	6.2	4.5	2.6	4.4	1.3
Oro Valley, AZ	16.2	10.6	10.3	4.1	4.4	2.5	3.1	2.3
Oviedo, FL	13.2	10.9	10.1	7.7	6.0	2.5	2.9	2.1
Palm Bch Grdns, FL	11.5	10.6	8.0	6.6	9.4	4.5	2.7	1.6
Parker, CO	21.3	12.5	11.5	4.5	4.9	2.5	3.4	2.5
Peachtree City, GA	8.3	8.5	8.8	10.4	2.7	1.4	1.8	2.0
Pflugerville, TX	15.3	9.3	9.7	5.3	2.5	1.5	2.9	2.4
Pleasanton, CA	10.2	8.8	7.9	2.5	5.4	1.5	2.3	1.8
Rapid City, SD	35.4	13.8	9.9	4.8	2.1	1.6	3.7	1.5
Redmond, WA	17.6	11.5	12.3	4.3	3.6	2.0	3.6	3.3
Richland, WA	17.7	9.8	11.5	6.8	2.4	1.2	3.2	2.2
Richmond, KY	12.4	11.5	12.5	16.0	2.1	1.1	1.9	2.2
Rio Rancho, NM	11.8	8.5	8.5	4.3	3.5	1.6	2.4	1.9
Rockaway, NJ	10.8	12.9	5.2	3.1	15.8	5.9	1.3	1.3
Rocklin, CA	14.4	10.7	10.7	4.6	5.4	1.4	3.3	2.2
Rogers, AR	14.4	11.4	10.7	13.0	2.0	1.0	2.6	1.9
Round Rock, TX	15.3	9.3	9.7	5.3	2.5	1.5	2.9	2.4
Sammamish, WA	17.6	11.5	12.3	4.3	3.6	2.0	3.6	3.3
San Ramon, CA	10.2	8.8	7.9	2.5	5.4	1.5	2.3	1.8
Santa Fe, NM	11.8	8.4	10.2	4.3	2.8	1.8	2.5	2.4
Saratoga, CA	9.2	7.1	7.2	2.3	5.2	1.5	2.2	1.6
Savage, MN	34.4	12.8	6.8	2.7	2.8	5.0	4.4	1.4
Schererville, IN	18.0	11.9	6.4	4.3	4.4	10.1	2.0	1.2
Shawnee, KS	21.8	13.2	11.2	8.1	3.2	1.7	2.8	2.0
Shrewsbury, MA	5.4	21.0	11.0	4.2	12.4	8.0	14.6	2.2
S Brunswick, NJ	12.8	15.0	5.7	2.9	17.2	9.8	1.5	1.3
S. Jordan, UT	12.0	6.2	27.4	6.4	2.8	0.8	2.3	4.3
S Kingstown, RI	4.6	17.6	11.7	3.0	16.9	4.1	11.9	1.8
Southaven, MS	6.3	7.5	7.2	8.6	2.2	0.7	1.6	1.5
Southlake, TX	11.4	9.2	9.1	9.7	2.0	1.2	2.4	1.9
Spanish Fork, UT	10.8	4.7	33.5	6.9	2.1	0.5	2.2	4.8
Sparks, NV	17.1	13.8	12.6	4.6	6.8	1.9	3.9	2.6
Stow, OH	24.5	14.3	10.7	6.6	9.0	4.9	2.4	2.1
Sugar Land, TX	9.2	6.6	6.6	5.9	2.2	1.4	2.6	1.3
Sun Prairie, WI	40.4	14.3	9.7	3.1	3.3	5.0	3.3	1.7
Tualatin, OR	20.8	11.8	12.7	5.5	3.5	1.8	3.7	3.1
Waimalu, HI	5.3	4.0	3.8	1.4	1.7	0.8	1.3	0.9
Wellington, FL	11.5	10.6	8.0	6.6	9.4	4.5	2.7	1.6
W Des Moines, IA	27.5	13.7	11.0	7.0	3.2	1.2	2.6	1.8
West Linn, OR	20.8	11.8	12.7	5.5	3.5	1.8	3.7	3.1
West Windsor, NJ	11.8	13.1	8.0	2.9	15.4	8.0	1.5	1.4
Weston, FL	9.1	9.0	5.7	6.5	9.5	3.7	2.2	1.2
Woodbury, MN	34.4	12.8	6.8	2.7	2.8	5.0	4.4	1.4
Woodridge, IL	16.1	12.1	4.9	2.4	7.2	10.1	1.7	1.0
Yorba Linda, CA	11.7	8.7	8.9	3.5	4.7	1.9	2.6	1.9
U.S.	15.2	10.9	8.7	7.3	5.6	3.2	3.0	1.7

Note: Figures cover the Metropolitan Statistical Area (MSA) - see Appendix A for areas included; Figures include multiple ancestry (e.g. if a person reported being Irish and Italian, they were included in both columns); (1) Includes Celtic; (2) Includes Alsatian but excludes Basque

Source: Census 2000, Summary File 3

Foreign-Born Population: City

City	Percent of Population Born in:							
	Any Foreign Country	Europe	Asia	Africa	Oceania[1]	Canada	Mexico	Latin America[2]
Allen, TX	7.3	1.3	2.6	0.6	0.1	0.9	1.1	0.8
Ankeny, IA	3.0	1.8	0.8	0.1	0.0	0.0	0.1	0.2
Apex, NC	7.3	1.6	3.1	0.5	0.0	0.7	0.3	1.2
Bangor, ME	3.4	0.8	1.1	0.2	0.0	1.1	0.0	0.2
Beavercreek, OH	4.7	1.1	3.1	0.1	0.0	0.2	0.0	0.3
Bellevue, NE	5.7	1.7	2.0	0.3	0.0	0.2	0.8	0.7
Bend, OR	3.7	0.8	0.5	0.1	0.1	0.5	1.1	0.6
Bernards, NJ	12.5	4.4	5.9	0.3	0.0	0.6	0.2	1.1
Bethlehem, NY	4.8	2.2	1.5	0.1	0.0	0.5	0.0	0.6
Bozeman, MT	3.7	1.3	1.6	0.0	0.1	0.5	0.0	0.1
Brentwood, TN	4.5	0.9	2.7	0.3	0.1	0.3	0.1	0.1
Brookfield, WI	6.3	3.1	2.4	0.1	0.1	0.3	0.2	0.2
Broomfield, CO	6.6	1.2	3.2	0.1	0.0	0.5	1.3	0.4
Burlington, VT	8.1	4.0	2.5	0.2	0.0	1.0	0.0	0.3
Carmel, IN	7.3	2.4	3.6	0.1	0.0	0.4	0.5	0.4
Cary, NC	14.0	2.8	6.5	1.1	0.1	0.8	1.8	1.0
Casper, WY	2.0	0.7	0.4	0.0	0.0	0.2	0.6	0.1
Cheshire, CT	6.4	2.6	2.6	0.1	0.0	0.3	0.2	0.6
Chino Hills, CA	22.7	1.2	14.3	0.4	0.1	0.3	4.6	1.9
Collierville, TN	2.8	0.5	1.1	0.3	0.0	0.4	0.2	0.3
Conway, AR	2.6	0.4	0.6	0.3	0.0	0.1	1.1	0.2
Coronado, CA	9.0	1.6	2.8	0.5	0.3	0.7	2.3	0.9
Cranberry, PA	3.2	1.1	1.5	0.1	0.1	0.1	0.2	0.0
Dover, DE	6.1	1.3	2.2	0.9	0.0	0.3	0.3	1.1
Draper, UT	3.7	1.2	0.9	0.0	0.2	0.5	0.7	0.2
Dublin, OH	9.1	1.5	6.6	0.3	0.0	0.5	0.0	0.1
Edmond, OK	5.2	0.7	3.1	0.4	0.0	0.2	0.5	0.3
Evesham, NJ	6.5	2.4	3.0	0.2	0.0	0.3	0.1	0.4
Fargo, ND	4.0	1.4	1.3	0.7	0.0	0.4	0.1	0.1
Farmington, CT	11.9	6.5	3.4	0.4	0.1	0.9	0.0	0.6
Fishers, IN	4.0	0.9	2.0	0.1	0.0	0.3	0.3	0.3
Flower Mound, TX	5.4	1.2	2.3	0.2	0.0	0.4	0.5	0.7
Franklin, MA	5.3	2.3	1.7	0.2	0.0	0.7	0.0	0.4
Frederick, MD	7.3	1.7	2.8	0.5	0.0	0.2	0.6	1.5
Frisco, TX	7.8	1.2	1.8	0.3	0.0	0.6	3.2	0.7
Goodyear, AZ	7.5	1.1	1.4	0.0	0.1	0.5	4.1	0.3
Grand Blanc, MI	3.9	1.0	1.8	0.3	0.1	0.4	0.2	0.1
Greenburgh, NY	21.0	5.3	7.5	0.7	0.1	0.3	0.8	6.2
Greenwich, CT	19.0	7.8	4.5	0.4	0.3	0.9	0.4	4.7
Hampden, PA	4.6	1.1	2.8	0.3	0.1	0.1	0.0	0.2
Hilliard, OH	4.2	0.6	3.1	0.2	0.0	0.2	0.0	0.3
Hoover, AL	6.4	0.8	2.5	0.3	0.0	0.1	2.0	0.7
Huntersville, NC	4.5	0.8	0.8	0.2	0.0	0.4	1.7	0.6
Juneau, AK	5.7	0.9	3.1	0.0	0.1	0.8	0.6	0.2
Keller, TX	5.2	1.9	1.8	0.0	0.0	0.7	0.3	0.6
Kenner, LA	11.3	0.7	2.3	0.1	0.0	0.0	0.6	7.6
Kennesaw, GA	7.5	0.9	2.3	0.7	0.0	0.3	1.8	1.5
League City, TX	8.9	1.3	2.6	0.2	0.1	0.5	2.9	1.4
Leawood, KS	3.6	1.3	1.6	0.1	0.0	0.4	0.0	0.2
Lee's Summit, MO	2.0	0.7	0.6	0.1	0.0	0.2	0.2	0.2
Leesburg, VA	8.6	2.1	2.6	0.3	0.1	0.3	0.3	3.0
Lehi, UT	3.1	0.3	0.4	0.2	0.0	0.7	1.0	0.4
Lwr Providence, PA	6.4	1.9	3.6	0.5	0.0	0.1	0.0	0.3
Madison, AL	5.6	1.0	3.3	0.5	0.0	0.4	0.1	0.3
Manhattan Bch, CA	9.1	2.7	3.7	0.3	0.1	1.0	0.4	1.0
Maple Grove, MN	4.3	1.3	1.8	0.4	0.1	0.4	0.0	0.3
Marion, IA	1.6	0.3	0.9	0.1	0.0	0.2	0.1	0.1

City	Percent of Population Born in: Any Foreign Country	Europe	Asia	Africa	Oceania[1]	Canada	Mexico	Latin America[2]
Marlboro, NJ	15.4	5.2	8.7	0.3	0.0	0.2	0.1	1.0
Matthews, NC	5.8	1.8	1.5	0.5	0.0	0.4	0.1	1.4
Meridian, ID	3.2	1.1	1.1	0.0	0.0	0.3	0.4	0.2
Merrimack, NH	5.0	1.4	1.6	0.1	0.0	1.5	0.0	0.4
Morgantown, WV	5.9	1.5	3.0	0.4	0.1	0.2	0.2	0.5
Mt Pleasant, SC	4.3	2.0	0.9	0.1	0.3	0.3	0.2	0.7
Northampton, PA	9.5	7.2	1.7	0.1	0.0	0.2	0.0	0.2
Northville, MI	9.6	2.8	4.4	0.2	0.0	1.6	0.3	0.3
Novi, MI	12.7	3.2	6.8	0.1	0.1	1.3	0.4	0.7
O'Fallon, MO	2.1	0.9	0.8	0.0	0.0	0.2	0.0	0.2
Oro Valley, AZ	6.2	2.2	1.2	0.1	0.1	1.1	1.0	0.5
Oviedo, FL	9.2	2.0	1.7	0.4	0.0	0.6	0.5	4.0
Palm Bch Grdns, FL	10.9	3.4	2.0	0.2	0.0	1.5	0.1	3.7
Parker, CO	3.6	1.2	1.4	0.0	0.1	0.5	0.3	0.0
Peachtree City, GA	7.8	2.3	2.9	0.4	0.0	0.8	0.1	1.4
Pflugerville, TX	6.4	0.7	3.5	0.8	0.0	0.1	0.9	0.5
Pleasanton, CA	14.3	3.3	7.8	0.3	0.2	0.6	1.3	0.8
Rapid City, SD	2.4	1.0	0.9	0.1	0.0	0.2	0.2	0.1
Redmond, WA	20.6	4.3	10.9	0.4	0.2	1.5	2.4	0.9
Richland, WA	7.2	2.7	2.9	0.1	0.1	0.5	0.5	0.5
Richmond, KY	2.1	0.2	1.1	0.1	0.0	0.2	0.4	0.1
Rio Rancho, NM	4.8	1.4	1.3	0.0	0.1	0.2	1.0	0.8
Rockaway, NJ	13.3	4.3	4.6	0.6	0.0	0.2	0.1	3.5
Rocklin, CA	5.2	1.4	1.9	0.2	0.0	0.5	0.7	0.5
Rogers, AR	13.0	0.3	0.6	0.0	0.0	0.2	8.5	3.5
Round Rock, TX	9.2	0.8	2.3	0.4	0.0	0.3	4.6	0.8
Sammamish, WA	9.9	1.9	5.3	0.3	0.2	1.8	0.1	0.3
San Ramon, CA	16.4	2.9	10.3	0.6	0.2	0.9	0.7	0.9
Santa Fe, NM	11.6	2.1	0.9	0.2	0.0	0.3	7.1	1.0
Saratoga, CA	25.6	5.1	18.6	0.3	0.4	0.7	0.2	0.4
Savage, MN	6.1	0.7	4.0	0.3	0.0	0.4	0.2	0.5
Schererville, IN	8.3	5.1	1.8	0.1	0.0	0.3	0.9	0.2
Shawnee, KS	5.2	0.8	2.5	0.3	0.0	0.2	0.8	0.6
Shrewsbury, MA	10.8	2.6	6.3	0.5	0.0	0.5	0.0	0.9
S Brunswick, NJ	21.6	3.4	14.0	1.6	0.0	0.4	0.1	2.1
S. Jordan, UT	3.1	1.0	0.8	0.0	0.2	0.4	0.3	0.3
S Kingstown, RI	5.8	1.8	2.9	0.2	0.0	0.3	0.1	0.5
Southaven, MS	2.2	0.3	0.7	0.0	0.0	0.0	1.1	0.1
Southlake, TX	5.1	1.8	1.7	0.1	0.0	0.5	0.4	0.7
Spanish Fork, UT	3.1	0.1	0.1	0.1	0.2	0.2	1.5	0.9
Sparks, NV	15.6	1.3	3.7	0.2	0.3	0.5	7.6	2.1
Stow, OH	3.7	1.2	1.9	0.1	0.0	0.2	0.1	0.2
Sugar Land, TX	23.5	1.9	17.6	1.1	0.0	0.6	0.8	1.5
Sun Prairie, WI	3.7	0.5	0.6	0.3	0.0	0.1	1.7	0.4
Tualatin, OR	12.5	1.4	3.2	0.0	0.0	0.8	6.5	0.6
Waimalu, HI	14.6	0.3	13.0	0.1	0.7	0.1	0.1	0.3
Wellington, FL	13.4	2.7	1.8	0.3	0.0	0.7	0.4	7.4
W Des Moines, IA	5.4	1.4	2.3	0.3	0.1	0.4	0.4	0.6
West Linn, OR	5.6	1.4	2.4	0.3	0.2	0.7	0.3	0.3
West Windsor, NJ	22.4	3.6	14.7	0.9	0.1	0.3	0.4	2.4
Weston, FL	28.0	2.5	2.8	0.6	0.1	0.8	0.8	20.5
Woodbury, MN	6.6	1.2	3.7	0.6	0.0	0.4	0.2	0.5
Woodridge, IL	17.3	3.0	8.9	0.5	0.1	0.2	3.7	1.0
Yorba Linda, CA	13.9	2.2	7.8	0.4	0.1	0.9	1.6	0.9
U.S.	11.1	1.7	2.9	0.3	0.1	0.3	3.3	2.5

Note: (1) Includes Australia, New Zealand subregion, Melanesia, Micronesia, Polynesia, and Oceania n.e.c.; (2) Includes Central America (excluding Mexico), South America, and the Caribbean.
Source: Census 2000, Summary File 3

Foreign-Born Population: Metro Area

Metro Area	Percent of Population Born in: Any Foreign Country	Europe	Asia	Africa	Oceania[1]	Canada	Mexico	Latin America[2]
Allen, TX	16.8	0.9	3.4	0.6	0.0	0.3	9.8	1.8
Ankeny, IA	5.3	1.3	1.7	0.3	0.0	0.1	1.3	0.6
Apex, NC	9.2	1.2	2.5	0.7	0.1	0.4	3.2	1.3
Bangor, ME	3.0	0.9	0.8	0.1	0.0	1.0	0.0	0.1
Beavercreek, OH	2.3	0.7	1.1	0.2	0.0	0.1	0.1	0.2
Bellevue, NE	4.8	0.8	1.3	0.3	0.0	0.1	1.8	0.5
Bend, OR	n/a	n/a	n/a	n/a	n/a	n/a	n/a	n/a
Bernards, NJ	20.8	4.4	8.9	1.1	0.0	0.2	1.1	5.1
Bethlehem, NY	4.7	1.9	1.5	0.2	0.0	0.3	0.1	0.7
Bozeman, MT	n/a	n/a	n/a	n/a	n/a	n/a	n/a	n/a
Brentwood, TN	4.7	0.7	1.5	0.4	0.0	0.2	1.3	0.6
Brookfield, WI	5.4	1.6	1.5	0.2	0.0	0.1	1.6	0.4
Broomfield, CO	11.1	1.7	2.3	0.4	0.1	0.4	5.5	0.7
Burlington, VT	5.7	2.1	1.5	0.1	0.0	1.7	0.0	0.2
Carmel, IN	3.4	0.7	1.0	0.2	0.0	0.1	1.0	0.4
Cary, NC	9.2	1.2	2.5	0.7	0.1	0.4	3.2	1.3
Casper, WY	1.8	0.6	0.4	0.0	0.0	0.2	0.5	0.1
Cheshire, CT	8.5	3.1	2.2	0.3	0.0	0.3	0.7	1.8
Chino Hills, CA	18.8	1.2	3.1	0.2	0.1	0.4	11.9	1.9
Collierville, TN	3.3	0.5	1.2	0.2	0.0	0.1	1.0	0.3
Conway, AR	2.4	0.5	0.9	0.1	0.0	0.1	0.6	0.2
Coronado, CA	21.6	2.0	7.0	0.4	0.1	0.5	10.4	1.0
Cranberry, PA	2.6	1.3	0.9	0.1	0.0	0.1	0.0	0.2
Dover, DE	4.0	1.1	1.3	0.3	0.0	0.2	0.2	0.8
Draper, UT	8.6	1.5	1.7	0.2	0.4	0.3	3.5	1.1
Dublin, OH	4.6	0.9	2.1	0.7	0.0	0.2	0.4	0.3
Edmond, OK	5.7	0.5	2.2	0.3	0.0	0.1	2.2	0.4
Evesham, NJ	7.0	2.3	2.8	0.4	0.0	0.2	0.3	1.1
Fargo, ND	3.0	0.9	1.0	0.4	0.0	0.3	0.2	0.1
Farmington, CT	10.2	4.2	1.9	0.3	0.0	0.8	0.2	2.8
Fishers, IN	3.4	0.7	1.0	0.2	0.0	0.1	1.0	0.4
Flower Mound, TX	16.8	0.9	3.4	0.6	0.0	0.3	9.8	1.8
Franklin, MA	14.9	4.3	4.2	0.9	0.1	0.7	0.2	4.7
Frederick, MD	16.9	2.1	6.1	1.9	0.1	0.2	0.7	5.9
Frisco, TX	16.8	0.9	3.4	0.6	0.0	0.3	9.8	1.8
Goodyear, AZ	14.1	1.5	1.8	0.2	0.1	0.6	9.2	0.8
Grand Blanc, MI	2.1	0.8	0.8	0.1	0.0	0.3	0.1	0.1
Greenburgh, NY	33.7	6.8	7.9	1.1	0.1	0.2	1.5	16.1
Greenwich, CT	20.4	6.5	3.4	0.4	0.1	0.6	0.8	8.6
Hampden, PA	3.3	1.0	1.3	0.2	0.0	0.1	0.2	0.4
Hilliard, OH	4.6	0.9	2.1	0.7	0.0	0.2	0.4	0.3
Hoover, AL	2.3	0.4	0.7	0.1	0.0	0.1	0.7	0.3
Huntersville, NC	6.7	0.9	1.5	0.4	0.0	0.2	2.3	1.4
Juneau, AK	n/a	n/a	n/a	n/a	n/a	n/a	n/a	n/a
Keller, TX	11.4	0.8	2.6	0.4	0.1	0.2	6.5	0.8
Kenner, LA	4.8	0.6	1.6	0.1	0.0	0.1	0.2	2.1
Kennesaw, GA	10.3	1.3	2.8	0.9	0.0	0.2	2.9	2.1
League City, TX	8.3	0.8	1.8	0.1	0.0	0.3	4.2	1.1
Leawood, KS	4.5	0.7	1.4	0.2	0.0	0.2	1.5	0.5
Lee's Summit, MO	4.5	0.7	1.4	0.2	0.0	0.2	1.5	0.5
Leesburg, VA	16.9	2.1	6.1	1.9	0.1	0.2	0.7	5.9
Lehi, UT	6.3	0.7	0.9	0.1	0.2	0.6	2.5	1.4
Lwr Providence, PA	7.0	2.3	2.8	0.4	0.0	0.2	0.3	1.1
Madison, AL	3.5	0.8	1.3	0.2	0.0	0.2	0.5	0.5
Manhattan Bch, CA	36.2	2.0	10.7	0.5	0.1	0.4	16.0	6.5
Maple Grove, MN	7.1	1.1	3.0	1.0	0.0	0.3	1.0	0.6
Marion, IA	2.6	0.6	1.3	0.1	0.0	0.1	0.3	0.1

Metro Area	Percent of Population Born in: Any Foreign Country	Europe	Asia	Africa	Oceania[1]	Canada	Mexico	Latin America[2]
Marlboro, NJ	8.6	3.2	2.3	0.2	0.0	0.2	0.8	1.9
Matthews, NC	6.7	0.9	1.5	0.4	0.0	0.2	2.3	1.4
Meridian, ID	5.6	1.3	1.0	0.1	0.0	0.3	2.6	0.3
Merrimack, NH	6.9	1.7	2.1	0.3	0.0	1.3	0.3	1.2
Morgantown, WV	n/a	n/a	n/a	n/a	n/a	n/a	n/a	n/a
Mt Pleasant, SC	3.3	1.0	1.0	0.1	0.1	0.2	0.6	0.4
Northampton, PA	7.0	2.3	2.8	0.4	0.0	0.2	0.3	1.1
Northville, MI	7.5	2.4	3.3	0.2	0.0	0.7	0.6	0.3
Novi, MI	7.5	2.4	3.3	0.2	0.0	0.7	0.6	0.3
O'Fallon, MO	3.1	1.1	1.2	0.2	0.0	0.1	0.3	0.2
Oro Valley, AZ	11.9	1.5	1.7	0.2	0.1	0.5	7.4	0.6
Oviedo, FL	12.0	1.6	2.2	0.4	0.0	0.5	1.0	6.3
Palm Bch Grdns, FL	17.4	3.5	1.5	0.3	0.0	0.9	1.5	9.7
Parker, CO	11.1	1.7	2.3	0.4	0.1	0.4	5.5	0.7
Peachtree City, GA	10.3	1.3	2.8	0.9	0.0	0.2	2.9	2.1
Pflugerville, TX	12.2	1.0	2.9	0.3	0.0	0.2	6.7	1.1
Pleasanton, CA	24.0	2.3	12.1	0.5	0.4	0.4	5.9	2.2
Rapid City, SD	2.1	0.8	0.7	0.1	0.0	0.2	0.2	0.1
Redmond, WA	13.8	2.8	6.9	0.7	0.2	1.0	1.5	0.6
Richland, WA	12.8	1.3	1.5	0.1	0.0	0.4	8.8	0.5
Richmond, KY	4.0	0.7	1.4	0.2	0.0	0.2	1.2	0.3
Rio Rancho, NM	7.9	1.0	1.2	0.1	0.0	0.3	4.7	0.6
Rockaway, NJ	19.0	4.9	3.3	0.9	0.0	0.2	0.4	9.2
Rocklin, CA	13.9	2.7	5.9	0.2	0.4	0.4	3.6	0.7
Rogers, AR	6.9	0.5	1.1	0.0	0.2	0.1	3.8	1.2
Round Rock, TX	12.2	1.0	2.9	0.3	0.0	0.2	6.7	1.1
Sammamish, WA	13.8	2.8	6.9	0.7	0.2	1.0	1.5	0.6
San Ramon, CA	24.0	2.3	12.1	0.5	0.4	0.4	5.9	2.2
Santa Fe, NM	9.7	1.8	0.9	0.1	0.1	0.3	5.7	0.8
Saratoga, CA	34.1	3.4	19.5	0.5	0.2	0.6	8.3	1.5
Savage, MN	7.1	1.1	3.0	1.0	0.0	0.3	1.0	0.6
Schererville, IN	4.8	1.7	0.8	0.1	0.0	0.1	1.8	0.2
Shawnee, KS	4.5	0.7	1.4	0.2	0.0	0.2	1.5	0.5
Shrewsbury, MA	8.3	2.6	2.5	0.8	0.0	0.6	0.1	1.8
S Brunswick, NJ	20.8	4.4	8.9	1.1	0.0	0.2	1.1	5.1
S. Jordan, UT	8.6	1.5	1.7	0.2	0.4	0.3	3.5	1.1
S Kingstown, RI	12.0	4.8	1.9	1.0	0.0	0.4	0.2	3.6
Southaven, MS	3.3	0.5	1.2	0.2	0.0	0.1	1.0	0.3
Southlake, TX	11.4	0.8	2.6	0.4	0.1	0.2	6.5	0.8
Spanish Fork, UT	6.3	0.7	0.9	0.1	0.2	0.6	2.5	1.4
Sparks, NV	14.1	1.4	3.4	0.1	0.3	0.5	6.7	1.7
Stow, OH	3.0	1.3	1.2	0.1	0.0	0.2	0.1	0.2
Sugar Land, TX	20.5	1.1	4.3	0.6	0.0	0.2	10.4	3.8
Sun Prairie, WI	6.3	1.1	2.8	0.3	0.0	0.3	1.2	0.6
Tualatin, OR	10.9	2.5	3.6	0.2	0.2	0.6	3.1	0.6
Waimalu, HI	19.2	0.8	16.4	0.1	1.2	0.3	0.2	0.4
Wellington, FL	17.4	3.5	1.5	0.3	0.0	0.9	1.5	9.7
W Des Moines, IA	5.3	1.3	1.7	0.3	0.0	0.1	1.3	0.6
West Linn, OR	10.9	2.5	3.6	0.2	0.2	0.6	3.1	0.6
West Windsor, NJ	13.9	3.8	3.8	0.9	0.0	0.3	0.4	4.7
Weston, FL	25.3	3.6	1.9	0.4	0.0	1.3	0.7	17.5
Woodbury, MN	7.1	1.1	3.0	1.0	0.0	0.3	1.0	0.6
Woodridge, IL	17.2	4.4	3.9	0.3	0.0	0.2	7.1	1.3
Yorba Linda, CA	29.9	2.0	10.9	0.4	0.2	0.6	13.7	2.1
U.S.	11.1	1.7	2.9	0.3	0.1	0.3	3.3	2.5

Note: Figures cover the Metropolitan Statistical Area - see Appendix A for areas included; (1) Includes Australia, New Zealand subregion, Melanesia, Micronesia, Polynesia, and Oceania n.e.c.; (2) Includes Central America (excluding Mexico), South America, and the Caribbean.

Source: Census 2000, Summary File 3

Marriage Status: City

Area	Never Married	Now Married (excluding Separated)	Separated	Widowed	Divorced
Allen, TX	18.0	72.2	0.9	1.6	7.4
Ankeny, IA	25.5	62.5	1.0	3.3	7.7
Apex, NC	20.0	68.9	1.9	2.4	6.9
Bangor, ME	32.4	44.1	1.7	8.2	13.6
Beavercreek, OH	19.1	68.6	0.7	4.8	6.8
Bellevue, NE	25.1	57.4	1.5	4.7	11.4
Bend, OR	23.9	55.8	2.0	5.7	12.5
Bernards, NJ	19.4	67.1	0.9	5.8	6.8
Bethlehem, NY	19.8	64.2	1.8	7.0	7.2
Bozeman, MT	44.9	42.4	0.9	3.9	8.0
Brentwood, TN	17.5	74.3	0.7	3.3	4.2
Brookfield, WI	18.6	69.9	0.5	6.3	4.8
Broomfield, CO	23.0	62.6	1.0	3.2	10.3
Burlington, VT	50.5	34.1	1.1	5.0	9.2
Carmel, IN	17.9	70.2	0.5	4.2	7.2
Cary, NC	23.5	65.7	1.5	2.5	6.7
Casper, WY	23.9	54.7	1.3	6.8	13.4
Cheshire, CT	24.2	62.3	0.9	6.0	6.5
Chino Hills, CA	23.6	65.8	1.2	3.0	6.4
Collierville, TN	19.1	71.1	0.9	3.2	5.7
Conway, AR	31.4	53.5	1.5	4.5	9.2
Coronado, CA	35.9	46.6	2.5	5.8	9.2
Cranberry, PA	18.0	69.9	1.3	4.9	5.9
Dover, DE	35.4	42.4	2.4	7.3	12.4
Draper, UT	25.5	60.4	1.5	2.3	10.2
Dublin, OH	18.9	71.5	0.7	2.9	6.0
Edmond, OK	24.5	61.5	0.9	4.8	8.5
Evesham, NJ	23.3	61.7	1.8	5.3	7.8
Fargo, ND	37.8	47.7	0.8	4.7	9.0
Farmington, CT	23.3	60.3	0.5	7.0	8.9
Fishers, IN	19.0	69.9	1.0	1.8	8.3
Flower Mound, TX	16.1	75.2	0.8	2.1	5.8
Franklin, MA	21.8	66.1	1.0	5.1	5.9
Frederick, MD	29.2	50.3	3.2	6.3	10.9
Frisco, TX	15.0	74.0	1.0	1.9	8.0
Goodyear, AZ	20.0	68.5	1.1	2.9	7.5
Grand Blanc, MI	22.5	62.0	1.0	4.8	9.7
Greenburgh, NY	24.8	60.1	1.6	6.8	6.8
Greenwich, CT	22.3	62.4	1.1	6.8	7.4
Hampden, PA	20.3	64.6	1.8	6.0	7.4
Hilliard, OH	19.8	67.7	0.4	3.6	8.4
Hoover, AL	22.1	63.7	0.7	5.2	8.3
Huntersville, NC	19.3	67.9	2.2	3.6	7.0
Juneau, AK	29.1	54.0	1.7	3.7	11.4
Keller, TX	15.1	77.0	0.5	2.1	5.3
Kenner, LA	28.7	51.0	2.8	6.2	11.3
Kennesaw, GA	21.0	62.2	1.8	4.1	11.0
League City, TX	19.3	66.6	1.4	3.5	9.2
Leawood, KS	16.5	74.2	0.3	3.7	5.2
Lee's Summit, MO	19.7	63.8	1.2	5.5	9.7
Leesburg, VA	22.3	59.5	3.0	4.4	10.8
Lehi, UT	18.4	72.9	1.0	2.4	5.3
Lwr Providence, PA	21.7	65.2	1.5	5.4	6.2
Madison, AL	20.7	64.3	1.4	3.0	10.5
Manhattan Bch, CA	30.6	55.6	1.0	4.1	8.7
Maple Grove, MN	22.6	67.1	0.6	2.3	7.3
Marion, IA	23.1	59.8	0.8	5.6	10.7
Marlboro, NJ	19.3	72.2	0.6	5.0	2.8

Area	Never Married	Now Married (excluding Separated)	Separated	Widowed	Divorced
Matthews, NC	19.6	68.4	1.2	4.5	6.4
Meridian, ID	18.4	67.0	0.7	3.2	10.6
Merrimack, NH	20.9	66.4	1.2	3.0	8.5
Morgantown, WV	58.0	30.3	0.8	5.1	5.7
Mt Pleasant, SC	22.1	61.6	1.4	5.6	9.2
Northampton, PA	21.9	67.6	1.4	4.4	4.8
Northville, MI	24.2	60.5	0.9	6.3	8.1
Novi, MI	25.1	61.4	0.6	4.3	8.6
O'Fallon, MO	19.5	68.4	0.9	3.5	7.6
Oro Valley, AZ	14.6	72.2	0.5	5.2	7.5
Oviedo, FL	22.9	66.1	0.9	3.1	6.9
Palm Bch Grdns, FL	18.4	59.3	0.9	8.1	13.4
Parker, CO	18.4	71.1	0.8	1.7	8.1
Peachtree City, GA	18.9	69.6	1.2	3.9	6.4
Pflugerville, TX	20.6	66.5	0.8	2.8	9.3
Pleasanton, CA	20.9	64.6	1.2	4.2	9.1
Rapid City, SD	27.3	52.5	1.6	6.5	12.1
Redmond, WA	28.1	55.2	1.4	4.4	10.9
Richland, WA	22.2	60.6	1.0	5.5	10.7
Richmond, KY	44.8	35.9	2.0	5.6	11.7
Rio Rancho, NM	22.1	60.5	1.1	5.7	10.5
Rockaway, NJ	20.7	67.0	1.2	4.4	6.7
Rocklin, CA	22.6	61.8	1.8	4.1	9.6
Rogers, AR	20.3	61.3	2.0	5.4	10.9
Round Rock, TX	23.3	62.7	1.8	3.1	9.1
Sammamish, WA	18.4	74.2	0.8	1.5	5.2
San Ramon, CA	22.3	62.8	1.1	3.3	10.5
Santa Fe, NM	30.3	44.7	1.6	6.6	16.9
Saratoga, CA	16.9	72.3	0.5	5.7	4.6
Savage, MN	17.8	72.9	0.7	1.7	6.9
Schererville, IN	23.0	61.6	1.0	5.9	8.5
Shawnee, KS	23.0	62.9	0.7	4.4	8.9
Shrewsbury, MA	21.4	63.4	1.3	6.6	7.3
S Brunswick, NJ	22.2	64.5	1.4	4.4	7.5
S. Jordan, UT	27.3	65.3	0.7	2.5	4.2
S Kingstown, RI	33.0	52.4	0.9	5.5	8.3
Southaven, MS	19.8	60.7	1.8	5.7	12.0
Southlake, TX	16.7	78.4	0.3	1.3	3.3
Spanish Fork, UT	22.4	66.4	1.3	3.8	6.2
Sparks, NV	23.9	53.5	1.6	5.7	15.2
Stow, OH	21.8	63.0	0.5	5.5	9.3
Sugar Land, TX	20.9	68.1	0.9	3.7	6.3
Sun Prairie, WI	26.1	58.3	1.6	4.8	9.2
Tualatin, OR	26.6	57.2	1.9	3.7	10.7
Waimalu, HI	29.5	56.0	1.3	3.8	9.4
Wellington, FL	20.3	66.3	1.3	3.8	8.3
W Des Moines, IA	27.3	57.4	1.0	3.9	10.3
West Linn, OR	20.9	63.4	1.4	3.3	11.1
West Windsor, NJ	19.5	71.0	1.2	3.3	5.0
Weston, FL	19.2	69.5	1.2	3.3	6.9
Woodbury, MN	21.7	67.8	0.5	2.8	7.1
Woodridge, IL	28.2	57.3	2.0	3.6	8.8
Yorba Linda, CA	22.2	66.1	1.2	3.6	6.9
U.S.	27.1	54.4	2.2	6.6	9.7

Note: Figures cover population 15 years of age and older
Source: Census 2000, Summary File 3

Marriage Status: Metro Area

Metro Area	Never Married	Now Married (excluding Separated)	Separated	Widowed	Divorced
Allen, TX	27.2	55.6	2.5	4.6	10.1
Ankeny, IA	25.0	57.6	1.3	5.5	10.7
Apex, NC	30.0	54.2	2.5	4.9	8.4
Bangor, ME	30.2	50.3	1.4	6.6	11.6
Beavercreek, OH	25.8	54.2	1.6	6.9	11.5
Bellevue, NE	27.6	54.8	1.4	5.7	10.5
Bend, OR	n/a	n/a	n/a	n/a	n/a
Bernards, NJ	26.3	58.8	1.6	6.2	7.0
Bethlehem, NY	28.3	52.9	2.8	7.6	8.5
Bozeman, MT	n/a	n/a	n/a	n/a	n/a
Brentwood, TN	26.3	54.8	1.8	5.6	11.5
Brookfield, WI	30.4	52.3	1.5	6.5	9.3
Broomfield, CO	27.8	54.2	1.7	4.6	11.7
Burlington, VT	31.6	52.9	1.2	5.0	9.5
Carmel, IN	25.8	55.0	1.6	6.0	11.6
Cary, NC	30.0	54.2	2.5	4.9	8.4
Casper, WY	23.2	55.9	1.3	6.1	13.5
Cheshire, CT	29.8	52.2	1.6	7.2	9.1
Chino Hills, CA	26.7	55.3	2.6	5.7	9.7
Collierville, TN	29.8	49.1	3.6	6.7	10.7
Conway, AR	24.0	56.0	1.8	6.2	12.0
Coronado, CA	30.2	52.0	2.3	5.3	10.2
Cranberry, PA	26.2	54.5	1.9	9.2	8.3
Dover, DE	26.0	54.5	2.2	6.4	10.9
Draper, UT	27.6	57.6	1.4	4.1	9.3
Dublin, OH	29.6	52.1	1.7	5.5	11.1
Edmond, OK	25.2	54.4	1.8	6.2	12.4
Evesham, NJ	30.6	51.3	2.7	7.6	7.8
Fargo, ND	33.8	52.2	0.8	5.0	8.2
Farmington, CT	27.7	54.3	1.7	6.8	9.6
Fishers, IN	25.8	55.0	1.6	6.0	11.6
Flower Mound, TX	27.2	55.6	2.5	4.6	10.1
Franklin, MA	33.4	50.6	1.8	6.6	7.5
Frederick, MD	30.9	52.7	2.8	5.1	8.5
Frisco, TX	27.2	55.6	2.5	4.6	10.1
Goodyear, AZ	26.5	55.0	1.9	5.6	11.0
Grand Blanc, MI	28.2	51.3	1.9	6.5	12.1
Greenburgh, NY	36.2	45.3	4.0	7.0	7.6
Greenwich, CT	25.7	58.6	1.5	6.5	7.7
Hampden, PA	25.3	56.5	2.0	7.3	8.8
Hilliard, OH	29.6	52.1	1.7	5.5	11.1
Hoover, AL	25.1	54.5	2.1	7.6	10.8
Huntersville, NC	25.5	57.0	2.7	5.8	8.9
Juneau, AK	n/a	n/a	n/a	n/a	n/a
Keller, TX	24.3	57.5	2.3	4.9	11.0
Kenner, LA	31.5	47.3	2.7	7.3	11.2
Kennesaw, GA	29.1	53.8	2.1	4.8	10.2
League City, TX	23.6	55.9	2.6	6.3	11.6
Leawood, KS	25.1	55.6	1.8	6.0	11.4
Lee's Summit, MO	25.1	55.6	1.8	6.0	11.4
Leesburg, VA	30.9	52.7	2.8	5.1	8.5
Lehi, UT	32.6	58.6	0.8	3.0	4.9
Lwr Providence, PA	30.6	51.3	2.7	7.6	7.8
Madison, AL	22.6	58.7	1.9	5.9	10.9
Manhattan Bch, CA	34.1	48.8	3.1	5.5	8.5
Maple Grove, MN	29.7	55.1	1.1	4.8	9.2
Marion, IA	26.1	57.0	1.1	5.9	10.1
Marlboro, NJ	23.3	58.6	1.6	8.9	7.6

Metro Area	Never Married	Now Married (excluding Separated)	Separated	Widowed	Divorced
Matthews, NC	25.5	57.0	2.7	5.8	8.9
Meridian, ID	23.4	58.9	1.2	4.7	11.7
Merrimack, NH	23.9	60.2	1.7	4.7	9.6
Morgantown, WV	n/a	n/a	n/a	n/a	n/a
Mt Pleasant, SC	29.5	51.6	3.3	6.3	9.3
Northampton, PA	30.6	51.3	2.7	7.6	7.8
Northville, MI	29.2	51.5	1.7	7.1	10.6
Novi, MI	29.2	51.5	1.7	7.1	10.6
O'Fallon, MO	27.3	53.3	1.9	7.1	10.3
Oro Valley, AZ	27.8	52.0	1.6	6.6	12.0
Oviedo, FL	26.6	54.0	2.4	6.0	11.0
Palm Bch Grdns, FL	21.6	56.2	2.0	9.5	10.8
Parker, CO	27.8	54.2	1.7	4.6	11.7
Peachtree City, GA	29.1	53.8	2.1	4.8	10.2
Pflugerville, TX	32.2	51.7	1.8	3.8	10.4
Pleasanton, CA	29.6	52.7	2.0	5.7	10.0
Rapid City, SD	25.5	55.8	1.5	5.7	11.6
Redmond, WA	29.2	53.2	1.5	4.8	11.3
Richland, WA	24.0	59.2	1.7	4.9	10.1
Richmond, KY	28.6	53.2	1.9	5.6	10.7
Rio Rancho, NM	28.6	51.5	1.6	5.6	12.6
Rockaway, NJ	29.8	53.1	2.8	7.1	7.2
Rocklin, CA	26.8	53.1	2.4	5.9	11.8
Rogers, AR	22.0	61.3	1.4	5.3	10.0
Round Rock, TX	32.2	51.7	1.8	3.8	10.4
Sammamish, WA	29.2	53.2	1.5	4.8	11.3
San Ramon, CA	29.6	52.7	2.0	5.7	10.0
Santa Fe, NM	26.6	53.3	1.4	5.0	13.7
Saratoga, CA	30.2	54.8	1.8	4.7	8.5
Savage, MN	29.7	55.1	1.1	4.8	9.2
Schererville, IN	27.9	52.7	1.8	7.5	10.1
Shawnee, KS	25.1	55.6	1.8	6.0	11.4
Shrewsbury, MA	28.2	53.7	1.9	7.0	9.1
S Brunswick, NJ	26.3	58.8	1.6	6.2	7.0
S. Jordan, UT	27.6	57.6	1.4	4.1	9.3
S Kingstown, RI	29.2	52.0	1.9	7.7	9.2
Southaven, MS	29.8	49.1	3.6	6.7	10.7
Southlake, TX	24.3	57.5	2.3	4.9	11.0
Spanish Fork, UT	32.6	58.6	0.8	3.0	4.9
Sparks, NV	25.7	52.1	1.9	5.4	14.9
Stow, OH	26.8	54.1	1.3	6.9	10.9
Sugar Land, TX	27.4	55.6	2.8	4.8	9.5
Sun Prairie, WI	34.8	51.0	1.1	4.0	9.1
Tualatin, OR	26.8	54.6	1.7	5.3	11.6
Waimalu, HI	30.7	53.4	1.6	5.9	8.4
Wellington, FL	21.6	56.2	2.0	9.5	10.8
W Des Moines, IA	25.0	57.6	1.3	5.5	10.7
West Linn, OR	26.8	54.6	1.7	5.3	11.6
West Windsor, NJ	29.9	52.9	2.4	7.0	7.8
Weston, FL	25.9	51.3	2.6	8.4	11.8
Woodbury, MN	29.7	55.1	1.1	4.8	9.2
Woodridge, IL	31.2	52.1	2.0	6.4	8.3
Yorba Linda, CA	28.4	55.4	2.1	5.1	9.1
U.S.	27.1	54.4	2.2	6.6	9.7

Note: Figures cover population 15 years of age and older in the Metropolitan Statistical Area - see Appendix A for areas included
Source: Census 2000, Summary File 3

Male/Female Ratio: City

City	Males	Females	Males per 100 Females
Allen, TX	36,601	36,429	100.5
Ankeny, IA	17,829	18,835	94.7
Apex, NC	14,148	14,252	99.3
Bangor, ME	14,702	16,122	91.2
Beavercreek, OH	19,755	20,039	98.6
Bellevue, NE	23,072	23,353	98.8
Bend, OR	35,799	36,540	98.0
Bernards, NJ	13,418	13,983	96.0
Bethlehem, NY	15,875	17,188	92.4
Bozeman, MT	17,728	15,984	110.9
Brentwood, TN	14,739	15,147	97.3
Brookfield, WI	19,082	20,275	94.1
Broomfield, CO	22,449	22,152	101.3
Burlington, VT	18,091	19,141	94.5
Carmel, IN	23,000	24,001	95.8
Cary, NC	54,786	55,007	99.6
Casper, WY	25,619	26,797	95.6
Cheshire, CT	15,655	13,644	114.7
Chino Hills, CA	37,831	38,225	99.0
Collierville, TN	18,710	19,247	97.2
Conway, AR	25,711	28,056	91.6
Coronado, CA	16,980	11,576	146.7
Cranberry, PA	13,640	14,000	97.4
Dover, DE	16,817	18,618	90.3
Draper, UT	20,294	16,509	122.9
Dublin, OH	17,806	18,056	98.6
Edmond, OK	37,544	39,581	94.9
Evesham, NJ	23,189	24,654	94.1
Fargo, ND	46,143	45,615	101.2
Farmington, CT	11,964	13,306	89.9
Fishers, IN	29,775	31,000	96.0
Flower Mound, TX	32,595	32,981	98.8
Franklin, MA	15,504	15,945	97.2
Frederick, MD	28,609	30,664	93.3
Frisco, TX	39,914	40,193	99.3
Goodyear, AZ	22,960	22,099	103.9
Grand Blanc, MI	17,687	18,601	95.1
Greenburgh, NY	42,658	46,799	91.2
Greenwich, CT	29,811	32,626	91.4
Hampden, PA	12,740	13,467	94.6
Hilliard, OH	13,390	13,753	97.4
Hoover, AL	34,137	35,756	95.5
Huntersville, NC	19,021	19,357	98.3
Juneau, AK	15,725	15,472	101.6
Keller, TX	19,084	19,191	99.4
Kenner, LA	32,431	34,909	92.9
Kennesaw, GA	15,388	15,865	97.0
League City, TX	32,458	32,916	98.6
Leawood, KS	14,887	15,455	96.3
Lee's Summit, MO	39,989	42,770	93.5
Leesburg, VA	18,846	19,184	98.2
Lehi, UT	15,158	15,213	99.6
Lwr Providence, PA	13,611	12,194	111.6
Madison, AL	18,192	18,613	97.7
Manhattan Bch, CA	18,878	18,717	100.9
Maple Grove, MN	30,554	31,164	98.0
Marion, IA	15,005	15,864	94.6
Marlboro, NJ	19,916	20,277	98.2
Matthews, NC	12,242	12,886	95.0

City	Males	Females	Males per 100 Females
Meridian, ID	27,151	27,861	97.5
Merrimack, NH	13,382	13,455	99.5
Morgantown, WV	14,941	14,021	106.6
Mt Pleasant, SC	28,142	30,365	92.7
Northampton, PA	20,176	21,150	95.4
Northville, MI	12,399	14,118	87.8
Novi, MI	27,082	27,776	97.5
O'Fallon, MO	33,076	33,748	98.0
Oro Valley, AZ	18,165	19,363	93.8
Oviedo, FL	15,961	16,211	98.5
Palm Bch Grdns, FL	23,767	26,084	91.1
Parker, CO	19,837	19,926	99.6
Peachtree City, GA	17,271	18,112	95.4
Pflugerville, TX	13,516	13,742	98.4
Pleasanton, CA	33,082	34,261	96.6
Rapid City, SD	30,416	31,526	96.5
Redmond, WA	24,418	24,136	101.2
Richland, WA	22,736	23,485	96.8
Richmond, KY	14,712	15,921	92.4
Rio Rancho, NM	34,534	36,750	94.0
Rockaway, NJ	12,923	13,150	98.3
Rocklin, CA	31,873	33,026	96.5
Rogers, AR	24,088	24,674	97.6
Round Rock, TX	42,678	42,597	100.2
Sammamish, WA	17,856	17,651	101.2
San Ramon, CA	25,476	26,089	97.7
Santa Fe, NM	34,169	36,694	93.1
Saratoga, CA	14,857	15,322	97.0
Savage, MN	13,861	13,661	101.5
Schererville, IN	14,326	14,905	96.1
Shawnee, KS	29,701	30,173	98.4
Shrewsbury, MA	16,334	17,056	95.8
S Brunswick, NJ	20,025	21,143	94.7
S. Jordan, UT	22,207	22,017	100.9
S Kingstown, RI	14,213	15,480	91.8
Southaven, MS	20,405	20,905	97.6
Southlake, TX	12,810	12,799	100.1
Spanish Fork, UT	14,060	13,866	101.4
Sparks, NV	42,688	43,610	97.9
Stow, OH	16,808	17,879	94.0
Sugar Land, TX	38,366	40,183	95.5
Sun Prairie, WI	12,560	13,380	93.9
Tualatin, OR	13,203	13,236	99.8
Waimalu, HI	15,165	15,079	100.6
Wellington, FL	27,649	28,880	95.7
W Des Moines, IA	26,237	28,390	92.4
West Linn, OR	12,646	12,783	98.9
West Windsor, NJ	13,568	13,824	98.1
Weston, FL	32,791	34,747	94.4
Woodbury, MN	26,546	27,857	95.3
Woodridge, IL	17,038	17,085	99.7
Yorba Linda, CA	32,759	33,896	96.6
U.S.	148,320,305	152,725,217	97.1

Note: Figures are 2007 estimates
Source: Claritas, Inc.

Male/Female Ratio: Metro Area

Metro Area	Males	Females	Males per 100 Females
Allen, TX	3,012,647	2,995,084	100.6
Ankeny, IA	261,341	273,780	95.5
Apex, NC	495,512	498,891	99.3
Bangor, ME	72,305	75,209	96.1
Beavercreek, OH	409,112	433,460	94.4
Bellevue, NE	408,561	419,147	97.5
Bend, OR	74,771	75,879	98.5
Bernards, NJ	9,117,706	9,769,899	93.3
Bethlehem, NY	417,318	438,019	95.3
Bozeman, MT	42,232	39,301	107.5
Brentwood, TN	719,926	738,189	97.5
Brookfield, WI	738,059	777,745	94.9
Broomfield, CO	1,209,653	1,199,727	100.8
Burlington, VT	101,581	105,085	96.7
Carmel, IN	821,473	850,887	96.5
Cary, NC	495,512	498,891	99.3
Casper, WY	35,077	35,811	98.0
Cheshire, CT	410,424	441,723	92.9
Chino Hills, CA	2,034,382	2,036,183	99.9
Collierville, TN	619,790	660,785	93.8
Conway, AR	318,269	335,906	94.7
Coronado, CA	1,526,061	1,495,860	102.0
Cranberry, PA	1,138,277	1,234,253	92.2
Dover, DE	72,542	77,478	93.6
Draper, UT	533,785	521,274	102.4
Dublin, OH	854,714	879,228	97.2
Edmond, OK	579,468	595,954	97.2
Evesham, NJ	2,831,289	3,031,364	93.4
Fargo, ND	93,192	94,572	98.5
Farmington, CT	580,819	616,784	94.2
Fishers, IN	821,473	850,887	96.5
Flower Mound, TX	3,012,647	2,995,084	100.6
Franklin, MA	2,141,463	2,264,097	94.6
Frederick, MD	2,624,053	2,743,412	95.6
Frisco, TX	3,012,647	2,995,084	100.6
Goodyear, AZ	2,031,917	2,001,964	101.5
Grand Blanc, MI	214,245	231,132	92.7
Greenburgh, NY	9,117,706	9,769,899	93.3
Greenwich, CT	441,280	465,302	94.8
Hampden, PA	255,654	270,057	94.7
Hilliard, OH	854,714	879,228	97.2
Hoover, AL	533,038	570,436	93.4
Huntersville, NC	778,817	801,262	97.2
Juneau, AK	15,725	15,472	101.6
Keller, TX	3,012,647	2,995,084	100.6
Kenner, LA	510,110	543,934	93.8
Kennesaw, GA	2,543,029	2,579,832	98.6
League City, TX	2,742,445	2,747,074	99.8
Leawood, KS	972,123	1,005,434	96.7
Lee's Summit, MO	972,123	1,005,434	96.7
Leesburg, VA	2,624,053	2,743,412	95.6
Lehi, UT	233,386	237,101	98.4
Lwr Providence, PA	2,831,289	3,031,364	93.4
Madison, AL	185,912	190,826	97.4
Manhattan Bch, CA	6,549,003	6,666,814	98.2
Maple Grove, MN	1,584,394	1,611,318	98.3
Marion, IA	122,923	126,138	97.5
Marlboro, NJ	9,117,706	9,769,899	93.3
Matthews, NC	778,817	801,262	97.2

Metro Area	Males	Females	Males per 100 Females
Meridian, ID	285,650	282,440	101.1
Merrimack, NH	201,221	205,022	98.1
Morgantown, WV	58,327	57,108	102.1
Mt Pleasant, SC	299,081	311,247	96.1
Northampton, PA	2,831,289	3,031,364	93.4
Northville, MI	2,193,132	2,300,204	95.3
Novi, MI	2,193,132	2,300,204	95.3
O'Fallon, MO	1,360,211	1,451,051	93.7
Oro Valley, AZ	470,818	491,233	95.8
Oviedo, FL	1,002,519	1,026,443	97.7
Palm Bch Grdns, FL	2,679,933	2,842,136	94.3
Parker, CO	1,209,653	1,199,727	100.8
Peachtree City, GA	2,543,029	2,579,832	98.6
Pflugerville, TX	762,780	741,092	102.9
Pleasanton, CA	2,094,712	2,133,687	98.2
Rapid City, SD	59,460	60,159	98.8
Redmond, WA	1,633,417	1,636,945	99.8
Richland, WA	115,828	113,000	102.5
Richmond, KY	47,062	49,587	94.9
Rio Rancho, NM	402,639	417,309	96.5
Rockaway, NJ	9,117,706	9,769,899	93.3
Rocklin, CA	1,033,092	1,069,120	96.6
Rogers, AR	211,981	211,400	100.3
Round Rock, TX	762,780	741,092	102.9
Sammamish, WA	1,633,417	1,636,945	99.8
San Ramon, CA	2,094,712	2,133,687	98.2
Santa Fe, NM	70,713	73,118	96.7
Saratoga, CA	913,801	881,514	103.7
Savage, MN	1,584,394	1,611,318	98.3
Schererville, IN	4,679,416	4,848,750	96.5
Shawnee, KS	972,123	1,005,434	96.7
Shrewsbury, MA	387,974	402,385	96.4
S Brunswick, NJ	9,117,706	9,769,899	93.3
S. Jordan, UT	533,785	521,274	102.4
S Kingstown, RI	785,710	840,524	93.5
Southaven, MS	619,790	660,785	93.8
Southlake, TX	3,012,647	2,995,084	100.6
Spanish Fork, UT	233,386	237,101	98.4
Sparks, NV	207,050	201,672	102.7
Stow, OH	340,261	363,186	93.7
Sugar Land, TX	2,742,445	2,747,074	99.8
Sun Prairie, WI	270,366	274,316	98.6
Tualatin, OR	1,065,621	1,072,892	99.3
Waimalu, HI	455,198	459,363	99.1
Wellington, FL	2,679,933	2,842,136	94.3
W Des Moines, IA	261,341	273,780	95.5
West Linn, OR	1,065,621	1,072,892	99.3
West Windsor, NJ	181,394	188,773	96.1
Weston, FL	2,679,933	2,842,136	94.3
Woodbury, MN	1,584,394	1,611,318	98.3
Woodridge, IL	4,679,416	4,848,750	96.5
Yorba Linda, CA	6,549,003	6,666,814	98.2
U.S.	148,320,305	152,725,217	97.1

Note: Figures are 2007 estimates and cover the Metropolitan Statistical Area (MSA) - see Appendix B for areas included
Source: Claritas, Inc.

Gross Metropolitan Product

MSA[1]	2002	2003	2004	2005	2005 Rank[2]
Allen, TX	229.2	238.6	260.0	284.5	5
Ankeny, IA	19.4	20.9	21.7	23.1	83
Apex, NC	31.2	32.8	35.3	38.4	55
Bangor, ME	4.5	4.6	5.0	5.2	268
Beavercreek, OH	30.4	31.3	32.7	33.7	59
Bellevue, NE	28.5	30.5	31.7	33.5	60
Bend, OR	3.8	4.0	4.7	5.2	270
Bernards, NJ	820.9	847.1	902.4	952.6	1
Bethlehem, NY	39.5	41.1	44.0	46.4	47
Brentwood, TN	48.8	51.8	56.3	60.3	40
Brookfield, WI	56.9	58.6	61.3	63.7	39
Broomfield, CO	98.7	102.4	108.5	116.4	19
Burlington, VT	7.4	7.8	8.4	8.7	188
Carmel, IN	58.6	62.4	66.1	69.1	36
Cary, NC	31.2	32.8	35.3	38.4	55
Casper, WY	2.6	2.9	3.4	3.8	323
Cheshire, CT	36.6	37.3	40.2	42.2	52
Chino Hills, CA	98.8	108.1	121.1	133.0	17
Collierville, TN	42.5	45.0	47.5	50.3	46
Conway, AR	19.6	20.5	22.3	23.7	81
Coronado, CA	117.0	124.4	134.5	143.4	16
Cranberry, PA	84.7	87.6	91.9	96.2	22
Dover, DE	5.4	5.8	6.6	7.1	213
Draper, UT	38.2	39.5	42.2	46.4	48
Dublin, OH	63.8	66.5	70.2	73.1	34
Edmond, OK	34.0	36.4	39.6	43.1	51
Evesham, NJ	227.1	236.5	250.3	264.8	6
Fargo, ND	6.3	6.7	7.3	7.8	204
Farmington, CT	62.8	64.3	69.1	73.8	33
Fishers, IN	58.6	62.4	66.1	69.1	36
Flower Mound, TX	229.2	238.6	260.0	284.5	5
Franklin, MA	210.9	218.1	230.5	241.1	8
Frederick, MD	238.6	256.3	280.1	300.4	4
Frisco, TX	229.2	238.6	260.0	284.5	5
Goodyear, AZ	120.3	128.0	136.2	153.2	14
Grand Blanc, MI	12.4	12.7	12.9	13.2	142
Greenburgh, NY	820.9	847.1	902.4	952.6	1
Greenwich, CT	44.5	45.9	48.8	52.0	45
Hampden, PA	23.7	24.6	25.9	27.2	70
Hilliard, OH	63.8	66.5	70.2	73.1	34
Hoover, AL	33.2	34.7	37.2	39.9	54
Huntersville, NC	60.6	63.1	66.1	71.3	35
Keller, TX	229.2	238.6	260.0	284.5	5
Kenner, LA	41.6	44.7	48.6	46.1	49
Kennesaw, GA	178.4	184.0	197.1	212.4	10
League City, TX	191.9	204.0	221.2	244.4	7
Leawood, KS	66.9	69.7	73.9	78.6	31
Lee's Summit, MO	66.9	69.7	73.9	78.6	31
Leesburg, VA	238.6	256.3	280.1	300.4	4
Lehi, UT	9.9	10.5	11.6	12.9	146
Lwr Providence, PA	227.1	236.5	250.3	264.8	6
Madison, AL	11.9	12.8	13.9	15.0	124
Manhattan Bch, CA	502.1	528.0	567.6	604.8	2
Maple Grove, MN	128.6	135.8	145.2	151.9	15
Marion, IA	8.9	9.3	9.7	10.2	170
Marlboro, NJ	820.9	847.1	902.4	952.6	1
Matthews, NC	60.6	63.1	66.1	71.3	35
Meridian, ID	14.5	15.3	17.3	19.2	97
Merrimack, NH	15.3	16.1	17.3	18.3	102
Morgantown, WV	3.1	3.3	3.6	3.8	321

MSA[1]	2002	2003	2004	2005	2005 Rank[2]
Mt Pleasant, SC	17.0	17.9	19.1	20.6	90
Northampton, PA	227.1	236.5	250.3	264.8	6
Northville, MI	165.2	171.9	172.9	177.5	12
Novi, MI	165.2	171.9	172.9	177.5	12
O'Fallon, MO	95.3	99.1	103.4	108.9	21
Oro Valley, AZ	25.7	27.1	28.7	31.1	67
Oviedo, FL	61.8	66.6	74.2	83.8	27
Palm Bch Grdns, FL	162.4	171.8	187.0	206.1	11
Parker, CO	98.7	102.4	108.5	116.4	19
Peachtree City, GA	178.4	184.0	197.1	212.4	10
Pflugerville, TX	52.0	54.3	59.7	66.2	38
Pleasanton, CA	186.1	190.8	201.5	213.5	9
Rapid City, SD	3.9	4.0	4.4	4.6	293
Redmond, WA	138.9	142.3	149.0	158.0	13
Richland, WA	6.7	7.2	7.7	8.0	198
Richmond, KY	15.3	15.9	16.7	17.7	109
Rio Rancho, NM	24.7	27.0	29.9	32.3	65
Rockaway, NJ	820.9	847.1	902.4	952.6	1
Rocklin, CA	73.5	78.8	85.3	91.6	24
Rogers, AR	11.2	12.0	13.3	14.5	130
Round Rock, TX	52.0	54.3	59.7	66.2	38
Sammamish, WA	138.9	142.3	149.0	158.0	13
San Ramon, CA	186.1	190.8	201.5	213.5	9
Santa Fe, NM	3.6	3.9	4.3	4.6	292
Saratoga, CA	82.6	82.8	87.6	93.6	23
Savage, MN	128.6	135.8	145.2	151.9	15
Schererville, IN	365.9	381.9	399.9	422.0	3
Shawnee, KS	66.9	69.7	73.9	78.6	31
Shrewsbury, MA	28.6	30.2	32.0	33.2	61
S Brunswick, NJ	820.9	847.1	902.4	952.6	1
S. Jordan, UT	38.2	39.5	42.2	46.4	48
S. Kingstown, RI	56.4	60.0	63.8	66.6	37
Southaven, MS	42.5	45.0	47.5	50.3	46
Southlake, TX	229.2	238.6	260.0	284.5	5
Spanish Fork, UT	9.9	10.5	11.6	12.9	146
Sparks, NV	15.4	16.6	18.2	19.9	94
Stow, OH	22.8	24.1	25.7	27.1	71
Sugar Land, TX	191.9	204.0	221.2	244.4	7
Sun Prairie, WI	20.9	21.9	23.5	24.9	80
Tualatin, OR	70.3	72.1	80.0	85.7	26
Waimalu, HI	33.0	35.1	38.0	40.9	53
Wellington, FL	162.4	171.8	187.0	206.1	11
W Des Moines, IA	19.4	20.9	21.7	23.1	83
West Linn, OR	70.3	72.1	80.0	85.7	26
West Windsor, NJ	19.0	19.7	21.1	22.4	86
Weston, FL	162.4	171.8	187.0	206.1	11
Woodbury, MN	128.6	135.8	145.2	151.9	15
Woodridge, IL	365.9	381.9	399.9	422.0	3
Yorba Linda, CA	502.1	528.0	567.6	604.8	2

Note: Figures are in billions of dollars; (1) Metropolitan Statistical Area - see Appendix A for areas included; (2) Rank ranges from 1 to 318
Source: The U.S. Conference of Mayors, "U.S. Metro Economies: GMP - The Engines of America's Growth," January 2007

Per Capita/Median/Average Income: City

City	Per Capita ($)	Median Household ($)	Average Household ($)
Allen, TX	34,198	90,467	104,107
Ankeny, IA	30,646	65,683	77,324
Apex, NC	36,968	88,470	100,123
Bangor, ME	22,539	33,667	48,266
Beavercreek, OH	36,713	80,790	94,104
Bellevue, NE	25,266	54,916	64,155
Bend, OR	26,849	48,521	63,681
Bernards, NJ	62,910	125,848	169,789
Bethlehem, NY	38,385	74,438	96,744
Bozeman, MT	20,583	39,908	49,508
Brentwood, TN	56,834	132,495	170,704
Brookfield, WI	42,903	83,387	113,622
Broomfield, CO	33,940	79,359	92,559
Burlington, VT	23,140	39,360	53,276
Carmel, IN	44,555	91,770	121,946
Cary, NC	39,555	89,187	107,966
Casper, WY	25,068	46,048	59,377
Cheshire, CT	39,369	91,466	115,245
Chino Hills, CA	32,360	96,655	110,790
Collierville, TN	38,765	96,045	116,893
Conway, AR	22,256	44,566	59,307
Coronado, CA	39,036	76,656	107,379
Cranberry, PA	34,011	82,173	95,426
Dover, DE	22,125	42,992	54,120
Draper, UT	29,513	90,650	107,497
Dublin, OH	47,352	102,571	130,187
Edmond, OK	32,769	65,921	86,535
Evesham, NJ	35,607	80,070	94,068
Fargo, ND	26,129	41,346	56,524
Farmington, CT	44,737	78,516	111,081
Fishers, IN	37,273	85,027	100,150
Flower Mound, TX	42,669	114,441	134,905
Franklin, MA	35,134	88,047	102,403
Frederick, MD	28,221	57,460	69,355
Frisco, TX	40,658	91,779	111,213
Goodyear, AZ	30,202	69,229	87,230
Grand Blanc, MI	31,666	65,848	78,473
Greenburgh, NY	50,392	93,433	131,190
Greenwich, CT	69,674	113,724	182,592
Hampden, PA	36,255	71,273	88,217
Hilliard, OH	35,419	86,024	100,215
Hoover, AL	41,544	75,167	102,252
Huntersville, NC	36,503	83,171	96,668
Juneau, AK	31,149	69,274	81,013
Keller, TX	37,653	103,011	119,511
Kenner, LA	22,062	43,266	58,646
Kennesaw, GA	29,971	69,762	78,958
League City, TX	32,106	77,025	89,026
Leawood, KS	55,451	111,226	153,602
Lee's Summit, MO	33,230	74,176	89,289
Leesburg, VA	35,052	85,215	99,084
Lehi, UT	18,036	58,449	66,846
Lwr Providence, PA	33,095	83,415	95,833
Madison, AL	33,894	76,260	88,796
Manhattan Bch, CA	69,587	119,359	165,334
Maple Grove, MN	37,767	90,675	106,715
Marion, IA	28,285	55,692	67,989
Marlboro, NJ	46,497	121,029	146,878
Matthews, NC	30,428	72,598	83,226

City	Per Capita ($)	Median Household ($)	Average Household ($)
Meridian, ID	25,369	64,976	72,666
Merrimack, NH	32,940	79,899	91,644
Morgantown, WV	16,489	24,121	40,296
Mt Pleasant, SC	40,488	76,073	98,366
Northampton, PA	40,164	96,608	119,232
Northville, MI	48,682	97,474	123,753
Novi, MI	44,075	83,218	110,239
O'Fallon, MO	27,759	73,455	81,553
Oro Valley, AZ	37,875	72,294	91,039
Oviedo, FL	29,399	77,575	91,356
Palm Bch Grdns, FL	48,198	68,646	106,463
Parker, CO	32,871	85,094	95,866
Peachtree City, GA	37,045	88,596	105,824
Pflugerville, TX	29,046	79,339	92,087
Pleasanton, CA	49,493	106,982	136,165
Rapid City, SD	23,223	41,561	55,227
Redmond, WA	41,714	76,315	95,190
Richland, WA	30,248	62,081	75,619
Richmond, KY	18,276	29,752	42,267
Rio Rancho, NM	24,050	55,331	64,576
Rockaway, NJ	41,360	95,282	115,612
Rocklin, CA	34,822	82,613	96,288
Rogers, AR	23,937	49,209	67,338
Round Rock, TX	28,157	66,571	80,468
Sammamish, WA	49,345	121,154	150,782
San Ramon, CA	51,814	111,949	135,179
Santa Fe, NM	29,679	46,730	65,312
Saratoga, CA	72,338	164,595	210,443
Savage, MN	31,888	91,310	100,198
Schererville, IN	32,849	66,614	83,169
Shawnee, KS	33,244	69,962	85,704
Shrewsbury, MA	39,261	79,578	99,421
S Brunswick, NJ	39,603	96,951	113,403
S. Jordan, UT	25,627	88,398	98,428
S Kingstown, RI	31,012	71,010	88,720
Southaven, MS	23,752	51,072	60,279
Southlake, TX	58,034	160,217	198,336
Spanish Fork, UT	17,508	54,761	63,950
Sparks, NV	25,147	55,562	68,563
Stow, OH	29,949	65,252	76,185
Sugar Land, TX	36,831	88,452	112,590
Sun Prairie, WI	29,646	63,838	74,576
Tualatin, OR	30,745	60,212	80,835
Waimalu, HI	31,257	70,286	84,383
Wellington, FL	34,004	76,632	99,534
W Des Moines, IA	36,187	61,303	82,528
West Linn, OR	41,068	83,695	109,846
West Windsor, NJ	58,426	142,859	178,147
Weston, FL	43,902	98,168	134,580
Woodbury, MN	40,456	90,550	110,143
Woodridge, IL	31,809	69,903	85,206
Yorba Linda, CA	42,184	104,776	129,129
U.S.	25,495	49,280	66,670

Note: Figures are 2007 estimates
Source: Claritas, Inc.

Per Capita/Median/Average Income: Metro Area

Metro Area	Per Capita ($)	Median Household ($)	Average Household ($)
Allen, TX	27,089	55,079	74,352
Ankeny, IA	28,482	55,557	70,397
Apex, NC	29,177	58,800	74,884
Bangor, ME	22,177	41,132	52,566
Beavercreek, OH	25,401	47,625	61,409
Bellevue, NE	26,544	53,433	67,682
Bend, OR	27,306	50,110	66,489
Bernards, NJ	30,292	58,080	82,491
Bethlehem, NY	27,300	51,760	66,055
Bozeman, MT	24,421	47,796	61,199
Brentwood, TN	26,706	50,679	67,062
Brookfield, WI	27,789	53,034	68,386
Broomfield, CO	31,164	61,038	79,383
Burlington, VT	27,214	55,036	69,063
Carmel, IN	27,888	53,907	70,098
Cary, NC	29,177	58,800	74,884
Casper, WY	24,676	46,421	59,372
Cheshire, CT	28,720	56,065	72,844
Chino Hills, CA	20,916	50,889	65,856
Collierville, TN	23,459	45,624	61,677
Conway, AR	24,219	45,499	59,603
Coronado, CA	28,074	57,444	77,474
Cranberry, PA	25,023	43,657	59,040
Dover, DE	22,806	48,826	59,583
Draper, UT	23,629	55,931	71,457
Dublin, OH	27,475	52,886	68,386
Edmond, OK	23,211	43,244	57,303
Evesham, NJ	29,121	57,357	75,797
Fargo, ND	25,033	45,767	59,349
Farmington, CT	31,210	61,837	79,024
Fishers, IN	27,888	53,907	70,098
Flower Mound, TX	27,089	55,079	74,352
Franklin, MA	33,809	65,038	86,341
Frederick, MD	37,288	76,534	97,910
Frisco, TX	27,089	55,079	74,352
Goodyear, AZ	25,647	52,519	69,851
Grand Blanc, MI	23,524	46,206	58,837
Greenburgh, NY	30,292	58,080	82,491
Greenwich, CT	41,302	73,085	111,709
Hampden, PA	27,040	51,772	65,721
Hilliard, OH	27,475	52,886	68,386
Hoover, AL	25,481	46,185	63,343
Huntersville, NC	27,995	53,758	71,403
Juneau, AK	31,149	69,274	81,013
Keller, TX	27,089	55,079	74,352
Kenner, LA	23,503	44,346	61,106
Kennesaw, GA	28,239	58,607	76,863
League City, TX	25,018	51,630	71,229
Leawood, KS	27,400	53,675	68,880
Lee's Summit, MO	27,400	53,675	68,880
Leesburg, VA	37,288	76,534	97,910
Lehi, UT	17,896	51,529	64,693
Lwr Providence, PA	29,121	57,357	75,797
Madison, AL	27,248	51,630	66,991
Manhattan Bch, CA	25,135	53,609	76,338
Maple Grove, MN	31,393	64,067	80,229
Marion, IA	26,168	51,830	63,419
Marlboro, NJ	30,292	58,080	82,491
Matthews, NC	27,995	53,758	71,403

Metro Area	Per Capita ($)	Median Household ($)	Average Household ($)
Meridian, ID	23,394	48,491	62,421
Merrimack, NH	29,843	62,027	77,121
Morgantown, WV	20,239	34,493	48,421
Mt Pleasant, SC	24,660	47,122	61,957
Northampton, PA	29,121	57,357	75,797
Northville, MI	28,321	55,940	72,671
Novi, MI	28,321	55,940	72,671
O'Fallon, MO	26,768	51,672	67,100
Oro Valley, AZ	24,035	43,759	59,634
Oviedo, FL	24,748	48,113	64,033
Palm Bch Grdns, FL	25,535	46,421	67,162
Parker, CO	31,164	61,038	79,383
Peachtree City, GA	28,239	58,607	76,863
Pflugerville, TX	27,754	55,339	72,712
Pleasanton, CA	36,196	70,740	96,428
Rapid City, SD	23,184	44,723	57,449
Redmond, WA	30,164	58,271	74,853
Richland, WA	22,982	53,002	65,657
Richmond, KY	19,663	37,030	48,372
Rio Rancho, NM	24,571	46,368	61,538
Rockaway, NJ	30,292	58,080	82,491
Rocklin, CA	26,930	55,569	72,043
Rogers, AR	22,121	44,376	57,802
Round Rock, TX	27,754	55,339	72,712
Sammamish, WA	30,164	58,271	74,853
San Ramon, CA	36,196	70,740	96,428
Santa Fe, NM	29,096	50,532	69,718
Saratoga, CA	36,203	83,628	108,587
Savage, MN	31,393	64,067	80,229
Schererville, IN	28,223	58,845	77,708
Shawnee, KS	27,400	53,675	68,880
Shrewsbury, MA	28,263	57,239	72,796
S Brunswick, NJ	30,292	58,080	82,491
S. Jordan, UT	23,629	55,931	71,457
S Kingstown, RI	26,302	51,397	66,195
Southaven, MS	23,459	45,624	61,677
Southlake, TX	27,089	55,079	74,352
Spanish Fork, UT	17,896	51,529	64,693
Sparks, NV	27,754	54,199	71,518
Stow, OH	26,172	49,020	64,123
Sugar Land, TX	25,018	51,630	71,229
Sun Prairie, WI	30,052	57,745	71,744
Tualatin, OR	26,987	53,775	68,909
Waimalu, HI	26,746	61,368	78,444
Wellington, FL	25,535	46,421	67,162
W Des Moines, IA	28,482	55,557	70,397
West Linn, OR	26,987	53,775	68,909
West Windsor, NJ	33,474	67,440	91,166
Weston, FL	25,535	46,421	67,162
Woodbury, MN	31,393	64,067	80,229
Woodridge, IL	28,223	58,845	77,708
Yorba Linda, CA	25,135	53,609	76,338
U.S.	25,495	49,280	66,670

Note: Figures are 2007 estimates and cover the Metropolitan Statistical Area (MSA) - see Appendix B for areas included
Source: Claritas, Inc.

Household Income Distribution: City

City	Percent of Households Earning							
	Under $15,000	$15,000 -24,999	$25,000 -34,999	$35,000 -49,999	$50,000 -74,999	$75,000 -99,000	$100,000 -149,999	$150,000 and up
Allen, TX	2.2	3.3	4.9	8.9	18.3	19.9	27.1	15.3
Ankeny, IA	6.2	7.0	8.9	13.6	21.9	17.8	18.1	6.4
Apex, NC	2.1	3.8	3.7	10.1	20.2	18.8	26.5	14.8
Bangor, ME	22.3	14.4	15.2	15.4	14.7	7.7	6.9	3.4
Beavercreek, OH	3.5	3.9	6.4	10.8	20.9	19.3	23.1	12.1
Bellevue, NE	6.7	8.3	11.8	17.9	25.7	14.5	11.8	3.3
Bend, OR	10.5	10.8	12.2	18.0	20.5	11.9	10.8	5.1
Bernards, NJ	2.9	3.1	2.4	6.1	11.6	11.5	20.8	41.7
Bethlehem, NY	3.4	6.0	7.3	14.7	19.0	14.8	20.8	14.0
Bozeman, MT	14.9	15.6	12.6	19.5	19.2	8.7	6.9	2.5
Brentwood, TN	3.1	1.9	2.7	5.4	10.5	11.0	23.3	42.2
Brookfield, WI	3.3	4.6	6.2	10.9	19.0	17.4	19.6	18.8
Broomfield, CO	4.7	3.5	6.4	11.4	20.7	18.7	23.1	11.5
Burlington, VT	17.0	13.4	13.8	17.8	17.3	9.3	7.8	3.6
Carmel, IN	3.6	4.8	5.6	10.3	16.0	14.4	21.2	24.0
Cary, NC	3.1	4.5	5.5	10.0	17.7	16.3	23.8	19.2
Casper, WY	11.8	12.5	12.2	17.4	20.5	12.2	9.5	3.9
Cheshire, CT	4.8	5.6	4.8	9.9	15.3	14.6	24.7	20.4
Chino Hills, CA	3.6	2.9	3.9	7.6	16.0	18.6	29.0	18.5
Collierville, TN	2.9	3.7	5.4	7.4	15.9	17.4	26.2	21.1
Conway, AR	16.8	11.6	11.1	15.8	18.4	11.0	10.8	4.4
Coronado, CA	5.7	5.8	7.4	12.9	17.3	14.1	18.2	18.6
Cranberry, PA	4.2	4.2	5.5	10.8	20.0	18.3	23.5	13.5
Dover, DE	15.6	13.8	11.5	17.4	18.3	10.8	9.3	3.3
Draper, UT	2.3	3.0	4.7	10.9	17.7	18.1	26.5	16.8
Dublin, OH	3.5	3.7	4.0	8.3	14.0	15.1	25.0	26.3
Edmond, OK	9.1	6.9	8.3	13.2	19.6	14.8	16.8	11.3
Evesham, NJ	4.1	4.2	5.4	12.8	19.8	17.8	23.5	12.3
Fargo, ND	14.3	14.0	13.4	17.9	18.7	9.3	8.0	4.2
Farmington, CT	6.6	5.8	7.0	12.1	16.5	14.3	18.5	19.2
Fishers, IN	2.2	3.1	4.8	10.9	20.4	21.6	24.0	13.1
Flower Mound, TX	1.8	1.8	1.9	5.8	12.3	16.8	30.8	28.9
Franklin, MA	4.9	5.7	4.5	9.6	16.4	16.8	24.9	17.1
Frederick, MD	7.9	8.6	9.9	16.0	22.8	15.1	13.9	5.7
Frisco, TX	3.4	3.0	4.4	8.2	17.2	20.6	25.5	17.8
Goodyear, AZ	3.3	3.8	8.7	14.7	24.1	16.7	17.1	11.5
Grand Blanc, MI	6.5	6.7	7.9	14.2	23.1	16.8	17.2	7.7
Greenburgh, NY	5.0	4.9	5.9	9.4	15.0	13.2	19.2	27.3
Greenwich, CT	5.8	4.9	4.4	7.7	12.3	10.1	15.6	39.3
Hampden, PA	4.2	6.7	8.9	12.6	20.6	15.6	19.5	11.9
Hilliard, OH	4.3	3.6	4.8	10.3	18.4	19.3	25.0	14.2
Hoover, AL	4.5	6.0	8.1	12.7	18.6	13.4	19.1	17.5
Huntersville, NC	5.2	4.7	6.2	11.6	16.7	17.4	25.3	13.0
Juneau, AK	6.0	7.3	8.2	13.3	19.7	18.0	19.3	8.2
Keller, TX	1.3	2.7	3.8	5.4	15.0	19.5	31.3	20.9
Kenner, LA	14.3	12.3	13.3	17.3	19.1	10.3	8.7	4.7
Kennesaw, GA	4.5	3.9	7.0	14.4	25.3	20.0	17.6	7.2
League City, TX	4.4	4.7	5.8	12.0	21.5	19.5	22.5	9.6
Leawood, KS	2.8	2.8	4.8	8.3	12.9	12.6	22.7	33.0
Lee's Summit, MO	5.1	5.3	7.1	11.6	21.6	17.6	20.7	11.0
Leesburg, VA	4.5	3.8	6.3	9.1	18.3	19.8	23.3	15.0
Lehi, UT	5.4	7.3	7.8	19.3	28.0	16.2	12.3	3.6
Lwr Providence, PA	4.5	5.1	6.7	12.0	15.6	18.3	23.4	14.4
Madison, AL	6.9	5.2	7.5	11.7	17.8	16.6	22.1	12.1
Manhattan Bch, CA	4.1	2.8	2.9	6.7	13.4	11.5	20.9	37.6
Maple Grove, MN	1.3	2.4	3.6	8.7	20.9	20.9	26.8	15.4
Marion, IA	6.8	10.4	10.0	16.8	23.1	15.1	12.5	5.3
Marlboro, NJ	3.4	3.5	3.6	6.2	10.7	12.5	23.2	36.8

City	Percent of Households Earning							
	Under $15,000	$15,000 -24,999	$25,000 -34,999	$35,000 -49,999	$50,000 -74,999	$75,000 -99,000	$100,000 -149,999	$150,000 and up
Matthews, NC	5.6	5.0	5.5	12.2	24.0	18.5	21.0	8.2
Meridian, ID	5.8	6.1	9.8	13.1	24.9	19.4	16.5	4.4
Merrimack, NH	3.0	4.0	5.5	10.1	23.5	19.3	22.7	11.8
Morgantown, WV	36.5	14.6	10.4	12.3	11.7	5.8	6.2	2.5
Mt Pleasant, SC	4.7	4.7	7.4	12.1	20.4	17.7	18.7	14.3
Northampton, PA	2.6	4.2	5.0	9.7	15.3	15.3	24.8	23.1
Northville, MI	3.7	4.9	5.2	9.1	14.6	13.8	23.2	25.4
Novi, MI	3.2	4.4	7.4	12.3	17.8	14.8	19.8	20.3
O'Fallon, MO	3.3	4.6	6.5	12.1	25.1	21.3	20.5	6.5
Oro Valley, AZ	4.3	5.3	7.6	12.4	22.9	17.2	19.4	11.0
Oviedo, FL	3.3	3.4	5.7	11.1	24.4	19.4	20.9	11.8
Palm Bch Grdns, FL	6.6	7.3	8.6	13.3	18.7	13.9	14.9	16.6
Parker, CO	2.5	3.2	3.1	9.7	22.6	22.1	25.6	11.3
Peachtree City, GA	3.6	4.6	4.9	9.4	18.4	16.8	23.7	18.6
Pflugerville, TX	2.0	3.2	5.0	11.1	24.8	22.8	22.0	9.2
Pleasanton, CA	3.0	3.7	3.1	7.1	14.7	14.7	24.7	29.0
Rapid City, SD	13.6	13.5	14.9	17.6	19.7	9.5	7.4	3.7
Redmond, WA	5.0	4.6	7.6	11.8	20.1	17.4	19.3	14.2
Richland, WA	9.0	8.3	8.5	14.4	19.9	15.5	16.9	7.5
Richmond, KY	27.5	15.5	14.6	13.7	14.6	7.3	4.5	2.3
Rio Rancho, NM	6.3	8.3	10.3	18.0	27.6	15.4	11.0	3.1
Rockaway, NJ	3.6	3.6	4.3	7.1	16.9	17.9	26.3	20.4
Rocklin, CA	5.0	5.7	6.7	9.5	18.2	16.4	23.9	14.6
Rogers, AR	10.8	11.5	11.7	16.9	21.9	10.8	9.6	6.9
Round Rock, TX	4.8	5.6	7.7	15.3	25.0	17.8	15.4	8.6
Sammamish, WA	1.9	1.6	2.5	5.8	11.5	14.2	27.8	34.8
San Ramon, CA	2.5	2.4	2.4	7.1	13.5	15.4	26.1	30.7
Santa Fe, NM	13.0	10.9	11.9	17.7	18.4	11.3	10.5	6.4
Saratoga, CA	3.9	3.1	2.6	4.0	7.5	7.3	17.2	54.5
Savage, MN	2.7	2.4	4.2	6.9	19.2	22.3	31.0	11.3
Schererville, IN	5.8	6.5	8.9	13.5	22.9	16.1	17.7	8.6
Shawnee, KS	5.1	5.8	7.1	14.1	22.3	17.1	18.5	10.0
Shrewsbury, MA	6.9	7.0	5.7	10.5	17.0	15.6	20.6	16.7
S Brunswick, NJ	3.4	3.2	4.3	7.8	16.2	17.1	26.6	21.3
S. Jordan, UT	2.1	3.2	3.5	8.1	21.1	22.3	29.2	10.5
S Kingstown, RI	6.8	6.5	7.2	12.5	20.0	16.3	18.4	12.3
Southaven, MS	9.3	9.3	10.0	20.2	26.0	13.7	8.6	3.0
Southlake, TX	2.0	1.7	2.7	3.1	8.0	7.8	21.2	53.6
Spanish Fork, UT	5.0	8.6	9.0	21.7	28.7	14.8	8.6	3.6
Sparks, NV	7.8	8.7	11.5	16.6	22.1	14.2	13.6	5.4
Stow, OH	7.2	6.4	7.1	14.8	23.7	17.6	16.0	7.2
Sugar Land, TX	4.4	4.4	4.8	10.7	17.6	15.2	22.7	20.3
Sun Prairie, WI	5.0	6.9	9.8	15.8	22.4	17.2	16.7	6.2
Tualatin, OR	6.1	6.9	12.0	15.6	20.3	13.9	15.8	9.5
Waimalu, HI	4.4	5.3	9.0	14.2	21.0	15.8	19.5	10.7
Wellington, FL	4.4	6.0	6.6	12.3	19.6	16.6	20.0	14.5
W Des Moines, IA	5.4	7.2	9.0	18.1	20.8	15.1	15.1	9.3
West Linn, OR	3.8	5.7	6.5	11.4	17.7	14.1	22.1	18.8
West Windsor, NJ	2.5	2.2	2.5	5.1	8.5	9.9	22.8	46.5
Weston, FL	5.3	4.9	4.6	8.9	14.2	13.1	21.5	27.5
Woodbury, MN	1.6	2.7	4.2	10.8	19.2	18.3	24.9	18.2
Woodridge, IL	5.0	5.2	8.0	14.9	21.2	16.9	19.2	9.4
Yorba Linda, CA	3.2	3.3	3.5	7.8	14.0	15.4	26.5	26.3
U.S.	13.1	10.9	11.2	15.6	19.5	11.9	11.3	6.6

Note: Figures are 2007 estimates
Source: Claritas, Inc.

Household Income Distribution: Metro Area

Metro Area	Percent of Households Earning							
	Under $15,000	$15,000 -24,999	$25,000 -34,999	$35,000 -49,999	$50,000 -74,999	$75,000 -99,000	$100,000 -149,999	$150,000 and up
Allen, TX	10.0	9.1	10.7	15.8	19.8	13.0	13.2	8.5
Ankeny, IA	8.9	9.0	10.9	15.9	22.1	14.2	12.8	6.2
Apex, NC	9.3	8.3	9.8	14.9	20.6	14.1	14.7	8.3
Bangor, ME	16.8	13.2	12.8	16.9	19.4	10.3	7.7	2.9
Beavercreek, OH	12.6	11.2	11.9	16.8	20.3	12.1	10.4	4.7
Bellevue, NE	9.6	9.8	11.3	16.1	21.7	13.6	12.3	5.6
Bend, OR	10.0	10.2	12.0	17.7	21.3	12.1	10.8	5.9
Bernards, NJ	14.0	8.8	8.7	12.6	17.1	12.3	14.5	12.0
Bethlehem, NY	11.5	10.4	11.0	15.5	20.3	13.1	12.4	5.8
Bozeman, MT	10.6	12.0	11.7	18.4	22.1	10.7	9.6	4.9
Brentwood, TN	11.8	10.0	11.2	16.3	21.0	12.3	11.1	6.3
Brookfield, WI	11.1	10.0	10.6	15.5	20.6	13.5	12.4	6.2
Broomfield, CO	8.0	7.5	9.6	15.1	21.0	14.5	15.2	9.2
Burlington, VT	9.3	9.3	10.2	16.2	21.9	14.3	13.0	5.8
Carmel, IN	10.0	9.9	10.8	15.8	20.7	13.3	12.7	6.7
Cary, NC	9.3	8.3	9.8	14.9	20.6	14.1	14.7	8.3
Casper, WY	11.8	12.5	12.0	17.5	20.6	12.3	9.4	3.9
Cheshire, CT	12.3	9.6	9.3	13.9	19.0	13.7	14.2	8.0
Chino Hills, CA	12.2	10.9	10.9	15.2	19.6	12.7	12.6	5.9
Collierville, TN	15.6	11.2	11.6	15.9	19.1	11.3	9.8	5.4
Conway, AR	13.7	11.8	12.2	17.2	20.4	10.9	9.2	4.5
Coronado, CA	9.7	9.3	10.2	14.6	19.4	13.1	14.3	9.5
Cranberry, PA	14.9	13.1	12.4	15.9	18.9	10.7	9.2	4.7
Dover, DE	11.3	11.5	11.3	17.1	22.0	12.2	10.6	3.8
Draper, UT	8.2	8.8	10.4	16.7	22.7	13.9	12.8	6.6
Dublin, OH	11.0	9.6	10.9	16.0	20.7	13.2	12.4	6.3
Edmond, OK	14.6	12.6	12.9	17.1	19.4	10.5	8.7	4.1
Evesham, NJ	11.8	8.9	9.4	13.9	19.0	13.4	14.6	8.9
Fargo, ND	12.7	12.3	12.4	17.0	20.9	11.4	9.0	4.2
Farmington, CT	10.0	8.4	8.8	13.5	19.1	14.6	16.2	9.4
Fishers, IN	10.0	9.9	10.8	15.8	20.7	13.3	12.7	6.7
Flower Mound, TX	10.0	9.1	10.7	15.8	19.8	13.0	13.2	8.5
Franklin, MA	10.6	7.8	8.0	12.3	18.4	14.0	16.7	12.1
Frederick, MD	6.7	5.2	6.7	11.9	18.7	15.4	19.8	15.7
Frisco, TX	10.0	9.1	10.7	15.8	19.8	13.0	13.2	8.5
Goodyear, AZ	10.0	10.1	11.2	16.4	20.6	12.6	12.2	7.0
Grand Blanc, MI	14.4	12.1	11.9	15.4	19.4	12.2	10.5	4.0
Greenburgh, NY	14.0	8.8	8.7	12.6	17.1	12.3	14.5	12.0
Greenwich, CT	8.9	7.0	7.4	11.4	16.5	12.7	15.9	20.2
Hampden, PA	10.0	10.3	11.5	16.4	21.6	13.2	11.9	5.1
Hilliard, OH	11.0	9.6	10.9	16.0	20.7	13.2	12.4	6.3
Hoover, AL	15.4	11.2	11.4	15.8	18.7	11.2	10.3	6.0
Huntersville, NC	10.4	9.1	10.9	16.1	21.1	13.0	12.0	7.3
Juneau, AK	6.0	7.3	8.2	13.3	19.7	18.0	19.3	8.2
Keller, TX	10.0	9.1	10.7	15.8	19.8	13.0	13.2	8.5
Kenner, LA	16.2	12.0	11.8	15.6	18.3	10.9	9.6	5.6
Kennesaw, GA	9.3	8.1	9.6	15.2	21.1	14.0	14.0	8.8
League City, TX	12.2	10.1	11.0	15.4	18.5	12.0	12.7	8.1
Leawood, KS	10.2	9.3	11.0	16.1	21.3	13.5	12.4	6.3
Lee's Summit, MO	10.2	9.3	11.0	16.1	21.3	13.5	12.4	6.3
Leesburg, VA	6.7	5.2	6.7	11.9	18.7	15.4	19.8	15.7
Lehi, UT	8.4	10.3	11.5	18.2	22.7	12.8	11.1	4.9
Lwr Providence, PA	11.8	8.9	9.4	13.9	19.0	13.4	14.6	8.9
Madison, AL	12.5	10.5	10.8	14.8	19.2	12.7	13.1	6.4
Manhattan Bch, CA	12.7	10.1	10.2	14.2	17.9	11.9	13.2	9.9
Maple Grove, MN	7.4	7.4	8.8	14.1	21.5	15.8	16.2	8.8
Marion, IA	9.4	10.2	11.4	17.1	23.1	13.8	10.8	4.1
Marlboro, NJ	14.0	8.8	8.7	12.6	17.1	12.3	14.5	12.0

Metro Area	Percent of Households Earning							
	Under $15,000	$15,000 -24,999	$25,000 -34,999	$35,000 -49,999	$50,000 -74,999	$75,000 -99,000	$100,000 -149,999	$150,000 and up
Matthews, NC	10.4	9.1	10.9	16.1	21.1	13.0	12.0	7.3
Meridian, ID	10.3	11.4	12.5	17.6	21.2	12.2	10.2	4.8
Merrimack, NH	8.2	8.0	8.9	14.1	21.7	15.3	15.4	8.3
Morgantown, WV	23.3	14.8	12.5	15.1	16.5	7.7	7.1	3.0
Mt Pleasant, SC	14.2	11.0	11.7	16.2	20.0	11.7	10.3	5.0
Northampton, PA	11.8	8.9	9.4	13.9	19.0	13.4	14.6	8.9
Northville, MI	11.4	9.4	10.0	14.2	19.4	13.6	14.1	7.8
Novi, MI	11.4	9.4	10.0	14.2	19.4	13.6	14.1	7.8
O'Fallon, MO	11.5	10.2	10.9	15.8	20.6	13.0	11.8	6.1
Oro Valley, AZ	14.1	12.5	12.9	17.0	18.9	10.3	9.3	5.0
Oviedo, FL	10.9	11.1	12.4	17.8	20.7	11.4	10.2	5.5
Palm Bch Grdns, FL	14.7	11.6	11.7	15.5	18.1	10.6	10.4	7.4
Parker, CO	8.0	7.5	9.6	15.1	21.0	14.5	15.2	9.2
Peachtree City, GA	9.3	8.1	9.6	15.2	21.1	14.0	14.0	8.8
Pflugerville, TX	10.7	8.9	10.4	15.4	20.3	13.4	13.0	8.0
Pleasanton, CA	9.3	6.9	7.3	11.9	17.6	13.9	17.5	15.8
Rapid City, SD	11.5	12.3	13.9	18.8	21.8	9.9	7.9	3.9
Redmond, WA	9.2	8.3	9.8	15.2	21.0	14.5	14.1	7.8
Richland, WA	10.5	10.6	10.2	16.1	20.5	13.8	13.5	4.9
Richmond, KY	20.7	13.6	13.3	15.9	17.9	9.4	6.5	2.5
Rio Rancho, NM	13.1	11.9	12.1	16.8	19.6	11.1	10.4	5.1
Rockaway, NJ	14.0	8.8	8.7	12.6	17.1	12.3	14.5	12.0
Rocklin, CA	10.7	9.3	10.0	15.1	20.0	13.3	14.1	7.5
Rogers, AR	13.3	12.2	13.0	17.7	21.4	10.0	7.9	4.5
Round Rock, TX	10.7	8.9	10.4	15.4	20.3	13.4	13.0	8.0
Sammamish, WA	9.2	8.3	9.8	15.2	21.0	14.5	14.1	7.8
San Ramon, CA	9.3	6.9	7.3	11.9	17.6	13.9	17.5	15.8
Santa Fe, NM	12.3	9.9	10.9	16.4	18.8	11.8	12.3	7.6
Saratoga, CA	6.5	5.3	6.0	10.1	17.0	14.6	20.3	20.1
Savage, MN	7.4	7.4	8.8	14.1	21.5	15.8	16.2	8.8
Schererville, IN	10.6	8.4	9.2	14.3	20.0	13.9	14.4	9.1
Shawnee, KS	10.2	9.3	11.0	16.1	21.3	13.5	12.4	6.3
Shrewsbury, MA	12.0	9.5	9.2	13.3	19.5	13.7	15.1	7.7
S Brunswick, NJ	14.0	8.8	8.7	12.6	17.1	12.3	14.5	12.0
S. Jordan, UT	8.2	8.8	10.4	16.7	22.7	13.9	12.8	6.6
S Kingstown, RI	14.2	10.8	9.8	14.0	19.4	13.0	12.7	6.0
Southaven, MS	15.6	11.2	11.6	15.9	19.1	11.3	9.8	5.4
Southlake, TX	10.0	9.1	10.7	15.8	19.8	13.0	13.2	8.5
Spanish Fork, UT	8.4	10.3	11.5	18.2	22.7	12.8	11.1	4.9
Sparks, NV	9.7	9.4	11.3	15.7	21.2	13.3	12.6	6.9
Stow, OH	12.5	10.9	11.4	16.2	20.6	12.3	10.6	5.5
Sugar Land, TX	12.2	10.1	11.0	15.4	18.5	12.0	12.7	8.1
Sun Prairie, WI	9.1	8.4	9.8	15.5	22.1	15.0	13.8	6.4
Tualatin, OR	9.9	9.4	10.7	16.4	21.6	13.4	12.3	6.3
Waimalu, HI	9.6	7.8	9.2	14.0	19.3	14.1	16.4	9.5
Wellington, FL	14.7	11.6	11.7	15.5	18.1	10.6	10.4	7.4
W Des Moines, IA	8.9	9.0	10.9	15.9	22.1	14.2	12.8	6.2
West Linn, OR	9.9	9.4	10.7	16.4	21.6	13.4	12.3	6.3
West Windsor, NJ	9.7	7.4	7.8	12.2	17.9	14.0	17.1	13.8
Weston, FL	14.7	11.6	11.7	15.5	18.1	10.6	10.4	7.4
Woodbury, MN	7.4	7.4	8.8	14.1	21.5	15.8	16.2	8.8
Woodridge, IL	10.6	8.4	9.2	14.3	20.0	13.9	14.4	9.1
Yorba Linda, CA	12.7	10.1	10.2	14.2	17.9	11.9	13.2	9.9
U.S.	13.1	10.9	11.2	15.6	19.5	11.9	11.3	6.6

Note: Figures are 2007 estimates and cover the Metropolitan Statistical Area (MSA) - see Appendix B for areas included
Source: Claritas, Inc.

Poverty Rates by Age: City

City	All Ages	Under 5 Years Old	5 to 17 Years Old	18 to 64 Years Old	65 Years and Over
Allen, TX	3.0	0.3	0.9	1.8	0.1
Ankeny, IA	4.0	0.5	0.7	2.7	0.2
Apex, NC	1.9	0.2	0.2	1.2	0.3
Bangor, ME	16.6	1.3	2.7	11.0	1.7
Beavercreek, OH	2.4	0.1	0.4	1.4	0.4
Bellevue, NE	5.9	0.6	1.7	3.2	0.3
Bend, OR	10.5	0.8	2.7	6.4	0.7
Bernards, NJ	1.3	0.2	0.2	0.6	0.3
Bethlehem, NY	3.1	0.2	0.9	1.6	0.4
Bozeman, MT	20.2	1.2	1.6	17.1	0.3
Brentwood, TN	2.0	0.1	0.8	0.8	0.3
Brookfield, WI	2.2	0.1	0.5	1.0	0.6
Broomfield, CO	4.2	0.3	1.1	2.4	0.4
Burlington, VT	20.0	0.9	2.7	15.4	1.1
Carmel, IN	2.5	0.1	0.8	1.5	0.2
Cary, NC	3.4	0.2	0.6	2.4	0.2
Casper, WY	11.4	1.5	2.6	6.3	1.0
Cheshire, CT	3.0	0.1	0.6	1.7	0.5
Chino Hills, CA	5.1	0.4	1.7	2.9	0.2
Collierville, TN	2.4	0.2	0.8	1.2	0.2
Conway, AR	16.3	1.4	2.5	11.5	0.9
Coronado, CA	5.0	0.4	0.8	3.4	0.4
Cranberry, PA	2.9	0.2	0.8	1.4	0.4
Dover, DE	13.8	1.9	3.1	7.4	1.3
Draper, UT	2.7	0.4	0.7	1.6	0.0
Dublin, OH	2.7	0.3	0.6	1.6	0.2
Edmond, OK	7.2	0.6	1.2	5.0	0.4
Evesham, NJ	2.8	0.2	0.6	1.7	0.3
Fargo, ND	11.8	1.0	1.4	8.7	0.7
Farmington, CT	4.5	0.3	0.5	2.6	1.1
Fishers, IN	1.8	0.2	0.3	1.2	0.0
Flower Mound, TX	2.5	0.2	0.7	1.5	0.0
Franklin, MA	2.8	0.3	0.6	1.4	0.4
Frederick, MD	7.4	0.8	1.6	4.3	0.7
Frisco, TX	3.4	0.4	0.7	2.2	0.1
Goodyear, AZ	6.1	0.9	1.5	3.4	0.4
Grand Blanc, MI	4.2	0.1	0.7	2.6	0.8
Greenburgh, NY	3.9	0.2	0.8	2.2	0.7
Greenwich, CT	4.0	0.2	0.8	2.5	0.5
Hampden, PA	2.8	0.2	0.6	1.6	0.5
Hilliard, OH	2.2	0.1	0.2	1.2	0.5
Hoover, AL	3.4	0.2	0.5	2.3	0.4
Huntersville, NC	3.1	0.1	0.6	1.9	0.4
Juneau, AK	6.0	0.6	1.6	3.5	0.2
Keller, TX	1.4	0.1	0.4	0.8	0.1
Kenner, LA	13.6	1.6	3.5	7.5	1.0
Kennesaw, GA	4.5	0.2	1.2	2.4	0.7
League City, TX	4.8	0.5	1.0	2.9	0.3
Leawood, KS	1.3	0.1	0.1	0.8	0.3
Lee's Summit, MO	3.8	0.4	1.0	2.0	0.4
Leesburg, VA	3.6	0.3	0.8	2.1	0.4
Lehi, UT	5.5	1.2	1.8	2.3	0.2
Lwr Providence, PA	4.4	0.6	0.8	2.7	0.4
Madison, AL	5.8	0.7	1.6	3.1	0.4
Manhattan Bch, CA	3.2	0.1	0.4	2.2	0.5
Maple Grove, MN	1.4	0.2	0.3	0.7	0.1
Marion, IA	5.2	0.7	1.3	2.6	0.6
Marlboro, NJ	3.5	0.3	0.9	2.1	0.2
Matthews, NC	4.0	0.2	0.7	2.4	0.7

City	All Ages	Under 5 Years Old	5 to 17 Years Old	18 to 64 Years Old	65 Years and Over
Meridian, ID	5.6	0.8	1.7	2.6	0.4
Merrimack, NH	1.9	0.1	0.7	0.9	0.2
Morgantown, WV	38.4	0.9	2.1	34.4	1.0
Mt Pleasant, SC	5.0	0.4	1.0	3.0	0.6
Northampton, PA	1.8	0.1	0.4	0.9	0.3
Northville, MI	2.5	0.2	0.4	1.5	0.5
Novi, MI	2.2	0.3	0.3	1.4	0.2
O'Fallon, MO	3.3	0.5	0.7	1.7	0.4
Oro Valley, AZ	3.1	0.2	0.2	2.2	0.5
Oviedo, FL	4.6	0.6	1.1	2.8	0.2
Palm Bch Grdns, FL	5.6	0.4	1.0	3.5	0.7
Parker, CO	2.3	0.3	0.5	1.5	0.1
Peachtree City, GA	2.3	0.1	0.9	1.0	0.3
Pflugerville, TX	1.7	0.3	0.5	0.9	0.0
Pleasanton, CA	2.6	0.1	0.6	1.5	0.3
Rapid City, SD	12.7	1.6	3.0	7.2	0.9
Redmond, WA	5.3	0.5	0.8	3.3	0.6
Richland, WA	8.2	0.7	2.3	4.4	0.7
Richmond, KY	25.0	2.0	3.5	17.5	2.0
Rio Rancho, NM	5.1	0.4	1.1	2.9	0.7
Rockaway, NJ	2.4	0.3	0.4	1.3	0.3
Rocklin, CA	4.5	0.3	1.1	2.8	0.3
Rogers, AR	12.8	1.6	3.6	6.4	1.1
Round Rock, TX	4.0	0.4	1.0	2.2	0.3
Sammamish, WA	2.0	0.2	0.5	1.2	0.1
San Ramon, CA	2.0	0.2	0.3	1.3	0.3
Santa Fe, NM	12.3	1.2	2.4	7.4	1.3
Saratoga, CA	2.8	0.2	0.7	1.5	0.4
Savage, MN	2.3	0.2	0.8	1.3	0.1
Schererville, IN	3.1	0.1	0.6	2.3	0.2
Shawnee, KS	3.3	0.3	0.5	2.2	0.3
Shrewsbury, MA	4.8	0.2	1.0	2.5	1.0
S Brunswick, NJ	3.1	0.2	0.7	1.9	0.3
S. Jordan, UT	1.7	0.2	0.7	0.7	0.1
S Kingstown, RI	5.3	0.3	1.1	3.3	0.6
Southaven, MS	6.7	0.4	1.8	4.0	0.6
Southlake, TX	1.8	0.0	0.7	1.0	0.1
Spanish Fork, UT	4.5	0.8	1.3	2.2	0.3
Sparks, NV	8.0	1.0	1.8	4.8	0.5
Stow, OH	4.0	0.1	0.9	2.3	0.6
Sugar Land, TX	3.8	0.2	0.9	2.1	0.6
Sun Prairie, WI	4.4	0.4	1.5	2.1	0.4
Tualatin, OR	5.5	0.4	1.0	3.9	0.2
Waimalu, HI	5.9	0.5	1.2	3.8	0.3
Wellington, FL	4.3	0.2	1.1	2.7	0.3
W Des Moines, IA	4.5	0.4	0.9	2.9	0.3
West Linn, OR	3.9	0.3	0.8	2.5	0.3
West Windsor, NJ	2.5	0.2	0.6	1.6	0.1
Weston, FL	5.0	0.3	1.4	2.9	0.4
Woodbury, MN	1.7	0.1	0.4	1.1	0.1
Woodridge, IL	3.8	0.4	0.9	2.3	0.2
Yorba Linda, CA	3.0	0.2	0.6	1.7	0.4
U.S.	12.4	1.2	3.0	6.9	1.2

Note: Figures are percent of population with income in 1999 below poverty level and only include population for whom poverty status is determined
Source: Census 2000, Summary File 3

Poverty Rates by Age: Metro Area

MSA[1]	All Ages	Under 5 Years Old	5 to 17 Years Old	18 to 64 Years Old	65 Years and Over
Allen, TX	11.1	1.3	2.8	6.3	0.7
Ankeny, IA	7.5	0.9	1.6	4.3	0.7
Apex, NC	10.2	1.0	1.9	6.4	1.0
Bangor, ME	13.4	1.0	2.2	8.8	1.4
Beavercreek, OH	10.3	1.1	2.4	5.8	1.0
Bellevue, NE	8.4	0.9	2.2	4.7	0.7
Bend, OR	n/a	n/a	n/a	n/a	n/a
Bernards, NJ	5.4	0.4	1.1	3.3	0.6
Bethlehem, NY	9.4	0.9	2.1	5.5	1.0
Bozeman, MT	n/a	n/a	n/a	n/a	n/a
Brentwood, TN	10.1	1.1	2.3	5.7	1.0
Brookfield, WI	10.6	1.3	3.0	5.5	0.8
Broomfield, CO	8.1	0.8	1.8	4.8	0.6
Burlington, VT	8.6	0.6	1.5	5.7	0.8
Carmel, IN	8.6	0.9	2.0	4.8	0.8
Cary, NC	10.2	1.0	1.9	6.4	1.0
Casper, WY	11.8	1.5	2.9	6.6	0.9
Cheshire, CT	9.7	0.9	2.4	5.4	1.1
Chino Hills, CA	15.0	1.8	4.5	7.9	0.8
Collierville, TN	15.3	1.9	4.3	7.7	1.3
Conway, AR	12.1	1.4	3.0	6.6	1.1
Coronado, CA	12.4	1.2	3.2	7.3	0.8
Cranberry, PA	10.8	0.9	2.4	5.9	1.6
Dover, DE	10.7	1.3	2.9	5.5	1.0
Draper, UT	7.7	1.0	1.9	4.4	0.4
Dublin, OH	10.1	1.1	2.2	6.0	0.8
Edmond, OK	13.5	1.5	3.3	7.8	0.9
Evesham, NJ	11.1	1.0	2.8	6.1	1.3
Fargo, ND	11.0	1.0	1.7	7.5	0.8
Farmington, CT	8.4	0.8	2.0	4.6	0.9
Fishers, IN	8.6	0.9	2.0	4.8	0.8
Flower Mound, TX	11.1	1.3	2.8	6.3	0.7
Franklin, MA	8.6	0.6	1.7	5.1	1.1
Frederick, MD	7.4	0.7	1.7	4.4	0.7
Frisco, TX	11.1	1.3	2.8	6.3	0.7
Goodyear, AZ	12.0	1.4	3.0	6.7	0.9
Grand Blanc, MI	13.1	1.6	3.7	6.9	0.9
Greenburgh, NY	19.5	1.8	4.9	10.9	1.9
Greenwich, CT	5.7	0.4	1.1	3.3	0.8
Hampden, PA	8.1	0.8	1.9	4.4	1.0
Hilliard, OH	10.1	1.1	2.2	6.0	0.8
Hoover, AL	13.1	1.3	3.2	7.1	1.6
Huntersville, NC	9.3	0.9	2.2	5.3	1.0
Juneau, AK	n/a	n/a	n/a	n/a	n/a
Keller, TX	10.3	1.2	2.6	5.7	0.8
Kenner, LA	18.4	1.9	5.1	9.8	1.6
Kennesaw, GA	9.4	1.0	2.3	5.4	0.7
League City, TX	13.2	1.4	3.4	7.3	1.1
Leawood, KS	8.5	0.9	2.1	4.7	0.8
Lee's Summit, MO	8.5	0.9	2.1	4.7	0.8
Leesburg, VA	7.4	0.7	1.7	4.4	0.7
Lehi, UT	12.0	1.1	1.9	8.6	0.3
Lwr Providence, PA	11.1	1.0	2.8	6.1	1.3
Madison, AL	10.9	1.2	2.6	5.9	1.2
Manhattan Bch, CA	17.9	1.9	4.9	10.1	1.0
Maple Grove, MN	6.7	0.6	1.7	3.8	0.6
Marion, IA	6.5	0.7	1.4	3.7	0.8
Marlboro, NJ	6.6	0.7	1.5	3.4	1.0
Matthews, NC	9.3	0.9	2.2	5.3	1.0

MSA[1]	All Ages	Under 5 Years Old	5 to 17 Years Old	18 to 64 Years Old	65 Years and Over
Meridian, ID	9.0	1.1	2.2	5.0	0.7
Merrimack, NH	4.6	0.4	1.1	2.5	0.5
Morgantown, WV	n/a	n/a	n/a	n/a	n/a
Mt Pleasant, SC	14.0	1.4	3.6	7.7	1.3
Northampton, PA	11.1	1.0	2.8	6.1	1.3
Northville, MI	10.7	1.1	2.9	5.7	1.0
Novi, MI	10.7	1.1	2.9	5.7	1.0
O'Fallon, MO	9.9	1.0	2.7	5.2	1.0
Oro Valley, AZ	14.7	1.4	3.5	8.6	1.2
Oviedo, FL	10.7	1.0	2.6	6.1	1.0
Palm Bch Grdns, FL	9.9	0.9	2.2	5.3	1.5
Parker, CO	8.1	0.8	1.8	4.8	0.6
Peachtree City, GA	9.4	1.0	2.3	5.4	0.7
Pflugerville, TX	11.1	1.0	2.1	7.4	0.6
Pleasanton, CA	9.7	0.8	2.3	5.8	0.8
Rapid City, SD	11.5	1.5	2.8	6.4	0.7
Redmond, WA	7.9	0.6	1.6	5.0	0.7
Richland, WA	12.6	1.9	3.7	6.3	0.7
Richmond, KY	12.6	1.2	2.3	8.0	1.1
Rio Rancho, NM	13.8	1.5	3.4	7.9	1.0
Rockaway, NJ	9.7	0.9	2.3	5.4	1.0
Rocklin, CA	12.2	1.2	3.5	6.8	0.7
Rogers, AR	12.3	1.3	2.8	7.2	1.0
Round Rock, TX	11.1	1.0	2.1	7.4	0.6
Sammamish, WA	7.9	0.6	1.6	5.0	0.7
San Ramon, CA	9.7	0.8	2.3	5.8	0.8
Santa Fe, NM	10.9	0.9	2.4	6.5	1.0
Saratoga, CA	7.5	0.6	1.6	4.7	0.6
Savage, MN	6.7	0.6	1.7	3.8	0.6
Schererville, IN	10.8	1.3	2.8	5.7	0.9
Shawnee, KS	8.5	0.9	2.1	4.7	0.8
Shrewsbury, MA	9.8	0.9	2.4	5.3	1.2
S Brunswick, NJ	5.4	0.4	1.1	3.3	0.6
S. Jordan, UT	7.7	1.0	1.9	4.4	0.4
S Kingstown, RI	11.8	1.1	2.9	6.2	1.6
Southaven, MS	15.3	1.9	4.3	7.7	1.3
Southlake, TX	10.3	1.2	2.6	5.7	0.8
Spanish Fork, UT	12.0	1.1	1.9	8.6	0.3
Sparks, NV	10.0	1.1	2.1	6.1	0.6
Stow, OH	9.8	1.1	2.3	5.6	0.9
Sugar Land, TX	13.9	1.6	3.7	7.7	0.9
Sun Prairie, WI	9.4	0.5	1.2	7.3	0.4
Tualatin, OR	9.5	0.9	2.0	5.7	0.7
Waimalu, HI	9.9	0.9	2.2	5.8	1.0
Wellington, FL	9.9	0.9	2.2	5.3	1.5
W Des Moines, IA	7.5	0.9	1.6	4.3	0.7
West Linn, OR	9.5	0.9	2.0	5.7	0.7
West Windsor, NJ	8.6	0.8	1.9	4.9	1.1
Weston, FL	11.5	1.0	2.7	6.2	1.6
Woodbury, MN	6.7	0.6	1.7	3.8	0.6
Woodridge, IL	10.5	1.1	2.7	5.8	0.9
Yorba Linda, CA	10.3	1.0	2.6	6.1	0.6
U.S.	12.4	1.2	3.0	6.9	1.2

Note: Figures are percent of population with income in 1999 below poverty level and only include population for whom poverty status is determined; (1) Metropolitan Statistical Area - see Appendix A for areas included
Source: Census 2000, Summary File 3

Personal Bankruptcy Filing Rate

City	Area Covered	2004	2005	2006
Allen, TX	Collin County	5.58	7.92	1.76
Ankeny, IA	Polk County	5.49	7.62	2.35
Apex, NC	Wake County	4.21	5.75	1.81
Bangor, ME	Penobscot County	3.76	6.22	0.99
Beavercreek, OH	Greene County	5.42	7.81	2.29
Bellevue, NE	Sarpy County	5.45	7.27	2.48
Bend, OR	Deschutes County	7.03	9.07	1.82
Bernards, NJ	Somerset County	2.29	2.93	0.81
Bethlehem, NY	Albany County	4.84	6.05	2.26
Bozeman, MT	Gallatin County	3.99	4.93	1.68
Brentwood, TN	Williamson County	3.44	3.92	1.60
Brookfield, WI	Waukesha County	2.99	4.39	1.35
Broomfield, CO	Broomfield County	n/a	n/a	n/a
Burlington, VT	Chittenden County	2.26	3.67	0.96
Carmel, IN	Hamilton County	5.85	8.27	2.22
Cary, NC	Wake County	4.21	5.75	1.81
Casper, WY	Natrona County	5.60	7.94	1.58
Cheshire, CT	New Haven County	4.61	5.53	1.89
Chino Hills, CA	San Bernardino County	3.87	4.26	0.87
Collierville, TN	Shelby County	19.73	21.75	11.58
Conway, AR	Faulkner County	8.39	10.95	2.64
Coronado, CA	San Diego County	3.55	4.98	1.32
Cranberry, PA	Butler County	4.28	5.94	1.90
Dover, DE	Kent County	4.46	5.51	n/a
Draper, UT	Salt Lake County	10.59	10.75	2.57
Dublin, OH	Franklin County	9.53	13.80	3.56
Edmond, OK	Oklahoma County	9.37	14.49	2.54
Evesham, NJ	Burlington County	6.40	6.10	2.16
Fargo, ND	Cass County	3.88	6.32	1.29
Farmington, CT	Hartford County	3.44	4.85	2.34
Fishers, IN	Hamilton County	5.85	8.27	2.22
Flower Mound, TX	Denton County	4.24	6.09	1.45
Franklin, MA	Norfolk County	2.00	2.90	1.00
Frederick, MD	Frederick County	3.41	4.03	1.17
Frisco, TX	Collin County	5.58	7.92	1.76
Goodyear, AZ	Maricopa County	6.03	7.24	1.30
Grand Blanc, MI	Genesee County	8.43	12.50	4.73
Greenburgh, NY	Westchester County	2.25	3.39	0.72
Greenwich, CT	Fairfield County	1.85	2.81	1.09
Hampden, PA	Cumberland County	4.03	5.21	1.95
Hilliard, OH	Franklin County	9.53	13.80	3.56
Hoover, AL	Jefferson County	14.11	16.95	6.76
Huntersville, NC	Mecklenburg County	3.47	5.07	1.61
Juneau, AK	Juneau Borough	2.35	4.02	0.78
Keller, TX	Tarrant County	6.46	8.04	2.34
Kenner, LA	Jefferson Parish	5.58	7.44	1.15
Kennesaw, GA	Cobb County	6.17	7.68	3.24
League City, TX	Galveston County	4.26	5.38	1.43
Leawood, KS	Johnson County	4.70	7.17	1.87
Lee's Summit, MO	Jackson County	8.00	11.51	3.89
Leesburg, VA	Loudoun County	1.87	2.13	0.84
Lehi, UT	Utah County	5.98	6.23	1.46
Lwr Providence, PA	Montgomery County	3.09	3.58	0.97
Madison, AL	Madison County	7.17	8.96	3.17
Manhattan Bch, CA	Los Angeles County	3.41	4.90	0.94
Maple Grove, MN	Hennepin County	3.45	5.27	1.41
Marion, IA	Linn County	4.40	6.82	1.43
Marlboro, NJ	Monmouth County	3.60	4.37	1.25
Matthews, NC	Mecklenburg County	3.47	5.07	1.61
Meridian, ID	Ada County	7.18	8.91	2.47

City	Area Covered	2004	2005	2006
Merrimack, NH	Hillsborough County	3.62	4.34	1.32
Morgantown, WV	Monongalia County	3.25	5.66	0.92
Mt Pleasant, SC	Charleston County	2.86	2.70	0.88
Northampton, PA	Bucks County	3.67	4.64	1.23
Northville, MI	Wayne County	9.39	12.56	5.34
Novi, MI	Oakland County	5.11	7.62	2.96
O'Fallon, MO	St. Charles County	5.12	7.31	2.06
Oro Valley, AZ	Pima County	4.75	6.24	1.28
Oviedo, FL	Seminole County	4.76	6.57	1.14
Palm Bch Grdns, FL	Palm Beach County	3.17	4.73	0.80
Parker, CO	Douglas County	4.74	7.49	1.64
Peachtree City, GA	Fayette County	5.29	6.50	2.75
Pflugerville, TX	Travis County	3.70	5.32	1.17
Pleasanton, CA	Alameda County	2.82	3.94	0.99
Rapid City, SD	Pennington County	4.28	5.41	1.66
Redmond, WA	King County	4.69	6.11	1.37
Richland, WA	Benton County	7.28	9.55	2.08
Richmond, KY	Madison County	6.40	8.52	2.51
Rio Rancho, NM	Sandoval County	6.03	7.43	1.27
Rockaway, NJ	Morris County	2.31	2.80	0.79
Rocklin, CA	Placer County	3.13	4.36	1.24
Rogers, AR	Benton County	5.91	7.58	2.12
Round Rock, TX	Williamson County	5.28	6.94	1.53
Sammamish, WA	King County	4.69	6.11	1.37
San Ramon, CA	Contra Costa County	2.68	3.41	1.02
Santa Fe, NM	Santa Fe County	3.34	5.05	1.00
Saratoga, CA	Santa Clara County	2.91	3.55	0.87
Savage, MN	Scott County	2.81	4.17	1.59
Schererville, IN	Lake County	10.59	15.11	4.91
Shawnee, KS	Johnson County	4.70	7.17	1.87
Shrewsbury, MA	Worcester County	3.44	5.14	1.68
S Brunswick, NJ	Middlesex County	3.23	4.29	0.98
S. Jordan, UT	Salt Lake County	10.59	10.75	2.57
S. Kingstown, RI	Washington County	2.67	3.25	1.00
Southaven, MS	DeSoto County	11.89	13.65	5.28
Southlake, TX	Tarrant County	6.46	8.04	2.34
Spanish Fork, UT	Utah County	5.98	6.23	1.46
Sparks, NV	Washoe County	6.08	7.62	1.47
Stow, OH	Summit County	8.53	13.63	3.51
Sugar Land, TX	Fort Bend County	4.41	5.28	1.63
Sun Prairie, WI	Dane County	3.45	4.80	1.50
Tualatin, OR	Washington County	6.30	8.43	1.83
Waimalu, HI	Honolulu County	2.44	3.45	0.82
Wellington, FL	Palm Beach County	3.17	4.73	0.80
W Des Moines, IA	Polk County	5.49	7.62	2.35
West Linn, OR	Clackamas County	6.44	8.04	1.96
West Windsor, NJ	Mercer County	4.49	5.13	1.50
Weston, FL	Broward County	4.48	5.85	1.23
Woodbury, MN	Washington County	2.78	4.18	1.57
Woodridge, IL	DuPage County	3.54	4.93	1.29
Yorba Linda, CA	Orange County	2.56	3.89	0.79
U.S.	U.S.	5.31	6.82	2.00

Note: Numbers are per 1,000 population and include Chapter 7 and Chapter 13 filings; n/a not available
Source: Federal Deposit Insurance Corporation (FDIC),
Regional Economic Conditions (RECON), 8/23/2007

Building Permits

City	Single-Family			Multi-Family			Total		
	2006	2007p	Pct. Chg.	2006	2007p	Pct. Chg.	2006	2007p	Pct. Chg.
Allen, TX	1,248	879	-29.6	348	184	-47.1	1,596	1,063	-33.4
Ankeny, IA	725	665	-8.3	120	13	-89.2	845	678	-19.8
Apex, NC	324	567	75.0	19	0	-100.0	343	567	65.3
Bangor, ME	72	57	-20.8	56	12	-78.6	128	69	-46.1
Beavercreek, OH	n/a	n/a	n/a	n/a	n/a	n/a	n/a	n/a	n/a
Bellevue, NE	317	354	11.7	20	248	1,140.0	337	602	78.6
Bend, OR	1,517	759	-50.0	162	152	-6.2	1,679	911	-45.7
Bernards, NJ	21	22	4.8	0	0	-	21	22	4.8
Bethlehem, NY	71	64	-9.9	14	10	-28.6	85	74	-12.9
Bozeman, MT	303	287	-5.3	348	463	33.0	651	750	15.2
Brentwood, TN	502	294	-41.4	0	0	-	502	294	-41.4
Brookfield, WI	39	33	-15.4	0	0	-	39	33	-15.4
Broomfield, CO	916	584	-36.2	166	476	186.7	1,082	1,060	-2.0
Burlington, VT	10	8	-20.0	0	0	-	10	8	-20.0
Carmel, IN	634	551	-13.1	42	206	390.5	676	757	12.0
Cary, NC	1,982	2,326	17.4	1,004	754	-24.9	2,986	3,080	3.1
Casper, WY	292	315	7.9	0	0	-	292	315	7.9
Cheshire, CT	68	51	-25.0	0	0	-	68	51	-25.0
Chino Hills, CA	32	26	-18.8	31	0	-100.0	63	26	-58.7
Collierville, TN	378	226	-40.2	0	0	-	378	226	-40.2
Conway, AR	407	312	-23.3	222	130	-41.4	629	442	-29.7
Coronado, CA	49	57	16.3	80	4	-95.0	129	61	-52.7
Cranberry, PA	87	96	10.3	0	0	-	87	96	10.3
Dover, DE	201	189	-6.0	168	48	-71.4	369	237	-35.8
Draper, UT	456	304	-33.3	156	140	-10.3	612	444	-27.5
Dublin, OH	253	131	-48.2	153	54	-64.7	406	185	-54.4
Edmond, OK	521	471	-9.6	0	265	-	521	736	41.3
Evesham, NJ	30	26	-13.3	0	0	-	30	26	-13.3
Fargo, ND	470	447	-4.9	383	537	40.2	853	984	15.4
Farmington, CT	77	44	-42.9	26	4	-84.6	103	48	-53.4
Fishers, IN	880	742	-15.7	174	171	-1.7	1,054	913	-13.4
Flower Mound, TX	174	87	-50.0	0	0	-	174	87	-50.0
Franklin, MA	75	87	16.0	53	14	-73.6	128	101	-21.1
Frederick, MD	231	167	-27.7	126	67	-46.8	357	234	-34.5
Frisco, TX	3,414	1,719	-49.6	0	1,198	-	3,414	2,917	-14.6
Goodyear, AZ	1,847	989	-46.5	260	1,218	368.5	2,107	2,207	4.7
Grand Blanc, MI	110	121	10.0	120	0	-100.0	230	121	-47.4
Greenburgh, NY	11	9	-18.2	0	0	-	11	9	-18.2
Greenwich, CT	214	191	-10.7	12	0	-100.0	226	191	-15.5
Hampden, PA	188	240	27.7	5	0	-100.0	193	240	24.4
Hilliard, OH	65	92	41.5	57	34	-40.4	122	126	3.3
Hoover, AL	720	613	-14.9	128	48	-62.5	848	661	-22.1
Huntersville, NC	n/a	n/a	n/a	n/a	n/a	n/a	n/a	n/a	n/a
Juneau, AK	70	57	-18.6	45	14	-68.9	115	71	-38.3
Keller, TX	369	254	-31.2	0	0	-	369	254	-31.2
Kenner, LA	15	27	80.0	2	2	0.0	17	29	70.6
Kennesaw, GA	253	35	-86.2	0	0	-	253	35	-86.2
League City, TX	1,510	1,345	-10.9	244	100	-59.0	1,754	1,445	-17.6
Leawood, KS	107	91	-15.0	0	0	-	107	91	-15.0
Lee's Summit, MO	621	496	-20.1	206	282	36.9	827	778	-5.9
Leesburg, VA	n/a	n/a	n/a	n/a	n/a	n/a	n/a	n/a	n/a
Lehi, UT	1,629	849	-47.9	0	33	-	1,629	882	-45.9
Lwr Providence, PA	21	17	-19.0	183	13	-92.9	204	30	-85.3
Madison, AL	630	364	-42.2	0	0	-	630	364	-42.2
Manhattan Bch, CA	176	146	-17.0	0	0	-	176	146	-17.0
Maple Grove, MN	365	219	-40.0	0	58	-	365	277	-24.1
Marion, IA	211	213	0.9	111	111	0.0	322	324	0.6
Marlboro, NJ	71	51	-28.2	0	0	-	71	51	-28.2

City	Single-Family			Multi-Family			Total		
	2006	2007p	Pct. Chg.	2006	2007p	Pct. Chg.	2006	2007p	Pct. Chg.
Matthews, NC	n/a	n/a	n/a	n/a	n/a	n/a	n/a	n/a	n/a
Meridian, ID	1,559	813	-47.9	74	32	-56.8	1,633	845	-48.3
Merrimack, NH	59	18	-69.5	24	0	-100.0	83	18	-78.3
Morgantown, WV	32	24	-25.0	6	70	1,066.7	38	94	147.4
Mt Pleasant, SC	829	361	-56.5	253	0	-100.0	1,082	361	-66.6
Northampton, PA	46	10	-78.3	0	0	-	46	10	-78.3
Northville, MI	218	98	-55.0	11	0	-100.0	229	98	-57.2
Novi, MI	248	176	-29.0	0	0	-	248	176	-29.0
O'Fallon, MO	680	648	-4.7	537	194	-63.9	1,217	842	-30.8
Oro Valley, AZ	354	334	-5.6	0	0	-	354	334	-5.6
Oviedo, FL	169	521	208.3	0	240	-	169	761	350.3
Palm Bch Grdns, FL	224	206	-8.0	274	128	-53.3	498	334	-32.9
Parker, CO	598	232	-61.2	6	0	-100.0	604	232	-61.6
Peachtree City, GA	106	73	-31.1	0	145	-	106	218	105.7
Pflugerville, TX	781	469	-39.9	560	42	-92.5	1,341	511	-61.9
Pleasanton, CA	136	47	-65.4	41	5	-87.8	177	52	-70.6
Rapid City, SD	320	253	-20.9	240	324	35.0	560	577	3.0
Redmond, WA	206	237	15.0	87	135	55.2	293	372	27.0
Richland, WA	318	296	-6.9	0	176	-	318	472	48.4
Richmond, KY	234	180	-23.1	50	63	26.0	284	243	-14.4
Rio Rancho, NM	1,935	1,147	-40.7	3	132	4,300.0	1,938	1,279	-34.0
Rockaway, NJ	23	21	-8.7	19	96	405.3	42	117	178.6
Rocklin, CA	231	251	8.7	435	0	-100.0	666	251	-62.3
Rogers, AR	1,042	368	-64.7	344	31	-91.0	1,386	399	-71.2
Round Rock, TX	1,307	796	-39.1	320	1,480	362.5	1,627	2,276	39.9
Sammamish, WA	0	0	-	0	0	-	0	0	-
San Ramon, CA	27	76	181.5	0	0	-	27	76	181.5
Santa Fe, NM	417	277	-33.6	0	0	-	417	277	-33.6
Saratoga, CA	27	25	-7.4	0	0	-	27	25	-7.4
Savage, MN	87	81	-6.9	62	111	79.0	149	192	28.9
Schererville, IN	103	73	-29.1	14	17	21.4	117	90	-23.1
Shawnee, KS	201	163	-18.9	70	179	155.7	271	342	26.2
Shrewsbury, MA	57	50	-12.3	215	7	-96.7	272	57	-79.0
S Brunswick, NJ	145	184	26.9	0	0	-	145	184	26.9
S. Jordan, UT	1,088	798	-26.7	0	36	-	1,088	834	-23.3
S. Kingstown, RI	95	57	-40.0	0	28	-	95	85	-10.5
Southaven, MS	854	491	-42.5	0	0	-	854	491	-42.5
Southlake, TX	129	96	-25.6	0	0	-	129	96	-25.6
Spanish Fork, UT	652	415	-36.3	10	12	20.0	662	427	-35.5
Sparks, NV	1,126	610	-45.8	28	13	-53.6	1,154	623	-46.0
Stow, OH	52	40	-23.1	9	3	-66.7	61	43	-29.5
Sugar Land, TX	502	500	-0.4	32	4	-87.5	534	504	-5.6
Sun Prairie, WI	167	71	-57.5	325	117	-64.0	492	188	-61.8
Tualatin, OR	101	48	-52.5	0	0	-	101	48	-52.5
Waimalu, HI	n/a	n/a	n/a	n/a	n/a	n/a	n/a	n/a	n/a
Wellington, FL	224	136	-39.3	0	6	-	224	142	-36.6
W Des Moines, IA	148	233	57.4	254	120	-52.8	402	353	-12.2
West Linn, OR	63	89	41.3	0	0	-	63	89	41.3
West Windsor, NJ	154	62	-59.7	0	0	-	154	62	-59.7
Weston, FL	11	12	9.1	0	0	-	11	12	9.1
Woodbury, MN	713	432	-39.4	0	0	-	713	432	-39.4
Woodridge, IL	63	38	-39.7	0	0	-	63	38	-39.7
Yorba Linda, CA	155	126	-18.7	83	4	-95.2	238	130	-45.4
U.S.	1,378,200	973,300	-29.4	460,700	407,200	-11.6	1,838,900	1,380,500	-24.9

Note: (p) Preliminary; Figures represent new, privately-owned housing units authorized (unadjusted data); All permit data are based on estimates with imputation; U.S. figures are based on the new 20,000-place series. Figures cover the city except where noted; (1) County level data

Source: U.S. Census Bureau, Manufacturing, Mining, and Construction Statistics

Homeownership and Housing Vacancies

MSA[1]	Homeownership Rate[2] (%)			Rental Vacancy Rate[3] (%)			Homeowner Vacancy Rate[4] (%)		
	2005	2006	2007	2005	2006	2007	2005	2006	2007
Allen, TX	62.3	60.7	60.9	13.6	11.7	11.0	2.2	2.3	2.5
Ankeny, IA	n/a	n/a	n/a	n/a	n/a	n/a	n/a	n/a	n/a
Apex, NC	71.4	71.1	72.8	10.7	9.0	11.2	2.3	1.6	1.6
Bangor, ME	n/a	n/a	n/a	n/a	n/a	n/a	n/a	n/a	n/a
Beavercreek, OH	66.1	64.6	64.2	14.6	16.4	16.6	3.9	3.1	1.2
Bellevue, NE	69.7	68.1	67.9	8.5	11.3	11.9	1.5	2.8	2.5
Bend, OR	n/a	n/a	n/a	n/a	n/a	n/a	n/a	n/a	n/a
Bernards, NJ	54.6	53.6	53.8	5.0	5.4	5.7	1.9	1.8	2.1
Bethlehem, NY	66.3	67.0	68.0	3.1	4.8	4.9	2.0	1.5	2.1
Bozeman, MT	n/a	n/a	n/a	n/a	n/a	n/a	n/a	n/a	n/a
Brentwood, TN	73.0	72.4	70.0	14.6	10.5	7.6	1.9	1.5	2.4
Brookfield, WI	65.7	65.2	64.8	11.6	7.8	8.3	1.3	1.1	1.4
Broomfield, CO	70.7	70.0	69.5	12.0	11.1	10.1	2.7	3.7	3.0
Burlington, VT	n/a	n/a	n/a	n/a	n/a	n/a	n/a	n/a	n/a
Carmel, IN	77.1	79.0	75.9	15.7	19.4	14.9	3.7	3.5	4.3
Cary, NC	71.4	71.1	72.8	10.7	9.0	11.2	2.3	1.6	1.6
Casper, WY	n/a	n/a	n/a	n/a	n/a	n/a	n/a	n/a	n/a
Cheshire, CT	66.9	63.9	64.6	9.9	8.4	8.6	1.7	1.2	2.2
Chino Hills, CA	68.5	68.3	66.6	8.6	7.1	8.9	1.2	1.8	3.8
Collierville, TN	64.8	61.6	60.6	10.2	9.5	12.8	1.9	1.9	2.8
Conway, AR	n/a	n/a	n/a	n/a	n/a	n/a	n/a	n/a	n/a
Coronado, CA	60.5	61.2	59.6	6.3	7.3	7.1	2.1	2.8	3.0
Cranberry, PA	73.1	72.2	73.6	10.0	13.4	9.3	2.1	2.3	3.0
Dover, DE	n/a	n/a	n/a	n/a	n/a	n/a	n/a	n/a	n/a
Draper, UT	68.8	69.6	71.8	7.0	4.7	5.3	1.5	2.7	2.2
Dublin, OH	68.9	65.8	66.1	13.8	13.1	13.3	3.0	3.4	2.8
Edmond, OK	72.9	71.8	68.2	13.5	10.9	7.4	2.5	2.5	2.5
Evesham, NJ	73.5	73.1	73.1	11.6	11.6	12.6	1.7	1.7	1.9
Fargo, ND	n/a	n/a	n/a	n/a	n/a	n/a	n/a	n/a	n/a
Farmington, CT	72.2	73.8	70.4	9.5	7.8	7.4	1.0	1.4	0.8
Fishers, IN	77.1	79.0	75.9	15.7	19.4	14.9	3.7	3.5	4.3
Flower Mound, TX	62.3	60.7	60.9	13.6	11.7	11.0	2.2	2.3	2.5
Franklin, MA	63.0	64.7	64.8	5.1	5.3	5.0	1.2	2.0	1.9
Frederick, MD	68.4	68.9	69.2	7.1	8.4	10.4	1.3	2.1	2.4
Frisco, TX	62.3	60.7	60.9	13.6	11.7	11.0	2.2	2.3	2.5
Goodyear, AZ	71.2	72.5	70.8	11.2	9.1	9.2	1.0	3.1	3.7
Grand Blanc, MI	n/a	n/a	n/a	n/a	n/a	n/a	n/a	n/a	n/a
Greenburgh, NY	54.6	53.6	53.8	5.0	5.4	5.7	1.9	1.8	2.1
Greenwich, CT	68.2	70.4	70.3	5.6	6.0	6.7	1.3	4.3	4.3
Hampden, PA	n/a	n/a	n/a	n/a	n/a	n/a	n/a	n/a	n/a
Hilliard, OH	68.9	65.8	66.1	13.8	13.1	13.3	3.0	3.4	2.8
Hoover, AL	75.1	76.1	75.0	13.8	17.2	17.5	1.6	2.9	2.5
Huntersville, NC	65.8	66.1	66.5	11.1	13.5	11.0	2.3	2.9	3.1
Juneau, AK	n/a	n/a	n/a	n/a	n/a	n/a	n/a	n/a	n/a
Keller, TX	62.3	60.7	60.9	13.6	11.7	11.0	2.2	2.3	2.5
Kenner, LA	71.2	70.3	67.8	9.0	8.6	9.1	2.2	2.6	4.0
Kennesaw, GA	66.4	67.9	66.4	15.3	12.3	14.7	3.4	3.8	4.7
League City, TX	61.7	63.5	64.5	15.4	16.8	17.3	3.5	2.8	3.1
Leawood, KS	71.3	69.5	71.3	15.6	14.1	15.8	2.6	4.1	2.5
Lee's Summit, MO	71.3	69.5	71.3	15.6	14.1	15.8	2.6	4.1	2.5
Leesburg, VA	68.4	68.9	69.2	7.1	8.4	10.4	1.3	2.1	2.4
Lehi, UT	n/a	n/a	n/a	n/a	n/a	n/a	n/a	n/a	n/a
Lwr Providence, PA	73.5	73.1	73.1	11.6	11.6	12.6	1.7	1.7	1.9
Madison, AL	n/a	n/a	n/a	n/a	n/a	n/a	n/a	n/a	n/a
Manhattan Bch, CA	54.6	54.4	52.3	4.4	4.0	4.7	0.9	1.2	1.6
Maple Grove, MN	74.9	73.4	70.7	10.6	8.4	6.9	1.7	2.6	3.2
Marion, IA	n/a	n/a	n/a	n/a	n/a	n/a	n/a	n/a	n/a
Marlboro, NJ	54.6	53.6	53.8	5.0	5.4	5.7	1.9	1.8	2.1

MSA[1]	Homeownership Rate[2] (%)			Rental Vacancy Rate[3] (%)			Homeowner Vacancy Rate[4] (%)		
	2005	2006	2007	2005	2006	2007	2005	2006	2007
Matthews, NC	65.8	66.1	66.5	11.1	13.5	11.0	2.3	2.9	3.1
Meridian, ID	n/a	n/a	n/a	n/a	n/a	n/a	n/a	n/a	n/a
Merrimack, NH	63.0	64.7	64.8	5.1	5.3	5.0	1.2	2.0	1.9
Morgantown, WV	n/a	n/a	n/a	n/a	n/a	n/a	n/a	n/a	n/a
Mt Pleasant, SC	n/a	n/a	n/a	n/a	n/a	n/a	n/a	n/a	n/a
Northampton, PA	73.5	73.1	73.1	11.6	11.6	12.6	1.7	1.7	1.9
Northville, MI	75.1	75.8	76.1	15.2	21.2	19.4	2.7	3.7	4.1
Novi, MI	75.1	75.8	76.1	15.2	21.2	19.4	2.7	3.7	4.1
O'Fallon, MO	74.4	72.8	72.1	15.5	12.6	10.7	2.1	2.2	1.7
Oro Valley, AZ	66.1	67.5	67.1	9.7	7.1	7.9	1.5	1.9	2.2
Oviedo, FL	70.5	71.1	71.8	10.3	6.9	11.3	2.0	5.2	7.4
Palm Bch Grdns, FL	69.2	67.4	66.6	7.3	7.3	10.4	2.3	3.4	4.4
Parker, CO	70.7	70.0	69.5	12.0	11.1	10.1	2.7	3.7	3.0
Peachtree City, GA	66.4	67.9	66.4	15.3	12.3	14.7	3.4	3.8	4.7
Pflugerville, TX	63.9	66.7	66.4	9.4	7.2	6.8	2.4	1.5	1.5
Pleasanton, CA	57.8	59.4	58.0	8.0	6.9	6.2	1.6	2.4	1.3
Rapid City, SD	n/a	n/a	n/a	n/a	n/a	n/a	n/a	n/a	n/a
Redmond, WA	64.5	63.7	62.8	6.9	5.6	4.9	1.0	0.9	1.8
Richland, WA	n/a	n/a	n/a	n/a	n/a	n/a	n/a	n/a	n/a
Richmond, KY	n/a	n/a	n/a	n/a	n/a	n/a	n/a	n/a	n/a
Rio Rancho, NM	69.2	70.0	70.5	7.9	8.3	8.8	1.8	2.0	2.6
Rockaway, NJ	54.6	53.6	53.8	5.0	5.4	5.7	1.9	1.8	2.1
Rocklin, CA	64.1	64.2	60.8	8.5	12.7	9.5	1.2	3.3	4.2
Rogers, AR	n/a	n/a	n/a	n/a	n/a	n/a	n/a	n/a	n/a
Round Rock, TX	63.9	66.7	66.4	9.4	7.2	6.8	2.4	1.5	1.5
Sammamish, WA	64.5	63.7	62.8	6.9	5.6	4.9	1.0	0.9	1.8
San Ramon, CA	57.8	59.4	58.0	8.0	6.9	6.2	1.6	2.4	1.3
Santa Fe, NM	n/a	n/a	n/a	n/a	n/a	n/a	n/a	n/a	n/a
Saratoga, CA	59.2	59.4	57.6	6.7	6.0	3.8	1.5	1.6	0.8
Savage, MN	74.9	73.4	70.7	10.6	8.4	6.9	1.7	2.6	3.2
Schererville, IN	70.0	69.6	69.0	13.1	13.0	11.0	1.9	2.3	2.7
Shawnee, KS	71.3	69.5	71.3	15.6	14.1	15.8	2.6	4.1	2.5
Shrewsbury, MA	65.3	71.0	67.8	8.9	9.6	7.0	1.4	1.5	0.5
S Brunswick, NJ	54.6	53.6	53.8	5.0	5.4	5.7	1.9	1.8	2.1
S. Jordan, UT	68.8	69.6	71.8	7.0	4.7	5.3	1.5	2.7	2.2
S. Kingstown, RI	63.1	65.5	64.1	7.0	8.6	9.2	1.4	1.8	1.6
Southaven, MS	64.8	61.6	60.6	10.2	9.5	12.8	1.9	1.9	2.8
Southlake, TX	62.3	60.7	60.9	13.6	11.7	11.0	2.2	2.3	2.5
Spanish Fork, UT	n/a	n/a	n/a	n/a	n/a	n/a	n/a	n/a	n/a
Sparks, NV	n/a	n/a	n/a	n/a	n/a	n/a	n/a	n/a	n/a
Stow, OH	78.1	77.1	74.6	9.3	7.7	8.4	2.1	3.2	4.5
Sugar Land, TX	61.7	63.5	64.5	15.4	16.8	17.3	3.5	2.8	3.1
Sun Prairie, WI	n/a	n/a	n/a	n/a	n/a	n/a	n/a	n/a	n/a
Tualatin, OR	68.3	66.0	61.2	9.7	7.1	4.8	1.6	1.7	2.3
Waimalu, HI	58.0	58.4	58.8	3.9	3.9	5.1	0.6	0.8	1.2
Wellington, FL	69.2	67.4	66.6	7.3	7.3	10.4	2.3	3.4	4.4
W Des Moines, IA	n/a	n/a	n/a	n/a	n/a	n/a	n/a	n/a	n/a
West Linn, OR	68.3	66.0	61.2	9.7	7.1	4.8	1.6	1.7	2.3
West Windsor, NJ	n/a	n/a	n/a	n/a	n/a	n/a	n/a	n/a	n/a
Weston, FL	69.2	67.4	66.6	7.3	7.3	10.4	2.3	3.4	4.4
Woodbury, MN	74.9	73.4	70.7	10.6	8.4	6.9	1.7	2.6	3.2
Woodridge, IL	70.0	69.6	69.0	13.1	13.0	11.0	1.9	2.3	2.7
Yorba Linda, CA	54.6	54.4	52.3	4.4	4.0	4.7	0.9	1.2	1.6
U.S.	68.9	68.8	68.1	9.8	9.8	9.7	1.9	2.4	2.7

Note: (1) Metropolitan Statistical Area - see Appendix B for areas included; (2) The proportion of households that are owners; (3) The proportion of the rental inventory that is vacant for rent; (4) The proportion of the homeowner inventory that is vacant for sale; n/a not available

Source: U.S. Census Bureau, Housing Vacancies and Homeownership Annual Statistics: 2007

Employment by Industry

Metro Area[1]	(A)	(B)	(C)	(D)	(E)	(F)	(G)	(H)	(I)	(J)	(K)	(L)	(M)
Allen, TX[2]	12.4	10.7	16.1	10.5	9.4	9.2	8.8	n/a	6.2	3.6	3.7	3.4	n/a
Ankeny, IA	13.1	11.9	11.6	11.6	6.0	8.9	15.8	n/a	5.5	3.9	3.3	2.9	n/a
Apex, NC	18.3	9.7	17.6	11.5	6.2	9.2	5.1	n/a	4.3	4.8	2.4	3.1	n/a
Bangor, ME[3]	20.9	20.3	8.2	16.8	4.5	8.3	3.4	4.6	3.1	2.7	4.6	2.2	0.4
Beavercreek, OH	16.1	16.6	12.9	10.9	13.0	9.1	4.9	n/a	3.5	3.9	2.9	2.7	n/a
Bellevue, NE	13.4	14.4	13.7	11.7	7.2	9.4	8.3	n/a	3.9	3.5	6.5	2.7	n/a
Bend, OR	11.5	12.5	10.7	15.3	7.6	13.9	7.4	n/a	2.4	3.3	2.1	2.4	n/a
Bernards, NJ[2]	14.6	13.3	17.2	13.0	7.0	7.5	5.8	n/a	5.8	4.6	3.9	2.9	n/a
Bethlehem, NY	24.3	18.1	12.1	11.6	5.0	7.1	5.7	n/a	3.3	4.0	3.0	2.2	n/a
Bozeman, MT	n/a	n/a	n/a	n/a	n/a	n/a	n/a	n/a	n/a	n/a	n/a	n/a	n/a
Brentwood, TN	13.1	14.3	13.4	11.9	10.1	10.5	6.0	n/a	4.8	3.9	4.0	2.5	n/a
Brookfield, WI	11.0	16.4	13.1	9.8	15.4	8.3	6.7	3.9	4.8	4.9	3.5	2.0	0.1
Broomfield, CO	13.8	10.4	17.1	10.7	5.7	10.2	7.8	n/a	5.3	3.7	4.1	3.9	n/a
Burlington, VT[3]	17.9	16.5	9.1	13.7	12.9	8.9	4.5	n/a	3.5	3.0	2.6	2.5	n/a
Carmel, IN	13.4	12.6	13.9	11.1	10.5	9.4	6.8	5.6	5.2	3.8	5.7	1.8	0.1
Cary, NC	18.3	9.7	17.6	11.5	6.2	9.2	5.1	n/a	4.3	4.8	2.4	3.1	n/a
Casper, WY	n/a	n/a	n/a	n/a	n/a	n/a	n/a	n/a	n/a	n/a	n/a	n/a	n/a
Cheshire, CT[3]	12.4	24.8	9.4	11.6	11.2	7.5	4.8	n/a	4.1	4.0	3.2	2.8	n/a
Chino Hills, CA	18.3	10.2	11.4	14.1	9.1	10.3	3.8	8.4	4.4	3.3	5.4	1.2	0.1
Collierville, TN	13.9	11.9	13.7	11.6	7.8	11.1	5.1	n/a	5.7	3.8	10.2	1.1	n/a
Conway, AR	19.8	13.7	12.4	10.9	7.0	8.2	5.9	n/a	4.9	4.0	4.8	2.8	n/a
Coronado, CA	17.1	10.0	16.5	11.8	7.8	12.2	5.9	6.2	3.5	3.8	2.3	3.0	<0.1
Cranberry, PA	11.2	20.0	13.4	11.8	8.7	9.1	5.9	4.9	4.3	4.6	3.9	1.9	0.4
Dover, DE	28.8	13.3	6.2	16.3	5.6	10.1	3.6	n/a	n/a	4.1	n/a	1.2	n/a
Draper, UT	14.3	9.4	15.5	11.5	9.0	9.3	8.0	n/a	4.8	3.0	4.8	2.9	n/a
Dublin, OH	16.6	11.8	16.0	11.4	8.0	9.2	7.7	n/a	4.1	3.9	5.5	1.9	n/a
Edmond, OK	19.9	12.8	13.1	11.4	6.4	9.7	6.0	4.9	4.1	3.9	3.0	2.1	2.6
Evesham, NJ[2]	16.4	14.5	13.4	13.7	8.2	7.4	6.0	n/a	5.9	4.5	3.8	1.7	n/a
Fargo, ND	14.9	14.1	10.6	12.8	7.7	9.9	7.4	n/a	6.2	4.2	3.5	2.7	n/a
Farmington, CT[3]	15.9	16.3	10.8	10.4	11.5	7.3	11.7	n/a	3.5	3.7	2.7	2.2	n/a
Fishers, IN	13.4	12.6	13.9	11.1	10.5	9.4	6.8	5.6	5.2	3.8	5.7	1.8	0.1
Flower Mound, TX[2]	12.4	10.7	16.1	10.5	9.4	9.2	8.8	n/a	6.2	3.6	3.7	3.4	n/a
Franklin, MA[4]	11.6	20.7	18.4	8.9	6.1	8.6	9.1	3.6	3.7	3.5	2.4	3.2	<0.1
Frederick, MD[2]	16.8	12.4	21.3	11.0	3.5	8.0	7.6	n/a	2.7	5.4	1.2	2.9	n/a
Frisco, TX[2]	12.4	10.7	16.1	10.5	9.4	9.2	8.8	n/a	6.2	3.6	3.7	3.4	n/a
Goodyear, AZ	13.1	10.9	16.9	12.5	7.0	9.9	7.9	8.2	4.7	3.6	3.5	1.6	0.2
Grand Blanc, MI	17.6	17.0	9.1	14.7	10.3	10.6	4.7	n/a	4.2	4.0	2.6	1.9	n/a
Greenburgh, NY[2]	14.8	18.2	15.2	9.3	3.7	7.7	10.9	n/a	4.6	4.2	3.6	4.0	n/a
Greenwich, CT[3]	11.1	14.8	16.7	12.5	9.5	7.8	10.7	n/a	3.4	4.1	2.8	2.9	n/a
Hampden, PA	18.7	13.9	11.9	10.7	7.2	8.4	7.4	n/a	4.3	5.0	6.8	2.0	n/a
Hilliard, OH	16.6	11.8	16.0	11.4	8.0	9.2	7.7	n/a	4.1	3.9	5.5	1.9	n/a
Hoover, AL	15.6	12.0	12.7	12.3	8.1	8.2	7.5	6.6	6.0	4.4	4.0	2.2	0.6
Huntersville, NC	12.3	9.1	15.5	11.5	9.3	9.6	8.9	n/a	5.7	4.5	4.2	2.5	n/a
Juneau, AK	n/a	n/a	n/a	n/a	n/a	n/a	n/a	n/a	n/a	n/a	n/a	n/a	n/a
Keller, TX[2]	13.4	11.2	11.9	12.1	11.3	9.7	5.5	n/a	4.8	3.7	7.3	1.9	n/a
Kenner, LA	15.6	12.3	13.0	11.5	7.0	12.9	5.2	6.5	4.6	3.7	4.7	1.4	1.6
Kennesaw, GA	13.5	10.4	16.6	11.6	7.0	9.5	6.5	5.6	6.5	3.9	5.3	3.5	0.1
League City, TX	13.7	11.1	14.9	10.6	9.1	8.8	5.6	7.8	5.2	3.6	4.9	1.4	3.3
Leawood, KS	14.8	11.8	14.7	10.9	8.0	9.1	7.4	n/a	5.1	4.0	4.8	4.2	n/a
Lee's Summit, MO	14.8	11.8	14.7	10.9	8.0	9.1	7.4	n/a	5.1	4.0	4.8	4.2	n/a
Leesburg, VA[2]	22.9	10.8	22.9	9.0	1.7	8.4	4.6	n/a	2.3	6.2	2.4	3.1	n/a
Lehi, UT	13.3	20.9	12.0	12.9	10.3	7.2	3.5	n/a	2.8	2.2	1.2	4.1	n/a
Lwr Providence, PA[2]	11.3	20.9	15.8	10.8	7.7	7.8	7.4	n/a	4.4	4.4	3.2	2.2	n/a
Madison, AL	20.5	7.5	20.8	11.7	15.3	8.2	3.0	n/a	2.8	3.5	1.5	1.3	n/a
Manhattan Bch, CA[2]	14.5	12.1	14.7	10.6	10.7	9.7	5.8	3.7	5.6	3.6	4.1	5.0	0.1
Maple Grove, MN	13.5	14.2	14.8	10.8	11.0	8.9	7.8	n/a	4.8	4.2	3.7	2.4	n/a
Marion, IA	11.7	12.5	9.2	11.9	16.2	7.9	7.6	n/a	3.9	3.8	6.0	3.8	n/a
Marlboro, NJ[2]	14.6	13.3	17.2	13.0	7.0	7.5	5.8	n/a	5.8	4.6	3.9	2.9	n/a
Matthews, NC	12.3	9.1	15.5	11.5	9.3	9.6	8.9	n/a	5.7	4.5	4.2	2.5	n/a
Meridian, ID	15.6	12.3	14.5	12.5	10.8	8.7	5.2	n/a	4.5	2.9	3.0	1.7	n/a

Metro Area[1]	(A)	(B)	(C)	(D)	(E)	(F)	(G)	(H)	(I)	(J)	(K)	(L)	(M)
Merrimack, NH[4]	11.5	12.6	11.0	15.7	18.7	7.7	6.5	n/a	4.6	3.2	3.0	1.6	n/a
Morgantown, WV	28.1	19.1	6.8	11.8	6.5	9.5	n/a	n/a	n/a	n/a	n/a	n/a	n/a
Mt Pleasant, SC	18.9	10.2	13.8	13.0	7.5	11.7	4.9	n/a	3.0	3.9	4.3	1.7	n/a
Northampton, PA[2]	11.3	20.9	15.8	10.8	7.7	7.8	7.4	n/a	4.4	4.4	3.2	2.2	n/a
Northville, MI[2]	14.5	16.0	14.9	9.4	11.9	10.0	4.6	n/a	4.3	4.5	5.5	1.7	n/a
Novi, MI[2]	9.9	13.4	19.5	12.4	13.6	8.4	6.3	n/a	4.7	4.5	1.8	1.7	n/a
O'Fallon, MO	12.7	15.3	14.2	11.2	9.9	10.1	5.9	n/a	4.6	4.2	3.7	2.2	n/a
Oro Valley, AZ	20.8	14.2	13.6	12.0	7.2	10.3	4.4	6.7	2.6	3.9	2.4	1.5	0.5
Oviedo, FL	10.8	10.1	18.1	11.7	3.8	17.4	6.1	6.9	4.3	5.3	3.0	2.4	<0.1
Palm Bch Grdns, FL[2]	11.3	13.2	20.7	12.9	3.1	12.7	6.7	7.3	4.0	4.2	1.8	1.9	n/a
Parker, CO	13.8	10.4	17.1	10.7	5.7	10.2	7.8	n/a	5.3	3.7	4.1	3.9	n/a
Peachtree City, GA	13.5	10.4	16.6	11.6	7.0	9.5	6.5	5.6	6.5	3.9	5.3	3.5	0.1
Pflugerville, TX	20.4	10.2	14.2	11.2	7.8	10.3	5.9	n/a	5.3	3.7	1.8	2.8	n/a
Pleasanton, CA[2]	18.0	11.9	14.8	11.3	8.8	8.3	5.7	6.8	4.6	3.4	3.5	2.7	0.1
Rapid City, SD	17.0	15.5	7.3	15.0	5.7	12.3	6.2	n/a	3.5	4.5	3.3	1.8	n/a
Redmond, WA[2]	13.7	10.4	14.7	10.3	11.5	9.3	6.0	6.7	4.9	3.3	3.6	5.5	0.1
Richland, WA	17.8	10.4	21.5	12.9	7.4	8.7	3.8	n/a	n/a	n/a	n/a	n/a	n/a
Richmond, KY	n/a	n/a	n/a	n/a	n/a	n/a	n/a	n/a	n/a	n/a	n/a	n/a	n/a
Rio Rancho, NM	20.4	12.4	16.0	11.8	5.8	9.9	4.8	n/a	3.3	3.1	2.8	2.3	n/a
Rockaway, NJ[2]	16.1	14.1	15.4	10.4	8.4	6.4	7.2	n/a	5.2	4.6	5.6	2.4	n/a
Rocklin, CA	26.1	10.9	12.3	11.4	4.3	9.7	6.8	7.1	3.1	3.2	2.9	2.2	0.1
Rogers, AR	13.5	9.3	15.7	11.0	15.4	8.4	4.2	n/a	4.6	3.1	8.1	1.3	n/a
Round Rock, TX	20.4	10.2	14.2	11.2	7.8	10.3	5.9	n/a	5.3	3.7	1.8	2.8	n/a
Sammamish, WA[2]	13.7	10.4	14.7	10.3	11.5	9.3	6.0	6.7	4.9	3.3	3.6	5.5	0.1
San Ramon, CA[2]	18.0	11.9	14.8	11.3	8.8	8.3	5.7	6.8	4.6	3.4	3.5	2.7	0.1
Santa Fe, NM	25.3	14.8	8.6	13.9	1.7	13.8	4.5	n/a	1.8	4.2	1.2	2.7	n/a
Saratoga, CA	10.7	11.3	19.4	10.0	18.3	8.2	4.0	5.1	4.4	2.8	1.5	4.4	<0.1
Savage, MN	13.5	14.2	14.8	10.8	11.0	8.9	7.8	n/a	4.8	4.2	3.7	2.4	n/a
Schererville, IN[2]	13.9	16.2	8.0	12.9	13.4	11.0	3.5	6.9	3.6	4.4	5.2	0.8	0.2
Shawnee, KS	14.8	11.8	14.7	10.9	8.0	9.1	7.4	n/a	5.1	4.0	4.8	4.2	n/a
Shrewsbury, MA[3]	15.3	20.0	11.3	11.6	11.5	8.5	5.4	n/a	4.0	3.6	3.3	1.6	n/a
S Brunswick, NJ[2]	14.6	13.3	17.2	13.0	7.0	7.5	5.8	n/a	5.8	4.6	3.9	2.9	n/a
S. Jordan, UT	14.3	9.4	15.5	11.5	9.0	9.3	8.0	n/a	4.8	3.0	4.8	2.9	n/a
S. Kingstown, RI[3]	12.8	19.8	10.8	12.1	11.0	10.0	6.4	4.6	3.6	4.5	2.3	2.0	0.1
Southaven, MS	13.9	11.9	13.7	11.6	7.8	11.1	5.1	n/a	5.7	3.8	10.2	1.1	n/a
Southlake, TX[2]	13.4	11.2	11.9	12.1	11.3	9.7	5.5	n/a	4.8	3.7	7.3	1.9	n/a
Spanish Fork, UT	13.3	20.9	12.0	12.9	10.3	7.2	3.5	n/a	2.8	2.2	1.2	4.1	n/a
Sparks, NV	13.4	9.3	13.2	11.3	6.5	17.6	4.4	8.8	4.8	3.2	6.1	1.2	0.2
Stow, OH	14.9	13.9	14.9	11.8	13.6	8.9	4.0	n/a	5.3	4.0	3.2	1.3	n/a
Sugar Land, TX	13.7	11.1	14.9	10.6	9.1	8.8	5.6	7.8	5.2	3.6	4.9	1.4	3.3
Sun Prairie, WI	23.4	10.1	10.7	11.9	9.2	8.4	7.6	n/a	3.6	5.0	2.5	2.7	n/a
Tualatin, OR	13.9	12.5	13.0	11.1	11.9	9.4	6.7	6.2	5.5	3.5	3.7	2.3	0.2
Waimalu, HI	21.5	12.5	13.3	10.5	2.5	13.8	4.9	n/a	3.2	4.5	5.3	1.9	n/a
Wellington, FL[2]	11.3	13.2	20.7	12.9	3.1	12.7	6.7	7.3	4.0	4.2	1.8	1.9	n/a
W Des Moines, IA	13.1	11.9	11.6	11.6	6.0	8.9	15.8	n/a	5.5	3.9	3.3	2.9	n/a
West Linn, OR	13.9	12.5	13.0	11.1	11.9	9.4	6.7	6.2	5.5	3.5	3.7	2.3	0.2
West Windsor, NJ	28.1	17.8	15.3	9.5	3.3	5.8	7.1	n/a	2.2	4.0	2.0	2.4	n/a
Weston, FL[2]	13.4	11.6	16.2	13.5	3.8	10.2	8.1	7.3	6.0	4.3	3.2	2.5	n/a
Woodbury, MN	13.5	14.2	14.8	10.8	11.0	8.9	7.8	n/a	4.8	4.2	3.7	2.4	n/a
Woodridge, IL[2]	12.3	13.1	17.1	10.5	9.8	8.5	7.5	4.4	5.4	4.4	4.7	2.1	<0.1
Yorba Linda, CA[2]	10.8	9.5	18.0	11.2	11.8	11.2	7.9	6.7	5.7	3.2	2.0	2.0	<0.1
U.S.	16.3	13.4	13.1	11.6	9.9	9.6	5.9	5.3	4.4	3.9	3.7	2.2	0.5

Note: All figures are percentages covering non-farm employment as of December 2007 and are not seasonally adjusted; (1) Figures cover the Metropolitan Statistical Area (MSA) except where noted. See Appendix B for areas included; (2) Metropolitan Division; (3) New England City and Town Area; (4) New England City and Town Area Division; (A) Government; (B) Education and Health Services; (C) Professional and Business Services; (D) Retail Trade; (E) Manufacturing; (F) Leisure and Hospitality; (G) Finance Activities; (H) Construction; (I) Wholesale Trade; (J) Other Services; (K) Transportation and Utilities; (L) Information; (M) Natural Resources and Mining; n/a not available

Source: Bureau of Labor Statistics, http://stats.bls.gov

Labor Force, Employment and Job Growth: City

City	Civilian Labor Force			Workers Employed		
	Dec. 2007	Dec. 2007	% Chg.	Dec. 2007	Dec. 2007	% Chg.
Allen, TX	39,657	40,015	0.9	38,247	38,503	0.7
Ankeny, IA	23,858	23,931	0.3	23,366	23,398	0.1
Apex, NC	16,610	16,609	0.0	16,197	16,210	0.1
Bangor, ME	17,163	17,131	-0.2	16,418	16,328	-0.5
Beavercreek, OH	20,972	20,762	-1.0	20,105	19,814	-1.4
Bellevue, NE	25,640	25,745	0.4	24,885	25,045	0.6
Bend, OR	40,907	41,919	2.5	39,278	39,568	0.7
Bernards, NJ	14,233	14,114	-0.8	13,939	13,803	-1.0
Bethlehem, NY	17,736	17,576	-0.9	17,272	17,035	-1.4
Bozeman, MT	20,466	22,395	9.4	20,027	21,892	9.3
Brentwood, TN	17,168	17,445	1.6	16,691	16,858	1.0
Brookfield, WI	20,496	20,184	-1.5	19,875	19,571	-1.5
Broomfield, CO	25,990	26,451	1.8	25,029	25,356	1.3
Burlington, VT	22,381	22,026	-1.6	21,795	21,451	-1.6
Carmel, IN	31,552	31,463	-0.3	30,816	30,771	-0.1
Cary, NC	61,948	62,051	0.2	60,456	60,503	0.1
Casper, WY	30,392	30,334	-0.2	29,535	29,419	-0.4
Cheshire, CT	14,544	14,701	1.1	14,121	14,181	0.4
Chino Hills, CA	42,444	42,254	-0.4	41,506	40,975	-1.3
Collierville, TN	20,546	20,685	0.7	19,711	19,859	0.8
Conway, AR	26,537	26,801	1.0	25,624	25,736	0.4
Coronado, CA	8,766	8,788	0.3	8,560	8,514	-0.5
Cranberry, PA	15,647	15,597	-0.3	15,279	15,172	-0.7
Dover, DE	17,111	17,057	-0.3	16,634	16,429	-1.2
Draper, UT	13,255	13,604	2.6	13,155	13,475	2.4
Dublin, OH	19,619	19,829	1.1	18,994	19,136	0.7
Edmond, OK	36,737	36,677	-0.2	35,919	35,799	-0.3
Evesham, NJ	27,561	27,529	-0.1	26,854	26,722	-0.5
Fargo, ND	58,778	60,004	2.1	57,372	58,480	1.9
Farmington, CT	12,817	13,007	1.5	12,456	12,570	0.9
Fishers, IN	37,185	37,172	0.0	36,322	36,269	-0.1
Flower Mound, TX	35,456	35,772	0.9	34,283	34,513	0.7
Franklin, MA	16,725	16,680	-0.3	16,108	16,131	0.1
Frederick, MD	32,504	32,237	-0.8	31,538	31,316	-0.7
Frisco, TX	44,667	45,258	1.3	43,173	43,462	0.7
Goodyear, AZ	20,876	21,194	1.5	20,416	20,630	1.0
Grand Blanc, MI	16,406	15,819	-3.6	15,775	15,159	-3.9
Greenburgh, NY	51,000	51,052	0.1	49,579	49,380	-0.4
Greenwich, CT	30,297	30,677	1.3	29,575	29,783	0.7
Hampden, PA	14,846	14,752	-0.6	14,517	14,386	-0.9
Hilliard, OH	15,366	15,548	1.2	14,877	14,988	0.7
Hoover, AL	39,552	39,486	-0.2	38,801	38,594	-0.5
Huntersville, NC	21,418	21,228	-0.9	20,838	20,572	-1.3
Juneau, AK	18,467	18,553	0.5	17,625	17,678	0.3
Keller, TX	19,617	19,725	0.6	18,993	19,077	0.4
Kenner, LA	34,655	35,315	1.9	33,704	34,306	1.8
Kennesaw, GA	17,636	17,854	1.2	17,066	17,273	1.2
League City, TX	35,670	36,403	2.1	34,483	35,123	1.9
Leawood, KS	15,704	15,847	0.9	15,325	15,432	0.7
Lee's Summit, MO	38,793	38,864	0.2	37,764	37,659	-0.3
Leesburg, VA	22,117	22,303	0.8	21,727	21,835	0.5
Lehi, UT	11,110	11,432	2.9	10,955	11,233	2.5
Lwr Providence, PA	13,408	13,361	-0.4	13,027	12,959	-0.5
Madison, AL	22,175	22,669	2.2	21,756	22,173	1.9
Manhattan Bch, CA	23,255	23,562	1.3	22,920	23,145	1.0
Maple Grove, MN	38,135	38,153	0.0	37,015	36,828	-0.5
Marion, IA	18,950	18,850	-0.5	18,418	18,269	-0.8
Marlboro, NJ	20,579	20,366	-1.0	20,073	19,878	-1.0
Matthews, NC	14,336	14,195	-1.0	13,926	13,749	-1.3

City	Civilian Labor Force			Workers Employed		
	Dec. 2007	Dec. 2007	% Chg.	Dec. 2007	Dec. 2007	% Chg.
Meridian, ID	21,835	31,933	46.2	21,516	31,093	44.5
Merrimack, NH	16,642	16,668	0.2	16,193	16,241	0.3
Morgantown, WV	16,000	16,212	1.3	15,510	15,698	1.2
Mt Pleasant, SC	34,022	34,405	1.1	33,048	33,246	0.6
Northampton, PA	22,865	22,846	-0.1	22,243	22,127	-0.5
Northville, MI	10,132	9,786	-3.4	9,971	9,610	-3.6
Novi, MI	26,065	25,506	-2.1	25,119	24,449	-2.7
O'Fallon, MO	29,912	29,748	-0.5	28,894	28,514	-1.3
Oro Valley, AZ	15,531	15,469	-0.4	15,161	15,014	-1.0
Oviedo, FL	18,142	18,658	2.8	17,734	18,093	2.0
Palm Bch Grdns, FL	27,072	27,309	0.9	26,513	26,449	-0.2
Parker, CO	20,798	21,165	1.8	20,331	20,597	1.3
Peachtree City, GA	17,816	18,071	1.4	17,298	17,509	1.2
Pflugerville, TX	17,247	17,526	1.6	16,755	16,982	1.4
Pleasanton, CA	36,074	36,257	0.5	35,366	35,379	0.0
Rapid City, SD	34,617	34,984	1.1	33,536	33,835	0.9
Redmond, WA	30,232	30,990	2.5	29,317	30,133	2.8
Richland, WA	23,081	24,395	5.7	22,121	23,396	5.8
Richmond, KY	17,058	16,771	-1.7	16,397	16,103	-1.8
Rio Rancho, NM	36,528	36,554	0.1	35,419	35,316	-0.3
Rockaway, NJ	14,741	14,648	-0.6	14,462	14,332	-0.9
Rocklin, CA	26,725	27,036	1.2	25,984	26,015	0.1
Rogers, AR	26,551	26,678	0.5	25,757	25,678	-0.3
Round Rock, TX	50,970	51,755	1.5	49,344	50,014	1.4
Sammamish, WA	19,320	19,816	2.6	18,744	19,266	2.8
San Ramon, CA	29,356	29,498	0.5	28,889	28,899	0.0
Santa Fe, NM	41,497	41,202	-0.7	40,526	40,338	-0.5
Saratoga, CA	13,224	13,397	1.3	12,961	13,070	0.8
Savage, MN	16,163	16,161	0.0	15,603	15,525	-0.5
Schererville, IN	16,027	15,786	-1.5	15,486	15,266	-1.4
Shawnee, KS	32,262	32,568	0.9	31,341	31,560	0.7
Shrewsbury, MA	17,418	17,224	-1.1	16,812	16,646	-1.0
S Brunswick, NJ	23,435	23,248	-0.8	22,869	22,645	-1.0
S. Jordan, UT	16,802	17,273	2.8	16,573	16,977	2.4
S. Kingstown, RI	16,278	16,166	-0.7	15,637	15,488	-1.0
Southaven, MS	22,378	22,564	0.8	21,672	21,651	-0.1
Southlake, TX	12,242	12,307	0.5	11,825	11,879	0.5
Spanish Fork, UT	11,938	12,297	3.0	11,721	12,018	2.5
Sparks, NV	47,759	49,063	2.7	45,974	46,587	1.3
Stow, OH	20,074	20,175	0.5	19,271	19,229	-0.2
Sugar Land, TX	41,536	42,328	1.9	40,232	40,978	1.9
Sun Prairie, WI	16,025	15,938	-0.5	15,428	15,296	-0.9
Tualatin, OR	15,125	15,300	1.2	14,611	14,748	0.9
Waimalu, HI	n/a	n/a	n/a	n/a	n/a	n/a
Wellington, FL	30,883	31,062	0.6	30,120	30,046	-0.2
W Des Moines, IA	33,558	33,639	0.2	32,845	32,890	0.1
West Linn, OR	13,636	13,808	1.3	13,193	13,317	0.9
West Windsor, NJ	14,348	14,339	-0.1	14,137	14,102	-0.2
Weston, FL	35,539	36,019	1.4	34,783	35,003	0.6
Woodbury, MN	31,686	31,657	-0.1	30,786	30,631	-0.5
Woodridge, IL	20,520	20,622	0.5	19,846	19,852	0.0
Yorba Linda, CA	36,900	36,422	-1.3	36,142	35,387	-2.1
U.S.	152,571,000	153,705,000	0.7	146,081,000	146,334,000	0.2

Note: Data is not seasonally adjusted and covers workers 16 years of age and older
Source: Bureau of Labor Statistics, http://stats.bls.gov

Labor Force, Employment and Job Growth: Metro Area

Metro Area	Civilian Labor Force			Workers Employed		
	Dec. 2007	Dec. 2007	% Chg.	Dec. 2007	Dec. 2007	% Chg.
Allen, TX[2]	2,068,085	2,086,426	0.9	1,984,055	1,997,359	0.7
Ankeny, IA	308,008	309,771	0.6	297,323	297,729	0.1
Apex, NC	541,158	542,390	0.2	522,867	523,302	0.1
Bangor, ME[3]	71,684	71,321	-0.5	68,390	68,017	-0.5
Beavercreek, OH	430,746	426,835	-0.9	407,083	401,192	-1.4
Bellevue, NE	447,220	449,040	0.4	432,928	435,011	0.5
Bend, OR	80,986	83,025	2.5	77,370	77,942	0.7
Bernards, NJ[2]	1,199,770	1,190,736	-0.8	1,157,810	1,146,507	-1.0
Bethlehem, NY	454,658	451,335	-0.7	438,693	432,686	-1.4
Bozeman, MT	49,878	50,152	0.5	48,826	48,872	0.1
Brentwood, TN	786,226	799,308	1.7	758,387	765,980	1.0
Brookfield, WI	807,173	797,111	-1.2	771,560	759,766	-1.5
Broomfield, CO	1,368,472	1,393,879	1.9	1,315,598	1,332,798	1.3
Burlington, VT[3]	112,948	111,157	-1.6	109,438	107,711	-1.6
Carmel, IN	896,028	894,741	-0.1	860,673	859,430	-0.1
Cary, NC	541,158	542,390	0.2	522,867	523,302	0.1
Casper, WY	40,541	40,469	-0.2	39,340	39,186	-0.4
Cheshire, CT[3]	308,799	312,248	1.1	296,386	297,642	0.4
Chino Hills, CA	1,797,226	1,807,573	0.6	1,711,443	1,689,570	-1.3
Collierville, TN	622,864	629,858	1.1	591,733	595,007	0.6
Conway, AR	337,587	340,290	0.8	323,028	324,442	0.4
Coronado, CA	1,544,056	1,555,276	0.7	1,485,911	1,478,027	-0.5
Cranberry, PA	1,200,792	1,196,486	-0.4	1,152,140	1,144,059	-0.7
Dover, DE	75,327	74,920	-0.5	73,290	72,388	-1.2
Draper, UT	596,424	614,462	3.0	583,449	597,668	2.4
Dublin, OH	955,896	967,649	1.2	914,318	921,121	0.7
Edmond, OK	572,031	571,342	-0.1	549,042	547,206	-0.3
Evesham, NJ[2]	663,461	661,003	-0.4	636,850	633,724	-0.5
Fargo, ND	116,907	118,806	1.6	113,760	115,497	1.5
Farmington, CT[3]	578,370	587,629	1.6	555,253	560,314	0.9
Fishers, IN	896,028	894,741	-0.1	860,673	859,430	-0.1
Flower Mound, TX[2]	2,068,085	2,086,426	0.9	1,984,055	1,997,359	0.7
Franklin, MA[4]	1,504,969	1,501,077	-0.3	1,447,425	1,449,468	0.1
Frederick, MD[2]	636,703	632,543	-0.7	620,675	616,311	-0.7
Frisco, TX[2]	2,068,085	2,086,426	0.9	1,984,055	1,997,359	0.7
Goodyear, AZ	2,044,802	2,080,380	1.7	1,980,437	2,001,144	1.0
Grand Blanc, MI	214,286	207,315	-3.3	198,026	190,298	-3.9
Greenburgh, NY[2]	5,532,850	5,580,260	0.9	5,306,749	5,313,071	0.1
Greenwich, CT[3]	470,388	476,955	1.4	454,621	457,828	0.7
Hampden, PA	282,110	280,672	-0.5	273,090	270,634	-0.9
Hilliard, OH	955,896	967,649	1.2	914,318	921,121	0.7
Hoover, AL	542,132	542,243	0.0	526,514	523,704	-0.5
Huntersville, NC	841,508	837,004	-0.5	804,473	796,443	-1.0
Juneau, AK	18,467	18,553	0.5	17,625	17,678	0.3
Keller, TX[2]	1,026,983	1,032,143	0.5	985,677	990,075	0.4
Kenner, LA	501,725	510,266	1.7	484,549	493,194	1.8
Kennesaw, GA	2,728,345	2,771,516	1.6	2,616,398	2,648,176	1.2
League City, TX	2,713,998	2,767,131	2.0	2,603,369	2,651,639	1.9
Leawood, KS	1,032,329	1,040,408	0.8	985,807	987,141	0.1
Lee's Summit, MO	1,032,329	1,040,408	0.8	985,807	987,141	0.1
Leesburg, VA[2]	2,328,726	2,347,351	0.8	2,260,232	2,273,004	0.6
Lehi, UT	225,624	232,573	3.1	221,015	226,628	2.5
Lwr Providence, PA[2]	1,938,477	1,934,718	-0.2	1,862,759	1,853,023	-0.5
Madison, AL	201,585	205,992	2.2	196,302	200,062	1.9
Manhattan Bch, CA[2]	4,890,873	4,987,766	2.0	4,681,530	4,727,423	1.0
Maple Grove, MN	1,848,336	1,850,202	0.1	1,776,526	1,767,152	-0.5
Marion, IA	143,219	142,295	-0.6	137,490	136,380	-0.8
Marlboro, NJ[2]	1,199,770	1,190,736	-0.8	1,157,810	1,146,507	-1.0
Matthews, NC	841,508	837,004	-0.5	804,473	796,443	-1.0

Metro Area	Civilian Labor Force			Workers Employed		
	Dec. 2007	Dec. 2007	% Chg.	Dec. 2007	Dec. 2007	% Chg.
Meridian, ID	294,054	297,681	1.2	286,914	288,783	0.7
Merrimack, NH[4]	179,695	179,719	0.0	173,427	173,813	0.2
Morgantown, WV	62,174	63,089	1.5	60,500	61,237	1.2
Mt Pleasant, SC	307,693	311,261	1.2	294,016	295,777	0.6
Northampton, PA[2]	1,938,477	1,934,718	-0.2	1,862,759	1,853,023	-0.5
Northville, MI[2]	895,900	873,116	-2.5	823,765	793,978	-3.6
Novi, MI[2]	1,277,144	1,254,310	-1.8	1,194,458	1,162,599	-2.7
O'Fallon, MO	1,448,868	1,445,887	-0.2	1,382,306	1,367,017	-1.1
Oro Valley, AZ	461,826	461,172	-0.1	445,862	441,543	-1.0
Oviedo, FL	1,070,483	1,105,205	3.2	1,036,944	1,057,903	2.0
Palm Bch Grdns, FL[2]	639,628	646,285	1.0	617,855	616,347	-0.2
Parker, CO	1,368,472	1,393,879	1.9	1,315,598	1,332,798	1.3
Peachtree City, GA	2,728,345	2,771,516	1.6	2,616,398	2,648,176	1.2
Pflugerville, TX	841,139	854,956	1.6	813,117	824,154	1.4
Pleasanton, CA[2]	1,280,696	1,294,351	1.1	1,229,498	1,229,939	0.0
Rapid City, SD	64,961	65,608	1.0	63,070	63,632	0.9
Redmond, WA[2]	1,422,350	1,458,732	2.6	1,366,226	1,404,277	2.8
Richland, WA	112,578	118,091	4.9	105,058	111,114	5.8
Richmond, KY	50,473	49,656	-1.6	48,225	47,361	-1.8
Rio Rancho, NM	409,444	407,506	-0.5	396,231	395,075	-0.3
Rockaway, NJ[2]	1,097,724	1,089,849	-0.7	1,055,293	1,045,749	-0.9
Rocklin, CA	1,050,405	1,066,472	1.5	1,002,259	1,003,441	0.1
Rogers, AR	227,442	228,321	0.4	219,999	219,291	-0.3
Round Rock, TX	841,139	854,956	1.6	813,117	824,154	1.4
Sammamish, WA[2]	1,422,350	1,458,732	2.6	1,366,226	1,404,277	2.8
San Ramon, CA[2]	1,280,696	1,294,351	1.1	1,229,498	1,229,939	0.0
Santa Fe, NM	79,300	78,727	-0.7	77,220	76,863	-0.5
Saratoga, CA	873,146	888,900	1.8	836,883	843,903	0.8
Savage, MN	1,848,336	1,850,202	0.1	1,776,526	1,767,152	-0.5
Schererville, IN[2]	333,266	328,031	-1.6	317,521	313,012	-1.4
Shawnee, KS	1,032,329	1,040,408	0.8	985,807	987,141	0.1
Shrewsbury, MA[3]	292,884	289,701	-1.1	279,509	276,906	-0.9
S Brunswick, NJ[2]	1,199,770	1,190,736	-0.8	1,157,810	1,146,507	-1.0
S. Jordan, UT	596,424	614,462	3.0	583,449	597,668	2.4
S. Kingstown, RI[3]	717,880	712,660	-0.7	682,575	674,551	-1.2
Southaven, MS	622,864	629,858	1.1	591,733	595,007	0.6
Southlake, TX[2]	1,026,983	1,032,143	0.5	985,677	990,075	0.4
Spanish Fork, UT	225,624	232,573	3.1	221,015	226,628	2.5
Sparks, NV	225,076	231,510	2.9	216,355	219,238	1.3
Stow, OH	389,238	390,380	0.3	369,201	368,396	-0.2
Sugar Land, TX	2,713,998	2,767,131	2.0	2,603,369	2,651,639	1.9
Sun Prairie, WI	339,368	336,874	-0.7	328,368	325,551	-0.9
Tualatin, OR	1,145,573	1,161,260	1.4	1,094,566	1,105,347	1.0
Waimalu, HI	454,662	451,111	-0.8	446,535	439,883	-1.5
Wellington, FL[2]	639,628	646,285	1.0	617,855	616,347	-0.2
W Des Moines, IA	308,008	309,771	0.6	297,323	297,729	0.1
West Linn, OR	1,145,573	1,161,260	1.4	1,094,566	1,105,347	1.0
West Windsor, NJ	196,855	196,495	-0.2	189,807	189,343	-0.2
Weston, FL[2]	990,435	1,007,268	1.7	961,413	967,505	0.6
Woodbury, MN	1,848,336	1,850,202	0.1	1,776,526	1,767,152	-0.5
Woodridge, IL[2]	4,091,326	4,131,401	1.0	3,926,789	3,927,892	0.0
Yorba Linda, CA[2]	1,648,462	1,634,033	-0.9	1,596,558	1,563,199	-2.1
U.S.	152,571,000	153,705,000	0.7	146,081,000	146,334,000	0.2

Note: Data is not seasonally adjusted and covers workers 16 years of age and older; (1) Figures cover the Metropolitan Statistical Area (MSA) except where noted. See Appendix B for areas included; (2) Metropolitan Division; (3) New England City and Town Area; (4) New England City and Town Area Division

Source: Bureau of Labor Statistics, http://stats.bls.gov

Unemployment Rate: City

City	2007											
	Jan.	Feb.	Mar.	Apr.	May	Jun.	Jul.	Aug.	Sep.	Oct.	Nov.	Dec.
Allen, TX	3.9	3.9	3.6	3.5	3.6	3.9	3.9	3.7	3.7	3.6	3.7	3.8
Ankeny, IA	2.4	2.3	2.2	2.0	2.1	2.4	2.1	2.3	2.3	2.1	2.1	2.2
Apex, NC	2.8	2.8	2.5	2.4	2.7	2.9	2.8	2.4	2.5	2.5	2.5	2.4
Bangor, ME	5.1	5.2	4.7	4.6	4.2	4.8	5.0	4.4	4.5	4.8	4.8	4.7
Beavercreek, OH	4.8	4.3	4.2	4.3	4.1	4.9	4.7	4.5	4.7	4.4	4.3	4.6
Bellevue, NE	4.0	3.7	3.1	2.7	2.9	3.3	3.7	3.3	3.1	3.0	3.0	2.7
Bend, OR	4.9	5.2	4.7	4.1	3.8	4.0	4.2	4.3	4.2	4.6	5.1	5.6
Bernards, NJ	2.4	2.3	2.3	2.1	2.2	2.3	2.5	2.1	2.2	2.1	2.2	2.2
Bethlehem, NY	3.3	3.2	3.0	2.7	2.9	3.0	3.1	2.7	3.0	2.8	3.0	3.1
Bozeman, MT	2.5	2.3	2.3	2.0	1.9	2.3	1.8	1.8	1.8	1.8	2.1	2.2
Brentwood, TN	2.9	2.8	2.5	2.5	2.9	3.2	2.9	3.5	3.6	3.5	3.5	3.4
Brookfield, WI	3.4	3.6	3.7	3.7	3.7	4.0	3.7	3.6	3.6	3.2	3.3	3.0
Broomfield, CO	4.2	3.9	3.9	3.4	3.3	3.9	3.9	3.8	3.9	3.7	3.9	4.1
Burlington, VT	3.3	3.0	2.9	3.0	2.7	3.5	3.2	2.9	3.2	3.1	2.8	2.6
Carmel, IN	2.5	2.4	2.5	2.4	2.3	2.5	2.2	2.3	2.3	2.3	2.5	2.2
Cary, NC	2.8	2.8	2.5	2.5	2.7	2.9	2.8	2.5	2.6	2.5	2.6	2.5
Casper, WY	3.5	3.0	2.9	2.6	2.6	2.5	2.5	2.2	2.1	2.1	2.5	3.0
Cheshire, CT	4.0	3.8	3.3	3.3	3.6	3.9	4.4	3.9	3.7	3.5	3.7	3.5
Chino Hills, CA	2.6	2.5	2.5	2.5	2.5	2.8	3.0	3.0	2.9	2.9	3.0	3.0
Collierville, TN	4.7	3.8	3.4	3.1	3.0	3.4	3.3	3.6	3.7	3.9	4.1	4.0
Conway, AR	4.0	4.2	3.7	3.5	3.7	3.8	4.4	3.7	3.8	3.6	3.6	4.0
Coronado, CA	2.8	2.7	2.6	2.6	2.6	2.9	3.1	3.0	3.0	3.0	3.1	3.1
Cranberry, PA	3.0	2.7	2.6	2.2	2.6	2.8	2.7	2.8	2.7	2.7	3.2	2.7
Dover, DE	3.9	3.5	3.4	3.7	3.1	3.8	3.7	3.7	3.5	3.6	3.4	3.7
Draper, UT	0.9	0.9	0.8	0.8	0.8	1.0	0.9	1.0	0.9	0.9	0.9	0.9
Dublin, OH	3.2	3.2	3.1	3.3	3.3	3.9	3.6	3.8	3.9	3.7	3.6	3.5
Edmond, OK	2.6	2.7	2.5	2.3	2.5	2.6	2.4	2.4	2.3	2.3	2.3	2.4
Evesham, NJ	3.2	3.0	2.8	2.7	2.9	3.2	3.3	2.7	2.9	2.7	2.8	2.9
Fargo, ND	3.1	3.0	3.1	2.8	2.4	2.8	2.4	2.4	2.3	1.9	2.1	2.5
Farmington, CT	3.8	3.7	3.3	3.2	3.5	3.9	3.8	3.5	3.8	3.6	3.6	3.4
Fishers, IN	2.5	2.4	2.3	2.3	2.3	2.5	2.3	2.6	2.4	2.4	2.4	2.4
Flower Mound, TX	3.7	3.6	3.3	3.1	3.1	3.7	3.7	3.4	3.4	3.3	3.5	3.5
Franklin, MA	4.6	4.4	4.0	3.7	3.9	4.0	4.1	3.6	3.6	3.2	3.2	3.3
Frederick, MD	3.6	3.5	3.1	2.8	3.0	3.3	3.4	3.1	3.0	2.9	2.8	2.9
Frisco, TX	4.0	3.8	3.6	3.3	3.4	3.7	3.7	3.5	3.7	3.7	3.9	4.0
Goodyear, AZ	2.5	2.2	2.2	2.1	1.9	2.2	2.3	2.2	2.3	2.4	2.5	2.7
Grand Blanc, MI	4.5	4.6	4.4	3.9	3.9	4.1	5.0	4.0	4.1	3.8	3.9	4.2
Greenburgh, NY	3.5	3.3	3.0	2.8	3.0	3.2	3.5	3.2	3.3	3.2	3.3	3.3
Greenwich, CT	3.0	2.9	2.6	2.6	3.0	3.3	3.1	2.9	3.2	3.2	3.3	2.9
Hampden, PA	2.7	2.4	2.5	2.1	2.4	2.8	2.8	2.6	2.4	2.5	2.5	2.5
Hilliard, OH	3.4	3.4	3.4	3.4	3.3	3.9	3.6	3.8	3.7	3.7	3.6	3.6
Hoover, AL	2.2	2.3	2.0	1.7	1.8	2.3	2.2	2.3	2.0	1.8	2.0	2.3
Huntersville, NC	3.1	3.0	2.7	2.7	2.9	3.3	3.4	3.2	3.1	3.1	3.1	3.1
Juneau, AK	5.3	5.2	4.7	4.4	3.8	4.4	3.9	3.9	4.2	4.1	4.4	4.7
Keller, TX	3.6	3.5	3.2	3.1	3.1	3.8	3.8	3.4	3.6	3.3	3.4	3.3
Kenner, LA	3.3	2.7	2.8	2.7	3.0	3.6	3.2	3.2	3.1	2.6	2.7	2.9
Kennesaw, GA	3.3	3.2	3.0	3.0	3.2	3.2	3.1	3.1	3.2	3.1	2.9	3.3
League City, TX	3.9	3.8	3.4	3.2	3.3	3.9	4.0	3.7	3.7	3.4	3.5	3.5
Leawood, KS	2.9	2.9	2.7	2.4	2.7	3.0	2.9	2.9	2.9	2.5	2.7	2.6
Lee's Summit, MO	2.8	2.9	2.8	2.6	2.6	3.0	2.9	3.0	3.0	3.0	2.8	3.1
Leesburg, VA	2.0	1.9	1.8	1.8	1.8	2.1	2.0	2.1	2.1	2.0	2.0	2.1
Lehi, UT	1.8	1.7	1.6	1.5	1.5	1.9	1.9	1.9	1.6	1.7	1.6	1.7
Lwr Providence, PA	3.5	3.4	3.2	2.9	3.2	3.3	3.1	3.1	2.9	2.9	3.0	3.0
Madison, AL	2.2	2.4	1.9	1.6	1.7	2.3	2.3	2.2	2.0	1.8	1.9	2.2
Manhattan Bch, CA	1.7	1.6	1.6	1.5	1.5	1.7	1.9	1.8	1.8	1.7	1.7	1.8
Maple Grove, MN	3.3	3.1	3.2	3.0	3.1	3.5	3.4	3.4	3.9	3.3	3.2	3.5
Marion, IA	3.5	3.4	3.1	2.9	2.9	3.1	2.9	3.1	3.2	2.8	2.7	3.1
Marlboro, NJ	3.0	2.7	2.5	2.4	2.6	2.8	3.3	2.8	2.7	2.4	2.5	2.4
Matthews, NC	3.3	3.4	3.1	3.0	3.2	3.4	3.6	3.2	3.2	3.3	3.3	3.1

City	2007											
	Jan.	Feb.	Mar.	Apr.	May	Jun.	Jul.	Aug.	Sep.	Oct.	Nov.	Dec.
Meridian, ID	2.2	2.4	2.5	2.3	1.8	2.0	2.2	2.4	2.1	2.2	2.7	2.6
Merrimack, NH	3.4	3.5	3.2	3.0	3.2	3.3	3.1	3.0	2.7	2.5	2.6	2.6
Morgantown, WV	3.5	4.1	4.6	3.6	4.0	4.1	3.9	4.5	4.1	3.9	3.7	3.2
Mt Pleasant, SC	3.1	3.2	2.8	2.6	2.5	3.2	3.2	3.4	3.4	3.5	3.2	3.4
Northampton, PA	3.3	3.1	3.0	2.6	3.0	3.3	3.6	3.5	3.0	3.2	3.3	3.1
Northville, MI	1.8	1.6	1.6	1.5	1.6	1.8	2.0	1.8	1.8	1.8	1.7	1.8
Novi, MI	4.1	3.7	3.9	3.6	3.7	4.2	4.3	4.0	4.1	3.8	3.8	4.1
O'Fallon, MO	4.4	4.3	3.9	3.4	3.5	4.3	4.2	3.9	4.1	4.2	3.9	4.1
Oro Valley, AZ	2.7	2.4	2.3	2.2	2.0	2.4	2.6	2.5	2.6	2.7	2.7	2.9
Oviedo, FL	2.7	2.6	2.6	2.7	2.6	3.1	2.9	2.8	2.9	2.6	2.8	3.0
Palm Bch Grdns, FL	2.5	2.4	2.3	2.3	2.5	2.8	3.0	3.1	3.0	2.9	3.0	3.1
Parker, CO	2.5	2.3	2.2	2.0	2.0	2.3	2.3	2.3	2.4	2.3	2.5	2.7
Peachtree City, GA	3.5	3.1	2.8	2.9	3.1	3.5	3.5	3.4	3.3	3.3	2.7	3.1
Pflugerville, TX	3.3	3.1	3.2	2.8	2.8	3.6	3.6	3.2	3.3	3.2	3.1	3.1
Pleasanton, CA	2.3	2.3	2.2	2.2	2.1	2.4	2.6	2.5	2.4	2.4	2.4	2.4
Rapid City, SD	4.0	3.7	3.5	2.9	3.0	2.9	2.8	2.7	2.9	2.8	3.0	3.3
Redmond, WA	3.3	3.4	3.2	2.7	3.0	3.1	2.8	2.8	3.1	3.0	2.9	2.8
Richland, WA	4.8	4.7	4.1	4.0	3.9	4.0	4.6	4.2	3.8	3.7	3.9	4.1
Richmond, KY	4.7	5.1	5.0	4.7	4.7	5.2	4.9	4.4	4.4	3.7	3.8	4.0
Rio Rancho, NM	3.6	3.5	3.1	3.2	3.1	3.9	4.0	3.2	3.9	3.5	3.6	3.4
Rockaway, NJ	2.6	2.4	2.4	2.2	2.2	2.2	2.7	2.3	2.2	2.0	2.1	2.2
Rocklin, CA	3.4	3.4	3.3	3.2	3.1	3.4	3.6	3.5	3.5	3.6	3.6	3.8
Rogers, AR	3.6	3.9	3.3	3.2	3.5	3.8	4.1	3.8	3.6	3.4	3.4	3.7
Round Rock, TX	3.7	3.7	3.3	3.0	3.1	3.6	3.4	3.2	3.4	3.2	3.3	3.4
Sammamish, WA	3.1	3.3	3.2	2.6	2.9	3.2	3.0	2.7	3.0	3.0	3.0	2.8
San Ramon, CA	1.9	1.8	1.8	1.8	1.7	1.9	2.1	2.0	2.0	1.9	2.0	2.0
Santa Fe, NM	2.9	2.8	2.5	2.6	2.7	2.9	3.0	2.5	2.5	2.3	2.3	2.1
Saratoga, CA	2.3	2.3	2.2	2.2	2.1	2.4	2.5	2.5	2.4	2.4	2.4	2.4
Savage, MN	3.9	3.7	3.7	3.3	3.1	3.4	3.5	3.4	4.0	3.3	3.3	3.9
Schererville, IN	4.2	4.2	4.1	3.5	3.3	3.5	3.3	3.4	2.9	3.0	3.4	3.3
Shawnee, KS	3.4	3.4	3.2	2.8	3.2	3.6	3.5	3.4	3.4	3.0	3.2	3.1
Shrewsbury, MA	4.3	4.0	3.6	3.6	3.9	4.1	4.1	3.8	3.8	3.3	3.2	3.4
S Brunswick, NJ	3.0	2.8	2.6	2.5	2.7	2.9	3.4	2.9	2.9	2.7	2.7	2.6
S. Jordan, UT	1.7	1.6	1.5	1.5	1.4	1.7	1.7	1.8	1.6	1.6	1.6	1.7
S. Kingstown, RI	5.5	5.1	4.5	4.2	3.9	4.0	4.7	4.2	3.5	3.4	4.0	4.2
Southaven, MS	3.7	3.7	3.0	3.2	3.7	3.5	3.6	3.7	3.9	3.8	4.1	4.0
Southlake, TX	4.0	3.9	3.5	3.3	3.4	4.1	4.0	3.6	3.6	3.5	3.6	3.5
Spanish Fork, UT	2.3	2.2	2.1	2.0	2.0	2.5	2.5	2.5	2.1	2.2	2.1	2.3
Sparks, NV	4.7	4.5	4.3	4.2	3.9	4.1	4.3	4.1	4.2	4.1	4.4	5.0
Stow, OH	4.7	4.5	4.3	4.3	4.2	4.8	4.6	4.4	4.5	4.4	4.2	4.7
Sugar Land, TX	3.8	3.8	3.5	3.2	3.2	3.9	3.7	3.4	3.4	3.1	3.2	3.2
Sun Prairie, WI	4.7	5.1	4.9	4.4	4.1	4.3	4.1	4.1	3.9	3.8	3.8	4.0
Tualatin, OR	3.8	3.9	3.8	3.6	3.2	3.8	3.9	3.8	3.7	3.8	3.7	3.6
Waimalu, HI	n/a	n/a	n/a	n/a	n/a	n/a	n/a	n/a	n/a	n/a	n/a	n/a
Wellington, FL	2.8	2.7	2.8	2.8	2.8	3.4	3.5	3.4	3.3	3.2	3.4	3.3
W Des Moines, IA	2.4	2.3	2.2	2.1	2.1	2.4	2.0	2.2	2.3	2.1	2.1	2.2
West Linn, OR	3.9	4.2	4.0	3.4	3.2	3.7	3.9	3.7	3.5	3.7	3.6	3.6
West Windsor, NJ	1.9	1.7	1.7	1.7	1.9	2.1	2.3	2.0	2.2	1.8	1.8	1.7
Weston, FL	2.4	2.4	2.4	2.5	2.5	3.0	3.2	3.0	2.9	2.8	2.9	2.8
Woodbury, MN	3.3	3.0	3.0	3.0	3.0	3.5	3.3	3.4	3.8	3.2	3.1	3.2
Woodridge, IL	3.8	3.8	3.5	4.0	4.0	4.6	4.4	4.3	4.2	3.8	3.7	3.7
Yorba Linda, CA	2.4	2.3	2.3	2.3	2.3	2.6	2.8	2.8	2.8	2.7	2.8	2.8
U.S.	5.0	4.9	4.5	4.3	4.3	4.7	4.9	4.6	4.5	4.4	4.5	4.8

Note: Data is not seasonally adjusted and covers workers 16 years of age and older; All figures are percentages
Source: Bureau of Labor Statistics, http://stats.bls.gov

Unemployment Rate: Metro Area

Metro Area[1]	2007											
	Jan.	Feb.	Mar.	Apr.	May	Jun.	Jul.	Aug.	Sep.	Oct.	Nov.	Dec.
Allen, TX[2]	4.7	4.5	4.1	4.0	4.0	4.6	4.6	4.3	4.4	4.1	4.2	4.3
Ankeny, IA	4.2	4.0	3.7	3.3	3.2	3.4	3.1	3.3	3.4	3.2	3.3	3.9
Apex, NC	3.7	3.7	3.4	3.3	3.5	3.8	3.8	3.5	3.4	3.5	3.5	3.5
Bangor, ME[3]	5.5	5.6	5.3	4.9	4.6	4.7	4.9	4.3	4.4	4.4	4.5	4.6
Beavercreek, OH	7.0	6.0	5.6	5.7	5.5	6.1	6.1	5.8	5.8	5.6	5.6	6.0
Bellevue, NE	4.1	3.7	3.3	3.1	3.3	3.6	3.7	3.3	3.1	3.1	3.3	3.1
Bend, OR	5.6	5.7	5.2	4.6	4.3	4.5	4.5	4.6	4.5	4.9	5.4	6.1
Bernards, NJ[2]	4.4	4.2	4.0	3.6	3.6	3.8	4.3	3.7	3.7	3.4	3.6	3.7
Bethlehem, NY	4.5	4.4	4.0	3.7	3.6	3.9	4.1	3.7	3.8	3.6	3.8	4.1
Bozeman, MT	2.7	2.5	2.5	2.3	2.1	2.3	1.8	1.8	1.7	2.0	2.6	2.6
Brentwood, TN	4.1	4.0	3.8	3.5	3.5	3.9	3.8	4.0	4.0	4.0	4.3	4.2
Brookfield, WI	5.1	5.4	5.2	5.3	5.0	5.5	5.4	5.2	4.9	4.6	4.7	4.7
Broomfield, CO	4.4	4.1	3.9	3.5	3.4	3.9	3.9	3.8	3.9	3.7	4.0	4.4
Burlington, VT[3]	4.0	3.8	3.6	3.6	3.0	3.5	3.3	3.0	3.3	3.1	3.0	3.1
Carmel, IN	4.5	4.5	4.2	3.9	3.7	4.0	3.8	4.0	3.7	3.7	3.7	3.9
Cary, NC	3.7	3.7	3.4	3.3	3.5	3.8	3.8	3.5	3.4	3.5	3.5	3.5
Casper, WY	3.7	3.1	3.0	2.8	2.8	2.6	2.7	2.3	2.2	2.2	2.6	3.2
Cheshire, CT[3]	5.2	4.9	4.5	4.5	4.6	4.9	5.2	4.9	4.8	4.5	4.8	4.7
Chino Hills, CA	5.4	5.4	5.2	5.2	5.2	5.9	6.5	6.4	6.3	6.3	6.3	6.5
Collierville, TN	5.8	5.3	5.1	4.6	4.6	5.3	5.2	5.1	5.2	5.2	5.3	5.5
Conway, AR	4.9	5.1	4.5	4.3	4.5	4.8	5.2	4.7	4.5	4.2	4.2	4.7
Coronado, CA	4.4	4.3	4.2	4.2	4.1	4.6	4.9	4.8	4.8	4.8	4.9	5.0
Cranberry, PA	5.1	4.9	4.4	3.8	4.1	4.4	4.6	4.4	3.9	3.9	4.0	4.4
Dover, DE	3.4	3.5	3.2	3.5	2.8	3.4	3.4	3.3	3.1	3.2	2.9	3.4
Draper, UT	2.7	2.6	2.4	2.3	2.3	2.7	2.7	2.9	2.6	2.6	2.6	2.7
Dublin, OH	4.9	4.8	4.6	4.7	4.5	5.1	4.8	4.8	4.8	4.6	4.5	4.8
Edmond, OK	4.7	4.7	4.4	4.0	4.4	4.6	4.3	4.2	4.0	4.1	4.0	4.2
Evesham, NJ[2]	4.8	4.7	4.3	4.1	4.1	4.3	4.9	4.1	4.2	3.9	3.9	4.1
Fargo, ND	3.5	3.4	3.5	3.1	2.6	3.2	2.6	2.5	2.4	2.1	2.2	2.8
Farmington, CT[3]	5.2	5.1	4.6	4.4	4.5	4.8	5.1	4.7	4.6	4.4	4.7	4.6
Fishers, IN	4.5	4.5	4.2	3.9	3.7	4.0	3.8	4.0	3.7	3.7	3.7	3.9
Flower Mound, TX[2]	4.7	4.5	4.1	4.0	4.0	4.6	4.6	4.3	4.4	4.1	4.2	4.3
Franklin, MA[4]	4.5	4.3	4.0	3.7	4.0	4.3	4.2	3.7	4.0	3.5	3.4	3.4
Frederick, MD[2]	3.1	2.9	2.6	2.5	2.6	3.0	3.0	2.7	2.7	2.7	2.6	2.6
Frisco, TX[2]	4.7	4.5	4.1	4.0	4.0	4.6	4.6	4.3	4.4	4.1	4.2	4.3
Goodyear, AZ	3.6	3.2	3.1	2.9	2.7	3.1	3.3	3.2	3.3	3.4	3.5	3.8
Grand Blanc, MI	8.9	9.1	8.6	7.8	7.7	8.1	9.7	7.9	8.0	7.5	7.7	8.2
Greenburgh, NY[2]	5.0	4.8	4.4	4.3	4.4	4.7	5.4	4.9	4.7	4.8	4.6	4.8
Greenwich, CT[3]	4.4	4.2	3.8	3.7	3.9	4.3	4.4	4.2	4.1	4.0	4.2	4.0
Hampden, PA	4.0	3.9	3.7	3.2	3.4	3.7	3.7	3.6	3.3	3.4	3.4	3.6
Hilliard, OH	4.9	4.8	4.6	4.7	4.5	5.1	4.8	4.8	4.8	4.6	4.5	4.8
Hoover, AL	3.3	3.4	2.9	2.5	2.6	3.5	3.5	3.6	3.2	3.0	3.1	3.4
Huntersville, NC	4.8	4.7	4.3	4.4	4.6	4.9	5.1	4.8	4.6	4.6	4.8	4.8
Juneau, AK	5.3	5.2	4.7	4.4	3.8	4.4	3.9	3.9	4.2	4.1	4.4	4.7
Keller, TX[2]	4.9	4.5	4.1	3.9	4.0	4.6	4.6	4.2	4.2	3.9	4.0	4.1
Kenner, LA	4.0	3.2	3.2	3.0	3.5	4.2	3.7	3.6	3.5	3.0	3.1	3.3
Kennesaw, GA	4.4	4.2	3.9	3.9	4.0	4.5	4.6	4.4	4.4	4.4	4.1	4.5
League City, TX	4.7	4.5	4.1	3.9	3.9	4.6	4.6	4.3	4.3	4.0	4.1	4.2
Leawood, KS	5.0	5.3	4.8	4.4	4.6	5.2	5.2	5.0	5.1	5.0	4.8	5.1
Lee's Summit, MO	5.0	5.3	4.8	4.4	4.6	5.2	5.2	5.0	5.1	5.0	4.8	5.1
Leesburg, VA[2]	3.3	3.2	3.0	2.8	2.9	3.3	3.3	3.2	3.1	3.0	3.1	3.2
Lehi, UT	2.6	2.5	2.4	2.2	2.2	2.8	2.8	2.8	2.4	2.5	2.4	2.6
Lwr Providence, PA[2]	4.7	4.5	4.3	3.9	4.3	4.5	4.6	4.5	4.3	4.3	4.2	4.2
Madison, AL	3.0	3.1	2.5	2.1	2.3	3.0	3.0	3.1	2.7	2.5	2.6	2.9
Manhattan Bch, CA[2]	5.0	4.8	4.7	4.6	4.5	4.9	5.6	5.3	5.2	5.0	5.1	5.2
Maple Grove, MN	4.7	4.4	4.4	4.2	4.0	4.4	4.2	4.1	4.5	3.9	3.9	4.5
Marion, IA	4.7	4.5	4.0	3.6	3.4	3.6	3.4	3.7	3.7	3.4	3.5	4.2
Marlboro, NJ[2]	4.4	4.2	4.0	3.6	3.6	3.8	4.3	3.7	3.7	3.4	3.6	3.7
Matthews, NC	4.8	4.7	4.3	4.4	4.6	4.9	5.1	4.8	4.6	4.6	4.8	4.8

Metro Area[1]	2007											
	Jan.	Feb.	Mar.	Apr.	May	Jun.	Jul.	Aug.	Sep.	Oct.	Nov.	Dec.
Meridian, ID	3.4	3.1	2.9	2.6	2.0	2.3	2.4	2.5	2.2	2.3	2.8	3.0
Merrimack, NH[4]	4.3	4.2	3.9	3.6	3.5	3.6	3.6	3.6	3.2	3.0	3.1	3.3
Morgantown, WV	3.3	4.0	3.8	3.2	3.2	3.5	3.4	3.6	3.1	3.1	2.9	2.9
Mt Pleasant, SC	4.8	4.8	4.2	3.9	3.8	4.6	4.7	4.8	4.8	4.8	4.6	5.0
Northampton, PA[2]	4.7	4.5	4.3	3.9	4.3	4.5	4.6	4.5	4.3	4.3	4.2	4.2
Northville, MI[2]	9.3	7.9	8.2	7.8	8.1	9.2	10.1	9.3	9.0	9.3	8.8	9.1
Novi, MI[2]	7.4	6.6	6.9	6.4	6.5	7.2	7.5	6.8	7.0	6.8	6.7	7.3
O'Fallon, MO	5.5	5.6	5.0	4.6	4.7	5.7	5.7	5.6	5.4	5.3	5.2	5.5
Oro Valley, AZ	4.0	3.5	3.4	3.3	3.0	3.5	3.8	3.7	3.8	3.9	4.0	4.3
Oviedo, FL	3.6	3.4	3.3	3.4	3.4	3.9	4.1	4.1	4.1	4.0	4.1	4.3
Palm Bch Grdns, FL[2]	3.9	3.6	3.5	3.6	3.7	4.5	4.9	4.9	5.0	4.7	4.6	4.6
Parker, CO	4.4	4.1	3.9	3.5	3.4	3.9	3.9	3.8	3.9	3.7	4.0	4.4
Peachtree City, GA	4.4	4.2	3.9	3.9	4.0	4.5	4.6	4.4	4.4	4.4	4.1	4.5
Pflugerville, TX	3.9	3.8	3.5	3.2	3.3	3.9	4.0	3.7	3.7	3.5	3.5	3.6
Pleasanton, CA[2]	4.7	4.6	4.4	4.4	4.3	4.8	5.2	5.0	4.9	4.9	4.9	5.0
Rapid City, SD	3.6	3.4	3.2	2.7	2.8	2.6	2.6	2.5	2.7	2.6	2.7	3.0
Redmond, WA[2]	4.2	4.3	4.0	3.4	3.7	3.8	3.5	3.4	3.8	3.7	3.7	3.7
Richland, WA	7.4	6.6	5.4	5.1	4.5	4.6	5.3	4.6	4.3	4.1	5.4	5.9
Richmond, KY	5.5	6.1	5.3	4.9	5.2	5.6	5.3	4.8	4.7	4.2	4.3	4.6
Rio Rancho, NM	3.8	3.6	3.3	3.3	3.3	3.8	4.0	3.5	3.4	3.2	3.3	3.1
Rockaway, NJ[2]	4.8	4.6	4.4	4.1	4.1	4.3	4.8	4.1	4.1	3.9	3.9	4.0
Rocklin, CA	5.5	5.4	5.1	5.0	4.8	5.3	5.6	5.4	5.4	5.5	5.6	5.9
Rogers, AR	3.8	4.2	3.6	3.5	3.7	4.1	4.4	4.0	3.9	3.6	3.6	4.0
Round Rock, TX	3.9	3.8	3.5	3.2	3.3	3.9	4.0	3.7	3.7	3.5	3.5	3.6
Sammamish, WA[2]	4.2	4.3	4.0	3.4	3.7	3.8	3.5	3.4	3.8	3.7	3.7	3.7
San Ramon, CA[2]	4.7	4.6	4.4	4.4	4.3	4.8	5.2	5.0	4.9	4.9	4.9	5.0
Santa Fe, NM	3.2	3.1	2.8	2.8	2.8	3.1	3.3	2.7	2.7	2.5	2.6	2.4
Saratoga, CA	4.8	4.7	4.5	4.5	4.4	4.8	5.1	5.0	4.9	4.9	4.9	5.1
Savage, MN	4.7	4.4	4.4	4.2	4.0	4.4	4.2	4.1	4.5	3.9	3.9	4.5
Schererville, IN[2]	6.0	5.8	5.5	4.7	4.4	4.6	4.5	4.7	4.3	4.2	4.6	4.6
Shawnee, KS	5.0	5.3	4.8	4.4	4.6	5.2	5.2	5.0	5.1	5.0	4.8	5.1
Shrewsbury, MA[3]	5.7	5.4	5.0	4.6	4.7	5.0	5.2	4.7	4.8	4.2	4.2	4.4
S Brunswick, NJ[2]	4.4	4.2	4.0	3.6	3.6	3.8	4.3	3.7	3.7	3.4	3.6	3.7
S. Jordan, UT	2.7	2.6	2.4	2.3	2.3	2.7	2.7	2.9	2.6	2.6	2.6	2.7
S. Kingstown, RI[3]	6.1	5.8	5.5	5.2	4.8	4.9	5.7	5.3	4.8	4.6	4.7	5.3
Southaven, MS	5.8	5.3	5.1	4.6	4.6	5.3	5.2	5.1	5.2	5.2	5.3	5.5
Southlake, TX[2]	4.9	4.5	4.1	3.9	4.0	4.6	4.6	4.2	4.2	3.9	4.0	4.1
Spanish Fork, UT	2.6	2.5	2.4	2.2	2.2	2.8	2.8	2.8	2.4	2.5	2.4	2.6
Sparks, NV	5.0	4.8	4.5	4.5	4.2	4.4	4.5	4.3	4.5	4.4	4.7	5.3
Stow, OH	6.0	5.8	5.5	5.5	5.1	5.6	5.3	5.2	5.2	5.0	5.0	5.6
Sugar Land, TX	4.7	4.5	4.1	3.9	3.9	4.6	4.6	4.3	4.3	4.0	4.1	4.2
Sun Prairie, WI	3.9	4.2	4.1	3.7	3.6	4.0	3.6	3.5	3.4	3.2	3.3	3.4
Tualatin, OR	5.3	5.4	5.0	4.7	4.5	4.9	5.0	5.0	4.6	4.6	4.7	4.8
Waimalu, HI	2.2	2.1	2.3	2.3	2.3	3.0	2.8	2.5	2.7	2.4	2.7	2.5
Wellington, FL[2]	3.9	3.6	3.5	3.6	3.7	4.5	4.9	4.9	5.0	4.7	4.6	4.6
W Des Moines, IA	4.2	4.0	3.7	3.3	3.2	3.4	3.1	3.3	3.4	3.2	3.3	3.9
West Linn, OR	5.3	5.4	5.0	4.7	4.5	4.9	5.0	5.0	4.6	4.6	4.7	4.8
West Windsor, NJ	4.4	4.1	3.9	3.6	3.6	3.9	4.4	3.7	3.7	3.4	3.5	3.6
Weston, FL[2]	3.4	3.2	3.1	3.1	3.2	3.7	3.9	3.9	3.9	3.8	3.9	3.9
Woodbury, MN	4.7	4.4	4.4	4.2	4.0	4.4	4.2	4.1	4.5	3.9	3.9	4.5
Woodridge, IL[2]	4.9	4.8	4.4	4.7	4.6	5.4	5.4	5.0	4.8	4.6	4.6	4.9
Yorba Linda, CA[2]	3.7	3.6	3.5	3.5	3.5	4.0	4.3	4.2	4.2	4.2	4.2	4.3
U.S.	5.0	4.9	4.5	4.3	4.3	4.7	4.9	4.6	4.5	4.4	4.5	4.8

Note: Data is not seasonally adjusted and covers workers 16 years of age and older; All figures are percentages; (1) Figures cover the Metropolitan Statistical Area (MSA) except where noted. See Appendix B for areas included; (2) Metropolitan Division; (3) New England City and Town Area; (4) New England City and Town Area Division
Source: Bureau of Labor Statistics, http://stats.bls.gov

Average Hourly Wages: Occupations A - C

MSA[1]	Accountants/ Auditors	Automotive Mechanics	Book-keepers	Carpenters	Cashiers	Clerks, Gen. Office	Clerks, Recep./Info.
Allen, TX	31.56	17.72	16.06	16.08	8.45	11.71	12.41
Ankeny, IA	26.79	18.60	15.64	18.98	8.82	12.96	11.59
Apex, NC	28.50	17.75	15.64	15.46	8.43	12.14	12.06
Bangor, ME	24.14	15.47	13.62	16.70	8.28	11.22	10.65
Beavercreek, OH	31.84	16.33	15.20	18.82	8.57	12.36	11.09
Bellevue, NE	29.32	17.96	14.94	16.38	8.46	12.25	11.77
Bend, OR	34.96	22.16	15.27	16.34	10.15	14.25	11.89
Bernards, NJ	36.27	18.30	17.66	24.94	9.35	13.14	12.50
Bethlehem, NY	29.53	19.14	15.93	19.56	8.88	12.87	12.27
Bozeman, MT	n/a	n/a	n/a	n/a	n/a	n/a	n/a
Brentwood, TN	27.01	16.48	15.40	15.07	8.35	13.38	12.23
Brookfield, WI	31.40	18.54	15.76	22.98	8.67	12.69	12.39
Broomfield, CO	32.43	18.37	17.08	18.93	10.58	14.13	13.05
Burlington, VT	29.76	17.08	16.16	19.20	9.33	12.69	12.42
Carmel, IN	29.75	19.13	16.39	19.61	8.44	12.31	11.71
Cary, NC	28.50	17.75	15.64	15.46	8.43	12.14	12.06
Casper, WY	28.60	15.11	15.03	15.09	8.47	11.15	10.54
Cheshire, CT	32.04	19.66	18.42	21.34	9.85	14.65	14.56
Chino Hills, CA	28.82	18.03	16.44	22.13	9.92	12.81	11.83
Collierville, TN	27.92	17.48	15.81	15.78	8.28	12.60	11.16
Conway, AR	24.80	16.97	14.69	15.35	8.10	10.43	10.30
Coronado, CA	30.67	20.30	17.38	22.28	10.53	13.39	12.30
Cranberry, PA	29.18	15.81	14.37	19.32	8.29	12.06	10.81
Dover, DE	27.33	16.69	13.89	21.01	8.55	12.46	10.96
Draper, UT	29.12	18.64	14.43	16.74	8.84	11.85	10.45
Dublin, OH	27.73	17.84	16.13	18.66	8.81	12.69	11.56
Edmond, OK	24.17	15.77	14.29	14.92	7.88	10.80	10.73
Evesham, NJ	31.23	19.04	17.35	23.99	9.30	13.09	12.12
Fargo, ND	23.50	17.82	14.33	15.85	8.06	11.48	11.17
Farmington, CT	30.36	19.27	18.74	22.22	9.79	14.94	13.63
Fishers, IN	29.75	19.13	16.39	19.61	8.44	12.31	11.71
Flower Mound, TX	31.56	17.72	16.06	16.08	8.45	11.71	12.41
Franklin, MA	32.24	20.89	18.85	25.87	9.66	14.82	12.89
Frederick, MD	36.38	23.39	19.34	22.13	10.11	15.24	13.24
Frisco, TX	31.56	17.72	16.06	16.08	8.45	11.71	12.41
Goodyear, AZ	26.47	18.93	16.16	16.77	9.90	13.10	12.13
Grand Blanc, MI	29.68	22.36	15.81	21.70	8.74	11.70	12.17
Greenburgh, NY	38.15	18.68	18.44	27.76	9.64	13.42	13.66
Greenwich, CT	37.43	21.24	19.84	23.74	9.89	14.84	14.56
Hampden, PA	29.42	17.03	15.55	19.13	8.35	13.47	11.45
Hilliard, OH	27.73	17.84	16.13	18.66	8.81	12.69	11.56
Hoover, AL	27.39	16.07	14.75	16.21	8.12	10.50	11.14
Huntersville, NC	29.49	19.44	15.42	16.09	8.59	12.19	11.98
Juneau, AK	n/a	n/a	n/a	n/a	n/a	n/a	n/a
Keller, TX	29.28	16.59	15.17	13.98	8.48	10.99	11.62
Kenner, LA	28.77	16.39	15.53	16.99	7.84	10.46	10.45
Kennesaw, GA	31.37	17.80	15.84	16.43	8.35	12.19	12.69
League City, TX	30.78	17.99	15.84	15.28	8.21	11.43	11.25
Leawood, KS	27.30	17.55	15.37	22.78	8.67	13.34	11.99
Lee's Summit, MO	27.30	17.55	15.37	22.78	8.67	13.34	11.99
Leesburg, VA	34.57	20.52	18.94	20.83	9.82	15.51	13.48
Lehi, UT	31.16	16.54	12.79	17.10	8.39	10.23	10.56
Lwr Providence, PA	34.90	18.52	16.93	22.94	8.79	13.93	12.36
Madison, AL	29.67	17.14	13.62	13.94	7.89	10.44	10.39
Manhattan Bch, CA	32.95	18.45	17.54	22.50	10.10	13.13	12.52
Maple Grove, MN	29.70	19.11	17.14	23.04	9.25	13.93	13.16
Marion, IA	26.88	16.01	14.16	16.84	8.48	12.68	11.30
Marlboro, NJ	36.27	18.30	17.66	24.94	9.35	13.14	12.50
Matthews, NC	29.49	19.44	15.42	16.09	8.59	12.19	11.98

MSA[1]	Accountants/ Auditors	Automotive Mechanics	Book-keepers	Carpenters	Cashiers	Clerks, Gen. Office	Clerks, Recep./Info.
Meridian, ID	24.63	16.02	14.23	14.87	9.08	12.15	11.48
Merrimack, NH	28.45	18.97	16.21	18.97	8.93	14.28	12.06
Morgantown, WV	24.51	13.46	14.32	15.18	7.22	11.50	9.24
Mt Pleasant, SC	29.42	15.95	14.53	16.55	7.59	11.06	11.12
Northampton, PA	34.90	18.52	16.93	22.94	8.79	13.93	12.36
Northville, MI	31.70	21.11	16.63	23.66	9.45	13.11	12.18
Novi, MI	29.47	23.73	17.04	23.15	9.50	12.35	12.59
O'Fallon, MO	29.51	18.40	15.74	25.19	8.96	13.49	11.15
Oro Valley, AZ	30.47	19.18	15.09	17.41	9.81	12.39	11.39
Oviedo, FL	27.43	17.52	14.65	16.72	8.48	11.38	11.13
Palm Bch Grdns, FL	31.27	18.32	16.28	17.66	8.77	11.79	12.04
Parker, CO	32.43	18.37	17.08	18.93	10.58	14.13	13.05
Peachtree City, GA	31.37	17.80	15.84	16.43	8.35	12.19	12.69
Pflugerville, TX	30.35	19.58	14.97	16.33	8.78	11.34	12.26
Pleasanton, CA	33.32	22.86	19.19	27.61	11.90	16.16	14.90
Rapid City, SD	24.46	16.11	12.03	14.28	7.98	9.68	9.96
Redmond, WA	31.35	21.38	17.84	24.42	12.05	14.59	13.02
Richland, WA	29.61	18.12	15.26	21.44	10.27	13.79	11.67
Richmond, KY	n/a	n/a	n/a	n/a	n/a	n/a	n/a
Rio Rancho, NM	28.23	16.96	14.47	15.73	8.29	10.83	10.91
Rockaway, NJ	37.05	18.93	18.48	25.61	9.46	13.55	12.56
Rocklin, CA	29.31	20.99	17.39	24.25	10.67	13.92	12.94
Rogers, AR	22.33	14.11	13.82	16.23	8.12	10.64	10.30
Round Rock, TX	30.35	19.58	14.97	16.33	8.78	11.34	12.26
Sammamish, WA	31.35	21.38	17.84	24.42	12.05	14.59	13.02
San Ramon, CA	33.32	22.86	19.19	27.61	11.90	16.16	14.90
Santa Fe, NM	24.56	19.43	16.15	18.56	9.93	12.03	12.49
Saratoga, CA	35.31	21.94	20.27	26.02	11.44	15.74	14.85
Savage, MN	29.70	19.11	17.14	23.04	9.25	13.93	13.16
Schererville, IN	24.74	15.57	15.62	21.78	8.40	11.36	10.65
Shawnee, KS	27.30	17.55	15.37	22.78	8.67	13.34	11.99
Shrewsbury, MA	30.28	17.58	17.32	20.37	9.50	13.85	12.52
S Brunswick, NJ	36.27	18.30	17.66	24.94	9.35	13.14	12.50
S. Jordan, UT	29.12	18.64	14.43	16.74	8.84	11.85	10.45
S. Kingstown, RI	30.86	17.76	16.96	21.25	9.24	12.54	12.34
Southaven, MS	27.92	17.48	15.81	15.78	8.28	12.60	11.16
Southlake, TX	29.28	16.59	15.17	13.98	8.48	10.99	11.62
Spanish Fork, UT	31.16	16.54	12.79	17.10	8.39	10.23	10.56
Sparks, NV	26.29	19.65	16.55	22.38	9.89	12.77	13.21
Stow, OH	28.21	17.08	15.07	20.99	8.38	11.72	10.79
Sugar Land, TX	30.78	17.99	15.84	15.28	8.21	11.43	11.25
Sun Prairie, WI	27.82	17.54	15.63	21.51	9.38	12.87	12.49
Tualatin, OR	29.64	17.89	16.85	19.99	10.54	13.95	12.61
Waimalu, HI	24.95	17.59	16.26	27.91	9.69	12.53	12.33
Wellington, FL	31.27	18.32	16.28	17.66	8.77	11.79	12.04
W Des Moines, IA	26.79	18.60	15.64	18.98	8.82	12.96	11.59
West Linn, OR	29.64	17.89	16.85	19.99	10.54	13.95	12.61
West Windsor, NJ	35.00	19.59	18.62	29.73	9.21	13.61	12.53
Weston, FL	30.90	16.41	15.53	16.04	8.66	11.59	11.86
Woodbury, MN	29.70	19.11	17.14	23.04	9.25	13.93	13.16
Woodridge, IL	33.07	20.14	17.24	29.18	9.09	13.35	12.73
Yorba Linda, CA	31.76	19.31	18.12	24.70	9.95	13.58	13.08

Notes: Wage data is for May 2007 and covers the Metropolitan Statistical Area - see Appendix A for areas included; n/a not available
Source: Bureau of Labor Statistics, May 2007 Metro Area Occupational Employment and Wage Estimates

Average Hourly Wages: Occupations C - E

MSA[1]	Clerks, Ship./Rec.	Computer Programmers	Computer Support Specialists	Computer Systems Analysts	Cooks, Restaurant	Dentists	Electrical Engineers
Allen, TX	12.87	38.32	22.07	39.12	10.19	n/a	44.17
Ankeny, IA	14.39	29.76	21.77	33.76	10.07	n/a	28.90
Apex, NC	13.35	34.06	22.45	36.64	10.48	n/a	39.57
Bangor, ME	12.62	n/a	18.22	29.59	10.86	n/a	34.08
Beavercreek, OH	13.78	31.08	20.08	34.39	9.42	n/a	36.90
Bellevue, NE	14.19	32.69	19.01	34.46	9.79	n/a	36.17
Bend, OR	14.13	30.08	17.51	32.67	11.39	n/a	33.07
Bernards, NJ	14.55	40.08	24.41	42.13	11.99	n/a	45.42
Bethlehem, NY	13.36	29.86	21.14	32.68	11.60	n/a	41.51
Bozeman, MT	n/a	n/a	n/a	n/a	n/a	n/a	n/a
Brentwood, TN	12.76	28.69	21.74	29.52	9.98	n/a	37.31
Brookfield, WI	14.32	31.44	21.28	32.67	10.50	n/a	43.48
Broomfield, CO	14.68	38.37	24.91	39.27	10.70	n/a	38.75
Burlington, VT	14.55	35.40	20.11	36.45	11.94	n/a	36.47
Carmel, IN	13.54	34.02	20.20	34.56	10.81	n/a	35.92
Cary, NC	13.35	34.06	22.45	36.64	10.48	n/a	39.57
Casper, WY	13.42	n/a	17.25	23.65	9.85	n/a	n/a
Cheshire, CT	14.11	42.99	24.04	34.02	13.12	n/a	36.59
Chino Hills, CA	13.32	26.85	22.40	32.85	11.14	n/a	38.49
Collierville, TN	13.19	33.09	22.63	30.71	9.83	n/a	34.55
Conway, AR	12.77	33.90	19.09	29.78	9.31	n/a	36.47
Coronado, CA	14.08	35.57	22.10	34.75	11.08	n/a	42.49
Cranberry, PA	13.36	30.79	19.22	31.81	10.70	n/a	37.60
Dover, DE	14.76	29.15	24.91	34.96	10.52	n/a	n/a
Draper, UT	12.84	38.00	20.31	33.25	10.53	n/a	39.78
Dublin, OH	14.07	32.85	18.75	35.78	10.26	n/a	33.98
Edmond, OK	12.91	31.00	16.71	30.84	8.93	n/a	30.21
Evesham, NJ	15.83	36.98	21.69	35.28	11.30	n/a	43.85
Fargo, ND	12.28	23.09	n/a	22.75	9.94	n/a	32.89
Farmington, CT	14.76	36.26	23.98	38.26	12.18	n/a	39.81
Fishers, IN	13.54	34.02	20.20	34.56	10.81	n/a	35.92
Flower Mound, TX	12.87	38.32	22.07	39.12	10.19	n/a	44.17
Franklin, MA	16.22	37.80	29.01	41.38	12.92	n/a	46.55
Frederick, MD	13.08	37.90	24.66	41.94	12.62	n/a	45.04
Frisco, TX	12.87	38.32	22.07	39.12	10.19	n/a	44.17
Goodyear, AZ	10.34	33.04	23.05	34.43	10.56	n/a	38.41
Grand Blanc, MI	16.53	31.57	19.95	n/a	10.94	n/a	25.61
Greenburgh, NY	14.18	37.83	26.98	42.64	13.59	n/a	43.02
Greenwich, CT	15.26	42.59	26.49	44.12	14.87	n/a	39.25
Hampden, PA	14.25	33.41	19.07	33.02	11.13	n/a	34.15
Hilliard, OH	14.07	32.85	18.75	35.78	10.26	n/a	33.98
Hoover, AL	13.30	33.14	20.62	31.91	8.95	n/a	37.83
Huntersville, NC	13.98	38.36	21.92	36.11	10.49	n/a	36.13
Juneau, AK	n/a	n/a	n/a	n/a	n/a	n/a	n/a
Keller, TX	13.23	37.02	19.60	34.67	9.77	n/a	37.06
Kenner, LA	12.77	27.00	19.63	30.92	9.82	n/a	42.56
Kennesaw, GA	13.08	35.22	21.37	37.70	10.70	n/a	37.14
League City, TX	13.07	38.89	22.23	36.57	9.19	n/a	44.72
Leawood, KS	13.88	33.59	20.83	32.40	10.23	n/a	38.61
Lee's Summit, MO	13.88	33.59	20.83	32.40	10.23	n/a	38.61
Leesburg, VA	14.76	39.31	25.22	41.55	12.09	n/a	43.07
Lehi, UT	11.56	30.38	17.10	33.42	10.71	n/a	n/a
Lwr Providence, PA	15.30	39.03	20.89	37.81	12.91	n/a	40.50
Madison, AL	12.42	33.29	18.76	34.13	9.62	n/a	39.50
Manhattan Bch, CA	13.95	35.84	21.70	37.61	10.99	n/a	41.57
Maple Grove, MN	15.43	32.34	22.55	36.00	10.99	n/a	40.00
Marion, IA	12.51	29.61	21.08	33.31	9.57	n/a	n/a
Marlboro, NJ	14.55	40.08	24.41	42.13	11.99	n/a	45.42

MSA[1]	Clerks, Ship./Rec.	Computer Programmers	Computer Support Specialists	Computer Systems Analysts	Cooks, Restaurant	Dentists	Electrical Engineers
Matthews, NC	13.98	38.36	21.92	36.11	10.49	n/a	36.13
Meridian, ID	12.38	28.38	19.11	31.25	9.90	n/a	36.12
Merrimack, NH	15.45	28.22	23.69	37.51	11.28	n/a	39.94
Morgantown, WV	14.72	24.62	21.87	25.29	8.85	n/a	34.75
Mt Pleasant, SC	14.71	25.14	20.61	30.05	10.35	n/a	37.01
Northampton, PA	15.30	39.03	20.89	37.81	12.91	n/a	40.50
Northville, MI	16.55	35.02	22.44	42.75	11.18	n/a	40.25
Novi, MI	15.34	33.46	21.63	35.79	11.42	n/a	36.34
O'Fallon, MO	13.89	31.38	20.34	34.29	10.50	n/a	34.97
Oro Valley, AZ	10.59	29.72	20.84	30.91	9.77	n/a	n/a
Oviedo, FL	11.88	32.85	17.98	33.90	11.17	n/a	34.71
Palm Bch Grdns, FL	13.57	35.31	19.13	36.03	12.00	n/a	32.35
Parker, CO	14.68	38.37	24.91	39.27	10.70	n/a	38.75
Peachtree City, GA	13.08	35.22	21.37	37.70	10.70	n/a	37.14
Pflugerville, TX	12.66	35.04	20.59	35.01	9.37	n/a	44.77
Pleasanton, CA	15.47	37.19	26.09	42.98	12.04	n/a	42.11
Rapid City, SD	12.07	22.53	15.20	28.02	9.57	n/a	31.71
Redmond, WA	16.08	41.77	24.97	38.87	11.86	n/a	38.33
Richland, WA	12.68	23.88	21.71	35.66	10.67	n/a	41.98
Richmond, KY	n/a	n/a	n/a	n/a	n/a	n/a	n/a
Rio Rancho, NM	12.29	37.38	21.82	34.19	9.72	n/a	41.09
Rockaway, NJ	15.52	43.47	23.16	43.80	11.82	n/a	n/a
Rocklin, CA	14.55	33.26	24.90	34.28	11.44	n/a	38.81
Rogers, AR	11.69	29.15	17.29	28.04	9.49	n/a	32.97
Round Rock, TX	12.66	35.04	20.59	35.01	9.37	n/a	44.77
Sammamish, WA	16.08	41.77	24.97	38.87	11.86	n/a	38.33
San Ramon, CA	15.47	37.19	26.09	42.98	12.04	n/a	42.11
Santa Fe, NM	13.09	n/a	20.49	29.20	10.80	n/a	38.70
Saratoga, CA	16.55	48.42	30.58	39.63	11.29	n/a	49.93
Savage, MN	15.43	32.34	22.55	36.00	10.99	n/a	40.00
Schererville, IN	13.80	25.96	16.87	33.04	9.66	n/a	35.81
Shawnee, KS	13.88	33.59	20.83	32.40	10.23	n/a	38.61
Shrewsbury, MA	14.41	42.36	24.20	36.08	11.75	n/a	38.33
S Brunswick, NJ	14.55	40.08	24.41	42.13	11.99	n/a	45.42
S. Jordan, UT	12.84	38.00	20.31	33.25	10.53	n/a	39.78
S. Kingstown, RI	13.98	32.40	20.47	39.49	12.00	n/a	39.84
Southaven, MS	13.19	33.09	22.63	30.71	9.83	n/a	34.55
Southlake, TX	13.23	37.02	19.60	34.67	9.77	n/a	37.06
Spanish Fork, UT	11.56	30.38	17.10	33.42	10.71	n/a	n/a
Sparks, NV	14.54	31.08	18.74	33.99	11.40	n/a	37.08
Stow, OH	13.13	30.07	20.32	31.58	9.97	n/a	31.28
Sugar Land, TX	13.07	38.89	22.23	36.57	9.19	n/a	44.72
Sun Prairie, WI	13.80	27.08	20.74	30.54	10.44	n/a	32.30
Tualatin, OR	14.61	34.48	21.32	35.96	10.94	n/a	40.20
Waimalu, HI	13.42	28.83	20.59	32.68	12.61	n/a	33.74
Wellington, FL	13.57	35.31	19.13	36.03	12.00	n/a	32.35
W Des Moines, IA	14.39	29.76	21.77	33.76	10.07	n/a	28.90
West Linn, OR	14.61	34.48	21.32	35.96	10.94	n/a	40.20
West Windsor, NJ	14.80	36.50	22.64	39.20	12.58	n/a	40.47
Weston, FL	12.97	34.05	16.81	26.39	11.14	n/a	41.45
Woodbury, MN	15.43	32.34	22.55	36.00	10.99	n/a	40.00
Woodridge, IL	14.24	36.56	24.95	39.57	9.57	n/a	40.54
Yorba Linda, CA	13.96	36.87	23.05	35.70	11.31	n/a	41.86

Notes: Wage data is for May 2007 and covers the Metropolitan Statistical Area - see Appendix A for areas included; n/a not available
Source: Bureau of Labor Statistics, May 2007 Metro Area Occupational Employment and Wage Estimates

Average Hourly Wages: Occupations E - I

MSA[1]	Electricians	Financial Managers	First-Line Supervisors/ Mgrs., Sales	Food Preparation Workers	General/ Oper. Mgrs.	Hairdressers/ Cosmetologists	Internists
Allen, TX	19.29	55.42	19.02	8.57	56.15	10.95	90.82
Ankeny, IA	22.05	47.40	19.83	9.05	48.35	12.05	n/a
Apex, NC	16.82	43.89	17.46	8.69	56.84	16.94	90.17
Bangor, ME	20.45	35.55	16.46	10.07	40.67	11.66	n/a
Beavercreek, OH	23.31	44.83	18.40	8.81	48.84	13.43	89.34
Bellevue, NE	21.28	48.80	19.83	8.75	47.85	12.38	78.53
Bend, OR	27.71	52.79	20.02	10.01	39.58	10.53	n/a
Bernards, NJ	28.34	59.33	21.41	10.15	70.21	14.36	87.25
Bethlehem, NY	20.82	49.70	19.96	9.39	51.23	11.80	80.21
Bozeman, MT	n/a	n/a	n/a	n/a	n/a	n/a	n/a
Brentwood, TN	17.73	38.73	18.42	9.15	44.34	17.11	77.72
Brookfield, WI	25.78	50.47	19.44	9.40	54.26	11.67	91.80
Broomfield, CO	22.34	54.01	20.48	9.73	51.87	12.76	97.38
Burlington, VT	20.05	52.94	21.97	9.98	51.69	16.81	n/a
Carmel, IN	23.60	51.94	19.87	8.90	51.45	12.72	78.03
Cary, NC	16.82	43.89	17.46	8.69	56.84	16.94	90.17
Casper, WY	21.06	36.80	17.04	9.00	38.10	11.77	n/a
Cheshire, CT	25.15	44.55	19.31	11.15	54.25	15.19	83.13
Chino Hills, CA	22.49	48.76	18.71	9.72	51.03	10.12	84.99
Collierville, TN	20.05	39.37	18.40	8.88	44.61	15.87	81.16
Conway, AR	17.62	40.13	17.60	8.36	46.77	10.45	n/a
Coronado, CA	23.07	53.32	19.28	9.44	55.20	11.70	66.34
Cranberry, PA	24.24	43.34	20.06	9.11	44.82	9.15	88.07
Dover, DE	18.80	41.68	17.46	8.51	47.94	11.29	n/a
Draper, UT	20.21	45.48	18.97	8.40	45.74	9.07	n/a
Dublin, OH	21.76	51.84	19.12	9.38	50.09	12.04	83.78
Edmond, OK	17.72	36.41	16.79	7.59	36.91	9.02	89.51
Evesham, NJ	32.31	52.60	20.44	9.66	64.05	15.22	84.98
Fargo, ND	20.05	42.23	17.45	9.81	46.34	11.14	n/a
Farmington, CT	25.75	51.77	18.63	10.55	50.07	14.84	63.18
Fishers, IN	23.60	51.94	19.87	8.90	51.45	12.72	78.03
Flower Mound, TX	19.29	55.42	19.02	8.57	56.15	10.95	90.82
Franklin, MA	28.75	56.92	20.61	10.47	58.04	14.39	88.15
Frederick, MD	23.30	54.86	21.64	9.93	59.34	16.36	80.45
Frisco, TX	19.29	55.42	19.02	8.57	56.15	10.95	90.82
Goodyear, AZ	19.11	42.80	20.47	10.96	47.62	13.17	84.25
Grand Blanc, MI	31.81	39.68	18.77	9.05	43.13	12.48	81.93
Greenburgh, NY	33.75	71.16	22.70	10.84	69.08	14.86	77.20
Greenwich, CT	25.38	61.60	21.73	10.94	71.24	15.41	79.66
Hampden, PA	22.89	42.17	19.09	8.94	43.52	9.47	75.95
Hilliard, OH	21.76	51.84	19.12	9.38	50.09	12.04	83.78
Hoover, AL	19.88	47.11	17.91	8.03	47.93	17.58	87.26
Huntersville, NC	17.73	56.20	17.63	8.52	56.26	13.95	87.33
Juneau, AK	n/a	n/a	n/a	n/a	n/a	n/a	n/a
Keller, TX	19.68	51.18	18.36	8.34	49.14	11.26	71.55
Kenner, LA	22.22	41.56	17.06	7.53	43.76	12.92	96.46
Kennesaw, GA	20.02	51.07	17.05	9.70	45.47	13.53	79.15
League City, TX	19.91	56.30	19.68	8.22	53.98	10.96	71.46
Leawood, KS	25.88	46.82	19.34	9.05	45.87	11.75	80.43
Lee's Summit, MO	25.88	46.82	19.34	9.05	45.87	11.75	80.43
Leesburg, VA	24.94	55.04	21.30	10.11	60.48	17.52	74.90
Lehi, UT	23.41	38.14	16.55	8.03	38.97	10.20	n/a
Lwr Providence, PA	31.80	55.12	22.15	9.82	55.09	11.88	63.10
Madison, AL	20.50	45.98	16.81	8.06	46.85	9.59	n/a
Manhattan Bch, CA	23.73	56.00	19.65	9.43	56.91	13.26	80.32
Maple Grove, MN	29.09	56.99	17.89	10.11	54.73	14.51	86.96
Marion, IA	23.67	49.42	18.56	8.90	49.12	11.62	n/a
Marlboro, NJ	28.34	59.33	21.41	10.15	70.21	14.36	87.25

MSA[1]	Electricians	Financial Managers	First-Line Supervisors/ Mgrs., Sales	Food Preparation Workers	General/ Oper. Mgrs.	Hairdressers/ Cosmetologists	Internists
Matthews, NC	17.73	56.20	17.63	8.52	56.26	13.95	87.33
Meridian, ID	20.29	36.86	17.51	9.04	35.00	9.10	n/a
Merrimack, NH	23.21	49.63	18.84	8.73	51.15	13.14	n/a
Morgantown, WV	16.39	31.80	14.20	8.80	34.97	10.92	n/a
Mt Pleasant, SC	18.29	40.17	18.45	7.90	41.26	15.02	101.73
Northampton, PA	31.80	55.12	22.15	9.82	55.09	11.88	63.10
Northville, MI	30.07	52.29	19.37	10.28	52.54	12.22	82.99
Novi, MI	30.19	48.35	23.46	10.22	54.27	13.23	81.98
O'Fallon, MO	28.06	52.64	19.65	8.86	51.53	12.40	77.59
Oro Valley, AZ	18.67	37.35	18.56	10.43	43.67	12.74	75.21
Oviedo, FL	16.86	48.91	21.44	9.24	46.72	13.37	72.04
Palm Bch Grdns, FL	19.37	51.61	23.14	10.56	50.88	12.69	90.36
Parker, CO	22.34	54.01	20.48	9.73	51.87	12.76	97.38
Peachtree City, GA	20.02	51.07	17.05	9.70	45.47	13.53	79.15
Pflugerville, TX	17.49	51.75	19.76	9.59	50.80	12.26	67.24
Pleasanton, CA	31.15	56.86	20.33	10.67	57.92	12.70	74.37
Rapid City, SD	19.10	44.49	19.42	7.73	46.54	12.24	n/a
Redmond, WA	26.80	55.55	24.17	11.38	66.79	15.06	76.35
Richland, WA	24.65	41.54	19.69	9.82	59.31	11.61	n/a
Richmond, KY	n/a	n/a	n/a	n/a	n/a	n/a	n/a
Rio Rancho, NM	19.56	38.02	18.34	8.77	44.73	8.79	n/a
Rockaway, NJ	31.84	61.75	22.55	10.27	69.48	15.37	78.14
Rocklin, CA	23.82	46.28	19.88	9.79	51.62	12.75	79.00
Rogers, AR	18.00	38.72	15.97	7.97	42.89	12.03	n/a
Round Rock, TX	17.49	51.75	19.76	9.59	50.80	12.26	67.24
Sammamish, WA	26.80	55.55	24.17	11.38	66.79	15.06	76.35
San Ramon, CA	31.15	56.86	20.33	10.67	57.92	12.70	74.37
Santa Fe, NM	18.41	45.08	19.34	9.73	43.97	11.14	n/a
Saratoga, CA	34.85	65.00	20.45	10.31	65.14	10.24	78.25
Savage, MN	29.09	56.99	17.89	10.11	54.73	14.51	86.96
Schererville, IN	28.53	40.08	19.44	9.05	47.87	10.18	96.55
Shawnee, KS	25.88	46.82	19.34	9.05	45.87	11.75	80.43
Shrewsbury, MA	24.84	42.84	18.32	10.67	50.06	14.07	66.35
S Brunswick, NJ	28.34	59.33	21.41	10.15	70.21	14.36	87.25
S. Jordan, UT	20.21	45.48	18.97	8.40	45.74	9.07	n/a
S. Kingstown, RI	24.17	49.18	19.46	9.85	53.03	12.72	83.10
Southaven, MS	20.05	39.37	18.40	8.88	44.61	15.87	81.16
Southlake, TX	19.68	51.18	18.36	8.34	49.14	11.26	71.55
Spanish Fork, UT	23.41	38.14	16.55	8.03	38.97	10.20	n/a
Sparks, NV	25.22	40.12	19.70	8.91	48.39	11.15	96.83
Stow, OH	22.70	46.19	18.28	9.19	45.02	10.63	85.19
Sugar Land, TX	19.91	56.30	19.68	8.22	53.98	10.96	71.46
Sun Prairie, WI	24.15	46.91	20.11	9.03	47.26	12.47	98.91
Tualatin, OR	27.91	51.13	20.11	10.45	52.07	11.12	86.78
Waimalu, HI	28.75	40.76	19.39	9.52	47.72	17.71	83.30
Wellington, FL	19.37	51.61	23.14	10.56	50.88	12.69	90.36
W Des Moines, IA	22.05	47.40	19.83	9.05	48.35	12.05	n/a
West Linn, OR	27.91	51.13	20.11	10.45	52.07	11.12	86.78
West Windsor, NJ	35.05	59.01	22.80	9.75	71.72	14.70	62.30
Weston, FL	19.43	46.73	21.94	9.79	50.64	11.71	85.78
Woodbury, MN	29.09	56.99	17.89	10.11	54.73	14.51	86.96
Woodridge, IL	32.23	56.99	20.23	9.29	57.02	12.15	68.09
Yorba Linda, CA	21.72	54.57	19.87	9.49	60.42	11.29	91.12

Notes: Wage data is for May 2007 and covers the Metropolitan Statistical Area - see Appendix A for areas included; n/a not available
Source: Bureau of Labor Statistics, May 2007 Metro Area Occupational Employment and Wage Estimates

Average Hourly Wages: Occupations J - N

MSA[1]	Janitors/ Cleaners	Landscapers	Lawyers	Maids/ House-keepers	Main-tenance Repairers	Marketing Managers	Nuclear Medicine Technologists
Allen, TX	9.02	10.25	65.73	8.23	15.14	60.78	30.51
Ankeny, IA	10.60	12.27	52.42	9.20	15.77	46.36	29.44
Apex, NC	9.89	10.29	52.93	8.67	16.95	52.72	27.80
Bangor, ME	10.80	10.40	40.08	9.46	14.71	30.30	n/a
Beavercreek, OH	12.05	11.76	54.67	8.93	15.53	49.71	30.58
Bellevue, NE	10.26	11.55	49.03	8.96	15.89	48.23	28.75
Bend, OR	13.05	12.20	29.85	9.46	16.64	42.07	n/a
Bernards, NJ	12.10	12.61	57.95	9.77	18.27	66.08	37.95
Bethlehem, NY	11.91	11.96	47.40	9.65	16.50	54.44	33.16
Bozeman, MT	n/a	n/a	n/a	n/a	n/a	n/a	n/a
Brentwood, TN	10.34	11.42	48.83	8.69	16.26	39.16	31.29
Brookfield, WI	11.18	12.74	51.41	9.63	17.88	53.15	33.06
Broomfield, CO	10.78	12.36	55.83	9.43	17.26	50.85	33.32
Burlington, VT	11.58	11.96	51.01	10.01	15.71	47.88	n/a
Carmel, IN	10.00	10.75	44.90	8.47	16.63	48.40	33.81
Cary, NC	9.89	10.29	52.93	8.67	16.95	52.72	27.80
Casper, WY	10.81	12.89	55.51	8.20	12.93	n/a	n/a
Cheshire, CT	13.47	13.42	55.00	11.33	19.79	45.67	33.58
Chino Hills, CA	12.50	11.03	55.48	9.26	17.54	51.62	38.64
Collierville, TN	9.98	10.91	54.48	8.00	16.62	45.35	29.44
Conway, AR	9.78	10.19	46.63	7.92	14.98	47.77	30.52
Coronado, CA	11.23	11.86	63.36	9.57	17.09	57.57	34.48
Cranberry, PA	10.92	11.75	50.18	9.13	16.19	46.08	24.86
Dover, DE	10.51	11.18	49.77	8.36	17.42	n/a	n/a
Draper, UT	10.00	10.87	58.49	8.69	16.60	43.33	27.43
Dublin, OH	11.24	11.53	43.34	9.14	16.76	49.33	30.45
Edmond, OK	9.24	9.80	48.28	7.84	15.04	32.72	32.14
Evesham, NJ	12.31	12.18	57.44	9.66	18.10	59.38	34.80
Fargo, ND	10.53	11.47	55.90	8.41	15.15	35.09	n/a
Farmington, CT	12.58	14.31	59.52	11.71	19.56	51.60	34.55
Fishers, IN	10.00	10.75	44.90	8.47	16.63	48.40	33.81
Flower Mound, TX	9.02	10.25	65.73	8.23	15.14	60.78	30.51
Franklin, MA	13.06	14.94	63.74	11.64	19.92	59.14	34.95
Frederick, MD	10.01	11.91	52.13	10.76	17.77	52.29	42.40
Frisco, TX	9.02	10.25	65.73	8.23	15.14	60.78	30.51
Goodyear, AZ	9.59	10.44	56.98	9.13	15.89	39.28	32.42
Grand Blanc, MI	13.26	12.33	55.85	10.52	17.42	35.91	21.93
Greenburgh, NY	13.14	13.87	70.39	14.67	18.01	69.31	34.59
Greenwich, CT	13.66	13.79	55.62	10.92	18.84	60.34	35.05
Hampden, PA	11.38	12.18	48.22	9.03	16.76	43.78	n/a
Hilliard, OH	11.24	11.53	43.34	9.14	16.76	49.33	30.45
Hoover, AL	8.63	10.44	54.63	8.17	15.96	45.64	27.32
Huntersville, NC	9.98	10.51	52.52	8.53	17.79	52.05	30.34
Juneau, AK	n/a	n/a	n/a	n/a	n/a	n/a	n/a
Keller, TX	9.36	10.75	51.71	7.99	14.88	50.62	32.29
Kenner, LA	8.91	10.64	50.80	8.42	15.18	40.15	30.22
Kennesaw, GA	10.14	10.99	66.49	8.56	16.50	51.22	31.29
League City, TX	8.74	9.47	62.17	7.73	14.25	57.18	35.31
Leawood, KS	10.75	12.12	48.93	9.27	16.50	49.69	31.54
Lee's Summit, MO	10.75	12.12	48.93	9.27	16.50	49.69	31.54
Leesburg, VA	10.88	11.76	66.79	11.09	20.39	58.72	31.27
Lehi, UT	9.07	9.31	45.25	8.88	12.97	43.94	n/a
Lwr Providence, PA	11.68	13.33	56.01	10.25	17.61	54.59	31.96
Madison, AL	8.84	9.71	50.92	7.88	15.54	50.00	29.83
Manhattan Bch, CA	11.33	12.95	67.81	10.17	17.82	60.53	33.92
Maple Grove, MN	12.02	13.28	57.16	10.86	19.22	57.19	32.80
Marion, IA	10.61	10.28	40.71	9.19	16.89	46.14	n/a
Marlboro, NJ	12.10	12.61	57.95	9.77	18.27	66.08	37.95

MSA[1]	Janitors/ Cleaners	Landscapers	Lawyers	Maids/ House-keepers	Main-tenance Repairers	Marketing Managers	Nuclear Medicine Technologists
Matthews, NC	9.98	10.51	52.52	8.53	17.79	52.05	30.34
Meridian, ID	10.23	11.46	52.46	8.30	14.37	41.52	29.83
Merrimack, NH	11.70	13.61	43.17	10.42	17.70	52.96	n/a
Morgantown, WV	9.34	8.93	39.43	8.20	13.91	n/a	n/a
Mt Pleasant, SC	8.19	10.04	49.30	8.37	15.73	40.72	27.17
Northampton, PA	11.68	13.33	56.01	10.25	17.61	54.59	31.96
Northville, MI	12.12	11.81	60.18	10.95	20.37	45.14	29.87
Novi, MI	12.54	12.27	53.86	9.99	18.74	52.43	32.28
O'Fallon, MO	10.77	12.59	55.08	9.67	17.82	53.86	30.23
Oro Valley, AZ	9.72	10.26	51.48	8.81	14.02	33.42	30.33
Oviedo, FL	9.67	11.17	58.00	8.94	13.73	44.79	29.44
Palm Bch Grdns, FL	9.95	10.33	47.03	9.11	15.21	54.26	28.60
Parker, CO	10.78	12.36	55.83	9.43	17.26	50.85	33.32
Peachtree City, GA	10.14	10.99	66.49	8.56	16.50	51.22	31.29
Pflugerville, TX	9.41	9.80	50.25	8.27	14.38	59.62	30.52
Pleasanton, CA	13.14	14.00	61.48	11.98	20.86	61.95	47.54
Rapid City, SD	9.75	9.63	33.88	7.98	13.61	n/a	n/a
Redmond, WA	12.93	13.94	n/a	11.18	19.22	61.63	37.17
Richland, WA	11.58	12.76	42.87	9.88	16.99	n/a	n/a
Richmond, KY	n/a	n/a	n/a	n/a	n/a	n/a	n/a
Rio Rancho, NM	9.31	9.54	43.08	7.91	13.92	44.75	20.37
Rockaway, NJ	12.49	13.47	59.41	10.91	18.38	62.55	37.51
Rocklin, CA	11.67	11.56	51.08	10.34	17.59	49.33	41.64
Rogers, AR	10.41	10.96	30.97	8.03	14.10	37.12	n/a
Round Rock, TX	9.41	9.80	50.25	8.27	14.38	59.62	30.52
Sammamish, WA	12.93	13.94	n/a	11.18	19.22	61.63	37.17
San Ramon, CA	13.14	14.00	61.48	11.98	20.86	61.95	47.54
Santa Fe, NM	10.91	11.79	52.30	10.21	13.57	n/a	n/a
Saratoga, CA	12.13	13.15	81.79	11.18	21.89	73.27	40.59
Savage, MN	12.02	13.28	57.16	10.86	19.22	57.19	32.80
Schererville, IN	10.70	11.14	49.57	9.16	21.74	42.18	34.03
Shawnee, KS	10.75	12.12	48.93	9.27	16.50	49.69	31.54
Shrewsbury, MA	12.44	13.10	52.49	10.50	17.45	52.83	28.39
S Brunswick, NJ	12.10	12.61	57.95	9.77	18.27	66.08	37.95
S. Jordan, UT	10.00	10.87	58.49	8.69	16.60	43.33	27.43
S. Kingstown, RI	12.47	12.87	48.82	10.96	17.05	44.47	35.70
Southaven, MS	9.98	10.91	54.48	8.00	16.62	45.35	29.44
Southlake, TX	9.36	10.75	51.71	7.99	14.88	50.62	32.29
Spanish Fork, UT	9.07	9.31	45.25	8.88	12.97	43.94	n/a
Sparks, NV	10.18	12.37	65.63	9.38	16.58	38.43	n/a
Stow, OH	11.94	11.04	49.22	8.48	16.84	48.33	31.13
Sugar Land, TX	8.74	9.47	62.17	7.73	14.25	57.18	35.31
Sun Prairie, WI	11.38	13.20	50.47	9.55	17.23	47.40	n/a
Tualatin, OR	11.32	11.77	48.06	9.80	17.31	51.55	34.64
Waimalu, HI	10.93	13.43	46.39	12.57	17.39	39.56	n/a
Wellington, FL	9.95	10.33	47.03	9.11	15.21	54.26	28.60
W Des Moines, IA	10.60	12.27	52.42	9.20	15.77	46.36	29.44
West Linn, OR	11.32	11.77	48.06	9.80	17.31	51.55	34.64
West Windsor, NJ	12.16	13.04	48.80	10.35	18.22	64.09	36.90
Weston, FL	10.04	11.51	51.59	8.94	15.01	54.56	34.08
Woodbury, MN	12.02	13.28	57.16	10.86	19.22	57.19	32.80
Woodridge, IL	11.95	12.46	62.73	9.85	19.67	51.81	30.99
Yorba Linda, CA	11.28	10.63	67.58	9.53	17.57	57.88	40.29

Notes: Wage data is for May 2007 and covers the Metropolitan Statistical Area - see Appendix A for areas included; n/a not available
Source: Bureau of Labor Statistics, May 2007 Metro Area Occupational Employment and Wage Estimates

Average Hourly Wages: Occupations N - R

MSA[1]	Nurses, Licensed Practical	Nurses, Registered	Nursing Aides/ Orderlies/ Attendants	Packers/ Packagers	Physical Therapists	Postal Mail Carriers	R.E. Brokers
Allen, TX	19.58	30.37	11.11	9.24	39.04	21.40	45.42
Ankeny, IA	17.89	24.66	11.94	8.45	30.11	21.28	29.10
Apex, NC	17.64	27.57	11.84	10.02	34.87	21.12	24.13
Bangor, ME	17.61	29.91	11.04	8.32	32.08	20.55	n/a
Beavercreek, OH	19.21	27.42	11.45	8.93	34.16	21.29	n/a
Bellevue, NE	17.96	26.45	11.61	9.33	30.10	21.58	22.06
Bend, OR	19.35	33.34	12.42	9.61	31.32	22.16	26.39
Bernards, NJ	23.49	33.79	12.60	9.76	37.21	21.31	50.65
Bethlehem, NY	18.43	26.94	11.78	11.87	29.26	21.03	26.53
Bozeman, MT	n/a	n/a	n/a	n/a	n/a	n/a	n/a
Brentwood, TN	17.89	27.94	11.30	9.60	34.28	21.34	27.53
Brookfield, WI	21.17	29.28	12.11	11.45	32.24	21.37	n/a
Broomfield, CO	20.66	30.87	13.13	9.22	29.98	21.28	36.66
Burlington, VT	19.82	31.18	12.56	11.68	27.94	21.21	16.70
Carmel, IN	19.33	28.57	12.34	10.42	33.87	21.23	43.47
Cary, NC	17.64	27.57	11.84	10.02	34.87	21.12	24.13
Casper, WY	17.12	25.83	10.79	7.87	n/a	21.64	n/a
Cheshire, CT	24.02	33.20	13.49	10.84	32.43	21.61	n/a
Chino Hills, CA	20.06	34.23	11.78	10.12	40.16	21.16	32.15
Collierville, TN	18.93	28.58	10.42	9.68	36.53	21.29	n/a
Conway, AR	17.19	27.67	9.92	8.39	30.85	21.13	41.82
Coronado, CA	20.34	35.78	11.75	9.27	35.40	21.15	55.79
Cranberry, PA	17.59	27.02	11.29	10.11	31.34	21.40	n/a
Dover, DE	20.27	27.26	12.98	12.40	n/a	20.73	n/a
Draper, UT	18.41	28.07	10.39	9.74	34.31	21.30	33.09
Dublin, OH	19.54	27.23	11.69	10.57	33.59	21.25	38.54
Edmond, OK	15.82	24.75	9.82	8.32	34.62	21.17	n/a
Evesham, NJ	22.75	31.33	12.33	10.57	34.89	21.27	50.94
Fargo, ND	16.04	26.19	11.19	8.14	32.04	21.22	n/a
Farmington, CT	24.83	32.76	14.62	9.85	35.61	21.36	n/a
Fishers, IN	19.33	28.57	12.34	10.42	33.87	21.23	43.47
Flower Mound, TX	19.58	30.37	11.11	9.24	39.04	21.40	45.42
Franklin, MA	24.04	38.48	13.78	10.39	33.56	21.36	30.18
Frederick, MD	22.17	36.90	14.60	10.88	37.15	21.36	35.57
Frisco, TX	19.58	30.37	11.11	9.24	39.04	21.40	45.42
Goodyear, AZ	19.92	29.18	11.45	9.20	30.41	21.09	38.67
Grand Blanc, MI	19.43	28.89	11.77	8.80	32.80	21.32	22.51
Greenburgh, NY	22.54	37.94	15.29	9.70	37.06	21.12	61.95
Greenwich, CT	25.97	31.65	14.33	10.62	36.56	21.48	n/a
Hampden, PA	18.91	n/a	12.08	9.31	38.30	21.49	42.99
Hilliard, OH	19.54	27.23	11.69	10.57	33.59	21.25	38.54
Hoover, AL	15.86	26.80	10.18	8.55	35.58	21.06	50.19
Huntersville, NC	18.99	27.81	10.87	9.44	33.80	21.00	28.24
Juneau, AK	n/a	n/a	n/a	n/a	n/a	n/a	n/a
Keller, TX	19.07	28.31	10.32	9.27	35.73	21.42	60.65
Kenner, LA	16.76	29.73	9.54	8.39	33.27	21.42	n/a
Kennesaw, GA	17.80	28.32	10.66	9.48	35.62	21.15	43.47
League City, TX	19.09	30.66	10.82	8.43	36.73	21.44	41.88
Leawood, KS	17.31	27.98	11.28	9.77	30.57	21.28	25.07
Lee's Summit, MO	17.31	27.98	11.28	9.77	30.57	21.28	25.07
Leesburg, VA	21.92	33.65	12.75	10.01	34.88	21.22	34.60
Lehi, UT	15.71	26.37	9.69	8.48	30.49	21.14	n/a
Lwr Providence, PA	22.50	32.05	12.59	10.09	34.98	21.45	n/a
Madison, AL	15.69	26.65	9.32	8.71	35.71	21.34	n/a
Manhattan Bch, CA	22.38	36.67	11.82	9.05	36.35	21.35	40.27
Maple Grove, MN	19.79	33.69	13.80	10.78	31.29	21.12	51.29
Marion, IA	17.22	23.55	11.48	9.55	28.68	21.07	n/a
Marlboro, NJ	23.49	33.79	12.60	9.76	37.21	21.31	50.65

MSA[1]	Nurses, Licensed Practical	Nurses, Registered	Nursing Aides/ Orderlies/ Attendants	Packers/ Packagers	Physical Therapists	Postal Mail Carriers	R.E. Brokers
Matthews, NC	18.99	27.81	10.87	9.44	33.80	21.00	28.24
Meridian, ID	18.67	26.23	11.30	9.63	32.52	20.90	15.77
Merrimack, NH	18.83	28.86	12.37	10.59	30.64	21.33	n/a
Morgantown, WV	14.80	n/a	9.70	8.12	38.81	20.85	n/a
Mt Pleasant, SC	18.16	26.87	9.83	8.24	30.53	21.06	55.68
Northampton, PA	22.50	32.05	12.59	10.09	34.98	21.45	n/a
Northville, MI	21.66	30.99	12.83	11.69	33.49	21.49	n/a
Novi, MI	21.73	31.18	12.51	11.78	35.40	21.46	35.92
O'Fallon, MO	17.79	26.61	10.58	9.97	28.59	21.24	39.66
Oro Valley, AZ	19.83	28.82	10.80	8.30	34.76	21.29	22.55
Oviedo, FL	18.06	27.29	10.92	9.99	33.39	21.31	31.98
Palm Bch Grdns, FL	20.15	30.71	10.74	10.11	35.10	21.13	63.34
Parker, CO	20.66	30.87	13.13	9.22	29.98	21.28	36.66
Peachtree City, GA	17.80	28.32	10.66	9.48	35.62	21.15	43.47
Pflugerville, TX	19.01	28.89	10.81	8.27	30.35	21.56	34.56
Pleasanton, CA	26.61	43.88	14.38	10.04	41.13	21.18	54.57
Rapid City, SD	15.86	26.78	10.59	8.15	28.45	21.46	n/a
Redmond, WA	22.15	34.79	13.26	10.80	33.99	21.09	47.61
Richland, WA	19.22	29.51	11.31	10.44	31.41	21.03	n/a
Richmond, KY	n/a	n/a	n/a	n/a	n/a	n/a	n/a
Rio Rancho, NM	25.26	29.56	11.17	8.46	29.38	21.02	n/a
Rockaway, NJ	23.64	35.63	12.34	9.65	40.68	21.18	29.99
Rocklin, CA	23.24	39.00	13.08	10.68	37.71	21.00	49.00
Rogers, AR	16.87	24.57	9.98	10.32	33.62	21.18	n/a
Round Rock, TX	19.01	28.89	10.81	8.27	30.35	21.56	34.56
Sammamish, WA	22.15	34.79	13.26	10.80	33.99	21.09	47.61
San Ramon, CA	26.61	43.88	14.38	10.04	41.13	21.18	54.57
Santa Fe, NM	20.59	27.65	11.91	10.50	35.57	21.16	52.51
Saratoga, CA	26.47	45.95	15.69	10.51	38.08	21.22	47.53
Savage, MN	19.79	33.69	13.80	10.78	31.29	21.12	51.29
Schererville, IN	18.29	28.11	10.83	9.63	37.16	21.36	n/a
Shawnee, KS	17.31	27.98	11.28	9.77	30.57	21.28	25.07
Shrewsbury, MA	23.91	34.66	13.84	10.52	30.16	20.99	n/a
S Brunswick, NJ	23.49	33.79	12.60	9.76	37.21	21.31	50.65
S. Jordan, UT	18.41	28.07	10.39	9.74	34.31	21.30	33.09
S. Kingstown, RI	22.50	31.20	13.02	9.73	36.50	21.38	n/a
Southaven, MS	18.93	28.58	10.42	9.68	36.53	21.29	n/a
Southlake, TX	19.07	28.31	10.32	9.27	35.73	21.42	60.65
Spanish Fork, UT	15.71	26.37	9.69	8.48	30.49	21.14	n/a
Sparks, NV	22.09	32.82	12.72	11.33	36.64	21.19	n/a
Stow, OH	18.47	27.23	11.06	10.53	34.59	21.47	24.62
Sugar Land, TX	19.09	30.66	10.82	8.43	36.73	21.44	41.88
Sun Prairie, WI	18.99	30.26	13.08	13.33	31.14	21.08	37.97
Tualatin, OR	22.13	33.48	12.60	10.04	31.83	21.24	42.80
Waimalu, HI	19.85	36.37	12.77	9.46	26.61	21.36	n/a
Wellington, FL	20.15	30.71	10.74	10.11	35.10	21.13	63.34
W Des Moines, IA	17.89	24.66	11.94	8.45	30.11	21.28	29.10
West Linn, OR	22.13	33.48	12.60	10.04	31.83	21.24	42.80
West Windsor, NJ	22.87	31.97	13.21	9.76	36.45	21.22	n/a
Weston, FL	19.53	29.84	10.91	9.42	36.14	21.37	33.28
Woodbury, MN	19.79	33.69	13.80	10.78	31.29	21.12	51.29
Woodridge, IL	20.89	31.26	11.47	9.48	37.38	21.39	33.59
Yorba Linda, CA	23.26	35.53	11.83	9.70	41.54	21.23	39.81

Notes: Wage data is for May 2007 and covers the Metropolitan Statistical Area - see Appendix A for areas included; n/a not available
Source: Bureau of Labor Statistics, May 2007 Metro Area Occupational Employment and Wage Estimates

Average Hourly Wages: Occupations R - T

MSA[1]	Retail Salespersons	Sales Reps., Except Tech./Scien.	Sales Reps., Tech./Scien.	Secretaries, Exc. Leg./ Med./Exec.	Security Guards	Surgeons	Teacher Assistants
Allen, TX	11.71	29.44	35.60	13.40	12.88	n/a	9.40
Ankeny, IA	12.09	26.34	40.88	14.48	13.02	100.28	9.40
Apex, NC	11.26	25.86	31.86	14.19	11.43	n/a	9.00
Bangor, ME	12.18	19.17	40.84	13.39	10.08	n/a	12.20
Beavercreek, OH	11.31	27.84	32.27	14.83	10.83	89.48	12.00
Bellevue, NE	12.39	27.52	35.47	13.73	13.01	67.93	9.50
Bend, OR	13.22	23.87	46.14	14.25	10.62	n/a	13.00
Bernards, NJ	12.69	35.27	44.40	16.38	12.84	n/a	12.40
Bethlehem, NY	12.12	26.24	31.12	15.51	12.56	97.53	11.90
Bozeman, MT	n/a	n/a	n/a	n/a	n/a	n/a	n/a
Brentwood, TN	11.48	29.65	34.46	13.47	11.58	n/a	9.70
Brookfield, WI	11.85	30.49	39.37	14.89	12.17	96.65	13.20
Broomfield, CO	12.45	29.26	40.42	15.50	11.98	88.25	12.30
Burlington, VT	12.46	25.50	26.45	14.05	12.67	n/a	11.20
Carmel, IN	11.38	28.51	34.51	13.77	11.89	97.63	11.20
Cary, NC	11.26	25.86	31.86	14.19	11.43	n/a	9.00
Casper, WY	10.94	20.49	32.75	12.08	12.00	n/a	12.30
Cheshire, CT	12.91	32.24	33.64	16.62	14.36	97.22	13.30
Chino Hills, CA	12.30	30.30	34.64	15.00	10.91	85.79	13.00
Collierville, TN	11.39	28.51	35.16	13.05	9.74	68.72	9.30
Conway, AR	10.12	23.90	31.04	12.43	11.22	n/a	8.80
Coronado, CA	12.26	31.31	35.34	16.06	11.48	81.87	13.40
Cranberry, PA	11.18	31.68	34.95	13.29	11.52	84.47	9.80
Dover, DE	12.28	23.02	42.96	15.76	10.72	79.16	17.20
Draper, UT	11.99	27.93	35.34	13.29	12.44	n/a	10.00
Dublin, OH	11.54	30.67	35.02	15.56	12.21	n/a	13.30
Edmond, OK	10.93	25.41	27.80	11.94	12.90	n/a	7.70
Evesham, NJ	12.32	33.54	38.64	16.18	11.36	n/a	10.80
Fargo, ND	10.63	25.26	33.90	14.59	10.01	64.17	12.00
Farmington, CT	13.09	32.98	36.90	16.91	13.42	83.68	12.80
Fishers, IN	11.38	28.51	34.51	13.77	11.89	97.63	11.20
Flower Mound, TX	11.71	29.44	35.60	13.40	12.88	n/a	9.40
Franklin, MA	12.44	34.15	44.45	18.04	12.73	99.69	12.00
Frederick, MD	12.32	33.72	42.58	17.33	15.03	n/a	12.50
Frisco, TX	11.71	29.44	35.60	13.40	12.88	n/a	9.40
Goodyear, AZ	12.50	26.27	30.15	14.07	11.21	81.15	10.30
Grand Blanc, MI	12.66	22.41	36.38	14.30	11.53	n/a	10.70
Greenburgh, NY	12.68	34.35	41.28	16.30	12.96	89.78	12.50
Greenwich, CT	14.01	37.45	47.36	17.35	11.77	95.57	12.80
Hampden, PA	11.12	34.06	31.84	14.65	11.38	87.58	9.90
Hilliard, OH	11.54	30.67	35.02	15.56	12.21	n/a	13.30
Hoover, AL	12.00	25.17	39.60	13.99	9.57	n/a	8.50
Huntersville, NC	11.53	29.39	30.02	13.82	10.86	n/a	9.70
Juneau, AK	n/a	n/a	n/a	n/a	n/a	n/a	n/a
Keller, TX	11.37	28.58	35.67	12.96	12.69	89.84	8.00
Kenner, LA	11.60	25.73	31.28	12.75	10.91	n/a	8.30
Kennesaw, GA	11.69	28.91	39.67	13.62	11.49	101.47	9.00
League City, TX	11.51	29.31	38.96	13.16	11.34	86.19	8.50
Leawood, KS	12.00	30.82	36.32	13.51	14.35	n/a	9.80
Lee's Summit, MO	12.00	30.82	36.32	13.51	14.35	n/a	9.80
Leesburg, VA	12.11	33.00	43.12	19.64	14.54	72.31	13.00
Lehi, UT	10.60	22.78	28.98	12.95	13.32	n/a	9.70
Lwr Providence, PA	12.34	32.29	42.06	14.99	10.80	78.71	10.60
Madison, AL	10.27	25.78	29.14	13.70	10.72	n/a	8.60
Manhattan Bch, CA	12.12	28.21	35.50	15.88	11.82	81.21	13.90
Maple Grove, MN	11.60	31.17	41.82	17.03	13.58	n/a	12.20
Marion, IA	12.36	26.76	30.45	13.07	9.87	n/a	10.50
Marlboro, NJ	12.69	35.27	44.40	16.38	12.84	n/a	12.40

MSA[1]	Retail Salespersons	Sales Reps., Except Tech./Scien.	Sales Reps., Tech./Scien.	Secretaries, Exc. Leg./ Med./Exec.	Security Guards	Surgeons	Teacher Assistants
Matthews, NC	11.53	29.39	30.02	13.82	10.86	n/a	9.70
Meridian, ID	11.24	23.40	35.13	12.96	11.14	n/a	8.90
Merrimack, NH	11.53	32.69	37.87	14.42	14.04	94.87	11.80
Morgantown, WV	9.68	25.64	28.97	11.81	9.55	n/a	10.10
Mt Pleasant, SC	11.14	25.85	28.77	14.11	10.39	96.67	9.90
Northampton, PA	12.34	32.29	42.06	14.99	10.80	78.71	10.60
Northville, MI	11.37	28.00	35.94	16.57	13.59	91.99	11.30
Novi, MI	12.32	33.57	40.82	16.27	12.09	93.21	12.30
O'Fallon, MO	11.94	30.38	37.59	14.45	12.29	90.90	10.60
Oro Valley, AZ	12.63	24.07	26.35	13.49	10.07	n/a	10.90
Oviedo, FL	12.35	28.72	32.96	12.64	10.80	91.49	10.70
Palm Bch Grdns, FL	14.77	27.39	38.25	13.72	11.15	82.20	9.20
Parker, CO	12.45	29.26	40.42	15.50	11.98	88.25	12.30
Peachtree City, GA	11.69	28.91	39.67	13.62	11.49	101.47	9.00
Pflugerville, TX	11.25	25.70	41.47	13.04	11.55	92.76	10.40
Pleasanton, CA	12.93	33.85	37.06	18.87	12.41	74.72	14.40
Rapid City, SD	10.77	21.49	29.42	11.06	10.12	n/a	10.80
Redmond, WA	14.03	29.85	38.80	17.07	14.57	96.01	14.10
Richland, WA	14.60	21.59	33.85	16.30	n/a	n/a	12.30
Richmond, KY	n/a	n/a	n/a	n/a	n/a	n/a	n/a
Rio Rancho, NM	11.68	23.60	30.37	13.04	11.23	102.33	9.00
Rockaway, NJ	12.70	33.22	37.22	16.96	13.59	96.86	11.20
Rocklin, CA	12.17	27.98	49.21	16.23	11.29	93.93	12.30
Rogers, AR	9.73	28.23	27.02	12.23	10.79	n/a	9.40
Round Rock, TX	11.25	25.70	41.47	13.04	11.55	92.76	10.40
Sammamish, WA	14.03	29.85	38.80	17.07	14.57	96.01	14.10
San Ramon, CA	12.93	33.85	37.06	18.87	12.41	74.72	14.40
Santa Fe, NM	11.90	26.14	n/a	13.35	13.51	n/a	9.40
Saratoga, CA	12.49	35.43	48.08	17.85	13.97	75.27	14.30
Savage, MN	11.60	31.17	41.82	17.03	13.58	n/a	12.20
Schererville, IN	10.83	28.10	41.27	13.57	12.06	83.81	9.30
Shawnee, KS	12.00	30.82	36.32	13.51	14.35	n/a	9.80
Shrewsbury, MA	13.20	31.61	39.46	15.90	12.23	n/a	11.70
S Brunswick, NJ	12.69	35.27	44.40	16.38	12.84	n/a	12.40
S. Jordan, UT	11.99	27.93	35.34	13.29	12.44	n/a	10.00
S. Kingstown, RI	11.84	29.18	35.68	16.01	12.34	n/a	12.20
Southaven, MS	11.39	28.51	35.16	13.05	9.74	68.72	9.30
Southlake, TX	11.37	28.58	35.67	12.96	12.69	89.84	8.00
Spanish Fork, UT	10.60	22.78	28.98	12.95	13.32	n/a	9.70
Sparks, NV	12.57	27.67	42.45	16.28	11.35	98.94	13.10
Stow, OH	11.54	29.35	32.23	13.90	11.76	n/a	12.60
Sugar Land, TX	11.51	29.31	38.96	13.16	11.34	86.19	8.50
Sun Prairie, WI	11.80	28.53	36.73	15.02	12.44	n/a	12.50
Tualatin, OR	13.03	31.76	39.10	15.08	11.51	88.60	13.00
Waimalu, HI	11.30	22.30	28.50	15.78	11.95	73.90	9.80
Wellington, FL	14.77	27.39	38.25	13.72	11.15	82.20	9.20
W Des Moines, IA	12.09	26.34	40.88	14.48	13.02	100.28	9.40
West Linn, OR	13.03	31.76	39.10	15.08	11.51	88.60	13.00
West Windsor, NJ	13.04	31.16	39.62	18.56	16.36	n/a	12.20
Weston, FL	13.76	27.39	31.11	13.38	10.19	53.01	10.00
Woodbury, MN	11.60	31.17	41.82	17.03	13.58	n/a	12.20
Woodridge, IL	12.05	34.26	34.82	15.30	12.29	75.92	10.80
Yorba Linda, CA	12.64	32.69	40.65	16.56	11.76	77.33	14.70

Notes: Wage data is for May 2007 and covers the Metropolitan Statistical Area - see Appendix A for areas included; hourly wages for teacher assistants were calculated by the editors from annual wage data assuming a 40 hour work week; n/a not available
Source: Bureau of Labor Statistics, May 2007 Metro Area Occupational Employment and Wage Estimates

Average Hourly Wages: Occupations T - Z

MSA[1]	Teachers, Elementary School	Teachers, Secondary School	Tele-marketers	Truck Driv., Heavy/ Trac. Trail.	Truck Drivers, Light	Waiters/ Waitresses
Allen, TX	22.00	21.40	13.10	19.27	14.20	8.06
Ankeny, IA	18.20	19.30	12.33	18.84	14.61	8.41
Apex, NC	19.30	21.70	11.27	17.38	14.17	8.50
Bangor, ME	19.30	20.60	n/a	17.50	14.55	8.42
Beavercreek, OH	25.00	25.70	10.11	18.78	14.53	7.76
Bellevue, NE	19.60	20.10	10.82	19.07	13.73	7.54
Bend, OR	22.10	n/a	13.26	17.61	13.64	11.17
Bernards, NJ	27.40	29.00	15.72	19.53	16.22	11.25
Bethlehem, NY	28.50	28.20	11.47	21.06	14.88	10.56
Bozeman, MT	n/a	n/a	n/a	n/a	n/a	n/a
Brentwood, TN	21.60	21.80	12.77	18.90	14.68	7.74
Brookfield, WI	27.50	26.70	10.89	18.43	14.35	8.37
Broomfield, CO	23.50	24.20	13.61	19.52	15.39	9.25
Burlington, VT	24.30	24.10	13.61	17.62	16.15	11.87
Carmel, IN	21.90	23.70	14.18	17.82	14.04	8.36
Cary, NC	19.30	21.70	11.27	17.38	14.17	8.50
Casper, WY	n/a	n/a	n/a	19.99	13.20	6.99
Cheshire, CT	27.00	27.20	14.06	20.29	14.87	10.56
Chino Hills, CA	29.50	29.30	12.45	20.62	14.25	9.15
Collierville, TN	19.60	20.60	12.04	19.75	13.85	8.00
Conway, AR	20.00	22.00	9.76	16.76	12.55	7.90
Coronado, CA	31.70	30.30	14.00	19.83	13.33	9.28
Cranberry, PA	25.20	25.70	13.31	18.09	13.86	7.84
Dover, DE	21.00	n/a	n/a	16.39	18.97	7.97
Draper, UT	22.00	24.90	10.80	18.36	11.70	9.43
Dublin, OH	27.20	26.20	10.27	18.23	14.86	8.21
Edmond, OK	17.10	17.80	9.29	17.44	12.61	7.51
Evesham, NJ	28.20	28.90	12.39	21.19	13.42	10.52
Fargo, ND	19.60	20.80	8.80	17.42	15.14	7.92
Farmington, CT	30.60	31.40	13.03	21.18	14.79	10.49
Fishers, IN	21.90	23.70	14.18	17.82	14.04	8.36
Flower Mound, TX	22.00	21.40	13.10	19.27	14.20	8.06
Franklin, MA	28.60	28.60	18.42	20.87	16.12	12.21
Frederick, MD	30.40	28.10	14.37	18.17	13.63	9.07
Frisco, TX	22.00	21.40	13.10	19.27	14.20	8.06
Goodyear, AZ	17.60	20.00	11.21	18.68	14.39	8.86
Grand Blanc, MI	27.80	26.60	12.22	17.66	13.48	8.57
Greenburgh, NY	30.30	31.90	15.56	21.15	16.73	13.25
Greenwich, CT	30.60	32.80	12.85	19.98	14.94	9.73
Hampden, PA	24.10	24.00	n/a	21.05	14.08	8.06
Hilliard, OH	27.20	26.20	10.27	18.23	14.86	8.21
Hoover, AL	20.60	22.00	10.01	18.64	13.03	7.18
Huntersville, NC	19.50	20.60	14.87	19.51	14.92	8.21
Juneau, AK	n/a	n/a	n/a	n/a	n/a	n/a
Keller, TX	22.40	23.80	9.61	17.47	13.97	7.67
Kenner, LA	20.50	20.60	13.98	16.36	12.54	8.01
Kennesaw, GA	23.70	24.30	11.59	19.07	14.07	8.18
League City, TX	22.00	23.30	10.47	16.73	13.11	7.74
Leawood, KS	20.50	20.40	12.15	19.11	12.83	7.90
Lee's Summit, MO	20.50	20.40	12.15	19.11	12.83	7.90
Leesburg, VA	29.20	30.90	13.27	18.31	14.58	9.91
Lehi, UT	21.10	23.30	11.47	18.39	10.60	7.93
Lwr Providence, PA	24.30	26.70	14.41	19.38	14.97	8.78
Madison, AL	21.60	23.40	10.36	17.62	14.18	7.57
Manhattan Bch, CA	27.40	29.10	12.61	18.78	14.13	9.31
Maple Grove, MN	24.10	24.40	12.00	19.78	15.00	10.49
Marion, IA	18.00	18.70	10.24	19.01	13.58	8.52
Marlboro, NJ	27.40	29.00	15.72	19.53	16.22	11.25

MSA[1]	Teachers, Elementary School	Teachers, Secondary School	Tele-marketers	Truck Driv., Heavy/ Trac. Trail.	Truck Drivers, Light	Waiters/ Waitresses
Matthews, NC	19.50	20.60	14.87	19.51	14.92	8.21
Meridian, ID	23.10	22.20	11.31	15.24	12.59	7.48
Merrimack, NH	23.60	24.70	13.92	20.51	14.51	9.62
Morgantown, WV	18.90	20.10	8.23	15.45	10.76	7.95
Mt Pleasant, SC	20.40	21.80	10.74	16.35	12.40	7.84
Northampton, PA	24.30	26.70	14.41	19.38	14.97	8.78
Northville, MI	25.40	26.30	11.27	19.80	16.05	8.59
Novi, MI	31.60	28.40	10.77	19.72	15.77	8.96
O'Fallon, MO	22.80	23.10	11.46	19.31	14.92	8.56
Oro Valley, AZ	19.60	17.40	9.33	18.33	13.44	8.08
Oviedo, FL	22.60	22.60	11.16	16.86	14.45	9.52
Palm Bch Grdns, FL	22.20	23.30	13.12	16.46	14.01	10.29
Parker, CO	23.50	24.20	13.61	19.52	15.39	9.25
Peachtree City, GA	23.70	24.30	11.59	19.07	14.07	8.18
Pflugerville, TX	20.40	21.60	10.37	15.67	14.09	7.58
Pleasanton, CA	30.10	30.10	14.79	20.41	15.66	9.36
Rapid City, SD	19.60	21.30	11.03	15.60	11.90	6.91
Redmond, WA	25.20	26.80	13.54	19.80	14.65	13.39
Richland, WA	24.30	26.50	n/a	19.74	12.01	12.54
Richmond, KY	n/a	n/a	n/a	n/a	n/a	n/a
Rio Rancho, NM	20.90	23.40	10.55	18.79	12.72	7.11
Rockaway, NJ	28.00	29.90	15.30	19.44	15.30	11.16
Rocklin, CA	26.80	28.10	12.43	19.23	14.57	8.79
Rogers, AR	20.00	23.10	12.28	20.48	11.74	8.02
Round Rock, TX	20.40	21.60	10.37	15.67	14.09	7.58
Sammamish, WA	25.20	26.80	13.54	19.80	14.65	13.39
San Ramon, CA	30.10	30.10	14.79	20.41	15.66	9.36
Santa Fe, NM	20.00	n/a	n/a	15.15	12.04	9.03
Saratoga, CA	28.30	31.80	15.17	19.03	15.15	9.34
Savage, MN	24.10	24.40	12.00	19.78	15.00	10.49
Schererville, IN	21.60	23.00	8.86	20.22	12.21	7.76
Shawnee, KS	20.50	20.40	12.15	19.11	12.83	7.90
Shrewsbury, MA	26.30	26.60	17.34	21.32	17.27	11.03
S Brunswick, NJ	27.40	29.00	15.72	19.53	16.22	11.25
S. Jordan, UT	22.00	24.90	10.80	18.36	11.70	9.43
S. Kingstown, RI	29.10	29.00	11.33	18.75	14.46	9.52
Southaven, MS	19.60	20.60	12.04	19.75	13.85	8.00
Southlake, TX	22.40	23.80	9.61	17.47	13.97	7.67
Spanish Fork, UT	21.10	23.30	11.47	18.39	10.60	7.93
Sparks, NV	n/a	n/a	12.53	19.98	14.92	7.31
Stow, OH	23.80	26.70	9.74	17.98	13.74	8.72
Sugar Land, TX	22.00	23.30	10.47	16.73	13.11	7.74
Sun Prairie, WI	22.70	23.10	11.70	19.40	15.61	7.99
Tualatin, OR	24.20	24.40	11.78	18.32	14.49	10.53
Waimalu, HI	19.40	26.60	11.42	18.58	13.40	11.52
Wellington, FL	22.20	23.30	13.12	16.46	14.01	10.29
W Des Moines, IA	18.20	19.30	12.33	18.84	14.61	8.41
West Linn, OR	24.20	24.40	11.78	18.32	14.49	10.53
West Windsor, NJ	27.50	29.40	19.95	19.05	14.13	10.89
Weston, FL	n/a	n/a	12.93	15.96	14.49	9.63
Woodbury, MN	24.10	24.40	12.00	19.78	15.00	10.49
Woodridge, IL	27.90	33.20	13.01	21.41	15.56	9.03
Yorba Linda, CA	30.90	32.90	14.21	19.35	13.45	9.16

Notes: Wage data is for May 2007 and covers the Metropolitan Statistical Area - see Appendix A for areas included; hourly wages for elementary and secondary school teachers were calculated by the editors from annual wage data assuming a 40 hour work week; n/a not available

Source: Bureau of Labor Statistics, May 2007 Metro Area Occupational Employment and Wage Estimates

Means of Transportation to Work: City

City	Car/Truck/Van		Public Transportation			Bicycle	Walked	Other Means	Worked at Home
	Drove Alone	Car-pooled	Bus	Subway	Railroad				
Allen, TX	86.1	7.7	1.0	0.0	0.0	0.0	0.5	0.3	4.3
Ankeny, IA	86.1	7.5	1.7	0.0	0.0	0.1	1.2	0.2	3.2
Apex, NC	87.5	7.4	0.3	0.0	0.0	0.1	0.5	0.8	3.4
Bangor, ME	76.6	10.2	1.6	0.0	0.0	0.4	5.3	1.4	4.4
Beavercreek, OH	90.0	5.8	0.1	0.0	0.0	0.0	0.6	0.3	3.2
Bellevue, NE	85.1	10.7	0.2	0.0	0.0	0.1	1.1	0.4	2.4
Bend, OR	74.6	12.7	1.2	0.0	0.0	1.9	2.8	1.1	5.7
Bernards, NJ	83.0	5.0	0.8	0.2	4.5	0.1	0.7	0.3	5.3
Bethlehem, NY	86.2	6.4	1.8	0.1	0.2	0.2	1.4	0.3	3.5
Bozeman, MT	67.6	11.9	0.3	0.0	0.0	4.0	10.7	0.7	4.8
Brentwood, TN	85.4	5.9	0.3	0.1	0.0	0.0	0.7	0.8	6.7
Brookfield, WI	89.4	5.4	0.5	0.0	0.0	0.1	0.4	0.3	3.8
Broomfield, CO	80.5	9.8	3.6	0.1	0.0	0.3	1.1	0.9	3.6
Burlington, VT	62.4	12.0	3.2	0.1	0.0	1.2	16.8	1.2	3.1
Carmel, IN	87.0	6.4	0.0	0.0	0.0	0.1	0.9	0.4	5.1
Cary, NC	84.2	8.9	0.2	0.0	0.0	0.1	0.8	0.8	4.9
Casper, WY	83.0	11.2	0.5	0.0	0.0	0.1	1.6	0.9	2.7
Cheshire, CT	88.4	5.6	0.5	0.0	0.2	0.0	0.9	0.4	4.1
Chino Hills, CA	80.1	13.4	0.8	0.1	1.1	0.2	0.3	0.8	3.3
Collierville, TN	88.4	6.6	0.0	0.1	0.0	0.0	0.3	0.8	3.7
Conway, AR	78.6	14.5	0.1	0.0	0.1	0.6	3.5	0.4	2.2
Coronado, CA	51.7	10.4	2.1	0.1	0.0	3.0	18.0	7.0	7.8
Cranberry, PA	87.5	7.2	0.4	0.0	0.0	0.1	0.8	0.4	3.7
Dover, DE	76.8	13.0	1.0	0.1	0.0	0.5	4.9	1.0	2.7
Draper, UT	81.6	8.9	0.5	0.3	0.8	0.1	0.7	0.8	6.4
Dublin, OH	89.4	4.0	0.4	0.0	0.0	0.0	0.5	0.4	5.4
Edmond, OK	84.7	8.3	0.2	0.0	0.0	0.2	1.9	0.7	4.0
Evesham, NJ	83.2	7.4	0.5	2.2	1.9	0.0	1.2	0.5	3.1
Fargo, ND	83.6	7.7	0.4	0.0	0.0	0.6	4.4	0.6	2.9
Farmington, CT	90.4	4.5	0.8	0.0	0.1	0.1	1.1	0.5	2.6
Fishers, IN	89.9	4.1	0.0	0.1	0.0	0.0	0.4	0.6	4.9
Flower Mound, TX	84.1	7.3	0.3	0.0	0.0	0.1	0.5	1.4	6.4
Franklin, MA	81.9	5.2	0.2	0.2	6.3	0.0	1.4	0.5	4.4
Frederick, MD	73.9	15.1	0.9	0.4	0.2	0.4	4.9	1.3	3.0
Frisco, TX	85.0	8.9	0.1	0.0	0.0	0.1	0.6	0.9	4.3
Goodyear, AZ	77.5	15.2	0.1	0.0	0.0	0.7	1.4	1.5	3.5
Grand Blanc, MI	90.6	7.2	0.1	0.0	0.0	0.0	0.2	0.2	1.8
Greenburgh, NY	63.3	7.5	3.1	0.7	17.5	0.1	2.7	0.7	4.3
Greenwich, CT	64.4	6.0	0.6	0.5	15.9	0.1	3.7	1.1	7.7
Hampden, PA	88.1	6.8	0.2	0.0	0.0	0.2	1.4	0.3	3.0
Hilliard, OH	88.2	5.6	0.7	0.0	0.0	0.0	0.7	0.4	4.4
Hoover, AL	86.8	8.4	0.0	0.0	0.0	0.0	0.5	0.4	3.9
Huntersville, NC	84.0	10.0	0.4	0.0	0.0	0.0	0.5	0.5	4.6
Juneau, AK	62.9	18.5	3.1	0.0	0.0	0.6	8.0	2.5	4.3
Keller, TX	85.2	6.9	0.0	0.1	0.0	0.0	1.0	0.7	6.2
Kenner, LA	77.2	14.5	2.2	0.0	0.0	0.4	2.1	1.5	2.2
Kennesaw, GA	84.6	10.0	0.2	0.0	0.0	0.1	1.2	0.7	3.3
League City, TX	83.7	10.2	1.0	0.0	0.0	0.2	0.8	1.1	3.0
Leawood, KS	88.0	4.1	0.2	0.0	0.0	0.0	0.4	0.7	6.7
Lee's Summit, MO	88.3	7.2	0.1	0.0	0.0	0.1	0.6	0.2	3.6
Leesburg, VA	82.4	10.0	0.5	0.0	0.1	0.1	1.6	0.6	4.6
Lehi, UT	76.2	14.6	1.5	0.2	0.1	0.3	0.8	0.8	5.6
Lwr Providence, PA	86.3	6.6	0.4	0.0	0.9	0.1	1.0	0.2	4.5
Madison, AL	87.1	9.9	0.1	0.0	0.0	0.0	0.4	0.4	2.2
Manhattan Bch, CA	84.5	6.9	0.3	0.0	0.0	0.3	1.3	0.8	6.0
Maple Grove, MN	85.4	7.0	3.0	0.0	0.0	0.1	0.7	0.4	3.5
Marion, IA	84.9	9.0	1.2	0.0	0.0	0.3	0.8	0.7	3.1
Marlboro, NJ	68.9	8.9	10.3	0.3	6.4	0.0	0.4	0.6	4.1

City	Car/Truck/Van		Public Transportation			Bicycle	Walked	Other Means	Worked at Home
	Drove Alone	Car-pooled	Bus	Subway	Railroad				
Matthews, NC	85.1	8.7	0.8	0.0	0.0	0.1	0.8	0.4	4.2
Meridian, ID	84.9	10.1	0.0	0.0	0.0	0.3	0.4	0.4	3.8
Merrimack, NH	87.5	7.8	0.1	0.0	0.0	0.2	0.5	0.4	3.5
Morgantown, WV	64.5	9.9	0.6	0.4	0.0	1.0	16.8	3.0	3.7
Mt Pleasant, SC	85.6	7.6	0.1	0.0	0.0	0.1	0.9	1.5	4.3
Northampton, PA	85.2	6.6	0.0	0.1	3.0	0.0	0.6	0.5	4.0
Northville, MI	92.4	3.2	0.1	0.0	0.0	0.0	0.7	0.4	3.2
Novi, MI	91.1	5.2	0.2	0.0	0.0	0.2	0.5	0.3	2.5
O'Fallon, MO	85.8	9.0	0.1	0.2	0.0	0.0	1.0	0.7	3.3
Oro Valley, AZ	82.5	9.3	0.6	0.0	0.0	0.0	0.8	1.4	5.4
Oviedo, FL	84.9	8.5	0.1	0.0	0.0	0.6	0.4	1.4	4.1
Palm Bch Grdns, FL	84.6	7.6	0.1	0.0	0.1	0.2	1.1	0.9	5.4
Parker, CO	79.7	9.1	1.4	0.1	0.0	0.4	0.8	0.6	7.9
Peachtree City, GA	83.4	8.8	0.3	0.4	0.1	0.1	0.3	1.8	4.8
Pflugerville, TX	85.9	9.6	0.1	0.1	0.0	0.0	0.5	0.8	3.0
Pleasanton, CA	80.0	8.0	0.6	2.8	1.4	0.5	1.3	0.9	4.6
Rapid City, SD	84.1	9.9	0.7	0.0	0.0	0.2	2.1	0.6	2.4
Redmond, WA	76.1	11.3	4.2	0.0	0.0	0.8	2.8	0.5	4.3
Richland, WA	80.5	11.8	1.1	0.0	0.0	0.6	2.0	0.9	3.1
Richmond, KY	76.3	13.4	0.1	0.0	0.0	0.3	7.2	0.8	2.0
Rio Rancho, NM	84.4	10.5	0.4	0.0	0.0	0.2	0.4	0.8	3.1
Rockaway, NJ	85.1	9.3	0.8	0.0	1.2	0.1	0.8	0.3	2.5
Rocklin, CA	81.4	9.4	0.6	0.0	0.2	0.5	1.4	0.6	6.0
Rogers, AR	79.8	15.0	0.1	0.0	0.0	0.3	1.6	1.4	1.8
Round Rock, TX	82.9	12.8	0.1	0.0	0.0	0.4	0.5	0.7	2.7
Sammamish, WA	79.7	8.6	2.1	0.0	0.0	0.2	0.9	1.0	7.6
San Ramon, CA	79.7	8.8	0.3	4.1	0.4	0.3	1.0	0.6	4.8
Santa Fe, NM	72.4	13.3	1.1	0.0	0.0	0.8	4.1	1.0	7.3
Saratoga, CA	85.4	5.0	0.4	0.1	0.2	0.2	0.9	0.6	7.1
Savage, MN	85.1	8.3	1.3	0.0	0.0	0.2	0.5	0.3	4.3
Schererville, IN	85.7	7.7	0.1	0.0	2.2	0.1	1.4	0.8	2.1
Shawnee, KS	88.1	6.9	0.1	0.0	0.0	0.0	0.5	0.4	3.9
Shrewsbury, MA	87.6	7.1	0.4	0.1	0.7	0.1	1.4	0.3	2.4
S Brunswick, NJ	81.1	7.7	3.3	0.3	3.0	0.1	1.1	0.4	2.9
S. Jordan, UT	81.8	9.3	1.1	0.2	0.4	0.1	0.4	0.8	6.0
S Kingstown, RI	76.0	8.0	0.5	0.0	0.1	0.1	10.2	0.5	4.6
Southaven, MS	86.6	10.3	0.1	0.0	0.1	0.1	0.3	0.6	2.0
Southlake, TX	84.8	6.1	0.0	0.0	0.0	0.1	0.7	1.7	6.6
Spanish Fork, UT	77.5	14.8	1.2	0.0	0.0	0.1	1.5	0.7	4.2
Sparks, NV	76.3	14.2	2.8	0.0	0.0	0.7	2.5	1.2	2.2
Stow, OH	89.9	5.6	0.3	0.0	0.0	0.2	0.6	0.5	2.9
Sugar Land, TX	84.3	9.3	1.4	0.0	0.0	0.2	0.2	0.4	4.1
Sun Prairie, WI	86.9	8.3	0.1	0.0	0.0	0.1	1.4	0.4	2.7
Tualatin, OR	77.3	10.1	4.4	0.2	0.0	0.9	2.4	0.3	4.6
Waimalu, HI	67.6	22.2	5.2	0.0	0.0	0.3	1.6	1.3	1.7
Wellington, FL	81.7	9.1	0.3	0.1	0.1	0.3	0.6	1.0	6.6
W Des Moines, IA	84.2	8.4	1.9	0.0	0.0	0.1	1.2	0.5	3.7
West Linn, OR	78.5	8.7	2.6	0.1	0.1	0.2	1.4	0.5	7.9
West Windsor, NJ	66.5	4.4	0.6	0.4	20.6	0.3	1.2	0.4	5.5
Weston, FL	82.9	9.0	0.2	0.0	0.3	0.2	0.8	0.9	5.7
Woodbury, MN	84.4	9.0	1.5	0.0	0.0	0.0	0.6	0.5	4.0
Woodridge, IL	80.1	8.1	1.1	0.1	5.8	0.3	1.4	0.3	2.7
Yorba Linda, CA	83.8	8.8	0.2	0.0	0.2	0.2	0.8	0.6	5.4
U.S.	75.7	12.2	2.5	1.5	0.5	0.4	2.9	1.0	3.3

Note: Figures shown are percentages and cover workers 16 years of age and older
Source: Census 2000, Summary File 3

Means of Transportation to Work: Metro Area

MSA[1]	Car/Truck/Van		Public Transportation			Bicycle	Walked	Other Means	Worked at Home
	Drove Alone	Car-pooled	Bus	Subway	Railroad				
Allen, TX	77.6	14.3	2.1	0.1	0.1	0.1	1.5	1.0	3.1
Ankeny, IA	81.8	10.7	1.5	0.0	0.0	0.2	2.1	0.5	3.3
Apex, NC	78.5	12.9	1.5	0.0	0.0	0.4	2.3	0.9	3.5
Bangor, ME	78.9	10.3	0.8	0.0	0.0	0.2	5.1	1.0	3.6
Beavercreek, OH	84.0	8.9	1.7	0.0	0.0	0.2	2.4	0.6	2.3
Bellevue, NE	82.9	10.5	1.1	0.0	0.0	0.1	1.9	0.6	2.9
Bend, OR	n/a	n/a	n/a	n/a	n/a	n/a	n/a	n/a	n/a
Bernards, NJ	77.2	9.9	2.7	0.2	3.6	0.2	2.4	0.9	2.9
Bethlehem, NY	79.4	9.9	2.8	0.0	0.1	0.2	3.8	0.8	3.0
Bozeman, MT	n/a	n/a	n/a	n/a	n/a	n/a	n/a	n/a	n/a
Brentwood, TN	80.7	12.8	0.9	0.0	0.0	0.1	1.5	0.8	3.2
Brookfield, WI	79.7	9.9	4.1	0.0	0.0	0.2	2.9	0.6	2.6
Broomfield, CO	76.1	11.6	4.4	0.1	0.0	0.4	2.1	0.8	4.5
Burlington, VT	75.7	11.8	1.1	0.0	0.0	0.5	6.1	0.7	4.1
Carmel, IN	82.8	10.5	1.2	0.0	0.0	0.2	1.7	0.7	2.9
Cary, NC	78.5	12.9	1.5	0.0	0.0	0.4	2.3	0.9	3.5
Casper, WY	82.7	11.3	0.4	0.0	0.0	0.1	1.4	0.8	3.3
Cheshire, CT	79.1	9.6	2.8	0.0	0.8	0.3	3.9	0.6	2.8
Chino Hills, CA	73.5	17.6	1.2	0.0	0.4	0.5	2.2	1.2	3.5
Collierville, TN	80.9	13.0	1.6	0.0	0.0	0.1	1.3	0.9	2.2
Conway, AR	81.6	13.2	0.7	0.0	0.0	0.2	1.3	0.9	2.3
Coronado, CA	73.9	13.0	2.9	0.0	0.2	0.6	3.4	1.6	4.4
Cranberry, PA	77.4	9.7	5.6	0.1	0.0	0.1	3.6	1.0	2.4
Dover, DE	79.7	12.9	0.8	0.0	0.0	0.2	2.3	1.0	3.1
Draper, UT	77.2	13.1	2.5	0.1	0.2	0.4	1.8	0.9	3.8
Dublin, OH	82.0	9.6	2.2	0.0	0.0	0.2	2.4	0.6	3.0
Edmond, OK	81.8	12.0	0.5	0.0	0.0	0.2	1.7	1.0	2.8
Evesham, NJ	72.3	10.1	5.5	1.8	2.1	0.3	4.1	0.9	2.9
Fargo, ND	81.8	8.6	0.4	0.0	0.0	0.5	4.7	0.5	3.5
Farmington, CT	82.5	9.0	2.7	0.0	0.0	0.2	2.5	0.6	2.5
Fishers, IN	82.8	10.5	1.2	0.0	0.0	0.2	1.7	0.7	2.9
Flower Mound, TX	77.6	14.3	2.1	0.1	0.1	0.1	1.5	1.0	3.1
Franklin, MA	68.2	8.2	4.1	6.5	2.1	0.5	5.3	1.6	3.4
Frederick, MD	67.8	13.4	4.0	6.5	0.4	0.3	3.0	0.9	3.7
Frisco, TX	77.6	14.3	2.1	0.1	0.1	0.1	1.5	1.0	3.1
Goodyear, AZ	74.6	15.3	1.8	0.0	0.0	0.9	2.1	1.4	3.7
Grand Blanc, MI	84.3	10.6	1.2	0.0	0.0	0.1	1.2	0.6	2.0
Greenburgh, NY	31.4	8.3	10.4	31.8	3.0	0.4	9.3	2.5	3.0
Greenwich, CT	69.1	8.4	2.6	0.2	9.9	0.1	2.9	0.9	5.9
Hampden, PA	80.2	11.0	1.0	0.0	0.0	0.2	3.6	0.8	3.1
Hilliard, OH	82.0	9.6	2.2	0.0	0.0	0.2	2.4	0.6	3.0
Hoover, AL	83.5	11.7	0.7	0.0	0.0	0.1	1.2	0.7	2.2
Huntersville, NC	80.9	12.9	1.3	0.0	0.0	0.1	1.2	0.8	2.8
Juneau, AK	n/a	n/a	n/a	n/a	n/a	n/a	n/a	n/a	n/a
Keller, TX	81.2	13.3	0.4	0.0	0.0	0.1	1.4	0.9	2.7
Kenner, LA	73.0	14.6	5.0	0.0	0.0	0.6	2.7	1.6	2.4
Kennesaw, GA	77.0	13.6	2.4	1.0	0.1	0.1	1.3	1.1	3.5
League City, TX	78.2	13.6	1.0	0.0	0.0	0.7	2.3	1.6	2.5
Leawood, KS	82.8	10.4	1.2	0.0	0.0	0.1	1.4	0.7	3.4
Lee's Summit, MO	82.8	10.4	1.2	0.0	0.0	0.1	1.4	0.7	3.4
Leesburg, VA	67.8	13.4	4.0	6.5	0.4	0.3	3.0	0.9	3.7
Lehi, UT	72.5	14.9	1.3	0.0	0.0	0.8	4.9	0.5	5.0
Lwr Providence, PA	72.3	10.1	5.5	1.8	2.1	0.3	4.1	0.9	2.9
Madison, AL	83.9	11.5	0.2	0.0	0.0	0.1	1.3	0.7	2.3
Manhattan Bch, CA	70.4	15.1	6.1	0.2	0.2	0.6	2.9	1.1	3.5
Maple Grove, MN	78.3	10.0	4.4	0.0	0.0	0.4	2.4	0.6	3.8
Marion, IA	82.3	10.3	0.9	0.0	0.0	0.3	2.6	0.6	2.9
Marlboro, NJ	78.7	9.8	3.0	0.1	2.3	0.3	1.8	1.1	3.0

MSA[1]	Car/Truck/Van Drove Alone	Car/Truck/Van Car-pooled	Public Transportation Bus	Public Transportation Subway	Public Transportation Railroad	Bicycle	Walked	Other Means	Worked at Home
Matthews, NC	80.9	12.9	1.3	0.0	0.0	0.1	1.2	0.8	2.8
Meridian, ID	79.9	11.4	0.6	0.0	0.0	1.0	2.2	0.8	4.1
Merrimack, NH	84.8	8.7	0.3	0.0	0.2	0.1	1.6	0.7	3.5
Morgantown, WV	n/a	n/a	n/a	n/a	n/a	n/a	n/a	n/a	n/a
Mt Pleasant, SC	78.1	13.0	1.1	0.0	0.0	0.5	3.5	1.6	2.2
Northampton, PA	72.3	10.1	5.5	1.8	2.1	0.3	4.1	0.9	2.9
Northville, MI	84.8	9.2	1.7	0.0	0.0	0.1	1.4	0.6	2.1
Novi, MI	84.8	9.2	1.7	0.0	0.0	0.1	1.4	0.6	2.1
O'Fallon, MO	82.6	9.9	2.1	0.2	0.0	0.1	1.6	0.7	2.8
Oro Valley, AZ	73.8	14.7	2.4	0.0	0.0	1.4	2.6	1.4	3.6
Oviedo, FL	80.6	12.1	1.6	0.0	0.0	0.4	1.3	1.2	2.9
Palm Bch Grdns, FL	79.6	11.9	1.1	0.0	0.1	0.5	1.4	1.2	4.1
Parker, CO	76.1	11.6	4.4	0.1	0.0	0.4	2.1	0.8	4.5
Peachtree City, GA	77.0	13.6	2.4	1.0	0.1	0.1	1.3	1.1	3.5
Pflugerville, TX	76.5	13.7	2.5	0.0	0.0	0.6	2.1	1.1	3.6
Pleasanton, CA	67.9	13.7	3.4	5.7	0.6	0.9	2.5	1.4	3.8
Rapid City, SD	82.9	10.4	0.5	0.0	0.0	0.1	2.3	0.6	3.1
Redmond, WA	70.4	12.6	7.8	0.0	0.0	0.7	3.2	0.9	4.4
Richland, WA	77.8	14.5	1.0	0.0	0.0	0.3	1.7	1.0	3.8
Richmond, KY	79.8	11.9	0.7	0.0	0.0	0.4	3.9	0.6	2.7
Rio Rancho, NM	77.7	13.3	1.2	0.0	0.0	0.8	2.3	0.9	3.9
Rockaway, NJ	71.8	10.6	6.1	0.7	3.6	0.2	3.0	1.0	3.0
Rocklin, CA	76.2	13.6	2.0	0.1	0.2	0.7	2.0	1.2	4.1
Rogers, AR	79.8	13.1	0.3	0.0	0.0	0.2	2.3	0.8	3.4
Round Rock, TX	76.5	13.7	2.5	0.0	0.0	0.6	2.1	1.1	3.6
Sammamish, WA	70.4	12.6	7.8	0.0	0.0	0.7	3.2	0.9	4.4
San Ramon, CA	67.9	13.7	3.4	5.7	0.6	0.9	2.5	1.4	3.8
Santa Fe, NM	72.7	15.0	0.5	0.0	0.0	0.7	3.0	1.0	6.9
Saratoga, CA	77.3	12.2	2.6	0.1	0.6	1.2	1.8	1.0	3.1
Savage, MN	78.3	10.0	4.4	0.0	0.0	0.4	2.4	0.6	3.8
Schererville, IN	81.9	10.4	0.8	0.1	1.7	0.2	2.0	0.7	2.1
Shawnee, KS	82.8	10.4	1.2	0.0	0.0	0.1	1.4	0.7	3.4
Shrewsbury, MA	82.3	9.3	1.2	0.0	0.4	0.1	3.3	0.7	2.6
S Brunswick, NJ	77.2	9.9	2.7	0.2	3.6	0.2	2.4	0.9	2.9
S. Jordan, UT	77.2	13.1	2.5	0.1	0.2	0.4	1.8	0.9	3.8
S Kingstown, RI	80.7	10.6	1.7	0.0	0.6	0.2	3.3	0.8	2.1
Southaven, MS	80.9	13.0	1.6	0.0	0.0	0.1	1.3	0.9	2.2
Southlake, TX	81.2	13.3	0.4	0.0	0.0	0.1	1.4	0.9	2.7
Spanish Fork, UT	72.5	14.9	1.3	0.0	0.0	0.8	4.9	0.5	5.0
Sparks, NV	75.3	13.8	3.0	0.0	0.0	0.7	3.2	1.2	2.9
Stow, OH	85.4	8.0	1.3	0.0	0.0	0.1	2.0	0.6	2.6
Sugar Land, TX	76.6	14.4	3.4	0.0	0.0	0.3	1.6	1.2	2.5
Sun Prairie, WI	74.1	9.5	4.0	0.0	0.0	1.7	6.2	0.6	3.8
Tualatin, OR	73.1	11.5	5.3	0.4	0.2	0.8	3.0	1.1	4.6
Waimalu, HI	61.4	19.4	8.1	0.0	0.0	0.9	5.6	1.7	2.9
Wellington, FL	79.6	11.9	1.1	0.0	0.1	0.5	1.4	1.2	4.1
W Des Moines, IA	81.8	10.7	1.5	0.0	0.0	0.2	2.1	0.5	3.3
West Linn, OR	73.1	11.5	5.3	0.4	0.2	0.8	3.0	1.1	4.6
West Windsor, NJ	73.3	11.0	2.9	0.1	3.7	0.5	4.5	0.8	3.2
Weston, FL	80.0	12.0	1.9	0.0	0.1	0.5	1.3	1.1	2.9
Woodbury, MN	78.3	10.0	4.4	0.0	0.0	0.4	2.4	0.6	3.8
Woodridge, IL	69.3	11.0	5.0	3.6	3.5	0.3	3.2	1.1	3.0
Yorba Linda, CA	76.5	13.3	2.5	0.0	0.2	0.8	2.0	0.9	3.7
U.S.	75.7	12.2	2.5	1.5	0.5	0.4	2.9	1.0	3.3

Note: Figures shown are percentages and cover workers 16 years of age and older; (1) Metropolitan Statistical Area - see Appendix A for areas included

Source: Census 2000, Summary File 3

Travel Time to Work: City

City	Less Than 15 Minutes	15 to 29 Minutes	30 to 44 Minutes	45 to 59 Minutes	60 Minutes or More
Allen, TX	19.8	32.0	25.1	13.3	9.8
Ankeny, IA	31.6	48.0	16.8	1.9	1.7
Apex, NC	19.8	39.3	32.5	5.5	2.8
Bangor, ME	62.1	27.4	4.5	2.3	3.6
Beavercreek, OH	32.1	54.2	9.5	1.7	2.5
Bellevue, NE	31.7	50.2	14.1	2.0	2.0
Bend, OR	58.6	29.8	7.0	2.0	2.5
Bernards, NJ	21.5	32.2	21.5	9.6	15.2
Bethlehem, NY	28.1	52.5	14.6	1.7	3.1
Bozeman, MT	69.1	23.3	3.1	1.0	3.5
Brentwood, TN	23.8	51.3	18.8	2.2	3.9
Brookfield, WI	32.3	49.7	13.6	2.5	1.9
Broomfield, CO	19.6	35.2	29.4	9.7	6.1
Burlington, VT	46.3	39.0	10.0	2.7	2.1
Carmel, IN	27.8	37.7	24.2	6.5	3.8
Cary, NC	23.7	47.6	21.5	4.1	3.1
Casper, WY	58.2	33.7	3.4	1.3	3.5
Cheshire, CT	25.0	36.7	27.5	6.7	4.2
Chino Hills, CA	12.7	23.5	23.5	16.7	23.6
Collierville, TN	23.4	31.3	31.5	10.4	3.4
Conway, AR	48.6	23.0	15.9	9.4	3.2
Coronado, CA	51.4	31.1	10.4	2.8	4.3
Cranberry, PA	27.2	24.3	32.1	11.5	4.9
Dover, DE	55.4	27.4	5.6	4.1	7.5
Draper, UT	24.8	35.8	28.5	6.1	4.8
Dublin, OH	28.2	37.4	26.3	4.4	3.7
Edmond, OK	29.2	44.0	21.0	2.6	3.1
Evesham, NJ	21.9	35.2	20.4	10.6	11.9
Fargo, ND	56.9	36.6	2.8	1.1	2.6
Farmington, CT	23.9	48.4	19.2	4.5	3.9
Fishers, IN	21.5	40.9	28.3	5.8	3.5
Flower Mound, TX	15.8	28.8	30.6	17.7	7.1
Franklin, MA	25.4	23.7	22.3	12.1	16.5
Frederick, MD	37.0	24.9	11.9	10.1	16.2
Frisco, TX	16.7	27.8	28.9	17.7	8.9
Goodyear, AZ	22.4	28.4	29.9	12.7	6.6
Grand Blanc, MI	29.0	38.7	12.7	9.8	9.9
Greenburgh, NY	20.9	30.4	18.9	9.6	20.1
Greenwich, CT	33.8	30.6	8.0	5.7	21.9
Hampden, PA	30.2	54.1	11.1	2.2	2.4
Hilliard, OH	28.8	43.7	19.4	4.4	3.7
Hoover, AL	21.5	49.6	22.1	3.6	3.2
Huntersville, NC	17.8	31.2	29.7	13.5	7.7
Juneau, AK	51.3	37.6	6.8	1.4	2.9
Keller, TX	15.6	32.4	30.0	14.1	7.9
Kenner, LA	22.3	35.9	25.5	10.2	6.1
Kennesaw, GA	17.0	24.1	23.8	15.5	19.5
League City, TX	18.6	37.4	23.4	11.8	8.8
Leawood, KS	32.2	44.0	19.3	2.3	2.3
Lee's Summit, MO	25.8	32.6	29.5	9.0	3.1
Leesburg, VA	27.5	28.0	21.7	12.8	10.0
Lehi, UT	30.2	39.0	19.8	6.7	4.3
Lwr Providence, PA	22.3	35.7	23.7	9.5	8.8
Madison, AL	30.9	56.0	10.4	1.2	1.5
Manhattan Bch, CA	25.1	29.0	21.9	14.5	9.4
Maple Grove, MN	19.6	38.6	30.4	8.3	3.1
Marion, IA	36.8	47.5	10.3	2.6	2.7
Marlboro, NJ	17.4	18.6	16.0	10.5	37.4
Matthews, NC	21.4	32.0	27.5	13.4	5.6

City	Less Than 15 Minutes	15 to 29 Minutes	30 to 44 Minutes	45 to 59 Minutes	60 Minutes or More
Meridian, ID	23.2	54.7	17.6	1.9	2.7
Merrimack, NH	23.0	45.4	14.5	7.3	9.8
Morgantown, WV	56.5	31.8	5.8	2.6	3.3
Mt Pleasant, SC	29.1	46.4	17.9	2.5	4.1
Northampton, PA	19.6	32.7	21.8	11.1	14.8
Northville, MI	22.5	31.3	33.4	9.0	3.7
Novi, MI	22.7	33.8	27.0	12.1	4.4
O'Fallon, MO	21.2	30.2	29.5	13.4	5.7
Oro Valley, AZ	15.2	29.5	34.2	16.3	4.8
Oviedo, FL	18.3	30.8	29.1	15.1	6.7
Palm Bch Grdns, FL	29.5	47.3	15.3	3.7	4.2
Parker, CO	14.2	38.3	31.4	9.8	6.3
Peachtree City, GA	30.0	19.3	26.4	13.4	11.0
Pflugerville, TX	19.2	41.6	27.7	6.0	5.6
Pleasanton, CA	29.0	23.2	16.4	10.2	21.2
Rapid City, SD	53.1	38.2	4.9	1.1	2.6
Redmond, WA	34.9	39.8	17.4	4.4	3.5
Richland, WA	45.6	36.0	11.3	4.6	2.5
Richmond, KY	48.6	22.8	16.9	7.6	4.0
Rio Rancho, NM	23.8	31.7	27.1	11.4	5.9
Rockaway, NJ	21.1	30.8	24.2	13.0	10.9
Rocklin, CA	28.6	30.1	24.5	10.2	6.7
Rogers, AR	46.2	38.8	10.9	1.7	2.4
Round Rock, TX	24.0	33.1	27.1	10.6	5.2
Sammamish, WA	11.3	33.1	38.4	12.2	4.9
San Ramon, CA	28.9	27.2	15.9	9.1	18.8
Santa Fe, NM	50.6	33.1	8.6	4.2	3.5
Saratoga, CA	17.3	39.7	32.0	7.4	3.6
Savage, MN	20.4	41.9	27.9	7.1	2.6
Schererville, IN	18.2	37.1	25.1	7.3	12.3
Shawnee, KS	24.3	53.5	18.7	2.1	1.4
Shrewsbury, MA	29.6	35.6	15.4	9.5	9.9
S Brunswick, NJ	19.0	32.0	21.2	9.3	18.5
S. Jordan, UT	20.4	38.9	28.6	6.9	5.2
S Kingstown, RI	41.0	27.0	18.1	8.3	5.5
Southaven, MS	21.6	45.3	25.6	4.4	3.2
Southlake, TX	18.3	29.9	33.1	12.6	6.1
Spanish Fork, UT	42.2	41.0	8.1	3.7	5.0
Sparks, NV	35.4	51.7	8.3	1.9	2.7
Stow, OH	27.1	42.0	19.1	7.5	4.3
Sugar Land, TX	18.9	29.5	29.4	15.2	7.0
Sun Prairie, WI	38.0	36.3	18.5	3.9	3.3
Tualatin, OR	32.4	36.3	23.8	4.9	2.6
Waimalu, HI	17.6	39.9	23.1	10.3	9.1
Wellington, FL	23.2	22.5	29.1	15.8	9.4
W Des Moines, IA	39.1	49.6	7.5	1.6	2.2
West Linn, OR	20.3	46.4	25.0	4.8	3.5
West Windsor, NJ	21.8	27.7	10.5	6.9	33.1
Weston, FL	17.3	25.9	29.6	16.9	10.4
Woodbury, MN	23.3	42.9	25.4	5.5	2.8
Woodridge, IL	18.5	35.2	23.1	10.1	13.0
Yorba Linda, CA	20.2	29.9	27.4	11.9	10.7
U.S.	29.4	36.1	19.1	7.4	8.0

Note: Figures are percentages and include workers 16 years old and over
Source: Census 2000, Summary File 3

Travel Time to Work: Metro Area

MSA[1]	Less Than 15 Minutes	15 to 29 Minutes	30 to 44 Minutes	45 to 59 Minutes	60 Minutes or More
Allen, TX	22.0	35.0	24.7	10.4	7.9
Ankeny, IA	35.2	46.7	13.0	2.8	2.3
Apex, NC	24.7	40.4	22.3	7.4	5.2
Bangor, ME	45.1	40.2	8.3	2.5	3.9
Beavercreek, OH	33.3	44.5	14.8	3.7	3.8
Bellevue, NE	33.9	48.4	12.9	2.2	2.5
Bend, OR	n/a	n/a	n/a	n/a	n/a
Bernards, NJ	23.3	31.2	20.7	10.3	14.6
Bethlehem, NY	30.8	41.0	18.4	5.5	4.2
Bozeman, MT	n/a	n/a	n/a	n/a	n/a
Brentwood, TN	23.9	38.6	23.0	8.8	5.7
Brookfield, WI	29.7	43.7	18.3	4.6	3.7
Broomfield, CO	21.6	38.4	25.3	8.6	6.1
Burlington, VT	36.8	40.9	15.9	3.6	2.9
Carmel, IN	27.0	40.8	21.6	6.1	4.4
Cary, NC	24.7	40.4	22.3	7.4	5.2
Casper, WY	53.7	36.5	4.6	1.4	3.8
Cheshire, CT	31.8	40.9	16.4	5.2	5.7
Chino Hills, CA	26.0	32.5	17.7	8.4	15.4
Collierville, TN	22.9	43.4	23.2	6.1	4.4
Conway, AR	29.4	41.1	19.3	6.1	4.1
Coronado, CA	24.7	40.7	21.6	6.7	6.4
Cranberry, PA	28.3	36.4	20.2	8.3	6.9
Dover, DE	36.4	37.5	13.2	5.5	7.4
Draper, UT	29.2	43.6	18.0	4.8	4.4
Dublin, OH	26.6	44.1	19.6	5.5	4.2
Edmond, OK	30.2	43.4	18.3	4.4	3.7
Evesham, NJ	23.7	33.2	22.6	10.4	10.0
Fargo, ND	51.2	37.9	6.1	2.0	2.8
Farmington, CT	29.9	41.0	19.3	5.3	4.5
Fishers, IN	27.0	40.8	21.6	6.1	4.4
Flower Mound, TX	22.0	35.0	24.7	10.4	7.9
Franklin, MA	23.3	31.4	24.3	11.0	10.1
Frederick, MD	16.3	30.3	25.7	13.7	14.0
Frisco, TX	22.0	35.0	24.7	10.4	7.9
Goodyear, AZ	23.8	37.0	24.1	8.8	6.3
Grand Blanc, MI	28.9	40.4	13.6	7.9	9.3
Greenburgh, NY	13.3	24.0	24.4	14.9	23.5
Greenwich, CT	31.7	33.8	13.7	5.1	15.7
Hampden, PA	32.7	41.3	15.7	5.9	4.4
Hilliard, OH	26.6	44.1	19.6	5.5	4.2
Hoover, AL	21.4	40.4	24.4	8.1	5.6
Huntersville, NC	23.8	38.7	23.0	8.5	6.1
Juneau, AK	n/a	n/a	n/a	n/a	n/a
Keller, TX	23.4	37.8	22.6	8.8	7.5
Kenner, LA	24.5	38.1	21.1	8.5	7.9
Kennesaw, GA	18.3	32.4	25.1	12.4	11.8
League City, TX	28.7	34.5	19.7	8.7	8.3
Leawood, KS	28.0	41.9	20.6	5.8	3.7
Lee's Summit, MO	28.0	41.9	20.6	5.8	3.7
Leesburg, VA	16.3	30.3	25.7	13.7	14.0
Lehi, UT	45.0	35.9	10.7	4.2	4.2
Lwr Providence, PA	23.7	33.2	22.6	10.4	10.0
Madison, AL	28.7	44.5	19.1	4.6	3.0
Manhattan Bch, CA	20.7	34.6	24.1	9.7	10.9
Maple Grove, MN	26.4	41.4	21.3	6.7	4.2
Marion, IA	43.6	42.0	9.9	2.1	2.5
Marlboro, NJ	26.3	28.3	16.7	9.0	19.8
Matthews, NC	23.8	38.7	23.0	8.5	6.1

MSA[1]	Less Than 15 Minutes	15 to 29 Minutes	30 to 44 Minutes	45 to 59 Minutes	60 Minutes or More
Meridian, ID	33.1	45.9	15.3	3.1	2.7
Merrimack, NH	29.5	33.8	17.9	8.4	10.4
Morgantown, WV	n/a	n/a	n/a	n/a	n/a
Mt Pleasant, SC	26.7	39.6	21.5	6.9	5.2
Northampton, PA	23.7	33.2	22.6	10.4	10.0
Northville, MI	23.4	38.4	23.3	8.5	6.4
Novi, MI	23.4	38.4	23.3	8.5	6.4
O'Fallon, MO	24.9	37.9	23.1	8.4	5.6
Oro Valley, AZ	25.8	42.4	21.5	5.6	4.7
Oviedo, FL	21.1	38.1	25.8	8.8	6.2
Palm Bch Grdns, FL	25.2	39.4	22.1	6.8	6.5
Parker, CO	21.6	38.4	25.3	8.6	6.1
Peachtree City, GA	18.3	32.4	25.1	12.4	11.8
Pflugerville, TX	24.5	38.6	22.5	8.3	6.1
Pleasanton, CA	20.9	30.0	21.5	11.7	15.9
Rapid City, SD	45.8	42.5	6.9	1.7	3.0
Redmond, WA	22.1	36.9	23.9	9.2	7.9
Richland, WA	37.3	38.3	13.8	6.0	4.7
Richmond, KY	35.1	40.6	15.7	4.8	3.8
Rio Rancho, NM	26.9	45.1	18.4	5.3	4.3
Rockaway, NJ	22.8	31.6	21.3	10.0	14.2
Rocklin, CA	25.2	39.3	21.7	6.9	6.8
Rogers, AR	39.5	38.8	14.9	3.8	3.0
Round Rock, TX	24.5	38.6	22.5	8.3	6.1
Sammamish, WA	22.1	36.9	23.9	9.2	7.9
San Ramon, CA	20.9	30.0	21.5	11.7	15.9
Santa Fe, NM	37.3	37.0	15.0	6.3	4.6
Saratoga, CA	21.1	40.8	23.4	7.9	6.8
Savage, MN	26.4	41.4	21.3	6.7	4.2
Schererville, IN	27.1	36.6	19.6	7.2	9.6
Shawnee, KS	28.0	41.9	20.6	5.8	3.7
Shrewsbury, MA	30.0	35.4	18.5	7.8	8.3
S Brunswick, NJ	23.3	31.2	20.7	10.3	14.6
S. Jordan, UT	29.2	43.6	18.0	4.8	4.4
S Kingstown, RI	32.2	39.9	16.3	5.4	6.2
Southaven, MS	22.9	43.4	23.2	6.1	4.4
Southlake, TX	23.4	37.8	22.6	8.8	7.5
Spanish Fork, UT	45.0	35.9	10.7	4.2	4.2
Sparks, NV	35.2	49.2	9.5	2.7	3.3
Stow, OH	30.1	41.0	17.9	6.4	4.6
Sugar Land, TX	20.3	33.8	25.5	11.1	9.3
Sun Prairie, WI	35.1	45.2	14.0	2.7	3.0
Tualatin, OR	26.3	40.0	21.1	7.0	5.5
Waimalu, HI	23.5	34.3	23.8	9.5	8.9
Wellington, FL	25.2	39.4	22.1	6.8	6.5
W Des Moines, IA	35.2	46.7	13.0	2.8	2.3
West Linn, OR	26.3	40.0	21.1	7.0	5.5
West Windsor, NJ	28.4	38.3	15.7	6.3	11.3
Weston, FL	20.9	36.5	26.0	9.5	7.1
Woodbury, MN	26.4	41.4	21.3	6.7	4.2
Woodridge, IL	20.4	29.8	24.0	12.2	13.6
Yorba Linda, CA	22.1	37.6	23.8	8.0	8.5
U.S.	29.4	36.1	19.1	7.4	8.0

Note: Figures are percentages and include workers 16 years old and over; (1) Metropolitan Statistical Area - see Appendix A for areas included
Source: Census 2000, Summary File 3

2004 Presidential Election Results

City	Area Covered	Bush	Kerry	Nader	Other
Allen, TX	Collin County	71.2	28.1	0.1	0.6
Ankeny, IA	Polk County	47.3	51.9	0.3	0.5
Apex, NC	Wake County	50.8	48.7	0.1	0.4
Bangor, ME	Penobscot County	49.1	49.2	1.0	0.7
Beavercreek, OH	Greene County	61.0	38.5	0.0	0.5
Bellevue, NE	Sarpy County	68.9	29.9	0.6	0.7
Bend, OR	Deschutes County	56.4	42.1	0.0	1.5
Bernards, NJ	Somerset County	51.7	47.4	0.6	0.4
Bethlehem, NY	Albany County	37.3	60.7	1.8	0.3
Bozeman, MT	Gallatin County	56.2	41.2	1.4	1.2
Brentwood, TN	Williamson County	72.1	27.3	0.3	0.3
Brookfield, WI	Waukesha County	67.3	32.0	0.4	0.4
Broomfield, CO	Broomfield County	51.7	47.1	0.6	0.6
Burlington, VT	Chittenden County	34.0	63.5	1.7	0.8
Carmel, IN	Hamilton County	74.2	25.2	0.0	0.6
Cary, NC	Wake County	50.8	48.7	0.1	0.4
Casper, WY	Natrona County	67.1	30.8	1.0	1.1
Cheshire, CT	New Haven County	43.8	54.3	0.9	1.0
Chino Hills, CA	San Bernardino County	55.3	43.6	0.0	1.1
Collierville, TN	Shelby County	41.9	57.5	0.3	0.3
Conway, AR	Faulkner County	58.6	39.6	0.6	1.1
Coronado, CA	San Diego County	52.5	46.4	0.1	1.0
Cranberry, PA	Butler County	64.3	35.2	0.0	0.4
Dover, DE	Kent County	56.4	42.6	0.6	0.3
Draper, UT	Salt Lake County	59.6	37.5	1.7	1.2
Dublin, OH	Franklin County	45.1	54.4	0.0	0.5
Edmond, OK	Oklahoma County	64.2	35.8	0.0	0.0
Evesham, NJ	Burlington County	46.1	53.1	0.5	0.3
Fargo, ND	Cass County	59.4	39.0	1.1	0.5
Farmington, CT	Hartford County	39.5	58.7	0.8	1.0
Fishers, IN	Hamilton County	74.2	25.2	0.0	0.6
Flower Mound, TX	Denton County	70.0	29.5	0.0	0.5
Franklin, MA	Norfolk County	38.6	60.2	0.2	1.0
Frederick, MD	Frederick County	59.6	39.3	0.5	0.7
Frisco, TX	Collin County	71.2	28.1	0.1	0.6
Goodyear, AZ	Maricopa County	57.0	42.3	0.1	0.6
Grand Blanc, MI	Genesee County	39.2	60.0	0.4	0.3
Greenburgh, NY	Westchester County	40.3	58.1	1.4	0.2
Greenwich, CT	Fairfield County	47.3	51.4	0.6	0.8
Hampden, PA	Cumberland County	63.8	35.8	0.0	0.5
Hilliard, OH	Franklin County	45.1	54.4	0.0	0.5
Hoover, AL	Jefferson County	54.2	45.2	0.3	0.3
Huntersville, NC	Mecklenburg County	48.0	51.6	0.1	0.3
Juneau, AK	Alaska	61.1	35.5	1.6	1.8
Keller, TX	Tarrant County	62.4	37.0	0.1	0.5
Kenner, LA	Jefferson Parish	61.5	37.6	0.5	0.4
Kennesaw, GA	Cobb County	62.1	37.2	0.1	0.6
League City, TX	Galveston County	57.8	41.4	0.2	0.5
Leawood, KS	Johnson County	61.1	37.8	0.5	0.5
Lee's Summit, MO	Jackson County	41.3	58.1	0.0	0.6
Leesburg, VA	Loudoun County	55.7	43.6	0.0	0.7
Lehi, UT	Utah County	86.0	11.6	0.9	1.5
Lwr Providence, PA	Montgomery County	44.0	55.6	0.0	0.5
Madison, AL	Madison County	58.9	40.2	0.4	0.5
Manhattan Bch, CA	Los Angeles County	35.6	63.1	0.1	1.2
Maple Grove, MN	Hennepin County	39.4	59.3	0.6	0.6
Marion, IA	Linn County	44.6	54.6	0.4	0.4
Marlboro, NJ	Monmouth County	54.6	44.6	0.6	0.3
Matthews, NC	Mecklenburg County	48.0	51.6	0.1	0.3
Meridian, ID	Ada County	61.0	37.7	0.2	1.0

City	Area Covered	Bush	Kerry	Nader	Other
Merrimack, NH	Hillsborough County	51.0	48.2	0.6	0.2
Morgantown, WV	Monongalia County	51.5	47.6	0.6	0.3
Mt Pleasant, SC	Charleston County	51.6	46.8	0.4	1.2
Northampton, PA	Bucks County	48.3	51.1	0.0	0.6
Northville, MI	Wayne County	29.8	69.4	0.4	0.4
Novi, MI	Oakland County	49.3	49.8	0.4	0.5
O'Fallon, MO	St. Charles County	58.6	40.9	0.0	0.5
Oro Valley, AZ	Pima County	46.6	52.6	0.1	0.7
Oviedo, FL	Seminole County	58.1	41.3	0.3	0.3
Palm Bch Grdns, FL	Palm Beach County	39.1	60.4	0.3	0.3
Parker, CO	Douglas County	66.5	32.7	0.3	0.4
Peachtree City, GA	Fayette County	71.1	28.3	0.1	0.5
Pflugerville, TX	Travis County	42.0	56.0	0.4	1.6
Pleasanton, CA	Alameda County	23.3	75.2	0.2	1.3
Rapid City, SD	Pennington County	66.7	31.6	1.2	0.5
Redmond, WA	King County	33.6	64.9	0.7	0.8
Richland, WA	Benton County	66.3	32.2	0.6	0.9
Richmond, KY	Madison County	61.6	37.5	0.6	0.3
Rio Rancho, NM	Sandoval County	50.8	48.1	0.5	0.6
Rockaway, NJ	Morris County	57.5	41.7	0.5	0.3
Rocklin, CA	Placer County	62.6	36.3	0.2	0.9
Rogers, AR	Benton County	68.4	30.5	0.6	0.6
Round Rock, TX	Williamson County	65.0	33.6	0.2	1.2
Sammamish, WA	King County	33.6	64.9	0.7	0.8
San Ramon, CA	Contra Costa County	36.5	62.3	0.2	1.0
Santa Fe, NM	Santa Fe County	27.9	71.1	0.5	0.5
Saratoga, CA	Santa Clara County	34.6	63.9	0.2	1.2
Savage, MN	Scott County	59.5	39.5	0.5	0.5
Schererville, IN	Lake County	38.2	61.0	0.0	0.7
Shawnee, KS	Johnson County	61.1	37.8	0.5	0.5
Shrewsbury, MA	Worcester County	42.3	56.4	0.1	1.2
S Brunswick, NJ	Middlesex County	42.8	56.3	0.6	0.3
S. Jordan, UT	Salt Lake County	59.6	37.5	1.7	1.2
S. Kingstown, RI	Washington County	42.4	55.4	1.3	1.0
Southaven, MS	DeSoto County	72.3	26.4	0.3	1.0
Southlake, TX	Tarrant County	62.4	37.0	0.1	0.5
Spanish Fork, UT	Utah County	86.0	11.6	0.9	1.5
Sparks, NV	Washoe County	51.3	47.0	0.6	1.1
Stow, OH	Summit County	42.9	56.7	0.0	0.4
Sugar Land, TX	Fort Bend County	57.4	42.1	0.1	0.4
Sun Prairie, WI	Dane County	33.0	66.0	0.5	0.5
Tualatin, OR	Washington County	46.4	52.4	0.0	1.3
Waimalu, HI	Honolulu County	48.3	51.1	0.0	0.6
Wellington, FL	Palm Beach County	39.1	60.4	0.3	0.3
W Des Moines, IA	Polk County	47.3	51.9	0.3	0.5
West Linn, OR	Clackamas County	50.1	48.8	0.0	1.1
West Windsor, NJ	Mercer County	37.9	61.3	0.6	0.3
Weston, FL	Broward County	34.6	64.2	0.5	0.6
Woodbury, MN	Washington County	51.2	47.8	0.5	0.5
Woodridge, IL	DuPage County	54.4	44.8	0.2	0.7
Yorba Linda, CA	Orange County	59.7	39.0	0.2	1.1
U.S.	U.S.	50.7	48.3	0.4	0.6

Note: Results are percentages and may not add to 100% due to rounding
Source: Dave Leip's Atlas of U.S. Presidential Elections, www.uselectionatlas.org

House Price Index (HPI)

Metro Area[1]	National Ranking[3]	Quarterly Change (%)	One-Year Change (%)	Five-Year Change (%)
Allen, TX[2]	97	0.16	2.95	15.82
Ankeny, IA	103	0.91	2.87	22.36
Apex, NC	24	0.73	6.04	26.41
Bangor, ME	n/a	n/a	n/a	n/a
Beavercreek, OH	191	0.50	0.07	11.11
Bellevue, NE	160	0.53	1.35	17.68
Bend, OR	236	-1.44	-2.84	84.37
Bernards, NJ[2]	214	-0.27	-1.48	54.92
Bethlehem, NY	59	1.22	4.31	64.06
Brentwood, TN	54	0.19	4.57	34.80
Brookfield, WI	156	0.72	1.44	35.71
Broomfield, CO	198	0.20	-0.49	10.13
Burlington, VT	155	-0.03	1.54	51.67
Carmel, IN	148	0.39	1.69	11.95
Cary, NC	24	0.73	6.04	26.41
Casper, WY	n/a	n/a	n/a	n/a
Cheshire, CT	167	0.09	0.91	47.99
Chino Hills, CA	267	-4.13	-7.14	91.68
Collierville, TN	159	0.80	1.36	18.47
Conway, AR	69	0.41	3.84	28.38
Coronado, CA	271	-2.57	-7.20	51.58
Cranberry, PA	105	0.55	2.80	22.52
Dover, DE	n/a	n/a	n/a	n/a
Draper, UT	7	0.49	9.68	59.84
Dublin, OH	190	0.33	0.10	13.49
Edmond, OK	51	0.63	4.59	29.80
Evesham, NJ[2]	163	-0.54	1.01	63.65
Fargo, ND	71	1.46	3.80	32.69
Farmington, CT	157	0.31	1.42	40.10
Fishers, IN	148	0.39	1.69	11.95
Flower Mound, TX[2]	97	0.16	2.95	15.82
Franklin, MA[2]	235	1.01	-2.83	26.95
Frederick, MD[2]	233	-0.53	-2.65	67.90
Frisco, TX[2]	97	0.16	2.95	15.82
Goodyear, AZ	247	-1.80	-3.42	82.76
Grand Blanc, MI	261	-1.54	-6.31	1.10
Greenburgh, NY[2]	169	0.07	0.85	60.20
Greenwich, CT	188	0.07	0.20	42.28
Hampden, PA	42	1.61	4.94	41.91
Hilliard, OH	190	0.33	0.10	13.49
Hoover, AL	98	1.06	2.92	29.39
Huntersville, NC	23	0.06	6.08	27.81
Keller, TX[2]	101	0.50	2.89	17.43
Kenner, LA	164	-0.29	1.01	43.74
Kennesaw, GA	151	0.67	1.63	19.43
League City, TX	44	1.38	4.79	25.12
Leawood, KS	172	0.16	0.81	19.37
Lee's Summit, MO	172	0.16	0.81	19.37
Leesburg, VA[2]	237	-1.91	-2.87	76.21
Lehi, UT	6	0.77	10.46	51.51
Lwr Providence, PA[2]	130	0.22	2.04	57.85
Madison, AL	15	2.73	7.34	33.66
Manhattan Bch, CA[2]	244	-2.69	-3.23	95.75
Maple Grove, MN	225	-0.01	-2.19	27.08
Marion, IA	95	0.84	2.97	16.11
Marlboro, NJ[2]	214	-0.27	-1.48	54.92
Matthews, NC	23	0.06	6.08	27.81
Meridian, ID	146	-0.16	1.74	65.24
Merrimack, NH	208	1.04	-1.09	31.30

Metro Area[1]	National Ranking[3]	Quarterly Change (%)	One-Year Change (%)	Five-Year Change (%)
Morgantown, WV	n/a	n/a	n/a	n/a
Mt Pleasant, SC	132	-0.03	1.99	55.55
Northampton, PA[2]	130	0.22	2.04	57.85
Northville, MI[2]	259	0.51	-6.13	-1.61
Novi, MI[2]	264	-0.51	-6.73	0.31
O'Fallon, MO	113	1.32	2.56	31.71
Oro Valley, AZ	193	0.31	-0.01	71.65
Oviedo, FL	238	-2.12	-2.95	82.17
Palm Bch Grdns, FL[2]	278	-4.05	-10.39	75.22
Parker, CO	198	0.20	-0.49	10.13
Peachtree City, GA	151	0.67	1.63	19.43
Pflugerville, TX	11	0.33	7.95	28.88
Pleasanton, CA[2]	268	-2.70	-7.17	48.77
Rapid City, SD	136	1.75	1.92	32.08
Redmond, WA[2]	28	-0.03	5.87	66.13
Richland, WA	112	3.55	2.69	21.32
Rio Rancho, NM	49	0.27	4.66	56.29
Rockaway, NJ[2]	170	0.38	0.83	54.03
Rocklin, CA	280	-3.57	-11.02	46.10
Rogers, AR	180	-0.75	0.42	38.19
Round Rock, TX	11	0.33	7.95	28.88
Sammamish, WA[2]	28	-0.03	5.87	66.13
San Ramon, CA[2]	268	-2.70	-7.17	48.77
Santa Fe, NM	40	0.90	4.99	57.28
Saratoga, CA	226	-2.12	-2.28	45.46
Savage, MN	225	-0.01	-2.19	27.08
Schererville, IN[2]	72	1.47	3.78	25.57
Shawnee, KS	172	0.16	0.81	19.37
Shrewsbury, MA	241	0.57	-3.10	27.97
S Brunswick, NJ[2]	214	-0.27	-1.48	54.92
S. Jordan, UT	7	0.49	9.68	59.84
S. Kingstown, RI	232	0.14	-2.57	46.05
Southaven, MS	159	0.80	1.36	18.47
Southlake, TX[2]	101	0.50	2.89	17.43
Spanish Fork, UT	6	0.77	10.46	51.51
Sparks, NV	273	-2.39	-7.83	65.05
Stow, OH	224	-0.08	-2.16	7.84
Sugar Land, TX	44	1.38	4.79	25.12
Sun Prairie, WI	126	0.76	2.15	33.23
Tualatin, OR	61	0.30	4.24	66.54
Waimalu, HI	56	-0.63	4.50	95.28
Wellington, FL[2]	278	-4.05	-10.39	75.22
W Des Moines, IA	103	0.91	2.87	22.36
West Linn, OR	61	0.30	4.24	66.54
West Windsor, NJ	199	0.07	-0.51	51.25
Weston, FL[2]	265	-2.64	-6.90	83.46
Woodbury, MN	225	-0.01	-2.19	27.08
Woodridge, IL[2]	152	0.39	1.62	40.78
Yorba Linda, CA[2]	258	-2.84	-6.11	75.74
U.S.[4]	-	0.10	0.84	41.37

Note: The HPI is a weighted repeat sales index. It measures average price changes in repeat sales or refinancings on the same properties. This information is obtained by reviewing repeat mortgage transactions on single-family properties whose mortgages have been purchased or securitized by Fannie Mae or Freddie Mac in January 1975; (1) figures cover the Metropolitan Statistical Area (MSA) unless noted otherwise - see Appendix B for areas included; (2) Metropolitan Division - see Appendix B for areas included; (3) Rankings are based on annual percentage change, for all MSAs containing at least 15,000 transactions over the last 10 years and ranges from 1 to 291; (4) figures based on a weighted division average; all figures are for the period ended December 31, 2007; n/a not available

Source: Office of Federal Housing Enterprise Oversight, House Price Index, February 26, 2008

Housing: Year Structure Built: City

City	1990 -2000	1980 -1989	1970 -1979	1960 -1969	1950 -1959	1940 -1949	Before 1940	Median Year
Allen, TX	58.3	24.0	14.0	2.5	0.9	0.2	0.0	1993
Ankeny, IA	36.3	13.4	26.5	14.5	5.3	2.1	2.0	1980
Apex, NC	78.5	10.6	3.5	3.1	1.8	0.6	1.8	1997
Bangor, ME	6.5	11.5	11.2	7.6	11.4	6.7	45.0	1948
Beavercreek, OH	21.7	10.6	24.9	20.2	17.2	3.0	2.4	1973
Bellevue, NE	9.3	13.2	30.2	23.6	13.6	4.8	5.2	1971
Bend, OR	38.3	14.3	23.8	6.8	5.7	3.8	7.2	1982
Bernards, NJ	35.9	25.8	8.8	12.2	6.5	3.7	7.0	1985
Bethlehem, NY	17.6	14.4	13.0	13.3	15.7	8.8	17.2	1966
Bozeman, MT	24.9	11.2	21.3	11.1	8.6	6.3	16.6	1973
Brentwood, TN	32.5	27.2	26.6	11.1	0.5	0.9	1.2	1984
Brookfield, WI	15.9	12.4	16.1	22.6	25.4	5.0	2.6	1968
Broomfield, CO	40.4	14.5	27.6	8.9	7.7	0.4	0.5	1983
Burlington, VT	7.9	10.3	10.0	11.0	13.2	8.8	38.8	1952
Carmel, IN	32.4	23.0	29.0	8.9	4.1	0.6	2.1	1982
Cary, NC	54.1	24.9	13.8	4.5	1.5	0.4	0.8	1991
Casper, WY	4.5	13.7	27.8	11.9	22.8	6.8	12.5	1967
Cheshire, CT	11.9	20.3	15.1	18.5	20.1	4.5	9.6	1969
Chino Hills, CA	42.6	37.1	13.3	3.5	2.1	0.6	0.8	1988
Collierville, TN	59.4	19.8	11.7	4.2	1.7	1.3	1.9	1992
Conway, AR	43.6	17.4	16.9	8.6	5.7	3.5	4.4	1986
Coronado, CA	8.1	13.0	28.6	9.5	14.3	8.2	18.3	1970
Cranberry, PA	40.1	24.6	21.9	5.4	4.9	1.3	1.8	1986
Dover, DE	22.7	17.2	17.9	18.6	11.5	5.3	6.9	1974
Draper, UT	80.5	4.7	4.7	3.0	2.4	1.3	3.4	1996
Dublin, OH	54.1	32.6	7.6	2.2	2.1	0.3	1.2	1991
Edmond, OK	26.1	31.1	25.3	9.2	3.7	1.6	2.9	1982
Evesham, NJ	25.0	35.2	21.3	12.3	4.4	0.9	1.1	1983
Fargo, ND	25.9	16.2	21.1	9.3	10.1	4.6	12.8	1976
Farmington, CT	15.9	22.9	20.1	10.5	15.8	5.6	9.4	1974
Fishers, IN	78.3	15.5	3.8	0.8	0.6	0.1	0.9	1995
Flower Mound, TX	69.6	21.3	6.6	1.3	0.7	0.2	0.3	1994
Franklin, MA	26.6	18.2	9.9	16.0	9.1	2.3	17.9	1975
Frederick, MD	26.4	21.9	16.4	7.3	6.9	4.7	16.4	1979
Frisco, TX	83.0	10.2	3.4	1.7	0.8	0.3	0.6	1997
Goodyear, AZ	78.5	5.1	6.6	2.9	3.3	2.7	0.9	1996
Grand Blanc, MI	22.5	13.8	24.6	21.8	10.5	3.7	3.1	1974
Greenburgh, NY	6.7	7.1	10.4	16.4	23.7	11.0	24.7	1956
Greenwich, CT	6.2	8.3	10.3	13.8	19.5	10.5	31.4	1954
Hampden, PA	26.8	19.0	24.3	14.1	11.2	2.5	2.0	1978
Hilliard, OH	53.5	16.0	7.0	5.9	14.5	1.3	1.8	1991
Hoover, AL	40.8	20.3	21.6	11.2	4.3	1.2	0.6	1985
Huntersville, NC	70.2	13.5	5.4	4.0	2.6	2.1	2.2	1995
Juneau, AK	15.0	29.1	28.4	10.4	5.5	3.3	8.3	1978
Keller, TX	52.2	26.9	14.2	2.7	1.4	1.9	0.6	1991
Kenner, LA	6.7	23.8	41.6	17.6	7.0	2.2	1.0	1975
Kennesaw, GA	57.9	22.8	9.5	5.5	2.9	0.3	1.1	1994
League City, TX	37.6	33.3	16.0	7.9	2.8	1.4	1.1	1986
Leawood, KS	32.2	23.7	12.8	10.5	16.8	3.4	0.5	1983
Lee's Summit, MO	36.4	24.4	21.1	9.3	5.3	1.3	2.3	1984
Leesburg, VA	42.5	27.5	17.1	6.1	2.8	0.7	3.4	1987
Lehi, UT	53.6	8.7	13.3	3.3	8.2	3.4	9.5	1991
Lwr Providence, PA	18.1	6.5	23.9	20.9	15.0	6.5	9.1	1969
Madison, AL	50.3	34.5	8.5	5.0	0.8	0.2	0.6	1990
Manhattan Bch, CA	10.2	12.9	12.5	15.2	28.8	13.1	7.3	1961
Maple Grove, MN	29.4	33.4	27.9	5.5	1.3	0.5	1.9	1984
Marion, IA	30.0	8.9	16.3	19.2	10.8	3.4	11.4	1973
Marlboro, NJ	32.4	33.3	16.4	11.9	2.5	0.8	2.6	1985
Matthews, NC	39.9	36.8	13.3	6.0	2.3	1.3	0.5	1987

City	1990 -2000	1980 -1989	1970 -1979	1960 -1969	1950 -1959	1940 -1949	Before 1940	Median Year
Meridian, ID	70.0	9.9	12.6	2.3	2.5	1.0	1.8	1994
Merrimack, NH	16.4	33.8	27.9	13.5	4.1	0.8	3.6	1980
Morgantown, WV	9.0	6.4	13.6	13.7	15.9	12.6	28.9	1955
Mt Pleasant, SC	39.1	28.8	16.7	6.9	5.0	1.5	2.0	1986
Northampton, PA	16.8	28.9	27.6	14.6	7.0	1.2	3.9	1978
Northville, MI	25.6	25.9	27.9	10.7	4.8	2.5	2.7	1981
Novi, MI	36.6	24.6	27.6	4.5	4.1	0.8	1.7	1985
O'Fallon, MO	64.8	16.8	6.7	7.0	3.5	0.4	0.7	1993
Oro Valley, AZ	69.7	19.6	7.5	2.1	0.9	0.0	0.2	1994
Oviedo, FL	60.2	30.0	4.9	2.3	1.4	0.4	0.7	1992
Palm Bch Grdns, FL	34.3	34.9	17.6	11.6	1.2	0.2	0.2	1986
Parker, CO	74.7	21.4	3.4	0.4	0.0	0.1	0.0	1996
Peachtree City, GA	45.8	36.7	15.2	1.7	0.2	0.1	0.2	1989
Pflugerville, TX	63.1	27.7	5.4	2.1	0.2	0.7	0.8	1993
Pleasanton, CA	25.3	26.7	25.9	15.8	3.3	1.1	1.9	1981
Rapid City, SD	14.1	13.9	23.6	13.6	20.5	6.4	7.9	1971
Redmond, WA	29.3	27.6	28.0	11.7	1.8	0.6	1.0	1982
Richland, WA	16.4	7.1	27.4	9.5	14.3	24.4	0.8	1970
Richmond, KY	34.8	16.6	17.2	10.1	8.9	4.4	7.9	1981
Rio Rancho, NM	42.0	38.2	16.4	2.8	0.3	0.1	0.2	1988
Rockaway, NJ	15.5	10.2	12.2	25.7	20.8	6.5	9.0	1965
Rocklin, CA	55.4	21.7	15.8	4.5	0.9	0.5	1.3	1991
Rogers, AR	34.8	21.8	22.6	8.4	4.6	2.7	4.9	1983
Round Rock, TX	48.1	32.3	15.7	1.6	0.9	0.5	1.0	1989
Sammamish, WA	38.6	34.3	17.4	4.5	1.9	1.4	2.0	1987
San Ramon, CA	30.7	32.1	25.6	10.5	0.5	0.3	0.2	1984
Santa Fe, NM	19.2	21.6	18.8	13.0	10.8	6.9	9.7	1975
Saratoga, CA	6.0	8.5	20.9	29.8	27.3	4.5	2.9	1965
Savage, MN	51.6	30.1	7.5	5.4	3.5	0.9	1.0	1990
Schererville, IN	29.5	24.2	29.7	7.9	5.3	1.9	1.6	1982
Shawnee, KS	23.8	20.0	25.4	15.2	10.0	3.2	2.5	1978
Shrewsbury, MA	23.4	14.5	16.6	11.3	15.0	5.4	13.7	1973
S Brunswick, NJ	34.7	27.6	14.1	9.1	10.4	1.0	3.1	1984
S. Jordan, UT	62.2	17.0	13.3	3.6	1.4	0.7	1.8	1992
S Kingstown, RI	18.2	17.5	16.8	10.4	11.9	5.6	19.5	1971
Southaven, MS	42.2	15.6	23.0	17.8	0.9	0.3	0.1	1985
Southlake, TX	67.5	19.3	6.8	3.3	1.9	0.8	0.5	1994
Spanish Fork, UT	41.1	5.9	18.3	6.9	9.0	6.3	12.5	1978
Sparks, NV	21.8	22.6	28.1	14.1	7.8	2.9	2.7	1978
Stow, OH	23.4	15.8	23.0	18.0	10.1	3.7	6.0	1975
Sugar Land, TX	32.3	44.1	18.0	2.4	1.7	0.5	1.0	1986
Sun Prairie, WI	32.1	14.9	21.5	16.4	7.8	2.5	4.7	1979
Tualatin, OR	41.1	27.4	27.1	2.4	1.0	0.6	0.4	1987
Waimalu, HI	5.5	24.6	52.4	10.1	6.2	1.0	0.3	1976
Wellington, FL	43.7	43.0	11.8	0.7	0.2	0.1	0.5	1989
W Des Moines, IA	36.2	22.1	18.1	8.0	7.8	2.9	4.8	1984
West Linn, OR	33.3	18.8	23.7	8.2	6.3	3.5	6.3	1981
West Windsor, NJ	28.7	35.1	12.1	9.9	6.9	1.6	5.6	1984
Weston, FL	74.4	17.9	6.8	0.6	0.2	0.0	0.0	1995
Woodbury, MN	60.6	20.6	11.3	4.2	2.3	0.2	0.9	1992
Woodridge, IL	13.9	23.4	34.1	24.5	3.4	0.4	0.4	1976
Yorba Linda, CA	17.0	36.7	29.4	12.5	2.9	0.7	0.8	1981
U.S.	17.0	15.8	18.5	13.7	12.7	7.3	15.0	1971

Note: Figures are percentages except for Median Year
Source: Census 2000, Summary File 3

Housing: Year Structure Built: Metro Area

MSA[1]	1990 -2000	1980 -1989	1970 -1979	1960 -1969	1950 -1959	1940 -1949	Before 1940	Median Year
Allen, TX	23.9	24.7	20.2	13.7	9.8	4.0	3.7	1979
Ankeny, IA	18.8	11.9	17.8	12.1	12.4	7.2	19.9	1969
Apex, NC	33.2	22.9	16.6	10.9	7.2	3.9	5.4	1983
Bangor, ME	12.0	13.8	15.5	9.6	10.7	6.2	32.1	1961
Beavercreek, OH	9.9	8.3	17.3	18.8	18.4	9.5	17.8	1962
Bellevue, NE	15.8	11.8	19.5	15.8	11.9	6.1	19.1	1968
Bend, OR	n/a	n/a	n/a	n/a	n/a	n/a	n/a	n/a
Bernards, NJ	15.2	18.7	13.3	16.8	16.2	6.8	13.0	1968
Bethlehem, NY	11.1	11.4	13.2	10.9	11.9	8.7	32.9	1957
Bozeman, MT	n/a	n/a	n/a	n/a	n/a	n/a	n/a	n/a
Brentwood, TN	25.8	20.1	19.1	13.8	9.8	4.9	6.6	1978
Brookfield, WI	12.6	8.2	14.8	13.7	18.6	9.2	22.9	1960
Broomfield, CO	19.4	18.0	23.7	13.2	12.4	4.4	9.0	1975
Burlington, VT	16.3	17.7	18.0	11.5	9.1	4.8	22.6	1971
Carmel, IN	20.9	12.9	16.1	14.7	12.8	7.1	15.5	1970
Cary, NC	33.2	22.9	16.6	10.9	7.2	3.9	5.4	1983
Casper, WY	6.8	14.1	31.4	11.4	18.9	6.3	11.1	1971
Cheshire, CT	7.8	12.8	14.6	15.7	16.8	9.2	23.1	1961
Chino Hills, CA	20.9	28.7	20.1	12.8	10.4	3.8	3.3	1980
Collierville, TN	21.3	16.3	20.1	16.1	13.2	6.6	6.4	1974
Conway, AR	22.7	18.7	23.1	14.8	10.1	5.2	5.4	1976
Coronado, CA	13.9	21.9	26.3	15.0	12.9	4.9	5.1	1975
Cranberry, PA	7.8	7.5	12.7	12.3	17.2	11.9	30.5	1954
Dover, DE	25.6	17.4	18.8	13.3	10.9	4.2	9.8	1976
Draper, UT	22.0	16.4	22.5	11.9	11.7	6.0	9.4	1975
Dublin, OH	20.7	13.5	17.5	15.0	12.8	6.3	14.2	1971
Edmond, OK	13.8	19.8	21.9	16.3	13.4	7.1	7.8	1972
Evesham, NJ	9.4	10.0	13.0	13.9	17.3	11.1	25.3	1958
Fargo, ND	21.7	14.3	22.9	11.3	11.4	4.8	13.6	1974
Farmington, CT	8.5	14.1	15.3	15.8	17.2	9.2	19.9	1962
Fishers, IN	20.9	12.9	16.1	14.7	12.8	7.1	15.5	1970
Flower Mound, TX	23.9	24.7	20.2	13.7	9.8	4.0	3.7	1979
Franklin, MA	7.0	9.3	11.6	11.8	13.2	8.5	38.6	1952
Frederick, MD	18.2	18.9	18.1	16.1	11.9	7.2	9.6	1973
Frisco, TX	23.9	24.7	20.2	13.7	9.8	4.0	3.7	1979
Goodyear, AZ	30.4	25.5	23.2	10.4	7.1	2.0	1.4	1982
Grand Blanc, MI	12.7	8.1	18.3	18.6	19.5	10.0	12.9	1964
Greenburgh, NY	4.5	5.4	9.2	15.5	16.2	14.6	34.7	1950
Greenwich, CT	7.4	11.4	12.9	17.1	20.2	9.2	21.9	1959
Hampden, PA	13.8	13.0	16.6	11.9	13.5	8.1	23.1	1965
Hilliard, OH	20.7	13.5	17.5	15.0	12.8	6.3	14.2	1971
Hoover, AL	20.3	15.4	19.6	15.3	13.3	7.7	8.4	1973
Huntersville, NC	30.3	19.1	16.3	12.7	10.0	5.5	6.1	1980
Juneau, AK	n/a	n/a	n/a	n/a	n/a	n/a	n/a	n/a
Keller, TX	21.4	26.8	19.2	12.5	11.1	4.9	4.1	1979
Kenner, LA	9.9	15.7	21.7	17.6	13.4	8.0	13.7	1968
Kennesaw, GA	30.8	24.6	18.0	12.0	7.1	3.2	4.2	1982
League City, TX	17.4	20.9	20.9	14.7	11.7	6.7	7.7	1974
Leawood, KS	17.2	15.0	18.1	15.5	14.1	7.1	12.9	1970
Lee's Summit, MO	17.2	15.0	18.1	15.5	14.1	7.1	12.9	1970
Leesburg, VA	18.2	18.9	18.1	16.1	11.9	7.2	9.6	1973
Lehi, UT	33.9	12.7	22.8	9.1	8.4	5.4	7.8	1978
Lwr Providence, PA	9.4	10.0	13.0	13.9	17.3	11.1	25.3	1958
Madison, AL	26.1	22.7	16.9	19.2	8.6	3.0	3.4	1979
Manhattan Bch, CA	6.9	12.3	15.6	17.8	22.3	12.2	12.9	1961
Maple Grove, MN	17.6	16.8	18.1	12.8	12.3	5.3	17.1	1971
Marion, IA	18.4	8.3	17.9	15.6	13.7	5.4	20.7	1967
Marlboro, NJ	14.7	18.3	19.9	17.2	13.4	5.8	10.8	1971
Matthews, NC	30.3	19.1	16.3	12.7	10.0	5.5	6.1	1980

MSA[1]	1990 -2000	1980 -1989	1970 -1979	1960 -1969	1950 -1959	1940 -1949	Before 1940	Median Year
Meridian, ID	33.8	12.7	24.4	8.3	8.1	5.2	7.4	1979
Merrimack, NH	12.9	25.3	21.8	12.5	7.1	3.7	16.7	1975
Morgantown, WV	n/a	n/a	n/a	n/a	n/a	n/a	n/a	n/a
Mt Pleasant, SC	22.0	23.9	21.3	14.0	8.4	4.7	5.9	1978
Northampton, PA	9.4	10.0	13.0	13.9	17.3	11.1	25.3	1958
Northville, MI	12.2	9.2	15.4	14.9	21.9	12.5	13.9	1961
Novi, MI	12.2	9.2	15.4	14.9	21.9	12.5	13.9	1961
O'Fallon, MO	14.0	13.4	15.6	16.0	15.2	8.8	17.0	1966
Oro Valley, AZ	23.2	22.4	25.6	11.7	10.4	3.7	3.0	1978
Oviedo, FL	31.0	28.1	18.7	9.7	7.7	2.3	2.4	1983
Palm Bch Grdns, FL	22.2	32.5	24.7	10.7	6.2	1.7	2.0	1981
Parker, CO	19.4	18.0	23.7	13.2	12.4	4.4	9.0	1975
Peachtree City, GA	30.8	24.6	18.0	12.0	7.1	3.2	4.2	1982
Pflugerville, TX	30.2	27.4	20.2	8.8	6.2	3.3	3.9	1983
Pleasanton, CA	11.7	14.8	18.2	17.0	15.4	9.2	13.8	1967
Rapid City, SD	17.1	15.6	25.8	12.1	15.9	5.7	7.8	1973
Redmond, WA	19.8	18.4	17.7	14.7	10.3	6.4	12.5	1973
Richland, WA	21.4	10.0	31.4	10.5	13.3	10.2	3.2	1974
Richmond, KY	24.4	16.8	20.0	14.0	10.0	4.9	9.9	1976
Rio Rancho, NM	24.3	20.3	22.0	12.5	12.0	5.1	3.7	1978
Rockaway, NJ	7.5	8.1	11.2	15.7	19.4	13.0	25.1	1956
Rocklin, CA	19.4	20.5	22.9	14.5	12.3	5.1	5.3	1976
Rogers, AR	34.7	18.6	20.2	10.6	5.8	3.5	6.5	1982
Round Rock, TX	30.2	27.4	20.2	8.8	6.2	3.3	3.9	1983
Sammamish, WA	19.8	18.4	17.7	14.7	10.3	6.4	12.5	1973
San Ramon, CA	11.7	14.8	18.2	17.0	15.4	9.2	13.8	1967
Santa Fe, NM	27.7	21.8	18.3	11.1	9.2	5.5	6.4	1980
Saratoga, CA	11.5	13.4	25.2	22.8	16.6	5.2	5.3	1970
Savage, MN	17.6	16.8	18.1	12.8	12.3	5.3	17.1	1971
Schererville, IN	13.5	8.0	17.6	16.6	18.0	11.2	15.0	1963
Shawnee, KS	17.2	15.0	18.1	15.5	14.1	7.1	12.9	1970
Shrewsbury, MA	11.0	12.9	12.8	10.3	13.0	8.5	31.5	1958
S Brunswick, NJ	15.2	18.7	13.3	16.8	16.2	6.8	13.0	1968
S. Jordan, UT	22.0	16.4	22.5	11.9	11.7	6.0	9.4	1975
S Kingstown, RI	8.7	11.1	13.3	12.7	13.7	9.8	30.7	1957
Southaven, MS	21.3	16.3	20.1	16.1	13.2	6.6	6.4	1974
Southlake, TX	21.4	26.8	19.2	12.5	11.1	4.9	4.1	1979
Spanish Fork, UT	33.9	12.7	22.8	9.1	8.4	5.4	7.8	1978
Sparks, NV	27.3	20.6	25.0	13.0	7.3	3.5	3.3	1979
Stow, OH	13.6	8.8	14.7	15.3	17.1	9.8	20.7	1962
Sugar Land, TX	19.8	23.0	26.6	13.6	9.4	4.3	3.4	1977
Sun Prairie, WI	21.1	13.1	20.0	14.6	10.6	5.6	15.1	1972
Tualatin, OR	24.6	13.0	20.9	11.3	9.1	6.5	14.7	1974
Waimalu, HI	14.7	13.1	26.5	22.5	13.2	5.6	4.4	1972
Wellington, FL	22.2	32.5	24.7	10.7	6.2	1.7	2.0	1981
W Des Moines, IA	18.8	11.9	17.8	12.1	12.4	7.2	19.9	1969
West Linn, OR	24.6	13.0	20.9	11.3	9.1	6.5	14.7	1974
West Windsor, NJ	10.2	12.4	12.5	15.2	16.6	9.6	23.5	1960
Weston, FL	19.5	21.2	29.8	17.2	9.5	1.7	1.0	1977
Woodbury, MN	17.6	16.8	18.1	12.8	12.3	5.3	17.1	1971
Woodridge, IL	12.4	9.8	15.9	15.3	16.1	9.2	21.3	1962
Yorba Linda, CA	14.1	17.5	27.6	22.6	12.8	3.0	2.5	1973
U.S.	17.0	15.8	18.5	13.7	12.7	7.3	15.0	1971

Note: Figures are percentages; (1) Metropolitan Statistical Area - see Appendix A for areas included
Source: Census 2000, Summary File 3

Highest Level of Education: City

Area	Less than H.S.	H.S. Diploma	Some College, No Deg.	Associate Degree	Bachelors Degree	Masters Degree	Profess. School Degree	Doctorate Degree
Allen, TX	3.9	13.3	24.5	7.7	38.0	10.5	1.2	0.9
Ankeny, IA	4.3	22.4	23.3	10.3	29.0	7.3	2.3	1.3
Apex, NC	4.1	11.7	17.0	8.3	41.9	12.5	2.0	2.6
Bangor, ME	13.1	31.2	20.2	9.0	16.3	6.2	2.3	1.6
Beavercreek, OH	7.3	21.9	20.7	6.2	22.6	16.4	2.4	2.5
Bellevue, NE	8.2	27.5	30.1	8.4	17.4	6.7	1.2	0.5
Bend, OR	9.7	23.7	28.4	8.4	20.5	6.0	2.6	0.8
Bernards, NJ	4.1	11.5	11.7	4.9	36.5	22.2	5.3	3.7
Bethlehem, NY	6.8	18.1	15.1	10.0	22.8	16.7	7.5	3.0
Bozeman, MT	5.8	15.4	24.9	4.6	33.7	9.7	2.2	3.6
Brentwood, TN	2.6	9.9	17.9	4.8	39.0	16.9	6.7	2.3
Brookfield, WI	5.9	19.0	19.8	6.3	31.3	10.7	5.3	1.7
Broomfield, CO	6.7	20.4	24.9	9.3	26.2	9.2	1.9	1.5
Burlington, VT	12.2	22.2	16.7	6.3	26.9	9.9	3.3	2.5
Carmel, IN	2.9	13.8	17.8	6.6	37.6	14.2	4.8	2.2
Cary, NC	4.6	10.6	15.9	7.2	38.7	16.2	3.0	3.9
Casper, WY	10.8	29.0	28.8	9.2	14.9	4.8	2.2	0.4
Cheshire, CT	7.5	20.9	16.0	7.4	26.8	14.7	4.3	2.2
Chino Hills, CA	9.8	16.1	26.0	9.9	27.5	7.9	2.1	0.8
Collierville, TN	5.9	18.2	26.9	6.3	30.6	9.1	1.9	1.0
Conway, AR	13.6	22.5	23.1	4.0	23.4	8.7	2.0	2.5
Coronado, CA	3.9	13.6	27.7	7.6	24.9	14.5	6.0	1.9
Cranberry, PA	4.9	23.0	17.4	7.4	32.1	11.1	2.8	1.3
Dover, DE	16.6	23.9	24.2	6.6	17.6	8.2	1.8	1.1
Draper, UT	7.9	16.9	31.5	8.2	25.2	7.3	2.0	1.1
Dublin, OH	2.8	11.6	16.8	5.3	41.4	15.4	4.9	2.0
Edmond, OK	5.5	16.3	25.0	4.2	31.0	11.3	4.8	1.9
Evesham, NJ	6.9	25.4	20.2	7.9	27.3	8.6	3.0	0.8
Fargo, ND	8.6	21.3	25.7	9.4	25.4	5.6	2.3	1.6
Farmington, CT	8.3	19.9	15.6	6.7	27.2	14.0	6.6	1.7
Fishers, IN	1.8	11.5	18.5	7.9	44.7	11.3	3.6	0.8
Flower Mound, TX	2.7	11.9	24.2	7.7	40.3	11.0	1.5	0.7
Franklin, MA	7.0	23.3	17.9	8.8	29.2	11.2	1.4	1.2
Frederick, MD	15.2	26.8	21.1	6.7	19.2	7.8	1.0	2.3
Frisco, TX	5.4	12.9	24.1	7.2	37.7	9.4	2.1	1.2
Goodyear, AZ	11.8	27.4	30.5	7.1	14.3	7.0	1.5	0.4
Grand Blanc, MI	7.6	25.4	24.9	9.7	20.6	8.2	2.5	1.1
Greenburgh, NY	9.1	17.1	14.9	5.5	26.2	17.5	7.0	2.7
Greenwich, CT	8.0	16.8	11.4	5.2	31.4	19.1	6.2	1.9
Hampden, PA	6.8	26.6	17.6	6.8	27.2	9.9	3.9	1.2
Hilliard, OH	7.5	20.8	19.3	6.5	31.6	9.0	3.3	2.1
Hoover, AL	5.1	15.2	21.6	5.1	36.0	11.0	4.2	1.9
Huntersville, NC	7.8	15.6	22.2	7.3	34.7	9.8	1.9	0.7
Juneau, AK	6.7	21.7	28.4	6.6	23.3	8.4	3.3	1.6
Keller, TX	4.1	15.9	27.5	8.7	32.9	8.8	1.1	1.0
Kenner, LA	21.1	29.0	23.4	4.8	14.6	4.3	2.2	0.5
Kennesaw, GA	8.1	23.6	25.9	6.8	26.6	6.3	1.7	0.9
League City, TX	9.1	19.7	27.2	8.5	24.0	7.9	1.7	1.9
Leawood, KS	2.0	7.7	17.7	4.7	40.3	15.2	9.9	2.6
Lee's Summit, MO	6.4	20.7	26.7	7.3	25.9	9.1	3.2	0.7
Leesburg, VA	9.7	19.2	22.8	7.3	27.9	10.7	1.5	0.9
Lehi, UT	8.3	25.6	30.1	9.1	19.9	5.3	1.0	0.7
Lwr Providence, PA	12.2	29.8	16.3	6.6	23.9	7.6	1.1	2.5
Madison, AL	5.5	12.6	23.3	6.1	35.0	14.8	1.2	1.5
Manhattan Bch, CA	3.2	8.1	15.4	5.6	39.0	16.9	8.7	3.0
Maple Grove, MN	3.3	19.5	23.6	9.9	32.8	8.0	2.2	0.7
Marion, IA	7.8	27.4	23.9	11.3	22.8	5.6	1.2	0.1
Marlboro, NJ	6.0	18.9	16.1	6.5	29.9	16.9	3.6	2.2

Area	Less than H.S.	H.S. Diploma	Some College, No Deg.	Associate Degree	Bachelors Degree	Masters Degree	Profess. School Degree	Doctorate Degree
Matthews, NC	6.9	17.9	24.8	8.3	29.7	9.3	2.3	0.7
Meridian, ID	7.8	26.2	30.5	8.1	21.4	4.1	1.3	0.7
Merrimack, NH	7.0	24.8	22.0	11.2	25.2	8.3	1.0	0.5
Morgantown, WV	11.0	19.7	18.5	3.0	21.5	14.5	5.2	6.6
Mt Pleasant, SC	5.4	13.6	19.2	7.9	34.8	11.4	5.5	2.3
Northampton, PA	5.3	26.7	18.4	6.2	26.4	11.4	3.9	1.6
Northville, MI	7.9	16.7	19.1	7.0	28.6	15.1	4.2	1.5
Novi, MI	6.3	17.1	21.5	6.8	29.4	14.5	3.3	1.1
O'Fallon, MO	8.9	27.8	27.1	8.2	20.7	6.2	0.8	0.3
Oro Valley, AZ	4.2	17.0	28.3	6.9	26.6	12.0	2.9	2.0
Oviedo, FL	6.6	19.5	23.3	9.7	27.6	9.7	1.9	1.6
Palm Bch Grdns, FL	5.8	20.1	21.5	8.4	26.5	9.9	6.3	1.5
Parker, CO	4.1	14.8	28.6	8.2	32.7	8.9	2.2	0.5
Peachtree City, GA	3.9	18.0	23.8	7.7	31.4	11.6	2.1	1.4
Pflugerville, TX	5.5	17.5	29.7	8.7	27.7	8.0	1.9	0.9
Pleasanton, CA	5.8	14.6	23.3	8.7	31.7	11.8	2.0	2.1
Rapid City, SD	12.9	27.4	25.6	7.7	17.8	5.6	2.2	0.9
Redmond, WA	5.6	11.6	22.3	7.7	35.9	12.7	2.2	1.9
Richland, WA	7.2	19.3	24.5	9.2	22.7	11.5	1.8	3.9
Richmond, KY	22.6	25.3	21.2	4.9	16.0	6.2	1.2	2.6
Rio Rancho, NM	8.1	27.0	29.7	9.5	17.7	6.3	1.1	0.6
Rockaway, NJ	7.1	24.9	19.1	7.2	29.2	9.5	2.1	0.8
Rocklin, CA	4.5	15.8	30.6	11.4	27.3	8.0	1.7	0.8
Rogers, AR	23.6	28.7	22.1	4.3	15.9	3.3	1.9	0.3
Round Rock, TX	9.3	21.1	27.9	7.8	24.7	6.9	1.3	1.0
Sammamish, WA	1.6	9.3	18.9	8.0	41.1	16.0	3.3	1.9
San Ramon, CA	3.3	11.6	23.8	8.1	36.1	12.3	2.7	2.0
Santa Fe, NM	15.9	17.3	22.3	5.3	21.2	11.1	4.0	2.8
Saratoga, CA	3.6	7.7	14.4	6.2	34.5	24.4	4.8	4.5
Savage, MN	4.1	19.8	23.4	9.4	34.8	7.3	0.8	0.3
Schererville, IN	8.0	33.1	22.9	6.3	18.7	7.3	2.7	0.9
Shawnee, KS	5.9	21.0	25.1	7.2	28.0	9.2	2.8	1.0
Shrewsbury, MA	8.2	20.7	16.8	7.8	26.7	13.4	3.8	2.5
S Brunswick, NJ	6.6	20.7	16.6	6.8	29.2	14.5	3.0	2.6
S. Jordan, UT	4.3	22.6	33.3	9.2	22.5	6.6	1.0	0.4
S Kingstown, RI	8.5	20.6	17.8	6.0	27.1	13.0	2.6	4.4
Southaven, MS	17.1	34.2	27.3	6.1	11.3	2.8	0.8	0.3
Southlake, TX	3.5	12.2	20.1	5.3	39.7	14.6	3.4	1.1
Spanish Fork, UT	7.9	24.7	32.7	11.2	17.2	4.5	1.5	0.4
Sparks, NV	16.3	27.4	29.0	7.6	13.9	3.8	1.5	0.6
Stow, OH	6.8	28.2	21.5	6.7	24.2	8.9	2.3	1.4
Sugar Land, TX	6.7	13.4	19.7	6.4	34.3	13.1	4.1	2.2
Sun Prairie, WI	9.2	21.2	22.5	11.6	27.9	5.7	1.6	0.4
Tualatin, OR	6.8	18.4	29.6	7.1	27.5	7.3	2.3	1.0
Waimalu, HI	9.5	25.0	23.5	9.7	22.2	7.1	2.1	0.8
Wellington, FL	7.7	21.3	23.1	10.3	24.2	8.1	4.3	1.0
W Des Moines, IA	3.4	17.1	21.9	7.5	35.8	8.4	4.6	1.3
West Linn, OR	4.6	13.5	26.0	6.9	32.4	11.4	4.0	1.2
West Windsor, NJ	3.1	7.7	10.1	5.2	35.0	25.4	6.7	6.8
Weston, FL	4.3	13.9	21.0	8.2	30.7	12.5	8.4	1.2
Woodbury, MN	3.3	15.4	22.3	8.7	33.5	10.4	4.1	2.3
Woodridge, IL	10.0	19.8	23.7	7.1	26.9	9.3	1.9	1.2
Yorba Linda, CA	6.7	15.2	26.7	10.0	26.3	11.0	3.0	1.3
U.S.	19.4	28.4	21.2	6.4	15.7	5.9	2.0	1.0

Figures are 2007 estimates and cover persons age 25 and over; (1) Metropolitan Statistical Area - see Appendix B for areas included
Source: Claritas, Inc.

Highest Level of Education: Metro Area

Area	Less than H.S.	H.S. Diploma	Some College, No Deg.	Associate Degree	Bachelors Degree	Masters Degree	Profess. School Degree	Doctorate Degree
Allen, TX	19.2	22.3	23.5	5.7	20.3	6.4	1.7	0.8
Ankeny, IA	10.8	30.3	22.1	7.5	21.0	5.3	2.4	0.8
Apex, NC	13.5	20.9	20.1	7.7	26.0	8.3	1.9	1.7
Bangor, ME	14.2	38.2	19.2	7.8	13.0	4.8	1.4	1.4
Beavercreek, OH	15.6	32.2	22.1	7.0	14.2	6.5	1.6	0.9
Bellevue, NE	11.6	28.4	25.0	6.9	19.6	5.8	2.0	0.8
Bend, OR	11.4	27.1	28.4	7.8	17.3	5.2	2.0	0.7
Bernards, NJ	21.5	26.4	16.5	5.6	17.7	8.2	3.0	1.2
Bethlehem, NY	13.7	29.5	17.4	10.1	16.3	9.0	2.5	1.5
Bozeman, MT	6.6	21.0	26.0	5.2	28.4	8.0	2.4	2.5
Brentwood, TN	19.1	28.7	21.1	5.1	17.8	5.5	1.9	0.9
Brookfield, WI	15.2	29.1	21.7	6.9	18.4	5.9	2.0	0.8
Broomfield, CO	13.2	21.8	23.8	6.8	23.2	7.8	2.3	1.0
Burlington, VT	11.5	27.9	16.8	8.9	21.7	9.0	2.6	1.7
Carmel, IN	14.9	31.2	20.2	6.1	18.4	6.3	2.0	0.9
Cary, NC	13.5	20.9	20.1	7.7	26.0	8.3	1.9	1.7
Casper, WY	11.7	30.5	28.7	9.1	13.4	4.3	1.9	0.4
Cheshire, CT	17.0	30.8	18.2	6.4	15.3	8.2	2.5	1.5
Chino Hills, CA	25.2	24.8	26.4	7.2	10.7	3.7	1.4	0.6
Collierville, TN	20.2	28.0	23.9	5.3	14.9	5.1	1.9	0.8
Conway, AR	16.6	30.4	23.7	4.7	16.1	5.4	2.2	0.9
Coronado, CA	17.2	19.6	25.4	7.7	19.1	6.9	2.6	1.5
Cranberry, PA	15.0	38.0	16.3	7.0	15.0	5.6	2.0	1.0
Dover, DE	20.8	33.0	21.4	6.5	11.5	5.1	1.2	0.6
Draper, UT	12.6	24.1	28.1	7.6	18.6	5.7	2.1	1.1
Dublin, OH	13.7	30.6	21.0	5.8	19.6	6.2	2.1	1.1
Edmond, OK	15.9	27.9	26.1	5.3	16.3	5.6	1.9	0.9
Evesham, NJ	17.3	31.4	17.5	5.8	17.4	6.8	2.5	1.3
Fargo, ND	9.9	24.3	26.6	9.6	21.7	4.8	1.8	1.3
Farmington, CT	16.0	28.6	17.8	7.0	18.1	8.9	2.4	1.2
Fishers, IN	14.9	31.2	20.2	6.1	18.4	6.3	2.0	0.9
Flower Mound, TX	19.2	22.3	23.5	5.7	20.3	6.4	1.7	0.8
Franklin, MA	13.4	26.0	16.8	7.1	21.5	10.4	2.9	2.0
Frederick, MD	12.9	20.4	19.4	5.1	23.5	12.4	3.9	2.4
Frisco, TX	19.2	22.3	23.5	5.7	20.3	6.4	1.7	0.8
Goodyear, AZ	18.1	23.4	26.6	7.1	16.6	5.7	1.8	0.8
Grand Blanc, MI	16.3	33.2	25.7	8.1	10.9	4.3	1.1	0.4
Greenburgh, NY	21.5	26.4	16.5	5.6	17.7	8.2	3.0	1.2
Greenwich, CT	16.1	23.7	15.4	5.6	22.7	11.9	3.4	1.1
Hampden, PA	15.6	37.6	16.0	6.2	15.7	5.8	2.4	0.7
Hilliard, OH	13.7	30.6	21.0	5.8	19.6	6.2	2.1	1.1
Hoover, AL	20.8	28.8	21.6	5.5	15.2	5.2	2.0	0.8
Huntersville, NC	17.9	24.6	21.9	6.9	20.8	5.7	1.6	0.6
Juneau, AK	6.7	21.7	28.4	6.6	23.3	8.4	3.3	1.6
Keller, TX	19.2	22.3	23.5	5.7	20.3	6.4	1.7	0.8
Kenner, LA	20.5	28.4	22.8	4.3	15.5	5.0	2.7	0.9
Kennesaw, GA	16.6	25.3	21.8	5.7	20.8	6.8	2.2	0.9
League City, TX	22.8	22.8	22.3	5.2	18.2	5.8	2.0	1.0
Leawood, KS	12.8	28.4	23.9	5.9	19.4	6.8	2.1	0.7
Lee's Summit, MO	12.8	28.4	23.9	5.9	19.4	6.8	2.1	0.7
Leesburg, VA	12.9	20.4	19.4	5.1	23.5	12.4	3.9	2.4
Lehi, UT	8.8	19.6	30.8	9.8	21.5	6.3	1.6	1.8
Lwr Providence, PA	17.3	31.4	17.5	5.8	17.4	6.8	2.5	1.3
Madison, AL	16.2	23.7	22.6	5.9	21.1	8.1	1.3	1.2
Manhattan Bch, CA	28.1	18.5	20.6	6.6	17.0	5.7	2.4	1.0
Maple Grove, MN	9.3	25.7	24.4	7.8	23.0	6.6	2.3	1.1
Marion, IA	10.0	32.5	23.0	9.1	18.8	4.7	1.4	0.4
Marlboro, NJ	21.5	26.4	16.5	5.6	17.7	8.2	3.0	1.2

Area	Less than H.S.	H.S. Diploma	Some College, No Deg.	Associate Degree	Bachelors Degree	Masters Degree	Profess. School Degree	Doctorate Degree
Matthews, NC	17.9	24.6	21.9	6.9	20.8	5.7	1.6	0.6
Meridian, ID	13.9	26.1	27.9	6.9	17.7	5.2	1.6	0.7
Merrimack, NH	13.0	27.4	20.4	9.1	20.1	7.6	1.6	0.8
Morgantown, WV	19.0	34.9	16.0	3.5	12.8	8.0	2.8	3.0
Mt Pleasant, SC	18.3	26.8	22.4	7.1	16.6	5.8	2.1	0.9
Northampton, PA	17.3	31.4	17.5	5.8	17.4	6.8	2.5	1.3
Northville, MI	17.2	28.9	23.6	6.8	14.8	6.3	1.8	0.6
Novi, MI	17.2	28.9	23.6	6.8	14.8	6.3	1.8	0.6
O'Fallon, MO	16.7	29.1	23.2	6.2	15.8	6.3	1.8	0.8
Oro Valley, AZ	16.2	23.3	27.0	6.8	16.0	7.2	2.0	1.6
Oviedo, FL	17.0	27.6	22.7	8.0	17.2	5.1	1.8	0.7
Palm Bch Grdns, FL	23.4	25.3	20.1	6.9	15.0	5.3	3.3	0.9
Parker, CO	13.2	21.8	23.8	6.8	23.2	7.8	2.3	1.0
Peachtree City, GA	16.6	25.3	21.8	5.7	20.8	6.8	2.2	0.9
Pflugerville, TX	14.9	20.1	23.0	5.6	24.3	8.2	2.1	1.7
Pleasanton, CA	16.1	17.6	21.3	6.8	24.0	9.1	3.3	1.9
Rapid City, SD	12.3	30.4	26.3	7.9	15.8	4.9	1.7	0.7
Redmond, WA	10.7	22.9	25.9	8.0	21.9	7.1	2.3	1.2
Richland, WA	20.2	23.2	24.0	8.7	15.1	6.2	1.1	1.6
Richmond, KY	27.6	31.0	17.6	4.1	11.8	5.3	1.1	1.5
Rio Rancho, NM	15.8	25.9	23.9	6.1	16.6	7.9	2.1	1.6
Rockaway, NJ	21.5	26.4	16.5	5.6	17.7	8.2	3.0	1.2
Rocklin, CA	14.9	22.0	27.0	8.9	18.0	5.8	2.3	1.0
Rogers, AR	21.0	32.1	21.5	4.1	14.1	4.5	1.6	1.1
Round Rock, TX	14.9	20.1	23.0	5.6	24.3	8.2	2.1	1.7
Sammamish, WA	10.7	22.9	25.9	8.0	21.9	7.1	2.3	1.2
San Ramon, CA	16.1	17.6	21.3	6.8	24.0	9.1	3.3	1.9
Santa Fe, NM	16.1	19.6	22.0	5.7	20.1	10.3	3.4	2.7
Saratoga, CA	17.4	16.2	19.9	7.4	23.4	11.1	2.2	2.4
Savage, MN	9.3	25.7	24.4	7.8	23.0	6.6	2.3	1.1
Schererville, IN	18.5	25.4	21.3	5.7	18.4	7.3	2.3	1.0
Shawnee, KS	12.8	28.4	23.9	5.9	19.4	6.8	2.1	0.7
Shrewsbury, MA	16.6	30.2	18.5	7.9	16.7	7.4	1.8	1.1
S Brunswick, NJ	21.5	26.4	16.5	5.6	17.7	8.2	3.0	1.2
S. Jordan, UT	12.6	24.1	28.1	7.6	18.6	5.7	2.1	1.1
S Kingstown, RI	23.8	28.4	17.1	7.1	15.0	6.0	1.7	0.8
Southaven, MS	20.2	28.0	23.9	5.3	14.9	5.1	1.9	0.8
Southlake, TX	19.2	22.3	23.5	5.7	20.3	6.4	1.7	0.8
Spanish Fork, UT	8.8	19.6	30.8	9.8	21.5	6.3	1.6	1.8
Sparks, NV	15.4	25.1	28.3	7.2	16.1	5.1	1.9	1.0
Stow, OH	14.0	34.6	21.4	5.2	16.4	5.5	1.8	1.0
Sugar Land, TX	22.8	22.8	22.3	5.2	18.2	5.8	2.0	1.0
Sun Prairie, WI	8.5	24.7	20.5	8.8	23.3	9.0	2.7	2.5
Tualatin, OR	12.7	23.9	27.7	7.0	19.2	6.5	2.0	0.9
Waimalu, HI	15.1	27.6	21.4	7.9	19.1	5.8	2.1	1.0
Wellington, FL	23.4	25.3	20.1	6.9	15.0	5.3	3.3	0.9
W Des Moines, IA	10.8	30.3	22.1	7.5	21.0	5.3	2.4	0.8
West Linn, OR	12.7	23.9	27.7	7.0	19.2	6.5	2.0	0.9
West Windsor, NJ	17.9	25.4	16.8	5.4	18.8	9.9	2.9	3.0
Weston, FL	23.4	25.3	20.1	6.9	15.0	5.3	3.3	0.9
Woodbury, MN	9.3	25.7	24.4	7.8	23.0	6.6	2.3	1.1
Woodridge, IL	18.5	25.4	21.3	5.7	18.4	7.3	2.3	1.0
Yorba Linda, CA	28.1	18.5	20.6	6.6	17.0	5.7	2.4	1.0
U.S.	19.4	28.4	21.2	6.4	15.7	5.9	2.0	1.0

Note: Figures cover persons age 25 and over; Figures are 2007 estimates and cover the Metropolitan Statistical Area (MSA) - see Appendix B for areas included
Source: Claritas, Inc.

School Enrollment by Race: City

City	Grades KG to 8 (%)				Grades 9 to 12 (%)			
	White	Black	Asian	Hisp.[1]	White	Black	Asian	Hisp.[1]
Allen, TX	86.8	3.9	3.0	8.3	86.1	7.1	1.1	7.3
Ankeny, IA	96.9	0.3	0.0	2.7	95.6	1.4	1.3	0.7
Apex, NC	86.5	6.5	3.6	2.7	83.2	11.0	2.1	2.1
Bangor, ME	0.6	0.0	0.0	6.1	0.0	0.0	0.0	0.0
Beavercreek, OH	92.6	2.4	2.2	1.8	93.1	1.4	4.0	0.8
Bellevue, NE	84.0	6.2	0.5	8.7	82.5	8.4	2.1	8.7
Bend, OR	89.4	0.5	1.2	6.9	90.3	0.9	1.2	7.5
Bernards, NJ	87.4	0.2	9.3	2.7	87.2	2.6	6.9	3.0
Bethlehem, NY	92.5	3.8	1.7	1.5	94.6	1.7	1.1	0.6
Bozeman, MT	89.7	0.0	3.8	5.0	95.0	0.0	1.5	3.0
Brentwood, TN	94.2	2.3	3.0	1.0	88.9	5.5	4.2	0.4
Brookfield, WI	94.6	0.3	3.1	0.8	91.3	0.8	6.7	0.3
Broomfield, CO	86.3	1.0	5.1	11.8	87.2	0.6	3.4	12.2
Burlington, VT	87.6	4.7	4.1	1.3	83.3	7.0	6.3	3.2
Carmel, IN	92.5	1.8	4.4	1.4	87.5	1.0	6.5	2.3
Cary, NC	81.3	6.3	7.9	4.2	81.6	7.6	6.9	3.3
Casper, WY	92.4	0.4	1.3	7.7	90.8	1.3	1.3	7.2
Cheshire, CT	93.3	1.0	4.3	2.8	80.0	10.8	1.1	9.0
Chino Hills, CA	54.7	6.2	18.9	28.8	56.1	6.9	17.2	32.2
Collierville, TN	88.5	7.4	1.4	1.4	91.6	5.9	0.3	0.9
Conway, AR	78.7	17.1	0.6	3.6	84.3	10.1	1.4	1.6
Coronado, CA	87.3	3.1	4.1	11.5	77.6	4.7	5.0	12.8
Cranberry, PA	97.1	0.3	0.5	1.7	98.0	0.8	0.0	0.9
Dover, DE	45.2	41.6	3.1	6.2	47.9	40.6	2.3	4.3
Draper, UT	95.5	0.7	1.0	3.6	88.1	0.8	0.9	7.4
Dublin, OH	86.7	2.1	8.2	1.1	91.6	0.5	5.1	0.4
Edmond, OK	86.8	4.9	1.5	3.6	86.9	5.0	0.8	2.8
Evesham, NJ	91.1	2.2	3.8	2.5	91.0	3.5	3.5	2.4
Fargo, ND	89.5	2.9	1.8	1.9	92.8	1.2	1.8	3.2
Farmington, CT	91.5	2.4	4.3	4.6	90.6	2.7	5.1	0.6
Fishers, IN	91.3	3.1	2.3	2.4	94.5	0.0	1.5	2.7
Flower Mound, TX	90.5	2.2	1.8	6.6	88.0	3.1	2.1	7.3
Franklin, MA	95.5	1.4	1.4	0.5	95.9	2.1	0.6	0.0
Frederick, MD	68.1	20.5	3.5	4.5	72.3	18.7	3.0	5.9
Frisco, TX	85.4	4.9	1.5	15.8	84.2	1.3	1.0	17.8
Goodyear, AZ	69.9	4.2	1.6	35.5	63.7	11.1	0.0	38.7
Grand Blanc, MI	85.5	7.5	1.2	2.7	88.1	6.4	2.8	5.0
Greenburgh, NY	67.1	15.0	10.0	9.7	63.6	17.4	9.2	11.9
Greenwich, CT	86.4	1.6	7.1	6.1	84.8	3.3	6.8	9.4
Hampden, PA	92.9	1.0	3.7	1.5	88.6	3.8	6.1	0.4
Hilliard, OH	91.9	1.4	4.9	1.4	93.8	0.8	5.5	1.0
Hoover, AL	87.1	7.1	2.8	3.1	88.3	6.5	3.0	2.6
Huntersville, NC	88.4	5.5	0.9	4.3	83.5	12.0	1.6	3.4
Juneau, AK	66.7	0.3	4.8	5.2	68.8	1.7	4.4	3.3
Keller, TX	90.4	1.5	1.7	7.0	93.7	0.8	0.6	5.8
Kenner, LA	59.3	30.9	2.6	14.2	59.3	28.4	2.7	14.2
Kennesaw, GA	80.3	13.9	0.0	8.9	77.9	14.6	1.9	3.3
League City, TX	83.1	6.4	3.3	15.3	82.6	5.9	2.3	18.9
Leawood, KS	94.0	1.4	2.9	0.8	97.3	0.5	1.7	1.3
Lee's Summit, MO	92.4	3.5	0.6	2.8	93.4	3.5	0.3	2.1
Leesburg, VA	79.9	10.4	2.8	6.2	81.7	12.3	1.5	5.1
Lehi, UT	92.5	0.3	1.1	2.6	98.0	0.0	0.0	2.7
Lwr Providence, PA	91.1	2.0	3.1	0.9	76.2	16.5	3.7	4.6
Madison, AL	78.0	13.1	3.5	3.7	78.8	15.9	1.5	3.2
Manhattan Bch, CA	86.8	1.0	5.2	3.7	85.7	0.2	6.6	11.5
Maple Grove, MN	93.0	2.1	2.2	1.8	94.0	1.6	1.8	0.7
Marion, IA	94.0	1.5	0.6	1.2	96.2	1.2	0.3	1.1
Marlboro, NJ	82.3	1.0	13.9	4.0	84.9	2.8	8.7	4.9
Matthews, NC	90.5	4.7	3.1	4.0	91.5	5.0	2.1	2.3

City	Grades KG to 8 (%)				Grades 9 to 12 (%)			
	White	Black	Asian	Hisp.[1]	White	Black	Asian	Hisp.[1]
Meridian, ID	94.3	0.1	0.7	4.4	92.7	0.0	1.2	3.3
Merrimack, NH	94.9	0.5	2.4	0.5	93.4	3.7	2.5	0.0
Morgantown, WV	85.2	8.0	2.2	2.2	92.9	2.3	2.3	1.8
Mt Pleasant, SC	89.3	7.0	1.3	0.8	86.0	10.2	0.3	4.1
Northampton, PA	96.9	0.3	2.3	0.2	96.4	0.0	3.6	0.5
Northville, MI	89.0	2.4	5.0	3.3	87.7	6.3	3.7	1.2
Novi, MI	85.6	1.5	9.6	2.2	86.0	2.0	6.9	4.0
O'Fallon, MO	94.8	3.2	0.5	1.2	95.2	2.2	0.3	1.1
Oro Valley, AZ	91.9	1.7	1.7	12.7	92.5	0.0	2.0	13.6
Oviedo, FL	84.0	8.4	1.7	12.5	80.7	10.2	1.7	13.2
Palm Bch Grdns, FL	90.9	3.3	2.6	8.6	88.0	5.5	4.6	7.9
Parker, CO	94.0	0.6	2.0	4.5	86.4	2.3	0.9	9.2
Peachtree City, GA	85.2	8.5	4.7	2.4	91.5	5.1	1.4	1.8
Pflugerville, TX	78.5	8.5	3.8	18.1	74.5	8.8	2.1	23.3
Pleasanton, CA	76.4	0.9	12.8	8.8	83.5	1.7	7.4	10.5
Rapid City, SD	74.2	0.7	1.4	4.3	82.5	0.9	1.4	4.1
Redmond, WA	74.3	2.6	12.6	8.6	83.5	0.0	9.8	7.3
Richland, WA	85.4	2.0	3.6	9.3	87.5	0.0	3.8	4.4
Richmond, KY	80.8	11.0	1.4	1.9	85.6	8.8	0.0	0.8
Rio Rancho, NM	73.6	2.5	1.2	34.5	75.3	0.6	2.0	32.9
Rockaway, NJ	86.2	3.0	6.8	6.5	90.9	1.1	4.8	7.1
Rocklin, CA	86.1	2.0	3.1	7.6	88.7	0.6	2.6	11.3
Rogers, AR	80.2	1.3	0.8	27.1	85.5	0.8	0.7	20.6
Round Rock, TX	72.8	9.6	2.1	27.1	75.1	8.7	3.6	23.9
Sammamish, WA	86.7	1.0	5.4	4.0	89.3	0.2	6.9	3.3
San Ramon, CA	72.2	1.5	17.8	7.4	75.6	3.3	10.7	9.8
Santa Fe, NM	67.9	0.2	0.8	63.8	69.2	0.6	0.9	64.1
Saratoga, CA	57.3	0.3	36.4	2.7	51.4	0.7	40.3	1.2
Savage, MN	89.7	1.5	3.6	3.4	88.3	1.5	4.8	2.1
Schererville, IN	88.0	2.8	3.7	7.1	91.2	2.8	1.7	6.6
Shawnee, KS	89.1	2.8	3.1	4.1	87.3	3.1	3.1	5.1
Shrewsbury, MA	84.1	2.1	10.1	2.0	89.8	0.0	8.1	0.6
S Brunswick, NJ	69.3	8.8	17.8	6.6	65.0	9.0	16.2	10.2
S. Jordan, UT	95.5	0.3	0.5	4.2	95.0	0.5	1.0	2.0
S Kingstown, RI	91.3	0.7	2.6	2.0	86.4	1.7	5.5	2.0
Southaven, MS	89.8	7.9	1.4	2.7	91.6	3.5	1.9	0.7
Southlake, TX	94.8	1.4	1.1	3.9	93.8	1.1	2.7	4.0
Spanish Fork, UT	93.7	0.0	0.2	4.9	94.1	0.0	1.0	3.2
Sparks, NV	72.4	3.2	4.6	28.0	75.3	3.0	4.7	23.4
Stow, OH	92.9	2.8	1.7	0.8	96.0	0.0	1.9	1.2
Sugar Land, TX	66.2	5.7	21.8	9.9	63.5	5.1	26.0	6.5
Sun Prairie, WI	86.6	5.0	2.8	6.2	94.1	2.5	1.8	1.1
Tualatin, OR	86.0	0.3	2.9	11.0	83.3	0.0	8.2	12.2
Waimalu, HI	6.3	0.2	48.1	7.8	8.3	1.0	45.9	8.5
Wellington, FL	88.8	5.7	1.8	11.6	86.8	9.2	1.7	8.7
W Des Moines, IA	89.7	2.3	2.5	4.8	92.1	1.7	2.2	6.1
West Linn, OR	91.0	1.0	2.6	3.5	93.0	0.0	2.9	2.8
West Windsor, NJ	70.8	2.3	22.3	4.7	63.0	3.3	27.1	5.7
Weston, FL	84.6	4.9	3.5	32.1	85.6	4.3	2.4	35.2
Woodbury, MN	86.8	1.6	6.5	3.7	84.9	3.9	6.7	3.2
Woodridge, IL	71.7	12.1	10.7	8.3	75.1	7.2	12.2	12.1
Yorba Linda, CA	77.4	1.7	11.2	12.4	78.3	1.1	11.7	11.1
U.S.	68.5	15.5	3.3	16.8	68.8	15.5	3.8	15.7

Note: Figures shown cover persons 3 years old and over; (1) people of Hispanic origin can be of any race; Source: Census 2000, Summary File 3

School Enrollment by Race: Metro Area

MSA[1]	Grades KG to 8 (%)				Grades 9 to 12 (%)			
	White	Black	Asian	Hisp.[2]	White	Black	Asian	Hisp.[2]
Allen, TX	60.7	18.0	3.6	28.9	61.2	18.7	4.0	25.8
Ankeny, IA	86.3	5.3	2.2	5.5	87.0	5.0	2.5	4.7
Apex, NC	63.0	28.2	2.6	6.1	64.9	27.9	2.6	4.7
Bangor, ME	0.6	0.0	0.0	4.2	0.6	0.0	0.0	0.3
Beavercreek, OH	76.7	18.4	1.0	1.3	79.2	17.1	1.1	1.0
Bellevue, NE	80.5	11.0	1.2	7.2	82.0	10.7	1.4	5.6
Bend, OR	n/a	n/a	n/a	n/a	n/a	n/a	n/a	n/a
Bernards, NJ	70.1	9.4	11.4	13.9	68.2	10.9	10.7	14.7
Bethlehem, NY	85.2	8.5	1.7	4.0	86.1	7.9	2.0	3.6
Bozeman, MT	n/a	n/a	n/a	n/a	n/a	n/a	n/a	n/a
Brentwood, TN	74.7	19.8	1.4	3.3	74.4	20.7	1.5	2.6
Brookfield, WI	64.7	24.8	2.4	8.9	68.9	21.5	2.4	7.6
Broomfield, CO	73.1	6.9	2.7	24.9	74.5	6.6	3.4	21.9
Burlington, VT	94.4	1.2	1.7	0.8	93.3	1.5	2.2	1.8
Carmel, IN	77.4	17.7	1.0	2.6	77.7	18.0	1.1	2.7
Cary, NC	63.0	28.2	2.6	6.1	64.9	27.9	2.6	4.7
Casper, WY	92.0	0.5	1.0	6.9	92.0	1.0	1.0	6.2
Cheshire, CT	69.3	18.2	2.2	14.8	68.9	18.3	2.0	14.4
Chino Hills, CA	54.0	9.0	3.3	48.1	54.7	9.0	4.3	44.9
Collierville, TN	43.1	53.1	1.2	2.2	44.0	52.4	1.3	1.9
Conway, AR	66.5	29.1	0.7	2.5	65.2	31.0	1.0	1.8
Coronado, CA	57.2	7.0	7.8	38.2	56.6	6.7	9.5	35.9
Cranberry, PA	84.8	11.9	1.0	0.9	87.2	9.9	0.9	1.0
Dover, DE	68.9	23.5	1.1	4.6	67.8	23.2	1.7	4.2
Draper, UT	85.4	1.1	1.7	12.7	87.1	1.0	2.1	10.6
Dublin, OH	76.5	17.1	2.0	2.1	77.3	16.8	1.9	2.0
Edmond, OK	67.3	13.6	2.2	9.9	69.2	14.0	2.4	7.6
Evesham, NJ	65.6	24.9	3.1	7.0	64.8	25.6	3.7	6.4
Fargo, ND	90.9	1.5	1.0	3.5	93.4	0.8	1.2	3.6
Farmington, CT	73.5	12.1	2.2	15.4	74.3	11.8	2.5	13.9
Fishers, IN	77.4	17.7	1.0	2.6	77.7	18.0	1.1	2.7
Flower Mound, TX	60.7	18.0	3.6	28.9	61.2	18.7	4.0	25.8
Franklin, MA	76.8	10.0	4.6	8.7	75.2	11.1	4.9	8.7
Frederick, MD	54.3	30.4	5.8	9.9	53.1	30.9	6.6	10.2
Frisco, TX	60.7	18.0	3.6	28.9	61.2	18.7	4.0	25.8
Goodyear, AZ	68.7	4.4	1.7	35.6	70.9	4.6	2.0	31.5
Grand Blanc, MI	66.6	26.9	0.5	3.4	69.5	24.4	0.8	3.2
Greenburgh, NY	39.1	30.1	8.0	32.0	37.2	31.2	9.0	31.3
Greenwich, CT	76.6	11.9	4.0	11.6	73.0	14.2	3.5	14.8
Hampden, PA	81.8	10.8	1.7	5.2	83.7	9.6	2.3	4.5
Hilliard, OH	76.5	17.1	2.0	2.1	77.3	16.8	1.9	2.0
Hoover, AL	60.1	37.1	0.6	2.0	59.8	38.0	0.6	1.3
Huntersville, NC	67.2	26.1	1.8	5.0	67.2	27.1	2.2	3.8
Juneau, AK	n/a	n/a	n/a	n/a	n/a	n/a	n/a	n/a
Keller, TX	69.1	12.9	2.8	23.7	69.0	14.1	3.6	19.9
Kenner, LA	46.8	47.2	2.2	4.2	47.3	46.8	2.4	4.1
Kennesaw, GA	56.5	35.2	3.0	6.2	56.3	35.5	3.6	5.3
League City, TX	67.0	17.8	2.1	22.4	66.0	19.7	1.7	22.0
Leawood, KS	75.5	16.1	1.3	6.4	75.6	16.7	1.9	5.5
Lee's Summit, MO	75.5	16.1	1.3	6.4	75.6	16.7	1.9	5.5
Leesburg, VA	54.3	30.4	5.8	9.9	53.1	30.9	6.6	10.2
Lehi, UT	91.8	0.5	0.6	7.5	93.6	0.2	0.6	6.1
Lwr Providence, PA	65.6	24.9	3.1	7.0	64.8	25.6	3.7	6.4
Madison, AL	70.7	23.3	1.3	2.8	68.7	25.2	1.6	2.8
Manhattan Bch, CA	41.8	10.5	9.1	57.7	39.8	10.3	11.2	55.9
Maple Grove, MN	79.3	7.7	6.0	4.4	80.8	7.1	6.3	3.8
Marion, IA	90.7	3.5	1.4	2.1	92.2	3.2	1.8	1.3
Marlboro, NJ	84.8	7.5	3.0	7.3	85.1	7.5	3.1	6.7
Matthews, NC	67.2	26.1	1.8	5.0	67.2	27.1	2.2	3.8

MSA[1]	Grades KG to 8 (%)				Grades 9 to 12 (%)			
	White	Black	Asian	Hisp.[2]	White	Black	Asian	Hisp.[2]
Meridian, ID	87.2	0.6	0.9	12.0	87.9	0.8	1.2	10.6
Merrimack, NH	92.3	1.2	2.0	5.0	92.0	1.8	1.9	4.3
Morgantown, WV	n/a	n/a	n/a	n/a	n/a	n/a	n/a	n/a
Mt Pleasant, SC	54.5	40.7	1.0	2.6	53.4	42.0	1.5	2.5
Northampton, PA	65.6	24.9	3.1	7.0	64.8	25.6	3.7	6.4
Northville, MI	63.6	29.2	2.2	3.7	66.4	26.8	2.3	3.2
Novi, MI	63.6	29.2	2.2	3.7	66.4	26.8	2.3	3.2
O'Fallon, MO	71.8	24.1	1.1	1.8	73.7	22.5	1.3	1.8
Oro Valley, AZ	65.5	3.4	1.5	42.8	65.7	3.6	1.9	40.6
Oviedo, FL	67.1	19.4	2.3	20.1	65.6	20.0	2.9	20.0
Palm Bch Grdns, FL	65.8	24.3	1.7	16.1	63.3	26.3	1.9	16.1
Parker, CO	73.1	6.9	2.7	24.9	74.5	6.6	3.4	21.9
Peachtree City, GA	56.5	35.2	3.0	6.2	56.3	35.5	3.6	5.3
Pflugerville, TX	66.6	9.5	2.7	34.2	67.3	10.3	2.5	31.0
Pleasanton, CA	47.5	15.0	15.4	24.8	47.7	15.0	16.9	22.8
Rapid City, SD	78.9	0.9	1.2	4.2	85.3	1.2	1.1	3.2
Redmond, WA	73.2	5.5	9.2	6.6	73.1	5.4	10.5	5.8
Richland, WA	73.9	1.5	1.5	30.9	75.8	1.1	2.6	26.1
Richmond, KY	83.1	11.8	1.4	2.6	82.8	12.4	1.3	2.0
Rio Rancho, NM	61.5	2.6	1.2	50.4	62.9	2.5	1.5	49.0
Rockaway, NJ	60.3	26.3	4.0	15.0	58.2	27.5	4.1	15.7
Rocklin, CA	61.7	9.9	9.5	19.4	63.2	9.0	11.1	17.1
Rogers, AR	85.6	1.6	1.1	12.1	87.7	1.2	1.2	10.1
Round Rock, TX	66.6	9.5	2.7	34.2	67.3	10.3	2.5	31.0
Sammamish, WA	73.2	5.5	9.2	6.6	73.1	5.4	10.5	5.8
San Ramon, CA	47.5	15.0	15.4	24.8	47.7	15.0	16.9	22.8
Santa Fe, NM	69.0	0.4	1.2	54.8	69.7	1.3	1.3	54.1
Saratoga, CA	47.3	2.6	24.3	32.8	45.3	3.1	25.2	33.5
Savage, MN	79.3	7.7	6.0	4.4	80.8	7.1	6.3	3.8
Schererville, IN	67.3	23.4	0.8	13.6	68.9	22.7	0.7	12.8
Shawnee, KS	75.5	16.1	1.3	6.4	75.6	16.7	1.9	5.5
Shrewsbury, MA	84.3	3.8	3.4	11.4	85.2	3.8	3.4	10.4
S Brunswick, NJ	70.1	9.4	11.4	13.9	68.2	10.9	10.7	14.7
S. Jordan, UT	85.4	1.1	1.7	12.7	87.1	1.0	2.1	10.6
S Kingstown, RI	79.3	5.8	2.7	12.8	79.8	5.6	3.6	11.5
Southaven, MS	43.1	53.1	1.2	2.2	44.0	52.4	1.3	1.9
Southlake, TX	69.1	12.9	2.8	23.7	69.0	14.1	3.6	19.9
Spanish Fork, UT	91.8	0.5	0.6	7.5	93.6	0.2	0.6	6.1
Sparks, NV	74.2	2.0	3.8	25.1	74.0	3.0	4.4	22.4
Stow, OH	80.1	15.1	1.2	1.1	81.6	14.8	1.3	0.8
Sugar Land, TX	56.0	19.6	4.3	36.5	56.0	19.8	5.4	32.8
Sun Prairie, WI	84.2	6.6	3.5	4.3	85.2	6.2	3.7	3.5
Tualatin, OR	80.1	3.1	4.4	9.9	81.9	3.4	4.8	7.7
Waimalu, HI	14.7	2.2	34.3	10.2	11.5	1.6	41.7	9.4
Wellington, FL	65.8	24.3	1.7	16.1	63.3	26.3	1.9	16.1
W Des Moines, IA	86.3	5.3	2.2	5.5	87.0	5.0	2.5	4.7
West Linn, OR	80.1	3.1	4.4	9.9	81.9	3.4	4.8	7.7
West Windsor, NJ	59.9	25.8	5.2	11.6	58.1	27.2	5.2	11.8
Weston, FL	59.2	30.1	2.2	19.3	55.9	32.4	2.4	19.4
Woodbury, MN	79.3	7.7	6.0	4.4	80.8	7.1	6.3	3.8
Woodridge, IL	58.6	23.4	3.9	22.2	58.7	23.2	4.6	20.2
Yorba Linda, CA	58.6	1.6	11.8	42.5	56.2	1.9	14.8	38.8
U.S.	68.5	15.5	3.3	16.8	68.8	15.5	3.8	15.7

Note: Figures shown cover persons 3 years old and over; (1) Metropolitan Statistical Area - see Appendix A for areas included; (2) people of Hispanic origin can be of any race
Source: Census 2000, Summary File 3

School Enrollment by Type: City

City	Grades KG to 8				Grades 9 to 12			
	Public		Private		Public		Private	
	Enrollment	%	Enrollment	%	Enrollment	%	Enrollment	%
Allen, TX	7,056	93.4	498	6.6	2,736	96.6	95	3.4
Ankeny, IA	3,497	96.8	117	3.2	1,577	97.6	39	2.4
Apex, NC	2,857	94.5	166	5.5	887	90.8	90	9.2
Bangor, ME	3,142	90.8	320	9.2	1,501	93.6	102	6.4
Beavercreek, OH	4,002	77.5	1,165	22.5	2,045	82.3	440	17.7
Bellevue, NE	5,032	84.2	943	15.8	2,744	91.7	247	8.3
Bend, OR	5,520	88.1	744	11.9	2,710	93.8	180	6.2
Bernards, NJ	3,187	87.9	439	12.1	1,074	91.3	102	8.7
Bethlehem, NY	3,700	83.5	731	16.5	1,815	88.2	242	11.8
Bozeman, MT	2,005	90.8	204	9.2	830	92.6	66	7.4
Brentwood, TN	3,230	79.5	835	20.5	1,531	74.3	530	25.7
Brookfield, WI	3,885	68.9	1,751	31.1	2,168	79.8	549	20.2
Broomfield, CO	5,316	89.2	641	10.8	2,247	95.2	113	4.8
Burlington, VT	2,896	89.9	325	10.1	1,355	89.3	162	10.7
Carmel, IN	4,939	83.0	1,015	17.0	2,024	83.3	405	16.7
Cary, NC	13,377	91.4	1,252	8.6	4,691	89.2	566	10.8
Casper, WY	6,305	97.0	192	3.0	2,969	98.8	36	1.2
Cheshire, CT	3,351	88.3	443	11.7	1,944	90.9	195	9.1
Chino Hills, CA	10,294	87.3	1,496	12.7	4,185	92.4	345	7.6
Collierville, TN	5,357	91.2	514	8.8	2,072	89.7	238	10.3
Conway, AR	4,464	85.9	730	14.1	1,870	92.3	155	7.7
Coronado, CA	1,705	82.8	353	17.2	868	88.8	109	11.2
Cranberry, PA	3,285	89.4	389	10.6	1,235	96.0	52	4.0
Dover, DE	3,587	90.5	378	9.5	1,390	96.1	57	3.9
Draper, UT	3,409	89.4	404	10.6	1,702	92.4	140	7.6
Dublin, OH	4,591	86.7	707	13.3	1,859	90.4	197	9.6
Edmond, OK	8,602	87.1	1,273	12.9	3,922	91.7	357	8.3
Evesham, NJ	5,186	86.6	801	13.4	2,095	88.9	261	11.1
Fargo, ND	8,463	90.9	845	9.1	3,834	92.9	294	7.1
Farmington, CT	2,913	93.2	213	6.8	1,177	85.4	202	14.6
Fishers, IN	5,055	88.1	686	11.9	1,400	91.1	136	8.9
Flower Mound, TX	8,124	92.4	664	7.6	2,937	95.4	143	4.6
Franklin, MA	4,340	96.9	137	3.1	1,378	87.4	198	12.6
Frederick, MD	6,143	89.8	701	10.2	2,188	92.0	189	8.0
Frisco, TX	3,964	90.7	405	9.3	1,258	92.5	102	7.5
Goodyear, AZ	1,890	92.5	153	7.5	872	96.1	35	3.9
Grand Blanc, MI	3,475	86.3	551	13.7	1,455	87.3	212	12.7
Greenburgh, NY	9,644	88.0	1,320	12.0	3,612	84.7	653	15.3
Greenwich, CT	6,337	75.5	2,059	24.5	2,160	75.3	710	24.7
Hampden, PA	2,644	84.9	471	15.1	1,299	82.7	272	17.3
Hilliard, OH	3,467	87.1	515	12.9	1,229	93.7	83	6.3
Hoover, AL	6,492	84.7	1,173	15.3	2,923	86.7	450	13.3
Huntersville, NC	2,744	81.5	622	18.5	1,235	94.6	70	5.4
Juneau, AK	4,001	92.0	349	8.0	1,782	95.8	78	4.2
Keller, TX	4,451	89.4	530	10.6	1,627	91.4	153	8.6
Kenner, LA	6,793	66.2	3,471	33.8	2,774	62.1	1,695	37.9
Kennesaw, GA	2,732	92.0	236	8.0	890	96.9	28	3.1
League City, TX	6,226	90.1	686	9.9	2,355	90.5	248	9.5
Leawood, KS	3,435	73.6	1,234	26.4	1,464	73.3	532	26.7
Lee's Summit, MO	9,780	90.7	1,006	9.3	3,820	92.9	294	7.1
Leesburg, VA	3,695	90.1	405	9.9	1,163	92.9	89	7.1
Lehi, UT	3,327	96.8	110	3.2	1,206	94.3	73	5.7
Lwr Providence, PA	2,661	87.2	390	12.8	1,168	79.5	301	20.5
Madison, AL	3,747	82.3	804	17.7	1,531	91.1	150	8.9
Manhattan Bch, CA	3,531	88.8	444	11.2	1,265	91.4	119	8.6
Maple Grove, MN	7,554	92.3	629	7.7	3,429	94.3	209	5.7
Marion, IA	3,167	89.1	388	10.9	1,440	95.4	69	4.6

City	Grades KG to 8				Grades 9 to 12			
	Public		Private		Public		Private	
	Enrollment	%	Enrollment	%	Enrollment	%	Enrollment	%
Marlboro, NJ	5,394	91.4	505	8.6	2,181	88.5	284	11.5
Matthews, NC	2,930	81.1	681	18.9	1,257	84.4	232	15.6
Meridian, ID	5,182	91.9	459	8.1	1,876	95.2	94	4.8
Merrimack, NH	3,659	87.8	508	12.2	1,419	88.2	190	11.8
Morgantown, WV	1,274	86.4	201	13.6	637	95.9	27	4.1
Mt Pleasant, SC	4,504	74.4	1,546	25.6	1,867	77.8	534	22.2
Northampton, PA	5,107	85.2	890	14.8	2,277	81.6	514	18.4
Northville, MI	2,115	87.4	305	12.6	969	80.9	229	19.1
Novi, MI	6,448	92.0	558	8.0	2,421	92.7	190	7.3
O'Fallon, MO	6,598	85.4	1,124	14.6	2,434	91.2	236	8.8
Oro Valley, AZ	3,058	88.7	391	11.3	1,467	94.2	90	5.8
Oviedo, FL	4,406	91.6	402	8.4	1,571	94.0	100	6.0
Palm Bch Grdns, FL	2,297	68.5	1,058	31.5	1,495	84.7	270	15.3
Parker, CO	3,535	93.1	262	6.9	1,234	93.4	87	6.6
Peachtree City, GA	4,977	88.1	674	11.9	2,329	92.9	179	7.1
Pflugerville, TX	2,990	93.8	196	6.2	946	99.3	7	0.7
Pleasanton, CA	9,203	91.3	878	8.7	3,374	95.9	143	4.1
Rapid City, SD	6,832	92.7	538	7.3	3,137	90.6	324	9.4
Redmond, WA	4,342	90.6	453	9.4	2,170	95.5	102	4.5
Richland, WA	4,874	87.7	685	12.3	2,475	95.7	110	4.3
Richmond, KY	2,056	92.5	166	7.5	787	92.2	67	7.8
Rio Rancho, NM	7,178	90.3	768	9.7	3,079	92.1	264	7.9
Rockaway, NJ	2,714	84.5	499	15.5	1,073	93.6	73	6.4
Rocklin, CA	5,319	91.3	505	8.7	2,281	95.2	115	4.8
Rogers, AR	5,305	90.1	580	9.9	1,942	96.7	66	3.3
Round Rock, TX	9,001	92.2	763	7.8	3,272	95.1	169	4.9
Sammamish, WA	5,474	89.5	641	10.5	2,321	95.1	119	4.9
San Ramon, CA	5,376	90.2	586	9.8	2,424	94.2	150	5.8
Santa Fe, NM	5,501	85.6	926	14.4	2,334	82.6	490	17.4
Saratoga, CA	3,364	75.7	1,082	24.3	1,547	87.0	232	13.0
Savage, MN	3,363	90.4	359	9.6	1,110	95.3	55	4.7
Schererville, IN	2,517	79.0	671	21.0	1,055	76.6	322	23.4
Shawnee, KS	5,112	80.6	1,233	19.4	2,480	86.7	381	13.3
Shrewsbury, MA	3,646	86.9	552	13.1	1,059	79.1	279	20.9
S Brunswick, NJ	5,224	90.3	564	9.7	2,038	96.5	75	3.5
S. Jordan, UT	5,718	96.3	220	3.7	3,230	97.2	93	2.8
S Kingstown, RI	3,218	93.3	231	6.7	1,363	94.3	82	5.7
Southaven, MS	3,742	90.1	409	9.9	1,270	86.4	200	13.6
Southlake, TX	4,093	92.0	355	8.0	1,749	96.1	71	3.9
Spanish Fork, UT	3,717	98.6	53	1.4	1,341	96.1	55	3.9
Sparks, NV	8,769	94.0	558	6.0	3,604	94.2	220	5.8
Stow, OH	3,608	80.2	892	19.8	1,633	88.0	223	12.0
Sugar Land, TX	9,478	85.9	1,559	14.1	4,778	90.1	525	9.9
Sun Prairie, WI	2,614	89.2	316	10.8	1,256	95.4	60	4.6
Tualatin, OR	2,875	92.4	236	7.6	1,394	93.7	93	6.3
Waimalu, HI	2,559	79.7	651	20.3	1,274	77.4	372	22.6
Wellington, FL	5,676	87.7	797	12.3	2,587	86.1	419	13.9
W Des Moines, IA	4,703	83.3	942	16.7	1,891	86.4	297	13.6
West Linn, OR	2,821	83.6	554	16.4	1,467	93.9	95	6.1
West Windsor, NJ	3,586	91.1	351	8.9	1,250	86.6	194	13.4
Weston, FL	7,065	82.0	1,553	18.0	2,176	76.1	684	23.9
Woodbury, MN	6,134	88.3	814	11.7	2,457	87.9	338	12.1
Woodridge, IL	3,719	88.8	469	11.2	1,656	90.5	174	9.5
Yorba Linda, CA	7,891	81.4	1,808	18.6	3,659	89.4	432	10.6
U.S.	33,526,011	88.7	4,285,121	11.3	14,848,628	90.6	1,532,323	9.4

Note: Figures shown cover persons 3 years old and over
Source: Census 2000, Summary File 3

School Enrollment by Type: Metro Area

MSA[1]	Grades KG to 8				Grades 9 to 12			
	Public		Private		Public		Private	
	Enrollment	%	Enrollment	%	Enrollment	%	Enrollment	%
Allen, TX	456,971	90.7	46,953	9.3	181,249	92.2	15,405	7.8
Ankeny, IA	53,644	90.8	5,417	9.2	23,513	92.7	1,860	7.3
Apex, NC	134,391	89.7	15,408	10.3	51,033	90.4	5,428	9.6
Bangor, ME	9,741	93.0	731	7.0	4,572	89.8	522	10.2
Beavercreek, OH	106,102	86.2	16,953	13.8	46,603	89.5	5,468	10.5
Bellevue, NE	82,606	83.0	16,937	17.0	37,494	86.1	6,066	13.9
Bend, OR	n/a	n/a	n/a	n/a	n/a	n/a	n/a	n/a
Bernards, NJ	129,755	87.7	18,130	12.3	53,556	88.7	6,806	11.3
Bethlehem, NY	99,443	89.7	11,383	10.3	43,264	91.7	3,921	8.3
Bozeman, MT	n/a	n/a	n/a	n/a	n/a	n/a	n/a	n/a
Brentwood, TN	136,243	86.5	21,347	13.5	56,641	85.6	9,515	14.4
Brookfield, WI	168,628	79.3	43,942	20.7	79,263	87.0	11,852	13.0
Broomfield, CO	250,673	90.0	27,814	10.0	104,095	91.3	9,939	8.7
Burlington, VT	19,471	91.8	1,745	8.2	8,141	89.3	975	10.7
Carmel, IN	187,223	86.2	29,909	13.8	76,997	89.2	9,345	10.8
Cary, NC	134,391	89.7	15,408	10.3	51,033	90.4	5,428	9.6
Casper, WY	8,473	96.0	356	4.0	3,988	98.8	47	1.2
Cheshire, CT	63,680	90.0	7,051	10.0	27,566	89.7	3,173	10.3
Chino Hills, CA	509,158	92.6	40,533	7.4	214,509	94.4	12,697	5.6
Collierville, TN	149,569	88.4	19,693	11.6	61,138	87.4	8,828	12.6
Conway, AR	65,034	85.4	11,160	14.6	29,770	87.3	4,344	12.7
Coronado, CA	345,699	90.9	34,480	9.1	149,710	93.8	9,945	6.2
Cranberry, PA	237,516	86.3	37,647	13.7	114,399	91.8	10,230	8.2
Dover, DE	16,252	91.1	1,594	8.9	7,065	94.7	392	5.3
Draper, UT	189,691	94.4	11,196	5.6	93,135	95.6	4,302	4.4
Dublin, OH	178,054	88.0	24,285	12.0	73,403	89.9	8,275	10.1
Edmond, OK	129,199	91.2	12,443	8.8	57,617	92.5	4,701	7.5
Evesham, NJ	544,674	79.7	138,763	20.3	248,356	81.5	56,489	18.5
Fargo, ND	19,637	92.4	1,620	7.6	8,982	94.6	515	5.4
Farmington, CT	142,203	92.0	12,379	8.0	60,214	91.1	5,862	8.9
Fishers, IN	187,223	86.2	29,909	13.8	76,997	89.2	9,345	10.8
Flower Mound, TX	456,971	90.7	46,953	9.3	181,249	92.2	15,405	7.8
Franklin, MA	347,941	87.2	51,024	12.8	147,396	85.5	25,007	14.5
Frederick, MD	556,504	85.7	92,990	14.3	239,684	88.0	32,576	12.0
Frisco, TX	456,971	90.7	46,953	9.3	181,249	92.2	15,405	7.8
Goodyear, AZ	414,735	93.4	29,200	6.6	163,065	93.8	10,740	6.2
Grand Blanc, MI	58,588	91.4	5,522	8.6	24,041	92.7	1,900	7.3
Greenburgh, NY	965,235	80.8	229,009	19.2	450,178	81.9	99,330	18.1
Greenwich, CT	39,768	84.9	7,049	15.1	14,756	83.9	2,827	16.1
Hampden, PA	68,133	87.0	10,192	13.0	29,993	89.6	3,475	10.4
Hilliard, OH	178,054	88.0	24,285	12.0	73,403	89.9	8,275	10.1
Hoover, AL	108,002	88.8	13,686	11.2	46,620	91.2	4,503	8.8
Huntersville, NC	176,153	88.3	23,233	11.7	71,217	91.1	6,951	8.9
Juneau, AK	n/a	n/a	n/a	n/a	n/a	n/a	n/a	n/a
Keller, TX	224,258	91.0	22,110	9.0	91,305	92.3	7,600	7.7
Kenner, LA	141,576	74.6	48,197	25.4	64,327	76.5	19,770	23.5
Kennesaw, GA	511,746	90.2	55,562	9.8	207,156	91.5	19,214	8.5
League City, TX	32,155	91.5	3,001	8.5	14,281	94.5	830	5.5
Leawood, KS	212,067	87.5	30,212	12.5	90,420	89.1	11,050	10.9
Lee's Summit, MO	212,067	87.5	30,212	12.5	90,420	89.1	11,050	10.9
Leesburg, VA	556,504	85.7	92,990	14.3	239,684	88.0	32,576	12.0
Lehi, UT	56,391	96.9	1,786	3.1	24,610	96.2	976	3.8
Lwr Providence, PA	544,674	79.7	138,763	20.3	248,356	81.5	56,489	18.5
Madison, AL	39,989	87.7	5,601	12.3	16,226	89.1	1,975	10.9
Manhattan Bch, CA	1,261,035	88.4	164,761	11.6	560,595	91.0	55,347	9.0
Maple Grove, MN	360,354	87.5	51,396	12.5	163,520	92.1	13,991	7.9
Marion, IA	21,662	86.5	3,372	13.5	9,839	93.7	663	6.3

MSA[1]	Grades KG to 8				Grades 9 to 12			
	Public		Private		Public		Private	
	Enrollment	%	Enrollment	%	Enrollment	%	Enrollment	%
Marlboro, NJ	127,771	85.7	21,328	14.3	52,824	88.1	7,144	11.9
Matthews, NC	176,153	88.3	23,233	11.7	71,217	91.1	6,951	8.9
Meridian, ID	55,566	91.3	5,311	8.7	24,072	92.7	1,882	7.3
Merrimack, NH	25,037	86.9	3,776	13.1	9,813	89.6	1,145	10.4
Morgantown, WV	n/a	n/a	n/a	n/a	n/a	n/a	n/a	n/a
Mt Pleasant, SC	65,879	86.6	10,174	13.4	27,841	87.9	3,845	12.1
Northampton, PA	544,674	79.7	138,763	20.3	248,356	81.5	56,489	18.5
Northville, MI	550,333	88.1	73,996	11.9	239,111	90.4	25,291	9.6
Novi, MI	550,333	88.1	73,996	11.9	239,111	90.4	25,291	9.6
O'Fallon, MO	288,749	80.5	70,107	19.5	129,252	83.7	25,180	16.3
Oro Valley, AZ	98,857	91.6	9,092	8.4	42,008	91.8	3,736	8.2
Oviedo, FL	186,352	87.2	27,385	12.8	83,562	92.0	7,301	8.0
Palm Bch Grdns, FL	108,192	84.8	19,420	15.2	50,042	88.8	6,287	11.2
Parker, CO	250,673	90.0	27,814	10.0	104,095	91.3	9,939	8.7
Peachtree City, GA	511,746	90.2	55,562	9.8	207,156	91.5	19,214	8.5
Pflugerville, TX	147,604	92.3	12,299	7.7	60,104	94.4	3,576	5.6
Pleasanton, CA	279,586	87.2	40,862	12.8	120,209	89.9	13,536	10.1
Rapid City, SD	11,127	92.5	903	7.5	4,868	91.5	454	8.5
Redmond, WA	260,622	88.3	34,672	11.7	116,866	91.1	11,446	8.9
Richland, WA	28,254	92.9	2,157	7.1	13,361	96.8	438	3.2
Richmond, KY	48,932	86.9	7,363	13.1	20,298	89.2	2,451	10.8
Rio Rancho, NM	84,412	88.0	11,536	12.0	37,748	89.6	4,358	10.4
Rockaway, NJ	234,826	86.3	37,148	13.7	99,591	86.8	15,189	13.2
Rocklin, CA	213,241	90.3	22,784	9.7	93,412	92.7	7,388	7.3
Rogers, AR	37,249	92.6	2,991	7.4	15,432	93.8	1,021	6.2
Round Rock, TX	147,604	92.3	12,299	7.7	60,104	94.4	3,576	5.6
Sammamish, WA	260,622	88.3	34,672	11.7	116,866	91.1	11,446	8.9
San Ramon, CA	279,586	87.2	40,862	12.8	120,209	89.9	13,536	10.1
Santa Fe, NM	16,469	87.1	2,449	12.9	7,133	86.2	1,143	13.8
Saratoga, CA	184,435	86.6	28,642	13.4	83,075	89.8	9,411	10.2
Savage, MN	360,354	87.5	51,396	12.5	163,520	92.1	13,991	7.9
Schererville, IN	75,543	88.7	9,602	11.3	36,767	91.9	3,234	8.1
Shawnee, KS	212,067	87.5	30,212	12.5	90,420	89.1	11,050	10.9
Shrewsbury, MA	62,097	90.2	6,767	9.8	24,009	86.7	3,682	13.3
S Brunswick, NJ	129,755	87.7	18,130	12.3	53,556	88.7	6,806	11.3
S. Jordan, UT	189,691	94.4	11,196	5.6	93,135	95.6	4,302	4.4
S Kingstown, RI	131,803	87.2	19,325	12.8	57,810	87.9	7,987	12.1
Southaven, MS	149,569	88.4	19,693	11.6	61,138	87.4	8,828	12.6
Southlake, TX	224,258	91.0	22,110	9.0	91,305	92.3	7,600	7.7
Spanish Fork, UT	56,391	96.9	1,786	3.1	24,610	96.2	976	3.8
Sparks, NV	41,138	94.0	2,646	6.0	17,229	93.4	1,216	6.6
Stow, OH	78,037	86.1	12,558	13.9	34,447	91.1	3,370	8.9
Sugar Land, TX	589,699	92.3	49,169	7.7	244,239	93.2	17,795	6.8
Sun Prairie, WI	44,489	89.8	5,034	10.2	20,659	94.4	1,235	5.6
Tualatin, OR	219,761	88.8	27,653	11.2	95,236	91.4	8,906	8.6
Waimalu, HI	89,045	82.9	18,407	17.1	38,196	79.4	9,908	20.6
Wellington, FL	108,192	84.8	19,420	15.2	50,042	88.8	6,287	11.2
W Des Moines, IA	53,644	90.8	5,417	9.2	23,513	92.7	1,860	7.3
West Linn, OR	219,761	88.8	27,653	11.2	95,236	91.4	8,906	8.6
West Windsor, NJ	37,980	86.3	6,027	13.7	16,206	85.8	2,692	14.2
Weston, FL	175,895	86.9	26,604	13.1	77,084	87.7	10,767	12.3
Woodbury, MN	360,354	87.5	51,396	12.5	163,520	92.1	13,991	7.9
Woodridge, IL	980,199	85.2	169,831	14.8	411,578	87.3	59,611	12.7
Yorba Linda, CA	358,527	88.6	45,927	11.4	154,346	93.5	10,681	6.5
U.S.	33,526,011	88.7	4,285,121	11.3	14,848,628	90.6	1,532,323	9.4

Note: Figures shown cover persons 3 years old and over; (1) Metropolitan Statistical Area - see Appendix A for areas included
Source: Census 2000, Summary File 3

Educational Attainment by Race: City

City	High School Graduate (%)					Bachelor's Degree (%)				
	Total	White	Black	Asian	Hisp.[1]	Total	White	Black	Asian	Hisp.[1]
Allen, TX	95.6	96.4	94.6	90.7	80.2	47.5	47.3	50.9	59.8	32.3
Ankeny, IA	95.5	95.8	100.0	68.9	96.8	39.1	39.4	53.6	31.7	12.7
Apex, NC	96.0	98.2	79.5	89.5	80.8	58.8	61.5	29.1	74.6	43.3
Bangor, ME	87.0	87.2	86.4	92.4	92.0	26.5	26.7	13.6	42.1	38.4
Beavercreek, OH	92.4	92.5	98.8	84.2	98.0	42.9	42.0	67.5	62.8	59.0
Bellevue, NE	91.5	92.4	90.7	82.6	76.5	25.2	25.3	26.8	36.6	8.8
Bend, OR	90.2	90.9	48.9	86.7	69.0	29.4	30.0	0.0	44.3	8.2
Bernards, NJ	95.8	96.7	69.6	94.9	78.1	67.4	66.2	43.5	89.5	45.6
Bethlehem, NY	93.1	93.2	92.4	91.2	88.3	50.0	49.9	45.2	59.8	67.6
Bozeman, MT	94.3	94.4	50.0	97.1	94.9	49.5	49.4	50.0	75.6	19.8
Brentwood, TN	97.4	97.5	100.0	92.4	95.1	64.7	64.7	77.1	58.6	65.7
Brookfield, WI	94.0	94.1	75.2	96.1	94.7	49.0	48.3	35.7	79.6	43.2
Broomfield, CO	93.1	94.3	91.0	76.3	84.1	37.9	38.2	66.7	47.5	21.5
Burlington, VT	87.7	88.7	76.2	61.9	87.9	42.0	42.7	33.6	35.2	43.8
Carmel, IN	97.0	97.3	100.0	92.1	100.0	58.4	58.4	48.7	67.6	74.6
Cary, NC	95.1	96.2	93.8	92.5	59.4	60.7	61.1	47.7	74.0	33.4
Casper, WY	89.1	89.9	74.9	73.4	72.3	22.1	22.7	23.4	38.0	6.7
Cheshire, CT	92.4	93.6	72.9	89.5	70.3	47.8	49.1	12.8	71.7	11.4
Chino Hills, CA	89.9	91.2	93.9	94.0	76.8	37.6	31.8	45.1	61.4	18.4
Collierville, TN	93.2	95.3	70.4	82.5	72.7	41.2	43.0	20.4	41.4	26.7
Conway, AR	85.9	87.4	77.3	89.3	59.6	36.0	38.3	16.5	53.4	15.8
Coronado, CA	96.1	96.4	100.0	86.8	86.8	48.2	50.3	9.9	45.3	27.7
Cranberry, PA	95.0	95.0	86.2	95.0	78.0	47.1	46.4	38.5	82.9	50.0
Dover, DE	83.3	88.1	76.1	73.6	70.5	28.8	33.0	21.3	39.4	11.1
Draper, UT	91.1	93.1	83.0	97.3	65.4	33.5	35.6	15.6	53.7	9.9
Dublin, OH	97.3	97.6	98.6	94.7	100.0	64.7	64.8	61.0	66.4	70.6
Edmond, OK	94.2	94.6	94.4	94.8	77.2	47.8	48.5	32.2	67.0	26.4
Evesham, NJ	93.3	93.8	95.4	83.3	80.7	39.7	39.4	34.1	57.9	41.2
Fargo, ND	91.0	91.3	94.3	82.6	78.8	34.4	34.7	23.2	61.3	19.4
Farmington, CT	91.6	91.7	84.6	93.1	89.2	49.2	48.3	33.5	74.0	54.1
Fishers, IN	98.2	98.7	96.4	91.7	83.5	60.1	60.3	58.3	70.7	49.1
Flower Mound, TX	97.4	97.6	99.2	92.9	94.6	53.1	53.1	57.5	69.2	46.7
Franklin, MA	92.9	93.3	93.8	81.6	67.5	42.7	42.4	40.4	57.5	30.8
Frederick, MD	84.2	85.8	76.5	90.5	76.4	29.9	32.6	9.9	55.3	23.1
Frisco, TX	94.5	96.1	96.2	98.7	66.5	49.8	50.8	47.0	75.9	25.5
Goodyear, AZ	83.6	87.4	77.9	95.2	56.1	22.6	24.9	13.8	31.6	7.3
Grand Blanc, MI	92.1	91.9	95.1	95.3	89.1	30.7	29.2	37.6	75.6	17.6
Greenburgh, NY	91.0	92.3	85.2	95.2	74.6	53.7	55.6	34.6	73.6	32.8
Greenwich, CT	92.1	92.9	78.8	91.4	73.8	58.8	60.0	15.3	67.7	23.6
Hampden, PA	93.1	93.7	87.9	80.3	82.5	41.7	41.7	21.0	50.5	22.7
Hilliard, OH	92.5	92.6	92.0	95.2	80.4	46.1	45.1	57.2	68.2	50.0
Hoover, AL	94.7	95.5	95.7	88.0	67.6	52.6	52.8	49.5	70.8	21.3
Huntersville, NC	91.6	93.4	78.7	86.4	68.5	46.5	47.5	36.7	42.4	26.3
Juneau, AK	93.2	95.3	94.8	84.9	86.9	36.0	41.1	23.0	34.5	19.9
Keller, TX	95.6	95.7	100.0	94.8	88.4	44.6	44.5	36.7	62.1	29.3
Kenner, LA	78.5	82.0	67.8	75.9	68.6	21.3	23.6	11.3	45.3	15.5
Kennesaw, GA	91.4	92.0	91.1	97.0	70.8	34.5	33.1	39.4	55.6	23.1
League City, TX	90.9	92.8	92.3	77.4	70.7	35.5	36.6	41.9	36.3	19.2
Leawood, KS	98.1	98.3	100.0	87.4	100.0	68.0	68.4	57.5	67.1	70.7
Lee's Summit, MO	93.1	93.3	93.3	86.3	83.0	37.3	37.0	51.8	45.7	33.7
Leesburg, VA	89.8	92.1	80.6	74.7	63.8	41.3	44.8	16.3	40.7	19.9
Lehi, UT	91.5	91.5	0.0	92.8	75.4	26.1	25.8	0.0	41.2	27.2
Lwr Providence, PA	87.5	90.5	54.0	94.8	62.4	34.8	34.0	16.2	80.2	37.1
Madison, AL	94.6	96.0	87.9	88.1	89.5	52.0	54.5	36.9	55.9	36.0
Manhattan Bch, CA	96.8	97.0	100.0	96.2	90.6	67.6	68.2	32.4	69.7	53.0
Maple Grove, MN	96.7	97.1	87.7	86.7	95.9	41.7	41.4	40.8	61.2	49.0
Marion, IA	92.0	92.1	95.1	92.2	76.8	29.1	29.0	23.5	59.3	18.1
Marlboro, NJ	94.0	94.4	85.4	92.2	82.8	52.3	49.4	30.3	76.1	34.9
Matthews, NC	93.2	93.5	96.3	85.8	83.7	42.3	42.3	49.9	33.2	42.5

City	High School Graduate (%)					Bachelor's Degree (%)				
	Total	White	Black	Asian	Hisp.[1]	Total	White	Black	Asian	Hisp.[1]
Meridian, ID	92.2	92.8	87.2	79.1	75.1	27.1	27.2	0.0	31.1	16.7
Merrimack, NH	92.9	92.9	94.2	90.7	94.6	35.0	34.5	34.5	59.7	60.0
Morgantown, WV	89.2	89.3	82.0	100.0	77.0	47.8	47.2	25.3	83.8	39.0
Mt Pleasant, SC	94.0	95.8	72.6	90.3	75.1	52.6	54.9	18.3	74.5	37.2
Northampton, PA	94.7	94.8	88.1	92.1	79.5	43.2	42.6	40.7	76.9	22.7
Northville, MI	91.7	93.4	66.2	93.0	75.7	48.1	48.7	14.9	83.9	40.7
Novi, MI	94.0	94.2	91.2	93.7	90.6	49.1	47.1	46.9	74.1	38.0
O'Fallon, MO	90.4	90.2	94.8	96.5	87.8	27.2	26.9	27.9	55.5	35.0
Oro Valley, AZ	95.7	95.9	100.0	99.7	87.8	43.5	43.9	30.6	62.5	32.2
Oviedo, FL	93.3	94.5	82.5	97.7	84.0	41.3	42.5	25.1	57.2	29.0
Palm Bch Grdns, FL	94.0	94.5	80.2	86.6	85.9	43.8	43.9	16.8	48.3	33.2
Parker, CO	97.0	97.4	100.0	86.1	86.9	45.3	45.8	47.7	49.6	19.5
Peachtree City, GA	96.2	96.6	91.3	96.9	88.4	46.2	47.7	32.2	45.6	24.5
Pflugerville, TX	94.7	95.8	98.2	80.7	87.4	38.3	39.0	42.7	36.1	24.5
Pleasanton, CA	94.2	94.7	92.3	96.5	81.3	47.3	44.7	50.4	71.2	24.6
Rapid City, SD	87.3	89.1	86.6	76.7	72.1	26.7	28.5	7.4	38.0	8.1
Redmond, WA	94.5	95.6	94.4	93.5	69.3	52.9	51.8	48.8	66.9	24.9
Richland, WA	92.6	93.3	90.6	92.4	74.1	38.9	38.3	30.7	62.8	20.7
Richmond, KY	76.9	77.2	70.3	100.0	67.3	25.7	26.4	10.0	75.3	2.5
Rio Rancho, NM	91.2	92.0	80.1	77.0	87.9	24.8	26.0	22.0	31.6	17.7
Rockaway, NJ	93.0	93.1	81.8	93.6	91.4	41.4	39.7	42.1	72.6	32.6
Rocklin, CA	94.4	94.6	93.8	92.5	90.9	36.1	35.3	37.8	57.5	29.4
Rogers, AR	76.1	80.4	72.2	54.4	27.7	21.1	22.7	28.3	18.5	4.3
Round Rock, TX	89.6	92.1	95.5	82.2	70.1	32.9	35.6	27.3	51.4	15.9
Sammamish, WA	98.3	98.5	100.0	98.7	96.5	61.5	60.3	43.1	78.3	47.5
San Ramon, CA	96.5	97.0	92.1	96.3	91.5	52.7	50.4	47.5	69.4	33.1
Santa Fe, NM	84.6	87.0	89.6	83.6	69.9	40.0	45.2	36.4	57.4	15.4
Saratoga, CA	96.5	96.5	100.0	96.6	88.8	68.2	65.1	44.0	79.8	41.0
Savage, MN	95.4	97.2	78.2	74.9	72.1	41.4	42.7	31.9	29.4	18.2
Schererville, IN	92.0	91.9	97.8	98.7	84.2	29.5	28.4	39.2	76.5	16.7
Shawnee, KS	93.5	94.2	95.6	77.7	78.3	39.5	39.9	42.7	43.8	21.2
Shrewsbury, MA	91.8	92.1	78.7	90.4	89.0	46.1	44.3	38.8	69.7	31.0
S Brunswick, NJ	93.3	93.3	92.4	94.1	85.4	49.0	43.5	36.0	78.5	29.8
S. Jordan, UT	95.8	96.3	80.9	89.9	84.1	30.9	31.1	29.8	46.8	15.2
S Kingstown, RI	91.3	92.1	87.7	89.3	83.3	46.8	47.3	19.2	70.7	37.3
Southaven, MS	82.6	83.9	71.2	76.0	35.2	14.3	14.5	9.8	24.5	6.8
Southlake, TX	96.6	96.9	94.5	90.1	87.1	59.2	59.5	48.6	69.3	49.5
Spanish Fork, UT	91.2	92.2	36.4	100.0	64.3	21.9	22.5	0.0	31.3	18.3
Sparks, NV	82.2	86.4	86.1	80.5	46.2	17.8	18.6	15.9	27.5	7.0
Stow, OH	93.0	93.1	95.7	89.9	85.0	36.2	36.0	30.1	67.1	16.8
Sugar Land, TX	93.4	95.8	93.7	87.9	83.7	53.7	52.7	51.2	60.7	33.0
Sun Prairie, WI	90.9	92.1	84.3	81.4	46.5	34.4	34.6	26.4	49.2	15.2
Tualatin, OR	92.9	94.5	100.0	90.7	71.8	37.5	38.9	0.0	45.5	17.5
Waimalu, HI	90.6	96.8	92.8	88.6	89.1	32.4	37.8	35.5	35.4	16.5
Wellington, FL	92.2	93.0	84.7	89.1	78.3	38.0	38.2	34.0	53.4	27.1
W Des Moines, IA	96.3	96.8	95.9	90.7	76.2	48.5	48.8	31.7	69.9	18.9
West Linn, OR	95.5	95.7	88.6	97.9	89.1	49.2	49.3	46.2	60.6	38.0
West Windsor, NJ	96.9	97.8	96.7	95.8	81.0	73.9	73.8	60.7	79.7	44.8
Weston, FL	95.5	95.9	95.4	91.1	92.9	50.9	50.7	49.8	61.5	46.2
Woodbury, MN	96.4	96.9	94.6	89.6	92.7	49.3	48.7	60.1	62.1	33.2
Woodridge, IL	90.0	91.9	87.1	90.1	61.0	39.0	36.9	30.6	65.0	16.5
Yorba Linda, CA	93.4	93.7	100.0	95.8	80.2	41.5	39.2	56.9	63.9	27.3
U.S.	80.4	83.6	72.3	80.4	52.4	24.4	26.1	14.3	44.1	10.4

Note: Figures shown cover persons 25 years old and over; (1) people of Hispanic origin can be of any race
Source: Census 2000, Summary File 3

Educational Attainment by Race: Metro Area

MSA[1]	High School Graduate (%)					Bachelor's Degree (%)				
	Total	White	Black	Asian	Hisp.[2]	Total	White	Black	Asian	Hisp.[2]
Allen, TX	79.4	84.4	78.9	83.4	41.5	30.0	34.0	18.5	52.2	8.7
Ankeny, IA	88.6	90.1	80.3	67.9	54.6	28.7	29.7	16.3	28.7	11.7
Apex, NC	85.4	89.4	76.6	91.6	43.0	38.9	43.7	22.2	70.0	15.3
Bangor, ME	88.7	88.7	87.9	94.4	95.1	26.4	26.5	15.4	57.2	31.7
Beavercreek, OH	83.7	84.6	78.0	86.5	80.2	22.1	22.7	15.5	53.9	28.0
Bellevue, NE	88.0	89.9	78.2	85.8	53.7	28.0	29.3	13.5	51.1	11.6
Bend, OR	n/a	n/a	n/a	n/a	n/a	n/a	n/a	n/a	n/a	n/a
Bernards, NJ	86.5	87.6	83.3	91.3	61.9	37.4	35.0	27.2	71.5	13.3
Bethlehem, NY	85.6	86.5	72.6	88.7	69.6	28.2	28.4	15.5	65.4	23.6
Bozeman, MT	n/a	n/a	n/a	n/a	n/a	n/a	n/a	n/a	n/a	n/a
Brentwood, TN	81.4	83.2	74.4	81.1	54.5	26.9	28.2	18.9	46.1	14.2
Brookfield, WI	84.5	88.2	68.3	77.2	52.4	27.0	29.7	10.3	46.6	10.7
Broomfield, CO	86.4	89.6	83.6	79.8	55.9	34.2	37.3	21.0	40.6	10.6
Burlington, VT	89.5	89.9	84.0	76.7	88.2	37.2	37.2	37.3	46.5	45.1
Carmel, IN	84.0	85.5	75.6	86.7	58.9	25.8	27.4	13.8	57.3	16.7
Cary, NC	85.4	89.4	76.6	91.6	43.0	38.9	43.7	22.2	70.0	15.3
Casper, WY	88.3	89.0	77.4	75.5	70.3	20.0	20.5	23.7	36.6	7.0
Cheshire, CT	84.3	86.6	75.8	92.3	59.5	31.4	33.6	15.0	69.6	11.8
Chino Hills, CA	74.6	80.2	81.9	84.0	49.7	16.3	17.7	14.9	41.7	6.1
Collierville, TN	79.8	87.1	69.6	78.7	52.4	22.7	29.2	12.1	48.4	14.1
Conway, AR	83.3	85.6	75.2	81.8	60.3	24.8	27.0	15.2	43.8	15.4
Coronado, CA	82.6	87.7	86.1	81.3	53.5	29.5	33.1	16.3	37.2	10.7
Cranberry, PA	85.1	85.5	78.2	90.5	80.7	23.8	24.2	12.8	70.8	31.6
Dover, DE	79.4	81.1	73.9	75.0	72.8	18.6	19.3	15.6	34.3	11.8
Draper, UT	87.5	89.9	83.0	78.2	56.5	26.5	27.6	19.5	34.8	9.4
Dublin, OH	85.8	87.2	78.1	86.1	67.9	29.1	30.4	15.4	59.7	21.6
Edmond, OK	83.6	85.7	80.7	76.8	50.1	24.4	26.1	15.6	37.3	9.6
Evesham, NJ	82.2	85.7	71.9	77.2	55.5	27.7	31.1	12.8	46.7	12.8
Fargo, ND	89.7	90.2	92.4	82.8	64.2	29.4	29.7	23.8	53.0	11.3
Farmington, CT	83.6	86.1	75.1	82.1	56.8	29.8	32.0	13.8	53.2	11.0
Fishers, IN	84.0	85.5	75.6	86.7	58.9	25.8	27.4	13.8	57.3	16.7
Flower Mound, TX	79.4	84.4	78.9	83.4	41.5	30.0	34.0	18.5	52.2	8.7
Franklin, MA	87.1	89.5	76.4	78.3	61.0	39.5	41.1	20.8	53.4	18.7
Frederick, MD	86.7	91.1	81.3	85.4	57.7	41.8	49.2	24.1	53.9	21.0
Frisco, TX	79.4	84.4	78.9	83.4	41.5	30.0	34.0	18.5	52.2	8.7
Goodyear, AZ	81.9	86.3	81.6	84.9	49.3	25.1	27.3	19.4	46.6	7.8
Grand Blanc, MI	83.1	85.2	74.7	88.7	75.6	16.2	17.3	10.3	59.6	10.1
Greenburgh, NY	74.0	81.2	70.8	70.9	53.9	29.2	37.9	16.3	38.1	11.0
Greenwich, CT	87.6	90.4	71.6	91.8	62.0	49.4	53.5	17.2	69.9	14.2
Hampden, PA	83.1	84.1	75.2	77.3	60.5	22.6	23.2	12.8	41.7	8.8
Hilliard, OH	85.8	87.2	78.1	86.1	67.9	29.1	30.4	15.4	59.7	21.6
Hoover, AL	80.6	83.2	74.2	87.6	57.9	24.7	28.3	14.6	65.5	17.3
Huntersville, NC	80.5	83.0	74.7	76.4	48.6	26.5	29.1	16.5	37.8	11.9
Juneau, AK	n/a	n/a	n/a	n/a	n/a	n/a	n/a	n/a	n/a	n/a
Keller, TX	81.0	84.9	80.2	72.4	46.6	25.1	27.3	16.8	36.3	9.2
Kenner, LA	77.7	83.6	67.6	64.8	71.0	22.6	27.4	12.7	33.5	20.8
Kennesaw, GA	84.0	86.8	81.0	80.0	51.7	32.0	36.1	21.9	46.4	16.1
League City, TX	80.9	85.1	71.3	76.9	58.0	22.7	25.4	10.7	48.1	10.1
Leawood, KS	86.7	88.8	77.4	80.9	61.4	28.5	30.6	14.6	46.6	13.3
Lee's Summit, MO	86.7	88.8	77.4	80.9	61.4	28.5	30.6	14.6	46.6	13.3
Leesburg, VA	86.7	91.1	81.3	85.4	57.7	41.8	49.2	24.1	53.9	21.0
Lehi, UT	90.9	92.2	78.7	91.5	62.8	31.5	32.1	25.7	48.7	16.2
Lwr Providence, PA	82.2	85.7	71.9	77.2	55.5	27.7	31.1	12.8	46.7	12.8
Madison, AL	83.3	84.9	76.4	85.1	68.7	30.9	32.8	21.8	53.4	22.4
Manhattan Bch, CA	69.9	77.0	79.3	82.4	42.1	24.9	29.3	17.8	42.9	6.8
Maple Grove, MN	90.6	92.5	79.9	70.9	61.5	33.3	34.4	19.1	36.3	16.7
Marion, IA	90.6	90.9	80.0	91.0	74.0	27.7	27.7	13.2	55.1	22.7
Marlboro, NJ	85.6	86.5	76.7	87.7	65.8	27.6	27.6	14.9	60.3	14.9
Matthews, NC	80.5	83.0	74.7	76.4	48.6	26.5	29.1	16.5	37.8	11.9

MSA[1]	High School Graduate (%)					Bachelor's Degree (%)				
	Total	White	Black	Asian	Hisp.[2]	Total	White	Black	Asian	Hisp.[2]
Meridian, ID	86.5	88.6	80.5	80.6	50.0	26.5	27.3	26.3	38.7	8.8
Merrimack, NH	89.4	89.7	93.7	90.1	67.9	33.2	32.7	29.5	67.2	23.8
Morgantown, WV	n/a	n/a	n/a	n/a	n/a	n/a	n/a	n/a	n/a	n/a
Mt Pleasant, SC	81.3	87.4	67.3	79.3	67.5	25.0	30.9	10.7	38.0	16.5
Northampton, PA	82.2	85.7	71.9	77.2	55.5	27.7	31.1	12.8	46.7	12.8
Northville, MI	82.1	84.8	73.9	85.9	63.2	22.8	24.6	12.8	62.6	14.7
Novi, MI	82.1	84.8	73.9	85.9	63.2	22.8	24.6	12.8	62.6	14.7
O'Fallon, MO	83.4	85.5	73.4	84.0	74.3	25.3	27.3	13.0	55.2	24.0
Oro Valley, AZ	83.4	87.1	81.9	80.5	62.8	26.7	29.7	16.8	43.3	10.9
Oviedo, FL	82.8	85.7	69.3	82.2	71.6	24.8	26.5	14.6	42.3	17.0
Palm Bch Grdns, FL	83.6	87.6	61.9	83.2	60.2	27.7	30.1	11.4	48.2	15.3
Parker, CO	86.4	89.6	83.6	79.8	55.9	34.2	37.3	21.0	40.6	10.6
Peachtree City, GA	84.0	86.8	81.0	80.0	51.7	32.0	36.1	21.9	46.4	16.1
Pflugerville, TX	84.8	89.7	80.0	88.5	58.6	36.7	41.1	20.1	62.2	14.7
Pleasanton, CA	84.2	89.0	81.7	83.0	58.0	35.0	38.6	18.6	46.8	12.6
Rapid City, SD	87.8	89.3	86.9	79.2	74.3	25.0	26.3	10.5	30.7	8.8
Redmond, WA	90.1	92.3	82.4	82.2	67.8	35.9	37.0	21.1	40.9	19.0
Richland, WA	80.1	86.0	73.0	78.4	32.8	23.3	25.1	17.7	45.1	4.7
Richmond, KY	82.1	82.9	75.1	91.2	52.8	28.7	29.7	13.5	66.5	13.9
Rio Rancho, NM	83.9	87.3	85.3	81.1	70.4	28.4	32.8	22.5	39.4	13.2
Rockaway, NJ	81.6	85.3	73.7	90.4	60.2	31.5	36.0	15.5	65.0	12.8
Rocklin, CA	85.0	88.7	83.1	73.8	63.6	25.9	27.8	16.2	31.6	12.3
Rogers, AR	80.0	81.7	82.5	80.0	33.1	22.4	22.8	25.5	48.7	6.1
Round Rock, TX	84.8	89.7	80.0	88.5	58.6	36.7	41.1	20.1	62.2	14.7
Sammamish, WA	90.1	92.3	82.4	82.2	67.8	35.9	37.0	21.1	40.9	19.0
San Ramon, CA	84.2	89.0	81.7	83.0	58.0	35.0	38.6	18.6	46.8	12.6
Santa Fe, NM	86.0	88.6	83.6	91.0	71.0	39.9	45.1	28.2	65.5	14.6
Saratoga, CA	83.4	88.4	88.6	84.8	55.1	40.5	42.5	29.7	51.3	11.0
Savage, MN	90.6	92.5	79.9	70.9	61.5	33.3	34.4	19.1	36.3	16.7
Schererville, IN	82.5	85.2	75.3	89.8	64.2	17.7	19.4	11.2	58.2	9.0
Shawnee, KS	86.7	88.8	77.4	80.9	61.4	28.5	30.6	14.6	46.6	13.3
Shrewsbury, MA	83.5	84.8	78.4	74.0	53.5	27.7	28.0	19.5	44.6	11.6
S Brunswick, NJ	86.5	87.6	83.3	91.3	61.9	37.4	35.0	27.2	71.5	13.3
S. Jordan, UT	87.5	89.9	83.0	78.2	56.5	26.5	27.6	19.5	34.8	9.4
S Kingstown, RI	76.0	77.8	70.5	68.3	50.2	23.6	24.5	16.8	35.4	8.5
Southaven, MS	79.8	87.1	69.6	78.7	52.4	22.7	29.2	12.1	48.4	14.1
Southlake, TX	81.0	84.9	80.2	72.4	46.6	25.1	27.3	16.8	36.3	9.2
Spanish Fork, UT	90.9	92.2	78.7	91.5	62.8	31.5	32.1	25.7	48.7	16.2
Sparks, NV	83.9	87.3	84.2	83.2	45.9	23.7	25.2	16.7	34.2	6.9
Stow, OH	85.7	86.9	75.7	88.7	80.3	24.3	25.2	10.9	64.0	25.7
Sugar Land, TX	75.9	81.4	77.5	80.1	43.6	27.2	31.4	18.4	47.7	8.5
Sun Prairie, WI	92.2	93.3	77.6	87.0	67.8	40.6	41.0	19.2	65.5	27.2
Tualatin, OR	87.2	89.4	80.4	79.1	53.7	28.8	29.6	18.0	38.3	11.8
Waimalu, HI	84.8	93.5	93.0	80.8	84.3	27.9	39.6	20.9	28.2	15.1
Wellington, FL	83.6	87.6	61.9	83.2	60.2	27.7	30.1	11.4	48.2	15.3
W Des Moines, IA	88.6	90.1	80.3	67.9	54.6	28.7	29.7	16.3	28.7	11.7
West Linn, OR	87.2	89.4	80.4	79.1	53.7	28.8	29.6	18.0	38.3	11.8
West Windsor, NJ	81.8	86.0	69.8	91.3	55.5	34.0	38.3	12.8	72.2	11.6
Weston, FL	82.0	85.5	69.2	81.0	75.7	24.5	26.8	14.7	38.8	23.0
Woodbury, MN	90.6	92.5	79.9	70.9	61.5	33.3	34.4	19.1	36.3	16.7
Woodridge, IL	81.0	85.8	74.3	86.9	47.8	30.1	34.1	15.6	57.5	8.9
Yorba Linda, CA	79.5	86.0	88.1	81.2	45.1	30.8	33.4	27.6	41.4	8.5
U.S.	80.4	83.6	72.3	80.4	52.4	24.4	26.1	14.3	44.1	10.4

Note: Figures shown cover persons 25 years old and over; (1) Metropolitan Statistical Area - see Appendix A for areas included; (2) people of Hispanic origin can be of any race
Source: Census 2000, Summary File 3

Cost of Living Index

Area	Composite	Groceries	Housing	Utilities	Transp.	Health	Misc.
Allen[1]	91.5	99.0	72.3	98.9	103.5	101.6	97.5
Ankeny[2]	90.6	87.1	87.2	96.7	94.2	89.8	92.0
Apex[3]	99.7	102.1	97.8	91.6	95.7	103.7	103.2
Bangor	103.8	101.9	98.1	131.9	102.2	106.0	101.3
Beavercreek[4]	93.9	91.9	81.4	101.1	103.5	93.8	99.8
Bellevue[5]	88.9	87.2	79.3	88.3	101.0	94.7	93.2
Bend	116.6	122.2	130.8	82.0	115.9	113.9	113.4
Bernards[6]	127.5	113.2	169.1	107.3	103.7	110.6	114.2
Bethlehem	n/a	n/a	n/a	n/a	n/a	n/a	n/a
Bozeman	104.5	97.1	119.8	102.2	94.5	100.9	98.9
Brentwood[7]	88.2	90.4	78.6	87.9	94.3	85.4	93.8
Brookfield[8]	100.3	95.3	106.4	96.5	100.2	111.1	97.2
Broomfield[9]	103.8	103.0	110.6	102.8	95.5	108.5	100.9
Burlington[10]	116.8	110.5	132.2	124.9	106.3	104.7	108.8
Carmel[11]	98.8	100.6	98.4	101.0	91.4	94.4	100.4
Cary[12]	99.7	102.1	97.8	91.6	95.7	103.7	103.2
Casper	n/a	n/a	n/a	n/a	n/a	n/a	n/a
Cheshire[13]	118.4	121.6	130.9	131.2	99.9	113.4	109.5
Chino Hills[14]	118.1	106.8	156.2	88.8	112.7	106.6	103.1
Collierville[15]	89.7	90.5	77.4	84.1	92.3	97.1	99.1
Conway	91.4	96.7	80.7	99.6	88.3	91.5	96.4
Coronado[16]	140.3	111.9	220.5	105.1	111.3	116.3	107.7
Cranberry[17]	99.3	98.3	93.7	108.6	105.8	87.3	101.1
Dover	103.1	110.6	94.1	133.3	101.1	104.7	99.4
Draper[18]	101.1	102.3	99.2	87.7	103.6	99.2	105.5
Dublin[19]	97.7	96.3	97.0	102.7	103.6	104.1	95.0
Edmond	90.4	88.6	81.2	90.3	98.6	96.0	95.3
Evesham[20]	124.1	124.4	146.1	116.5	105.9	110.9	115.3
Fargo[21]	95.8	97.5	82.9	123.0	101.9	97.8	95.6
Farmington[22]	119.4	115.8	134.8	134.4	110.0	113.8	107.3
Fishers[23]	98.8	100.6	98.4	101.0	91.4	94.4	100.4
Flower Mound[24]	88.5	95.3	74.9	98.3	97.7	90.1	91.2
Franklin[25]	135.4	120.1	165.9	129.6	104.8	136.0	127.0
Frederick[26]	132.8	107.1	190.3	128.3	114.6	109.5	105.6
Frisco[27]	91.5	99.0	72.3	98.9	103.5	101.6	97.5
Goodyear[28]	101.0	100.5	102.1	93.9	100.8	101.0	102.6
Grand Blanc	n/a	n/a	n/a	n/a	n/a	n/a	n/a
Greenburgh	n/a	n/a	n/a	n/a	n/a	n/a	n/a
Greenwich[29]	148.4	118.4	224.7	130.1	119.0	117.2	115.7
Hampden	n/a	n/a	n/a	n/a	n/a	n/a	n/a
Hilliard[30]	97.7	96.3	97.0	102.7	103.6	104.1	95.0
Hoover[31]	92.4	96.6	78.5	99.1	96.2	99.4	98.1
Huntersville[32]	90.0	99.2	76.5	83.5	92.4	104.3	96.9
Juneau	134.7	135.6	150.6	138.2	127.1	144.4	121.8
Keller[33]	88.5	95.3	74.9	98.3	97.7	90.1	91.2
Kenner[34]	100.0	108.5	99.5	90.2	99.9	96.4	100.4
Kennesaw[35]	96.5	98.7	92.9	85.2	103.6	103.4	98.9
League City[36]	88.0	83.1	74.4	101.0	96.2	101.2	93.1
Leawood[37]	96.1	91.5	88.2	104.2	100.2	97.9	100.4
Lee's Summit[38]	96.1	91.5	88.2	104.2	100.2	97.9	100.4
Leesburg[39]	137.2	106.6	213.0	111.8	109.9	110.0	106.1
Lehi	n/a	n/a	n/a	n/a	n/a	n/a	n/a
Lower Providence[40]	124.1	124.4	146.1	116.5	105.9	110.9	115.3
Madison[41]	92.8	93.7	79.8	84.3	97.0	95.0	104.0
Manhattan Beach[42]	145.4	111.8	254.0	78.9	113.6	103.8	104.0
Maple Grove[43]	110.6	112.1	122.7	101.6	108.0	102.9	104.5
Marion[44]	91.4	87.4	78.8	95.8	99.2	108.8	97.4
Marlboro[45]	127.5	113.2	169.1	107.3	103.7	110.6	114.2
Matthews[46]	90.0	99.2	76.5	83.5	92.4	104.3	96.9
Meridian	n/a	n/a	n/a	n/a	n/a	n/a	n/a

Area	Composite	Groceries	Housing	Utilities	Transp.	Health	Misc.
Merrimack[47]	114.7	106.3	124.4	107.0	102.4	125.2	114.5
Morgantown	100.5	95.3	107.8	107.4	99.1	103.9	94.7
Mount Pleasant[48]	98.1	100.5	91.4	102.3	97.9	110.3	100.2
Northampton[49]	124.1	124.4	146.1	116.5	105.9	110.9	115.3
Northville[50]	98.6	97.6	97.9	107.9	100.7	99.2	96.1
Novi[51]	98.6	97.6	97.9	107.9	100.7	99.2	96.1
O'Fallon[52]	91.8	106.2	78.8	91.2	96.1	97.2	95.2
Oro Valley[53]	100.7	105.4	97.0	96.6	100.5	102.3	102.8
Oviedo[54]	103.8	98.2	100.3	109.9	105.9	98.2	106.9
Palm Bch Grdns[55]	121.6	102.7	169.5	103.1	104.9	107.2	102.1
Parker[56]	103.8	103.0	110.6	102.8	95.5	108.5	100.9
Peachtree City[57]	96.5	98.7	92.9	85.2	103.6	103.4	98.9
Pflugerville[58]	94.8	89.9	81.8	95.0	99.3	98.0	105.4
Pleasanton[59]	147.3	138.4	213.4	88.0	118.3	121.2	126.0
Rapid City	n/a	n/a	n/a	n/a	n/a	n/a	n/a
Redmond[60]	121.5	113.0	155.0	94.9	106.2	124.0	109.7
Richland[61]	94.2	94.1	85.3	89.6	106.5	116.4	96.5
Richmond[62]	98.6	95.4	91.1	109.3	97.4	99.4	102.8
Rio Rancho	95.8	100.9	90.0	86.5	100.2	106.0	98.7
Rockaway[63]	127.1	111.2	165.9	107.8	104.1	107.0	116.2
Rocklin[64]	125.3	130.7	155.3	102.2	104.8	114.1	113.0
Rogers[65]	91.1	91.4	78.3	105.5	98.8	92.2	94.9
Round Rock	92.4	85.0	76.4	108.7	95.3	106.3	100.9
Sammamish[66]	121.5	113.0	155.0	94.9	106.2	124.0	109.7
San Ramon[67]	147.3	138.4	213.4	88.0	118.3	121.2	126.0
Santa Fe	n/a	n/a	n/a	n/a	n/a	n/a	n/a
Saratoga[68]	155.0	143.9	254.3	99.3	113.2	122.6	111.4
Savage[69]	110.6	112.1	122.7	101.6	108.0	102.9	104.5
Schererville[70]	110.8	108.4	126.5	108.2	113.2	104.3	100.0
Shawnee[71]	96.1	91.5	88.2	104.2	100.2	97.9	100.4
Shrewsbury[72]	109.2	94.8	124.7	125.8	105.3	115.1	97.8
South Brunswick[73]	127.5	113.2	169.1	107.3	103.7	110.6	114.2
South Jordan[74]	101.1	102.3	99.2	87.7	103.6	99.2	105.5
South Kingstown[75]	121.1	116.5	136.3	119.4	101.2	115.7	117.4
Southaven[76]	89.7	90.5	77.4	84.1	92.3	97.1	99.1
Southlake[77]	88.5	95.3	74.9	98.3	97.7	90.1	91.2
Spanish Fork	n/a	n/a	n/a	n/a	n/a	n/a	n/a
Sparks[78]	108.3	104.3	115.1	86.8	111.3	109.0	109.4
Stow[79]	94.0	98.8	81.7	100.0	101.9	92.4	98.2
Sugar Land[80]	88.0	83.1	74.4	101.0	96.2	101.2	93.1
Sun Prairie	n/a	n/a	n/a	n/a	n/a	n/a	n/a
Tualatin[81]	121.4	124.3	135.8	104.0	111.1	107.9	118.2
Waimalu[82]	164.0	159.3	249.3	140.3	117.6	110.3	123.8
Wellington[83]	121.6	102.7	169.5	103.1	104.9	107.2	102.1
West Des Moines[84]	90.6	87.1	87.2	96.7	94.2	89.8	92.0
West Linn[85]	121.4	124.3	135.8	104.0	111.1	107.9	118.2
West Windsor	n/a	n/a	n/a	n/a	n/a	n/a	n/a
Weston[86]	121.6	102.7	169.5	103.1	104.9	107.2	102.1
Woodbury[87]	110.6	112.1	122.7	101.6	108.0	102.9	104.5
Woodridge[88]	99.5	107.2	94.7	90.6	105.9	102.6	100.9
Yorba Linda[89]	155.9	122.5	265.4	103.6	108.9	114.1	113.9
U.S.	100.0	100.0	100.0	100.0	100.0	100.0	100.0

Note: In cases where data is not available for the city, data for the metro area or for a neighboring city has been provided and noted below; (1) Dallas TX; (2) Des Moines IA; (3) Raleigh NC; (4) Dayton OH; (5) Omaha NE; (6) Middlesex-Monmouth NJ; (7) Nashville-Franklin TN; (8) Milwaukee-Waukesha WI; (9) Denver CO; (10) Burlington-Chittenden County VT; (11) Hamilton County IN; (12) Raleigh NC; (13) New Haven CT; (14) Riverside City CA; (15) Memphis TN; (16) San Diego CA; (17) Pittsburgh PA; (18) Salt Lake City UT; (19) Columbus OH; (20) Philadelphia PA; (21) Fargo-Moorhead ND-MN; (22) Hartford CT; (23) Hamilton County IN; (24) Ft. Worth TX; (25) Boston MA; (26) Bethesda-Gaithersburg-Frederick MD; (27) Dallas TX; (28) Phoenix AZ; (29) Stamford CT; (30) Columbus OH; (31) Birmingham AL; (32) Charlotte NC; (33) Ft. Worth TX; (34) Slidell-St. Tammany Parish LA; (35) Atlanta GA; (36) Houston TX; (37) Kansas City MO-KS; (38) Kansas City MO-KS; (39) Washington-Arlington-Alexandria DC-VA; (40) Philadelphia PA; (41) Huntsville AL; (42) Los Angeles-Long Beach CA; (43) Minneapolis MN; (44) Cedar Rapids IA; (45) Middlesex-Monmouth NJ; (46) Charlotte NC; (47) Manchester NH; (48) Charleston-N Charleston SC; (49) Philadelphia PA; (50) Detroit MI; (51) Detroit MI; (52) St. Louis MO-IL; (53) Tucson AZ; (54) Orlando FL; (55) Ft. Lauderdale FL; (56) Denver CO;

(57) Atlanta GA; (58) Austin TX; (59) Oakland CA; (60) Seattle WA; (61) Kennewick-Richland-Pasco WA; (62) Lexington KY; (63) Newark-Elizabeth NJ; (64) Sacramento CA; (65) Fayetteville AR; (66) Seattle WA; (67) Oakland CA; (68) San Jose CA; (69) Minneapolis MN; (70) Chicago IL; (71) Kansas City MO-KS; (72) Fitchburg-Leominster MA; (73) Middlesex-Monmouth NJ; (74) Salt Lake City UT; (75) Providence RI; (76) Memphis TN; (77) Ft. Worth TX; (78) Reno-Sparks NV; (79) Akron OH; (80) Houston TX; (81) Portland OR; (82) Honolulu HI; (83) Ft. Lauderdale FL; (84) Des Moines IA; (85) Portland OR; (86) Ft. Lauderdale FL; (87) Minneapolis MN; (88) Joliet-Will County IL; (89) Orange County CA
Source: The Council for Community and Economic Research (formerly ACCRA), Cost of Living Index, 2007

Grocery Prices

Area	T-Bone Steak ($/pound)	Frying Chicken ($/pound)	Whole Milk ($/half gal.)	Eggs ($/dozen)	Orange Juice ($/64 oz.)	Coffee ($/11.5 oz.)
Allen[1]	8.81	1.24	2.26	1.40	3.17	3.43
Ankeny[2]	7.42	1.17	1.75	1.31	2.99	3.03
Apex[3]	9.44	1.21	2.58	1.74	3.45	2.91
Bangor	10.03	1.08	2.41	1.42	3.52	2.93
Beavercreek[4]	9.08	1.09	1.57	1.34	2.93	3.32
Bellevue[5]	8.33	1.04	1.84	1.17	2.96	3.07
Bend	10.42	1.36	1.92	1.95	4.02	4.44
Bernards[6]	9.68	1.09	2.24	2.25	3.07	3.46
Bethlehem	n/a	n/a	n/a	n/a	n/a	n/a
Bozeman	7.42	1.04	2.04	1.34	3.11	3.62
Brentwood[7]	8.50	0.91	1.72	1.22	3.07	3.04
Brookfield[8]	8.52	1.00	2.11	1.19	3.18	3.23
Broomfield[9]	9.05	1.06	2.20	1.31	3.14	4.08
Burlington[10]	7.97	1.32	2.38	1.78	3.36	3.04
Carmel[11]	10.32	1.36	2.03	1.32	2.83	3.34
Cary[12]	9.44	1.21	2.58	1.74	3.45	2.91
Casper	n/a	n/a	n/a	n/a	n/a	n/a
Cheshire[13]	8.73	1.51	2.46	1.88	3.50	3.59
Chino Hills[14]	7.99	1.14	2.19	1.98	3.41	3.92
Collierville[15]	9.96	0.85	2.07	1.33	2.93	3.13
Conway	8.25	0.87	2.22	1.50	2.89	3.31
Coronado[16]	8.80	1.23	2.18	2.09	3.37	4.33
Cranberry[17]	9.43	1.32	1.80	1.45	3.10	3.30
Dover	9.37	1.37	2.38	1.75	3.47	3.58
Draper[18]	9.29	1.29	1.89	1.46	3.19	3.56
Dublin[19]	10.75	1.29	1.79	1.27	3.13	3.26
Edmond	8.76	0.91	2.01	1.38	2.97	3.12
Evesham[20]	9.62	1.53	2.16	1.94	4.33	3.81
Fargo[21]	8.91	1.35	2.52	1.30	3.11	3.25
Farmington[22]	10.65	1.35	2.13	2.08	3.31	3.65
Fishers[23]	10.32	1.36	2.03	1.32	2.83	3.34
Flower Mound[24]	9.03	0.96	2.28	1.50	3.11	3.04
Franklin[25]	9.82	1.59	2.39	2.33	3.31	3.61
Frederick[26]	10.32	1.32	2.20	1.85	3.00	3.20
Frisco[27]	8.81	1.24	2.26	1.40	3.17	3.43
Goodyear[28]	8.95	1.30	1.79	1.58	3.07	3.58
Grand Blanc	n/a	n/a	n/a	n/a	n/a	n/a
Greenburgh	n/a	n/a	n/a	n/a	n/a	n/a
Greenwich[29]	10.20	1.54	2.29	2.05	3.28	3.47
Hampden	n/a	n/a	n/a	n/a	n/a	n/a
Hilliard[30]	10.75	1.29	1.79	1.27	3.13	3.26
Hoover[31]	9.22	1.00	2.37	1.29	2.97	2.77
Huntersville[32]	9.41	1.04	2.59	1.65	3.26	2.92
Juneau	11.07	1.60	2.89	2.06	4.35	4.07
Keller[33]	9.03	0.96	2.28	1.50	3.11	3.04
Kenner[34]	9.48	1.06	2.70	1.50	3.39	3.35
Kennesaw[35]	9.37	1.17	2.14	1.30	3.43	3.44
League City[36]	6.49	0.96	2.13	1.33	2.90	2.90
Leawood[37]	8.38	1.16	1.97	1.40	3.03	3.05
Lee's Summit[38]	8.38	1.16	1.97	1.40	3.03	3.05
Leesburg[39]	10.62	1.39	2.16	1.75	3.08	3.58
Lehi	n/a	n/a	n/a	n/a	n/a	n/a
Lower Providence[40]	9.62	1.53	2.16	1.94	4.33	3.81
Madison[41]	8.65	1.06	2.10	1.35	3.10	3.05
Manhattan Beach[42]	7.98	1.32	2.40	2.10	3.32	3.92
Maple Grove[43]	12.80	1.76	2.37	1.95	3.62	3.74
Marion[44]	8.13	1.11	1.80	1.24	2.86	3.19
Marlboro[45]	9.68	1.09	2.24	2.25	3.07	3.46

Area	T-Bone Steak ($/pound)	Frying Chicken ($/pound)	Whole Milk ($/half gal.)	Eggs ($/dozen)	Orange Juice ($/64 oz.)	Coffee ($/11.5 oz.)
Matthews[46]	9.41	1.04	2.59	1.65	3.26	2.92
Meridian	n/a	n/a	n/a	n/a	n/a	n/a
Merrimack[47]	9.51	1.14	2.10	1.47	3.03	3.04
Morgantown	7.98	1.24	2.05	1.45	2.98	3.39
Mount Pleasant[48]	10.31	1.08	2.52	1.55	3.39	2.73
Northampton[49]	9.62	1.53	2.16	1.94	4.33	3.81
Northville[50]	10.16	1.12	1.90	1.32	2.84	3.08
Novi[51]	10.16	1.12	1.90	1.32	2.84	3.08
O'Fallon[52]	10.07	1.25	2.14	1.73	3.16	3.49
Oro Valley[53]	8.31	1.11	2.01	1.56	3.35	3.67
Oviedo[54]	8.67	1.13	2.43	1.49	3.22	3.03
Palm Bch Grdns[55]	9.96	0.98	2.32	1.61	3.37	2.94
Parker[56]	9.05	1.06	2.20	1.31	3.14	4.08
Peachtree City[57]	9.37	1.17	2.14	1.30	3.43	3.44
Pflugerville[58]	8.24	1.02	2.09	1.94	3.19	3.22
Pleasanton[59]	9.46	1.58	2.64	3.54	5.79	5.19
Rapid City	n/a	n/a	n/a	n/a	n/a	n/a
Redmond[60]	9.50	1.47	2.33	2.00	3.47	4.32
Richland[61]	8.93	1.08	1.92	1.70	2.93	3.15
Richmond[62]	9.15	1.39	2.23	1.41	3.13	3.05
Rio Rancho	8.37	1.05	2.04	1.62	3.25	3.44
Rockaway[63]	9.72	1.14	2.22	2.18	3.13	3.22
Rocklin[64]	8.07	1.43	2.57	2.36	4.49	5.09
Rogers[65]	9.14	0.84	2.02	1.27	3.11	3.22
Round Rock	7.08	0.84	2.35	1.02	2.56	3.22
Sammamish[66]	9.50	1.47	2.33	2.00	3.47	4.32
San Ramon[67]	9.46	1.58	2.64	3.54	5.79	5.19
Santa Fe	n/a	n/a	n/a	n/a	n/a	n/a
Saratoga[68]	10.66	1.34	2.56	2.63	5.64	4.90
Savage[69]	12.80	1.76	2.37	1.95	3.62	3.74
Schererville[70]	10.37	1.23	2.05	1.56	3.46	4.14
Shawnee[71]	8.38	1.16	1.97	1.40	3.03	3.05
Shrewsbury[72]	8.21	1.06	1.72	1.37	2.89	2.94
South Brunswick[73]	9.68	1.09	2.24	2.25	3.07	3.46
South Jordan[74]	9.29	1.29	1.89	1.46	3.19	3.56
South Kingstown[75]	10.08	1.42	2.22	2.05	3.12	3.27
Southaven[76]	9.96	0.85	2.07	1.33	2.93	3.13
Southlake[77]	9.03	0.96	2.28	1.50	3.11	3.04
Spanish Fork	n/a	n/a	n/a	n/a	n/a	n/a
Sparks[78]	9.09	1.13	2.09	1.80	3.38	4.24
Stow[79]	8.89	1.37	1.98	1.13	3.10	3.24
Sugar Land[80]	6.49	0.96	2.13	1.33	2.90	2.90
Sun Prairie	n/a	n/a	n/a	n/a	n/a	n/a
Tualatin[81]	9.78	1.92	1.95	2.66	3.96	3.98
Waimalu[82]	9.96	1.69	3.43	2.80	5.12	6.20
Wellington[83]	9.96	0.98	2.32	1.61	3.37	2.94
West Des Moines[84]	7.42	1.17	1.75	1.31	2.99	3.03
West Linn[85]	9.78	1.92	1.95	2.66	3.96	3.98
West Windsor	n/a	n/a	n/a	n/a	n/a	n/a
Weston[86]	9.96	0.98	2.32	1.61	3.37	2.94
Woodbury[87]	12.80	1.76	2.37	1.95	3.62	3.74
Woodridge[88]	8.29	1.43	1.98	1.47	3.05	3.66
Yorba Linda[89]	9.23	1.37	2.43	1.83	3.25	4.24
Average[90]	8.93	1.12	2.13	1.52	3.26	3.31
Minimum[90]	5.88	0.71	1.33	0.83	2.30	2.20
Maximum[90]	12.80	2.07	3.43	3.54	5.79	6.20

*Note: **T-Bone Steak** (price per pound); **Frying Chicken** (price per pound, whole fryer); **Whole Milk** (half gallon carton); **Eggs** (price per dozen, Grade A, large); **Orange Juice** (64 oz. Tropicana or Florida Natural); **Coffee** (11.5 oz. can, vacuum-packed, Maxwell House, Hills Bros, or Folgers); n/a not available; In cases where data is not available for the city, data for the metro area or for a neighboring city has been provided and noted below; (1) Dallas TX; (2) Des Moines IA; (3) Raleigh NC; (4) Dayton OH; (5) Omaha*

NE; (6) Middlesex-Monmouth NJ; (7) Nashville-Franklin TN; (8) Milwaukee-Waukesha WI; (9) Denver CO; (10) Burlington-Chittenden County VT; (11) Hamilton County IN; (12) Raleigh NC; (13) New Haven CT; (14) Riverside City CA; (15) Memphis TN; (16) San Diego CA; (17) Pittsburgh PA; (18) Salt Lake City UT; (19) Columbus OH; (20) Philadelphia PA; (21) Fargo-Moorhead ND-MN; (22) Hartford CT; (23) Hamilton County IN; (24) Ft. Worth TX; (25) Boston MA; (26) Bethesda-Gaithersburg-Frederick MD; (27) Dallas TX; (28) Phoenix AZ; (29) Stamford CT; (30) Columbus OH; (31) Birmingham AL; (32) Charlotte NC; (33) Ft. Worth TX; (34) Slidell-St. Tammany Parish LA; (35) Atlanta GA; (36) Houston TX; (37) Kansas City MO-KS; (38) Kansas City MO-KS; (39) Washington-Arlington-Alexandria DC-VA; (40) Philadelphia PA; (41) Huntsville AL; (42) Los Angeles-Long Beach CA; (43) Minneapolis MN; (44) Cedar Rapids IA; (45) Middlesex-Monmouth NJ; (46) Charlotte NC; (47) Manchester NH; (48) Charleston-N Charleston SC; (49) Philadelphia PA; (50) Detroit MI; (51) Detroit MI; (52) St. Louis MO-IL; (53) Tucson AZ; (54) Orlando FL; (55) Ft. Lauderdale FL; (56) Denver CO; (57) Atlanta GA; (58) Austin TX; (59) Oakland CA; (60) Seattle WA; (61) Kennewick-Richland-Pasco WA; (62) Lexington KY; (63) Newark-Elizabeth NJ; (64) Sacramento CA; (65) Fayetteville AR; (66) Seattle WA; (67) Oakland CA; (68) San Jose CA; (69) Minneapolis MN; (70) Chicago IL; (71) Kansas City MO-KS; (72) Fitchburg-Leominster MA; (73) Middlesex-Monmouth NJ; (74) Salt Lake City UT; (75) Providence RI; (76) Memphis TN; (77) Ft. Worth TX; (78) Reno-Sparks NV; (79) Akron OH; (80) Houston TX; (81) Portland OR; (82) Honolulu HI; (83) Ft. Lauderdale FL; (84) Des Moines IA; (85) Portland OR; (86) Ft. Lauderdale FL; (87) Minneapolis MN; (88) Joliet-Will County IL; (89) Orange County CA; (90) Values for the local area are compared with the average, minimum, and maximum values for all 331 areas in the Cost of Living Index report

Source: The Council for Community and Economic Research (formerly ACCRA), Cost of Living Index, 2007

Housing and Utility Costs

Area	New Home Price ($)	Apartment Rent ($/month)	All Electric ($/month)	Part Electric ($/month)	Other Energy ($/month)	Telephone ($/month)
Allen[1]	213,140	715	-	107.07	50.72	26.67
Ankeny[2]	282,800	595	-	65.80	90.67	25.56
Apex[3]	301,390	739	141.03	-	-	26.00
Bangor	272,848	1,066	-	102.61	163.55	21.47
Beavercreek[4]	248,709	666	-	98.40	85.79	21.55
Bellevue[5]	240,408	690	-	59.92	78.98	24.31
Bend	442,674	603	118.95	-	-	25.00
Bernards[6]	531,339	1,321	-	82.61	85.27	29.75
Bethlehem	n/a	n/a	n/a	n/a	n/a	n/a
Bozeman	390,928	707	-	58.70	106.05	27.11
Brentwood[7]	238,782	687	-	67.29	76.50	23.08
Brookfield[8]	332,179	773	-	72.78	93.32	23.01
Broomfield[9]	351,968	797	-	101.34	74.30	24.78
Burlington[10]	395,295	1,083	-	85.71	147.39	25.21
Carmel[11]	307,497	768	-	63.03	121.06	20.87
Cary[12]	301,390	739	141.03	-	-	26.00
Casper	n/a	n/a	n/a	n/a	n/a	n/a
Cheshire[13]	384,954	1,271	-	124.53	130.51	23.91
Chino Hills[14]	498,526	1,084	-	108.21	59.02	17.52
Collierville[15]	226,932	750	-	67.56	62.99	23.57
Conway	255,867	599	-	54.50	99.13	28.17
Coronado[16]	692,277	1,569	-	129.62	51.13	25.15
Cranberry[17]	282,911	780	-	69.34	129.37	22.90
Dover	285,792	825	-	91.79	130.18	33.64
Draper[18]	307,604	777	-	53.08	73.82	26.91
Dublin[19]	303,182	778	-	68.02	97.08	27.36
Edmond	248,942	670	-	69.74	66.55	26.33
Evesham[20]	424,647	1,385	-	55.44	112.57	35.89
Fargo[21]	259,475	658	-	54.21	171.86	25.67
Farmington[22]	408,570	1,233	-	111.39	152.31	23.91
Fishers[23]	307,497	768	-	63.03	121.06	20.87
Flower Mound[24]	213,267	815	-	112.12	50.83	24.95
Franklin[25]	495,140	1,479	-	110.12	119.46	29.26
Frederick[26]	594,130	1,474	-	85.54	133.84	30.95
Frisco[27]	213,140	715	-	107.07	50.72	26.67
Goodyear[28]	316,545	788	161.96	-	-	22.27
Grand Blanc	n/a	n/a	n/a	n/a	n/a	n/a
Greenburgh	n/a	n/a	n/a	n/a	n/a	n/a
Greenwich[29]	663,847	2,153	-	113.76	138.40	23.91
Hampden	n/a	n/a	n/a	n/a	n/a	n/a
Hilliard[30]	303,182	778	-	68.02	97.08	27.36
Hoover[31]	236,911	717	-	80.78	90.22	23.57
Huntersville[32]	235,835	658	130.06	-	-	23.29
Juneau	467,818	1,097	-	110.30	173.29	20.56
Keller[33]	213,267	815	-	112.12	50.83	24.95
Kenner[34]	283,249	1,099	151.54	-	-	22.44
Kennesaw[35]	288,758	781	127.25	-	-	25.13
League City[36]	214,931	812	-	130.96	44.20	23.71
Leawood[37]	272,160	756	-	63.78	124.13	22.69
Lee's Summit[38]	272,160	756	-	63.78	124.13	22.69
Leesburg[39]	650,190	1,773	-	67.37	133.18	24.59
Lehi	n/a	n/a	n/a	n/a	n/a	n/a
Lower Providence[40]	424,647	1,385	-	55.44	112.57	35.89
Madison[41]	247,572	677	114.55	-	-	27.75
Manhattan Beach[42]	818,583	1,564	-	85.28	49.15	18.92
Maple Grove[43]	367,020	1,107	-	59.81	114.60	24.72
Marion[44]	245,994	621	-	94.19	79.90	20.54
Marlboro[45]	531,339	1,321	-	82.61	85.27	29.75

Area	New Home Price ($)	Apartment Rent ($/month)	All Electric ($/month)	Part Electric ($/month)	Other Energy ($/month)	Telephone ($/month)
Matthews[46]	235,835	658	130.06	-	-	23.29
Meridian	n/a	n/a	n/a	n/a	n/a	n/a
Merrimack[47]	378,952	1,014	-	75.57	91.72	29.93
Morgantown	336,973	782	-	46.48	124.66	29.01
Mount Pleasant[48]	272,635	902	182.59	-	-	22.75
Northampton[49]	424,647	1,385	-	55.44	112.57	35.89
Northville[50]	303,819	840	-	81.18	84.60	30.71
Novi[51]	303,819	840	-	81.18	84.60	30.71
O'Fallon[52]	227,673	811	-	61.74	91.66	22.61
Oro Valley[53]	295,018	841	-	98.49	69.59	22.57
Oviedo[54]	303,978	820	170.01	-	-	31.01
Palm Bch Grdns[55]	544,498	1,197	177.65	-	-	24.52
Parker[56]	351,968	797	-	101.34	74.30	24.78
Peachtree City[57]	288,758	781	127.25	-	-	25.13
Pflugerville[58]	228,613	946	-	94.41	54.62	26.29
Pleasanton[59]	683,330	1,457	-	70.83	74.32	22.55
Rapid City	n/a	n/a	n/a	n/a	n/a	n/a
Redmond[60]	454,300	1,434	142.92	-	-	27.27
Richland[61]	263,727	701	137.79	-	-	25.49
Richmond[62]	282,480	753	-	46.03	120.76	31.39
Rio Rancho	274,224	720	-	60.41	73.39	24.38
Rockaway[63]	518,648	1,322	-	84.58	84.80	29.75
Rocklin[64]	499,367	1,071	-	150.60	36.92	21.49
Rogers[65]	248,720	570	-	66.12	105.74	27.56
Round Rock	219,990	803	-	138.72	50.24	25.43
Sammamish[66]	454,300	1,434	142.92	-	-	27.27
San Ramon[67]	683,330	1,457	-	70.83	74.32	22.55
Santa Fe	n/a	n/a	n/a	n/a	n/a	n/a
Saratoga[68]	818,997	1,262	-	103.36	62.30	24.97
Savage[69]	367,020	1,107	-	59.81	114.60	24.72
Schererville[70]	354,224	1,443	-	59.10	113.53	29.15
Shawnee[71]	272,160	756	-	63.78	124.13	22.69
Shrewsbury[72]	397,219	812	-	92.38	122.05	30.51
South Brunswick[73]	531,339	1,321	-	82.61	85.27	29.75
South Jordan[74]	307,604	777	-	53.08	73.82	26.91
South Kingstown[75]	409,494	1,155	-	80.37	101.22	34.45
Southaven[76]	226,932	750	-	67.56	62.99	23.57
Southlake[77]	213,267	815	-	112.12	50.83	24.95
Spanish Fork	n/a	n/a	n/a	n/a	n/a	n/a
Sparks[78]	371,493	705	-	73.83	86.10	18.04
Stow[79]	246,770	699	-	82.72	92.62	22.98
Sugar Land[80]	214,931	812	-	130.96	44.20	23.71
Sun Prairie	n/a	n/a	n/a	n/a	n/a	n/a
Tualatin[81]	434,461	946	-	88.95	85.14	25.99
Waimalu[82]	767,846	2,086	271.14	-	-	25.95
Wellington[83]	544,498	1,197	177.65	-	-	24.52
West Des Moines[84]	282,800	595	-	65.80	90.67	25.56
West Linn[85]	434,461	946	-	88.95	85.14	25.99
West Windsor	n/a	n/a	n/a	n/a	n/a	n/a
Weston[86]	544,498	1,197	177.65	-	-	24.52
Woodbury[87]	367,020	1,107	-	59.81	114.60	24.72
Woodridge[88]	267,435	989	-	68.38	76.00	24.45
Yorba Linda[89]	858,654	1,569	-	110.53	56.77	27.44
Average[90]	309,605	782	146.13	78.67	90.16	26.14
Minimum[90]	189,877	n/a	82.03	37.41	33.15	17.08
Maximum[90]	1,202,800	3,481	271.14	150.60	257.67	37.45

Note: ***New Home Price*** *(2,400 sf living area, 8,000 sf lot, in urban area with full utilities);* ***Apartment Rent*** *(950 sf 2 bedroom/1.5 or 2 bath, unfurnished, excluding all utilities except water);* ***All Electric*** *(average monthly cost for an all-electric home);* ***Part Electric*** *(average monthly cost for a part-electric home);* ***Other Energy*** *(average monthly cost for natural gas, fuel oil, coal, wood, and any other forms of energy except electricity);* ***Telephone*** *(price includes basic monthly rate for a private residential line plus additional* *local usage charges incurred by a family of four); n/a not available; In cases where data is not available for the city, data for the metro area or for a neighboring city has been provided and noted below; (1) Dallas TX; (2) Des Moines IA; (3) Raleigh NC; (4) Dayton OH; (5) Omaha NE; (6) Middlesex-Monmouth NJ; (7) Nashville-Franklin TN; (8) Milwaukee-Waukesha WI; (9) Denver CO; (10) Burlington-Chittenden County VT; (11) Hamilton County IN; (12) Raleigh NC; (13) New Haven CT; (14) Riverside City CA; (15) Memphis TN; (16) San Diego CA; (17) Pittsburgh PA; (18) Salt Lake City UT; (19) Columbus OH; (20) Philadelphia PA; (21) Fargo-Moorhead ND-MN; (22) Hartford CT; (23) Hamilton County IN; (24) Ft. Worth TX; (25) Boston MA; (26) Bethesda-Gaithersburg-Frederick MD; (27) Dallas TX; (28) Phoenix AZ; (29) Stamford CT; (30) Columbus OH; (31) Birmingham AL; (32) Charlotte NC; (33) Ft. Worth TX; (34) Slidell-St. Tammany Parish LA; (35) Atlanta GA; (36) Houston TX; (37) Kansas City MO-KS; (38) Kansas City MO-KS; (39) Washington-Arlington-Alexandria DC-VA; (40) Philadelphia PA; (41) Huntsville AL; (42) Los Angeles-Long Beach CA; (43) Minneapolis MN; (44) Cedar Rapids IA; (45) Middlesex-Monmouth NJ; (46) Charlotte NC; (47) Manchester NH; (48) Charleston-N Charleston SC; (49) Philadelphia PA; (50) Detroit MI; (51) Detroit MI; (52) St. Louis MO-IL; (53) Tucson AZ; (54) Orlando FL; (55) Ft. Lauderdale FL; (56) Denver CO; (57) Atlanta GA; (58) Austin TX; (59) Oakland CA; (60) Seattle WA; (61) Kennewick-Richland-Pasco WA; (62) Lexington KY; (63) Newark-Elizabeth NJ; (64) Sacramento CA; (65) Fayetteville AR; (66) Seattle WA; (67) Oakland CA; (68) San Jose CA; (69) Minneapolis MN; (70) Chicago IL; (71) Kansas City MO-KS; (72) Fitchburg-Leominster MA; (73) Middlesex-Monmouth NJ; (74) Salt Lake City UT; (75) Providence RI; (76) Memphis TN; (77) Ft. Worth TX; (78) Reno-Sparks NV; (79) Akron OH; (80) Houston TX; (81) Portland OR; (82) Honolulu HI; (83) Ft. Lauderdale FL; (84) Des Moines IA; (85) Portland OR; (86) Ft. Lauderdale FL; (87) Minneapolis MN; (88) Joliet-Will County IL; (89) Orange County CA; (90) Values for the local area are compared with the average, minimum, and maximum values for all 331 areas in the Cost of Living Index report*

Source: The Council for Community and Economic Research (formerly ACCRA), Cost of Living Index, 2007

Health Care, Transportation, and Other Costs

Area	Doctor ($/visit)	Dentist ($/visit)	Optometrist ($/visit)	Gasoline ($/gallon)	Beauty Salon ($/visit)	Men's Shirt ($)
Allen[1]	74.44	77.38	77.68	2.52	26.77	22.20
Ankeny[2]	82.00	59.88	73.33	2.52	23.65	20.61
Apex[3]	80.88	74.02	77.14	2.58	34.02	27.67
Bangor	82.33	76.19	94.65	2.65	24.24	19.94
Beavercreek[4]	68.00	64.85	83.48	2.67	30.26	22.74
Bellevue[5]	87.33	61.27	66.73	2.70	23.89	23.13
Bend	98.90	85.19	99.05	3.04	32.06	33.30
Bernards[6]	70.73	93.52	88.50	2.52	31.67	35.87
Bethlehem	n/a	n/a	n/a	n/a	n/a	n/a
Bozeman	83.00	71.00	86.22	2.69	34.00	17.13
Brentwood[7]	65.55	58.81	64.80	2.56	26.11	18.26
Brookfield[8]	96.11	92.91	43.95	2.68	26.87	22.55
Broomfield[9]	94.44	80.78	84.24	2.57	32.28	19.40
Burlington[10]	92.72	69.03	86.33	2.72	30.11	34.30
Carmel[11]	78.63	60.30	93.84	2.33	26.45	23.25
Cary[12]	80.88	74.02	77.14	2.58	34.02	27.67
Casper	n/a	n/a	n/a	n/a	n/a	n/a
Cheshire[13]	87.67	85.89	110.08	2.71	37.22	21.50
Chino Hills[14]	70.20	81.53	83.33	2.89	35.06	29.22
Collierville[15]	68.14	68.95	79.93	2.54	31.67	24.94
Conway	74.47	59.39	71.83	2.53	22.80	22.72
Coronado[16]	83.44	94.54	106.28	2.97	41.60	28.03
Cranberry[17]	64.33	53.95	68.25	2.61	29.93	31.57
Dover	69.68	78.67	94.22	2.54	27.35	19.78
Draper[18]	77.80	72.35	75.47	2.62	32.00	27.88
Dublin[19]	70.09	85.33	88.04	2.79	33.60	26.22
Edmond	72.01	69.00	81.93	2.54	33.49	26.33
Evesham[20]	100.28	80.89	94.67	2.70	54.67	37.35
Fargo[21]	86.50	68.10	55.67	2.69	23.93	22.93
Farmington[22]	94.18	84.45	101.62	2.78	28.03	20.50
Fishers[23]	78.63	60.30	93.84	2.33	26.45	23.25
Flower Mound[24]	61.32	67.49	47.44	2.46	30.46	21.38
Franklin[25]	132.33	112.88	79.33	2.54	49.33	37.99
Frederick[26]	90.47	85.53	76.80	2.78	50.80	30.06
Frisco[27]	74.44	77.38	77.68	2.52	26.77	22.20
Goodyear[28]	74.63	76.33	96.07	2.61	35.73	24.10
Grand Blanc	n/a	n/a	n/a	n/a	n/a	n/a
Greenburgh	n/a	n/a	n/a	n/a	n/a	n/a
Greenwich[29]	93.58	93.17	104.08	2.97	35.10	25.60
Hampden	n/a	n/a	n/a	n/a	n/a	n/a
Hilliard[30]	70.09	85.33	88.04	2.79	33.60	26.22
Hoover[31]	61.57	78.39	96.95	2.51	28.94	20.89
Huntersville[32]	79.40	81.33	80.65	2.60	24.70	22.39
Juneau	104.95	126.27	154.38	3.48	31.86	35.26
Keller[33]	61.32	67.49	47.44	2.46	30.46	21.38
Kenner[34]	70.83	75.47	59.50	2.55	30.98	31.39
Kennesaw[35]	84.67	81.25	58.11	2.59	34.57	26.85
League City[36]	81.72	76.13	82.50	2.51	31.37	23.16
Leawood[37]	77.43	68.40	82.50	2.55	25.58	26.96
Lee's Summit[38]	77.43	68.40	82.50	2.55	25.58	26.96
Leesburg[39]	91.47	86.20	75.13	2.64	49.27	30.72
Lehi	n/a	n/a	n/a	n/a	n/a	n/a
Lower Providence[40]	100.28	80.89	94.67	2.70	54.67	37.35
Madison[41]	64.55	65.32	96.39	2.59	34.97	25.37
Manhattan Beach[42]	77.13	75.78	86.49	2.95	46.34	21.95
Maple Grove[43]	97.82	75.19	72.40	2.79	36.54	22.41
Marion[44]	80.04	92.91	72.20	2.66	21.26	19.06
Marlboro[45]	70.73	93.52	88.50	2.52	31.67	35.87

Area	Doctor ($/visit)	Dentist ($/visit)	Optometrist ($/visit)	Gasoline ($/gallon)	Beauty Salon ($/visit)	Men's Shirt ($)
Matthews[46]	79.40	81.33	80.65	2.60	24.70	22.39
Meridian	n/a	n/a	n/a	n/a	n/a	n/a
Merrimack[47]	148.44	89.04	82.59	2.49	35.00	34.09
Morgantown	72.93	86.20	59.93	2.66	30.80	24.50
Mount Pleasant[48]	76.00	92.42	84.50	2.48	42.73	27.11
Northampton[49]	100.28	80.89	94.67	2.70	54.67	37.35
Northville[50]	68.35	73.50	75.82	2.66	42.97	24.09
Novi[51]	68.35	73.50	75.82	2.66	42.97	24.09
O'Fallon[52]	79.17	71.38	62.87	2.62	33.33	23.06
Oro Valley[53]	75.25	79.71	81.26	2.57	36.00	25.47
Oviedo[54]	70.38	75.59	64.21	2.56	36.93	22.30
Palm Bch Grdns[55]	77.27	86.68	73.13	2.65	38.07	20.27
Parker[56]	94.44	80.78	84.24	2.57	32.28	19.40
Peachtree City[57]	84.67	81.25	58.11	2.59	34.57	26.85
Pflugerville[58]	68.27	74.11	78.25	2.59	55.00	25.94
Pleasanton[59]	101.50	91.45	117.40	3.09	39.67	41.93
Rapid City	n/a	n/a	n/a	n/a	n/a	n/a
Redmond[60]	99.96	100.52	105.07	2.94	28.75	24.28
Richland[61]	85.27	91.73	141.00	2.83	33.93	20.75
Richmond[62]	80.73	76.28	55.62	2.59	35.05	28.51
Rio Rancho	80.27	79.94	97.26	2.63	32.33	25.29
Rockaway[63]	76.17	84.13	78.93	2.52	34.33	33.55
Rocklin[64]	86.80	86.83	112.05	2.53	34.28	26.51
Rogers[65]	73.21	64.87	69.13	2.62	29.87	26.10
Round Rock	79.44	89.00	88.00	2.58	30.83	29.94
Sammamish[66]	99.96	100.52	105.07	2.94	28.75	24.28
San Ramon[67]	101.50	91.45	117.40	3.09	39.67	41.93
Santa Fe	n/a	n/a	n/a	n/a	n/a	n/a
Saratoga[68]	115.73	88.67	103.33	2.99	25.78	36.36
Savage[69]	97.82	75.19	72.40	2.79	36.54	22.41
Schererville[70]	83.03	82.13	74.22	2.95	27.91	20.63
Shawnee[71]	77.43	68.40	82.50	2.55	25.58	26.96
Shrewsbury[72]	100.67	88.58	84.83	2.54	25.67	20.99
South Brunswick[73]	70.73	93.52	88.50	2.52	31.67	35.87
South Jordan[74]	77.80	72.35	75.47	2.62	32.00	27.88
South Kingstown[75]	110.33	82.47	79.17	2.56	42.67	35.34
Southaven[76]	68.14	68.95	79.93	2.54	31.67	24.94
Southlake[77]	61.32	67.49	47.44	2.46	30.46	21.38
Spanish Fork	n/a	n/a	n/a	n/a	n/a	n/a
Sparks[78]	75.42	90.43	91.54	2.94	29.25	24.25
Stow[79]	64.27	67.39	68.73	2.59	38.52	26.46
Sugar Land[80]	81.72	76.13	82.50	2.51	31.37	23.16
Sun Prairie	n/a	n/a	n/a	n/a	n/a	n/a
Tualatin[81]	96.67	79.62	90.50	2.92	32.87	40.65
Waimalu[82]	95.04	73.00	101.81	3.04	42.43	47.06
Wellington[83]	77.27	86.68	73.13	2.65	38.07	20.27
West Des Moines[84]	82.00	59.88	73.33	2.52	23.65	20.61
West Linn[85]	96.67	79.62	90.50	2.92	32.87	40.65
West Windsor	n/a	n/a	n/a	n/a	n/a	n/a
Weston[86]	77.27	86.68	73.13	2.65	38.07	20.27
Woodbury[87]	97.82	75.19	72.40	2.79	36.54	22.41
Woodridge[88]	85.00	72.77	82.11	2.76	30.93	25.15
Yorba Linda[89]	104.96	81.39	84.80	2.92	54.33	28.22
Average[90]	79.48	71.93	79.55	2.64	29.52	25.77
Minimum[90]	52.08	44.80	43.95	2.19	15.58	16.19
Maximum[90]	148.44	126.27	158.83	3.48	60.62	48.53

Note: ***Doctor*** *(general practitioners routine exam of an established patient);* ***Dentist*** *(adult teeth cleaning and periodic oral examination);* ***Optometrist*** *(full vision eye exam for established adult patient);* ***Gasoline*** *(one gallon regular unleaded, national brand, including all taxes, cash price at self-service pump if available);* ***Beauty Salon*** *(woman's shampoo, trim, and blow-dry);* ***Men's Shirt*** *(cotton/polyester dress shirt, pinpoint weave, long sleeves); n/a not available; In cases where data is not available for the city, data for*

the metro area or for a neighboring city has been provided and noted below; (1) Dallas TX; (2) Des Moines IA; (3) Raleigh NC; (4) Dayton OH; (5) Omaha NE; (6) Middlesex-Monmouth NJ; (7) Nashville-Franklin TN; (8) Milwaukee-Waukesha WI; (9) Denver CO; (10) Burlington-Chittenden County VT; (11) Hamilton County IN; (12) Raleigh NC; (13) New Haven CT; (14) Riverside City CA; (15) Memphis TN; (16) San Diego CA; (17) Pittsburgh PA; (18) Salt Lake City UT; (19) Columbus OH; (20) Philadelphia PA; (21) Fargo-Moorhead ND-MN; (22) Hartford CT; (23) Hamilton County IN; (24) Ft. Worth TX; (25) Boston MA; (26) Bethesda-Gaithersburg-Frederick MD; (27) Dallas TX; (28) Phoenix AZ; (29) Stamford CT; (30) Columbus OH; (31) Birmingham AL; (32) Charlotte NC; (33) Ft. Worth TX; (34) Slidell-St. Tammany Parish LA; (35) Atlanta GA; (36) Houston TX; (37) Kansas City MO-KS; (38) Kansas City MO-KS; (39) Washington-Arlington-Alexandria DC-VA; (40) Philadelphia PA; (41) Huntsville AL; (42) Los Angeles-Long Beach CA; (43) Minneapolis MN; (44) Cedar Rapids IA; (45) Middlesex-Monmouth NJ; (46) Charlotte NC; (47) Manchester NH; (48) Charleston-N Charleston SC; (49) Philadelphia PA; (50) Detroit MI; (51) Detroit MI; (52) St. Louis MO-IL; (53) Tucson AZ; (54) Orlando FL; (55) Ft. Lauderdale FL; (56) Denver CO; (57) Atlanta GA; (58) Austin TX; (59) Oakland CA; (60) Seattle WA; (61) Kennewick-Richland-Pasco WA; (62) Lexington KY; (63) Newark-Elizabeth NJ; (64) Sacramento CA; (65) Fayetteville AR; (66) Seattle WA; (67) Oakland CA; (68) San Jose CA; (69) Minneapolis MN; (70) Chicago IL; (71) Kansas City MO-KS; (72) Fitchburg-Leominster MA; (73) Middlesex-Monmouth NJ; (74) Salt Lake City UT; (75) Providence RI; (76) Memphis TN; (77) Ft. Worth TX; (78) Reno-Sparks NV; (79) Akron OH; (80) Houston TX; (81) Portland OR; (82) Honolulu HI; (83) Ft. Lauderdale FL; (84) Des Moines IA; (85) Portland OR; (86) Ft. Lauderdale FL; (87) Minneapolis MN; (88) Joliet-Will County IL; (89) Orange County CA; (90) Values for the local area are compared with the average, minimum, and maximum values for all 331 areas in the Cost of Living Index report
Source: The Council for Community and Economic Research (formerly ACCRA), Cost of Living Index, 2007

Distribution of Physicians[1]

City (Area Covered)	Total	Family/ General Practice	Specialties	
			Medical	Surgical
Allen (Collin County)	19.2	4.9	7.1	4.1
Ankeny (Polk County)	17.9	4.3	6.0	4.7
Apex (Wake County)	21.0	5.0	8.1	4.9
Bangor (Penobscot County)	25.5	5.6	9.1	5.8
Beavercreek (Greene County)	16.4	7.3	5.2	2.6
Bellevue (Sarpy County)	9.8	4.6	3.1	2.2
Bend (Deschutes County)	23.3	7.4	5.8	6.8
Bernards (Somerset County)	30.1	5.0	12.3	6.6
Bethlehem (Albany County)	32.9	3.7	12.4	9.4
Bozeman (Gallatin County)	20.3	9.8	4.9	4.7
Brentwood (Williamson County)	43.1	6.8	15.4	8.0
Brookfield (Waukesha County)	32.6	7.7	11.5	5.7
Broomfield (Broomfield County)	14.0	8.7	5.3	1.2
Burlington (Chittenden County)	40.8	10.1	14.4	8.6
Carmel (Hamilton County)	37.9	7.8	12.2	8.7
Cary (Wake County)	21.0	5.0	8.1	4.9
Casper (Natrona County)	19.8	7.0	5.2	5.4
Cheshire (New Haven County)	29.2	1.7	12.9	6.5
Chino Hills (San Bernardino County)	11.5	3.5	3.9	2.6
Collierville (Shelby County)	24.7	4.2	10.3	5.8
Conway (Faulkner County)	12.2	5.6	3.4	3.5
Coronado (San Diego County)	21.8	5.2	7.5	4.9
Cranberry (Butler County)	10.3	2.4	4.0	1.9
Dover (Kent County)	12.9	2.6	4.8	3.1
Draper (Salt Lake County)	22.3	4.5	7.9	5.2
Dublin (Franklin County)	22.7	6.0	8.0	5.4
Edmond (Oklahoma County)	25.4	5.3	8.5	6.2
Evesham (Burlington County)	20.0	4.2	7.7	4.0
Fargo (Cass County)	32.1	9.5	12.1	6.7
Farmington (Hartford County)	25.7	2.7	10.9	6.5
Fishers (Hamilton County)	37.9	7.8	12.2	8.7
Flower Mound (Denton County)	12.3	4.1	4.5	2.8
Franklin (Norfolk County)	36.8	2.8	16.4	7.3
Frederick (Frederick County)	14.6	5.4	5.3	2.8
Frisco (Collin County)	19.2	4.9	7.1	4.1
Goodyear (Maricopa County)	16.6	3.8	6.0	3.8
Grand Blanc (Genesee County)	13.5	4.6	5.8	2.5
Greenburgh (Westchester County)	44.6	3.4	20.0	9.7
Greenwich (Fairfield County)	25.9	2.2	11.4	6.4
Hampden (Cumberland County)	20.4	5.6	6.6	5.6
Hilliard (Franklin County)	22.7	6.0	8.0	5.4
Hoover (Jefferson County)	32.6	3.7	12.8	9.0
Huntersville (Mecklenburg County)	23.2	4.9	8.8	5.9
Juneau (Juneau Borough)	22.3	13.9	3.5	4.5
Keller (Tarrant County)	13.9	3.6	4.6	3.7
Kenner (Jefferson Parish)	27.4	3.5	11.4	7.3
Kennesaw (Cobb County)	15.7	2.7	6.2	4.0
League City (Galveston County)	22.0	4.8	7.1	4.6
Leawood (Johnson County)	31.7	7.0	10.9	7.2
Lee's Summit (Jackson County)	16.6	3.6	6.4	4.0
Leesburg (Loudoun County)	13.8	4.1	5.4	3.1
Lehi (Utah County)	10.6	4.4	2.9	2.8
Lower Providence (Montgomery County)	38.5	5.4	15.0	7.8
Madison (Madison County)	21.7	7.4	6.8	5.5
Manhattan Beach (Los Angeles County)	0.0	3.9	7.6	4.4
Maple Grove (Hennepin County)	30.4	8.8	10.6	6.9
Marion (Linn County)	16.2	7.4	4.0	3.6
Marlboro (Monmouth County)	27.3	2.3	12.1	6.6

City (Area Covered)	Total	Family/ General Practice	Specialties	
			Medical	Surgical
Matthews (Mecklenburg County)	23.2	4.9	8.8	5.9
Meridian (Ada County)	23.5	7.9	6.6	6.8
Merrimack (Hillsborough County)	17.9	4.4	7.1	4.1
Morgantown (Monongalia County)	46.1	8.5	14.1	12.4
Mount Pleasant (Charleston County)	43.4	7.5	14.6	10.7
Northampton (Bucks County)	17.3	3.6	7.1	3.8
Northville (Wayne County)	12.5	2.3	5.2	2.7
Novi (Oakland County)	33.8	5.3	14.0	7.6
O'Fallon (St. Charles County)	8.1	2.3	3.6	2.2
Oro Valley (Pima County)	23.1	4.7	7.6	5.0
Oviedo (Seminole County)	14.9	4.3	5.5	3.0
Palm Beach Gardens (Palm Beach County)	22.6	2.9	9.5	5.9
Parker (Douglas County)	13.6	4.0	4.9	3.6
Peachtree City (Fayette County)	20.5	5.8	8.2	4.8
Pflugerville (Travis County)	23.8	6.0	7.7	5.6
Pleasanton (Alameda County)	22.4	4.0	9.4	4.5
Rapid City (Pennington County)	25.2	7.1	8.1	6.5
Redmond (King County)	30.8	9.2	10.4	6.2
Richland (Benton County)	16.4	5.3	5.7	3.9
Richmond (Madison County)	10.9	3.5	4.0	3.1
Rio Rancho (Sandoval County)	11.1	6.0	3.4	1.0
Rockaway (Morris County)	27.9	2.7	12.6	6.4
Rocklin (Placer County)	22.4	7.6	7.9	4.8
Rogers (Benton County)	10.3	5.7	2.9	2.6
Round Rock (Williamson County)	9.9	5.3	3.0	2.0
Sammamish (King County)	30.8	9.2	10.4	6.2
San Ramon (Contra Costa County)	20.9	4.4	8.3	4.5
Santa Fe (Santa Fe County)	26.6	10.8	7.3	5.0
Saratoga (Santa Clara County)	25.4	3.8	10.8	5.7
Savage (Scott County)	8.5	9.6	1.8	0.9
Schererville (Lake County)	15.7	4.2	5.9	4.0
Shawnee (Johnson County)	31.7	7.0	10.9	7.2
Shrewsbury (Worcester County)	21.4	4.7	9.6	4.2
South Brunswick (Middlesex County)	22.1	2.6	11.0	4.5
South Jordan (Salt Lake County)	22.3	4.5	7.9	5.2
South Kingstown (Washington County)	20.6	3.6	9.2	4.4
Southaven (DeSoto County)	5.8	1.8	2.3	2.0
Southlake (Tarrant County)	13.9	3.6	4.6	3.7
Spanish Fork (Utah County)	10.6	4.4	2.9	2.8
Sparks (Washoe County)	21.3	5.5	6.0	5.5
Stow (Summit County)	19.4	4.9	7.0	4.4
Sugar Land (Fort Bend County)	15.5	5.4	5.6	2.7
Sun Prairie (Dane County)	32.7	9.8	10.8	6.7
Tualatin (Washington County)	21.0	4.8	8.0	4.8
Waimalu (Honolulu County)	24.9	4.0	10.0	5.5
Wellington (Palm Beach County)	22.6	2.9	9.5	5.9
West Des Moines (Polk County)	17.9	4.3	6.0	4.7
West Linn (Clackamas County)	17.3	3.5	5.7	4.0
West Windsor (Mercer County)	26.4	2.5	11.4	6.3
Weston (Broward County)	19.3	3.0	8.2	4.5
Woodbury (Washington County)	18.0	10.3	5.0	3.9
Woodridge (DuPage County)	32.6	6.6	12.6	6.8
Yorba Linda (Orange County)	22.8	5.8	8.3	5.1
U.S. Average	17.7	4.6	6.9	4.3

Note: Data as of 2005; Figures are the number of physicians per 10,000 population; (1) Includes all non-federal, patient-care, office-based MDs

Source: Area Resource File (ARF). June 2007. U.S. Department of Health and Human Services, Health Resources and Services Administration, Bureau of Health Professions, Rockville, MD.

Crime Rate: City

City	All Crimes	Violent Crimes: Murder	Violent Crimes: Forcible Rape	Violent Crimes: Robbery	Violent Crimes: Aggrav. Assault	Property Crimes: Burglary	Property Crimes: Larceny -Theft	Property Crimes: Motor Vehicle Theft
Allen, TX	2,712.7	0.0	9.8	22.5	50.6	467.8	2,062.3	99.7
Ankeny, IA	2,283.3	0.0	16.3	16.3	65.1	379.7	1,697.6	108.5
Apex, NC	2,013.2	3.6	7.2	25.0	128.7	332.5	1,426.7	89.4
Bangor, ME	6,271.7	6.4	3.2	77.2	80.4	695.1	5,254.9	154.5
Beavercreek, OH	3,143.3	0.0	15.1	37.8	55.4	304.8	2,569.1	161.2
Bellevue, NE	2,737.9	0.0	21.0	42.0	77.7	292.1	2,078.1	226.9
Bend, OR	4,484.8	1.5	32.2	46.9	137.7	716.5	3,213.0	337.0
Bernards, NJ	630.6	3.7	11.1	0.0	11.1	155.8	426.6	22.3
Bethlehem, NY	1,794.4	0.0	3.0	15.2	54.6	263.7	1,406.4	51.5
Bozeman, MT	4,610.7	0.0	38.4	38.4	174.3	389.9	3,627.1	342.6
Brentwood, TN	1,793.7	0.0	9.1	15.2	60.9	268.0	1,403.9	36.5
Brookfield, WI	2,869.3	0.0	0.0	15.1	5.0	316.6	2,469.8	62.8
Broomfield, CO	3,338.6	0.0	18.1	20.3	51.9	288.9	2,713.3	246.0
Burlington, VT	4,455.2	2.6	59.6	41.5	298.1	673.9	3,265.6	114.0
Carmel, IN	1,747.3	0.0	10.1	21.8	11.7	218.0	1,396.8	88.9
Cary, NC	2,137.0	0.0	12.9	38.7	69.1	510.3	1,400.1	105.9
Casper, WY	5,181.8	0.0	38.2	22.9	187.3	842.9	3,866.7	223.6
Cheshire, CT	877.7	0.0	10.3	10.3	6.9	141.1	657.4	51.6
Chino Hills, CA	1,755.1	1.3	9.2	34.0	121.7	359.9	1,015.7	213.3
Collierville, TN	2,255.4	0.0	10.5	57.8	89.4	291.8	1,648.2	157.7
Conway, AR	4,957.0	5.7	66.6	116.0	167.3	747.3	3,504.3	349.9
Coronado, CA	2,021.6	0.0	11.3	33.8	41.3	251.3	1,421.5	262.5
Cranberry, PA	1,504.2	0.0	0.0	51.7	114.6	85.0	1,219.6	33.3
Dover, DE	5,738.9	5.8	49.0	135.5	642.8	409.3	4,136.3	360.3
Draper, UT	3,058.2	0.0	16.5	19.3	35.8	581.9	2,197.8	206.8
Dublin, OH	2,051.0	0.0	17.1	31.4	2.9	402.8	1,539.7	57.1
Edmond, OK	2,716.4	1.3	39.7	18.5	60.9	489.8	1,984.3	121.8
Evesham, NJ	1,627.8	0.0	12.8	17.0	59.6	195.8	1,291.6	51.1
Fargo, ND	3,204.2	2.2	76.0	20.9	155.3	578.1	2,125.1	246.6
Farmington, CT	2,714.6	0.0	12.0	40.2	4.0	232.9	2,248.8	176.7
Fishers, IN	1,163.2	0.0	8.7	24.3	13.9	135.4	920.2	60.8
Flower Mound, TX	1,258.3	3.1	12.2	6.1	36.7	206.7	943.0	50.5
Franklin, MA	379.7	0.0	9.7	3.2	12.9	54.7	257.4	41.8
Frederick, MD	3,916.2	6.9	29.3	261.8	614.8	609.7	2,216.4	177.4
Frisco, TX	4,508.3	1.4	15.1	19.2	98.9	1,006.9	3,267.9	98.9
Goodyear, AZ	6,060.8	0.0	30.7	59.2	107.4	3,163.0	1,889.5	811.0
Grand Blanc, MI	2,406.3	2.9	28.5	22.8	139.9	459.6	1,547.1	205.5
Greenburgh, NY	1,882.2	0.0	0.0	43.8	39.2	184.5	1,503.9	110.7
Greenwich, CT	867.4	3.2	1.6	16.1	19.3	93.3	688.8	45.1
Hampden, PA	1,392.9	0.0	11.9	11.9	7.9	119.0	1,206.3	35.7
Hilliard, OH	3,499.7	0.0	11.2	71.2	30.0	573.3	2,712.8	101.2
Hoover, AL	3,695.7	2.9	25.0	119.0	42.6	458.3	2,815.8	232.1
Huntersville, NC	3,452.6	0.0	29.6	80.9	161.7	722.3	2,312.5	145.5
Juneau, AK	5,107.9	6.4	102.3	28.8	255.7	620.1	3,915.6	179.0
Keller, TX	1,566.0	5.4	19.1	10.9	32.7	269.6	1,173.8	54.5
Kenner, LA	4,629.8	13.6	25.7	172.0	347.1	837.5	2,566.9	667.0
Kennesaw, GA	2,054.0	0.0	0.0	24.8	95.8	322.8	1,411.9	198.7
League City, TX	2,784.9	0.0	28.5	38.0	64.8	540.9	1,975.2	137.6
Leawood, KS	1,485.6	0.0	13.2	13.2	128.5	230.6	1,073.9	26.4
Lee's Summit, MO	3,015.1	2.5	18.5	28.4	105.0	388.0	2,293.5	179.2
Leesburg, VA	2,336.9	0.0	32.8	51.9	114.7	182.9	1,823.6	131.0
Lehi, UT	2,109.0	0.0	18.3	6.1	54.9	653.2	1,254.4	122.1
Lwr Providence, PA	1,230.0	4.0	8.0	16.0	16.0	208.3	925.5	52.1
Madison, AL	2,323.4	0.0	23.3	55.4	104.9	466.4	1,548.0	125.4
Manhattan Bch, CA	2,572.7	0.0	19.0	65.2	43.5	556.9	1,725.1	163.0
Maple Grove, MN	2,608.3	0.0	33.2	33.2	36.6	518.7	1,913.4	73.1
Marion, IA	1,812.9	3.3	23.0	3.3	62.5	332.3	1,283.1	105.3

City	All Crimes	Violent Crimes				Property Crimes		
		Murder	Forcible Rape	Robbery	Aggrav. Assault	Burglary	Larceny -Theft	Motor Vehicle Theft
Marlboro, NJ	1,045.5	0.0	2.5	20.2	17.6	183.9	788.5	32.7
Matthews, NC	4,742.2	3.9	23.2	81.4	124.0	743.9	3,475.3	290.6
Meridian, ID	2,596.7	1.9	26.1	16.8	158.6	503.7	1,742.3	147.4
Merrimack, NH	1,132.6	0.0	0.0	3.7	7.5	112.1	990.5	18.7
Morgantown, WV	3,976.4	3.5	91.8	102.4	201.3	822.8	2,609.7	144.8
Mt Pleasant, SC	2,459.5	0.0	18.7	37.4	283.9	324.6	1,692.9	102.0
Northampton, PA	988.9	0.0	4.9	17.1	17.1	192.4	721.0	36.5
Northville, MI	2,244.6	0.0	23.8	23.8	31.7	503.6	1,499.0	162.6
Novi, MI	2,374.3	0.0	9.4	20.8	64.2	200.1	1,993.1	86.8
O'Fallon, MO	2,602.5	0.0	8.5	14.2	61.3	253.6	2,205.0	59.8
Oro Valley, AZ	1,929.5	2.5	5.0	12.5	52.6	253.1	1,448.4	155.4
Oviedo, FL	1,736.4	0.0	3.3	23.1	204.3	270.2	1,179.5	56.0
Palm Bch Grdns, FL	3,926.5	0.0	14.1	86.3	184.7	732.7	2,661.8	246.9
Parker, CO	1,981.9	2.6	15.3	0.0	43.4	380.5	1,399.6	140.5
Peachtree City, GA	1,122.6	2.8	5.6	14.0	22.5	103.8	799.8	174.0
Pflugerville, TX	2,409.0	0.0	49.5	31.8	67.1	480.4	1,706.1	74.2
Pleasanton, CA	2,410.4	0.0	9.0	37.6	55.6	321.6	1,774.8	211.9
Rapid City, SD	3,866.1	0.0	89.4	60.7	220.3	649.7	2,680.1	166.0
Redmond, WA	3,723.4	0.0	24.8	41.3	66.1	429.8	2,752.2	409.1
Richland, WA	3,411.9	0.0	22.2	31.1	168.6	625.6	2,371.4	193.0
Richmond, KY	4,377.7	6.4	32.1	51.4	215.2	934.6	2,881.0	256.9
Rio Rancho, NM	2,746.5	0.0	23.7	22.2	346.6	717.0	1,370.3	266.7
Rockaway, NJ	1,944.5	0.0	11.7	23.5	23.5	148.7	1,658.9	78.3
Rocklin, CA	2,734.0	0.0	14.0	41.9	91.9	549.2	1,795.4	241.6
Rogers, AR	5,359.4	0.0	90.0	26.6	90.0	597.1	4,390.1	165.6
Round Rock, TX	2,334.3	0.0	25.9	34.9	56.3	312.1	1,849.9	55.2
Sammamish, WA	1,338.9	0.0	14.3	2.9	14.3	283.2	941.2	83.0
San Ramon, CA	1,924.7	2.0	2.0	49.6	73.3	335.0	1,306.3	156.6
Santa Fe, NM	6,520.4	12.6	58.7	145.3	368.8	3,085.6	2,547.8	301.7
Saratoga, CA	1,841.0	0.0	6.7	6.7	73.5	537.9	1,152.7	63.5
Savage, MN	2,926.1	0.0	14.9	7.5	93.4	508.2	2,212.3	89.7
Schererville, IN	2,851.4	0.0	3.5	31.5	14.0	286.9	2,302.1	213.4
Shawnee, KS	2,472.6	0.0	25.8	29.3	120.6	337.7	1,683.5	275.7
Shrewsbury, MA	1,108.7	0.0	27.0	6.0	44.9	89.9	889.9	50.9
S Brunswick, NJ	1,550.7	0.0	4.9	29.5	41.8	349.5	1,028.9	96.0
S. Jordan, UT	2,194.2	0.0	16.9	14.5	53.0	315.5	1,620.9	173.4
S. Kingstown, RI	1,196.2	0.0	17.2	10.3	41.2	189.0	900.6	37.8
Southaven, MS	4,586.6	2.6	25.8	100.8	111.1	617.6	3,328.2	400.5
Southlake, TX	2,323.5	0.0	0.0	11.7	39.1	413.9	1,776.8	82.0
Spanish Fork, UT	2,507.9	0.0	29.1	3.6	40.0	458.6	1,900.0	76.4
Sparks, NV	4,519.2	3.5	47.2	146.2	251.2	1,053.1	2,481.3	536.6
Stow, OH	2,705.7	0.0	26.1	34.8	14.5	325.1	2,264.4	40.6
Sugar Land, TX	2,195.1	0.0	7.7	57.8	64.2	272.1	1,697.0	96.3
Sun Prairie, WI	1,824.6	0.0	23.5	19.6	78.5	153.0	1,467.5	82.4
Tualatin, OR	3,269.3	0.0	7.6	49.4	68.4	463.8	2,395.0	285.1
Waimalu, HI	n/a	n/a	n/a	n/a	n/a	n/a	n/a	n/a
Wellington, FL	3,454.0	0.0	38.5	62.4	198.2	513.9	2,362.0	279.0
W Des Moines, IA	3,666.5	0.0	37.7	17.0	130.1	454.3	2,899.3	128.2
West Linn, OR	1,270.3	0.0	19.6	19.6	58.8	239.2	886.1	47.0
West Windsor, NJ	2,157.3	3.8	3.8	26.9	30.8	203.8	1,815.0	73.1
Weston, FL	1,591.6	0.0	9.0	24.0	110.8	235.1	1,121.5	91.3
Woodbury, MN	2,212.8	0.0	13.3	18.9	18.9	299.1	1,773.6	89.0
Woodridge, IL	1,906.5	0.0	56.0	35.4	50.1	285.8	1,411.4	67.8
Yorba Linda, CA	1,600.1	0.0	6.1	24.6	47.7	325.9	1,074.4	121.4
U.S.	3,808.1	5.7	30.9	149.4	287.5	729.4	2,206.8	398.4

Note: Figures are crimes per 100,000 population; n/a not available
Source: FBI Uniform Crime Reports 2006

Crime Rate: Metro Area

Metro Area[1]	All Crimes	Violent Crimes				Property Crimes		
		Murder	Forcible Rape	Robbery	Aggrav. Assault	Burglary	Larceny -Theft	Motor Vehicle Theft
Allen, TX	4,891.4	4.6	25.7	78.1	270.1	850.6	3,288.2	374.1
Ankeny, IA	4,378.7	1.5	23.2	82.8	240.7	675.7	3,093.7	261.0
Apex, NC	3,249.1	3.3	20.9	112.1	194.6	778.4	1,934.0	205.8
Bangor, ME	3,220.8	2.0	9.5	22.4	41.5	533.1	2,515.0	97.2
Beavercreek, OH	4,069.6	5.3	43.5	136.5	139.9	867.0	2,459.7	417.6
Bellevue, NE	4,495.5	4.8	37.6	118.0	255.9	642.9	2,880.5	555.9
Bend, OR	3,774.5	1.4	29.9	33.4	153.1	670.8	2,624.2	261.7
Bernards, NJ[2]	2,085.6	2.0	10.1	69.3	103.0	365.7	1,408.9	126.5
Bethlehem, NY	3,115.1	2.1	24.3	113.3	232.2	569.7	2,034.2	139.3
Bozeman, MT	n/a	n/a	n/a	n/a	n/a	n/a	n/a	n/a
Brentwood, TN	4,699.8	7.2	41.2	204.6	604.8	792.2	2,717.1	332.8
Brookfield, WI	4,506.0	7.4	14.2	266.9	291.1	583.2	2,723.9	619.3
Broomfield, CO	4,111.3	4.4	47.9	109.3	266.1	745.4	2,323.5	614.6
Burlington, VT	n/a	n/a	n/a	n/a	n/a	n/a	n/a	n/a
Carmel, IN	4,722.8	9.4	41.1	220.0	276.4	913.4	2,629.6	632.9
Cary, NC	3,295.3	3.8	21.0	111.4	223.6	777.1	1,947.1	211.3
Casper, WY	4,753.3	2.8	29.8	22.7	184.2	838.7	3,472.6	202.6
Cheshire, CT	n/a	n/a	n/a	n/a	n/a	n/a	n/a	n/a
Chino Hills, CA	3,920.7	6.9	26.7	167.3	288.3	840.7	1,866.4	724.4
Collierville, TN	7,275.5	13.7	46.3	458.5	744.2	1,700.3	3,647.3	665.1
Conway, AR	6,547.1	14.3	57.9	209.3	623.9	1,426.3	3,751.7	463.6
Coronado, CA	3,612.7	4.3	26.3	145.7	282.5	603.2	1,738.4	812.4
Cranberry, PA	2,694.4	4.4	18.9	130.4	206.1	470.7	1,660.3	203.6
Dover, DE	3,709.8	5.5	63.2	96.1	440.0	618.5	2,257.9	228.6
Draper, UT	5,195.3	2.2	44.3	88.4	210.6	743.9	3,535.6	570.4
Dublin, OH	5,125.8	6.6	51.1	246.4	122.2	1,252.1	2,989.9	457.5
Edmond, OK	5,128.7	7.0	46.5	124.4	337.4	1,214.1	2,853.8	545.3
Evesham, NJ[2]	3,008.6	4.7	24.5	134.3	188.5	530.8	1,886.0	240.0
Fargo, ND	n/a	1.1	n/a	16.2	116.2	442.0	1,732.5	186.4
Farmington, CT	3,464.5	3.8	18.0	143.9	149.7	510.9	2,262.2	376.0
Fishers, IN	4,722.8	9.4	41.1	220.0	276.4	913.4	2,629.6	632.9
Flower Mound, TX[2]	4,972.8	6.4	32.8	219.6	300.8	1,025.0	2,827.7	560.5
Franklin, MA	n/a	n/a	n/a	n/a	n/a	n/a	n/a	n/a
Frederick, MD[2]	2,698.5	2.3	15.6	125.2	122.1	417.2	1,767.2	248.7
Frisco, TX[2]	4,972.8	6.4	32.8	219.6	300.8	1,025.0	2,827.7	560.5
Goodyear, AZ	5,388.0	8.7	31.6	167.4	302.1	978.7	2,875.2	1,024.3
Grand Blanc, MI	5,077.7	15.4	70.0	195.1	649.1	1,259.1	2,305.9	583.1
Greenburgh, NY[2]	2,422.6	5.9	12.0	250.7	282.9	289.2	1,382.2	199.7
Greenwich, CT	n/a	n/a	n/a	n/a	n/a	n/a	n/a	n/a
Hampden, PA	2,604.3	2.9	31.4	115.4	156.8	411.8	1,771.7	114.4
Hilliard, OH	5,125.8	6.6	51.1	246.4	122.2	1,252.1	2,989.9	457.5
Hoover, AL	4,878.4	12.5	44.3	233.8	271.8	1,051.4	2,860.3	404.3
Huntersville, NC	n/a	8.3	36.7	269.5	n/a	1,405.5	3,220.5	622.0
Juneau, AK	n/a	n/a	n/a	n/a	n/a	n/a	n/a	n/a
Keller, TX[2]	4,914.1	4.1	36.5	143.0	299.9	984.4	3,066.3	379.9
Kenner, LA	3,888.7	21.7	23.9	138.1	372.2	912.8	1,930.7	489.3
Kennesaw, GA	4,607.2	6.9	22.2	195.9	267.1	936.9	2,570.6	607.7
League City, TX	4,829.8	9.6	34.6	279.6	383.4	964.9	2,570.8	586.9
Leawood, KS	4,771.9	8.9	43.7	159.0	384.3	850.3	2,740.9	584.7
Lee's Summit, MO	4,771.9	8.9	43.7	159.0	384.3	850.3	2,740.9	584.7
Leesburg, VA[2]	3,553.3	8.8	20.0	233.7	275.2	411.1	2,001.8	602.8
Lehi, UT	2,591.3	0.6	23.3	13.5	56.0	465.1	1,896.2	136.4
Lwr Providence, PA[2]	3,647.7	11.8	35.0	332.8	377.0	486.7	2,008.3	396.1
Madison, AL	4,436.4	1.7	39.4	119.9	237.9	819.7	2,866.1	351.7
Manhattan Bch, CA[2]	3,335.5	10.1	23.4	276.6	338.7	553.6	1,487.7	645.4
Maple Grove, MN	n/a	3.5	n/a	157.6	206.9	654.5	2,542.0	338.2
Marion, IA	3,218.1	2.8	23.8	56.9	130.8	599.1	2,248.9	155.8

Metro Area[1]	All Crimes	Violent Crimes				Property Crimes		
		Murder	Forcible Rape	Robbery	Aggrav. Assault	Burglary	Larceny -Theft	Motor Vehicle Theft
Marlboro, NJ[2]	2,085.6	2.0	10.1	69.3	103.0	365.7	1,408.9	126.5
Matthews, NC	n/a	8.3	36.7	269.5	n/a	1,405.5	3,220.5	622.0
Meridian, ID	3,009.0	2.7	46.6	33.3	205.8	589.5	1,916.8	214.4
Merrimack, NH	2,212.0	1.2	23.3	57.3	75.5	376.4	1,548.1	130.1
Morgantown, WV	2,668.3	3.5	36.6	48.9	151.0	601.2	1,656.2	171.0
Mt Pleasant, SC	5,177.5	12.6	48.2	202.9	566.7	892.2	2,931.9	523.0
Northampton, PA[2]	3,647.7	11.8	35.0	332.8	377.0	486.7	2,008.3	396.1
Northville, MI[2]	6,212.6	23.0	48.4	426.4	779.5	1,229.5	2,216.7	1,489.2
Novi, MI[2]	2,856.5	1.9	34.5	68.3	234.8	483.4	1,678.0	355.6
O'Fallon, MO	4,297.4	6.6	22.8	167.1	369.6	678.7	2,565.0	487.5
Oro Valley, AZ	n/a	7.5	41.7	205.7	336.9	871.2	n/a	999.0
Oviedo, FL	5,200.2	8.1	40.3	263.4	567.3	1,098.9	2,693.2	529.0
Palm Bch Grdns, FL[2]	4,940.9	7.1	35.7	225.4	450.6	997.6	2,756.5	468.1
Parker, CO	4,111.3	4.4	47.9	109.3	266.1	745.4	2,323.5	614.6
Peachtree City, GA	n/a	7.4	21.6	209.2	289.0	n/a	2,341.6	563.4
Pflugerville, TX	4,288.0	1.9	35.0	104.8	203.5	765.2	2,951.7	225.9
Pleasanton, CA[2]	4,823.4	10.6	29.0	326.4	325.3	803.1	2,185.7	1,143.2
Rapid City, SD	2,708.3	0.0	80.6	31.9	157.0	495.3	1,820.1	123.4
Redmond, WA	5,424.5	3.6	39.4	143.9	229.0	972.1	3,026.7	1,009.7
Richland, WA	3,516.7	2.7	30.7	39.6	216.7	662.9	2,318.5	245.6
Richmond, KY	n/a	n/a	n/a	n/a	n/a	n/a	n/a	n/a
Rio Rancho, NM	5,602.7	8.9	51.9	174.3	542.7	1,109.3	2,885.3	830.3
Rockaway, NJ[2]	2,759.4	8.7	13.8	198.2	194.6	442.2	1,384.0	517.9
Rocklin, CA	4,566.1	5.4	31.7	212.4	386.1	930.8	2,100.0	899.7
Rogers, AR	3,472.9	2.2	63.5	27.8	225.8	666.7	2,295.5	191.4
Round Rock, TX	4,288.0	1.9	35.0	104.8	203.5	765.2	2,951.7	225.9
Sammamish, WA[2]	5,365.3	3.3	37.4	141.0	193.3	933.0	3,021.9	1,035.4
San Ramon, CA[2]	4,823.4	10.6	29.0	326.4	325.3	803.1	2,185.7	1,143.2
Santa Fe, NM	4,182.3	6.3	47.6	81.2	310.3	2,084.5	1,493.3	159.0
Saratoga, CA	3,033.9	2.3	19.1	87.8	207.5	517.6	1,623.6	576.1
Savage, MN	n/a	3.5	n/a	157.6	206.9	654.5	2,542.0	338.2
Schererville, IN	n/a	n/a	n/a	n/a	n/a	n/a	n/a	n/a
Shawnee, KS	4,771.9	8.9	43.7	159.0	384.3	850.3	2,740.9	584.7
Shrewsbury, MA	n/a	1.1	38.7	74.7	n/a	448.6	1,208.9	212.7
S Brunswick, NJ[2]	2,085.6	2.0	10.1	69.3	103.0	365.7	1,408.9	126.5
S. Jordan, UT	5,195.3	2.2	44.3	88.4	210.6	743.9	3,535.6	570.4
S. Kingstown, RI	n/a	n/a	n/a	n/a	n/a	n/a	n/a	n/a
Southaven, MS	7,275.5	13.7	46.3	458.5	744.2	1,700.3	3,647.3	665.1
Southlake, TX[2]	4,914.1	4.1	36.5	143.0	299.9	984.4	3,066.3	379.9
Spanish Fork, UT	2,591.3	0.6	23.3	13.5	56.0	465.1	1,896.2	136.4
Sparks, NV	4,522.6	7.4	34.6	164.8	302.9	889.4	2,553.3	570.1
Stow, OH	n/a	n/a	n/a	n/a	n/a	n/a	n/a	n/a
Sugar Land, TX	4,829.8	9.6	34.6	279.6	383.4	964.9	2,570.8	586.9
Sun Prairie, WI	3,097.2	0.7	25.8	100.6	134.7	510.8	2,173.8	150.8
Tualatin, OR	3,968.4	2.3	39.7	98.5	183.3	619.1	2,574.8	450.7
Waimalu, HI	4,498.2	1.9	25.1	104.7	169.1	600.6	2,907.9	689.0
Wellington, FL[2]	4,940.9	7.1	35.7	225.4	450.6	997.6	2,756.5	468.1
W Des Moines, IA	4,378.7	1.5	23.2	82.8	240.7	675.7	3,093.7	261.0
West Linn, OR	3,968.4	2.3	39.7	98.5	183.3	619.1	2,574.8	450.7
West Windsor, NJ	2,692.0	5.7	18.0	236.5	225.6	507.5	1,474.1	224.5
Weston, FL[2]	4,166.5	4.8	26.4	203.9	360.4	731.2	2,447.4	392.3
Woodbury, MN	n/a	3.5	n/a	157.6	206.9	654.5	2,542.0	338.2
Woodridge, IL	n/a	n/a	n/a	n/a	n/a	n/a	n/a	n/a
Yorba Linda, CA[2]	2,519.7	2.7	15.8	101.7	157.2	422.2	1,470.3	349.9
U.S.	3,808.1	5.7	30.9	149.4	287.5	729.4	2,206.8	398.4

Note: Figures are crimes per 100,000 population; n/a not available; (1) Figures cover the Metropolitan Statistical Area (MSA) except where noted; (2) Metropolitan Division (MD); See Appendix B for counties included in MSAs and MDs
Source: FBI Uniform Crime Reports 2006

Temperature & Precipitation: Yearly Averages and Extremes

City	Extreme Low (°F)	Average Low (°F)	Average Temp. (°F)	Average High (°F)	Extreme High (°F)	Average Precip. (in.)	Average Snow (in.)
Allen, TX	-2	56	67	77	112	33.9	3
Ankeny, IA	-24	40	50	60	108	31.8	33
Apex, NC	-9	48	60	71	105	42.0	8
Bangor, ME	-33	32	n/a	54	99	43.2	78.4
Beavercreek, OH	-25	42	52	62	102	37.4	29
Bellevue, NE	-23	40	51	62	110	30.1	29
Bend, OR	-12	42	53	63	108	47.3	7
Bernards, NJ	-8	46	55	63	105	43.5	27
Bethlehem, NY	-28	37	48	58	100	35.8	63
Bozeman, MT	-32	36	47	59	105	14.6	59
Brentwood, TN	-17	49	60	70	107	47.4	11
Brookfield, WI	-26	38	47	55	103	32.0	49
Broomfield, CO	-25	37	51	64	103	15.5	63
Burlington, VT	-30	35	45	54	100	34.0	79
Carmel, IN	-23	42	53	62	104	40.2	25
Cary, NC	-9	48	60	71	105	42.0	8
Casper, WY	-41	32	46	59	104	12.2	80
Cheshire, CT	-7	44	52	60	103	41.4	25
Chino Hills, CA	24	53	66	78	114	n/a	n/a
Collierville, TN	0	52	65	77	107	54.8	1
Conway, AR	-5	51	62	73	112	50.7	5
Coronado, CA	29	57	64	71	111	9.5	Trace
Cranberry, PA	-18	41	51	60	103	37.1	43
Dover, DE	-14	45	55	64	102	41.5	20
Draper, UT	-22	40	52	64	107	15.6	63
Dublin, OH	-19	42	52	62	104	37.9	28
Edmond, OK	-8	49	60	71	110	32.8	10
Evesham, NJ	-7	45	55	64	104	41.4	22
Fargo, ND	-36	31	41	52	106	19.6	40
Farmington, CT	-26	40	50	60	102	44.2	46
Fishers, IN	-23	42	53	62	104	40.2	25
Flower Mound, TX	-2	56	67	77	112	33.9	3
Franklin, MA	-12	44	52	59	102	42.9	41
Frederick, MD	-5	49	58	67	104	39.5	18
Frisco, TX	-2	56	67	77	112	33.9	3
Goodyear, AZ	17	59	72	86	122	7.3	Trace
Grand Blanc, MI	-25	38	47	57	101	30.5	47
Greenburgh, NY	-2	47	55	62	104	47.0	23
Greenwich, CT	-7	44	52	60	103	41.4	25
Hampden, PA	-9	44	53	62	107	39.0	35
Hilliard, OH	-19	42	52	62	104	37.9	28
Hoover, AL	-6	51	63	74	106	53.5	2
Huntersville, NC	-5	50	61	71	104	42.8	6
Juneau, AK	-22	34	41	47	90	55.2	102
Keller, TX	-1	55	66	76	113	32.3	3
Kenner, LA	11	59	69	78	102	60.6	Trace
Kennesaw, GA	-8	52	62	72	105	49.8	2
League City, TX	7	58	69	79	107	46.9	Trace
Leawood, KS	-23	44	54	64	109	38.1	21
Lee's Summit, MO	-23	44	54	64	109	38.1	21
Leesburg, VA	-18	43	54	65	104	40.3	23
Lehi, UT	-22	40	52	64	107	15.6	63
Lwr Providence, PA	-7	45	55	64	104	41.4	22
Madison, AL	-11	50	61	71	104	56.8	4
Manhattan Bch, CA	27	55	63	70	110	11.3	Trace
Maple Grove, MN	-34	35	45	54	105	27.1	52
Marion, IA	-34	36	47	57	105	34.4	33
Marlboro, NJ	-8	46	55	63	105	43.5	27
Matthews, NC	-5	50	61	71	104	42.8	6

City	Extreme Low (°F)	Average Low (°F)	Average Temp. (°F)	Average High (°F)	Extreme High (°F)	Average Precip. (in.)	Average Snow (in.)
Meridian, ID	-25	39	51	63	111	11.8	22
Merrimack, NH	-33	34	46	57	102	36.9	63
Morgantown, WV	-24	38	50	62	99	44.4	73
Mt Pleasant, SC	6	55	66	76	104	52.1	1
Northampton, PA	-7	45	55	64	104	41.4	22
Northville, MI	-21	39	49	58	104	32.4	41
Novi, MI	-21	39	49	58	104	32.4	41
O'Fallon, MO	-18	46	56	66	115	36.8	20
Oro Valley, AZ	16	55	69	82	117	11.6	2
Oviedo, FL	19	62	72	82	100	47.7	Trace
Palm Bch Grdns, FL	30	69	76	83	98	57.1	0
Parker, CO	-25	37	51	64	103	15.5	63
Peachtree City, GA	-8	52	62	72	105	49.8	2
Pflugerville, TX	-2	58	69	79	109	31.1	1
Pleasanton, CA	27	52	59	66	106	17.6	Trace
Rapid City, SD	-30	34	47	60	110	16.1	40
Redmond, WA	0	44	52	59	99	38.4	13
Richland, WA	-25	36	50	63	110	8.2	24
Richmond, KY	-21	45	55	65	103	45.1	17
Rio Rancho, NM	-17	43	57	70	105	8.5	11
Rockaway, NJ	-8	46	55	63	105	43.5	27
Rocklin, CA	18	48	61	73	115	17.3	Trace
Rogers, AR	-10	49	61	73	111	41.8	6
Round Rock, TX	-2	58	69	79	109	31.1	1
Sammamish, WA	0	44	52	59	99	38.4	13
San Ramon, CA	27	52	59	66	106	17.6	Trace
Santa Fe, NM	-17	43	57	70	105	8.5	11
Saratoga, CA	21	50	59	68	105	13.5	Trace
Savage, MN	-34	35	45	54	105	27.1	52
Schererville, IN	-27	40	49	59	104	35.4	39
Shawnee, KS	-23	44	54	64	109	38.1	21
Shrewsbury, MA	-13	38	47	56	99	47.6	62
S Brunswick, NJ	-8	46	55	63	105	43.5	27
S. Jordan, UT	-22	40	52	64	107	15.6	63
S. Kingstown, RI	-13	42	51	60	104	45.3	35
Southaven, MS	0	52	65	77	107	54.8	1
Southlake, TX	-1	55	66	76	113	32.3	3
Spanish Fork, UT	-22	40	52	64	107	15.6	63
Sparks, NV	-16	33	50	67	105	7.2	24
Stow, OH	-24	40	50	59	101	36.7	47
Sugar Land, TX	7	58	69	79	107	46.9	Trace
Sun Prairie, WI	-37	35	46	57	104	31.1	42
Tualatin, OR	-3	45	54	62	107	37.5	7
Waimalu, HI	52	70	77	84	94	22.4	0
Wellington, FL	30	69	76	83	98	57.1	0
W Des Moines, IA	-24	40	50	60	108	31.8	33
West Linn, OR	-3	45	54	62	107	37.5	7
West Windsor, NJ	-7	45	55	64	104	41.4	22
Weston, FL	30	69	76	83	98	57.1	0
Woodbury, MN	-34	35	45	54	105	27.1	52
Woodridge, IL	-27	40	49	59	104	35.4	39
Yorba Linda, CA	27	55	63	70	110	11.3	Trace

Source: National Climatic Data Center, International Station Meteorological Climate Summary, 9/96

Weather Conditions

City	Temperature			Daytime Sky			Precipitation		
	10°F & below	32°F & below	90°F & above	Clear	Partly cloudy	Cloudy	.01 inch or more precip.	1.0 inch or more snow/ice	Thunder-storms
Allen, TX	1	34	102	108	160	97	78	2	49
Ankeny, IA	n/a	137	26	99	129	137	106	25	46
Apex, NC	n/a	n/a	39	98	143	124	110	3	42
Bangor, ME	n/a	180	27	n/a	n/a	n/a	n/a	n/a	16
Beavercreek, OH	18	117	17	80	121	164	133	28	40
Bellevue, NE	n/a	139	35	100	142	123	97	20	46
Bend, OR	n/a	n/a	15	75	115	175	136	4	3
Bernards, NJ	n/a	90	24	80	146	139	122	16	46
Bethlehem, NY	n/a	147	11	58	149	158	133	36	24
Bozeman, MT	n/a	149	29	75	163	127	97	41	27
Brentwood, TN	5	76	51	98	135	132	119	8	54
Brookfield, WI	n/a	141	10	90	118	157	126	38	35
Broomfield, CO	24	155	33	99	177	89	90	38	39
Burlington, VT	n/a	156	7	49	146	170	154	55	22
Carmel, IN	19	119	19	83	128	154	127	24	43
Cary, NC	n/a	n/a	39	98	143	124	110	3	42
Casper, WY	n/a	179	28	103	141	121	97	53	34
Cheshire, CT	n/a	n/a	7	80	146	139	118	17	22
Chino Hills, CA	0	4	82	124	178	63	n/a	n/a	5
Collierville, TN	1	53	86	101	152	112	104	2	59
Conway, AR	1	57	73	110	142	113	104	4	57
Coronado, CA	0	< 1	4	115	126	124	40	0	5
Cranberry, PA	n/a	121	8	62	137	166	154	42	35
Dover, DE	6	99	20	86	135	144	116	11	29
Draper, UT	n/a	128	56	94	152	119	92	38	38
Dublin, OH	n/a	118	19	72	137	156	136	29	40
Edmond, OK	5	79	70	124	131	110	80	8	50
Evesham, NJ	5	94	23	81	146	138	117	14	27
Fargo, ND	n/a	180	15	81	145	139	100	38	31
Farmington, CT	n/a	134	18	69	151	145	126	26	20
Fishers, IN	19	119	19	83	128	154	127	24	43
Flower Mound, TX	1	34	102	108	160	97	78	2	49
Franklin, MA	n/a	97	12	88	127	150	253	48	18
Frederick, MD	2	71	34	84	144	137	112	9	30
Frisco, TX	1	34	102	108	160	97	78	2	49
Goodyear, AZ	0	10	167	186	125	54	37	< 1	23
Grand Blanc, MI	n/a	143	8	74	122	169	133	47	33
Greenburgh, NY	n/a	n/a	18	85	166	114	120	11	20
Greenwich, CT	n/a	n/a	7	80	146	139	118	17	22
Hampden, PA	n/a	106	22	83	134	148	124	20	31
Hilliard, OH	n/a	118	19	72	137	156	136	29	40
Hoover, AL	1	57	59	91	161	113	119	1	57
Huntersville, NC	1	65	44	98	142	125	113	3	41
Juneau, AK	n/a	139	n/a	40	78	247	219	50	1
Keller, TX	1	40	100	123	136	106	79	3	47
Kenner, LA	0	13	70	90	169	106	114	1	69
Kennesaw, GA	1	49	38	98	147	120	116	3	48
League City, TX	n/a	n/a	96	83	168	114	101	1	62
Leawood, KS	22	110	39	112	134	119	103	17	51
Lee's Summit, MO	22	110	39	112	134	119	103	17	51
Leesburg, VA	9	115	30	79	141	145	117	12	28
Lehi, UT	n/a	128	56	94	152	119	92	38	38
Lwr Providence, PA	5	94	23	81	146	138	117	14	27
Madison, AL	2	66	49	70	118	177	116	2	54
Manhattan Bch, CA	0	< 1	5	131	125	109	34	0	1
Maple Grove, MN	n/a	156	16	93	125	147	113	41	37
Marion, IA	n/a	156	16	89	132	144	109	28	42

City	Temperature			Daytime Sky			Precipitation		
	10°F & below	32°F & below	90°F & above	Clear	Partly cloudy	Cloudy	.01 inch or more precip.	1.0 inch or more snow/ice	Thunder-storms
Marlboro, NJ	n/a	90	24	80	146	139	122	16	46
Matthews, NC	1	65	44	98	142	125	113	3	41
Meridian, ID	n/a	124	45	106	133	126	91	22	14
Merrimack, NH	n/a	171	12	87	131	147	125	32	19
Morgantown, WV	23	144	3	48	133	184	174	49	42
Mt Pleasant, SC	< 1	33	53	89	162	114	114	1	59
Northampton, PA	5	94	23	81	146	138	117	14	27
Northville, MI	n/a	136	12	74	134	157	135	38	32
Novi, MI	n/a	136	12	74	134	157	135	38	32
O'Fallon, MO	13	100	43	97	138	130	109	14	46
Oro Valley, AZ	0	18	140	177	119	69	54	2	42
Oviedo, FL	n/a	n/a	90	76	208	81	115	0	80
Palm Bch Grdns, FL	n/a	n/a	55	48	263	54	128	0	74
Parker, CO	24	155	33	99	177	89	90	38	39
Peachtree City, GA	1	49	38	98	147	120	116	3	48
Pflugerville, TX	< 1	20	111	105	148	112	83	1	41
Pleasanton, CA	0	< 1	3	99	168	98	59	0	6
Rapid City, SD	n/a	169	31	89	168	108	98	37	40
Redmond, WA	n/a	38	3	57	121	187	157	8	8
Richland, WA	n/a	149	32	102	133	130	70	18	6
Richmond, KY	11	96	22	86	136	143	129	17	44
Rio Rancho, NM	4	114	65	140	161	64	60	9	38
Rockaway, NJ	n/a	90	24	80	146	139	122	16	46
Rocklin, CA	0	21	73	175	111	79	58	< 1	2
Rogers, AR	3	76	76	117	121	127	98	5	59
Round Rock, TX	< 1	20	111	105	148	112	83	1	41
Sammamish, WA	n/a	38	3	57	121	187	157	8	8
San Ramon, CA	0	< 1	3	99	168	98	59	0	6
Santa Fe, NM	4	114	65	140	161	64	60	9	38
Saratoga, CA	0	5	5	106	180	79	57	< 1	6
Savage, MN	n/a	156	16	93	125	147	113	41	37
Schererville, IN	n/a	132	17	83	136	146	125	31	38
Shawnee, KS	22	110	39	112	134	119	103	17	51
Shrewsbury, MA	n/a	141	4	81	144	140	131	32	23
S Brunswick, NJ	n/a	90	24	80	146	139	122	16	46
S. Jordan, UT	n/a	128	56	94	152	119	92	38	38
S. Kingstown, RI	n/a	117	9	85	134	146	123	21	21
Southaven, MS	1	53	86	101	152	112	104	2	59
Southlake, TX	1	40	100	123	136	106	79	3	47
Spanish Fork, UT	n/a	128	56	94	152	119	92	38	38
Sparks, NV	14	178	50	143	139	83	50	17	14
Stow, OH	n/a	129	8	67	134	164	153	48	38
Sugar Land, TX	n/a	n/a	96	83	168	114	101	1	62
Sun Prairie, WI	n/a	161	14	88	119	158	118	38	40
Tualatin, OR	n/a	37	11	67	116	182	152	4	7
Waimalu, HI	n/a	n/a	23	25	286	54	98	0	7
Wellington, FL	n/a	n/a	55	48	263	54	128	0	74
W Des Moines, IA	n/a	137	26	99	129	137	106	25	46
West Linn, OR	n/a	37	11	67	116	182	152	4	7
West Windsor, NJ	5	94	23	81	146	138	117	14	27
Weston, FL	n/a	n/a	55	48	263	54	128	0	74
Woodbury, MN	n/a	156	16	93	125	147	113	41	37
Woodridge, IL	n/a	132	17	83	136	146	125	31	38
Yorba Linda, CA	0	< 1	5	131	125	109	34	0	1

Note: Figures are average number of days per year

Source: National Climatic Data Center, International Station Meteorological Climate Summary, 9/96

Air Quality Index

Area (Days[1])	Percent of Days when Air Quality was...				AQI Statistics	
	Good	Moderate	Unhealthy for Sensitive Groups	Unhealthy	Maximum	Median
Allen, TX (365)	67.1	27.7	4.4	0.8	177	44
Ankeny, IA (365)	74.0	25.8	0.3	0.0	101	38
Apex, NC (365)	53.7	38.1	8.2	0.0	142	47
Bangor, ME (123)	89.4	10.6	0.0	0.0	74	25
Beavercreek, OH (365)	69.0	26.3	4.4	0.3	151	40
Bellevue, NE (365)	46.6	51.5	1.9	0.0	123	52
Bend, OR (362)	96.7	3.3	0.0	0.0	70	13
Bernards, NJ (365)	71.0	20.8	7.4	0.8	166	39
Bethlehem, NY (365)	74.5	21.4	4.1	0.0	135	37
Bozeman, MT (365)	88.5	10.7	0.3	0.5	171	21
Brentwood, TN (365)	49.6	40.0	9.9	0.5	172	51
Brookfield, WI (365)	74.5	21.6	3.8	0.0	142	38
Broomfield, CO (365)	47.9	45.5	6.0	0.5	156	51
Burlington, VT (361)	94.5	5.5	0.0	0.0	86	8
Carmel, IN (365)	40.8	49.3	9.9	0.0	150	55
Cary, NC (365)	53.7	38.1	8.2	0.0	142	47
Casper, WY (115)	100.0	0.0	0.0	0.0	42	18
Cheshire, CT (365)	73.2	24.9	1.9	0.0	129	36
Chino Hills, CA (365)	16.7	31.8	35.3	16.2	501	104
Collierville, TN (365)	47.9	41.6	9.9	0.5	182	52
Conway, AR (365)	59.5	37.3	3.0	0.3	235	44
Coronado, CA (365)	43.6	46.6	8.8	1.1	257	54
Cranberry, PA (365)	34.0	50.1	13.7	2.2	159	58
Dover, DE (263)	72.2	26.2	1.5	0.0	109	42
Draper, UT (365)	41.6	45.5	10.4	2.5	166	55
Dublin, OH (365)	64.9	26.8	8.2	0.0	147	42
Edmond, OK (365)	72.9	25.5	1.6	0.0	135	41
Evesham, NJ (365)	44.9	44.1	9.0	1.9	203	54
Fargo, ND (365)	95.9	3.3	0.3	0.5	162	29
Farmington, CT (365)	76.4	19.2	3.0	1.4	190	36
Fishers, IN (365)	40.8	49.3	9.9	0.0	150	55
Flower Mound, TX (365)	67.1	27.7	4.4	0.8	177	44
Franklin, MA (365)	58.1	35.9	5.5	0.5	169	46
Frederick, MD (365)	49.6	38.4	11.2	0.8	187	51
Frisco, TX (365)	67.1	27.7	4.4	0.8	177	44
Goodyear, AZ (365)	7.4	36.4	30.4	25.8	501	109
Grand Blanc, MI (292)	80.1	16.8	3.1	0.0	137	37
Greenburgh, NY (365)	52.1	40.3	6.6	1.1	164	49
Greenwich, CT (365)	81.6	14.2	4.1	0.0	150	30
Hampden, PA (365)	57.3	37.5	5.2	0.0	127	46
Hilliard, OH (365)	64.9	26.8	8.2	0.0	147	42
Hoover, AL (365)	17.3	69.3	11.5	1.9	182	69
Huntersville, NC (365)	40.8	43.8	13.7	1.6	205	55
Juneau, AK (135)	91.1	7.4	1.5	0.0	112	13
Keller, TX (365)	65.2	29.0	5.2	0.5	203	43
Kenner, LA (365)	62.2	33.2	4.4	0.3	154	45
Kennesaw, GA (365)	35.1	49.3	11.5	4.1	204	61
League City, TX (365)	77.5	19.7	2.2	0.5	156	37
Leawood, KS (365)	52.1	42.5	4.9	0.5	159	49
Lee's Summit, MO (365)	52.1	42.5	4.9	0.5	159	49
Leesburg, VA (365)	49.6	38.4	11.2	0.8	187	51
Lehi, UT (365)	57.5	35.6	5.2	1.6	156	46
Lwr Providence, PA (365)	44.9	44.1	9.0	1.9	203	54
Madison, AL (364)	69.2	27.5	3.0	0.3	156	42
Manhattan Bch, CA (365)	28.8	43.8	22.7	4.7	201	66
Maple Grove, MN (365)	62.5	34.8	2.7	0.0	138	44
Marion, IA (365)	85.5	12.9	1.6	0.0	126	34
Marlboro, NJ (365)	76.7	17.5	5.8	0.0	140	36

Area (Days[1])	Percent of Days when Air Quality was...				AQI Statistics	
	Good	Moderate	Unhealthy for Sensitive Groups	Unhealthy	Maximum	Median
Matthews, NC (365)	40.8	43.8	13.7	1.6	205	55
Meridian, ID (365)	62.5	33.4	3.8	0.3	163	44
Merrimack, NH (359)	94.7	5.0	0.3	0.0	127	21
Morgantown, WV (365)	79.7	18.4	1.9	0.0	116	36
Mt Pleasant, SC (365)	74.5	24.1	1.1	0.3	154	41
Northampton, PA (365)	44.9	44.1	9.0	1.9	203	54
Northville, MI (365)	52.1	41.9	4.9	1.1	161	49
Novi, MI (365)	52.1	41.9	4.9	1.1	161	49
O'Fallon, MO (365)	29.0	59.2	10.7	1.1	195	58
Oro Valley, AZ (365)	65.8	34.0	0.3	0.0	127	46
Oviedo, FL (365)	80.5	16.4	2.7	0.3	160	39
Palm Bch Grdns, FL (365)	92.1	7.1	0.8	0.0	134	32
Parker, CO (365)	47.9	45.5	6.0	0.5	156	51
Peachtree City, GA (365)	35.1	49.3	11.5	4.1	204	61
Pflugerville, TX (365)	81.1	17.8	1.1	0.0	145	36
Pleasanton, CA (365)	80.5	17.5	1.9	0.0	140	36
Rapid City, SD (362)	80.4	19.6	0.0	0.0	78	31
Redmond, WA (365)	76.7	20.5	2.5	0.3	155	36
Richland, WA (365)	88.5	11.2	0.3	0.0	119	21
Richmond, KY (117)	70.1	29.1	0.9	0.0	109	38
Rio Rancho, NM (365)	34.2	63.8	1.6	0.3	178	54
Rockaway, NJ (365)	54.8	39.2	5.5	0.5	151	47
Rocklin, CA (365)	52.1	32.3	14.5	1.1	203	50
Rogers, AR (365)	94.5	5.5	0.0	0.0	100	32
Round Rock, TX (365)	81.1	17.8	1.1	0.0	145	36
Sammamish, WA (365)	76.7	20.5	2.5	0.3	155	36
San Ramon, CA (365)	80.5	17.5	1.9	0.0	140	36
Santa Fe, NM (365)	95.3	4.7	0.0	0.0	71	27
Saratoga, CA (365)	76.7	21.1	2.2	0.0	134	38
Savage, MN (365)	62.5	34.8	2.7	0.0	138	44
Schererville, IN (365)	40.5	52.6	6.3	0.5	182	54
Shawnee, KS (365)	52.1	42.5	4.9	0.5	159	49
Shrewsbury, MA (365)	74.8	19.5	5.5	0.3	151	36
S Brunswick, NJ (365)	71.0	20.8	7.4	0.8	166	39
S. Jordan, UT (365)	41.6	45.5	10.4	2.5	166	55
S. Kingstown, RI (365)	72.1	22.7	4.9	0.3	161	39
Southaven, MS (365)	47.9	41.6	9.9	0.5	182	52
Southlake, TX (365)	65.2	29.0	5.2	0.5	203	43
Spanish Fork, UT (365)	57.5	35.6	5.2	1.6	156	46
Sparks, NV (365)	75.3	24.7	0.0	0.0	100	42
Stow, OH (365)	73.2	20.8	5.8	0.3	154	39
Sugar Land, TX (365)	40.0	49.3	9.9	0.8	174	56
Sun Prairie, WI (365)	69.9	27.7	2.5	0.0	143	40
Tualatin, OR (365)	76.4	20.5	3.0	0.0	150	34
Waimalu, HI (365)	98.6	1.4	0.0	0.0	61	19
Wellington, FL (365)	92.1	7.1	0.8	0.0	134	32
W Des Moines, IA (365)	74.0	25.8	0.3	0.0	101	38
West Linn, OR (365)	76.4	20.5	3.0	0.0	150	34
West Windsor, NJ (362)	70.7	24.3	4.4	0.6	177	40
Weston, FL (365)	87.9	9.9	1.9	0.3	155	35
Woodbury, MN (365)	62.5	34.8	2.7	0.0	138	44
Woodridge, IL (365)	40.5	52.6	6.3	0.5	182	54
Yorba Linda, CA (365)	28.8	43.8	22.7	4.7	201	66

Note: The Air Quality Index (AQI) is an index for reporting daily air quality. EPA calculates the AQI for five major air pollutants regulated by the Clean Air Act: ground-level ozone, particle pollution (also known as particulate matter), carbon monoxide, sulfur dioxide, and nitrogen dioxide. The AQI runs from 0 to 500. The higher the AQI value, the greater the level of air pollution and the greater the health concern. There are six AQI categories: "Good" The AQI is between 0 and 50. Air quality is considered satisfactory; "Moderate" The AQI is between 51 and 100. Air quality is acceptable; "Unhealthy for Sensitive Groups" When AQI values are between 101 and 150, members of sensitive groups may experience health effects; "Unhealthy" When AQI values are between 151 and 200 everyone may begin to experience health effects; "Very Unhealthy" AQI values between 201 and 300 trigger a health alert; "Hazardous" AQI values over 300 trigger health warnings of emergency conditions; Figures cover the Metropolitan Statistical Area - see Appendix A for areas included; (1) Number of days with AQI data in 2007.
Source: U.S. Environmental Protection Agency, Air Quality Index Report, 2007

Air Quality Index Pollutants

Area (Days[1])	Percent of Days when AQI Pollutant was...					
	Carbon Monoxide	Nitrogen Dioxide	Ozone	Sulfur Dioxide	Particulate Matter 2.5	Particulate Matter 10
Allen, TX (365)	0.0	0.0	61.6	0.3	38.1	0.0
Ankeny, IA (365)	4.7	0.0	38.6	0.0	54.8	1.9
Apex, NC (365)	0.0	0.0	52.3	0.0	47.7	0.0
Bangor, ME (123)	0.0	0.0	0.0	0.0	88.6	11.4
Beavercreek, OH (365)	21.9	0.0	51.5	4.7	21.9	0.0
Bellevue, NE (365)	0.3	0.0	11.2	1.4	67.7	19.5
Bend, OR (362)	0.0	0.0	0.0	0.0	92.3	7.7
Bernards, NJ (365)	0.0	0.0	64.1	0.0	35.9	0.0
Bethlehem, NY (365)	0.0	0.0	66.6	0.0	33.4	0.0
Bozeman, MT (365)	1.4	0.0	0.0	0.0	98.6	0.0
Brentwood, TN (365)	0.0	0.0	46.0	0.0	54.0	0.0
Brookfield, WI (365)	0.0	0.0	64.1	0.0	24.9	11.0
Broomfield, CO (365)	0.0	0.0	66.0	0.0	18.9	15.1
Burlington, VT (361)	66.2	0.0	0.0	0.0	33.5	0.3
Carmel, IN (365)	0.3	0.0	33.4	0.8	65.5	0.0
Cary, NC (365)	0.0	0.0	52.3	0.0	47.7	0.0
Casper, WY (115)	0.0	0.0	0.0	0.0	0.0	100.0
Cheshire, CT (365)	0.8	0.0	33.2	1.4	64.4	0.3
Chino Hills, CA (365)	0.0	0.0	71.8	0.0	16.4	11.8
Collierville, TN (365)	0.0	0.0	42.5	0.3	57.3	0.0
Conway, AR (365)	0.0	0.0	35.3	0.0	64.4	0.3
Coronado, CA (365)	1.1	0.0	66.3	0.0	28.5	4.1
Cranberry, PA (365)	0.0	0.0	17.5	0.3	81.1	1.1
Dover, DE (263)	0.0	0.0	71.9	0.0	28.1	0.0
Draper, UT (365)	1.6	0.0	42.7	0.0	37.0	18.6
Dublin, OH (365)	10.7	0.0	52.1	2.7	18.9	15.6
Edmond, OK (365)	0.0	0.0	58.6	0.0	41.1	0.3
Evesham, NJ (365)	0.8	0.0	47.7	0.0	50.4	1.1
Fargo, ND (365)	0.0	0.0	78.9	0.0	14.2	6.8
Farmington, CT (365)	12.9	0.0	45.8	0.0	41.1	0.3
Fishers, IN (365)	0.3	0.0	33.4	0.8	65.5	0.0
Flower Mound, TX (365)	0.0	0.0	61.6	0.3	38.1	0.0
Franklin, MA (365)	0.0	0.0	32.1	0.3	67.7	0.0
Frederick, MD (365)	0.0	0.0	60.0	0.0	39.7	0.3
Frisco, TX (365)	0.0	0.0	61.6	0.3	38.1	0.0
Goodyear, AZ (365)	0.0	0.0	14.0	0.0	3.0	83.0
Grand Blanc, MI (292)	0.0	0.0	58.9	17.8	23.3	0.0
Greenburgh, NY (365)	0.0	0.0	40.0	0.0	60.0	0.0
Greenwich, CT (365)	10.4	0.0	46.6	23.8	18.9	0.3
Hampden, PA (365)	0.0	0.0	37.5	0.5	59.5	2.5
Hilliard, OH (365)	10.7	0.0	52.1	2.7	18.9	15.6
Hoover, AL (365)	6.6	0.0	18.1	0.0	51.2	24.1
Huntersville, NC (365)	0.0	0.0	59.2	0.0	40.8	0.0
Juneau, AK (135)	0.0	0.0	0.0	0.0	95.6	4.4
Keller, TX (365)	0.0	0.0	59.2	0.0	40.8	0.0
Kenner, LA (365)	0.0	0.0	49.6	6.6	43.6	0.3
Kennesaw, GA (365)	0.0	0.0	34.8	0.3	64.9	0.0
League City, TX (365)	0.0	0.0	63.0	0.0	35.9	1.1
Leawood, KS (365)	0.0	0.0	44.9	3.6	49.3	2.2
Lee's Summit, MO (365)	0.0	0.0	44.9	3.6	49.3	2.2
Leesburg, VA (365)	0.0	0.0	60.0	0.0	39.7	0.3
Lehi, UT (365)	0.8	0.0	38.1	0.0	54.0	7.1
Lwr Providence, PA (365)	0.8	0.0	47.7	0.0	50.4	1.1
Madison, AL (364)	0.0	0.0	81.6	0.0	18.1	0.3
Manhattan Bch, CA (365)	0.8	0.0	55.3	0.0	41.6	2.2
Maple Grove, MN (365)	0.0	0.0	39.2	0.0	56.4	4.4
Marion, IA (365)	9.3	0.0	53.4	20.8	14.8	1.6
Marlboro, NJ (365)	6.0	0.0	54.8	0.0	39.2	0.0

Area (Days[1])	Percent of Days when AQI Pollutant was...					
	Carbon Monoxide	Nitrogen Dioxide	Ozone	Sulfur Dioxide	Particulate Matter 2.5	Particulate Matter 10
Matthews, NC (365)	0.0	0.0	59.2	0.0	40.8	0.0
Meridian, ID (365)	0.8	0.0	32.3	0.0	60.5	6.3
Merrimack, NH (359)	25.6	0.0	51.0	15.9	0.0	7.5
Morgantown, WV (365)	0.0	0.0	46.0	29.3	24.7	0.0
Mt Pleasant, SC (365)	0.0	0.0	57.8	0.0	42.2	0.0
Northampton, PA (365)	0.8	0.0	47.7	0.0	50.4	1.1
Northville, MI (365)	0.0	0.0	32.6	0.8	55.6	11.0
Novi, MI (365)	0.0	0.0	32.6	0.8	55.6	11.0
O'Fallon, MO (365)	0.0	0.0	30.1	2.7	49.6	17.5
Oro Valley, AZ (365)	0.0	0.0	76.4	0.0	3.6	20.0
Oviedo, FL (365)	0.3	0.0	83.3	0.0	16.4	0.0
Palm Bch Grdns, FL (365)	0.0	0.0	80.5	0.0	17.8	1.6
Parker, CO (365)	0.0	0.0	66.0	0.0	18.9	15.1
Peachtree City, GA (365)	0.0	0.0	34.8	0.3	64.9	0.0
Pflugerville, TX (365)	0.0	0.0	63.6	0.0	36.2	0.3
Pleasanton, CA (365)	0.0	0.0	72.6	0.0	27.1	0.3
Rapid City, SD (362)	0.0	0.0	0.0	0.0	11.0	89.0
Redmond, WA (365)	0.0	0.0	44.4	0.0	54.8	0.8
Richland, WA (365)	0.0	0.0	0.0	0.0	63.3	36.7
Richmond, KY (117)	0.0	0.0	0.0	0.0	100.0	0.0
Rio Rancho, NM (365)	0.0	0.0	43.0	0.0	23.8	33.2
Rockaway, NJ (365)	0.0	0.0	42.2	0.0	57.8	0.0
Rocklin, CA (365)	0.0	0.0	82.5	0.0	17.5	0.0
Rogers, AR (365)	0.0	0.0	100.0	0.0	0.0	0.0
Round Rock, TX (365)	0.0	0.0	63.6	0.0	36.2	0.3
Sammamish, WA (365)	0.0	0.0	44.4	0.0	54.8	0.8
San Ramon, CA (365)	0.0	0.0	72.6	0.0	27.1	0.3
Santa Fe, NM (365)	1.6	0.0	49.9	0.0	44.4	4.1
Saratoga, CA (365)	0.0	0.0	57.8	0.0	42.2	0.0
Savage, MN (365)	0.0	0.0	39.2	0.0	56.4	4.4
Schererville, IN (365)	0.0	0.0	33.7	0.3	60.3	5.8
Shawnee, KS (365)	0.0	0.0	44.9	3.6	49.3	2.2
Shrewsbury, MA (365)	4.9	0.0	41.1	1.9	50.7	1.4
S Brunswick, NJ (365)	0.0	0.0	64.1	0.0	35.9	0.0
S. Jordan, UT (365)	1.6	0.0	42.7	0.0	37.0	18.6
S. Kingstown, RI (365)	0.3	0.0	40.3	4.4	55.1	0.0
Southaven, MS (365)	0.0	0.0	42.5	0.3	57.3	0.0
Southlake, TX (365)	0.0	0.0	59.2	0.0	40.8	0.0
Spanish Fork, UT (365)	0.8	0.0	38.1	0.0	54.0	7.1
Sparks, NV (365)	4.9	0.0	84.9	0.0	5.2	4.9
Stow, OH (365)	12.6	0.0	50.7	15.1	21.6	0.0
Sugar Land, TX (365)	0.0	0.0	30.1	0.0	58.6	11.2
Sun Prairie, WI (365)	0.0	0.0	48.2	0.0	51.8	0.0
Tualatin, OR (365)	0.5	0.0	44.1	0.0	55.1	0.3
Waimalu, HI (365)	1.9	0.0	35.9	0.0	11.2	51.0
Wellington, FL (365)	0.0	0.0	80.5	0.0	17.8	1.6
W Des Moines, IA (365)	4.7	0.0	38.6	0.0	54.8	1.9
West Linn, OR (365)	0.5	0.0	44.1	0.0	55.1	0.3
West Windsor, NJ (362)	0.0	0.0	62.7	0.0	36.7	0.6
Weston, FL (365)	0.0	0.0	72.6	0.0	22.5	4.9
Woodbury, MN (365)	0.0	0.0	39.2	0.0	56.4	4.4
Woodridge, IL (365)	0.0	0.0	33.7	0.3	60.3	5.8
Yorba Linda, CA (365)	0.8	0.0	55.3	0.0	41.6	2.2

Note: The Air Quality Index (AQI) is an index for reporting daily air quality. EPA calculates the AQI for five major air pollutants regulated by the Clean Air Act: ground-level ozone, particle pollution (also known as particulate matter), carbon monoxide, sulfur dioxide, and nitrogen dioxide. The AQI runs from 0 to 500. The higher the AQI value, the greater the level of air pollution and the greater the health concern; Figures cover the Metropolitan Statistical Area - see Appendix A for areas included; (1) Number of days with AQI data in 2007.

Source: U.S. Environmental Protection Agency, Air Quality Index Report, 2007

Air Quality Index Trends

Area (# trend sites)	1999	2000	2001	2002	2003	2004	2005	2006
Allen, TX (7)	16	20	14	7	5	9	10	13
Apex, NC (6)	27	8	4	18	5	1	3	0
Beavercreek, OH (8)	17	9	10	25	7	2	9	1
Bellevue, NE (14)	5	1	2	0	1	1	1	0
Bernards, NJ (4)	23	9	13	20	8	6	12	5
Bethlehem, NY (5)	6	1	11	8	5	2	3	1
Brentwood, TN (19)	37	20	7	16	7	1	10	6
Brookfield, WI (16)	18	5	20	10	9	6	16	4
Broomfield, CO (24)	3	2	8	7	17	0	1	6
Carmel, IN (27)	23	8	13	24	11	1	17	2
Cary, NC (6)	27	8	4	18	5	1	3	0
Cheshire, CT (5)	18	8	15	25	16	3	13	8
Chino Hills, CA (44)	121	144	153	146	138	116	103	97
Collierville, TN (14)	35	28	15	17	9	2	12	9
Conway, AR (7)	6	16	4	9	1	0	8	4
Coronado, CA (29)	33	31	30	20	20	16	7	15
Cranberry, PA (45)	40	32	50	50	37	39	48	36
Draper, UT (13)	12	19	25	27	10	37	24	11
Dublin, OH (7)	24	12	14	21	9	1	8	1
Edmond, OK (9)	4	7	2	2	2	0	2	11
Evesham, NJ (45)	33	21	34	35	19	9	21	18
Farmington, CT (7)	18	7	18	23	8	6	11	6
Fishers, IN (27)	23	8	13	24	11	1	17	2
Flower Mound, TX (7)	16	20	14	7	5	9	10	13
Franklin, MA (13)	4	0	3	9	8	1	4	1
Frederick, MD (41)	41	20	27	33	12	10	18	18
Frisco, TX (7)	16	20	14	7	5	9	10	13
Goodyear, AZ (26)	9	14	8	10	8	1	6	7
Greenburgh, NY (20)	22	19	19	27	11	6	15	11
Hampden, PA (9)	19	16	22	20	9	5	11	7
Hilliard, OH (7)	24	12	14	21	9	1	8	1
Hoover, AL (21)	51	49	29	16	9	13	29	20
Huntersville, NC (11)	34	22	13	27	4	5	11	8
Keller, TX (7)	19	17	17	23	25	11	22	19
Kenner, LA (15)	18	20	6	2	8	5	4	4
Kennesaw, GA (19)	73	39	24	20	12	12	11	18
League City, TX (24)	51	42	28	21	31	22	28	18
Leawood, KS (16)	3	10	4	7	11	0	9	11
Lee's Summit, MO (16)	3	10	4	7	11	0	9	11
Leesburg, VA (41)	41	20	27	33	12	10	18	18
Lwr Providence, PA (45)	33	21	34	35	19	9	21	18
Manhattan Bch, CA (47)	54	63	81	81	88	65	43	34
Maple Grove, MN (21)	0	6	6	1	1	0	2	0
Marlboro, NJ (4)	27	11	21	32	13	8	16	10
Matthews, NC (11)	34	22	13	27	4	5	11	8
Merrimack, NH (13)	4	0	3	9	8	1	4	1
Mt Pleasant, SC (12)	5	7	0	3	0	1	4	1
Northampton, PA (45)	33	21	34	35	19	9	21	18
Northville, MI (32)	23	15	31	26	19	5	24	6
Novi, MI (32)	23	15	31	26	19	5	24	6
O'Fallon, MO (42)	31	20	20	33	13	2	27	12
Oro Valley, AZ (20)	7	0	0	3	1	0	1	0
Oviedo, FL (13)	4	3	4	1	0	0	5	1
Palm Bch Grdns, FL (5)	1	1	1	0	0	0	0	0
Parker, CO (24)	3	2	8	7	17	0	1	6
Peachtree City, GA (19)	73	39	24	20	12	12	11	18
Pflugerville, TX (1)	8	6	0	5	3	2	1	3
Pleasanton, CA (19)	17	10	11	21	7	7	5	10
Redmond, WA (17)	6	8	6	7	2	1	3	5
Rio Rancho, NM (18)	1	0	2	4	2	2	0	1

Area (# trend sites)	1999	2000	2001	2002	2003	2004	2005	2006
Rockaway, NJ (17)	26	12	18	29	11	7	11	13
Rocklin, CA (22)	65	41	47	57	36	26	39	43
Round Rock, TX (1)	8	6	0	5	3	2	1	3
Sammamish, WA (17)	6	8	6	7	2	1	3	5
San Ramon, CA (19)	17	10	11	21	7	7	5	10
Saratoga, CA (5)	17	20	12	9	6	2	6	5
Savage, MN (21)	0	6	6	1	1	0	2	0
Schererville, IN (45)	19	13	33	20	10	9	23	5
Shawnee, KS (16)	3	10	4	7	11	0	9	11
S Brunswick, NJ (4)	23	9	13	20	8	6	12	5
S. Jordan, UT (13)	12	19	25	27	10	37	24	11
S. Kingstown, RI (8)	8	5	14	13	3	2	6	2
Southaven, MS (14)	35	28	15	17	9	2	12	9
Southlake, TX (7)	19	17	17	23	25	11	22	19
Stow, OH (7)	25	9	22	24	6	6	13	0
Sugar Land, TX (24)	51	42	28	21	31	22	28	18
Tualatin, OR (14)	5	6	2	6	0	3	2	2
Waimalu, HI (12)	2	2	2	2	2	2	2	1
Wellington, FL (5)	1	1	1	0	0	0	0	0
West Linn, OR (14)	5	6	2	6	0	3	2	2
Weston, FL (13)	4	3	3	3	0	0	0	2
Woodbury, MN (21)	0	6	6	1	1	0	2	0
Woodridge, IL (45)	19	13	33	20	10	9	23	5
Yorba Linda, CA (47)	54	63	81	81	88	65	43	34

Note: An AQI value greater than 100 indicates that air quality would have been in the unhealthful range on that day; (1) Metropolitan Statistical Area - see Appendix A for areas included; n/a not available.
Source: U.S. Environmental Protection Agency, Office of Air and Radiation, Air Trends, Factbook and Related Information, Air Pollution Trends in Selected Metropolitan Areas 2006

Maximum Air Pollutant Concentrations

Area	Particulate Matter 10 (ug/m³)	Particulate Matter 2.5 (ug/m³)	Ozone 1-hour (ppm)	Carbon Monoxide (ppm)	Sulfur Dioxide (ppm)	Nitrogen Dioxide (ppm)	Lead (ug/m³)
Allen, TX	56	23	0.115	2	0.02	0.016	0.77 (c)
Ankeny, IA	53	24	0.079	2	n/a	0.01	n/a
Apex, NC	43	41	0.097	3	0.006	n/a	n/a
Bangor, ME	42	21	n/a	n/a	n/a	n/a	n/a
Beavercreek, OH	45	31	0.097	2	0.013	n/a	n/a
Bellevue, NE	129	26	0.08	2	0.019	n/a	n/a
Bernards, NJ	n/a	33	0.125	2	0.014	0.014	n/a
Bethlehem, NY	n/a	n/a	0.086	2	0.014	n/a	n/a
Brentwood, TN	50	32	0.104	3	0.009	0.017	n/a
Brookfield, WI	54	44	0.1	2	0.008	0.015	0
Broomfield, CO	111	26	0.103	3	0.009	0.029	0.16
Burlington, VT	45	28	n/a	1	n/a	0.011	n/a
Carmel, IN	59	38	0.093	2	0.026	0.015	0.03 (d)
Cary, NC	43	41	0.097	3	0.006	n/a	n/a
Casper, WY	70	n/a	n/a	n/a	n/a	n/a	n/a
Cheshire, CT	44	38	0.117	2	0.019	0.02	n/a
Chino Hills, CA	155	54	0.165	2	0.005	0.031	0.01
Collierville, TN	67	31	0.125	3	0.035	0.012	n/a
Conway, AR	39	27	0.119	2	0.006	0.012	n/a
Coronado, CA	117	31	0.115	3	0.009	0.024	n/a
Cranberry, PA	128	58	0.103	2	0.054	0.018	0.18
Dover, DE	n/a	n/a	0.104	n/a	n/a	n/a	n/a
Draper, UT	164	40	0.104	3	0.007	0.022	n/a
Dublin, OH	64	34	0.094	2	0.011	n/a	0.01 (b)
Edmond, OK	51	22	0.101	2	0.003	0.01	n/a
Evesham, NJ	159	39	0.124	3	0.024	0.021	0.05
Fargo, ND	55	19	0.071	n/a	0.002	0.006	n/a
Farmington, CT	36	31	0.117	4	0.012	0.013	n/a
Fishers, IN	59	38	0.093	2	0.026	0.015	0.03 (d)
Flower Mound, TX	56	23	0.115	2	0.02	0.016	0.77 (c)
Franklin, MA	46	29	0.097	2	0.016	0.023	0.01
Frederick, MD	61	34	0.142	3	0.017	0.02	n/a
Frisco, TX	56	23	0.115	2	0.02	0.016	0.77 (c)
Goodyear, AZ	794	29	0.109	5	0.007	0.031	n/a
Grand Blanc, MI	37	27	0.089	n/a	0.007	n/a	0.01
Greenburgh, NY	n/a	41	0.114	3	0.034	0.034	0.02
Greenwich, CT	61	37	0.136	n/a	0.021	n/a	n/a
Hampden, PA	53	37	0.096	1	0.014	0.013	n/a
Hilliard, OH	64	34	0.094	2	0.011	n/a	0.01 (b)
Hoover, AL	169	40	0.12	10	0.017	n/a	0.03
Huntersville, NC	62	32	0.115	2	0.013	0.013	0
Keller, TX	34	23	0.114	1	n/a	0.014	n/a
Kenner, LA	n/a	37	0.101	n/a	n/a	0.01	0.1
Kennesaw, GA	53	34	0.147	2	0.018	0.018	0.1
League City, TX	173	32	0.15	3	0.023	0.016	0.01
Leawood, KS	85	25	0.109	2	0.044	0.019	n/a
Lee's Summit, MO	85	25	0.109	2	0.044	0.019	n/a
Leesburg, VA	61	34	0.142	3	0.017	0.02	n/a
Lehi, UT	90	32	0.101	3	n/a	0.029	n/a
Lwr Providence, PA	159	39	0.124	3	0.024	0.021	0.05
Madison, AL	47	30	0.099	n/a	n/a	n/a	n/a
Manhattan Bch, CA	113	44	0.155	6	0.008	0.031	0.02
Maple Grove, MN	70	30	0.086	3	0.03	0.011	0.32
Marion, IA	47	24	0.073	1	0.032	n/a	n/a
Marlboro, NJ	n/a	33	0.125	2	0.014	0.014	n/a
Matthews, NC	62	32	0.115	2	0.013	0.013	0
Meridian, ID	96	22	0.104	2	n/a	n/a	n/a
Merrimack, NH	31	n/a	0.086	3	0.014	0.01	n/a

Area	Particulate Matter 10 (ug/m³)	Particulate Matter 2.5 (ug/m³)	Ozone 1-hour (ppm)	Carbon Monoxide (ppm)	Sulfur Dioxide (ppm)	Nitrogen Dioxide (ppm)	Lead (ug/m³)
Mt Pleasant, SC	37	25	0.099	0	0.009	0.009	0
Northampton, PA	159	39	0.124	3	0.024	0.021	0.05
Northville, MI	79	43	0.1	3	0.049	0.016	0.11
Novi, MI	79	43	0.1	3	0.049	0.016	0.11
O'Fallon, MO	284	36	0.117	3	0.075	0.015	1.93
Oro Valley, AZ	95	16	0.086	2	0.003	0.016	n/a
Oviedo, FL	61	18	0.1	2	0.003	0.009	n/a
Palm Bch Grdns, FL	43	20	0.103	2	0.001	0.013	n/a
Parker, CO	111	26	0.103	3	0.009	0.029	0.16
Peachtree City, GA	53	34	0.147	2	0.018	0.018	0.1
Pflugerville, TX	32	n/a	0.099	1	n/a	0.004	n/a
Pleasanton, CA	61	37	0.121	2	0.008	0.015	n/a
Rapid City, SD	125	20	0.069	n/a	n/a	n/a	n/a
Redmond, WA	63	37	0.129	3	n/a	n/a	n/a
Richland, WA	85	n/a	n/a	n/a	n/a	n/a	n/a
Rio Rancho, NM	266	28	0.091	3	n/a	0.016	n/a
Rockaway, NJ	n/a	41	0.114	3	0.034	0.034	0.02
Rocklin, CA	101	55	0.134	4	0.002	0.016	n/a
Rogers, AR	n/a	n/a	0.063	n/a	n/a	n/a	n/a
Round Rock, TX	32	n/a	0.099	1	n/a	0.004	n/a
Sammamish, WA	63	37	0.129	3	n/a	n/a	n/a
San Ramon, CA	61	37	0.121	2	0.008	0.015	n/a
Santa Fe, NM	29	9	n/a	1	n/a	n/a	n/a
Saratoga, CA	97	36	0.119	3	n/a	0.018	n/a
Savage, MN	70	30	0.086	3	0.03	0.011	0.32
Schererville, IN	82	33	0.105	3	0.02	0.031	0.06
Shawnee, KS	85	25	0.109	2	0.044	0.019	n/a
Shrewsbury, MA	40	30	0.099	2	0.013	0.015	n/a
S Brunswick, NJ	n/a	33	0.125	2	0.014	0.014	n/a
S. Jordan, UT	164	40	0.104	3	0.007	0.022	n/a
S. Kingstown, RI	50	30	0.123	3	0.02	0.015	n/a
Southaven, MS	67	31	0.125	3	0.035	0.012	n/a
Southlake, TX	34	23	0.114	1	n/a	0.014	n/a
Spanish Fork, UT	90	32	0.101	3	n/a	0.029	n/a
Sparks, NV	104	27	0.092	3	n/a	n/a	n/a
Stow, OH	n/a	32	0.09	2	0.038	n/a	n/a
Sugar Land, TX	173	32	0.15	3	0.023	0.016	0.01
Sun Prairie, WI	n/a	33	0.076	n/a	n/a	n/a	n/a
Tualatin, OR	45	39	0.092	8	0.006	n/a	n/a
Waimalu, HI	64	9	0.044	2	0.006	0.005	0.01
Wellington, FL	43	20	0.103	2	0.001	0.013	n/a
W Des Moines, IA	53	24	0.079	2	n/a	0.01	n/a
West Linn, OR	45	39	0.092	8	0.006	n/a	n/a
West Windsor, NJ	44	36	0.118	n/a	n/a	0.012	n/a
Weston, FL	83	20	0.095	3	0.012	0.008	n/a
Woodbury, MN	70	30	0.086	3	0.03	0.011	0.32
Woodridge, IL	82	33	0.105	3	0.02	0.031	0.06
Yorba Linda, CA	95	41	0.129	3	0.004	0.022	n/a
NAAQS[2]	150	35	0.125	9	0.140	0.053	1.50

Note: (1) Metropolitan Statistical Area - see Appendix A for areas included; (2) National Ambient Air Quality Standard; n/a not available; (a) Localized impact from an industrial source in Cleveland. Concentration from highest nonpoint source site is 0.03 ug/m³ in Cuyahoga County; (b) Localized impact from an industrial source in Columbus; (c) Localized impact from an industrial source in Dallas. Concentration from highest nonpoint source site is 0.14 ug/m³ in Collin County; (d) Localized impact from an industrial source in Indianapolis. Concentration from highest nonpoint source site is 0.01 ug/m³ in Marion County; (e) Localized impact from an industrial source in Tampa. Concentration from highest nonpoint source site is 0.01 ug/m³ in Pinellas County;
Concentrations: Particulate Matter 10 (coarse particulate) - highest second maximum 24-hour concentration; Particulate Matter 2.5 (fine particulate) - highest 98th percentile 24-hour concentration; Ozone - highest second daily maximum 1-hour concentration; Carbon Monoxide - highest second maximum non-overlapping 8-hour concentration; Sulfur Dioxide - highest second maximum 24-hour concentration; Nitrogen Dioxide - highest arithmetic mean concentration; Lead - highest quarterly maximum concentration
Units: ppm = parts per million; ug/m³ = micrograms per cubic meter
Source: U.S. Environmental Protection Agency, MSA Factbook 2006, Air Quality Statistics by City

The Directory of Business Information Resources, 2008

With 100% verification, over 1,000 new listings and more than 12,000 updates, *The Directory of Business Information Resources* is the most up-to-date source for contacts in over 98 business areas – from advertising and agriculture to utilities and wholesalers. This carefully researched volume details: the Associations representing each industry; the Newsletters that keep members current; the Magazines and Journals - with their "Special Issues" - that are important to the trade, the Conventions that are "must attends," Databases, Directories and Industry Web Sites that provide access to must-have marketing resources. Includes contact names, phone & fax numbers, web sites and e-mail addresses. This one-volume resource is a gold mine of information and would be a welcome addition to any reference collection.

"This is a most useful and easy-to-use addition to any researcher's library." –The Information Professionals Institute

Softcover ISBN 978-1-59237-193-8, 2,500 pages, $195.00 | Online Database $495.00

Hudson's Washington News Media Contacts Directory, 2008

With 100% verification of data, Hudson's Washington News Media Contacts Directory is the most accurate, most up-to-date source for media contacts in our nation's capital. With the largest concentration of news media in the world, having access to Washington's news media will get your message heard by these key media outlets. Published for over 40 years, Hudson's Washington News Media Contacts Directory brings you immediate access to: News Services & Newspapers, News Service Syndicates, DC Newspapers, Foreign Newspapers, Radio & TV, Magazines & Newsletters, and Freelance Writers & Photographers. The easy-to-read entries include contact names, phone & fax numbers, web sites and e-mail and more. For easy navigation, Hudson's Washington News Media Contacts Directory contains two indexes: Entry Index and Executive Index. This kind of comprehensive and up-to-date information would cost thousands of dollars to replicate or countless hours of searching to find. Don't miss this opportunity to have this important resource in your collection, and start saving time and money today. Hudson's Washington News Media Contacts Directory is the perfect research tool for Public Relations, Marketing, Networking and so much more. This resource is a gold mine of information and would be a welcome addition to any reference collection.

Softcover ISBN 978-1-59237-393-2, 800 pages, $289.00

Nations of the World, 2009 A Political, Economic and Business Handbook

This completely revised edition covers all the nations of the world in an easy-to-use, single volume. Each nation is profiled in a single chapter that includes Key Facts, Political & Economic Issues, a Country Profile and Business Information. In this fast-changing world, it is extremely important to make sure that the most up-to-date information is included in your reference collection. This edition is just the answer. Each of the 200+ country chapters have been carefully reviewed by a political expert to make sure that the text reflects the most current information on Politics, Travel Advisories, Economics and more. You'll find such vital information as a Country Map, Population Characteristics, Inflation, Agricultural Production, Foreign Debt, Political History, Foreign Policy, Regional Insecurity, Economics, Trade & Tourism, Historical Profile, Political Systems, Ethnicity, Languages, Media, Climate, Hotels, Chambers of Commerce, Banking, Travel Information and more. Five Regional Chapters follow the main text and include a Regional Map, an Introductory Article, Key Indicators and Currencies for the Region. As an added bonus, an all-inclusive CD-ROM is available as a companion to the printed text. Noted for its sophisticated, up-to-date and reliable compilation of political, economic and business information, this brand new edition will be an important acquisition to any public, academic or special library reference collection.

"A useful addition to both general reference collections and business collections." –RUSQ

Softcover ISBN 978-1-59237-273-7, 1,700 pages, $155.00

The Directory of Venture Capital & Private Equity Firms, 2008

This edition has been extensively updated and broadly expanded to offer direct access to over 2,800 Domestic and International Venture Capital Firms, including address, phone & fax numbers, e-mail addresses and web sites for both primary and branch locations. Entries include details on the firm's Mission Statement, Industry Group Preferences, Geographic Preferences, Average and Minimum Investments and Investment Criteria. You'll also find details that are available nowhere else, including the Firm's Portfolio Companies and extensive information on each of the firm's Managing Partners, such as Education, Professional Background and Directorships held, along with the Partner's E-mail Address. *The Directory of Venture Capital & Private Equity Firms* offers five important indexes: Geographic Index, Executive Name Index, Portfolio Company Index, Industry Preference Index and College & University Index. With its comprehensive coverage and detailed, extensive information on each company, The Directory of Venture Capital & Private Equity Firms is an important addition to any finance collection.

"The sheer number of listings, the descriptive information and the outstanding indexing make this directory a better value than …Pratt's Guide to Venture Capital Sources. Recommended for business collections in large public, academic and business libraries." –Choice

Softcover ISBN 978-1-59237-272-0, 1,300 pages, $565/$450 Library | Online Database $889.00

The Encyclopedia of Emerging Industries

*Published under an exclusive license from the Gale Group, Inc.

The fifth edition of the *Encyclopedia of Emerging Industries* details the inception, emergence, and current status of nearly 120 flourishing U.S. industries and industry segments. These focused essays unearth for users a wealth of relevant, current, factual data previously accessible only through a diverse variety of sources. This volume provides broad-based, highly-readable, industry information under such headings as Industry Snapshot, Organization & Structure, Background & Development, Industry Leaders, Current Conditions, America and the World, Pioneers, and Research & Technology. Essays in this new edition, arranged alphabetically for easy use, have been completely revised, with updated statistics and the most current information on industry trends and developments. In addition, there are new essays on some of the most interesting and influential new business fields, including Application Service Providers, Concierge Services, Entrepreneurial Training, Fuel Cells, Logistics Outsourcing Services, Pharmacogenomics, and Tissue Engineering. Two indexes, General and Industry, provide immediate access to this wealth of information. Plus, two conversion tables for SIC and NAICS codes, along with Suggested Further Readings, are provided to aid the user. *The Encyclopedia of Emerging Industries* pinpoints emerging industries while they are still in the spotlight. This important resource will be an important acquisition to any business reference collection.

"This well-designed source...should become another standard business source, nicely complementing Standard & Poor's Industry Surveys. It contains more information on each industry than Hoover's Handbook of Emerging Companies, is broader in scope than The Almanac of American Employers 1998-1999, but is less expansive than the Encyclopedia of Careers & Vocational Guidance. Highly recommended for all academic libraries and specialized business collections." –Library Journal

Hardcover ISBN 978-1-59237-242-3, 1,400 pages, $325.00

Encyclopedia of American Industries

*Published under an exclusive license from the Gale Group, Inc.

The Encyclopedia of American Industries is a major business reference tool that provides detailed, comprehensive information on a wide range of industries in every realm of American business. A two volume set, Volume I provides separate coverage of nearly 500 manufacturing industries, while Volume II presents nearly 600 essays covering the vast array of services and other non-manufacturing industries in the United States. Combined, these two volumes provide individual essays on every industry recognized by the U.S. Standard Industrial Classification (SIC) system. Both volumes are arranged numerically by SIC code, for easy use. Additionally, each entry includes the corresponding NAICS code(s). The *Encyclopedia's* business coverage includes information on historical events of consequence, as well as current trends and statistics. Essays include an Industry Snapshot, Organization & Structure, Background & Development, Current Conditions, Industry Leaders, Workforce, America and the World, Research & Technology along with Suggested Further Readings. Both SIC and NAICS code conversion tables and an all-encompassing Subject Index, with cross-references, complete the text. With its detailed, comprehensive information on a wide range of industries, this resource will be an important tool for both the industry newcomer and the seasoned professional.

"Encyclopedia of American Industries contains detailed, signed essays on virtually every industry in contemporary society. ... Highly recommended for all but the smallest libraries." -American Reference Books Annual

Two Volumes, Hardcover ISBN 978-1-59237-244-7, 3,000 pages, $650.00

Encyclopedia of Global Industries

*Published under an exclusive license from the Gale Group, Inc.

This fourth edition of the acclaimed *Encyclopedia of Global Industries* presents a thoroughly revised and expanded look at more than 125 business sectors of global significance. Detailed, insightful articles discuss the origins, development, trends, key statistics and current international character of the world's most lucrative, dynamic and widely researched industries – including hundreds of profiles of leading international corporations. Beginning researchers will gain from this book a solid understanding of how each industry operates and which countries and companies are significant participants, while experienced researchers will glean current and historical figures for comparison and analysis. The industries profiled in previous editions have been updated, and in some cases, expanded to reflect recent industry trends. Additionally, this edition provides both SIC and NAICS codes for all industries profiled. As in the original volumes, *The Encyclopedia of Global Industries* offers thorough studies of some of the biggest and most frequently researched industry sectors, including Aircraft, Biotechnology, Computers, Internet Services, Motor Vehicles, Pharmaceuticals, Semiconductors, Software and Telecommunications. An SIC and NAICS conversion table and an all-encompassing Subject Index, with cross-references, are provided to ensure easy access to this wealth of information. These and many others make the *Encyclopedia of Global Industries* the authoritative reference for studies of international industries.

"Provides detailed coverage of the history, development, and current status of 115 of "the world's most lucrative and high-profile industries." It far surpasses the Department of Commerce's U.S. Global Trade Outlook 1995-2000 (GPO, 1995) in scope and coverage. Recommended for comprehensive public and academic library business collections." -Booklist

Hardcover ISBN 978-1-59237-243-0, 1,400 pages, $495.00

The Directory of Mail Order Catalogs, 2008

Published since 1981, *The Directory of Mail Order Catalogs* is the premier source of information on the mail order catalog industry. It is the source that business professionals and librarians have come to rely on for the thousands of catalog companies in the US. Since the 2007 edition, *The Directory of Mail Order Catalogs* has been combined with its companion volume, *The Directory of Business to Business Catalogs*, to offer all 13,000 catalog companies in one easy-to-use volume. Section I: Consumer Catalogs, covers over 9,000 consumer catalog companies in 44 different product chapters from Animals to Toys & Games. Section II: Business to Business Catalogs, details 5,000 business catalogs, everything from computers to laboratory supplies, building construction and much more. Listings contain detailed contact information including mailing address, phone & fax numbers, web sites, e-mail addresses and key contacts along with important business details such as product descriptions, employee size, years in business, sales volume, catalog size, number of catalogs mailed and more. Three indexes are included for easy access to information: Catalog & Company Name Index, Geographic Index and Product Index. *The Directory of Mail Order Catalogs*, now with its expanded business to business catalogs, is the largest and most comprehensive resource covering this billion-dollar industry. It is the standard in its field. This important resource is a useful tool for entrepreneurs searching for catalogs to pick up their product, vendors looking to expand their customer base in the catalog industry, market researchers, small businesses investigating new supply vendors, along with the library patron who is exploring the available catalogs in their areas of interest.

"This is a godsend for those looking for information." –Reference Book Review

Softcover ISBN 978-1-59237-202-7, 1,700 pages, $350/$250 Library | Online Database $495.00

Sports Market Place Directory, 2008

For over 20 years, this comprehensive, up-to-date directory has offered direct access to the Who, What, When & Where of the Sports Industry. With over 20,000 updates and enhancements, the *Sports Market Place Directory* is the most detailed, comprehensive and current sports business reference source available. In 1,800 information-packed pages, *Sports Market Place Directory* profiles contact information and key executives for: Single Sport Organizations, Professional Leagues, Multi-Sport Organizations, Disabled Sports, High School & Youth Sports, Military Sports, Olympic Organizations, Media, Sponsors, Sponsorship & Marketing Event Agencies, Event & Meeting Calendars, Professional Services, College Sports, Manufacturers & Retailers, Facilities and much more. The Sports Market Place Directory provides organization's contact information with detailed descriptions including: Key Contacts, physical, mailing, email and web addresses plus phone and fax numbers. *Sports Market Place Directory* provides a one-stop resources for this billion-dollar industry. This will be an important resource for large public libraries, university libraries, university athletic programs, career services or job placement organizations, and is a must for anyone doing research on or marketing to the US and Canadian sports industry.

"Grey House is the new publisher and has produced an excellent edition...highly recommended for public libraries and academic libraries with sports management programs or strong interest in athletics." -Booklist

Softcover ISBN 978-1-59237-348-2, 1,800 pages, $225.00 | Online Database $479.00

Food and Beverage Market Place, 2008

Food and Beverage Market Place is bigger and better than ever with thousands of new companies, thousands of updates to existing companies and two revised and enhanced product category indexes. This comprehensive directory profiles over 18,000 Food & Beverage Manufacturers, 12,000 Equipment & Supply Companies, 2,200 Transportation & Warehouse Companies, 2,000 Brokers & Wholesalers, 8,000 Importers & Exporters, 900 Industry Resources and hundreds of Mail Order Catalogs. Listings include detailed Contact Information, Sales Volumes, Key Contacts, Brand & Product Information, Packaging Details and much more. *Food and Beverage Market Place* is available as a three-volume printed set, a subscription-based Online Database via the Internet, on CD-ROM, as well as mailing lists and a licensable database.

"An essential purchase for those in the food industry but will also be useful in public libraries where needed. Much of the information will be difficult and time consuming to locate without this handy three-volume ready-reference source." –ARBA

3 Vol Set, Softcover ISBN 978-1-59237-198-3, 8,500 pages, $595 | Online Database $795 | Online Database & 3 Vol Set Combo, $995

The Grey House Performing Arts Directory, 2007

The Grey House Performing Arts Directory is the most comprehensive resource covering the Performing Arts. This important directory provides current information on over 8,500 Dance Companies, Instrumental Music Programs, Opera Companies, Choral Groups, Theater Companies, Performing Arts Series and Performing Arts Facilities. Plus, this edition now contains a brand new section on Artist Management Groups. In addition to mailing address, phone & fax numbers, e-mail addresses and web sites, dozens of other fields of available information include mission statement, key contacts, facilities, seating capacity, season, attendance and more. This directory also provides an important Information Resources section that covers hundreds of Performing Arts Associations, Magazines, Newsletters, Trade Shows, Directories, Databases and Industry Web Sites. Five indexes provide immediate access to this wealth of information: Entry Name, Executive Name, Performance Facilities, Geographic and Information Resources. *The Grey House Performing Arts Directory* pulls together thousands of Performing Arts Organizations, Facilities and Information Resources into an easy-to-use source – this kind of comprehensiveness and extensive detail is not available in any resource on the market place today.

"Immensely useful and user-friendly … recommended for public, academic and certain special library reference collections." –Booklist

Softcover ISBN 978-1-59237-138-9, 1,500 pages, $185.00 | Online Database $335.00

New York State Directory, 2008/09

The New York State Directory, published annually since 1983, is a comprehensive and easy-to-use guide to accessing public officials and private sector organizations and individuals who influence public policy in the state of New York. *The New York State Directory* includes important information on all New York state legislators and congressional representatives, including biographies and key committee assignments. It also includes staff rosters for all branches of New York state government and for federal agencies and departments that impact the state policy process. Following the state government section are 25 chapters covering policy areas from agriculture through veterans' affairs. Each chapter identifies the state, local and federal agencies and officials that formulate or implement policy. In addition, each chapter contains a roster of private sector experts and advocates who influence the policy process. The directory also offers appendices that include statewide party officials; chambers of commerce; lobbying organizations; public and private universities and colleges; television, radio and print media; and local government agencies and officials.

"This comprehensive directory covers not only New York State government offices and key personnel but pertinent U.S. government agencies and non-governmental entities. This directory is all encompassing... recommended." -Choice

New York State Directory - Softcover ISBN 978-1-59237-358-1, 800 pages, $145.00
New York State Directory with *Profiles of New York* – 2 Volumes, Softcover ISBN 978-1-59237-359-8, 1,600 pages, $225.00

The Grey House Homeland Security Directory, 2008

This updated edition features the latest contact information for government and private organizations involved with Homeland Security along with the latest product information and provides detailed profiles of nearly 1,000 Federal & State Organizations & Agencies and over 3,000 Officials and Key Executives involved with Homeland Security. These listings are incredibly detailed and include Mailing Address, Phone & Fax Numbers, Email Addresses & Web Sites, a complete Description of the Agency and a complete list of the Officials and Key Executives associated with the Agency. Next, *The Grey House Homeland Security Directory* provides the go-to source for Homeland Security Products & Services. This section features over 2,000 Companies that provide Consulting, Products or Services. With this Buyer's Guide at their fingertips, users can locate suppliers of everything from Training Materials to Access Controls, from Perimeter Security to BioTerrorism Countermeasures and everything in between – complete with contact information and product descriptions. A handy Product Locator Index is provided to quickly and easily locate suppliers of a particular product. This comprehensive, information-packed resource will be a welcome tool for any company or agency that is in need of Homeland Security information and will be a necessary acquisition for the reference collection of all public libraries and large school districts.

"Compiles this information in one place and is discerning in content. A useful purchase for public and academic libraries." –Booklist

Softcover ISBN 978-1-59237-196-6, 800 pages, $195.00 | Online Database $385.00

The Grey House Safety & Security Directory, 2008

The Grey House Safety & Security Directory is the most comprehensive reference tool and buyer's guide for the safety and security industry. Arranged by safety topic, each chapter begins with OSHA regulations for the topic, followed by Training Articles written by top professionals in the field and Self-Inspection Checklists. Next, each topic contains Buyer's Guide sections that feature related products and services. Topics include Administration, Insurance, Loss Control & Consulting, Protective Equipment & Apparel, Noise & Vibration, Facilities Monitoring & Maintenance, Employee Health Maintenance & Ergonomics, Retail Food Services, Machine Guards, Process Guidelines & Tool Handling, Ordinary Materials Handling, Hazardous Materials Handling, Workplace Preparation & Maintenance, Electrical Lighting & Safety, Fire & Rescue and Security. Six important indexes make finding information and product manufacturers quick and easy: Geographical Index of Manufacturers and Distributors, Company Profile Index, Brand Name Index, Product Index, Index of Web Sites and Index of Advertisers. This comprehensive, up-to-date reference will provide every tool necessary to make sure a business is in compliance with OSHA regulations and locate the products and services needed to meet those regulations.

"Presents industrial safety information for engineers, plant managers, risk managers, and construction site supervisors…" –Choice

Softcover ISBN 978-1-59237-205-8, 1,500 pages, $165.00

The Grey House Transportation Security Directory & Handbook

This is the only reference of its kind that brings together current data on Transportation Security. With information on everything from Regulatory Authorities to Security Equipment, this top-flight database brings together the relevant information necessary for creating and maintaining a security plan for a wide range of transportation facilities. With this current, comprehensive directory at the ready you'll have immediate access to: Regulatory Authorities & Legislation; Information Resources; Sample Security Plans & Checklists; Contact Data for Major Airports, Seaports, Railroads, Trucking Companies and Oil Pipelines; Security Service Providers; Recommended Equipment & Product Information and more. Using the *Grey House Transportation Security Directory & Handbook*, managers will be able to quickly and easily assess their current security plans; develop contacts to create and maintain new security procedures; and source the products and services necessary to adequately maintain a secure environment. This valuable resource is a must for all Security Managers at Airports, Seaports, Railroads, Trucking Companies and Oil Pipelines.

"Highly recommended. Library collections that support all levels of readers, including professionals/practitioners; and schools/organizations offering education and training in transportation security." -Choice

Softcover ISBN 978-1-59237-075-7, 800 pages, $195.00

The Grey House Biometric Information Directory

This edition offers a complete, current overview of biometric companies and products – one of the fastest growing industries in today's economy. Detailed profiles of manufacturers of the latest biometric technology, including Finger, Voice, Face, Hand, Signature, Iris, Vein and Palm Identification systems. Data on the companies include key executives, company size and a detailed, indexed description of their product line. Information in the directory includes: Editorial on Advancements in Biometrics; Profiles of 700+ companies listed with contact information; Organizations, Trade & Educational Associations, Publications, Conferences, Trade Shows and Expositions Worldwide; Web Site Index; Biometric & Vendors Services Index by Types of Biometrics; and a Glossary of Biometric Terms. This resource will be an important source for anyone who is considering the use of a biometric product, investing in the development of biometric technology, support existing marketing and sales efforts and will be an important acquisition for the business reference collection for large public and business libraries.

"This book should prove useful to agencies or businesses seeking companies that deal with biometric technology. Summing Up: Recommended. Specialized collections serving researchers/faculty and professionals/practitioners." -Choice

Softcover ISBN 978-1-59237-121-1, 800 pages, $225.00

The Environmental Resource Handbook, 2008/09

The Environmental Resource Handbook is the most up-to-date and comprehensive source for Environmental Resources and Statistics. Section I: Resources provides detailed contact information for thousands of information sources, including Associations & Organizations, Awards & Honors, Conferences, Foundations & Grants, Environmental Health, Government Agencies, National Parks & Wildlife Refuges, Publications, Research Centers, Educational Programs, Green Product Catalogs, Consultants and much more. Section II: Statistics, provides statistics and rankings on hundreds of important topics, including Children's Environmental Index, Municipal Finances, Toxic Chemicals, Recycling, Climate, Air & Water Quality and more. This kind of up-to-date environmental data, all in one place, is not available anywhere else on the market place today. This vast compilation of resources and statistics is a must-have for all public and academic libraries as well as any organization with a primary focus on the environment.

"...the intrinsic value of the information make it worth consideration by libraries with environmental collections and environmentally concerned users." –Booklist

Softcover ISBN 978-1-59237-195-2, 1,000 pages, $155.00 | Online Database $300.00

The Rauch Guide to the US Adhesives & Sealants, Cosmetics & Toiletries, Ink, Paint, Plastics, Pulp & Paper and Rubber Industries

The Rauch Guides save time and money by organizing widely scattered information and providing estimates for important business decisions, some of which are available nowhere else. Within each Guide, after a brief introduction, the ECONOMICS section provides data on industry shipments; long-term growth and forecasts; prices; company performance; employment, expenditures, and productivity; transportation and geographical patterns; packaging; foreign trade; and government regulations. Next, TECHNOLOGY & RAW MATERIALS provide market, technical, and raw material information for chemicals, equipment and related materials, including market size and leading suppliers, prices, end uses, and trends. PRODUCTS & MARKETS provide information for each major industry product, including market size and historical trends, leading suppliers, five-year forecasts, industry structure, and major end uses. Next, the COMPANY DIRECTORY profiles major industry companies, both public and private. Information includes complete contact information, web address, estimated total and domestic sales, product description, and recent mergers and acquisitions. *The Rauch Guides* will prove to be an invaluable source of market information, company data, trends and forecasts that anyone in these fast-paced industries.

"An invaluable and affordable publication. The comprehensive nature of the data and text offers considerable insights into the industry, market sizes, company activities, and applications of the products of the industry. The additions that have been made have certainly enhanced the value of the Guide." –Adhesives & Sealants Newsletter of the Rauch Guide to the US Adhesives & Sealants Industry

Paint Industry: Softcover ISBN 978-1-59237-127-3 $595 | Plastics Industry: Softcover ISBN 978-1-59237-128-0 $595 | Adhesives and Sealants Industry: Softcover ISBN 978-1-59237-129-7 $595 | Ink Industry: Softcover ISBN 978-1-59237-126-6 $595 | Rubber Industry: Softcover ISBN 978-1-59237-130-3 $595 | Pulp and Paper Industry: Softcover ISBN 978-1-59237-131-0 $595 | Cosmetic & Toiletries Industry: Softcover ISBN 978-1-59237-132-7 $895

Research Services Directory: Commercial & Corporate Research Centers

This ninth edition provides access to well over 8,000 independent Commercial Research Firms, Corporate Research Centers and Laboratories offering contract services for hands-on, basic or applied research. Research Services Directory covers the thousands of types of research companies, including Biotechnology & Pharmaceutical Developers, Consumer Product Research, Defense Contractors, Electronics & Software Engineers, Think Tanks, Forensic Investigators, Independent Commercial Laboratories, Information Brokers, Market & Survey Research Companies, Medical Diagnostic Facilities, Product Research & Development Firms and more. Each entry provides the company's name, mailing address, phone & fax numbers, key contacts, web site, e-mail address, as well as a company description and research and technical fields served. Four indexes provide immediate access to this wealth of information: Research Firms Index, Geographic Index, Personnel Name Index and Subject Index.

"An important source for organizations in need of information about laboratories, individuals and other facilities." –ARBA

Softcover ISBN 978-1-59237-003-0, 1,400 pages, $465.00

International Business and Trade Directories

Completely updated, the Third Edition of *International Business and Trade Directories* now contains more than 10,000 entries, over 2,000 more than the last edition, making this directory the most comprehensive resource of the worlds business and trade directories. Entries include content descriptions, price, publisher's name and address, web site and e-mail addresses, phone and fax numbers and editorial staff. Organized by industry group, and then by region, this resource puts over 10,000 industry-specific business and trade directories at the reader's fingertips. Three indexes are included for quick access to information: Geographic Index, Publisher Index and Title Index. Public, college and corporate libraries, as well as individuals and corporations seeking critical market information will want to add this directory to their marketing collection.

"Reasonably priced for a work of this type, this directory should appeal to larger academic, public and corporate libraries with an international focus." –Library Journal

Softcover ISBN 978-1-930956-63-6, 1,800 pages, $225.00

TheStreet.com Ratings Guide to Health Insurers

TheStreet.com Ratings Guide to Health Insurers is the first and only source to cover the financial stability of the nation's health care system, rating the financial safety of more than 6,000 health insurance providers, health maintenance organizations (HMOs) and all of the Blue Cross Blue Shield plans – updated quarterly to ensure the most accurate information. The Guide also provides a complete listing of all the major health insurers, including all Long-Term Care and Medigap insurers. Our *Guide to Health Insurers* includes comprehensive, timely coverage on the financial stability of HMOs and health insurers; the most accurate insurance company ratings available–the same quality ratings heralded by the U.S. General Accounting Office; separate listings for those companies offering Medigap and long-term care policies; the number of serious consumer complaints filed against most HMOs so you can see who is actually providing the best (or worst) service and more. The easy-to-use layout gives you a one-line summary analysis for each company that we track, followed by an in-depth, detailed analysis of all HMOs and the largest health insurers. The guide also includes a list of TheStreet.com Ratings Recommended Companies with information on how to contact them, and the reasoning behind any rating upgrades or downgrades.

"With 20 years behind its insurance-advocacy research [the rating guide] continues to offer a wealth of information that helps consumers weigh their healthcare options now and in the future." -Today's Librarian

Issues published quarterly, Softcover, 550 pages, $499.00 for four quarterly issues, $249.00 for a single issue

TheStreet.com Ratings Guide to Life & Annuity Insurers

TheStreet.com Safety Ratings are the most reliable source for evaluating an insurer's financial solvency risk. Consequently, policy-holders have come to rely on TheStreet.com's flagship publication, *TheStreet.com Ratings Guide to Life & Annuity Insurers*, to help them identify the safest companies to do business with. Each easy-to-use edition delivers TheStreet.com's independent ratings and analyses on more than 1,100 insurers, updated every quarter. Plus, your patrons will find a complete list of TheStreet.com Recommended Companies, including contact information, and the reasoning behind any rating upgrades or downgrades. This guide is perfect for those who are considering the purchase of a life insurance policy, placing money in an annuity, or advising clients about insurance and annuities. A life or health insurance policy or annuity is only as secure as the insurance company issuing it. Therefore, make sure your patrons have what they need to periodically monitor the financial condition of the companies with whom they have an investment. The TheStreet.com Ratings product line is designed to help them in their evaluations.

"Weiss has an excellent reputation and this title is held by hundreds of libraries. This guide is recommended for public and academic libraries." -ARBA

Issues published quarterly, Softcover, 360 pages, $499.00 for four quarterly issues, $249.00 for a single issue

TheStreet.com Ratings Guide to Property & Casualty Insurers

TheStreet.com Ratings Guide to Property and Casualty Insurers provides the most extensive coverage of insurers writing policies, helping consumers and businesses avoid financial headaches. Updated quarterly, this easy-to-use publication delivers the independent, unbiased TheStreet.com Safety Ratings and supporting analyses on more than 2,800 U.S. insurance companies, offering auto & homeowners insurance, business insurance, worker's compensation insurance, product liability insurance, medical malpractice and other professional liability insurance. Each edition includes a list of TheStreet.com Recommended Companies by type of insurance, including a contact number, plus helpful information about the coverage provided by the State Guarantee Associations.

"In contrast to the other major insurance rating agencies...Weiss does not have a financial relationship worth the companies it rates. A GAO study found that Weiss identified financial vulnerability earlier than the other rating agencies." -ARBA

Issues published quarterly, Softcover, 455 pages, $499.00 for four quarterly issues, $249.00 for a single issue

TheStreet.com Ratings Consumer Box Set

Deliver the critical information your patrons need to safeguard their personal finances with *TheStreet.com Ratings' Consumer Guide Box Set*. Each of the eight guides is packed with accurate, unbiased information and recommendations to help your patrons make sound financial decisions. TheStreet.com Ratings Consumer Guide Box Set provides your patrons with easy to understand guidance on important personal finance topics, including: *Consumer Guide to Variable Annuities, Consumer Guide to Medicare Supplement Insurance, Consumer Guide to Elder Care Choices, Consumer Guide to Automobile Insurance, Consumer Guide to Long-Term Care Insurance, Consumer Guide to Homeowners Insurance, Consumer Guide to Term Life Insurance, and Consumer Guide to Medicare Prescription Drug Coverage*. Each guide provides an easy-to-read overview of the topic, what to look out for when selecting a company or insurance plan to do business with, who are the recommended companies to work with and how to navigate through these often-times difficult decisions. Custom worksheets and step-by-step directions make these resources accessible to all types of users. Packaged in a handy custom display box, these helpful guides will prove to be a much-used addition to any reference collection.

Issues published twice per year, Softcover, 600 pages, $499.00 for two biennial issues

TheStreet.com Ratings Guide to Stock Mutual Funds

TheStreet.com Ratings Guide to Stock Mutual Funds offers ratings and analyses on more than 8,800 equity mutual funds – more than any other publication. The exclusive TheStreet.com Investment Ratings combine an objective evaluation of each fund's performance and risk to provide a single, user-friendly, composite rating, giving your patrons a better handle on a mutual fund's risk-adjusted performance. Each edition identifies the top-performing mutual funds based on risk category, type of fund, and overall risk-adjusted performance. TheStreet.com's unique investment rating system makes it easy to see exactly which stocks are on the rise and which ones should be avoided. For those investors looking to tailor their mutual fund selections based on age, income, and tolerance for risk, we've also assigned two component ratings to each fund: a performance rating and a risk rating. With these, you can identify those funds that are best suited to meet your - or your client's – individual needs and goals. Plus, we include a handy Risk Profile Quiz to help you assess your personal tolerance for risk. So whether you're an investing novice or professional, the *Guide to Stock Mutual Funds* gives you everything you need to find a mutual fund that is right for you.

"There is tremendous need for information such as that provided by this Weiss publication. This reasonably priced guide is recommended for public and academic libraries serving investors." -ARBA

Issues published quarterly, Softcover, 655 pages, $499 for four quarterly issues, $249 for a single issue

TheStreet.com Ratings Guide to Exchange-Traded Funds

TheStreet.com Ratings editors analyze hundreds of mutual funds each quarter, condensing all of the available data into a single composite opinion of each fund's risk-adjusted performance. The intuitive, consumer-friendly ratings allow investors to instantly identify those funds that have historically done well and those that have under-performed the market. Each quarterly edition identifies the top-performing exchange-traded funds based on risk category, type of fund, and overall risk-adjusted performance. The rating scale, A through F, gives you a better handle on an exchange-traded fund's risk-adjusted performance. Other features include Top & Bottom 200 Exchange-Traded Funds; Performance and Risk: 100 Best and Worst Exchange- Traded Funds; Investor Profile Quiz; Performance Benchmarks and Fund Type Descriptions. With the growing popularity of mutual fund investing, consumers need a reliable source to help them track and evaluate the performance of their mutual fund holdings. Plus, they need a way of identifying and monitoring other funds as potential new investments. Unfortunately, the hundreds of performance and risk measures available, multiplied by the vast number of mutual fund investments on the market today, can make this a daunting task for even the most sophisticated investor. This Guide will serve as a useful tool for both the first-time and seasoned investor.

Editions published quarterly, Softcover, 440 pages, $499.00 for four quarterly issues, $249.00 for a single issue

TheStreet.com Ratings Guide to Bond & Money Market Mutual Funds

TheStreet.com Ratings Guide to Bond & Money Market Mutual Funds has everything your patrons need to easily identify the top-performing fixed income funds on the market today. Each quarterly edition contains TheStreet.com's independent ratings and analyses on more than 4,600 fixed income funds – more than any other publication, including corporate bond funds, high-yield bond funds, municipal bond funds, mortgage security funds, money market funds, global bond funds and government bond funds. In addition, the fund's risk rating is combined with its three-year performance rating to get an overall picture of the fund's risk-adjusted performance. The resulting TheStreet.com Investment Rating gives a single, user-friendly, objective evaluation that makes it easy to compare one fund to another and select the right fund based on the level of risk tolerance. Most investors think of fixed income mutual funds as "safe" investments. That's not always the case, however, depending on the credit risk, interest rate risk, and prepayment risk of the securities owned by the fund. TheStreet.com Ratings assesses each of these risks and assigns each fund a risk rating to help investors quickly evaluate the fund's risk component. Plus, we include a handy Risk Profile Quiz to help you assess your personal tolerance for risk. So whether you're an investing novice or professional, the *Guide to Bond and Money Market Mutual Funds* gives you everything you need to find a mutual fund that is right for you.

"Comprehensive... It is easy to use and consumer-oriented, and can be recommended for larger public and academic libraries." -ARBA

Issues published quarterly, Softcover, 470 pages, $499.00 for four quarterly issues, $249.00 for a single issue

TheStreet.com Ratings Guide to Banks & Thrifts

Updated quarterly, for the most up-to-date information, *TheStreet.com Ratings Guide to Banks and Thrifts* offers accurate, intuitive safety ratings your patrons can trust; supporting ratios and analyses that show an institution's strong & weak points; identification of the TheStreet.com Recommended Companies with branches in your area; a complete list of institutions receiving upgrades/downgrades; and comprehensive coverage of every bank and thrift in the nation – more than 9,000. TheStreet.com Safety Ratings are then based on the analysts' review of publicly available information collected by the federal banking regulators. The easy-to-use layout gives you: the institution's TheStreet.com Safety Rating for the last 3 years; the five key indexes used to evaluate each institution; along with the primary ratios and statistics used in determining the company's rating. *TheStreet.com Ratings Guide to Banks & Thrifts* will be a must for individuals who are concerned about the safety of their CD or savings account; need to be sure that an existing line of credit will be there when they need it; or simply want to avoid the hassles of dealing with a failing or troubled institution.

"Large public and academic libraries most definitely need to acquire the work. Likewise, special libraries in large corporations will find this title indispensable." -ARBA

Issues published quarterly, Softcover, 370 pages, $499.00 for four quarterly issues, $249.00 for a single issue

TheStreet.com Ratings Guide to Common Stocks

TheStreet.com Ratings Guide to Common Stocks gives your patrons reliable insight into the risk-adjusted performance of common stocks listed on the NYSE, AMEX, and Nasdaq – over 5,800 stocks in all – more than any other publication. TheStreet.com's unique investment rating system makes it easy to see exactly which stocks are on the rise and which ones should be avoided. In addition, your patrons also get supporting analysis showing growth trends, profitability, debt levels, valuation levels, the top-rated stocks within each industry, and more. Plus, each stock is ranked with the easy-to-use buy-hold-sell equivalents commonly used by Wall Street. Whether they're selecting their own investments or checking up on a broker's recommendation, TheStreet.com Ratings can help them in their evaluations.

"Users... will find the information succinct and the explanations readable, easy to understand, and helpful to a novice." -Library Journal

Issues published quarterly, Softcover, 440 pages, $499.00 for four quarterly issues, $249.00 for a single issue

TheStreet.com Ratings Ultimate Guided Tour of Stock Investing

This important reference guide from TheStreet.com Ratings is just what librarians around the country have asked for: a step-by-step introduction to stock investing for the beginning to intermediate investor. This easy-to-navigate guide explores the basics of stock investing and includes the intuitive TheStreet.com Investment Rating on more than 5,800 stocks, complete with real-world investing information that can be put to use immediately with stocks that fit the concepts discussed in the guide; informative charts, graphs and worksheets; easy-to-understand explanations on topics like P/E, compound interest, marked indices, diversifications, brokers, and much more; along with financial safety ratings for every stock on the NYSE, American Stock Exchange and the Nasdaq. This consumer-friendly guide offers complete how-to information on stock investing that can be put to use right away; a friendly format complete with our "Wise Guide" who leads the reader on a safari to learn about the investing jungle; helpful charts, graphs and simple worksheets; the intuitive TheStreet.com Investment rating on over 6,000 stocks — every stock found on the NYSE, American Stock Exchange and the NASDAQ; and much more.

"Provides investors with an alternative to stock broker recommendations, which recently have been tarnished by conflicts of interest. In summary, the guide serves as a welcome addition for all public library collections." -ARBA

Issues published quarterly, Softcover, 370 pages, $499.00 for four quarterly issues, $249.00 for a single issue

TheStreet.com Ratings' Reports & Services

- Ratings Online — An on-line summary covering an individual company's TheStreet.com Financial Strength Rating or an investment's unique TheStreet.com Investment Rating with the factors contributing to that rating; available 24 hours a day by visiting www.thestreet.com/tscratings or calling (800) 289-9222.
- Unlimited Ratings Research — The ultimate research tool providing fast, easy online access to the very latest TheStreet.com Financial Strength Ratings and Investment Ratings. Price: $559 per industry.

Contact TheStreet.com for more information about Reports & Services at www.thestreet.com/tscratings or call (800) 289-9222

TheStreet.com Ratings' Custom Reports

TheStreet.com Ratings is pleased to offer two customized options for receiving ratings data. Each taps into TheStreet.com's vast data repositories and is designed to provide exactly the data you need. Choose from a variety of industries, companies, data variables, and delivery formats including print, Excel, SQL, Text or Access.

- Customized Reports - get right to the heart of your company's research and data needs with a report customized to your specifications.
- Complete Database Download – TheStreet.com will design and deliver the database; from there you can sort it, recalculate it, and format your results to suit your specific needs.

Contact TheStreet.com for more information about Custom Reports at www.thestreet.com/tscratings or call (800) 289-9222

The Value of a Dollar 1600-1859, The Colonial Era to The Civil War

Following the format of the widely acclaimed, *The Value of a Dollar, 1860-2004, The Value of a Dollar 1600-1859, The Colonial Era to The Civil War* records the actual prices of thousands of items that consumers purchased from the Colonial Era to the Civil War. Our editorial department had been flooded with requests from users of our *Value of a Dollar* for the same type of information, just from an earlier time period. This new volume is just the answer – with pricing data from 1600 to 1859. Arranged into five-year chapters, each 5-year chapter includes a Historical Snapshot, Consumer Expenditures, Investments, Selected Income, Income/Standard Jobs, Food Basket, Standard Prices and Miscellany. There is also a section on Trends. This informative section charts the change in price over time and provides added detail on the reasons prices changed within the time period, including industry developments, changes in consumer attitudes and important historical facts. This fascinating survey will serve a wide range of research needs and will be useful in all high school, public and academic library reference collections.

"The Value of a Dollar: Colonial Era to the Civil War, 1600-1865 will find a happy audience among students, researchers, and general browsers. It offers a fascinating and detailed look at early American history from the viewpoint of everyday people trying to make ends meet. This title and the earlier publication, The Value of a Dollar, 1860-2004, complement each other very well, and readers will appreciate finding them side-by-side on the shelf." -Booklist

Hardcover ISBN 978-1-59237-094-8, 600 pages, $145.00 | Ebook ISBN 978-1-59237-169-3 www.gale.com/gvrl/partners/grey.htm

The Value of a Dollar 1860-2004, Third Edition

A guide to practical economy, *The Value of a Dollar* records the actual prices of thousands of items that consumers purchased from the Civil War to the present, along with facts about investment options and income opportunities. This brand new Third Edition boasts a brand new addition to each five-year chapter, a section on Trends. This informative section charts the change in price over time and provides added detail on the reasons prices changed within the time period, including industry developments, changes in consumer attitudes and important historical facts. Plus, a brand new chapter for 2000-2004 has been added. Each 5-year chapter includes a Historical Snapshot, Consumer Expenditures, Investments, Selected Income, Income/Standard Jobs, Food Basket, Standard Prices and Miscellany. This interesting and useful publication will be widely used in any reference collection.

"Business historians, reporters, writers and students will find this source... very helpful for historical research. Libraries will want to purchase it." –ARBA

Hardcover ISBN 978-1-59237-074-0, 600 pages, $145.00 | Ebook ISBN 978-1-59237-173-0 www.gale.com/gvrl/partners/grey.htm

Working Americans 1880-1999
Volume I: The Working Class, Volume II: The Middle Class, Volume III: The Upper Class

Each of the volumes in the *Working Americans* series focuses on a particular class of Americans, The Working Class, The Middle Class and The Upper Class over the last 120 years. Chapters in each volume focus on one decade and profile three to five families. Family Profiles include real data on Income & Job Descriptions, Selected Prices of the Times, Annual Income, Annual Budgets, Family Finances, Life at Work, Life at Home, Life in the Community, Working Conditions, Cost of Living, Amusements and much more. Each chapter also contains an Economic Profile with Average Wages of other Professions, a selection of Typical Pricing, Key Events & Inventions, News Profiles, Articles from Local Media and Illustrations. The *Working Americans* series captures the lifestyles of each of the classes from the last twelve decades, covers a vast array of occupations and ethnic backgrounds and travels the entire nation. These interesting and useful compilations of portraits of the American Working, Middle and Upper Classes during the last 120 years will be an important addition to any high school, public or academic library reference collection.

"These interesting, unique compilations of economic and social facts, figures and graphs will support multiple research needs. They will engage and enlighten patrons in high school, public and academic library collections." –Booklist

Volume I: The Working Class Hardcover ISBN 978-1-891482-81-6, 558 pages, $145.00 | Volume II: The Middle Class Hardcover ISBN 978-1-891482-72-4, 591 pages, $145.00 | Volume III: The Upper Class Hardcover ISBN 978-1-930956-38-4, 567 pages, $145.00 | Ebooks www.gale.com/gvrl/partners/grey.htm

Working Americans 1880-1999 Volume IV: Their Children

This Fourth Volume in the highly successful *Working Americans* series focuses on American children, decade by decade from 1880 to 1999. This interesting and useful volume introduces the reader to three children in each decade, one from each of the Working, Middle and Upper classes. Like the first three volumes in the series, the individual profiles are created from interviews, diaries, statistical studies, biographies and news reports. Profiles cover a broad range of ethnic backgrounds, geographic area and lifestyles – everything from an orphan in Memphis in 1882, following the Yellow Fever epidemic of 1878 to an eleven-year-old nephew of a beer baron and owner of the New York Yankees in New York City in 1921. Chapters also contain important supplementary materials including News Features as well as information on everything from Schools to Parks, Infectious Diseases to Childhood Fears along with Entertainment, Family Life and much more to provide an informative overview of the lifestyles of children from each decade. This interesting account of what life was like for Children in the Working, Middle and Upper Classes will be a welcome addition to the reference collection of any high school, public or academic library.

Hardcover ISBN 978-1-930956-35-3, 600 pages, $145.00 | Ebook ISBN 978-1-59237-166-2 www.gale.com/gvrl/partners/grey.htm

Working Americans 1880-2003 Volume V: Americans At War

Working Americans 1880-2003 Volume V: Americans At War is divided into 11 chapters, each covering a decade from 1880-2003 and examines the lives of Americans during the time of war, including declared conflicts, one-time military actions, protests, and preparations for war. Each decade includes several personal profiles, whether on the battlefield or on the homefront, that tell the stories of civilians, soldiers, and officers during the decade. The profiles examine: Life at Home; Life at Work; and Life in the Community. Each decade also includes an Economic Profile with statistical comparisons, a Historical Snapshot, News Profiles, local News Articles, and Illustrations that provide a solid historical background to the decade being examined. Profiles range widely not only geographically, but also emotionally, from that of a girl whose leg was torn off in a blast during WWI, to the boredom of being stationed in the Dakotas as the Indian Wars were drawing to a close. As in previous volumes of the *Working Americans* series, information is presented in narrative form, but hard facts and real-life situations back up each story. The basis of the profiles come from diaries, private print books, personal interviews, family histories, estate documents and magazine articles. For easy reference, *Working Americans 1880-2003 Volume V: Americans At War* includes an in-depth Subject Index. The Working Americans series has become an important reference for public libraries, academic libraries and high school libraries. This fifth volume will be a welcome addition to all of these types of reference collections.

Hardcover ISBN 978-1-59237-024-5, 600 pages, $145.00 | Ebook ISBN 978-1-59237-167-9 www.gale.com/gvrl/partners/grey.htm

Working Americans 1880-2005 Volume VI: Women at Work

Unlike any other volume in the *Working Americans* series, this Sixth Volume, is the first to focus on a particular gender of Americans. *Volume VI: Women at Work*, traces what life was like for working women from the 1860's to the present time. Beginning with the life of a maid in 1890 and a store clerk in 1900 and ending with the life and times of the modern working women, this text captures the struggle, strengths and changing perception of the American woman at work. Each chapter focuses on one decade and profiles three to five women with real data on Income & Job Descriptions, Selected Prices of the Times, Annual Income, Annual Budgets, Family Finances, Life at Work, Life at Home, Life in the Community, Working Conditions, Cost of Living, Amusements and much more. For even broader access to the events, economics and attitude towards women throughout the past 130 years, each chapter is supplemented with News Profiles, Articles from Local Media, Illustrations, Economic Profiles, Typical Pricing, Key Events, Inventions and more. This important volume illustrates what life was like for working women over time and allows the reader to develop an understanding of the changing role of women at work. These interesting and useful compilations of portraits of women at work will be an important addition to any high school, public or academic library reference collection.

Hardcover ISBN 978-1-59237-063-4, 600 pages, $145.00 | Ebook ISBN 978-1-59237-168-6 www.gale.com/gvrl/partners/grey.htm

Working Americans 1880-2005 Volume VII: Social Movements

Working Americans series, Volume VII: Social Movements explores how Americans sought and fought for change from the 1880s to the present time. Following the format of previous volumes in the Working Americans series, the text examines the lives of 34 individuals who have worked -- often behind the scenes --- to bring about change. Issues include topics as diverse as the Anti-smoking movement of 1901 to efforts by Native Americans to reassert their long lost rights. Along the way, the book will profile individuals brave enough to demand suffrage for Kansas women in 1912 or demand an end to lynching during a March on Washington in 1923. Each profile is enriched with real data on Income & Job Descriptions, Selected Prices of the Times, Annual Incomes & Budgets, Life at Work, Life at Home, Life in the Community, along with News Features, Key Events, and Illustrations. The depth of information contained in each profile allow the user to explore the private, financial and public lives of these subjects, deepening our understanding of how calls for change took place in our society. A must-purchase for the reference collections of high school libraries, public libraries and academic libraries.

Hardcover ISBN 978-1-59237-101-3, 600 pages, $145.00 | Ebook ISBN 978-1-59237-174-7 www.gale.com/gvrl/partners/grey.htm

Working Americans 1880-2005 Volume VIII: Immigrants

Working Americans 1880-2007 Volume VIII: Immigrants illustrates what life was like for families leaving their homeland and creating a new life in the United States. Each chapter covers one decade and introduces the reader to three immigrant families. Family profiles cover what life was like in their homeland, in their community in the United States, their home life, working conditions and so much more. As the reader moves through these pages, the families and individuals come to life, painting a picture of why they left their homeland, their experiences in setting roots in a new country, their struggles and triumphs, stretching from the 1800s to the present time. Profiles include a seven-year-old Swedish girl who meets her father for the first time at Ellis Island; a Chinese photographer's assistant; an Armenian who flees the genocide of his country to build Ford automobiles in Detroit; a 38-year-old German bachelor cigar maker who settles in Newark NJ, but contemplates tobacco farming in Virginia; a 19-year-old Irish domestic servant who is amazed at the easy life of American dogs; a 19-year-old Filipino who came to Hawaii against his parent's wishes to farm sugar cane; a French-Canadian who finds success as a boxer in Maine and many more. As in previous volumes, information is presented in narrative form, but hard facts and real-life situations back up each story. With the topic of immigration being so hotly debated in this country, this timely resource will prove to be a useful source for students, researchers, historians and library patrons to discover the issues facing immigrants in the United States. This title will be a useful addition to reference collections of public libraries, university libraries and high schools.

Hardcover ISBN 978-1-59237-197-6, 600 pages, $145.00 | Ebook ISBN 978-1-59237-232-4 www.gale.com/gvrl/partners/grey.htm

The Religious Right, A Reference Handbook

Timely and unbiased, this third edition updates and expands its examination of the religious right and its influence on our government, citizens, society, and politics. From the fight to outlaw the teaching of Darwin's theory of evolution to the struggle to outlaw abortion, the religious right is continually exerting an influence on public policy. This text explores the influence of religion on legislation and society, while examining the alignment of the religious right with the political right. A historical survey of the movement highlights the shift to "hands-on" approach to politics and the struggle to present a unified front. The coverage offers a critical historical survey of the religious right movement, focusing on its increased involvement in the political arena, attempts to forge coalitions, and notable successes and failures. The text offers complete coverage of biographies of the men and women who have advanced the cause and an up to date chronology illuminate the movement's goals, including their accomplishments and failures. This edition offers an extensive update to all sections along with several brand new entries. Two new sections complement this third edition, a chapter on legal issues and court decisions and a chapter on demographic statistics and electoral patterns. To aid in further research, *The Religious Right*, offers an entire section of annotated listings of print and non-print resources, as well as of organizations affiliated with the religious right, and those opposing it. Comprehensive in its scope, this work offers easy-to-read, pertinent information for those seeking to understand the religious right and its evolving role in American society. A must for libraries of all sizes, university religion departments, activists, high schools and for those interested in the evolving role of the religious right.

" Recommended for all public and academic libraries." - Library Journal

Hardcover ISBN 978-1-59237-113-6, 600 pages, $135.00 | Ebook ISBN 978-1-59237-226-3 www.gale.com/gvrl/partners/grey.htm

From Suffrage to the Senate, America's Political Women

From Suffrage to the Senate is a comprehensive and valuable compendium of biographies of leading women in U.S. politics, past and present, and an examination of the wide range of women's movements. Up to date through 2006, this dynamically illustrated reference work explores American women's path to political power and social equality from the struggle for the right to vote and the abolition of slavery to the first African American woman in the U.S. Senate and beyond. This new edition includes over 150 new entries and a brand new section on trends and demographics of women in politics. The in-depth coverage also traces the political heritage of the abolition, labor, suffrage, temperance, and reproductive rights movements. The alphabetically arranged entries include biographies of every woman from across the political spectrum who has served in the U.S. House and Senate, along with women in the Judiciary and the U.S. Cabinet and, new to this edition, biographies of activists and political consultants. Bibliographical references follow each entry. For easy reference, a handy chronology is provided detailing 150 years of women's history. This up-to-date reference will be a must-purchase for women's studies departments, high schools and public libraries and will be a handy resource for those researching the key players in women's politics, past and present.

"An engaging tool that would be useful in high school, public, and academic libraries looking for an overview of the political history of women in the US." –Booklist

Two Volumes, Hardcover ISBN 978-1-59237-117-4, 1,160 pages, $195.00 | Ebook ISBN 978-1-59237-227-0
www.gale.com/gvrl/partners/grey.htm

An African Biographical Dictionary

This landmark second edition is the only biographical dictionary to bring together, in one volume, cultural, social and political leaders – both historical and contemporary – of the sub-Saharan region. Over 800 biographical sketches of prominent Africans, as well as foreigners who have affected the continent's history, are featured, 150 more than the previous edition. The wide spectrum of leaders includes religious figures, writers, politicians, scientists, entertainers, sports personalities and more. Access to these fascinating individuals is provided in a user-friendly format. The biographies are arranged alphabetically, cross-referenced and indexed. Entries include the country or countries in which the person was significant and the commonly accepted dates of birth and death. Each biographical sketch is chronologically written; entries for cultural personalities add an evaluation of their work. This information is followed by a selection of references often found in university and public libraries, including autobiographies and principal biographical works. Appendixes list each individual by country and by field of accomplishment – rulers, musicians, explorers, missionaries, businessmen, physicists – nearly thirty categories in all. Another convenient appendix lists heads of state since independence by country. Up-to-date and representative of African societies as a whole, An African Biographical Dictionary provides a wealth of vital information for students of African culture and is an indispensable reference guide for anyone interested in African affairs.

"An unquestionable convenience to have these concise, informative biographies gathered into one source, indexed, and analyzed by appendixes listing entrants by nation and occupational field." –Wilson Library Bulletin

Hardcover ISBN 978-1-59237-112-9, 667 pages, $135.00 | Ebook ISBN 978-1-59237-229-4 www.gale.com/gvrl/partners/grey.htm

American Environmental Leaders, From Colonial Times to the Present

A comprehensive and diverse award winning collection of biographies of the most important figures in American environmentalism. Few subjects arouse the passions the way the environment does. How will we feed an ever-increasing population and how can that food be made safe for consumption? Who decides how land is developed? How can environmental policies be made fair for everyone, including multiethnic groups, women, children, and the poor? *American Environmental Leaders* presents more than 350 biographies of men and women who have devoted their lives to studying, debating, and organizing these and other controversial issues over the last 200 years. In addition to the scientists who have analyzed how human actions affect nature, we are introduced to poets, landscape architects, presidents, painters, activists, even sanitation engineers, and others who have forever altered how we think about the environment. The easy to use A–Z format provides instant access to these fascinating individuals, and frequent cross references indicate others with whom individuals worked (and sometimes clashed). End of entry references provide users with a starting point for further research.

"Highly recommended for high school, academic, and public libraries needing environmental biographical information." –Library Journal/Starred Review

Two Volumes, Hardcover ISBN 978-1-59237-119-8, 900 pages $195.00 | Ebook ISBN 978-1-59237-230-0
www.gale.com/gvrl/partners/grey.htm

World Cultural Leaders of the Twentieth & Twenty-First Centuries

World Cultural Leaders of the Twentieth & Twenty-First Centuries is a window into the arts, performances, movements, and music that shaped the world's cultural development since 1900. A remarkable around-the-world look at one-hundred-plus years of cultural development through the eyes of those that set the stage and stayed to play. This second edition offers over 120 new biographies along with a complete update of existing biographies. To further aid the reader, a handy fold-out timeline traces important events in all six cultural categories from 1900 through the present time. Plus, a new section of detailed material and resources for 100 selected individuals is also new to this edition, with further data on museums, homesteads, websites, artwork and more. This remarkable compilation will answer a wide range of questions. Who was the originator of the term "documentary"? Which poet married the daughter of the famed novelist Thomas Mann in order to help her escape Nazi Germany? Which British writer served as an agent in Russia against the Bolsheviks before the 1917 revolution? A handy two-volume set that makes it easy to look up 450 worldwide cultural icons: novelists, poets, playwrights, painters, sculptors, architects, dancers, choreographers, actors, directors, filmmakers, singers, composers, and musicians. *World Cultural Leaders of the Twentieth & Twenty-First Centuries* provides entries (many of them illustrated) covering the person's works, achievements, and professional career in a thorough essay and offers interesting facts and statistics. Entries are fully cross-referenced so that readers can learn how various individuals influenced others. An index of leaders by occupation, a useful glossary and a thorough general index complete the coverage. This remarkable resource will be an important acquisition for the reference collections of public libraries, university libraries and high schools.

"Fills a need for handy, concise information on a wide array of international cultural figures."-ARBA

Two Volumes, Hardcover ISBN 978-1-59237-118-1, 900 pages, $195.00 | Ebook ISBN 978-1-59237-231-7
www.gale.com/gvrl/partners/grey.htm

Political Corruption in America: An Encyclopedia of Scandals, Power, and Greed

The complete scandal-filled history of American political corruption, focusing on the infamous people and cases, as well as society's electoral and judicial reactions. Since colonial times, there has been no shortage of politicians willing to take a bribe, skirt campaign finance laws, or act in their own interests. Corruption like the Whiskey Ring, Watergate, and Whitewater cases dominate American life, making political scandal a leading U.S. industry. From judges to senators, presidents to mayors, *Political Corruption in America* discusses the infamous people throughout history who have been accused of and implicated in crooked behavior. In this new second edition, more than 250 A–Z entries explore the people, crimes, investigations, and court cases behind 200 years of American political scandals. This unbiased volume also delves into the issues surrounding Koreagate, the Chinese campaign scandal, and other ethical lapses. Relevant statutes and terms, including the Independent Counsel Statute and impeachment as a tool of political punishment, are examined as well. Students, scholars, and other readers interested in American history, political science, and ethics will appreciate this survey of a wide range of corrupting influences. This title focuses on how politicians from all parties have fallen because of their greed and hubris, and how society has used electoral and judicial means against those who tested the accepted standards of political conduct. A full range of illustrations including political cartoons, photos of key figures such as Abe Fortas and Archibald Cox, graphs of presidential pardons, and tables showing the number of expulsions and censures in both the House and Senate round out the text. In addition, a comprehensive chronology of major political scandals in U.S. history from colonial times until the present. For further reading, an extensive bibliography lists sources including archival letters, newspapers, and private manuscript collections from the United States and Great Britain. With its comprehensive coverage of this interesting topic, *Political Corruption in America: An Encyclopedia of Scandals, Power, and Greed* will prove to be a useful addition to the reference collections of all public libraries, university libraries, history collections, political science collections and high schools.

"...this encyclopedia is a useful contribution to the field. Highly recommended." - CHOICE
"Political Corruption should be useful in most academic, high school, and public libraries." Booklist

Two Volumes, Hardcover ISBN 978-1-59237-297-3, 500 pages, $195.00

Religion and Law: A Dictionary

This informative, easy-to-use reference work covers a wide range of legal issues that affect the roles of religion and law in American society. Extensive A–Z entries provide coverage of key court decisions, case studies, concepts, individuals, religious groups, organizations, and agencies shaping religion and law in today's society. This *Dictionary* focuses on topics involved with the constitutional theory and interpretation of religion and the law; terms providing a historical explanation of the ways in which America's ever increasing ethnic and religious diversity contributed to our current understanding of the mandates of the First and Fourteenth Amendments; terms and concepts describing the development of religion clause jurisprudence; an analytical examination of the distinct vocabulary used in this area of the law; the means by which American courts have attempted to balance religious liberty against other important individual and social interests in a wide variety of physical and regulatory environments, including the classroom, the workplace, the courtroom, religious group organization and structure, taxation, the clash of "secular" and "religious" values, and the relationship of the generalized idea of individual autonomy of the specific concept of religious liberty. Important legislation and legal cases affecting religion and society are thoroughly covered in this timely volume, including a detailed Table of Cases and Table of Statutes for more detailed research. A guide to further reading and an index are also included. This useful resource will be an important acquisition for the reference collections of all public libraries, university libraries, religion reference collections and high schools.

Hardcover ISBN 978-1-59237-298-0, 500 pages, $135.00

Human Rights in the United States: A Dictionary and Documents

This two volume set offers easy to grasp explanations of the basic concepts, laws, and case law in the field, with emphasis on human rights in the historical, political, and legal experience of the United States. Human rights is a term not fully understood by many Americans. Addressing this gap, the new second edition of *Human Rights in the United States: A Dictionary and Documents* offers a comprehensive introduction that places the history of human rights in the United States in an international context. It surveys the legal protection of human dignity in the United States, examines the sources of human rights norms, cites key legal cases, explains the role of international governmental and non-governmental organizations, and charts global, regional, and U.N. human rights measures. Over 240 dictionary entries of human rights terms are detailed—ranging from asylum and cultural relativism to hate crimes and torture. Each entry discusses the significance of the term, gives examples, and cites appropriate documents and court decisions. In addition, a Documents section is provided that contains 59 conventions, treaties, and protocols related to the most up to date international action on ethnic cleansing; freedom of expression and religion; violence against women; and much more. A bibliography, extensive glossary, and comprehensive index round out this indispensable volume. This comprehensive, timely volume is a must for large public libraries, university libraries and social science departments, along with high school libraries.

"...invaluable for anyone interested in human rights issues ... highly recommended for all reference collections."
- American Reference Books Annual

Two Volumes, Hardcover ISBN 978-1-59237-290-4, 750 pages, $225.00

The Comparative Guide to American Elementary & Secondary Schools, 2008

The Complete Learning Disabilities Directory, 2008

Educators Resource Directory, 2007/08

The Comparative Guide to American Suburbs, 2007/08

The Comparative Guide to American Suburbs is a one-stop source for Statistics on the 2,000+ suburban communities surrounding the 50 largest metropolitan areas – their population characteristics, income levels, economy, school system and important data on how they compare to one another. Organized into 50 Metropolitan Area chapters, each chapter contains an overview of the Metropolitan Area, a detailed Map followed by a comprehensive Statistical Profile of each Suburban Community, including Contact Information, Physical Characteristics, Population Characteristics, Income, Economy, Unemployment Rate, Cost of Living, Education, Chambers of Commerce and more. Next, statistical data is sorted into Ranking Tables that rank the suburbs by twenty different criteria, including Population, Per Capita Income, Unemployment Rate, Crime Rate, Cost of Living and more. *The Comparative Guide to American Suburbs* is the best source for locating data on suburbs. Those looking to relocate, as well as those doing preliminary market research, will find this an invaluable timesaving resource.

"Public and academic libraries will find this compilation useful...The work draws together figures from many sources and will be especially helpful for job relocation decisions." – Booklist

Softcover ISBN 978-1-59237-180-8, 1,700 pages, $130.00 | Ebook ISBN 978-1-59237-235-5 www.gale.com/gvrl/partners/grey.htm

The American Tally: Statistics & Comparative Rankings for U.S. Cities with Populations over 10,000

This important statistical handbook compiles, all in one place, comparative statistics on all U.S. cities and towns with a 10,000+ population. *The American Tally* provides statistical details on over 4,000 cities and towns and profiles how they compare with one another in Population Characteristics, Education, Language & Immigration, Income & Employment and Housing. Each section begins with an alphabetical listing of cities by state, allowing for quick access to both the statistics and relative rankings of any city. Next, the highest and lowest cities are listed in each statistic. These important, informative lists provide quick reference to which cities are at both extremes of the spectrum for each statistic. Unlike any other reference, *The American Tally* provides quick, easy access to comparative statistics – a must-have for any reference collection.

"A solid library reference." -Bookwatch

Softcover ISBN 978-1-930956-29-2, 500 pages, $125.00 | Ebook ISBN 978-1-59237-241-6 www.gale.com/gvrl/partners/grey.htm

The Asian Databook: Statistics for all US Counties & Cities with Over 10,000 Population

This is the first-ever resource that compiles statistics and rankings on the US Asian population. *The Asian Databook* presents over 20 statistical data points for each city and county, arranged alphabetically by state, then alphabetically by place name. Data reported for each place includes Population, Languages Spoken at Home, Foreign-Born, Educational Attainment, Income Figures, Poverty Status, Homeownership, Home Values & Rent, and more. Next, in the Rankings Section, the top 75 places are listed for each data element. These easy-to-access ranking tables allow the user to quickly determine trends and population characteristics. This kind of comparative data can not be found elsewhere, in print or on the web, in a format that's as easy-to-use or more concise. A useful resource for those searching for demographics data, career search and relocation information and also for market research. With data ranging from Ancestry to Education, *The Asian Databook* presents a useful compilation of information that will be a much-needed resource in the reference collection of any public or academic library along with the marketing collection of any company whose primary focus in on the Asian population.

"This useful resource will help those searching for demographics data, and market research or relocation information... Accurate and clearly laid out, the publication is recommended for large public library and research collections." -Booklist

Softcover ISBN 978-1-59237-044-3, 1,000 pages, $150.00

The Hispanic Databook: Statistics for all US Counties & Cities with Over 10,000 Population

Previously published by Toucan Valley Publications, this second edition has been completely updated with figures from the latest census and has been broadly expanded to include dozens of new data elements and a brand new Rankings section. The Hispanic population in the United States has increased over 42% in the last 10 years and accounts for 12.5% of the total US population. For ease-of-use, *The Hispanic Databook* presents over 20 statistical data points for each city and county, arranged alphabetically by state, then alphabetically by place name. Data reported for each place includes Population, Languages Spoken at Home, Foreign-Born, Educational Attainment, Income Figures, Poverty Status, Homeownership, Home Values & Rent, and more. Next, in the Rankings Section, the top 75 places are listed for each data element. These easy-to-access ranking tables allow the user to quickly determine trends and population characteristics. This kind of comparative data can not be found elsewhere, in print or on the web, in a format that's as easy-to-use or more concise. A useful resource for those searching for demographics data, career search and relocation information and also for market research. With data ranging from Ancestry to Education, *The Hispanic Databook* presents a useful compilation of information that will be a much-needed resource in the reference collection of any public or academic library along with the marketing collection of any company whose primary focus in on the Hispanic population.

"This accurate, clearly presented volume of selected Hispanic demographics is recommended for large public libraries and research collections."-Library Journal

Softcover ISBN 978-1-59237-008-5, 1,000 pages, $150.00

Ancestry in America: A Comparative Guide to Over 200 Ethnic Backgrounds

This brand new reference work pulls together thousands of comparative statistics on the Ethnic Backgrounds of all populated places in the United States with populations over 10,000. Never before has this kind of information been reported in a single volume. Section One, Statistics by Place, is made up of a list of over 200 ancestry and race categories arranged alphabetically by each of the 5,000 different places with populations over 10,000. The population number of the ancestry group in that city or town is provided along with the percent that group represents of the total population. This informative city-by-city section allows the user to quickly and easily explore the ethnic makeup of all major population bases in the United States. Section Two, Comparative Rankings, contains three tables for each ethnicity and race. In the first table, the top 150 populated places are ranked by population number for that particular ancestry group, regardless of population. In the second table, the top 150 populated places are ranked by the percent of the total population for that ancestry group. In the third table, those top 150 populated places with 10,000 population are ranked by population number for each ancestry group. These easy-to-navigate tables allow users to see ancestry population patterns and make city-by-city comparisons as well. This brand new, information-packed resource will serve a wide-range or research requests for demographics, population characteristics, relocation information and much more. *Ancestry in America: A Comparative Guide to Over 200 Ethnic Backgrounds* will be an important acquisition to all reference collections.

"This compilation will serve a wide range of research requests for population characteristics ... it offers much more detail than other sources." –Booklist

Softcover ISBN 978-1-59237-029-0, 1,500 pages, $225.00

Weather America, A Thirty-Year Summary of Statistical Weather Data and Rankings

This valuable resource provides extensive climatological data for over 4,000 National and Cooperative Weather Stations throughout the United States. Weather America begins with a new Major Storms section that details major storm events of the nation and a National Rankings section that details rankings for several data elements, such as Maximum Temperature and Precipitation. The main body of Weather America is organized into 50 state sections. Each section provides a Data Table on each Weather Station, organized alphabetically, that provides statistics on Maximum and Minimum Temperatures, Precipitation, Snowfall, Extreme Temperatures, Foggy Days, Humidity and more. State sections contain two brand new features in this edition – a City Index and a narrative Description of the climatic conditions of the state. Each section also includes a revised Map of the State that includes not only weather stations, but cities and towns.

"Best Reference Book of the Year." –Library Journal

Softcover ISBN 978-1-891482-29-8, 2,013 pages, $175.00 | Ebook ISBN 978-1-59237-237-9 www.gale.com/gvrl/partners/grey.htm

Crime in America's Top-Rated Cities

This volume includes over 20 years of crime statistics in all major crime categories: violent crimes, property crimes and total crime. *Crime in America's Top-Rated Cities* is conveniently arranged by city and covers 76 top-rated cities. Crime in America's Top-Rated Cities offers details that compare the number of crimes and crime rates for the city, suburbs and metro area along with national crime trends for violent, property and total crimes. Also, this handbook contains important information and statistics on Anti-Crime Programs, Crime Risk, Hate Crimes, Illegal Drugs, Law Enforcement, Correctional Facilities, Death Penalty Laws and much more. A much-needed resource for people who are relocating, business professionals, general researchers, the press, law enforcement officials and students of criminal justice.

"Data is easy to access and will save hours of searching." –Global Enforcement Review

Softcover ISBN 978-1-891482-84-7, 832 pages, $155.00

The Comparative Guide to American Hospitals, Second Edition

This new second edition compares all of the nation's hospitals by 24 measures of quality in the treatment of heart attack, heart failure, pneumonia, and, new to this edition, surgical procedures and pregnancy care. Plus, this second edition is now available in regional volumes, to make locating information about hospitals in your area quicker and easier than ever before. The Comparative Guide to American Hospitals provides a snapshot profile of each of the nations 4,200+ hospitals. These informative profiles illustrate how the hospital rates when providing 24 different treatments within four broad categories: Heart Attack Care, Heart Failure Care, Surgical Infection Prevention (NEW), and Pregnancy Care measures (NEW). Each profile includes the raw percentage for that hospital, the state average, the US average and data on the top hospital. For easy access to contact information, each profile includes the hospital's address, phone and fax numbers, email and web addresses, type and accreditation along with 5 top key administrations. These profiles will allow the user to quickly identify the quality of the hospital and have the necessary information at their fingertips to make contact with that hospital. Most importantly, *The Comparative Guide to American Hospitals* provides easy-to-use Regional State by State Statistical Summary Tables for each of the data elements to allow the user to quickly locate hospitals with the best level of service. Plus, a new 30-Day Mortality Chart, Glossary of Terms and Regional Hospital Profile Index make this a must-have source. This new, expanded edition will be a must for the reference collection at all public, medical and academic libraries.

"These data will help those with heart conditions and pneumonia make informed decisions about their healthcare and encourage hospitals to improve the quality of care they provide. Large medical, hospital, and public libraries are most likely to benefit from this weighty resource."-Library Journal

Four Volumes Softcover ISBN 978-1-59237-182-2, 3,500 pages, $325.00 | Regional Volumes $135.00 |
Ebook ISBN 978-1-59237-239-3 www.gale.com/gvrl/partners/grey.htm

Older Americans Information Directory, 2008

Completely updated for 2008, this sixth edition has been completely revised and now contains 1,000 new listings, over 8,000 updates to existing listings and over 3,000 brand new e-mail addresses and web sites. You'll find important resources for Older Americans including National, Regional, State & Local Organizations, Government Agencies, Research Centers, Libraries & Information Centers, Legal Resources, Discount Travel Information, Continuing Education Programs, Disability Aids & Assistive Devices, Health, Print Media and Electronic Media. Three indexes: Entry Index, Subject Index and Geographic Index make it easy to find just the right source of information. This comprehensive guide to resources for Older Americans will be a welcome addition to any reference collection.

"Highly recommended for academic, public, health science and consumer libraries…" –Choice

1,200 pages; Softcover ISBN 978-1-59237-357-4, $165.00 | Online Database $215.00 | Online Database & Directory Combo $300.00

The Complete Directory for Pediatric Disorders, 2008

This important directory provides parents and caregivers with information about Pediatric Conditions, Disorders, Diseases and Disabilities, including Blood Disorders, Bone & Spinal Disorders, Brain Defects & Abnormalities, Chromosomal Disorders, Congenital Heart Defects, Movement Disorders, Neuromuscular Disorders and Pediatric Tumors & Cancers. This carefully written directory offers: understandable Descriptions of 15 major bodily systems; Descriptions of more than 200 Disorders and a Resources Section, detailing National Agencies & Associations, State Associations, Online Services, Libraries & Resource Centers, Research Centers, Support Groups & Hotlines, Camps, Books and Periodicals. This resource will provide immediate access to information crucial to families and caregivers when coping with children's illnesses.

"Recommended for public and consumer health libraries." –Library Journal

Softcover ISBN 978-1-59237-150-1, 1,200 pages, $165.00 | Online Database $215.00 | Online Database & Directory Combo $300.00

The Directory of Drug & Alcohol Residential Rehabilitation Facilities

This brand new directory is the first-ever resource to bring together, all in one place, data on the thousands of drug and alcohol residential rehabilitation facilities in the United States. The Directory of Drug & Alcohol Residential Rehabilitation Facilities covers over 1,000 facilities, with detailed contact information for each one, including mailing address, phone and fax numbers, email addresses and web sites, mission statement, type of treatment programs, cost, average length of stay, numbers of residents and counselors, accreditation, insurance plans accepted, type of environment, religious affiliation, education components and much more. It also contains a helpful chapter on General Resources that provides contact information for Associations, Print & Electronic Media, Support Groups and Conferences. Multiple indexes allow the user to pinpoint the facilities that meet very specific criteria. This time-saving tool is what so many counselors, parents and medical professionals have been asking for. *The Directory of Drug & Alcohol Residential Rehabilitation Facilities* will be a helpful tool in locating the right source for treatment for a wide range of individuals. This comprehensive directory will be an important acquisition for all reference collections: public and academic libraries, case managers, social workers, state agencies and many more.

"This is an excellent, much needed directory that fills an important gap…" –Booklist

Softcover ISBN 978-1-59237-031-3, 300 pages, $135.00

Canadian Almanac & Directory, 2008

The Canadian Almanac & Directory contains sixteen directories in one – giving you all the facts and figures you will ever need about Canada. No other single source provides users with the quality and depth of up-to-date information for all types of research. This national directory and guide gives you access to statistics, images and over 100,000 names and addresses for everything from Airlines to Zoos - updated every year. It's Ten Directories in One! Each section is a directory in itself, providing robust information on business and finance, communications, government, associations, arts and culture (museums, zoos, libraries, etc.), health, transportation, law, education, and more. Government information includes federal, provincial and territorial - and includes an easy-to-use quick index to find key information. A separate municipal government section includes every municipality in Canada, with full profiles of Canada's largest urban centers. A complete legal directory lists judges and judicial officials, court locations and law firms across the country. A wealth of general information, the *Canadian Almanac & Directory* also includes national statistics on population, employment, imports and exports, and more. National awards and honors are presented, along with forms of address, Commonwealth information and full color photos of Canadian symbols. Postal information, weights, measures, distances and other useful charts are also incorporated. Complete almanac information includes perpetual calendars, five-year holiday planners and astronomical information. Published continuously for 160 years, *The Canadian Almanac & Directory* is the best single reference source for business executives, managers and assistants; government and public affairs executives; lawyers; marketing, sales and advertising executives; researchers, editors and journalists.

Hardcover ISBN 978-1-59237-220-1, 1,600 pages, $315.00

Associations Canada, 2008

The Most Powerful Fact-Finder to Business, Trade, Professional and Consumer Organizations
Associations Canada covers Canadian organizations and international groups including industry, commercial and professional associations, registered charities, special interest and common interest organizations. This annually revised compendium provides detailed listings and abstracts for nearly 20,000 regional, national and international organizations. This popular volume provides the most comprehensive picture of Canada's non-profit sector. Detailed listings enable users to identify an organization's budget, founding date, scope of activity, licensing body, sources of funding, executive information, full address and complete contact information, just to name a few. Powerful indexes help researchers find information quickly and easily. The following indexes are included: subject, acronym, geographic, budget, executive name, conferences & conventions, mailing list, defunct and unreachable associations and registered charitable organizations. In addition to annual spending of over $1 billion on transportation and conventions alone, Canadian associations account for many millions more in pursuit of membership interests. *Associations Canada* provides complete access to this highly lucrative market. *Associations Canada* is a strong source of prospects for sales and marketing executives, tourism and convention officials, researchers, government officials - anyone who wants to locate non-profit interest groups and trade associations.

Hardcover ISBN 978-1-59237-277-5, 1,600 pages, $315.00

Financial Services Canada, 2008/09

Financial Services Canada is the only master file of current contacts and information that serves the needs of the entire financial services industry in Canada. With over 18,000 organizations and hard-to-find business information, Financial Services Canada is the most up-to-date source for names and contact numbers of industry professionals, senior executives, portfolio managers, financial advisors, agency bureaucrats and elected representatives. Financial Services Canada incorporates the latest changes in the industry to provide you with the most current details on each company, including: name, title, organization, telephone and fax numbers, e-mail and web addresses. *Financial Services Canada* also includes private company listings never before compiled, government agencies, association and consultant services - to ensure that you'll never miss a client or a contact. Current listings include: banks and branches, non-depository institutions, stock exchanges and brokers, investment management firms, insurance companies, major accounting and law firms, government agencies and financial associations. Powerful indexes assist researchers with locating the vital financial information they need. The following indexes are included: alphabetic, geographic, executive name, corporate web site/e-mail, government quick reference and subject. *Financial Services Canada* is a valuable resource for financial executives, bankers, financial planners, sales and marketing professionals, lawyers and chartered accountants, government officials, investment dealers, journalists, librarians and reference specialists.

Hardcover ISBN 978-1-59237-278-2, 900 pages, $315.00

Directory of Libraries in Canada, 2008/09

The Directory of Libraries in Canada brings together almost 7,000 listings including libraries and their branches, information resource centers, archives and library associations and learning centers. The directory offers complete and comprehensive information on Canadian libraries, resource centers, business information centers, professional associations, regional library systems, archives, library schools and library technical programs. *The Directory of Libraries in Canada* includes important features of each library and service, including library information; personnel details, including contact names and e-mail addresses; collection information; services available to users; acquisitions budgets; and computers and automated systems. Useful information on each library's electronic access is also included, such as Internet browser, connectivity and public Internet/CD-ROM/subscription database access. The directory also provides powerful indexes for subject, location, personal name and Web site/e-mail to assist researchers with locating the crucial information they need. *The Directory of Libraries in Canada* is a vital reference tool for publishers, advocacy groups, students, research institutions, computer hardware suppliers, and other diverse groups that provide products and services to this unique market.

Hardcover ISBN 978-1-59237-279-9, 850 pages, $315.00

Canadian Environmental Directory, 2008 /09

The Canadian Environmental Directory is Canada's most complete and only national listing of environmental associations and organizations, government regulators and purchasing groups, product and service companies, special libraries, and more! The extensive Products and Services section provides detailed listings enabling users to identify the company name, address, phone, fax, e-mail, Web address, firm type, contact names (and titles), product and service information, affiliations, trade information, branch and affiliate data. The Government section gives you all the contact information you need at every government level – federal, provincial and municipal. We also include descriptions of current environmental initiatives, programs and agreements, names of environment-related acts administered by each ministry or department PLUS information and tips on who to contact and how to sell to governments in Canada. The Associations section provides complete contact information and a brief description of activities. Included are Canadian environmental organizations and international groups including industry, commercial and professional associations, registered charities, special interest and common interest organizations. All the Information you need about the Canadian environmental industry: directory of products and services, special libraries and resource, conferences, seminars and tradeshows, chronology of environmental events, law firms and major Canadian companies, *The Canadian Environmental Directory* is ideal for business, government, engineers and anyone conducting research on the environment.

Softcover ISBN 978-1-59237-224-9, 900 pages, $315.00

Canadian Parliamentary Guide, 2008

An indispensable guide to government in Canada, the annual *Canadian Parliamentary Guide* provides information on both federal and provincial governments, courts, and their elected and appointed members. The Guide is completely bilingual, with each record appearing both in English and then in French. The Guide contains biographical sketches of members of the Governor General's Household, the Privy Council, members of Canadian legislatures (federal, including both the House of Commons and the Senate, provincial and territorial), members of the federal superior courts (Supreme, Federal, Federal Appeal, Court Martial Appeal and Tax Courts) and the senior staff for these institutions. Biographies cover personal data, political career, private career and contact information. In addition, the Guide provides descriptions of each of the institutions, including brief historical information in text and chart format and significant facts (i.e. number of members and their salaries). The Guide covers the results of all federal general elections and by-elections from Confederations to the present and the results of the most recent provincial elections. A complete name index rounds out the text, making information easy to find. No other resources presents a more up-to-date, more complete picture of Canadian government and her political leaders. A must-have resource for all Canadian reference collections.

Hardcover ISBN 978-1-59237-310-9, 800 pages, $184.00